One of the best, if not the best, class dictionaries available

Higher Education Journal

TEACH YOURSELF BOOKS

SPANISH DICTIONARY

Spanish-English/English-Spanish

Margaret H. Raventós
M.A.

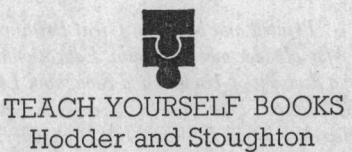

TEACH YOURSELF BOOKS
Hodder and Stoughton

First printed 1953
First printed in this form 1963
Eighth impression 1982

This volume is published in the U.S.A. by David McKay Inc., 750 Third Avenue, New York, N.Y. 10017.

ISBN 0 340 32401 5

Printed and bound in Great Britain
for Hodder and Stoughton Educational,
a division of Hodder and Stoughton Ltd,
Mill Road, Dunton Green, Sevenoaks, Kent,
by Hazell Watson & Viney Ltd, Aylesbury, Bucks

SPANISH-ENGLISH

A

a, *f.* name of the letter A

a, *prep.* to; at; on; by; in, into; up to; according to; if, etc. 1. Denotes the direct complement of verb before objects representing specified persons or animals, personified nouns, pronouns referring to persons (**alguien, entrambos, cualquiera,** etc.), demonstrative or relative pronouns, collective nouns representing persons (**el público, la muchedumbre,** etc.), names of countries, cities, rivers, etc., except where these invariably take the def. art., e.g. **Dejé a Varsovia,** I left Warsaw, *but* **Dejé el Perú,** I left Peru. 2. Introduces indirect obj. when this is a noun governed by a verb implying motion, or an emphatic pers. pron., e.g. **Nos conviene a tí y a mí,** It suits both you and me. It is also used before indirect obj. to avoid ambiguity when there is both an indirect and direct obj. 3. Denotes the complement of verb when this is an infin., e.g. **Enseñó a pintar a María,** He taught Mary to paint. 4. Indicates direction or destination, e.g. **Vamos a Edimburgo,** We are going to Edinburgh. 5. Signifies location, or point of time when action takes place, e.g. **Vinieron a las doce.** They came at twelve o'clock. 6. Describes position of persons or things, e.g. **Se sentaron a la puerta,** They sat down at the door. **La casa está a la derecha,** The house is on the right. 7. Denotes interval of time or place between one thing and another, e.g. **de tres a cinco de la tarde,** from three to five in the afternoon, **de calle a calle,** from street to street. 8. Expresses manner or mode of action, e.g. **a la francesa,** in the French way, **bordado a mano,** embroidered by hand. 9. Indicates rate or price, e.g. **a cuatro pesetas la libra,** at four pesetas the lb. 10. Indicates difference or comparison, e.g. **Va mucho de querer a hacer,** There's a difference between wishing and doing. 11. Sometimes means **hasta, según, hacia** and governs almost all parts of speech. Has many idiomatic uses. 12. Before infin. sometimes has conditional sense, e.g. **A haber sabido las noticias no lo hubiéramos hecho,** If we had known the news we should not have done it. 13. With nouns and adjectives forms adverbial phrases, e.g. **poco a poco,** little by little, **a veces,** sometimes, **a ciegas,** blindly, etc. 14: Used to turn adjectives into verbs, e.g. **ablandar (blando).** A + **el** becomes **al,** e.g. **al rey,** to the king. **Al** + infin. means when or on, e.g. **al marcharme yo,** when I went away (on my going away)

abacería, *f.* grocery, or provision shop

abacero (-ra), *s.* grocer

abacial, *a.* abbatial

ábaco, *m.* (*arch.*) abacus; counting frame

abad, *m.* abbot

abadejo, *m.* codfish; golden-crested wren

abadengo, *a.* abbatial

abadesa, *f.* abbess

abadía, *f.* abbacy; abbey

abadiato, *m.* abbacy

abajamiento, *m.* lowering; letting down

abajar, *v.t.* to lower

abajo, *adv.* under; underneath; below; down. Used immediately after noun in adverbial phrases, e.g. **cuesta a, escalera a,** downhill, downstairs. *interj.* Down with'l **venirse a,** to fall down; (*fig.*) collapse

abalanzamiento, *m.* balancing; rushing upon; dashing

abalanzar, *v.t.* to balance; impel violently; *v.r.* throw oneself upon; attack, rush upon; (*with prep. a*) rush into, risk. **Se abalanzó hacia ellos,** He rushed upon them

abalaustrado, *a.* balustered

abalear, *v.t.* (*agr.*) to winnow

abaleo, *m.* (*agr.*) winnowing; winnowing fan

abalizar, *v.t.* (*naut.*) to lay down buoys

abalorio, *m.* glass bead; bead work

abanderado, *m.* standard-bearer; ensign

abanderamiento, *m.* (*naut.*) registration; (*mil.*) enlistment

abanderar, *v.t.* to register (a ship)

abanderizar, *v.t.* to organize in groups; *v.r.* band together

abandonado, *a.* deserted; forlorn; helpless; indolent, careless; slovenly

abandonamiento, *m.* desertion; forlornness; helplessness; carelessness; slovenliness

abandonar, *v.t.* to forsake, desert; neglect; leave; give up; renounce; *v.r.* neglect oneself; grow discouraged; (*with prep. a*) give oneself over to

abandono, *m.* abandonment; defencelessness; forlornness; dilapidation; renunciation; neglect; slovenliness; debauchery

abanicamiento, *m.* fanning

abanicar, *v.t.* to fan

abanicazo, *m.* tap or blow with a fan

abanico, *m.* fan; anything fanshaped; (*fam.*) sword; railway signal; (*naut.*) derrick. **en a.,** fanshaped

abaniqueo, *m.* fanning; swinging, oscillation; gesticulation

abaniquería, *f.* fan factory or shop

abaniquero (-ra), *s.* fan maker or seller

abaratar, *v.t.* to cheapen, make less expensive; *v.r.* fall in price

abarca, *f.* leather sandal, worn chiefly in the Basque provinces

abarcador(-ra), *s.* one who clasps or embraces; monopolist

abarcadura, *f.* **abarcamiento,** *m.* inclusion; scope

abarcar, *v.t.* to clasp, encircle; include, comprise; undertake, attempt; monopolize

abarloar, *v.t.* (*naut.*) to bring alongside

abarquillado, *a.* rolled, curled, tubular

abarquillar, *v.t.* to shape into a roll; roll; curl

abarracar(se), *v.i.* and *v.r.* (*mil.*) to go into barracks

abarrancadero, *m.* rough road; ravine, precipice; (*fig.*) difficult situation

abarrancar, *v.t.* to ditch; make a ravine; *v.r.* fall into a pit; stick (in the mud, etc.); get into difficulties; (*naut.*) run aground

abastar, *v.t.* see **abastecer**

abastecedor (-ra), *a.* provisioning, supplying. *s.* provider; purveyor, supplier; caterer

abastecer, *v.t. irr.* to supply, provide; purvey. See **conocer**

abastecimiento, *m.* providing; supply, provision; catering; supplies

abastionar, *v.t.* (*mil.*) to fortify with bastions

abasto, *m.* provisions, food; (*com.*) supply. *adv.* plentifully, abundantly

abatanadura, *f.* fulling (of cloth)

abatanar, *v.t.* to full (cloth)

abate, *m.* abbé

abatido, *a.* dejected, depressed; spiritless; discouraged; crushed, humbled; (*com.*) depreciated

abatimiento, *m.* dejection, depression; humiliation; discouragement; falling; lowering; (*aer.,* *naut.*) drift

abatir, *v.t.* to knock down; overthrow; demolish; lower, take down; droop; humiliate; discourage; (*naut.*) dismantle; *v.i.* (*naut., aer.*) drift; *v.r.* be despondent, despair; humble oneself; swoop down (of birds)

abdicación, *f.* abdication

abdicar, *v.t.* to abdicate; revoke, cancel; give up (rights, opinions)

abdomen, *m.* abdomen

abdominal, *a.* abdominal

abducción, *f.* (*anat., phil.*) abduction

abductor, *m.* (*anat.*) abducent muscle

abecedario, *m.* ABC, alphabet; reading book, primer. **a. manual,** deaf-and-dumb alphabet

abedul, *m.* birch tree; birch wood

abeja, *f.* bee. **a. maestra,** queen bee. **a. obrera,** worker

abejar, *m.* bee-hive

abejero (-ra), *s.* beekeeper

abejón, *m.* drone; hornet

abejorro, *m.* bumble-bee

abejuno, *a.* bee, pertaining to bees

abellacar, *v.t.* to make a rogue of; *v.r.* become a rogue

abellotado, *a.* acorn-shaped

aberenjenado, *a.* having dark purple colour, or shape, of egg-plant

aberración, *f.* deviation; error, lapse; (*ast., phys., biol.*) aberration

abertura, *f.* opening; aperture, gap, hole; fissure, cleft; mountain pass; naturalness, frankness

abetal, *m.* fir grove

abeto, *m.* yew-leaved fir

abetunado, *a.* bituminous

abiertamente, *adv.* openly; frankly.

abierto, *a.* free, unobstructed; open, not enclosed; open, full-blown (flowers); frank, sincere. *adv.* openly

abigarrado, *a.* variegated; varied; speckled

abigarrar, *v.t.* to variegate; vary; speckle; fleck; spot; dapple

abigotado, *a.* having a thick moustache

abintestato, *a.* (*law*) intestate

abiselar, *v.t.* to bevel

abisinio (-ia), *a.* and *s.* Abyssinian. *m.* Abyssinian language

abismal, *a.* abysmal

abismar, *v.t.* to plunge into an abyss; depress, sadden; *v.r.* despair; be plunged in thought, be abstracted: be amazed

abismo, *m.* chasm, abyss, gulf; hell

abizcochado, *a.* biscuit-like

abjuración, *f.* abjuration

abjurar, *v.t.* to forswear, retract

ablación, *f.* ablation

ablactación, *f.* weaning

ablactar, *v.t.* to wean

ablandamiento, *m.* softening; placating

ablandante, *a.* softening; placatory

ablandar, *v.t.* to soften; appease, placate; loosen; relax; *v.i.* and *v.r.* be softened; be appeased; grow less stormy; decrease in force (elements)

ablandecer, *v.t.* *irr.* to soften. See **conocer**

ablativo, *a.* and *m.* (*gram.*) ablative

ablución, *f.* ablution

abnegación, *f.* abnegation, self-sacrifice

abnegado, *a.* self-sacrificing

abnegarse, *v.r.* *irr.* to deprive oneself, sacrifice oneself. See **cegar**

abobado, *a.* bewildered; foolish-looking, silly

abobamiento, *m.* bewilderment; silliness, stupidity

abobar, *v.t.* to daze, bewilder; make stupid

abocado, *a.* full-flavoured, pleasant (of wine)

abocar, *v.t.* to seize with the mouth; bring nearer; transfer contents of one jug to another; *v.r.* meet, assemble; *v.i.* (*naut.*) enter a channel, port, etc.

abocetado, *a.* (*art*) unfinished; sketchy

abochornado, *a.* flushed (of the face); ashamed; embarrassed

abochornar, *v.t.* to overheat, make flushed; shame; embarrass; *v.r.* dry up (plants)

abofetear, *v.t.* to slap, hit; buffet

abogacía, *f.* profession and practice of law; advocacy

abogado (-da), *s.* lawyer, solicitor; mediator; barrister

abogar, *v.i.* to defend at law; intercede for; advocate, champion

abolengo, *m.* lineage, descent, family; inheritance

abolible, *a.* abolishable

abolición, *f.* abolition

abolicionismo, *m.* abolitionism

abolicionista, *m.* and *f.* abolitionist

abolir, *v.t.* to abolish; cancel; annul

abolladura, *f.* bruise; dent; embossment

abollar, *v.t.* to bruise; dent

abollonar, *v.t.* to emboss, do raised work on; *v.r.* sprout (vines)

abombado, *a.* convex; domed

abombar, *v.t.* to make convex; (*fam.*) deafen, bewilder; *v.r.* begin to putrefy; get intoxicated

abominable, *a.* abominable

abominación, *f.* abomination; loathing, detestation

abominar, *v.t.* to abominate, loathe, detest

abonable, *a.* subscribable; payable

abonado (-da), *a.* trustworthy, reliable; ready, prepared, inclined. *s.* subscriber; season ticket holder (for concerts, etc.)

abonanzar, *v.i. impers.* to clear up, be fine (weather)

abonar, *v.t.* to guarantee; go surety for; improve, better; manure; ratify, confirm; pay; (*com.*) place to the credit of; *v.r.* subscribe, become a subscriber; take out (season tickets, etc.)

abonaré, *m.* (*com.*) due bill; promissory note, I.O.U.

abono, *m.* subscription; voucher; guarantee; manure. *a.* verde, leaf-mould

aboquillado, *a.* tipped (of cigarettes)

abordaje, *m.* (*naut.*) boarding of a ship

abordar, *v.t.* (*naut.*) to board a ship; (*naut.*) collide, run into; accost, tackle; undertake; *v.i.* (*naut.*) put into port

aborigen, *a.* aboriginal

aborígenes, *m. pl.* aborigines

aborrachado, *a.* bright red; highly coloured; flushed

aborrascarse, *v.r.* to grow stormy

aborrecedor (-ra), *a.* hateful. *s.* hater, loather

aborrecer, *v.t. irr.* to hate, loathe; desert offspring (animals, birds). See conocer

aborrecible, *a.* hateful, detestable

aborrecimiento, *m.* hate, detestation; dislike

abortar, *v.t.* to abort; *v.i.* (*med.*) miscarry; fail, go awry

abortivo, *a.* abortive

aborto, *m.* abortion; miscarriage; monster; failure

abotagarse, *v.r.* to swell up, become bloated

abotonador, *m.* button-hook

abotonar, *v.t.* to button; *v.i.* bud, sprout

abovedar, *v.t.* to vault, arch

aboyar, *v.t.* (*naut.*) to lay down buoys

abozalar, *v.t.* to muzzle

abra, *f.* cove, small bay; narrow gorge; fissure, cleft

abrasador, *a.* burning, flaming

abrasamiento, *m.* burning; ardour, heat

abrasar, *v.t.* to burn; dry up, parch (plants); squander, waste; shame; *v.i.* burn; *v.r.* be very hot, glow; burn with passion

abrasión, *f.* abrasion

abrasivo, *a.* and *m.* abrasive

abrazadera, *f.* clasp; clamp

abrazamiento, *m.* embracing

abrazar, *v.t.* to embrace, clasp in one's arms; follow, adopt; engage in; seize, take advantage of; comprise, include; surround; take in hand; clamp; clasp.

abrazarse a, to clutch, hang on to

abrazo, *m.* embrace

abrebocas, *m.* mouth gag

ábrego, *m.* south-west wind

abrelatas, *m.* tin opener

abrenuncio, *interj.* Begone!

abrevadero, *m.* watering place for cattle

abrevar, *v.t.* to water cattle; irrigate, water; soak skins (in tanning)

abreviación, *f.* abbreviation, shortening; summary; hastening

abreviadamente, *adv.* shortly, in brief

abreviador, *m.* abridger, condenser

abreviar, *v.t.* to abbreviate, shorten; hasten, accelerate; condense, abridge. Y para a . . . And, to cut a long story short . . .

abreviatura, *f.* abbreviation, contraction; shorthand

abridor, *m.* opener; ear-ring (for keeping holes in ears open). *a.* de guantes, glove-stretcher. *a.* de láminas, engraving needle. *a.* de latas, tin-opener

abrigada, *f.* **abrigadero,** *m.* sheltered place

abrigar, *v.t.* to shelter, protect (against the cold, etc.); defend, help; hold (opinions); nurse (a hope, etc.); cover; *v.r.* take shelter; wrap oneself up

abrigo, *m.* shelter; defence; protection; help; sheltered place; wrap, coat; (*naut.*) haven

abril, *m.* April; youth; *pl.* (*poet.*) years

abrileño, *a.* April

abrillantar, *v.t.* to cut in facets like a diamond; polish, burnish; cause to shine; (*fig.*) improve, add lustre to

abrir, *v.t.* to open; reveal; unlock; slide the bolt of; extend, spread out; cleave; engrave; clear (the way, etc.); begin; head, lead; separate; dig; inaugurate. *v.i.* unfold (flowers); expand; *v.r.* open; expand; (*with con*) confide in. **abrirse camino,** to make one's way (*also fig.*)

abrochador, *m.* button-hook

abrochamiento, *m.* buttoning; fastening

abrochar, *v.t.* to button; fasten, clasp; hook up (a dress, etc.); buckle

abrogación, *f.* repeal, annulment

abrogar, *v.t.* to repeal, annul

abrojo, *m.* thistle; (*bot.*) caltrops; thorn, prickle; *pl.* submerged rocks in sea

abroncar, *v.t.* (*fam.*) to bore, annoy

abrumador, *a.* burdensome, crushing, oppressive; troublesome, tiresome; exhausting

abrumar, *v.t.* to weigh down; overwhelm, oppress; weary, exhaust; *v.r.* grow misty

abrupto, *a.* steep; rough, broken (ground); rugged

absceso, *m.* abscess

abscisa, *f.* (*geom.*) abscissa

abscisión, *f.* (*med.*) incision

absentismo, *m.* absenteeism

ábside, *m.* or *f.* (*arch.*) apse. *m.* (*ast.*) apsis

absolución, *f.* (*ecc.* and *law*) absolution; remission, pardon

absoluta, *f.* (*mil.*) discharge

absolutismo, *m.* absolutism

absolutista, *m.* and *f.* absolutist

absoluto, *a.* absolute; categori-

cal; (*fam.*) despotic. **en a.,** absolutely

absolver, *v.t. irr.* to absolve; acquit (of a charge). (*law*) **a. de la instancia,** to dismiss a case. See **mover**

absorbente, *a.* and *m.* absorbent

absorber, *v.t.* to absorb; consume, use up; attract, hold (the attention, etc.); imbibe

absorción, *f.* absorption

absortar, *v.t.* to amaze, dumbfound

absorto, *a.* amazed, astounded; abstracted, lost in thought

abstemio, *a.* abstemious; (*fam.*) teetotal

abstención, *f.* abstention

abstenerse, *v.r. irr.* to refrain; abstain. See **tener**

abstinencia, *f.* abstinence; fasting

abstinente, *a.* abstemious; temperate

abstracción, *f.* abstraction; preoccupation; absent-mindedness

abstracto, *a.* abstract. **en a.,** in the abstract

abstraer, *v.t. irr.* to abstract; consider separately; *v.i.* (*with de*) do without, exclude; *v.r.* be preoccupied; let one's thoughts wander. See **traer**

abstraído, *a.* retired, recluse; preoccupied; absent-minded

abstruso, *a.* abstruse

absurdidad, *f.* absurdity; folly, nonsense

absurdo, *a.* ridiculous, absurd. *m.* piece of folly, nonsense

abuela, *f.* grandmother; old woman, dame

abuelo, *m.* grandfather; ancestor (*gen. pl.*); old man; *pl.* grandparents

abulia, *f.* lack of will-power, abulia

abúlico, *a.* abulic, lacking will-power

abultado, *a.* bulky, large; voluminous; exaggerated

abultamiento, *m.* bulkiness; enlargement, increase; mound; exaggeration

abultar, *v.t.* to enlarge, increase; exaggerate; model in rough (sculpture); *v.i.* be bulky; be large

abundancia, *f.* abundance, plenty

abundante, *a.* abundant, plentiful; abounding (in)

abundar, *v.i.* to be plentiful, abound

abundoso, *a.* See **abundante**

¡**abur!** *interj.* (*fam.*) So long! Bye-bye!

aburrido, *a.* boring, tedious, dull; tired, weary

aburrimiento, *m.* boredom, dullness; wearisomeness, tediousness

aburrir, *v.t.* to bore; (*fam.*) spend (time, money); desert the nest (birds); *v.r.* grow bored; be weary

abusar, *v.i.* to abuse; exceed one's rights, go too far; (*with de*) take advantage of

abusivo, *a.* abusive

abuso, *m.* abuse. **a. de confianza,** abuse of trust

abyección, *f.* degradation, misery; abjectness, servility

abyecto, *a.* abject, wretched; servile

acá, *adv.* hither, here; at this time, now. **a. y acullá,** hither and thither. **desde ayer a.,** from yesterday until now

acabable, *a.* terminable, finishable; achievable

acabado, *a.* complete; perfect; expert, consummate; old, worn out; ill, infirm. *m.* finish

acabador (-ra), *a.* end, final, finishing. *s.* finisher

acabàmiento, *m.* finishing, completion; end; death, decease

acabar, *v.t.* to end, terminate; finish; complete, perfect; kill; (*with con*) destroy, finish off; suppress; squander; *v.i.* end; die; be destroyed; (*with de +* *infin.*) to have just (e.g. **Acaba de salir,** He has just gone out); *v.r.* end, be exhausted, run out of (e.g. **Se le acabó el dinero,** His money ran out); fade, grow weak; be destroyed

acachetear, *v.t.* to slap, cuff

acacia, *f.* (*bot.*) acacia

academia, *f.* academy; literary association; school

académico (-ca), *a.* academic. *s.* academician

acaecer, *v.i. irr.* to happen, occur. See **conocer**

acaecimiento, *m.* happening, occurrence, event

acalenturarse, *v.r.* to grow feverish

acaloradamente, *adv.* excitedly, vehemently

acalorado, *a.* hot; fervent; (*fig.*) heated

acaloramiento, *m.* excitement, agitation, vehemence; ardour

acalorar, *v.t.* to warm; aid, encourage; excite, stimulate; stir, move (to enthusiasm); inflame, rouse; tire (by exercise); *v.r.* grow hot; become agitated or excited; become heated (arguments)

acallar, *v.t.* to quieten, hush; soothe, appease

acamar, *v.t.* to lay flat (plants by the wind); *v.r.* be flattened (plants); lie down (animals); go rotten (fruit)

acampanado, *a.* bell-shaped

acampar, *v.i.* and *v.t.* to encamp

acanalado, *a.* grooved; fluted, striated; furrowed; corrugated

acanalar, *v.t.* to groove; striate, flute; corrugate; furrow, channel

acanelado, *a.* cinnamon-coloured

acantilado, *a.* steep, precipitous; shelving (ocean-bed). *m.* cliff

acanto, *m.* (*arch.*, *bot.*) acanthus

acantonamiento, *m.* billeting; cantonment

acantonar, *v.t.* to billet or quarter troops

acaparador (-ra), *s.* monopolist

acaparar, *v.t.* (*com.*) to monopolize, corner; seize, take possession of

acaracolado, *a.* spiral, winding, twisting

acardenalar, *v.t.* to bruise; *v.r.* be bruised; be covered with livid marks

acarear, *v.t.* to face; face up to, meet with courage

acariciador (-ra), *a.* caressing, loving. *s.* fondler

acariciar, *v.t.* to caress; brush, touch lightly; cherish, treat affectionately; toy with (a suggestion)

ácaro, *m.* (*ent.*) acarid, mite, tick

acarreadizo, *a.* transportable

acarreador (-ra), *s.* carrier, carter

acarreamiento, acarreo, *m.* cartage, carting; transport, carriage; occasioning

acarrear, *v.t.* to cart, transport; occasion, bring (gen. evil). **La**

guerra acarreó la carestía,
The war·brought scarcity

acartonado, *a.* shrivelled; shrunken; of cardboard

acaso, *m.* chance. *adv.* by chance; perhaps, perchance. **por si a.,** in case (e.g. **Por si a. venga,** In case he comes)

acatable, *a.* venerable, worthy

acatadamente, *adv.* with respect, humbly

acatamiento, *m.* respect; reverence; observance

acatar, *v.t.* to treat with respect, honour, revere; observe

acatarrarse, *v.r.* to catch a cold

acaudalado, *a.* wealthy, well-to-do

acaudalar, *v.t.* to make money; hoard up wealth; acquire (learning, etc.)

acaudillar, *v.t.* (*mil.*) to command, lead; head (a party, etc.)

acceder, *v.i.* (*with prep. a*) to concede, grant; accede to, agree to

accesibilidad, *f.* accessibility; approachableness

accesible, *a.* accessible; approachable

accesión, *f.* agreement, acquiescence; accession; accessory; feverish attack

acceso, *m.* access; paroxysm, outburst; (*med.*) attack

accesorio, *a.* accessory

accesorios, *m. pl.* accessories; (*theat.*) properties

accidentado, *a* rough, uneven; stormy, troubled (life, etc.)

accidental, *a.* accidental; *m.* (*mus.*) accidental

accidentalmente, *adv.* accidentally, by chance

accidentar, *v.t.* to cause an accident to; *v.r.* be the victim of an accident; be seized by a fit or an illness

accidente, *m.* chance; accident, mishap; illness, indisposition; (*med.*) fit; (*gram.*) accidence; (*mus.*) accidental. **a. del trabajo,** industrial accident. **por a.,** by chance, accidentally

acción, *f.* action; battle; skirmish; (*mech.*) drive; (*com.*) share; gesture; lawsuit; (*lit.*) action (of play, etc.); (*art*) posture, pose. **a. de gracias,** thanksgiving;

(*com.*) **a. liberada,** paid-up share. **a. privilegiada,** preference share

accionar, *v.i.* to gesture, gesticulate

accionista, *m.* and *f.* (*com.*) shareholder

acebal, acebo, *m.* holly tree

acebuche, *m.* wild olive tree; olive wood

acecinar, *v.t.* to salt and dry meat; *v.r.* wither, dry up (persons)

acechar, *v.t.* to spy upon, watch; lie in ambush for

acecho, *m.* spying upon, watch; waylaying, ambush. **al a.,** in ambush; on the watch

acechona, *f.* waylaying; ambush

acedar, *v.t.* to make bitter, sour; embitter, displease; *v.r.* turn sour; wither (plants)

acéfalo, *a.* acephalous

aceitar, *v.t.* to oil, lubricate; rub with oil

aceite, *m.* olive oil; oil. **a. de hígado de bacalao,** cod-liver oil. **a. de linaza,** linseed oil. **a. de ricino,** castor-oil. **a. de trementina,** oil of turpentine

aceitera, *f.* woman who sells oil; oil can; oil bottle; *pl.* cruet

aceitería, *f.* oil shop

aceitero, *m.* oil seller. **a.** oil

aceitoso, *a.* oily

aceituna, *f.* (*bot.*) olive

aceitunado, *a.* olive-coloured

aceitunero (-ra), *s.* olive picker or seller. *m.* warehouse for storing olives

aceituno, *m.* olive tree

aceleración, *f.* speed, haste; acceleration

aceleradamente, *adv.* hastily, swiftly

acelerador, *a.* accelerating. *m.* hastener; (*aut.*) accelerator

acelerar, *v.t.* to hasten, speed up; accelerate

acelga, *f.* (*bot.*) saltwort

acémila, *f.* beast of burden, mule; (*ant.*) tax

acemilero, *m.* muleteer

acendrado, *a.* pure, unblemished, spotless

acendrar, *v.t.* to refine (metals); purify, make spotless

acento, *m.* accent; tone, inflection; (*poet.*) voice, words. **a.**

agudo, acute accent. **a. circun-flejo,** circumflex accent. **a. grave,** grave accent. **a. tónico,** tonic accent

acentuación, *f.* accentuation, stress; emphasis

acentuar, *v.t.* to accent; stress, emphasize; *v.r.* become evident, be noticeable

aceña, *f.* water-mill; irrigation water-wheel; chain-well

acepción, *f.* meaning, significance, acceptation. **a. de personas,** partiality, preference

acepilladura, *f.* sweeping, brushing; planing; wood-shaving

acepillar, *v.t.* to sweep, brush; plane; (*fam.*) brush up, polish up

aceptabilidad, *f.* acceptability

aceptable, *a.* acceptable

aceptación, *f.* acceptance; popularity; approval

aceptador (-ra), *a.* accepting. *s.* acceptor

aceptar, *v.t.* to accept; approve; accept a challenge; (*com.*) honour

acepto, *a.* agreeable, acceptable

acequia, *f.* ditch, trench; irrigation channel

acequiero, *m.* keeper of irrigation ditches

acera, *f.* sidewalk, pavement

acerado, *a.* steel; steel-like; strong, tough; mordant, incisive

acerar, *v.t.* to steel; treat (liquids) with steel; harden, make obdurate

acerbidad, *f.* bitterness, acerbity, sourness; harshness, cruelty

acerbo, *a.* sour, tart, bitter; cruel, harsh

acerca de, *adv.* concerning, about

acercamiento, *m.* approach

acercar, *v.t.* to bring nearer; *v.r.* be near at hand, draw near; (*with prep. a*) approach

acerico, *m.* small cushion; pincushion

acerino, *a.* (*poet.*) steel, steel-like

acero, *m.* steel; blade, sword; *pl.* bravery, spirit; (*fam.*) good appetite. **a. inoxidable,** stainless steel

acerola, *f.* (*bot.*) haw, fruit of hawthorn

acérrimo, *a. sup.* extremely strong, mighty; most harsh; most resolute, unflinching; very strong (taste, smell)

acerrojar, *v.t.* to lock, padlock; bolt

acertado, *a.* well-aimed; fitting, suitable; wise; successful

acertar, *v.t. irr.* to hit the mark; find, come across; succeed (in), achieve; guess, find out; *v.i.* be successful; thrive (of plants); (*with prep. a + infin.*) happen, occur, come to pass. *Pres. Ind.* **acierto, aciertas, acierta, aciertan.** *Pres. Subjunc.* **acierte, aciertes, acierte, acierten**

acertijo, *m.* riddle

acervo, *m.* pile, heap

acetato, *m,* acetate

acético, *a.* acetic

acetileno, *m.* acetylene

acetona, *f.* acetone

acetoso, *a.* acetous; sour

acetre, *m.* small pail; holy water stoup

aciago, *a.* unhappy, ill-omened; fateful

aciano, *m.* corn-flower

acíbar, *m.* aloe tree; bitter aloes; sorrow, bitterness

acibarar, *v.t.* to add bitter aloes to; embitter, sadden

acicalado, *a.* polished; neat; well-groomed. *m.* polishing, burnishing (of weapons)

acicalador (-ra), *a.* polishing. *s.* polisher. *m.* burnisher (machine)

acicalar, *v.t.* to burnish (weapons); adorn, deck; *v.r.* dress oneself with care

acicate, *m.* Moorish spur; incitement, stimulus

acidez, *f.* acidity, bitterness

acidia, *f.* indolence; sluggishness

acidificar, *v.t.* to acidify

ácido, *a.* acid; sour; harsh. *m.* acid. **a. fénico,** carbolic acid. **a. graso,** fatty acid

acidular, *v.t.* (*chem.*) to acidulate

acídulo, *a.* (*chem.*) acidulous

acierto, *m.* good hit, bull's-eye; success; achievement; cleverness; dexterity, skill; wisdom, sense; tact

acimut, *m.* (*ast.*) azimuth

aclamación, *f.* acclamation; shout of acclamation. **por a.,** unanimously

aclamador (-ra), *a.* acclaiming. *s.* applauder, acclaimer

aclamar, *v.t.* to acclaim; applaud

aclaración, *f.* explanation; elucidation

aclarado, *m.* rinse; rinsing

aclarador, aclaratorio, *a.* explanatory

aclarar, *v.t.* to clarify, purify; clear; rinse (clothes); explain; thin; *v.i.* clear; clear up (sky); dawn

aclimatación, *f.* acclimatization

aclimatar, *v.t.* to acclimatize

aclocar(se), *v.i.* and *v.r.* to be broody (hens)

acne, *m.* acne

acobardar, *v.t.* to intimidate, frighten

acoceamiento, *m.* kicking; (*fam.*) insulting

acocear, *v.t.* to kick; (*fam.*) insult, humiliate

acocharse, *v.r.* to squat, crouch

acodalar, *v.t.* to prop

acodiciar, *v.t.* to yearn for, covet, desire

acodo, *m.* (*agr.*) sucker, scion

acogedizo, *a.* gathered haphazardly

acogedor (-ra), *a.* welcoming, friendly. *s.* protector

acoger, *v.t.* to receive, welcome, admit; protect, harbour; *v.r.* take refuge; (*with prep. a*) make use of, resort to

acogida, *f.* reception, welcome; protection, shelter; meeting place; confluence (of waters). **tener buena a.,** to be well received

acogollar, *v.t.* to protect, cover (plants); *v.i.* sprout, shoot

acogotar, *v.t.* to fell by a blow on the neck; (*fam.*) knock out

acolada, *f.* accolade

acolchar, *v.t.* (*sew.*) to quilt

acólito, *m.* acolyte

acolmillado, *a.* fanged (of teeth); tusked

acollador, *m.* (*naut.*) lanyard

acometedor (-ra), *a.* capable, enterprising; aggressive. *s.* aggressor, attacker

acometer, *v.t.* to attack furiously; undertake; take in hand; overcome (of sleep, etc.)

acometida, *f.* **acometimiento,** *m.* assault, onrush; undertaking

acometividad, *f.* aggressiveness

acomodable, *a.* easily arranged

acomodación, *f.* adjustment;

adaptation; accommodation

acomodadizo, *a.* accommodating, easy-going

acomodado, *a.* suitable; convenient; wealthy, well-off; comfort-loving; moderate, low (of price)

acomodador (-ra), *s.* theatre attendant, usher

acomodamiento, *m.* agreement, transaction; accommodation

acomodar, *v.t.* to arrange, adjust, accommodate; adapt; appoint; place; reconcile; employ, take on; equip, provide; lodge; *v.i.* suit, be convenient; *v.r.* compromise, agree

acomodaticio, *a.* accommodating

acomodo, *m.* post, employment; arrangement; settlement

acompañamiento, *m.* accompaniment; following, retinue; (*mus.*) accompaniment; (*theat.*) crowd, chorus

acompañanta, *f.* chaperon; maid, servant

acompañante, *m.* (*mus.*) accompanist

acompañar, *v.t.* to accompany; follow, escort; enclose (a letter, etc.); (*mus.*) accompany

acompasado, *a.* rhythmic; deliberate, slow

acondicionado, *a.* conditioned; (*with bien or mal*) in good or bad condition; of good or bad quality; good- or ill-natured. **reflejo acondicionado** (*med.*) conditioned reflex

acondicionar, *v.t.* to prepare; mend, repair; *v.r.* condition oneself

acongojar, *v.t.* to sadden, grieve; oppress

acónito, *m.* (*bot.*) aconite

aconsejable, *a.* advisable

aconsejar, *v.t.* to advise; *v.r.* (*with con*) consult, ask advice of

aconsonantar, *v.t.* and *v.i.* to rhyme

acontecedero, *a.* possible

acontecer, *v.i. irr. impers.* to happen. See **conocer**

acontecimiento, *m.* event, occurrence

acopado, *a.* cup-shaped, cup-like

acopiar, *v.t.* to collect, amass, gather

acopio, *m.* collection, store; accumulation, gathering

acopladura, *f.* **acoplamiento,** *m.* (*carp.*, *mech.*) joint; coupling; yoking; mating (of animals)

acoplar, *v.t.* to join, couple; yoke; mate (animals); reconcile (opinions); *v.r.* (*fam.*) fall in love

acoplo, *m.* coupling

acoquinar, *v.t.* (*fam.*) to intimidate, terrify

acorazado, *a.* (*nav.*, *mil.*) armoured, iron-clad. *m.* iron-clad, battleship

acorazar, *v.t.* (*nav.*, *mil.*) to armour

acorazonado, *a.* heart-shaped

acorcharse, *v.r.* to dry up, shrivel; go numb (limbs)

acordada, *f.* (*law*) resolution

acordadamente, *adv.* by common consent, unanimously; deliberately, after due thought

acordar, *v.t. irr.* to decide unanimously; resolve; remind; tune; harmonize (colours); *v.i.* agree; *v.r.* remember; come to an agreement. **Si mal no me acuerdo,** If my memory does not deceive me. *Pres. Ind.* **acuerdo, acuerdas, acuerda, acuerdan.** *Pres. Subjunc.* **acuerde, acuerdes, acuerde, acuerden**

acorde, *a.* agreed; in harmony; in agreement. *m.* (*mus.*) chord; harmony

acordeón, *m.* accordion

acordonar, *v.t.* to lace; cordon off, surround; mill (coins)

acornear, *v.t.* to butt, toss (bulls)

acorralamiento, *m.* corralling, penning

acorralado, *a.* at bay, intimidated

acorralar, *v.t.* to corral, pen; confine; corner, silence (in argument); frighten

acorrer, *v.t.* to aid, assist; *v.i.* run, hasten; *v.r.* take refuge

acortamiento, *m.* shortening

acortar, *v.t.* to shorten; *v.r.* be speechless, be shy. **a. las velas,** to take in sail

acosador (-ra), *a.* persecuting. *s.* persecutor

acosamiento, *m.* persecution

acosar, *v.t.* to persecute relentlessly; annoy, harass

acostado, *a.* in bed; stretched out; (*her.*) couchant

acostar, *v.t. irr.* to lay down, stretch out; put to bed; *v.i.* lean, tilt; *v.r.* lie down; go to bed; (*naut.*) come alongside. See **contar**

acostumbrado, *a.* accustomed, usual

acostumbrar, *v.t.* to habituate, accustom; *v.i.* be in the habit of (e.g. **Acostumbramos ir a la playa en el verano,** We generally go to the seaside in summer); *v.r.* (*with prep. a*) become used to

acotiacón, *f.* noting; marginal note; stage direction; ordnance survey number

acotar, *v.t.* to annotate; mark out boundaries; fix, establish; accept; (*fam.*) choose; testify; fill in elevation figures on a map; *v.r.* seek refuge

acotillo, *m.* sledge-hammer

acre, *a.* bitter, sour; harsh; biting, mordant. *m.* acre (land measure)

acrecencia, *f.* **acrecentamiento,** *m.* increase; addition

acrecentar, *v.t. irr.* to increase; augment; promote, prefer. See **acertar**

acrecer, *v.t. irr.* to increase; augment. See **conocer**

acreción, *f.* accretion

acreditado, *a.* accredited, well-reputed; respected

acreditar, *v.t.* to prove; verify; accredit; recommend; sanction, authorize; vouch for, guarantee; (*com.*) credit

acreedor (-ra), *s.* creditor; claimant. *a.* deserving. **a. hipotecario,** mortgagee

acreencia, *f.* debt; (*com.*) claim

acribillar, *v.t.* to riddle with holes; wound repeatedly; pelt; torment; (*fam.*) pester, harass

acriminación, *f.* accusation

acriminador (-ra), *a.* incriminating. *s.* accuser

acriminar, *v.t.* to accuse, charge

acrimonia, *f.* acrimony

acrisolar, *v.t.* to refine, purify (metals); perfect; clarify, elucidate

acrobacia, *f.* acrobatics

acróbata, *m.* and *f.* acrobat

acrobático, *a.* acrobatic

acromático, *a.* achromatic

acrómico, *a.* achromic

acrópolis, *f.* acropolis

acróstico, *a.* and *m.* acrostic

acta, *f.* minutes, record; certificate of election (as deputy to Cortes, etc.); *pl.* deeds (of a martyr). a. matrimonial, marriage register

actitud, *f.* attitude

activar, *v.t.* to stimulate, make active; accelerate, hasten

actividad, *f.* activity; movement, bustle. en a., in action; at work

activo, *a.* active. *m.* (*com.*) assets

acto, *m.* act, deed, action; act, law; act (of a play); public ceremony; *pl.* minutes (of a meeting, etc.). a. continuo *or* a. seguido, immediately afterwards. los Actos de los Apóstoles, Acts of the Apostles. en a., in the act (of doing). en el a., in the act; immediately

actor, *m.* actor; (*law*) plaintiff

actriz, *f.* actress

actuación, *f.* operation, functioning; action; *pl.* legal functions, judicial acts

actual, *a.* present; contemporary

actualidad, *f.* present, present time; topic of interest. Actualidades, current events; News Reel (cinema). en la a., at the present time

actuar, *v.t.* to operate, set in motion; *v.i.* act; exercise legal functions

actuario, *m.* (*law*) clerk of Assize. a. de seguros, actuary

acuadrillar, *v.t.* to get together an armed band *or* to lead it

acuarela, *f.* water-colour painting

acuarelista, *m.* and *f.* water-colour painter

acuario, *m.* aquarium; Aquarius

acuartelamiento, *m.* billeting (of troops); billet, quarters

acuartelar, *v.t.* to billet

acuático, acuátil, *a.* aquatic

acuatinta, *f.* aquatint

acucia, *f.* fervour, zeal; yearning, longing

acuciar, *v.t.* to incite; goad; stimulate; encourage

acucioso, *a.* zealous, fervent, keen

acuclillarse, *v.r.* to squat, crouch

acucharado, *a.* spoon-shaped

acuchillado, *a.* taught by experience, schooled; slashed (of Elizabethan garments, etc.)

acuchillar, *v.t.* to hack, cut about; stab, put to the sword; slash (sleeves, etc.); *v.r.* fight with swords, daggers

acudir, *v.i.* to go, repair (to); come; go or come to the aid of; attend, be present; resort (to), seek protection; reply, respond

acueducto, *m.* aqueduct

ácueo, *a.* aqueous, watery

acuerdo, *m.* motion, resolution; decision; harmony, agreement; opinion, belief; remembrance; report; meeting of members of a tribunal; (*art*) harmony (of colours). de a., in agreement, in conformity; unanimously. ponerse de a., to come to an understanding

acuitar, *v.t.* to distress, trouble; grieve

acullá, *adv.* afar, yonder, in the distance

acumulación, *f.* accumulation, collection

acumulador (-ra), *a.* accumulative. *m.* accumulator, storage battery. *s.* collector, accumulator

acumular, *v.t.* to accumulate, amass, collect; accuse, charge with

acuñación, *f.* minting, coining; wedging

acuñador (-ra), *s.* coiner, stamper; wedge. *m.* coining machine

acuñar, *v.t.* to mint, stamp, coin; wedge

acuosidad, *f.* wateriness

acuoso, *a.* aqueous, watery

acurrucarse, *v.r.* to huddle; curl up; crouch

acusación, *f.* accusation; (*law*) charge; (*law*) prosecution

acusado (-da), *a.* accused; prominent; well-defined; *s.* accused; (*law*) defendant

acusador (-ra), *a.* accusing. *s.* accuser; (*law*) prosecutor

acusar, *v.t.* to accuse; blame; denounce; (*com.*) acknowledge receipt; (*law*) prosecute; (*law*) charge

acusativo, *m.* (*gram.*) accusative

acusatorio, *a.* accusatory

acusón (-ona), s. (fam.) tell-tale, sneak, informer

acústica, f. acoustics

acústico, a. acoustic

acutángulo, a. (geom.) acute-angled

achacar, v.t. to attribute, impute, assign

achacoso, a. ailing, ill, sickly

achantarse, v.r. (fam.) to hide from danger; put up with, bear

achaparrado, a. stocky

achaque, m. ailment, illness (permanent); (fam.) period, menstruation; pregnancy; matter, affair; pretext; failing, bad habit

achatamiento, m. flattening

achatar, v.t. to flatten, make flat

achicado, a. childish

achicador, m. (naut.) boat-scoop

achicar, v.t. to make smaller, diminish; drain, bail out; depreciate, belittle

achicarse, (fam.) to sing small

achicoria, f. chicory

achicharrar, v.t. (cul.) to overcook; overheat; annoy, importune

achinelado, a. slipper-shaped

achique, m. bailing, draining

achispado, a. (fam.) tipsy

achubascarse, v.r. to become overcast, grow stormy

achuchar, v.t. (fam.) to squeeze, hug; jostle, push against

achuchón, m. (fam.) shove, push; hug, squeeze

achulado, a. (fam.) brazen, tough

adagio, m. proverb, saw; (mus.) adagio

adalid, m. chieftain; head, leader

adamado, a. effeminate; refined; genteel

adamantino, a. adamantine

adamascado, a. damask-like

adaptabilidad, f. adaptability

adaptación, f. adaptation

adaptar, v.t. to adapt, make suitable; v.r. adapt oneself

adarga, f. leather shield

adarme, m. 179 centigrammes, ½ drachm; tittle, jot

adecentar, v.t. to make decent; tidy up; v.r. tidy oneself

adecuación, f. adequacy; suitability

adecuado, a. adequate; suitable

adecuar, v.t. to proportion, fit

adefesio, m. (fam.) folly, absurdity (gen. pl.); extravagant attire; guy, sight

adehala, f. tip, gratuity

adehesar, v.t. to turn into pasture (land)

adelantado, a. precocious; forward, pert; fast (clocks); early (of fruit); excellent; capable, proficient. m. (ant.) provincial governor or chief justice or captain-general (Spanish history). por a., in advance

adelantamiento, m. promotion, furtherance; progress, advancement; betterment; improvement; (ant.) office of adelantado; anticipation

adelantar, v.t. to advance, move on; hasten; forestall; overtake; put on (the hands of clocks); improve; better; beat, excel; place in front; v.i. progress, advance; be fast (clocks); grow, develop; v.r. come forward

adelante, adv. on, forward; further on; straight ahead. ¡A.! Onward! Come in! de hoy en a., henceforth, from to-day forward

adelanto, m. anticipation; progress; (com.) payment in advance. el a. de la hora, the putting forward of the clock

adelfa, f. (bot.) rose-bay, oleander

adelgazamiento, m. loss of weight; slenderness; thinness

adelgazar, v.t. to make slender or thin; (fig.) split hairs; whittle, taper; v.i. grow slender or thin

ademán, m. posture, attitude; gesture; pl. behaviour, manners

además, adv. besides, in addition; moreover. a. de, as well as

adentellar, v.t. to bite, sink the teeth into

adentro, adv. inside, within

adentros, m. pl. private thoughts (e.g. Pensé por mis adentros, I thought in my own mind). Interj. ¡Adentro! Come in!; Go in!

adepto, a. affiliated; adept, proficient

aderezamiento, m. dressing; seasoning; embellishment

aderezar, v.t. to deck, embellish; cook; (cul.) season; (cul.) dress;

prepare; repair, mend; guide, direct; dress (cloth)

aderezo, *m.* dressing, adornment; beautifying; finery, ornament; preparation; seasoning; set of jewels; horse's trappings; gum starch (for dressing cloth); equipment

adeudar, *v.t.* to owe; be dutiable (goods); (*com.*) debit; *v.i.* become related (by marriage); *v.r.* run into debt

adeudo, *m.* debt; customs duty; (*com.*) debit

adherencia, *f.* adherence; adhesion (also *med.*)

adherente, *a.* adhesive; connected, attached. *m.* and *f.* adherent, follower; *m. pl.* adherentes, accessories, requisites

adherirse, *v.r. irr.* to adhere, stick; follow; believe (in). See herir

adhesión, *f.* adhesion; adherence

adhesividad, *f.* adhesiveness

adhesivo, *a.* adhesive

adiamantado, *a.* diamond-like, diamantine

adición, *f.* addition

adicional, *a.* additional, extra

adicionar, *v.t.* to add up; add to

adicto (-ta), *a.* addicted, fond; joint. *s.* addict; follower, disciple

adiestrador (-ra), *s.* trainer, coach; guide, teacher

adiestrar, *v.t.* to train, coach; guide, teach; lead; *v.r.* practise, perfect oneself

adietar, *v.t.* (*med.*) to put on a diet

adinerado, *a.* wealthy, well-off, rich

adiós, *interj.* Good-bye!; Hello, God be with you! (used as greeting). *m.* farewell

adiposidad, *f.* adiposity

adiposo, *a.* adipose

aditamento, *m.* addition

adive, *m.* jackal

adivinación, *f.* divination; guess

adivinador (-ra), *a.* prophesying, divining. *s.* soothsayer

adivinanza, *f.* divination; riddle; puzzle

adivinar, *v.t.* to prophesy, foretell; divine, guess; solve, guess (riddles, etc.)

adivino (-na), *s.* soothsayer, prophet

adjetival, *a.* adjectival

adjetivo, *a.* adjectival. *m.* adjective

adjudicación, *f.* adjudication, award

adjudicador (-ra), *s.* adjudicator

adjudicar, *v.t.* to adjudge; award; *v.r.* appropriate

adjudicatario (-ia), *s.* recipient (of a prize, etc.); grantee

adjuntar, *v.t.* to enclose (with a letter, etc.)

adjunto, *a.* attached; enclosed, accompanying; assistant, deputy; adjectival. *m.* addition, supplement

administración, *f.* administration; direction, control; administratorship

administrador (-ra), *a.* administrative. *s.* administrator. **a. de correos,** postmaster

administrar, *v.t.* to control, manage; provide, supply; administer

administrativo, *a.* administrative, executive

admirable, *a.* admirable

admirablemente, *adv.* admirably, excellently

admiración, *f.* amazement; admiration; wonder; exclamation mark

admirador (-ra), *a.* admiring. *s.* admirer

admirar, *v.t.* to admire; surprise, amaze (e.g. **Me admira su acción,** His action surprises me); *v.r.* (*with de*) be surprised at or by

admirativo, *a.* admiring; admirable, excellent

admisibilidad, *f.* allowability, permissibility

admisible, *a.* admissible; permissible

admisión, *f.* admission; acceptance; allowance

admitir, *v.t.* to admit; receive, accept; tolerate, brook; allow, permit

admonición, *f.* admonition, warning; reprimand

adobado, *m.* pickled pork (or other meat)

adobar, *v.t.* to prepare; (*cul.*) garnish; pickle (meat): cook; dress (hides)

adobo, *m.* repairing; dressing (for cloth, leather); (*cul.*) savoury sauce; pickling sauce; make-up, cosmetic

adocenado, *a.* ordinary; narrow-minded

adoctrinar, *v.t.* to instruct

adolecer, *v.i. irr.* to fall ill;. (*with de*) suffer from (diseases, defects); *v.r.* be sorry for, regret. See **conocer**

adolescencia, *f.* adolescence

adolescente, *a.* and *m.* and *f.* adolescent

adonde, *adv.* (*interr.* **adónde**) where to, whither (e.g. ¿ **Adónde fuiste ?** Where did you go to?)

adondequiera, *adv.* wherever

adopción, *f.* adoption

adoptador (-ra), *a.* adopting. *s.* adopter

adoptar, *v.t.* to adopt (children); make one's own, embrace (opinions); take (decisions)

adoptivo, *a.* adoptive

adoquín, *m.* cobble-stone; (*fig.*) blockhead

adoquinado, *m.* cobbling, paving. *m.* cobbled pavement

adoquinar, *v.t.* to pave with cobble-stones

ador, *m.* time for watering land (in irrigation districts)

adorable, *a.* adorable

adoración, *f.* worship, adoration. A. de los Reyes, Adoration of the Magi; Epiphany

adorador (-ra), *a.* adoring. *s.* adorer

adorar, *v.t.* to adore; worship; (*with en*) dote on; *v.i.* pray

adormecedor, *a.* soporific, drowsy

adormecer, *v.t. irr.* to make drowsy; soothe, lull; hush to sleep; *v.r.* go to sleep; go numb (limbs); (*with en*) persist in. See **conocer**

adormecimiento, *m.* sleepiness; lulling asleep; numbness

adormidera, *f.* poppy

adormitarse, *v.r.* to doze, take a nap, snooze

adornamiento, *m.* adornment, decoration

adornar, *v.t.* to deck, beautify; decorate; trim, embellish; adorn (of virtues, etc.)

adornista, *m.* decorator

adorno, *m.* decoration, adornment; ornament; trimming. **de**

a., ornamental; flowering (of shrubs)

adosar, *v.t.* to lean against

adquiridor (-ra), *a.* acquiring. *s.* acquirer

adquirir, *v.t. irr.* to acquire, get; achieve, obtain. *Pres. Ind.* adquiero, adquieres, adquiere, adquieren. *Pres. Subjunc.* adquiera, adquieras, adquiera, adquieran

adquisición, *f.* acquirement; acquisition. **poder de a.,** purchasing power

adquisidor (-ra), *a.* acquiring. *s.* acquirer, obtainer

adquisitivo, *a.* acquisitive

adquisividad, *f.* acquisitiveness

adrazo, *m.* salt-water still

adrede, *adv.* on purpose, intentionally

adrenalina, *f.* (*chem., med.*) adrenalin

adriático, *a.* Adriatic

adscribir, *v.t.* to ascribe, attribute; appoint (to a post, etc.)

adscripción, *f.* ascription, attribution; appointment

aduana, *f.* customs house, customs. **pasar por la a.,** to go through the customs

aduanero, *a.* customs, excise. *m.* customs officer; excise officer

aduar, *m.* small town composed of huts; gypsy encampment; Red Indian settlement

aducir, *v.t. irr.* to adduce, allege, cite; add. See **conducir**

aduendado, *a.* fairy-like, elfish

adueñarse, *v.r.* to appropriate, take possession (of)

adujar, *v.t.* (*naut.*) to coil (a rope, etc.)

adulación, *f.* adulation, flattery

adulador (-ra), *a.* fawning. *s.* flatterer

adular, *v.t.* to flatter, fawn upon, adulate

adularia, *f.* moonstone

adulteración, *f.* adulteration; falsification

adulterador (-ra), *a.* adulterant. *s.* adulterator; falsifier; coiner

adulterar, *v.i.* to commit adultery; *v.t.* adulterate; falsify

adulterino, *a.* adulterous; false

adulterio, *m.* adultery

adúltero (-ra), *a.* adulterous; corrupt. *s.* adulterer adulto (-ta), *a.* and *s.* adult

adunar, *v.t.* to join, unite; unify, combine

adusto, *a.* extremely hot (of countries); grave, austere; stand-offish, reserved

advenedizo, *a.* foreign, alien; strange, unknown; upstart; newly rich

advenimiento, *m.* advent, arrival; ascension (of throne)

advenir, *v.i. irr.* to come, arrive; happen, befall. See venir

adventicio, *a.* casual, accidental; (*bot.*) adventitious

adverbial, *a.* adverbial

adverbio, *m.* adverb

adversario (-ia), *s.* adversary, rival; opponent

adversidad, *f.* adversity, misfortune, sorrow

adverso, *a.* unfavourable, contrary, adverse; opposite

advertencia, *f.* warning; introduction, preface; remark

advertido, *a.* capable, clever; experienced; expert

advertir, *v.t. irr.* to observe, notice; warn; advise; feel, be conscious of; point out, indicate; inform; discover. See sentir

Adviento, *m.* (*ecc.*) Advent

adyacente, *a.* adjacent, near-by, neighbouring

aeración, *f.* aeration

aéreo, *a.* aerial; airborne; airy; air; aeronautic; unsubstantial, fantastic. correo a., air-mail. Líneas aéreas, Air Lines

aeriforme, *a.* aeriform

aerodinámica, *f.* aerodynamics

aeródromo, *m.* aerodrome

aerograma, *m.* wireless message; airgraph

aerolito, *m.* aerolite

aeronauta, *m.* and *f.* aeronaut, balloonist

aeronáutica, *f.* aeronautics

aeronáutico, *a.* aeronautic

aeronave, *f.* airship

aeroplano, *m.* aeroplane. a. de reacción, jet-propelled 'plane. a. sin motor, glider

aeropuerto, *m.* airport

aerostática, *f.* aerostatics

aerostático, *a.* aerostatic

aeróstato, *m.* dirigible

aeroterapia, *f.* (*med.*) aerotherapy

afabilidad, *f.* affability, geniality, friendliness

afable, *a.* affable, genial, pleasant

afamado, *a.* famous, well-known

afamar, *v.t.* to make famous

afán, *m.* effort; manual labour; desire, anxiety

afanar, *v.t.* to press, urge on; filch; *v.r.* toil, labour; (*with por*) work hard to, try to

afanoso, *a.* hard, laborious; hard-working; eager, anxious

afasia, *f.* (*med.*) aphasia

afear, *v.t.* to make ugly; distort, deform; blame; criticize

afección, *f.* fondness, affection; complaint, disease

afectación, *f.* affectation

afectado, *a.* affected

afectar, *v.t.* to feign, assume; affect; move, touch; (*law*) encumber

afectivo, *a.* affective

afecto, *a.* fond, affectionate; (*law*) encumbered; (*with prep. a*) addicted to. *m.* emotion, sentiment; affection

afectuosidad, *f.* affectionateness

afectuoso, *a.* affectionate, fond

afeitada, *f.* shave, shaving

afeitar, *v.t.* to shave; make up (complexion); adorn, beautify

afeite, *m.* cosmetic; make-up (for the complexion)

afelpado, *a.* velvet-like, plushy

afeminación, *f.* effeminacy; weakness, languor

afeminado, *a.* effeminate

afeminar, *v.t.* to make effeminate; weaken; *v.r.* grow effeminate

aferente, *a.* afferent

aféresis, *f.* (*gram.*) aphæresis

aferradamente, *adv.* tenaciously, persistently, obstinately

aferramiento, *m.* seizing, clutching; (*naut.*) furling; (*naut.*) grappling; mooring, anchoring; obstinacy

aferrar, *v.t.* to seize, clutch; (*naut.*) take in, furl; (*naut.*) grapple; *v.i.* (*naut.*) anchor; *v.r.* (*with con, en, a*) persist in, insist on

afestonado, *a.* festooned

afgano (-na), *a.* and *s.* Afghan

afianzamiento, *m.* fastening, fixing; propping; grasping; guarantee, security

afianzar, *v.t.* to fasten, fix; prop; guarantee, be security for; grasp

afición, *f.* propensity, inclination; fondness. **tomar a (a.)**, to take a liking for

aficionado (-da), *a.* amateur. *s.* amateur, fan, enthusiast. **ser a a.**, to be fond of, have a liking for

aficionar, *v.t.* to inspire liking or affection; *v.r.* (*with prep. a*) take a liking for, grow fond of; become an enthusiast for

afijo, *m.* (*gram.*) affix (prefix or suffix)

afiladera, *f.* whetstone, grindstone

afilado, *a.* sharp, keen (of edges)

afilador, *m.* grinder (of scissors, etc.); razor strop

afilalápices, *m.* pencil-sharpener

afilar, *v.t.* to sharpen; grind, whet; taper; *v.r.* grow thin; taper

afiliación, *f.* affiliation

afiliar, *v.t.* (*with prep. a*) to affiliate with; *v.r.* (*with prep. a*) become affiliated with; join, become a member of

afiligranado, *a.* filigree; delicate, fine; slender

afilón, *m.* steel, knife-sharpener; razor-strop

afín, *a.* near-by, contiguous; similar, related. *m.* and *f.* relation by marriage

afinador, *m.* tuning-key; tuner (of pianos, etc.)

afinar, *v.t.* to finish, perfect; (*fig.*) polish, refine; tune (musical instruments); refine (metals); *v.i.* sing in tune; *v.r.* grow refined

afinidad, *f.* affinity, analogy; relationship (by marriage); (*chem.*) affinity

afirmación, *f.* affirmation, statement

afirmadamente, *adv.* firmly

afirmar, *v.t.* to make firm; fix, fasten; affirm; *v.r.* steady oneself; hold on to

afirmativa, *f.* affirmative

afirmativo, *a.* affirmative

aflicción, *f.* affliction, grief

aflictivo, *a.* sorrowful, grievous

afligidamente, *adv.* sorrowfully

afligir, *v.t.* to sadden; afflict, trouble; *v.r.* lament, mourn

aflojamiento, *m.* slackening; loosening; diminution

aflojar, *v.t.* to slacken; loosen; *v.i.* relax, weaken; abate, diminish. **a. el paso**, to slow down

afluencia, *f.* crowd, concourse; eloquence, fluency

afluente, *a.* fluent, eloquent. *m.* tributary (river)

afluir, *v.i. irr.* to crowd, swarm; flow (into). See **huir**

aflujo, *m.* (*med.*) afflux

afonía, *f.* (*med.*) aphonia, loss of voice

aforar, *v.t.* to award privileges; value (goods); measure (water). *Irr. in first meaning only.* See **contar**

aforismo, *m.* aphorism

aforo, *m.* valuation (of goods); measurement (of water)

aforrador (-ra), *s.* one who lines jackets, etc.

aforrar, *v.t.* to line (clothes, etc.); *v.r.* wrap oneself up; (*fam.*) gormandize

afortunadamente, *adv.* luckily, fortunately

afortunado, *a.* lucky, fortunate; happy; stormy

afortunar, *v.t.* to bring luck to, make happy

afrancesado (-da), *a.* Francophile; Frenchified. *s.* Francophile

afrancesamiento, *m.* adoption of the French way of life; servile imitation of everything French

afrancesar, *v.t.* to make French, gallicize; Frenchify; *v.r.* become Francophile

afrenta, *f.* insult, affront; disgrace

afrentar, *v.t.* to insult; *v.r.* be ashamed

afrentoso, *a.* insulting, outrageous; disgraceful

africano (-na), *a.* and *s.* African

áfrico, *m.* south-west wind

afrodisíaco, *a.* and *m.* aphrodisiac

afrontar, *v.t.* to place opposite; confront; face (danger, etc.)

afuera, *adv.* outside, out.

afueras, *f. pl.* suburbs, outskirts

agachada, *f.* crouch, duck; jerk

agachadiza, *f.* (*orn.*) snipe

agachar, *v.t.* (*fam.*) bend, bow; *v.r.* (*fam.*) crouch down; lie low, hide

agalla, *f.* oak-apple; tonsil (gen. *pl.*); (*zool.*) gill (gen. *pl.*); *pl.* (*fam.*) gall, cheek

ágape, *m.* agape; banquet, feast
agareno, *a.* Mohammedan
agárico, *m.* (*bot.*) agaric
agarrada, *f.* (*fam.*) brawl, scuffle
agarradero, *m.* handle; heft; (*fam.*) influence, " pull "
agarrado, *a.* (*fam.*) tight-fisted, mean
agarrar, *v.t.* to grip, grasp; seize, take; (*fam.*) nab (jobs); *v.r.* grip, hold on
agarro, *m.* hold; grip, grasp
agarrotar, *v.t.* to garrotte; tighten (ropes, etc.); press, squeeze; *v.r.* go numb (limbs)
agasajar, *v.t.* to indulge, spoil, pet; receive kindly; entertain; caress
agasajo, *m.* indulgence, kindness; affability, geniality; entertainment; gift, offering
ágata, *f.* (*min.*) agate
agavillar, *v.t.* to bind in sheaves
agazapar, *v.t.* (*fam.*) to nab, catch; *v.r.* (*fam.*) squat, crouch
agencia, *f.* influence, agency
agenciar, *v.t.* to negotiate, arrange; procure, manage
agenda, *f.* notebook; agenda
agente, *m.* agent. a. de bolsa *or* a. de cambio, bill-broker. a. de negocios, business agent. a. de policía, policeman. a. fiscal, revenue officer
agestado, *a.* used generally with advs. bien *or* mal, well *or* ill-featured
agigantado, *a.* enormous, gigantic; outstanding, extraordinary
ágil, *a.* agile, nimble
agilidad, *f.* agility, nimbleness
agitación, *f.* shaking; agitation, excitement
agitador (-ra), *a.* stirring; agitating. *s.* agitator. *m.* stirrer, stirring rod
agitar, *v.t.* to stir; shake; agitate, excite
aglomeración, *f.* agglomeration
aglomerado, *m.* briquette
aglomerar, *v.t.* to agglomerate, amass
aglutinación, *f.* agglutination
aglutinar(se),*v.t.* and *v.r.* to stick, agglutinate
agnación, *f.* agnation
agnado (-da), *a.* and *s.* agnate
agnosticismo, *m.* agnosticism

agnóstico (-ca), *a.* and *s.* agnostic
agnusdéi, *m.* Agnus Dei; (*ant.*) small Spanish coin
agobiar, *v.t.* to bow, bend down; (*fig.*) weigh down, oppress; *v.r.* bend (beneath a weight)
agobio, *m.* bowing, bending down; oppression, burden, weight
agolparse, *v.r.* to rush, crowd, swarm
agonía, *f.* agony, anguish
agónico, *a.* dying; agonizing
agonizante, *a.* dying. *m.* monk of an Order which attends the dying
agonizar, *v.t.* to attend a dying person; (*fam.*) pester, annoy; *v.i.* be dying (gen. estar agonizando)
agorar, *v.t.* to prophesy, foretell
agorero (-ra), *a.* prophetic; ill-boding. *s.* seer, augur
agostarse, *v.t.* and *v.r.* to dry up, shrivel
agosto, *m.* August; harvest. (*fam.*) hacer su a., to make hay while the sun shines
agotable, *a.* exhaustible
agotado, *a.* exhausted; out of print (of books)
agotador, *a.* exhausting; exhaustive
agotamiento, *m.* exhaustion
agotar, *v.t.* to drain off (water); empty (a glass); exhaust; run through (money)
agraciado, *a.* graceful; pretty
agraciar, *v.t.* to lend grace to; make pretty; favour
agradable, *a.* agreeable, pleasant
agradar, *v.i.* to be pleasing, like, please (e.g. Me agrada su sinceridad, I like his sincerity
agradecer, *v.t. irr.* to be grateful for; thank for; (*fig.*) repay, requite. See conocer
agradecido, *a.* grateful; thankful
agradecimiento, *m.* gratitude; thankfulness
agrado, *m.* pleasure; desire, liking; amiability, affability
agrandar, *v.t.* to enlarge
agrario, *a.* agrarian
agravación, *f.* agravamiento, *m.* aggravation, worsening
agravador, *a.* aggravating; worsening; increasing
agravar, *v.t.* to aggravate, in-

crease; oppress (taxes, responsibilities); make worse; exaggerate; *v.r.* grow worse

agraviador (-ra), *a.* offensive. *s.* offender

agraviar, *v.t.* to offend; wrong; *v.r.* take offence, be insulted

agravio, *m.* offence, insult; wrong, injury

agraz, *m.* unripened grape; verjuice; *(fig.)* bitterness

agredir, *v.t.* to attack

agregación, *f.* association, aggregation; total, collection, aggregate

agregado, *m.* aggregate; assistant; attaché

agregar, *v.t.* to add; collect, amass; appoint (to a post)

agresión, *f.* aggression

agresivo, *a.* aggressive

agresor (-ra), *a.* and *s.* aggressor

agreste, *a.* rural, rustic; wild; uncouth, rude

agriar, *v.t.* to make bitter or sour; exasperate, provoke

agrícola, *a.* agricultural; *m.* and *f.* agriculturalist, farmer

agricultura, *f.* agriculture

agridulce, *a.* bitter-sweet

agrietarse, *v.r.* to crack, split

agrifolio, *m.* holly tree

agrimensor, *m.* land surveyor

agrimensura, *f.* land surveying

agrio, *a.* bitter, sour; rough, uneven (ground); brittle; sharp (of colour contrast); unsociable; disagreeable

agrisado, *a.* greyish

agrisetado, *a.* flowered (of materials)

agronomía, *f.* agronomy

agrónomo, *a.* agronomic. *m.* agronomist

agrupación, *f.* congregation, assembly; group; crowd; crowding, grouping

agrupar, *v.t.* to assemble, group; *v.r.* crowd, cluster

agrura, *f.* bitterness; sourness; asperity

agua, *f.* water; rain; slope of a roof; *pl.* shot or watered effect on silks, etc.; medicinal waters; waves; water (of precious stones). **a. abajo,** down-stream. **a. arriba,** upstream. **a. bendita,** holy water. **a. cruda,** hard water.

a. de colonia, eau de Cologne. **a. dulce,** fresh water. **a. fresca,** cold water. **a. nieve,** sleet. **a. oxigenada,** hydrogen peroxide. *(fig., fam.)* **estar con el a. al cuello,** to be in low water. *(fig., fam.)* **estar entre dos aguas,** to be between two fires. *(naut.)* **hacer a.,** to leak

aguacero, *m.* heavy fall of rain, shower

aguada, *f.* water supply on board ship; flood (in mines); watering station; *(art)* water colour

aguadero, *m.* animals' drinking or watering place

aguado, *a.* watery; abstemious; watered

aguador (-ra), *s.* water carrier or seller; drawer (of water)

aguafiestas, *m.* and *f. (fig., fam.)* wet blanket

aguafuerte, *f.* etching

aguaje, *m.* tide, waves; sea current; water supply on board ship; wake (of a ship)

aguamanil, *m.* wash-stand; water-jug, pitcher, ewer

aguamanos, *m.* water for washing the hands; pitcher

aguamarina, *f.* aquamarine

aguamiel, *f.* honey and water, hydromel

aguantable, *a.* tolerable, bearable

aguantar, *v.t.* to bear, tolerate, endure; restrain, resist, oppose; *v.r.* bear in silence, keep quiet

aguante, *m.* patience, endurance; resistance

aguar, *v.t.* to water down (wine, etc.); spoil (fun, etc.); *v.r.* be filled with water; be flooded; become watery or thin

aguardar, *v.t.* to await; expect; allow time to (debtors)

aguardentería, *f.* liquor shop, spirits store

aguardentoso, *a.* spirituous, containing aguardiente; hoarse, husky (of the voice)

aguardiente, *m.* spirituous liquor. **a. de caña,** rum

aguardo, *m.* ambush (for a hunter)

aguarrás, *m.* oil of turpentine

aguatinta, *f.* aquatint

aguatocha, *f.* pump (for water, etc.)

aguaturma, f. Jerusalem artichoke

agudeza, f. sharpness; keenness; distinctness; alertness, cleverness; witty sally, repartee; wit; swiftness

agudo, a. sharp; alert, clever; (geom., med.) acute; fine, keen; rapid; high-pitched; strong (of scents, etc.)

agüero, m. omen, sign; prophecy, prediction

aguerrido, a. veteran, war-hardened

aguerrir, v.t. defective, to harden to war; toughen

aguijada, f. goad, spur

aguijar, v.t. to prick with the goad; urge on, encourage (animals); incite, instigate; spur on; v.i. walk swiftly

aguijón, m. goad; sting; thorn, prickle; spur; incitement, stimulus. **tener aguijones,** to suffer from pins and needles

aguijonazo, m. prick with a goad

águila, f. eagle; master mind. **a. caudal** or **a. real,** royal eagle

aguileña, f. (bot.) columbine

aguileño, a. aquiline

aguilón, m. (arch.) gable; boom of a crane

aguilucho, m. eaglet

aguinaldo, m. Christmas present; New Year gift

aguja, f. needle; hand, pointer; hatpin; engraver's burin; switch; (r.w.) point; (r.w.) rail; obelisk; spire; bodkin; knitting needle; crochet hook; compass needle. pl. (bot.) plumelet. **a. capotera, a. de zurcir,** darning-needle. **a. de marear** (naut.), binnacle; mariner's compass. **a. de media,** knitting-needle. **a. espartera, a.** packing-needle

agujerear, v.t. to perforate, make holes in

agujero, m. hole, aperture; needle maker or seller; needle-case

agujeta, f. lace (for shoes, etc.); pl. muscular pains, aches; tip, gratuity

¡agur! interj. (fam.) Good-bye! Cheerio!

agusanarse, v.r. to become worm-infested

agustino (-na), a. and s. (ecc.) Augustinian

aguzadura, f. sharpening, grinding, whetting

aguzanieves, f. (orn.) wagtail

aguzar, v.t. to sharpen; grind, whet; stimulate, encourage; urge on, incite

ahebrado, a. fibrous

ahechadura, f. chaff (of grain)

ahembrado, a. effeminate

aherrojar, v.t. to put (a prisoner) in irons; oppress

aherrumbrar, v.t. to give the colour or taste of iron to; v.r. taste or look like iron; go rusty

ahí, adv. there; over there. **de a.,** thus, so. **por a.,** somewhere about; near at hand. (fam.) **a. te pudras,** dicky-seat

ahidalgado, a. gentlemanly; noble, generous

ahijado (-da), s. godchild; protégé

ahijar, v.t. to adopt (children); mother (animals); attribute, impute; v.i. bring forth offspring; (bot.) sprout

ahincado, a. earnest, eager

ahincar, v.t. to urge, press; v.r. hurry, hasten

ahinco, m. earnestness, eagerness

ahitar, v.t. to stuff with food; bore, disgust

ahito, a. full of food; (fig.) fed up. m. indigestion

ahogado (-da), a. drowned; suffocated; stuffy, unventilated; stifling. s. drowned person; one dead through suffocation

ahogamiento, m. drowning; suffocation

ahogar, v.t. to drown; suffocate; put out (the fire); stifle (yawns, etc.); suppress, extinguish; tire; over-water (plants); v.r. (naut.) sink, founder; drown; suffocate

ahogo, m. anxiety, grief; difficulty in breathing, oppression; asthma; embarrassment; suffocation; straitened circumstances

ahondar, v.t. to deepen; excavate, dig; go into thoroughly; go deep into, penetrate; v.r. subside (earth)

ahora, adv. now; very soon; just now, a short time ago. conjunc. whether; now. **a. bien,** well now, given that. **a. mismo,** immediately, at once. **por a.,** for the present

ahorcado (-da), s. hanged man

ahorcar, v.t. to execute by hanging, hang. (fam.) **a. los hábitos**, to cease to be an ecclesiastic or abandon the idea of being one

ahormar, v.t. to adjust, shape; break in new shoes; make a person see reason

ahorquillar, v.t. to prop up with forks (trees); v.r. grow forked

ahorrar, v.t. to free (slaves); save, economize; avoid, eschew; v.r. avoid; remove clothing

ahorro, m. economy, thrift; pl. savings

ahuchar, v.t. to hoard; expel, drive away

ahuecar, v.t. to hollow out; loosen; shake out; puff out, inflate; put on a solemn voice; hoe, dig; (fam.) v.r. puff oneself out; put on airs

ahumada, f. smoke signal

ahumado, a. smoked; smoky

ahumar, v.t. to smoke (herrings, etc.); fill with smoke; v.i. smoke, burn; v.r. be full of smoke; taste smoked; (fam.) get drunk

ahusado, a. spindle-shaped

ahuyentar, v.t. to frighten off; drive away; dismiss, banish (anxiety, etc.); v.r. flee

aína, adv. soon; easily; almost

airadamente, adv. wrathfully, angrily

airado, a. angry

airar, v.t. to annoy, anger; v.r. grow annoyed

aire, m. air; atmosphere (sometimes pl.); breeze, wind; bearing, appearance; vanity; horse's gait; futility, frivolity; grace, charm; gracefulness; (mus.) air; (mus.) tempo. a. **popular**, popular song. **al a. libre**, in the open air, out of doors. (fam.) **beber los aires (por)**, to yearn (for)

aireación, f. airing; ventilation

airear, v.t. to air; ventilate; aerate; v.r. take the air; catch a chill

airosidad, f. gracefulness; jauntiness

airoso, a. airy, open; windy, breezy, fresh; graceful; handsome; jaunty; victorious, successful

aislacionista, m. and f. (pol.) isolationist

aislado, a. isolated; remote; individual; single; (elec.) insulated

aislador, m. (phys.) insulator

aislamiento, m. isolation; (phys.) insulation

aislante, a. isolating; insulating

aislar, v.t. to isolate; (elec.) insulate; v.r. become a recluse; become isolated

¡ajá! interj. (fam.) Aha! Good!

ajaquecarse, v.r. to have a headache

ajar, v.t. to crease, crumple, spoil; humiliate; v.r. fade, wither (flowers)

ajedrecista, m. and f. chess player

ajedrez, m. chess

ajenjo, m. (bot.) wormwood; absinthe

ajeno, a. alien; belonging to another; various, diverse; free, exempt; unsuitable; irrelevant

ajetrear, v.t. to tire out, exhaust; v.r. be over-tired

ajetreo, m. exhaustion, fatigue

ajimez, m. (arch.) arched window divided by a pillar

ajo, m. garlic; (fam.) make up, paint; disreputable affair, shady business; curse, oath. (fam.) **revolver el a.**, to stir up trouble

ajorca, f. bracelet; slave bangle

ajornalar, v.t. to hire by the day

ajuar, m. trousseau; household equipment

ajustado, a. exact; tight-fitting; trim

ajustador (-ra), a. adjusting. s. adjuster. m. tight-fitting jacket

ajustamiento, m. adjustment; agreement

ajustar, v.t. to adjust; fit; arrange; make an agreement about; reconcile; settle (accounts); engage, employ; retain (a barrister); regulate; tune up (a motor); v.i. fit; v.r. adapt oneself. (fam.) a. **cuentas viejas**, to pay off old scores

ajuste, m. fitting; adjustment; agreement; arrangement; (print.) making-up. reconciliation; settlement; regulation; engagement, appointment

ajusticiado (-da), s. executed person

ajusticiar, v.t. to put to death

al (contraction of a + el). **1.** prep.

a + *m. def. art.*, to the, e.g. **Han ido al mar,** They have gone to the sea. 2. *prep. a* + *el* used as *dem. pron.*, to that, to the one, e.g. **Mi sombrero se parece mucho al que tiene Vd.,** My hat is very similar to the one you have. *al* + *infin.* means when, as, at the same time as, e.g. **Al llamar a la puerta la vi en el jardín,** As I was knocking at the door, I saw her in the garden

ala, *f.* (*zool.*) wing; row, line; brim (of a hat); eaves; (*arch., aer., mil., bot.*) wing; blade (of propeller); fin (of fish); *pl.* courage. **a. del corazón,** (*anat.*) auricle. **arrastrar el a.,** to woo, flirt with. (*fig.*) **cortar** (or **quebrar) las alas (a),** to clip a person's wings

Alá, *m.* Allah

alabador (-ra), *s.* praiser, extoller

alabanza, *f.* praise; eulogy

alabar, *v.t.* to praise; *v.r.* brag, boast

alabarda, *f.* halberd

alabardero, *m.* halberdier; (*theat.*) claque, clapper

alabastrino, *a.* alabastrine, alabaster

alabastro, *m.* alabaster

alacena, *f.* cupboard; recess; closet; safe (for food)

alacrán, *m.* scorpion

alacridad, *f.* alacrity, eagerness

alado, *a.* winged; feathered; (*fig.*) soaring

alambicado, *a.* sparing, frugal; subtle; euphuistic

alambicar, *v.t.* to distil; examine carefully, scrutinise; make over-subtle or euphuistic (of style)

alambique, *m.* still

alambrada, *f.* (*mil.*) wire-entanglement

alambrado, *m.* wire-netting; (*mil.*) wire-entanglement; wire cover

alambrar, *v.t.* to wire (fence)

alambre, *m.* wire; sheep bells. **a. espinoso,** barbed wire

alambrera, *f.* wire fence; wire-netting; wire cover

alambrista, *m.* and *f.* tight-rope walker

alameda, *f.* poplar wood or grove; avenue of poplars

álamo, *m.* poplar. **a. temblón,** aspen tree

alancear, *v.t.* to lance, spear

alano, *m.* mastiff

alarde, *m.* (*mil.*) parade; display, ostentation. **hacer a. de,** to brag about

alargamiento, *m.* lengthening; stretching

alargar, *v.t.* to lengthen; prolong; pass, hand (things); pay out (ropes, etc.); increase; *v.r.* go away, depart; be wordy, spread oneself; lengthen

alarido, *m.* yell, shout; shriek, scream; howl; yelp; cry (of a seagull)

alarma, *f.* alarm. **a. aérea,** air-raid warning

alarmante, *a.* alarming

alarmar, *v.t.* to give the alarm; frighten; *v.r.* be alarmed

alarmista, *m.* and *f.* alarmist

alazán, *a.* sorrel-coloured. *m.* sorrel horse

alazo, *m.* flap or stroke of the wings

alba, *f.* dawn; (*ecc.*) alb, vestment. **al a.,** at dawn

albacea, *m.* and *f.* executor, executrix; testator

albahaca, *f.* (*bot.*) sweet basil

albanega, *f.* hair-net; rabbit snare

albanés (-esa), *a.* and *s.* Albanian. *m.* Albanian language

albañal, *m.* common sewer

albañil, *m.* mason, bricklayer

albañilería, *f.* masonry; brick-laying

albar, *a.* white

albarda, *f.* pack-saddle

albardilla, *f.* small saddle; pad; small pillow; (*arch.*) coping

albaricoque, *m.* apricot

albaricoquero, *m.* apricot tree

albarrada, *f.* stone wall; mud fence

albatros, *m.* albatross

albayalde, *m.* white lead

albear, *v.i.* to become white, whiten

albedrío, *m.* free will; fancy, caprice

albéitar, *m.* veterinary surgeon; farrier

alberca, *f.* reservoir, tank; vat; artificial lake

albergar, *v.t.* to shelter; nourish,

harbour; *v.i.* and *v.r.* take refuge or shelter; lodge

albergue, *m.* shelter, refuge; den, lair; hospitality; lodging; asylum

albigense, *a.* and *m.* and *f.* Albigensian

albinismo, *m.* albinism

albo, *a.* pure white

albóndiga, *f.* forced meat ball, rissole

albor, *m.* whiteness; dawnlight, dawn. **a. de la vida,** life's dawning, childhood

alborada, *f.* dawn; réveillé; (*mil.*) dawn attack; (*mus.*) aubade

alborear, *v.i.* to grow light, dawn

albornoz, *m.* burnouse

alborotado, *a.* impulsive; turbulent; noisy; excitable

alborotar, *v.t.* to disturb; *v.i.* make a noise; be gay; *v.r.* riot; grow rough (sea)

alboroto, *m.* noise; confusion; tumult; riot; rejoicing, gaiety

alborozar, *v.t.* to overjoy, gladden; *v.r.* rejoice, be glad

alborozo, *m.* gladness, rejoicing, joy

albricias, *f. pl.* reward for bringer of good tidings. *interj.* ¡A.! Joy!

albufera, *f.* salt-lagoon

álbum, *m.* album

albúmina, *f.* albumin

albuminoso, *a.* albuminous

albur, *m.* (*icht.*) dace; chance, risk

alcabala, *f.* ancient tax on sales

alcachofa, *f.* artichoke

alcahueta, *f.* procuress, go-between

alcahuete, *m.* procurer, go-between, pimp, pander; (*fig., fam.*) protector, screen; (*fam.*) scandalmonger

alcahuetear, *v.t.* to procure, act as a go-between for; *v.i.* be a pimp or a procuress

alcaide, *m.* governor of a fortress (*ant.*); governor of a prison

alcalde, *m.* mayor; magistrate. (*fam.*) **tener el padre a,** to have a friend at court

alcaldesa, *f.* mayoress

alcaldía, *f.* office or authority of an alcalde

álcali, *m.* (*chem.*) alkali

alcalino, *a.* alkaline

alcaloide, *m.* (*chem.*) alkaloid

alcance, *m.* reaching, attainment; range (of firearms, etc.); scope; arm's length or reach; pursuit; stop press *or* extra edition (newspapers); (*com.*) deficit; importance; *pl.* talent; capacity. **al a. de la voz,** within call. **hombre de cortos alcances,** a limited, dull man

alcancía, *f.* money-box

alcanfor, *m.* camphor

alcanforado, *a.* camphorated

alcantarilla, *f.* little bridge; sewer; culvert; bed for electric cable

alcantarillado, *m.* sewage system; main sewer

alcanzable, *a.* obtainable; attainable

alcanzadizo, *a.* attainable, easily reached

alcanzar, *v.t.* to overtake; reach; range (of guns, etc.); attain, achieve; understand; (*fig.*) equal (in attainments); live at the same time as, be contemporaneous with; be capable of, be able; *v.i.* reach; share, participate in; be enough

alcaparra, *f.* (*bot.*) caper; caper bush

alcázar, *m.* fortress; royal residence, castle; (*naut.*) quarterdeck

alción, *m.* (*orn.*) kingfisher

alcista, *m.* and *f.* speculator (on Stock Exchange)

alcoba, *f.* bedroom; alcove, recess; Moorish flute

alcohol, *m.* alcohol; galena; eyeblack (cosmetic); spirits of wine. **a. desnaturalizado,** industrial alcohol, methylated spirit. **a. metílico,** wood alcohol

alcohólico, *a.* alcoholic

alcoholismo, *m.* (*med.*) alcoholism

alcoholizar, *v.t.* to alcoholize

alcor, *m.* hill; slope

Alcorán, *m.* Koran

alcornoque, *m.* cork tree; dunderhead, dolt

alcorza, *f.* (*cul.*) icing, sugarpaste

alcorzar, *v.t.* (*cul.*) to ice, cover with sugar; decorate, adorn

alcotana, *f.* pickaxe

alcubilla, *f.* reservoir, tank

alcurnia, *f.* lineage, family, descent

alcuza, *f.* oil-bottle; oil-can; cruet

aldaba, *f.* door knocker; bolt, latch; *pl.* protectors, influential helpers. (*fam.*) **tener buenas aldabas,** to have plenty of "pull"

aldabada, *f.* rap with the knocker; sudden shock

aldabeo, *m.* knocking

aldea, *f.* village

aldeano (-na), *a.* village; country, ignorant. *s.* villager; countryman, peasant

aldehído, *m.* (*chem.*) aldehyde

aleación, *f.* alloy

alear, *v.i.* to flutter, beat the wings; flap one's arms; recuperate, grow well; *v.t.* alloy

aleatorio, *a.* accidental, fortuitous

aleccionamiento, *m.* teaching, training, coaching

aleccionar, *v.t.* to teach, train, coach

aledaño, *a.* adjoining; border. *m.* boundary, border

alegación, *f.* allegation, statement

alegar, *v.t.* to allege, state; cite; *v.i.* (*law*) bring forward, adduce

alegato, *m.* (*law*) speech (for the prosecution or defence)

alegoría, *f.* allegory

alegórico, *a.* allegorical

alegorizar, *v.t.* to interpret allegorically, treat as an allegory

alegrar, *v.t.* to make happy, gladden, rejoice; adorn, beautify; stir (fires); *v.r.* be glad, rejoice; (*fam.*) be merry (tipsy)

alegre, *a.* joyful, glad; cheerful, gay; bright (colours, etc.); pretty, attractive; (*fam.*) risqué; (*fam.*) flirtatious, light

alegría, *f.* joy, gladness; cheerfulness, gaiety; *pl.* public rejoicings

alegrón, *m.* sudden unexpected joy; (*fam.*) flash of light. *a.* (*fam.*) flirtatious

alejamiento, *m.* placing at a distance, removal; withdrawal

alejandrino (-na), *a.* and *s.* Alexandrian (Egypt). *a.* and *m.* Alexandrine (metre)

alejar, *v.t.* to place at a distance, remove; withdraw; ward off (dangers, etc.); *v.r.* depart, go away; withdraw

alelar, *v.t.* to make silly or stupid

aleluya, *m.* or *f.* alleluia. *m.* Eastertide. *f.* small Easter cake; (*fam.*) daub, poor painting; (*fam.*) doggerel; joy, rejoicing

alemán (-ana), *a.* and *s.* German. *m.* German language. **a. sudete,** Sudeten German

alentada, *f.* deep breath

alentado, *a.* valiant, spirited; proud

alentador, *a.* encouraging, inspiring, stimulating

alentar, *v.i. irr.* to breathe; *v.t.* encourage, inspire; *v.r.* be encouraged. See **sentar**

alerce, *m.* larch tree and wood

alergia, *f.* allergy

alero, *m.* projecting roof; splashboard (of carriages); eaves; gable end

alerón, *m.* (*aer.*) aileron

alerta, *adv.* watchfully. *interj.* Take care! Look out! **estar ojo a.,** to be on the watch

alerto, *a.* watchful, alert

aleta, *f. dim.* small wing; fin

aletargado, *a.* lethargic; comatose

aletargamiento, *m.* lethargy

aletargar, *v.t.* to cause lethargy; *v.r.* become lethargic

aletazo, *m.* flapping, beating (of wings); (*fam.*) theft

aletear, *v.i.* to flap the wings, flutter; move the arms up and down; become convalescent

aleteo, *m.* fluttering, flapping of wings; beating, palpitation (of heart)

aleve, *a.* See **alevoso**

alevosía, *f.* (*law*) malice; treachery

alevoso, *a.* (*law*) malicious; treacherous

alfabético, *a.* alphabetical

alfabeto, *m.* alphabet. **a. manual,** deaf-and-dumb alphabet

alfalfa, *f.* (*bot.*) lucerne

alfanje, *m.* cutlass

alfaque, *m.* (gen. *pl.*) sand-bank, bar

alfar, *m.* potter's workshop; pottery, earthenware

alfarería, *f.* pottery shop; potter's workshop; potter's craft

alfarero, *m.* potter

alféizar, *m.* (*arch.*) embrasure, recess; sill, ledge (of a window, etc.)

alfeñique, *m.* (*cul.*) icing, sugar-paste; (*fam.*) affectation

alferecía, *f.* epilepsy

alférez, *m.* (*mil.*) ensign; second lieutenant; lieutenant. (*nav.*) **a. de fragata,** sub-lieutenant. (*nav.*) **a. de navío,** lieutenant

alfil, *m.* bishop (in chess)

alfiler, *m.* pin; brooch with a pin; tiepin; *pl.* pin-money, dress-allowance; (*fig., fam.*) **no estar uno con sus alfileres,** to have a slate loose. (*fam.*) **vestido de veinticinco alfileres,** dressed up to the nines

alfilerazo, *m.* pin-prick

alfiletero, *m.* needle-case

alfombra, *f.* carpet; rug

alfombrado, *m.* carpeting

alfombrar, *v.t.* to carpet

alfombrilla eléctrica, *f.* electric pad or blanket

alfombrista, *m.* carpet merchant; layer of carpets

alfonsino, *a.* Alphonsine (from Spanish kings named Alphonso)

alforfón, *m.* buckwheat

alforja, *f.* saddle-bag; (*mil.*) knapsack

alforza, *f.* (*sew.*) tuck; (*fam.*) scar

alforzar, *v.t.* (*sew.*) to tuck

alga, *f.* alga, seaweed

algalia, *f.* civet

algarabía, *f.* Arabic; (*fam.*) gibberish; din of voices, uproar

algarada, *f.* troop of horse; uproar, hubbub; outcry

algarroba, *f.* (*bot.*) carob bean

algazara, *f.* Moorish war cry; rejoicing, merriment; noise, clamour

álgebra, *f.* algebra; art of bone setting

algebraico, *a.* algebraic

algidez, *f.* icy coldness

álgido, *a.* icy cold

algo, *indef. pron.* some, something (e.g. **Se ve que hay a. que le molesta,** You can see that something is irritating him). *adv.* somewhat, a bit

algodón, *m.* cotton plant; cotton flower; cotton fabric. **a. en rama,** cotton-wool. **a. hidró-filo,** absorbent cotton wool. **a. pólvora,** nitro cellulose

algodonal, *m.* cotton plantation

algodonero (-ra), *a.* cotton. *s.* cotton merchant

alguacil, *m.* policeman, constable; (*ant.*) city governor; short-legged spider

alguien, *indef. pron.* someone, somebody, e.g. **Dime si viene a.,** Tell me if anyone comes

algún, *abb.* of **alguno** bef. *m. sing.* noun, e.g. **a. libro**

alguno, *a.* (*abb.* **algún** bef. *m. sing.*) some, any. *indef. pron.* someone, somebody; *pl.* some, some people. **alguno que otro,** a few

alhaja, *f.* jewel; ornament; treasure, precious object; (*fam.*) gem, excellent person (also ironic, e.g. **Es una a.,** He's a fine fellow)

alhajar, *v.t.* to adorn with jewels, bejewel; furnish, equip

alharaca, *f.* vehemence, demonstration, fuss (gen. *pl.*)

alhelí, *m.* wallflower

alheña, *f.* (*bot.*) privet; henna

alhóndiga, *f.* corn exchange; public granary

aliacán, *m.* jaundice

aliado (-da), *a.* allied. *s.* ally

alianza, *f.* alliance; pact, agreement; relationship (by marriage); sum total, whole (of factors, etc.); wedding-ring

aliarse, *v.r.* to join together, become allies; be associated

alicaído, *a.* drooping; (*fam.*) weak, exhausted; discouraged, downhearted; come down in the world

alicates, *m. pl.* pincers, pliers

aliciente, *m.* attraction, inducement

alícuota, *a.* (*f.*) aliquot; proportional. **partes alícuotas,** aliquot parts

alienación, *f.* alienation

alienado, *a.* insane, mad

alienar, *v.t.* See **enajenar**

alienista, *m.* and *f.* (*med.*) alienist

aliento, *m.* breathing; breath; courage, spirit; encouragement. **cobrar a.,** to regain one's breath; take heart. **de un a.,** in one breath; without stopping

alifafe, *m.* (*fam.*) ailment; tumour on horse's hock

aligación, *f.* binding together, alligation

aligátor, *m.* alligator

aligeramiento, *m.* lightening, reduction in weight

aligerar, *v.t.* to lighten, make less heavy; quicken, hasten; ease, alleviate; moderate; shorten, abbreviate

alígero, *a.* (*poet.*) winged; fleet, swift

alimaña, *f.* destructive animal

alimentación, *f.* nourishment; feeding

alimentar, *v.t.* to feed; nourish; encourage, foment; assist, aid; keep, support

alimenticio, *a.* nourishing; feeding

alimento, *m.* food, nourishment; stimulus, encouragement; *pl.* alimony; allowance

alindar, *v.t.* to mark the boundary of; beautify, adorn; *v.i.* border, be contiguous

alineación, *f.* alignment

alinear, *v.t.* to align, range in line; dress (troops); *v.r.* fall into line

aliñar, *v.t.* to decorate, adorn; (*cul.*) season; prepare; set (bones)

aliño, *m.* decoration, ornament; preparation; condiment, seasoning; setting (bones)

aliquebrado, *a.* broken-winged; (*fam.*) down in the mouth

alisador (-ra), *a.* smoothing; polishing. *s.* polisher

alisar, *v.t.* to smooth; polish; sleek; plane; comb lightly

alisios, *m. pl.* trade winds

aliso, *m.* alder tree and wood

alistador, *m.* enroller

alistamiento, *m.* enlistment; conscription; enrolment

alistar, *v.t.* to enrol, list; enlist; conscript; prepare, get ready; *v.r.* enrol; (*mil.*) enlist; get ready

aliviar, *v.t.* to lighten; alleviate, mitigate; relieve; ease; quicken (one's step); hasten, speed up; steal

alivio, *m.* lightening; relief; alleviation; ease

aljaba, *f.* quiver (for arrows)

aljamía, *f.* Moorish name for Spanish language; work written in Spanish language, but transcribed in Arabic characters

aljibe, *m.* tank, cistern; watership or tanker

aljófar, *m.* small irregular shaped pearl; dew-drop, raindrop. tear drop

aljofarar, *v.t.* to dew

aljofifa, *f.* floorcloth.

alma, *f.* soul; living person; essence, core; vivacity, animation; energy, vitality; spirit, ghost; core (of a rope). a. **de Dios,** simple soul, kind person. a. **en pena,** soul in purgatory. ¡**A. mía!** My darling! con todo **el a.,** with all my heart. **Lo siento en el a.,** I feel it deeply

almacén, *m.* warehouse; store, shop

almacenaje, *m.* cost of storage

almacenar, *v.t.* to store; put in store; hoard

almacenero, *m.* warehouseman, storekeeper

almacenista, *m.* and *f.* owner of a store; assistant, salesman (saleswoman)

almáciga, *f.* mastic; tree plantation or nursery

almadraba, *f.* tunny fishery; net for tunny fishing

almagre, *m.* (*min.*) red ochre; stain, mark

almanaque, *m.* calendar, almanac

almeja, *f.* (*icht.*) clam

almena, *f.* merlon (of a battlement)

almenaje, *m.* battlements, merlons

almenara, *f.* beacon fire

almendra, *f.* almond; kernel; crystal drop (of chandeliers, etc.); cocoon; bean (of cocoa tree, etc.). a. **garapiñada,** sugar almond

almendrado, *a.* almond-shaped

almendro, *m.* almond tree

almendruco, *m.* green almond

almete, *m.* casque, helmet; helmeted soldier

almiar, *m.* haystack, hayrick

almíbar, *m.* sugar syrup; nectar

almibarado, *a.* syrupy; (*fam.*) sugary

almibarar, *v.t.* to coat with sugar; preserve (fruit) in syrup; flatter with sweet words

almidón, *m.* starch

almidonado, *a.* starched; (*fig.*, *fam.*) stiff, unbending; prim

almidonar, *v.t.* to starch

alminar, *m.* minaret (of mosque)

almiranta, *f.* admiral's wife; flagship

almirantazgo, *m.* Admiralty; admiralship; Admiralty Court

almirante, *m.* admiral

almirez, *m.* brass mortar

almizcle, *m.* musk

almizcleño, *a.* musk (of scents)

almizclero, *a.* musky. *m.* (*zool.*) musk-deer

almocafre, *m.* (*agr.*) hoe; trowel, dibble

almohada, *f.* pillow; pillowcase; cushion. (*fam.*) aconsejarse *or* consultar, con la a., to think over (a matter) carefully, sleep on it.

almohadilla, *f.*, *dim.* small cushion; lace or sewing cushion; pin cushion

almohadillado, *a.* cushioned; padded

almohaza, *f.* curry-comb

almoneda, *f.* auction; furniture sale

almonedear, *v.t.* to auction; sell off (furniture)

almorranas, *f. pl.* (*med.*) hæmorrhoids

almorávid, *a.* and *m.* and *f.* Almoravide (name of a powerful Moorish tribe)

almorzar, *v.i.* *irr.* to lunch; breakfast. See forzar

almuecín, almuédano, *m.* muezzin

almuerzo, *m.* luncheon;· breakfast (not so usual)

alocado, *a.* feather-brained, reckless; crazy, wild

alocución, *f.* allocution, address, harangue

áloe, *m.* (*bot.*) aloe

alojado (-da), *m.* billeted soldier. *s.* lodger

alojamiento, *m.* lodging; dwelling; (*mil.*) billeting; (*naut.*) steerage; camp, encampment

alojar, *v.t.* to lodge; billet, quarter (troops); insert, introduce; *v.i.* and *v.r.* lodge; live, dwell

alón, *m.* plucked wing of a bird

alondra, *f.* (*orn.*) lark

alópata, *a.* (*med.*) allopathic. *m.* and *f.* allopathist

alopatía, *f.* (*med.*) allopathy

alpaca, *f.* alpaca (animal and fabric); nickel silver

alpargata, *f.* sandal with hemp sole

alpargatero (-ra), *s.* manufacturer or seller of alpargatas

alpestre, *a.* Alpine (also *bot.*); rock (of plants); mountainous, lofty

alpinismo, *m.* mountaineering

alpinista, *m.* and *f.* mountaineer, climber

alpino, *a.* Alpine

alpiste, *m.* bird seed

alquería, *f.* farmstead

alquiladizo, *a.* rentable, hirable

alquilador (-ra), *s.* hirer

alquilamiento, *m.* See alquiler

alquilar, *v.t.* to rent; hire out; hire; *v.r.* hire oneself out, serve on a wage basis

alquiler, *m.* hiring out; renting; rental; hire; wages. de a., for hire, on hire

alquimia, *f.* alchemy

alquímico, *a.* alchemic

alquimista, *m.* alchemist

alquitrán, *m.* tar, pitch. a. mineral, coal tar

alquitranado, *a.* tarred. *m.* (*naut.*) tarpaulin

alrededor, *adv.* around, round about. a. de, around; approximately, about (e.g. a. de dos libras, about £2)

alrededores, *m. pl.* environs, surrounding country

alsaciano (-na), *a.* and *s.* Alsatian

alta, *f.* certificate of discharge from hospital

altanería, *f.* hawking; haughtiness, disdain; superciliousness

altanero, *a.* soaring, high-flying (of birds); supercilious; haughty, disdainful

altar, *m.* altar. a. mayor, high altar

altavoz, *m.* loudspeaker; megaphone

altearse, *v.r.* to rise, grow steep (of land)

alterabilidad, *f.* alterability, changeability

alteración, *f.* alteration, change; debasement (of coinage); agitation

alterar, *v.t.* to change, alter; debase (coinage); disturb, agitate; *v.r.* grow angry; become excited

altercación, *f.*, altercado, *m.* altercation, quarrel

altercar(se), *v.i.* and *v.r.* to quarrel, dispute, altercate

alternación, *f.* alternation

alternado, *a.* alternate

alternador, *a.* alternating. *m.* (*elec.*) alternator

alternante, *a.* alternating

alternar, *v.t.* to alternate; make one's début as a **matador;** *v.i.* alternate; (*with con*) have dealings with, know

alternativa, *f.* alternative, option; service performed by turns; alternation

alternativo, *a.* alternative

alterno, *a.* alternative; (*bot.*) alternate

alteza, *f.* altitude, height; sublimity, perfection; (**A.**) Highness (title)

altibajo, *m.* embossed velvet; *pl.* (*fam.*) rough ground; (*fam.*) vicissitudes of fortune

altillo, *m.* hillock, eminence; garret, attic

altímetro, *m.* (*aer.*) altimeter

altiplanicie, *f.* plateau; highland

altisonante, *a.* sonorous; sublime; high-flown, pompous

altitud, *f.* altitude, height

altivez, *f.* arrogance, haughtiness

altivo, *a.* arrogant, haughty

alto, *a.* high; tall; difficult, arduous; sublime; deep; most serious (of crimes, etc.); dear (of price); small, early (hours). *m.* height; eminence, hill; storey, floor; (*mil.*) halt. *adv.* up, above, on high; loudly. *interj.* ¡ A.! (*mil.*) Halt! (*mil.*) A. Mando, High Command. **las altas horas de la noche,** the small (or early) hours. **en alta voz,** in a loud voice. **en alto,** on high; up above. **hacer alto,** to halt, stop

altoparlante, *m.* (*rad.*) loudspeaker

altozano, *m.* mound, hillock; view-point, open space

altramuz, *m.* (*bot.*) lupin

altruismo, *m.* altruism

altruista, *a.* altruistic. *m.* and *f.* altruist

altura, *f.* height; altitude; (*geom.*) altitude or height; top, peak; sublimity; tallness

alubia, *f.* (*bot.*) French bean

alucinación, *f.*, **alucinamiento,** *m.* hallucination

alucinador, *a.* hallucinatory, deceptive

alucinar, *v.t.* to dazzle, fascinate; deceive

alud, *m.* avalanche

aludir, *v.i.* to allude (to); refer (to), cite

alumbrado, *m.* lighting; *pl.* illuminati

alumbramiento, *m.* lighting, supply of light; childbirth

alumbrar, *v.t.* to light, illuminate; give sight to the blind; instruct, teach; inflict (blows); hoe vine roots; *v.i.* give birth to a child; *v.r.* (*fam.*) grow tipsy

alumbre, *m.* alum

aluminio, *m.* aluminium

alumno (-na), *s.* ward, adopted child; pupil. **a. externo,** day pupil. **a. interno,** boarder

alusión, *f.* allusion

alusivo, *a.* allusive, suggestive; hinting

aluvial, *a.* alluvial

aluvión, *m.* alluvium. **de a.,** alluvial

alvéolo, *m.* alveolus; socket (of a tooth)

alza, *f.* rise (of temperature, etc.); increase (in price); front sight (of guns)

alzacuello, *m.* high collar, clergyman's collar; neck-stock

alzada, *f.* horse's stature mountain pasture; (*law*) appeal

alzado, *a.* fraudulent (of bankruptcy); fixed (of price). *m.* theft; (*arch.*) front elevation

alzamiento, *m.* raising, lifting; higher bid (at auction); rising, rebellion; fraudulent bankruptcy

alzapaño, *m.* curtain holder

alzaprima, *f.* lever; wedge; bridge (of string instruments)

alzar, *v.t.* to raise; lift up; elevate (the Host); steal, remove; hide; gather in the harvest; build, construct; (*naut.*) heave; *v.r.* rise (of temperature, mercury, price, etc.); make a fraudulent bankruptcy; (*law*) appeal; (*with con*) run off with, steal. (*naut.*) a. la vela, to set sail

allá, *adv.* there; to that place. **más a.,** farther on, beyond. Used in conjunction with phrases of time, indicates remoteness, e.g. A. en tiempos de los Reyes Católicos, Long ago in the time of the Catholic Monarchs

allanamiento, *m.* levelling, flattening; condescension, affability; acceptance of a judicial finding

allanar, *v.t.* to level, flatten; overcome (difficulties); soothe; break into (a house, etc.); give entrance to the police; *v.r.* collapse (buildings, etc.); abide by, adapt oneself (to); condescend, be affable

allegado (-da), *a.* near, allied; related. *s.* follower, ally

allegar, *v.t.* to gather, collect; draw nearer; (*agr.*) reap; add; *v.i.* arrive

allende, *adv.* beyond; besides. **de a. el mar,** from beyond the sea

allí, *adv.* there; to that place, thereto; thereupon, then. **por a.,** through there; that way

ama, *f.* mistress of the house; owner; housekeeper; wet nurse. **a. de leche,** foster-mother. **a. de llaves** *or* **a. de gobierno,** housekeeper. **a. seca,** children's nurse

amabilidad, *f.* lovableness; kindness; niceness, goodness, helpfulness

amable, *a.* lovable; kind; nice, good, helpful

amador (-ra), *a.* loving. *s.* lover, admirer

amadrigar, *v.t.* to welcome, receive well; *v.r.* go into a burrow or lair; go into seclusion

amaestrar, *v.t.* to train, instruct; tame; break in (horses)

amagar, *v.t.* and *v.i.* to threaten; *v.t.* show signs of (diseases, etc.); *v.r.* (*fam.*) hide

amainar, *v.t.* (*naut.*) to take in the sails; *v.i.* drop (of the wind); *v.i.* and *v.t.* relax (efforts, etc.)

amaine, *m.* dropping, abatement (of the wind)

amalgama, *f.* (*chem.*) amalgam (also *fig.*)

amalgamación, *f.* amalgamation

amalgamar, *v.t.* to amalgamate; *v.r.* be amalgamated

amamantamiento, *m.* suckling, nursling

amamantar, *v.t.* to suckle

amancebamiento, *m.* liaison, concubinage

amancebarse, *v.r.* to form a liaison

amancillar, *v.t.* to discredit, dishonour; tarnish; stain

amanecer, *v.i. irr.* to dawn; arrive *or* be somewhere *or* be doing, at dawn (e.g. **Amanecimos en el barco,** Dawn came while we were in the ship. **Amanecimos escribiendo la carta,** The day broke as we were writing the letter); appear at daybreak; begin to appear. *m.* dawn, daybreak. See **conocer**

amanerado, *a.* mannered; affected

amaneramiento, *m.* manneredness; mannerism

amanerarse, *v.r.* to acquire mannerisms or tricks of style; become affected

amanojar, *v.t.* to make into bunches

amansador (-ra), *a.* soothing, calming. *s.* appeaser

amansamiento, *m.* taming; appeasement; soothing; breaking in (horses)

amansar, *v.t.* to tame; appease, moderate; soothe, pacify; break in (horses)

amante, *a.* loving. *m.* and *f.* lover

amanuense, *m.* and *f.* amanuensis, secretary, clerk

amañar, *v.t.* to execute with skill; *v.r.* grow skilful

amaño, *m.* skill, dexterity; *pl.* schemes, intrigues; tools, equipment

amapola, *f.* poppy

amar, *v.t.* to love

amaranto, *m.* (*bot.*) amaranth

amarar, *v.i.* to alight on the water (of hydroplanes)

amargar, *v.i.* to taste or be bitter; *v.t.* make bitter; embitter

amargo, *a.* bitter; embittered; grievous, sad. *m.* bitterness; *pl.* bitters

amargor, *m.,* **amargura,** *f.* bitter taste, bitterness; trouble, affliction, pain

amaricado, *a.* (*fam.*) effeminate

amarilis, *f.* (*bot.*) amaryllis; (*poet.*) shepherdess

amarillear, *v.i.* to look yellow; turn yellow; tend to yellow

amarillento, *a.* yellowish, turning yellow

amarilleo, *m.* yellowing

amarillez, *f.* yellowness

amarillo, *a.* and *m.* yellow

amarra, *f.* (*naut.*) cable, thick rope

amarradero, *m.* (*naut.*) mooring berth; mooring-post; hitching-post or ring

amarraje, *m.* (*naut.*) mooring charge

amarrar, *v.t.* to tie up, hitch; moor

amarre, *m.* mooring; hitching

amartelar, *v.t.* to make jealous; court, woo, make love to; *v.r.* be jealous; fall madly in love

amartillar, *v.t.* to hammer, knock; cock (firearms)

amasadera, *f.* kneading-trough

amasador (-ra), *a.* kneading. *s.* kneader

amasar, *v.t.* to knead; massage; scheme, plot

amasijo, *m.* (*cul.*) dough; kneading; portion of plaster or mortar; (*fam.*) hotchpotch, mixture; scheme, plot

amatista, *f.* amethyst

amatividad, *f.* amativeness

amatorio, *a.* amatory

amayorazgar, *v.t.* (*law*) to entail

amazacotado, *a.* heavy, dense; (*fig.*) stodgy (of writings, etc.)

amazona, *f.* Amazon; independent woman; woman rider; woman's riding habit

ambages, *m. pl.* maze, intricate paths; circumlocutions

ámbar, *m.* amber. **a. gris,** ambergris

ambarino, *a.* amber

ambición, *f.* ambition

ambicionar, *v.t.* to long for; desire eagerly; be ambitious to

ambicioso, *a.* ambitious; eager, desirous

ambidextro, *a.* ambidextrous

ambiente, *a.* ambient, surrounding. *m.* air, atmosphere; environment

ambigú, *m.* cold buffet; buffet (in theatres, etc.)

ambigüedad, *f.* ambiguity

ambiguo, *a.* ambiguous

ámbito, *m.* precincts; boundary, limit; compass, scope

amblar, *v.i.* to pace (of a horse)

ambos, *a., m. pl.* **ambas,** *a. f. pl.*

both, e.g. **ambas casas,** both houses

ambrosíaco, *a.* ambrosial

ambrosiano, *a.* Ambrosian

ambulancia, *f.* ambulance. **a. de correos,** train post office. **a. fija,** field-hospital

ambulante, *a.* walking; travelling, wandering

amedrentador, *a.* frightening; terrible; intimidating

amedrentar, *v.t.* to frighten, scare; intimidate

ameliorar, *v.t.* to better, improve

amelonado, *a.* melon-shaped; (*fam.*) madly in love

amén, *m.* amen, so be it. **a. de,** besides, in addition to. (*fam.*) **en un decir a.,** in a trice

amenaza, *f.* threat

amenazador, amenazante, *a.* menacing, threatening

amenazar, *v.t.* to threaten; *v.t.* and *v.i.* presage, be pending

amenguamiento, *m.* lessening, diminution; discredit; loss of prestige

amenguar, *v.t.* to lessen, decrease; dishonour, discredit

amenidad, *f.* amenity; agreeableness

amenizar, *v.t.* to make pleasant or attractive

ameno, *a.* pleasant; entertaining; agreeable, delightful

amento, *m.* (*bot.*) catkin

americana, *f.* (man's) jacket

americanismo, *m.* Americanism

americano, *a.* American

ametrallador, *m.* machine-gunner

ametralladora, *f.* machine-gun

ametrallar, *v.t.* to machine-gun

amianto, *m.* (*min.*) amianthus, asbestos

amiba, *f.* (*zool.*) amœba

amicísimo, *a. sup.* **amigo,** most friendly

amiga, *f.* woman friend; mistress, lover; dame, schoolmistress; dame school

amigabilidad, *f.* friendliness, amicability

amigable, *a.* friendly, amicable; harmonious; suitable

amígdala, *f.* tonsil

amigdalitis, *f.* tonsillitis

amigo (-ga), *a.* friendly; fond, addicted. *s.* friend. *m.* lover.

(*fam.*) **ser muy a. de,** to be very friendly with; be very keen on or fond of

amilanado, *a.* cowed, spiritless

amilanar, *v.t.* to terrify, intimidate; *v.r.* grow discouraged

aminorar, *v.t.* to diminish, lessen

amir, *m.* ameer, Arab prince or chief

amistad, *f.* friendship; liaison; favour; *pl.* acquaintances, friends

amistar, *v.t.* to introduce, make known to each other; bring about a reconciliation between or with

amistoso, *a.* friendly

amito, *m.* (*ecc.*) amice

amnesia, *f.* amnesia

amnistia, *f.* amnesty

amnistiar, *v.t.* to concede an amnesty, pardon

amo, *m.* head of the house; master; owner; overlord: overseer. **Nuestro A.** Our Lord. (*fam.*) **ser el a. del cotarro,** to rule the roost

amodorramiento, *m.* stupor, deep sleep

amodorrarse, *v.r.* to fall into a stupor; fall into a heavy sleep

amoladera, *f.* whetstone

amolador, *m.* scissor-grinder; knife-grinder; sharpener

amoladura, *f.* grinding, whetting, sharpening

amolar, *v.t. irr.* to grind, sharpen; (*fam.*) pester, annoy. See **colar**

amoldar, *v.t.* to mould; adjust; *v.r.* adapt oneself

amonedación, *f.* coinage, minting

amonedar, *v.t.* to coin, mint

amonestación, *f.* warning; advice. **correr las amonestaciones,** to publish banns of marriage

amonestador (-ra), *a.* warning, admonitory. *s.* admonisher

amonestar, *v.t.* to warn; advise; rebuke; (*ecc.*) publish bans of marriage

amoníaco, *m.* ammonia

amontillado, *m.* kind of pale, dry sherry

amontonamiento, *m.* accumulation; gathering, collection; piling up, heaping

amontonar, *v.t.* to pile up, heap; gather; collect; accumulate; *v.r.* (*fam.*) fly into a rage

amor, *m.* love; beloved; willingness, pleasure; *pl.* love affairs; caresses. **a. propio,** self-esteem; vanity. (*fam.*) **con mil amores,** with great pleasure. **por a. de,** for love of; for the sake of

amoral, *a.* amoral

amoralidad, *f.* amorality

amoratado, *a.* livid, bluish

amorcillo, *m.,* *dim.* little love; unimportant love affair; Cupid

amordazamiento, *m.* muzzling; gagging

amordazar, *v.t.* to muzzle; gag; prevent speaking

amorfo, *a.* amorphous

amorío, *m.* (*fam.*) wooing, love making; *pl.* love affairs

amoroso, *a.* loving; gentle; mild, balmy

amorrar, *v.i.* (*fam.*) to hang one's head; sulk, be sullen

amortajar, *v.t.* to wrap in a shroud; enshroud

amortiguador, *m.* (*mech.*) shock absorber. (*aut.*) **a. de los muelles,** shock-absorber

amortiguamiento, *m.* softening, deadening; mitigation, lessening

amortiguar, *v.t.* to soften, deaden; absorb (shocks); moderate, mitigate; soften (colours)

amortización, *f.* amortization

amortizar, *v.t.* to amortize; recover, redeem; suppress, abolish (posts)

amoscarse, *v.r.* (*fam.*) to be piqued or annoyed; become agitated

amostazar, *v.t.* (*fam.*) to annoy; *v.i.* become peeved

amotinador (-ra), *a.* mutinous, rebellious. *s.* rebel, mutineer; rioter

amotinar, *v.t.* to incite to rebellion; unbalance, unhinge (mind); *v.r.* rebel; riot; (*fig.*) unhinged

amovible, *a.* movable, removable; removable (of officials, etc.)

amovilidad, *f.* movability, removability; liability to discharge or dismissal

amparador (-ra), *a.* protective; sheltering. *s.* protector, defender, helper; shelterer

amparar, *v.t.* to protect, favour, help; shelter; *v.r.* take refuge, take shelter; defend oneself

amparo, *m.* shelter, refuge; protection, favour, help; defence

amper, *m.* (*elec.*) ampere

amperímetro, *m.* (*elec.*) ammeter

amperio, *m.* (*elec.*) ampere

ampliable, *a.* amplifiable

ampliación, *f.* enlargement, increase, extension; (*phot.*) enlargement

ampliador (**-ra**), *a.* enlarging. *s.* enlarger

ampliadora, *f.* (*phot.*) enlarger

ampliar, *v.t.* to extend, enlarge, increase; (*phot.*) enlarge

amplificación, *f.* extension, amplification; (*phot.*) enlargement

amplificar, *v.t.* to enlarge; extend; increase; amplify, expatiate upon

amplio, *a.* wide; extensive; roomy, ample; prolix

amplitud, *f.* extension; width; spaciousness, amplitude

ampolla, *f.* blister; ampoule; bubble; (*elec.*) bulb

ampulosidad, *f.* pomposity, redundancy (of style)

ampuloso, *a.* pompous, high-flown (style)

amputación, *f.* amputation

amputar, *v.t.* to amputate

amuchachado, *a.* boyish

amueblar, *v.t.* to furnish; provide with furniture

amulatado, *a.* mulatto-like

amuleto, *m.* amulet, charm

amura, *f.* (*naut.*) bow; (*naut.*) tack

amurallar, *v.t.* to surround with a wall, wall

amusgar, *v.t.* and *v.i.* to flatten the ears (animals); *v.t.* screw up the eyes (to see better)

ana, *f.* ell (measure)

anabaptismo, *m.* Anabaptism

anabaptista, *m.* and *f.* Anabaptist

anacardo, *m.* cashew (nut)

anacoreta, *m.* and *f.* anchorite, hermit

anacreóntico, *a.* Anacreontic

anacrónico, *a.* anachronous

anacronismo, *m.* anachronism

ánade, *m.* and *f.* duck

anadear, *v.i.* to waddle (like a duck)

anadeo, *m.* waddle

anadino (**-na**), *s.* duckling

anadón, *m.* drake

anáfora, *f.* anaphora

anafrodisíaco, *a.* anaphrodisiac

anagrama, *m.* anagram

analectas, *f. pl.* analects

anales, *m. pl.* annals

analfabetismo, *m.* illiteracy

analfabeto (**-ta**), *a.* and *s.* illiterate

analgesia, *f.* analgesia

analgésico, *a.* and *m.* (*med.*) analgesic

análisis, *m.* or *f.* analysis; (*gram.*) parsing

analista, *m.* and *f.* analyst

analizar, *v.t.* to analyse

analogía, *f.* analogy

analógico, **análogo**, *a.* analogous

ananás, *m.* pine-apple

anaquel, *m.* shelf, ledge

anaranjado, *a.* and *m.* orange (colour)

anarquía, *f.* anarchy

anárquico, *a.* anarchical

anarquismo, *m.* anarchism

anarquista, *m.* and *f.* anarchist

anatema, *m.* or *f.* anathema

anatematizar, *v.t.* to anathematize, denounce

anatomía, *f.* anatomy

anatómico, *a.* anatomical

anatomista, *m.* and *f.* anatomist

anca, *f.* croup, hindquarters of a horse

ancianidad, *f.* old age; seniority; oldness

anciano (**-na**), *a.* old; ancient. *s.* old person

ancla, *f.* anchor. **a. de la esperanza**, sheet anchor. **echar anclas**, to anchor

ancladero, **anclaje**, *m.* anchorage

anclar, *v.i.* to anchor

áncora, *f.* anchor; refuge, haven

ancho, *a.* wide, broad. *m.* width, breadth. (*fam.*) **a mis** (**tus**, **sus**, etc.) **anchas** *or* **anchos**, at my (your, his, etc.) ease, with complete freedom

anchoa, *f.* anchovy

anchura, *f.* width, breadth; ease, freedom; extent

anchuroso, *a.* very wide; extensive; spacious

andada, *f.* wandering, roving;

hard bread roll; pasture; *pl.*
trail, tracks. *(fig., fam.)* **volver a
las andadas,** to return to one's
old tricks

andaderas, *f. pl.* go-cart (for
learning to walk)

andador, *a.* walking; swift walking; wandering. *m.* walker; garden path; *pl.* leading-strings, reins

andadura, *f.* walk, gait; pace,
step

andaluz (-za), *a.* and *s.* Andalusian

andaluzada, *f. (fam.)* exaggeration, tall story

andamio, *m.* scaffolding; stand,
platform

andanada, *f. (naut.)* broadside;
cheapest priced seat in a bull-
ring; *(fam.)* dressing-down, scolding

andante, *a.* walking, strolling;
errant (of knights). *a.* and *m.*
(mus.) andante

andanza, *f.* happening, occurrence; *pl.* doings, deeds. **buena
a.,** good fortune

andar, *v.i. irr.* to walk; move;
work, operate, run (machines,
etc.); progress, get along (negotiations, etc.); be, feel; elapse (of
time); be occupied; behave;
(with prep. a) administer (blows,
etc.); *(with en)* upset, turn over
(papers, etc.); ride in or on (cars,
bicycles, etc.); be engaged in;
(with con) use, handle; *v.t.* traverse. *m.* gait, walk. **a. tras,** to
follow, go after; persecute;
desire ardently (things). **andarse a la flor del berro,** to
sow one's wild oats. *(fig., fam.)*
andarse por las ramas, to beat
about the bush. **¡Anda!** Get
along with you!; Hurry up!;
You don't say so! *Preterite*
anduve, etc. *Imperf. subjunc.*
anduviese, etc.

andariego, *a.* swift walking;
wandering, vagrant

andarín (-ina), *s.* good walker;
professional walker

andas, *f. pl.* kind of stretcher;
bier

andén, *m.* railway platform

andero, *m.* bearer (of a bier)

andino, *a.* Andean

andorrano (-na), *a.* and *s.* Andorran

andrajo, *m.* rag, wisp of cloth,
tatter

andrajoso, *a.* ragged, tattered

andurriales, *m. pl.* byways, unfrequented paths; remote places

anécdota, *f.* anecdote

anecdótico, *a.* anecdotal

anegación, *f.* drowning; flooding, inundation

anegar, *v.t.* to drown; inundate;
shipwreck; *v.r.* drown; be flooded

anejo, *a.* attached, annexed. *m.*
annexed borough

anemia, *f.* anæmia

anémico, *a.* anæmic

anemómetro, *m.* anemometer

anémona, anémone, *f.* anemone.
anémone de mar, sea-anemone

anestesia, *f.* anæsthesia

anestesiador (-ra), *s.* anæsthetist

anestesiar, *v.t.* to anæsthetize

anestésico, *a.* and *m.* anæsthetic

aneurisma, *m.* or *f. (med.)* aneurism

anexar, *v.t.* to annex

anexión, *f.* annexation

anexo, *a.* attached, joined. *m.*
annexe

anfibio, *a. (zool., bot., mil.)*
amphibious. *m.* amphibian

anfiteatro, *m.* amphitheatre;
operating theatre; *(theat.)* dress-
circle

anfitrión, *m. (fam.)* host, one who
entertains guests

ánfora, *f.* amphora

angarillas, *f. pl.* hand barrow;
table cruet; yoke and panniers

ángel, *m.* angel. **á. de la
guarda,** guardian angel

angélica, *f.* angelica

angelical, angélico, *a.* angelic;
divine, excellent

ángelus, *m.* angelus

angina, *f. (med.)* angina, tonsillitis.
a. de pecho, angina pectoris

anglicanismo, *m.* Anglicanism

anglicano (-na), *a.* and *s.* Anglican

anglicismo, *m.* anglicism

anglo (-la), *a.* and *s.* Angle. *a.*
Anglo-

angloamericano (-na), *a.* and *s.*
Anglo-American

anglófilo (-la), *s.* Anglophile

anglosajón (-ona), *a.* and *s.*
Anglo-Saxon. *m.* Anglo-Saxon
language

angostar, *v.i.* and *v.t.* to narrow; tighten

angosto, *a.* narrow; tight

angostura, *f.* narrowness; tightness; narrow pass; strait; (*fig.*) tight corner, fix

anguila, *f.* (*icht.*) eel; *pl.* (*naut.*) slipway, slips

angula, *f.* (*icht.*) elver (young eel)

angular, *a.* angular

ángulo, *m.* angle. **a. recto,** right angle

anguloso, *a.* angulate; angular, gaunt; cornered

angustia, *f.* anguish, grief

angustiar, *v.t.* to grieve; afflict; *v.r.* be full of anguish

anhelación, *f.* panting, hard breathing; yearning, longing

anhelar, *v.i.* to pant, breathe with difficulty; *v.i.* and *v.t.* long for, yearn for, desire

anhélito, *m.* pant, hard breathing

anhelo, *m.* longing, desire

anheloso, *a.* difficult, laboured (of breathing); anxious, longing

anhidro, *a.* (*chem.*) anhydrous

anidar, *v.i.* to nest (birds); swell; *v.t.* shelter, protect; *v.r.* nest; dwell; nestle

anilina, *f.* (*chem.*) aniline

anilla, *f.* curtain ring; *pl.* gymnastic rings

anillo, *m.* finger ring; small ring; coil (of serpents and ropes). (*fam.*) **venir como a. al dedo,** to fit like a glove; come just at the right moment

ánima, *f.* soul, spirit; soul in purgatory; bore (of firearms); *pl.* prayer bell for the souls of the departed

animación, *f.* liveliness, gaiety; animation, vivacity; bustle, movement

animal, *m.* animal; (*fam.*) dolt, brute. *a.* animal; (*fam.*) brutish, doltish

animalada, *f.* (*fam.*) stupidity, foolishness

animalidad, *f.* animalism

animar, *v.t.* to animate; encourage, incite; invigorate, enliven; make gay, cheer up; make attractive, adorn; *v.r.* take heart; make up one's mind; cheer up; grow gay

animismo, *m.* animism

ánimo, *m.* soul, spirit; courage; endurance, fortitude; will, intention; mind. ¡Á.! Courage!

animosidad, *f.* hatred, animosity, dislike

animoso, *a.* spirited, lively; valiant

aniñado, *a.* childlike, childish

aniquilable, *a.* destructible

aniquilación, *f.* destruction, annihilation; suppression; decay

aniquilador (-ra), *a.* destructive, annihilating. *s.* destroyer

aniquilamiento, *m.* See **aniquilación**

aniquilar, *v.t.* to annihilate, destroy completely; *v.r.* waste away, decay

anís, *m.* aniseed, anise; anisette (liqueur)

anisar, *v.t.* to flavour with aniseed

anisete, *m.* anisette

aniversario, *a.* annual. *m.* anniversary

ano, *m.* (*anat.*) anus

anoche, *adv.* last night; the previous night

anochecer, *v.i.* *irr.* to grow night; become dark; be in a place *or* be doing something at nightfall (e.g. **Anochecimos en Lérida,** We were in Lerida at nightfall). *v.r.* (*poet.*) be obscured or darkened. *m.* nightfall, dusk. See **conocer**

anochecida, *f.* dusk, late twilight

anodino, *a.* (*med.*) anodyne; ineffective, useless; inoffensive. *m.* anodyne

ánodo, *m.* (*elec.*) anode

anomalía, *f.* anomaly, inconstancy, irregularity; (*ast.*) anomaly

anómalo, *a.* anomalous, abnormal, unusual

anonadación, *f.* **anonadamiento,** *m.* destruction, annihilation; despair, melancholy; suppression

anonadar, *v.t.* to destroy, annihilate; suppress; (*fig.*) overwhelm, depress; humble

anónimo, *a.* anonymous. *m.* anonymity; anonymous letter; unsigned literary work

anormal, *a.* abnormal; irregular, unusual. *m.* and *f.* abnormal person

anormalidad, *f.* abnormality; irregularity, inconsistency

anotación, f. annotation

anotador (-ra), s. annotator

anotar, v.t. to annotate; note down

anquilosis, f. (med.) ankylosis

anquilostoma, m. (med.) hookworm

ánsar, m. goose; drake

ansarero (-ra), s. gooseherd

ansarino, a. goose. m. gosling

anseático, a. Hanseatic

ansia, f. anxiety, trouble; grief; longing, desire; greed

ansiar, v.t. to long for, yearn for; covet, desire

ansiedad, f. anxiety, anguish, worry

ansioso, a. anxious; grievous, painful; eager, desirous; greedy

anta, f. (zool.) elk; obelisk

antagónico, a. antagonistic

antagonismo, m. antagonism

antagonista, m. and f. antagonist, adversary

antaño, adv. last year, yesteryear; long ago

antártico, a. antarctic

ante, m. (zool.) elk; suède; buffalo

ante, prep. in the presence of, before; regarding, in the face of (e.g. a. deber tan alto, in the face of so noble a duty)

anteado, a. beige, buff-coloured, fawn

antealtar, m. (arch.) chancel

anteanoche, adv. the night before last

anteayer, adv. the day before yesterday

antebrazo, m. forearm

antecámara, f. ante-chamber

antecedente, m. antecedent

antecedentemente, adv. previously

anteceder, v.t. to precede

antecesor (-ra), a. previous. s. predecessor. m. forebear, ancestor

antecoger, v.t. to carry in front, lead before; pick too soon

antedata, f. antedate

antedatar, v.t. to antedate

antedicho, a. aforementioned, aforesaid

antediluviano, a. antediluvian

antelación, f. advance, anticipation

antemano, de, adv. in advance, beforehand

antemeridiano, a. antemeridian, forenoon

antena, f. antenna; (rad.) aerial

antenacido, a. born prematurely

antenombre, m. title (placed before name)

anteojera, f. horse's blinker; spectacle-case

anteojo, m. spy-glass, small telescope; pl. horse's blinkers; spectacles; goggles

antepagar, v.t. to pay in advance

antepalco, m. vestibule of a box in a theatre

antepasado, a. previous, past. m. ancestor (gen. pl.)

antepecho, m. parapet; windowsill; railing, balustrade; front (of a theatre box, etc.); (naut.) bulwark

antepenúltimo, a. antepenultimate

anteponer, v.t. irr. to place before; prefer, favour. See poner

anteproyecto, m. first sketch, preliminary work or plan

antepuerta, f. door-curtain, portière; (mil.) anteport

antepuerto, m. (naut.) anteport

antera, f. (bot.) anther

anterior, a. previous, former; anterior; aforementioned, preceding

anteriormente, adv. beforehand, previously

antes, adv. before; rather, on the contrary; previously. a. bien, rather, sooner. a. con a. or cuanto a., as soon as possible

antesala, f. ante-chamber

antevíspera, f. two days previously

antiaéreo, a. anti-aircraft. m. pl. (cañones) antiaéreos, A.A. guns

anticición, m. anticyclone

anticipación, f. anticipation; advance

anticipada, f. foul thrust (in fencing, etc.)

anticipadamente, adv. in advance; prematurely

anticipado, a. in advance; premature

anticipador, a. anticipatory

anticipar, v.t. to anticipate; foresee; forestall; advance (money); lend; v.r. happen before time;

(with prep. a) act in advance, of, anticipate

anticipo, *m.* anticipation, advance; advance payment; sum of money lent

anticlerical, *a.* anticlerical

anticlímax, *m.* anticlimax

anticonstitucional, *a.* unconstitutional

Anticristo, *m.* Antichrist

anticuado, *a.* antiquated, ancient

anticuario, *m.* antiquarian, antique dealer

antídoto, *m.* antidote (also *fig.*)

antiesclavista, *a.* antislavery. *m.* and *f.* antislavist

antiespasmódico, *a.* and *m.* (*med.*) antispasmodic

antiestético, *a.* unæsthetic

antifaz, *m.* mask; face-covering

antiflogístico, *a.* and *m.* (*med.*) antiphlogistic

antífona, *f.* anthem, antiphony

antigramatical, *a.* ungrammatical

antigualla, *f.* antique; ancient custom; anything out-of-date

antiguamente, *adv.* in time past, formerly

antigüedad, *f.* antiquity (in ancients; length of service (in an employment); *pl.* antiquities

antiguo, *a.* ancient, very old; antique; senior (in an employment); former. *m.* senior member (of a community, etc.). *m pl.* ancients. A. Testamento, Old Testament. de a., from ancient times

antihelmíntico, *a.* (*med.*) anthelminthic

antílope, *m.* antelope

antillano (-na), *a.* and *s.* of or from the Antilles

antimacasar, *m.* antimacassar

antimilitarismo, *m.* antimilitarism

antimilitarista, *a.* antimilitaristic

antimonárquico, *a.* antimonarchical

antimonio, *m.* (*met.*) antimony

antioqueño (-ña), *a.* and *s.* Antiochian (from Syria or Colombia)

antipalúdico, *a.* anti-malarial

antipapa, *m.* antipope

antipara, *f.* screen, shield

antiparras, *f. pl* (*fam.*) spectacles, glasses

antipatía, *f.* antipathy

antipático, *a.* disagreeable; unattractive

antipatriótico, *a.* unpatriotic

antípoda, *a.* and *m.* or *f.* antipode

antiquísimo, *a.* *sup.* antiguo, most ancient

antirrepublicano, *a.* anti-republican

antisemita, *a.* anti-semitic. *m.* and *f.* anti-semite

antisemitismo, *m.* anti-semitism

antiséptico, *a.* and *m.* antiseptic

antisifilítico, *a.* (*med.*) antisyphilitic

antisocial, *a.* anti-social

antítesis, *f.* antithesis

antitético, *a.* antithetic, contrasted

antitoxina, *f.* (*med.*) antitoxin

antófago, *a.* anthophagous, flower-eating

antojadizo, *a.* capricious, fanciful, whimsical

antojarse, *v.r.* to have a fancy for, want (e.g. Se me antoja marcharme al campo, I have a fancy to go into the country); suspect, imagine

antojo, *m.* caprice, fancy, whim; desire, will; *pl.* birthmark

antología, *f.* anthology

antólogo, *m.* anthologist

antonomasia, *f.* antonomasia. por a., by analogy, by transference

antorcha, *f.* torch, flambeau

antracita, *f.* anthracite

ántrax, *m.* (*med.*) anthrax

antro, *m.* cave, cavern; (*anat.*) antrum

antropofagia, *f.* cannibalism, anthropophagy

antropófago (-ga), *a.* cannibalistic. *s.* cannibal

antropología, *f.* anthropology

antropológico, *a.* anthropological

antropólogo, *m.* anthropologist

antropometría, *f.* anthropometry

antropomorfo, *a.* anthropomorphous

antroposofía, *f.* anthroposophy

antruejo, *m.* three days of carnival before Lent

anual, *a.* yearly, annual

anualidad, *f.* annuity

anuario, *m.* directory, year-book, handbook

anubarrado, *a.* covered with clouds, cloudy

anublado, *a.* lowering, overcast; clouded

anublar, *v.t.* to cloud; darken, obscure; blight (plants); *v.r.* cloud over; become blighted or mildewed

anudar, *v.t.* to knot; tie, fasten; join; continue; *v.r.* grow stunted

anulable, *a.* annulable, voidable

anulación, *f.* annulment, abrogation

anular, *a.* annular, ring-shaped. *v.t.* to annul; (*math.*) cancel out

anuloso, *a.* annulate, formed of rings

anunciación, *f.* (*ecc.*) Annunciation; announcement

anunciador (-ra), *s.*, anunciante, *m.* and *f.* announcer; advertiser

anunciar, *v.t.* to announce; publish, proclaim; advertise; foretell, presage

anuncio, *m.* announcement; publication, proclamation; advertisement; presage, omen. *a.* luminoso, sky-sign

anverso, *m.* obverse, face

anzuelo, *m.* fish-hook; (*cul.*) fritter; (*fam.*) attraction, inducement

añadido, *m.* hair-switch; make-weight

añadidura, *f.* addition; make-weight, extra

añadir, *v.t.* to add; increase

añagaza, *f.* decoy bird; enticement, lure

añejo, *a.* very old

añicos, *m. pl.* fragments, small pieces. hacer a., to break into fragments

añil, *m.* indigo; indigo blue

año, *m.* year; *pl.* birthday. *a.* bisiesto, leap-year. *a.* económico, fiscal year. A. Nuevo, New Year. tener (siete) años, to be (seven) years old

añoranza, *f.* homesickness, loneliness; nostalgia

añorar, *v.i.* to be homesick or lonely

añoso, *a.* very old, full of years

añublo, *m.* mildew

aojamiento, *m.* evil eye, wicked spell

aojar, *v.t.* to bewitch, place under a spell; spoil, frustrate

aojo, *m.* evil eye; magic spell

aorta, *f.* (*anat.*) aorta

aovado, *a.* oval; ovoid

aovar, *v.i.* to lay eggs

aovillarse, *v.r.* to roll oneself into a ball; curl up

apacentadero, *m.* grazing land, pasture

apacentamiento, *m.* pasturage; grazing

apacentar, *v.t. irr.* to put out to grass; teach, instruct; satisfy (one's desires); *v.r.* graze (cattle). See acertar

apacibilidad, *f.* agreeableness; mildness; peaceableness

apacible, *a.* agreeable; mild; peaceable; calm, peaceful

apaciguamiento, *m.* appeasement, soothing, pacification

apaciguar, *v.t.* to appease, pacify; calm

apadrinar, *v.t.* to act as godfather to; be best man to (at a wedding); act as a second for (in a duel); sponsor; favour

apagable, *a.* extinguishable

apagado, *a.* timid, nervous; pale (of colours); dull, lustreless

apagador (-ra), *a.* quenching. *s.* extinguisher. *m.* candle-snuffer; damper (of a piano)

apagaincendios, *m.* ship's fire-extinguisher

apagamiento, *m.* quenching, extinguishment

apagar, *v.t.* to extinguish, put out; (*fig.*) quench, moderate; slake (lime); (*art*) tone down (colours); shut off (engines)

apagavelas, *m.* candle-snuffer

apaisado, *a.* elongated

apalabrar, *v.t.* to make an appointment with; discuss, consider

apalancar, *v.t.* to lever

apaleamiento, *m.* beating, thrashing

apalear, *v.t.* to beat, thrash; knock down with a stick

apandillarse, *v.r.* to form a gang or group

apantanar, *v.t.* to make marshy; flood

apañar, *v.t.* to take away, remove; seize; steal; dress, get ready; (*fam.*) wrap up; patch, repair; *v.r.* (*fam.*) grow skilful

apaño, *m.* dexterity, skill; craft, guile

aparador, *m.* shop window; sideboard; workshop; (*ecc.*) credence (table)

aparato, *m.* apparatus; equipment, utensils; pomp, ostentation; symptoms; sign, circumstance, token

aparatoso, *a.* showy, ostentatious

aparcería, *f.* partnership (in a farm)

aparear, *v.t.* to match, make equal; pair; mate (animals); *v.r.* form up in pairs

aparecer(se), *v.i.* and *v.r. irr.* to appear; seem; be. See **conocer**

aparecido, *m.* apparition, spectre

aparejador, *m.* overseer, foreman; (*naut.*) rigger

aparejar, *v.t.* to prepare, make ready; saddle (horses); prime, size; rig (a ship)

aparejo, *m.* preparation, arrangement; harness, trappings; (*naut.*) rigging; (*naut.*) gear; priming, sizing; (*mech.*) tackle; *pl.* equipment

aparentar, *v.t.* to pretend, simulate

aparente, *a.* seeming, apparent; obvious, visible; suitable, proper

aparición, *f.* appearance, arrival; apparition, phantom

apariencia, *f.* appearance, looks, probability, likelihood; outward semblance; *pl.* (*theat.*) scenery

apartadamente, *adv.* apart, in private; secretly

apartadero, *m.* passing place for cars; railway siding; grass verge. *a.* **ferroviario**, railway marshalling yard

apartado, *a.* distant, far off; secluded; different. *m.* post office box; secluded room; smelting house; sorting of cattle

apartamiento, *m.* separation; withdrawal, retiral; seclusion; apartment, flat; (*law*) withdrawal of an action

apartar, *v.t.* to separate; remove, take away; (*r.w.*) shunt; dissuade;·sort; *v.r.* obtain a divorce; (*law*) withdraw an action

aparte, *adv.* aside, on one side; separately; (*theat.*) aside; besides; beyond. *m.* (*theat.*) aside;

paragraph; space between words

apasionado (**-da**), *a.* impassioned; fervent, devoted; passionate; enthusiastic. *s.* admirer, lover; enthusiast

apasionamiento, *m.* passion

apasionar, *v.t.* to arouse to passion; pain; *v.r.* (*with por*) grow passionately fond of; become enthusiastic for

apatía, *f.* apathy

apático, *a.* apathetic

apeadero, *m.* mounting-block; halt, stopping place; wayside railway station; pied à terre, occasional dwelling

apear, *v.t.* to dismount; hobble (horse); survey, map out; fell a tree; (*fig.*) overcome (difficulties); (*fam.*) dissuade; prop; remove, bring down; scotch (a wheel); *v.r.* dismount; alight, step off

apechugar, *v.i.* to push with the breast; (*fam.*) put up with reluctantly

apedazar, *v.t.* to tear; break; mend, repair

apedreamiento, **apedreo**, *m.* stoning, lapidation

apedrear, *v.t.* to stone; stone to death; *v.i. impers.* hail; *v.r.* be damaged by hail (crops)

apegarse, *v.r.* to grow fond (of), become attached (to)

apego, *m.* fondness, inclination; affection, attachment

apelación, *f.* (*law*) appeal; (*fam.*) doctor's consultation

apelante, *a.* and *m.* and *f.* (*law*) appellant

apelar, *v.i.* (*law*) to appeal; (*with prep. a*) have recourse to; *v.i.* be of the same colour (horses)

apelotonar, *v.t.* to make into balls, ball

apellidar, *v.t.* to name, call; acclaim; call to arms; *v.r.* be named

apellido, *m.* surname; nickname; call to arms; clamour; name

apenar, *v.t.* to grieve, afflict; cause sorrow

apenas, *adv.* scarcely; immediately, as soon as; with trouble or difficulty

apéndice, *m.* appendix, supplement; (*anat.*) appendix

apendicitis, *f.* (*med.*) appendicitis

apeo, *m.* survey; scaffolding; prop, support

apercibimiento, *m.* preparation; provision; warning; (*law*) summons

apercibir, *v.t.* to prepare, furnish; warn; (*law*) summon

apergaminado, *a.* parchment; parchment-like

apergaminarse, *v.r.* (*fam.*) to shrivel, dry up (with old age, etc.)

aperitivo, *a.* aperitive. *m.* aperient; aperitive, appetiser

apertura, *f.* opening; inauguration; reading (of a will)

apesadumbrar, *v.t.* to sadden, afflict, grieve

apestar, *v.t.* to infect with the plague; catch the plague; (*fig.*) corrupt; (*fam.*) pester, annoy; *v.i.* stink

apestoso, *a.* stinking, putrid

apetecer, *v.t. irr.* to want, desire; attract. See **conocer**

apetecible, *a.* attractive, desirable

apetencia, *f.* appetite; desire

apetito, *m.* appetite

apetitoso, *a.* appetising; tasty, savoury; attractive

apiadarse, *v.r.* (*with de*) to have compassion on, be sorry for

ápice, *m.* apex; peak, summit, top; orthographic accent; iota, tittle; crux (of a problem)

apícola, *a.* apiarian, bee-keeping

apicultor (-ra), *s.* apiarist, beekeeper

apicultura, *f.* apiculture, beekeeping

apilar, *v.t.* to pile, heap

apimpollarse, *v.r.* to sprout

apiñado, *a.* crowded, serried

apiñamiento, *m.* crowding; congestion

apiñar, *v.t.* to group together, crowd; *v.r.* crowd

apio, *m.* celery

apisonadora, *f.* steam-roller; roller

apisonar, *v.t.* to roll, stamp, flatten, ram down

apizarrado, *a.* slate-coloured

aplacable, *a.* appeasable, placable

aplacamiento, *m.* appeasement

aplacar, *v.t.* to appease, calm; moderate, mitigate

aplacible, *a.* agreeable, pleasant

aplanar, *v.t.* to flatten, level; roll (pastry); (*fam.*) dumbfound, overwhelm; *v.r.* collapse (buildings); lose heart

aplastar, *v.t.* to flatten, squash, crush; (*fam.*) squash flat, floor

aplaudir, *v.t.* to applaud, clap; praise, commend, approve

aplauso, *m.* applause; clapping, plaudit; approbation, commendation

aplazamiento, *m.* postponement; appointment, summons

aplazar, *v.t.* to summon, arrange a meeting; postpone; adjourn

aplicabilidad, *f.* applicability

aplicable, *a.* applicable

aplicación, *f.* application; diligence, assiduity; appliqué, ornamentation

aplicado, *a.* diligent, hardworking; appliqué

aplicar, *v.t.* to apply; impute; intend, destine (for processions); (*law*) adjudge; *v.r.* engage in; apply oneself. **a. sanciones,** (*pol.*) to impose sanctions

aplomado, *a.* self-possessed, dignified; leaden, lead-coloured

aplomar, *v.t.* and *v.i.* to plumb, test with a plumb-line; *v.r.* collapse, fall down

aplomo, *m.* self-possession, dignity; sang-froid

apocado, *a.* spiritless, timid; base, mean

Apocalipsis, *m.* Apocalypse

apocalíptico, *a.* apocalyptic

apocamiento, *m.* timidity, pusillanimity; depression, discouragement; shyness; baseness, meanness

apocar, *v.t.* to diminish, reduce, humiliate, scorn

apócrifo, *a.* fictitious, false, apocryphal. **Apócrifos,** Apocrypha

apodar, *v.t.* to nickname

apoderado, *a.* authorized. *m.* attorney; deputy; proxy

apoderar, *v.t.* to authorize, grant powers of attorney to; *v.r* (*with de*) seize, take possession of

apodo, *m.* nickname

apófisis, *f.* (*anát.*) apophysis

apogeo, *m.* (*ast.*) apogee; (*fig.*) zenith, peak (of fame, etc.)

apolillar, *v.t.* to eat clothes (moths); *v.r.* be moth-eaten

apologético, *a.* apologetic

apologista, *m.* and *f.* apologist

apólogo, *m.* apologue, moral fable

apoltronarse, *v.r.* to grow idle

apoplegía, *f.* apoplexy

apoplético (-ca), *a.* and *s.* apoplectic

aporrear, *v.t.* to beat, cudgel; *v.r.* work hard, slog away

aportación, *f.* contribution; occasioneer

aportar, *v.t.* to cause, occasion; contribute; *v.i.* (*naut.*) reach port; arrive at an unexpected place

aposentador, *m.* usher; (*mil.*) billeting officer

aposentar, *v.t.* to lodge, give hospitality to; *v.r.* lodge, settle down

aposento, *m.* room; suite, apartments; lodging, accommodation; (*theat.*) box (in old theatres)

aposición, *f.* (*gram.*) apposition

apósito, *m.* poultice, external application

apostadero, *m.* (*naut.*) naval station; placing or stationing (of soldiers)

apostar, *v.t.* irr. to bet; station (soldiers); *v.i.* compete, rival. See contar

apostasía, *f.* apostasy

apóstata, *m.* and *f.* apostate

apostatar, *v.i.* to apostatize

apostilla, *f.* marginal note, gloss

apóstol, *m.* apostle

apostólico, *a.* apostolic

apostrofar, *v.t.* to apostrophize

apóstrofe, *m.* or *f.* apostrophe, hortatory exclamation

apóstrofo, *m.* (*gram.*) apostrophe

apostura *f.* neatness, spruceness

apotegma, *m.* apothegm, maxim

apoteosis, *f.* apotheosis

apoyar, *v.t.* (*with en*) to lean against; rest upon; *v.t.* uphold, favour; confirm, bear out; droop the head (horses); second (a motion); *v.i.* (*with en*) rest on; lean against; *v.r.* (*with en*) rest on; lean against; be upheld by; (*fig.*) be founded on; (*fig.*) depend on, lean on

apoyo, *m.* support, prop; assistance; backing, support

apreciable, *a.* appreciable; estimable; important

apreciación, *f.* appreciation; valuation, estimate

apreciador (-ra), *a.* appreciatory. *s.* appreciator

apreciar, *v.t.* to estimate (values); appreciate; like, esteem, have a regard for

apreciativo, *a.* appreciative

aprecio, *m.* valuation; appreciation, regard

aprehender, *v.t.* to apprehend, catch; seize (contraband); understand, grasp

aprehensión, *f.* seizure, apprehension

apremiador, apremiante, *a.* urgent, pressing

apremiar, *v.t.* to hurry; urge, press; force, oblige; burden, oppress (with taxes)

apremio, *m.* insistence, pressure; compulsion; demand note

aprendedor (-ra), *s.* learner

aprender, *v.t.* to learn. a. de memoria, to learn by heart

aprendiz (-za), *s.* apprentice

aprendizaje, *m.* apprenticeship. hacer el a., to serve an apprenticeship

aprensión, *f.* capture; fear, apprehension; suspicion, fancy; prejudice, scruple

aprensivo, *a.* apprehensive, nervous, fearful

apresar, *v.t.* to nab, catch; capture (a ship); imprison; fetter

aprestar, *v.t.* to prepare, arrange; dress (fabrics)

apresto, *m.* preparation, arrangement; dressing (for cloth)

apresurar, *v.t.* to quicken; *v.r.* hasten, be quick

apretado, *a.* difficult, dangerous; tight; crabbed (of handwriting); (*fam.*) mean, close-fisted. *m.* small close handwriting

apretadura, *f.* tightening, compression

apretar, *v.t.* irr. to tighten; compress; urge on, press; harass, vex; trouble, worry; speed up; squeeze; press (bells, gun triggers, etc.); *v.i.* increase, grow worse (storms, heat, etc.); pinch, hurt (shoes). (*fam.*) a. a correr, to take to one's heels. ¡ Aprieta ¡

(*fam.*) Nonsense! It can't be! See acertar

apretón, *m.* squeeze, grip, pressure; (*fam.*) sprint, spurt; (*fam.*) fix, pickle. a. de manos, handshake

apretujar, *v.t.* (*fam.*) to squeeze, hug

aprieto, *m.* crowd, crush; urgency; (*fam.*) jam, trouble, fix

aprisa, *adv.* quickly, in a hurry

aprisco, *m.* cattle-shed; sheepfold

aprisionar, *v.t.* to imprison; bind, fetter; tie

aprobación, *f.* approbation, approval, commendation; ratification (of a bill); pass (in an examination)

aprobado, *m.* pass certificate (in examinations)

aprobar, *v.t. irr.* to approve; pass (in an examination). See contar

apropiación, *f.* appropriation; application; adaptation

apropiado, *a.* appropriate, suitable, proper

apropiar, *v.t.* to appropriate; adapt, fit; *v.r.* appropriate, take possession

aprovechable, *a.* usable, available

aprovechado, *a.* advantageous; assiduous, conscientious; capable; thrifty

aprovechamiento, - *m.* utilization, employment; exploitation; profitable use

aprovechar, *v.t.* to be advantageous or useful; be beneficial; make progress (in studies, etc.); *v.t.* use; profit by; *v.r.* take advantage of, make use of. ¡Qué aproveche! May it do you good! (said to anyone eating)

aprovisionar, *v.t.* to provision, supply

aproximación, *f.* approximation; consolation prize (in a lottery)

aproximadamente, *adv.* approximately; nearly, almost

aproximar, *v.t.* to bring or draw nearer; *v.r.* approach; be almost, be approximately

aptitud, *f.* aptitude, ability; fitness; propensity

pto, *a.* suitable, fitting; competent. No apta para menores,

Not suitable for children (of films, etc.)

apuesta, *f.* bet, wager; competition

apuestas benéficas de fútbol, football pools

apuesto, *a.* elegant; handsome, well set-up

apuntación, *f.* noting down; note; (*mus.*) notation

apuntador (-ra), *s.* note-taker; observer. *m.* (*theat.*) prompter; (*theat.*) stage-manager

apuntalar, *v.t.* to prop up

apuntamiento, *m.* summary; (*law*) indictment, minute

apuntar, *v.t.* to aim (a gun, etc.); point to, indicate; note down; mark; sketch; sharpen; bet (at cards); fasten temporarily; (*fam.*) mend; (*theat.*) prompt; suggest, hint; *v.i.* begin to appear. (*fam.*) a. y no dar, to promise and do nothing

apunte, *m.* abstract; note; annotation; sketch; (*theat.*) prompt *or* prompter *or* prompt book *or* cue; stake in a card game)

apuñalado, *a.* dagger-shaped

apuñalar, *v.t.* to stab, attack with a dagger

apurado, *a.* poor, needy; dangerous; difficult; accurate, exact; hurried

apurar, *v.t.* to purify; drain; exhaust; finish, conclude; examine closely, scrutinize; irritate, make impatient; urge on, hasten; *v.r.* be anxious, fret

apuro, *m.* difficulty, fix; poverty, want; anxiety, worry. pasar apuros, to have a hard time

aquejar, *v.t.* to grieve, afflict, sadden

aquel, *a. m.,* **aquella,** *a. f.,* **aquellos,** *a. m. pl.,* **aquellas,** *a. f. pl.* that, those; that or those over there (farther off than ese)

aquel, *m.* charm, attraction, "it"

aquél, **aquélla,** **aquéllos,** **aquéllas,** *dem. pron., m., f.* sing. and pl., that, the one, those, those ones; the former. e.g. La casa que ve usted a lo lejos aquélla es la vivienda de mi tío, The house that you see in the distance, that is my uncle's dwelling. Éste no me gusta

pero aquél sí, I do not like the latter, but I like the former

aquelarre, *m.* witches' sabbath

aquello, *dem. pron., neut.* that; the fact; the matter, the affair, the former (remark, idea, etc.). e.g. **Todo a. por fin acabó,** All that came to an end at last. **a. de,** the fact that

aquende, *adv.* on this side (rarely used)

aquí, *adv.* here. **de a.,** hence the fact that. ¡He a.! Behold!

aquiescencia, *f.* consent, acquiescence

aquietar, *v.t.* to calm, soothe

aquilatar, *v.t.* to assay; scrutinize; examine, weigh up (persons)

aquilino, *a.* (*poet.*) aquiline

aquilón, *m.* north

aquistar, *v.t.* to attain, acquire

ara, *f.* altar

árabe, *a.* Arab, Arabic. *m. and f.* Arab. *m.* Arabic (language)

arabesco, *a.* Arabic. *m.* (*art*) arabesque

arábigo, *a.* Arabic. *m.* Arabic (language)

arabista, *m. and f.* Arabist

arácnido, *m.* (*zool.*) arachnid

arado, *m.* plough

arador, *a.* ploughing. *m.* ploughman. **a. de la sarna,** (*ent.*) scabies mite

aragonés (**-esa**), *a. and s.* Aragonese

arancel, *m.* tariff, duty, tax

arancelario, *a.* tariff, tax; customs

arándano, *m.* (*bot.*) bilberry

arandela, *f.* candle-dripper; (*mech.*) washer; wall candelabrum

araña, *f.* spider; chandelier

arañar, *v.t.* to scratch; (*fam.*) scrape together; hoard

arañazo, *m.* scratch

arar, *v.t.* to plough. **a. en el mar,** to labour in vain

arbitrador (**-ra**), *s.* arbitrator

arbitraje, *m.* arbitration; arbitrament, decision

arbitrar, *v.t.* to judge freely; (*law*) arbitrate, mediate; devise; invent; *v.r.* make shift, contrive

arbitrariedad, *f.* arbitrariness

arbitrario, *a.* arbitral, mediatory; arbitrary, capricious

arbitrio, *m.* free will; arbitration; means, way; discretion; arbitrament, judgment; *pl.* rates, municipal taxes

árbitro (**-ra**), *a.* arbitrary. *s.* arbiter. *m.* (*sport*) umpire; referee

árbol, *m.* tree; (*mech.*) shaft; (*naut.*) mast; axis of a winding stair. **a. de amor** *or* **a. de Judas,** Judas tree. **a. de la ciencia** (**del bien y del mal**), Tree of Knowledge (of good and evil). **a. de levas,** (*mech.*) camshaft. **a. del pan,** breadfruit tree. (*naut.*) **a. mayor,** mainmast. **a. motor** (*mech.*), driving-shaft

arbolado, *a.* tree-covered, wooded. *m.* copse, woodland

arboladura, *f.* (*naut.*) masts and spars

arbolar, *v.t.* to hoist (flags); (*naut.*) fit with masts; place upright; *v.r.* rear, prance (horses)

arboleda, *f.* copse, grove, spinney

arbóreo, *a.* arboreal, tree

arboricultura, *f.* arboriculture

arbotante, *m.* flying-buttress

arbusto, *m.* shrub, woody plant

arca, *f.* chest; money-box, coffer; ark; *pl.* (treasury) vaults. **a. caudal,** strong box. **a. de agua,** water-tower. **a. de la alianza.** *or* **a. del testamento,** Ark of the Covenant (Bible). **a. de Noé,** Noah's Ark; lumber box

arcabucero, *m.* arquebusier; maker of arquebuses

arcabuz, *m.* arquebus

arcada, *f.* arcade; series of arches; *pl.* sickness, nausea

árcade, *a. and m. and f.* Arcadian (Greece)

arcaico, *a.* archaic

arcaísmo, *m.* archaism

arcángel, *m.* archangel

arcano, *a.* secret. *m.* mystery, arcanum

arce, *m.* (*bot.*) maple tree

arcedianato, *m.* archdeaconate

arcediano, *m.* archdeacon

arcilla, *f.* clay

arcilloso, *a.* clayey, like or full of clay

arcipreste, *m.* archpriest

arco, *m.* (*geom.*) arc; (*mil.*) bow; bow (of a stringed instrument); hoop (of casks, etc.); (*arch.*) arch. **a. del cielo** *or* **a. de San Martín**

or a. iris, rainbow. **a. voltaico,** electric arc. (*mus.*) **para a.,** for strings

archiduque, *m.* archduke

archiduquesa *f.* archduchess

archimillonario (-ia), *a.* and *s.* multi-millionaire

archipiélago, *m.* archipelago

archivar, *v.t.* to place in an archive; file (papers)

archivero, *m.* archivist, keeper of the archives; librarian; registrar

archivo, *m.* archives

archivolta, *f.* (*arch.*) archivolt

arder, *v.i.* to burn; shine, gleam; (*fig.*) burn (with passion, etc.); *v.t.* to set alight, burn

ardid, *a.* crafty. *m.* trick, stratagem

ardiente, *a.* burning; ardent, passionate; vehement; enthusiastic; flame-coloured; fiery-red

ardilla, *f.* squirrel

ardite, *m.* ancient Spanish coin of very small value; (*fig.*) farthing, fig, straw. **no valer un a.,** to be not worth a straw

ardor, *m.* great heat; zeal, earnestness; passion, ardour; courage

ardoroso, *a.* ardorous

arduo, *a.* arduous

área, *f.* area; small plot of ground; arc (surface measure)

arena, *f.* sand; arena; grit, gravel. **a. movediza,** quicksand

arenal, *m.* quicksand; sand pit; sandy place

arenero (-ra), *s.* sand merchant. *m.* sand-box (carried by railway engines)

arenga, *f.* harangue, discourse

arenilla, *f.* sand (for drying writing)

arenisca, *f.* sandstone

arenisco, *a.* sandy

arenque, *m.* herring

areómetro, *m.* (*phys.*) areometer

arete, *m.* earring

argamasa, *f.* mortar

argelino (-na), *a.* and *s.* Algerian

argentado, *a.* silvered; silvery

argénteo, *a.* silver; silvery

argentífero, *a.* silver-yielding

argentino (-na), *a.* silvery. *a.* and *s.* Argentinian. *m.* Argentinian gold coin

argento, *m.* silver. **a. vivo,** mercury

argolla, *f.* thick metal ring (for hitching, etc.); croquet (game); stocks, pillory; hoop, iron arch

argonauta, *m.* (*myth.*) Argonaut; (*zool.*) paper nautilus, argonaut

argucia, *f.* sophism, quibble; subtlety

argüir, *v.t. irr.* to deduce, imply; prove; reveal, manifest; accuse; *v.i.* argue, debate; dispute, oppose. See **huir**

argumentador (-ra), *a.* argumentative. *s.* arguer

argumentar, *v.i.* to argue; dispute; oppose

argumento, *m.* contention, case; theme (of a book, etc.); argument, discussion

aridez, *f.* aridity, dryness; drought; sterility, barrenness; dullness, lack of interest

árido, *a.* dry, arid; sterile, barren; uninteresting, dull

ariete, *m.* (*mil.*) battering-ram

ario (-ia), *a.* and *s.* Aryan

arisco, *a.* unsociable, surly; wild, shy (animals)

arista, *f.* (*bot.*) arista, awn, beard; pebble; edge, side

aristocracia, *f.* aristocracy

aristócrata, *m.* and *f.* aristocrat

aristocrático, *a.* aristocratic

aristotélico, *a.* Aristotelian

aristotelismo, *m.* Aristotelianism

aritmética, *f.* arithmetic

aritmético (-ca), *a.* arithmetical. *s.* arithmetician

arlequín, *m.* harlequin; (*fam.*) fool, buffoon; Neapolitan ice-cream

arlequinada, *f.* harlequinade; buffoonery

arma, *f.* weapon; (*mil.*) arm, branch; bull's horn; *pl.* troops, army; means, way; arms, coat of arms. **a. arrojadiza,** missile. **a. blanca,** steel weapon. **a. de fuego,** fire-arm. **¡Armas al hombro!** Shoulder Arms! **armas portátiles,** small arms. (*fam.*) **de armas tomar,** belligerent; resolute. **pasar por las armas,** (*mil.*) to shoot. **presentar las armas,** (*mil.*) to present arms. **ser a. de dos filas,** (*fig.*) to cut both ways

armada, *f.* navy, armada; fleet, squadron

armadía, *f.* raft, pontoon

armador (-ra), *s.* supplier, outfitter. *m.* shipowner; pirate, privateer; jacket; assembler, fitter

armadura, *f.* armature, armour; frame, framework; skeleton (of a building); skeleton (of vertebrates); (*phys.*) armature; plate-armour (of persons)

armamento, *m.* (*mil.*) armament; arms, military equipment

armar, *v.t.* to arm; (*mech.*) mount; man (guns); put together, assemble; reinforce (concrete); (*fam.*) arrange, prepare; (*fam.*) occasion (quarrels); (*fam.*) outfit; (*naut.*) equip; commission (a ship) *v.r.* prepare oneself, arm oneself. **a. caballero,** to knight. **a. los remos,** to ship the oars. (*fam.*) **armarla,** to cause a row or quarrel

armario, *m.* cupboard; wardrobe. **a. de luna,** wardrobe with a mirror

armatoste, *m.* unwieldy piece of furniture; (*fig..fam.*) dead weight, clumsy person; snare

armazón, *f.* frame, framework; ship's hulk. *m.* (*anat.*) skeleton

armenio (**-ia**),*a.* and *s.* Armenian. *m.* Armenian language

armería, *f.* armoury; heraldry; gunsmith's craft or shop

armero, *m.* gunsmith, armourer; stand for weapons. **a. mayor,** Royal Armourer

armiño, *m.* ermine

armipotente, *a.* mighty in arms

armisticio, *m.* armistice

armón (*m.*) **de artillería,** gun-carriage

armonía, *f.* harmony; friendship; concord; (*mus.*) harmony

armónica (**de boca**), *f.* mouth-organ

armónico, *a.* harmonious. *a.* and *m.* (*mus.*) harmonic

armonio, *m.* harmonium

armonioso, *a.* harmonious

armonización, *f.* (*mus.*) harmonization

armonizar, *v.t.* to bring into harmony; (*mus.*) harmonize

arnés, *m.* armour; harness; *pl.* horse trappings; (*fam.*) equipment, tools

árnica, *f.* arnica

aro, *m.* hoop; rim (of wheel, etc.); napkin-ring; croquet hoop; (*bot.*)

wild arum; child's hoop. **a. de empaquedura,** (*mech.*) gasket

aroma, *m.* aroma, fragrance; balsam; sweet-smelling herb

aromático, *a.* aromatic

arpa, *f.* harp. **a. eolia,** Æolian harp

arpar, *v.t.* to scratch, claw; tear, rend

arpegio, *m.* (*mus.*) arpeggio

arpeo, *m.* (*naut.*) grappling-iron

arpía, *f.* harpy

arpicordio, *m.* harpsichord

arpista, *m.* and *f.* harpist, harp player

arpón, *m.* harpoon

arponear, *v.t.* to harpoon

arponero, *m.* harpooner; harpoon maker

arquear, *v.t.* to arch; bend; beat (wool); gauge (ship's capacity); *v.i.* retch

arqueo, *m.* arching; bending, curving; (*naut.*) tonnage; gauging (of ship's capacity); (*com.*) examination of deposits and contents of safe

arqueología, *f.* archæology

arqueológico, *a.* archæological

arqueólogo, *m.* archæologist

arquero, *m.* (*com.*) cashier, treasurer; (*mil.*) archer

arquitecto, *m.* architect. **a. de jardines,** landscape gardener

arquitectónico, *a.* architectural

arquitectura, *f.* architecture

arquitrabe, *m.* (*arch.*) architrave

arrabal, *m.* suburb, district; *pl.* outskirts

arracada, *f.* pendant-earring

arracimarse, *v.r.* to cluster; group

arráez, *m.* Moorish or Arab chieftain; (*naut.*) captain

arraigadamente, *adv.* deeply, firmly

arraigado, *a.* deep-rooted; firm; convinced

arraigar, *v.i.* to take root; *v.i.* and *v.r.* (*fig.*) become established, take hold; *v.r.* settle; take up residence

arraigo, *m.* rooting; settlement; establishment; landed property

arrancaclavos, *m.* nail-puller

arrancadero, *m.* (*sport*) starting-point

arrancar, *v.t.* to uproot; pull out; wrench; tear off; extirpate;

obtain by threats; clear one's throat; *v.t.* and *v.i.* (*naut.*) put on speed; *v.i.* start (a race); (*fam.*) leave, quit; derive, originate

arranque, *m.* uprooting; extirpation; wrenching, pulling, seizing; stimulus (of passion); sudden impulse; (*mech.*) start; (*mech.*) starter. **a. automático,** self-starter

arras, *f. pl.* dowry; coins given by bridegroom to his bride; earnest money, token

arrasamiento, *m.* demolition, destruction; levelling

arrasar, *v.t.* to demolish, destroy; level; fill to the brim; *v.i.* and *v.r.* clear up (sky). **ojos arrasados de lágrimas,** eyes brimming with tears

arrastrado, *a.* (*fam.*) poverty-stricken, wretched; (*fam.*) knavish; unhappy, unfortunate

arrastrar, *v.t.* to drag; trail; convince; haul; *v.i.* trail along or touch the ground; trump (at cards); *v.r.* crawl, creep; shuffle along; humble oneself

arrastre, *m.* dragging, trailing; haulage; trumping (at cards)

arrayán, *m.* (*bot.*) myrtle

¡arre! *interj.* Gee up! Get along!

arrear, *v.t.* to spur on, whip up (horses, etc.). *interj.* (*fam.*) **¡Arrea!** Hurry up! Get on!

arrebañar, *v.t.* to pick clean, clear; eat or drink up

arrebatado, *a.* precipitate, headlong; rash; flushed, red

arrebatador, *a.* overwhelming; violent; bewitching, captivating; delightful

arrebatamiento, *m.* abduction; seizure; fury; ecstasy

arrebatar, *v.t.* to abduct, carry off; seize, grab; attract, charm; grip (the attention); *v.r.* be overcome with rage

arrebatiña, *f.* grab; scuffle, scrimmage

arrebato, *m.* fit (gen. of anger); ecstasy, rapture

arrebol, *m.* red flush in the sky; rouge; *pl.* red clouds

arrebozar, *v.t.* to muffle; envelop

arrebujarse, *v.r.* to huddle; wrap oneself up

arreciar, *v.i.* to increase in intensity; *v.r.* grow strong

arrecife, *m.* reef (in the sea); stone-paved road

arrechucho, *m.* (*fam.*) fit of rage; sudden slight ailment

arredrar, *v.t.* to separate, remove; force back, repel; terrify

arregazar(se), *v.t.* and *v.r.* to tuck up one's skirts

arreglado, *a.* regular; regulated; ordered; methodical

arreglar, *v.t.* to regulate; arrange; adjust, put right; tidy; make up (the face); *v.r.* (*with prep. a*) conform to; (*with con*) reach an agreement with. **Me voy a a.,** I am going to make myself presentable. (*fam.*) **arreglárselas,** to shift for oneself

arreglo, *m.* arrangement; rule; regulation; method, order; agreement; adjustment; compromise

arrellanarse, *v.r.* to settle comfortably in one's chair; be happy in one's work

arremangar, *v.t.* to roll up (sleeves, trousers, etc.); *v.r.* (*fam.*) make a decision

arremango, *m.* rolling or tucking up (of sleeve, etc.)

arremetedor (**-ra**), *s.* attacker, assailant

arremeter, *v.t.* to attack, assail; *v.i.* launch oneself (at); (*fig.*) spoil the view, shock the eye

arremetida, *f.* attack, assault

arremolinarse, *v.r.* to crowd, cluster, group

arrendador (**-ra**), *s.* landlord; renter; hirer; tenant

arrendamiento, *m.* letting, renting; hiring; rental; agreement, lease

arrendar, *v.t. irr.* to let, lease; hire; rent (as a tenant); train (horses); tie up (horses); restrain; mimic, imitate. See **recomendar**

arrendatario (**-ia**), *a.* rent, lease. *s.* tenant; lessee; hirer

arreo, *m.* ornament; apparel; *pl.* horse trappings; appurtenances, equipment

arrepentimiento, *m.* repentance

arrepentirse, *v.r. irr.* to repent. See **sentir**

arrequesonarse, *v.r.* to go sour, curdle

arrestado, *a.* courageous, audacious, bold

arrestar, *v.t.* to arrest, detain; *v.r.* be bold, dare

arresto, *m.* arrest; detention; imprisonment; audacity, boldness

arriada, *f.* lowering (of a boat); taking in (of sail)

arriar, *v.t.* (*naut.*) to strike (colours); take in (sail); pay out (ropes, etc.); lower (boats) · flood, inundate

arriate, *m.* garden border; avenue, walk; trellis (for plants)

arriba, *adv.* up, above; overhead; upstairs; earlier, before; upwards (with prices). *interj.* ¡A.! Up with!; Long live! **de a. abajo,** from head to foot, from one end to the other; completely, wholly

arribada, *f.* (*naut.*) arrival. **de a.,** emergency (port)

arribar, *v.i.* (*naut.*) to arrive; put into an emergency port; reach, arrive at; (*fam.*) convalesce; attain; (*naut.*) drift

arribo, *m.* arrival

arriero, *m.* farrier; muleteer

arriesgado, *a.* dangerous, risky; rash, daring

arriesgar, *v.t.* to risk; *v.r.* run into danger; dare, risk

arrimar, *v.t.* to bring or draw near; abandon (professions, etc.); lay aside, discard; (*fam.*) administer (blows); (*naut.*) stow (cargo); *v.r.* (*with prep. a*) lean against, rest on; join, go with; seek the protection of. **Cada cual se arrima a su cada cual,** Birds of a feather flock together

arrimo, *m.* bringing or placing near; leaning or resting against; abandonment, giving up; protection; staff, support

arrinconado, *a.* remote, secluded; forgotten, neglected

arrinconar, *v.t.* to discard, lay aside; corner, besiege; set aside, dismiss; forsake; *v.r.* go into retirement, withdraw

arriscado, *a.* craggy, rugged; bold, resolute; sprightly, handsome

arrivista, *m. and f.* social climber

arrizar, *v.t.* (*naut.*) to reef; lash

arroba, *f.* weight of 25 lb.; variable liquid measure

arrobamiento, *m.* ecstasy, rapture; trance

arrobar, *v.t.* to charm, entrance; *v.r.* be enraptured; be in ecstasy

arrodillar, *v.t.* to cause to kneel down; *v.i.* and *v.r.* kneel down

arrogancia, *f.* arrogance; courage; majesty, pride

arrogante, *a.* arrogant, haughty; courageous; proud, majestic

arrogar, *v.t.* to adopt (as a son); *v.r.* usurp, appropriate

arrojadizo, *a.* easily cast or hurled; projectile

arrojado, *a.* bold, determined; rash

arrojar, *v.t.* to throw, hurl, cast; shed (light, etc.); (*com.*) show (a balance, etc.); put out (sprouts); dismiss, send away; *v.r.* cast oneself; (*with prep. a*) hurl oneself against or upon; undertake, venture upon. **a. de sí (a),** to get rid of, dismiss

arrojo, *m.* daring, intrepidity; boldness

arrollar, *v.t.* to roll; make into a roll, roll up; defeat (the enemy); silence, confound; rock to sleep; bear along, carry off

arromar, *v.t.* to blunt; flatten

arropamiento, *m.* wrapping up, covering, muffling

arropar, *v.t.* to wrap up, cover

arrostrar, *v.t.* to confront, defy, face up to; *v.r.* fight hand to hand. **a. las consecuencias,** (*fig.*) to face the music

arroyada, *f.* gorge, gully; course, channel; flood

arroyo, *m.* stream, brook; street gutter; road, street; (*fig.*) flood, plenty

arroz, *m.* rice

arrozal, *m.* rice field

arruga, *f.* wrinkle; fold, pleat; crease

arrugamiento, *m.* wrinkling; fold, pleating; crumpling, creasing; corrugation

arrugar, *v.t.* to wrinkle; pleat; corrugate; crumple, crease

arruinamiento, *m.* ruin, decay, decline

arruinar, *v.t.* to ruin; destroy, damage severely

arrullar, *v.t.* to bill and coo (doves); lull to sleep; (*fam.*) whisper sweet words to, make love to

arrullo, *m.* cooing of doves; lulla-by

arrumaco, *m.* (*fam.*) embrace, caress (gen. *pl.*); ornament in bad taste

arrumaje, *m.* (*naut.*) stowage; clouds on the horizon

arrurruz, *m.* arrowroot

arsenal, *m.* dockyard; arsenal; (*fig.*) store (of information, etc.)

arsénico, *m.* arsenic

arte, *m.* or *f.* art; skill; ability, talent; guile, craftiness. **las bellas artes,** Fine Arts. (*fam.*) **no tener a. ni parte en,** to have nothing to do with, have no part in

artefacto, *m.* machine, mechanism, apparatus; device, appliance. **a. atómico,** atomic bomb

artería, *f.* (*med.*) artery; main line (of communication)

artería, *f.* craftiness, guile

arterial, *a.* arterial

artesa, *f.* wooden trough; kneading bowl

artesano (-na), *s.* artisan; mechanic

artesiano, *a.* artesian

artesón, *m.* bucket, pail; (*arch.*) curved ceiling-panel; panelled ceiling

artesonado, *a.* (*arch.*) panelled (ceiling). *m.* panelled ceiling

ártico, *a.* Arctic

articulación, *f.* joint, articulation; jointing; enunciation, pronunciation

articular, *v.t.* to joint, articulate; enunciate, pronounce clearly

articulista, *m.* and *f.* article writer

artículo, *m.* finger knuckle; heading; article; (*anat.*) joint; (*gram.*) article; *pl.* goods, things. **a. de fondo,** leading article (in a newspaper). **a. de primera necesidad,** prime necessity, essential

artífice, *m.* and *f.* craftsman, artificer; author, creator; forger

artificial, *a.* artificial

artificio, *m.* skill, art; appliance, contraption, mechanism; trick, cunning device; guile, craftiness

artificioso, *a.* skilful; artificial; crafty, cunning

artillar, *v.t.* to mount guns upon

artillería, *f.* artillery. **a. de costa,** coastal guns. **a. ligera, a. montada, a. rodada** *or* **a. volante,** field artillery

artillero, *m.* gunner

artimaña, *f.* trick, ruse, stratagem

artista, *m.* and *f.* artist; performer

artístico, *a.* artistic

artrítico, *a.* (*med.*) arthritic

artritis, *f.* (*med.*) arthritis

arveja, *f.* (*bot.*) vetch

arzobispado, *m.* archbishopric

arzobispal, *a.* archiepiscopal

arzobispo, *m.* archbishop

arzón, *m.* saddle-tree

as, *m.* Roman copper coin; ace (*aer.*, cards, etc.)

asa, *f.* handle; pretext, excuse

asación, *f.* roasting

asado, *m.* (*cul.*) roast

asador, *m.* (*cul.*) roasting-spit; roaster

asadura, *f.* (*cul.*) chitterlings; offal

asaetear, *v.t.* to attack with arrows

asalariar, *v.t.* to fix a salary for

asaltador (-ra), *a.* attacking. *s.* assailant, attacker

asaltar, *v.t.* to storm, besiege; assault, attack; occur to (ideas); come on suddenly (illness)

asalto, *m.* storming, besieging; assault, attack; bout (in fencing, boxing, wrestling); round (in a fight)

asamblea, *f.* congregation, assembly; meeting; legislative assembly; (*mil.*) assembly (bugle call)

asambleísta, *m.* and *f.* member of an assembly

asar, *v.t.* (*cul.*) to roast; grill; *v.r.* be burning-hot; (*fig.*) burn (with enthusiasm)

asaz, *adv.* sufficiently, enough; very; in abundance. *a.* sufficient; many

asbesto, *m.* asbestos

ascalonia, *f.* (*bot.*) shallot

ascendencia, *f.* lineage, ancestry, origin

ascendente, *a.* ascending

ascender, *v.i. irr.* to ascend, climb; be promoted; (*with prep. a*) amount to (bills, etc.); *v.t.* promote. See **entender**

ascendiente, *m.* and *f.* ancestor, forbear. *m.* influence, ascendancy

ascensión, *f.* ascension; promotion; (*ast.*) exaltation

ascenso, *m.* ascent; promotion, preferment

ascensor, *m.* lift, elevator

ascensorista, *m.* and *f.* lift worker

asceta, *m.* and *f.* ascetic

ascético, *a.* ascetic

ascetismo, *m.* asceticism

asco, *m.* nausea; repugnance, loathing; revolting thing. (*fam.*) Me da a., It sickens me

ascua, *f.* live coal, ember. **estar como una a. de oro,** to be as bright as a new pin. **estar en ascuas,** (*fig.*) to be on pins

aseado, *a.* clean, tidy

asear, *v.t.* to tidy, make neat; clean up; decorate, adorn

asechanza, *f.* ambush; trick, snare, stratagem

asechar, *v.t.* to ambush, waylay; (*fig.*) lay snares for

asediador (-ra), *s.* besieger

asediar, *v.i.* to besiege; pester, importune

asedio, *m.* siege; importunity

asegundar, *v.t.* to do again, repeat

asegurado (-da), *a.* insured. *s.* insured person

asegurador (-ra), *a.* insuring. *s.* insurer

asegurar, *v.t.* to fasten, make secure; pinion, grip; reassure, soothe; assert, state; (*com.*) insure; guarantee; ensure, secure; *v.r.* (*com.*) insure oneself; (*with de*) make sure of

asemejar, *v.t.* to imitate, copy; make similar to; *v.r.* (*with prep. a*) be like, be similar to

asenderear, *v.t.* to make a pathway through; persecute, harass

asenso, *m.* assent. **dar a.,** to believe, give credence (to)

asentaderas, *f. pl.* (*fam.*) buttocks, seat

asentado, *a.* prudent, circumspect; permanent, stable

asentamiento, *m.* seating; settlement, residence; prudence, judgment

asentar, *v.t. irr.* to seat; place; fasten, fix; found; plant (flags); pitch (a tent); establish, make firm; smooth; hone (razors); estimate, budget, arrange, set forth; note down; affirm, believe; (*com.*) enter (in an account); *v.i.* fit (clothes); *v.r.* seat oneself; alight (birds); settle (liquids); (*arch.*) settle, subside. a. la **mano en,** to strike hard. See **acertar**

asentimiento, *m.* assent; consent, approval

asentir, *v.i. irr.* to assent, agree; (*with en*) consent to. See **sentir**

aseñorado, *a.* refined, gentlemanly; ladylike; presumptuous

aseo, *m.* cleanliness, neatness

asepsia, *f.* (*med.*) asepsis

asequible *a.* attainable; obtainable

aserción, *f.* assertion

aserradero, *m.* saw-mill; saw-pit

aserrador (-ra), *s.* sawyer

aserrar, *v.t. irr.* to saw. See **acertar**

aserrín, *m.* sawdust

asertivo, *a.* assertive

aserto, *m.* assertion

asesinar, *v.t.* to assassinate, murder

asesinato, *m.* assassination, murder

asesino, *m.* and *f.* assassin, murderer; murderess

asesor (-ra), *s.* assessor

asesorar, *v.t.* to give advice; *v.r.* take legal advice; seek advice

asestar, *v.t.* to aim (firearms); fire; deal (a blow)

aseveración, *f.* assertion, statement

aseveradamente, *adv.* affirmatively

aseverar, *v.t.* to affirm, assert

asfaltado, *m.* asphalting; asphalt pavement

asfaltar, *v.t.* to asphalt

asfalto, *m.* asphalt

asfixia, *f.* (*med.*) asphyxia

asfixiante, *a.* asphyxiating

asfixiar, *v.t.* to asphyxiate

asfódelo, *m.* (*bot.*) asphodel

así, *adv.* thus, so, in this way; even if; so that, therefore. a. a., middling, so-so. a. como a., as well as; as soon as. a. que, as soon as, immediately; consequently, thus

asiático (-ca), *a.* and *s.* Asiatic

asidero, *m.* hold, grasp; handle, haft; pretext, excuse

asiduidad, *f.* assiduity
asiduo, *a.* assiduous
asiento, *m.* seat; place, position; site; base (of a vase, etc.); lees, sediment; (*arch.*) subsidence, settling; treaty, pact; contract; note, reminder; (*com.*) entry; permanence, stability; prudence; bit (of a bridle); *pl.* buttocks, seat. estar de .a., to be established (in a place)
asignación, *f.* assignation; salary; portion, share
asignar, *v.t.* to assign; apportion; destine, intend; appoint
asignatura, *f.* subject (of study in schools, etc.)
asilar, *v.t.* to give shelter to, receive; put into an institution
asilo, *m.* shelter, refuge; sanctuary, asylum; (*fig.*) protection, defence; home, institution
asimetría, *f.* asymmetry
asimétrico, *a.* asymmetrical
asimiento, *m.* hold, grasp; attachment, affection
asimilable, *a.* assimilable
asimilación, *f.* assimilation
asimilar, *v.t.* to compare, liken; (*bot., zool., gram.*) assimilate; *v.i.* resemble, be like; (*fig.*) assimilate, digest (ideas)
asimismo, *adv.* similarly, likewise
asir, *v.t. irr.* to grasp, take hold of; seize; *v.i.* take root (plants); *v.r.* (*with de*) lay hold of; take advantage of; make an excuse to. *Pres. Ind.* asgo, ases, etc. *Pres. Subjunc.* asga, etc.
asirio (-ia), *a.* and *s.* Assyrian. *m.* Assyrian language
asistencia, *f.* presence, attendance; assistance, help; service, attendance; medical treatment; remuneration; *pl.* allowance. a. pública, Public Assistance. a. social, social work
asistenta, *f.* daily maid; waiting-maid
asistente, *m.* assistant; (*mil.*) orderly
asistir, *v.t.* to accompany; assist, help; attend, treat; (*with de*) act as; *v.i.* (*with prep. a*) be present at, attend; follow suit (in cards)
asma, *f.* asthma
asmático (-ca), *a.* asthmatic. *s.* sufferer from asthma

asnal, *a.* asinine; brutish, stupid
asno, *m.* ass
asociación, *f.* association; company, partnership; society, fellowship
asociado (-da), *s.* associate; member; partner
asociar, *v.t.* to associate; *v.r.* associate oneself; join together; form a partnership
asolación, *f.* asolamiento, *m.* destruction, ruin
asolanar, *v.t.* to shrivel (plants by wind)
asolar, *v.t. irr.* to destroy, devastate, lay flat; *v.r.* wither; settle (liquids). See contar
asoldar, *v.t. irr.* to employ, engage, hire. See contar
asolear, *v.t.* to expose to the sun; *v.r.* sun oneself; become sunburnt
asomada, *f.* brief appearance; vantage point
asomar, *v.t.* to show, allow to appear, put forth; *v.i.* begin to show; *v.r.* show oneself, appear; (*fam.*) be flushed (with wine); (*with prep. a, por*) look out of. asomarse a la ventana, to show oneself at, or look out of, the window
asombrar, *v.t.* to shade, shadow; darken (a colour); terrify; amaze
asombro, *m.* fright, terror; amazement; wonder, marvel
asombroso, *a.* amazing; marvellous, wonderful
asonancia, *f.* assonance; congruity, harmony
asonante, *a.* and *m.* assonant
asordar, *v.t.* to deafen
aspa, *f.* cross; sail of a windmill
aspaviento, *m.* exaggerated display of emotion; gesture (of horror, etc.)
aspecto, *m.* look, appearance; aspect, outlook
aspereza, *f.* roughness, harshness; ruggedness, rockiness; severity, asperity
áspero, *a.* rough, harsh; uneven, rocky; jarring, grating; hard, severe
aspersión, *f.* (*ecc.*) aspersion; sprinkling
áspid, *m.* asp, viper
aspillera, *f.* embrasure, loophole

aspiración, *f.* breath; breathing; aspiration, desire; (*mus.*) pause

aspirador de polvo, *m.* vacuum cleaner

aspirante, *m.* aspirant, novice; office-seeker; applicant

aspirar, *v.t.* to breathe in, inhale; (*gram.*) aspirate; (*with prep. a*) aspire to, desire

aspirina, *f.* aspirin

asquear, *v.i.* and *v.t.* to hate, loathe

asquerosidad, *f.* filthiness, loathsomeness; vileness, hatefulness

asqueroso, *a.* nauseating; loathsome, revolting; vile, hateful

asta, *f.* lance, spear, pike; horn (of bull); antler; flagstaff; shaft. **a media a.,** at half-mast

asterisco, *m.* asterisk

astigmático, *a.* astigmatic

astigmatismo, *m.* astigmatism

astil, *m.* handle, pole, shaft; bar of a balance; beam feather

astilla, *f.* splinter

astillar, *v.t.* to splinter, chip

astillero, *m.* shipyard; rack for lances and pikes

astilloso, *a.* splintery, fragile

astracán, *m.* astrakhan

astringente, *a.* astringent

astringir, *v.t.* to tighten up; compress; constrain

astro, *m.* heavenly body

astrología, *f.* astrology

astrológico, *a.* astrological

astrólogo (-ga), *s.* astrologist

astronomía, *f.* astronomy

astronómico, *a.* astronomical

astrónomo, *m.* astronomer

astucia, *f.* astuteness, guile, craftiness

asturiano (-na), *a.* and *s.* Asturian

astuto, *a.* guileful, crafty, astute

asueto, *m.* day's holiday

asumir, *v.t.* to assume; adopt, appropriate

asunción, *f.* assumption

asunto, *m.* matter, theme, subject; business, affair

asustadizo, *a.* timid, nervous, easily-frightened

asustar, *v.t.* to frighten; *v.r.* be frightened

atabal, *m.* kettle-drum

atabanado, *a.* with white spots (horses)

atablar, *v.t.* to roll, flatten (earth)

atacado, *a.* (*fam.*) hesitant; mean, stingy

atacador (-ra), *a.* attacking. *s.* aggressor, attacker

atacar, *v.t.* to attack; fasten; button; fit (clothes); ram (guns); (*fig.*) press hard, corner (persons). **a. a los nervios,** to jar on the nerves

atadero, *m.* rope, tie, cord; hook, ring, etc. (for hitching); hindrance, impediment; hitching or fastening point

atado, *m.* bundle, rol.

atadura, *f.* tying, stringing, fastening, tie; knot; connection

atajar, *v.i.* to take a short cut; *v.t.* intercept, cut off; screen off, divide; impede, stop; interrupt (people); *v.r.* be overcome (by fear, shame, etc.)

atajo, *m.* short cut, quick way; cutting, abbreviation; division. (*fam.*) **echar por el a.,** to go to the root of (a matter)

atalaya, *f.* look-out, watch-tower; observation point. *m.* look-out

atalayar, *v.t.* to scan, watch; spy upon

atalón, *m.* atoll, coral island

atañer, *v.i. impers.* to concern, affect; belong, pertain

ataque, *m.* (*mil., med.*) attack; quarrel, fight

atar, *v.t.* to tie; fasten; lace; stop, paralyse; *v.r.* get in a fix; confine oneself. **a. cabos,** to put two and two together

atardecer, *v.i. irr. impers.* to grow dusk. See conocer

atardecer, *m.* dusk, evening

atarear, *v.t.* to set to work, assign work to; *v.r.* work hard

atarugar, *v.t.* to wedge; stop up; plug; block; (*fam.*) silence, shut up; stuff, cram; *v.r.* (*fig., fam.*) lose one's head

atasajar, *v.t.* to cut up, jerk (beef, etc.)

atascadero, *m.* deep rut, boggy place; impediment, obstacle

atascar, *v.t.* to plug; block up; stop (a leak); hinder, obstruct; *v.r.* stick in the mud; be held up or delayed; (*fam.*) get stuck in a speech

atasco, *m.* obstruction, block

ataúd, *m.* coffin

ataviar, *v.t.* to deck, apparel, adorn

atavío, *m.* get-up, dress, apparel; *pl.* ornaments

atavismo, *m.* atavism

ateísmo, *m.* atheism

atelaje, *m.* team, yoke (of horses); trappings, harness; (*fam.*) trousseau

atemperación, *f.* moderation, mitigation; tempering

atemperar, *v.t.* to moderate, mitigate; adapt, adjust; temper, cool

atenazar, *v.t.* to grip, grasp; torture

atención, *f.* attention; solicitude, kindness; courtesy, civility; *pl.* business affairs. *interj.* ¡A.! Take care! Look out!; (*mil.*) Attention! en a. (a), taking into consideration

atender, *v.t. irr.* to await, expect; take care of, look after; *v.i.* (*with prep. a*) attend to, listen to; *v.i.* remember. See entender

ateneo, *m.* athenæum. *a.* Athenian

atenerse, *v.r. irr.* (*with prep. a*) to abide by; resort to, rely on. See tener

ateniense, *a.* and *m.* and *f.* Athenian

atentado, *a.* prudent, sensible; secret, silent. *m.* infringement, violation; attempt (on a person's life); crime

atentar, *v.t. irr.* to do illegally; attempt a crime; *v.r.* proceed cautiously; restrain oneself. See acertar

atento, *a.* attentive; courteous, civil. *adv.* taking into consideration. su atenta (atta), (*com.*) your favour

atenuación, *f.* attenuation, diminution

atenuante, *a.* attenuating; extenuating (of circumstances)

atenuar, *v.t.* to attenuate, diminish; extenuate

ateo (-ea), *a.* atheistic. *s.* atheist

aterciopelado, *a.* velvety

aterirse, *v.r. defective.* to grow stiff with cold

aterrador, *a.* terrifying, dreadful

aterraje, *m.* (*aer., naut.*) landing

aterramiento, *m.* horror, terror; terrorization; (*naut.*) landing; ruin, demolition

aterrar, *v.t. irr.* to demolish; discourage; cover with earth; *v.i.* land; *v.r.* (*naut.*) draw near to land. See acertar

aterrizaje, *m.* (*aer.*) landing. a. forzoso, forced landing. campo de a., landing-field

aterrizar, *v.i.* (*aer.*) to land, touch down

aterrorizar, *v.t.* to terrify; terrorize

atesorar, *v.t.* to hoard, treasure up

atestación, *f.* attestation, affidavit

atestar, *v.t. irr.* to stuff, cram; insert; (*fam.*) stuff with food; crowd, fill with people. See acertar

atestar, *v.t.* to attest, testify

atestiguación, *f.* deposition, testimony

atestiguar, *v.t.* to testify, attest

atetar, *v.t.* to suckle; *v.i.* suck

atezado, *a.* bronzed, sunburnt; black

atezar, *v.t.* to blacken

ático, *a.* Attic

atiesar, *v.t.* to stiffen

atigrado, *a.* tigerish; tiger (of cats)

atildar, *v.t.* to place a tilde over; blame, criticize; decorate, ornament

atinado, *a.* pertinent, relevant

atinar, *v.i.* to find by touch; discover by chance; guess; hit the mark

atisbadura, *f.* watching, spying, prying

atisbar, *v.t.* to spy upon, watch

atisbo, *m.* prying, watching; suspicion, hint

atizador, *m.* poker (for the fire)

atizar, *v.t.* to poke (the fire); dowse, snuff; trim (lamps); excite, rouse; (*fam.*) slap, wallop

atlántico, *a.* Atlantic. *m.* Atlantic Ocean

atleta, *m.* athlete

atlético, *a.* athletic

atletismo, *m.* athletics

atmósfera, *f.* atmosphere

atmosférico, *a.* atmospheric

atolón, *m.* atoll, coral island

atolondrado, *a.* scatter-brained, flighty

atolondramiento, *m.* rashness, recklessness; bewilderment

atolondrar, *v.t.* to bewilder, confuse

atolladero, *m.* rut; mud; bog

atómico, *a.* atomic

átomo, *m.* atom; speck, particle

atónito, *a.* amazed, astounded

atontar, *v.t.* to confuse, daze; make stupid; stun

atormentador (-ra), *a.* torturing. *s.* tormentor; torturer

atormentar, *v.t.* to torment; torture; grieve, harass

atornillar, *v.t.* to screw; fasten with screws

atracadero, *m.* jetty, landing-stage

atracar, *v.t.* (*fam.*) to stuff with food; (*naut.*) tie up, moor; hold up, rob; *v.i.* (*naut.*) moor, stop; *v.r.* (*fam.*) guzzle, gorge

atracción, *f.* attraction

atraco, *m.* hold up, ambush

atracón, *m.* (*fam.*) gorge, fill; surfeit

atractivo, *a.* attractive. *m.* attraction, charm

atraer, *v.t. irr.* to attract; charm, enchant. See **traer**

atragantarse, *v.r.* to choke; (*fam.*) be at a loss, dry up (in conversation)

atraíble, *a.* attractable, able to be attracted

atrancar, *v.t.* to bar the door; obstruct, block; hinder; *v.i.* (*fam.*) stride; skip (in reading)

atrapar, *v.t.* (*fam.*) grab, seize, catch; net, obtain; deceive

atrás, *adv.* behind, back; past; previously. ¡A.¡ Back¡ años a., years ago

atrasado, *a.* slow (of clocks); backward; old-fashioned; hard-up, poor

atrasar, *v.t.* to delay, retard; fix a later date than the true one; put back (clocks). *v.i.* be slow (clocks); *v.r.* be late; be left behind

atraso, *m.* delay; backwardness, dullness; slowness (clocks); lateness; *pl.* arrears. El reloj lleva cinco minutos de a., The watch is five minutes slow

atravesado, *a.* slightly squint-eyed; mongrel, crossbreed; half-caste; ill-intentioned

atravesar, *v.t. irr.* to lay across, put athwart; cross, traverse; pierce; obstruct; (*naut.*) lie to; *v.r.* be among, mingle (with); interrupt; interfere, take part; quarrel; occur, arise. See **confesar**

atrayente, *a.* attractive

atreverse, *v.r.* to dare, risk, venture; be overbold or insolvent

atrevido, *a.* bold, audacious; hazardous, dangerous; brazen, impudent

atribuible, *a.* attributable

atribución, *f.* attribution; perquisite, attribute

atribuir, *v.t. irr.* to impute, attribute; assign, turn over to; *v.r.* take upon oneself, assume. See **huir**

atributo, *m.* attribute; quality

atril, *m.* lectern, reading-desk; music stand

atrincherar, *v.t.* to protect with entrenchments; *v.r.* entrench oneself

atrio, *m.* atrium; hall, vestibule; (*arch.*) parvis

atrocidad, *f.* atrocity, cruelty; (*fam.*) terrific amount; enormity, crime

atrofia, *f.* atrophy

atrofiarse, *v.r.* to atrophy

atronado, *a.* hare-brained, foolish

atronar, *v.t. irr.* to deafen, stun with noise; confuse, daze. See **tronar**

atropelladamente, *adv.* in disorder, helter-skelter

atropellado, *a.* rash, foolhardy

atropellar, *v.t.* to trample upon; thrust out of the way; knock down; disregard, violate (feelings); insult, abuse; transgress; do hastily; *v.r.* act rashly

atropello, *m.* trampling; road accident; knocking over; upsetting; violation; outrage

atropina, *f.* (*chem.*) atropine

atroz, *a.* atrocious, savage; monstrous, outrageous; (*fam.*) terrific, enormous

atufar, *v.t.* to irritate, vex; *v.r.* grow irritated; turn sour (wine, etc.)

atún, *m.* tunny fish

aturdido, *a.* scatter-brained, silly

aturdimiento, *m.* daze; confusion, bewilderment

aturdir, *v.t.* to daze; confuse, bewilder; amaze; stun

atusar, *v.t.* to trim (hair, beard); (*agr.*) prune; smooth down (hair); *v.r.* dress over-carefully

audacia, *f.* audacity

audaz, *a.* audacious, daring

audibilidad, *f.* audibility

audición, *f.* audition

audiencia, *f.* audience, hearing; (*law*) audience; audience chamber

audífono, *m.* deaf aid, hearing apparatus

auditivo, *a.* auditory

auditor, *m.* magistrate, judge

auditorio, *a.* auditory. *m.* audience

auge, *m.* (*fig.*) zenith, height; (*ast.*) apogee

augusto, *a.* august, awesome

aula, *f.* lecture or class room; (*poet.*) palace

aulaga, *f.* (*bot.*) gorse, whin

aullador, *a.* howling

aullar, *v.i.* to howl; bay

aullido, *m.* howl; baying

aumentar(se), *v.t.*, *v.i.*, *v.r.* to increase, augment

aumentativo, *a.* (*gram.*) augmentative

aumento, *m.* increase; progress; enlargement. ir en a., to increase; advance, progress; prosper

aun (aún), *adv.* even; yet; still. *conjunc.* aun cuando, even if, although. Tendency in modern Spanish is to use aun and aún interchangeably

aunque, *conjunc.* although, even if, even though. It takes the Indicative referring to statement of fact and Subjunctive referring to a hypothesis, e.g. A. vino, no lo hizo, Although he came, he did not do it. A. él cantase yo no iría allí, Even though he sang (were to sing), I should not go there

aura, *f.* zephyr, gentle breeze; popularity, approbation; aura. a. epiléptica, (*med.*) epileptic aura

áureo, *a.* gold, gilt; golden

aureola, *f.* aureole

aurícula, *f.* (*anat.*) auricle

auricular, *a.* auricular. *m.* little finger; receiver, ear-piece (of a telephone); earphone (wireless)

aurífero, *a.* gold-yielding, auriferous

auriga, *m.* charioteer

aurora, *f.* dawn; genesis, beginnings. a. boreal, aurora borealis, Northern Lights

auscultación, *f.* (*med.*) auscultation

auscultar, *v.t.* (*med.*) to auscultate

ausencia, *f.* absence

ausentar, *v.t.* to send away; *v.r.* absent oneself

ausente, *a.* absent. *m.* and *f.* absent person

auspicio, *m.* augury, prediction; favour, patronage; *pl.* auspices

austeridad, *f.* austerity; mortification of the flesh

austero *a.* austere, ascetic; severe, harsh; honest, upright

austral, *a.* southerly, austral

australiano (-na), *a.* and *s.* Australian

austríaco (-ca), *a.* and *s.* Austrian

autenticación, *f.* authentication

autenticar, *v.t.* to authenticate, attest; prove genuine

autenticidad, *f.* authenticity

auténtico, *a.* authentic

autillo, *m.* brown owl

auto, *m.* (*law*) sentence, decision; (*theat.*) one-act allegory (gen. religious); *pl.* proceedings. a. de fe, auto-da-fé. a. de reconocimiento, search-warrant. a. sacramental, one-act religious drama on theme of mystery of the Eucharist. hacer a. de fe de, to burn

autobiografía, *f.* autobiography

autobús, *m.* motor bus, bus

autoclave, *m.* pressure cooker

autocracia, *f.* autocracy

autócrata, *m.* and *f.* autocrat

autocrático, *a.* autocratic

autodidacto, *a.* self-educating

autódromo, *m.* motor-racing track, speedway

autógeno, *a.* autogenous, self-generating

autogiro, *m.* (*aer.*) autogyro

autografía, *f.* autography

autográfico, *a.* autographic, in lithographic reproduction

autógrafo, *a.* autographical. *m.* autograph

autoinducción, *f.* self-induction

autómata, *m.* automaton

automático, *a.* automatic. *m.* (*sew.*) press stud

automatismo, *m.* automatism

automóvil, *m.* automobile, motor car. *a.* automatic

automovilismo, *m.* motoring

automovilista, *m.* and *f.* motorist

autonomía, *f.* autonomy

autónomo, *a.* autonomous

autopista, *f.* motor road

autopsia, *f.* (*med.*) autopsy, post-mortem

autor (**-ra**), *s.* agent, originator; author; inventor; (*law*) perpetrator

autoridad, *f.* authority; pomp, show

autoritario, *a.* authoritarian; authoritative

autorización, *f.* authorization

autorizado, *a.* approved, authorized, responsible

autorizar, *v.t.* to authorize; (*law*) attest, testify; cite, prove by reference; approve; exalt

autorretrato, *m.* self-portrait

autosugestión, *f.* auto-suggestion

auxiliador (**-ra**), *a.* assistant; helpful. *s.* helper, assistant

auxiliar, *v.t.* to help, aid; attend (the dying). *m.* (*univ.*) lecturer. *a.* assisting

auxiliaría, *f.* (*univ.*) lectureship

auxilio, *m.* help, aid, assistance

aval, *m.* (*com.*) endorsement; voucher

avalentado, *a.* boastful, bragging

avalorar, *v.t.* to value, estimate; put spirit into, encourage

avance, *m.* advance; advance payment; balance sheet; attack

avanzada, *f.* (*mil.*) advance guard

avanzado, *a.* advanced, progressive

avanzar, *v.t.* to advance; promote; *v.i.* advance; attack; grow late (time)

avanzo, *m.* balance sheet; price estimate

avaricia, *f.* greed, avarice

avaricioso, avariento, *a.* avaricious, greedy

avaro (**-ra**), *a.* miserly; greedy. *s.* miser

avasallador, *a.* dominating; (*fig.*) overwhelming

avasallar, *v.t.* to subdue, domi-

nate; *v.r.* become a vassal; surrender, yield

ave, *f.* bird. **a. de paso,** migratory bird; (*fig.*) bird of passage. **a. de rapiña,** bird of prey. **a. fría,** (*orn.*) plover. **aves cantoras,** singing birds

avecindar, *v.t.* to domicile; *v.r.* take up residence; approach

avechucho, *m.* hideous bird; (*fig., fam.*) scarecrow, sight

avellana, *f.* hazel nut

avellanarse, *v.r.* to shrivel

avellano, *m.* (*bot.*) hazel

avemaría, *f.* Hail Mary (prayer); Angelus; rosary bead. (*fam.*) **en un a.,** in a trice

avena, *f.* oats; (*poet.*) oaten pipe. **a. loca,** wild oats

avenal, *m.* oatfield

avenar, *v.t.* to drain (land); drain off· (liquids)

avenencia, *f.* agreement, arrangement; transaction; conformity, harmony

avenida, *f.* flood, spate; avenue; abundance; way, approach (to a place)

avenido, *a.* (*with bien or mal*) well *or* ill-suited

avenidor (**-ra**), *s.* arbitrator, mediator

avenir, *v.t. irr.* to reconcile; *v.i.* happen (used in infinitive and third singular and plural); *v.r.* be reconciled; agree; compromise, give way; harmonize (things); (*with con*) get on with, agree with. See **venir**

aventador, *m.* (*agr.*) winnower; pitchfork

aventajado, *a.* outstanding, talented; advantageous. *m.* (*mil.*) private who enjoys extra pay

aventajar, *v.t.* to improve, better; promote, prefer; excel; *v.r.* (*with prep. a*) surpass, excel

aventamiento, *m.* winnowing

aventar, *v.t. irr.* to fan; air, ventilate; winnow; (*fam.*) drive away, expel; *v.r.* be inflated; (*fam.*) flee; smell (bad meat). See **sentar**

aventura, *f.* adventure; chance, luck; risk, danger

aventurar, *v.t.* to risk, hazard

aventurero (**-ra**), *a.* adventurous; unscrupulous, intriguing;

undisciplined (of troops). *s.* adventurer

avergonzar, *v.t. irr.* to shame; make shy, abash; *v.r.* be ashamed; be shy or sheepish. *Pres. Ind.* avergüenzo, avergüenzas, avergüenza, avergüenzan. *Pres. Subjunc.* avergüence, avergüences, avergüence, avergüencen

avería, *f.* aviary; damage (to merchandise); loss, harm; (*elec.*) fault; breakdown. a. gruesa, general average (marine insurance)

averiarse, *v.r.* to be damaged; deteriorate; break down

averiguable, *a.* examinable, investigable; discoverable

averiguación, *f.* inquiry, investigation; discovery

averiguar, *v.t.* to investigate, inquire into; discover, ascertain

averío, *m.* flock of birds

Averno, *m.* (*poet.*) Avernus, Hades

aversión, *f.* aversion, repugnance

avestruz *m.* ostrich

avetado, *a.* veined, mottled, streaked

avezar, *v.t.* to accustom; *v.r.* grow accustomed (to)

aviación, *f.* aviation

aviador, *m.* aviator

aviar, *v.t.* to outfit, equip; prepare, make ready; (*fam.*) speed up; caulk (ship). (*fig., fam.*) estar aviado, to be in a mess

avicultura, *f.* aviculture

avidez, *f.* avidity, greed; longing, desire

ávido, *a.* avid, greedy

avieso, *a.* twisted, crooked; ill-natured; sinister

avilés (-esa), *a.* and *s.* of or from Ávila (Castile)

avillanado, *a.* countrified; gross, vulgar; boorish

avinagrado, *a.* (*fam.*) crabbed, sour, testy

avío, *m.* preparation, provision; picnic lunch; money advanced (to miners or labourers); *pl.* (*fam.*) equipment, tools

avión, *m.* aeroplane; (*orn.*) martin or swift. a. de bombardeo, bombing aircraft. a. de caza, fighter aircraft. a. de combate nocturno, night fighter aircraft. a. de hostigamiento, inter-

ceptor aircraft. a. de transporte, (*aer.*) transport. a. en picado, dive-bomber. a. taxi, air taxi. por a., by air-mail

avisado, *a.* shrewd, sensible. mal·a., ill-advised, imprudent

avisar, *v.t.* to inform, acquaint; warn; advise

aviso, *m.* notice, announcement; warning; advice; care, caution; attention; shrewdness, prudence. estar sobre a., to be on call; be on the alert

avispa, *f.* wasp

avispado, *a.* (*fam.*) smart, clever, quick; wide-awake

avispar, *v.t.* to goad, prick; (*fam.*) rouse, incite; *v.r.* be uneasy, fret

avispero, *m.* wasp's nest; swarm of wasps; (*fig., fam.*) hornet's nest

avispón, *m.* hornet

avituallar, *v.t.* to victual, supply with food

avivar, *v.t.* to enliven; stimulate, encourage; stir (fire); trim (wicks); brighten (colours); inflame; vivify, invigorate; *v.i.* revive, recover

avizor, *m.* watcher, spy. *a.* watchful, vigilant

avizorar, *v.t.* to watch, spy upon

avolcanado, *a.* volcanic (of a region)

avutarda, *f.* (*orn.*) bustard

axila, *f.* (*bot.*) axil; (*anat.*) axilla, arm-pit

axilar, *a.* axillary

axioma, *m.* axiom

axiomático, *a.* axiomatic

¡ay! *interj.* Alas! Woe is me! *m.* complaint, sigh

aya, *f.* governess

ayer, *adv.* yesterday; a short while ago; in the past. *m.* past

ayo, *m.* tutor

ayuda, *f.* help, assistance; enema; clyster; watch dog. *m.* a. de cámara, valet

ayudador (-ra), *a.* helping, assisting. *s.* helper

ayudante, *m.* assistant; assistant teacher; (*mil.*) adjutant. a. a cátedra, (*univ.*) assistant lecturer

ayudar, *v.t.* to assist; help, aid; *v.r.* make an effort; avail oneself of another's help

ayunador (-ra), *a.* fasting. *s.* faster; abstainer

ayunar, *v.i.* to fast

ayuno, *m.* fast. *a.* fasting; ignorant, unaware. **en a.** *or* **en ayunas,** before breakfast, fasting; (*fam.*) ignorant, unaware

ayuntamiento, *m.* meeting, assembly; municipal government; town hall; sexual union

azabache, *m.* (*min.*) jet

azada, *f.* (*agr.*) spade; hoe

azadón, *m.* (*agr.*) hoe

azafata, *f.* queen's waiting-maid (*ant.*); air-hostess

azafate, *m.* flat basket; small tray

azafrán, *m.* (*bot.*) saffron; crocus

azafranado, *a.* saffron-coloured

azagaya, *f.* assegai, spear

azahar, *m.* flower of orange, lemon or sweet lime tree

azalea, *f.* (*bot.*) azalea

azar, *m.* chance, hazard; unexpected misfortune; losing card or throw of dice

azararse, *v.r.* to go wrong, fail (negotiations, etc.); grow nervous; become confused; blush

azaroso, *a.* unlucky, ill-omened; hazardous

ázimo, *a.* unleavened (bread)

ázoe, *m.* (*chem.*) nitrogen

azogar, *v.t.* to silver (mirrors, etc.); slake lime; *v.r.* suffer from mercury poisoning; (*fam.*) grow uneasy, be agitated

azogue, *m.* (*min.*) mercury, quicksilver; market-place

azor, *m.* (*orn.*) goshawk

azoramiento, *m.* alarm, terror; confusion, stupefaction; incitement

azorar, *v.t.* to alarm, terrify; confuse, stun, dumbfound; excite, stimulate; encourage

azotacalles, *m.* and *f.* (*fam.*) idler, street loafer

azotaina, *f.* (*fam.*) whipping, spanking

azotamiento, *m.* flogging, beating, whipping

azotar, *v.t.* to whip, beat, flog; scourge; knock against or strike repeatedly

azotazo, *m.* spank

azote, *m.* whip; scourge; lash, blow with a whip; spank, slap; misfortune, disaster. (*fam.*) **azotes y galeras,** monotonous diet

azotea, *f.* flat terrace roof

azteca, *a.* and *m.* and *f.* Aztec

azúcar, *m.* sugar. **a. blanco** *or* **a. de flor,** white sugar. **a. de pilón,** loaf sugar. **a. moreno,** brown sugar. **a. quebrado,** brown sugar. **a. y canela,** sorrel grey (of horses)

azucarado, *a.* sugary; sugared, sugar-coated; (*fam.*) honeyed, flattering

azucarar, *v.t.* to coat with sugar; sweeten; (*fam.*) soften, mitigate; *v.r.* crystallize; go sugary (jam)

azucarera, *f.* sugar-basin

azucarillo, *m.* (*cul.*) bar made of white of egg and sugar for sweetening water

azucena, *f.* white lily. **a. de agua,** water-lily

azud, *m.* water-wheel; weir

azuela, *f.* adze

azufrar, *v.t.* to sulphurate

azufre, *m.* sulphur

azufroso, *a.* sulphurous

azul, *a.* and *m.* blue. **a. celeste,** sky blue, azure. **a. de mar** *or* **a. marino,** navy blue. **a. de ultramar,** ultramarine. **a. turquí,** indigo

azulado, *a.* bluish, blue

azulear, *v.i.* to look bluish, have a blue tint

azulejo, *m.* ornamental glazed tile

azumbre, *f.* liquid measure (just over 2 litres)

azuzar, *v.t.* to set on (dogs); irritate, provoke; incite, urge

B

baba, *f.* saliva; secretion (of snails, etc.); viscous fluid (of plants). (*fam.*) **caérsele (a uno) la b.,** to ooze satisfaction; be dumbfounded

babador, babero, *m.* bib, feeder

babear, *v.i.* to dribble, slaver; (*fig.*, *fam.*) slobber over, be sloppy

babel, *m.* babel

Babia, estar en, to be daydreaming

babieca, *m.* and *f.* (*fam.*) stupid person. *f.* name of the Cid's horse

babilónico, *a.* Babylonian

bable, *m.* Asturian dialect

babor, *m.* (*naut.*) larboard, port

babosa, *f.* slug; young onion

baboso, *a.* slavering; (*fig., fam.*) "sloppy"; (*fam.*) incompetent, useless

babucha, *f.* heelless slipper, babouche

babuino, *m.* (*zool.*) baboon

baca, *f.* luggage carrier on roof of bus, etc.

bacalao, *m.* codfish

bacanales, *f. pl.* Bacchanalia

bacante, *f.* Bacchante

bacará, *m.* baccarat (card game)

baceta, *f.* pool (in card games)

bacía, *f.* bowl; barber's circular shaving-dish; barber's trade sign

bacilar, *a.* bacillary

bacilo, *m.* bacillus

bacinete, *m.* headpiece (armour)

baconiano, *a.* Baconian

bacterial, bacteriano, *a.* bacterial

bactericida, *m.* bactericide

bacteriología, *f.* bacteriology

bacteriológico, *a.* bacteriological

bacteriólogo, *m.* bacteriologist

báculo, *m.* staff; walking-stick; (*fig.*) support. **b. episcopal,** bishop's crozier

bache, *m.* rut (in road); pothole

bachiller, *m.* and *f.* Bachelor (first university degree). *m.* (*fam.*) babbler. *f.* **bachillera,** (*fam.*) blue-stocking; garrulous woman

bachillerarse, *v.r.* to graduate as a Bachelor

bachillerato, *m.* baccalaureate, Bachelor's degree

badajo, *m.* clapper (of a bell); chatterbox, gossip

badana, *f.* cured sheepskin, chamois leather, washleather; (*fam.*) **zurrar (a uno) la b.,** to take the hide off; insult

badén, *m.* channel made by rain, furrow; conduit

badil, *m.* fire-shovel

badulaque, *m.* (*fam.*) good-for-nothing fellow

bagaje, *m.* (*mil.*) baggage; beast of burden, transport animal; luggage

bagatela, *f.* trifle, oddment, bagatelle

bagazo, *m.* oilcake, bagasse

bahía, *f.* bay, harbour

bailable, *a.* dance (of music). *m.* (*theat.*) dance number

bailador (-ra), *s.* dancer

bailar, *v.i.* to dance; spin round

bailarín, *a.* dancing. *m.* professional dancer

bailarina, *f.* ballerina

baile, *m.* dance; ball; ballet. **b. de mascaras, b. de trajos,** fancy-dress ball. **b. de San Vito,** St. Vitus' dance. **b. ruso,** ballet

bailotear, *v.i.* to jig about; dance

baja, *f.* drop, diminution; fall (in price, etc.); (*mil.*) casualty; discharge. (*fam.*) **darse de b.,** to leave an employment

bajá, *m.* pasha

bajada, *f.* descent, fall; slope, incline; hollow, depression. **b. de aguas,** roof gutter

bajamar, *f.* low tide

bajamente, *adv.* basely, abjectly

bajar, *v.i.* to descend; go down; get off; drop; fall, decrease; *v.t.* lower, take down, bring down; let down; dismount, alight; bend, droop; drop; reduce (price); (*fig.*) lower (voices); humiliate, humble; *v.r.* alight, dismount; humble oneself

bajel, *m.* (*naut.*) galley, ship

bajeza, *f.* base action; meanness; (*fig.*) humble estate, lowliness. **b. de ánimo,** timorousness

bajío, *m.* (*naut.*) shallows, shoal; depression, hollow

bajista, *m.* and *f.* speculator, bear (Stock Exchange)

bajo, *a.* low; short, not tall; downcast; under; subordinate; pale (of colours); humble (origin); base; coarse, vulgar; cheap (price); low (sounds). *m.* depth; shoal, sand-bank; (*mus.*) bass; *pl.* petticoats, skirts; horses' hoofs. *adv.* beneath, below. *prep.* under, beneath. **b. juramento,** upon oath. **en voz baja,** in a low voice. **planta baja,** ground floor. **por lo b.,** in a whisper; in secret, on the sly

bajón, *m.* (*mus.*) bassoon; bassoon player; (*fig., fam.*) downfall

bajonista, *m.* and *f.* bassoon player

bajorrelieve, *m.* bas-relief

bakelita, *f.* bakelite

bala, *f.* bullet, ball; bale. **b. fría,** spent bullet. **b. luminosa,**

tracer bullet. **b. perdida;** stray
bullet. (*fam.*) **como una b.,**
like a shot
balada, *f.* ballad, song
baladí, *a.* worthless, insignificant
baladre, *m.* (*bot.*) oleander
baladro, *m.* yell, outcry, shout
baladrón, *a.* braggart
baladronada, *f.* bravado, bragging
balagar, *m.* straw rick
bálago, *m.* straw; soap-ball;
straw rick
balance, *m.* balance; swinging,
oscillation; rolling, rocking (of a
ship, etc.); doubt, insecurity,
(*com.*) balance; (*com.*) balance
sheet
balancear, *v.i.* to swing; oscillate; vacillate, hesitate; *v.t.*
balance; *v.r.* balance oneself;
rock or swing oneself
balanceo, *m.* balancing; rocking;
swinging; rolling (of a ship, etc.)
balancín, *m.* swing-bar; whipple-
tree; tight-rope dancer's pole;
minting-mill; yoke (for carrying
pails); *pl.* (*naut.*) lifts
balandra, *f.* (*naut.*) sloop, cutter
balanza, *f.* balance; scale; judgment; comparison. **b. de
comercio,** balance of trade.
en balanzas, in doubt or danger,
in the balance
balar, *v.i.* to bleat (sheep)
balasto, *m.* (*r.w.*) ballast
balaustrada, *f.* balustrade
balaustrado, *a.* balustered
balaustre, *m.* baluster
balazo, *m.* shot; bullet wound
balbuceo, *m.* stammering; babbling; lisping
balbuciente, *a.* stammering; babbling; lisping
balbucir, *v.i. irr. defective* to
stammer; lisp; babble; read
hesitantly. See **lucir**
balcánico, *a.* Balkan
balcón, *m.* balcony
baldaquín, *m.* canopy, baldachin
baldar, *v.t.* to cripple; impede,
obstruct
balde, *m.* bucket
balde (en), *adv.* in vain. **de b.,**
gratis, free of charge
baldear, *v.t.* (*naut.*) to wash the
decks
baldío, *a.* untilled; fallow; useless,
worthless; vagrant

baldón, *m.* insult; dishonour
baldonar, *v.t.* to insult
baldosa, *f.* paving stone; tile
balduque, *m.* red tape
baleárico, *a.* Balearic
balido, *m.* bleat, bleating
balín, *m.* small bullet
balística, *f.* (*mil.*) ballistics
baliza, *f.* (*naut.*) buoy, beacon
balneario, *a.* pertaining to public
baths; bathing; holiday; spa.
m. watering place, spa
balompié, *m.* football (game)
balón, *m.* large ball; football;
(*chem.*) balloon; bundle; bale.
b. de ensayo, (*fig.*) feeler
baloncesto, *m.* (*sport*) basket ball
balota, *f.* ballot
balotar, *v.i.* to ballot
balsa, *f.* pond; raft
balsadera, *f.* ferry
balsámico, *a.* balmy
bálsamo, *m.* balm
balsero, *m.* ferryman
balso, *m.* (*naut.*) sling
báltico, *a.* Baltic
baluarte, *m.* bulwark; bastion;
protection, defence
balumbo, *m.* bulkiness
ballena, *f.* whale; whalebone
ballenero, *a.* whaling. *m.* whaler
ballesta, *f.* crossbow; spring (of
carriages)
ballestería, *f.* archery; crossbow-
men
ballestero, *m.* archer; crossbow-
man; crossbow maker
bambalina, *f.* fly (theatrical
scenery)
bambolearse, *v.r.* to sway; swing;
totter; be shaky; stagger
bamboleo, *m.* rocking; swinging;
tottering; staggering; reeling
bambolla, *f.* (*fam.*) ostentation,
swank
bambú, *m.* bamboo
banal, *a.* banal, commonplace
banana, *f.* banana
banasta, *f.* big basket
banastero (-ra), *s.* basket maker
or dealer
banasto, *m.* big round basket
banca, *f.* bench; card game; stall;
(*com.*) banking
bancada, *f.* rowing seat
bancal, *m.* oblong garden-plot;
terrace
bancario, *a.* banking, bank

bancarrota, *f.* bankruptcy. **hacer b.,** to go bankrupt

banco, *m.* form, bench; rowing seat; settle; seat; (*carp.*) bench; (*com.*) bank; (*naut.*) bar, shoal; school (of fish). **b. azul,** Government benches in Spanish Parliament. **b. de arena,** sand-bank. **b. de hielo,** iceberg

banda, *f.* wide ribbon; sash; ribbon, insignia; strip; border; party, group; gang; flock (of birds); zone, belt; side (of ship); (*mus.*) band; cushion (billiards); (*her.*) bar, bend. (*naut.*) **dar a la b.,** to lie along

bandada, *f.* flock (of birds)

bandeja, *f.* tray, salver

bandera, *f.* banner, flag; colours, standard. **b. de popa,** ensign. **jurar la b.,** (*mil., nav.*) to take the oath of allegiance

banderilla, *f.* banderilla (bull-fighting)

banderillear, *v.t.* to put banderillas on bulls

banderillero, *m.* man who puts banderillas on bulls

banderín, *m. dim.* small flag; recruiting post

banderizo, *a.* factious; vehement, excitable

banderola, *f.* banderole, pennon; bannerole

bandido (-da), *a.* and *s.* outlaw, fugitive. *m.* bandit; highwayman; rogue, desperado

bando, *m.* proclamation, order; faction, group, party

bandola, *f.* (*mus.*) pandora, pandore

bandolerismo, *m.* brigandage

bandolero, *m.* robber, footpad, brigand

bandolín, *m.* mandolin

bandurria, · *f.* (*mus.*) mandolin

banjo, *m.* banjo

banquero, *m.* banker

banqueta, *f.* three-legged stool; seat; footstool

banquete, *m.* banquet, feast

banquetear, *v.t.* and *v.i.* to banquet

bañador (-ra), *a.* bathing. *s.* bather. *m.* bathing dress; bath, vat

bañar, *v.t.* to bathe; coat, cover; dip; lave, wash; (*fig.*) bathe (of

sunlight, etc.). *v.r.* take a bath; bathe

bañera, *f.* bath attendant; bath-tub

bañista, *m.* and *f.* bather; one who takes spa waters

baño, *m.* bathing; bath; bathroom; bath-tub; bagnio, Turkish prison; covering, coat; *pl.* mineral baths, spa. **b. de mar,** sea bath. **b. de María,** double saucepan. **b. de sol,** sunbath. **casa de baños,** public baths. **cuarto de b.,** bathroom

bao, *m.* (*naut.*) beam

baptisterio, *m.* baptistery; (*ecc.*) font

baqueta, *f.* ramrod; *pl.* drumsticks; (*mil.*) gauntlet

báquico, *a.* Bacchic

bar, *m.* bar; café

barahunda, *f.* uproar, confusion

baraja, *f.* pack (of cards); game of cards

barajar, *v.t.* to shuffle (cards); jumble, mix; *v.i.* quarrel

baranda, *f.* handrail, banister; cushion (of billiard table)

barandilla, *f. dim.* railing

baratija, *f.* (gen. *pl.*) trifle, oddment

baratillo, *m.* second-hand article, frippery; second-hand shop or stall; bargain counter

barato, *a.* cheap; easy. *m.* bargain sale. *adv.* cheaply

baratura, *f.* cheapness

baraúnda, *f.* See **barahunda**

barba, *f.* chin; beard; whiskers; fin; barb (of a feather); *m.* actor who plays old men. *f. pl.* fibres of plants. **b. bien poblada,** a thick beard. **barbas de ballena,** whalebone. (*fig., fam.*) **echar a las barbas,** to throw in a person's face. **hacer la b.,** to shave; (*fam.*) annoy

barbacana, *f.* (*mil.*) barbican

barbacoa, *f.* (*S.A.*) barbecue; trellis (for climbing plants)

barbado, *a.* bearded. *m.* shoot; sucker; transplanted plant

barbárico, *a.* barbarian; barbaric

barbaridad, *f.* barbarity; blunder; atrocity; outrage; (*fam.*) huge amount. **¡Qué b.!** How awful! You don't say so!

barbarie, *f.* barbarism; barbarity; cruelty

barbarismo, *m.* barbarism; cruelty; barbarians

bárbaro (-ra), *a.* and *s.* barbarian. *a.* fierce; headstrong; uncivilized

barbechar, *v.t.* to plough; leave fallow

barbecho, *m.* (*agr.*) fallow; first ploughing

barbería, *f.* barber's shop

barbero, *m.* barber

barbicano, *a.* grey-bearded

barbihecho, *a.* fresh-shaved

barbilampiño, *a.* smooth-faced, beardless, clean-shaven

barbilindo, *a.* dandified. *m.* dandy

barbilla, *f.* point of the chin; chin. acariciar la b. (de), to .chuck under the chin

barbiquejo, *m.* (*naut.*) bobstay; hat-guard

barbo, *m.* (*icht.*) barbel

barboquejo, *m.* hat-guard

barbudo, *a.* heavily bearded

barbulla, *f.* (*naut.*) babble, chatter, murmur of voices

barca, *f.* small boat, bark; barge. b. de pasaje, ferry-boat

barcada, *f.* boat-load; ferry crossing

barcaje, *m.* ferriage

barcarola, *f.* barcarolle

barcaza, *f.* (*naut.*) lighter; barge. b. de desembarco, landing-craft

barcelonés (-esa), *a.* and *s.* of or from Barcelona

barcino, *a.* ruddy (of animals); fawn and white; (*fam.*) turncoat (of politicians)

barco, *m.* boat; ship; hollow, rut. b. barredero, trawler. b. siem-braminas, minelayer

barda, *f.* horse armour; thatch; (*carp.*) shingle

bardal, *m.* thatched wall; mud wall

bardar, *v.t.* to thatch

bardo, *m.* poet, bard

bario, *m.* (*chem.*) barium

barita, *f.* (*chem.*) baryta

baritono, *m.* baritone

barloventear, *v.i.* (*naut.*) to tack; ply to·windward; (*fam.*) wander about

barlovento, *m.* (*naut.*) windward

barnacla, *m.* barnacle

barniz, *m.* varnish; glaze; smattering, veneer

barnizar, *v.t.* to varnish; glaze

barométrico, *a.* barometric

barómetro, *m.* barometer

barón, *m.* baron

baronesa, *f.* baroness

baronía, *f.* barony

barquero, *m.* boatman; bargee; (*ent.*) water-boatman

barquillero, *m.* seller of wafers; waffle-iron

barquillo, *m.* wafer, cornet

barquín, *m.* furnace bellows

barra, *f.* bar; ingot; railing (in courtroom); sand-bank; fault (in cloth); lever, ·cross-bar; (in cricket) bail; (*mus.*) bar. b. de jabón de afeitar, shaving-stick.· a barras derechas, without deceit

barrabasada, *f.* (*fam.*) wilfulness, escapade

barraca, *f.* cabin, hut; stall; side-show

barracón, *m.* side-show; stall

barragana, *f.* concubine, mistress

barranca, *f.*, **barranco**, *m.* furrow, channel, rut; gorge; difficulty, fix

barrancoso, *a.* rutty, uneven

barredor (-ra), *s.* sweeper

barredura, *f.* sweeping; *pl.* sweepings; rubbish

barrena, *f.* borer, gimlet, drill, auger. (*aer.*) b. de cola, tail-spin

barrenar, *v.t.* to drill, bore; blast (in quarries)

barrendero (-ra), *s.* sweeper, scavenger

barrenero, *m.* driller; blaster

barreno, *m.* blast hole; bore, drill; vanity

barreño, *m.* earthenware bowl (for dish washing, etc.)

barrer, *v.t.* to sweep; (*fig.*) clear, make a clean sweep

barrera, *f.* barrier; barricade; (*fig.*) obstacle. b. de golpe, automatic gate (at level crossings, etc.). b. de minas, minefield

barriada, *f.* district; quarter (of a city)

barrica, *f.* cask; barrel

barricada, *f.* barricade

barriga, *f.* (*fam.*) belly

barrigón, **barrigudo**, *a.* pot-bellied

barril, *m.* barrel; cask; water-butt

barrilero, *m.* cooper

barrilete, *m. dim.* keg; clamp; (*naut.*) mouse

barrio, *m.* district, quarter; suburb. **barrios bajos,** slums, back streets. **el otro b.,** the other world, Eternity

barritar, *v.i.* to trumpet (of elephants)

barrizal, *m.* muddy place; clay-pit

barro, *m.* mud; clay; earthenware drinking vessel; (*fam.*) money

barroco, *a.* baroque

barroso, *a.* muddy; pimpled; mud-coloured

barrote, *m.* thick iron bar; stave, bond

barruntar, *v.t.* to conjecture; suspect

barrunto, *m.* conjecture; indication, sign

bártulos, *m. pl.* household goods; (*fig.*) means, wherewithal

barullo, *m.* (*fam.*) confusion, disorder; mob

basa, *f.* base; (*arch.*) pedestal; foundation, basis

basalto, *m.* basalt

basar, *v.t.* to base, place on a base; (*fig.*) found, base; *v.r.* (*with en*) rely upon, base oneself on

basca, *f.* (gen. *pl.*) nausea; retching; wave of anger

báscula, *f.* weighing-machine, platform-scale; weigh-bridge

base, *f.* base; (*chem., geom., mil.*) base; basis; (*arch.*) pedestal; (*mus.*) root. **sin b.,** baseless

básico, *a.* basic

basílica, *f.* palace; church, basilica

basilisco, *m.* basilisk; antique cannon

basquear, *v.i.* to retch; feel squeamish

basquiña, *f.* skirt (gen. black)

bastante, *a.* sufficient, enough. *adv.* sufficiently; enough; fairly; a good deal; somewhat. **Hace b. calor,** It is quite hot. **Tengo b.,** I have enough. **Tenemos b. tiempo,** We have sufficient time

bastar, *v.i.* to suffice. ¡**Basta!** Enough! No more! Stop!

bastardía, *f.* bastardy, illegitimacy; baseness, meanness

bastardilla, *f.* (*print.*) italics

bastardo (**-da**), *a.* bastard; spurious. *s.* bastard

bastear, *v.t.* (*sew.*) to baste

bastidor, *m.* embroidery frame; (*art*) stretcher (for canvas); (*theat.*) wing; (*mech.*) underframe; chassis, carriage; frame (of a window). (*fig.*) **entre bastidores,** behind the scenes

bastilla, *f.* (*sew.*) hem; bastille

bastimentar, *v.t.* to provision; supply

bastimento, *m.* supplies; provisioning

bastión, *m.* bastion

basto, *m.* pack-saddle; ace of clubs; clubs (cards). *a.* rude; tough; (*fig.*) unpolished, rough

bastón, *m.* walking-stick; rod (of office); truncheon. **b. de junquillo,** Malacca cane. **empuñar el b.,** to take control, take over. **meter el b.,** to mediate

bastoncillo, *m.* narrow lace for trimming

bastonear, *v.t.* to cane; stir with a stick

basura, *f.* rubbish, refuse; dung; sweepings

basurero, *m.* dustman; dunghill, rubbish dump; dust-bin

bata, *f.* dressing-gown; smoking-jacket; old-fashioned dress; overall, smock

batacazo, *m.* bump, noise of a fall

batahola, *f.* (*fam.*) hurly-burly, hubbub

batalla, *f.* battle; (*fig.*) struggle, conflict; tournament; (*art*) battle-piece. **b. campal,** pitched battle

batallador, *a.* fighting, warlike

batallar, *v.i.* to battle, fight; dispute, argue; hesitate

batallón, *m.* battalion

batán, *m.* fulling-mill; scutcheon (textile industry)

batanero, *m.* fuller

batata, *f.* sweet potato

bátavo (**-va**), *a.* and *s.* Batavian

batayola, *f.* (*naut.*) rail

batea, *f.* wooden tray; punt

batería, *f.* (*mil., elec., naut.*) battery. **b. de cocina,** kitchen utensils. **b. de pilas secas,** dry battery. **b. de teatro,** stage lights. **b. eléctrica,** electric battery

baticola, *f.* crupper

batida, *f.* game drive; attack; (*met.*) beating

batido, *a.* beaten (of metals); shot (of silk); trodden, worn (roads, etc.). *m.* (*cul.*) batter

batidor, *m.* beater; scout; outrider; hair comb; (*cul.*) whisk. **b. de oro** (*or* **de plata**), gold (*or* silver) beater

batiente, *m.* jamb (of door, etc.); damper (piano); leaf (of door); place where sea beats against cliffs, etc.

batihoja, *m.* gold beater; metal worker

batimiento, *m.* beating

batín, *m.* smoking-jacket; man's dressing-gown

batintín, *m.* Chinese gong

batir, *v.t.* to beat, slap; demolish; dismantle, take down (stall, etc.); hammer, flatten; batter (*fig.*) beat (of sun, etc.); stir; pound; churn; comb (hair); vanquish, defeat; coin; reconnoitre, beat; throw down or drop; *v.r.* fight; swoop (birds of prey). **b. palmas,** to clap, applaud

batista, *f.* cambric, batiste

baturrillo, *m.* hotchpotch (gen. food); (*fam.*) farrago, medley

batuta, *f.* baton, conductor's wand. **llevar la b.,** (*fam.*) to rule the roost

baúl, *m.* trunk; (*fam.*) belly. **b. escaparate** *or* **b. mundo,** wardrobe trunk

bauprés, *m.* (*naut.*) bowsprit

bausán (**-ana**), *s.* guy, strawman; puppet; fool, idiot; lazybones

bautismal, *a.* baptismal

bautismo, *m.* baptism

bautista, *m.* baptizer, baptist. **San Juan B.,** St. John the Baptist

bautisterio, *m.* baptistery

bautizar, *v.t.* to baptize, christen; (*fam.*) nickname; (*fam.*) water (wine); accidentally shower with water

bautizo, *m.* baptism; christening party

bávaro(**-ra**), *a.* and *s.* Bavarian

baya, *f.* berry

bayadera, *f.* Indian dancing-girl

bayeta, *f.* baize; flannel

bayo (**-ya**), *a.* bay (of horses)

bayoneta, *f.* bayonet. **b. calada,** fixed bayonet

bayonetazo, *m.* bayonet thrust

baza, *f.* tricks taken (playing cards). (*fig., fam.*) meter b., to stick one's oar in

bazar, *m.* bazaar; shop, store

bazo, *m.* (*anat.*) spleen. *a.* yellow-brown

bazucar, bazuquear, *v.t.* to shake or stir (liquids)

bazuqueo, *m.* shaking or stirring of liquids

be, *f.* letter B. *m.* baa

beata, *f.* devout woman; (*fam.*) pious hypocrite, prude; Sister of Mercy; over-religious woman

beatería, *f.* sanctimoniousness; bigotry

beatificación, *f.* beatification

beatificar, *v.t.* to make happy; sanctify; beatify

beatífico, *a.* beatific

beatitud, *f.* blessedness, beatitude; happiness

beato (**-ta**), *a.* happy; blessed, beatified; devout; prudish. *s.* devout person; over-pious person

bebé, *m.* baby

bebedero, *a.* drinkable. *m.* drinking trough or place

bebedizo, *a.* drinkable. *m.* draught of medicine; love-potion; poisonous drink

bebedor (**-ra**), *a.* drinkable. *s.* drinker; toper

beber, *v.t.* to drink; absorb; *v.i.* toast, drink to the health (of); tipple. *m.* drinking; drink

bebida, *f.* drink; beverage; alcoholic liquor

beca, *f.* academic scarf or sash; scholarship, exhibition

becario, *m.* exhibitioner, scholarship holder

becerra, *f.* calf; (*bot.*) snapdragon

becerro, *m.* bullock; bull calf; calf-skin. **b. marino,** (*zool.*) seal

becuadro, *m.* (*mus.*) natural

bedel, *m.* beadle; servitor, university porter

beduino (**-na**), *a.* and *s.* Bedouin. *m.* savage, bloodthirsty man

befar, *v.t.* to mock, ridicule

befo, *a.* thick-lipped; knock-kneed. *m.* animal's lip

begonia, *f.* (*bot.*) begonia

bejín, *m.* (*bot.*) puff-ball; spoilt child

bejuco, *m.* rattan

bejuquillo, *m.* thin gold chain (for ornament)

beldad, *f.* beauty; belle

beldar, *v.t.* (*agr.*) to winnow

belén, *m.* nativity, manger; (*fam.*) bedlam; (*fam.*) gossip

beleño, *m.* (*bot.*) henbane

belfo, *a.* blobber-lipped

belga, *a.* and *m.* and *f.* Belgian

bélgico, *a.* Belgian

bélico, *a.* war-like, military

belicosidad, *f.* bellicosity

belicoso, *a.* bellicose, aggressive; warlike

beligerancia, *f.* belligerency

beligerante, *a.* and *m.* and *f.* belligerent

belitre, *a.* (*fam.*) knavish, cunning

bellaco (-ca), *a.* artful, cunning. *s.* knave

belladona, *f.* belladonna

bellaquería, *f.* roguery, knavery, cunning

belleza, *f.* beauty, loveliness, fairness

bello, *a.* beautiful

bellota, *f.* acorn; carnation bud; ornamental button, knob

bellote, *m.* round-headed nail

bemol, *a.* and *m.* (*mus.*) flat. (*fam.*) tener bemoles, to be thorny, be difficult

bencina, *f.* benzine; petrol

bendecir, *v.t. irr.* to praise, extol; bless; dedicate, consecrate. See decir

bendición, *f.* benediction; blessing; consecration; *pl.* marriage ceremony. b. de la mesa, grace before meat

bendito, *a.* holy, blessed; fortunate; simple. ser un b., to be a simpleton; be a good soul

benedictino (-na), *a.* and *s.* Benedictine. *m.* Benedictine liqueur

beneficencia, *f.* beneficence; charitable institutions

beneficiación, *f.* benefaction

beneficiado (-da), *s.* beneficiary. *m.* incumbent of a benefice

beneficiador (-ra), *s.* benefactor

beneficiar, *v.t.* to benefit; improve; cultivate (land); exploit (mine); purchase (directorship, etc.); sell at a loss (bonds, etc.)

beneficiario (-ia), *s.* beneficiary

beneficiencia, *f.* beneficence, charity

beneficio, *m.* benefit; profit; cultivation (land, etc.); working (mine); (*ecc.*) benefice; (*theat.*) benefit

beneficioso, *a.* beneficial; useful

benéfico, *a.* beneficent; kind, helpful; charitable

benemérito, *a.* benemeritus, worthy, meritorious

beneplácito, *m.* approbation; consent

benevolencia, *f.* benevolence, goodwill

benévolo, *a.* benevolent, kind

bengalí, *a.* and *m.* and *f.* Bengali

benignidad, *f.* kindness; mildness (of the weather, etc.)

benigno, *a.* kind; benign; mild; balmy

beodo (-da), *a.* drunk, intoxicated. *s.* drunkard

bérbero, *m.* (*bot.*) barberry

ereber, *a.* and *m.* and *f.* Berber

erenjena, *f.* egg-plant

bergante, *m.* rascal, rogue

bergantín, *m.* (*naut.*) brig, brigantine

berilo, *m.* beryl

berlina, *f.* berlin, closed carriage

berlinés (-esa), *a.* and *s.* of or from Berlin

bermejear, *v.i.* to be or look reddish

bermejo, *a.* reddish; red; redgold; carroty (of hair)

bermellón, *m.* vermilion

bernardina, *f.* lie; boast; gibberish

bernardo (-da), *a.* and *s.* (*ecc.*) Bernardine (Order of St. Bernard)

berrear, *v.i.* to low, bellow; yell, squall; shriek; *v.r.* reveal, confess

berrido, *m.* lowing, bellowing; (*fam.*) yell

berrinche, *m.* (*fam.*) tantrum, fit of sulks

berro, *m.* watercress

berroqueña, *f.* granite

berza, *f.* cabbage

besamanos, *m.* ceremony of kissing royal hand, levee; kissing fingers (in salute)

besar, *v.t.* to kiss; (*fam.*) brush against, touch (of things); *v.r* kiss one another; (*fam.*) bang into, knock against one another

beso, *m.* kiss; knock, collision

bestia, *f.* quadruped (especially horses or mules); beast. *m.* and *f.* (*fam.*) nasty piece of work. **b. de carga,** beast of burden

bestial, *a.* bestial; brutal; beastly

bestialidad, *f.* brutality; bestiality; beastliness

besugo, *m.* (*icht.*) sea-bream

besuquear, *v.t.* (*fam.*) to cover with kisses; *v.r.* (*fam.*) spoon, make love

besuqueo, *m.* (*fam.*) kissing and spooning

bético, *a.* Andalusian

betún, *m.* bitumen; shoe blacking; kind of cement. **b. de Judea** *or* **b. judaico,** asphalt

bey, *m.* bey

bezo, *m.* blubber lip; proud flesh (of a wound)

bezudo, *a.* thick-lipped

biberón, *m.* feeding bottle

Biblia, *f.* Bible

bíblico, *a.* biblical

bibliófilo, *m.* bibliophile

bibliografía, *f.* bibliography

bibliográfico, *a.* bibliographical

biblioteca, *f.* library; book series. **b. por subscripción,** circulating library

bibliotecario (-ia), *s.* librarian

bicarbonato, *m.* bicarbonate

bíceps, *m.* biceps

bicicleta, *f.* bicycle. **ir** (*or* **andar** *or* **montar**) **en b.,** to bicycle

bicloruro, *m.* bichloride

bicoca, *f.* (*fam.*) trifle, bagatelle

bicolor, *a.* bicoloured

bichero, *m.* (*naut.*) boat-hook

bicho, *m.* any small animal or reptile; quadruped; fighting bull; scarecrow, sight. **b. viviente,** (*fam.*) living soul. **mal b.,** rogue

bidé, *m.* bidet

biela, *f.* axle-tree; connecting-rod; big-end

bielda, *f.* pitchfork; (*agr.*) winnowing

bien, *m.* ideal goodness, perfection; benefit, advantage; welfare; *pl.* property, wealth. *adv.* well; willingly; happily; perfectly; easily; enough, sufficient; all right! very well! **b. que,** although. **bienes muebles,** movables, goods and chattels. **bienes raíces,** real estate. **el B. y**

el Mal, Good and Evil. **¡ Está b.!** All right! **no b.,** scarcely, as soon as. **si b.,** although, even if. **¿ Y b.?** And so what? Well, then; What next?

bienal, *a.* biennial

bienamado, *a.* dearly beloved

bienandante, *a.* prosperous; happy

bienandanza, *f.* happiness, welfare; prosperity

bienaventurado, *a.* blessed, holy; happy; (*fam.*) over-simple, innocent, foolish

bienaventuranza, *f.* blessedness

bienestar, *m.* well-being; ease; comfort

bienhablado, *a.* well-spoken; civil, polite

bienhadado, *a.* fortunate, happy

bienhechor (-ra), *a.* kind, helpful. *s.* benefactor

bienintencionado, *a.* well-meaning

bienio, *m.* space of two years

bienquisto, *a.* respected; generally esteemed

bienvenida, *f.* safe or happy arrival; welcome. **dar la b.,** to welcome

bienvivir, *v.i.* to live comfortably; live decently or uprightly

bies, *m.* bias, cross; slant

biftec, *m.* beefsteak

bifurcación, *f.* bifurcation; fork, branch, junction

bifurcarse, *v.r.* to fork, branch

bigamia, *f.* bigamy

bígamo (-ma), *a.* bigamous. *s.* bigamist

bigornia, *f.* anvil

bigote, *m.* moustache; *pl.* whiskers

bigotudo, *a.* moustached, whiskered

bikini, *m.* two-piece bathing suit

bilateral, *a.* bilateral

bilbaíno, *a.* pertaining to or native of Bilbao

bilingüe, *a.* bilingual

bilioso, *a.* bilious

bilis, *f.* bile

billar, *m.* billiards; billiard table

billete, *m.* note, short letter; ticket; bank-note. **b. de abono,** season ticket. **b. de andén,** platform ticket. **b. de banco,** bank-note. **b. de favor,** free ticket. **b. de ida y vuelta,**

return ticket. **b. entero,** full fare. **b. kilométrico,** tourist ticket. **b. sencillo,** single ticket. **medio b.,** half-fare

billón, *m.* billion

bimestral, *a.* bimonthly

bimestre, *a.* bimonthly. *m.* two months' duration; money paid or received at two-monthly intervals

bimetalismo, *m.* bimetallism

bimotor, *a.* two-motor. *m.* twin-engined aircraft

binario, *a.* binary

binóculo, *m.* opera glasses

binomio, *a.* and *m.* binomial

biofísica, *f.* biophysics

biografía, *f.* biography

biográfico, *a.* biographical

biógrafo (-fa), *s.* biographer

biología, *f.* biology

biológico, *a.* biological

biólogo, *m.* biologist

biombo, *m.* screen

bioquímica, *f.* biochemistry

bioquímico, *m.* biochemist

bipartido, *a.* bipartite

bípedo, *a.* and *m.* biped

biplano, *m.* biplane

biplaza, *a.* two-seater

birimbao, *m.* Jew's harp

birla, *f.* skittle

birlar, *v.t.* to bowl from where the bowl stopped; (*fam.*) knock down; snatch away; (*fam.*) rob

birlocha, *f.* child's kite

birlocho, *m.* barouche

birmano (-na), *a.* and *s.* Burmese

bironiano, *a.* Byronic

birreta, *f.* biretta

birrete, *m.* biretta; university cap; cap

birretina, *f.* busby, bearskin

bis, *adv.* twice; repeat; encore. *a.* duplicate

bisabuela, *f.* great-grandmother. **bisabuelo,** *m.* great-grandfather

bisagra, *f.* hinge; shoemaker's polisher

bisbís, *m.* game of chance

bisbisar, *v.t.* (*fam.*) to mutter; whisper

bisbiseo, *m.* (*fam.*) muttering; murmuring; whispering

bisecar, *v.t.* to bisect

bisección, *f.* (*geom.*) bisection

bisectriz, *f.* bisector

bisel, *m.* bevel, chamfer

bisiesto, *a.* and *m.* Leap (Year)

bisílabo, *a.* two-syllabled

bismuto, *m.* bismuth

bisnieto (-ta), *s.* great-grandchild

bisonte, *m.* bison

bisoño (-ña), *a.* inexperienced, raw. *s.* recruit; (*fam.*) greenhorn

bistec, *m.* beef steak

bisturí, *m.* surgical knife

bisunto, *a.* grubby, greasy

bisutería, *f.* imitation jewellery

bitas, *f. pl.* (*naut.*) bitts

bituminoso, *a.* bituminous

bivalvo, *a.* bivalve

bizantino, *a.* Byzantine

bizarría, *f.* handsomeness; dash; verve; gallantry, courage; magnificence; liberality; whim, caprice

bizarro, *a.* handsome; dashing; gallant, courageous; liberal; splendid, magnificent

bizco, *a.* squint-eyed, cross-eyed

bizcocho, *m.* biscuit; sponge-cake; bisque

bizma, *f.* poultice. **poner bizmas,** to poultice

biznieto, *s.* See **bisnieto**

blanca, *f.* old Spanish coin; (*fam.*) penny; (*mus.*) minim. **sin b.,** penniless

blanco, *a.* white; fair-skinned; blank, vacant; (*fam.*) cowardly. *m.* target; blank left in writing; white person; interval. **b. de España,** whiting. **b. de la uña,** half-moon of the nail. **dar en el b.,** to hit the mark. **en b.,** blank, unused; (*fam.*) in vain; uncomprehendingly; (of nights) sleepless

blancor, *m.,* **blancura,** *f.* whiteness; fairness (of skin)

blandear, *v.t.* to moderate, soothe; brandish; *v.i.* (*fig.*) give way, yield

blandir, *v.t.* to brandish, wield, flourish

blando, *a.* soft; mild (weather); delicate; kind; peaceable; delicate, effeminate; (*fam.*) cowardly

blandón, *m.* wax taper

blandura, *f.* softness; poultice; blandishment, compliment; mildness (of weather); gentleness, affability; luxury

blanquear, *v.t.* to bleach; whitewash; whiten; *v.i.* appear white; show white

blanquecino, *a.* whitish

blanqueo, *m.* whitening; white-washing; bleaching

blanquizal, *m.* pipe-clay

blasfemador (**-ra**), *a.* blaspheming. *s.* blasphemer

blasfemar, *v.i.* to blaspheme; curse, swear

blasfemia, *f.* blasphemy; insult

blasfemo (**-ma**), *s.* blasphemer. *a.* blasphemous

blasón, *m.* heraldry; escutcheon; glory, honour

blasonar, *v.t.* to blazon; *v.i.* boast, brag, blazon abroad

bledo, *m.* blade, leaf. **no importar un b.,** not to matter a straw

blenda, *f.* (*min.*) blende

blindado, *a.* (*nav.*) armoured, iron-clad

blindaje, *m.* (*nav.*) armour-plating; (*mil.*) blindage

blindar, *v.t.* to plate with armour, to case with steel

blocao, *m.* (*mil.*) block-house

blonda, *f.* blonde (of lace)

blondo, *a.* fair, blond, flaxen-haired

bloque, *m.* block, slab

bloquear, *v.t.* to blockade; besiege

bloqueo, *m.* blockade; siege; blocking; freezing (of assets). **violar el b.,** to run the blockade

blusa, *f.* blouse

boa, *f.* boa, large snake. *m.* boa (fur)

boato, *m.* outward show, ostentation

bobería, *f.* foolishness, stupidity

bobilis, bobilis. (de), *adv.* (*fam.*) free of charge; without effort

bobina, *f.* bobbin, spool, reel; (*elec.*) coil; spool (of fishing rod)

bobo (**-ba**), *a.* stupid, idiotic; simple, innocent. *s.* fool. *m.* clown, jester

boca, *f.* mouth; pincers (of crustaceans); entrance or exit; mouth (of a river); orifice, opening; muzzle (of guns); cutting edge (of tools); taste (of wine, etc.). **b. arriba,** on one's back. **b. del estómago,** pit of the stomach. **b. rasgada,** large mouth. **a b.,** verbally. **a b. de jarro,** point-blank. **a pedir de b.,** just as one would wish. **de b.,** by word of mouth. (*fam.*) **sin decir esta b. es mía,** without a word, in silence

bocacalle, *f.* entrance to a street; street junction

bocadillo, *m.* narrow ribbon; sandwich

bocado, *m.* mouthful; snack; bite; horse's bit; bridle; *pl.* preserved fruit cut up

bocamanga, *f.* wrist of sleeve

bocanada, *f.* mouthful (of liquid); cloud (of smoke). **b. de aire,** gust of wind

boceto, *m.* sketch; outline; rough-cast model

bocina, *f.* trumpet; megaphone; fog-horn; hooter; (*aut.*) horn; horn (of gramophone); (*ast.*) Ursa Minor

bocio, *m.* (*med.*) goitre

bocoy, *m.* hogshead; large cask

bocha, *f.* (*sport*) bowl; *pl.* bowls

bochorno, *m.* sultry weather; heat, stuffiness; blush, hot flush; shame

bochornoso, *a.* sultry; shameful

boda, *f.* wedding, marriage. **bodas de oro,** fiftieth (golden) anniversary. **bodas de plata,** twenty-fifth (silver) anniversary

bodega, *f.* wine-cellar; store-room; granary; (*naut.*) hold (of ship)

bodegón, *m.* eating-house; tavern; (*art.*) still-life; genre picture

bóer, *a.* and *m.* and *f.* Boer

bofes, *m. pl.* lungs, lights. (*fam.*) **echar los b.,** to work oneself to death

bofetada, *f.,* **bofetón,** *m.* blow, slap; box on the ear

boga, *f.* rowing; fashion, vogue; (*mech.*) bogie. *m.* and *f.* oarsman, rower. **estar en b.,** to be fashionable

bogada, *f.* rowing stroke

bogador (**-ra**), *s.* rower, oarsman

bogar, *v.i.* to row

bogavante, *m.* lobster

bogotano (**-na**), *a.* and *s.* of or from Bogotá (Colombia)

bohemio (**-ia**), *a.* and *s.* gipsy; bohemian; Bohemian. *m.* archer's short cloak

boicotear, *v.t.* to boycott

boicot, boicoteo, *m.* boycott

boina, *f.* Basque cap; beret

boj, *m.* box tree; boxwood, box oak; shoemaker's tool

bola, *f.* globe; ball; (*sport*) bowl; (*arch.*) balloon; (*fam.*) trick, lie. **b. de nieves,** snowball. (*fam.*) **dejar rodar la b.,** to let things slide

bolardo, *m.* bollard

bolchevique, *a.* and *m.* and *f.* bolshevist

bolchevismo, *m.* Bolshevism

bolchevista, *m.* and *f.* bolshevist

bolchevización, *f.* bolshevization

bolea, *f.* (tennis) volley; throw

bolera, *f.* skittle alley

bolero, *m.* bolero; dancer; (*fam.*) top hat

boleta, *f.* admission ticket; billet ticket; warrant, voucher

boletín, *m.* bulletin; admission ticket; (*com.*) price list; learned periodical. **b. de noticias,** news bulletin. **b. meteorológico,** weather report

boliche, *m.* jack (in bowls); cup and ball toy; small oven (for charcoal); drag-net. **juego de b.,** bowls

bólido, *m.* (*ast.*) bolide, meteor

bolillo, *m.* bobbin (lace making)

bolina, *f.* (*naut.*) bowline; (*naut.*) sounder; (*fam.*) uproar, tumult

boliviano (-na), *a.* and *s.* Bolivian. *m.* silver coin

bolo, *m.* skittle, ninepin; pillow (for lace making); Cuban coin; (*med.*) large pill; (*fig., fam.*) blockhead; *pl.* skittles (game of)

boloñés (-esa), *a.* and *s.* Bolognese

bolsa, *f.* purse; bag; footmuff; fold, pucker; pouch; Exchange; Stock Exchange; capital, money; prize money; (*med.*) sac; (*min.*) pocket. **b. de estudio,** scholarship grant. **B. de Trabajo,** Labour Exchange. **bajar** (*or* **subir) la b.,** to fall (or rise) (of Stock Exchange quotations). **jugar a la b.,** to speculate on the Stock Exchange

bolsear, *v.t.* to pouch

bolsillo, *m.* pocket; purse; money

bolsista, *m.* stock-broker; speculator (on the Stock Exchange)

bollo, *m.* bread roll; bun; bulge, bruise (in metal); (*med.*) lump

bollón, *m.* round-headed or brass-headed nail; (*bot.*) bud (especially vines)

bomba, *f.* (*mech.*) pump; pump-ing engine; bomb; (*mil.*) shell; lamp globe; (*fam.*) improvised verses; (*fam.*) drinking bout. **¡B.!** Listen! Here goes! **b. de incendios,** fire-engine. **b. marina,** waterspout. **b. volante,** flying-bomb. **a prueba de b.,** bomb-proof. **arrojar bombas,** to bomb. (*fam.*) **caer como una b.,** to be a bomb-shell

bombachos, *m. pl.* plus fours

bombardear, *v.t.* to bombard; bomb; shell

bombardeo, *m.* bombardment, bombing; shelling

bombardero, *m.* gunner, bombardier; (*aer.*) bomber. **b. pesado,** (*aer.*) heavy bomber. **Servicio de b.,** Bomber Command

bombástico, *a.* bombastic, high sounding

bombazo, *m.* bombshell; bomb crater; noise of an exploding bomb

bombear, *v.t.* to pump; bombard, shell; praise

bombero, *m.* worker of a pressure pump; fireman; mortar, howitzer

bombilla, *f.* (*naut.*) lantern; (*elec., phys.*) bulb; small pump; straw for drinking Maté (*S.A.*)

bombillo, *m.* w.c. siphon; hand-pump

bombo, *m.* big drum or player of it; (*naut.*) barge, ferry; ballot box; exaggerated praise

bombón, *m.* bonbon, sweet

bombonera, *f.* box for toffee, etc.

bonachón, *a.* (*fam.*) genial, good-natured

bonaerense, *a.* and *m.* and *f.* of or from Buenos Aires

bonancible, *a.* calm (of weather, sea)

bonanza, *f.* fair weather; prosperity

bondad, *f.* goodness; kindness, helpfulness. **Tenga la b. de . . .,** Be good enough to . . ., Please . .

bondadoso, *a.* good, kind

bonete, *m.* academic cap; (*zool.*) reticulum (ruminants); (*ecc.*) biretta. **gran b.,** important person. (*fam.*) **a tente b.,** insistently

bonetero (-ra), *s.* seller or maker of caps and birettas

bonificación, *f.* bonus; allowance, discount

bonísimo, *a. sup.* bueno, extremely good

bonito, *a.* pretty; graceful; (ironical) fine. *m.* (*icht.*) striped tunny

bono, *m.* voucher; (*com.*) bond; certificate. **b. postal,** money-order. **bonos del Gobierno,** Government bonds

boñiga, *f.* cow-dung, animal manure

boqueada, *f.* gasp, opening of the mouth

boquear, *v.i.* to gasp; be dying; (*fam.*) be at last gasp (of things); *v.i.* say, utter

boquera, *f.* sluice (in irrigation canal)

boquerón, *m.* large opening; (*icht.*) anchovy (fish); whitebait

boquete, *m.* narrow entrance, aperture; gap, breach; hole

boquiabierto, *a.* open-mouthed; amazed

boquiancho, *a.* wide-mouthed

boquiduro, *a.* hard-mouthed

boquilla, *f. dim.* small mouth; mouthpiece (of wind instruments, etc.); cigar- or cigarette-holder; gas-burner; nozzle; tip (of cigarettes)

boquirroto, *a.* (*fam.*) loquacious, indiscreet

borbollar, *v.i.* to bubble, foam, froth

borbollón, borbotón, *m.* gushing, bubbling, welling up. **a borbollones,** in a torrent; hastily, impetuously

borbónico, *a.* Bourbon

borbotar, *v.i.* to gush out, well up

borceguí, *m.* buskin, boot

borda, *f.* hut, cabin; (*naut.*) gunwale

bordada, *f.* (*naut.*) tack

bordado, *m.* embroidery

bordador (-ra), *s.* embroiderer

bordar, *v.i.* to embroider; (*fig.*) perform perfectly

borde, *m.* edge; fringe; verge; rim; mount (of a picture); brim (of a hat); side (of ship). *a.* wild (of plants); illegitimate. **estar lleno hasta los bordes,** to be full to the brim

bordelés (-esa), *a.* and *s.* of or from Bordeaux

bordillo, *m.* kerb-stone, kerb

bordo, *m.* side (of ships); border, edge. **a b.,** on board

bordón, *m.* pilgrim's staff; monotonous repetition; refrain; (*mus.*) bass string; (*fig.*) guide, stay

bóreas, *m.* north wind

borgoña, *m.* Burgundy wine

borgoñón (-ona), *a.* and *s.* Burgundian

bórico, *a.* boric

borla, *f.* tassel; puff (for powder). (*fig.*) **tomar la b.,** to take one's doctorate, graduate

borne, *m.* tip (of lance); (*elec.*) terminal

bornear, *v.i.* to bend, twist; (*arch.*) hoist into position; *v.r.* warp (wood)

borra, *f.* yearling ewe; thickest wool; wad-stuffing; lees, sediment; fluff, dust; (*fam.*) trash. **b. de algodón,** cotton-waste

borrachera, *f.* drunkenness; orgy, carousal; (*fam.*) blunder

borrachín (-ina), *s.* tippler, toper

borracho (-cha), *a.* drunk, intoxicated; (*fam.*) blind (with rage, etc.). *s.* tippler, drunkard

borrador, *m.* rough draft

borradura, *f.* erasure

borrajear, *v.i.* to scribble

borrar, *v.i.* to erase; cross out; blot out; (*fig.*) obliterate

borrasca, *f.* storm, tempest; peril, danger; (*fam.*) orgy

borrascosidad, *f.* storminess

borrascoso, *a.* stormy; disordered, turbulent

borrego (-ga), *s.* lamb; (*fam.*) nincompoop, simpleton; *m. pl.* fleecy clouds; white horses (waves)

borrico (-ca), *s.* donkey; fool. *m.* (*carp.*) sawing-horse

borrón, *m.* blot; rough draft; defect; (*fig.*) stigma

borroso, *a.* blurred, indistinct; full of dregs, muddy

boscaje, *m.* grove, group of trees, thicket

bosque, *m.* wood, forest

bosquejar, *v.i.* (*art*) to sketch; sketch out, draft; model in rough (sculpture); outline

bosquejo, *m.* outline, sketch;

rough plan or idea; unfinished work

bostezar, v.i. to yawn

bostezo, m. yawning; yawn

bota, f. small wineskin; barrel; butt; boot. **b. de montar,** riding boot. **botas de campaña,** top-boots. **botas de vadear,** waders

botada, botadura, f. launching (of a ship)

botador, m. thrower; boating-pole; (carp.) nail-puller

botafuego, m. (mil.) linstock; (fam.) quick-tempered, irascible person

botalón, m. (naut.) boom. **b. de foque,** jib-boom

botánica, f. Botany

botánico (-ca), a. botanical. s. botanist

botar, v.t. to fling; launch (boat); (naut.) shift the helm; v.i. jump; bounce, rebound; rear, prance (horses)

botarate, m. (fam.) madcap, devil-may-care

botarel, m. (arch.) flying-buttress

botarga, f. motley; harlequin

botavara, f. (naut.) boom

bote, m. thrust (with lance, etc.); rearing (of horse); rebound; (aer.) bump; open boat; small bottle, jar. **b. salvavidas,** life-boat. (fam.) **de b. en b.,** chock-full

botella, f. bottle; bottleful; flask

botica, f. chemist's shop; medicines, remedies; physic; store, shop; medicine chest

boticario, m. apothecary, chemist

botijo, m. earthenware jar with spout and handle

botillería, f. ice-cream bar

botín, m. gaiter; buskin; booty·

botiquín, m. first aid kit; medicine chest

botón, m. bud; button; knob, handle; switch (electric); press button (bell); (bot.) centre; button (on a foil); (mech.) stud

botonero (-ra), s. button maker or seller

bóveda, f. (arch.) vault, arch; crypt; cavern. **b. celeste,** sky

bovino, a. bovine

boxeador, m. boxer

boxear, v.i. (sport) to box

boxeo, m. (sport) boxing

boya, f. (naut.) buoy; float

boyante, a. floating; light, buoyant; prosperous

boyar, v.i. (naut.) to float

boyera, f. ox-stall

boyero, m. cowherd

boza, f. painter (of a boat)

bozal, m. muzzle; nosebag; harness bells. m. and f. (fam.) greenhorn; a. wild, untamed (horses)

bozo, m. down which precedes beard; muzzle; headstall; lips, snout

bracero, m. one who offers his arm (to a lady); day labourer; strong man. **de b.,** arm-in-arm

bracete, m. small arm. **de b.,** arm-in-arm

bracmán, m. Brahmin

bráctea, f. (bot.) bract

braga, f. (gen. pl.) breeches; knickerbockers; hoist or pulley rope

bragazas, m. (fam.) weak-willed, fellow, soft specimen

braguero, m. (med.) truss

bragueta, f. fly (of breeches)

brahmanismo, m. Brahmanism

bramante, a. roaring. m. twine, pack-thread

bramar, v.i. to roar; rage; (fig.) howl (of the wind, etc.)

bramido, m. bellowing; roaring; yell of rage; (fig.) howling (wind, sea, etc.)

brancada, f. drag net

branquia, f. (gen. pl.) (icht.) gill

branquial, a. branchiate

braquiotomía, f. (surg.) brachiotomy, amputation of the arms

brasa, f. live coal. **estar como en brasas,** to be like a cat on hot bricks

brasero, m. brazier

brasileño (-ña), a. and s. Brazilian

bravata, f. bravado; threat

braveza, f. ferocity, savageness; valour; violence, fury (of elements)

bravío, a. savage, untamed; wild (plants); uncultured

bravo, a. valiant; surly, rude; independent, strong-minded, good, excellent; savage (animals); stormy (sea); rough, rugged; violent, angry; (fam.) sumptuous, magnificent.

bravura, *f.* ferocity (animals); courage (persons); boastful threat

braza, *f.* (*naut.*) fathom; stroke (in swimming)

brazado, *m.* armful

brazal, *m.* armlet, brassard

brazalete, *m.* bracelet; brassard

brazo, *m.* arm; upper arm; front paw; (*mech.*) arm; branch (of chandelier, etc.); bough; arm (of chair); power, courage; *pl.* protectors; workmen, hands. **b. de mar,** firth, arm of the sea. **a b. partido,** in unarmed fight, man to man. **con los brazos abiertos,** welcomingly; willingly, gladly. **dar los brazos (a),** to embrace. (*fam.*) **hecho un b. de mar,** dressed up to the nines

brea, *f.* pitch, tar; sacking, canvas

brebaje, *m.* beverage; unpleasant drink; (*naut.*) draught (of beer, grog, etc.)

brécol, *m.* (*bot.*) broccoli

brecha, *f.* (*mil.*) breach; opening; (*fig.*) impression (on mind). **morir en la b.,** to fight to the last ditch; die in harness

brega, *f.* fight; quarrel; disappointment, trick. **andar a la b.,** to work hard. **dar b.,** to play a trick

bregar, *v.i.* to fight; work hard; (*fig.*) struggle

breña, *f.* rough ground, bramble patch

breñal, *m.* scrub, brushwood

breñoso, *a.* rugged, rocky

bretón (-ona), *a.* and *s.* Breton. *m.* Breton dialect

breva, *f.* early fig; early acorn; (*fig.*) advantage, " plum "; (*fam.*) peach (girl); (*fam.*) windfall, piece of luck; Havana cigar

breve, *a.* brief; concise. *m.* papal brief. *f.* (*mus.*) breve. **en b.,** shortly, concisely; in a short while, soon

brevedad, *f.* brevity

breviario, *m.* breviary

brezal, *m.* heath, moor

brezo, *m.* (*bot.*) heath

bribón (-ona), *s.* rogue, ruffian. *a.* knavish, dishonest; lazy

bribonada, *f.* knavery, mischievous trick

bribonear, *v.i.* to idle; play tricks, be a rogue

bribonería, *f.* rascality, vagrant life

brida, *f.* bridle

bridón, *m.* snaffle-bridle

brigada, *f.* (*mil.*) brigade; (*naut.*) division of fleet; beasts of burden

brigadier, *m.* brigadier-general

brillante, *a.* sparkling, brilliant; (*fig.*) outstanding. *m.* diamond

brillantez, *f.* brightness, lustre; fame; (*fig.*) brilliance

brillantina, *f.* brilliantine

brillar, *v.i.* to shine, sparkle, gleam, glisten; (*fig.*) be brilliant or outstanding

brillo, *m.* brilliancy, brightness, shine; fame, glory; distinction, brilliance, splendour

brincar, *v.i.* to spring, leap, skip, frisk; (*fig., fam.*) skip, omit; (*fam.*) grow angry; *v.t.* jump a child up and down

brinco, *m.* leap, spring; skip, frolicking

brindar, *v.i.* to invite, provoke (of things); (*with prep. a or por*) drink the health of, toast; *v.t.* and *v.i.* give, present; offer; *v.r.* offer one's services

brindis, *m.* toast (drink)

brío, *m.* vigour; spirit, courage; gusto, verve

brioso, *a.* vigorous, enterprising; spirited, courageous; dashing, lively

briqueta, *f.* briquette

brisa, *f.* breeze; grape pressings

británico, *a.* British

británo (-na), *a.* British. *s.* Briton

brizna, *f.* shred, paring; blade (grass); filament, fibre; string (of bean-pod, etc.); splinter, chip

broca, *f.* reel; tack (shoemaker's); (*mech.*) drill, bit

brocado, *m.* brocade. *a.* brocade or embroidered like brocade

brocal, *m.* puteal (of a well); mouthpiece (of wineskin); metal ring (of sword-sheath)

brocamantón, *m.* large jewelled brooch

brocatel, *m.* imitation brocade

brocha, *f.* brush. **b. de afeitar,** shaving-brush. **de b. gorda,** crudely painted. **pintor de b. gorda,** decorator

brochada, *f.* stroke of the brush

brochado, *a.* brocaded, embossed

brochadura, *f.* fastening, set of hooks and eyes

broche, *m.* clasp, fastening; brooch; hooks and eyes

brochón, *m.* whitewash brush

broma, *f.* merriment; joke, jest; ship-worm

bromear(se), *v.i.* and *v.r.* to joke, make fun

bromista, *a.* joking, jesting; mischievous. *m.* and *f.* genial person; player of practical jokes, tease

bromo, *m.* bromine

bromuro, *m.* bromide

bronca, *f.* (*fam.*) shindy

bronce, *m.* bronze; brass; (*poet.*) gun, bell, trumpet; bronze statue; sunburn

bronceado, *a.* bronzed; sunburnt. *m.* sunburn

broncear, *v.t.* to bronze; sunburn

bronco, *a.* rough, coarse; brittle; (of metals); harsh (voice, musical instruments); rigid, stiff; surly

bronconeumonía, *f.* bronchopneumonia

bronquial, *a.* bronchial

bronquio, *m.* (gen. *pl.*) bronchi

bronquitis, *f.* bronchitis

broquel, *m.* shield; (*fig.*) protection

broquelero, *m.* shield maker; quarrelsome man

broqueta, *f.* skewer

brotadura, *f.* budding

brotar, *v.i.* to germinate, sprout; gush forth (water); issue forth, burst out; (*fig.*) appear (of rash); (*fig.*) begin to appear; *v.t.* to bring forth; produce (of earth)

brote, *m.* bud, sprout; (*fig.*) germ, genesis; iota, jot, atom

broza, *f.* garden rubbish; débris; thicket

bruces (a *or* **de),** *adv.* face downwards. **caer de b.,** to fall flat. Also with other verbs: *dar, echarse,* etc.

bruja, *f.* witch; owl; (*fam.*) hag

brujear, *v.i.* to practise witchcraft

brujería, *f.* witchcraft

brujo, *m.* magician, wizard

brújula, *f.* magnetic needle; compass; mariner's compass. **b. de bolsillo,** pocket compass. **b. giroscópica,** gyro-compass

brulote, *m.* fire-ship

bruma, *f.* haze; sea-mist

brumoso, *a.* misty, hazy

bruno, *a.* dark brown

bruñido, *m.* polishing; burnish

bruñidor (-ra), *a.* polishing. *s.* burnisher. *m.* polisher (instrument)

bruñir, *v.t.* to polish, burnish; (*fam.*) apply make up

brusco, *a.* brusque, rude; blunt; sudden, unexpected; sharp (of bends)

bruselense, *a.* and *m.* and *f.* of or from Brussels

brusquedad, *f.* brusquerie, rudeness; bluntness; suddenness, unexpectedness; sharpness (of a bend)

brutal, *a.* brutal

brutalidad, *f.* brutality; (*fig.*) brutishness; viciousness

bruto, *a.* stupid, unreasonable; vicious; unpolished, rough. *m.* animal (gen. quadruped). **en b.,** in the rough; (*com.*) in bulk. **diamante en b.,** an uncut diamond

bruza, *f.* strong brush; scrubbing brush

bu, *m.* (*fam.*) bogey man

buba, *f.* pustule; *pl.* buboes

bubónico, *a.* bubonic

bucal, *a.* buccal

bucanero, *m.* buccaneer

bucarda, *f.* cockle (bivalve)

búcaro, *m.* arsenican clay; jar made of this

bucear, *v.i.* to work as a diver; swim under water; (*fig.*) investigate

bucéfalo, *m.* bucephalus; (*fam.*) fool, blockhead

buceo, *m.* diving; dive; (*fig.*) investigation

bucle, *m.* ringlet, curl

bucólico, *a.* bucolic

buche, *m.* craw or crop; mouthful; wrinkle, pleat; (*fam.*) stomach, belly. (*fig.,* *fam.*) inmost heart

búdico, *a.* Buddhist

budismo, *m.* Buddhism

budista, *a.* and *m.* and *f.* Buddhist

budín, *m.* pudding

buen, *a. abb.* of **bueno,** good. Used before *m.* singular nouns and infinitives used as nouns, e.g. **un b. libro,** a good book. **el b. cantar,** good singing

buenamente, *adv.* easily; comfortably, conveniently; willingly

buenaventura, *f.* good luck; fortune told from hand

bueno (see **buen**), *a.* good; kind; useful; convenient; pleasant; healthy; large (drink, etc.); simple, innocent; suitable; sufficient; opportune. ¡B.! Good!; Enough!; All right! **a buenas**, willingly. **de buenas a primeras**, at first sight, from the beginning

buey, *m.* ox. **b. suelto**, (*fam.*) freelance; bachelor

búfalo (-la), *s.* buffalo

bufanda, *f.* scarf

bufar, *v.i.* to bellow; snort; (*fam.*) snort with rage

bufete, *m.* desk, writing-table; lawyer's office or practice; sideboard

bufido, *m.* snort; bellow

bufo, *a.* comic. *m.* clown, buffoon

bufón, *m.* buffoon, clown; jester. *a.* comical, clownish

bufonada, *f.* buffoonery, clowning; raillery, taunt

bufonear(se), *v.r.* and *v.i.* to joke, jest, parody

bufonería. See **bufonada**

buhardilla, *f.* garret; sky-light

buho, *m.* owl; (*fam.*) hermit, unsociable person

buhonería, *f.* peddling, hawking; peddler's wares

buhonero, *m.* peddler

buido, *a.* sharp-pointed; sharp

buitre, *m.* vulture

bujía, *f.* candle; candlestick; (*elec.*) candle-power; (*aut.*) sparking plug

bula, *f.* Papal bull or seal

bulbo, *m.* (*bot.*) bulb. **b. dentario**, pulp (of teeth)

bulboso, *a.* bulbous

bulevar, *m.* boulevard, promenade

búlgaro (-ra), *a.* and *s.* Bulgarian

bulla, *f.* noise; bustle; confusion; fuss. (*fam.*) **meter a b.**, to throw into great confusion

bullebulle, *m.* and *f.* busybody; madcap

bullicio, *m.* noise, bustle; rioting; uproar

bullicioso, *a.* noisy, merry, boisterous; rebellious; lively, restless

bullir, *v.i.* to boil; foam, bubble; (*fig.*) seethe; (*fig.*) swarm (insects); bustle; *v.t.* move, stir; *v.r.* stir, give signs of life

bulto, *m.* bulk, mass, size; form of person, etc., seen indistinctly; swelling; bust, statue; bundle, package, piece of luggage; pillowcase. (*fig., fam.*) **escurrir el b.**, to get out from under. **poner de b.**, to put clearly, emphasize. **ser de b.**, to be obvious

bumerang, *m.* boomerang

buñolería, *f.* bun or waffle shop

buñuelo, *m.* bun; waffle, fritter; (*fig.*) botch

buque, *m.* ship, vessel; capacity of ship; ship's hull. **b. barreminas**, mine-sweeper. **b. de guerra**, battle-ship, man-of-war. **b. de vapor**, steamer. **b. de vela**, sailing ship. **b. escuela**, training-ship. **b. mercante**, merchant vessel. **b. submarino**, submarine. **b. transbordador**, train-ferry

burbuja, *f.* bubble

burbujear, *v.i.* to bubble

burda, *f.* (*naut.*) backstay

burdel, *m.* brothel; (*fam.*) untidy, noisy place. *a.* lascivious

burdo, *a.* coarse, tough

burgalés (-esa), *a.* and *s.* of or from Burgos

burgo, *m.* borough, burgh

burgomaestre, *m.* burgomaster

burgués (-esa), *a.* and *s.* bourgeois, middle class (person)

burguesía, *f.* middle class, bourgeoisie

buriel, *a.* dark red

buril, *m.* burin, engraver's tool

burla, *f.* mockery; joke, jest; trick. **b. burlando**, without effort; negligently. **de burlas**, in fun. **entre burlas y veras**, half-jokingly

burlador, *a.* mocking. *m.* libertine, rake; deceiver

burlar, *v.t.* to play a trick on; deceive; disappoint; *v.r.* and *v.i.* (*with de*) make fun of, laugh at, ridicule

burlesco, *a.* jocular, comic, burlesque

burlón (-ona), *a.* joking; mocking, scoffing. *s.* joker; scoffer

buró, *m.* bureau, writing-desk

burocracia, *f.* bureaucracy

burócrata, *m.* and *f.* bureaucrat

burocrático, *a.* bureaucratic

burra, *f.* she-ass; foolish, un-teachable woman; painstaking, patient woman

burrajo, *m.* dry stable dung used as fuel

burro, *m.* ass, donkey; sawing-horse; card game

bursátil, *a.* (com.) relating to the Exchange; financial

busca, *f.* search; hunting party; research; pursuit

buscador (-ra), *s.* searcher; investigator. *m.* finder (of a camera, etc.)

buscapié, *m.* hint or suggestion; (*fig.*) feeler

buscapiés, *m.* squib, cracker

buscar, *v.t.* to search, look for; research; pursue. **ir a b.,** to go to look for; bring, fetch

buscarruidos, *m.* and *f.* (fam.) quarrel maker

buscavidas, *m.* and *f.* (fam.) busy-body; (fam.) go-getter

buscón (-ona), *s.* searcher; pick-pocket, thief, swindler, rogue

buscona, *f.* prostitute

busilis, *m.* (fam.) knotty problem, snag; core, main point

búsqueda, *f.* search

busto, *m.* (art) bust, head and shoulders

butaca, *f.* armchair; (theat.) orchestra stall; seat (in cinemas, etc.)

butifarra, *f.* sausage made principally in Catalonia and Balearic Islands; (fam.) badly fitting stocking

buz, *m.* respectful kiss

buzo, *m.* diver

buzón, *m.* pillar-box; letter-box; canal, channel; sluice

C

¡ca! *interj.* Fancy! Oh no!

cabal, *a.* just, exact; perfect; complete; faultless. *interj.* Exactly! **por sus cabales,** according to plan; perfectly

cábala, *f.* cabala; divination; (fam.) intrigue

cabalgada, *f.* cavalcade; foray, raid

cabalgador (-ra), *s.* rider, horse-man

cabalgadura, *f.* riding-horse; beast of burden

cabalgar, *v.i.* to ride a horse; ride in procession

cabalgata, *f.* cavalcade; troop of horse

cabalístico, *a.* cabalistic; mysterious

caballa, *f.* mackerel

caballada, *f.* pack of horses; stud (of horses)

caballar, *a.* equine, horse

caballeresco, *a.* gentlemanly; knightly; chivalrous

caballerete, *m.* dim. (fam.) foppish young man, dandy

caballería, *f.* riding-animal; cavalry; knightly deed or quest; any of Spanish Military Orders; knight-errantry; knighthood; chivalry; share of the spoils of war; horsemanship. **c. andante,** knight-errantry. **c. ligera,** (mil.) light horse. **c. mayor,** horses, mares, mules. **c. menor,** asses, donkeys

caballeriza, *f.* stable; stud of horses; staff of a stable

caballerizo, *m.* head stable-groom. **c. mayor del rey,** Master of the King's Horse

caballero, *m.* gentleman; cavalier; knight. **c. andante,** knight-errant. (fam.) **c. de industria,** adventurer, sharper. **c. del hábito,** knight of one of the Spanish Military Orders. **c. novel,** untried knight. **armar c.,** to dub a knight

caballerosidad, *f.* gentlemanliness; nobility; generosity; chivalry

caballeroso, *a.* gentlemanly; noble; generous; chivalrous

caballete, *m.* ridge (of a roof); (mil.) wooden horse; brake (for flax and hemp); (agr.) furrow; easel; sawing-frame; trestle; bridge (of the nose)

caballito, *m.* dim. little horse; *pl.* merry-go-round; automatic horse gambling game; circus equestrian act. **c. del diablo,** dragon-fly

caballo, *m.* horse; (chess) knight; (Spanish cards) queen; sawing-frame; *pl.* cavalry. **c. balancín,** rocking-horse. **c. de batalla,** war-horse; (fig.) hobby-horse;

forte; crux. **c. de cartón**, hobby-horse; rocking-horse. **c. de carrera**, racehorse. **c. de tiro**, draught-horse. **c. de vapor**, horse-power. **c. marino**, sea-horse. **a c.**, on horseback. A c. regalado no le mires el diente, Never look a gift horse in the mouth. **caer bien a c.**, to have a good seat (on a horse). **ser un c.** loco en una cacharrería, to be like a bull in a china shop

caballuno, a. pertaining to horses; horselike; horsy

cabaña, f. hut, cabin, cottage; flock (of sheep); drove (of mules); (art) pastoral scene; balk (billiards)

cabecear, v.i. to nod; shake the head in disapproval; move the head from side to side; toss the head (horses); (aer., naut.) pitch; sway (of a carriage); lean; v.t. refoot (socks); head (wine)

cabeceo, m. nod, shake (of head); (naut., aer.) pitching; lurching (of a carriage, etc.); bight (of river)

cabecera, f. top, upper portion, head; seat of honour; bed-head; river source; capital (country·or county); illustrated chapter heading; pillow; inscription, heading

cabecilla, dim. f. small head. m. and f. (fam.) hothead. m. rebel leader

cabellera, f. head of long hair; hair-switch; tail (of comet)

cabello, m. hair; head of hair; silk (of maize). (fig., fam.) asirse de un c., to clutch at a straw

cabelludo, a. hairy; (bot.) fibrous

caber, v.i. irr. to be room for, contain; fit into, go into (e.g. No cabemos todos en este coche, There is not room for all of us in this car); happen, befall, have (e.g. No les cupo tal suerte, They did not have such luck—Such luck did not befall them); be possible (e.g. Todo cabe en Dios, All things are possible with God). No cabe más, There's no room for anything else; (fig.) That's the limit. (fig.) no c. en sí, to be beyond

oneself (with joy, pride, etc.). No cabe duda de que, There's no doubt that. . . . *Pres. Ind.* quepo, cabes, etc. *Fut.* cabré, etc. *Conditional* cabría, etc. *Preterite* cupe, cupiste, etc. *Pres. Subjunc.* quepa, quepas, etc. *Imperf. Subjunc.* cupiese, etc.

cabestrar, v.t. to halter

cabestrillo, m. sling; thin chain (for ornament)

cabestro, m. halter; sling; leading ox

cabeza, f. head; top, upper end; nail-head; brain; mind; judgment; self-control; edge (of book); peak, summit; source, origin; individual, person; head of cattle; capital city. m. leader, chief, head. (mech.) c. de biela, big-end. (fam.) c. de chorlito, scatter-brain (person). (mil.) c. de puente, bridgehead. c. de partido, principal town of a region. c. de turco, scapegoat. irse la c. (a alguien), to feel giddy. (fig., fam.) meter a uno en la c., to put into someone's head. (fam.) quebrarse la c., to rack one's brains. (fam.) quitar a uno de la c. (una cosa), to dissuade; get an idea out of someone's head

cabezada, f. blow with or on the head; nod; headshake; headstall; (naut.) pitching. dar cabezadas, to nod, go to sleep

cabezal, m. small head pillow; (surg.) pad; bolster; narrow mattress; (mech.) head

cabezo, m. summit (of mountain); hill; (naut.) reef

cabezón, m. tax-register; collar-band; head-opening (of a garment)

cabezudo, a. large-headed; (fam.) obstinate; (fam.) heady (of wine). m. carnival grotesque

cabida, f. space, capacity; extent, area

cabildear, v.i. to canvass votes, lobby

cabildo, m. (ecc.) chapter; municipal council; meeting, or meeting place of council

cabilla, f. (naut.) belaying pin

cabina, f. cabin. c. del teléfono, (telephone) call-box

cabizbajo, *a.* crestfallen; pensive, melancholy

cable, *m.* cable; string (of bridge); cable's length; c. aéreo, overhead cable. c. eléctrico, electric cable

cablegrafiar, *v.t.* to cable

cablegrama, *m.* cablegram

cabo, *m.* end, extremity; stump, stub; handle, shaft, haft; leader; (*geog.*) cape; end, conclusion; (*naut.*) rope; ply (of wool, etc.); (*mil.*) corporal; *pl.* accessories (clothes); horse's tail and mane. c. de maestranza, foreman. c. de mar, naval quartermaster. c. furriel, (*mil.*) quartermaster. al c., in the end. llevar a c., to finish

cabotaje, *m.* (*naut.*) coasting trade

cabra, *f.* nanny-goat; goat. c. montesa, wild goat

cabrahigo, *m.* wild fig; wild fig tree

cabrerizo (-za), *a.* goatish. *m.* goatherd

cabrero (-ra), *m.* goatherd

cabrestante, *m.* (*naut.*) capstan

cabria, *f.* winch, hoist

cabrilla, *f.* (*carp.*) saw-horse; *pl.* (*ast.*) Pleiades; burn marks on legs from sitting too near fire; white crests (of waves)

cabrillear, *v.i.* to foam, froth (the sea)

cabrío, *a.* goatish. *m.* herd of goats. macho c., male goat, he-goat

cabriola, *f.* fouetté (in dancing); spin in air (acrobats); curvet (horses); caper

cabriolar, *v.i.* to curvet; caper, skip

cabriolé, *m.* cabriolet; short cape with or without sleeves

cabritilla, *f.* dressed kid; lambskin, etc.

cabrito, *m.* (*zool.*) kid; *pl.* toasted maize, popcorn

cabrón, *m.* he-goat; (*fam.*) complaisant husband

cabruno, *a.* goatish

cabujón, *m.* (*min.*) uncut gem; unpolished ruby; *pl.* vignettes

cacahual, *m.* cacao plantation

cacahuete, *m.* (*bot.*) peanut, monkey nut

cacao, *m.* (*bot.*) cacao tree; cacao-nut

cacarear, *v.i.* to crow, cackle; *v.t.* (*fam.*) boast

cacareo, *m.* crowing, cackling; (*fam.*) boast

cacatúa, *f.* cockatoo

cacera, *f.* irrigation channel

cacería, *f.* hunting party; hunting bag, booty; (*art*) hunting scene

cacerola, *f.* stew-pot, casserole

cacillo, *m.* ladle; basting spoon

cacique, *m.* Indian chief, cacique; (*fam.*) political " boss "

caciquismo, *m.* political " bossism "

caco, *m.* pickpocket, thief; (*fam.*) poltroon

cacofonía, *f.* cacophony

cacto, *m.* cactus

cacumen, *m.* (*fam.*) brains, acumen

cachalote, *m.* sperm whale

cachar, *v.t.* to break in fragments; split (wood)

cacharrería, *f.* crockery store

cacharro, *m.* coarse earthenware vessel; (*fam.*) decrepit, worthless object

cachazudo, *a.* phlegmatic, slow

cachear, *v.t.* to search (a person) for weapons

cachemira, *f.* cashmere

cacheo, *m.* search (of persons) for weapons

cachete, *m.* blow on the head or face with fist; cheek (especially fat one)

cachetero, *m.* dagger

cachetina, *f.* hand-to-hand fight

cachipolla, *f.* (*ent.*) mayfly

cachiporra, *f.* club, bludgeon

cachivache, *m.* (*fam.*) (gen. *pl.*) trash; pots, pans, utensils

cacho, *m.* small slice (gen. of bread or fruit)

cachón, *m.* breaker, wave; small waterfall

cachorro (-rra), *s.* puppy; cub. *m.* small pistol

cachuela, *f.* Extremaduran pork stew

cada, *a.* every, each. c. cual, each. c. que, whenever; every time that. c. y cuando que, whenever

cadalso, *m.* scaffold; platform, stand

cadarzo, *m.* floss (of a cocoon)

cadáver, *m.* corpse

cadavérico, *a.* cadaverous, ghastly

cadena, *f.* chain; link, tie; (*fig.*) bond; (*fig.*) sequence (of events); (*law*) imprisonment; (*arch.*) buttress; grand chain (dancing); **c. de montañas,** range of mountains. **c. perpetua,** penal servitude for life

cadencia, *f.* cadence; rhythm; (*mus.*) measure, time; (*mus.*) cadenza

cadencioso, *a.* rhythmic

cadeneta, *f.* (*sew.*) chain-stitch

cadente, *a.* falling, declining; decaying, dying; rhythmic

cadera, *f.* hip; flank

caderillas, *f. pl.* bustle, panniers

cadete, *m.* (*mil.*) cadet

cadmio, *m.* (*chem.*) cadmium

caducar, *v.i.* to become senile; become invalid, be annulled; expire, lapse; (*fig.*) be worn out

caduceo, *m.* Mercury's wand

caducidad, *f.* decrepitude; lapse, expiry

caduco, *a.* senile; decrepit; perishable; lapsed

caduquez, *f.* senility

caedizo, *a.* ready to fall; timid, cowardly, weak

caer, *v.i. irr.* to fall, drop; drop out or off; suit, fit, become; fail; fade (colours); (*fig.*) drop (voice); (*with sobre*) attack, fall upon; (*with en*) fall in or on to; decay, collapse; understand; (*with preps. a, hacia*) (*fig.*) look on to, face; (*with por, en*) (*fig.*) fall on, occur on; *v.r.* (*aer.*) crash; fly off (buttons, etc.). **c. de cabeza,** to fall head foremost. **c. en gracia,** to make a good impression, arouse affection. **caerse de suyo,** to be self-evident. **Cayó enfermo,** He was taken ill. *Pres. Ind.* **caigo, caes,** etc. *Pres. Part.* **cayendo.** *Preterite* **cayó cayeron.** *Pres. Subjunc.* **caiga,** etc.

café, *m.* coffee (tree, berry, drink); café, coffee-house

cafeína, *f.* caffeine

cafetal, *m.* coffee plantation

cafetera, *f.* coffee-pot

cafeto, *m.* coffee tree

cafre, *a.* Kaffir. *m.* savage, cruel person; lout, boor

cagaaceite, *m.* missel thrush

cagadas, *f. pl.* droppings, dung

cagafierro, *m.* iron-dross

cagar(se), *v.i., v.t., v.r.* to evacuate (bowels); *v.t.* (*fam.*) spoil, make a botch of

cagarruta, *f.* dung of sheep, deer, rabbits, etc.

caída, *f.,* falling; fall; ruin; failure; close (of day); (*fig.*) falling off; hanging (curtains, etc.); diminution; incline; *pl.* coarse wool; (*fam.*) repartee. **a la c. de la tarde,** at the end of the afternoon. **a la c. del sol,** at sunset

caído (-da), *a.* debilitated, languid; lapsed; (of a shoulder) sloping. **los caídos,** the fallen, the dead (in war, etc.)

caimán, *m.* alligator; (*fam.*) shark, astute person

caja, *f.* box; safe, cash box; coffin; (of a vehicle) body; (*mus.*) drum; case (of piano, watch, etc.); cavity; well (of a stair); (*com.*) cash; cash-desk; cashier's office; (*bot.*) sheath. **c. de ahorros,** savings bank. **c. de caudales,** strong-box. (*print.*) **c. de imprenta,** type case. **c. de música,** musical box. **c. de reclutamiento,** recruiting office. **c. de velocidades,** gear-box. **c. registradora,** cash register

cajero (-ra), *m.* boxmaker; *s.* (*com.*) cashier; peddler

cajetilla, *f.* packet (for cigarettes, etc.)

cajista, *m.* and *f.* (*print.*) compositor

cajón, *m.* chest, locker, case; drawer. **c. de municiones,** ammunition-box

cajonada, *f.* (*naut.*) lockers

cajonera, *f.* (*ecc.*) chest of drawers in sacristy; (*agr.*) frame

cal, *f.* lime. **c. muerta,** slaked lime. **c. viva,** quicklime. (*fig., fam.*) **de c. y canto,** tough, strong

cala, *f.* sample slice (of fruit); (*naut.*) hold; (*surg.*) probe; cove, small bay; (*bot.*) iris

calabacera, *f.* (*bot.*) pumpkin or gourd plant

calabacín, *m.* kind of vegetable marrow; (*fam.*) dolt

calabaza, *f.* (*bot.*) pumpkin (plant and fruit); gourd; (*fam.*) dolt.

dar calabazas, to refuse (suitor); fail (in an examination). (*fam.*) **llevar calabazas,** to get the sack; be jilted

calabobos, *m.* (*fam.*) drizzle

calabocero, *m.* gaoler

calabozo, *m.* dungeon; prison cell; pruning knife

calabrés (-esa), *a.* and *s.* Calabrian

calabrote, *m.* (*naut.*) hawser

calada, *f.* soaking, wetting through; flight of bird of prey; swoop. **dar una c.,** (*fig.*, *fam.*) to dress down

calado, *a.* soaked, wet through. *m.* (*sew.*) open-work; fretwork; (*naut.*) draught of a ship; water level; *pl.* lace. **c. hasta los huesos,** soaked to the skin; madly in love

calador, *m.* one who does open or fretwork; caulking iron; borer; (*surg.*) probe

calafate, *m.* caulker

calafatear, *v.t.* (*naut.*) to caulk

calamar, *m.* (*zool.*) squid, calamary

calambre, *m.* cramp. **c. del escribiente,** writer's cramp

calamidad, *f.* misfortune, calamity

calamina, *f.* (*min.*) calamine

calamitoso, *a.* calamitous; unfortunate, unhappy

cálamo, *m.* ancient flute; stalk (of grass); (*poet.*) pen

calamocano, *a.* maudlin, tipsy

calandrar, *v.t.* (*mech.*) to calender

calandria, *f.* (*orn.*) calender, lark; (*mech.*) calender; treadmill. *m.* and *f.* (*fam.*) malingerer

calaña, *f.* sample; model; pattern; kind, quality; temperament; cheap fan

calar, *v.t.* to . permeate, soak through; pierce; do openwork (in cloth, paper, metal); cut a sample slice from fruit; pull (hat, etc.) well down on head; fix (bayonets, etc.); (*fam.*) understand (persons); (*fam.*) guess, realize; (*naut.*) let down; *v.i.* (*naut.*) draw (water); *v.r.* be drenched, wet through; swoop (birds of prey); (*fam.*) sneak in. *a.* calcareous

calar, *m.* limestone deposit or region

calavera, *f.* skull. *m.* dare-devil, madcap; roué

calaverada, *f.* (*fam.*) dare-devilment, foolishness; escapade

calcañar, *m.* heel (of foot)

calcar, *v.t.* to trace (drawing); press with foot; copy servilely, imitate

calcáreo, *a.* calcareous

calce, *m.* rim of a wheel; wedge; tyre

calcedonia, *f.* chalcedony

calcés, *m.* (*naut.*) mast-head

calceta, *f.* stocking; fetter. (*fam.*) **hacer c.,** to knit

calcetería, *f.* hosiery shop; hosiery trade

calcetero (-ra), *s.* hosier; hose maker or darner

calcetín, *m.* sock

calcificación, *f.* (*med.*) calcification

calcinación, *f.* calcination

calcinar, *v.t.* to calcine

calcio, *m.* calcium

calco, *m.* tracing (drawing)

calcografía, *f.* chalcography

calcografiar, *v.t.* to transfer; make chalcographies of

calcomanía, *f.* transfer

calculación, *f.* calculation

calculadamente, *adv.* calculatedly

calculado, *a.* calculated

calculador, *a.* calculating. *m.* calculating machine, comptometer

calcular, *v.t.* to calculate

cálculo, *m.* calculation; (*math.*) estimate; investigation; conjecture; (*math.*, *med.*) calculus. **c. hepático,** (*med.*) gall-stone

calda, *f.* heating; *pl.* hot mineral baths

caldear, *v.t.* to heat

caldeo (-ea), *a.* and *s.* Chaldean

caldeo, *m.* heating

caldera, *f.* cauldron; cauldron full; (*S.A.*) teapot; (*eng.*) boiler. **c. de vapor,** steam-boiler

calderería, *f.* copper-smith's trade and shop

calderero, *m.* boiler maker; copper-smith; tinker

calderilla, *f.* holy water stoup; any copper coin

caldero, *m.* small cauldron; casserole; kettle

calderón, *m.* large cauldron;

(*mus.*) rest; (*mus.*) **trill;** pause
calderoniano, *a.* Calderonian
(from Calderon de la Barca,
seventeenth-century S p a n i s h
dramatist)
caldo, *m.* broth; salad dressing;
pl. (*agr.*) oil, wine, vegetable
juices
calefacción, *f.* heating. **c. central,** central heating
calendario, *m.* calendar. **c. deportivo,** fixture card. **c. gregoriano,** Gregorian calendar
caléndula, *f.* marigold
calentador, *a.* heating, warming.
m. heater; warming-pan
calentamiento, *m.* heating,
warming
calentar, *v.t. irr.* to heat, warm;
rev-up (an engine); hasten; (*fam.*)
spank; *v.r.* warm oneself; be- in
heat (animals); grow excited.
See **acertar**
calentura, *f.* fever
calenturiento, *a.* feverish
calera, *f.* lime-pit; lime-kiln; fishing smack
calesa, *f.* calash (carriage)
calesín, *m.* fly (carriage)
caleta, *f.* cove, creek
caletre, *m.* (*fam.*) discernment,
head, sense
calibrar, *v.t.* to calibrate;
gauge
calibre, *m.* (*mech.*) gauge; bore,
calibre; diameter (tubes, pipes,
etc.)
calicata, *f.* (*min.*) sounding
calidad, *f.* quality; rôle; character, temperament; condition,
requisite; importance, gravity;
personal particulars; nobility; *pl.*
qualities of the mind. **en c. de,**
in the capacity of
cálido, *a.* warm, hot; warming,
heating; vehement, ardent; (*art*)
warm
calidoscópico, *a.* kaleidoscopic
calidoscopio, *m.* kaleidoscope
calientapiés, *m.* footwarmer
calientaplatos, *m.* hot-plate,
plate-warmer
caliente, *a.* warm, hot; excited;
(*art*) warm
califa, *m.* caliph
califato, *m.* caliphate
calificable, *a.* classifiable; qualifiable

calificación, *f.* classification;
qualification; judgment; mark,
place (examinations)
calificar, *v.t.* to class; authorize;
judge (qualities); (*fig.*) ennoble;
v.r. prove noble descent
calificativo, *a.* (*gram.*)'qualifying.
m. epithet
californio (-ia), *a.* and *s.* Californian
caliginoso, *a.* murky, dark
caligrafía, *f.* calligraphy
calígrafo, *m.* calligraphist
calinoso, *a.* hazy
caliqueño, *m.* cheroot
calistenia, *f.* callisthenics
cáliz, *m.* chalice; (*poet.*) cup;
(*bot.*) calyx
caliza, *f.* limestone
calizo, *a.* calcareous
calma, *f.* calm, airlessness; serenity, composure; quiet, tranquillity, peace. **c. chicha,** dead
calm. **en c.,** at peace; tranquil;
calm (of the sea)
calmante, *a.* calming, soothing.
(*med.*) *a.* and *m.* sedative
calmar, *v.t.* to. soothe, calm;
moderate; mitigate; pacify;
quench (thirst); *v.i.* grow calm;
moderate; be becalmed
calmoso, *a.* calm, tranquil; (*fam.*)
sluggish, lazy; imperturbable
caló, *m.* Romany; argot
calor, *m.* heat; ardour, vehemence; cordiality; (*fig.*) heat (of
battle); excitement
caloría, *f.* (*phys.*) calorie
calórico, *a.* (*phys.*) caloric,
thermic
calorífero, *a.* heat-giving. *m.*
heater, radiator
calorífico, *a.* calorific
calumnia, *f.* calumny; (*law*)
slander
calumniador (-ra), *a.* slandering.
s. calumniator, slanderer
calumniar, *v.t.* to calumniate;
(*law*) slander
calumnioso, *a.* calumnious, slanderous
caluroso, *a.* hot, warm; cordial,
friendly; enthusiastic; ardent,
impassioned; excited
calva, *f.* bald patch on head; worn
place (cloth, etc.); bare spot,
clearing (trees, etc.)
Calvario, *m.* Calvary; (*fam.*)
series of disasters; (*fam.*) debts

calvero, *m.* clearing (in a wood); chalk or marl pit

calvicie, *f.* baldness

calvinismo, *m.* Calvinism

calvinista, *m.* and *f.* Calvinist. *a.* Calvinistic

calvo, *a.* bald; bare, barren (land); worn (cloth, etc.)

calza, *f.* breeches (gen. *pl.*); wedge; (*fam.*) stocking. (*fam.*) **tomar calzas,** to beat it

calzada, *f.* roadway. **c. romana,** Roman road

calzado, *m.* footwear, shoes

calzador, *m.* shoehorn

calzadura, *f.* wedging (of a wheel); act of putting on shoes; felloe of a wheel

calzar, *v.t.* to put on shoes; wear (spurs, gloves, etc.); wedge, block (wheel); scotch (a wheel). (*fig., fam.*) **calzarse a una persona,** to have a person in one's pocket

calzón, *m.* breeches (gen. *pl.*). (*fig., fam.*) **ponerse los calzones,** to wear the breeches (of a woman)

calzonazos, *m.* (*fam.*) weak-willed, easily-led fellow

calzoncillos, *m. pl.* drawers, pants

callado, *a.* silent; reserved; secret

callar(se), *v.i.* and *v.r.* to say nothing, keep silent; stop speaking; stop making any sound (persons, animals, things); *v.t.* conceal, keep secret; omit, leave out; (*fam.*) *interj.* ¡Calle! You don't say so! **Quien calla otorga,** Silence gives consent

calle, *f.* street. (*fam.*) **abrir c.,** to clear the way. (*fam.*) **dejar en la c.,** to leave destitute. (*fam.*) **echar a la c.,** to throw out of the house. **ponerse en la c.,** to go out

calleja, callejuela, *f.* small street, alley, side street

callejear, *v.i.* to wander about the streets

callejero, *a.* fond of gadding. *m.* street directory

callejón, *m.* alley, lane. **c. sin salida,** cul-de-sac; (*fig.*) impasse

callicida, *m.* corn cure

callista, *m.* and *f.* chiropodist

callo, *m.* corn, callosity; (*med.*) callus; *pl.* tripe

callosidad, *f.* callosity

calloso, *a.* callous, horny

cama, *f.* bed; bedstead; bed-hanging; lair, form; floor (of a cart); check (of bridle) (gen. *pl.*). **c. de campaña,** camp-bed. **c. de matrimonio,** double bed. **c. de monja,** single bed. **c. turca,** settee-bed. **guardar c.,** to stay in bed

camada, *f.* brood, litter; (*fam.*) gang

camafeo, *m.* cameo

camaleón, *m.* chameleon; (*fam.*) changeable person

cámara, *f.* chamber; hall; house (of deputies); granary; (*naut.*) state room; chamber (firearms, mines); (*phys.*) camera; human excrement; (*aut.*) inner tube. **c. acorazada,** strong-room. **C. alta,** Upper House, House of Lords. **C. baja** or **C. de los Comunes,** Lower House, House of Commons. **C. de comercio,** Chamber of Commerce. **c. oscura,** (optics) dark room

camarada, *m.* and *f.* pal, companion, comrade

camaradería, *f.* comradeship, companionship

camarera, *f.* waiting-maid; waitress; chamber-maid; stewardess. **c. mayor,** mistress of queen's wardrobe

camarero, *m.* papal chamberlain; chamberlain; steward; waiter; valet. **c. mayor,** Lord Chamberlain

camarilla, *f.* palace or other clique, coterie; (*fam.*) back-scratch

camarín, *m.* (*theat.*) dressing-room; closet; boudoir; cage (of a lift); niche

camarón, *m.* prawn, shrimp; tip, reward

camarote, *m.* cabin; berth

cambalachear, *v.t.* (*fam.*) to barter

cámbaro, *m.* sea-crab

cambiable, *a.* exchangeable; changeable

cambiante, *a.* exchanging; changing. *m.* sheen, lustre (gen. *pl.*); money changer

cambiar, *v.t.* to exchange; convert. *v.t.* and *v.i.* change, alter; *v.i.* and *v.r.* to veer (wind). **c. de frente,** to face about; (*fig.*) change front

cambija, *f.* reservoir

cambín, *m.* lobster-pot

cambio, *m.* exchange; change; (*com.*) rate of exchange; money change; (*com.*) premium on bills of exchange. **en c.,** instead, on the other hand. **c. de velocidad,** (*aut.*) gear-changing. **letra de c.,** bill of exchange. **Libre c.,** Free Trade

cambista, *m.* and *f.* money changer. *m.* banker

camelar, *v.t.* (*fam.*) to woo; seduce

camelia, *f.* camelia. **c. japonesa,** japonica

camelo, *m.* (*fam.*) eyewash

camellero, *m.* camel keeper or driver

camello, *m.* camel. **c. pardal,** giraffe

camellón, *m.* furrow; drinking trough

camilla, *f.* couch; small round skirted table with brazier underneath; stretcher, litter

camillero, *m.* (*mil.*) stretcherbearer

caminador, *a.* in the habit of walking a great deal

caminante, *m.* and *f.* walker, traveller

caminar, *v.i.* to travel; walk; (*fig.*) move on, go (inanimate things). (*fig., fam.*) **c. derecho,** to walk uprightly

caminata, *f.* long, tiring walk; excursion

camino, *m.* road; route; journey; way, means; **c. de hierro,** railway. **c. de mesa,** table-runner. **c. de sirga,** tow-path. **c. real,** highway, main road. **de c.,** on the way, in passing. **ponerse en c.,** to set out

camión, *m.* lorry, truck

camionaje, *m.* truckage

camisa, *f.* shirt, stiff shirt; thin skin (of fruit); sloughed skin of snakes; coat (of whitewash, etc.); (*mech.*) jacket; mantle (gas). **c. de fuerza,** strait jacket. **c. pantalón,** cami-knickers. **dejar sin c.,** (*fam.*) to leave penniless

camisería, *f.* shirt shop or factory

camisero (-ra), *s.* shirt maker or seller

camiseta, *f.* vest. **c. de fútbol,** football jersey

camisola, *f.* stiff shirt; ruffled shirt

camisolín, *m.* stiff front (of shirt)

camisón, *m.* large wide shirt; night shirt

camomila, *f.* camomile

camorra, *f.* (*fam.*) brawl, shindy. **armar c.,** to start a row

campal, *a.* field, country

campamento, *m.* camping; (*mil.*) encampment; camp

campana, *f.* bell; anything bell-shaped; church, parish. **c. de chimenea,** mantelpiece. **c. de hogar,** hood, shutter (of a fire-place)

campanada, *f.* peal of a bell; scandal

campanario, *m.* belfry, bell tower

campanear, *v.i.* to ring bells frequently

campaneo, *m.* bell-ringing; chime

campanero, *m.* bell-founder; bell ringer

campanil, *m.* small belfry, campanile

campanilla, *f.* hand-bell; bubble; any bell-shaped flower

campanillazo, *m.* loud peal of a bell

campante, *a.* outstanding; (*fam.*) proud, satisfied

campanudo, *a.* bell-shaped; sonorous (of words); pompous (of speech)

campánula, *f.* (*bot.*) campanula

campaña, *f.* level country; campaign. (*naut.*) voyage, cruise. **correr la c.,** to reconnoitre

campar, *v.i.* to camp. (*fam.*) **c. por sus respetos,** to stand on one's own feet

campeador, *a.* mighty in battle (used especially of the Cid)

campear, *v.i.* to go out to graze; grow green (crops); excel; (*mil.*) be engaged in a campaign, reconnoitre

campechano, *a.* (*fam.*) hearty; frank; cheerful; generous

campeche, *m.* (*bot.*) logwood

campeón, *m.* champion; advocate, defender

campeonato, *m.* championship

campesino (-na), *a.* rural, rustic. *s.* country dweller

campestre, *a.* rural

campiña, *f.* expanse of cultivated land; countryside, landscape

campo, *m.* country (as opposed to town); field; (*fig.*) sphere, province; (*phys., her., mil.*) field; (*art*) ground; (*mil.*) camp, army; plain ground (of silks, etc.). **c. de aterrizaje,** (*aer.*) landing-field. **c. de batalla,** battlefield. **c. de concentración,** concentration camp. **c. de golf,** golf course. **c. de prisioneros** (*mil.*) prison camp. **c. de tiro,** rifle-range. **c. santo,** graveyard. **c. visual,** field of vision. **a c. abierto,** in the open air. **a c. travieso,** cross-country

camuesa, *f.* pippin apple

camuflaje, *m.* camouflage

camuflar, *v.t.* to camouflage

can, *m.* dog; trigger; (*arch.*) modillion; (*ast.*) Dog Star

cana, *f.* (gen. *pl.*) white hair

canadiense, *a.* and *m.* and *f.* Canadian

canal, *m.* canal. *m.* or *f.* (*geol.*) subterranean waterway; channel; (*anat.*) canal, duct; defile, narrow valley; gutter; drinking trough; animal carcass. **abrir en c.,** to open up, split open

canalera, *f.* roof gutter

canalete, *m.* paddle

canalización, *f.* canalization; (*elec.*) main, mains; piping, tubing

canalizar, *v.t.* to make canals or channels; regulate waters of rivers, etc.; canalize

canalizo, *m.* (*naut.*) fairway

canalón, *m.* gutter, spout; shovel hat; pantile

canalla, *f.* (*fam.*) mob, rabble. *m.* (*fam.*) scoundrel

canallesco, *a.* scoundrelly, knavish; despicable

canana, *f.* cartridge-belt

canapé, *m.* sofa

canario (-ia), *m.* canary bird. *a.* and *s.* pertaining to or native of the Canary Islands. **c. de raza flauta,** a roller canary

canasta, *f.* hamper, basket; card game

canastilla, *f.* small basket; layette

canastillo, *m.* basket-work tray

cáncamo, *m.* ring-bolt

cancamusa, *f.* (*fam.*) trick, deception

cancel, *m.* draught-screen; (*ecc.*) screen

cancela, *f.* wrought-iron door

cancelación, *f.* cancellation; expunging

cancelar, *v.t.* to cancel; expunge, annul; abolish, blot out; pay off, clear (a mortgage)

cancelaría, *f.* papal chancery

cancelario, *m.* chancellor (universities)

cáncer, *m.* cancer

cancerar, *v.t.* to consume; weaken; mortify; *v.r.* suffer from cancer; become cancerous

cancerbero, *m.* (*myth.*) Cerberus; (*fig.*) unbribable guard

canceroso, *a.* cancerous

canciller, *m.* chancellor; assistant vice-consul

cancillería, *f.* chancellorship; chancellery

canción, *f.* song; lyric poem; musical accompaniment; old name for any poetical composition. **volver a la misma c.,** (*fig.*) to be always harping on the same theme

cancionero, *m.* collection of songs and verses; song-book

cancionista, *m.* and *f.* singer; song writer

cancha, *f.* (*sport*) frontón; (tennis) court; cockpit; yard; hippodrome; widest part of a river; road; toasted maize

candado, *m.* padlock; earring

candeal, *a.* white (of bread)

candela, *f.* candle; horse-chestnut flower; candlestick; (*fam.*) fire. **en c.,** (*naut.*) vertical (of masts, etc.)

candelabro, *m.* candelabrum

candelaria, *f.* Candlemas

candelero, *m.* candlestick; lamp; candle maker or seller; (*naut.*) stanchion

candente, *a.* candescent, red-hot

candidato (-ta), *s.* candidate

candidatura, *f.* candidature

candidez, *f.* simplicity, ingenuousness; candidness

cándido, *a.* white; simple, ingenuous; candid, frank

candil, *m.* oil lamp; Greek lamp; tips of stag's horns; (*fam.*) cock of a hat

candileja, *f.* oil reservoir of lamp; *pl.* footlights, floats

candor, *m.* extreme whiteness; sincerity, candour; simplicity, innocence

candoroso, *a.* candid, open; simple, honest

canela, *f.* (*bot.*) cinnamon; (*fig.*) anything exquisitely perfect

canelo, *m.* cinnamon tree. *a.* cinnamon-coloured

canesú, *m.* yoke (of a dress, etc.); corset-cover

caney, *m.* log-cabin

cangilón, *m.* pitcher, jar; bucket (for water); dredging bucket

cangreja, *f.* (*naut.*) gaffsail. **c. de mesana,** (*naut.*) jigger

cangrejo, *m.* crab. **c. de mar,** sea-crab. **c. ermitaño,** hermit crab

canguro, *m.* kangaroo

caníbal, *a.* and *m.* and *f.* cannibal

canibalismo, *m.* cannibalism

canica, *f.* marble (for playing with)

canícula, *f.* dog days; (*ast.*) Dog star

canicular, *a.* canicular

caniculares, *m. pl.* dog days

canijo, *a.* (*fam.*) delicate, sickly; anæmic, stunted

canilla, *f.* long bone of leg or arm; any principal bones in bird's wing; tap, faucet; spool, reel; fault (in cloth)

canino, *a.* canine

canje, *m.* (diplomacy, *mil.*, *com.*) exchange, substitution. **c. de prisioneros,** exchange of prisoners

canjear, *v.t.* to exchange

cano, *a.* white-haired, hoary; ancient; (*poet.*) white

canoa, *f.* canoe; launch. **c. automóvil,** motor launch

canoero (-ra), *s.* canoeist

canón, *m.* rule; (*ecc.*, *print.*) canon; catalogue; part of the Mass; (*mus.*) canon, catch; tax. *pl.* canon law

canonesa, *f.* canoness

canónico, *a.* canonic, canonical

canónigo, *m.* canon; prebendary

canonización, *f.* canonization

canonizar, *v.t.* to canonize; extol, exalt; approve, acclaim

canonjía, *f.* canonry, canonship; (*fam.*) sinecure

canoso, *a.* white-haired, hoary

cansado (-da), *a.* tired; weary; exhausted; decadent; tiresome; (*fam.*) fed up. *s.* bore, tedious person

cansancio, *m.* fatigue, weariness

cansar, *v.t.* to tire, weary; (*agr.*) exhaust soil; bore; badger, annoy; *v.r.* be tired; grow weary

cansino, *a.* worn-out (of horses, etc.)

cantable, *a.* singable; (*mus.*) cantabile

cantábrico (-ca), *a.* and *s.* Cantabrian

cantante, *a.* singing. *m.* and *f.* professional singer

cantar, *v.i.* to sing; twitter, chirp; extol; (*fam.*) squeak, creak; (*fig.*) call (cards); (*fam.*) squeal, confess. *m.* song. **C. de los Cantares,** Song of Songs. **cantarlas claras,** to call a spade a spade

cántara, *f.* pitcher, jug

cantárida, *f.* Spanish fly

cántaro, *m.* pitcher, jug; jugful; varying wine measure; ballot box; tax on spirits and oil

cantata, *f.* cantata

cantatriz, *f.* singer, prima donna

cante, *m.* song; singing

cantera, *f.* (*min.*) quarry; capacity, talent

cantería, *f.* stone-cutting; quarrying; building made of hewn stone

cantero, *m.* stone-cutter; quarryman

cántico, *m.* (*ecc.*) canticle; (*poet.*) poem

cantidad, *f.* quantity; large part; portion; sum of money; quantity (prosody). **c. llovida,** rainfall

cantiga *or* **cántiga,** *f.* old poetic form designed to be sung

cantil, *m.* cliff; steep rock

cantimplora, *f.* water cooler; water bottle; siphon

cantina, *f.* wine cellar; canteen; refreshment room

cantinera, *f.* vivandière

cantinero, *m.* sutler; owner of a canteen

canto, *m.* singing; song; canto; epic or other poem; end, rim, edge; non-cutting edge (knives, swords); pebble, stone; angle (of a building). (*mus.*) **c. llano,** plain-song. **al c. del gallo,** at cockcrow. **de c.,** on edge

cantón, *m.* province, region;

corner (of a street); cantonment; (*her.*) canton, quartering

cantonera, *f.* corner-piece (books, furniture, etc., as ornament); angle-iron; bracket, small shelf

cantor (-**ra**), *a.* singing. *s.* singer; song-bird

canturía, *f.* singing exercise; vocal music; monotonous song; droning; (*mus.*) execution, technique

canturreo, *m.,* **canturria,** *f.* humming; droning

canturriar, *v.i.* (*fam.*) to hum, sing under the breath

caña, *f.* stalk; reed; bone of arm or leg; leg (of a trouser, stocking, boot, etc.); marrow; (*bot.*) cane; tumbler, glass; wine measure; gallery (of mine); *pl.* mock battle on horseback, using **cañas** as spears. **c. de azúcar,** sugar-cane. **c. de pescar,** fishing rod. **c. del timón,** tiller (*naut.*)

cañada, *f.* glen, ravine, cattle track

cañal, *m.* cane-break; weir (for fish)

cañamazo, *m.* hempen canvas; embroidery canvas; embroidered canvas

cañamelar, *m.* sugar-cane plantation

cáñamo, *m.* hemp

cañamón, *m.* hemp-seed

cañaveral, *m.* cane-brake; (*S.A.*) bamboo field

cañazo, *m.* blow with a cane

cañería, *f.* conduit; pipe; piping

cañero, *m.* pipe layer

caño, *m.* pipe, tube, sewer; organ pipe; jet (of water); mine gallery

cañón, *m.* pipe, cylindrical tube; flue; quill (of birds); cannon; soft down; (*arch.*) shaft (of column); stack (of a chimney). **c. antiaéreo,** A.A. gun. **c. antitanque,** anti-tank gun. **c. de escalera,** well of a staircase

cañonazo, *m.* cannon shot; roar of a cannon

cañonear, *v.t.* to bombard

cañoneo, *m.* cannonade; bombardment

cañonera, *f.* embrasure (for cannon)

cañonería, *f.* (*mil.*) group of cannon; (*mus.*) set of organ pipes

cañonero, *m.* gunboat

cañuto, *m.* (*bot.*) internode; small pipe or tube; (*fam.*) tale-bearer

caoba, *f.* (*bot.*) mahogany

caolín, *m.* kaolin

caos, *m.* chaos; confusion

caótico, *a.* chaotic

capa, *f.* cloak; cape; (*ecc.*) cope; coating; layer; cover; coat (animals); (*fig.*) cloak, disguise; (*geol.*) stratum. **la c. del cielo,** the canopy of heaven. (*fig., fam.*) **echar la c. al toro,** to throw one's cap over the windmill. (*naut.*) **estarse** (*or* **ponerse**) **a la c.,** to lie to

capacete, *m.* helmet

capacidad, *f.* capacity; extension, space; mental capacity; talent; opportunity, means; (*law*) capacity. **c. de producción,** output

capacitar, *v.t.* to capacitate, qualify, enable

capacho, *m.* frail; tool-bag

capadura, *f.* castration

capar, *v.t.* to castrate, geld; (*fam.*) diminish, reduce

caparazón, *m.* caparison, horse blanket; waterproof cover; hood (of carriages); nosebag; shell (insects, crustaceans)

caparrosa, *f.* copperas

capataz, *m.* foreman; steward; overseer

capaz, *a.* capacious; large, spacious; capable, competent; (*law*) able

capcioso, *a.* deceitful, artful; captious, carping

capear, *v.t.* to steal a cape; play the bull with a cape (bullfighting); (*fam.*) put off with excuses, deceive; (*naut.*) lie to

capelina, *f.* poke-bonnet

capelo, *m.* cardinal's hat; cardinalate

capellán, *m.* chaplain; any ecclesiastic

capellanía, *f.* chaplaincy

capeo, *m.* playing the bull with a cape (bullfighting)

caperuza, *f.* hood, pointed cap; (*arch.*) coping-stone

capigorrón, *a.* (*fam.*) loafing. *m.* loafer, idler

capilar, *a.* capillary

capilaridad, *f.* capillarity

capilla, *f.* cowl, hood; chapel; (*ecc.*) chapter; (*ecc.*) choir.

c. ardiente, chapelle ardente. estar en c., to await execution (criminals); (fam.) be in suspense, await anxiously

capillero, m. sexton; churchwarden

capillo, m. baby's bonnet; cocoon of silkworm; flowerbud

capirotazo, m. box on the ear; fillip

capirote, m. academic hood and cap; hood (falconry); tall pointed cap. ser tonto de c., (fam.) to be a complete fool

capitación, f. poll-tax, capitation

capital, a. relating to the head; capital (sins, etc.); main, principal. m. capital, patrimony; (com.) capital stock. f. capital city

capitalismo, m. capitalism

capitalista, a. capitalistic. m. and f. capitalist

capitalización, f. capitalization

capitalizar, v.t. to capitalize

capitán, m. captain, skipper; chief, leader; ringleader. (aer.) c. de aviación, group captain. c. de fragata, (nav.) commander. c. de puerto, harbour master. c. general de ejército, field-marshal

capitana, f. admiral's ship; (fam.) captain's wife

capitanear, v.t. to captain, command; (fig.) guide, lead

capitanía, f. captaincy; captainship

capitel, m. (arch.) capital

capitolio, m. dignified building; (arch.) acropolis; Capitol

capitulación, f. agreement, pact; capitulation; pl. marriage articles

capitular, a. capitulary, belonging to a Chapter. m. capitular, member of a Chapter. v.i. to make an agreement; capitulate; sing prayers; arrange order

capítulo, m. (ecc.) Chapter; meeting of town council, etc.; chapter of book; determination, decision

capó, m. (aut.) bonnet

capón, a. castrated; gelded. m. capon; bundle of firewood or vines

caponera, f. coop for fattening capons; (fam.) gaol; (fam.) place

where one lives well free of charge

capota, f. (bot.) head of teasel; bonnet; hood (of vehicles)

capote, m. short, brightly coloured cape (used by bullfighters); cape coat; (cards) slam; (fam.) scowl

capotillo, m. short cape

Capricornio, m. (ast.) Capricorn

capricho, m. caprice, fancy; strong desire

caprichoso, a. capricious; whimsical

caprichudo, a. headstrong; capricious

cápsula, f. cartridge-case; bottle-cap; (bot., med., chem., zool.) capsule

captar, v.t. gain, attract (goodwill, attention, etc.); (mech.) collect

captor, m. capturer

captura, f. (law) capture; seizing, arrest

capturar, v.t. to capture; arrest, apprehend

capucha, f. hood; cowl; (print.) circumflex accent

capuchina, f. Capuchin nun; (bot.) nasturtium; table-lamp with an extinguisher

capuchino (-na), a. and s. Capuchin

capucho, m. cowl

capullo, m. cocoon; flower bud; acorn cup; (anat.) prepuce

caqui, m. khaki; khaki colour

cara, f. face; likeness, aspect; façade, front; surface; side (of metal, etc.); mien. c. a c. face to face; frankly; openly. (fam.) c. de juez, severe face. (fam.) c. de pascua, smiling face. (fam.) c. de vinagre, sour face. c. o cruz, heads or tails. de c., opposite. hacer a dos caras, to be deceitful, be two-faced. hacer c. (a), to stand up to

cárabe, m. amber

carabela, f. (naut.) carave

carabina, f. carbine; rifle

carabinazo, m. report of a carbine

carabinero, m. carabineer; customs' guard

caracol, m. snail; snail's shell; cure; (zool.) cochlea; winding stair. c. marino, periwinkle. ¡Caracoles! Fancy!

caracola, *f.* conch shell used as a horn

caracolear, *v.i.* to prance from side to side (horses)

carácter, *m.* sign, mark; character, writing (gen. *pl.*); style of writing; brand (animals); nature, temperament; character, individuality, strong-mindedness, energy, firmness; condition, state, capacity. **comedia de c.,** psychological play. **caracteres de imprenta,** printing types

característica, *f.* quality, characteristic; (*math.*) characteristic; actress who plays the part of an old woman

característico, *a.* characteristic, distinctive. *m.* actor who plays rôles of old men

caracterización, *f.* characterization; (*theat.*) make-up

caracterizar, *v.t.* to characterize; confer an office, honour, dignity, on; (*theat.*) create a character; (*theat.*) to make up, dress as, a character

¡ **caramba!** *interj.* gosh!; blast!

carámbano, *m.* icicle

carambola, *f.* cannon (billiards); (*fam.*) double effect; (*fam.*) trick, deception

caramelo, *m.* caramel; toffee

caramillo, *m.* flageolet; small flute, pipe; gossip, intrigue

carantamaula, *f.* (*fam.*) hideous mask; ugly person

carapacho, *m.* carapace, shell

carátula, *f.* mask; (*fig.*) dramatic art, the theatre

caravana, *f.* caravan, group of traders, pilgrims, etc. (especially in East); (*fam.*) crowd of excursionists, picnickers, etc.

¡ **caray!** *interj.* blast!; gosh!

carbólico, *a.* carbolic

carbón, *m.* coal; charcoal; black chalk, crayon. **c. bituminoso,** soft coal. **c. de coque,** coke. **c. de leña,** charcoal. **c. mineral,** coal, anthracite. **mina de c.,** coal-mine

carbonato, *m.* (*chem.*) carbonate

carboncillo, *m.* charcoal crayon

carbonear, *v.t.* to turn into charcoal; (*naut.*) coal

carboneo, *m.* coaling

carbonera, *f.* coal-cellar, coalhouse, etc.; coal-scuttle; woman who sells charcoal or coal; charcoal burner

carbonería, *f.* coal or charcoal merchant's office

carbonero, *a.* relating to coal or charcoal. *m.* collier; charcoal maker; coal merchant; (*naut.*) coal-ship

carbónico, *a.* (*chem.*) carbonic

carbonífero, *a.* carboniferous

carbonización, *f.* carbonization

carbonizar, *v.t.* to carbonize

carbono, *m.* (*chem.*) carbon

carbonoso, *a.* carbonaceous; coaly

carbunco, *m.* (*med.*) carbuncle

carbúnculo, *m.* carbuncle, ruby

carburador, *m.* carburettor

carburo, *m.* (*chem.*) carbide

carcaj, *m.* quiver (for arrows)

carcajada, *f.* burst of laughter. **reírse a carcajadas,** to roar with laughter

carcamal, *m.* (*fam.*) dotard

cárcel, *f.* prison, gaol

carcelario, *a.* prison, gaol

carcelero (-ra), *a.* gaol. *s.* gaoler

cárcola, *f.* treadle (of a loom)

carcoma, *f.* wood-worm; dry rot; (*fig.*) gnawing care; spendthrift

carcomer, *v.t.* to gnaw wood (worms); (*fig.*) undermine (health, etc.); *v.r.* be worm-eaten

carda, *f.* card, carding; teasel head; card brush; (*fam.*) reprimand

cardador (-ra), *s.* carder, comber

cardadura, *f.* carding; carding frame

cardar, *v.t.* to card, tease; brush up (felt, etc.)

cardenal, *m.* cardinal; cardinal bird; bruise

cardenalato, *m.* cardinalate, cardinalship

cardenalicio, *a.* pertaining to cardinals

cardencha, *f.* (*bot.*) teasel; card comb

cardenillo, *m.* verdigris; (*art*) verditer

cárdeno, *a.* livid

cardíaco, *a.* (*med.*) cardiac

cardinal, *a.* principal; cardinal (point); (*gram.*) cardinal (number)

cardiógrafo, *m.* (*med.*) cardiograph

cardiograma, *m.* (*med.*) cardiogram

cardizal, *m.* waste land covered with thistles and weeds

cardo, *m.* (*bot.*) thistle

carear, *v.t.* to confront; compare; *v.i.* turn towards, face; *v.r.* meet; come together

carecer, *v.i.* *irr.* to be short; lack, need (e.g. **Carece de las condiciones necesarias,** It lacks the necessary conditions). See **conocer**

carena, *f.* (*naut.*) bottom; careening

carenar, *v.t.* to careen

carencia, *f.* shortage, lack

carestía, *f.* shortage, scarcity; famine; dearness, high price

careta, *f.* mask; beekeeper's veil; fencing mask. (*fig.*) **quitar la c.** (**a**), to unmask

carey, *m.* (*zool.*) shell turtle; tortoise-shell

carga, *f.* loading; (*elec.*) charging, charge; load (*also elec.*); burden, weight; cargo; explosive charge; (*fig.*) imposition; tax; duty, obligation. (*naut.*) **c. de profundidad,** depth charge

cargadero, *m.* place where goods are loaded or unloaded

cargado, *a.* loaded; heavy, sultry; strong (tea, coffee). **c. de espaldas,** round-shouldered

cargador, *m.* loader; porter; dockhand; pitchfork; rammer; (*mech.*) stoker; (*elec.*) charger

cargamento, *m.* (*naut.*) cargo, freight, shipload

cargar, *v.t.* to load; charge (guns, etc.); stoke; overburden; tax, impose; blame for, charge with; (*fam.*) annoy, bore; (*com.*) charge, book; (*mil.*) attack; (football) tackle; *v.i.* tip, slope; (*with con*) carry away; be loaded with (fruit); assume responsibility; (*with sobre*) importune, urge; lean against; *v.r.* turn (head, etc.); (*with de*) be abundant (in or with); load oneself with

cargazón, *f.* cargo; loading; heaviness; darkness (of the sky)

cargo, *m.* loading; load, weight; post, office; duty, obligation; management, charge; care; (*com.*) debit; accusation. (*com.*)

el c. y la data, debit and credit. **hacerse c. de,** to take charge of; understand; consider carefully. **ser en c.** (**a**), to be debtor (to)

cariancho, *a.* (*fam.*) broadfaced

cariacontecido, *a.* crestfallen, disappointed; glum

cariarse, *v.r.* to become carious

cariátide, *f.* (*arch.*) caryatid

caribe, *a.* Caribbean. *m.* and *f.* cannibal, savage

caricatura, *f.* caricature

caricaturesco, *a.* caricaturish

caricaturista, *m.* and *f.* caricaturist

caricaturizar, *v.t.* to caricature

caricia, *f.* caress

caridad, *f.* charity; charitableness; alms

caries, *f.* caries

carilargo, *a.* (*fam.*) long-faced

carilla, *f.* *dim.* small face; mask; page (of a book)

carilleno, *a.* (*fam.*) plump-faced, round-faced

carillón, *m.* peal (of bells)

cariño, *m.* affection; love; caress (gen. *pl.*); fondness, inclination

cariñoso, *a.* affectionate; loving; kind

carirredondo, *a.* (*fam.*) round-faced

caritativo, *a.* charitable

cariz, *m.* appearance of the sky; look, face; aspect; (*fam.*) outlook (for a business deal, etc.)

carlismo, *m.* Carlism (Spanish politics, nineteenth century)

carlista, *a.* and *m.* and *f.* Carlist

carmelita, *a.* and *m.* and *f.* Carmelite

carmen, *m.* country house and garden (Granada); song; poem

carmesí, *a.* crimson. *m.* crimson colour; cramoisy

carmín, *m.* red, carmine colour; red wild rose-tree and flower

carnada, *f.* bait

carnaje, *m.* salted meat

carnal, *a.* carnal; lascivious; materialistic; worldly; related by blood

carnalidad, *f.* carnality

carnaval, *m.* carnival. **martes de c.,** Shrove Tuesday

carnavalesco, *a.* carnival

carne, *f.* flesh; meat; pulpy part of fruit; carnality, **c. concen-**

trada, meat extract. **c. congelada,** frozen meat. **c. de
gallina,** (*fig.*) gooseflesh. **c. de
membrillo,** quince cheese or
conserve. **c. y hueso,** (*fig.*) flesh
and blood. (*fam.*) **cobrar
carnes,** to put on weight. **poner
toda la c. en el asador,** (*fam.*)
to put all one's eggs in one
basket

carnerada, *f.* flock of sheep

carnerero (-ra), *s.* shepherd

carnero, *m.* sheep; mutton;
mortuary; charnel-house; family
burial vault. **c. marino,** (*zool.*)
seal

carnestolendas, *f. pl.* three days
of carnival before Ash Wednesday

carnet, *m.* note-book, diary;
identity card; membership card,
pass. **c. de chófer,** driving
licence

carnicería, *f.* butcher's shop;
carnage, slaughter

carnicero, *a.* carnivorous; inhuman, cruel. *m.* butcher

carnívoro, *a.* carnivorous. *m.*
carnivore

carnosidad, *f.* proud flesh; local
fat; fatness

carnoso, *a.* meaty; fleshy; full of
marrow; (*bot.*) pulpy, juicy

caro, *a.* beloved; expensive; dear.
adv. expensively; dear

carolingio (-ia), *a.* and *s.* Carolingian

carótida, *f.* carotid artery

carpa, *f.* (*icht.*) carp. **c. dorada,**
goldfish

carpanta, *f.* (*fam.*) violent hunger

carpelo, *m.* (*bot.*) carpel

carpeta, *f.* table or chest cover;
writing case; portfolio; docket,
letter file

carpetazo, dar, *v.t.* to shelve (a
project, etc.)

carpintear, *v.i.* to carpenter

carpintería, *f.* carpenter's shop;
carpentry

carpinteril, *a.* carpentering

carpintero, *m.* carpenter, joiner;
(*theat.*) scene-shifter. **c. de
carretas,** wheelwright. **c. de
ribera,** shipwright

carraca, *f.* rattle; ratchet-drill

carrasca, *f.* (*bot.*) pin-oak.

carrascal, *m.* field of pin-
oaks

carraspear, *v.i.* to clear one's
throat, cough

carraspera, *f.* (*fam.*) hoarseness

carraspique, *m.* (*bot.*) candytuft

carrera, *f.* run; race; racing;
racecourse; (*ast.*) course; high
road; route; (*mas.*) layer, course;
line, row; (*fig.*) ladder (in stockings, etc.); course; duration (of
life); career, profession; conduct;
girder. **c. de fondo,** long-distance
race. **c. de relevos, c. de
equipos,** relay race

carrerista, *m.* and *f.* racing enthusiast; professional racer

carreta, *f.* long, narrow two-
wheeled cart; waggon; tumbril

carretada, *f.* cart-load; (*fam.*)
great deal, mass

carretaje, *m.* cartage; carriage,
transport

carrete, *m.* spool, reel, bobbin;
fishing reel; (*elec.*) coil; (*phot.*)
film spool

carretear, *v.t.* to cart; drive a
cart

carretela, *f.* calash

carretera, *f.* high road

carretería, *f.* number of carts;
carting trade; cartwright's yard

carretero, *m.* cartwright; carter,
driver

carretilla, *f.* wheelbarrow; hand
cart; railway truck; squib. **de
c.,** (*fam.*) mechanically, without thought; (*with saber, repetir,* etc.) by rote

carretón, *m.* truck, trolley; hand
cart

carricoche, *m.* old-fashioned
coach; dog-cart; brougham; go-
cart

carril, *m.* wheel mark; furrow,
rut; cart road, narrow road; rail
(railways, etc.)

carrillera, *f.* jaw (of some animals); chin strap; *pl.* bonnet
strings, etc.

carrillo, *m.* cheek; jowl

carriola, *f.* truckle bed; curricle

carro, *m.* cart; cartload; car,
chariot; carriage (of a typewriter,
etc.); chassis; (*ast.*) Plough, Great
Bear. (*mil.*) **c. blindado,** armoured car. (*mil.*) **c. de asalto,**
tank. **c. de mudanzas,** removal van. **c. de regar,** water-
cart

carrocería, *f.* place where carriages are made, sold, repaired; (*aut.*) coachwork, body

carrocha, *f.* eggs (of insects)

carrochar, *v.i.* to lay eggs (insects)

carromato, *m.* road waggon; covered waggon

carroña, *f.* putrid flesh, carrion

carroza, *f.* elegant coach; state coach; carriage; float (for tableaux, etc.); (*naut.*) awning

carruaje, *m.* carriage ; any vehicle

carta, *f.* letter; charter; royal order; playing card; chart, map. **c. certificada,** registered letter. **c. de amparo,** safe-conduct. **c. de crédito,** (*com.*) letter of credit. **c. de marear,** sea chart. **c. de naturaleza,** naturalization papers. **c. de venta,** (*com.*) bill of sale. **poner las cartas boca arriba,** (*fig.*) to lay one's cards on the table

cartabón, *m.* set-square ; shoemaker's slide; quadrant

cartaginés (-esa), *a.* and *s.* Carthaginian

cartapacio, *m.* note-book; school-bag, satchel; file, batch of papers

cartear, *v.i.* (*cards*) to play low; *v.r.* to correspond by letter

cartel, *m.* placard, poster; cartel; pasquinade, lampoon. **fijar carteles,** to placard

cartela, *f.* tablet (for writing); slip (of paper, etc.); (*arch.*) console, bracket

cartelera, *f.* advertisement hoarding

cartelero, *m.* bill sticker

carteo, *m.* correspondence (by letter)

cartera, *f.* pocket-book; wallet; dispatch-case; portfolio; note-book; pocket flap; office of a cabinet minister; (*com.*) shares

cartería, *f.* sorting room in a post-office

carterista, *m.* pickpocket

cartero, *m.* postman

cartesiano (-na), *a.* and *s.* Cartesian

cartilaginoso, *a.* cartilaginous

cartílago, *m.* cartilage

cartilla, *f.* first reading book; primer; certificate of ordination; note-book ; liturgical calendar.

c. de racionamiento, ration book

cartista, *a.* and *m.* and *f.* Chartist

cartografía, *f.* cartography

cartógrafo, *m.* map maker

cartomancia, *f.* cartomancy

cartón, *m.* pasteboard, cardboard; (*arch.*) bracket; (*art*) cartoon, design

cartuchera, *f.* cartridge-pouch; cartridge-belt

cartucho, *m.* cartridge; paper cone

cartuja, *f.* Carthusian Order or monastery

cartujano, *a.* Carthusian

cartujo, *m.* Carthusian monk; (*fam.*) taciturn, reserved man

cartulina, *f.* Bristol board, pasteboard, card

carúncula, *f.* caruncle, comb of cock, etc.

casa, *f.* house; home; household; residence, dwelling; family house; (*com.*) firm. **c. consistorial,** town hall. **c. cuna,** crèche. **c. de campo,** country-house. **c. de empeño,** pawnshop. **c. de huéspedes,** lodging-house. **c. de moneda,** mint. **c. de socorro,** First Aid Post. **c. de vecindad,** tenement. **c. solar** or **c. solariego,** family seat. **casas baratas,** council houses. **en c.,** at home (also sport usage). **poner c.,** to set up house

casaca, *f.* dress coat. **volver la c.,** to become a turncoat, change one's allegiance

casación, *f.* (*law*) cassation

casadero, *a.* marriageable

casamata, *f.* (*mil.*) casemate

casamiento, *m.* marriage; wedding

casar, *v.t.* to marry (of a priest); (*law*) repeal; (*fam.*) marry off; join; match, harmonize; *v.i.* and *v.r.* (*with con*) to get married.

casar, *m.* group of houses

casca, *f.* grape skin; tan (bark); shell, peel, rind

cascabel, *m.* small bell (for harness, etc.). **serpiente de c.,** rattlesnake. (*fam.*) **ser un c.,** to be feather-brained

cascabeleo, *m.* jingling of bells

cascabillo, *m.* husk (of cereals)

cascada, *f.* cascade; waterfall

cascadura, *f.* cracking, crack

cascajo, *m.* gravel, shingle; (*fam.*) broken, old things, junk; nuts

cascanueces, *m.* nutcrackers

cascar, *v.t.* to crack, split, break; (*fam.*) beat; (*fig.*, *fam.*) break down (of health); *v.i.* (*fam.*) talk, chatter

cáscara, *f.* shell; peel, rind; bark. (*med.*) c. sagrada, cascara

cascarón, *m.* eggshell; (*arch.*) vault

cascarrabias, *m.* and *f.* (*fam.*) spitfire

casco, *m.* cranium; broken fragment of china, glass, etc.; crown of hat; helmet; tree of saddle; bottle; tank, pipe; barrel; (*naut.*) hull; hoof; quarter (of fruit); *pl.* (*fam.*) head. c. colonial, sun-helmet. c. respiratorio, smoke-helmet

cascote, *m.* rubble, ruins

caseoso, *a.* cheesy

caserío, *m.* group of houses; country house

casero, *a.* home made; home bred; familiar; informal; (*fam.*) domesticated, home-loving; domestic. *m.* landlord; caretaker; tenant

caserón, *m.* large tumbledown house, mansion, hall

caseta, *f.* hut; cottage; booth, stall. c. de baños, bathing van

casi, *adv.* almost, nearly. c. c., very nearly

casilla, *f.* hut; cabin; lodge; ticket office; pigeon-hole. (*aer.*) c. del piloto, cockpit

casino, *m.* casino; club

caso, *m.* happening, event; chance, hazard; occasion, opportunity; case, matter; (*med.*, *gram.*) case. en tal c., in such a case. en todo c., in any case. no hacer c. de, to take no notice of. venir al c., to be opportune

caspa, *f.* dandruff; scab

caspio, *a.* Caspian

¡cáspita! *interj.* Amazing! Wonderful!

casquete, *m.* helmet; skull cap; half wig

casquijo, *m.* gravel

casquillo, *m.* tip, cap, ferrule; socket; arrow-head; metal cartridge-case

casquivano, *a.* (*fam.*) giddy, feather-brained

casta, *f.* race; caste; breed (animals); kind, species, quality

castaña, *f.* (*bot.*) chestnut; knot, bun of hair

castañar, *m.* chestnut plantation or grove

castañetear, *v.i.* to play the castanets; snap one's fingers; chatter (of teeth); knock together (of knees)

castaño, *a.* chestnut-coloured. *m.* chestnut tree; chestnut wood. c. de Indias, horse-chestnut tree

castañuela, *f.* castanet. tocar las castañuelas, to play the castanets

castellán, *m.* castellan

castellano (-na), *s.* Castilian; Spaniard. *m.* Spanish language; castellan. *a.* Castilian; Spanish

casticismo, *m.* purity (of language); Spanish spirit; traditionalism

castidad, *f.* chastity

castigador, *a.* punishing. *m.* punisher; (*fam.*) lady-killer

castigadora, *f.* (*fam.*) man-hunter

castigar, *v.t.* to punish; chastise; chasten, advise; pain, grieve; correct, edit; decrease (expenses); (*com.*) allow a discount

castigo, *m.* punishment; emendation, correction

castillo, *m.* castle; howdah. c. de naipes, house of cards. c. de proa, (*naut.*) forecastle. (*fam.*) hacer castillos en el aire, to build castles in the air or in Spain

castizo, *a.* pure-blooded; prolific; pure (of language); typically Spanish; traditional

casto, *a.* chaste; pure, unsullied

castor, *m.* (*zool.*) beaver (animal and fur); soft, woollen cloth

castración, *f.* castration, gelding

castrado, *a.* castrated. *m.* (*fam.*) eunuch

castrador, *m.* castrator, gelder

castrar, *v.t.* to castrate, geld; prune; remove honeycomb from hives; weaken

castrense, *a.* military

casual, *a.* accidental, casual

casualidad, *f.* chance. por c., by chance

casuario, *m.* (*orn.*) cassowary
casucha, *f.* (*fam.*) tumbledown
hut
casuista, *a.* casuistic. *m.* and *f.*
casuist
casuística, *f.* casuistry
casulla, *f.* chasuble
cata, *f.* tasting; taste, sample
catabolismo, *m.* katabolism
cataclismo, *m.* cataclysm
catacumbas, *f. pl.* catacombs
catador, *m.* taster, sampler
catadura, *f.* tasting; look, countenance (gen. qualified)
catafalco, *m.* catafalque
catalán (-ana), *a.* and *s.* Catalan,
Catalonian. *m.* Catalan language
catalejo, *m.* telescope
catalepsia, *f.* (*med.*) catalepsy
cataléptico, *a.* cataleptic
catálisis, *f.* (*chem.*) catalysis
catalítico, *a.* catalytic
catalogar, *v.t.* to catalogue, list
catálogo, *m.* catalogue, list
cataplasma, *m.* cataplasm
catapulta, *f.* catapult
catar, *v.t.* to taste, sample; see,
examine; inspect; regard
catarata, *f.* cataract, waterfall;
(*med.*) cataract (of the eyes)
catarral, *a.* catarrhal
catarro, *m.* catarrh; common
cold
catástrofe, *f.* (*lit.*) tragic climax;
catastrophe
catastrófico, *a.* catastrophic
cataviento, *m.* (*naut.*) dog-vane,
cone
catavino, *m.* taster (cup)
catavinos, *m.* professional wine
taster; (*fam.*) tippler, tavern
haunter
catecismo, *m.* catechism
catecúmeno (-na), *s.* catechumen
cátedra, *f.* university chair; chair
in a Spanish instituto; professorship; university lecture room;
subject taught by professor;
reading desk, lectern; (*ecc.*)
throne; (*ecc.*) see. **c. del espíritu
santo,** pulpit. **c. de San Pedro,**
Holy See
catedral, *f.* and *a.* cathedral
catedrático (-ca), *s.* professor
categoría, *f.* (*phil.*) category;
class, rank
categórico, *a.* categorical, downright
catequismo, *m.* catechism;

question and answer method of
teaching
catequista, *m.* and *f.* catechist
catequizar, *v.t.* to catechize; persuade, induce
caterva, *f.* crowd, throng; jumble,
collection
catéter, *m.* (*surg.*) probe; catheter
catódico, *a.* (*elec.*) cathodic
cátodo, *m.* cathode
catolicidad, *f.* catholicity; catholic world
catolicismo, *m.* Catholicism
católico (-ca), *a.* universal, catholic; infallible. *a.* and *s.* Catholic
(by religion)
catorce, *a.* fourteen; fourteenth.
m. number fourteen; fourteenth
(of days of month)
catorzavo, *a.* fourteenth
catre, *m.* camp-bed; truckle-bed;
cot
caucáseo (-ea), *a.* and *s.* Caucasian
cauce, *m.* river or stream bed;
ditch, irrigation canal
caución, *f.* caution, precaution;
surety; security
cauchal, *m.* rubber plantation
cauchera, *f.* rubber tree
cauchero, *m.* rubber planter
caucho, *m.* caoutchouc, rubber
caudal, *m.* wealth, capital; flow,
volume (of water); plenty, abundance
caudaloso, *a.* carrying much
water; wealthy; abundant
caudillo, *m.* head, leader; chief
tain
causa, *f.* cause; reason, motive;
lawsuit; (*law*) trial. **c. final,**
(*phil.*) final cause. **c. pública,**
public welfare
causador (-ra), *a.* motivating. *s.*
occasioner, originator
causalidad, *f.* causality
causante, *a.* causative, causing.
m. (*law*) principal
causar, *v.t.* to cause; occasion
causticidad, *f.* causticity; mordacity
cáustico, *a.* burning, caustic;
scathing; mordant; (*surg.*) caustic
cautela, *f.* caution; astuteness,
cunning
cauteloso, *a.* cautious; cunning
cauterio, *m.* (*surg.*) cautery
cauterización, *f.* cauterization
cauterizar, *v.t.* (*surg.*) to cauterize

cautivar, *v.t.* to capture; captivate, charm; attract; *v.i.* become a prisoner

cautiverio, *m.* captivity

cautivo (-va), *a.* and *s.* captive

cauto, *a.* cautious; prudent; sly

cava, *f.* digging (especially vines); wine cellar in royal palaces

cavador (-ra), *s.* digger, hoer

cavadura, *f.* digging, hoeing; sinking (wells)

cavar, *v.t.* to dig, hoe; sink (wells); *v.i.* hollow; (*fig.*) go deeply into a thing

caverna, *f.* cavern, cave; (*med.*) cavity (generally in the lung)

cavernícola, *a.* cave. **hombre c.**, cave-man

cavernoso, *a.* cavernous; caverned; (*fig.*) hollow (cough, etc.)

cavidad, *f.* cavity; sinus; cell

cavilación, *f.* cavilling

cavilar, *v.t.* to cavil; criticize

caviloso, *a.* captious

cayado, *m.* crook; bishop's crozier

caz, *m.* channel, canal; head-race, flume

caza, *f.* hunting; hunt, chase; game. *m.* (*aer.*) fighter. (*aer.*) **c. lanzacohetes**, rocket-launching aircraft. **c. nocturno**, night fighter. (*naut.*) **dar c.**, to pursue

cazabombardero, *m.* (*aer.*) fighter bomber

cazadero, *m.* hunting ground

cazador, *a.* hunting. *m.* (*mil.*) chasseur; huntsman

cazadora, *f.* huntress; jacket; forage cap

cazar, *v.t.* to hunt, chase; (*fig., fam.*) run to earth; (*fig., fam.*) catch out; (*fam.*) overcome by flattery

cazasubmarino, *m.* submarine chaser

cazatorpedero, *m.* (*naut.*) torpedo-boat destroyer

cazcarria, *f.* (gen. *pl.*) mud splash

cazo, *m.* ladle; dipper

cazolada, *f.* panful

cazoleta, *f.* small pan; bowl (of pipe, etc.); sword guard; boss of a shield; pan (of a firelock)

cazón, *m.* (*icht.*) dogfish

cazuela, *f.* earthenware cooking dish; stew-pot; part of theatre formerly reserved for women; (*theat.*) gallery

cazumbrón, *m.* cooper

cazurro, *a.* (*fam.*) unsociable; surly, boorish

ce, *f.* name of the letter C. *interj.* Look! Chist! **ce por be**, in detail

cebada, *f.* barley (plant and grain). **c. perlada**, pearl barley

cebadal, *m.* barley field

cebadera, *f.* nose-bag; barley bin

cebadero, *m.* barley dealer

cebar, *v.t.* to feed or fatten (animals); fuel, feed (furnace, etc.); prime, charge (fire-arms, etc.); start up (machines); bait (fish hook); stimulate (passion, etc.); *v.i.* stick in, penetrate (nails, screws, etc.); *v.r.* put one's mind to; grow angry

cebo, *m.* fodder; detonator; encouragement, food; bait

cebolla, *f.* onion; onion bulb; any bulbous stem; oil bulb (of lamp). **c. escalonia**, shallot

cebollana, *f.* (*bot.*) chive

cebollero (-ra), *s.* onion seller

cebolleta, *f.* (*bot.*) leek; young onion

cebollino, *m.* onion seed; onion bed; chive

cebra, *f.* (*zool.*) zebra

ceca, *f.* mint (for coining money); name of mosque at Cordova. **de C. en Meca**, from pillar to post, hither and thither

cecear, *v.i.* to lisp

ceceo, *m.* lisping

ceceoso, *a.* lisping

cecial, *m.* dried fish

cecina, *f.* dried salt meat

cedazo, *m.* sieve, strainer

ceder, *v.t.* to cede, give up; transfer; *v.i.* give in, yield; diminish, decrease (fever, storm, etc.); fail, end; happen, turn out; sag, give, stretch

cedro, *m.* cedar tree; cedar wood. **c. dulce**, red cedar

cédula, *f.* document, certificate, card. (*ecc.*) **c. de comunión**, Communion card. **c. personal**, identity card. **c. real**, royal letters patent

cefalalgia, *f.* (*med.*) cephalalgia

cefálico, *a.* (*anat.*) cephalic

céfiro, *m.* west wind; (*poet.*) zephyr

cegajoso, *a.* blear-eyed

cegar, *v.i. irr.* to become blind; *v.t.* to put out the eyes; (*fig.*)

blind; wall up, close up, stop up; infatuate. *Pres. Ind.* **ciego, ciegas, ciega, ciegan.** *Pres. Subjunc.* **ciegue, ciegues, ciegue, cieguen**

cegato, *a.* (*fam.*) short-sighted

ceguedad, ceguera, *f.* blindness; delusion; ignorance

ceja, *f.* eyebrow; cloud cap; mountain peak; (*mus.*) bridge (of stringed instruments). (*fig.*) **quemarse las cejas,** to burn the midnight oil

cejar, *v.i.* to go backwards; give way, hesitate

cejijunto, *a.* having eyebrows that almost meet, beetle-browed

cejo, *m.* river mist

cejudo, *a.* having long thick eyebrows

celada, *f.* helmet; ambush; fraud, trick

celador (-ra), *a.* watchful, zealous. *s.* supervisor; caretaker

celaje, *m.* sky with scudding clouds (gen. *pl.*); skylight, window; promising sign, presage

celar, *v.t.* to be zealous in discharge of duties; spy upon; watch; oversee, superintend; conceal; engrave

celda, *f.* cell

celdilla, *f.* cell (bees, wasps, etc.); (*zool., bot.*) cell; (*bot.*) capsule

celebérrimo, *a. sup.* **célebre,** most celebrated

celebración, *f.* celebration; applause

celebrador (-ra), *s.* celebrator; applauder

celebrante, *a.* celebrating. *m.* (*ecc.*) celebrant

celebrar, *v.t.* to celebrate; applaud; praise; venerate; hold, conduct; *v.t.* and *v.i.* (*ecc.*) officiate; *v.r.* take place

célebre, *a.* famous

celebridad, *f.* fame, celebrity; magnificence, show, pomp

celeridad, *f.* celerity

celeste, *a.* celestial, heavenly

celestial, *a.* celestial, heavenly; perfect, delightful; (*fam.*) foolish (ironical)

celestina, *f.* procuress (allusion to *Tragicomedia de Calixto y Melibea*)

celibato, *m.* celibacy; (*fam.*) bachelor

célibe, *a.* celibate, unmarried. *m.* and *f.* unmarried person

celo, *m.* enthusiasm, ardour; religious zeal; devotion; jealousy; heat, rut; *pl.* jealousy, suspicion. **dar celos (a),** to make jealous

celosía, *f.* lattice; Venetian blind

celoso, *a.* zealous; jealous; suspicious

celta, *a.* Celtic. *m.* and *f.* Celt

celtibérico (-ca), *a.* and *s.* Celtiberian

célula, *f.* cell (*bot., biol.,* etc.)

celular, *a.* cellular

celuloide, *f.* celluloid

celulosa, *f.* (*chem.*) cellulose

celuloso, *a.* cellular

cementación, *f.* cementation

cementar, *v.t.* to cement

cementerio, *m.* cemetery

cemento, *m.* cement

cena, *f.* evening meal; supper; Last Supper

cenáculo, *m.* cenacle

cenacho, *m.* marketing bag

cenador, *m.* diner out; arbour, pergola

cenagal, *m.* quagmire; (*fig.*) impasse

cenagoso, *a.* miry, muddy

cenar, *v.i.* to dine, sup; *v.t.* eat for evening meal, sup off

cenceño, *a.* slim, thin

cencerrada, *f.* noisy mock serenade given to widows or widowers on the first night of their new marriage

cencerrear, *v.i.* to jingle; (*fam.*) play out of tune; bang in the wind, rattle; squeak

cencerreo, *m.* jingling; jangle; rattling; squeaking

cencerro, *m.* cow-bell

cendal, *m.* gauze; (*ecc.*) stole; barbs of a feather

cendra, *f.* bone ash

cenefa, *f.* border; valance, flounce; edging

cenicero, *m.* ash-pan; ash-pit; ash-tray

ceniciento, *a.* ash coloured, ashen. **la cenicienta,** Cinderella

cenit, *m.* (*ast.*) zenith; (*fig.*) peak, summit

ceniza, *f.* ash, cinders

cenotafio, *m.* cenotaph

censatario, *m.* lessee; payer of an annuity. *a.* leasehold

censo, *m.* census; agreement for

settlement of an annuity; annual ground rent; leasehold

censor, *m.* censor; censorious person; (*univ.*) proctor

censual, *a.* pertaining to census, annuity, rents

censualista, *m.* and *f.* annuitant

censura, *f.* censorship; criticism; blame, reproach; scandal, gossip; (*psy.*) censorship

censurable, *a.* reprehensible; censorable

censurar, *v.t.* to judge; censure; criticize

centaura, *f.* (*bot.*) centaury

centauro, *m.* (*myth.*) centaur

centavo, *m.* hundredth part; cent

centella, *f.* lightning; spark; flash; (*fig.*) spark (of anger, affection, etc.)

centellador, *a.* flashing

centellear, *v.i.* to flash; twinkle; sparkle

centelleo, *m.* scintillation; sparkle; flash

centena, *f.* hundred

centenal, centenar, *m.* hundred; centenary; rye field. **a centenares,** by the hundred, in crowds

centenario (-ia), *a.* centenary. *s.* centenarian. *m.* centenary

centeno, *m.* (*bot.*) rye

centésimo, *a.* and *m.* hundredth

centígrado, *a.* centigrade

centigramo, *m.* centigramme

centilitro, *m.* centilitre

centímetro, *m.* centimetre. **c. cúbico,** cubic centimetre, millilitre

céntimo, *a.* hundredth. *m.* centime (coin)

centinela, *m.* and *f.* (*mil.*) sentry, sentinel; person on watch. **estar de c.,** to be on sentry duty; be on guard

centiplicado, *a.* centuple

centolla, *f.* marine crab

centón, *m.* patchwork quilt

central, *a.* central; centric. *f.* head office; central depôt; mother house. **c. de fuerza,** power-house. **c. telefónica,** telephone exchange

centralismo, *m.* centralism

centralista, *a.* centralistic. *m.* and *f.* centralist

centralización, *f.* centralization

centralizador, *a.* centralizing

centralizar, *v.t.* to centralize

centrar, *v.t.* to centre

céntrico, *a.* central, centric

centrífugo, *a.* centrifugal

centrípeto, *a.* centripetal

centro, *m.* centre; headquarters, meeting place, club; centre, hub; middle; core (of a rope); (*fig.*) focus. (*phys.*) **c. de gravedad,** centre of gravity. **c. de mesa,** table centre-piece. (*anat.*) **centros nerviosos,** nervous centres

centroamericano (-na), *a.* and *s.* Central American

centunviro, *m.* centumvir

centuplicar, *v.t.* to centuplicate

céntuplo, *a.* centuple

centuria, *f.* century

centurión, *m.* centurion

ceñido, *a.* thrifty; wasp-waisted, slender waisted; fitting (of garments)

ceñidor, *m.* girdle, belt

ceñir, *v.t. irr.* to girdle; surround; shorten, abbreviate; *v.r.* be moderate (speech, expenditure, etc.); conform, confine oneself (to). *Pres. Ind.* **ciño, ciñes, ciñen.** *Pres. Part.* **ciñendo.** *Preterite* **ciñó, ciñeron.** *Pres. Subjunc.* **ciña,** etc. *Imperf. Subjunc.* **ciñese,** etc.

ceño, *m.* band, hoop; frown; (*fig.*) dark outlook

ceñudo, *a.* frowning

cepillar, *v.t.* to brush; plane; smooth

cepa, *f.* stump; vine-stock; root (tails, antlers, etc.); (*fig.*) origin, trunk (of a family); (*biol.*) strain

cepillo, *m.* brush; (*carp.*) plane; poor-box, offertory-box. **c. para los dientes,** toothbrush. **c. para ropa,** clothes-brush. **c. para el suelo,** scrubbing-brush. **c. para las uñas,** nail-brush

cepo, *m.* bough; wooden stocks; snare; trap; poor-box; collecting-box

cera, *f.* beeswax; wax; wax candles, etc., used at a function. (*fam.*) **ser como una c.,** to be like wax (in the hands of)

cerámica, *f.* ceramics; ceramic art, pottery

cerámico, *a.* ceramic

cerbatana, *f.* blow-pipe, pop-gun; pea-shooter; ear-trumpet

cerca, *f.* fence, wall

cerca, *adv.* near. **c. de,** near to;

almost, nearly (e.g. **c. de las once,** nearly eleven o'clock)

cercado, *m.* enclosure, fenced in place; fence

cercanía, *f.* nearness, proximity; (gen. *pl.*) outskirts, surroundings

cercano, *a.* near, neighbouring; impending, early

cercar, *v.t.* to enclose; build a wall or fence round; to lay siege to; crowd round; (*mil.*) surround

cercenar, *v.t.* to lop off the ends, clip; curtail, diminish; abridge; whittle

cerciorar, *v.t.* to assure, confirm; *v.r.* make sure

cerco, *m.* ring, hoop; fence; siege; small conversational circle; spin, circling; halo (sun, moon); frame; sash (of a window). **poner c.** (a), to lay siege to, blockade

cerda, *f.* sow; bristle

cerdo, *m.* pig, hog

cerdoso, *a.* bristly

cereal, *a.* and *m.* cereal

cerebelo, *m.* (*anat.*) cerebellum

cerebral, *a.* cerebral

cerebro, *m.* (*anat.*) cerebrum; brain; intelligence

cerebro-espinal, *a.* cerebrospinal

ceremonia, *f.* ceremony; function, display; formality. **de c.,** ceremonial; formally. **por c.,** for politeness' sake

ceremonial, *a.* ceremonial. *m.* ceremony; rite

ceremonioso, *a.* ceremonious, formal, over-courteous

cerería, *f.* wax-chandler's shop

cerero, *m.* wax-chandler

cereza, *f.* cherry

cerezal, *m.* cherry orchard

cerezo, *m.* cherry tree; cherry wood

cerilla, *f.* wax taper; match; ear wax

cerneja, *f.* (gen. *pl.*) fetlocks (of horse)

cerner, *v.t. irr.* to sieve; watch, observe; (*fig.*) sift, clarify; *v.i.* bolt (of plants); drizzle; *v.r.* waddle; hover; threaten (of evil, etc.). *Pres. Ind.* **cierno, ciernes, cierne, ciernen.** *Pres. Subjunc.* **cierna, ciernas, cierna, ciernan**

cernícalo, *m.* (*orn.*) kestrel; (*fam.*) lout

cernidillo, *m.* drizzle; teetering walk

cernido, *m.* sifting, sieving; sifted flour

cerniduras, *f. pl.* siftings

cero, *m.* (*math.*) nought; zero; (tennis) love. (*fig., fam.*) **ser un c.,** to be a mere cipher

cerote, *m.* cobbler's wax. (*fam.*) fear

cerquillo, *m.* tonsure; welt (of a shoe)

cerquita, *adv.* very near, hard by

cerradero, *m.*, **cerradera,** *f.* bolt staple; catch of a lock; clasp or strings of a purse

cerradizo, *a.* closable, lockable

cerrado, *a.* closed; compact; incomprehensible, obscure; overcast, cloudy; (*fam.*) taciturn; secretive. *m.* enclosure

cerradura, *f.* fastening, lock; closing, locking

cerraja, *f.* lock of a door; bolt

cerrajería, *f.* locksmith's craft; locksmith's workshop or shop

cerrajero, *m.* locksmith

cerramiento, *m.* closing, locking up; fence; enclosure, shooting preserve; partition wall

cerrar, *v.t. irr.* to close; lock, fasten, bolt; shut up; (*mech.*) shut off, turn off; fold up; block or stop up; seal (letters, etc.); close down; terminate; obstruct; (*with con*) attack; *v.i.* close; close in (of night, etc.); *v.r.* heal up (wounds); close (flowers); (*rad.*) close down; crowd together; (*fig.*) stand firm. (*fam.*) **cerrarse la espuela,** to take a nightcap, have a last drink. **c. la marcha,** to bring up the rear. **al c. la edición,** stop press. See **acertar**

cerrazón, *f.* dark, overcast sky heralding a storm

cerril, *a.* rough, rocky; wild, untamed (cattle, horses); (*fam.*) boorish

cerrillar, *v.t.* to mill coins

cerro, *m.* neck of an animal; spine, backbone; hill. (*fig.*) **irse por los cerros de Úbeda,** to go off the track, indulge in irrelevancies

cerrojo, *m.* bolt (of a door, etc.); lock (of a door, gun, etc.)

certamen, *m.* literary competition; match

certero, *a.* well-aimed; sure, well-timed; knowledgeable, sure

certeza, certidumbre, *f.* certitude, assurance

certificación, *f.* certification; certificate; affidavit

certificado, *a.* certified; registered. *m.* registered letter; certificate

certificar, *v.t.* to certify; register (letter, etc.)

certificatorio, *a.* certifying or serving to certify

certitud, *f.* certitude

cerúleo, *a.* cerulean

cervantino, *a.* Cervantine (from Cervantes)

cervato, *m.* fawn

cervecería, *f.* brewery; ale-house

cervecero (-ra), *s.* brewer; beer seller

cerveza, *f.* beer, ale. **c. negra,** stout

cerviz, *f.* cervix, nape of neck. **doblar** (*or* **bajar**) **la c.,** to humble oneself

cervuno, *a.* pertaining to a deer; deer-coloured

cesación, *f.* cessation, stopping

cesante, *a.* dismissed; pensioned off. **declarar c. (a),** to dismiss (a person from a post). **estar c.,** to be out of a job

cesantía, *f.* status of dismissed or retired official; retirement pension

cesar, *v.i.* to cease, stop, end; leave an employment; desist; retire

cesáreo, *a.* Cæsarean; imperial

cese, *m.* from *subjunc.* of cesar, "let it cease," stopping of payment for an employment

cesión, *f.* cession; transfer; resignation; (*law*) release

cesionario (-ia), *s.* cessionary, transferee

cesionista, *m.* and *f.* grantor, transferer

césped, *m.* grass, sward; sod, lawn

cesta, *f.* basket, hamper; (*sport*) racket; cradle (for a wine bottle)

cestada, *f.* basketful

cestería, *f.* basket factory or shop; craft of basket making

cestero (-ra), *s.* basket maker or seller

cesto, *m.* hamper, skip

cesura, *f.* cæsura

cetáceo, *a.* and *m.* (*zool.*) cetacean

cetrería, *f.* falconry

cetrino, *a.* greenish-yellow; sallow; citrine; melancholy; reserved, aloof

cetro, *m.* sceptre; verge; reign

cianuro, *m.* (*chem.*) cyanide

ciar, *v.i.* to go backwards; (*naut.*) row backwards; (*fig.*) make no headway (negotiations)

ciática, *f.* (*med.*) sciatica

ciático, *a.* sciatic

ciborio, *m.* (*archæol., arch.*) ciborium

cicatería, *f.* niggardliness, avarice

cicatero, *a.* avaricious, niggardly, mean

cicatriz, *f.* cicatrice; (*fig.*) scar, mark, impression

cicatrización, *f.* cicatrization

cicatrizar, *v.t.* to cicatrize, heal; *v.r.* scar over

ciclamino, *m.* cyclamen

ciclamor, *m.* (*bot.*) Judas tree

cíclico, *a.* cyclic, cyclical

ciclismo, *m.* bicycling

ciclista, *m.* and *f.* cyclist

ciclo, *m.* cycle (of time, etc.)

cicloide, *f.* (*geom.*) cycloid

ciclón, *m.* cyclone

ciclópeo, *a.* cyclopean

ciclostilo, *m.* cyclostyle

cicuta, *f.* (*bot.*) hemlock

cid, *m.* great warrior, chief. **Cid,** national hero of Spanish wars against the Moors

cidra, *f.* (*bot.*) citron

cidro, *m.* citron tree

ciego, *a.* blind; dazed, blinded; choked up. *m.* blind man; (*anat.*) cæcum. **a ciegas,** blindly; heedlessly

cielo, *m.* sky, firmament; atmosphere; climate; paradise (also *pl.*); Providence (also *pl.*); bliss, glory; roof, canopy; (*fam.*) darling. **a c. abierto,** in the open air

ciempiés, *m.* centipede

cien, *a.* abb. **ciento,** hundred. Used always before substantives (e.g. **c. hombres,** 100 men)

ciénaga, *f.* swamp; morass

ciencia, *f.* science; knowledge; erudition, ability. **ciencias naturales,** natural science. **a c.**

cierta, for certain, without doubt (gen. with *saber*)

cienmilésimo, *a.* hundred-thous-andth ·

cienmillonésimo, *a.* hundred-millionth

cieno, *m.* slime, mud; silt

científico, *a.* scientific. *m.* scientist

ciento, (cf. **cien**). *a.* hundred; hundredth. *m.* hundred. **por c.,** per cent.

cierne, en, in flower; (*fig.*) in the early stages, in embryo

cierre, *m.* closing, shutting; closing time of shops, etc.; fastening; fastener; clasp (of a necklace, handbag, etc.). **c. cremallera,** zip fastener. **c. metálico,** door-shutter

ciertamente, *adv.* certainly; undoubtedly; indeed

cierto, *a.* certain, sure; true; particular (e.g. **c. hombre,** a certain man (note no *def. art.*)). **no, por c.,** no, certainly not. **por c.,** truly, indeed

cierva, *f.* hind

ciervo, *m.* stag. **c. volante,** stag-beetle

cierzo, *m.* northerly wind

cifra, *f.* number; figure; sum total; cipher, code; monogram; abbreviation

cifrar, *v.t.* to write in cipher; summarize, abridge; (*with en*) be dependent on; depend on

cigarra, *f.* (*ent.*) cicada, harvest fly

cigarral, *m.* (Toledo) country-house and garden or orchard

cigarrera, *f.* woman who makes or sells cigars; cigar-cabinet; cigar-case

cigarrillo, *m.* cigarette

cigarro, *m.* cigar

cigüeña, *f.* (*orn.*) stork; (*mech.*) crank

ciliar, *a.* ciliary

cilicio, *m.* hair-shirt

cilindrar, *v.t.* to roll; calender; bore

cilíndrico, *a.* cylindrical

cilindro, *m.* cylinder; roller

cima, *f.* summit; top of trees; apex; (*arch.*) coping; head (thistle, etc.); (*fig.*) aim, goal, end

cimbalero (-ra), *s.* (*mus.*) cymbalist

címbalo, *m.* cymbal

cimborrio, *m.* (*arch.*) cupola; cimborium

cimbra, *f.* (*arch.*) centre scaffolding; centering

cimbrar, cimbrear, *v.t.* to bend; brandish; *v.r.* sway (in walking)

cimbreño, *a.* willowy, graceful

cimbreo, *m.* swaying, bending

cimentar, *v.t. irr.* to lay foundations; refine (gold, metals, etc.); found; (*fig.*) ground (in virtue, etc.). See **acertar**

cimera, *f.* crest of helmet

cimiento, *m.* foundation (of a building); bottom; groundwork; origin, base. **abrir los cimientos,** to lay the foundations

cimitarra, *f.* scimitar

cinabrio, *m.* cinnabar; vermilion

cinc, *m.* zinc

cincel, *m.* chisel; burin, engraver

cincelador (-ra), *s.* engraver; chiseller

cincelar, *v.t.* to chisel; carve; engrave

cinco, *a.* and *m.* five; fifth. **a las c.,** at five o'clock

cincuenta, *a.* and *m.* fifty; fiftieth

cincuentavo, *a.* fiftieth

cincuentenario, *m.* fiftieth anniversary

cincuentón (-ona), *a.* and *s.* fifty years old (person)

cincha, *f.* girth of a saddle

cinchar, *v.t.* to tighten the saddle girths

cincho, *m.* belt, girdle; iron hoop

cine, cinema, *m.* cinema. **c. sonoro,** sound film

cinemática, *f.* (*phys.*) kinematics

cinematografía, *f.* cinematography

cinematografiar, *v.t.* to film

cinematográfico, *a.* cinematographic

cinematógrafo, *m.* cinematograph; cinema

cingalés (-esa), *s.* Cingalese

cínico, *a.* cynical; impudent; untidy. *m.* cynic

cinismo, *m.* cynicism

cinta, *f.* ribbon; tape; strip; film (cinematograph). **c. métrica,** tape-measure

cinteado, *a.* decorated with ribbons

cintería, *f.* collection of ribbons; ribbon trade

cintillo, *m.* hatband; small ring set with gems

cinto, *m.* belt, girdle. **c. de pistolas,** pistol-belt

cintura, *f.* waist; belt; girdle

cinturón, *m.* large waist; belt girdle; sword-belt; that which encircles or surrounds

cipayo, *m.* Sepoy

ciprés, *m.* (*bot.*) cypress tree or wood

cipresal, *m.* cypress grove

cipresino, *a.* cypress; cypresslike

circasiano (-na), *a.* and *s.* Circassian

circo, *m.* circus; amphitheatre

circón, *m.* (*min.*) zircon

circuir, *v.t. irr.* to surround, encircle. See **huir**

circuito, *m.* periphery; contour; (*elec., phys.*) circuit. **corto c.,** short circuit

circulación, *f.* circulation; traffic. **c. de la sangre,** circulation of the blood. **calle de gran c.,** busy street

circular, *a.* circular. *f.* circular. *v.t.* to pass round; *v.i.* circle; circulate; move in a circle; move about; run, travel (traffic)

circulatorio, *a.* circulatory

círculo, *m.* circle; circumference; circuit; casino, social club

circuncidar, *v.t.* to circumcise; modify, reduce

circuncisión, *f.* circumcision

circunciso, *a.* circumcised

circundar, *v.t.* to surround

circunferencia; *f.* circumference

circunflejo, *a.* circumflex. **acento c.,** circumflex accent

circunlocución, *f.* circumlocution

circunnavegación, *f.* circumnavigation

circunnavegar, *v.t.* to circumnavigate; sail round the world

circunscribir, *v.t.* to circumscribe. *Past Part.* **circunscrito**

circunscripción, *f.* circumscription

circunspección, *f.* circumspection; seriousness, dignity

circunspecto, *a.* circumspect; serious, dignified

circunstancia, *f.* circumstance; incident, detail; condition. **c. agravante,** aggravating circumstance. **c. atenuante,** extenuating circumstance. **bajo las circunstancias,** under the circumstances. **estar al nivel de las circunstancias,** to rise to the occasion

circunstanciado, *a.* circumstantiated, detailed

circunstancial, *a.* circumstantial

circunstante, *a.* surrounding; present. *m.* and *f.* person present, bystander

circunvecino, *a.* adjacent, neighbouring

circunvolución, *f.* circumvolution

cirial, *m.* processional candlestick

cirio, *m.* wax candle

cirro, *m.* (*med.*) scirrhus; (*bot.*) tendril; (*zool.*) cirrus

cirrosis, *f.* cirrhosis

cirroso, *a.* (*med.*) scirrhous; (*zool., bot.*) cirrose

ciruela, *f.* plum; prune. **c. claudia, c. verdal,** greengage. **c. damascena,** damson

ciruelo, *m.* plum tree

cirugía, *f.* surgery

cirujano, *m.* surgeon

cisco, *m.* coal dust, slack coal; (*fam.*) hubbub, quarrel

cisma, *m.* or *f.* schism; disagreement, discord

cismático, *a.* schismatic; discordant, inharmonious

cisne, *m.* swan

císter, *m.* Cistercian Order

cisterciense, *a.* Cistercian

cisterna, *f.* water-tank, cistern

cístico, *a.* (*anat.*) cystic

cistitis, *f.* cystitis

cita, *f.* appointment; quotation, citation

citable, *a.* quotable

citación, *f.* quotation; (*law*) summons

citar, *v.t.* to make an appointment; cite, quote; (*law*) summons

cítara, *f.* (*mus.*) zither

citerior, *a.* hither, nearer

citrato, *m.* (*chem.*) citrate

cítrico, *a.* citric

ciudad, *f.* city; municipal body

ciudadanía, *f.* citizenship

ciudadano (-na), *a.* city; civic, born in or belonging to a city.

s. citizen; burgess; bourgeois.
c. de honor, freeman (of a city)

ciudadela, *f.* citadel

cívico, *a.* civic; patriotic

civil, *a.* civil; civilian; polite

civilidad, *f.* politeness, civility

civilización, *f.* civilization

civilizador, *a.* civilizing

civilizar, *v.t.* to civilize; educate; *v.r.* grow civilized; be educated

civismo, *m.* civism; patriotism; civics

cizalla, *f.* shears, shearing machine; metal filings

cizaña, *f.* (*bot.*) darnel, tare; vice, evil; dissension, discord (gen. with *meter* and *sembrar*)

clac, *m.* opera-hat; tricorne

clamar, *v.i.* to cry out; (*fig.*) demand (of inanimate things); vociferate; speak solemnly

clamor, *m.* outcry, shouting; shriek, complaint; knell, tolling of bells

clamorear, *v.t.* to implore, clamour (for); *v.i.* toll (of bells)

clamoroso, *a.* noisy, clamorous

clandestino, *a.* clandestine, secret

clangor, *m.* (*poet.*) blare, bray (of trumpet)

claque, *f.* (*fam.*) claque (in a theatre)

claqué, *m.* tap-dance

clara, *f.* white of egg; bald patch (in fur); (*fam.*) fair interval on a rainy day

claraboya, *f.* skylight; (*arch.*) clerestory

claramente, *adv.* clearly, evidently

clarear, *v.t.* to clear; give light to; *v.i.* to dawn; grow light; *v.r.* be transparent; (*fam.*) reveal secrets unwittingly

clarete, *m.* claret (wine); claret colour. *a.* claret; claret-coloured

claridad, *f.* clearness; transparency; lightness, brightness; distinctness; clarity; good reputation, renown; plain truth, home truth (gen. *pl.*)

clarificación, *f.* clarification; purifying, refining

clarificar, *v.t.* to illuminate; clarify, purify; refine (sugar, etc.)

clarín, *m.* bugle; clarion; organ stop; bugler

clarinete, *m.* clarinet; clarinet player

clarión, *m.* white chalk, crayon

clarividencia, *f.* perspicuity, clear-sightedness

clarividente, *a.* perspicacious, clear-sighted

claro, *a.* clear; light, bright; distinct; pure, clean; transparent, translucent; light (of colours); easily understood; evident, obvious; frank; cloudless; shrewd, quick-thinking; famous. *m.* skylight; space between words; break in a speech; space in procession, etc.; (*art*) (gen. *pl.*) high lights. *interj.* **¡C.!** or **¡C. está!** Of course! **a las claras,** openly, frankly

claroscuro, *m.* chiaroscuro; monochrome

clase, *f.* class, group; kind, sort, quality; class (school, university); lecture room; lecture lesson; order, family. **c. media,** middle class. **c. social,** social class

clasicismo, *m.* classicism

clasicista, *a.* and *m.* and *f.* classicist

clásico, *a.* classic; notable; classical. *m.* classic

clasificación, *f.* classification

clasificador (-ra), *s.* classifier. **c. de billetes,** ticket-punch

clasificar, *v.t.* to classify, arrange. **c. correspondencia,** to file letters

claudicación, *f.* limping; negligence; hesitancy, weakness

claudicar, *v.i.* to limp; be negligent; hesitate, give way

claustral, *a.* cloistral

claustro, *m.* cloister; council, faculty, senatus (of university); monastic rule

claustrofobia, *f.* claustrophobia

cláusula, *f.* (*law, gram.*) clause

clausura, *f.* sanctum of convent; claustration; solemn ending ceremony of tribunal, etc. **la vida de c.,** monastic or conventual life

clava, *f.* club, truncheon; (*naut.*) scupper

clavadizo, *a.* nail-studded (doors, etc.)

clavar, *v.t.* to nail; fasten with nails; pierce, prick; set gems.

(jeweller); spike (guns); (*fig.*) fix (eyes, attention, etc.); (*fam.*) cheat

clave, *m.* clavichord. *f.* code, key; commentary, explanation; (*mus.*) clef; (*arch.*) keystone; plug (telephones); (*mus.*) **c. de sol,** treble clef

clavel, *m.* (*bot.*) carnation plant and flower

clavelito, *m.* (*bot.*) pink plant and flower

clavero (-ra), *s.* keeper of the keys. *m.* clove tree

clavetear, *v.t.* to stud with nails; (*fig.*) round off (business affairs)

clavicordio, *m.* (*mus.*) clavichord

clavícula, *f.* (*anat.*) clavicle

clavija, *f.* peg, pin; plug; peg of stringed instrument; axle-pin

clavo, *m.* nail, spike, peg; corn (on foot); anguish. **c. de especia,** clove. **c. de herradura,** hob-nail

clemátide, *f.* (*bot.*) clematis

clemencia, *f.* mildness; clemency; mercy

clemente, *a.* mild; clement; merciful

cleptomanía, *f.* kleptomania

cleptómano (-na), *a.* and *s.* kleptomaniac

clerecía, *f.* clergy

clerical, *a.* belonging to the clergy; clerical

clericalismo, *m.* clericalism

clericato, *m.* state and dignity of a cleric

clericatura, *f.* clerical state

clerigalla, *f.* (*contemptuous*) priesthood

clérigo, *m.* cleric, clergyman; clerk (in Middle Ages)

clero, *m.* clergy

cliente, *m.* and *f.* client, customer; protégé, ward

clientela, *f.* patronage, protection; clientèle

clima, *m.* climate, clime

climatérico, *a.* climacteric

climático, *a.* climatic

climatología, *f.* climatology

clímax, *m.* climax

clínica, *f.* clinic, nursing home; department of medicine or surgery

clínico, *a.* clinical

clíper, *m.* (*aer.* and *naut.*) clipper

clisar, *v.t.* (*print.*) to cast from a mould, stereotype

clisé, *m.* (*print.*) stereotype plate

clivoso, *a.* (*poet.*) sloping

cloaca, *f.* sewer, drain; (*zool.*) cloaca

cloquear, *v.i.* to go broody (hen); cluck

cloqueo, *m.* cluck, clucking

cloquera, *f.* broodiness (hens)

cloral, *m.* (*chem.*) chloral

clorato, *m.* (*chem.*) chlorate

clorhidrato, *m.* (*chem.*) hydrochloride

clorhídrico, *a.* (*chem.*) hydrochloric

cloro, *m.* chlorine

clorófila, *f.* chlorophyll

cloroformizar, *v.t.* to chloroform

cloroformo, *m.* chloroform

clorosis, *f.* (*med.*) chlorosis

cloruro, *m.* (*chem.*) chloride

club, *m.* club

clueca, *f.* broody hen

clueco, *a.* broody (hens); (*fam.*) doddering

coacción, *f.* coercion

coactivo, *a.* coercive

coadjutor, *m.* co-worker, assistant

coadunar, *v.t.* to join or mingle together

coadyuvar, *v.t.* to assist

coagulación, *f.* coagulation

coagular, *v.t.* to coagulate; clot; curdle

coágulo, *m.* clot; coagulation; congealed blood

coalición, *f.* coalition

coartada, *f.* alibi. **probar la c.,** to prove an alibi

coartar, *v.t.* to limit, restrict

coautor (-ra), *s.* co-author

cobalto, *m.* cobalt

cobarde, *a.* cowardly; irresolute. *m.* coward

cobardía, *f.* cowardice

cobayo, *m.* guinea-pig

cobertera, *f.* lid, cover

cobertizo, *m.* overhanging roof; shack, shed, hut. **c. de aeroplanos,** (*aer.*) hangar

cobertura, *f.* covering; coverlet; wrapping

cobija, *f.* imbrex tile; cover

cobijar, *v.t.* to cover; shelter

cobra, *f.* (*zool.*) cobra; rope or thong for yoking oxen; retrieval (of game) cobradero, *a.* that which can be collected, recoverable

cobrador, *m.* collector, receiver. *a.* collecting. **c. de tranvía,** tram conductor

cobranza, *f.* receiving, collecting; collection of fruit or money

cobrar, *v.t.* to collect (what is owed); charge; earn; regain, recover; feel, experience (emotions); wind, pull in (ropes, etc.); gain, acquire; retrieve (game); *v.r.* recuperate. **c. ánimo,** to take courage. **c. cariño (a),** to grow fond of. **c. fuerzas,** to gather strength. ¿Cuánto cobra Vd.? How much do you charge?; How much do you earn?

cobre, *m.* (*min.*) copper; copper kitchen utensils; *pl.* (*mus.*) brass

cobreño, *a.* made of copper

cobrizo, *a.* containing copper; copper-coloured

cocaína, *f.* cocaine

coccíneo, *a.* purple

cocción, *f.* coction

coceador, *a.* inclined to kick; kicking (animals)

coceadura, *f.* kicking

cocear, *v.i.* to kick; (*fam.*) kick against, oppose

cocedero, *a.* easily cooked

cocer, *v.t. irr.* to boil; cook; bake (bricks, etc.); digest; (*surg.*) suppurate; *v.i.* boil (of a liquid); ferment; *v.r.* suffer pain or inconvenience over a long period. *Pres. Ind.* **cuezo, cueces, cuece, cuecen.** *Pres. Subjunc.* **cueza, cuezas, cueza, cuezan**

cocido, *a.* boiled, cooked, baked. *m.* dish of stewed meat, pork, chicken, with peas, etc.

cociente, *m.* quotient

cocimiento, *m.* cooking; decoction

cocina, *f.* kitchen; pottage; broth; cookery. **c. de campaña,** field-kitchen. **c. económica,** cooking range

cocinar, *v.t.* to cook; *v.i.* (*fam.*) meddle, interfere

cocinería, *f.* (*naut.*) galley

cocinero (-ra), *s.* cook, chef

cocinilla, *f.* spirit-stove

coco, *m.* (*bot.*) coco-nut tree and fruit; coco-nut shell; grub, maggot; bogeyman; hobgoblin; (*fam.*)

grimace. (*fam.*) **ser un c.,** to be hideously ugly

cocodrilo, *m.* crocodile

cócora, *m.* and *f.* (*fam.*) bore, nosey Parker

cocotal, *m.* grove of coco palms

cocotero, *m.* coco palm

coctel, *m.* cocktail

cocuyo, *m.* firefly

coche, *m.* carriage, car. **c. camas,** sleeping-car. **c. cerrado,** (*aut.*) saloon. **c. de muchos caballos,** high-powered car. **c. de plaza,** hackney-carriage. **c. fúnebre,** hearse

cochera, *f.* coach house; tramway depôt

cochero, *m.* coachman; driver. *a.* easily cooked

cochina, *f.* sow

cochinería, *f.* (*fam.*) filthiness; mean trick

cochinilla, *f.* wood louse; cochineal insect; cochineal

cochinillo, *m.* sucking-pig. **c. de Indias,** guinea-pig

cochino, *m.* pig; (*fam.*) filthy person. *a.* filthy

codal, *a.* cubital. *m.* shoot of a vine; prop, strut; frame of a hand-saw

codazo, *m.* blow or nudge of the elbow. **dar codazos,** to elbow, shoulder out of the way

codear, *v.i.* to jostle; elbow, nudge; *v.r.* be on terms of equality with

codeína, *f.* (*med.*) codeine

codelincuente, *m.* and *f.* partner in crime, accomplice

codera, *f.* elbow rash; elbow-piece or patch

codeso, *m.* (*bot.*) laburnum

códice, *m.* codex

codicia, *f.* covetousness; greed

codiciar, *v.t.* to covet

codicilar, *a.* pertaining to a codicil

codicilo, *m.* codicil

codicioso (-sa), *a.* covetous; (*fam.*) hardworking. *s.* covetous person

codificación, *f.* codification

codificar, *v.t.* to codify, compile

código, *m.* code of laws. **c. civil,** civil laws. **c. de la vía pública,** highway code. (*naut.*) **c. de señales,** signal code. **c. penal,** criminal laws

codillo, *m.* knee of quadrupeds; shaft of branch; bend (pipe, tube); stirrup

codo, *m.* elbow; angle, bend (pipe, tube); cubit. (*fam.*) **hablar por los codos,** to chatter

codorniz, *f.* (*orn.*) quail

coeducación, *f.* co-education

coeficiente, *m.* coefficient

coercer, *v.t.* to restrain, coerce

coerción, *f.* (*law*) coercion

coercitivo, *a.* coercive

coetáneo (-ea), *a.* contemporaneous. *s.* contemporary

coevo, *a.* coeval

coexistencia, *f.* co-existence

coexistir, *v.i.* to co-exist

cofa, *f.* (*naut.*) top

cofia, *f.* hair-net; coif

cofín, *m.* basket

cofradía, *f.* confraternity, brotherhood or sisterhood

cofre, *m.* trunk, chest (for clothes); coffer

cogedor, *m.* collector, gatherer; dustpan; coal-shovel

coger, *v.t.* to seize, hold; catch; take, collect, gather; have room for; take up or occupy space; find; catch in the act; attack, surprise; reach; *v.i.* have room, fit

cogida, *f.* gathering, picking; (*fam.*) fruit harvest; toss (bull-fighting)

cogido, *m.* pleat, fold; crease

cogitabundo, *a.* very pensive

cognación, *f.* cognation; kinship

cognoscitivo, *a.* cognitive

cogollo, *m.* heart (of lettuce, etc.); shoot; topmost branches of pine tree

cogote, *m.* nape of neck

cogulla, *f.* monk's habit

cohabitación, *f.* cohabitation

cohabitar, *v.t.* to cohabit

cohechador (-ra), *a.* bribing. *s.* briber

cohechar, *v.t.* to bribe, corrupt, suborn

cohecho, *m.* bribing; bribe

coheredero (-ra), *s.* co-heir

coherencia, *f.* coherence, connection

coherente, *a.* coherent

cohesión, *f.* cohesion

cohesivo, *a.* cohesive

cohete, *m.* rocket

cohetero, *m.* firework manufacturer

cohibir, *v.t.* to restrain; repress

cohombrillo, *m. dim.* gherkin

cohombro, *m.* cucumber

cohonestar, *v.t.* (*fig.*) to gloss over, cover up; make appear decent (actions, etc.)

cohorte, *f.* cohort

coincidencia, *f.* coincidence

coincidir, *v.t.* to coincide

coito, *m.* coitus

cojear, *v.i.* to limp; wobble, be unsteady (of furniture); (*fig.*, *fam.*) go wrong or astray; (*fam.*) suffer from (vice, bad habit)

cojera, *f.* lameness, limp

cojijoso, *a.* peevish

cojín, *m.* cushion; pad; pillow (for lace-making)

cojinete, *m.* small cushion; (*mech.*) bearing. **c. de bolas,** ball-bearing

cojo, *a.* lame; unsteady, wobbly (of furniture, etc.)

col, *f.* cabbage. **c. de Bruselas,** Brussels sprout

cola, *f.* tail; train (of gown); shank (of a button); queue; tailpiece (of a violin, etc.); appendage; glue. **c. de milano,** (*carp.*) dovetail. **c. de pescado,** isinglass. **formar c.,** to queue up

colaboración, *f.* collaboration

colaboracionista, *m.* and *f.* collaborationist

colaborador (-ra), *s.* collaborator

colaborar, *v.t.* to collaborate

colación, *f.* conferment of a degree; collation (of texts); light repast; cold supper; area of a parish

colada, *f.* wash; bleaching; mountain path; (*met.*) casting; (*fam.*) trusty sword (allusion to name of one of the Cid's swords)

coladero, *m.* colander, sieve; strainer; narrow path

colador, *m.* colander

coladura, *f.* straining, filtration; (*fam.*) untruth; (*fam.*) howler, mistake

colanilla, *f.* small bolt

colapso, *m.* (*med.*) prostration, collapse

colar, *v.t. irr.* to filter, strain; bleach; (*met.*) cast; *v.i.* go through a narrow place; (*fam.*) drink wine; *v.r.* thread one's way; (*fam.*) enter by stealth, steal in; (*fam.*) tell untruths.

Pres. Ind. **cuelo, cuelas, cuela, cuelan.** *Pres. Subjunc.* **cuele, cueles, cuele, cuelen**

colateral, *a.* collateral

colcha, *f.* bedspread, counterpane, quilt

colchadura, *f.* quilting

colchero, *m.* quilt maker

colchón, *m.* mattress. **c. de muelles,** spring-mattress. **c. de viento,** air-bed

colchonero, *m.* mattress maker or seller

colchoneta, *f.* pad, thin mattress

coleada, *f.* wag of the tail

colear, *v.i.* to wag the tail

colección, *f.* collection

coleccionador (-ra), *s.* collector

coleccionar, *v.t.* to collect

coleccionista, *m.* and *f.* collector

colecta, *f.* assessment; collection (of donations); (*ecc.*) collect; voluntary offering

colectividad, *f.* collectivity; body of people

colectivismo, *m.* collectivism

colectivista, *a.* collectivist

colectivo, *a.* collective

colector, *m.* gatherer; collector; tax-collector; water-pipe; water-conduit; (*elec.*) commutator, collector

colega, *m.* colleague

colegatario, *m.* (*law*) co-legatee

colegiado, *a.* collegiate

colegial (-la), *a.* college, collegiate. *s.* student; pupil; (*fig., fam.*) novice.

colegiarse, *v.r.* to meet as an association (professional, etc.)

colegiata, *f.* college church

colegiatura, *f.* exhibition or fellowship of a college

colegio, *m.* college; school; academy; association (professional); council, convocation; college or school buildings. **c. de cardenales,** College of Cardinals. **c. electoral,** polling-booth. **c. militar,** military academy

colegir, *v.t. irr.* to collect, gather; deduce, infer. See **elegir**

coleóptero, *a.* coleopterous

cólera, *f.* bile, anger. *m.* cholera. **montar en c.,** to fly into a rage

colérico, *a.* angry; choleric; suffering from cholera

colesterina, *f.* (*chem.*) cholesterol

coleta, *f.* pigtail; queue; (*fam.*) postscript

coleto, *m.* leather jerkin; (*fam.*) body of a man

colgadero, *a.* able to be hung up. *m.* coat-hanger, hook

colgadizo, *a.* hanging. *m.* overhanging roof

colgadura, *f.* hangings, drapery, tapestries. **c. de cama,** bed-hangings

colgajo, *m.* tatter; bunch (of grapes, etc.); (*surg.*) skin lap

colgar, *v.t. irr.* to hang up; decorate with hangings; (*fam.*) hang, kill; *v.i.* hang, be suspended; (*fig.*) be dependent. See **contar**

colibrí, *m.* humming-bird

cólico, *m.* (*med.*) colic

colicuar, *v.t.* to dissolve

coliflor, *f.* cauliflower

coligarse, *v.r.* to confederate, unite

colilla, *f.* stub of a cigar or cigarette

colina, *f.* hill; cabbage seed; (*chem.*) choline

colindante, *a.* adjacent, contiguous

coliseo, *m.* coliseum; theatre

colisión, *f.* collision; abrasion; bruise; (*fig.*) clash (of ideas)

colitis, *f.* colitis

colmado, *a.* abundant. *m.* provision shop

colmar, *v.t.* to fill to overflowing; bestow generously, heap upon

colmena, *f.* bee hive

colmenar, *m.* apiary

colmenero (-ra), *s.* bee-keeper

colmillo, *m.* canine tooth; tusk; fang

colmilludo, *a.* having large canine teeth; tusked; fanged; sagacious

colmo, *m.* overflow; highest point; completion, limit, end. **ser el c.,** (*fam.*) to be the last straw

colocación, *f.* placing, putting; situation, place; employment; (*sport*) placing; order, arrangement

colocar, *v.t.* to place, put, arrange; place in employment; *v.r.* place oneself

colodra, *f.* wooden milking-pail

colofón, *m.* (*print.*) colophon

colofonia, *f.* solid resin (for bows of stringed instruments, etc.)

coloide, *a.* and *m.* (*chem.*) colloid

colombiano (-na), *a.* and *s.* Colombian

colombina, *f.* columbine

colonia, *f.* colony; plantation

colonial, *a.* colonial

colonización, *f.* colonization

colonizador (-ra), *a.* colonizing. *s.* colonizer

colonizar, *v.t.* to colonize; settle

colono, *m.* settler, colonist; farmer

coloquio, *m.* colloquy, conversation

color, *m.* colour; dye; paint; rouge; colouring; pretext, excuse; character, individuality; *pl.* natural colours. **c. estable, c. sólido,** fast colour. **mudar de c.,** to change colour. **de c.,** coloured. **so c.,** under the pretext. **ver las cosas c. de rosa,** to see things through rose-coloured spectacles

coloración, *f.* colouration, painting

colorado, *a.* coloured. (*S.A.*) red, reddish; (*fam.*) blue, obscene; specious

colorante, *a.* colouring. *m.* dyestuff; colouring (substance)

colorar, *v.t.* to colour; dye

colorear, *v.t.* to colour; pretext; (*fig.*) whitewash, excuse; *v.i.* show colour; be reddish; grow red, ripe (tomatoes, cherries, etc.)

colorete, *m.* rouge

colorido, *m.* colouring, colour

colorímetro, *m.* colorimeter

colorín, *m.* goldfinch; bright colour

colorista, *a.* and *m.* and *f.* colourist

colosal, *a.* colossal, enormous; extraordinary, excellent

coloso, *m.* colossus; (*fig.*) outstanding person or thing, giant

columbino, *a.* pertaining to a dove; dovelike; candid, innocent; purply-red

columbrar, *v.t.* to discern in the distance, glimpse; conjecture, guess

columna, *f.* (*mil., arch., print.*) column; (*fig.*) protection, shelter; (*naut.*) stanchion. **c. cerrada,** (*mil.,* etc.) mass formation. **c.**

de los suspiros, agony column (in a newspaper)

columnata, *f.* colonnade

columpiar, *v.t.* to swing; *v.r.* (*fam.*) sway in walking; swing

columpio, *m.* swing

colusión, *f.* (*law*) collusion

colusorio, *a.* (*law*) collusive

collado, *m.* hill, hillock

collar, *m.* necklace; chain of office or honour; collar (dogs, etc.)

collarín, *m.* ecclesiastical collar

collera, *f.,* **collerón,** *m.* horse collar

coma, *f.* (*gram.*) comma. *m.* (*med.*) coma

comadre, *f.* midwife; (*fam.*) procuress, go-between; (*fam.*) pal, gossip

comadrear, *v.i.* (*fam.*) to gossip

comadreja, *f.* (*zool.*) weasel

comadrón, *m.* accoucheur

comadrona, *f.* midwife

comandancia, *f.* (*mil.*) command; commandant's H.Q.

comandante, *m.* commandant; commander; major; squadron-leader. *a.* (*mil.*) commanding. **c. en jefe,** commanding officer

comandar, *v.t.* (*mil.*) to command

comandita, *f.* (*com.*) sleeping partnership; private company

comando, *m.* (*mil.*) commando

comarca, *f.* district, region

comatoso, *a.* comatose

comba, *f.* bend, warping; skipping-rope; camber (of road)

combadura, *f.* curvature; warping; camber (of a road)

combar, *v.t.* to bend; twist; warp; camber

combate, *m.* fight, combat; mental strife; contradiction, opposition. **dejar fuera de c.,** (a) (boxing) to knock out

combatiente, *m.* combatant, soldier

combatir, *v.i.* to fight; *v.t.* attack; struggle against (winds, water, etc.); contradict, oppose; (*fig.*) disturb, trouble (emotions)

combés, *m.* (*naut.*) waist

combinación, *f.* combination; list of words beginning with same letter; project; concurrence; underskirt, petticoat

combinar, *v.t.* to combine; (*mil., nav.*) join forces; arrange, plan; (*chem.*) combine

combustible, *a.* combustible. *m.* fuel

combustión, *f.* combustion. **c. activa,** rapid combustion. **c. espontánea,** spontaneous combustion

comedero, *a.* edible. *m.* feeding-trough; dining-room

comedia, *f.* comedy; play; theatre; comic incident; (*fig.*) play-acting, theatricalism. **c. de costumbres,** comedy of manners. **c. de enredo,** play with very involved plot. (*fam.*) **hacer la c.,** to play-act, pretend

comediante, *m.* actor; (*fam.*) dissembler.

comedianta, *f.* actress

comedido, *a.* courteous; prudent; moderate

comedimiento, *m.* courtesy; moderation; prudence

comedir, *v.t. irr.* to prepare, premeditate; *v.r.* restrain oneself, be moderate; offer one's services. See **pedir**

comedor, *a.* voracious. *m.* dining-room

comendador, *m.* knight commander

comendatorio, *a.* commendatory (of letters)

comensal, *m.* and *f.* table companion

comentador (-ra), *s.* commentator

comentar, *v.t.* explain (document); (*fam.*) comment

comentario, *m.* commentary

comentarista, *m.* and *f.* commentator

comento, *m.* comment; commentary

comenzante, *m.* and *f.* beginner, novice. *a.* initial

comenzar, *v.t., v.i., irr.* to begin, commence. See **empezar**

comer, *m.* eating; food. *v.i.* to eat; feed; dine. *v.t.* eat; (*fam.*) enjoy an income; waste (patrimony); consume, exhaust; fade (of colours); *v.r.* be troubled, uneasy, remorseful. **ser de buen c.,** to have a good appetite; taste good. **tener que c.,** to be obliged to eat; have to eat; have enough to eat

comerciable, *a.* marketable; sociable, pleasant (of persons)

comercial, *a.* commercial

comerciante, *a.* trading. *m.* and *f.* merchant, trader

comerciar, *v.i.* to trade; have dealings (with)

comercio, *m.* trade, commerce; intercourse, traffic; illicit sexual intercourse; shop, store; tradesmen; commercial quarter of town

comestible, *a.* edible, eatable. *m.* (gen. *pl.*) provisions

cometa, *m.* (*ast.*) comet. *f.* kite (toy). **c. celular,** box-kite

cometedor (-ra), *s.* perpetrator

cometer, *v.t.* to entrust, hand over to; commit (crime, sins, etc.); (*com.*) order

cometido, *m.* charge, commission; moral obligation; function

comezón, *f.* itching, irritation; hankering, longing

comicidad, *f.* comic element; comic spirit

cómico, *a.* comic; funny, comical. *m.* actor; comedian. **c. de la legua,** strolling player

comida, *f.* food; meal; dinner; eating. **c. de gala,** state banquet. **c. de prueba,** (*med.*) test meal

comienzo, *m.* beginning, origin

comilón (-ona), *a.* (*fam.*) gluttonous. *s.* glutton

comillas, *f. pl.* (*gram.*) inverted commas

comino, *m.* (*bot.*) cumin. **no valer un c.,** to be not worth a jot

comisar, *v.t.* to confiscate, sequestrate

comisaría, *f.* commissaryship; commissariat. **c. de policía,** police station

comisario, *m.* deputy, agent; commissary, head of police; commissioner. **alto c.,** High Commissioner

comisión, *f.* perpetration, committal; commission; committee; (*com.*) commission

comisionado (-da), *a.* commissioned. *m.* commissary

comisionar, *v.t.* to commission

comisionista, *m.* and *f.* (*com.*) commission agent

comiso, *m.* (*law*) confiscation, sequestration; contraband

comité, *m.* committee

comitiva, *f.* retinue, following

como, *adv.* like, as; in the same way; thus, accordingly; in the capacity of; so that; since. *conjunc.* if (*followed by subjunc.*); because. **c. no**, unless. *¿* **Cómo ?** How?; In what way?; Why?; Pardon? What did you say? *interj.* ¡Cómo! What!; You don't say! ¡Cómo no! Why not! Of course! Surely!

cómo, *m.* the wherefore. **no saber el por qué ni el c.**, not to know the why or wherefore

cómoda, *f.* chest of drawers

comodidad, *f.* comfort; convenience; advantage; utility; interest

comodín, *m.* (in cards) joker

cómodo, *a.* comfortable; convenient; opportune

comodón, *a.* (*fam.*) comfort-loving; easy-going; egoistical

comodoro, *m.* (*naut.*) commodore

compacidad, *f.* compactness

compacto, *a.* compact, dense; close (type)

compadecer, *v.t.* irr. to pity; *v.r.* (*with de*) sympathize with; pity; harmonize, agree with. See **conocer**

compadre, *m.* (*fam.*) pal

compaginación, *f.* joining, fixing; (*print.*) making-up

compaginar, *v.t.* to fit together; join, put in order; (*print.*) make up

compañerismo, *m.* comradeship

compañero (-ra), *s.* companion, comrade; fellow-member; partner (games); (*fig.*) pair, fellow, mate (things)

compañía, *f.* company; society; association; theatrical company; (*com.*, *mil.*) company. **C. de Jesús**, Order of Jesus. **c. de navegación**, shipping-company. **c. por acciones**, joint stock company

comparable, *a.* comparable

comparación, *f.* comparison

comparar, *v.t.* to compare; collate

comparativo, *a.* comparative

comparecencia, *f.* (gen. *law*) appearance

comparecer, *v.i.* irr. (*law*) to appear (before tribunal, etc.); present oneself. See **conocer**

comparendo, *m.* (*law*) summons

comparsa, *f.* retinue; (*theat.*) chorus; troop of carnival revellers dressed alike. *m.* and *f.* (*theat.*) supernumerary actor

comparte, *m.* and *f.* (*law*) partner; accomplice

compartimiento, *m.* share, division; railway carriage. (*naut.*) **c. estanco**, compartment

compartir, *v.t.* to share out, divide; participate

compás, *m.* compasses; callipers; size; compass, time; range of voice; (*naut.*, *min.*) compass; (*mus.*) time, rhythm, bar, marking time. **c. de mar**, mariner's compass. **c. de puntas**, dividers, callipers. **fuera de c.**, (*mus.*) out of time; out of joint (of the times); (*mus.*) **llevar el c.**, to beat time

compasar, *v.t.* to measure with compasses; arrange or apportion accurately; (*mus.*) put into bars

compasillo, *m.* (*mus.*) ¼ measure

compasivo, *a.* compassionate; tender-hearted

compatibilidad, *f.* compatibility

compatible, *a.* compatible

compatriota, *m.* and *f.* compatriot

compeler, *v.t.* to compel, force

compendiador (-ra), *a.* abridging. *s.* abridger

compendiar, *v.t.* to abridge, summarize

compendio, *m.* compendium. **en c.**, briefly

compendioso, *a.* summary, condensed; compendious

compenetración, *f.* co-penetration; intermingling

compenetrarse, *v.r.* to co-penetrate; intermingle

compensación, *f.* compensating; compensation

compensar, *v.t.* to equalize, counterbalance; compensate

compensatorio, *a.* compensatory; equalizing

competencia, *f.* competition, contest; rivalry; competence; aptitude; (*law*) jurisdiction

competente, *a.* adequate, opportune; rightful, correct; apt, suitable; learned, competent

competer, *v.i.* irr. to belong to; devolve on; concern. See **pedir**

competición, *f.* competition

competidor (-ra), *s.* competitor

competir, *v.i. irr.* to compete, contest; be equal (to), vie (with). See **pedir**

compilación, *f.* compilation

compilador (-ra), *s.* compiler. *a.* compiling

compilar, *v.t.* to compile

compinche, *m.* and *f.* (*fam.*) pal, chum

complacencia, *f.* satisfaction, pleasure

complacer, *v.t. irr.* to oblige, humour; *v.r.* (*with en*) be pleased or satisfied with; delight in, like to. See **nacer**

complaciente, *a.* pleasing; obliging, helpful

complejidad, *f.* complexity

complejo, *a.* complex; intricate. *m.* complex. **c. de inferioridad,** inferiority complex

complementario, *a.* complementary

complemento, *m.* complement (all meanings)

completar, *v.t.* to complete; perfect

completas, *f. pl.* (*ecc.*) Compline

completo, *a.* full; finished; perfect

complexión, *f.* physical constitution

complexo, *a.* complex; intricate

complicación, *f.* complication

complicar, *v.t.* to complicate; muddle, confuse; *v.r.* be complicated; be muddled or confused

cómplice, *m.* and *f.* accomplice

complicidad, *f.* complicity

complot, *m.* (*fam.*) conspiracy, plot, intrigue

complutense, *a.* native of, or belonging to, Alcalá de Henares (Cervantes's birthplace)

componedor (-ra), *s.* repairer; arbitrator; bone-setter; (*mus.*) composer; writer, author, compiler; (*print.*) compositor

componenda, *f.* mending, repair; (*fam.*) settlement; compromise, arbitration; (*fam.*) shady business

componente, *a.* and *m.* component

componer, *v.t. irr.* to construct, form; (*mech.*) resolve; compose, create; (*print.*) compose; prepare, concoct, mend, repair;

settle (differences); remedy; trim; correct, adjust; (*lit., mus.*) compose; add up to, amount to; *v.i.* write (verses); (*mus.*) compose; *v.r.* dress oneself up; **c. el semblante,** to compose one's features; (*fam.*) **componérselas,** to fix matters, use one's wits. See **poner**

componible, *a.* reparable, mendable; able to be arranged or adjusted

comportamiento, *m.* conduct; deportment

comportar, *v.t.* to tolerate; *v.r.* behave, comport oneself

composición, *f.* composition; repair; arrangement, compromise; (*print.*) composition; (*gram.*) compound; (*chem.*) constitution; (*mech.*) resolution

compositor (-ra), *s.* (*mus.*) composer; (*print.*) compositor

compostura, *f.* composition, structure; repair; neatness (of person); adulteration; arrangement, agreement; discretion, modesty

compota, *f.* fruit preserve, compôte; thick sauce

compotera, *f.* jam or preserve dish

compra, *f.* buying; marketing, shopping; purchase. **ir de compras,** to go shopping

comprable, *a.* purchasable

comprador (-ra), *a.* purchasing. *s.* purchaser; buyer; shopper

comprar, *v.t.* to buy; bribe

comprender, *v.t.* to encircle, surround; include, comprise, contain; understand

comprensible, *a.* comprehensible

comprensión, *f.* comprehension, understanding

comprensivo, *a.* understanding; comprehensive

compresa, *f.* (*med.*) compress, swab; pack (for the face, etc.)

compresión, *f.* compression; squeeze

compresivo, *a.* compressive

compresor, *m.* compressor; (*aut., aer.*) supercharger

comprimido, *m.* tablet, pill

comprimir, *v.t.* to compress; squeeze; restrain; *v.r.* restrain oneself

comprobación, *f.* verification; checking; proof

comprobante, *a.* verifying; confirmatory

comprobar, *v.t. irr.* to verify, check; confirm, prove. See **probar**

comprobatorio, *a.* confirmatory; verifying; testing

comprometedor, *a.* (*fam.*) compromising; jeopardizing

comprometer, *v.t.* to submit to arbitration; compromise; imperil, jeopardize; *v.r.* pledge oneself; (*fam.*) compromise oneself

compromiso, *m.* compromise, agreement, arbitration, commitment, obligation; appointment, engagement; jeopardy; difficulty

compuerta, *f.* half-door, wicket, hatch; floodgate, sluice. **c. flotante,** floating dam

compuesto, *a.* and *past part.* made-up, built-up; composite; circumspect; (*bot., gram.*) compound. *m.* composite; preparation, compound

compulsar, *v.t.* to collate; (*law*) make a transcript of

compulsivo, *a.* compelling

compunción, *f.* compunction

compungir, *v.t.* to cause remorse or pity; *v.r.* repent; sympathize with, pity

computable, *a.* computable

computación, *f.*, **cómputo;** *m.* calculation, computation

computar, *v.t.* to compute

computista, *m.* and *f.* computer

cómputo, *m.* computation; estimate

comulgar, *v.t.* to administer Holy Communion; *v.i.* receive Holy Communion

comulgatorio, *m.* (*ecc.*) altar-rail

común, *a.* general, customary, ordinary; public, communal; universal, common; vulgar, low. *m.* community, population; water-closet. **en c.,** in common; generally. **por lo c.,** generally. **sentido c.,** common sense

comunal, *a.* communal; common. *m.* commonalty

comunero, *a.* popular, affable, democratic. *m.* joint owner; commoner; (*hist.*) commune (Spanish, sixteenth-century)

comunicable, *a.* communicable; communicative, sociable

comunicación, *f.* communication; (telephone) call, message; letter (to the press); (*mil.*) communiqué; *pl.* lines of communication, transport

comunicado, *m.* official communication, communiqué; letter (to the press)

.comunicante, *a.* communicating

comunicar, *v.t.* to communicate; transmit; impart, share; *v.r.* lead into each other (rooms); communicate, converse, correspond with each other

comunicativo, *a.* communicative; talkative, not reserved

comunidad, *f.* the common people; community; generality, majority; *pl.* (*hist.*) Commune

comunión, *f.* communion; intercourse, fellowship; (*ecc.*) Communion

comunismo, *m.* Communism

comunista, *a.* and *m.* and *f.* Communist

comúnmente, *adv.* commonly, generally; frequently

con, *prep.* with; by means of; in the company of; towards, to; although (followed by *infin.* in Spanish, but generally translated by a tense, e.g. **C. ser almirante, no le gusta el mar,** Although he is an admiral, he doesn't like the sea); by (followed by *infin.* and generally translated by a gerund, e.g. **c. hacer todo esto,** by doing all this). **c. que,** so, then. **c. tal que,** provided that, on condition that. **c. todo,** nevertheless

conato, *m.* effort, endeavour; tendency; (*law*) attempted crime

concatenación, *f.* concatenation

concausa, *f.* joint cause

concavidad, *f.* concavity; hollow

cóncavo, *a.* concave. *m.* concavity; hollow

concebible, *a.* conceivable

concebimiento, *m.* See **concepción**

concebir, *v.i. irr.* to become pregnant; conceive, imagine; understand; *v.t.* conceive, acquire (affection, etc.). See **pedir**

concedente, *a.* conceding

conceder, *v.t.* to confer, grant; concede; agree to

concejal, *m.* councillor; alderman·

concejil, *a.* pertaining to a municipal council; public

concejo, *m.* town council; .town hall; council meeting

concentración, *f.* concentration

concentrado, *a.* concentrated; (of persons) reserved

concentrar, *v.t.* to concentrate

concéntrico, *a.* (*geom.*) concentric·

concepción, *f.* conception; idea, concept; (*ecc.*) Immaculate Conception

conceptismo, *m.* (*lit.*) Concettism (cf. *Euphuism*)

conceptista, *a.* and *m.* and *f.* concettist

concepto, *m.* idea, concept; epigram; opinion; judgment

conceptualismo, *m.* conceptualism

conceptuar, *v.t.* to judge, take to be; believe; imagine

conceptuoso, *a.* witty, ingenious

concernencia, *f.* respect, relation

concerniente, *a.* concerning

concernir, *v.i. irr. defective* to concern. See **discernir**

concertadamente, *adv.* methodically, orderly; by arrangement, or agreement

concertar, *v.t. irr.* to arrange, settle, adjust; bargain; conclude (business deal); harmonize (also *mus.*); compare, correlate; tune instruments; *v.i.* reach an agreement. See **acertar**

concertina, *f.* concertina

concesión, *f.* conceding, grant; concession; lease

concesionario, *m.* (*law*) concessionaire, lease-holder

conciencia, *f.* consciousness; conscience; conscientiousness. **c. doble,** dual personality. **ancho de c.,** broad-minded. **a c.,** conscientiously

concienzudo, *a.* of a delicate conscience, scrupulous; conscientious

concierto, *m.* methodical arrangement; agreement; (*mus.*) concert; (*mus.*) concerto. **de c.,** by common consent

conciliable, *a.* reconcilable compatible

conciliábulo, *m.* conclave, private meeting; secret meeting

conciliación, *f.* conciliation; similarity, affinity; protection, favour

conciliador, *a.* conciliatory

conciliar, *m.* councillor. *v.t.* to conciliate; (*fig.*) reconcile (opposing theories, etc.); woo (sleep); *v.r.* win liking (or sometimes dislike)

concilio, *m.* council; (*ecc.*) assembly; conciliary decree; findings of council

concisión, *f.* conciseness, brevity

conciso, *a.* concise

concitar, *v.t.* to stir up, foment

conciudadano (-na), *s.* fellowcitizen; fellow-countryman

cónclave, *m.* conclave; meeting

concluir, *v.t. irr.* to conclude, finish; come to a conclusion, decide; infer, deduce; convince by reasoning; (*law*) close legal proceedings; *v.r.* expire, terminate. See **huir**

conclusión, *f.* finish, end; decision; close, dénouement; theory, proposition (gen. *pl.*); deduction, inference; (*law*) close. **en c.,** in conclusion

conclusivo, *a.* final; conclusive

concluyente, *a.* concluding; convincing; conclusive

concomitancia, *f.* concomitance

concomitante, *a.* and *m.* concomitant

concordable, *a.* conformable

concordador (-ra), *a.* peacemaking. *s.* peacemaker

concordancia, *f.* harmony, agreement; (*mus., gram.*) concord; *pl.* concordance

concordar, *v.t. irr.* to bring to agreement; *v.i.* agree (also *gram.*). See **acordar**

concordato, *m.* concordat

concorde, *a.* agreeing; harmonious

concordia, *f.* concord, agreement, harmony; written agreement

concreción, *f.* concretion

concretar, *v.t.* to combine, bring together; make concise; resume; *v.r.* (*fig.*) confine oneself (to a subject)

concreto, *a.* concrete, real, not abstract. **en c.,** in definite terms; finally, to sum up

concubina, *f.* concubine, mistress

concubinato, *m.* concubinage

concupiscencia, *f.* concupiscence, lust; greed

concupiscente, *a.* concupiscent, lustful; greedy

concurrencia, *f.* assembly; coincidence; attendance; help, influence

concurrido, *a.* crowded; busy; frequented

concurrir, *v.i.* to coincide; contribute; meet together; agree, be of same opinion; compete (in an examination, etc.)

concurso, *m.* crowd, concourse; conjunction, coincidence; help; competition; (tennis) tournament; competitive examination; invitation to offer tenders. **c. de acreedores,** creditors' meeting

concusión, *f.* concussion; shock; extortion

concha, *f.* shell; turtle-shell; prompter's box; cove, creek; anything shell-shaped. *(fig.)* **meterse en su c.,** to retire into one's shell. *(fam.)* **tener más conchas que un galápago,** to be very cunning

conchado, *a.* scaly, having a shell

condado, *m.* earldom; county

conde, *m.* earl; king of the gypsies

condecoración, *f.* conferment of an honour, decoration; medal

condecorar, *v.t.* to confer a decoration or medal

condena, *f.* *(law)* sentence; punishment; penalty

condenable, *a.* culpable, guilty; worthy of damnation

condenado (-da), *a.* damned; wicked, harmful. *s.* *(law)* convicted criminal

condenador, *a.* condemning; incriminating; blaming

condenar, *v.t.* *(law)* to pronounce sentence (on), convict; condemn; disapprove; wall or block or close up; *v.r.* blame oneself; be eternally damned

condenatorio, *a.* condemnatory; incriminating

condensación, *f.* condensation

condensador, *a.* condensing. *m.* *(elec., mech., chem.)* condenser

condensante, *a.* condensing

condensar, *v.t.* to condense; thicken; abridge

condesa, *f.* countess

condescendencia, *f.* affability, graciousness

condescender, *v.i.* *irr.* to be obliging, helpful, agreeable. See **entender**

condescendiente, *a.* affable, gracious

condestable, *m.* *(hist.)* constable, commander-in-chief

condición, *f.* condition; quality; temperament, character; (social) position; rank, family; nobility, circumstance; stipulation, condition, requirement. **no estar en condiciones de,** to be in no condition to

condicional, *a.* conditional

condicionar, *v.i.* to come to an agreement, arrange; *v.t.* impose conditions

condigno, *a.* condign

condimentación, *f.* *(cul.)* seasoning

condimentar, *v.t.* to flavour, season (food)

condimento, *m.* condiment, flavouring

condiscípulo, *m.* schoolfellow

condolencia, *f.* compassion; condolence

condolerse, *v.r.* *(with de)* to sympathize with, be sorry for. See **doler**

condonación, *f.* condonation

condonar, *v.t.* to condone

conducción, *f.,* **conducencia,** *f.* transport, conveyance, carriage; guiding; direction, management; *(phys.)* conduction; *(mech.)* control-gear. *(aut.)* **c. a izquierda,** left-hand drive

conducente, *a.* conducting, conducive

conducir, *v.t.* *irr.* to transport, convey, carry; *(phys.)* conduct; guide, lead; manage, direct; *(aut.)* drive; conduce; *v.i.* be suitable; *v.r.* behave, conduct oneself. *Pres. Ind.* **conduzco, conduces,** etc. *Preterite* **conduje, condujiste,** etc. *Pres. Subjunc.* **conduzca, conduzcas,** etc. *Imperf. Subjunc.* **condujese,** etc.

conducta, *f.* transport, conveyance; management, conduct, direction; behaviour

conductibilidad, *f.* *(phys.)* conductivity

conductivo, a. (phys.) conductive

conducto, m. pipe, conduit, drain, duct; (fig.) channel, means; (anat.) tube

conductor (-ra), s. guide; leader; driver (vehicles); m. (phys.) conductor. c. de entrada, (rad.) lead-in. c. del calor, heat-conductor. c. eléctrico, electric wire or cable

conectar, v.t. (elec.) to connect, switch on; couple; attach, join

conectivo, a. connective; (elec., mech.) connecting

conejar, m. rabbit-warren

conejera, f. rabbit-warren; (fam.) low dive or haunt

conejillo de Indias, m. guinea-pig

conejo, m. rabbit

conejuno, a. rabbit, rabbit-like

conejuna, f. rabbit fur, coney

conexión, f. connection; (elec.) switching on, connection; joint; joining; pl. friends, connections; (elec.) wiring

conexo, a. connected

confabulación, f. confabulation, conspiracy

confabular, v.i. to confer; v.r. scheme, plot

confalón, m. standard, banner

confección, f. making; confection; making-up; concoction, remedy; ready-made garment

confeccionador (-ra), s. maker (of clothes, etc.)

confeccionar, v.t. to make; prepare; make up (pharmaceuticals)

confederación, f. alliance, pact; confederacy, federation

confederarse, v.r. to confederate, be allied

conferencia, f. conference, meeting; lecture; (telephone) trunk call

conferenciante, m. and f. lecturer

conferenciar, v.i. to confer

conferir, v.t. irr. to grant, concede; consider, discuss; compare, correlate. See herir

confesable, a. acknowledgeable, avowable

confesar, v.t. irr. to avow, declare; acknowledge, admit; (ecc.) hear confession; v.r. (ecc.) confess. Pres. Ind. confieso, confiesas, confiesa, con-

fiesan. Pres. Subjunc. confiese, confieses, confiese, confiesen

confesión, f. confession

confesional, a. confessional

confesionario, confesonario, confesorio, m. (ecc.) confessional

confeso, a. confessed; converted (of Jews). m. (ecc.) lay brother

confesor, m. confessor

confeti, m. confetti

confianza, f. confidence, trust; assurance, courage; over-confidence, conceit; intimacy; familiarity. en c., in confidence, confidentially

confianzudo, a. (fam.) over-confident

confiar, v.i. (with en) to trust in, hope; v.t. (with prep. a or en) entrust, commit to the care of; confide in

confidencia, f. trust; confidence; confidential information

confidencial, a. confidential

confidente (-ta), a. trustworthy, true. m. seat for two. s. confidant(e); spy

configuración, f. configuration, form, lie

configurar, v.t. to shape

confín, m. boundary, frontier; limit. a. boundary

confinado, a. banished. m. (law) prisoner

confinar, v.i. (with con) to be bounded by, contiguous to; v.t. banish; place in confinement

confirmación, f. corroboration; (ecc.) confirmation

confirmar, v.t. to corroborate; uphold; (ecc.) confirm

confirmatorio, a. confirmatory

confiscación, f. confiscation

confiscar, v.t. to confiscate

confitar, v.t. to candy, crystallize or preserve (fruit, etc.); (fig.) sweeten

confite, m. bon-bon, sugared almond, etc.

confitería, f. confectionery

confitero (-ra), s. confectioner

confitura, f. preserve, jam

conflagración, f. conflagration, blaze; uprising, rebellion

conflicto, m. strife, struggle; spiritual conflict; (fig.) difficult situation

confluencia, f. confluence; crowd

confluir, v.i. irr. to meet, flow

together (rivers); run together (roads); crowd. See **huir**

conformación, *f.* conformation

conformar, *v.t.* to fit, adjust; *v.r.* agree, be of the same opinion; submit, comply

conforme, *a.* similar, alike; consistent; in agreement; long-suffering, resigned. *adv.* according (to), in proportion (to)

conformidad, *f.* conformity; similarity; resignation; agreement, harmony; proportion, symmetry. **de c.,** by common consent. **en c.,** according to

confort, *m.* comfort

confortante, *a.* comforting; consoling; strengthening (of beverages)

confortar, *v.t.* to comfort, reassure; encourage; console

confortativo, *a.* comforting; comfortable; strengthening, warming (of beverages); encouraging, cheering

confrontación, *f.* confrontment; comparison (of texts, etc.)

confrontar, *v.t.* to bring face to face; compare, correlate; *v.i.* face; (*with* **con**) be contiguous to, border on

confucianismo, *m.* Confucianism

confundible, *a.* mistakable, liable to be confused

confundimiento, *m.* confounding; mistaking; confusion

confundir, *v.t.* to mix, confuse; jumble together; mistake; (*fig.*) confound (in argument); humble; bewilder, perplex; *v.r.* be mixed together; mistake, confuse; be ashamed; be bewildered

confusión, *f.* confusion; perplexity; shame; jumble

confuso, *a.* mixed, upset; jumbled; obscure; indistinct; blurred; bewildered

confutación, *f.* confutation

confutar, *v.t.* to confute

congelación, *f.* freezing; congealment. **punto de c.,** freezing point

congelar, *v.t.* to congeal; freeze

congeniar, *v.i.* to be congenial

congénito, *a.* congenital

congestión, *f.* (*med.*) congestion

congestionar, *v.t.* to congest; *v.r.* (*med.*) be overcharged (with blood)

conglomeración, *f.* conglomeration

conglomerar, *v.t.* to conglomerate

congoja, *f.* anguish, anxiety, grief

congraciarse (*con*), *v.r.* to ingratiate oneself (with), get into the good graces (of)

congratulación, *f.* congratulation

congratular, *v.t.* to congratulate; *v.r.* congratulate oneself

congratulatorio, *a.* congratulatory

congregación, *f.* gathering, meeting, congregation; brotherhood, guild

congregar(se), *v.t.* and *v.r.* to meet, assemble

congresista, *m.* and *f.* member of a congress

congreso, *m.* congress; conference, meeting; sexual intercourse

congrio, *m.* conger-eel

congruencia, *f.* suitability, convenience; (*math.*) congruence

congruente, *a.* convenient, opportune; (*math.*) congruent

cónico, *a.* conical, tapering; (*math.*) conic

conífera, *f.* conifer

conífero, *a.* (*bot.*) coniferous

conjetura, *f.* conjecture

conjetural, *a.* conjectural

conjeturar, *v.t.* to conjecture, surmise

conjugación, *f.* (*gram.*) conjugation

conjugar, *v.t.* (*gram.*) to conjugate

conjunción, *f.* connection, union, association; (*ast., gram.*) conjunction

conjuntivitis, *f.* conjunctivitis

conjunto, *a.* united, associated; adjoining; mingled, mixed (with); bound, affiliated. *m.* whole

conjura, conjuración, *f.* conspiracy, plot

conjurador (-ra), *s.* conspirator, plotter; exorcist

conjurar, *v.i.* to conspire, plot; *v.t.* swear, take an oath; exorcise; implore, beg; ward off (danger)

conjuro, *m.* plot, conspiracy; spell, incantation; entreaty

conllevar, *v.t.* to share (troubles); bear, put up with; endure

conmemoración, *f.* commemoration

conmemorar, *v.t.* to commemorate

conmemorativo, *a.* commemorative

conmensurable, *a.* commensurable

conmigo, *pers. pron.* 1st pers. sing. *m.* and *f.* with myself, with me

conminar, *v.t.* to threaten

conminatorio, *a.* threatening

conmiseración, *f.* commiseration, compassion, pity

conmoción, *f.* disturbance (mind or body); upheaval, commotion. **c. eléctrica**, electric shock

conmovedor, *a.* moving, pitiful; stirring, thrilling

conmover, *v.t. irr.* to perturb, stir; move to pity; *v.r.* be emotionally moved. See **mover**

conmutable, *a.* commutable

conmutación, *f.* commutation (*also elec.*)

conmutador, *m.* (*elec.*) commutator; change-over switch

conmutar, *v.t.* to commute (also *law*); (*elec.*) switch, convert

conmutatriz, *f.* (*elec.*) converter

connato, *a.* contemporary

connatural, *a.* innate, inborn

connivencia, *f.* connivance

connotación, *f.* connotation

connotar, *v.t.* to connote

connubial, *a.* connubial

cono, *m.* (*geom., bot.*) cone

conocedor (-ra), *s.* one who knows; connoisseur; expert

conocer, *v.t. irr.* to know; understand; observe, perceive; be acquainted (with); conjecture; confess, acknowledge; know carnally; *v.r.* know oneself; know one another. *Pres. Ind.* conozco, conoces, etc. *Pres. Subjunc.* conozca, etc.

conocido (-da), *a.* illustrious, distinguished. *s.* acquaintance

conocimiento, *m.* knowledge; understanding; intelligence; acquaintance (*not* friend); consciousness; (*com.*) bill of lading; *pl.* knowledge, learning

conoide, *m.* (*geom.*) conoid

conque, *conjunc.* so, so that (e.g. ¿ C. Juan se va ? So John's going away?)

conquista, *f.* conquest

conquistador (-ra), *a.* conquering. *s.* conqueror

conquistar, *v.t.* to conquer; (*fig.*) captivate, win

conreinar, *v.i.* to reign jointly

consabido, *a.* aforesaid, beforementioned

consagración, *f.* consecration; dedication

consagrar, *v.t.* to consecrate; dedicate, devote; deify; *v.r.* (*with prep.* a) dedicate oneself to, engage in

consanguíneo, *a.* consanguineous

consanguinidad, *f.* consanguinity

consciente, *a.* conscious; aware; sane. *m.* (*psy.*) conscious

conscripción, *f.* conscription

conscripto, *m.* conscript

consecución, *f.* obtainment; attainment

consecuencia, *f.* consequence, outcome; logical consequence, conclusion; importance; consistence (of people)

consecuente, *a.* consequent, resultant; consistent. *m.* consequence; (*math.*) consequent

consecutivo, *a.* consecutive, successive

conseguir, *v.t. irr.* to obtain, achieve. See **seguir**

conseja, *f.* story, fairy-tale; old wives' tale

consejero (-ra), *s.* adviser; member of council. **m. c. de estado**, counsellor of state

consejo, *m.* advice; council, commission, board; council chamber or building. **c. de administración**, board of directors. **c. de guerra**, council of war. **c. privado**, Privy Council

consenso, *m.* consensus of opinion, unanimity

consentido, *a.* complaisant (of husband); spoilt, over-indulged

consentimiento, *m.* consent; assent

consentir, *v.t. irr.* to permit, allow; believe; tolerate, put up with; over-indulge, spoil; *v.r.* crack, give way (furniture, etc.). **c. en**, to consent to; to agree to. See **sentir**

conserje, *m.* concierge, porter; warden or keeper (of castle, etc.)

conserjería, f. conciergerie, porter's lodge; warden's dwelling (in castles, etc.)

conserva, f. jam; preserve; pickles; (naut.) convoy. en c., preserved, tinned

conservación, f. upkeep; preservation, maintenance; (cul.) preserving; conservation. c. refrigerada, cold-storage

conservador (-ra), a. keeping, preserving. a. and s. preserver; (pol.) Conservative; traditionalist. m. curator

conservadurismo, m. conservatism

conservar, v.t. to keep, maintain, preserve; keep up (custom, etc.); guard; (cul.) preserve. c. en buen estado, to keep in repair

conservatorio, m. conservatoire; academy. C. de Música, Academy of Music, Conservatoire

considerable, a. considerable; worthy of consideration, powerful; numerous; large; important

consideración, f. consideration, attention; reflection, thought; civility; importance. en c. de, considering

considerado, a. considerate; prudent; distinguished; important

considerar, v.t. to consider, reflect upon; treat with consideration (persons); judge, estimate

consigna, f. (mil.) watchword; left luggage office

consignador (-ra), s. (com.) consigner, sender

consignar, v.t. to assign, lay aside; deposit; (com.) consign; entrust, commit · put in writing; (law) deposit in trust

consignatario, m. (law) trustee; mortgagee; (com.) consignee. c. de buques, shipping-agent

consigo, pers. pron. 3rd sing. and pl. m. and f. with himself, herself, oneself, yourself, yourselves, themselves

consiguiente, a. consequent, resulting. m. consequence. por c., in consequence

consistencia, f. solidity; consistence, density; consistency, congruity; relevance

consistente, a. of a certain consistency; solid

consistir, v.i. (with en) to consist in; be comprised of; be the result of

consistorio, m. consistory; municipal council (in some Spanish towns); town hall

consola, f. console table; piertable; (mech.) bracket

cónsola, f. radio cabinet

consolable, a. consolable

consolación, f. consolation

consolador (-ra), s. comforter, consoler

consolar, v.t. irr. to comfort, console. See contar

consolidación, f. consolidation; stiffening

consolidar, v.t. to consolidate; strengthen; combine, unite; v.r. (law) unite

consonancia, f. harmony; agreement

consonante, a. consonant, consistent. m. rhyme. f. (gram.) consonant

consorcio, m. partnership; trust; intimacy, common life

consorte, m. and f. consort; companion, associate, partner; spouse

conspicuo, a. outstanding, distinguished; conspicuous

conspiración, f. conspiracy

conspirador (-ra), s. conspirator

conspirar, v.i. to conspire; plot, scheme; tend, combine

constancia, f. constancy, steadfastness; stability, steadiness

constante, a. constant; durable; (mech.) steady, non-oscillating. m. constant

constar, v.i. to be evident, be clear; (with de) be composed of, consist of, comprise

constelación, f. (ast.) constellation; climate

consternación, f. dismay, alarm

consternarse, v.r. to be dismayed or alarmed

constipado, m. (med.) cold; chill

constiparse, v.r. to catch a cold or chill

constitución, f. constitution (also pol., med., law)

constitucional, a. constitutional

constituir, v.t. to constitute, form; found, establish; (with en) appoint, nominate; (fig.) place in

(a difficult situation, etc.); *v.r.*
(*with en* or *por*) be appointed or
authorized; be under (an obligation). See **huir**

constituyente, constitutivo, *a.*
and *m.* constituent

constreñir, *v.t. irr.* to constrain,
oblige; constrict; constipate. See
ceñir

constricción, *f.* constriction; contraction, shrinkage

construcción, *f.* construction;
art or process of construction;
fabric, structure; (*gram.*) -con-
struction; building, erection. **c.
de caminos,** road making. **c.
naval,** shipbuilding

constructor (**-ra**), *a.* building,
constructive. *s.* builder; constructor

construir, *v.t. irr.* to construct;
build, make; (*gram.*) construct.
See **huir**

consuelo, *m.* consolation; comfort, solace; joy, delight

cónsul, *m.* consul

consulado, *m.* consulate. **C.
general,** Consulate General

consular, *a.* consular

consulta, *f.* deliberation, consideration; advice; reference;
conference, consultation

consultar, *v.t.* to discuss, consider; seek advice, consult. **c.
con la almohada,** (*fig.*) to sleep
on (a problem, etc.)

consultor (**-ra**), *a.* consultative,
advisory; consulting. *s.* consultant; adviser

consultorio, *m.* (*med.*) consulting
rooms; surgery; technical information bureau

consumación, *f.* consummation;
completion, attainment; extinction, end

consumado, *a.* consummate;
(*fam.*) thorough, perfect

consumar, *v.t.* to consummate;
complete, accomplish, perfect

consumido, *a.* (*fam.*) emaciated,
wasted away; timid, spiritless

consumidor (**-ra**), *a.* consuming.
s. consumer, user

consumir, *v.t.* to destroy; consume, use; waste away, wear
away; (*ecc.*) take communion;
(*fam.*) grieve; *v.r.* be destroyed;
(*fam.*) be consumed with grief

consumo, *m.* consumption; de-

mand. **c. de combustible,** fuel
consumption

contabilidad, *f.* book-keeping;
accounts; accounting

contable, *m.* book-keeper

contacto, *m.* contact (also *elec.,
mil.*)

contado, *a.* few; infrequent; rare.
al c., (*com.*) cash down. **por de
c.,** presumably; of course, naturally

contador, *a.* counting. *m.* accountant; (*law*) auditor; counter (in banks); (*elec.*) meter,
counter; (*naut.*) purser

contaduría, *f.* accountancy;
counting house; accountant's
office; auditorship; (*theat.*) box-
office; (*naut.*) purser's office

contagiar, *v.t.* to infect; corrupt,
pervert; *v.r.* (*with con, de* or *por*)
be infected by or through

contagio, *m.* infection; contagious
disease; (*fig.*) contagion, perversion, corruption

contagiosidad, *f.* infectiousness;
(*fig.*) contagiousness

contagioso, *a.* infectious; (*fig.*)
catching, contagious

contaminación, *f.* contamination

contaminar, *v.t.* to pollute, contaminate; infect; (*fig.*) corrupt

contante, *a.* ready (of money)

contar, *v.t. irr.* to count; recount, tell; place to account;
include, count among; *v.i.* calculate, compute. **c. con,** to
rely upon; reckon upon. *Pres.
Ind.* **cuento, cuentas, cuenta,
cuentan.** *Pres. Subjunc.* **cuente,
cuentes, cuente, cuenten**

contemplación, *f.* meditation,
contemplation; consideration

contemplar, *v.t.* to consider, reflect upon; look at, contemplate;
indulge, please

contemplativo, *a.* (*ecc.*) contemplative; reflective, thoughtful; kind, indulgent

contemporáneo (**-ea**), *a.* contemporaneous. *s.* contemporary

contemporización, *f.* temporizing

contemporizador, *a.* temporizing

contemporizar, *v.i.* to temporize, gain time

contencioso, *a.* contentious, argumentative; (*law*) litigious

contender, *v.i. irr.* to contain; restrain, hold back; comprise; *v.r.* control oneself. See **entender**

contendiente, *m.* and *f.* contestant

contener, *v.t. irr.* to contain; include; comprise; hold back; restrain; check, repress; hold down, subdue; suppress, put down; *v.r.* contain oneself; keep one's temper; keep quiet; refrain. See **tener**

contenido, *m.* contents. *a.* contained; (*fig.*) restrained; reserved (of persons)

contentamiento, *m.* contentment

contentar, *v.t.* to satisfy, please; (*com.*) endorse; *v.r.* be pleased or satisfied

contento, *a.* happy; content; satisfied; pleased. *m.* pleasure; contentment. **no caber de c.,** to be overjoyed

contera, *f.* ferrule (of umbrella, etc.); refrain

contestación, *f.* reply, answer; discussion, argument, dispute

contestar, *v.t.* to reply, answer; confirm, attest; *v.i.* accord, harmonize

contexto, *m.* context

contextura, *f.* structure; context; physique, frame

contienda, *f.* struggle, fight; quarrel, dispute; discussion

contigo, *pers. pron.* 2nd sing. *m.* and *f.* with thee, with you

contigüidad, *f.* proximity, nearness

contiguo, *a.* adjacent, near

continencia, *f.* moderation, self-restraint; continence; chastity; containing

continental, *a.* continental. *m.* express messenger service

continente, *a.* continent. *m.* container; demeanour, bearing; (*geog.*) continent; mainland

contingencia, *f.* contingency; risk, danger

contingente, *a.* incidental; fortuitous; dependent; *m.* (*mil.*) task-force, contingent

continuación, *f.* continuation; prolongation; sequel (of a story, etc.)

continuador (-ra), *s.* continuer

continuar, *v.t.* to continue; *v.i.*

continue; last, remain, go on; *v.r.* be prolonged

continuidad, *f.* continuity

continuo, *a.* continuous, steady, uninterrupted; persevering; tenacious; persistent, lasting, unremitting. *m.* a united whole. **de c.,** continuously

contonearse, *v.r.* to swing the hips (in walking); strut

contorno, *m.* contour, outline; (gen. *pl.*) environs, surrounding district

contorsión, *f.* contortion

contorsionista, *m.* contortionist

contra, *prep.* against, counter, athwart; opposed to, hostile to; in front of, opposite; towards. *m.* opposite view or opinion. *f.* (*fam.*) difficulty, trouble. **c. la corriente,** upstream. **el pro y el c.,** the pros and cons. **en c.,** in opposition, against

contraalmirante, *m.* rear-admiral

contraataque, *m.* (*mil.*) counter-attack

contraaviso, *m.* countermand

contrabajo, *m.* (*mus.*) double-bass; player of this instrument; deep bass voice

contrabalancear, *v.t.* to counterbalance; (*fig.*) compensate

contrabandista, *a.* smuggling. *m.* and *f.* smuggler

contrabando, *m.* contraband; smuggling

contracción, *f.* contraction; shrinkage; abridgment; abbreviation

contráctil, *a.* contractile

contradanza, *f.* square dance

contradecir, *v.t. irr.* to contradict; *v.r.* contradict oneself. See **decir**

contradicción, *f.* contradiction

contradictorio, *a.* contradictory

contraer, *v.t. irr.* to shrink, reduce in size, shorten; abridge; contract (matrimony, obligations); (*fig.*) acquire (diseases, habits); *v.r.* shorten, contract, shrink. See **traer**

contrafuerte, *m.* buttress, counterfort, abutment; (*geog.*) spur

contrahacer, *v.t. irr.* to forge, counterfeit; mimic; imitate. See **hacer**

contrahecho, *a.* deformed

contralto, *m.* contralto (voice)

contraluz, *f.* counterlight

contramaestre, *m.* (*naut.*) boatswain; overseer, superintendent, foreman

contramarcha, *f.* retrogression; (*mil.*) countermarch

contramedida, *f.* counter-measure

contraorden, *f.* countermand

contrapedalear, *v.i.* to backpedal

contrapelo, *a. adv.* the wrong way of the hair, against the grain; (*fam.*) reluctantly, distastefully

contrapeso, *m.* counterpoise, counterweight; balancing-pole (acrobats); (*fig.*) counterbalance; makeweight

contraponer, *v.t. irr.* to compare; place opposite; oppose. See poner

contraproducente, *a.* counteractive, self-deceiving

contrapuesto, *a.* opposing, divergent

contrapunto, *m.* (*mus.*) counterpoint

contrariar, *v.t.* to counter, oppose; impede; vex, annoy

contrariedad, *f.* contrariety, opposition; obstacle; vexation, trouble

contrario (-ia), *a.* opposite; hostile, opposed; harmful; adverse, contrary. *s.* adversary; opponent. *m.* obstacle. *f.* contraria, contrary opposite. al contrario, on the contrary. llevar la contraria (a), to oppose; contradict

Contrarreforma, *f.* Counter-Reformation

contrasentido, *m.* wrong sense, opposite sense (of words); contradiction of initial premise; nonsense

contraseña, *f.* countersign; (*mil.*) password

contrastar, *v.t.* to contrast; oppose, resist; check (weights and measures); assay; (*mech.*) calibrate, gauge; *v.i.* contrast

contraste, *m.* contrast; opposition, difference; weights and measures inspector; dispute, clash

contrata, *f.*, contrato, *m.* contract. contrato de arrendamiento, lease

contratación, *f.* hiring; (*com.*) transaction; commerce, trade

contratar, *v.t.* to contract, enter into an agreement; make a bargain (with), deal (with); hire, contract

contratiempo, *m.* mishap, accident

contratista, *m.* and *f.* contractor

contratorpedero, *m.* torpedo-boat destroyer

contravención, *f.* contravention

contraveneno, *m.* (*med.*) antidote; remedy, precaution

contravenir, *v.t. irr.* to infringe, contravene. See venir

contraventana, *f.* shutter (for windows)

contravidriera, *f.* storm-window

contrayente, *a.* contracting. *m.* and *f.* contracting party (used of matrimony)

contribución, *f.* contribution; tax. c. sobre la propiedad, property tax

contribuir, *v.t. irr.* to pay (taxes); contribute. See huir

contribuyente, *a.* contributing; contributory. *m.* and *f.* contributor; taxpayer

contrición, *f.* contrition

contrincante, *m.* competitor, candidate (public examinations); rival, opponent

contrito, *a.* contrite

control, *m.* control; checking. c. de precios, price control

controlar, *v.t.* to control

controversia, *f.* controversy

controvertir, *v.i.* and *v.t. irr.* to dispute, argue against, deny. See sentir

contumacia, *f.* obstinacy; (*law*) contumacy

contumaz, *a.* stubborn; impenitent; (*law*) contumacious; (*med.*) obstinate, resistant (to cure)

contumelia, *f.* contumely

conturbar, *v.t.* to perturb, make anxious, disturb; *v.r.* be perturbed

contuso, *a.* contused, bruised

convalecencia, *f.* convalescence; convalescent home

convalecer, *v.i. irr.* to convalesce, get better; (*fig.*) recover, regain (influence, etc.). See **conocer**

convaleciente, *a*. and *m*. and *f*. convalescent

convalidar, *v.t.* to ratify, confirm

convecino, *a*. nearby; neighbouring

convencedor, *a*. convincing

convencer, *v.t.* to convince; prove beyond doubt, demonstrate to (persons); *v.r.* be convinced

convencimiento, *m*. conviction, belief, assurance

convención, *f*. pact, formal agreement; harmony, conformity; convention (also *pol.*)

convencional, *a*. conventional (all meanings)

convencionalismo, *m*. conventionality

convenido, *a*. agreed

conveniencia, *f*. conformity, harmony, adjustment; experience, suitability, convenience; advantage; agreement, pact; post as domestic; ease, comfort; *pl.* income; social conventions

conveniente, *a*. convenient, opportune; suitable, fitting; profitable; useful; decorous

convenio, *m*. pact, treaty; (*com.*) agreement, contract

convenir, *v.i. irr.* to agree; assemble, congregate; belong; be suitable; *v.r.* agree; suit oneself. **No me conviene salir esta tarde,** It does not suit me to go out this afternoon. **Me convendría pasar un mes allí,** It would be a good idea (or a wise plan) for me to spend a month there. See **venir**

convento, *m*. convent; monastery; religious community

conventual, *a*. conventual; monastic. *m*. (*ecc.*) conventual

convergencia, *f*. convergence

convergir, *v.i.* to converge; (*fig.*) coincide (views, etc.)

conversación, *f*. conversation; intercourse, company; (*law*) criminal conversation

conversar, *v.i.* to converse; chat; live with others; know socially

conversión, *f*. conversion; change, transformation; (*com.*) conversion; (*mil.*) wheel; wheeling

converso (-sa), *s*. convert

convertible, *a*. convertible

convertir, *v.t. irr.* to change, transform; convert; reform; *v.r.* be transformed; be converted; be reformed. See **sentir**

convexidad, *f*. convexity

convexo, *a*. convex

convicción, *f*. conviction; certitude; (*law*) conviction

convicto (-ta), *a*. and *s*. (*law*) convict

convidado (-da), *s*. guest

convidar, *v.t.* to invite (persons); encourage, provoke; entice, attract; *v.r.* invite oneself; offer one's services

convincente, *a*. convincing

convite, *m*. invitation; banquet; party

convivencia, *f*. common life, life together

convivial, *a*. convivial

convivir, *v.i.* to live together, live under the same roof

convocación, *f*. convocation

convocar, *v.t.* to convene, convoke

convoy, *m*. convoy; escort; following; cruet-stand

convoyar, *v.t.* to convoy, escort

convulsión, *f*. convulsion

convulsivo, *a*. convulsive

conyugal, *a*. conjugal

cónyuge, *m*. and *f*. husband or (and) wife (used gen. in *pl.*)

coñac, *m*. brandy

cooperación, *f*. co-operation

coöperador (-ra), *a*. co-operative. *s*. co-operator, collaborator

cooperar, *v.t.* to co-operate

cooperativa, *f*. co-operative society

cooperativo, *a*. co-operative

coordenada, *f*. (*math.*) co-ordinate

coordinación, *f*. co-ordination

coordinar, *v.t.* to co-ordinate, classify

copa, *f*. wineglass, goblet; glassful; top branches (of trees); crown (of hat); (*cards*) heart; gill (liquid measure); (*fam.*) drink, glass; *pl.* (*cards*) hearts (in Spanish pack, goblets)

copartícipe, *m*. and *f*. co-partner, partaker, participant

copec, *m*. kopeck

copernicano, *a*. Copernican

copero, *m.* cupbearer; sideboard; cocktail cabinet

copete, *m.* lock, tress (hair); tuft, crest; forelock (horses); head, top (ice-cream, drinks); (*fam.*) **de alto c.,** aristocratic; socially prominent

copia, *f.* abundance, plenty; copy, reproduction; transcript; imitation

copiador (-ra), *a.* copying. *s.* copier; transcriber. *m.* copybook

copiar, *v.t.* to copy

copioso, *a.* abundant, plentiful

copla, *f.* couplet; popular four-line poem; couple, pair; *pl.* (*fam.*) verses

coplero (-ra), *s.* balladmonger; poetaster

copo, *m.* cop (of a spindle); snowflake

copón, *m.* large goblet; (*ecc.*) ciborium, chalice

copropietario (-ia), *s.* co-proprietor

cóptico, *a.* Coptic. *m.* Coptic language

copto (-ta), *s.* Copt

cópula, *f.* connection; coupling; joining; copulation

copularse, *v.r.* to copulate

coque, *m.* coke

coqueluche, *f.* whooping cough

coqueta, *f.* coquette, flirt

coquetear, *v.i.* to flirt

coqueteo, *m.* coquetry; flirtation

coquetería, *f.* coquetry

coquetón, *a.* coquettish

coracero, *m.* cuirassier

coraje, *m.* **courage, valour;** anger

coral, *m.* coral. *f.* coral snake. *m.* (*bot.*) coral tree; *pl.* coral beads

coral, *a.* choral

coralina, *f.* coral (polyp).

coraza, *f.* cuirass; shell (of tortoise); armour-plate, armour (ships, etc.)

corazón, *m.* heart; courage, spirit; love, tenderness; goodwill, benevolence; core (of a fruit); (*fig.*) pith. **de c.,** sincerely. **tener el c. en la mano,** to wear one's heart on one's sleeve

corazonada, *f.* feeling, instinct; presentiment, apprehension

corbata, *f.* necktie; scarf; ribbon (insignia)

corbatería, *f.* necktie shop

corbatero (-ra), *s.* tie seller

corbeta, *f.* (*naut.*) corvette

corcel, *m.* charger or battle horse

corcova, *f.* hump, abnormal protuberance

corcovado (-da), *a.* hunchbacked, crooked. *s.* hunchback

corcovear, *v.i.* to curvet, caper

corchea, *f.* (*mus.*) quaver

corchete, *m.* (*sew.*) hook and eye; hook

corcho, *m.* (*bot.*) cork, cork bark; stopper, cork; cork mat; bee hive

cordaje, *m.* (*naut.*) cordage, tackling, rope

cordel, *m.* cord; (*naut.*) line. **a c.,** in a straight line

cordelería, *f.* rope making; ropeyard; cordage

cordelero (-ra), *s.* rope maker

cordera, *f.* ewe lamb; sweet, gentle woman

cordero, *m.* lamb; dressed lambskin; peaceable, mild man; Jesus (gen. **Divino C.**)

cordial, *a.* warming, invigorating; affectionate, loving, friendly. *m.* (*med.*) cordial

cordialidad, *f.* cordiality, friendliness

cordillera, *f.* mountain range

cordobán, *m.* cured goatskin; Cordovan leather, Spanish leather

cordobés (-esa), *a.* and *s.* Cordovan

cordón, *m.* cord; cordon; (*ecc.*) rope girdle; (*arch.*) string-course

cordoncillo, *m.* rib (in cloth); ridge, milling (of coins); (*sew.*) piping

cordura, *f.* good sense, prudence

coreografía, *f.* choreography; art of dancing

coreográfico, *a.* choreographic

coreógrafo, *m.* choreographer

coriambo, *m.* choriamb

corintio (-ia), *a.* and *s.* Corinthian

corista, *m.* (*ecc.*) chorister. *m.* and *f.* (*theat.*) member of the chorus

coriza, *f.* (*med.*) coryza

cormorán, *m.* (*orn.*) cormorant

cornada, *f.* horn thrust or wound (bulls, etc.)

cornalina, *f.* (*min.*) cornelian

cornamenta, *f.* horns (bulls, deer, etc.)

córnea, *f.* cornea

corneja, *f.* (*orn.*) carrion or black crow

córneo, *a.* horny, corneous

corneta, *f.* (*mus.*) bugle; (*mus.*) cornet; swineherd's horn; (*mil.*) pennon. *m.* bugler; (*mil.*) cornet. **c. de monte**, hunting horn

cornetín, *m. dim.* **corneta**, (*mus.*) cornet; cornet player

cornezuelo, *m. dim.* little horn; (*med.*) ergot; (*bot.*) variety of olive

cornisa, *f.* (*arch.*) cornice

cornucopia, *f.* cornucopia, horn of plenty; sconce; mirror

cornudo, *a.* horned. *m.* cuckold

coro, *m.* choir; chorus; (*arch.*) choir. **hacer c. (a)**, to listen to, support. **saber de c.**, to know by heart

corola, *f.* (*bot.*) corolla

corolario, *m.* corollary

corona, *f.* garland, wreath; halo; (*ast., arch.*) corona; crown (of tooth); crown (of head); tonsure; crown (coin); royal power; kingdom; triumph; reward; summit, height, peak; circlet (for candles)

coronación, *f.* coronation; coping-stone

coronamiento, *m.* coronation; coping-stone; (*fig.*) crowning touch; (*naut.*) taffrail

coronar, *v.t.* to crown; crown (in draughts); complete, round off; *v.r.* be crowned; crown oneself; be tipped or capped

coronel, *m.* colonel

coronela, *f.* (*fam.*) colonel's wife

coronelía, *f.* colonelcy

coronilla, *f. dim.* small crown; crown of head; (*fig., fam.*) **estar hasta la c.**, to be fed up

coroza, *f.* dunce's cap

corpiño, *m.* bodice

corporación, *f.* corporation, body, association

corporal, *a.* and *m.* (*ecc.*) corporal

corporativo, *a.* corporate, corporative

corpóreo, *a.* corporeal

corpulento, *a.* corpulent, stout

Corpus, *m.* (*ecc.*) Corpus Christi

corpúsculo, *m.* corpuscle

corral, *m.* yard; pen, enclosure, corral; old-time theatre. **c. de madera**, timber yard. (*fam.*) **hacer corrales**, to play truant

correa, *f.* leather strap or thong;

flexibility; (*mech.*) belt, band

corrección, *f.* correction; correctness; punishment; emendation

correcional, *a.* correctional. *m.* reformatory

correctivo, *a.* and *m.* corrective

correcto, *a.* correct; well-bred; unexceptionable, irreproachable; regular (of features)

corredera, *f.* link (engines); (*mech.*) slide; (*naut.*) log; race-course; (*fam.*) procuress

corredizo, *a.* easy to untie; running (of knots); sliding

corredor (-ra), *s.* runner. *m.* (*com.*) broker; corridor; (*fam.*) meddler; (*fam.*) procurer, pimp. *a.* running. **c. de bolsa**, stock-broker

corregible, *a.* corrigible

corregidor, *m.* Spanish magistrate; (*ant.*) mayor

corregidora, *f.* wife of corregidor; mayoress

corregir, *v.t. irr.* to correct; scold, punish; moderate, counteract; (*mech.*) adjust; *v.r.* mend one's ways. *Pres. Ind.* **corrijo**, **corriges**, **corrige**, **corrigen**. *Pres. Part.* **corrigiendo**. *Pres. Subjunc.* **corrija**, **corrijas**, etc. *Imperf. Subjunc.* **corrigiese**, etc.

correlación, *f.* correlation

correligionario (-ia), *s.* co-religionist; fellow-supporter or believer

correo, *m.* courier; mail (also *pl.*); post-office; post, letters. **c. aéreo**, air-mail. **c. certificado**, registered post. **a vuelta de c.**, by return of post. **tren c.**, mail train

correoso, *a.* leathery, tough

correr, *v.i.* to run; race; sail, steam; flow; blow; flood; extend, stretch; pass (of time); fall due (salary, etc.); be current or general; (*with con*) be in charge of or responsible for; *v.t.* run (a horse); fasten, slide (bolts, etc.); draw (curtains); undergo, suffer; sell, auction; (*fam.*) steal; (*fig.*) embarrass; spread (a rumour, etc.); *v.r.* slide, glide, slip; run (of colours); (*fam.*) spread oneself, talk too much

correría, *f.* raid, foray; excursion, trip

correspondencia, *f.* relationship;

connection; intercourse, communication; correspondence, letters; equivalence, exact translation

corresponder, *v.i.* to requite, repay; be grateful; belong to, concern; devolve upon, fall to; suit, harmonize (with); fit; *v.r.* correspond by letters; like or love each other

correspondiente, *a.* suitable; proportionate; corresponding. *m.* and *f.* correspondent

corresponsal, *m.* and *f.* correspondent (especially professional); (*com.*) agent

corretear, *v.i.* to wander about the streets; gad

correveidile, *m.* and *f.* (*fam.*) tale-bearer, gossip

corrida, *f.* race, run; (*aer.*) taxying; bull fight (abb. for **c. de toros**)

corrido, *a.* extra, over (of weight); embarrassed; experienced

corriente, *a.* current, present; well-known; usual, customary; fluent (style); ordinary, average; easy. *f.* flow, stream; (*fig.*) course (of events, etc.); (*elec.*) current. *adv.* quite, exactly. (*elec.*) **c. alterna,** alternating current. **c. continua,** direct current. **c. de aire,** draught. **estar al c.,** to be informed (of something)

corrillo, *m.* knot, group, huddle (of people)

corro, *m.* circle, group; ring (for children's games)

corroboración; *f.* corroboration, confirmation

corroborar, *v.t.* to fortify; corroborate, support

corroborativo, *a.* corroborative

corroer, *v.t. irr.* to corrode, waste away; (*fig.*) gnaw. See roer

corromper, *v.t.* to rot; mar; spoil, ruin; seduce; corrupt (texts); bribe; (*fig.*) contaminate, corrupt; *v.i.* stink; *v.r.* putrefy, rot; be spoilt; (*fig.*) be corrupted

corrosión, *f.* corrosion

corrosivo, *a.* corrosive

corrugación, *f.* corrugation, wrinkling

corrupción, *f.* rot, putrefaction; corruption, depravity; decay; stink; bribery; falsification (of texts); corruption (of language, etc.)

corrupto, *a.* corrupt

corruptor (-ra), *s.* corrupter

corsario, *m.* pirate; privateer

corsé, *m.* corset

corsetería, *f.* corset shop or manufactory

corso (-sa), *a.* and *s.* Corsican

corta, *f.* felling, cutting

cortacircuitos, *m.* (*elec.*) circuit breaker, cut-out; disconnecting switch

cortado, *a.* fitting, proportioned; disjointed (style); confused, shamefaced

cortador, *m.* cutter; cutter-out (dresses, etc.); butcher

cortadura, *f.* cut, wound; cutting (from periodicals); defile; *pl.* clippings, cuttings

cortafrío, *m.* cold chisel; (*carp.*) hammer-head chisel

cortalápices, *m.* pencil-sharpener

cortante, *a.* cutting; sharp; piercing (of wind, etc.); trenchant

cortapapel, *m.* paper-knife

cortapisa, *f.* condition, stipulation

cortaplumas, *m.* penknife

cortapuros, *m.* cigar cutter

cortar, *v.t.* to cut; cut out (dresses, etc.); switch off, shut off (water, electricity, etc.); cleave, divide; cut (cards); pierce (wind, etc.); interrupt, impede; omit, cut; (*fig.*) interrupt (conversation); decide, determine; *v.r.* be confused or shamefaced; curdle; split, fray; chap

cortavidrios, *m.* diamond, glass-cutter

cortaviento, *m.* windscreen

corte, *f.* court (royal); retinue; yard; *pl.* Spanish parliament. *m.* cutting, cut; blade, cutting edge; cutting out, dressmaking; length, material required for garment, shoes, etc.; cut, fit; style; book edge; (*arch.*) section; means, expedient

cortedad, *f.* shortness, brevity; smallness; stupidity, dullness; timidity, shyness

cortejar, *v.t.* to accompany, escort; woo, court

cortejo, *m.* courtship, wooing; suite, accompaniment; gift, present; homage, attention; (*fam*) lover, beau

cortés, *a*. polite, attentive, courteous, civil

cortesana, *f*. courtesan

cortesano, *a*. court; courtly. *m*. courtier

cortesía, *f*. politeness, courtesy; attentiveness; civility; gift, present; favour

corteza, *f*. (*bot*.) bark; (*anat*.) cortex; skin, peel, crust; aspect, appearance; roughness

cortijo, *m*. farmhouse and land

cortina, *f*. curtain; (*fig*.) veil; (*fam*.) heel taps; (*mil*.) curtain, screen. **c. de fuego de artillería**, anti-aircraft barrage. **c. de globos de intercepción**, balloon barrage. **c. de humo**, smoke screen

cortinaje, *m*. curtains, hangings

corto, *a*. short, brief; timid, bashful; concise; defective; stupid, dull; tongue-tied, inarticulate. **c. circuito**, (*elec*.) short-circuit. **c. de alcances**, dull-witted. **c. de vista**, short-sighted

coruscar, *v.i.* to glitter, shine

corva, *f*. bend of the knee

corvadura, *f*. bend; curvature

corveta, *f*. curvet, prancing

corvetear, *v.i.* to curvet

corzo, *m*. (*zool*.) roe-deer, fallow-deer

cosa, *f*. thing. **c. rara**, strange to relate; an extraordinary thing. **como si tal c.**, as though nothing had happened. (*fam*.) **poquita c.**, a person of no account

cosaco (-ca), *a*. and *s*. Cossack

coscorrón, *m*. blow on the head, cuff

cosecha, *f*. harvest; harvest time; reaping, gathering, lifting; yield, produce; crop, shower (of honours, etc.). **c. de vino**, vintage

cosechar, *v.i.* and *v.t.* to harvest, reap

coseno, *m*. (*math*.) cosine

coser, *v.t.* to sew, stitch; join, unite; press together (lips, etc.). **c. a puñaladas**, to stab repeatedly

cosmético, *a*. and *m*. cosmetic

cósmico, *a*. cosmic

cosmografía, *f*. cosmography

cosmógrafo, *m*. cosmographer

cosmopolita, *a*. and *m*. and *f*. cosmopolitan

cosmopolitismo, *m*. cosmopolitanism

cosmos, *m*. cosmos

cosquillas, *f. pl*. tickling. **hacer c.** (a), to tickle

cosquillear, *v.t.* to tickle

cosquilleo, *m*. tickle, tickling

cosquilloso, *a*. ticklish; hypersensitive, touchy

costa, *f*. cost; expense; coast; *pl*. (*law*) costs. **a c. de**, by dint of; at the cost of. **a toda c.**, at all costs

costado, *m*. (*anat*.) side; (*mil*.) flank; side; *pl*. line of descent, genealogy. (*naut*.) **dar el c.**, to be broadside on

costal, *m*. sack, bag

costanero, *a*. sloping; coast, coastal

costar, *v.i.* *irr*. to cost; cause. See **contar**

costarriqueño (-ña), *a*. and *s*. Costa-Rican

coste, *m*. cost, price

costear, *v.t.* to pay for, defray the expense of; (*naut*.) coast; *v.r.* pay (for itself)

costilla, *f*. (*anat*., *aer*., *naut*., *arch*.) rib; (*fig*., *fam*.) better half, wife; *pl*. (*fam*.) back, behind

costillaje, **costillar**, *m*. (*anat*.) ribs; (*naut*.) ship's frame

costoso, *a*. expensive, costly; valuable; dear, costly, difficult

costra, *f*. crust; scab; rind (of cheese)

costumbre, *f*. habit; custom

costumbrista, *m*. and *f*. writer on everyday life and customs. *a*. (of literary work) dealing with life and customs

costura, *f*. sewing; seam; needlework; (*carp*.) joint; riveting

costurera, *f*. seamstress

costurero, *m*. work-box, sewing-bag

cota, *f*. (*surv*.) elevation, height; coat (of mail); quota. **c. de malla**, chain-mail

cotangente, *f*. (*math*.) cotangent

cotejar, *v.t.* to compare; collate

cotejo, *m*. comparison; collation

cótel, *m*. cocktail, drink

cotelera, *f*. cocktail shaker

cotí, *m*. ticking (cloth)

cotidiano, *a*. daily

cotiledón, *m*. (*bot*.) cotyledon

cotillón, *m*. cotillion (dance)

cotizable, *a.* valued at; (of prices, shares) quoted

cotización, *f.* (*com.*) quotation; (*com.*) rate. **boletín de c.,** price list (of shares, etc.)

cotizar, *v.t.* (*com.*) to quote (prices, rates)

coto, *m.* enclosed ground; boundary stone; preserve, covert; hand's breadth; end, stop, limit. **c. de caza,** game preserve

cotorra, *f.* small green parrot; magpie; (*fam.*) chatterbox

cotufa, *f.* earthnut; titbit; (*fam.*) **pedir cotufas en el golfo,** to ask for the moon

coturno, *m.* buskin

coy, *m.* (*naut.*) hammock

coyuntura, *f.* (*anat.*) joint; juncture, occasion

coz, *f.* kick, recoil (of gun); butt (of a rifle); (*fam.*) slap in the face, unprovoked rudeness. **dar coces,** to kick

craneal, *a.* cranial

cráneo, *m.* cranium, skull

crápula, *f.* drunkenness; depravity, immorality, debauchery

crasitud, *f.* greasiness; fatness; crassness

craso, *a.* fat, greasy; thick; unpardonable, crass (often with *ignorancia*). *m.* fatness; ignorance

creación, *f.* creation; universe, world; foundation, establishment; appointment (dignitaries)

creador (-ra), *s.* creator, originator. *m.* God. *a.* creative

crear, *v.t.* to create; found, institute, establish; make, appoint

crecer, *v.i. irr.* to grow; grow up; increase in size; grow longer; wax (moon); come in (of the tide); increase in value (money); *v.r.* become more sure of oneself; swell with pride; grow in authority. See **nacer**

creces, *f. pl.* increase, interest. **con c.,** fully, amply. **pagar con c.,** (*fig.*) to pay with interest

crecida, *f.* swollen river or stream; flood; rising (of the tide)

crecido, *a.* grown up; considerable; abundant, plentiful; large; full; serious, important

crecidos, *m. pl.* widening stitches (knitting)

creciente, *a.* growing; rising (of the tide); crescent (moon). *m.* (*her.*) crescent. *f.* rising of the tide; crescent moon

crecimiento, *m.* growing; growth, development; increase (in value, money); waxing (of moon)

credencial, *a.* accrediting

credenciales, *f. pl.* credentials

credibilidad, *f.* credibility

crédito, *m.* belief, credence; assent, acquiescence; reputation, name; favour, popularity, acceptance; (*com.*) credit; (*com.*) letter of credit. **créditos activos,** assets. **créditos pasivos,** liabilities. **a c.,** on credit

credo, *m.* creed. (*fam.*) **en un c.,** in a jiffy

credulidad, *f.* credulity

crédulo, *a.* credulous

creencia, *f.* belief; religion, sect, faith

creer, *v.t. irr.* to believe; think, consider, opine; think likely or probable. **¡Ya lo creo!** I should just think so! Rather! *Pres. Part.* creyendo. *Preterite* creyó, creyeron. *Imperf. Subjunc.* creyese, etc.

creíble, *a.* credible

crema, *f.* cream (off milk); custard mould, cream, shape; face cream; cold cream; elect, flower (of society, etc.)

cremación, *f.* cremation; burning, incineration

cremallera, *f.* (*mech.*) rack, ratch; zip fastener. **colgar la c.,** to give a house-warming

crematorio, *m.* crematorium. *a.* burning; cremating

cremor, *m.* (*chem.*) cream of tartar

cremoso, *a.* creamy

crencha, *f.* parting (of the hair); each side of parting

creosota, *f.* creosote

crepitación, *f.* crackling, sputtering; hissing; roar (of a fire); (*med.*) crepitation

crepitar, *v.i.* to crackle; sputter; hiss; roar (of a fire); (*med.*) crepitate

crepuscular, *a.* twilight

crepúsculo, *m.* twilight, half light

cresa, *f.* maggot; cheese-mite; fly's egg

crespo, *a.* curly, frizzy (hair);

rough (of animal's fur); curled (leaves); artificial, involved (style)

crespón, *m.* crape

cresta, *f.* comb (of cock, etc.); tuft, topknot (birds); plume; summit, top (of mountains); crest (of a wave); (*her.*) crest

crestado, *a.* crested

creta, *f.* chalk

cretáceo, *a.* chalky

cretense, *a.* Cretan

cretinismo, *m.* (*med.*) cretinism

cretino (-na), *a.* and *s.* cretin

cretona, *f.* cretonne

creyente, *a.* believing; religious. *m.* and *f.* believer

cría, *f.* rearing; bringing up; nursing; suckling; breeding; brood; litter

criada, *f.* servant, maid

criadero, *m.* (*min.*) vein, deposit; tree nursery, plantation; breeding farm or place. *a.* prolific

criado, *m.* servant. *a.* bred, brought up (used with *bien* or *mal*, well *or* badly brought up)

criador (-ra), *s.* breeder, keeper, raiser. *a.* creating; rearing; creative; fertile, rich

crianza, *f.* feeding, suckling; lactation; manners. **buena (or mala) c.,** good (or bad) breeding or upbringing

criar, *v.t.* to create; procreate; rear, educate, bring up; feed, nurse, suckle; raise (birds, animals); inspire, give rise to. **Me crié raquítico,** I grew up delicate

criatura, *f.* being, creature; man, human being; infant; small child; fœtus; (*fig.*) puppet, tool

criba, *f.* sieve, cribble

cribar, *v.t.* to sieve; riddle (earth, etc.)

crimen, *m.* crime

criminal, *a.* and *m.* criminal

criminalidad, *f.* guilt; crime ratio; delinquency

criminalista, *m.* criminal lawyer; criminologist

criminología, *f.* criminology

crin, *f.* horsehair; (gen. *pl.*) mane

crinolina, *f.* crinoline

crío, *m.* (*fam.*) kid, brat

criollo (-lla), *a.* and *s.* creole. *a.* indigenous, native

cripta, *f.* crypt

criptografía, *f.* cryptography

criquet, *m.* (*sport*) cricket

crisálida, *f.* chrysalis

crisantemo, *m.* chrysanthemum

crisis, *f.* crisis. **c. de vivienda,** housing shortage

crisma, *m.* or *f.* (*eco.*) chrism

crisol, *m.* crucible; melting-pot

crispar, *v.t.* to cause to contract or twitch; *v.r.* twitch. (*fam.*) Se me crispan los nervios, My nerves are all on edge

cristal, *m.* crystal; glass; window-pane; mirror; water. **c. tallado,** cut glass

cristalería, *f.* glassware; glass manufacture; glass panes; glass and china shop

cristalino, *a.* crystalline. *m.* lens (of the eye)

cristalización, *f.* crystallization

cristalizar, *v.i.* to crystallize; (*fig.*) take shape; *v.t.* cause to crystallize

cristalografía, *f.* crystallography

cristiandad, *f.* Christendom

cristianismo, *m.* Christianity; Christendom

cristianizar, *v.t.* to convert to Christianity, christianize

cristiano (-na), *a.* and *s.* Christian. *a.* (*fam.*) watered (of wine). *m.* (*fam.*) Spanish (contrasted with other languages); (*fam.*) soul, person

cristino (-na), *a.* and *s.* (Spanish history, nineteenth century) supporting, or follower of, Queen Regent Maria Cristina during Carlist wars

cristo, *m.* Christ; crucifix. (*fam.*) donde C. dió las tres voces, in the middle of nowhere

cristus, *m.* Christ-cross; alphabet. no saber el c., to be extremely ignorant

criterio, *m.* criterion, standard; judgment, discernment

crítica, *f.* criticism (all meanings)

criticar, *v.t.* to criticize; censure, find fault with, blame

crítico, *a.* critical; censorious; dangerous, difficult; (*med.*) critical. *m.* critic; fault-finder

criticón (-ona), *a.* censorious, hyper-critical. *s.* fault-finder

croar, *v.i.* to croak (frogs)

croata, *a.* and *m.* and *f.* Croatian

croché, *m.* crochet work

cromado, *a.* chromium-plated

cromático, *a.* (*mus.*, *phys.*) chromatic

cromato, *m.* (*chem.*) chromate

crómico, *a.* chromic

cromo, *m.* chrome; chromium; chromo-lithograph

crónica, *f.* chronicle; diary of events

crónico, *a.* chronic; inveterate

cronista, *m.* and *f.* chronicler

cronología, *f.* chronology

cronológico, *a.* chronological

cronómetro, *m.* stop-watch

croqueta, *f.* (*cul.*) croquette

croquis, *m.* sketch, outline, drawing. **c. de nivel,** (optical) foresight

crótalo, *m.* rattlesnake; snapper (kind of castanet)

cruce, *m.* crossing; point of intersection; crossroads

crucero, *m.* (*ecc.*) cross-bearer; crossroads; (*arch.*) transept; (*ast.*) Cross; (*naut.*) cruiser

crucificar, *v.t.* to crucify; (*fig.*, *fam.*) torment, torture

crucifijo, *m.* crucifix

crucifixión, *f.* crucifixion

cruciforme, *a.* cruciform

crucigrama, *m.* crossword puzzle

crudelísimo, *a.* *sup.* cruel, most or exceedingly cruel

crudeza, *f.* rawness, uncookedness; unripeness; rawness (silk, etc.); crudeness; harshness; (*fam.*) boasting

crudo, *a.* uncooked, raw; green, unripe; indigestible; raw, natural, unbleached; harsh, cruel; cold, raw; (*fam.*) boastful

crueldad, *f.* cruelty; harshness

cruento, *a.* bloody

crujía, *f.* passage, corridor; (*naut.*) midship gangway

crujido, *m.* creak, crack, crackling, rustle

crujir, *v.i.* to creak, crackle, rustle

crup, *m.* (*med.*) croup

crupié, *m.* croupier

crustáceo, *a.* and *m.* crustacean

cruz, *f.* cross; tails (of coin); withers (of animals); insignia, decoration; affliction, trouble; (*ast.*) Southern Cross; (*print.*) dagger. **c. de mayo,** May cross. **c. gamada,** swastika. (*fam.*) ¡C. y raya! An end to this! **en c.,**

in the shape of a cross. (*fam.*) **hacerse cruces,** to be left speechless, be dumbfounded

cruzada, *f.* crusade; crossroads; campaign

cruzado, *a.* cross; double-breasted (of coats). *m.* crusader; member of military order

cruzamiento, *m.* crossing; intersection

cruzar, *v.t.* to cross; intersect; interbreed; bestow a cross upon; (*naut.*) cruise; *v.r.* take part in a crusade; cross one another; coincide; (*geom.*) intersect

cu, *f.* name of the letter Q

cuaderna, *f.* (*naut.*) ship's frame, timber; double fours (backgammon)

cuaderno, *m.* note-book, jotter, account book; (*fam.*) card pack. (*naut.*) **c. de bitácora,** log-book

cuadra, *f.* stable; ward, dormitory; hall, large room; quarter of a mile

cuadrado, *a.* square; perfect, exact. *m.* square; (*carp.*, *mil.*, *math.*) square; window-frame; clock (of a stocking)

cuadragenario, *a.* forty years old

cuadragésima, *f.* Quadragesima

cuadragésimo, *a.* fortieth

cuadrangular, *a.* quadrangular

cuadrángulo, *m.* quadrangle

cuadrante, *m.* quadrant; dial, face

cuadrar, *v.t.* (*math.*, *carp.*) to square; make square; *v.i.* correspond, tally. *v.r.* (*mil.*) stand at attention; (*fig.*, *fam.*) dig one's heels in

cuadrática, *f.* quadratic equation

cuadrático, *a.* quadratic

cuadratura, *f.* squareness; (*math.*, *ast.*) quadrature

cuadrienal, *a.* quadrennial

cuadrienio, *m.* space of four years

cuadriga, *f.* quadriga

cuadrilátero, *m.* quadrilateral; boxing-ring. *a.* quadrilateral

cuadrilongo, *a.* and *m.* oblong

cuadrilla, *f.* gang; company, band, group; police patrol; quadrille (dance); matadors and their assistants (at a bull fight)

cuadrimotor, *a.* (*aer.*) four-engined

cuadrivio, *m.* quadrivium

cuadro, *m.* square; picture-frame; frame (of bicycle); flowerbed; (*theat.*) tableau, scene; spectacle, sight; board (of instruments); description (in novel, etc.); (*mil.*) command, officers; square (of troops). **c. de distribución,** (*elec.*) main switchboard. **c. enrejado,** play-pen. **cuadros de costumbres,** word-pictures of everyday life and customs. **cuadros vivos,** tableaux vivants. **a cuadros,** checked, in squares

cuadrúpedo (-da), *a.* and *s.* quadruped

cuadruple, *a.* quadruple

cuadruplicación, *f.* quadruplication

cuadruplicar, *v.t.* to quadruple

cuajada, *f.* curd (of milk)

cuajar, *m.* maw (of a ruminant)

cuajar, *v.t.* to coagulate; curdle; *v.i.* (*fam.*) achieve, get away with; *v.r.* be coagulated or curdled; (*fam.*) be packed or chock full

cuajarón, *m.* clot (of blood, etc.)

cuajo, *m.* rennet; coagulation; curdling; (*anat.*) abomasum

cual, *rel. pron.* sing. *m.* and *f.* and *neut. pl.* **cuales,** which; who; such as (e.g. Le detuvieron sucesos cuales suelen ocurrir, He was detained by events such as usually happen). **a c. mas,** vying (with) (e.g. Los dos canónigos a c. más grueso, The two canons each fatter (vying in fatness) than the other). **c.** is used with *def. art.* **el (la, lo, los, las) cual(es),** who; which, when the antecedent is a noun (e.g. Juan saltó en el barco, el c. zarpó en seguida, John jumped into the boat which sailed at once). **por lo c.,** for which reason. *adv.* like (gen. literary or poet.). **¿cuál?** *interr. pron.* (no article) which? what? e.g. ¿Aquí tienes dos cuadros, cuál de ellos te gusta? Here are two pictures, which one do you like? Also expresses an implicit question, e.g. No sé cuál te guste, I don't know which you will like. **¡cuál!** *adv. interj.* how! **c. ... c.** *indef. pron.* some ... some

cualesquier, *a. pl.* of **cualquier**

cualesquiera, *a. pl.* of **cualquiera**

cualidad, *f.* quality; characteristic; talent

cualitativo, *a.* qualitative

cualquier, *abb.* of **cualquiera,** any; *pl.* **cualesquier.** Only used as abb. *before* noun

cualquiera, *a.* (*m.* and *f.*) any, e.g. una canción c., any song. *pron.* anybody, each, anyone whatsoever, whoever (e.g. ¡C. diría que no te gusta! Anyone would say you don't like it!) (*fam.*) un c., a nobody

cuán, *adv.* how (e.g. ¡C. bello es! How beautiful it is). Used only before *a.* or *adv.* Abb. of cuánto

cuando, *adv.* when; if. *interr.* **¿cuándo?** *abb. conjunc.* although; since; sometimes; followed by a noun means at the time of (e.g. c. la guerra, at the time of the war). **c. más,** at most, at best. **c. menos,** at the least. **de c. en c.,** from time to time

cuandoquiera, *adv.* whenever

cuantía, *f.* quantity, amount; importance, rank, distinction

cuantiar, *v.t.* to value, estimate; tax

cuantidad, *f.* quantity

cuantioso, *a.* large, considerable; numerous; plentiful, abundant

cuantitativo, *a.* quantitative

cuanto, *a.* as much as, all the; *pl.* as many as, all the (e.g. Te daré cuantas muñecas veas allí, I'll give you all the dolls you see there). *a. correlative* the ... the, as ... as (e.g. C. más tanto, mejor, The more the better). **cuánto,** *a.* and *pron. interr.* and *interj.* how much; *pl.* how many (e.g. ¡Cuánto tiempo sin verla! How long without seeing her!) *pron. neut.* cuanto, as much as, all that (e.g. Te daré c. quieras, I shall give you all that you wish). *adv.* cuanto, as soon as. **c. antes,** as soon as possible. **c. a** or en **c. a,** concerning. *adv.* and *conjunc.* **c. más,** all the more (e.g. Se lo diré c. más que tenía esa intención, I shall tell him all the more because I meant to do so). *adv.* **en c.,** as soon as, immediately (e.g. Lo haré en c. venga,

I shall do it immediately he comes). **en c. a,** with regard to. **por c.,** inasmuch, for this reason. *adv. interr.* ¿ Cuánto ? How much? How long? *adv. interj.* How! How much! (e.g. ¡ Cuánto me gustaría ir! How much I should like to go!)

cuaquerismo, *m.* Quakerism

cuáquero (-ra), *s.* Quaker

cuarenta, *a.* and *m.* forty; fortieth

cuarentena, *f.* fortieth; period of forty days, months or years; Lent; quarantine

cuarentón (-ona), *s.* person forty years old

cuaresma, *f.* Lent

cuaresmal, *a.* Lenten

cuarta, *f.* quarter, fourth; hand's breadth; *(mus.)* fourth; *(ast.)* quadrant

cuartago, *m.* pony, nag

cuartana, *f.* quartan (fever)

cuartear, *v.t.* to quarter, divide into quarters; cut or divide into pieces

cuartel, *m.* barracks; *(naut.)* hatch; quarter, fourth; *(her.)* quarter; district, ward; flower-bed; *(fam.)* house, accommodation; *(mil.)* quarter, mercy; *(mil.)* billet, station. *(mil.)* **c. general,** general headquarters

cuartelada, *f. (naut.)* quarter; military rebellion

cuartelar, *v.t. (her.)* to quarter

cuarterón (-ona), *s.* quadroon

cuarteta, *f.* quatrain

cuarteto, *m. (mus.)* quartet; *(poet.)* quatrain

cuartilla, *f.* sheet of paper; liquid measure; quarter of an arroba; pastern (horses)

cuarto, *m.* room; quarter, fourth; point (of compass); watch (on battleships); *(ast.)* quarter, phase; portion, quarter; joint (of meat); *pl.* quarters (of animals); *(fam.)* penny, farthing. *a.* quarter, fourth. **c. creciente,** first phase (of moon). **c. de hora,** quarter of an hour. **en c.,** *(print.)* in quarto. *(fam.)* **no tener un c.,** to be broke

cuarzo, *m.* quartz

cuasi, *adv.* almost, nearly, quasi

cuasidelito, *m. (law)* technical offence

cuasimodo, *m. (ecc.)* Low Sunday, Quasimodo

cuaterna, *f.* quaternion

cuatrillón, *m.* quadrillion

cuatrimestre, *a.* of four months' duration. *m.* space of four months

cuatrimotor, *m. (aer.)* four-engined aeroplane

cuatrisílabo, *a.* quadrisyllabic

cuatro, *a.* four; fourth. *m.* figure four; fourth (of days of months); playing-card with four spots; *(mus.)* quartet. **el c. de mayo,** the fourth of May. **Son las c.,** It is four o'clock

cuatrocientos, *a.* four hundred; four hundredth. *m.* figure four hundred

cuba, *f.* barrel, cask; tub, vat; *(fam.)* pot-bellied person; *(fam.)* drunkard, toper

cubano (-na), *a.* and *s.* Cuban

cubería, *f.* cooperage

cubeta, *f. dim.* keg, small cask; bucket, pail; *(phot.)* developing dish

cubicar, *v.t. (math.)* to cube; *(geom.)* measure the volume of

cúbico, *a.* cubic

cubículo, *m.* cubicle

cubierta, *f.* cover; envelope; casing; deck (of ship); tyre cover; book-jacket; pretext, excuse. **c. de escotilla,** *(naut.)* companion-hatch. **c. de paseo,** promenade deck

cubierto, *m.* cover, place at table; course (of a meal); table d'hôte, complete meal; roof. **un c. de cinco pesetas,** a five-peseta meal

cubil, *m.* lair, den (of animals)

cubilete, *m. (cul.)* mould; dice box; conjurer's cup

cubismo, *m.* Cubism

cubista, *m.* and *f.* cubist. *a.* Cubistic

cubo, *m.* bucket, pail; *(mech.)* socket; *(math.)* cube; hub (of a wheel); mill-pond

cubrecama, *m.* bedspread

cubrecorsé, *m.* camisole

cubreplatos, *m.* dish-cover

cubrimiento, *m.* covering

cubrir, *v.t.* to cover; *(mil.)* defend; spread over, extend over; conceal, hide; *(com.)* cover; dissemble; *(arch.)* roof; *v.r.* cover one's head; pay, meet (debts, etc.); cover or protect oneself (by insurance, etc.). *Past Part.* **cubierto**

cucaña, *f.* greasy pole; (*fam.*) snip, cinch, bargain

cucaracha, *f.* cockroach

cuclillas, en, *adv.* in a squatting position

cuclillo, *m.* (*orn.*) cuckoo; (*fam.*) cuckold

cuco, *a.* (*fam.*) pretty, cute; crafty, smart

cucú, *m.* cry of the cuckoo

cuculla, *f.* cowl, hood

cucurucho, *m.* paper cornet

cuchara, *f.* spoon; ladle; (*naut.*) boat scoop; scoop, dipper. (*fig.*) **meter c.**, to stick one's oar in

cucharada, *f.* spoonful; ladleful

cuchicheador (-ra), *s.* whisperer

cuchichear, *v.i.* to whisper

cuchicheo, *m.* whisper; whispering; murmur

cuchillada, *f.* knife thrust or wound; *pl.* (in sleeves, etc.) slashes; fight, blows

cuchillería, *f.* cutlery; cutler's shop

cuchillero, *m.* cutler

cuchillo, *m.* knife; (*sew.*) gore, gusset (gen. *pl.*); authority, power; anything triangular in shape. **pasar a c.**, to put to the sword

cuello, *m.* (*anat.*) neck; neck (of bottle, etc.); (*sew.*) neck; collar; necklet (of fur, etc.)

cuenca, *f.* socket (of eye); (*geog.*) catchment-basin; gorge, deep valley. **c. de un río**, river-basin

cuenta, *f.* count, counting; calculation; account; bead; charge, responsibility; reckoning; explanation, reason; (*com.*) bill. **c. corriente**, current account. **c. pendiente**, outstanding account. (*fam.*) **caer en la c.**, to tumble to, realize. **llevar la c.**, to reckon, keep account. **sin c.**, countless. **tener en c.**, to bear in mind

cuentacorrentista, *m.* and *f.* one who has a bank account

cuentagotas, *m.* dropper, dropping tube

cuentakilómetros, *m.* speedometer

cuentapasos, *m.* pedometer

cuentista, *m.* and *f.* story-teller; (*fam.*) gossip

cuento, *m.* story, tale; narrative; calculation; (*fam.*) gossip, fairytale; (*math.*) million. **c. de viejas**, old wives' tale. (*fig., fam.*) **dejarse de cuentos**, to go straight to the point. (*fam.*) **Va de c.**, It is told, they say

cuerda, *f.* rope; cord; string; (*geom.*) chord; (*mus.*) string; catgut; chain (of clock); (*mus.*) chord; vocal range. **dar c.** (a), to wind up (a watch); lead on, make talk. **de cuerdas cruzadas**, overstrung (of a piano)

cuerdo, *a.* sane; prudent; level-headed

cuerno, *m.* (*anat.*) horn; feeler, antenna; (*mus.*) horn; horn (of the moon). **c. de abundancia**, horn of plenty. (*fam.*) **poner en los cuernos de la luna**, to praise to the skies

cuero, *m.* hide, pelt; leather. **c. charolado**, patent leather. **en cueros**, stark naked

cuerpo, *m.* (*anat.*) body or trunk; flesh (as opposed to spirit); bodice; volume, book; main portion; collection; size, volume; physical appearance; corpse; group, assembly; corporation, association; (*geom.*) solid; (*chem.*) element; thickness, density; (*mil.*) corps. **c. de bomberos**, fire brigade. **c. de guardia**, guard-house. (*fam.*) **dar con el c. en tierra**, to fall flat. **de c. entero**, (*art.*) full-length (portrait). **en c.**, without a coat, lightly clad. **un c. a c.**, a clinch (in wrestling)

cuervo, *m.* raven; crow

cuesco, *m.* stone, seed, pip

cuesta, *f.* slope, incline, gradient. **c. abajo (arriba)**, down (up) hill. **a cuestas**, on one's back; having the responsibility of

cuestión, *f.* problem, question; quarrel, disagreement; affair, matter; torture

cuestionable, *a.* doubtful, questionable

cuestionar, *v.t.* to discuss, debate

cuestionario, *m.* questionnaire

cueva, *f.* cave, cavern; basement, cellar. (*fig.*) **c. de ladrones**, den of thieves cuévano, *m.* hamper, basket

cuezo, *m.* mortar hod

cuidado, *m.* carefulness, pains; attention; charge, care, responsibility; anxiety, fear. *interj.* ¡ C. ! Careful! Look out! **Me tiene sin c. su opinión,** I am not interested in his opinion. (*fam.*) **estar de c.,** to be dangerously ill

cuidadoso, *a.* careful; watchful; conscientious

cuidar, *v.t.* to care for; tend; take care of, look after; mind, be careful of; *v.r.* look after oneself

cuita, *f.* misfortune, anxiety, trouble

cuitado, *a.* unfortunate, worried; timid, bashful, humble

culata, *f.* (*anat.*) haunch; butt (of fire-arms); back, rear; (*aut.*) sump

culatazo, *m.* recoil (of fire-arms)

culebra, *f.* snake; (*fam.*) trick, joke; (*fam.*) sudden uproar. **hacer c.,** to stagger along

culebrear, *v.i.* to wriggle; grovel; meander, wind

culebreo, *m.* wriggling; meandering, winding

culebrina, *f.* (*mil.*) culverin

culí, *m.* coolie

culinario, *a.* culinary

culminación, *f.* culmination, peak; (*ast.*) zenith

culminante, *a.* culminating; (*fig.*) outstanding

culminar, *v.i.* to culminate (in)

culo, *m.* buttocks, seat; rump; anus; base, bottom. **c. de lámpara,** (*arch.*) pendant; (*print.*) tail-piece

culpa, *f.* fault; blame. **echar la c.** (a), to blame. **tener la c.,** to be to blame

culpabilidad, *f.* guilt

culpable, *a.* culpable

culpado (-da), *s.* culprit

culpar, *v.t.* to blame, accuse; criticize, censure

culteranismo, **cultismo,** *m.* involved literary style (cf. *Euphuism*)

cultivable, *a.* cultivable

cultivación, *f.* cultivation; culture

cultivador (-ra), *s.* cultivator; planter

cultivar, *v.t.* to cultivate; develop; exercise, practise (professions); culture (bacteriology)

cultivo, *m.* cultivation; farming; culture (bacteriological)

culto, *a.* cultivated; educated; cultured; elegant, artificial (style). *m.* worship; cult; religion, creed; homage

cultura, *f.* cultivation; culture

cultural, *a.* cultural

cumbre, *f.* peak, crest, summit; (*fig.*) zenith, acme

cumpleaños, *m.* birthday

cumplidamente, *adv.* fully, completely

cumplido, *a.* complete; thorough; long; plentiful; courteous, punctilious; fulfilled. *m.* courtesy, attention; formality. **gastar cumplidos,** to stand on ceremony; be formal

cumplimentar, *v.t.* to congratulate; perform, carry out

cumplimentero, *a.* over-complimentary; (*fam.*) gushing

cumplimiento, *m.* fulfilment, performance; courtesy, formality; completion; complement

cumplir, *v.t.* to perform, carry into effect; reach (of age); keep (promises); *v.i.* perform a duty; expire, fall due; serve the required term of military service; be necessary, behove; *v.r.* be fulfilled, come true. **por c.,** as a matter of form

cumulativo, *a.* cumulative

cúmulo, *m.* mass, cumulus; heap, pile

cuna, *f.* cradle; foundling hospital; birthplace; origin, genesis; *pl.* cat's cradle (game)

cundir, *v.i.* to extend, spread (gen. liquids); be diffused (news); expand, grow

cuneiforme, *a.* wedge-shaped, cuneiform

cunero (-ra), *s.* foundling, orphan

cuneta, *f.* gutter (of roads)

cuña, *f.* wedge; (*mech.*) quoin. (*mil.*) **practicar una c.,** to make a wedge

cuñada, *f.* sister-in-law

cuñado, *m.* brother-in-law

cuño, *m.* die, stamp; (*fig.*) impression; mark on silver, hallmark

cuota, *f.* quota; share; subscription; fee

cupé, *m.* coupé

Cupido, *m.* Cupid; philanderer

cuplé, *m.* couplet; song

cupo, *m.* quota; share; tax rate; (*mil.*) contingent

cupón, *m.* coupon

cúprico, *a.* (*chem.*) cupric

cuproso, *a.* (*chem.*) cuprous

cúpula, *f.* (*arch.*) dome, cupola; (*bot.*) cup

cuquería, *f.* craftiness, smartness; cuteness, prettiness

cura, *m.* parish priest; (*fam.*) Roman Catholic priest. *f.* cure (e.g. La enfermedad tiene c., The illness can be cured); healing; remedy. c. de almas, cure of souls. primera c., first aid. un c. de misa y olla, an ignorant priest

curabilidad, *f.* curableness

curable, *a.* curable

curación, *f.* cure, remedy; healing

curador (-ra), *s.* curer, salter. *m.* (*Scots law*) curator. *a.* curing; healing

curaduría, *f.* (*law*) guardianship

curanderismo, *m.* quackery, charlatanism; quack medicine

curandero (-ra), *s.* quack doctor; charlatan

curar, *v.i.* to heal, cure; (*with de*) take care of; care about, mind; *v.t.* cure, salt; treat medically (bandage, give medicines, etc.); cure (leather); bleach (cloth); season (timber); (*fig.*) remedy (an evil)

curare, *m.* (*med.*) curare

curasao, *m.* curaçao (drink)

curativo, *a.* curative

curato, *m.* (*ecc.*) parish, cure

cúrcuma, *f.* turmeric

curdo, (-da) *a.* Kurdish. *s.* Kurd

cureña, *f.* gun-carriage

curia, *f.* (*law*) bar; tribunal; (*ecc.*) curia; care, attention

curiana, *f.* cockroach

curiosamente, *adv.* curiously; carefully, attentively; neatly

curiosear, *v.i.* to pry; be curious (about); meddle, be a busybody

curiosidad, *f.* curiosity; inquisitiveness, meddlesomeness; neatness; carefulness, conscientiousness; curio

curioso, *a.* curious; inquisitive; interesting, odd; neat, clean; conscientious, careful

cursado, *a.* experienced, versed

cursante, *m.* student

cursar, *v.t.* to frequent, visit; do repeatedly; study, attend classes in; expedite (public admin.)

cursi, *a.* (*fam.*) vulgar, in bad taste; loud, crude

cursilería, *f.* (*fam.*) vulgarity, bad taste

cursivo, *a.* cursive

curso, *m.* course, direction; duration, passage (time); progress; route; course of study; academic year; succession, series; (*com.*) tender

curtido, *m.* tanning; leather; tanned leather (gen. *pl.*)

curtidor, *m.* tanner

curtiduría, *f.* tannery

curtimiento, *m.* tanning; effect of weather on the complexion; toughening-up; hardening

curtir, *v.t.* to tan; (*fig.*) bronze (complexions); make hardy, harden up; *v.r.* be weather-beaten; be hardy. (*fam.*) estar curtido en, to be experienced in; be expert at

curva, *f.* curve; bend. (*surv.*) c. de nivel, contour line

curvatura, curvidad, *f.* curvature

curvilíneo, *a.* curvilinear

curvo, *a.* curved; bent. *m.* curve

cúspide, *f.* peak, summit; (*geom., arch.*) cusp

custodia, *f.* custody; guardianship, care; (*ecc.*) monstrance; custodian, keeper; guardian; guard

custodiar, *v.t.* to watch, guard; look after, care for; (*naut.*) convoy

custodio, *a.* guardian; guarding; custodial. *m.* custodian; guard. angel c., guardian angel

cutáneo, *a.* cutaneous, skin

cúter, *m.* (*naut.*) cutter

cutícula, *f.* cuticle

cutis, *m.* complexion; skin (sometimes *f.*)

cuyo (cuya, cuyos, cuyas), *rel. pron. poss.* whose, of which (e.g. El viejo cuya barba era más blanca que la nieve, The old man whose beard was whiter than snow). *interr.* ¿ Cúyo ? Whose ? (e.g. ¿ Cúyos son estos lápices ? Whose pencils are these ?) (gen. de quien is used rather than cuyo). *m.* beau, lover

CH

chabacanería, f. bad taste; vulgarity

chabacano, a. vulgar, common; rude, uncouth

chacal, m. (zool.) jackal

chacó, m. (mil.) shako

chacolotear, v.i. to clatter, clink (loose horse-shoe)

chacoloteo, m. clatter (of horse-shoes)

chacota, f. merriment, mirth

chacotear, v.i. (fam.) to be merry, have fun

cháchara, f. (fam.) empty chatter; verbiage

chacharear, v.i. to chatter; gabble, cackle

chacharero, a. (fam.) chattering; talkative

chafallar, v.t. (fam.) to mend carelessly, botch

chafandín, m. vain fool

chafar, v.t. to flatten; crumple, crease (clothes); (fam.) heckle

chafarrinar, v.t. to stain, mark, blot

chaflán, m. bevel edge, chamfer

chagrén, m. shagreen leather

chal, m. shawl

chalán, m. horse-dealer

chalana, f. (naut.) wherry, lighter

chalanear, v.t. to bargain; indulge in sharp practice

chalar, v.t. to drive mad; enamour

chaleco, m. waistcoat; cardigan

chalina, f. flowing scarf, artist's bow

chalote, m. (bot.) shallot

chalupa, f. (naut.) shallop; launch; canoe; long boat, ship's boat

chamar, v.t. (fam.) to palm off, barter

chamarasca, f. brushwood, tinder

chamarilero (-ra), s. second-hand dealer

chamarreta, f. vest

chambelán, m. court chamberlain

chambergo, a. pertaining to the Chambergo regiment. m. broad-brimmed hat

chambón, a. (fam.) awkward, clumsy; lucky

chambonada, f. (fam.) blunder; fluke, chance

chambra, f. dressing-jacket, peignoir

chamicera, f. piece of scorched earth (woodland, etc.)

chamorro, a. close-cropped, shorn (hair)

champán, m. sampan (boat)

champaña, m. champagne

champar, v.t. (fam.) to cast in a person's face, remind

champú, m. shampoo

chamuscar, v.t. to scorch; singe

chamusquina, f. scorching; singeing; (fam.) brawl

chanada, f. (fam.) trick, mischievous act

chancearse, v.r. to joke

chancero, a. joking, facetious

canciller, m. chancellor

chancillería, f. chancery

chancla, f. down at heel shoe; heelless slipper

chancleta, f. heelless slipper, babouche. m. and f. (fam.) ninny

chancleteo, m. clicking of heelless slippers

chanclo, m. overshoe; Wellington

chanchullo, m. (fam.) fraud

chanfaina, f. (cul.) savoury fricassee

chanflón, a. tough, coarse; ungainly

chantaje, m. blackmail

chantajista, m. and f. blackmailer

chantar, v.t. to put on, clothe; (fam.) tell plainly. (fam.) ch. sus verdades, to tell home-truths

chantre, m. (ecc.) cantor

chanza, f. joke, jest

chanzoneta, f. canzonetta; (fam.) joke

chapa, f. plate, sheet; veneer; clasp; (fam.) prudence, common sense; rouge. ch. de hierro, sheet-iron. ch. de identidad, number plate

chapado a la antigua, a. old-fashioned

chapalear, v.i. to dabble in water; splash; clatter (of a horse-shoe)

chapaleo, m. dabbling, paddling; splash; clattering, clink (of a horse-shoe)

chapaleteo, m. lapping of water; splashing (of rain)

chaparrear, v.i. to pour with rain

chaparrón, *m.* heavy shower of rain, downpour

chapear, *v.t.* to veneer; *v.i.* clatter (loose horse-shoe)

chapeo, *m.* hat

chaperón, *m.* hood

chapeta, *f. dim.* clasp; red flush or spot on cheek

chapetón (-ona), *s. (S.A.)* recently arrived European, especially Spaniard

chapín, *m.* cork-soled leather overshoe (for women) (*ant.*)

chapitel, *m.* (*arch.*) capital; spire

chapodar, *v.t.* to prune, lop off branches; cut down, reduce

chapotear, *v.t.* to sponge, moisten, damp; *v.i.* paddle, splash; dabble or trail the hands (in water)

chapoteo, *m.* moistening, sponging; paddling, splashing; dabbling

chapucear, *v.t.* to botch, do badly; bungle

chapucería, *f.* roughness, poor workmanship; botch

chapucero, *a.* rough, badly finished; bungling, clumsy, awkward

chapurrar, chapurrear, *v.t.* to speak badly (a language); jabber; (*fam.*) mix (drinks)

chapuz, *m.* ducking, submerging; plunge; unimportant job; clumsiness

chapuzar, *v.t.* to duck, submerge; plunge

chaqué, *m.* morning coat; morning suit

chaqueta, *f.* jacket; (*mech.*) casing

chaquete, *m.* backgammon

chaquetilla, *f.* short jacket; coatee; blazer

chaquetón, *m.* short coat. **ch. de piloto,** (*aer.*) pea-jacket

charabán, *m.* charabanc

charada, *f.* charade

charanga, *f.* brass band

charanguero, *a.* rough, badly finished; clumsy. *m.* Andalusian boat

charca, *f.* pond, pool; reservoir

charco, *m.* puddle; (*fam.*) sea

charla, *f.* (*fam.*) chatter; conversation; talk, informal lecture

charlar, *v.i.* (*fam.*) to prattle, chatter; chat, converse; give a talk (on)

charlatán (-ana), *a.* loquacious, garrulous; indiscreet; fraudulent, false. *s.* charlatan; chatterer

charlatanería, *f.* loquacity, garrulity; quackery

charlatanismo, *m.* charlatanism, quackery

charnela, *f.* hinge; hinged joint

charol, *m.* japan, varnish; patent leather

charolar, *v.t.* to japan, varnish

charolista, *m.* varnisher

charpa, *f.* pistol-belt; (*med.*) sling

charrán (-ana), *s.* rogue, trickster

charranada, *f.* roguery, knavery

charrería, *f.* tawdriness; gaudiness

charretera, *f.* (*mil.*) epaulet; garter

charro, *a.* churlish, coarse; flashy, tawdry

chasca, *f.* brushwood, firewood

chascar, *v.i.* to creak, crack; clack (the tongue); swallow

chascarrillo, *m.* (*fam.*) amusing anecdote, good story

chasco, *m.* trick, practical joke; disappointment. **llevarse un ch.,** to meet with a disappointment

chasis, *m.* (*aut.*) chassis; (*phot.*) plate-holder; (*mech.*) underframe

chasquear, *v.t.* to play a trick on; crack (a whip); break a promise, disappoint; *v.i.* creak, crack; meet with a disappointment

chasquido, *m.* crack (of whip); creaking (of wood); click (of the tongue)

chatarra, *f.* scrap iron; junk

chato, *a.* flat-nosed; flat

chauvinismo, *m.* chauvinism

chaval, *a.* (*fam.*) young. *m.* lad

chaveta, *f.* (*mech.*) bolt, pin, peg, cotter, key

che, *f.* name of the letter Ch

checo (-ca), *a.* and *s.* Czech. *m.* Czech language

checoslovaco (-ca), *a.* Czecho-Slovakian. *s.* Czecho-Slovak

chelín, *m.* shilling

chepa, *f.* (*fam.*) hunch (back); hump

cheque, *m.* cheque. **ch. cruzado,** crossed cheque

chibalete, *m.* (*print.*) cabinet composing frame

chibuquí, *m.* chibouk (Turkish pipe)

chica, f. girl; (fam.) dear
chicana, f. chicanery
chicle, m. chewing-gum
chico, a. little, small; young. m. little boy; youth; (fam.) old boy, dear. Es un buen ch., He's a good fellow
chicoleo, m. (fam.) compliment
chicote, m. and f. sturdy child. m. (fam.) cigar
chicuelo (-la), s., dim. chico, little boy
chícharo, m. (bot.) pea
chicharrón, m. (cul.) crackling; burnt meat; (fam.) sunburnt person
chichón, m. bruise, bump
chichonera, f. child's protective hat (something like a straw crash-helmet)
chifla, f. whistling, whistle; tanner's paring knife
chiflado, a. (fam.) cracked, daft; crack-brained
chifladura, f. whistling; (fam.) whim, mania, hobby
chiflar, v.i. to whistle; v.t. to make fun of, hiss; pare or scrape leather; (fam.) swill, tipple; v.r. (fam.) have a slate loose; be slightly mad; (fam.) lose one's head over, adore
chifle, m. whistle, whistling; decoy call (birds)
chilaba, f. Moorish gown with a hood
chile, m. (bot.) red pepper, chilli
chileno (-na), a. and s. Chilean
chillador, a. screaming, shrieking
chillar, v.i. to scream, shriek; creak; squeak; jabber (monkeys, etc.); (art) be strident (of colours)
chillería, f. shrieking, screaming
chillido, m. scream, shriek; squeak (of mice, etc.); jabber (of monkeys, etc.)
chillón, a. (fam.) screaming, yelling; strident, piercing; crude, loud (colours)
chimenea, f. chimney; funnel; fireplace; kitchen range
chimpancé, m. chimpanzee
china, f. pebble; porcelain, china; Chinese silk
chinche, f. bed-bug; drawing-pin. m. and f. (fam.) bore
chinchona, f. quinine
chinchorrería, f. (fam.) impertinence, tediousness; gossip

chinela, f. mule, slipper; overshoe, patten (ant.)
chinero, m. china cupboard
chinesco, a. Chinese. a la chinesca, in the Chinese fashion
chino (-na), a. and s. Chinese. m. Chinese language
chipriota, a. and m. and f. Cypriot
chiquero, m. pig-sty; stable for bulls
chiquillada, f. childishness, puerility
chiquillería, f. (fam.) crowd of children
chiquillo (-lla), s. small boy
chiquito (-ta), a. dim. chico, tiny, very small. s. little one, small boy
chirimía, f. flageolet. m. flageolet player
chiripa, f. (billiards) fluke; (fam.) happy coincidence, stroke of luck
chirivía, f. (bot.) parsnip; (orn.) wagtail
chirla, f. round clam (shell fish)
chirlar, v.i. (fam.) to gabble, talk loudly
chirlo, m. knife wound, sabre cut; knife scar
chirona, f. (fam.) gaol
chirriador, a. sizzling, crackling; creaking, squeaking
chirriar, v.i. to sizzle, crackle; creak, squeak; squawk; (fam.) croak, sing out of tune
chirrido, m. squawk; croaking; noise of grasshoppers; squeaking; creaking, creak
¡chis! interj. Shh! Silence!
chisme, m. gossip, tale; (fam.) small household utensil, trifle
chismear, v.t. to tell tales, gossip
chismero (-ra), chismoso (-sa), a. gossiping, talebearing. s. gossip, tale bearer
chispa, f. spark; ember; (elec.) spark; tiny diamond; small particle; wit; quickwittedness; (fam.) drunkenness. ch. del encendido, ignition spark
chispazo, m. flying out of a spark, sparking; damage done by spark; (fam.) gossip, rumour
chispeante, a. sparking; sparkling; (fig.) scintillating (with wit, etc.)
chispear, v.i. to throw out sparks, spark; sparkle, gleam;

(*fig.*) scintillate; drizzle gently

chisporrotear, *v.i.* (*fam.*) to sputter; fizz

chisporroteo, *m.* (*fam.*) sputtering; fizz

chisposo, *a.* sputtering, throwing out sparks

chistar, *v.i.* to speak, break silence (gen. used negatively)

chiste, *m.* witticism, bon mot; amusing incident; joke

chistera, *f.* creel (for fish); (*fam.*) top-hat, tile

chistoso, *a.* joking; amusing, funny

chiticallando, *adv.* quietly, stealthily; (*fam.*) on the quiet, in secret

¡chito! ¡chitón! *interj.* Hush! Sh!

chivo (-va), *s.* (*zool.*) kid

chocante, *a.* colliding; provoking; shocking; surprising

chocar, *v.i.* to collide; strike (against); run into; fight, clash; *v.t.* clink (glasses); provoke, annoy; surprise, shock

chocarrería, *f.* coarse joke

choco, *m.* small hump, hunchback

chocolate, *m.* chocolate; drinking chocolate. **ch. a la española,** thick chocolate. **ch. a la francesa,** French drinking chocolate

chocolatería, *f.* chocolate factory or shop

chocolatero (-ra), *a.* fond of chocolate. *s.* chocolate maker or seller

chocha, *f.* (*orn.*) woodcock

chochear, *v.i.* to be senile; (*fig.*, *fam.*) dote (on)

chocho, *a.* senile; (*fig.*, *fam.*) doting

chófer, *m.* chauffeur; driver

chopera, *f.* grove or plantation of black poplar trees

chopo, *m.* (*bot.*) black poplar; (*fam.*) gun

choque, *m.* collision; shock; jar; (*med.*) concussion; fight; clink (of glasses); clash; (*mil.*) skirmish

choricera, *f.* sausage-making machine

choricero (-ra), *s.* sausage maker

chorizo, *m.* kind of pork sausage; counterweight

chorlito, *m.* (*orn.*) plover

chorrear, *v.i.* to spout, jet; drip; (*fig.*, *fam.*) trickle, arrive slowly

chorreo, *m.* drip, dripping; spouting, gushing

chorrera, *f.* spout; drip; jabot, lace front

chorro, *m.* jet; stream (of water, etc.); (*fig.*) shower. **a chorros,** in a stream; in abundance, plentifully

chotacabras, *f.* (*orn.*) goatsucker

choucroute, *f.* (*cul.*) sauerkraut

chova, *f.* (*orn.*) rook; carrion-crow; jackdaw

choza, *f.* hut, cabin; cottage

chubasco, *m.* squall, storm; transitory misfortune

chuchería, *f.* gewgaw, trinket; savoury tit-bit; snaring, trapping

chueca, *f.* round head of a bone; small ball; game like shinty; (*fam.*) practical joke

chufa, *f.* (*bot.*) chufa; (*fam.*) joke, trick

chufería, *f.* place where drink made of chufas is sold

chufleta, *f.* (*fam.*) joke; taunt

chulada, *f.* mean trick, base action; drollery

chulería, *f.* drollness; attractive personality

chuleta, *f.* (*cul.*) cutlet, chop; mutton-chop; (*fam.*) slap

chulo, *a.* droll, amusing; attractive. *m.* slaughter-house worker; bull-fighter's assistant; pimp; rogue

chumacera, *f.* rowlock

chumbera, *f.* prickly pear; Indian fig

chunga, *f.* (*fam.*) banter, teasing

chupada, *f.* sucking; suck; suction

chupador, *a.* sucking. *m.* baby's comforter or dummy

chupar, *v.t.* to suck; absorb (of plants); (*fig.*, *fam.*) drain, rob; *v.r.* grow thin. **chuparse los dedos,** (*fam.*) to lick one's lips; be delighted

chupatintas, *m.* (*fam.*) scrivener, clerk (scornful)

churdón, *m.* raspberry cane; raspberry; raspberry vinegar

churrería, *f.* place where churros are made or sold

churrero (-ra), *s.* maker or seller of churros

churrigueresco, *a.* (*arch.*) Churrigueresque

churro, *a.* coarse (of wool). *m.* (*cul.*) a kind of fritter eaten with chocolate, coffee, etc.

churumbela, *f.* (*mus.*) pipe; reed for drinking mate (*S.A.*)

chusco, *a.* droll, witty, amusing

chusma, *f.* galley hands, crew; rabble, mob

chutar, *v.t.* (*sport*) to shoot (a goal)

chuzo, *m.* (*mil.*) pike

chuzón, *a.* wily, suspicious, cunning

D

dable, *a.* practicable, possible

daca (da *or* **dame, acá**) Give me!

dactílico, *a.* dactylic

dáctilo, *m.* dactyl

dactilografía, *f.* typewriting

dactilógrafo (-fa), *s.* typist

dactilología, *f.* dactylology

dactiloscopia, *f.* dactyloscopy

dádiva, *f.* gift, present

dadivosidad, *f.* generosity

dadivoso, *a.* generous, liberal

dado, *m.* die; (*arch.*) **dado.** *conjunc.* **d. que**, given that, supposing that. **cargar los dados**, to load the dice

dador (-ra), *s.* giver, donor. *m.* (*com.*) bearer; (*com.*) drawer (of a bill of exchange)

daga, *f.* dagger

daguerrotipo, *m.* daguerreotype

daifa, *f.* concubine

¡dale! *interj.* Stop! No more about . . .!

dalia, *f.* (*bot.*) dahlia

dálmata, *a.* and *m.* and *f.* Dalmatian

dalmática, *f.* dalmatic, loose tunic or vestment

dalmático (-ca), *a.* and *s.* Dalmatian

daltoniano, *a.* colour-blind

daltonismo, *m.* colour-blindness

daltonismo, *m.* daltonism

dallador, *m.* wielder of a scythe

dallar, *v.t.* to scythe (grass)

dalle, *m.* scythe

dama, *f.* lady; noblewoman; lady-in-waiting; lady-love; mistress, concubine; queen (chess); king (draughts); (*theat.*) **d. primera**, leading lady

damajuana, *f.* demijohn

damas, *f. pl.* draughts (game)

damasceno (-na), *a.* and *s.* Damascene

damasco, *m.* damask

damasquino, *a.* damascened (swords, etc.)

damería, *f.* prudery, affectation

damisela, *f.* damsel; (*fam.*) woman of the town

damnificar, *v.t.* to injure

dandi, *m.* dandy

dandismo, *m.* dandyism

danés (-esa), *a.* Danish. *s.* Dane. *m.* Danish language

danta, *f.* (*zool.*) tapir

dantesco, *a.* Dantesque

danubiano, *a.* Danubian

danza, *f.* dance; set (of dancers); (*fig., fam.*) dirty business. **d. de arcos**, dance of the arches. **d. de cintas**, maypole dance

danzador (-ra), *s.* dancer. *a.* dancing

danzante (-ta), *s.* dancer; (*fig., fam.*) live wire; (*fam.*) busybody

danzar, *v.t.* and *v.i.* to dance; *v.i.* jump up and down, rattle; (*fam.*) interfere, meddle

danzarín (-ina), *s.* good dancer; (*fam.*) meddler; (*fam.*) playboy

danzón, *m.* Cuban dance

dañable, *a.* harmful; worthy of condemnation

dañado, *a.* evil, perverse; damned; spoiled, damaged

dañador (-ra), *a.* harmful. *s.* injurer, offender

dañar, *v.t.* to hurt, harm; damage, spoil; *v.r.* spoil, deteriorate

dañino, *a.* destructive (often of animals); hurtful, harmful. **animales dañinos**, vermin, pests

daño, *m.* hurt; damage; loss. (*law*) **daños y perjuicios**, damages. **hacerse d.**, to hurt oneself

dañoso, *a.* hurtful, harmful

dar, *v.t. irr.* to give; wish, express (congratulations, etc.); hand over; concede, grant; inspire; produce, yield; cause, create; sacrifice; propose, put forward; take (a walk); believe, consider; deliver (blows, etc.); administer (medicine); provide with; apply, coat with; occasion; perform (plays); propose (a toast); give forth, emit; render (thanks, etc.); hold (banquets, etc.); proffer, hold out; *v.i.* to strike (clocks); (*with prep. a*) overlook, look on to (e.g. **Su ventana da a la calle,** His window looks on to the street); (*with con*) find, meet (things, persons); (*with de*) fall on, fall down (e.g. **Dió de cabeza,** He fell head first. **Dió de espaldas,** He fell on his back); (*with en*) fall into, incur; insist on or persist in (doing something); acquire the habit of (e.g. **Dieron en no venir a vernos,** They took to not coming to see us); solve, guess (riddles, etc.); strike, wound, hurt (e.g. **La bala le dió en el brazo,** The bullet struck him in the arm); (*with por*) decide on (e.g. **Di por no hacerlo,** I decided not to do it). *v.r.* to yield, give in; (*with prep. a*) engage in, devote oneself to; (*with por*) think or consider oneself (e.g. **Me di por muerto,** I gave myself up for dead). **darse a la vela,** to set sail. **darse la mano,** to shake hands. **darse por buenos,** to make up a quarrel, be friends. **darse prisa,** to hurry up, make haste. **darse uno a conocer,** to make oneself known. **darse uno por entendido,** to show that one understands; be grateful. **No se me da un bledo,** I don't care a straw. **d. abajo,** to fall down. **d. a conocer,** to make known. **d. a entender,** to suggest, hint. **d. a luz,** to give birth; publish, issue. **d. cuenta de,** to give an account of. **d. de baja,** (*mil.*) to muster out, discharge. **d. de comer,** to feed. **d. de sí,** to stretch, expand; produce, yield; give of itself (oneself, himself, themselves) (either in good or bad sense). **d. diente con diente,** to chatter (of. teeth), shiver. **d. el pésame,** to tender condolences. **d. en cara,** (*fig., fam.*) to throw in one's face. **d. en el clavo,** (*fig.*) to hit the mark. **d. en qué pensar,** to make suspicious, cause to think. **d. fe,** to certify, attest. **d. fiado,** to

give on credit. **d. fianza,** to give security. **d. fin a,** to finish. **d. licencia,** to permit, allow. **d. los buenos días,** to wish good day or good morning. **d. mal,** to have bad luck at cards. **d. parte de,** to announce; issue a communiqué about (e.g. **Dieron parte de la pérdida del buque,** They announced the loss of the ship). **d. prestado,** to lend. **d. que decir,** to cause a scandal. **d. que hacer,** to cause trouble. **d. razón de,** to give an account of. **d. sobre uno,** to assault a person. **d. un abrazo,** to embrace. **d. voces,** to shriek; call out. (*fam.*) **Donde las dan las toman,** It's only tit-for-tat. (*fam.*) **No me da la real gana,** I darn well don't want to. *Pres. Ind.* **doy, das,** etc. *Preterite* **di, diste,** etc. *Pres. Subjunc.* **dé,** etc. *Imperf. Subjunc.* **diese,** etc.

dardo, *m.* (*mil., sport*) dart; (*icht.*) dáce; lampoon

dares y tomares, *m. pl.* give and take; (*fam.*) hard words. Generally used with *andar, haber* or *tener*

dársena, *f.* (*naut.*) dock

darviniano, *a.* Darwinian

darvinismo, *m.* Darwinism

darvinista, *m. and f.* Darwinian

data, *f.* date (calendar); (*com.*) credit

datar, *v.t.* to date; *v.i.* (*with de*) date from; *v.r.* (*com.*) credit

dátil, *m.* (*bot.*) date

datilado, *a.* date-like or date-coloured

datilera, *f.* (*bot.*) date-palm

dativo, *m.* (*gram.*) dative

dato, *m.* datum; basis, fact

davídico, *a.* Davidic

de, *f.* name of letter D. *prep.* of (possessive) (e.g. **Este cuadro es de Vd.,** This picture is yours); from (place and time) (e.g. **Vengo de Madrid,** I come from Madrid. **de vez en cuando,** from time to time); with, of, from, as the result of (e.g. **Lloraban de miedo,** They were crying with fright. **Murió de un ataque del corazón,** He died from a heart attack); for, to (e.g. **Es hora de marchar,** It is time to leave); with (of characteristics) (e.g. **El señor de los lentes,** The gentleman with the eyeglasses. **El cuarto de la alfombra azul,** The room with the blue carpet); when, as (e.g. **De niños nos gustaban los juguetes,** When we were children we liked toys); by (e.g. **Es un ensayo del mismo autor,** It is an essay by the same author. **Fué amado de todos,** He was loved by all. **Es hidalgo de nacimiento,** He is a gentleman by birth). Indicates the material of which a thing is made (e.g. **La mesa es de mármol,** The table is marble). Indicates contents of a thing (e.g. **un vaso de leche,** a glass of milk). Shows manner in which an action is performed (e.g. **Lo hizo de prisa,** He did it hurriedly). Shows the use to which an article is put (e.g. **una mesa de escribir,** a writing-table. **una máquina de coser,** a sewing-machine. **un caballo de batalla,** a war-horse). Sometimes used for emphasis (e.g. **El tonto de tu secretario,** That fool of a secretary of yours). Used by Spanish married women before husband's surname (e.g. **Señora Martinez de Cabra,** Mrs. Cabra (née Martinez)). Used after many adverbs (generally of time or place) to form prepositional phrases (e.g. **detrás de,** behind. **enfrente de,** opposite to; in front of. **además de,** besides, etc.). Used at beginning of various adverbial phrases (e.g. **de noche,** at night. **de día,** by day. **de antemano,** previously, etc.) Used partitively before nouns, pronouns, adjectives (e.g. **Estas historias tienen algo de verdad,** These stories have some truth in them. **¿ Qué hay de nuevo ?** What's the news ? Forms many compound words (e.g. **deponer, denegar,** etc.). With **" uno "** means "at" (e.g. **Lo cogió de un salto,** He caught it at one bound). **de a** is used before expressions of price, weight, etc. (e.g. **un libro de a cinco pesetas,** a five-peseta book)

dea, *f.* (*poet.*) goddess
deán, *m.* dean

deanato, deanazgo, *m.* deanship; deanery
debajo, *adv.* underneath; below
debate, *m.* discussion, debate; dispute
debatible, *a.* debatable
debatir, *v.t.* to discuss, debate, argue
debe, *m.* (*com.*) debtor (Dr.)
debelación, *f.* conquest
debelador (-ra), *a.* conquering. *s.* conqueror
debelar, *v.t.* to conquer, overthrow
deber, *v.t.* to owe (e.g. **Le debo cien pesetas,** I owe him one hundred pesetas. Used as auxiliary verb followed by infinitive, ought to, be obliged to (e.g. **Debía haberlo hecho,** I ought to have done it. **Deberá hacerlo,** He will have to do it); be destined to (e.g. **La princesa que más tarde debió ser reina,** The princess who later was destined to be queen); be essential, must (e.g. **La cuestión debe ser resuelta,** The question must be settled); (*with de + infin.*) be probable (indicates supposition) (e.g. **Debe de tener cincuenta años,** He is probably about fifty. **Debía de sufrir del corazón,** He probably suffered from heart trouble); (preceded by a negative *with de + infin.*) be impossible (e.g. **No debe de ser verdad,** It can't be true)
deber, *m.* duty, obligation; debt. **hacer su d.,** to do one's duty
debidamente, *adv.* justly, rightly; duly
debido, *a.* correct, due. **d. a,** owing to, because of
débil, *a.* weak; (*fig.*) spineless; frail
debilidad, *f.* weakness; feebleness
debilitación, *f.* debilitation
debilitamiento, *m.* weakening
debilitante, *a.* weakening
debilitar, *v.t.* to weaken; *v.r.* become weak
débito, *m.* debit, debt; duty
debutar, *v.i.* to appear for the first time, make one's début
década, *f.* decade
decadencia, *f.* decadence, decline

decadente, *a.* decadent, decaying

decaedro, *m.* (*geom.*) decahedron

decaer, *v.i. irr.* to fail (persons); decay, decline. See **caer**

decágono, *m.* (*geom.*) decagon

decágramo, *m.* decagramme

decaimiento, *m.* decadence; (*med.*) prostration

decalaje, *m.* (*aer.*) stagger

decalitro, *m.* decalitre

decálogo, *m.* decalogue, the Ten Commandments

decámetro, *m.* decametre

decampar, *v.i.* (*mil.*) to decamp

decanato, *m.* deanery; (*univ.*) dean's rooms

decano, *m.* senior member; (*univ.*) dean

decantación, *f.* decantation

decantar, *v.t.* to decant (wines); praise

decapitación, *f.* decapitation

decapitar, *v.t.* to decapitate, behead

decasílabo, *a.* ten-syllable

decena, *f.* ten; (*mus.*) tenth

decenal, *a.* decennial

decenario, *m.* decade

decencia, *f.* propriety, decency; decorum, modesty

decenio, *m.* decade

deceno, *a.* tenth

decentar, *v.t. irr.* to begin, cut (loaves, etc.); (*fig.*) undermine (health, etc.); *v.r.* suffer from bedsores. See **acertar**

decente, *a.* decent, honest; respectable; suitable; tidy

decenvirato, *m.* decemvirate

decepción, *f.* disillusionment, disappointment

decible, *a.* expressible

decidero, *a.* that which can be safely said

decidido, *a.* decided; resolute, determined

decidir, *v.t.* to resolve, decide; *v.r.* make up one's mind

decidor (-ra), *a.* talkative, fluent, eloquent. *s.* good talker

decigramo, *m.* decigramme

décima, *f.* tenth; tithe; ten-line stanza of eight-syllable verse

decimal, *a.* decimal; pertaining to tithes. **sistema d.,** metric system

decímetro, *m.* decimetre

décimo, *a.* tenth. *m.* tenth part; tenth of a lottery ticket

décimoctavo, *a.* eighteenth

décimocuarto, *a.* fourteenth

décimonono, *a.* nineteenth

décimoquinto, *a.* fifteenth

décimoséptimo, *a.* and *m.* seventeenth

décimosexto, *a.* sixteenth

décimotercio, *a.* thirteenth

decir, *v.t. irr.* to say; name; indicate, show; tell. **d. bien,** to go with, suit; speak the truth; be eloquent. **d. entre** (*or* **para**) **sí,** to say to oneself. (*fam.*) **d. nones,** to refuse. **¡ Diga!** Hello! (telephone). (*fam.*) **el qué dirán,** public opinion (what will people say!). **Es d.,** That is to say. **Se dice,** It is said, people say. *Pres. Ind.* **digo,** **dices,** etc. *Pres. Part.* **diciendo.** *Past Part.* **dicho.** *Fut.* **diré,** etc. *Condit.* **diría,** etc. *Preterite* **dije,** etc. *Pres. Subjunc.* **diga,** etc. *Imperf. Subjunc.* **dijese,** etc.

decir, *m.* saying, saw; maxim, witticism (often *pl.*)

decisión, *f.* decision, resolution; (*law*) judgment; firmness, strength (of character)

decisivo, *a.* decisive

declamación, *f.* declamation; oration; (*theat.*) delivery; recitation

declamador (-ra), *a.* declamatory. *s.* reciter; orator

declamar, *v.i.* to make a speech, declaim; recite

declamatorio, *a.* declamatory, rhetorical

declaración, *f.* declaration; exposition, explanation; confession; statement; (*law*) deposition

declaradamente, *adv.* avowedly

declarante, *a.* declaring. *m.* and *f.* (*law*) deponent

declarar, *v.t.* to declare; make clear, explain; (*law*) find; *v.i.* (*law*) give evidence; *v.r.* avow, confess (one's sentiments, etc.); show, reveal itself

declarativo, declaratorio, *a.* explanatory, declaratory

declinación, *f.* fall, descent; decadence, decay; (*ast.*) declination; (*gram.*) declension. (*fam.*) **no saber las declinaciones,** not to know one's ABC, be very ignorant

declinante, *a.* declining; sloping

declinar, *v.i.* to slope; diminish, fall; decline, deteriorate; (*fig.*) near the end; *v.t.* (*gram.*) decline

declive, *m.,* **declividad,** *f.* slope, incline; gradient

decocción, *f.* decoction

decoloración, *f.* decolouration; decolourization

decomisar, *v.t.* to confiscate, seize

decoración, *f.* decoration; ornament, embellishment; (*theat.*) scenery

decorado, *m.* (*theat.*) scenery, décor

decorador, *m.* decorator

decorar, *v.t.* to adorn, ornament; (*poet.*) decorate, honour

decorativo, *a.* decorative

decoro, *m.* respect, reverence; prudence, circumspection; decorum, propriety; integrity, decency; (*arch.*) decoration

decoroso, *a.* decorous, honourable, decent

decrecer, *v.i.* *irr.* to decrease, grow less. See **conocer**

decreciente, *a.* decreasing

decrepitación, *f.* (*chem.*) decrepitation, crackling

decrepitar, *v.i.* (*chem.*) to decrepitate, crackle

decrépito, *a.* decrepit

decrepitud, *f.* decrepitude

decretar, *v.t.* to decree, decide; (*law*) give a judgment (in a suit)

decreto, *m.* decree, order; judicial decree

decuplar, decuplicar, *v.t.* to multiply by ten

décuplo, *a.* tenfold

decurso, *m.* course, lapse (of time)

decuso, *a.* (*bot.*) decussate

dechado, *m.* model, ideal; (*sew.*) sampler; exemplar, ideal

dedada, *f.* thimbleful, finger; pinch

dedal, *m.* thimble; finger-stall

dedalera, *f.* (*bot.*) foxglove

dédalo, *m.* labyrinth

dedeo, *m.* (*mus.*) touch

dedicación, *f.* dedication (all meanings)

dedicar, *v.t.* to dedicate; devote; consecrate; *v.r.* (*with prep. a*) dedicate oneself to, engage in

dedicatoria, *f.* dedication (of a book, etc.)

dedicatorio, *a.* dedicatory

dedil, *m.* finger-stall

dedillo, *m.* saber al, (*fig.*) to have at one's finger-tips, know perfectly

dedo, *m.* finger; toe; finger's breadth. **d. anular,** third (ring) finger. **d. de en medio** *or* **del corazón,** middle finger. **d. índice,** forefinger. **d. meñique,** little finger. **d. pulgar,** thumb or big toe. (*fig., fam.*) **a dos dedos de,** within an inch of. (*fig., fam.*) **chuparse los dedos,** to smack one's lips over. (*fam.*) **estar unidos como los dedos de la mano,** to be as thick as thieves

deducción, *f.* inference, deduction; derivation; (*mus.,* *math.*) progression

deduciente, *a.* deductive

deducir, *v.t.* *irr.* to deduce, infer; deduct, subtract; (*law*) plead, allege in pleading. See **conducir**

deductivo, *a.* deductive

defecación, *f.* purification; defecation

defecar, *v.t.* to clarify, purify; defecate

defección, *f.* defection

defectible, *a.* deficient; imperfect

defecto, *m.* defect, fault; imperfection

defectuoso, *a.* imperfect, defective

defender, *v.t.* *irr.* to defend, protect; maintain, uphold; forbid; hinder; *v.r.* defend oneself. See **entender**

defendible, *a.* defensible

defensa, *f.* defence; protection; (hockey) pad; (*law*) defence; (*sport*) back; *pl.* (*mil.*) defences; (*naut*) fenders **d. química,** chemical warfare. (*mil.*) **defensas costeras,** coastal defences

defensiva, *f.* defensive

defensivo, *a.* defensive. *m.* safeguard

defensor (-ra), *s.* defender. *m.* (*law*) counsel for the defence

defensorio, *m.* manifesto, apologia

deferencia, *f.* deference

deferente, *a.* deferential

deferir, *v.i.* *irr.* to defer, yield. *v.t.* delegate. *Pres. Ind.* **defiero, defieres, defiere, defieren.** *Pres. Part.* **defiriendo.** *Preterite*

defirió, defirieron. *Pres. Subjunc.* **defiera,** etc. *Imperf. Subjunc.* **defiriese,** etc.

deficiencia, *f.* defect, deficiency

deficiente, *a.* faulty, deficient

déficit, *m.* (*com.*) deficit

definible, *a.* definable

definición, *f.* definition; decision

definido, *a.* definite

definir, *v.t.* to define; decide

definitivo, *a.* definitive. **en definitiva,** in conclusion

deflagración, *f.* sudden blaze, deflagration

deflagrador, *m.* (*elec.*) deflagrator

deflagrar, *v.i.* to go up in flames

deformación, *f.* deformation; (*rad.*) distortion

deformado, *a.* deformed; misshapen

deformador (-ra), *a.* disfiguring, deforming. *s.* disfigurer

deformar, *v.t.* to deform; *v.r.* become deformed or misshapen

deformidad, *f.* deformity; gross error; vice, lapse

defraudación, *f.* defrauding; deceit

defraudador (-ra), *s.* defrauder

defraudar, *v.t.* to defraud; usurp; frustrate, disappoint; impede

defuera, *adv.* outwardly, externally

defunción, *f.* decease, death

degaullista, *a.* (*pol.*) De Gaullist

degeneración, *f.* degeneration. **d. grasienta,** fatty degeneration

degenerado (-da), *a.* and *s.* degenerate

degenerar, *v.i.* to degenerate

deglución, *f.* swallowing, deglutition

deglutir, *v.i.* and *v.t.* to swallow

degollación, *f.* decollation, throat slitting

degolladero, *m.* slaughter-house; execution block

degollador, *m.* executioner

degolladura, *f.* slitting of the throat

degollar, *v.t. irr.* to behead; slit the throat; (*fig.*) destroy; (*fig., theat.*) murder; (*fam.*) annoy, bore. *Pres. Ind.* **degüello, degüellas, degüella, degüellan.** *Pres. Subjunc.* **degüelle, degüelles, degüelle, degüellen**

degollina, *f.* (*fam.*) massacre

degradación, *f.* degradation; humiliation, debasement; (*art*) gradation, shading (colours, light)

degradante, *a.* degrading, humiliating

degradar, *v.t.* to degrade; humiliate; (*art*) grade, blend; *v.r.* degrade oneself

degüello, *m.* decollation; havoc, destruction; haft (of swords, etc.)

degustación, *f.* act of tasting or sampling

dehesa, *f.* pasture, meadow

dehiscencia, *f.* dehiscence

deicida, *m.* and *f.* deicide (person)

deicidio, *m.* deicide (act)

deidad, *f.* divinity; deity, idol

deificación, *f.* deification

deificar, *v.t.* to deify; overpraise

deífico, *a.* deific, divine

deísmo, *m.* Deism

deísta, *m.* and *f.* deist. *a.* deistic

dejación, *f.* relinquishment, abandonment

dejadez, *f.* slovenliness; neglect; laziness; carelessness

dejado, *a.* lazy; neglectful; slovenly; discouraged, depressed

dejamiento, *m.* relinquishment; negligence; lowness of spirits; indifference

dejar, *v.t.* to leave; omit, forget; allow, permit (e.g. **Déjame salir,** Let me go out); yield, produce; entrust, leave in charge; believe, consider; intend, appoint; cease, stop; forsake, desert; renounce, relinquish; bequeath; give away; *v.r.* neglect oneself; engage (in); lay oneself open to, allow oneself; abandon oneself (to), fling oneself (into); (*fig.*) be depressed or languid; (*with de* + *infin.*) cease to (e.g. **Se dejó de hacerlo,** He stopped doing it); *v.i.* (*with de* + *adjective*) be none the less, be rather (e.g. **No deja de ser sorprendente,** It isn't any the less surprising). **d. aparte,** to omit, leave out. **d. atrás,** to overtake; (*fig.*) leave behind, beat. **d. caer,** to let fall. **dejarse caer,** to let oneself fall; (*fig., fam.*) to let fall, utter; appear suddenly. **dejarse vencer,** to give way, allow oneself to be persuaded

dejo, *m.* relinquishment; end; accent (of persons); savour, after-taste; negligence; (*fig.*) touch, flavour

del, contraction of **de + el,** (*def. art. m.*) of the (e.g. **del perro,** of the dog)

delación, *f.* accusation, denunciation

delantal, *m.* apron

delante, *adv.* before, in front, in the presence (of)

delantera, *f.* front, front portion; (*theat.*) orchestra stall, front seat; front (of garment). **tomar la d.,** to take the lead; (*fam.*) steal a march on

delantero, *a.* fore, front. *m.* postilion; (*sport*) forward. **d. centro,** (*sport*) centre-forward

delatable, *a.* impeachable; blameworthy

delatar, *v.t.* to inform against, accuse; impeach

delator (-ra), *a.* denunciatory, accusing. *s.* denouncer, informer

delectación, *f.* delectation, pleasure

delegación, *f.* delegation; proxy

delegado (-da), *s.* delegate; proxy

delegar, *v.t.* to delegate

deleitable, *a.* delightful

deleitar, *v.t.* to delight, charm, please; *v.r.* delight (in)

deleite, *m.* delight; pleasure

deleitoso, *a.* delightful, pleasant

deletéreo, *a.* deleterious; poisonous

deletrear, *v.i.* to spell; (*fig.*) decipher

deletreo, *m.* spelling; (*fig.*) decipherment

deleznable, *a.* fragile, brittle; slippery; brief, fugitive, transitory

délfico, *a.* Delphic

delfín, *m.* (*icht., ast.*) dolphin; dauphin

delfina, *f.* dauphiness

delgadez, *f.* thinness; slenderness, leanness

delgado, *a.* slim; thin; scanty; poor (of land); sharp, perspicacious

delgaducho, *a.* slenderish, somewhat thin

deliberación, *f.* deliberation; consideration; discussion

deliberadamente, *adv.* deliberately

deliberante, *a.* deliberative, considering

deliberar, *v.i.* to deliberate, consider; *v.t.* decide after reflection; discuss

deliberativo, *a.* deliberative

delicadez, *f.* weakness; delicacy; hypersensitiveness; amiability

delicadeza, *f.* delicacy; fastidiousness; refinement, subtlety; sensitiveness; consideration, tact; scrupulosity

delicado, *a.* courteous; tactful; fastidious; weak, delicate; fragile, perishable; delicious, tasty; exquisite; difficult, embarrassing; refined, discriminating, sensitive; scrupulous; subtle; hypersensitive, suspicious

delicia, *f.* pleasure, delight; sensual pleasure

delicioso, *a.* delightful, agreeable, pleasant

delicuescencia, *f.* (*chem.*) deliquescence.

delicuescente, *a.* (*chem.*) deliquescent

delimitar, *v.t.* to delimit

delincuencia, *f.* delinquency

delincuente, *a.* and *m.* and *f.* delinquent

delineación, *f.* delineation; diagram, design, plan

delineador (-ra), *s.,* **delineante,** *m.* draftsman, designer

delineamiento, *m.* delineation

delinear, *v.t.* to delineate; sketch; describe

delinquimiento, *m.* delinquency. crime

delinquir, *v.i. irr.* to commit a crime. *Pres. Ind.* **delinco.** *Pres. Subjunc.* **delinca**

deliquio, *m.* faint, swoon

delirante, *a.* delirious

delirar, *v.i.* to be delirious; act or speak foolishly

delirio, *m.* delirium; frenzy; foolishness, nonsense

delito, *m.* delict, offence against the law, crime

delta, *f.* fourth letter of Greek alphabet. *m.* delta (of a river)

delusorio, *a.* deceptive

demacración, *f.* emaciation

demacrado, *a.* emaciated

demacrarse, *v.r.* to become emaciated

demagogia, *f.* demagogy

demagógico, *a.* demagogic

demagogo (-ga), *s.* demagogue

demanda, *f.* petition, request; collecting (for charity); collecting box; " wanted " advertisement; question; search; undertaking; (*com.*) order or demand; (*law*) claim

demandadero (-ra), *s.* convent or prison messenger; errand-boy

demandado (-da), *s.* (*law*) defendant; (*law*) respondent

demandante, *m.* and *f.* (*law*) plaintiff

demandar, *v.t.* to ask, request; desire, yearn for; question; (*law*) claim

demarcación, *f.* demarcation, limit

demarcar, *v.t.* to fix boundaries, demarcate

demás, *a.* other. *adv.* besides. **lo d.,** the rest. **los (las) d.,** the others. **por d.,** useless; superfluous. **por lo d.,** otherwise; for the rest

demasía, *f.* excess; daring; insolence; guilt, crime. **en d.,** excessively

demasiado, *a.* too; too many; too much. *adv.* excessively

demencia, *f.* madness, insanity

dementar, *v.t.* to render insane; *v.r.* become insane

demente, *a.* insane, mad. *m.* and *f.* lunatic

demérito, *m.* demerit, fault

demeritorio, *a.* undeserving, without merit

demisión, *f.* submission, acquiescence

democracia, *f.* democracy

demócrata, *m.* and *f.* democrat

democrático, *a.* democratic

democratizar, *v.t.* to make democratic

demoledor (-ra), *a.* demolition. *s.* demolisher

demoler, *v.t. irr.* to demolish, destroy, dismantle. See **moler**

demolición, *f.* demolition, destruction, dismantling

demoníaco, *a.* devilish; possessed by a demon

demonio, *m.* devil; evil spirit. *interj.* ¡Demonios! Deuce take it! (*fam.*) **tener el d. en el cuerpo,** to be always on the move, be very energetic

demonología, *f.* demonology

demontre, *m.* (*fam.*) devil

demora, *f.* delay; (*naut.*) bearing; (*com.*) demurrage

demorar, *v.t.* to delay; *v.i.* stay, remain, tarry; (*naut.*) bear

demostrable, *a.* demonstrable

demostración, *f.* demonstration; proof

demostrador (-ra), *a.* demonstrating. *s.* demonstrator

demostrar, *v.t. irr.* to demonstrate, explain; prove; teach. See **mostrar**

demostrativo, *a.* demonstrative. (*gram.*) **pronombre d.,** demonstrative pronoun

demudación, *f.* change; alteration

demudar, *v.t.* to change, vary; alter, transform; *v.r.* change suddenly (colour, facial expression, etc.); grow angry

demulcente, *a.* and *m.* (*pharmacy*) demulcent

denario, *a.* denary. *m.* denarius

denegación, *f.* denial; refusal

denegar, *v.t. irr.* to deny, refuse. See **acertar**

dengoso, *a.* fastidious, finicky

dengue, *m.* affectation, faddiness, fastidiousness

denigración, *f.* slander, defamation (of character)

denigrante, *a.* slanderous

denigrar, *v.t.* to slander; insult

denodado, *a.* valiant, daring

denominación, *f.* denomination

denominador, *a.* denominating. *m.* (*math.*) denominator

denominar, *v.t.* to name, designate

denostada, *f.* insult

denostar, *v.t. irr.* to revile, insult. See **acordar**

denotar, *v.t.* to denote, indicate

densidad, *f.* density; closeness, denseness; (*phys.*) specific gravity; obscurity

denso, *a.* compact, close; thick, dense; crowded; dark, confused

dentado, *a.* toothed; pronged; dentate

dentadura, *f.* set of teeth (real or false). **d. postiza,** false teeth

dental, *a.* dental

dentar, *v.t. irr.* to provide with teeth, prongs, etc.; *v.i.* cut teeth. See **sentar**

dentellada, *f.* gnashing or chattering of teeth; bite; toothmark

dentellar, *v.i.* to chatter, grind, gnash (teeth)

dentellear, *v.t.* to bite, sink the teeth into

dentera, *f.* (dar) to set one's teeth on edge; (*fig., fam.*) make one's mouth water

dentición, *f.* teething, dentition

denticular, *a.* dentiform

dentífrico, *m.* toothpaste

dentista, *m.* and *f.* dentist

dentro, *adv.* within, inside. **d. de poco,** soon, shortly. **por d.,** from the inside; on the inside

dentudo, *a.* having large teeth

denudación, *f.* denudation; (*geol.*) erosion

denudar, *v.t.* to denude

denuedo, *m.* courage, daring

denuesto, *m.* insult

denuncia, *f.* denunciation, accusation

denunciante, *a.* accusing. *m.* and *f.* (*law*) denouncer

denunciar, *v.t.* to give notice, inform; herald, presage; declare, proclaim; denounce; (*law*) accuse

denunciatorio, *a.* denunciatory

deparar, *v.t.* to furnish, offer, present

departamental, *a.* departmental

departamento, *m.* department; compartment (railway); branch, section

departir, *v.i.* to converse

depauperación, *f.* impoverishment; (*med.*) emaciation

depauperar, *v.t.* to impoverish; *v.r.* (*med.*) grow weak, become emaciated

dependencia, *f.* d e p e n d e n c e; subordination; dependency; (*com.*) branch; firm, agency; business affair; kinship or affinity; *pl.* (*arch.*) offices; (*com.*) staff; accessories

depender, *v.i.* (*with de*) to be subordinate to; depend on; be dependent on, need

dependiente (-ta), *a.* and *s.*, dependent, subordinate. *m.* employee; shop-assistant

depilación, *f.* depilation

depilar, *v.t.* to depilate

depilatorio, *m.* depilatory

deplorar, *v.t.* to deplore, lament

deponente, *a.* deposing; affirming. *m.* and *f.* deponent. (*gram.*) **verbo d.,** deponent verb

deponer, *v.t. irr.* to lay aside; depose, oust; affirm, testify; remove, take from its place; (*law*) depose. See **poner**

deportación, *f.* deportation.

deportar, *v.t.* to exile; deport

deporte, *m.* sport; *pl.* games. **d. de vela,** yachting; boating

deportismo, *m.* sport

deportista, *a.* sporting. *m.* and *f.* sportsman (woman)

deportivo, *a.* sporting

deposición, *f.* affirmation, statement; (*law*) deposition; degradation, removal (from office, etc.)

depositador (-ra), *a.* depositing. *s.* depositor

depositar, *v.t.* to deposit; place in safety; entrust; lay aside, put away; *v.r.* (*chem.*) settle

depositaría, *f.* depository; trusteeship; accounts office

depositario (-ia), *a.* pertaining to a depository. *s.* depositary, trustee

depósito, *m.* deposit; depository; (*com.*) depôt, warehouse; (*chem.*) deposit, sediment; tank, reservoir; (*mil.*) depôt. **d. de bencina, d. de gasolina,** petrol tank; filling station. **d. de municiones,** munition dump. (*com.*) **en d.,** in bond. **Queda hecho el d. que marca la ley,** Copyright reserved

depravación, *f.* depravity

depravar, *v.t.* to deprave, corrupt; *v.r.* become depraved

deprecación, *f.* supplication, petition; deprecation

deprecar, *v.t.* to supplicate, petition; deprecate

depreciación, *f.* depreciation, fall in value

depreciar, *v.t.* to depreciate, reduce the value (of)

depredación, *f.* depredation, robbery

depredar, *v.t.* to pillage

depresión, *f.* depression

depresivo, *a.* depressive; humiliating

deprimir, *v.t.* to depress, compress, press down; depreciate, belittle; *v.r.* be compressed

depuración, *f.* cleansing, purification; (*pol.*) purge

depurar, *v.t.* to cleanse, purify; (*pol.*) purge

derecha, *f.* right hand; (*pol.*) (*gen. pl.*) Right, Conservative party; (*mil.*) ¡D.! Right Turn! **a la d.,** on the right

derechamente, *adv.* straight, directly; prudently; justly; openly, frankly

derechera, *f.* direct road

derechista, *m.* and *f.* (*pol.*) Conservative

derecho, *a.* straight; upright; right (not left); just, reasonable; (*sport*) forehand. *adv.* straightaway. *m* right; law; just claim; privilege; justice, reason; exemption; right side (cloth, etc.); *pl.* dues, taxes; fees. **d. a la vía,** right of way. **d. de visita,** (international law) right of search. **derechos de aduana,** customhouse duties. **derechos de entrada,** import duties. **según d.,** according to law. **usar de su d.,** to exercise one's right

derechura, *f.* directness, straightness; uprightness

deriva, *f.* (*naut., aer.*) drift, leeway

derivación, *f.* origin, derivation; inference, consequence; (*gram.*) derivation

derivar, *v.i.* to originate; (*naut.*) drift; *v.t.* conduct, lead; (*gram.*) derive; (*elec.*) tap

derivativo, *a.* derivative

dermatitis, *f.* dermatitis

dermatología, *f.* dermatology

dermatólogo, *m.* dermatologist

derogación, *f.* repeal, annulment; deterioration

derogar, *v.t.* to annul, repeal; destroy, suppress

derogatorio, *a.* (*law*) repealing

derrama, *f.* apportionment of tax

derramado, *a.* **extravagant,** wasteful

derramamiento, *m.* pouring out; spilling; scattering

derramar, *v.t.* to pour out; spill; scatter; apportion (taxes); publish abroad, spread; *v.r.* be scattered; overflow

derrame, *m.* spilling; leakage; overflow; scattering; slope

derredor, *m.* circumference. **al** (*or* **en**) **d.,** round about

derrelicto, *a.* abandoned; derelict. *m.* (*naut.*) derelict

derrengado, *a.* crooked; crippled

derretimiento, *m.* melting; thaw; liquefaction; (*fam.*) burning passion

derretir, *v.t. irr.* to melt, liquefy; waste, dissipate; *v.r.* be very much in love; (*fam.*) be susceptible (to love); (*fam.*) long, be impatient. See **pedir**

derribar, *v.t.* to demolish; knock down; fell; throw down; (*aer.*) shoot down; throw (in wrestling); (*fig.*) overthrow; control (emotions); *v.r.* fall down; prostrate oneself; throw oneself down

derribo, *m.* demolition; débris, rubble; throw (in wrestling)

derrocadero, *m.* rocky precipice

derrocar, *v.t.* to throw down from a rock; demolish (buildings); overthrow, oust

derrochador (-ra), *a.* wasteful, extravagant. *s.* spendthrift

derrochar, *v.t.* to waste, squander

derroche, *m.* squandering

derrota, *f.* road; route, path; (*naut.*) course; (*mil.*) defeat

derrotar, *v.t.* to squander; destroy, harm; (*mil.*) defeat; *v.r.* (*naut.*) drift, lose course

derrotero, *m.* (*naut.*) course; (*naut.*) ship's itinerary; number of sea charts; means to an end, course of action

derrotismo, *m.* defeatism

derrotista, *m.* and *f.* defeatist

derruir, *v.t. irr.* to demolish (a building). See **huir**

derrumbadero, *m.* precipice; risk, danger

derrumbamiento, *m.* landslide; collapse, downfall

derrumbar, *v.t.* to precipitate; *v.r.* throw oneself down, collapse, tumble down (buildings, etc.)

derrumbe, *m.* collapse; subsidence

derviche, *m.* dervish

desabarrancar, *v.t.* to pull out of a ditch or rut; extricate (from a difficulty)

desabillé, *m.* deshabillé

desabor, *m.* insipidity

desabotonar, *v.t.* to unbutton; *v.i.* open (flowers)

desabrido, *a.* insipid, poor-tasting; inclement (weather); disagreeable; unsociable

desabrigar, *v.t.* to uncover; leave without shelter

desabrigo, *m.* want of clothing or shelter; poverty, destitution

desabrimiento, *m.* insipidity; harshness, disagreeableness; melancholy, depression

desabrir, *v.t.* to give a bad taste (to food); annoy, trouble

desabrochar, *v.t.* to unbutton, untie; open; *v.r.* (*fam.*) confide, open up

desacatar, *v.t.* to behave disrespectfully (towards); lack reverence

desacato, *m.* irreverence; disrespect

desacertado, *a.* wrong, erroneous; imprudent

desacertar, *v.i.* *irr.* to be wrong; act imprudently. See **acertar**

desacierto, *m.* mistake, miscalculation, blunder

desacomodado, *a.* lacking means of subsistence; poor; unemployed (servants); troublesome

desacomodar, *v.t.* to incommode, make uncomfortable, inconvenience; dismiss, discharge

desaconsejado, *a.* ill-advised

desaconsejar, *v.t.* to advise against, dissuade

desacoplar, *v.t.* to disconnect

desacordar, *v.t.* *irr.* (*mus.*) to put out of tune; *v.r.* (with *de*) forget. See **acordar**

desacorde, *a.* discordant, inharmonious; (*mus.*) out of tune

desacostumbrado, *a.* unaccustomed; unusual

desacostumbrar, *v.t.* to break of a habit

desacotar, *v.t.* to remove (fences); refuse, deny; *v.i.* withdraw (from agreement, etc.)

desacreditar, *v.t.* to discredit

desacuerdo, *m.* disagreement, discord; mistake; forgetfulness; swoon, loss of consciousness

desadeudar, *v.t.* to free from debt

desadornar, *v.t.* to denude of ornaments

desadorno, *m.* lack of ornaments; bareness

desafecto, *a.* disaffected; hostile. *m.* disaffection

desaferrar, *v.t.* *irr.* to untie, unfasten; (*fig.*) wean from; (*naut.*) weigh anchor. See **acertar**

desafiador (-ra), *a.* challenging. *s.* challenger. *m.* duellist

desafiar, *v.t.* to challenge; compete with; oppose

desafinar, *v.i.* (*mus.*) to go out of tune; (*fig.*, *fam.*) speak out of turn

desafío, *m.* challenge; competition; duel

desaforado, *a.* lawless· outrageous; enormous

desaforar, *v.t.* to infringe (laws, etc.); *v.r.* be disorderly

desaforrar, *v.t.* to remove the lining of or from

desafortunado, *a.* unfortunate

desafuero, *m.* act of injustice; outrage, excess

desagarrar, *v.t.* (*fam.*) to release, loosen; unhook

desagraciado, *a.* ugly, unsightly

desagraciar, *v.t.* to disfigure, make ugly

desagradable, *a.* disagreeable; unpleasant

desagradar, *v.i.* to be disagreeable, displease (e.g. Me desagrada su voz, His voice is unpleasant to me)

desagradecer, *v.t.* *irr.* to be ungrateful (for). See **conocer**

desagradecido, *a.* ungrateful

desagradecimiento, *m.* ingratitude

desagrado, *m.* displeasure, dislike, dissatisfaction

desagraviar, *v.t.* to make amends, apologize; indemnify

desagravio, *m.* satisfaction, reparation; compensation

desagregar(se), *v.t.* and *v.r.* to separate

desaguadero, *m.* drain, waste pipe

desaguar, *v.t.* to drain off; dissipate; *v.i.* flow (into sea, etc.)

desagüe, *m.* drainage; outlet, drain; catchment

desaguisado, *a.* outrageous, lawless. *m.* offence, insult

desahogado, *a.* brazen, insolent; clear, unencumbered; in comfortable circumstances

desahogar, *v.t.* to ease, relieve; *v.r.* unburden oneself; recover (from illness, heat, etc.); get out of debt; speak one's mind

desahogo, *m.* relief, alleviation; ease; comfort, convenience; freedom, frankness; unburdening (of one's mind). (*fam.*) **vivir con d.,** to be comfortably off

desahuciar, v.t. to banish all hope; give up, despair of the life of; put out (tenants)

desahucio, m. ejection, dispossession (of tenants)

desahumar, v.t. to clear of smoke

desairado, a. unattractive, graceless, ugly; unsuccessful, crestfallen; slighted

desairar, v.t. to disdain, slight, disregard; underrate (things)

desaire, m. gracelessness, ugliness; insult, slight

desalabanza, f. disparagement; criticism

desalabar, v.t. to censure, disparage

desalado, a. anxious, precipitate, hasty

desalar, v.t. to remove the salt from; take off wings; v.r. walk or run at great speed; long for, yearn

desalentar, v.t. irr. to make breathing difficult (work, fatigue); discourage; v.r. be depressed or sad. See sentar

desaliento, m. depression, discouragement, dismay

desalinear, v.t. to throw out of the straight

desaliñado, a. slovenly; slipshod

desaliñar, v.t. to disarrange, make untidy, crumple

desaliño, m. untidiness, slovenliness; negligence, carelessness

desalmado, a. soulless, conscienceless; cruel

desalmamiento, m. inhumanity, consciencelessness; cruelty

desalmidonar, v.t. to remove starch from

desalojamiento, m. dislodgement, ejection

desalojar, v.t. to dislodge, remove, eject; v.i. move out, remove

desalquilado, a. untenanted, vacant

desalquilar, v.t. to leave, or cause to leave, rented premises

desalterar, v.t. to soothe, calm

desamar, v.t. to cease to love; hate

desamarrar, v.t. to untie; separate; (naut.) unmoor

desamor, m. indifference; lack of sentiment or affection; hatred

desamortización, f. disentail

desamortizar, v.t. to disentail

desamotinarse, v.r. to cease from rebellion; submit

desamparar, v.t. to abandon, forsake; leave (a place)

desamparo, m. desertion; need

desamueblado, a. unfurnished

desamueblar, v.t. to empty of furniture

desancorar, v.t. (naut.) to weigh anchor

desandar, v.t. irr. to retrace one's steps. See andar

desangrar, v.t. (med.) to bleed; drain (lake, etc.); impoverish, bleed; v.r. lose much blood

desanidar, v.i. to leave the nest; v.t. eject, expel

desanimado, a. downhearted; (of places) dull, quiet

desanimar, v.t. to discourage, depress

desanublar, v.t., desanublarse, v.r. to clear up (weather)

desanudar, v.t. to untie; disentangle

desaojar, v.t. to cure of the " evil eye "

desapacibilidad, f. disagreeableness, unpleasantness

desapacible, a. disagreeable; unpleasant; unsociable

desaparecer, v.t. irr. to cause to disappear; v.i. and v.r. disappear. See conocer

desaparecido, a. (mil.) missing

desaparejar, v.t. to unharness

desaparición, f. disappearance

desapegar, v.t. to unstick, undo; v.r. be indifferent, cast off a love or affection

desapego, m. lack of affection or interest, coolness

desapercibido, a. unnoticed; unprovided, unprepared

desapercibir iento, m. unpreparedness

desapestar, v.t. to disinfect

desapiadado, a. merciless

desaplicación, f. laziness, lack of application; carelessness, negligence

desaplicado, a. lazy; careless

desapoderado, a. precipitate, uncontrolled; furious, violent

desapoderar, v.t. to dispossess, rob; remove from office

desapolillar, v.t. to free from moths; v.r. (fam.) take an airing

desaposentar, *v.t.* to evict; drive away

desapreciar, *v.t.* to scorn

desaprender, *v.t.* to unlearn

desaprensivo, *a.* unscrupulous

desapretar(se), *v.t.* and *v.r.* *irr.* to slacken. See **acertar**

desaprisionar, *v.t.* to release from prison

desaprobación, *f.* disapproval

desaprobar, *v.t.* *irr.* to disapprove; disagree with. See **probar**

desapropiamiento, *m.* renunciation or transfer of property

desapropiarse, *v.r.* to renounce or transfer (property)

desaprovechado, *a.* unprofitable; backward; unintelligent

desaprovechar, *v.t.* to take no advantage of, waste; *v.i.* (*fig.*) lose ground, lose what one has gained

desapuntalar, *v.t.* to remove supports (of buildings)

desapuntar, *v.t.* to unstitch; lose one's aim

desarbolar, *v.t.* (*naut.*) to unmast

desarenar, *v.t.* to clear of sand

desarmar, *v.t.* to disarm; dismantle, dismount; appease

desarme, *m.* disarming; disarmament

desarraigar, *v.t.* to pull up by root (plants); extirpate, suppress; eradicate (opinion, etc.); exile

desarraigo, *m.* uprooting; extirpation; eradication; exile

desarrebujar, *v.t.* to disentangle, uncover; explain

desarreglado, *a.* disarranged; untidy; intemperate, immoderate

desarreglar, *v.t.* to disarrange

desarreglo, *m.* disorder; disarrangement; irregularity

desarrendar, *v.t.* *irr.* to unbridle a horse; end a tenancy or lease. See recomendar

desarrollar, *v.t.* to unroll; increase, develop, grow, unfold; explain (theory); *v.r.* develop, grow

desarrollo, *m.* unrolling; development, growth; explanation

desarropar, *v.t.* to uncover, remove the covers, etc. from

desarrugar, *v.t.* to take out wrinkles or creases

desarticulación, *f.* disarticulation

desarticular, *v.t.* to disarticulate; (*mech.*) disconnect

desaseado, *a.* dirty; unkempt, slovenly

desaseo, *m.* dirtiness; slovenliness

desasimiento, *m.* loosening; liberality; disinterestedness; indifference, coldness

desasir, *v.t.* *irr.* to loosen, undo. *v.r.* disengage oneself. See asir

desasnar, *v.t.* (*fam.*) to instruct, educate, polish

desasosegar, *v.t.* *irr.* to disturb, make anxious. See cegar

desasosiego, *m.* uneasiness, disquiet

desastre, *m.* disaster, calamity

desastroso, *a.* unfortunate, calamitous

desatacar, *v.t.* to unfasten, undo, unbutton

desatadura, *f.* untying

desatar, *v.t.* to untie; melt, dissolve; elucidate, explain; *v.r.* loosen the tongue; lose self control; lose all reserve; unbosom oneself

desatascar, *v.t.* to pull out of the mud; free from obstruction; extricate from difficulties

desataviar, *v.t.* to strip of ornaments

desatavío, *m.* carelessness in dress, slovenliness

desatención, *f.* inattention, abstraction; incivility

desatender, *v.t.* *irr.* to pay no attention to; disregard, ignore. See entender

desatentado, *a.* imprudent, illadvised; excessive, immoderate

desatento, *a.* inattentive, abstracted; discourteous

desatinado, *a.* foolish, imprudent, wild

desatinar, *v.t.* to bewilder; *v.i.* behave foolishly; lose one's bearings

desatino, *m.* imprudence, rashness; blunder, mistake

desatracar, *v.i.* (*naut.*) to push off

desatrancar, *v.t.* to unbar the door; remove obstacles

desaturdir, *v.t.* to rouse (from torpor, etc.)

desautorizar, *v.t.* to remove from authority; discredit

desavenencia, *f.* disharmony, disagreement

desavenido, *a.* disagreeing, discordant

desavenir, *v.t. irr.* to upset. See venir

desaventajado, *a.* disadvantageous; unfavourable, inferior

desaviar, *v.t.* to lead astray; deprive of a necessity; *v.r.* lose one's way

desavisado, *a.* unaware, unprepared

desavisar, *v.t.* to take back one's previous advice

desayunarse, *v.r.* to have breakfast

desayuno, *m.* breakfast

desazón, *f.* insipidity, lack of flavour; poorness (soil); anxiety, trouble; vexation

desazonar, *v.t.* to make insipid; make anxious, worry; vex; *v.r.* feel out of sorts

desbancar, *v.t.* to break the bank (gambling); supplant

desbandada, *f.* dispersal, rout. **a la d.,** in confusion or disorder

desbandarse, *v.r.* to disband, retreat in disorder; (*mil.*) desert

desbaratado, *a.* (*fam.*) corrupt, vicious

desbaratar, *v.t.* to spoil, destroy; dissipate, waste; thwart; (*mil.*) rout; *v.i.* talk foolishly; *v.r.* go too far, behave badly

desbarbado, *a.* beardless

desbastadura, *f.* (*carp.*) planing

desbastar, *v.t.* (*carp.*) to plane, dress; polish, refine, civilize

desbocado, *a.* (of tools) blunt; runaway (of a horse); (*fam.*) foul-tongued

desbocar, *v.t.* to break the spout or neck (of jars, etc.); *v.i.* run (into) (of streets, etc.); *v.r.* bolt (horses); curse, swear

desboquillar, *v.t.* to remove or break a stem or mouthpiece

desbordamiento, *m.* overflowing, flood

desbordarse, *v.r.* to overflow; lose self-control

desbravar, *v.t.* to break in (horses, etc.); *v.i.* grow less savage; lose force, decrease

desbrozar, *v.t.* to free of rubbish, clear up

descabalgadura, *f.* alighting (from horses, etc.)

descabalgar, *v.i.* to alight (from horse); *v.t.* dismantle (gun)

descabellado, *a.* dishevelled; ridiculous, foolish

descabellar, *v.t.* to disarrange, ruffle (hair)

descabezado, *a.* headless; rash, impetuous

descabezar, *v.t.* to behead; cut the top off (trees, etc.); (*fig., fam.*) break the back of (work); *v.i.* abut, join; *v.r.* (*with con* or *en*) rack one's brains about

descalabazarse, *v.r.* (*fam.*) to rack one's brains

descalabradura, *f.* head wound or scar

descalabrar, *v.t.* to wound in the head; wound; harm

descalabro, *m.* misfortune, mishap

descalzar, *v.t.* to remove the shoes and stockings; undermine; *v.r.* remove one's shoes and stockings; lose a shoe (horses)

descalzo, *a.* barefoot

descamación, *f.* (*med.*) desquamation

descaminar, *v.t.* to lead astray; pervert, corrupt

descamisado (-da), *a.* (*fam.*) shirtless; ragged, poor. *s.* (*fam.*) down and out, outcast; vagabond

descansadero, *m.* resting place

descansado, *a.* rested, refreshed; tranquil

descansar, *v.i.* to rest, repose oneself; have relief (from anxiety, etc.); sleep; (*agr.*) lie fallow; sleep in death; (*with en*) trust, have confidence in; (*with sobre*) lean on or upon; *v.t.* (*with sobre*) rest (a thing) on another. **¡Quién en paz descanse!** May he rest in peace!

descanso, *m.* rest, repose; relief (from care); landing of stairs; (*mech.*) bench, support; (*mil.*) stand easy

descarado, *a.* impudent, brazen

descararse, *v.r.* to behave impudently

descarbonizar, *v.t.* to decarbonize

descarburación, *f.* decarbonization

descarga, *f.* unloading; (*naut.*) discharge of cargo; (*elec.*) discharge; (*mil.*) volley. **d. cerrada,** fusillade

descargadero, *m.* wharf

descargador, *m.* unloader, docker; (*elec.*) discharger

descargar, *v.t.* to unload; (*mil.*) fire; unload (fire-arms); (*elec.*) discharge; rain (blows) upon; (*fig.*) free, exonerate; *v.i.* disembogue (of rivers); burst (clouds); *v.r.* relinquish (employment); shirk responsibility; (*law*) clear oneself

descargo, *m.* unlbading; (*com.*) acquittance; (*law*) answer to an impeachment

descargue, *m.* unloading

descarnado, *a.* fleshless; scraggy; spare, lean

descarnador, *m.* dental scraper; tanner's scraper

descarnar, *v.t.* to scrape off flesh; corrode; inspire indifference to earthly things

descaro, *m.* impudence

descarriar, *v.t.* to lead astray; *v.r.* be lost, be separated (from others); (*fig.*) go astray

descarrilamiento, *m.* derailment

descarrilar, *v.i.* to run off the track, be derailed

descarrío, *m.* losing one's way

descartar, *v.t.* to put aside; *v.r.* discard (cards); shirk, make excuses

descarte, *m.* discard (cards); excuse, pretext

descascarar, *v.t.* to peel; shell; *v.r.* peel off

descendencia, *f.* descendants, offspring; lineage, descent

descender, *v.i. irr.* to descend; flow (liquids); (*with de*) descend from, derive from; *v.t.* lower, let down. See **entender**

descendiente, *m.* and *f.* descendant, offspring. *a.* descending

descendimiento, *m.* descent

descenso, *m.* descent; lowering, letting down; degradation

descentralización, *f.* decentralization

descentralizar, *v.t.* to decentralize

desceñir(se), *v.t.* and *v.r. irr.* to ungird, remove a girdle, etc. See **ceñir**

descepar, *v.t.* to tear up by the roots; (*fig.*) extirpate

descercado, *a.* unfenced, open

descercar, *v.t.* to pull down a wall or fence; (*mil.*) raise a siege

descerrajar, *v.t.* to remove the locks (of doors, etc.)

descifrable, *a.* decipherable

descifrador, *m.* decipherer, decoder

descifrar, *v.t.* to decipher; decode

descinchar, *v.t.* to loosen or remove girths (of horse)

desclavar, *v.t.* to remove nails; unnail, unfasten

descoagular, *v.t.* to liquefy, dissolve, melt

descobijar, *v.t.* to uncover; undress

descocado, *a.* (*fam.*) brazen, saucy

descoco, *m.* (*fam.*) impudence

descogollar, *v.t.* to prune a tree of shoots; remove hearts (of lettuces, etc.)

descolar, *v.t. irr.* to cut off or dock an animal's tail. See **colar**

descolgar, *v.t. irr.* to unhang; lower; *v.r.* lower oneself (by rope, etc.); come down, descend; (*fam.*) come out (with), utter. See **volcar**

descoloramiento, *m.* discolouration

descolorar, *v.t.* to discolour; *v.r.* be discoloured

descolorido, *a.* discoloured; pale-coloured; pallid

descollar, *v.i. irr.* to excel, be outstanding. See **degollar**

descomedido, *a.* excessive, disproportionate; rude

descomedimiento, *m.* disrespect, lack of moderation, rudeness

descomedirse, *v.r. irr.* to be disrespectful or rude. See **pedir**

descompasarse, *v.r.* See **descomedirse**

descomponer, *v.t. irr.* to disorder, disarrange; (*chem.*) decompose; unsettle; *v.r.* go out of order; rot, putrefy; be ailing; lose one's temper. See **poner**

descomposición, *f.* disorder, confusion; discomposure; (*chem.*) decomposition; putrefaction

descompostura, *f.* decomposition; slovenliness, dirtiness, untidiness; impudence, rudeness

descompuesto, *a.* rude, impudent

descomunal, *a.* enormous, extraordinary

desconcertar, *v.t. irr.* to disorder, disarrange; dislocate (bones); disconcert, embarrass; *v.r.* disagree; be impudent. See **acertar**

desconcierto, *m.* disorder, disarrangement; dislocation; embarrassment; disagreement; impudence

desconchadura, *f.* flaking (off), peeling (off)

desconcharse, *v.r.* to flake off, peel

desconectar, *v.t.* to disconnect; switch off

desconfianza, *f.* lack of confidence

desconfiar, *v.i.* to lack confidence

desconformidad, *f.* See **disconformidad**

desconocer, *v.t. irr.* to forget; be unaware of; deny, disown; pretend ignorance; not to understand (persons, etc.). See **conocer**

desconocido (-da), *a.* unknown; ungrateful. *s.* stranger; ingrate

desconocimiento, *m.* unawareness; ignorance; ingratitude

desconsiderado, *a.* inconsiderate; discourteous; rash

desconsolación, *f.* affliction, trouble

desconsolar, *v.t. irr.* to afflict, make disconsolate; *v.r.* grieve, despair. See **colar**

desconsuelo, *m.* anguish, affliction, despair

descontar, *v.t. irr. (com.)* to make a discount; ignore, discount; take for granted, leave aside. See **contar**

descontentadizo, *a.* discontented, difficult to please; fastidious, finicky

descontentar, *v.t.* to displease; *v.r.* be dissatisfied

descontento, *m.* discontent, dissatisfaction

desconveniencia, *f.* inconvenience, unsuitability, disagreement

desconvenir, *v.i. irr.* to disagree; be unsuitable, unsightly or odd (things). See **venir**

descorazonamiento, *m.* depression, despair

descorazonar, *v.t.* to tear out the heart; depress, discourage.

descorchar, *v.t.* to take the cork from cork tree; draw a cork (bottles); force, break into (safes)

descorrer, *v.t.* to re-run (race, etc.); draw back (curtains, etc.); *v.i.* run, flow (liquids)

descorrimiento, *m.* overflow (liquids)

descortés, *a.* impolite

descortesía, *f.* impoliteness, discourtesy

descortezadura, *f.* peeling (of bark)

descortezar, *v.t.* to decorticate; remove crust (bread, etc.); polish, civilize

descoser, *v.t. (sew.)* to unpick; *v.r.* be unpicked; be indiscreet or tactless

descosido, *a.* tactless, talkative; *(fig.)* disjointed; desultory; unsewn. *m. (sew.)* rent, hole

descoyuntamiento, *m.* dislocation (bones); irritation, bore; ache, pain

descoyuntar, *v.t.* to dislocate (bones); bore, annoy; *v.r.* be dislocated

descrédito, *m.* fall in value (things); discredit (persons)

descreer, *v.t. irr.* to disbelieve; depreciate, disparage (persons). See **creer**

descreído (-da), *a.* unbelieving. *s.* unbeliever; infidel

describir, *v.t.* to describe; outline, sketch. *Past Part.* **descrito**

descripción, *f.* description; *(law)* inventory

descriptible, *a.* describable

descriptivo, *a.* descriptive

descuajar, *v.t.* to liquefy; *(fam.)* discourage; *(agr.)* pull up by the root

descuajo, *m. (agr.)* pulling up by the root

descuartizar, *v.t.* to quarter; joint (meat); *(fam.)* carve, cut into pieces, break up

descubierto, *a.* bareheaded; exposed. *m.* deficit. **al d.,** openly; in the open, without shelter.

girar en d., to overdraw (a bank account)

descubridero, *m.* viewpoint, lookout

descubridor (-ra), *s.* discoverer; inventor; explorer. *m.* (*mil.*) scout

descubrimiento, *m.* find; discovery; revelation; newly-discovered territory

descubrir, *v.t.* to reveal; show; discover; learn; unveil (memorials, etc.); *v.r.* remove one's hat; show oneself, reveal one's whereabouts. *Past Part.* descubierto

descuello, *m.* extra height; (*fig.*) pre-eminence; arrogance

descuento, *m.* reduction; (*com.*) rebate, discount

descuidado, *a.* negligent; careless; untidy; unprepared

descuidar, *v.t.* to relieve (of responsibility, etc.); distract, occupy (attention, etc.); *v.i.* and *v.r.* be careless; *v.r.* (*with de* or *en*) neglect

descuido, *m.* carelessness, negligence; oversight, mistake; incivility; forgetfulness; shameful act

desde, *prep.* since, from (time or space); after (e.g. **d. hoy**, from to-day). **d. la ventana**, from the window. **d. aquella época**, since that time

desdecir, *v.i. irr.* (*with de*) to degenerate, be less good than; be discordant, clash; be unworthy of; *v.r.* unsay one's words, retract. See **decir**

desdén, *m.* indifference, coldness; disdain, scorn

desdentado, *a.* toothless; (*zool.*) edentate

desdentar, *v.t.* to remove teeth

desdeñar, *v.t.* to scorn; *v.r.* (*with de*) dislike, be reluctant

desdeñoso, *a.* disdainful, scornful

desdevanar, *v.t.* to unwind thread, etc.

desdibujado, *a.* badly drawn; blurred, confused

desdicha, *f.* misfortune; extreme poverty, misery. **por d.**, unfortunately

desdichado, *a.* unfortunate; (*fam.*) timid, weak-kneed

desdoblar, *v.t.* to unfold

desdorar, *v.t.* to remove the gilt; (*fig.*) tarnish, sully

desdoro, *m.* discredit, dishonour

deseable, *a.* desirable

desear, *v.t.* to desire; yearn or long for

desecación, *f.* desiccation

desecar, *v.t.* to dry; *v.r.* be desiccated

desechar, *v.t.* to reject, refuse; scorn; cast out, expel; put away (thoughts, etc.); cast off (old clothes); turn (key); give up

desecho, *m.* residue, rest; remains; cast-off; scorn

desembalaje, *m.* unpacking

desembalar, *v.t.* to unpack

desembanastar, *v.t.* to take out of a basket; (*fam.*) unsheath (sword); *v.r.* break loose (animals); (*fam.*) get out, alight

desembarazar, *v.t.* to clear of obstruction; disembarrass, free; vacate; *v.r.* (*fig.*) rid oneself of obstacles

desembarazo, *m.* freedom, insouciance, naturalness

desembarcadero, *m.* landing-stage

desembarcar, *v.t.* to unload; *v.i.* disembark; alight from vehicle

desembarco, *m.* disembarkation, landing; staircase landing

desembargar, *v.t.* to free of obstacles or impediments; (*law*) remove an embargo

desembargo, *m.* (*law*) removal of an embargo

desembarque, *m.* disembarkation, landing

desembarrancar, *v.t.* and *v.i.* (*naut.*) to re-float

desembaular, *v.t.* to unpack from a trunk; disinter, empty; (*fam.*) unbosom oneself

desembocadero, *m.* exit, way out; mouth (rivers, etc.)

desembocadura, *f.* mouth (rivers, etc.); street opening

desembocar, *v.i.* (*with en*) to lead to, end in; flow into (rivers)

desembolsar, *v.t.* to take out of a purse; pay, spend

desembolso, *m.* disbursement; expenditure

desemboscarse, *v.r.* to get out of the wood; extricate oneself from an ambush

desembozar, *v.t.* to unmuffle

desembozo, *m.* uncovering of the face

desembragar, *v.t.* (*mech.*) to disengage (the clutch, etc.)

desembravecer, *v.t. irr.* to tame, domesticate. See **conocer**

desembriagar(se), *v.t.* and *v.r.* to sober up (after a drinking bout)

desembrollar, *v.t.* (*fam.*) to disentangle, unravel

desemejanza, *f.* unlikeness

desemejar, *v.i.* to be unlike; *v.t.* disfigure, deform

desempacar, *v.t.* to unpack

desempapelar, *v.t.* to unwrap, remove the paper from; remove wall-paper

desempaquetar, *v.t.* to unpack

desemparejar, *v.t.* to split (a pair); make unequal

desemparentado, *a.* without relatives

desempedrar, *v.t. irr.* to take up the flags (of a pavement). See **acertar**

desempeñar, *v.t.* to redeem (pledges); free from debt; fulfil (obligations, etc.); take out of pawn; hold, fill (an office); extricate (from difficulties, etc.); perform, carry out; (*theat.*) act

desempeño, *m.* redemption of a pledge; fulfilment (of an obligation, etc.); performance, accomplishment; (*theat.*) acting of a part

desempolvar, *v.t.* to free from dust, dust

desenamorar, *v.t.* to kill the affection of; *v.r.* fall out of love

desencadenar, *v.t.* to unchain, unfetter; (*fig.*) unleash, let loose; *v.r.* (*fig.*) break loose

desencajamiento, *m.* disjointedness, dislocation; ricketiness, broken-down appearance

desencajar, *v.t.* to disconnect, disjoint; dislocate; *v.r.* be out of joint; be contorted (of the face); be tired looking

desencaje, *m.* See **desencajamiento**

desencallar, *v.t.* (*naut.*) to float a grounded ship

desencantar, *v.t.* to disenchant

desencanto, *m.* disenchantment; disillusionment

desencerrar, *v.t. irr.* to set at liberty; unlock; disclose, reveal. See **acertar**

desenclavijar, *v.t.* to remove the pegs or pins; disconnect, disjoint

desencoger, *v.t.* to unfold, spread out; *v.r.* grow bold

desencolar, *v.t. irr.* to unglue. See **colar**

desencolerizar, *v.t.* to placate; *v.r.* lose one's anger, grow calm

desenconar, *v.t.* to reduce (inflammation); appease (anger, etc.); *v.r.* become calm

desencono, *m.* reduction of inflammation; appeasement (of anger, etc.)

desencordelar, *v.t.* to untie the ropes (of), unstring

desencorvar, *v.t.* to straighten (curves, etc.)

desenchufar, *v.t.* to disconnect, unplug (electric plugs, etc.)

desenfadado, *a.* expeditious; natural, at ease; gay; forward, bold; wide, spacious

desenfadar, *v.t.* to appease, make anger disappear

desenfado, *m.* freedom; ease; unconcern, frankness

desenfardar, *v.t.* to unpack bales

desenfrailar, *v.i.* to leave the cloister, become secularized; (*fam.*) emancipate oneself

desenfrenar, *v.t.* to unbridle (horses); *v.r.* give rein to one's passions, etc.; break loose (storms, etc.)

desenfreno, *m.* licence, lasciviousness; complete freedom from restraint

desengalanar, *v.t.* to strip of ornaments

desenganchar, *v.t.* to unhook; uncouple; unfasten; unharness

desengañador, *a.* undeceiving

desengañar, *v.t.* to undeceive, disillusion

desengaño, *m.* undeceiving, disabuse; disillusionment

desengarzar, *v.t.* to loosen from its setting; unlink, unhook, unclasp

desengastar, *v.t.* to remove from its setting (jewellery, etc.)

desengrasar, *v.t.* to remove the grease from, clean; *v.i.* (*fam.*) grow thin

desenlace, *m.* loosening, untying;

(lit.) dénouement, climax (of play, etc.)

desenlazar, v.t. to untie, unloose; (lit.) unravel (a plot)

desenlosar, v.t. to remove flagstones

desenmarañar, v.t. to disentangle; (fig) straighten out

desenmascarar, v.t. to remove the mask from; (fig.) unmask

desenmudecer, v.i. irr. to be freed of a speech impediment; break silence, speak. See **conocer**

desenojar, v.t. to soothe, appease; v.r. distract oneself, amuse oneself

desenojo, m. relenting, abatement of anger

desenredar, v.t. to disentangle; (fig.) set right; straighten out; v.r. extricate oneself, get out of a difficulty

desenredo, m. disentanglement; (lit.) climax

desenseñar, v.t. to unteach

desentablar, v.t. to tear up planks or boards; disorder, disrupt

desentenderse, v.r. irr. (with de) to pretend to be ignorant of; take no part in. See **entender**

desenterrador, m. disinterrer, unearther

desenterramiento, m. disinterment; (fig.) unearthing, recollection

desenterrar, v.t. irr. to unbury, disinter; rummage out; (fig.) unearth, bring up, recall. See **acertar**

desentoldar, v.t. to take away an awning; (fig.) strip of ornament

desentonar, v.t. to humiliate; v.i. (mus.) be out of tune; speak rudely; v.r. be inharmonious; raise the voice (anger, etc.), behave badly

desentono, m. bad behaviour, rudeness; (mus.) discord; grating quality or harshness (of voice)

desentorpecer, v.t. irr. to restore feeling to (numbed limbs); free from torpor; v.r. become bright and intelligent. See **conocer**

desentramparse, v.r. (fam.) free oneself from debt

desentrañar, v.t. to disembowel;

(fig.) unravel, penetrate; v.r. give away one's all

desentronizar, v.t. to dethrone; dismiss from office

desentumecer, v.t. irr. to free from numbness (limbs); v.r. be restored to feeling (numb limbs). See **conocer**

desenvainar, v.t. to unsheath; (fam.) reveal, bring into the open

desenvoltura, f. naturalness, ease, freedom; eloquence, facility (of speech); effrontery, audacity, shamelessness (especially in women)

desenvolver, v.t. irr. to unroll; unfold; (fig.) unravel, explain; (fig.) develop, work out (theories, etc.); v.r. unroll; unfold; lose one's timidity, blossom out; be over-bold; extricate oneself (from a difficulty). See **resolver**

desenvuelto, a. natural, easy; impudent, bold

deseo, m. desire, will, wish

deseoso, a. desirous, wishful

desequilibrar(se), v.t. and v.r. to unbalance

desequilibrio, m. lack of balance; confusion, disorder; mental instability

deserción, f. (mil.) desertion

desertar, v.t. (mil.) to desert; (fam.) quit

desertor, m. (mil.) deserter; (fam.) quitter

deservicio, m. disservice

desesperación, f. desperation, despair; frenzy, violence

desesperado, a. desperate, hopeless; frenzied

desesperanza, f. despair; hopelessness

desesperanzar, v.t. to render hopeless; v.r. despair, lose hope

desesperar, v.t. to make hopeless; (fam.) annoy, make furious; v.r. lose hope, despair; be frenzied

desestañar, v.t. to unsolder

desestimación, f. disrespect, lack of esteem; rejection

desestimar, v.t. to scorn; reject

desfachatado, a. (fam.) impudent, brazen

desfachatez, f. (fam.) effrontery, cheek

desfalcador (-ra), a. embezzling. s. embezzler

desfalcar, *v.t.* to remove a part of; embezzle

desfalco, *m.* diminution, reduction; embezzlement

desfallecer, *v.t. irr.* to weaken; *v.i.* grow weak; faint, swoon. See **conocer**

desfallecimiento, *m.* weakness, languor; depression, discouragement; faint, swoon

desfavorable, *a.* unfavourable; hostile, contrary

desfavorecer, *v.t. irr.* to withdraw one's favour, scorn; disfavour; oppose. See **conocer**

desfiguración, *f.* deformation; disfigurement

desfigurar, *v.t.* to deform, misshape; disfigure; (*fig.*) disguise, mask; obscure, darken; distort, misrepresent; *v.r.* be disfigured (by rage, etc.)

desfijar, *v.t.* to unfix, pull off, remove

desfiladero, *m.* defile, gully

desfilar, *v.i.* to walk in file; (*fam.*) file out; (*mil.*) file or march past

desfile, *m.* (*mil.*) march past; parade; walk past; procession

desfloración, *f.* defloration

desflorar, *v.t.* to tarnish, stain; deflower, violate; (*fig.*) touch upon, deal lightly with

desfortalecer, *v.t. irr.* (*mil.*) to dismantle a fortress. See **conocer**

desfruncir, *v.t.* to unfold, shake out

desgaire, *m.* untidiness, slovenliness; affectation of carelessness (in dress); scornful gesture. **al d.,** with an affectation of carelessness, negligently

desgajadura, *f.* tearing off of a tree branch

desgajar, *v.t.* to tear off a tree branch; break; *v.r.* break off; dissociate oneself (from)

desgalgar, *v.t.* to throw headlong

desgana, *f.* lack of appetite; lack of interest, indifference; reluctance

desganar, *v.t.* to dissuade; *v.r.* lose one's appetite; become bored or indifferent, lose interest

desgarbado, *a.* slovenly, slatternly; gawky, graceless

desgarrado, *a.* dissolute, vicious; impudent, brazen

desgarrador, *a.* tearing; heart-rending

desgarrar, *v.t.* to tear; *v.r.* leave, tear oneself away

desgarro, *m.* tearing; rent, breach; boastfulness, impudence, effrontery

desgastar, *v.t.* to corrode, wear away; spoil, corrupt; *v.r.* lose one's vigour, grow weak; wear away

desgaste, *m.* attrition; wearing down or away; corrosion; wear and tear

desgobernado, *a.* uncontrolled (of persons)

desgobernar, *v.t. irr.* to upset or rise against the government; dislocate (bones); (*naut.*) neglect the tiller; *v.r.* affect exaggerated movements in dancing. See **recomendar**

desgobierno, *m.* misgovernment; mismanagement; maladministration; disorder, tumult

desgomar, *v.t.* to ungum (fabrics)

desgoznar, *v.t.* to unhinge; *v.r.* (*fig.*) lose one's self-control

desgracia, *f.* misfortune, adversity; mishap, piece of bad luck; disgrace, disfavour; disagreeableness, brusqueness; ungraciousness. **por d.,** unhappily, unfortunately

desgraciado, *a.* unfortunate, unhappy; unlucky; dull, boring; disagreeable

desgraciar, *v.t.* to displease; spoil the development (of), destroy; maim; *v.r.* fall out of friendship; be out of favour; turn out badly, fail; be destroyed or spoiled; be maimed

desgranar, *v.t.* (*agr.*) to thresh, flail; *v.r.* break (string of beads, etc.)

desgreñar, *v.t.* to dishevel the hair; *v.r.* (*fam.*) pull each other's hair, come to blows

desguarnecer, *v.t. irr.* to strip of trimming; (*mil.*) de-militarize; (*mil.*) disarm; dismantle; unharness. See **conocer**

desguazar, *v.t.* to break up (ships)

deshabitado, *a.* uninhabited, empty

deshabitar, *v.t.* to desert, quit, leave (a place)

deshabituar, *v.t.* to disaccustom; *v.r.* lose the habit, become un-accustomed

deshacer, *v.t. irr.* to undo; destroy; (*mil.*) rout, defeat; take to pieces; melt; pulp (paper); untie (knots, etc.); open (parcels); diminish, decrease; break in pieces, smash; (*fig.*) obstruct, spoil; *v.r.* be wasted or spoiled; be full of anxiety; vanish; try or work very hard; injure oneself; be emaciated, grow extremely thin; (*with de*) part with. **d. agravios,** to right wrongs. See **hacer**

desharrapado, *a.* tattered, shabby

deshebillar, *v.t.* to unbuckle

deshebrar, *v.t.* to unravel; shred

deshecha, *f.* pretence, evasion; courteous farewell; obligatory departure

deshechizar, *v.t.* to disenchant

deshelar, *v.t. irr.* to thaw, melt. See **acertar**

desherbar, *v.t. irr.* to pull up weeds. See **acertar**

desheredación, *f.* disinheritance

desheredar, *v.t.* disinherit; *v.r.* (*fig.*) lower oneself

deshermanar, *v.t.* to unmatch; *v.r.* fail in brotherly love

desherrar, *v.t. irr.* to unfetter, unchain; strike off horseshoes; *v.r.* lose a shoe (horses). See **acertar**

desherrumbrar, *v.t.* to remove the rust from; clean off rust from

deshidratación, *f.* dehydration

deshidratar, *v.t.* to dehydrate

deshielo, *m.* thaw

deshilado, *a.* in single file. *m.* (*sew.*) drawn-thread work (gen. *pl.*). **a la deshilada,** (*mil.*) in file formation; secretly

deshiladura, *f.* unravelling

deshilar, *v.t.* to unravel; (*sew.*) draw threads; (*cul.*) shred, grate

deshilvanado, *a.* (*fig.*) disjointed, disconnected

deshilvanar, *v.t.* (*sew.*) to remove the tacking threads

deshincar, *v.t.* to pull out, remove, draw out

deshinchar, *v.t.* to remove a swelling; deflate; lessen the anger of; *v.r.* decrease, subside (swellings); deflate; (*fam.*) grow humble

deshojar, *v.t.* to strip off leaves or petals

deshollejar, *v.t.* to skin, peel (fruit); shell (peas, etc.)

deshollinador, *m.* chimney-sweep; wall-brush; chemical chimney cleaner

deshollinar, *v.t.* to sweep chimneys; clean down walls; (*fam.*) examine closely

deshonestidad, *f.* immodesty, shamelessness; indecency

deshonesto, *a.* shameless, immodest; dissolute, vicious; indecent

deshonor, *m.* dishonour; disgrace, insult

deshonra, *f.* dishonour

deshonrabuenos, *m.* and *f.* (*fam.*) slanderer; degenerate

deshonrador (-ra), *a.* dishonourable. *s.* dishonourer

deshonrar, *v.t.* to dishonour; insult; seduce (women)

deshonroso, *a.* dishonourable, insulting, indecent

deshora, *f.* inconvenient time. **a d.,** *or* **a deshoras,** at an inconvenient time, unseasonably; extempore

deshuesar, *v.t.* to remove the bone (from meat); stone (fruit)

deshumedecer, *v.t. irr.* to dry; *v.r.* become dry. See **conocer**

desidia, *f.* negligence; laziness

desidioso, *a.* negligent; lazy

desierto, *a.* deserted, uninhabited, solitary. *m.* desert; wilderness

designación, *f.* designation; appointment

designar, *v.t.* to plan, intend; designate; appoint

designio, *m.* intention, idea

desigual, *a.* unequal; uneven (ground); rough; arduous, difficult; changeable

desigualar, *v.t.* to make unequal; *v.r.* prosper

desigualdad, *f.* inequality; unevenness, rockiness; (*fig.*) changeability; variability

desilusión, *f.* disillusionment; disappointment

desilusionar, *v.t.* to disillusion; *v.r.* become disillusioned; be undeceived

desinclinar, *v.t.* to dissuade

desinfección, *f.* disinfection

desinfectante, *a.* and *m.* disinfectant

desinfectar, *v.t.* to disinfect

desinflación, *f.* deflation

desinflar, *v.t.* to deflate

desinterés, *m.* disinterestedness

desinteresado, *a.* disinterested; generous

desinteresarse, *v.r.* to lose interest, grow indifferent

desistencia, *f.,* **desistimiento,** *m.* desistance, ceasing

desistir, *v.i.* to desist; cease; (*law*) renounce

desjuntamiento, *m.* separation; division

desjuntar(se), *v.t.* and *v.r.* to separate; divide

deslavado, *a.* brazen, impudent

deslavar, *v.t.* to wash superficially; spoil by washing, take away the body of (cloth, etc.)

desleal, *a.* disloyal, treacherous

deslealtad, *f.* disloyalty

desleír, *v.t.* *irr.* to dissolve; dilute. See **reír**

deslenguado, *a.* shameless, foul-mouthed

deslenguar, *v.t.* to remove the tongue; *v.r.* (*fam.*) be insolent

desliar, *v.t.* to untie, undo, unloose

desligadura, *f.* untying, loosening

desligar, *v.t.* to unfasten, unbind; (*fig.*) solve, unravel; relieve of an obligation; (*mus.*) play staccato; *v.r.* come unfastened, grow loose

deslindador, *m.* one who fixes boundaries or limits

deslindar, *v.t.* to fix the boundaries (of); limit, circumscribe

deslinde, *m.* demarcation, boundary

desliz, *m.* slipping, slip, slide; skid; indiscretion, slip; peccadillo, trifling fault

deslizadero, *m.* slippery place; chute

deslizadizo, *a.* slippery

deslizar, *v.t.* to slip, slide; skid; *v.r.* commit an indiscretion; speak or act unwisely; escape, slip away; slip; skid

deslucido, *a.* fruitless, vain; stupid, clumsy, awkward; discoloured; tarnished, dull; unsuccessful

deslucimiento, *m.* clumsiness, gracelessness; failure, lack of success

deslucir, *v.t.* *irr.* to fade; discolour, stain; tarnish; spoil; sully the reputation of; *v.r.* do a thing badly, fail at. See **lucir**

deslumbrador, *a.* dazzling

deslumbramiento, *m.* brilliant light, glare, dazzle; bewilderment, confusion

deslumbrar, *v.t.* to dazzle; confuse, bewilder; (*fig.*) daze (with magnificence)

deslustrar, *v.t.* to dull, dim, tarnish; frost (glass); discredit, sully (reputation)

deslustre, *m.* dullness, tarnish; frosting (of glass); disgrace, stigma

deslustroso, *a.* ugly, unsuitable, unbecoming

desmadejamiento, *m.* debility, languor; untidiness, dishevelment

desmadejar, *v.t.* to debilitate, enervate

desmán, *m.* outrageous behaviour; disaster, misfortune

desmandado, *a.* disobedient

desmandar, *v.t.* to cancel, revoke (orders); withdraw (an offer). *v.r.* behave badly; stray

desmantelado, *a.* dismantled, dilapidated

desmantelamiento, *m.* dismantling; dilapidation

desmantelar, *v.t.* to dismantle; abandon, forsake

desmaña, *f.* lack of. dexterity, clumsiness, awkwardness

desmañado, *a.* clumsy, awkward, unhandy

desmayado, *a.* pale, faint (of colours); weak (of a voice)

desmayar, *v.t.* to cause to faint; *v.i.* grow discouraged, lose heart; *v.r.* swoon, faint

desmayo, *m.* depression, discouragement; faint, swoon

desmedido, *a.* disproportionate; excessive

desmedirse, *v.r.* to misbehave, go too far

desmedrado, *a.* thin, emaciated; deteriorated, spoilt

desmedrar, *v.t.* to spoil, ruin; *v.i.* deteriorate; decline

desmejora, *f.* deterioration

desmejorar, *v.t.* to spoil, impair,

cause to deteriorate; *v.r.* deteriorate; *v.i.* and *v.r.* decline in health; lose one's beauty

desmelenar, *v.t.* to ruffle or dishevel the hair

desmembración, *f.* dismemberment

desmembrar, *v.t.* to dismember; separate, divide

desmemoriarse, *v.r.* to forget, lose one's memory

desmenguar, *v.t.* to reduce, decrease; (*fig.*) diminish

desmentida, *f.* action of giving the lie to

desmentir, *v.t. irr.* to give the lie to; contradict, deny; lower oneself; behave unworthily; *v.i.* deviate (from right direction, etc.). See **sentir**

desmenuzar, *v.t.* to crumble, break into small pieces; (*fig.*) examine in detail; *v.r.* be broken up

desmeollar, *v.t.* to remove the marrow of

desmerecedor, *a.* unworthy

desmerecer, *v.t. irr.* to become undeserving of; *v.i.* deteriorate; be inferior to. See **conocer**

desmesura, *f.* insolence; disproportion; excess

desmesurado, *a.* disproportionate; excessive, enormous; insolent, uncivil

desmesurar, *v.t.* to disarrange, disorder; *v.r.* be insolent

desmigajar(se), *v.t.* and *v.r.* to crumble

desmigar, *v.t.* (*cul.*) to make breadcrumbs

desmilitarizar, *v.t.* to demilitarize

desmochar, *v.t.* to lop off the top; pollard (trees)

desmoche, *m.* lopping, removal of the top or head

desmonetización, *f.* demonetization; conversion of coin into bullion

desmonetizar, *v.t.* to convert money into bullion; demonetize; *v.r.* depreciate (shares, etc.)

desmontable, *a.* movable; sectional

desmontar, *v.t.* to clear wholly or partially of trees or shrubs; clear up (rubbish); level (ground); dismantle; dismount; uncock

(fire-arms); *v.i.* and *v.r.* dismount (from horse, etc.)

desmonte, *m.* clearing of trees and shrubs; clearing, cleared ground; timber remaining

desmoralización, *f.* demoralization, corruption

desmoralizador, *a.* demoralizing

desmoralizar, *v.t.* to demoralize, corrupt

desmoronamiento, *m.* crumbling; decay, ruin

desmoronar, *v.t.* to destroy, decay; crumble; *v.r.* crumble away, fall into ruin; decline, decay; wane, fade (power, etc.)

desmovilización, *f.* demobilization

desmovilizar, *v.t.* to demobilize

desnacificación, *f.* denazification

desnatar, *v.t.* to skim; (*fig.*) take the cream or best

desnaturalización, *f.* denaturalization

desnaturalizar, *v.t.* to denaturalize; exile; deform, disfigure, pervert; *v.r.* give up one's country

desnivel, *m.* unevenness; slope, drop

desnivelar(se), *v.i.* and *v.r.* to become uneven

desnudar, *v.t.* to undress; (*fig.*) despoil, strip, denude; *v.r.* undress oneself; deprive oneself

desnudez, *f.* nudity; nakedness; bareness; plainness

desnudo, *a.* nude; ill-clad; bare, naked; clear, patent; (*fig.*) destitute (of grace, etc.). *m.* (*art*) nude

desnutrición, *f.* malnutrition

desobedecer, *v.t. irr.* to disobey. See **conocer**

desobediencia, *f.* disobedience

desobediente, *a.* disobedient

desobligar, *v.t.* to free from obligation; offend, hurt

desocupación, *f.* lack of occupation; leisure

desocupado, *a.* idle; vacant, unoccupied

desocupar, *v.t.* to empty; vacate; *v.r.* give up an employment or occupation

desodorante, *a.* and *m.* deodorant

desoír, *v.t. irr.* to pay no attention, pretend not to hear. See **oír**

desojar, *v.t.* to break the eye of (needles, etc.); *v.r.* gaze intently desolación, f. destruction, desolation; affliction

desolador, a. desolate; grievous

desolar, v.t. irr. to lay waste, destroy; v.r. grieve, be disconsolate. See contar

desoldar, v.t. to unsolder; v.r. become unsoldered

desolladero, m. slaughter-house

desollado, a. (fam.) impertinent, barefaced. m. carcass

desolladura, f. flaying, skinning; (fam.) slander

desollar, v.t. irr. to flay, skin; harm, discredit. d. vivo, (fam.) to extort an exorbitant price; slander. See contar

desopinado, a. discredited

desopinar, v.t. to discredit, defame

desorden, m. disorder, disarray; confusion; excess

desordenado, a. disordered; vicious; licentious

desordenar, v.t. to disorder; confuse; v.r. go beyond the just limits; behave badly; be impertinent

desorganización, f. disorganization

desorganizador, a. disorganizing

desorganizar, v.t. to disorganize; disband

desorientación, f. disorientation, loss of bearings; lack of method, confusion

desorientar, v.t. to disorientate; perplex, confuse; v.r. lose one's way; be disorientated

desovar, v.i. to spawn

desove, m. spawning; spawning season

desovillar, v.t. to unwind; uncoil; uncurl; explain, clarify

despabiladeras, f. pl. snuffers

despabilado, a. alert, wide-awake; watchful, vigilant

despabiladura, f. snuff of a candle, lamp, etc.

despabilar, v.t. to snuff (a candle); trim (lamps); hasten, expedite; finish quickly; steal, rob; (fig.) quicken (intelligence, etc.); (fam.) kill; v.r. rouse oneself, wake up

despacio, adv. slowly, little by little; deliberately, leisurely. interj. Careful! Gently now!

despacito, adv. (fam.) very slowly

despachador (-ra), s. dispatcher, sender

despachar, v.t. to expedite; dispatch, conclude; forward, send; attend to correspondence; sell; dismiss; (fam.) serve in a shop; (fam.) kill; v.i. hasten; carry letters to be signed (in offices, etc.); v.r. get rid of

despacho, m. transaction, execution; study; office, room; department; booking-office; dispatch, shipment; expedient; commission, warrant; dispatch (diplomatic); telegram; telephone message. d. particular, private office

despachurrar, v.t. (fam.) to crush, squash; recount in a muddled fashion; (fig.) squash flat, confound

despalmador, m. dockyard

despalmar, v.t. (naut.) to careen, caulk

despampanar, v.t. (agr.) to prune vines; (fam.) amaze, stun, astound; v.i. (fam.) relieve one's feelings; v.r. (fam.) receive a serious injury (through falling)

desparejar, v.t. to break a pair

desparpajar, v.t. to spoil; v.i. (fam.) chatter

desparpajo, m. (fam.) loquaciousness, pertness; disorder, muddle

desparramar, v.t. to disperse, scatter; squander, waste (money, etc.); v.r. amuse oneself; be dissipated

despavorido, a. terrified, panic-stricken

despectivo, a. contemptuous, depreciatory

despechar, v.t. to anger; make despair; (fam.) wean; v.r. be angry; be in despair

despecho, m. rancour, malice; despair. a d. de, in spite of

despechugar, v.t. to cut off the breast (fowls); v.r. (fam.) show the bosom

despedazar, v.t. to cut or break into pieces; (fig.) break (heart, etc.)

despedida, f. dismissal, discharge; seeing off (a visitor, etc.); farewell, good-bye

despedir, v.t. irr. to throw out, emit, cast up; dismiss, discharge;

see off (on a journey or after a visit); banish (from the mind); get rid of; *v.r.* say good-bye; leave (employment). See pedir

despedregar, *v.t.* to clear of stones

despegadamente, *adv.* uninterestedly, unconcernedly, indifferently

despegado, *a.* (*fam.*) indifferent, unconcerned, cold

despegar, *v.t.* to unstick; unglue; separate, detach; *v.r.* become estranged; come apart or unstuck; *v.i.* (*aer.*) take off

despegue, *m.* (*aer.*) take-off

despeinar, *v.t.* to disarrange the hair; undo the coiffure

despejado, *a.* lively, sprightly; logical, clear-cut; cloudless; spacious, unobstructed, clear

despejar, *v.t.* to clear, free of obstacles; (*fig.*) elucidate, solve; (*math.*) find the value of; *v.r.* smarten up, grow gay; amuse oneself; clear up (weather, sky, etc.); improve (a patient)

despejo, *m.* freeing of obstacles; smartness, gaiety; grace, elegance; perkiness; clear-sightedness, intelligence

despeluzar, *v.t.* to disorder the hair; cause the hair to stand on end; horrify; *v.r.* stand on end (hair); be horrified or terrified

despeluznante, *a.* hair-raising, terrifying

despellejar, *v.t.* to flay, skin; slander

dependedor (-ra), *s.* spendthrift, waster

despender, *v.t.* to spend; waste

despensa, *f.* larder, pantry; store (of food); (*naut.*) steward's room; stewardship

despensero (-ra), *s.* steward; caterer; victualler; (*naut.*) steward

despeñadero, *m.* precipice, crag; dangerous undertaking, risk. *a.* steep, precipitous

despeñar, *v.t.* to precipitate, fling down from a height, hurl down; *v.r.* fling oneself headlong; throw oneself into (vices, etc.)

despeño, *m.* precipitation; headlong fall; (*fig.*) collapse, ruin

despepitar, *v.t.* to remove seeds

or pips; *v.r.* vociferate; act wildly; (*fam.*) desire, long (for)

desperdiciador (-ra), *a.* squandering, wasting. *s.* squanderer

desperdiciar, *v.t.* to squander; (*fig.*) misspend, waste

desperdicio, *m.* waste; remains, left-overs (gen. *pl.*)

desperdigar, *v.t.* to separate, sever; scatter

desperecerse, *v.r. irr.* to crave, yearn (for). See conocer

desperezarse, *v.r.* to stretch oneself

desperfecto, *m.* imperfection, flaw; slight deterioration

despernado, *a.* weary, footsore

despertador (-ra), *a.* awakening. *s.* awakener. *m.* alarm clock; incentive, stimulus

despertamiento, *m.* awakening

despertar, *v.t. irr.* to awaken; bring to mind, recall; incite, stimulate; *v.i.* waken; (*fig.*) wake up, become more intelligent. See acertar

despiadado, *a.* cruel, merciless

despicar, *v.t.* to satisfy, content; *v.r.* revenge oneself

despierto, *a.* wide-awake, clever

despilfarrado, *a.* ragged, shabby; wasteful; spendthrift

despilfarrar, *v.t.* to squander, waste

despilfarro, *m.* slovenliness, waste, extravagance; mismanagement, maladministration

despintar, *v.t.* to paint out; wash off the paint; efface, blot out; disfigure, deform; *v.i.* be unlike or unworthy (of); *v.r.* fade (colours); forget

despiojar, *v.t.* to remove lice, delouse; (*fam.*) rescue from misery

despique, *m.* vengeance, revenge

despistar, *v.t.* to throw off the scent; mislead

desplacer, *v.t. irr.* to displease. *m.* disgust, displeasure, sorrow. See placer

desplantar(se), *v.t.* and *v.r.* to deviate from the vertical

desplazamiento, *m.* (*naut.*) displacement

desplegadura, *f.* unfolding

desplegar, *v.t. irr.* to unfold; spread open; (*fig.*) reveal, disclose, explain; evince, display;

(mil.) deploy troops; *v.r.* unfold, open (flowers, etc.); *(mil.)* deploy. See **cegar**

despliegue, *m.* unfolding; spreading out; evincing, demonstration; *(mil.)* deployment

desplomar, *v.t.* to put out of the straight, cause to lean (walls, buildings); *v.r.* lean, tilt (buildings); topple, fall down (walls, etc.); collapse (people); be ruined

desplome, *m.* collapse

desplomo, *m.* tilt, cant, deviation from vertical

desplumar, *v.t.* to remove feathers, pluck; rob, despoil

despoblación, *f.* depopulation

despoblado, *m.* wilderness; deserted place

despoblar, *v.t.* to depopulate; despoil, rob; *v.r.* become depopulated

despojador (-ra), *a.* robbing, despoiling, *s.* despoiler

despojar, *v.t.* to plunder, despoil; dispossess; *v.r. (with de)* remove (garments, etc.); relinquish, give up

despojo, *m.* pillaging, spoliation; booty, plunder; butcher's offal; *pl.* remains, leavings; débris, rubble; corpse

despolvorear, *v.t.* to remove dust; *(fig.)* shake off

desposado, *a.* recently married; fettered, handcuffed. **los desposados**, the newly-weds

desposar, *v.t.* to perform the marriage ceremony; *v.r.* become betrothed; marry

desposeer, *v.t.* to dispossess; *v.r.* renounce one's possessions. See **creer**

desposeimiento, *m.* dispossession

desposorio, *m.* betrothal, promise of marriage; (gen. *pl.*) wedding, marriage

déspota, *m.* despot, tyrant

despótico, *a.* tyrannical

despotismo, *m.* despotism

despotricarse, *v.r.* to rave (against), rail (against)

despreciable, *a.* worthless, contemptible

despreciar, *v.t.* to scorn, despise; *v.r.* despise oneself

despreciativo, *a.* contemptuous, scornful

desprecio, *m.* contempt, scorn

desprender, *v.t.* to loosen, remove, unfix; give off (gases, etc.); *v.r.* work loose, give way; deduce, infer; give away, deprive oneself (of)

desprendido, *a.* disinterested; generous

desprendimiento, *m.* loosening; removal, separation; emission; indifference, lack of interest; generosity; impartiality

despreocupación, *f.* fair mindedness, impartiality; lack of interest

despreocupado, *a.* unprejudiced, broad-minded; indifferent, uninterested

despreocuparse, *v.r.* to shake off prejudice; *(with de)* pay no attention to; set aside

desprestigiar, *v.t.* to discredit; *v.r.* lose prestige; lose caste

desprestigio, *m.* loss of prestige, discredit

desprevenido, *a.* unprepared, improvident

desproporción, *f.* disproportion

desproporcionado, *a.* disproportionate; out of proportion

despropósito, *m.* nonsense, absurdity

desproveer, *v.t. irr.* to deprive of necessities. See **creer**

despueble, *m.* depopulation

después, *adv.* afterwards, after, next (of time and place) (e.g. **Vendrá d. de Pascua**, He will come after Easter. **Zaragoza viene d. de Madrid**, Saragossa comes after Madrid)

despuntar, *v.t.* to blunt the point; *(naut.)* double, sail round; *v.i.* show green, sprout; appear (the dawn); grow clever; *(fig.)* stand out, excel

desquiciamiento, *m.* unhinging; disconnecting; *(fig.)* upsetting, throwing out of gear; downfall, fall from favour

desquiciar, *v.t.* to unhinge; disconnect; *(fig.)* throw out of gear, upset; banish from favour; *v.r.* become unhinged; *(fig.)* be disordered; upset

desquitar(se), *v.t. and v.r.* to retrieve a loss; take revenge, retaliate

desquite, *m.* compensation; revenge

destacamento, *m.* (*mil.*) detachment

destacar, *v.t.* (*mil.*) to detach; *v.r.* excel; be prominent; be conspicuous; (*art*) stand out

destajador, *m.* smith's hammer

destajar, *v.t.* to cut (cards); set forth conditions, stipulate, contract

destajista, *m.* and *f.* pieceworker; jobber (workman)

destajo, *m.* piece-work; job. a d., quickly and diligently. (*fam.*) hablar a d., to chatter, talk too much

destapar, *v.t.* to remove the cover or lid; reveal, uncover; *v.r.* be uncovered; reveal oneself

destartalado, *a.* tumble-down, rickety; poverty-stricken

destejar, *v.t.* to remove tiles or slates; leave unprotected

destejer, *v.t.* to unweave, unravel; (*fig.*) undo, spoil

destello, *m.* gleam, sparkle, brilliance; flash, beam, ray; (*fig.*) gleam (of talent)

destemplado, *a.* out of tune; inharmonious; intemperate; (*art*) inharmonious: (*fam.*) out of sorts, indisposed

destemplanza, *f.* inclemency, rigour (weather); intemperance, excess, abuse; (*fam.*) indisposition; lack of moderation (actions, speech)

destemplar, *v.t.* to disturb, upset, alter; (*mus.*) put out of tune; put to confusion; *v.r.* be unwell; (*fig.*) go too far, behave badly; lose temper (metals)

destemple, *m.* (*mus.*) being out of tune; (*med.*) indisposition; uncertainty (weather); lack of temper (metals); disturbance, disorder; intemperance, excess, confusion

desternillarse de risa, to shake with laughter

desterrado (-da), *a.* exiled. *s.* exile

desterrar, *v.t.* *irr.* to exile; shake off the soil; (*fig.*) discard, lay aside. See **recomendar**

desterronar, *v.t.* to break sods

destetar, *v.t.* to wean

destete, *m.* weaning

destiempo, a, *adv.* untimely, inopportunely

destierro, *m.* banishment, exile; place of exile; remote place

destilación, *f.* distillation

destilador (-ra), *s.* distiller. *m.* still

destilar, *v.t.* to distil; filter; *v.i.* to drip

destilatorio, *a.* distilling. *m.* distillery; still

destilería, *f.* distillery

destinación, *f.* destination

destinar, *v.t.* to destine; appoint; assign

destino, *m.* fate, destiny; post, appointment; destination. con d. a, going to, bound for

destitución, *f.* destitution; discharge, dismissal

destituir, *v.t.* *irr.* (*with de*) to dismiss or discharge from (employment); deprive of. See **huir**

destorcer, *v.t.* *irr.* to untwist; straighten out; *v.r.* (*naut.*) drift. See **torcer**

destornillado, *a.* reckless; (*fig.*, *fam.*) with a screw loose

destornillador, *m.* screwdriver

destornillamiento, *m.* unscrewing

destornillar, *v.t.* to unscrew; *v.r.* act rashly

destrenzar, *v.t.* to unplait

destreza, *f.* dexterity; agility

destrón, *m.* blind man's guide

destronamiento, *m.* dethronement

destronar, *v.t.* to dethrone, depose; oust

destroncamiento, *m.* detruncation

destroncar, *v.t.* to lop, detruncate (trees); dislocate, disjoint; mutilate; (*fig.*) ruin, seriously harm; tire out; *v.r.* be exhausted or tired

destrozar, *v.t.* to destroy; break in pieces, shatter; (*mil.*) wipe out, annihilate; squander, dissipate

destrozo, *m.* destruction, ruin; shattering; (*mil.*) rout; dissipation, waste

destrozón, *a.* hard on wearing apparel, shoes, etc.

destrucción, *f.* destruction; ruin, irreparable loss

destructible, *a.* destructible

destructivo, *a.* destructive

destructor (-ra), *a.* destructive. *s.* destroyer. *m.* (*nav.*) destroyer

destruible, *a.* destructible

destruir, *v.t. irr.* to destroy, ruin, annihilate; frustrate, blast, disappoint; deprive of means of subsistence; squander, waste; *v.r.* (*math.*) cancel. See **huir**

desuello, *m.* flaying, skinning; forwardness, impertinence; extortion, fleecing. (*fig., fam.*) ¡ Es un d.! It's daylight robbery!

desuncir, *v.t.* to unyoke

desunión, *f.* disunion, separation; (*fig.*) discord, disharmony

desunir, *v.t.* to disunite, separate; (*fig.*) cause discord or disharmony

desusarse, *v.r.* to fall into disuse, become obsolete

desuso, *m.* disuse

desvaído, *a.* gaunt, lanky; pale, faded, dull (of colours)

desvainar, *v.t.* to shell (peas, beans)

desvalido, *a.* unprotected, helpless

desvalijar, *v.t.* to rifle (a suitcase, etc.); swindle

desvalimiento, *m.* defencelessness, lack of protection; lack of favour; desertion, abandonment

desvalorización, *f.* devaluation

desván, *m.* garret

desvanecer, *v.t. irr.* to cause to disappear; disintegrate; make vain; remove; *v.r.* evaporate; faint, swoon; grow vain or conceited. See **conocer**

desvanecimiento, *m.* faintness, loss of consciousness; vanity, conceit

desvarar, *v.t.* to slip, slide; (*naut.*) refloat

desvariar, *v.i.* to be delirious; rave, talk wildly

desvarío, *m.* foolish action, absurdity; delirium; monstrosity; whim, caprice

desvedar, *v.t.* to raise a ban or prohibition

desvelar, *v.t.* to keep awake; *v.r.* be sleepless; (*with por*) take great care over

desvelo, *m.* sleeplessness, vigil; care, attention, vigilance; anxiety. con d., watchfully

desvencijar, *v.t.* to loosen, disconnect, disjoint; *v.r.* work loose, become disjointed

desventaja, *f.* disadvantage

desventajoso, *a.* disadvantageous

desventura, *f.* misfortune

desventurado, *a.* unfortunate; timid, faint-hearted; miserly

desvergonzado, *a.* shameless, brazen, impudent

desvergonzarse, *v.r. irr.* to be brazen, be impudent. See **avergonzar**

desvergüenza, *f.* insolence; shamelessness

desvestir(se), *v.t.* and *v.r. irr.* to undress. See **pedir**

desviación, *f.* deviation, deflection

desviadero, *m.* diversion; (*r.w.*) siding

desviar, *v.t.* to divert, deflect; dissuade

desvío, *m.* deviation; indifference, coldness; repugnance

desvirgar, *v.t.* to deflower

desvirtuar, *v.t.* to decrease in strength or merit

desvivirse, *v.r.* (*with por*) to adore, love dearly; yearn for, be dying to; do one's best to please, (e.g. **Juan se desvive por servirme,** John does his best to help me)

detallar, *v.t.* to retail in detail; relate

detalle, *m.* detailed account; detail, particular

detective, *m.* detective

detector, *m.* detector; (*rad.*) cat-whisker

detención, *f.* stop, halt; delay; prolixity; arrest, detention

detener, *v.t. irr.* to detain, stop; arrest; retain, keep; *v.r.* go slowly; tarry; halt, stop; (*with en*) pause over, stop at. See **tener**

detenido, *a.* timid, irresolute; miserable, mean

deterioración, *f.* deterioration

deteriorar(se), *v.t.* and *v.r.* to deteriorate

determinación, *f.* determination; daring; decision

determinado, *a.* resolute, determined

determinar, *v.t.* to determine, limit; discern, distinguish; specify, appoint; decide, resolve; (*law*) define, judge; *v.r.* make up one's mind

determinativo, *a.* determining

determinismo, *m.* determinism

determinista, *m.* and *f.* determinist. *a.* deterministic

detersorio, *a.* and *m.* detergent

detestable, *a.* detestable

detestación, *f.* detestation

detestar, *v.t.* to abominate, detest

detonación, *f.* detonation

detonador, *m.* detonator

detonar, *v.t.* to detonate

detracción, *f.* detraction

detractor (-ra), *a.* slandering. *s.* detractor, slanderer

detraer, *v.t. irr.* to detract, take away; separate; slander. See **traer**

detrás, *adv.* behind, after (place). **por d.,** in the rear; (*fig.*) behind one's back

detrimento, *m.* detriment; moral harm

deuda, *f.* debt; fault, offence; sin. **d. exterior,** foreign debt. **Perdónanos nuestras deudas,** Forgive us our trespasses

deudo, *m.* relative, kinsman; kinship, relationship

deudor (-ra), *a.* indebted. *s.* debtor. **d. hipotecario,** mortgagor

devanadera, *f.,* bobbin, reel, spool; winder (machine)

devanador (-ra), *s.* winder (person). *m.* spool, bobbin

devanar, *v.t.* to reel, wind. (*fam.*) **devanarse los sesos,** to rack one's brains

devanear, *v.i.* to rave, talk nonsense

devaneo, *m.* delirium; foolishness, nonsense; dissipation; love-affair

devastación, *f.* devastation

devastar, *v.t.* to devastate, lay waste; (*fig.*) destroy, ruin

devengar, *v.t.* to have a right to, earn (salary, interest, etc.)

devoción, *f.* piety; affection, love; pious custom; prayer

devocionario, *m.* prayer book

devolución, *f.* restitution, return; devolution

devolutivo, *a.* (*law*) returnable

devolver, *v.t. irr.* to restore to original state; return, give back; repay. See **resolver**

devorador (-ra), *a.* devouring. *s.* devourer

devorar, *v.t.* to devour; destroy, consume

devoto (-ta), *a.* devout, pious; devoted, fond. *s.* devotee. *m.* object of devotion

dextrina, *f.* dextrine

día, *m.* day; daylight; *pl.* name or saint's day; birthday (e.g. **Hoy son los días de María,** This is Mary's saint day (or birthday)). **d. de Año Nuevo,** New Year's Day. **d. de ayuno** or **de vigilia,** Fast Day. **d. del juicio,** Day of Judgment. **d. de los difuntos,** All Souls' Day. **d. de recibo,** At Home Day. **d. de Reyes,** Epiphany (when Spanish children receive their Christmas presents). **d. de trabajo** or **d. laborable,** working day. **días caniculares,** dog days. **d. por d.,** day by day. **al d.,** up to date; per day. **al otro d.,** next day. **¡Buenos días !** Good morning! Good day! **de d.,** by day. **de d. en d.,** from day to day. **de un d. a otro,** any time now, very soon. **el d. de mañana,** tomorrow, the near future. **un d. sí y otro no,** every other day. **vivir al d.,** to live up to one's income

diabético, *a.* diabetic

diablillo, *m. dim.* devilkin, imp; (*fam.*) madcap

diablo, *m.* devil; Satan; (*fig.*) fiend. (*fam.*) **d. cojuelo,** mischievous devil; (*fig., fam.*) imp. (*fam.*) **Anda el d. suelto,** The Devil's abroad, there's trouble. (*fam.*) **tener el d. en el cuerpo,** to be as clever as the Devil; be mischievous

diablura, *f.* mischief, prank; devilry

diabólico, *a.* diabolical, devilish; (*fam.*) fiendish, iniquitous

diaconato, *m.* deaconship

diaconisa, *f.* deaconess

diácono, *m.* deacon

diacústica, *f.* diacoustics

diadema, *f.* diadem; crown; tiara

diafanidad, *f.* transparency

diáfano, *a.* transparent, diaphanous

diafragma, *m.* (*anat., mech.*) diaphragm; sound-box (of a gramophone)

diagnosticar, *v.t.* (*med.*) to diagnose

diagnóstico, *a.* diagnostic. *m.* diagnosis

diagonal, *a.* diagonal; oblique

diagrama, *m.* diagram

dialectal, *a.* dialect

dialéctica, *f.* dialectic

dialéctico, *a.* dialectic. *m.* logician

dialecto, *m.* dialect

dialogar, *v.i.* to hold a dialogue, converse; *v.t.* write dialogue

diálogo, *m.* dialogue

diamante, *m.* diamond; miner's lamp; glass-cutting diamond. **d. bruto,** rough diamond

diamantífero, *a.* diamond-bearing

diamantino, *a.* diamantine; (*poet.*) **adamant**

diamantista, *m.* and *f.* diamondcutter; diamond merchant

diametral, *a.* diametrical

diámetro, *m.* diameter

diana, *f.* (*mil.*) reveille; bull's-eye (of a target); the moon

¡diantre! *interj.* (*fam.*) the deuce!

diapasón, *m.* (*mus.*) tuning-fork; diapason; neck (of violins, etc.). **d. normal,** tuning-fork. **d. vocal,** pitch-pipe

diapositiva, *f.* (*phot.*) diapositive; lantern slide

diario, *a.* daily. *m.* diary; daily paper; daily expenses. **d. de navegación,** ship's log

diarista, *m.* and *f.* journalist, diarist

diarrea, *f.* diarrhœa

diatónico, *a.* (*mus.*) diatonic

diatriba, *f.* diatribe

diávolo, *m.* diabolo (game)

dibujante, *m.* sketcher; draftsman; designer

dibujar, *v.t.* (*art*) to draw; describe, depict; *v.r.* appear, be revealed; be outlined, stand out

dibujo, *m.* drawing; sketch, design, pattern; depiction, description. **d. a la pluma,** pen-and-ink drawing. **d. a pulso,** free-hand drawing. **d. del natural,** drawing from life

dicción, *f.* word; diction, language, style

diccionario, *m.* dictionary

diciembre, *m.* December

dicotiledóneo, *a.* (*bot.*) dicotyledonous

dictado, *m.* title of honour; dictation; *pl.* promptings (of heart, etc.). **escribir al d.,** to write to dictation

dictador, *m.* dictator

dictadura, *f.* dictatorship

dictáfono, *m.* dictaphone

dictamen, *m.* judgment, opinion

dictaminar, *v.i.* to give judgment or opinion

dictar, *v.t.* to dictate; suggest, inspire

dictatorial, dictatorio, *a.* dictatorial

dicterio, *m.* taunt, insult

dicha, *f.* happiness; good fortune. **por d.,** by chance; fortunately

dicharacho, *m.* (*fam.*) vulgar expression, slangy expression

dicho, *m.* saying, phrase, expression; witty remark; (*law*) declaration; (*fam.*) insult. *a.* said, aforementioned. *past part.* **decir,** "said." **D. y hecho,** No sooner said than done. **Del d. al hecho hay muy gran trecho,** There's many a slip 'twixt the cup and the lip. **Lo d. d.,** The agreement stands

dichoso, *a.* happy; lucky; (*fam.*) blessed, wretched, darn

didáctica, *f.* didactics

didáctico, *a.* didactic

diecinueve, *a.* and *m.* nineteen

diecinuevavo, *a.* and *m.* nineteenth

dieciochavo, *a.* and *m.* eighteenth

dieciocheno, *a.* See **décimoctavo**

dieciocho, *a.* and *m.* eighteen

dieciséis, *a.* and *m.* sixteen

dieciseisavo, *a.* and *m.* sixteenth

dieciseiseno, *a.* See **décimosexto**

diecisiete, *a.* and *m.* seventeen

diecisieteavo, *a.* and *m.* seventeenth

diente, *m.* tooth; tooth (of saw, etc.); tusk; cog (of wheel); prong (of fork); tongue (of a buckle). **d. de leche,** milk-tooth. (*bot.*) **d. de león,** dandelion. **d. de perro,** (*sew.*) feather-stitch. (*fam.*) **dar d. con d.,** to chatter (teeth). (*fig., fam.*) **enseñar** (*or* **mostrar**) **los dientes,** to show one's teeth; threaten. (*fam.*) **estar a d.,** to be famished. **hablar entre dientes,** to mutter;

fume, grumble. (*fam.*) **tener buen d.**, to have a good appetite.

traer a uno entre dientes, to loathe someone; speak scandal of

diestra, *f.* right hand; protection

diestro, *a.* right (hand); skilful, dextrous; shrewd; astute, cunning; favourable, happy. *m.* expert fencer; bull-fighter; halter; bridle

dieta, *f.* (*med.*) diet; (*fam.*) fast, abstinence; legislative assembly; travelling subsistence allowance (gen. *pl.*); day's journey of ten leagues; daily fee (gen. *pl.*)

dietario, *m.* household accounts' book

dietética, *f.* dietetics

dietético, *a.* dietetic

dietista, *m.* and *f.* dietician

diez, *a.* ten; tenth. *m.* ten; decade of rosary

diezmar, *v.t.* to tithe; decimate; punish every tenth man

diezmero (-ra), *s.* tax-gatherer

diezmesino, *a.* ten months old

diezmilésimo, *a.* ten-thousandth

diezmillonésimo, *a.* ten-millionth

diezmo, *m.* ten per cent. tax; tithe

difamación, *f.* defamation, libel

difamador (-ra), *a.* libelling. *s.* libeller

difamar, *v.t.* to libel; denigrate

difamatorio, *a.* libellous, defamatory

diferencia, *f.* unlikeness, dissimilarity; (*math.*) difference; dissension, disagreement. **a d. de**, unlike; in contrast to

diferenciación, *f.* differentiation

diferencial, *a.* differential

diferenciar, *v.t.* to differentiate; change the function (of); *v.i.* dissent, disagree; *v.r.* be different, differ; distinguish oneself

diferente, *a.* different, various

diferir, *v.t. irr.* to delay, retard; postpone; suspend, interrupt; *v.i.* be different. See **discernir**

difícil, *a.* difficult

dificultad, *f.* difficulty; impediment, obstacle; objection

dificultar, *v.t.* to raise difficulties; put obstacles in the way; *v.i.* think difficult (of achievements)

dificultoso, *a.* difficult; (*fam.*) ugly (face, figure, etc.)

difidencia, *f.* mistrust; lack of faith, doubt

difidente, *a.* mistrustful

difracción, *f.* diffraction

difractar, *v.t.* to diffract

difteria, *f.* diphtheria

diftérico, *a.* diphtheric

difundir, *v.t.* to diffuse (fluids); spread, publish, divulge; (*rad.*) broadcast

difunto (-ta), *a.* and *s.* deceased. *m.* corpse

difusión, *f.* diffusion; prolixity; (*rad.*) broadcasting

difusivo, *a.* diffusive

difuso, *a.* widespread, diffuse; prolix, wordy

digerible, *a.* digestible

digerir, *v.t. irr.* to digest; bear patiently; consider carefully; (*chem.*) digest. See **sentir**

digestible, *a.* easily digested

digestivo, *a.* digestive

digesto, *m.* (*law*) digest

digitación, *f.* (*mus.*) fingering

digital, *a.* digital. *f.* (*bot.*) foxglove, digitalis

dígito, *a.* digital. *m.* (*ast., math.*) digit

dignación, *f.* condescension

dignarse, *v.r.* to deign, condescend

dignatario, *m.* dignitary

dignidad, *f.* dignity, stateliness; serenity, loftiness; high office or rank; high repute, honour; (*ecc.*) dignitary

dignificar, *v.t.* to dignify

digno, *a.* worthy, deserving; upright, honourable; fitting, suitable, appropriate

digresión, *f.* digression

dije, *m.* charm; trinket, any small piece of jewellery; (*fam.*) person of excellent qualities, jewel

dilacerar, *v.t.* to lacerate, tear flesh; (*fig.*) discredit

dilación, *f.* delay

dilapidación, *f.* waste, dissipation, squandering

dilapidar, *v.t.* to waste, squander

dilatación, *f.* expansion; enlargement, widening; prolongation; (*surg.*) dilatation; respite (in trouble)

dilatador, *a.* dilating. *m.* (*surg.*) dilater

dilatar, *v.t.* to dilate, enlarge; expand; delay, postpone; spread, publish abroad; prolong; *v.r.* expand; be prolix, spread oneself

dilatorio, *a.* procrastinating, dilatory

dilección, *f.* affection, love

dilema, *m.* dilemma

diletantismo, *m.* dilettantism

diligencia, *f.* care, conscientiousness, industry; haste, briskness; diligence (coach); (*fam.*) business, occupation. **hacer sus diligencias,** to try one's best

diligenciar, *v.t.* to set on foot, put into motion

diligente, *a.* diligent, conscientious, industrious; speedy, prompt

dilucidación, *f.* elucidation, clarification

dilucidar, *v.t.* to elucidate, clarify

dilución, *f.* dilution

diluir, *v.t. irr.* to dilute. See **huir**

diluviano, *a.* diluvian

diluviar, *v.i.* to teem with rain

diluvio, *m.* flood, inundation; (*fam.*) very heavy rain, deluge; over-abundance

dimanación, *f.* emanation, source

dimanar, *v.i.* (*with de*) to rise in (rivers); proceed from, originate in

dimensión, *f.* dimension; size, extent

dimes y diretes, *m. pl.* (*fam.*) back-chat

diminutivo, *a.* diminutive; diminishing; (*gram.*) diminutive

diminuto, *a.* defective, incomplete; minute, very small

dimisión, *f.* resignation (of office, etc.)

dimisorias, *f. pl.* (*ecc.*) letter dimissory. (*fam.*) **dar d. a uno,** to give a person his marching orders, dismiss

dimitente, *a.* resigning; retiring. *m.* and *f.* résigner (of a post)

dimitir, *v.t.* to resign (office, post, etc.)

dinamarqués (-esa), *a.* Danish. *s.* Dane

dinámica, *f.* dynamics

dinámico, *a.* dynamic

dinamita, *f.* dynamite

dínamo, *f.* dynamo

dinasta, *m.* dynast

dinastía, *f.* dynasty

dinástico, *a.* dynastic

dineral, *m.* large amount of money, fortune

dinero, *m.* money; Peruvian coin; wealth, fortune; currency. **d. contante, ready cash. Poderoso caballero es Don D.,** Money talks

dinosauro, *m.* (*zool.*) dinosaur

dintel, *m.* (*arch.*) lintel

diocesano, *a.* diocesan

diócesis, *f.* diocese

Dios, *m.* God; deity. ¡ D. le guarde! God keep you! ¡ D. lo quiera! God grant it! D. mediante, God willing (D.V.). ¡ D. mío! Good gracious! De menos nos hizo D., Nothing is impossible, Never say die. (*fam.*) haber (*or* armarse) la de D. es Cristo, to be the deuce of a row. ¡ No lo quiera D.! God forbid! ¡ Plegue a D.! Please God! ¡ Por D.! For goodness sake! Heavens! ¡ Válgame D.! Bless me! ¡ Vaya Vd con D.! Goodbye! Off with you! Depart! ¡ Vive D.! By God!

diosa, *f.* goddess

diploma, *m.* licence, bull; diploma

diplomacia, *f.* diplomacy; tactfulness; (*fam.*) astuteness

diplomático, *a.* diplomatic; tactful; (*fam.*) astute. *m.* diplomat. cuerpo d., diplomatic corps

dipsomanía, *f.* dipsomania

dipsómano (-na), *s.* dipsomaniac

diptongo, *m.* diphthong

diputación, *f.* deputation; mission

diputado (-da), *s.* deputy, delegate. **d. a Cortes,** Member of Spanish Parliament, Congressman

diputar, *v.t.* to appoint, depute; delegate; empower

dique, *m.* dike; dam; dry dock; (*fig.*) bulwark, check; **d. flotante,** floating dock

dirección, *f.* direction; management, control, guidance; directorate; instruction; information; order, wish, command; editorial board; directorship, managership; postal address; managerial office

directiva, *f.* board, governing body

directivo, *a.* directive, controlling, guiding, managing

directo, *a.* direct; straight

director (-ra), *a.* directing, controlling. *s.* director; manager; principal, head (schools, etc.); editor. **d. de escena,** stage-manager. **d. espiritual,** *(ecc.)* Father Confessor. **d. gerente,** managing director

directorio, *a.* directory, advising. *m.* directory; directorate, board of directors

dirigible, *m.* airship

dirigir, *v.t.* to direct; regulate; govern; supervise; guide; *(mus.)* conduct; address (an envelope, etc.); keep (a shop, etc.); edit; put (a question); point (a gun); cast (a glance); *v.r.* go; wend one's way. **d. la palabra** (a), to speak to, address. **dirigirse a,** to go towards; make one's way to

dirimir, *v.t.* to annul, make void; break, dissolve; settle (disputes, etc.)

discante, *m.* (*mus.*) descant

discernidor (-ra), *s.* discerner. *a.* discerning

discernimiento, *m.* discernment; judgment; discrimination

discernir, *v.t. irr.* to discern, distinguish. *Pres. Ind.* **discierno, disciernes, discierne, disciernen.** *Pres. Subjunc.* **discierna, disciernas, discierna, disciernan**

disciplina, *f.* discipline; system, philosophy, education; submission, obedience; subject (arts or science); *pl.* scourge

disciplinante, *a.* disciplinary. *m.* scourge

disciplinar, *v.t.* to train; educate; scourge, beat; discipline; *v.r.* scourge oneself

disciplinario, *a.* disciplinary

discipulado, *m.* pupilship, studentship; education, teaching; discipleship; body of pupils (of a school, etc.)

discípulo (-la), *s.* pupil, student; disciple, follower

disco, *m.* discus; disk; gramophone record; (*ast.*) disk. **d. de señales,** railway signal. **d. giratorio,** turn-table (of a gramophone)

discóbolo, *m.* discus thrower

díscolo, *a.* wilful, unmanageable

disconformidad, *f.* disagreement; disconformity

discontinuo, *a.* intermittent, discontinuous

discordancia, *f.* discord, disagreement

discordar, *v.i.* to be discordant; disagree; (*mus.*) be out of tune

discorde, *a.* discordant; (*mus.*) dissonant

discordia, *f.* discord, disagreement

discreción, *f.* discretion; circumspection; prudence, good sense; shrewdness; pithy or clever saying. **a d.,** at discretion; at will; voluntarily. (*mil.*) **darse** (*or* **entregarse**) **a d.,** to surrender unconditionally

discrecional, *a.* optional, voluntary

discrepancia, *f.* discrepancy; disagreement

discrepar, *v.i.* to be discrepant; differ; disagree

discreto, *a.* discreet; ingenious, witty

disculpa, *f.* excuse

disculpabilidad, *f.* pardonableness

disculpable, *a.* excusable

disculpar, *v.t.* to excuse; forgive, pardon; *v.r* apologize; excuse oneself

discurrir, *v.i.* to wander, roam, flow, run (rivers, etc.); (*with en*) consider, think about; (*with sobre*) discourse on; *v.t.* invent; conjecture

discursivo, *a.* discursive; thoughtful, reflective

discurso, *m.* reasoning power; oration, discourse; consideration, reflection; speech, conversation; dissertation

discusión, *f.* discussion

discutible, *a.* debatable; disputable

discutir, *v.t.* to discuss, debate, consider

disecar, *v.t.* (*anat.*) to dissect; stuff animals; mount plants

disección, *f.* dissection

disector, *m.* dissector, anatomist

diseminación, *f.* dissemination

diseminar, *v.t.* to disseminate; spread

disensión, *f.* dissension

disentería, *f.* (*med.*) dysentery

disentimiento, *m.* dissent

disentir, *v.i. irr.* to dissent; disagree. See **sentir**

diseñador, *m.* delineator, drawer

diseñar, *v.t.* to outline, sketch

diseño, *m.* outline, sketch; plan; description

disertación, *f.* dissertation

disertar, *v.i. (with sobre)* to discourse on, discuss, treat of

diserto, *a.* eloquent

disfavor, *m.* disfavour, discourtesy, slight

disforme, *a.* deformed; ugly; enormous

disfraz, *m.* disguise; mask; fancy dress, pretence

disfrazar, *v.t.* to disguise; dissemble, misrepresent; *v.r.* disguise oneself; wear fancy dress

disfrutar, *v.t.* to enjoy (health, comfort, friendship, etc.); reap the benefit of; *v.i.* take pleasure in, enjoy

disfrute, *m.* enjoyment, use, benefit

disgregación, *f.* separation, disjunction

disgregar, *v.t.* to separate, disjoin

disgustado, *a.* annoyed; discontented, dissatisfied; melancholy, depressed

disgustar, *v.t.* to displease, dissatisfy; annoy; *(fig.)* depress; *v.r.* quarrel, fall out. **Me disgusta la idea de marcharme,** I don't like the idea of going away

disgusto, *m.* displeasure, dissatisfaction; discontent; annoyance; affliction, sorrow, trouble; quarrel; boredom; repugnance

disidente, *a.* dissenting. *m.* and *f.* dissenter, nonconformist

disidir, *v.i.* to dissent

disímil, *a.* dissimilar, different, unlike

disimulación, *f.* dissimulation, pretence

disimulado, *a.* feigned, pretended

disimular, *v.t.* to dissemble; pretend, feign; put up with, tolerate; misrepresent, misinterpret

disimulo, *m.* pretence, dissimulation; tolerance, patience

disipación, *f.* dispersion; dissipation, frivolity; immorality

disipado, *a.* spendthrift; dissipated, frivolous

disipar, *v.t.* to disperse; squander; *v.r.* evaporate; vanish, fade, disappear

dislate, *m.* absurdity, nonsense

dislocación, *f.* dislocation

dislocar, *v.t.* to dislocate; *v.r.* dislocate; sprain

disminución, *f.* diminution. **ir (una cosa) en d.,** to diminish, decrease; taper, grow to a point

disminuir, *v.t.* and *v.i. irr.* to diminish, decrease. See **huir**

disociación, *f.* dissociation

disociar, *v.t.* to dissociate, separate; *(chem.)* dissociate

disoluble, *a.* dissoluble

disolución, *f.* dissolution; immorality, laxity; disintegration; loosening, relaxation

disolutivo, *a.* dissolvent, solvent

disoluto, *a.* dissolute, vicious

disolvente, *m.* dissolvent, solvent

disolver, *v.t. irr.* to loosen, undo; *(chem.)* dissolve; separate, disintegrate; annul. See **resolver**

disonancia, *f.* dissonance; disagreement; *(mus.)* dissonant

disonante, *a.* dissonant; discordant, inharmonious

disonar, *v.i. irr.* to be inharmonious; disagree. See **sonar**

dísono, *a.* dissonant

dispar, *a.* unequal; unlike, different

disparadero, *m.* trigger of a firearm

disparador, *m.* shooter, firer; trigger (of firearms); ratchet (of watch)

disparar, *v.t.* to shoot, fire; throw or discharge with violence; *v.r.* run precipitately; rush (towards); bolt (horses); race (of a machine); explode, go off; *(fam.)* go too far, misbehave

disparatado, *a.* foolish; absurd, unreasonable

disparatar, *v.i.* to act or speak foolishly

disparate, *m.* foolishness, nonsense

disparidad, *f.* disparity, dissimilarity

disparo, *m.* shooting; explosion; racing (of an engine); discharge; foolishness

dispendio, *m.* squandering, extravagance

dispendioso, *a.* costly, expensive

dispensa, *f.* dispensation; privilege

dispensable, *a.* dispensable; excusable

dispensación, *f.* dispensation; exemption

dispensar, *v.t.* to grant, concede, distribute; exempt; excuse, forgive

dispensario, *m.* dispensary

dispepsia, *f.* (*med.*) dyspepsia

dispéptico (**-ca**), *a.* and *s.* dyspeptic

dispersar, *v.t.* to disperse, scatter, separate; (*mil.*) rout

dispersión, *f.* dispersion

disperso, *a.* dispersed, scattered; (*mil.*) separated from regiment

displicencia, *f.* disagreeableness, coldness; hesitation, lack of enthusiasm

displicente, *a.* unpleasant, disagreeable; difficult, peevish

disponer, *v.t. irr.* to arrange, dispose; direct, order; decide; prepare, get ready; *v.i.* (*with de*) dispose of, make free with; possess; have at one's disposal; *v.r.* prepare oneself to die; make one's will; get ready. See **poner**

disponible, *a.* disposable; available

disposición, *f.* arrangement; order, instruction; decision; preparation; aptitude, talent; disposal; condition of health; temperament; grace of bearing; promptitude, competence; measure, step, preliminary; (*arch.*) plan; proviso, stipulation; symmetry. **A la d. de Vd,** I (we, he, it, etc.) am at your disposal. **hallarse en d. de hacer una cosa,** to be ready to do something. **última d.,** last will and testament

dispositivo, *a.* directory, advisory

dispuesto, *a.* ready, prepared; handsome, gallant; clever, wideawake. **bien d.,** well-disposed; well, healthy. **mal d.,** ill-disposed; disinclined; out of sorts, indisposed

disputa, *f.* dispute. **sin d.,** undoubtedly

disputar, *v.t.* to argue, debate; dispute, question; (*fig.*) fight for

disquisición, *f.* disquisition

distancia, *f.* distance; interval of time; difference, dissimilarity; unfriendliness, coolness

distanciar, *v.t.* to separate, place farther apart

distante, *a.* separated; distant; far off

distar, *v.i.* to be distant (time and place); be different, unlike

distender(se), *v.t.* and *v.r.* (*med.*) to distend, swell

dístico, *m.* distich

distinción, *f.* distinction, differentiation; difference, individuality; privilege, honour; clarity, order; distinction (of bearing or mind). **a d. de,** unlike, different from

distinguible, *a.* distinguishable

distinguido, *a.* distinguished, illustrious

distinguir, *v.t.* to distinguish, discern; differentiate; characterize; esteem, honour, respect; discriminate; see with difficulty; make out; *v.r.* be different; excel, distinguish oneself

distintivo, *a.* distinguishing; distinctive. *m.* distinguishing mark

distinto, *a.* different; distinct; clear

distracción, *f.* distraction; abstraction, heedlessness, absentmindedness; pleasure, amusement; licentiousness

distraer, *v.t. irr.* to lead astray; distract (attention); influence for bad; amuse. *v.r.* be absentminded; amuse oneself. See **traer**

distraído, *a.* abstracted, absentminded; inattentive; licentious

distribución, *f.* distribution; (gen. *pl.*) share

distribuidor (**-ra**), *a.* distributing. *s.* distributor

distribuir, *v.t. irr.* to distribute; share out, divide. See **huir**

distributivo, *a.* distributive

distrito, *m.* district

disturbar, *v.t.* to disturb

disturbio, *m.* disturbance

disuadir, *v.t.* to dissuade

disuasión, *f.* dissuasion

disuasivo, *a.* dissuasive

disyunción, *f.* disjunction

disyuntivo, *a.* disjunctive. **pronombre d.,** disjunctive pronoun

ditirambo, *m.* dithyramb; excessive praise

diurético, *a.* diuretic
diurno, *a.* diurnal
diva, *f.* prima donna; woman singer
divagación, *f.* wandering, roaming; digression
divagar, *v.i.* to wander, roam; digress
diván, *m.* divan (Turkish supreme council); divan, sofa; collection of Arabic, Persian or Turkish poems
divergencia, *f.* divergence; disagreement
divergente, *a.* divergent; conflicting, dissentient
divergir, *v.i.* to diverge; dissent
diversidad, *f.* diversity, unlikeness, difference; variety
diversificar, *v.t.* to differentiate; vary
diversión, *f.* pastime, amusement; (*mil.*) diversion
diverso, *a* diverse, unlike; *pl.* various, many
divertido, *a.* amusing, funny, entertaining
divertir, *v.t. irr.* to lead astray, turn aside; entertain; (*mil.*) create a diversion. *v.r.* amuse oneself. See **sentir**
dividendo, *m.* dividend. (*com.*) **d. activo,** dividend
dividir, *v.t.* to divide; distribute; stir up discord; *v.r.* (*with de*) part company with, leave
divieso, *m.* (*med.*) boil
divinamente, *adv.* divinely; excellently, admirably, perfectly
divinidad, *f.* divinity, Godhead; person or thing of great beauty
divinizar, *v.t.* to deify; sanctify; extol
divino, *a.* divine; excellent, admirable, superb
divisa, *f.* badge, emblem; (*her.*) motto
divisar, *v.t.* to glimpse, descry
divisibilidad, *f.* divisibility
divisible, *a.* divisible
división, *f.* division, partition; discord; (*math., mil.*) division; hyphen; apportionment; district, ward
divisor (-ra), *a.* dividing, separating. *m.* (*math.*) divisor. *s.* divider, separator
  visoria, *f.* dividing line
  visorio, *a.* dividing

divorciar, *v.t.* to divorce; separate; *v.r.* be divorced, be separated
divorcio, *m.* divorce
divulgación, *f.* spreading, publication, propagation
divulgar(se), *v.t.* and *v.r.* to spread abroad, publish
do, *m.* (*mus.*) doh, C. (*poet.*) **donde,** where
dobladillo, *m.* (*sew.*) hem; turn-up (of a trouser)
doblado, *a.* stocky, thickset, sturdy; rocky, rough, uneven; dissembling. *m.* garret
dobladura, *f.* fold, crease; crease mark
doblamiento, *m.* doubling; folding
doblar, *v.t.* to double, multiply by two; fold, double; bend; persuade, induce; (*naut.*) double, sail round; turn, walk round; *v.i.* (*ecc.*) ring the passing bell, (*theat.*) double a rôle; *v.r.* fold, double; bend; bow; stoop: allow oneself to be persuaded
doble, *a.* double, twofold; duplicate; insincere, false; thick (cloth); (*bot.*) double (flowers); hardy, robust. *m.* fold, crease; (*ecc.*) passing-bell; Spanish dance step. *adv.* double, twice. (*ecc.*) **rito d.,** full rites
doblegar, *v.t.* to fold; bend; brandish; dissuade in favour of another proposition; *v.r.* submit, give way, acquiesce
doblete, *a.* of medium thickness. *m.* imitation jewel
doblez, *m.* fold, crease; fold mark. *m.* or *f.* double dealing, treachery
doblón, *m.* doubloon
doce, *a.* twelve. *m.* twelve; twelfth (of the month). **las d.,** twelve o'clock
docena, *f.* dozen. **la d. del fraile,** baker's dozen
docente, *a.* teaching
dócil, *a.* docile; obedient; flexible, easily worked (metals, etc.)
docilidad, *f.* docility; obedience; flexibility
docto, *a.* learned, erudite
doctor (-ra), *s.* doctor; physician, teacher. *f.* (*fam.*) blue-stocking
doctorado, *m.* doctorate
doctorarse, *v.r.* to graduate as a doctor in a university
doctrina, *f.* doctrine; instruction,

teaching; theory, conception; (*ecc.*) sermon

doctrinar, *v.t.* to teach, instruct

documentación, *f.* documentation; collection of documents, papers

documental, *a.* documental. *m.* documentary film

documentar, *v.t.* to document

dodecaedro, *m.* dodecahedron

dodecasílabo, *a.* twelve-syllabled

dogal, *m.* halter; noose; slipknot. (*fig.*) **estar con el d. a la garganta,** to be in a fix

dogma, *m.* dogma

dogmático, *a.* dogmatic

dogmatizar, *v.t.* to teach heretical doctrines; dogmatize

dólar, *m.* dollar

dolencia, *f.* ailment; pain; ache

doler, *v.i. irr.* to be in pain; be reluctant; *v.r.* be sorry, regretful; grieve; sympathize, be compassionate; complain. *Pres. Ind.* **duelo, dueles, duele, duelen.** *Pres. Subjunc.* **duela, duelas, duela, duelan**

doliente, *a.* suffering; ill; afflicted, sad. *m.* and *f.* sufferer, ill person. *m.* chief mourner

dolo, *m.* fraud; deception; deceit; (*law*) premeditation

dolor, *m.* pain, ache; mental suffering. **d. sordo,** dull pain

dolorido, *a.* painful; afflicted, sad

doloroso, *a.* sad, regrettable; mournful, sorrowful; pitiful; painful

doloso, *a.* deceitful, fraudulent

domable, *a.* tamable; controllable

domador (-ra), *s.* subduer, controller; wild animal tamer; horse-breaker

domadura, *f.* taming, breaking in; controlling (emotions)

domar, *v.t.* to tame, break in; control, repress (emotions)

domesticable, *a.* tamable; domesticable

domesticar, *v.t.* to tame; domesticate; *v.r.* grow tame; become domesticated

domesticidad, *f.* domesticity

doméstico (-ca), *a.* domestic, domesticated; tame. *s.* domestic worker

domiciliar, *v.t.* to domicile; *v.r.* become domiciled, settle down

domiciliario, *a.* domiciliary

domicilio, *m.* domicile; house

dominación, *f.* domination; power, authority; command (of a military position, etc.); (*mil.*) high ground; *pl.* dominions, angels

dominador, *a.* dominating; overbearing

dominante, *a.* dominating; overbearing, domineering; dominant. *f.* (*mus.*) dominant

dominar, *v.t.* to dominate; repress, subdue; (*fig.*) master (branch of knowledge); *v.i.* stand out; *v.r.* control oneself

dómine, *m.* (*fam.*) teacher; pedant, know-all

domingo, *m.* Sunday. **d. de Cuasimodo,** Low Sunday. **d. de Pentecostés,** Whitsuntide Sunday. **d. de Ramos,** Palm Sunday. **d. de Resurrección,** Easter Sunday

dominguero, *a.* (*fam.*) Sunday; special, excursion (trains)

dominicano (-na), *a.* and *s.* Dominican, of O.S.B.; native of Santo Domingo

dominio, *m.* authority, power; rule, sovereignty; dominion (country); domain

dominó, *m.* domino; game of dominoes

don, *m.* gift; quality, characteristic; talent. **d. de gentes,** the human touch; charm

don, *m.* Spanish title equivalent to English Mr. or Esquire. Used only before Christian name and *not* before surnames., e.g. don **Juan Martínez,** *never* don **Martínez**

donación, *f.* donation, gift, grant

donador (-ra), *a.* donating. *s.* donor

donaire, *m.* discretion, wit; witticism; gracefulness, elegance

donar, *v.t.* to bestow, give; transfer; grant

donatario, *m.* recipient, grantee

donativo, *m.* gift, present, donation

doncel, *m.* squire, youth not yet armed; knight; male virgin; King's page

doncella, *f.* virgin, maid; maid-servant; lady's maid

doncellez, *f.* virginity; maidenhood

donde, *adv.* where, wherein. Sometimes used as relative pronoun " in which " (e.g. La casa d. (en la que) estaba, The house in which I was). *interrog.* ¿ dónde ? ¿ A dónde va Vd ? Where are you going to? ¿ De dónde viene Vd ? Where do you come from? ¿ Por dónde se va a Madrid ? Which is the way to Madrid ?

dondequiera, *adv.* wherever, anywhere, everywhere

donoso, *a.* witty; graceful

donostiarra, *a.* and *m.* and *f.* of or from San Sebastian (N. Spain)

donosura, *f.* wit; grace; dash, verve

doña, *f.* Spanish title equivalent to English Mrs. or Miss, but used only before Christian names (e.g. D. Catalina Palacios)

dorado, *a.* golden, gilded; fortunate, happy. *m.* gilding

dorador, *m.* gilder

doradura, *f.* gilding

dorar, *v.t.* to gild; make golden; (*fig.*) gild the pill; (*cul.*) toast lightly; *v.r.* become golden

dórico, *a.* Doric

dormán, *m.* dolman

dormidero, *a.* soporiferous, narcotic

dormilón (-ona), *a.* (*fam.*) sleepy. *s.* sleepyhead

dormir, *v.i. irr.* to sleep; spend the night; (*fig.*) grow calm; sleep (tops) ; (*with* sobre) sleep on, consider; *v.t.* put to sleep; *v.r.* go to sleep; go slow over, neglect; be dormant; go numb (limbs). d. como un lirón, to sleep like a top. (*fam.*) d. la mona, to sleep oneself sober. entre duerme y vela, half-awake. *Pres. Ind.* duermo, duermes, duerme, duermen. *Pres. Part.* durmiendo. *Preterite* durmió, durmieron. *Pres. Subjunc.* duerma, duermas, duerma, duerman

dormitar, *v.i.* to doze

dormitivo, *a.* and *m.* sedative

dormitorio, *m.* dormitory; bedroom

dorsal, *a.* dorsal

dorso, *m.* back; dorsum

dos, *a.* two. *m.* two; second (of the month). las d., two o'clock.

d. a d., two against two. de d. en d., two by two. (*fam.*) en un d. por tres, in a twinkling

dosalbo, *a.* having two white stockings (horses)

doscientos, *a.* and *m.* two hundred; two hundredth

dosel, *m.* canopy; dais

dosis, *f.* dose; quantity

dotación, *f.* endowment; (*naut.*) crew; staff, workers; equipment

dotar, *v.t.* to give as dowry; endow, found; (*fig.*) endow (with talents, etc.); equip; apportion (salary)

dote, *m.* or *f.* dowry. *f.* (gen. *pl.*) gifts, talents. dotes de mando, capacity for leadership

dovela, *f.* (*arch.*) keystone

dozavo, *a.* and *m.* twelfth

dracma, *f.* drachma; dram

draga, *f.* dredger

dragado, *m.* dredging

dragaminas, *m.* (*nav.*) minesweeper

dragar, *v.t.* to dredge

dragón, *m.* dragon; (*bot.*) snapdragon; (*mil.*) dragoon; (*zool.*) dragon, giant lizard; (*ast.*) Draco

dragona, *f.* female dragon; (*mil.*) shoulder-strap

drama, *m.* play; drama. d. lírico, opera

dramática, *f.* dramatic art

dramático, *a.* dramatic; vivid, unexpected, moving

dramaturgo, *m.* dramatist, playwright

drenaje, *m.* drainage (of land and wounds)

dril, *m.* drill, cotton cloth

driza, *f.* (*naut.*) halyard

droga, *f.* drug; falsehood, deception; nuisance

droguería, *f.* chemist's shop; drug trade

droguero (-ra), *s.* chemist, druggist

dromedario, *m.* (*zool.*) dromedary

druida, *m.* Druid

druídico, *a.* druidical

drupa, *f.* (*bot.*) drupe

dualidad, *f.* duality

dualismo, *m.* (*phil.*) dualism

ducado, *m.* dukedom; duchy; ducat

ducentésimo, *a.* two hundredth

dúctil, *a.* ductile (metals); adaptable, docile, flexible

ductilidad, *f.* ductility; adaptability

ducha, *f.* shower-bath; douche; stripe in cloth; furrow

ducho, *a.* experienced, skilful

duda, *f.* doubt, hesitation; problem. **sin d.,** doubtless

dudable, *a.* doubtful

dudar, *v.i.* to be in doubt; *v.t.* doubt, disbelieve

dudoso, *a.* doubtful; uncertain, not probable

duela, *f.* hoop, stave

duelista, *m.* duellist

duelo, *m.* sorrow, grief; mourning; mourners; duel; (*gen. pl.*) troubles, trials. **duelos y quebrantos,** (*cul.*) fried offal. **sin d.,** in abundance

duende, *m.* imp, elf, sprite, ghost

dueña, *f.* owner, proprietress, mistress; duenna; married lady (*ant.*)

dueño, *m.* owner, proprietor; master (of servants). **d. de sí mismo,** self-controlled

duetista, *m.* and *f.* duettist

dula, *f.* common pasture ground or herds

dulce, *a.* sweet; fresh, pure; fresh, not salty; fragrant; melodious; pleasant, agreeable; tender, gentle; soft (metals). *m.* sweetmeat, bonbon. **d. de almíbar,** preserved fruit.

dulcedumbre, *f.* sweetness; softness

dulcémele, *m.* dulcimer

dulcera, *f.* preserve dish, fruit dish

dulcería, *f.* See **confitería**

dulcificar, *v.t.* to make sweet; alleviate, sweeten

dulcinea, *f.* (*fam.*) sweetheart; ideal

dulzaina, *f.* (*mus.*) flageolet

dulzura, *f.* sweetness; gentleness; pleasure; meekness; agreeableness

duna, *f.* (*gen. pl.*) sand dune

dúo, *m.* (*mus.*) duet

duodécimo, *a.* twelfth

duodeno, *a.* twelfth. *m.* (*anat.*) duodenum

duplicación, *f.* duplication

duplicado, *m.* duplicate

duplicar, *v.t.* to duplicate; double

duplicidad, *f.* duplicity, falseness

duplo, *a.* double

duque, *m.* duke

duquesa, *f.* duchess

duración, *f.* duration; durability

duradero, *a.* lasting; durable

durante, *adv.* during

durar, *v.i.* to continue; endure, last

dureza, *f.* hardness; (*med.*) callosity; severity, harshness

durmiente, *a.* sleeping. *m.* and *f.* sleeper; *m.* (*arch.*) dormant

duro, *a.* hard; firm, unyielding; vigorous, robust; severe, inclement; exacting, cruel; (*mus.*) metallic, harsh; (*art*) crude, too sharply defined; miserly, avaricious; obstinate; self-opinionated; unbearable, intolerable; merciless, hard; harsh (style). *m.* Spanish coin worth five pesetas

dux, *m.* doge

E

e, *f.* letter E. *conjunc.* used instead of "y" (and) before words beginning with "i" or "hi," provided this last is not followed by a diphthong (e.g. **e invierno, e hijos,** *but* **y hierro**)

¡ea! *interj.* Well!; Come on!; Let's see! (often used with *pues*)

ebanista, *m.* cabinet-maker

ebanistería, *f.* cabinet-maker's shop; cabinet-making or work

ébano, *m.* ebony

ebonita, *f.* ebonite, vulcanite

ebrio, *a.* intoxicated, inebriated

ebullición, *f.* boiling, ebullition

ebúrneo, *a.* eburnine, ivory-like

eclecticismo, *m.* eclecticism

ecléctico (-ca), *a.* and *s.* eclectic

eclesiástico, *a.* ecclesiastical. *m.* ecclesiastic, clergyman; Ecclesiasticus

eclipsar, *v.t.* (*ast.*) to eclipse; surpass, outvie; *v.r.* (*ast.*) be in eclipse; disappear

eclipse, *m.* (*ast.*) eclipse; retirement, withdrawal

eclíptica, *f.* (*ast.*) ecliptic

écloga, *f.* eclogue

eco, *m.* echo; verse-echo; muffled sound; slavish imitation or imitator

economato, *m.* trusteeship; co-operative store

economía, f. economy, thrift;
structure, organization; poverty,
shortage; saving (of time, labour,
etc.); pl. savings. e. dirigida,
planned economy. e. doméstica, domestic economy. e.
política, political economy

económico, a. economic; thrifty;
avaricious; cheap

economista, m. and f. economist

economizar, v.t. to economize;
save

ecónomo, m. trustee, guardian

ectoplasma, m. ectoplasm

ecuable, a. equable

ecuación, f. (math. and ast.) equation. e. personal, personal
equation

ecuador, m. equator

ecuánime, a. calm, unruffled;
impartial

ecuanimidad, f. calmness, serenity; impartiality

ecuatorial, a. equatorial

ecuatoriano (-na), a. and s.
Ecuadorian

ecuestre, a. equestrian

ecuménico, a. oecumenical

eczema, m. eczema

echada, f. throw, cast, pitch,
fling; length of a man

echador (-ra), s. thrower m.
(fam.) chucker-out

echadura, f. sitting on eggs to
hatch them; (gen. pl.) gleanings

echamiento, m. throw, fling;
throwing, casting; expulsion;
rejection

echar, v.t. to throw, fling; eject,
drive away; cast out, expel; put
forth, sprout; emit, give forth;
cut (teeth); dismiss, discharge;
couple (animals); pour (liquids);
place, apply; put into, fill; turn
(keys, locks); impute; attribute;
impose (penalty, taxes, etc.);
play (game); try one's luck; distribute; publish, make known;
perform (plays); (with por) go in
direction of; (with prep. a +
infin.) begin to (e. a andar, to
begin to walk); v.r. throw oneself down, lie down; sit on eggs
(birds); abate, calm (wind);
apply oneself, concentrate on;
rush (towards), fling oneself
(upon). e. abajo, to overthrow;
demolish. e. a perder, to spoil,

deteriorate. (naut.) e. a pique,
to sink. e. a vuelo, to ring
(bells). e. carnes, to put on
weight, grow fat. e. cuentas, to
reckon up. e. de menos, to
miss; mourn absence of. e. de
ver, to notice. (fig.) e. en cara,
to throw in one's face, reproach.
e. las cartas al correo, to post
the letters. e. las cartas, to tell
fortunes. e. el pie atrás, (fig.)
to climb down; (fig.) back out.
e. raíces, to take root; (fig.) become established. e. suertes,
to draw lots. echarlo todo a
rodar, to spoil everything. e.
una mano, to lend a hand

echazón, f. throw, cast; jetsam

edad, f. age; epoch; period. e. de
piedra, Stone Age. e. media,
Middle Ages. de cierta e.,
middle-aged. ser mayor de e.,
to have attained one's majority.
ser menor de e., to be a
minor

edecán, m. (mil.) aide-de-camp

edema, m. (med.) œdema

Edén, m. Eden; (fig.) paradise

edición, f. edition. e. diamante,
miniature edition. e. príncipe,
first edition

edicto, m. edict, decree, public
notice

edificación, f. building, construction; edification

edificador (-ra), a. uplifting,
edifying; building. s. builder

edificante, a. building, construc-
ting; edifying

edificar, v.t. to build, construct;
edify

edificio, m. building, structure,
fabric

editar, v.t. (of a publisher) to
publish; edit

editor (-ra), s. publisher; editor

editorial, a. publishing; editorial.
m. editorial, leading article

edredón, m. down of an eider-
duck; eider-down, quilt

eduardiano (-na), a. and s. Edwardian

educable, a. educable

educación, f. upbringing; education; good breeding, good manners

educado, a. educated. ser mal e.,
to be badly brought up; be ill-
mannered

educador (-ra), *a.* educating. *s.* educator

educando (-da), *s.* pupil

educar, *v.t.* to educate; bring up, train, teach, develop

educativo, *a.* educational, educative

educción, *f.* eduction; inference, deduction

educir, *v.t. irr.* to educe; infer, deduce. See conducir

efe, *f.* name of letter F

efectismo, *m.* sensationalism; striving after effect

efectista, *a. (art., lit.)* striking, sensational

efectivo, *a.* effective; real. *m.* cash. hacer é., to put into effect

efecto, *m.* effect, result; purpose, intent; impression; *pl.* assets; goods, chattels. efectos de escritorio, stationery. efectos públicos, public securities. en e., in fact, actually. llevar a e., to put into effect; make effective

efectuación, *f.* accomplishment, execution

efectuar, *v.t.* to accomplish, effect; make (a payment); *v.r* be effected; happen, take place

eferente, *a.* efferent

efervescencia, *f.* effervescence; excitement, enthusiasm

efervescente, *a.* effervescent

efesio (-ia), *a.* and *s.* Ephesian

eficacia, *f.* efficacy; effectiveness

eficaz, *a.* efficacious; effective

eficiencia, *f.* efficiency

eficiente, *a.* efficient, effective

efigie, *f.* effigy; image, representation, symbol

efímero, *a.* ephemeral; brief

eflorescencia, *f. (chem.)* efflorescence

efluvio, *m.* effluvium; exhalation

efugio, *m.* subterfuge, evasion

efusión, *f.* effusion; *(fig.)* spate (of words, etc.)

efusivo, *a.* effusive, expansive

égida, *f.* shield; ægis, protection

egipcíaco (-ca), egipcio (-ia), *a.* and *s.* Egyptian

egiptólogo (-ga), *s.* Egyptologist

égloga, *f.* eclogue

egoísmo, *m.* egoism

egoísta, *a.* egoistic. *m.* and *f.* egoist

egolatría, *f.* self-love

egotismo, *m.* egotism

egotista, *a.* egotistical. *m.* and *f.* egotist

egregio, *a.* distinguished, celebrated

eje, *m.* axis; axle-tree; shaft; pivot, fundamental; idea. e. trasero, rear-axle

ejecución, *f.* accomplishment, performance; execution, technique; death penalty

ejecutable, *a.* feasible, practicable

ejecutante, *m.* and *f. (mus.)* executant, performer

ejecutar, *v.t.* to discharge, perform; put to death; *(art., mus.)* execute; serve (a warrant, etc.); *(law)* seize (property)

ejecutivo, *a.* executive; urgent

ejecutor, *m.* executor

ejecutoria, *f.* letters patent of nobility; *(law)* judgment, sentence

ejecutoría, *f.* executorship

ejemplar, *a.* exemplary. *m.* copy, specimen; precedent; example; warning

ejemplificar, *v.t.* to exemplify

ejemplo, *m.* example, precedent; illustration, instance; specimen. dar e., to set an example. por e., for example

ejercer, *v.t.* to practise (a profession); perform, fulfil; exercise, use

ejercicio, *m.* exercise; practice; performance; exertion, effort; *(mil.)* exercises (gen. *pl.*). ejercicios espirituales, spiritual exercises. ejercicios físicos, physical training

ejercitar, *v.t.* to exercise; train, teach; *v.r.* exercise; practise

ejército, *m.* army

el, *def. art. m. sing.*, the

él, *pers. pron. sing.*, *m.*, he; it *(f.* ella. *neut.* ello) (e.g. Él lo hizo, He did it). Also used with prep. (e.g. Lo hicimos para él, We did it for him)

elaboración, *f.* elaboration, working out

elaborado, *a.* elaborate

elaborar, *v.t.* to elaborate; produce, work out

elasticidad, *f.* elasticity; adaptability

elástico, *a.* elastic; adaptable. *m.* elastic tape; elastic material

ele, *f.* name of letter L
eléboro, *m.* (*bot.*) hellebore
elección, *f.* choice; election; selection; discrimination
electivo, *a.* elective
electo, *m.* elect, candidate elect
elector (-ra), *s.* elector, voter. *m.* German prince (*ant.*)
electorado, *m.* electorate
electoral, *a.* electoral
electricidad, *f.* electricity
electricista, *m.* electrician
eléctrico, *a.* electric; electrical
electrificación, *f.* electrification
electrificar, *v.t.* to electrify
electrizar, *v.t.* to electrify; startle; *v.r.* be electrified
electrocución, *f.* electrocution
electrocutar, *v.t.* to electrocute
electrodinámica, *f.* electro-dynamics
electrodo, *m.* electrode
electroimán, *m.* electro-magnet
electrólisis, *f.* electrolysis
electrólito, *m.* electrolyte
electrolizar, *v.t.* to electrolyze
electromagnético, *a.* electromagnetic
electromotriz, *a.* electromotive. fuerza e., electromotive force
electrón, *m.* electron
electroquímica, *f.* electro-chemistry
electroscopio, *m.* electroscope
electrotecnia, *f.* electrical engineering
electroterapia, *f.* (*med.*) electrotherapy
electrotipia, *f.* electrotyping; electrotype
elefante (-ta), *s.* elephant
elefantíasis, *f.* (*med.*) elephantiasis
elefantino, *a.* elephantine
elegancia, *f.* elegance, grace; fashionableness; (*lit.*) beauty of style
elegante, *a.* elegant; graceful, lovely; fashionable, stylish
elegía, *f.* elegy
elegíaco, *a.* elegiac
elegibilidad, *f.* eligibility
elegible, *a.* eligible
elegir, *v.t. irr.* to select, prefer; elect. *Pres. Ind.* elijo, eliges, elige, eligen. *Pres. Part.* eligiendo. *Preterite* eligió, eligieron. *Pres. Subj.* elija, etc.

elemental, *a.* elemental; fundamental; elementary
elemento, *m.* element; component, constituent; (*elec.*) element; *pl.* rudiments. (*mil.*) **elementos de choque,** shock troops
elevación, *f.* lifting, raising; height, high ground; elevation; altitude; (*fig.*) eminence; elevation, advancement; ecstasy; raising (of the voice)
elevado, *a.* sublime, lofty
elevar, *v.t.* to raise, lift; (*fig.*) exalt; *v.r.* be in ecstasy, be transported
elfo, *m.* elf
elidir, *v.t.* (phonetics) to elide
eliminación, *f.* elimination
eliminador, *a.* eliminatory. *m.* eliminator
eliminar, *v.t.* to eliminate
elipse, *f.* (*geom.*) ellipse
elipsis, *f.* (*gram.*) ellipsis
elíptico, *a.* (*geom., gram.*) elliptic
elíseo, *m.* Elysium. *a.* Elysian. campos elíseos, Elysian fields
elocución, *f.* elocution; style of speech
elocuencia, *f.* eloquence
elocuente, *a.* eloquent
elogiador (-ra), *a.* eulogistic. *s.* eulogist
elogiar, *v.t.* to eulogize, praise
elogio, *m.* eulogy, praise
elucidación, *f.* elucidation, explanation
elucidar, *v.t.* to elucidate, clarify
eludible, *a.* escapable, avoidable
eludir, *v.t.* to elude, avoid
ella, *pers. pron.* 3rd sing. *f.* she; it. See él
elle, *f.* name of letter LL
ello, *pers. pron.* 3rd sing. *neut.* that, the fact, it. ello es que ..., the fact is that ... No tengo tiempo para ello, I have no time for that
ellos, ellas, *pers. pron.* 3rd *pl. m.* and *f.* they. See él
emaciación, *f.* emaciation
emanación, *f.* emanation; effluvium
emanar, *v.i.* to emanate (from), originate (in)
emancipación, *f.* emancipation; enfranchisement
emancipador (-ra), *a.* emancipatory. *s.* emancipator

emancipar, *v.t.* to emancipate, free; enfranchise; *v.r.* emancipate oneself; become independent; free oneself

emasculación, *f.* emasculation

emascular, *v.t.* to emasculate

embadurnar, *v.t.* to smear, smudge, daub

embajada, *f.* embassy; ambassadorship; embassy building; (*fam.*) message

embajador, *m.* ambassador; emissary

embajadora, *f.* wife of ambassador; woman ambassador

embalador, *m.* packer

embalaje, *m.* packing; bale; wrapper; packing charge

embalar, *v.t.* to pack

embaldosado, *m.* tiled pavement or floor

embaldosar, *v.t.* to tile, pave with tiles

embalsamador, *a.* embalming. *m.* embalmer

embalsamamiento, *m.* embalmment

embalsamar, *v.t.* to embalm; perfume

embalse, *m.* dam; damming, impounding (of water)

embanastar, *v.t.* to place in a basket; crowd, squeeze

embarazada, *a.* (*f.*) pregnant

embarazar, *v.t.* to impede, hinder, embarrass; *v.r.* be hindered or embarrassed; be pregnant

embarazo, *m.* difficulty, impediment; pregnancy; timidity, embarrassment

embarazoso, *a.* embarrassing; inconvenient; difficult, troublesome

embarcación, *f.* ship, vessel; embarkation

embarcadero, *m.* wharf, dock; quay; pier; jetty

embarcador, *m.* shipper

embarcar, *v.t.* to embark, ship; board (boat, train, etc.); *v.r.* embark; board

embarco, *m.* embarking, embarkation

embargar, *v.t.* to obstruct, impede; (*law*) seize; suspend, paralyse

embargo, *m.* (*law*) seizure; embargo. sin e., nevertheless, however

embarque, *m.* loading, embarkation (goods)

embarrancar, *v.i.* (*naut.*) to run aground; *v.r.* (*naut.*) be stuck on a reef or in the mud

embarrilar, *v.t.* to barrel

embarullar, *v.t.* (*fam.*) to mix up, muddle; do hastily and badly

embasamiento, *m.* (*arch.*) foundation

embastar, *v.t.* (*sew.*) to baste; tack

embaste, *m.* (*sew.*) basting; tacking stitch

embate, *m.* beating of the waves; sudden attack; unexpected misfortune

embaucamiento, *m.* trick, deception

embaucar, *v.t.* to deceive, hoodwink

embaular, *v.t.* to pack in a trunk; (*fam.*) stuff with food

embazar, *v.t.* to dye brown; hinder; amaze; *v.r.* be amazed; be tired or bored; be satiated

embebecer, *v.t. irr.* to entertain, amuse; engross, fascinate; *v.r.* be dumbfounded. See conocer

embebecimiento, *m.* astonishment; absorption, engrossment

embeber, *v.t.* to absorb; contain; shrink, contract; saturate; insert, introduce; incorporate; *v.i.* shrink; *v.r.* be amazed; master or absorb (a subject)

embelecar, *v.t.* to dupe, deceive, trick

embeleco, *m.* deception, fraud

embelesar, *v.t.* to astonish; fascinate, enchant; *v.r.* be astonished or fascinated

embeleso, *m.* astonishment; fascination; charm

embellecer, *v.t. irr.* to embellish; *v.r.* beautify oneself. See conocer

embellecimiento, *m.* beautifying, embellishment

emberizo, *m.* (*orn.*) yellowhammer

embermejecer, *v.t. irr.* to dye red; shame, make blush; *v.i.* turn red or reddish; *v.r.* blush. See conocer

embestida, *f.* assault, attack, onrush; (*fam.*) importunity

embestir, *v.t. irr.* to rush upon, assault; (*fam.*) importune, be a nuisance to; *v.i.* (*fig., fam.*) clash, be inharmonious. See **pedir**

emblema, *m.* emblem; symbol; badge

emblemático, *a.* emblematic; symbolical

embobamiento, *m.* stupefaction, amazement

embobar, *v.t.* to entertain, fascinate; *v.r.* be dumbfounded

embobecer, *v.t. irr.* to make stupid. See **conocer**

embobecimiento, *m.* stupefaction

embocadero, *m.* narrow entrance, bottle-neck; mouth of a channel

embocadura, *f.* entrance by a narrow passage; (*mus.*) mouthpiece; flavour (of wine); estuary, mouth of river; proscenium (of theatre)

embocar, *v.t.* to put in the mouth; go through narrow passage; deceive; (*fam.*) devour, wolf; initiate business deal

embolia, *f.* (*med.*) embolism

émbolo, *m.* (*mech.*) piston, plunger

embolsar, *v.t.* to place money in a purse; collect (a debt, etc.)

emborrachar, *v.t.* to intoxicate; daze, stupefy; *v.r.* become intoxicated; run (dyes)

emborrascarse, *v.r.* to be furious; become stormy (weather); (*fig.*) go downhill (business concern)

emborronar, *v.t.* to blot; scribble, write hastily

emboscada, *f.* ambuscade, ambush; intrigue, spying

emboscar, *v.t.* (*mil.*) to place in ambush; *v.r.* lie in ambush

embosquecer, *v.i. irr.* to become wooded. See **conocer**

embotamiento, *m.* blunting or bluntness (of weapons, etc.)

embotar, *v.t.* to blunt (cutting edge); *v.i.* (*fig.*) weaken; *v.r.* become blunt

embotellado, *m.* bottling; (*fig.*) bottle-neck

embotellador (-ra), *s.* bottler. *f.* **embotelladora,** bottling outfit

embotellar, *v.t.* to bottle; bottle up, prevent from escaping

embotijar, *v.t.* to put into jars; *v.r.* (*fam.*) be enraged

embozar, *v.t.* (*fig.*) to cloak, dis-

semble; muffle; *v.r.* muffle oneself up

embozo, *m.* anything used to cover or muffle the face; pretence, pretext; facings (gen. *pl.*); yashmak

embragar, *v.t.* to sling, lift; (*mech.*) let in the clutch

embrague, *m.* hoisting, slinging; (*mech.*) clutch

embravecer, *v.t. irr.* to infuriate; *v.r.* be enraged; be boisterous (sea). See **conocer**

embravecimiento, *m.* fury, rage

embrazadura, *f.* grasping, clasping; handle, clasp

embreadura, *f.* tarring

embrear, *v.t.* to tar, paint with pitch

embriagador, *a.* intoxicating

embriagar, *v.t.* to intoxicate; enrapture; *v.r.* become inebriate

embriaguez, *f.* intoxication, inebriation; rapture

embriología, *f.* embryology

embrión, *m.* embryo; germ, first rough idea

embrionario, *a.* embryonic

embrocación, *f.* (*med.*) embrocation

embrollar, *v.t.* to entangle; embroil

embrollo, *m.* tangle; falsehood; difficult situation

embromar, *v.t.* to tease, chaff; trick, deceive; waste the time of; annoy; harm

embrujar, *v.t.* to bewitch

embrutecer, *v.t. irr.* to make brutish or stupid; *v.r.* become brutish. See **conocer**

embudo, *m.* (*chem.*) funnel

embuste, *m.* lie, fraud; *pl.* trinkets

embustero (-ra), *a.* deceitful, knavish. *s.* liar, cheat, trickster

embutido, *m.* inlaid work; (*cul.*) salamé

embutir, *v.t.* to inlay; stuff full, cram; *v.t.* and *v.r.* (*fam.*) stuff with food

eme, *f.* name of letter M

emergencia, *f.* emergence; accident, emergency

emergente, *a.* emergent.

emerger, *v.i.* to emerge; have its source (rivers, etc.)

emérito, *a.* emeritus

emético, *a.* and *m.* emetio

emigración, f. emigration; migration; number of emigrants

emigrado, m. emigrant, emigré

emigrante, a. and m. and f. emigrant

emigrar, v.i. to emigrate; migrate

emigratorio, a. emigration

eminencia, f. high land; importance, prominence; outstanding personality, genius; title given to cardinals

eminente, a. high, elevated; prominent, illustrious

emisario (-ia), s. emissary

emisión, f. emission; (rad.) broadcast; (com.) issue (bonds, etc.); floating (of a loan)

emisor, m. (elec.) transmitter.

emisora, f. (rad.) wireless station

emitir, v.t. to emit; (rad.) broadcast; (com.) issue (bonds, paper money, etc.); utter, give voice to

emoción, f. emotion

emocional, a. emotional; emotive

emocionante, a. moving, causing emotion; thrilling

emocionar, v.t. to cause emotion, move; v.r. be stirred by emotion; be thrilled

emoliente, a. and m. emollient

emolumento, m. emolument (gen. pl.)

emotivo, a. emotive

empachado, a. awkward, clumsy

empachar, v.t. to hinder, impede; disguise, dissemble; v.r. overeat, stuff; be bashful

empacho, m. bashfulness, timidity; embarrassment, impediment; indigestion, satiety

empadronamiento, m. census

empadronar, v.t. to take the census

empalagar, v.t. to cloy (of food); tire, annoy

empalagoso, a. sickly, oversweet; cloying; (fig.) sugary, honeyed

empalar, v.t. to impale

empalizada, f. stockade, fencing

empalmar, v.t. to dovetail; splice (ropes); clamp; (fig.) combine (plans, actions, etc.); v.i. join (railway lines); couple (railway carriages); v.r. palm (as in conjuring)

empalme, m. connection; splicing; (fig.) combination (of plans, etc.); railway junction; continuation; palming, secreting

empanada, f. savoury pasty or pie; secret negotiations, intrigue

empanar, v.t. to bake in paste; (cul.) cover with breadcrumbs; (agr.) sow grain

empantanar, v.t. to turn into marsh; embog; delay, embarrass

empañar, v.t. to swaddle; tarnish, dim; blur; (fig.) sully (fame, etc.)

empapar, v.t. to saturate; absorb; impregnate; v.r. be saturated; absorb; (fig.) be imbued

empapelado, m. paper hanging; wall-paper

empapelador, m. paper hanger

empapelar, v.t. to wrap in paper; paper (room)

empaque, m. packing; panelling; (fam.) mien, air; pomposity

empaquetador (-ra), s. packer

empaquetar, v.t. to pack; make up parcels or packages; overcrowd

emparedado (-da), a. cloistered, recluse. s. recluse. m. (cul.) sandwich

emparedar, v.t. to shut up, immure; v.r. become a recluse

emparejar, v.t. to pair, match; equalize, make level; v.i. come abreast (of); be equal

emparentar, v.i. irr. to become related by marriage. See acertar

emparrado, m. vine arbour; vine prop; pergola

empastadura, f. filling, stopping (of teeth)

empastar, v.t. to cover with glue or paste; bind in boards (books); fill (teeth)

empaste, m. pasting, gluing; filling (teeth)

empatar, v.t. to equal, tie with

empate, m. tie, draw; dead heat

empecatado, a. wilful, evilminded, wicked; incorrigible, impenitent; extremely unlucky

empecer, v.t. irr. to harm, damage; v.i. hinder. See conocer

empedernido, a. stony-hearted, cruel

empedrado, a. dappled (horses); (fig.) flecked (with clouds). m. paving; pavement

empedrador, *m.* stone paver

empedrar, *v.t. irr.* to pave with stones. See **acertar**

empegadura, *f.* coat of pitch

empegar, *v.t.* to coat with pitch; mark with pitch (sheep)

empeine, *m.* groin; instep

empellar, *v.t.* to push, jostle

empellón, *m.* hard push. *(fam.)* **a empellones,** by pushing and shoving

empenachado, *a.* plumed

empeñado, *a.* violent, heated (of disputes)

empeñar, *v.t.* to pledge, leave as surety; pawn; oblige, compel; appoint as mediator; *v.r.* bind oneself, be under an obligation; (*with en*) insist on; persist in; *v.r* intercede; mediate; *(mil.)* begin (a battle)

empeño, *m.* pledge, surety; obligation, engagement; fervent desire; purpose, intention, determination, resolve; guarantor; *(fam.)* influence, favour

empeoramiento, *m.* worsening; deterioration

empeorar, *v.t.* to make worse; *v.i.* and *v.r.* deteriorate, grow worse

empequeñecer, *v.t. irr.* to diminish, lessen; make smaller; belittle. See **conocer**

emperador, *m.* emperor

emperatriz, *f.* empress

emperezar, *v.t.* to obstruct, hinder; *v.r.* be lazy

empergaminar, *v.t.* to cover or bind in parchment

empernar, *v t* to peg, bolt

empero, *conjunc.* but; nevertheless

empezar, *v.t. irr.* to begin, commence; initiate; *v.i.* begin. *Pres. Ind.* **empiezo, empiezas, empieza, empiezan.** *Preterite* **empecé, empezaste,** etc. *Pres. Subjunc.* **empiece, empieces, empiece, empecemos, empecéis, empiecen**

empicotar, *v.t.* to pillory

empinado, *a.* steep; lofty; arrogant; exalted

empinar, *v.t.* to raise; tip, tilt (drinking vessels); *v.r.* stand on tiptoe; rear, prance; tower, rise; *(aer.)* zoom, climb steeply. *(fam.)* **e. el codo,** to lift the elbow, tipple

empingorotado, *a.* important, prominent; *(fam.)* stuck-up

empíreo, *a.* empyreal; heavenly, divine. *m.* empyrean

empírico (-ca), *a.* empiric. *s.* quack, charlatan

empirismo, *m.* empiricism

empizarrado, *m.* slate roof

empizarrar, *v.t.* to roof with slates

emplastar, *v.t. (med.)* to apply plasters; make up; paint; *(fam.)* hinder, obstruct; *v.r.* be smeared

emplasto, *m. (med.)* plaster; poultice; *(fam.)* put-up job, fraud

emplazamiento, *m.* placing, location; site; *(law)* summons; *(naut.)* berth

emplazar, *v.t.* to convene, arrange a meeting; *(law)* summon

empleado (-da), *s.* employee; clerk. **e. público,** Civil Servant

emplear, *v.t.* to employ; lay out, invest (money); use; *v.r.* be employed or occupied

empleo, *m.* employment; investment, laying out (of money); occupation; post, office

emplomar, *v.t.* to lead, solder or cover with lead; affix lead seals on or to; weight (a stick, etc.)

emplumar, *v.t.* to feather; decorate with feathers; tar and feather

emplumecer, *v.i. irr.* to fledge, grow feathers. See **conocer**

empobrecer, *v.t. irr.* to impoverish; *v.i.* and *v.r.* become poor; decay. See **conocer**

empobrecimiento, *m.* impoverishment

empolvar, *v.t.* to cover with dust; powder

empollar, *v.t.* to hatch; *v.i.* produce brood (bees); *(fam.)* brood on, consider; *(fam.)* swot (of students)

empollón (-ona), *s. (fam.)* plodder, swot

emponzoñamiento, *m.* poisoning

emponzoñar, *v.t.* to poison; pervert, corrupt

emporio, *m.* emporium

empotrar, *v.t.* to embed, implant; fix down

emprendedor, *a.* capable, efficient, enterprising

emprender, *.v.t.* to undertake;

(with *prep. a* or *con*) (*fam.*) accost, tackle, buttonhole

empresa, *f.* undertaking, task; motto, device; intention, design; management, firm; enterprise, deal

empresario, *m.* contractor; theatrical manager

empréstito, *m.* loan

empujar, *v.t.* to push; (*fig.*) exert pressure, influence

empuje, *m.* push; (*arch.*) pressure; energy; power, influence

empujón, *m.* violent thrust or push. (*fam.*) **a empujones**, by pushing and shoving; intermittently

empuñadura, *f.* hilt (of sword); (*fam.*) preamble

empuñar, *v.t.* to grasp; grip; clutch

emu, *m.* emu

emulación, *f.* emulation, competition, rivalry

emulador, *a.* emulative

emular, *v.t.* to emulate, rival, compete with

émulo (**-la**), *a.* emulative, rival. *s.* competitor, rival

emulsión, *f.* emulsion

emulsivo, *a.* emulsive

en, *prep.* in; into; on, upon; at; by. **en Madrid**, in Madrid. **en junio**, in June. **Se echó en un sillón**, He threw himself into an armchair. **Se transformó en mariposa**, It turned into a butterfly. **Hay un libro en la mesa**, There is a book on the table. **María está en casa**, Mary is at home. **en un precio muy alto**, at a very high price. **El número de candidatos ha disminuido en un treinta por ciento**, The number of candidates has decreased by thirty per cent. **En** appears in a number of adverbial phrases, e.g. **en particular**, in particular, **en secreto**, in secret, **en seguida**, immediately. When it is used with a gerund, it means after, as soon as, when, e.g. **En llegando a la puerta llamó**, When he arrived at the door, he knocked. In compound verbs **en** becomes **em** before **b** or **p**, e.g. **empobrecer**

enagua, *f.* underskirt, petticoat

enajenación, *f.* transference, alienation (property); abstraction, absent-mindedness. **e. mental**, lunacy

enajenar, *v.t.* to transfer (property)

enaltecer, *v.t. irr.* to elevate, raise; exalt. See **conocer**

enamoradizo, *a.* susceptible, easily enamoured; fickle

enamorado, *a.* in love, love-sick; easily enamoured

enamorar, *v.t.* to arouse love in; court, make love to; *v.r.* fall in love; (with *de*) become fond of (things)

enano (**-na**), *a.* small, dwarf. *s.* dwarf

enarbolar, *v.t.* to hoist (flags); *v.r.* prance (horses); become angry

enardecer, *v.t. irr.* to kindle, stimulate (passion, quarrel, etc.); *v.r.* be afire (with passion); (*med.*) be inflamed. See **conocer**

enastado, *a.* horned; antlered

encabestrar, *v.t.* to halter; lead, dominate

encabezamiento, *m.* census-taking; tax register; tax assessment; heading, inscription, running title

encabezar, *v.t.* to take the census of; put on the tax register; open a subscription list; put a heading or title to; lead, head; *v.r.* compound, settle by agreement (taxes, etc.)

encabritarse, *v.r.* to rear, prance (horses)

encadenamiento, *m.* fettering, chaining; connection, link, relation

encadenar, *v.t.* to chain, fetter; (*fig.*) link up, connect; (*fig.*) paralyse

encajar, *v.t.* to insert, fit one thing inside another; force in; fit tightly; (*fam.*) be opportune, fit in (often *bien*); *v.r.* squeeze or crowd in; (*fam.*) butt in, interfere

encaje, *m.* fitting, insertion; socket, groove; joining; lace; inlay, mosaic

encajera, *f.* lace-maker or seller

encaladura, *f.* whitewashing

encalar, *v.t.* to whitewash

encalmado, *a.* calm; (*com.*) dull

encalmarse, *v.r.* to become calm (wind, weather)

encalvecer, *v.i.* *irr.* to grow bald. See **conocer**

encalladero, *m.* (*naut.*) sand-bank, reef, shoal

encallar, *v.i.* (*naut.*) to run aground; (*fig.*) be held up (negotiations, etc.)

encamarse, *v.r.* to go to bed (gen. illness); be laid flat (grain, etc.); crouch

encaminar, *v.t.* to guide; direct; regulate; manage; promote, advance; *v.r.* (*with prep. a*) make for, go in the direction of

encandecer, *v.t.* *irr.* to make incandescent. See **conocer**

encandilar, *v.t.* to dazzle; mislead; (*fam.*) poke (the fire); *v.r.* be bloodshot (eyes)

encanecer, *v.i.* *irr.* to grow grey or white haired; grow mould; grow old. See **conocer**

encanijar, *v.t.* to make weak, sickly (gen. babies); *v.r.* be delicate or ailing

encantado, *a.* (*fam.*) day-dreaming, abstracted; haunted; rambling (houses)

encantador, *a.* captivating, bewitching, delightful. *m.* sorcerer, magician. **e. de serpientes**, snake-charmer

encantamiento, *m.* enchantment, spell, charm

encantar, *v.t.* to enchant, weave a spell; delight, captivate, charm

encanutar, *v.t.* to flute

encañada, *f.* gorge, ravine

encañado, *m.* trellis; pipe line

encañar, *v.t.* to run water through a pipe; stake plants; wind thread on a spool.

encañonar, *v.t.* to run into pipes; pleat, fold

encapotarse, *v.r.* to muffle oneself in a cloak; scowl; be overcast; lower (sky)

encapricharse, *v.r.* to take a fancy (for); insist on having one's own way, be stubborn

encapuchar, *v.t.* to cover or hide with a hood

encaramar, *v.t.* to raise, lift; climb; praise, extol. **encaramarse por**, to climb up

encarar, *v.t.* to place face to face;

aim (at); *v.t.* and *v.r.* face; come face to face

encarcelación, *f.* incarceration

encarcelar, *v.t.* to imprison, gaol; (*carp.*) clamp

encarecer, *v.t.* *irr.* to raise the price; overpraise, exaggerate; recommend strongly; *v.i.* and *v.r.* increase in price. See **conocer**

encarecimiento, *m.* increase (in price); enhancement; exaggeration. **con e.**, insistently, earnestly

encargado, *m.* man in charge; manager; agent, representative. **e. de negocios**, chargé d'affaires

encargar, *v.t.* to enjoin; commission; recommend; advise; (*com.*) order

encargo, *m.* charge, commission; order; office, employ; responsibility

encariñarse (*con*), *v.i.* to become fond (of)

encarnación, *f.* incarnation

encarnadino, *a.* incarnadine

encarnado, *a.* incarnate; flesh-coloured; red

encarnar, *v.i.* to incarnate; pierce the flesh; (*fig.*) leave a strong impression; *v.t.* symbolize, personify; *v.r.* mingle, blend

encarnizado, *a.* blood-shot (eyes); flesh-coloured; bloody, cruel (gen. battles)

encarnizamiento, *m.* cruelty, fury

encarnizar, *v.t.* to infuriate; *v.r.* devour flesh (animals); persecute, ill-treat

encaro, *m.* stare, gaze; aim

encarrilar, *v.t.* to set on the track or rails (vehicles); (*fig.*) put right, set on the right track

encartamiento, *m.* proscription; charter

encartar, *v.t.* to proscribe, outlaw; place on the tax register; (*law*) summons, cite

encartonar, *v.t.* to cover with cardboard; bind in boards (books)

encasar, *v.t.* (*surg.*) to set (a bone)

encasillado, *m.* set of pigeon-holes

encasillar, *v.t.* to pigeon-hole; file, classify

encasquetar(se), *v.t.* and *v.r.* to pull a hat well down on the head; *v.r.* get a fixed idea

encastillar, *v.t.* to fortify with castles; *v.r.* retire to a castle; be headstrong, obstinate

encauzamiento, *m.* channelling; (*fig.*) direction

encauzar, *v.t.* to channel; (*fig.*) direct, guide

encefalitis, *f.* (*med.*) encephalitis. **e. letárgica**, encephalitis lethargica, sleeping sickness

encéfalo, *m.* (*anat.*) brain

encenagarse, *v.r.* to wallow in mire; muddy oneself; take to vice

encendedor, *a.* lighting. *m.* lighter. **e. de bolsillo**, pocket lighter

encender, *v.t.* irr. to light; switch on; set fire to, kindle; arouse (emotions); inflame, incite; *v.r.* blush. See **entender**

encendido, *a.* high-coloured; inflamed; ardent. *m.* (*aut.*) ignition

encerado, *a.* wax-coloured. *m.* oilskin; sticking-plaster; blackboard; tarpaulin

enceramiento, *m.* waxing

encerar, *v.t.* to wax, varnish with wax; stain with wax; inspissate (lime)

encerotar, *v.t.* to wax (thread)

encerrar, *v.t.* irr. to shut up, imprison; include, contain; *v.r.* go into seclusion. See **acertar**

encerrona, *f.* (*fam.*) voluntary retreat; (*fig., fam.*) tight corner

encespedar, *v.t.* to cover with sods

encía, *f.* gum (of mouth)

encíclica, *f.* encyclical

enciclopedia, *f.* encyclopædia

enciclopédico, *a.* encyclopædic

encierro, *m.* act of closing or shutting up; prison; retreat, confinement

encima, *adv.* over; above; at the top; besides; (*with de*) on, on top of. **por e. de esto**, over and above this, besides this

encina, *f.* (*bot.*) evergreen or holm-oak

encinar, *m.* grove of evergreen or holm-oaks

encinta, *a.* (*f.*) pregnant

encintar, *v.t.* to decorate with ribbons

enclaustrar, *v.t.* to cloister

enclavar, *v.t.* to nail; pierce; embed; (*fam.*) deceive

enclenque, *a.* ailing, weak; puny, anæmic

enclocar, *v.i.* irr. to go broody (hens). See **contar**

encobar, *v.i.* to hatch eggs

encoger, *v.t.* to shrink, contract, recoil; discourage; *v.i.* shrink (wood, cloth, etc.); *v.r.* shrink from, recoil; be discouraged; be timid or bashful

encogimiento, *m.* shrinkage; contraction; depression, discouragement; timidity; bashfulness

encoladura, *f.*, **encolamiento**, *m.* gluing; sizing

encolar, *v.t.* to glue, size

encolerizar, *v.t.* to anger; *v.r.* be angry

encomendar, *v.t.* irr. to charge with, entrust; recommend, commend; *v.r.* (*with prep. a*) put one's trust in; send greetings to. See **acertar**

encomiar, *v.t.* to eulogize, praise

encomiástico, *a.* encomiastic

encomienda, *f.* commission, charge; knight commandership; insignia of knight commander; land formerly granted in America to **conquistadores**; recommendation, commendation; protection, defence; *pl.* greetings, compliments, messages

encomio, *m.* eulogy; strong recommendation

enconar, *v.t.* to irritate, exasperate; *v.r.* (*med.*) be inflamed; be exasperated; (*with en*) burden one's conscience by

encono, *m.* rancour, resentment, ill-will

encontrado, *a.* facing, opposite, in front; hostile, inimical, opposed (to)

encontrar, *v.t.* irr. to meet; find; *v.i.* meet; encounter unexpectedly; (*with con*) run into, collide with; *v.r.* be antagonistic; find; feel, be; differ, disagree (opinions); (*with con*) meet, come across. ¿ **Cómo se encuentra Vd ?** How are you? *Pres. Ind.* **encuentro**, etc. *Pres. Subjunc.* **encuentre**, etc.

encontrón, *m.* collision, violent impact

encopetado, *a.* conceited, proud; of noble descent; prominent, important

encorajar, *v.t.* to encourage, inspire, hearten; *v.r.* be angry

encordelar, *v.t.* to cord, rope

encorsetar, *v.t.* to correct

encorvadura, *f.* bending, curving

encorvar, *v.t.* to bend, curve; *v.r.* have a leaning towards, favour

encostrar, *v.t.* to cover with a crust; *v.r.* form a crust

encrespador, *m.* curling-tongs

encrespar, *v.t.* to curl (hair); enrage; *v.r.* be curly (hair); stand on end (hair, feathers, from fright); be angry; grow rough (sea); become complicated, entangled

encrestado, *a.* crested; haughty, arrogant

encrestarse, *v.r.* to stiffen the comb or crest (birds)

encrucijada, *f.* crossroad, intersection; ambush

encrudecer, *v.t. irr.* to make raw-looking; annoy; *v.r.* be annoyed. See **conocer**

encuadernación, *f.* bookbinding; binding (of a book); bookbinder's workshop

encuadernador (-ra), *s.* bookbinder

encuadernar, *v.t.* to bind (a book)

encuadrar, *v.t.* to frame; fit one thing into another; insert; limit; (*mil.*) enlist

encubar, *v.t.* to put into casks (wine, etc.)

encubiertamente, *adv.* secretly; deceitfully

encubierto, *a.* concealed; secret

encubridor (-ra), *a.* concealing, hiding. *s.* hider; harbourer; accomplice; receiver (stolen goods); (*law*) accessory after the fact

encubrimiento, *m.* hiding, concealment; (*law*) accessory before (after) the fact; receiving (of stolen goods)

encubrir, *v.t.* to conceal; receive (stolen goods); (*law*) prosecute as an accessory. *Past. Part.* **encubierto**

encuentro, *m.* collision; meeting, encounter; opposition, hostility; (*mil.*) fight, skirmish; (*arch.*) angle. **ir al e de,** to go in search of. **salir al e. (de),** to go to meet; resist

encuesta, *f.* investigation, examination

encumbrado, *a.* elevated, high

encumbramiento, *m.* act of elevating; height; aggrandizement; advancement

encumbrar, *v.t.* to raise, elevate; exalt, promote; ascend, climb to the top; *v.r.* be proud; be lofty, tower

encurtido, *m.* pickle (often *pl.*)

encurtir, *v.t.* to pickle

enchufar, *v.t.* to connect tubes; (*fig.*) combine (jobs, etc.); (*elec.*) plug, connect

enchufe, *m.* joint, fitting together (of tubes); (*elec.*) wall-socket, plug; part-time post; (*fam.*) cushy job. **e. de reducción,** (*elec.*) adapter

ende, *adv.* (*ant.*) there. **por e.,** therefore

endeble, *a.* weak, frail

endeblez, *f.* weakness

endecasílabo, *a.* hendecasyllabic

endecha, *f.* dirge (often *pl.*)

endémico, *a.* (*med.*) endemic

endemoniado, *a.* devil-possessed; (*fam.*) fiendish, malevolent

endemoniar, *v.t.* to possess of a devil; (*fam.*) enrage

endentar, *v.t. irr.* (*mech.*) to cut the cogs (of a wheel); engage, interlock (gears, wheels, etc.). See **regimentar**

endentecer, *v.i. irr.* to cut teeth. See **conocer**

enderezamiento, *m.* straightening; directing, guiding; putting right, correction

enderezar, *v.t.* to straighten; direct, guide; put right, correct; *v.i.* take the right road; *v.r.* straighten oneself; prepare to

endeudarse, *v.r.* to contract debts; be under an obligation

endiablado, *a.* ugly, monstrous; (*fam.*) fiendish

endiosar, *v.t.* to deify; *v.r.* be puffed up with pride; be abstracted or lost in ecstasy

endocrino, *a.* endocrine

endocrinología, *f.* endocrinology

endomingarse, *v.r.* to put on one's Sunday best

endosante, *m.* endorser

endosar, *v.t.* (*com.*) to endorse; transfer, pass on

endoso, *m.* (*com.*) endorsement

endrina, *f.* (*bot.*) sloe

endrino, *m.* sloe tree. *a.* blue-black, sloe-coloured

endulzar, *v.t.* to sweeten; soften, mitigate

endurecer, *v.t. irr.* to harden; toughen, inure; make severe or cruel; *v.r.* grow hard; become hardened or robust; be harsh or cruel. endurecerse al trabajo, to become hardened to work. See conocer

endurecimiento, *m.* hardness; obstinacy, tenacity

ene, *f.* name of letter N

enebro, *m.* (*bot.*) common juniper tree

enemiga, *f.* hostility, enmity

enemigo (-ga), *a.* hostile. *s.* enemy; antagonist. *m.* Devil

enemistad, *f.* enmity, hostility

enemistar, *v.t.* to make enemies of; *v.r.* (*with con*) become an enemy of; cease to be friendly with

energía, *f.* energy, vigour

enérgico, *a.* energetic, vigorous

energúmeno (-na), *s.* energumen

enero, *m.* January

enervación, *f.* enervation

enervar, *v.t.* to enervate, weaken; (*fig.*) take the force out of (reasons, etc.)

enfadar, *v.t.* to make angry; *v.r.* become angry

enfado, *m.* anger; annoyance; trouble, toil

enfadoso, *a.* vexatious; trouble-some, wearisome

enfaldar, *v.t.* to tuck up the skirts; lop off lower branches (of trees)

enfangarse, *v.r.* to cover oneself with mud; (*fam.*) dirty one's hands, sully one's reputation; wallow in vice

enfardar, *v.t.* to pack; make bales or bundles.

énfasis, *m.* or *f.* emphasis

enfático, *a.* emphatic

enfermar, *v.i.* to fall ill; *v.t.* cause illness; (*fig.*) weaken. Enfermó del corazón, He fell ill of heart trouble

enfermedad, *f.* illness; (*fig.*) mal-ady, distemper. e. del sueño, sleeping sickness

enfermera, *f.* nurse

enfermería, *f.* infirmary; hospital; first-aid post

enfermero, *m.* male nurse

enfermizo, *a.* ailing, delicate; unhealthy, unwholesome

enfermo (-ma), *a.* ill; (*fig.*) corrupt, diseased; delicate, sickly. *s.* patient

enfeudar, *v.t.* to enfeoff

enfilar, *v.t.* to place in line; string; (*mil.*) enfilade

enflaquecer, *v.t. irr.* to make thin; weaken, enervate; *v.i.* grow thin; lose heart. See conocer

enflaquecimiento, *m.* loss of flesh; discouragement

enfocar, *v.t.* to focus; envisage

enfoque, *m.* focus

enfoscado, *a.* ill-humoured; immersed in business matters

enfrascar, *v.t.* to bottle; *v.r.* (*with en*) plunge into, entangle oneself in (undergrowth, etc.); become engrossed or absorbed in

enfrenar, *v.t.* to bridle; curb (a horse); restrain, repress; check

enfrente, *adv.* in front, opposite, facing; in opposition

enfriadero, *m.* cooling place, cold cellar

enfriamiento, *m.* cooling

enfriar, *v.t.* to cool; (*fig.*) chill, make indifferent; *v.r.* grow cold; (*fig.*) grow stormy (weather)

enfurecer, *v.t. irr.* to enrage. See conocer

enfurecimiento, *m.* fury

enfurruñarse, *v.r.* (*fam.*) to fume, be angry; be disgruntled

engalanar, *v.t.* to decorate, embellish

enganchar, *v.t.* to hook; couple, connect; hitch, harness, yoke; (*fam.*) seduce, hook; (*mil.*) bribe into army; *v.r.* be hooked or caught on a hook; (*mil.*) enlist

enganche, *m.* hooking; coupling (of railway coaches, etc.); connection; yoke, harness; hook; (*fam.*) enticement; (*mil.*) enlistment

engañadizo, *a.* easily deceived, simple

engañador (-ra), *a.* deceiving; deceptive. *s.* deceiver, impostor

engañar, *v.t.* to deceive; defraud, cheat; beguile, while away; hoax, humbug; *v.r.* be mistaken; deceive oneself. **e. como a un chino**, *(fam.)* to pull the wool over a person's eyes. **Las apariencias engañan**, Appearances are deceptive

engañifa, *f. (fam.)* swindle, fraud

engaño, *m.* deceit; deception, illusion; fraud; falsehood

engañoso, *a.* deceitful, false; fraudulent; deceptive, misleading

engarabatar, *v.t. (fam.)* to hook; *v.r.* become hooked, curved, crooked

engarce, *m.* hooking; coupling; setting (of jewels)

engarzar, *v.t.* to link, couple, enchain; hook; curl; set (precious stones)

engastar, *v.t.* to set (precious stones)

engaste, *m.* setting (of jewels)

engatusar, *v.t. (fam.)* to wheedle, coax, flatter

engendrador (-ra), *a.* engendering; original. *s.* begetter

engendrar, *v.t.* to procreate; engender, produce, cause

engendro, *m.* fœtus; abnormal embryo; literary monstrosity

englobar, *v.t.* to include, comprise, embrace

engolfarse, *v.r.* to sail out to sea; *(with en) (fig.)* be absorbed in

engomar, *v.t.* to gum

engordar, *v.t.* to fatten; *v.i.* grow fat; *(fam.)* prosper, grow rich

engorde, *m.* fattening (stock)

engorro, *m.* impediment, obstacle, difficulty

engorroso, *a.* difficult, troublesome

engranaje, *m. (mech.)* gearing, gear; *(fig.)* connection, link

engrandecer, *v.t. irr.* to enlarge; augment; eulogize; promote, exalt. See **conocer**

engrandecimiento, *m.* enlargement; increase; exaggeration, eulogization; advancement, promotion

engrasado, *m.* oiling; greasing

engrasador, *m.* greaser, lubricator; oil-box

engrasar, *v.t.* to grease; lubri-

cate, oil; manure; stain with grease

engreimiento, *m.* conceit, vanity

engreír, *v.t. irr.* to make conceited; *v.r.* become vain or conceited. See **reír**

engrescar(se) *v.t.* and *v.r.* to start a quarrel

engrosar, *v.t. irr.* to fatten, thicken; *(fig.)* increase, swell; manure; *v.i.* put on weight, grow fat. See **contar**

engrudar, *v.t.* to paste, glue

engrudo, *m.* paste, gloy

enguantarse, *v.r.* to put on one's gloves

enguijarrado, *a.* pebbled. *m.* pebbled path

engullir, *v.t.* to gobble, swallow

enhebrar, *v.t.* to thread (needles); string

enhestar, *v.t. irr.* to erect; set upright; *v.r.* rise; rear up; straighten oneself up. See **acertar**

enhiesto, *a.* upright, erect

enhorabuena, *f.* congratulation. *adv.* well and good. **dar la e.**, congratulate

horamala, *adv.* in an evil hour. *(fam.)* ¡Vete e! Go to the Devil!

enhornar, *v.t.* to place in the oven

enhuerar, *v.t.* to addle; *v.i.* become addled

enigma, *m.* enigma

enigmático, *a.* enigmatical

enjabonar, *v.t.* to soap; *(fam.)* soap down, flatter

enjaezar, *v.t.* to harness (a horse)

enjalbegar, *v.t.* to whitewash

enjambrar, *v.t.* to hive bees; *v.i.* multiply, increase

enjambre, *m.* swarm (of bees); crowd

enjaretado, *m.* lattice work

enjaular, *v.t.* to cage; *(fam.)* gaol

enjoyar, *v.t.* to adorn with jewels; beautify; set with precious stones

enjuagadura, *f.* rinsing (the mouth); rinsing water; mouthwash

enjuagar, *v.t.* to rinse; *v.r.* rinse the mouth

enjuague, *m.* rinse; rinsing; mouth-wash; tooth-mug; scheme, plan

enjugar, *v.t.* to dry; cancel, write

off; wipe, mop (perspiration, tears, etc.); *v.r.* grow lean

enjuiciar, *v.t.* to submit a matter to arbitration; (*law*) prosecute; (*law*) give judgment; (*law*) carry on (a case)

enjundia, *f.* animal fat or grease; (*fig.*) substance, meat; strength, vigour; constitution, temperament

enjuto, *a.* dry; lean. *m. pl.* brushwood; (*cul.*) canapés, savouries

enlace, *m.* connection; link; tie; (*chem.*) bond; alliance, relationship; marriage

enladrillado, *m.* brick floor or pavement

enlardar, *v.t.* (*cul.*) to baste

enlazar, *v.t.* to tie, bind; join, link; lasso; *v.r.* marry; be allied, related. e. con, to connect with (of trains); link up with

enlodar, *v.t.* to muddy; (*fig.*) smirch, sully

enloquecer, *v.t. irr.* to drive insane; *v.i.* go mad. See conocer

enlosado, *m.* tile floor

enlosar, *v.t.* to pave with flags

enlucir, *v.t. irr.* to plaster (walls); polish (metals). See lucir

enlutar, *v.t.* to put in mourning, drape with crape; darken, obscure; sadden; *v.r.* go into mourning; become dark

enmaderar, *v.t.* to panel in wood, board up

enmarañar, *v.t.* to tangle, disorder (hair, etc.); complicate, confuse; *v.r.* be tangled; be sprinkled with clouds

enmaridar, *v.i.* to become a wife

enmarillecerse, *v.r. irr.* to grow yellow. See conocer

enmascarar, *v.t.* to mask; disguise, dissemble; *v.r.* be masked

enmasillar, *v.t.* to putty

enmendar, *v.t. irr.* to correct, improve; reform; compensate, indemnify; (*law*) repeal; *v.r.* be improved or corrected; mend one's ways. See acertar

enmienda, *f.* correction; reform; indemnity; compensation; amendment; *pl.* (*agr.*) fertilizers

enmohecer, *v.t. irr.* to rust; *v.r.* go mouldy. See conocer

enmudecer, *v.t. irr.* to silence; *v.i.* become dumb; be silent. See conocer

enmugrecer, *v.t. irr.* to cover with grime; *v.r.* be grimy, dirty. See conocer

ennegrecer, *v.t. irr.* to dye black; make black; *v.r.* become black; become dark or cloudy. See conocer

ennoblecer, *v.t. irr.* to ennoble; enrich, embellish; adorn, befit. See conocer

ennoblecimiento, *m.* ennoblement; enrichment

enojadizo, *a.* irritable, peevish

enojar, *v.t.* to anger; annoy irritate; *v.r.* be angry; rage, be rough (wind, sea)

enojo, *m.* anger; resentment; vexations, troubles, trials (gen. *pl.*)

enojoso, *a.* annoying; troublesome, tiresome

enorgullecer, *v.t. irr.* to make proud; *v.r.* be proud. See conocer

enorme, *a.* enormous, huge; monstrous, heinous

enormidad, *f.* hugeness; enormity; wickedness

enramada, *f.* bower; thickness of foliage

enramar, *v.t.* to intertwine branches; embower; *v.i.* branch (trees)

enranciarse, *v.r.* to grow rancid

enrarecer, *v.t. irr.* to rarefy; *v.r.* become rarefied; grow rare. See conocer

enrarecimiento, *m.* rarefaction

enrayar, *v.t.* to put spokes (in a wheel)

enredadera, *f.* (*bot.*) convolvulus. *a.* (*f.*) (*bot.*) climbing, twining (plant)

enredador (-ra), *a.* mischievous, wilful; intriguing, scheming; (*fam.*) gossiping, meddlesome. *s.* intriguer; (*fam.*) meddler

enredar, *v.t.* to catch in a net; put down nets or snares; entangle; sow discord; compromise, involve (in difficulties); *v.i.* be mischievous; *v.r.* be entangled; be involved (in difficulties)

enredo, *m.* tangle; mischief; prank; intrigue, malicious falsehood; difficult situation; plot

enredoso, *a.* tangled; fraught with difficulties

enrejado, *m.* railing, paling;

trellis or latticework; (sew.) openwork

enrejar, v.t. to fence with a railing; cover with grating

enriquecer, v.t. irr. to enrich; exalt, aggrandize; v.i. grow rich; prosper, flourish. See conocer

enriscado, a. craggy, rocky

enriscar, v.t. to raise; v.r. hide among crags

enristrar, v.t. to couch (the lance); string (onions, etc.); (fig.) surmount (difficulties); go straight to (a place)

enrojecer, v.t. irr. to redden; make blush; v.r. grow red; blush. See conocer

enroscar, v.t. to twist, twine; v.r. turn (screw); twist; coil

ensaimada, f. Spanish pastry cake

ensalada, f. salad; hotchpotch

ensaladera, f. salad bowl

ensalmar, v.t. (surg.) to set (bones); salad; hotchpotch

ensalmo, m. spell, charm. por e., as if by magic, rapidly

ensalobrarse, v.r. to become brackish (water)

ensalzar, v.t. to exalt, promote; praise

ensamblador, m. joiner, assembler

ensambladura, f. assemblage, joinery; joining; dovetailing

ensamblar, v.t. to assemble; join, dovetail, mortise

ensanchador, m. glove-stretcher

ensanchar, v.t. to widen, enlarge, extend; (sew.) let out, stretch; v.r. put on airs

ensanche, m. dilatation, widening; stretch; extension; (sew.) turnings, letting out; (city) extension

ensangrentar, v.t. irr. to stain with blood; v.r. be bloodstained; be over-hasty. See regimentar

ensañar, v.t. to irritate, infuriate; v.r. be merciless (with vanquished)

ensartar, v.t. to string (beads); thread (needles); spit, pierce; tell a string (of falsehoods)

ensayador, m. metal assayer

ensayar, v.t. to try out; (chem.) test; (theat.) rehearse; assay

ensaye, m. assaying (of metals)

ensayista, m. and f. essayist

ensayo, m. test, trial; (lit.) essay; assay; experiment; rehearsal. e. general, dress rehearsal

ensenada, f. cove, inlet

enseña, f. ensign, standard

enseñanza, f. teaching; education; example, experience. e. primaria, elementary education. e. secundaria, secondary education. e. superior, higher education

enseñar, v.t. to teach, instruct; train; point out; exhibit, show; v.r. become accustomed. e. la oreja, (fig.) to show the cloven hoof

enseñorearse, v.r. to take possession (of)

enseres, m. pl. household goods; utensils; equipment

ensillar, v.t. to saddle

ensimismarse, v.r. to be lost in thought

ensoberbecer, v.t. irr. to make haughty; v.r. become arrogant; grow rough (sea). See conocer

ensordecedor, a. deafening

ensordecer, v.t. irr. to deafen; v.i. become deaf; keep silent, refuse to reply. See conocer

ensuciar, v.t. to soil, dirty; (fig.) sully; v.r. be dirty; (fam.) accept bribes

ensueño, m. dream; illusion, fancy

entablado, m. stage, dais; wooden floor; planking

entablar, v.t. to plank, floor with boards; board up; (surg.) splint; undertake, initiate (negotiations, etc.); begin (conversations, etc.); v.r. settle (winds)

entalegar, v.t. to put into sacks or bags; hoard (money)

entalladura, f. carving; sculpture; (carp.) mortise, notch

entallar, v.t. to carve; sculpture; engrave; notch, groove; tap (trees); fit (well or ill) at the waist

entallecer, v.i. irr. to sprout (plants). See conocer

entapizar, v.t. to hang with tapestry; upholster; (fig.) cover, carpet

entarimado, m. wooden floor; dais

ente, m. entity, being; (fam.) object, individual

enteco, *a.* sickly, ailing, delicate

entendederas, *f. pl. (fam.)* understanding

entendedor (-ra), *a.* understanding, comprehending. *s.* one who understands. **A buen e. pocas palabras,** A word is enough to the wise

entender, *v.t. irr.* to comprehend, understand; know; deduce, infer; intend; believe; *(with de)* be familiar with or knowledgeable about; *(with en)* have as a profession or trade; be engaged in; have authority in; *v.r.* understand oneself; have a reason (for behaviour); understand each other; have an amatory understanding; be meant, signify; *(with con)* have an understanding with. **a mi entender,** in my opinion, as I see it. *Pres. Ind.* **entiendo, entiendes, entiende, entienden.** *Pres. Subjunc.* **entienda, entiendas, entienda, entiendan**

entendido, *a.* learned, knowledgeable

entendimiento, *m.* understanding; mind, reason, intelligence

enteramente, *adv.* completely, entirely, wholly

enterar, *v.t.* to inform, advise

entereza, *f.* entirety; completeness; impartiality, integrity; fortitude, constancy; strictness, rigour

enternecer, *v.t. irr.* to soften, make tender; move to pity; *v.r.* be touched by compassion. See **conocer**

enternecimiento, *m.* compassion, pity; tenderness

entero, *a.* entire; whole; robust, healthy; upright, just; constant, loyal; virgin; pure; *(fam.)* strong, tough (cloth); *(math.)* integral

enterrador, *m.* grave-digger

enterrar, *v.t. irr.* to inter; outlive; bury, forget. See **acertar**

entibiar *v.t.* to make lukewarm; *(fig.)* cool, temper

entidad, *f.* entity; value, importance

entierro, *m.* interment, burial; grave; funeral; buried treasure

entoldar, *v.t.* to cover with an awning; hang with tapestry, etc., drape; cover (sky, clouds)

entomología, *f.* entomology

entomológico, *a.* entomological

entomólogo, *m.* entomologist

entonación, *f.* intonation; modulation (voice); conceit

entonador (-ra), *a.* intoning. *s.* organ-blower

entonar, *v.t.* to modulate (voice); intone; blow (organ bellows); lead (song); *(med.)* tone up; *(art)* harmonize; *v.r.* become conceited; *(com.)* improve, harden (stock, etc.)

entonces, *adv.* then, at that time; in that case, that being so

entonelar, *v.t.* to put in barrels or casks

entontecer, *v.t. irr.* to make stupid or foolish; *v.r.* become stupid. See **conocer**

entornar, *v.t.* to leave ajar; half close; upset, turn upside down

entorpecer, *v.t. irr.* to numb, make torpid; confuse, daze; obstruct, delay; *v.r.* go numb; be confused. See **conocer**

entorpecimiento, *m.* numbness, torpidity; stupidity, dullness; delay, obstruction

entrada, *f.* entrance; door, gate; admission; *(cul.)* entrée; admission ticket; *(theat.)* house; takings, gate; *(mil.)* entry; beginnings (of month, etc.); intimacy; right of entry. **entradas y salidas,** comings and goings; collusion; *(com.)* ingoing and outgoing

entrambos, *a. m. pl.* both. *f. pl.* **entrambas**

entrampar, *v.t.* to trap (animals); swindle; *(fig., fam.)* entangle (business affairs); *(fam.)* load with debts; *v.r.* be embogged; *(fam.)* be in debt

entrante, *a.* incoming, entrant; next, coming (month)

entraña, *f.* entrail; *pl.* heart; *(fig.)* centre, core; humaneness; temperament; *(fam.)* **no tener entrañas,** to be heartless, be without feeling

entrañable, *a.* intimate; dearly loved

entrar, *v.i. (with en)* to enter, go into, come in; flow into; *(fig.)* have access to; join, become a member; *(fig.)* be taken by (fever, panic, etc.); *(mil.)* enter; be an ingredient of; (with por, en) penetrate, pierce; (with de) embrace (professions, etc.); (with prep. , a + infin.) begin to; (with en + noun) begin to be (e.g. e. en calor, begin to be hot) or begin to take part in (e.g. e. en lucha, begin to fight); v.t. introduce, make enter; (mil.) (with en) occupy; v.r. (with en) squeeze in. (fam.) no entrar ni salir en, to take no part in. (fam.) No me entra, I don't understand it

entre, prep. between; among; to. e. joyas, among jewels. E. las dos se escribió la carta, Between them they wrote the letter. Dije e. mí, I said to myself. los días de esemana, week-days. e. tanto, in the meanwhile. Used in some verbs, entrelazar, to interlace, entrecoger, to intercept; and in some substantives, entredicho, interdiction, etc.

entreabrir, v.t. to leave ajar; half open. Past Part. entreabierto

entreacto, m. interval, entr'acte; small cigar

entrecano, a. going grey, greyish (hair)

entrecejo, m. space between eyebrows; frown

entrecoger, v.t. to intercept, catch; constrain, compel

entrecoro, m. (arch.) chancel

entrecortado, a. intermittent (sounds); faltering, broken (voice)

entrecubiertas, f. pl. (naut.) between decks

entredicho, m. prohibition; (ecc.) interdiction

entredós, m. (sew.) insertion

entrefino, a. middling or fairly fine

entrega, f. handing over; delivery; (lit.) part, serial; instalment. por entregas, as a serial, serial (of stories)

entregar, v.t. to hand over; deliver; surrender; v.r. give oneself up; surrender; submit; (with prep. a) engage in, be absorbed in; (with prep. a or en) give oneself over to (vice, etc.)

entrelazar, v.t. to interlace, intertwine; interweave

entrelistado, a. striped

entrelucir, v.i. irr. to show

through, be glimpsed. See lucir

entremedias, adv. in between, half way; in the meantime

entremés, m. hors-d'œuvres (gen. pl.); interlude, farce

entremesista, m. and f. author of, or actor in, one-act farces

entremeter, v.t. to place between or among; v.r. intrude; meddle, pry

entremetido (-da), a. meddlesome. s. busybody, meddler

entremetimiento, m. meddlesomeness

entremezclar, v.t. to intermingle

entrenador (-ra), s. trainer; (sport) coach

entrenamiento, m. training, exercise

entrenar(se), v.t. and v.r. to train; exercise; (sport) coach

entreoír, v.t. to overhear; hear imperfectly

entrepaño, m. (arch.) panel; pier (between windows, etc.)

entrepiernas, f. pl. (anat.) crotch; gusset (of breeches)

entrepuente, m. (naut.) betweendecks; steerage quarters

entresacar, v.t. to choose or pick out; thin out (plants); thin (hair)

entresuelo, m. mezzanine, entresol; ground floor

entretalladura, f. bas-relief

entretallar, v.t. to carve in basrelief; engrave; (sew.) do openwork; intercept; v.r. connect, dovetail

entretejer, v.t. to interweave; interlace; (lit.) insert

entretela, f. (sew.) interlining

entretener, v.t. irr. to keep waiting; make more bearable; amuse, entertain; delay, postpone; maintain, upkeep; v.r. amuse oneself. See tener

entretenido, a. amusing, entertaining

entretenimiento, m. amusement; pastime, diversion; upkeep, maintenance

entretiempo, m. between seasons, spring or autumn

entreventana, f. space between windows

entreverado, a. variegated; streaky (of bacon)

entreverar, v.t. to intermingle

entrevía, f. railway gauge

entrevista, f. meeting, interview

entristecer, v.t. irr. to sadden; v.r. grieve. See **conocer**

entristecimiento, m. sadness

entrometer, v.t. See **entremeter**

entronar, v.t. See **entronizar**

entroncar, v.t. to prove descent; v.i. be related, or become related (by marriage)

entronerar, v.t. to pocket (in billiards)

entronización, f. enthronement

entronizar, v.t. to enthrone; exalt

entronque, m. blood-relationship, cognation; junction

entumecer, v.t. irr. to numb; v.r. go numb; swell, rise (sea, etc.). See **conocer**

enturbiar, v.t. to make turbid or cloudy; confuse, disorder; v.r. become turbid; be in disorder

entusiasmar, v.t. to inspire enthusiasm; v.r. be enthusiastic

entusiasmo, m. enthusiasm

entusiasta, a. enthusiastic. m. and f. enthusiast

enumeración, f. enumeration

enumerar, v.t. to enumerate

enunciación, f. statement, declaration, enunciation

enunciar, v.t. to state clearly, enunciate

envainar, v.t. to sheathe

envalentonamiento, m. boldness; braggadocio, bravado

envalentonar, v.t. to make bold (gen. in bad sense); v.r. strut, brag; take courage

envanecer, v.t. irr. to make vain or conceited; v.r. be vain; be conceited

envanecimiento, m. conceit, vanity

envasador (-ra), s. packer. m. funnel

envasar, v.t. to bottle; barrel; sack (grain, etc.); pack in any container; pierce (with sword)

envase, m. bottling; filling; container; packing

envejecer, v.t. irr. to make old, wear out; v.i. grow old. See **conocer**

envenenador (-ra), s. poisoner

envenenamiento, m. poisoning

envenenar, v.t. to poison; corrupt, pervert; put a malicious

interpretation on; embitter; v.r. take poison

envergadura, f. (zool. and aer.) wing span

envés, m. wrong side of anything; (fam.) back. **al e.,** wrong side out

enviado, m. messenger; envoy. **e. extraordinario,** special envoy

enviar, v.t. to send, dispatch

enviciar, v.t. to corrupt, make vicious; v.r. (with con, en) take to (drink, etc.)

envidia, f. envy; emulation; desire (to possess)

envidiable, a. enviable

envidiar, v.t. to envy, grudge; emulate

envidioso, a. envious

envilecer, v.t. irr. to debase; v.r. degrade oneself. See **conocer**

envío, m. (com.) remittance; consignment

envite, m. stake (at cards); offer; push, shove

enviudar, v.i. to become a widow or widower

envoltorio, m. bundle

envoltura, f. swaddling clothes (also pl.); covering; wrapping

envolver, v.t. irr. to enfold; envelop; wrap up, parcel; (fig.) contain, enshrine; swaddle, swathe; roll into a ball; confound (in argument); (mil.) outflank; implicate (person). See **mover**

enyesado, m. plastering; stucco

enyesar, v.t. to plaster; (surg.) apply a plaster bandage

enyugar, v.t. to yoke

enzarzar, v.t. to fill or cover with brambles; v.r. be caught on brambles; set off one person against another; get in difficulties; quarrel

eñe, f. name of letter Ñ

eolio, a. æolian

eperlano, m. (icht.) smelt

épica, f. epic

epicarpio, m. (bot.) epicarp

épico, a. epic

epicúreo (-ea), a. epicurean; sensual, voluptuous. s. epicure

epidemia, f. epidemic

epidémico, a. epidemic

epifanía, f. Epiphany, Twelfth Night

epigastrio, m. (anat.) epigastrium

epiglotis, f. (anat.) epiglottis

epígrafe, *m.* epigraph, inscription; title, motto

epigrafía, *f.* epigraphy

epigrama, *m.* inscription; epigram

epigramático (-ca), *a.* epigrammatic. *s.* epigrammatist

epilepsia, *f.* (*med.*) epilepsy

epiléptico (-ca), *a.* and *s.* epileptic

epilogar, *v.t.* to summarize, recapitulate

epílogo, *m.* recapitulation; summary, digest; epilogue

episcopado, *m.* episcopate; bishopric

episódico, *a.* episodic

episodio, *m.* episode; digression

epístola, *f.* epistle

epistolar, *a.* epistolary

epitafio, *m.* epitaph

epitalamio, *m.* epithalamium, bridal song

epíteto, *m.* epithet

epítome, *m.* epitome; summary, abstract

época, *f.* epoch, period; space of time. **en aquella é.,** at that time

épodo, *m.* (*poet.*) epode

epopeya, *f.* epic poem; (*fig.*) epic

equidad, *f.* fairness; reasonableness; equity

equidistancia, *f.* equidistance

equidistante, *a.* equidistant

equilátero, *a.* (*geom.*) equilateral

equilibrar, *v.t.* to balance; (*fig.*) maintain in equilibrium, counterbalance

equilibrio, *m.* equilibrium; equanimity; (*fig.*) balance

equilibrista, *m.* and *f.* equilibrist, tight-rope walker

equino, *a.* equine. *m.* (*arch.*) echinus; (*zool.*) sea-urchin

equinoccial, *a.* equinoctial

equinoccio, *m.* (*ast.*) equinox

equipaje, *m.* luggage, baggage; (*naut.*) crew

equipar, *v.t.* to equip, furnish

equipo, *m.* outfitting, furnishing; equipment; team; trousseau

equis, *f.* name of letter X

equitación, *f.* horsemanship, riding

equitativo, *a.* equitable, just, fair

equivalencia, *f.* equivalence, equality

equivalente, *a.* equivalent

equivaler, *v.i. irr.* to be equivalent; (*geom.*) be equal. See **valer**

equivocación, *f.* error, mistake

equivocadamente, *adv.* mistakenly, by mistake

equivocar, *v.t.* to mistake; *v.r.* be mistaken or make a mistake

equívoco, *a.* equivocal, ambiguous. *m.* equivocation

era, *f.* era; threshing floor; vegetable or flower bed

erario, *m.* Exchequer, public treasury

erección, *f.* raising; erection, elevation; foundation, institution

eréctil, *a.* erectile

eremita, *m.* hermit

ergio, *m.* (*phys.*) erg

erguir, *v.t. irr.* to raise; straighten; lift up; *v.r.* straighten up; tower; grow proud. *Pres. Ind.* **irgo** (or **yergo**), **irgues, irguen.** *Pres. Part.* **irguiendo.** *Preterite* **irguió, irguieron.** *Pres. Subjunc.* **irga** or **yerga,** etc.

erial, *m.* uncultivated land

erigir, *v.t.* to found, establish; promote, exalt

erisipela, *f.* (*med.*) erysipelas

erizado, *a.* standing on end (of hair); prickly, covered with bristles or quills. **e. de espinas,** bristling with thorns; covered with bristles or quills

erizar, *v.t.* to set on end (hair); beset with difficulties; *v.r.* stand on end, bristle (hair, quills, etc.)

erizo, *m.* (*zool.*) hedgehog; husk (of some fruits); (*fam.*) touch-me-not, unsociable person; (*mech.*) sprocket-wheel. **e. de mar,** sea-urchin

ermita, *f.* hermitage

ermitaño, *m.* hermit

erosión, *f.* erosion

erótico, *a.* erotic

errabundo, *a.* wandering, errant, vagrant

erradamente, *adv.* erroneously

erradicable, *a.* eradicable

erradicación, *f.* eradication

erradicar, *v.t.* to eradicate

errante, *a.* wandering; erring; errant

errar, *v.i. irr.* to err, fail; rove, roam; wander (attention, etc.); *v.r.* be mistaken. (*aut.*) **e. el encendido,** to misfire. *Pres. Ind.* **yerro, yerras, yerra, yerran.** *Pres. Subjunc.* **yerre, yerres, yerre, yerren**

errata, *f.* misprint

errático, *a.* wandering, vagrant; (*med.*) erratic

erre, *f.* name of letter R

erróneo, *a.* erroneous, mistaken

error, *m.* error

eructar, *v.i.* to eructate

eructo, *m.* eructation, belching

erudición, *f.* erudition

erudito, *a.* learned, erudite. *m.* scholar. **e. a la violeta,** pseudo-learned

erupción, *f.* (*med.*) rash; eruption

eruptivo, *a.* eruptive

es, *irr. 3rd pers. sing. Pres. Ind.* of **ser,** is

esa, *f. dem. a.* that. **ésa,** *f. dem. pron.* that one; the former; the town in which you are (e.g. **Vendré a é. mañana,** I shall come to your town to-morrow). Used generally in letters. See **ése**

esbeltez, *f.* slenderness

esbelto, *a.* tall and slim and graceful, willowy

esbozar, *v.t.* to sketch, outline

esbozo, *m.* sketch; outline, rough plan, first draft

escabechar, *v.t.* to pickle; dye (the hair, etc.); (*fam.*) kill in anger; (*fam.*) plough, fail (an examination)

escabeche, *m.* (*cul.*) pickle; hair dye

escabechina, *f.* (*fam.*) heavy plough (in an examination)

escabel, *m.* footstool; small backless chair; (*fig.*) stepping stone

escabiosa, *f.* (*bot.*) wild scabious

escabioso, *a.* (*med.*) scabby, scabious

escabro, *m.* scab, mange

escabroso, *a.* rough; rocky; uneven; rude, unpolished, uncivil; risqué, improper

escabullirse, *v.r. irr.* to escape; run away; slip out unnoticed. See **mullir**

escafandra, *f.* diving-dress

escala, *f.* ladder; (*mus., math.*) scale; dial (machines); proportion, ratio; stage, stopping place; measuring rule; (*naut.*) port of call. **e. de toldilla,** companion-ladder. (*mus.*) **e. mayor,** major scale. **e. menor,** minor scale. (*naut.*) **hacer e. en un puerto,** to call at a port

escalada, *f.* escalade

escalafón, *m.* salary promotion scale; roll, list

escalamiento, *m.* scaling, climbing; storming

escalar, *v.t.* to scale; climb, ascend; storm, assail, enter or leave violently

escaldadura, *f.* scalding; scald

escaldar, *v.t.* to scald; make red hot; *v.r.* scald or burn oneself. **Gato escaldado del agua fría huye,** A scalded cat dreads cold water, (A burnt child dreads the fire)

escalera, *f.* staircase; stair. **e. abajo,** below stairs. **e. de caracol,** spiral stair. **e. de mano,** ladder. **e. de tijera,** step-ladder. **e. móvil,** escalator

escalfar, *v.t.* to poach (eggs); burn (bread)

escalinata, *f.* outside staircase or flight of steps, perron

escalofrío, *m.* (gen. *pl.*) shiver, shudder

escalón, *m.* step, stair; rung (of a ladder); (*fig.*) stepping stone; grade, rank. **en escalones,** in steps

escalpar, *v.t.* to scalp

escalpelo, *m.* (*surg.*) scalpel

escama, *f.* (*zool.*) scale; anything scale shaped; flake; suspicion, resentment

escamar, *v.t.* to scale (fish); make suspicious. *v.r.* (*fam.*) be suspicious or disillusioned

escamondar, *v.t.* (*agr.*) to prune

escamoso, *a.* scaly

escamotear, *v.t.* to make disappear; palm (conjurers); steal

escamoteo, *m.* disappearance; stealing

escampada, *f.* (*fam.*) clear interval on a rainy day

escampar, *v.i.* to cease raining; clear up (of the weather, sky); stop (work, etc.)

escamujar, *v.t.* (*agr.*) to cut out superfluous wood (olive trees, etc.)

escanciar, *v.t.* to pour out wine; *v.i.* drink wine

escandalizar, *v.t.* to shock, scandalize; disturb with noise; *v.r.* be vexed or irritated

escándalo, *m.* scandal; commotion, uproar; bad example; viciousness; astonishment

escandaloso, *a.* disgraceful, scandalous; turbulent

escandallo, *m.* (*naut.*) deep-sea lead; random test

escandínavo (-va), *a.* and *s.* Scandinavian

escandir, *v.t.* to scan (of verse)

escansión, *f.* scansion

escantillón, *m.* templet, pattern; rule

escaño, *m.* bench with a back

escapada, *f.* escape; escapade

escapar, *v.t.* to spur on (horse); *v.i.* escape; flee; avoid, evade; *v.r.* escape; leak (gas, etc.). Se me escapó su nombre, His name escaped me. e. por un pelo, to have a narrow escape

escaparate, *m.* showcase, cabinet; show-window

escapatoria, *f.* escape, flight; (*fam.*) way-out, loophole

escape, *m.* flight; evasion; escape (gas, etc.); (*aut.*) exhaust. a e., at full speed

escápula, *f.* (*anat.*) scapula

escapulario, *m.* scapulary

escaque, *m.* square (chess or draughts board); *pl.* chess

escaqueado, *a.* checked, worked in squares

escara, *f.* (*surg.*) scar

escarabajo, *m.* beetle, scarab; (*fig., fam.*) dwarf; *pl.* (*fam.*) scrawl

escaramujo, *m.* (*bot.*) dog-rose; rose-hip; goose barnacle

escaramuza, *f.* skirmish

escaramuzar, *v.i.* to skirmish

escarapela, *f.* cockade, rosette; brawl

escarbar, *v.t.* to scratch, scrabble (fowls); rootle, dig; rake out (the fire); inquire into

escarcha, *f.* hoar-frost

escarchar, *v.t.* (*cul.*) to frost, ice; sprinkle with frosting; *v.i.* freeze lightly

escarda, *f.* weeding; (*fig.*) weeding out

escardador (-ra), *s.* weeder

escardar, *v.t.* to weed; (*fig.*) separate good from bad

escarificación, *f.* (*surg.*) scarification

escarlata, *f.* scarlet; scarlet cloth

escarlatina, *f.* (*med.*) scarlet fever

escarmentar, *v.t.* *irr.* to reprehend or punish severely; *v.i.* learn from experience, be warned. See acertar

escarmiento, *m.* disillusionment, experience; warning; punishment, fine

escarnecedor (-ra), *a.* mocking. *s.* mocker

escarnecer, *v.t.* *irr.* to mock. See conocer

escarnio, *m.* gibe, jeer

escarola, *f.* (*bot.*) endive; frilled ruff

escarpa, *f.* steep slope, declivity; escarpment

escarpado, *a.* steep, precipitous

escarpia, *f.* hook, spike, nail

escarpín, *m.* pump, slipper

escasear, *v.t.* to dole out, give grudgingly; save, husband; *v.i.* be scarce or short; grow less

escasez, *f.* meanness, frugality; want; shortage, scarcity

escaso, *a.* scarce; short; bare; parsimonious

escatimar, *v.t.* to cut down, curtail

escatimoso, *a.* malicious, guileful

escayola, *f.* plaster of Paris

escena, *f.* (*theat.*) stage; scene; scenery; theatre, drama; spectacle, sight; episode, incident. director de e., producer. poner en e., (*theat.*) to produce

escenario, *m.* (*theat.*) stage; scenario

escénico, *a.* scenic

escenografía, *f.* scenography

escenógrafo (-fa), *s.* scenographer, scene-painter

escepticismo, *m.* scepticism

escéptico (-ca), *a.* sceptical. *s.* sceptic

escindir, *v.t.* to split

escisión, *f.* cleavage, split; splitting; schism; disagreement

esclarecer, *v.t.* *irr.* to illuminate; ennoble, make illustrious; (*fig.*) enlighten; elucidate; *v.i.* dawn. See conocer

esclarecido, *a.* distinguished, illustrious

esclavina, *f.* short cape

esclavitud, *f.* slavery; fraternity

esclavizar, *v.t.* to enslave

esclavo (-va), *s.* slave; member of a brotherhood. *a.* enslaved. *f.* slave bangle

esclerosis, *f.* (*med.*) sclerosis

esclerótica, *f.* (*anat.*) sclerotic

esclusa, *f.* lock; sluice-gate; weir

esclusero, *m.* lock keeper

escoba, *f.* broom, sweeping brush; (*bot.*) yellow broom

escobada, *f.* sweep, stroke (of broom)

escobar, *v.t.* to sweep with broom

escobazo, *m.* brush with a broom

escobero, *m.* brush maker or seller

escobilla, *f.* brush

escobina, *f.* metal filing; wood-shaving

escocer, *v.i.* *irr.* to smart; (*fig.*) sear; *v.r.* hurt, smart; be chafed. See **mover**

escocés (-esa), *a.* Scots, Scottish. *s.* Scot

escoda, *f.* claw hammer

escofina, *f.* rasp, file

escoger, *v.t.* to choose, select

escogido, *a.* choice, select

escolapio (-ia), *a.* and *s.* (*ecc.*) Escolapian

escolar, *a.* school; pupil. *m.* pupil

escolasticismo, *m.* Scholasticism

escolástico, *a.* scholastic

escolopendra, *f.* (*ent.*) centipede; (*bot.*) hart's tongue fern

escolta, *f.* escort, guard

escoltar, *v.t.* to escort; guard, conduct

escollera, *f.* breakwater, sea-wall, jetty

escollo, *m.* reef; danger, risk; difficulty, obstacle

escombrar, *v.t.* to remove obstacles, free of rubbish; (*fig.*) clean up

escombro, *m.* débris, rubble, rubbish; mackerel

esconder, *v.t.* to hide, conceal; (*fig.*) contain, embrace; *v.r.* hide

escondidas, a. *adv.* secretly

escondite, escondrijo, *m.* hiding-place. **jugar al escondite,** to play hide-and-seek

escopeta, *f.* shotgun. **e. de aire comprimido,** air-gun, pop-gun. **e. de viento,** air-gun

escopetazo, *m.* gunshot; gunshot wound; (*fig.*) bomb-shell

escopetear, *v.t.* to shoot repeatedly

escopetero, *m.* musketeer; gun-smith; man with a gun

escoplear, *v.t.* (*carp.*) to notch; chisel; gouge

escoplo, *m.* chisel

escorbútico, *a.* (*med.*) scorbutic

escorbuto, *m.* (*med.*) scurvy

escoria, *f.* dross, slag; scoria, volcanic ash; (*fig.*) dregs

escorial, *m.* slag heap

escorpión, *m.* scorpion; Scorpio

escorzo, *m.* (*art.*) foreshortening

escotado, a low-cut (of dresses)

escotadura, *a.* low neck (of dress); piece cut out of something; (*theat.*) large trap-door; recess

escotar, *v.t.* to cut low in the neck (dresses); pay one's share (of expenses)

escote, *m.* low neck (of dress); shortness (of sleeves); share (of expenses); lace yoke

escotilla, *f.* (*naut.*) hatch

escotillón, *m.* trap-door

escozor, *m.* smart, pricking pain; irritation, prickle; heartache

escriba, *m.* (*Jewish hist.*) scribe

escribanía, *f.* secretaryship; notaryship; bureau, office; writing case; inkstand

escribano, *m.* notary public; secretary

escribiente, *m.* and *f.* clerk

escribir, *v.t.* to write; *v.r.* enlist; enrol; correspond by writing. *Past Part.* **escrito**

escrito, *m.* writing, manuscript; literary or scientific work; (*law*) writ. **por e.,** in writing

escritor (-ra), *a.* writer, author

escritorio, *m.* escritoire; office

escritura, *f.* writing; handwriting; (*law*) deed; literary work. **Sagrada E.,** Holy Scripture

escrófula, *f.* (*med.*) scrofula

escrofuloso, *a.* (*med.*) scrofulous

escroto, *m.* (*anat.*) scrotum

escrúpulo, *m.* scruple, qualm; conscientiousness; scruple (pharmacy)

escrupulosidad, *f.* conscientiousness, scrupulousness

escrupuloso, *a.* scrupulous; exact, accurate

escrutador (-ra), *s.* scrutinizer. *a.* examining, inspecting

escrutar, *v.t.* to scrutinize, examine; count (votes)

escrutinio, *m.* scrutiny, examination; count (votes)

escuadra, *f.* carpenter's square; architect's square; (*nav.*) fleet; (*aer.*) squadron; (*mil.*) squad. **e. de agrimensor,** (*surv.*) cross-staff

escuadrar, *v.t.* (*carp.* and *mas.*) to square

escuadrilla, *f.* squadron (aeroplanes, small ships)

escuadrón, *m.* (*mil.*) squadron

escualidez, *f.* squalor, sordidness

escuálido, *a.* filthy, squalid; sordid; thin

escucha, *f.* listening; peephole; (*mil.*) sentinel

escuchar, *v.t.* to listen; attend to, heed; *v.r.* like the sound of one's own voice

escudar, *v.t.* to shield, protect

escuderear, *v.t.* to squire, serve

escuderil, *a.* squirely

escudero, *m.* squire, page; gentleman; shield maker

escudete, *m.* escutcheon; shield; gusset; white water-lily

escudilla, *f.* bowl

escudo, *m.* shield; escudo; escutcheon; protection, defence; ward (of keyhole)

escudriñador (-ra), *a.* searching; curious, prying. *s.* scrutinizer; pryer

escudriñar, *v.t.* to scrutinize; scan; investigate; pry into

escuela, *f.* school; school building; style; (*lit.* and *art*) school. **e. de artes y oficios,** industrial school. **e. industrial,** technical school. **e. normal,** normal school

escueto, *a.* dry, bare, unadorned; simple, exact; unencumbered

esculpir, *v.t.* to sculpture; engrave

escultor (-ra), *s.* sculptor

escultórico, *a.* sculptural

escultura, *f.* sculpture; carving; modelling

escultural, *a.* sculptural

escupidera, *f.* spittoon

escupir, *v.i.* to expectorate; *v.t.* (*fig.*) spit out; cast away, throw out

escurreplatos, *m.* plate-draining rack

escurrido, *a.* narrow-hipped; skin-tight (of skirts)

escurridor, *m.* colander, sieve; plate-draining rack; draining-board

escurriduras, *f. pl.* lees, dregs

escurrir, *v.t.* to drain to the dregs; wring, press out, drain; *v.i.* trickle, drip; slip, slide; *v.r.* slip away, edge away; escape, slip out; skid

esdrújulo, *a.* (*gram.*) of words where the accent falls on the antepenultimate syllable

ese, *f.* name of letter S; S-shaped link in chain. (*fam.*) **andar haciendo eses,** to reel about drunkenly

ese, *m. dem. a.* (*f.* **esa.** *pl.* **esos, esas**) that; those. **ése,** *m. dem. pron.* (*f.* **ésa.** *neut.* **eso.** *pl.* **ésos, ésas**) that one; the former (e.g. Me gusta éste, pero ése no me gusta, I like this one, but I do not like that one; I like the latter, but I do not like the former)

esencia, *f.* essence, nature, character; extract; (*chem.*) essence

esencial, *a.* essential

esfera, *f.* (*geom.*) sphere, globe, ball; sky; rank; face, dial; province, scope

esférico, *a.* (*geom.*) spherical

esferoidal, *a.* spheroidal

esferoide, *m.* (*geom.*) spheroidal

esfinge, *f.* sphinx

esforzado, *a.* valiant, courageous; spirited

esforzador, *a.* encouraging

esforzar, *v.t. irr.* to encourage; invigorate; *v.r.* make an effort. See **contar**

esfuerzo, *m.* effort; courage; spirit; vigour; exertion, strain; (*mech.*) stress. **sin e.,** effortless

esfumar, *v.t.* (*art*) shade; (*art*) stump; dim; *v.r.* disappear

esfumino, *m.* (*art*) stump

esgrima, *f.* (art of) fencing

esgrimidor, *m.* fencer, swordsman

esgrimir, *v.t.* to fence; fend off

esguazar, *v.t.* to ford (a river)

esguince, *m.* dodging, twist; expression or gesture of repugnance; (*med.*) sprain

eslabón, *m.* link (in a chain); steel for producing fire. **e. perdido,** (*fig.*) missing link

eslabonar, *v.t.* to link; connect, unite

eslavo (-va), *a.* and *s.* Slav

eslora, *f.* (*naut.*) length (of a ship)

eslovaco (-ca), *a.* Slovakian. *s.* Slovak

esloveno (-na), *a.* and *s.* Slovene

esmaltador (-ra), *s.* enameller

esmaltar, *v.t.* to enamel; decorate, adorn

esmalte, *m.* enamel; enamel work; smalt; brilliance

esmerado, *a.* careful, painstaking

esmeralda, *f.* emerald

esmerar, *v.t.* to polish; *v.r.* (with *en*) take great pains with (or to)

esmeril, *m.* emery

esmerilar, *v.t.* to polish with emery

esmero, *m.* great care, conscientiousness

esmoladera, *f.* grindstone

esnob, *a.* snobbish. *m.* and *f.* snob

eso, *neut. dem. pron.* that; the fact that; that idea, affair, etc.; about (of time) (e.g. Vendrá a e. de las nueve, He will come about nine o'clock). Eso refers to an abstraction, never to one definite object. No me gusta e., I don't like that kind of thing. e. es, that's it. por e., therefore, for that reason

esófago, *m.* (anat.) œsophagus

esotérico, *a.* esoteric

esotro, *dem. pron.* and *a.* that other. *m. pl.* esotros. *f. pl.* esotras, those others; those other

espaciar, *v.t.* to space; (print.) lead; *v.r.* spread oneself, enlarge (upon)

espacio, *m.* space; capacity; interval, duration; slowness; (print.) lead

espaciosidad, *f.* spaciousness; capacity

espada, *f.* sword; matador (also *m.*); swordsman; (cards) spade. entre la e. y la pared, (fig.) in a cleft stick

espadachín, *m.* good swordsman; bully, quarrelsome fellow

espadaña, *f.* open belfry; (bot.) gladiolus

espadería, *f.* sword cutler's workshop or shop

espadero, *m.* sword cutler

espadilla, *f.* insignia of Order of Santiago; swingle; ace of spades

espadín, *m.* small dress-sword

espahí, *m.* Spahi

espalda, *f.* (anat.) back (often *pl.*); *pl.* rear, . back portion; (mil.)

rearguard. de espaldas, with one's (its, his, etc.) back turned; on one's (its, etc.) back

espaldar, *m.* backpiece of cuirass; back (of chair); garden trellis, espalier

espaldarazo, *m.* accolade

espaldera, *f.* espalier, trellis

espantadizo, *a.* easily frightened

espantapájaros, *m.* scarecrow

espantar, *v.t.* to frighten, terrify; chase off; *v.r.* be amazed; be scared

espanto, *m.* terror, panic; dismay; amazement; threat

espantoso, *a.* horrible, terrifying, awesome; amazing

español (-la), *a.* Spanish. *s.* Spaniard. *m.* Spanish language. a la española, in the Spanish fashion

españolismo, *m.* love of things Spanish; Hispanism

españolizar, *v.t.* to hispanize; *v.r.* adopt Spanish customs

esparadrapo, *m.* court plaster

esparaván, *m.* (orn.) sparrowhawk; (vet.) spavin

esparavel, *m.* casting net

esparcimiento, *m.* scattering; naturalness, frankness; geniality

esparcir, *v.t.* to scatter, sprinkle, disperse; spread, publish abroad; entertain; *v.r.* be scattered; amuse oneself

espárrago, *m.* (bot.) asparagus

esparraguera, *f.* asparagus plant; asparagus bed; asparagus dish

espartano (-na), *a.* and *s.* Spartan

espartería, *f.* esparto industry or shop

esparto, *m.* (bot.) esparto grass

espasmo, *m.* spasm

espasmódico, *a.* spasmodic

espato, *m.* (min.) spar

espátula, *f.* spatula; palette knife

especia, *f.* spice. nuez de e., nutmeg

especial, *a.* special; particular

especialidad, *f.* speciality; branch (of learning)

especialista, *m.* and *f.* specialist

especialización, *f.* specialization

especializarse, *v.r.* to specialize

especie, *f.* class, kind; species; affair, matter, case; idea, image; news; pretext, appearance

especiería, *f.* spice trade; spice shop

especiero (-ra), *s.* spice merchant; spice cupboard

especificación, *f.* specification.
e. normalizada, standard specification

especificar, *v.t.* to specify, particularize

específico, *a.* and *m.* specific, patent medicine

espécimen, *m.* specimen, sample

especioso, *a.* lovely, perfect; specious

espectacular, *a.* spectacular

espectáculo, *m.* spectacle, sight; show, display

espectador (-ra), *s.* spectator

espectral, *a.* spectral; faint, dim

espectro, *m.* phantom, spectre; (*phys.*) spectrum

especulación, *f.* conjecture; (*com.*) speculation

especulador (-ra), *s.* speculator

especular, *v.t.* to examine, look at; (*with en*) reflect on, consider; *v.i.* (*com.*) speculate

especulativo, *a.* speculative; thoughtful, meditative

espéculo, *m.* (*surg.*) speculum

espejería, *f.* mirror shop or factory

espejero, *m.* mirror manufacturer or seller

espejismo, *m.* mirage; illusion

espejo, *m.* mirror; (*fig.*) model.
e. de cuerpo entero, full-length mirror. **e. retrovisor,** driving mirror

espejuelo, *m.* small mirror; (*min.*) selenite; (*min.*) sheet of talc; *pl.* lenses, eyeglasses

espeluznante, *a.* hair-raising

espeluznar, *v.t.* to dishevel; untidy (hair, etc.); *v.r.* stand on end (hair)

espera, *f.* waiting; expectation; (*law*) adjournment; caution, restraint; (*law*) respite

esperantista, *m.* and *f.* Esperantist

esperanto, *m.* Esperanto

esperanza, *f.* hope

esperanzar, *v.t.* to inspire hope in

esperar, *v.t.* to hope; expect; await; (*with en*) have faith in.
e. sentado, (*fig., fam.*) to whistle for

esperma, *f.* (*anat.*) sperm, semen.
e. de ballena, spermaceti

esperpento, *m.* (*fam.*) scarecrow, grotesque; folly, madness; fantastic dramatic composition

espesar, *v.t.* to thicken; make closer; tighten (fabrics); *v.r.* thicken; grow denser or thicker

espeso, *a.* thick; dense; greasy, dirty

espesor, *m.* thickness; density

espesura, *f.* thickness; density; thicket; filth

espetar, *v.t.* (*cul.*) to spit, skewer; pierce; (*fam.*) utter, give; *v.r.* be stiff or affected; (*fam.*) push oneself in, intrude

espetera, *f.* kitchen or pan rack

espetón, *m.* (*cul.*) spit; poker; large pin

espía, *m.* and *f.* spy. *f.* (*naut.*) warp

espiar, *v.t.* to spy upon, watch; *v.i.* (*naut.*) warp

espicanardo, *m.* (*bot.*) spikenard

espiche, *m.* sharp-pointed weapon or instrument; spit, spigot

espiga, *f.* (*bot.*) spike, ear; sprig; (*carp.*) peg; tang, shank (of sword); (*carp.*) tenon, dowel; (*naut.*) masthead; (*her.*) garb

espigador (-ra), *s.* gleaner

espigar, *v.t.* to glean; (*carp.*) tenon; *v.i.* (*bot.*) begin to show the ear or spike; *v.r.* (*bot.*) bolt; shoot up, grow (persons)

espigón, *m.* sting; sharp point; breakwater; bearded spike (maize, etc.)

espigueo, *m.* gleaning

espín, *m.* porcupine

espina, *f.* thorn; prickle; splinter; fishbone; (*anat.*) spine; suspicion, doubt

espinaca, *f.* (*bot.*) spinach

espinal, *a.* spinal

espinar, *m.* thorn-brake; (*fig.*) awkward position. *v.t.* to prick, wound, hurt

espinazo, *m.* (*anat.*) backbone

espinela, *f.* (*min.*) spinel ruby

espineta, *f.* (*mus.*) spinet; virginals

espinilla, *f.* shinbone; blackhead

espinillera, *f.* (cricket) pad

espino, *m.* (*bot.*) hawthorn

espinoso, *a.* thorny; difficult, intricate

espión, *m.* See **espía**

espionaje, *m.* espionage; spying

espira, *f.* (*geom., arch.*) helix; turn, twist (of winding stair); whorl (of shell)

espiración, *f.* expiration; respiration

espiral, *a.* spiral. *f.* (*geom.*) spiral; spiral watch spring

espirar, *v.t.* to exhale, breathe out; inspire; encourage; *v.i.* breathe; breathe out; (*poet.*) blow (wind)

espiritismo, *m.* Spiritualism

espiritista, *a.* spiritualist. *m.* and *f.* spiritualist

espiritoso, *a.* lively, active, spirited; spirituous

espíritu, *m.* spirit; apparition, spectre; soul; intelligence, mind; mood, temper, outlook; underlying principle, spirit; devil (gen. *pl.*) vigour, ardour, vivacity; (*chem.*) essence; (*chem.*) spirits; turn of mind. **E. Santo,** Holy Ghost

espiritual, *a.* spiritual

espiritualidad, *f.* spirituality

espiritualismo, *m.* (*phil.*) Spiritualism

espiritualizar, *v.t.* to spiritualize

espita, *f.* spigot, tap; (*fam.*) tippler

esplender, *v.i.* (*poet.*) to shine

esplendidez, *f.* liberality, abundance; splendour, pomp

espléndido, *a.* magnificent; liberal; resplendent (gen. *pl.*)

esplendor, *m.* splendour, brilliance; distinction, nobility

esplendoroso, *a.* splendid, brilliant, radiant

esplénico, *a.* (*anat.*) splenic

espliego, *m.* (*bot.*) lavender

esplín, *m.* spleen, melancholy

espolada, *f.* prick with the spur

espolear, *v.t.* to prick with the spur; encourage, stimulate

espoleta, *f.* fuse (of explosives); breast-bone (of fowls); wishbone. **e. de tiempo, e. graduada,** time fuse. **e. de seguridad,** safety-fuse

espolio, *m.* (*ecc.*) spolium

espolón, *m.* spur (of a bird or mountain range); (*naut.*) ram; breakwater; buttress; (*naut.*) fender

espolvorear, *v.t.* to scatter with powder

espondeo, *m.* (metrical foot) spondee

esponja, *f.* sponge

esponjadura, *f.* sponging

esponjar, *v.t.* to make spongy; sponge; *v.r.* swell with pride; (*fam.*) bloom with health

esponjera, *f.* sponge-holder

esponjosidad, *f.* sponginess

esponjoso, *a.* spongy, porous

esponsales, *m. pl.* betrothal; betrothal contract

espontaneidad, *f.* spontaneity

espontáneo, *a.* spontaneous

espora, *f.* (*bot.*) spore

esporádico, *a.* sporadic

esportillo, *m.* bass, frail

esposa, *f.* wife; *pl.* handcuffs

esposo, *m.* husband; *pl.* husband and wife

espuela, *f.* spur; stimulus; spur (of a bird or flower). **e. de caballero,** (*bot.*) larkspur

espuerta, *f.* bass, frail

espulgar, *v.t.* to delouse; examine carefully

espuma, *f.* froth, foam; (*cul.*) scum; (*fig.*) the best of anything, flower; (*fig., fam.*) **crecer como la e.,** to flourish like weeds

espumadera, *f.* skimming ladle

espumajear, *v.i.* to foam at the mouth

espumajoso, *a.* frothy, foaming

espumar, *v.t.* to skim (soup, etc.); *v.i.* foam; increase rapidly

espumoso, *a.* frothy, foaming

espurio, *a.* bastard; spurious

esputo, *m.* sputum

esqueje, *m.* (*agr.*) cutting

esquela, *f.* note; printed card

esqueleto, *m.* skeleton; (*fam.*) skinny person; framework

esquema, *f.* diagram, layout sketch; scheme, plan. **e. de una máquina,** drawing of a machine

esquemático, *a.* schematic; diagrammatic

esquematizar, *v.t.* to plan, outline

esquí, *m.* ski, snow-shoe

esquiador, *m.* skier

esquiar, *v.i.* to ski

esquife, *m.* skiff

esquila, *f.* cattle bell; small bell, hand-bell; sheep-shearing; (*icht., bot.*) squill

esquilador, *a.* shearing. *m.* sheepshearer

esquiladora, *f.* shearing machine

esquilar, *v.t.* to shear, clip (sheep, etc.)

esquileo, *m.* shearing; shearing time or place

esquilmar, *v.t.* to harvest; impoverish

esquilmo, *m.* harvest

esquimal, *a.* and *m.* and *f.* Eskimo

esquina, *f.* corner

esquinado, *a.* having corners; *(fig.)* difficult of approach (people)

esquirla, *f.* splinter (of a bone); shrapnel

esquirol, *m.(fam.)* blackleg, strikebreaker

esquisto, *m.* *(min.)* slate; shale

esquivar, *v.t.* to avoid; *v.r.* slip away, disappear; excuse oneself

esquivez, *f.* unsociableness; unfriendliness, aloofness

esquivo, *a.* unsociable, elusive, aloof

esquizado, *a.* mottled (marble)

estabilidad, *f.* stability; fastness (of colours)

estabilizar, *v.t.* to stabilize

estable, *a.* stable; fast (of colours)

establecer, *v.t. irr.* to establish, found, institute; decree; *v.r.* take up residence; open (a business firm). See **conocer**

establecimiento, *m.* law, statute; foundation, institution; establishment

establero, *m.* stable-groom

establo, *m.* stable

estabulación, *f.* stabling

estaca, *f.* stake, pole; *(agr.)* cutting; cudgel

estacada, *f.* fence; *(mil.)* palisade; place fixed for duel

estacar, *v.t.* to stake; fence; tie to a stake; *v.r. (fig.)* be as still as a post

estación, *f.* position, situation; season; station (railway, etc.); depôt; time, period; stop, halt; building, headquarters; *(bot.)* habitat; *(surv., geom., ecc.)* station

estacional, *a.* seasonal; *(ast.)* stationary

estacionamiento, *m.* stationariness; *(aut.)* parking

estacionar, *v.t.* to station, place; *(aut.)* park (a car); *v.r.* remain stationary; place oneself

estacionario, *a.* motionless; *(ast.)* stationary. *m.* stationer

estada, *f.* sojourn

estadía, *f.* stay, sojourn; *(art)* sitting (of model)

estadio, *m.* racecourse; stadium; furlong

estadista, *m.* statistician; statesman

estadística, *f.* statistics

estadístico, *a.* statistical

estadizo, *a.* stagnant

estado, *m.* state; condition; rank, position; *(pol.)* state; profession; status; *(com.)* statement. **e. de guerra,** state of war; martial law. **e. mayor central,** *(nav., mil.)* General Staff. **e. tapón,** *(pol.)* buffer state. **tomar e.,** to marry; *(ecc.)* profess; be ordained priest

estadounidense, *a.* United States

estafa, *f.* swindle

estafador (-ra), *s.* swindler

estafar, *v.t.* to swindle

estafeta, *f.* courier; branch postoffice; diplomatic postbag

estafetero, *m.* postmaster

estafilococo, *m.* *(med.)* staphylococcus

estagnación, *f.* stagnation

estalactita, *f.* stalactite

estalagmita, *f.* stalagmite

estallar, *v.i.* to explode; burst; *(fig.)* break out

estallido, *m.* explosion, report; crash, crack; *(fig.)* outbreak; *(aut.)* **e. de un neumático,** tyre-burst

estambre, *m.* woollen yarn, worsted; *(bot.)* stamen

estameña, *f.* serge

estampa, *f.* illustration, picture; print; aspect; printing press; track, step; *(met.)* boss

estampación, *f.* stamping; printing; imprinting. **e. en seco,** tooling (of a book)

estampado, *a.* printed (of textiles). *m.* textile printing; printed or figured fabric

estampar, *v.t.* to print, stamp; leave the print (of); bestow, imprint. **e. en relieve,** to emboss. **e. en seco,** to tool (a book)

estampería, *f.* print or picture shop; trade in prints

estampero, *m.* print dealer, picture dealer

estampido, *m.* report, bang, detonation; crash

estampilla, *f.* rubber stamp; seal

estampillar, *v.t.* to stamp, imprint

estancación, *f.* stagnation

estancado, *a.* stagnant; blocked, held up

estancar, *v.t.* to check, stem; set up a monopoly; (*fig.*) hold up (negotiations, etc.); *v.r.* be stagnant

estancia, *f.* stay, residence; dwelling; lounge, living-room; stanza; (*S.A.*) farm

estanciero, *m.* (*S.A.*) farmer

estanco, *a.* (*naut.*) watertight. *m.* monopoly; shop which sells Government monopoly goods; archive

estandarte, *m.* standard, flag. **e. real,** royal standard

estanque, *m.* tank; pool; reservoir

estanquero (-ra), *s.* seller of monopoly goods (tobacco, matches, etc.)

estante, *a.* present; extant; permanent. *m.* shelf; bookcase; bin (for wine)

estantería, *f.* shelving; shelves, bookcase

estantigua, *f.* hobgoblin, spectre; (*fig., fam.*) scarecrow

estañador, *m.* tinsmith

estañar, *v.t.* to tin; solder

estaño, *m.* tin (metal)

estaquilla, *f.* peg, cleat

estar, *v.i. irr.* to be. Indicates: 1. Position or place (e.g. **Está a la puerta,** He is at the door). 2. State (e.g. **Las flores están marchitas,** The flowers are faded). 3. Used to form the continuous or progressive tense (e.g. **Siempre está (estaba) escribiendo,** He is (was) always writing). 4. In contrast to verb *ser,* indicates impermanency (e.g. **Está enfermo,** He is ill). 5. **Estar** forms an apparent passive where no action is implied (e.g. **El cuadro está pintado al óleo,** The picture is painted in oils). 6. Used in some impersonal expressions (e.g. **¡ Bien está !** All right! **¡ Claro está !** Of course! etc.). **e.**

de, to be in, or on, or acting as (e.g. **e. de prisa,** to be in a hurry. **e. de capitán,** to be acting as a captain). **e. para,** tó be on the point of; to be nearly; to be in the mood for. **e. para llover,** to be on the point of raining. **e. por,** to remain to be done; have a mind to (e.g. **La historia está por escribir,** The story remains to be written). **e. bien,** to be well (in health). (*mech.*) **e. bajo presión,** to have the steam up. (*pol.*) **e. en el poder,** to be in office. **¿ A cómo** (*or* **a cuántos) estamos ?** What is the date? *Pres. Ind.* **estoy, estás, está, estamos, estáis, están.** *Preterite* **estuve,** etc. *Pres. Subjunc.* **esté, estés, esté, estén.** *Imperf. Subjunc.* **estuviese,** etc.

estarcir, *v.t.* to stencil

estatal, *a.* state

estática, *f.* (*mech.*) statics

estático, *a.* static

estatua, *f.* statue

estatuaria, *f.* statuary

estatuario, *a.* statuary

estatuir, *v.t. irr.* to establish, order. See **huir**

estatura, *f.* stature, height (of persons)

estatuto, *m.* statute, law

estay, *m.* (*naut.*) stay. **e. mayor,** (*naut.*) mainstay

este, *m.* east

este, *m. dem. a.* this (*f.* **esta,** *pl.* **estos, estas,** these). **éste,** *m. dem. pron.* this one; the latter. (*f.* **ésta,** *neut.* **esto,** *pl.* **éstos, éstas,** these ones; the latter) (e.g. **Aquel cuadro no es tan hermoso como éste,** That picture is not as beautiful as this one)

estela, *f.* wake, track (of a ship)

esteliforme, *a.* star-shaped

estenodactilógrafo (-fa), *s.* shorthand-typist

estenografía, *f.* shorthand

estenográfico, *a.* shorthand

estenógrafo (-fa), *s.* stenographer

estenordeste, *m.* East-North-East

estentóreo, *a.* stentorian

estepa, *f.* steppe, arid plain

estera, *f.* matting

esterar, *v.t.* to cover with matting; *v.i* (*fam.*) muffle oneself up

estercoladura, *f.* manuring

estercolar, *v.t.* to manure

estercolero, *m.* manure heap; driver of a dung cart

estereoscópico, *a.* stereoscopic

estereoscopio, *m.* stereoscope

estereotipar, *v.t.* to stereotype (printing)

estereotipia, *f.* stereotypography

esterería, *f.* matting factory or shop

esterero (-ra), *s.* matting maker or fitter or seller

estéril, *a.* sterile, barren; unfruitful, unproductive

esterilidad, *f.* sterility; barrenness, unfruitfulness

esterilización, *f.* sterilization

esterilizador, *a.* sterilizing. *m.* sterilizer

esterilizar, *v.t.* to make barren; *(med.)* sterilize

esterilla, *f.* mat, matting

esterlina, *a.* *(f.)* sterling. **libra e.,** pound sterling

esternón, *m.* *(anat.)* sternum

estero, *m.* salt marsh

estertor, *m.* stertorous breathing, rattle

estertoroso, *a.* stertorous

estesudeste, *m.* East-South-East

estética, *f.* æsthetics

estético, *a.* æsthetic. *m.* æsthete

estetoscopio, *m.* *(med.)* stethoscope

esteva, *f.* plough handle

estevado, *a.* bandy-legged

estiaje, *m.* low water level (rivers)

estiba, *f.* *(naut.)* stowage

estibador, *m.* stevedore, dockworker

estibar, *v.t.* *(naut.)* to stow

estiércol, *m.* dung; manure

estigio, *a.* Stygian; *(fig., poet.)* infernal

estigma, *m.* stigma (also *fig.*)

estigmatizar, *v.t.* to brand; stigmatize; insult

estilar, *v.i.* to be accustomed; *v.t.* draw up (document)

estilete, *m.* stiletto, dagger; needle, hand, pointer; *(med.)* stylet

estilista, *m.* and *f.* stylist

estilística, *f.* stylism

estilizar, *v.t.* to stylize

estilo, *m.* *(art, arch., lit.)* style, writing instrument; gnomon, pointer; manner, way; *(bot.)*

style. **por el e.,** in some such way, like that

estilográfico, *a.* stylographic. **pluma estilográfica,** fountain pen

estima, *f.* appreciation, esteem, consideration

estimable, *a.* estimable

estimación, *f.* valuation, estimate; regard, esteem. **e. prudente,** conservative estimate

estimar, *v.t.* to value, estimate; esteem, judge

estimulante, *m.* *(med.)* stimulant. *a.* stimulating

estimular, *v.t.* to stimulate, excite; goad on, encourage, incite

estímulo, *m.* stimulus; incitement, encouragement

estío, *m.* summer

estipendiar, *v.t.* to pay a stipend to

estipendiario, *m.* stipendiary

estipendio, *m.* stipend, pay, remuneration

estípula, *f.* *(bot.)* stipule

estipulación, *f.* stipulation; *(law)* clause, condition

estipular, *v.t.* to stipulate; arrange terms; *(law)* covenant

estirado, *a.* stretched out; tight, stiff; wiredrawn (metals); stiff, pompous; parsimonious

estirador, *m.* wiredrawer

estirar, *v.t.* to stretch; iron roughly (clothes); *(met.)* wiredraw; dole out (money); *(fig.)* stretch, go beyond the permissible; *v.r.* stretch oneself

estirpe. *f.* race, stock, lineage

estival, *a.* summer

esto, *dem. pron. neut.* this, this matter, this idea, etc. Always refers to abstractions, never to a definite object. **e. es,** that's it; namely. **por e.,** for this reason. **a todo e.,** meanwhile

estocada, *f.* sword thrust

estofa, *f.* *(sew.)* quilting; kind, quality

estofado, *m.* stew. *a.* *(sew.)* quilted; stewed

estofar, *v.t.* *(sew.)* to quilt; make a stew

estoicismo, *m.* stoicism

estoico (-ca), *s.* stoic. *a.* stoical

estola, *f.* *(ecc.)* stole

estolidez, *f.* idiocy

estólido (-da), *a.* idiotic. *s.* idiot

estolón, *m.* (*bot.*) stolen

estoma, *m.* (*bot.*) stomata

estomacal, *a.* stomach

estómago, *m.* stomach

estomático, *a.* pertaining to the mouth, oral

estomatitis, *f.* (*med.*) stomatitis

estonio (-ia), *a.* and *s.* Esthonian. *m.* Esthonian language

estopa, *f.* tow; oakum

estopilla, *f.* batiste, lawn; calico, cotton cloth

estopín, *m.* (*mil.*) quick match

estoque, *m.* rapier; sword-stick

estoquear, *v.t.* to wound or kill with a rapier

estoqueo, *m.* sword-play

estorbador (-ra), *a.* obstructive. *s.* obstructor

estorbar, *v.t.* to obstruct, impede; hinder

estorbo, *m.* obstruction; hindrance, nuisance

estornino, *m.* (*orn.*) starling

estornudar, *v.i.* to sneeze

estornudo, *m.* sneezing; sneeze

estrabismo, *m.* (*med.*) strabismus, squint, cast

estrada, *f.* road, highway

estrado, *m.* dais

estrafalario, *a.* (*fam.*) slovenly, untidy; (*fam.*) eccentric, odd

estragar, *v.t.* to corrupt, spoil, vitiate; ruin, destroy

estrago, *m.* devastation, destruction, ruin, havoc

estragón, *m.* (*bot.*) tarragon

estrambote, *m.* refrain

estrambótico, *a.* (*fam.*) eccentric

estrangul, *m.* (*mus.*) mouthpiece

estrangulación, *f.* strangulation; (*aut.*) throttling

estrangulador (-ra), *a.* strangling. *s.* strangler. *m.* (*aut.*) throttle

estrangular, *v.t.* to strangle

estraperlista, *m.* and *f.* black marketeer

estraperlo, *m.* black market

estratagema, *f.* stratagem, trick

estrategia, *f.* strategy

estratégico, *a.* strategic

estratego, *m.* strategist

estratificación, *f.* stratification

estrato, *m.* (*geol.*) stratum

estratosfera, *f.* stratosphere

estraza, *f.* rag. **papel de e.,** brown paper

estrechar, *v.t.* to make narrower, tighten; hold tightly, clasp; compel, oblige; *v.r.* tighten oneself up; reduce one's expenses; (*fig.*) tighten the bonds (of friendship, etc.). **e. la mano,** to shake hands

estrechez, *f.* narrowness; tightness; scantiness; poverty, want. **e. de miras,** narrow-mindedness

estrecho, *a.* narrow; tight; intimate, close; austere, rigid; mean-spirited. *m.* (*geog.*) strait

estregadera, *f.* shoe-scraper; scourer

estregar, *v.t. irr.* to rub, scour, scrub, scrape, scratch. See **cegar**

estrella, *f.* star; fortune, fate; anything star-shaped; (*fig.*) star. **e. de la pantalla,** movie star. **e. de mar,** star-fish. **e. de rabo,** comet. **e. fugaz,** shooting star. **tener e.,** to be born under a lucky star

estrellado, *a.* star-shaped; full of stars, starry; shattered, broken; fried (eggs)

estrellamar, *f.* star-fish

estrellar, *v.t.* (*fam.*) to shatter, break into fragments; fry (eggs); *v.r.* be starry or sprinkled with stars; be dashed against; fail in, come up against

estrellón, *m.* large artificial star (painted or otherwise); firework like a star

estremecer, *v.t. irr.* to cause to tremble; perturb; *v.r.* shudder, tremble. See **conocer**

estremecimiento, *m.* shudder, trembling; agitation

estrenar, *v.t.* to use or do for the first time; inaugurate; give the first performance of (plays, etc.); *v.r.* do for the first time; (*com.*) make first sale of the day

estreno, *m.* commencement, inauguration; first appearance; (*theat.*) dress rehearsal or first night

estrenque, *m.* strong esparto rope

estrenuo, *a.* strong, energetic, agile

estreñimiento, *m.* (*med.*) constipation

estreñir, *v.t.* to constipate

estrépito, *m.* clamour, din, great noise; fuss, show

estrepitoso, a. noisy, clamorous

estreptococo, m. (med.) streptococcus

estreptomicina, f. (med.) streptomycine

estría, f. (arch.) fluting, stria

estribadero, m. prop, support, strut

estribar, v.i. (with en) to lean on, rest on, be supported by; (fig.) be based on

estribillo, m. refrain

estribo, m. stirrup; footboard, step (of vehicles); (arch.) buttress or pier; (fig.) stay, support; (anat.) stapes; (mech., carp.) stirrup-piece. perder los estribos, to lose patience, forget oneself

estribor, m. (naut.) starboard

estricnina, f. strychnine

estricto, a. strict, exact; unbending, severe

estridente, a. strident, shrill

estridor, m. strident harsh sound; screech; creak

estro, m. inspiration

estrofa, f. strophe; verse, stanza

estroma, f. (biol., anat.) stroma

estropajo, m. scourer, dish-cloth; worthless person or thing

estropajoso, a. (fam.) indistinct, stammering; dirty and ragged; tough (meat, etc.)

estropear, v.t. to spoil, damage; ruin, undo, spoil (plans, effects, etc.); ill treat, maim; v.r. hurt oneself, be maimed; spoil, deteriorate

estropicio, m. (fam.) crash (of china, etc.)

estructura, f. fabric, structure; (fig.) construction

estructural, a. structural

estruendo, m. din, clatter; clamour, noise; ostentation

estruendoso, a. noisy

estrujar, v.t. to squeeze, crush (fruit); hold tightly, press, squeeze, bruise; (fig., fam.) squeeze dry

estrujón, m. squeeze, pressure; final pressing (grapes)

estuario, m. estuary

estucado, m. stucco

estucar, v.t. to stucco

estuco, m. stucco; plaster

estuche, m. case; casket, box; cover; sheath

estudiante, m. and f. student

estudiantil, a. (fam.) student

estudiantina, f. strolling band of students playing and singing, generally in aid of charity

estudiantino, a. (fam.) student

estudiantón, m. (fam.) swot

estudiar, v.t. to study; learn; (art) copy

estudio, m. study; sketch; disquisition, dissertation; studio; diligence; (art) study; reading-room, den

estudiosidad, f. studiousness

estudioso, a. studious

estufa, f. heating stove; hot-house; hot room (in baths); drying chamber; (elec.) heater

estufador, m. stew-pan or casserole

estufilla, f. muff; small brazier

estufista, m. stove maker or repairer. m. and f. stove seller

estulto, a. foolish

estupefacción, f. stupefaction

estupefacto, a. stupefied, stunned, amazed

estupendo, a. wonderful, marvellous

estupidez, f. stupidity

estúpido, a. stupid

estupor, m. (med.) stupor; astonishment

estupro, m. (law) rape

estuque, m. stucco

estuquería, f. stucco work

esturión, m. (icht.) sturgeon

etapa, f. (mil.) field ration; (mil.) halt, camp; stage, juncture. a pequeñas etapas, by easy stages (of a journey)

etcétera, etcetera

éter, m. ether; (poet.) sky

etéreo, a. etheric; ethereal

eterizar, v.t. (med.) to etherize

eternidad, f. eternity

eternizar, v.t. to drag out, prolong; eternize, perpetuate

eterno, a. eternal, everlasting; lasting, enduring

ética, f. ethics

ético, a. ethical. m. moralist

etileno, m. (chem.) ethylene

etilo, m. (chem.) ethyl

etimología, f. etymology

etimológico, a. etymological

etimologista, m. and f. etymologist

etimólogo, m. etymologist

etiología, f. ætiology
etiope, a. and m. and f. Ethiopian
etiqueta, f. etiquette; label
etiquetero, a. ceremonious, stiff; prim
étnico, a. ethnic; heathen
etnografía, f. ethnography
etnográfico, a. ethnographic
etnología, f. ethnology
etnólogo, m. ethnologist
etrusco (-ca), a. and s. Etruscan
eubolia, f. discretion in speech
eucalipto, m. (bot.) eucalyptus
Eucaristía, f. Eucharist
eucarístico, a. eucharistic
euclídeo, a. Euclidean
eufemismo, m. euphemism
eufonía, f. euphony
eufónico, a. euphonious
euforia, f. resistance to disease; buoyancy, well-being
eufuismo, m. euphuism
eugenesia, f. Eugenics
eugenésico, a. eugenic
eunuco, m. eunuch
euritmia, f. eurythmics
eurítmico, a. eurythmic
euro, m. (poet.) east wind
europeizar, v.t. to europeanize
europeo (-ea), a. and s. European
éuscaro, a. Basque. m. Basque language
eutanasia, f. euthanasia
evacuación, f. evacuation
evacuar, v.t. to vacate; evacuate, empty; finish, conclude (business deal, etc.)
evadir, v.t. to avoid, elude; v.r. escape; elope
evaluación, f. valuation; estimation
evaluar, v.t. to evaluate, estimate; gauge; value
evangélico, a. evangelical
evangelio, m. Gospel; Christianity; (fam.) indisputable truth
evangelista, m. evangelist
evangelizar, v.t. to evangelize
evaporación, f. evaporation
evaporar(se), v.t. and v.r. to evaporate; disappear, vanish
evasión, evasiva, f. subterfuge; evasion; flight, escape
evasivo, a. evasive
evento, m. happening, event; contingency
eventual, a. possible, fortuitous; accidental (expenses); extra (emoluments)

eventualidad, f. eventuality
evicción, f. (law) eviction
evidencia, f. proof, evidence. ponerse en e., to put oneself forward
evidenciar, v.t. to show, make obvious
evidente, a. obvious, evident
evitable, a. avoidable
evitación, f. avoidance
evitar, v.t. to avoid; shun, eschew
evocación, f. evocation
evocador, a. evocative
evocar, v.t. to evoke
evolución, f. evolution; development; (mil., nav.) manœuvre; change; (geom.) involution
evolucionar, v.i. to evolve; (nav., mil.) manœuvre; change, alter
evolucionismo, m. evolutionism
evolutivo, a. evolutional
ex, prefix out of; from; formerly
exacción, f. exaction; tax
exacerbación, f. exacerbation
exacerbar, v.t. to exasperate; exacerbate
exactitud, f. exactitude; correctness; punctuality
exacto, a. exact; correct; punctual
exactor, m. tax-gatherer; tyrant, oppressor
exageración, f. exaggeration
exagerador (-ra), a. given to exaggerating. s. exaggerator
exagerar, v.t. to exaggerate
exaltación, f. exaltation
exaltar, v.t. to exalt, elevate; extol; v.r. grow excited or agitated
examen, m. inquiry; investigation, research; examination; (geol.) survey
examinador (-ra), s. examiner
examinando (-da), s. candidate, examinee
examinar, v.t. to inquire into; investigate; inspect; examine; v.r. sit an examination
exangüe, a. bloodless, pale; exhausted, weak; dead
exánime, a. lifeless; spiritless, weak
exasperación, f. exasperation
exasperador, exasperante, a. exasperating
exasperar, v.t. to exasperate; irritate, annoy

excarcelar, *v.t.* to release from gaol

excavación, *f.* excavation

excavador (-ra), *s.* excavator. *f.* (*mech.*) excavator

excavar, *v.t.* to hollow; excavate; (*agr.*) hoe (roots of plants)

excedente, *a.* exceeding; excessive; surplus

exceder, *v.t.* to exceed; *v.r.* forget oneself, go too far

excelencia, *f.* excellence, superiority; excellency (title)

excelente, *a.* excellent; (*fam.*) first-rate

excelso, *a.* lofty, high; eminent, mighty; sublime

excentricidad, *f.* eccentricity

excéntrico, *a.* unconventional; erratic; (*geom.*) eccentric

excepción, *f.* exception

excepcional, *a.* exceptional

exceptuar, *v.t.* to except

excerpta, excerta, *f.* excerpt, extract

excesivo, *a.* excessive

exceso, *m.* excess; (*com.*) surplus; *pl.* crimes, excesses. **e. de peso** *or* **e. de equipaje**, excess baggage

excipiente, *m.* (*med.*) excipient

excisión, *f.* excision

excitabilidad, *f.* excitability

excitable, *a.* excitable, highly-strung

excitación, *f.* excitation; excitement

excitador, *a.* exciting, stimulating. *m.* (*phys.*) exciter

excitar, *v.t.* to excite, stimulate, provoke; (*elec.*) energize; *v.r.* become agitated or excited

exclamación, *f.* exclamation, interjection

exclamar, *v.i.* to exclaim

exclamatorio, *a.* exclamatory

exclaustrado (-da), *s.* secularized religious

exclaustrar, *v.t.* to drive out of the cloister, secularize

excluir, *v.t. irr.* to exclude, keep out; reject, bar. See **huir**

exclusiva, *f.* exclusion; special privilege, sole right

exclusive, *adv.* exclusively; excluded

exclusivismo, *m.* exclusivism

exclusivista, *a.* exclusive. *m.* and *f.* exclusivist

exclusivo, *a.* exclusive

excomulgado (-da), *a.* and *s.* (*ecc.*) excommunicate; (*fam.*) wicked (person)

excomulgar, *v.t.* (*ecc.*) to excommunicate

excomunión, *f.* (*ecc.*) excommunication

excoriar, *v.t.* to flay, excoriate; *v.r.* graze oneself

excrecencia, *f.* excrescence

excreción, *f.* excretion

excremento, *m.* excrement

excretar, *v.i.* to excrete

excretorio, *a.* (*anat.*) excretory

exculpación, *f.* exoneration

exculpar(se), *v.t.* and *v.r.* to exonerate

excursión, *f.* excursion, trip; (*mil.*) incursion

excursionismo, *m.* sightseeing; hiking

excursionista, *m.* and *f.* excursionist; hiker

excusa, *f.* excuse

excusabaraja, *f.* basket with a lid

excusable, *a.* excusable

excusado, *a.* excused; exempt; unnecessary, superfluous; reserved, private. *m.* water-closet

excusar, *v.t.* to excuse; avoid, ward off, prevent; exempt; *v.r.* excuse oneself

execración, *f.* execration

execrar, *v.t.* to execrate; denounce; loathe

exención, *f.* exemption

exentar, *v.t.* to exempt

exento, *a.* exempt; free, liberated; open (of buildings, etc.)

exequias, *f. pl.* obsequies

exfoliar, *v.t.* to strip off; *v.r.* flake off

exhalación, *f.* exhalation; shooting star; lightning; emanation, effluvium

exhalar, *v.t.* to exhale, give off; (*fig.*) give vent to

exhausto, *a.* exhausted

exhibición, *f.* exhibition

exhibicionismo, *m.* exhibitionism

exhibicionista, *m.* and *f.* exhibitionist

exhibir, *v.t.* to exhibit, show

exhortación, *f.* exhortation

exhortar, *v.t.* to exhort

exhumación, *f.* exhumation

exhumar, *v.t.* to exhume, disinter

exigencia, *f.* exigency; demand

exigente, *a.* exigent

exigir, *v.t.* to exact, collect; need, require; demand

exigüidad, *f.* exiguousness

exiguo, *a.* exiguous, meagre

eximio, *a.* most excellent; illustrious

eximir, *v.t.* to exempt

existencia, *f.* existence; *pl.* (*com.*) stock-in-hand

existir, *v.i.* to exist, be; live

éxito, *m.* success; result, conclusion

éxodo, *m.* Exodus; exodus, emigration

exoneración, *f.* exoneration

exonerar, *v.t.* to exonerate; discharge (from employment)

exorbitancia, *f.* exorbitance

exorbitante, *a.* exorbitant, excessive

exorcismo, *m.* exorcism

exorcista, *m.* exorcist

exorcizar, *v.t.* to exorcize

exordio, *m.* exordium, introduction

exornar, *v.t.* to adorn; embellish (lit. style)

exotérico, *a.* exoteric

exótico, *a.* exotic, rare

expandir, *v.t.* to expand

expansibilidad, *f.* (*phys.*) expansibility

expansión, *f.* expansion (also *fig.*); recreation, hobby

expansivo, *a.* expansive; communicative, frank

expatriación, *f.* expatriation

expatriarse, *v.r.* to emigrate, quit one's country

expectación, *f.* expectation; expectancy

expectante, *a.* expectant

expectativa, *f.* expectancy; expectation.

expectoración, *f.* expectoration

expectorar, *v.t.* to expectorate

expedición, *f.* expedition; speed, promptness; (*eco.*) bull, dispensation; excursion; forwarding, dispatch

expediente, *m.* (*law*) proceedings; file of documents; expedient, device, means; expedition, promptness; motive, reason; provision

expedir, *v.t. irr.* to expedite; forward, send, ship; issue, make out (cheques, receipts, etc.); draw up (documents); dispatch, deal with. See pedir

expedito, *a.* expeditious, speedy

expeler, *v.t.* to expel, discharge, emit

expendedor (-ra), *a.* spending. *s.* spender; agent; retailer; seller; (*law*) e. de moneda falsa, distributor of counterfeit money

expenduría, *f.* shop where Government monopoly goods are sold, i.e. tobacco, stamps, etc.

expender, *v.t.* to spend (money); (*com.*) retail; (*com.*) sell on commission; (*law*) distribute counterfeit

expensas, *f. pl.* costs, charges

experiencia, *f.* experience; practice, experiment

experimentación, *f.* experiencing

experimentar, *v.t.* to test, try; experience; feel

experimento, *m.* experiment

experto (-ta), *a.* practised, expert. *s.* expert; (*fam.*) dab

expiación, *f.* expiation

expiar, *v.t.* to expiate, atone for; pay the penalty of; (*fig.*) purify

expiatorio, *a.* expiatory

expiración, *f.* expiration

expirar, *v.i.* to die; (*fig.*) expire; die down; exhale, expire

explanación, *f.* levelling; explanation, elucidation

explanada, *f.* esplanade; (*mil.*) glacis

explanar, *v.t.* to level; explain

explayar, *v.t.* to extend, enlarge; *v.r.* spread oneself, enlarge (upon); enjoy an outing; confide (in)

expletivo, *a.* expletive

explicación, *f.* explanation; elucidation

explicar, *v.t.* to explain; expound; interpret, elucidate; *v.r.* explain oneself.

explicativo, *a.* explanatory

explícito, *a.* explicit, clear

exploración, *f.* exploration

explorador, *a.* exploring. *m.* explorer; prospector; boy scout; (*mil.*) scout

explorar, *v.t.* to explore; investigate; (*med.*) probe

exploratorio, *a.* exploratory

explosión, *f.* explosion; outburst, outbreak. hacer falsas explosiones, (*mech.*) to misfire

explosivo, *a.* and *m.* explosive. **e. violento**, high explosive

explotación, *f.* development, exploitation

explotar, *v.t.* to work (mines); (*fig.*) exploit

expoliación, *f.* spoliation

expoliar, *v.t.* to despoil

exponente, *a.* and *m.* and *f.* exponent. *m.* (*math.*) index

exponer, *v.t. irr.* to show, expose; expound, interpret; risk, jeopardize; abandon (child). See **poner**

exportación, *f.* exportation; export

exportador (-ra), *a.* export. *s.* exporter

exportar, *v.t.* to export

exposición, *f.* exposition, demonstration; petition; exhibition; (*lit.*) exposition; (*phot.*) exposure; orientation, position

expósito (-ta), *a.* and *s.* foundling

expositor (-ra), *a.* and *s.* exponent. *s.* exhibitor

expremijo, *m.* cheese vat

exprés, *a.* express. *m.* messenger or carrier service; express train; transport office

expresar, *v.t.* to express (all meanings)

expresión, *f.* statement, utterance; phrase, wording; expression; presentation; manifestation; gift, present; squeezing; pressing (fruits, etc.)

expresivo, *a.* expressive; affectionate

expreso, *a.* express; clear, obvious. *m.* courier

exprime limones, *m.*, **exprimidera**, *f.* lemon-squeezer

exprimidor de la ropa, *m.* wringing machine, mangle

exprimir, *v.t.* to squeeze, press (fruit); press, hold tightly; express, utter

expropiación, *f.* expropriation

expropiar, *v.t.* to expropriate; commandeer

expugnar, *v.t.* (*mil.*) to take by storm

expulsar, *v.t.* to expel, eject, dismiss

expulsión, *f.* expulsion

expurgación, *f.* expurgation

expurgar, *v.t.* to cleanse, purify; expurgate

expurgatorio, *a.* expurgatory. *m.* (*ecc.*) index

exquisitez, *f.* exquisiteness

exquisito, *a.* exquisite, choice; delicate, delicious

extasiarse, *v.r.* to fall into ecstasy; marvel (at), delight (in)

éxtasis, *m.* ecstasy; rapture

extático, *a.* ecstatic

extemporáneo, *a.* untimely; inopportune, inconvenient

extender, *v.t. irr.* to spread; reach, extend; elongate; enlarge, amplify; unfold, open out, stretch; draw up (documents); make out (cheques, etc.); *v.r.* stretch out; lie down; spread, be generalized; extend; last (of time); record; (*fig.*, *fam.*) put on side; stretch, open out. **extenderse en**, to expatiate on. See **entender**

extensión, *f.* extension; expanse; length; extent; duration; extension (logic)

extensivo, *a.* extensive, spacious; extensible

extenso, *a.* extensive, vast

extensor, *a.* extensor. *m.* chest expander

extenuación, *f.* emaciation, weakness; extenuation

extenuar, *v.t.* to exhaust, weaken; *v.r.* become weak

exterior, *a.* external; foreign (trade, etc.). *m.* outside, exterior; outward appearance

exterioridad, *f.* outward appearance; outside, externality; *pl.* ceremonies, forms; ostentation

exteriorizar, *v.t.* to exteriorize, reveal

exterminador (-ra), *a.* exterminating. *s.* exterminator

exterminar, *v.t.* to exterminate; devastate

exterminio, *m.* extermination; devastation

externado, *m.* day school

externo (-na), *a.* external. *s.* day scholar

extinción, *f.* extinction; extinguishment; abolition, cancellation

extinguir, *v.t.* to extinguish; destroy

extintor, *m.* fire-extinguisher

extirpación, *f.* extirpation

extirpador (-ra), *a.* extirpating. *s.* extirpator

extirpar, *v.t.* to extirpate; (*fig.*) eradicate

extorsión, *f.* extortion

extorsionar, *v.t.* to extort

extra, *prefix* outside, without, beyond. *prep.* besides. *a.* extremely, most. *m.* (*fam.*) extra

extracción, *f.* extraction; drawing (numbers in lottery); origin, lineage; exportation

extractar, *v.t.* to abstract, summarize

extracto, *m.* abstract, summary; (*chem.*) extract

extractor, *a.* extracting. *m.* extractor (also *mech.*)

extradición, *f.* extradition

extraer, *v.t. irr.* to extract; draw out; export; (*chem.*) extract. See traer

extranjero (-ra), *a.* alien, foreign. *s.* foreigner. *m.* abroad, foreign land

extrañar, *v.t.* to exile; alienate, estrange; wonder at; miss, feel loss of; *v.r.* be exiled; be estranged; be amazed (by); refuse (to do a thing)

extrañeza, *f.* strangeness; estrangement; surprise

extraño, *a.* strange, unusual; foreign, extraneous

extraoficial, *a.* unofficial

extraordinario, *a.* extraordinary; special. *m.* (*cul.*) extra course

extraterritorialidad, *f.* exterritoriality

extravagancia, *f.* eccentricity; queerness; folly

extravagante, *a.* eccentric; queer, strange; absurd

extravasarse, *v.r.* (*med.*) to extravasate

extravertido, *m.* (*psy.*) extrovert

extraviar, *v.t.* to mislead; mislay; *v.r.* lose one's way; be lost (of things); (*fig.*) go astray

extravío, *m.* deviation, divergence; error; aberration, lapse

extremado, *a.* extreme

extremar, *v.t.* to take to extremes; *v.r.* do one's best

extremaunción, *f.* (*ecc.*) extreme unction

extremeño (-ña), *a.* and *s.* native or belonging to Extremadura (Sp. province)

extremidad, *f.* end; extremity; remotest part; edge; limit; *pl.* extremities

extremista, *a.* and *m.* and *f.* extremist

extremo, *a.* last, ultimate; extreme; farthest; great, exceptional; utmost. *m.* end, extreme; highest degree; extreme care; *pl.* excessive emotional display

extremoso, *a.* immoderate, exaggerated; very affectionate

extrínseco, *a.* extrinsic

exuberancia, *f.* abundance; exuberance

exuberante, *a.* abundant, copious; exuberant

exudar, *v.i.* and *v.t.* to exude

exultación, *f.* exultation; rejoicing

exultante, *a.* exultant

exultar, *v.i.* to exult

exvoto, *m.* (*ecc.*) votive offering

eyaculación, *f.* (*med.*) ejaculation

eyacular, *v.t.* (*med.*) to ejaculate

F

fa, *m.* (*mus.*) fa, F

fabada, *f.* dish of broad beans, pork and sausage and bacon

fábrica, *f.* manufacture; making; factory, works; fabric, structure, building; creation; invention. **f. de papel,** paper-mill. **marca de f.,** trade-mark

fabricación, *f.* make; making; construction. **f. en serie,** mass production

fabricador (-ra), *a.* creative, inventive. *s.* fabricator; maker

fabricante, *a.* manufacturing. *m.* manufacturer; maker

fabricar, *v.t.* to manufacture; make; construct, build; devise; invent, create

fabril, *a.* manufacturing

fabriquero, *m.* manufacturer; churchwarden; charcoal burner

fábula, *f.* rumour; gossip; fiction; fable; story, plot; mythology; myth; laughing-stock; falsehood.

fabulista, *m.* and *f.* fabulist; mythologist

fabulosidad, *f.* fabulousness

fabuloso, *a.* fabulous; fictitious; incredible, amazing

faca, *f.* jack-knife

facción, *f.* rebellion; faction, party, band; feature (of the face) (gen. *pl.*); military exploit; any military routine duty

faccionario, *a.* factional

faccioso (-sa), *a.* factional; factious, seditious. *s.* rebel

faceta, *f.* facet (gems); aspect, view

facial, *a.* facial; intuitive

fácil, *a.* easy; probable; easily-led; docile; of easy virtue (women). *adv.* easy

facilidad, *f.* easiness; facility, aptitude; ready compliance; opportunity

facilitación, *f.* facilitation

facilitar, *v.t.* to facilitate, expedite; provide, deliver

facineroso, *a.* criminal, delinquent. *m.* criminal; villain

facistol, *m.* (*ecc.*) lectern; chorister's stand

facsímile, *m.* facsimile

factibilidad, *f.* feasibility, practicability

factible, *a.* feasible, practicable

facticio, *a.* factitious, artificial

factor, *m.* (*com.*) factor, agent; baggage master (railway); (*math.*) factor; element; consideration

factoría, *f.* agency; factorage; merchants' trading station, especially in foreign country; manufactory

factótum, *m.* (*fam.*) factotum, handyman; (*fam.*) busybody; confidential agent or deputy

factura, *f.* (*com.*) invoice, bill, account; (*art*) execution; workmanship; making

facturar, *v.t.* (*com.*) to invoice; register (luggage on railway)

facultad, *f.* faculty; mental or physical aptitude, capability; authority, right; science, art; (*univ.*) faculty; licence

facultar, *v.t.* to authorize, permit

facultativo, *a.* belonging to a faculty; optional, permissive. *m.* physician

facundia, *f.* eloquence

facundo, *a.* eloquent

facha, *f.* (*fam.*) countenance, look, face; guy, scarecrow. (*naut.*) **ponerse en f.,** to lie to

fachada, *f.* façade, front (building, ship, etc.); (*fam.*) build,

presence (of person); frontispiece of book

fachenda, *f.* (*fam.*) boastfulness, vanity

faena, *f.* manual labour; mental work; business affairs (gen. *pl.*)

faetón, *m.* phæton

fagocito, *m.* (*med.*) phagocyte

fagot, *m.* bassoon

fagotista, *m.* bassoon player

faisán (-ana), (*orn.*) cock (hen) pheasant

faisanera, *f.* pheasantry

faja, *f.* belt, girdle; sash, scarf; corset; (*geog.*) zone; newspaper wrapper; (*arch.*) fascia; swathing band

fajar, *v.t.* to swathe; swaddle (child)

fajero, *m.* swaddling band

fajín, *m.* ceremonial ribbon or sash worn by generals, etc.

fajina, *f.* stook, stack; brushwood; (*fort.*) fascine

fajo, *m.* bundle, sheaf; *pl.* swaddling-clothes

falacia, *f.* fraud, deceit; deceitfulness; fallacy

falange, *f.* (*mil.*) phalanx; (*anat.*) phalange; (*Spanish pol.*) Falange

falangista, *a.* and *m.* and *f.* (*Spanish pol.*) Falangist

falaz, *a.* deceitful; fallacious

falda, *f.* skirt; lap, flap, panel (of dress); slope (of hill); the lap; loin (beef, etc.); brim of hat; *pl.* (*fam.*) petticoats, women. **f. escocesa,** kilt

faldellín, *m.* skirt; underskirt

faldero, *a.* (of a dog) lap; fond of the company of women

faldillas, *f. pl.* coat-tails

faldistorio, *m.* faldstool

faldón, *m.* long flowing skirt; shirt-tail; coat-tail

falibilidad, *f.* fallibility

falible, *a.* fallible

fálico, *a.* (*anat.*) phallic

falo, *m.* (*anat.*) phallus

falsario, *a.* falsifying, forging, counterfeiting; deceiving, lying. *m.* falsifier, forger, counterfeiter

falseamiento, *m.* falsifying; forging

falsear, *v.t.* to falsify; forge; counterfeit; penetrate; *v.i.* weaken; (*mus.*) be out of tune (strings)

falsedad, *f.* falseness; falsehood

falsete, *m.* spigot; (*mus.*) falsetto voice

falsificación, *f.* falsification; forgery

falsificador, *a.* falsifying; forging. *m.* falsifier; forger

falsificar, *v.t.* to forge, counterfeit; falsify

falso, *a.* false; forged, counterfeit; treacherous, untrue, deceitful; incorrect; sham; vicious (horses). **de f.,** falsely; deceitfully

falta, *f.* lack, shortage; defect; mistake; (*sport*) fault; shortcoming; non-appearance, absence; deficiency in legal weight of coin; (*law*) offence. **f. de éxito,** failure. **hacer f.,** to be necessary. **sin f.,** without fail

faltar, *v.i.* to be lacking; fail, die; fall short; be absent from appointment; not to fulfil one's obligations. **f. a,** to be unfaithful to, break (e.g. **Faltó a su palabra,** He broke his promise). (*fam.*) ¡**No faltaba más!** I should think not!; That's the limit!

falto, *a.* lacking, wanting; defective; wretched, mean, timid. **f. de personal,** short-handed

faltriquera, *f.* pocket; hip-pocket

falúa, *f.* (*naut.*) tender; longboat

falucho, *m.* (*naut.*) felucca

falla, *f.* deficiency, defect; failure; (*geol.*) displacement; bonfire (Valencia); (*min.*) slide

fallar, *v.t.* (*law*) to pass sentence; *v.i.* be deficient

falleba, *f.* shutter-bolt

fallecer, *v.i. irr.* to die; fail. See **conocer**

fallecimiento, *m.* death, decease

fallido, *a.* frustrated; bankrupt

fallo, *m.* (*law*) verdict; judgment

fama, *f.* rumour, report; reputation; fame

famélico, *a.* ravenous

familia, *f.* family; household; kindred

familiar, *a.* family; familiar; well-known; unceremonious; plain, simple; colloquial (language). *m.* (*ecc.*) familiar; servant; intimate friend; familiar spirit

familiaridad, *f.* familiarity

familiarizar, *v.t.* to familiarize;

v.r. become familiar; accustom oneself

familiarmente, *adv.* familiarly

famoso, *a.* famous; notorious; (*fam.*) excellent, perfect; (*fam.*) conspicuous

fámula, *f.* (*fam.*) maidservant

fámulo, *m.* servant of a college; (*fam.*) servant

fanal, *m.* lantern of lighthouse; (*naut.*) poop lantern; lantern; lamp glass

fanático (**-ca**), *a.* fanatical. *s.* fanatic; (*fam.*) fan, enthusiast

fanatismo, *m.* fanaticism

fanatizar, *v.t.* to make fanatical; turn into a fanatic

fandango, *m.* lively Andalusian dance

fanega, *f.* grain measure about the weight of an English bushel; land measure (about 1½ acres)

fanerógama, *f.* (*bot.*) phanerogamous

fanfarrón (**-ona**), *a.* (*fam.*) boastful; swaggering. *s.* swashbuckler; boaster

fanfarronear, *v.i.* to swagger; brag

fanfarronería, *f.* bragging

fango, *m.* mud, mire; degradation

fangoso, *a.* muddy, miry

fantasear, *v.i.* to let one's fancy roam; boast

fantasía, *f.* fancy, imagination; fantasy; caprice; fiction; (*fam.*) presumption; (*mus.*) fantasia

fantasma, *m.* ghost, phantom; vision; image, impression; presumptuous person. *f.* (*fam.*) scarecrow; apparition

fantasmagoría, *f.* phantasmagoria

fantasmagórico, *a.* phantasmagoric

fantástico, *a.* fanciful, imaginary; fantastic, imaginative; presumptuous, conceited

fantoche, *m.* puppet; (*fam.*) yes-man, mediocrity

faquín, *m.* porter, carrier

faquir, *m.* fakir

faradio, *m.* (*elec.*) farad

faralá, *m.* flounce, frill

farándula, *f.* profession of low comedian; troupe of strolling players; cunning trick

farandulero, *m.* actor, strolling player. *a.* (*fam.*) plausible

faraón, *m.* Pharaoh; faro (card game)

fardel, *m.* bag, knapsack; bundle

fardo, *m.* bundle, bale, package

fárfara, *f.* (*bot.*) colt's-foot

farfulla, *f.* (*fam.*) mumbling; gibbering. *m.* and *f.* (*fam.*) mumbler

farfullar, *v.t.* (*fam.*) to mumble; gibber; (*fam.*) act in haste

farináceo, *a.* farinaceous

faringe, *f.* (*anat.*) pharynx

faríngeo, *a.* pharyngeal

faringitis, *f.* (*med.*) pharyngitis

farisaico, *a.* pharisaical

fariseísmo, *m.* cant, hypocrisy

fariseo, *m.* Pharisee; hypocrite

farmacéutico, *a.* pharmaceutical. *m.* pharmacist

farmacia, *f.* pharmacy; chemist's shop

farmacología, *f.* pharmacology

farmacológico, *a.* pharmacological

farmacólogo, *m.* pharmacologist

farmacopea, *f.* pharmacopœia

faro, *m.* lighthouse; beacon, guide; (*aut.*) headlight

farol, *m.* lantern, lamp; street lamp; cresset

farola, *f.* lamp post (generally with several branches); lantern

farolero, *m.* lantern maker; lamp lighter; lamp tender. *a.* (*fam.*) swaggering, braggart

fárrago, *m.* hotchpotch

farsa, *f.* old name for a play; farce; theatrical company; poor, badly constructed play; sham, trick, deception

farsante, *m.* comedian; (*ant.*) actor; (*fig., fam.*) humbug

fas (por) o por nefas, *adv.* by fair means or foul; at any cost

fascinación, *f.* evil eye; enchantment, fascination

fascinador (-ra), *a.* bewitching; fascinating. *s.* charmer

fascinante, *a.* fascinating

fascinar, *v.t.* to bewitch, place under a spell; deceive, impose upon; attract, fascinate

fascismo, *m.* Fascism

fascista, *a.* and *m.* and *f.* Fascist

fase, *f.* phase (also *ast.*); aspect

fastidiar, *v.t.* to disgust, bore; annoy; *v.r.* be bored

fastidio, *m.* sickness, squeamishness; annoyance, boredom, dislike, repugnance

fastidioso, *a.* disgusting, sickening; annoying; boring, tiresome

fastuoso, *a.* ostentatious; pompous

fatal, *a.* fatal, mortal; predetermined, inevitable; ill-fated, unhappy, disastrous; evil

fatalidad, *f.* fatality; inevitability; disaster, ill-fatedness

fatalismo, *m.* fatalism

fatalista, *a.* fatalistic. *m.* and *f.* fatalist

fatalmente, *adv.* inevitably, unavoidably; unhappily, unfortunately; extremely badly

fatídico, *a.* prophetic (gen. of evil)

fatiga, *f.* fatigue; toil; difficult breathing; hardship, troubles (gen. *pl.*)

fatigar, *v.t.* to tire; annoy; *v.r.* be tired

fatigoso, *a.* tired; tiring; tiresome, annoying

fatuidad, *f.* fatuousness, inanity, foolishness; conceit; priggishness

fatuo, *a.* fatuous, foolish; conceited; priggish. *m.* self-satisfied fool. fuego f., will o' the wisp

fauces, *f. pl.* (*anat.*) gullet

fauna, *f.* fauna

fauno, *m.* faun

fausto, *m.* pomp, magnificence, ostentation. *a.* fortunate, happy

fautor, *m.* protector, helper; accomplice

favonio, *m.* (*poet.*) zephyr, westerly wind

favor, *m.* aid, protection, support; favour, honour, service; love favour, sign of favour. a f. de, in favour of; on behalf of

favorable, *a.* kind, helpful; favourable

favorecedor (-ra), *a.* favouring, helping. *s.* helper; protector

favorecer, *v.t. irr.* to aid, protect, support; favour; do a service, grant a favour. See conocer

favoritismo, *m.* favouritism

favorito (-ta), *a.* and *s.* favourite

fayenza, *f.* faience

faz, *f.* face; external surface of a thing, side; frontage. f. de las aguas, face of the waters

fe, *f.* faith; confidence, trust, good opinion; belief; solemn promise; assertion; certificate, attestation; faithfulness. **f. de erratas,** (*print.*) errata. **dar f.,** (*law*) to testify. **de buena f.,** in good faith. **en f.,** in proof

fealdad, *f.* ugliness; base action

febo, *m.* Phœbus; (*poet.*) sun

febrero, *m.* February

febril, *a.* feverish; ardent, violent; passionate

fecal, *a.* fæcal

fécula, *f.* fecula; starch

feculento, *a.* starchy; dreggy

fecundación, *f.* fecundation

fecundar, *v.t.* to fertilize; fecundate

fecundidad, *f.* fecundity; fertility, fruitfulness

fecundizar, *v.t.* to fertilize; make fruitful

fecundo, *a.* fertile, fecund, prolific; abundant

fecha, *f.* date. **a la f.,** at present, now. **hasta la f.,** up to the present (day)

fechar, *v.t.* to date, write the date

federación, *f.* federation, league

federal, *a.* federal. *m.* and *f.* federalist

federalismo, *m.* federalism

federalista, *a.* federal, federalist. *m.* and *f.* federalist

federativo, *a.* federative

fehaciente, *a.* (*law*) authentic, attested

feldespato, *m.* (*min.*) feldspar

felicidad, *f.* happiness; contentment, satisfaction; good fortune

felicitación, *f.* congratulation

felicitar, *v.t.* to congratulate; wish well; *v.r.* congratulate oneself

feligrés (-esa), *s.* parishioner

feligresía, *f.* parish

felino, *a.* and *m.* feline

feliz, *a.* happy; fortunate; skilful, felicitous (of phrases, etc.)

felón (-ona), *s.* felon

felonía, *f.* felony

felpa, *f.* plush; (*fam.*) drubbing, beating

felpilla, *f.* chenille

felpudo, *a.* plushy

femenino, *a.* feminine; female; (*fig.*) weak

fementido, *a.* sly, false, treacherous, unfaithful

feminismo, *m.* feminism

feminista, *a.* feministic. *m.* and *f.* feminist

fémur, *m.* (*anat.*) femur

fenecer, *v.t. irr.* to conclude, finish; *v.i.* die; be ended. See **conocer**

fenecimiento, *m.* end; death

fenicio (-ia), *a.* and *s.* Phœnician

fénico, *a.* phenic, carbolic

fénix, *f.* phœnix

fenol, *m.* (*chem.*) phenol

fenomenal, *a.* phenomenal; (*fam.*) terrific

fenómeno, *m.* phenomenon; (*fam.*) something of great size

feo, *a.* ugly; alarming, horrid; evil. *m.* (*fam.*) slight, insult

feraz, *a.* fruitful, fertile

féretro, *m.* coffin; bier

feria, *f.* fair, market; working day; holiday; rest

feriar, *v.t.* to buy at a fair; bargain; give fairings; *v.i.* cease work, take a holiday

fermentación, *f.* fermentation

fermentar, *v.i.* to ferment; be agitated; *v.t.* cause to ferment

fermento, *m.* ferment; leaven; (*chem.*) enzyme

ferocidad, *f.* ferocity, cruelty

feroz, *a.* ferocious, cruel

férreo, *a.* ferrous; hard, tenacious. **línea férrea,** railway

ferrería, *f.* ironworks

ferrete, *m.* marking iron

ferretería, *f.* ironworks; ironmonger's shop; iron ware, hardware

férrico, *a.* ferric

ferrocarril, *m.* railway; railway train. **f. de cremallera,** rack railway. **f. funicular,** funicular railway

ferroso, *a.* (*chem.*) ferrous

ferroviario, *a.* railway. *m.* railway employee

ferruginoso, *a.* ferruginous

fértil, *a.* fertile; fruitful, productive

fertilidad, *f.* fertility

fertilización, *f.* fertilization

fertilizar, *v.t.* to fertilize, make fruitful

férula, *f.* ferule; (*surg.*) splint; (*fig.*) yoke, rule

fervor, *m.* intense heat; fervour, devotion; zeal

fervoroso, *a.* fervent, zealous, devoted

festejar, *v.t.* to feast, entertain; woo; celebrate; *v.r.* amuse oneself

festejo, *m.* feast, entertainment; courtship, wooing; *pl.* public celebrations

festín, *m.* private dinner or party; sumptuous banquet

festival, *m.* musical festival; festival

festividad, *f.* festivity; *(ecc.)* celebration, solemnity; witticism

festivo, *a.* joking, witty; happy, gay; solemn, worthy of celebration. **día f.,** holiday

festón, *m.* garland, wreath; festoon; border; scalloped edging

festonear, *v.t.* to garland, festoon; border

fetal, *a.* fœtal

fetiche, *m.* fetish

fetichismo, *m.* fetishism

fetidez, *f.* fetidness, stink

fétido, *a.* stinking, fetid

feto, *m.* fœtus

feudal, *a.* feudal; despotic

feudalismo, *m.* feudalism

feudatario (-ia), *a.* and *s.* feudatory

feudo, *m.* fief; fee. **f. franco,** freehold

fez, *m.* fez

fiado, al, *adv.* on credit. **en f.,** on bail

fiador (-ra), *s.* guarantor; bail. *m.* fastener, loop (of coat, clock, etc.); safety-catch, bolt. **salir f.,** to be surety (for); go bail

fiambre, *m.* cold meat, cold dish; *(fam.)* stale, out-of-date news, etc.; *(fam.)* corpse

fiambrera, *f.* luncheon pail

fianza, *f.* guarantee, bail; surety; security. *(law)* **dar f.,** to guarantee; go bail

fiar, *v.t.* to go surety for, go bail; sell on credit; trust; confide; *v.r.* *(with de)* confide in; trust

fibra, *f.* fibre; filament; energy, strength; *(min.)* vein; grain (of wood)

fibroso, *a.* fibrous; fibroid

ficción, *f.* falsehood; invention; fiction, imaginative creation; pretence

ficticio, *a.* fictitious

ficha, *f.* chip, counter; domino; index card, filing card. **f. antropométrica,** personal particulars card

fichar, *v.t.* to record personal particulars on filing card; file, index

fichero, *m.* filing cabinet; card-index

fichú, *m.* fichu

fidedigno, *a.* trustworthy, bona-fide

fideicomisario, *m.* *(law)* fiduciary, trustee

fideicomiso, *m.* *(law)* trust

fidelidad, *f.* fidelity, honesty; loyalty; punctiliousness

fideos, *m. pl.* vermicelli. *m.* *(fam.)* scraggy person

fiduciario, *a.* *(law)* fiduciary. *m.* *(law)* trustee

fiebre, *f.* fever; great agitation, excitement. **f. palúdica,** malarial fever. **f. puerperal,** puerperal fever. **f. tifoidea,** typhoid fever

fiel, *a.* faithful, loyal; true, exact. *m.* axis; pointer (of a scale or balance)

fielato, *m.* octroi, local customs duties office

fieltro, *m.* felt

fiera, *f.* wild beast; cruel person

fiereza, *f.* savageness, wildness; cruelty, fierceness; deformity

fiero, *a.* wild, savage; ugly; huge, enormous; horrible, alarming; haughty

fiesta, *f.* merriment, gaiety; entertainment, feast; *(fam.)* joke; festivity, celebration; public holiday; caress, cajolery (gen. *pl.*); *pl.* holidays. **f. fija** *(ecc.)* immovable feast. *(fam.)* **estar de f.,** to be making merry. **hacer f.,** to take a holiday. *(fam.)* **Se acabó la f.,** It's all over and done with

figón, *m.* eating-house

figulino, *a.* fictile, made of terra cotta

figura, *f.* shape, form; face; *(art)* image, figure; *(law)* form; court-card; *(mus.)* note; *(theat.)* character, rôle; *(geom., gram., dancing)* figure. **f. de nieve,** snow-man. *(naut.)* **f. de proa,** figure-head. *(fig.)* **f. decorativa,** figure-head. *(fig.)* **hacer f.,** to cut a figure

figurado, *a.* figurative; rhetorical

figurar, *v.t.* to shape, mould; simulate, pretend; represent; *v.i.* be numbered among; cut a figure; *v.r.* imagine

figurativo, *a.* figurative; symbolical

FIG 213 FIN

figurilla, *m.* and *f.* (*fam.*) ridiculous, dwarfish figure. *f.* (*art*) statuette

figurín, *m.* fashion plate or model; fashion book

fijación, *f.* fixing; nailing; sticking, posting; attention, fixity; (*chem.*) fixation; firmness, stability

fijador, *m.* (*med.*, *phot.*) fixative; setting lotion; (*art*) varnish. *a.* fixing

fijamente, *adv.* firmly; attentively

fijar, *v.t.* to fix; glue, stick; nail; make firm; settle, appoint (date); fix, concentrate (attention, gaze); (*phot.*, *med.*) fix; *v.r.* decide; notice (e.g. **No me había fijado,** I hadn't noticed). **f. anuncios,** to post bills

fijeza, *f.* fixedness; firmness, stability; constancy, steadfastness

fijo, *a.* firm; fixed; stable; steadfast; permanent; exact. **de f.,** certainly, without doubt

fila, *f.* line, row; (*mil.*) rank; antipathy, hatred. **en f.,** in a line

filacteria, *f.* phylactery

filamento, *m.* filament

filantropía, *f.* philanthropy

filantrópico, *a.* philanthropic

filántropo, *m.* philanthropist

filarmónico, *a.* philharmonic

filástica, *f.* (*naut.*) rope-yarn

filatelia, *f.* philately

filatélico, *a.* philatelic

filatelista, *m.* and *f.* philatelist

filete, *m.* (*arch.*) fillet; (*cul.*) small spit; fillet (of meat or fish); thread of screw; (*sew.*) hem

filiación, *f.* filiation; affiliation, relationship; (*mil.*) regimental register

filial, *a.* filial; affiliated

filibustero, *m.* filibuster

filiforme, *a.* filamentous

filigrana, *f.* filigree; watermark (of paper); (*fig.*) delicate creation

filípica, *f.* philippic

filipino (-na), *a.* and *s.* Philippine

filisteo (-ea), *a.* and *s.* Philistine

film, *m.* (cinematograph) film

filmar, *v.t.* to film

filo, *m.* cutting edge; dividing line

filología, *f.* philology

filológico, *a.* philological

filólogo, *m.* philologist

filomela, *f.* (*poet.*) nightingale

filón, *m.* (*min.*) vein, lode; (*fig.*) goldmine

filosofar, *v.i.* to philosophize

filosofía, *f.* philosophy. **f. moral,** moral philosophy. **f. natural,** natural philosophy

filosófico, *a.* philosophic

filósofo, *m.* philosopher. *a.* philosophic

filoxera, *f.* phylloxera

filtración, *f.* filtration

filtrar, *v.t.* to filter; *v.i.* filter through, percolate; *v.r.* (*fig.*) disappear (of money, etc.)

filtro, *m.* filter, strainer; love potion, philtre

fin, *m.* finish, end, conclusion; purpose, goal, aim; limit, extent. **a f. de,** in order to, so that. **a fines de,** towards the end of (with months, years, etc.) (e.g. **a fines de octubre,** towards the end of October). **en f.,** at last; **in fine;** well then! **por f.,** finally. **un sin f. de cosas,** innumerable things

finado (-da), *s.* deceased, dead person

final, *a.* final. *m.* end, finish; (*sport*) final (gen. *pl.*)

finalidad, *f.* finality; purpose

finalista, *m.* and *f.* (*sport*) finalist

finalizar, *v.t.* to conclude, finish; *v.i.* be finished; close (Stock Exchange)

finalmente, *adv.* finally

financiar, *v.t.* to finance

financiero, *a.* financial. *m.* financier

finanzas, *f. pl.* finance

finar, *v.i.* to die; *v.r.* desire, long for a thing

finca, *f.* land, real estate; house property, country-house, ranch

fineza, *f.* fineness; excellence, goodness; kindness, expression of affection; good turn, friendly act; gift; beauty, delicacy

fingido, *a.* pretended; assumed; feigned; sham

fingimiento, *m.* pretence; affectation, assumption

fingir, *v.t.* to pretend, feign; imagine

finiquitar, *v.t.* to close and pay up an account; (*fam.*) end

finiquito, *m.* closing of an ac-

flaco, *a.* thin; weak, feeble; (*fig.*) weak-minded; dispirited. *m.* failing, weakness. (*fam.*) hacer un **f.** servicio, to do an ill turn

flagelación, *f.* flagellation

flagelante, *m.* flagellant

flagelar, *v.t.* to scourge; (*fig.*) lash

flagelo, *m.* whip, scourge

flagrante, *a.* (*poet.*) refulgent; present; actual. en **f.**, in the very act, flagrante delicto

flagrar, *v.i.* (*poet.*) to blaze, be refulgent

flamante, *a.* resplendent; brand new; fresh, spick and span

flamenco (-ca), *m.* (*orn.*) flamingo. *a.* and *s.* Flemish. *a.* Andalusian; gipsy; buxom, fresh

flan, *m.* baked custard

flanco, *m.* side; (*mil.*) flank

flanquear, *v.t.* (*mil.*) to flank

flanqueo, *m.* (*mil.*) outflanking

flaquear, *v.i.* to grow weak; weaken; totter (buildings, etc.); be disheartened, flag

flaqueza, *f.* weakness; thinness; faintness, feebleness; frailty, fault; loss of zeal

flato, *m.* flatulence

flatulento, *a.* flatulent

flauta, *f.* flute

flautín, *m.* piccolo

flautista, *m.* and *f.* flautist

flebitis, *f.* (*med.*) phlebitis

flebotomía, *f.* phlebotomy

fleco, *m.* fringe; fringe (of hair)

flecha, *f.* arrow, dart

flechar, *v.t.* to shoot an arrow or dart; wound or kill with arrows; (*fam.*) inspire love; *v.i.* bend a bow to shoot

flechazo, *m.* wound with an arrow; (*fam.*) love at first sight

flechero, *m.* archer; arrow maker

fleje, *m.* iron hoop (for barrels, etc.)

flema, *f.* phlegm; sluggishness

flemático, *a.* phlegmatic; sluggish

flemón, *m.* gumboil; abscess

flequillo, *m.* fringe (of hair)

fletamento, *m.* chartering (a ship)

fletar, *v.t.* to charter a ship; embark merchandise or people

flete, *m.* freightage; cargo, freight

flexibilidad, *f.* flexibility; suppleness, adaptability

flexible, *a.* pliant, supple; flex-

---

count; final receipt, quittance; quietus

finito, *a.* finite

finlandés (-esa), *a.* Finnish. *s.* Finn. *m.* Finnish language

fino, *a.* fine; excellent, good; slim, slender, thin; delicate, subtle; dainty (of people); cultured, polished; constant, loving; sagacious, shrewd; (*min.*) refined

finta, *f.* feint (fencing); menace, threat

finura, *f.* fineness; excellence; delicacy; courtesy

fiordo, *m.* fjord

firma, *f.* signature; act of signing; (*com.*) firm name, firm

firmamento, *m.* firmament

firmante, *a.* signing. *m.* and *f.* signatory

firmar, *v.t.* to sign

firme, *a.* firm; hard; steady, solid; constant, resolute, loyal. *m.* foundation base. (*mil.*) ¡Firmes! Attention! batir de f., to strike hard

firmeza, *f.* stability, firmness; constancy, resoluteness, loyalty

fiscal, *a.* fiscal. *m.* attorney-general; public prosecutor; meddler. f. de quiebras, Official Receiver

fiscalizar, *v.t.* to prosecute; pry into; meddle with; censure, criticize

fisco, *m.* national exchequer, revenue

fisgar, *v.t.* to harpoon; pry; *v.i.* mock, make fun of

fisgón (-ona), *a.* prying; mocking. *s.* pryer; mocker; eavesdropper

fisgoneo, *m.* prying; eavesdropping

física, *f.* physics

físico, *a.* physical. *m.* physicist; physician; physique

fisiología, *f.* physiology

fisiológico, *a.* physiological

fisiólogo, *m.* physiologist

fisioterapia, *f.* physiotherapy

fisonomía, *f.* physiognomy

fisonomista, *m.* and *f.* physiognomist

fístula, *f.* pipe, conduit; (*mus.*) pipe; (*surg.*) fistula

fisura, *f.* (*anat.*, *geol.*) fissure

flaccidez, *f.* flabbiness

fláccido, *a.* flaccid, soft, flabby

ible, adaptable. *m.* (*elec.*) flex

flexión, *f.* flexion; bend, bending; deflection

flirtear, *v.i.* to flirt

flirteo, *m.* flirtation

flogístico, *a.* (*chem.*) phlogistic

flogisto, *m.* phlogiston

flojedad, *f.* flabbiness; weakness, feebleness; laziness, negligence

flojo, *a.* flabby; slack, loose; weak, feeble; lazy, slothful; poor (of a literary work, etc.)

floqueado, *a.* fringed

flor, *f.* flower; best of anything; bloom on fruit; virginity; grain (of leather); compliment (gen. *pl.*); menstruation (gen. *pl.*). **f. de especia,** mace. **f. de la edad,** prime, youth. **f. del cuclillo,** may-flower. **f. del estudiante,** French marigold. **flores de mano,** artificial flowers. **flores de oblón,** hops. **a f. de,** on the surface of, level with. **andarse en flores,** (*fig.*) to beat about the bush. **echar flores,** to pay compliments. **en f.,** in bloom

flora, *f.* flora

floración, *f.* flowering

floral, *a.* floral. **juegos florales,** poetical contest

florear, *v.t.* to adorn with flowers; *v.i.* execute a flourish on the guitar

florecer, *v.i. irr.* to flower, bloom; flourish, prosper; *v.r.* grow mould (cheese, etc.). See **conocer**

floreciente, *a.* flowering; prosperous

florecimiento, *m.* flowering; prosperity

florentino (-na), *a.* and *s.* Florentine

floreo, *m.* witty conversation; flourish on the guitar or in fencing

florero, *m.* flower vase; plant pot; (*art*) flower-piece

florescencia, *f.* (*bot.*) flowering; flowering season, florescence

floresta, *f.* grove, wooded park, woodland; (*fig.*) collector of beautiful things; anthology

florete, *m.* fencing foil

floricultor (-ra), *s.* floriculturist

floricultura, *f.* floriculture

floridamente, *adv.* elegantly, with a flourish

florido, *a.* flowery; best, most select; florid, ornate

florilegio, *m.* anthology, collection

florín, *m.* florin

florista, *m.* and *f.* artificial flower maker; florist; flower seller

florón, *m.* large flower; (*arch.*) fleuron; honourable deed

flósculo, *m.* (*bot.*) floret, floscule

flota, *f.* fleet of merchant ships. **f. aérea,** air force

flotación, *f.* floating. (*naut.*) **línea de f.,** water-line

flotador, *a.* floating. *m.* float

flotamiento, *m.* floating

flotante, *a.* floating

flotar, *v.i.* to float on water or in air

flote, *m.* floating. **a f.,** afloat; independent, solvent

flotilla, *f.* flotilla; fleet of small ships. **f. aérea,** air fleet

fluctuación, *f.* fluctuation; hesitation, vacillation

fluctuante, *a.* fluctuating

fluctuar, *v.i.* to fluctuate; be in danger (things); vacillate, hesitate; undulate; oscillate

fluidez, *f.* fluidity

flúido, *a.* fluid; fluent. *m.* fluid; (*elec.*) current

fluir, *v.i. irr.* to flow. See **huir**

flujo, *m.* flow, flux; rising tide. **f. de sangre,** hæmorrhage

fluor, *m.* (*chem.*) fluorine

fluorescencia, *f.* fluorescence

fluorescente, *a.* fluorescent

fluorita, *f.* fluorite

fluvial, *a.* fluvial

flux, *m.* flush (in cards)

foca, *f.* (*zool.*) seal

focal, *a.* focal

foco, *m.* focus; centre; origin; source; (*theat.*) spotlight; core (of an abscess)

fofo, *a.* spongy, soft; flabby

fogata, *f.* bonfire

fogón, *m.* fire, cooking place, kitchen range, kitchen stove; furnace of a steam-boiler; vent of fire-arm

fogonazo, *m.* powder flash

fogonero, *m.* stoker

fogosidad, *f.* enthusiasm; vehemence; ardour

fogoso, *a.* ardent; vehement; enthusiastic

folgo, *m.* footmuff

foliar, *v.t.* to number pages of a book

folículo, *m.* (*bot., anat.*) follicle

folio, *m.* leaf of a book or manuscript, folio. **en f.,** in folio

folklórico, *a.* pertaining to folklore

folklorista, *m.* and *f.* folklorist

follaje, *m.* foliage; leafy ornamentation; crude unnecessary decoration; verbosity

folletín, *m.* feuilleton, literary article; serial story; (*fam.*) penny dreadful

folletinista, *m.* and *f.* pamphleteer

folleto, *m.* pamphlet, leaflet

follón, *a.* lazy; caddish; craven

fomentación, *f.* (*med.*) fomentation, poultice

fomentador, *a.* fomenting. *m.* fomenter

fomentar, *v.t.* to warm, foment; incite, instigate; (*med.*) apply fomentations

fomento, *m.* heat, shelter; fuel; protection, encouragement; (*med.*) fomentation

fonda, *f.* inn; railway buffet; restaurant

fondeadero, *m.* (*naut.*) anchorage, anchoring ground

fondear, *v.t.* (*naut.*) to sound; search a ship; examine carefully; *v.i.* (*naut.*) anchor

fondillos, *m. pl.* seat (of trousers)

fondista, *m.* and *f.* owner of an inn or restaurant

fondo, *m.* bottom (of a well, etc.); bed (of sea, etc.); depth; rear, portion at the back; ground (of fabrics); background; (*com.*) capital; (*com.*) stock; (*fig.*) fund (of humour, etc.); character, nature; temperament; (*fig.*) substance, core, essence; (*naut.*) bottom; *pl.* (*com.*) resources, funds. **f. de amortización,** sinking fund. **f. doble** *or* **f. secreto,** false bottom. **f. muerto, f. perdido** *or* **f. vitalicio,** life annuity. (*com.*) **fondos inactivos,** idle capital. **a fondo,** completely, thoroughly. **artículo de f.,** leading article. (*sport*) **carrera de f.,** long distance race. (*naut.*) **irse a f.,** to sink, founder

fonética, *f.* phonetics

fonético, *a.* phonetic

fonetista, *m.* and *f.* phoneticist

fonógrafo, *m.* phonograph

fonología, *f.* phonology

fonológico, *a.* phonological

fontanar, *m.* spring, stream

fontanería, *f.* pipe laying, plumbing

fontanero, *m.* pipe layer; plumber

foque, *m.* (*naut.*) jib; (*fam.*) high stiff collar

forajido (-da), *a.* fugitive, outlawed. *s.* robber, fugitive

forastero (-ra), *a.* strange, foreign; alien, exotic. *s.* stranger

forcejear, *v.i.* to struggle; try, strive; oppose, contradict

forcejo, *m.* struggle; endeavour; opposition, hostility

fórceps, *m. pl.* forceps

forense, *a.* forensic

forestal, *a.* forestal

forillo, *m.* (*theat.*) backcloth

forja, *f.* forge

forjador, *m.* smith, iron-worker

forjar, *v.t.* to forge; fabricate; create; counterfeit

forma, *f.* shape, form; arrangement; method; style; manifestation, expression; formula, formulary; ceremonial; (*print.*) forme; manner; means, way; mould, matrix; style of handwriting; (*law*) **en debida f.,** in due form

formación, *f.* formation; form, contour, shape; (*mil., geol.*) formation

formador, *a.* forming, shaping

formal, *a.* apparent, formal; serious, punctilious, steady; truthful, reliable; sedate; orderly, regular, methodical

formaldehido, *m.* formaldehyde

formalidad, *f.* orderliness, propriety; formality; requirement, requisite; ceremony; seriousness, sedateness; punctiliousness

formalismo, *m.* formalism; bureaucracy, red-tape

formalizar, *v.t.* to put into final form; legalize; formulate, enunciate; *v.r.* take seriously (a joke)

formar, *v.t.* to shape; form; educate, mould; (*mil.*) form; *v.r.* develop, grow

formativo, *a.* formative

formato, *m.* (*print.*) format; (*chem.*) formate

formidable, *a.* formidable, awe-inspiring; huge, enormous

fórmula, *f.* formula; prescription; mode of expression. (*math.*, *chem.*) **f. clásica,** standard formula

formular, *v.t.* to formulate; prescribe

formulario, *m.* (*law*) formulary; handbook

formulismo, *m.* formulism; bureaucracy, red-tape

fornicación, *f.* fornication

fornicador (-ra), *a.* and *s.* fornicator

fornicar, *v.i.* to fornicate

fornido, *a.* stalwart, muscular, strong

foro, *m.* forum; law courts; law, bar, legal profession; (*theat.*) back scenery; leasehold

forraje, *m.* forage, fodder; foraging

forrajeador, *m.* forager

forrajear, *v.t.* to gather forage, go foraging

forrajera, *f.* (*mil.*) shako guard

forrar, *v.t.* (*sew.*) to line; cover, encase, make a cover for

forro, *m.* lining, inner covering; cover of a book

fortalecedor, *a.* fortifying

fortalecer, *v.t. irr.* to fortify. See **conocer**

fortaleza, *f.* vigour; fortitude; fortress; natural defence. (*aer.*) **f. volante,** flying fortress

fortificable, *a.* fortifiable

fortificación, *f.* fortification

fortificador, *a.* fortifying

fortificar, *v.t.* to fortify

fortísimo, *a. sup.* **fuerte,** extremely strong

fortuito, *a.* fortuitous, chance

fortuna, *f.* fate, destiny; fortune, capital, estate; tempest. **por f.,** fortunately. **probar f.,** to try one's luck

forzado, *a.* forced, obliged. *m.* convict condemned to the galleys

forzador, *m.* violator, seducer

forzar, *v.t. irr.* to force, break open; take by force; rape, ravish; oblige, compel. *Pres. Ind.* **fuerzo, fuerzas, fuerza, fuerzan.** *Preterite* **forcé, forzaste,** etc. *Pres. Subjunc.* **fuerce, fuerces, fuerce, forcemos, forcéis, fuercen**

forzoso, *a.* obligatory, unavoidable, necessary

forzudo, *a.* brawny, stalwart

fosa, *f.* grave; socket (of a joint)

fosar, *v.t.* to undermine; dig a trench around

fosfato, *m.* phosphate

fosforecer, *v.i. irr.* to phosphoresce. See **conocer**

fosforera, *f.* match-box

fosforero (-ra), *s.* match seller

fosforescencia, *f.* phosphorescence

fosforescente, *a.* phosphorescent

fosfórico, *a.* (*chem.*) phosphoric

fosforita, *f.* (*min.*) phosphorite

fósforo, *m.* phosphorus; match; morning star

fosgeno, *m.* (*chem.*) phosgene

fósil, *a.* and *m.* fossil; (*fam.*) antique

fosilizarse, *v.r.* to become fossilized

foso, *m.* hole, hollow, pit; trench; pit (in garages); (*theat.*) room under stage

foto, *f.* snapshot, photo

fotocopia, *f.* blue print

fotogénico, *a.* photogenic

fotograbado, *m.* photogravure

fotografía, *f.* photography; photograph

fotografiar, *v.t.* to photograph

fotográfico, *a.* photographic

fotógrafo, *m.* photographer

fotograma, *m.* (cinema) shot

fotoquímica, *f.* photochemistry

fotostato, *m.* photostat

frac, *m.* dress-coat

fracasar, *v.i.* to break, crumble, be shattered; collapse (of plans, etc.); fail; be disappointed

fracaso, *m.* shattering; collapse (of plans, etc.); disaster; failure, disappointment, downfall

fracción, *f.* division into parts; fraction. **f. impropia,** (*math.*) improper fraction

fractura, *f.* fracture. **f. conminuta,** compound fracture

fracturar, *v.t.* to fracture

fragancia, *f.* fragrance, perfume; renown, good name

fragante, *a.* fragrant; perfumed; flagrant

fragata, *f.* (*naut.*) frigate

frágil, *a.* fragile, brittle; perishable, frail; weak, sinful

fragilidad, *f.* fragility; frailty, sinfulness

fragmentario, *a.* fragmentary

fragmento, *m.* fragment

fragor, *m*. noise, crash

fragosidad, *f*. roughness, rockiness, unevenness

fragoso, *a*: craggy, rocky; rough; noisy, clamorous

fragua, *f*. forge

fraguado, *m*. forging; (*mas*.) setting

fraguar, *v.t.* to forge, work; plot, scheme; *v.i.* set (concrete, etc.)

fraile, *m*. friar, monk. (*fam*.) **f. de misa y olla**, ignorant friar

frailesco, *a*. (*fam*.) pertaining to friars, friar-like

frambuesa, *f*. raspberry

frambueso, *m*. raspberry-cane

francachela, *f*. (*fam*.) binge

francés (-esa), *a*. French. *s*. Frenchman (woman). *m*. French language. **a la francesa**, in the French fashion

francesilla, *f*. (*cul*.) French roll

franciscano (-na), *a*. and *s*. Franciscan

francmasón (-ona), *s*. Freemason

francmasonería, *f*. Freemasonry

franco, *a*. generous, liberal; exempt; sincere, genuine, frank; duty-free; Frank; Franco (in compound words). *m*. franc (coin). **f. de porte**, post-free; carriage-free; prepaid

francotirador, *m*. sharp-shooter, franc tireur

franela, *f*. flannel

frangir, *v.t.* to divide, quarter

frangollar, *v.t.* to scamp, skimp (work)

franja, *f*. fringe; border, trimming; stripe. (*rad*.) **f. undosa**, wave-band

franjar, *v.t.* (*sew*.) to fringe, trim

franquear, *v.t.* to exempt; make free, make a gift of; clear the way (also *fig*.); stamp, prepay; free (slaves); *v.r.* fall in easily with others' plans; make confidences

franqueo, *m*. exemption; bestowal, making free; postage, **stamping**; enfranchisement (slaves)

franqueza, *f*. exemption, freedom; generosity, liberality; sincerity, frankness

franquicia, *f*. exemption from excise duties

franquista, *m*. and *f*. (Spanish *pol*.) supporter of General Franco

frasco, *m*. bottle, flask; powder flask or horn. **f. cuentagotas**, drop bottle

frase, *f*. sentence; phrase; epigram; idiom, style. **f. hecha**, cliché

frasear, *v.t.* to phrase

fraseología, *f*. phraseology; wording

fratás, *m*. plastering trowel

fraternal, *a*. brotherly

fraternidad, *f*. fraternity, brotherhood

fraternizar, *v.i.* to fraternize

fraterno, *a*. fraternal

fratricida, *a*. fratricidal. *m*. and *f*. fratricide

fratricidio, *m*. fratricide (act)

fraude, *m*. fraud, deception

fraudulento, *a*. fraudulent

fray, *m*. abb. fraile. Always used in conjunction with a name (e.g. F. Bartolomé, Friar Bartholomew)

frazada, *f*. blanket

frecuencia, *f*. frequency. **f. radioeléctrica**, radiofrequency

frecuentación, *f*. frequenting, visiting

frecuentador (-ra), *s*. frequenter

frecuentar, *v.t.* to frequent

frecuente, *a*. frequent

fregadero, *m*. kitchen sink

fregado, *m*. scrubbing; rubbing; scouring; washing; (*fam*.) murky business

fregador, *m*. kitchen sink; scrubbing-brush; dish-cloth. **f. mecánico de platos**, washing-up machine

fregar, *v.t.* *irr*. to rub; scour; wash (dishes). See **cegar**

fregona, *f*. kitchen-maid

fregotear, *v.t.* (*fam*.) to clean or scour inefficiently

freiduría, *f*. fried fish shop

freír, *v.t.* *irr*. (*cul*.) to fry. See **reír**

fréjol, *m*. kidney-bean

frenar, *v.t.* to restrain, hold back; bridle, check; (*mech*.) brake

frenesí, *m*. madness, frenzy; vehemence, exaltation

frenético, *a*. mad, frenzied; vehement, exalted

freno, *m*. bridle; (*mech*.) brake; restraint, check. **f. de pedal**, foot brake. **f. neumático**, vacuum brake

frenología, *f.* phrenology
frenólogo, *m.* phrenologist
frenópata, *m.* phrenopathist
frenopatía, *f.* phrenopathy
frente, *f.* brow, forehead; front portion; countenance; head; heading; beginning (of letter, etc.). *m.* (*mil.*) front. *m.* or *f.* façade; front; obverse (coins). *adv.* in front, opposite. **f. a f.,** face to face. **con la f. levantada,** with head held high; proudly; insolently. **de f.,** abreast
freo, *m.* (*naut.*) strait, narrow channel
fresa, *f.* strawberry plant and fruit (especially small or wild varieties); (*mech.*) milling cutter, miller
fresadora, *f.* milling machine
fresal, *m.* strawberry bed
fresca, *f.* cool air; fresh air; (*fam.*) home truth
fresco, *a.* cool; fresh, new; recent; buxom, freshly-coloured; calm, serene; (*fam.*) cheeky, bold; thin (cloths). *m.* coolness; fresh air; (*art*) fresco. **al f.,** in the open air. **hacer f.,** to be cool or fresh
frescote, *a.* (*fam.*) ruddy and corpulent
frescura, *f.* coolness; freshness; pleasant verdure and fertility; (*fam.*) cheek, nerve; piece of insolence; unconcern, indifference; calmness, serenity
fresero (-ra), *s.* strawberry seller
fresneda, *f.* ash grove
fresno, *m.* (*bot.*) ash
fresón, *m.* strawberry (large, cultivated varieties)
fresquera, *f.* meat-safe; cool place
fresquista, *m.* fresco painter
friable, *a.* brittle; friable, powdery
frialdad, *f.* coldness, chilliness; (*med.*) frigidity; indifference, lack of interest; foolishness; negligence
fríamente, *adv.* coldly; coolly, with indifference; dully, flatly
fricativo, *a.* (*gram.*) fricative
fricción, *f.* friction
friccionar, *v.t.* to rub; give a friction, massage
friega, *f.* friction, massage
frigidez, *f.* See **frialdad**

frígido, *a.* frigid
frigio, *a.* and *s.* Phrygian
frigorífico, *a.* refrigerative. *m.* refrigerator, cold-storage chamber
frío, *a.* cold; (*med.*) frigid; indifferent, uninterested; dull, uninteresting; inefficient. *m.* coldness, chill; cold
friolera, *f.* bagatelle, trifle, mere nothing
friolero, *a.* sensitive to cold
frisa, *f.* frieze cloth
frisar, *v.t.* to frizz, curl (cloth); scrub, rub; *v.i.* approach, be nearly (e.g. **Frisa en los dieciséis años,** He's nearly sixteen)
friso, *m.* frieze; dado, border
frisón (-ona), *a.* and *s.* Frisian
fritada, *f.* (*cul.*) fry, fried dish
fritilaria, *f.* (*bot.*) fritillary
frito, *a.* fried
fritura, *f.* frying; fry
frivolidad, *f.* frivolity
frivolité, *m.* (*sew.*) tatting
frívolo, *a.* frivolous, superficial; futile, unconvincing
fronda, *f.* (*bot.*) leaf; frond (of ferns); *pl.* foliage
frondosidad, *f.* luxuriance of foliage
frondoso, *a.* leafy
frontera, *f.* frontier; façade
fronterizo, *a.* frontier; facing, opposite
frontero, *a.* facing, opposite. *m.* (*ant., mil.*) frontier commander
frontispicio, *m.* frontispiece; façade; (*fig., fam.*) face, dial
frontón, *m.* pelota court; fives court; (*arch.*) pediment
frotamiento, frote, *m.* rubbing, friction
frotar, *v.t.* to rub
frotis, *m.* (*med.*) smear
fructífero, *a.* fruitful, fructiferous
fructuoso, *a.* fruitful, fertile; useful
frufrú, *m.* rustle (of a silk dress, etc.)
frugal, *a.* frugal; saving, economical
frugalidad, *f.* frugality, abstemiousness, moderation
frugívoro, *a.* frugivorous
fruición, *f.* enjoyment; fruition; satisfaction
fruir, *v.i. irr.* to enjoy what one has long desired. See **huir**

frunce, *m.* (*sew.*) shirring; gather; ruffling; tuck; pucker; wrinkle

fruncimiento, *m.* wrinkling; puckering; (*sew.*) shirring

fruncir, *v.t.* to frown; purse (the lips); pucker; (*sew.*) shirr, pleat, gather; reduce in size; conceal the truth; *v.r.* pretend to be prudish. **f. el ceño,** to scowl

fruslería, *f.* trifle, nothing

frustración, *f.* frustration

frustrar, *v.t.* to disappoint; frustrate, thwart

fruta, *f.* fruit; (*fam.*) consequence, result. **f. de hueso,** stone fruit. (*cul.*) **f. de sartén,** fritter

frutal, *a.* fruit bearing. *m.* fruit tree

frutar, *v.i.* to bear fruit

frutería, *f.* fruit shop

frutero (-ra), *a.* fruit. *s.* fruit vendor. *m.* fruit dish; (*art*) painting of fruit; basket of imitation fruit

frútice, *m.* (*bot.*) bush, shrub

fruticultura, *f.* fruit farming

fruto, *m.* fruit; product, result; profit, proceeds; (*agr.*) grain

fu, spitting (of cats). *interj.* expression of scorn. (*fam.*) **ni f. ni fa,** neither one thing nor the other

fucilazo, *m.* heat lightning

fucsia, *f.* (*bot.*) fuchsia

fucsina, *f.* (*chem.*) fuchsine

fuego, *m.* fire; conflagration; firing (of fire-arms); beacon; hearth; home; rash; ardour; heat (of an argument, etc.); *interj.* ¡ **F.** ! (*mil.*) Fire! **fuegos artificiales,** fireworks. **a sangre y f.,** by fire and sword. (*mil.*) **hacer f.,** to fire. **pegar f.,** to set on fire

fuelle, *m.* bellows; bag (of bag-pipe); (*sew.*) pucker, wrinkle; hood (of carriage, etc.); wind cloud; (*fam.*) tale bearer. **f. de pie,** foot-pump

fuente, *f.* stream, spring; fountain; meat dish; genesis, origin; source, headwaters; tap

fuera, *adv.* outside, out. *interj.* get out! **f. de,** beside, in addition to. **f. de alcance,** out of reach. **f. de sí,** beside oneself (with rage, etc.). **de f.,** from the outside. **por f.,** on the outside, externally

fuero, *m.* municipal charter; jurisdiction; compilation of laws; legal right or privilege; *pl.* (*fam.*) arrogance. **los fueros de León,** the laws of León

fuerte, *a.* strong, resistant; robust; spirited, vigorous; hard (diamonds, etc.); rough, uneven; impregnable; terrible, tremendous; overweight (coins); active; efficacious, effective; expert, knowledgeable; (*gram.*) strong; intense; loud; tough. *m.* fort; talent, strong point; (*mus.*) forte. *adv.* strongly; excessively. **tener genio f.,** to be quick-tempered

fuerza, *f.* strength; power, might; force; efficacy; fortress; (*sew.*) stiffening; (*mech.*) power; violence; toughness, durability, solidity; potency; authority; courage; vigour; *pl.* (*fig., fam.*) live wires, influential people. **a f. de,** by means of, by dint of. **a la f.,** forcibly. **en f. de,** because of, on account of. **por f. mayor,** by main force. **ser f.,** to be necessary

fuga, *f.* flight, escape, running away; leak (gas, etc.); elopement; (*mus.*) fugue; ardour, strength

fugarse, *v.r.* to run away; elope; escape

fugaz, *a.* fugitive; fleeting, brief

fugitivo (-va), *a.* fugitive; runaway, escaping; transient. *s.* fugitive

fulano (-na), *s.* so-and-so, such a person. **F., Zutano y Mengano,** (*fam.*) Tom, Dick and Harry

fulcro, *m.* (*mech.*) fulcrum

fulgente, fúlgido, *a.* brilliant, shining

fulgor, *m.* brilliance, brightness

fulgurar, *v.i.* to shine, be resplendent, scintillate; flare

fulguroso, *a.* shining, sparkling

fúlica, *f.* (*orn.*) coot

fulminante, *a.* (*med.*) fulminant; fulminating; thundering. *m.* percussion cap

fulminar, *v.t.* to fulminate (all meanings)

fulminato, *m.* (*chem.*) fulminate

fulmíneo, fulminoso, *a.* fulminous, connected with lightning

fullería, *f.* cheating at play; craftiness, low guile

fullero (-ra), *a.* cheating; crafty, astute. *s.* cheat, card-sharper

fumadero, *m.* smoke-room

fumador (-ra), *a.* smoking. *s.* smoker. **"No fumadores," "Non-smoking"** (compartment)

fumar, *v.i.* to smoke; *v.r.* (*fam.*) dissipate, waste

fumarola, *f.* fumarole, place where smoke escapes in cone of volcano

fumigación, *f.* fumigation

fumigador (-ra), *s.* fumigator

fumigar, *v.t.* to fumigate

fumigatorio, *a.* fumigatory. *m.* perfume burner

fumista, *m.* stove maker or seller

fumistería, *f.* stove works or shop

funámbulo, *s.* tight-rope walker, acrobat

función, *f.* function; working, operation; (*theat.*) performance; activity, duty; ceremony; celebration; (*math.*) function; (*mil.*) battle

funcional, *a.* functional

funcionamiento, *m.* functioning

funcionar, *v.i.* to function, work. **"No funciona," "Out of order"**

funcionario, *m.* functionary, official; civil servant

funda, *f.* case, cover, sheath; hold-all. **f. de almohada,** pillow-case

fundación, *f.* foundation

fundadamente, *adv.* with reason, on good evidence

fundador (-ra), *s.* founder, creator; originator

fundamental, *a.* fundamental

fundamento, *m.* (*mas.*) foundation; basis; basic principle, reason; origin, root

fundar, *v.t.* to build, erect; base; found, institute; create, establish; *v.r.* (*with en*) found, base upon. **f. una compañía,** (*com.*) to float a company

fundición, *f.* foundry; smelting, founding, casting; cast-iron; (*print.*) fount

fundidor, *m.* founder, smelter. **f. de letras de imprenta,** type-founder

fundir, *v.t.* to melt; found, smelt; cast (metals); *v.r.* join together, unite; (*elec.*) blow (fuses)

fúnebre, *a.* funeral; dismal, lugubrious, mournful

funeral, *a.* funeral

funerales, *m.* *pl.* funeral; (*ecc.*) commemoration masses

funerala, (a la) *adv.* (*mil.*) with reversed arms

funeraria, *f.* funeral furnishers

funerario, *a.* funeral

funéreo, *a.* funereal, mournful

funesto, *a.* unlucky, unfortunate; mournful, melancholy, sad

fungoso, *a.* spongy, fungous

funicular, *a.* funicular

furgón, *m.* waggon; van; guard's van, luggage van. **f. postal,** mail van

furia, *f.* (*myth.*) fury; rage, wrath; fit of madness; raging, violence (of elements); speed, haste

furibundo, *a.* frantic, furious; raging

furioso, *a.* furious, enraged; mad, insane; violent, terrible; enormous, excessive

furor, *m.* fury, rage; poetic frenzy; violence; furore

furriel, *m.* (*mil.*) quartermaster

furtivo, *a.* furtive; covert, clandestine; (of editions) pirate

fusa, *f.* (*mus.*) demisemiquaver

fuscia, *f.* (*bot.*) fuchsia

fusco, *a.* dark

fuselado, *a.* stream-lined

fuselaje, *m.* (*aer.*) fuselage

fusible, *a.* fusible. *m.* (*elec.*) fuse; fuse wire

fusil, *m.* rifle

fusilamiento, *m.* execution by shooting

fusilar, *v.t.* to execute by shooting; (*fam.*) plagiarize

fusilazo, *m.* rifle shot

fusilero, *m.* (*mil.*) fusilier

fusión, *f.* melting, liquefying; fusion, blending; mixture, union; (*com.*) merger, amalgamation

fusionar, *v.t.* to blend, fuse, merge; *v.r.* (*com.*) combine, form a merger

fusta, *f.* brushwood; whip

fuste, *m.* wood, timber; (*poet.*) saddle; (*fig.*) core, essence; importance, substance; shaft of lance; (*arch.*) fust, shaft. **hombre de buen f.,** a man with a good constitution (physical)

fustigar, *v.t.* to whip, lash; rebuke harshly

fútbol, *m.* football, soccer

futbolista, *m.* footballer, soccer player

fútil, *a.* futile, ineffectual, worthless

futilidad, *f.* futility, worthlessness

futura, *f.* (*law*) reversion (of offices); (*fam.*) fiancée

futurismo, *m.* futurism

futurista, *m.* and *f.* futurist

futurístico, *a.* futuristic

futuro (-ra), *a.* future. *m.* future. *s.* (*fam.*) betrothed

G

gabacho (-cha), *a.* and *s.* (*fam.*, scornful) Frenchman

gabán, *m.* overcoat; cloak

gabardina, *f.* gabardine; weatherproof coat

gabarra, *f.* (*naut.*) lighter, gabbard, barge

gabarrero, *m.* (*naut.*) lighter man

gabarro, *m.* flaw (in cloth); knot (in stone); snag, drawback; slip, error (in accounts)

gabela, *f.* duty, tax; imposition, burden

gabinete, *m.* study, library; sitting-room; den; (*pol.*) cabinet; collection, museum, gallery; laboratory; boudoir; studio; display cabinet. **g. de lectura**, reading-room

gablete, *m.* (*arch.*) gable

gacel, *m.*, **gacela**, *f.* (*zool.*) gazelle

gaceta, *f.* bulletin, review, record; newspaper; gazette (official Spanish Government organ); (*fam.*) news hound

gacetero (-ra), *s.* news vendor. *m.* news reporter

gacetilla, *f.* news in brief, miscellany column, society news; gossip column; (*fam.*) news hound

gacetillero, *m.* paragrapher, penny-a-liner; reporter

gacha, *f.* unglazed crock; *pl.* pap; porridge

gaché, *m.* name gypsies give the Andalusians; (*fam.*) fellow

gacho, *a.* drooping, bent downwards; slouch (hat); (of ears) lop

gachón, *a.* (*fam.*) attractive, charming

gaditano (-na), *a.* and *s.* native of, or pertaining to, Cadiz

gaélico, *a.* and *m.* Gaelic

gafas, *f. pl.* spectacles; goggles; spectacle ear-hooks; grapplehooks

gafar, *v.t.* to claw; seize with a hook, hook; mend with a bracket (pottery)

gafete, *m.* hook and eye; clasp

gaita, *f.* bagpipe; hand organ; kind of clarinet; (*fam.*) neck. **g. gallega**, bagpipe

gaitería, *f.* crude, gaudy garment or ornament

gaitero, *a.* (*fam.*) over-merry; loud, crude. *m.* piper

gajes, *m. pl.* salary; emoluments; perquisites

gajo, *m.* branch, bough (gen. cut); little cluster (of grapes); bunch (of fruit); quarter (of oranges, etc.); prong (of forks, etc.)

gala, *f.* evening or full dress; grace, wit; flower, cream, best; gala; *pl.* finery; trappings; wedding presents. **de g.**, full dress. **hacer g. de**, to glory in, boast of

galactita, *f.* fuller's earth

galaico, *a.* See **gallego**

galán, *m.* handsome well-made man; lover, wooer, gallant; (*theat.*) leading man or one of leading male rôles

galancete, *m.* handsome little man; (*theat.*) male juvenile lead

galano, *a.* smart, well-dressed; agreeable, pleasing; beautiful; ornamented; (*fig.*) elegant (speech, style, etc.)

galante, *a.* gallant, courtly, attentive; flirtatious (of women); licentious

galanteador, *a.* flirtatious. *m.* philanderer; wooer

galantear, *v.t.* to court; flirt with; make love to; (*fig.*) procure assiduously

galanteo, *m.* courtship; flirtation; love-making; wooing

galantería, *f.* courtesy; attention, compliment; elegance, grace; gallantry; generosity, liberality

galantina, *f.* (*cul.*) galantine

galanura, *f.* showiness, gorgeousness; elegance, grace; prettiness

galápago, *m.* fresh-water tortoise; cleat

galardón, *m.* reward, recompense, prize

galardonar, *v.t.* to reward, recompense

gálata, *a.* and *m.* and *f.* Galatian

galbana, *f.* (*fam.*) laziness, inertia

galbanoso, *a.* (*fam.*) slothful

galénico, *a.* Galenic

galenismo, *m.* Galenism

galeón, *m.* (*naut.*) galleon

galeota, *f.* (*naut.*) galliot

galeote, *m.* galley-slave

galera, *f.* van, waggon, cart; (*naut.*) galley; prison for women; (*print.*) galley. **echar a galeras**, to condemn to the galleys

galerada, *f.* (*print.*) galley-proof

galería, *f.* gallery; corridor, passage; collection of paintings; (*min.*) gallery, drift; (*theat.*) gallery

galerín, *m.* (*print.*) wooden galley

galerna, *f.* tempestuous northwest wind (gen. on Spanish north coast)

galés (-esa), *a.* Welsh. *s.* Welshman. *m.* Welsh language

galga, *f.* boulder, rolling stone; greyhound bitch

galgo, *m.* greyhound. **g. ruso**, borzoi (dog)

gálibo, *m.* (*naut.*) mould; elegance

galicado, *a.* gallicized

galicismo, *m.* gallicism

gálico, *m.* syphilis. *a.* gallic

galileo (-ea), *a.* and *s.* Galilean

galimatías, *m.* (*fam.*) gibberish, nonsense

galocha, *f.* patten, clog; cap with ear flaps

galón, *m.* galloon, braid; (*mil.*) stripe; gallon (measure)

galoneadura, *f.* braiding, trimming

galonear, *v.t.* to trim with braid

galop, *m.* galop; gallopade

galopante, *a.* galloping (of consumption, etc.)

galopar, *v.i.* to gallop; (*mech.*) wabble

galope, *m.* gallop. **a or de g.**, at the gallop; at the run, quickly. **andar a g. corto**, to canter

galopillo, *m.* scullion

galopín, *m.* ragamuffin, urchin; rogue, knave; (*fam.*) clever rogue; (*naut.*) cabin boy

galvánico, *a.* (*elec.*) galvanic

galvanismo, *m.* (*phys.*) galvanism

galvanización, *f.* (*phys.*) galvanization

galvanizar, *v.t.* (*elec.*) to galvanize; electroplate; (*fig.*) shock into life

galvanómetro, *m.* (*phys.*) galvanometer

gallardear, *v.i.* to behave with ease and grace

gallardete, *m.* (*naut.*) pennant; bunting

gallardía, *f.* grace, dignity; spirit, dash; courage; liveliness

gallardo, *a.* handsome, upstanding; gallant; spirited; fine, noble; lively

gallear, *v.i.* (*fam.*) to put on airs; be a bully; shout, bawl (with anger, etc.); (*fig., fam.*) stand out

gallego (-ga), *a.* and *s.* Galician (from Galicia in N.W. Spain). *m.* Galician dialect

galleta, *f.* biscuit; (*fam.*) slap; anthracite, lump coal; small jar or vessel

gallina, *f.* hen. *m.* and *f.* (*fam.*) coward. **g. ciega**, blind man's buff. (*fam.*) **acostarse con las gallinas**, to go early to bed

gallinaza, *f.* hen dung

gallinero (-ra), *s.* poultry dealer. *m.* hen-house; brood of hens; (*theat.*) gallery; babel, noisy place

gallito, *m.* small cock; cock-o'-the-walk; bully

gallo, *m.* (*orn.*) cock; (*fam.*) false note (in singing); (*fam.*) boss, chief. (*fam.*) **alzar el g.**, to put on side, boast. **Cada g. canta en su muladar**, Every man is boss in his own house. (*fam.*) **Otro g. nos cantara**, Our lot (or fate) would have been very different

gallofero (-ra), *a.* mendicant, vagabond. *s.* beggar

gama, *f.* (*mus.*) scale; gamut, range; (*zool.*) doe

gambito, *m.* gambit (in chess)

gamella, *f.* trough (for washing, feeding animals, etc.)

gamo, *m.* (*zool.*) buck (of the fallow deer)

gamuza, *f.* (*zool.*) chamois; chamois leather

gamuzado, *a.* chamois-coloured

gana, *f.* appetite; wish, desire. **de buena g.**, willingly. **de**

mala g., reluctantly. tener g.
(de), to wish, desire, want. no
tener g., to have no appetite, be
not hungry. No me da la g., I
don't want (to), I won't

ganable, a. attainable; earnable

ganadería, f. live-stock; strain
(of cattle); cattle raising; stock
farm; cattle dealing

ganadero, m. cattle raiser or
dealer; herdsman

ganado, m. live-stock, herd;
flock; hive (of bees); (fam.) mob.
g. mayor, cattle, mules, horses.
g. menor, cattle, sheep, goats, etc.
g. moreno, hogs, swine. g.
vacuno, cattle

ganador (-ra), a. winning. s.
winner

ganancia, f. winning; gain, profit

ganancial, ganancioso, a. gainful, profitable; lucrative

ganapán, m. labourer; porter;
(fam.) boor

ganar, v.t. to gain; win; conquer; arrive at; earn; surpass,
beat; achieve; acquire; v.i.
prosper

ganchero, m. lumber-jack

ganchillo, m. crochet-hook; crochet. hacer g., to crochet

gancho, m. hook; stump (of a
branch); shepherd's crook; crochet-hook; (fam.) trickster,
pimp; (fam.) scribble

ganchoso, a. hooked; bent;
curved

gandujar, v.t. (sew.) to pleat,
tuck, shirr. .

gandul (-la), a. (fam.) lazy. s.
lazybones, loafer

gandulería, f. loafing, idleness

ganga, f. (min.) gangue, matrix;
bargain, cinch

ganglio, m. (anat.) ganglion

gangoso, a. nasal; with a twang
(of speech)

gangrena, f. (med.) gangrene

gangrenarse, v.r. to become gangrenous, mortify

gangrenoso, a. (med.) gangrenous

ganguear, v.i. to speak nasally,
or with a twang

ganoso, a. wishful, desirous,
anxious

gansada, f. (fam.) impertinence,
foolishness

ganso (-sa), s. goose, gander;

slow-moving person; yokel,
bumpkin

ganzúa, f. skeleton key; (fam.)
picklock, burglar; (fam.) pumper,
inquisitive person

gañán, m. farm labourer; day
labourer; brawny fellow

gañido, m. yowl, yelp, howl

gañir, v.i. irr. to yowl, yelp,
howl (dogs, etc.); crow, croak;
(fam.) talk hoarsely. See mullir

garabatear, v.i. to hook, catch
with hooks; scribble; (fig., fam.)
beat about the bush

garabateo, m. hooking; scribbling

garabato, m. hook; (agr.) weed
clearer; scrawl, scribble; (fam.)
charm, sex-appeal; pothook;
boat-hook; pl. gestures, movements (with hands)

garaje, m. garage

garambaina, f. tawdry finery,
gaudiness; pl. (fam.) grimaces of
affectation; (fam.) scribble,
scrawl

garante, m. and f. guarantor;
reference (person). a. responsible,
guaranteeing

garantía, f. guarantee; security,
pledge; (law) warranty

garantir, v.t. to guarantee; warrant, vouch for

garapiñar, v.t. to ice, freeze
(drinks, syrups, etc.); (cul.)
candy, coat with sugar

garapiñera, f. ice-cream freezer

garbanzo, m. chick-pea. g.
negro, (fig.) black sheep

garbillar, v.t. (agr.) to sift; (min.)
riddle

garbo, m. jaunty air; grace, elegance; frankness; generosity,
liberality

garbón, m. (orn.) male partridge

garboso, a. attractive; handsome, sprightly, gay; graceful;
munificent

garduña, f. (zool.) weasel; marten

garduño (-ña), s. (fam.) sneak
thief

garete, (ir or irse al) (naut.) to be
adrift

garfa, f. claw (of a bird or animal)

garfear, v.i. to catch with a
hook, hook

garfio, m. grappling iron, hook,
drag-hook, cramp; gaff

gargajear, v.i. to expectorate

gargajo, *m.* phlegm

garganta, *f.* throat; gullet; instep; defile; neck, shaft, narrowest part

gargantear, *v.i.* to warble, trill

gárgara, *f.* gargling (gen. *pl.*). hacer gárgaras, to gargle

gargarismo, *m.* gargling; gargle (liquid)

gárgol, *a.* addled (eggs). *m.* groove, mortise

gárgola, *f.* (*arch.*) gargoyle; linseed

garguero, *m.* (*anat.*) windpipe; œsophagus

garita, *f.* sentry-box; porter's lodge; hut; cabin. g. de señales, (railway) signal-box

garitero, *m.* gambling-house keeper; gambler

garito, *m.* gambling-house; profits of a gambling-house

garra, *f.* paw with claws; talon; hand; (*mech.*) clamp, claw. (*fig.*) caer en las garras, to fall into the clutches (of)

garrafa, *f.* decanter, carafe; carboy

garrapata, *f.* (*ent.*) tick

garrapatear, *v.i.* to scribble

garrapato, *m.* scribble, scrawl

garrar, *v.i.* (*naut.*) to trail, drag (the anchor)

garrido, *a.* handsome; gallant; elegant; graceful

garroba, *f.* carob bean

garrocha, *f.* goad. salto a la g., pole-jumping

garrotazo, *m.* blow with a truncheon or cudgel. dar garrotazos de ciego, to lay about one

garrote, *m.* truncheon, club; (*med.*) tourniquet; garrotte. dar g. (a), to strangle

garrotillo, *m.* (*med.*) croup

garrucha, *f.* pulley; (*mech.*) gin block

garrulidad, *f.* garrulity, loquaciousness

gárrulo, *a.* twittering, chirping (birds); garrulous; murmuring, babbling (wind, water, etc.)

garza, *f.* (*orn.*) heron

garzo, *a.* blue (generally of eyes)

gas, *m.* gas; fumes. g. asfixiante, poison gas. cámara de g., gas-bag, gas-chamber

gasa, *f.* gauze. tira de g., black mourning-band

gascón (-ona), *a.* and *s.* Gascon

gasconada, *f.* bravado, gasconade

gaseosa, *f.* aerated water

gaseoso, *a.* gaseous

gasista, *m.* gas-fitter; gas-man

gasolina, *f.* gasolene, petrol

gasómetro, *m.* gas-meter; gasometer

gastado, *a.* worn; worn-out; exhausted

gastador (-ra), *a.* extravagant, wasteful. *s.* spendthrift. *m.* (*mil.*) sapper; convict condemned to hard labour

gastar, *v.t.* to spend (money); wear out; exhaust; ruin, destroy; display or have habitually; possess, use, wear; *v.r.* wear out; run down (of a battery)

gasto, *m.* spending; expenditure; consumption (of gas, etc.); expense, cost, charge; wear (and tear). g. suplementario, extra charge

gástrico, *a.* gastric

gastritis, *f.* gastritis

gastronomía, *f.* gastronomy

gastronómico, *a.* gastronomic

gastrónomo (-ma), *s.* gastronome

gata, *f.* she-cat; wreath of mist; (*fam.*) Madrilenian woman. a gatas, on all fours

gatada, *f.* (*fam.*) sly trick

gatear, *v.i.* to climb like a cat; (*fam.*) crawl on all fours; *v.t.* (*fam.*) scratch (of a cat); steal, pinch

gatera, *f.* cat-hole (in a door, etc.)

gatillo, *m.* dim. small-cat; dental forceps; trigger (of gun); (*fam.*) juvenile petty thief

gato, *m.* cat; tomcat; money-bag or its contents; (*mech.*) jack; mouse-trap; (*fam.*) cat burglar, sneak thief; (*fam.*) man from Madrid; (*carp.*) clamp. g. atigrado, tiger cat. g. de algalia, civet cat. g. de Angora, Persian cat. g. montés, wild cat. g. romano, tabby cat. dar g. por liebre, to serve cat for hare, to deceive; misrepresent. (*fam.*) Hay g. encerrado, There's a cat imprisoned (here) (There's more in this than meets the eye)

gatuno, *a.* feline

gaucho (-cha), s. Gaucho; cowboy, rider

gaveta, f. drawer (of desk)

gavia, f. (naut.) main top-sail; pl. top-sails; (naut.) crow's nest

gaviero, m. (naut.) ship's look-out

gavilán, m. (orn.) sparrow-hawk; (bot.) thistle flower

gavilla, f. sheaf (of corn, etc.); gang, rabble

gaviota, f. (orn.) sea-gull

gavota, f. gavotte

gayo, a. gay, happy; showy, attractive. **gaya ciencia,** minstrelsy, art of poetry

gazapera, f. rabbit-warren; (fam.) thieves' kitchen; (fam.) brawl

gazapo, m. young rabbit; (fam.) cunning fellow; fib, lie; slip, blunder

gazmoñería, f. prudery, priggish affectation

gazmoño, a. hypocritical, prudish, priggish

gaznápiro (-ra), s. ninny, simpleton

gaznate, m. (anat.) windpipe

gazpacho, m. (cul.) cold dish containing bread, onions, vinegar, olive oil, garlic, etc.

ge, f. name of the letter G

gehena, m. gehenna, hell

geiser, m. (geol.) geyser

gelatina, f. gelatine. **g. seca,** cooking gelatine

gelatinoso, a. gelatinous

gélido, a. (poet.) icy; very cold

gema, f. gem; (bot.) bud

gemelo (-la), a. and s. twin. m. pl. field or opera glasses, binoculars; cuff-links; (ast.) Gemini

gemido, m. groan, lament, moan

gemidor, a. groaning, moaning; wailing (of the wind, etc.)

gemir, v.i. irr. to moan, groan, lament; (fig.) wail, howl. See pedir

genciana, f. (bot.) gentian

gene, m. (biol.) gene

genealogía, f. genealogy

genealógico, a. genealogical

genealogista, m. and f. genealogist

generación, f. generation, reproduction; species; generation

generador, a. generative. m. (mech.) generator

general, a. general; universal; widespread; common, usual. m.

(mil., ecc.) general. **g. de división,** (mil.) major-general. **en** or **por lo g.,** generally

generalato, m. generalship

generalidad, f. majority, bulk; generality

generalísimo, m. generalissimo, commander-in-chief

generalización, f. generalization

generalizar, v.t. to generalize; v.r. become widespread or general

generar, v.t. to generate

genérico, a. generic

género, m. kind; class; way, mode; (com.) goods; species, genus; (gram.) gender; cloth, material. **g. chico,** short theatrical pieces (gen. one act). **g. humano,** mankind

generosidad, f. hereditary nobility; generosity, magnanimity; liberality, munificence; courage

generoso, a. noble (by birth); magnanimous; generous (of wine); munificent; courageous; excellent

genésico, a. genetic

génesis, m. Genesis. f. beginning, origin

genial, a. of genius; highly talented; brilliant; characteristic, individual; pleasant; cheerful

genialidad, f. genius; talent; brilliance; eccentricity, oddity

genio, m. nature, individuality, temperament; temper; character; talent; genius; genie, spirit. **corto de g.,** unintelligent. **mal g.,** bad temper

genital, a. genital. m. (anat.) testicle (gen. pl.)

genitivo, a. reproductive, generative. m. (gram.) genitive

genovés (-esa), a. and s. Genoese

gente, f. people, a crowd; nation; army; (fam.) family; followers, adherents. **g. baja,** rabble. **g. de bien,** honest folk; respectable people. **g. de paz,** friends (reply to sentinel's challenge). **g. fina,** nice, cultured people. **g. menuda,** children, small fry

gentecilla, f. dim. (fam.) rabble; contemptible people

gentil, a. pagan, idolatrous; spirited, dashing, handsome; notable, extraordinary; graceful, charming

gentileza, f. grace; elegance; beauty; verve, sprightliness; courtesy; show, ostentation

gentilhombre, m. gentleman; handsome man; kind sir! **gentileshombres de cámara,** gentlemen in waiting

gentilicio, a. gentilitial; national; family

gentílico, a. pagan, idolatrous

gentilidad, f. idolatry, paganism; heathendom

gentío, m. crowd, throng

gentualla, gentuza, f. (fam.) canaille, rabble

genuflexión, f. genuflexion

genuino, a. pure; authentic, genuine

geodesia, f. geodesy

geodésico, a. geodesic

geofísico, m. geophysicist

geografía, f. geography

geográfico, a. geographical

geógrafo, m. geographer

geología, f. geology.

geológico, a. geological

geólogo, m. geologist

geometría, f. geometry. **g. del espacio,** solid geometry

geométrico, a. geometrical

geranio, m. (bot.) geranium

gerencia, f. (com.) managership; manager's office; management

gerente, m. (com.) manager

gerifalte, m. (orn.) gerfalcon

germanía, f. thieves' slang; association of thieves; sixteenth-century political brotherhood

germánico, a. germanic

germanófilo (-la), a. and s. germanophile

germen, m. germ, sprout; (bot.) embryo; genesis, origin

germinación, f. germination

germinar, v.i. to germinate, sprout; develop, grow

germinativo, a. germinative

gerundio, m. (gram.) gerund; (fam.) pompous ass; (fam.) tub-thumper

gesta, f. heroic deed. **cantar de g.,** heroic epic or poem

gestación, f. gestation

gestear, v.i. to gesture or grimace

gesticulación, f. gesticulation; grimace

gesticular, v.i. to grimace or gesticulate. a. gesticulatory

gestión, f. negotiation; management, conduct; effort, exertion; measure

gestionar, v.t. to negotiate; conduct; undertake; take steps to attain

gesto, m. gesture; facial expression; grimace; face, visage

gestor (-ra), s. manager; partner; promoter. a. managing

giba, f. hump, hunchback; (fam.) nuisance, inconvenience

gibelino, a. Ghibelline

gibón, m. (zool.) gibbon

giboso, a. hunchbacked

gibraltareño, a. Gibraltarian

gigante, a. gigantic. m. giant.

giganta, f. giantess

gigantesco, a. giant, gigantic; (fig.) outstanding

gigantez, f. gigantic size

gigantón (-ona), s. enormous giant; carnival grotesque

gimnasia, f. gymnastics

gimnasio, m. gymnasium; school, academy

gimnasta, m. gymnast

gimnástico, a. gymnastic

gimotear, v.i. (fam.) to whine (often used scornfully)

gimoteo, m. (fam.) whining, whimpering

ginebra, f. gin (drink); confusion; babble, din

ginebrés (-esa), **ginebrino** (-na), a. and s. Genevan

gineceo, m. (bot., and in ancient Greece) gynæcium

ginecología, f. gynæcology

ginecológico, a. gynæcological

ginecólogo (-ga), s. gynæcologist

girado, m. (com.) drawee

girador, m. (com.) drawer

giralda, f. weathercock in shape of a person or animal; tower at Seville

girar, v.i. to revolve; deal (with), concern; turn, branch (streets, etc.); (com.) trade; (mech.) turn on, revolve; v.t. and v.i. (com.) draw, cash. **g. en descubierto,** (com.) to overdraw

girasol, m. (bot.) sunflower

giratorio, a. revolving, gyrating; swivelling

giro, m. revolution, turn; revolving; trend; course (of affairs);

style, turn (of phrase); threat;
knife gash; (com.) draft, drawing;
(com.) line of business, speciality.
g. postal, postal order

giroscopio, m. (phys.) gyroscope

gitanería, f. cajolery, wheedling;
gypsies; gypsy saying or action

gitanesco, a. gypsy, gypsy-like

gitano (-na), a. gypsy; gypsy-like;
seductive, attractive; sly. s.
gypsy

glaciar, m. glacier

gladiador, m. gladiator

gladiatorio, a. gladiatorial

glándula, f. (anat., bot.) gland

glasé, m. glacé silk

glicerina, f. glycerine, glycerol

glicocola, f. (chem.) glycine

globo, m. (geom.) sphere; globe,
world; globe (elec., gas); balloon.
g. aerostático, air-balloon. g.
terrestre, world; geographical
globe

globular, a. globular

glóbulo, m. dim. globule.

globuloso, a. globulous

gloria, f. heavenly bliss; fame,
glory; delight, pleasure; magnificence, splendour; (art) apotheosis, glory. m. (ecc.) doxology

gloriar, v.t. to praise; v.r. (with
de or en) boast about; be proud
of, rejoice in

glorieta, f. bower, arbour; open
space in a garden; street square

glorificación, f. glorification

glorificador, a. glorifying

glorificar, v.t. to exalt, raise up;
glorify, extol; v.r. (with de or en)
be proud of; glory in; boast of

glorioso, a. glorious; (ecc.)
blessèd; boastful, bragging

glosa, f. gloss; explanation, note

glosador (-ra), s. glossator;
commentator. a. explanatory

glosar, v.t. (lit.) to gloss

glosario, m. glossary

glosopeda, f. foot-and-mouth
disease

glotón (-ona), a. greedy, gluttonous. s. glutton

glotonería, f. gluttony, greed

glucosa, f. (chem.) glucose

glúteo, a. gluteal

glutinoso, a. glutinous

gnomo, m. gnome

gnóstico (-ca), a. and s. gnostic

gobernación, f. government;
governor's office or building;

Home Office (abb. for Ministerio de G.)

gobernador (-ra), a. governing.
s. governor

gobernalle, m. (naut.) helm

gobernante, a. governing. m.
(fam.) self-appointed director or
manager

gobernar, v.t. irr. to govern,
rule; lead, conduct; manage;
steer; control; v.i. govern; (naut.)
obey the tiller. See recomendar

gobierno, m. government (all
meanings); (naut.) helm; control (of machines, business, etc.)

goce, m. enjoyment; possession

godo (da), a. Gothic; aristocratic,
noble. s. Goth; aristocrat

gol, m. (sport) goal

gola, f. throat; gullet; gorget;
tucker, bib

goleta, f. schooner

golf, m. golf. palo de g., golf-
club

golfear, v.i. to loaf

golfería, f. loafing; vagabondage;
loafers

golfo (-fa), m. (geog.) gulf; sea,
ocean. s. ragamuffin, urchin.
m. (fam.) loafer; lounge-lizard;
waster

golilla, f. ruff; m. (fam.) magistrate

golondrina, f. (orn.) swallow.
g. de mar, tern

golosina, f. tit-bit, delicacy;
desire, caprice; pleasant useless
thing

goloso, a. fond of sweet things;
greedy, desirous; appetizing

golpe, m. blow, knock; pull (at
the oars); ring (of a bell); (mech.)
stroke; crowd; fall (of rain, etc.);
mass, torrent; misfortune; shock,
collision; spring lock; beating (of
heart); flap (of pocket); (sew.)
passementerie; surprise; point,
wit; bet. g. de Estado, coup
d'état. g. de fortuna, stroke of
fortune. g. de mano, rising,
insurrection. g. en vago, blow
in the air; disappointment. g.
franco, (sport) free kick. de g.,
suddenly; quickly

golpeadura, f., golpeo, m. knocking, striking; beating, throbbing

golpear, v.t. and v.i. to knock,
strike; beat, throb

gollería, *f.* dainty, tit-bit; (*fam.*) affectation, pernicketiness

gollete, *m.* gullet; neck (of bottle, etc.); (*mech.*) nozzle

goma, *f.* gum, rubber; india-rubber; rubber band

gomero, *a.* gum; rubber. *m.* rubber planter (*S.A.*)

gomorresina, *f.* gum resin

gomoso, *a.* gummy; gum

gonada, *f.* gonad

góndola, *f.* gondola

gondolero, *m.* gondolier

gongorino, *a.* gongoristic, euphuistic

gongorismo, *m.* gongorism

gonorrea, *f.* gonorrhœa

gordo, *a.* fat, stout; greasy, oily; thick (thread, etc.). *m.* animal fat, suet. (*fam.*) **ganar el g.,** to win the fat prize (in a lottery, etc.)

gordura, *f.* grease, fat; stoutness, corpulence

gorgojo, *m.* (*ent.*) weevil; (*fig.*) dwarf

gorgoritear, *v.i.* (*fam.*) to trill, quaver

gorgorito, *m.* (*fam.*) quaver, tremolo, trill (gen. *pl.*)

gorgoteo, *m.* gurgle

gorjear, *v.i.* to trill, warble; twitter; *v.r.* crow (of a baby)

gorjeo, *m.* trill, shake; warbling, twitter; crowing, lisping (of child)

gorra, *f.* cap; bonnet; (*mil.*) busby; hunting-cap. **vivir de g.,** (*fam.*) to sponge

gorrión, *m.* (*orn.*) sparrow

gorrista, *m.* and *f.* (*fam.*) parasite; sponger

gorro, *m.* cap; bonnet

gorrón, *m.* smooth round pebble; (*mech.*) pivot, gudgeon; sponger, waster. *a.* parasitical

gota, *f.* drop (of liquid); (*med.*) gout

gotear, *v.i.* to drop, trickle, drip; leak; drizzle; give or receive in driblets

goteo, *m.* trickling, dripping

gotera, *f.* dripping; trickle; leak; leakage; valance

gótico, *a.* Gothic; noble, illustrious

gotoso (**-sa**), *a.* gouty. *s.* sufferer from gout

goyesco, *a.* Goyesque

gozar, *v.t.* to enjoy, have; take pleasure (in), delight (in); know carnally; *v.i.* (*with de*) enjoy; have, possess

gozne, *m.* hinge

gozo, *m.* enjoyment, possession; gladness, joy; *pl.* couplets in honour of the Virgin or a Saint. (*fam.*) **¡Mi g. en el pozo!** I'm sunk! All is lost!

gozoso, *a.* glad, happy. *adv.* gladly; with pleasure

grabado, *m.* engraver's art; engraving; illustration, picture. **g. al agua fuerte,** etching. **g. al agua tinta,** aquatint

grabador (**-ra**), *s.* engraver

grabadura, *f.* act of engraving

grabar, *v.t.* to engrave; (*fig.*) leave a deep impression

gracejo, *m.* humour, wit; cheerfulness

gracia, *f.* grace; attraction, grace; favour; kindness; jest, witticism; pardon, mercy; pleasant manner; obligingness, willingness; *pl.* thanks, thank you. **gracias a,** thanks to. **¡Gracias a Dios!** Thank God! Thank goodness! **las Gracias,** the Three Graces

grácil, *a.* slender; small

graciosidad, *f.* beauty, perfection, grace

gracioso (**-sa**), *a.* attractive, graceful, elegant; witty, humorous; free, gratis. *s.* (*theat.*) comic rôle; *m.* (*theat.*) fool

grada, *f.* step, stair; gradin, seat, stand, gallery; (*agr.*) harrow; (*naut.*) runway; *pl.* perron, flight of stairs

gradación, *f.* gradation; climax

gradería, *f.* flight of steps

grado, *m.* step, stair; degree (of relationship); university degree; grade, class (in schools); (*fig.*, *geom.*, *phys.*) degree; will, desire. **de buen g.,** willingly. **en sumo g.,** in the highest degree

graduación, *f.* graduation; (*mil.*) rank; rating (of a ship's company). **g. de oficial,** (*mil.*) commission

graduado, *a.* graded; (*mil.*) brevet. *m.* graduate

gradual, *a.* gradual

graduar, *v.t.* to classify; (*mil.*) grade; confer a degree on; measure; test; (*com.*) standardize; (*mech.*) calibrate; *v.r.* graduate, receive a degree. **g. la vista**, to test the eyes. **graduarse de oficial**, (*mil.*) to get one's commission

gráfica, *f.* graph

gráfico, *a.* graphic; vivid

grafito, *m.* (*min.*) graphite

grafología, *f.* graphology

grajear, *v.i.* to caw; gurgle, burble (infants)

grajo, *m.* (*orn.*) rook

gramática, *f.* grammar. (*fam.*) **g. parda**, horse-sense

gramático, *a.* grammatical. *m.* grammarian

gramíneo, *a.* (*bot.*) graminaceous

gramo, *m.* gramme

gramófono, *m.* gramophone

gran, *a. abb.* See **grande**. Used only before *m.* and *f.* singular nouns. big; great; grand

grana, *f.* grain, seed; seed-time; cochineal; kermes; red

granada, *f.* (*mil.*) grenade, shell; pomegranate

granadero, *m.* grenadier; (*fam.*) very tall person

granadilla, *f.* (*bot.*) passion-flower

granadina, *f.* grenadine

granar, *v.i.* (*agr.*) to seed; run to seed

granate, *m.* garnet; dark red

grande, *a.* big, large; great, illustrious; grand. *m.* great man; grandee. **en g.**, in a large size; as a whole; in style, lavishly

grandeza, *f.* largeness; greatness, magnificence; grandeeship; vastness, magnitude

grandilocuencia, *f.* grandiloquence

grandílocuo, *a.* grandiloquent

grandiosidad, *f.* grandeur, greatness

grandioso, *a.* grandiose, magnificent

grandor, *m.* size

granear, *v.t.* (*agr.*) to sow; grain (leather)

granero, *m.* granary; grain-producing country

granito, *m. dim.* small grain; (*min.*) granite; small pimple

granizar, *v.i.* to hail, sleet; *v.i.* and *v.t.* (*fig.*) shower down, deluge

granizo, *m.* hail, sleet; hailstorm; (*fig.*) shower, deluge

granja, *f.* farm; farmhouse; dairy-farm, dairy

granjear, *v.t.* to trade, profit, earn; obtain, acquire; *v.r.* gain, win

granjería, *f.* farming; agricultural profits; earnings, profits

granjero (-ra), *s.* farmer

grano, *m.* (*agr.*) grain; seed; bean (of coffee, etc.); particle; markings, grain (wood, etc.); pimple; grain (measure). (*fig.*, *fam.*) **ir al g.**, to go to the root of the matter; come to the point

granuja, *f.* grape-stone. *m.* (*fam.*) urchin, scamp; knave, rogue

granulación, *f.* (*chem.*, *med.*) granulation

gránulo, *m. dim.* granule

granuloso, *a.* granulous

grapa, *f.* cramp, dowel, clamp; block hook; (*elec.*) cleat; staple

grasa, *f.* fat; grease; oil; dripping, suet

grasiento, *a.* greasy; grubby, dirty

gratificación, *f.* monetary reward; fee, remuneration; gratuity

gratificar, *v.t.* to recompense; please, gratify

gratis, *a.* and *adv.* gratis

gratitud, *f.* gratitude

grato, *a.* pleasing, agreeable; free, gratuitous

gratuito, *a.* gratuitous, free; baseless, unfounded

grava, *f.* gravel; stone-chip, pebble; metal (of a road)

gravamen, *m.* obligation; burden; tax

gravar, *v.t.* to burden, weigh upon; tax

grave, *a.* heavy; important, momentous; grave; dignified, serious; sedate; tiresome; low pitched, low; (*gram.*) grave (accent)

gravedad, *f.* (*phys.*) gravity

gravitación, *f.* (*phys.*) gravitation; seriousness; sedateness; importance; enormity, gravity

gravitar, *v.i.* to gravitate; lean or rest (upon)

gravoso, *a.* grievous, oppressive; onerous; costly

graznar, *v.i.* to caw; cackle; quack; croak; sing stridently, screech

graznido, *m.* caw; cackle; croaking; quack; screech

greca, *f.* Greek Key design

greco (-ca), *a.* and *s.* Greek

grecorromano, *a.* Græco-Roman

gregario, *a.* gregarious

gregoriano, *a.* Gregorian

gregüescos, *m. pl.* wide breeches (sixteenth and seventeenth centuries)

gremial, *a.* pertaining to a guild, union or association. *m.* member of above

gremio, *m.* guild, corporation, union; society, association; general council (universities)

greña, *f.* tangled lock (of hair) (gen. *pl.*); tangle, confused mass

gresca, *f.* uproar, tumult; fight, row

grey, *f.* flock, drove, herd; (*ecc.*) flock, company; people, nation

grial, *m.* grail

griego (-ga), *a.* and *s.* Greek. *m.* Greek language; (*fam.*) gibberish

grieta, *f.* fissure; crevice; chink; split; flaw; vein (in stone, etc.); (*mech.*) leak

grietado, *a.* fissured; cracked

grifo, *m.* griffin; tap; cock

grillo, *m.* (*ent.*) cricket; (*bot.*) shoot; *pl.* fetters, irons, chains; (*fig.*) shackles

grima, *f.* revulsion, horror

gringo (-ga), *s.* (*fam.*) foreigner (scornful)

gripe, *f.* (*med.*) influenza; grippe

gris, *a.* and *m.* grey

grisáceo, *a.* greyish; grizzled (of hair)

grisú, *m.* (*min.*) fire-damp

gritador (-ra), *a.* shouting. *s.* shouter

gritar, *v.i.* to shout, yell, scream; howl down; hoot

gritería, *f.* shouting, yelling, clamour

grito, *m.* shout, yell, shriek, scream. (*fam.*) **poner el g. en el cielo**, to cry to high heaven, complain

groenlandés (-esa), *a.* Greenland. *s.* Greenlander

grog, *m.* grog

grosella, *f.* (*bot.*) currant. **g. blanca**, gooseberry

grosellero, *m.* (*bot.*) currant-bush

grosería, *f.* rudeness; roughness

(of workmanship); ignorance; rusticity

grosero, *a.* coarse; rough; thick; unpolished, rude

grotesco, *a.* grotesque, absurd

grúa, *f.* (*mech.*) crane, hoist, derrick. **g. de pescante**, jib crane. **g. móvil**, travelling crane

gruesa, *f.* twelve dozen, gross

grueso, *a.* stout, corpulent; large. *m.* bulk, body; major portion, majority; thick stroke (of letter); thickness, density. **en g.**, in bulk

grulla, *f.* (*orn.*) crane

grumete, *m.* ship's boy, cabin boy

grumo, *m.* clot; heart (of vegetables); bunch, cluster; bud

gruñido, *m.* grunt; growl

gruñidor, *a.* grunting; growling

gruñir, *v.i.* to grunt; growl; grumble; squeak, creak (doors, etc.). *Pres. Part.* **gruñendo**. *Pres. Ind.* **gruño**, **gruñes**, etc.

grupa, *f.* croup (of a horse); pillion (of a motor-cycle)

grupera, *f.* pillion (of a horse, etc.)

grupo, *m.* knot, cluster; band, group; (*art*) group; (*mech.*) set

gruta, *f.* cavern, grotto

guacamayo, *m.* (*orn.*) macaw

guadamecí, *m.* embossed decorated leather

guadaña, *f.* scythe

guadañar, *v.t.* to cut with a scythe

gualdo, *a.* yellow, golden

gualdrapa, *f.* saddle-cloth, trappings; (*fam.*) tatter, rag

guante, *m.* glove. **g. con puño**, gauntlet glove. **g. de boxeo**, boxing glove. **g. de cabritilla**, kid glove. **arrojar el g.**, to throw down the glove; challenge, defy

guantelete, *m.* gauntlet

guantería, *f.* glove trade, shop or factory

guantero (-ra), *s.* glove maker or seller, glover

guapear, *v.i.* (*fam.*) to make the best of a bad job; (*fam.*) pride oneself on being well dressed

guapeza, *f.* prettiness; (*fam.*) resolution, courage; (*fam.*) smartness or showiness of dress; boastful act or behaviour

guapo, *a.* pretty; handsome; (*fam.*) daring, enterprising; (*fam.*) smart, well dressed, foppish; (*fam.*) handsome. *m.* braggart, brawler; beau, lover; (*fam.*) fine fellow, son-of-a-gun

guarda, *m.* and *f.* keeper, guard. *f.* guarding, keeping, custodianship, preservation; guardianship; observance, fulfilment; fly-leaf, end page (books); ward (of locks or keys); (*mech.*) guard; guard (of fan)

guardabarrera, *m.* and *f.* gate-keeper at a level crossing (railway)

guardabarro, *m.* mudguard

guardabosque, *m.* gamekeeper

guardabrisa, *m.* (*aut.*) wind-screen; glass candle shield

guardacostas, *m.* coast-guard; (*naut.*) revenue cutter

guardafrenos, *m.* brakeman (railway)

guardagujas, *m.* pointsman (railway)

guardainfante, *m.* farthingale, crinoline

guardalmacén, *m.* and *f.* store-keeper

guardameta, *m.* goalkeeper

guardamuebles, *m.* furniture repository

guardapelo, *m.* locket

guardapolvo, *m.* dust-sheet; light overcoat; inner case of a pocket watch

guardar, *v.t.* to keep; preserve, retain; maintain, observe; save, put aside, lay up; defend, protect; guard; *v.r.* (*with de*) avoid. **guard against**. **g. silencio**, to keep silence. **¡Guarda!** Take care! **¡Guárdate del agua mansa!** Still waters run deep!

guardarropa, *m.* cloak-room. *m.* and *f.* cloak-room attendant; keeper of the wardrobe. *m.* wardrobe, clothes press

guardarropía, *f.* theatrical wardrobe

guardavía, *m.* signalman (railway)

guardería, *f.* day nursery

guardia, *f.* guard, escort; protection; (*mil.*, *naut.*) watch; regiment, body (of troops); guard (fencing). *m.* guardsman; policeman. **g. de asalto**, armed police.

g. de corps, royal bodyguard. **g. civil**, Civil Guard. **g. marina**, midshipman. **g. municipal**, city police. (*mil.*) **montar la g.**, to mount guard

guardián (-ana), *s.* keeper; custodian; warden. *m.* watchman; gaoler

guardilla, *f.* attic, garret

guarecer, *v.t. irr.* to shelter, protect, aid; preserve, keep; cure; *v.r.* take shelter. See conocer

guarida, *f.* lair, den; refuge, shelter; haunt, resort

guarismo, *m.* (*math.*) figure; number, numeral

guarnecer, *v.t. irr.* to decorate, adorn; (*sew.*) trim, face, border; (*mil.*) garrison; (*mas.*) plaster. See conocer

guarnecido, *m.* (*mas.*) plastering

guarnición, *f.* (*sew.*) trimming, ornament, border, fringe; (*mech.*) packing; (*mil.*) garrison; setting (jewels); guard (of sword, etc.); *pl.* harness; fittings

guarnir, (*naut.*) *v.t.* to reeve

guasa, *f.* (*fam.*) dullness, boringness; joke. **de g.**, jokingly

guasón, *a.* (*fam.*) dull, tedious; humorous, jocose

guatemalteco (-ca), *a.* and *s.* Guatemalan

guau, *m.* bow-wow, bark of a dog

guayaba, *f.* (*bot.*) guava; guava jelly

gubernamental, *a.* governmental

gubernativo, *a.* governmental; administrative

gubia, *f.* (*carp.*) chisel; gouge

guedeja, *f.* long tress or lock of hair; forelock; lion's mane

güelfo (-fa), *a.* and *s.* Guelph

guerra, *f.* war; struggle, fight; (*fig.*) hostility. (*fam.*) **dar g.**, to give trouble, annoy. **en g. con**, at war with

guerrear, *v.i.* to make war, fight; oppose

guerrero (-ra), *a.* war, martial; warrior; (*fam.*) troublesome, annoying. *s.* fighter. *m.* warrior, soldier

guerrillear, *v.i.* to wage guerrilla warfare; fight as a guerrilla

guerrillero, *m.* guerrilla fighter

guía, *m.* and *f.* guide, conductor; adviser, director. *f.* guide, aid; guide book; (*mech.*) guide, slide;

directory; signpost. **g. de ferro-carriles,** railway time-table. **g. de teléfonos,** telephone directory

guiar, *v.t.* to guide; lead, conduct; *(mech.)* work, control; *(aut.)* drive; pilot; teach, direct, govern

guija, *f.* pebble

guijarro, *m.* smooth, round pebble; boulder; cobblestone

guijarroso, *a.* pebbly, cobbled

guijo, *m.* gravel; granite chips; pebble

guillotina, *f.* guillotine; paper-cutting machine

guillotinar, *v.t.* to guillotine, decapitate

guinda, *f.* *(bot.)* mazard cherry; *(naut.)* height of masts

guindo, *m.* mazard cherry tree

guinea, *f.* guinea

guinga, *f.* gingham

guiñada, *f.* wink; blink; *(naut.)* yaw

guiñapo, *m.* rag, tatter; sloven, ragamuffin

guiñar, *v.t.* to wink; blink; *(naut.)* yaw; *v.r.* wink at each other

guiño, *m.* wink

guión, *m.* royal standard; banner; summary; leader of a dance; *(gram.)* hyphen; subtitle (in films)

guipuzcoano (-na), *a.* and *s.* Guipuzcoan (from Spanish province of Guipuzcoa)

guirigay, *m.* *(fam.)* gibberish; uproar, babble

guirnalda, *f.* garland, wreath

guisa, *f.* way, manner; will, desire. **a g. de,** in the manner or fashion of

guisado, *m.* *(cul.)* stew; cooked dish

guisante, *m.* *(agr.)* pea; pea plant. **g. de olor,** sweet-pea

guisar, *v.t.* to cook; stew; *(cul.)* prepare, dress; adjust, arrange

guiso, *m.* cooked dish

guitarra, *f.* guitar

guitarrista, *m.* and *f.* guitar player

guito, *a.* vicious (horses, mules)

gula, *f.* greed, gluttony

gusaniento, *a.* worm-eaten; maggoty

gusano, *m.* worm; caterpillar; maggot; meek, downtrodden person. **g. de seda,** silkworm

gusanoso, *a.* wormy

gustar, *v.t.* to taste, savour; try; *v.i.* be pleasing, give pleasure; like. Notice impersonal construction (e.g. **Me gusta el libro,** I like the book (the book is pleasing to me). **La película no me gustó,** I didn't like the film). **g. de,** to like, is used only when a person is the subject

gusto, *m.* taste; flavour, savour; pleasure, delight; will, desire; discrimination, taste, style, fashion, manner; whim, caprice. **a g.,** to taste; according to taste. **con mucho g.,** with great pleasure. **dar g.,** to please. **de buen g.,** in good taste

gustoso, *a.* savoury, palatable; willingly, with pleasure; pleasant, agreeable

gutagamba, *f.* gamboge (yellow)

gutapercha, *f.* gutta-percha

H

haba, *f.* broad bean; bean (coffee, cocoa, etc.). **h. de las Indias,** sweet-pea. **Esas son habas contadas,** That's a certainty

habanero (-ra), habano (-na), *a.* and *s.* Havanese, from Havana. *m.* **habano,** Havana cigar

habar, *m.* bean field

haber, *m.* estate, property (gen. *pl.*); income; *(com.)* credit balance. **h. monedado,** specie

haber, *v.t. irr.* to have; catch, lay hands on (e.g. **El reo fué habido,** The criminal was caught). *v. aux.* (e.g. **Hemos escrito la carta,** We have written the letter). *v. impers.* to happen, take place; be. *3rd pers. sing., Pres. Ind.* **ha** is replaced by **hay,** meaning there is or there are (e.g. **No hay naranjas en las tiendas,** There are no oranges in the shops). In certain weather expressions, **hay** means it is (e.g. **Hay luna,** It is moonlight). Used of expressions of time, **haber** means to elapse and **ha** (*3rd pers. sing., Pres. Ind.*) has adverbial force of " ago " (e.g.

muchos días ha, many days ago). **h. de,** to be necessary (less strong than **h. que**) (e.g. **Hemos de verle mañana,** We must see him to-morrow. **He de hacer el papel de Manolo,** I am to play the part of Manolo). **h. que,** to be unavoidable, be essential. With this construction the form **hay** is used (e.g. **Hay que darse prisa,** We (or one) must hurry. **No hay que enojarse,** There's no need to get annoyed). **no h., más que pedir,** to leave nothing to be desired. **no h. tal,** to be no such thing. (*fam.*) **habérselas con,** to quarrel or fall out with. **Hubo una vez,** ... Once upon a time ... **No hay de qué,** Don't mention it!; Not at all!; You're welcome! **No hay para que** ... There's no point in ... **poco tiempo ha,** a little while ago. ¿ **Qué hay ?** What's the matter ?; What's the news ? ¿ **Qué hay de nuevo ?** What's the news ? *Pres. Ind.* **he, has, ha, hemos, habéis, han.** *Fut.* **habré,** etc. *Condit.* **habría,** etc. *Preterite* **hube, hubiste, hubo, hubimos, hubisteis, hubieron.** *Pres. Subjunc.* **haya,** etc. *Imperf. Subjunc.* **hubiese,** etc.

habichuela, *f.* kidney-bean

hábil, *a.* clever; skilful; able; lawful

habilidad, *f.* ability; skill; accomplishment; craftsmanship, workmanship

habilidoso, *a.* accomplished; able; skilful

habilitación, *f.* habilitation; paymastership; equipment; furnishing

habilitado, *m.* paymaster

habilitar, *v.t.* to qualify; equip: furnish; habilitate; enable; (*com.*) capitalize

habitabilidad, *f.* habitableness

habitable, *a.* habitable

habitación, *f.* habitation, dwelling; room in a house; residence; (*bot., zool.*) habitat; caretaking

habitante, *m.* inhabitant

habitar, *v.t.* to inhabit, reside in

hábito, *m.* attire; (*ecc.*) habit; use, custom; skill, facility; *pl.* vestments; gown, robe. **tomar el h.,** to become a monk or nun

habitual, *a.* habitual, usual

habituar, *v.t.* to accustom; *v.r.* accustom oneself; grow used (to)

habitud, *f.* habit, custom; connection, relationship

habla, *f.* speech; language; dialect; discourse. **al h.,** within speaking distance

hablado, *a.* spoken. **bien h.,** well-spoken; courteous. **mal h.,** ill-spoken; rude

hablador (-ra), *a.* talkative; gossiping. *s.* chatterbox; gossip

habladuría, *f.* gossip; impertinent chatter

hablanchín, *a.* (*fam.*) chattering, gossiping

hablar, *v.i.* to speak; converse; express oneself; arrange; (*with de*) speak about, discuss; gossip about, criticize; (*with por*) intercede on behalf of; *v.t.* speak (a language); say, speak; *v.r.* speak to one another. **no hablarse,** to be not on speaking terms. **h. a gritos,** to shout. **h. alto,** to speak loudly or in strong terms. **h. bien** (*or* **mal**), to be well (or ill) spoken; be polite (or rude). **h. claro,** to speak frankly. **h. consigo** *or* **h. entre sí,** to talk to oneself. (*fam.*) **h. cristiano,** to speak clearly or intelligibly (gen. in the mother tongue of the listener). **hablarlo todo,** to talk too much. **h. por h.,** to talk for talking's sake. (*fam.*) **h. por los codos,** to chatter. **h. sin ton ni son,** to speak foolishly

hablilla, *f.* rumour, tittle-tattle, gossip

hablista, *m.* and *f.* stylist

hacecillo, *m.* small sheaf; small bundle; (*bot.*) fascicle; beam (of light)

hacedero, *a.* feasible, practicable

hacedor, *m.* maker; steward, manager; Creator

hacendado (-da), *a.* landed. *s.* land-owner; (*S.A.*) cattle-owner

hacendista, *m.* political economist

hacendoso, *a.* diligent, hardworking

hacer, *v.t. irr.* to make; fashion, form, construct; do, perform; cause, effect; arrange, put right; contain; accustom, harden; pack (luggage); **imagine, invent,**

create; improve, perfect; compel, oblige; deliver (speeches); compose; earn; (*math.*) add up to; suppose, imagine (e.g. **Sus padres hacían a María en casa,** Her parents imagined that Mary was at home); put into practice, execute; play the part of or act like (e.g. **h. el gracioso,** to play the buffoon); shed, cast (e.g. **El roble hace sombra,** The oak casts a shadow); assemble, convoke (meetings gatherings); give off, produce (e.g. **La chimenea hace humo,** The chimney is smoking); perform (plays); (*with el, la, lo and some nouns*) pretend to be (e.g. **Se hizo el desconocido,** He pretended to be ignorant). (h. followed by infin. in Spanish sometimes becomes past participle in English (e.g. **Lo hice h.,** I had it done).) *v.i.* to matter, be important, signify (e.g. **Su llegada no hace nada al caso,** His arrival makes no difference to the case. **Se me hace muy poco** . . . It matters to me very little . . .); be fitting or suitable; concern, be pertinent; match, go with; agree, be in harmony; (*with de*) act as, discharge duties of temporarily (e.g. **h. de camarero,** to be a temporary waiter); (*with por*) try to, attempt to (e.g. **Haremos por decírselo,** We shall try to tell him). *v.i. impers.* Used in expressions concerning: 1. the weather. 2. lapse of time. English uses verb " to be " in both cases, e.g.:

1. **hace buen** (*or* **mal**) **tiempo,** it is fine (or bad) weather. **hace mucho frío,** it is very cold. **hace sol,** it is sunny. **hace viento,** it is windy. **¿Qué tiempo hace?** What is the weather like?

2. **hace** + an expression of time is followed by **que** introducing a clause (e.g. **Hace dos horas que llegamos,** It is two hours since we arrived) or **hace** + an expression of time may be followed by **desde** + a noun (e.g. **Hace dos años desde aquel día,** It is two years since that day)

When an action or state which has begun in the past is still continuing in the present, the Spanish verb is in the Pres. Ind., whereas the English verb is in the Perfect (e.g. **Hace un mes que la veo todos los días,** I have been seeing her every day for a month). This rule holds good with other tenses. English Pluperfect, Future Perfect, Conditional Perfect become in Spanish Imperfect, Future, Conditional respectively. (*naut.*) **h. agua,** to leak. **h. alarde de,** to boast of. **h. a todo,** to have many uses; be adaptable. **h. bancarrota,** to go bankrupt. (*fam.*) **h. calceta,** to knit. **h. cara** *or* **frente a,** to face; resist. **h. caso,** to take notice, mind (e.g. **¡No hagas caso!** Never mind!). (*fig., fam.*) **h. buena,** to justify. **h. cuentas,** to reckon up. **h. daño,** to harm. (*fam.*) **h. de las suyas,** to behave in his usual manner or play one of his usual tricks. **h. diligencias por,** to endeavour to. **h. fiesta,** to take a holiday. **h. fuerza,** to struggle. **h. fuerza a,** (*fig.*) to do violence to (e.g. **Hizo fuerza a sus creencias,** He did violence to his beliefs). **h. h.,** to cause to be made (e.g. **He hecho hacer un vestido,** I have had a dress made). **h. juego,** to make a set, match (e.g. **El sombrero hace juego con el traje,** The hat goes with the dress). **h. la corte (a),** to court, woo. (*fig., fam.*) **h. la vista gorda,** to turn a blind eye. **h. mal,** to do wrong; be harmful (food, etc.). **h. pedazos,** to break (also *fig.*). **h. pinos** (*or* **pinitos**) to totter; toddle; stagger. (*aer.*) **h. rizos,** to loop the loop. **h. saber,** to make known; notify. **h. seguir,** to forward (letters). **h. señas,** to make signs (wave, beckon, etc.). (*fam.*) **h. una que sea sonada,** to cause a big scandal. (*fam.*) **haberla hecho buena,** to have made a bloomer. **¡Hágame el favor!** Please! *Pres. Ind.* **hago,** etc. *Fut.* **haré,** etc. *Condit.* **haría,** etc. *Imperat.* **haz, haga, hagamos, haced,**

hagan. *Preterite* **hice, hiciste, hizo, hicimos, hicisteis, hicieron.** *Pres. Subjunc.* **haga,** etc. *Imperf. Subjunc.* **hiciese,** etc.

hacerse, *v.r. irr.* to become (e.g. **Se ha hecho muy importante,** It (or he) has become very important); grow up (e.g. **Miguel se ha hecho hombre,** Michael has grown up (become a man)); develop, mature; pass oneself off as, pretend to be; (*with prep. a*) become accustomed to or used to (e.g. **Me haré a este clima,** I shall grow used to this climate); withdraw or retire to (of places); (*with de or con*) provide oneself with. **h. a la vela,** to set sail. **h. a (uno),** to seem (e.g. **Eso que me cuentas se me hace increíble,** What you tell me seems incredible). (*fam.*) **h. chiquito,** to sing small, be modest. **h. tarde,** to grow late; (*fig.*) be too late. See **hacer**

hacia, *prep.* towards, near, about. **h. adelante,** forward, onward

hacienda, *f.* country estate, land; property; *pl.* domestic tasks; cattle. **h. pública,** public funds. (**Ministerio de**) **H.,** The Exchequer

hacina, *f.* (*agr.*) stack; heap, pile

hacinamiento, *m.* stacking, piling; accumulation

hacinar, *v.t.* (*agr.*) to stack sheaves; accumulate, amass; pile up, heap

hacha, *f.* large candle; torch; axe. **h. pequeña,** hatchet

hachazo, *m.* stroke of an axe

hache, *f.* name of the letter H

hachero, *m.* candlestick; woodcutter, axe-man

hacho, *m.* torch; beacon

hada, *f.* fairy

hado, *m.* fate; destiny

hagiografía, *f.* hagiography

hagiógrafo, *m.* hagiographer

haitiano (-na), *a.* and *s.* of or from Haiti

halagar, *v.t.* to caress; flatter; coax; please, delight

halago, *m.* flattery; coaxing; caress; source of pleasure, delight

halagüeño, *a.* flattering; pleasing; caressing; hopeful, promising

halar, *v.t.* (*naut.*) to haul, tow

halcón, *m.* (*orn.*) falcon

halconero, *m.* hawker, hunter

hálito, *m.* breath; vapour; (*poet.*) breeze

halitosis, *f.* halitosis

halo, *m.* halo

hallado, *a.* and *Past Part.* found, met. **bien h.,** welcome; happy, contented. **mal h.,** unwelcome; uneasy, discontented

hallador (-ra), *s.* finder

hallar, *v.t.* to find; meet; observe; discover; find out; *v.r.* be present; be, find oneself

hallazgo, *m.* finding; thing found; finder's reward

hamaca, *f.* hammock

hamadríade, *f.* hamadryad

hambre, *f.* hunger; famine; desire, yearning. **tener h.,** to be hungry

hambriento, *a.* hungry; famished; (*fig.*) starved (of affection, etc.)

hamburgués (-esa), *a.* and *s.* of or from Hamburg

hamo, *m.* fish-hook

hampa, *f.* rogue's life; gang of rogues; underworld, slum

hangar, *m.* hangar

hanseático, *a.* Hanseatic

haragán (-ana), *a.* lazy, idle. *s.* idler, lazybones

harapiento, *a.* ragged

harapo, *m.* tatter, rag

haraposo, *a.* ragged

harén, *m.* harem

harina, *f.* flour; powder; farina. (*fam.*) **ser h. de otro costal,** to be a very different matter

harinero, *a.* relating to flour. *m.* flour merchant; flour bin

harinoso, *a.* floury, mealy; farinaceous

harmónica, *f.* (*phys., math.*) harmonic

harnero, *m.* sieve

harón, *a.* slothful, slow; lazy, idle

harpillera, *f.* sackcloth, sacking

hartar, *v.t.* to satiate; tire, annoy; satisfy the appetite; shower (with blows, etc.)

hartazgo, *m.* satiety

harto, *a.* satiated; tired (of). *adv.* enough

hartura, *f.* satiety; abundance

hasta, *prep.* until; as far as; down

or up to. *conjunc.* also, even. **h. la vista**, au revoir. **h. mañana**, until to-morrow

hastial, *m.* gable, end wall; boor, lout

hastío, *m.* loathing; distaste; nausea

hato, *m.* personal clothing; herd of cattle; gang (of suspicious characters); crowd, mob; (*fam.*) group, party. (*fam.*) **liar el h.**, to pack up

hay, there is; there are. See **haber**

haya, *f.* beech tree; beech wood

hayal, *m.* wood of beech trees, plantation of beech

hayuco, *m.* beechmast

haz, *m.* bundle, sheaf; (*mil.*) file; *pl.* fasces. *f.* visage; surface, face. **h. de la tierra**, face of the earth. **h. de luz**, beam of light. (*fig.*) **ser de dos haces**, to be two-faced

haz, 2*nd pers. Imperat.* hacer

hazaña, *f.* exploit, prowess

hazañoso, *a.* heroic, dauntless, courageous

hazmerreír, *m.* (*fam.*) laughing-stock

he, *interj.* and *adv.* halloa! hist!; behold! ¡**Heme aquí!** Here I am. **he aquí**, here is . . .

hebilla, *f.* buckle

hebra, *f.* thread; fibre; flesh; (*min.*) vein, streak; filament (textiles); grain (wood); *pl.* (*poet.*) hair. (*fam.*) **pegar la h.**, to start a conversation

hebraísmo, *m.* Hebraism

hebraísta, *m.* Hebraist

hebreo (**-ea**), *a.* Hebraic, Jewish. *s.* Jew. *m.* Hebrew (language)

hecatombe, *f.* hecatomb; slaughter, massacre

hectárea, *f.* hectare

hectógrafo, *m.* hectograph

hectogramo, *m.* hectogramme

hectolitro, *m.* hectolitre

hectovatio, *m.* (*elec.*) hectowatt

hechicería, *f.* sorcery; spell, enchantment

hechicero, *a.* bewitching, magic; charming, attractive

hechizar, *v.t.* to bewitch; charm, attract, delight

hechizo, *m.* magic spell; fascination, charm; delight, pleasure

hecho, *a.* developed, mature; accustomed, used; perfected, finished; ready-made. **h. una furia**, like a fury, very angry. **bien h.**, well-made, well-proportioned; well or rightly done

hecho, *m.* deed, action; fact; happening, event. **Los Hechos de los Apóstoles**, The Acts of the Apostles

hechura, *f.* making, make; creation; form; figure, statue; (*lit.*) composition; build (of body); (*fig.*) puppet, creature; *pl.* price paid for work done. **de h. sastre**, *a.* tailor-made

heder, *v.i. irr.* to stink; be intolerable. See **entender**

hediondez, *f.* stink, stench

hediondo, *a.* stinking; intolerable, pestilential; obscene

hedonismo, *m.* hedonism

hedonista, *m.* and *f.* hedonist

hegelianismo, *m.* Hegelianism

hegeliano, *a.* Hegelian

hegemonía, *f.* hegemony

helada, *f.* frost. **h. blanca**, hoar-frost

heladera, *f.* refrigerator

helado, *a.* frozen; ice-cold; astounded, disdainful. *m.* iced drink; water ice, ice-cream

helamiento, *m.* icing; freezing

helar, *v.t. irr.* to freeze; ice, chill; astound; discourage; *v.r.* become iced; freeze; become ice-cold. *v. impers.* to freeze. See **acertar**

helecho, *m.* (*bot.*) fern

helénico, *a.* Hellenic

helenismo, *m.* Hellenism

helenista, *m.* and *f.* Hellenist

helenizar, *v.t.* to Hellenize

hélice, *f.* spiral, helical line; screw, propeller; (*geom.*) helix; (*ast.*) Ursa Major

helicón, *m.* helicon

helicóptero, *m.* (*aer.*) helicopter

helio, *m.* (*chem.*) helium

heliógrafo, *m.* heliograph

helioscopio, *m.* helioscope

helióstato, *m.* heliostat

helioterapia, *f.* (*med.*) heliotherapy

heliotropismo, *m.* (*bot.*) heliotropism

heliotropo, *m.* (*bot.*) heliotrope; (*min.*) agate

helvecio (**-ia**), *a.* and *s.* Swiss, Helvetian

hembra, *f.* female; (*fam.*) woman; nut of a screw; eye of a hook. (*fam.*) **una real h.,** a fine figure of a woman

hemiciclo, *m.* hemicycle; centre space of Spanish Congress Hall

hemisférico, *a.* hemispherical

hemisferio, *m.* hemisphere

hemistiquio, *m.* hemistitch

hemofilia, *f.* (*med.*) hæmophilia

hemoglobina, *f.* hæmoglobin

hemorragia, *f.* hæmorrhage

hemorroides, *f.* (*med.*) hæmorrhoids

henchido, *a.* swollen

henchimiento, *m.* swelling; inflation; filling

henchir, *v.t. irr.* to fill; stuff; swell. *Pres. ·Ind.* **hincho, hinches, hinche, hinchen.** *Pres. Part.* **hinchiendo.** *Pres. Subjunc.* **hincha,** etc. *Imperf. Subjunc.* **hinchiese,** etc. *Imperat.* **hinche, hincha, hinchamos, henchid, hinchan**

hendecasílabo, *a.* hendecasyllabic

hendedura, *f.* fissure; rift

hender, *v.t. irr.* to split, crack; (*fig.*) cleave (air, water, etc.); make one's way through. See **entender**

hendidura, *f.* split, fissure, crack, chink

henil, *m.* hayloft

heno, *m.* hay

hepático, *a.* hepatic

heptágono, *m.* (*geom.*) heptagon

heptarquía, *f.* heptarchy

heráldica, *f.* heraldry

heráldico, *a.* heraldic

heraldo, *m.* herald; King-of-Arms; harbinger

herbáceo, *a.* herbaceous

herbaje, *m.* herbage; pasture, grass; thick woollen cloth

herbario, *m.* herbalist, botanist; herbarium. *a.* herbal

herbívoro, *a.* herbivorous

herbolaria, *f.* herbal

herborizar, *v.i.* to botanize

hercúleo, *a.* Herculean

heredad, *f.* landed property; country estate

heredar, *v.t.* to inherit; make a deed of gift to; inherit characteristics, etc.; take as heir

heredera, *f.* heiress

heredero, *m.* heir; inheritor. **h.**

aparente, heir apparent. **presunto h.,** heir presumptive

hereditario, *a.* hereditary

hereje, *m.* and *f.* heretic

herejía, *f.* heresy

herencia, *f.* inheritance; heredity; heritage

heresiarca, *m.* heresiarch

herético, *a.* heretical

herida, *f.* wound; insult; anguish. **h. contusa,** contusion. **h. penetrante,** deep wound

herir, *v.t. irr.* .to wound; strike, harm; (*fig.*) pierce (of sun's rays); (*fig.*) pluck (strings of a musical instrument); impress (senses); affect (emotions); offend (gen. words). *Pres. Part.* **hiriendo.** *Pres. Ind.* **hiero, hieres, hiere, hieren.** *Preterite* **hirió, hirieron.** *Pres. Subjunc.* **hiera, hieras, hiera, hiramos, hiráis, hieran.** *Imperf. Subjunc.* **hiriese,** etc.

hermafrodita, *a.* and *m.* and *f.* hermaphrodite

hermafroditismo, *m.* hermaphroditism

hermana, *f.* sister; twin, pair (of things). **h. de leche,** fostersister. **h. política,** sister-in-law

hermanar, *v.t.* to join; mate; harmonize; *v.t.* and *v.r.* be spiritual brother of, be compatible

hermanastra, *f.* stepsister

hermanastro, *m.* stepbrother

hermandad, *f.* brotherhood; friendship, intimacy; relationship (one thing to another); confraternity. **Santa H.,** Spanish rural police force instituted in the fifteenth century

hermano, *m.* brother; pair, twin (of things); (*ecc.*) brother. **h. político,** brother-in-law

hermético, *a.* hermetic

hermosear, *v.t.* to embellish, beautify, adorn

hermoso, *a.* beautiful; shapely; handsome; fine, wonderful (weather, view, etc.)

hermosura, *f.* beauty; pleasantness, attractiveness, perfection of form; belle

hernia, *f.* hernia

héroe, *m.* hero

heroicidad, *f.* heroism

heroico, *a.* heroic

heroína, *f.* heroine

heroismo, *m.* heroism

herpes, *m. pl.* or *f. pl.* herpes

herrada, *f.* pail

herradero, *m.* branding of live-stock

herrador, *m.* farrier

herradura, *f.* horseshoe

herraje, *m.* ironwork

herramienta, *f.* tool; set of tools

herrar, *v.t. irr.* to shoe horses; brand (cattle); decorate with iron. See **acertar**

herrería, *f.* forge; ironworks; blacksmith's shop; clamour, tumult, confusion

herrero, *m.* smith

herrete, *m.* ferrule, tag

herrumbre, *f.* rust; taste of iron

herrumbroso, *a.* rusty

hertziano, *a.* Hertzian

hervidero, *m.* boiling, bubbling; (*fig.*) ebullition; swarm, crowd

hervir, *v.i. irr.* to boil; foam and froth (sea); seethe (emotions); surge (crowds); (*with en*) abound in, swarm with. See **sentir**

hervor, *m.* boiling; ebullition, vigour, zest; seething, agitation

hesitación, *f.* hesitation, doubt, uncertainty

hesitar, *v.i.* to hesitate, vacillate

Héspero, *m.* (*ast.*) Hesperus

heteo (-ea), *a.* and *s.* Hittite

heterodina, *a.* (*f.*) (*rad.*) heterodyne

heterodoxia, *f.* heterodoxy

heterodoxo, *a.* heterodox

heterogeneidad, *f.* heterogeneity

heterogéneo, *a.* heterogeneous

hético, *a.* hectic, consumptive

hexaedro, *m.* (*geom.*) hexahedron

hexagonal, *a.* hexagonal

hexágono, *m.* hexagon

hexámetro, *m.* hexameter

hez, *f.* (gen. *pl.* **heces**) lees, dregs

hiato, *m.* hiatus

hibernal, *a.* wintry

hibernés, *a.* Hibernian, Irish

hibisco, *m.* (*bot.*) hibiscus

hibridación, *f.* hybridization

hibridismo, *m.* hybridism

híbrido, *a.* and *m.* hybrid

hidalgo (-ga), *s.* noble, aristocrat. *a.* noble; illustrious; generous

hidalguía, *f.* nobility; generosity, nobility of spirit

hidra, *f.* (*zool.*) hydra; poisonous snake; (*ast.*) Hydra

hidratar, *v.t.* (*chem.*) to hydrate

hidrato, *m.* hydrate. **h. de carbono,** carbo-hydrate

hidráulica, *f.* hydraulics

hidráulico, *a.* hydraulic

hidroavión, *m.* flying-boat

hidrocarburo, *m.* (*chem.*) hydro-carbon

hidrocéfalo, *a.* (*med.*) hydrocephalic

hidrodinámica, *f.* hydrodynamics

hidroeléctrico, *a.* hydroelectric

hidrofobia, *f.* hydrophobia; rabies

hidrógeno, *m.* hydrogen

hidrografía, *f.* hydrography

hidrología, *f.* hydrology

hidromancia, *f.* hydromancy

hidropático, *a.* hydropathic

hidropesía, *f.* dropsy

hidrópico, *a.* dropsical

hidroplano, *m.* seaplane

hidroquinona, *f.* (*chem.*) hydroquinone

hidroscopio, *m.* hydroscope

hidrostática, *f.* hydrostatics

hidroterapia, *f.* hydrotherapy

hiedra, *f.* ivy

hiel, *f.* gall, bile, bitterness, affliction; *pl.* troubles

hielo, *m.* ice, frost; freezing, icing; stupefaction; indifference, coldness; (*fam.*) **estar hecho un h.,** to be as cold as ice

hiena, *f.* hyena

hierático, *a.* hieratical

hierba, *f.* grass; small plant; herb. **h. cana,** groundsel. **mala h.,** weed

hierbabuena, *f.* (*bot.*) mint

hierofante, *m.* hierophant

hierro, *m.* iron; brand with hot iron; iron or steel head of lance, etc.; instrument or shape made of iron; weapon of war. *pl.* fetters. **h. colado,** cast-iron. **h. dulce,** wrought-iron. **h. en planchas,** sheet-iron. **h. viejo,** scrap-iron

hígado, *m.* liver; courage

higiene, *f.* hygiene; cleanliness, neatness. **h. privada,** personal hygiene. **h. pública,** public health

higiénico, *a.* hygienic

higo, *m.* fig. **h. chumbo,** prickly pear

higrómetro, *m.* hygrometer

higuera, *f.* fig tree

hija, *f.* daughter; native of a place; offspring

hijastro (-ra), *s.* stepchild

hijo, *m.* son; child; native of a place; offspring; shoot, sprout; *pl.* descendants. **h. de la cuna,** foundling. **h. de leche,** foster-child. **h. natural,** illegitimate child. **h. político,** son-in-law

hijuela, *f.* little daughter; small mattress; small drain; side road; accessory, subordinate thing; piece of material for widening a garment

hila, *f.* row, line; gut; (*surg.*) lint (gen. *pl.*)

hilacha, *f.* thread ravelled from cloth; fibre, filament. **h. de vidrio,** spun glass

hilado, *m.* spinning; thread, yarn

hilandería, *f.* spinning; spinning-mill; mill. **h. de algodón,** cotton mill

hilandero (-ra), *s.* spinner

hilar, *v.t.* to spin; reason, infer, discourse

hilaridad, *f.* hilarity; quiet happiness

hilaza, *f.* yarn

hilera, *f.* line, file, row; fine yarn; (*mil.*) file, rank; (*met.*) wire drawer; (*mas.*) course (of bricks)

hilo, *m.* thread; linen; wire; mesh (spiders, silkworm's web, etc.); edge (of a blade); thin stream (of liquid); thread (of discourse)

hilván, *m.* (*sew.*) basting; tack

hilvanar, *v.t.* (*sew.*) to baste

himalayo, *a.* Himalayan

himen, *m.* (*anat.*) hymen

himeneo, *m.* marriage, wedding

himnario, *m.* hymnal

himno, *m.* hymn

hin, *m.* whinny, neigh

hincapié, *m.* foothold. **hacer h.,** to insist, make a stand

hincar, *v.t.* to thrust in; drive in, sink; *v.r.* kneel. **h. el diente,** to bite. **h. la uña,** to scratch. **hincarse de rodillas,** to kneel down

hinchado, *a.* puffed up, vain; pompous, high-flown, redundant (style)

hinchar, *v.t.* to inflate; puff out (the chest); swell (river, etc.); exaggerate (events); *v.r.* swell, grow vain, be puffed up

hinchazón, *f.* swelling; vanity,

presumption; pomposity, euphuism (style)

hiniesta, *f.* Spanish broom

hinojo, *m.* (*bot.*) fennel; knee. **de hinojos,** on bended knee

hipar, *v.i.* to hiccough; pant (of dogs); be over-anxious; be over-tired; sob, cry

hipérbole, *f.* hyperbole

hiperbólico, *a.* hyperbolical

hipercrítico, *m.* hypercritic. *a.* hypercritical

hipertrofiarse, *v.r.* to hyper-trophy

hípico, *a.* equine

hipnosis, *f.* hypnosis

hipnótico, *a.* hypnotic. *m.* hypnotic drug

hipnotismo, *m.* hypnotism

hipnotización, *f.* hypnotization

hipnotizar, *v.t.* to hypnotize

hipo, *m.* hiccough; sob; longing, desire; dislike, disgust

hipocondría, *f.* hypochondria

hipocondríaco (-ca), *a.* hypochondriacal. *s.* hypochondriac

hipocrático, *a.* Hippocratic

hipocresía, *f.* hypocrisy

hipócrita, *a.* hypocritical. *m.* and *f.* hypocrite

hipodérmico, *a.* hypodermic

hipódromo, *m.* hippodrome, race-course

hipofosfato, *m.* hypophosphate

hipógrifo, *m.* (*myth.*) hypogryph

hipopótamo, *m.* hippopotamus

hipostático, *a.* hypostatic

hipoteca, *f.* mortgage

hipotecable, *a.* mortgageable

hipotecar, *v.t.* to mortgage

hipotecario, *a.* belonging to a mortgage

hipotenusa, *f.* (*geom.*) hypote-nuse

hipótesis, *f.* hypothesis

hipotético, *a.* hypothetical

hirsuto, *a.* hirsute, hairy

hirviente, *a.* boiling

hisca, *f.* bird-lime

hisopear, *v.t.* (*ecc.*) to sprinkle, asperse

hisopo, *m.* (*bot.*) hyssop; (*ecc.*) hyssop, sprinkler

hispánico, *a.* Spanish

hispanismo, *m.* Hispanism

hispanista, *m.* and *f.* Hispanist

hispanoamericano (-na), *a.* and *s.* Hispano-American

histeria, *f.* hysteria

histérico, *a.* hysterical; hysteric

histerismo, *m.* (*med.*) hysteria

histología, *f.* histology

histólogo, *m.* histologist

historia, *f.* history; narrative, story; tale; (*fam.*) gossip (gen. *pl.*); (*art*) historical piece. **h. natural**, natural history. **h. sagrada**, biblical history. (*fig., fam.*) **dejarse de historias**, to stop beating about the bush.

historiador (-ra), *s.* historian

historiar, *v.t.* to narrate, relate; record, chronicle

histórico, *a.* historical; historic

historieta, *f.* short story; anecdote

historiografía, *f.* historiography

historiógrafo, *m.* historiographer

histriónico, *a.* histrionic

hitlerismo, *m.* Hitlerism

hito, *m.* milestone; boundary mark; (*fig.*) mark, target. **de h. en h.**, from head to foot

hocico, *m.* snout; (*fam.*) face, mug; (*fam.*) angry gesture; (*naut.*) prow. **meter el h.**, to stick one's nose into other people's business

hogaño, *adv.* (*fam.*) during this year; at the present time

hogar, *m.* hearth, fireplace; home, house; family life; fire-box (of a railway engine)

hoguera, *f.* bonfire

hoja, *f.* (*bot.*) leaf; petal; sheet (metal, paper, etc.); page (of book); blade (sharp instruments); leaf (door, window); sword. **h. de servicios**, service or professional record. **h. de tocino**, flitch of bacon. **h. extraordinaria**, extra, special edition (of a newspaper). **h. volante**, hand-bill, supplement. **volver la h.**, to turn over (pages); change one's opinion; turn the conversation

hojalata, *f.* tin-plate

hojalatería, *f.* tin ware; tin shop

hojalatero, *m.* tinsmith

hojaldre, *m.* or *f.* puff pastry

hojarasca, *f.* withered leaves; excessive foliage; rubbish, trash

hojear, *v.t.* to turn leaves of a book; skip, skim, read quickly; *v.i.* exfoliate

hojuela, *f.* *dim.* little leaf; (*bot.*) leaflet; pancake

hola! *interj.* Hallo! Goodness!

holandés (-esa), *a.* and *s.* Dutch (man). *m.* Dutch language

holgado, *a.* leisured, free; loose, wide; comfortable; well off, rich

holganza, *f.* repose, leisure, ease; idleness; pleasure

holgar, *v.i.* *irr.* to rest; be idle; be glad; be unused or unnecessary (things). *v.r.* enjoy oneself, amuse oneself; be glad. See **contar**

holgazán (-ana), *a.* idle. *s.* idler

holgazanear, *v.i.* to idle

holgazanería, *f.* idleness, sloth

holgorio, *m.* rejoicing, festivity, merriment

holgura, *f.* enjoyment, merry-making; width; comfort, ease; (*mech.*) free play

holocausto, *m.* holocaust

hológrafo, *m.* holograph

hollar, *v.t.* *irr.* to trample under foot; humiliate. See **degollar**

hollejo, *m.* peel, thin skin (fruit); ·(*agr.*) chaff

hollín, *m.* soot

hombradía, *f.* manliness; courage

hombre, *m.* man; adult; ombre (cards). *interj.* **¡h.!** (*fam.*) Old fellow; You don't say so! **¡h. al agua!** Man overboard! **h. de bien**, honest, honourable man. **h. de Estado**, statesman. **h. de muchos oficios**, Jack of all trades. **h. de negocios**, business man; man of many affairs. **h. de pro**, worthy man; famous man. **ser muy h.**, to be a real man, be very manly

hombrera, *f.* epaulette; shoulder-pad

hombro, *m.* shoulder. **echar al h.**, to shoulder; undertake, take the responsibility of. **encogerse de hombros**, to shrug one's shoulders; be indifferent or uninterested

hombruno, *a.* (*fam.*) mannish (of a woman)

homenaje, *m.* allegiance; homage; veneration, respect

homeópata, *a.* homœopathic. *m.* and *f.* homœopath

homeopatía, *f.* homœopathy

homérico, *a.* Homeric

homicida, *a.* murderous, homicidal. *m.* and *f.* murderer(-ess)

homicidio, *m.* homicide (act)

homilía, *f.* (*ecc.*) homily

homogeneidad, *f.* homogeneity
homogéneo, *a.* homogeneous
homólogo, *a.* homologous
homónimo, *a.* homonymous. *m.* homonym
homosexual, *a.* and *m.* and *f.* homosexual
honda, *f.* sling, catapult
hondear, *v.t.* (*naut.*) to sound, plumb; (*naut.*) unload
hondo, *a.* deep; low; (*fig.*) profound; deep, intense (emotion). *m.* depth
hondón, *m.* depth, recess
hondonada, *f.* hollow; glen; valley
hondura, *f.* depth
hondureño (-ña), *a.* and *s.* Honduran
honestidad, *f.* honourableness; virtue; respectability; modesty; courtesy
honesto, *a.* honourable, virtuous; modest; honest, just
hongo, *m.* fungus; toadstool; bowler hat
honor, *m.* honour; fame; reputation (women); modesty (women); praise; *pl.* rank, position; honours
honorable, *a.* honourable
honorario, *a.* honorary. *m.* honorarium, fee
honorífico, *a.* honorary; honourable
honra, *f.* self-respect, honour, personal dignity; reputation; chastity and modesty (women); *pl.* obsequies
honradez, *f.* honesty; honourableness, integrity; respectability
honrado, *a.* honest; honourable
honrar, *v.t.* to respect; honour; *v.r.* be honoured
honroso, *a.* honour-giving, honourable
hora, *f.* hour; opportune moment; *pl.* book of hours. **horas hábiles,** working hours. **horas muertas,** small hours; wasted time. **última h.,** Stop Press. **a última h.,** at the last minute. **dar la h.,** to strike the hour. **¿ Qué h. es ?** What time is it ?
horaciano, *a.* Horatian
horadar, *v.t.* to bore, pierce
horario, *a.* hourly. *m.* time-table; hour-hand of clock; watch
horca, *f.* gibbet, gallows; (*agr.*) pitchfork; fork; prop for trees
horcajadas, (a) *adv.* astride
horcajadura, *f.* (*anat.*) crutch
horchata, *f.* drink made of chufas or crushed almonds
horda, *f.* horde
horizontal, *a.* horizontal
horizonte, *m.* horizon. **nuevos horizontes,** new opportunities
horma, *f.* mould; cobbler's last; stone wall. (*fig., fam.*) **hallar la h. de su zapato,** to find what suits one; meet one's match
hormiga, *f.* ant
hormigón, *m.* concrete. **h. armado,** ferro-concrete
hormiguear, *v.i.* to itch; crowd, swarm
hormiguero, *m.* ant-hill; crowd, swarm
hormona, *f.* hormone
hornacina, *f.* (*arch.*) vaulted niche
hornero (-ra), *s.* baker
horno, *m.* oven; furnace; kiln; bakery. **h. alfarero,** firing oven (pottery). **h. de cocina,** kitchen stove. **h. de cuba,** blast-furnace. **h. de ladrillo,** brick-kiln. **alto h.,** iron smelting-furnace
horóscopo, *m.* horoscope
horquilla, *f.* forked stick; hairpin; hatpin; (*agr.*) fork; hook. **viraje en h.,** hairpin bend
horrendo, *a.* horrible, frightful
hórreo, *m.* granary, barn
horribilidad, *f.* horribleness
horribilísimo, *a.* *sup.* most or exceedingly horrible
horrible, *a.* horrible
horrífico, *a.* horrific
horripilante, *a.* hair-raising, horrifying
horrísono, *a.* (*poet.*) horrid-sounding, terrifying
horror, *m.* horror; horribleness; atrocity, enormity
horrorizar, *v.t.* to horrify; *v.r.* be horrified or terrified
horroroso, *a.* dreadful, horrible; horrid; (*fam.*) hideous, most ugly
hortaliza, *f.* green vegetable, garden produce
hortelano, *m.* market-gardener
hortensia, *f.* (*bot.*) hydrangea
horticultor (-ra), *s.* horticulturalist
horticultura, *f.* horticulture
horticultural, *a.* horticultural
hosanna, *m.* hosanna

hosco, *a.* dark brown; unsociable. sullen; crabbed

hospedaje, *m.* lodging; board, payment

hospedar, *v.t.* to lodge, receive as a guest; *v.r.* and *v.i.* lodge, stay

hospedería, *f.* hostelry, inn; lodging

hospedero (-ra), *s.* innkeeper

hospicio, *m.* hospice; almshouse, workhouse; lodging; orphanage

hospital, *m.* hospital; hospice. **h. de sangre,** field-hospital

hospitalario, *a.* hospitable

hospitalidad, *f.* hospitality; hospitableness; stay in hospital

hostelero (-ra), *s.* innkeeper

hostería, *f.* hostelry; inn

hostia, *f.* (*ecc.*) wafer, Host; sacrificial victim

hostigar, *v.t.* to chastise; harass; tease, annoy

hostil, *a.* hostile

hostilidad, *f.* hostility

hostilizar, *v.t.* to commit hostile acts against; antagonize

hotel, *m.* hotel; villa

hotelero (-ra), *s.* hotel keeper

hotentote (-ta), *a.* and *s.* Hottentot

hoy, *adv.* to-day; at present. **h. día** *or* **h. en día,** today. **h. por h.,** day by day; at the present time. **de h. en adelante,** from today forward

hoya, *f.* hole; grave; valley, glen; bed (of river)

hoyo, *m.* hole; pock-mark; grave; hollow

hoyuelo, *m.* *dim.* little hole; dimple

hoz, *f.* sickle; defile

hozar, *v.t.* to root, rootle (pigs, etc.)

hucha, *f.* large chest; money-box; money savings

hueco, *a.* empty; hollow; vain; hollow (sound); pompous (style); spongy, soft; inflated. *m.* hollow; interval of time or place; (*fam.*) vacancy; gap in wall, etc.

huelga, *f.* strike; leisure; lying fallow; merrymaking. **h. de brazos caídos,** sit-down strike. **h. patronal,** lock-out strike

huelguista, *m.* and *f.* striker

huella, *f.* footprint, track; footstep; tread (of stairs); impres-

sion (printing); vestige, trace. **h. digital,** finger-mark; finger-print

huérfano (-na), *s.* orphan. *a.* unprotected, uncared for

huero, *a.* addled; empty, hollow

huerta, *f.* kitchen garden; orchard; irrigation land

huerto, *m.* orchard; kitchen garden

hueso, *m.* bone; stone (of fruit); kernel, core; drudgery; cheap, useless thing of poor quality. **la sin h.,** the tongue. (*fam.*) **no dejar un h. sano,** to tear (a person) to pieces. **tener los huesos molidos,** to be tired out; be bruised

huésped (-da), *s.* guest; host; innkeeper

hueste, *f.* (gen. *pl.*) army on the march, host; party, supporters

huesudo, *a.* bony

hueva, *f.* fish roe

huevera, *f.* egg seller; egg-cup

huevo, *m.* egg. **h. duro,** hard-boiled egg. **h. estrellado,** fried egg. **h. pasado por agua,** soft-boiled egg. **huevos revueltos,** scrambled eggs

hugonote (-ta), *a.* and *s.* Huguenot

huida, *f.* flight, escape; bolting (of a horse); outlet

huir, *v.i.* *irr.* to flee; fly (of time); elope; run away, bolt; (*with de*) avoid. *Pres. Part.* huyendo. *Pres. Ind.* huyo, huyes, huyen. *Pretérito* huyó, huyeron. *Pres. Subjunc.* huya, etc. *Imperf. Subjunc.* huyese, etc.

hule, *m.* oilcloth; rubber

hulla, *f.* coal, soft coal

hullera, *f.* colliery

humanidad, *f.* humanity; human nature; human weakness; compassion; affability; (*fam.*) stoutness; *pl.* study of humanities

humanismo, *m.* humanism

humanista, *m.* and *f.* humanist. *a.* humanistic

humanitario, *a.* humanitarian

humanizar, *v.t.* to humanize

humano, *a.* human; understanding, sympathetic. *m.* human being

humareda, *f.* cloud of smoke

humeante, *a.* smoking; smoky

humear, *v.i.* to give forth smoke; give oneself airs

humedad, *f.* humidity; dampness; moisture

humedecer, *v.t. irr.* to moisten, wet, damp; *v.r.* grow moist. See **conocer**

húmedo, *a.* humid; damp; wet

húmero, *m.* (*anat.*) humerus

humildad, *f.* humility; lowliness; humbleness

humilde, *a.* meek; lowly; humble

humillación, *f.* humiliation

humillante, *a.* humiliating; debasing; mortifying

humillar, *v.t.* to humble; humiliate; *v.r.* humble oneself

humo, *m.* smoke; vapour, fume; *pl.* homes; vanity, airs

humor, *m.* (*med.*) humour; temperament, disposition; mood. **de buen h.,** good-tempered. **de mal h.,** ill-tempered

humorada, *f.* humorous saying, extravagance, witticism

humorismo, *m.* humour, comic sense; humorousness

humorista, *m.* and *f.* humorist

humorístico, *a.* humorous

humoso, *a.* smoky, reeky

hundible, *a.* sinkable

hundido, *a.* sunken (of cheeks, etc.); hollow, deep-set (of eyes)

hundimiento, *m.* sinking; collapse; subsidence (of earth)

hundir, *v.t.* to sink; oppress; confound; destroy, ruin; *v.r.* collapse (building); sink; (*fig.,* *fam.*) disappear

húngaro (-ra), *a.* and *s.* Hungarian. *m.* Hungarian language

huno (-na), *s.* Hun

huracán, *m.* hurricane

huraña, *f.* shyness, unsociableness; diffidence; wildness (of birds, etc.)

huraño, *a.* shy, unsociable; diffident; wild (of animals, etc.)

hurgar, *v.t.* to stir; poke, rake; touch; rouse, incite. *v.r.* pick one's nose

hurgón, *m.* fire-rake, poker; (*fam.*) sword

hurgonada, *f.* raking (of the fire, etc.)

hurí, *f.* houri

hurón (-ona), *s.* ferret. *a.* shy, unsociable

¡hurra! *interj.* hurrah!

hurtadillas (a), *adv.* by stealth, secretly

hurtar, *v.t.* to steal; encroach (sea, river); plagiarize; *v.r.* hide oneself

hurto, *m.* theft. **coger con el h. en las manos,** (*fig.*) to catch redhanded

húsar, *m.* hussar

husmear, *v.t.* to sniff out; (*fam.*) pry; *v.i.* smell high (of meat)

huso, *m.* spindle; bobbin

¡huy! *interj.* denoting pain or surprise. Oh!

I

ibérico, *a.* Iberian

ibero (-ra), *a.* and *s.* Iberian

íbice, *m.* (*zool.*) ibex

icnografía, *f.* (*arch.*) ichnography

icnográfico, *a.* ichnographical

icono, *m.* icon

iconoclasta, *a.* iconoclastic. *m.* and *f.* iconoclast

iconografía, *f.* iconography

icosaedro, *m.* (*geom.*) icosahedron

ictericia, *f.* (*med.*) jaundice

ictiófago, *a.* fish-eating, ichthyophagous

ictiología, *f.* ichthyology

ictiólogo, *m.* ichthyologist

ictiosauro, *m.* ichthyosaurus

ida, *f.* setting out, departure, going; impetuous action; precipitancy; track, trail (of animals). **de i. y vuelta,** return, out and home (of railway tickets, etc.)

idea, *f.* idea. (*fam.*) **¡Qué ideas tienes!** What (odd) ideas you have!

ideación, *f.* (*phil.*) ideation

ideal, *a.* ideal; perfect. *m.* model; ideal

idealidad, *f.* ideality

idealismo, *m.* idealism

idealista, *a.* idealistic. *m.* and *f.* idealist

idealización, *f.* idealization

idealizar, *v.t.* to idealize

idealmente, *adv.* ideally

idear, *v.t.* to imagine; devise; plan; design; draft, draw up

ídem, *adv.* idem

idéntico, *a.* identical

identidad, *f.* identity

identificable, *a.* identifiable

identificación, *f.* identification

identificar, *v.t.* to identify; recognize; *v.r.* (*with con*) identify oneself with

ideografía, *f.* ideography

ideograma, *m.* ideogram, ideograph

ideología, *f.* ideology. **i. racista,** racial ideology

ideológico, *a.* ideological

ideólogo (**-ga**), *s.* ideologist; dreamer, planner

idílico, *a.* idyllic

idilio, *m.* idyll

idioma, *m.* language, tongue

idiomático, *a.* idiomatic

idiosincrasia, *f.* idiosyncrasy

idiosincrásico, *a.* idiosyncratic

idiota, *a.* idiot; idiotic. *m.* and *f.* idiot

idiotez, *f.* idiocy

idiotismo, *m.* (*gram.*) idiom; ignorance

idólatra, *a.* idolatrous; adoring. *m.* and *f.* idolater, heathen

idolatrar, *v.t.* to idolize; worship, love excessively

idolatría, *f.* idolatry; adoration, idolization

ídolo, *m.* idol

idoneidad, *f.* fitness, suitability; competence; capacity

idóneo, *a.* suitable; competent, fit

idus, *m. pl.* ides

iglesia, *f.* church. **i. colegial,** collegiate church. **cumplir con la i.,** to discharge one's religious duties. **llevar a una mujer a la i.,** to lead a woman to the altar

ígneo, *a.* igneous

ignición, *f.* ignition

ignominia, *f.* ignominy, disgrace

ignominioso, *a.* ignominious

ignorancia, *f.* ignorance. **pretender i.,** to plead ignorance

ignorante, *a.* ignorant; unaware, uninformed. *m.* and *f.* ignoramus

ignorar, *v.t.* to be unaware of, not to know

ignoto, *a.* unknown, undiscovered

igual, *a.* equal; level; even, smooth; very similar; alike; uniform;' proportionate; unchanging; constant; indifferent; same. *m.* and *f.* equal. *m.* (*math.*) equal sign. **al i.,** equally. **sin i.,** peerless, without equal. **Me es completamente i.,** It's all the same to me

iguala, *f.* equalizing; levelling; agreement, arrangement; cash adjustment

igualación, *f.* equalization; levelling; arrangement, agreement; matching; (*math.*) equation

igualador, *a.* equalizing; levelling

igualar, *v.t.* to equalize, make equal; match; pair; level, flatten; smooth; adjust; arrange. agree upon; weigh, consider; (*math.*) equate; *v.i.* be equal

igualdad, *f.* equality; uniformity, harmony; evenness; smoothness; identity, sameness. **i. de ánimo,** equability, equanimity

igualitario, *a.* equalizing; equalitarian

igualmente, *adv.* equally; the same, likewise

ijada, *f.* (*anat.*) side, flank; pain in the side

ijadear, *v.i.* to pant

ijar, *m.* See ijada

ilación, *f.* connection, reference

ilegal, *a.* illegal

ilegalidad, *f.* illegality

ilegible, *a.* illegible, unreadable

ilegitimidad, *f.* illegitimacy

ilegítimo, *a.* illegitimate; false

íleon, *m.* (*anat.*) ileum

ileso, *a.* unharmed, unhurt

iletrado, *a.* unlettered, uncultured

Ilíada, *f.* Iliad

iliberal, *a.* illiberal; narrowminded

iliberalidad, *f.* illiberality; narrow-mindedness

ilícito, *a.* illicit

ilicitud, *f.* illicitness

ilimitado, *a.* unlimited, boundless

ilirio (**-ia**), *a.* and *s.* Illyrian

iliterato, *a.* illiterate, uncultured

ilógico, *a.* illogical

ilota, *m.* and *f.* helot

iluminación, *f.* illumination; lighting. **i. intensiva,** floodlighting

iluminador (**-ra**), *a.* lighting; illuminating. *s.* (*art*) illuminator

iluminar, *v.t.* to illuminate; light; (*art*) illuminate; enlighten

iluminativo, *a.* illuminating

ilusión, *f.* illusion; illusoriness; hope; dream

ilusionarse, *v.r.* to harbour illusions

ilusivo, *a.* deceptive, illusive

iluso, *a.* deceived, deluded; dreamy; visionary

ilusorio, *a.* illusory; deceptive; null

ilustración, *f.* illustration, picture; enlightenment; explanation; picture paper, illustrated journal; erudition, knowledge; example, illustration

ilustrado, *a.* erudite, learned; knowledgeable, well-informed

ilustrador (-ra), *a.* illustrative. *s.* illustrator

ilustrar, *v.t.* to explain, illustrate; enlighten, instruct; illustrate (books); make illustrious; inspire with divine light

ilustrativo, *a.* illustrative

ilustre, *a.* illustrious, distinguished

ilustrísimo, *a. sup.* most illustrious (title of bishops, etc.)

imagen, *f.* image; effigy, statue; idea; metaphor, simile. **i. nítida,** sharp image

imaginable, *a.* imaginable

imaginación, *f.* imagination

imaginar, *v.i.* to imagine; *v.t.* suppose, conjecture; discover, invent; imagine. **¡Imagínese Vd!** Just imagine!

imaginario, *a.* imaginary

imaginativa, *f.* imagination; common sense

imaginativo, *a.* imaginative

imaginería, *f.* imagery

imán, *m.* magnet; attraction, charm; imaum

imanación, *f.* magnetization

imanar, *v.t.* to magnetize

imbécil, *a.* imbecile; stupid, idiotic. *m.* and *f.* imbecile

imbecilidad, *f.* imbecility; folly, stupidity

imberbe, *a.* beardless. (*fam.*) **un joven i.,** a stripling

imbibición, *f.* imbibing, absorption

imborrable, *a.* ineffaceable

imbuir, *v.t. irr.* to imbue. See **huir**

imitable, *a.* imitable

imitación, *f.* imitation; reproduction; copy

imitado, *a.* imitation; imitated

imitador (-ra), *a.* imitation; imitative. *s.* imitator

imitar, *v.t.* to imitate; counterfeit

imitativo, *a.* imitative

impacción, *f.* impact

impaciencia, *f.* impatience

impacientar, *v.t.* to make impatient, annoy; *v.r.* grow impatient

impaciente, *a.* impatient

impacto, *m.* impact. **i. de lleno,** direct hit

impalpabilidad, *f.* impalpability

impalpable, *a.* impalpable

impar, *a.* odd; unpaired; single, uneven. **números impares,** odd numbers

imparcial, *a.* impartial

imparcialidad, *f.* impartiality

imparisilábico, *a.* imparisyllabic

impartible, *a.* indivisible

impasibilidad, *f.* impassivity, indifference

impasible, *a.* impassive

impavidez, *f.* dauntlessness; serenity in the face of danger

impávido, *a.* dauntless; calm, composed, imperturbable

impecabilidad, *f.* impeccability, perfection

impecable, *a.* impeccable, perfect

impedido, *a.* disabled

impedimento, *m.* obstacle; hindrance; (*law*) impediment

impedir, *v.t. irr.* to impede; obstruct; prevent; thwart; disable; delay; (*poet.*) amaze. See **pedir**

impeler, *v.t.* to push; incite; drive; urge

impender, *v.t.* to spend money

impenetrabilidad, *f.* impenetrability; imperviousness; obscurity, difficulty

impenetrable, *a.* impenetrable, dense; impervious; (*fig.*) unfathomable; obscure

impenitencia, *f.* impenitence

impenitente, *a.* impenitent

impensado, *a.* unexpected, unforeseen

imperante, *a.* ruling, dominant

imperar, *v.i.* to rule; command

imperativo, *a.* commanding. *a.* and *m.* (*gram.*) imperative

imperatorio, *a.* imperial, imperatorial

imperceptible, *a.* imperceptible

imperdible, *m.* safety-pin

imperdonable, *a.* unpardonable, inexcusable

imperecedero, *a.* undying; eternal, everlasting

imperfección, *f.* imperfection, inadequacy; fault, blemish; weakness

imperfecto, *a.* imperfect; inadequate; faulty. *a.* and *m.* (*gram.*) imperfect

imperial, *a.* imperial. *f.* upper deck of omnibus or tram-car

imperialismo, *m.* imperialism

imperialista, *a.* imperialistic. *m.* and *f.* imperialist

impericia, *f.* inexpertness; unskilfulness, unhandiness

imperio, *m.* empire; rule, reign; command, sway; imperial dignity; arrogance, haughtiness. (*fig., fam.*) **valer un i.,** to be priceless

imperioso, *a.* imperious

imperito, *a.* inexpert; clumsy, unskilled

impermeabilidad, *f.* watertightness; imperviousness; impermeability

impermeabilizar, *v.t.* to waterproof

impermeable, *a.* watertight, impermeable; impervious. *m.* rainproof, mackintosh

impersonal, *a.* impersonal

impertérrito, *a.* unafraid, dauntless

impertinencia, *f.* impertinence, insolence; peevishness; fancy, whim; over-exactness, meticulosity; interference, intrusion

impertinente, *a.* impertinent; irrelevant; inopportune; officious, interfering

impertinentes, *m. pl.* lorgnettes

imperturbabilidad, *f.* imperturbability

imperturbable, *a.* calm, imperturbable

impetrar, *v.t.* to obtain by entreaty; implore

ímpetu, *m.* impetus, momentum; speed, swiftness; violence

impetuosidad, *f.* impetuosity

impetuoso, *a.* impetuous; precipitate

impiedad, *f.* cruelty, harshness; irreligion

impío, *a.* impious, wicked; irreverent, irreligious

implacabilidad, *f.* implacability, relentlessness

implacable, *a.* implacable

implantación, *f.* inculcation, implantation

implantar, *v.t.* to inculcate, implant (ideas, etc.)

implicación, *f.* implication; contradiction (in terms); complicity

implicar, *v.t.* to implicate; imply, infer; involve, entangle; *v.i.* imply contradiction (gen. with negatives)

implicatorio, *a.* contradictory; implicated (in crime)

implícito, *a.* implicit; implied

implorante, *a.* imploring

implorar, *v.t.* to implore, entreat

implume, *a.* without feathers, unfeathered

impolítico, *a.* impolitic; unwise, inexpedient; tactless

impoluto, *a.* unpolluted, spotless, pure

imponderabilidad, *f.* imponderability

imponderable, *a.* imponderable, immeasurable; most excellent

imponente, *a.* imposing; awe-inspiring

imponer, *v.t. irr.* to exact; impose; malign, accuse falsely; instruct, acquaint; (*fig.*) impress (with respect, etc.); invest or deposit (money); (*print.*) impose; (a name) give, bestow. *v.r.* assert oneself. See **poner**

imponible, *a.* taxable; ratable

impopular, *a.* unpopular

impopularidad, *f.* unpopularity

importable, *a.* importable

importación, *f.* (*com.*) importation; import

importador (-ra), *a.* import, importing. *s.* importer

importancia, *f.* importance; magnitude

importante, *a.* important

importar, *v.i.* to matter; be important; concern, interest; *v.t.* amount to; import; include, comprise. **¡No importa!** It doesn't matter! Never mind!

importe, *m.* amount; value, cost. **i. bruto,** gross or total amount. **i. líquido** *or* **neto,** net amount

importunación, *f.* importuning; importunity

importunadamente, *adv.* importunately

importunar, *v.t.* to importune, pester

importunidad (*also* **importunación**), *f.* importunity

importuno, *a.* importunate, inopportune, ill-timed; persistent; tedious

imposibilidad, *f.* impossibility

imposibilitado, *a.* d i s a b l e d , crippled; incapable, unable

imposibilitar, *v.t.* to disable; render unable; make impossible

imposible, *a.* impossible

imposición, *f.* imposition; exaction; tax, duty, tribute; (*print.*) make-up. (*ecc.*) **i. de manos**, laying on of hands

impostor (**-ra**), *s.* impostor

impostura, *f.* swindle, imposture; aspersion, slur, imputation

impotable, *a.* undrinkable

impotencia, *f.* impotence

impotente, *a.* impotent; powerless

impracticabilidad, *f.* impracticability; impassibility (of roads, etc.)

impracticable, *a.* impracticable; impossible; impassable (roads, etc.)

imprecación, *f.* i m p r e c a t i o n ; curse, malediction

imprecar, *v.t.* to imprecate, curse

imprecatorio, *a.* imprecatory

impregnación, *f.* impregnation, permeation, saturation

impregnar, *v.t.* impregnate; to permeate; *v.r.* become impregnated

impremeditado, *a.* unpremeditated

imprenta, *f.* printing; printing house or office; print; letterpress

imprescindible, *a.* indispensable, essential

impresión, *f.* printing; impression; effect; influence; imprint, stamp; (*print.*) impression; print. **impresiones digitales**, finger-prints

impresionable, *a.* impressionable, susceptible

impresionante, *a.* imposing; moving, affecting

impresionar, *v.t.* to impress; affect; fix in the mind; (*fig.*) move deeply, stir; (*rad.*, cinema) record

impresionismo, *m.* (*art*) impressionism

impresionista, *m.* and *f.* impressionist. *a.* impressionistic

impreso, *m.* (gen. *pl.*) printed matter

impresor, *m.* printer

imprevisión, *f.* lack of foresight; improvidence

imprevisto, *a.* unforeseen, unexpected, sudden

imprevistos, *m. pl.* incidental expenses

imprimación, *f.* priming (of paint, etc.)

imprimar, *v.t.* (*art*) to prime

imprimir, *v.t.* to print; stamp; impress upon (the mind)

improbabilidad, *f.* improbability

improbable, *a.* improbable

improbo, *a.* vicious, corrupt; dishonest; hard, arduous

improductivo, *a.* unproductive; unprofitable, fruitless

impronta, *f.* (*art*) cast, mould

impronunciable, *a.* unpronounceable; ineffable

improperio, *m.* insult, affront

impropiedad, *f.* inappropriateness; unsuitableness; impropriety

impropio, *a.* unsuitable; inappropriate; inadequate; improper

improporcionado, *a.* disproportionate, out of proportion

impróvido, *a.* improvident, heedless

improvisación, *f.* improvisation

improvisador (**-ra**), *s.* improviser

improvisamente, *adv.* unexpectedly, suddenly

improvisar, *v.t.* to improvise

improviso, improvisto, *a.* unexpected, unforeseen. **al** (*or* **de**) **improviso**, unexpectedly

imprudencia, *f.* i m p r u d e n c e , rashness, indiscretion

imprudente, *a.* imprudent, unwise, rash

impúbero, *a.* below the age of puberty

impudencia, *f.* impudence, impertinence

impudente, *a.* brazen, impudent

impudicia, *f.* immodesty, brazenness

impúdico, *a.* immodest, brazen

impuesto, *m.* tax; duty. **i. de utilidades,** income-tax

impugnable, *a.* impugnable, refutable

impugnación, *f.* refutation; contradiction

impugnar, *v.t.* to refute, contradict; oppose; criticize

impulsar, *v.t.* to impel; prompt, cause; drive, operate, propel

impulsión, *f.* impulse; impetus; (*mech.*) operation, driving; propulsion

impulsivo, *a.* impulsive; irreflexive, precipitate

impulso, *m.* stimulus, incitement; impulse, desire; (*mech.*) drive, impulse

impulsor (**-ra**), *a.* driving, impelling. *s.* driver, operator

impune, *a.* unpunished

impunemente, *adv.* with impunity

impunidad, *f.* impunity

impureza, *f.* impurity; lack of chastity; obscenity, indecency

impurificar, *v.t.* to defile; make impure; adulterate

impuro, *a.* impure; adulterated; polluted; immoral, unchaste

imputable, *a.* imputable

imputación, *f.* imputation

imputador (**-ra**), *s.* imputer, attributer

imputar, *v.t.* to impute; attribute

inacabable, *a.* endless, interminable, ceaseless; wearisome

inaccesibilidad, *f.* inaccessibility

inaccesible, *a.* inaccessible; incomprehensible

inacción, *f.* inaction

inaceptable, *a.* unacceptable

inactividad, *f.* inactivity; quiescence; idleness

inactivo, *a.* inactive; idle; unemployed; (*naut.*) laid up

inadaptable, *a.* inadaptable

inadecuado, *a.* inadequate, insufficient

inadmisible, *a.* inadmissible

inadvertencia, *f.* inadvertence; oversight, mistake, slip

inadvertido, *a.* unnoticed; inattentive; inadvertent, unintentional; negligent

inafectado, *a.* unaffected, natural

inagotable, *a.* inexhaustible, unfailing; abundant

inaguantable, *a.* unbearable, intolerable

inajenable, *a.* inalienable

inalámbrica, *f.* wireless station

inalienable, *a.* inalienable

inalterable, *a.* unalterable

inamovibilidad, *f.* immovability

inamovible, *a.* immovable

inanición, *f.* (*med.*) inanition

inanimado, *a.* inanimate

inapagable, *a.* inextinguishable

inapelable, *a.* unappealable; irremediable, inevitable

inapetencia, *f.* lack of appetite

inaplazable, *a.* undeferable, unable to be postponed

inaplicable, *a.* inapplicable

inaplicación, *f.* laziness, inattention, negligence

inaplicado, *a.* lazy; inattentive; careless

inapreciable, *a.* inappreciable; invaluable

inarmónico, *a.* unharmonious, discordant

inarticulado, *a.* inarticulate

inasequible, *a.* unattainable; out of reach

inaudible, *a.* inaudible

inaudito, *a.* unheard of, unprecedented; extraordinary, strange

inauguración, *f.* inauguration; induction; inception, commencement

inaugural, *a.* inaugural

inaugurar, *v.t.* to inaugurate; induct

inaveriguable, *a.* unascertainable

inca, *m.* Inca

incaico, *a.* Inca

incalculable, *a.* incalculable; innumerable

incalificable, *a.* indescribable, unclassable; vile

incandescencia, *f.* incandescence, white heat

incandescente, *a.* incandescent

incansable, *a.* indefatigable; unflagging; unwearying

incapacidad, *f.* incapacity; incompetence

incapacitar, *v.t.* to incapacitate; disable

incapaz, *a.* incapable, incompetent; inefficient

incasable, *a.* unmarriageable; anti-marriage

incautarse, *v.r.* to seize, take possession (of)

incauto, *a.* incautious; unwary

incendiar, *v.t.* to set on fire, set alight

incendiario (-ia), *a.* and *s.* incendiary

incendiarismo, *m.* incendiarism

incendio, *m.* conflagration, fire; consuming passion

incensar, *v.t. irr.* (*ecc.*) to cense, incense; flatter. See **acertar**

incensario, *m.* incense burner, incensory

incentivo, *m.* incentive; encouragement

incertidumbre, *f.* uncertainty, incertitude

incesable, incesante, *a.* incessant, continuous

incesto, *m.* incest

incestuoso, *a.* incestuous

incidencia, *f.* incidence

incidental, *a.* incidental

incidente, *a.* incidental. *m.* incident, event, occurrence

incidir, *v.i.* (*with* en) to incur, fall into (e.g. **Incidió en el pecado,** He fell into sin)

incienso, *m.* incense; flattery

incierto, *a.* untrue, false; uncertain; unknown

incineración, *f.* incineration

incinerador, *m.* incinerator

incinerar, *v.t.* incinerate, reduce to ashes

incipiente, *a.* incipient

incircunciso, *a.* uncircumcised

incircunscripto, *a.* uncircumscribed

incisión, *f.* incision

incisivo, *a.* sharp, keen; incisive, sarcastic, caustic

inciso, *m.* clause; comma

incitación, *f.* incitement; (*fig.*) spur, stimulus

incitar, *v.t.* to incite; stimulate, encourage

incivil, *a.* rude, discourteous, uncivil

incivilidad, *f.* rudeness, incivility

inclasificable, *a.* unclassifiable

inclemencia, *f.* harshness, severity; inclemency (of the weather). **a la i.,** at the mercy of the elements

inclemente, *a.* inclement

inclinación, *f.* inclination; slope;

slant; tendency, propensity; predilection, fondness; bow (in greeting); (*geom.*) inclination

inclinar, *v.t.* to incline, tilt, slant; bow; bend; influence; persuade; *v.i.* resemble; *v.r.* lean; stoop; tilt; tend, incline (to), view favourably (e.g. **Me inclino a creerlo,** I am inclined to believe it)

ínclito, *a.* famous, celebrated

incluir, *v.t. irr.* to comprise, embrace, contain; include, take into account. See **huir**

inclusa, *f.* foundling home

inclusión, *f.* inclusion; relationship, intercourse, friendship

inclusive, *adv.* including

inclusivo, *a.* inclusive

incluso, *adv.* including, inclusive. *prep.* even

incoar, *v.t.* to begin (especially lawsuits, etc.)

incoativo, *a.* inceptive

incobrable, *a.* irrecoverable; irredeemable

incógnita, *f.* (*math.*) X; unknown quantity; secret motive; unknown lady

incógnito, *a.* unknown. *m.* incognito, assumed name, disguise

incoherencia, *f.* incoherence

incoherente, *a.* incoherent, disconnected, illogical

íncola, *m.* resident, dweller, inhabitant

incoloro, *a.* colourless, uncoloured

incólume, *a.* unharmed, unscathed; untouched, undamaged

incombustibilidad, *f.* incombustibility

incomodar, *v.t.* to disturb, incommode, inconvenience; annoy; *v.r.* disturb oneself, put oneself out; grow angry. ¡No se incomode Vd! Please don't move! Please don't be angry!

incomodidad, *f.* discomfort; inconvenience; trouble, upset; annoyance

incómodo, *a.* uncomfortable; inconvenient; troublesome, tiresome. *m.* discomfort; inconvenience

incomparable, *a.* incomparable

incompartible, *a.* indivisible

incompasivo, *a.* unsympathetic, hard

incompatibilidad, *f.* incompatibility

incompatible, *a.* incompatible

incompetencia, *f.* incompetence

incompetente, *a.* incompetent

incomplejo, incomplexo, *a.* noncomplex, simple

incompleto, *a.* incomplete

incomponible, *a.* unrepairable, unmendable

incomprensibilidad, *f.* incomprehensibility

incomprensible, *a.* incomprehensible

incomprensión, *f.* incomprehension

incomunicado, *a.* in solitary confinement (of a prisoner)

incomunicar, *v.t.* to sentence to solitary confinement; isolate, deprive of means of communication; *v.r.* become a recluse

inconcebible, *a.* inconceivable

inconciliable, *a.* irreconcilable

incondicional, *a.* unconditional

inconexión, *f.* disconnectedness

inconexo, *a.* unconnected; incoherent

inconfeso, *a.* unconfessed

incongruencia, *f.* incongruity

incongruente, *a.* incongruous, inappropriate

inconmensurabilidad, *f.* incommensurability

inconmovible, *a.* immovable; unflinching, unshakable

inconmutable, *a.* unalterable, immutable, unchangeable

inconquistable, *a.* unconquerable; (*fig.*) resolute, inflexible

inconsciencia, *f.* unconsciousness; subconscious

inconsciente, *a.* unconscious, involuntary; subconscious

inconsecuencia, *f.* inconsequence; inconsistency

inconsecuente, *a.* inconsequential; inconsistent

inconsideración, *f.* thoughtlessness

inconsiderado, *a.* thoughtless; heedless, selfish

inconsiguiente, *a.* illogical, inconsistent

inconsistencia, *f.* inconsistency

inconsistente, *a.* inconsistent

inconsolable, *a.* inconsolable

inconstancia, *f.* inconstancy, infidelity

inconstante, *a.* inconstant, fickle

inconstitucional, *a.* unconstitutional

incontaminado, *a.* uncontaminated

incontestable, *a.* undeniable, unquestionable

incontinencia, *f.* incontinence

incontinente, *a.* incontinent

incontrastable, *a.* insuperable, invincible; undeniable, unanswerable; (*fig.*) unshakable, inconvincible

incontrovertible, *a.* undeniable, incontrovertible

inconvencible, *a.* inconvincible

inconveniencia, *f.* discomfort; inconvenience; unsuitability

inconveniente, *a.* awkward, inconvenient; uncomfortable; inappropriate. *m.* inconvenience; obstacle, impediment; disadvantage

inconvertible, *a.* inconvertible

incorporación, *f.* incorporation

incorporar, *v.t.* to incorporate; cause to sit up, lift up; *v.r.* sit up, raise oneself; become a member, join (associations); be incorporated; blend, mix

incorporeidad, *f.* incorporeity

incorpóreo, *a.* incorporeal; immaterial

incorrección, *f.* incorrectness; indecorum, impropriety

incorrecto, *a.* incorrect; indecorous, unbecoming, improper

incorregible, *a.* incorrigible

incorrupción, *f.* incorruption; purity; integrity; wholesomeness

incorrupto, *a.* incorrupt; pure; chaste

incredibilidad, *f.* incredibility

incredulidad, *f.* incredulity, scepticism

incrédulo (-la), *a.* incredulous; atheistic. *s.* atheist; unbeliever, sceptic

increíble, *a.* incredible; marvellous, extraordinary

incremento, *m.* increment, increase

increpación, *f.* scolding, harsh rebuke

increpar, *v.t.* to scold, rebuke harshly

incriminante, *a.* incriminating

incriminar, *v.t.* to incriminate,

accuse; exaggerate (a charge, etc.)

incruento, *a.* bloodless, unstained with blood

incrustación, *f.* incrustation; (*art*) inlay

incubación, *f.* hatching; (*med.*) incubation

incubadora, *f.* incubator (for chickens)

incubar, *v.i.* to sit upon eggs (hens); *v.t.* hatch; (*med.*) incubate

inculcación, *f.* inculcation, instilment

inculcar, *v.t.* to press one thing against another; instil, inculcate; *v.r.* grow more fixed in one's views

inculpable, *a.* blameless, innocent

inculpar, *v.t.* to blame; accuse

incultivable, *a.* uncultivable; untillable

inculto, *a.* uncultivated, untilled; uncultured; uncivilized

incultura, *f.* lack of cultivation; lack of culture

incumbencia, *f.* obligation, moral responsibility, duty

incumbir, *v.i.* to be incumbent on; concern

incumplimiento, *m.* non-fulfilment

incurable, *a.* incurable; inveterate, hopeless

incuria, *f.* negligence, carelessness

incurioso, *a.* incurious

incurrir, *v.i.* (*with en*) to fall into (error, etc.); incur (dislike, etc.)

incursión, *f.* incursion; inroad

indagación, *f.* investigation, inquiry

indagador (-ra), *a.* investigating, inquiring. *s.* investigator

indagar, *v.t.* to investigate, examine; inquire. **i. precios,** to inquire prices

indebido, *a.* undue, immoderate improper; illegal, illicit

indecencia, *f.* indecency; obscenity; impropriety

indecente, *a.* indecent; obscene; improper

indecible, *a.* unutterable, ineffable, unspeakable

indeciso, *a.* undecided; hesitant, irresolute; vague; non-committal

indeclinable, *a.* obligatory; unavoidable; (*gram.*) indeclinable, uninflected

indecoro, *m.* impropriety, indecorum

indecoroso, *a.* indecorous, unbecoming; base, mean

indefectible, *a.* unfailing; perfect

indefendible, *a.* indefensible

indefenso, *a.* unprotected, defenceless

indefinible, *a.* indefinable, vague; indescribable

indefinido, *a.* indefinite, vague; undefined; (*gram.*) indefinite

indeleble, *a.* indelible

indeliberado, *a.* unpremeditated; unconsidered

indemne, *a.* unharmed, undamaged

indemnidad, *f.* indemnity

indemnización, *f.* compensation, indemnification; indemnity

indemnizar, *v.t.* to indemnify, compensate

indemostrable, *a.* indemonstrable, incapable of demonstration

independencia, *f.* independence

independiente, *a.* independent; self-contained

indescifrable, *a.* undecipherable; illegible

indestructibilidad, *f.* indestructibility

indestructible, *a.* indestructible

indeterminado, *a.* indeterminate; vague, doubtful, uncertain; hesitant, irresolute; (*math.*) indeterminate

indiano (-na), *a. and s.* Indian; East Indian; West Indian. *m.* nouveau-riche, one who returns rich from America

indicación, *f.* indication; sign, evidence; intimation, hint

indicador, *a.* indicative. *m.* indicator. **i. del nivel de gasolina,** petrol-gauge

indicar, *v.t.* to indicate; show point out; imply, suggest; intimate

indicativo, *a.* indicative. *a. and m.* (*gram.*) indicative

índice, *m.* index; indication, sign; library catalogue; catalogue room; hand (of a clock); pointer, needle (of instruments); gnomon (of a sundial); (*math.*) index;

forefinger. **I. expurgatorio,** The
Index
indicio, *m.* indication; sign; evidence. **indicios vehementes,**
circumstantial evidence
índico, *a.* Indian
indiferencia, *f.* indifference
indiferente, *a.* indifferent
indígena, *a.* native, indigenous.
m. and *f.* native
indigencia, *f.* destitution, indigence; impecuniosity
indigente, *a.* destitute, indigent;
impecunious
indigestión, *f.* indigestion
indigesto, *a.* indigestible; (*lit.*)
muddled, confused; unsociable,
brusque
indignación, *f.* indignation, anger
indignado, *a.* indignant
indignar, *v.t.* to anger, make indignant; *v.r.* grow angry
indignidad, *f.* unworthiness; indignity; personal affront
indigno, *a.* unworthy; base, despicable
índigo, *m.* indigo
indio (-ia), *a.* Indian; blue. *s.*
Indian. *m.* (*chem.*) indium
indirecta, *f.* hint, covert suggestion, innuendo. (*fam.*) **i. del
padre Cobos,** strong hint
indirecto, *a.* indirect
indisciplina, *f.* indiscipline
indisciplinado, *a.* undisciplined
indiscreción, *f.* indiscretion
indiscreto, *a.* indiscreet
indiscutible, *a.* unquestionable,
undeniable
indisoluble, *a.* indissoluble
indispensable, *a.* indispensable
indisponer, *v.t. irr.* to make unfit or incapable; indispose, make
ill; (*with* con *or* contra) set
against, make trouble with; *v.r.*
be indisposed; (*with* con *or*
contra) quarrel with. See **poner**
indisposición, *f.* reluctance, disinclination; indisposition; short
illness
indisputable, *a.* indisputable
indistinguible, *a.* undistinguishable
indistinto, *a.* indistinct; indeterminate; vague
individual, *a.* individual; peculiar, characteristic. *m.* (tennis)
single
individualidad, *f.* individuality

individualismo, *m.* individualism
individualista, *a.* individualistic.
m. and *f.* individualist
individuo (-ua), *a.* individual;
indivisible. *m.* individual; member, associate; (*fam.*) self. *s.*
(*fam.*) person
indivisibilidad, *f.* indivisibility
indivisible, *a.* indivisible
indiviso, *a.* undivided
indócil, *a.* unmanageable; disobedient; brittle, unpliable
(of metals)
indocilidad, *f.* indocility; disobedience; brittleness (of metals)
indochino (-na), *a.* and *s.* Indo-
Chinese
indoeuropeo, *a.* Indo-European
indoísmo, *m.* Hinduism
índole, *f.* temperament, nature;
kind, sort
indolencia, *f.* idleness, indolence
indolente, *a.* non-painful; indifferent, insensible; idle, indolent
indoloro, *a.* painless
indomable, *a.* untamable; invincible; indomitable; ungovernable, unmanageable
indomado, *a.* untamed
indómito, *a.* untamed; untamable; unmanageable, unruly; indomitable
indonesio (-ia), *a.* and *s.* Indo-
nesian
indostanés, *a.* Hindustani
indostani, *m.* Hindustani (language)
indubitable, *a.* unquestionable
inducción, *f.* persuasion; (*phys.*)
induction
inducir, *v.t. irr.* to persuade,
prevail upon; induce; infer,
conclude. See **conducir**
inductivo, inductor, *a.* inductive
indudable, *a.* indubitable
indulgencia, *f.* over-kindness,
tenderness; (*ecc.*) indulgence
indulgente, *a.* indulgent, tender;
tolerant
indultar, *v.t.* to pardon; exempt
indulto, *m.* amnesty; exemption;
forgiveness; (*ecc.*) indult
indumentaria, *f.* clothing; outfit
(of clothes)
industria, *f.* assiduity, industriousness; pains, effort, ingenuity; industry. **i. pesada,** heavy
industry

industrial, *a.* industrial. *m.* industrialist

industrialismo, *m.* industrialism

industrialización, *f.* industrialization

industriar, *v.t.* to teach, train; *v.r.* find a way, manage, succeed in

industrioso, *a.* industrious; diligent, assiduous

inédito, *a.* unpublished; unedited

inefable, *a.* ineffable

ineficacia, *f.* inefficiency; ineffectiveness

ineficaz, *a.* ineffective; inefficient

ineludible, *a.* unavoidable

ineptitud, *f.* ineptitude

inepto, *a.* inept, incompetent; unfit, unsuitable

inequívoco, *a.* unequivocal

inercia, *f.* inertia

inerme, *a.* defenceless, unprotected; (*bot., zool.*) unarmed

inerte, *a.* inert

inescrutable, *a.* inscrutable, unfathomable

inesperado, *a.* unexpected, sudden

inestabilidad, *f.* instability

inestable, *a.* unstable

inestimable, *a.* inestimable

inevitable, *a.* inevitable

inexactitud, *f.* inexactitude, inaccuracy; error, mistake

inexacto, *a.* inexact, inaccurate; erroneous

inexcusable, *a.* inexcusable, unforgivable; indispensable

inexhausto, *a.* inexhaustible

inexistente, *a.* non-existent

inexorabilidad, *f.* inexorability

inexorable, *a.* inexorable

inexperiencia, *f.* inexperience

inexperto, *a.* inexperienced; inexpert

inexplicable, *a.* inexplicable

inexplorado, *a.* unexplored

inexplosible, *a.* inexplosive

inexpresivo, *a.* inexpressive; reticent

inexpugnable, *a.* impregnable; (*fig.*) unshakable, firm; obstinate

inextinguible, *a.* inextinguishable; everlasting, perpetual

infalibilidad, *f.* infallibility

infalible, *a.* infallible

infamación, *f.* defamation

infamador (-ra), *a.* slandering. *s.* slanderer

infamar, *v.t.* to defame, slander

infame, *a.* infamous, vile

infamia, *f.* infamy; baseness, vileness

infancia, *f.* infancy, babyhood; childhood

infanta, *f.* female child under seven years; infanta, any Spanish royal princess; wife of a Spanish royal prince

infantado, *m.* land belonging to an **infante** *or* **infanta**

infante, *m.* male child under seven years; infante, any of Spanish royal princes except heir-apparent; infantryman. **i. de coro,** choir boy

infantería, *f.* infantry

infanticida, *a.* infanticidal. *m. and f.* infanticide (person)

infanticidio, *m.* infanticide (act)

infantil, *a.* infantile, baby; innocent, candid

infanzón, *m.* nobleman, landed gentleman (*ant.*)

infatigable, *a.* unwearying, indefatigable

infatuación, *f.* infatuation

infatuar, *v.t.* to infatuate; *v.r.* become infatuated

infausto, *a.* unlucky, unfortunate

infección, *f.* infection

infeccioso, *a.* infectious

infectar, *v.t.* to infect; corrupt, pervert; *v.r.* become infected; be corrupted

infecto, *a.* infected; corrupt, perverted; tainted

infecundidad, *f.* sterility

infecundo, *a.* sterile, barren

infelice, *a.* (*poet.*) unhappy, unfortunate

infelicidad, *f.* unhappiness

infeliz, *a.* unhappy; unfortunate; (*fam.*) simple, good-hearted

inferencia, *f.* inference, connection

inferior, *a.* inferior; lower; second-rate; subordinate. *m. and f.* inferior, subordinate

inferioridad, *f.* inferiority

inferir, *v.t. irr.* to infer, deduce; involve, imply; occasion; inflict. See **sentir**

infernáculo, *m.* hopscotch (game)

infernal, *a.* infernal; devilish, fiendish; wicked, inhuman; (*fam.*) confounded

inferno, *a.* (*poet.*) infernal

infértil, a. infertile
infestación, f. infestation
infestar, v.t. to infest, swarm in; infect; injure, damage
infesto, a. (poet.) harmful, dangerous
inficionar, v.t. to infect; pervert, corrupt
infidelidad, f. faithlessness, infidelity; disbelief in Christian religion; unbelievers, infidels
infidelísimo, a. sup. infiel, most disloyal; most incorrect; most incredulous, or faithless
infidencia, f. disloyalty, faithlessness
infiel, a. unfaithful, disloyal; inaccurate, incorrect; infidel, unbelieving. m. and f. infidel, unbeliever
infierno, m. hell; hades (gen. pl.); (fig., fam.) inferno. en el quinto i., very far off, at the end of the world
infiltración, f. infiltration; inculcation, implantation
infiltrar, v.t. to infiltrate; imbue, inculcate
ínfimo, a. lowest; meanest, vilest, most base; cheapest, poorest (in quality)
infinidad, f. infinity; infinitude; great number
infinitivo, a. and m. (gram.) infinitive
infinito, a. infinite; endless; boundless; countless. m. (math.) infinite. adv. excessively, immensely
infinitud, f. See infinidad
inflación, f. inflation; distension; pride, vanity
inflacionismo, m. inflationism
inflacionista, m. and f. inflationist
inflamabilidad, f. inflammability
inflamable, a. inflammable
inflamación, f. inflammation; (eng.) ignition
inflamador, a. inflammatory
inflamar, v.t. to set on fire; (fig.) inflame, excite; v.r. take fire; (med.) become inflamed; grow hot or excited
inflamatorio, a. (med.) inflammatory
inflar, v.t. to inflate; blow up, distend; throw out (the chest); exaggerate; make haughty or

vain; v.r. be swollen or inflated; be puffed up with pride
inflexibilidad, f. inflexibility; rigidity; immovability, constancy
inflexible, a. inflexible
inflexión, f. bending, flexion; diffraction (optics); inflection
infligir, v.t. to impose, inflict (penalties)
inflorescencia, f. (bot.) inflorescence
influencia, f. influence; power, authority; (elec.) charge
influir, v.t. irr. to influence; affect; (with en) co-operate in, assist with. See huir
influjo, m. influence; flux, inflow of the tide
influyente, a. influential
infolio, m. folio
información, f. information; legal inquiry; report; research, investigation
informador (-ra), a. informing, acquainting. s. informant
informal, a. informal, irregular; unreliable (of persons); unconventional
informalidad, f. irregularity; unconventionality; unreliability
informante, m. and f. informant
informar, v.t. to inform, acquaint with; v.i. (law) plead; v.r. (with de, en, sobre) find out about, investigate
informativo, a. informative
informe, ɜ. formless, shapeless. m. report, statement; information; (law) plea; pl. data, particulars; references
infortificable, a. unfortifiable
infortuna, f. (astrol.) evil influence
infortunado, a. unfortunate
infortunio, m. misfortune; unhappiness, adversity; mischance, ill-luck
infracción, f. transgression, infringement
infracto, a. imperturbable
infractor (-ra), a. infringing. s. transgressor, infringer
infrangible, a. unbreakable
infranqueable, a. insuperable, unsurmountable
infrarrojo, a. (phys.) infra-red
infrascrito, a. undersigned; undermentioned
infrecuente, a. infrequent

infringir, *v.t.* to infringe, transgress, break

infructífero, *a.* unfruitful; worthless, useless

infructuosidad, *f.* unfruitfulness; worthlessness, uselessness

infructuoso, *a.* fruitless; useless, worthless

infumable, *a.* unsmokable (tobacco)

infundado, *a.* unfounded, groundless

infundio, *m.* (*fam.*) nonsense, untruth

infundir, *v.t.* to infuse, imbue with

infusión, *f.* infusion

ingeniar, *v.t.* to devise, concoct, plan; *v.r.* contrive, find a way, manage

ingeniería, *f.* engineering

ingeniero, *m.* engineer. **i. agrónomo**, agricultural engineer. **i. de caminos, canales y puertos**, civil engineer. **i. radiotelegrafista**, wireless engineer. **Cuerpo de Ingenieros**, Royal Engineers

ingenio, *m.* mind; inventive capacity; imaginative talent; man of genius; talent, cleverness; ingeniousness; machine; guillotine (bookbinding)

ingeniosidad, *f.* ingeniousness; witticism, clever remark

ingenioso, *a.* talented, clever; ingenious

ingénito, *a.* unengendered, unconceived; innate, inborn

ingente, *a.* huge, enormous

ingenuidad, *f.* ingenuousness, naïveté

ingenuo, *a.* ingenuous, naïve, artless, unaffected

ingle, *f.* (*anat.*) groin

inglés (-esa), *a.* English; British. *s.* Englishman; Briton. *m.* English language; (*fam.*) creditor. **a la inglesa**, in the English fashion. **marcharse a la inglesa**, (*fam.*) to take French leave

inglesismo, *m.* anglicism

inglete, *m.* (*carp.*) mitre

ingobernable, *a.* ungovernable, unruly

ingratitud, *f.* ingratitude

ingrato, *a.* ungrateful; irksome, thankless; disagreeable

ingrávido, *a.* light (in weight)

ingrediente, *m.* ingredient

ingresar, *v.i.* to return, come in (money); (*with en*) join, become a member of, enter

ingreso, *m.* joining, entering, admission; (*com.*) money received; opening, commencement; *pl.* earnings, takings, revenue

ingurgitación, *f.* (*med.*) ingurgitation

ingurgitar, *v.t.* to ingurgitate, swallow

inhábil, *a.* unskilful; unpractised; incompetent, unfit; unsuitable; ill-chosen

inhabilidad, *f.* unskilfulness; incompetence; unsuitability; inability

inhabilitación, *f.* incapacitation; disqualification; disablement

inhabilitar, *v.t.* to make ineligible; disqualify; incapacitate, makeunfit; *v.r.* become ineligible; be incapacitated

inhabitable, *a.* uninhabitable

inhabitado, *a.* uninhabited, deserted

inhalación, *f.* inhalation

inhalador, *m.* (*med.*) inhaler

inhalar, *v.t.* to inhale

inhereditable, *a.* uninheritable

inherencia, *f.* inherency

inherente, *a.* inherent, innate

inhestar, *v.t. irr.* to raise, lift up; erect. See **acertar**

inhibición, *f.* inhibition

inhibir, *v.t.* (*law*) to inhibit; *v.r.* inhibit or restrain oneself

inhibitorio, *a.* (*law*) inhibitory

inhonesto, *a.* indecent, obscene; immodest

inhospedable, inhospitalario, *a.* inhospitable; bleak, uninviting; exposed

inhospitalidad, *f.* inhospitality

inhumación, *f.* inhumation, burial

inhumanidad, *f.* inhumanity; brutality

inhumano, *a.* inhuman; brutal, barbarous

inhumar, *v.t.* to bury, inter

iniciación, *f.* initiation

iniciador (-ra), *a.* initiating; *s.* initiator

inicial, *a.* and *f.* initial

iniciar, *v.t.* to initiate; admit, introduce; originate; *v.r.* be initiated; (ecc.) take minor or first orders

iniciativa, f. initiative

inicuo, a. iniquitous, most unjust, wicked

inimaginable, a. inconceivable

inimicísimo, a. sup. **enemigo,** most hostile

inimitable, a. inimitable

ininteligible, a. unintelligible

iniquidad, f. iniquity, wickedness

injerir, v.t. irr. to insert, place within, introduce; interpolate; v.r. meddle. See **sentir**

injertar, v.t. (agr.) to graft

injerto, m. (agr.) graft; grafting; grafted plant, briar or tree

injuria, f. insult; slander; outrage; wrong, injustice; harm, damage

injuriador (-ra), a. insulting. s. offender, persecutor

injuriar, v.t. to insult; slander; outrage; wrong, persecute; harm, damage

injurioso, a. insulting; slanderous; offensive, abusive; harmful

injusticia, f. injustice; lack of justice; unjust action

injustificable, a. unjustifiable

injustificado, a. unjustified

injusto, a. unjust; unrighteous

inllevable, a. unbearable, intolerable

inmaculado, a. immaculate, pure

inmanejable, a. unmanageable; uncontrollable

inmanencia, f. immanence

inmanente, a. immanent

inmarcesible, inmarchitable, a. unfading, imperishable

inmaterial, a. incorporeal; immaterial

inmaterialidad, f. incorporeity; immateriality

inmaturo, a. immature; unripe

inmediación, f. nearness, proximity; contact; pl. outskirts, neighbourhood, environs

inmediatamente, adv. near; immediately, at once

inmediato, a. adjoining, close, near by; immediate, prompt

inmejorable, a. unsurpassable, unbeatable

inmemorable, inmemorial, a. immemorial

inmensidad, f. vastness, huge extent; infinity; infinite space; immensity; huge number

inmenso, a. vast; infinite; immense; innumerable

inmensurable, a. immeasurable, incalculable

inmerecido, a. undeserved, unmerited

inmérito, a. wrongful, unjust

inmeritorio, a. unmeritorious, unpraiseworthy

inmersión, f. immersion (also ast.); dip

inmigración, f. immigration

inmigrante, a. and m. and f. immigrant

inmigrar, v.i. to immigrate

inminencia, f. imminence

inminente, a. imminent

inmiscuir, v.t. to mix; v.r. meddle

inmisión, f. inspiration

inmobiliario, a. concerning real estate

inmoble, a. immovable; motionless, immobile, stationary; (fig.) unshakable, unflinching

inmoderación, f. immoderateness, excess

inmoderado, a. immoderate; unrestrained, excessive

inmodestia, f. immodesty

inmodesto, a. immodest

inmolación, f. immolation

inmolador (-ra), a. sacrificing. s. immolator

inmolar, v.t. to immolate; (fig.) sacrifice, give up; v.r. (fig.) sacrifice oneself

inmoral, a. immoral

inmoralidad, f. immorality

inmortal, a. immortal

inmortalidad, f. immortality

inmortalizar, v.t. to immortalize

inmotivado, a. unfounded, without reason

inmoto, a. motionless, stationary

inmóvil, a. immovable, fixed; motionless; steadfast, constant

inmovilidad, f. immovability; immobility; constancy, steadfastness

inmovilizar, v.t. to immobilize

inmueble, m. (law) immovable estate (also pl.)

inmundicia, f. filth, nastiness; dirt; rubbish, refuse; obscenity, indecency

inmundo, *a.* dirty, filthy; obscene, indecent; unclean

inmune, *a.* exempt; (*med.*) immune

inmunidad, *f.* exemption; immunity

inmunizar, *v.t.* to immunize

inmutabilidad, *f.* immutability, changelessness; imperturbability

inmutable, *a.* immutable, unchangeable; imperturbable

inmutación, *f.* change, alteration, difference

inmutar, *v.t.* to change, alter, vary; *v.r.* change one's expression (through fear, etc.)

innato, *a.* innate; inherent; instinctive, inborn

innatural, *a.* unnatural

innavegable, *a.* unnavigable; unseaworthy (of ships)

innecesario, *a.* unnecessary

innegable, *a.* undeniable; indisputable, irrefutable

innoble, *a.* plebeian; ignoble

innocuo, *a.* harmless, innocuous

innovación, *f.* innovation

innovador (-ra), *a.* innovatory. *s.* innovator

innovar, *v.t.* to introduce innovations

innumerabilidad, *f.* countless number, multitude

innumerable, *a.* innumerable, countless

innúmero, *a.* countless, innumerable

inobediencia, *f.* disobedience

inobediente, *a.* disobedient

inobservable, *a.* unobservable

inobservancia, *f.* inobservance

inobservante, *a.* unobservant

inocencia, *f.* innocence; simplicity, candour; harmlessness

inocentada, *f.* (*fam.*) naïve remark or action; fool's trap; practical joke

inocente, *a.* innocent; candid, simple; harmless; easily deceived

inocentón, *a.* (*fam.*) extremely credulous and easily hoaxed

inocuidad, *f.* innocuousness

inoculación, *f.* inoculation

inoculador, *m.* inoculator

inocular, *v.t.* to inoculate; pervert, corrupt; contaminate

inodoro, *a.* odourless. *m.* watercloset

inofensivo, *a.* inoffensive, harmless

inolvidable, *a.* unforgettable

inoperable, *a.* inoperable

inopia, *f.* poverty; scarcity

inopinable, *a.* indisputable, unquestionable

inopinado, *a.* unexpected, sudden

inoportunidad, *f.* inopportuneness, unseasonableness; unsuitability

inoportuno, *a.* inopportune, untimely

inordenado, *a.* inordinate, immoderate, excessive

inorgánico, *a.* inorganic

inoxidable, *a.* rustless

inquebrantable, *a.* unbreakable; final, irrevocable

inquietador (-ra), *a.* disturbing. *s.* disturber

inquietar, *v.t.* to disturb; trouble, make anxious, worry; *v.r.* be disquieted, worry

inquieto, *a.* restless; unquiet; fidgety; disturbed; anxious, worried, uneasy

inquietud, *f.* restlessness; uneasiness; worry; trouble, care, anxiety

inquilinato, *m.* tenancy; (*law*) lease; rates (of a house)

inquilino (-na), *s.* tenant; lessee

inquina, *f.* dislike, grudge

inquinar, *v.t.* to contaminate, corrupt, infect

inquiridor (-ra), *a.* inquiring, examining. *s.* investigator

inquirir, *v.t. irr.* to inquire; examine, look into. See **adquirir**

inquisición, *f.* inquiry, investigation; (*ecc.*) Inquisition

inquisidor (-ra), *a.* inquiring, investigating. *s.* investigator. *m.* (*ecc.*) Inquisitor; judge

inquisitorial, *a.* inquisitorial

insaciabilidad, *f.* insatiability

insaciable, *a.* insatiable

insacular, *v.t.* to ballot

insalivación, *f.* insalivation

insalubre, *a.* unhealthy

insanable, *a.* incurable

insania, *f.* insanity

insano, *a.* insane, mad

inscribir, *v.t.* to inscribe; record; enter (a name on a list, etc.), register, enrol; engrave; (*geom.*) inscribe. *Past Part.* **inscrito**

inscripción, *f.* inscription; record, enrolment; registration; government bond

insecable, *a.* unable to be dried

insecticida, *a.* insecticide

insectívoro, *a.* insectivorous

insecto, *m.* insect

inseguridad, *f.* insecurity

inseguro, *a.* insecure; unsafe; uncertain

insensatez, *f.* folly, foolishness

insensato, *a.* foolish, stupid, mad

insensibilidad, *f.* insensibility; imperception; callousness, hardheartedness

insensibilizar, *v.t.* to make insensible (to sensations)

insensible, *a.* insensible; imperceptive, insensitive; unconscious, senseless; imperceptible, inappreciable; callous

inseparabilidad, *f.* inseparability

inseparable, *a.* inseparable

insepulto, *a.* unburied (of the dead)

inserción, *f.* insertion; interpolation; grafting

insertar, *v.t.* to insert; introduce; interpolate; *v.r.* (*bot.*, *zool.*) become attached

inservible, *a.* useless; unfit; unsuitable

insidia, *f.* insidiousness; snare, ambush

insidiador (-ra), *a.* ensnaring. *s.* schemer, ambusher

insidiar, *v.t.* to waylay, ambush; set a trap for; scheme against

insidioso, *a.* insidious; treacherous; scheming, guileful

insigne, *a.* illustrious, famous; distinguished

insignia, *f.* symbol; badge; token; banner, standard; (*naut.*) pennant; *pl.* insignia

insignificancia, *f.* meaninglessness; unimportance, triviality; insignificance, insufficiency

insignificante, *a.* meaningless; unimportant; insignificant, small

insinuación, *f.* insinuation; hint; implication; suggestion

insinuador, *a.* insinuating; suggestive, implicative

insinuar, *v.t.* to insinuate; suggest, hint; *v.r.* ingratiate oneself; creep in (also *fig.*)

insinuativo, *a.* insinuative

insipidez, *f.* tastelessness, insipidity; (*fig.*) dullness

insípido, *a.* tasteless, insipid; dull, uninteresting, boring

insistencia, *f.* insistence

insistente, *a.* insistent

insistir, *v.i.* (*with en or sobre*) to lay stress upon, insist on; persist in

insito, *a.* inherent, innate

insociabilidad, *f.* unsociability

insociable, *a.* unsociable

insolación, *f.* insolation, exposure to the sun; sunstroke

insolar, *v.t.* to expose to the sun's rays; *v.r.* contract sunstroke

insoldable, *a.* unsolderable, unable to be soldered

insolencia, *f.* insolence; impudence, impertinence

insolentarse, *v.r.* to grow insolent; be impudent

insolente, *a.* insolent; impudent, impertinent

insólito, *a.* unaccustomed; infrequent; unusual; unexpected

insolubilidad, *f.* insolubility

insoluble, *a.* insoluble

insoluto, *a.* unpaid, outstanding

insolvencia *f.* insolvency

insolvente, *a.* insolvent

insomne, *a.* sleepless

insomnio, *m.* insomnia

insondable, *a.* unfathomable, bottomless; inscrutable, secret

insoportable, *a.* intolerable, unbearable

insostenible, *a.* indefensible; arbitrary, baseless

inspección, *f.* inspection; supervision; examination; inspectorship; inspector's office

inspeccionar, *v.t.* to inspect; survey, examine. **i. una casa,** to view a house

inspector (-ra), *a.* inspecting, examining. *s.* supervisor. *m.* inspector; surveyor

inspiración, *f.* inspiration; inhalation

inspirador (-ra), *a.* inspiring. *s.* inspirer

inspirar, *v.t.* to breathe in, inhale; blow (of the wind); inspire; *v.r.* be inspired; (*with en*) find inspiration in, imitate

instabilidad, *f.* instability; unsteadiness; shakiness; unreliability, inconstancy

instable, *a.* unstable

instalación, *f.* plant, apparatus; erection, fitting; induction; instalment, settling in

instalador (-ra), *s.* fitter; one who installs (electricity, etc.)

instalar, *v.t.* to appoint, induct; erect (plant, etc.); install, put in; lay on; wire (of electricity); *v.r.* install oneself, settle down

instancia, *f.* instance (also *law*); argument; suggestion; supplication; request; formal petition. de primera i., in the first instance, firstly

instantánea, *f.* (*phot.*) snapshot

instantáneo, *a.* instantaneous

instante, *a.* urgent. *m.* second; instant, moment. a cada i., every minute; frequently. al i., at once, immediately. por instantes, continually; immediately

instar, *v.t.* to press; persuade; insist upon; *v.i.* be urgent, press

instauración, *f.* restoration; renewal; renovation

instaurador (-ra), *a.* renovating, renewing. *s.* restorer, renovator

instaurar, *v.t.* to restore; repair; renovate, renew

instaurativo, *a.* restorative

instigación, *f.* instigation, incitement

instigador (-ra), *s.* instigator

instigar, *v.t.* to instigate, incite; induce

instilación, *f.* instilment, pouring drop by drop; inculcation, implantation

instilar, *v.t.* (*chem.*) instil; implant, inculcate

instintivo, *a.* instinctive

instinto, *m.* instinct. por i., by instinct, naturally

institución, *f.* setting up, establishment; institution; teaching, instruction; *pl.* institutes, digest

institucional, *a.* institutional

instituir, *v.t. irr.* to found, establish; institute; instruct, teach. See huir

instituto, *m.* institute; secondary school. i. de belleza, beauty parlour

institutor, *m.* founder, instituter; tutor

institutriz, *f.* governess

instrucción, *f.* teaching, instruction; knowledge, learning; education; *pl.* orders; rules; instruction. i. primaria, primary education. i. pública, state education

instructivo, *a.* instructive

instructor (-ra), *a.* instructive. *s.* instructor

instruido, *a.* cultured, well-educated; knowledgeable

instruir, *v.t. irr.* to teach, instruct; train; inform, acquaint with; (*law*) formulate. See huir

instrumentación, *f.* (*mus.*) instrumentation

instrumental, *a.* instrumental

instrumentar, *v.t.* (*mus.*) to score

instrumentista, *m.* (*mus.*) instrumentalist; instrument maker

instrumento, *m.* tool, implement; machine, apparatus; (*mus.*) instrument; means, medium; legal document. i. de cuerda, string instrument. i. de percusión, percussion instrument. i. de viento, wind instrument

insuave, *a.* unpleasant (to the senses); rough

insubordinación, *f.* insubordination, rebellion

insubordinado, *a.* insubordinate, unruly

insubordinar, *v.t.* to rouse to rebellion; *v.r.* become insubordinate, rebel

insubsistencia, *f.* instability

insubsistente, *a.* unstable; groundless, unfounded

insubstancial, *a.* insubstantial, unreal, illusory; pointless, worthless, superficial

insubstancialidad, *f.* superficiality, worthlessness

insuficiencia, *f.* insufficiency, shortage; incompetence, inefficiency

insuficiente, *a.* insufficient, scarce, inadequate

insuflación, *f.* (*med.*) insufflation

insuflar, *v.t.* (*med.*) to insufflate

insufrible, *a.* insufferable, unbearable, intolerable

ínsula, *f.* island

insular, *a.* insular

insulina, *f.* (*med.*) insulin

insulsez, *f.* insipidity, tastelessness; dullness; tediousness

insulso, *a.* insipid, tasteless; tedious; dull

insultador (-ra), *a.* insulting. *s.* insulter

insultante, *a.* insulting

insultar, *v.t.* to insult; call names; *v.r.* take offence

insulto, *m.* insult; sudden attack; sudden illness, fit

insumable, *a.* incalculable; excessive, exorbitant

insumergible, *a.* unsinkable

insumiso, *a.* rebellious

insuperable, *a.* insuperable

insurgente, *a.* insurgent, rebellious. *m.* rebel

insurrección, *f.* insurrection

insurreccionar, *v.t.* to incite to rebellion; *v.r.* rise in rebellion

insurrecto (-ta), *s.* rebel

insustancial, *a.* See **insubstancial**

insustituible, *a.* indispensable

intacto, *a.* untouched; intact, uninjured; whole, entire; complete; pure

intachable, *a.* irreproachable; impeccable, perfect

intangibilidad, *f.* intangibility

intangible, *a.* intangible

integración, *f.* (*math.*) integration

integral, *a.* integral

integrar, *v.t.* to integrate (also *math.*); (*com.*) repay

integridad, *f.* wholeness; completeness; integrity, probity, honesty; virginity

íntegro, *a.* integral, whole; upright, honest

integumento, *m.* integument; pretence, simulation

intelectiva, *f.* understanding

intelecto, *m.* intellect

intelectual, *a.* intellectual

intelectualidad, *f.* understanding, intellectuality; intelligentsia

intelectualismo, *m.* intellectualism

inteligencia, *f.* intelligence; intellect; mental alertness; mind; meaning, sense; experience, skill; understanding, secret agreement; information, knowledge; Intelligence, Secret Service

inteligente, *a.* intelligent; clever; skilful; capable, competent

inteligibilidad, *f.* intelligibility

inteligible, *a.* intelligible; understandable; able to be heard

intemperancia, *f.* intemperance, lack of moderation

intemperante, *a.* intemperate

intemperie, *f.* stormy weather. **a la i.,** at the mercy of the elements; in the open air

intempestivo, *a.* inopportune, ill-timed

intención, *f.* intention; determination, purpose; viciousness (of animals); caution. (*fam.*) **con segunda i.,** with a double meaning, slyly

intencionado, *a.* intentioned, disposed

intencional, *a.* intentional, designed, premeditated

intendencia, *f.* management; supervision; administration; (*pol.*) intendancy. (*mil.*) **Cuerpo de I.,** Army Supply Corps

intendente, *m.* director; manager; (*pol.*) intendant. **i de. ejército,** quartermaster-general

intensar, *v.t.* to intensify

intensidad, *f.* intensity; ardour; vehemence

intensificar, *v.t.* to intensify

intensivo, *a.* intensive

intenso, *a.* intense; ardent; fervent, vehement

intentar, *v.t.* to intend, mean; propose; try, endeavour; initiate

intento, *m.* intention, determination; purpose. **de i.,** on purpose; knowingly

intentona, *f.* (*fam.*) foolhardy attempt

interacción, *f.* interaction; reciprocal effect; (*chem.*) reaction

intercalación, *f.* interpolation; insertion

intercalar, *v.t.* to intercalate; interpolate, include, insert

intercambiable, *a.* interchangeable

intercambio, *m.* interchange

interceder, *v.i.* to intercede, plead for

interceptación, *f.* interception

interceptar, *v.t.* to intercept; interrupt; hinder

intercesión, *f.* intercession

intercesor (-ra), *a.* interceding. *s.* intercessor

intercolumnio, *m.* (*arch.*) intercolumniation

intercutáneo, *a.* intercutaneous

interdecir, *v.t. irr.* to forbid, prohibit. See **decir**

interdicción, *f.* interdiction, prohibition

interdicto, *m.* interdict

interés, *m.* interest; yield, profit; advantage; (*com.*) interest; inclination, fondness; attraction, fascination; *pl.* money matters. **i. compuesto,** compound interest. **intereses creados,** bonds of interest; vested interests

interesado, *a.* involved, concerned; biassed; selfish

interesante, *a.* interesting

interesar(se), *v.i.* and *v.r.* to be interested; *v.t.* (*com.*) invest; interest

interfecto (-ta), *s.* (*law*) victim (of murder)

interferencia, *f.* (*phys.*) interference

interfoliar, *v.t.* to interleave (of a book)

ínterin, *m.* interim. *adv.* meanwhile, in the meantime

interinamente, *adv.* in the interim; provisionally

interinar, *v.t.* to discharge (duties) provisionally, act temporarily as

interino, *a.* acting, provisional, temporary

interior, *a.* interior; inner; inside; indoor; inland; internal, domestic (policies, etc.); inward, spiritual. *m.* interior, inside; mind, soul; *pl.* entrails

interjección, *f.* (*gram.*) interjection, exclamation

interlínea, *f.* (*print.*) lead

interlinear, *v.t.* to write between the lines; (*print.*) lead

interlocución, *f.* dialogue, conversation

interlocutorio, *a.* (*law*) interlocutory

intérlope, *a.* interloping. *m.* and *f.* interloper

interludio, *m.* interlude

intermediario (-ia), *a.* and *s.* intermediary. *m.* (*com.*) middleman

intermedio, *a.* intermediate. *m.* interim; (*theat.*) interval. **por i. de,** through, by the mediation of

intermisión, *f.* intermission, interval

intermitencia, *f.* intermittence

intermitente, *a.* intermittent

intermitir, *v.t.* to interrupt, suspend, discontinue

internación, *f.* going inside; penetration; taking into

internacional, *a.* international

internacionalismo, *m.* internationalism

internacionalista, *m.* and *f.* internationalist

internacionalización, *f.* internationalization

internado, *m.* boarding-school

internamiento, *m.* internment

internar, *v.t.* to take or send inland; *v.i.* penetrate; *v.r.* (*with en*) go into the interior of (a country); get into the confidence of; study deeply (a subject)

interno (-na), *a.* interior; internal; inner; inside; boarding (pupil). *s.* boarding-school pupil; (*med.*) interne

internodio, *m.* internode

internuncio, *m.* (*ecc.*) internuncio; interlocutor; representative

interoceánico, *a.* interoceanic

interpaginar, *v.t.* to interleave (of books)

interpelación, *f.* (*law*) interpellation; appeal

interpelar, *v.t.* (*law*) to interpellate; appeal to, ask protection from

interpolación, *f.* interpolation, insertion; interruption

interpolador (-ra), *s.* interpolator; interrupter

interpolar, *v.t.* to interpolate; interject

interponer, *v.t. irr.* to interpose, insert, intervene; designate as an arbitrator; *v.r.* intervene. See **poner**

interposición, *f.* interposition; intervention; mediation, arbitration

interpresa, *f.* (*mil.*) surprise attack

interpretación, *f.* interpretation; translation

interpretador (-ra), *a.* interpretative. *s.* interpreter

interpretar, *v.t.* to interpret; translate; attribute; expound, explain. **i. mal,** to misconstrue; translate wrongly

interpretativo, *a.* interpretative

intérprete, *m.* and *f.* interpreter (all meanings)

interregno, *m.* interregnum. **i. parlamentario,** parliamentary recess

interrogación, *f.* interrogation, question; (*print.*) question-mark

interrogador (-ra), *s.* questioner

interrogante, *a.* interrogating. *m.* (*print.*) question-mark

interrogar, *v.t.* to interrogate, question

interrogativo, *a.* interrogative

interrogatorio, *m.* interrogatory

interrumpir, *v.t.* to interrupt; hinder, obstruct; (*elec.*) break contact

interrupción, *f.* interruption; stoppage (of work); (*elec.*) break

interruptor (-ra), *a.* interrupting. *s.* interrupter. *m.* (*elec.*) switch, interruptor. **i. de dos direcciones,** (*elec.*) two-way switch

intersecarse, *v.r.* (*geom.*) to intersect

intersección, *f.* (*geom.*) intersection

intersticio, *m.* interstice, crack, crevice; interval, intervening space

intervalo, *m.* interval (also *mus.*)

intervención, *f.* intervention; mediation, intercession; auditing of accounts

intervenir, *v.i. irr.* to take part (in); intervene, interfere; arbitrate, mediate; happen, occur; *v.t.* (*com.*) audit. See **venir**

interventor (-ra), *a.* intervening. *s.* one who intervenes. *m.* auditor; inspector

interviev, *m.* interview

intervocálico, *a.* intervocalic

intestado (-da), *a.* and *s.* (*law*) intestate

intestinal, *a.* intestinal

intestino, *a.* intestinal. *m.* intestine

íntima, intimación, *f.* intimation, notification

intimar, *v.t.* to intimate; inform, notify; *v.r.* penetrate; *v.r.* and *v.i.* become intimate or friendly

intimidación, *f.* intimidation, terrorization

intimidad, *f.* intimacy

intimidar, *v.t.* to intimidate, terrorize, cow

íntimo, *a.* intimate; deep-seated, inward; private, personal

intitular, *v.t.* to give a title to, entitle, call; *v.r.* call oneself

intolerable, *a.* intolerable; unbearable

intolerancia, *f.* narrow-mindedness, intolerance, bigotry

intolerante, *a.* narrow-minded, illiberal; (*med.*) intolerant

intonso, *a.* long-haired, unshorn; boorish, ignorant

intoxicación, *f.* poisoning

intoxicar, *v.t.* to poison

intraducible, *a.* untranslatable

intramuros, *adv.* within the town walls, within the city

intranquilidad, *f.* disquiet, restlessness; anxiety

intranquilizador, *a.* disquieting, perturbing

intranquilizar, *v.t.* to disquiet, make uneasy, worry

intranquilo, *a.* uneasy, anxious

intransferible, *a.* untransferable, not transferable

intransigencia, *f.* intolerance, intransigence

intransigente, *a.* intolerant, intransigent

intransitable, *a.* impassable; unsurmountable

intransitivo, *a.* (*gram.*) intransitive

intratable, *a.* intractable; impassable; rough; unsociable, difficult

intrauterino, *a.* (*med.*) intrauterine

intravenoso, *a.* (*med.*) intravenous

intrepidez, *f.* intrepidity, dauntlessness, gallantry

intrépido, *a.* intrepid, dauntless, gallant

intriga, *f.* scheme, intrigue; entanglement; (*lit.*) plot

intrigante, *m.* and *f.* intriguer, schemer

intrigar, *v.i.* to intrigue, scheme, plot

intrincación, *f.* intricacy

intrincado, *a.* intricate

intrincar, *v.t.* to complicate; obscure, confuse

intríngulis, *m.* (*fam.*) ulterior motive

intrínseco, *a.* intrinsic, inherent; essential

introducción, *f.* introduction (all meanings)

introducir, *v.t. irr.* to introduce; insert; fit in; drive in; present, introduce; bring into use; cause, occasion; show in, bring in; *v.r.* interfere, meddle; enter. See **conducir**

introductor (**-ra**), *s.* introducer

introito, *m.* preamble, introduction; (*ecc.*) introit; (*theat., ant.*) prologue

intromisión, *f.* intromission; interference; (*geol.*) intrusion

introspección, *f.* introspection

introverso, *a.* (*psy.*) introvert

intruso (**-sa**), *a.* intruding, intrusive. *s.* intruder

intubación, *f.* (*surg.*) intubation

intuición, *f.* intuition

intuir, *v.t. irr.* to know by intuition. See **huir**

intuitivo, *a.* intuitive

intuito, *m.* glance, look, view

intumescencia, *f.* intumescence

inulto, *a.* (*poet.*) unavenged, unpunished

inundación, *f.* flood; flooding; excess, superabundance

inundar, *v.t.* to flood; swamp; (*fig.*) inundate, overwhelm

inurbanidad, *f.* discourtesy, impoliteness

inurbano, *a.* discourteous, uncivil, impolite

inusitado, *a.* unusual, unaccustomed; rare

inútil, *a.* useless

inutilidad, *f.* uselessness

inutilizar, *v.t.* to render useless; disable, incapacitate; spoil, damage

invadeable, *a.* impassable, unfortlable

invadir, *v.t.* to invade

invaginación, *f.* (*med.*) invagination

invalidación, *f.* invalidation

invalidar, *v.t.* to invalidate

invalidez, *f.* invalidity; disablement; infirmity

inválido (**-da**), *a.* weak, infirm; invalid, null; disabled. *s.* invalid; disabled soldier

invariabilidad, *f.* invariability

invariable, *a.* invariable

invariación, *f.* invariableness

invariante, *m.* (*math.*) invariant

invasión, *f.* invasion, encroachment, incursion

invasor (**-ra**), *a.* invading; (*med.*) attacking. *s.* invader

invectiva, *f.* invective

invencibilidad, *f.* invincibility

invencible, *a.* invincible

invención, *f.* invention, discovery; deception, fabrication, lie; creative imagination; finding (e.g. **i. de la Santa Cruz,** Invention of the Holy Cross)

invencionero (**-ra**), *s.* inventor; schemer, deceiver

invendible, *a.* unsalable

inventar, *v.t.* to invent; create; imagine; concoct, fabricate (lies, etc.)

inventariar, *v.t.* to make an inventory of; (*com.*) take stock of

inventario, *m.* inventory; (*com.*) stock-taking

inventiva, *f.* inventiveness, ingenuity; creativeness

inventivo, *a.* inventive

invento, *m.* See **invención**

inventor (**-ra**), *s.* inventor, discoverer; liar, story-teller

inverecundia, *.f.* impertinence, impudence

inverecundo, *a.* shameless, brazen

inverisímil, *a.* See **inverosímil**

invernáculo, *m.* greenhouse; conservatory

invernada, *f.* winter season; hibernation

invernadero, *m.* winter quarters; greenhouse

invernal, *a.* wintry; winter

invernar, *v.i. irr.* to winter; hibernate; be winter time. See **acertar**

invernizo, *a.* wintry, winter

inverosímil, *a.* unlikely, improbable

inverosimilitud, *f.* improbability

inversamente, *adv.* inversely

inverso, *a.* inverse; inverted

invertebrado, *a.* and *m.* invertebrate

invertir, *v.t. irr.* to invert, transpose; reverse; (*com.*) invest; spend (time). See **sentir**

investidura, *f.* investiture

investigación, *f.* investigation examination; research; inquiry

investigador (**-ra**), *a.* investigating. *s.* investigator; research worker

investigar, *v.t.* to investigate, examine; research on

investir, *v.t.* *irr.* to confer upon, decorate with; invest, appoint. See **pedir**

inveterado, *a.* inveterate

invicto, *a.* invincible; unconquered

invierno, *m.* winter; rainy season

inviolabilidad, *f.* inviolability. **i. parlamentaria**, parliamentary immunity

inviolable, *a.* inviolable; infallible

inviolado, *a.* inviolate

invisibilidad, *f.* invisibility

invisible, *a.* invisible

invitación, *f.* invitation

invitado (-da), *s.* guest

invitar, *v.t.* to invite; urge, request; allure, attract

invocación, *f.* invocation

invocador (-ra), *s.* invoker

invocar, *v.t.* to invoke

involucro, *m.* (*bot.*) involucre

involuntariedad, *f.* involuntariness

involuntario, *a.* involuntary

invulnerabilidad, *f.* invulnerability

invulnerable, *a.* invulnerable

inyección, *f.* injection

inyectado, *a.* bloodshot (of eyes)

inyectar, *v.t.* to inject

ionización, *f.* (*chem.*) ionization

ipecacuana, *f.* (*bot.*) ipecacuanha

iperita, *f.* mustard gas

ir, *v.i.* *irr.* to go; bet (e.g. **Van cinco pesetas que no lo hace**, I bet five pesetas he doesn't do it); be different, be changed (e.g. **¡Qué diferencia va entre esto y aquello!** What a difference there is between this and that!); suit, be becoming, fit (e.g. **El vestido no te va bien**, The dress doesn't suit you); extend; lead, go in the direction of (e.g. **Este camino va a Lérida**, This road leads to Lerida); get along, do, proceed, be (e.g. **¿Cómo te va estos días?** How are you getting along these days?); come (e.g. **Ahora voy**, I'm coming now); (*math.*) carry (e.g. **siete y van cuatro**, seven, and four to carry); (*math.*) leave (e.g. **De quince a seis van nueve**, Six from fifteen leaves nine). With a

gerund, **ir** indicates the continuance of the action, or may mean to become or to grow (e.g. **Iremos andando hacia el mar**, We shall go on walking towards the sea, or **Entre tanto iba amaneciendo**, In the meanwhile it was growing light). With a past participle, **ir** means to be (e.g. **Voy encantado de lo que he visto**, I am delighted with what I have seen). With *prep.* *a + infin*, **ir** means to prepare (to do) or to intend (to do) or to be on the point of doing (e.g. **Van a cantar la canción que te gusta**, They are going (or preparing) to sing the song you like). With *prep.* *a + noun*, **ir** indicates destination (e.g. **Voy al cine**, I'm going to the cinema. **¿Adónde vamos?** Where are we going to?). **ir + con** means to go in the company of or to do a thing in a certain manner (e.g. **Hemos de ir con cuidado**, We must go carefully). **ir + en** means to concern, interest (e.g. **¿Qué le va a él en este asunto?** What has this affair to do with him?). **ir + por** means to follow the career of, become (e.g. **Juan va por abogado**, John is going to be a lawyer). It also means to go and bring, or to go for (e.g. **Iré por agua**, I shall go and bring (or for) water). *v.r.* to go away, leave, depart; die; leak (of liquids); evaporate; overbalance, slip (e.g. **Se le fueron los pies**, He slipped (and lost his balance)); be worn out, grow old, deteriorate; (*med.*) be incontinent; (*fig.*, *fam.*) **írsele a uno una cosa**, not to notice or not to understand a thing. (*naut.*) **irse a pique**, to founder, sink. **Se le fueron los ojos tras María**, He couldn't keep his eyes off Mary. **i. a caballo**, to ride, go on horseback. **i. adelante**, to go on ahead, lead; (*fig.*, *fam.*) forge ahead, go ahead. **i. a una**, to co-operate in. **i. bien** (*fig.*, *fam.*) to go on well; be well. **i. de brazo**, to walk arm-in-arm. **i. de compras**, to go shopping. **i. de juerga** (*fam.*) to go on the binge. **i. de bicicleta** *or* **en** coche, to go by bicycle or to ride (in a car or carriage). (*fig.*, *fam.*) i. tirando, to carry on, manage. ¿ Cómo le va ? How are things with you ? How are you getting along? (*fam.*) no irle ni venirle a uno nada en un asunto, to be not in the least concerned in (an affair). ¡ Qué va! Rubbish! Nothing of the sort! ¿ Quién va ? (*mil.*) Who goes there? Vamos, Let's go (also used as exclamation : Good gracious! You don't say so! Well!) Vamos a ver ..., Let's see ... ¡ Vaya! What a . . . !; Come now! Never mind! Vaya Vd a paseo *or* Vaya con su música a otra parte, Take yourself off! Get out! ¡ Vaya Vd con Dios! God keep you! Good-bye! *Pres. Ind.* voy, vas, va, vamos, váis, van. *Pres. Part.* yendo. *Preterite* fuí, fuiste, fué, fuimos, fuisteis, fueron. *Imperf.* iba, etc. *Pres. Subjunc.* vaya, etc. *Imperf. Subjunc.* fuese, etc. *Imperat.* vé

ira, *f.* wrath, anger; vengeance; raging, fury (of elements); *pl.* cruelties, acts of vengeance

iracundia, *f.* irascibility, irritability; anger

iracundo, *a.* irascible, irritable, choleric; angry; raging, tempestuous

iranio (-ia), *a.* and *s.* Iranian (Asia)

irascibilidad, *f.* irascibility; petulance

iridio, *m.* (*chem.*) iridium

iridiscencia, *f.* iridescence

iridiscente, *a.* iridescent

iris, *m.* rainbow; (*anat.*) iris (of eye)

irisación, *f.* irisation

irisar, *v.i.* to be iridescent

irlandés (-esa), *a.* and *s.* Irish (man)

ironía, *f.* irony

irónico, *a.* ironical

iroqués (-esa), *a.* and *s.* Iroquois

irracional, *a.* irrational; illogical, unreasonable; (*math.*) irrational, absurd

irracionalidad, *f.* irrationality, unreasonableness

irradiación, *f.* radiation, irradiation

irradiar, *v.t.* to radiate, irradiate

irrazonable, *a.* unreasonable

irreal, *a.* unreal

irrealidad, *f.* unreality

irrealizable, *a.* unachievable, unattainable

irrebatible, *a.* irrefutable, evident

irreconciliable, *a.* irreconcilable, intransigent

irrecuperable, *a.* irretrievable

irredimible, *a.* irredeemable

irreemplazable, *a.* irreplaceable

irreflexión, *f.* thoughtlessness; impetuosity

irreflexivo, *a.* thoughtless; rash, impetuous

irreformable, *a.* unreformable

irrefragable, *a.* indisputable, unquestionable

irrefrenable, *a.* unmanageable, uncontrollable

irrefutable, *a.* irrefutable

irregular, *a.* irregular; infrequent, rare

irregularidad, *f.* irregularity; abnormality; (*fam.*) moral lapse

irreligión, *f.* irreligion

irreligiosidad, *f.* impiety, godlessness

irreligioso, *a.* irreligious, impious

irremediable, *a.* irremediable

irremediablemente, *adv.* unavoidably; hopelessly

irremisible, *a.* unpardonable, inexcusable

irremunerado, *a.* unremunerated, gratuitous

irreparable, *a.* irreparable

irreprensible, *a.* blameless, unexceptionable

irreprochable, *a.* irreproachable

irresistible, *a.* irresistible; ravishing

irresolución, *f.* vacillation, indecision

irresoluto, *a.* hesitant, irresolute

irrespetuoso, *a.* disrespectful

irresponsabilidad, *f.* irresponsibility

irresponsable, *a.* irresponsible

irreverencia, *f.* irreverence

irreverente, *a.* irreverent

irrevocabilidad, *f.* irrevocability, finality

irrevocable, *a.* irrevocable

irrigación, *f.* irrigation

irrigador, *m.* spray, sprinkler; (*med.*) syringe, spray

irrigar, *v.t.* (*med.*, *agr.*) to irrigate

irrisible, *a.* ridiculous, laughable, absurd

irrisión, *f.* derision; laughing-stock

irrisorio, *a.* ridiculous; derisive

irritabilidad, *f.* irritability, petulance, irascibility

irritable, *a.* irritable

irritación, *f.* (*med.*) irritation; petulance, exasperation

irritador, *a.* irritating; exasperating. *m.* irritant

irritante, *a.* irritating; exasperating

irritar, *v.t.* to exasperate, annoy; provoke, inflame; (*med.*, *law*) irritate

irrito, *a.* (*law*) null, void

irrogar, *v.t.* to occasion (damage, harm)

irrompible, *a.* unbreakable

irrumpir, *v.i.* to enter violently, break in

irrupción, *f.* irruption, incursion, invasion

irruptor, *a.* invading, attacking

isabelino, *a.* Isabelline. Pertaining to Spanish Queen Isabella II (reigned 1830–68); bay (of horses)

isla, *f.* island; block (of houses)

islacionismo, *m.* (*pol.*) isolationism

islámico, *a.* Islamic

islamismo, *m.* Mohammedanism

islamita, *a.* and *m.* and *f.* Mohammedan

islandés (-esa), islándico (-ca), *a.* Icelandic. *s.* Icelander. *m.* Icelandic (language)

isleño (-ña), *a.* island. *s.* islander; native of the Canary Isles

isleta, *f.* islet

islote, *m.* barren islet

ismaelita, *a.* and *m.* and *f.* Arab

isobárico, *a.* isobaric

isocronismo, *m.* isochronism

isomería, *f.* (*chem.*) isomerism

isómero, *a.* (*chem.*) isomeric

isométrico, *a.* isometric

isomorfo, *a.* isomorphic

isotermo, *a.* isothermal

isotope, isotopo, *m.* isotope

israelita, *m.* and *f.* Israelite. *a.* Israelitish

istmeño (-ña), *s.* native of an isthmus

ístmico, *a.* isthmian

istmo, *m.* isthmus

italianismo, *m.* Italianism

italianizar, *v.t.* to italianize

italiano (-na), *a.* and *s.* Italian. *m.* Italian language

itálico, *a.* Italic

iteración, *f.* iteration, repetition

iterar, *v.t.* to repeat, reiterate

iterativo, *a.* iterative, repetitive

itinerario, *a.* and *m.* itinerary

izar, *v.t.* (*naut.*) to hoist

izote, *m.* (*bot.*) yucca

izquierda, *f.* left, left-hand side; (*pol.*) left wing party, Left. **¡I.!** (*mil.*) Left face! **a la i.**, on the left

izquierdo, *a.* left, left-hand; left-handed; bent, twisted, crooked

J

jabalí, *m.* wild boar

jabalina, *f.* sow of wild boar; javelin

jabato, *m.* young wild boar

jabón, *m.* soap. **j. ,blando,** soft soap. **j. de olor** *or* **j. de tocador,** toilet soap. **j. de sastre,** French chalk, steatite

jabonadura, *f.* soaping; *pl.* soap-suds, lather

jabonar, *v.t.* to soap; wash; (*fam.*) dress down, scold

jaboncillo, *m.* toilet soap; steatite

jabonera, *f.* soap-dish or box; (*bot.*) soapwort

jabonería, *f.* soap factory or shop

jabonoso, *a.* soapy

jaca, *f.* pony; filly

jácara, *f.* gay roguish ballad; song and dance

jácena, *f.* (*arch.*) beam, girder

jacinto, *m.* (*bot.*) hyacinth; (*min.*) jacinth. **j. de ceilán,** zircon. **j. occidental,** topaz. **j. oriental,** ruby

jaco, *m.* short coat of mail; hack, jade

jacobinismo, *m.* Jacobinism

jacobino (-na), *s.* Jacobin

jactancia, *f.* bragging, boasting

jactancioso (-sa), *a.* boastful. *s.* braggart

jactarse, *v.r.* to brag, boast

jaculatoria, *f.* ejaculatory prayer

jaculatorio, *a.* ejaculatory

jade, *m.* (*min.*) jade

jadeante, *a.* panting

jadear, *v.i.* to pant

jadeo, *m.* pant; panting; hard breathing

jacz, *m.* harness (gen. *pl.*); kind, sort; *pl.* trappings

jaguar, *m.* jaguar

¡ja, ja, ja! *interj.* ha! ha! ha!

jalbegar, *v.t.* to whitewash; make up the face

jalbegue, *m.* whitewashing

jalde, *a.* bright yellow

jalea, *f.* jelly. **j. de membrillo,** quince jelly

jalear, *v.t.* to encourage, urge on (by shouts, etc.)

jaleo, *m.* act of encouraging dancers by clapping, shouting, etc.; Andalusian song and dance, (*fam.*) uproar

jalifa, *m.* (in Morocco) lieutenant, substitute

jalón, *m.* surveying rod

jamaicano (-na), *a.* and *s.* Jamaican

jamás, *adv.* never. **nunca j.,** never. **por siempre j.,** for always, for ever

jamba, *f.* (*arch.*) jamb of door or window

jamelgo, *m.* sorry nag, miserable hack

jamón, *m.* ham

jamona, *f.* (*fam.*) nicely covered, plumpish, woman

jansenismo, *m.* Jansenism

jansenista, *m.* and *f.* and *a.* Jansenist

japonés (-esa), *a.* and *s.* Japanese. *m.* Japanese language

jaque, *m.* check (in chess); braggart. **j. mate,** checkmate. **en j.,** at bay

jaquear, *v.t.* to check (in chess); (*mil.*) harass the enemy

jaqueca, *f.* migraine, sick-headache. (*fam.*) **dar una j.,** to annoy

jarabe, *m.* syrup

jarana, *f.* round-house; (*fam.*) revelry; fight, rough house; trick, deception

jarcia, *f.* equipment; (*naut.*) tackle, rigging (gen. *pl.*); fishing tackle; (*fam.*) heap, mixture, medley

jardín, *m.* garden

jardinera, *f.* plant stand, jardinière; open tramcar

jardinería, *f.* gardening

jardinero, *m.* gardener

jareta, *f.* (*sew.*) running hem; (*naut.*) netting

jarra, *f.* jar, jug. **en jarras,** arms akimbo

jarrero, *m.* jug seller or manufacturer

jarrete, *m.* calf of leg

jarretera, *f.* garter. **Orden de la J.,** Order of the Garter

jarro, *m.* pitcher; jug; jar; vase

jarrón, *m.* garden urn; vase

jaspe, *m.* (*min.*) jasper

jaspeado, *a.* marbled, mottled; dappled; frosted (of glass)

jauja, *f.* (*fig.*) paradise, land of milk and honey

jaula, *f.* cage; crate; miner's cage

jauría, *f.* pack of hounds

javanés (-esa), *a.* and *s.* Javanese

jazmín, *m.* (*bot.*) jasmine. **j. amarillo,** yellow jasmine. **j. de la India,** gardenia

jedive, *m.* Khedive

jefa, *f.* forewoman; manageress; leader, head

jefatura, *f.* chieftainship; managership; leadership. **j. de policía,** police station or headquarters

jefe, *m.* chief; head, leader; manager; (*mil.*) commanding officer. (*mil.*) **j. de Estado Mayor,** Chief of Staff. **j. del tren,** railway guard

jengibre, *m.* (*bot.*) ginger

jenízaro, *m.* janissary

jeque, *m.* sheikh

jerarca, *m.* hierarch

jerarquía, *f.* hierarchy

jerárquico, *a.* hierarchical

jeremiada, *f.* lamentation

jerez, *m.* sherry

jerga, *f.* thick frieze cloth; jargon

jergón, *m.* straw or hay mattress, pallet; misfit (garments); (*fam.*) fat, lazy person

jerife, *m.* Shereef

jerigonza, *f.* jargon; gibberish

jeringa, *f.* syringe

jeringar, *v.t.* to inject; syringe; (*fam.*) annoy

jeringuilla, *f.* (*bot.*) mock-orange

jeroglífico, *a.* hieroglyphic. *m.* hieroglyph

jersey, *m.* jersey, sweater

jesuita, *m.* Jesuit

jesuita, jesuítico, *a.* jesuitical

Jesús, *m.* Jesus. *interj.* goodness!; bless you! (said to someone sneezing). ¡ay J.! Alas! (*fam.*) **en un decir J.,** in a trice

jeta, *f.* hog's snout; blubber lip; (*fam.*) face, mug

jibia, *f.* (*zool.*) cuttle-fish

jícara, *f.* small cup

jifa, *f.* meat offal

jifero, *m.* butcher, slaughterer

jifía, *f.* sword-fish

jilguero, *m.* (*orn.*) goldfinch

jinete, *m.* horseman, rider; horse soldier, cavalryman

jingoísmo, *m.* jingoism

jip, *m.* (*mil.*) jeep

jipijapa, *f.* very fine straw. **sombrero de j.,** panama hat

jira, *f.* strip of cloth; picnic; tour

jirafa, *f.* giraffe

jirón, *m.* rag; piece off a dress, etc.; portion of whole

jiujitsu, *m.* jj-jutsu

jocosidad, *f.* pleasantry, jocularity; joke

jocoso, *a.* waggish; jocose, joyous

jocundidad, *f.* jocundity

jocundo, *a.* jocund

jofaina, *f.* wash-bowl

jónico (-ca), *a.* Ionic. *s.* Ionian. *m.* (metrics) Ionic foot

jornada, *f.* day's journey; journey, trip; (*mil.*) expedition; duration of working day; opportunity; span of life; act of a drama. **a grandes jornadas,** by forced marches, rapidly

jornal, *m.* day's wage or labour

jornalero (-ra), *s.* day labourer; wage earner

joroba, *f.* hump; (*fam.*) impertinence, nuisance

jorobado (-da), *a.* humpbacked. *s.* hunchback

jota, *f.* name of letter J; popular Spanish dance; jot, tittle (always used negatively). **no saber j.,** to be completely ignorant

joven, *a.* young. *m.* and *f.* young man or woman

jovenzuelo (-la), *s.* youngster, boy

jovialidad, *f.* joviality, cheerfulness

joya, *f.* jewel; present; (*arch.*) astragal; (*fig.*) a jewel of a person

joyería, *f.* jeweller's shop or workshop

joyero, *m.* jeweller; jewel-case

juanete, *m.* bunion; prominent cheekbone; (*naut.*) topgallant sail

juanetudo, *a.* having bunions; with prominent cheekbones

jubilación, *f.* retirement; pensioning off; pension

jubilado, *a.* retired

jubilar, *v.t.* to pension off; excuse from certain duties; (*fam.*) put aside as useless (things); *v.r.* rejoice; retire or be pensioned off

jubileo, *m.* jubilee

júbilo, *m.* rejoicing, merriment

jubiloso, *a.* jubilant, happy

jubón, *m.* doublet; bodice

judaico, *a.* Judaic

judaísmo, *m.* Judaism

judas, *m.* Judas; traitor

judería, *f.* ghetto; Jewry

judía, *f.* Jewess; (*bot.*) haricot bean. **judías verdes,** string beans

judicatura, *f.* judicature; judgeship; judiciary

judío (-ía), *a.* Jewish. *s.* Jew. **j. errante,** wandering Jew

juego, *m.* play, sport; gambling; hand (of cards); set; suite; (*mech.*) play, working. **j. de café,** coffee-set. **j. de los cientos,** piquet. **j. de manos,** sleight of hand, conjuring. **j. de naipes,** game of cards. **j. limpio,** fair play. **j. sencillo,** single (at tennis). **j. sucio,** foul play. **juegos florales,** floral games. **juegos malabares,** jugglery. **en j.,** in operation; at stake. **entrar en j.,** to come into play. **hacer j.,** to match. **hacer juegos malabares,** to juggle

juerga, *f.* (*fam.*) spree, binge. **ir de j.,** (*fam.*) to go on the binge

jueves, *m.* Thursday. ¡No es cosa del otro j.! (*fam.*) It's no great shakes!

juez, *m.* judge. **j. arbitrador,** arbitrator; referee. **j. municipal,** magistrate

jugada, *f.* play; playing; move, throw; (*fig.*) bad turn

jugador (-ra), *a.* gambling; playing. *s.* gambler; player. **j. de manos,** conjurer

jugar, *v.i. irr.* to play; frolic; take part in a game; gamble; make a move (in a game); (*mech.*) work; handle (weapon); (*com.*) intervene; *v.t.* play (match); bet; handle (weapon); risk. **j. el 'lance**, (*fig.*) to play one's cards well. **j. limpio**, to play fair; (*fig.*, *fam.*) be straightforward. **j. sucio**, to play foul. **jugarse el todo por el todo**, to stake one's all. *Pres. Ind.* **juego, juegas, juega, juegan**. *Pres. Subjunc.* **juegue, juegues, juegue, jueguen**

jugarreta, *f.* (*fam.*) bad play; dirty trick

juglar, *m.* entertainer; buffoon, juggler; minstrel

juglaresco, *a.* pertaining to minstrels

jugo, *m.* sap; juice; (*fig.*) essence. **j. de muñeca**, elbow-grease

jugosidad, *f.* juiciness, succulence; (*fig.*) pithiness

jugoso, *a.* juicy, succulent; (*fig.*) pithy

juguete, *m.* toy; plaything; (*fig.*) puppet

juguetear, *v.i.* to frolic, gambol

jugueteo, *m.* gambolling; play, dalliance

juguetería, *f.* toy trade; toyshop

juguetón, *a.* playful

juicio, *m.* judgment; wisdom, prudence; sanity, right mind; opinion; horoscope. **j. final**, Last Judgment. **j. sano**, right mind. **asentar el j.**, to settle down, become sensible. **estar fuera de j.**, to be insane. **pedir en j.**, to sue at law

juicioso, *a.* judicious; prudent

julio, *m.* July; (*elec.*) joule

jumento, *m.* ass; beast of burden

juncal, *a.* reedy; rushy; (*fam.*) slim, lissom

juncar, *m.* reedy ground

junco, *m.* (*bot.*) rush, reed; (*naut.*) junk

juncoso, *a.* reed-like; rushy; reedy

junio, *m.* June

junquillo, *m.* (*bot.*) jonquil; (*arch.*) reed moulding

junta, *f.* joint; assembly, council; committee; union, association; session, sitting; entirety, whole; board, management. **j. de comercio**, Board of Trade. **j. directiva**, managerial board

juntamente, *adv.* jointly; simultaneously

juntar, *v.t.* to join, unite (*with prep. a* or *con*); couple; assemble; amass; leave ajar (door); *v.r.* (*with con*) frequent company of; meet; join; copulate

junto, *a.* united, together. *adv.* (*with prep. a*) near; *adv.* together, simultaneously. **en j.**, altogether in all

juntura, *f.* joining; joint; seam; juncture

jura, *f.* solemn oath; swearing

jurado, *m.* juryman; jury

juramentar, *v.t.* to swear in; *v.r.* take an oath

juramento, *m.* oath; curse, imprecation. **j. falso**, perjury. **prestar j.**, to take the oath

jurar, *v.i.* to swear an oath; swear allegiance; *v.i.* curse, be profane

jurídico, *a.* juridical, legal

jurisconsulto, *m.* jurisconsult

jurisdicción, *f.* (*law*) jurisdiction; boundary; authority

jurisprudencia, *f.* jurisprudence

jurista, *m.* jurist

justa, *f.* joust; tournament; contest

justar, *v.i.* to joust

justicia, *f.* justice; equity, right; penalty, punishment; righteousness; court of justice; (*fam.*) death penalty, execution. **administrar j.**, to dispense justice

justiciero, *a.* just

justificable, *a.* justifiable

justificación, *f.* justification, impartiality, fairness; convincing proof

justificar, *v.t.* to justify, vindicate; adjust, regulate; prove innocent; *v.r.* justify oneself; prove one's innocence

justillo, *m.* jerkin

justipreciar, *v.t.* to appraise, value

justiprecio, *m.* appraisement, valuation

justo, *a.* just; righteous, virtuous; exact, accurate; tight-fitting, close. *adv.* justly; exactly; tightly

juvenil, *a.* young

juventud, *f.* youthfulness, youth; younger generation

juzgado, *m.* court of law; jurisdiction; judgeship

juzgar, *v.t.* to judge, pass sentence on; decide, consider

K

ka, *f.* name of the letter K
káiser, *m.* Kaiser
kan, *m.* Khan
kantiano, *a.* Kantian
kantismo, *m.* Kantianism
kermese, *f.* kermess, festival
keroseń, *m.* kerosene
kilo, *prefix* meaning a thousand. *m. abb.* kilogramme
kilociclo, *m.* (*elec.*) kilocycle
kilogramo, *m.* kilogramme (2·17 lb.)
kilolitro, *m.* kilolitre
kilometraje, *m.* number of kilometres; mileage
kilométrico, *a.* kilometric. **billete k.,** tourist ticket
kilómetro, *m.* kilometre (about ⅝ mile)
kilovatio, *m.* (*elec.*) kilowatt
kiosco, *m.* kiosk
krausismo, *m.* Krausism
krausista, *a.* and *m.* and *f.* Krausist

L

la, *def. art. f. sing.* the, (e.g. **la mesa,** the table). **la** is replaced by **el** (*m. sing.*) before feminine noun beginning with stressed *a* or *ha* (e.g. **el hambre,** hunger). **la** is sometimes used before names of famous women (e.g. **la Juana de Arco, la Melba** (Joan of Arc, Melba)) and is generally not translated. *pers. pron. acc. f. sing.* her; it (e.g. **La veo venir,** I see her coming). *dem. pron.* followed by *de,* or by *que* introducing relative clause, that of, that which, the one that, she who (e.g. **La casa está lejos de la en que escribo,** The house is far from the one in which I write). **la de** is used familiarly for Mrs. (e.g. **la de Jiménez,** Mrs. Jimenez). **la** means some, any, one, as substitution for noun already given (e.g. **Su hija lo haría si la tuviera,** Her daughter would do it if she had one)
lábaro, *m.* labarum, standard
laberíntico, *a.* labyrinthine

laberinto, *m.* labyrinth; (*fig.*) tangle, complication; (*anat.*) labyrinth of the ear
labia, *f.* (*fam.*) blarney, gab
labial, *a.* labial
labihendido, *a.* hare-lipped
labio, *m.* lip; rim, edge. **l. leporino,** hare-lip. **cerrar los labios,** to close one's lips; keep silent
labor, *f.* work, toil; sewing; needlework; husbandry, farming; silkworm egg; (*min.*) working; trimming; ploughing, harrowing
laborable, *a.* workable; cultivable, tillable. **día l.,** workday
laborar, *v.t.* to work; till; plough; construct; *v.i.* scheme, plot, plan
laboratorio, *m.* laboratory
laborear, *v.t.* to work; till, cultivate; (*naut.*) reeve
laboreo, *m.* tilling, cultivation; working, development (of mines, etc.)
laboriosidad, *f.* laboriousness, diligence
laborioso, *a.* industrious, diligent; laborious, tedious, hard
laborista, *a.* and *m.* and *f.* socialist, belonging to the Labour Party
labra, *f.* stone-cutting; carving or working (metal, stone or wood)
labrada, *f.* fallow land ready for sowing
labradero, *a.* workable; cultivable, tillable
labrado, *a.* and *past part.* worked; fashioned; carved; embroidered; figured, patterned. *m.* (gen. *pl.*) cultivated ground
labrador, *m.* labourer, worker; farmer; peasant
labradora, *f.* peasant girl; farm girl
labradoresco, labradoril, *a.* rustic, peasant, farming
labrandera, *f.* seamstress
labrantío, *a.* tillable, cultivable. *m.* farming
labranza, *f.* tillage, cultivation; farm; farm lands; farming; employment, work
labrar, *v.t.* to work, do; carve; fashion, construct, make; (*agr.*) cultivate, till; plough; embroider; sew; bring about, cause; *v.i.* (*fig.*) impress deeply, leave a strong impression

labriego (-ga), s. agricultural labourer; peasant

laca, f. lac; lacquer, varnish; (art.) lake (pigment)

lacayo, m. groom; lackey, footman

lacear, v.t. (sew.) to trim with bows; tie, lace; snare, trap

lacedemonio (-ia), a. and s. Lacedemonian

laceración, f. laceration

lacerado, a. unhappy, unfortunate; leprous

lacerar, v.t. to lacerate, mangle, tear; distress, wound the feelings of

lacería, f. poverty, misery; toil, drudgery; trouble, affliction

lacero, m. cowboy, one who uses a lasso; poacher

lacio, a. drooping, limp; withered, faded; straight (hair)

lacónico, a. laconic; concise; Laconian

laconismo, m. laconicism

lacra, f. after-effect, trace (of illness); vice; fault

lacrar, v.t. to impair the health; infect with an illness; injure, prejudice (the interests, etc.); seal with sealing-wax

lacre, m. sealing-wax. a. red

lacrimal, a. lachrymal

lacrimoso, a. tearful, lachrymose

lactancia, f. lactation

lactar, v.t. to suckle; feed with milk; v.i. take or drink milk

lactato, m. (chem.) lactate

lácteo, a. lacteal; milky

láctico, a. (chem.) lactic

lactosa, f. (chem.) lactose

lacustre, a. lacustrine, lake

ladear, v.t. to incline; tilt; turn aside, twist; skirt, pass close to; reach by a roundabout way, go indirectly to; v.r. tilt; be in favour of, incline to; be equal to

ladeo, m. tilt; sloping; turning aside

ladera, f. slope, incline; hill-side

ladería, f. terrace on a hill-side

ladero, a. lateral

ladilla, f. (ent.) crab-louse

ladino, a. eloquent; versatile linguistically; wily, crafty

lado, m. side; edge, margin; slope, declivity; faction, party; side, flank; face (of a coin); (fig.) aspect, view; line of descent; means, way; favour, protection; pl. helpers, protectors; advisers. al l., near at hand. (fam.) dar de l. (a), to cool off, fall out with. dejar a un l. (una cosa), to omit, pass over (a thing). mirar de l. or de medio l., to look upon with disapproval; steal a look at

ladrador, a. barking

ladrar, v.i. to bark; (fam.) threaten without hurting

ladrido, m. bark, barking; slander, gossip

ladrillado, m. brick floor or pavement

ladrillar, v.t. to floor or pave with bricks. m. brick yard; brick kiln

ladrillero (-ra), s. brick maker

ladrillo, m. brick; tile

ladrón (-ona), a. robbing, thieving. s. thief, robber; burglar. m. (fam.) thief, flaw in candlewick. m. l. de corazones, ladykiller

ladronera, f. thieves' den; thieving, pilfering; money-box

lagar, m. wine or olive press

lagarta, f. female lizard; (fam.) she-serpent, cunning female

lagartera, f. lizard hole

lagartija, f. wall lizard, small lizard

lagarto, m. lizard; (fam.) sly, artful person, fox; (fam.) insignia of Spanish Military Order of Santiago

lago, m. lake

lagotear, v.i. (fam.) to wheedle, play up to

lagotería, f. wheedling, coaxing, flattery

lágrima, f. tear; drop (of liquid); exudation, oozing (from trees)

lagrimal, a. lachrymal

lagrimear, v.i. to shed tears

lagrimeo, m. weeping, crying; watering of the eyes

lagrimoso, a. tearful; watery (of eyes); sad, tragic

laguna, f. small lake, lagoon; lacuna; gap, hiatus

lagunoso, a. boggy, marshy

laical, a. lay, secular

laicismo, m. secularism

laico, a. lay, secular

lama, f. ooze, slime. m. lama, Buddhist priest

lamaísmo, *m.* Lamaism
lameculos, *m.* and *f.* (*fam.*) toady
lamedura, *f.* licking; lapping
lamentable, *a.* lamentable
lamentación, *f.* lamentation; lament
lamentador (-ra), *a.* lamenting, wailing. *s.* wailer, mourner
lamentar, *v.t.* to mourn, lament, bewail; *v.r.* bemoan, bewail
lamento, *m.* lament
lamentoso, *a.* lamenting, afflicted; lamentable
lamer, *v.t.* to lick; pass the tongue over; touch lightly; lap
lámina, *f.* sheet (of metal); lamina; engraving; illustration, picture; engraving plate
laminación, *f.* lamination, rolling (of metals)
laminado, *a.* laminate; rolled (metals). *m.* rolling (of metals)
laminador, *m.* rolling-mill (for metals)
laminar, *a.* laminate; laminated. *v.t.* to roll (metals); laminate; lick
lámpara, *f.* lamp; radiance, light, luminous body; grease spot. l. de los mineros *or* l. de seguridad, safety-lamp. l. de soldar, blow-pipe. l. termiónica, (*rad.*) thermionic valve. atizar la l., to trim the lamp; (*fam.*) refill drinking glasses
lamparería, *f.* lamp factory; lamp shop
lamparero (-ra), *s.* lamparista, *m.* and *f.* lamp-lighter; lamp maker or seller
lamparilla, *f.* night-light; (*bot.*) aspen; hand-torch
lamparón, *m.* King's evil; tumour (disease of horses)
lampiño, *a.* beardless, clean-shaven; smooth-faced; (*bot.*) non-hirsute
lampista, *m.* and *f.* See lamparero
lamprea, *f.* (*icht.*) lamprey
lana, *f.* wool; fleece; woollen garments or cloth; woollen trade (gen. *pl.*)
lanar, *a.* wool; wool-bearing. ganado l., sheep
lance, *m.* throw, cast; casting a fishing line; catch of fish; crisis, difficult moment; (*lit.*) episode; quarrel; move (in a game). (*fig.*)

l. apretado, difficult position, tight corner. l. de fortuna, chance, fate. l. de honor, affair of honour; duel
lancear, *v.t.* to wound with a lance; lance
lancero, *m.* (*mil.*) lancer; *pl.* lancers (dance and music)
lanceta, *f.* (*med.*) lancet
lancetada, *f.* (*med.*) lancing
lancinar, *v.t.* (*med.*) to lance
lancha, *f.* (*naut.*) launch; lighter; ship's boat; small boat; flagstone. l. bombardera *or* l. cañonera, gunboat. l. de salvamento, ship's life-boat. l. escampavía, patrol boat
landa, *f.* lande
landó, *m.* landau
lanero, *a.* woollen. *m.* woollen merchant; woollen warehouse
langosta, *f.* locust; lobster. l. migratoria, locust
langostín, *m.* crayfish
languidecer, *v.i. irr.* to languish, pine. See conocer
languidez, *f.* lassitude, inertia, languor
lánguido, *a.* listless, weak, languid; half-hearted; languishing, languorous
lanolina, *f.* (*chem.*) lanoline
lanosidad, *f.* woolliness; down (on leaves, etc.)
lanoso, lanudo, *a.* woolly
lanza, *f.* lance, spear; lancer; nozzle (of hosepipe). correr lanzas, to joust (in a tournament). estar con la l. en ristre, to have the lance in rest; be prepared or ready. (*fam.*) ser una l., to be very clever
lanzabombas, *m.* (*aer.*, *nav.*) bomb-release
lanzada, *f.* lance or spear thrust
lanzadera, *f.* weaver's shuttle; sewing-machine shuttle. (*fam.*) parecer una l., to be constantly on the go
lanzador (-ra), *m.* batsman. *s.* thrower, caster, tosser
lanzallamas, *m.* (*mil.*) flame thrower
lanzamiento, *m.* throwing; cast; throw; (*law*) dispossession; (*naut.*) launching
lanzaminas, *m.* (*nav.*) mine layer
lanzar, *v.t.* to throw, cast, hurl;

(*naut.*) launch; vomit; (*law*) dispossess; (*agr.*) take root; *v.r.* hurl oneself, rush; take (to), embark (upon)

lanzatorpedos, (tubo) *m.* torpedo tube

lañar, *v.t.* to clamp; clean fish (for salting)

lapa, *f.* barnacle, limpet

lapicero, *m.* pencil-holder or case; automatic pencil

lápida, *f.* memorial tablet; gravestone

lapidación, *f.* lapidation, stoning

lapidar, *v.t.* to stone, lapidate; throw stones at

lapidario, *a.* lapidary

lapislázuli, *m.* (*min.*) lapis lazuli

lápiz, *m.* graphite; pencil; crayon l. **para los labios,** lip-stick

lapizar, *m.* graphite mine. *v.t.* to pencil

lapón (-ona), *a.* Lappish. *s.* Laplander. *m.* Lappish (language)

lapso, *m.* lapse, period, passage; slip, error, failure

laquear, *v.t.* to lacquer, paint

lar, *m.* home; *pl.* lares

lardear, *v.t.* (*cul.*) to baste

lardo, *m.* lard; animal fat

lardoso, *a.* greasy; fat; oily

larga, *f.* longest billiard cue; delay (gen. *pl.*). **a la l.,** in the long run

largamente, *adv.* fully, at length; generously; widely, extensively; comfortably

largar, *v.t.* to slacken, loosen; (*naut.*) unfurl; set at liberty; (*fig., fam.*) let fly (oaths, etc.); administer (blows, etc.); *v.r.* (*fam.*) quit, leave (in a hurry or secretly); (*naut.*) set sail

largo, *a.* long; generous, liberal; abundant, plentiful; protracted; prolonged; expeditious; *pl.* many long (e.g. **por largos años,** for many long years). *m.* (*mus.*) largo; length. (*fam.*) ¡**L. de aquí!** Get out! **a la larga,** in length; eventually, finally; slowly; with many digressions. **a lo l.,** lengthwise; along the length (of); in the distance, far off; along, the length (of). (*fig.*) **ponerse de l.,** to " come out," put one's hair up

largor, *m.,* **largura,** *f.* length

largueza, *f.* length; generosity, munificence

largura, *f.* length

lárice, *m.* larch tree

laringe, *f.* larynx

laríngeo, *a.* laryngeal

laringitis, *f.* laryngitis

larva, *f.* larva; worm, grub; spectre, phantom

las, *def. art. f. pl.* of **la,** the. *pers. pron. acc. f. pl.* of **la,** them

lascivia, *f.* lasciviousness

lascivo, *a.* lascivious, lewd; wanton

lasitud, *f.* lassitude, weariness, exhaustion

laso, *a.* weary, exhausted; weak; untwisted (of silk, etc.)

lástima, *f.* compassion, pity; pitiful sight; complaint, lamentation. **dar l.,** to cause pity. **Es l.,** It's a pity. **tener l.** (a *or* de) to be sorry for (persons)

lastimador, *a.* harmful, injurious; painful

lastimar, *v.t.* to hurt, harm, injure; pity; (*fig.*) wound, distress; *v.r.* (*with de*) be sorry for or about; complain, lament

lastimero, *a.* pitiful; mournful; injurious, harmful

lastimoso, *a.* pitiful, heart-breaking; mournful

lastrar, *v.t.* to ballast

lastre, *m.* ballast; good sense, prudence

lata, *f.* tin, can; tin-plate; tin of food. **en l.,** tinned (of food). (*fam.*) **Es una l.,** It's a bore, It's an awful nuisance

latamente, *adv.* extensively, at length; broadly

latente, *a.* latent

lateral, *a.* lateral

latido, *m.* yelp, bark; beat; throb; palpitation

latifundios, *m. pl.* latifundia

latigazo, *m.* lash; crack of a whip; sudden blow of fate; (*fam.*) draught (of wine, etc.); harsh scolding; (*naut.*) jerk or flapping (of sails)

látigo, *m.* whip, lash; cinch, girth of a saddle

latín, *m.* Latin. **bajo l.,** low Latin. (*fam.*) **saber l.,** to know how many beans make five

latinajo, *m.* (*fam.*) bad Latin

latinidad, *f.* Latinity

latinismo, *m.* Latinism
latinista, *m.* and *f.* Latinist
latinizar, *v.t.* to latinize; *v.i.* (*fam.*) use Latin phrases
latino, *a.* Latin; lateen
latinoamericano (-na), *a.* and *s.* Latin American
latir, *v.i.* to yelp, howl; bark; throb, palpitate, beat
latitud, *f.* latitude; area, extent; breadth
latitudinario, *a.* latitudinarian
lato, *a.* extensive; large; broad (of word meanings)
latón, *m.* brass
latonería, *f.* brass works; brass shop
latoso, *a.* boring, troublesome, annoying
latrocinio, *m.* larceny
latvio (-ia), *a.* and *s.* Latvian
laúd, *m.* lute
laudable, *a.* praiseworthy, laudable
láudano, *m.* laudanum
laudatorio, *a.* laudatory
laudes, *f. pl.* (*ecc.*) lauds
laurear, *v.t.* to crown with laurel; honour, reward
laurel, *m.* bay tree. **l.** cerezo, laurel. **l.** rosa, rose-bay, oleander
láureo, *a.* laurel
lauréola, *f.* laurel wreath
lauro, *m.* bay tree; glory, triumph
lava, *f.* lava
lavable, *a.* washable
lavabo, *m.* washstand; cloakroom, lavatory
lavadedos, *m.* finger-bowl
lavadero, *m.* washing place; laundry
lavado, *m.* washing; cleaning; wash. **l.** al seco, dry-cleaning
lavadura, *f.* washing
lavamanos, *m.* wash-stand; lavatory
lavamiento, *m.* washing, cleansing, ablution
lavanda, *f.* lavender
lavandera, *f.* laundress; washerwoman
lavandería, *f.* laundry
lavandero, *m.* laundry; laundry man
lavar, *v.t.* to wash; (*fig.*) wipe out, purify; paint in water colours. **l.** al seco, to dry clean
lavativa, *f.* enema; syringe,

clyster; (*fam.*) nuisance, bore
lavatorio, *m.* washing, lavation; (*ecc.*) lavabo; lavatory, washing place; (*ecc.*) maundy
lavazas, *f. pl.* dirty soapy water
laxante, *a.* and *m.* (*med.*) laxative
laxar, *v.t.* to loosen, relax; soften
laxitud, *f.* laxity
laxo, *a.* lax; slack
laya, *f.* (*agr.*) fork; kind, sort, class
layar, *v.t.* (*agr.*) to fork
lazar, *v.t.* to lasso
lazareto, *m.* leper hospital; quarantine hospital
lazarillo, *m.* boy who guides a blind person
lazarino, *a.* leprous
lázaro, *m.* lazar, beggar
lazo, *m.* bow; knot of ribbons; tie; ornamental tree; figure (in dancing); lasso; rope, bond; lace (of a shoe); (*fig.*) trap, snare; bond, obligation; slip-knot. **l.** corredizo, running knot. (*fig.*, *fam.*) armar **l.**, to set a trap. (*fam.*) caer en el **l.**, to fall into the trap, be deceived
le, *pers. pron. dat. m.* or *f.* 3*rd pers. sing.* to him, to her, to it, to you (e.g. María le dió el perro, Mary gave him (her, you) the dog). Clarity may require the addition of a él, a ella, a usted (e.g. Le dió el perro a ella, etc.). *pers. pron. acc. m.* 3*rd pers. sing.* him (e.g. Le mandé a casa, I sent him home)
leal, *a.* loyal; faithful (animals)
lealtad, *f.* loyalty; faithfulness; sincerity, truth
lebrel, *m.* greyhound
lección, *f.* reading; lesson; oral test; warning, example. **l.** práctica, object lesson. dar **l.**, to give a lesson. tomar la **l.**, to hear a lesson
leccionista, *m.* and *f.* private teacher, coach, tutor
lector (-ra), *s.* reader; lecturer
lectura, *f.* reading; lecture; culture, knowledge
lechas, *f. pl.* soft roes
leche, *f.* milk; milky fluid of some plants and seeds. (*fam.*) estar con la **l.** en los labios, to be young and inexperienced
lechera, *f.* milkmaid; milk can or jug

lechería, *f.* dairy; dairy shop

lechero (-ra), *a.* dairy, milk; milky; milch, milk-giving. *s.* milk vendor. **industria lechera,** dairy-farming

lecho, *m.* bed; couch; animal's bed, litter; river-bed; bottom of the sea; layer; (*geol.*) stratum

lechón, *m.* sucking-pig; hog; (*fam.*) slovenly man

lechoso, *a.* milky

lechuga, *f.* lettuce; frill, flounce. (*fam.*) **como una l.,** as fresh as a daisy

lechuguero (-ra), *s.* lettuce seller

lechuguilla, *f.* ruff; ruche

lechuguina, *f.* (*fam.*) affected, over-dressed young woman

lechuguino, *m.* lettuce plant; (*fam.*) young blood, gallant; (*fam.*) foppish young man

lechuza, *f.* barn owl

ledo, *a.* happy, content

leer, *v.t. irr.* to read; explain, interpret; teach; take part in an oral test. See **creer**

lega, *f.* (*ecc.*) lay sister

legacía, *f.* (*ecc.*) legateship

legación, *f.* (*ecc.*) legateship; legation

legado, *m.* legacy; legate

legajo, *m.* bundle, docket; file

legal, *a.* legal; legitimate; upright, trustworthy

legalidad, *f.* legality

legalización, *f.* legalization

legalizar, *v.t.* to legalize

legamente, *adv.* ignorantly, stupidly

légamo, *m.* mud, slime

legamoso, *a.* slimy

legaña, *f.* bleariness (in eyes)

legañoso, *a.* bleary-eyed

legar, *v.t.* to bequeath; send as a legate

legatario (-ia), *s.* legatee (one to whom a legacy is bequeathed)

legendario, *a.* legendary

legibilidad, *f.* legibility

legible, *a.* legible

legión, *f.* legion

legionario, *a.* and *m.* legionary

legislación, *f.* legislation

legislador (-ra), *a.* legislative. *s.* legislator

legislar, *v.t.* to legislate

legislativo, *a.* legislative

legislatura, *f.* legislature

legista, *m.* jurist; student of law

legítima, *f.* portion of a married man's estate which cannot be willed away from his wife and children

legitimación, *f.* legitimation

legitimar, *v.t.* to legitimize

legitimidad, *f.* legitimacy

legítimo, *a.* legitimate; real, true

lego, *a.* lay, secular. *m.* layman

legua, *f.* league (approximately 5·573 metres). **a la l., de cien leguas, desde media l.,** from afar off

legumbre, *f.* (*bot.*) pulse; vegetable

leguminoso, *a.* leguminous

leído, *a.* well-read

leila, *f.* nocturnal Moorish merry-making or dance

lejanía, *f.* distance

lejano, *a.* distant, remote, far off

lejía, *f.* lye; bleaching solution; (*fam.*) dressing down, scolding

lejos, *adv.* far off, far, distant. *m.* perspective, view from afar; (*art*) background. **a lo l.,** far off, in the distance. **de** *or* **desde l.,** from afar, from a distance

lelo, *a.* stupid; fatuous, inane

lema, *m.* (*lit.*) chapter heading, argument, summary; motto; theme, subject

lémur, *m.* (*zool.*) lemur

lencería, *f.* linen goods; linen-draper's shop; linen room

lencero, *m.* linen-draper

lene, *a.* smooth, soft; kind, sweet, gentle; light in weight

lengua, *f.* (*anat.*) tongue; mother tongue, language; clapper of a bell; information. *m.* or *f.* spokesman. **l. de escorpión** *or* **mala l.,** scandalmonger, back-biter. **l. de fuego,** (*ecc.*) tongue of fire, flame. **l. del agua,** water-line, tide mark. **l. de oc,** langue d'oc. **l. de oil,** langue d'oil. **l. de tierra,** neck of land, promontory. **l. viva,** modern language. (*fam.*) **andar en lenguas,** to be on every lip, be famous. (*fam.*) **hacerse lenguas de,** to praise to the skies. (*fam.*) **irse** (a uno) **la l.,** to be indiscreet, talk too much. **poner l.** *or* **lenguas en,** to gossip about. (*fam.*) **tener mucha l.,** to be very talkative. **tomar l.** *or* **lenguas,** to find out about, inform oneself on

lenguado, *m.* (*icht.*) sole

lenguaje, *m.* language; style; speech, idiom. **l. vulgar,** common speech

lengüeta, *f. dim.* little tongue; (*mus.*) tongue (of wind instruments); barb (of an arrow);— needle (of a balance)

lenidad, *f.* lenience, indulgence, mercy

lenitivo, *a.* lenitive; soothing. *m.* (*med.*) lenitive; (*fig.*) balm (of sorrow, etc.)

lente, *m.* lens; *pl.* eyeglasses. **l. de aumento,** magnifying glass

lenteja, *f.* (*bot.*) lentil; lentil plant

lentejuela, *f.* sequin

lentitud, *f.* lentitude; slowness, deliberation

lento, *a.* slow, deliberate; sluggish, heavy; (*med.*) glutinous, adhesive

leña, *f.* firewood; (*fam.*) beating, birching. (*fig.*) **echar l. al fuego,** to add fuel to the flame. (*fig.*) **llevar l. al monte,** to take coal to Newcastle

leñador (-ra), *s.* wood-cutter; firewood dealer

leñera, *f.* wood pile; woodshed

leño, *m.* wood log; wood, timber; (*poet.*) ship; (*fam.*) blockhead

leñoso, *a.* woody, ligneous

león, *m.* lion. (*ast.*) Leo; valiant man. **l. marino,** sea-lion

leona, *f.* lioness

leonado, *a.* tawny

leonera, *f.* lion cage; lion's den; (*fam.*) gambling den; (*fam.*) lumber room

leonero (-ra), *s.* lion keeper; (*fam.*) keeper of a gambling-house

leonés (-esa), *a.* and *s.* of or from León (Spanish province)

leonino, *a.* leonine (also *law*)

leopardo, *m.* leopard

leporino, *a.* hare-like

lepra, *f.* leprosy

leproso, *a.* leprous

lerdo, *a.* slow, lumbering (gen. horses); stupid, slow-witted, dull

les, *pers. pron. dat.* 3*rd pers. pl. m.* or *f.* to them (e.g. **Les dimos las flores,** We gave them flowers. **Les hablé del asunto,** I spoke to them about the matter)

lesbio (-ia), *a.* and *s.* Lesbian

lesión, *f.* lesion, wound; (*fig.*) injury

lesionar, *v.t.* to wound; (*fig.*) injure

lesna, *f.* awl

leso, *a.* wounded, hurt; offensive, injurious; (*fig.*) unbalanced, perturbed (the mind). **crimen de lesa majestad,** crime of lèse-majesté

letal, *a.* lethal; deadly

letanía, *f.* (*ecc.*) litany

letargia, *f.* (*med.*) lethargy

letárgico, *a.* lethargic

letargo, *m.* lethargy; indifference, apathy

letra, *f.* letter (of alphabet); (*print.*) type; penmanship, hand; (*fig.*) letter, literal meaning; words (of a song); inscription; (*com.*) bill, draft; cunning, shrewdness; *pl.* learning, knowledge. **l. abierta,** (*com.*) open credit. **l. de cambio,** (*com.*) bill of exchange. **l. gótica,** Gothic characters. **l. itálica,** italics. **l. mayúscula,** capital letter. **l. paladial,** palatal. **Facultad de Letras,** Faculty of Arts. **La l. con sangre entra,** Learning is acquired with pain. **primeras letras,** early education, first letters

letrado, *a.* learned, educated; (*fam.*) presumptuous; pedantic. *m.* lawyer

letrero, *m.* label; inscription; poster, bill; sign, indicator. **l. luminoso,** illuminated sign

letrilla, *f.* short poem, often set to music

letrina, *f.* latrine

leucocito, *m.* (*med.*) leucocyte

leva, *f.* (*naut.*) weighing anchor; (*mil.*) levy, forced enrolment; tappet; (*mech.*) lever; (*mech.*) cam; *pl.* fishing floats. (*fam.*) **irse a l. y a monte,** to flee, beat it, quit

levadizo, *a.* able to be raised or lowered (bridges). **puente l.,** drawbridge

levadura, *f.* leaven, yeast; rising (of bread)

levantada, *f.* act of rising from bed

levantamiento, *m.* raising, lifting; rebellion, revolt; ennoblement, elevation; settlement of accounts

levantar, *v.t.* to raise, lift; pick

up; build, construct; cançel, remove; encourage, rouse; recruit,
enlist; cut (cards); leave, abandon; survey; disturb (game);
produce, raise (a swelling); found,
institute; increase (prices); raise
(the voice); (*fig.*) ennoble, elevate; cause, occasion; libel,
accuse falsely; *v.r.* rise; get up;
stand up; stand out, be prominent; rebel; leave one's bed
after illness. **l. bandera, to** rebel.
l. el campo, to break camp.
levantarse de l izquierdo, (*fam.*)
to get out of bed on the wrong
side

levante, *m.* east; Levant; east
wind

levantino (-na), *a.* and *s.* Levantine

levar, *v.t.* (*naut.*) to weigh
anchor; *v.r.* set sail

leve, *a.* light (in weight); unimportant, trifling

levedad, *f.* lightness (in weight);
unimportance, levity, flippancy

leviatán, *m.* leviathan

levita, *m.* Levite; deacon. *f.*
frock-coat

levitación, *f.* levitation

levítico, a. Levitical. *m.* Leviticus

levitón, *m.* frock-coat

léxico, *m.* lexicon; dictionary

lexicografía, *f.* lexicography

lexicógrafo, *m.* lexicographer

lexicólogo, *m.* lexicologist

ley, *f.* law; precept; regulation,
rule; doctrine; loyalty, faithfulness; affection, love; legal standard (weights, measures, quality); ratio of gold or silver in
coins, jewellery; statute, ordinance; *pl.* the Law. **l. de préstamo y arriendo,** Lease-Lend
Bill. **leyes suntuarias,** sumptuary laws. (*fam.*) **a la l.,** with
care and decorum. **a l. de
caballero,** on the word of a
gentleman. **de buena l.,** *a.* excellent; *adv.* genuinely; in good
faith. **de mala l.,** *a.* disreputable, base; *adv.* in bad faith

leyenda, *f.* legend; inscription;
story, tale

leyente, *a.* reading. *m.* and *f.*
reader

lezna, *f.* awl

lía, *f.* plaited esparto rope; *pl.*
lees, dregs

liar, *v.t.* to fasten or tie up; wrap
up, parcel; roll (a cigarette);
(*fam.*) entangle, embroil; *v.r.*
take a lover, enter on a liaison.
(*fam.*) **liarlas,** to quit, sneak off;
(*fam.*) kick the bucket, die

libación, *f.* libation

libar, *v.t.* to suck; perform a
libation; sip, taste; sacrifice

libelista, *m.* libeller

libelo, *m.* libel; (*law*) petition

libélula, *f.* dragon-fly

liberación, *f.* liberation, freeing;
receipt, quittance; (*law*) re-
conveyance (of mortgages)

liberador (-ra), *a.* liberating,
freeing. *s.* liberator

liberal, *a.* generous, open-handed;
liberal, tolerant; learned (of
professions). *a.* and *m.* and *f.*
(*pol.*) liberal

liberalidad, *f.* generosity, magnanimity

liberalismo, *m.* liberalism

liberalizar, *v.t.* to liberalize,
make liberal

liberar, *v.t.* to liberate

libérrimo, *a. sup.* extremely, or
most, free

libertad, *f.* liberty, freedom; independence; privilege, right
(gen. *pl.*); exemption; licentiousness; forwardness, familiarity;
naturalness, ease of manner;
facility, capacity; immunity. **l.
de cultos,** freedom of worship;
religious toleration. **l. vigilada,**
(*law*) probation. **poner en l.,**
to set at liberty; (*with de*) (*fig.*)
free from

libertador (-ra), *a.* liberating,
freeing. *s.* liberator, deliverer

libertar, *v.t.* to liberate, free;
save, deliver; exempt

libertario (-ia), *a.* anarchistic. *s*
anarchist

libertinaje, *m.* libertinage, licentiousness

libertino (-na), *a.* debauched,
licentious. *m.* libertine. *s.* child
of a freed slave

liberto (-ta), *s.* freed slave, freedman

libídine, *f.* lust

libidinoso, *a.* libidinous, lustful

libio (-ia), *a.* and *s.* Libyan

libra, *f.* pound (measure, coinage); (*ast.*) Libra. **l. esterlina,**

pound sterling. **l. medicinal,** pound troy

libración, *f.* oscillation; (*ast.*) libration

librador (-ra), *a.* freeing, liberating. *s.* deliverer, liberator. *m.* (*com.*) drawer (of bill of exchange, etc.)

libramiento, *m.* liberation, deliverance; (*com.*) delivery; order of payment

libranza, *f.* (*com.*) draft

librar, *v.t.* to liberate, free; protect (from misfortune); (*com.*) draw (a draft); (*com.*) deliver; place confidence in; issue, enact; *v.i.* bring forth children; (*with de*) escape from; get rid of

libre, *a.* free; at liberty, disengaged; unhampered, untrammelled; independent; bold, brazen; dissolute, vicious; exempt; vacant, unoccupied; unmarried; clear, free; mutinous, rebellious; isolated, remote; innocent; unharmed. **l. cambio,** free trade

librea, *f.* livery

librecambio, *m.* free trade

librecambista, *a.* free trade. *m.* and *f.* free trader

librepensador (-ra), *a.* free thinking. *s.* free thinker

librepensamiento, *m.* free thought

librería, *f.* book-shop; book trade, bookselling; bookcase; library

librero, *m.* bookseller

libreta, *f.* (*cul.*) 1-lb. loaf; note-book; pass-book, bank-book

libretista, *m.* and *f.* librettist

libreto, *m.* libretto

librillo, *m.* dim. small book; book of cigarette papers; tub, pail; (*zool.*) omasum

libro, *m.* book; (*mus.*) libretto; (*zool.*) omasum. **l. copiador,** (*com.*) letter-book. **l. de actas,** minute-book. **l. de caja,** (*com.*) cash-book. **l. de cheques,** cheque-book. **l. de facturas,** (*com.*) invoice-book. **l. de texto,** text-book. **l. diario,** (*com.*) day-book. **l. mayor,** ledger. **l. talonario,** receipt-book. (*fig.*, *f*)*am.* **hacer l. nuevo,** to turn over a new leaf; introduce innovations

licencia, *f.* permission, licence; licentiousness; over-boldness, insolence; (*univ.*) degree of bachelor, licentiate. **l. absoluta,** (*mil.*) discharge

licenciado (-da), *a.* pedantic; free, exempt; licensed. *s.* (*univ.*) bachelor; licentiate. *m.* discharged soldier

licenciar, *v.t.* to allow, permit; license; dismiss, discharge; confer degree of bachelor or licentiate; (*mil.*) discharge; *v.r* become licentious; receive degree of bachelor or licentiate

licenciatura, *f.* degree of licentiate or bachelor; graduation as such; licentiate course of study

licencioso, *a.* licentious, dissolute

liceo, *m.* lyceum

licitación, *f.* bidding (at auction)

licitador, *m.* bidder (at auction)

licitar, *v.t.* to bid for (at auction)

lícito, *a.* permissible, lawful

licor, *m.* liquor, alcoholic drink; liquid

licorera, *f.* liqueur set; decanter

licoroso, *a.* aromatic, generous (wines)

licuar, *v.t.* to liquefy

licuefacción, *f.* liquefaction

lid, *f.* combat, fight; dispute, controversy. **en buena l.,** in fair fight; by fair means

líder, *m.* leader; chief

lidia, *f.* fighting; bull fight

lidiador (-ra), *s.* combatant fighter

lidiar, *v.i.* to fight; (*fig.*) struggle; (*with contra or con*) oppose, fight against; *v.t.* fight (a bull). **¡Cuánto tienen que l. con Juan!** (*fig.*) What a struggle they have with John!

lidio (-ia), *a.* and *s.* Lydian

liebre, *f.* (*zool.*) hare

liendre, *f.* (*ent.*) nit

lienza, *f.* narrow strip (of cloth)

lienzo, *m.* linen; cotton; cambric; hemp cloth; (*art*) canvas

liga, *f.* garter; bandage; bird-lime; mixture, blend; (*met.*) alloy; alliance, coalition; league (football, etc.)

ligación, *f.* tying; binding; union

ligado, *m.* (*mus.*) legato; (*mus.*) tie

ligadura, *f.* bond, tie; binding, fastening; (*fig.*) shackle, link;

(*surg.*, *mus.*) ligature; (*naut.*) lashing

ligamento, *m.* tie, bond; mixture; (*anat.*) ligament

ligar, *v.t.* to tie, bind; (*met.*) alloy; join, connect; render impotent by sorcery; (*mus.*) slur (notes); *v.r.* ally, join together; (*fig.*) bind oneself

ligazón, *f.* fastening; union; bond

ligereza, *f.* lightness (of weight); swiftness, nimbleness; fickleness; tactless remark, indiscretion

ligero, *a.* light (in weight); swift, nimble; light (sleep); unimportant, insignificant; easily digested (food); thin (fabrics, etc.); fickle, changeable. **l. de cascos,** frivolous, gay. **a la ligera,** lightly; quickly; without fuss. **de l.,** impetuously, thoughtlessly; easily, with ease

lignito, *m.* lignite

ligurino (-na), *a.* and *s.* Ligurian

lija, *f.* (*icht.*) dog-fish; sand-paper

lijar, *v.t.* to sand-paper

lila, *f.* (*bot.*) lilac bush and flower; lilac colour. *a.* (*fam.*) foolish, vain

liliputiense, *a.* and *m.* and *f.* Lilliputian

lima, *f.* sweet lime, citron fruit; lime tree; file (tool); filing, polishing

limadura, *f.* filing; polishing; *pl.* filings

limar, *v.t.* to file, smooth with a file; (*fig.*) touch up, polish

limazo, *m.* slime, viscosity (especially of snails, etc.)

limbo, *m.* limbo; edge, hem; (*ast., bot.*) limb; limb (of quadrant, etc.). (*fam.*) **estar en el l.,** to be bewildered or abstracted

limen, *m.* (*poet.*) threshold; (*psy.*) limen

limeño (-ña), *a.* and *s.* native of or belonging to Lima (Peru)

limero (-ra), *s.* seller of sweet limes. *m.* sweet lime tree (citron)

limitación, *f.* limitation; limit, extent, bound; district, area

limitado, *a.* dull-witted, limited

limitáneo, *a.* limitrophe

limitar, *v.t.* to limit; curb, restrict; bound

límite, *m.* limit, extent; boundary, border; end, confine

limítrofe, *a.* limitrophe, contiguous

limo, *m.* mud, mire, slime

limón, *m.* lemon; lemon tree

limonada, *f.* lemonade. **l. seca,** lemonade powder

limonar, *m.* lemon grove

limonero (-ra), *s.* lemon seller. *m.* lemon tree

limosna, *f.* alms

limosnear, *v.i.* to beg, ask alms

limosnero, *a.* charitable, generous. *m.* almoner

limoso, *a.* slimy, muddy

limpiabarros, *m.* shoe-scraper

limpiabotas, *m.* shoe-black (person)

limpiachimeneas, *m.* chimney-sweep

limpiador (-ra), *a.* cleaning. *s.* cleaner

limpiadura, *f.* cleaning; *pl.* rubbish

limpiamente, *adv.* cleanly; dexterously, neatly; sincerely, candidly; generously, charitably

limpiametales, *m.* metal polish

limpiaparabrisas, *m.* windscreen wiper

limpiapipas, *m.* pipe-cleaner

limpiaplumas, *m.* pen-wiper

limpiar, *v.t.* to clean; (*fig.*) cleanse, clear; empty, free (from); (*agr.*) thin out; (*fam.*) steal, pinch; (*fam.*) win (gambling); *v.r.* clean oneself

limpiauñas, *m.* orange-stick (for finger-nails)

limpidez, *f.* (*poet.*) limpidity

límpido, *a.* (*poet.*) limpid

limpieza, *f.* cleanliness; cleaning; chastity; purity; altruism; uprightness, integrity; neatness, tidiness; dexterity, skill, precision; fair play. **l. de sangre,** (doctrine of) blood purity

limpio, *a.* clean; pure, unalloyed, unmixed; neat, tidy; pure-blooded (having no Moorish, Jewish or heretical ancestors); unharmed, free. **en l.,** in substance; as a fair copy; clearly; (*com.*) net

linaje, *m.* lineage, family; offspring; kind; sort, quality

linajudo (-da), *a.* high-born. *s.* noble, aristocrat; one who alleges his noble descent

linar, *m.* field of flax

linaza, *f.* (*bot.*) linseed

lince, *m.* lynx; fox, crafty person

linchamiento, *m.* lynching

linchar, *v.t.* to lynch

lindar, *v.i.* to run together, be contiguous

linde, *m.* or *f.* limit, extent; boundary

lindero, *a.* bordering, contiguous. *m.* boundary. (*fam.*) **con linderos y arrabales,** with many digressions

lindeza, *f.* beauty, loveliness; witticism; *pl.* (*fam., ironical*) insults

lindo, *a.* lovely, beautiful; perfect, exquisite. *m.* (*fam.*) fop (generally **lindo don Diego**)

línea, *f.* line; kind, class; ancestry, lineage; limit, extent; (*mil.*) file; equator. **l. aérea,** air-line. (*naut.*) **l. de flotación,** water-line. **l. de toque,** touchline (in football). **l. recta,** direct line (of descent)

lineal, *a.* lineal

lineamento, *m.* lineament

linear, *a.* linear. *v.t.* to line, mark with lines; (*art*) sketch

linfa, *f.* (*med.*) lymph; vaccine; (*poet.*) water

linfático, *a.* lymphatic

lingote, *m.* ingot; bar (of iron). **l. de fundición,** pig-iron

lingüista, *m.* and *f.* linguist

lingüística, *f.* linguistics

lingüístico, *a.* linguistic

linimento, *m.* liniment

lino, *m.* (*bot.*) flax; linen; (*poet.*) ship's sail, canvas

linóleo, *m.* linoleum

linotipia, *f.* linotype

linterna, *f.* lantern; lighthouse; lamp. **l. sorda,** dark lantern

lío, *m.* bundle; (*fam.*) muddle, imbroglio; (*fam.*) liaison, amour. (*fam.*) **armar un l.,** to make a muddle, cause trouble. (*fam.*) **hacerse un l.,** to get in a fix; get in a muddle

lionés (-esa), *a.* and *s.* of or from Lyons

liquen, *m.* (*bot.*) lichen

liquidable, *a.* liquefiable

liquidación, *f.* liquefaction; (*com.*) clearance, sale; (*com.*) settlement

liquidar, *v.t.* to liquefy; (*com.*) settle; (*com.*) liquidate; finish; *v.r.* liquefy

liquidez, *f.* liquidness

líquido, *a.* liquid; (*com.*) net. *m.* liquid; (*com.*) net profit

lira, *f.* (*mus.*) lyre; (*ast.*) Lyra; lira (coin)

lírica, *f.* lyrical verse, lyric

lírico, *a.* lyrical

lirio, *m.* lily. **l. cárdeno,** yellow flag (iris). **l. de los valles,** lily of the valley

lirismo, *m.* lyricism

lirón, *m.* (*zool.*) dormouse; (*fam.*) sleepy-head

lisbonense, *a.* and *m.* and *f.* **lisbonés (-esa),** *a.* and *s.* of or from Lisbon

lisiado, *a.* lame, crippled

lisiar, *v.t.* to cripple, lame; *v.r.* be disabled; be lame

liso, *a.* smooth; sleek; unadorned, plain; unicoloured

lisonja, *f.* flattery, adulation

lisonjear, *v.t.* to flatter; fawn upon; (*fig.*) delight (the ear)

lisonjero (-ra), *a.* flattering; sweet, pleasant (sounds). *s.* flatterer

lista, *f.* strip of cloth; streak; rib; stripe; catalogue, list. **l. de correos,** poste restante. **l. de platos,** bill of fare. **pasar l.,** to call the roll; check the list

listado, *a.* streaked; striped; ribbed

listo, *a.* clever; expeditious, diligent; ready, prepared

listón, *m.* ribbon; strip (of wood)

lisura, *f.* smoothness; sleekness; flatness; sincerity

litera, *f.* litter; (*naut.*) berth

literal, *a.* literal

literalidad, *f.* literalness

literario, *a.* literary

literatear, *v.i.* to write on literary subjects

literato (-ta), *a.* literary *s.* writer, litterateur

literatura, *f.* literature

litigación, *f.* litigation

litigante, *m.* and *f.* litigant

litigar, *v.t.* to litigate; *v.i.* dispute, argue

litigio, *m.* lawsuit; dispute, argument

litigioso, *a.* litigious; quarrelsome, disputatious

litisexpensas, *f. pl.* (*law*) costs of a suit; legal expenses

litografía, *f.* lithography

litografiar, *v.t.* to lithograph

litográfico, *a.* lithographic

litoral, *a.* and *m.* littoral

litro, *m.* litre (metric unit of capacity)

lituano (-na), *a.* and *s.* Lithuanian. *m.* Lithuanian language

liturgia, *f.* (*ecc.*) liturgy

litúrgico, *a.* liturgical

liviandad, *f.* lightness (of weight); fickleness; unimportance; frivolity; lewdness; act of folly, indiscretion

liviano, *a.* light (of weight); fickle; unimportant, trifling, frivolous; lascivious

lividez, *f.* lividness

lívido, *a.* livid

liza, *f.* list (at a tournament); arena

lo, *def. art. neut.* the thing, part, fact, what, that which. Used before adjectives, past participles, sometimes before nouns and adverbs (e.g. *Lo barato es caro,* Cheap things are dear (in the long run). *Lo mío es mío, pero lo tuyo es de ambos nosotros,* What's mine is mine, but what is yours belongs to both of us. *Juan siente mucho lo ocurrido,* John is very sorry for what has happened. *a lo lejos,* in the distance). *lo ... que,* how (e.g. *No sabes lo bueno que es,* You don't know how good he is). *pers. pron. acc. m.* or *neut.* him, it; that; it (e.g. *Lo harán mañana,* They will do it tomorrow). Means some, any, one, as substitute for noun already mentioned (e.g. *Carecemos de azúcar, no lo hay,* We are short of sugar, there isn't any)

loa, *f.* praise, eulogy; (*theat.*) prologue; short dramatic piece (*ant.*); dramatic eulogy

loable, *a.* praiseworthy

loador (-ra), *a.* eulogizing. *s.* eulogist

loar, *v.t.* to praise; commend

lobanillo, *m.* wen

lobelia, *f.* (*bot.*) lobelia

lobero, *a.* wolf; wolfish

lobezno, *m.* wolf-cub

lobo (-ba), *s.* wolf. *m.* (*bot., anat.*) lobe; (*fam.*) drinking fit. **l. marino,** (*zool.*) seal. (*fam.*) **pillar un l.,** to get drunk

lóbrego, *a.* murky, dark; dismal; mournful, lugubrious

lobreguez, *f.* obscurity, gloom, darkness

lóbulo, *m.* (*anat., bot., arch.*) lobe

lobuno, *a.* wolf, wolfish

locación, *f.* (*law*) lease; agreement, contract

local, *a.* local. *m.* premises; place, spot, scene

localidad, *f.* location; locality; place, spot; seat (in theatres, etc.)

localización, *f.* localization, placing; place

localizar, *v.t.* to localize

locamente, *adv.* insanely, madly; extraordinarily, extremely

loción, *f.* lotion

loco (-ca), *a.* insane, mad; rash, foolish, crazy; excessive, enormous; amazing; extraordinary; infatuated. *s.* lunatic; rash person. (*fig., fam.*) **Es un l. de atar,** He's completely crazy!

locomoción, *f.* locomotion

locomotor, *a.* locomotive

locomotora, *f.* railway engine; locomotive

locomóvil, *a.* locomotive. *f.* locomotive

locuacidad, *f.* loquacity

locuaz, *a.* loquacious

locución, *f.* style of speech; phrase, idiom; (*gram.*) locution

locuelo (-la), *s.* madcap

locura, *f.* insanity, lunacy; madness, fury; folly, foolishness

locutor (-ra), *s.* (radio) announcer

locutorio, *m.* locutory; telephone box

lodazal, lodazar, *m.* muddy place; quagmire

lodo, *m.* mud

lodoso, *a.* muddy

logarítmico, *a.* logarithmic

logaritmo, *m.* (*math.*) logarithm

logia, *f.* freemason's lodge

lógica, *f.* logic. (*fam.*) **l. parda,** common sense

lógico (-ca), *a.* logical. *s.* logician

logística, *f.* logistics

lograr, *v.t.* to achieve, attain, obtain; enjoy; (*with infin.*) succeed in; *v.r.* succeed in, achieve; reach perfection

logrear, *v.i.* to borrow or lend at interest

logrero (-ra), *s.* money-lender; monopolist, profiteer

logro, *m.* achievement, attainment; profit, gain; usury, money-lending

loma, *f.* knoll, hillock

lombarda, *f.* red cabbage

lombardo (-da), *a.* of or from Lombardy. *s.* native of Lombardy (Italy). *m.* mortgage bank

lombriguera, *f.* worm hole

lombriz, *f.* earthworm, common worm. **l. intestinal,** intestinal worm. **l. solitaria,** tapeworm

lomo, *m.* loin, back of a book; ridge between furrows; *pl.* ribs; loins

lona, *f.* canvas, sailcloth

londinense, *a.* London. *m.* and *f.* Londoner

longanimidad, *f.* longanimity, fortitude

longaniza, *f.* (*cul.*) salamé

longevidad, *f.* longevity

longevo, *a.* long-lived

longísimo, *a.* *sup.* **luengo,** exceedingly long

longitud, *f.* length; longitude. **l. de onda,** (*rad.*) wave-length

lonja, *f.* (*com.*) exchange; sale room; grocer's shop; woollen warehouse; slice

lonjista, *m.* and *f.* provision merchant, grocer

lontananza, *f.* distance (also *art*). **en l.,** in the distance, far off

loor, *m.* praise

loquear, *v.i.* to play the fool; romp

lord, *m.* lord; *pl.* **lores,** lords

loriga, *f.* cuirass

loro, *m.* (*orn.*) parrot

los, *def. art. m. pl.* the (e.g. **l. sombreros,** the hats). *pers. pron. acc. 3rd pers. m. pl.* them. **Tus cigarrillos no están sobre la mesa, los tengo en mi bolsillo,** Your cigarettes are not on the table, I have them in my pocket. Means some, any, ones, as substitution for noun already stated (e.g. **Los cigarros están en la caja si los hay,** The cigars are in the box, if there are any). Used demonstratively followed by *de* or *que* introducing relative clause, those of; those which, those who; the ones that (who) (e.g. **Estaba leyendo algunos libros de los que tienes en tu cuarto,** I was reading some

books from among those which you have in your room)

losa, *f.* flagstone; slab; tombstone

lote, *m.* lot, portion, share

lotería, *f.* lottery; lotto (game); lottery office

lotero (-ra), *s.* seller of lottery tickets

loto, *m.* (*bot.*) lotus; lotus flower or fruit

lovaniense, *a.* and *m.* and *f.* of or from Louvain (Belgium)

loza, *f.* porcelain, china; china ware

lozanía, *f.* luxuriance (of vegetation); vigour, lustiness; arrogance

lozano, *a.* luxuriant, exuberant; vigorous, lusty; arrogant

lubricación, *f.* lubrication

lubricador, *m.* lubricator

lubricante, *a.* lubricant

lubricar, *v.t.* to lubricate

lubrico, *a.* slippery, smooth; lascivious, lustful

lucera, *f.* skylight

lucerna, *f.* large chandelier; skylight

lucero, *m.* evening star; any bright star; white star (on horse's head); brilliance, radiance; *pl.* (*poet.*) eyes, orbs. **l. del alba,** (the) morning star

lucidez, *f.* brilliance, shine; lucidity, clarity

lucido, *a.* splendid, brilliant, sumptuous; fine, elegant

lúcido, *a.* (*poet.*) brilliant; lucid clear

luciente, *a.* bright, shining

luciérnaga, *f.* glowworm

lucimiento, *m.* brilliance, lustre, success, triumph; elegance; display, ostentation

lucir, *v.i. irr.* to shine, scintillate, excel, outshine; be successful, *v.t.* illuminate; display, show off, show; *v.r.* dress elegantly; be successful; excel, be brilliant. *Pres. Ind.* luzco, luces, etc. *Pres. Subjunc.* luzca, etc.

lucrativo, *a.* lucrative

lucro, *m.* gain, profit

lucroso, *a.* profitable

luctuoso, *a.* lugubrious, mournful

lucubración, *f.* lucubration

lucha, *f.* fight; struggle; wrestling match; argument, disagreement.

l. grecorromana, wrestling. **l. igualada,** close fight. **l. libre,** catch-as-catch²can

luchador (-ra), s. fighter; struggler

luchar, v.i. to fight hand to hand; wrestle; fight; struggle; argue

ludibrio, m. mockery, ridicule

luego, adv. immediately; afterwards, later; then; soon, presently. conjunc. therefore. **l. que,** as soon as. **desde l.,** immediately, at once; of course, naturally; in the first place. **hasta l.,** au revoir, good-bye for the present

luengo, a. long

lugar, m. place; spot; village, town, city; region, locality; office, post; passage, text; opportunity, occasion; cause, motive; place on a list; room, space; seat. **l. común,** commonplace. **en l. de,** instead of. **en primer l.,** firstly, in the first place. **hacer l.,** to make room, make way. **No ha l.,** The petition is refused. **tener l.,** to take place; have the time or opportunity (to)

lugarejo, m. hamlet

lugareño (-ña), a. peasant, regional. s. villager, peasant

lugartenencia, f. lieutenancy

lugarteniente, m. lieutenant; substitute, deputy

lúgubre, a. lugubrious, dismal, mournful

luis, m. louis (French coin)

lujo, m. luxury; abundance, profusion. **artículos de l.,** luxury goods

lujoso, a. luxurious; abundant, profuse

lujuria, f. lasciviousness; excess, intemperance

lujuriante, a. luxuriant, abundant, profuse

lujurioso, a. lascivious, voluptuous

luliano (-na), a. and s. Lullian (from Ramón Llull)

lumbago, m. lumbago

lumbre, f. fire; light; splendour, lustre; transom-window, opening, skylight; pl. tinder box

lumbrera, f. luminary; skylight; dormer-window; eminent authority

luminar, m. luminary (also fig.)

luminaria, f. fairy-light, small light; lamp burning before the Sacrament in Catholic churches

luminosidad, f. luminosity

luminoso, a. luminous; bright

luna, f. moon; mirror; satellite; sheet of plate-glass. **l. creciente,** new or rising moon. **l. de miel,** honeymoon. **l. llena,** full moon. **l. menguante,** waning moon. **media l.,** crescent moon

lunado, a. half-moon, crescent

lunar, m. beauty spot; (fig.) stain, blot (on reputation, etc.); blemish, slight imperfection. a. lunar

lunático (-ca), a. and s. lunatic

lunes, m. Monday

luneta, f. lens (of eyeglasses); (theat.) orchestra stall; (arch., mil.) lunette

lupa, f. magnifying glass

lupanar, m. brothel

lupino, a. wolf-like, lupine. m. (bot.) lupin

lúpulo, m. (bot.) hop

lusitano (-na), a. and s. Lusitanian; Portuguese

lustrador, m. polisher. **l. de piso,** floor polisher

lustrar, v.i. to lustrate, purify; polish, burnish; roam, journey

lustre, m. polish, sheen, gloss; glory, lustre

lustro, m. lustrum, period of five years; chandelier

lustroso, a. shining, glossy; brilliant; glorious, noble

luteranismo, m. Lutheranism

luterano (-na), a. and s. Lutheran

luto, m. mourning; grief, affliction; pl. mourning draperies. **estar de l.,** to be in mourning

luxación, f. (surg.) luxation, dislocation

luz, f. light; glow; brightness, brilliance; information, news; (fig.) luminary; day, daylight; pl. culture, learning; windows. **luces de estacionamiento,** parking lights. **a buena l.,** in a good light; in a favourable light; after due consideration. **a primera l.,** at dawn. **dar a l.,** to publish (a book); bring forth (children); reveal. **entre dos luces,** in the dawn light; in the twilight; (fam.) tipsy. **media l.,** half-light, twilight

LL

llaga, *f.* ulcer; sore; grief, affliction; (*fig.*) thorn in the flesh

llagar, *v.t.* to ulcerate; make or produce sores; (*fig.*) wound; *v.r.* be covered with sores

llama, *f.* flame; ardour, vehemence; marsh; (*zool.*) llama

llamada, *f.* call; (*mil.*) call-to-arms *or* call

llamado, *a.* called; so-called

llamador (-ra), *s.* caller. *m.* door knocker; bell push

llamamiento, *m.* calling; call; divine summons, inspiration; invocation, appeal; summons, convocation

llamar, *v.t.* to call; invoke, call upon; summon, convoke; name; attract; *v.i.* knock (at a door); ring (a bell); *v.r.* be named, be called; (*naut.*) veer (wind). **Se llama Pedro,** He is called Peter

llamarada, *f.* flame, flash; blaze, flare (of anger, etc.)

llamativo, *a.* striking, showy; provocative

llamear, *v.i.* to throw out flames, blaze

llana, *f.* mason's trowel; plain; surface of a page

llanada, *f.* plain

llanamente, *adv.* frankly, plainly; naturally, simply; candidly, sincerely

llanero (-ra), *s.* plain dweller

llaneza, *f.* naturalness; candour; familiarity; simplicity (of style)

llano, *a.* flat, level; smooth, even; shallow (of receptacles); unaffected, homely, natural; plain (of dresses); manifest, evident; easy; straightforward, candid; informal; simple (of style). *m.* plain; level stretch of ground

llanta, *f.* (*aut.*) tyre; rim, felloe. **ll. de rueda,** wheel-band, rim

llanto, *m.* weeping, flood of tears

llanura, *f.* smoothness, evenness, levelness; plain

llar, *m.* hearth

llave, *f.* key; spigot, faucet, tap; spanner, wrench; (*elec.*) switch; clock-winder; (*mus.*) key, clef; (*arch.*) keystone; (*print.*) brace; (*mech.*) wrench; lock (of a gun); tuning-key; piston (of musical instruments); lock (in wrestling); (*fig.*) key (of a problem or a study). **ll. de transmisión,** sender (telegraphy). **ll. inglesa,** monkey-wrench, spanner. **ll. maestra,** master key, skeleton key. **echar la ll.,** to lock. **torcer la ll.,** to turn the key

llavero (-ra), *s.* keeper of the keys. *m.* key-ring. **ll. de cárcel,** turnkey

llavín, *m.* yale key, latch-key

llegada, *f.* arrival, advent

llegar, *v.i.* to arrive; last, endure; reach; achieve a purpose; be sufficient, suffice; amount (to), make; *v.t.* bring near, draw near; gather; *v.r.* come near, approach; adhere. **ll. a ser,** to become. **ll. a un punto muerto,** to reach a dead-lock. **ll. hasta . .,** to stretch as far as . .

llena, *f.* spate, overflow

llenar, *v.t.* to fill; occupy (a post); satisfy, please; fulfil; satiate; pervade; fill up (a form); *v.i.* be full (of the moon); *v.r.* (*fam.*) stuff, over-eat; (*fig., fam.*) be fed-up

lleno, *a.* full; replete; abundant; complete. *m.* full moon; (*theat.*) full house; (*fam.*) glut, abundance; perfection. **de ll., de ll. en ll.,** entirely, completely

llenura, *f.* abundance, plenty

lleva, llevada, *f.* carrying, bearing

llevadero, *a.* tolerable, bearable

llevar, *v.t.* to carry, transport; charge (a price); yield, produce, carry off, take away; endure, bear; persuade; guide, take; direct; wear (clothes); carry (a handbag, etc.); introduce, present; gain, achieve; manage (a horse); pass, spend (of time); (*with past part.*) have (e.g. **Llevo escrita la carta,** I have written the letter); (*math.*) carry; (*with prep. a*) surpass, excel. **ll. a cabo,** to accomplish. **ll. a cuestas,** to carry on one's back; support. **ll. la correspondencia,** to look after the correspondence. **ll. la delantera,** to take the lead. **llevarse bien,** to get on well, agree

llorar, *v.i.* to weep, cry; drip; water (eyes); *v.t.* lament, mourn; bewail one's troubles

lloriquear, v.i. to whine, snivel

lloriqueo, m. whining, snivelling

lloro, m. weeping, crying; flood of tears

llorón, a. weeping; snivelling, whining. m. long plume. **niño llorón,** cry-baby

lloroso, a. tearful; grievous, sad; sorrowful

llovedizo, a. leaky; rainy

llover, v.i. impers. irr. to rain, come in abundance (of troubles, etc.); v.r. leak (roofs, etc.). **ll. a cántaros,** to rain in torrents. **como llovido,** unexpectedly See **mover**

llovido, m. stowaway

llovizna, f. drizzle, fine rain

lloviznar, v.i. to drizzle

lluvia, f. rain; rainwater; (fig.) shower; rose (of watering-can)

lluvioso, a. rainy, showery

M

maca, f. bruise or blemish on fruit; defect, flaw; (fam.) fraud, swindle

macabro, a. macabre

macadán, m. macadam

macadanizar, v.t. to macadam-ize

macagua, f. (orn.) macaw

macanudo, a. (fam. Sp. Am.) extraordinary; enormous; ro-bust; fine, excellent

macareno (-na), s. inhabitant of the Macarena district of Seville. m. (fam.) braggart

macarrones, m. pl. macaroni, (naut.) stanchions

macarrónico, a. macaronic, re-condite, stylized

macarse, v.r to go bad, rot (fruit)

macedón (-ona), macedonio (-ia), a. and s. Macedonian

maceración, f. maceration; steep-ing, soaking; mortification of the flesh

macerar, v.t. to macerate; steep, soak; mortify

macero, m. mace-bearer

maceta, f. dim. small mace; handle, haft (of tools); stone-cutter's hammer; flower-pot

macetero, m. flower-pot stand

macicez, f. solidity; massiveness; thickness

macilento, a. thin, lean, emaci-ated

macillo, m. dim. small mace; hammer (of a piano)

macis, f. (cul.) mace

macizar, v.t. to block up, fill up

macizo, a. massive; compact, solid; (fig.) well-founded, unas-sailable; thick; strong. m. solid-ity, compactness; bulk, volume; flowerbed; solid tyre

macrocéfalo, a. (med.) macro-cephalous

macrocosmo, m. macrocosm

mácula, f. stain, spot; (fig.) blot, blemish; (fam.) trick, deception; (ast.) macula

macuquero, m. unauthorized worker of abandoned mines

machaca, f. pestle; pulverizer. m. and f. (fam.) bore, tedious person

machacador (-ra), a. crushing, pounding. s. beater, crusher, pounder

machacar, v.t. to crush, pound, v.i. importune; harp on a subject

machacón, a. tiresome, prolix

machado, m. hatchet, axe

machetero, m. one who cuts sugar-cane with a **machete**

machihembrar, v.t. (carp.) to dovetail

machina, f derrick, crane; pile-driver

macho, m. male; male animal (he-goat, stallion, etc.); male plant; hook (of hook and eye) screw; (met.) core; tap (tool), (fam.) dunderhead, fool; (arch.) buttress. a. male; stupid, ignor-ant; vigorous, strong. m. ca-brío, he-goat

machucadura, f., **machuca-miento,** m. pounding, crushing bruising

machucar, v.t. to crush, pound bruise

machucho, a. prudent, sensible; adult, mature

madama, f. madam

madeja, f. skein, hank; lock of hair; (fam.) dummy, useless person

madera, f. wood; timber; (fam.) kind, sort; (mus.) wind instru-ments. **m. contrachapada,**

plywood. **m. de construcción,**
timber. **maderas de sierra,**
lumber wood. (*fam.*) **ser de
mala m.,** to be a ne'er do well

maderada, *f.* lumber wood

maderaje, *m.* woodwork, timber
work

maderero, *m.* timber merchant;
lumber jack; carpenter

madería, *f.* timber yard

madero, *m.* wooden beam; log,
piece of lumber; ship, vessel;
(*fam.*) blockhead or insensible
person

madrastra, *f.* stepmother; anything unpleasant

madraza, *f.* (*fam.*) over-indulgent
mother

madre, *f.* mother; matron; cause,
genesis; (*fam.*) dame, mother;
river-bed; dam; womb; main
sewer; chief irrigation channel.
m. de familia, mother; housewife. **m. de leche,** wet-nurse.
m. política, mother-in-law;
stepmother. (*fam.*) **sacar de
m.** (a), to provoke, irritate (a
person)

madreperla, *f* mother-of-
pearl

madrépora, *f.* white coral,
madrepore

madreselva, *f.* (*bot.*) honeysuckle

madrigado, *a.* twice-married
(women); (*fam.*) experienced,
wide-awake

madrigal, *m.* madrigal

madriguera, *f.* rabbit-warren;
burrow, den, hole, lair; haunt of
thieves, etc.

madrileño (-ña), *a.* and *s.*
Madrilenian

madrina, *f.* godmother; matron
of honour or bridesmaid; sponsor; patroness; prop; stanchion

madroncillo, *m.* strawberry

madroño, *m.* strawberry tree;
tuft, spot; tassel

madrugada, *f.* dawn, daybreak;
early rising. **de m.,** at dawn

madrugador (-ra), *a.* early-
rising. *s.* early riser

madrugar, *v.i.* to get up early;
gain time; anticipate, be beforehand

maduración, *f.* ripening; mellowing; preparation; ripeness;
maturity

madurador, *a.* ripening; ma-
turing

maduramente, *adv.* maturely;
sensibly

madurar, *v.t.* to ripen; mature;
think out; *v.i.* ripen; grow
mature, learn wisdom

madurez, *f.* ripeness; maturity;
mellowness; wisdom

maduro, *a.* ripe; mature; mellow;
adult; wise

maestra, *f.* schoolmistress;
teacher, instructor; queen bee;
guide, model

maestral, *a.* referring to the
Grand Master of one of the
Spanish Military Orders; teaching, pedagogic. *m.* mistral
(wind); cell of queen bee

maestrante, *m.* member of a
maestranza

maestranza, *f.* society of knights
devoted to equestrian exercises;
arsenal; staff of an arsenal

maestrazgo, *m.* Grandmaster-
ship of one of the Spanish
Military Orders

maestre, *m.* Grand Master of
Military Order. **m. de raciones**
or **m. de víveres,** quartermaster

maestrear, *v.t.* to direct, control,
manage; prune vines; *v.i.* (*fam.*)
bully, domineer

maestría, *f.* mastery, skill; (*univ.*)
Master's degree

maestril, *m.* queen cell (bees)

maestro, *a.* masterly; excellent;
chief, main; midship. *m.* master,
expert; teacher; instructor;
master craftsman; (*univ.*)
Master; (*mus.*) composer; (*naut.*)
mainmast. **m. de armas,** fencing master. **m. de capilla,** (*ecc.*)
choir master. **m. de obras,**
building contractor; master
builder. **El ejercicio hace m.,**
Practice makes perfect

magdalena, *f.* madeleine (cake),
magdalen, penitent. (*fam.*) **estar
hecha una M.,** to be inconsolable

magia, *f.* magic

magiar, *a.* and *m.* and *f.* Magyar.
m. Magyar language

mágica, *f.* magic; enchantress,
sorceress

mágico, *a.* magic; marvellous,
wonderful. *m.* magician; enchanter, wizard

magín, *m.* (*fam.*) imagination; head, mind

magisterio, *m.* teaching profession; teaching diploma; teaching post; pedantry, pompousness

magistrado, *m.* magistrate; magistracy

magistral, *a.* magistral; authoritative, magisterial; pedantic, pompous

magistratura, *f.* magistracy

magnanimidad, *f.* magnanimity; generosity, liberality

magnánimo, *a.* magnanimous, generous, noble

magnate, *m.* magnate

magnesia, *f.* magnesia

magnesio, *m.* magnesium

magnético, *a.* magnetic

magnetismo, *m.* magnetism

magnetización, *f.* magnetization; mesmerization

magnetizar, *v.t.* to magnetize; mesmerize

magneto, *m.* magneto

magnificar, *v.t.* to magnify, enlarge; praise, extol

magnificencia, *f.* magnificence, pomp, splendour

magnífico, *a.* magnificent; splendid, wonderful, fine; excellent

magnitud, *f.* magnitude (also *ast.*); quantity; importance

magno, *a.* great; famous. **Alejandro el M.,** Alexander the Great*

magnolia, *f.* (*bot.*) magnolia

mago, *m.* magician; *pl.* magi

magra, *f.* rasher (of bacon, ham)

magrez, magrura, *f.* leanness; scragginess

magro, *a.* lean; scraggy. *m.* (*fam.*) lean pork

magulladura, *f.,* **magullamiento,** *m.* bruising; bruise, contusion

magullar, *v.t.* to bruise

mahometano (-na), *a.* and *s.* Mohammedan

mahometismo, *m.* Mohammedanism

mahonesa, *f.* (*cul.*) mayonnaise

maitines, *m. pl.* (*ecc.*) matins

maíz, *m.* maize

maizal, *m.* maize field

maja, *f.* belle

majada, *f.* sheepfold; dung

majadería, *f.* impertinence, insolence

majadero, *a.* persistent, tedious. *m.* bobbin (for lace making); pestle. *s.* fool, bore

majador, *m.* pestle

majar, *v.t.* to pound, crush; (*fam.*) importune, annoy

majestad, *f.* majesty (title); dignity; stateliness

majestuosidad, *f.* majesty; dignity

majestuoso, *a.* majestic; stately; dignified

majo, *a.* arrogant, aggressive; gaudily attired, smart; dashing, handsome; attractive, pretty; elegant, well-dressed. *m.* beau, gallant, lad of the town

majuelo, *m.* new vine; species of white hawthorn

mal, *a. abb.* **malo.** Used only before *m. sing.* nouns (e.g. **un m. cuarto de hora,** a bad quarter of an hour). *m.* evil; damage; harm; misfortune; illness, disease; trouble (e.g. **El m. es,** The trouble is). **m. de altura,** air sickness. **m. de ojo,** evil eye. **m. de piedra,** lithiasis, stone. **m. francés,** syphilis. *interj.* ¡ **M. haya !** A curse upon! **echar a m.,** to scorn (things); waste, squander. **llevar a m.** (**una cosa**), to take (a thing) badly, complain. **No hay m. que por bien no venga,** It's an ill-wind that blows no one any good. **parar en m.,** to come to a bad end

mal, *adv.* badly; unfavourably; wrongly; wickedly; with difficulty; scarcely, barely. **m. que bien,** willingly or unwillingly; rightly or wrongly. **de m. en peor,** from bad to worse

mala, *f.* mail, post. **m. real,** royal mail

malabarista, *m.* and *f.* juggler

malaconsejado, *a.* ill-advised, imprudent

malacostumbrado, *a.* badly trained, spoilt; having bad habits

malagueña, *f.* popular song of lament

malagueño, *a.* of or from Málaga

malandante, *a.* evil-doing; unfortunate, miserable; poor

malandanza, *f.* evil doing; misfortune, misery; poverty

malandrín, *a.* wicked, ill-disposed. *m.* scoundrel, miscreant

malaquita, *f.* malachite

malaria, *f.* malaria

malaventura, *f.* misfortune, adversity, ill-luck

malaventurado, *a.* unfortunate, unlucky

malayo (-ya), *a.* Malay. *s.* Malayan

malbaratador (-ra), *a.* wasteful, spendthrift. *s.* squanderer, spendthrift

malbaratar, *v.t.* to squander, waste; sell at a loss

malcasado, *a.* adulterous, unfaithful

malcasar(se), *v.t.* and *v.r.* to marry badly

malcomido, *a.* underfed

malcontento (-ta), *a.* dissatisfied, discontented; rebellious. *s.* malcontent, rebel

malcriado, *a.* badly brought up; ill-bred; spoilt, peevish

maldad, *f.* badness; depravity, wickedness

maldecidor (-ra), *a.* slanderous. *s.* scandalmonger, slanderer

maldecir, *v.t. irr.* to curse; *v.t.* and *v.i.* slander, backbite. See **decir**

maldiciente, *a.* defamatory, slanderous; cursing, reviling. *m.* slanderer; curser

maldición, *f.* malediction; curse, imprecation

maldispuesto, *a.* indisposed, ill; reluctant

maldita, *f. (fam.)* tongue. *(fam.)* **soltar la m.,** to say too much, go too far

maldito, *a.* accursed; wicked; damned; poor (of quality); *(fam.)* **not a . . .**

maleabilidad, *f.* malleability, flexibility

maleable, *a.* malleable, flexible

maleante, *a.* rascally, villainous. *m.* and *f.* evildoer

malecón, *m.* breakwater

maledicencia, *f.* slander, abuse, backbiting; cursing

maleficencia, *f.* wrongdoing

maleficio, *m.* (magic) curse; spell; charm

maléfico, *a.* malefic, harmful. *m.* sorcerer

malestar, *m.* indisposition, slight illness; discomfort

maleta, *f.* suit-case, valise, grip; *m. (fam.)* clumsy matador; duffer (at games, etc.). **hacer la m.,** to pack a suit-case; *(fam.)* prepare for a journey, get ready to leave

maletero, *m.* seller or maker of travelling bags; porter

maletín, *m.* small suitcase or valise

malevolencia, *f.* malevolence, hatred, malice

malévolo, *a.* malevolent, malicious

maleza, *f.* weeds; undergrowth; thicket

malgache, *a.* and *m.* and *f.* of or from Madagascar

malgastador (-ra), *a.* thriftless, wasteful. *s.* squanderer

malgastar, *v.t.* to waste (time); squander, throw away (money)

malhablado, *a.* foul-tongued, indecent

malhadado, *a.* ill-fated, unhappy

malhecho, *a.* deformed, twisted (persons). *m.* evil deed, wrongdoing

malhechor (-ra), *s.* malefactor; evil-doer

malhumorado, *a.* ill-humoured, bad-tempered

malicia, *f.* wickedness, evil; malice, maliciousness; acuteness, subtlety, shrewdness; craftiness, guile; *(fam.)* suspicion

maliciar, *v.t.* to suspect; spoil, damage; hurt, harm

malicioso, *a.* malicious; vindictive; wicked; shrewd, clever; *(fam.)* suspicious; artful

malignidad, *f.* malignancy, spite, ill-will

maligno, *a.* malignant, spiteful; wicked; *(med.)* malignant

malintencionado, *a.* ill-intentioned, badly disposed

malmandado, *a.* disobedient; reluctant, unwilling

malmaridada, *f.* adultress, faithless wife

malo, *a.* bad; wicked; evil; injurious, harmful; illicit; licentious; ill; difficult; troublesome, annoying; *(fam.)* mischievous; knavish; rotten, decaying. *interj.* **¡ M. !** That's bad!; You shouldn't have done that!; That's a bad sigal **de malas,** unluckily, unhappily. **el M.,** the Evil One, the Devil. **estar m.,** to be ill. **Lo m. es,** The trouble is, The worst of it is . . . **por malas o por buenas,** willy-nilly, willingly or unwillingly. **ser m.,** to be wicked; be evil; behave badly (children)

malograr, *v.t.* to lose (time); waste, throw away (opportunities); *v.r.* fall through, fail; wither, fade; die early, come to an untimely end

malogro, *m.* loss, waste (time, opportunity); frustration; decline, fading; untimely death

malparar, *v.t.* to ill-treat; damage. **quedar malparado,** to get the worst of

malparir, *v.t.* (*med.*) to miscarry

malparto, *m.* miscarriage; abortion

malquerencia, *f.* ill-will, aversion, dislike

malquistar, *v.t.* to stir up trouble; make unpopular; estrange; *v.r.* make oneself disliked

malquisto, *a.* unpopular, disliked

malsano, *a.* unhealthy

malta, *m.* malt

maltés (-esa), *a.* and *s.* Maltese

maltraer, *v.t.* *irr.* to ill-treat; insult. See **traer**

maltratamiento, *m.* abuse, ill usage; damage, deterioration

maltratar, *v.t.* to ill-treat; abuse, insult; misuse, spoil, damage

maltrato, *m.* maltreatment; misuse

maltrecho, *a.* ill-treated, bruised; abused, insulted; damaged

maltusianismo, *m.* Malthusianism

maltusiano, *a.* Malthusian

malucho, *a.* (*fam.*) off-colour, below par, not well

malva, *f.* (*bot.*) mallow. **m. real, m. rosa,** *or* **m. loca,** hollyhock. **ser como una m.,** (*fig., fam.*) to be a clinging vine

malvado, *a.* evil, malevolent, fiendish. *s.* villain, fiend

malvarrosa, *f.* (*bot.*) hollyhock

malvasía, *f.* (*bot.*) malvasia; malmsey (wine)

malvavisco, *m.* (*bot.*) marshmallow

malvender, *v.t.* to sell at a loss

malversación, *f.* malversation, maladministration; misappropriation (of funds)

malversador (-ra), *s.* bad or corrupt administrator

malversar, *v.t.* to misappropriate (funds)

malvís, *m.* (*orn.*) mavis

malla, *f.* mesh (of a net); coat of mail; *pl.* (*theat.*) tights. **m. de alambre,** wire-netting. **cota de m.,** coat of mail

mallorquín (-ina), *a.* and *s.* Majorcan. **m.** Majorcan dialect

mama, *f.* (*fam.*) mamma, mummy; breast; udder

mamá, *f.* mamma

mamar, *v.t.* to suck (the breast); (*fam.*) wolf, swallow; learn from an early age; enjoy, obtain unfairly; *v.r.* get drunk

mamario, *a.* (*anat.*) mammary

mamarracho, *m.* (*fam.*) scarecrow, dummy; anything grotesque looking

mameluco, *m.* mameluke; (*fam.*) ninny, fool

mamífero, *a.* (*zool.*) mammalian. **m.** mammal

mamotreto, *m.* note-book, memorandum; (*fam.*) large book or bulky file of papers

mampara, *f.* folding screen; screen; partition

mamparo, *m.* (*naut.*) bulkhead

mampostería, *f.* masonry, stone masonry

mampostero, *m.* stone-mason

mamut, *m.* (*zool.*) mammoth

maná, *m.* manna

manada, *f.* handful; herd, flock; group, drove, crowd

manadero, *m.* herdsman, drover; spring, stream

manantial, *m.* fountain, source, spring; head (of river)

manar, *v.i.* to flow, stream; be plentiful

manatí, *m.* (*zool.*) sea-cow, manatee

mancar, *v.t.* to injure, maim; *v.i.* grow calm (elements)

manceba, *f.* concubine; girl

mancebía, *f.* brothel; youth, young days

mancebo, *m.* youth, stripling; bachelor; shop assistant

mancilla, *f.* stain; slur

mancillar, *v.t.* to stain; (*fig.*) smirch

manco (-ca), *a.* maimed, disabled; one-handed; one-armed; armless; handless; incomplete, faulty. *s.* disabled person

mancomunidad, *f.* association, society; community, union; commonwealth; regional legislative assembly

mancha, *f.* spot, smear, stain; blotch; plot of ground; patch of vegetation; stigma, disgrace

manchar, *v.t.* to stain; smear; spot; speckle; disgrace; tarnish

manchego (-ga), *a.* and *s.* of or from La Mancha (Spain)

manchuriano (-na), *a.* and *s.* Manchurian

manda, *f.* offer, suggestion, proposition; legacy

mandadero (-ra), *s.* convent or prison messenger; errand-boy (girl)

mandado, *m.* order, command; errand

mandamiento, *m.* order, command; (*ecc.*) commandment; (*law*) writ; *pl.* (*fam.*) one's five fingers

mandar, *v.t.* to order, command; bequeath, will; send; control, drive; promise, offer; order (e.g. **Mandó hacerse un traje,** He ordered a suit to be made); *v.r.* walk unaided (convalescents, etc.); lead into one another (rooms, etc.); **¿Quién manda aquí?** Who is in charge here?

mandarín, *m.* mandarin; (*fam.*) bureaucrat

mandarina, *f.* mandarin (Classical Chinese); mandarin orange

mandatario, *m.* mandatary

mandato, *m.* mandate; command; (*ecc.*) maundy. (*pol.*) **cuarto m.,** Fourth Term (*U.S.A.*)

mandíbula, *f.* jaw; jaw-bone, mandible

mandil, *m.* long leather apron; apron; freemason's apron; close-meshed fishing-net

mandilón, *m.* (*fam.*) coward, nincompoop

mandioca, *f.* (*bot.*) manioc, cassava; tapioca

mando, *m.* authority, power; (*mil.*, *nav.*) command; (*eng.*)

regulation; controls (of a machine, etc.). **m. a distancia,** remote control. (*aer.*) **m. de dos pilotos,** dual-controlled. **mandos gemelos,** dual-control. **al m. de,** under the command of; under the direction of

mandolín, *m.,* **mandolina,** *f.* mandolin

mandón, *a.* domineering, bossy

mandrágora, *f.* (*bot.*) mandrake

mandril, *m.,* (*mech.*) mandrel, chuck; (*zool.*) mandrill

manear, *v.t.* to hobble (a horse); manage, control

manecilla, *f.* *dim.* little hand; hand of a clock; (*print.*) fist

manejable, *a.* manageable, controllable

manejar, *v.t.* to handle; use, wield; control; manage, direct; ride. (horses); *v.r.* manage to move around (after accident, illness).

manejo, *m.* handling; use, wielding; control; management, direction; horsemanship; intrigue

maneota, *f.* hobble, shackle

manera, *f.* manner, way, means; behaviour, style (gen. *pl.*); class (of people); (*art*) style, manner. **a la m. de,** like, in the style of. **de esa m.,** in that way; according to that, in that case. **de m. que,** so that. **en gran m.,** to a great extent. **sobre m.,** exceedingly

manga, *f.* sleeve; gripsack; handle; pipe (of a hose); strainer; jelly bag; waterspout; body of troops; beam, breadth of a ship; *pl.* profits. **m. de viento,** whirlwind. **echar de m. a,** to make use of a person. (*fam.*) **estar de m.,** to be in league. **tener m. ancha,** to be broad-minded. (*fig.*, *fam.*) **traer (una cosa) en la m.,** to have (something) up one's sleeve

mangana, *f.* lasso

manganeso, *m.* manganese

manganilla, *f.* sleight of hand; hoax, trick

mangle, *m.* (*bot.*) mangrove tree

mango, *m.* handle, haft, stock; (*bot.*) mango. **m. de cuchillo,** knife-handle

mangonear, *v.i.* (*fam.*) to loaf, roam about; interfere, meddle mangonero, a. (fam.) meddle-some

mangosta, f. (zool.) mongoose

mangote, m. (fam.) long wide sleeve; black oversleeve

manguera, f. hose-pipe; sleeve, tube; air-shaft; waterspout

manguero, m. fireman; hoseman

manguito, m. muff; black oversleeve; wristlet, cuff; (mech.) bush, sleeve

manía, f. mania, obsession; whim, fancy

maníaco (-ca), a. maniacal; capricious, extravagant. s. maniac

maniatar, v.t. to handcuff; hobble (a cow, etc.)

maniático (-ca), a. maniacal; capricious; faddy, fussy. s. crank

manicomio, m. lunatic asylum

manicura, f. manicure

manicuro (-ra), s. manicurist

manida, f. lair, den; dwelling, habitation

manifestación, f. declaration, statement; exhibition; demonstration; (ecc.) exposition (of the Blessed Sacrament)

manifestante, m. and f. demonstrator

manifestar, v.t. irr. to declare, make known, state; exhibit, show; (ecc.) to expose (the Blessed Sacrament). See acertar

manifiesto, a. obvious, evident. m. manifesto; (naut.) manifest; (ecc.) exposition of Blessed Sacrament. poner de m., to show; make public; reveal

manigua, f. thicket, jungle (in Cuba)

manija, f. handle, stock, haft; hand-lever; clamp; hopple (for horses, etc.)

manileño (ña), a. and s. of or from Manila

manilla, f. bracelet; handcuff, manacle

maniobra, f. operation, process; (mil.) manœuvre; intrigue; tackle, gear; handling, management; (naut.) working of a ship; pl. shunting (trains)

maniobrar, v.i. (mil.) to manœuvre; (naut.) handle, work (ships)

manipulación, f. handling; manipulation; control, management

manipulador, a. manipulative. m. sending-key (telegraphy)

manipular, v.t. to handle; manipulate; manage, direct

manípulo, m. maniple

maniqueo (-ea), a. Manichæan. s. Manichee

maniquete, m. black lace mitten

maniquí, m. mannequin; dummy; (fam.) puppet, weak person

manirroto (-ta), a. wasteful, extravagant. s. spendthrift

manivela, f. (mech.) crank, lever

manjar, m. dish, food; pastime, recreation, pleasure. m. blanco, blancmange

mano, f. hand; coat, coating; quire (of paper); front paw (animals); elephant's trunk; side, hand; hand (of a clock); game (of cards, etc.); lead (at cards); way, means; ability; power; protection, favour; compassion; aid, help; scolding; (mus.) scale; pestle; workers. (fam.) m. de gato, hare's foot (for make-up); (fam.) make-up; editing, correction of a literary work (gen. by person more skilled than author). m. de mortero, pestle. m. de obra, (manual) labour. manos muertas, (law) mortmain. m. sobre m., with folded hands; lazily, indolently. a la m., at hand, near by; within one's grasp. a manos llenas, in abundance, abundantly. bajo m., in an underhand manner, secretly. buenas manos, cleverness, ability; dexterity. de primera m., first-hand, new. estar dejado de la m. de Dios, to be very unlucky; be very foolish. poner la m. en, to ill-treat; slap, buffet. Si a m. viene . . ., If by chance . . . tender la m., to put out one's hand, shake hands. traer entre manos, to have on hand, be engaged in

manojo, m. bunch, handful. a manojos, in handfuls; plentifully, in abundance

manolo (-la), s. inhabitant of low quarters of Madrid noted for pride, gaiety, quarrelsomeness and wit

manómetro, *m.* pressure-gauge, manometer

manopla, *f.* gauntlet

manoseado, *a.* hackneyed

manosear, *v.t.* to handle; paw, touch repeatedly; finger

manoseo, *m.* handling; fingering; (*fam.*) pawing, feeling

manotada, *f.* slap, cuff

manotear, *v.t.* to slap, cuff; *v.i.* gesticulate, gesture with the hands

manoteo, *m.* gesticulation with the hands

manquedad, *f.* disablement of hand or arm; lack of one of these; defect; incompleteness

mansalva, (a) *adv.* without danger

mansedumbre, *f.* meekness; kindness; gentleness

mansión, *f.* stay, visit; dwelling, abode; mansion

manso, *a.* soft, gentle; meek, mild; tame; peaceable, amiable; calm

manta, *f.* blanket; horse blanket; travelling rug; (*fam.*) hiding, thrashing. **m. de viaje,** travelling rug. (*fam.*) **a m. de Dios,** in abundance. **dar una m.,** to toss in blanket. (*fig., fam.*) **tirar de la m.,** to let the cat out of the bag

manteamiento, *m.* tossing in a blanket

mantear, *v.t.* to toss in a blanket

manteca, *f.* lard; cooking fat; grease. **como m.,** as mild as milk, as soft as butter

mantecada, *f.* buttered toast

mantecado, *m.* French ice-cream

mantecoso, *a.* greasy

manteísta, *m.* day student (of a seminary)

mantel, *m.* table-cloth; altar-cloth

mantelería, *f.* table-linen

mantelete, *m.* (*ecc., mil.*) mantlet

mantener, *v.t. irr.* to maintain; keep, feed; support; continue, persevere with; uphold, affirm; keep up; *v.r.* support oneself; remain in a place; (*with en*) continue to uphold (views, etc.), persevere in. **mantenerse firme,** (*fig.*) to stand one's ground. See **tener**

mantenimiento, *m.* maintenance; support; sustenance, nou-

rishment; affirmation; upkeep; livelihood

manteo, *m.* tossing in a blanket; long cloak

mantequera, *f.* churn; dairymaid; butter-dish

mantequero, *m.* dairyman; butter-dish

mantequilla, *f.* butter

mantero, *m.* blanket seller or maker

mantilla, *f.* mantilla; saddle cloth. *pl.* baby's long clothes. **estar en mantillas,** to be in swaddling-clothes; (*fig.*) be in first infancy

manto, *m.* cloak; cover, disguise; (*zool.*) mantle; (*min.*) layer

mantón, *m.* shawl. **m. de Manila,** Manila shawl

mantuano (-na), *a.* and *s.* Mantuan (Italy)

manuable, *a.* easy to handle or use, handy

manual, *a.* manual; handy, easy to use; docile, peaceable. *m.* manual, text-book; (*ecc.*) book of ritual; note-book

manubrio, *m.* handle, crank

manuela, *f.* open carriage (Madrid)

manufactura, *f.* manufacture; manufactured article; factory

manufacturar, *v.t.* to manufacture

manufacturero, *a.* manufacturing

manumisión, *f.* freeing (of a slave)

manumitir, *v.t.* (*law*) to free, enfranchise (slaves)

manuscrito, *a.* and *m.* manuscript

manutención, *f.* maintenance; upkeep; protection

manzana, *f.* apple; block (of houses); city square; Adam's apple (in throat)

manzanal, *m.* apple orchard; apple tree

manzanar, *m.* apple orchard

manzanilla, *f.* white sherry wine; (*bot.*) camomile; camomile tea; knob, ball (on furniture); pad (on an animal's foot)

manzano, *m.* apple tree

maña, *f.* skill, dexterity; craftiness, guile; vice, bad habit (gen. *pl.*). **darse m. para,** to contrive to

mañana, f. morning; tomorrow. *m.* future, tomorrow. *adv.* tomorrow; in time to come; soon. ¡M.! Tomorrow! Another day! Not now! (generally to beggars). de m., early in the morning. muy de m., very early in the morning. pasado m., the day after tomorrow

mañanica, f. early morning

mañear, v.t. to arrange cleverly; v.i. behave shrewdly

mañero, a. shrewd, clever; easily worked; handy

mañoso, a. clever, skilful; crafty; vicious, with bad habits

mañuela, f. low guile

mapa, m. map; card. m. en relieve, relief map. m. del estado mayor, ordnance map. (fam.) no estar en el m., to be off the map; be most unusual (of things)

mapache, m. (zool.) raccoon

mapamundi, m. map of the world

maqueta, f. (art, arch.) model

maquiavélico, a. Machiavellian

maquiavelismo, m. Machiavellism

maquillaje, m. make-up, cosmetics; making-up (of the face)

maquillar(se), v.t. and v.r. to make up (the face, etc.)

máquina, f. machine, mechanism; engine; apparatus; plan, scheme; machine, puppet; (fam.) mansion, palace; plenty; railway engine; fantasy, product of the imagination. m. a vapor, steam engine. m. de arrastre, traction-engine; tractor. m. de coser, sewing-machine. m. de escribir, typewriter. m. fotográfica, camera. m. de impresionar, movie camera. m. de imprimir, printing machine. m. herramienta, machine-tool. m. neumática, air pump

maquinación, f. intrigue, machination

maquinador (-ra), s. intriguer, schemer

maquinal, a. mechanical

maquinar, v.t. to intrigue, scheme, plot

maquinaria, f. machinery; applied mechanics; mechanism

maquinista, m. and f. driver, engine-man; mechanic; machinist; railway engine driver

mar, m. or f. sea; great many, abundance. m. bonanza or m. en calma, calm sea. m. de fondo or m. de leva, swell. alta m., high seas. a mares, plentifully. arar en el m., to labour in vain. (naut.) hacerse a la m., to put out to sea. la m. de historias, a great number of stories

marabú, m. marabou

maraña, f. undergrowth; tangle; (fig.) difficult position; intrigue; silk waste

marasmo, m. (med.) marasmus, atrophy; inactivity, paralysis

maravedí, m. old Spanish coin of fluctuating value

maravilla, f. marvel, wonder; admiration; amazement; (bot.) marigold. a m., wonderfully. a las mil maravillas, to perfection, excellently. por m., by chance; occasionally

maravillar, v.t. to amaze, cause admiration; v.r. (with de) marvel at, admire; be amazed by

maravilloso, a. marvellous, wonderful

marbete, m. label, tag; edge, border

marca, f. mark, sign; brand; frontier zone, border country; standard, norm (of size); make, brand; measuring rule; (sport) record. m. de fábrica, brand, trade-mark. m. de ley, hallmark. m. registrada, registered name. de m., excellent, of excellent quality

marcado, a. marked; pronounced; strong (of accents)

marcador, a. marking. m. marker; scoring board; bookmark

marcar, v.t. to mark; brand; embroider initials on linen; tell the time (watches); show the amount (cash register, etc.); dial (an automatic telephone); (sport) score (a goal); notice, observe; set aside, earmark; v.r. (naut.) check the course. m. el compás to beat time

marcasita, f. marcasite

marcial, a. martial; courageous, militant

marcialidad, f. warlike spirit, militancy

marciano, a. Martian

marco, m. mark (German coin); boundary mark; frame (of a picture, etc.). **m. de ventana,** window-frame

marcha, f. departure; running, working; (mil.) march; speed (of trains, ships, etc.); (mus.) march; progress, course (of events). **m. atrás,** backing, reversing. **m. de ensayo,** trial run. **m. forzada,** (mil.) forced march. **a largas marchas,** with all speed. **a toda m.,** at top speed; full speed ahead; by forced marches; (mil.) **batir la m.,** to strike up a march. **en m.,** under way; working; in operation

marchamero, m. customs official who checks goods and marks them

marchamo, m. customs mark on checked goods

marchar, v.i. to run; work; function; go; leave, depart; progress, proceed; (mil.) march; go (clocks); v.r. leave, go away

marchitable, a. perishable, fragile

marchitamiento, m. withering

marchitar, v.t. to wither, fade; blight, spoil; weaken; v.r. wither; be blighted

marchitez, f. witheredness; fadedness

marchito, a. withered; faded; blighted, frustrated

marea, f. tide; strand, water's edge; light breeze; drizzle; dew; street dirt. **m. creciente,** flood-tide. **m. menguante,** ebb-tide. **m. muerta,** neap-tide

mareaje, m. seamanship; ship's course

marear, v.t. to navigate; sell; sell publicly; (fam.) annoy; v.r. be seasick; feel faint; feel giddy; be damaged at sea (goods)

marejada, f. surge, swell; high sea; tidal wave; commotion, uproar

mareo, m. sea-sickness; nausea, dizziness; (fam.) irritation, tediousness

mareta, f. movement of the waves; sound, noise (of a crowd)

marfil, m. ivory

marfileño, a. ivory; ivory-like

marfuz, a. spurned, rejected; deceitful

marga, f. loam, marl

margarina, f. margarine

margarita, f. pearl; marguerite, ox-eye daisy; daisy; periwinkle

margen, m. or f. edge, fringe, border, verge; margin (of a book); opportunity; marginal note. **dar m. para,** to provide an opportunity for; give rise to

marginal, a. marginal

margoso, a. loamy, marly

mariano, a. (ecc.) Marian

marica, f. magpie. m. (fam.) pansy, homosexual; milksop

maricón, m. (fam.) pansy, homosexual

maridable, a. marital, matrimonial

maridaje, m. conjugal union and harmony; intimate relationship (between things)

maridar, v.i. to get married; mate, live as husband and wife; v.t. unite, link, join together

marido, m. husband

marimacho, m. (fam.) mannish woman

marina, f. coast, seashore; (art) seascape; seamanship; navy, fleet. **M. de guerra,** Navy. **M. mercante,** Merchant Navy

marinaje, m. seamanship; sailors

marinera, f. sailor blouse

marinería, f. profession of a sailor; seamanship; crew of a ship; sailors (as a class)

marinero, m. sailor, seaman. **m. de agua dulce,** freshwater sailor (a novice). **m. práctico,** able seaman. **a la marinera,** in a seamanlike fashion

marinesco, a. seamanly

marinismo, m. (ecc.) Marianism

marino, a. marine, sea; seafaring; shipping. m. sailor, mariner

marioneta, f. marionette, puppet

mariposa, f. butterfly; night-light

mariposear, v.i. to flutter, flit, fly about; flirt, be fickle; follow about, dance attendance on

mariquita, f. (ent.) lady-bird; parakeet. m. (fam.) homosexual, pansy

marisabidilla, f. (fam.) blue-stocking, know-all

mariscal, *m.* (*mil.*) marshal; field-marshal; farrier

mariscalía, *f.* marshalship

marisco, *m.* shellfish

marisma, *f.* bog, morass, swamp

marital, *a.* marital

marítimo, *a.* maritime, sea

maritornes, *f.* (*fam.*) plain, unattractive maid-of-all-work

marjal, *m.* marshland, fen

marlota, *f.* Moorish gown

marmita, *f.* stew-pot; copper, boiler

marmitón, *m.* kitchen-boy, scullion

mármol, *m.* marble; work executed in marble

marmolería, *f.* marble works; work executed in marble

marmolista, *m.* marble cutter; dealer in marble

marmóreo, *a.* marble; (*poet.*) marmoreal

marmosete, *m.* (*print.*) tail-piece

marmota, *f.* (*zool.*) marmot; sleepy-head, dormouse

maroma, *f.* rope, hawser

marqués, *m.* marquis

marquesa, *f.* marchioness

marquesado, *m.* marquisate

marquesina, *f.* marquee

marquetería, *f.* marqueterie

marrana, *f.* sow; (*fam.*) slattern, slut

marrano, *m.* pig, hog

marras, (de) *adv.* long ago, in the dim past

marrasquino, *m.* maraschino (liqueur)

marro, *m.* tick, tag (game)

marrón, *a.* maroon; brown. *m.* brown colour; maroon colour; quoit

marroquí, *a.* and *m.* and *f.* Moroccan. *m.* Morocco leather

marroquín (-ina), marrueco (-ca), *a.* and *s.* Moroccan

marrullería, *f.* flattery, cajolery

marrullero (-ra), *a.* wheedling, flattering. *s.* wheedler, cajoler

marsellés (-esa), *a.* and *s.* of or from Marseilles. *f.* **marsellesa,** Marseillaise (French anthem)

marsopa, *f.* (*icht.*) porpoise

marta, *f.* (*zool.*) sable; (*zool.*) marten

marte, *m.* (*ast.*) Mars

martes, *m.* Tuesday. **m. de carnaval,** mardi gras

martillar, *v.t.* to hammer; oppress

martillazo, *m.* hammer blow

martilleo, *m.* hammering; noise of the hammer; clink, clatter

martillo, *m.* hammer; oppressor, tyrant; auction rooms. **a m.,** by hammering. **de m.,** wrought (of metals)

martín pescador, *m.* kingfisher

martinete, *m.* hammer (of a pianoforte); pile-driver; drop-hammer. **m. de báscula,** tilt-hammer

mártir, *m.* and *f.* martyr

martirio, *m.* martyrdom

martirizar, *v.t.* to martyr; torture, torment, martyrize; tease, annoy

martirologio, *m.* martyrology

marxismo, *m.* Marxism

marxista, *a.* and *m.* and *f.* Marxist

marzo, *m.* March

mas, *conjunc.* but; yet

más, *adv. comp.* more; in addition, besides; rather, preferably. *m.* (*math.*) plus. **el (la, etc.) mas,** *adv. sup.* the most, etc. **m. bien,** more; rather; preferably. **m. que,** only; but; more than; although, even if. **a lo m.,** at the most; at the worst. **a m.,** besides, in addition. **de m.,** superfluous, unnecessary, unwanted. **no ... m. que,** only. **por m. que,** however; even if. **sin m. ni m.,** without more ado

masa, *f.* mass; dough; whole, aggregate; majority (of people); mortar. **en la m. de la sangre,** (*fig.*) in the blood, in a person's nature

masada, *f.* farmhouse and stock

masadero, *m.* farmer; farm labourer

masaje, *m.* massage

masajista, *m.* and *f.* masseur; masseuse

mascadura, *f.* chewing

mascar, *v.t.* to chew; masticate; (*fam.*) mumble, mutter

máscara, *f.* mask; fancy-dress; pretext, excuse. *m.* and *f.* masquerader, reveller; *pl.* masquerade. **m. para gases,** gas mask

mascarada, *f.* masquerade; company of revellers

mascarero (-ra), *s.* theatrical

costumier, fancy-dress dealer

mascarilla, f. death-mask

mascarón, m. large mask; (*arch.*) gargoyle. **m. de proa,** (*naut.*) figure-head

mascota, f. mascot

masculinidad, f. masculinity

masculino, a. masculine; male; manly, vigorous

mascullar, v.t. (*fam.*) to chew; mutter, mumble

masera, f. kneading-trough or bowl; cloth for covering the dough

masilla, f. mastic, putty

masón (-ona), s. freemason

masonería, f. freemasonry

masónico, a. masonic

masoquismo, m. masochism

mastelero, m. (*naut.*) topmast

masticación, f. mastication

masticar, v.t. to masticate, eat; (*fam.*) chew upon, consider

masticatorio, a. masticatory

mástil, m. (*naut.* and wireless) mast; upright, stanchion; pole (of a tent); stem, trunk; neck (of a guitar, etc.)

mastín, m. mastiff

mastodonte, m. (*zool.*) mastodon

mastoides, a. (*med.*) mastoid

mastuerzo, m. watercress; fool, blockhead

masturbación, f. masturbation

masturbarse, v.r. to masturbate

mata, f. (*bot.*) plant, shrub; stalk, sprig; grove, copse. **m. de pelo,** mat of hair

matacandelas, m. candle-snuffer

matachín, m. mummer; butcher; (*fam.*) swashbuckler

matadero, m. slaughter-house, abattoir

matadura, f. sore (on animals)

matafuego, m. fire extinguisher; fireman

matalotaje, m. ship's supplies, stores; (*fam.*) hodge-podge

matamoros, a. swashbuckling, swaggering

matamoscas, m. fly swatter

matanza, f. killing, massacre, slaughter; butchery (animals); (*fam.*) persistence, determination

matar, v.t. to kill; quench (thirst); put out (fire, light); slake (lime); tarnish (metal); bevel (corners, etc.); pester, importune; suppress; compel; (*art*) tone down; v.r. kill oneself; be disappointed, grieve; overwork. **estar a m.,** to be at daggers drawn. **matarse por,** to try hard to; work hard for

matasanos, m. (*fam.*) quack (doctor); bad doctor

matasellos, m. postmark

mate, a. matt, unpolished, dull. m. checkmate (chess); maté, Paraguayan tea; gourd; vessel made from gourd, coconut, etc. **maté,** m. maté, Paraguayan tea

matemáticas, f. pl. mathematics. **m. prácticas,** applied mathematics. **m. teóricas,** pure mathematics

matemático, a. mathematical; exact. m. mathematician

materia, f. matter; theme, subject-matter; subject (of study); matter, stuff, substance; pus, matter; question, subject; reason, occasion. **m. colorante,** dye-stuff. **materias plásticas,** plastics. **materias primas,** raw materials. **en m. de,** concerning; in the matter of

material, a. material; dull, stupid, limited. m. material; ingredient; plant, factory; equipment. **m. móvil ferroviario,** rolling-stock (railway)

materialidad, f. materiality; external appearance (of things)

materialismo, m. materialism

materialista, a. materialistic. m. and f. materialist

materializar, v.t. to materialize; v.r. materialize; grow materialistic, grow less spiritual

maternidad, f. maternity, motherhood

materno, a. maternal

matiz, m. combination of colours; tone, hue; shade (of meaning, etc.)

matizar, v.t. to combine, harmonize (colours); tint, shade; tinge (words, etc.)

matojo, m. shrub, bush

matorral, m. thicket, bush, undergrowth

matraca, f. rattle; (*fam.*) scolding, dressing-down; insistence, importunity

matraquear, v.i. to make a noise with a rattle; (*fam.*) scold

matraz, m. (*chem.*) matrass

matriarcado, *m.* matriarchy

matricida, *m.* and *f.* matricide (person)

matricidio, *m.* matricide (crime)

matrícula, *f.* list, register; matriculation; registration number (of a car, etc.). **m. de buques,** maritime register. **m. de mar,** mariner's register; **maritime register**

matriculación, *f.* matriculation; registration

matricular, *v.t.* to matriculate; enrol; (*naut.*) register; *v.r.* matriculate; enrol, register

matrimonial, *a.* matrimonial

matrimonio, *m.* marriage, matrimony; married couple. **m. a yuras,** secret marriage. **m. de la mano izquierda** *or* **m. morganático,** morganatic marriage. **contraer m.,** to get married

matritense, *a.* and *m.* and *f.* Madrilenian

matriz, *f.* uterus, womb; matrix, mould; (*min.*) matrix; nut, female screw

matrona, *f.* married woman; matron; midwife; female customs officer

matronal, *a.* matronal

matusalén, *m.* Methuselah, very old man

matute, *m.* smuggling; contraband; gaming-house

matutero (-ra), *s.* smuggler, contrabandist

matutino, *a.* matutinal

maula, *f.* trash; remnant; deception. fraud, trick. *m.* and *f.* (*fam.*) bad payer; lazybones. (*fam.*) **ser buena m.,** to be a trickster or a fraud

maulería, *f.* remnant stall; trickery

maullar, *v.i.* to miaow, mew (cats)

maullido, *m.* miaow, cry of the cat

mauritano (-na), *a.* and *s.* Mauritian

mausoleo, *m.* mausoleum, stately tomb

maxilar, *a.* maxillary. *m.* jaw

máxima, *f.* maxim, rule, precept, principle

máxime, *adv.* principally, chiefly

máximo, *a. sup.* **grande,** great-

est, maximum, top. *m.* maximum

maya, *f.* common daisy; May queen

mayal, *m.* flail

mayo, *m.* May (month); maypole; bouquet, wreath of flowers; *pl.* festivities on eve of May day

mayólica, *f.* majolica (china)

mayonesa, *f.* mayonnaise

mayor, *a. comp.* **grande,** bigger; greater; elder; main, principal; older; high (Mass, etc.); (*mus.*) major. *m.* and *f.* major (of full age). *a. sup.* **grande. el, la, lo mayor, los (las) mayores,** the biggest, greatest; eldest; chief, principal. **por m.,** in short, briefly; (*com.*) wholesale

mayor, *m.* head, director; chief clerk; (*mil.*) major; *pl.* ancestors

mayoral, *m.* head shepherd; coachman, driver; foreman, overseer, supervisor, steward

mayorazgo, *m.* (*law*) entail; entailed estate; heir (to an entail); eldest son; right of primogeniture

mayordoma, *f.* steward's wife; housekeeper; stewardess

mayordomía, *f.* stewardship; butlership

mayordomo, *m.* steward, superintendent; butler; major-domo, royal chief steward

mayoría, *f.* majority

mayormente, *adv.* chiefly; especially

mayúscula, *f.* capital letter

mayúsculo, *a.* large; capital (letters). **letra mayúscula,** capital letter

maza, *f.* mallet; club, bludgeon; mace; bass drum stick; pile driver; bone, stick, etc.; tied to dog's tail in carnival; (*fam.*) pedant, bore; important person, authority. **m. de polo,** polo mallet

mazacote, *m.* concrete; rough-hewn work of art; (*fam.*) stodgy over-cooked dish; bore, tedious person

mazamorra, *f.* dish made of maize flour; biscuit crumbs; broken fragments, remains

mazapán, *m.* marzipan

mazmorra, *f.* dungeon

mazo, *m.* mallet; bundle, bunch; importunate person; clapper of a bell

mazonería, *f.* stone-masonry

mazonero, *m.* stone-mason

mazorca, *f.* spindleful; spike, ear (of corn); cocoa berry; camarilla, group

mazurca, *f.* mazurka

me, *pers. pron., acc.* or *dat., 1st sing., m.* and *f.* me; to me

meandro, *m.* meandering, twisting, winding; wandering

meato, *m.* (*anat.*) meatus

mecánica, *f.* mechanics; mechanism, machinery; (*fam.*) worthless thing; mean action

mecánico, *a.* mechanical; power-operated; base, ill-bred. *m.* mechanician; engineer; mechanic

mecanismo, *m.* mechanism; works, machinery

mecanizar, *v.t.* to mechanize

mecanografía, *f.* typewriting

mecanografiar, *v.t.* to typewrite

mecanográfico, *a.* typewriting; typewritten

mecanografista, *m.* and *f.*, **mecanógrafo (-fa)**, *s.* typist

mecedor, *a.* rocking, swaying. *m.* swing

mecedora, *f.* rocking-chair

mecenas, *m.* Maecenas, patron

mecer, *v.t.* to stir, mix; shake; rock; swing

mecha, *f.* wick; bit, drill; fuse (of explosives); match (for guns); fat bacon (for basting); lock of hair; skein, twist

mechar, *v.t.* (*cul.*) to baste, lard

mechero, *m.* gas-burner; pocket lighter; socket of a candlestick

mechón, *m.* tuft, skein, bundle; lock of hair; wisp

medalla, *f.* medal; medallion; plaque, round panel; (*fam.*) piece of eight (coin)

medallón, *m.* large medal; medallion; locket

médano, *m.* sand dune

media, *f.* stocking

mediación, *f.* mediation, arbitration; intercession

mediado, *a.* half-full. **a mediados (del mes,** etc.**),** towards the middle (of the month, etc.)

mediador (-ra), *s.* mediator, arbitrator; intercessor

medianamente, *adv.* moderately; passably, fairly well

medianero (-ra), *a.* middle; intervening, intermediate; mediatory. *s.* mediator. *m.* owner of a semi-detached house or of one in a row

medianía, *f.* average; medium. mediocrity; moderate wealth or means

mediano, *a.* medium, average; moderate; (*fam.*) middling, passable, fair

medianoche, *f.* midnight

mediante, *a.* mediatory. *adv.* by means of, by, through

mediar, *v.i.* to reach the middle; get half-way; elapse half a given time; intercede, mediate; arbitrate; be in between or in the middle; intervene, take part

medicación, *f.* medication

medicamento, *m.* medicament, medicine, remedy

medicar, *v.t.* to medicate

medicastro, *m.* unskilled physician; quack, charlatan

medicina, *f.* medicine; medicament

medicinal, *a.* medicinal

medicinar, *v.t.* to attend; treat (patients)

medición, *f.* measuring; measurements; survey (land); (metrics) scansion

médico (-ca), *a.* medical. *s.* doctor of medicine. **m. de cabecera,** family doctor. **m. general,** general practitioner

medida, *f.* measurement; measuring stick; measure, precaution (gen. with *tomar, adoptar,* etc.); gauge; judgment; wisdom; (metrics) metre; standard. **a m. que,** while, at the same time as. **tomar las medidas, (a)** (*fig.*) to take a person's measure, sum him up. **tomar sus medidas,** to take his (their) measurements; take the necessary measures. **un traje hecho a m.,** a suit made to measure

medidor, *m.* measurer; meter

medieval, *a.* medieval

medio, *a.* half; middle; intermediate; half-way. *m.* half; middle; (*art*) medium; spiritualist medium; proceeding, measure,

precaution; environment, medium; middle way, mean; (*sport*)
half-back. **m.** galope, canter.
m. tiempo, (*sport*) half-time.
a medias, by halves; half,
partially. de por m., by halves;
in between; in the way. estar
de por m., to be in the way;
take part in. (*fam.*) quitar de
en m., to get rid of. (*fam.*)
quitarse de en m., to go away,
remove oneself

mediocre, *a.* mediocre

mediocridad, *f.* mediocrity; insignificance

mediodía, *m.* noon, meridian;
south

medioeval, *a.* mediæval

mediquillo, *m.* (*fam.*) quack; (in
the Philippines) medicine man

medir, *v.t.* *irr.* to measure;
(metrics) scan; survey (land);
compare; *v.r.* measure one's
words; act with restraint. See
pedir

meditabundo, *a.* pensive, meditative, thoughtful

meditación, *f.* meditation; consideration, reflection

meditador, *a.* meditative,
thoughtful

meditar, *v.t.* to meditate, consider, muse

meditativo, *a.* meditative

mediterráneo, *a.* mediterranean;
inland

médium, *m.* (*spirit.*) medium

medo (-da), *s.* Mede

medra, *f.* progress; improvement,
betterment; growth; prosperity

medrar, *v.i.* to flourish, grow;
become prosperous or improve
one's position

medro, *m.* improvement, progress. See medra

medroso, *a.* timid, frightened;
frightful, horrible

médula, *f.* (*anat.*) marrow; (*bot.*)
pith; (*fig.*) essence, core

medusa, *f.* jelly-fish

mefistofélico, *a.* Mephistophelian

mefítico, *a.* noxious, mephitic;
poisonous

megáfono, *m.* megaphone

megalítico, *a.* megalithic

megalito, *m.* megalith

megalómano (-na), *s.* megalomaniac

mejicano (-na), *a.* and *s.* Mexican

mejilla, *f.* (*anat.*) cheek

mejillón, *m.* sea mussel

mejor, *a.* *comp.* bueno, better.
adv. better; rather; sooner; preferably. *a.* *sup.* bueno. el, la,
lo mejor; los, las mejores, the
best; most preferable. **m.** que
m., better and better. (*fam.*) a
lo m., probably, in all probability. tanto m., so much the
better

mejora, *f.* improvement; bettering; progress; higher bid (at
auctions)

mejorable, *a.* improvable

mejoramiento, *m.* betterment,
improvement

mejorana, *f.* (*bot.*) marjoram

mejorar, *v.t.* to improve; better;
outbid; *v.i.* grow better (in
health); improve (weather);
make progress; rally (of markets).
Mejorando lo presente, Present
company excepted

mejoría, *f.* improvement, progress; betterment; superiority;
advantage, profit

mejunje, *m.* (*fam.*) brew, potion,
cure-all, stuff

melado, *a.* honey-coloured. *m.*
cane-syrup

melancolía, *f.* melancholia; sadness, depression, melancholy

melancólico, *a.* melancholy, sad;
depressing

melaza, *f.* molasses

melena, *f.* long side-whiskers;
loose flowing hair (in women);
over-long hair (in men); lion's
mane. (*fam.*) andar a la m., to
start a fight or quarrel. (*fam.*)
traer a la m., to drag by the
hair, force

melifluidad, *f.* mellifluence,
sweetness

melifluo, *a.* mellifluous, sweet-
voiced; honeyed

melindre, *m.* honey fritter; affectation, scruple, fastidiousness;
narrow ribbon

melindroso, *a.* over-fastidious,
affected, prudish

melocotón, *m.* peach; peach tree

melocotonero, *m.* peach tree

melodía, *f.* melody, tune; melodiousness

melódico, *a.* melodic, melodious

melodioso, *a.* melodious, tuneful, sweet-sounding

melodrama, *m.* melodrama

melodramático, *a.* melodramatic

melón, *m.* melon

melosidad, *f.* sweetness

meloso, *a.* honeyed; sweet; gentle; mellifluous

mella, *f.* nick, notch; dent; gap; harm, damage (to reputation, etc.). hacer m., (*fig.*) to make an impression (on the mind); (*mil.*) breach, drive a wedge

mellar, *v.t.* to nick, notch; dent; damage

mellizo (-za), *a.* and *s.* twin

membrana, *f.* membrane

membrete, *m.* note, memorandum; note or card of invitation; superscription, heading; address (of person)

membrillo, *m.* quince tree; quince; quince jelly

membrudo, *a.* brawny, strong, muscular

memo, *a.* silly, stupid

memorable, *a.* memorable

memorándum, *m.* note-book, jotter; memorandum (diplomatic)

memorar(se), *v.t.* and *v.r.* to remember, recall

memoria, *f.* memory; remembrance, recollection; monument; memorial; report; essay, article; codicil; memorandum; record, chronicle; *pl.* regards, compliments, greetings; memoirs; memoranda. (*fam.*) m. de grillo, poor memory. de m., by heart. flaco de m., forgetful. hacer m., to remember

memorial, *m.* note-book; memorial, petition

memorialista, *m.* secretary, amanuensis

memorioso, *a.* mindful, unforgetful

mena, *f.* (*min.*) ore

ménade, *f.* mænad, bacchante

menaje, *m.* household or school equipment or furniture

mención, *f.* mention. m. honorífica, honorary mention. hacer m. de, to mention

mencionar, *v.t.* to mention

mendacidad, *f.* mendacity, untruthfulness

mendaz, *a.* mendacious, untruthful

mendelismo, *m.* Mendelism

mendicante, *a.* begging; (*ecc.*) mendicant. *m.* and *f.* beggar

mendicidad, *f.* mendicancy, begging

mendigar, *v.t.* to beg for alms; entreat, supplicate

mendigo (-ga), *s.* beggar

mendoso, *a.* mendacious, untruthful; mistaken

mendrugo, *m.* crust of bread

menear, *v.t.* to sway, move; wag; shake; manage, control, direct; *v.r.* (*fam.*) get a move on; sway, move; wriggle .

meneo, *m.* swaying movement; wagging; shaking; wriggling; management, direction; (*aer.*) bump; (*fam.*) spanking

menester, *m.* lack, shortage; necessity; occupation, employment; *pl.* physical necessities; (*fam.*) tools, implements, equipment. haber m., to need, require. ser m., to be necessary or requisite

menesteroso, *a.* indigent, poverty-stricken, needy

menestra, *f.* vegetable soup; dried vegetable (gen. *pl.*)

menestral (-la), *s.* artisan; worker; mechanic

mengano (-na), *s.* so-and-so (used instead of name of person)

mengua, *f.* decrease; lack, shortage; waning (of the moon, etc.); dishonour, disgrace; poverty

menguado (-da), *a.* timid, cowardly; silly, stupid; mean, avaricious. *s.* coward; fool; skinflint. *m.* narrowing stitch when knitting socks

menguante, *a.* ebb; waning; decreasing. *f.* ebb tide; decadence, decline. m. de la luna, waning of the moon

menguar, *v.i.* to decrease; decline, decay; wane; ebb; narrow (socks); *v.t.* diminish; disgrace, discredit

menina, *f.* child attendant on Spanish royalty

meníngeo, *a.* (*med.*) meningeal

menino, *m.* Spanish royal page; little dandy

menjurje, *m.* See mejunje

menopausia, *f.* menopause

menor, *a.* comp. pequeño, less, smaller; younger; minor; (*mus.*) minor. *m.* minor. *f.* (logic) minor. *a. sup.* pequeño. el, la, lo m.; los, las menores, the least; smallest; youngest. m. de edad, minor (in age). por m., at retail; in detail

menoría, *f.* subordination, dependence; inferiority; minority (under age); childhood, youth

menos, *adv.* less; minus; least;. except. m. de *or* m..que, less than. al m., por lo m.; at least. a m. que, unless. De m. nos hizo Dios, Never say die, Nothing is impossible. poco más ó m., more or less, about

menoscabar, *v.t.* to lessen, diminish, decrease; deteriorate, damage; disgrace, discredit

menoscabo, *m.* decrease, diminishment; harm, damage, loss

menospreciable, *a.* despicable, contemptible

menospreciador (-ra), *a.* scornful. *s.* scorner, despiser

menospreciar, *v.t.* to despise, scorn; under-estimate, have a poor opinion of

menospreciativo, *a.* scornful, slighting, derisive

menosprecio, *m.* scorn, derision; under-estimation

mensaje, *m.* message; official communication

mensajería, *f.* carrier service; steamship line

mensajero (-ra), *s.* messenger; errand-boy

menstruación, *f.* menstruation

menstruar, *v.i.* to menstruate

mensual, *a.* monthly

mensualidad, *f.* monthly salary or payment

ménsula, *f.* (*arch.*) corbel

mensurable, *a.* measurable

mensurar, *v.t.* to measure

menta, *f.* menthe, mint; peppermint

mentado, *a.* celebrated, distinguished, famous

mental, *a.* mental

mentalidad, *f.* mentality

mentalmente, *adv.* mentally

mentar, *v.t. irr.* to mention. See sentar

mente, *f.* mind; intelligence, understanding; will, intention

mentecatería, *f.* folly, stupidity

mentecato (-ta), *a.* foolish, silly;

feeble-minded, simple. *s.* fool, idiot

mentir, *v.i. irr.* to lie, be untruthful; deceive, mislead; falsify; (*poet.*) belie; disagree, be incompatible; *v.t.* break a promise, disappoint. See sentir

mentira, *f.* lie, falsehood; error (in writing); (*fam.*) white spot on finger-nail; cracking of finger-joints. m. oficiosa, white lie. Parece m., It seems incredible

mentiroso, *a.* lying, false; full of errors (literary works); deceptive

mentís, *m.* giving the lie (literally, you lie); proof, demonstration (of error)

mentol, *m.* menthol

mentón, *m.* chin

mentonera, *f.* (*mus.*) chin rest

menú, *m.* menu

menudamente, *adv.* minutely; in detail, circumstantially

menudear, *v.t.* to do frequently; do repeatedly; *v.i.* happen frequently; describe in detail; (*com.*) sell by retail

menudencia, *f.* minuteness, smallness; exactness, care, accuracy; trifle, worthless object; small matter; *pl.* offal; pork sausages

menudeo, *m.* repetition; description in detail; (*com.*) retail. al m., at retail

menudillos, *m. pl.* giblets; offal

menudo, *a.* minute, tiny; despicable; thin; small; vulgar; meticulous, exact; small (money). m. small coal; m. *pl.* offal, entrails; small change (money). a m., often, frequently. por m., in detail, carefully; (*com.*) in small lots

meñique, *a.* (*fam.*) very small. m. little finger (in full, dedo m.)

meollo, *m.* brain; (*anat.*) marrow; (*fig.*) essence, core, substance; understanding; (*fam.*) no tener m. (una cosa), to be worthless, unsubstantial (things)

mequetrefe, *m.* (*fam.*) coxcomb, whipper-snapper

meramente, *adv.* solely, simply, merely

mercachifle, *m.* pedlar; small merchant

mercadear, *v.i.* to trade, traffic

mercader, *m.* dealer, merchant,

trader. **m. de grueso,** wholesaler

mercadería, *f.* See **mercancía**

mercado, *m.* market; market place

mercancía, *f.* goods, merchandise; commerce, trade, traffic

mercante, *a.* trading; commercial. *m.* merchant, dealer, trader

mercantil, *a.* mercantile, commercial

mercantilismo, *m.* mercantilism

merced, *f.* salary, remuneration; favour, benefit, kindness; will, desire, pleasure; mercy, grace; courtesy title given to untitled person (e.g. **vuestra m.,** your honour. Has now become **usted** and is universally used). **m. a,** thanks to. **estar uno a m. de,** to live at someone else's expense, be dependent on

mercenario (-ia), *s.* (*ecc.*) member of Order of la Merced. *m.* (*mil.*) mercenary; day labourer. *a.* mercenary

mercería, *f.* haberdashery, mercery

mercerizar, *v.t.* to mercerize

mercero, *m.* haberdasher, mercer

mercurial, *a.* mercurial

mercurio, *m.* mercury, quicksilver; (*ast.*) Mercury

merecedor, *a.* deserving, worthy

merecer, *v.t. irr.* to deserve, be worthy of; attain, achieve; be worth; *v.i.* deserve, be deserving. **·m. bien de,** to deserve well of; have a claim on the gratitude of. See **conocer**

merecido, *m.* due reward

merecimiento, *m.* desert; merit

merendar, *v.i. irr.* to have tea; lunch; pry into another's affairs; *v.t.* have (a certain food) for tea or lunch. (*fam.*) **merendarse (una cosa),** to obtain (a thing), have it in one's pocket. See **recomendar**

merendero, *m.* tea-room, place for taking tea; lunch room

merengue, *m.* (*cul.*) meringue

meretriz, *f.* prostitute

meridiana, *f.* day-bed, chaise longue; siesta

meridiano, *a.* meridian. *m.* meridian. **a la meridiana,** at noon

meridional, *a.* meridional, southern

merienda, *f.* tea, snack; lunch; (*fam.*) hunchback. **m. de negros,** (*fam.*) bear-garden, confusion. (*fam.*) **juntar meriendas,** to join forces, combine interests

merino, *a.* merino. *m.·* merino fabric; shepherd of merino sheep

meritísimo, *a. sup.* most worthy, most deserving

mérito, *m.* merit; desert; worth, excellence. **de m.,** excellent, notable. **hacer m. de,** to mention

meritorio, *a.* meritorious. *m.* unpaid worker, learner

merlango, *m.* (*icht.*) whiting

merlón, *m.* merlon

merluza, *f.* (*icht.*) hake; (*fam.*) drinking bout. (*fam.*) **pescar una m.,** to get drunk

merma, *f.* decrease, drop; loss, waste, reduction; leakage

mermar, *v.i.* to diminish, waste away, decrease; evaporate; leak; *v.t.* filch, pilfer; reduce, decrease

mermelada, *f.* conserve, preserve; jam; marmalade

mero, *a.* mere; simple; plain

merodeador, *a.* marauding. *m.* marauder, raider

merodear, *v.i.* to maraud, raid

merodeo, *m.* raiding, marauding

merovingio (-ia), *a.* and *s.* Merovingian

mes, *m.* month; menses, menstruation

mesa, *f.* table; board, directorate; meseta, tableland; staircase landing; flat (of a sword, etc.); game of billiards. **m. de batalla,** post-office sorting-table. **m. de caballete,** trestle-table. **m. de noche,** bedside-table. **m. de tijeras,** folding-table. **m. giratoria,** turn-table. **alzar** (*or* **levantar**) **la m.,** to clear the table. **cubrir** (*or* **poner**) **la m.,** to set the table

mesada, *f.* monthly wages or other payment

mesadura, *f.* tearing of the hair or beard

mesana, *f.* (*naut.*) mizzen mast; mizzen sail

mesarse, *v.r.* to tear one's hair or beard

mesenterio, *m.* (*anat.*) mesentery

meseta, *f.* staircase landing; plateau, tableland

mesiánico, *a.* Messianic

Mesías, *m.* Messiah

mesilla, *f.* small table; laughing admonition; landing (of a stair).

mesmerismo, *m.* mesmerism

mesnada, *f.* association, company, society; body of armed men (*ant.*)

mesocarpio, *m.* (*bot.*) mesocarp

mesocracia, *f.* mesocracy; middle class, bourgeoisie

mesón, *m.* inn, tavern

mesonero (-ra), *s.* innkeeper

mesonil, *a.* pertaining to an inn or innkeeper, inn

mesta, *f.* ancient order of sheep farmers; *pl.* confluence, meeting (of rivers)

mester, *m.* craft, occupation. m. de clerecía, learned poetic metre of Spanish Middle Ages. m. de juglaría, popular poetry and troubadour songs

mestizo, *a.* half-breed; hybrid; cross-breed

mesura, *f.* sedateness; dignity; courtesy; moderation

mesurado, *a.* sedate; dignified; moderate, restrained, temperate

meta, *f.* winning post; (*fig.*) aim, end; goal; goalkeeper; (cricket) wicket; (cricket) bye

metabolismo, *m.* metabolism

metacarpo, *m.* metacarpus

metafísica, *f.* metaphysics

metafísico, *a.* metaphysical. *m.* metaphysician

metáfora, *f.* metaphor

metafórico, *a.* metaphorical

metal, *m.* metal; brass; timbre of the voice; state, condition; quality, substance; (*her.*) gold or silver; (*mus.*) brass (instruments)

metalario, *m.* metal worker

metálico, *a.* metallic. *m.* metal worker; coin, specie; bullion

metalífero, *a.* metalliferous

metalistería, *f.* metal work

metalizar, *v.t.* to metallize, make metallic; *v.r.* become metallized; grow greedy of money

metaloide, *m.* (*chem.*) metalloid

metalurgia, *f.* metallurgy

metalúrgico, *a.* metallurgical. *m.* metallurgist

metamorfosis, *f.* metamorphosis

metano, *m.* (*chem.*) methane

metatarso, *m.* (*anat.*) metatarsus

metátesis, *f.* metathesis

metedor (-ra), *s.* placer, inserter; smuggler, contrabandist

metempsicosis, *f.* metempsychosis

metemuertos, *med.* scene-shifter; meddler, nosey Parker

meteórico, *a.* meteoric

meteorito, *m.* meteorite

meteoro, *m.* meteor

meteorología, *f.* meteorology

meteorológico, *a.* meteorological

meteorologista, *m.* and *f.* meteorologist; weather-prophet

meter, *v.t.* to place; put; introduce, insert; stake (gambling); smuggle; cause, occasion; place close together; persuade to take part in; (*sew.*) take in fullness; deceive, humbug; cram in, pack tightly; (*naut.*) take in sail; *v.r.* interfere, butt in; meddle (with); take up, follow (occupations); be over-familiar; disembogue, empty itself (rivers, etc.); attack with the sword; (*with prep. a*) follow (occupations); become, turn (e.g. meterse a predicar, to turn preacher); (*with con*) pick a quarrel with. (*fam.*) meterse en todo, to be very meddlesome

metesillas y sacamuertos, *m.* scene-shifter, stage-hand

meticulosidad, *f.* meticulosity; timorousness

meticuloso, *a.* meticulous, fussy; timid, nervous

metido, *a.* tight; crowded; crabbed (of handwriting). *m.* material for letting out (in seams)

metílico, *a.* (*chem.*) methylic

metimiento, *m.* insertion, introduction; influence, sway

metódico, *a.* methodical

metodismo, *m.* Methodism

metodista, *a.* methodistic. *m.* and *f.* Methodist

método, *m.* method

metodología, *f.* methodology

metralla, *f.* (*mil.*) grapeshot, shrapnel

métrica, *f.* metrics

métrico, *a.* metric; metrical

metro, *m.* (verse) metre; metre (measurement); tube, underground railway

metrología, *f.* metrology, science of weights and measures

metrónomo, *m.* metronome

metrópoli, f. metropolis, capital; see of a metropolitan bishop; mother country

metropolitano, a. metropolitan. m. metropolitan bishop

mezcla, f. mixture; blend, combination; mixed cloth, tweed; mortar

mezclar, v.t. to mix, blend, combine; v.r. mix, mingle; take part; interfere, meddle; intermarry

mezcolanza, f. (fam.) hotchpotch

mezquindad, f. poverty; indigence; miserliness; paltriness; meanness, poorness

mezquino, a. needy, impoverished; miserly, stingy; small, diminutive; unhappy; mean, paltry

mezquita, f. mosque

mi, poss. pron. my. m. (mus.) mi, E

mí, pers. pron. acc., gen., dat., 1st pers. sing. me. Used only after prepositions (e.g. **Lo hicieron para mí,** They did it for me)

miaja, f. See **migaja**

miasma, m. miasma

miasmático, a. miasmatic, malarious

miau, m. miaow

mica, f. (min.) mica; coquette, flirt

Micado, m. Mikado

micción, f. micturition

micología, f. mycology

micra, f. micron, thousandth part of millimetre

microbiano, a. microbial, microbic

microbio, m. microbe

microbiología, f. micro-biology

microcéfalo, a. (med.) microcephalous

microcosmo, m. microcosm

micrófono, m. microphone

microscópico, a. microscopic

microscopio, m. microscope

micho (-cha), s. (fam.) puss, pussycat

miedo, m. fear, apprehension, terror. **m. al público,** stagefright. **tener m.,** to be afraid

miedoso, a. (fam.) fearful, nervous

miel, f. honey. **m. de caña,** sugar-cane syrup. (fam.) **quedarse a media m.,** to see one's pleasure snatched away. (fam.)

ser de mieles, to be most pleasant or agreeable

mielitis, f. myelitis

miembro, m. (anat.) limb; penis; member, associate; part, portion, section; (math.) member

miente, f. thought, imagination, mind. **parar** or **poner mientes en,** to consider, think about. **venírsele a las mientes,** to occur to one's mind

mientras, adv. while. **m. más ...,** the more ... **m. que,** while (e.g. **M. que esperaba en el jardín,** while he was waiting in the garden). **m. tanto,** in the meanwhile

miércoles, m. Wednesday. **m. de ceniza,** Ash Wednesday

mierda, f. excrement; (fam.) filth

mies, f. cereal plant, grain; harvest time; pl. grain lands

miga, f. breadcrumb; crumb; (fam.) essence, core; substance; bit, scrap; pl. fried breadcrumbs. (fam.) **hacer buenas** (or **malas**) **migas,** to get on well (or badly) together

migaja, f. breadcrumb; bit, scrap; trifle, mere nothing; pl. crumbs (from the table); remains, remnants

migajón, m. crumb (of a loaf); (fig., fam.) essence, substance, core

migración, f. migration; emigration

migraña, f. migraine

migratorio, a. migratory

mijo, m. (bot.) millet; maize

mil, a. thousand; thousandth; many, large number. m. thousand; thousandth. (fam.) **Son las m. y quinientas,** It's extremely late (of the hour)

miladi, f. my lady

milagrero, a. miracle-mongering; (fam.) miraculous

milagro, m. miracle; marvel, wonder. **¡M.!** Amazing! Just fancy!

milagroso, a. miraculous; marvellous, wonderful

milanés (-esa), a. and s. Milanese

milano, m. (orn.) kite

mildeu, m. mildew

milenario, a. millenary; millennial. m. millenary; millennium

milenrama, f. (bot.) yarrow

milésimo, *a.* thousandth

milicia, *f.* **militia;** military; art of war; military profession

miliciano, *a.* military. *m.* militiaman

miligramo, *m.* milligramme

mililitro, *m.* millilitre

milímetro, *m.* millimetre

militante, *a.* militant

militar, *a.* military. *m.* soldier. *v.i.* to fight in the army; struggle (for a cause); (*fig.*) be in favour of or against (e.g. **Las circunstancias militan en favor de** (*or* **contra**) **sus ideas,** Circumstances favour (*or* are against) his ideas)

militarismo, *m.* militarism

militarista, *a.* militaristic. *m.* and *f.* militarist

militarizar, *v.t.* to militarize; make warlike

milmillonésimo, *a.* billionth

milord, *m.* my lord. *pl.* **milores,** my lords

milla, *f.* mile

millar, *m.* thousand; vast number (gen. *pl.*)

millón, *m.* million

millonario (-ia), *a.* and *s.* millionaire

millonésimo, *a.* millionth

mimar, *v.t.* to spoil, over-indulge; caress, fondle

mimbre, *m.* or *f.* (*bot.*) osier; willow tree. *m.* wicker

mimbrear, *v.i.* to sway, bend

mimbrera, *f.* (*bot.*) osier; osier bed; willow

mimetismo, *m.* mimesis (animals, plants, etc.)

mímica, *f.* mimicry; mime

mímico, *a.* mimic

mimo, *m.* mimic, buffoon; mime; caress, expression of affection, tenderness; over-indulgence

mimosa, *f.* (*bot.*) mimosa

mimoso, *a.* affectionate, demonstrative

mina, *f.* mine; excavation, mining; underground passage; lead (in a pencil); (*mil., nav.*) mine; (*fig.*) gold-mine. (*mil.*) **m. terrestre,** land-mine

minador, *m.* excavator; (*nav.*) minelayer; (*mil.*) sapper

minar, *v.t.* to excavate, mine; (*fig.*) undermine; (*mil., nav.*) mine; work hard for

minarete, *m.* minaret

mineraje, *m.* exploitation of a mine, mining; mineral products

mineral, *a.* and *m.* mineral

mineralogía, *f.* mineralogy

mineralógico, *a.* mineralogical

mineralogista, *m.* mineralogist

minería, *f.* mining, mine working; mine workers

minero, *a.* mining. *m.* miner, mine worker; source, origin

miniar, *v.t.* (*art*) to illuminate

miniatura, *f.* miniature

miniaturista, *m.* and *f.* miniaturist

mínima, *f.* (*mus.*) minim; very small thing or portion

mínimo, *a. sup.* **pequeño,** smallest; minimum; meticulous, precise. *m.* minimum; (meteorological) trough

ministerial, *a.* ministerial

ministerio, *m.* office, post; (*pol.*) cabinet; ministry; government office; government department. **M. de Abastecimientos y Transportes,** Ministry of Food and Transport. **M. de Estado,** Department of State; State Department. **M. de Fomento,** (*ant.*) Ministry of Public Works, Education, Commerce, Agriculture. **M. de Gobernación,** Home Office; Ministry of the Interior. **M. de Gracia y Justicia,** (*ant.*) Department of Justice and Ecclesiastical Affairs. **M. de la Guerra,** War Office; War Department. **M. de Hacienda,** Exchequer; Treasury Department. **M. de la Marina,** Admiralty; Navy Department. **M. del Trabajo,** Ministry of Labour. **M. de Relaciones Extranjeras,** Foreign Office

ministrar, *v.t.* and *v.i.* to fill, administer (an office); *v.t.* minister to; give, provide

ministro, *m.* instrument, agency; minister of state, cabinet minister; clergyman, minister; minister plenipotentiary; policeman. **M. de Estado,** Secretary of State. **M. de Gobernación,** Home Secretary. **M. de Hacienda,** Chancellor of the Exchequer. **M. de Relaciones Extranjeras,** Foreign Secretary

minoración, *f.* reduction, decrease

minorar, *v.t.* to diminish, decrease

minoría, *f.* minority, smaller number; minority (of age)

minoridad, *f.* minority (of age)

minucia, *f.* smallness; morsel, mite; *pl.* details, trifles, minutiæ

minuciosidad, *f.* meticulousness, minuteness, precision

minucioso, *a.* meticulous, precise, minute

minué, *m.* minuet (dance)

minúsculo, *a.* minute, very small

minuta, *f.* memorandum, minute; note; list, catalogue

minutario, *m.* minute-book

minutero, *m.* minute hand (of a clock)

minuto, *a.* minute, very small. *m.* minute

mío, *m.,* **mía,** *f.* (*m. pl.* **míos,** *f. pl.* **mías**) *poss. pron.* mine (e.g. **Las flores son mías,** The flowers are mine). **Mi** is used before nouns, *not* **mío.** Also used with article (e.g. **Este sombrero no es el mío,** This hat is not mine (my one)). **de mío,** by myself, without help. (*fam.*) **¡Esta es la mía!** This is my chance!

miope, *a.* myopic. *m.* and *f.* myope

miopía, *f.* short-sightedness

miosota, *f.* myosotis, forget-me-not

mira, *f.* sight (optical instruments, guns); intention, design; (*mil.*) watchtower; care, precaution. **andar, estar** *or* **quedar a la m.,** to be vigilant, be on the look-out

mirada, *f.* look; gaze. **lanzar miradas de carnero degollado (a),** to cast sheep's eyes at

miradero, *m.* object of attention, cynosure; observation post, lookout

mirador (-ra), *s.* spectator. *m.* (*arch.*) oriel; enclosed balcony; observatory

miraguano, *m.* kapok

miramiento, *m.* observation, gazing; scruple, consideration; precaution, care; thoughtfulness

mirar, *v.t.* to look at, gaze at; observe, behold; watch; consider, look after; value, appreciate; concern; believe, think; (*with prep. a*) overlook, look on to; face; (*with por*) care for, protect; look after, consider. **m. contra el gobierno,** (*fam.*) to be squint-eyed. **m. de hito en hito,** to look over, stare at. **mirarse en (una cosa),** to consider (a matter) carefully

miríada, *f.* myriad, huge number

mirilla, *f.* peep-hole

miriñaque, *m.* trinket, ornament; crinoline

mirlarse, *v.r.* (*fam.*) to give oneself airs

mirlo, *m.* blackbird; (*fam.*) pompous air

mirón, *a.* inquisitive, curious

mirra, *f.* myrrh

mirto, *m.* (*bot.*) myrtle

misa, *f.* (*ecc., mus.*) mass. **m. de difuntos,** Requiem Mass. **m. del gallo,** Midnight Mass. **m. mayor,** High Mass. **m. rezada,** Low Mass. **como en m.,** in profound silence. **oír m.,** to attend Mass

misal, *m.* (*ecc.*) missal

misantropía, *f.* misanthropy

misantrópico, *a.* misanthropic

misántropo, *m.* misanthrope

miscelánea, *f.* medley, assortment, miscellany

misceláneo, *a.* assorted, miscellaneous, mixed

miscible, *a.* mixable

miserable, *a.* miserable, unhappy; timid, pusillanimous; miserly, mean; despicable

miseria, *f.* misery; poverty, destitution; avarice, miserliness; (*fam.*) poor thing, trifle

misericordia, *f.* mercy, compassion

misericordioso, *a.* merciful, compassionate

misero, *a.* (*fam.*) fond of church-going

misérrimo, *a. sup.* most miserable

misión, *f.* mission; vocation; commission, duty, errand

misionar, *v.i.* to missionize, act as a missionary; (*ecc.*) conduct a mission

misionero, *m.* missioner; missionary

misiva, *f.* missive

mismo, *a.* same; similar; self (e.g. **ellos mismos,** they themselves); very, same (e.g. **Ahora m. voy,** I'm going this very minute). **Me da lo m.,** It makes no difference to me. **por lo m.,** for that self-same reason

misógamo (-ma), *s.* misogamist

misógino, *m.* misogynist

misterio, *m.* mystery

misterioso, *a.* mysterious

mística, *f.*, **misticismo,** *m.* mysticism

místico, *a.* mystic

mistificación, *f.* mystification; mystery; deception

mistificar, *v.t.* to mystify; deceive

mitad, *f.* half; middle, centre. (*fig., fam.*) **cara m.,** better half. (*fam.*) **mentir por la m. de la barba,** to lie barefacedly

mítico, *a.* mythical

mitigación, *f.* mitigation

mitigador (-ra), *a.* mitigatory. *s.* mitigator

mitigar, *v.t.* to mitigate, moderate, alleviate; appease

mitigativo, *a.* mitigatory

mitin, *m.* meeting

mito, *m.* myth

mitología, *f.* mythology

mitológico, *a.* mythological

mitologista, mitólogo, *m.* mythologist

mitón, *m.* mitten

mitra, *f.* mitre; bishopric; archbishopric

mitrado, *a.* mitred

mixedema, *m.* (*med.*) myxœdema

mixto, *a.* mixed, blended; hybrid; composite; mongrel. *m.* mixed train (carrying freight and passengers); sulphur match

mixtura, *f.* mixture, blend; compound; mixture (medicine)

¡miz, miz! puss, puss!

mnemotecnia, *f.* mnemonics

moabita, *m.* and *f.* Moabite

mobiliario, *a.* movable (goods). *m.* furniture

moblaje, *m.* household goods and furniture

mocasín, *m.* moccasin

mocedad, *f.* youth, adolescence; mischief, prank. (*fig., fam.*) **correr sus mocedades,** to sow one's wild oats

moción, *f.* motion, movement;

impulse, tendency; divine inspiration; motion (of a debate)

moco, *m.* mucus from the nose; candle droppings; snuff of a candle. **m. de pavo,** turkey's snood. (*fam.*) **caérsele el m.,** to be very simple, be easily deceived

mocoso (-sa), *a.* running at the nose, snuffly; unimportant, insignificant. *s.* coxcomb, stripling

mochila, *f.* knapsack; nosebag; military rations for a march

mocho, *a.* blunted, topless, lopped; (*fam.*) shorn, cropped. *m.* butt, butt-end

mochuelo, *m.* owl; (*fam.*) difficult job

moda, *f.* fashion. **estar** *or* **ser de m.,** to be fashionable, be in fashion. **la última m.,** the latest fashion

modal, *a.* modal

modales, *m. pl.* manners, behaviour

modalidad, *f.* form, nature; (*mus.*) modality

modelado, *m.* (*art*) modelling

modelar, *v.t.* (*art*) to model; *v.r.* model oneself (on), copy

modelo, *m.* example, pattern; model. *m.* and *f.* (*art*) life model

moderación, *f.* moderation; restraint, temperance, equability

moderado, *a.* moderate; restrained, temperate

moderador (-ra), *a.* moderating. *s.* moderator

moderantismo, *m.* moderate opinion; moderate political party

moderar, *v.t.* to moderate; temper, restrain; *v.r.* regain one's self-control; behave with moderation

modernidad, *f.* modernity

modernismo, *m.* modernism

modernista, *a.* modernistic; modern. *m.* and *f.* modernist

modernización, *f.* modernization

modernizar, *v.t.* to modernize

moderno, *a.* modern. *m.* modern, man of our time. **a la moderna,** in the modern fashion

modestia, *f.* modesty

modesto, *a.* modest

módico, *a.* moderate (of prices, etc.)

modificable, *a.* modifiable

modificación, *f.* modification

modificador, modificante, *a.* modifying, moderating

modificar, *v.t.* to modify; moderate

modillón, *m.* (*arch.*) modillion

modismo, *m.* idiom

modista, *m.* and *f.* dressmaker; couturier; milliner

modo, *m.* mode, method, style; manner, way; moderation, restraint; civility, politeness (often *pl.*); (*mus.*) mode; (*gram.*) mood. **m. de ser,** nature, temperament. **de m. que,** so that. **de ningún m.,** not at all, by no means. **de todos modos,** in any case

modorra, *f.* deep sleep, stupor

modorro, *a.* drowsy, heavy

modoso, *a.* demure; well-behaved

modulación, *f.* (*mus.*) modulation

modulador (-ra), *a.* modulative. *s.* modulator. *m.* (*mus.*) modulator

modular, *v.t.* and *v.i.* (*mus.*) to modulate

mofa, *f.* mockery, ridicule, jeering

mofador (-ra), *a.* jeering. *s.* scoffer, mocker

mofarse, *v.r.* (*with de*) to make fun of, jeer at

mofeta, *f.* noxious gas, mofette; damp (gas); (*zool.*) skunk

moflete, *m.* (*fam.*) plump cheek

mofletudo, *a.* plump-cheeked

mogol (-la), *a.* and *s.* Mongolian. **el Gran Mogol,** the Great Mogul

mogote, *m.* hillock; pyre, stack

mohicanos, *m. pl.* Mohicans

mohín, *m.* grimace

mohina, *f.* grudge, rancour; sullenness; sulkiness

mohino, *a.* depressed, gloomy; sulky; black or black-nosed (animals)

moho, *m.* mould, fungoid growth; mouldiness; moss. (*fam.*) **no criar m.,** to be always on the move (A rolling stone gathers no moss)

mohoso, *a.* mossy; mouldy

mojada, *f.* wetting; (*fam.*) stab; sop of bread

mojador (-ra), *s.* wetter. *m.* stamp-moistener

mojar, *v.t.* to wet; moisten; (*fam.*) stab, wound with a dagger;

v.i. take part in; meddle, interfere; **v.r.** get wet

mojicón, *m.* kind of sponge-cake; (*fam.*) slap in the face

mojiganga, *f.* masquerade, mummer's show; farce; funny sight, figure of fun

mojigatería, *f.* hypocrisy; sanctimoniousness; prudery

mojigato (-ta), *a.* hypocritical; sanctimonious; prudish. *s.* hypocrite; bigot; prude

mojón, *m.* boundary stone; milestone; heap. **m. kilométrico,** milestone

molar, *a.* molar

moldavo (-va), *a.* and *s.* Moldavian

molde, *m.* mould, matrix; (*fig.*) model, pattern; worm-cast. **de m.,** printed; suitably, conveniently; perfectly. **letra de m.,** printed letters, print

moldeador (-ra), *s.* moulder

moldear, *v.t.* to mould, cast

moldura, *f.* moulding

moldurar, *v.t.* (*carp.*) to mould

molécula, *f.* molecule

molecular, *a.* molecular

moler, *v.t. irr.* to grind, crush; tire, exhaust; ill-treat; pester, annoy. **m. a palos,** to beat black and blue. *Pres. Ind.* **muelo, mueles, muele, muelen.** *Pres. Subjunc.* **muela, muelas, muela, muelan**

molestia, *f.* inconvenience, trouble; annoyance; discomfort, pain; bore, nuisance. **Es una m.,** It's a nuisance

molesto, *a.* inconvenient, troublesome; annoying; painful; uncomfortable; boring, tedious

moletón, *m.* flannelette

molicie, *f.* softness, smoothness; effeminacy, weakness

molienda, *f.* milling; grinding; mill; portion ground at one time; (*fam.*) exhaustion, fatigue; (*fam.*) nuisance

molificar, *v.t.* to mollify, appease

molimiento, *m.* milling; grinding; exhaustion, fatigue

molinera, *f.* woman miller; miller's wife

molinero, *a.* mill. *m.* miller

molinillo, *m.* hand-mill, small grinder; mincing machine; beater. **m. de café;** coffee-mill molino, *m.* mill; harum-scarum, rowdy; bore, tedious person; (*fam.*) mouth. **m. de rueda de escalones**, treadmill. **m. de viento**, windmill

molusco, *m.* mollusc

molleja, *f.* gizzard

mollera, *f.* crown of the head; brains, sense. (*fam.*) **ser duro de m.**, to be obstinate; be stupid

momentaneidad, *f.* momentariness

momentáneo, *a.* momentary, brief; instantaneous, immediate

momento, *m.* moment, minute; importance; (*mech.*) moment. **al m.**, immediately. **a cada m.**, all the time; frequently. **por momentos**, continually; intermittently

momería, *f.* mummery

momero (-ra), *s.* mummer

momia, *f.* mummy, corpse

momificación, *f.* mummification

momificar, *v.t.* to mummify; *v.r.* become mummified

mona, *f.* female monkey; (*fam.*) imitator; drinking bout; drunk. (*fam.*) **Aunque la m. se vista de seda, m. se queda**, Breeding will out. (*fam.*) **ser la última m.**, to be of no account, be unimportant

monacal, *a.* monkish, monastic

monacillo, *m.* (*ecc.*) acolyte

monada, *f.* mischievous prank; affected gesture or grimace; small pretty thing; childish cleverness; flattery; rash act; *pl.* monkey tricks

monarca, *m.* monarch, sovereign

monarquía, *f.* monarchy

monárquico (-ca), *a.* monarchic. *s.* monarchist

monarquismo, *m.* monarchism

monasterio, *m.* monastery; convent

monástico, *a.* monastic

monda, *f.* skinning, peeling; (*agr.*) pruning; cleansing

mondadientes, *m.* toothpick

mondar, *v.t.* to skin, peel; (*agr.*) prune; cut the hair; cleanse; free of rubbish; (*fam.*) deprive of possessions; *v.r.* pick one's teeth

mondo, *a.* simple, plain; bare; unadulterated, pure

moneda, *f.* coin, piece of money; coinage; (*fam.*) wealth; cash. **m.**

corriente, currency. **m. metálica**, specie. **pagar en buena m.**, to give entire satisfaction. **pagar en la misma m.**, to pay back in the same coin, return like for like. (*fam.*) **ser m. corriente**, to be usual or very frequent

monedero, *m.* coiner, minter; handbag; purse

monería, *f.* mischievous trick; unimportant trifle; pretty thing; childish cleverness, pretty ways

monetario, *a.* monetary. *m.* collection of coins and medals

monetización, *f.* monetization

monigote, *m.* (*ecc.*) lay brother; (*fam.*) boor; grotesque, puppet

monitor, *m.* monitor

monitorio, *a.* monitory

monja, *f.* nun; *pl.* sparks

monje, *m.* monk

monjil, *a.* nun-like. *m.* nun's habit

mono, *a.* (*fam.*) pretty, attractive; amusing, funny. *m.* monkey; person given to grimacing; rash youth; boiler suit. (*fam.*) **estar de monos**, to be on bad terms

monocotiledóneo, *a.* (*bot.*) monocotyledonous

monocromo, *a.* monochrome; monochromatic

monóculo, *m.* monocle

monogamia, *f.* monogamy

monógamo, *a.* monogamous. *s.* monogamist

monografía, *f.* monograph

monograma, *m.* monogram

monolítico, *a.* monolithic

monolito, *m.* monolith

monólogo, *m.* monologue

monomanía, *f.* monomania

monomaníaco (-ca), *s.* monomaniac

monopatín, *m.* scooter

monoplano, *m.* monoplane

monopolio, *m.* monopoly

monopolista, *m. and f.* monopolist

monopolizar, *v.t.* to monopolize

monosilábico, *a.* monosyllabic

monosílabo, *m.* monosyllable

monoteísmo, *m.* monotheism

monoteísta, *m. and f.* monotheist

monotipia, *f.* monotype

monotonía, *f.* monotony; monotone

monótono, *a.* monotonous

monóxido, *m.* monoxide

monroísmo, *m.* Monroe doctrine

monseñor, *m.* Monseigneur

monserga, *f.* (*fam.*) rigmarole; jargon

monstruo, *m.* monster; freak, monstrosity; cruel person; hideous person or thing

monstruosidad, *f.* monstrousness, monstrosity

monstruoso, *a.* monstrous, abnormal; enormous; extraordinary; atrocious, outrageous

monta, *f.* mounting a horse; total; (*mil.*) mounting signal; breeding station (horses)

montacargas, *m.* hoist, goods-lift

montador, *m.* mounter; mounting block

montadura, *f.* mounting; mount, setting (of jewels)

montaje, *m.* assembling, setting up (machines); presentation (of a book); (cinema) montage

montano, *a.* hilly, mountainous

montante, *m.* upright, stanchion; tent pole

montaña, *f.* mountain; mountainous country. montañas rusas, switchback (in a fun fair)

montañés (-esa), *a.* mountain. *s.* mountain dweller; native of Santander (N. Spain)

montañoso, *a.* mountainous; hilly

montar, *v.i.* to ascend, climb up, get on top; mount (a horse); ride (a horse); be important; *v.t.* get on top of; ride (a horse); total, amount to; set up (apparatus, machinery); (*naut.*) sail round, double; set, mount (gems); cock (firearms); fine for trespassing; wind (a clock); command (a ship); (*naut.*) carry, be fitted with (guns, etc.). m. a horcajadas en, to mount astride; straddle. montarse en cólera, to fly into a rage

montaraz, *a.* mountain-dwelling; wild, savage; rude, uncivilized, uncouth. *m.* gamekeeper, forester

montazgo, *m.* toll payable for cattle moving from one province to another

monte, *m.* mount, hill; woodland; obstacle, impediment. m. de

piedad, pawnshop. m. pío, savings fund

montenegrino (-na), *a.* and *s.* Montenegran

montera, *f.* cap; glass roof

montería, *f.* hunt, chase; art of hunting

montero (-ra), *s.* hunter, huntsman

montés, *a.* wild, savage, untamed

montevideano (-na), *a.* and *s.* Montevidean

montículo, *m.* mound, hillock

montón, *m.* heap, pile; (*fam.*) abundance, lot. (*fam.*) a, de or en m., all jumbled up together. a montones, in abundance

montuoso, *a.* mountainous

montura, *f.* riding animal, mount; horse trappings; setting up, mounting (artillery, etc.)

monumental, *a.* monumental

monumento, *m.* monument; document, record; tomb

monzón, *m.* or *f.* monsoon

moña, *f.* doll; dressmaker's model; bow for the hair; bullfighter's black bow; baby's bonnet; (*fam.*) drinking bout

moño, *m.* bun, chignon; top-knot (birds); bunch of ribbons; *pl.* tawdry trimmings

moqueta, *f.* moquette

moquete, *m.* slap in the face

moquillo, *m.* distemper (of animals)

mora, *f.* blackberry; mulberry; bramble; Moorish girl

morada, *f.* dwelling, abode; sojourn, stay

morado, *a.* purple

morador (-ra), *s.* dweller; sojourner

moral, *a.* moral, ethical. *f.* morality, ethics; morale. *m.* blackberry bush

moraleja, *f.* moral, lesson

moralidad, *f.* morality

moralista, *m.* moralist

moralización, *f.* moralization

moralizador (-ra), *a.* moralizing. *s.* moralizer

moralizar, *v.t.* to reform, correct; *v.i.* moralize

morar, *v.i.* to dwell, live

moratoria, *f.* moratorium

moravo (-va), *a.* and *s.* Moravian

morbidez, *f.* (*art*) morbidezza; softness

mórbido, *a.* morbid, diseased; (*art*) delicate (of flesh tones); soft

morbo, *m.* illness. m. gálico, syphilis

morboso, *a.* ill; morbid, unhealthy

morcilla, *f.* (*cul.*) black pudding; (*fam., theat.*) gag

morcillero (-ra), *s.* seller of black puddings; (*fam., theat.*) actor who gags

mordacidad, *f.* corrosiveness; mordacity, sarcasm; (*cul.*) piquancy

mordaz, *a.* corrosive; sarcastic, caustic, mordant; (*cul.*) piquant

mordaza, *f.* gag

mordedor, *a.* biting; scandalmongering

mordedura, *f.* bite, biting

morder, *v.t. irr.* to bite; nibble, nip; seize, grasp; corrode, eat away; slander; etch. *Pres. Ind.* muerdo, muerdes, muerde, muerden. *Pres. Subjunc.* muerda, muerdas, muerda, muerdan

mordiente, *m.* fixative (for dyeing); mordant. *a.* mordant (of acid)

mordiscar, *v.t.* to nibble, bite gently; bite

mordisco, *m.* nibble; nibbling; bite; biting; piece bitten off

morena, *f.* moraine (débris left by a glacier)

moreno (-na), *a.* dark brown; swarthy complexioned; dark (of people). *s.* (*fam.*) negro, mulatto

morera, *f.* mulberry bush

moreral, *m.* mulberry plantation

morería, *f.* Moorish quarter; Moorish territory

morfina, *f.* morphine

morfinómano (-na), *s.* morphine addict

morfología, *f.* morphology

morfológico, *a.* morphological

morganático, *a.* morganatic

moribundo (-da), *a.* moribund, dying. *s.* dying person

morillo, *m.* andiron, fire-dog

morir, *v.i. irr.* to die; fade, wither; decline, decay; disappear; yearn (for); long (to); go out (lights, fire); *v.r.* die; go numb (limbs); (*with por*) adore,

be mad about. (*fam.*) m. vestido, to die a violent death. ¡ Muera ! Down with! *Past Part.* muerto. For other tenses see dormir

morisco (-ca), *a.* Moorish. *s.* Morisco, Moor converted to Christianity

morisma, *f.* Mohammedanism; multitude of Moors

mormón (-ona), *s.* Mormon

mormónico, *a.* Mormon

mormonismo, *m.* Mormonism

moro (-ra), *a.* Moorish. *s.* Moor; Mohammedan. (*fam.*) haber moros y cristianos, to be the deuce of a row. (*fam.*) Hay moros en la cósta, The coast is not clear; There's trouble in the offing

morosidad, *f.* slowness, delay; sluggishness, sloth

moroso, *a.* slow, dilatory; sluggish, lazy

morra, *f.* crown of the head

morral, *m.* nose-bag; knapsack; game-bag; (*fam.*) lout

morriña, *f.* cattle plague, murrain; (*fam.*) depression, blues; homesickness

morrión, *m.* morion (sixteenthcentury helmet)

morro, *m.* anything round; hummock, hillock; round pebble; headland, cliff

morsa, *f.* walrus

mortaja, *f.* winding sheet, shroud

mortal, *a.* mortal; fatal, deadly; on the point of death; great, tremendous; certain, sure. *m.* and *f.* mortal

mortalidad, *f.* humanity, human race; mortality, death-rate

mortandad, *f.* mortality, number of deaths

mortecino, *a.* dead from natural causes (animals); weak; fading; dull, dead (of eyes); flickering; on the point of death or extinction. (*fam.*) hacer la mortecina, to sham dead

mortero, *m.* mortar (for building); (*mil.*) mortar; pounding mortar

mortífero, *a.* deadly, mortal

mortificación, *f.* (*med.*) gangrene; humiliation, wounding; mortification (of the flesh)

mortificar, *v.t.* (*med.*) to mortify; humiliate, wound, hurt; mortify (the flesh); *v.r.* become gangrenous

mortuorio, *a.* mortuary. *m.* funeral, obsequies

mosaico, *a.* and *m.* mosaic

mosca, *f.* fly; *(fam.)* nuisance; bore, pest; cash; *pl.* sparks. *(fam.)* **m. muerta,** underhand person. *(fam.)* **papar moscas,** to gape, be dumbfounded. *(fam.)* **soltar la m.,** to give or spend money unwillingly

moscardón, *m.* gad-fly

moscatel, *a.* muscatel. *m.* muscatel (grapes and wine); *(fam.)* pest, tedious person

moscón, *m.* *(ent.)* bluebottle

moscovita, *a.* and *m.* and *f.* Muscovite

mosén, *m.* ancient title of nobles in N.-E. Spain (Aragon, etc.); title of priests in same area

mosquear, *v.t.* to drive off flies; reply crossly; whip; *v.r.* be exasperated; brush aside obstacles

mosquero, *m.* fly-trap

mosquete, *m.* musket

mosquetería, *f.* musketry; *(ant., theat.)* male members of the audience who stood at the back of the pit

mosquetero, *m.* musketeer; (Spanish theatre of sixteenth and seventeenth centuries) male member of the audience who stood at the back of the pit

mosquitero, *m.* mosquito net

mosquito, *m.* mosquito; midge, gnat; *(fam.)* tippler, drunkard

mostacera, *f.* mustard pot

mostacho, *m.* moustache, whiskers; *(fam.)* smudge on the face

mostaza, *f.* mustard plant or seed; *(cul.)* mustard

mostela, *f.* sheaf (of corn, etc.)

mosto, *m.* must, unfermented wine

mostrador (-ra), *s.* one who shows, exhibitor. *m.* shop counter; face of a watch

mostrar, *v.t.* *irr.* to show; indicate, point out; demonstrate, prove; manifest, reveal; *v.r.* show oneself, be (e.g. **Se mostró bondadoso,** He showed himself kind). *Pres. Ind.* **muestro, muestras, muestra, muestran.** *Pres. Subjunc.* **muestre, muestres, muestre, muestren**

mostrenco, *a.* *(fam.)* stray, vagrant, homeless; *(fam.)* dull, ignorant; *(fam.)* fat, heavy

mota, *f.* fault in cloth; mote, defect, fault; mound, hillock; thread of cotton, speck of dust, etc.; fleck (of the sun, etc.); spot

mote, *m.* maxim, saying; motto, device; catchword, slogan; nickname

motear, *v.t.* to speckle, dot, variegate, spot

motejar, *v.t.* to nickname, call names, dub

motete, *m.* *(mus.)* motet

motín, *m.* mutiny; riot

motivar, *v.t.* to motivate, cause; explain one's reasons

motivo, *a.* motive. *m.* cause, motive; *(mus.)* motif. **con m. de,** on account of, because of. **de m. propio,** of one's own free will

motocicleta, *f.* motor-cycle

motociclista, *m.* and *f.* motorcyclist

motor (-ra), *a.* motive, driving. *m.* motor, engine. *s.* (person) mover, motive force. **m. de combustión interna,** internal combustion engine. **m. de retroacción,** jet-propelled engine

motorista, *m.* and *f.* motorist, driver

movedizo, *a.* movable; insecure, unsteady; shaky; changeable, vacillating

mover, *v.t.* *irr.* to move; operate, drive; sway; wag; persuade, induce; excite; move (to pity, etc.); *(with prep. a)* cause; *v.i.* sprout (plants); *v.r.* move. *Pres. Ind.* **muevo, mueves, mueve, mueven.** *Pres. Subjunc.* **mueva, muevas, mueva, muevan**

movible, *a.* movable; insecure, shaky. *m.* motive, cause, incentive

movilidad, *f.* mobility; changeableness, inconstancy

movilización, *f.* mobilization

movilizar, *v.t.* to mobilize

movimiento, *m.* movement; perturbation, excitement; *(mus.)* movement; *(lit.)* fire, spirit; *(mech.)* motion, movement. *(mil.)* **m. envolvente,** encircling movement

moza, *f.* maidservant; prostitute; dolly-peg. **m. de partido,**

prostitute. **buena m.,** well-set-up young woman

mozalbete, *m.* lad, stripling, boy

mozárabe, *a.* Mozarabic. *m.* and *f.* Mozarab

mozo, *a.* young, unmarried. *m.* boy, youth; bachelor; waiter; porter. **m. de cordel** *or* **m. de esquina,** street porter, message boy. **m. de estación,** railway porter. **buen m.,** fine upstanding young man

muaré, *m.* moiré silk

muceta, *f.* (*univ.*) hood, short cape (of a graduate's gown)

mucilaginoso, *a.* mucilaginous

mucílago, *m.* mucilage, gum

mucosidad, *f.* mucosity

mucosa, *f.* mucous membrane

mucoso, *a.* mucous

muchacha, *f.* girl, lass; serving maid

muchachada, *f.* childish prank

muchachez, *f.* boyhood; girlhood

muchachil, *a.* boyish; girlish

muchacho, *m.* boy, youth; male servant

muchedumbre, *f.* abundance, plenty; crowd, multitude; mass, mob

muchísimo, *a. sup.* very much. *adv.* very great deal, very much

mucho, *a.* much; plenty of; very; long (time); *pl.* many, numerous. *adv.* a great deal; much; very much; yes, certainly; frequently, often; very (e.g. **Me alegro m.,** I am very glad); to a great extent; long (time). **con m.,** by far, easily. **ni con m.,** nor anything like it, very far from it. **ni m. menos,** and much less. **por m. que,** however much

muda, *f.* change, transformation; change of clothes; moulting season; moult, sloughing of skin (snakes, etc.); change of voice (in boys)

mudable, *a.* changeable, inconstant

mudanza, *f.* change; furniture removal; step, figure (in dancing); changeability, inconstancy

mudar, *v.t.* to change; alter, transform; exchange; remove; dismiss (from employment); moult; slough the skin (snakes, etc.); change the voice (boys); *v.r.* alter one's behaviour; change

one's clothes; change one's residence; change one's expression; (*fam.*) go away, depart. **mudarse por el aire,** (*fam.*) to do a moonlight flit

mudéjar, *m.* (*arch.*) style containing Moorish and Christian elements. *m.* and *f.* Moor who remained in Spain under Christian rule

mudez, *f.* dumbness; silence, muteness

mudo, *a.* dumb; silent, mute, quiet

mueblaje, *m.* household goods and furniture

mueble, *m.* piece of furniture; furnishing

mueblería, *f.* furniture shop or factory

mueblista, *m.* and *f.* furniture maker; furniture dealer

mueca, *f.* grimace

muela, *f.* grindstone; molar (tooth); millstone; flat-topped hill. **m. del juicio,** wisdom tooth. **dolor de muelas,** toothache

muellaje, *m.* wharfage, dock dues

muelle, *a.* soft, smooth; voluptuous, sensuous; luxurious. *m.* spring (of a watch, etc.); wharf, quay; freight platform (railway). **m. real,** mainspring (of a watch). **m. del volante,** hair-spring.

muérdago, *m.* mistletoe

muermo, *m.* glanders (disease of horses)

muerte, *f.* death; destruction, annihilation; end, decline. (*fam.*) **una m. chiquita,** a nervous shudder. **a m.,** to the death, with no quarter. **de m.,** implacably, inexorably (of hatred); very seriously (of being ill). **dar m. (a),** to kill. **estar a la m.,** to be on the point of death

muerto (**-ta**), *a.* dead; slaked (lime); (*mech.*) neutral; faded, dull (colours); languid, indifferent. **m.** is used in familiar speech as *past part.* **matar** (e.g. **Le ha muerto,** He has killed him). *s.* corpse. (*fam.*) **desenterrar los muertos,** to speak ill of the dead. (*fam.*) **echarle a uno el m.,** to pass the buck, transfer the responsibility. (*fam.*) **estar m. por,** to be dying, yearning for. **ser el m.**, to be dummy (at cards)

muesca, *f.* notch, mortise, groove

muestra, *f.* shop sign; sample, specimen; pattern, model; demeanour; watch or clock face; sign, indication; poster, placard; (*mil.*) muster-roll. **hacer m.**, to show

muestrario, *m.* sample book, collection of samples

mufla, *f.* muffler (furnace)

mugido, *m.* mooing or lowing of cattle

mugir, *v.i.* to low or moo (cattle); bellow, shout; rage (elements)

mugre, *f.* grease, grime, dirt

mugriento, *a.* grimy, greasy

mugrón, *m.* (*bot.*) sucker, tiller; (*bot.*) shoot

muguete, *m.* lily of the valley

mujer, *f.* woman; wife. **m. de la vida airada** *or* **m. del partido** *or* **m. pública**, prostitute. **m. de la luna**, man in the moon. **m. de su casa**, good housewife. **tomar m.**, to take a wife

mujeriego, *a.* womanly, feminine; (of men) dissolute, given to philandering. **cabalgar a mujeriegas**, to ride side-saddle

mujeril, *a.* womanly, feminine

mújol, *m.* (*icht.*) grey mullet

mula, *f.* female mule; mule (heelless slipper). (*fam.*) **Se me fué la m.**, My tongue ran away with me

muladar, *m.* refuse heap, dunghill

mular, *a.* mule; mulish ·

mulatero, *m.* mule hirer; muleteer

mulato (-ta), *a.* and *s.* mulatto

muleta, *f.* crutch; bullfighter's red flag; support, prop

mulo, *m.* mule

multa, *f.* fine

multar, *v.t.* to impose a fine on

multicolor, *a.* multicoloured

multiforme, *a.* multiform

multilátero, *a.* multilateral

multimillonario (-ia), *a.* and *s.* multi-millionaire

multiplicación, *f.* multiplication

multiplicador (-ra), *s.* multiplier. *m.* (*math.*) multiplier

multiplicando, *m.* multiplicand

multiplicar(se), *v.t.* and *v.r.* to multiply; reproduce

multiplicidad, *f.* multiplicity

múltiplo, *a.* and *m.* multiple

multitud, *f.* multitude, great number; crowd; rabble, masses, mob

mullir, *v.t. irr.* to make soft, shake out (wool, down, etc.); (*fig.*) prepare the way; (*agr.*) hoe the roots (vines, etc.). *Pres. Part.* **mullendo.** *Preterite* **mulló, mulleron.** *Imperf. Subjunc.* **mullese**, etc.

mundanal, mundano, *a.* worldly, mundane

mundanalidad, *f.* worldliness

mundial, *a.* world, world-wide

mundo, *m.* world, universe; human race; earth; human society; world (of letters, scientific, etc.); secular life; (*ecc.*) vanities of the flesh; geographical globe. **echar al m.**, to give birth to; produce, bring forth. **el Nuevo M.**, the New World, America. (*fam.*) **medio m.**, half the earth, a great crowd. (*fam.*) **ponerse el m. por montera**, to treat the world as one's oyster. **ser hombre del m.**, to be a man of the world. (*fam.*) **tener m.** *or* **mucho m.**, to be very experienced, know the world. **todo el m.**, everyone. **venir al m.**, to be born. **ver m.**, to travel, see the world

mundología, *f.* worldliness, experience of the world

munición, *f.* (*mil.*) munition; small shot. (*mil.*) **m. de boca**, fodder and food supplies

municionar, *v.t.* to munition, furnish with munitions

municionero (-ra), *s.* purveyor, supplier

municipal, *a.* municipal. *m.* policeman

municipalidad, *f.* municipality

municipio, *m.* municipality, town council

munificencia, *f.* munificence, generosity

munífico, *a.* munificent, generous

muñeca, *f.* (*anat.*) wrist; doll; puppet; dressmaker's dummy; polishing pad; mannequin doll; boundary stone; (*fam.*) flighty young woman

muñeco, *m.* boy doll; puppet; (*fam.*) play-boy

muñeira, *f.* popular Galician dance (N. Spain)

muñir, *v.t. irr.* to summon, convoke; arrange, dispose. See **mullir**

muñón, *m.* (*surg.*) stump of an amputated limb; (*mech.*) gudgeon

mural, *a.* mural

muralla, *f.* town wall; rampart, fortification

murar, *v.t.* to surround with a wall, wall in

murciano (-na), *a.* and *s.* of or from Murcia (S. Spain)

murciélago, *m.* (*zool.*) bat

murga, *f.* band of street musicians

murmullo, *m.* whisper; whispering; rustling; purling, lapping, splashing; mumbling, muttering

murmuración, *f.* slander, backbiting, gossip

murmurador (-ra), *a.* gossiping, slanderous. *s.* gossip, backbiter

murmurar, *v.i.* to rustle (leaves, etc.); purl, lap, splash (water); whisper; mumble, mutter; *v.i.* and *v.t.* (*fam.*) slander, backbite

murmurio, *m.* rustling; lapping (of water); whispering; murmur; (*fam.*) slander

muro, *m.* wall; defensive wall, rampart

musa, *f.* Muse

musaraña, *f.* (*zool.*) shrew; any small animal; (*fam.*) ridiculous effigy, guy. (*fam.*) **mirar a las musarañas,** to be absentminded

muscular, *a.* muscular

musculatura, *f.* musculature

músculo, *m.* muscle; strength, brawn

musculoso, *a.* muscular; strong, brawny

muselina, *f.* muslin

museo, *m.* museum. **m. de pintura,** art gallery

musgo, *m.* moss

musgoso, *a.* mossy, moss-grown

música, *f.* music; melody, harmony; musical performance; musical composition; team of musicians; sheet music. (*fam.*) **m. celestial,** vain words, moonshine. (*fam.*) **m. ratonera,** badly played music. (*fam.*) **¡Vaya con su m. a otra parte!** Get out! Go to blazes!

musical, *a.* musical

músico (-ca), *a.* music. *s.* musician. **m. mayor,** bandmaster

musitar, *v.i.* to mutter, mumble

muslo, *m.* thigh

mustio, *a.* sad, disheartened, depressed; faded, withered

musulmán (-ana), *a.* and *s.* Mohammedan, Mussulman

mutabilidad, *f.* mutability, changeability

mutación, *f.* change, mutation; sudden change in weather; (*theat.*) change of scene

mutilación, *f.* mutilation; damage; defacement

mutilar, *v.t.* to mutilate; spoil, deface, damage; cut short; reduce

mutis, *m.* (*theat.*) exit. **hacer m.** (*theat.*) to exit; keep quiet, say nothing

mutismo, *m.* mutism, dumbness; silence, speechlessness

mutualidad, *f.* reciprocity, mutuality, interdependence; principle of mutual help; mutual help association

mutualismo, *m.* mutualism, organized mutual help

mutualista, *m.* and *f.* member of a mutual help association

mutuante, *m.* and *f.* (*com.*) lender

mutuo, *a.* reciprocal, mutual, interdependent

muy, *adv.* very; very much; much. Used to form absolute superlative (e.g. **m. rápidamente,** very quickly). Can modify adjectives, nouns used adjectivally, adverbs, participles (e.g. **María es m. mujer,** Mary is very much of a woman (very womanly)). **m. temprano,** very early). **m. señor mío,** dear sir (in letters)

N

naba, *f.* swede, turnip

nabar, *m.* turnip field

nabo, *m.* turnip; turnip root; any root-stem; (*naut.*) mast; stock (of horse's tail)

nácar, *m.* mother-of-pearl

nacarado, nacáreo, *a.* nacreous, mother-of-pearl

nacer, *v.i. irr.* to be born; rise

(rivers, etc.); sprout; grow (plumage, fur, leaves, etc.); descend (lineage); appear (stars, etc.); originate; (*fig.*) issue forth; appear suddenly; (*with prep. a* or *para*) be destined for, have a natural leaning towards; *v.r.* grow; sprout; (*sew.*) split at the seams. *Pres. Ind.* **nazco, naces,** etc. *Pres. Subjunc.* **nazca,** etc.

nacido, *a.* and *past part.* born; suitable, fit. *m.* (gen. *pl.*) the living and the dead. **bien n.,** noble, well-born; well-bred. **mal n.,** base-born; ill-bred

naciente, *a.* growing; naissant. *m.* east

nacimiento, *m.* birth; source (rivers, etc.); birthplace; origin; lineage; (*ast.*) rising; Nativity crib, manger. **de n.,** from birth; by birth; born

nación, *f.* nation; country; (*fam.*) birth

nacional, *a.* national; native. *m.* and *f.* citizen, national

nacionalidad, *f.* nationality

nacionalismo, *m.* nationalism

nacionalista, *a.* and *m.* and *f.* nationalist

nacionalización, *f.* naturalization; nationalization; acclimatization

nacionalizar, *v.t.* to naturalize; nationalize

nacionalsindicalismo, *m.* (*pol.*) national-syndicalism

nacionalsocialismo, *m.* (*pol.*) national-socialism, nazism

nada, *f.* void, nothingness. *pron. indef.* nothing. *adv.* by no means. **casi n.,** very little, practically nothing. **¡De n.!** Not at all! Don't mention it! **No vale para n.,** He (It, She) is no use

nadaderas, *f. pl.* water-wings (for swimming)

nadador (-ra), *s.* swimmer. *a.* swimming

nadar, *v.i.* to swim; float; have an abundance (of); (*fam.*) be too large (garments, etc.). **n. y guardar la ropa,** (*fig.*) to sit on the fence

nadería, *f.* trifle

nadie, *pron. indef.* no one. *m.* (*fig.*) a nobody

nadir, *m.* (*ast.*) nadir

nado, a, by swimming; afloat

nafta, *f.* naphtha

naftalina, *f.* naphthalene

naipe, *m.* playing-card; card-pack

naire, *m.* elephant keeper and trainer

nalga, *f.* (gen. *pl.*) buttock(s)

nana, *f.* (*fam.*) grandma; lullaby

nansú, *m.* nainsook

nao, *f.* ship

napoleónico, *a.* Napoleonic

napolitano (-na), *a.* and *s.* Neapolitan

naranja, *f.* orange. **n. dulce,** blood-orange. **n. mandarina,** tangerine orange. (*fam.*) **media n.,** better half

naranjada, *f.* orangeade

naranjal, *m.* orange grove

naranjero (-ra), *s.* orange seller

naranjo, *m.* orange tree; (*fam.*) lout, blockhead

narciso, *m.* narcissus; dandy, fop. **n. trompón,** daffodil

narcótico, *a.* and *m.* narcotic

narcotizar, *v.t.* to narcotize

nardo, *m.* (*bot.*) tuberose, spikenard, nard

narguile, *m.* hookah, hubble-bubble, narghile

narigudo, *a.* large-nosed; nose-shaped

nariz, *f.* nose; nostril; snout; nozzle; sense of smell; bouquet (of wine). **n. perfilada,** well-shaped nose. **n. respingona,** snub nose. (*fam.*) **meter las narices,** to meddle, interfere

narración, *f.* narration, account

narrador (-ra), *a.* narrative. *s.* narrator

narrar, *v.t.* to narrate, tell, relate

narrativa, *f.* narrative; account; narrative skill

narrativo, narratorio, *a.* narrative

nasa, *f.* fish-trap; lobster-pot

nasal, *a.* nasal

nata, *f.* cream; (*fig.*) the flower, élite; *pl.* whipped cream with sugar

natación, *f.* swimming. **n. a la marinera,** trudgeon stroke

natal, *a.* natal; native. *m.* birth; birthday

natalicio, *a.* natal. *a.* and *m.* birthday

natalidad, *f.* birth-rate

natatorio, *a.* swimming. *m.* swimming pool

natillas, *f. pl.* custard

natividad, *f.* nativity; birth; Christmas

nativo, *a.* indigenous; native; innate

nato, *a.* born; inherent; ex-officio

natura, *f.* nature; (*mus.*) major scale

natural, *a.* natural; native; indigenous; spontaneous; sincere, candid; physical; usual, ordinary; (*mus.*) natural; unadulterated, pure; (*her.*) proper. *m.* and *f.* native, citizen. *m.* temperament; disposition; instinct (animals); natural inclination. **al n.,** naturally, without art. **del n.,** (*art*) from life

naturaleza, *f.* nature; character; disposition; instinct; temperament; nationality, origin; naturalization; kind, class; constitution, physique. **n. humana,** mankind. **n. muerta,** (*art*) still life

naturalidad, *f.* **naturalness;** nationality

naturalismo, *m.* (*phil., lit.*) naturalism

naturalista, *m.* and *f.* naturalist (also scientific)

naturalización, *f.* naturalizatión; acclimatization

naturalizar, *v.t.* to naturalize; acclimatize; *v.r.* become naturalized; become acclimatized

naturalmente, *adv.* naturally; of course

naturismo, *m.* Nature Cure

naufragar, *v.i.* to be shipwrecked; fail, be unsuccessful

naufragio, *m.* shipwreck; disaster, loss

náufrago (-ga), *s.* shipwrecked person. *m.* shark

náusea, *f.* nausea (*pl.* more usual); repugnance

nauseabundo, nauseoso, *a.* nauseous; nauseating, repugnant

nauta, *m.* mariner

náutica, *f.* navigation; yachting; seamanship

náutico, *a.* nautical

navaja, *f.* razor; clasp-knife; boar-tusk; sting; (*fam.*) slanderous tongue. **n. de afeitar,** (shaving) razor

navajada, *f.* slash with a razor

navajero, *m.* razor-case

naval, *a.* naval

navarro (-ra), *a.* and *s.* Navarrese

nave, *f.* ship; (*arch.*) nave. **n. aérea,** airship. (*arch.*) **n.** lateral, aisle. **n. principal,** (*arch.*) nave

navegable, *a.* navigable

navegación, *f.* navigation; sea voyage

navegante, *a.* voyaging; navigating. *m.* navigator

navegar, *v.i.* to navigate; sail; fly

navidad, *f.* nativity; Christmas; *pl.* Christmastide

naviero, *a.* shipping. *m.* ship-owner

navío, *m.* warship; ship. **n. de transporte,** transport. **n. de tres puentes,** three-decker

náyade, *f.* naiad, water-nymph

nazareno (-na), *a.* and *s.* Nazarene; Christian

nazismo, *m.* nazism

neblí, *m.* (*orn.*) falcon gentle

neblina, *f.* fog; mist

nebulosidad, *f.* nebulousness; cloudiness

nebuloso, *a.* foggy; misty; cloudy; sombre, melancholy; confused, nebulous

necedad, *f.* silliness

necesario, *a.* necessary; unavoidable

neceser, *m.* dressing-case. **n. de costura,** work-box

necesidad, *f.* necessity; poverty, want; shortage, need; emergency. **de n.,** necessarily

necesitado (-da), *a.* needy, poor. *s.* poor person

necesitar, *v.t.* to necessitate; compel, oblige; *v.i.* be necessary, need

necio, *a.* stupid; senseless; unreasonable

necrología, *f.* necrology, obituary

necrológico, *a.* necrological

necromancía, *f.* necromancy

nectario, *m.* (*bot.*) nectary

neerlandés, *a.* Dutch

nefando, *a.* iniquitous

nefario, *a.* nefarious

nefasto, *a.* disastrous, ill-omened

nefrítico, *a.* (*med.*) nephritic

nefritis, *f.* (*med.*) nephritis

negable, *a.* deniable

negación, *f.* negation; privation;

negative; nay; (*gram.*) negative particle; (*law*) traverse

negado, *a.* inept, unfitted; stupid

negar, *v.t. irr.* to deny; refuse; prohibit; disclaim; dissemble; disown; (*law*) traverse; *v.r.* refuse, avoid; decline (to receive visitors). See acertar

negativa, *f.* denial; refusal; (*phot.*) negative

negativo, *a.* negative

negligencia, *f.* negligence; omission; carelessness; forgetfulness

negligente, *a.* negligent; careless; neglectful

negociable, *a.* negotiable

negociación, *f.* negotiation; business affair, deal

negociado, *m.* department, section (of ministry, etc.); business

negociante, *m.* business man. *a.* negotiating; trading

negociar, *v.i.* to trade, traffic; negotiate

negocio, *m.* occupation; trade; business; employment; transaction; *pl.* business affairs. hombre de negocios, business man

negra, *f.* negress; (*fam.*) honey, sweetheart (*S.A.*)

negrecer, *v.i. irr.* to become black. See conocer

negrero (-ra), *s.* slave-trader

negro, *a.* black; dark; melancholy; disastrous; (*her.*) sable. *m.* negro; black (colour). **n.** de humo, lamp-black

negrura, *f.* blackness

negruzco, *a.* blackish

nene (-na), *s.* (*fam.*) baby; darling

nenúfar, *m.* white water lily

neo, *m.* (*chem.*) neon

neófito (-ta), *s.* neophyte

neoguineano, *a.* New Guinea

neolítico, *a.* Neolithic

neologismo, *m.* neologism

neoyorquino (-na), *a.* New York. *s.* New Yorker

neozelandés (-esa), *a.* New Zealand. *s.* New Zealander

nepotismo, *m.* nepotism

neptuno, *m.* (*ast.*) Neptune; (*poet.*) sea

nereida, *f.* nereid, sea-nymph

nervio, *m.* nerve; sinew; (*bot.*) vein; vigour; string (musical instruments). **n. ciático,** sciatic nerve

nervioso, *a.* nervous; overwrought, agitated; vigorous; neural; sinewy; (of style, etc.) jerky

nervosidad, *f.* nervousness; nervosity; flexibility (metals); (of style, etc.) jerkiness; force, efficacy

nervudo, *a.* strong-nerved, vigorous

nesga, *f.* (*sew.*) gore

neto, *a.* neat; clean; pure; (*com.*) net. *m.* (*arch.*) dado

neumático, *a.* pneumatic. *m.* rubber tyre

neumococo, *m.* (*med.*) pneumococcus

neurálgico, *a.* neuralgic

neurastenia, *f.* neurasthenia

neurasténico (-ca), *a.* and *s.* neurasthenic

neurología, *f.* neurology

neurólogo, *m.* neurologist

neurona, *f.* (*anat.*) neurone

neurópata, *m.* neuropath

neurosis, *f.* neurosis. **n.** de guerra, war neurosis; shell shock

neurótico (-ca), *a.* and *s.* neurotic

neutral, *a.* neutral; indifferent

neutralidad, *f.* neutrality; impartiality, indifference

neutralizar, *v.t.* to neutralize; counteract, mitigate

neutro, *a.* neuter; (*chem.*) neutral; (*mech.*) neuter; sexless

nevada, *f.* snowfall

nevar, *v.i. irr. impers.* to snow. *Pres. Ind.* nieva. *Pres. Subjunc.* nieve

nevera, *f.* refrigerator; ice-house

nevero, *m.* ice-cream man; ice man

nevisca, *f.* light snowfall

nevoso, *a.* snowy

nexo, *m.* nexus; connection, union

ni, *conjunc.* neither, nor. **ni bien ni mal,** neither good nor bad. **ni siquiera,** not even

niara, *f.* haystack, rick

nicaragüeño (-ña), *a.* and *s.* Nicaraguan

nicotina, *f.* nicotine

nicho, *m.* niche; recess (in wall)

nidada, *f.* nest of eggs; brood, clutch

nidal, *m.* nest; nest-egg; haunt; cause, foundation

nido, *m.* nest; den; hole; dwelling; haunt. **n. de ametralladoras,** (*mil.*) pill-box niebla, *f.* fog; mist; cloud; mildew; haze

nieto (-ta), *s.* grandchild; descendant

nieve, *f.* snow; whiteness. deportes de n., winter sports

nigromancia, *f.* necromancy

nigromante, *m.* necromancer

nihilismo, *m.* nihilism

nihilista, *m. and f.* nihilist

nimbo, *m.* halo, nimbus

nimiedad, *f.* prolixity; (*fam.*) fussiness; fastidiousness, delicacy

nimio, *a.* prolix; (*fam.*) fussy; fastidious; (*fam.*) parsimonious

ninfa, ‹ nymph; (*ent.*) chrysalis

ningún, *a. abb.* of ninguno. Used before *m. sing.* nouns only. De n. modo, In no way; Certainly not!

niña, *f.* girl. n. del ojo, pupil of the eye. n. de los ojos, apple of one's eye, darling

niñada, *f.* childishness, foolish act

niñera, *f.* nursemaid

niñería, *f.* childish act; trifle; childishness, folly

niñez, *f.* childhood; beginning, early days; (*fig.*) cradle

niño (-ña), *a.* childish; young; inexperienced; imprudent. *s.* child; young or inexperienced person. n. de la doctrina, charity child. desde n., from childhood

nipón (-ona), *a. and s.* Japanese

níquel, *m.* (*chem.*) nickel

niquelar, *v.t.* to chromium-plate

nirvana, *m.* nirvana

níspero, *m.* medlar tree; medlar

níspola, *f.* medlar

nitidez, *f.* brightness, neatness, cleanliness

nítido, *a.* bright, neat, clean (often *poet.*)

nitrato, *m.* (*chem.*) nitrate

nítrico, *a.* (*chem.*) nitric

nitrito, *m.* (*chem.*) nitrite

nitrógeno, *m.* nitrogen

nivel, *m.* level; levelness. n. de albañil, plummet. n. de burbuja, spirit-level. a n., on the level. estar al n. de las circunstancias, to rise to the occasion; save the situation

nivelación, *f.* levelling

nivelador (-ra), *a.* levelling. *s.* leveller

nivelar, *v.t.* to level; (*fig.*) make equal

níveo, *a.* snowy; snow-white

no, *adv.* no; not. no bien, no sooner. no sea que, unless. no tal, no such thing

noble, *a.* noble, illustrious; generous; outstanding, excellent; aristocratic. *m. and f.* nobleman (woman)

nobleza, *f.* nobility

noción, *f.* notion, idea; *pl.* elementary knowledge

nocividad, *f.* noxiousness

nocivo, *a.* noxious

nocturnal, *a.* nocturnal

nocturno, *a.* nocturnal; melancholy. *m.* (*mus.*) nocturne

noche, *f.* night; darkness; confusion, obscurity. (*fam.*) n. toledana, restless night. ¡Buenas noches! Good night! de n., by night. esta n., tonight

nochebuena, *f.* Christmas Eve

nochebueno, *m.* yule log; Christmas cake

nocherniego, *a.* night, nocturnal

nodriza, *f.* wet-nurse

nogal, *m.* walnut tree; walnut wood

nómada, *a.* nomadic

nomadismo, *m.* nomadism

nombradía, *f.* renown

nombramiento, *m.* naming; appointment; nomination

nombrar, *v.t.* to name; nominate; appoint; mention (in dispatches, etc.)

nombre, *m.* name; title; reputation; proxy; (*gram.*) noun; (*mil.*) password. n. de pila, Christian name. por n., called; by name

nomenclatura, *f.* nomenclature

nómina, *f.* list, register; pay roll; amulet

nominación, *f.* nomination, appointment

nominador (-ra), *a.* nominating. *s.* nominator

nominal, *a.* nominal

nominalismo, *m.* nominalism

nominalista, *a.* nominalistic. *m. and f.* nominalist

nominativo, *m.* (*gram.*) nominative

non, *a.* odd (of numbers)

nona, *f.* (*ecc.*) nones

nonada, *f.* nothing, practically nothing

nonagenario (-ia), *a.* and *s.* nonagenarian

nonagésimo, *m.* north-east

nones, *m. pl.* certainly not, definitely no

nopal, *m.* (*bot.*) nopal, prickly Indian pear tree

noque, *m.* tanner's vat

noquear, *v.t.* (*boxing*) to knock out

norabuena, *f.* congratulation

nordeste, *m.* north-east

nórdico (-ca), *a.* and *s.* Nordic

noria, *f.* draw-well; chain-pump; (*fam.*) hard, monotonous work

norma, *f.* square (used by builders, etc.); (*fig.*) norm, standard, model

normal, *a.* normal, usual; standard, average. *f.* Normal school (also escuela n.)

normalidad, *f.* normality

normalista, *m.* and *f.* student of a Normal school

normalización, *f.* normalization; standardization

normalizar, *v.t.* to make normal; standardize

normando (-da), *a.* Norman. *s.* Northman; Norman

nornordeste, *m.* north-north-east

nornorueste, *m.* north-north-west

noroeste, *m.* north-west

norte, *m.* north pole; north; north wind; pole-star; (*fig.*) guide

norteamericano (-na), *a.* and *s.* North American; American (*U.S.A.*)

norteño, *a.* northerly, northern

noruego (-ga), *a.* and *s.* Norwegian. *m.* Norwegian language

nos, *pers. pron. pl. m.* and *f. acc.* and *dat.* (direct and indirect object) of nosotros, us; to us (e.g. Nos lo dió, He gave it to us)

nosotros, nosotras, *pers. pron. pl. m.* and *f.* we; us. Also used with preposition (e.g. Lo hicieron para nosotros, They did it for us)

nostalgia, *f.* nostalgia

nostálgico, *a.* nostalgic; melancholy; homesick

nota, *f.* mark, sign; annotation, comment; (*mus.*) note; memoran-

dum; (*com.*) bill, account; criticism, imputation; mark (in exams.); repute, renown; note (diplomatic)

notabilidad, *f.* notability

notable, *a.* notable, remarkable; outstanding, prominent; with distinction (examination mark). *m. pl.* notabilities

notación, *f.* (*mus., math.*) notation; annotation

notar, *v.t.* to mark, indicate; observe, notice; note down; annotate; dictate, read out; criticize, reproach; discredit

notaría, *f.* profession of a notary; notary's office

notarial, *a.* notarial

notario, *m.* notary public

noticia, *f.* rudiment, elementary knowledge; information; news (gen. *pl.*); *pl.* knowledge. (*fig.*) atrasado de noticias, behind the times

noticiar, *v.t.* to inform, give notice

noticiero, *m.* newspaper reporter

noticioso, *a.* informed; learned; newsy

notificación, *f.* (*law*) notification

notificar, *v.t.* to notify officially; inform; warn

noto, *a.* known. *m.* south wind

notoriedad, *f.* notoriety, publicity; flagrancy; fame, renown

notorio, *a.* well-known; notorious, obvious; flagrant

novatada, *f.* (*fam.*) ragging (of a freshman); blunder

novato (-ta), *a.* new, inexperienced. *s.* novice, beginner

novecientos, *a.* and *m.* nine hundred

novedad, *f.* newness, novelty; change, alteration; latest news; surprise; *pl.* novelties. sin n., no change; all well (or as usual); safely, without incident

novel, *a.* new; inexperienced

novela, *f.* novel; tale; falsehood. n. caballista, Western, cowboy story. n. por entregas, serial (story)

novelero (-ra), *a.* fond of novelty and change; fond of novels; fickle. *s.* newshound, gossip

novelesco, *a.* novelistic; imaginary

novelista, *m.* and *f.* novelist

novelística, f. art of novel writing

novena, f. (ecc.) novena, religious services spread over nine days

noveno, a. and m. ninth

noventa, a. and m. ninety; ninetieth

novia, f. bride; fiancée

noviazgo, m. engagement, betrothal

noviciado, m. novitiate; training, apprenticeship

novicio (-ia), s. (ecc.) novice; beginner, apprentice; unassuming person

noviembre, m. November

novilunio, m. new moon

novillada, f. herd of young bulls; bullock baiting

novillo, m. bullock. hacer novillos, to play truant

novio, m. bridegroom; fiancé; novice, beginner

novísimo, a. sup. nuevo, newest; latest, most recent

nubada, f. cloud-burst, rainstorm; abundance, plenty

nubarrón, m. dense lowering cloud, storm-cloud

nube, f. cloud (also fig.); (fig.) screen, impediment. n. de verano, summer cloud; passing annoyance

nublado, a. cloudy; overcast. m. storm-cloud; menace, threat; multitude, crowd

nublarse, v.r. to cloud over

nubloso, a. cloudy; unfortunate, unhappy

nuca, f. nape

núcleo, m. kernel; stone, pip (of fruit); nucleus; (fig.) core, essence

nudillo, m. knuckle; (mas.) plug

nudo, m. knot; (bot., med.) node; joint; (naut.) knot; (fig.) bond, tie; (fig.) crux, knotty point. n. al revés, granny knot. n. de comunicaciones, communication centre. n. de marino, reefknot. n. de tejedor, sheet bend (knot). n. en la garganta, (fig.) a lump in the throat (from emotion)

nudoso, a. knotted, knotty; gnarled

nuera, f. daughter-in-law

nuestro, nuestra, poss. pron., 1st pers. pl., m. and f. our; ours. los

nuestros, our friends, supporters, party, profession, etc.

nueva, f. news

nueve, a. nine; ninth. m. number nine; ninth (of days of month) (e.g. el nueve de marzo, March 9th). a las nueve, at nine o'clock

nuevo, a. new; fresh; newly-arrived; inexperienced; unused, scarcely worn. de n., again. ¿ Qué hay de n. ? What's the news?

nuez, f. walnut; (anat.) Adam's apple. n. moscada, nutmeg

nulidad, f. nullity; incompetence, ineptitude; worthlessness

nulo, a. null, void; incapable; worthless

numen, m. divinity; inspiration

numeración, f. calculation; numbering

numerador, m. (math.) numerator

numeral, a. numeral

numerar, v.t. to number; enumerate; calculate

numerario, a. numerary. m. cash

numérico, a. numerical

número, m. number; figure; numeral; size (of gloves, etc.); quantity; issue, copy; rhythm; (gram.) number; item (of a programme); pl. (ecc.) Numbers. n. quebrado, (math.) fraction. sin n., numberless

numeroso, a. numerous; harmonious

numismática, f. numismatics

nunca, adv. never. n. jamás, nevermore

nunciatura, f. nunciature

nuncio, m. messenger; papal nuncio; (fig.) harbinger

nupcial, a. nuptial

nupcialidad, f. marriage rate

nupcias, f. pl. nuptials, marriage

nutria, f. (zool.) otter, nutria

nutrición, f. nourishment; nutrition

nutrido, a. abundant; numerous

nutrimento, m. nutriment; nourishment; nutrition; (fig.) food, encouragement

nutrir, v.t. to nourish; encourage; (fig.) fill

nutritivo, a. nourishing, nutritive

Ñ

ñaques, *m. pl.* odds and ends, rubbish

ñiquiñaque, *m.* (*fam.*) good-for-nothing, wastrel; (*fam.*) trash

ñoñería, *f.* (*fam.*) drivel; folly, stupidity

ñoño (-ña), *a.* (*fam.*) sentimental; foolish, idiotic. *s.* fool.

O

o, *f.* letter O. *conjunc.* or, either. O becomes U before words beginning with O or Ho (e.g. **gloria u honor**)

oasis, *m.* oasis; (*fig.*) refuge, haven

obcecación, *f.* blindness; obstinacy; obsession

obcecar, *v.t.* to blind; obsess; (*fig.*) dazzle; darken

obduración, *f.* obstinacy, stubbornness, obduracy

obedecer, *v.t. irr.* to obey; (*fig.*) respond; bend, yield (metals, etc.); *v.i.* result (from), arise (from). See **conocer**

obedecimiento, *m.* obediencia, *f.* obedience

obediente, *a.* obedient; docile

obelisco, *m.* obelisk

obenque, *m.* (*naut.*) shroud; *pl.* (*naut.*) rigging

obertura, *f.* (*mus.*) overture

obesidad, *f.* obesity

obeso, *a.* obese

óbice, *m.* obstacle, impediment

obispado, *m.* bishopric

obispal, *a.* episcopal

obispalía, *f.* bishop's palace; bishopric

obispo, *m.* bishop. **o. sufragáneo,** suffragan bishop

óbito, *m.* death, demise

obitorio, *m.* mortuary, morgue

obituario, *m.* obituary; obituary column (newspaper)

objeción, *f.* objection

objetar, *v.t.* to object to, oppose

objetivar, *v.t.* to view objectively

objetividad, *f.* objectivity

objetivo, *a.* objective. *m.* (*opt.*) eye-piece; object-finder; aim, goal

objeto, *m.* object; subject, theme; purpose; aim, goal. **sin o.,** without object; aimlessly

oblación, *f.* oblation

oblea, *f.* seal, wafer

oblicuidad, *f.* obliqueness

oblicuo, *a.* slanting, oblique

obligación, *f.* obligation; (*com.*) bond; (*com.*) debenture; *pl.* responsibilities; (*com.*) liabilities

obligacionista, *m.* and *f.* (*com.*) bond holder, debenture holder

obligado, *m.* contractor (to borough, etc.); (*mus.*) obbligato

obligar, *v.t.* to compel, oblige, constrain; lay under an obligation; (*law*) mortgage; *v.r.* bind oneself, promise

obligatorio, *a.* obligatory

oblongo, *a.* oblong

oboe, *m.* (*mus.*) oboe; oboe player

óbolo, *m.* obol

obra, *f.* work; anything made; literary, artistic, scientific production; structure, construction; repair, alteration (to buildings, etc.); means, influence, power; labour, or time spent; action, behaviour. **o. de caridad,** charitable act. **o. maestra,** masterpiece. **Obras Públicas,** Public Works. **poner por o.,** to put into effect; to set to work on. **o. de,** about, approximately

obrar, *v.t.* to work; make, do; execute, perform; affect; construct, build; *v.i.* be, exist (things); act, behave. **o. mal,** to behave badly, do wrong

obrero (-ra), *a.* working. *s* workman; *pl.* workers

obscenidad, *f.* obscenity

obsceno, *a.* obscene

obscurantismo, *m.* obscurantism

obscurantista, *a.* and *m.* and *f.* obscurantist

obscurecer, *v.t. irr.* to darken; (*fig.*) tarnish, dim, sully; confuse, bewilder; express obscurely; (*art*) shade; *v.n.* grow dark; *v.r.* cloud over (sky); (*fam.*) disappear (things, gen. by theft). See **conocer**

obscuridad, *f.* darkness; gloom, blackness; humbleness; obscurity, abstruseness

obscuro, *a.* dark; humble, unknown; abstruse, involved; uncertain, dangerous. **a obscuras,** in the dark; ignorant

obsequiar, *v.t.* to entertain, be attentive (to); give presents (to); court, make love to. **Me obsequia con un reloj,** He is presenting me with a watch

obsequio, *m.* attention; gift; deference. **en o. de,** as a tribute to

obsequioso, *a.* obliging, courteous, attentive

observable, *a.* observable

observación, *f.* observation; remark

observador (-ra), *a.* observing. *s.* observer

observancia, *f.* observance; respect, reverence

observar, *v.t.* to notice; inspect, examine; fulfil; remark; watch, spy upon; (*ast.*) observe

observatorio, *m.* observatory

obsesión, *f.* obsession

obsesionar, *v.t.* to obsess

obseso, *a.* obsessed

obsidiana, *f.* (*min.*) obsidian

obsoleto, *a.* obsolete

obstáculo, *m.* impediment; obstacle

obstante, no, *adv.* in spite of; nevertheless

obstar, *v.i.* to impede, hinder

obstetricia, *f.* (*med.*) obstetrics

obstétrico, *a.* (*med.*) obstetrical

obstinación, *f.* obstinacy

obstinado, *a.* obstinate, stubborn

obstinarse, *v.r.* (*with en*) to persist in, insist on, be stubborn about

obstinaz, *a.* obstinate

obstrucción, *f.* obstruction

obstruccionismo, *m.* obstructionism

obstruccionista, *m.* and *f.* obstructionist

obstruir, *v.t. irr.* to obstruct; block; hinder; *v.r.* become choked or stopped up (pipes, etc.). See **huir**

obtención, *f.* obtainment; attainment, realization

obtener, *v.t. irr.* to obtain; attain; maintain, preserve. See **tener**

obturador, *m.* stopper; shutter (of a camera)

obturar, *v.t.* to stopper, plug; block, obstruct

obtuso, *a.* blunt, dull; (*geom.* and *fig.*) obtuse

obús, *m.* (*mil.*) howitzer; (*mil.*) shell

obviar, *v.t.* to obviate

obvio, *a.* obvious, evident, apparent

oca, *f.* goose

ocarina, *f.* (*mus.*) ocarina

ocasión, *f.* occasion; opportunity; motive, cause; danger, risk; (*fam.*) **asir la o. por la melena,** to take Time by the forelock. **de o.,** second-hand

ocasional, *a.* chance, fortuitous; occasional

ocasionar, *v.t.* to cause, occasion; excite, provoke; risk, endanger

ocaso, *m.* sunset; west; dusk; decadence, decline

occidental, *a.* western

occidente, *m.* west, occident

occipital, *a.* (*anat.*) occipital

occipucio, *m.* (*anat.*) occiput

occiso, *a.* murdered; killed

oceánico, *a.* oceanic

océano, *m.* ocean; immensity, abundance

oceanografía, *f.* oceanography

ocelote, *m.* (*zool.*) ocelot

ocio, *m.* leisure, idleness; *pl.* pastimes; leisure moments

ociosidad, *f.* idleness, laziness; leisure

ocioso (-sa), *a.* idle; useless, worthless; unprofitable, fruitless. *s.* idle fellow

oclusión, *f.* (*med.*) occlusion

oclusivo, *a.* (*med.*) occlusive

ocre, *m.* ochre

octaedro, *m.* (*geom.*) octahedron

octagonal, *a.* octagonal

octágono, *m.* (*geom.*) octagon

octava, *f.* (*ecc., prosody, mus.*) octave

octaviano, *a.* Octavian

octavo, *a.* eighth. *m.* an eighth. **en o.,** in octavo

octeto, *m.* (*mus.*) octet

octogenario (-ia), *a.* and *s.* octogenarian

octogésimo, *a.* eightieth

octosilábico, *a.* eight-syllabled

octubre, *m.* October

óctuple, *a.* octuple, eightfold

ocular, *a.* ocular. *m.* eyepiece

oculista, *m.* and *f.* oculist

ocultación, *f.* hiding, concealment

ocultamente, *adv.* secretly
ocultar, *v.t.* to hide, conceal; disguise; keep secret
ocultismo, *m.* occultism
oculto, *a.* hidden; secret; occult. en o., secretly, quietly
ocupación, *f.* occupancy; occupation, pursuit; employment, office, trade
ocupado, *a.* occupied; busy
ocupante, *m.* occupant
ocupar, *v.t.* to take possession of; obtain or hold (job); occupy, fill; inhabit; employ; hinder, embarrass; hold the attention (of); *v.r.* (with en) be engaged in, be occupied with; (with con) concentrate on (business affair, etc.)
ocurrencia, *f.* occurrence, incident; bright idea; witty remark
ocurrir, *v.i.* to anticipate; happen, take place; occur, strike (ideas)
ochava, *f.* eighth; (*ecc.*) octave
ochavo, *m.* small Spanish copper coin (*ant.*)
ochenta, *a.* and *m.* eighty; eightieth
ochentón (-ona), *s.* octogenarian
ocho, *a.* eight; eighth. *m.* figure eight; playing-card with eight pips; eight; eighth day (of the month). las o., eight o'clock
ochocientos, *a.* and *m.* eight hundred; eight hundredth
oda, *f.* ode
odalisca, *f.* odalisk
odiar, *v.t.* to hate
odio, *m.* hatred; malevolence
odioso, *a.* hateful, odious
odisea, *f.* odyssey
odontología, *f.* odontology
odontólogo, *m.* odontologist
odorífero, *a.* odoriferous, fragrant
odre, *m.* goatskin, wineskin; (*fam.*) wine-bibber
oesnorueste, *m.* west-north-west
oessudueste, *m.* west-south-west
oeste, *m.* west
ofender, *v.t.* to ill-treat, hurt; offend, insult; anger, annoy; *v.r.* be offended
ofendido, *a.* offended; resentful
ofensa, *f.* injury, harm; offence, crime
ofensiva, *f.* (*mil.*) offensive. tomar la o., to take the offensive

ofensivo, *a.* offensive
ofensor (-ra), *s.* offender
oferta, *f.* offer; gift; proposal; (*com.*) tender. o. y demanda, supply and demand
ofertorio, *m.* (*ecc.*) offertory
oficial, *a.* official. *m.* official; officer; clerk; executioner; workman
oficiala, *f.* trained worker (woman)
oficialidad, *f.* officialdom; officers
oficiar, *v.t.* (*ecc.*) to celebrate or serve (mass); communicate officially, inform; (*fam.*) (with de) act as
oficina, *f.* workshop; office; pharmaceutical laboratory; *pl.* cellars, basement (of house)
oficinesco, *a.* bureaucratic. red-tape
oficinista, *m.* clerk, office employee
oficio, *m.* occupation, employment; office, function, capacity; craft; operation; trade, business; official communication; office, bureau; (*ecc.*) office. Santo O., Inquisition. (*fig.*) buenos oficios, good offices
oficiosidad, *f.* diligence, conscientiousness; helpfulness, friendliness; officiousness
oficioso, *a.* conscientious; helpful, useful; officious; meddlesome; (*dip.*) unofficial, informal
ofrecer, *v.t. irr.* to offer; present; exhibit; consecrate, dedicate; *v.r.* occur, suggest itself; volunteer. ¿Qué se le ofrece? What do you require? See conocer
ofrecimiento, *m.* offer, offering
ofrenda, *f.* (*ecc.*) offering; gift, present
oftalmia, *f.* (*med.*) ophthalmia
oftalmología, *f.* ophthalmology
oftalmólogo, *m.* oculist, ophthalmologist
ofuscación, *f.*, **ofuscamiento**, *m.* obfuscation, dazzle, dimness of sight; mental confusion, bewilderment
ofuscar, *v.t.* to dazzle, daze; dim, obfuscate; confuse, bewilder
ogro, *m.* ogre
ohmio, *m.* (*elec.*) ohm
oídas, de, *adv.* by hearsay
oído, *m.* sense of hearing; ear.

de o., by ear. decir al o., to whisper in a person's ear. (*mus.*) duro de o., hard of hearing; having a bad ear (for music). estar sordo de un o., to be deaf in one ear

oidor, *m.* hearer; judge, magistrate (*ant.*)

oír, *v.t.* *irr.* to hear; give ear to, listen; understand. *Pres. Part.* oyendo. *Pres. Ind.* oigo, oyes, oye, oyen. *Preterite* oyó, oyeron. *Pres. Subjunc.* oiga, etc. *Imperf. Subjunc.* oyese, etc.

oíslo, *m.* and *f.* (*fam.*) better-half

ojal, *m.* buttonhole; slit, hole

¡ ojalá ! *interj.* Would to Allah! God grant!

ojeada, *f.* glance

ojear, *v.t.* to look at, stare at; bewitch; scare, startle

ojera, *f.* dark shadow under the eye; eye-bath

ojeriza, *f.* ill-will, spite

ojeroso, *a.* having dark shadows under the eyes, wan, haggard

ojete, *m.* eyelet

ojinegro, *a.* black-eyed

ojiva, *f.* (*arch.*) ogive

ojival, *a.* ogival

ojo, *m.* eye; hole; slit; socket; keyhole; eye (of a needle); span (of a bridge); core (of a corn); attention, care; mesh; spring, stream; well (of a staircase); *pl.* darling. ¡ Ojo ! Take care! o. avizor, sharp watch; lynx eye. Ojos que no ven corazón que no siente, Out of sight, out of mind. ojos saltones, prominent eyes. ojos vivos, bright eyes. a o. de buen cubero, at a guess. a ojos vistas, visibly; patently

ola, *f.* billow; wave (atmospheric)

¡ ole ! *interj.* Bravo! *m.* Andalusian dance

oleada, *f.* big wave, breaker; swell of the sea; (*fig.*) surge (of a crowd)

oleaginoso, *a.* oleaginous

oleaje, *m.* swell, surge, billowing

olear, *v.t.* to administer extreme unction

óleo, *m.* oil; (*ecc.*) holy oil (gen. *pl.*). al ó., in oils

oleoducto, *m.* oil pipe line

oleografía, *f.* oleograph

oler, *v.t.* *irr.* to smell; guess, discover; pry, smell out; *v.i.* smell; (*with prep. a*) smell of; smack of, be reminiscent of. *Pres. Ind.* huelo, hueles, huele, huelen. *Pres. Subjunc.* huela, huelas, huela, huelan

olfatear, *v.t.* to sniff, snuff, smell; (*fam.*) pry into

olfativo, olfatorio, *a.* olfactory

olfato, *m.* sense of smell; shrewdness

olfatorio, *a.* olfactory

oliente, (mal), *a.* evil-smelling

oligarquía, *f.* oligarchy

oligárquico, *a.* oligarchic

olímpico, *a.* Olympic; Olympian

oliva, *f.* olive tree; olive; barn owl; peace

olivar, *m.* olive grove

olivo, *m.* olive tree

olmeda, *f.*, olmedo, *m.* elm grove

olmo, *m.* elm tree

olor, *m.* odour, scent, smell; hope, promise; suspicion, hint; reputation. o. de santidad, odour of sanctity

oloroso, *a.* fragrant, perfumed

olvidadizo, *a.* forgetful

olvidar(se), *v.i.* and *v.r.* to forget; neglect, desert. Se me olvidó el libro, I forgot the book. Me olvidé de lo pasado, I forgot the past

olvido, *m.* forgetfulness; indifference, neglect; oblivion

olla, *f.* stewpot; Spanish stew; whirlpool. o. podrida, rich Spanish stew containing bacon, fowl, meat, vegetables, ham, etc. las ollas de Egipto, the fleshpots of Egypt, luxury

ombligo, *m.* navel; (*fig.*) core, centre

ominoso, *a.* ominous

omisión, *f.* omission; carelessness, negligence; neglect

omiso, *a.* omitted; remiss; careless. hacer caso o. de, to set aside, ignore

omitir, *v.t.* to omit

ómnibus, *m.* omnibus

omnímodo, *a.* all-embracing

omnipotencia, *f.* omnipotence

omnipotente, *a.* omnipotent, all-powerful

omnisciencia, *f.* omniscience

omniscio, *a.* omniscient

omnívoro, *a.* (*zool.*) omnivorous

omoplato, *m.* *(anat.)* scapula, shoulder-blade

once, *a.* eleven; eleventh. *m.* eleven; eleventh (of the month). **las o.,** eleven o'clock

onceno, *a.* eleventh

onda, *f.* wave; *(fig.)* flicker (flames); *(sew.)* scallop; *(phys.)* wave; ripple; *pl.* waves (in hair). *(rad.)* **o. corta,** short wave. **o. etérea,** ether wave. **o. sonora,** sound wave

ondeado, *a.* undulating; wavy; scalloped

ondeante, *a.* waving; flowing

ondear, *v.i.* to wave; ripple; undulate; roll (of the sea); float, flutter, stream; *(sew.)* scallop; *v.r.* swing, sway

ondeo, *m.* waving; undulation

ondina, *f.* undine, water-sprite

ondulación, *f.* undulation; wave; wriggling; twisting. **o. permanente,** permanent wave

ondulado, *a.* wavy; undulating; scalloped

ondular, *v.i.* to writhe, squirm, wriggle; twist; coil; *v.t.* wave (hair)

oneroso, *a.* onerous, heavy; troublesome

ónice, *m.* *(min.)* onyx

onomástico, *a.* onomastic. **día o.,** saint's day

onomatopeya, *f.* onomatopœia

ontogenia, *f.* *(biol.)* ontogenesis

onza, *f.* ounce; *(zool.)* ounce. **por onzas,** by ounces; sparingly

onzavo, *a.* and *m.* eleventh

opacidad, *f.* opacity; obscurity; gloom

opaco, *a.* opaque; dark; gloomy, sad

opalescente, *a.* opalescent

opalino, *a.* opaline

ópalo, *m.* *(min.)* opal

opción, *f.* option; choice, selection; *(law)* option

ópera, *f.* opera

operación, *f.* *(surg.)* operation; execution, performance; *(com.)* transaction

operar, *v.t.* *(surg.)* to operate; *v.i.* act, have an effect; operate, control; *(com.)* transact

operario (-ia), *s.* worker, hand; operator; mechanic

opereta, *f.* operetta, light opera

opiata, *f.* *(med.)* opiate

opinar, *v.i.* to have or form an opinion, think; judge, consider

opinión, *f.* opinion, view; reputation

opio, *m.* opium. **fumadero de o.,** opium den

opiófago (-ga), *s.* opium-eater

opíparo, *a.* magnificent, sumptuous (banquets, etc.)

oponer, *v.t. irr.* to oppose; resist, withstand; protest against; *v.r.* oppose; be contrary or hostile (to); face, be opposite; object (to), set oneself against; compete (in public exams.). See **poner**

oporto, *m.* port wine

oportunidad, *f.* opportunity, occasion

oportunismo, *m.* opportunism

oportunista, *a.* and *m.* and *f.* opportunist

oportuno, *a.* opportune, timely

oposición, *f.* opposition; resistance; antagonism; public competitive exam. for post; *(ast., pol.)* opposition

opositor (-ra), *s.* opponent; competitor

opresión, *f.* oppression; hardship; pressure. **o. de pecho,** difficulty in breathing

opresor (-ra), *a.* oppressive. *s.* oppressor

oprimir, *v.t.* to oppress; treat harshly; press, crush; choke

oprobio, *m.* opprobrium

optar, *v.t.* to take possession of; *(with por)* choose

óptica, *f.* *(phys.)* optics; peepshow

óptico, *a.* optic, optical. *m.* optician

optimismo, *m.* optimism

optimista, *m.* and *f.* optimist. *a.* optimistic

óptimo, *a.* *sup.* **bueno,** best, optimum

opugnar, *v.t.* to resist violently; *(mil.)* assault, attack; impugn, challenge

opulencia, *f.* opulence, riches; excess, superabundance

opulento, *a.* opulent, rich

opúsculo, *m.* monograph, opuscule

oquedad, *f.* hollow, cavity; superficiality, banality

ora, *abb.* **ahora,** now

oración, *f.* oration, speech; prayer; (*gram.*) sentence

oráculo, *m.* oracle

orador (-ra), *s.* orator; speechmaker. *m.* preacher

oral, *a.* oral; verbal; buccal

orangután, *m.* (*zool.*) orangoutang

orar, *v.i.* to harangue, make an oration; pray; *v.t.* request, beg

orate, *m.* and *f.* lunatic

oratoria, *f.* oratory, eloquence

oratorio, *a.* oratorical. *m.* oratory, chapel; (*mus.*) oratorio

orbe, *m.* sphere; orb; world

órbita, *f.* (*ast.*) orbit; (*fig.*) sphere; (*anat.*) orbit, eye-socket

ordalía, *f.* (medieval hist.) ordeal

orden, *m.* or *f.* order, mode of arrangement; succession, sequence; group; system; orderliness, neatness; coherence, plan; (*ecc.*) order, brotherhood; (*zool.*, *bot.*) group, class; (*arch.*) order; (*math.*) degree. *f.* precept, command; (*com.*) order; *pl.* (*ecc.*) ordination. (*mil.*, *naut.*) o. de batalla, battle array. o. de caballería, Order of Knighthood. o. del día, order of the day. (*ecc.*) dar órdenes, to ordain. en o., in order; with regard (to). por su o., in its turn; successively

ordenación, *f.* order, orderly arrangement, disposition; ordinance, precept; (*ecc.*) ordination

ordenamiento, *m.* ordaining; ordinance; edict

ordenancista, *m.* (*mil.*) martinet; disciplinarian

ordenando, *m.* (*ecc.*) ordinand

ordenanza, *f.* order, method; command, instruction; ordinance, regulation (gen. *pl.*). *m.* (*mil.*) orderly

ordenar, *v.t.* to put in order, arrange; command, give instructions to; decree; direct, regulate; (*ecc.*) ordain; *v.r.* (*with de*) (*ecc.*) be ordained as

ordeñadero, *m.* milk pail

ordeñar, *v.t.* to milk

ordinal, *a.* ordinal. *m.* ordinal number

ordinariez, *f.* rudeness, uncouthness; vulgarity

ordinario, *a.* ordinary, usual; vulgar, coarse, uncultured; rude;

commonplace, average, mediocre. *m.* (*ecc.*) ordinary; carrier; courier. de o., usually, ordinarily

oréade, *f.* wood-nymph, oread

orear, *v.t.* to ventilate; *v.r.* dry; air; take the air

orégano, *m.* (*bot.*) wild marjoram

oreja, *f.* external ear; lug; tab, flap; tongue (of a shoe). (*fam.*) con las orejas caídas, down in the mouth, depressed

orejera, *f.* ear-flap; mould-board (of a plough)

orejudo, *a.* large or long-eared

oreo, *m.* zephyr; ventilation; airing

orfanato, *m.* orphanage, orphan asylum

orfandad, *f.* orphanhood; defencelessness, lack of protection

orfebre, *m.* gold- or silver-smith

orfebrería, *f.* gold or silver work

orfeón, *m.* choral society

organdí, *m.* organdie

orgánico, *a.* organic; harmonious; (*fig.*) organized

organillero(-ra), *s.* organ-grinder

organillo, *m.* barrel-organ

organismo, *m.* organism; organization, association

organista, *m.* and *f.* organist

organización, *f.* organization; order, arrangement

organizador (-ra), *a.* organizing. *s.* organizer

organizar, *v.t.* to organize; regulate; constitute

órgano, *m.* (*mus.*) organ; (*anat.*, *bot.*) organ; means, agency. o. de manubrio, barrel-organ

orgasmo, *m.* orgasm

orgía, *f.* orgy

orgullo, *m.* pride; arrogance

orgulloso, *a.* proud; haughty

orientación, *f.* orientation; exposure, prospect; bearings

oriental, *a.* oriental, eastern. *m.* an Oriental

orientalismo, *m.* orientalism

orientalista, *m.* and *f.* Orientalist

orientar, *v.t.* to orientate; *v.r.* find one's bearings; familiarize oneself (with)

oriente, *m.* Orient, the East; lustre (of pearls); youth, childhood; origin, source

orificio, *m.* (*anat.*) orifice; hole

oriflama, *f.* oriflamme; standard, flag

origen, *m.* origin, source, root; stock, extraction; reason, genesis. **dar o. a,** to give rise to. **país de o.,** native land

original, *a.* original; earliest, primitive; new, first-hand; novel, fresh; inventive, creative; eccentric; quaint. *m.* original manuscript; original; sitter (portraits); eccentric

originalidad, *f.* originality

originar, *v.t.* to cause, originate; set on foot; invent; *v.r.* spring from, originate (in)

originario, *a.* original, primary; primitive; native (of)

orilla, *f.* limit, edge; hem, border; selvage; shore, margin; bank (rivers, etc.); side-walk; brink, edge. **a la o.,** on the brink; nearly

orillar, *v.t.* to settle, arrange, conclude; *v.i.* reach the shore or bank; (*sew.*) leave a hem;.(*sew.*) border; leave a selvage on cloth

orillo, *m.* selvage (of cloth)

orín, *m.* rust; *pl.* urine

orinal, *m.* chamber-pot, urinal

orinar, *v.i.* to urinate

oriundo, *a.* native (of); derived (from)

orla, *f.* border, fringe; selvage (cloth, garments); ornamental border (on diplomas, etc.)

orlar, *v.t.* to border; edge, trim

ornamentación, *f.* ornamentation

ornamental, *a.* ornamental

ornamentar, *v.t.* to ornament; embellish

ornamento, *m.* ornament; decoration; gift, virtue, talent; *pl.* (*ecc.*) vestments

ornar, *v.t.* to ornament, adorn, embellish

ornato, *m.* decoration, ornament

ornitología, *f.* ornithology

ornitológico, *a.* ornithological

ornitólogo, *m.* ornithologist

oro, *m.* gold; gold coins or jewellery; (*fig.*) riches; *pl.* diamonds (cards). **o. batido,** gold leaf. **o. en polvo,** gold dust. (*fig.*) **como un o.,** shining with cleanliness. **el as de oros,** the ace of diamonds

orondo, *a.* hollow; (*fam.*) pompous; (*fam.*) swollen, spongy

oropel, *m.* brass foil; showy cheap thing; trinket; tinsel

oropéndola, *f.* (*orn.*) oriole

orquesta, *f.* orchestra

orquestación, *f.* orchestration

orquestal, *a.* orchestral

orquestar, *v.t.* to orchestrate

orquídea, *f.* (*bot.*) orchid

orquitis, *f.* (*med.*) orchitis

ortega, *f.* (*orn.*) grouse

ortiga, *f.* (*bot.*) nettle

orto, *m.* rising (of sun, stars)

ortocromático, *a.* (*phot.*) orthochromatic

ortodoxia, *f.* orthodoxy

ortodoxo, *a.* orthodox

ortografía, *f.* orthography

ortográfico, *a.* orthographical

ortopedia, *f.* orthopædics

ortopédico (-ca), *a.* orthopædic. *s.* orthopædist

ortopedista, *m.* and *f.* orthopædist

oruga, *f.* caterpillar

orzuelo, *m.* (*med.*) sty; trap (for wild animals)

os, *pers. pron., 2nd pl., m.* and *f., dat.* and *acc.* of **vos** and **vosotros,** you, to you

osa, *f.* (*zool.*) she-bear; (*ast.*) **o. mayor,** Great Bear; **o. menor,** Little Bear

osadía, *f.* boldness, audacity

osado, *a.* daring, bold

osamenta, *f.* skeleton; bones (of skeleton)

osar, *v.i.* to dare; risk, venture

osario, *m.* charnel-house, ossuary

oscilación, *f.* oscillation

oscilante, *a.* oscillating

oscilar, *v.i.* to oscillate, sway; hesitate, vacillate

ósculo, *m.* kiss, osculation

oscuridad, *f.* darkness; obscurity

oscuro, *a.* dark; obscure

óseo, *a.* osseous

osera, *f.* bear's den

osezno, *m.* bear cub

osificación, *f.* ossification

osificarse, *v.r.* to ossify

osmio, *m.* (*chem.*) osmium

ósmosis, *f.* (*phys., chem.*) osmosis

oso, *m.* (*zool.*) bear. **o. blanco,** polar bear

ostensible, *a.* ostensible; obvious

ostensión, *f.* show, display, manifestation

ostensivo, *a.* ostensive

ostentación, *f.* manifestation; ostentation

ostentar, *v.t.* to exhibit, show; boast, show off

ostentoso, *a.* magnificent, showy, ostentatious

osteología, *f.* osteology

osteópata, *m. and f.* osteopath

osteopatía, *f.* osteopathy

ostra, *f.* oyster. **vivero de ostras,** oyster bed

ostracismo, *m.* ostracism

otear, *v.t.* to observe; look on to

otero, *m.* hill, height, eminence

otología, *f.* otology

otólogo, *m.* otologist

otomana, *f.* ottoman, couch

otomano, *a.* Ottoman, Turkish

otoñal, *a.* autumnal

otoño, *m.* autumn

otorgamiento, *m.* granting; consent, approval; licence. award

otorgar, *v.t.* to grant; concede, approve; (*law*) grant, stipulate, execute

otro (-ra), *a.* other, another. *s.* another one

otrosí, *adv.* besides, moreover

ovación, *f.* ovation, triumph; applause

ovacionar, *v.t.* to applaud

oval, *a.* oval

óvalo, *m.* oval

ovario, *m.* (*anat. and bot.*) ovary

ovariotomía, *f.* (*surg.*) ovariotomy

oveja, *f.* ewe

ovejuno, *a.* relating to ewes or sheep, sheep-like

ovillar, *v.i.* to wind thread into a ball; *v.r.* curl up; huddle

ovillo, *m.* ball, bobbin (thread); tangled heap (of things)

ovíparo, *a.* oviparous

ovulación, *f.* (*med.*) ovulation

óvulo, *m.* ovule

oxálico, *a.* (*chem.*) oxalic

oxidación, *f.* (*chem.*) oxidation

oxidar, *v.t.* (*chem.*) oxidize; *v.r.* become oxidized

óxido, *m.* (*chem.*) oxide. **ó de carbono,** carbon monoxide. **ó de cinc,** zinc oxide

oxígeno, *m.* oxygen

oyente, *m. and f.* hearer; *pl.* audience

ozono, *m.* (*chem.*) ozone

P

pabellón, *m.* pavilion; colours, flag; bell-tent. **p. británico,** Union Jack. **en p.,** stacked (of arms)

pábulo, *m.* food; (*fig.*) pabulum

pacedero, *a.* (*agr.*) grazing, meadow

pacer, *v.i. irr.* (*agr.*) to graze; *v.t.* nibble away; eat away. See **nacer**

paciencia, *f.* patience

paciente, *a.* patient; long-suffering; complaisant (husband). *m. and f.* (*med.*) patient

pacienzudo, *a.* extremely patient or long-suffering

pacificación, *f.* pacification; serenity, peace of mind

pacificador (-ra), *a.* peacemaking; pacifying. *s.* peacemaker

pacificar, *v.t.* to pacify; *v.i.* make peace; *v.r.* grow quiet, become calm (sea, etc.)

pacífico, *a.* pacific, meek, mild; peace-loving, peaceful

pacifismo, *m.* pacifism

pacifista, *a. and m. and f.* pacifist

pacotilla, *f.* goods. (*fam.*) **hacer su p.,** to make one's packet or fortune. **ser de p.,** to be poor stuff; be jerry-built (of houses)

pactar, *v.t.* to stipulate, arrange; contract

pacto, *m.* agreement, contract; pact

padecer, *v.t. irr.* to suffer; feel keenly; experience, undergo; tolerate. See **conocer**

padecimiento, *m.* suffering

padrastro, *m.* stepfather; cruel father; (*fig.*) impediment, obstacle; hang-nail

padrazo, *m.* (*fam.*) indulgent father

padre, *m.* father; stallion; head (of family, etc.); (*ecc.*) father; genesis, source; author, creator; *pl.* parents; ancestors. **p. adoptivo,** foster father. **p. de familia, paterfamilias. P. Eterno,** Eternal Father, God. **p. nuestro,** Lord's Prayer. **P. Santo,** Holy Father, the Pope

padrear, *v.i.* to take after one's father; (*zool.*) reproduce, breed

padrino, *m.* godfather; sponsor; second (duels, etc.); patron; best man

padrón, *m.* census; pattern, model; memorial stone

paella, *f.* (*cul.*) savoury rice dish of shellfish, chicken and meat

paga, *f.* payment; amends, restitution; pay; payment of fine; reciprocity (in love, etc.)

pagadero, *a.* payable. *m.* date and place when payment·is due

pagador (-ra), *s.* payer. *m.* teller; wages clerk; paymaster

pagaduría, *f.* pay office

paganismo, *m.* paganism; heathenism

pagano (-na), *a.* and *s.* pagan; heathen

pagar, *v.t.* to pay; make restitution, expiate; return, requite (love, etc.); *v.r.* (*with de*) become fond of; be proud of. **p. adelantado**, to prepay. (*com.*) **p. al contado**, to pay cash

pagaré, *m.* (*com.*) promissory note, note of hand, I.O.U.

página, *f.* page (of book); episode, occurrence

paginación, *f.* pagination

paginar, *v.t.* to paginate

pago, *m.* payment; recompense, reward; region of vineyards, olive groves, etc.

pagoda, *f.* pagoda, temple; idol

paguro, *m.* hermit crab

pailebote, *m.* (*naut.*) schooner

país, *m.* country, nation; region; (*art*) landscape. **del p.**, typical of the country of origin (gen. food)

paisaje, *m.* countryside; landscape, scenery

paisajista, paisista, *m.* and *f.* (*art*) landscape painter

paisano (-na), *s.* compatriot; peasant; civilian

paja, *f.* straw; chaff; trash; (*fig.*) padding. **ver la p. en el ojo del vecino y no la viga en el nuestro**, to see the mote in our neighbour's eye and not the beam in our own

pajar, *m.* barn

pájara, *f.* hen bird; kite (toy); (*fam.*) jay; prostitute. **p. pinta**, game of forfeits

pajarear, *v.t.* to snare birds; loaf, idle about

pajarera, *f.* aviary

pajarero, *m.* bird catcher or vendor. *a.* (*fam.*) frivolous, giddy; (*fam.*) gaudy (colours)

pájaro, *m.* bird. **p. bobo**, penguin. **p. carpintero**, woodpecker. (*fig., fam.*) **p. gordo**, big gun. **p. mosca**, humming-bird

pajarota, *f.* (*fam.*) canard, false report

paje, *m.* buttons, page; (*naut.*) cabin boy

pajera, *f.* straw-loft

pajizo, *a.* made of straw; covered or thatched with straw; straw-coloured

pala, *f.* paddle; blade (of an oar); shovel; spade; baker's peel (long-handled shovel); cutting edge of spade, hoe, etc.; (*sport*) racquet; vamp, upper (of a shoe); pelota racquet; tanner's knife; (*fam.*) guile, cunning; cleverness, dexterity. **p. de hélice**, propeller blade. **p. para pescado**, fish server. (*fam.*) **corta p.**, ignoramus; blockhead

palabra, *f.* word; power of speech; eloquence; offer, promise; *pl.* magic formula, spell. **p. de clave**, code word. **p. de matrimonio**, promise of marriage. **palabras cruzadas**, cross-word puzzle. **bajo p. de**, under promise of. **cuatro palabras**, a few words; short conversation. **de p.**, verbally, by word of mouth. **dirigir la p. a**, to address, speak to. **faltar a su p.**, to break one's promise. **llevar la p.**, to be spokesman. **medias palabras**, half words; hint, insinuation. **tener la p.**, to have the right to speak (in meetings, etc.) (e.g. **El señor Martínez tiene la p.**, Mr. Martinez is going to speak)

palabrería, *f.* verbosity, wordiness

palabrota, *f.* (*fam.*) coarse language; long word

palaciego (-ga), *a.* pertaining to palaces; (*fig.*) courtesan. *s.* courtier

palacio, *m.* palace; mansion

palada, *f.* shovelful, spadeful; oar-stroke

paladar, *m.* (*anat.*) palate; taste; discernment, sensibility paladear, *v.t.* to taste with pleasure, savour; enjoy, relish

paladial, *a.* palatal

paladín, *m.* paladin

paladino, *a.* public, clear, open

paladio, *m.* (*min.*) palladium

palafrén, *m.* palfrey

palafrenero, *m.* groom; stable-boy

palanca, *f.* (*mech.*) lever; handle; bar; (high) diving board. **p. de arranque,** starting gear. **p. de cambio de velocidad,** gear-changing lever. **p. de mando,** (*aer.*) control stick

palangana, *f.* wash-basin

palanganero, *m.* wash-stand

palanqueta, *f. dim.* small lever; jemmy

palastro, *m.* sheet iron or steel

palatinado, *m.* Palatinate

palatino, *a.* palatine

palatizar, *v.t.* to palatilize

palazón, *f.* woodwork

palco, *m.* (*theat.*) box; stand, raised platform, enclosure. **p. de platea,** orchestra box

palenque, *m.* enclosure; stand; platform; palisade

paleografía, *f.* palæography

paleógrafo, *m.* palæographer

paleolítico, *a.* palæolithic

paleología, *f.* palæology

paleontología, *f.* palæontology

palestra, *f.* tilt yard

paleta, *f. dim.* little shovel; trowel; (*art*) palette; fire shovel; mason's trowel; (*anat.*) shoulder blade; blade (of propeller, ventilator, etc.); (*chem.*) spatula

paliación, *f.* palliation; excuse

paliar, *v.t.* to dissemble, excuse; palliate, mitigate

paliativo, *a.* palliative; extenuating

palidecer, *v.i. irr.* to turn pale. See **conocer**

palidez, *f.* pallor, paleness

pálido, *a.* pale, pallid

paliducho, *a.* somewhat pale, palish; sallow

palillo, *m. dim.* small stick; toothpick; bobbin (for lacemaking); drumstick; (*fig.*) chatter; *pl.* castanets

palimpsesto, *m.* palimpsest

palinodia, *f.* palinode. **cantar la p.,** to eat one's words, recant

palio, *m.* Greek mantle; cape; (*ecc.*) pallium; canopy, awning

palique, *m.* (*fam.*) chat. **estar de p.,** to be having a chat

paliquear, *v.i.* to chat

paliza, *f.* caning, beating

palizada, *f.* paling, fence; palisade, stockade. **p. de tablas,** hoarding

palma, *f.* palm tree; palm leaf; date palm; palm (of hand); hand; triumph. **llevarse la p.,** to bear away the palm; take the cake

palmada, *f.* slap; *pl.* hand-clapping

palmado, *a.* web (of feet); palmy

palmar, *a.* palmaceous; palmar; clear, obvious. *m* palm grove

palmatoria, *f.* ferule, ruler; candlestick

palmear, *v.i.* to clap hands

palmera, *f.* palm tree

palmeta, *f.* ferule, ruler

palmetazo, *m.* slap on the hand with a ferule; (*fig.*) slap in the face

palmípedo, *a.* (*zool.*) web-footed

palmo, *m.* span; hand's breadth

palmotear, *v.t.* to applaud; clap

palo, *m.* stick; rod; pole; timber, wood; wood log; (*naut.*) mast; blow with a stick; execution by hanging; suit (of playing cards); fruit-stalk; (*her.*) pale. **p. Campeche** *or* **p. de Campeche,** logwood. **p. de hule,** rubber tree. **p. de rosa,** tulip wood. (*naut.*) **p. mayor,** mainmast. (*naut.*) **a p. seco,** under bare poles. **De tal p., tal astilla,** A chip off the old block, Like father like son. **estar del mismo p.,** to be of the same way of thinking, agree

paloma, *f.* dove; pigeon; gentle person; *pl.* (*naut.*) white horses. **p. buchona,** pouter-pigeon. **p. mensajera,** carrier-pigeon. **p. torcaz,** wood-pigeon

palomar, *m.* dove-cot; pigeon-loft

palomero (-ra), *s.* pigeon fancier; pigeon dealer

palomino, *a.* young pigeon

palomo, *m.* male pigeon; wood pigeon

palotes, *m. pl.* drumsticks; pothooks (writing)

palpabilidad, *f.* palpability

palpable, *a.* palpable, tangible

palpación, *f.* (*med.*) palpation

palpar, *v.t.* to palpate, examine by touch; grope, walk by touch; (*fig.*) see clearly

palpitación, *f.* beating (of a heart); (*med.*) palpitation; convulsive movement

palpitante, *a.* palpitating; quivering; beating; (of a question) burning

palpitar, *v.i.* to beat (heart); throb, palpitate; shudder, move convulsively; (*fig.*) manifest itself (passions, etc.)

palpo, *m.* palp, feeler

palúdico, *a.* marshy, swampy; malarial

paludismo, *m.* (*med.*) paludism; malaria

palurdo (-da), *a.* (*fam.*) gross, rude, boorish. *s.* boor

palustre, *m.* mason's trowel. *a.* marshy, swampy

pamela, *f.* wide-brimmed straw sailor (woman's hat)

pamema, *f.* (*fam.*) unimportant trifle; (*fam.*) caress

pampa, *f.* pampa, treeless plain

pámpano, *m.* young vine shoot; vine leaf

pamplina, *f.* (*fam.*) nonsense, rubbish

pan, *m.* bread; loaf; (*cul.*) piecrust; (*fig.*) food; wheat; gold leaf; *pl.* cereals. **p. ázimo**, unleavened bread. **p. de oro**, gold leaf. **llamar al p. p. y al vino vino**, to call a spade a spade. **venderse como p. bendito**, to sell like hot cakes

pana, *f.* velveteen, velours

panacea, *f.* panacea; cure-all

panadería, *f.* bakery trade or shop; bakery, bakehouse

panadero (-ra), *s.* baker. *m. pl.* Spanish dance

panadizo, *m.* (*med.*) whitlow; (*fam.*) crock, ailing person

panal, *m.* honeycomb; wasp's nest

panameño (-ña), *a.* and *s.* native of Panama

panamericanismo, *m.* Pan-Americanism

panarra, *m.* (*fam.*) simpleton

páncreas, *m.* pancreas

pancreático, *a.* pancreatic

pancromático, *a.* (*chem.*) panchromatic

panda, *f.* gallery of a cloister. *m.* and *f.* (*zool.*) panda

pandémico, *a.* pandemic

pandemónium, *m.* pandemonium

pandereta, *f.* tambourine

pandero, *m.* tambourine; (*fam.*) windbag

pandilla, *f.* league, group; gang (of burglars, etc.); party, crowd, band

pane, *f.* (*aut.*) breakdown

panecillo, *m.* *dim.* roll (of bread)

panegírico, *a.* and *m.* panegyric

panegirista, *m.* panegyrist; eulogizer

panel, *m.* panel

panetela, *f.* (*cul.*) panada

pánfilo (-la), *a.* sluggish, phlegmatic, slow-moving. *s.* sluggard

panfleto, *m.* pamphlet

paniaguado, *m.* servant; favourite, protégé

pánico, *a.* and *m.* panic

panoja, *f.* (*bot.*) panicle; (*bot.*) ear, beard, awn

panoli, *a.* (*fam.*) doltish, stupid

panoplia, *f.* panoply; collection of arms

panorama, *m.* panorama; view

panorámico, *a.* panoramic

pantalón, *m.* trouser (gen. *pl.*); knickers. **p. de corte**, striped trousers. **pantalones bombachos**, plus fours

pantalla, *f.* lamp-shade; face screen; cinema screen; shade, reflector

pantano, *m.* marsh, swamp; impediment; artificial pool

pantanoso, *a.* marshy, swampy; (*fig.*) awkward, full of pitfalls

panteísmo, *m.* pantheism

panteísta, *a.* pantheistic. *m.* and *f.* pantheist

panteón, *m.* pantheon

pantera, *f.* (*zool.*) panther

pantógrafo, *m.* pantograph

pantomima, *f.* pantomime; mime

pantoque, *m.* (*naut.*) bilge

pantorrilla, *f.* (*anat.*) calf (of the leg)

pantuflo, *m.* house slipper

panza, *f.* paunch, stomach; belly (of jugs, etc.). (*fam.*) **un cielo de p. de burra**, a dark grey sky

panzudo, *a.* paunchy

pañal, *m.* infant's napkin; shirt tail; *pl.* long clothes, swaddling clothes; infancy

pañería, *f.* drapery stores; drapery

pañero (-ra), *s.* draper

paño, *m.* woollen material; cloth, fabric; drapery, hanging; tapestry; linen, bandage; tarnish or other mark; (*naut.*) canvas; (*sew.*) breadth, width (of cloth); panel (in a dress); floor-cloth, duster; livid mark on the face; *pl.* garments. **p. de lágrimas,** consoler, sympathizer. **p. mortuorio,** pall (on a coffin). **paños menores,** underwear. (*theat.*) **al p.,** from the wings, from without. (*fam.*) **poner el p. al púlpito,** to hold forth, spread oneself

pañol, *m.* (*naut.*) bunker, store room

pañoleta, *f.* kerchief, triangular scarf; fichu

pañuelo, *m.* kerchief; handkerchief

papa, *m.* pope; (*fam.*) papa, daddy. *f.* (*fam.*) potato; stupid rumour; nonsense; *pl.* pap; (*cul.*) sop; food

papá, *m.* (*fam.*) papa, daddy

papada, *f.* double chin; dewlap

papado, *m.* papacy

papagayo, *m.* (*orn.*) parrot

papamoscas, *m.* (*orn.*) flycatcher; (*fam.*) simpleton

papanatas, *m.* (*fam.*) simpleton

papar, *v.t.* to sip, take soft food; (*fam.*) eat; neglect, be careless about

paparrucha, *f.* (*fam.*) stupid rumour; nonsense

papel, *m.* paper; document; manuscript; (*theat.*) rôle, part; pamphlet; sheet of paper; paper, monograph, essay; guise, rôle; (*theat.*) character. **p. carbón,** carbon paper. **p. celofán,** Cellophane. **p. cuadriculado,** cartridge paper. **p. de calcar,** carbon paper; tracing-paper. **p. de escribir,** writing-paper. **p. de estaño,** tin-foil. **p. de estraza,** brown paper. **p. de fumar,** cigarette paper. **p. de lija,** emery- or sand-paper. **p. de paja de arroz,** rice paper. **p. de seda,** tissue-paper. **p. de tornasol,** litmus paper. **p. del estado,** Government bonds. **p. higiénico,** toilet-paper. **p.**

moneda, paper money. **p. pintado,** wall-paper. **p. secante,** blotting-paper. **p. sellado,** official stamped paper. **hacer buen** (*or* **mal**) **p.,** to do well (*or* badly). **hacer el p. (de),** (*theat.*) to act the part (of); feign, pretend

papelear, *v.i.* to turn over papers, search among them; (*fam.*) cut a dash

papelera, *f.* mass of papers; desk (for keeping papers)

papelería, *f.* heap of papers; stationer's shop; stationery

papelero (-ra), *a.* paper, stationery. *s.* paper maker; stationer

papeleta, *f.* slip or scrap of paper

papelista, *m.* paper maker; stationer; paper-hanger

papelucho, *m.* old or dirty piece of paper; trash, worthless writing; (*fam.*) rag (newspaper)

papera, *f.* (*med.*) mumps

papilar, *a.* papillary

papilla, *f.* pap; guile, wiliness

papillote, *m.* curl-paper

papiro, *m.* papyrus

papista, *a.* and *m.* and *f.* papist

papo, *m.* dewlap; gizzard (of a bird); goitre. **p. de cardo,** thistle-down

paquebote, *m.* (*naut.*) packet; mail boat; liner

paquete, *m.* packet; parcel, package

paquidermo, *m.* pachyderm

par, *a.* equal; alike; corresponding. *m.* pair, couple; team (of oxen, mules); peer (title); rafter (of a roof); (*mech.*) torque, couple; (*elec.*) cell. *f.* par. **a la p.,** jointly; simultaneously; (*com.*) at par. **a pares,** two by two. **de p. en p.,** wide-open (doors, etc.). **sin p.,** peerless, excellent

para, *prep.* in order to; for; to; for the sake of (e.g. **Lo hice p. ella,** I did it for her sake); enough to (gen. with *bastante,* etc.); in the direction of, towards; on the point of (e.g. **Está p. salir,** He is on the point of going out). Expresses:

1. *Purpose* (e.g. **La educan p. bailarina,** They are bringing her up to be a dancer. **Lo dije p. ver lo que harías,** I said it to

(in order to) see what you would do)

2. *Destination* (e.g. **Salió p. Londres,** He left for London)

3. *Use* (e.g. **seda p. medias,** silk for stockings. **un vaso p. flores,** a vase for flowers)

4. *An appointed time* (e.g. **Lo pagaré p. navidad,** I shall pay it at Christmas)

p. con, towards (a person) (e.g. **Ha obrado muy bien p. con mi hermano,** He has behaved very well towards my brother)

p. que, in order to, so that (e.g. **Lo puse en la mesa p. que lo vieses,** I put it on the table so that you should see it)

¿ P. qué ? Why? For what reason?

p. siempre, for ever. **decir p. sí,** to say to oneself. **sin qué ni p. qué,** without rhyme or reason

parábola, *f.* parable; (*geom.*) parabola

parabrisas, *m.* (*aut.*) wind-screen

paracaídas, *m.* (*aer.*) parachute

paracaidista, *m.* parachutist

paráclito, *m.* Paraclete

parachoques, *m.* (*aut.*) bumper; buffer (railway)

parada, *f.* stopping, halting; stop; stoppage, suspension; halt; (*mil.*) review; interval, pause; cattle-stall; dam; gambling stakes; parry (in fencing); relay of horses. **p. de coches,** taxi rank. **p. de tranvía,** tram stop. **p. discrecional,** request stop (buses, etc.)

paradero, *m.* railway station; stopping place; end, conclusion; whereabouts

paradisíaco, *a.* paradisiac

parado, *a.* still; indolent, lazy; unoccupied, leisured; silent, reserved; timid; unemployed

paradoja, *f.* paradox

paradójico, *a.* paradoxical

parador, *m.* inn, tavern, hostelry

parafina, *f.* (*chem.*) paraffin

parafinar, *v.t.* to paraffin

parafrasear, *v.t.* to paraphrase

paráfrasis, *f.* paraphrase

paraguas, *m.* umbrella

paraguayo (-ya), *a.* and *s.* Paraguayan

paragüería, *f.* umbrella shop

paragüero (-ra), *s.* umbrella maker or seller. *m.* umbrella stand

paraíso, *m.* paradise; garden of Eden; heaven; (*fam., theat.*) gallery, gods

paraje, *m.* place, locality, spot; state, condition

paralela, *f.* (*mil.*) parallel; *pl.* parallel bars (for gymnastic exercises)

paralelismo, *m.* parallelism

paralelo, *a.* parallel; analogous; similar. *m.* parallel, similarity; (*geog.*) parallel

paralelogramo, *m.* (*geom.*) parallelogram

parálisis, *f.* paralysis

paralítico (-ca), *a.* and *s.* paralytic

paralización, *f.* paralysis; cessation; (*com.*) dullness, quietness

paralizar, *v.t.* to paralyze; stop

paramento, *m.* ornament; trappings (of a horse); face (of a wall); facing (of a building). **paramentos sacerdotales,** liturgical vestments or ornaments

páramo, *m.* paramo, treeless plain; desert, wilderness

parangón, *m.* comparison; similarity

parangonar, *v.t.* to compare

paraninfo, *m.* (*arch.*) paranymph, university hall; best man (weddings); messenger of good

paranoico, *m.* paranoiac

parapetarse, *v.r.* to shelter behind a parapet; take refuge behind

parapeto, *m.* (*arch.* and *mil.*) parapet

parapoco, *m.* and *f.* (*fam.*) ninny, numskull

parar, *v.i.* to stop, halt; end, finish; lodge; come into the hands of; *v.t.* stop; detain; prepare; bet, stake; point (game dogs); parry (fencing); *v.r.* halt; be interrupted. **p. mientes en,** to notice; consider. **sin p.,** immediately, at once; without stopping

pararrayos, *m.* lightning-conductor

parasitario, parasítico, *a.* parasitic

parásito, *m.* parasite; (*fig.*) sponger; *pl.* (*rad.*) interference. *a.* parasitic

parasitología, *f.* parasitology

parasol, *m.* sunshade; (*bot.*) umbel

paratifoidea, *f.* paratyphoid

parca, *f.* Fate; (*poet.*) death. **las Parcas,** the Three Fates

parcela, *f.* plot, parcel (of land); atom, particle

parcial, *a.* partial, incomplete; biassed, prejudiced; factional, party; participatory

parcialidad, *f.* partiality, bias, prejudice; party, faction, group; intimacy, friendship

parco, *a.* scarce, scanty; temperate, moderate; frugal

parche, *m.* (*med.*) plaster; (*aut.*) patch; drum; drum-head, parchment of drum; patch, mend

¡pardiez! *interj.* (*fam.*) By gad!

pardo, *a.* brown; grey, drab, dun-coloured; cloudy, dark; husky (voices). *m.* leopard

pardusco, *a.* greyish; fawnish

parear, *v.t.* to pair, match; put in pairs; compare

parecer, *v.i. irr.* to appear; look, seem; turn up (be found). *impers.* believe, think (e.g. **Me parece,** It seems to me, I think, My opinion is); *v.r.* look alike, resemble one another. **See conocer**

parecer, *m.* opinion, belief; appearance, looks

parecido, *a.* (*with bien or mal*) good or bad looking. *m.* resemblance

pared, *f.* wall; partition wall; side, face. **p. maestra,** main wall. **p. medianera,** party-wall. **Las paredes oyen,** Walls have ears. (*fam.*) **pegado a la p.,** confused, taken aback

pareja, *f.* pair; dance partner; couple. **parejas mixtas,** mixed doubles (in tennis). **correr parejas or correr a las parejas,** to be equal; go together, happen simultaneously; be on a par

parejo, *a.* equal; similar; smooth, flat; even, regular

parénquima, *m.* (*bot., anat.*) parenchyma

parentela, *f.* relatives, kindred; parentage

parentesco, *m.* kinship; relationship; affinity; (*fig.*) connection, link

paréntesis, *m.* parenthesis; digression. **entre p.,** incidentally

paresa, *f.* peeress

paria, *m.* and *f.* pariah; outcast

parida, *a.* (*f.*) newly-delivered of child

paridad, *f.* parity; analogy, similarity

pariente (-ta), *s.* relative, relation; (*fam.*) husband (wife)

parihuela, *f.* hand-barrow; stretcher

parir, *v.t.* to give birth to; (*fig.*) bring forth; reveal, publish; *v.i.* lay eggs

parisiense, *a.* and *m.* and *f.* Parisian

parisílabo, *a.* parisyllabic

parla, *f.* speech; loquaciousness, eloquence; verbiage

parlamentar, *v.i.* to converse; discuss (contracts, etc.); (*mil.*) parley

parlamentario, *a.* parliamentarian. *m.* member of parliament

parlamentarismo, *m.* parliamentarianism

parlamento, *m.* legislative assembly; parliament; discourse, speech; (*theat.*) long speech; (*mil.*) parley

parlanchín, *a.* (*fam.*) talkative, chattering, loquacious

parlar, *v.t.* and *v.i.* to speak freely or easily; chatter; reveal, speak indiscreetly; babble (of streams, etc.)

parlero, *a.* talkative; gossiping, indiscreet; talking (birds); (*fig.*) expressive (eyes, etc.); prattling, babbling (brook, etc.)

parlotear, *v.i.* (*fam.*) to chatter, gossip

parloteo, *m.* chattering, gossip

parmesano (-na), *a.* and *s.* Parmesan

parnaso, *m.* Parnassus; verse anthology

paro, *m.* (*fam.*) stoppage of work; lock-out; (*orn.*) tit. **p. forzoso,** unemployment

parodia, *f.* parody

parodiar, *v.t.* to parody

parodista, *m.* and *f.* parodist

parótida, *f.* (*anat.*) parotid gland; (*med.*) parotitis, mumps

parotiditis, *f.* parotitis, mumps

paroxismo, *m.* (*med.*) paroxysm; frenzy, ecstasy, fit

parpadear, v.i. to blink

parpadeo, m. blinking

párpado, m. eyelid

parque, m. park; depôt, park; paddock, pen. p. de atracciones, pleasure-ground. p. de (or para) automóviles, car park

parquedad, f. scarcity; moderation, temperance; parsimony, frugality

parra, f. vine. hoja de p., (fig.) fig-leaf

párrafo, m. paragraph; (gram.) paragraph sign. p. aparte, new paragraph. echar un p., to chat, gossip

parranda, f. (fam.) binge; strolling orchestra. ir de p., to go on the binge

parricida, m. and f. parricide (person)

parricidio, m. parricide (act)

parrilla, f. (cul.) griller, broiler; grill, gridiron; (eng.) grate. (cul.) a la p., grilled

párroco, m. parish priest; parson

parroquia, f. parish church; parish; clergy of a parish; clientèle, customers

parroquial, a. parochial

parroquiano (-na), a. parochial. s. parishioner; client, customer

parsi, m. Parsee; Parseeism, religion of Parsees

parsimonia, f. frugality, thrift; prudence, moderation

parsimonioso, a. parsimonious

parte, f. part; share; place; portion; side, faction; (law) party; (theat.) part, rôle. m. communication, message; telegraph or telephone message; (mil., nav.) communiqué. f. pl. parts, talents. p. actora, (law) prosecution. p. de la oración, part of speech. partes litigantes, (law) contending parties. dar p., to notify; (mil., naut.) report; give a share (in a transaction). de algún tiempo a esta p., for some time past. de p. de, in the name of, from. en p., partly. por todas partes, on all sides, everywhere. ser p. a or ser p. para que, to contribute to. tener de su p. (a), to count on the favour of. la quinta p., one-fifth, etc.

partear, v.i. to assist in childbirth

partenogénesis, f. parthenogenesis

partera, f. midwife

partero, m. accoucheur

partición, f. partition, distribution; (aer., naut.) accommodation

participación, f. participation; notice, warning; announcement (of an engagement, etc.); (com.) share

participante, a. and m. and f. participant

participar, v.i. to participate, take part (in), share; v.t. inform; announce (an engagement, etc.)

participe, a. sharing. m. and f. participant

participio, m. (gram.) participle

partícula, f. particle, grain; (gram.) particle

particular, a. private; peculiar; special, particular; unusual; individual. m. and f. private individual. m. matter, subject. en p., especially; privately

particularidad, f. individuality; speciality; rareness, unusualness; detail, circumstance; intimacy, friendship

particularizar, v.t. to detail, particularize; single out, choose; v.r. (with en) be characterized by

partida, f. departure; entry, record (of birth, etc.); certificate (of marriage, etc.); (com.) item; (com.) lot, allowance; (mil.) guerrilla; armed band; expedition, excursion; game (of cards, etc.); rubber (at bridge, etc.); (fam.) conduct, behaviour; place, locality; death. (com.) p. doble, double entry. Las siete Partidas, Code of Spanish laws compiled by Alfonso X (1252–84)

partidarismo, m. partisanship

partidario (-ia), a. partisan. s. adherent, disciple. m. partisan, guerrilla

partido, m. party, group, faction; profit; (sport) match; team; agreement, pact. p. conservador, (pol.) Conservative party. p. obrero or p. laborista, (pol.) Labour party. buen p. (fig.) good match, catch. sacar p. de, to take advantage of, make the most of. tomar p., to enlist; join, become a supporter (of)

partidor, *m.* divider, apportioner; cleaver, chopper; hewer

partir, *v.t.* to divide; split; crack, break; separate; (*math.*) divide; *v.i.* go, depart; start (from); *v.r.* disagree, become divided; leave, depart

partitivo, *a.* partitive

partitura, *f.* (*mus.*) score

parto, *m.* parturition, birth; newborn child; (*fig.*) creation, offspring; important event

parturienta, *a.* (*f.*) and *f.* parturient

parva, *f.* light breakfast; threshed or unthreshed grain; heap, mass

parvedad, *f.* smallness; scarcity; light breakfast (taken on fast days)

parvo, *a.* little, small

párvulo (-la), *s.* child. *a.* small; innocent, simple; lowly, humble. **escuela de párvulos,** infant school

pasa, *f.* raisin; (*naut.*) channel; passage, flight (of birds). **p. de Corinto,** currant

pasacalle, *m.* (*mus.*) gay, popular march

pasada, *f.* passing, passage; money sufficient to live on; passage, corridor. **dar p.,** to let pass, put up with. (*fam.*) **mala p.,** bad turn, dirty trick

pasadera, *f.* stepping stone

pasadero, *a.* passable, traversable; fair (health); tolerable, passable. *m.* stepping stone

pasadizo, *m.* narrow corridor or passage; alley, narrow street; (*naut.*) alley-way

pasado, *m.* past; *pl.* ancestors. **lo p., p.,** What's past is past

pasador, *m.* bolt, fastener; (*mech.*) pin, coupler; hair-slide; pin (of brooches, etc.); colander; (*naut.*) marlin-spike; shirt stud

pasajaretas, *m.* bodkin

pasaje, *m.* passing; passage; fare; passage money; (*naut.*) complement of passengers; channel, strait; (*mus., lit.*) passage; (*mus.*) modulation, transition (of voice); voyage; passage; covered way; road

pasajero (-ra), *a.* crowded, public (thoroughfares); transitory, fugitive; passing; temporary. *s.* passenger

pasamanería, *f.* passementerie work, industry or shop

pasamano, *m.* passementerie; banister, hand-rail; (*naut.*) gangway

pasante, *a.* (*her.*) passant. *m.* pupil teacher; articled clerk; apprentice; student. **p. de pluma,** solicitor's clerk

pasaporte, *m.* passport; licence, permission. **dar el p. (a),** (*fam.*) to give the sack (to)

pasar, *v.t.* to pass; carry, transport; cross over; send; go beyond, overstep; run through, pierce; upset; overtake; transfer; suffer, undergo; sieve; study; dry (grapes, etc.); smuggle; surpass; omit; swallow (food); approve; dissemble; transform; spend (time); *v.i.* pass; be transferred; be infectious; have sufficient to live on; cease; last; die; pass away; pass (at cards); be transformed; be current (money); be salable (goods); (*with prep.*) (*with a + infin.*) begin to; (*with por*) pass as; have a reputation as; visit; (*with sin*) do without. *impers.* happen, occur. *v.r.* end; go over to another party; forget; go stale or bad; (*fig.*) go too far, overstep the mark; permeate. **p. por alto (de),** to omit, overlook. **p. de largo,** to go by without stopping. **pasarse de listo,** to be too clever. **¡No pases cuidado!** Don't worry!

pasarela, *f.* gang-plank

pasatiempo, *m.* pastime, hobby, amusement

pasavante, *m.* (*naut.*) safe-conduct; navicert

pascua, *f.* Passover; Easter; Christmas; Twelfth Night; Pentecost; *pl.* twelve days of Christmas. **P. florida,** Easter Sunday. **dar las pascuas,** to wish a merry Christmas. **¡Felices pascuas!** Merry Christmas!

pascual, *a.* Paschal

pase, *m.* pass (with the hands and in football, etc.); safe-conduct; free pass; thrust (in fencing)

paseante, *m.* and *f.* stroller, promenader, passer-by

pasear, *v.t.* to take a walk; parade up and down, display;

v.i. take a walk; go for a drive; go for a ride (on horseback, etc.); stroll up and down; *v.r.* touch upon lightly, pass over; loaf, be idle; drift; float

paseo, *m.* walk, stroll; drive; outing, expedition; promenade; boulevard. **p. a caballo,** ride on horseback

pasiega, *f.* wet-nurse

pasillo, *m.* gallery; corridor; lobby; railway corridor; (*sew.*) basting stitch

pasión, *f.* suffering; passivity; passion; desire; (*ecc.*) passion. **con p.,** passionately

pasional, *a.* passionate; of passion

pasionaria, *f.* passion-flower

pasiva, *f.* (*gram.*) passive

pasividad, *f.* passivity

pasivo, *a.* passive; inactive; (*com.*) sleeping (partner); (*gram.*) passive. *m.* (*com.*) liabilities

pasmar, *v.t.* to freeze to death (plants); dumbfound, amaze, stun; chill; *v.r.* be stunned or amazed

pasmo, *m.* amazement, astonishment; wonder, marvel; (*med.*) tetanus, lockjaw

pasmoso, *a.* astounding, amazing; wonderful

paso, *a.* dried (fruit)

paso, *m.* step; pace; passage, passing; way; footstep; progress, advancement; passage (in a book); (*sew.*) tacking stitch; occurrence, event; (*theat.*) short play; gait, walk; strait, channel; migratory flight (birds); (*mech.*) pitch; event or scene from the Passion; armed combat; death; *pl.* measures, steps. *adv.* softly, in a low voice; gently. **p. a nivel,** level crossing. **p. a p.,** step by step. **p. doble,** quick march; Spanish dance. **p. volante,** (gymnastics) giant-stride. **a cada p.,** at every step; often. **al p.,** without stopping; on the way, in passing. **ceder el p.,** to allow to pass. **de p.,** in passing; incidentally. **llevar el p.,** to keep in step. **marcar el p.,** to mark time. **salir al p. (a),** to waylay, confront; oppose. **seguir los pasos (a),** to follow; spy upon

pasquín, *m.,* **pasquinada,** *f.* pasquinade, lampoon

pasta, *f.* (*cul.*) dough; paste; pastry; piecrust; batter; (*cul.*) noodle paste; paper pulp; board (bookbinding). **ser de buena p.,** to be good-natured

pastar, *v.t.* to take to pasture; *v.i.* graze, pasture

pastel, *m.* cake; (*art*) pastel; pie; (*fam.*) plot, secret understanding; cheating (at cards); (*print.*) pie; (*fam.*) fat, stocky person

pastelear, *v.i.* (*fam.*) to indulge in shady business (especially in politics)

pastelería, *f.* cake bakery; cake shop; confectioner's art; confectionery

pastelero (-ra), *s.* confectioner, pastry-cook; (*fig., fam.*) spineless person, jellyfish

pastelillo, *m.* (*cul.*) turnover

pastelista, *m.* and *f.* pastelist

pastelón, *m.* meat or game pie

pasteurización, *f.* pasteurization

pasteurizar, *v.t.* to pasteurize

pastilla, *f.* tablet, cake; lozenge; pastille, drop; tread (of a tyre)

pasto, *m.* grazing land, pasture; fodder; (*fig.*) fuel, food; spiritual food. **a p.,** in plenty, abundantly. **de p.,** of daily use

pastor (-ra), *s.* shepherd. *m.* (*ecc.*) pastor

pastoral, *a.* rustic, country; (*ecc.*) pastoral. *f.* pastoral poem; (*ecc.*) pastoral letter

pastorear, *v.t.* to graze, put to grass; (*ecc.*) have charge of souls

pastorela, *f.* (*poet., mus.*) pastoral

pastoreo, *m.* pasturage, grazing

pastoría, *f.* pastorate

pastoril, *a.* shepherd, pastoral

pastoso, *a.* doughy; mealy; pasty; mellow

pasturaje, *m.* pasturage

pata, *f.* paw and leg (animals); foot (of table, etc.); duck; (*fam.*) leg. **p. de gallo,** blunder; crow's-foot, wrinkle. **meter la p.,** to interfere, put one's foot in it. (*fam.*) **tener mala p.,** to be unlucky

patada, *f.* kick, stamp; (*fam.*) step, pace

patagón (-ona), *a.* and *s.* Patagonian

patalear, v.i. to stamp (with the feet)

pataleo, m. kicking; stamping

pataleta, f. (fam.) convulsion; feigned hysterics

patán, m. (fam.) yokel; boor, churl

patanería, f. (fam.) boorishness, churlishness

patarata, f. trash, useless thing; extravagant courtesy

patata, f. potato

patatal, patatar, m. potato patch

patatús, m. (fam.) petty worry; mishap; (med.) stroke, fit

patear, v.t. (fam.) to stamp; (fig.) walk on, treat badly; v.i. (fam.) stamp the feet; be furiously angry; (golf) putt

patena, f. engraved medal worn by country women; (ecc.) paten

patentar, v.t. to issue a patent; take out a patent, patent

patente, a. obvious, patent; f. patent; warrant, commission; letters patent. **p. de invención,** patent. **p. de sanidad,** clean bill of health

patentizar, v.t. to make evident

paternidad, f. paternity

paterno, a. paternal

patético, a. pitiable; pathetic, moving

patiabierto, a. (fam.) knock-kneed

patibulario, a. heartrending, harrowing

patíbulo, m. scaffold

paticojo, a. (fam.) lame; wobbly; unsteady

patilla, f. side whisker (gen. pl.); pl. old Nick, the Devil

patín, m. skate; runner (of a sledge); (aer. and of vehicles) skid; (mech.) shoe. **p. de ruedas,** roller skate

patinador (-ra), s. skater

patinaje, m. skating; skidding (of planes and vehicles)

patinar, v.i. to skate; slip, lose one's footing; skid (vehicles and planes)

patinazo, m. skid (of a vehicle)

patinete, m. child's scooter

patio, m. courtyard; (theat.) pit

patitieso, a. (fam.) paralyzed in the hands or feet; open-mouthed, amazed; stiff, unbending, proud

patituerto, a. crooked-legged; pigeon-toed; (fam.) lop-sided

patizambo, a. knock-kneed

pato, m. duck; (fam.) **pagar el p.,** to be a scapegoat

patógeno, a. (med.) pathogenic

patojo, a. waddling

patología, f. pathology

patológico, a. pathological

patólogo, m. pathologist

patoso, a. (fig.) heavy, pedestrian, tedious

patraña, f. nonsense, rubbish, fairy tale

patria, f. motherland, native country; native place. **p. chica,** native region

patriarca, m. patriarch

patriarcado, m. patriarchy

patriarcal, a. patriarchal

patricio (-ia), a. and s. patrician

patrimonio, m. patrimony

patriota, m. and f. patriot

patriótico, a. patriotic

patriotismo, m. patriotism

patrocinar, v.t. to protect, defend; favour, sponsor; patronize

patrocinio, m. protection, defence; sponsorship; patronage

patrón (-ona), s. patron, sponsor; patron saint; landlord; employer. m. coxswain; (naut.) master, skipper; pattern, model; standard. **p. de oro,** gold standard

patronato, m. patronage, protection; employers' association; charitable foundation. **P. de Turismo,** Tourist Bureau

patronímico, a. and m. patronymic

patrono (-na), s. protector; sponsor; patron; patron saint; employer

patrulla, f. (mil.) patrol; group, band

patrullar, v.i. (mil.) patrol; march about

patudo, a. (fam.) large-footed

paulatinamente, adv. slowly, by degrees

pauperismo, m. destitution, pauperism

paupérrimo, a. sup. pobre, exceedingly poor

pausa, f. pause, interruption; delay; (mus.) rest; (mus.) pause. **a. pausas,** intermittently

pausado, a. deliberate, slow. adv. slowly, deliberately

pausar, *v.i.* to pause
pauta, *f.* standard, norm, design; (*fig.*) guide, model
pavada, *f.* flock of turkeys
pavana, *f.* pavan, stately dance
pavero (-ra), *a.* vain; strutting. *s.* turkey keeper or vendor. *m.* broad-brimmed Andalusian hat
pavimentación, *f.* paving, flagging
pavimento, *m.* pavement
pavo (-va), *s.* (*orn.*) turkey. **p. real**, peacock. (*fam.*) **pelar la pava**, to serenade, court
pavón, *m.* (*orn.*) peacock; peacock butterfly; preservative paint (for steel, etc.); gun-metal
pavonear, *v.i.* to strut, peacock (also *v.r.*); (*fam.*) hoodwink, dazzle
pavor, *m.* terror, panic
pavoroso, *a.* fearful, awesome, dreadful
payasada, *f.* clowning, practical joke; clown's patter
payaso, *m.* clown
paz, *f.* peace; harmony, concord; peaceableness. ¡**P. sea en esta casa!** Peace be upon this house! (salutation). **estar en p.,** to be at peace; be quits, be even. **poner** (*or* **meter**) **p.,** to make peace (between dissentients). **venir de p.,** to come with peaceful intentions
pazguato (-ta), *s.* simpleton, booby
pazpuerca, *f.* slattern
pe, *f.* name of the letter P. (*fam.*) **de pe a pa**, from beginning to end
peaje, *m.* toll (on bridges, roads, etc.)
peana, *f.* base; pedestal
peatón, *m.* pedestrian; walker; country postman
pebete, *m.* joss-stick; fuse; (*fam.*) stench
peca, *f.* mole, freckle
pecado, *m.* sin; fault; excess; defect; (*fam.*) the Devil. **p. capital**, mortal sin
pecador, *a.* sinful. *m.* sinner. ¡**P. de mí!** Poor me!
pecadora, *f.* sinner; (*fam.*) prostitute
pecaminoso, *a.* sinful
pecar, *v.i.* to sin; trespass, transgress; (*with de*) be too ... (e.g. **El**

libro peca de largo, The book is too long)
peceño, *a.* pitch-black (horses, etc.); tasting of pitch
pecera, *f.* goldfish bowl; aquarium
pecio, *m.* flotsam
pécora, *f.* sheep, head of sheep; wily woman, serpent
pecoso, *a.* freckled; spotted (with warts)
pectina, *f.* (*chem.*) pectin
pecuario, *a.* (*agr.*) stock; cattle
peculiar, *a.* peculiar, individual
peculiaridad, *f.* peculiarity
peculio, *m.* private money or property
pecunia, *f.* (*fam.*) cash
pecuniario, *a.* pecuniary
pechera, *f.* shirt front; chest protector; bib, tucker; shirt-frill; (*fam.*) bosom
pecho, *m.* (*anat.*) chest; breast; bosom; mind, conscience; courage, endurance; (*mus.*) quality (of voice); incline, slope. **p. arriba**, uphill. **abrir su p. a** (*or* **con**), to unbosom oneself to. **dar el p.** (a), to suckle. **de pechos**, leaning on. **echar el p. al agua**, (*fig.*) to embark courageously upon. **tomar a pechos** (una cosa), to take (a thing) very seriously; take to heart
pechuga, *f.* breast (of a bird); (*fam.*) breast, bosom; slope, incline
pedagogía, *f.* education, pedagogy
pedagógico, *a.* educational, pedagogic
pedagogo, *m.* schoolmaster; educationalist; (*fig.*) mentor
pedal, *m.* (*mech.*) treadle, lever; (*mus.*) pedal; (*mus.*) sustained harmony. (*aut.*) **p. de embrague**, clutch pedal
pedalear, *v.i.* to pedal
pedante, *a.* pedantic. *m.* and *f.* pedant
pedantería, *f.* pedantry
pedazo, *m.* bit, piece; lump; fragment, portion. (*fam.*) **p. del alma, p. del corazón, p. de las entrañas**, loved one, dear one. **a pedazos** *or* **en pedazos**, in pieces, in bits. **hacer pedazos**, to break into fragments

pedernal, *m.* flint, silex; anything very hard

pedestal, *m.* pedestal; base; stand; (*fig.*) foundation

pedestre, *a.* pedestrian; dull, uninspired

pediatra, *m.* and *f.* pediatrician

pedicuro, *m.* chiropodist

pedido, *m.* (*com.*) order; request, petition

pedigüeño, *a.* importunate, insistent

pedimento, *m.* petition, demand; (*law*) claim; (*law*) motion

pedir, *v.t. irr.* to ask, request; (*com.*) order; demand; necessitate; desire; ask in marriage. **p. en juicio,** (*law*) to bring an action against. (*fam.*) **pedírselo (a uno) el cuerpo,** to desire (something) ardently. **a p. de boca,** according to one's wish. *Pres. Part.* **pidiendo.** *Pres. Ind.* **pido, pides, pide, piden.** *Preterite* **pidió, pidieron.** *Pres. Subjunc.* **pida,** etc. *Imperf. Subjunc.* **pidiese,** etc.

pedo, *m.* fart

pedómetro, *m.* pedometer

pedrada, *f.* casting a stone; blow with a stone; innuendo

pedrea, *f.* stone throwing; fight with stones; shower of hailstones

pedregal, *m.* stony ground

pedregoso, *a.* stony

pedrera, *f.* stone-quarry

pedrería, *f.* precious stones

pedrisco, *m.* hailstone; shower of stones; pile of stones

pedrusco, *m.* (*fam.*) rough, unpolished stone

pedúnculo, *m.* (*bot.*) peduncle, stalk

pega, *f.* sticking; cementing; joining; pitch; varnish; (*fam.*) joke; beating; (*orn.*) magpie

pegadizo, *a.* sticky, gummy, adhesive; detachable, removable; (*fig.*) clinging, importunate (of people)

pegado, *m.* sticking-plaster; patch

pegajoso, *a.* sticky, gluey; viscid; contagious, catching; (*fam.*) oily, unctuous; (*fig., fam.*) cadging, sponging

pegar, *v.t.* to stick; cement; join, fasten; press (against); infect with (diseases); hit, strike; give

(a shout, jump, etc.); patch; *v.i.* spread, catch (fire, etc.); (*fig.*) make an impression, have influence; be opportune; *v.r.* (*cul.*) stick, burn; meddle; become enthusiastic about; take root in the mind. **p. un tiro** (a). to shoot

pegaso, *m.* (*ast.*) Pegasus

pegote, *m.* sticking-plaster; (*fig., fam.*) sponger; (*fam.*) patch

peinado, *m.* hairdressing or style; head-dress. *a.* (*fam.*) effeminate, over-elegant (men); over-careful (style). **un p. al agua,** a finger-wave

peinador (**-ra**), *m.* peignoir, dressing gown. *s.* hairdresser

peinadura, *f.* brushing or combing of hair; *pl.* hair combings

peinar, *v.t.* to comb, dress the hair; card (wool); cut away (rock)

peine, *m.* comb; (*mech.*) hackle, reed; instep; (*fam.*) crafty person

peinería, *f.* comb factory or shop

peinero, *m.* comb manufacturer or seller

peineta, *f.* high comb (for mantillas, etc.)

peladilla, *f.* sugared almond; smooth, small pebble

pelado, *a.* plucked; bare, unadorned; needy, poor; hairless; skinned; peeled; without shell; treeless

peladura, *f.* peeling; shelling; skinning; plucking (feathers)

pelafustán, *m.* (*fam.*) good-for-nothing, scamp

pelagatos, *m.* (*fam.*) miserable wretch

pelágico, *a.* pelagian, oceanic

pelagra, *f.* (*med.*) pellagra

pelaje, *m.* fur, wool

pelamesa, *f.* brawl, fight; lock, tuft (of hair)

pelapatatas, *m.* potato peeler

pelar, *v.t.* to tear out or cut the hair; pluck; skin; peel; shell; rob, fleece; *v.r.* lose one's hair

peldaño, *m.* step, stair, tread, rung

pelea, *f.* battle; quarrel, dispute; fight (among animals); effort, exertion; (*fig.*) struggle

peleador, *a.* fighting; quarrelsome, aggressive

pelear, *v.i.* to fight; quarrel; struggle, strive; *v.r.* come to blows; fall out, become enemies

pelechar, *v.i.* to get a new coat (animals); grow new feathers (birds); (*fam.*) prosper, flourish; grow well

pelele, *m.* guy, effigy; (*fam.*) nincompoop

peletería, *f.* furriery; fur shop

peletero, *m.* furrier; skinner

peliagudo, *a.* long-haired (animals); (*fam.*) complicated, difficult; wily, downy

peliblanco, *a.* white-haired

pelícano, *m.* (*orn.*) pelican

pelicorto, *a.* short-haired

película, *f.* film. **p. fotográfica,** roll-film. **p. sonora,** sound film

peligrar, *v.i.* to be in danger

peligro, *m.* danger, peril. **correr p.** *or* **estar en p.,** to be in danger

peligroso, *a.* dangerous, perilous, risky

pelilargo, *a.* long-haired

pelirrojo, *a.* red-haired

pelmazo, *m.* squashed mass; (*fam.*) idler, sluggard; (*fam.*) bore

pelo, *m.* hair; down (on birds and fruit); fibre, filament; hair-trigger (fire-arms); hairspring (watches); kiss (in billiards); nap (of cloth), grain (of wood); flaw (in gems); raw silk. **p. a la garçonne,** Eton crop. **p. de camello,** camel's hair. **a p.,** in the nude; without hat; opportunely. **en p.,** bareback (of horses). **hacerse el p.,** to do one's hair; have one's hair cut. (*fam.*) **no tener p. de tonto,** to be smart, clever. (*fam.*) **no tener pelos en la lengua,** to be outspoken. (*fam.*) **tomar el p. (a),** to pull a person's leg. **venir a p.,** to be apposite; come opportunely

pelón, *a.* hairless; (*fig., fam.*) broke, fleeced

pelonería, *f.* (*fam.*) poverty, misery

peloponense, *a.* and *m.* and *f.* Peloponnesian

pelota, *f.* ball; ball game; (*sport*) pelota. **p. base,** baseball. **p. vasca,** pelota. **en p.,** stark naked

pelotari, *m.* professional pelota player

pelotazo, *m.* knock or blow with a ball

pelotear, *v.t.* to audit accounts;

v.i. play ball; throw, cast; quarrel; argue

pelotera, *f.* (*fam.*) brawl

pelotón, *m.* big ball; lump of hair; crowd, multitude; (*mil.*) platoon. **p. de castigo,** fatigue-party. **p. de ejecución,** firing-squad

peltre, *m.* pewter

peluca, *f.* wig; periwig; (*fam.*) wigging, scolding

peludo, *a.* hairy. *m.* long-haired rug

peluquería, *f.* hairdressing establishment; hairdressing trade

peluquero (-ra), *s.* hairdresser

peluquín, *m.* small wig, top wig; bag wig

pelusa, *f.* down, soft hair; fluff, nap

pelviano, pélvico, *a.* (*anat.*) pelvic

pelleja, *f.* hide, skin (of animals); sheepskin

pellejo, *m.* hide; pelt; skin; wineskin; (*fam.*) drunkard, winebag; peel, skin (of fruit)

pelliza, *f.* fur or fur-trimmed coat

pellizcar, *v.t.* to pinch, tweak, nip; pilfer

pellizco, *m.* pinch, nip, tweak; pilfering, pinching; bit, pinch

pena, *f.* punishment, penalty; grief; pain, suffering; difficulty, trouble; mourning veil; hardship; anxiety; embarrassment; tail feather. **p. capital** *or* **p. de la vida,** capital punishment. **a duras penas,** with great difficulty. **so p. de,** under penalty of. **valer** (*or* **merecer**) **la p.,** to be worth while

penable, *a.* punishable

penacho, *m.* topknot, crest (birds); plume, panache; (*fam.*) pride, arrogance

penado (-da), *a.* difficult, laborious; painful, troubled, afflicted. *s.* convict

penal, *a.* penal; punitive

penalidad, *f.* trouble, labour, difficulty; (*law*) penalty

penar, *v.t.* to penalize; punish; *v.i.* suffer; undergo purgatorial pains; *v.r.* suffer anguish. **p. por,** to long for

penca, *f.* (*bot.*) fleshy leaf; lash, strap, cat-o'-nine-tails

penco, *m.* (*fam.*) wretched nag

pendejo, *m.* pubic hair; (*fam.*) poltroon

pendencia, *f.* fight; quarrel

pendenciar, *v.i.* to fight; quarrel

pendenciero, *a.* quarrelsome, aggressive

pender, *v.i.* to hang; depend; be pending

pendiente, *a.* pending; hanging; (*com.*) outstanding. *m.* earring; pendant. *f.* slope, incline; gradient

péndola, *f.* feather, plume; quill pen; pendulum (of clock)

pendolista, *m.* and *f.* calligraphist

pendolón, *m.* king-post

pendón, *m.* pennon, banner; (*bot.*) shoot; (*fam.*) lanky, slatternly woman; *pl.* reins

péndulo, *a.* pendulous, hanging. *m.* pendulum

pene, *m.* (*anat.*) penis

penetrabilidad, *f.* penetrability

penetración, *f.* penetration; understanding, perspicuity; sagacity, shrewdness

penetrador, *a.* penetrating, perspicacious; sagacious, acute

penetrante, *a.* penetrating; deep; piercing (of sounds); acute, shrewd

penetrar, *v.t.* to penetrate; permeate; master, comprehend; (*with en*) enter

penetrativo, *a.* piercing

penicilina, *f.* (*med.*) penicillin

península, *f.* peninsula

penique, *m.* penny

penitencia, *f.* penitence, repentance; penance

penitencial, *a.* penitential

penitenciaria, *f.* penitentiary

penitenciario, *a.* penitentiary

penitente, *a.* penitent, repentant. *m.* and *f.* penitent

penol, *m.* (*naut.*) yard-arm

penoso, *a.* laborious, difficult; grievous; painful; troublesome; (*fam.*) foppish

pensado, *a.* premeditated, deliberate. **de p.**, intentionally. **mal p.**, malicious, evil-minded

pensador, *a.* thinking; pensative. *m.* thinker

pensamiento, *m.* mind; thought; idea; suspicion, doubt; heartsease pansy; maxim; intention, project

pensar, *v.t. irr.* to think; purpose, intend; (*with en, sobre*) reflect upon; think about; *v.i.* feed (animals). **p. entre sí**, **p. para consigo** *or* **p. para sí**, to think to oneself. See **acertar**

pensativo, *a.* reflective, pensative

pensil, *a.* hanging. *m.* hanging garden; delightful garden

pensilvano (-na), *a.* and *s.* Pennsylvanian

pensión, *f.* pension, allowance; boarding-house, private hotel; scholarship grant; cost of board; trouble, drudgery

pensionado (-da), *a.* pensioned; retired. *s.* exhibitioner, scholarship holder. *m.* boarding-school

pensionar, *v.t.* to pension, grant a pension to; charge a pension on

pensionista, *m.* and *f.* pensioner; boarder

pentaedro, *m.* (*geom.*) pentahedron

pentágono, *m.* (*geom.*) pentagon. *a.* pentagonal

pentagrama, *m.* (*mus.*) pentagram, stave

pentámetro, *m.* pentameter

pentano, *m.* (*chem.*) pentane

pentateuco, *m.* Pentateuch

Pentecostés, *m.* Pentecost, Whitsuntide

penúltimo, *a.* penultimate

penuria, *f.* scarcity; want, penury

peña, *f.* crag, rock; boulder; group of friends; club. **ser una p.**, to be stony-hearted

peñasco, *m.* craggy peak

peñascoso, *a.* craggy, rocky

peñón, *m.* rock; cliff; peak

peón, *m.* pedestrian; casual labourer; top (toy); piece (chess, draughts); (*mech.*) axle; infantryman. **p. caminero**, navvy, roadmender. **p. de ajedrez**, pawn (in chess)

peonada, *f.* day's manual labour; gang of labourers

peonía, *f.* (*bot.*) peony

peonza, *f.* whipping top; teetotum

peor, *a. comp.* **malo**, worse. *adv. comp.* **mal**, worse. *a. sup.* **el** (**la**, **lo**) **peor**; **los** (**las**) **peores**, the worst. **p. que p.**, worse and worse. **tanto p.**, so much the worse

pepino, *m.* cucumber plant; cucumber; (*fig.*) pin, straw

pepita, *f.* (*min.*) nugget; pip, seed (of fruit)

peplo, *m.* Greek tunic, peplum

pepsina, *f.* (*chem.*) pepsin

péptico, *a.* peptic

peptona, *f.* (*chem.*) peptone

pequeñez, *f.* littleness, smallness; pettiness; childhood; infancy; trifle, insignificant thing; meanness, baseness

pequeño, *a.* little, small; petty; very young; short, brief; humble, lowly

pera, *f.* pear; goatee; (*fig.*) plum, sinecure

peral, *m.* pear tree; pear wood

perca, *f.* (*icht.*) perch

percal, *m.* percale, calico

percalina, *f.* percaline, binding cloth

percance, *m.* perquisite, attribute (gen. *pl.*); disaster, mischance

percebe, *m.* (gen. *pl.*) goose barnacle

percentaje, *m.* percentage

percepción, *f.* perception; idea, conception

perceptible, *a.* perceptible

perceptivo, *a.* perceptive

perceptor (-ra), *a.* perceptive. *s.* observer

percibir, *v.t.* to collect, draw, receive; perceive; understand, grasp

percibo, *m.* perceiving; collecting, drawing, receiving

percolador, *m.* coffee percolator

percusión, *f.* percussion; shock, vibration

percusor, *m.* hammer (of firearms)

percutir, *v.t.* to percuss, strike

percha, *f.* stake, pole; coat hanger; perch (for birds); rack (for hay); hall-stand, coat-and-hat-stand

perchero, *m.* hall-stand; row of perches (for fowls, etc.)

perdedor (-ra), *a.* losing. *s.* loser

perder, *v.t.* to lose; throw away, squander; spoil, destroy; *v.i.* fade (colours); *v.r.* lose one's way, be lost; be confused or perplexed; be shipwrecked; take to vice; be spoiled or destroyed; disappear; love madly. **p. la ocasión,** to let the chance slip.

p. los estribos, to lose patience. **p. terreno,** to lose ground. **perderse de vista,** to be lost to sight. **echarse a p.,** to spoil, be damaged. See **entender**

perdición, *f.* loss; perdition, ruin; damnation; depravity, viciousness

pérdida, *f.* loss; waste. (*mil.*) **pérdidas cuantiosas,** heavy losses

perdidamente, *adv.* ardently, desperately; uselessly

perdigón, *m.* young partridge; decoy partridge; hailshot, pellet, shot

perdigonada, *f.* volley of hailshot; hailshot wound

perdiguero (-ra), *s.* game dealer; setter, retriever

perdiz, *f.* partridge. **p. blanca,** ptarmigan

perdón, *m.* pardon, forgiveness; remission. **con p.,** with your permission; excuse me

perdonable, *a.* pardonable, excusable

perdonar, *v.t.* to pardon, forgive; remit, excuse; exempt; waste, lose; give up (a privilege)

perdonavidas, *m.* (*fam.*) bully, braggart

perdulario, *a.* careless, negligent; slovenly; vicious, depraved

perdurable, *a.* perpetual, everlasting; enduring, lasting

perdurar, *v.i.* to last, endure

perecedero, *a.* brief, fugitive, transient; perishable. *m.* (*fam.*) poverty, want

perecer, *v.i. irr.* to end, finish; perish, die; suffer (damage, grief, etc.); be destitute; *v.r.* (*with por*) long for, crave; desire ardently. See **conocer**

peregrinación, *f.* journey, peregrination; pilgrimage

peregrinamente, *adv.* rarely, not often; beautifully, perfectly

peregrinar, *v.i.* to journey, travel; make a pilgrimage

peregrino (-na), *a.* and *s.* pilgrim. *a.* migrant (birds); rare, unusual; extraordinary. strange; beautiful, perfect

perejil, *m.* parsley; (*fam.*) ornament or apparel (gen. *pl.*); *pl.* honours, titles

perengano (-na), *s.* so-and-so, such a one

perenne, *a.* incessant, constant; (*bot.*) perennial

perennidad, *f.* perpetuity

perentoriedad, *f.* peremptoriness; urgency

perentorio, *a.* peremptory; conclusive, decisive; urgent, pressing

pereza, *f.* laziness; languor, inertia; slowness, deliberateness

perezoso, *a.* lazy; languid; slothful; slow, deliberate. *m.* (*zool.*) sloth

perfección, *f.* perfection; perfecting, perfect thing, virtue, grace

perfeccionamiento, *m.* perfecting; progress, improvement

perfeccionar, *v.t.* to perfect; – complete

perfectamente, *adv.* perfectly; quite, entirely

perfectible, *a.* perfectible

perfecto, *a.* perfect; excellent, very good; complete; whole; (*gram.*) perfect

perfidia, *f.* perfidy, treachery

pérfido, *a.* perfidious, treacherous

perfil, *m.* ornament, decoration; outline, contour; profile; section (of metal); fine stroke (of letters); *pl.* finishing touches; politeness, attention, courtesy. **de p.,** in profile; sideways on

perfilado, *a.* long, elongated (of faces, etc.)

perfilar, *v.t.* to draw in profile; outline; *v.r.* place oneself sideways, show one's profile; (*fam.*) hess up, titivate

perforación, *f.* perforation, boring; hole

perforador, *a.* perforating, boring. *m.* (*mech.*) drill

perforar, *v.t.* to perforate, pierce; bore, drill, make a hole in

perfumador (-ra), *a.* perfuming. *s.* perfumer. *m.* perfume burner

perfumar, *v.t.* to perfume; *v.r.* give off perfume

perfume, *m.* perfume; scent, fragrance

perfumería, *f.* scent factory; perfumery; perfume shop

perfumista, *m.* and *f.* perfumer

perfunctorio, *a.* perfunctory

pergamino, *m.* parchment, vellum; document; diploma; *pl.* aristocratic descent

periantio, *m.* (*bot.*) perianth

pericardio, *m.* (*anat.*) pericardium

pericarpio, *m.* (*bot.*) pericarp

pericia, *f.* expertness; skilled workmanship

pericial, *a.* expert, skilful

perico, *m.* (*orn.*) parakeet

periferia, *f.* periphery

periférico, *a.* peripheral

perifollos, *m. pl.* (*fam.*) frills, flounces, finery

perifrástico, *a.* periphrastic

perigonio, *m.* (*bot.*) perianth

perilla, *f.* pear-shaped ornament; goatee; imperial. **p. de la oreja,** lobe of the ear. **venir de p.,** to be most opportune

perillán, *m.* (*fam.*) rascal, rogue

perímetro, *m.* perimeter; precincts

perínclito, *a.* distinguished, illustrious; heroic

perineo, *m.* (*anat.*) perineum

perinola, *f.* teetotum

periódicamente, *adv.* periodically

periodicidad, *f.* periodicity

periódico, *a.* periodic. *m.* newspaper; periodical publication

periodismo, *m.* journalism

periodista, *m.* and *f.* journalist

periodístico, *a.* journalistic

período, *m.* period; (*phys.*) cycle; menstruation period; (*gram.*) clause; age, era

periostio, *m.* (*anat.*) periosteum

peripatético, *a.* peripatetic

peripecia, *f.* peripetia, sudden change of fortune, vicissitude

peripuesto, *a.* (*fam.*) over-elegant, spruce, too well-dressed; smart

periquete, *m.* (*fam.*) jiffy, trice

periquito, *m.* (*orn.*) budgerigar. (*fam.*) **P. entre ellos,** ladies' man

periscopio, *m.* periscope

peristilo, *m.* (*arch.*) peristyle

perito (-ta), *a.* expert; skilful, experienced. *s.* expert

peritoneo, *m.* (*anat.*) peritoneum

perjudicador (-ra), *a.* injurious, prejudicial. *s.* injurer

perjudicar, *v.t.* to harm, damage, injure; prejudice

perjudicial, *a.* injurious, noxious, harmful; prejudicial

perjuicio, *m.* injury, damage; harm; (*law*) prejudice

perjurador (-ra), *s.* perjurer

perjurar, *v.i.* to perjure oneself, commit perjury; swear, curse

perjurio, *m.* perjury

perjuro (-ra), *a.* perjured, forsworn. *s.* perjurer

perla, *f.* pearl; (*arch.*) bead; (*fig.*) treasure, jewel, dear. **de perlas,** excellent; exactly right

perlero, *a.* pearl

perlesía, *f.* paralysis; palsy

perlino, *a.* pearly, pearl-coloured

permanecer, *v.i.* *irr.* to stay, remain. **p. en posición de firmes,** to stand to attention. See **conocer**

permanencia, *f.* stay, sojourn; permanence

permanente, *a.* permanent; lasting, enduring

permanganato, *m.* permanganate

permeabilidad, *f.* permeability

permisible, *a.* permissible, allowable

permisivo, *a.* permissive

permiso, *m.* permission, leave; permit; (*mil.*, etc.) pass. **¡Con p.!** Excuse me!; Allow me!

permitir, *v.t.* to permit, allow

permuta, *f.* exchange

permutación, *f.* permutation, interchange

permutar, *v.t.* to exchange

pernear, *v.i.* to kick; (*fam.*) bustle; fret, be impatient

pernetas, en, *adv.* barelegged

perniciosidad, *f.* perniciousness

pernicioso, *a.* pernicious

pernil, *m.* (*anat.*) hock; ham; leg (of pork, etc.); leg of breeches

pernio, *m.* hinge (doors, windows)

perniquebrar, *v.t.* *irr.* to break the legs of. See **quebrar**

perno, *m.* bolt, pin, spike

pernoctar, *v.i.* to spend the night (away from home)

pero, *conjunc.* but. *m.* (*fam.*) defect; difficulty, snag

perogrullada, *f.* (*fam.*) truism

perol, *m.* (*cul.*) cooking utensil similar to a preserving pan

peroné, *m.* (*anat.*) fibula

peroración, *f.* peroration

perorar, *v.i.* to make a speech; (*fam.*) speak pompously; ask insistently

peróxido, *m.* peroxide

perpendicular, *a.* perpendicular. *f.* perpendicular

perpendicularidad, *f.* perpendicularity

perpetración, *f.* perpetration

perpetrar, *v.t.* to perpetrate

perpetua, *f.* (*bot.*) immortelle

perpetuación, *f.* perpetuation

perpetuar, *v.t.* to perpetuate; *v.r.* last, endure

perpetuidad, *f.* perpetuity

perpetuo, *a.* everlasting; lifelong

perplejidad, *f.* perplexity, bewilderment, doubt

perplejo, *a.* perplexed, bewildered, doubtful

perquirir, *v.t.* *irr.* to search carefully. See **adquirir**

perra, *f.* bitch; (*fam.*) sot, drunkard; tantrums. **p. chica,** five cent coin. **p. gorda,** ten cent coin

perrada, *f.* pack of dogs; (*fam.*) dirty trick

perrengue, *m.* (*fam.*) short-tempered person; negro

perrera, *f.* dog-kennel; useless toil; (*fam.*) bad payer; tantrums

perrería, *f.* pack of dogs; (*fam.*) dirty trick; fit of anger

perrero, *m.* dog fancier; kennel man

perro, *m.* dog. **p. danés,** Great Dane. **p. de aguas,** French poodle; spaniel. **p. de casta,** thoroughbred dog. **p. de muestra,** pointer. **p. de presa** *or* **p. dogo,** bulldog. **p. de San Bernardo,** St. Bernard dog. **p. de Terranova,** Newfoundland dog. **p. del hortelano,** dog-in-the-manger. **p. faldero,** lap-dog. **p. lobo,** wolfhound. **p. pachón,** dachshund. **p. pastor alemán** *or* **p. policía,** Alsatian. **p. pequinés,** Pekingese. **p. perdiguero,** pointer. **p. pomerano,** Spitz, Pomeranian dog. **p. sabueso español,** spaniel. **p. zorrero,** foxhound. (*fam.*) **A p. viejo no hay tus tus,** You can't deceive an old dog. **vivir como perros y gatos,** (*fam.*) to live like cat and dog

perruno, *a.* dog, dog-like

persa, *a.* and *m.* and *f.* Persian. *m.* Persian language

persecución, *f.* pursuit; persecution; annoyance, importuning

perseguidor (-ra), *a.* pursuing; tormenting. *s.* pursuer; tormentor, persecutor

perseguimiento, *m.* pursuit

perseguir, *v.i. irr.* to pursue; persecute, torment; importune. See **seguir**

perseverancia, *f.* perseverance

perseverante, *a.* persevering; constant

perseverar, *v.i.* to persevere; last, endure

persiana, *f.* Venetian blind; flowered silk material

pérsico, *a.* Persian. *m.* peach tree; peach

persignar, *v.t.* to sign; make the sign of the cross over; *v.r.* cross oneself

persistencia, *f.* persistence

persistente, *a.* persistent

persistir, *v.i.* to persist

persona, *f.* person; personage; (in a play, etc.) character; *(gram., ecc.)* person. **de p. a p.,** in private, face to face

personaje, *m.* important person, personage; (in a play, etc.) character

personal, *a.* personal. *m.* staff, personnel

personalidad, *f.* personality

personalismo, *m.* personality; personal question

personalizar, *v.t.* to become personal, be offensive

personalmente, *adv.* personally

personarse, *v.r.* to present oneself, call, appear

personificación, *f.* personification

personificar, *v.t.* to personify

perspectiva, *f.* perspective; view; outlook; aspect, appearance. **p. aérea,** bird's-eye view

perspicacia, *f.* perspicacity, shrewdness

perspicaz, *a.* perspicacious, clear-sighted

perspicuidad, *f.* perspicuity

perspicuo, *a.* lucid, clear

persuadir, *v.t.* to persuade

persuasible, *a.* persuadable

persuasión, *f.* persuasion; belief, conviction, opinion

persuasiva, *f.* persuasiveness

persuasivo, *a.* persuasive

pertenecer, *v.i. irr.* to belong; relate, concern. See **conocer**

perteneciente, *a.* belonging (to), pertaining (to)

pertenencia, *f.* ownership, proprietorship; property, accessory

pértica, *f.* (*agr.*) perch (measure)

pértiga, *f.* long rod; pole (of cart, trolley, etc.). **salto de p.,** pole-jumping

pertiguero, *m.* verger

pertinacia, *f.* pertinacity, doggedness

pertinaz, *a.* pertinacious, stubborn, dogged

pertinencia, *f.* relevance, appropriateness

pertinente, *a.* relevant, apposite; appropriate

pertrechar, *v.t.* to supply, equip; prepare, make ready

pertrechos, *m. pl.* (*mil.*) armaments, stores; equipment, appliances

perturbación, *f.* disturbance; agitation

perturbador (-ra), *a.* disturbing. *s.* disturber; heckler

perturbar, *v.t.* to disturb; agitate

peruano (-na), *a.* and *s.* Peruvian

perversidad, *f.* wickedness, depravity

perversión, *f.* perversion; wickedness, evil

perversivo, *a.* perversive

perverso, *a.* wicked, iniquitous, depraved

pervertir, *v.t. irr.* to pervert, corrupt; distort. See **sentir**

pesa, *f.* weight; clock weight; gymnast's weight. **pesas y medidas,** weights and measures

pesacartas, *m.* letter-balance

pesada, *f.* weighing

pesadez, *f.* heaviness; obesity; tediousness, tiresomeness; slowness; fatigue

pesadilla, *f.* nightmare

pesado, *a.* heavy; obese; deep (of sleep); close (of weather); slow; unwieldy; tedious; impertinent; dull, boring; offensive

pesadumbre, *f.* heaviness; grief, sorrow; trouble, anxiety

pésame, *m.* expression of condolence. **dar el p.,** to present one's condolences

pesantez, *f.* weight, heaviness; seriousness, gravity

pesar, *m.* grief, sorrow; remorse. **a p. de,** in spite of

pesar, *v.i.* to weigh; be heavy; be important; grieve, cause regret (e.g. **Me pesa mucho,** I am very sorry); influence, affect; *v.t.* weigh; consider.. **Mal que me (te, etc.) pese ...,** Much as I regret ...

pesario, *m.* (*surg.*) pessary

pesaroso, *a.* regretful, remorseful; sorrowful

pesca, *f.* fishery; angling, fishing; catch of fish. **p. a la rastra,** trawling. **p. mayor,** deep-sea fishing

pescadería, *f.* fishing ground; fishery; fishmonger's shop; fish market

pescadilla, *f.* (*icht.*) whiting

pescado, *m.* fish (out of the water); salted cod

pescador (-ra), *s.* fisherman; angler

pescante, *m.* driving seat; coach-box; jib (of a crane)

pescar, *v.t.* to fish; (*fam.*) catch in the act; acquire. **p. a la rastra,** to trawl

pescozón, *m.* slap on the neck or head

pescuezo, *m.* neck; throat; haughtiness, arrogance. **torcer el p.,** to wring the neck (of chickens, etc.)

pesebre, *m.* manger, stable; feeding trough

pesimamente, *adv.* extremely badly

pesimismo, *m.* pessimism

pesimista, *a.* pessimistic. *m.* and *f.* pessimist

pésimo, *a. sup.* **malo,** extremely bad

peso, *m.* weighing; weight; heaviness; gravity; importance; influence; load; peso (coin); scale, balance. **p. bruto,** gross weight. **p. de joyería,** troy weight. **p. específico,** (*phys.*) specific gravity. **p. pluma,** (*boxing*) feather weight

pespunte, *m.* (*sew.*) backstitch

pesquera, *f.* fishing ground, fishery

pesquería, *f.* fishing, angling; fisherman's trade; fishing ground, fishery

pesquero, *a.* fishing (of boats, etc.)

pesquisa, *f.* investigation, examination; search

pesquisar, *v.t.* to investigate, look into; search

pestaña, *f.* eyelash; (*sew.*) edging, fringe; ear, lug; (*naut.*) fluke

pestañear, *v.i.* to wink; blink; flutter the eyelashes

pestañeo, *m.* winking; blinking

peste, *f.* plague, pestilence; nauseous smell; epidemic; pest; vice; *pl.* oaths, curses. **p. bubónica,** bubonic plague. **p. de las abejas,** foul brood. **echar pestes,** to swear; fume

pestífero, *a.* noxious

pestilencia, *f.* plague, pestilence

pestilente, *a.* pestilential

pestillo, *m.* latch, falling latch; lock bolt. **p. de golpe,** safety-latch

petaca, *f.* cigarette or cigar-case; tobacco-pouch

pétalo, *m.* petal

petardista, *m.* and *f.* swindler, impostor

petardo, *m.* detonator; torpedo; squib, cracker; fraud

petición, *f.* petition, request

peticionario (-ia), *s.* petitioner. *a.* petitionary

petimetra, *f.* stylish and affected young woman

petimetre, *m.* fop

petirrojo, *m.* (*orn.*) robin

petitorio, *a.* petitionary. *m.* (*fam.*) importunity

peto, *m.* breastplate; front (of a shirt); bib

petrarquista, *a.* Petrarchan. *m.* and *f.* Petrarchist

pétreo, *a.* petrous

petrificación, *f.* petrifaction

petrificar, *v.t.* to petrify; *v.r.* become petrified

petrografía, *f.* petrology (study of rocks)

petróleo, *m.* petroleum; oil, mineral oil. **p. bruto,** crude oil. **p. de lámpara,** kerosene

petrolero (-ra), *a.* oil, petroleum. *s.* petroleum seller; incendiarist. *m.* (*naut.*) oil tanker

petrolífero, *a.* oil-bearing

petroso, *a.* stony, rocky

petulancia, *f.* insolence; vanity

petulante, *a.* insolent; vain

pez, *m.* fish; *pl.* Pisces. *f.* (*chem.*) pitch. **p. sierra,** sword-fish pezón, *m.* (*bot.*) stalk; nipple; axle pivot; point (of land, etc.)

pezonera, *f.* linchpin

pezuña, *f.* cloven hoof (of cows, pigs, etc.)

piada, *f.* chirping, twittering

piadoso, *a.* compassionate; kind, pitiful; pious, religious

piafar, *v.i.* to stamp, paw the ground (horses)

piamontés (-esa), *a.* and *s.* Piedmontese

pianista, *m.* and *f.* piano maker; piano dealer; pianist

piano, *m.* pianoforte. **p. de cola,** grand piano. **p. de media cola,** baby grand. **p. vertical,** upright piano

piante, *a.* chirping, twittering

piar, *v.i.* to chirp, twitter

piara, *f.* herd of swine; pack (of horses, etc.)

pica, *f.* (*mil.*) pike; bullfighter's goad; pike soldier; stonecutter's hammer. **a p. seca,** in vain. **pasar por las picas,** to suffer hardship. **poner una p. en Flandes,** to triumph over great difficulties

picacho, *m.* peak, summit

picada, *f.* prick; bite; peck; (*aer.*) dive

picadero, *m.* riding school; paddock (of a racecourse)

picado, *a.* (*sew.*) pinked. *m.* (*cul.*) hash

picador, *m.* horse trainer; meat chopper; horseman armed with a goad (bullfights)

picadura, *f.* puncture; prick; sting; (*sew.*) pinking; peck (birds); cut tobacco; black tobacco; beginning of caries in teeth

picajoso, *a.* hypersensitive, touchy, peevish

picamaderos, *m.* woodpecker

picante, *a.* piquant; mordant; hot, highly seasoned. *m.* mordancy; pungency

picapleitos, *m.* (*fam.*) shady lawyer, pettifogger

picaporte, *m.* latch, door-catch; door-knocker

picar, *v.t.* to prick; sting; peck; bite; chop fine; mince; nibble (fish); irritate (skin); (*sew.*) pink; burn (the tongue); eat (grapes); goad; spur; stipple (walls); stimulate, encourage; split, cleave;

(*mil.*) harass; vex; (*mus.*) play staccato; *v.i.* burn (sun); smart (of cuts, etc.); eat sparingly; (*aut.*) knock; (*with en*) knock at (doors, etc.); *v.r.* be moth-eaten; go rotten (fruit, etc.); grow choppy (sea); be piqued; boast

picaramente, *adv.* knavishly, cunningly

picardear, *v.i.* to play the rogue; behave mischievously

picardía, *f.* knavery, roguery; mischievousness; practical joke; wantonness

picaresco, *a.* roguish, picaresque, knavish

pícaro (-ra), *a.* knavish; base, vile; astute; mischievous. *s.* rogue

picatoste, *m.* (*cul.*) kind of fritter

picaza, *f.* magpie

picazo, *m.* blow with a pike or anything pointed; peck, tap with a beak; sting

picazón, *f.* itch, irritation; annoyance

pícea, *f.* (*bot.*) spruce

píceo, *a.* piscine, fish-like

Picio (ser más feo que), (*fam.*) to be as ugly as sin

pico, *m.* beak (of birds); peak; pick-axe; woodpecker; odd amount (e.g. **treinta y p.,** thirty-odd); sharp point; spout (of jug, etc.); (*fam.*) mouth; blarney, gab. **p. de cigüeña,** (*bot.*) crane's bill. **p. de oro,** silver-tongued orator

picor, *m.* burning sensation in mouth; smarting; itching, irritation

picoso, *a.* pitted, marked by smallpox

picota, *f.* pillory; peak; spire

picotazo, *m.* peck; dab; sting, bite

picoteado, *a.* peaked, having points

picotear, *v.t.* to peck (of a bird); *v.i.* toss the head (horses); (*fam.*) chatter senselessly; *v.r.* (*fam.*) slang each other

picotero, *a.* (*fam.*) chattering, talkative; indiscreet

picrato, *m.* (*chem.*) picrate

pícrico, *a.* (*chem.*) picric

pictografía, *f.* picture writing

pictórico, *a.* pictorial

picudo, *a.* pointed, peaked; having a spout; (*fam.*) chattering

pichel, *m.* tankard

pichón (-ona), *m.* male pigeon. *s.* (*fam.*) darling

pie, *m.* foot; stand, support; stem (of a glass, etc.); standard (of a lamp); (*bot.*) trunk, stem; sapling; lees, sediment; (*theat.*) cue; foot (measure); custom; (metrics) foot; motive, cause; pretext; (metrics) metre. **p. de cabra,** crowbar. **p. de imprenta,** printer's mark, printer's imprint. **p. de piña,** club-foot. **p. de rey,** calliper. **p. palmado,** web-foot. **A los pies de usted,** At your service (said by a gentleman to a lady). **al p. de la letra,** au pied de la lettre, punctiliously. (*fam.*) **andar con pies de plomo,** to walk warily. **a p.,** on foot. **a p. firme,** without budging; steadfastly. (*fam.*) **buscar tres pies al gato,** to look for something that isn't there; twist a person's words. **de a p.,** on foot. **en p. de guerra,** on a wartime footing. (*fam.*) **poner pies en polvorosa,** to quit, bunk

piedad, *f.* piety; pity, compassion; (*art*) pietà

piedra, *f.* stone; tablet; (*med.*) gravel. **p. de amolar,** whetstone, grindstone. **p. angular,** corner-stone (also *fig.*). **p. caliza,** limestone. **p. clave,** keystone. **p. de construcción,** building stone; child's brick. **p. de toque,** touchstone, test. **p. filosofal,** philosopher's stone. **p. fundamental,** foundation stone. **p. miliaria,** milestone. **p. mortuoria,** tombstone. (*fig., fam.*) **no dejar p. sin remover,** to leave no stone unturned. **no dejar p. sobre p.,** to demolish, destroy completely

piel, *f.* skin; fur; hide; leather; peel (of some fruits); rind (of bacon). **p. de gallina,** (*fig.*) goose-flesh. **p. de rata,** horse blanket. **p. de Rusia,** Russian leather. *m. pl.* **pieles rojas,** Red Skins, Red Indians

piélago, *m.* high seas; sea, ocean; glut, superabundance

pienso, *m.* (*agr.*) fodder

pierna, *f.* (*anat.*) leg; (*mech.*) shank; leg of a compass. (*fam.*) **a p. suelta,** at one's ease. **en piernas,** barelegged

pietismo, *m.* pietism

pietista, *a.* pietistic. *m.* and *f.* pietist

pieza, *f.* portion; piece; component part; room; (*theat.*) play; roll (of cloth); man (in chess, etc.); coin; piece (of music). **p. de recambio** *or* **p. de repuesto,** spare part. **p. de recibo,** reception room. (*fam.*) **quedarse en una. p.,** to be struck dumb

piezómetro, *m.* (*phys.*) piezometer

pífano, *m.* (*mus.*) fife; fife player, fifer

pigmentación, *f.* pigmentation

pigmentario, *a.* pigmentary

pigmento, *m.* pigment

pigmeo (-ea), *a.* and *s.* pygmy

pignoración, *f.* hypothecation; pawning; mortgage

pignorar, *v.t.* to hypothecate; pawn; mortgage

pigre, *a.* lazy; negligent, careless

pigricia, *f.* laziness; negligence

pijama, *m.* pyjamas

pila, *f.* trough, basin; heap, pile; (*elec.*) battery; (*ecc.*) parish; pier, pile; (*phys.*) cell. **p. atómica,** atomic pile. **p. bautismal,** (*ecc.*) font

pilar, *m.* fountain basin; milestone; pillar

pilastra, *f.* pier, pile; pilaster

píldora, *f.* (*med.*) pill; (*fam.*) disagreeable news

pilón, *m.* fountain basin; pestle; loaf-sugar; pylon

pilongo, *a.* thin, lean

píloro, *m.* (*anat.*) pylorus

pilotaje, *m.* (*naut., aer.*) pilotage; piling, pile work. **examen de p.,** (*aer.*) flying test

pilotar, *v.t.* (*naut., aer.*) to pilot

pilote, *m.* (*eng.*) pile

pilotear, *v.t.* (*naut., aer.*) to pilot

piloto, *m.* pilot; mate (in merchant ships). **p. de pruebas,** (*aer.*) test pilot

pillador (-ra), *a.* pillaging, plundering. *s.* plunderer

pillaje, *m.* pillaging, looting; robbery; theft

pillar, *v.t.* to pillage; steal, rob; seize, snatch; (*fam.*) surprise, find out (in a lie, etc.)

pillastre, *m.* (*fam.*) rogue, raga-muffin:

pillear, *v.i.* (*fam.*) to lead a rogue's life

pillería, *f.* (*fam.*) gang of rogues; (*fam.*) rogue's trick

pillo, *m.* rogue, knave

pimentero, *m.* pepper plant; pepper-castor

pimentón, *m.* red pepper, cayenne

pimienta, *f.* pepper. **p. húngara,** paprika. (*fam.*) ser como una p., to be as sharp as a needle

pimiento, *m.* pimento; capsicum; red pepper; pepper plant. **p. de cornetilla,** chili

pimpinela, *f.* (*bot.*) pimpernel

pimpollo, *m.* sapling; sprout, shoot; rosebud

pina, *f.* conical stone; felloe (of a wheel)

pinacoteca, *f.* picture gallery

pináculo, *m.* pinnacle, summit; climax, culmination; (*arch.*) finial

pinar, *m.* pine wood

pinaza, *f.* (*naut.*) pinnace

pincarrasco, *m.* (*bot.*) pin oak

pincel, *m.* paint-brush; artist, painter; painting technique. **p. para las cejas,** eyebrow-pencil

pincelada, *f.* brush stroke. **dar la última p.,** to give the finishing touch

pincelero (-ra), *s.* seller or maker of paint brushes; brush box

pinchadura, *f.* prick, puncture; piercing; sting; nipping, biting

pinchar, *v.t.* to prick; puncture; pierce; sting; nip, bite. **no p. ni cortar,** to be ineffective (of persons)

pinchazo, *m.* prick; puncture; sting; incitement

pinche, *m.* scullion

pindárico, *a.* Pindaric

pineda, *f.* pine wood

pingajo, *m.* (*fam.*) tatter, rag

pingajoso, *a.* (*fam.*) tattered, ragged

pingo, *m.* (*fam.*) tatter, rag; *pl.* (*fam.*) cheap clothes, duds

pingüe, *a.* fat, greasy; fertile, rich

pingüino, *m.* penguin

pino, *a.* steep. *m.* (*bot.*) pine, deal; (*poet.*) ship. **p. de tea,** pitch-pine. **p. silvestre, red fir**

pinocha, *f.* pine needle

pinta, *f.* spot; marking; mark; fleck; look, appearance; pint (measure); drop, drip; (in billiards) spot ball

pintamonas, *m.* and *f.* (*fam.*) dauber

pintar, *v.t.* to paint; describe; picture; exaggerate; *v.i.* show, manifest itself; *v.r.* make up (one's face). (*fam.*) **pintarse solo para,** to be very good at, excel at

pintiparado, *a.* most similar, very alike; fitting, apposite

pintiparar, *v.t.* (*fam.*) to compare

pintor (-ra), *s.* painter, artist. **p. callejero,** pavement-artist. **p. de brocha gorda,** house painter

pintoresco, *a.* picturesque, quaint, pretty

pintoresquismo, *m.* picturesqueness

pintorrear, *v.t.* (*fam.*) to daub, paint badly

pintura, *f.* painting; paint, pigment; picture, painting; description. **p. a la aguada,** water-colour painting. **p. al fresco,** fresco. **p. al óleo,** oil painting. **p. al pastel,** pastel drawing

pinturero, *a.* (*fam.*) affected, conceited; dandified, over-dressed

pinza, *f.* clamp. **p. de la ropa,** clothes-peg

pinzas, *f. pl.* pincers; pliers, tweezers; forceps. **p. hemostáticas,** arterial forceps

pinzón, *m.* (*orn.*) chaffinch

piña, *f.* pine-apple; cluster, knot (of people, etc.); pine-cone

piñón, *m.* pine-kernel; (*mech.*) pinion, chain-wheel

pío, *a.* pious; compassionate; good; piebald. *m.* chirping, cheep; (*fam.*) longing

piojo, *m.* louse

piojoso, *a.* lousy; avaricious, stingy

pionero, *m.* pioneer

piorrea, *f.* pyorrhœa

pipa, *f.* barrel, cask; tobacco pipe; pip (of fruits)

pipar, *v.i.* to smoke a pipe

pipeta, *f.* (*chem.*) pipette

pipiar, *v.i.* to chirp, twitter

pique, *m.* pique, resentment. **a p. de,** on the verge of, about to. **echar a p.,** (*naut.*) to sink;

destroy. **irse a p.,** to sink, founder

piquero, m. pike soldier

piqueta, f. pick, mattock; mason's hammer

piquete, m. puncture, small wound; (mil.) picket; pole, stake; small hole (in garments); picket (in strikes)

pira, f. funeral pyre; bonfire

piragua, f. (naut.) piragua, canoe

piramidal, a. pyramidal

pirámide, f. pyramid

pirarse, v.r. (fam.) to bunk, slip away

pirata, a. piratical. m. pirate; savage, cruel person

piratear, v.i. to play the pirate

piratería, f. piracy; plunder, robbery

pirático, a. piratical

pirenaico, pirineo, a. Pyrenean

pirético, a. pyretic

piriforme, a. pear-shaped

pirita, f. (min.) pyrites

pirograbado, m. poker work

piromancia, f. pyromancy

pirómetro, m. pyrometer

piropear, v.t. (fam.) to pay compliments to

piropo, m. carbuncle; (fam.) compliment. **echar piropos,** to pay compliments

pirotecnia, f. pyrotechnics

pirotécnico, a. pyrotechnical. m. pyrotechnist

pirrarse, v.r. (fam.) to desire ardently

pírrico, a. Pyrrhic

pirueta, f. pirouette, twirl

pisada, f. treading, stepping; footprint, footstep; stepping on a person's foot. **seguir las pisadas de alguien,** (fig.) to follow in someone's footsteps, imitate them

pisano (-na), a. and s. of or from Pisa

pisapapeles, m. paper-weight

pisar, v.t. to tread upon; trample upon; crush; (mus.) press (strings); trespass upon

pisaverde, m. (fam.) fop, dandy

piscatorio, a. piscatorial

piscicultura, f. pisciculture, fish rearing

piscina, f. fishpond; bathing pool; (ecc.) piscina

piscolabis, m. (fam.) snack, light meal

piso, m. treading, trampling; storey, floor; flooring; flat, apartment. **p. bajo,** ground floor

pisón, m. rammer, ram

pisotear, v.t. to trample; crush under foot; tread on; step on; humiliate, treat inconsiderately

pisoteo, m. trampling under foot; treading

pista, f. track, trail (of animals); circus ring; race-track, · race-course. **p. de patinar,** skating-rink. **p. de vuelo,** (aer.) landing field. (fam.) **seguir la p. a,** to spy upon

pistacho, m. pistachio

pistar, v.a. to pestle, pound

pistero, m. feeding cup

pistilo, m. (bot.) pistil

pistola, f. pistol. **p. ametralladora,** sub-machine-gun. **p. de arzón,** horse pistol

pistolera, f. holster; pistol-case

pistolero, m. gangster

pistoletazo, m. pistol shot; pistol wound

pistón, m. (mus.) piston; (mil.) percussion cap; (mech.) piston

pitada, f. blast on the whistle, whistling; impertinence

pitagórico (-ca), a. and s. Pythagorean

pitanza, f. alms, charity; (fam.) daily food; pittance, scanty remuneration

pitar, v.i. to play the whistle; v.t. pay (debts); smoke; give alms to

pitido, m. blast on a whistle; whistling (of birds)

pitillera, f. cigarette-case; girl cigarette maker

pitio, a. (myth.) Pythian

pito, m. whistle; (mus.) fife. (fam.) **Cuando pitos flautas, cuando flautas pitos,** It's always the unexpected that happens. (fam.) **no valer un p.,** to be not worth a straw

pitoflero (-ra), s. mediocre performer (gen. on wind instruments); (fam.) tale-bearer, gossip

pitón, m. (zool.) python; nascent horn (of goats, etc.); spout; protuberance; (bot.) sprout

pitonisa, f. (myth.) pythoness; witch, enchantress

pitorrearse, *v.r.* to ridicule, mock

pituitario, *a.* pituitary

pituso, *a.* small and amusing (of children)

pivote, *m.* pivot, swivel, gudgeon

piyama, *m.* pyjamas

pizarra, *f.* slate; blackboard

pizarral, *m.,* **pizarrería,** *f.* slate quarry

pizarrero, *m.* slater

pizarrín, *m.* slate pencil

pizca, *f.* (*fam.*) atom, speck, crumb; jot, whit. ¡ Ni p. ! Not a scrap !

pizpireta, *a.* (*f.*) (*fam.*) coquettish; smart; dressed-up

placa, *f.* plate, disk; (*art*) plaque; (*phot.*) plate; star (insignia)

placabilidad, *f.* placability, appeasability

placativo, *a.* placatory

pláceme, *m.* congratulation

placentero, *a.* agreeable, pleasant

placer, *v.t. irr.* to please, give pleasure to, gratify (e.g. Que me place, It pleases me). *m.* (*naut.*) reef, sand-bank; pleasure; wish, desire; permission, consent; entertainment, diversion. a p., at one's convenience; at leisure. *Pres. Ind.* plazco, places, etc. *Preterite* plugo, pluguieron. *Pres. Subjunc.* plazca, etc. *Imperf. Subjunc.* pluguiese, etc.

placibilidad, *f.* agreeableness, pleasantness

placible, *a.* agreeable, pleasant

placidez, *f.* placidity, calmness, serenity

plácido, *a.* placid, calm, serene

placiente, *a.* pleasing, attractive

plácito, *m.* decision, judgment, opinion

plafón, *m.* ceiling light; (*arch.*) panel

plaga, *f.* plague; disaster, calamity; epidemic; glut; pest; grief

plagar, *v.t.* (*with de*) to infect with; *v.r.* (*with de*) be covered with; be overrun by; be infested with

plagiar, *v.t.* to plagiarize, copy; kidnap, hold for ransom

plagiario (-ia), *s.* plagiarist

plagio, *m.* plagiary; kidnapping

plan, *m.* plan; scheme; plane.

P. Quinquenal, Five Year Plan

plana, *f.* sheet, page; mason's trowel; plain. p. mayor, (*mil., nav.*) Staff

plancha, *f.* sheet, slab, plate; flat iron; horizontal suspension (in gymnastics); (*naut.*) gangway, gang-board; (*fam.*) howler

planchado, *m.* ironing; ironing to be done or already finished

planchador (-ra), *s.* ironer

planchamangas, *m.* sleeve-board

planchar, *v.t.* to iron, press with an iron

planchear, *v.t.* to plate (with metal)

planeador, *m.* (*aer.*) glider

planear, *v.t.* to plan out; make plans for; *v.i.* (*aer.*) glide; (*aer.*) plane

planeo, *m.* (*aer.*) glide

planeta, *m.* planet

planetario, *a.* planetary. *m.* planetarium

planicie, *f.* levelness, evenness; plain

plano, *a.* flat, level; plane. *m.* (*geom.*) plane; plan, map; (*aer.*) aileron, wing

planta, *f.* (*bot.*) plant; sole (of the foot); plantation; layout, plan; position of the feet (in dancing, fencing); scheme, project. p. baja, ground floor. p. vivaz, perennial plant. (*fam.*) buena p., good appearance

plantación, *f.* planting; plantation, nursery

plantador (-ra), *s.* planter. *m.* (*agr.*) dibbler. *f.* **plantadora,** mechanical planter

plantar, *v.t.* to plant; erect; place; found, set up; pose (a problem); raise (a question, etc.); (*fam.*) leave in the lurch; *v.r.* take up one's position; jib (of horses); oppose

planteamiento, *m.* execution; putting into practice; planning; statement (of problems)

plantel, *m.* nursery garden; training school, nursery

plantilla, *f.* young plant; insole (of shoes); sock (in a shoe); (*mech.*) template, jig

plantío, *m.* plantation, afforestation; planting. *a.* planted or ready for planting (ground)

plantón, *m.* plant or sapling ready

for transplanting; (*bot.*) cutting;
doorkeeper, porter. **dar un p.**
(a), to keep (a person) waiting
a long time

plañidera, *f.* paid mourner

plañidero, *a.* mournful, piteous,
anguished

plañido, *m.* lament, weeping,
wailing

plañir, *v.i.* and *v.t. irr.* to lament,
wail, weep. See **tañer**

plasma, *m.* plasma

plasmar, *v.t.* to mould, throw
(pottery)

plasmático, *a.* plasmic

plástica, *f.* art of clay modelling;
plastic

plasticidad, *f.* plasticity

plástico, *a.* plastic; flexible,
malleable, soft

plata, *f.* silver; silver (coins);
money; white. **p. labrada**,
silver ware

plataforma, *f.* platform; run-
ning-board (of a train); (*r.w.*)
turn-table

plátano, *m.* banana (tree and
fruit); plane tree

platea, *f.* (*theat.*) pit. **butaca de
p.**, pit stall

plateado, *a.* silvered; silver-
plated; silvery

plateador, *m.* plater

platear, *v.t.* to electro-plate, silver

plateresco, *a.* (*arch.*) plateresque

platería, *f.* silversmith's art or
trade; silversmith's shop or
workshop

platero, *m.* silversmith; jeweller

plática, *f.* conversation; exhortation, sermon; address, discourse

platicar, *v.t.* and *v.i.* to converse
(about)

platija, *f.* (*icht.*) plaice

platillo, *m.* saucer; kitty (in card
games); pan (of a scale); *pl.*
cymbals

platinado, *m.* plating

platino, *m.* platinum

plato, *m.* plate; dish; (*cul.*)
course, dish; pan (of a scale). **p.
sopero**, soup-plate. **p. trinchero**, meat-dish. (*fam.*) **comer
en un mismo p.**, to be on
intimate terms. **nada entre
dos platos**, much ado about
nothing

platónico, *a.* Platonic

platonismo, *m.* Platonism

plausibilidad, *f.* plausibility

plausible, *a.* plausible, reasonable

playa, *f.* beach, seashore, strand

plaza, *f.* square (in a town, etc.);
market place; fortified town;
space; duration; employment,
post.; (*com.*) market. **p. de
armas**, garrison town; military
camp. **p. de toros**, bull ring.
p. fuerte, strong place, fortress.
sentar p., to enlist in the army

plazo, *m.* term, duration; expiration of term, date of payment;
instalment. **a plazos**, (*com.*)
by instalments, on the instalment system

plazoleta, *f.* small square (in
gardens, etc.)

pleamar, *f.* (*naut.*) high water

plebe, *f.* common people; rabble,
mob

plebeyo (-ya), *a.* plebeian. *s.*
commoner, plebeian

plebiscito, *m.* plebiscite

plectro, *m.* (*mus.*) plectrum

plegable, *a.* foldable

plegadera, *f.* folder; folding knife;
paper-folder

plegadizo, *a.* folding; collapsible;
jointed

plegado, *m.* pleating; folding

plegador, *a.* folding. *m.* folding
machine

plegadura, *f.* folding, doubling;
fold, pleat

plegar, *v.t. irr.* to fold; pleat;
(*sew.*) gather; *v.r.* submit, give
in. See **acertar**

plegaria, *f.* fervent prayer

pleitear, *v.t.* to go to law about;
indulge in litigation

pleitista, *a.* quarrelsome, litigious

pleito, *m.* action, lawsuit; dispute, quarrel; litigation. **ver el
p.**, (*law*) to try a case

plenamente, *adv.* fully, entirely

plenario, *a.* full; complete; (*law*)
plenary

plenilunio, *m.* full moon

plenipotencia, *f.* full powers
(diplomatic, etc.)

plenipotenciario, *a.* and *m.* plenipotentiary

plenitud, *f.* fullness, completeness; plenitude, abundance

pleno, *a.* full. *m.* general meeting

pleonasmo, *m.* (*gram.*) pleonasm,
redundancy

pleonástico, *a.* pleonastic

plétora, f. (med.) plethora; excess

pleuresía, f. (med.) pleurisy

plexo, m. (anat.) plexus

pléyades, f. pl. Pleiades

pliego, m. sheet (of paper); letter or packet of papers

pliegue, m. fold, pleat; (sew.) gather

plinto, m. (arch.) plinth (of column); skirting-board

plisar, v.t. to pleat; fold

plomada, f. plummet; sounding-lead; plumb, lead

plombagina, f. plumbago, black-lead, graphite

plomería, f. plumbing; plumbing business; lead roofing

plomero, m. plumber

plomizo, a. lead-like; lead-coloured, grey

plomo, m. lead (metal); plummet; bullet; (fam.) bore, tedious person

pluma, f. feather; pen; plumage; quill; penmanship; writer; writing profession. **p. estilográfica,** fountain pen. **a vuela p.,** as the pen writes, written in a hurry

plumado, a. feathered

plumaje, m. plumage, feathers; plume

plúmbeo, a. plumbeous, leaden

plúmbico, a. (chem.) plumbic

plúmeo, a. feathered, plumed

plumero, m. feather duster; plume, feather; plumage

plumón, m. down; feather-bed

plumoso, a. feathered

plural, a. and m. plural

pluralidad, f. plurality; multitude, number

pluralizar, v.t. to pluralize

pluscuamperfecto, m. (gram.) pluperfect

plusmarquista, m. and f. (sport) record-holder

plutocracia, f. plutocracy

plutócrata, m. and f. plutocrat

plutocrático, a. plutocratic

plutónico, a. (geol.) Plutonic

pluviómetro, m. rain-gauge, pluviometer

población, f. peopling; population; town

poblacho, m. miserable town or village

poblado, m. inhabited place; town; village

poblador (-ra), a. populating. s. colonist, settler

poblar, v.t. irr. to colonize; people, populate; breed fast; stock, supply; v.r. put forth leaves (trees). See **contar**

pobre, a. poor; indigent, needy; mediocre; unfortunate; humble, meek. m. and f. beggar, pauper, needy person. (fam.) **ser p. de solemnidad,** to be down and out

pobrero, m. (ecc.) distributor of alms

pobretería, f. poverty; needy people

pobretón, a. extremely needy

pobreza, f. poverty, need; shortage; timidity; (min.) baseness; poorness (of soil, etc.)

pocero, m. well-sinker; sewage man; turncock

pocilga, f. pigsty; (fam.) filthy place

poción, f. potion, drink; mixture, dose

poco, a. little, scanty; pl. few. m. small amount, a little. adv. little; shortly, in a little while. **p. a p.,** by degrees, little by little; slowly. **p. más o menos,** more or less, approximately. **por p.,** almost, nearly. **tener en p. (a),** to have a poor opinion of; undervalue

poda, f. (agr.) pruning; pruning season

podadera, f. pruning knife

podar, v.t. (agr.) to prune, trim

poder, m. power; authority, jurisdiction; (law) power of attorney; strength; ability; proxy; efficacy; possession; pl. authority; power of attorney. **p. de adquisición,** purchasing power. **casarse por poderes,** to be married by proxy

poder, v.t. irr. to be able to (e.g. **Podemos comprar estas naranjas,** We can (are able to) buy these oranges. **Dice que la calamidad podía haberse evitado,** He says that the disaster could have been averted). **p.** also expresses possibility (e.g. **Pueden haber ido a la ciudad,** They may have gone to the city. **¡Qué distinta pudo haber sido su vida!** How different his life might have been!). *impers.* be possible. **a más no p.,** of necessity, without being able to help it; to the utmost. **no p. con,** to be unable to control or manage. **no p. hacer más,** to have no alternative, have to; be unable to do more. **no p. menos de,** to be obliged to, have no alternative but. **no p. ver a,** to hate (persons). *impers.* **Puede que venga esta tarde,** He may come (perhaps he will come) this afternoon. *Pres. Part.* **pudiendo.** *Pres. Ind.* **puedo, puedes, puede, pueden.** *Fut.* **podré,** etc. *Condit.* **podría,** etc. *Preterite* **pude, pudiste,** etc. *Pres. Subjunc.* **pueda, puedas, pueda, puedan.** *Imperf. Subjunc.* **pudiese,** etc.

poderío, *m.* power, authority; sway, rule; dominion; wealth

poderoso, *a.* powerful; opulent; effective, efficacious; mighty, magnificent

podredumbre, *f.* decay; pus; (*fig.*) canker, anguish

podredura, podrición, *f.* putrefaction; decay

podrido, *a.* rotten; putrid; corrupt; decayed

podrir, *v.t.* See **pudrir**

poema, *m.* poem. **p. sinfónico,** (*mus.*) tone poem

poesía, *f.* poetry, verse; lyric, poem

poeta, *m.* poet

poetastro, *m.* poetaster

poética, *f.* poetics

poético, *a.* poetical

poetisa, *f.* poetess

poetizar, *v.i.* to write verses; *v.t.* poeticize

polaco (-ca), *a.* Polish. *s.* Pole. *m.* Polish language

polainas, *f. pl.* leggings, puttees, gaiters

polar, *a.* polar

polaridad, *f.* polarity; polarization

polarímetro, *m.* polarimeter

polarización, *f.* polarization

polarizar, *v.t.* to polarize

polca, *f.* polka

polea, *f.* pulley; (*naut.*) block

polémica, *f.* polemic, controversy, dispute

polémico, *a.* polemical

polemista, *m.* and *f.* disputant, controversialist

polen, *m.* (*bot.*) pollen

poliandria, *f.* polyandry (also *bot.*)

policía, *f.* police; government, polity, administration; civility, courtesy; cleanliness, tidiness. *m.* policeman. **p. urbana,** city police

policíaco, *a.* police; detective

policromo, *a.* polychrome

polichinela, *m.* Punchinello

poliedro, *m.* (*geom.*) polyhedron

polifacético, *a.* many-sided

polifonía, *f.* (*mus.*) polyphony

polifónico, *a.* polyphonic

poligamia, *f.* polygamy

polígamo (-ma), *a.* polygamous. *s.* polygamist

polígloto (-ta), *s.* polyglot. *f.* polyglot Bible

polígono, *a.* polygonal. *m.* polygon

polilla, *f.* moth; moth grub; destroyer, ravager

polimorfismo, *m.* (*chem.*) polymorphism

polimorfo, *a.* polymorphous

polinesio (-ia), *a.* and *s.* Polynesian

polinización, *f.* pollination

polinomio, *m.* (*math.*) polynome

poliomielitis, *f.* (*med.*) poliomyelitis

pólipo, *m.* (*zool.*) polyp; octopus; (*med.*) polypus

polisílabo, *a.* polysyllabic. *m.* polysyllable

polista, *m.* and *f.* polo player

polistilo, *a.* (*arch.*) polystyle

politécnico, *a.* polytechnic

politeísmo, *m.* polytheism

politeísta, *a.* polytheistic. *m.* and *f.* polytheist

política, *f.* politics; civility, courtesy; diplomacy; tact; policy

politicastro, *m.* corrupt politician

político, *a.* political; civil, courteous; in-law, by marriage (relationships). *m.* politician

politiquear, *v.i.* (*fam.*) to dabble in politics, talk politics

póliza, *f.* (*com.*) policy; (*com.*) draft; share certificate; revenue stamp; admission ticket; lampoon. **p. a prima fija,** fixed premium policy. **p. de seguros.**

insurance policy. **p. dotal**, endowment policy

polizón, *m.* loafer, tramp; stowaway; bustle (of a dress)

polo, *m.* pole (all meanings); (*fig.*) support; popular Andalusian song; (*sport*) polo. **de p. a p.**, from pole to pole

polonés (-esa), *a.* Polish. *s.* Pole

polonesa, *f.* polonaise; short coat

poltrón, *a.* lazy, idle

poltronería, *f.* idleness, laziness

polución, *f.* (*med.*) ejaculation

poluto, *a.* filthy, unclean

Pólux, *m.* (*ast.*) Pollux

polvareda, *f.* dust cloud; storm, agitation

polvera, *f.* powder bowl; powder puff; powder compact

polvo, *m.* dust; powder; pinch (of snuff, etc.); *pl.* face or toilet powder. **Se hizo como por polvos de la madre celestina**, It was done as if by magic. (*fam.*) **limpio de p. y paja**, gratis, for nothing; net (of profit)

pólvora, *f.* gunpowder; bad temper. **p. de algodón**, gun-cotton. **descubrir la p.**, (*fig.*) to set the Thames on fire

polvorear, *v.t.* to powder, dust with powder

polvoriento, *a.* dusty; powdery; covered with powder

polvorín, *m.* very fine powder; powder-magazine; powder-flask

polvoroso, *a.* dusty; covered with powder

polla, *f.* pullet; (*fam.*) flapper, girl

pollada, *f.* brood, hatch (especially chickens)

pollastro (-ra), *s.* pullet. *m.* (*fam.*) downy bird

pollera, *f.* poultry breeder or seller (woman); chicken-coop; go-cart

pollería, *f.* poultry market or shop

pollero, *s.* poultry breeder; poulterer. *m.* hen-coop

pollino (-na), *s.* young ass; donkey

pollo, *m.* chicken; (*fam.*) youth, stripling; (*fig.*, *fam.*) downy bird. (*fam.*) **p. pera**, young blood, lad. **sacar pollos**, to hatch chickens

pomada, *f.* pomade; salve, ointment

pomar, *m.* orchard (especially apple orchard)

pómez, *f.* pumice stone (**piedra p.**)

pomo, *m.* (*bot.*) pome; pomander; nosegay; pommel, hilt (of sword); handle; rose (of watering can)

pomología, *f.* pomology, art of fruit growing

pompa, *f.* pomp, splendour; ceremonial procession; air bubble; peacock's outspread tail; (*naut.*) pump; billowing of clothes in the wind

pompeyano, *a.* Pompeian

pomposidad, *f.* pomposity

pomposo, *a.* stately, ostentatious, magnificent; inflated, pompous; florid, bombastic

pómulo, *m.* cheek-bone

ponche, *m.* punch, toddy

ponchera, *f.* punch-bowl

poncho, *a.* lazy, negligent. *m.* military cloak; poncho, cape

ponderación, *f.* weighing; reflection, consideration; exaggeration

ponderador, *a.* reflective, deliberate; exaggerated

ponderar, *v.t.* to weigh; consider, ponder; exaggerate; overpraise

ponderosidad, *f.* heaviness; ponderousness, dullness

ponderoso, *a.* heavy; ponderous; circumspect

ponedero, *a.* egg-laying (hens). *m.* nest

ponencia, *f.* clause, section; office of referee or arbitrator; report, referendum

poner, *v.t.* *irr.* to place, put; arrange; set (the table); bet, stake; appoint (to an office); call, name; lay (eggs); set down (in writing); calculate, count; suppose; leave to a person's judgment; risk; contribute; prepare; need, take; cause, inspire (emotions); make, cause; adapt; add; cause to become (angry, etc.); insult; praise; (*with prep. a + infin.*) begin to. **p. al corriente**, to bring up to date, inform. **p. a prueba**, to test. **p. casa**, to set up house. (*fam.*) **p. colorado a**, to make blush. **p. coto a**, to put a stop to, check. **p. en limpio**, to make a fair copy (of). **p. en marcha**, to start, set in motion. **p. en práctica**, to put into effect. **p. por encima (de)**, to prefer. *v.r.* to place oneself; become; put on (garments, etc.); dirty or stain oneself; set (sun, stars); oppose; deck oneself, dress oneself up; arrive; (*with prep. a + infin.*) begin to. **ponerse al corriente**, to bring oneself up to date. **ponerse bien**, to improve; get better (in health). **ponerse colorado**, to blush, flush. *Pres. Ind.* **pongo**, **pones**, etc. *Fut.* **pondré**, etc. *Condit.* **pondría**, etc. *Imperat.* **pon**. *Past Part.* **puesto**. *Preterite* **puse**, **pusiste**, etc. *Pres. Subjunc.* **ponga**, etc. *Imperf. Subjunc.* **pusiese**, etc.

ponientada, *f.* steady west wind

poniente, *m.* west; west wind

pontazgo, *m.* bridge toll

pontear, *v.t.* to bridge; make bridges

pontificado, *m.* pontificate, papacy

pontífice, *m.* pontifex; pope, pontiff; archbishop; bishop

pontificial, *a.* and *m.* pontifical

pontificio, *a.* pontifical

pontón, *m.* (*mil.*) pontoon; hulk used as prison, hospital, store, etc.; wooden bridge

pontonero, *m.* pontoneer, military engineer

ponzoña, *f.* poison, venom

ponzoñoso, *a.* poisonous, venomous; noxious; harmful

popa, *f.* (*naut.*) stern, poop. **en p.**, abaft

popelina, *f.* poplin

populachería, *f.* cheap popularity with the rabble

populachero, *a.* mob, vulgar

populacho, *m.* mob, rabble

popular, *a.* popular

popularidad, *f.* popularity

popularizar, *v.t.* to popularize; *v.r.* grow popular

popularmente, *adv.* popularly

populoso, *a.* populous, crowded

popurrí, *m.* (*cul.*) stew; potpourri; miscellany

poquedad, *f.* paucity, scarcity; timidity, cowardice; trifle, mere nothing

poquísimo, *a. sup.* **poco**, very little

poquito, *a. dim.* **poco**, very little

por, *prep.* for; by; through, along; during; because, as (e.g. **Lo desecharon p. viejo**, They threw it away because it was old); however (e.g. **P. bonito que sea**, However pretty it is); during; in order to (e.g. **Lo hice p. no ofenderla**, I did it in order not to offend her); towards, in favour of, for; for the sake of; on account of, by reason of (e.g. **No pudo venir p. estar enfermo**, He could not come on account of his illness); via, by (e.g. **p. correo aéreo**, by air-mail); as for (e.g. **P. mí, lo rechazo**, As for me, I refuse it); in exchange for (e.g. **Me vendió dos libros p. un chelín**, He sold me two books for a shilling); in the name of; as a substitute for, instead of (e.g. **Hace mi trabajo p. mí**, He is doing my work for me); per. **Por** has many uses: 1. Introduces the agent after a Passive (e.g. **La novela fué escrita p. él**, The novel was written by him). 2. Expresses movement through, along or about (e.g. **Andaban p. la calle**, They were walking along (or down) the street). 3. Denotes time at or during which an action occurs (e.g. **Ocurrió p. entonces un acontecimiento de importancia**, About that time an important event occurred). 4. Expresses rate or proportion (e.g. **seis por ciento**, six per cent). 5. With certain verbs means to be and expresses vague futurity (e.g. **El libro queda p. escribir**, The book remains to be written). **p. escrito**, in writing. **p. mucho que**, however great, however much; in spite of, notwithstanding. **¿p. qué?** Why? **p. si acaso**, in case, if by chance. **estar p.**, to be about to; be inclined to

porcelana, *f.* porcelain, china; china ware

porcentaje, *m.* percentage

porcino, *a.* porcine. *m.* young pig; bruise

porción, *f.* portion; (*com.*) share; (*fam.*) crowd; allowance, pittance

porcionista, *m.* and *f.* shareholder; sharer; boarding-school pupil

porcuno, *a.* porcine, hoggish

porche, *m.* porch, portico

pordiosear, *v.i.* to ask alms, beg

pordioseo, *m.* asking alms, begging

pordiosero (-ra), *a.* begging. *s.* beggar

porfía, *f.* obstinacy; importunity; tenacity. **a p.,** in competition

porfiadamente, *adv.* obstinately

porfiado, *a.* obstinate, obdurate, persistent

porfiar, *v.i.* to be obstinate, insist; persist

pórfido, *m.* porphyry

pormenor, *m.* particular, detail (gen. *pl.*); secondary matter

pormenorizar, *v.t.* to describe in detail

pornografía, *f.* pornography

pornográfico, *a.* pornographic, obscene

poro, *m.* pore

porosidad, *f.* porosity, permeability

poroso, *a.* porous, leaky

porque, *conjunc.* because, for; in order that

porqué, *m.* reason, wherefore, why; (*fam.*) money. **el cómo y el p.,** the why and the wherefore

porquería, *f.* (*fam.*) filth, nastiness; dirty trick; rudeness, gross act; trifle, thing of no account

porquerizo, porquero, *m.* swineherd

porra, *f.* club, bludgeon; last player (children's games); (*fam.*) vanity, boastfulness; bore, tedious person

porrada, *f.* blow with a club; buffet, knock, fall; (*fam.*) folly; glut, abundance

porrazo, *m.* blow with a club; buffet, knock, fall

porrear, *v.i.* (*fam.*) to insist, harp on

porrería, *f.* (*fam.*) folly; obduracy, persistence

porreta, *f.* green leaves of leek, onions and cereals. (*fam.*) **en p.,** stark-naked

porrino, *m.* seed of leeks; young leek plant

porrón, *m.* winebottle with a spout; earthenware jug

porta, *f.* (*naut.*) port, gun embrasure

portaaviones, *m.* aircraft carrier

portacartas, *m.* mail bag

portachuelo, *m.* defile, narrow mountain pass

portada, *f.* front, façade; frontispiece, title page; portal, doorway

portado (bien *or* **mal),** *a.* well- or ill-dressed or behaved

portador (-ra), *s.* carrier. *m.* (*com.*) bearer; (*mech.*) carrier

portaestandarte, *m.* standard bearer; colour-sergeant

portafolio, *m.* portfolio (*gallicism*)

portafusil, *m.* (*mil.*) rifle sling

portal, *m.* entrance, porch; portico; city gate

portalámpara, *f.* lamp holder; (*elec.*) socket

portalero, *m.* octroi officer

portalibros, *m.* bookstrap

portalón, *m.* (*naut.*) gangway

portamantas, *m.* rug strap

portamanteo, *m.* grip, travelling bag

portamonedas, *m.* pocket-book; hand-bag, purse

portanuevas, *m. and f.* bringer of news, newsmonger

portaobjetos, *m.* stage (of a microscope)

portaplumas, *m.* pen-holder

portar, *v.t.* to retrieve (of dogs); carry (arms); *v.r.* behave (well or badly); bear oneself, act; be well, or ill (in health)

portátil, *a.* portable

portatostadas, *m.* toast-rack

portavoz, *m.* megaphone; spokesman, mouthpiece

portazgo, *m.* toll tax; tolbooth

portazguero, *m.* toll gatherer

portazo, *m.* bang of the door; slamming the door in a person's face

porte, *m.* transport; (*com.*) carriage; postage; freight, transport cost; porterage; behaviour, conduct; bearing, looks; capacity, volume; size, dimension; nobility (of descent); (*naut.*) tonnage. **p. debido,** carriage-forward. **p. pagado,** charges prepaid; carriage paid

porteador, *m.* carrier; porter; carter

portear, *v.t.* to carry, transport; *v.r.* migrate (birds) portento, *m.* marvel, prodigy, portent

portentoso, *a.* marvellous, portentous

porteo, *m.* porterage, cartage

portería, *f.* porter's lodge; porter's employment; (*sport*) goal

portero (-ra), *s.* door-keeper; porter; concierge; janitor; (*sport*) goal-keeper

portezuela, *f. dim.* small door; carriage door; pocket flap

pórtico, *m.* portico, piazza; porch; vestibule, hall

portillo, *m.* breach, opening; wicket gate; defile, narrow pass; octroi gate; (*fig.*) loophole

portón, *m.* hall door, inner door

portorriqueño (-ña), *a.* and *s.* Porto-Rican

portuario, *a.* dock, port

portugués (-esa), *a.* and *s.* Portuguese. *m.* Portuguese language

portuguesada, *f.* exaggeration

porvenir, *m.* future time

¡Porvida! *interj.* By the Saints! By the Almighty!

pos, *prefix* after; behind. Also *adv.* en p., with the same meanings

posa, *f.* tolling, passing bell; *pl.* buttocks

posada, *f.* dwelling; inn, tavern; lodging; hospitality

posaderas, *f. pl.* buttocks.

posadero (-ra), *s.* innkeeper; lodging-house keeper

posar, *v.i.* to lodge, live; rest; alight, perch; *v.t.* set down (a burden); *v.r.* settle (liquids); (*with en* or *sobre*) perch upon

posdata, *f.* P.S., postscript

pose, *f.* (*phot.*) time exposure; (*fam.*) pose

poseedor (-ra), *s.* possessor, holder

poseer, *v.t. irr.* to own, possess; know (a language, etc.); *v.r.* restrain oneself. estar poseído por, to be possessed by (passion, etc.); be thoroughly convinced of. See creer

posesión, *f.* ownership, occupancy; possession; property, territory (often *pl.*)

posesionarse, *v.r.* to take possession; lay hold (of)

posesivo, *a.* possessive

poseso, *a.* possessed of an evil spirit

posesor (-ra), *s.* owner, possessor

posfecha, *f.* post-date

posibilidad, *f.* possibility; probability; opportunity, means. chance; *pl.* property, wealth

posibilitar, *v.t.* to make possible, facilitate

posible, *a.* possible. *m. pl.* property, personal wealth. hacer lo p. *or* hacer todo lo p., to do everything possible; do one's best

posición, *f.* placing; position; situation; status

positivamente, *adv.* positively, definitely

positivismo, *m.* positivism

positivista, *a.* positivistic. *m.* and *f.* positivist

positivo, *a.* positive; certain, definite; (*math., elec.*) plus; true, real

pósito, *m.* public granary; co-operative association

posma, *f.* (*fam.*) sluggishness, sloth

poso, *m.* sediment; lees, dregs; repose, quietness

posponer, *v.t. irr.* (*with prep. a*) to place after; make subordinate to; value less than. See poner

posta, *f.* post-horse; stage, post; stake (cards)

postal, *a.* postal. *f.* post card

poste, *m.* post, stake

postema, *f.* tumour, abscess; bore, tedious person

postergación, *f.* delay; delaying; relegation; disregard of seniority (in promotion)

postergar, *v.t.* to delay; disregard a senior claim to promotion

posteridad, *f.* descendants; posterity

posterior, *a.* back, rear; hind; subsequent

posterioridad, *f.* posteriority

posteriormente, *adv.* later, subsequently

postguerra, *f.* post-war period

postigo, *m.* secret door; wicket; half-door; grating, hatch; postern; shutter (window)

postillón, *m.* postilion

postizo, *a.* false, artificial, not natural. *m.* switch of false hair

postmeridiano, *a.* and *m.* postmeridian

postor, *m.* bidder (at auctions)

postración, *f.* prostration; exhaustion; depression, distress

postrar, *v.t.* to cast down, demolish; prostrate, exhaust; *v.r.* kneel down; be prostrated or exhausted

postre, *a.* last (in order). *m.* (*cul.*) dessert. **a la p.,** at last, finally

postrero, *a.* last (in order); rearmost, hindermost

postrimeramente, *adv.* lastly, finally

postrimería, *f.* (*ecc.*) last period of life

postulación, *f.* entreaty, request

postulado, *m.* assumption; supposition; working hypothesis; (*geom.*) postulate

postulante (-ta), *s.* (*ecc.*) postulant, applicant, candidate

postular, *v.t.* to postulate

póstumo, *a.* posthumous

postura, *f.* posture, bearing; laying (of an egg); bid (at auction); position; agreement, pact; bet, stake; planting; transplanted tree

potable, *a.* drinkable. **agua p.,** drinking water

potación, *f.* potation, drink

potaje, *m.* stew, potage; dried vegetables; mixed drink; hotch potch

potasa, *f.* potash

potásico, *a.* potassic

potasio, *m.* potassium

pote, *m.* pot; jar; flower-pot; (*cul.*) cauldron; (*cul.*) stew

potencia, *f.* power; potency; (*mech.*) performance, capacity; strength, force; (*math.*) power; rule, dominion

potencial, *a.* potential

potencialidad, *f.* potentiality

potentado, *m.* potentate

potente, *a.* potent; powerful; (*fam.*) enormous

poterna, *f.* (*mil.*) postern

potestad, *f.* authority, power; podesta, Italian magistrate; potentate; (*math.*) power; *pl.* angelic powers

potestativo, *a.* (*law*) facultative

potingue, *m.* (*fam.*) brew; mixture; lotion; medicine; filthy place, pigsty

potra, *f.* filly

potrada, *f.* herd of colts

potrear, *v.t.* (*fam.*) to tease, annoy

potro, *m.* colt, foal; rack (for torture); vaulting-horse. **p. mesteño,** mustang

poyo, *m.* stone seat

pozal, *m.* pail, bucket

pozo, *m.* well; shaft (in a mine). (*aut.*) **p. colector,** sump

práctica, *f.* practice; custom, habit; method; exercise

practicabilidad, *f.* feasibility

practicable, *a.* feasible, practicable

practicaje, *m.* (*naut.*) pilotage

prácticamente, *adv.* practically, in practice

practicante, *m.* medical practitioner; medical student; (*med.*) interne; first-aider

practicar, *v.t.* to execute, perform; practise; make

práctico, *a.* practical; experienced, expert; workable. *m.* (*naut.*) pilot

pradeño, *a.* meadow, prairie

pradera, *f.* meadow, field; lawn

pradería, *f.* meadowland, prairie

prado, *m.* meadow; grassland; field; lawn; walk (in cities)

pragmatismo, *m.* pragmatism

pragmatista, *a.* pragmatic. *m.* and *f.* pragmatist

pravedad, *f.* wickedness, immorality, depravity

pravo, *a.* wicked, immoral, depraved

pre, *m.* (*mil.*) daily pay. *prep. insep.* pre-

preámbulo, *m.* preamble, preface; importunate digression

prebenda, *f.* (*ecc.*) prebend, benefice; (*fam.*) sinecure

prebendado, *m.* (*ecc.*) prebendary

prebostazgo, *m.* provostship

preboste, *m.* provost

precario, *a.* precarious, uncertain, insecure

precaución, *f.* precaution, safeguard

precaucionarse, *v.r.* to take precautions, safeguard oneself

precautelar, *v.t.* to forewarn; take precautions

precaver, *v.t.* to prevent, avoid; *v.r.* (*with de* or *contra*) guard against

precavido, *a.* cautious, forewarned

precedencia, *f.* priority, precedence; superiority; preference, precedence

precedente, *a.* preceding. *m.* antecedent; precedent

preceder, *v.t.* to precede; have precedence over, be superior to

preceptivo, *a.* preceptive; didactic

precepto, *m.* precept; order, injunction; rule, commandment. **de p.,** obligatory

preceptor (-ra), *s.* teacher, instructor, tutor, preceptor

preces, *f. pl. (ecc.)* prayers; entreaties

preciado, *a.* excellent, esteemed, precious; boastful

preciar, *v.t.* to esteem, value; valuate, price; *v.r.* boast

precintar, *v.t.* to seal; rope, string, tie up

precinto, *m.* sealing; roping, tying up; strap

precio, *m.* price, cost; recompense, reward; premium; rate; reputation, importance; esteem. **p. de tasa,** controlled price

preciosidad, *f.* preciousness; exquisiteness, fineness; richness; wittiness; *(fam.)* loveliness, beauty; thing of beauty

precioso, *a.* precious; exquisite, fine, rare; rich; witty; *(fam.)* lovely, delicious, attractive

precipicio, *m.* precipice; heavy fall; ruin, disaster

precipitación, *f.* precipitancy, haste; rashness; *(chem.)* precipitation

precipitadamente, *adv.* precipitately, in haste; rashly, foolishly

precipitado, *a.* precipitate; rash, thoughtless. *m. (chem.)* precipitate

precipitar, *v.t.* to precipitate, hurl headlong; hasten; *(chem.)* precipitate; *v.r.* hurl oneself headlong; hasten, rush

precipitoso, *a.* precipitous; rash, heedless

precisamente, *adv.* exactly, precisely, just; necessarily. **Y p. en aquel instante llegó,** And just at that moment he arrived

precisar, *v.t.* to fix, arrange; set forth, draw up, state; compel, force, oblige

precisión, *f.* accuracy, precision; necessity, conciseness, clarity; compulsion, obligation

preciso, *a.* necessary, unavoidable; concise, clear; precise, exact

precitado, *a.* aforementioned

preclaro, *a.* illustrious, distinguished, celebrated

precocidad, *f.* precocity

precognición, *f.* foreknowledge

preconcebido, *a.* preconceived

preconizar, *v.t.* to eulogize, praise publicly

preconocer, *v.t. irr.* to know beforehand; foresee. See **conocer**

precoz, *a.* precocious

precursor (-ra), *a.* precursory; preceding, previous. *s.* precursor

predecesor (-ra), *s.* predecessor

predecir, *v.t. irr.* to foretell, prophesy. See **decir**

predestinación, *f.* predestination

predestinado (-da), *a.* predestined; foreordained. *s.* one of the predestined

predestinar, *v.t.* to predestine, foreordain

predeterminación, *f.* predetermination

predeterminar, *v.t.* to predetermine

prédica, *f. (fam.,* contemptuous*)* sermon

predicación, *f.* preaching; homily, sermon

predicadera, *f.* pulpit; *pl. (fam.)* talent for preaching

predicado, *m. (gram., phil.)* predicate

predicador (-ra), *a.* preaching. *s.* preacher

predicamento, *m.* predicament; reputation

predicar, *v.t.* to publish; manifest; preach; *v.i.* overpraise; *(fam.)* lecture, scold

predicción, *f.* prediction, prophecy

predilección, *f.* predilection, preference, partiality

predilecto, *a.* favourite, preferred

predisponer, *v.t. irr.* to predispose. See **poner**

predisposición, *f.* predisposition; tendency, prejudice

predominación, *f.* predominance

predominante, *a.* predominant; prevailing

predominar, *v.i.* and *v.t.* to predominate; prevail; tower above; overlook

predominio, *m.* predominance, ascendancy, preponderance

preeminencia, *f.* pre-eminence

preeminente, *a.* pre-eminent

preexistencia, *f.* pre-existence

preexistente, *a.* pre-existent

preexistir, *v.i.* to pre-exist, exist before

prefacio, *m.* introduction, preface, prologue; (*ecc.*) preface

prefecto, *m.* prefect

prefectura, *f.* prefecture

preferencia, *f.* preference; superiority. de p., preferred, favourite; preferably

preferente, *a.* preferable; preferential; preferred (of shares)

preferible, *a.* preferable

preferir, *v.t. irr.* to prefer; excel, exceed. *Pres. Part.* prefiriendo. *Pres. Ind.* prefiero, prefieres, prefiere, prefieren. *Preterite* prefirió, prefirieron. *Pres. Subjunc.* prefiera, prefieras, prefiera, prefieran. *Imperf. Subjunc.* prefiriese, etc.

prefijar, *v.t.* to prefix

prefijo, *m.* (*gram.*) prefix

prefinir, *v.t.* to fix a time limit for

prefulgente, *a.* brilliant, shining, resplendent

pregón, *m.* public proclamation; marriage banns

pregonar, *v.t.* to proclaim publicly; cry one's wares; publish abroad; eulogize, praise; proscribe, outlaw. p. a los cuatro vientos, (*fam.*) to shout from the housetops

pregonería, *f.* office of the town crier

pregonero, *m.* town crier

preguerra, *f.* pre-war period

pregunta, *f.* question; (*com.*) inquiry; questionnaire, interrogation. (*fam.*) andar (*or* estar) a la cuarta p., to be very hard up, be on the rocks. hacer una p., to ask a question

preguntador (-ra), *a.* questioning; inquisitive. *s.* questioner; inquisitive person

preguntar, *v.t.* to question, ask; (*with por*) inquire for; *v.r.* ask oneself, wonder

prehistoria, *f.* prehistory

prehistórico, *a.* prehistoric

prejuicio, *m.* prejudice

prejuzgar, *v.t.* to prejudge, judge hastily

prelacía, *f.* prelacy

prelación, *f.* preference

prelado, *m.* (*ecc.*) prelate

preliminar, *a.* preliminary, prefatory. *m.* preliminary

preludiar, *v.i.* and *v.t.* (mus.) to play a prelude (to); *v.t.* prepare, initiate

preludio, *m.* introduction, prologue; (*mus.*) prelude; (*mus.*) overture

prematuro, *a.* premature, untimely; unseasonable; immature, unripe

premeditación, *f.* premeditation

premeditar, *v.t.* to premeditate, plan in advance

premiador (-ra), *a.* rewarding. *s.* rewarder

premiar, *v.t.* to reward, requite

premio, *m.* prize; reward; premium; (*com.*) interest. p. en metálico, cash prize. (*fam.*) p. gordo, the fat prize (in a lottery)

premioso, *a.* tight; troublesome, annoying; stern, strict; slow-moving; burdensome, hard; laboured (of speech or style)

premisa, *f.* premise; sign, indication

premonitorio, *a.* premonitory

premura, *f.* urgency, haste

prenda, *f.* pledge; token, sign; jewel; article of clothing; talent, gift; loved one; *pl.* game of forfeits

prendador (-ra), *s.* pledgor

prendamiento, *m.* pawning

prendar, *v.t.* to pawn; charm, delight; *v.r.* (*with de*) take a liking for

prender, *v.t.* to seize; arrest; capture, catch. *v.i.* take root (plants); catch fire; be infectious

prendería, *f.* second-hand shop

prendero (-ra), *s.* second-hand dealer

prendimiento, *m.* seizure, capture; arrest

prenombre, *m.* prenomen, christian name

prensa, *f.* press; printing press;

newspapers, Press. **dar a la p.**, to publish

prensado, *m.*, **prensadura**, *f.* pressing; flattening; squeezing

prensar, *v.t.* to press; squeeze

prensil, *a.* prehensile

preñado, *a.* pregnant; bulging, sagging (walls, etc.); swollen. *m.* pregnancy

preñez, *f.* pregnancy; suspense

preocupación, *f.* anxiety, preoccupation; prejudice

preocupadamente, *adv.* preoccupiedly, absentmindedly; with prejudice.

preocupar, *v.t.* to preoccupy; make anxious; bias, prejudice; *v.r.* be anxious; be prejudiced

preordinar, *v.t.* (*ecc.*) to predestine

preparación, *f.* preparation; treatment; compound, specific

preparado, *a.* ready, prepared. *m.* preparation, patent food, etc.

preparar, *v.t.* to prepare; (*met.*) dress; *v.r.* prepare oneself; qualify

preparativo, *a.* preparatory. *m.* preparation

preparatorio, *a.* preparatory

preponderancia, *f.* preponderance

preponderante, *a.* preponderant; dominant

preponderar, *v.i.* to preponderate; dominate; outweigh

preponer, *v.t. irr.* to put before. See **poner**

preposición, *f.* (*gram.*) preposition

preposicional, *a.* prepositional

prepósito, *m.* chairman, head, president; (*ecc.*) provost

prepucio, *m.* (*anat.*) prepuce

prerrafaelista, *a.* and *m.* and *f.* Pre-Raphaelite

prerrogativa, *f.* prerogative

presa, *f.* hold, grasp; seizure, capture; booty; dam; lock (on rivers, canals); weir; ditch, trench; embankment; slice, bit. **hacer p.**, to seize; take advantage of (circumstances)

presagiar, *v.t.* to prophesy, presage, bode

presagio, *m.* presage, sign; presentiment, foreboding

présbita, *a.* long-sighted

presbiterado, *m.* priesthood; holy orders

presbiteriano (**-na**), *a.* and *s.* Presbyterian

presbiterio, *m.* chancel; presbytery

presbítero, *m.* priest

presciencia, *f.* prescience, foresight

presciente, *a.* prescient, farsighted

prescindible, *a.* non-essential, able to be dispensed with

prescindir, *v.i.* (*with de*) to pass over, omit; do without. **Prescindiendo de esto . . .**, Leaving this aside

prescribir, *v.t.* to prescribe, order

prescripción, *f.* prescription

presea, *f.* jewel, object of value

presencia, *f.* presence, attendance; appearance, looks; ostentation. **p. de ánimo**, presence of mind

presenciar, *v.t.* to be present at; witness, behold

presentación, *f.* presentation; introduction

presentar, *v.t.* to show; present, make a gift of; introduce (persons); *v.r.* occur; present oneself; offer one's services

presente, *a.* present. *m.* gift; present time. (*law*) **Por estas presentes . . .**, By these presents . . . **tener p.**, to remember

presentimiento, *m.* presentiment, apprehension

presentir, *v.t. irr.* to have a presentiment of. See **sentir**

preservación, *f.* preservation, protection, saving

preservar, *v.t.* to preserve, protect, save

preservativo, *a.* preservative. *m.* preservative, safeguard, protection

presidencia, *f.* presidency; chairmanship; presidential seat or residence

presidencial, *a.* presidential

presidenta, *f.* woman president; president's wife; woman chairman

presidente, *m.* president; chairman; head, director; presiding judge

presidiar, *v.t.* (*mil.*) to garrison

presidiario, *m.* convict

presidio, *m.* (*mil.*) garrison;

garrison town; fortress; péni-
tentiary; imprisonment; (law)
hard labour; assistance, protection

presidir, v.t. to preside over;
act as chairman for; influence,
determine

presilla, f. loop, shank, noose;
press stud

presión, f. pressure

preso (-sa), s. prisoner, captive;
convict

prestación, f. lending, loan

prestador (-ra), a. lending, loan.
s. lender

prestamente, adv. expeditiously,
promptly

prestamista, m. and f. money-
lender; pawnbroker

préstamo, m. loan; lending.
casa de préstamos, pawn-
shop

prestar, v.t. to lend; assist; pay
(attention); give; v.i. be useful;
give, expand; v.r. be suitable;
lend itself; offer oneself. tomar
prestado, to borrow

prestatario (-ia), s. money borrower

preste, m. celebrant of High Mass.
p. Juan, title of Emperor of
Abyssinia, Prester John

presteza, f. speed; promptness,
dispatch

prestidigitación, f. prestidigitation

prestidigitador (-ra), s. juggler,
conjurer

prestigio, m. magic spell, sorcery; trick, illusion (of conjurers, etc.); influence, prestige

prestigioso, a. illusory; influential

presto, a. quick, speedy; prompt,
ready. adv. immediately; soon;
quickly. de p., speedily

presumido, a. conceited, vain;
presumptuous

presumir, v.t. to suppose, presume; v.i. be conceited

presunción, f. supposition, presumption; vanity, presumptuousness

presuntivo, a. presumptive

presuntuosidad, f. presumptuousness

presuntuoso, a. presumptuous,
vain

presuponer, v.t. irr. to presup-

pose, assume; budget, estimate.
See poner

presuposición, f. presupposition

presupuesto, m. motive, reason;
supposition, assumption; estimate; (com.) tender; national
budget

presuroso, a. swift, speedy

pretal, m. breastplate

pretencioso, a. pretentious, vain

pretender, v.t. to seek, solicit;
claim; apply for; attempt, try;
woo, court

pretendiente (-ta), s. pretender;
candidate; petitioner; suitor

pretensión, f. pretension; claim;
pl. ambitions

pretérito, a. past. m. (gram.)
preterite

pretextar, v.t. to allege as a pretext or excuse

pretexto, m. pretext, excuse

pretina, f. waist-band; belt

prevalecer, v.i. irr. to prevail; be
dominant; take root (plants).
See conocer

prevaleciente, a. prevailing; prevalent

prevaricación, f. prevarication

prevaricador (-ra), s. prevaricator

prevaricar, v.i. to prevaricate

prevención, f. prevention; precaution; prejudice; policestation;
(mil.) guard-room; foresight, prevision; preparation. de p., as a
precaution

prevenido, a. prepared; cautious,
forewarned

prevenir, v.t. irr. to prepare;
prevent, avoid; warn; prejudice;
occur, happen; (fig.) overcome
(obstacles); v.r. be ready; be
forewarned. See venir

preventivo, a. preventive

prever, v.t. irr. to foresee, forecast, anticipate. See ver

previamente, adv. previously, in
advance

previo, a. previous, advance

previsión, f. forecast; foresight,
prevision, prescience. p. social,
social insurance

previsor, a. far-sighted, provident

prieto, a. almost black, blackish;
tight; mean, avaricious

prima, f. (ecc.) prime; (com.)
premium; female cousin

primacía, *f.* supremacy, pre-eminence; primacy; primateship

primada, *f.* (*fam.*) act of sponging upon, taking advantage of

primado, *m.* primate; primate-ship

primario, *a.* primary. *m.* professor who gives first lecture of the day

primavera, *f.* spring-tide; prim-rose; figured silk material; beautifully coloured thing; youth; prime

primaveral, *a.* spring, springlike

primeramente, *adv.* firstly; in the first place

primerizo (-za), *s.* novice; beginner; apprentice; first-born

primero, *a.* first; former; excellent, first-rate. *adv.* first; in the first place. primera enseñanza, primary education. primera materia, raw material. primer plano, (*art*) foreground. primera cura, first aid. de buenas a primeras, all at once, suddenly

primicia, *f.* first fruits; offering of these; *pl.* first effects

primitivo, *a.* original, early; primitive

primo (-ma), *a.* first; excellent, fine. *s.* cousin; (*fam.*) simpleton; (*fam.*) pigeon, dupe. p. carnal, first cousin. (*fam.*) hacer el p., to be a dupe. (*fam.*) ser prima hermana de, to be the twin of (of things)

primogénito (-ta), *a.* and *s.* first-born

primogenitura, *f.* primogeniture

primor, *m.* exquisite care; beauty, loveliness; thing of beauty

primoroso, *a.* beautiful; exquisitely done; dexterous, skilful

primula, *f.* (*bot.*) cowslip; primula

princesa, *f.* princess

principado, *m.* principality; princedom; superiority, pre-eminence

principal, *a.* chief, principal; illustrious; fundamental, first. *m.* head, principal (of a firm); (*com.*) capital, principal; first floor

principalmente, *adv.* principally, chiefly

príncipe, *m.* leader; prince. p. de Asturias, Prince of Asturias, (heir to Spanish throne). p. de la sangre, prince of the blood royal

principesco, *a.* princely

principiante (-ta), *s.* beginner, novice; apprentice

principiar, *v.t.* to begin, commence

principio, *m.* beginning; principle; genesis, origin; rudiment; axiom; constituent. al p., at first. a. principios, at the beginning (of the month, year, etc.). en p., in principle

pringar, *v.t.* (*cul.*) to soak in fat; stain with grease; (*fam.*) wound; take part in a business deal; slander; *v.r.* (*fam.*) appropriate, misuse (funds, etc.)

pringoso, *a.* greasy

pringue, *m.* or *f.* animal fat, lard; grease spot

prior, *m.* prior; parish priest

priora, *f.* prioress

priorato, *m.* priorship; priory

prioridad, *f.* priority

prisa, *f.* haste, speed; skirmish, foray. a toda p., with all speed. correr p., to be urgent. dar p., to hasten, speed up. darse (*or* estar de) p., to hurry

prisión, *f.* prison, gaol; seizure; captivity, imprisonment; (*fig.*) bond; obstacle, shackle; *pl.* fetters

prisionero (-ra), *s.* prisoner; (*fig.*) victim (of passion, etc.)

prisma, *m.* prism

prismático, *a.* prismatic

prismáticos, *m. pl.* field glasses

pristino, *a.* pristine

privación, *f.* privation; lack, shortage; deprivation; degradation

privada, *f.* water-closet

privadamente, *adv.* privately; individually, separately

privado, *a.* private; individual, personal. *m.* favourite; confidant

privanza, *f.* court favour, intimacy of princes

privar, *v.t.* to deprive; dismiss (from office); interdict, forbid; *v.i.* prevail, be in favour; *v.r.* swoon; deprive oneself

privilegiar, *v.t.* to privilege; bestow a favour on

privilegio, *m.* privilege; prerogative; concession; copyright; patent

pro, *m.* or *f.* advantage, benefit.
el p. y el contra, the pros and
cons. en p., in favour

proa, *f.* (*naut.*) prow, bow

probabilidad, *f.* probability

probable, *a.* probable; likely;
provable

probación, *f.* proof, test; novitiate, probation

probado, *a.* tried, tested, proved

probar, *v.t. irr.* to prove; test;
taste; try on (clothes); *v.i.* suit;
(*with prep.* a + *infin.*) try to.
p. fortuna, to try one's luck.
Pres. Ind. pruebo, pruebas,
prueba, prueban. *Pres. Subjunc.* pruebe, pruebes, prueben

probatorio, *a.* probationary

probeta, *f.* (*chem.*) measurement
cylinder; (*mech.*) test piece; pressure gauge

probidad, *f.* probity, trustworthiness, honesty

problema, *m.* problem

problemático, *a.* problematical,
uncertain

probo, *a.* honest, trustworthy

procacidad, *f.* insolence, pertness

procaz, *a.* insolent, pert, brazen

procedencia, *f.* origin, source;
parentage, descent; (*naut.*) port
of sailing or call

procedente, *a.* arriving or coming
from

proceder, *v.i.* to proceed; behave; originate, arise; continue,
go on; act. (*law*) p. contra,
to proceed against (a person)

procedimiento, *m.* proceeding,
advancement; procedure; legal
practice; process

proceloso, *a.* tempestuous

prócer, *a.* exalted, eminent;
lofty. *m.* exalted personage

procesado (-da), *s.* (*law*) defendant

procesamiento, *m.* suing, suit;
indictment

procesar, *v.t.* (*law*) to proceed
against, sue

procesión, *f.* proceeding, emana-
ting; procession; (*fam.*) train,
string. andar (*or* ir) por
dentro la p., to feel keenly
without betraying one's emotion

procesional, *a.* processional

proceso, *m.* process; progress;
advancement; lapse of time;
lawsuit

proclama, *f.* proclamation; announcement; publication of marriage banns

proclamación, *f.* proclamation;
acclaim, applause

proclamar, *v.t.* to proclaim;
acclaim; publish abroad; reveal,
show

proclividad, *f.* proclivity, tendency

procomún, *m.* social or public
welfare

procreación, *f.* procreation

procreador (-ra), *a.* procreative.
s. procreator

procrear, *v.t.* to procreate, beget,
engender

procuración, *f.* procurement;
assiduity, care; (*law*) power of
attorney; (*law*) solicitorship;
(*law*) attorneyship

procurador (-ra), *m.* proxy;
(*law*) solicitor; (*law*) attorney;
proctor. *s.* procurer

procurar, *v.t.* to try, attempt;
procure, get; exercise the profession of a solicitor

prodigalidad, *f.* prodigality,
lavishness; waste, extravagance

prodigar, *v.t.* to waste, squander;
lavish, bestow freely; *v.r.* make
oneself cheap

prodigio, *m.* marvel, wonder;
prodigy; monster; miracle

prodigiosidad, *f.* prodigiousness

prodigioso, *a.* wonderful; prodigious; monstrous; miraculous

pródigo (-ga), *a.* wasteful, extravagant; lavish, generous. *s.*
spendthrift, wastrel, prodigal

producción, *f.* production; output, yield; generation (of heat,
etc.); crop

producir, *v.t. irr.* to produce;
generate; yield, give; cause,
occasion; publish; *v.r.* explain
oneself; arise, appear, be pro-
duced. p. efecto, to have effect;
take effect. See conducir

productividad, *f.* productivity

productivo, *a.* productive; fertile; profitable

producto, *m.* produce; product;
profit; yield, gain; (*math.*) product. (*chem.*) p. derivado, by-
product

productor (-ra), *a.* productive.
s. producer

proemio, *m.* prologue, preface, introduction

proeza, *f.* prowess, gallantry; skill

profanación, *f.* profanation

profanador (-ra), *s.* profaner, transgressor

profanar, *v.t.* to profane

profanidad, *f.* profanity

profano, *a.* profane; dissolute; pleasure-loving, worldly; immodest; lay, ignorant

profecía, *f.* prophecy; (*ecc.*) Book of the Prophets; opinion, view

proferir, *v.t. irr.* to utter, pronounce. See **herir**

profesar, *v.t.* to exercise, practise (professions); (*ecc.*) profess; believe in; teach

profesión, *f.* profession; trade, occupation; avowal, admission

profesional, *a.* professional

profesionalismo, *m.* professionalism

profeso (-sa), *a.* (*ecc.*) professed. *s.* professed monk

profesor (-ra), *s.* teacher; professor

profesorado, *m.* teaching staff; teaching profession; professorship; professoriate

profeta, *m.* prophet; seer

profético, *a.* prophetic

profetisa, *f.* prophetess

profetizar, *v.t.* to prophesy; imagine, suppose

proficiente, *a.* proficient

profiláctico, *a.* and *m.* (*med.*) prophylactic

prófugo (-ga), *a.* and *s.* fugitive from justice. *m.* (*mil.*) one who evades military service

profundamente, *adv.* profoundly; acutely, deeply

profundidad, *f.* depth; profundity, obscurity; (*geom.*) depth; concavity; intensity (of feeling); vastness (of knowledge, etc.)

profundizar, *v.t.* to deepen; hollow out; (*fig.*) go into deeply, fathom

profundo, *a.* deep; low; (*fig.*) intense, acute; abstruse, profound; (*fig.*) vast, extensive; high. *m.* depth, profundity; (*poet.*) ocean, the deep; (*poet.*) hell

profuso, *a.* profuse, abundant; extravagant, wasteful

progenie, *f.* descendants

prognosis, *f.* prognosis; forecast

programa, *m.* programme; edict, public notice; plan, scheme; (*univ.*) calendar; syllabus; timetable

progresar, *v.t.* and *v.i.* to make progress; progress, advance

progresión, *f.* progression (also *math.*); advancement, progress

progresista, *a.* (*pol.*) progressive. *m.* and *f.* progressive

progresivo, *a.* progressive; advancing

progreso, *m.* progress, advancement; growth; improvement, development

prohibente, *a.* prohibitory, prohibitive

prohibición, *f.* forbidding, prohibition

prohibicionista, *m.* and *f.* prohibitionist. *a.* prohibitionist

prohibir, *v.t.* to forbid, prohibit. Prohibido el paso, No thoroughfare

prohibitivo, prohibitorio, *a.* prohibitive

prohijador (-ra), *s.* adopter (of a child)

prohijamiento, *m.* child adoption; fathering (of a bill, etc.)

prohijar, *v.t.* to adopt (children, ideas); (*fig.*) father

prohombre, *m.* master of a guild; respected, well-liked man

prójimo, *m.* fellow-man, brother, neighbour. A tu p. como a tí, Do to others as you would be done by

prole, *f.* progeny, young offspring

proletariado, *m.* proletariat

proletario, *a.* poor; common, vulgar. *m.* plebeian; pauper; proletarian

prolífico, *a.* prolific; abundant, fertile

prolijidad, *f.* verbosity, prolixity; nicety, scruple; importunity, tediousness

prolijo, *a.* verbose, prolix; fussy, fastidious; tedious, importunate

prologar, *v.t.* to prologue; provide with a preface

prólogo, *m.* preface; (*theat.*) prologue; introduction

prolongación, *f.* lengthening; prolongation, protraction; extension

prolongado, *a.* prolonged; oblong, long

prolongar, *v.t.* to lengthen; (*geom.*) produce; prolong, spin out

promediar, *v.t.* to distribute or divide into two equal portions; average; *v.i.* arbitrate; place oneself between two people; reach half time

promedio, *m.* average; middle, centre

promesa, *f.* promise; augury, favourable sign

prometedor (-ra), *a.* promising. *s.* promiser

prometer, *v.t.* to promise; attest, certify; *v.i.* promise well, look hopeful; *v.r.* devote oneself to service of God; anticipate confidently, expect; become engaged (marriage). (*fam.*) **prometérselas muy felices**, to have high hopes

prometido (-da), *s.* affianced, betrothed. *m.* promise

prometimiento, *m.* promise; promising

prominencia, *f.* prominence, protuberance; eminence, hill

prominente, *a.* prominent, protuberant; eminent, elevated

promiscuar, *v.i.* to eat meat and fish on fast days

promiscuidad, *f.* promiscuity; ambiguity

promiscuo, *a.* indiscriminate, haphazard, promiscuous; ambiguous

promisión, *f.* promise

promisorio, *a.* promissory

promoción, *f.* promotion; batch, class, year (of recruits, students, etc.)

promontorio, *m.* headland; promontory; cumbersome object

promotor (-ra), *a.* promotive. *s.* promoter; supporter

promover, *v.t. irr.* to promote, further, advance; promote (a person). See **mover**

promulgación, *f.* promulgation

promulgar, *v.t.* to publish officially, proclaim; promulgate. (*law*) **p. sentencia**, to pass judgment

pronombre, *m.* (*gram.*) pronoun

pronosticación, *f.* prognostication; presage

pronosticar, *v.t.* to prognosticate, forecast; presage

pronóstico, *m.* omen, prediction; almanac; (*med.*) prognosis; sign, indication. **p. del tiempo**, weather-forecast

prontitud, *f.* quickness, promptness; quick-wittedness; (*fig.*) sharpness, liveliness; celerity, dispatch

pronto, *a.* quick, speedy; prompt; ready, prepared. *m.* (*fam.*) sudden decision. *adv.* immediately; with all speed; soon. **de p.**, suddenly; without thinking. **por lo p.**, temporarily, provisionally

prontuario, *m.* compendium, handbook; summary

pronunciación, *f.* pronunciation

pronunciamiento, *m.* military rising; political manifesto; (*law*) pronouncement of sentence

pronunciar, *v.t.* to pronounce, articulate; decide, determine; (*law*) pronounce judgment; give, make (a speech)

propagación, *f.* propagation; dissemination; transmission

propagador, *a.* propagative. *m.* propagator

propaganda, *f.* propaganda organization; propaganda

propagandista, *m.* and *f.* propagandist

propagar, *v.t.* to reproduce; propagate, disseminate; *v.r.* reproduce, multiply; propagate, spread

propalar, *v.t.* to disseminate, spread abroad

propasarse, *v.r.* to go too far, forget oneself; overstep one's authority

propender, *v.i.* to be inclined, have a leaning to

propensión, *f.* propensity, inclination; tendency

propenso, *a.* inclined, disposed; liable

propiamente, *adv.* properly, suitably

propiciación, *f.* propitiation

propiciador (-ra), *a.* propitiatory. *s.* propitiator

propiciar, *v.t.* to propitiate, appease

propiciatorio, *a.* propitiatory

propicio, *a.* propitious, auspicious; kind, favourable

propiedad, *f.* estate, property; ownership; landed property; attribute, quality, property; (*art*) resemblance, naturalness

propietario (-ia), *a.* proprietary. *s.* proprietor, owner

propina, *f.* gratuity, tip. (*fam.*) **de p.,** in addition, extra

propinar, *v.t.* to treat to a drink; administer (medicine); (*fam.*) give (slaps, etc.)

propincuidad, *f.* propinquity, proximity

propincuo, *a.* near, contiguous, adjacent

propio, *a.* own, one's own; typical, characteristic; individual, peculiar; suitable, apt; natural, real; same. *m.* messenger; *pl.* public lands

proponente, *a.* proposing. *m.* proposer; (*com.*) tenderer

proponer, *v.t. irr.* to propose, suggest; make a proposition; propose (for a post, office, etc.); (*math.*) state; *v.r.* intend, purpose. **proponerse para un empleo,** to apply for a post. See **poner**

proporción, *f.* proportion; chance, opportunity; size; (*math.*) proportion

proporcionado, *a.* fit, suitable; proportionate; symmetrical

proporcional, *a.* proportional

proporcionar, *v.t.* to allot, proportion; supply, provide, give; adapt

proposición, *f.* proposition; motion (in a debate)

propósito, *m.* proposal; intention, aim; subject, question, matter. **a p.,** suitable, apropos; by the way, incidentally. **de p.,** with the intention, proposing. **fuera de p.,** irrelevant

propuesta, *f.* proposal, tender

propugnar, *v.t.* to defend, protect

propulsar, *v.t.* to repulse, throw back; propel, drive

propulsión, *f.* repulse; propulsion

propulsor, *a.* driving, propelling. *m.* propeller

prorrata, *f.* quota, share, apportionment. **a p.,** in proportion

prorratear, *v.t.* to apportion, distribute proportionately

prorrogación, *f.* prorogation, ad-

journment; extension (of time); renewal (of a lease, etc.)

prorrogar, *v.t.* to extend, prolong; defer, suspend, prorogue; renew (leases, etc.)

prorrumpir, *v.t.* (*with en*) to burst out; utter, give vent to, burst into

prosa, *f.* prose; prosaism, prosaic style; (*fam.*) dull verbosity; monotony, tediousness

prosaico, *a.* prosaic; prosy; monotonous, tedious; matter-of-fact

prosapia, *f.* family, lineage, descent

proscenio, *m.* (*theat.*) proscenium

proscribir, *v.t.* to proscribe, outlaw; forbid, prohibit. *Past Part.* **proscrito**

proscripción, *f.* proscription

proscrito (-ta), *s.* outlaw, exile

prosecución, *f.* prosecution, performance; pursuit

proseguir, *v.t. irr.* to continue, proceed with. See **pedir**

proselitismo, *m.* proselytism

prosélito, *m.* convert, proselyte

prosificar, *v.t.* to turn verse into prose

prosista, *m.* and *f.* prose writer

prosodia, *f.* prosody

prospecto, *m.* prospectus

prosperar, *v.t.* to prosper; protect; *v.i.* flourish, prosper

prosperidad, *f.* prosperity; wealth; success

próspero, *a.* favourable, propitious, fortunate; prosperous

próstata, *f.* (*anat.*) prostate

prostitución, *f.* prostitution

prostituir, *v.t. irr.* to prostitute; *v.r.* become a prostitute; sell oneself, debase oneself. See **huir**

prostituta, *f.* prostitute

protagonista, *m.* and *f.* hero or heroine, principal character; leading figure, protagonist

protección, *f.* protection, defence; favour, aid

proteccionismo, *m.* (*pol.*) protectionism

proteccionista, *m.* and *f.* (*pol.*) protectionist

protector, *a.* protective. *m.* protector; guard

protectorado, *m.* protectorate

protectriz, *f.* protectress

proteger, *v.t.* to protect, defend; favour, assist

protegido (-da), *s.* protégé

proteico, *a.* protean

proteína, *f.* protein

proteo, *a.* Protean

protervia, *f.* depravity, perversity

protervo, *a.* depraved, perverse

protesta, protestación, *f.* protest; protestation, declaration

protestante, *a.* and *m.* and *f.* Protestant

protestantismo, *m.* Protestant

protestar, *v.t.* to declare, attest; (*with* contra) protest against; (*with* de) affirm vigorously

protesto, *m.* (*com.*) protest; objection

protocolizar, *v.t.* to protocol, draw up

protocolo, *m.* protocol

protoplasma, *m.* protoplasm

prototipo, *m.* model, prototype

protuberancia, *f.* protuberance, projection, swelling

provecto, *a.* ancient, venerable; mature, experienced

provecho, *m.* gain, benefit; profit; advantage; progress, proficiency. ¡ **Buen p.!** May it do you good! (said to those eating or drinking). **ser de p.,** to be advantageous or useful

provechoso, *a.* beneficial; profitable; advantageous; useful

proveedor (-ra), *s.* provider; purveyor, supplier

proveer, *v.t.* *irr.* to provide; furnish; supply; confer (honour, office); transact, arrange. **p. de,** to furnish or supply with; fit with. See **creer**

provenir, *v.i.* *irr.* (*with* de) to originate in, proceed from. See **venir**

provenzal, *a.* and *m.* and *f.* Provencal. *m.* Provencal language

proverbio, *m.* proverb; omen; *pl.* Book of Proverbs

providencia, *f.* precaution, foresight; provision, furnishing; measure, preparation. **la Divina P.,** Providence

providencial, *a.* providential

próvido, *a.* provident, thrifty, careful; kind, favourable

provincia, *f.* province; (*fig.*) sphere

provincial, *a.* provincial. *m.* (*ecc.*) provincial

provincialismo, *m.* provincialism

provinciano (-na), *a.* provincial. *s.* provincial, rustic, countryman; native of Spanish province of Biscay

provisión, *f.* stock, store; provision; supply; food supply (gen. *pl.*); catering; means, way

provisional, *a.* temporary, provisional

provisor, *m.* purveyor, supplier; (*ecc.*) vicar-general

provocación, *f.* provocation

provocador (-ra), *a.* provocative. *s.* provoker; instigator

provocar, *v.t.* to provoke; incite; irritate; help, assist; (*fam.*) vomit

provocativo, *a.* provocative

próximamente, *adv.* proximately; soon; approximately

proximidad, *f.* nearness, proximity (time or space)

próximo, *a.* near, neighbouring; next; not distant (of time)

proyección, *f.* projection (all meanings)

proyectante, *a.* projecting, jutting

proyectar, *v.t.* to throw, cast; plan, contrive; design; project; *v.r.* jut out; be cast (a shadow, etc.)

proyectil, *m.* projectile

proyectista, *m.* and *f.* planner

proyecto, *a.* placed in perspective. *m.* project, plan, scheme; planning; intention, idea

proyector (-ra), *s.* designer, planner. *m.* searchlight; spotlight; projector

prudencia, *f.* prudence, sagacity, caution; moderation

prudencial, *a.* prudent, discreet; safe

prudente, *a.* prudent, cautious; provident

prueba, *f.* proof; test; testing; trial; fitting (on) (of garments); sample; taste; (*law*) evidence; (*phot.*, *print.*) proof. (*law*) **p. de indicios** *or* **p. indiciaria,** circumstantial evidence. (*phot.*) **p. negativa,** negative. (*com.*) **a p.,** on approval; on trial; up to standard, perfect. **a p. de,** proof against (water, etc.). **poner a p.,** to put to the test, try out

prurito, *m.* (*med.*) pruritus; desire, longing

pseudónimo, *m.* pseudonym

psicoanálisis, *m.* psycho-analysis

psicoanalista, *m.* and *f.* psychoanalyst

psicoanalizar, *v.t.* to psycho-analyse

psicología, *f.* psychology

psicológico, *a.* psychological

psicólogo (-ga), *s.* psychologist

psicopático, *a.* psychopathic

psicosis, *f.* (*med.*) psychosis

psicoterapia, *f.* psychotherapy

psiquiatra, psiquiatro, *m.* psychiatrist

psiquiatría, *f.* psychiatry

psíquico, *a.* psychic

púa, *f.* prong; tooth (of a comb); quill (of porcupine); (*agr.*) graft; plectrum (for playing mandolin, etc.); anxiety, grief; (*bot.*) pine needle; (*fam.*) crafty person

púber, *a.* pubescent

pubertad, *f.* puberty

púbico, *a.* pubic

publicación, *f.* publication; announcement, proclamation; revelation; publishing of marriage banns

publicador (-ra), *a.* publishing. *s.* publisher; announcer

publicar, *v.t.* to publish; reveal; announce, proclaim; publish (marriage banns)

publicidad, *f.* publicity; advertising, propaganda

publicista, *m.* and *f.* publicist

público, *a.* well-known, universal; common, general; public. *m.* public; audience; gathering, attendance. **dar al p.** *or* **sacar al p.,** to publish

pucherazo, *m.* (*fam.*) electoral fraud, vote-cooking

puchero, *m.* (*cul.*) kind of stew; stew-pot; (*fam.*) daily food; puckering of the face preceding tears

pudendo, *a.* shameful, monstrous, obscene

pudicia, *f.* modesty; bashfulness; chastity

púdico, *a.* modest; bashful; chaste

pudiente, *a.* rich, wealthy; powerful

pudín, *m.* pudding

pudor, *m.* modesty; bashfulness, shyness

pudoroso, *a.* modest; shy

pudrición, *f.* putrefaction

pudrir, *v.t.* to rot, putrefy; irritate, worry, provoke; *v.i.* rot in the grave; *v.r.* rot; be consumed with anxiety

puebla, *f.* town; population; gardener's seed setting

pueblo, *m.* town; village, hamlet; people, population, inhabitants; common people; working-classes; nation

puente, *m.* or *f.* bridge; (*mus.*) bridge (of stringed instruments); (*naut.*) bridge; (*carp.*) cross-beam, transom. **p. colgante,** suspension-bridge. **p. levadizo,** drawbridge. **hacer p. de plata (a),** to remove obstacles for, make plain sailing

puerca, *f.* sow; (*fam.*) slattern; harridan, termagant

puerco, *m.* pig; wild boar. *a.* filthy; rough, rude; low, mean. **p. espín** *or* **p. espino,** porcupine. **p. marino,** dolphin. **p. montés** *or* **p. salvaje,** wild boar

puericultura, *f.* child welfare

pueril, *a.* childish, puerile; foolish, silly; trivial

puerilidad, *f.* puerility; foolishness; triviality

puerro, *m.* (*bot.*) leek

puerta, *f.* door; gate; goal (football, hockey); octroi duty; means, way. **p. caediza,** trap-door. **p. corrediza,** sliding-door. **p. de servicio,** tradesmen's entrance. **p. falsa** *or* **p. secreta,** secret door; side door. **p. trasera,** back door. **a p. cerrada,** in camera; in secret. (*fam.*) **dar con la p. en las narices (de),** to slam the door in a person's face; offend, insult. **llamar a la p.,** to knock at the door; be on the verge of happening. **tomar la p.,** to depart, go away

puerto, *m.* harbour; port; defile, narrow pass; refuge, haven. **p. fluvial,** river port. **p. franco,** free port. **tomar p.,** to put into port; take refuge

pues, *conjunc.* then; since, as; for, because; well. *adv.* yes, certainly. *conjunc.* **p. que,** since, as

puesta, *f.* (*ast.*) setting, sinking; stake (gambling). **p. de largo,**

coming of age; coming-out party. **p. del sol**, sunset

puesto, *m.* post, job; booth, stall; beat, pitch; place, position; state, condition; (*mil.*) encampment or barracks; office, position. **p. de los testigos**, witness-box. **p. de mando**, command, position of authority; saluting base. **p. de socorro**, dressing station

puesto, *a.* (*with bien* or *mal*) well or badly dressed. *conjunc.* **p. que**, since, as; although

púgil, *m.* pugilist, boxer

pugilato, *m.* boxing; boxing match

pugilista, *m.* boxer

pugna, *f.* fight, struggle; rivalry, conflict

pugnante, *a.* hostile, conflicting, rival

pugnar, *v.i.* to fight; quarrel; (*with con, contra*) struggle against, oppose; (*with por, para*) strive to

pugnaz, *a.* pugnacious

puja, *f.* outbidding (at auctions); higher bid; push, thrust

pujador (**-ra**), *s.* bidder or outbidder (at an auction)

pujante, *a.* strong, powerful, vigorous

pujanza, *f.* strength, vigour

pujar, *v.t.* to push on; bid or outbid (at auctions); *v.i.* stutter; hesitate, falter; (*fam.*) show signs of weeping

pujo, *m.* irresistible impulse; desire; will; purpose, intention

pulcritud, *f.* beauty, loveliness, delicacy; fastidiousness, subtlety

pulcro, *a.* beautiful, lovely; delicate, fine; fastidious, subtle

pulchinela, *m.* Punchinello

pulga, *f.* flea; small top (toy). **el juego de la p.**, tiddly-winks. (*fam.*) **tener malas pulgas**, to be irritable

pulgada, *f.* inch

pulgar, *m.* thumb

pulgón, *m.* aphis, greenfly

pulgoso, *a.* full of fleas

pulidez, *f.* elegance, fineness; polish, smoothness; neatness

pulido, *a.* elegant, fine; polished, smooth; neat

pulidor, *m.* polisher (machine)

pulimentar, *v.t.* to polish, burnish

pulir, *v.t.* to polish, burnish; give the finishing touch to; beautify, decorate; (*fig.*) polish up, civilize; *v.r.* beautify oneself; become polished and polite

pulmón, *m.* (*anat.*) lung

pulmonar, *a.* pulmonary

pulmonía, *f.* pneumonia

pulpa, *f.* fleshy part of fruit; (*anat.*) pulp; wood-pulp

pulpejo, *m.* (*anat.*) fleshy part, fat portion (of thumbs, etc.)

pulpería, *f.* drug store (*S.A.*)

púlpito, *m.* pulpit

pulpo, *m.* octopus. (*fam.*) **poner como un p.**, to beat to a pulp

pulposo, *a.* pulpy, pulpous

pulquérrimo, *a. sup.* **pulcro**, most lovely, most exquisite

pulsación, *f.* pulsation; throb, beat

pulsar, *v.t.* to touch, feel; take the pulse of; (*fig.*) explore (a possibility); *v.i.* beat (the heart, etc.)

pulsátil, pulsativo, *a.* pulsatory

pulsera, *f.* bracelet; wrist bandage. **p. de pedida**, betrothal bracelet

pulso, *m.* pulse; steadiness of hand; tact, diplomacy, circumspection. **a p.**, free-hand (drawing). **tomar a p.** (**una cosa**), to try a thing's weight. **tomar el p.** (**a**), to take a person's pulse

pulular, *v.i.* to pullulate, sprout; abound, be plentiful; swarm, teem; multiply (of insects)

pulverización, *f.* pulverization; atomization

pulverizador, *m.* atomizer, sprayer; scent-spray

pulverizar, *v.t.* to pulverize, grind, make into powder; atomize; spray

pulla, *f.* lewd remark; strong hint; witty comment

¡pum! *interj.* bang! thump!

pundonor, *m.* (**punto de honor**) point of honour, sense of honour

pundonoroso, *a.* careful of one's honour; honourable, punctilious

pungir, *v.t.* to prick, pierce; revive an old sorrow; (*fig.*) wound, sting (passions)

punible, *a.* punishable

púnico, *a.* Punic

punitivo, *a* punitive, punitory

punta, *f.* sharp end, point; butt (of a cigarette); end, point, tip; cape, headland; trace, touch, suspicion; nib (of a pen); pointing (pointer dogs); (*her.*) point; *pl.* point lace. **p. de París,** wire nail. **p. seca,** dry-point, engraving needle. **sacar p.,** to sharpen; (*fam.*) twist (a remark)

puntación, *f.* dotting, placing dots over (letters)

puntada, *f.* (*sew.*) stitch; innuendo, hint

puntal, *m.* (*naut.*) draught, depth; stanchion, prop, brace, pile; (*fig.*) basis, foundation

puntapié, *m.* kick

punteado, *m.* plucking the strings of a guitar, etc.; sewing

puntear, *v.t.* to make dots; (*mus.*) pluck the strings of; play the guitar; sew; (*art*) stipple; *v.i.* (*naut.*) tack

puntera, *f.* mend in the toe of a stocking; toe-cap; new piece on toe of shoe; (*fam.*) kick

puntería, *f.* aiming (of a fire-arm); aim, sight (fire-arm); marksmanship

puntero, *a.* of a good aim, having a straight eye. *m.* pointer, wand, tally-man; stone-cutter's chisel

puntiagudo, *a.* pointed, sharp-pointed

puntilla, *f.* narrow lace edging; headless nail, wire nail; brad, tack. **de puntillas,** on tip-toe

puntillismo, *m.* (*art*) pointillisme

puntilloso, *a.* punctilious; over-fastidious, fussy

punto, *m.;* dot; point; pen-nib; gun-sight; stitch (sewing, knitting); dropped stitch, hole; weaving stitch, mesh; (*gram.*) full stop, period; hole (in belts for adjustment); place, spot; point, mark; subject matter; (*mech.*) cog; degree, extent; taxi rank; instant; infinitesimal amount; opportunity, chance; vacation, recess; aim, goal; point of honour, pundonor. **p. de congelación,** freezing point. **p. de ebullición,** boiling point. **p. de fuga,** vanishing point. **p. de fusión,** melting point. **p. de mira,** foresight (of a gun). **p. de partida,** starting-point. **p. de vista,** point of view. **p. final,**

(*gram.*) full stop. **p. interrogante,** question-mark. **p. menos,** a little less. **p. y coma,** (*gram.*) semicolon. **puntos cardinales,** cardinal points. **puntos suspensivos,** (*gram.*) suspension points, dots. **a p.,** in readiness; immediately. **en p.,** sharp, prompt (e.g. **a las seis en p.,** at six o'clock sharp)

puntoso, *a.* many-pointed

puntuación, *f.* punctuation; (*sport*) score

puntual, *a.* punctual; punctilious; certain, indubitable; suitable, convenient

puntualidad, *f* punctuality; punctiliousness; certainty; exactitude, accuracy

puntualizar, *v.t.* to describe in detail; give the finishing touch to, perfect; impress on the mind

puntualmente, *adv.* punctually; carefully, diligently; exactly

puntuar, *v.t.* to punctuate

punzada, *f.* prick, sting; puncture, piercing; sudden pain, twinge, stitch; (*fig.*) anguish, pain

punzar, *v.t.* to pierce, puncture; prick; punch, perforate; *v.i.* revive, make itself felt (pain or sorrow)

punzón, *m.* awl; punch; die; engraver's burin

puñado, *m.* handful; a few, some, a small quantity. **a puñados,** in handfuls; liberally, lavishly

puñal, *m.* dagger

puñalada, *f.* dagger thrust; stab, wound; (*fig.*) unexpected blow (of fate). **p. por la espalda,** stab in the back

puñalero, *m.* dagger maker or seller

puñetazo, *m.* blow with the fist

puño, *m.* fist; handful; cuff (of sleeve); wristband; handle, head, haft; hilt (of a sword); *pl.* (*fam.*) guts, courage. **p. de amura,** (*naut.*) tack. **p. de un manillar,** handle-bar grip. (*fam.*) **meter en un p.,** to over-awe. (*fam.*) **ser como un p.,** to be tight-fisted; be small (in stature)

pupila, *f.* female child ward; (*anat.*) pupil; (*fam.*) cleverness, talent

pupilaje, *m.* pupilage, minority; boarding-house, guest house; boarding-school; price of board residence; dependence, bondage

pupilo (-la), *s.* ward, minor; boarder; boarding-school pupil

pupitre, *m.* desk, school desk

puramente, *adv.* purely; simply, solely; (*law*) unconditionally, without reservation

puré, *m.* (*cul.*) purée, thick soup

pureza, *f.* purity; perfection, excellence; chastity; disinterestedness, genuineness; clearness

purga, *f.* laxative, purge; waste product

purgación, *f.* purging; menstruation; gonorrhoea

purgante, *a.* purgative. *m.* purge, cathartic

purgar, *v.t.* to cleanse, purify; expiate, atone for; (*med., law*) purge; suffer purgatorial pains; clarify, refine; *v.r.* rid oneself, purge oneself

purgativo, *a.* purgative

purgatorio, *m.* purgatory. *a.* purgatorial

puridad, *f.* purity; secrecy, privacy. en p., openly, without dissembling; secretly, in private

purificación, *f.* purification; cleansing

purificador (-ra), *a.* purifying; cleansing. *s.* purifier; cleanser

purificar, *v.t.* to purify; cleanse; *v.r.* be purified

purificatorio, *a.* purificatory

Purísima (la), *f.* (*ecc.*) the Most Blessed Virgin

purista, *m.* and *f.* purist

puritanismo, *m.* Puritanism

puritano (-na), *a.* puritanical. *s.* Puritan

puro, *a.* pure; undiluted; unalloyed; unmixed; disinterested, honest; virgin; absolute, sheer; mere, simple. *m.* cigar. de p., by sheer . . . , by dint of

púrpura, *f.* purple; (*poet.*) blood; purpura; (*her.*) purpure; purple (cloth); dignity of an emperor, cardinal, consul

purpurear, *v.i.* to look like purple; be tinged with purple

purpúreo, purpurino, *a.* purple

purulencia, *f.* purulence

purulento, *a.* purulent

pus, *m.* pus, matter

pusilánime, *a.* pusillanimous, timid, cowardly

pusilanimidad, *f.* pusillanimity, timidity, cowardice

pústula, *f.* (*med.*) pustule

puta, *f.* prostitute, whore

putativo, *a.* putative

putrefacción, *f.* putrefaction; rottenness, putrescence

putrefacto, *a.* rotten, decayed

pútrido, *a.* putrid, rotten

puya, *f.* goad

puyazo, *m.* prick with a goad

Q

quanta, (Teoría de la), *f.* Quantum Theory

quasimodo, *m.* (*ecc.*) Low Sunday

que, *pron. rel.* all genders sing. and pl. who; which; that; whom; when (e.g. Un poema en que habla de su juventud, A poem in which he speaks of his youth. El libro que tengo aquí, The book (that) I have here. No es oro todo lo que reluce, All that glitters is not gold. Un día que nos vimos, One day when we met. *interr.* ¿ qué ? what? *interj.* what a ——! what! how! (e.g. ¿ Qué hay ? What's the matter? ¡ Qué día más hermoso! What a lovely day! ¿ qué de... ? how many? ¿ qué tal ? how? (*fam.*) ¿ Qué tal estás hoy ? How are you today? ¿ qué tanto ? how much?) ¿ a qué ? why? for what reason? (e.g. ¿ A qué negarlo ? Why deny it ?). *conjunc.* that (e.g. Me dijo que vendría, He said (that) he would come). Means *so that, that, for,* in commands (e.g. Mandó que le trajesen el libro, He ordered that they should bring him the book (He ordered them to bring him the book)). Note that the translation of que is often omitted in English.

In compound tenses where the participle is placed first, que means *when* (e.g. Llegado que hube, When I had arrived). In comparisons, que means *than* (e.g. más joven que yo, younger than I).

With subjunctives and expressing commands or wishes, **que**
means *let* (e.g. ¡ Que venga !
Let him come!) Preceding a
subjunctive, **que** is generally
translated by *to* (e.g. Quiero,
que venga *or* que llueva, I want
him to come *or* I want it to rain).
Also means *may* (e.g. ¡Que Vd
lo pase bien ! May you enjoy
yourself! (I hope you . . .)). es
(era) que, the fact is (was)
that . . . que . . . que, whether . . .
or . . .

quebrada, *f.* mountain gorge;
(*com.*) bankruptcy

quebradizo, *a.* brittle, fragile;
ailing, infirm; delicate, frail;
flexible (voice)

quebrado (-da), *m.* (*math.*) fraction; *s.* (*com.*) bankrupt. *a.*
rough, uneven (ground); (*med.*)
ruptured; bankrupt; ailing,
broken down

quebradura, *f.* snap, breaking;
gap, crevice; hernia

quebraja, *f.* split, crack; flaw (in
wood, metal, etc.)

quebrantahuesos, *m.* sea-eagle,
osprey; (*fam.*) bore, tedious person

quebrantamiento, *m.* crushing;
splitting, cleaving; fracture, rupture; profanation, desecration;
burglary; violation, breaking, infringement; fatigue; (*law*) annulment; exhaustion

quebrantanueces, *m.* nut-crac-
kers

quebrantaolas, *m.* (*naut.*) breakwater

quebrantapiedras, *f.* (*bot.*) saxifrage, stone-break

quebrantar, *v.t.* to break, shatter; crush, pound; transgress;
infringe; break out, force (a
prison, etc.); tone down, soften;
moderate, lessen; bore, exhaust;
move to pity; (*fam.*) break in
(horses); profane; overcome
(difficulties); assuage, placate;
(*law*) revoke (wills); *v.r.* be
shaken or bruised, suffer from
after-effects

quebranto, *m.* breaking, shattering; crushing, pounding; infringement; breaking out (from
prison); weakness, exhaustion;
compassion, pity; loss, damage;
pain, suffering

quebrar, *v.t. irr.* to break, shatter; crush; impede, hinder;
make pale (colour, gen. of complexion); mitigate, moderate;
bend, twist; overcome (difficulties); *v.i.* break off (a friendship); weaken, give way; go
bankrupt; *v.r.* (*med.*) suffer from
hernia; be interrupted (mountain ranges). quebrarse los
ojos, to strain one's eyes.
Pres. Ind. quiebro, quiebras,
quiebra, quiebran. *Pres.
Subjunc.* quiebre, quiebres,
quiebre, quiebren

queche, *m.* (*naut.*) ketch

queda, *f.* curfew; curfew bell

quedada, *f.* stay, sojourn

quedar, *v.i.* to stay, sojourn; remain; be left over; (*with por* +
infin.) remain to be (e.g. Queda
por escribir, It remains to be
written); (*with por*) be won by or
be knocked down to; be, remain
in a place; end, cease; (*with en*)
reach an agreement (e.g. Que-
damos en no ir, We have decided not to go). *v.r.* remain;
abate (wind); grow calm (sea);
(*with con*) keep, retain possession
of. q. bien o mal, to behave well
or badly, come off well or badly
(in business affairs, etc.). quedarse muerto, to be astounded

quedo, *a.* still, motionless; quiet,
tranquil. *adv.* in a low voice;
quietly, noiselessly. de q., slowly, gradually. *interj.* ¡Q.! Quiet!

quehacer, *m.* odd job; task;
business (gen. *pl.*)

queja, *f.* lamentation, grief;
complaint, grudge; quarrel

quejarse, *v.r.* to lament; complain, grumble; (*law*) lodge an
accusation (against)

quejido, *m.* complaint, moan

quejoso, *a.* querulous, complaining

quejumbre, *f.* complaint, whine;
querulousness

quejumbroso, *a.* complaining,
grumbling

quema, *f.* burn; burning; fire,
conflagration

quemadero, *a.* burnable. *m.*
stake (for burning people)

quemado, *m.* burnt patch of
forest; (*fam.*) anything burnt or
burning

quemador (-ra), *m.* jet, burner. *s.* incendiary

quemadura, *f.* burn; scald; burning

quemajoso, *a.* smarting, burning, pricking

quemar, *v.t.* to burn; dry up; parch; scorch; tan, bronze; scald; throw away, sell at a loss; *v.i.* burn, be excessively hot; *v.r.* be very hot; be dried up with the heat; burn with (passions); (*fam.*) be near attainment of desired end. **quemarse las cejas,** to burn the midnight oil, study too hard

quemazón, *f.* burning; conflagration; intense heat; (*fam.*) smarting; (*fam.*) hurtful remark; (*fam.*) vexation, soreness

quepis, *m.* képi

querella, *f.* complaint; quarrel; fight; (*law*) plaint

querellarse, *v.r.* to complain; lament, bemoan; (*law*) lodge an accusation; (*law*) contest a will

querelloso, *a.* complaining, grumbling, querulous

querencia, *f.* love, affection; homing instinct; lair; natural inclination or desire

querer, *v.t. irr.* to desire, wish; want, will; attempt, endeavour; (*with a*) love. *impers.* be on the point of. **como quiera que,** by any means that, anyway; whereas, given that. **cuando quiera,** whenever. **q. decir,** to mean. **¿Qué quiere decir esto?** What does this mean? **sin q.,** unintentionally. See *entender*

querer, *m.* affection, love

querido (-da), *s.* lover; beloved; darling. *a.* dear

quermes, *m.* (*ent.*) kermes

querub, querube, (*poet.*) **querubín,** *m.* cherub

querúbico, *a.* cherubic

quesera, *f.* dairymaid; dairy; cheese-vat; cheese-board; cheesedish

quesería, *f.* dairy; cheese shop; season for making cheese

queso, *m.* cheese. **q. de bola,** Dutch cheese. **q. rallado,** grated cheese

quetzal, *m.* (*orn.*) quetzal

quevedos, *m. pl.* glasses, eyeglasses; pince-nez

¡quia! *interj.* (*fam.*) You don't say so!

quianti, *m.* chianti (wine)

quicial, *m.* door jamb

quicio, *m.* threshold; hinge; (*mech.*) bushing. **fuera de q.,** out of order; unhinged. **sacar de q.,** to displace (things); annoy, irritate; drive crazy

quiebra, *f.* breach, crack; rut, fissure; loss; bankruptcy

quiebro, *m.* twisting of the body, dodging; (*mus.*) trill

quien, *rel. pron. m.* and *f. pl.* **quienes.** *interr.* **quién, quiénes,** who; whom; he (she, etc.) who, anyone who, whoever; which; whichever (e.g. **Mis padres a quienes respeto,** My parents whom I respect. **Quien te quiere te hará llorar,** Whoever (he, those, who) love(s) you will make you weep. **¿Quién está a la puerta?** Who is at the door? **¿De quién es?** Whose is it?). *indef. pron.* one (*pl.* some)

quienquiera, *indef. pron. m.* and *f. pl.* **quienesquiera,** whosoever, whichever, whomsoever

quietación, *f.* quieting, soothing

quietador (-ra), *a.* tranquillizing, soothing. *s.* soother

quietismo, *m.* quietism

quietista, *m.* and *f.* quietist. *a.* quietistic

quieto, *a.* quiet, still; peaceful, tranquil; virtuous, respectable

quietud, *f.* stillness, repose; peacefulness; rest, quietness

quif, *m.* hashish, marihuana

quijada, *f.* jawbone, jaw; (*mech.*) jaw

quijo, *m.* (*min.*) ore (of gold or silver)

quijotada, *f.* quixotic action, quixotism

quijote, *m.* cuisse; thigh-guard; quixotic person

quijotesco, *a.* quixotic

quijotería, *f.*, **quijotismo,** *m.* quixotism

quilate, *m.* carat; degree of excellence (gen. *pl.*). (*fam.*) **por quilates,** in small bits, parsimoniously

quilla, *f.* (*naut.*) keel; breast bone (of birds)

quillotrar, *v.t.* (*fam.*) to encourage, incite; woo, make love to;

consider; *v.r.* (*fam.*) fall in love;
dress up; whine, complain

quillotro, *m.* (*fam.*) incentive;
indication, sign; love affair;
puzzle, knotty point; compliment; dressing up

quimera, *f.* chimæra; fancy,
vision; quarrel, dispute

quimérico, *a.* chimerical, fanciful

quimerista, *m.* and *f.* dreamer,
visionary; quarreller, disputant

química, *f.* chemistry

químico, *a.* chemical. *m.* chemist.
productos químicos, chemicals

quimono, *m.* kimono

quina, *f.* cinchona; quinine; *pl.*
Arms of Portugal. (*fam.*) tragar
q., to suffer in patience, put up
with

quinario, *a.* quinary.

quincalla, *f.* cheap jewellery;
fancy goods

quincallería, *f.* cheap jewellery
shop; hardware factory or industry; cheap jewellery; fancy goods

quince, *a.* and *m.* fifteen; fifteenth

quincena, *f.* fortnight; bi-
monthly pay; (*mus.*) fifteenth

quincenal, *a.* fortnightly; lasting
a fortnight

quinceno, *a.* fifteenth

quincuagenario, *a.* quinquagen-
arian

quincuagésima, *f.* (*ecc.*) Quinquagesima Sunday

quincuagésimo, *a.* fiftieth

quindécimo, *a.* fifteenth

quinientos, *a.* five hundred; five
hundredth. *m.* five hundred

quinina, *f.* quinine

quinqué, *m.* oil lamp, student's
lamp, table-lamp; perspicuity,
talent

quinquefolio, *m.* (*bot.*) common
cinquefoil

quinquenal, *a.* quinquennial

quinquenio, *m.* period of five
years, lustrum

quinquerreme, *f.* quinquereme

quinta, *f.* country house; (*mus.*)
fifth; conscripting men into
army by drawing lots; (*mil.*) draft

quintaesencia, *f.* quintessence

quintal, *m.* hundredweight

quintante, *m.* (*ast.*) quintant

quintar, *v.t.* to draw one out of
every five; draw lots for conscription into the army; *v.i.* reach
the fifth (day, etc., gen. of moon)

quintería, *f.* farm

quintero, *m.* farmer; farm
labourer

quinteto, *m.* quintet

quintilla, *f.* five-line stanza of
eight syllables

Quintín, San. armarse (*or*
haber) **la de San Q.,** to quarrel,
make trouble; be a row

quinto, *a.* fifth. *m.* one-fifth;
(*mil.*) conscript; duty of 20 per
cent.; (*law*) fifth part of estate.
(*pol.*) quinta columna, fifth
column. quinta esencia, quintessence

quintuplicación, *f.* quintuplica-
tion

quintuplicar, *v.t.* to quintuplicate

quíntuplo, *a.* fivefold, quintuple

quinzavo, *a.* and *m.* fifteenth

quiñón, *m.* share of land owned
jointly, share of profits

quiosco, *m.* kiosk, stand; pavilion, pagoda. q. de música,
bandstand

quiquiriquí, *m.* cock-a-doodle-
doo; (*fig., fam.*) cock of the walk

quiromancia, *f.* chiromancy, palmistry

quiromántico (-ca), *s.* chiroman-
cer, palmist

quirúrgico, *a.* surgical

quirurgo, *m.* surgeon

quisicosa, *f.* (*fam.*) riddle, puzzle,
enigma

quisquilla, *f.* trifle, quibble,
scruple; prawn, shrimp

quisquilloso, *a.* quibbling, over-
scrupulous, fastidious; hypersensitive; irascible, touchy

quistarse, *v.r.* to make oneself
well-liked or loved

quiste, *m.* (*med.*) cyst

quita, *f.* (*law*) discharge (of part
of debt)

quitaesmalte, *m.* varnish remover (for nails)

quitamanchas, *m.* or *f.* dry
cleaner, clothes cleaner

quitamotas, *m.* and *f.* (*fam.*)
flatterer, adulator

quitanieve, *m.* snow-plough

quitanza, *f.* quittance; quietus

quitapesares, *m.* (*fam.*) consolation, solace, comfort

quitapón, *m.* coloured woollen
headstall for horses, mules, etc.

quitar, *v.t.* to remove; take off or
away; clear (the table); rob,

steal; prevent, impede; parry
(fencing); separate; redeem
(pledges); forbid; annul, repeal
(laws, etc.); free from (obligations); *v.r.* shed, take off, remove; get rid of; leave, quit.
qiutarse de encima (a), to get
rid of someone or something.
q. el polvo, to dust. **de quita y
pon,** detachable, removable; adjustable

quitasol, *m.* parasol, sunshade

quitasueño, *m. (fam.)* sleep-ban-
isher, anxiety

quite, *m.* hindering, impeding;
obstruction; parry (fencing).
estar al q., to be ready to protect someone

quizá, quizás, *adv.* perhaps. **q.
y sin q.,** without doubt, certainly

R

rabadán, *m.* head shepherd or
herdsman

rabadilla, *f.* rump, croup

rábano, *m. (bot.)* radish. **r.
picante,** horse-radish

rabel, *m. (mus.)* rebec; *(fam.)* backside, seat

rabera, *f.* tail-end; chaff, siftings

rabí, *m.* rabbi

rabia, *f.* rabies, hydrophobia;
anger, fury. *(fam.)* **tener r. (a),** to
hate

rabiar, *v.i.* to suffer from hydrophobia; groan with pain; be
furious; *(with por)* yearn for,
desire. **a r.,** excessively

rabicorto, *a.* short-tailed

rabieta, *f. (fam.)* tantrum

rabilargo, *a.* long-tailed

rabínico, *a.* rabbinical

rabinismo, *m.* rabbinism

rabino, *m.* rabbi. **gran r.,** grand
rabbi

rabioso, *a.* rabid; furious, angry;
vehement. **perro r.,** mad dog

rabo, *m.* tail; *(bot.)* stalk; *(fam.)*
train (of a dress); shank (of a
button). **r. del ojo,** corner of the
eye. *(fig., fam.)* **ir r. entre
piernas,** to have one's tail between one's legs

rabón, *a.* tailless, docked; bob-
tailed

rabudo, *a.* big-tailed

racimo, *m.* bunch (of grapes
and other fruits); cluster; *(bot.)*
racime

racimoso, *a.* racemose

raciocinación, *f.* ratiocination

raciocinar, *v.i.* to reason

raciocinio, *m.* reasoning; ratiocination; discourse, speech

ración, *f.* ration; portion (in a
restaurant); meal allowance;
(ecc.) prebendary. *(fam.)* **r. de
hambre,** starvation diet; pittance, starvation wage

racional, *a.* reasonable, logical;
rational

racionalidad, *f.* reasonableness;
rationality

racionalismo, *m.* rationalism

racionalista, *a.* and *m.* and *f.*
rationalist. *a.* rationalistic

racionalización, *f.* rationalization

racionamiento, *m.* rationing.
f. **cartilla de r.,** ration book

racionar, *v.t.* to ration

rada, *f.* bay, cove; *(naut.)* road,
roadstead

radar, *m.* radar

radiación, *f.* radiation (also
geom.); *(rad.)* broadcasting

radiactivo, *a.* radioactive

radiador, *m.* radiator (for heating); *(aut.)* radiator

radial, *a.* radial

radiante, *a. (phys.)* radiating;
brilliant, shining; *(fig.)* beaming
(with satisfaction)

radiar, *v.i. (phys.)* to radiate;
v.t. broadcast (by radio)

radical, *a.* radical; fundamental;
(pol.) radical. *m. (gram.)* root;
(math., chem.) radical. *m.* and *f.*
(pol.) radical

radicalismo, *m.* radicalism

radicar(se), *v.i.* and *v.r.* to take
root; *v.i.* be (in a place)

radio, *m. (geom., anat.)* radius;
(chem.) radium. *f.* radio, wireless

radioactividad, *f.* radioactivity

radioaficionado (-da), *s.* radio
amateur; *(fam.)* wireless fan or
enthusiast

radioaudición, *f.* radio broadcast

radiocomunicación, *f.* wireless
transmission

radiodifundir, *v.t. (rad.)* to
broadcast

radiodifusión, radioemisión, *f.*
(*rad.*) broadcast; broadcasting

radioemisora, *f.* wireless station

radioescucha, *m.* and *f.* radio listener

radiofotografía, *f.* radiophotography; X-ray photograph. **tomar una r. de,** to X-ray

radiofrecuencia, *f.* radiofrequency

radiogonómetro, *m.* radiogonionometer

radiografía, *f.* radiography

radiografiar, *v.t.* to X-ray, radiograph

radiografista, *m.* and *f.* radiographer

radiograma, *m.* radiogram, cable

radiogramola, *f.* radiogram (gramophone)

radiolocación, *f.* radiolocation

radiología, *f.* radiology

radiólogo, *m.* radiologist

radiometría, *f.* radiometry

radiómetro, *m.* radiometer

radiooyente, *m.* and *f.* listener (to radio)

radiorreceptor, *m.* receiver, wireless set

radioscopia, *f.* radioscopy

radiotelefonía, *f.* radiotelephony

radiotelegrafía, *f.* radiotelegraphy.

radiotelegrafiar, *v.t.* to wireless

radiotelegráfico, *a.* radiotelegraphic, wireless

radiotelegrafista, *m.* and *f.* wireless operator

radiotelegrama, *m.* radiogram, radiotelegram

radiotransmisor, *m.* transmitter (radio)

raditerapia, *f.* radiotherapy, radiotherapeutics

raedera, *f.* scraper

raedor, *a.* scraping; abrasive

raedura, *f.* scraping; rubbing; fraying

raer, *v.t. irr.* to scrape; abrade; fray; (*fig.*) extirpate. See **caer**

ráfaga, *f.* gust or blast of wind; light cloud; flash (of light)

rafe, *m.* (*arch.*) eaves

rafia, *f.* raffia

raído, *a.* frayed, threadbare; brazen, barefaced

raíz, *f.* root. **r. cuadrada (cúbica),** square (cubed) root.

r. pivotante, (*bot.*) tap-root. **a r.,** close to the root, closely. **a r. de,** as a result of; after. **de r.,** from the root, entirely. **echar raíces,** to take root

raja, *f.* split, crack; chip, splinter (of wood); slice (of fruit, etc.)

rajá, *m.* rajah

rajadura, *f.* splitting; crack, split, crevice; (*geol.*) break

rajar, *v.t.* to crack, split; slice; *v.i.* (*fam.*) boast, crack oneself up; chatter; *v.r.* crack, split; (*fam.*) take back one's words

ralea, *f.* kind, quality; (*fam.,* scornful) race, lineage

ralear, *v.i.* to grow thin (cloth, etc.); behave true to type (gen. in a bad sense)

ralo, *a.* sparse, thin

rallador, *m.* (*cul.*) grater

rallar, *v.t.* (*cul.*) to grate; (*fam.*) bother, annoy

rallo, *m.* (*cul.*) grater; rasp

rama, *f.* (*bot.*) bough, branch; (*fig.*) branch (of family). (*fig., fam.*) **andarse por las ramas,** to beat about the bush. **en r.,** (*com.*) raw; unbound (books)

ramaje, *m.* thickness of branches, denseness of foliage

ramal, *m.* strand (of rope); halter; (*r.w.*) branch-line; fork (of road, etc.); flight (of locks); ramification, division

ramalazo, *m.* blow with a rope; mark left by this; bruise

rambla, *f.* bed, channel, course; boulevard (in Catalonia)

ramera, *f.* prostitute, whore

ramificación, *f.* ramification; (*anat.*) bifurcation

ramificarse, *v.r.* to branch, fork; (*fig.*) spread

ramillete, *m.* bouquet; table centre-piece; (*bot.*) cluster

ramo, *m.* (*bot.*) branch; twig, spray; bouquet, bunch; wreath; (*fig.*) branch (of learning, etc.); (*com.*) line (of business); (*fig.*) touch, slight attack. **Domingo de Ramos,** Palm Sunday

ramoso, *a.* branchy, thick with branches

rampa, *f.* gradient, incline; (*mil.*) ramp; launching site

rampante, *a.* (*her.*) rampant

ramplón, *a.* stout, heavy (shoes); coarse; vulgar; bombastic

rana, f. frog. **r. de San Antonio,** tree-frog

rancidez, f. rancidness; staleness; rankness; antiquity

ranciedad, f. rancidness; antiquity, oldness; mustiness

rancio, a. rancid, rank; mellow (of wine); ancient; traditional; musty

ranchero, m. (mil.) cook; small farmer; (S.A.) rancher

rancho, m. mess, rations; settlement, camp; hut, cabin; (fam.) group, huddle; (S.A.) ranch; (naut.) gang. (fam.) **hacer r.,** to make room

rango, m. grade, class; range; (mil., nav. and social) rank; file, line

ranúnculo, m. buttercup

ranura, f. groove; rabbet; slot, notch

rapa, f. (bot.) flower of the olive tree

rapacidad, f. rapacity, avidity, greed

rapador, a. scraping. m. (fam.) barber

rapapiés, m. squib

rapapolvo, m. (fam.) severe scolding, dressing down

rapar(se), v.t. and v.r. to shave; v.t. crop, cut close (hair); (fam.) steal, pinch

rapaz, a. rapacious. m. young boy. **ave r.,** bird of prey

rapaza, f. young girl

rape, m. (fam.) hasty shave or hair-cut. **al r.,** close cropped

rapé, m. snuff

rapidez, f. speed, swiftness, rapidity

rápido, a. quick, swift; express (trains). m. torrent, rapid; express train

rapiña, f. robbery, plundering, sacking

rapiñar, v.t. (fam.) to steal, pinch

raposa, f. vixen, fox; (fam.) wily person

raposo, m. male fox

raposear, v.i. to behave like the fox

rapsodia, f. rhapsody

raptar, v.t. to abduct; rob

rapto, m. abduction, rape; snatching, seizing; ecstasy, trance; (med.) loss of consciousness

raptor, m. kidnapper, abductor

raquero, a. pirate. m. wrecker; pickpocket, dock rat

raqueta, f. racquet (tennis, badminton, squash racquets); croupier's rake. **r. de nieve,** snowshoe

raquianestesia, f. spinal anæsthesia

raquídeo, a. spinal

raquítico, a. (med.) rachitic; small, minute; weak, feeble; rickety

raquitismo, m. (med.) rickets

rarefacción, f. rarefaction

rarefacer(se), v.t. and v.r. irr. to rarefy. See **satisfacer**

rareza, f. rareness, unusualness; eccentricity, whim; oddity, curio

raridad, f. rarity; thinness; scarcity

raro, a. rare, unusual, uncommon; notable, outstanding; odd, eccentric, queer; rarefied (gases, etc.). **rara vez,** seldom

ras, m. level. **a r.,** flush (with), nearly touching

rasa, f. worn place in cloth; clearing, glade

rasar, v.t. to level with a strickle; graze, brush, touch lightly; v.r. grow clear (sky, etc.)

rascacielos, m. sky-scraper

rascador, m. scraper; ornamental hairpin

rascadura, f. scraping; scratching

rascar, v.t. to scratch; claw; scrape; twang (guitar, etc.). (fam.) **¡Que se rasque!** Let him put up with it, Let him lump it!

rascatripas, m. (fam.) caterwauler, squeaker (of violinists, etc.)

rascón, a. sour, tart

rasgadura, f. tearing; tear, rip, rent

rasgar(se), v.t. and v.r. to tear, rip; v.t. thrum the guitar

rasgo, m. flourish (of the pen); felicitous expression; characteristic, quality; pl. features (of face)

rasgón, m. rip, tear

rasguear, v.t. to thrum, twang (the guitar); v.i. write with a flourish

rasgueo, m. flourish (on the guitar); scratch (of the pen)

rasguñar, *v.t.* to scratch, scrape; claw; (*art*) sketch

rasguño, *m.* scratch; (*art*) sketch, outline

raso, *a.* flat; free of obstacles; glossy; clear (sky, etc.); plain; undistinguished; backless (chairs). *m.* satin. **al r.,** in the open air

raspa, *f.* (*bot.*) beard (cereals); hair (on the pen); fishbone; bunch of grapes; (*bot.*) husk; (*carp.*) scraper

raspador, *m.* eraser; scraper, rasp

raspadura, *f.* scraping; erasing; shavings, filings

raspar, *v.t.* to scrape; erase; rob, steal; burn, bite (wine, etc.)

rastra, *f.* trace, sign; sled; string of onions, etc.; anything dragging; (*agr.*) harrow; (*agr.*) rake. **a la r.,** dragging; reluctantly. **pescar a la r.,** to trawl

rastreador, *m.* (*naut.*) minesweeper. *a.* dragging

rastrear, *v.t.* to trace, trail; drag, trawl; surmise, conjecture, investigate; *v.i.* (*agr.*) rake; fly low

rastreo, *m.* dragging (of lakes, etc.)

rastrero, *a.* dragging, trailing; low-flying; servile, abject; (*bot.*) creeping. *m.* slaughterhouse employee

rastrillador (-ra), *s.* raker; hackler

rastrilladora, *f.* **mechanical harrow**

rastrillaje, *m.* raking

rastrillar, *v.t.* to rake; dress, hackle (flax)

rastrillo, *m.* (*agr.*) rake; hackle; portcullis; (*agr.*) rack; ward (of a lock)

rastro, *m.* (*agr.*) rake; track, trail; wholesale meat market; slaughter-house; trace, vestige; second-hand market in Madrid

rastrojo, *m.* stubble; stubble field

rasura, *f.* shaving

rasurar(se), *v.t.* and *v.r.* to shave

rata, *f.* rat. *m.* (*fam.*) pickpocket. **r. almizclera,** musk-rat; musquash. (*fam.*) **más pobre que las ratas,** poorer than a church mouse

rataplán, *m.* rub-a-dub-dub, beating of a drum

ratear, *v.t.* to rebate pro rata;

apportion; thieve on a small scale, filch; *v.i.* crawl, creep

ratería, *f.* filching, petty theft, picking pockets; meanness, parsimony

ratero (-ra), *s.* pilferer, petty thief, pickpocket

ratificación, *f.* ratification

ratificador (-ra), *s.* ratifier

ratificar, *v.t.* to ratify

ratificatorio, *a.* ratifying, confirmatory

rato, *m.* short interval of time, while. **buen (mal) r.,** pleasant (unpleasant) time. **ratos perdidos,** leisure moments. **a ratos,** sometimes, occasionally. **de r. en r.,** from time to time. (*fam.*) **pasar el r.,** to while away the time

ratón (-ona), *s.* mouse

ratonera, *f.* mouse-trap; mousehole; mouse nest. (*fig.*) **caer en la r.,** to fall into a trap

ratonero, ratonesco, ratonil, *a.* mousy

rauco, *a.* (*poet.*) hoarse

raudal, *m.* torrent, cascade; (*fig.*) flood, abundance

raudo, *a.* swift, rapid

ravioles, *m. pl.* (*cul.*) ravioli

raya, *f.* stripe, streak; limit, end; parting (of hair); boundary; (*gram.*) dash; score (some games). *m.* (*icht.*) ray. **pasar de r.,** to go too far; misbehave

rayadillo, *m.* striped cotton

rayano, *a.* neighbouring; border; almost identical, very similar

rayar, *v.t.* to draw lines; streak; stripe; cross out; underline; rifle (a gun); *v.i.* verge (on), border (on); appear (of dawn, daylight); excel; be similar. **Raya en los catorce años,** He is about fourteen

rayo, *m.* (*phys.*) beam, ray; thunderbolt; flash of lightning; spoke; quick-witted person; capable, energetic person; sudden pain; disaster, catastrophe. **r. de sol,** sunbeam. **rayos catódicos,** cathode rays. **rayos x,** X-rays. (*fig.*) **echar rayos,** to breathe forth fury

rayón, *m.* rayon

raza, *f.* race; breed; lineage; family; kind, class; crack, crevice. **de r.,** pure bred

razón, *f.* reason; reasoning; word, expression; speech, argument; motive, cause; order, method; justice, equity; right, authority; explanation; (*math.*) ratio, proportion. **r. de estado,** raison d'état, reasons of state. (*com.*) **r. social,** firm, trade-name. **a r. de,** at a rate of. **dar la r.** (a), to agree with. **estar puesto en r.,** to stand to reason. **tener r.,** to be in the right

razonable, *a.* reasonable; moderate

razonador (-ra), *s.* reasoner

razonamiento, *m.* reasoning

razonar, *v.i.* to reason; speak; *v.t.* attest, confirm

razzia, *f.* foray; pillaging, sacking; police raid

re, *m.* (*mus.*) re, D

reabsorción, *f.* reabsorption

reacción, *f.* reaction (all meanings)

reaccionar, *v.i.* to react

reaccionario (-ia), *a.* and *s.* reactionary

reaccionarismo, *m.* reactionism

reacio, *a.* recalcitrant

reactivo, *m.* (*chem.*) reagent. *a.* reactive; reacting

readmisión, *f.* readmission

readmitir, *v.t.* to readmit

reajustar, *v.t.* to readjust

real, *a.* actual, real; kingly; royal; royalist; (*fig.*) regal; (*fam.*) fine, handsome. *m.* silver coin, real; *m. pl.* encampment, camp. **alzar el r.,** (*mil.*) to strike camp. **asentar el r.,** (*mil.*) to encamp. **los sitios reales,** the royal residences. (*fam.*) **un r., sobre otro,** cash down in full

realce, *m.* raised or embossed work; renown, glory; (*art*) high light

realeza, *f.* royalty, royal majesty

realidad, *f.* reality; sincerity, truth. **en r.,** in fact, actually

realismo, *m.* realism; regalism; royalism

realista, *a.* realistic; royalist. *m.* and *f.* realist; royalist; regalist

realizable, *a.* realizable; practicable

realización, *f.* realization; performance, execution

realizar, *v.t.* to perform, execute, carry out; (*com.*) realize. **r. beneficio,** to make a profit

realmente, *adv.* really, truly; actually

realzar, *v.t.* to heighten, raise; emboss; exalt; enhance; (*art*) intensify (colours, etc.)

reanimar, *v.t.* to reanimate; revive, restore, resuscitate; encourage

reanudación, *f.* resumption, renewal

reanudar, *v.t.* to resume, continue

reaparecer, *v.i. irr.* to reappear. See **conocer**

reaparición, *f.* reappearance

rearmamento, *m.* rearmament

rearmar, *v.t.* to re-arm

reasegurador, *m.* underwriter

reasegurar, *v.t.* to reinsure, underwrite

reaseguro, *m.* reinsurance, underwriting

reasumir, *v.t.* to reassume; resume

reasunción, *f.* reassumption; resumption

reata, *f.* string of horses or mules. **de r.,** in single file; (*fam.*) blindly, unquestioningly; (*fam.*) at once

rebaba, *f.* (*mech.*) burr, fash

rebaja, *f.* diminution; (*com.*) discount, rebate; remission

rebajar, *v.t.* to lower; curtail, lessen; remit; (*com.*) reduce in price; (*mech.*) file; (*elec.*) step down; humble, humiliate; *v.r.* cringe, humble oneself

rebajo, *m.* reduction (in price, etc.); rabbet

rebanada, *f.* slice, piece (of bread, etc.)

rebanar, *v.t.* to cut into slices; split

rebaño, *m.* flock, drove, herd; (*ecc.*) flock

rebasar, *v.t.* to exceed, go beyond; (*mil.*) by-pass

rebate, *m.* altercation, dispute, quarrel

rebatiña, *f.* grab; scrimmage. **andar a la r.,** to scuffle

rebatir, *v.t.* to repulse, repel; fight again; fight hard; oppose, resist; (*com.*) deduct; refuse, reject

rebato, *m.* alarm, tocsin; (*mil.*) surprise attack; panic, dismay

rebeca, *f.* cardigan, jersey

rebeco, *m.* (*zool.*) chamois

rebelarse, *v.r.* to mutiny, rebel; oppose, resist

rebelde, *a.* mutinous, rebellious; wilful, disobedient; stubborn. *m.* and *f.* rebel

rebeldía, *f.* rebelliousness; wilfulness; stubbornness; (*law*) non-appearance

rebelión, *f.* insurrection, revolt

rebenque, *m.* hide whip; horsewhip; (*naut.*) ratlin

rebién, *adv.* very or extremely well

rebisabuelo (-la), *s.* See **tatarabuelo.**

reblandecer, *v.t.* irr. to soften; *v.r.* become soft. See **conocer**

reblandecimiento, *m.* softening; (*med.*) flabbiness

reborde, *m.* rim, edge; (*mech.*) flange. **r. de acera,** kerbstone

rebordear, *v.t.* (*mech.*) to flange

rebosar, *v.i.* to overflow, run over; (*fig.*) abound in; express one's feelings

rebotar, *v.i.* to rebound; clinch (nails, etc.); refuse; *v.r.* change colour; (*fam.*) be vexed

rebote, *m.* rebounding; rebound

rebotica, *f.* back room to a chemist's shop; back shop

rebozar, *v.t.* to muffle up; (*cul.*) coat with batter

rebozo, *m.* muffling up, hiding the face; head-shawl; pretence, excuse. (*fig.*) **sin r.,** openly

rebramo, *m.* barking of deer, stags, etc.

rebueno, *a.* (*fam.*) extremely good, fine

rebullicio, *m.* uproar, clamour

rebullir, *v.i.* to stir, show signs of movement; (*fig.*) swarm, seethe

rebusca, *f.* close search; gleaning; remains

rebuscado, *a.* affected, unnatural (of style)

rebuscar, *v.t.* to search for; glean

rebuznar, *v.i.* to bray

rebuzno, *m.* braying

recabita, *m.* and *f.* Rechabite

recadero (-ra), *s.* messenger, errand-boy

recado, *m.* message; greeting, note; gift, present; daily market-

ing; outfit, implements; precaution, safeguard

recaer, *v.i.* irr. to fall again; (*med.*) relapse; lapse, backslide; devolve, fall upon. See **caer**

recaída, *f.* falling again; (*med.*) relapse; lapse

recalar, *v.t.* to impregnate; (*naut.*) call at, come within sight of land

recalcada, *f.* pressing down, squeezing; emphasis; (*naut.*) list

recalcar, *v.t.* to press down, squeeze; pack tight; stress, emphasize; *v.i.* (*naut.*) list; *v.r.* (*fam.*) say over and over, savour one's words

recalcitrante, *a.* obdurate, recalcitrant

recalentador, *m.* (*mech.*) superheater

recalentar, *v.t.* irr. to overheat; superheat; re-heat. See **sentar**

recamado, *m.* raised embroidery

recámara, *f.* dressing-room; explosives chamber; breech of a gun; (*fam.*) caution

recambio, *m.* spare, spare part; (*com.*) re-exchange

recantación, *f.* retraction, recantation

recapacitar, *v.i.* to search one's memory; think over

recapitulación, *f.* summary, résumé

recapitular, *v.t.* to recapitulate, summarize

recargar, *v.t.* to recharge; load again; re-accuse; overcharge; over-dress or over-decorate; *v.r.* (*med.*) become more feverish. **r. acumuladores,** to charge accumulators

recargo, *m.* charge; new load; (*law*) new accusation; overcharge, extra cost; (*med.*) temperature increase

recatado, *a.* prudent, discreet, circumspect; modest, shy

recatar, *v.t.* to hide; conceal; *v.r.* be prudent or cautious

recato, *m.* caution, prudence; modesty, shyness, reserve

recauchatar, *v.t.* to retread (tyres)

recaudación, *f.* collecting; collection (of taxes, etc.); tax-collector's office

recaudador, *m.* tax-collector

recaudar, *v.t.* to collect, recover (taxes, debts, etc.); deposit, place in custody

recaudo, *m.* collecting; collection (taxes, etc.); precaution, safeguard; (*law*) surety

recelar, *v.t.* to suspect, fear, mistrust; *v.r.* (*with de*) be afraid or suspicious of

recelo, *m.* suspicion, mistrust, doubt, fear

receloso, *a.* suspicious, distrustful, doubtful

recepción, *f.* receiving, reception; admission, acceptance; reception, party; (*law*) cross-examination

receptáculo, *m.* receptacle, container; (*fig.*) refuge; (*bot.*) receptacle

receptador (-ra), *s.* receiver (of stolen goods); accomplice

receptivo, *a.* receptive

receptor (-ra), *a.* receiving. *s.* recipient. *m.* (*elec.*) receiver; wireless set. **r. a galena,** crystal set. **r. telefónico,** telephone receiver

receta, *f.* (*med.*) prescription; (*cul.*) recipe

recetar, *v.t.* (*med.*) to prescribe; (*fam.*) demand

reciamente, *adv.* hard; strongly, firmly, vigorously

recibí, *m.* (*com.*) receipt (literally I received)

recibidor (-ra), *a.* receiving. *s.* recipient. *m.* reception room

recibiente, *a.* receiving

recibimiento, *m.* reception; welcome, greeting; reception or waiting room; hall, vestibule

recibir, *v.t.* to obtain, receive; support, bear; suffer, experience (attack, injury); approve; accept, receive; entertain; stand up to (attack); *v.r.* (*with de*) graduate as, take office as

recibo, *m.* reception; (*com.*) receipt; reception room, waiting-room; hall, vestibule. (*com.*) **acusar r.,** to acknowledge receipt

recidiva, *f.* (*med.*) relapse

recién, *adv.* recently, newly. Used before past participles instead of **reciente** (e.g. **r. llegado,** newly arrived)

reciente, *a.* recent; new; fresh

recinto, *m.* precincts; neighbourhood; premises, place

recio, *a.* strong; robust; bulky, thick; rough, uncouth; grievous, hard; severe (weather); impetuous, precipitate

recipiente, *a.* receiving. *m.* receptacle, container, vessel

reciprocar, *v.t.* to reciprocate

reciprocidad, *f.* reciprocity; reciprocation

recíproco, *a.* reciprocal (also *gram.*)

recitación, *f.* recitation

recitado, *m.* (*mus.*) recitative

recitador (-ra), *s.* elocutionist, reciter

recitar, *v.t.* to recite, declaim

reclamación, *f.* reclamation; objection, opposition; (*com.*) claim

reclamar, *v.i.* to oppose, object to; (*poet.*) resound; *v.t.* call repeatedly; (*com.*) claim; decoy (birds)

reclamo, *m.* decoy bird; enticement, allurement; (*law*) reclamation; advertisement. (*com.*) **objetos de r.,** free gifts (for advertisement). **venta de r.,** bargain sale

reclinación, *f.* reclining; leaning

reclinatorio, *m.* couch; prie-dieu

recluir, *v.t. irr.* to immure, shut up; detain, arrest. See **huir**

reclusión, *f.* confinement, seclusion; prison

recluso (-sa), *s.* recluse

recluta, *f.* recruiting. *m.* (*mil.*) recruit

reclutador, *m.* recruiting office

reclutamiento, *m.* recruiting

reclutar, *v.t.* to enlist recruits, recruit

recobrar, *v.t.* to recover, regain; *v.r.* recuperate; recover consciousness

recobro, *m.* recovery; (*mech.*) pick-up

recocer, *v.t. irr.* to re-boil; re-cook; over-boil; over-cook; anneal (metals); *v.r.* (*fig.*) be tormented (by emotion), be all burnt up. See **cocer**

recodo, *m.* bend, turn, loop

recogedor, *a.* sheltering. *m.* (*agr.*) gleaner

recoger, *v.t.* to gather, pick; pick up; re-take; collect (letters from a pillar box, etc.); amass;

shrink, narrow; keep; hoard; shelter; reap, pick; *v.r.* withdraw, retire; go home; go to bed; retrench, economize; give oneself to meditation

recogida, *f.* collection (of letters from a pillar box); withdrawal; retirement; harvest

recogido, *a.* recluse; cloistered, confined

recogimiento, *m.* gathering, picking; collection, accumulation; seclusion; shelter; reformatory (for women)

recolección, *f.* summary, résumé; harvest; collection (taxes, etc.); (*ecc.*) convent of reformed order; mystic ecstasy

recoleto, *a.* (*ecc.*) reformed (religious orders); recluse

recomendable, *a.* commendable, recommendable

recomendación, *f.* recommendation (all meanings)

recomendar, *v.t. irr.* to recommend (all meanings); entrust, commend. *Pres. Ind.* recomiendo, recomiendas, recomienda, recomiendan. *Pres. Subjunc.* recomiende, recomiendes, recomiende, recomienden

recompensa, *f.* compensation; recompense, reward

recompensar, *v.t.* to compensate; requite; reward, recompense

recomposición, *f.* recomposition

recomprar, *v.t.* to repurchase

reconcentrar, *v.t.* to concentrate; dissemble; *v.r.* withdraw into oneself, meditate

reconciliable, *a.* reconcilable

reconciliación, *f.* reconciliation

reconciliador (-ra), *a.* reconciliatory. *s.* reconciler

reconciliar, *v.t.* to reconcile; (*ecc.*) re-consecrate; (*ecc.*) hear a short confession; *v.r.* become reconciled; (*ecc.*) make an additional confession

recondicionar, *v.t.* to rebuild, overhaul, recondition

recóndito, *a.* recondite

reconocer, *v.t. irr.* to examine, inspect; recognize; admit, acknowledge; own, confess; search; (*pol.*) recognize; (*mil.*) reconnoitre; (*with por*) adopt as (son, etc.); recognize as; *v.r.* be seen;

show; acknowledge, confess; know oneself. **Bien se reconoce que no está aquí,** It's easily seen he's not here. See **conocer**

reconocido, *a.* grateful

reconocimiento, *m.* examination, inspection; recognition; acknowledgement, admission; search; (*mil.*) reconnoitring; adoption; gratitude

reconquista, *f.* reconquest

reconquistar, *v.t.* to reconquer; (*fig.*) recover, win back

reconstitución, *f.* reconstitution

reconstituir, *v.t. irr.* to reconstitute. See **huir**

reconstituyente, *m.* (*med.*) tonic

reconstrucción, *f.* reconstruction

reconstruir, *v.t. irr.* to reconstruct, rebuild; re-create. See **huir**

reconvención, *f.* rebuke, reproof; recrimination; (*law*) countercharge

reconversión, *f.* reconversion

recopilación, *f.* summary, compendium; collection (of writings); digest (of laws)

recopilador, *m.* compiler

recopilar, *v.t.* to compile, collect

recordar, *v.t. irr.* to cause to remember, remind; remember; *v.i.* remember; awake. See **acordar**

recordatorio, *m.* reminder

recorrer, *v.t.* to travel over; pass through; wander about; examine, inspect; read hastily; overhaul, renovate

recorrido, *m.* journey, run; (*mech.*) stroke; overhaul. **r. de despegue,** (*aer.*) take-off run

recortado, *a.* (*bot.*) jagged, incised. *m.* paper cut-out

recortar, *v.t.* to clip, trim, pare; cut out; (*art*) outline; *v.r.* stand out (against), be outlined (against)

recorte, *m.* clipping, paring; cutting; cut-out; (*art*) outline; *pl.* snippets, clippings. **un r. de periódico,** a newspaper cutting

recostar, *v.t. irr.* (*with en* or *contra*) to lean, rest against; *v.r.* (*with en* or *contra*) lean against, rest on; lean back; recline. See **contar**

recova, *f.* purchase of dairy stock; poultry market

recreación, f. recreation, hobby

recrear, v.t. to entertain, amuse; v.r. amuse oneself; delight (in), enjoy

recreo, m. recreation, hobby; playtime (in schools); place of amusement. salón de r., recreation hall

recriminación, f. recrimination

recriminador, a. recriminatory

recriminar, v.t. to recriminate

recrudecer(se), v.i. and v.r. irr. to recur, return. See conocer

recrudescencia, f. recrudescence, recurrence

rectangular, a. rectangular

rectángulo, m. rectangle. a. rectangular

rectificable, a. rectifiable

rectificación, f. rectification; (mech.) grinding

rectificador, m. (elec.) rectifier

rectificar, v.t. to rectify; (mech.) grind; v.r. mend one's ways; (mil.) r. el frente, to straighten the line

rectilíneo, a. rectilinear

rectitud, f. straightness; rectitude, integrity; exactness; righteousness

recto, a. straight; upright; erect; literal (meaning); just, fair; single-breasted (of coats); m. right angle; (anat.) rectum

rector (-ra), s. director; principal, headmaster. m. (ecc.) rector

rectorado, m. principalship, headmaster- (mistress-) ship, directorship; (ecc.) rectorship

rectoría, f. rectorate, rectorship

recua, f. drove of beasts of burden; (fam.) string or line of things

recubrir, v.t. to re-cover, lag; coat; plate. Past Part. recubierto

recuento, m. calculation; recount; inventory

recuerdo, m. memory, remembrance; memento; pl. greetings, regards

reculada, f. drawing back; recoil

recular, v.i. to recoil, draw back; (fam.) go back on, give up

recuperable, a. recoverable, recuperable

recuperación, f. recovery, recuperation; (chem.) recovery

recuperativo, a. recuperative

recurrente, a. recurrent

recurrir, v.i. to recur; (with prep. a) have recourse to; appeal to

recurso, m. recourse, resort; choice, option; reversion; petition; (law) appeal; pl. means of livelihood; (fig.) way out, last hope

recusar, v.t. to refuse; challenge the authority (of)

rechapear, v.t. to re-plate

rechazar, v.t. to repulse; resist; refuse; oppose, deny (the truth of); contradict

rechazo, m. recoil; rebound; refusal

rechinamiento, rechino, m. squeaking, creaking; gnashing (of teeth)

rechinar, v.i. to squeak, creak; gnash (teeth); chatter (teeth); do with a bad grace

rechoncho, a. squat, stocky

red, f. net; network; hair-net; railing, grating; (fig.) snare; system (of communications, etc.); (fig.) combination (of events, etc.); (elec.) mains. r. de arrastre, trawl-net. (fig., fam.) caer en la r., to fall into the trap

redacción, f. phrasing; editorial office; editing; editorial board

redactar, v.t. to write, phrase; draw up; edit

redactor (-ra), a. editorial. s. editor

redada, f. cast (of a fishing net); haul, catch

redecilla, f. dim. small net; netting; hair-net

redención, f. redemption; ransom; deliverance, salvation; redeeming, paying off (mortgage, etc.)

redentor (-ra), a. redeeming, redemptive. s. redeemer

redifusión, f. (rad.) relay

redil, m. sheepfold

redimible, a. redeemable

redimir, v.t. to ransom; redeem, buy back; pay off (mortgage, etc.); deliver, free; (ecc.) redeem

rédito, m. (com.) income, revenue, interest, profit

redoblamiento, m. redoubling; bending back (of nails, etc.); rolling (of a drum)

redoblar, *v.t.* to redouble; repeat; bend back (nails, etc.); *v.i.* roll (a drum)

redoble, *m.* doubling; redoubling; repetition; roll (of a drum)

redoma, *f.* flask, phial

redomado, *a.* astute, crafty, sly; complete, perfect

redonda, *f.* district; pasture ground; (*naut.*) square sail; (*mus.*) semibreve. **a la r.,** round about, around

redondear, *v.t.* to make round; round; free (from debt, etc.); *v.r.* acquire a fortune; clear oneself (of debts, etc.)

redondel, *m.* (traffic) roundabout

redondez, *f.* roundness

redondo, *a.* round; circular; unequivocal, plain. *m.* round, circle; (*fam.*) cash. **en r.,** round about; in plain words

reducción, *f.* reduction; (*mil.*) defeat, conquest; decrease; (*com.*) rebate; (*math., chem.*) reduction

reducible, *a.* reducible

reducir, *v.t. irr.* to reduce; decrease, cut down; break up; (*art*) scale down; (*elec.*) step down; subdue; (*chem., math., surg.*) reduce; exchange; divide into small fragments; persuade; *v.r.* be obliged to, have to; live moderately. See **conducir**

reducto, *m.* (*mil.*) redoubt (of fortifications)

redundancia, *f.* redundance

redundante, *a.* redundant

redundar, *v.i.* to overflow; be excessive or superfluous; (*with en*) redound to

reduplicación, *f.* reduplication

reduplicar, *v.t.* to reduplicate

reedificar, *v.t.* to rebuild

reeditar, *v.t.* to reprint, reissue

reelección, *f.* re-election

reelegir, *v.t. irr.* to re-elect. See **elegir**

reembarcar, *v.t.* to re-embark, re-ship

reembarque, *m.* re-embarkation, reshipment

reembolsable, *a.* repayable

reembolsar, *v.t.* to recover (money); refund, return (money)

reembolso, *m.* repayment. **contra r.,** cash on delivery, C.O.D.

reemitir, *v.t.* (*elec.*) to relay

reemplazar, *v.t.* to replace; exchange, substitute; succeed, take the place of

reemplazo, *m.* replacement; exchange, substitute; successor; (*mil.*) replacement

reencarcelar, *v.t.* to reimprison

reencarnación, *f.* reincarnation

reencarnar(se), *v.i.* and *v.r.* to be reincarnated

reencuadernar, *v.t.* to rebind (books)

reencuentro, *m.* collision; (*mil.*) encounter, clash

reenganchar(se), *v.t.* and *v.r.* (*mil.*) to re-enlist

reenganche, *m.* (*mil.*) re-enlistment

reexaminación, *f.* re-examination

reexaminar, *v.t.* to re-examine

reexpedir, *v.t.* to forward, send on

reexportación, *f.* re-export

reexportar, *v.t.* (*com.*) to re-export

refacción, *f.* refection, light meal; compensation, reparation

refajo, *m.* skirt, underskirt

refección, *f.* refection, light meal

refectorio, *m.* refectory

referencia, *f.* report, account; allusion; regard, relation; (*com.*) reference (gen. *pl.*); consideration

referente, *a.* concerning, related (to)

referir, *v.t. irr.* to narrate; describe; direct, guide; relate, refer, concern; *v.r.* allude (to); refer (to); concern. See **sentir**

refinación, *f.* refining

refinado, *a.* refined; polished, cultured; crafty

refinador, *m.* refiner

refinamiento, *m.* refinement, subtlety, care

refinar, *v.t.* to refine, purify; polish, perfect

refinería, *f.* refinery

reflector, *a.* reflecting. *m.* reflector; searchlight; shade (for lamps, etc.)

reflejar, *v.i.* (*phys.*) to reflect; *v.t.* consider; show, mirror; *v.r.* (*fig.*) be reflected, be seen

reflejo, *m.* reflection; image; glare. *a.* reflex; considered, judicious

reflexión, f. (*phys.*) reflection; consideration, thought

reflexionar, v.t. (*with en* or *sobre*) to consider, reflect upon

reflexivo, a. (*phys.*) reflective; thoughtful

reflorecer, v.i. *irr.* to flower again; return to favour (ideas, etc.). See **conocer**

reflujo, m. reflux, refluence; ebb-tide

refocilar, v.t. to warm up, brace up; give pleasure to; v.r. enjoy oneself

reforma, f. reform; improvement; reformation; (*hist.*) Reformation

reformación, f. reform, improvement

reformador (-ra), a. reformatory, reforming. s. reformer

reformar, v.t. to remake; reshape; repair, mend, restore; improve, correct; (*ecc.*) reform; reorganize; v.r. mend one's ways, improve; control oneself

reformatorio, m. reformatory. a. reforming, reformatory

reformista, m. and f. reformist, reformer. a. reformatory

reforzador, m. (*phot.*) reinforcing bath; (*elec.*) booster

reforzamiento, m. stiffening, reinforcing

reforzar, v.t. *irr.* to reinforce, strengthen, stiffen; encourage, inspirit. See **forzar**

refracción, f. (*phys.*) refraction

refractar, v.t. to refract

refractario, a. stubborn; (*phys.*, *chem.*) refractory; unmanageable, unruly; fireproof

refrán, m. proverb, saying

refranero, m. collection of proverbs

refregamiento, m. rubbing; scrubbing, scouring

refregar, v.t. *irr.* to rub; scrub, scour; (*fig.*, *fam.*) rub in, insist on. See **cegar**

refrenamiento, m. curbing; control, restraint

refrenar, v.t. to curb, check (horses); control, restrain

refrendar, v.t. to countersign, endorse, legalize

refrescante, a. refreshing, cooling

refrescar, v.t. to cool, chill; repeat; (*fig.*) brush up, revise; v.i.

be rested or refreshed; grow cooler; take the air; freshen (wind); take a cool drink; v.r. grow cooler; take the air; take a cool drink

refresco, m. refreshment; cool drink

refriega, f. affray, scuffle, rough-and-tumble

refrigeración, f. refrigeration

refrigerador, m. refrigerator

refrigerante, a. refrigerative; chilling; cooling. m. cooling chamber, cooler

refrigerar, v.t. to chill; cool; freeze, refrigerate; refresh

refrigerio, m. coolness; consolation; refreshment, food

refringente, a. (*phys.*) refringent

refuerzo, m. reinforcement, strengthening; aid, help

refugiado (-da), a. and s. refugee

refugiar, v.t. to protect, shelter; v.r. take refuge

refugio, m. refuge, shelter, protection; street island. **r. antiaéreo**, air-raid shelter. **r. para peatones**, traffic island

refulgencia, f. resplendence, splendour, brilliance

refulgente, a. resplendent, refulgent, dazzling

refulgir, v.i. to shine, be dazzling

refundición, f. recasting (of metals); adaptation; rehash, refurbishing

refundir, v.t. to recast (metals); include, comprise; adapt; (*lit.*) rehash, refurbish; v.i. (*fig.*) promote, contribute to

refunfuñador, a. grumbling, fuming

refunfuñar, v.i. to grumble, growl, fume

refunfuño, m. grumble, fuming; snort

refutable, a. refutable

refutación, f. refutation

refutar, v.t. to refute

regadera, f. watering-can; irrigation canal; sparger

regadío, m. irrigated land; irrigation, watering. a. irrigated

regajal, **regajo**, m. pool, puddle; stream, brook

regala, f. (*naut.*) gunwale

regalado, a. delicate, highly-bred; luxurious, delightful

regalar, *v.t.* to make a gift of, give; caress, fondle; indulge, cherish; entertain, regale; *v.r.* live in luxury

regalía, *f.* royal privilege; right, exemption; perquisite, emolument

regalismo, *m.* regalism

regalista, *a.* and *m.* and *f.* regalist

regaliz, *m.*, **regaliza,** *f.* (*bot.*) liquorice

regalo, *m.* gift, present; satisfaction, pleasure; entertainment, regalement; luxury, comfort

regalón, *a.* (*fam.*) pampered

regañadientes, a, *adv.* unwillingly, grumblingly

regañar, *v.i.* to snarl (dogs); crack (skin of fruits); grumble, mutter; (*fam.*) quarrel; *v.t.* (*fam.*) scold

regaño, *m.* angry look or gesture; (*fam.*) scolding

regañón (-ona), *a.* (*fam.*) grumbling, complaining; scolding. *s.* (*fam.*) grumbler

regar, *v.t. irr.* to water, sprinkle with water; flow through, irrigate; spray; (*fig.*) shower (with), strew. See **cegar**

regata, *f.* regatta; small irrigation channel (gardens, etc.)

regate, *m.* twist of the body, side step; dribbling (football); (*fam.*) dodging, evasion

regatear, *v.t.* to haggle about, beat down (prices); resell, retail; dribble (a ball); (*fig., fam.*) dodge, avoid; *v.i.* bargain, haggle; (*naut.*) take part in a regatta, race

regateo, *m.* haggling, bargaining

regatero (-ra), *a.* retail. *s.* retailer

regatón (-ona), *m.* ferrule, tip. *a.* haggling, bargaining. *s.* haggler; retailer

regatonear, *v.t.* to resell at retail

regazo, *m.* lap, knees; (*fig.*) heart, bosom

regencia, *f.* regency

regeneración, *f.* regeneration.

regenerador (-ra), *s.* regenerator. *a.* regenerative, reforming

regenerar, *v.t.* to regenerate, reform

regenta, *f.* wife of president of a court of session

regentar, *v.t.* to fill temporarily (offices); rule, govern; manage, run (businesses)

regente, *a.* ruling. *m.* and *f.* regent. *m.* president of a court of session; manager

regicida, *m.* and *f.* regicide (person)

regicidio, *m.* regicide

regidor, *a.* ruling, governing. *m.* magistrate, alderman

régimen, *m.* administration, management; régime; (*med., gram.*) regimen; (*mech.*) rating

regimentación, *f.* regimentation

regimentar, *v.t. irr.* to form into regiments; regiment. *Pres. Ind.* **regimiento, regimientas, regimienta, regimientan.** *Pres. Subjunc.* **regimiente, regimientes, regimiente, regimienten**

regimiento, *m.* (*mil.*) regiment; administration, rule

regio, *a.* royal; magnificent, regal

región, *f.* region, country; area, tract, space. **r. industrial,** industrial area

regionalismo, *m.* regionalism

regionalista, *m.* and *f.* regionalist. *a.* regional

regir, *v.t. irr.* to govern, rule; administer, conduct; (*gram.*) govern; *v.i.* be in force (laws, etc.); work, function; (*naut.*) obey the helm. See **pedir**

registrador, *a.* recording. *m.* registrar, keeper of records; recorder. **caja registradora,** cash register

registrar, *v.t.* to examine, inspect; search; copy, record; mark the place (in a book); observe, note; (of thermometers, etc.) record, show; look on to (houses, etc.); *v.r.* register (hotels, etc.)

registro, *m.* search; registration, entry; record; recording; reading (of a thermometer, etc.); (*mech.*) damper; registry; register (book); (*mus.*) range, compass (voice); (*mus.*) register (organ); (*mech., print.*) register; book mark. **r. civil,** register of births, marriages and deaths

regla, *f.* ruler, measuring rod; rule, principle, guide, precept; system, policy; (*med.*) period; moderation; method, order. **r. de cálculo,** slide-rule. **r. T,** T-square. **en r.,** in due form. **por r.,** general, generally

reglamentación, *f.* regulation; rules and regulations

reglamentar, *v.t.* to regulate

reglamento, *m.* by-law; regulation, ordinance

reglar, *v.t.* to rule (lines); regulate; govern; control; *v.r.* restrain oneself, mend one's ways

regleta, *f.* (*print.*) reglet

regocijado, *a.* merry, joyful, happy

regocijar, *v.t.* to cheer, delight; *v.r.* enjoy oneself, rejoice

regocijo, *m.* happiness, joy; cheer, merriment

regordete, *a.* (*fam.*) chubby

regresar, *v.i.* to return

regresión, *f.* return; retrogression; regression

regreso, *m.* return

reguera, *f.* irrigation channel or ditch

reguero, *m.* trickle. **r. de pólvora,** train of gunpowder

regulación, *f.* regulation; (*mech.*) control, timing

regulador, *m.* (*mech.*) governor, regulator. *a.* regulating, controlling

regular, *v.t.* to adjust, regulate; (*mech.*) govern. *a.* methodical, ordered; moderate; average, medium; (*ecc., mil., geom., gram.*) regular; so-so, not bad; probable. **por lo r.,** generally

regularidad, *f.* regularity

regularización, *f.* regularization; regulation

regularizar, *v.t.* to regularize; regulate

regurgitar, *v.i.* to regurgitate

rehabilitación, *f.* rehabilitation

rehabilitar, *v.t.* to rehabilitate; *v.r.* rehabilitate oneself

rehacer, *v.t. irr.* to remake; repair, mend; *v.r.* recover one's strength; control one's emotions; (*mil.*) rally. See **hacer**

rehén, *m.* hostage (gen. *pl.*); (*mil.*) pledge, security

rehenchir, *v.t. irr.* to restuff; refill, recharge. See **henchir**

reherir, *v.t. irr.* to repulse. See **herir**

rehilar, *v.t.* to spin too much or twist the yarn; *v.i.* totter, stagger; whizz (arrows, etc.)

rehuir, *v.t. irr.* to withdraw; avoid; reject. See **huir**

rehusar, *v.t.* to refuse, reject

reimponer, *v.t. irr.* to reimpose. See **poner**

reimportación, *f.* reimportation

reimpresión, *f.* reprint

reimprimir, *v.t.* to reprint

reina, *f.* queen; queen (chess); queen bee; peerless beauty, belle

reinado, *m.* reign; heyday, fashion

reinante, *a.* reigning; prevalent

reinar, *v.i.* to reign; influence; endure, prevail

reincidencia, *f.* relapse (into crime, etc.), recidivism

reincidente, *m.* and *f.* backslider

reincidir, *v.i.* to relapse (into crime, etc.)

reincorporación, *f.* re-incorporation

reincorporar, *v.t.* to re-incorporate; *v.r.* join again, become a member once more

reingresar, *v.i.* to re-enter

reingreso, *m.* re-entry

reino, *m.* kingdom (all meanings)

reinstalación, *f.* reinstatement

reinstalar, *v.t.* to reinstate; *v.r.* be reinstalled

reintegración, *f.* reintegration

reintegrar, *v.t.* to reintegrate; *v.r.* be reinstated, recuperate, recover

reír, *v.i. irr.* to laugh; sneer, jeer; (*fig.*) smile (nature); *v.t.* laugh at; *v.r.* (*fam.*) (*with de*) scorn. **reírse a carcajadas,** to shout with laughter. *Pres. Part.* **riendo.** *Pres. Ind.* **río, ríes, ríe, ríen.** *Preterite* **rió, rieron.** *Pres. Subjunc.* **ría,** etc. *Imperf. Subjunc.* **riese,** etc.

reiteración, *f.* reiteration, repetition

reiteradamente, *adv.* repeatedly, reiteratively

reiterar, *v.i.* to reiterate, repeat

reiterativo, *a.* reiterative

reivindicación, *f.* (*law*) recovery

reivindicar, *v.t.* (*law*) to recover

reja, *f.* coulter, ploughshare; ploughing, tilling; grating, grille

rejado, *m.* railing, grating

rejilla, *f.* grating; grill, lattice; rack (for luggage in a train); cane (for chairs, seats, etc.); wire-mesh; small brazier; (*elec.*) grid; (*mech.*) grate

rejuntar, *v.t.* to point (a building)

rejuvenecer, *v.t. irr.* to rejuvenate; (*fig.*) revive; bring up to date; *v.i.* and *v.r.* be rejuvenated, grow young again, rejuvenesce. See **conocer**

rejuvenecimiento, *m.* rejuvenation

relación, *f.* relation; connection (of ideas); report, statement; narrative, account; (*math.*) ratio; (*law*) brief; intercourse, association, dealings (gen. *pl.*); list; analogy, relation. **tener relaciones con,** to have dealings with; be engaged or betrothed to; woo, court

relacionar, *v.t.* to recount, narrate, report; connect, relate; *v.r.* be connected

relajación, *f.* relaxation (all meanings); recreation; laxity, dissoluteness

relajar, *v.t.* to relax (all meanings); recreate, amuse; make less rigorous; (*law*) remit; *v.r.* become relaxed; be dissolute, lax or vicious

relamer, *v.t.* to lick again; *v.r.* lick one's lips; (*fig.*) over-paint, make up too much; ooze satisfaction, brag

relamido, *a.* over-dressed; affected

relámpago, *m.* lightning; flash, gleam; streak of lightning (of quick persons or things); shaft of wit, witticism

relampaguear, *v.i.* to lighten (of lightning); flash, gleam

relapso, *a.* relapsed, lapsed (into error, vice)

relatar, *v.t.* to relate, narrate, report

relatividad, *f.* relativeness; (*phys.*) relativity

relativismo, *m.* (*phil.*) relativism

relativo, *a.* relevant, pertinent; relative, comparative; (*gram.*) relative

relato, *m.* narration, account, report

relator (-ra), *a.* narrating. *s.* narrator. *m.* (*law*) reporter

relavar, *v.t.* to re-wash, wash again

releer, *v.t. irr.* to re-read; revise. See **creer**

relegación, *f.* relegation

relegar, *v.t.* to banish; relegate, set aside

relente, *m.* night dew, dampness; (*fam.*) cheek, impudence

relevación, *f.* (*art*) relief; release; remission, exemption

relevar, *v.t.* (*art*) to work in relief; emboss; relieve, free; dismiss; excuse, pardon; aid, succour; (*fig.*) aggrandize; (*mil.*) relieve; *v.i.* carve in relief

relevo, *m.* relay; (*mil.*) relief

relicario, *m.* reliquary

relieve, *m.* (*art*) relief; *pl.* leftovers, remains (food). **alto r.,** high relief. **bajo r.,** low relief

religar, *v.t.* to re-tie, fasten again; fasten more securely; solder

religión, *f.* religion; creed, faith, philosophy; devotion, religious practice. **r. reformada,** Protestantism. **entrar en r.,** (*ecc.*) to profess

religionario, *m.* Protestant

religiosidad, *f.* religiosity; religiousness; conscientiousness, punctiliousness

religioso (-sa), *a.* religious; punctilious, conscientious; moderate. *s.* religious

relinchar, *v.i.* to whinny, neigh (horses)

relincho, *m.* neigh, whinny

reliquia, *f.* residue (gen. *pl.*); (*ecc.*) relic; vestige, remnant, memento; permanent disability or ailment

reloj, *m.* clock; watch. **r. de arena,** hour-glass. **r. de bolsillo,** watch. **r. de la muerte,** death-watch beetle. **r. de péndulo,** grandfather clock. **r. de pulsera,** wrist-watch. **r. de repetición,** repeater. **r. de sol** or **r. solar,** sundial

relojera, *f.* clock stand; watch case

relojería, *f.* watch or clock making; jewellers, watchmaker's shop

relojero (-ra), *s.* watchmaker or repairer

reluciente, *a.* shining, sparkling; shiny

relucir, *v.i. irr.* to glitter, sparkle, gleam; (*fig.*) shine, excel. See **lucir**

reluctante, *a.* unruly, refractory, disobedient

relumbrante, *a.* resplendent, dazzling

relumbrar, *v.i.* to be resplendent, shine, glitter

rellanar, *v.t.* to make level again; *v.r.* stretch oneself at full length

rellano, *m.* landing (of a staircase); level stretch (of ground)

rellenar, *v.t.* to refill, replenish; fill up; (*mas.*) plug, point; (*cul.*) stuff; (*fam.*) cram with food (gen. *v.r.*)

relleno, *m.* (*cul.*) stuffing; replenishing; filling; (*fig.*) padding (of speeches, etc.)

remachadora, *f.* riveting machine

remachar, *v.t.* to rivet; (*fig.*) clinch

remache, *m.* riveting; rivet

remanente, *m.* remains, residue

remanso, *m.* backwater; stagnant water; sloth, dilatoriness

remar, *v.i.* to row, paddle, scull; toil, strive

rematadamente, *adv.* completely, entirely, absolutely

rematado, *a.* beyond hope, extremely ill; utterly lost; (*law*) convicted

rematar, *v.t.* to end, finish; finish off, kill; knock down at auction; (*sew.*) finish; *v.i.* end; *v.r.* be ruined or spoiled

remate, *m.* end, conclusion; extremity; (*arch.*) coping; (*arch.*) terminal; highest bid; auction. **de r.,** utterly hopeless

remedar, *v.t.* to copy, imitate; mimic

remediable, *a.* remediable

remediador (-ra), *a.* remedying. *s.* benefactor, helper

remediar, *v.t.* to remedy; aid, help; save from danger; prevent (trouble)

remedio, *m.* remedy; emendation, correction; help; refuge, protection; (*med.*) remedy. **No hay más r.,** There's nothing else to do, It's the only way open. **no tener más r.,** to be unable to help (doing something), be obliged to

remedo, *m.* imitation; poor copy

remembranza, *f.* remembrance, memory

rememorar, *v.t.* to remember, recall to mind

remendar, *v.t. irr.* to mend, patch; darn; repair; correct. See **recomendar**

remendón (-ona), *s.* cobbler; mender of old clothes

remero (-ra), *s.* oarsman, rower; sculler

remesa, *f.* remittance; consignment, shipment

remesar(se), *v.t.* and *v.r.* to pluck out (hair); *v.t.* (*com.*) remit; consign

remiendo, *m.* (*sew.*) patch; mend, darn; emendation; (*fam.*) insignia of one of Spanish Military Orders. **a remiendos,** (*fam.*) piecemeal

remilgarse, *v.r.* to preen oneself, be overdressed

remilgo, *m.* affectation; mannerism; prudery, squeamishness

reminiscencia, *f.* reminiscence; memory, recollection

remirado, *a.* wary, cautious, prudent, circumspect

remirar, *v.t.* to revise, go over again; *v.r.* take great care over; behold with pleasure

remisión, *f.* sending; remission; pardon, forgiveness; foregoing, relinquishment; abatement, diminution; (*lit.*) reference, allusion

remiso, *a.* timid, spiritless; languid, slow

remitente, *m.* and *f.* sender. *a.* sending

remitir, *v.t.* to remit, send; pardon, forgive; defer, postpone; abate, diminish; relinquish, forgo; (*lit.*) refer; *v.r.* remit, submit, consult; refer (to), cite

remo, *m.* oar, scull, paddle; arm or leg (men or animals. gen. *pl.*); wing (gen. *pl.*); hard, continuous toil; galleys. **al r.,** by dint of rowing; (*fam.*) struggling with hardships

remojar, *v.t.* to soak, steep; celebrate by drinking

remojo, *m.* soaking, steeping

remolacha, *f.* (*bot.*) beet

remolcador, *m.* (*naut.*) tow, tug. *a.* (*naut.*) towing remolcar, v.t. (naut., aut.) to tow; (fig.) press into service, use

remolinar, v.i. to spin, whirl, eddy; v.r. throng, swarm

remolino, m. whirlwind; eddy, swirl; whirlpool; crowd, throng, swarm; disturbance, riot

remolonear, v.i. (fam.) to loiter, lag; avoid work; be lax or dilatory

remolque, m. towage, towing; tow-line; barge; (aut.) trailer. a r., on tow

remonta, f. resoling (shoes); leather gusset (riding breeches); (mil.) remount

remontar, v.t. to scare off (game); (mil.) supply with fresh horses; resole (shoes); (fig.) rise to great heights (oratory, etc.); v.r. soar (birds); (with prep. a) date from, go back to; originate in

remoquete, m. blow with the fist; witticism; (fam.) flirtation, courtship

rémora, f. (icht.) remora; delay, hindrance

remorder, v.t. irr. to bite again or repeatedly; (fig.) gnaw, nag, cause uneasiness or remorse; v.r. show one's feelings. See morder

remordimiento, m. remorse

remotamente, adv. distantly, remotely; unlikely; vaguely, confusedly

remoto, a. distant, remote; unlikely, improbable

remover, v.t. irr. to remove, move; stir; turn over; dismiss, discharge. See mover

remozar, v.t. to cause to appear young; freshen up, bring up to date; v.r. look young

remuda, f. replacement, exchange

remudar, v.t. to replace

remuneración, f. remuneration; reward

remunerador (-ra), a. remunerative, recompensing. s. remunerator

remunerar, v.t. to recompense, reward

remusgar, v.i. to suspect, imagine

renacentista, a. renaissance

renacer, v.i. irr. to be reborn. See nacer

renacimiento, m. rebirth; Renaissance

renacuajo, m. tadpole; (mech.) frog; (fam.) twirp

renano, a. Rhenish

rencilla, f. grudge, grievance, resentment

rencilloso, a. peevish, easily offended, touchy

rencor, m. rancour, spite, old grudge. guardar r., to bear malice

rencoroso, a. rancorous, malicious, spiteful

rendición, f. surrender; yield, profit

rendido, a. submissive, obsequious

rendija, f. crevice, cleft, crack, fissure

rendimiento, m. weariness, fatigue; submissiveness, obsequiousness; yield, profit; (mech.) efficiency

rendir, v.t. irr. (mil.) to cause to surrender; defeat; overcome, conquer; give back, return; yield, provide; tire, exhaust; vomit; pay, render; v.r. be exhausted, worn out; surrender. (mil.) r. el puesto, to retire from or give up a post. See pedir

renegado (-da), s. renegade, apostate; turncoat; (fam.) malignant person. a. renegade

renegador (-ra), s. blasphemer; foul-mouthed person

renegar, v.t. irr. to deny, disown; loathe, hate; v.i. (with de) apostatize; blaspheme; (fam.) curse. See cegar

renglón, m. (print.) line; pl. writing, composition

reniego, m. blasphemy; (fam.) foul language, cursing

renitencia, f. repugnance

reno, m. reindeer

renombrado, a. illustrious, famous

renombre, m. surname; renown, reputation, fame

renovable, a. renewable, replaceable

renovación, f. replacement; renewal; renovation; transformation, reform

renovador (-ra), s. reformer; renovator. a. renovating; reforming renovar, *v.t. irr.* to renew; renovate; replace; exchange; reiterate, repeat. See contar

renta, *f.* yield, profit; income; revenue; Government securities; rent; tax

rentar, *v.t.* to yield, produce an income

rentero (-ra), *s.* farmer tenant. *m.* one who farms out land

rentista, *m.* and *f.* financier; bond-holder; person who lives on a private income, rentier

rentístico, *a.* revenue, financial

renuente, *a.* refractory, wilful

renuevo, *m.* (*bot.*) shoot; renewal

renuncia, renunciación, *f.* renunciation; resignation; abandonment, relinquishment

renunciar, *v.t.* to renounce; refuse; scorn; abandon, relinquish; resign; revoke (at cards). r. a, to give up

renuncio, *m.* revoke (cards); (*fam.*) falsehood

reñidamente, *adv.* strongly, stubbornly, fiercely

reñir, *v.i. irr.* to quarrel, dispute; fight; be on bad terms, fall out; *v.t.* scold; fight (battles, etc.). See ceñir

reo, *m.* and *f.* criminal; offender, guilty party; (*law*) defendant

reojo, *m.* (mirar de) to look out of the corner of the eye; (*fig.*) look askance

reómetro, *m.*-(*phys.*) rheometer

reorganización, *f.* reorganization

reorganizador (-ra), *a.* reorganizing. *s.* reorganizer

reorganizar, *v.t.* to reorganize

reóstato, *m.* (*elec.*) rheostat

repantigarse, *v.r.* to stretch out one's legs, make oneself comfortable

reparable, *a.* remediable, reparable; worthy of note

reparación, *f.* repair, mending; reparation, satisfaction; indemnity, compensation

reparada, *f.* shying (of horses)

reparador, *a.* repairing, mending; fault-finding; restoring; satisfying, compensating

reparar, *v.t.* to repair; restore; consider; correct, remedy; atone for, expiate; indemnify; hold up; detain; protect, guard; (*with en*)

notice; *v.i.* halt, be detained; *v.r.* control oneself

reparo, *m.* repair; restoration; remedy; note, reflection; warning; doubt, scruple; guard, protection; parry (fencing)

repartición, *f.* distribution

repartidero, *a.* distributable

repartidor (-ra), *a.* distributing. *s.* distributor; tax-assessor

repartimiento, *m.* distribution, allotment; assessment

repartir, *v.t.* to distribute; share out; allot; deal (at cards); assess; (*com.*) deliver

reparto, *m.* distribution; assessment; delivery (of letters, etc.); (*theat.*) cast; deal (at cards)

repasar, *v.t.* to pass by again; peruse, re-examine; brush up, revise; skim, glance over; mend, repair (garments); edit, revise; hone

repaso, *m.* second passage through; re-examination, perusal; revision, editing; brushing up, revision; repair, mending; (*fam.*) dressing down, scolding

repatriación, *f.* repatriation

repatriado (-da), *s.* repatriate

repatriar, *v.t.* to repatriate; *v.i.* and *v.r.* return to one's own country

repecho, *m.* steep slope. a r., uphill

repelar, *v.t.* to pull by the hair; put through its paces (horse); clip, cut; remove, diminish

repeler, *v.t.* to repel, throw back; reject, refute

repelo, *m.* anything against the grain; wrong way of hair; (*fam.*) skirmish; reluctance, repugnance

repente, *m.* (*fam.*) sudden or unexpected movement. de r., suddenly

repentino, *a.* sudden, unexpected

repentizar, *v.i.* (*mus.*) to read at sight

repercusión, *f.* repercussion; vibration

repercutir, *v.i.* to recoil, rebound; *v.r.* reverberate; re-echo; (*fig.*) have repercussions; *v.t.* (*med.*) repel

repertorio, *m.* repertory

repesar, *v.t.* to re-weigh, weigh again

repetición, *f.* repetition; (*art*) replica, copy; repeater (in clocks); recital

repetidamente, *adv.* repeatedly

repetidor, *a.* repeating

repetir, *v.t.* *irr.* to repeat, do over again; reiterate; (*art*) copy, make a replica of; recite. See **pedir**

repicar, *v.t.* to chop, mince; peal (bells); prick again; *v.r.* pride oneself (on), boast

repique, *m.* chopping, mincing; peal, pealing (bells); disagreement, grievance

repisa, *f.* (*arch.*) bracket; ledge; shelf. **r. de chimenea,** mantelpiece

replantar, *v.t.* to replant; transplant

repleción, *f.* repletion, satiety

replegar, *v.t.* *irr.* to re-fold, fold many times; *v.r.* (*mil.*) retreat in good order. See **cegar**

repleto, *a.* replete

réplica, *f.* reply, answer; replica

replicar, *v.i.* to contradict, dispute; answer, reply. (*fam.*) **¡No me repliques!** Don't answer back!

repliegue, *m.* double fold, crease; doubling, folding; (*mil.*) withdrawal

repoblación, *f.* repeopling, repopulation

repoblar, *v.t.* to repeople, repopulate

repollo, *m.* white cabbage; heart (of lettuces, etc.)

reponer, *v.t.* *irr.* to replace; reinstate; restore; reply; *v.r.* recover, regain (possessions); grow well again; grow calm. See **poner**

reportación, *f.* serenity, moderation

reportaje, *m.* journalistic report

reportar, *v.t.* to restrain, moderate; achieve, obtain; carry; bring; *v.r.* control oneself

reporte, *m.* report, news; rumour

reporterismo, *m.* newspaper reporting

reportero (-ra), *a.* news, report. *s.* reporter

reposado, *a.* quiet, peaceful, tranquil

reposar, *v.i.* to rest, repose oneself; sleep, doze; lie in the grave; settle (liquids); rest (on)

reposición, *f.* replacement; restoration; renewal; recovery (of health); (*theat.*) revival

repositorio, *m.* repository

reposo, *m.* rest, repose; peace, tranquillity; sleep

repostería, *f.* confectioner's shop; pantry; butler's pantry

repostero, *m.* confectioner, pastry-cook

repregunta, *f.* (*law*) cross-examination

repreguntar, *v.t.* (*law*) to cross-examine

reprender, *v.t.* to scold, reprimand, rebuke

reprensible, *a.* reprehensible, censurable

reprensión, *f.* scolding, reprimand, rebuke

represa, *f.* damming, holding back (water); dam, lock; restraining, controlling

represalia, *f.* reprisal (gen. *pl.*); retaliation

represar, *v.t.* to dam, harness (water); (*naut.*) retake, recapture; (*fig.*) restrain, control

representación, *f.* representation; (*theat.*) performance; authority; dignity; (*com.*) agency; portrait, image; depiction, expression; petition

representador, *a.* representative

representante, *a.* representative. *m.* and *f.* representative; actor; performer

representar, *v.t.* to represent; (*theat.*) perform; depict, express; describe, portray; *v.r.* imagine, picture to oneself

representativo, *a.* representative

represión, *f.* repression; recapture

represivo, *a.* repressive

reprimenda, *f.* rebuke, reprimand

reprimir, *v.t.* to repress, restrain, control; *v.r.* restrain oneself

reprobación, *f.* censure; reprobation

reprobar, *v.t.* *irr.* to reprove; censure; fail (in an exam.). See **probar**

réprobo (-ba), *s.* reprobate

reprochar, *v.t.* to reproach

reproche, *m.* reproaching; rebuke, reproach

reproducción, *f.* reproduction. **r. gran escala,** large-scale model

reproducir, *v.t. irr.* to reproduce. See **conducir**

reproductor (-ra), *a.* reproductive. *s.* breeding animal

reps, *m.* rep (fábric)

reptil, *a.* reptilian; crawling. *m.* reptile

república, *f.* republic; state, commonwealth. **r. de las letras,** (the) republic of letters

republicanismo, *m.* republicanism

republicano (-na), *a.* and *s.* republican

repudiación, *f.* repudiation

repudiar, *v.t.* to cast off (a wife); repudiate, renounce

repuesto, *a.* retired, hidden. *m.* stock, provision; serving table; pantry; stake (cards, etc.). **de r.,** spare, extra

repugnancia, *f.* inconsistency, contradiction; aversion, dislike; reluctance; repugnance

repugnante, *a.* repugnant, loathsome

repugnar, *v.t.* to contradict, be inconsistent with; hate, be averse to (e.g. **La idea me repugna,** I hate the idea)

repujado, *m.* repoussé work

repujar, *v.t.* to work in repoussé

repulir, *v.t.* to repolish, reburnish; *v.t.* and *v.r.* make up too much, overdress

repulsa, *f.* snub, rebuff; rejection; repulse

repulsar, *v.t.* to decline, reject; repulse; deny, refuse; rebuff

repulsión, *f.* repulsion; rebuff; aversion, dislike

repulsivo, *a.* repellent

repunta, *f.* headland, cape; (*fig.*) first sign; (*fam.*) disgust; caprice; fight

reputación, *f.* reputation

reputar, *v.t.* to believe, consider (e.g. **Le reputo por honrado,** I believe him to be an honourable man); appreciate, esteem

requebrar, *v.t. irr.* to break into smaller pieces; make love to, woo; compliment, flatter. See **quebrar**

requemado, *a.* sunburnt; brown

requemar, *v.t.* to burn again; overcook; dry up, parch (plants, etc.); burn (the mouth) (of curry, etc.); *v.r.* (*fig.*) suffer inwardly

requerimiento, *m.* requirement, demand; (*law*) summons

requerir, *v.t. irr.* to inform, notify; examine; need, necessitate; require; summon; woo; persuade. See **sentir**

requesón, *m.* cream cheese; curd

requetebién, *adv.* (*fam.*) exceedingly well

requiebro, *m.* compliment, expression of love; wooing, flirtation

requisa, *f.* inspection, visitation; (*mil.*) requisitioning

requisar, *v.t.* (*mil.*) to requisition

requisito, *m.* requisite

res, *f.* animal, beast; head of cattle

resabiar, *v.t.* to make vicious, cause bad habits; *v.r.* contract bad habits or vices; be discontented; relish

resabio, *m.* disagreeable aftertaste; bad habit, vice

resaca, *f.* surf, surge; (*com.*) redraft

resalado, *a.* (*fam.*) very witty; most attractive

resaltar, *v.i.* to rebound; project, jut out; grow loose, fall out; (*fig.*) stand out, be prominent

resalto, *m.* rebound; projection

resarcir, *v.t.* to compensate, indemnify

resbaladizo, *a.* slippery; difficult, delicate (situation)

resbalar, *v.i.* to slip; slide; skid; err, fall into sin

resbalón, *m.* slip; slide; skid; temptation, error

rescatador (-ra), *s.* ransomer; rescuer

rescatar, *v.t.* to ransom; redeem, buy back; barter; free, rescue; (*fig.*) redeem (time, etc.)

rescate, *m.* ransom; redemption; barter; amount of ransom

rescindir, *v.t.* to annul, repeal, rescind

rescisión, *f.* annulment, abrogation

rescoldo, *m.* ember, cinder; scruple, qualm, doubt

resección, *f.* (*surg.*) resection

reseda, *f.* (*bot.*) mignonette

resentimiento, *m.* deterioration, impairment; animosity, resentment

resentirse, *v.r.* *irr.* to deteriorate, be impaired; be hurt or offended. See **sentir**

reseña, *f.* (*mil.*) review; short description; (book) review

reseñar, *v.t.* (*mil.*) to review; describe briefly, outline

reserva, *f.* store, stock; exception, qualification; reticence; restraint, moderation; (*ecc.* and *law*) reservation; (*mil.*, *naut.*) reserve. **sin r.,** frankly, without reserve

reservación, *f.* reservation; scruple

reservado, *a.* reserved, reticent; prudent, moderate; kept, reserved. *m.* reserved compartment; private apartment, garden, etc.

reservar, *v.t.* to keep, hold; postpone; reserve (rooms, etc.); exempt; keep secret; withhold (information); (*ecc.*) reserve; *v.r.* await a better opportunity; be cautious

reservista, *a.* (*mil.*, *nav.*) reserved. *m.* reservist

resfriado, *m.* (*med.*) cold, chill

resfriar, *v.t.* to chill; (*fig.*) cool, moderate; *v.i.* grow cold; *v.r.* catch a cold; (*fig.*) cool off (love, etc.)

resguardar, *v.t.* to protect; shelter; *v.r.* take refuge; (*with de*) guard against; (*with con*) shelter by

resguardo, *m.* protection, guard; (*com.*) guarantee, security; (*com.*) voucher; preservation; vigilance (to prevent smuggling); contraband guards

residencia, *f.* stay, residence; home, domicile; (*ecc.*) residence

residencial, *a.* residential; resident, residentiary

residente, *a.* resident. *m.* and *f.* inhabitant. *m.* resident or minister resident (diplomatic)

residir, *v.i.* to live, inhabit; reside officially; be found, be, exist

residuo, *m.* residuum; remainder; (*math.*) remainder; (*chem.*) residue

resignación, *f.* resignation; fortitude, submission

resignar, *v.t.* to resign, relinquish; *v.r.* submit, resign oneself

resina, *f.* resin

resinoso, *a.* resinous

resistencia, *f.* resistance; opposition; endurance; (*phys.*, *mech.*, *psy.*) resistance

resistente, *a.* resistant; tough; (of plants) hardy

resistir, *v.i.* to resist, oppose; reject; *v.t.* endure, bear; resist; *v.r.* fight, resist.

resma, *f.* ream (paper)

resolución, *f.* decision; boldness, daring; determination, resolution; decree

resoluto, *a.* resolute, bold; brief, concise; able, expert

resolver, *v.t.* *irr.* to determine, decide; summarize; solve; dissolve; analyse; (*phys.*, *med.*) resolve; *v.r.* decide, determine; be reduced to, become; (*med.*) resolve. *Pres. Ind.* **resuelvo, resuelves, resuelve, resuelven.** *Past Part.* **resuelto.** *Pres. Subjunc.* **resuelva, resuelvas, resuelva, resuelvan**

resollar, *v.i.* *irr.* to breathe; pant. See **degollar**

resonancia, *f.* resonance, sonority, ring; fame, reputation

resonante, *a.* resonant; resounding

resonar, *v.i.* *irr.* to resound, echo. See **tronar**

resoplido, resoplo, *m.* heavy breathing, pant, snort

resorber, *v.t.* to re-absorb

resorción, *f.* reabsorption

resorte, *m.* (*mech.*) spring; elasticity; (*fig.*) means, instrument

respaldo, *m.* back (of chairs, etc.); reverse side of a piece of paper

respectivo, *a.* respective

respecto, *m.* relation, regard, reference. **con r. a,** *or* **r. a,** with regard to, concerning

respetabilidad, *f.* respectability; worthiness

respetable, *a.* worthy of respect; respectable; (*fig.*) considerable, large

respetar, *v.t.* to respect, revere

respeto, *m.* respect, honour; consideration, reason. **de r.,** spare, extra; special, ceremonial respetuoso, *a.* venerable, worthy of honour; respectful, courteous

respingar, *v.i.* to flinch, wince, kick; (*fam.*) be uneven, rise (hem of garments); (*fam.*) do (a thing) grumblingly

respingo, *m.* wincing; jerk, shake; (*fam.*) gesture of reluctance or dislike

respirable, *a.* breathable

respiración, *f.* breathing, respiration; ventilation

respiradero, *m.* ventilator; air-hole, vent; rest, breathing space

respirador, *a.* breathing; respiratory. *m.* respirator

respirar, *v.i.* to breathe; exhale, give off; take courage; have a breathing space, rest; (*fam.*) speak. sin r., continuously, without stopping for breath

respiratorio, *a.* respiratory

respiro, *m.* breathing; breathing space, respite

resplandecer, *v.i. irr.* to glitter, gleam; shine, excel. See conocer

resplandeciente, *a.* glittering, resplendent, shining

resplandor, *m.* radiance, brilliance; glitter, gleam; majesty, splendour

responder, *v.t.* to reply; satisfy, answer; *v.i.* re-echo; requite, return; produce, provide; (*fig.*) answer, have the desired effect; (*com.*) (*with de*) answer for, guarantee; (*com.*) correspond

respondón, *a.* (*fam.*) pert, cheeky, given to answering back

responsabilidad, *f.* responsibility

responsable, *a.* responsible

responso, *m.* (*ecc.*) response, responsory

respuesta, *f.* answer, reply; response; refutation; repartee

resquebradura, *f.* fissure, crevice, crack

resquebrajarse, *v.r.* to crack, split

resquemar, *v.t.* (of hot dishes) to bite, sting

resquicio, *m.* crack, chink, slit; opportunity

resta, *f.* (*math.*) subtraction; (*math.*) remainder

restablecer, *v.t. irr.* to re-establish; restore; *v.r.* recover one's health; re-establish oneself. See conocer

restablecimiento, *m.* re-establishment; restoration

restañar, *v.t.* to re-tin; staunch

restar, *v.t.* (*math.*) to subtract; deduct; return (ball); *v.i.* remain. No me resta más que decir adiós, It only remains for me to say good-bye

restauración, *f.* restoration; renovation

restaurador (-ra), *a.* restorative. *s.* restorer

restaurante, *m.* restaurant

restaurar, *v.t.* to recover, recuperate; renovate, repair; restore

restaurativo, *a.* and *m.* restorative

restinga, *f.* sand-bank, bar

restitución, *f.* restitution

restituible, *a.* returnable, replaceable

restituir, *v.t. irr.* to return, give back; restore; re-establish; *v.r.* return to one's place of departure. See huir

resto, *m.* rest, balance; (*math.*) remainder; *pl.* remains

restorán, *m.* restaurant

restricción, *f.* limitation, restriction

restrictivo, *a.* restrictive; restraining

restringir, *v.t.* to limit, restrict; contract

resucitar, *v.t.* to raise from the dead; (*fig., fam.*)—revive; *v.i.* resuscitate

resuelto, *a.* audacious, daring; resolute, capable

resuello, *m.* breathing; panting, hard breathing

resulta, *f.* consequence, result; decision, resolution; vacant post. de resultas de, as the result of; in consequence of

resultado, *m.* result, consequence, outcome

resultante, *a.* resulting. *f.* (*mech.*) resultant

resultar, *v.i.* to result, follow; turn out, happen; result (in); (*fam.*) turn out well. El vestido no me resulta, The dress isn't a success on me

resumen, *m.* summary. en r., in short

resumir, *v.t.* to summarize, abridge; sum up, recapitulate; *v.r.* be contained, be included

resurgimiento, *m.* resurgence, revival

resurgir, *v.i.* to reappear, rise again, revive; resuscitate

resurrección, *f.* resurrection

resurtir, *v.i.* to rebound

retablo, *m.* (*arch.*) altar-piece, retable; frieze; series of pictures

retaguardia, *f.* rear-guard. **a r.,** in the rear. **picar la r.,** to harass the rear-guard

retajar, *v.t.* to cut in the round; circumcise

retal, *m.* clipping; filing, shaving; remnant

retama, *f.* (*bot.*) broom. **r. común** *or* **r. de olor,** Spanish broom. **r. de escobas,** common broom

retar, *v.t.* to challenge; (*fam.*) reproach, accuse

retardación, *f.* retardment

retardar, *v.t.* to retard, delay

retardo, *m.* delay, retardment

retazo, *m.* remnant, cutting; excerpt, fragment

retemblar, *v.i.* to quiver, tremble constantly

retén, *m.* stock, reserve, provision; (*mil.*) reserve

retención, *f.* retention

retener, *v.t. irr.* to keep, retain; recollect, remember; keep back; (*law*) detain; deduct. See **tener**

retenidamente, *adv.* retentively

retentiva, *f.* retentiveness, memory

retentivo, *a.* retentive

reticencia, *f.* reticence

reticente, *a.* reticent

reticular, *a.* reticulate

retículo, *m.* reticulum, network; (*phys.*) reticle

retina, *f.* retina (of the eye)

retintín, *m.* ringing; tinkling; (*fam.*) sarcastic tone

retiñir, *v.i.* to tinkle, clink; jingle

retirada, *f.* withdrawal; retirement; seclusion, refuge; (*mil.*) retreat

retirado, *a.* remote, secluded; (*mil.*) retired

retirar, *v.t.* to withdraw; remove; repel, throw back; hide, put aside; *v.r.* withdraw; retire; (*mil.*) retreat

retiro, *m.* withdrawal; removal; seclusion, privacy; (*mil.*) retreat;

retirement; (*ecc.*) retreat. **dar el r. (a),** to place on the retired list

reto, *m.* challenge; threat

retocar, *v.t.* to touch again or repeatedly; (*phot.*) retouch; restore (pictures); (*fig.*) put the finishing touch to

retoñar, *v.i.* to sprout, shoot; (*fig.*) revive, resuscitate

retoño, *m.* sprout, shoot

retoque, *m.* frequent touching; finishing touch; touch, slight attack

retorcer, *v.t. irr.* to twist; contort; confound with own argument; misconstrue, distort; *v.r.* contort; writhe. See **torcer**

retórica, *f.* rhetoric; *pl.* (*fam.*) quibbling

retórico (-ca), *a.* rhetorical. *s.* rhetorician

retornar, *v.t.* to return, give back; turn, twist; turn back; *v.i.* and *v.r.* return, go back

retorno, *m.* return, going back; recompense, repayment; exchange; return journey

retorsión, *f.* twisting, writhing; (*fig.*) misconstruction

retorta, *f.* (*chem.*) retort

retortijón, *m.* twisting, curling. **r. de tripas,** stomach-ache

retozar, *v.i.* to skip, frisk, frolic, gambol; romp; (*fig.*) be aroused (passions)

retozón, *a.* frolicsome

retracción, *f.* drawing back, retraction

retractación, *f.* retractation, recantation

retractar, *v.t.* to retract, recant, withdraw

retráctil, *a.* retractile

retraer, *v.t. irr.* to bring back again; dissuade; buy back, redeem; *v.r.* take refuge; retire; withdraw; go into seclusion. See **traer**

retraído, *a.* fugitive, refugee; retired, solitary; timid, nervous, unsociable

retraimiento, *m.* withdrawal; seclusion, privacy; refuge, asylum; sanctuary; timidity, unsociability

retrasar, *v.t.* to postpone, delay; put back (the clock); *v.i.* be slow (clocks); *v.r.* be behind time, be late; be backward (persons)

retraso, *m.* lateness; delay, dilatoriness; loss of time (clocks); putting back (of the clock) (e.g. **El reloj lleva cinco minutos de r.,** The clock is five minutes slow)

retratar, *v.t.* to paint (draw) the portrait of; portray, describe; photograph; copy, imitate

retratista, *m.* and *f.* portrait painter; photographer; portrayer

retrato, *m.* portrait; portrayal; (*fig.*) image, likeness

retrechería, *f.* (*fam.*) craftiness, evasiveness

retreta, *f.* (*mil.*) retreat; tattoo

retrete, *m.* water-closet

retribución, *f.* recompense, reward

retribuir, *v.t. irr.* to recompense, reward. See **huir**

retroactivo, *a.* retroactive

retroceder, *v.i.* to withdraw, move back, draw back; recede

retroceso, *m.* retrocedence, withdrawal; (*med.*) retrogression

retrogradación, *f.* retrogression

retrógrado, *a.* retrogressive, retrograde; (*pol.*) reactionary

retronar, *v.i. irr.* to bang, thunder, resound with noise. See **tronar**

retrospección, *f.* retrospection

retrospectivo, *a.* retrospective

retrotraer, *v.t. irr.* to antedate. See **traer**

retruécano, *m.* antithesis; play upon words, pun

retumbante, *a.* resounding; pompous, high-flown

retumbar, *v.i.* to resound, echo, reverberate; roll (of thunder); roar (of cannon)

retumbo, *m.* reverberation, echo; rumble; roll (of thunder); roar (of cannon, etc.)

reuma, *m.* rheumatism

reumático, *a.* rheumatic

reumatismo, *m.* rheumatism

reunión, *f.* reunion, union; meeting; assembly, gathering

reunir, *v.t.* to reunite; unite; join; gather, assemble; *v.r.* meet, assemble; unite

revacunación, *f.* revaccination

revacunar, *v.t.* to revaccinate

revalidación, *f.* ratification, confirmation

revalidar, *v.t.* to ratify, confirm; *v.r.* pass final examination (gen. universities)

revejido, *a.* prematurely old

revelación, *f.* revelation; (*phot.*) developing

revelador, *a.* revealing. *m.* (*phot.*) developer

revelar, *v.t.* to reveal; (*phot.*) develop

revendedor (-ra), *a.* reselling, retail. *s.* retailer

revender, *v.t.* to resell; retail (goods)

reventa, *f.* resale; retail

reventar, *v.i. irr.* to burst, explode; break in foam (waves); burst forth; (*fig.*) burst (with impatience, etc.); (*fam.*) explode (with anger, etc.); *v.t.* break, crush; (*fig.*) wear out, exhaust; (*fam.*) irritate, vex; *v.r.* burst; (*fig.*) be exhausted. See **sentar**

reventón, *a.* bursting. *m.* explosion, bursting; steep hill; hole, fix, difficulty; uphill work, heavy toil

rever, *v.t. irr.* to look at again, revise; (*law*) retry. See **ver**

reverberación, *f.* reflection (of light); reverberation, resounding

reverberar, *v.i.* to reflect; resound, reverberate

reverbero, *m.* reverberation; reflector; reverberatory furnace

reverdecer, *v.i. irr.* to grow green again; revive, acquire new vigour. See **conocer**

reverencia, *f.* respect, veneration; bow; curtsy; reverence (*ecc.* title)

reverencial, *a.* reverential, respectful

reverenciar, *v.t.* to revere; honour; respect

reverendo, *a* reverend; venerable; (*fam.*) over-prudent

reversibilidad, *f.* reversibility

reversión, *f.* reversion

reverso, *m.* wrong side, back; reverse side (of coins)

reverter, *v.i. irr.* to overflow. See **entender**

revertir, *v.i.* (*law*) to revert

revés, *m.* wrong side, back, reverse; cuff, slap; backstroke (ball games); check, setback, reverse; disaster, misfortune. **al**

r., on the contrary; wrong side out. **de r.,** from left to right, anticlockwise

revesado, *a.* complicated, difficult; wilful

revestimiento, *m.* (*mas.*) lining, coating

revestir, *v.t. irr.* to dress; (*mas.*) coat, line; (*fig.*) cover, clothe; *v.r.* be dressed or dress oneself; (*fig.*) be captivated (by an idea); become haughty or full of oneself; rise to the occasion, develop qualities necessary. See **pedir**

reviejo, *a.* very old. *m.* dead branch (trees)

revisar, *v.t.* to revise; examine

revisión, *f.* revision; re-examination; (*law*) retrial

revisor, *a.* revising, examining. *m.* reviser; ticket inspector

revista, *f.* re-examination, revision; review, periodical; (*theat.*) revue; re-inspection; review (of books, etc.); (*law*) fresh trial; (*mil.*) review. **pasar r.,** to inspect; review

revistero (-ra), *s.* reviewer, writer of reviews

revivificación, *f.* revivification

revivificar, *v.t.* to revivify, revive

revivir, *v.i.* to resuscitate; revive

revocación, *f.* revocation, cancellation, annulment

revocar, *v.t.* to revoke, annul; dissuade; repel, throw back; wash (walls); (*law*) discharge

revolcadero *m.* animals' bathing place

revolcar, *v.t. irr.* to knock down, trample underfoot; lay flat (in argument); *v.r.* wallow; stick one's heels in, be obstinate. See **volcar**

revolotear, *v.i.* to flutter, fly around; twirl; *v.t.* hurl, toss

revoltillo, *m.* jumble, hotchpotch; confusion, tangle

revoltoso, *a.* rebellious; mischievous, wilful; intricate

revolución, *f.* turn, revolution; rebellion, uprising; revolution

revolucionar, *v.t.* to revolutionize

revolucionario (-ia), *a.* and *s.* revolutionary

revolver, *v.t. irr.* to turn over; turn upside down; wrap up; revolve; stir; reflect upon, consider; upset, cause disharmony; search through, disorder (papers, etc.); *v.r.* move from side to side; change (weather). See **resolver**

revólver, *m.* revolver

revoque, *m.* (*mas.*) washing, whitewashing; plastering

revuelco, *m.* wallowing

revuelo, *m.* second flight (birds); irregular course of flight; disturbance, upset

revuelta, *f.* second turn or revolution; revolt, rebellion; quarrel, fight; turning point; change of direction, turn; change (opinions, posts, etc.)

revueltamente, *adv.* in confusion, higgledy-piggledy

revulsión, *f.* revulsion

revulsivo, *a.* (*med.*) revulsive

rey, *m.* king (cards, chess); queen bee; (*fam.*) swineherd; (*fig.*) king, chief. (*her.*) **r. de armas,** King-of-Arms. **reyes magos,** magi. **dia de Reyes,** Twelfth Night. **servir al r.,** to fight for the king

reyerta, *f.* quarrel, shindy

reyezuelo, *m.* kinglet, petty king; (*orn.*) golden-crested wren

rezagar, *v.t.* to leave behind; postpone, delay; *v.r.* lag behind, straggle

rezar, *v.t.* to pray, say prayers; say (Mass); (*fam.*) state, say; *v.i.* pray; (*fam.*) fume, grumble. **El edicto reza así,** The edict runs like this

rezo, *m.* prayer; devotions

rezongar, *v.i.* to grouse, grumble

rezumar(se), *v.r.* and *v.i.* to percolate, ooze through; (*fam.*) leak out, be known

ría, *f.* firth, estuary, river mouth

riachuelo, *m.* rivulet, stream

riada, *f.* flood. (*aer.*) **r. de acero,** rain of flak

ribaldería, *f.* ribaldry

ribaldo, *a.* ribald. *m.* knave

ribazo, *m.* slope, incline

ribera, *f.* bank, margin, shore, strand

ribereño (-ña), *a.* and *s.* riparian

ribero, *m.* embankment, wall

ribete, *m.* binding, border, trimming; stripe; increase, addition; dramatic touch, exaggeration; *pl.* indications, signs

ribetear, *v.t.* (*sew.*) to bind, trim, edge

ricacho (-cha), *s.* (*fam.*) newly rich person

ricahembra, *f.* lady; daughter or wife of a Spanish noble (*ant.*)

ricamente, *adv.* richly, opulently; beautifully, splendidly; luxuriously

ricino, *m.* castor-oil plant

rico, *a.* wealthy, rich; abundant; magnificent, splendid; delicious

ricohombre, *m.* nobleman (*ant.*)

ricura, *f.* (*fam.*) richness, wealth

ridiculez, *f.* absurd action or remark; ridiculousness; affectation; folly

ridiculizar, *v.t.* to ridicule, poke fun at

ridículo, *a.* ridiculous, absurd; grotesque; preposterous, outrageous. *m.* reticule

riego, *m.* watering, spraying; irrigation

riel, *m.* ingot; rail (of a railway, tramcar)

rielar, *v.i.* to glimmer, glisten; glitter; shimmer

rienda, *f.* rein (gen. *pl.*); restraint; *pl.* administration, government. **a r. suelta,** swiftly; without restraint

riesgo, *m.* risk, danger

rifa, *f.* raffle; quarrel, disagreement

rifar, *v.t.* to raffle; *v.i.* quarrel, fall out

rifeño (-ña), *a.* and *s.* Riffian (Morocco)

rifle, *m.* rifle

rigidez, *f.* stiffness; rigidity; harshness

rígido, *a.* stiff; rigid; inflexible; severe, harsh

rigodón, *m.* rigadoon (dance)

rigor, *m.* severity, sternness; rigour; hardness; inflexibility; (*med.*) rigor. **en r.,** strictly speaking. **ser de r.,** to be essential, be indispensable

rigorista, *m.* and *f.* martinet

riguroso, *a.* rigorous; harsh, cruel; austere, rigid; strict, exact, scrupulous

rijoso, *a.* quarrelsome; lascivious

riksha, *m.* ricksha

rima, *f.* rhyme; heap; *pl.* lyrics

rimador (-ra), *a.* rhyming. *s.* rhymer

rimar, *v.i.* to compose verses; *v.i.* and *v.t.* rhyme

rimbombo, *m.* reverberation of a sound

rimero, *m.* heap, pile

rincón, *m.* corner, angle; retreat, hiding place; (*fam.*) home, nest, nook

rinconada, *f.* corner, angle

rinconera, *f.* corner cupboard; corner table

ringlera, *f.* file, line, row

ringlero, *m.* guiding line for writing

ringorrangos, *m. pl.* (*fam.*) exaggerated flourishes in writing; (*fam.*) unnecessary frill or ornaments

rinoceronte, *m.* rhinoceros

riñón, *m.* (*anat.*) kidney; (*fig.*) centre, heart; *pl.* (*anat.*) back

río, *m.* river; (*fig.*) stream, flood

rioja, *m.* red wine from Rioja (province of Logroño, N.E. Spain)

ripio, *m.* remains, rest; débris, rubbish; (*lit.*) padding; verbiage, prolixity. **no perder r.,** to lose no occasion or opportunity

riqueza, *f.* riches, wealth; abundance; richness, magnificence

risa, *f.* laugh; laughter; cause of amusement, joke

risco, *m.* crag

riscoso, *a.* craggy

risibilidad, *f.* risibility

risible, *a.* laughable

risoles, *m. pl.* (*cul.*) rissoles

risotada, *f.* loud laugh

ristra, *f.* string (of onions, etc.); file, line, row

ristre, *m.* rest (of a lance)

risueño, *a.* smiling; cheerful; pleasant, agreeable; favourable, hopeful

rítmico, *a.* rhythmic

ritmo, *m.* rhythm

rito, *m.* rite

ritualismo, *m.* ritualism

ritualista, *m.* and *f.* ritualist

rivalidad, *f.* rivalry, competition; hostility

rivalizar, *v.i.* to compete, rival

rizado, *m.* curling; pleating, crimping; rippling, ruffling

rizar, *v.t.* to curl (hair); ripple, ruffle (water); pleat, crimp; *v.r.* be naturally wavy (hair)

rizo, *m.* curl, ringlet; cut velvet. (*aer.*) **hacer el r.,** to loop the loop; (*naut.*) to take in reefs

rizoma, *m.* (*bot.*) rhizome

rizoso, *a.* naturally curly or wavy (hair)

ro, ro, *m.* lullabye, lullabye

roano, *a.* roan (horses)

robador (-ra), *a.* robbing. *s.* robber, thief. *m.* abductor

robar, *v.t.* to rob; abduct; wash away, eat away (of rivers, sea); remove honey from the hive; draw (cards, dominoes); (*fig.*) capture (love, etc.)

roblar, *v.t.* to reinforce, strengthen; clinch

roble, *m.* oak tree; oak; (*fig.*) bulwark, tower of strength

robledo, *m.* oak grove

roblón, *m.* rivet

robo, *m.* theft, robbery; booty

robustecer, *v.t. irr.* to strengthen. See **conocer**

robustez, *f.* strength, robustness

robusto, *a.* vigorous, robust, hearty, strong

roca, *f.* rock; (*fig.*) pillar of strength

roce, *m.* rubbing, brushing, touching, friction; social intercourse

rociada, *f.* dewing; sprinkling; dew-wet grass given as medicine to horses and mules; (*fig.*) shower; general slander; harsh rebuke

rociar, *v.i.* to fall in dew; drizzle; *v.t.* sprinkle, spray; (*fig.*) shower (with)

rocín, *m.* sorry nag; hack; (*fam.*) ignoramus, boor

rocinante, *m.* poor nag (alluding to Don Quixote's horse)

rocío, *m.* dew; dew-drop; drizzle, light shower; (*fig.*) sprinkling, spray

rocoso, *a.* rocky

rocho, *m.* (*orn.*) roc

rodaballo, *m.* (*icht.*) turbot; (*fam.*) crafty man

rodada, *f.* wheel mark or track

rodado, *a.* dappled (of horses)

rodaje, *m.* wheeling; shooting (of a cinematograph film)

rodante, *a.* rolling

rodar, *v.i.* to roll; revolve, turn; run on wheels; wander, roam; be moved about; be plentiful, abound; happen successively; (*with por*) fall down, roll down

rodear, *v.i.* to walk round; go by a roundabout way; (*fig.*) beat about the bush; *v.t.* encircle, surround; besiege; round up (cattle) (*S.A.*)

rodela, *f.* round shield; buckler

rodeno, *a.* red (rocks, earth, etc.)

rodeo, *m.* encirclement; indirect and longer way; trick to evade pursuit; (*S.A.*) rodeo, round-up; stock-yard, cattle enclosure; (*fig.*) beating about the bush; evasive reply

rodera, *f.* rail, track, line; cart rut or track

rodilla, *f.* knee; floor-cloth. **de rodillas,** on one's knees. **ponerse de rodillas,** *or* **hincar las rodillas,** to kneel down

rodillazo, *m.* push with the knee

rodillera, *f.* knee cap or pad; mend at the knee of garments; bagginess of trouser knees

rodillo, *m.* roller; traction engine; (*print.*) inking-roller; garden roller. **r. de pastas,** (*cul.*) rolling-pin

rodio (-ia), *a.* and *s.* Rhodian

rododafne, *f.* (*bot.*) daphne, rose-bay

rododendro, *m.* rhododendron

rodrigar, *v.t.* to stake (plants)

rodrigón, *m.* stake, prop (for plants); (*fam.*) old retainer who acted as ladies' escort

roedor, *a.* gnawing; (*fig.*) nagging; biting. *a.* and *m.* rodent

roedura, *f.* biting, gnawing; corrosion

roer, *v.t. irr.* to gnaw, nibble, eat; corrode, wear away; trouble, afflict. *Pres. Ind.* **roigo, roes,** etc. *Preterite* **royó, royeron.** *Imperf. Subjunc.* **royese,** etc.

rogación, *f.* request, supplication, entreaty; (*ecc.*) rogation

rogador (-ra), *a.* requesting; beseeching. *s.* suppliant

rogar, *v.t. irr.* to request; beseech, beg. See **contar**

rogativa, *f.* (*ecc.*) rogation (gen. *pl.*)

rogativo, *a.* supplicatory, petitioning

roído, *a.* gnawed, eaten; (*fam.*) miserable, stingy

rojal, *a.* red (of soil, etc.). *m.* red earth.

rojear, *v.i.* to appear red; be reddish

rojete, *m.* rouge

rojez, *f.* redness

rojizo, *a.* reddish

rojo, *a.* red; fair; red-gold (of hair); (*pol.*) radical, red

rol, *m.* roll, list

roldana, *f.* pulley wheel

rollizo, *a.* round; plump, sturdy. *m.* log

rollo, *m.* roll; (*cul.*) rolling-pin; log; town cross or pillar; anything rolled (paper, etc.); twist (of tobacco)

romaico, *a.* and *m.* Romaic, modern Greek

romana, *f.* steelyard

romance, *a.* and *m.* romance (language). *m.* Spanish; ballad; romance of chivalry; *pl.* (*fig.*) fairy-tales, excuses. **en buen r.,** (*fig.*) in plain words

romancear, *v.t.* to translate from Latin into the vulgar tongue; translate into Spanish; paraphrase the Spanish to assist translation

romancero (-ra), *s.* ballad singer. *m.* collection of ballads

romancista, *m.* and *f.* romancist

románico, *a.* (*arch.*) Romanesque

romanista, *m.* and *f.* expert in Roman law, or Romance languages and literature

romanizar, *v.t.* to romanize; *v.r.* become romanized

romano (-na), *a.* and *s.* Roman. **a la romana,** in the Roman way. (*fam.*) **cabello a la romana,** bobbed hair

romanticismo, *m.* romanticism

romántico (-ca), *a.* romantic; emotional; fanciful. *s.* romantic; romanticist

rombo, *m.* (*geom.*) rhombus

romboedro, *m.* (*geom.*) rhombohedron

romboide, *m.* (*geom.*) rhomboid

romería, *f.* pilgrimage; excursion, picnic (made on saint's day)

romero (-ra), *m.* (*bot.*) rosemary. *s.* pilgrim

romo, *a.* blunt, dull, unsharpened; flat (noses)

rompecabezas, *m.* bludgeon; knuckle-duster; (*fam.*) teaser, puzzle, riddle; jig-saw puzzle

rompeolas, *m.* jetty, breakwater

romper, *v.t.* to break; shatter, break into fragments; spoil, ruin; break up, plough; (*fig.*) cut, divide (of water, etc.); (*fig.*) end, break; interrupt; infringe, break; *v.i.* break; break (waves); sprout, flower; (*with prep.* **a**) begin to. **Rompió a hablar,** He broke into speech. *Past Part.* **roto**

rompiente, *a.* breaking. *m.* reef, shoal

rompimiento, *m.* break, rupture; crack, split; breakage; infringement; ploughing up; (*fig.*) dividing (water, etc.); spoiling, ruining; opening (buds, etc.)

ron, *m.* rum

roncar, *v.i.* to snore; bell (deer); (*fig.*) roar, howl (sea, wind, etc.); (*fam.*) brag

roncear, *v.i.* to be dilatory or unwilling; (*fam.*) flatter, cajole; (*naut.*) lag behind, sail slowly

roncero, *a.* dilatory, slow; grumbling, complaining; cajoling, flattering

ronco, *a.* hoarse, husky

roncha, *f.* wheal; bruise, bump; (*fam.*) money lost through trickery; thin round slice

ronda, *f.* round, beat, patrol; serenading party; (*fam.*) round (of drinks)

rondador, *m.* watchman; roundsman; serenader; night wanderer

rondalla, *f.* tale, fairy-tale

rondar, *v.i.* to patrol, police; walk the streets by night; serenade; *v.t.* haunt; hover about; (*fam.*) overcome (of sleep, etc.)

rondó, *m.* (*mus.*) rondo

ronquear, *v.i.* to be hoarse

ronquera, *f.* hoarseness

ronquido, *m.* snore; hoarse sound

ronronear, *v.i.* to purr (cats)

ronzal, *m.* halter

ronzar, *v.t.* to munch, crack with the teeth

roña, *f.* mange (in sheep); grime, filth; mould; moral corruption; (*fam.*) stinginess; (*fam.*) trick, deception

roñería, *f.* (*fam.*) meanness, stinginess

roñoso, *a.* scabby; filthy; rusty; (*fam.*) mean, stingy

ropa, *f.* fabric, material, stuff; clothes, wearing apparel; garment, outfit; robe (of office). **r. blanca,** underclothes; (domestic) linen. **r. hecha,** ready-made clothing. **r. talar,** long gown; cassock

ropaje, *m.* clothes, garments; vestments; drapery; (*fig.*) form, outline

ropavejería, *f.* old clothes' shop

ropavejero (-ra), *s.* old clothes' dealer

ropería, *f.* clothier's shop or trade; wardrobe; cloakroom

ropero (-ra), *s.* clothier; keeper of the wardrobe. *m.* wardrobe; charitable organization

ropilla, *f.* doublet

ropón, *m.* a loosely-fitting gown generally worn over clothes

roque, *m.* rook (in chess)

roqueño, *a.* rocky; hard as rock

roquete, *m.* (*ecc.*) rochet; barb of lance

rorro, *m.* (*fam.*) infant, baby

ros, *m.* (*mil.*) képi

rosa, *f.* rose; anything rose-shaped; artificial rose; red spot on body; (*arch.*) rose-window; *pl.* rosettes. *m.* rose colour. **r. de los vientos,** mariner's compass. **r. laurel,** oleander

rosáceo, *a.* rose-coloured; (*bot.*) rosaceous

rosado, *a.* rose-coloured; rose; rosé (wines)

rosal, *m.* rose-tree. **r. de tallo,** standard rose-tree

rosaleda, rosalera, *f.* rose-garden

rosario, *m.* rosary; (*fig.*) string; chain pump; (*fam.*) backbone

rosbif, *m.* roast beef

rosca, *f.* screw and nut; (*cul.*) twist (of bread or cake); spiral

roscado, *a.* twisted, spiral

rosear, *v.i.* to turn to rose, become rose-coloured

róseo, *a.* rose-coloured

roseta, *f.* *dim.* small rose; rosette; rose of a watering can; rosette copper; *pl.* toasted maize

rosetón, *m.* large rosette; (*arch.*) rose window

rosicler, *m.* rose pink (first flush of dawn)

rosillo, *a.* light red; roan (horses)

rosmaro, *m.* (*zool.*) manatee, sea-cow

roso, *a.* bald, worn; red

rosquilla, *f.* cake shaped like a ring

rosquillero (-ra), *s.* seller of rosquillas

rostrituerto, *a.* (*fam.*) wry-faced (sadness or anger)

rostro, *m.* bird's beak; face, visage. **conocer de r.,** to know by sight. **dar en r.,** (*fig.*) to throw in one's face

rota, *f.* (*mil.*) defeat; (*ecc.*) Rota; (*bot.*) rattan

rotación, *f.* rotation. **r. de cultivos,** rotation of crops

rotativa, *f.* rotary printing press

rotativo, *a.* rotary

rotatorio, *a.* rotatory

roto, *a.* shabby, ragged; vicious, debauched

rotograbado, *m.* rotogravure

rotonda, *f.* (*arch.*) rotunda

rótula, *f.* (*anat.*) rotula, patella

rotular, *v.t.* to label; give a title or heading to

rótulo, *m.* title; poster, placard; label

rotundamente, *adv.* tersely, roundly, plainly

rotundidad, *f.* rotundity; roundness; finality (of words, etc.)

rotundo, *a.* round; rotund; sonorous; final, plain (of words, etc.)

rotura, *f.* breaking, shattering; ploughing up; breakage; rupture

roturar, *v.t.* (*agr.*) to break up, plough up

roya, *f.* rust, mildew; tobacco

roza, *f.* (*agr.*) clearing (of weeds, etc.); ground ready for sowing. **de r. abierta,** open cast (of mining)

rozadura, *f.* rubbing, friction; abrasion, chafing

rozagante, *a.* long and elaborate (dresses); upstanding; handsome; strapping, fine

rozamiento, *m.* grazing, brushing, rubbing; discord, disharmony, disagreement; (*mech.*) friction

rozar, *v.t.* (*agr.*) to clear of weeds; crop, nibble; scrape; brush against, touch; *v.i.* brush, rub, touch; *v.r.* have dealings with, know; stammer; be like, resemble rúa, f. village street; high road

ruar, v.i. to walk or ride through the streets; parade the streets flirting with the ladies

rubefacción, f. (med.) rubefaction

rubeola, f. (med.) German measles

rubí, m. ruby; jewel (of a watch)

rubia, f. (bot.) madder; blonde (girl)

rubicundez, f. rubicundity, ruddiness, redness

rubicundo, a. red-gold; ruddy-complexioned; reddish

rubidio, m. (chem.) rubidium

rubio, a. red-gold; gold; fair, blond

rublo, m. rouble (coin)

rubor, m. blush, flush; bashfulness

ruborizarse, v.r. to blush; be shamefaced

ruboroso, a. shamefaced; blushing

rúbrica, f. rubric; personal mark, flourish added to signature

rubricar, v.t. to sign and seal; sign with an X or other symbol; sign with a flourish

rubro, a. red

rucio, a. fawn, light-grey (of animals); (fam.) going grey, grey-haired

rudamente, adv. rudely, abruptly, churlishly; roughly

rudeza, f. roughness; rudeness, uncouthness; stupidity

rudimentario, a. rudimentary

rudimento, m. embryo; pl. rudiments

rudo, a. rough; unfinished; uncouth, boorish, rude; stupid

rueca, f. distaff (spinning); spinning-wheel; curve, twist

rueda, f. wheel; group, circle; spread of a peacock's tail; roller, castor; round piece or slice; turn, chance; succession (of events); wheel (torture). r. libre, freewheeling; (fam.) hacer la r. (a), to flatter, make a fuss of

ruedero, m. wheelwright

ruedo, m. turning, rotation; circumference; lined hem of a cassock; circuit

ruego, ml request, entreaty

rufián, m. ruffian; pimp

rufianesco, a. ruffianly

rufo, a. fair; red-haired; curly-haired

rugido, m. roaring, roar; creaking; gnashing; rumbling

rugir, v.i. to roar; squeak, creak; gnash (the teeth)

ruibarbo, m. rhubarb

ruido, m. noise, din; disturbance; rumour. hacer (meter) r., to cause a sensation; (fam.) ser más el r. que las nueces, to be much ado about nothing

ruidoso, a. noisy; notable

ruin, a. base, vile; despicable; mean; puny

ruina, f. ruin, downfall; financial ruin; fall, decline; pl. ruins

ruinar, v.t. to ruin

ruindad, f. baseness; meanness; pettiness, unworthiness; mean trick, despicable action

ruinoso, a. half-ruined; ruinous; useless, worthless

ruiseñor, m. nightingale

ruleta, f. roulette

rumano (-na), a. and s. Rumanian. m. Rumanian language

rumbo, m. (naut.) course, way, route; direction; (fam.) swank. con r. a, headed for, in the direction of. hacer r. a, to sail for; make for

rumboso, a. (fam.) pompous, dignified; open-handed, generous

rumia, f. rumination; cud

rumiante, a. and m. and f. (zool.) ruminant. a. (fam.) reflective, meditative

rumiar, v.t. (zool.) to ruminate; (fam.) reflect upon, chew on; (fam.) fume, rage

rumor, m. noise; rumour; murmur, babble; dull sound

runa, f. rune

rúnico, a. runic

runrunearse, v. impers. to be rumoured

rupestre, a. rupestrian

rupia, f. rupee

ruptura, f. (fig.) rupture; (surg.) hernia

rural, a. rustic, rural

ruralmente, adv. rurally

rusificar, v.t. to russianize

ruso (-sa), a. and s. Russian. m. Russian language

rusticación, f. rustication

rusticar, v.i. to rusticate

rusticidad, f. rusticity; boorishness, coarseness

rústico, *a.* rustic, country; boorish, uncouth. *m.* countryman; yokel; peasant. **en rústica,** in paper covers (of books)

ruta, *f.* route; (*fig.*) way. **r. de evitación,** by-pass

rutenio, *m.* (*chem.*) ruthenium

ruteno (-na), *a.* and *s.* Ruthenian. *m.* Ruthenian language

rutilante, *a.* (*poet.*) sparkling, glowing

rutilar, *v.i.* (*poet.*) to gleam, sparkle

rutina, *f.* routine

rutinario, *a.* routine

rutinero (-ra), *a.* routinistic. *s.* routinist

S

sábado, *m.* Saturday; Jewish sabbath. **s. de gloria,** Easter Saturday

sábalo, *m.* (*icht.*) shad

sabana, *f.* savannah

sábana, *f.* bed sheet; altar-cloth. (*fam.*) **pegársele (a uno) las sábanas,** to be tied to the bed, get up late

sabandija, *f.* any unpleasant insect or reptile; (*fig.*) vermin

sabanero (-ra), *s.* savannah dweller.—*a.* savannah

sabanilla, *f.* small piece of linen (kerchief, towel, etc.); altar-cloth

sabañón, *m.* chilblain

sabatario, *a.* sabbatarian

sabático, *a.* sabbatical

sabatino, *a.* Saturday

sabedor, *a.* aware; knowledge-able, knowing

sabélico, *a.* pertaining to the Samnites or Sabines

sábelotodo, *m.* and *f.* (*fam.*) know-all

sabeo (-ea), *a.* and *s.* of or from Sheba (Yemen), Sabæan

saber, *m.* learning; wisdom

saber, *v.t. irr.* to know; be able to, know how; *v.i.* know; be shrewd, be well aware of; (*with prep. a*) taste of; be like or similar to. **s. al dedillo,** (*fig.*) to have at one's finger-tips. **a s.,** viz., namely; (*fam.*) **no s. cuántas son cinco,** not to know how many beans make five. **no**

s. dónde meterse, to be overcome by shame (lit. not to know where to put oneself); have the jitters. **No sé cuántos,** I don't know who (which person). **No sé qué,** I don't know what. **un no sé qué,** a certain something; a touch (of). **Quién sabe!** Who knows!; Time will tell. *Pres. Ind.* **sé, sabes,** etc. *Fut.* **sabré,** etc. *Condit.* **sabría,** etc. *Preterite* **supe,** etc. *Pres. Subjunc.* **sepa,** etc. *Imperf. Subjunc.* **supiese,** etc.

sabiamente, *adv.* wisely, prudently

sabidillo (-lla), *a.* and *s.* (*fam.*) know-all

sabiduría, *f.* prudence, wisdom; erudition, learning; knowledge, awareness. **Libro de la s. de Salomón,** Book of Wisdom

sabiendas, a, *adv.* knowingly, consciously

sabihondo (-da), *s.* (*fam.*) know-all

sabino (-na), *a.* and *s.* Sabine. *a.* roan (horses)

sabio (-ia), *a.* wise; learned, erudite; prudent, sagacious; knowing (animals); performing (animals). *s.* wise person; scholar, erudite person

sablazo, *m.* sabre thrust or wound; (*fam.*) sponging, taking advantage of. **dar un s. (a),** (*fam.*) to sponge on; touch for money

sable, *m.* sabre; (*her.*) sable; (*fam.*) talent for sponging on people. *a.* (*her.*) sable

sablear, *v.i.* (*fam.*) to touch for invitations, loans, etc.; cadge

sablista, *m.* and *f.* (*fam.*) sponger, cadger

saboneta, *f.* hunting case watch, hunter

sabor, *m.* taste, flavour; impression, effect. **a s.,** to taste; at pleasure

saboreamiento, *m.* savouring; relishing, enjoyment

saborear, *v.t.* to flavour, season; relish, savour; appreciate, enjoy; *v.r.* relish, savour; enjoy

saboreo, *m.* tasting; savouring; relishing

sabotaje, *m.* sabotage

saboteador, *m.* saboteur

saboyano (-na), *a.* and *s.* Savoyard

sabroso, *a.* tasty, savoury, well-seasoned; delightful, delicious; (*fam.*) piquant, racy

sabuco, *m.* (*bot.*) elder

sabueso, *m.* cocker spaniel. **s. de artois,** hound

sabuloso, *a.* sandy

saburra, *f.* fur (on the tongue)

saca, *f.* drawing out, removing; export, transport, shipping; removal, extraction; legal copy of a document. **estar de s.,** to be on sale; (*fam.*) be marriageable (women)

sacabocados, *m.* punch (tool); (*fam.*) cinch, easy matter

sacabotas, *m.* bootjack

sacabrocas, *m.* tack-puller

sacabuche, *m.* (*mus.*) sackbut; sackbut player; (*fam.*) insignificant little man; (*naut.*) hand pump

sacacorchos, *m.* corkscrew

sacacuartos, *m.* (*fam.*) catch-penny

sacada, *f.* territory cut off from a province

sacadineros, *m.* (*fam.*) catch-penny

sacamanchas, *m.* or *f.* See **quitamanchas**

sacamantas, *m.* (*fam.*) tax-collector

sacamiento, *m.* removing or taking out

sacamuelas, *m.* and *f.* dentist; charlatan, quack; (*fam.*) windbag

sacanete, *m.* lansquenet (card game)

sacapotras, *m.* (*fam.*) unskilled surgeon

sacar, *v.t.* to draw out; extract; pull out; take out; remove; dispossess, turn out; free from, relieve; examine, investigate; extort (the truth); extract (sugar, etc.); win (prizes, games); copy; discover, find out; elect by ballot; obtain, achieve; exclude; show, exhibit; quote, mention; produce, invent; manufacture; note down; put forth; unsheath (swords); bowl (in cricket); serve (in tennis). **s. a bailar,** to invite, to dance. **s. à luz,** to publish, print; reveal, bring out. **s. a paseo,** to take for a walk. **s. de pila,** to be a godfather or godmother to. **s. en claro** *or* **s. en limpio,** to copy; conclude, infer, gather

sacarificar, *v.t.* to saccharify

sacarina, *f.* saccharine

sacasillas, *m.* (*fam.*) (*theat.*) stage-hand

sacerdocio, *m.* priesthood

sacerdotal, *a.* priestly

sacerdote, *m.* priest

sacerdotisa, *f.* priestess. **sumo s.,** high priest

saciable, *a.* satiable

saciar, *v.t.* to satisfy; satiate; *v.r.* be satiated

saciedad, *f.* satiety, surfeit

saco, *m.* handbag; sack, bag; sackful; sack-coat; (*biol.*) sac; (*mil.*) sack, plundering. **s. de noche,** dressing-case, week-end case. (*fam.*) **no echar en s. roto,** not to forget, to remember

sacramental, *a.* sacramental

sacramentalmente, *adv.* sacramentally; in confession

sacramentar, *v.t.* to consecrate; administer the Blessed Sacrament; hide, conceal

sacramentario (-ia), *s.* sacramentalist; sacramentarian

sacramento, *m.* sacrament; (*ecc.*) Host; (*ecc.*) mystery. **s. del altar,** Eucharist. **con todos los sacramentos,** with all the sacraments; done in order, complete with all formalities. **recibir los sacramentos,** to receive the last sacraments

sacratísimo, *a. sup.* sagrado, most sacred

sacre, *m.* (*orn.*) saker, kind of falcon; saker, small cannon (sixteenth century)

sacrificadero, *m.* place of sacrifice

sacrificador (-ra), *a.* sacrificing. *s.* sacrificer

sacrificar, *v.t.* to sacrifice; slaughter; *v.r.* consecrate oneself to God; sacrifice oneself; devote or dedicate oneself (to)

sacrificio, *m.* sacrifice; offering, dedication; surrendering, forgoing; compliance, submission. **s. del altar,** sacrifice of the Mass

sacrilegio, *m.* sacrilege

sacrílego, *a.* sacrilegious

sacristán, *m.* sacristan; sexton; hoop (for dresses). (*fam.*) **s. de amén,** a yes-man. (*fam.*) **ser gran s.,** to be very crafty

sacristana, *f.* wife of a sacristan or sexton; nun in charge of a convent sacristy

sacristanía, *f.* office of a sacristan or sexton

sacristía, *f.* sacristy; vestry; office of a sacristan or sexton

sacro, *a.* sacred; (*anat.*) sacral

sacrosanto, *a.* sacrosanct

sacudida, *f.* shake, shaking; jerk, jar, jolt; twitch, pull; (*aer.*) bump

sacudido, *a.* unsociable; difficult, wayward; determined, bold

sacudidor (-ra), *a.* shaking; jerking. *s.* shaker. *m.* carpet beater; duster

sacudidura, *f.* shaking (especially to remove dust); jerking

sacudimiento, *m.* shake, shaking; jerk; twitch, pull; jolt

sacudir, *v.t.* to shake; flap, wave; jerk, twitch; beat, bang; shake off; *v.r.* shake off, avoid

sachar, *v.t.* (*agr.*) to weed

sacho, *m.* (*agr.*) weeder

sadismo, *m.* sadism

sadista, *m.* and *f.* sadist

sadístico, *a.* sadistic

saduceo (-ea), *a.* Sadducean. *s.* Sadducee

saeta, *f.* arrow, dart; clock or watch hand; magnetic needle; short sung expression of religious ecstasy; (*ast.*) Sagitta

saetada, *f.*, **saetazo,** *m.* arrow wound

saetera, *f.* loophole; small window

saetero, *a.* arrow, arrow-like. *m.* archer, bowman

saetín, *m.* mill-course

sáfico, *a.* Sapphic

saga, *f.* saga

sagacidad, *f.* sagacity

sagaz, *a.* sagacious, shrewd; far-seeing; quick on the scent (dogs)

sagital, *a.* arrow-shaped

sagitario, *m.* archer; (*ast.*) Sagittarius

sagrado, *a.* sacred; holy; sacrosanct, venerable; accursed, detestable. *m.* sanctuary, refuge; haven

sagrario, *m.* sanctuary; sacrarium

sagú, *m.* sago

sahornarse, *v.r.* to chafe, grow sore

sahorno, *m.* chafing, abrasion

sahumado, *a.* improved, rendered more excellent; perfumed; fumigated

sahumador, *m.* perfumer; fumigating vessel

sahumar, *v.t.* to perfume; fumigate

sahumerio, *m.* perfuming; fumigation; fume, smoke

saín, *m.* fat, grease; sardine oil (for lamps); grease spot (on clothes)

sainar, *v.t.* to fatten up (animals)

sainete, *m.* (*cul.*) sauce; (*theat.*) one-act parody or burlesque; farce; delicacy, tit-bit; delicate taste (of food)

sainetero, *m.* writer of sainetes

sainetesco, *a.* pertaining to sainetes; burlesque, satirical

sajar, *v.t.* (*surg.*) to scarify

sajón (-ona), *a.* and *s.* Saxon

sal, *f.* salt; wit; grace, gracefulness. **s. de cocina,** common kitchen-salt. **s. de la Higuera,** Epsom salts. **s. gema,** rock-salt. **s. marina,** sea-salt. **sales inglesas,** smelling-salts. (*fam.*) **estar hecho de s.,** to be full of wit. (*fam.*) **hacerse s. y agua,** to melt away, disappear (riches, etc.)

sala, *f.* drawing-room; large room, hall; (*law*) court-room; (*law*) bench; **s. de apelación,** court of appeal. **s. de hospital,** hospital ward. **s. de justicia,** court of justice. **s. de lectura,** reading-room. (*law*) **guardar s,** to respect the court

salacidad, *f.* lewdness, salaciousness

saladar, *m.* salt-marsh

saladero, *m.* salting or curing place; (*S.A.*) meat packing factory

saladillo, *m.* salt pork

salado, *a.* salty, briny; brackish; witty; attractive, amusing

salador (-ra), *a.* salting, curing. *s.* salter, curer. *m.* curing place

saladura, *f.* salting, curing

salamandra, *f.* salamander; fire sprite

salamanquesa, *f.* star-lizard

salangana, *f.* (*orn.*) Chinese swallow

salar, *v.t.* to salt; season with salt; over-salt; cure, pickle (meat, etc.)

salario, *m.* salary

salaz, *a.* lewd, lecherous.

salazón, *f.* salting, curing; salt meat or fish trade

salazonero, *a.* salting, curing

salchicha, *f.* sausage

salchichería, *f.* shop which sells sausages

salchichero (-ra), *s.* sausage maker or seller

salchichón, *m.* (*cul.*) salamé, kind of sausage

saldar, *v.t.* (*com.*) to settle, pay in full; sell out cheap; balance

saldista, *m.* remnant buyer

saldo, *m.* (*com.*) balance; closing of an account; bargain sale. **s. acreedor,** credit balance. **s. deudor,** debit balance. **s. líquido,** net balance

salero, *m.* salt-cellar; salt storage warehouse; (*fam.*) wit

salesiano (-na), *a.* and *s.* (*ecc.*) Salesian

saleta, *f. dim.* small hall; royal ante-chamber; court of appeal

salicilato, *m.* (*chem.*) salicylate

sálico, *a.* Salic

salida, *f.* going out; leaving; departure; sailing; exit, way out; projection, protrusion; (*fig.*) escape, way out; outcome, result; witty remark; (*mil.*) sally; (*com.*) outlay, expense; (*com.*) opening, sale, salability; environs, outskirts; (*fam.*) **s. de tono,** an impertinent remark. (*com.*) **dar s.,** to enter on the credit side

salidero, *a.* fond of going about and amusements. *m.* exit, way out

salidizo, *m.* (*arch.*) projection. *a.* projecting

saliente, *a.* outgoing; salient, projecting. *m.* east; projection; salient

salificar, *v.t.* (*chem.*) to salify

salina, *f.* salt mine; salt works

salinero, *m.* salt merchant; salter; salt worker

salino, *a.* saline. *m.* (*med.*) saline

salir, *v.i. irr.* to go out; depart, leave; succeed in getting out; escape; appear (sun, etc.); sprout, show green; fade, come out (stains); project, stand out; grow, develop; turn out, result; happen, take place; cost; sail; end (seasons, time); lead off, start (some games); be published (books); do (well or badly), succeed or fail; appear, show oneself; be drawn, win (lottery tickets); balance, come out right (accounts); be elected; become; give up (posts); lead to (streets, etc.); (*naut.*) overtake; (*with prep. a*) guarantee, be surety for; resemble, be like; (*with con*) utter, come out with; commit, do inopportunely; succeed in, achieve (e.g. **Salió con la suya,** He got his own way); (*with de*) originate in; break away from (traditions, conventions); get rid of; (*with por*) stand up for, protect; go surety for, guarantee. *v.r.* leak; boil over; overflow; (*with con*) achieve, get; (*with de*) (*fig.*) break away from. (*theat.*) **s. a la escena,** to enter, come on to the stage. **s. de estampía,** to stampede (of animals). (*fam.*) **s. pitando,** to get out in a hurry. **Esta idea no salió de Juan,** This wasn't John's idea. (*fam.*) **salga lo que saliere,** come what may ... *Pres.Ind.* **salgo, sales,** etc. *Fut.* **saldré,** etc. *Condit.* **saldría,** etc. *Pres. Sub-junc.* **salga,** etc.

salitral, *a.* nitrous. *m.* saltpetre bed

salitre, *m.* saltpetre

salitrería, *f.* saltpetre works

salitrero, *s.* saltpetre worker or dealer

saliva, *f.* saliva. (*fam.*) **tragar s.,** to put up with; be unable to speak through emotion

salivación, *f.* salivation

salival, *a.* salivary

salivar, *v.i.* to salivate; spit

salma, *f.* ton, 20 cwt.

salmantino (-na), *a.* and *s.* of or concerning Salamanca (Old Castile)

salmear, *v.i.* to intone psalms

salmista, *m.* psalmist; psalmodist, psalm chanter

salmo, *m.* psalm

salmodia, *f.* psalmody; (*fam.*) drone; psalter

salmodiar, *v.i.* to chant psalms; *v.t.* drone

salmón, *m.* salmon

salmonado, *a.* salmon-like

salmonera, *f.* salmon net

salmonete, *m.* (*icht.*) red mullet

salmuera, *f.* brine

salobre, *a.* salt, salty; brackish

salobridad, *f.* saltiness

saloma, *f.* (*naut.*) chantey

salomar, *v.i.* (*naut.*) to sing chanteys

salón, *m.* drawing-room; large room or hall; reception room; salon, reception, social gathering. **s. de muestras,** showroom

saloncillo, *m. dim.* small room; (*theat.*) greenroom; rest room

salpicadura, *f.* sprinkling, spattering, splashing

salpicar, *v.t.* to sprinkle, scatter; bespatter, splash

salpicón, *m.* (*cul.*) kind of salmagundi; (*fam.*) hotchpotch; spattering

salpimentar, *v.t. irr.* to season with pepper and salt; sprinkle; (*fig.*) leaven, enliven (a speech, etc.). See **regimentar**

salpresar, *v.t.* to preserve in salt, salt

salpullido, *m.* rash, skin eruption

salsa, *f.* sauce; gravy. **s. mahonesa** *or* **s. mayonesa,** mayonnaise sauce. **s. mayordoma,** sauce maître d'hôtel

salsera, *f.* sauce-boat, gravy-boat

salsifí, *m.* (*bot.*) salsify

saltabanco, *m.* mountebank; street entertainer, juggler

saltabarrancos, *m.* and *f.* (*fam.*) madcap, harum-scarum

saltable, *a.* jumpable

saltadero, *m.* jumping ground; fountain, jet

saltador (-ra), *a.* jumping. *s.* jumper; acrobat. *m.* skipping-rope

saltamontes, *m.* grasshopper

saltaojos, *m.* peony

saltaparedes, *m.* and *f.* (*fam.*) madcap, romp

saltar, *v.i.* to jump, leap, spring; prance; frisk, gambol; rebound; blow up; burst, break asunder; pop (of corks); fly off, come off (buttons, etc.); gush out, shoot up (liquids); break apart, be shattered; be obvious, stand out; come to mind, suggest itself;

show anger; (*fig.*) let slip, come out with (remarks); *v.t.* leap or jump over; poke out (eyes); cover (the female); omit, pass over; blow up, explode. **s. a la cuerda,** to play with a skipping-rope. **s. a la vista,** to be obvious, leap to the eye. **s. diciendo,** (*fam.*) to come out with, say

saltarín (-ina), *a.* dancing. *s.* dancer

saltatriz, *f.* ballet-dancer, girl acrobat

saltatumbas, *m.* (*fam.,* contemptuous) cleric who makes his living off funerals

salteador, *m.* highwayman

salteamiento, *m.* highway robbery, hold-up; assault, attack

saltear, *v.t.* to hold up and rob; assault, attack; jump from one thing to another, do intermittently; forestall; surprise, amaze

salterio, *m.* psaltery

saltimbanco, saltimbanqui, *m.* (*fam.*). See **saltabanco**

salto, *m.* jump, leap, bound; leap-frog (game); precipice, ravine; waterfall; assault; important promotion; omission (of words). **s. de agua,** waterfall. **s. de cama,** peignoir, morning gown. **s. de campana,** overturning. (*fam.*) **s. de mal año,** sudden improvement in circumstances. **s. de mata,** flight, escape. **s. mortal,** leap of death; somersault. **dar un s.,** to leap. **en un s.,** at one jump; swiftly

saltón, *a.* jumping, leaping; prominent (teeth, eyes). *m.* grasshopper

salubérrimo, *a. sup.* salubre, most healthy

salubre, *a.* salubrious, healthful

salubridad, *f.* healthfulness

salud, *f.* health; salvation; welfare, well-being; (*ecc.*) state of grace; *pl.* civilities, greetings. ¡**S. y pesetas!** Here's to your good health and prosperity! (on drinking). **gastar s.,** to enjoy good health. (*fam.*) **vender** (*or* **verter**) **s.,** to look full of health

saludable, *a.* healthy, wholesome

saludador (-ra), *a.* greeting, saluting. *s.* greeter. *m.* charlatan, quack

saludar, *v.t.* to greet, salute; hail (as king, etc.); send greetings to; bow; (*mil.*) fire a salute; (*naut.*) dip the colours

saludo, *m.* greeting, salutation; bow (*mil., nav.*) salute

salutación, *f.* greeting, salutation; Ave Maria

salutífero, *a.* salubrious

salva, *f.* salutation, greeting; (*mil., nav.*) salvo, volley; salute (of guns); salver; ordeal (to establish innocence); solemn assurance, oath; sampling, tasting (of food, drink)

salvación, *f.* liberation, deliverance; salvation

salvado, *m.* bran

salvador (-ra), *a.* saving, redeeming. *s.* deliverer. *m.* redeemer

salvadoreño (-ña), *a.* and *s.* Salvadorean (from El Salvador, Central America)

salvaguardia, *m.* guard, watch. *f.* safeguard; protection, defence; safe-conduct, passport

salvajada, *f.* savagery, brutal action

salvaje, *a.* wild (plants, animals); rough, uncultivated; uncultured, uncivilized. *m.* and *f.* savage

salvajismo, *m.* savagery

salvamano, a, *adv.* safely

salvamente, *adv.* safely, securely

salvamento, *m.* salvation; deliverance, security, safety; place of safety; salvage

salvante, *adv.* (*fam.*) except, save

salvar, *v.t.* to save; (*ecc.*) redeem; avoid (difficulty, danger); exclude, except; leap, jump; pass over, clear; (*law*) prove innocent; (*naut.*) salve; *v.i.* taste, sample (food and drink); *v.r.* be saved from danger; (*ecc.*) be redeemed

salvavidas, *m.* life-belt; safety-belt; (*aut.*) cow-catcher; life preserver; traffic island

**¡salve! ***interj.* (*poet.*) hail! Hail Mary, Salve Regina

salvedad, *f.* qualification, reservation

salvia, *f.* (*bot.*) sage

salvilla, *f.* salver

salvo, *a.* safe, unharmed; excepting, omitting. *adv.* except. **a s.,** safely, without harm. **a su s.,** to his (her, their) satis-

faction; at his (her, etc.) pleasure. **dejar a s.,** to exclude, leave aside. **en s.,** in safety

salvoconducto, *m.* safe-conduct, pass

sallar, *v.t.* (*agr.*) to weed

sámara, *f.* key-fruit (of sycamore, etc.)

samarita, *a.* and *m.* and *f.* **samaritano (-na),** *a.* and *s.* Samaritan

sambenito, *m.* penitent's gown (Inquisition); disgrace, dishonour

samio (-ia), *a.* and *s.* of or from Samos (Greece); Samian

samotracio (-ia), *a.* and *s.* Samothracian

samoyedo (-da), *s.* Samoyed

san, *a.* *abb.* of **santo.** Used before masculine singular names of saints except **Santos Tomás** (*or* **Tomé**), **Domingo, Toribio**

sanable, *a.* curable

sanador (-ra), *a.* healing, curing. *s.* healer

sánalotodo, *m.* (*fam.*) cure-all, universal remedy

sanar, *v.t.* to cure, heal; *v.i.* recover, get well; heal

sanatorio, *m.* sanatorium; convalescent home

sanción, *f.* authorization, consent; sanction; penalty

sancionable, *a.* sanctionable

sancionar, *v.t.* to authorize, approve; sanction

sancochar, *v.t.* (*cul.*) to parboil, half cook

sanchopancesco, *a.* like or pertaining to Sancho Panza (Don Quixote's squire)

sandalia, *f.* sandal

sándalo, *m.* sandal-wood

sandáraca, *f.* sandarach gum

sandez, *f.* foolishness, stupidity; folly

sandía, *f.* water-melon

sandiar, *m.* water-melon bed

sandío, *a.* foolish, inane

sandunga, *f.* (*fam.*) attractiveness, winsomeness, grace

sandunguero, *a.* (*fam.*) attractive, appealing, winsome

saneado, *a.* unencumbered, untaxable, free

saneamiento, *m.* guarantee, security; indemnity; stabilization (of currency); drainage

sanear, *v.t.* (*com.*) to guarantee, secure; indemnify; stabilize (currency); drain (land, etc.)

sanedrín, *m.* sanhedrim

sangradera, *f.* lancet; channel, sluice, drain

sangrador, *m.* phlebotomist; outlet, drainage

sangradura, *f.* inner bend of the arm; (*surg.*) bleeding; draining off

sangrar, *v.t.* (*surg.*) to bleed; drain off; (*fam.*) extort money, bleed; (*print.*) indent; draw off resin (from pines, etc.); *v.i.* bleed; *v.r.* bleed; have oneself bled; run (of colours)

sangre, *f.* blood; lineage, family. **s. fría,** sang-froid. **a s. fría,** in cold blood, premeditated. **a s. y fuego,** by fire and sword, without quarter. (*fam.*) **bullir la s.,** to have youthful blood in one's veins. **llevar en la s.,** (*fig.*) to be in the blood. **subírsele la s. a la cabeza,** to grow excited. (*fig., fam.*) **tener s. de horchata,** to have milk and water in one's veins

sangría, *f.* (*surg.*) blood-letting; resin cut (on pines, etc.)

sangriento, *a.* bloody, bloodstained; bloodthirsty, cruel; mortal (insults, etc.); (*poet.*) bloodcoloured

sangüesa, *f.* raspberry

sanguijuela, *f.* leech; (*fig., fam.*) sponger

sanguina, *f.* red crayon drawing, sanguine

sanguinaria, *f.* bloodstone

sanguinario, *a.* vengeful, bloody, cruel

sanguíneo, *a.* blood; sanguineous; sanguine, fresh-complexioned; blood-coloured

sanguinolento, *a.* See **sangriento**

sanidad, *f.* safety, security; healthiness; health department. **S. Interior,** Public Health. **S. Militar,** Army Medical Corps

sanitario, *a.* sanitary, hygienic. *m.* (*mil.*) Medical Officer

sano, *a.* healthy; safe, secure; healthful, wholesome; unhurt, unharmed; upright, honest; sincere; (*fam.*) entire, undamaged; sane. **s. y salvo,** safe and sound.

(*fam.*) **cortar por lo s.,** to cut one's losses

sánscrito, *a.* and *m.* Sanscrit

santa, *f.* female saint

santabárbara, *f.* (*nav.*) magazine

santamente, *adv.* in a saintly manner; simply

santanderino (-na), *a.* and *s.* of or from Santander (N. Spain)

santero (-ra), *a.* given to image-worship. *s.* accomplice (to a burglar); caretaker (of a hermitage); beggar

¡Santiago! St. James! (Spanish war cry). *m.* attack, assault

santiamén, *m.* (*fam.*) trice, twinkling

santidad, *f.* sanctity; saintliness; godliness. **Su S.,** His Holiness (the Pope)

santificación, *f.* sanctification

santificador (-ra), *a.* sanctifying. *s.* sanctifier

santificar, *v.t.* to sanctify, make holy; consecrate; dedicate; keep (feast days)

santiguada, *f.* crossing oneself; rough treatment, harsh reproof. **¡Por mi s.!** By the rood!

santiguar, *v.t.* to make the sign of the cross over; (*fam.*) beat, rain blows on; *v.r.* cross oneself; (*fam.*) be dumbfounded

santísimo, *a. sup.* most saintly, most holy

santo, *a.* holy; saintly; saint (see **san**); · consecrated; inviolate, sacred; (*fam.*) simple, sincere, ingenuous. *m.* saint; image of a saint; saint's day, name day (of a person); (*mil.*) password. **Santa Hermandad,** Holy Brotherhood (formerly name of Spanish rural police force). **S. Oficio,** Holy Office, Inquisition. **S. y bueno,** Well and good, All right! (*fam.*) **alzarse con el s. y la limosna,** to take the lot, make off with everything. **llegar y besar el s.,** to do in a trice. (*fam.*) **No es s. de mi devoción,** I'm not very keen on him. (*fam.*) **todo el s. día,** the whole blessed day

santón, *m.* dervish, santon. (*fam.*) hypocrite, sham saint

santonina, *f.* (*med.*) santonine

santoral, *m.* book of saints; calendar of saints; choir book

santuario, *m.* sanctuary

santurrón (-ona), *a.* sanctimonious; hypocritical; prudish. *s.* hypocrite

santurronería, *f.* sanctimoniousness

saña, *f.* fury, blind rage; lust for revenge, cruelty

sañoso, sañudo, *a.* furious, blind with rage; cruel

sapidez, *f.* flavour, sapidity

sápido, *a.* tasty, savoury

sapiencia, *f.* wisdom; knowledge; erudition

sapino, *m.* (*bot.*) fir tree

sapo, *m.* toad

saponáceo, *a.* saponaceous, soapy

saponificar, *v.t.* to make soapy, saponify

saque, *m.* (*sport*) service; service or bowling line; (*sport*) server; (*sport*) bowler; bowling (in cricket)

saqueador (-ra), *a.* looting, pillaging. *s.* pillager, plunderer

saquear, *v.t.* to pillage, plunder, sack

saqueo, *m.* plundering, pillage, sacking

saquilada, *f.* small sackful (especially of grain)

sarampión, *m.* (*med.*) measles

sarao, *m.* soirée, evening party

sarapia, *f.* (*bot.*) tonka bean

sarasa, *f.* (*fam.*) pansy, effeminate man

sarcasmo, *m.* sarcasm

sarcástico, *a.* sarcastic

sarcia, *f.* load, cargo

sarcófago, *m.* tomb; sarcophagus

sarda, *f.* mackerel

sardana, *f.* traditional Catalonian dance

sardina, *f.* sardine. **s. arenque,** herring. (*fig.*) **como sardinas en banasta,** packed like sardines

sardinal, *m.* sardine net

sardinero (-ra), *a.* sardine. *s.* vendor or dealer in sardines. *m.* famous district of Santander (N. Spain)

sardineta, *f.* (*icht.*) sprat; small sardine; (*mil.*) chevron

sardo (-da), *a.* and *s.* Sardinian

sardónice, *f.* (*min.*) sardonyx

sardónico, *a.* sardonic

sarga, *f.* (silk) serge; (*bot.*) willow

sargenta, *f.* sergeant's wife; (*fam.*) mannish, overbearing woman

sargentear, *v.t.* to be in charge as a sergeant; command, captain; (*fam.*) boss

sargentía, *f.* sergeantcy

sargento, *m.* (*mil.*) sergeant

sarmentoso, *a.* vine-like; twining

sarmiento, *m.* vine shoot

sarna, *f.* (*med.*) scabies. **s. perruna,** mange. (*fam.*) **más viejo que la s.,** older than the plague

sarnoso, *a.* itchy; mangy

sarraceno (-na), *a.* Saracen; Moorish. *s.* Saracen; Moor

sarracina, *f.* scuffle

sarrillo, *m.* death-rattle, râle; arum lily

sarro, *m.* furry encrustation, scale; film; tartar (teeth)

sarta, *f.* string, link (of pearls, etc.); file, line

sartén, *f.* frying-pan. (*fam.*) **tener la s. por el mango,** to be top dog

sastra, *f.* tailoress; tailor's wife

sastre, *m.* tailor. (*fam.*) **ser buen s.,** to be an expert (in)

sastrería, *f.* tailoring; tailor's shop

Satanás, *m.* Satan; devil

satánico, *a.* Satanic

satélite, *m.* satellite; follower, admirer, sycophant

satén, *m.* sateen

satinar, *v.t.* to calender; glaze; satin (paper)

sátira, *f.* satire

satírico, *a.* satiric

satirizar, *v.i.* to write satires; *v.t.* satirize

sátiro, *m.* satyr. (*theat.*) indecent play

satisfacción, *f.* settlement, payment; atonement, expiation; satisfaction; gratification; amends; complacency, conceit; contentment; apology. **tomar s.,** to avenge oneself

satisfacer, *v.t. irr.* to pay, settle; atone for, expiate; gratify; quench; fulfil, observe; compensate, indemnify; discharge, meet; convince, persuade; allay, relieve; reward; explain; answer, satisfy; *v.r.* avenge oneself; satisfy oneself. *Pres. Ind.* **satisfago, satisfaces,** etc. *Fut.* **satisfaré,** etc. *Condit.* **satisfaría,** etc. *Preterite* **satisfice,**

etc. *Past Part.* **satisfecho.**
Pres. Subjunc. **satisfaga,** etc.
Imperf. Subjunc. **satisficiese,**
etc.

satisfactorio, *a.* satisfactory

satisfecho, *a.* self-satisfied, complacent; happy, contented

sátrapa, *m.* satrap; (*fam.*) cunning fellow

saturación, *f.* saturation

saturar, *v.t.* to satiate, fill; saturate

saturnal, *a.* Saturnian. *f.* Saturnalia; orgy

saturnino, *a.* saturnine, melancholy, morose

saturnismo, *m.* (*med.*) saturnism, lead poisoning

Saturno, *m.* (*ast.*) Saturn

sauce, *m.* (*bot.*) willow. **s. llorón,** weeping willow

saúco, *m.* (*bot.*) elder tree

saurio, *a.* and *m.* (*zool.*) saurian

savia, *f.* sap; energy, zest

sáxeo, *a.* stone, stony

saxífrage, *f.* (*bot.*) saxifrage

saxófono, *m.* saxophone

saya, *f.* skirt; long tunic

sayal, *m.* thick woollen material

sayo, *m.* loose smock; (*fam.*) any garment. (*fam.*) **cortar un s. (a),** to gossip behind a person's back

sayón, *m.* executioner; (*fam.*) hideous-looking man

sazón, *f.* ripeness, maturity; season; perfection, excellence; opportunity; taste, flavour; seasoning. **a la s.,** at that time, then. **en s.,** in season; opportunely

sazonador (-ra), *a.* seasoning. *s.* seasoner

sazonar, *v.t.* (*cul.*) to season; mature; *v.r.* mature, ripen

se, *object pron. reflexive, 3rd sing. and pl., m.* and *f.* 1. Used as accusative (direct object) himself, herself, yourself, themselves, yourselves (e.g. **Juan se ha cortado,** John has cut himself). 2. Used as dative or indirect object to himself, at himself, herself, themselves, etc. (e.g. **María se mira al espejo,** Mary looks at herself in the mirror). Reciprocity is also expressed by reflexive (e.g. **No se hablan,** They do not speak to one another). When a direct object pron. (accusative) and an indirect object pron., both in the 3rd pers. (sing. or pl.), are used together, the indirect object pron. becomes se (instead of **le** or **les)** (e.g. **Se lo doy,** I give it to him). Many Spanish verbs are reflexive in form and not in meaning (e.g. **desayunarse,** to breakfast, **arrepentirse,** to repent, **quejarse,** to complain). Some intransitive (neuter) verbs have a modified meaning when used reflexively (e.g. **marcharse,** to go away, **dormirse,** to fall asleep). The passive may be formed by using **se** + 3rd pers. sing. of verb (e.g. **Se dice,** It is said, People say). A number of impersonal phrases are also formed in this way (e.g. **Se alquila,** To Let, **Se vende,** For Sale). The imperative is used in the same way (e.g. **Véase la página dos,** See page two)

sebáceo, *a.* sebaceous

sebo, *m.* tallow; candle-grease; fat, grease

seboso, *a.* tallowy; fat, greasy

seca, *f.* drought; (*naut.*) unsubmerged sand-bank

secadero, *m.* drying place, drying room

secadora, *f.* drying-machine, clothes-dryer. **s. de cabello,** hair-dryer

secafirmas, *m.* blotting-pad

secamente, *adv.* tersely, brusquely; curtly; dryly

secamiento, *m.* drying

secano, *m.* non-irrigated land; (*naut.*) unsubmerged sand-bank; anything very dry

secante, *a.* drying. *a.* and *f.* (*geom.*) secant. **papel s.,** blotting-paper

secar, *v.t.* to dry; desiccate; annoy, bore; *v.r.* dry; dry up (streams, etc.); wilt, fade (plants); become parched; grow thin, become emaciated; be very thirsty; become hard-hearted

sección, *f.* act of cutting; section, part, portion; (*geom., mil.*) section. **s. cónica,** conic section. (*mil.*) **s. de reserva,** Reserve List

seccionar, *v.t.* to divide into sections, section

seccionario, *a.* sectional

secesión, *f.* secession

secesionista, *a.* and *m.* and *f.* secessionist

seco, *a.* dry; dried up, parched; faded, wilted; dead (plants); dried (fruits); thin, emaciated; unadorned; barren, arid; brusque, curt; severe, strict; indifferent, unenthusiastic; sharp (sounds); dry (wines). **a secas,** only; solely; simply, just. **'en s.,** on dry land; curtly. (*fam.*) **dejar s. (a),** to dumbfound, petrify

secreción, *f.* segregation, separation; (*med.*) secretion

secreta, *f.* (*law*) secret trial or investigation; (*ecc.*) secret(s); water-closet

secretar, *v.t.* (*med.*) to secrete

secretaría, *f.* secretaryship; secretary's office, secretariat

secretario (-ia), *s.* secretary; amanuensis, clerk. *m.* actuary; registrar. **S. de Asuntos Exteriores** *or* **S. de Asuntos Extranjeros,** Foreign Secretary. **s. particular,** private secretary

secretear, *v.i.* (*fam.*) to whisper, have secrets

secreteo, *m.* (*fam.*) whispering, exchanging of secrets

secreter, *m.* secrétaire, bureau

secreto, *m.* secret; secrecy, silence; confidential information; mystery; secret drawer. *a.* secret; private, confidential. **en s.,** in secret, confidentially. **s. a voces,** open secret

secretorio, *a.* (*med.*) secretory

secta, *f.* sect

sectario (-ia), *a.* and *s.* sectarian. *s.* fanatical believer

sectarismo, *m.* sectarianism

sector, *m.* sector

secuaz, *m.* and *f.* follower, disciple

secuela, *f.* sequel, result

secuencia, *f.* (*ecc.*) sequence; sequence (cinema)

secuestrador (-ra), *a.* sequestrating. *s.* sequestrator

secuestrar, *v.t.* to sequestrate; kidnap

secuestro, *m.* sequestration; kidnapping; (*surg.*) sequestrum

secular, *a.* secular, lay; centennial; age-old, ancient; (*ecc.*) secular

secularización, *f.* secularization

secularizar, *v.t.* to secularize; *v.r.* become secularized

secundar, *v.t.* to second, aid

secundario, *a.* secondary; accessory, subordinate; (*geol.*) mesozoic

sed, *f.* thirst; desire, yearning, appetite. **apagar** (*or* **matar**) **la s.,** to satisfy one's thirst. **tener s.,** to be thirsty

seda, *f.* silk; bristle (boar, etc.). **s. cordelada,** twist silk. **s. ocal,** floss silk. **s. vegetal** *or* **s. artificial,** artificial silk. (*fam.*) **como una s.,** as smooth as silk; sweet-tempered; achieved without any trouble

sedación, *f.* calming, soothing

sedal, *m.* fishing-line

sedar, *v.t.* to soothe, calm

sedativo, *a.* and *m.* (*med.*) sedative

sede, *f.* (*ecc.*) see; bishop's throne; (*fig.*) seat (of government, etc.); Holy See (also **Santa S.**)

sedentario, *a.* sedentary

sedeño, *a.* silky; silken, made of silk

sedería, *f.* silk merchandise; silks; silk shop

sedero (-ra), *a.* silk. *s.* silk weaver or worker; silk merchant

sedición, *f.* sedition

sedicioso, *a.* seditious

sediento, *a.* thirsty; parched, dry (land); eager (for), desirous (of)

sedimentación, *f.* sedimentation

sedimentar, *v.t.* to leave a sediment; *v.r.* settle, form a sediment

sedimento, *m.* sediment; dregs, lees; scale (on boilers)

sedoso, *a.* silky, silk-like

seducción, *f.* seduction; temptation, blandishment, wile; charm, allurement

seducir, *v.t. irr.* to seduce; tempt, lead astray; charm, attract; corrupt, bribe. See **conducir**

seductivo, *a.* tempting; seductive, charming

seductor (-ra), *a.* tempting; charming. *s.* seducer; charming person

sefardí, *m.* and *f.* Spanish Jew or Jewess; *pl.* Sephardim

segadera, *f.* (*agr.*) sickle

segadero, *a.* reapable, able to be reaped

segador, *m.* reaper, harvester

segadora, *f.* mowing machine, harvester; woman harvester

segar, *v.t. irr.* to scythe, cut down; reap, harvest; mow. See **cegar**

seglar, *a.* secular, lay. *m.* and *f.* layman

segmento, *m.* segment; (*geom.*) segment. **s. de émbolo,** piston ring

segoviano (-na), *a.* and *s.* Segovian (N. Spain)

segregación, *f.* segregation

segregar, *v.t.* to segregate, separate; (*med.*) secrete

seguida, *f.* continuation, prolongation. **de s.,** continuously; immediately. **en s.,** at once, immediately

seguidamente, *adv.* continuously; immediately

seguidilla, *f.* popular Spanish tune and dance and verse sung to them; (*fam.*) diarrhœa

seguido, *a.* continuous, successive; direct, straight

seguidor (-ra), *a.* following. *s.* follower, disciple

seguimiento, *m.* following, pursuit; continuation, resumption

seguir, *v.t. irr.* to follow; go after, pursue; prosecute, execute; continue, go on; accompany, go with; exercise (a profession); subscribe to, believe in; agree with; persecute, pester, annoy; imitate; (*law*) institute (a suit); handle, manage; *v.r.* result, follow as a consequence; follow in order, happen by turn; originate. *Pres. Part.* **siguiendo.** *Pres. Ind.* **sigo, sigues, sigue, siguen.** *Pres. Subjunc.* **siga,** etc. *Imperf. Subjunc.* **siguiese**

según, *adv.* according to; as. **s. y como,** as, according to

segunda, *f.* (*mus.*) second

segundar, *v.t.* to repeat, do again; *v.i.* be second, follow the first

segundero, *a.* (*agr.*) of the second flowering or fruiting. *m.* seconds hand (of watch)

segundo, *a.* second. *m.* second in command, deputy head; (*ast., geom.*) second. **segunda intención,** double meaning. **segunda velocidad,** (*aut.*) second gear. **de**

segunda mano, second-hand. **sin s.,** without peer or equal

segundogénito (-ta), *a.* and *s.* second-born

segundón, *m.* second son; any son but the eldest

segurador, *m.* surety, security (person)

seguramente, *adv.* securely, safely; surely, of course, naturally

seguridad, *f.* security; safety; certainty; trustworthiness; (*com.*) surety. **con toda s.,** with complete safety. **de s.,** *a.* safety

seguro, *a.* secure; safe; certain; sure; firm, fixed; reliable, trustworthy; unfailing. *m.* certainty; haven, place of safety; (*com.*) insurance; permit; (*mech.*) ratchet. **s. contra incendio, accidentes, robo,** insurance against fire, accident, burglary. **s. sobre la vida,** life-insurance. **de s.,** surely, certainly. **en s.,** in safety

seis, *a.* six; sixth. *m.* six; sixth (of days of month); playing-card or domino with six spots. **Son las s.** It is six o'clock

seisavo, *a.* and *m.* sixth. *m.* hexagon

seiscientos, *a.* six hundred; six hundredth. *m.* six hundred

seise, *m.* one of the six choirboys who dance in Seville cathedral on certain religious festivals

selección, *f.* selection, choice. **s. natural,** natural selection

seleccionar, *v.t.* to select, choose

selectivo, *a.* selective

selecto, *a.* choice, select, excellent

selenio, *m.* (*chem.*) selenium

selenografía, *f.* selenography

selva, *f.* forest, wood; jungle

selvático, *a.* sylvan, wood, forest; wild

selvoso, *a.* wooded, sylvan

sellador (-ra), *a.* sealing, stamping. *s.* sealer, stamper

selladura, *f.* sealing, stamping

sellar, *v.t.* to seal; stamp; end, conclude; close

sello, *m.* seal; stamp; cachet. **s. fiscal,** stamp-duty. **s. postal,** postage-stamp

semafórico, *a.* semaphoric

semáforo, *m.* semaphore

semana, *f.* week; week's salary. **S. Mayor** *or* **S. Santa,** Holy Week. **entre s.,** any day except Saturday and Sunday

semanal, *a.* weekly; of a week's duration

semanario, *a.* weekly. *m.* weekly periodical

semanero, *a.* employed by the week

semántica, *f.* semantics

semántico, *a.* semantic

semblante, *m.* facial expression, countenance; face; appearance, look, aspect. **componer el s.,** to pull oneself together, straighten one's face. **mudar de s.,** to change colour, change one's expression; alter (of circumstances)

semblanza, *f.* biographical sketch. **semblanzas literarias,** short biographies of writers

sembradera, *f.* (*agr.*) sowing machine

sembradío, *a.* (*agr.*) ready for sowing

sembrado, *m.* sown land

sembrador (-ra), *a.* sowing. *s.* sower

sembradura, *f.* (*agr.*) sowing

sembrar, *v.t. irr.* (*agr.*) to sow; scatter, sprinkle; spread, disseminate. See **sentar**

semeja, *f.* resemblance, similarity; indication, sign (gen. *pl.*)

semejante, *a.* like, similar; such a; (*math.*) similar. *m.* similarity, imitation. *m.* and *f.* fellow man

semejanza, *f.* similarity, likeness. **a s. de,** in the likeness of; like

semejar(se), *v.i.* and *v.r.* to resemble

semen, *m.* semen; (*bot.*) seed

semental, *a.* (*agr.*) seed; breeding (of male animals). *m.* stallion

sementar, *v.t.* (*agr.*) to sow

sementera, *f.* (*agr.*) sowing; sown land; seed-bed; seed-time; (*fig.*) hotbed, nursery, genesis

sementero, *m.* seed-bag; seed-bed

semestral, *a.* bi-annual, half-yearly; lasting six months

semestre, *a.* bi-annual. *m.* half-year, period of six months; six months' salary; semester

semicircular, *a.* semicircular

semicírculo, *m.* semicircle

semicorchea, *f.* (*mus.*) semi-quaver

semicromático, *a.* (*mus.*) semi-chromatic

semidifunto, *a.* half-dead

semidiós, *m.* demi-god

semidiosa, *f.* demi-goddess

semidítono, *m.* (*mus.*) semidi-tone

semidormido, *a.* half-asleep

semieje, *m.* (*geom.*) semi-axis

semiesférico, *a.* hemispherical

semifusa, *f.* (*mus.*) double demi-semiquaver

semilunio, *m.* (*ast.*) half-moon

semilla, *f.* (*bot.*) seed; (*fig.*) germ, genesis

semillero, *m.* seed-bed; nursery; (*fig.*) hotbed, origin

seminario, *m.* seed-bed; nursery; genesis, origin; seminary; tutorial. **s. conciliar,** theological seminary

seminarista, *m.* seminarist

semínima, *f.* (*mus.*) crotchet

semiótica, *f.* (*med.*) symptomatology

semita, *m.* and *f.* Semite. *a.* semitic

semítico, *a.* semitic

semitismo, *m.* Semitism

semitono, *m.* (*mus.*) semitone

semitransparente, *a.* semi-transparent

semivivo, *a.* half-alive

sémola, *f.* semolina

sempiterna, *f.* everlasting flower; thick woollen material

sempiterno, *a.* eternal

sen, *m.* (*bot.*) senna

sena, *f.* (*bot.*) senna; six-spotted die

senado, *m.* senate; senate-house; any grave assembly

senador, *m.* senator

senaduría, *f.* senatorship

senario, *a.* senary

senatorio, *a.* senatorial

sencillez, *f.* simplicity; naturalness; easiness; ingenuousness, candour

sencillo, *a.* simple; unmixed; natural; thin, light (fabric); easy; ingenuous, candid; unadorned, plain; single; sincere

senda, *f.* path, footpath; way; means

senderear, *v.t.* to conduct along a path; make a pathway; *v.i.* attain by tortuous means

sendero, *m.* footpath, path

sendos, sendas, *a. m.* and *f. pl.* one each (e.g. **Les dió sendos lápices,** He gave them each a pencil)

senectud, *f.* old age

senegalés (-esa), *a.* and *s.* Senegalese

senescal, *m.* seneschal

senil, *a.* senile

senilidad, *f.* senility

seno, *m.* hollow; hole; concavity; bosom, breast; chest; uterus, womb; any internal cavity of body; bay, cove; lap (of women); interior of anything, heart; gulf; (*math.*) sine; (*anat.*, etc.) sinus

sensación, *f.* sensation

sensacional, *a.* sensational

sensacionalista, *a.* sensationalist; yellow (of Press)

sensatez, *f.* prudence, good sense

sensato, *a.* prudent, wise

sensibilidad, *f.* sensibility

sensibilizar, *v.t.* (*phot.*) to sensitize

sensible, *a.* sensible, sensitive; tender, feeling; perceptible; noticeable, definite; sensitive; sad, regrettable

sensiblemente, *adv.* appreciably; perceptibly; painfully, sadly

sensiblería, *f.* sentimentality, sentimentalism

sensiblero, *a.* over-sentimental

sensitiva, *f.* sensitive plant

sensitivo, *a.* sensuous; sensitive, sensible

sensorio, *a.* sensory. *m.* sensorium

sensual, *a.* sensual; sensitive, sensible; carnal, voluptuous

sensualidad, *f.* sensuality; sensualism

sensualismo, *m.* sensualism; (*phil.*) sensationalism

sensualista, *m.* and *f.* (*phil.*) sensationalist; sensualist

sensualmente, *adv.* sensually

sentadero, *m.* resting place, improvised seat

sentado, *a.* prudent, circumspect

sentar, *v.t.* *irr.* to seat; *v.i.* (*fam.*) suit, agree with (e.g. **No me sienta este clima** (este plato),This climate (dish) doesn't suit me); fit, become; (*fam.*)

please, satisfy, be agreeable to; *v.r.* sit down; (*fam.*) leave a mark on the skin. *Pres. Ind.* **siento, sientas, sienta, sientan.** *Pres. Subjunc.* **siente, sientes, siente, sienten**

sentencia, *f.* opinion, belief; maxim; (*law*) verdict, sentence; decision, judgment. (*law*) **fulminar** (*or* **pronunciar**) **la s.,** to pass sentence

sentenciador, *a.* (*law*) sentencing

sentenciar, *v.t.* (*law*) to sentence; (*fam.*) destine, intend

sentencioso, *a.* sententious

sentidamente, *adv.* feelingly; sadly, regretfully

sentido, *m.* one of the five senses; understanding, sense; meaning, interpretation, signification; perception, discrimination; judgment; direction, way. *a.* and *past part.* felt; expressive; hypersensitive, touchy. **s. común,** common sense. (*fig., fam.*) **costar un s.,** to cost a fortune. **perder el s.,** to lose consciousness

sentimental, *a.* emotional; sentimental; romantic

sentimentalismo, *m.* emotional quality; sentimentalism

sentimiento, *m.* feeling, sentiment; sensation, impression; grief, sorrow. **Le acompaño a Vd en su s.,** I sympathize with you in your sorrow (bereavements)

sentina, *f.* well (of a ship); (*naut.*) bilge; cesspool; sink of iniquity

sentir, *v.t.* *irr.* to feel, experience; hear; appreciate; grieve, regret; believe, consider; envisage, foresee; *v.r.* complain; suffer; think or consider oneself; crack; feel, be; go rotten, decay (gen. with *estar* + *past part.*). *m.* view, opinion; feeling. **sin s.,** without feeling; without noticing. *Pres. Part.* **sintiendo.** *Pres. Ind.* **siento, sientes, siente, sienten.** *Preterite* **sintió, sintieron.** *Pres. Subjunc.* **sienta, sientas, sienta, sintamos, sintáis, sientan.** *Imperf. Subjunc.* **sintiese,** etc.

seña, *f.* sign, mark; gesture; (*mil.*) password; signal; *pl.* address, domicile. **señas mortales,** definite or unmistakable signs.

dar señas, to show signs, manifest. **hablar por señas,** to converse by signs

señal, *f.* mark, sign; boundary stone; landmark; scar; signal; trace, vestige; indication, symptom, token; symbol, sign; image, representation; prodigy, marvel; deposit, advance payment. **s. de aterrizaje,** (*aer.*) landing signal. **s. de niebla,** fog-signal. **señales horarias,** (*rad.*) time signal. **en s.,** as a sign, in proof of. **las señales luminosas de la circulación,** traffic lights, traffic robot

señaladamente, *adv.* especially, particularly, notably

señalado, *a.* famous, distinguished; important, notable

señalamiento, *m.* marking; pointing out; appointment, designation

señalar, *v.t.* to mark; indicate, point out; fix, arrange; wound; signal; stamp; appoint (to an office); *v.r.* excel

señero, *a.* solitary, isolated

señor, *a.* (*fam.*) gentlemanly. *m.* owner, master; mister, esquire; (S.) the Lord; lord, sire. **s. de horca y cuchillo,** feudal lord, lord of life and death

señora, *f.* lady; owner, mistress; madam; wife. **s. de compañía,** chaperon; lady-companion. **Nuestra S.,** Our Lady

señorear, *v.t.* to control, run, manage; master; domineer; appropriate, seize; dominate, overlook; restrain (emotions); *v.r.* behave with dignity

señoría, *f.* lordship (title and person); lordship, jurisdiction; area, territory; control, restraint

señoría, *f.* dignity, sedateness; self-control

señorial, *a.* manorial; noble, dignified, lordly

señoril, *a.* lordly, noble, aristocratic

señorío, *m.* lordship; jurisdiction, dominion

señorita, *f.* young lady; miss; (*fam.*) mistress of the house

señorito, *m.* young gentleman; (*fam.*) master of the house; master (address); (*fam.*) young man about town

señuelo, *m.* decoy; bait; allurement, attraction. (*fig., fam.*) **caer en el s.,** to fall into the trap

sépalo, *m.* (*bot.*) sepal

sepancuantos, *m.* (*fam.*) scolding, rebuke; spanking

separación, *f.* separation

separado, *a.* separate

separador (-ra), *a.* separating. *s.* separator. *m.* filter. **s. de aceite,** oil filter

separar, *v.t.* to separate; divide; dismiss (from a post); lay aside; *v.r.* retire, resign; separate

separatismo, *m.* separatism

separatista, *a.* and *m.* and *f.* separatist

sepia, *f.* cuttlefish; sepia (colour)

sepsia, *f.* sepsis

septena, *f.* heptad

septenario, *a.* septenary. *m.* heptad

septenio, *m.* septennium, space of seven years

septeno, *a.* See **séptimo**

septentrión, *m.* (*ast.*) Great Bear; north

septentrional, *a.* north; northern

septeto, *m.* (*mus.*) septet

septicemia, *f.* (*med.*) septicæmia

séptico, *a.* (*med.*) septic

septiembre, *m.* September

septilio, *m.* (*mus.*) septuplet

séptima, *f.* (*mus.*) seventh

séptimo, *a.* and *m.* seventh

septuagenario (-ia), *a.* and *s.* septuagenarian

septuagésimo, *a.* seventieth; septuagesimal. *m.* seventieth

septuplicar, *v.t.* to multiply by seven

séptuplo, *a.* sevenfold

sepulcral, *a.* sepulchral

sepulcro, *m.* sepuchre, tomb

sepultador (-ra), *a.* burying. *s.* grave-digger; burier

sepultar, *v.t.* to inter, bury; hide, cover up

sepultura, *f.* interment; grave; tomb

sepulturero, *m.* grave-digger

sequedad, *f.* dryness, barrenness; acerbity, sharpness

sequía, *f.* drought

séquito, *m.* following, suite, retinue; general approval, popularity

ser, *m.* essence, nature; being; existence, life. **El S. Supremo,** The Supreme Being, God

ser, *v.i. irr.* to be (e.g. **El sombrero es azul,** The hat is blue). **Ser** may agree with either subject or complement, though when latter is *pl.* the verb tends to be so too (e.g. **Son las once,** (horas), It is eleven o'clock. **Cien libras son poco dinero,** A hundred pounds is a small amount). If verbal complement is pers. pron., **ser** agrees with it both in number and person (e.g. **Son ellos,** It is they. **Soy yo,** It is I). In impers. phrases the pron. is not expressed (e.g. **Es difícil,** It is difficult. **Es sorprendente,** It is surprising). **ser** means to exist (e.g. **Pienso luego soy,** I think, therefore I exist). **ser** (also ser de with nouns or obj. prons.) means to belong to, be the property of (e.g. **Este gato es mío,** This cat is mine. **El libro es de Juan,** The book belongs to John). Signifies to happen, occur (e.g. **¿Cómo fué eso?** How did that happen?). Means to be suitable or fitting (e.g. **Este vestido no es para una señora mayor,** This dress is not suitable for an elderly lady). Expresses price, to be worth (e.g. **¿A cuánto es la libra?** How much is it a pound?; How much is the pound (sterling) worth?). Means to be a member of, belong to (e.g. **Es de la Academia Española,** He is a member of the Spanish Academy). Means to be of use, be useful for (e.g. **Esta casa no es para una familia numerosa,** This house is no use for a large family). **Ser** expresses nationality (e.g. **Son francesas,** They are French women. **Somos de Londres,** We are from London). *Auxiliary verb* used to form Passive Tense (e.g. **Esta historia ha sido leída por muchos,** This story has been read by many. **Fueron mandados al Japón,** They were sent to Japan. **s. de ver,** to be worth seeing. **s. para poco,** to be of little use, amount to little.

s. testigo de, to witness. **¡Cómo es eso!** How can that be! Surely not! **¡Cómo ha de ser!** How should it be!; One must resign oneself. **Érase una vez** or **Érase que érase,** Once upon a time. **es a saber,** viz., that is to say. **un sí es no es,** a touch of, a suspicion of). *Pres. Part.* **siendo.** *Pres. Ind.* **soy, eres, es, somos, sois, son.** *Fut.* **seré,** etc. *Condit.* **sería,** etc. *Preterite* **fui, fuiste, fué, fuimos, fuisteis, fueron.** *Imperf.* **era,** etc. *Past Part.* **sido.** *Pres. Subjunc.* **sea,** etc. *Imperf. Subjunc.* **fuese,** etc. *Imperat.* **sé**

sera, *f.* large frail

seráfico, *a.* seraphic

serafín, *m.* seraphim

serbal, *m.* (*bot.*) service tree

serena, *f.* serenade; (*fam.*) dew

serenar, *v.t.* to calm; soothe; clear; *v.r.* grow calm; clear up (weather); clear (liquids); be soothed or pacified

serenata, *f.* serenade

serenidad, *f.* serenity, composure, tranquillity; Serene Highness (title)

sereno, *a.* cloudless, fair; composed, serene. *m.* dew; night-watchman

sergas, *f. pl.* deeds, prowess

sericultor, *m.* silk cultivator, sericulturist

sericultura, *f.* silk culture

serie, *f.* series, sequence, succession; (*math.*) progression; (*biol., elec.*) series; break (in billiards)

seriedad, *f.* seriousness, earnestness; gravity; austerity; sternness; importance; sincerity; solemnity

serio, *a.* serious, earnest; grave; austere; stern; important; sincere, genuine; solemn. **en s.,** seriously

sermón, *m.* sermon; scolding. **dar un s.,** to give a sermon; scold

sermonar, *v.i.* to preach

sermonear, *v.i.* to preach sermons; *v.t.* scold

sermoneo, *m.* (*fam.*) scolding

seroja, *f.* withered leaves; brushwood

serosidad, *f.* (*med.*) serosity

seroso, *a.* serous

seroterapia, *f.* serotherapy

serpear, *v.i.* to wind, twist; wriggle, squirm; coil

serpenteado, *a.* winding

serpentear, *v.i.* to wind, twist, meander; stagger along; wriggle; coil; (*aer.*) yaw

serpenteo, *m.* winding, twisting; wriggling; coiling; (*aer.*) yaw

serpentín, *m.* (*chem.*) worm; coil (in industry); (*min.*) serpentine

serpentina, *f.* (*min.*) serpentine; paper streamer

serpentino, *a.* serpentine; (*poet.*) winding, sinuous

serpentón, *m.* (*mus.*) serpent

serpiente, *f.* ·snake, serpent; Satan, the Devil; (*ast.*) Serpent. **s. de anteojos,** cobra. **s. de cascabel,** rattlesnake

serpol, *m.* wild thyme

serpollo, *m.* (*bot.*) shoot, new branch; sprout; sucker

serrado, *a.* serrate

serrallo, *m.* harem, seraglio; brothel

serrana, serranilla, *f.* pastoral poem

serranía, *f.* mountainous territory

serrano (-na), *a.* mountain, highland. *s.* highlander, mountain dweller

serrucho, *m.* handsaw. **s. de calar,** fretsaw

servible, *a.* serviceable; useful

servicial, *a.* useful, serviceable; obliging, obsequious

servicio, *m.* service, domestic service; cult, devotion; care, attendance; military service; set, service; department, section; present of money; cover (cutlery, etc., at table); domestic staff, servants. **s. informativo,** news service. **s. nocturno permanente,** all-night service. (*fam.*) **hacer un flaco s. (a),** to do someone an ill-turn. **prestar servicios,** to render service, serve

servidor (-ra), *s.* servant, domestic; name by which one refers to oneself (e.g. **Un s. lo hará con mucho gusto,** I (your servant) will do it with much pleasure). *m.* wooer, lover; bowler (in cricket). **los servidores de una ametralladora,** the crew (of a gun). **Quedo de**

Vd atento y seguro s., I remain your obedient servant (in letters), Yours faithfully

servidumbre, *f.* serfdom; servitude; servants, domestic staff; obligation, duty; enslavement (by passions); right-of-way; use, service

servil, *a.* servile; humble

servilismo, *m.* servility; abjectness; absolutism (Spanish history)

servilleta, *f.* table napkin. **s. higiénica,** sanitary towel

servilletero, *m.* napkin-ring

servio (-ia), *a.* and *s.* Serbian

servir, *v.i. irr.* to be employed (by), be in the service (of); serve (as), perform the duties (of); be of use; wait (on), be subject to. (*mil.*) serve in the forces; wait at table; be suitable or favourable; (*sport*) serve; perform a service; follow the lead (cards); (*with de*) act as, be a deputy for; be a substitute for; *v.t.* serve; worship; do a favour to; woo, court; serve (food, drink); *v.r.* be pleased or willing, deign; help oneself to (food); (*with de*) make use of. **no s. para nada,** to be good for nothing, be useless. **No sirves para tales cosas,** You are no good at this sort of thing. **Para s. a Vd,** At your service. **¡Sírvase de . . .!** (followed by infin.), Please! See **pedir**

sésamo, *m.* (*bot.*) sesame

sesear, *v.i.* to pronounce *c* as *s* (said of Andalusians and Spanish Americans)

sesenta, *a.* and *m.* sixty; sixtieth

sesentavo, *a.* and *m.* sixtieth

sesentón (-ona), *s.* (*fam.*) person of sixty

sesga, *f.* (*sew.*) gore

sesgadamente, *adv.* on the slant; askew; obliquely

sesgado, *a.* oblique, slanting

sesgar, *v.t.* (*sew.*) to cut on the cross; slant, slope; place askew, twist to one side

sesgo, *a.* slanting, oblique; serious-faced. *m.* slope, slant, obliquity; compromise, middle way. **al s.,** on the slant

sésil, *a.* (*bot.*) sessile

sesión, *f.* session, meeting; conference, consultation; (*law*) sitting; term. **abrir la s.,** to open the meeting. **levantar la s.,** to adjourn the meeting

seso, *m.* brain; prudence; *pl.* brains. **perder el s.,** to go mad; (*fig.*) lose one's head

sestear, *v.i.* to take an afternoon nap; rest; settle

sesudez, *f.* prudence, shrewdness

sesudo, *a.* sensible, prudent

seta, *f.* mushroom. **s. venenosa,** poisonous toadstool

setal, *m.* mushroom bed, patch or field

setecientos, *a.* and *m.* seven hundred; seven hundredth

setenta, *a.* and *m.* seventy; seventieth

setentavo, *a.* and *m.* seventieth

setentón (-ona), *s.* septuagenarian

setiembre, *m.* September

seto, *m.* fence; hedge

sétter, *m.* setter (dog)

seudo, *a.* pseudo

seudónimo, *m.* pseudonym

severamente, *adv.* severely, harshly

severidad, *f.* severity; harshness; strictness, rigour; austerity, seriousness

severo, *a.* severe; harsh; strict, rigid, scrupulous, exact; austere, serious

sevillanas, *f. pl.* Sevillian dance and its music

sevillano (-na), *a.* and *s.* of or from Seville, Sevillian

sexagenario (-ia), *s.* sexagenarian

sexagésimo, *a.* sixtieth

sexo, *m.* sex. **el s. débil,** the weaker sex

sexología, *f.* sexology

sexólogo (-ga), *s.* sexologist

sexta, *f.* (*ecc.*) sext; (*mus.*) sixth

sextante, *m.* (*math.*) sextant

sexteto, *m.* (*mus.*) sextet

sexto, *a.* sixth

sextuplicación, *f.* multiplication by six

sextuplicar, *v.t.* to multiply by six, sextuple

séxtuplo, *a.* sixfold

sexualidad, *f.* sexuality

si, *m.* (*mus.*) B, seventh note of scale. *conjunc.* if; whether; even if, although. In conditional clause, **si,** meaning if, is followed by indicative tense unless statement be contrary to fact (e.g. **Si**

pierdes el tren, volverás a casa, If you miss your train you will return home, *but* **Si hubieran venido habríamos ido al campo,** If they had come (but they didn't) we should have gone to the country). **Si** is used at beginning of clause to make expressions of doubt, desire or affirmation more emphatic (e.g. ¡ **Si lo sabrá él, con toda su experiencia!** Of course he knows it, with all his experience. ¡ **Si será falsa la noticia ?** Can the news be false?) **Si** also means whether (e.g. **Me preguntaron si era médico o militar,** They asked me whether I was a doctor or a soldier). Sometimes means even if, although (e.g. **Si viniesen no lo harían,** Even if they came they would not do it. **como si,** as if. **por si acaso,** in case, in the event of. **si bien,** although)

sí, *pers. pron. reflexive,* 3rd *pers.,* *m.* and *f.,* *sing.* and *pl.* himself, herself, itself, themselves. Always used with prep. (e.g. **para sí,** for himself, herself, etc. **de por sí,** separately, on its own. **decir para sí,** to say to oneself)

sí, *adv.* yes. **sí** *or* **sí que** is frequently used to emphasize a verb generally in contrast to previous negative (e.g. **Ellos no lo harán, pero yo sí,** They won't do it but I shall). Often translated by " did" (e.g. **No lo vi todo, pero lo que sí vi,** I didn't see it all, but what I did see ...). *m.* assent; yes; consent. **dar el sí,** to say yes; agree; accept an offer of marriage

siamés (-esa), *a.* and *s.* Siamese. *m.* Siamese language

sibarita, *a.* sybaritic. *m.* and *f.* sybarite

sibarítico, *a.* sybaritic; sensual

sibaritismo, *m.* sybaritism

siberiano (-na), *a.* and *s.* Siberian

sibila, *f.* sibyl

sibilante, *a.* sibilant

sibilino, *a.* sibylline

sicario, *m.* paid assassin

siciliano (-na), *a.* and *s.* Sicilian

sicofanta, sicofante, *m.* sycophant

sicomoro, *m.* (*bot.*) sycamore

sideral, sidéreo, *a.* sidereal

siderosa, *f.* (*min.*) siderite

siderurgia, *f.* (*met.*) siderurgy

sidonio (-ia), *a.* and *s.* Sidonian

sidra, *f.* cider

siega, *f.* reaping, harvesting; harvest time; harvest, crop

siembra, *f.* (*agr.*) sowing; seed-time; sown field

siempre, *adv.* always. **s. que,** provided that; whenever. **para s.,** for ever. **por s. jamás,** for always, for ever and ever

siempreviva, *f.* (*bot.*) everlasting flower. **s. mayor,** houseleek

sien, *f.* (*anat.*) temple

sienés (-esa), *s.* Sienese

sierpe, *f.* serpent, snake; anything that wriggles; kite (toy); (*bot.*) sucker; hideous person

sierra, *f.* (*carp.*) saw; ridge of mountains; (*icht.*) sawfish; slope; hillside. **s. de cerrojero,** hacksaw. **s. de cinta,** handsaw

siervo (-va), *s.* slave; servant; serf

siesta, *f.* noonday heat; afternoon nap

siete, *a.* seven; seventh. *m.* seven; seventh (of days of month); playing-card with seven spots; number seven. **las s.,** seven o'clock. (*fam.*) **más que s.,** more than somewhat, extremely

sietemesino (-na), *s.* seven-months' child; (*fig., fam.*) young cock

sífilis, *f.* syphilis

sifilítico (-ca), *a.* and *s.* syphilitic

sifilografía, *f.* syphilography

sifón, *m.* siphon; siphon bottle; soda-water; (*mech.*) trap

sigilar, *v.t.* to seal; hide; conceal

sigilo, *m.* seal; secrecy, concealment; silence, reserve

sigiloso, *a.* secret, silent

sigla, *f.* abbreviation in writing

siglo, *m.* century; long time, age; social intercourse, society, world. **s. de oro,** golden age. **en** *or* **por los siglos de los siglos,** for ever and ever

signar, *v.t.* to sign; make the sign of the cross over; *v.r.* cross oneself

signatario (-ia), *a.* and *s.* signatory

signatura, *f.* (*print.*) signature; mark, sign; (*mus.*) signature

significación, *f.,* **significado,** *m.* meaning; importance, significance

significante, *a.* significant

significar, *v.t.* to signify, indicate; mean; publish, make known; *v.i.* represent, mean; be worth

significativo, *a.* significant

signo, *m.* sign, indication, token; sign, character; (*math.*) symbol; sign of the zodiac; (*mus.*) sign; (*med.*) symptom; (*ecc.*) gesture of benediction; destiny, fate

síguemepollo, *m.* (*fam.*) follow-me-lads, streamer

siguiente, *a.* following; next, subsequent. **el día s.,** the next day

sílaba, *f.* syllable

silabario, *m.* spelling-book

silabear, *v.i.* and *v.t.* to pronounce by syllables, syllabize

silabeo, *m.* pronouncing syllable by syllable, syllabication

silábico, *a.* syllabic

sílabo, *m.* syllabus, list

silba, *f.* hissing (as sign of disapproval)

silbador (-ra), *a.* whistling; hissing. *s.* whistler; one who hisses

silbar, *v.i.* to whistle; whizz, rush through the air; *v.i.* and *v.t.* (*theat.*) hiss

silbato, *m.* whistle; air-hole

silbido, silbo, *m.* whistle, whistling; hiss, hissing

silenciador, *m.* (*aut.*, and of fire-arms) silencer

silenciar, *v.t.* to silence; keep secret

silenciario, *a.* vowed to perpetual silence

silencio, *m.* silence; noiselessness, quietness; omission, disregard; (*mus.*) rest. **en s.,** in silence; quietly; uncomplainingly. **pasar en s. (una cosa),** to pass over (something) in silence, omit

silencioso, *a.* silent; noiseless; tranquil, quiet. *m.* silencer (*aut.*, fire-arms)

silepsis, *f.* (*gram.*) syllepsis

silesio (-ia), *a.* and *s.* Silesian

sílfide, *f.,* **silfo,** *m.* sylph

silicato, *m.* (*chem.*) silicate

sílice, *f.* (*chem.*) silica

silicio, *m.* (*chem.*) silicium

silo, *m.* (*agr.*) silo; dark cavern or cave

silogismo, *m.* syllogism

silogístico, *a.* syllogistic

silueta, *f.* silhouette; figure

silúrico, *a.* (*geol.*) silurian

siluro, *m.* (*icht.*) catfish; (*nav.*) self-propelling torpedo

silva, *f.* literary miscellany; metrical form

silvestre, *a.* (*bot.*) wild; sylvan; uncultivated; savage

silvicultor, *m.* forester

silvicultura, *f.* forestry

silla, *f.* chair; riding-saddle; (*mech.*) rest, saddle; (*ecc.*) see. s. de manos, sedan-chair. s. de montar, riding-saddle. s. de posta, post-chaise. s. de ruedas, wheel-chair. s. de tijera, deck-chair; camp stool. s. giratoria, swivel chair. s. poltrona, easy-chair. (*fam.*) pegársele la s., to overstay one's welcome

sillar, *m.* ashlar, quarry stone; horseback

sillería, *f.* set of chairs; pew, choir stalls; chair factory; shop where chairs are sold; chair making; (*mas.*) ashlar masonry

sillero (-ra), *s.* chair maker or seller; saddler

silleta, *f. dim.* small chair; bedpan; fireman's lift

silletero, *m.* runner, sedan-chair carrier

sillín, *m.* light riding-saddle; seat, saddle (bicycles, etc.)

sillón, *m.* armchair; side-saddle. s. de mimbres, cane chair

sima, *f.* abyss, chasm

simbiosis, *f.* symbiosis

simbólico, *a.* symbolical

simbolismo, *m.* symbolism

simbolista, *m.* and *f.* symbolist

simbolización, *f.* symbolization

simbolizar, *v.t.* to symbolize, represent

símbolo, *m.* symbol. s. de la fe, (*ecc.*) Creed

simetría, *f.* symmetry

simétrico, *a.* symmetric; symmetrical

simetrizar, *v.t.* to make symmetrical

símico, *a.* simian

simiente, *f.* seed; semen; germ, genesis, origin

simiesco, *a.* apish

símil, *a.* similar. *m.* comparison; (*gram.*) simile

similar, *a.* similar

similitud, *f.* similarity

simio (-ia), *s.* ape

simón, *m.* horse cab; cabman

simonía, *f.* simony

simoníaco, *a.* simoniacal

simpatía, *f.* liking, understanding, affection; fellow-feeling; sympathy (also *med.*)

simpático, *a.* friendly, nice, decent, congenial; sympathetic. (*anat.*) gran s., sympathetic

simpatizar, *v.i.* to get on well, be congenial

simple, *a.* simple; single, not double; insipid; easy; plain, unadorned; stupid, silly; pure, unmixed; easily deceived, simple; naïve, ingenuous; mere; mild, meek. *m.* and *f.* simpleton; fool

simpleza, *f.* foolishness, stupidity; simplicity

simplicidad, *f.* simplicity; candour, ingenuousness

simplicísimo, *a. sup.* simple, most or exceedingly simple

simplificable, *a.* simplifiable

simplificación, *f.* simplification, simplifying

simplificador, *a.* simplifying

simplificar, *v.t.* to simplify

simplista, *m.* and *f.* herbalist

simulación, *f.* pretence, simulation

simulacro, *m.* image, simulacrum; vision, fancy; (*mil.*) mock battle

simuladamente, *adv.* pretendedly

simulador (-ra), *a.* feigned. *s.* dissembler

simular, *v.t.* to feign, pretend

simultanear, *v.t.* to perform simultaneously

simultaneidad, *f.* simultaneousness

simultáneo, *a.* simultaneous

simún, *m.* simoom

sin, *prep.* without (e.g. Lo hizo s. hablar, He did it without speaking). s. embargo, nevertheless. s. fin, endless. s. hilos, wireless

sinagoga, *f.* synagogue

sinalefa, *f.* (*gram.*) synalepha

sinapismo, *m.* (*med.*) mustard plaster; (*fam.*) pest, bore

sincerarse, *v.r.* to justify oneself; vindicate one's actions

sinceridad, *f.* sincerity

sincero, *a.* sincere

síncopa, *f.* (*mus.*) syncopation; (*gram.*) syncope

sincopado, *a.* (*mus.*) syncopated

sincopar, *v.t.* to syncopate; abbreviate

síncope, *m.* (*med., gram.*) syncope

sincrónico, *a.* synchronous

sincronismo, *m.* synchronism

sincronizar, *v.t.* to synchronize; (*rad.*) tune in

sindéresis, *f.* discretion, good sense

sindicación, *f.* syndication

sindicado, *m.* syndicate

sindical, *a.* syndical

sindicalismo, *m.* syndicalism, trade unionism

sindicalista, *m.* and *f.* syndicalist, trade-unionist. *a.* syndicalistic, trade-unionist

sindicar, *v.t.* to accuse, charge; censure; syndicate

sindicato, *m.* syndicate; trade union. **s. gremial,** trade union

sindicatura, *f.* (official) receivership

síndico, *m.* (*com.*) receiver or trustee

síndrome, *m.* (*med.*) syndrome

sinecura, *f.* sinecure

sinéresis, *f.* synæresis

sinergia, *f.* (*med.*) synergy

sinfín, *m.* countless number

sínfisis, *f.* symphisis

sinfonía, *f.* symphony

sinfónico, *a.* symphonic

sinfonista, *m.* and *f.* composer of symphonies, player in a symphony orchestra

singladura, *f.* (*naut.*) day's sailing; nautical twenty-four hours (beginning at midday)

singlar, *v.i.* (*naut.*) to sail a given course

singular, *a.* singular, single; individual; extraordinary, remarkable. *a.* and *m.* (*gram.*) singular

singularidad, *f.* individuality, peculiarity; strangeness, remarkableness; oddness, eccentricity

singularizar, *v.t.* to particularize, single out; (*gram.*) make singular, singularize; *v.r.* distin-

guish oneself, stand out; be distinguished (by)

sinhueso, *f.* (*fam.*) tongue (organ of speech)

sínico, *a.* Chinese (of things)

siniestra, *f.* left, left-hand

siniestro, *a.* left (side); vicious, perverse; sinister; unlucky. *m.* viciousness, depravity (gen. *pl.*); shipwreck, sinking; disaster, catastrophe; (*com.*) damage, loss

sinnúmero, *m.* countless number

sino, *m.* fate, destiny. *conjunc.* but; except (e.g. **No lo hicieron ellos s. yo,** They didn't do it (but) I did. **no . . . s.,** not . . ., but); only (e.g. **No sólo lo dijo él s. ella,** Not only he said it, but she did too)

sinodal, *a.* (*ecc.*) synodic

sínodo, *m.* (*ecc., ast.*) synod; council

sinología, *f.* sinology

sinólogo, *m.* sinologist

sinonimia, *f.* synonymy

sinónimo, *a.* synonymous. *m.* synonym

sinopsis, *f.* synopsis

sinóptico, *a.* synoptic

sinovia, *f.* (*anat.*) synovia

sinrazón, *f.* injustice, wrong

sinsabor, *m.* unpleasantness, trouble; grief, anxiety

sintáctico, *a.* (*gram.*) syntactic

sintaxis, *f.* (*gram.*) syntax

síntesis, *f.* synthesis

sintético, *a.* synthetic

sintetizar, *v.t.* to synthesize

sintoísmo, *m.* Shintoism

síntoma, *m.* symptom

sintomático, *a.* symptomatic

sintomatología, *f.* (*med.*) symptomatology

sintonización, *f.* (*rad.*) tuning-in

sintonizador, *m.* (*rad.*) tuner

sintonizar, *v.t.* (*rad.*) to tune in

sinuosidad, *f.* sinuosity

sinuoso, *a.* sinuous, winding

sinvergüenza, *m.* and *f.* rascal, knave, rogue

sionismo, *m.* Zionism

sionista, *a.* and *m.* and *f.* Zionist

siquiera, *conjunc.* although, even if. **s. . . . s.,** whether . . . or. *adv.* at least; even (e.g. **Hay que pedir mucho para tener s. la mitad,** One must ask a great deal to get even half). **ni s.,** not even (e.g. **No había nadie, ni s.**

un perro, There was no one, not even a dog)

siracusano (-na), *a.* and *s.* Syracusan

sirena, *f.* mermaid, syren; siren; foghorn

sirga, *f.* (*naut.*) towline

sirgar, *v.t.* (*naut.*) to track, tow

siríaco (-ca), *a.* and *s.* Syrian

sirio (-ia), *a.* and *s.* Syrian. *m.* (*ast.*) Sirius

siroco, *m.* sirocco

sirte, *f.* sand-bank, submerged rock

sirvienta, *f.* maidservant

sirviente, *a.* serving. *m.* servant

sisa, *f.* pilfering; (*sew.*) dart. **s. dorada,** gold lacquer

sisador (-ra), *s.* filcher, pilferer

sisar, *v.t.* to pilfer, filch, steal; (*sew.*) take in, make darts in

sisear, *v.i.* and *v.t.* to hiss (disapproval); sizzle

sísmico, *a.* seismic

sismógrafo, *m.* seismograph

sismología, *f.* seismology

sismológico, *a.* seismological

sismómetro, *m.* seismometer

sistema, *m.* system. **s. ferroviario,** railway system. **s. métrico,** decimal system

sistemático, *a.* systematic

sistematización, *f.* systematization

sistematizar, *v.t.* to systematize

sístole, *f.* systole

sitiador, *a.* besieging. *m.* besieger

sitial, *m.* ceremonial chair

sitiar, *v.t.* (*mil.*) to lay siege to; surround, besiege

sitio, *m.* place, spot; room, space; site; locality; (*mil.*) siege, blockade; country-seat. **No hay s.,** There's no room

sito, *past part.* situated, located

situación, *f.* situation; position; circumstances; condition, state; location

situado, *past part.* situated, placed. *m.* income, interest

situar, *v.t.* to situate, locate, place; assign funds; *v.r.* place oneself

smoking, *m.* dinner-jacket

snobismo, *m.* snobbery

so, *prep.* under (used only with **color, pena, pretexto, capa**) (e.g. **so color de,** under the pretext of). *interj.* ¡So! Whoa! (to horses)

soba, *f.* rubbing; kneading; massaging; drubbing, beating; handling, touching

sobacal, *a.* underarm, axillary

sobaco, *m.* armpit; (*bot.*) axil

sobajar, *v.t.* to squeeze, press

sobaquera, *f.* (*sew.*) arm hole; dress-protector

sobar, *v.t.* to rub; knead; massage; beat, thrash; handle, touch, paw (persons); soften

soberanear, *v.i.* to tyrannize, domineer

soberanía, *f.* sovereignty; dominance, sway, rule; dignity, majesty

soberano (-na), *a.* sovereign; superb; regal, majestic. *s.* ruler, lord. *m.* sovereign (coin)

soberbia, *f.* arrogance, haughtiness; conceit, presumption; ostentation, pomp; rage, anger

soberbio, *a.* haughty, arrogant; conceited; superb, magnificent; lofty, soaring; spirited (horses)

sobón, *a.* (*fam.*) over-demonstrative, sloppy; (*fam.*) lazy

sobordo, *m.* (*naut.*) manifest, freight list

sobornación, *f.* bribing; bribery

sobornador (-ra), *a.* bribing. *s.* briber

sobornar, *v.t.* to bribe

soborno, *m.* bribing; bribe; inducement

sobra, *f.* excess, surplus; insult, outrage; *pl.* left-overs (from meal); remains, residue; rubbish, trash. **de s.,** in abundance; in excess, surplus; unnecessary, superfluous; too well

sobradamente, *adv.* abundantly; in excess

sobrado, *a.* excessive; brazen, bold; wealthy, rich. *m.* garret

sobrante, *a.* surplus, left-over, remaining. *m.* remainder, surplus, excess

sobrar, *v.t.* to exceed; have too much of (e.g. **Me sobran mantas,** I have too many blankets); *v.i.* be superfluous; remain, be left. (*fam.*) **Aquí sobro yo,** I am in the way here (My presence is superfluous)

sobrasada, *f.* (*cul.*) savoury sausage

sobre, *prep.* upon, on; above, over; concerning, about; apart from, besides; about (e.g. **s. las nueve,** about nine o'clock) (indicates approximation); towards; after. *m.* envelope; address, superscription. **s. cero,** above freezing point. **s. el nivel del mar,** above sea-level. **s. manera,** excessively, extremely. **s. todo,** especially

sobreabundancia, *f.* superabundance, excess

sobreabundante, *a.* superabundant

sobreabundar, *v.i.* to be superabundant

sobreagudo, *a.* and *m.* (*mus.*) treble (pitch)

sobrealiento, *m.* heavy, painful breathing

sobrealimentación, *f.* overfeeding; (*aut.*) supercharge

sobrealimentar, *v.t.* (*aut.*) to supercharge

sobrearco, *m.* (*arch.*) relieving arch

sobreasar, *v.t.* to roast or cook again

sobrecama, *f.* bedspread, quilt

sobrecarga, *f.* overload; rope, etc., for securing bales and packs; additional trouble or anxiety

sobrecargar, *v.t.* to overload; weigh down; (*sew.*) oversew, fell

sobrecargo, *m.* (*naut.*) purser

sobrecarta, *f.* envelope (for a letter)

sobrecebadera, *f.* (*naut.*) sprit topsail

sobreceja, *f.* brow, lower forehead; frown

sobrecejo, *m.* frown

sobrecielo, *m.* canopy

sobrecoger, *v.t.* to take by surprise; *v.r.* be frightened or apprehensive

sobrecogimiento, *m.* fright, apprehension

sobrecomida, *f.* dessert, sweet

sobrecoser, *v.t.* (*sew.*) to oversew, whip

sobrecrecer, *v.i. irr.* to grow too much. See **conocer**

sobrecubierta, *f.* second lid or cover; dust jacket (of a book); (*naut.*) upper deck

sobrecuello, *m.* over-collar; loose collar

sobredicho, *a.* aforementioned, aforesaid

sobredorar, *v.t.* to gild (metals); make excuses for

sobreedificar, *v.t.* to build upon or above

sobreexcitar, *v.t.* to over-excite

sobrefaz, *f.* surface, exterior

sobreganar, *v.t.* to make an excess profit

sobreguarda, *m.* head guard; extra or second guard

sobreherido, *a.* lightly wounded

sobrehilar, *v.t.* to oversew or overcast

sobrehumano, *a.* superhuman

sobrejuanete, *m.* (*naut.*) royal

sobrellenar, *v.t.* to fill full

sobrellevar, *v.t.* to help in the carrying of a burden; endure, bear; make excuses for, overlook; help

sobremesa, *f.* tablecloth; afterdinner conversation while still at table. (*fig.*) **de s.,** over the dinner table

sobremesana, *f.* (*naut.*) mizzen topsail

sobrenadar, *v.i.* to float

sobrenatural, *a.* supernatural; extraordinary, singular

sobrenombre, *m.* additional surname; nickname

sobrentender, *v.t. irr.* to take for granted, understand as a matter of course; *v.r.* go without saying. See **entender**

sobrepaga, *f.* overpayment; extra pay

sobreparto, *m.* time after parturition; afterbirth

sobrepasar, *v.t.* to exceed; outdo, excel

sobrepelliz, *f.* (*ecc.*) surplice

sobreponer, *v.t. irr.* to place over; overlap; *v.r.* rise above (circumstances); dominate (persons). See **poner**

sobreprecio, *m.* extra charge, rise in price

sobreproducción, *f.* over-production

sobrepuerta, *f.* curtain pelmet; door curtain

sobrepujar, *v.t.* to excel, surpass, outdo

sobrequilla, *f.* (*naut.*) keelson

sobresaliente, *a.* overhanging; projecting; distinctive, outstanding; excellent, remarkable. *m.* mark " excellent " in examinations. *m.* and *f.* (*theat.*, etc.) understudy

sobresalir, *v.i. irr.* to overhang, project; stand out; be conspicuous or noticeable; excel; distinguish oneself. See **salir**

sobresaltar, *v.t.* to assail, rush upon; startle, frighten suddenly; *v.i.* (*art*) stand out, be striking; *v.r.* be startled or frightened

sobresalto, *m.* sudden attack; unexpected shock; agitation; sudden fear. **de s.,** unexpectedly

sobresanar, *v.i.* to heal superficially but not deeply; conceal, dissemble

sobrescribir, *v.t.* to label; address, superscribe. *Past Part.* **sobrescrito**

sobrescrito, *m.* address, superscription

sobresello, *m.* second seal

sobrestadía, *f.* (*com.*) demurrage

sobrestante, *m.* overseer; supervisor; foreman; inspector

sobresueldo, *m.* additional salary, bonus

sobresuelo, *m.* second flooring

sobretarde, *f.* early evening, late afternoon

sobretodo, *m.* overcoat

sobrevenida, *f.* sudden arrival

sobrevenir, *v.i. irr.* occur, take place; supervene. See **venir**

sobrevidriera, *f.* storm-window; wire-mesh window-guard; fly-window

sobrevienta, *f.* gust of wind, fury, violence; shock, surprise. **a s.,** suddenly

sobreviviente, *a.* surviving. *m.* and *f.* survivor

sobrevivir, *v.i.* to survive

sobriedad, *f.* sobriety, moderation

sobrina, *f.* niece

sobrino, *m.* nephew

sobrio, *a.* sober, moderate, temperate

socaire, *m.* (*naut.*) slatch

socaliña, *f.* cunning, sharp practice

socaliñero (**-ra**), *a.* cunning. *s.* trickster

socalzar, *v.t.* (*mas.*) to underpin

socapa, *f.* blind, pretext. **a s.,** secretly; cautiously

socarra, *f.* scorching, singeing; craftiness

socarrón, *a.* cunning, deceitful; malicious, sly (of humour, etc.)

socarronería, *f.* cunning, craftiness; slyness (of humour, etc.); knavish action

socava, *f.* undermining; (*agr.*) hoeing round tree roots

socavar, *v.t.* to undermine

sociabilidad, *f.* sociability

sociable, *a.* sociable; social

social, *a.* social

socialdemócrata, *a.* and *m.* and *f.* (*pol.*) social-democrat

socialismo, *m.* socialism

socialista, *m.* and *f.* socialist. *a.* socialistic

socialización, *f.* socialization

socializar, *v.t.* to socialize

sociedad, *f.* society; association; (*com.*) partnership; (*com.*) company. (*com.*) **s. anónima,** joint stock company, limited company. **S. de las Naciones,** League of Nations. **s. de socorros mutuos,** mutual aid society. **s. en comandita,** private company

socio (**-ia**), *s.* associate, partner; member. **s. comanditario,** (*com.*) sleeping partner

sociología, *f.* sociology

sociológico, *a.* sociological

sociólogo (**-ga**), *s.* sociologist

socolor, *m.* pretext. *adv.* (also **so c.**) under pretext

socollada, *f.* (*naut.*) flapping (of sails); pitching (of ship)

socorredor (**-ra**), *a.* aiding, succouring. *s.* helper

socorrer, *v.t.* to aid, succour, assist; pay on account

socorrido, *a.* helpful, generous, prompt to assist; well-equipped or furnished; well-supplied

socorro, *m.* aid, help, assistance; payment on account; (*mil.*) relieving force; relief (provisions or arms)

socrático, *a.* socratic

sochantre, *m.* (*ecc.*) choir master

sódico, *a.* (*chem.*) sodic

sodio, *m.* sodium

sodomía, *f.* sodomy

sodomita, *m.* and *f.* sodomite. *a.* sodomitic

soez, *a.* base, vile; vulgar

sofá, *m.* sofa, couch

sofaldar, *v.t.* to tuck up the skirts; disclose, reveal

sofisma, *m.* sophism, fallacy

sofista, *a.* sophistical. *m.* sophist. *m.* and *f.* quibbler

sofistería, *f.* sophistry

sofístico, *a.* sophistic, fallacious

soflama, *f.* thin flame; glow; flush, blush; specious promise, deception

soflamar, *v.t.* to shame, put to the blush; promise with intent to deceive, swindle; *v.r.* (*cul.*) burn

sofocación, *f.* suffocation, smothering; shame; anger

sofocador, sofocante, *a.* suffocating; stifling

sofocar, *v.t.* to suffocate, smother; extinguish; dominate, oppress; pester, importune; shame, make blush, make angry; agitate; *v.r.* be ashamed; be angry

sofocleo, *a.* Sophoclean

sofoco, *m.* mortification, chagrin; shame; anger; suffocation, smothering; hot flush

sofreír, *v.t. irr.* (*cul.*) to fry lightly. See **reír**

sofrenada, *f.* sudden check, pulling up short (horses); harsh scolding; moral restraint

sofrenar, *v.t.* to pull up, check suddenly (horses); scold harshly; restrain, repress (emotions)

soga, *f.* rope; land measure (varies in length). *m.* (*fam.*) rogue, knave

soguería, *f.* rope making; rope walk; rope shop; ropes

soguero, *m.* rope maker or seller

soja, *f.* soya bean

sojuzgador (-ra), *a.* conquering, oppressive. *s.* conqueror, oppressor

sojuzgar, *v.t.* to conquer, oppress, subdue

sol, *m.* sun; sunlight; day; Peruvian coin; (*mus.*) G, fifth note of scale, soh. **de s. a s.,** from sunrise to sunset. **hacer s.,** to be sunny. (*fam.*) **morir uno sin s. sin luz y sin moscas,** to die abandoned by all. (*fam.*) **no dejar a s. ni a sombra,** to follow everywhere; pester constantly. **tomar el s.,** to bask in the sun; (*naut.*) take, shoot the sun

solado, *m.* paving; tile floor

solador, *m.* tiler

solamente, *adv.* only; exclusively; merely, solely. **s. que,** only that; nothing but

solana, *f.* sunny corner; sun room

solanera, *f.* sunburn; sun trap, sunny spot

solanina, *f.* (*chem.*) solanin

solapa, *f.* lapel; excuse, pretext. (*fam.*) **de s.,** secretly, on the quiet

solapado, *a.* cunning, sly

solapar, *v.t.* (*sew.*) to provide with lapels; (*sew.*) cause to overlap; dissemble; *v.i.* (*sew.*) overlap

solapo, *m.* lapel; (*fam.*) slap, buffet. **a s.,** (*fam.*) secretly, slyly

solar, *v.t. irr.* to pave; sole (shoes). *m.* family seat, manor house; building site; lineage, family. *a.* solar. See **colar**

solariego, *a.* memorial; of an old and noble family

solas, a, *adv.* alone, in private

solaz, *m.* consolation; pleasure; relief, relaxation. **a s.,** enjoyably, pleasantly

solazar, *v.t.* to solace, comfort; amuse, entertain; rest; *v.r.* be comforted; find pleasure (in)

soldada, *f.* salary, wage, emoluments; (*nav., mil.*) pay

soldadesca, *f.* soldiering, military profession; troops. **a la s.,** in a soldier-like way

soldadesco, *a.* military, soldier

soldado, *m.* soldier; defender, partisan. **s. raso,** (*mil.*) private

soldador, *m.* solderer, welder; soldering iron

soldadura, *f.* welding, soldering; correction, emendation

soldar, *v.t. irr.* to weld; mend by welding; correct, put right; (*mil.*) wipe out, liquidate. See **contar**

solecismo, *m.* solecism

soledad, *f.* solitude; loneliness; homesickness; *pl.* melancholy Andalusian song and dance (also *f. pl.* **soleares**)

solemne, *a.* solemn; magnificent; formal; serious, grave, important; pompous; (*fam.*) downright, complete

solemnidad, *f.* solemnity; magnificence; formality; gravity, seriousness; solemn ceremony; religious ceremony; legal formality

solemnización, *f.* solemnization

solemnizar, *v.t.* to solemnize, celebrate; extol

solenoide, *m.* (*elec.*) solenoid

soler, *v.i. irr. defective* to be in the habit, be used; happen frequently (e.g. **Solía hacerlo los sábados,** I generally did it on Saturdays. **Suele llover mucho aquí,** It rains a great deal here). See **moler**

solercia, *f.* shrewdness, ability, astuteness

solevantado, *a.* agitated; restless

solevantar, *v.t.* to raise, push up; incite to rebellion. **s. con gatos,** (*mech.*) to jack up

solfa, *f.* (*mus.*) sol-fa

solfear, *v.t.* (*mus.*) to sing in solfa; (*fam.*) buffet, spank; (*fam.*) scold

solfeo, *m.* (*mus.*) sol-fa; (*fam.*) drubbing, spanking

solicitación, *f.* request; application; solicitation; wooing; search (for a post); attraction, inducement

solicitador (**-ra**), *a.* soliciting. *s.* solicitor. *m.* agent; applicant

solicitante, *m. and f.* applicant, candidate

solicitar, *v.t.* to solicit; request; apply for; make love to, court; seek (posts, etc.); try to, attempt to; manage (business affairs); (*phys.*) attract; appeal to

solícito, *a.* solicitous; conscientious; careful

solicitud, *f.* diligence, conscientiousness; solicitude; request; application; appeal, entreaty; petition; (*com.*) demand. **a s.,** on request

solidaridad, *f.* solidarity

solidario, *a.* (*law*) jointly responsible or liable

solideo, *m.* (*ecc.*) calotte, small skull-cap

solidez, *f.* solidity; (*fig.*) force, weight (of arguments, etc.)

solidificación, *f.* solidification

solidificar(se), *v.t. and v.r.* to solidify; jelly

sólido, *a.* compact, solid; thick; fast or lasting (of colours); indisputable, convincing. *m.* (*geom., phys.*) solid; solidus (ancient coin)

soliloquiar, *v.i.* (*fam.*) to soliloquize, talk to oneself

soliloquio, *m.* soliloquy

solio, *m.* throne

solista, *m. and f.* (*mus.*) soloist

solitario (**-ia**), *a.* abandoned, deserted; solitary; secluded; solitude-loving. *s.* recluse. *m.* solitaire diamond; hermit; solitaire, patience. **hacer solitarios,** to play patience

sólito, *a.* accustomed, wonted; customary, habitual

soliviantar, *v.t.* to rouse, incite, excite

soliviar, *v.t.* to help to lift up; *v.r.* half get up, raise oneself

solo, *a.* sole, only; alone; lonely; deserted, forsaken. *m.* solo performance; (cards) solo; solitaire (game). **a solas,** alone; without help, unaided

sólo, *adv.* only; merely, solely; exclusively

solomillo, *m.* (*cul.*) sirloin; fillet (of meat)

solsticio, *m.* (*ast.*) solstice. **s. hiemal,** winter solstice. **s. vernal,** summer solstice

soltar, *v.t. irr.* to loosen; let go; disengage; untie; release; let drop; let out (a laugh, etc.); solve; (*fam.*) utter; turn on (taps); set free; *v.r.* work loose; grow skilful; (*with prep.* **a** + *infin.*) begin to do (something). See **contar**

soltera, *f.* spinster

soltería, *f.* bachelorhood; spinsterhood

soltero, *a.* unmarried, single. *m.* bachelor

solterón, *m.* confirmed bachelor

solterona, *f.* confirmed old maid

soltura, *f.* loosening; untying; freedom from restraint; ease, independence; impudence; immorality, viciousness; facility of speech; (*law*) release

solubilidad, *f.* solubility

soluble, *a.* soluble, dissolvable; solvable

solución, *f.* dissolution, loosening; (*math., chem.*) solution; answer, solution; payment, satisfaction; (*lit.*).climax; conclusion, end (of negotiations)

solucionar, *v.t.* to solve, find a solution for

solvencia, *f.* (*com.*) solvency

solventar, *v.t.* to pay or settle accounts; solve (problems, difficulties)

solvente, a. (com.) solvent

sollado, m. (naut.) orlop

sollastre, m. scullion; brazen rogue

sollozante, a. sobbing

sollozar, v.i. to sob

sollozo, m. sob

somático, a. somatic, corporeal

somatología, f. somatology

sombra, f. shadow; shade; darkness, dimness; spectre, phantom; defence, refuge, protection; resemblance, likeness; defect; (fam.) luck; gaiety, charm; trace, vestige; (art) shading, shadow. **sombras chinescas,** shadow show. **a la s.,** in the shade; (fam.) in gaol. **hacer s.,** to shade; (fig.) stand in the light, be an obstacle; protect. **ni por s.,** by no means; without warning. **no tener s. de,** to have not a trace of .... (fam.) **tener buena s.,** to be witty or amusing and agreeable. (fam.) **tener mala s.,** to bring bad luck, exert an evil influence upon; be dull and disagreeable

sombrear, v.t. to shadow, shade; (art) shade; v.i. begin to show (moustaches)

sombrerera, f. milliner; hatbox

sombrerería, f. hat shop or trade; hat factory

sombrerero, m. hatter; hat manufacturer

sombrerete, m. (mech.) bonnet, cap; cowl

sombrero, m. hat; (mech.) cap, cowl; sounding board; head (mushrooms, toadstools). **s. calañés,** Andalusian hat. **s. chambergo,** broad-brimmed plumed hat. **s. de canal,** or **s. de teja,** shovel-hat (worn by ecclesiastics). **s. de copa,** top-hat. **s. de jipijapa,** panama hat. **s. de tres picos,** three-cornered hat, cocked hat. **s. flexible,** soft felt hat. **s. hongo,** bowler hat

sombría, f. shady spot

sombrilla, f. sunshade

sombrío, a. dark; shadowy; overcast; (art) shaded; gloomy, melancholy

someramente, adv. superficially; briefly, summarily

somero, a. superficial, shallow; summary, rudimentary, brief

someter, v.t. to put down, defeat; submit, place before; subject; v.r. yield, surrender; (with prep. a) undergo

sometimiento, m. defeat; submission (to arbitration or plans, etc.); subjection

somnambulismo, m. somnambulism

somnámbulo (-la), a. somnambulistic. s. somnambulist

somnífero, a. soporiferous

somnílocuo, a. somniloquous, sleep-talking

somnolencia, f. somnolence

son, m. sound; rumour; reason, motive; means, way; guise, manner. **al s. de,** to the sound of; to the music of. **en s. de,** in the manner of, as, like, under pretext of

sonadera, f. nose blowing

sonado, a. famous; much admired or talked of. (fam.) **hacer una que sea sonada,** to cause a great scandal; do something noteworthy

sonaja, f. metal jingles on tambourine; baby's rattle

sonajero, m. baby's rattle

sonar, v.i. irr. to sound; be quoted or mentioned; ring; (fam.) be familiar, remember (e.g. **No me suena el nombre,** I don't remember the name); (with prep. a) be reminiscent of; v.t. sound; ring; play on; clink; v.r. be rumoured; be reported; blow one's nose. Pres. Ind. **sueno, suenas, suena, suenan.** Pres. Subjunc. **suene, suenes, suene, suenen**

sonata, f. (mus.) sonata

sonda, f. (naut.) taking of soundings, heaving the lead; sound, plummet, lead; (aer.) drag-rope; probe, sound

sondar, v.t. (naut.) to take soundings; probe; (fam.) sound, try to find out; bore, drill

sondeable, a. fathomable

sondeo, m. (naut.) sounding; (min.) drilling; probing

sonetear, sonetizar, v.i. to write sonnets

sonetista, m. and f. writer of sonnets

soneto, *m.* sonnet

sonido, *m.* sound; literal meaning; rumour, report

sonochar, *v.i.* to keep vigil in the early hours of the night

sonoridad, *f.* sonorousness

sonoro, *a.* sounding; resonant, loud; sonorous

sonreír(se), *v.i.* and *v.r. irr.* to smile; *v.i.* look pleasant (landscape, etc.); look favourable (circumstances). See **reír**

sonriente, *a.* smiling

sonrisa, *f.* smile

sonrojar, *v.t.* to cause to blush; *v.r.* blush

sonrojo, *m.* blush, flushing

sonrosado, *a.* rosy, rose-coloured, pink

sonrosar, *v.t.* to make rose-coloured; *v.r.* blush, flush

sonroseo, *m.* blush, flush

sonsaca, *f.* removal by stealth; pilfering; enticement; (*fig.*) pumping (persons)

sonsacar, *v.t.* to remove by stealth; steal, pilfer; entice away; (*fig.*) pump, draw out (persons)

sonsonete, *m.* rhythmic tapping or drumming; monotonous sound (gen. unpleasant); sarcastic tone of voice

soñador (-ra), *a.* dreamy, sleepy. *s.* dreamer

soñar, *v.t.* to dream; imagine, conjure up; (*with con*) dream of; (*with prep. a, of persons*) fear

soñoliento, *a.* sleepy, drowsy; soothing; slow, leisurely

sopa, *f.* sop, piece of bread; soup. **s. boba,** beggar's portion; life of ease at others' expense. **andar a la s.,** to beg one's way. (*fam.*) **hecho una s.,** wet through

sopalancar, *v.t.* to lever

sopanda, *f.* joist

sopapo, *m.* chuck under the chin; (*fam.*) slap; valve

sopera, *f.* soup-tureen

sopero, *m.* soup-plate. *a.* fond of soup

sopesar, *v.t.* to try the weight of

sopetón, *m.* blow, cuff. **de s.,** suddenly

soplada, *f.* puff of wind

soplado, *a.* (*fam.*) over-elegant; haughty, stiff. *m.* fissure, chasm

soplador (-ra), *a.* instigatory. *m.* blower, blowing-fan. *s.* instigator; blower

soplar, *v.i.* to blow; *v.t.* blow; blow away; inflate, blow up; filch, steal; instigate, inspire; accuse; fan; prompt, help out; *v.r.* (*fam.*) eat and drink too much; (*fam.*) be puffed up, grow haughty. *interj.* (*fam.*) ¡Sopla! You don't say so!

soplete, *m.* blow-pipe

soplo, *m.* blow; blowing; instant, trice; (*fam.*) hint, tip; (*fam.*) accusation; (*fam.*) tale-bearer; puff, breath (of wind)

soplón (-ona), *a.* (*fam.*) tale-bearing, back-biting. *s.* tale-bearer. *m.* (*aut.*) scavenger

soponcio, *m.* (*fam.*) fainting fit

sopor, *m.* stupor; deep sleep

soporífero, *a.* soporiferous

soportable, *a.* bearable

soportador (-ra), *a.* supporting. *s.* supporter

soportal, *m.* (*arch.*) portico

soportar, *v.t.* to bear; carry, support; put up with, tolerate

soporte, *m.* rest, support; (*mech.*) bearing; (*mech.*) bracket, support

sopuntar, *v.t.* to underline in dots

sor, *f.* (*ecc.*) sister (used of nuns)

sorbedor (-ra), *a.* supping, sipping. *s.* sipper

sorber, *v.t.* to suck; imbibe; swallow; (*fig.*) absorb eagerly (ideas); sip

sorbete, *m.* sherbet, iced drink; French ice-cream

sorbo, *m.* sucking; imbibition; swallow; sip; mouthful, gulp

sordamente, *adv.* secretly, quietly

sordera, *f.* deafness

sordidez, *f.* sordidness

sórdido, *a.* dirty, squalid; mean, niggardly; sordid

sordina, *f.* (*mus.*) sordine, mute; (*mus.*) damper. **a la s.,** on the quiet, in secret

sordo, *a.* deaf; silent, quiet; dull, muted (sounds); insensible, inanimate; obdurate, uncompliant. **a la sorda** *or* **a lo s.** *or* **a sordas,** in silence, quietly

sordomudez, *f.* deaf-mutism

sordomudo (-da), *a.* and *s.* deaf-and-dumb (person)

sorna, *f.* slowness, sluggishness; craftiness, guile, knavery; malice

sorprendente, *a.* surprising, amazing

sorprender, *v.t.* to surprise, amaze

sorpresa, *f.* surprise; amazement; shock

sortear, *v.t.* to raffle; draw lots for; avoid artfully (difficulties, etc.); fight (bulls)

sorteo, *m.* raffle; casting lots

sortero (-ra), *s.* sorcerer; holder of a draw ticket

sortija, *f.* ring (for finger); ring (for curtains, etc.); curl

sortilegio, *m.* sorcery, magic

sortílego (-ga), *a.* magic. *s.* sorcerer, fortune-teller

sosa, *f.* (*chem.*) soda ash. **s. cáustica,** caustic soda, soda

sosegado, *a.* tranquil, peaceful, calm

sosegador (-ra), *a.* soothing, calming. *s.* appeaser, soother

sosegar, *v.t.* *irr.* to soothe, quieten; reassure; appease, moderate; *v.i.* grow still; rest, sleep; *v.r.* grow quiet; calm down, be appeased; grow still. See **cegar**

sosería, *f.* insipidness; lack of wit, dullness; stupidity

sosia, *m.* double, exact likeness (of persons)

sosiego, *m.* calm; peace, tranquility

soslayar, *v.t.* to slant, place in an oblique position; (*fig.*) go round (a difficulty)

soslayo, *a.* slanting. **al s.,** obliquely, on the slant; askance

soso, *a.* saltless, insipid; dull, uninteresting; heavy (of people)

sospecha, *f.* suspicion

sospechar, *v.t.* and *v.i.* to suspect

sospechoso, *a.* suspicious. *m.* suspect

sostén, *m.* support; (*mech.*) stand, support; brassière, bust bodice; steadiness (of a ship)

sostenedor (-ra), *a.* supporting. *s.* supporter

sostener, *v.t.* *irr.* to support; defend, uphold; bear, tolerate; help, aid; maintain, support. See **tener**

sostenido, *a.* (*mus.*) sostenuto, sustained. *a.* and *m.* (*mus.*) sharp

sostenimiento, *m.* support; defence; toleration, endurance; maintenance, sustenance

sota, *f.* knave, jack (cards); (*fam.*) baggage, hussy. *m.* foreman, supervisor. *prep.* deputy, substitute (e.g. **sotamontero,** deputy huntsman)

sotabanco, *m.* attic, garret

sotana, *f.* gown, cassock, robe

sótano, *m.* basement, cellar

sotavento, *m.* (*naut.*) leeward. **a s.,** on the lee

sotechado, *m.* hut, shed

soterrar, *v.t.* *irr.* to bury in the ground; hide, conceal. See **acertar**

sotileza, *f.* fine cord for fishing (used in Santander province)

soto, *m.* thicket, grove, coppice

soviético, *a.* soviet

sovietismo, *m.* sovietism

sovietizar, *v.t.* to sovietize, russianize

sovoz, a, *adv.* in a low voice

su, sus, *poss. pron.,* *3rd pers.,* *m.* and *f., sing.* and *pl.* his, her, its, one's, your, their (e.g. **Sus libros están sobre la mesa,** Their (his, her, your) books are on the table)

suasorio, *a.* suasive, persuasive

suave, *a.* soft, smooth; sweet; pleasant, harmonious, quiet; slow, gentle; meek; delicate, subtle

suavidad, *f.* softness, smoothness; sweetness; pleasantness; quietness; gentleness; meekness; delicacy

suavizador, *a.* softening, smoothing; soothing, quietening. *m.* razor strop

suavizar, *v.t.* to soften; smooth; strop (a razor); moderate, temper; (*mech.*) steady; quieten; ease

subalcaide, *m.* subwarden (in prisons)

subalpino, *a.* sub-alpine

subalternar, *v.t.* to put down, subdue

subalterno, *a.* subordinate. *m.* subordinate; (*mil.*) subaltern

subarrendar, *v.t.* *irr.* to sublet. See **recomendar**

subarrendatario (-ia), *s.* sublessee

subarriendo, *m.* sublease, sublet

subasta, *f.* auction sale. **sacar a pública s.,** to sell by auction

subastar, *v.t.* to auction

subcentral, *f.* (*elec.*) sub-station

subclase, *f.* (*zool., bot.*) sub-class

subcolector, *m.* assistant collector

subcomendador, *m.* lieut.-commander (Spanish Military Orders)

subcomisión, *f.* sub-committee

subconsciencia, *f.* subconscious

subcutáneo, *a.* subcutaneous

subdelegación, *f.* sub-delegation

subdelegado (-da), *s.* sub-delegate

subdelegar, *v.t.* to sub-delegate

subdiácono, *m.* sub-deacon

subdirector (-ra), *s.* deputy or assistant director

súbdito (-ta), *a.* dependent, subject. *s.* subject (of a state)

subdividir, *v.t.* to subdivide

subdominante, *f.* (*mus.*) subdominant

subgénero, *m.* (*zool., bot.*) sub-genus

subgobernador, *m.* deputy or lieutenant-governor

subida, *f.* ascension, ascent; upgrade; rise; carrying up; rising (of the curtain in a theatre)

subidero, *m.* uphill road; mounting-block; way up (to a higher level)

subido, *a.* strong (scents); deep (colours); expensive, highly-priced; best, finest

subidor, *m.* porter, carrier; elevator

subintendente, *m.* deputy or assistant intendant

subir, *v.i.* to ascend, climb, go up; mount; rise; (*com.*) amount (to), reach; prosper, advance, be promoted; grow more acute (illnesses); intensify; (*mus.*) raise the pitch (of instrument or voice); *v.t.* ascend, climb; pick up, take up; raise up; place higher; build up, make taller; straighten up, place in a vertical position; increase, raise (price, value); *v.r.* ascend, climb. **s. a caballo,** to mount a horse. (*fam.*) **subirse a la cabeza,** to go to one's head (alcohol, etc.)

subitáneo, *a.* sudden

súbito, *a.* unexpected, unforeseen; sudden; precipitate, impulsive. *adv.* suddenly (also **de s.**)

subjefe, *m.* deputy chief, second-in-command

subjetividad, *f.* subjectivity

subjetivismo, *m.* subjectivism

subjetivo, *a.* subjective

subjuntivo, *a.* and *m.* (*gram.*) subjunctive

sublevación, *f.,* **sublevamiento,** *m.* rebellion, mutiny, rising

sublevar, *v.t.* to rouse to rebellion; excite (indignation, etc.); *v.r.* rebel

sublimación, *f.* sublimation

sublimado, *m.* (*chem.*) sublimate

sublimar, *v.t.* to exalt, raise up; (*chem.*) sublimate

sublime, *a.* sublime

sublimidad, *f.* sublimity, majesty, nobility

submarino, *a.* submarine. *m.* submarine. **s. de bolsillo** *or* **s. enano,** midget submarine

suboficial, *m.* (*mil.*) subaltern; (*nav.*) petty-officer

subordinación, *f.* dependence, subordination

subordinado (-da), *a.* and *s.* subordinate

subordinar, *v.t.* to subordinate

subpolar, *a.* subpolar

subprefecto, *m.* sub-prefect

subproducto, *m.* (*chem.*) by-product

subrayar, *v.t.* to underline; emphasize

subrepción, *f.* underhand dealing; (*law*) subreption

subrepticio, *a.* surreptitious; clandestine

subrogación, *f.* surrogation

subrogar, *v.t.* (*law*) to surrogate, elect as a substitute

subsanar, *v.t.* to make excuses for; remedy, put right; indemnify

subscribir, *v.t.* to sign; agree to; *v.r.* subscribe, contribute; take out a subscription (to periodicals, etc.). *Past Part.* **subscrito**

subscripción, *f.* subscription; agreement, accession

subscriptor (-ra), *s.* subscriber

subsección, *f.* subsection

subsecretaría, *f.* assistant secretaryship; assistant secretary's office

subsecretario (-ia), *s.* assistant secretary

subsecuente, *a.* subsequent

subsidiario, *a.* subsidized; subsidiary

subsidio, *m.* subsidy

subsiguiente, *a.* subsequent; next

subsistencia, *f.* permanence; stability; subsistence, maintenance; livelihood

subsistir, *v.i.* to last, endure; subsist, live; make a livelihood

substancia, *f.* substance, juice; extract, essence; (*fig.*) core, pith; (*fig.*) meat; wealth, estate; worth, importance; nutritive part; (*fam.*) common sense. (*anat.*) s. gris, grey matter. en s.; in short

substanciación, *f.* substantiation

substancial, *a.* substantial, real; important, essential; nutritive; solid

substanciar, *v.t.* to substantiate; summarize, extract, abridge

substancioso, *a.* substantial; nutritive

substantivo, *a.* and *m.* (*gram.*) substantive, noun

substitución, *f.* substitution

substituible, *a.* susceptible of substitution, replaceable

substituir, *v.t. irr.* to substitute. See **huir**

substitutivo, *a.* substitutive

substituto (-ta), *s.* substitute

substracción, *f.* subtraction

substraendo, *m.* (*math.*) subtrahend

substraer, *v.t. irr.* to remove, separate; rob, steal; (*math.*) subtract; *v.r.* depart, remove oneself; avoid. See **traer**

substrato, *m.* substratum

subsuelo, *m.* subsoil, substratum

subteniente, *m.* (*mil.*) second-lieutenant

subterfugio, *m.* subterfuge, trick

subterráneo, *a.* underground, subterranean. *m.* subterranean place

subtítulo, *m.* subtitle; (cinema) caption

subtropical, *a.* subtropical

suburbano (-na), *a.* suburban. *s.* suburbanite, dweller in a suburb

suburbio, *m.* suburb

subvención, *f.* subsidy, subvention, grant

subvencionar, *v.t.* to subsidize

subvenir, *v.t. irr.* to help, succour; subsidize. See **venir**

subversivo, *a.* subversive

subvertir, *v.t. irr.* to subvert, overturn, ruin. See **sentir**

subyugación, *f.* subjugation

subyugador (-ra), *a.* subjugating. *s.* conqueror

subyugar, *v.t.* to subjugate, overcome

succión, *f.* suction

sucedáneo, *m.* (*med.*) succedaneum

suceder, *v.i.* to follow, come after; inherit, succeed. *impers.* happen, occur

sucedido, *m.* (*fam.*) event, occurrence

sucesión, *f.* succession; series; offspring, descendants; (*law*) estate

sucesivo, *a.* successive. en lo s., in future

suceso, *m.* happening, occurrence; course (of time); outcome, result

sucesor (-ra), *a.* succeeding. *s.* successor

suciedad, *f.* dirt; filth, nastiness; obscenity

sucinto, *a.* succinct, brief, concise

sucio, *a.* dirty, unclean; stained; easily-soiled; (*fig.*) sullied, spotted; obscene; dirty (of colours); (*fig.*) tainted, infected. (*sport*) jugar s., to play in an unsporting manner

suco, *m.* juice

sucoso, *a.* juicy

suculencia, *f.* succulence; juiciness

suculento, *a.* succulent; juicy

sucumbir, *v.i.* to yield, give in; die, succumb; (*law*) lose a suit

sucursal, *a.* branch. *f.* (*com.*) branch (of firm)

sud, *m.* south (gen. **sur**). Used in combinations like **sudamericano**

sudadero, *m.* horse blanket; sudatory, sweating bath

sudafricano (-na), *a.* and *s.* South African

sudamericano (-na), *a.* and *s.* South American

sudanés (-esa), *a.* and *s.* Sudanese

sudante, *a.* sweating, perspiring

sudar, *v.i.* and *v.t.* to perspire, sweat; ooze; *v.i.* (*fam.*) toil; *v.t.* bathe in sweat; (*fam.*) give reluctantly. **s. la gota gorda,** (*fig., fam.*) to be in a stew

sudario, *m.* shroud

sudeste, *m.* south-east; south-east wind

sudexpreso, *m.* southern express

sudoeste, *m.* south-west; south-west wind

sudor, *m.* sweat, perspiration; toil; juice, moisture, sap, gum

sudorífico, *m.* (*med.*) sudorific

sudoroso, *a.* sweaty

sudsudeste, *m.* south-south-east

sudsudoeste, *m.* south-south-west

sueco (-ca), *a.* Swedish. *s.* Swede. *m.* Swedish (language)

suegra, *f.* mother-in-law

suegro, *m.* father-in-law

suela, *f.* sole (of a shoe); (*icht.*) sole; tanned leather; base. (*fam.*) **no llegarle a uno a la s. del zapato,** to be not fit to hold a candle to

sueldo, *m.* salary, wages; (*ant.*) Spanish coin. **s. por libra,** shilling in the £. **a s.,** for a salary, salaried

suelo, *m.* ground, earth; soil; bottom, base; sediment, dregs; site, plot; floor; flooring; storey; land, territory; hoof (horses); earth, world; *pl.* chaff of grain. **s. natal,** native land; (*fam.*) **besar el s.,** to fall flat. **dar consigo en el s.,** to fall down. **dar en el s. con,** to throw down; damage, spoil. (*fam.*) **estar (una cosa) por los suelos,** to be dirt cheap

suelta, *f.* loosening, unfastening; hobble (for horses); relay of oxen. **dar s. a,** to let loose, allow to go out for a time

suelto, *a.* swift; competent, efficient; odd, separate; licentious; flowing, easy (style); loose, unbound. *m.* single copy (of a newspaper); loose change; newspaper paragraph

sueño, *m.* dream; sleep; drowsiness, desire for sleep; vision, fancy. **s. pesado,** deep sleep. **conciliar el s.,** to court sleep. (*fam.*) **echar un s.,** to take a nap. **en sueños,** in a dream; while asleep. **entre sueños,** between sleeping and waking. (*fam.*) **¡Ni por sueño!** Certainly not! I wouldn't dream of it!

suero, *m.* serum. **s. de la leche,** whey

suerte, *f.* chance, luck; good luck; destiny, fate; condition, state; kind, species, sort; way, manner; bullfighter's manœuvre; parcel of ground. **de s. que,** so that; as a result. **echar suertes,** to draw lots. **tener buena s.,** to be lucky. **tocarle (a uno) la s.,** to draw, fall to one's lot (lottery, raffle)

sueste, *m.* south-east; sou'wester (cap)

suevo (-va), *a.* and *s.* Swabian

suficiencia, *f.* sufficiency; talent, aptitude; pedantry. **a s.,** enough

suficiente, *a.* sufficient, enough; suitable

sufijo, *m.* suffix

sufismo, *m.* Sufism

sufragáneo, *a.* and *m.* (*ecc.*) suffragan

sufragar, *v.t.* to assist, aid; favour; pay, defray

sufragio, *m.* aid, assistance; (*ecc.*) suffragium, pious offering; vote; suffrage

sufragista, *f.* suffragette

sufrible, *a.* bearable, endurable

sufrido, *a.* long-suffering, resigned; complaisant (husbands); dirt-resisting (colours)

sufrimiento, *m.* suffering, pain; affliction; tolerance

sufrir, *v.t.* to suffer, undergo, experience; bear, endure; tolerate, put up with; allow, permit; resist, oppose; expiate; *v.i.* suffer

sugerir, *v.t. irr.* to suggest. See sentir

sugestión, *f.* suggestion

sugestionable, *a.* easily influenced, open to suggestion

sugestionador, *a.* suggestive

sugestionar, *v.t.* to suggest hypnotically; dominate, influence

sugestivo, *a.* suggestive, stimulating

suicida, *a.* suicidal, fatal. *m.* and *f.* suicide (person)

suicidarse, *v.r.* to commit suicide

suicidio, *m.* suicide

suiza, *f.* shindy, scrap

suizo (-za), *a.* and *s.* Swiss
sujeción, *f.* subjection, domination; fastening, fixture; obedience, conformity
sujetador, *m.* clamp; clip
sujetar, *v.t.* to fasten, fix; hold down; grasp, clutch; subdue; *v.r.* (*with prep. a*) conform to, obey. **s. con alfileres,** to pin up. **s. con tornillos,** to screw down
sujeto, *a.* liable, subject. *m.* topic, subject; person, individual; (*gram., phil.*) subject
sulfanilamida, *f.* (*med.*) sulphanilamide
sulfatar, *v.t.* to sulphate
sulfato, *m.* sulphate
sulfito, *m.* (*chem.*) sulphite
sulfonal, *m.* (*chem.*) sulphonal
sulfurar, *v.t.* to sulphurate; *v.r.* grow irritated, become angry
sulfúrico, *a.* (*chem.*) sulphuric
sulfuro, *m.* (*chem.*) sulphide
sulfuroso, *a.* sulphurous
sultán, *m.* sultan
sultana, *f.* sultana
sultanía, *f.* sultanate
suma, *f.* total; amount, sum; (*math.*) addition; summary, digest; computation. **en s.,** in brief, in short, finally
sumador (-ra), *s.* summarizer; computator, adder
sumamente, *adv.* extremely, most
sumar, *v.t.* to sum up, summarize; (*math.*) add up
sumaria, *f.* (*law*) written indictment
sumariamente, *adv.* concisely, in brief; (*law*) summarily
sumario, *a.* brief, concise, abridged; (*law*) summary. *m.* summary, résumé, digest
sumergible, *a.* sinkable; submergible. *m.* submarine
sumergir, *v.t.* to dip, immerse; sink, submerge; (*fig.*) overwhelm (grief, etc.); *v.r.* sink; dive; be submerged
sumersión, *f.* immersion, dive, submersion
sumidero, *m.* cesspool; drain; sink; pit, gully
sumiller, *m.* head of various departments in royal household. **s. de cortina,** royal chaplain
suministración, *f.* See **suministro**

suministrador (-ra), *s.* purveyor
suministrar, *v.t.* to purvey, supply, provide
suministro, *m.* purveyance; provision; supply
sumir, *v.t.* to sink; submerge; (*ecc.*) consummate; (*fig.*) overwhelm (grief, etc.); *v.r.* fall in, become sunken (cheeks, etc.); sink; be submerged
sumisión, *f.* submission, obedience; (*com.*) estimate, tender
sumiso, *a.* submissive, docile
sumista, *m.* and *f.* quick reckoner, computator. *m.* condenser, summarizer, abridger
sumo, *a.* supreme; high; tremendous, extraordinary. **a lo s.,** at the most; even if, although. **en s. grado,** in the highest degree
suntuosidad, *f.* magnificence, luxury
suntuoso, *a.* magnificent, luxurious, sumptuous
supeditación, *f.* subjection
supeditar, *v.t.* to oppress; overcome, conquer; subordinate
superabundancia, *f.* superabundance, excess; glut
superabundante, *a.* superabundant, excessive
superádito, *a.* superadded
superar, *v.t.* to overcome, conquer; surpass; do better than
superávit, *m.* (*com.*) balance, surplus
superconsciencia, *f.* (*psy.*) higher consciousness
superchería, *f.* trickery, guile
superchero, *a.* guileful, wily
superdominante, *f.* (*mus.*) superdominant
supereminencia, *f.* supereminence, greatest eminence
supereminente, *a.* supereminent
superentender, *v.t. irr.* to supervise, superintend. See **entender**
supererogación, *f.* supererogation
superestructura, *f.* superstructure
superficial, *a.* surface, shallow; superficial, rudimentary; futile
superficialidad, *f.* superficiality; futility; shallowness
superficie, *f.* area; surface; outside, exterior. **s. de rodadura,** tread (of a tyre)

superfino, *a.* superfine

superfluidad, *f.* superfluity

superfluo, *a.* superfluous, redundant

superfortaleza volante, *f.* *(aer.)* superfortress

superhombre, *m.* superman

superintendencia, *f.* supervision; superintendentship; higher administration

superintendente, *m.* and *f.* superintendent; supervisor

superior, *a.* higher, upper; excellent, fine; superior; higher (education, etc.). *m.* head, director; superior

superiora, *f.* *(ecc.)* Mother Superior

superioridad, *f.* superiority

superlativo, *a.* and *m.* superlative

superno, *a.* supreme

supernumerario (-ia), *a.* and *s.* supernumerary

superposición, *f.* superposition

superproducción, *f.* super production (cinema)

superrealismo, *m.* surrealism

superrealista, *a.* surrealist

superstición, *f.* superstition

supersticioso, *a.* superstitious

supervención, *f.* *(law)* supervention

supervivencia, *f.* survival

superviviente, *a.* surviving. *m.* and *f.* survivor

supino, *a.* supine; foolish, stupid. *m.* *(gram.)* supine

suplantación, *f.* supplanting

suplantador (-ra), *a.* supplanting. *s.* supplanter

suplantar, *v.t.* to forge, alter (documents); supplant

suplefaltas, *m.* and *f.* *(fam.)* scapegoat

suplementario, *a.* supplementary, additional

suplemento, *m.* s u p p l e m e n t; supply, supplying; newspaper supplement; *(geom.)* supplement

suplente, *m.* substitute, proxy; *(fig.)* makeweight

súplica, *f.* supplication, prayer; request

suplicación, *f.* entreaty, supplication; *(law)* petition

suplicante, *a.* supplicatory; *(law)* petitioning. *m.* and *f.* supplicator; *(law)* petitioner

suplicar, *v.t.* to beg, supplicate; request; *(law)* appeal

suplicio, *m.* torment, torture; execution; place of torture or execution; affliction, anguish. **último s.,** capital punishment

suplir, *v.t.* to supply, furnish; substitute, take the place of; overlook, forgive

suponer, *v.t.* *irr.* to suppose, take for granted; simulate; comprise, include; *v.i.* carry weight, wield authority. See **poner**

suposición, *f.* supposition; conjecture, assumption; distinction, talent, importance; falsity, falsehood

supositorio, *m.* *(med.)* suppository

suprasensible, *a.* supersensible

supremacía, *f.* supremacy

supremo, *a.* supreme; matchless, incomparable; last

supresión, *f.* suppression; destruction, eradication; omission

suprimir, *v.t.* to suppress; destroy, eradicate; omit, leave out

suprior, *m.* *(ecc.)* sub-prior

supriora, *f.* sub-prioress

supuesto, *a.* supposed; so-called; reputed. *m.* supposition, hypothesis. **por s.,** presumably; doubtless

supuración, *f.* suppuration

supurar, *v.i.* to suppurate

suputar, *v.t.* to calculate, compute

sur, *m.* south; south wind

surcador, *m.* ploughman

surcar, *v.t.* to plough furrows; furrow, line; cut, cleave (water, etc.)

surco, *m.* furrow; wrinkle, line; groove, channel; rut

surgidero, *m.* *(naut.)* road, roadstead

surgir, *v.i.* to spout, gush, spurt; *(naut.)* anchor; appear, show itself; come forth, turn up

surrealismo, *m.* surrealism

surrealista, *a.* and *m.* and *f.* surrealist

surtida, *f.* hidden exit; false door; *(naut.)* slipway

surtidero, *m.* outlet, drain; jet, fountain

surtido, *a.* mixed, assorted. *m.* variety, assortment; stock, range. **de s.,** in everyday use

surtidor (-ra), *s.* purveyor, supplier. *m.* fountain, jet. **s. de gasolina,** petrol pump

surtimiento, *m.* assortment; stock

surtir, *v.t.* to provide, supply, furnish; *v.i.* spurt, gush

surto, *a.* calm, reposeful; *(naut.)* anchored

¡sus! *interj.* Come on! Hurry up!

susceptibilidad, *f.* susceptibility

susceptible, *a.* susceptible, open to; touchy, over-sensitive

suscitar, *v.t.* to cause, originate; provoke, incite; *v.r.* arise, take place

susodicho, *a.* aforesaid

suspender, *v.t.* to suspend, hang up; postpone, defer, stop; amaze, dumbfound; suspend (from employment); fail (in an examination); adjourn (meetings); *v.r.* rear (horses)

suspensión, *f.* suspension; postponement, stoppage, deferment; amazement; failure (in an examination); adjournment (of a meeting); springs (of a car). *(com.)* **s. de pagos,** suspension of payments. **con mala s.,** badly sprung (of a car)

suspensivo, *a.* suspensive

suspensivos, *m. pl. (gram.)* suspension points

suspenso, *a.* amazed, bewildered. *m.* failure slip (in an examination). **en s.,** in suspense

suspensorio, *a.* suspensory

suspicacia, *f.* suspiciousness; mistrust, uneasiness

suspicaz, *a.* suspicious, mistrustful

suspirado, *a.* eagerly desired, longed for

suspirar, *v.t.* and *v.i.* to sigh. **s por,** to long for

suspiro, *m.* sigh; breath; glass whistle; *(mus.)* brief pause or pause sign. *(fam.)* **último s.,** last kick, end

suspirón, *a.* given to sighing

sustancia, *f.* See **substancia**

sustentable, *a.* arguable, defensible

sustentación, *f.* maintenance; defence

sustentar, *v.t.* to sustain, keep; support, bear; nourish, feed; uphold, advocate

sustento, *m.* maintenance, preservation; nourishment, sustenance; support

sustitución, *f.* See **substitución**

sustituible, *a.* substitutive

susto, *m.* fright, shock; apprehension. **dar un s.** (a), to scare

susurrador (-ra), *a.* whispering; murmuring; rustling. *s.* whisperer

susurrante, *a.* whispering; murmuring; rustling

susurrar, *v.i.* to whisper; murmur; rustle; babble, purl, prattle (water); *v.i.* and *v.r.* be whispered abroad

susurro, *m.* whispering, whisper; murmur; rustle; lapping

sutil, *a.* fine, thin; penetrating, subtle, keen

sutileza, sutilidad, *f.* fineness, thinness; subtlety, penetration. **sutileza de manos,** dexterity; light fingeredness; sleight of hand

sutilizar, *v.t.* to make thin, refine; *(fig.)* finish, perfect; *(fig.)* split hairs, make subtle distinctions

sutura, *f. (bot., surg., anat.)* suture

suyo, suya, *m.* and *f., pl.* **suyos, suyas,** *poss. pron.* and *a., 3rd pers.* his; hers; its; yours; theirs; of his, of hers, etc. (e.g. **Este libro es suyo,** This book is his (yours, theirs). **Este libro es uno de los suyos,** This book is one of his). (suyo is often used with def. art. **el, la,** etc.) **los suyos,** his (yours, etc.) family, following, adherents, etc. **de suya,** of its very nature, of itself; spontaneously. **salirse con la suya,** to get one's own way. *(fam.)* **ver uno la suya,** to see one's opportunity

svástica, *f.* swastika

T

tabacal, *m.* tobacco plantation

tabacalero (-ra), *a.* tobacco. *s.* tobacco merchant; tobacco planter

tabaco, *m.* tobacco plant or leaf; tobacco; cigar. **t. de pipa,** pipe

TAB 443 TAC

tobacco. **t. flojo,** mild tobacco.
t. rubio, Virginian tobacco

tabalear(se), *v.t.* and *v.r.* to rock, sway, swing; *v.i.* drum with the fingers

tabaleo, *m.* swaying, rocking; drumming with the fingers

tabanco, *m.* market stall

tábano, *m.* (*ent.*) horse-fly

tabanque, *m.* potter's wheel

tabaque, *m.* small osier basket (for fruit, sewing, etc.); large tack

tabaquera, *f.* tobacco jar or tin; bowl of tobacco-pipe; tobacco-pouch; snuff-box

tabaquería, *f.* tobacconist's shop

tabaquero (-ra), *s.* worker in a tobacco factory; tobacconist

tabaquismo, *m.* nicotinism

tabaquista, *m.* and *f.* tobacco expert; heavy smoker

tabardillo, *m.* fever. **t. de tripas,** typhoid. **t. pintado,** typhus

tabardo, *m.* tabard

taberna, *f.* public-house, tavern

tabernáculo, *m.* tabernacle

tabernario, *a.* public-house, tavern; low, vulgar

tabernera, *f.* publican's wife; bar-maid

tabernero, *m.* publican; barman, drawer

tabicar, *v.t.* to wall or board up; hide, cover up

tabique, *m.* partition wall, inside wall; thin wall

tabla, *f.* plank of wood, board; (*met.*) plate; slab; flat side, face (of wood); (*sew.*) box-pleat; table (of contents, etc.); (*art*) panel; vegetable plot; butcher's slab; butcher's stall; *pl.* tablets (for writing); (*math.,* etc.) tables; stalemate (chess, draughts); draw (in an election); (*theat.*) boards, stage. **t. de armonía,** sounding-board (of musical instruments). **t. de lavar,** washing-board. **t. de materias,** table of contents. **t. de multiplicación,** multiplication table. **t. rasa,** clean sheet (of paper, etc.); complete ignorance. **T. Redonda,** Round Table (of King Arthur). **escapar** *or* **salvarse en una t.,** to have a narrow escape, escape in the nick of time

tablacho, *m.* sluice-gate. (*fam.*) **echar el t.,** to interrupt the flow of someone's remarks

tablado, *m.* flooring; platform; (*theat.*) stage; gibbet; scaffold. **sacar al t.,** to produce, put on the stage; to make known, publish abroad

tablazón, *f.* planks, boards; flooring; (*naut.*) deck planks or sheathing

tablear, *v.t.* to saw into planks; (*sew.*) make box-pleats in; hammer iron into sheets

tablero, *m.* board (of wood); panelling; boarding; slab; shop counter; board (draughts, chess). **t. de instrumentos,** dashboard; instrument board

tableta, *f. dim.* tablet; pastille, lozenge

tablilla, *f. dim.* small board; tablet; notice board

tablón, *m.* thick plank; wooden beam; (*fam.*) drinking bout

tabú, *m.* taboo

tabuco, *m.* miserable little room; hovel

taburete, *m.* stool; taboret

tacada, *f.* stroke (at billiards)

tacañería, *f.* miserliness, niggardliness; craftiness

tacaño, *a.* miserly, niggardly; crafty

tácito, *a.* silent, unexpressed; tacit, implied

taciturnidad, *f.* taciturnity; reserve; melancholy

taciturno, *a.* taciturn; reserved; dismal, gloomy, melancholy

taco, *m.* stopper, plug; billiard cue; rammer; wad, wadding (in a gun); pop-gun; tear-off calendar; (*fam.*) snack; obscenity, oath. **t. de papel,** writing-tablet

tacón, *m.* heel of a shoe

taconazo, *m.* stamp with the heel

taconear, *v.i.* to stamp with the heels; walk heavily on the heels; walk arrogantly

taconeo, *m.* drumming or stamping of the heels (gen. in dancing)

táctica, *f.* method, technique; (*mil.*) tactics; policy, way, means

táctico, *a.* tactical. *m.* (*mil.*) tactician

táctil, *a.* tactile

tacto, *m.* sense of touch; touch, feel; touching; skill; tact

tacha, *f.* imperfection, defect; spot, stain; fault; large tack. **poner t.,** to criticize, object to

tachable, *a.* censurable, blameworthy

tachar, *v.t.* to criticize, blame; cross out, erase; charge, accuse

tachón, *m.* round-headed ornamental nail; *(sew.)* gold or silver studs, trimming; crossing out, erasure

tachonar, *v.t.* to stud with round-headed nails; *(sew.)* trim with gold or silver studs or trimming

tachoso, *a.* imperfect, defective, faulty; spotted, stained

tachuela, *f.* *(carp.)* tack

tafetán, *m.* taffeta; *pl.* flags, standards. **t. de heridas** *or* **t. inglés,** court-plaster

tafilete, *m.* morocco leather

tahalí, *m.* sword shoulder-belt

tahona, *f.* horse-mill; bakery; baker's shop

tahonero (-ra), *s.* miller; baker

tahur, *m.* gambler; card-sharper

tahurería, *f.* gambling-den; gambling; cheating at cards

taimado, *a.* knavish, crafty; obstinate, headstrong

taimería, *f.* cunning, craftiness

taita, *m.* daddy

taja, *f.* cut, cutting; slice; washing-board

tajada, *f.* slice; strip, portion; steak, fillet; *(fam.)* cough; drinking bout; hoarseness

tajadera, *f.* cheese-knife; chisel; *pl.* sluice-gate

tajado, *a.* steep, sheer (of cliffs, etc.)

tajadura, *f.* cutting, dividing, dissection

tajamar, *m.* cutwater; break-water; raft

tajar, *v.t.* to cut, chop; sharpen, trim (quill pens)

tajea, *f.* culvert; aqueduct; drain; watercourse

tajo, *m.* cut, incision; task; cutting (in mountain, etc.); cut, thrust (of sword); executioner's block; chopping-board; washing-board; steep cliff, precipice

tajón, *m.* butcher's block; chopping-board

tal, *a.* *pl.* **tales,** such; said (e.g. **el t. Don Juan,** the said Don Juan). **tal** is always used before

nouns and (except meaning "the said") without def. art. **un t.,** a certain (e.g. **un t. hombre,** a certain man). *pron.* some, some people; someone; such a thing. *adv.* so, thus. **t. para cual,** two of a kind, a well-matched pair; tit for tat. **con t. que,** *conjunc.* on condition that, provided that. **No hay t.,** There isn't such a thing. *(fam.)* **¿Qué t.?** How are you? What's the news?

tala, *f.* felling or cutting down (of trees); cropping of grass (ruminants)

talabarte, *m.* sword-belt

talabartería, *f.* saddlery

talabartero, *m.* saddler

talador (-ra), *a.* felling, cutting; destructive. *s.* feller, cutter; destroyer

taladrar, *v.t.* to drill, bore, gouge holes; pierce, perforate; clip (a ticket); assail or hurt the ear (sounds); *(fig.)* go into deeply (a subject)

taladro, *m.* drill, gimlet, gouge; drill hole, bore; punch (for tickets, etc.)

tálamo, *m.* marriage bed; *(bot., anat.)* thalamus

talán, *m.* peal, or tolling, of a bell

talanquera, *f.* barricade; parapet, fence, wall; refuge, asylum; safety, security

talante, *m.* mode of execution, technique; personal appearance, mien; disposition, temperament; wish, desire; aspect, appearance. **de buen (mal) t.,** willingly (unwillingly)

talar, *a.* full-length, long (of robes, etc.)

talar, *v.t.* to fell, chop down (trees); ravage, lay waste; prune (gen. olive tree)

talares, *m.* *pl.* talaria, wings on Mercury's heels

talaverano (-na), *a.* and *s.* of or from Talavera (Spain)

talco, *m.* *(min.)* talc; sequin, tinsel

talcualillo, *a.* *(fam.)* not too bad, fairly good; slightly better (of health)

taled, *m.* tallith

talega, *f.* sack, bag; sackful; money-bag; *pl.* *(fam.)* cash wealth

talego, *m.* narrow sack; (*fam.*) dumpy person

talento, *m.* talent (Greek coin); talent, gift, quality; intelligence, understanding; cleverness

talentoso, *a.* talented

tálero, *m.* thaler (old German coin)

talio, *m.* (*min.*) thallium

talión, *m.* (ley de) law of retaliation

talismán, *m.* talisman

talmúdico, *a.* Talmudic

talón, *m.* heel; heel of a shoe; (*com.*) counterfoil; luggage receipt; (*com.*) sight-draft; coupon; heel (of violin bow). (*fam.*) **apretar los talones,** to take to one's heels. (*fam.*) **pisarle (a uno) los talones,** to follow on a person's heels; rival successfully

talonada, *f.* dig with the spurs

talonario, *m.* stub-book

talla, *f.* carving (especially wood); cutting (of gems); reward for apprehension of a criminal; ransom; stature, height, size; height measuring rod

tallado, *a.* **bien** (or **mal**), well (or badly) carved; well (or badly) proportioned, of a good (or bad) figure

tallado, *m.* carving

tallador, *m.* metal engraver; die-sinker

tallar, *v.t.* (*art*) to carve; engrave; cut (gems); value, estimate; measure height (of persons)

tallarín, *m.* (gen. *pl.*) (*cul.*) noodle

talle, *m.* figure, physique; waist; fit (of clothes); appearance, aspect. (*fam.*) **largo de t.,** long-waisted; long drawn out, overlong. **tener buen t.,** to have a good figure

tallecer, *v.i.* *irr.* (*bot.*) to sprout, shoot. See **conocer**

taller, *m.* workshop; factory; mill; work-room, atelier; industrial school; school of arts and crafts; studio

tallista, *m.* and *f.* engraver; wood carver; sculptor

tallo, *m.* (*bot.*) stalk; shoot; slice of preserved fruit; cabbage. **t. rastrero,** (*bot.*) runner

talludo, *a.* long-stalked; lanky, overgrown; no longer young, ageing (women); habit-ridden

tamaño, *a. comp.* so big; so small (e.g. **La conocí tamaña,** I knew her when she was so high) (indicating her size with a gesture); so great, so large (e.g. **tamaña empresa,** so great an undertaking). *m.* size

tamarindo, *m.* (*bot.*) tamarind

tamarisco, *m.* (*bot.*) tamarisk

tambaleante, *a.* tottering, rickety; staggering

tambalear(se), *v.i.* and *v.r.* to totter, sway, shake; reel, stagger

tambaleo, *m.* swaying; tottering; rocking; shaking; staggering, reeling

tambarillo, *m.* chest with an arched lid

también, *adv.* also, too; in addition, as well

tambor, *m.* (*mus.*) drum; drummer; embroidery frame; (*mech.*) drum, cylinder; roaster (for coffee, chestnuts, etc.). **t. mayor,** drum-major. **a t.** (or **con t.**) **batiente,** with drums beating; triumphantly, with colours flying

tamborear, *v.i.* to totter, sway; stagger, reel

tamboreo, *m.* tottering, swaying; staggering, reeling

tamboril, *m.* (*mus.*) tabor

tamborilada, *f.* (*fam.*) slap on the back or face; (*fam.*) fall on the bottom

tamborilear, *v.i.* to play the tabor; *v.t.* eulogize, extol

tamborilero, *m.* tabor player

tamborín, *m.* tabor

tamiz, *m.* sieve

tamizar, *v.t.* to sieve

tamo, *m.* fluff; chaff

tampoco, *adv.* neither, not . . . either, nor . . . either; no more. **No lo ha hecho María t.,** Mary hasn't done it either

tampón, *m.* stamp moistener; (*surg.*) tampon

tan, *adv. abb. tanto,* so, as. Used before adjectives and adverbs, excepting **más, mejor, menos, peor** which need **tanto. t. . . . como,** as . . . as. **t. siquiera,** even (see **siquiera**). **t. sólo,** only, solely (e.g. **No vengo t. sólo para saludarte,** I do not come merely to greet you). **qué ... t.,** what a ... (e.g. ¡**Qué día t.hermoso!** What a lovely day!)

tanaceto, *m.* (*bot.*) tansy

tanda, *f.* turn; opportunity; task; shift, relay; game (of billiards); bad habit; collection, batch, group; round (of a game); (*dance*) set

tándem, *m.* tandem

tandeo, *m.* allowance of irrigation water, turn for using water

tangente, *a.* and *f.* (*geom.*) tangent

tangerino (-na), *a.* and *s.* of or from Tangier, Tangerine

tánico, *a.* (*chem.*) tannic

tanino, *m.* (*chem.*) tannin

tanque, *m.* (*mil.*) tank; cistern, tank, reservoir; ladle, dipper

tanteador, *m.* (*sport*) scorer, marker; scoreboard

tantear, *v.t.* to measure, compare; consider fully; test, try out; (*fig.*) probe, pump (persons); estimate roughly; (*art*) sketch, block in; *v.t.* and *v.i.* (*sport*) keep the score of

tanteo, *m.* measurement, comparison; test; rough estimate; (*sport*) score

tanto, *a.* so much; as much; very great; as great; *pl.* **tantos,** so many; as many (e.g. **Tienen tantas flores como nosotros,** They have as many flowers as we). In comparisons **tanto** is used before **más, mejor, menos, peor,** but generally **tan** is used before adjectives and adverbs (e.g. ¡**Tanto peor!** So much the worse!). *pron. dem.* that (e.g. **por lo t.,** therefore, on that account); *m.* so much, certain amount; copy of a document; counter (in games); point (score in games); (*com.*) rate (e.g. **el t. por ciento,** the percentage, the rate per cent.); *pl.* approximation, odd (e.g. **Llegaron cien hombres y tantos,** A hundred-odd men arrived). *adv.* so much; as much; so, in such a way. **t. ... como,** the same as, as much as. **t. ... cuanto,** as much as. **t. más,** the more. **t. menos,** the less (e.g. **Cuanto más (menos) dinero tiene t. más (menos) quiere,** The more

(less) money he has, the more (less) he wants). **t. más (menos) ... cuanto que,** all the more (less) ... because. **algún t.,** a certain amount, somewhat. **al t. de (una cosa),** aware of, acquainted with (a thing). **en t. or entre t.,** meanwhile. (*fam.*) **las tantas,** late hour, small hours. (*fam.*) **No es para t.,** It's not as bad as that; there's no need to make such a fuss; he (she, it) isn't equal to it. **otro t.,** the same, as much; as much more. **por lo t.,** therefore, so. **un t.,** a bit, somewhat

tañedor (-ra), *s.* (*mus.*) player

tañer, *v.t. irr.* (*mus.*) to play; *v.i.* sway, swing. **t. la occisa,** to sound the death (hunting). *Pres. Part.* **tañendo.** *Preterite* **tañó, tañeron.** *Imperf. Subjunc.* **tañese,** etc.

tañido, *m.* tune, sound, note; toll, peal; ring

taoísmo, *m.* Taoism

taoísta, *m.* and *f.* Taoist

tapa, *f.* lid; cover; cover (of books)

tapaboca, *m.* blow on the mouth; *f.* muffler, scarf; (*fam.*) remark which silences

tapada, *f.* veiled lady, one whose face is hidden

tapadera, *f.* loose lid, top, cover

tapadero, *m.* stopper

tapador (-ra), *a.* covering. *s.* coverer. *m.* stopper; lid; cover

tapagujeros, *m.* (*fam.*) unskilled mason or bricklayer; (*fig., fam.*) stopgap (person)

tapar, *v.t.* to cover; cover with a lid; muffle up, veil; hide, keep secret; close up, stop up

taparrabo, *m.* loin-cloth; swimming-trunks

tapete, *m.* rug; table cover. (*fam.*) **t. verde,** gaming-table. (*fig.*) **estar sobre el t.,** to be on the carpet, be under consideration

tapia, *f.* adobe; mud wall; fence. (*fam.*) **más sordo que una t.,** as deaf as a post

tapiar, *v.t.* to wall up; put a fence round

tapicería, *f.* set of tapestries; tapestry work; art of tapestry making; upholstery; tapestry storehouse or shop

tapicero, *m.* tapestry weaver or maker; upholsterer; carpet layer; furnisher

tapioca, *f.* tapioca

tapir, *m.* (*zóol.*) tapir

tapiz, *m.* tapestry; carpet

tapizar, *v.t.* to cover with tapestry; cover, clothe; upholster; carpet; hang with tapestry; furnish with hangings or drapery

tapón, *m.* stopper; cork (of a bottle); plug; (*surg.*) tampon

taponar, *v.t.* to stopper, cork; plug; (*surg.*) tampon; (*mil.*) seal off

taponazo, *m.* pop of a cork

tapujarse, *v.r.* to wrap oneself up, muffle oneself

tapujo, *m.* muffler, scarf, face covering; disguise; (*fam.*) pretence, subterfuge

taquera, *f.* rack for billiard cues

taquigrafía, *f.* shorthand

taquigrafiar, *v.t.* to write in shorthand

taquigráfico, *a.* shorthand

taquígrafo (-fa), *s.* shorthand writer, stenographer

taquilla, *f.* booking office; box office; grill, window (in banks, etc.); roll-top desk, cupboard for papers; (*theat.*) takings, cash

taquillero (-ra), *s.* booking-office clerk

taquimetría, *f.* tachymetry

taquímetro, *m.* tachymeter

tara, *f.* tally stick; (*com.*) tare

taracea, *f.* inlaid work, marquetry

taracear, *v.t.* to inlay

tarambana, *m.* and *f.* (*fam.*) madcap

tarantela, *f.* tarantella

tarántula, *f.* tarantula

tararear, *v.t.* to hum a tune

tarareo, *m.* humming, singing under one's breath

tarasca, *f.* figure of a dragon carried in Corpus Christi processions; (*fam.*) hag; trollop

tarascada, *f.* bite, nip; (*fam.*) insolent reply

tarascar, *v.t.* to bite; wound with the teeth

tardanza, *f.* delay, tardiness; slowness

tardar, *v.i.* to delay; be tardy, arrive late; take a long time. **a más t.,** at the latest

tarde, *f.* afternoon. *adv.* late. **¡Buenas tardes!** Good afternoon! **de t. en t.,** from time to time, sometimes. **hacerse t.,** to grow late. **Más vale t. que nunca,** Better late than never

tardecer, *v.i. impers. irr.* to grow dusk. See **conocer**

tardecica, tardecita, *f.* dusk, late afternoon

tardíamente, *adv.* late; too late

tardío, *a.* late; backward; behindhand; slow, deliberate

tardo, *a.* slow, slothful, tardy; late; dilatory; stupid, slow-witted; badly-spoken, inarticulate

tarea, *f.* task, work

tarifa, *f.* price-list; tariff

tarifar, *v.t.* to put a tariff on

tarima, *f.* stand, raised platform

tarín barín, *adv.* (*fam.*) more or less, about

tarja, *f.* large shield; ancient coin; tally stick. (*fam.*) **beber sobre t.,** to drink on credit

tarjar, *v.t.* to reckon by tally

tarjeta, *f.* buckler, small shield; (*arch.*) tablet bearing inscription; title (of maps and charts); visiting card; invitation card. **t. de visita,** visiting card. **t. postal,** post card

tarjetero, *m.* (visiting) card-case

tarlatana, *f.* tarlatan

tarquín, *m.* mud, mire

tarraconense, *a.* and *m.* and *f.* of or from Tarragona (province of Cataluña, Spain)

tárraga, *f.* old Spanish dance

tarro, *m.* jar, pot

tarso, *m.* (*anat.*) tarsus, ankle; (*zool.*) hock; (*orn.*) shank

tarta, *f.* cake tin; cake; tart

tártago, *m.* (*bot.*) spurge; (*fam.*) misfortune, disappointment

tartajear, *v.i.* to stammer; stutter

tartajeo, *m.* stammering; stutter

tartajoso (-sa), *a.* stammering; stuttering. *s.* stutterer

tartalear, *v.i.* (*fam.*) to stagger; totter; be speechless, be dumbfounded

tartamudear, *v.i.* to stammer, stutter

tartamudeo, *m.,* **tartamudez,** *f.* stammering; stuttering

tartamudo (-da), *s.* stammerer

tartán, *m.* tartan

tartana, *f.* (*naut.*) tartan; covered two-wheeled carriage

tartáreo, *a.* (*poet.*) infernal, hellish

tártaro (-ra), *m.* (*chem.*) cream of tartar; tartar (on teeth); (*poet.*) hell, hades. *a.* and *s.* Tartar

tartrato, *m.* (*chem.*) tartrate, salt of tartaric acid

tártrico, *a.* (*chem.*) tartaric

tartufo, *m.* hypocrite

tarugo, *m.* thick wooden peg; stopper; wood block

tasa, *f.* assessment, valuation; valuation certificate; fixed price; standard rate; measure, rule

tasación, *f.* valuation; assessment

tasador, *m.* public assessor; valuer

tasajo, *m.* salt meat; piece of meat

tasar, *v.t.* to value; price; fix remuneration; tax; regulate; rate; dole out sparingly

tasca, *f.* gambling-den; tavern

tascar, *v.t.* to dress (hemp, etc.); graze, crop the grass

tasquera, *f.* (*fam.*) quarrel, shindy

tasquil, *m.* wood splinter, chip

tata, *m.* (*fam.*) daddy (*S.A.*)

tatarabuela, *f.* great-great-grandmother

tatarabuelo, *m.* great-great-grandfather

tataradeudo (-da), *s.* very old relative; ancestor

tataranieta, *f.* great-great-granddaughter

tataranieto, *m.* great-great-grandson

tatas, andar a, *v.t.* to go on all fours

¡tate! *interj.* Stop!; Be careful!; Go slowly!; Now I understand!, Of course!

tatuaje, *m.* tattooing

tatuar, *v.t.* to tattoo

taumaturgia, *f.* thaumaturgy, wonder-working

taumaturgo, *m.* thaumaturge, magician

taurino, *a.* taurine; concerning bullfights

Tauro, *m.* (*ast.*) Taurus

tauromaquia, *f.* bull fighting, tauromachy

tautología, *f.* tautology

taxi, *m.* taxi

taxidermia, *f.* taxidermy

taxidermista, *m.* and *f.* taxidermist

taxímetro, *m.* taximeter; taxi

taxonomía, *f.* taxonomy

taz a taz, *adv.* in exchange, without payment; even

taza, *f.* cup; cupful; bowl of a fountain

tazar(se), *v.t.* and *v.r.* to fray (of cloth)

tazmía, *f.* tithe contribution; share of tithes; tithe register

tazón, *m.* large cup; bowl

te, *f.* name of the letter T. *m.* and *f.* dat. and acc. of *pers. pron.*, *2nd pers. sing.* thee; you; to thee, to you. Never used with a preposition

té, *m.* tea

tea, *f.* torch; fire-brand

teatino, *a.* and *m.* (*ecc.*) Theatin

teatral, *a.* theatrical

teatralidad, *f.* theatricality

teatro, *m.* theatre; stage; dramatic works; dramatic art; drama, plays. **t. de variedades,** music-hall

tebano (-na), **tebeo** (-ea), *a.* and *s.* Theban.

teca, *f.* (*bot.*) teak

tecla, *f.* key (of keyed instruments); typewriter, linotype or calculating machine key; (*fig.*) difficult or delicate point; (*fam.*) **dar en la t.,** to hit on the right way of doing a thing

teclado, *m.* (*mus.*) keyboard

tecleado, *m.* (*mus.*) fingering

teclear, *v.i.* to finger the keyboard; run one's fingers over the keyboard; (*fam.*) drum or tap with the fingers; *v.t.* tap (the keys, etc.); (*fam.*) try out various schemes

tecleo, *m.* fingering the keys; (*fam.*) drumming with the fingers; scheme, means

técnica, *f.* technique

tecnicismo, *m.* technical jargon; technicality, technical term

técnico, *a.* technical. *m.* technician

tecnicolor, *m.* technicolour

tecnología, *f.* technology

tecnológico, *a.* technological

tecnólogo, *m.* technologist

techado, *m.* ceiling; roof

techador, *m.* roofer

techar, *v.t.* to roof

techo, *m.* roof; ceiling; dwelling, habitation

techumbre, *f.* ceiling; roof

tedero, *m.* torch seller; torch holder

tedio, *m.* tedium, boredom, ennui

tedioso, *a.* tedious, boring

tegumento, *m.* integument, tegument

teísmo, *m.* theism

teísta, *a.* theistic. *m.* and *f.* theist

teja, *f.* tile, slate. (*fam.*) **de tejas abajo,** in the normal way; in the world of men. **de tejas arriba,** in a supernatural way; in heaven

tejadillo, *m.* roof (of a motor car, bus, etc.)

tejado, *m.* roof

tejar, *m.* tile works. *v.t.* to roof with tiles

tejavana, *f.* penthouse, open shed

tejedor (-ra), *a.* weaving; (*fam.*) scheming. *s.* weaver; (*fam.*) schemer

tejedura, *f.* weaving; fabric; texture

tejeduría, *f.* art of weaving; weaving shed or mill

tejemaneje, *m.* (*fam.*) cleverness, knack

tejer, *v.t.* to weave; plait; spin a cocoon; arrange, regulate; concoct, hatch (schemes); wind in and out (in dancing)

tejero, *m.* tile manufacturer

tejido, *m.* texture, weaving; textile; (*anat.*) tissue; fabric, material

tejo, *m.* quoit, discus; metal disk; (*bot.*) yew tree

tejón, *m.* (*zool.*) badger

tela, *f.* fabric, material, cloth; membrane; film (on liquids); web (spider's); inner skin (fruit, vegetables); film over the eye; matter, subject; scheme, plot. **t. metálica,** wire gauze. **en t. de juicio,** under consideration, in doubt. **llegarle a uno a las telas del corazón,** to hurt deeply, cut to the quick

telar, *m.* loom, weaving machine; (*theat.*) gridiron

telaraña, *f.* cobweb; mere trifle, bagatelle. (*fam.*) **mirar las telarañas,** to be absent-minded

telarañoso, *a.* cobwebby

telecomunicación, *f.* telecommunication

telefonear, *v.t.* to telephone

telefonema, *m.* telephone dispatch

telefonía, *f.* telephony. **t. sin hilos,** wireless telephony, broadcasting

telefónico, *a.* telephonic

telefonista, *m.* and *f.* telephonist

teléfono, *m.* telephone. **t. automático,** dial telephone. **llamar por t. (a),** to telephone, ring up

telegrafía, *f.* telegraphy. **t. sin hilos,** wireless telegraphy

telegrafiar, *v.t.* to telegraph

telegráfico, *a.* telegraphic

telegrafista, *m.* and *f.* telegraphist

telégrafo, *m.* telegraph. **t. sin hilos,** wireless telegraph. (*fam.*) **hacer telégrafos,** to talk by signs

telegrama, *m.* telegram

telemetría, *f.* telemetry

telémetro, *m.* telemeter, rangefinder

teleología, *f.* teleology

telepatía, *f.* telepathy

telepático, *a.* telepathic

telescópico, *a.* telescopic

telescopio, *m.* telescope

teletipo, *m.* teleprinter

televisión, *f.* television

telilla, *f.* film (on liquids); thin fabric

telón, *m.* (*theat.*) curtain; drop scene. **t. contra incendios, t. de seguridad,** (*theat.*) safety-curtain. **t. de boca,** drop curtain. **t. de foro,** drop scene

telúrico, *a.* tellural

tema, *m.* theme, subject; (*mus.*) motif, theme; thesis, argument. *f.* obstinacy; obsession, mania; hostility, grudge, rancour

temático, *a.* thematic; pigheaded, obstinate

temblador (-ra), *a.* trembling, shaking. *s.* Quaker

temblante, *a.* shaking; quivering. *m.* bracelet

temblar, *v.i. irr.* to tremble, shake; wave, quiver; shiver with fear. See acertar

temblequear, tembletear, *v.i.* (*fam.*) tremble; shake with fear

temblón, *a.* (*fam.*) trembling, shaking. *m.* (*fam.*) aspen

temblor, *m.* shake, trembling, shiver. **t. de tierra,** earthquake

tembloroso, tembloso, *a.* trembling, shaking, shivering, quivering

temedero, *a.* fearsome, dread

temedor (-ra), *a.* fearful. *s.* fearer, dreader

temer, *v.t.* to fear, dread; suspect, imagine; *v.i.* be afraid

temerario, *a.* reckless, impetuous; thoughtless, hasty

temeridad, *f.* recklessness, impetuosity, temerity; thoughtlessness; act of folly; rash judgment

temerón, *a.* (*fam.*) swaggering, bombastic

temeroso, *a.* frightening, dread; fearful, timid; afraid, suspicious

temible, *a.* dread, awesome

temor, *m.* fear

temoso, *a.* obstinate, headstrong

témpano, *m.* (*mus.*) tabor; drumhead; block, flat piece; side of bacon. **t. de hielo,** iceberg, ·ice floe

temperación, *f.* tempering

temperamento, *m.* temperament, nature; compromise, agreement

temperar, *v.t.* to temper

temperatura, *f.* temperature

temperie, *f.* weather conditions

tempestad, *f.* storm

tempestividad, *f.* opportuneness, seasonableness

tempestivo, *a.* opportune, seasonable

tempestuoso, *a.* stormy

templa, *f.* (*art*) tempera; *pl.* (*anat.*) temples

templado, *a.* moderate; temperate (of regions); lukewarm; (*mus.*) in tune; restrained (of style); (*fam.*) brave, long-suffering. (*fam.*) **estar bien** (*or* **mal**) **templado,** to be well (or badly) tuned (of musical instruments); be in a good (*or* bad) temper; be good (*or* ill) natured

templador (-ra), *s.* tuner. *m.* tuning key

templadura, *f.* tuning; tempering

templanza, *f.* moderation; sobriety; mildness of climate

templar, *v.t.* to tune; (*met.*) temper; moderate; warm; allay, appease; anneal; (*art*) harmonize, blend; (*naut.*) trim the sails; *v.r.* control oneself, be moderate; *v.i.* grow warm

templario, *m.* Templar

temple, *m.* weather conditions; temperature; temper (of metals, etc.); nature, disposition; bravery; mean, average; (*mus.*) tuning. (*art*) **al t.,** in tempera

templete, *m. dim.* shrine; niche (for statues); kiosk, pavilion

templo, *m.* temple, church

temporada, *f.* space of time, season, while. **de t.,** seasonal; temporary. **estar de t.,** to be out of town, on holiday

temporal, *a.* temporal; temporary; secular, lay; transient, fugitive. *m.* storm, tempest; rainy period; seasonal labourer

temporalidad, *f.* secular character; temporality secular possession (gen. *pl.*)

temporáneo, temporario, *a.* temporary, impermanent, fleeting

témporas, *f. pl.* (*ecc.*) ember days

temporejar, *v.t.* (*naut.*) to lie to in a storm

temporero, *a.* temporary (of labour)

temporizar, *v.i.* to while away the time; temporize

tempranal, *a.* (*agr.*) early fruiting

tempranero, *a.* early

temprano, *a.* early. *adv.* in the early hours; prematurely, too soon

temulento, *a.* intoxicated, drunken

ten con ten, *m.* (*fam.*) tact, diplomacy

tenacear, *v.i.* to insist, be obstinate

tenacero, *m.* manufacturer or vendor of tongs

tenacidad, *f.* adhesiveness; resistance, toughness; obstinacy, tenacity

tenacillas, *f. pl. dim.* small tongs; candle snuffers; sugar tongs; curling tongs; tweezers

tenaz, *a.* adhesive; hard, resistant, unyielding; tenacious, obstinate

tenaza, *f.* claw (lobster's, etc.); *pl.* tongs; pincers; pliers; dental forceps

tenazada, *f.* seizing with the tongs; strong bite, snap; rattle of the tongs

tenazón, (a or de) *adv.* without taking aim, wildly; unexpectedly

tenca, *f.* (*icht.*) tench

tención, *f.* retention, holding; grip

tendal, *m.* awning; sheet for catching olives

tendedero, *m.* drying ground

tendedura, *f.* laying out; stretching

tendencia, *f.* tendency

tendencioso, *a.* tendencious, biassed

tender, *v.t. irr.* to hang out; unfold, spread out; extend, hold out; (*mas.*) plaster; *v.i.* tend, incline; *v.r.* lie down at full length; place one's cards on the table; gallop hard (horses). See **entender**

tendero (-ra), *s.* shopkeeper; retailer. *m.* tent maker

tendido, *m.* row of seats in bull-fight arena; clothes hung out to dry; clear sky; (*mas.*) plaster

tendón, *m.* (*anat.*) tendon

tenducha, *f.* (*fam.*) wretched little shop

tenebrosidad, *f.* gloom, darkness, obscurity

tenebroso, *a.* dark, gloomy

tenedero, *m.* (*naut.*) anchoring ground, anchorage

tenedor, *m.* table fork; possessor, retainer; (*com.*) holder; payee. **t. de libros,** book-keeper

teneduría, *f.* employment of a book-keeper. **t. de libros,** book-keeping

tenencia, *f.* possession; tenancy, occupation; lieutenancy

tener, *v.t. irr.* to have; hold; grasp; possess, own; uphold, maintain; contain; include; hold fast, grip; stop; keep (promises); lodge, accommodate; (*with en*) value, estimate (e.g. **Le tengo en poco,** I have a poor opinion of him); (*with para*) be of the opinion that (e.g. **Tengo para mí,** My opinion is); (*with por*) believe, consider; *v.i.* be wealthy; *v.r.* steady oneself; hold on to; lean (upon); rest (on); defend oneself; uphold; rely upon; (*with por*) consider oneself as. **tener** is used to express: 1. *Age* (e.g. ¿ **Cuántos años tiene Vd ?** How old are you ?). 2. *Possession* (e.g. **Tenemos muchos sombreros,** We have a great many hats).

3. *Measurements* (e.g. **El cuarto tiene 18 metros de largo,** The room is 18 metres long). Means to be when describing some physical and mental states (e.g. **Tenemos miedo,** We are afraid. **Tengo sueño,** I am sleepy. **Tienen frío (calor),** They are cold (hot)). *Used as auxiliary verb replacing haber* in compound tenses of transitive verbs (e.g. **Tengo escritas las cartas,** I have written the letters). **tener a bien,** to think fit, please, judge convenient. **t. a menos de hacer (una cosa),** to scorn to do (a thing). **t. en cuenta,** to bear in mind. **t. en menos (a),** to despise (a person). **t. gana,** to want, wish; feel disposed; have an appetite. **t. lugar,** to take place, occur. **t. presente,** to remember. **t. que,** to have to (e.g. **tengo que hacerlo,** I must do it). **t. que ver (con),** to have something to do (with), be related. **no tenerlas todas consigo,** (*fam.*) to have the jitters. *Pres. Ind.* **tengo, tienes, tiene, tenemos, tenéis, tienen.** *Preterite* **tuve,** etc. *Fut.* **tendré,** etc. *Condit.* **tendría,** etc. *Pres. Subjunc.* **tenga,** etc. *Imperf. Subjunc.* **tuviese,** etc.

tenguerengue, en, *adv.* (*fam.*) rickety, insecure

tenia, *f.* tapeworm; (*arch.*) fillet, narrow moulding

tenientazgo, *m.* lieutenancy

teniente, *a.* owning, holding; unripe (fruit); (*fam.*) slightly deaf; stingy, mean. *m.* deputy, substitute; (*mil.*) first-lieutenant, lieutenant. **t. coronel,** lieut.-colonel. **t. de navío,** naval lieutenant. **t. general,** (*mil.*) lieutenant-general. **t. general de aviación,** air marshal

tenis, *m.* tennis

tenor, *m.* import, contents (of letter, etc.); constitution, composition; (*mus.*) tenor

tenorio, *m.* rake, Don Juan, philanderer

tensar, *v.t.* to tighten; tense

tensión, *f.* tautness; tension; strain, stress; (*elec.*) tension

tenso, *a.* taut; tight; tense

tensor, *a.* tensile

tentación, *f.* temptation; attraction, inducement

tentáculo, *m.* tentacle; feeler

tentadero, *m.* yard for trying out bullocks for bull fighting

tentador (-ra), *a.* tempting; attractive. *s.* tempter. *m.* the Devil

tentalear, *v.t.* to examine by touch

tentar, *v.t.* *irr.* to touch, feel; examine by touch; incite, encourage; try, endeavour; test; tempt; (*surg.*) probe. See **sentar**

tentativa, *f.* endeavour, attempt; preliminary examinations (some univs.)

tentativo, *a.* tentative, experimental

tentemozo, *m.* support, prop; tumbler (toy)

tentempié, *m.* (*fam.*) snack, bite

tenue, *a.* thin; slender, delicate; trivial, worthless, insignificant; pale; faint

tenuidad, *f.* slenderness; delicacy; triviality, insignificance; paleness; faintness

teñidura, *f.* dyeing, staining

teñir, *v.t.* *irr.* to dye; (*art*) darken; colour, tinge; *v.r.* be dyed; be tinged or coloured. See **ceñir**

teocracia, *f.* theocracy

teocrático, *a.* theocratic

teodolito, *m.* theodolite

teodosiano, *a.* Theodosian

teologal, *a.* theological

teología, *f.* theology, divinity

teológico, *a.* theological

teologizar, *v.i.* to theologize

teólogo, *a.* theological. *m.* theologian, divine; student of theology

teorema, *m.* theorem

teoría, *f.* theory

teórica, *f.* theory

teórico, *a.* theoretical, speculative. *m.* theorist

teorizar, *v.i.* to consider theoretically, theorize about

teoso, *a.* resinous, gummy

teosofía, *f.* theosophy

teosófico, *a.* theosophical

teósofo, *m.* theosophist

tepe, *m.* sod, cut turf

terapeuta, *m.* and *f.* therapeutist

terapéutica, *f.* therapeutics

terapéutico, *a.* therapeutic

terapia, *f.* therapy

teratología, *f.* teratology

tercena, *f.* warehouse for storing monopoly goods (tobacco, etc.)

tercenista, *m.* and *f.* person in charge of **tercena**

tercer, *a.* *abb.* of **tercero,** third. Used before *m. sing.* nouns

tercera, *f.* procuress; (*mus.*) third

tercería, *f.* arbitration, mediation; temporary occupation of a fortress, etc.

tercero (-ra), *a.* third; mediatory. *s.* third; mediator. *m.* pimp; (*ecc.*) tertiary; tithes collector; third person. ¡A la tercera va la vencida! Third time lucky!

terceto, *m.* tercet, triplet

tercia, *f.* one-third; (*ecc.*) tierce, third hour; storehouse for tithes. **tercias reales,** royal share of ecclesiastical tithes

terciado, *m.* short broad sword; ribbon

terciana, *f.* (*med.*) tertian fever

terciar, *v.t.* to slant; sling sideways; divide into three; equalize weight (on beasts of burden); (*agr.*) plough or dig for third time; (*agr.*) prune; *v.r.* be opportune, come at the right time. *v.i.* mediate, arbitrate; make up a number (for cards, etc.); reach the third day (moon); take part, participate

terciario, *a.* third, tertiary; (*geol.*) tertiary. *m.* (*ecc.*) tertiary

tercio, *a.* third. *m.* one-third; (*mil.*) infantry regiment (*ant.*); division of Spanish Guardia Civil; (*mil.*) body of foreign volunteers; fishermen's association; *pl.* brawny limbs of a man. **hacer t.,** to take part in; make up the number of. **hacer buen** (*or* **mal**) **t. a alguien,** to do someone a good (*or* bad) turn

terciopelo, *m.* velvet; velveteen

terco, *a.* pigheaded, obstinate; hard, tough

terenciano, *a.* Terentian, of Terence

teresiana, *f.* kind of képi

tergiversación, *f.* tergiversation, vacillation

tergiversar, *v.t.* to tergiversate, shuffle, vacillate

termal, *a.* thermal

termas, *f. pl.* thermal springs, hot mineral baths; thermal

térmico, *a.* thermic

terminable, *a.* terminable

terminación, *f.* conclusion, termination; end, finish; ending of a word; (*gram.*) termination

terminador (-ra), *a.* concluding. *s.* finisher

terminal, *a.* terminal; final. *m.* (*elec.*) terminal

terminante, *a.* conclusive, definite; categorical

terminar, *v.t.* to end, conclude; complete; *v.r.* and *v.i.* end

término, *m.* limit, end; term, expression; boundary stone; district, suburb; space, period; state, condition; boundary; object, aim; appearance, demeanour, behaviour (gen. *pl.*); completion; (*mus.*) tone; (*math., law, logic*) term. **t. medio,** (*math.*) average; compromise, middle way. **correr el t.,** to lapse (of time). **en primer t.,** (*art*) in the foreground. **medios términos,** evasions, excuses. **primer t.,** (cinema) close-up

terminología, *f.* terminology

termita, *f.* (*chem.*) thermite. *m.* (*ent.*) termite

termodinámica, *f.* thermodynamics

termoeléctrico, *a.* thermoelectric

termómetro, *m.* thermometer

termos, *m.* thermos, vacuum flask

termoscopio, *m.* thermoscope

termóstato, *m.* thermostat

termostático, *a.* thermostatic

terna, *f.* triad, trio; set of dice

ternario, *a.* ternal, ternary

terne, *a.* (*fam.*) bullying, braggartly; persistent, obstinate; robust. *m.* and *f.* bully

ternera, *f.* female calf; veal

ternero, *m.* male calf

terneza, *f.* tenderness, kindness; softness; softheartedness; endearment, caress, compliment (gen. *pl.*)

ternilla, *f.* cartilage, gristle

ternísimo, *a. sup.* **tierno,** most tender

terno, *m.* triad; suit of clothes, threepiece; oath, curse

ternura, *f.* softness; softheartedness; tenderness, kindness, sweetness

terquedad, terquería, terqueza, *f.* obstinacy, obduracy

terracota, *f.* terra-cotta

terrado, *m.* flat roof

terraja, *f.* screw-tap

terraplén, *m.* embankment; (*mil.*) terreplein

terraplenar, *v.t.* to fill up with earth; fill in (a hollow); make into an embankment; terrace

terráqueo, *a.* terraqueous

terrateniente, *m.* and *f.* land-owner

terraza, *f.* terrace; flat roof; garden flower border

terrazgo, *m.* tillable land; rent for farming land

terregoso, *a.* lumpy, full of clods (land)

terremoto, *m.* earthquake

terrenal, *a.* terrestrial

terreno, *a.* terrestrial. *m.* ground, land; (*fig.*) sphere; region; soil; plot of land. (*fig.*) **ganar t.,** to win ground, make progress. **medir el t.,** (*fig.*) to feel one's way

térreo, *a.* earthy

terrero, *a.* earthly; low-flying, almost touching the ground; humble. *m.* flat roof; pile or mound of earth; deposit of earth, alluvium; target; mineral refuse

terrestre, *a.* terrestrial, earthly

terrezuela, *f.* poor soil

terribilidad, *f.* terribleness, horribleness; rudeness

terribilísimo, *a. sup.* most terrible

terrible, *a.* terrible, horrible; rude, unsociable, ill-humoured; enormous, huge

terrífico, *a.* terrible, frightful

territorial, *a.* territorial

territorialidad, *f.* territoriality

territorio, *m.* territory; jurisdiction. **territorios bajo mandato,** mandated territory

terrizo, *a.* earthen

terrón, *m.* clod of earth; lump; *pl.* lands, landed property. **t. de azúcar,** lump of sugar

terrorismo, *m.* terrorism

terrorista, *m.* terrorist

terrosidad, *f.* earthiness

terroso, *a.* earthy; earthen

terruño, *m.* plot of ground; native earth; country; soil

terso, *a.* smooth, shiny, glossy; (*lit.*) elegant, polished (style)

tersura, *f.* smoothness, glossiness; elegance (of style)

tertulia, *f.* regular social meeting (gen. in cafés); conversational group; party; part of Spanish cafés set apart for players of chess, etc. hacer t., to meet for conversation

tertuliano (-na), *s.*, tertuliante, *m.* and *f.*, tertulio (-ia), *s.* member of a tertulia

terzuelo, *m.* third, third part

tesaliense, *a.* and *m.* and *f.*, tesalónico (-ca), *a.* and *s.* Thessalonian

tesar, *v.t.* (*naut.*) to make taut; *v.i.* step backwards, back (oxen)

tesela, *f.* tessera, square used in mosaic work

teselado, *a.* tessellated

tesis, *f.* thesis

teso, *a.* tight, taut, tensed. *m.* hilltop; bulge, lump

tesón, *m.* persistence, obstinacy, tenacity

tesonería, *f.* stubbornness, obstinacy

tesorería, *f.* treasury; treasuryship

tesorero (-ra), *s.* treasurer

tesoro, *m.* treasure; public exchequer; hoard; (*fig.*) gem, excellent person; thesaurus. t. de duende, fairy-gold

tespíades, *f. pl.* the Muses

testa, *f.* head; face, front; (*fam.*) sense, acumen. t. coronada, crowned head

testación, *f.* erasure, crossing out

testado, *a.* testate

testador (-ra), *s.* testator

testaferro, *m.* (*fig.*) figure-head, proxy

testamentar, *v.t.* to bequeath

testamentaria, *f.* execution of a will; (*law*) estate; executors' meeting

testamentario, *a.* testamental, testamentary

testamento, *m.* (*law*) will; testament. Antiguo T., Old Testament. ordenar (*or* otorgar) su t., to make one's will

testar, *v.i.* to make a will; *v.t.* erase, cross out

testarada, *f.* a blow with the head; pigheadedness, stubbornness

testarrón, *a.*.(*fam.*) pigheaded

testarudez, *f.* obstinacy, obduracy

testarudo, *a.* stubborn, obstinate

teste, *m.* (*anat.*) testicle

testera, *f.* front, face; front seat (in vehicle); upper half of animal's face; tester, canopy

testículo, *m.* (*anat.*) testicle

testificación, *f.* testification

testificar, *v.t.* to testify; affirm, assert; attest, prove

testigo, *m.* and *f.* witness. *m.* proof, evidence. (*law*) t. de cargo, witness for the prosecution. (*law*) t. de descargo, witness for the defence. t. de vista, eye-witness. (*law*) hacer testigos, to bring forward witnesses

testimonial, *a.* confirmatory, proven

testimoniar, *v.t.* to attest, confirm, bear witness to

testimoniero (-ra), *a.* slanderous; hypocritical. *s.* slanderer, hypocrite

testimonio, *m.* testimony, proof; slander; affidavit

testuz, *m.* front of head (some animals); nape (animals)

teta, *f.* mammary gland, breast; teat, dug, udder. dar la t. (a), to suckle

tétano, tétanos, *m.* (*med.*) tetanus

tetera, *f.* tea-pot; tea-kettle

tetilla, *f. dim.* rudimentary teat or nipple; feeding-bottle teat

tetracordio, *m.* (*mus.*) tetrachord

tetraedro, *m.* (*geom.*) tetrahedron

tetrarca, *m.* tetrarch

tetravalente, *a.* (*chem.*) quadrivalent

tétrico, *a.* gloomy; sombre

tetuaní, *a.* and *m.* and *f.* of or from Tetuan

teurgia, *f.* theurgy

teutón (-ona), *s.* teuton. *a.* teutonic

teutónico, *a.* teutonic

textil, *a.* and *m.* textile

texto, *m.* text; quotation, citation; text-book

textorio, *a.* textile

textual, *a.* textual

textualista, *m.* textualist

textura, *f.* texture; weaving; structure (of novel, etc.); animal structure

tez, *f.* complexion, skin

ti, *pers. pron., 2nd sing., m.* and *f., dat., acc., abl.,* thee, you. Always used with prep. (e.g. **por.ti,** by thee (you).)

tía, *f.* aunt; (*fam.*) wife, mother, dame; (*fam.*) coarse creature. **t. abuela,** great-aunt. (*fam.*) **quedarse para t.,** to be left an old maid

tiara, *f.* ancient Persian head-dress; papal tiara; coronet; dignity and power of Papacy

tiberino, *a.* Tiberine

tibetano (-na), *a.* and *s.* Tibetan. *m.* Tibetan language

tibia, *f.* flute; (*anat.*) tibia

tibieza, *f.* tepidity; indifference, lack of enthusiasm

tibio, *a.* tepid, warm; indifferent, unenthusiastic

tiburón, *m.* (*icht.*) shark

ticket, *m.* ticket; pass, membership card

tictac, *m.* tick-tock (of a clock)

tiempo, *m.* time; season; epoch, period; chance, opportunity; leisure, free time; weather; (*mus.*) tempo; (*gram.*) tense; (*naut.*) storm. **t. ha,** many years ago, long ago. **t. medio** *or* **medio t.,** (*sport*) half-time. **abrir el t.,** to clear up (weather). **ajustar los tiempos,** to fix the date (chronology). **a largo t.,** after a long time. **andando el t.,** in the course of time. **a su t.,** in due course, at the proper time. **a t.,** in time, at the right time. **a un t.,** simultaneously, at the same time. **cargarse el t.,** to cloud over (sky). **con t.,** in advance, with time; in time. **correr el t.,** to pass, move on (time). **de t. en t.,** from time to time. **engañar** (*or* **entretener**) **el t.,** to kill time, while away the hours. (*fam.*) **en t., de Maricastaña** *or* **del rey Perico,** long, long ago. **fuera de t.,** unseasonably, inopportunely; out of season. **ganar t.,** to gain time; (*fam.*) hurry. **hacer t.,** to wait, kick one's heels; (*fig.*)

mark time. **perder el t.,** to waste time; misspend or lose time. **sentarse el t.,** to clear up (weather). **tomarse t.** (para), to postpone, take time for (or to)

tienda, *f.* tent; (*naut.*) awning, canopy; shop. **t. de antigüedades,** antique shop. **t. de campaña,** bell-tent, pavilion. **t. oxígena,** oxygen tent

tienta, *f.* astuteness; cleverness; (*surg.*) probe; trying out bullocks for the bull-ring. **a tientas,** by touch, gropingly

tientaparedes, *m.* and *f.* one who gropes his (her) way

tiento, *m.* touching, feeling; touch, feel; blind man's stick; tight-rope walker's pole; manual control, steady hand; caution, care, tact; (*mus.*) preliminary flourish; (*fam.*) buffet, slap; (*zool.*) tentacle. **a t.,** by the touch; unsurely, gropingly

tierno, *a.* soft; tender; kind; sweet; delicate; softhearted; fresh, recent; affectionate

tierra, *f.* world, planet; earth; soil; ground; cultivated ground, land; fatherland, native land; region; district, territory. **t. adentro,** inland. **t. de batán,** fuller's earth. **t. de Promisión,** Promised Land. **t. de Siena,** sienna. (*fam.*) **besar la t.,** to fall down. **dar en t. con,** to throw down; demolish. (*naut.*) **echar en t.,** to put ashore, land. **echar por t.,** (*fig.*) to overthrow, destroy. **echar t. a,** (*fig.*) to bury, forget. (*fam.*) **la t. de María Santísima,** Andalusia. **por t.,** overland. **saltar en t.,** to land, disembark. **venir** (*or* **venirse**) **a t.,** to fall down, topple over

tieso, *a.* hard, rigid, stiff; healthy, robust; taut; spirited, courageous; obstinate, stiff-necked; distant, formal. *adv.* firmly, strongly

tiesto, *m.* flowerpot; broken piece of earthenware

tiesura, *f.* hardness, rigidity, stiffness; physical fitness; courageousness; obstinacy; formality, stiffness

tifoidea, *f.* typhoid

tifón, *m.* typhoon

tifus, m. (med.) typhus. **t. exantemático,** trench-fever

tigre, m. tiger; ferocious person

tigresa, f. tigress

tigridia, f. tiger-lily

tijera, f. scissors (gen. pl.); any scissor-shaped instrument; shears; drainage channel; carpenter's horse; scandalmonger, gossip

tijereta, f. dim. vine tendril; earwig

tijeretada, f. cut or snip with scissors

tijeretear, v.t. to cut with scissors; (fam.) interfere arbitrarily

tijereteo, m. scissor cut; click of the scissors

tila, f. lime or linden tree or flower; infusion made of lime flowers

tílburi, m. tilbury (carriage)

tildar, v.t. to cross out, erase; stigmatize; place a tilde over a letter

tilde, m. or f. bad reputation; tilde (on ñ); f. jot, iota

tilín, m. tinkle, peal (of bell)

tilo, m. lime tree

tillar, v.t. to lay wood floors

timador (-ra), s. (fam.) swindler, sharper, cheat

tímalo, m. (icht.) grayling

timar, v.t. to swindle, cheat, deceive; v.r. (fam.) exchange looks or winks

timba, f. (fam.) gambling-den; game of chance

timbal, m. kettle-drum

timbalero, m. kettle-drum player

timbrador, m. stamper; stamping machine; rubber stamp

timbrar, v.t. to stamp; place the crest over a coat of arms

timbre, m. postage-stamp; heraldic crest; excise stamp; bell, press-button; (mus.) timbre; noble deed; personal merit

timidez, f. timidity, nervousness

tímido, a. timid, nervous

timo, m. (fam.) swindling, trick; (anat.) thymus

timol, m. thymol

timón, m. (naut.) helm; rudder; management, direction; stick of a rocket. **t. de dirección,** (aer.) tail-fin

timonear, v.i. (naut.) to steer

timonel, timonero, m. (naut.) helmsman, coxswain

timorato, a. godfearing; timid, vacillating

tímpano, m. (anat.) ear-drum; tympanum; (mus.) kettle-drum; (arch.) tympanum; (print.) tympan

tina, f. vat; flour bin; large earthenware jar; wooden tub; bath

tinada, f. wood pile; byre, cattle shed

tinaja, f. large earthenware jar; jarful

tinajero, m. vendor of earthenware jars

tinelo, m. servants' hall

tinerfeño (-ña), a. and s. of or from Teneriffe

tinglado, m. overhanging roof; open shed; penthouse; intrigue

tiniebla, f. gloom, darkness (gen. pl.); pl. profound ignorance; confusion of mind; (ecc.) tenebræ

tino, m. skilled sense of touch; good eye, accurate aim; judgment, shrewdness; vat. **sacar de t. (a),** to bewilder, confuse; irritate, exasperate. **sin t.,** without limit, excessively

tinta, f. colour, tint; ink; staining, dyeing; dye, stain; pl. shades, colours; (art) colours, mixed ready for painting. **t. china,** Indian ink. **t. simpática,** invisible ink. **recargar las tintas,** (fig.) to over-paint, lay the colours on too thick. (fam.) **saber de buena t. (una cosa),** to learn (a thing) from a reliable source

tintar, v.t. to dye; colour, tinge, stain

tinte, m. dyeing, staining; colour; dye; stain; dye-house; pretext, disguise

tintero, m. ink-well. (fam.) **dejar** (or **quedársele a uno) en el t.,** to forget, omit (to say, write)

tintín, m. ring, peal; clink; chink

tintinar, v.i. to ring, tinkle; clink; jingle

tintineo, m. ringing, tinkling; clinking; jingle

tintirintín, m. bray of a trumpet

tinto, *a.* red (of wine). *m.* red wine; dark red

tintorería, *f.* dyeing industry; dyeing and dry-cleaning shop

tintorero (-ra), *s.* dyer; dry cleaner

tintura, *f.* dyeing, staining; colour, tint; dye; stain; tincture; smattering, slight knowledge

tinturar, *v.t.* to dye; colour, tinge, stain; give a superficial notion of

tiña, *f.* (*med.*) ringworm; (*fam.*) meanness, stinginess

tiñoso, *a.* mangy; afflicted with ringworm; (*fam.*) mean, stingy, scurvy

tiñuela, *f.* ship-worm

tío, *m.* uncle; gaffer; fellow, chap; fool; stepfather; father-in-law. **t. abuelo,** great-uncle

tiovivo, *m.* merry-go-round

tipiadora, *f.* typewriter

típico, *a.* typical

tiple, *m.* soprano or treble voice. *m.* and *f.* soprano

tipo, *m.* model, pattern; type; print, type; species, group (of animals, etc.); (*fam.*) guy, chap

tipografía, *f.* typography, art of printing

tipográfico, *a.* typographical

tipógrafo, *m.* printer, typographer

típula, *f.* (*ent.*) daddy-long-legs

tiquismiquis, *m. pl.* ridiculous scruples; affected courtesies. *a.* (*fam.*) faddy, fussy

tira, *f.* strip, band, ribbon; stripe, rib

tirabotas, *m.* button-hook

tirabuzón, *m.* corkscrew; ringlet, curl; hair-curler

tirada, *f.* throwing; drawing, pulling; cast, throw; distance, space; (*print.*) edition, issue; circulation (of a newspaper, etc.); stroke (golf); lapse, interval (of time). **t. aparte,** reprint (of an article, etc.)

tiradero, *m.* shooting butt

tirado, *a.* (*fam.*) dirt-cheap. *m.* wiredrawing

tirador (-ra), *s.* thrower, caster; drawer, puller; marksman. *m.* handle, knob; (*mech.*) trigger; bell-rope, bell-pull; (*print.*) pressman. **t. de bota,** boot tag. **t. de gomas,** catapult. **t. de oro,** gold wiredrawer

tiralíneas, *m.* ruling-pen

tiramiento, *m.* pulling; stretching

tiramira, *f.* long, narrow mountain range; long line of persons or things; distance

tirana, *f.* old Spanish popular song

tiranía, *f.* tyranny, despotism

tiranicida, *m.* and *f.* tyrannicide (person)

tiranicidio, *m.* tyrannicide (act)

tiránico, *a.* tyrannical

tiranización, *f.* tyranny, tyrannization

tiranizar, *v.t.* to tyrannize over

tirano (-na), *a.* tyrannous, tyrannical; (*fig.*) overwhelming, dominating. *s.* tyrant

tirante, *a.* taut; tense, strained. *m.* trace (of harness); shoulder-strap; brace, suspender (gen. *pl.*); (*arch.*) tie

tirantez, *f.* tautness; tension, strain; straight distance between two points. **estado de t.,** (*pol.*) strained relations

tirar, *v.t.* to throw, cast; fling, aim, toss; throw down, overthrow; pull; draw; discharge, shoot; stretch, pull out; rule, draw (lines); squander, waste; (*print.*) print; *v.i.* attract; pull; (*with prep. a*) turn to, turn in the direction of; incline, tend to; incline towards; have a tinge of (colours); try, aspire to; (*with de*) wield, unsheath, draw out (fire-arms, arms); *v.r.* cast oneself, precipitate oneself; throw oneself on. (*fam.*) **ir tirando,** to carry on, get along somehow

tirilla, *f.* (*sew.*) shirt neckband

tirio (-ia), *a.* and *s.* Tyrian

tiritaña, *f.* thin silk material; (*fam.*) mere nothing, trifle

tiritar, *v.i.* to shiver with cold

tiritón, *m.* shiver, shudder

tiro, *m.* throwing; throw, cast; toss, fling; try (in football); shooting; piece of artillery; report, shot (of a gun); discharge (fire-arms); shooting range or gallery; team (of horses); range (of fire-arms, etc.); hoisting cable; flight (of stairs); (*min.*) shaft; (*fam.*) trick; robbery, theft; innuendo, insinuation; grave harm or injury; *pl.* sword-belt.

t. de pichón, pigeon shooting.
t. par, four-in-hand. a t.,
within firing range; within reach.
(fam.) de tiros largos, in full
regalia
tirocinio, m. apprenticeship
tiroideo, a. thyroid
tiroides, f. thyroid gland
tirolés (-esa), a. and s. Tyrolese
tirón, m. novice, beginner; pull,
tug, heave. de un t., with one
tug; at one stroke, at one blow
tiroriro, m. (fam.) sound of a wind-
instrument; pl. (fam.) wind-
instruments
tirotearse, v.r. (mil.) to exchange
fire; indulge in repartee
tiroteo, m. shooting, exchange of
shots; crackle (of rifle fire)
tirreno, a. Tyrrhenian; Etruscan
tirria, f. (fam.) hostility, grudge,
dislike
tirso, m. thyrsus; (bot.) panicle
tirulato, a. dumbfounded, stupefied
tisana, f. tisane
tísico (-ca), a. (med.) phthisical,
tuberculous. s. sufferer from
tuberculosis, consumptive
tisis, f. (med.) phthisis, tuberculosis
tisú, m. silver or gold tissue
titánico, a. titanesque; colossal,
huge
títere, m. puppet; (fig., fam.)
dummy, grotesque; (fam.) fool;
obsession, fixed idea; pl. (fam.)
circus; Punch and Judy show.
(fam.) echar los títeres a
rodar, to upset the whole show;
quarrel, fall out with. (fam.) no
dejar t. con cabeza, to destroy
entirely, smash up completely;
leave no one
titerero (-ra), titiritero (-ra), s.
titerista, m. and f. puppet showman; acrobat; juggler
tití, m. marmoset
titilación, f. quiver, tremor;
twinkling, winking, gleam
titilador, titilante, a. quivering,
trembling; twinkling
titilar, v.i. to quiver, tremble;
twinkle
titiritaina, f. (fam.) muffled
strains of musical instruments;
merrymaking, uproar
titiritar, v.i. to tremble, shiver,
shudder

titiritero (-ra), s. puppet-master;
acrobat
titubear, v.i. to totter, sway,
rock; stutter, stammer; toddle;
hesitate, vacillate
titubeo, m. tottering, swaying;
stuttering; hesitation
titulado, m. titled person; one
who holds an academic title
titular, a. titular. v.t. to entitle,
call; v.i. obtain a title (of nobility); v.r. style oneself, call
oneself
título, m. title; heading; inscription; pretext, excuse; diploma,
certificate; claim, right; noble
title and its owner; section,
clause; (univ.) degree; (com.)
share certificate, bond; (com.)
title; caption; qualification,
right, merit; basis of a claim or
privilege; pl. (com.) securities,
stocks. t. de la columna,
(print.) running title. títulos de
propiedad, title-deeds. t. del
reino, title of nobility. a t., under
pretext
tiza, f. chalk; whiting; calcined
stag's antler
tiznar, v.t. to make sooty; dirty,
stain, begrime; (fig.) sully, tarnish
tizne, m. (sometimes f.) soot;
charcoal; stain (on one's honour,
etc.); (agr.) blight
tizón, m. fire-brand; (agr.) blight;
(fig.) stain (on honour, etc.)
tizona, f. (fam.) sword (by allusion to name of that of the Cid)
tizonear, v.i. to poke or rake
together the fire
toalla, f. towel. t. continua,
roller-towel. t. rusa, Turkish
towel
toallero, m. towel-rail
tobillera, f. (fam.) girl, flapper
tobillo, m. ankle
tobogán, m. toboggan; chute (in
flats and fun fairs)
toca, f. head-dress; toque;
wimple; coif
tocable, a. touchable
tocado, a. (fig.) touched half-
crazy. m. head-dress; coiffure,
hairdressing
tocador (-ra), s. (mus.) player.
m. dressing-table; kerchief; boudoir; cloak-room; dressing-room;
dressing-case

tocamiento, *m.* touching, feeling; touch; (*fig.*) inspiration

tocante, *a.* touching. **t. a,** concerning, with regard to

tocar, *v.t.* to touch, feel; (*mus.*) play; knock, rap; summon; ring, peal; brush against; discover by experience; persuade, inspire; mention, touch upon; (*naut.*) touch bottom; (*art*) retouch, touch up. *v.i.* belong; stop (at), touch at; be one's turn; concern, interest; be one's lot; adjoin, be near to; be opportune; be allied or closely related to; find the scent (dogs). (*naut.*) **t. en un puerto,** to touch at a port. **Ahora me toca a mí,** Now it's my turn. **Es un problema que me toca de cerca,** It is a problem that touches me very nearly. (*fam.*) **a toca teja,** in ready cash

tocayo (-ya), *s.* namesake

tocinería, *f.* pork-butcher's shop

tocinero, *m.* pork butcher

tocino, *m.* bacon; salt pork

tocología, *f.* tokology, obstetrics

tocón, *m.* stump of a tree; stump of an amputated limb

tochedad, *f.* boorishness, loutishness

tocho, *a.* boorish, loutish, countrified. *m.* iron bar

todavía, *adv.* still; even; nevertheless; yet. **No han venido t.,** They have not come yet. **Queda mucho que hacer t.,** There is still much to be done

todo, *a.* all; whole, entire; every, each. *m.* whole, entirety; whole word (charades); all; *pl.* all; everyone. *adv.* wholly, entirely. **t. lo posible,** everything possible; all one can, one's best. **t. lo que,** all that which. **ante t.,** in the first place; especially, particularly. **así y t.,** nevertheless. **a t. esto,** in the meanwhile. **con t.** *or* **con t. esto,** nevertheless, in spite of this. **del t.,** wholly, completely. **jugar el t. por el t.,** to risk everything on the outcome. **sobre t.,** especially. **y t.,** in addition, as well

todopoderoso, *a.* all-powerful, almighty. *m.* the Almighty, God

.toga, *f.* toga; robe, gown

toisón, *m.* fleece. **t. de oro,** Golden Fleece

tojo, *m.* (*bot.*) gorse, furze

toldadura, *f.* awning; canopy; hanging, curtain

toldilla, *f.* (*naut.*) awning

toldillo, *m.* covered litter or sedan-chair; mosquito net (*S.A.*)

toldo, *m.* awning; canopy; pomp, show

tole, *m.* outcry, uproar, tumult

toledano (-na), *a.* and *s.* Toledan, of or from Toledo (Old Castile)

tolerable, *a.* bearable, tolerable

tolerancia, *f.* tolerance, forbearance; permission

tolerante, *a.* tolerant, broad-minded

tolerantismo, *m.* religious toleration

tolerar, *v.t.* to put up with, bear, tolerate; overlook, allow, forgive

tolmo, *m.* tor

tolondro, *a.* stupid, heedless, reckless. *m.* bump, bruise

tolonés (-esa), *a.* and *s.* of or from Toulon (France)

tolva, *f.* chute (for grain, etc.)

tolla, *f.* marsh, bog

tollina, *f.* (*fam.*) spanking, whipping

toma, *f.* taking; receiving; conquest, capture; dose (of medicine)

tomada, *f.* taking; take; capture

tomadero, *m.* handle, haft

tomadura, *f.* taking; receiving; dose (of medicine). (*fam.*) **t. de pelo,** leg-pull, joke

tomar, *v.t.* to take; pick up; conquer; eat; drink; adopt, employ; contract (habits); engage (employees); rent; understand; steal; remove; buy; suffer; (*fig.*) overcome (of laughter, sleep, etc.); choose; possess physically; *v.i.* (*with por*) go in the direction of; *v.r.* grow rusty; go mouldy; (*with con*) quarrel with. **t. a pechos,** to take to heart. **t. el fresco,** to take the air. **tomarla con,** to contradict, oppose; bear a grudge. **t. la delantera,** to take the lead; excel, beat. (*fam.*) **t. las de Villadiego,** to quit, show a clean pair of heels. **t. por su cuenta,** to undertake, take charge of; take upon oneself. **Más vale un toma que**

dos te daré, A little help is worth a lot of promises. (*fam.*)
¡Toma! Fancy! You don't say!; Of course! There's nothing new about that!

tomatal, *m.* tomato bed or patch

tomate, *m.* tomato; tomato plant; (*fam.*) hole, potato (in stockings, etc.)

tomatera, *f.* tomato plant

tomatero (-ra), *s.* tomato seller

tómbola, *f.* raffle (gen. for charity); jumble-sale

tomillo, *m.* thyme

tomismo, *m.* Thomism

tomista, *a.* and *m.* and *f.* Thomist

tomo, *m.* volume, book; importance, worth

ton, *m.* abb. **tono**. (*fam.*) **sin t. ni son**, without rhyme or reason

tonada, *f.* words of a song and its tune

tonadilla, *f. dim.* short song; comic song; (*theat.*) musical interlude (*ant.*)

tonadillero (-ra), *s.* composer or singer of tonadillas

tonal, *a.* tonal

tonalidad, *f.* tonality

tonar, *v.i.* (*poet.*) to thunder or lighten

tonel, *m.* barrel; cask; butt

tonelada, *f.* ton

tonelería, *f.* cooperage; collection or stock of casks and barrels

tonelero, *m.* cooper

tonga, **tongada**, *f.* layer, stratum; (*fam.*) task

tónica, *f.* (*mus.*) keynote

tónico, *a.* tonic. *m.* (*med.*) tonic; pick-me-up

tonificador, **tonificante**, *a.* strengthening, invigorating, tonic

tonillo, *m. dim.* monotonous sing-song voice; regional accent

tonina, *f.* tunny fish; dolphin

tono, *m.* inflection, modulation; (*mus.*, *med.*, *art*) tone; pitch, resonance; energy, strength; style; manner, behaviour; (*mus.*) key; mode of speech. **bajar el t.**, (*fig.*, *fam.*) to change one's tune. (*fam.*) **darse t.**, to put on side, give oneself airs. **de buen (mal) t.**, in good (bad) taste

tonsila, *f.* (*anat.*) tonsil

tonsilitis, *f.* tonsillitis

tonsura, *f.* shearing; hair cutting; (*ecc.*) tonsure

tonsurar, *v.t.* to shear, clip; cut the hair off; (*ecc.*) tonsuré

tontaina, *m.* and *f.* (*fam.*) ninny, fool

tontear, *v.i.* to behave foolishly; play the fool

tontería, *f.* foolishness, stupidity; piece of folly; trifle, bagatelle

tontiloco, *a.* (*fam.*) crazy, daft

tontillo, *m.* dress bustle; hoop (for dresses)

tontina, *f.* (*com.*) tontine

tontivano, *a.* vain, conceited

tonto (-ta), *a.* silly, stupid, simple; foolish, absurd. *s.* fool, idiot. *m.* short coat, stroller. (*fam.*) **t. de capirote**, an utter fool. **a tontas y a locas**, without rhyme or reason, topsyturvy. (*fig.*, *fam.*) **volver t. (a)**, to drive crazy

topacio, *m.* topaz

topar, *v.t.* (*with con*) to run into, collide with, hit; meet unexpectedly; come across, find; *v.i.* butt (horned animals); take a bet (cards); consist in (obstacles); meet with (difficulties); (*fam.*) be successful

tope, *m.* projection, part which juts out; obstacle, impediment; collision, bump; crux, difficult point; quarrel, fight; (*mech.*) stop; (*naut.*) mast-head; (*r.w.*) buffer. **hasta el t.**, completely full, full to the brim

topera, *f.* molehill

topetada, *f.* butt (from horned animal); (*fam.*) knock, bang

topetar, *v.t.* and *v.i.* to butt (of horned animals); *v.t.* meet, run into

topetón, *m.* butt; collision, impact, bump; blow on the head

tópico, *a.* topical. *m.* topic, theme

topo, *m.* (*zool.*) mole; (*fam.*) clumsy or short-sighted person; dolt, ninny

topografía, *f.* topography

topográfico, *a.* topographical

topógrafo, *m.* topographer

toque, *m.* touch, touching; pealing, ringing (bells); crux, essence; test, proof; touchstone; (*met.*) assay; warning; (*fam.*) tap (on the shoulder, etc.); (*art*) touch. (*art*) **t. de luz**, light (in a picture). (*art*) **t. de obscuro**, shade (in a picture). **t. de queda**, curfew.

t. de tambor, beating of a drum. (*fam.*) **dar un t. a,** to put to the test; pump (for information)

toquero (-ra), *s.* manufacturer of head-dresses

toquetear, *v.t.* to keep touching, handle repeatedly

toquilla, *f.* hatband or trimming; kerchief; small shawl

torácico, *a.* thoracic

toral, *a.* principal, chief, main

tórax, *m.* thorax

torbellino, *m.* whirlwind; spate of things; (*fam.*) madcap

torcecuello, *m.* (*orn.*) wry-neck

torcedero, *a.* twisted, crooked

torcedor, *a.* twisting. *m.* twister; cause of continual anxiety

torcedura, *f.* twisting; sprain, wrench

torcer, *v.t. irr.* to twist; bend; turn, bear (roads, etc.); slant, slope, incline; misconstrue, pervert; dissuade; wrench, sprain (muscles); corrupt (justice); *v.r.* turn sour (wine, milk); (*fig.*) go astray; turn out badly (negotiations). *Pres. Ind.* **tuerzo, tuerces,** etc. *Pres. Subjunc.* **tuerza, tuerzas, tuerza, tuerzan**

torcida, *f.* wick (of lamps, etc.)

torcido, *a.* bent, crooked, sloping, inclined; curved; dishonest, tortuous. *m.* silk twist

torcijón, *m.* stomach-ache

torcimiento, *m.* twisting; twist, turn; circumlocution; digression

tordo, *a.* piebald, black and white. *m.* (*orn.*) thrush. **t. de campanario** *or* **t. de Castilla,** starling

toreador, *m.* bull fighter

torear, *v.i.* and *v.t.* to fight bulls; *v.t.* ridicule; exasperate, provoke; (*fam.*) string along, deceive

toreo, *m.* bull fighting

torera, *f.* bull fighter's jacket

torero, *a.* (*fam.*) bull fighting. *m.* bull fighter

torete, *m. dim.* small bull; (*fam.*) problem, difficult question; engrossing topic of conversation

toril, *m.* pen for fighting bulls

torio, *m.* thorium

tormenta, *f.* storm; misfortune, calamity; indignation, agitation

tormento, *m.* torment; torture; pain; anxiety, anguish. **dar t. (a),** to torture; inflict pain (on)

tormentoso, *a.* stormy, tempestuous; (*naut.*) pitching, rolling

torna, *f.* return; restitution; backwater

tornaboda, *f.* day after a wedding; rejoicings of this day

tornada, *f.* return home; return visit, revisit; (*poet.*) envoy

tornadizo (-za), *a.* (*fam.*) changeable. *s.* turncoat

tornaguía, *f.* (*com.*) merchandise receipt, landing certificate

tornamiento, *m.* return; change, transformation

tornar, *v.t.* to return, give back; change, transform; *v.i.* return, go back; continue

tornasol, *m.* sunflower; sheen, changing light; (*chem.*) litmus

tornasolado, *a.* shot (of silk, etc.)

tornasolar, *v.t.* to look iridescent; change the colour of, cause to appear variegated

tornátil, *a.* turned (in a lathe); inconstant, changeable; (*poet.*) spinning, revolving

tornatrás, *m.* and *f.* half-caste

tornaviaje, *m.* return journey

tornavoz, *m.* sound-board

torneador, *m.* turner; jouster, fighter in a tournament

tornear, *v.t.* (*sport*) to put a spin on (balls); turn in a lathe; *v.i.* turn round, spin; fight in a tournament; turn over in the mind

torneo, *m.* tournament

tornera, *f.* sister portress (in a nunnery)

tornería, *f.* turnery

tornero, *m.* turner; lathe maker; convent messenger

tornillero, *m.* (*fam., mil.*) deserter

tornillo, *m.* screw; (*fam., mil.*) desertion

torniquete, *m.* turnstile; (*surg.*) tourniquet. **dar t. (a),** to pervert, misinterpret (meanings)

torniscón, *m.* (*fam.*) slap, buffet, blow; pinch

torno, *m.* lathe; turn-table (of a convent, etc.); turn, rotation; windlass; dumb-waiter; axletree; spinning-wheel; bend, loop (in a river). **en t.,** round about, around; in exchange

toro, *m.* bull; (*ast.*) Taurus; *pl.* bull fight. (*fam.*) **t. corrido,** tough nut to crack, wise guy.

(fam.) Ciertos son los toros, So it's true (generally bad news)

toronja, f. grape-fruit

toronjil, m. (bot.) balm gentle

toroso, a. strong, vigorous, robust

torpe, a. heavy, slow, encumbered; torpid; clumsy, unskilled; stupid, dull-witted; obscene, indecent; base, infamous; ugly

torpedeamiento, m. torpedoing, sinking

torpedear, v.t. to torpedo

torpedeo, m. torpedoing

torpedero, m. torpedo-boat

torpedo, m. (icht.) torpedo fish, electric ray; torpedo; sports car. **t. automóvil,** self-propelling torpedo

torpeza, f. slowness, heaviness; torpidity; stupidity; lack of skill, clumsiness; indecency; ugliness; baseness, infamy

tórpido, a. torpid

torrar, v.t. to toast, brown

torre, f. tower; belfry, steeple; turret; rook (chess); (naut.) gun turret; stack, pile (of chairs, etc.); country house with a garden. **t. del tráfico,** traffic robot. **t. de viento,** castle in the air, castle in Spain

torrefacción, f. toasting (of coffee, etc.)

torrencial, a. torrential

torrente, m. torrent; (fig.) spate, rush; crowd

torreón, m. large fortified tower

torrero, m. lighthouse keeper; gardener

torreznero (-ra), s. (fam.) lazybones, idler

torrezno, m. rasher of bacon

tórrido, a. torrid

torsión, f. twisting, torsion

torta, f. cake; pastry, tart; (fam.) slap. **t. de reyes,** traditional Twelfth Night cake

tortada, f. meat or game pie

tortedad, f. twistedness, crookedness

tortera, f. cake-tin; baking-dish; whorl (of a spindle)

tortícolis, m. crick (in the neck)

tortilla, f. omelette. **t. a la española,** potato omelette. **hacer t.,** to smash to atoms. **Se volvió la t.,** (fam.) The tables are turned

tórtola, f. turtle-dove

tórtolo, m. turtle-dove (male); (fam.) devoted lover

tortuga, f. turtle; tortoise. **a paso de t.,** at a snail's pace

tortuosidad, f. tortuousness; winding; indirectness; deceitfulness

tortuoso, a. tortuous; winding; disingenuous, deceitful

tortura, f. twistedness; torture, torment; anguish, grief

torturador, a. torturing, tormenting

torturar, v.t. to torture

torva, f. squall of rain or snow

torzal, m. sewing silk; twist, plait

tos, f. cough. **t. ferina,** whooping-cough

toscano (-na), a. and s. Tuscan. m. Italian language

tosco, a. rough, unpolished; coarse; boorish, uncouth

toser, v.i. to cough

tósigo, m. poison, venom; anguish; affliction

tosigoso, a. poisoned, venomous

tosquedad, f. roughness, lack of polish; coarseness; boorishness, uncouthness

tostada, f. (cul.) toast

tostadera, f. toasting-fork

tostado, a. golden brown, tanned. m. roasting (coffee, etc.)

tostador (-ra), s. toaster of peanuts, etc. m. toaster (utensil); coffee or peanut roaster

tostadura, f. toasting; roasting (coffee, etc.)

tostón, m. (cul.) buttered toast; anything over-toasted; roast pig; (fam.) nuisance, blow, bore

total, a. total, entire, whole; general. m. total. adv. in short; so, therefore

totalidad, f. whole; aggregate, entirety

totalitario, a. totalitarian

tótem, m. totem

totemismo, m. totemism

toxicidad, f. toxicity

tóxico, a. toxic. m. toxic substance

toxicología, f. toxicology

toxicológico, a. toxicological

toxicólogo, m. toxicologist

toxina, f. toxin

tozo, a. dwarfish, small

tozudez, f. obstinacy

tozudo, a. obstinate, obdurate

tozuelo, *m.* scruff, fat nape (of animals)

traba, *f.* setting (of a saw's teeth); hobble (for horses); difficulty, obstacle; fastening; bond, tie; shackle; (*law*) distraint

trabacuenta, *f.* mistake in accounts; argument, difference of opinion

trabajado, *a.* and *past part.* wrought; fashioned; laboured, exhausted, weary

trabajador (-ra), *a.* working; conscientious. *s.* worker

trabajar, *v.i.* to work; function; stand the strain, resist (machines, etc.); exert oneself, strive; toil, labour; operate, work; produce, yield (the earth fruits, etc.); *v.t.* work; till, cultivate; exercise (a horse); worry, annoy, weary; operate, drive; *v.r.* make every effort, work hard

trabajo, *m.* work; toil, labour; operation, working; difficulty, obstacle; literary work; hardship, trouble; process; *pl.* poverty; hardship. **t. al ralenti,** go-slow tactics. (*law*) **trabajos forzados** (*or* **forzosos**), hard labour. **pasar trabajos,** to go through hardship

trabajoso, *a.* difficult, hard; ailing, delicate; needy; afflicted

trabalenguas, *m.* (*fam.*) tongue-twister, jaw-breaker

trabamiento, *m.* joining, fastening; uniting; initiation, commencement; shackling; hobbling (horses)

trabar, *v.t.* to join, unite, fasten; grasp, seize; set the teeth (of a saw); thicken; begin, initiate; hobble (horses); reconcile, bring together, harmonize; shackle; (*law*) distrain; *v.r.* speak with an impediment; stutter, hesitate. **t. amistad,** to make friends. **t. conversación,** to get into conversation. **Se me trabó la lengua,** I began to stutter

trabazón, *f.* join, union, fastening; connection; thickness, consistency

trabilla, *f.* waistcoat strap; dropped (knitting) stitch

trabuca, *f.* squib, Chinese cracker, rip-rap

trabucar, *v.t.* to turn upside down, upset; confuse, bewilder; mix up, confuse (news, etc.); pronounce or write incorrectly

trabucazo, *m.* shot or report of a blunderbuss; (*fam.*) calamity, unexpected misfortune

trabuco, *m.* (*mil.*) catapult; blunderbuss

trabuquete, *m.* catapult

tracamundana, *f.* (*fam.*) barter, exchange of trash; hubbub, uproar

tracción, *f.* pulling; traction

tracería, *f.* (*arch.*) tracery

traciano (-na), **tracio** (-ia), *a.* and *s.* Thracian

tracoma, *f.* (*med.*) trachoma

tracto, *m.* tract, area, expanse; lapse of time

tractor, *m.* tractor. **t. de orugas,** caterpillar tractor

tradición, *f.* tradition

tradicional, *a.* traditional

tradicionalismo, *m.* traditionalism

tradicionalista, *a.* traditionalistic. *m.* and *f.* traditionalist

traducción, *f.* translation; interpretation, explanation

traducible, *a.* translatable

traducir, *v.t. irr.* to translate; interpret, explain; express. See **conducir**

traductor (-ra), *s.* translator; interpreter

traedizo, *a.* portable, movable

traer, *v.t. irr.* to bring; attract; cause, occasion; wear, have on; quote, cite (as proof); compel, force; persuade; conduct, lead (persons); be engaged in; *v.r.* dress (well *or* badly). **t. consigo,** to bring with it; have *or* carry *or* bring with one. **t. entre manos,** to have on hand. *Pres. Ind.* **traigo, traes,** etc. *Pres. Part.* **trayendo.** *Preterite* **traje, tra-. jiste,** etc. *Pres. Subjunc.* **traiga,** etc. *Imperf. Subjunc.* **trajese,** etc.

trafagador, *m.* dealer, trafficker, merchant

tráfago, *m.* traffic, trade; toil, drudgery

trafalmejas, *a.* (*fam.*) rowdy, crazy. *m.* and *f.* (*fam.*) rowdy

traficante, *m.* and *f.* dealer, merchant, trader

traficar, *v.i.* to trade; travel

tráfico, *m.* traffic; trade, commerce

tragaderas, *f. pl.* throat, gullet. (*fam.*) **tener buenas t.,** to be very credulous; be tolerant (of evil)

tragadero, *m.* gullet, throat; sink, drain; hole, plug

tragador (-ra), *s.* glutton, guzzler

tragahombres, *m.* (*fam.*) braggart, bully

trágala, *m.* (**trágala tú, servilón),** title of Spanish Liberal song aimed at Absolutists; (*fam.*) take that!

tragaleguas, *m.* and *f.* (*fam.*) fast walker

tragaluz, *m.* skylight; fan-light

tragantón (-ona), *a.* (*fam.*) guzzling, greedy. *s.* glutton

tragantona, *f.* (*fam.*) spread, large meal; swallowing with difficulty; (*fig., fam.*) hard pill to swallow

tragaperras, *m.* (*fam.*) automatic machine, catchpenny

tragar, *v.t.* to swallow; eat ravenously, devour; engulf, swallow up; believe, take in; tolerate, put up with; dissemble; consume, absorb

tragedia, *f.* tragedy

trágico (-ca), *a.* tragic. *s.* tragedian; writer of tragedies

tragicomedia, *f.* tragi-comedy

tragicómico, *a.* tragi-comic

trago, *m.* draught, swallow, gulp; (*fig., fam.*) bitter pill. (*fam.*) **a tragos,** little by little, slowly

tragón (-ona), *a.* (*fam.*) greedy, gluttonous. *s.* glutton

tragonear, *v.t.* (*fam.*) to devour, eat avidly

traición, *f.* treason, treachery. **a t.,** treacherously

traicionar, *v.t.* to betray

traicionero (-ra), *a.* treacherous. *s.* traitor

traída, *f.* conduction. **t. de aguas,** water supply

traidor (-ra), *a.* treacherous. *s.* traitor

trailla, *f.* lead, leash (for dogs)

traje, *m.* dress, apparel; outfit, costume; suit. **t. de americana,** lounge-suit. **t. de ceremonia** *or* **t. de etiqueta,** full dress uniform; evening dress (men). **t. de luces,** bull fighter's gala out-

fit. **t. de montar,** riding-habit. **t. de noche,** evening dress (women). **t. paisano,** civilian dress; lounge-suit

trajín, *m.* carriage, transport; busyness, moving around; bustle; clatter

trajinar, *v.t.* to carry, transport; *v.i.* be busy, go about on one's affairs

tralla, *f.* rope, cord; lash (of a whip); whip

trama, *f.* woof (of cloth); twisted silk; intrigue, scheme; (*lit.*) plot; olive flower

tramar, *v.t.* to weave; prepare, hatch (plots); (*fig.*) prepare the way for; *v.i.* flower (trees, especially olive)

tramitación, *f.* transaction, conduct; procedure, method

tramitar, *v.t.* to transact, conduct, settle

trámite, *m.* transit; negotiation, phase of a business deal; requirement, condition

tramo, *m.* plot of ground; flight of stairs, staircase; stretch, expanse, reach, tract

tramontana, *f.* north wind; arrogance, haughtiness

tramontano, *a.* ultramontane, from beyond the mountains

tramontar, *v.i.* to cross the mountains; sink behind the mountains (sun); *v.r.* run away, escape

tramoya, *f.* (*theat.*) stage machinery; trick, deception, hoax

tramoyista, *m.* stage-carpenter; stage-hand; scene-shifter. *m.* and *f.* trickster, impostor, swindler

trampa, *f.* trap, snare; trapdoor; flap of a shop counter; trouser fly; trick, swindle; overdue debt. (*fig., fam.*) **caer en la t.,** to fall into the trap. (*fam.*) **coger en la t.,** to catch in a trap; catch in the act

trampal, *m.* bog, marsh

trampantojo, *m.* (*fam.*) optical illusion, swindle

trampeador, *a.* (*fam.*) swindling. *s.* trickster, swindler

trampear, *v.i.* (*fam.*) to obtain money on false pretences; struggle on (against illness, etc.); keep oneself alive, make shift; *v.t.* defraud, swindle

trampolín, *m.* spring-board; diving-board; (*fig.*) jumping-off place

tramposo (-sa), *s.* debtor; cardsharper; swindler

tranca, *f.* thick stick, cudgel; bar (of a window, etc.)

trancada, *f.* stride

trancar, *v.t.* to bar the door; *v.i.* (*fam.*) oppose, resist

trancazo, *m.* blow with a stick; influenza

trance, *m.* crisis, difficult juncture; danger, peril. **t.** de armas, armed combat. **a todo t.,** at all costs, without hesitation

tranco, *m.* stride; threshold. (*fam.*) **en dos trancos,** in a trice

tranquera, *f.* stockade, palisade

tranquilar, *v.t.* (*com.*) to check off

tranquilidad, *f.* tranquillity, peace, quietness; composure, serenity

tranquilizador, *a.* tranquillizing, soothing

tranquilizar, *v.t.* to calm, quieten; soothe

tranquilo, *a.* tranquil, quiet, peaceful; serene, composed

transacción, *f.* compromise, arrangement; transaction, negotiation, deal

transalpino, *a.* transalpine

transandino, *a.* transandean

transatlántico, *a.* transatlantic. *m.* (transatlantic) liner

transbordar, *v.t.* to trans-ship; transfer, remove goods from one vehicle to another

transbordo, *m.* trans-shipment, trans-shipping; transfer, removal

transcendencia, *f.* See **trascendencia**

transcendental, *a.* See **trascendental**

transcribir, *v.t.* to transcribe (also *mus.*); copy. *Past Part.* **transcrito**

transcripción, *f.* transcription (also *mus.*); copy, transcript

transcurrir, *v.i.* to elapse, pass (time)

transcurso, *m.* passage, lapse, course (of time)

transepto, *m.* (*arch.*) transept

transeúnte, *a.* transient, temporary. *m.* and *f.* passer-by; visitor, sojourner

transferencia, *f.* transfer (from one place to another); (*law*) conveyance, transference

transferidor (-ra), *a.* transferring. *s.* transferrer; (*law*) transferor

transferir, *v.t.* *irr.* to transfer, move from one place to another; (*law*) convey (property, etc.); postpone. See **sentir**

transfiguración, *f.* transfiguration

transfigurar, *v.t.* to transfigure

transfijo, *a.* transfixed

transfixión, *f.* transfixion

transformable, *a.* transformable

transformación, *f.* transformation

transformador, *a.* transformative. *m.* (*elec.*) transformer

transformar, *v.t.* to transform; reform (persons); *v.r.* be transformed; reform, mend one's ways

transfregar, *v.t.* *irr.* to rub, scrub. See **cegar**

transfretar, *v.t.* (*naut.*) to cross the sea; *v.i.* spread

tránsfuga, *m.* and *f.*, **tránsfugo,** *m.* fugitive; political turncoat

transfundir, *v.t.* to transfuse, pour from one vessel to another; imbue, transmit

transfusor, *a.* transfusive

transgredir, *v.t.* to transgress, infringe

transgresión, *f.* infringement, violation, transgression

transgresor (-ra), *a.* infringing. *s.* transgressor, violator

transiberiano, *a.* trans-Siberian

transición, *f.* transition, change

transido, *a.* exhausted, worn-out, spent; niggardly, mean

transigencia, *f.* tolerance, forbearance, indulgence

transigente, *a.* tolerant, forbearing

transigir, *v.i.* to be tolerant; be broad-minded. *v.t.* put up with, tolerate

transilvano (-na), *a.* and *s.* Transylvanian

transitable, *a.* passable, traversable

transitar, *v.i.* to cross, pass through; travel

transitivo, *a.* (*gram.*) transitive

tránsito, *m.* passage, crossing; transit; stopping place; transition, change; gallery of a cloister; (ecc.) holy death. **de t.,** temporarily; in transit (of goods). **hacer tránsitos,** to break one's journey, stop

transitorio, a. transitory, fugitive, fleeting

translimitación, f. trespass; bad behaviour; armed intervention in neighbouring state

translimitar, v.t. to overstep the boundaries (of a state, etc.); overstep the limits (of decency, etc.)

translucidez, f. translucence, semi-transparency

translúcido, a. translucent, semitransparent

transmarino, a. transmarine

transmigración, f. transmigration

transmigrar, v.i. to migrate; transmigrate (of the soul)

transmisión, f. transmission. **t. del pensamiento,** thought-transference

transmisor, a. transmitting. m. (elec.) transmitter, sender

transmitir, v.t. to transmit; (mech.) drive

transmutable, a. transmutable

transmutación, f. transmutation, transformation, change

transmutar, v.t. to transmute, transform, change

transmutativo, a. transmutative

transoceánico, a. transoceanic

transpacífico, a. transpacific

transparencia, f. transparency; obviousness

transparentarse, v.r. to be transparent; show through; (fig.) reveal, give away (secrets)

transparente, a. transparent; translucent; evident, obvious. m. window-shade, blind

transpiración, f. transpiration; perspiration

transpirar, v.i. to perspire; transpire

transpirenaico, a. trans-Pyrenean

transponer, v.t. irr. to move, transfer; transplant; transpose; v.r. hide behind; sink behind the horizon (sun, stars); be half-asleep. See **poner**

transportable, a. transportable

transportación, f. See **transporte**

transportador (-ra), a. transport. s. transporter. m. (geom.) protractor

transportamiento, m. See **transporte**

transportar, v.t. to transport; (mus.) transpose; carry; v.r. (fig.) be carried away by (anger, rapture)

transporte, m. transport, carriage; cartage; (naut.) transport; strong emotion, transport, ecstasy

transposición, f. transposition

transpositivo, a. transpositive

transubstanciación, f. transubstantiation

transubstanciar, v.t. to transubstantiate, transmute

transversal, transverso, a. transverse

tranvía, m. street railway; tramcar. **t. de sangre,** horse tram

tranviario, a. tram, tram-car. m. tramway employee

trapacear, v.i. to cheat, swindle

trapacete, m. (com.) day-book

trapacista, m. and f. trickster, swindler, knave

trapajoso, a. ragged, shabby, tattered

trápala, f. noise, confusion, hubbub; noise of horse's hoofs, gallop; (fam.) trick, swindle; prattling, babbling. m. and f. (fam.) babbler, prattler; trickster

trapalear, v.i. to walk noisily, tramp; (fam.) chatter, babble

trapatiesta, f. (fam.) brawl, row, quarrel

trapaza, f. hoax, swindle

trapecio, m. trapeze; (geom.) trapezium, trapezoid

trapense, a. and m. (ecc.) Trappist

trapería, f. old-clothes shop; old clothes, rags, trash, frippery

trapero (-ra), s. old-clothes seller; rag merchant; rag-picker

trapezoide, m. (geom.) trapezium, trapezoid

trapichear, v.i. (fam.) to make shift, endeavour

trapiento, a. ragged, shabby

trapillo, m. (fam.) poverty-stricken lover; nest-egg, savings. (fam.) **de t.,** in undress, in négligé

trapío, *m.* (*fam.*) spirit of a fighting bull; verve, dash, independent air (women)

trapisonda, *f.* (*fam.*) uproar, brawl; hubbub, bustle; snare, fix

trapisondear, *v.i.* (*fam.*) to be given to brawling; scheme, intrigue

trapisondista, *m.* and *f.* brawler; schemer, trickster

trapo, *m.* rag; (*naut.*) canvas; bull fighter's cape; *pl.* garments, bits and pieces. (*fam.*) **poner como un t.** (a), to dress down, scold. (*fam.*) **soltar el t.**, to burst out crying or laughing

trapujo, *m.* (*fam.*) trick; subterfuge

traque, *m.* report, bang (of a rocket, etc.); fuse (of a firework)

tráquea, *f.* (*anat.*) trachea

traqueal, *a.* (*anat.*) tracheal

traqueotomía, *f.* (*surg.*) tracheotomy

traquetear, *v.i.* to crack, bang, go off with a report; rattle; jolt (of trains, etc.). *v.t.* shake, stir; (*fam.*) paw, handle too much

traqueteo, *m.* banging (of fireworks); creaking; rattling; jolting (of trains, etc.)

traquido, *m.* report (of a gun); crack (of a whip); creak

tras, *prep.* after; behind; following, in pursuit of; trans- (in compounds). *m.* (*fam.*) buttock; sound of a blow, bang, bump. **t. t.**, knocking (at a door); banging

trasalcoba, *f.* dressing-room

trasbarrás, *m.* bang, bump, noise

trascendencia, *f.* transcendence, excellence; consequence, result

trascendental, *a.* transcendental; important, far-reaching

trascender, *v.i. irr.* to spread to, influence; become known, leak out; exhale a scent; *v.t.* investigate, discover. See **entender**

trascocina, *f.* back kitchen

trascolar, *v.t. irr.* to filter, strain; cross over, traverse. See **colar**

trascordarse, *v.r. irr.* to mix up, make a muddle of, forget. See **acordar**

trasechar, *v.t.* to ambush, waylay

trasegar, *v.t. irr.* to upset, turn upside down; transfer, move from one place to another;

empty, pour out, upset (liquids). See **cegar**

traseñalar, *v.t.* to re-mark, mark again

trasera, *f.* rear, back, rear portion

trasero, *a.* rear, back. *m.* hindquarters, rump; buttocks, seat; *pl.* (*fam.*) ancestors

trasgo, *m.* imp, sprite, puck

trashumante, *a.* nomad (of flocks)

trashumar, *v.i.* to go from winter to summer pasture (or vice versa) (flocks)

trasiego, *m.* emptying, pouring out, upsetting (liquids); decanting (of wines)

traslación, *f.* removal, transfer; alteration (of date for meeting); metaphor

trasladable, *a.* removable, movable, transferable

trasladar, *v.t.* to remove, transfer; move from one place to another; alter (the date of a meeting); translate; copy, transcribe; *v.r.* remove (from a place)

traslado, *m.* removal; transfer; transcription

traslapar, *v.t.* to cover, overlap

traslapo, *m.* overlap, overlapping

traslucirse, *v.r. irr.* to be transparent or translucent; shine through; come out (of secrets); infer, gather. See **lucir**

traslumbramiento, *m.* dazzle, glare, brilliance

traslumbrar, *v.t.* to dazzle; *v.r.* flicker, glimmer; fade quickly, disappear

trasluz, *m.* reflected light. **al t.**, against the light

trasmañana, *adv.* the day after tomorrow

trasmañanar, *v.t.* to put off from day to day

trasminar, *v.t.* to undermine, excavate; *v.i.* percolate, ooze; penetrate, spread

trasnochada, *f.* previous night, last night; night's vigil; sleepless night; (*mil.*) night attack

trasnochado, *a.* stale, old; weary; hackneyed; drawn, pinched

†**trasnochador** (-ra), *s.* one who watches by night or stays up all night; (*fam.*) night-bird, reveller

trasnochar, *v.i.* to stay up all night; watch through the night;

spend the night; *v.t.* sleep on, leave for following day

trasnoche, trasnocho, *m.* (*fam.*) night out; night vigil

trasoír, *v.t. irr.* to hear incorrectly, misunderstand. See **oír**

trasojado, *a.* haggard, tired-eyed

trasoñar, *v.t. irr.* to imagine, mistake a dream for reality. See **contar**

traspalar, *v.t.* to fork (grain); shovel; transfer, move

trasparencia, *f.* See **transparencia**

traspasar, *v.t.* to transfer, move; cross; (*law*) convey, make over to; pierce; transgress, flout; exceed one's authority; (*fig.*) go too far; reexamine, go over again; give intolerable pain (illness, grief). **Se traspasa,** To be disposed of (houses, etc.)

traspaso, *m.* transport, transfer; (*law*) conveyance; property transferred; price agreed upon

traspié, *m.* slip, catching of the foot, stumble; heel of the foot; (*fam.*) **dar traspiés,** to blunder

trasplantación, *f.,* **trasplante,** *m.* transplantation; emigration

trasplantar, *v.t.* (*agr.*) to transplant; *v.r.* emigrate

trasplante, *m.* planting out

traspuesta, *f.* transposition; back quarters; rear (of a house); back yard

traspunte, *m.* (*theat.*) prompter

traspuntín, *m.* (*aut.*) folding seat

trasquilar, *v.t.* to cut the hair unevenly; shear (sheep); (*fam.*) cut down, diminish

trasquilón, *m.* cropping (hair); shearing; (*fam.*) money stolen by pilfering

trastada, *f.* (*fam.*) dirty trick, mean act

traste, *m.* fret (of stringed instruments); tasting cup. **dar al t. con,** to spoil, upset, damage. (*fam.*) **sin trastes,** topsyturvy, without method

trastear, *v.t.* to play well (mandolin, etc.); (*fam.*) manage tactfully; *v.i.* move around, change (furniture, etc.); discuss excitedly

trastejar, *v.t.* to repair the roof; renew slates; overhaul

trastienda, *f.* back of a shop; room behind a shop; (*fam.*) wariness, caution

trasto, *m.* piece of furniture; (household) utensil; lumber, useless furniture; (*theat.*) wing or set piece; (*fam.*) useless person, ne'er-do-well; oddment, thing; *pl.* implements, equipment

trastornable, *a.* easily overturned or upset; easily agitated

trastornar, *v.t.* to turn upside down; perturb, disturb; (*fig.*) overpower (scents, etc.); disorder, upset; dissuade; send mad; derange the mind

trastorno, *m.* upset; perturbation, anxiety; disorder; mental derangement; confusion (of the senses)

trastrabillar, *v.i.* to stumble, slip; totter, sway; hesitate; stutter, be tongue-tied

trastrás, *m.* (*fam.*) last but one (in games)

trastrocamiento, *m.* alteration, change; disarrangement

trastrocar, *v.t. irr.* to alter, change; disarrange; change the order of. See **contar**

trasudar, *v.i.* to perspire

trasudor, *m.* light perspiration

trasuntar, *v.t.* to copy, transcribe; summarize

trasunto, *m.* copy, transcript; imitation

trasver, *v.t. irr.* to see through or between, glimpse; see incorrectly. See **ver**

trasverter, *v.i. irr.* to overflow. See **entender**

trata, *f.* slave-trade. **t. de blancas,** white-slave traffic

tratable, *a.* easily accessible, sociable, unpretentious

tratadista, *m.* writer of a treatise; expert, writer on special subjects

tratado, *m.* pact, agreement; treaty; treatise

tratador (-ra), *s.* arbitrator

tratamiento, *m.* treatment; courtesy title; address, style; (*med.*) treatment; process

tratante, *m.* merchant, dealer

tratar, *v.t.* to handle, use; conduct, manage; have dealings with, meet, know (e.g. **Yo no le trato,** I don't know him); behave well or badly towards; care for, treat; discuss, deal with (e.g. ¿ De qué trata el libro? What is the book about?); propose, suggest; (*chem.*) treat; (*with de*) address as, call; *v.i.* have amorous relations; (*with de*) try to, endeavour to; (*with en*) trade in; *v.r.* look after oneself, treat oneself; conduct oneself

trato, *m.* use, handling; management; conduct, behaviour; manner, demeanour; appellation, title; commerce, traffic; dealings, intercourse; treatment; agreement, arrangement. **t. colectivo,** collective bargaining

traumático, *a.* (*med.*) traumatic

traumatismo, *m.* traumatism

través, *m.* slant, slope; mishap; (*mil., arch.*) traverse. **a t.** *or* **al t.,** across; through. **de t.,** athwart; through

travesaño, *m.* crossbar; bolster; rung (of a ladder); (*carp.*) traverse

travesear, *v.i.* to run about, romp, be mischievous; lead a vicious life; speak wittily; move ceaselessly (water, etc.)

travesía, *f.* crossing; traverse; crossroad; side road or street; distance, space; sea crossing; crosswise position; stretch of road within a town

travestido, *a.* disguised, dressed up

travesura, *f.* romping, frolic; mischief; prank; quick-wittedness

traviesa, *f.* sleeper (railway); (*arch.*) rafter; distance between two points

travieso, *a.* transverse, crosswise; mischievous, wilful; debauched; clever, subtle; evermoving (streams, etc.)

trayecto, *m.* run, distance, journey; stretch, expanse, tract; fare-stage

trayectoria, *f.* trajectory; journey

traza, *f.* plan, design, draft; scheme, project; idea, proposal; aspect, appearance; means, manner. **Hombre pobre todo es trazas,** A poor man is full of schemes (for bettering himself)

trazado, *m.* designing, drawing; design, draft, model, plan; course, direction (of a canal, etc.)

trazador (-ra), *s.* draftsman, designer; planner, schemer

trazar, *v.t.* to plan, draft, design; make a drawing of; trace; describe; map out, arrange

trazo, *m.* line, stroke; outline, contour, form, line; (*art*) fold in drapery; stroke of the pen

trébedes, *f. pl.* (*cul.*) trivet

trebejar, *v.i.* to frolic, skip, play

trebejo, *m.* chessman; utensil, article (gen. *pl.*); plaything

trébol, *m.* (*bot.*) clover

trece, *a.* and *m.* thirteen, thirteenth. *m.* thirteenth (day of the month)

trecemesino, *a.* thirteen months old

trecenario, *m.* period of thirteen days

trecho, *m.* distance, space; interval (of time). **a trechos,** at intervals. **de t. en t.,** from time to time

trefe, *a.* pliable, flexible; light; spurious (coins)

tregua, *f.* truce, respite, rest. **dar treguas,** to afford relief, give a respite; give time

treinta, *a.* and *m.* thirty; thirtieth. *m.* thirtieth (day of month)

treintañal, *a.* thirty years old

treintavo, *a.* thirtieth

treintena, *f.* thirtieth (part)

tremebundo, *a.* fearsome, dread

tremedal, *m.* bog; quagmire

tremendo, *a.* fearful, formidable; awesome; (*fam.*) tremendous, enormous

trementina, *f.* turpentine

tremesino, *a.* three months old

tremolar, *v.t.* and *v.i.* to wave, fly (banners); (*fig.*) make a show of

tremolina, *f.* noise of the wind; (*fam.*) hubbub, confusion

trémulo, *a.* trembling, tremulous

tren, *m.* supply, provision; outfit; equipment; pomp, show; railway train; following, train. **t. ascendente,** up train (from coast to interior). (*fam.*) **t. botijo,** excursion train. **t. con coches corridos,** corridor train. **t. correo,** mail train. **t. descendente,** down train (from interior to coast). **t. mixto,** train carrying passengers and freight. **t. ómnibus,** slow stopping train. **t. rápido,** express

trencilla, *f.* braid, trimming

trencillar, *v.t.* to trim with braid, braid

treno, *m.* threnody

trenza, *f.* plait, braid; plait of hair; bread-twist. **en t.,** in plaits, plaited (hair)

trenzadera, *f.* linen tape

trenzar, *v.t.* to plait, braid; *v.i.* curvet, prance

trepa, *f.* perforation, boring, piercing; climbing; creeping; (*fam.*) half-somersault; grain, surface (of wood); craftiness, slyness; deception, fraud; beating, drubbing

trepador, *a.* climbing; crawling; (*bot.*) creeping, climbing. *m.* climbing place

trepanación, *f.* (*surg.*) trepanning

trepanar, *v.t.* (*surg.*) to trepan

trepante, *a.* creeping; (*bot.*) twining, climbing

trepar, *v.i.* to climb, ascend; (*bot.*) climb or creep; bore, perforate

trepidación, *f.* trepidation, dread; vibration; jarring; shaking

trepidar, *v.i.* to shiver, shudder; vibrate; shake; jar

trépido, *a.* shuddering, shivering; vibrating

tres, *a.* three; third. *m.* figure three; third (of days of month); three (of playing cards); trio. (*fam.*) **Como t. y dos son cinco,** As sure as two and two make four (lit. three and two make five)

trescientos, *a.* and *m.* three hundred; three hundredth

tresillo, *m.* ombre (card game); (*mus.*) triplet

tresnal, *m.* (*agr.*) stook, cock, sheaf

treta, *f.* scheme; trick, hoax; feint (fencing)

trezavo, *a.* thirteenth

tría, *f.* selection, choice; worn place (in cloth)

triangulación, *f.* (*surv.*) triangulation

triángulo, *a.* triangular. *m.* (*geom., mus.*) triangle. **t. acutángulo,** acute-angled triangle. **t. obtusángulo,** obtuse-angled triangle. **t. rectángulo,** right-angled triangle

triar, *v.t.* to select, pick out; *v.i.* fly in and out of the hive (bees); *v.r.* grow threadbare, become worn

tribu, *f.* tribe; species, family

tribulación, *f.* tribulation, suffering

tribuna, *f.* tribune; platform, rostrum, pulpit; spectators' gallery; stand. **t. de la prensa,** press-gallery. **t. del jurado,** jury-box. **t. del órgano,** organ-loft

tribunado, *m.* tribunate

tribunal, *m.* law court; (*law*) bench; judgment seat; tribunal; board of examiners. **t. de menores,** juvenile court. (*naut.*) **t. de presas,** prize court. **t. de primera instancia,** (*law*) petty sessions. **t. militar,** court-martial

tribúnico, *a.* tribunary

tribuno, *m.* tribune; political speaker

tributar, *v.t.* to pay taxes; offer, render (thanks, homage, etc.)

tributario (-ia), *a.* tributary; tax-paying, contributive. *s.* tax-payer. *m.* tributary (of a river)

tributo, *m.* contribution; tax; tribute, homage; census

tricenal, *a.* of thirty years' duration; occurring every thirty years

tricentésimo, *a.* three-hundredth

triciclo, *m.* tricycle

triclinio, *m.* triclinium

tricolor, *a.* three-coloured

tricorne, *a.* (*poet.*) three-cornered, three-horned

tricornio, *a.* three-cornered. *m.* three-cornered hat

tricotomía, *f.* trichotomy, division into three

tricromía, *f.* three-colour process

tridente, *a.* tridentate, three-pronged. *m.* trident

tridentino, *a.* Tridentine

trienal, *a.* triennial

trienio, *m.* space of three years

trifásico, *a.* (*elec.*) three-phase

trifolio, *m.* trefoil

triforme, *a.* triform

trigal, *m.* wheat-field

trigésimo, *a.* thirtieth

triglifo, *m.* (*arch.*) triglyph

trigo, *m.* wheat plant; ear of

wheat; wheat field (gen. *pl.*); wealth, money. **t. sarraceno,** buckwheat. **t. tremés, t. trechel, t. tremesino** *or* **t. de marzo,** summer wheat

trigonometría, *f.* trigonometry

trigueño, *a.* brunette, dark

triguero, *a.* wheat; wheat-growing. *m.* grain-sieve; grain merchant

trilátero, *a.* three-sided, trilateral

trilingüe, *a.* trilingual

trilogía, *f.* trilogy

trilla, *f.* (*icht.*) red mullet; (*agr.*) harrow; threshing; threshing season

trillado, *a.* frequented, trodden, worn (paths); hackneyed

trilladora, *f.* threshing machine

trillar, *v.t.* (*agr.*) to thresh; (*fam.*) frequent; ill-treat

trillo, *m.* threshing machine; harrow

trillón, *m.* trillion

trimestral, *a.* quarterly; terminal (in schools, etc.)

trimestre, *a.* quarterly; terminal. *m.* quarter, three months; term (in schools, etc.); quarterly payment; quarter's rent

trinado, *m.* (*mus.*) trill; twittering, shrilling (of birds)

trinar, *v.i.* (*mus.*) to trill; twitter, shrill; (*fam.*) get in a temper, be furious

trincapiñones, *m.* (*fam.*) scatterbrained youth

trincar, *v.t.* to fasten securely; tie tightly; pinion; (*naut.*) lash, make fast; cut up, chop; (*fam.*) tipple; *v.i.* (*naut.*) sail close to the wind

trincha, *f.* waistcoat strap

trinchante, *m.* table-carver; carving-fork; stone-cutter's hammer

trinchar, *v.t.* to carve (at table); (*fam.*) decide, dispose

trinchera, *f.* (*mil.*) trench; cutting (for roads, etc.); trench coat

trinchero, *m.* trencher, platter; serving-table, side-table

trineo, *m.* sledge, sleigh

trinidad, *f.* trinity

trinitaria, *f.* (*bot.*) heartsease

trinitario (-ia), *a.* and *s.* (*ecc.*) Trinitarian

trino, *a.* triune; ternary. *m.* (*mus.*) trill

trinomio, *m.* (*math.*) trinomial

trinquete, *m.* (*naut.*) mainmast; mainsail; (*sport*) rackets; (*mech.*) ratchet

trinquis, *m.* (*fam.*) draught, drink

trío, *m.* (*mus.*) trio

tripa, *f.* entrail, gut; (*fam.*) belly; inside (of some fruits). (*fam.*) **hacer de tripas corazón,** to take heart, buck up. (*fig., fam.*) **revolver las tripas (a),** to make one sick

tripartición, *f.* tripartition

tripartir, *v.t.* to divide into three

tripartito, *a.* tripartite

tripicallos, *m. pl.* (*cul.*) tripe

triplano, *m.* (*aer.*) triplane

triple, *a.* triple; (of yarn) three-ply

triplicación, *f.* trebling

triplicar, *v.t.* to treble

trípode, *m.* (sometimes *f.*) three-legged stool or table; tripod; trivet

tripolino (-na), **tripolitano** (-na), *a.* and *s.* of or from Tripoli

tríptico, *m.* triptych

triptongo, *m.* triphthong

tripulación, *f.* crew (ships and aircraft)

tripulante, *m.* member of a crew

tripular, *v.t.* to provide with a crew, man; equip, furnish; serve in, work as the crew of

trique, *m.* crack, creak. (*fam.*) **a cada t.,** at every moment

triquiñuela, *f.* (*fam.*) evasion, subterfuge

triquitraque, *m.* tap, rap; crack; rip-rap (firework)

trirreme, *m.* (*naut.*) trireme

tris, *m.* crack, noise of glass, etc., cracking; (*fam.*) instant, trice. **estar en un t. (de),** to be on the verge (of), within an ace (of)

trisar, *v.t.* to crack, break, splinter (glass); *v.i.* chirp, twitter (especially swallows)

trisca, *f.* cracking, crushing, crackling (of nuts, etc.); noise, tumult

triscar, *v.i.* to make a noise with the feet; gambol, frolic; creak, crack; *v.t.* blend, mingle; set the teeth of a saw

trisecar, *v.t.* (*geom.*) to trisect

trisección, *f.* trisection

trisemanal, *a.* three times weekly; every three weeks

trisílabo, *a.* trisyllabic

trismo, *m.* lock-jaw, trismus

triste, *a.* unhappy, sorrowful; melancholy, gloomy; sad; piteous, unfortunate; useless, worthless

tristeza, tristura, *f.* unhappiness; melancholy, gloom; sadness; piteousness

tritón, *m.* merman

triturar, *v.t.* to crumble, crush; chew; masticate; ill-treat, bruise; refute, contradict

triunfada, *f.* trumping at cards

triunfador (-ra), *a.* triumphant. *s.* victor

triunfal, *a.* triumphal

triunfante, *a.* triumphant

triunfar, *v.i.* to triumph; be victorious, win; trump (at cards); spend ostentatiously

triunfo, *m.* triumph; victory; trump-card; success; booty, spoils of war; conquest

triunvirato, *m.* triumvirate

triunviro, *m.* triumvir

trivial, *a.* well-known, hackneyed; frequented, trodden; commonplace, mediocre; trivial, unimportant

trivialidad, *f.* banality, triteness; mediocrity; triviality

trivio, *m.* road junction

triza, *f.* fragment, bit; (*naut.*) rope. **hacer trizas,** to smash to bits

trizar, *v.t.* to smash up, destroy

trocable, *a.* exchangeable

trocada, a la, *adv.* contrariwise; in exchange

trocador (-ra), *s.* exchanger

trocaico, *a.* and *m.* trochaic

trocar, *v.t.* *irr.* to exchange; vomit; distort, misconstrue, mistake; *v.r.* change, alter one's behaviour; change places with another; be transferred. See **contar**

trocear, *v.t.* to divide into pieces

trocha, *f.* short cut; trail, path, track

trochemoche, a, *adv.* (*fam.*) without rhyme or reason, pell-mell

trofeo, *m.* trophy; victory; military booty

troglodita, *a.* and *m.* and *f.* troglodyte. *m.* (*fig.*) savage, barbarian. *m.* and *f.* glutton

troglodítico, *a.* troglodytic

troj, *f.* granary

trojero, *m.* granary keeper

trola, *f.* (*fam.*) lie, nonsense, hoax

trole, *m.* electric trolley

trolebús, *m.* trolley-bus

trolero, *a.* (*fam.*) deceiving, lying

tromba, *f.* waterspout

trombón, *m.* (*mus.*) trombone; trombone player

trombosis, *f.* (*med.*) thrombosis

trompa, *f.* elephant's trunk; (*mus.*) horn; proboscis (of insects); waterspout; humming-top. **t. de Falopio,** (*anat.*) Fallopian tube

trompada, *f.* (*fam.*) bang, bump; blow, buffet, slap; collision

trompazo, *m.* heavy blow, knock, bang

trompear, *v.i.* to play with a top; *v.t.* knock about

trompero, *m.* top-maker. *a.* deceiving, swindling

trompeta, *f.* trumpet; bugle. *m.* trumpeter; bugler; (*fam.*) ninny. **t. de amor,** (*bot.*) sunflower

trompetada, *f.* (*fam.*) stupid remark, piece of nonsense

trompetazo, *m.* bray of trumpet; bugle-blast; (*fam.*) stupid remark

trompetear, *v.i.* (*fam.*) to play the trumpet or bugle

trompeteo, *m.* trumpeting, trumpet-call; sound of the bugle

trompetería, *f.* collection of trumpets; metal organ-pipes

trompetero, *m.* trumpet or bugle maker or player

trompetilla, *f.* *dim.* little trumpet; ear-trumpet

trompicar, *v.t.* to make stumble, trip. *v.i.* stumble, trip up

trompicón, *m.* stumble

trompo, *m.* humming or spinning-top; (*fam.*) dolt, idiot

tronada, *f.* thunderstorm

tronado, *a.* worn-out; threadbare, old; poor, poverty-stricken; down-at-heel

tronar, *v.* *impers.* *irr.* to thunder; *v.i.* growl, roar (guns); (*fam.*) go bankrupt, be ruined; (*fam.*) protest against, attack; (*with* con) quarrel with. *Pres. Ind.* **trueno, truenas, truena, truenan.** *Pres.*

Subjunc. **truene, truenes, truene, truenen**

troncal, *a.* trunk; main, principal

tronco, *m. (anat., bot.)* ·trunk;
main body or line (of communications); trunk-line; common
origin, stock; *(fam.)* blockhead,
dolt; callous person. *(fig.)* **estar
hecho un t.,** to lie like a log;
sleep like a log

tronchar, *v.t.* to break off, lop
off (branches)

troncho, *m. (bot.)* stem, stalk,
branch

tronera, *f. (naut.)* porthole; embrasure; slit window; pocket of a
billiard table. *m.* and *f. (fam.)*
madcap, harum-scarum

tronido, *m.* roll of thunder

trono, *m.* throne; *(ecc.)* tabernacle; shrine; kingly might; *pl.*
thrones, hierarchy of angels

tronzador, *m.* two-handled saw

tronzar, *v.t.* to smash, break in
bits; *(sew.)* pleat; exhaust, overtire

tropa, *f.* crowd (of people);
troops, military; *(mil.)* call to
arms; *pl.* army. **t. de línea,**
regiment of the line. **tropas de
asalto,** storm troops. **tropas
de refresco,** fresh troops. **en
t.,** in a crowd; in groups

tropel, *m.* rush, surge (of crowds,
etc.); bustle, confusion; crowd,
multitude; heap, jumble (of
things). **en t.,** in a rush; in a
crowd

tropelía, *f.* rush, dash; violence;
outrage

tropezar, *v.i. irr.* to stumble,
slip; *(with con)* meet unexpectedly or accidentally come up
against, be faced with (difficulties); quarrel with or oppose;
fall into (bad habits). See
empezar

tropezón, *m.* stumbling, slipping;
stumbling block, obstacle. *(fam.)*
a tropezones, stumblingly; by
fits and starts

tropical, *a.* tropical

trópicos, *m. pl. (geog., ast.)*
tropics

tropiezo, *m.* stumble; stumbling-
block, obstacle; hitch; impediment; slip, peccadillo, fault;
difficulty, embarrassment; fight,
skirmish; quarrel

tropismo, *m.* tropism

tropo, *m.* trope, figure of speech

troquel, *m.* die, mould

troqueo, *m.* trochee

trotaconventos, *f. (fam.)* go-
between, procuress

trotamundos, *m. (fam.)* globe
trotter

trotar, *v.i.* to trot; *(fam.)* hurry,
get a move on

trote, *m.* trot; toil, drudgery.
t. corto, jog-trot. **al t.,** with all
speed

trotón (-ona), *a.* trotting. *m.*
horse. *f.* chaperon

trova, *f.* verse; song, lay, ballad;
love song

trovador (-ra), *m.* troubador,
minstrel. *s.* poet

trovadoresco, *a.* pertaining to
minstrels, troubador

trovar, *v.i.* to compose verses;
write ballads; misconstrue, misinterpret

troyano (-na), *a.* and *s.* Trojan

trozo, *m.* part, fragment; piece,
portion; *(lit.)* selection. *(nav.)*
t. de abordaje, landing party

truco, *m.* trick, deception

truculencia, *f.* harshness, cruelty,
truculence

truculento, *a.* fierce, harsh, truculent

trucha, *f. (icht.)* trout. **t. asalmonada,** salmon trout

truchuela, *f. dim.* small trout;
dried cod

trueco, *m.* exchange. **a t. de,** in
exchange for; on condition that

trueno, *m.* thunder; report, noise.
(of fire-arms); *(fam.)* rake, scapegrace

trueque, *m.* exchange. **a. (or en)
t.,** in exchange

trufa, *f. (bot.)* truffle; nonsense,
idle talk

trufar, *v.t. (cul.)* to stuff with
truffles; *v.i. (fam.)* lie, tell fibs

truhán (-ana), *a.*knavish,roguish,
comic. *s.* knave, rogue; clown,
buffoon

truhanear, *v.i.* to be a trickster,
behave like a knave; play the
clown

truhanería, *f.* knavery, act of a
rogue; clowning, buffoonery; collection of rogues

truhanesco, *a.* knavish, scoundrelly; clownish

trujal, *m.* oil or grape-press; oil mill; vat for soap making

trujar, *v.t.* to partition off

trulla, *f.* uproar, tumult; crowd, throng

truncar, *v.t.* to shorten, detruncate; decapitate, mutilate; omit, cut out (words, etc.); curtail, abridge; mutilate, deform (texts, etc.)

truque, *m.* card game; kind of hopscotch

trust, *m.* (*com.*) trust

tú, *pers. pron.,* 2*nd sing., m.* and *f.* thou, you. **tratar de t.** (a), to address familiarly; be on intimate terms with

tu, *poss. pron., m.* and *f.* thy, your. *Abb.* of **tuyo, tuya, tuyos, tuyas.** Used only before nouns

tuberculina, *f.* tuberculin

tubérculo, *m.* (*zool., med.*) tubercle; (*bot.*) tubercle, tuber

tuberculoso, *a.* tubercular, tuberculous

tubería, *f.* piping, tubing; pipe system; pipe factory

tuberosa, *f.* (*bot.*) tuberose

tuberosidad, *f.* tuberosity

tuberoso, *a.* tuberous

tubo, *m.* pipe, tube; lamp-chimney; flue; (*anat.*) duct, canal. **t. acústico,** speaking-tube. **t. de ensayo,** test-tube. **t. de escape,** exhaust pipe. **t. lanzatorpedos,** torpedo-tube. **t. termiónico,** (*rad.*) thermionic valve

tubular, *a.* tubular

tucán, *m.* (*orn.*) toucan

tudesco, *a.* German

tueco, *m.* stump (of a tree); wormhole in wood

tuerca, *f.* nut (of a screw)

tuerto, *a.* one-eyed. *m.* (*law*) tort; *pl.* after-pains. **a t.,** unjustly

tueste, *m.* toasting

tuétano, *m.* marrow. (*fam.*) **hasta los tuétanos,** to the depths of one's being

tufillas, *m.* and *f.* (*fam.*) easily irritated person

tufo, *m.* strong smell, poisonous vapour; (*fam.*) stink; side, airs, conceit (often *pl.*); lock of hair over the ears

tugurio, *m.* shepherd's hut; miserable little room; (*fam.*) haunt, low dive

tul, *m.* tulle

tulipa, *f.* small tulip; lamp-shade

tulipán, *m.* (*bot.*) tulip

tullido, *a.* partially paralysed; maimed, crippled

tullir, *v.t. irr.* to maim, cripple; paralyse; *v.r.* become paralysed; be crippled. See **mullir**

tumba, *f.* tomb; tumble, overbalancing; somersault; Catherine-wheel

tumbar, *v.t.* to knock down; kill, drop; (*fam.*) overpower, overcome (odours, wine). *v.i.* fall down; (*naut.*) run aground; *v.r.* (*fam.*) lie down, stretch oneself out

tumbo, *m.* tumble, overbalancing; undulation (of ground); rise and fall of sea waves; imminent danger; book containing deeds and privileges of monasteries and churches

tumbón, *a.* (*fam.*) crafty, sly; idle, lazy. *m.* trunk with an arched lid

tumefacción, *f.* swelling

tumefacto, túmefacto, *a.* swollen

tumor, *m.* tumour

túmulo, *m.* tumulus; catafalque; mound of earth

tumulto, *m.* riot, uprising; tumult, commotion, disturbance

tumultuario, tumultuoso, *a.* noisy, tumultuous, confused

tuna, *f.* prickly pear (tree and fruit); vagrant life; strolling student musicians (playing to raise money for charity)

tunante, ... rascally, roguish. *m.* and *f.* ra. , scoundrel

tunantuelo (-la), *s.* (*fam.*) imp, little rascal

tunda, *f.* shearing of cloth; (*fam.*) sound beating, hiding

tundear, *v.t.* to beat, drub, buffet

tundidora, *f.* woman who shears cloth; cloth shearing machine; lawn mower

tundir, *v.t.* to shear (cloth); mow (grass); (*fam.*) beat, wallop

tunecino (-na), *a.* and *s.* Tunisian

túnel, *m.* tunnel

tungro (-ra), *a.* and *s.* Thuringian

tungsteno, *m.* tungsten

túnica, *f.* tunic, chiton; tunicle; robe

tuno (-na), *a.* knavish, rascally. *s.* rascal, scoundrel

tupé, *m.* forelock (of horse); toupee; (*fam.*) cheek, brass neck

tupido, *a.* thick, dense; obtuse, dull, stupid

tupir, *v.t.* to thicken, make dense; press tightly; *v.r.* stuff oneself with food or drink

turba, *f.* crowd, multitude; peat

turbación, *f.* disturbance; upset; perturbation; bewilderment, confusion; embarrassment

turbador (-ra), *a.* disturbing, upsetting. *s.* disturber, upsetter

turbamulta, *f.* (*fam.*) mob; rabble

turbante, *a.* upsetting, perturbing. *m.* turban

turbar, *v.t.* to disturb, upset; make turbid, muddy; bewilder, confuse; embarrass

turbera, *f.* peat-bog

turbiedad, *f.* muddiness (of liquids); obscurity

turbina, *f.* turbine

turbio, *a.* turbid, muddy; troublous; turbulent, disturbed; obscure, confused (style); indistinct, blurred. *m. pl.* lees, sediment (of oil)

turbión, *m.* brief storm, squall; (*fig.*) shower, rush

turbulencia, *f.* turbidity, muddiness; turbulence, commotion; disturbance, confusion

turbulento, *a.* muddy, turbid; turbulent, disturbed; confused

turca, *f.* (*fam.*) drinking bout

turco (-ca), *a.* Turkish. *s.* Turk. *m.* Turkish (language)

turgencia, *f.* swelling, turgidity

turgente, *a.* (*med.*) turgescent; (*poet.*) turgid, prominent, swollen

turismo, *m.* touring, tourist industry. **coche de t.,** touring car

turista, *m.* and *f.* tourist

turmalina, *f.* (*min.*) tourmalin

turno, *m.* turn. **por t.,** in turn

turquesa, *f.* (*min.*) turquoise

turquesco, *a.* Turkish

turrón, *m.* kind of nougat; almond paste; (*fam.*) soft job, sinecure; Civil Service job

turulato, *a.* (*fam.*) dumbfounded, speechless, inarticulate

tus! word for calling dogs. (*fam.*) **sin decir t. ni mus,** without saying anything

tutear, *v.t.* to address as **tú** (instead of formal **Vd**); treat familiarly

tutela, *f.* guardianship; tutelage; protection, defence

tuteo, *m.* the use in speaking to a person of the familiar **tú** instead of the formal **usted**

tutor (-ra), *s.* guardian. *m.* stake (for plants); protector, defender

tutoría, *f.* See **tutela**

tuyo, tuya, tuyos, tuyas, *poss. pron.,* 2*nd sing.* and *pl., m.* and *f.* thine, yours. Used sometimes with def. art. (e.g. **Este sombrero es el tuyo,** This hat is yours (your one))

U

u, *f.* letter U. *conjunc.* Used instead of **o** or before words beginning with **o** or **Ho** (e.g. **fragante u oloroso**)

ubérrimo, *a. sup.* most fruitful; very abundant

ubicación, *f.* situation, position, location

ubicar, *v.t.* to place, situate; *v.i.* and *v.r.* be situated

ubicuidad, *f.* ubiquity

ubicuo, *a.* omnipresent; ubiquitous

ubre, *f.* udder

ucranio (-ia), *a.* and *s.* Ukrainian

¡ uf ! *interj.* ugh!

ufanarse, *v.r.* to pride oneself, put on airs

ufanía, *f.* pride, conceit

ufano, *a.* conceited, vain; satisfied, pleased; expeditious, masterly

ujier, *m.* usher

ukelele, *m.* (*mus.*) ukulele

ulano, *m.* uhlan

úlcera, *f.* (*med.*) ulcer

ulceración, *f.* ulceration

ulcerar(se), *v.t.* and *v.r.* to ulcerate

ulceroso, *a.* ulcerous

ulterior, *a.* farther, ulterior; subsequent

ulteriormente, *adv.* subsequently, later

ultimación, *f.* ending, finishing

ultimar, *v.t.* to end, conclude

ultimátum, *m.* ultimatum

último, *a.* last; farthermost; ultimate; top; final, definitive; most valuable, best; latter; recent.

Última Hora, Stop Press. **a última hora,**(*fig.*)at the eleventh hour. **en estos últimos años,** in recent years. **a últimos de mes,** towards the end of the month. **el ú piso,** the top flat; the top floor. **por ú.,** finally. (*fam.*) **estar en las últimas,** to be at the end, be finishing

ultra, *adv.* besides; (with words like *mar*) beyond; (as prefix) excessively

ultrajar, *v.t.* to insult; scorn, despise

ultraje, *m.* insult, outrage

ultrajoso, *a.* offensive, insulting, abusive

ultramar, *m.* overseas, abroad

ultramarino, *a.* oversea; ultramarine. *m.* foreign produce (gen. *pl.*)

ultramontano, *a.* ultramontane

ultrarrojo, *a.* (*phys.*) infra-red

ultratumba, *adv.* beyond the grave

ultravioleta, *a.* (*phys.*) ultra-violet

úlula, *f.* screech-owl

ululación, *f.* screech, howl; hoot of an owl

ulular, *v.i.* to howl, shriek, screech; hoot (of an owl)

ululato, *m.* ululation

umbela, *f.* (*bot.*) umbel

umbelífero, *a.* (*bot.*) umbelliferous

umbilical, *a.* umbilical

umbral, *m.* threshold; (*fig.*) starting-point; (*arch.*) lintel. **atravesar** (*or* **pisar**) **los umbrales,** to cross the threshold

umbría, *f.* shady place

umbrío, *a.* shady, dark

umbroso, *a.* shady

un, *abb.* of **uno,** *a,* one. Used before *m. sing. f.* **una,** *indef. art.* a, an; a; one

unánime, *a.* unanimous

unanimidad, *f.* unanimity. **por u.,** unanimously

unción, *f.* anointing; (*ecc.*) Extreme Unction; unction, fervour

uncir, *v.t.* to yoke

undécimo, *a.* eleventh

undísono, *a.* (*poet.*) sounding, sonorous (waves, etc.)

undoso, *a.* wavy, rippling

undulación, *f.* undulation; (*phys.*) wave

undular, *v.i.* to undulate; wriggle; float, wave (flags, etc.)

undulatorio, *a.* undulatory

ungimiento, *m.* anointment

ungir, *v.t.* to anoint

ungüento, *m.* ointment; lotion; (*fig.*) balm, unguent

unicelular, *a.* unicellular

único, *a.* unique; sole, solitary, only. **Lo ú. que se puede hacer es . . .,** The only thing one can do is . . .

unicolor, *a.* of one colour

unicornio, *m.* unicorn

unidad, *f.* unity; unit; (*math., mil.*) unit. (of drama) **u. de lugar,** unity of place. **u. de tiempo,** unity of time

unidamente, *adv.* jointly; harmoniously

unificación, *f.* unification

unificar(se), *v.t.* and *v.r.* to unify, unite

uniformar, *v.t.* to make uniform; put into uniform; *v.r.* become uniform

uniforme, *a.* uniform; same, similar. *m.* uniform

uniformidad, *f.* uniformity

unigénito, *a.* only-begotten. *m.* Christ

unilateral, *a.* one-sided, unilateral

unión, *f.* union; correspondence, conformity; agreement; marriage; alliance, federation; composition, mixture; combination; proximity, nearness; (mystic) union

unionista, *m.* and *f.* (*pol.*) unionist

unir, *v.t.* to unite, join; mix, combine; bind, fasten; connect; couple; bring together; marry; (*fig.*) harmonize, conciliate; *v.r.* join together, unite; be combined; marry; (*with prep. a or con*) be near to; associate with

unísono, *a.* unisonant. **al u.,** in unison; unanimously

unitario (-ia), *a.* and *s.* Unitarian

universal, *a.* universal; well-informed; widespread

universalidad, *f.* universality

universalizar, *v.t.* to make universal, generalize

universidad, *f.* university; universality; universe

universitario, *a.* university

universo, *a.* universal. *m.* universe

uno (*f.* **una**), *a.* a, one; single, only; same; *pl.* some; about, nearly. *m.* one (number). **Tiene unos doce años,** He is about twelve. **unas pocas manzanas,** a few apples. *pron.* someone; one thing, same thing; *pl.* some people. **No sabe uno qué creer,** One doesn't know what to believe. **Unos dicen que no, otros que sí,** Some (people) say no, others yes. **Juan no tiene libros y le voy a dar uno,** John has no books and I am going to give him one. **Todo es uno,** It's all the same. **u. a u.,** one by one. **u. que otro,** a few. **u. y otro,** both. **unos cuantos,** a few, some. **Es la una,** It is one o'clock

untar, *v.t.* to anoint; grease, oil; (*fam.*) bribe; *v.r.* smear oneself with grease or similar thing; (*fig., fam.*) line one's pockets. **u. el carro,** (*fig.*) to grease the wheels

unto, *m.* grease; animal fat; (*fig.*) balm

untuoso, *a.* fat, greasy

uña, *f.* nail of fingers or toes; hoof, trotter, claw; stinging tail of scorpion; thorn; stump of tree branch; (*naut.*) fluke; (*fig., fam.*) light fingers (gen. *pl.*). **afilarse las uñas,** to sharpen one's claws, prepare for trouble. **comerse las uñas,** to bite one's nails. **caer en las uñas de,** to fall into the clutches of. **hincar la u.** (en), to stick the claws into; to defraud, overcharge. **ser u. y carne,** to be devoted friends

uñarada, *f.* scratch with nails

uñero, *m.* ingrowing nail

¡upa! *interj.* Up you get! (gen. to children)

uranio, *m.* (*chem.*) uranium

urbanidad, *f.* civility, good manners, urbanity

urbanismo, *m.* town planning; housing scheme

urbanización, *f.* urbanization

urbanizar, *v.t.* to civilize, polish; urbanize

urbano, *a.* urban, city; urbane

urbe, *f.* city, metropolis

urbícola, *m.* and *f.* city dweller

urdemalas, *m.* schemer, intriguer

urdidera, *f.* warping-frame

urdimbre, *f.* warp; scheming, plotting

urdir, *v.t.* to warp; weave; scheme, intrigue

uréter, *m.* (*anat.*) ureter

uretra, *f.* (*anat.*) urethra

urgencia, *f.* urgency; necessity; compulsion

urgente, *a.* urgent

urgir, *v.i.* to be urgent; be valid, be in force (laws)

úrico, *a.* uric

urinario, *a.* urinary. *m.* urinal

urna, *f.* urn; ballot box; glass case

urraca, *f.* (*orn.*) magpie

uruguayo (-ya), *a.* and *s.* Uruguayan

usado, *a.* worn out; accustomed, efficient. (*com.*) **al u.,** in the usual form. **ropa usada,** second-hand or worn clothing

usanza, *f.* custom, usage

usar, *v.t.* to use; wear, make use of; follow (trade, occupation); *v.i.* be accustomed

usarcé, usarced, *m.* and *f.* (*ant.*) *abb.* **vuestra merced,** Your Honour

usencia, *m.* and *f.* *abb.* **vuesa reverencia,** Your reverence

useñoría, *m.* and *f.* *abb.* **vue-señoría,** Your ladyship or lordship

usía, *m.* and *f.* *abb.* **usiría,** Your lord or ladyship

uso, *m.* use; custom; fashion; habit; wear and tear. **al u.,** according to custom. **al u. de,** in the manner of

usted, *m.* and *f.* you. *pl.* **ustedes.** Often abbreviated to Vd, V, Vds, VV. Derives from Vues-tra merced

usual, *a.* usual; general, customary; sociable

usufructo, *m.* (*law*) usufruct; life-interest; profit

usura, *f.* usury; profiteering. **pagar con u.,** to pay back a thousandfold

usurario, *a.* usurious

usurear, *v.i.* to lend or borrow with usury; profiteer, make excess profits

usurero (-ra), *s.* usurer; profiteer

usurpación, *f.* usurpation

usurpador (-ra), *a.* usurping. *s.* usurper

usurpar, *v.t.* to usurp

utensilio, *m.* utensil; tool, implement (gen. *pl.*)

uterino, *a.* uterine

útero, *m.* uterus

útil, *a.* useful; profitable; *(law)* lawful (of days, etc.). *m.* usefulness, profit; *pl.* útiles, utensils, tools

utilidad, *f.* utility; usefulness; profit

utilitario, *a.* utilitarian

utilitarismo, *m.* utilitarianism

utilizable, *a.* utilizable

utilización, *f.* utilization

utilizar, *v.t.* to utilize

utillaje, *m.* machinery

utópico, *a.* Utopian

uva, *f.* grape. u. espina, kind of gooseberry. u. moscatel, muscatel grape. *(fam.)* hecho una u., dead-drunk

uvero (-ra), *a.* pertaining or relating to grapes, grape. *s.* grape seller

uxoricidio, *m.* uxoricide (crime)

uxorio, *a.* uxorious

V

v, *f.* letter V. v doble *or* doble v, letter W. V *or* Vd, VV, *abbs.* vuestra(s) merced(es), *m.* and *f.*, *sing.* and *pl.* you

vaca, *f.* cow. v. de San Antón, *(ent.)* lady-bird

vacación, *f.* holiday, vacation (gen. *pl.*); vacancy; act of vacating (employment). vacaciones retribuidas, holidays with pay

vacada, *f.* herd of cows

vacancia, *f.* vacancy

vacante, *a.* vacant. *f.* vacancy

vacar, *v.i.* to be vacant; take a holiday; retire temporarily; *(with prep. a)* dedicate oneself to, engage in

vaciadero, *m.* rubbish-dump; sewer, drain

vaciado, *m.* plaster cast; *(arch.)* excavation

vaciamiento, *m.* emptying; moulding, casting; depletion

vaciar, *v.t.* to empty; drain, drink; mould, cast; *(arch.)* excavate; hone; copy; *v.i.* flow (into) (rivers); *v.r.* *(fam.)* blurt out

vaciedad, *f.* emptiness; foolishness, inanity

vacilación, *f.* swaying; tottering; staggering; hesitation, perplexity

vacilante, *a.* swaying; tottering; staggering; hesitating, vacillating

vacilar, *v.i.* to sway; totter; stagger; flicker; hesitate

vacío, *a.* empty, void; fruitless, vain; unoccupied, vacant, deserted; imperfect; hollow, empty; conceited, immature. *m.* hollow; *(anat.)* flank; vacancy; shortage; *(phys.)* vacuum. v. de aire, airpocket. de v., unloaded (carts, etc.). en v., in vacuo. *(fam.)* hacer el v. (a), to send to Coventry

vacuidad, *f.* emptiness; vacuity

vacuna, *f.* cow-pox; vaccine

vacunación, *f.* vaccination

vacunar, *v.t.* to vaccinate; inoculate

vacuno, *a.* bovine

vacuo, *a.* empty; vacant. *m.* void; vacuum

vadeable, *a.* fordable (rivers, etc.); *(fig.)* surmountable

vadear, *v.t.* to ford, wade; *(fig.)* overcome (obstacles); *(fig.)* sound, find out the opinion (of); *v.r.* behave

vademécum, *m.* vade-mecum; school satchel

vado, *m.* ford; expedient, help

vagabundear, *v.i.* to wander, roam, loiter

vagabundeo, *m.* vagabondage

vagabundo (-da), *a.* roving, wandering; vagrant. *s.* tramp, vagabond

vagamundear, *v.i.* See vagabundear

vagancia, *f.* vagrancy

vagar, *m.* leisure; interval, pause. *v.i.* be idle or at leisure; wander, roam

vagido, *m.* cry, wail (infants)

vagneriano, *a.* Wagnerian

vago (-ga), *a.* vagrant, idle; vague; *(art)* indefinite, blurred. *s.* idler. *m.* tramp; loafer. en v., unsuccessfully, vainly

vagón, *m.* waggon; (railway) coach. v. comedor, dining-car

vagoneta, *f.* open truck (railways, mines, etc.)

vaguear, *v.i.* to roam, wander; loaf

vaguedad, *f.* vagueness; vague remark

vaharada, *f.* whiff, exhalation

vahido, *m.* vertigo

vaho, *m.* vapour, fume

vaina, *f.* scabbard; (*bot.*) sheath, pod; case (scissors, etc.)

vainilla, *f.* (*bot.*) vanilla; (*sew.*) drawn-thread work

vaivén, *m.* swing, sway, see-saw; instability, fluctuation

vajilla, *f.* china; dinner-service

val, *m. abb.* **valle**

Valdepeñas, *m.* red wine from Valdepeñas (New Castile)

vale, *m.* (*com.*) bond, I.O.U., promissory note; voucher; valediction

valedero, *a.* valid, binding

valedor (-ra), *s.* protector, sponsor

valencia, *f.* (*chem.*) valency

valenciano (-na), *a.* and *s.* Valencian

valentía, *f.* bravery; heroic deed; boast; (*art, lit.*) dash, imagination, fire; superhuman effort

valentón, *a.* boastful, blustering

valer, *v.t. irr.* to protect; defend; produce (income, etc.); cost; *v.i.* be worth; deserve; have power or authority; be of importance or worth; be a protection; be current (money); be valid; *v.r.* (*with de*) make use of. *m.* value, worth. **v. la pena,** to be worth while. **¡Válgame Dios!** Heavens! Bless me! **Más vale así,** It's better thus. *Pres. Ind.* **valgo, vales,** etc. *Fut.* **valdré,** etc. *Condit.* **valdría,** etc. *Pres. Subjunc.* **valga,** etc.

valeriana, *f.* (*bot.*) valerian

valeroso, *a.* active, energetic; courageous; powerful

valetudinario, *a.* valetudinarian

valía, *f.* value, price; influence, worth; faction, party. **a las valías,** at the highest price

validación, *f.* validation; force, soundness

validar, *v.t.* to make strong; validate

validez, *f.* validity

valido, *a.* favourite, esteemed. *m.* court favourite; prime minister

válido, *a.* firm, sound, valid; strong, robust.

valiente, *a.* strong, robust; courageous; active; excellent; excessive; enormous (gen. *iron.*); boastful

valija, *f.* valise, suitcase, grip; mail bag; mail

valimiento, *m.* value; favour; protection, influence

valioso, *a.* valuable; powerful; wealthy

valisoletano (-na), *a.* and *s.* of or from Valladolid (Castile)

valón, *a.* Walloon

valona, *f.* Vandyke collar

valor, *m.* worth, value; price; courage; validity; power; yield, income; insolence; *pl.* (*com.*) securities

valoración, *f.* valuation; appraisement

valorar, *v.t.* to value; appraise

valorización, *f.* valuation

valquiria, *f.* Valkyrie

vals, *m.* waltz

valsar, *v.i.* to waltz

valuación, *f.* See **valoración**

valuar, *v.t.* to value; appraise; assess

valva, *f.* (*zool.*) valve

válvula, *f.* (*mech.*) valve. (*aut.*) **v. de cámara (del neumático),** tyre-valve. **v. de seguridad,** safety-valve

valla, *f.* barricade, paling; stockade; (*fig.*) obstacle

vallado, *m.* stockade; enclosure

valle, *m.* valley; vale; river-basin

vampiro, *m.* vampire; (*fig.*) bloodsucker

vanagloria, *f.* vaingloriousness, conceit

vanagloriarse, *v.r.* to be conceited

vanaglorioso (-sa), *a.* conceited. *s.* boaster

vanamente, *adv.* vainly; without foundation; superstitiously; arrogantly

vandálico, *a.* Vandal

vandalismo, *m.* vandalism; destructiveness

vándalo (-la), *a.* and *s.* Vandal

vanguardia, *f.* vanguard; *pl.* outerworks. **a v.,** in the forefront

vanidad, *f.* vanity; ostentation; empty words; illusion. (*fam.*) **ajar la v. de,** to take (a person) down a peg

vanidoso (-sa), *a.* vain; ostentatious. *s.* conceited person

vano, *a.* vain; hollow, empty; useless, ineffectual; unsubstantial, illusory. *m.* span (bridge). **v. único,** single span. **en v.,** uselessly, in vain

vapor, *m.* steam, vapour; fainting fit; steamboat; *pl.* hysterics. **v. de ruedas, v. de paleta,** paddle-steamer. **v. volandero,** tramp-steamer. **al v.,** full steam ahead; (*fam.*) with all speed

vaporable, *a.* vaporizable

vaporación, *f.* evaporation

vaporización, *f.* vaporization

vaporizador, *m.* vaporizer; spray, sprayer

vaporizar, *v.t.* to vaporize; spray

vaporoso, *a.* vaporous; ethereal; gauzy

vapulación, *f.,* **vapulamiento,** *m.* whipping

vapular, *v.t.* to whip

vapuleo, *m.* whipping, spanking

vaquería, *f.* herd of cattle; dairy; dairy-farm

vaquero (-ra), *s.* cowherd

vaquilla, *f.* heifer

vara, *f.* staff; rod; wand (of authority); vara (nearly one yard); shaft (of cart). **v. de aforar,** water-gauge

varada, *f.* (*naut.*) running aground

varadero, *m.* shipyard

varar, *v.i.* (*naut.*) to run aground; (*fig.*) be held up (negotiations, etc.); *v.t.* (*naut.*) put in dry dock

varear, *v.t.* to knock down (fruit from tree); beat (with a rod); measure with a rod; sell by the rod; *v.r.* grow thin

várgano, *m.* stake, rail, slat (of fence)

variabilidad, *f.* variableness

variable, *a.* variable; changeable, inconsistent

variación, *f.* variation (also *mus.*)

variado, *a.* varied; variegated

variante, *a.* varying. *f.* variant; discrepancy

variar, *v.t.* to vary; change; *v.i.* change; be different

varice, *f.* (*med.*) varix

varicela, *f.* (*med.*) chicken-pox

varicoso, *a.* (*med.*) varicose

variedad, *f.* variety; change; inconstancy, instability; alteration; variation; (*biol.*) variety

varilla, *f. dim.* rod; rib (fan, umbrella). **v. de virtudes,** conjurer's wand. (*mech.*) **v. percusora,** tappet rod

vario, *a.* different, diverse; inconstant, changeable; variegated; *pl.* some, a few

variómetro, *m.* (*elec.*) variometer

varón, *m.* male; man

varonil, *a.* male; manly

varsoviano (-na), *a.* and *s.* of or from Warsaw

vasallaje, *m.* vassalage; dependence; tribute money

vasallo (-lla), *s.* vassal. *a.* vassal; dependent

vasco (-ca), **vascongado** (-da), *a.* and *s.* Basque

vascuence, *m.* Basque language; (*fam.*) gibberish

vaselina, *f.* vaseline

vasija, *f.* vessel, receptacle, jar

vaso, *m.* receptacle; glass, tankard, mug; glassful; (*naut., anat., bot.*) vessel; garden-urn; vase

vástago, *m.* stem, shoot; offspring, descendant; piston rod

vastedad, *f.* extensiveness, largeness, vastness

vasto, *a.* vast, extensive

vate, *m.* bard; seer

vaticano, *a.* and *m.* Vatican

vaticinar, *v.t.* to prophesy, foretell

vaticinio, *m.* prediction

vatímetro, *m.* water-meter

vatio, *m.* (*elec.*) watt. **v. hora,** watt hour

ve, *f.* name of the letter V. **v. doble** *or* **doble v.,** name of the letter W

vecinal, *a.* neighbouring

vecindad, *f.* neighbourhood. **buena v.,** good neighbourliness. **hacer mala v.,** to be a nuisance to one's neighbours

vecindario, *m.* neighbourhood; population of a district

vecino (-na), *a.* neighbouring; near; similar. *s.* neighbour; citizen; inhabitant

vector, *m.* carrier (of disease)

veda, *f.* close season; prohibition

vedamiento, *m.* prohibition

vedar, *v.t.* to forbid; prevent

vedija, *f.* tangled lock of hair; piece of matted wool; curl (of smoke)

veedor (-ra), *a.* prying. *s.* busy-body. *m.* inspector; overseer

vega, *f.* fertile lowland plain; meadow

vegada, *f.* See vez

vegetable, *a.* and *m.* vegetable

vegetación, *f.* vegetation

vegetal, *a.* vegetal; plant. *m.* vegetable, plant

vegetar, *v.i.* to flourish, grow (plants); (*fig.*) vegetate

vegetarianismo, *m.* vegetarianism

vegetariano (-na), *a.* and *s.* vegetarian

vegetativo, *a.* vegetative

vehemencia, *f.* vehemence

vehemente, *a.* vehement; vivid

vehículo, *m.* vehicle; means, instrument

veinte, *a.* and *m.* twenty; twentieth

veintena, *f.* a score

veinticinco, *a.* and *m.* twenty-five; twenty-fifth

veinticuatro, *a.* and *m.* twenty-four; twenty-fourth

veintidós, *a.* and *m.* twenty-two; twenty-second

veintinueve, *a.* and *m.* twenty-nine; twenty-ninth

veintiocho, *a.* and *m.* twenty-eight; twenty-eighth

veintiséis, *a.* and *m.* twenty-six; twenty-sixth

veintisiete, *a.* and *m.* twenty-seven; twenty-seventh

veintitrés, *a.* and *m.* twenty-three; twenty-third

veintiuno, *a.* and *m.* twenty-one; twenty-first. Abbreviates to **veintiún** when placed before noun

vejación, *f.* ill-treatment, persecution

vejamen, *m.* irritation, provocation; taunt; lampoon

vejar, *v.t.* to ill-treat, persecute; plague

vejatorio, *a.* vexing, annoying

vejete, *m.* (*fam.*) silly old man

vejez, *f.* oldness; old age; platitude. (*fam.*) **a la v., viruelas**, the older the madder

vejiga, *f.* bladder; blister. **v. natatoria**, float (of a fish)

vela, *f.* vigil; watch; pilgrimage; sentinel, watchman; candle; (*naut.*) sail; awning; night work,

overtime. **v. de cangreja**, boom sail. **v. de mesana**, mizzen sail. **v. de trinquete**, foresail. **v. latina**, lateen sail. **a toda v.**, with all speed. **alzar velas**, to hoist sail. **en v.**, wakeful, without sleep. (*fam.*) **estar entre dos velas**, to be tipsy

velación, *f.* vigil; watch; marriage ceremony of veiling (gen. *pl.*)

velada, *f.* vigil; watch; evening party

velado, *a.* veiled; dim; (of voice) thick, indistinct

velador (-ra), *a.* watchful; vigilant. *m.* candlestick; small round table. *s.* watcher, guard

velamen, *m.* (*naut.*) canvas

velar, *v.i.* to watch, be wakeful; work overtime or at night; (*ecc.*) watch; (*fig.*) (*with por*) watch over, defend; *v.t.* veil (also *ecc.*); conceal; (*phot.*) blur; (*with prep. a*) wake (corpse); sit with (patient at night)

veleidad, *f.* velleity; fickleness

veleidoso, *a.* inconstant, changeable

velero (-ra), *m.* sailing ship; sailmaker. *s.* candle-maker

veleta, *f.* weathercock; float, quill (fishing). *m.* and *f.* changeable person

velo, *m.* veil; curtain; (*ecc.*) humeral veil; excuse, pretext; (*zool.*) velum. **v. del paladar**, soft palate. **correr el v.**, to disclose a secret. **tomar el v.**, to take the veil, become a nun

velocidad, *f.* speed; (*mech.*) velocity. (*aer.*) **v. ascensional**, rate of climb. (*mech.*) **v. del choque**, speed of impact. **en gran v.**, by passenger train. **en pequeña v.**, by goods train

velocípedo, *m.* velocipede

velódromo, *m.* velodrome

velón, *m.* oil lamp

veloz, *a.* swift; quick-thinking or acting

vello, *m.* down, soft hair

vellocino, *m.* wool; fleece

vellón, *m.* fleece; copper and silver alloy formerly used in sense of " sterling "; (*ant.*) copper coin

vellosidad, *f.* downiness, hairiness

velloso, *a.* downy, hairy

velludo, *a.* hairy, downy. *m.* plush, velvet

vena, *f.* (*bot.*, *anat.*) vein; streak, veining (in wood or stone); (*min.*) seam; underground spring; inspiration. **estar de v.,** to be in the mood; be inspired

venablo, *m.* javelin

venado, *m.* venison; deer

venal, *a.* venous; saleable; venal

venalidad, *f.* saleableness; venality

venatorio, *a.* pertaining to hunting

vencedor (-ra), *a.* conquering. *s.* conqueror

vencejo, *m.* (*orn.*) swift; (*orn.*) martin

vencer, *v.t.* to conquer; defeat; overcome, rise above; outdo, excel; restrain, control (emotions); convince, persuade; *v.i.* succeed, triumph; (*com.*) fall due, mature; (*com.*) expire; *v.r.* control oneself; twist, incline

vencible, *a.* conquerable; superable

vencimiento, *m.* defeat; conquest, victory; bend, twist (of things); (*com.*) expiration; (*com.*) maturity (of a bill)

venda, *f.* bandage; fillet. **tener una v. en los ojos,** to be blind (to the truth)

vendaje, *m.* bandage

vendar, *v.t.* to bandage; (*fig.*) blind (generally passions)

vendaval, *m.* strong wind

vendedor (-ra), *a.* selling. *s.* seller

vender, *v.t.* to sell; betray; *v.r.* sell oneself; be sold; risk all (for someone); (*fig.*) give away (secret); (*with por*) sell under false pretences. **v. al contado,** to sell for cash. **v. al por mayor,** to sell wholesale. **v. al por menor,** to sell retail. **venderse caro,** to be unsociable

vendí, *m.* (*com.*) certificate of sale

vendible, *a.* purchasable; saleable

vendimia, *f.* vintage; profit, fruits

vendimiador (-ra), *s.* vintager

vendimiar, *v.t.* to harvest the grapes; take advantage of; (*fam.*) kill

veneciano (-na), *a.* and *s.* Venetian

veneno, *m.* poison; venom; danger (to health or soul); evil passion

venenosidad, *f.* poisonousness

venenoso, *a.* poisonous, venomous

venera, *f.* scallop-shell (pilgrim's badge); badge, decoration

veneración, *f.* respect, veneration

venerador (-ra), *a.* venerating. *s.* venerator, respector

venerar, *v.t.* to venerate; worship

venéreo, *a.* venereal

venero, *m.* spring of water; horary line on sundial; origin, genesis; (*min.*) bed

venezolano (-na), *a.* and *s.* Venezuelan

vengador (-ra), *a.* avenging. *s.* avenger

venganza, *f.* revenge

vengar, *v.t.* to avenge; *v.r.* avenge oneself

vengativo, *a.* vindictive

venia, *f.* pardon, forgiveness; permission; inclination of head (in greeting); (*law*) licence issued to minors to manage own estate

venial, *a.* venial

venialidad, *f.* veniality

venida, *f.* arrival, coming; return; attack (fencing); precipitancy

venidero, *a.* future

venideros, *m. pl.* successors; posterity

venir, *v.i.* *irr.* to come; arrive; turn up (at cards); fit, suit; consent, agree; (*agr.*) grow; follow, come after, succeed; result, originate; occur (to the mind); feel, experience; (*with prep. a + infin.*) happen finally, come to pass; (*with en*) decide, resolve; *v.r.* ferment. **v. a menos,** to deteriorate, decline; come upon evil days. **v. a pelo,** to come opportunely, be just right. **v. a ser,** to become. **venirse abajo,** to fall, collapse. **¿A qué viene este viaje?** What is the purpose of this journey? **el mes que viene,** next month. **El vestido te viene muy ancho,** The dress is too wide for you. **Me vino la idea de marcharme,** It occurred to me to go away. **en lo por venir,** in the future. *Pres. Ind.* **vengo, vienes, viene, venimos, venís, vienen.** *Pres. Part.* **viniendo.**

Fut. vendré, etc. *Condit.* vendría, etc. *Preterite* vine, viniste, vino, vinimos, vinisteis, vinieron. *Pres. Subjunc.* venga, etc. *Imperf. Subjunc.* viniese, etc.

venoso, *a.* veined; venous

venta, *f.* selling; sale; inn; (*fam.*) wilderness; *pl.* (*com.*) turnover. v. pública, auction. a la v., on sale

ventada, *f.* gust of wind

ventaja, *f.* advantage; profit

ventajoso, *a.* advantageous

ventana, *f.* window. v. de guillotina, sash window. v. saledíza, bay window. echar algo por la v., to waste a thing

ventanal, *m.* large window

ventanilla, *f.* small window (as in railway compartments); grill (ticket office, bank, etc.); nostril

ventarrón, *m.* high wind

ventear, *v. impers.* to blow (of the wind); *v.t.* sniff air (animals); air, dry; investigate; *v.r.* be spoiled by air (tobacco, etc.)

ventero (-ra), *s.* innkeeper

ventilación, *f.* ventilation; ventilator; current of air

ventilador, *m.* ventilating fan; ventilator

ventilar, *v.t.* to ventilate; shake, winnow; air; discuss

ventisca, *f.* snowstorm

ventiscar, ventisquear, *v. impers.* to snow with a high wind

ventisquero, *m.* glacier; snowfield, snow-drift; snowstorm

ventolera, *f.* gust of wind; (*fam.*) boastfulness; whim, caprice

ventor (-ra), *s.* pointer (dog)

ventosa, *f.* vent (pipes, etc.); (*zool.*) sucker; (*surg.*) cupping glass

ventosidad, *f.* flatulence

ventoso, *a.* windy; flatulent

ventrículo, *m.* (*anat.*) ventricle

ventrílocuo (-ua), *a.* ventriloquial. *s.* ventriloquist

ventriloquia, *f.* ventriloquism

ventrudo, *a.* big-bellied

ventura, *f.* happiness; chance, hazard; risk, danger. a la v., at a venture. buena v., good luck. por v., perhaps; by chance; fortunately

venturoso, *a.* fortunate

Venus, *m.* (*ast.*) Venus. *f.* beautiful woman, beauty

ver, *v.t. irr.* to see; witness, behold; visit; inspect, examine; consider; observe; know, understand; (*with de + infin.*) try to; *v.r.* be seen; show oneself, appear; experience, find oneself; exchange visits; meet. v. mundo, to travel. V. y creer, Seeing is believing. A mi v., In my opinion. ¡A v.! Let's see!; Wait and see! no tener nada que v. con, to have no connection with, nothing to do with. Veremos, Time will tell. Ya se ve, Of course, Naturally. *Pres. Ind.* veo, ves, etc. *Imperf.* veía, etc. *Past Part.* visto. *Pres. Subjunc.* vea, etc. *Imperf. Subjunc.* viese, etc.

vera, *f.* edge; border; shore. a la v., on the edge, on the verge

veracidad, *f.* truthfulness, veracity

veranadero, *m.* summer pasture

veraneante, *m.* and *f.* summer resident, holiday-maker

veranear, *v.i.* to spend the summer

veraneo, *m.* summer holidays, summering

veraniego, *a.* summer; light, unimportant

verano, *m.* summer; dry season (*S.A.*)

veras, *f. pl.* reality, truth; fervour, earnestness. de v., really; in earnest

veraz, *a.* truthful, veracious

verbal, *a.* verbal; oral

verbalismo, *m.* verbalism

verbena, *f.* (*bot.*) verbena, vervain; fair held on eve of Saint's day

verbigracia, *adv.* for instance. *m.* example

verbo, *m.* word; vow; (*gram.*) verb. v. activo *or* v. transitivo, active or transitive verb. v. auxiliar, auxiliary verb. v. intransitivo *or* v. neutro, intransitive or neuter verb. v. reflexivo *or* v. recíproco, reflexive verb

verbosidad, *f.* verbosity

verboso, *a.* verbose, prolix

verdad, *f.* truth, veracity; reality. a la v., indeed; without doubt. en v., in truth; indeed. contar cuatro verdades a alguien, to tell someone a few home truths. **la pura v.,** the plain truth

verdadero, *a.* true; real; sincere; truthful

verdal, *a.* green. **ciruela v.,** greengage

verde, *a.* green; unripe; fresh (vegetables); youthful; immature, undeveloped; obscene, dissolute. *m.* green (colour); verdure, foliage

verdear, *v.i.* to look green; be greenish; grow green

verdecer, *v.i. irr.* to grow green, be verdant. See **conocer**

verdegay, *a.* and *m.* bright green

verdemar, *a.* and *m.* sea-green

verderón, *m.* (*orn.*) linnet

verdín, *m.* verdure; mould; verdigris

verdinegro, *a.* dark green

verdor, *m.* verdure; greenness; strength; youth (also *pl.*)

verdoso, *a.* greenish

verdugo, *m.* hangman, executioner; wale, mark; shoot of tree; switch; whip; (*fig.*) scourge; tyrant

verdulera, *f.* greengrocer; market woman; (*fam.*) harridan

verdulería, *f.* greengrocer's shop

verdulero, *m.* greengrocer

verdura, *f.* verdure; green garden produce, vegetables (gen. *pl.*); (*art*) foliage; obscenity

verecundo, *a.* bashful

vereda, *f.* footpath; sheep track

veredicto, *m.* (*law*) verdict; judgment, considered opinion

verga, *f.* steel bow of crossbow; (*naut.*) yard; (*fam.*) penis

vergajo, *m.* rod (for punishment)

vergel, *m.* orchard

vergonzoso (-sa), *a.* shameful; bashful, shamefaced. *s.* shy person

vergüenza, *f.* shame; self-respect; bashfulness, timidity; shameful act; public punishment

vericueto, *m.* narrow, stony path

verídico, *a.* veracious; true, exact

verificación, *f.* verification, checking; (*law*) **v. de un testamento,** probate

verificador (-ra), *a.* verifying, checking. *s.* inspector, checker

verificar, *v.t.* to prove; verify; *v.r.* take place, happen; check;

come true. (*elec.*) **v. las conexiones,** to check the connections

verisímil, *a.* credible, probable

verisimilitud, *f.* credibility

verismo, *m.* realism; truthfulness

verja, *f.* grating, grill; railing

vermiforme, *a.* vermiform

vermífugo, *a.* and *m.* vermifuge

verminoso, *a.* verminous

vermut, *m.* Vermouth

vernáculo, *a.* native, vernacular

vernal, *a.* vernal

veronés (-esa), *a.* and *s.* Veronese

verónica, *f.* (*bot.*) speedwell; veronica (bull fighting)

verosímil, *a.* credible, probable

verosimilitud, *f.* verisimilitude, probability

verraco, *m.* boar

verruga, *f.* (*med.*) wart; (*fam.*) bore; defect

versar, *v.i.* to revolve; (*with sobre*) concern, deal with (book, etc.); *v.r.* become versed (in)

versátil, *a.* (*zool.*) versatile; changeable; fickle

versatilidad, *f.* (*zool.*) versatility; changeableness; fickleness

versículo, *m.* versicle

versificación, *f.* versification

versificador, (-ra), *s.* versifier

versificar, *v.i.* to write verses; *v.t.* put into verse, versify

versión, *f.* translation; version; account

verso, *m.* poetry, verse; stanza; line (of a poem). **v. suelto,** blank verse

vertebrado, *a.* and *m.* (*zool.*) vertebrate

vertedor, *m.* drain, sewer; chute

verter, *v.t. irr.* to pour, spill; empty; translate; *v.i.* flow. See **entender**

vertical, *a.* and *f.* vertical

verticalidad, *f.* verticality

vértice, *m.* (*geom., anat.*) vertex

verticilo, *m.* (*bot.*) whorl

vertiente, *a.* emptying. *m.* or *f.* slope, incline; watershed

vertiginoso, *a.* giddy; vertiginous

vértigo, *m.* giddiness, faintness

vesícula, *f.* blister; (*anat., bot.*) vesicle

vespertino, *a.* evening

vestíbulo, *m.* hall, vestibule foyer

vestido, *m.* dress; clothes

vestidura, *f.* garment; *pl.* vestments

vestigio, *m.* footmark; trace, mark; remains; (*fig.*) vestige

vestir, *v.t. irr.* to clothe, dress; adorn; embellish (ideas); (*fig.*) disguise (truth); simulate, pretend; *v.i.* be dressed; *v.r.* dress oneself; (*fig.*) be covered. See **pedir**

vestuario, *m.* clothing, dress; (*theat.*) wardrobe or dressing-room; (*ecc.*) vestry; (*mil.*) uniform

veta, *f.* vein; stripe, rib (fabric)

veterano (-na), *a.* and *s.* veteran

veterinaria, *f.* veterinary science

veterinario, *a.* veterinary. *m.* veterinary surgeon

veto, *m.* veto; prohibition

vetustez, *f.* antiquity, oldness

vetusto, *a.* ancient, very old

vez, *f.* time, occasion; turn; *pl.* proxy, deputy, substitute. **a la v.,** simultaneously. **alguna v.,** sometime. **a su v.,** in its (her, his, their) turn. **a veces,** sometimes. **de una v.,** at the one time. **de v. en cuando,** from time to time. **en v.,** instead of. **hacer las veces de,** to be a substitute for. **otra v.,** again. **Su cuarto es dos veces más grande que éste,** His room is twice as large as this one

veza, *f.* (*bot.*) vetch

vía, *f.* way; road; carriage track; railway track or gauge; (*anat.*) tract; (mystic) way; route; conduct; *pl.* procedure. **v. ancha,** broad gauge (railway). **v. angosta,** narrow gauge. **v. de agua,** (*naut.*) leak. (*law*) **v. ejecutiva,** seizure, attachment. **v. férrea,** railway. **v. láctea,** Milky Way. **v. muerta,** railway siding. **v. principal,** main line. **v. pública,** public thoroughfare. **v. romana,** Roman road. **v. secundaria,** (*r.w.*) side line. **por v. aérea,** by air or aeroplane

viabilidad, *f.* viability

viable, *a.* viable; practicable; workable; passable

viaducto, *m.* viaduct

viajante, *m.* and *f.* commercial traveller

viajar, *v.i.* to travel, journey, voyage

viaje, *m.* journey; voyage; water-supply; travel journal; (*naut.*) **v. de ensayo,** trial trip. **v. redondo,** circular tour. **¡ Buen v.!** Bon voyage!

viajero (-ra), *a.* travelling. *s.* traveller; passenger

vianda, *f.* viand, victual (gen. *pl.*); meal

viático, *m.* (*ecc.*) viaticum; provisions for a journey

víbora, *f.* viper

viborezno, *m.* young viper

vibración, *f.* vibration; jar, jolt; thrill

vibrante, *a.* shaking; vibrant; thrilling

vibrar, *v.t.* to shake, oscillate; *v.i.* vibrate; jar, jolt; quiver, thrill

vibratorio, *a.* vibratory, vibrative

vicaría, *f.* vicarage; vestry

vicario, *a.* vicarious. *m.* vicar; curate; deputy

vicealmirante, *m.* vice-admiral

vicecanciller, *m.* vice-chancellor

vicecónsul, *m.* vice-consul

viceconsulado, *m.* vice-consulate

vicepresidente (-ta), *s.* vice-president

vicesecretario (-ia), *s.* assistant secretary

viciar, *v.t.* to corrupt; adulterate; forge; annul; interpret maliciously, misconstrue; *v.r.* become vicious

vicio, *m.* vice; defect; error, fraud; bad habit; excess, exaggerated desire; viciousness (animals); overgrowth (plants); peevishness (children). **tener el v. de,** to have the bad habit of

vicioso, *a.* vicious; vigorous, overgrown; abundant; (*fam.*) spoilt (children)

vicisitud, *f.* vicissitude

víctima, *f.* victim

¡ víctor! ¡ víctor! *interj.* Victor!; Long live!; Hurrah!

victoria, *f.* victory, triumph; victoria

victoriano (-na), *a.* and *s.* Victorian

victorioso, *a.* victorious

vid, *f.* vine

vida, *f.* life; livelihood; human being; biography; vivacity. **v. airada,** gay life. **de por v.,** for life. **darse buena v.**, to live comfortably; enjoy one's life. **dar mala v.**, to ill-treat. **en la v.**, in life; never. **ganarse la v.**, to make one's living

vidente, *m.* clairvoyant; seer

vidriar, *v.t.* to glaze (earthenware)

vidriera, *f.* glass window (gen. stained or coloured)

vidriero, *m.* glazier. *a.* made of glass

vidrio, *m.* glass; anything made of glass; fragile thing; touchy person. **v. inastillable**, safetyglass. **v. jaspeado**, frosted glass. **v. pintado** *or* **v. de color**, stained-glass. **v. plano**, plate-glass

vidrioso, *a.* brittle; slippery; fragile; hypersensitive; (*fig.*) glazed (eyes)

vieja, *f.* old woman

viejo, *a.* old; ancient; former; old-fashioned; worn out. *m.* old man

vienés (-esa), *a.* and *s.* Viennese

viento, *m.* wind; scent (of game, etc.); guy (rope); upheaval; vanity. **v. en popa**, (*naut.*) following wind; without a hitch, prosperously. **vientos alisios**, trade-winds. **v. terral**, land wind. **a los cuatro vientos**, in all directions. **contra v. y marea**, (*fig.*) against all obstacles. **correr malos vientos**, to be unfavourable (of circumstances). **refrescar el v.**, to stiffen (of the breeze)

vientre, *m.* stomach; belly; vitals; (*law*) venter

viernes, *m.* Friday. **V. Santo**, Good Friday

viga, *f.* beam, rafter; girder; joist; mill beam. **v. maestra**, main beam or girder

vigente, *a.* valid; in force (laws, customs)

vigésimo, *a.* twentieth

vigía, *f.* watch tower; (gen. *m.*) look-out, watch

vigilancia, *f.* watchfulness, vigilance; watch patrol

vigilante, *a.* watchful. *m.* watcher; watchman

vigilar, *v.i.* to watch over; supervise

vigilia, *f.* vigil; wakefulness; night study; (*ecc.*) vigil, eve;

wake; (*mil.*) watch. **día de v.**, fast-day

vigor, *m.* strength; **activity**; vigour, efficiency; validity

vigorizar, *v.t.* to invigorate; exhilarate; encourage

vigorosidad, *f.* vigorousness.

vigoroso, *a.* strong, vigorous

vihuela, *f.* (*mus.*) lute

vil, *a.* vile, infamous; base; despicable; untrustworthy

vilano, *m.* (*bot.*) down, filament; thistle flower

vileza, *f.* baseness; vileness, infamy

vilipendiar, *v.t.* to revile

vilipendio, *m.* vilification; contempt

vilo, en, *adv.* hanging in the air; (*fig.*) in suspense

vilorta, *f.* hoop; (*mech.*) washer

villa, *f.* villa; country-house; town

villancico, *m.* carol

villanesco, *a.* peasant; rustic, country

villanía, *f.* humbleness of birth; vileness; villainy

villano (-na), *s.* peasant. *a.* rustic, country; boorish; base

vinagre, *m.* vinegar

vinagrera, *f.* vinegar bottle; table cruet

vinagreta, *f.* vinegar sauce

vinagroso, *a.* vinegary; (*fam.*) bad-tempered, acid

vinatero (-ra), *s.* wine merchant. *a.* wine

vincapervinca, *f.* (*bot.*) periwinkle

vinculación, *f.* (*law*) entail

vincular, *v.t.* (*law*) to entail; (*fig.*) base; *v.r.* perpetuate. *a.* (*law*) entail

vínculo, *m.* tie, bond; (*law*) entail

vindicación, *f.* vindication; justification; excuse

vindicador (-ra), *s.* vindicator. *a.* vindicative

vindicar, *v.t.* to avenge; vindicate; justify; excuse

vindicativo, *a.* avenging; vindicatory

vinícola, *a.* wine-growing; wine

vinicultor (-ra), *s.* wine grower, viniculturalist

vinicultura, *f.* wine-growing, viniculture

vinificación, *f.* vinification

vinillo, *m.* thin, weak wine

vino, *m.* wine; fermented fruit juice. **v. de Oporto,** port wine. **v. generoso,** well-matured wine. **v. tinto,** red wine

vinosidad, *f.* vinosity

vinoso, *a.* vinous; fond of wine

viña, *f.* vineyard

viñador, *m.* vineyard-keeper; vine-cultivator

viñedo, *m.* vineyard

viñeta, *f.* (*art*) vignette

viola, *f.* (*mus.*) viola; (*bot.*) viola, pansy. *m.* and *f.* viola player

violación, *f.* violation; infringement

violado, *a.* violet

violador (-ra), *s.* violator. *m.* seducer

violar, *v.t.* to violate; infringe; rape; spoil, harm

violencia, *f.* violence; outrage; rape

violentar, *v.t.* to force; falsify; misinterpret; force an entrance; *v.r.* force oneself

violento, *a.* violent; repugnant; impetuous, hasty-tempered; unnatural, false; unreasonable

violeta, *f.* (*bot.*) violet. *m.* violet colour. **v. de febrero,** snowdrop

violín, *m.* violin

violinista, *m.* and *f.* violinist

violón, *m.* (*mus.*) double-bass, bass viol; double-bass player

violoncelista, *m.* and *f.* (*mus.*) 'cellist

violoncelo, *m.* 'cello

viperino, *a.* viperine; venomous, evil

vira, *f.* welt (of a shoe); dart

viraje, *m.* (*aut.*) change of direction; bend, turn

virar, *v.t.* (*naut.*) to put about; (*phot.*) tone; *v.i.* (*naut.*) tack; (*aut.*) change direction. **v. de bordo,** (*naut.*) to lay off

virgen, *m.* and *f.* virgin. *f.* (*ast.*) Virgo; Mother of God

virgiliano, *a.* Virgilian (from poet Virgil)

virginal, *a.* virginal; pure, unspotted

virginidad, *f.* virginity

virgulilla, *f.* comma; cedilla; accent; apostrophe; fine line

viril, *a.* manly, virile. *m.* clear glass screen

virilidad, *f.* virility

virote, *m.* arrow; shaft; (*fam.*) young blood

virreina, *f.* vicereine

virreinato, *m.* viceroyship

virrey, *m.* viceroy

virtual, *a.* virtual; implicit

virtualidad, *f.* virtuality

virtualmente, *adv.* virtually; tacitly

virtud, *f.* virtue; power; strength, courage; efficacy. **en v. de,** in virtue of

virtuosidad, *f.* virtuosity

virtuoso, *a.* virtuous; powerful, efficacious. *m.* virtuoso, artist

viruela, *f.* (*med.*) smallpox (gen. *pl.*)

virulencia, *f.* virulence

virulento, *a.* virulent

virus, *m.* virus

viruta, *f.* wood-shaving

vis cómica, *f.* the comic spirit

visaje, *m.* grimace

visar, *v.t.* to visé; endorse

viscosidad, *f.* viscosity

viscoso, *a.* viscous, sticky

visera, *f.* visor; eye-shade; peak (of a cap)

visibilidad, *f.* visibility

visigodo (-da), *a.* Visigothic. *s.* Visigoth

visigótico, *a.* Visigothic

visillo, *m.* window-blind

visión, *f.* seeing, sight; queer sight; vision; hallucination; (*fam.*) scarecrow, sight

visionario (-ia), *a.* and *s.* visionary

visir, *m.* vizier. **gran v.,** Turkish Prime Minister, Grand Vizier

visita, *f.* visit; visitor; inspection. **v. de cumplido,** formal call. **v. de sanidad,** health inspection. **hacer una v.,** to pay a call

visitación, *f.* visitation; visit

visitador (-ra), *s.* regular visitor. *m.* inspector. *a.* visiting; inspecting

visitar, *v.t.* to visit; inspect; (*med.*) attend; (*ecc.*) examine. **v. los monumentos,** to see the sights

visiteo, *m.* receiving or paying of visits

vislumbrar, *v.t.* to glimpse; surmise, conjecture

vislumbre, *f.* glimmer, glimpse; surmise, glimmering (gen. *pl.*); semblance, appearance

viso, *m.* view point, elevation; glare; shimmer, gleam; coloured slip under transparent dress; semblance. **de v.,** prominent (persons)

visón, *m.* mink

víspera, *f.* eve; *(ecc.)* day before festival; prelude, preliminary. *pl. (ecc.)* vespers. **en vísperas de,** on the eve of

vista, *f.* vision, sight; view; eyes; eyesight; meeting, interview; *(law)* hearing (of a case); apparition; picture of a view; clear idea; connection (of things); proposition, intention; glance; *pl.* window, door, skylight, opening for light. **v. corta,** short sight. **v. de lince,** sharp eyes. **a primera v.,** at first sight. **a v. de,** in sight of; in the presence of. **conocer de v.,** to know by sight. **dar una v.,** to take a look. **doble v.,** second sight; clairvoyance. **en v. de,** in view of, considering. **estar a la v.,** to be evident. *(fam.)* **hacer la v. gorda,** to turn a blind eye. **¡Hasta la v.!** Good-bye! **perder de v.** (a), to lose sight of

vistazo, *m.* glance. **echar un v.,** to cast a glance

visto, *past part. irr.* **ver.** *(law)* whereas. **bien v.,** approved. **mal v.,** disapproved. **V. Bueno** (V° B°) Approved, Passed. **v. que,** since

vistoso, *a.* showy, gaudy; beautiful

visual, *a.* visual

vital, *a.* vital; essential

vitalicio, *a.* lifelong. *m.* life-insurance

vitalidad, *f.* vitality

vitalismo, *m.* vitalism

vitalizar, *v.t.* to vitalize

vitamina, *f.* vitamin

vitando, *a.* odious; bad; vital

vitela, *f.* vellum

vitícola, *a.* viticultural. *m.* and *f.* viticulturist

viticultura, *f.* viticulture

¡vítor! *interj.* Victor!; Hurrah!; Long live!

vitorear, *v.t.* to cheer; applaud, acclaim

vítreo, *a.* glassy, vitreous

vitrificar(se), *v.t.* and *v.r.* to vitrify

vitrina, *f.* show-case; display cabinet

vitriólico, *a.* vitriolic

vitriolo, *m.* vitriol

vitualla, *f.* (gen. *pl.*) victuals, provisions

vituperable, *a.* blameworthy, vituperable

vituperador (-ra), *a.* vituperative. *s.* vituperator

vituperar, *v.t.* to censure, blame, vituperate

vituperio, *m.* vituperation

viuda, *f.* widow

viudedad, *f.* widow's pension

viudez, *f.* widowhood, widowerhood

viudo, *m.* widower

¡viva! *interj.* Long live!; Hurrah!

vivacidad, *f.* vivacity, gaiety; ardour, warmth; brightness

vivamente, *adv.* quickly, lively

vivandera, *f.* vivandière

vivandero, *m.* sutler

vivaque, *m.* *(mil.)* bivouac

vivaquear, *v.i.* to bivouac

vivar, *m.* warren; aquarium; breeding ground; well (of a fishing boat)

vivaracho, *a.* *(fam.)* sprightly, cheery, lively

vivaz, *a.* vigorous; quick-witted; sprightly; *(bot.)* perennial; vivid, bright

víveres, *m.* *pl.* provisions; *(mil.)* stores

vivero, *m.* *(bot.)* nursery; vivarium; small marsh

viveza, *f.* quickness, briskness; vehemence; perspicuity; witticism; resemblance; brightness (eyes, colours); thoughtless word or act

vividero, *a.* habitable

vívido, *a.* *(poet.)* vivid

vividor (-ra), *a.* frugal, thrifty; dissolute. *s.* liver; long-liver; libertine, rake

vivienda, *f.* dwelling

viviente, *a.* living

vivificación, *f.* vivification

vivificante, *a.* vivifying

vivificar, *v.t.* to vivify; comfort

vivir, *v.i.* to be alive, live; last, endure; *(with en)* inhabit. *m.* life. **¿Quién vive?** *(mil.)* Who goes there?

vivisección, *f.* vivisection

vivo, *a.* alive; intense, strong; bright; (*mil.*) active; subtle, ingenious; precipitate; (*fig.*) lasting, enduring; diligent; hasty; persuasive; expressive. *m.* edge. **al v.,** **a lo v.,** to the life; vividly

vizcaíno (-na), *a.* and *s.* Biscayan

vizcondado, *m.* viscounty

vizconde, *m.* viscount.

vizcondesa, *f.* viscountess

vocablo, *m.* word

vocabulario, *m.* vocabulary

vocación, *f.* vocation; trade, profession

vocal, *a.* vocal; oral. *f.* (*gram.*) vowel. *m.* and *f.* voter (committees, etc.)

vocalización, *f.* (*mus.*, *phon.*) vocalization

vocalizar, *v.i.* (*mus.*, *phon.*) to vocalize

vocativo, *m.* (*gram.*) vocative

vocear, *v.i.* to cry out, shout; *v.t.* proclaim; call for; acclaim

vocerío, *m.* shouting; clamour, outcry.

vociferación, *f.* vociferation, outcry

vociferar, *v.t.* to boast (of); *v.i.* shout, vociferate

vocinglería, *f.* clamour; babble, chatter

vocinglero, *a.* vociferous; prattling, babbling

vodca, *m.* vodka

volada, *f.* short flight. (*mech.*) **v. de grúa,** jib

voladura, *f.* explosion; blasting

volandas, en, **volandillas, en,** *adv.* in the air, as though flying; (*fam.*) in a trice

volante, *a.* flying; wandering, restless. *m.* frill, flounce; screen; fan (of a windmill); (*mech.*) flywheel; (*mech.*) balance wheel (watches); coiner's stamp mill; shuttle-cock. (*aut.*) **v. de dirección,** steering-wheel

volantón (-ona), *s.* fledgeling

volar, *v.i. irr.* to fly (birds, insects, aviation); float in the air; hurry; disappear suddenly; burst, explode; jut out (buttresses, etc.); cleave (air) (arrows, etc.); (*fig.*) spread (rumours); *v.t.* explode; blast; anger. See **contar**

volatería, *f.* fowling; fowls; poultry; flock of birds; (*fig.*) crowd (of ideas)

volátil, *a.* volatile; inconstant

volatilizar, *v.t.* to volatilize

volatinero (-ra), *s.* tight-rope walker, acrobat

volcán, *m.* volcano; violent passion. **v. extinto,** extinct volcano

volcánico, *a.* volcanic

volcar, *v.t. irr.* to overturn, capsize; make dizzy; cause a change (of opinion); annoy; *v.i.* overturn. *Pres.Ind.* vuelco, vuelcas, vuelca, vuelcan. *Preterite* volqué, volcaste, etc. *Pres. Subjunc.* vuelque, vuelques, vuelque, vuelquen

volear, *v.t.* to strike in the air, volley; (*agr.*) sow broadcast

voleo, *m.* volley (tennis, etc.); high kick; straight punch

volframio, *m.* wolfram, tungsten

volición, *f.* volition

volquete, *m.* tip-cart

voltaico, *a.* (*elec.*) voltaic

voltaje, *m.* (*elec.*) voltage

voltario, *a.* versatile; capricious, headstrong

volteador (-ra), *s.* acrobat

voltear, *v.t.* to whirl, turn; overturn; change place (of); (*arch.*) construct an arch or vault; *v.i.* revolve; tumble, twirl (acrobats)

volteo, *m.* turning, revolution; whirl; overturning; twirling; (*elec.*) voltage

voltereta, *f.* somersault

volteriano, *a.* Voltairian

voltímetro, *m.* (*elec.*) voltmeter

voltío, *m.* (*elec.*) volt

volubilidad, *f.* inconstancy, fickleness

voluble, *a.* easily turned; inconstant, changeable; (*bot.*) twining

volumen, *m.* bulk, size; volume, book

volumétrico, *a.* volumetric

voluminoso, *a.* voluminous, bulky

voluntad, *f.* will, volition; wish; decree; free will; intention; affection; free choice; consent. **a v.,** at will; by choice. **de buena v.,** of good will; willingly, with pleasure. **de su propia v.,** of one's own free will. **mala v.,** hostility, ill-will

voluntario (-ia), *a.* voluntary; strong-willed. *s.* volunteer

voluntarioso, *a.* self-willed

voluptuosidad, *f.* voluptuousness

voluptuoso, *a.* voluptuous

voluta, f. (arch.) volute

volver, v.t. irr. to turn; turn over; return; pay back; direct, aim; translate; restore; change, alter; close (doors, etc.); vomit; reflect, repercuss; v.i. come back; continue (speech, etc.); bend, turn (roads); (with prep. a + infin.) do something again (e.g. v. a leer, to read over again); (with por + noun) protect; v.r. become; go sour; turn. **v. a las filas,** (mil.) to reduce to the ranks. **v. en sí,** to regain consciousness. **v. la cabeza,** to turn one's head. **volverse atrás,** (fig.) to back out. **volverse loco,** to go mad. See **resolver**

vomitar, v.t. to vomit; (fig.) vomit forth; (fig.) spit out (curses, etc.); (fam.) burst into confidences

vomitivo, a. and m. emetic

vómito, m. vomit

voracidad, f. voracity

vorágine, f. vortex, whirlpool

voraz, a. voracious

vórtice, m. whirlpool; (fig.) vortex

vortiginoso, a. vortical

vos, pers. pron., 2nd pers. sing. and pl. you. In modern usage, limited to poetical and biblical style or to indicate great respect

vosotros, vosotras, pers. pron., 2nd pers. pl., m. and f. you, ye

votación, f. voting

votador (-ra), s. voter; swearer

votar, v.i. and v.t. to vote; make a vow; curse, swear. **v. una proposición de confianza,** to pass a vote of confidence

votivo, a. votive

voto, m. vote; vow; voter; prayer; curse; desire; opinion. **v. de calidad,** casting-vote. **v. de confianza,** vote of confidence

voz, f. voice; sound, noise; cry, shout (gen. pl.); word; expression; (mus.) singer or voice; (gram.) mood; vote; rumour; instruction, order. **v. común,** general opinion. **a voces,** in a shout, loudly. **llevar la v. cantante,** (fam.) to have the chief say

vuecelencia, vuensencia, m. and f. abb. of **vuestra excelencia,** Your Excellency

vuelco, m. overturning

vuelo, m. flight; wing; (sew.) skirt-fullness; ruffle, frill; (arch.) buttress. **v. a ciegas,** (aer.) blind flying. **v. de distancia,** long-distance flight. **v. de patrulla,** patrol or reconnaissance flight. **v. de reconocimento,** reconnaissance flight. **v. nocturno,** (aer.) night flying. **v. sin parar,** non-stop flight. **al v.,** on the wing; in passing; quickly. **alzar** (or **levantar**) **el v.,** to take flight

vuelta, f. revolution, turn; bend, curve; return; restitution; recompense; repetition; wrong side; beating; (sew.) facing, cuff; change (money); conning (lessons, etc.); stroll, walk; change; vault, ceiling; (sport) round; (mech.) **vueltas por minuto,** revolutions per minute. **a v. de correo,** by return of post. **a la v.,** on returning; overleaf. **dar la v.,** to turn round, make a détour. **dar una v.,** to take a stroll. **dar vueltas,** to revolve; search (for); consider. **media v.,** half turn

vuesarced, m. and f. **vuestra merced,** your honour, you

vueseñoría, m. and f. your lord or ladyship

vuestro, vuestra, vuestros, vuestras, poss. pron., 2nd pl., m. and f. your, yours

vulcanita, f. vulcanite

vulcanización, f. vulcanization

vulcanizar, v.t. to vulcanize

vulgar, a. popular; general, common; vernacular; mediocre

vulgaridad, f. vulgarity

vulgarismo, m. vulgarism

vulgarización, f. vulgarization; popularization

vulgarizar, v.t. to vulgarize; popularize; translate into the vernacular; v.r. grow vulgar

vulgata, f. Vulgate

vulgo, m. mob

vulnerabilidad, f. vulnerability

vulnerable, a. vulnerable

vulpeja, f. vixen

vulpino, a. vulpine; crafty

W

This letter does not form part of the Spanish alphabet, but it is found in a few foreign words.

wagneriano, *a.* Wagnerian
water, *m.* water-closet
whisky, *m.* whisky

X

xenofobia, *f.* xenophobia, hatred of foreigners
xifoides, *a.* (*anat.*) xiphoid
xilófago, *a.* xylophagous, wood-boring. *m.* wood-borer
xilófono, *m.* xylophone
xilografía, *f.* xylography

Y

y, *conjunc.* and. Is replaced by "e" before words beginning with "i" or "hi."
ya, *adv.* already; formerly; soon; now; finally; immediately; well, yes, quite. Used of past, present and future time, and in various idiomatic ways. **Ha venido ya,** He has already come. **Ya vendrá,** He will come soon. **¡Ya voy!** Coming! **¡Ya lo creo!** Of course! I should think so! **¡Ya! ¡Quite!** I understand. **ya no,** no longer. **ya que,** since
yacente, *a.* recumbent, reclining (statues, etc.)
yacer, *v.i. irr.* to be lying at full length; lie (in the grave); be situated, be; lie (with), sleep (with); graze by night. *Pres. Ind.* **yazgo** *or* **yazco, yaces,** etc. *Pres. Subjunc.* **yazga** *or* **yazca,** etc.
yaciente, *a.* recumbent
yacija, *f.* bed; couch; tomb
yacimiento, *m.* (*geol.*) bed, deposit
yacio, *m.* (*bot.*) india-rubber tree
yak, *m.* (*zool.*) yak
yámbico, *a.* and *m.* (metrics) iambic
yanqui, *a.* and *m.* and *f.* North American (gen. U.S.A.)
yarda, *f.* yard (English measure)
yatagán, *m.* yataghan, Turkish sword

yate, *m.* (*naut.*) yacht
ye, *f.* name of the letter **Y**
yegua, *f.* mare
yelmo, *m.* helmet
yema, *f.* bud; yolk (of egg); sweetmeat; (*fig.*) best of anything. **y. del dedo,** finger-tip
yermo, *a.* uninhabited, deserted; uncultivated. *m.* **w i l d e r n e s s,** desert
yerno, *m.* son-in-law
yero, *m.* (*bot.*) tare
yerro, *m.* error; mistake; fault
yerto, *a.* stiff, rigid
yesca, *f.* tinder; fuel, stimulus
yeso, *m.* gypsum, calcium sulphate; plaster; plaster cast
yo, *pers. pron., 1st sing., m.* and *f.* **I. el yo,** the ego
yodo, *m.* (*chem.*) iodine
yodoformo, *m.* (*chem.*) iodoform
yoduro, *m.* (*chem.*) iodide
yola, *f.* (*naut.*) yawl
yuca, *f.* (*bot.*) yucca
yucateco (-ca), *a.* and *s.* from or pertaining to Yucatan
yugo, *m.* yoke; nuptial tie; oppression; (*naut.*) transom; (*fig.*) **sacudir el y.,** to throw off the yoke
yugoeslavo (-va), *a.* and *s.* Jugo-Slav
yugular, *a.* (*anat.*) jugular. *m.* jugular vein
yunque, *m.* anvil; patient, undaunted person; hard worker; (*anat.*) incus
yunta, *f.* yoke (of oxen, etc.)
yute, *m.* jute fibre or fabric
yuxtaponer, *v.t. irr.* to juxtapose. See **poner**
yuxtaposición, *f.* juxtaposition

Z

zabarcera, *f.* vegetable seller
zaborda, *f.* **zabordamiento,** *m.* (*naut.*) grounding, stranding
zabordar, *v.i.* (*naut.*) to run aground, strand
zacatín, *m.* street or square where clothes are sold
zafar, *v.t.* to embellish, garnish, adorn; (*naut.*) lighten (a ship); *v.r.* escape, hide oneself; (*with de*) excuse oneself, avoid; get rid of
zafarrancho, *m.* (*naut.*) clearing the decks; (*fam.*) damage; (*fam.*) scuffle

zafiedad, *f.* rudeness, ignorance, boorishness

zafio, *a.* rude, unlettered, boorish

zafiro, *m.* sapphire

zafra, *f.* olive oil container; sugar crop or factory; (*min.*) waste

zafre, *m.* (*min.*) zaffre

zaga, *f.* rear. *m.* last player. en z., behind. (*fam.*) no quedarse en z.,'not to be left behind; be not inferior

zagal, *m.* youth; strong, handsome lad; young shepherd; full skirt

zagala, *f.* maiden, girl; young shepherdess

zagual, *m.* paddle

zaguán, *m.* entrance hall; vestibule

zaguero, *a.* loitering, straggling. *m.* (*sport*) back

zahareño, *a.* untamable, wild (birds); unsociable, disdainful

zaherimiento, *m.* upbraiding; nagging

zaherir, *v.t. irr.* to upbraid, reprehend; nag. See herir

zahina, *f.* (*bot.*) sorghum

zahón, *m.* leather apron (worn by cowboys)

zahorí, *m.* soothsayer; waterfinder; sagacious person

zahurda, *f.* pigsty

zaino, *a.* treacherous; vicious (horses); chestnut (horses); black (cows)

zalagarda, *f.* ambush; skirmish; snare, trap; (*fam.*) trick, ruse; (*fam.*) mock battle

zalamería, *f.* adulation, flattery

zalamero (-ra), *a.* wheedling, flattering. *s.* flatterer

zalea, *f.* sheepskin

zalear, *v.t.* to shake; frighten away (dogs)

zalema, *f.* salaam

zamacuco, *m.* (*fam.*) oaf, dolt; (*fam.*) drinking bout

zamarra, *f.* sheepskin jacket

zamarrear, *v.t.* to worry, shake (prey); (*fig., fam.*) beat up; (*fam.*) floor, confound

zambo, *a.* knock-kneed

zambomba, *f.* rustic drum

zambra, *f.* Moorish festival; (*fam.*) merrymaking; Moorish boat

zambuco, *m.* (*fam.*) concealment (especially of cards)

zambullida, *f.* plunge, submersion; thrust (in fencing)

zambullir, *v.t.* to plunge in water, submerge; *v.r.* dive; hide oneself, cover oneself

zampar, *v.t.* to conceal (one thing in another); eat greedily; (*with en*) arrive suddenly

zampatortas, *m.*. and·*f.* (*fam.*) glutton

zampoña, *f,* rustic flute; (*fam.*) unimportant work

zanahoria, *f.* (*bot.*) carrot

zanca, *f.* long leg (birds); (*fam.*) long thin leg; (*arch.*) stringboard (of stairs)

zancada, *f.* swift stride

zancadilla, *f.* trip (wrestling); (*fam.*) trick, deceit. echar la z. (a), to trip up

zancajear, *v.i.* to stride about

zancajo, *m.* heel-bone; torn heel (stocking, shoe); (*fam.*) ill-shaped person. (*fam.*) no llegarle al z., to be immensely inferior to someone

zancajoso, *a.* splay-footed; slovenly

zanco, *m.* stilt. (*fig., fam.*) andar ·(*or* estar) en zancos, to have gone up in the·world

zancudo, *a.* long-legged

zangandungo (-ga), *s.* (*fam.*) loafer

zanganear, *v.i.* (*fam.*) to loaf

zángano, *m.* (*ent.*) drone; (*fam.*) idler, parasite

zangolotear, *v.t.* (*fam.*) to shake violently; *v.i.* fuss about, bustle; *v.r.* rattle (windows, etc.)

zangoloteo, *m.* shaking; rattling

zanguango, *m.* (*fam.*) lazybones

zanja, *f.* trench, ditch; drain; furrow

zanjar, *v.t.* to excavate; (*fig.*) remove (obstacles)

zapa, *f.* shovel, spade; (*mil.*) sap; sand-paper

zapador, *m.* (*mil.*) sapper

zapapico, *m.* pick-axe; mattock

zapaquilda, *f.* (*fam.*) she-cat

zapar, *v.i.* (*mil.*) to sap

zaparrastrar, *v.i.* (*fam.*) to trail along the floor (dresses)

zapata, *f.* half-boot; piece of leather used to stop creaking of a hinge; (*arch.*) lintel; (*naut., mech.*) shoe

zapatazo, *m.* blow with a shoe; fall, thud; stamping (horses); flap (of sail)

zapateado, *m.* dance in which rhythmic drumming of heels plays important part

zapatear, *v.t.* to hit with a shoe; stamp feet; drum heels (in dancing); (*fam.*) ill-treat; thump ground (rabbits); *v.i.* stamp (horses); (*naut.*) flap (sails); *v.r.* (*fig.*) stand one's ground

zapateo, *m.* stamping; rhythmic drumming of heels

zapatera, *f.* cobbler's wife; woman who makes or sells shoes

zapatería, *f.* shoemaking; shoe shop

zapatero, *m.* shoemaker; shoe seller. z. remendón, cobbler

zapateta, *f.* caper, leap

zapatilla, *f.* slipper; trotter, hoof

zapato, *m.* shoe

¡zape! *interj.* (*fam.*) shoo! Used for frightening away cats; exclamation of surprise or warning

zapear, *v.t.* to scare away cats; (*fam.*) frighten off

zaque, *m.* leather bottle, wineskin; (*fam.*) drunkard, sot

zaquizamí, *m.* garret; dirty little house or room

zar, *m.* czar

zarabanda, *f.* saraband; (*fam.*) racket, row

zaragata, *f.* (*fam.*) fight, brawl

zaragozano (-na), *a.* and *s.* Saragossan

zaragüelles, *m. pl.* wide pleated breeches

zaranda, *f.* sieve, strainer, colander

zarandajas, *f. pl.* (*fam.*) odds and ends

zarandar, *v.t.* to sieve (grapes, grain); strain; (*fam.*) pick out the best; *v.r.* (*fam.*) move quickly

zarandillo, *m.* small sieve, strainer; (*fam.*) a live wire, energetic person; Spanish dance

zaraza, *f.* chintz

zarcillo, *m.* earring; (*bot.*) tendril; (*agr.*) trowel

zarco, *a.* light blue (generally eyes or water)

zarina, *f.* czarina

zarpa, *f.* (*naut.*) weighing anchor; paw

zarpada, *f.* blow with a paw

zarpar, *v.t.* and *v.i.* (*naut.*) to weigh anchor, sail

zarza, *f.* (*bot.*) bramble, blackberry bush

zarzal, *m.* bramble patch

zarzamora, *f.* (*bot.*) blackberry

zarzaparrilla, *f.* (*bot.*) sarsaparilla

zarzo, *m.* hurdle; wattle

zarzoso, *a.* brambly

zarzuela, *f.* comic opera; musical comedy

zarzuelista, *m.* and *f.* writer or composer of comic operas

¡zas! *m.* sound of a bang or blow

zascandil, *m.* (*fam.*) busybody

zatara, *f.* raft

zeda, *f.* name of the letter Z

zedilla, *f.* cedilla

zenit, *m.* See **cenit**

zepelín, *m.* Zeppelin

zeta, *f.* See **zeda**

zigzag, *m.* zigzag

zigzaguear, *v.i.* to zigzag

zinc, *m.* zinc

zíngaro (-ra), *a.* and *s.* Tzigany

zipizape, *m.* (*fam.*) row, quarrel

zoca, *f.* square

zócalo, *m.* (*arch.*) socle

zoclo, *m.* clog, sabot

zoco, *m.* square; market; clog, sabot.

zodíaco, *m.* zodiac

zona, *f.* girdle, band; strip (of land); zone; (*med.*) shingles. z. de depresión, air-pocket. z. templada, temperate zone. z. tórrida, torrid zone

zonal, *a.* zonal

zoófito, *m.* (*zool.*) zoophyte

zoología, *f.* zoology

zoológico, *a.* zoological

zoólogo, *m.* zoologist

zootecnia, *f.* zootechnics

zopenco, *a.* (*fam.*) oafish

zopo, *a.* maimed, deformed (hands, feet)

zoquete, *m.* (*carp.*) block; dowel; hunk of bread; (*fam.*) short, ugly man; (*fam.*) dunderhead

zorcico, *m.* Basque song and dance

zorra, *f.* vixen; fox; (*fam.*) cunning person; (*fam.*) prostitute; (*fam.*) drinking-bout; truck, dray

zorrera, *f.* fox-hole

zorrería, *f.* foxyness; (*fam.*) cunning

zorro, *m.* fox; · fox-skin; (*fam.*) knave

zóster, *f.* (*med.*) shingles

zote, *a.* dull, ignorant

zozobra, *f.* (*naut.*) foundering, capsizing; anxiety

zozobrar, *v.i.* (*naut.*) to founder, sink; (*naut.*) plunge, shiver; be anxious, vacillate

zuavo, *m.* zouave

zueco, *m.* sabot, clog

zulú, *a.* and *m.* and *f.* Zulu

zumaque, *m.* (*bot.*) sumach tree; (*fam.*) wine

zumba, *f.* cow bell; jest

zumbar, *v.i.* to buzz, hum; ring (of the ears); whizz; twang (of a guitar, etc.); (*fig., fam.*) be on the brink

zumbido, *m.* buzzing, humming; ringing (in the ears); whizz; twanging (of a guitar, etc.); (*fam.*) slap, blow

zumbón, *a.* waggish, jocose

zumo, *m.* sap; juice; profit, advantage ·

zumoso, *a.* succulent, juicy

zupia, *f.* wine lees; cloudy wine; (*fig.*) dregs

zurcido, *m.* (*sew.*) darn; mend

zurcidor (-ra), *s.* darner, mender

zurcidura, *f.* darning; mending; darn

zurcir, *v.t.* to darn; mend, repair; join; (*fig.*) concoct, weave

zurdo, *a.* left-handed

zurra, *f.* (*tan.*) currying; (*fam.*) spanking; (*fam.*) quarrel

zurrador, *m.* (*tan.*) currier, dresser

zurrapa, *f.* (gen. *pl.*) sediment, lees, dregs

zurrar, *v.t.* to curry (leather); (*fam.*) spank; (*fam.*) dress down, scold

zurriagazo, *m.* lash with a whip; (*fig.*) blow of fate

zurriago, *m.* whip

zurribanda, *f.* (*fam.*) whipping; fight, quarrel

zurriburri, *m.* (*fam.*) ragamuffin; mob; uproar

zurrido, *m.* (*fam.*) blow; dull noise

zurrir, *v.i.* to have a confused sound, hum, rattle

zurrón, *m.* shepherd's pouch; leather bag; (*bot.*) husk

zutano (-na), *s.* (*fam.*) so-and-so, such a one

Abisinia, Abyssinia; Ethiopia
Adriático, el, the Adriatic
Afganistán, Afghanistan
África, Africa
Alejandría, Alexandria
Alemania, Germany
Alpes, los, the Alps
Alsacia, Alsace
Amazonas, el Río de las, the River Amazon
Amberes, Antwerp
América, America
América española, Spanish America
América del Norte,. North America
América del Sur, South America
Andalucía, Andalusia
Antillas, las, the Antilles
Apeninos, los, the Apennines
Argel, Algiers
Argelia, Algeria
Asia Menor, Asia Minor
Atenas, Athens
Atlántico, el, the Atlantic
Atlántida, Atlantis
Babilonia, Babylon
Balcanes, los, the Balkans
Baleares, las Islas, the Balearic Islands
Báltico, el Mar, the Baltic Sea
Barbados, Isla de, Barbados
Basilea, Basle
Bayona, Bayonne
Belén, Bethlehem
Belga, el Congo, the Belgian Congo
Bélgica, Belgium
Belgrado, Belgrade
Bengala, Bengal
Berbería, Barbary
Berlín, Berlin
Berna, Berne
Birmania, Burma
Bizancio, Byzantium
Bolonia, Boulogne
Bona, Bonn
Borgoña, Burgundy
Bósforo, el, the Bosphorus
Brema, Bremen
Bretaña, Brittany
Brujas, Bruges
Bruselas, Brussels
Bucarest, Bucharest
Cabo de Buena Esperanza, Cape of Good Hope
Cabo de Hornos, Cape Horn
Cachemira, Cashmere
Cádiz, Cadiz
Calcuta, Calcutta
Caldea, Chaldea
Camarones, los, the Cameroons
Cambrige, Cambridge
Canadá, Canada
Canal de la Mancha, English Channel
Canarias, las Islas, the Canary Islands
Cantorbery, Canterbury
Caribe, el Mar, Caribbean Sea
Cárpatos, los Montes, the Carpathian Mountains

Cartago, Carthage
Caspio, el Mar, the Caspian Sea
Castilla, Castile
Cataluña, Catalonia
Caúcaso, el, the Caucasus
Ceilán, Ceylon
Cerdeña, Sardinia
Cevenes, los, the Cevennes
Constantinopla, Constantinople
Copenhague, Copenhagen
Córcega, Corsica
Córdoba, Cordova
Corea, Korea
Corinto, Corinth
Corriente del Golfo, Gulf Stream
Costa del Oro, la, the Gold Coast
Creta, Crete
Croacia, Croatia
Checoeslovaquia, Czechoslovakia
Chipre, Isla de, Cyprus
Damasco, Damascus
Danubio, el, the Danube
Dardanelos, los, the Dardanelles
Delfos, Delphi
Diepa, Dieppe
Dinamarca, Denmark
Dodecaneso, el, the Dodecanese
Dresde, Dresden
Duero, el, the Douro
Dunas, las, the Downs
Dunquerque, Dunkirk
Edimburgo, Edinburgh
Éfeso, Ephesus
Egipto, Egypt
Escandinavia, Scandinavia
Escocia, Scotland
España, Spain
Esparta, Sparta
Estados Unidos de América, United States of America
Estrasburgo, Strasburg
Etiopía, Ethiopia; Abyssinia
Filipinas, las Islas, the Philippines
Finlandia, Finland
Flandes, Flanders
Florencia, Florence
Francia, France
Franco-Condado, Franche-Comté
Frisia, Friesland
Gales, País de, Wales
Galia, Gaul
Galilea, Galilee
Gante, Ghent
Génova, Genoa
Getsemaní, Gethsemane
Gran Bretaña, Great Britain
Gran Lago Salado, el, the Great Salt Lake
Grecia, Greece
Groenlandia, Greenland
Guayana, Guiana
Guernesey, Guernsey
Habana, la, Havana
Haití, Haiti
Hamburgo, Hamburg
Hawai, Hawaii
Haya, La, The Hague

Hébridas, las, the Hebrides
Hendaya, Hendaye
Holanda, Holland
Hungría, Hungary
Inglaterra, England
Irak, Iraq
Irlanda, Ireland
Istmo de Suez, el, the Suez Canal
Itaca, Ithaca
Italia, Italy
Japón, Japan
Jerusalén, Jerusalem
Jutlandia, Jutland
Laponia, Lapland
Lausana, Lausanne
Leningrado, Leningrad
Letonia, Lithuania
Levante, el, the Levant
Libia, Libya
Líbano, el, the Lebanon
Lombardía, Lombardy
Londres, London
Lucerna, Lucerne
Luxemburgo, Luxembourg
Magallanes, Estrecho de, Straits of Magellan
Malasia, Malaya
Malayo, Archipiélago, Malaya
Mallorca, Majorca
Malucas, las, the Moluccas
Mar Muerto, Dead Sea
Mar del Norte, North Sea
Marruecos, Morocco
Marsella, Marseilles
Mauricio, Isla de, Mauritius
Meca, la, Mecca
Mediterráneo, el, the Mediterranean
Méjico, Mexico
Menorca, Minorca
Misisipí, el, the Mississippi
Misuri, el, the Missouri
Moscú, Moscow
Nápoles, Naples
Navarra, Navarre
Nazaret, Nazareth
Nilo, el, the Nile
Nínive, Nineveh
Niza, Nice
Normandía, Normandy
Noruega, Norway
Nueva Escocia, Nova Scotia
Nueva Gales del Sur, New South Wales.
Nueva Guinea, New Guinea
Nueva Orleans, New Orleans
Nueva York, New York
Nueva Zelandia, New Zealand
Órcades, las, the Orkneys
Ostende, Ostend
Pacífico, el Océano, the Pacific Ocean
Países Bajos, los, the Low Countries, the Netherlands
Palestina, Palestine
Palmira, Palmyra
Panamá, Panama
París, Paris
Península Ibérica, la, the Iberian Peninsula
Perú, Peru

494a

Pirineos, los, the Pyrenees
Polinesia, Polynesia
Polonia, Poland
Pompeya, Pompeii
Praga, Prague
Provenza, Provence
Prusia, Prussia
Puerto Rico, Porto Rico
Rin, el, the Rhine
Rodas, Rhodes
Rodesia, Rhodesia
Roma, Rome
Rosellón, Rousillon
Rusia, Russia
Saboya, Savoy
Sáhara, el, the Sahara
Sajonia, Saxony
Samotracia, Samothrace
Selva Negra, la, the Black
　　Forest
Sena, el, the Seine
Sicilia, Sicily
Singapur, Singapore
Sión, Zion

Siracusa, Syracuse
Siria, Syria
Sudán, el, the Sudan
Suecia, Sweden
Suiza, Switzerland
Tajo, el, the Tagus
Támesis, el, the Thames
Tanganica, Tanganyika
Tánger, Tangier
Tartaria, Tartary
Tebas, Thebes
Termópilas, Thermopylæ
Terranova, Newfoundland
Tesalia, Thessaly
Tierra Santa, Holy Land
Tiro, Tyre
Tirol, el, the Tyrol
Tirreno, el Mar, the Tyrrhen-
　　ian Sea
Tokio, Tokyo
Tolosa, Toulouse
Toscana, Tuscany
Tracia, Thrace
Transjordania, Transjordan

Trento, Trent. Concilio de T.,
　　Council of Trent
Trípoli, Tripoli
Troya, Troy
Túnez, Tunis
Turingia, Thuringia
Turquía, Turkey
Ucrania, Ukraine
Unión Soviética, Soviet Union
Unión Sudafricana, Union of
　　South Africa
Urales, los, the Urals
Varsovia, Warsaw
Venecia, Venice
Vesubio, Vesuvius
Viena, Vienna
Vizcaya, el Golfo de, the Bay
　　of Biscay
Yugoeslavia, Yugoslavia
Yukón, el, the Yukon
Zanzíbar, Zanzibar
Zaragoza, Saragossa
Zululandia, Zululand
Zuyderzée, el, the Zuyder Zee

PROPER NAMES OF PERSONS AND ANIMALS, AND MYTHOLOGICAL NAMES

Abelardo, Abelard
Abrahán, Abraham
Absalón, Absalom
Adán, Adam
Adolfo, Adolphus
Agustín, Augustine
Aladino, Aladdin
Alberto, Albert
Alejandro, Alexander
Alicia, Alice
Ambrosio, Ambrose
Amílcar, Hamilcar
Ana, Anne, Hannah
Andrés, Andrew
Andrómaca, Andromache
Aníbal, Hannibal
Antonio, Anthony
Apolo, Apollo
Apuleyo, Apuleius
Aquiles, Achilles
Aquino, Santo Tomás de, St.
　　Thomas Aquinas
Arco, Juana de, Joan of Arc
Argonautas, los, the Argon-
　　auts
Aristófanes, Aristophanes
Aristóteles, Aristotle
Arlequín, Harlequin
Arturo, Arthur
Augusto, Augustus
Baco, Bacchus
Barba Azul, Blue Beard
Bárbara, Barbara
Bartolomé, Bartholomew
Basilio, Basil
Beatriz, Beatrice
Belcebú, Beelzebub
Benedicto, Benito, Benedict
Bernardo, Bernard
Berta, Bertha
Blanca, Blanche
Bocacio, Boccaccio
Boecio, Boetius
Bonifacio, Boniface
Borbón, la Casa de, the House
　　of Bourbon
Brígida, Bridget
Bruto, Brutus
Bucéfalo, Bucephalus

Buda, Buddha
Caifás, Caiaphas
Caín, Cain
Calvino, Calvin
Camila, Camilla
Canuto, Canute
Caperucita Roja, Little Red
　　Riding Hood
Caribdis, Charybdis
Carlomagno, Charlemagne
Carlos, Charles
Carlota, Charlotte
Carolina, Caroline
Caronte, Charon
Casandra, Cassandra
Catalina, Catherine
Catilina, Catiline
Catón, Cato
Cecilia, Cicely
Cenicienta, la, Cinderella
Cerbero, Cerberus
César, Cæsar
Cicerón, Cicero
Cíclope, Cyclops
Cipriano, Cyprian
Cirilo, Cyril
Claudio, Claude, Claudius
Clemente, Clement
Colón, Columbus
Columbina, Columbine
Constantino, Constantine
Constanza, Constance
Cornelio, Cornelius
Creso, Crœsus
Cupido, Cupid
Dafnis, Daphne
Dálila, Delilah
Darío, Darius
Débora, Deborah
Dédalo, Dædalus
Demócrito, Democritus
Demóstenes, Demosthenes
Diocleciano, Diocletian
Diógenes, Diogenes
Dionisio, Dionysus
Domingo, Dominic
Dorotea, Dorothy, Dorothea
Edipo, Œdipus
Edmundo, Edmund

Eduardo, Edward
Elena, Helen
Elías, Elijah
Eliseo, Elisha
Emilia, Emily
Endimión, Endymion
Engracia, Grace
Enoc, Enoch
Enrique, Henry, Harry
Enriqueta, Henrietta
Epicteto, Epictetus
Epicuro, Epicurus
Erasmo, Erasmus
Ernesto, Ernest
Esaú, Esau
Escila, Scylla
Escipión, Scipio
Esdras, Ezra
Esopo, Æsop
Esquilo, Æschylus
Ester, Esther
Estuardo, Stuart
Etelredo, Ethelred
Euclides, Euclid
Eugenio, Eugen
Eustaquio, Eustace
Eva, Eve
Ezequías, Hezekiah
Ezequiel, Ezekiel
Faraón, Pharaoh
Fausto, Faust
Federico, Frederick
Felipe, Philip
Fernando, Ferdinand
Fidias, Phidias
Florencia, Florence
Francisca, Frances
Francisco, Francis
Galaor, Galahad
Ganimedes, Ganymede
Gaspar, Jasper
Gengis Kan, Genghis Khan
Geofredo, Geoffrey
Gertrudis, Gertrude
Gil, Giles
Gilberto, Gilbert
Godofredo, Godfrey
Gorgonas, las, the Gorgons
Gracos, los, the Gracchi

494b

Gregorio, Gregory
Gualterio, Walter
Guillermo, William
Habacuc, Habakkuk
Habsburgos, los, the Hapsburgs
Heráclito, Heraclitus
Herodes, Herod
Heródoto, Herodotus
Hilario, Hilary
Homero, Homer
Horacio, Horace
Huberto, Hubert
Hugo, Hugh
Icaro, Icarus
Ifigenia, Iphigenia
Ignacio, Ignatius
Inés, Agnes, Inez
Isabel, Elizabeth, Isabel
Isaías, Isaiah
Isidoro, Isidro, Isidore
Jafet, Japheth
Jaime, James
Jenofonte, Jenophon
Jeremías, Jeremiah
Jerónimo, Jerome
Jesús, Jesucristo, Jesus
Jonás, Jonah
Jonatán, Jonathan
Jorge, George
José, Joseph
Juana, Jane, Jéan, Joan
Julián, Julian
Julieta, Juliet
Julio, Julius
Lanzarote, Launcelot
Lázaro, Lazarus
Leandro, Leander
Leonor, Eleanor
Leopoldo, Leopold
Leticia, Lettice
Licurgo, Lycurgus
Livio, Livy
Lorenzo, Lawrence
Lucano, Lucan
Lucas, Luke
Lucía, Lucy
Lucrecia, Lucretia
Lucrecio, Lucretius
Luis, Louis
Luisa, Louise
Lutero, Luther
Magdalena, Magdalen
Mahoma, Mahomet
Manuel, Emmanuel

Marcial, Martial
Marco Aurelio, Marcus Aurelius
Marcos, Mark
Margarita, Margaret
María, Mary
Mariana, Marion
Mario, Marius
Marte, Mars
Mateo, Matthew
Matilde, Matilda
Mauricio, Maurice
Maximiliano, Maximilian
Mefistófeles, Mephistopheles
Mercurio, Mercury
Miguel, Michael
Miguel Angel, Michelangelo
Moisés, Moses
Morfeo, Morpheus
Napoleón, Napoleon
Natan: el, Nathaniel
Neptuno, Neptune
Nerón, Nero
Nicolás, Nicholas
Noé, Noah
Octavio, Octavius
Orfeo, Orpheus
Orlando, Roland
Otón, Otto
Ovidio, Ovid
Pablo, Paul
Patillas, Old Nick, the Devil
Patricio, Patrick
Paula, Pauline
Pedro, Peter
Pegaso, Pegasus
Perséfone, Persephone
Petrarca, Petrarch
Píndaro, Pindar
Pío, Pius
Pitágoras, Pythagoras
Platón, Plato
Plinio, Pliny
Plutarco, Plutarch
Plutón, Pluto
Pompeyo, Pompey
Poncio Pilatos, Pontius Pilate
Prometeo, Prometheus
Proserpina, Proserpine
Psique, Psyche
Ptolomeo, Ptolemy
Pulgarcito, Tom Thumb
Quijote, Don, Don Quixote
Quintiliano, Quintilian
Rafael, Raphael

Raimundo, Raymond
Raquel, Rachel
Rebeca, Rebecca
Ricardo, Richard
Roberto, Robert
Rolando, Roland
Rómulo, Romulus
Rosa, Rose
Rodolfo, Rudolfo, Rudolph
Ruperto, Rupert
Safo, Sappho
Saladino, Saladin
Salomón, Solomon
Salusto, Sallustus
Sansón, Samson
Satanás, Satan
Saturno, Saturn
Saúl, Saul
Sebastián, Sebastian
Séneca, Seneca
Silvia, Sylvia
Sofía, Sophia
Sófocles, Sophocles
Suetonio, Suetonius
Susana, Susan
Tácito, Tacitus
Tamerlán, Tamerlane
Temístocles, Themistocles
Teobaldo, Theobald
Teócrito, Theocritus
Teodoro, Theodore
Teresa, Theresa
Teseo, Theseus
Tiberio, Tiberius
Ticiano, Titian
Timoteo, Timothy
Tito, Titus
Tobías, Tobias
Tolomeo, Ptolemy
Tomás, Thomas
Trajano, Trajan
Tristán, Tristram
Tucídides, Thucydides
Ulises, Ulysses
Urbano, Urban
Urías, Uriah
Valentín, Valentine
Vespasiano, Vespasian
Vespucio, Vespucci
Vicente, Vincent
Virgilio, Virgil
Vulcano, Vulcan
Yago, Iago
Zwinglio, Zwingli

ABBREVIATIONS COMMONLY USED IN SPANISH WHICH DIFFER FROM THOSE FOUND IN ENGLISH

A

A.: Alteza
(a.): alias
A.A.: Altezas; Autores
abr.: abreviatura
a/c: (com.) a cuenta (on account)
admón.: administración
admor.: administrador
a/f: (com.) a favor (in favour)
afmo or afmº: afectísimo
afto or aftº: afecto
a la v/ or a/v: (com.) a la vista (at sight)
alcde: alcalde
Almte.: almirante
alt.: altura
ap.: aparte; apóstol
A.R.: Alteza Real

art. or artº: artículo
arz. or arzbpo.: arzobispo
atto. or attº: atentísimo
Audª: Audiencia
Av.: Avenida

B

B.: Beato; Bueno
Barna.: Barcelona
B.L.M. or b.l.m.: besa la mano
B.L.P. or b.l.p.: besa los pies
B.p.: bendición papal

C

c/: cargo; contra
c.a.: (elec.) corriente alterna (a.c.)
cª: compañía

c/a: (*com.*) cuenta abierta (open account)
C.A.E.: Cóbrese al entregar (C.O.D.)
cap.ª: capítulo; capitán
cappª: capellán
Card¹: cardenal
c.c.: (*elec.*) corriente continua (d.c.)
c/c: (*com.*) cuyo cargo (whose account); (*com.*) cuenta corriente (current account)
c/cta: (*com.*) cuya cuenta (whose account)
c/d: (*com.*) cuenta de (account of)
C. de J.: Compañía de Jesús (S.J.)
C. en C.: (*com.*) Compañía en comandita (Limited Company)
c.f.: caballo de fuerza (h.p.); coste de flete
Cía: Compañía
C.M.B. or c.m.b.: cuyas manos besa
cnel.: coronel
col. or colª: columna; colonia
conso: consejo
Const.: Constitución
constl: constitucional
conto: (*com.*) conocimiento (B/L)
corrte: corriente
C.P.B. or c.p.b.: cuyos pies besa
c/r: (*com.*) cuenta y riesgo (own risk)
c.s.f.: (*com.*) coste, seguro y flete (c.i.f.)
cta. corrte: (*com.*) cuenta corriente
cts.: céntimos
c/u: cada uno
cuad.: cuadrado
c/v or c/vta: (*com.*) cuenta de ventas (bill of sale; account sales)

CH

ch/: cheque

D

D or Dⁿ: Don
Dª: Doña
DD.: doctores
descto or dº: (*com.*) descuento
d/f or d/fha: (*com.*) días fecha (d.f.)
dho.: dicho
dna. or doc.: docena
domo: domingo
d/p: (*com.*) días plazo (days' time)
drcha. or dcha.: derecha
dro.: derecho
d/v: (*com.*) días vista (days after sight, d.s.)

E

ecoo: eclesiástico
EE.UU.: Estados Unidos (U.S.A.)
E.M.: (*mil.*) Estado Mayor
Emmo. or Emmo: Eminentísimo
E.P.D.: En paz descanse
escs.: escudos
E.U.A.: Estados Unidos de América
Evangº: Evangelio
Excª: Excelencia
Excmo.: Excelentísimo

F

f.: (*com.*) franco (free)
fab.: fabricante
f.a.b.: (*com.*) franco a bordo (f.o.b.)
factª: factura
farm.: farmacia
F.C. or f.c.: ferrocarril
F.E.M.: fuerza electromotriz (E.M.F.)
fha.: fecha
foo or fo or fol.: folio
Fr.: Fray
frs.: francos
fund.: fundador

G

g/: (*com.*) giro (draft)
gnte.: gerente
gobo or gobno: gobierno
gobr: gobernador
graL: general

H

h.: habitantes
hect.: hectárea
Hnos.: Hermanos
hta.: hasta

iglª: iglesia
Ill: Ilustre
Ilmo or Illmo: Ilustrísimo
inf.: informe (report)
I.P.: Indulgencia plenaria
izqa or izqda: izquierda

J

J.C.: Jesucristo
Jhs.: Jesús

L

l.: ley; litro; libro
L/: (*com.*) letra (draft, letter)
Ldo or L.: Licenciado

M

M.: Majestad; Merced; Maestro; Madre (religiosa)
m.: murió; metro; minuto
m/: mes; mi
maymo: mayordomo
M.C.M.: (*math.*) mínimo común múltiplo (L.C.M.)
mcos.: marcos
m/ft: (*com.*) mi favor; (*com.*) meses fecha (months after date)
minº: ministro
Mons.: Monseñor
M.P.S.: Muy Poderoso Señor
ms as: muchos años

N

n.: nacido; noche
n/: nuestro
Nª Sª: Nuestra Señora
nro. or ntro.: nuestro
N.S.: Nuestro Señor
nto.: (*com.*) neto

O

O.: Oeste
o/ or ord.: (*com.*) orden (order)
obo or obpo.: obispo

P

P.: Padre; Papa; pregunta
pbro. or presb.: presbítero
P.D.: Posdata (P.S.)
p. ej.: por ejemplo (e.g.)
perg.: pergamino
P.P.: Porte pagado (prepaid, carriage paid); (*law*) por poder (by power of attorney; by proxy)
priv.: privilegio
provª: provincia
provor: provisor
próxo: próximo
ptas. or pts.: pesetas
pte: parte
pza: pieza

ABBREVIATIONS

Q

q.: que
Q.B.S.M. or q.b.s.m.: que besa su mano
Q.B.S.P. or q.b.s.p.: que besa sus pies
Q.D.G.: que Dios guarde
q.e.p.d.: que en paz descanse
q.e.s.m.: que estrecha su mano

R

R.; Reverendo; Real; respuesta
Rbⁱ: (com.) Recibí (receipt)
R.D.: Real Decreto
Rda. M. or R.M.: Reverenda Madre
Rdo. P. or R.P.: Reverendo Padre
R.O.: Real Orden
R.S.: Real Servicio
rúst.: rústica

S

S.: San; Santo; Sur
Sª: Señora
S.A.: Su Alteza; (com.) Sociedad Anónima
(Limited Company); South America
S.E.: Su Excelencia
servº: servicio
servᵒʳ: servidor
s.e.u.o.: (com.) salvo error u omisión (E. &
O.E.)
sigⁱᵉ: siguiente
S.M. or S.R.M.: Su (Real) Majestad
Sⁿ: San
Sr.: Señor
Sra.: Señora
Sres.: Señores

T

Srta.: Señorita
S.S.: Su Santidad
S.Sª: Su Señoría
SS. AA.: Sus Altezas
SSmo P.: Santísimo Padre
S.S.S. or s.s.s.: Su seguro servidor
Sta.: Santa; Señorita

tente: teniente
testmto: testamento
testo: testigo
tit.: título
tº or tom.: tomo
tribl: tribunal

U

U. or Ud.: usted
Uds. or UU.: ustedes
U.R.S.S.: Unión de las Repúblicas Soviéticas
Socialistas (U.S.S.R.)

V

V.: usted; venerable; valor; versículo; véase
v.: vapor (s.s.)
Vª: Vigilia
Vd.: usted
Vds.: ustedes
V.E.: Vuestra Excelencia
Vo Bo: Visto bueno (O.K.)
vol.: volumen
vta: vuelta
VV.: ustedes

WEIGHTS AND MEASURES (Pesos y Medidas)

Spain adopted the metric system in 1871 and all official calculations are based on this. Many of the traditional weights and measures still survive, however, in some Spanish provinces, especially in the country districts, and a list of these is therefore also given.

Pesos

Sistema métrico

1 gramo = 15·4 grains
1 kilogramo = 1000 gramos = 2·2 lb.
1 quintal métrico = 100 kilogramos

Pesos tradicionales

1 libra = 16 onzas = 460 gramos
1 onza = 28·7 gramos
1 arroba = 25 libras = 11·5 kilogramos
1 quintal = 4 arrobas = 46 kilogramos

Medidas

Medidas longitudinales (Linear Measure)

Sistema métrico

1 milímetro = 0·04 inches
1 centímetro = 0·4 inches
1 metro = (approx.) 3 feet 3 inches
1 kilómetro = 0·62 miles

Medidas longitudinales tradicionales

1 vara = 3 pies (feet) = 0·83 metros
1 braza = 1·67 metros
1 legua = 3894 metros
1 milla (española) = 1298 metros

Medidas de superficie (Square Measure)

Sistema métrico

1 metro cuadrado = 10½ square feet
1 kilómetro cuadrado = 0·46 square miles

Medidas tradicionales de superficie

1 área = 100 metros cuadrados
1 hectárea = 100 áreas = 10,000 metros cuadrados
1 fanega = 6460 metros cuadrados

Medidas para líquidos (Liquid Measure)

Sistema métrico

1 litro = 1·7 pints = 35 fluid ounces
1 metro cúbico = 1000 litros = 35 cubic feet

Medidas tradicionales para líquidos

1 cuartillo = 0·54 litros
1 azumbre = 2·01 litros
1 cántara = 16·1 litros

Medidas para áridos (Dry Measure)

Sistema métrico. See Pesos

Medidas tradicionales para áridos

1 fanega = 55·5 litros
1 celemín = 4·62 litros

CURRENCY (Monedas)

The standard coin is the peseta, but the rate of this to the £ varies owing to Spain's adoption of the multiple exchange system. In 1952 the tourist Exchange Rate was 110·90 pts. to the £.

1 peseta = 100 céntimos.

There are coins of 5, 10, 25 céntimos and of 1, 5 pesetas. Bank notes are issued for 1, 5, 25, 50, 100, 500 and 1000 pesetas.

A coin of 5 céntimos is often called "un perro chico," one of 10 céntimos "un perro gordo," one of 25 céntimos "un real," and a 5 peseta piece "un duro."

Coins not now in circulation: 1 onza = 80 pesetas oro, 1 doblón = 20 pesetas oro.

ENGLISH-SPANISH

A

a, *s.* (letter) a, *f.*; (*mus.*) la, *m.* **symphony in A major**, sinfonía en la mayor, *f.* **A1**, de primera clase; de primera calidad, excelente

a, **an**, *indef. art.* (one) un, *m.*; una, *f.*; (with weights, quantities) el, *m.*; la, *f.*; (with weeks, months, years, etc.) por, al, *m.*; a la, *f.* The indef. art. is omitted in Spanish before nouns expressing nationality, profession, rank, and generally before a noun in apposition. It is omitted also before certain words such as **mil, ciento, otro, semejante, medio,** etc. Other more subtle omissions also occur, some of them due to reasons of style. *prep.* **a.** In phrases such as **to go a hunting,** ir a cazar. As prefix, see **abed, ashore,** etc. **Madrid, a Spanish city,** Madrid, ciudad de España. **six shillings a pound,** seis chelines la libra. **three times a month,** tres veces al mes. **ten shillings an hour,** diez chelines por hora. **thirty miles an hour,** treinta millas por hora. **a certain Mrs. Brown,** una tal Sra. Brown. **a thousand soldiers,** mil soldados. **half an hour later,** media hora después

aback, *adv.* (*naut.*) en facha; (*fig.*) sorprendido, desconcertado. **to take a.,** desconcertar, coger desprevenido (a)

abacus, *s.* ábaco, *m.*

abaft, *adv.* (*naut.*) hacia la popa, en popa; atrás

abandon, *v.t.* abandonar; dejar; desertar, desamparar; renunciar; entregar. *s.* entusiasmo, fervor, *m.*; naturalidad, *f.* **to a. oneself to,** (despair, vice, etc.) entregarse a

abandoned, *a.* entregado a los vicios, vicioso

abandonment, *s.* abandono, *m.*; renunciación, *f.*; deserción, *f.*

abase, *v.t.* humillar; degradar; abatir

abasement, *s.* humillación, degradación, *f.*; abatimiento, *m.*

abash, *v.t.* avergonzar; confundir, desconcertar

abashed, *a.* avergonzado, confuso, consternado

abate, *v.t.* disminuir, reducir; (a price) rebajar; (suppress) suprimir, abolir; (remit) condonar, remitir; (annul) anular; (moderate) moderar; (of pride, etc.) humillar; (of pain) aliviar. *v.i.* disminuir; moderarse; (of the wind and *fig.*) amainar; cesar; apaciguarse, calmarse

abatement, *s.* disminución, *f.*; reducción, *f.*; mitigación, *f.*; (of price) rebaja, *f.*; supresión, *f.*; remisión, *f.*; (annulment) anulación, *f.*; (of pride) humillación, *f.*; (of the wind and of enthusiasm, etc.) amaine, *m.*; (of pain, etc.) alivio, *m.*

abattoir, *s.* matadero, *m.*

abbacy, *s.* abadía, *f.*

abbatial, *a.* abacial

abbé, *s.* abate, *m.*

abbess, *s.* abadesa, *f.*

abbey, *s.* abadía, *f.*

abbot, *s.* abad, *m.*

abbreviate, *v.t.* abreviar; condensar, resumir

abbreviation, *s.* abreviación, *f.*; resumen, *m.*, condensación, *f.*; (of a word) abreviatura, *f.*

abdicate, *v.t.* renunciar; (a throne) abdicar

abdication, *s.* renuncia, *f.*; abdicación, *f.*

abdomen, *s.* abdomen, *m.*

abdominal, *a.* abdominal

abduct, *v.t.* raptar, secuestrar

abduction, *s.* rapto, *m.*; (*anat., phil.*) abducción, *f.*

abductor, s. (*anat.*) abductor, *m.*; raptor, *m.*

abeam, *adv.* (*naut.*) por el través

abed, *adv.* en cama

aberration, s. aberración (also *ast.*, *phys.*, *biol.*) f.

abet, *v.t.* ayudar, apoyar, favorecer; incitar, alentar; (in bad sense) ser cómplice de

abetment, s. ayuda, f., apoyo, *m.*; instigación, f.

abettor, s. instigador (-ra); cómplice, *m.* and f.

abeyance, s. suspensión, f.; expectativa, esperanza, f. **in a.,** en suspenso; vacante; latente

abhor, *v.t.* detestar, odiar, aborrecer; repugnar

abhorrence, s. detestación, f., odio, aborrecimiento, *m.*; repugnancia, f.

abhorrent, *a.* detestable, odioso, aborrecible; repugnante

abide, *v.i.* morar, quedar. *v.t.* aguardar; (*fam.*) aguantar, sufrir. **to a. by,** atenerse a, cumplir; sostener

abiding, *a.* permanente, constante, perenne

ability, s. habilidad, facultad, f., poder, *m.*; talento, *m.*, capacidad, f. **To the best of my a.,** Lo mejor que yo pueda

abject, *a.* abyecto, miserable; despreciable, vil; servil

abjectly, *adv.* miserablemente; abyectamente; servilmente

abjectness, s. abyección, f.; humildad, f.; servilismo, *m.*

abjuration, s. abjuración, f.; renuncia, f.

abjure, *v.t.* abjurar; renunciar; retractar

ablactation, s. ablactación, f.

ablation, s. ablación, f.

ablative, *a.* a nd s. ablativo (*m.*). **in the a.,** en el ablativo. **a. case,** ablativo, *m.*

ablaze, *adv.* en llamas, ardiendo. *a.* brillante; (with, of anger, etc.) dominado por

able, *a.* capaz (de); (clever) hábil; competente; en estado (de); (*law*) apto legalmente, capaz; bueno, excelente. **to be a. to,** poder; ser capaz de; (know how) saber. **a.-bodied,** fuerte, fornido. **a.-bodied seaman,** marinero práctico, *m.*

abloom, *adv.* en flor

ablution, s. ablución, f.

ably, *adv.* hábilmente; competentemente

abnegation, s. abnegación, f.

abnormal, *a.* anormal; irregular

abnormality, s. anormalidad, f.; irregularidad, f.

abnormally, *adv.* anormalmente; demasiado

aboard, *adv.* a bordo. *prep.* a bordo de. **to go a.,** embarcarse, ir a bordo. **All a.!** ¡Viajeros a bordo!; (a train) ¡Viajeros al tren!

abode, s. morada, habitación, f.; residencia, f.; (stay) estancia, f.

abolish, *v.t.* abolir; suprimir; anular

abolition, s. abolición, supresión, f.; anulación, f.

abolitionism, s. abolicionismo, *m.*

abolitionist, s. abolicionista, *m.* and f.

abomasum, s. (of ruminants) abomaso, cuajar, *m.*

abominable, *a.* abominable, aborrecible; repugnante, execrable; (*fam.*) horrible

abominably, *adv.* abominablemente

abominate, *v.t.* abominar, aborrecer, detestar

abomination, s. abominación, f.; aborrecimiento, *m.*; horror, *m.*

aboriginal, *a.* aborigen; primitivo

aborigines, s. *pl.* aborígenes, *m. pl.*

abort, *v.i.* abortar, malparir; (*fig.*) malograrse

abortifacient, s. abortifaciente, *m.*

abortion, s. aborto, *m.*; (*fig.*) fracaso, malogro, *m.*

abortive, *a.* abortivo

abound, *v.i.* abundar (en)

about, *adv.* (around) alrededor; (round about) a la redonda, en torno; (all over) por todas partes; (up and down) acá y acullá; por aquí, por ahí; en alguna parte; por aquí; (in circumference) en circunferencia; (almost) casi, aproximadamente; (by turns) por turnos, en rota-

ción. *prep.* alrededor de; en torno; por; (near to) cerca de; (on
one's person) sobre; (on the subject of) sobre; (concerning) acerca
de; (over) por, a causa de; en;
(of) de; (with time by the clock)
a eso de, sobre; (towards) hacia;
(engaged in) ocupado en; (on the
point of) a punto de. **a. here,**
por aquí. **a. nothing,** por nada.
a. supper time, hacia la hora de
cenar. **a. three o'clock,** a eso
de las tres. **A. turn!** ¡Media
vuelta! (a la izquierda or a la
derecha). **He wandered a. the
streets,** Vagaba por las calles.
Is Mr. Martínez a.? ¿Está el
Sr. Martínez por aquí? **some-**
where a., en alguna parte.
to be a. to, estar para, estar a
punto de. **to bring a.,** ocasionar.
to come a., suceder. **to set a.,**
empezar, iniciar; (a person)
acometer. **What are you think-**
ing a.? ¿En qué piensas?
above, *adv.* arriba; en lo alto;
encima; (superior) superior;
(earlier) antes; (higher up on a
page, etc.) más arriba; (in
heaven) en el cielo. *prep.* encima de; por encima de; sobre;
(beyond) fuera de; fuera del
alcance de; (superior to) superior
a; (more than) más de; (too
proud to) demasiado orgulloso
para; (too good to) demasiado
bueno para; (in addition to)
además de, en adición a; (with
degrees of temperature) sobre.
a. anterior; (with past participles)
antes. **from a.,** desde arriba.
a. all, sobre todo. **over and a.,**
además de. **a.-board,** *adv.*
abiertamente, con las cartas
boca arriba. *a.* franco y abierto.
a.-mentioned, susodicho, antes
citado
abrasion, *s.* abrasión, *f.*; rozadura, *f.*; (*geol.*) denudación, *f.*
abrasive, *a.* abrasivo. *s.* substancia abrasiva, *f.*, abrasivo,
m.
abreast, *adv.* de frente, al lado
uno de otro; (*naut.*) por el
través. **to keep a. of the
times,** mantenerse al día. **to
ride six a.,** cabalgar a seis de
frente. **a. with,** al nivel de, a la
altura de

abridge, *v.t.* abreviar; resumir,
condensar, compendiar; disminuir; reducir
abridgment, *s.* abreviación, *f.*;
resumen, *m.*, sinopsis, *f.*; disminución, *f.*; reducción, *f.*
abroad, *adv.* (out) fuera, afuera;
(gone out) salido; ausente; (everywhere) en todas partes; (in
foreign lands) en el extranjero.
to go a., salir de casa, echarse
a la calle; ir al extranjero; (of
rumours, etc.) propagarse, ru-
morearse
abrogation, *s.* abrogación, anulación, *f.*
abrupt, *a.* (precipitous) escarpado, precipitado, abrupto;
(unexpected) repentino, inés-
perado; (of persons) brusco,
descortés; (of style) seco
abruptly, *adv.* bruscamente;
repentinamente
abruptness, *s.* precipitación, *f.*;
brusquedad, *f.*
abscess, *s.* absceso, *m.*
abscond, *v.i.* evadirse, huir,
escaparse; (with money) desfalcar
absconder, *s.* prófugo, *m.*; desfalcador, *m.*
absence, *s.* ausencia, *f.*; alejamiento, *m.*; (of mind) abstracción, *f.*, ensimismamiento, *m.*;
(lack) falta, *f.* **leave of a.,**
permiso para ausentarse, *m.*;
(*mil.*) licencia, *f.*, permiso, *m.*
absent, *a.* ausente; alejado (de);
(in mind) abstraído, ensimismado, distraído. *v.t.* ausentarse;
alejarse. **the a.,** los ausentes.
a.-mindedness, ensimismamiento, *m.*, abstracción, *f.*
absentee, *s.* ausente, *m.* and *f.*
absenteeism, *s.* absentismo, *m.*
absently, *adv.* distraídamente
absinth, *s.* ajenjo, *m.*
absolute, *a.* absoluto; perfecto;
puro; (unconditional) incondicional; (downright) categórico;
completo; (true) verdadero; (unlimited) ilimitado. **the a.,** lo
absoluto
absolutely, *adv.* absolutamente;
enteramente, completamente;
realmente; categóricamente
absolution, *s.* (*ecc. law*) absolución, *f.*
absolutism, *s.* absolutismo, despotismo, *m.*

absolutist, s. absolutista, m. and f.

absolve, v.t. absolver; (free) exentar, eximir; librar; exculpar

absorb, v.t. absorber; (drink) beber; (use) gastar; (of shocks) amortiguar; (fig., digest) asimilar; (engross) ocupar (el pensamiento, etc.). **to be absorbed in,** (fig.) enfrascarse en, engolfarse en, estar entregado a

absorbent, a. and s. absorbente (m.). **a. cotton-wool,** algodón hidrófilo, m.

absorbing, a. absorbente; (fig.) sumamente interesante

absorption, s. absorción, f.; (fig., digestion) asimilación, f.; (engrossment) enfrascamiento m., preocupación, abstracción, f.

abstain, v.i. abstenerse (de); evitar

abstainer, s. el (la) que se abstiene de bebidas alcohólicas

abstemious, a. abstemio, abstinente; sobrio; moderado

abstemiousness, s. abstinencia, f.; sobriedad, f.; moderación, f.

abstention, s. abstención, f.; abstinencia, f.; privación, f.

abstinence, s. abstinencia, f. **day of a.,** día de ayuno, m.

abstinent, a. abstinente; sobrio

abstract, a. abstracto. s. extracto, resumen, m.; abstracción, f. v.t. abstraer; separar; extraer; (précis) resumir; (steal) substraer. **in the a.,** en abstracto

abstracted, a. distraído, desatento, absorto, ensimismado

abstractedly, adv. distraídamente

abstraction, s. abstracción, f.; (of mind) preocupación, desatención, f.; (stealing) substracción, f.

abstruse, a. abstruso, ininteligible; obscuro; recóndito

abstruseness, s. obscuridad, dificultad, f.; reconditez, f.

absurd, a. absurdo, grotesco; ridículo, disparatado; cómico

absurdity, s. absurdidad, ridiculez, f.; disparate, m., tontería, f.

absurdly, adv. absurdamente

abundance, s. abundancia, copia, f.; muchedumbre (de) multitud (de), f.; riqueza, f.; prosperidad, f.

abundant, a. abundante, copioso; rico. **to be a. in,** abundar en

abundantly, adv. en abundancia, abundantemente

abuse, s. abuso, m.; (bad language) insulto, m., injuria, f. v.t. (ill-use) maltratar; (misuse) abusar (de); (revile) insultar, injuriar; (deceive) engañar

abuser, s. abusador (-ra); injuriador (-ra); (defamer) denigrante, m. and f.

abusive, a. abusivo; (scurrilous) insultante, injurioso, ofensivo

abusively, adv. insolentemente, ofensivamente

abusiveness, s. insulto, m., injuria, f.; vituperación, f.

abut (on), v.i. lindar con; terminar en; estar adosado a

abysmal, a. abismal

abyss, s. abismo, m., sima, f.; (hell) infierno, m.

Abyssinian, a. abisinio (-ia), etíope; (language) abisinio, m.

acacia, s. acacia, f.

academic, a. académico

academician, s. académico, miembro de la Academia, m.

academy, s. academia, f.; conservatorio, m.; (school) colegio, m.; (of riding, etc.) escuela, f. **A. of Music,** Conservatorio de Música, m.

acanthus, s. (arch., bot.) acanto, m.

acarid, s. (ent.) ácaro, m.

accede, v.i. (to a throne) ascender (al trono); tomar posesión (de); (join) hacerse miembro (de); aceptar; (agree) acceder (a), consentir (en), convenir (en)

accelerate, v.t. acelerar; apresurar; (shorten) abreviar

acceleration, s. aceleración, f.

accelerator, s. (of a vehicle) acelerador, m.

accent, s. acento (all meanings), m. v.t. acentuar

accentuate, v.t. acentuar; dar énfasis a

accentuation, s. acentuación, f.

accept, v.t. aceptar; (believe) creer; recibir; admitir; (welcome) acoger

acceptability, s. aceptabilidad; f.; mérito, m.

acceptable, a. aceptable; admisible; agradable; (welcome) bien acogido

acceptably, adv. aceptablemente; agradablemente

acceptance, s. aceptación, f.; (approval) aprobación, f.; (welcome) buena acogida, f.; (com.) aceptación, f.

acceptation, s. acepción, f.

access, s. acceso, m.; entrada, f.; (way) camino, m.; (med.) ataque, m.; (fit) transporte, m.; (advance) avance, m. **easy of a.,** accesible; fácil de encontrar

accessibility, s. accesibilidad, f.

accessible, a. accesible; asequible

accession, s. (to the throne, etc.) advenimiento, m.; aumento, m.; (acquisition) adición, f.; adquisición, f.; (law) accesión, f.

accessory, a. accesorio; secundario; suplementario, adicional. s. accesorio, m.; (law) cómplice, m. and f. **a. before the fact,** instigador (-ra). **a. after the fact,** encubridor (-ra)

accidence, s. (gram.) accidente, m.; rudimentos, m. pl.

accident, s. accidente, m.; (chance) casualidad, f.; (mishap) contratiempo, m. **by a.,** por casualidad, accidentalmente. **a. insurance,** seguro contra accidentes, m.

accidental, a. accidental, casual, fortuito. s. (mus.) accidente, m.

accidentally, adv. accidentalmente; por casualidad; sin querer

acclaim, v.t. aclamar; proclamar; vitorear, aplaudir

acclaimer, s. aclamador (-ra)

acclamation, s. aclamación, f.; aplauso, vítor, m.

acclamatory, a. aclamador

acclimatization, s. aclimatación, f.

acclimatize, v.t. aclimatar

acclivity, s. cuesta, f.

accolade, s. acolada, f., espaldarazo, m.

accommodate, v.t. acomodar; ajustar; adaptar; (reconcile) reconciliar; (provide) proveer, proporcionar; (oblige) complacer;

(fit) poner, instalar; (lodge) hospedar; (lend) prestar; (hold) tener espacio para, contener; (give a seat to) dar un sitio a. **to a. oneself to,** adaptarse a

accommodating, a. acomodadizo; (obliging) servicial

accommodation, s. acomodación, f.; ajuste, m.; adaptación, f.; (arrangement) arreglo, m.; (reconciliation), reconciliación, f.; (lodging) alojamiento, m.; (aer., naut.) partición, f.; (space, room or seat) sitio, m.; (loan) préstamo, m. **We found the a. good in this hotel,** Estuvimos muy bien en este hotel. **a. ladder,** escalera real, f.

accompaniment, s. acompañamiento, m.

accompanist, s. acompañante (-ta)

accompany, v.t. acompañar

accompanying, a. anexo. s. acompañamiento, m.

accomplice, s. cómplice, comparte, m. and f.

accomplish, v.t. llevar a cabo, efectuar; terminar; (fulfil) cumplir; perfeccionar; (achieve) conseguir, lograr

accomplished, a. consumado; perfecto; culto; (talented) talentoso

accomplishment, s. efectuación, f.; realización, f., logro, m.; (fulfilment) cumplimiento, m.; (gift) prenda, f., talento, m.; pl. **accomplishments,** partes, dotes, f. pl.; conocimientos, m. pl.

accord, s. acuerdo, m.; unión, f.; consentimiento, m.; concierto, m., concordia, f.; voluntad, f. v.t. otorgar, conceder. v.i. estar de acuerdo · (con); armonizar (con). **of one's own a.,** espontáneamente. **with one a.,** unánimemente

accordance, s. acuerdo, m., conformidad, f.; arreglo, m. **in a. with,** de acuerdo con, según, con arreglo a

according, adv. según, conforme. **a. as,** conforme, a medida que. **a. to,** según

accordingly, adv. en consecuencia, por consiguiente; pues

accordion, s. acordeón, m. **to a. pleat,** v.t. plisar

accost, *v.t.* abordar, acercarse a; dirigirse a, hablar

accoucheur, *s.* comadrón, *m.*

account, *v.t.* (judge) considerar, creer, juzgar, tener por. *v.i.* (for) explicar; (understand) comprender; (be responsible) responder de, dar razón de; justificar

account, *s.* (bill) cuenta, *f.*; factura, *f.*; (narrative) narración, relación, *f.*; (description) descripción, *f.*; historia, *f.*; versión, *f.*; (list) enumeración, *f.*; (reason) motivo, *m.*, causa, *f.*; (importance) importancia, *f.*; (weight) peso, *m.*; (news) noticias, *f. pl.*; (advantage) provecho, *m.*, ventaja, *f.* **in a.** with, en cuenta con. **by all accounts,** según lo que se oye, según voz pública. **current a.,** cuenta corriente, *f.* **outstanding a.,** cuenta pendiente, *f.* **on a.,** a cuenta. **on a. of,** a causa de, por motivo de. **on no a.,** de ninguna manera. **on that a.,** por lo tanto. **to be of no a.,** ser insignificante; ser de poca importancia; (*fam.*) ser la última mona. **to give an a.,** contar, hacer una relación (de). **to give an a. of oneself,** explicarse. **to keep a.,** llevar la cuenta. **to settle accounts,** ajustar cuentas. **to take into a.,** considerar. **to turn to a.,** sacar provecho de. **a.-book,** libro de cuentas, *m.*

accountability, *s.* responsabilidad, *f.*

accountable, *a.* responsable

accountancy, *s.* contabilidad, *f.*

accountant, *s.* contador, *m.* **chartered a.,** contador autorizado, *m.* **accountant's office,** contaduría, *f.*

accoutre, *v.t.* ataviar, vestir; equipar; armar

accoutrement, *s.* atavío, *m.*; equipo, *m.*

accredit, *v.t.* acreditar

accretion, *s.* acrecentamiento, aumento, *m.*; (*law*) accesión, *f.*

accrue, *v.i.* resultar (de), proceder (de); originarse (en); aumentar

accumulate, *v.t.* acumular; amontonar, atesorar. *v.i.* acumularse; aumentarse, crecer

accumulation, *s.* acumulación, *f.*; amontonamiento, *m.*

accumulative, *a.* acumulador; adquisitivo, ahorrador

accumulator, *s.* (*elec.*) acumulador, *m.*

accuracy, *s.* exactitud, corrección

accurate, *a.* exacto, correcto, fiel; (of persons) exacto, minucioso; (of apparatus) de precisión

accurately, *adv.* con exactitud, correctamente; con precisión

accursed, *a.* maldito. **A. be!** ¡Mal haya!

accusation, *s.* acusación, *f.* **to lodge an a.,** querellarse ante el juez

accusative, *s.* acusativo, *m.* **in the a.,** en el acusativo

accusatory, *a.* acusatorio

accuse, *v.t.* acusar

accused, *s.* (*law*) acusado (-da)

accuser, *s.* acusador (-ra)

accusing, *a.* acusador

accustom, *v.t.* acostumbrar (a), habituar (a)

accustomed, *a.* acostumbrado, usual; general; característico

ace, *s.* as, *m.*; (*fig.*) pelo, *m.* **to be within an ace of,** estar a dos dedos de

acephalous, *a.* acéfalo

acerbity, *s.* acerbidad, *f.*; (*fig.*) aspereza, *f.*; severidad, *f.*; sequedad, *f.*

acetate, *s.* acetato, *m.*

acetic, *a.* acético

acetone, *s.* acetona,

acetous, *a.* acetoso

acetylene, *s.* acetileno, *m.* **a. lamp,** lámpara de acetileno, *f.*

ache, *s.* dolor, *m.*; pena, *f.* *v.i.* doler. **My head aches,** Me duele la cabeza, Tengo un dolor de cabeza

achievable, *a.* alcanzable, asequible; factible

achieve, *v.t.* conseguir, lograr; (reach) alcanzar; (obtain) obtener, ganar

achievement, *s.* logro, *m.*, realización, *f.*; obtención, *f.*; (deed) hazaña, *f.*; (work) obra, *f.*; (success) éxito, *m.*; (discovery) descubrimiento, *m.*; (victory) victoria, *f.*

aching, *s.* dolor, *m.*; pena, angustia, *f.* *a.* doliente; afligido

achromatic, *a.* acromático
achromic, *a.* acrómico
acid, *a.* and *s.* ácido (*m.*). fatty a.,
ácido graso, *m.*
acidify, *v.t.* acidificar
acidity, *s.* acidez, *f.*
acidosis, *s.* (*med.*) acidismo, *m.*
acidulate, *v.t.* acidular
acidulous, *a.* acídulo
acknowledge, *v.t.* reconocer;
confesar; (reply to) contestar a;
(appreciate) agradecer. to a.
receipt, (*com.*) acusar recibo
acknowledgment, *s.* reconocimiento, *m.*; confesión, *f.*; (appreciation) agradecimiento, *m.*; (reward) recompensa, *f.*; (of a
letter) acuse de recibo, *m.*
acme, *s.* cumbre, *f.*; (*fig.*) auge,
apogeo, *m.*
acne, *s.* acne, *m.*
acolyte, *s.* acólito, monacillo, *m.*
aconite, *s.* (*bot.*) acónito, *m.*
acorn, *s.* bellota, *f.* a. cup,
capullo de bellota, *m.* a.-
shaped, en forma de bellota,
abellotado
acotyledonous, *a.* (*bot.*) acotile-
dóneo
acoustic, *a.* acústico
acoustics, *s. pl.* acústica, *f.*
acquaint, *v.t.* dar a conocer,
comunicar, informar (de), dar
parte (de); familiarizar (con).
to be acquainted with,
conocer; saber. to make oneself acquainted with, familiarizarse con; entablar amistad
con
acquaintance, *s.* conocimiento,
m.; (person) conocido (-da) *pl.*
acquaintances, amistades, *f. pl.*
to make their a., conocer (a),
llegar a conocer (a)
acquiesce, *v.i.* asentir (en), consentir (a)
acquiescence, *s.* acquiescencia,
f., consentimiento, *m.*
acquiescent, *a.* conforme; resignado
acquire, *v.t.* adquirir, obtener;
(diseases, habits) contraer;
ganar; (learn) aprender
acquirement, *s.* adquisición, *f.*;
(learning) conocimiento, *m.*;
(talent) talento, *m.*
acquirer, *s.* adquisidor (-ra)
acquisition, *s.* adquisición, *f.*
acquisitive, *a.* adquisitivo

acquisitiveness, *s.* adquisividad,
f.
acquit, *v.t.* (a debt) pagar;
exonerar; (*law*) absolver; (a
duty) cumplir. to a. oneself
well (badly), portarse bien (mal);
salir bien (mal)
acquittal, *s.* (of a debt) pago, *m.*;
(*law*) absolución, *f.*; (of a duty)
cumplimiento, *m.*
acquittance, *s.* descargo, *m.*;
quitanza, *f.*
acre, *s.* (measure) acre, *m.*; *pl.*
acres, terrenos, campos, *m. pl.*
acreage, *s.* acres, *m. pl.*
acrid, *a.* acre
acridness, *s.* acritud, *f.*
acrimonious, *a.* acrimonioso,
áspero; mordaz, sarcástico
acrimoniously, *adv.* con aspereza; sarcásticamente
acrimony, *s.* acrimonia, acritud,
f.; sarcasmo, *m.*
acrobat, *s.* acróbata, *m.* and *f.*
acrobatic, *a.* acrobático
acrobatics, *s. pl.* acrobacia, *f.*
acropolis, *s.* acrópolis, *f.*
across, *adv.* a través, de través,
transversalmente; (on the other
side) al otro lado; de una parte a
otra; (of the arms, etc.) cruzados
(*m. pl.*). *prep.* a través de;
al otro lado de; (upon) sobre;
por. He went a. the road,
Cruzó la calle. to run a.,
correr por; tropezar con; dar
con. a. country, a campo travieso. a. the way, en frente
acrostic, *s.* (poema) acróstico,
m. a. acróstico
act, *s.* acción, obra, *f.*, hecho, *m.*;
acto, *m.*; (*law*) ley, *f.*; (*theat.*)
acto, *m.* in the act, en el acto.
in the act (of doing), en acto de
(hacer algo). in the very act,
en flagrante. the Acts of the
Apostles, los Actos de los
Apóstoles. act of God, fuerza
mayor, *f.* act of indemnity,
bill de indemnidad, *m.*
act, *v.t.* (a play) representar,
hacer; (a part) desempeñar,
hacer (un papel); (pretend)
simular, fingir. *v.i.* obrar,
actuar; (behave) portarse, conducirse; (function) funcionar;
producir su efecto; (feign) fingir;
(as a profession) ser actor.
to act as, hacer de; cumplir las

funciones de. **to act as a second**, (in a duel) apadrinar. **to act for**, representar; ser el representante de. **to act upon**, obrar sobre; afectar; influir en

acting, *s.* (of a play) representación (de una comedia), *f.*; (of an actor) interpretación (de un papel), *f.*; (as a hobby) el hacer comedia; (dramatic art) arte dramática, *f.* *a.* interino, suplente; comanditario. **He is a. captain**, Está de capitán. **a. partner**, socio (-ia) comanditario (-ia)

actinic rays, *s. pl.* rayos actínicos, *m. pl.*

action, *s.* acción, *f.*; función, *f.*; operación, *f.*; (movement) movimiento, *m.*; (effect) efecto, *m.*; influencia, *f.*; (law) proceso, *m.*; (mil.) batalla, acción, *f.*; (lit.) acción, *f.* **in a.**, en actividad; en operación; (mil.) en el campo de batalla. **man of a.**, hombre de acción, *m.* **to be killed in a.**, morir en el campo de batalla. **to bring an a. against**, pedir en juicio, entablar un pleito contra. **to bring into a.**, emplear, poner en práctica. **to put into a.**, hacer funcionar; introducir. **to take a.**, tomar medidas (para). **to take a. against**, prevenirse contra; (law) proceder contra

actionable, *a.* procesable, punible

active, *a.* activo; ágil; diligente; (mil.) vivo; enérgico; (gram.) activo. **to make a.**, activar, estimular

actively, *adv.* activamente

activity, *s.* actividad, *f.*

actor, *s.* actor, *m.*; (in comedy) comediante, *m.*

actress, *s.* actriz, *f.*; (in comedy) comedianta, *f.*

actual, *a.* actual, existente; real, verdadero

actuality, *s.* realidad, *f.*

actually, *adv.* en efecto, realmente, en realidad

actuary, *s.* actuario de seguros, *m.*

actuate, *v.t.* mover, animar, excitar

acumen, *s.* cacumen, *m.*, agudeza, sagacidad, *f.*

acute, *a.* agudo; (shrewd) perspicaz; (of a situation) crítico. **a. accent**, acento agudo, *m.* **a.-angled**, acutángulo

acutely, *adv.* agudamente; (deeply) profundamente

acuteness, *s.* agudeza, *f.*; (shrewdness) perspicacia, penetración, *f.*

adage, *s.* refrán, proverbio, decir, *m.*

adagio, *s.* adagio, *m.*

Adam, *s.* Adán, *m.* **Adam's apple**, nuez de la garganta, *f.*

adamant, *s.* diamante, *m.*; (fig.) piedra, *f.*

adamantine, *a.* de diamante; (fig.) adamantino

adapt, *v.t.* adaptar; ajustar; acomodar; aplicar; (a play, etc.) refundir, arreglar; (mus.) arreglar

adaptability, *s.* adaptabilidad, *f.*

adaptable, *a.* adaptable

adaptation, *s.* adaptación, *f.*; (of a play, etc.) refundición, *f.*; (mus., etc.) arreglo, *m.*

adapter, *s.* (of a play, etc.) refundidor (-ra); (elec.) enchufe de reducción, *m.*

add, *v.t.* añadir; juntar; (up) sumar. **to add to**, añadir a; (increase) aumentar, acrecentar. **to add up**, sumar. **to add up to**, subir a; (mean) querer decir.

adder, *s.* víbora, serpiente, *f.*

addict, *s.* adicto (-ta). **to a. oneself to**, dedicarse a, entregarse a

addicted, *a.* aficionado (a), amigo (de), dado (a); adicto (a)

addiction, *s.* afición, propensión, *f.*; adicción, *f.*

adding, *s.* añadidura, *f.*; (up) suma, adición, *f.* **a. machine**, máquina de sumar, *f.*

addition, *s.* añadidura, *f.*; (math.) adición, suma, *f.* **in a. (to)**, además (de), también

additional, *a.* adicional

addled, *a.* huero, podrido; (fig.) confuso

address, *s.* (on a letter) sobrescrito, *m.*; (of a person) dirección, *f.*, señas, *f. pl.*; (speech) discurso, *m.*; (petition) memorial, *m.*, petición, *f.*; (dedication) dedicatoria, *f.*; (invocation) invocación, *f.*; (deportment) presencia, *f.*; (tact) diplomacia, habilidad,

f.; *pl.* **addresses**, corte, *f.*
v.t. (a ball) golpear; (a letter)
dirigir, poner el sobrescrito a;
(words, prayers) dirigir (a);
hablar, hacer un discurso. **to
a. oneself to a task,** dedicarse a
(or entregarse a or emprender)
una tarea. **to deliver an a.,**
pronunciar un discurso. **to pay
one's addresses to,** cortejar,
hacer la corte (a), galantear
addressee, *s.* destinatario (-ia)
addressing machine, *s.*
máquina para dirigir sobres, *f.*
adduce, *v.t.* aducir, alegar; aportar
adenoids, *s. pl.* amígdalas, *f. pl.*
adept, *a.* adepto, versado, consumado. *s.* adepto, *m.*
adequacy, *s.* adecuación, *f.*;
suficiencia, *f.*; competencia, *f.*
adequate, *a.* adecuado; proporcionado; suficiente; competente;
a la altura (de)
adequately, *adv.* adecuadamente
adhere, *v.i.* adherirse; pegarse;
ser fiel (a); persistir (en)
adherence, *s.* (*fig.*) adhesión, *f.*
adherent, *s.* partidario (-ia)
adhesion, *s.* adherencia, *f.*; (to a
party, etc.) adhesión, *f.*
adhesive, *a.* adhesivo; (sticky)
pegajoso. **a. tape,** esparadrapo,
m.; (*elec.*) cinta aisladora adherente, *f.*
adipose, *a.* adiposo
adiposity, *s.* adiposidad, *f.*
adjacency, *s.* proximidad, contigüidad, vecindad, *f.*
adjacent, *a.* próximo, contiguo,
adyacente, vecino
adjectival, *a.* adjetivo
adjective, *s.* adjetivo, *m.*
adjoin, *v.t.* estar contiguo a,
lindar con; juntar. *v.i.* colindar
adjoining, *a.* vecino, de al lado,
adyacente; cercano
adjourn, *v.t.* aplazar, diferir;
(a meeting, etc.) suspender,
levantar. *v.i.* retirarse. **The
debate was adjourned,** Se
suspendió el debate. **to a. a
meeting,** levantar la sesión
adjournment, *s.* aplazamiento,
m.; (of a meeting) suspensión (de
la sesión), *f.*
adjudicate, *v.t.* adjudicar; (*law*)
declarar; juzgar. *v.i.* ejercer las
funciones del juez; fallar, dictar
sentencia

adjudication, *s.* adjudicación, *f.*;
(*law*) fallo, *m.*, sentencia, *f.*;
(of bankruptcy) declaración (de
quiebra), *f.*; concesión, *f.*,
otorgamiento, *m.*
adjudicator, *s.* adjudicador (-ra)
adjunct, *s.* atributo; *m.*; accesorio,
m.; adjunto, *m.*; (*gram.*) adjunto,
m.
adjure, *v.t.* conjurar; rogar encarecidamente
adjust, *v.t.* ajustar; regular;
arreglar; (correct) corregir;
adaptar
adjustable, *a.* ajustable; regu-
lable; desmontable; de quita y
pon
adjustment, *s.* ajuste, *m.*; regulación, *f.*; arreglo, *m.*; (correction) corrección, *f.*; adaptación,
f.; (*com.*) prorrateo, *m.*
adjutant, *s.* (*mil.*) ayudante, *m.*
administer, *v.t.* administrar;
(laws) aplicar; (blows, etc.) dar;
(an office) ejercer; (govern) regir,
gobernar; (provide) suministrar;
(an oath) tomar; (justice) hacer;
(the sacraments) administrar;
(with to) contribuir a. **to a.
an oath,** tomar juramento (a)
administration, *s.* administración, *f.*; (government) gobierno,
m.; dirección, *f.*; (of laws)
aplicación, *f.*; distribución, *f.*
administrative, *a.* administrativo; gubernativo
administrator, *s.* administrador,
m.
administratrix, *s.* administradora, *f.*
admirable, *a.* admirable
admirably, *adv.* admirablemente
admiral, *s.* almirante, *m.* **A. of
the Fleet,** almirante supremo, *m.*
admiral's ship, capitana, *f.*
Admiralty, *s.* almirantazgo, *m.*
First Lord of the A., Ministro
de Marina, *m.*
admiration, *s.* admiración, *f.*
admire, *v.t.* sentir admiración
por; (love) amar; (like) gustar;
(respect) respetar
admirer, *s.* admirador (-ra);
(amateur) aficionado (-da).
apasionado (-da); (partisan) satélite, *m.*; (lover) enamorado,
amante, *m.*
admiring, *a.* admirativo, de
admiración

admissible, *a.* admisible; aceptable; lícito, permitido

admission, *s.* admisión, *f.;* recepción, *f.;* entrada, *f.;* confesión, *f.,* reconocimiento, *m.* **No a.!** Entrada prohibida. **right of a.,** derecho de entrada, *m.* **A. free!** Entrada libre. a. ticket, entrada, *f.*

admit, *v.t.* admitir; recibir; dejar entrar; hacer entrar, introducir; (hold) contener; (concede) conceder; (acknowledge) reconocer, confesar. **to a. of,** permitir; sufrir

admittance, *s.* admisión, *f.;* entrada, *f.* **No a.!** Prohibida la entrada. **to gain a.,** lograr entrar

admittedly, *adv.* según opinión general; sin duda

admonish, *v.t.* (advise) aconsejar; amonestar, advertir; (reprimand) reprender

admonition, *s.* amonestación, *f.;* advertencia, *f.;* admonición, *f.*

admonitory, *a.* amonestador

ado, *s.* (noise) ruido, *m.;* (trouble) trabajo, *m.,* dificultad, *f.;* (fuss) barahunda, *f.* **Much ado about nothing,** Mucho ruido y pocas nueces, Nada entre dos platos. **without more ado,** sin más ni más

adolescence, *s.* adolescencia, *f.*

adolescent, *a.* and *s.* adolescente (*m.* and *f.*)

adopt, *v.t.* adoptar

adopted, *a.* adoptivo

adopter, *s.* adoptador (-ra)

adoption, *s.* adopción, *f.;* (choice) elección, *f.*

adoptive, *a.* adoptivo

adorable, *a.* adorable.

adorableness, *s.* lo adorable

adorably, *adv.* adorablemente

adoration, *s.* adoración, *f* **A. of the Magi,** Adoración de los Reyes, *f.*

adore, *v.t.* adorar

adorer, *s.* adorador (-ra); amante, *m.*

adoringly, *adv.* con adoración

adorn, *v.t.* adornar, embellecer; (*fig.,* of persons) adornar con su presencia

adornment, *s.* adorno, *m.;* ornamento, *m.;* embellecimiento, *m.*

adrenalin, *s.* adrenalina, *f.*

Adriatic, *a.* adriático

adrift, *a.* and *adv.* a merced de las olas; a la ventura. **to turn a.,** (*fam.*) poner de patitas en la calle

adroit, *a.* hábil

adroitly, *adv.* hábilmente

adroitness, *s.* habilidad, *f.*

adulate, *v.t.* adular

adulation, *s.* adulación, *f.*

adulatory, *a.* adulador

adult, *a.* and *s.* adulto (-ta)

adulterate, *v.t.* adulterar; falsificar; contaminar. *a.* adulterado; falsificado; impuro

adulteration, *s.* adulteración, *f.;* falsificación, *f.;* impureza, *f.;* contaminación, *f.*

adulterer, *s.* adúltero, *m.*

adulteress, *s.* adúltera, *f.*

adulterous, *a.* adúltero

adulterously, *adv.* por adulterio

adultery, *s.* adulterio, *m.* **to commit a.,** cometer adulterio, adulterar

advance, *s.* avance, *m.;* (progress) progreso, adelantamiento, *m.;* (improvement) mejora, *f.;* (of shares) alza, *f.;* (of price) subida, *f.;* (loan) préstamo, *m.;* (in rank) ascenso, *m.; pl.* **advances,** (overtures) avances, *m. pl.;* (proposals) propuestas, *f. pl.;* (of love) requerimientos amorosos, *m. pl.* **in a.,** de antemano, con tiempo, previamente; (of money) por adelantado. a. guard, (*mil.*) avanzada, *f.* **a. payment,** anticipo, *m.,* paga por adelantado, *f.*

advance, *v.t.* avanzar; (suggest) sugerir, proponer; (encourage) fomentar; (a person) ascender; (improve) mejorar; (of events, dates) adelantar; (of prices, stocks) hacer subir; (money) anticipar; (of steps) tomar. *v.i.* avanzar; (progress) progresar; (in rank, studies, etc.) adelantar; (of prices) subir

advanced, *a.* avanzado; (developed) desarrollado; (mentally, of children) precoz. **a. views,** ideas avanzadas, *f. pl.*

advancement, *s.* adelantamiento, *m.;* progreso, *m.;* (encouragement) fomento, *m.;* (in employment) promoción, *f.;* prosperidad, *f.*

advancing, *a.* que avanza; (of years) que pasan

advantage, *s.* ventaja, *f.*; superioridad, *f.*; (benefit) provecho, beneficio, *m.*; interés, *m.*; ocasión favorable, oportunidad, *f.*; (tennis) ventaja, *f.* **to have the a. of,** tener la ventaja de. **to show to a.,** embellecer, realzar; aumentar la belleza (etc.) de. **to take a. of,** sacar ventaja de, aprovecharse de; (deceive) engañar. **to take a. of the slightest pretext,** asirse de un cabello

advantageous, *a.* ventajoso, provechoso. **to be a.,** ser de provecho

advent, *s.* advenimiento, *m.*, llegada, *f.*; (ecc.) Adviento, *m.*

adventitious, *a.* adventicio (all uses)

adventure, *s.* aventura, *f.*; riesgo, *m.*; (chance) casualidad, *f.*; (com.) especulación, *f.* *v.t.* aventurar, arriesgar. *v.i.* arriesgarse, osar

adventurer, *s.* aventurero, *m.*; (one living by his wits) caballero de industria, *m.*; (in commerce) especulador, *m.*

adventuress, *s.* aventurera, *f.*

adventurous, *a.* aventurero; osado, audaz; (dangerous) peligroso, arriesgado

adverb, *s.* adverbio, *m.*

adverbial, *a.* adverbial

adversary, *s.* adversario (-ia)

adverse, *a.* adverso; hostil (a); malo; desfavorable; (opposite) opuesto

adversity, *s.* adversidad, *f.*

advertise, *v.t.* anunciar. *v.i.* poner un anuncio; (oneself) llamar la atención

advertisement, *s.* anuncio, *m.*; (poster) cartel, *m.*; (to attract attention) reclamo, *m.* **to put an a. in the paper,** poner un anuncio en el periódico. **a. hoarding,** cartelera, *f.*

advertiser, *s.* anunciante, *m.* and *f.*

advertising, *s.* anuncios, *m. pl.*; publicidad, propaganda, *f.*

advice, *s.* consejo, *m.*; (warning) advertencia, amonestación, *f.*; (news) noticia, *f.*, aviso, *m.*; (com.) comunicación, *f.*; (belief) parecer, *m.*, opinión, *f.* **piece of a.,** consejo, *m.* **to follow the a. of,** seguir los consejos de. **to give a.,** dar consejos

advisability, *s.* conveniencia, *f.*; prudencia, *f.*

advisable, *a.* conveniente, aconsejable; prudente

advise, *v.t.* aconsejar; (inform) avisar, informar

advised, *a.* avisado; premeditado. **ill-a.,** mal aconsejado; imprudente. **well-a.,** bien aconsejado; prudente

adviser, *s.* consejero (-ra)

advisory, *a.* consultivo

advocacy, *s.* defensa, *f.*; apología, *f.*; abogacía, intercesión, *f.*

advocate, *s.* (law) abogado (-da); defensor (-ra); (champion) campeón, *m.* *v.t.* abogar, defender; sostener, apoyar; recomendar

adze, *s.* azuela, *f.*

ægis, *s.* égida, *f.*; protección, *f.*

Æolian, *a.* eolio. **Æ. harp,** arpa eolia, *f.*

æon, *s.* eón, *m.*

aerated, *a.* aerado; (of lemonade, etc.) gaseoso. **a. waters,** aguas gaseosas, *f. pl.*

aeration, *s.* aeración, *f.*

aerial, *a.* aéreo, de aire; etéreo; fantástico. *s.* (radio) antena, *f.* **indoor a.,** antena interior, *f.*

aerodrome, *s.* aeródromo, aeropuerto, *m.*

aerodynamics, *s.* aerodinámica, *f.*

aerolite, *s.* aerolito, *m.*

aeronaut, *s.* aeronauta, *m.* and *f.*

aeronautical, *a.* aeronáutico

aeronautics, *s.* aeronáutica, *f.*

aeroplane, *s.* aeroplano, avión, *m.* **interceptor a.,** avión de hostigamiento, *m.* **jet-propelled a.,** aeroplano de reacción, *m.* **model a.,** aeroplano en miniatura, *m.* **night fighter a.,** avión de combate nocturno, *m.*

aerostatic, *a.* aerostático

aerostatics, *s.* aerostática, *f.*

aerotherapy, *s.* aeroterapia, *f.*

æsthete, *s.* estético, *m.*

æsthetic, *a.* estético

æsthetically, *adv.* estéticamente

æsthetics, *s.* estética, *f.*

afar, *adv.* a lo lejos, en la distancia. **from a.,** desde lejos

affability, *s.* afabilidad, condescendencia, urbanidad, *f.*

affable, *a.* afable, condescendiente

affably, *adv.* afablemente

affair, *s.* asunto, *m.*, cosa, *f.*; cuestión, *f.*; (business) negocio, *m.*; (*fam.*, applied to a machine, carriage, etc.) artefacto, *m.*; (of the heart) amorío, *m.* **a. of honour,** lance de honor, *m.*

affect, *v.t.* afectar; influir; (*med.*) atacar; (move) impresionar, conmover; enternecer; (harm) perjudicar; (frequent) frecuentar; (like) gustar de; (love) amar; (wear) vestir; (use) gastar, usar; (feign) aparentar; (boast) hacer alarde de

affectation; *s.* afectación, *f.*

affected, *a.* afectado; influido; (*med.*) atacado; (moved) conmovido, impresionado; enternecido; (inclined) dispuesto, inclinado; (artificial) artificioso; amanerado, afectado; (of style) rebuscado, artificial

affecting, *a.* conmovedor, emocionante

affection, *s.* afecto, cariño, *m.*; amor, *m.*; apego, *m.*; simpatía, *f.*; (emotion) emoción, *f.*, sentimiento, *m.*; (*med.*) afección, enfermedad, *f.*

affectionate, *a.* afectuoso, cariñoso; mimoso; (tender) tierno; expresivo

affectionately, *adv.* afectuosamente. **Yours a., tu cariñoso . . ., tu . . ., que te quiere**

affective, *a.* afectivo

afferent, *a.* aferente

affianced, *a.* and *s.* prometido (-da). **a. bride,** novia, prometida, *f.*

affidavit, *s.* declaración jurada, atestiguación, *f.*

affiliate, *v.t.* afiliar; adoptar; (law) imputar; (law) legitimar

affiliation, *s.* afiliación, *f.*; adopción, *f.*; legitimación de un hijo, *f.*

affinity, *s.* afinidad, *f.*

affirm, *v.t.* afirmar, aseverar, declarar; confirmar. *v.i.* (law) declarar ante un juez

affirmation, *s.* afirmación, aserción, *f.*; confirmación, *f.*; (law) declaración, deposición, *f.*

affirmative, *a.* afirmativo. *s.* afirmativa, *f.*

affix, *v.t.* fijar; pegar; añadir; (seal, one's signature) poner. *s.* (*gram.*) afijo, *m.*

afflict, *v.t.* afligir, atormentar, aquejar

affliction, *s.* aflicción, *f.*; tribulación, pesadumbre, *f.*; calamidad, *f.*; miseria, *f.*; (ailment) achaque, *m.*

affluence, *s.* afluencia, *f.*; abundancia, *f.*; riqueza, *f.*; opulencia, *f.*

affluent, *a.* abundante; rico; opulento

afflux, *s.* afluencia, *f.*; (*med.*) aflujo, *m.*

afford, *v.t.* dar, proporcionar; producir; ofrecer; (bear) soportar; poder con; (financially) tener medios para; permitirse el lujo de; (be able) poder. **I could not a. to pay so much,** No puedo (podía) pagar tanto

afforest, *v.t.* convertir en bosque

afforestation, *s.* conversión en bosque, *f.*; plantación de un bosque, *f.*

affray, *s.* riña, refriega, *f.*

affront, *s.* afrenta, *f.*, insulto, agravio, *m.* *v.t.* insultar, ultrajar, afrentar; (offend) ofender

Afghan, *a.* and *s.* afgano (-na)

afield, *adv.* en el campo; lejos. **to go far a.,** ir muy lejos

afire, *adv.* en fuego, en llamas; (*fig.*) ardiendo

aflame, *adv.* en llamas; (*fig.*) encendido

afloat, *adv.* a flote; (*naut.*) a bordo; (solvent) solvente; en circulación; (floating) flotante; (swamped) inundado; (in full swing) en marcha, en movimiento

afoot, *adv.* a pie; en marcha, en movimiento; en preparación. **to set a.,** iniciar, poner en marcha

aforementioned, *a.* antedicho, ya mencionado

aforesaid, *a.* consabido, dicho, susodicho

afraid, *a.* espantado; temeroso, miedoso. **I'm a. that . . .,** Me temo que. . . . **to be a.,** tener miedo. **to make a.,** dar miedo (a)

afresh, *adv.* de nuevo, otra vez

African, *a.* and *s.* africano (-na)

Afrikander, *s.* bóer, *m.* and *f.*

aft, *adv.* en popa; a popa. **fore and aft,** de proa a popa

after, *prep.* (of place). detrás de; (of time) después de; (behind) en pos de; (following) tras; (in spite of) a pesar de; (in consequence of) después de, a consecuencia de; (in accordance with) según; (in the style of) al estilo de, en imitación de. *adv.* (later) después, más tarde; (subsequently) . después (que); (when) cuando. *a.* futuro, venidero. **day a.** day, día tras día. **on the day a.,** al día siguiente. **soon a.,** poco después. **to look a.,** cuidar de. **to go a.,** ir a buscar; seguir. **the day a. to-morrow,** pasado mañana. **What are you a. ?** ¿Qué buscas? **a. all,** después de todo. **a. the manner of,** a la moda de, según la moda de; al estilo de. **a.-dinner conversation,** conversación de sobremesa, *f.* **a.-glow,** resplandor crepuscular, reflejo del sol poniente en el cielo, *m.* **a.-life,** vida futura, *f.* **a.-pains,** dolores de sobreparto, *m. pl.* **a.-taste,** dejo, resabio, *m.*

afterbirth, *s.* placenta, *f.*

aftermath, *s.* consecuencias, *f. pl.*, resultado, *m.*

afternoon, *s.* tarde, *f.* **Good a.!** ¡Buenas tardes! **a. nap,** siesta, *f.* **a. tea,** el té de las cinco

afterthought, *s.* reflexión tardía, *f.*; segunda intención, *f.* **to have an a.,** pensar en segundo lugar

afterwards, *adv.* después; más tarde

again, *adv.* (once more) otra vez, de nuevo; por segunda vez, dos veces; (on the other hand) por otra parte; (moreover) además; (likewise) también; (returned) de vuelta. Sometimes translated by prefix **re** in verbs. **as much a.,** otro tanto. **never a.,** nunca más. **not a.,** no más. **now and a.,** de vez en cuando. **to do a.,** volver a hacer, hacer de nuevo. **a. and a.,** repetidas veces

against, *prep.* (facing) enfrente de; contra; (in preparation for) para; (contrary to) contrario a; (opposed to) opuesto a; (near)

cerca de. **to be a.,** oponer; estar enfrente de. **a. the grain,** a contrapelo

agaric, *s.* (*bot.*) agárico, *m.*

agate, *s.* ágata, *f.*; heliotropo, *m.*

age, *s.* edad, *f.*; (generation) generación, *f.*; (epoch) siglo, período, *m.*; época, *f.*; (old age) vejez, *f.*; (majority) mayoría de edad, *f.* *v.i.* envejecer. **at any age,** a cualquier edad. **the golden age,** la edad de oro; (in literature, etc.) el siglo de oro. **from age to age,** por los siglos de los siglos. **to be of age,** ser mayor de edad. **to be under age,** ser menor de edad. **to come of age,** llegar a la mayoría de edad. **She is six years of age,** Ella tiene seis años. **What age are you?** ¿Qué edad tienes? **age-old,** secular

aged, *a.* de la edad de; (old) anciano, viejo. **A girl a. four,** Una niña de cuatro años

ageless, *a.* siempre joven; eterno

agency, *s.* órgano, *m.*, fuerza, *f.*; acción, *f.*; influencia, *f.*; intervención, *f.*; mediación, *f.*; (*com.*) agencia, *f.* **through the a. of,** por la mediación (or influencia) de

agenda, *s.* agenda, *f.*

agent, *s.* agente, *m.*; (*com.*) representante, *m. and f.*; (*law*) apoderado (-da). **business a.,** agente de negocios, *m.*

agglomerate, *v.t.* and *v.i.* aglomerar(se)

agglomeration, *s.* aglomeración, *f.*

agglutinate, *v.t.* and *v.i.* aglutinar(se)

agglutination, *s.* aglutinación, *f.*

aggrandize, *v.t.* engrandecer

aggrandizement, *s.* engrandecimiento, *m.*

aggravate, *v.t.* agravar, hacer peor; intensificar; (annoy) irritar, exasperar

aggravating, *a.* agravante, agravador; (tiresome) molesto; (annoying) irritante. **a. circumstance,** circunstancia agravante, *f.*

aggravation, *s.* agravación, *f.*; intensificación, *f.*; (annoyance) irritación, *f.*

aggregate, *a.* total. *s.* agregado, conjunto, *m.* **in the a., en** conjunto

aggression, *s.* agresión, *f.*

aggressive, *a.* agresivo

aggressively, *adv.* agresivamente

aggressiveness, *s.* carácter agresivo, *m.,* belicosidad, *f.*

aggressor, *a.* and *s.* agresor (-ra)

aggrieved, *a.* afligido; ofendido; lastimero

aghast, *a.* horrorizado, espantado; (amazed) estupefacto

agile, *a.* ágil; ligero; vivo

agility, *s.* agilidad, *f.*; ligereza, *f.*

agitate, *v.t.* agitar; excitar; inquietar, perturbar; discutir. **to a. for,** luchar por; excitar la opinión pública en favor de

agitating, *a.* agitador

agitation, *s.* agitación, *f.*; perturbación, *f.*; discusión, *f.*

agitator, *s.* agitador (-ra); (apparatus) agitador, *m.*

aglow, *a.* and *adv.* brillante, fulgente; encendido

agnate, *a.* and *s.* agnado (-da)

agnation, *s.* agnación, *f.*

agnostic, *a.* and *s.* agnóstico (-ca)

agnosticism, *s.* agnosticismo, *m.*

ago, *adv.* hace, ha. **a short while ago,** hace poco. **How long ago?** ¿Cuánto tiempo ha? **long ago,** hace mucho. **many years ago,** muchos años ha. **I last saw him ten years ago,** La última vez que le vi fué hace diez años

agog, *a.* agitado; ansioso; excitado; impaciente; curioso. *adv.* con agitación; con ansia; con curiosidad

agonize, *v.t.* atormentar. *v.i.* sufrir intensamente; retorcerse de dolor

agonizing, *a.* (of pain) intenso, atormentador

agonizingly, *adv.* dolorosamente

agony, *s.* agonía, *f.*; angustia, *f.*; paroxismo, *m.* **a. column,** columna de los suspiros, *f.*

agrarian, *a.* agrario

agree, *v.i.* estar de acuerdo; convenir (en); acordar; ponerse de acuerdo, entenderse; (suit) sentar bien, probar; (consent) consentir (en); (*gram.*) concordar,

(get on well) llevarse bien; (correspond) estar conforme (con). **to a. to,** convenir en, consentir en. **to a. with,** estar de acuerdo con, apoyar; dar la razón a; (suit) sentar bien; (*gram.*) concordar

agreeable, *a.* agradable; afable; amable; (pleasant) ameno, grato; conforme; dispuesto a (hacer algo); conveniente

agreeableness, *s.* (of persons) afabilidad, amabilidad, *f.*; amenidad, *f.*; deleite, *m.*; conformidad, *f.*

agreeably, *adv.* agradablemente; de acuerdo (con), conforme (a)

agreed, *a.* convenido, acordado; (approved) aprobado. *interj.* ¡ convenido! ¡ de acuerdo!

agreement, *s.* acuerdo, *m.*; pacto, *m.*; acomodamiento, concierto, *m.*; contrato, *m.*; (*com.*) convenio, *m.*; conformidad, *f.*; consentimiento, *m.*; (*gram.*) concordancia, *f.* **in a.,** conforme. **in a. with,** de acuerdo con; según. **to reach an a.,** ponerse de acuerdo

agricultural, *a.* agrícola. **a. engineer,** ingeniero agrónomo, *m.* **a. labourer,** labriego, *m.* **a. show,** exposición agrícola, *f.*

agriculturalist, *s.* agrícola, *m.* and *f.*

agriculture, *s.* agricultura, *f.*

agronomic, *a.* agrónomo

agronomist, *s.* agrónomo, *m.*

agronomy, *s.* agronomía, *f.*

aground, *adv.* (*naut.*) varado, encallado. **running a.,** varada, *f.* **to run a.,** varar

ague, *s.* fiebre intermitente, *f.*; (*fig.*) escalofrío, *m.*

ah! *interj.* ¡ah! ¡ay!

aha! *interj.* ¡ajá!

ahead, *adv.* delante; enfrente; al frente (de); a la cabeza (de); adelante; hacia delante; (*naut.*) por la proa. **Go a.!** ¡Adelante! **It is straight a.,** Está directamente enfrente. **to go straight a.,** ir hacia delante; seguir (haciendo algo)

ahoy! *interj.* ¡ah del barco!

aid, *s.* ayuda, *f.*; socorro, auxilio, *m.*; subsidio, *m.* *v.t.* ayudar; socorrer, auxiliar. **in aid of,** pro, en beneficio de. **first aid,** primera cura, *f.* **first aid**

post, puesto de socorro, *m.*
to come or go to the aid of,
acudir en defensa de
aide-de-camp, *s.* edecán, *m.*
aigrette, *s.* (*orn.*) garzota, *f.*;
penacho, *m.*
ail, *v.t.* afligir, doler; pasar. *v.i.*
estar indispuesto (or enfermo).
What ails you? (*fam.*) ¿Qué te
pasa?
aileron, *s.* (*aer.*) alerón, *m.*
ailing, *a.* enfermizo, enclenque,
achacoso
ailment, *s.* enfermedad, *f.*,
achaque, *m.*
aim, *s.* (of firearms) puntería, *f.*;
(mark) blanco, *m.*; (*fig.*) objeto,
fin, *m.*; (*fig.*) intención, *f.*,
propósito, *m.* *v.t.* (a gun) apuntar; dirigir; (throw) lanzar;
(a blow) asestar. *v.i.* apuntar
(a); (a remark at) decir por;
aspirar (a); intentar, proponerse.
Is your remark aimed at me?
¿Lo dices por mí? to aim high,
apuntar alto; (*fam.*) picar alto.
to miss one's aim, errar el
tiro. to take aim, apuntar.
with the aim of, con objeto de,
a fin de
aimless, *a.*, aimlessly, *adv.* sin
objeto, a la ventura
air, *s.* aire, *m.* (all meanings).
by air, en avión; (of mail) por
avión; (of goods) por vía aérea.
in the air, al aire; al aire libre;
(as though flying) en volandas.
in the open air, al aire libre, al
fresco, a la intemperie. to be on
the air, (*rad.*) hablar por radio.
to give oneself airs, darse tono,
tener humos. to take the air,
tomar el fresco; despegar. air
balloon, globo aerostático, *m.*;
(toy) globo, *m.* air-base, base
aérea, *f.* air-bed, colchón de
viento, *m.* air-borne (to become), levantar el vuelo, despegar. air-brake, (*mech.*) freno
neumático, *m.* air-chamber,
cámara de aire, *f.* air chief
marshal, general del ejército
del aire, *m.* air-cock, válvula
de escape de aire, *f.* air
commodore, general de brigada
de aviación, *m.* air condition-
ing, purificación de aire, *f.*
air-cooled, enfriado por aire.
air crash, accidente de aviación,

m. air current, corriente de
aire, *f.* air-cushion, almohadilla neumática, *f.* air-field,
campo de aviación, *m.* air
fleet, flotilla aérea, *f.* air force,
fuerza aérea, flota aérea, *f.* air-
gun, escopeta de viento, *f.*
air-hole, respiradero, *m.* air-
hostess, azafata, *f.* air-lift,
puente aéreo, *m.* air-liner, avión
de pasajeros, *m.* air lines, líneas
aéreas, *f. pl.* air-mail, correo
aéreo, *m.* by air-mail, por avión.
air marshal, teniente general de
aviación, *m.* air-pocket, bolsa
(or vacío, *m.*) de aire, *f.* airport, aeropuerto, *m.* air pump,
bomba neumática, *f.* air raid,
bombardeo aéreo, *m.* air-raid
shelter, refugio antiaéreo, *m.*
air-raid warning, alarma aérea,
f. air-route, vía aérea, *f.* air-
screw, hélice de avión, *f.* air-
shaft, respiradero de mina, *m.*
air-sickness, mal de altura, *m.*
air squadron, escuadrilla aérea,
f. air taxi, avión taxi, *m.* air-
tight, herméticamente cerrado.
air valve, válvula de aire, *f.*
air vice-marshal, general de
división de aviación, *m.*
air, *v.t.* airear, orear; secar al
aire; ventilar; (*fig.*) sacar a
lucir, emitir; (*fig.*) ostentar
aircraft, *s.* aparato, avión, *m.*
a. barrage, cortina de fuego de
artillería, *f.* a.-carrier, porta-
aviones, *m.* a. factory, fábrica
de aeroplanos, *f.*
aircraftsman, *s.* soldado de
aviación, *m.*
airgraph, *s.* aerograma, *m.*
airily, *adv.* ligeramente, sin preocuparse; alegremente
airiness, *s.* airosidad, *f.*; ventilación, *f.*; situación airosa, *f.*;
(lightness) ligereza, *f.*; alegría, *f.*;
frivolidad, *f.*
airing, *s.* aireación, *f.*; ventilación, *f.*; secamiento, *m.*; (walk)
vuelta, *f.*, paseo, *m.* to take
an a., dar una vuelta
airless, *a.* sin aire; falto de
ventilación; sofocante
airman, *s.* aviador, *m.*
airship, *s.* aeronave, nave aérea,
f.
airway, *s.* vía aérea, *f.*
airwoman, *s.* aviadora, *f.*

airy, *a.* aéreo; (breezy) airoso; ligero; vaporoso; alegro; (vain) vano; (flippant) frívolo

aisle, *s.* nave lateral, ala, *f.*

ajar, *a.* entreabierto, entornado. **to leave a.,** dejar entreabierto, entornar

akimbo, *adv.* en jarras. **with arms a.,** con los brazos en jarras

akin, *a.* consanguíneo, emparentado; análogo, relacionado; semejante

alabaster, *s.* alabastro, *m.* *a.* alabastrino

alacrity, *s.* alacridad, *f.*

alarm, *s.* alarma, *f.*; toque de alarma, *m.*; (tocsin) rebato, *m.*; sobresalto, *m.*, alarma, *f.* *v.t.* alarmar; (*mil.*) dar la alarma (a); asustar. **to give the a.,** dar la alarma. **a. bell,** timbre de alarma, *m.* **a. clock,** despertador, *m.* **a. signal,** señal de alarma, *f.*

alarming, *a.* alarmante

alarmingly, *adv.* de un modo alarmante; espantosamente

alarmist, *s.* alarmista, *m.* and *f.*

alas! *interj.* ¡ay!

alb, *s.* alba, *f.*

Albanian, *a.* and *s.* albanés (-esa); (language) albanés, *m.*

albatross, *s.* albatros, *m.*

albeit, *conjunc.* aunque, si bien; sin embargo

Albigensian, *a.* and *s.* albigense (*m.* and *f.*)

albinism, *s.* albinismo, *m.*

albino, *a.* albino

album, *s.* álbum, *m.*

albumin, *s.* albúmina, *f.*

albuminous, *a.* albuminoso, *m.*

alchemic, *a.* alquímico

alchemist, *s.* alquimista, *m.*

alchemy, *s.* alquimia, *f.*

alcohol, *s.* alcohol, *m.* **industrial a.,** alcohol desnaturalizado, *m.* **wood a.,** alcohol metílico, alcohol de madera, *m.*

alcoholic, *a.* alcohólico

alcoholism, *s.* alcoholismo, *m.*

alcoholize, *v.t.* alcoholizar

alcove, *s.* alcoba, *f.*; nicho, *m.*

aldehyde, *s.* aldehido, *m.*

alder, *s.* (tree and wood) aliso, *m.*

alderman, *s.* concejal, *m.*

ale, *s.* cerveza, *f.* **ale-house,** cervecería, *f.*

alert, *a.* alerto; vigilante; despierto; vivo. *s.* sirena, *f.* **to be on the a.,** estar sobre aviso; estar vigilante

alertly, *adv.* alertamente

alertness, *s.* vigilancia, *f.*; viveza, *f.*; prontitud, *f.*

Alexandrian, *a.* alejandrino

Alexandrine, *a.* and *s.* alejandrino (*m.*)

alga, *s.* alga, *f.*

algebra, *s.* álgebra, *f.*

algebraic, *a.* algebraico

Algerian, *a.* and *s.* argelino (-na) *a.* alias, por otro nombre.

alias, *adv.* alias, por otro nombre. *s.* nombre falso, seudónimo, *m.*

alibi, *s.* (*law*) coartada, *f.* **to prove an a.,** probar la coartada

alien, *a.* ajeno; (foreign) extranjero; extraño; contrario. *s.* extranjero (-ra). *a.* **to,** ajeno a; repugnante a. **Aliens Department,** Sección de Extranjeros, *f.*

alienable, *a.* enajenable

alienate, *v.t.* alejar, hacer indiferente; (property) enajenar, traspasar

alienation, *s.* desvío, *m.*; enajenación, *f.*; traspaso, *m.*; enajenación mental, *f.*

alienist, *s.* alienista, *m.* and *f.*

alight, *v.i.* apearse (de), bajar (de); desmontar (de); (of birds, etc.) posarse (sobre)

alight, *a.* encendido, iluminado; en llamas

align, *v.t.* alinear

alignment, *s.* alineación, *f.*

alike, *a.* semejante; igual. *adv.* del mismo modo; igualmente

alimentary, *a.* nutritivo; alimenticio. **a. canal,** tubo digestivo, *m.*

alimentation, *s.* alimentación, *f.*

alimony, *s.* (*law*) alimentos, *m. pl.*

aliquant, *a.* (*f.*) alicuanta. *s.* parte alicuanta, *f.*

aliquot, *a.* (*f.*) alícuota. *s.* parte alícuota, *f.*

alive, *a.* viviente; vivo; del mundo; (busy) animado, concurrido; (aware) sensible; (alert) lleno de vida, enérgico, despierto. **He is still a.,** Aún vive. **He is the best man a.,** Es el mejor hombre que existe. Es el mejor hombre del mundo. **half-a.,** semivivo. **while a.,** en

vida. a. to, consciente de, sensible
de. a. with, plagado de, lleno de
alkali, s. álcali, m.
alkaline, a. alcalino
alkaloid, s. alcaloide, m.
all, a. todo, m.; toda, f.; todos,
m. pl.; todas, f. pl.; (in games)
iguales. adv. enteramente, completamente; del todo; absolutamente. after all, después de
todo; sin embargo. at all, nada;
de ninguna manera; en absoluto.
fifteen all, (tennis) quince
iguales. for good and all,
para siempre. If that's all,
Si no es más que eso. in all, en
conjunto. It is all one to
me, Me es igual. not at all,
de ningún modo, nada de
eso; nada; (never) jamás; (as
a polite formula) no hay de
qué. once for all, una vez por
todas; por última vez. that is
all, eso es todo. all along, (of
time) siempre, todo el tiempo;
(of place) a lo largo de, de un
extremo a otro de. all but,
(almost) casi, por poco; (except)
todo menos. all of them, todos
ellos, m. pl.; todas ellas, f.
pl. All right! ¡Bien! ¡Está
bien!; ¡Entendido! all that,
todo eso; (as much as) cuanto.
all that which, todo lo que.
all those who, todos los que,
m. pl.; todas las que, f. pl. all
the more, cuanto más. all the
same, sin embargo, a pesar
de todo. all the worse, tanto
peor
all, s. todo, m.; todos, m. pl.;
todas, f. pl.; (everyone, all men)
todo el mundo. to lose one's
all, perder todo lo que se tiene.
All is lost, Todo se ha perdido.
all told, en conjunto
all, (in compounds) all-absorb-
ing, que todo lo absorbe;
sumamente interesante. all-
bountiful, de suma bondad.
all-conquering, invicto. all-
consuming, que todo lo consume; irresistible; ardiente. all-
enduring, resignado a todo.
All Fools' Day, Día de Inocentes,
m. (December 28th). all-fours,
a cuatro patas; a gatas. to go
on all fours, andar a gatas.
All hail! ¡Salud! ¡Bienvenido!

all-important, sumamente importante. all-in insurance,
seguro contra todo riesgo, m.
all-in wrestling, lucha libre, f.
all-loving, de un amor infinito.
all-merciful, de una compasión
infinita, sumamente misericordioso. all-powerful, omnipotente, todo poderoso. all-
round, completo, cabal; universal. an all-round athlete,
un atleta completo. All Souls'
Day, Día de las Ánimas, Día
de difuntos, m. all-wise,
omniscio
Allah, s. Alá, m.
allay, v.t. calmar; (relieve)
aliviar; apaciguar
allaying, s. alivio m.; apaciguamiento, m.
allegation, s. alegación, f.
allege, v.t. afirmar, declarar;
alegar
allegiance, s. lealtad, f.; fidelidad, f.; obediencia, f. oath of
a., jura de la bandera, f.
allegorical, a. alegórico
allegory, s. alegoría, f.
alleluia, s. aleluya, m. or f.
allergic, a. alérgico
allergy, s. alergia, f.
alleviate, v.t. aliviar
alleviation, s. alivio, m.; mitigación, f.
alley, s. callejuela, f., callejón,
m.; avenida, f.; (skittle a.) pista
de bolos, f. a.-way, (naut.) pasadizo, m.
alliance, s. alianza, f.; parentesco,
m.
allied, a. aliado; allegado
alligator, s. caimán, m. a. pear,
avocado, m.
alliteration, s. aliteración, f.
alliterative, a. aliterado
allocate, v.t. asignar, destinar;
distribuir, repartir
allocation, s. asignación, f.; distribución, f., repartimiento, m.
allocution, s. alocución, f.
allopathy, s. alopatía, f.
allotment, s. repartimiento, m.,
distribución, f.; porción, f.;
lote, m.; parcela de tierra,
huerta, f.
allow, v.t. permitir; autorizar;
dejar; tolerar, sufrir; (provide)
dar; conceder, otorgar; (acknowledge) admitir; confesar;

(discount) descontar; (a pension)
hacer; deducir. to a. for, tener en
cuenta; ser indulgente con;
deducir; dejar (espacio, etc.)
para

allowable, a. admisible, permisible; lícito, legítimo

allowably, adv. legitimamente

allowance, s. ración, f.; (discount) descuento, m.; pensión, f.;
concesión, f.; excusa, f.; (subsidy) subsidio, m.; (bonus) abono,
m.; (monthly) mesada, f. to
make a. for, tener presente;
hacer excusas para, ser indulgente con

alloy, s. aleación, f.; liga, f.;
mezcla, f. v.t. alear, ligar;
mezclar

allspice, s. guindilla de Indias, f.

allude, v.i. aludir (a), referirse (a)

allure, v.t. convidar, provocar;
atraer; seducir, fascinar

allurement, s. (snare) añagaza,
f.; atracción, f.; tentación,
seducción, f.

alluring, a. atractivo, seductor,
tentador; (promising) halagüeño

allusion, s. alusión, referencia,
f.; insinuación, f.

allusive, a. alusivo

alluvial, a. aluvial, de aluvión

alluvium, s. aluvión, m.

ally, s. aliado (-da), allegado (-da);
asociado (-da); (state) aliado, m.
v.t. unir. to become allies,
aliarse

almanac, s. almanaque, m.

almighty, a. omnipotente

almond, s. almendra, f.; (tree)
almendro, m. bitter a., almendra amarga, f. green a., almendruco, m. milk of al-
monds, horchata de almendras,
f.; (for the hands) loción de
almendras, f. sugar a., almendra garapiñada, f. a.-eyed, con,
or de, ojos rasgados. a. paste,
pasta de almendras, f. a.-
shaped, en forma de almendra,
almendrado

almoner, s. limosnero, m.

almost, adv. casi; por poco

alms, s. limosna, f. to ask a.,
pedir limosna, mendigar. to
give a., dar limosna. a.-box,
cepillo de limosna, m.

almsgiving, s. caridad, f.

almshouse, s. asilo, m.

aloe, s. áloe, m.; pl. aloes, (med.)
acíbar, m.

aloft, adv. arriba, en alto

alone, a. solo; solitario. adv. a
solas, sin compañía; solamente;
únicamente. to leave a., dejar
solo; dejar en paz

along, adv. adelante; a lo largo;
todo el tiempo. prep. a lo largo
de; por; al lado (de); en compañía (de). Come a.! ¡Ven!
all a., todo el tiempo, desde el
principio; a lo largo de. a.
with, junto con; en compañía de

alongside, adv. al lado; (naut.)
al costado. prep. junto a, al lado
de; (naut.) al costado de. to
bring a., (naut.) abarloar. to
come a., (naut.) acostarse

aloof, adv. a distancia; lejos.
a. altanero, esquivo; reservado.
to keep a., mantenerse alejado

aloofness, s. alejamiento, m.;
esquivez, f.; reserva, f.

alopecia, s. alopecia, f.

aloud, adv. en alta voz, alto

alpaca, s. alpaca, f.

alphabet, s. alfabeto, m.;
abecedario, m.

alphabetical, a. alfabético

Alpine, a. alpestre, alpino

already, adv. ya; previamente

Alsatian, a. and s. alsaciano
(-na). A. dog, perro policía,
perro pastor alemán, perro lobo,
m.

also, adv. también, igualmente,
además

altar, s. altar, m. high a., altar
mayor, m. to lead a woman
to the a., llevar a una mujer a
la iglesia. a.-cloth, mantel del
altar, m. a.-piece, retablo, m.
a.-rail, mesa del altar, f.

alter, v.t. cambiar; alterar; modificar; corregir; transformar;
(clothes) arreglar. v.i. cambiar

alterable, a. alterable

alteration, s. cambio, m., alteración, f.; modificación, f.; corrección, f.; innovación, f.; (to
buildings, etc.) reforma, f.;
renovación, f.; arreglo, m.

altercation, s. altercación, f.

alternate, a. alternativo; (bot., and
of rhymes) alterno. v.t. and v.i.
alternar

alternately, adv. alternativa-
mente; por turno

alternating, a. alternador. a.
current, (elec.) corriente alterna,
f.
alternation, s. alternación, f.;
(of time) transcurso, m.; turno,
m.
alternative, s. alternativa, f.
a. alternativo, alterno; to have
no a. but, no poder menos de
alternatively, adv. alternativa-
mente
alternator, s. (elec.) alternador, m.
although, conjunc. aunque, bien
que; si bien; no obstante, a pesar
de
altimeter, s. (aer.) altímetro, m.
altitude, s. altitud, elevación, f.;
altura, f.
alto, s. (voice) contralto, m.;
(singer) contralto, m. and f.;
viola, f.
altogether, adv. completamente;
del todo; en conjunto
alto-relievo, s. alto-relieve, m.
altruism, s. altruísmo, m.
altruist, s. altruista, m. and f.
altruistic, a. altruista
alum, s. alumbre, m.
aluminium, s. aluminio, m.
alveole, s. alvéolo, m.
always, adv. siempre
amalgam, s. amalgama, f.;
mezcla, f.
amalgamate, v.t. amalgamar;
combinar, unir. v.i. amalga-
marse; combinarse, unirse
amalgamation, s. amalgamación,
f.; combinación, f.; mezcla, f.
amanuensis, s. amanuense, m.
and f.; secretario (-ia)
amaranth, s. (bot.) amaranto, m.
amaryllis, s. (bot.) amarilis, f.
amass, v.t. acumular, amontonar
amateur, a. and s. aficionado
(-da). a. theatricals, función de
aficionados, f.
amateurish, a. no profesional;
de aficionado; superficial;
(clumsy) torpe
amatory, a. amatorio
amaze, v.t. asombrar, sorprender; pasmar; confundir
amazed, a. asombrado; sorprendido; admirado; asustado
amazement, s. asombro, pasmo,
m.; sorpresa, f.; (wonderment)
admiración, f.; estupor, m.
amazing, a. asombroso, pasmoso;
sorprendente

amazingly, adv. asombrosamente
Amazon, s. amazona, f.
ambassador, s. embajador, m.
ambassadorial, a. de embajador
ambassadorship, s. embajada,
f.
ambassadress, s. embajadora, f.
amber, s. ámbar, m. a. ambarino
ambergris, s. ámbar gris, m.
ambidextrous, a. ambidextro
ambiguity, s. ambigüedad, f.
ambiguous, a. ambiguo, equívoco
ambition, s. ambición, f.
ambitious, a. ambicioso. to be
a. to, ambicionar
amble, s. (of a horse) paso de
andadura, m.; paso lento, m.
v.i. (of a horse) andar a paso de
andadura; andar lentamente
ambrosia, s. ambrosía, f.
ambrosial, a. ambrosíaco
ambulance, s. ambulancia, f.
a. corps, cuerpo de sanidad, m.
a. man, sanitario, m.
ambulatory, s. paseo, m.;
claustro, m. a. ambulante
ambush, s. acecho, m., asechanza,
f.; (mil.) emboscada, f. v.t.
acechar, asechar; (mil.) emboscar; sorprender. to be in
a., emboscarse, estar en acecho
amelioration, s. mejora, f.
amen, s. amén, m.
amenable, a. sujeto (a); responsable; dócil; fácil de convencer,
dispuesto a ser razonable; dispuesto a escuchar. to make a.
to reason, hacer razonable
amend, v.t. enmendar; modificar. v.i. reformarse
amendment, s. enmienda, f.;
modificación, f.
amends, s. pl. reparación, f.;
satisfacción, f.; compensación, f.
to make a., dar satisfacción
amenity, s. amenidad, f.
American, s. americano (-na);
(U.S.A.) norteamericano (-na). a.
americano, de América; norteamericano, de los Estados
Unidos. Central A., a. and s.
centroamericano (-na). A. bar,
bar americano, m. A. Indian,
piel roja, m.
Americanism, s. americanismo,
m.
Americanize, v.t. americanizar
amethyst, s. amatista, f.

amiability, *s.* amabilidad, afabilidad, cordialidad, *f.*

amiable, *a.* amable, afable, cordial.

amiably, *adv.* amablemente, con afabilidad

amianthus, *s.* amianto, *m.*

amicable, *a.* amigable, amistoso

amicably, *adv.* amigablemente

amice, *s.* amito, *m.*

amid, amidst, *prep.* en medio de; entre; rodeado por

amidships, *adv.* en el centro del buque, en medio del navío

amiss, *adv.* mal; de más; (ill) indispuesto, enfermo; (inopportunely) inoportunamente. *a.* malo. It would not come a., No vendría mal. to take a., llevar a mal

ammeter, *s.* (*elec.*) amperímetro, *m.*

ammonia, *s.* amoníaco, *m.*

ammoniacal, *a.* amoniacal

ammunition, *s.* munición, *f.* a. box, cajón de municiones, *m.*

amnesia, *s.* amnesia, *f.*

amnesty, *s.* amnistía, *f.* to concede an a. to, amnistiar

amœba, *s.* amiba, *f.*

amok (to run a.), atacar a ciegas

among, *prep.* en medio de; entre; con

amoral, *a.* amoral

amorality, *s.* amoralidad, *f.*

amorous, *a.* amoroso; (tender) tierno

amorousness, *s.* erotismo, *m.*, galantería, *f.*

amorphous, *a.* amorfo

amortization, *s.* amortización, *f.*

amortize, *v.t.* amortizar

amount, *s.* importe, *m.*, suma, *f.*; cantidad, *f. v.i.* (to) subir a, ascender a, llegar a; valer; reducirse a. **gross a.,** importe bruto, *m.* **net a.,** importe líquido, importe neto, *m.* It amounts to the same thing, then, Es igual entonces, Viene a ser lo mismo pues. What he says amounts to this, Lo que dice se reduce a esto

amperage, *s.* amperaje, *m.*

ampère, *s.* amper, amperio, *m.*

amphibian, *s.* anfibio, *m.*

amphibious, *a.* anfibio

amphitheatre, *s.* anfiteatro, *m.*

amphora, *s.* ánfora, *f.*

ample, *a.* amplio; abundante; extenso, vasto; (sufficient) bastante, suficiente

amplification, *s.* amplificación, *f.*

amplifier, *s.* amplificador, *m.*

amplify, *v.t.* amplificar; aumentar, ampliar

amplitude, *s.* amplitud, *f.*; abundancia, *f.*; extensión, *f.*

amply, *adv.* ampliamente; abundantemente; suficientemente

amputate, *v.t.* amputar

amputation, *s.* amputación, *f.*

amulet, *s.* amuleto, *m.*

amuse, *v.t.* divertir, entretener, distraer. to a. oneself, divertirse; pasarlo bien

amusement, *s.* diversión, *f.*, entretenimiento, *m.*; (hobby) pasatiempo, *m.* a. park, parque de atracciones, *m.*

amusing, *a.* divertido, entretenido; (of people) salado

amusingly, *adv.* de un modo divertido, entretenidamente

an. See a

Anabaptism, *s.* anabaptismo, *m*

Anabaptist, *s.* anabaptista, *m.* and *f.*

anachronism, *s.* anacronismo, *m.*

anachronistic, *a.* anacrónico

anæmia, *s.* anemia, *f.*

anæmic, *a.* anémico

anæsthesia, *s.* anestesia, *f.*

anæsthetic, *a.* and *s.* anestésico (*m.*)

anæsthetist, *s.* anestesiador (-ra)

anæsthetize, *v.t.* anestesiar

anagram, *s.* anagrama, *m.*

analects, *s. pl.* analectas, *f. pl.*

analgesia, *s.* analgesia, *f.*

analgesic, *a.* and *s.* analgésico (*m.*)

analogous, *a.* análogo

analogy, *s.* analogía, *f*

analyse, *v.t.* analizar

analysis, *s.* análisis, *m.* or *f.*

analyst, *s.* analista, *m.* and *f.*

analytical, *a.* analítico

anaphora, *s.* anáfora, *f.*

anaphrodisiac, *a.* anafrodisíaco

anarchic, *a.* anárquico

anarchism, *s.* anarquismo, *m.*

anarchist, *s.* anarquista, *m.* and *f.*

anarchy, *s.* anarquía, *f.*

anastigmatic, *a.* anastigmático

anathema, *s.* anatema, *m.* or *f.*

anathematize, *v.t.* anatematizar
anatomic, *a.* anatómico
anatomically, *adv.* anatómicamente; físicamente
anatomist, *s.* anatomista, *m.* and *f.*
anatomy, *s.* anatomía, *f.*
ancestor, *s.* antepasado, abuelo, *m.*
ancestral, *a.* de sus antepasados; de familia; hereditario. **a. home,** casa solariega, *f.*
ancestry, *s.* antepasados, *m. pl.*; linaje, abolengo, *m.*; estirpe, *f.*; nacimiento, *m.*; origen, *m.*
anchor, *s.* ancla, *f.*; *(fig.)* áncora, *f. v.t.* sujetar con el ancla. *v.i.* anclar, echar anclas, fondear. **at a.,** al ancla. **drag a.,** ancla flotante, ancla de arrastre, *f.* **sheet a.,** ancla de la esperanza, *f.*; *(fig.)* ancla de salvación, *f.* **to drop a.,** anclar. **to ride at a.,** estar al ancla. **to weigh a.,** levar el ancla
anchorage, *s.* anclaje, *m.*; ancladero, fondeadero, *m.*; derechos de anclaje, *m. pl.*
anchorite, *s.* anacoreta, *m.* and *f.*
anchovy, *s.* anchoa, *f.,* boquerón, *m.*
ancient, *a.* anciano; antiguo. *s. pl.* **ancients,** los antiguos. **From a. times,** de antiguo. **most a.,** antiquísimo
and, *conjunc.* y; (before stressed i or hi) e; (after some verbs and before infin.) de, a; que; (with) con; (often not translated before infins.). **Better and better,** Mejor que mejor. **I shall try and do it,** Trataré de hacerlo. **to come and see,** venir a ver. **We shall try and speak to him,** Procuraremos hablarle
Andalusian, *a.* andaluz. *s.* andaluz (-za). **A. hat,** sombrero calañés, *m.*
Andean, *a.* andino
andiron, *s.* morillo, *m.*
Andorran, *a.* and *s.* andorrano (-na)
androgynous, *a.* andrógino
anecdotal, *a.* anecdótico
anecdote, *s.* anécdota, *f.*
anemone, *s.* anémona, anémone, *f.*
anemometer, *s.* anemómetro, *m.*
aneroid, *a.* aneroide. *s.* barómetro aneroide, *m.*

aneurism, *s.* aneurisma, *m.* or *f.*
angel, *s.* ángel, *m.*
angelic, *a.* angélico
angelica, *s.* angélica, *f.*
angelus, *s.* ángelus, *m.*
anger, *s.* cólera, ira, *f.,* enojo, *m. v.t.* enojar, encolerizar; hacer rabiar
angina, *s.* angina, *f.* **a. pectoris,** angina de pecho, *f.*
angle, *s.* ángulo, *m.*; rincón, *m.*; esquina, *f.*; (of a roof) caballete, *m.*; *(fig.)* punto de vista, *m. v.i.* pescar con caña. **at an a.,** a un lado. **a.-iron,** hierro angular, *m.* **to a. for,** pescar; *(fig.)* procurar obtener
Angle, *a.* and *s.* anglo (-la)
angler, *s.* pescador (-ra) de caña
Anglican, *a.* and *s.* anglicano (-na)
Anglicanism, *s.* anglicanismo, *m.*
Anglicism, *s.* anglicismo, inglesismo, *m.*
Anglicize, *v.t.* inglesar
angling, *s.* pesca con caña, *f.*
Anglo-, (in compounds) anglo-. **A.-American,** *a.* and *s.* angloamericano (-na). **A.-Indian,** *a.* and *s.* angloindio (-ia). **A.-Saxon,** *a.* and *s.* anglosajón (-ona); (language) anglosajón, *m.*
anglomania, *s.* anglomanía, *f.*
anglophile, *s.* anglófilo (-la)
anglophobia, *s.* anglofobia, *f.*
angora, *s.* angora, *f.* **a. cat,** gato de angora, *m.* **a. rabbit,** conejo de angora, *m.*
angrily, *adv.* airadamente
angry, *a.* (of persons) enfadado, enojado, airado; (of waves, etc.) furioso; *(med.)* inflamado; (red) rojo; (scowling) ceñudo; (dark) obscuro. **to be a.,** estar enojado. **to grow a.,** enojarse, enfadarse; (of waves) encresparse; (of the sky) obscurecerse. **to make a.,** enojar
anguish, *s.* agonía, *f.,* dolor, *m.*; angustia, *f. v.t.* angustiar
angular, *a.* angular; (of features, etc.) anguloso
angularity, *s.* angulosidad, *f.*
anhydrous, *a.* anhidro
aniline, *s.* anilina, *f.*
animal, *a.* and *s.* animal (*m.*) **a. fat,** grasa animal, *f.* **a. kingdom,** reino animal, *m.* **a.**

spirits, (*phil.*) espíritus animales, *m. pl.*; brío, *m.*, energía, *f.*

animalism, *s.* animalidad, *f.*; sensualidad, *f.*

animate, *v.t.* animar; inspirar. *a.* animado; viviente

animated, *a.* animado; vivo, lleno de vida

animation, *s.* animación, *f.*; vivacidad, *f.*; calor, fuego, *m.*

animism, *s.* animismo, *m.*

animosity, *s.* animosidad, hostilidad, *f.*

aniseed, *s.* anís, *m.*

anisette, *s.* (liqueur) anisete, *m.*

ankle, *s.* tobillo, *m.* a. bone, hueso del tobillo, *m.* a. sock, calcetín corto, *m.*

anklet, *s.* brazalete para el tobillo, *m.*; (support) tobillera, *f.*

ankylosis, *s.* anquilosis, *f.*

annals, *s. pl.* anales, *m. pl.*

anneal, *v.t.* (metals) recocer; (glass) templar; (with oil) atemperar

annex, *v.t.* unir, juntar; anexar. *s.* anexo, *m.*

annexation, *s.* anexión, *f.*

annihilate, *v.t.* aniquilar, destrozar por completo, destruir

annihilation, *s.* aniquilación, destrucción completa, *f.*

anniversary, *a.* and *s.* aniversario (*m.*)

annotate, *v.t.* anotar, acotar, comentar

annotation, *s.* anotación, *f.*; nota, *f.*

annotator, *s.* anotador (-ra), comentador (-ra)

announce, *v.t.* proclamar; declarar; publicar; anunciar

announcement, *s.* proclama, *f.*; declaración, *f.*; publicación, *f.*; anuncio, *m.*; (of a betrothal) participación, *f.*

announcer, *s.* anunciador (-ra); (radio) locutor (-ra)

annoy, *v.t.* exasperar, irritar, disgustar; molestar, incomodar

annoyance, *s.* disgusto, *m.*, exasperación, *f.*; molestia, *f.*, fastidio, *m.*

annoying, *a.* enojoso, molesto, fastidioso

annual, *a.* anual. *s.* anuario, *m.*; calendario, *m.*; planta anual, *f.*

annually, *adv.* anualmente, cada año

annuitant, *s.* censualista; *m.* and *f.*

annuity, *s.* anualidad, pensión vitalicia, *f.*

annul, *v.t.* anular

annulable, *a.* anulable

annulate, *a.* anuloso

annulment, *s.* anulación, *f.*

annunciation, *s.* anunciación, *f.* The A., la Anunciación

anode, *s.* ánodo, *m.*

anodyne, *a.* and *s.* anodino (*m.*)

anoint, *v.t.* untar; (before death) olear; (a king, etc.) ungir

anointing, *s.* unción, *f.*

anomalous, *a.* anómalo

anomaly, *s.* anomalía, *f.* (also *ast.*)

anon, *adv.* pronto, en seguida. ever and a., de vez en vez

anonymity, *s.* anónimo, *m.*

anonymous, *a.* anónimo. a. letter, anónimo, *m.*

anonymously, *adv.* anónimamente

another, *a.* otro; (different) distinto. *s.* otro, *m.*; otra, *f.* For one thing . . . and for a., En primer lugar . . . y además (y por otra cosa). one after a., uno después de otro. They love one a., Ellos se aman. They sent it from one to a., Lo mandaron de uno a otro

answer, *s.* contestación, respuesta, *f.*; (refutation) refutación, *f.*; (pert reply) réplica, *f.*; (solution) solución, *f.*; (*math.*) resultado, *m.*; (*law*) contestación a la demanda, *f.*

answer, *v.t.* responder, contestar; (a letter, etc.) contestar a; (refute) refutar; (reply pertly) replicar; (write) escribir; (return) devolver; (suit) servir; (a bell, etc.) acudir a; (the door) abrir. *v.i.* contestar; (succeed) tener éxito; dar resultado. to a. by return, contestar a vuelta de correo. to a. back, replicar. to a. for, ser responsable por; ser responsable de; (speak for) hablar por; (guarantee) garantizar, responder de

answerable, *a.* responsable; refutable; (adequate) adecuado. to make a. for, hacer responsable de

ant, s. hormiga, f. ant-eater, oso hormiguero, m. ant-hill, hormiguero, m.

antagonism, s. antagonismo, m., hostilidad, oposición, f.

antagonist, s. antagonista, m. and f.

antagonistic, a. antagónico, hostil

antagonize, v.t. contender; hacer hostil (a)

antarctic, a. antártico. s. polo antártico, m.

antecedent, a. and s. antecedente (m.)

antechamber, s. antecámara, antesala, f.

antedate, v.t. antedatar; anticipar

antediluvian, a. antediluviano

antelope, s. antílope, m.

ante meridiem, adv. antes del mediodía

antenatal, a. antenatal

antenna, s. antena, f.

antepenultimate, a. antepenúltimo

anteport, s. (mil.) antepuerta, f.; (naut.) antepuerto, m.

anterior, a. anterior

anthelminthic, a. antihelmíntico

anthem, s. antífona, f.

anther, s. antera, f.

anthologist, s. antólogo, m.

anthology, s. antología, f.

anthracite, s. antracita, f., carbón mineral, m.

anthrax, s. ántrax, m.

anthropoid, s. antropoide, m.

anthropological, a. antropológico

anthropologist, s. antropólogo, m.

anthropology, s. antropología, f.

anthropometry, s. antropometría, f.

anthropophagous, a. antropófago

anti-aircraft, a. antiaéreo. A.A. guns, cañones antiaéreos, m. pl.

antibody, s. anticuerpo, m.

antic, s. travesura, f.

Antichrist, s. Anticristo, m.

antichristian, a. anticristiano

anticipate, v.t. (foresee) prever; anticipar; adelantarse a; (hope) esperar; (frustrate) frustrar; (enjoy) disfrutar con anticipación de

anticipation, s. anticipación, f.; adelantamiento, m.; esperanza, expectación, f. in a. of, en espera de

anticipatory, a. anticipador

anticlerical, a. anticlerical

anticlericalism, s. anticlericalismo, m.

anticlimax, s. anticlímax, m.

anticlockwise, a. de izquierda a derecha, de revés

anti-comintern, a. anticómintern

anticyclone, s. anticiclón, m.

antidote, s. antídoto, m.

antifreeze, s. anticongelante, m.

antimacassar, s. antimacasar, m.

anti-malarial, a. antipalúdico

anti-militarism, s. antimilitarismo, m.

anti-militaristic, a. antimilitarista

anti-monarchical, a. antimonárquico

antimony, s. antimonio, m.

antipathetic, a. antipático

antipathy, s. antipatía, f.

antiphon, s. antífona, f.

antipode, s. pl. antípodas, m. or f. pl.

antipope, s. antipapa, m.

antipyretic, a. and s. antipirético (m.)

antiquarian, a. anticuario

antiquary, s. anticuario, m.

antiquated, a. anticuado

antique, a. antiguo. s. antigüedad, antigualla, f. a. dealer, anticuario, m. a. shop, tienda de antigüedades, f.

antiquity, s. antigüedad, f.; ancianidad, f.

anti-religious, a. antirreligioso

anti-republican, a. antirrepublicano

antirrhinum, s. boca de dragón, f.

anti-semitic, a. antisemita

anti-semitism, s. antisemitismo, m.

antiseptic, a. and s. antiséptico (m.)

anti-slavery, a. antiesclavista

anti-social, a. antisocial

anti-syphilitic, a. antisifilítico

anti-tank, a. antitanque

antithesis, s. antítesis, f.

antithetic, a. antitético

antitoxin, s. antitoxina, f.

anti-trust, a. antimonopolio

anti-vivisectionist, *a.* and *s.* antiviviseccionista (*m.* and *f.*)

antler, *s.* asta, *f.*

antonomasia, *s.* antonomasia, *f.*

antrum, *s.* antro, *m.*

anus, *s.* ano, *m.*

anvil, *s.* yunque, *m.*, bigornia, *f.*

anxiety, *s.* inquietud, intranquilidad, *f.*; preocupación, *f.*; ansiedad, *f.*; curiosidad, *f.*; impaciencia, *f.*; (wish) deseo, afán, *m.*

anxious, *a.* inquieto, intranquilo; preocupado; ansioso; impaciente; deseoso. to be a., estar inquieto; apurarse. to be a. to, ansiar, tener deseos de. to make a., preocupar, inquietar, intranquilizar

anxiously, *adv.* con inquietud; ansiosamente; impacientemente

any, *a.* cualquiera; (before the noun only) cualquier; (some) algún, *m.*; alguna, *f.*; (every) todo; (expressing condition or with interrogatives or negatives; following the noun) alguno, *m.*; alguna, *f.* (Any is often omitted in translation in a partitive sense, e.g. Have you any butter ? ¿ Tienes mantequilla ?) *pron.* algo; (with the relevant noun) alguno, etc.; lo, *m.* and *neut.*; la, *f.*; los, *m. pl.*; las, *f. pl.* He hasn't any pity, No tiene piedad alguna. at any rate, de todos modos; por lo menos. If there is any, Si lo (la, etc.) hay. in any case, venga lo que venga. not any, ninguno, *m.*; ninguna, *f.* Whether any of them . . ., Si alguno de ellos . . . any further, más lejos. any longer, más largo; (of time) más tiempo. any more, nada más; nunca más

anybody, *s.* and *pron.* (someone) alguien; cualquiera, *m.* and *f.*; (everyone) todo el mundo; (with a negative) nadie; (of importance) persona de importancia, *f.* hardly a., casi nadie

anyhow, *adv.* de cualquier modo; (with a negative) de ningún modo; de cualquier manera; (at least) por lo menos, en todo caso; (carelessly) sin cuidado

anyone, *s.* See anybody

anything, *s.* algo, *m.*, alguna cosa, *f.*; (negative) nada; cualquier cosa, *f.*; todo (lo que). a. but, todo menos

anyway, *adv.* de todos modos, con todo; venga lo que venga; (anyhow) de cualquier modo

anywhere, *adv.* en todas partes, dondequiera; en cualquier parte; (after a negative) en (or a) ninguna parte

aorta, *s.* aorta, *f.*

apart, *adv.* aparte; a un lado; separadamente; separado (de); apartado (de). a. from, aparte de, dejando a un lado. to keep a., mantener aislado; distinguir (entre). to take a., desarmar. wide a., muy distante

apartment, *s.* cuarto, *m.*, habitación, *f.*; (flat) piso, *m.*

apathetic, *a.* apático; indiferente

apathy, *s.* apatía, *f.*; indiferencia, *f.*

ape, *s.* simio, *m.*

aperient, *s.* aperitivo, *m.*

aperitive, *a.* and *s.* aperitivo (*m.*)

aperture, *s.* abertura, *f.*; agujero, *m.*; orificio, *m.*

apex, *s.* ápice, *m.*

aphæresis, *s.* aféresis, *f.*

aphasia, *s.* afasia, *f.*

aphis, *s.* pulgón, *m.*

aphonia, *s.* afonía, *f.*

aphorism, *s.* aforismo *m.*

aphrodisiac, *a.* and *s.* afrodisíaco (*m.*)

apiarist, *s.* apicultor (-ra)

apiary, *s.* colmenar, *m.*

apiculture, *s.* apicultura, *f.*

apiece, *adv.* cada uno; por persona

apish, *a.* simiesco, de simio; (affected) afectado; (foolish) tonto

aplomb, *s.* confianza en sí, *f.*, aplomo, *m.*

apocalypse, *s.* Apocalipsis, *m.*

apocalyptic, *a.* apocalíptico

apocopate, *v.t.* apocopar

Apocrypha, *s.* libros apócrifos, *m. pl.*

apocryphal, *a.* apócrifo

apodosis, *s.* apódosis, *f.*

apogee, *s.* apogeo, *m.*

apologetic, *a.* apologético

apologetically, *adv.* apologéticamente

apologist, *s.* apologista, *m.* and *f.*

apologize, *v.i.* presentar sus excusas; disculparse, excusarse; (regret) sentir

apologue, *s.* apólogo, *m.*

apology, *s.* excusa, disculpa, *f.*; defensa, apología, *f.*; (make-shift) substituto, *m.*

apophysis, *s.* apófisis, *f.*

apoplectic, *a.* and *s.* apoplético (-ca)

apoplexy, *s.* apoplegía, *f.*

apostasy, *s.* apostasía, *f.*

apostate, *s.* apóstata, *m.* and *f.*, renegado (-da)

apostatize, *v.i.* apostatar, renegar

apostle, *s.* apóstol, *m.* Apostles' Creed, el Credo de los Apóstoles

apostolate, *s.* apostolado, *m.*

apostolic, *a.* apostólico

apostrophe, *s.* apóstrofe, *m.* or *f.*; (punctuation mark) apóstrofo, *m.*

apostrophize, *v.t.* apostrofar

apothecary, *s.* apotecario, *m.* Apothecaries weight, peso de boticario, *m.*

apothegm, *s.* apotegma, *m.*

apotheosis, *s.* apoteosis, *f.*

appal, *v.t.* horrorizar, espantar, aterrar

appalling, *a.* espantoso, horrible

apparatus, *s.* aparato, *m.*; máquina, *f.*; instrumentos, *m. pl.*

apparel, *s.* ropa, *f.*; vestiduras, *f. pl.*; ornamento, *m. v.t.* vestir

apparent, *a.* aparente; visible; evidente, manifiesto; (of heirs) presunto. to become a., manifestarse

apparently, *adv.* al parecer, aparentemente

apparition, *s.* aparición, *f.*, fantasma, espectro, *m.*

appeal, *s.* súplica, *f.*; llamamiento, *m.*; (charm) atracción, *f.*, encanto, *m.*; (law) apelación, alzada, *f. v.i.* (to) suplicar (a); hacer llamamiento (a); poner por testigo (a); recurrir a; llamar la atención de; interesar (a); (attract) atraer, encantar; (law) apelar. It doesn't a. to him, No le atrae, No le gusta. to allow an a., revocar una sentencia apelada. without a., inapelable

appealing, *a.* suplicante; atrayente

appealingly, *adv.* de un modo suplicante

appear, *v.i.* (of persons and things) aparecer; (seem) parecer; (before a judge) comparecer; presentarse (ante el juez); (of books) publicarse; (of lawyers) representar; (of the dawn) rayar; (of the sun, etc.) salir; (show itself) manifestarse. to cause to a., hacer presentarse; (show) hacer ver; (prove) demostrar, probar

appearance, *s.* aparición, *f.*; (show, semblance or look, aspect) apariencia, *f.*; presencia, *f.*; aspecto, *m.*; (in court of law) comparecencia, *f.*; (of a book) publicación, *f.*; (arrival) llegada, *f.*; (view) perspectiva, *f.*; (ghost) aparición, *f.*, fantasma, *m.* first a., (of an actor, etc.) debut, *m.*; (of a play) estreno, *m.* to all appearances, según las apariencias. to make one's first a., aparecer por primera vez; (theat.) debutar. Appearances are deceptive, Las apariencias engañan

appease, *v.t.* apaciguar, aplacar, pacificar; satisfacer

appeasement, *s.* apaciguamiento, aplacamiento, *m.*, pacificación, *f.*; satisfacción, *f.*

appellant, *a.* and *s.* (law) apelante (*m.* and *f.*)

appellation, *s.* nombre, *m.*; título, *m.*

append, *v.t.* añadir; (a seal) poner; (enclose) incluir, anexar

appendage, *s.* accesorio, *m.*; (bot., zool.) apéndice, *m.*

appendicitis, *s.* apendicitis, *f.*

appendix, *s.* apéndice, *m.*

appertain, *v.i.* pertenecer (a)

appetite, *s.* apetito, *m.*; (fig.) hambre, *f.*; deseo, *m.* to have a bad a., no tener apetito, estar desganado. to have a good a., tener buen apetito. to whet the a., abrir el apetito

appetizer, *s.* aperit.vo, *m.*

appetizing, *a.* apetitoso

applaud, *v.t.* and *v.i.* aplaudir; aclamar, ovacionar; celebrar

applause, *s.* aplauso, *m.*; ovación, *f.*; aprobación, alabanza, *f.*

apple, s. manzana, f. **the a. of
one's eye,** la niña de los ojos.
a. orchard, manzanar, m. **a.
sauce,** compota de manzanas, f.
a. tart, pastel de manzanas, m.
a. tree, manzano, m.

appliance, s. aparato, m.; instrumento, m.; utensilio, m.; máquina, f.

applicability, s. aplicabilidad, f.

applicable, a. aplicable

applicant, s. candidato, m.; aspirante, m.; solicitante, m. and f.

application, s. aplicación, f.;
solicitud, f.; petición, f.; empleo,
m. **on a.,** a solicitar

appliqué, a. aplicado. s. aplicación, f.

apply, v.t. aplicar; (use) emplear; (place) poner; (give) dar;
(the brakes) frenar; v.i. ser
aplicable; ser a propósito; dirigirse (a)'; acudir (a); (for a post)
proponerse para. **to a. for,** solicitar, pedir; (a post) proponerse
para. **to a. oneself to,** ponerse
a; dedicarse a, consagrarse a

appoint, v.t. (prescribe) prescribir, ordenar; señalar; asignar;
(furnish) amueblar; equipar;
(create) crear, establecer; (to a
post) nombrar, designar; (manage) gobernar; organizar. **at
the appointed hour,** a la hora
señalada. **well-appointed,** bien
amueblado; bien equipado

appointment, s. (assignation)
cita, f.; (to a post) nombramiento, m.; (post, office) cargo,
m.; creación, f. **By Royal A.,**
Proveedor de la Real Casa.
to make an a. with, citar

apportion, v.t. dividir; distribuir; prorratear; (taxes) derramar

apportionment, s. repartimiento,
m., distribución, f.; división, f.;
prorrateo, m.

apposite, a. a propósito, pertinente, oportuno; justo

appositeness, s. pertinencia,
oportunidad, f.

apposition, s. aposición, f.

appraisal, s. valoración, valuación, f.; estimación, f.

appraise, v.t. valorar, tasar;
estimar

appreciable, a. apreciable, perceptible

appreciably, adv. sensiblemente

appreciate, v.t. (understand)
darse cuenta de, comprender;
estimar; apreciar; (distinguish)
distinguir. v.i. encarecer, aumentar en valor; (of shares)
subir, estar en alza

appreciation, s. (understanding)
comprensión, f.; apreciación, f.;
(recognition, etc.) aprecio, reconocimiento, m.; (in value)
aumento (en valor), m.; subida
de precio, f.

appreciative, a. apreciativo

appreciatively, adv. con aprecio

appreciator, s. apreciador (-ra)

apprehend, v.t. aprehender,
prender; comprender, aprehender; (fear) temer

apprehension, s. aprehensión,
comprensión, f.; (fear) aprensión,
f.; (seizure) aprehensión, presa, f.

apprehensive, a. aprehensivo;
(fearful) aprensivo

apprehensiveness, s. aprehensión, f.; (fear) aprensión, f.,
temor, m.

apprentice, s. aprendiz (-za). **to
bind a.,** poner de aprendiz

apprenticeship, s. aprendizaje,
m. **to serve an a.,** hacer el
aprendizaje

apprise, v.t. dar parte (de),
informar (de)

approach, v.t. acercarse a;
aproximarse a; (pull, etc. nearer)
acercar, aproximar; (resemble)
parecerse a, ser semejante a;
(speak to) hablar con; entablar
negociaciones con. v.i. acercarse, aproximarse. s. acercamiento, m.; (arrival) llegada, f.;
aproximación, f.; (of night, etc.)
avance, m.; (entrance) entrada,
f.; avenida, f.; vía, f.; (step)
paso, m.; (to a subject) punto de
vista (sobre), concepto (de), m.;
(introduction) introducción, f.;
pl. **approaches,** (environs)
alrededores, m. pl., inmediaciones, f. pl.; (seas) mares,
m. pl.; (overtures) avances,
m. pl.

approachable, a. accesible

approaching, a. venidero,
próximo, cercano

approbation, s. asentimiento, m.;
aprobación, f.

appropriate, *a.* apropiado; conveniente; *v.t.* adueñarse de, tomar posesión de, apropiar

appropriately, *adv.* propiamente; convenientemente; justamente

appropriateness, *s.* conveniencia, *f.*; justicia, *f.*

appropriation, *s.* apropiación, *f.*; aplicación, *f.*; empleo, *m.*

approval, *s.* aprobación, *f.*; consentimiento, *m.* **on a.,** a prueba

approve, *v.t.* aprobar; confirmar; (sanction) autorizar, sancionar; ratificar; estar contento (de); (oneself) demostrarse. *v.i.* aprobar

approved, *a.* aprobado; ·bien visto; (on documents) Visto Bueno (Vº Bº)

approximate, *a.* aproximado. *v.t.* acercar. *v.i.* aproximarse (a)

approximately, *adv.* aproximadamente, poco más o menos

approximation, *s.* aproximación, *f.*

appurtenance, *s.* accesorio, *m.*, pertenencia, *f.*

apricot, *s.* albaricoque, *m.* **a. tree,** albaricoquero, *m.*

April, *s.* abril, *m.* *a.* abrileño. **A. Fool's Day,** el 1º de abril; (in Spain) el día de los Inocentes (December 28th)

apron, *s.* delantal, *m.*; (of artisans and freemasons) mandil, *m.* **to be tied to a mother's a.-strings,** estar cosido a las faldas de su madre. **a.-stage,** proscenio, *m.* **a.-string,** cinta del delantal, *f.*

apse, *s.* ábside, *m.* or *f.*

apsis, *s.* (*ast.*) ábside, *m.*

apt, *a.* apto, listo; propenso (a), inclinado (a); expuesto (a); (suitable) apropiado, oportuno

aptitude, *s.* aptitud, disposición, facilidad, *f.*

aptly, *adv.* apropiadamente; justamente, bien

aquamarine, *s.* aguamarina, *f.*

aquarelle, *s.* acuarela, *f.*

aquarellist, *s.* acuarelista, *m.* and *f.*

aquarium, *s.* acuario, *m.*

Aquarius, *s.* Acuario, *m.*

aquatic, *a.* acuático

aquatint, *s.* acuatinta, *f.*

aqueduct, *s.* acueducto, *m.*

aqueous, *a.* ácueo, acuoso

aquiline, *a.* aguileño

Arab, *a.* árabe. *s.* árabe, *m.* and *f.*

arabesque, *s.* arabesco, *m.*

Arabian, *a.* árabe, arábigo. The A. nights, las mil y una noches

Arabic, *a.* arábigo. *s.* (language) arábigo, árabe, *m.*

Arabist, *s.* arabista, *m.* and *f.*

arable, *a.* cultivable, labrantío

arachnid, *s.* arácnido, *m.*

Aragonese, *a.* and *s.* aragonés (-esa)

arbiter, *s.* árbitro (-ra), arbitrador (-ra)

arbitrariness, *s.* arbitrariedad, *f.*

arbitrary, *a.* arbitrario

arbitrate, *v.i.* arbitrar, juzgar como árbitro; someter al arbitraje

arbitration, *s.* arbitraje, *m.*

arbitrator. See arbiter

arboriculture, *s.* arboricultura, *f.*

arbour, *s.* glorieta, *f.*, emparrado, *m.*

arbutus, *s.* madroño, *m.*

arc, *s.* arco, *m.* **arc-light,** lámpara de arco, *f.*

arcade, *s.* arcada, *f.*; galería, *f.*; pasaje, *m.*

Arcadian, *a.* árcade

arch, *s.* arco, *m.*; (vault) bóveda, *f.* *v.t.* abovedar; arquear; encorvar

arch, *a.* (roguish) socarrón; (coy) coquetón

arch-, *prefix* archi-

archæological, *a.* arqueológico

archæologist, *s.* arqueólogo, *m.*

archæology, *s.* arqueología, *f.*

archaic, *a.* arcaico

archaism, *s.* arcaísmo, *m.*

archangel, *s.* arcángel, *m.*

archbishop, *s.* arzobispo, *m.*

archbishopric, *s.* arzobispado, *m.*

archdeacon, *s.* arcediano, *m.*

archdeaconate, *s.* arcedianato, *m.*

archducal, *a.* archiducal

archduchess, *s.* archiduquesa, *f.*

archduke, *s.* archiduque, *m.*

arch-enemy, *s.* mayor enemigo (-ga); Demonio, *m.*

archer, *s.* flechero, saltero, *m.*; (*mil.*) arquero, *m.*

archery, *s.* ballestería, *f.*

archfiend, *s.* demonio, *m.*

archiepiscopal, *a.* arzobispal

arching, s. arqueo, m.
archipelago, s. archipiélago, m.
architect, s. arquitecto, m.
architectural, s. arquitectónico
architecturally, adv. arquitectó-
nicamente; desde el punto de
vista arquitectónico
architecture, s. arquitectura, f.
architrave, s. arquitrabe, m.
archive, s. archivo, m.
archivist, s. archivero, m.
archivolt, s. archivolta, f.
archness, s. coquetería, f.;
malicia, f.
archpriest, s. arcipreste, m.
archway, s. arcada, f., pasaje
abovedado, m.; arco, m.
arctic, a. ártico; muy frío.
A. Circle, Círculo ártico, m.
ardent, a. ardiente; apasionado,
vehemente; fogoso
ardently, adv. ardientemente;
con vehemencia, apasionadamente
ardour, s. ardor, m.
arduous, a. arduo, difícil
arduousness, s. dificultad,
arduidad, f.
are, pl. of present indicative of
be. See be. There are, Hay
area, s. área, f.; superficie, f.;
(extent) extensión, f.; espacio,
m.; región, f.; (of a house) patio,
m.; (of a concert hall, etc.)
sala, f.
arena, s. arena, f.
areometer, s. areómetro, m.
argent, s. (poet.) blancura, f.;
(her.) argén, m.
Argentinian, a. and s. argentino
(-na)
argonaut, s. (zool. and myth.)
argonauta, m.
argot, s. jerga, f.; (thieves')
germanía, f.
arguable; a. discutible
argue, v.t. discutir; persuadir; (prove) demostrar. v.i.
argüir, discutir; sostener. to a.
against, hablar en contra de,
oponer
arguing, s. razonamiento, m.;
argumentación, f.; discusión, f.
argument, s. argumento, m.
argumentative, a. argumentador;
contencioso
arid, a. árido, seco
aridity, s. aridez, f.
Aries, s. Aries, m.

arise, v.i. levantarse; (appear)
surgir, aparecer; ofrecerse,
presentarse; (of sound) hacerse
oír; provenir (de); proceder
(de); (result) hacerse sentir;
(rebel) sublevarse
aristocracy, s. aristocracia, f.
aristocrat, s. aristócrata, m. and
f.
aristocratic, a. aristocrático
Aristotelian, a. aristotélico
Aristotelianism, s. aristotelismo,
m.
arithmetic, s. aritmética, f.
arithmetical, a. aritmético
arithmetician, s. aritmético (-ca)
ark, s. arca, f. Noah's ark,
arca de Noé, f. Ark of the
Covenant, arca de la alianza, f.
arm, s. (anat., geog., mech. of a
chair, a cross, and fig.) brazo, m.;
(lever) palanca, f.; (of a tree)
rama, f., brazo, m.; (sleeve)
manga, f.; (naut.) cabo de una
verga, m.; (weapon) arma, f.;
(of army, navy, etc.) ramo, m.
pl. arms, (her.) armas, f. pl.,
escudo, m. in arms, en brazos;
armado; en oposición. To arms!
¡A las armas! to keep at arm's
length, guardar las distancias;
tratar fríamente. to lay down
arms, rendir las armas. to present arms, presentar las armas.
to receive with open arms,
recibir con los brazos abiertos.
to take up arms, alzarse en
armas, empuñar las armas.
under arms, sobre las armas.
with folded arms, con los
brazos cruzados. arm in arm,
del bracete, de bracero. arm of
the sea, brazo de mar, m.
arm-rest, brazo, m.
arm, v.t. armar; proveer (de);
(fig., fortify) fortificar. v.i.
armarse
armada, s. armada, f.
armament, s. armamento, m.
armchair, s. sillón, m., silla
poltrona, f.
armed, a. armado
Armenian, a. and s. armenio
(-ia); (language) armenio, m.
armful, s. brazado, m.
armhole, s. sobaquera, f.
arming, s. armamento, m.
armistice, s. armisticio, m.
armless, a. sin brazos

armlet, s. brazal, m.

armorial, a. heráldico

armour, s. armadura, f.; (for ships, etc.) blindaje, m. v.t. blindar, acorazar. (to) a.-plate, v.t. blindar. s. coraza, plancha blindada, f.

armoured, a. blindado, acorazado. a. car, carro blindado, m. a. cruiser, crucero acorazado, m.

armourer, s. armero, m.

armoury, s. armería, f.

army, s. ejército, m.; multitud, muchedumbre, f. to be in the a., ser del ejército. to go into the a., alistarse. a. corps, cuerpo del ejército, m. a. estimates, presupuesto del ejército, m. a. list, escalafón del ejército, m. A. Medical Corps, Sanidad Militar, f. A. Supply Corps, Cuerpo de Intendencia, m.

arnica, s. árnica, f.

aroma, s. aroma, m.

aromatic, a. aromático

around, prep. alrededor de; por todas partes de; cerca de; (with words like corner) a la vuelta de. adv. alrededor; a la redonda, en torno; por todas partes; de un lado para otro

arouse, v.t. despertar; excitar

arpeggio, s. arpegio, m.

arquebus, s. arcabuz, m.

arquebusier, s. arcabucero, m.

arraign, v.t. acusar; (law) procesar

arraignment, s. acusación, f.; (law) procesamiento, m.

arrange, v.t. arreglar; acomodar; poner en orden, clasificar; (place) colocar; (order) disponer; (contrive) agenciar; organizar; preparar; (mus.) adaptar; (of differences) concertar, ajustar. v.i. convenir, concertarse; arreglar; hacer preparativos

arrangement, s. arreglo, m.; clasificación, f.; disposición, f.; (agreement) acuerdo, m.; (mus.) adaptación, f.; pl. arrangements, preparativos, m. pl.

arras, s. tapicería, f.

array, s. (of troops) orden de batalla, m. or f.; formación, f.; colección, f.; (dress) atavío, m. v.t. poner en orden de batalla;

formar (las tropas, etc.); ataviar, adornar

arrears, s. pl. atrasos, m. pl. in a., atrasado

arrest, v.t. detener, impedir; (the attention) atraer; (capture) arrestar, prender; (judgment) suspender. s. (stop) interrupción, parada, f.; (hindrance) estorbo, m.; (detention) arresto, m., detención, f.; (of a judgment) suspensión, f. under a., bajo arresto

arresting, a. que llama la atención, notable, muy interesante; asombroso, chocador

arrival, s. llegada, venida, f., advenimiento, m.; (naut.) arribada, f.; entrada, f.; el, m. (f. la) que llega. on a., al llegar, a la llegada. the new arrivals, los recién llegados

arrive, v.i. llegar; aparecer; (happen) suceder; (naut.) arribar; entrar. to a. at, (a place or conclusion) llegar a

arrogance, s. arrogancia altivez, soberbia, f.

arrogant, a. altivo, arrogante, soberbio

arrogate, v.t. arrogar

arrow, s. saeta, flecha, f. a.-head, punta de flecha, f. a.-shaped, en forma de flecha, sagital. a. wound, flechazo, saetazo, m.

arrowroot, s. arrurruz, m.

arsenal, s. arsenal, m.

arsenic, s. arsénico, m.

arsenical, a. arsenical

arson, s. incendio premeditado, m.

art, s. arte, m. or f.; (cleverness) habilidad, f.; (cunning) artificio, m. Faculty of Arts, Facultad de Letras, f. fine arts, bellas artes, f. pl. art exhibition, exposición de pinturas, f. art gallery, museo de pinturas, m. art school, colegio de arte, m.

arterial, a. arterial; (of roads) de primera clase. a. forceps, pinzas hemostáticas, f. pl.

artery, s. arteria, f.

artesian, a. artesiano

artful, a. hábil, ingenioso; (crafty) astuto

artfully, adv. ingeniosamente; con astucia

artfulness, *s.* habilidad, ingeniosidad, *f.*; astucia, maña, *f.*

arthritic, *a.* artrítico

arthritis, *s.* artritis, *f.*

artichoke, *s.* alcachofa, *f.* **Jerusalem a.,** aguaturma, *f.*

article, *s.* artículo, *m.*; (object) objeto, *m.*, cosa, *f.*; *pl.* **articles;** escritura, *f.*; contrato, *m.*; estatutos, *m. pl. v.t.* escriturar; contratar. **leading a.,** artículo de fondo, *m.* **articles of apprenticeship,** contrato de aprendizaje, *m.* **articles of association,** estatutos de asociación, *m. pl.* **articles of war,** código militar, *m.*

articulate, *v.t.* articular; pronunciar, articular. *v.i.* estar unido por articulación; articular. *a.* articulado; claro; expresivo

articulation, *s.* articulación, *f.* (all meanings)

artifice, *s.* artificio, *m.*; arte, *m.* or *f.*, habilidad, *f.*

artificer, *s.* artífice, *m.* and *f.*

artificial, *a.* artificial; falso, fingido; afectado. **a. flowers,** flores de mano, *f. pl.* **a. silk,** seda artificial, seda vegetal, *f.*

artificiality, *s.* artificialidad, *f.*; falsedad, *f.*; afectación, *f.*

artificially, *adv.* artificialmente; con afectación

artillery, *s.* artillería, *f.* **field a.,** artillería volante (or ligera or montada), *f.* **a. practice,** ejercicio de cañón, *m.*

artilleryman, *s.* artillero, *m.*

artisan, *s.* artesano (-na)

artist, *s.* artista, *m.* and *f.*; (painter) pintor (-ra)

artiste, *s.* artista, *m.* and *f.*

artistic, *a.* artístico

artistically, *adv.* artísticamente

artistry, *s.* habilidad artística, *f.*, arte, *m.* or *f.*

artless, *a.* natural; sencillo, cándido, inocente

artlessly, *adv.* con naturalidad; con inocencia

artlessness, *s.* naturalidad, *f.*; sencillez, candidez, inocencia, *f.*

arum, *s.* aro, sarrillo, *m.*

Aryan, *a.* ario

as, *adv., conjunc., rel. pron.* como; así como; (followed by infin.) de; (in comparisons) tan . . . como; (while) mientras; a

medida que; (when) cuando, al (followed by infin.); (since) puesto que, visto que; (because) porque; (although) aunque; por; (according to) según; en; (in order that) para (que). **as a rule,** por regla general. **Once as he was walking,** Una vez mientras andaba. **as . . . as,** tan . . . como. **as far as,** hasta; en cuanto a. **as from,** desde. **as good as,** tan bueno como. **as if,** como si. **as it were,** por decirlo así, en cierto modo. **as many as,** tanto . . . como; todos los que. **as soon as,** en cuanto, luego que, así que. **as soon as possible,** cuanto antes. **as sure as can be,** sin duda alguna. **as to,** en cuanto a. **as usual,** como de costumbre. **as well,** también. **as well as,** (besides) además de; tan bien como. **as yet,** todavía.

asbestos, *s.* asbesto, amianto, *m.*

ascend, *v.t.* and *v.i.* subir; (on, in) subir a; ascender; (rise) elevarse; (a river) remontar. **to a. the stairs,** subir las escaleras. **to a. the pulpit,** subir al púlpito. **to a. the throne,** subir al trono

ascendancy, *s.* ascendiente, influjo, *m.*

ascendant, *s.* elevación, *f. a.* ascendente; predominante. **to be in the a.,** (*fig.*) ir en aumento; predominar

ascending, *a.* ascendente

ascension, *s.* subida, ascensión, *f.*; (of the throne) advenimiento (al trono), *m.* **The A.,** La Ascensión

ascent, *s.* subida, *f.*, ascenso, *m.*; elevación, *f.*; (slope) cuesta, pendiente, *f.*

ascertain, *v.t.* averiguar, descubrir

ascertainable, *a.* averiguable, descubrible

ascertainment, *s.* averiguación, *f.*

ascetic, *a.* ascético. *s.* asceta, *m.* and *f.*

asceticism, *s.* ascetismo, *m.*

ascribable, *a.* imputable, atribuible

ascribe, *v.t.* atribuir, adscribir, imputar

ascription, *s.* atribución, adscripción, *f.*

asepsis, *s.* asepsia, *f.*

aseptic, *a.* aséptico

asexual, *a.* asexual

ash, *s.* ceniza, *f.*; cenizas, *f. pl.*; (tree and wood) fresno, *m.*; *pl.* ashes, cenizas, *f. pl.*; restos mortales, *m. pl.* mountain ash, serbal, *m.* ash-bin, basurero, *m.* ash-coloured, ceniciento. ash grove, fresneda, *f.* ashtray, cenicero, *m.* Ash Wednesday, miércoles de ceniza, *m.*

ashamed, *a.* avergonzado. to be a. of, avergonzarse de. to be a. of oneself, avergonzarse, tener vergüenza de sí mismo

ashen, *a.* ceniciento; (of ash wood) de fresno; pálido como un muerto

ashlar, *s.* sillar, *m.*

ashore, *adv.* a tierra; en tierra. to go or put a., desembarcar

Asiatic, *a.* and *s.* asiático (-ca)

aside, *adv.* a un lado; aparte. *s.* (*theat.*) aparte, *m.* to set a., poner a un lado; (omit) dejar aparte; descontar; abandonar; (a judgment) anular. to take a., llevar aparte

asinine, *a.* asnal

ask, *v.t.* (a question; enquire) preguntar; (request; demand) pedir; (beg) rogar; (invite) invitar. to ask a question, hacer una pregunta. to ask about, preguntar acerca de. to ask after, preguntar por. to ask down, invitar a bajar; invitar a visitar (a alguien). to ask for, pedir; preguntar por. to ask in, invitar (a alguien) a entrar

askance, *adv.* al (or de) soslayo, de reojo; con recelo

askew, *adv.* oblicuamente; al lado; a un lado; sesgadamente

aslant, *prep.* al través de

asleep, *a.* and *adv.* dormido. to be a., estar dormido. to fall a., dormirse

asp, *s.* áspid, *m.*

asparagus, *s.* espárrago, *m.* a. bed, esparraguera, *f.*

aspect, *s.* aspecto, *m.*; vista, *f.*; apariencia, *f.*, semblante, *m.* to have a southern a., dar (mirar) al sur.

aspen, *s.* álamo temblón, *m.*

asperity, *s.* aspereza, *f.*

aspersion, *s.* (*ecc.*) aspersión, *f.*; calumnia, *f.*; insinuación, *f.*

asphalt, *s.* asfalto, *m.* *v.t.* asfaltar

asphodel, *s.* asfódelo, *m.*

asphyxia, *s.* asfixia, *f.*

asphyxiate, *v.t.* asfixiar

asphyxiating, *a.* asfixiante

aspidistra, *s.* aspidistra, *f.*

aspirant, *s.* aspirante, candidato, *m.*

aspirate, *v.t.* aspirar. *s.* letra aspirada, *f.*

aspiration, *s.* aspiración, ambición, *f.*; deseo, anhelo, *m.*; (*gram.*) aspiración, *f.*

aspire, *v.i.* aspirar (a), pretender, ambicionar; alzarse

aspirin, *s.* aspirina, *f.*

ass, *s.* asno, *m.*

assail, *v.t.* atacar, acometer, arremeter

assailable, *a.* atacable

assailant, *s.* asaltador (-ra)

assassin, *s.* asesino, *m.* and *f.*

assassinate, *v.t.* asesinar

assassination, *s.* asesinato, *m.*

assault, *s.* asalto, *m.*; acometida, embestida, *f.*; (*fig.*) ataque, *m.* *v.t.* asaltar; acometer, embestir; atacar. to take by a., tomar por asalto

assay, *s.* ensayo, *m.* *v.t.* ensayar, aquilatar

assayer, *s.* ensayador, *m.*

assaying, *s.* ensaye, *m.*

assegai, *s.* a azagaya, *f.*

assemblage, *s.* reunión, *f.*; (of a machine) montaje, *m.*; (of people) muchedumbre, *f.*, concurso, *m.*; (of things) colección, *f.*, grupo, *m.*

assemble, *v.t.* (persons) reunir, convocar; (things and persons) juntar; (a machine, etc.) armar, ensamblar. *v.i.* reunirse, congregarse; acudir

assembly, *s.* asamblea, *f.*; reunión, *f.*; (*ecc.*) concilio, *m.* a. line, línea de montaje, *f.*; a. room, sala de reuniones, *f.*; sala de baile, *f.*

assent, *s.* asentimiento, consentimiento, *m.*; aprobación, *f.*; (parliamentary, *law*) sanción, *f.* *v.i.* asentir (a), consentir (en); aprobar

assert, *v.t.* mantener, defender; declarar, afirmar; hacer valer, reclamar. **to a. oneself,** imponerse, hacerse sentir; hacer valer sus derechos

assertion, *s.* aserción, afirmación, *f.*; defensa, *f.*; reclamación, *f.*

assertive, *a.* afirmativo; dogmático

assess, *v.t.* tasar, valorar; fijar, señalar; repartir (contribuciones, etc.)

assessment, *s.* tasación, *f.*; fijación, *f.*; repartimiento, *m.*

assessor, *s.* (*law*) asesor (-ra); (of taxes) repartidor (-ra); (valuer) tasador, *m.* **public a.,** tasador, *m.*

asset, *s.* ventaja, *f.*; adquisición, *f.*; cualidad, *f.*; *pl.* **assets,** fondos, *m. pl.*; (*com.*) activo, *m.*, créditos activos, *m. pl.*

assiduity, *s.* asiduidad, *f.*

assiduous, *a.* asiduo

assiduously, *adv.* asiduamente, con asiduidad

assign, *v.t.* (*law*) ceder; señalar, asignar; (appoint) destinar; fijar; atribuir, imputar. *s.* cesionario (-ia)

assignation, *s.* asignación, *f.*; cita, *f.*; (*law*) cesión, *f.*

assignment, *s.* (*law*) cesión, *f.*; escritura de cesión, *f.*; atribución, *f.*; parte, porción, *f.*

assimilable, *a.* asimilable

assimilate, *v.t.* asimilar; incorporarse. *v.i.* mezclarse

assimilation, *s.* asimilación, *f.*; incorporación, *f.*

assimilative, *a.* asimilativo

assist, *v.t.* ayudar; auxiliar, socorrer; (uphold) apoyar; (further) promover, fomentar. *v.i.* (be present) asistir (a)

assistance, *s.* ayuda, *f.*; auxilio, socorro, *m.*; apoyo, *m.*; (furtherance) fomento, *m.* **public a.,** asistencia pública, *f.*

assistant, *s.* ayudante, *m.*; (*ecc.*) asistente, *m.*; (in a shop) dependiente (-ta); colaborador (-ra); (university) auxiliar, *m.*; sub-. **a. secretary,** subsecretario (-ia). **a. secretaryship,** subsecretaría, *f.*

assize, *s.* sesión, de tribunal de justicia, *f.*

associate, *s.* asociado (-da); miembro, *m.*; socio (-ia); compañero (-ra); amigo (-ga); colega, *m.*; colaborador (-ra); (confederate) cómplice, *m.* and *f.* *a.* asociado: auxiliar. *v.t.* asociar; unir, juntar. **to a. oneself with,** asociarse con; asociarse a. **to a. with,** frecuentar la compañía de, ir con

association, *s.* asociación, *f.*; unión, *f.*; sociedad, *f.*; compañía, corporación, *f.*; (connection) relación, *f.* **a. football,** fútbol, *m.*

assonance, *s.* asonancia, *f.*

assonant, *a.* and *s.* asonante (*m.*)

assort, *v.t.* clasificar; mezclar

assorted, *a.* surtido, mezclado. **They are a well-a. pair,** Ellos son una pareja bien avenida

assortment, *s.* . clasificación, *f.*, arreglo, *m.*; surtido, *m.*, mezcla, *f.*

assuage, *v.t.* mitigar; suavizar, calmar; aliviar

assume, *v.t.* asumir; tomar; apropiarse; (wear) revestir; (suppose) suponer; poner por caso

assumed, *a.* fingido, falso; supuesto

assumption, *s.* asunción, *f.*; apropiación, arrogación, *f.*; suposición, *f.* **Feast of the A.,** Fiesta de la Asunción, *f.*

assurance, *s.* garantía, *f.*; promesa, *f.*; confianza, seguridad, *f.*; (in a good sense) aplomo, *m.*, naturalidad, *f.*; (in a bad sense) presunción frescura, *f.*, descaro, *m.*; (*com.*) seguro, *m.*

assure, *v.t.* asegurar

assured, *a.* asegurado; seguro

assuredly, *adv.* seguramente

Assyrian, *a.* and *s.* asirio (-ia); (language) asirio, *m.*

aster, *s.* áster, *m.*

asterisk, *s.* asterisco, *m.*

astern, *adv.* a popa; de popa; en popa; atrás

asthma, *s.* asma, *f.*

asthmatic, *a.* asmático

astigmatic, *a.* astigmático ¡

astigmatism, *s.* astigmatismo, *m.*

astir, *adv.* en movimiento; (out of bed) levantado; excitado

astonish, *v.t.* sorprender, asombrar

astonished, *a.* atónito, estupefacto

astonishing, *a.* sorprendente, asombroso

astonishment, *s.* asombro, *m.*, sorpresa; estupefacción, *f.*

astound, *v.t.* aturdir, pasmar. **to be astounded,** (*fam.*) quedarse muerto

astounding, *a.* asombroso

astrakhan, *s.* astracán, *m.*

astral, *a.* astral

astray, *adv.* desviado, extraviado; por el mal camino. **to go a.,** errar el camino, perderse; (*fig.*) descarriarse

astride, *adv.* a horcajadas. *prep.* a horcajadas sobre; a ambos lados de

astringent, *a.* astringente

astrologer, *s.* astrólogo (-ga)

astrological, *a.* astrológico

astrology, *s.* astrología, *f.*

astronomer, *s.* astrónomo, *m.*

astronomical, *a.* astronómico

astronomy, *s.* astronomía, *f.*

astrophysics, *s.* astrofísica, *f.*

astute, *a.* astuto, sagaz; (with knave, etc.) redomado, pícaro

astuteness, *s.* astucia, sagacidad, *f.*

asunder, *adv.* en dos; separadamente; lejos uno de otro

asylum, *s.* asilo, *m.*; (for the insane) manicomio, *m.*

asymmetrical, *a.* asimétrico

asymmetry, *s.* asimetría, *f.*

at, *prep.* a; en casa de; en; de; con; por; (before) delante de. Sometimes forms part of verb, e.g. to aim at, apuntar. to look at, mirar. May be translated by using pres. part., e.g. They were at play, Estaban jugando. at a bound, de un salto. at peace, en paz. at the doctor's, en casa del médico. at the head, a la cabeza. John is at Brighton, Juan está en Brighton. at first, al principio. at last, por fin. at no time, jamás. at once, en seguida. at most, a lo más. at all events, en todo caso. What is he getting at? ¿Qué quiere saber? at home, en casa. at-home day, día de recibo, *m.*

atavism, *s.* atavismo, *m.*

atavistic, *a.* atávico

ataxia, *s.* ataxia, *f.*

atheism, *s.* ateísmo, *m.*

atheist, *s.* ateo (-ea)

atheistic, *a.* ateo

Athenæum, *s.* ateneo, *m.*

Athenian, *a.* and *s.* ateniense (*m.* and *f.*)

athlete, *s.* atleta, *m.*

athletic, *a.* atlético

athletics, *s.* atletismo, *m.*

athwart, *adv.* de través. *prep.* al través de; contra

Atlantic, *a.* and *s.* atlántico (*m.*). **A. Charter,** Carta del Atlántico, *f.* **A. liner,** transatlántico, *m.*

atlas, *s.* atlas, *m.*

atmosphere, *s.* aire, *m.*; atmósfera, *f.*; (*fig.*) ambiente, *m.*

atmospheric, *a.* atmosférico

atmospherics, *s.pl.* perturbaciones eléctricas atmosféricas, *f.pl.*

atoll, *s.* atalón, *m.*

atom, *s.* átomo, *m.* **splitting of the a.,** escisión del átomo, *f.*

atomic, *a.* atómico. **a. bomb,** bomba atómica, *f.* **a. pile,** pila atómica, *f.* **a. theory,** teoría atómica, *f.*

atomize, *v.t.* pulverizar

atomizer, *s.* pulverizador, *m.*

atone, *v.i.* (for) expiar

atonement, *s.* expiación, *f.*

atonic, *a.* átono, atónico

atrocious, *a.* atroz; horrible

atrocity, *s.* atrocidad, *f.*

atrophy, *s.* atrofia, *f.* *v.i.* atrofiarse

atropine, *s.* atropina, *f.*

attach, *v.t.* (*law,* of goods) embargar; (*law,* of persons) arrestar; (fix) fijar; (tie) atar; (join) juntar; (stick) pegar; (connect) conectar; (hook) enganchar; (with a brooch, etc.) prender; (blame, etc.) imputar; (importance, etc.) dar, conceder; (assign) asignar; (attract) atraer; (enclose) adjuntar, incluir. *v.i.* pertenecer (a), ser indivisible (de). **to a. oneself to,** pegarse a; adherirse a, asociarse con; acompañar; hacerse inseparable de

attaché, *s.* agregado, *m.* **a. case,** maletín, *m.*

attachment, *s.* (*law,* of goods) embargo, *m.*, vía ejecutiva, *f.*; (*law,* of persons) arresto, *m.*; unión, *f.*; conexión, *f.*; (hooking) enganche, *m.*; (with a brooch, etc.) prendimiento, *m.*; (tying) atadura, f.; (fixing) fijación, f.; (affection) apego, cariño, m.; (friendship) amistad, f.

attack, s. ataque, m.; (mil.) ofensiva, f.; (access) acceso, m. v.t. atacar

attacker, s. atacador (-ra), asaltador (-ra)

attain, v.t. alcanzar, conseguir, lograr. v.i. llegar a; alcanzar

attainable, a. asequible, realizable; accesible

attainment, s. consecución, obtención, f.; logro, m.; pl. attainments, prendas, dotes, f. pl.

attempt, v.t. (try) procurar, tratar de, intentar; ensayar; querer; (law) hacer una tentativa (de), atentar. s. tentativa, prueba, f.; esfuerzo, ensayo, m.; (criminal) atentado, m., tentativa f.

attend, v.i. prestar atención (a); escuchar; (look after) cuidar (de); (serve) servir; (accompany) acompañar; (await) esperar. v.t. (be present) asistir (a); (of a doctor) visitar; (accompany) acompañar; (bring) acarrear, traer; (follow) seguir. to be attended with, traer consigo, acarrear

attendance, s. asistencia, presencia, f.; (those present) público, m., concurrencia, f.; servicio, m.; (train) acompañamiento, m.; (med.) asistencia, f., tratamiento médico, m. to be in a., acompañar (a)

attendant, a. que acompaña; que sigue; concomitante. s. criado (-da); (keeper) guardián (-ana); (nurse) enfermero (-ra); (in a cloakroom) guardarropa, f.; (in a theatre) acomodador (-ra); (on a train) mozo, m.; (waiter) camarero, m.; (at baths) bañero (-ra)

attention, s. atención, f.; cuidado, m. A.! ¡Atención!; (mil.) ¡Firmes! to pay a., prestar atención. to stand to a., cuadrarse, permanecer en posición de firmes

attentive, a. atento; solícito; cortés, obsequioso

attentively, adv. con atención, atentamente; solícitamente

attentiveness, s. cuidado, m.; cortesía, f.

attenuate, v.t. atenuar

attenuating, a. atenuante. a. circumstance, circunstancia atenuante, f.

attenuation, s. atenuación, f.

attest, v.t. atestar. v.i. atestiguar, deponer, dar fe

attestation, s. atestación, deposición, f.; (certificate) certificado, m., fe, f.

attic, s. buhardilla, guardilla, f., desván, sotabanco, m.

Attic, a. ático

attire, s. atavío, m.; (dress) traje, m.; (finery) galas, f. pl. v.t. ataviar, vestir; engalanar

attitude, s. actitud, f.; postura, f.; posición, f.

attorney, s. (solicitor) abogado (-da); (agent) apoderado (-da); (public) procurador, m. power of a., poderes, m. pl., procuración, f. A.-general, fiscal, m.

attract, v.t. atraer; (charm) seducir, cautivar, apetecer; (invite) convidar; (goodwill, etc.) captar

attraction, s. atracción, f.; atractivo, aliciente, encanto, m.

attractive, a. atrayente; atractivo, seductivo; apetecible; encantador

attractively, adv. atractivamente

attributable, a. imputable, atribuible

attribute, v.t. atribuir (a), achacar (a), imputar (a). s. atributo, m.

attribution, s. atribución, imputación, f.; atributo, m.

attributive, a. atributivo

attrition, s. atrición, f.

aubergine, s. berenjena, f.

auburn, a. castaño, rojizo

auction, s. subasta, almoneda, f.; venta pública, pública subasta, f. v.t. subastar. to put up to a., sacar a pública subasta

auctioneer, s. subastador (-ra)

audacious, a. atrevido, audaz, osado, temerario; (shameless) descarado, impudente

audaciously, adv. osadamente; descaradamente

audacity, s. audacia, osadía, temeridad, f.; atrevimiento, m.; (shamelessness) descaro, m., desvergüenza, f.

audibility, s. audibilidad, f.

audible, a. audible, oíble

audibly, *adv.* en forma audible, perceptiblemente, en alta voz

audience, *s.* (interview and·*law*) audiencia, *f.*; oyentes, *m. pl.*, auditorio, público, *m.* **to give a.,** dar audiencia. **a. chamber,** sala de recepción, *f.*

audiofrequency, *s.* audiofrecuencia, *f.*

audit, *v.t.* intervenir, examinar (cuentas). *s.* intervención, *f.*, ajuste (de cuentas), *m.*

audition, *s.* audición, *f.*

auditor, *s.* (hearer) oyente, *m.* and *f.*; interventor, contador, *m.*

auditorium, *s.* sala de espectáculos, *f.*

auditory, *a.* auditivo, auditorio

Augean, *a.* de Augeas; muy sucio

auger, *s.* taladro, *m.*

aught; *s.* algo. **For a. I know,** Por lo que yo sepa

augment, *v.t.* aumentar, acrecentar. *v.i.* aumentarse, acrecentarse

augmentation, *s.* aumento, acrecentamiento, *m.*; añadidura, *f.*

augmentative, *a.* aumentativo

augur, *s.* agorero (-ra). *v.t.* and *v.i.* presagiar, anunciar; pronosticar, agorar

augury, *s.* predicción, *f.*; agüero, presagio, pronostico, *m.*

August, *s.* agosto, *m.*

august, *a.* augusto

Augustan, *a.* (of Roman emperor) augustal. **A. Age,** siglo de Augusto, *m.*

Augustinian, *a.* and *s.* (*ecc.*) agustino (-na)

aunt, *s.* tía, *f.* **great-a.,** tía abuela, *f.* **A. Sally,** el pim, pam, pum

aura, *s.* exhalación, *f.*; influencia psíquica, *f.*; (*med.*) aura, *f.*

aural, *a.* auricular. **a. surgeon,** otólogo, *m.*

aureole, *s.* aureola, *f.*

auricle, *s.* (of the heart)·aurícula, ala del corazón, *f.*; oreja, *f.*, pabellón de la oreja, *m.*

auricula, *s.* (*bot.*) oreja de oso, *f.*

auricular, *a.* auricular

aurist, *s.* otólogo, *m.*

aurora, *s.* aurora, *f.* **a. borealis,** aurora boreal, *f.*

auscultate, *v.t.* auscultar

auscultation, *s.* auscultación, *f.*

auspice, *s.* auspicio, *m.*

auspicious, *a.* propicio, favorable, feliz

auspiciously, *adv.* prósperamente, felizmente

auspiciousness, *s.* buenos auspicios, *m. pl.*; felicidad, *f.*

austere, *a.* severo, austero, adusto; ascético; (of style) desnudo

austerity, *s.* austeridad, severidad, *f.*; ascetismo, *m.*; (of style) desnudez, *f.*

Australian, *a.* and *s.* australiano (-na)

Austrian, *a.* and *s.* austríaco (-ca)

Austro-Hungarian, *a.* austrohúngaro

autarchy, *s.* autarquía, *f.*

authentic, *a.* auténtico

authenticate, *v.t.* autenticar

authentication, *s.* autenticación, *f.*

authenticity, *s.* autenticidad, *f.*

author, *s.* autor, *m.*

authoress, *s.* autora, *f.*

authoritarian, *a.* autoritario

authoritative, *a.* autoritario

authority, *s.* autoridad, *f.*; poder, *m.* **to have on the best a.,** tener de muy buena fuente

authorization, *s.* autorización, *f.*

authorize, *v.t.* autorizar

authorship, *s.* profesión de autor, *f.*; paternidad (literaria), *f.*; origen, *m.*

autobiographical, *a.* autobiográfico

autobiography, *s.* autobiografía, *f.*

autobus, *s.* autobús, ómnibus, *m.*

autocar, *s.* coche automóvil, *m.*

autocracy, *s.* autocracia, *f.*

autocrat, *s.* autócrata, *m.* and *f.*

autocratic, *a.* autocrático

auto-da-fé, *s.* auto de fe, *m.*

autogenous, *a.* autógeno

autograph, *s.* autógrafo, *m.*

autography, *s.* autografía, *f.*

autogyro, *s.* autogiro, *m.*·

automatic, *a.* automático. **a. gate,** (at level crossings, etc.) barrera de golpe, *f.* **a. machine,** máquina automática, *f.*; (*fam.*) tragaperras, *m.* **a. pencil,** lapicero, *m.*

automatically, *adv.* automáticamente

automatism, *s.* automatismo, *m.*

automaton, *s.* autómata, *m.*

automobile, *s.* automóvil, *m.*

autonomous, *a.* autónomo

autonomy, *s.* autonomía, *f.*

autopsy, *s.* autopsia, *f.*

auto-suggestion, *s.* autosugestión, *f.*

autumn, *s.* otoño, *m.*

autumnal, *a.* otoñal, de otoño

auxiliary, *a.* auxiliar. *s.* auxiliador, *m.*

avail, *v.i.* servir; valer; importar. *v.t.* aprovechar. **to a. oneself of,** valerse de, aprovecharse de. **to no a.,** en balde

availability, *s.* utilidad, *f.*; disponibilidad, *f.*; provecho, *m.*; (validity) validez, *f.*

available, *a.* útil; disponible; aprovechable; válido

avalanche, *s.* alud, *m.*

avarice, *s.* avaricia, *f.*

avaricious, *a.* avaro, avaricioso

ave, *interj.* ¡ave! *s.* avemaría, *f.*; despedida, *f.*

avenge, *v.t.* vengar; vindicar. **to a. oneself for,** vengarse de

avenger, *s.* vengador (-ra)

avenging, *a.* vengador

avenue, *s.* avenida, *f.*

aver, *v.t.* afirmar, asegurar

average, *s.* promedio, término medio, *m.*; (marine insurance) avería, *f.*; *a.* de promedio; típico; corriente; normal. *v.t.* hallar el término medio (de); prorratear, proporcionar; ser por término medio. **general a.,** (marine insurance) avería gruesa, *f.* **on the a.,** por término medio

averse, *a.* opuesto (a); desinclinado (a); enemigo (de); repugnante. **to be a. to,** no gustar de; oponerse a; estar desinclinado a; ser enemigo de; repugnar

aversion, *s.* aversión, *f.*; repugnancia, *f.*

avert, *v.t.* apartar; (avoid) evitar

aviary, *s.* avería, pajarera, *f.*

aviation, *s.* aviación, *f.*

aviator, *s.* aviador (-ra)

aviculture, *s.* avicultura, *f.*

avid, *a.* ávido

avidity, *s.* avidez, *f.*

avidly, *adv.* ávidamente, con avidez

avocation, *s.* pasatiempo, *m.*, distracción, *f.*; ocupación, *f.*; profesión, *f.*

avoid, *v.t.* evitar; (pursuit) evadir, eludir; guardarse (de), rehuir; (*law*) anular

avoidable, *a.* evitable, eludible

avoidance, *s.* evitación, *f.*

avow, *v.t.* confesar; declarar

avowal, *s.* confesión, admisión, *f.*

avowedly, *adv.* por confesión propia

avuncular, *a.* avuncular

await, *v.t.* aguardar, esperar

awake, *v.t.* despertar. *v.i.* despertarse. *a.* despierto; vigilante; consciente (de); atento (a)

awakening, *s.* despertamiento, *m.*

award, *s.* sentencia, decisión, *f.*; adjudicación, *f.*; (prize) premio, *m.* *v.t.* adjudicar; otorgar, conceder

aware, *a.* consciente, sabedor. **to be well a. of,** saber muy bien. **to make a. of,** hacer saber

awash, *adv.* a flor de agua

away, *adv.* a distancia, a lo lejos, lejos; (absent) ausente; (out) fuera; (unceasingly) sin parar, continuamente; (wholly) completamente; (visibly) a ojos vistas. In verbs of motion a. is rendered by the reflexive, e.g. **to go a.,** marcharse. Sometimes not translated, e.g. **to take a.,** quitar. *interj.* ¡fuera de aquí! ¡márchese Vd.!; ¡vámonos! ¡adelante! **nine miles a.,** a nueve millas de distancia. **a. in the distance,** allá a lo lejos. **She sang a.,** Ella seguía cantando

awe, *s.* temor reverente, *m.*; horror, *m.*; respeto, *m.*; reverencia, *f.* *v.t.* intimidar, aterrar; infundir respeto (a). **to stand in awe of,** tener respeto (a), reverenciar

awesome, *a.* pavoroso, temible, aterrador; terrible; (august) augusto; (imposing) imponente

awestruck, *a.* espantado, aterrado

awful, *a.* terrible, pavoroso; horrible; temible; atroz; (*fam.*) enorme. **How a.!** (*fam.*) ¡Qué barbaridad!

awfully, *adv.* terriblemente; horriblemente; (*fam.*) muy

awfulness, *s.* lo terrible; lo horrible; atrocidad, *f.*; (of a crime, etc.) enormidad, *f.*

awkward, *a.* difícil; peligroso; delicado; embarazoso; (of time, etc.) inconveniente, inoportuno; (of things) incómodo; (clumsy) torpe, desmañado; desagradable; (ungraceful) sin gracia. **the a. age,** la edad difícil

awkwardly, *adv.* torpemente; incómodamente; mal; con dificultad; sin gracia. **He is a. placed,** Se encuentra en una situación difícil

awkwardness, *s.* dificultad, *f.*; peligro, *m.*; delicadeza, *f.*; inconveniencia, inoportunidad, *f.*; (clumsiness) torpeza, desmaña, *f.*; (ungracefulness) falta de gracia, *f.*

awl, *s.* lezna, *f.*, punzón, *m.*

awn, *s.* arista, panoja, *f.*

awning, *s.* toldo, palio, *m.*; (naut.) toldilla, *f.*

awry, *adv.* a un lado; oblicuamente; (fig.) mal. *a.* torcido; (fig.) descarriado

axe, *s.* hacha, *f.*

axil, *s.* axila, *f.*

axilla, *s.* axila, *f.*, sobaco, *m.*

axillary, *a.* axilar, sobacal

axiom, *s.* axioma, *m.*

axiomatic, *a.* axiomático

axis, *s.* eje, *m.*; (zool.) axis, *m.* **A. powers,** las naciones del Eje

axle, *s.* eje, *m.*; peón, árbol (de una rueda), *m.* **back a.,** eje trasero, *m.* **differential a.,** eje diferencial, *m.* **front a.,** eje delantero, *m.*

ay, *interj.* sí. *s.* voto afirmativo, *m.*

aye, *adv.* siempre. **for aye,** por (or para) siempre

azalea, *s.* azalea, *f.*

azimuth, *s.* acimut, *m.*

Aztec, *a.* and *s.* azteca (*m.* and *f.*)

azure, *s.* azul celeste, *m.*

B

b, *s.* (letter) be, *f.*; (mus.) si, *m.*

baa, *s.* balido, be, *m.* *v.i.* balar, dar balidos

babble, *s.* (chatter) charla, *f.*; (of a child) gorjeo, *m.*; (confused sound) vocinglería, barbulla, *f.*, rumor, *m.*; (of water) murmullo, susurro, *m.* *v.i.* charlar; (of children) gorjearse; (incoherently) balbucir; (water) murmurar, susurrar; (a secret) descubrir

babbler, *s.* charlatán (-ana)

babbling, *s.* garrulería, locuacidad, *f.*; (incoherent speech) balbuceo, *m.*; (of water) murmullo, *m.* *a.* gárrulo, locuaz; balbuciente; murmurante

babel, *s.* babel, *m.*

baboon, *s.* babuino, *m.*

babouche, *s.* babucha, chancleta, *f.*

baby, *s.* bebé, crío, *m.*; niño (-ña) de pecho; (fig.) gran bebé, *m.*; niño mimado, *m.* *a.* infantil. **b. blue,** azul claro, *m.* **b. doll,** muñeca bebé, *f.* **b. grand piano,** piano de media cola, *m.*

babyhood, *s.* infancia, niñez, *f.*

babyish, *a.* infantil, aniñado, pueril

Babylonian, *a.* babilónico

baccalaureate, *s.* bachillerato, *m.*

baccarat, *s.* bacará, *m.*

Bacchanalia, *s. pl.* bacanales, *f. pl.*

Bacchante, *s.* bacante, ménade, *f.*

Bacchic, *a.* báquico

bachelor, *s.* soltero, célibe, *m.*; (of a university) licenciado, bachiller, *m.*; (as a title) caballero, *m.* **confirmed b.,** solterón, *m.* **degree of b.,** licenciatura, *f.* **to receive the degree of b.,** licenciarse, bachillerarse

bachelorhood, *s.* soltería, *f.*, celibato, *m.*

bacillary, *a.* bacilar

bacillus, *s.* bacilo, *m.*

back, *s.* (anat.) espalda, *f.*; (of an animal) lomo, espinazo, *m.*; (reins, loins) riñones, *m. pl.*; (of chairs, sofas) respaldo, *m.*; (of a book) lomo, *m.*; (back, bottom) fondo, *m.*; parte posterior, parte de atrás, *f.*; (of a hand, brush and many other things) dorso, *m.*; (of a coin) reverso, *m.*; el otro lado de alguna cosa; (in football, hockey) defensa, *m.*; (theat.) foro, *m.*; (of fire-arms) culata, *f.*; (of a knife) canto, *m.*; (upper portion) parte superior, *f.* *a.* posterior, trasero; de atrás;

(remote) alejado, apartado; inferior; (overdue) past; out of date) atrasado; (earlier) anterior; (*anat.*) dorsal. **at the b.**, detrás; en el fondo; en la última fila. **at the b. of one's back**, por sus adentros, en el fondo del pensamiento. **behind one's b.**, a espaldas de uno, en ausencia de uno. **half-b.**, medio, *m.* **on one's b.**, boca arriba; a cuestas. **to see the b. of,** (*fam.*) ver por última vez, desembarazarse de. **to turn one's b. on,** volver la espalda (a). **with one's b. to the engine,** de espaldas a la máquina. **b. to b.,** espalda con espalda

back, *v.t.* empujar hacia atrás; (a vehicle) dar marcha atrás; hacer retroceder; (line) reforzar; (support) apoyar; (sign) endosar; (bind) forrar; (bet on) apostar a; (a sail) fachear. *v.i.* retroceder; dar marchar atrás; (of the wind) girar; (with on to) dar sobre, dominar; (with down) abandonar (una pretensión, etc.). **to b. out,** salir, marcharse; volverse atrás; (retract) desdecirse

back, *adv.* detrás; atrás; otra vez, de nuevo; (returned) de vuelta; a alguna distancia; (at home) en casa. *interj.* ¡atrás! **A few weeks b.,** Hace unas semanas, Unas semanas atrás. **It stands b. from the road,** Está a alguna distancia del camino. **to go b. to,** (of families, etc.) remontar a. **to come b.,** regresar. **to come b. again,** regresar de nuevo, regresar por segunda vez

back-axle, *s.* eje trasero, *m.*
backbite, *v.t.* cortar (a uno) un sayo, desollarle (a uno) vivo, murmurar de
backbiter, *s.* mala lengua, *f.,* murmurador (-ra)
backbiting, *s.* murmuración, detracción, maledicencia, *f. a.* murmurador, detractor
backbone, *s.* espinazo, *m.,* columna vertebral, *f.* **to the b.,** hasta la médula
back-chat, *s.* dimes y diretes, *m. pl.;* insolencia, *f.* **to indulge in b.-c.,** andar en dimes y diretes

backcloth, *s.* (*theat.*) forillo, *m.;* (for horses) sudadero, *m.*
back-comb, *s.* peineta, *f.*
back-door, *s.* puerta trasera, puerta de servicio, *f.*
backed, *a.* (lined) forrado; (in compounds; of persons) de espalda; (of chairs) de respaldo
backer, *s.* (better) apostador, *m.;* protector (-ra, -triz)
back-fire, *s.* falsa explosión, *f.*
backgammon, *s.* chaquete, *m.*
back-garden, *s.* jardín de atrás, *m.*
background, *s.* fondo, *m.;* (*art*) último término, *m.* **in the b.,** en el fondo; (*art*) en último término; (*fig.*) en las sombras; alejado, a distancia
backhand, *s.* (*sport*) revés, *m.*
backhanded, *a.* de revés, dado con el revés de la mano; (*fig.*) ambiguo, equívoco
backing, *s.* forro, *m.;* (lining) refuerzo, *m.;* (of a vehicle) marcha atrás, *f.;* retroceso, *m.;* (betting) el apostar (a); (wagers) apuestas, *f. pl.;* (*fig.,* support) apoyo, *m.,* ayuda, *f.;* garantía, *f.*
back-number, *s.* (of a periodical) número atrasado, *m.*
back-pedal, *v.i.* contrapedalear
back-premises, *s.* parte trasera (de una casa, etc.), *f.*
backroom, *s.* cuarto interior, *m.,* habitación trasera, *f.* **b. boys,** investigadores ocupados en trabajos secretos para el gobierno, *m. pl.*
back-seat, *s.* asiento trasero, *m.;* fondo, *m.* **to take a b.-s.,** permanecer en el fondo, ceder el paso
back-shop, *s.* trastienda, *f.*
backside, *s.* trasero, *m.,* posaderas, nalgas, *f. pl.*
backslide, *v.i.* recaer, reincidir
backslider, *s.* (in religion or politics) apóstata, *m. and f.;* reincidente, *m.* and *f.*
backsliding, *s.* apostasía, *f.;* reincidencia, *f.*
back-stage, *s.* foro, fondo del escenario, *m. adv.* hacia el foro; detrás de bastidores
back-staircase, *s.* escalera de servicio, *f.;* escalera secreta, *f.*
backstairs, *s.* escalera de servicio, *f.;* (*fig.*) vías secretas, *f. pl. a.* de cocina; (*fig.*) secreto

backstay, s. (*naut.*) burda, f.

backstitch, s. (*sew.*) pespunte, m. v.t. and v.i. pespuntar

back-street, s. calle secundaria, callejuela, f.; pl. **back-streets,** barrios bajos, m. pl.

backstroke, s. reculada, f.; (*sport*) revés, m.

back-tooth, s. muela, f.

back-view, s. vista de detrás, f.

backward, a. hacia atrás; vuelto hacia · atrás; (in development) atrasado, poco avanzado; lento; negligente; (shy) modesto; (late) tardío; atrasado; retrógrado; (dull) torpe; retrospectivo. adv. hacia atrás; atrás; al revés; (of falling) de espaldas; (of time) al pasado. **to go b. and forward,** ir y venir. **b. and forward,** de acá para allá

backwardness, s. atraso, m.; lentitud, f.; negligencia, f.; modestia, f.; (lateness) tardanza, f.; atraso, m.; (dullness) torpeza, f.; falta de progreso, f.

backwards, adv. See **backward**

backwash, s. agua de rechazo, f.

backwater, s. remanso, m.

back-wheel, s. rueda trasera, f. v.i. contrapedalear

backwoods, s. monte, m., selva, f.

back-yard, s. corral, m.

bacon, s. tocino, m.

Baconian, a. baconiano

bacteria, s. bacteria, f.

bacterial, a. bacterial, bacteriano

bactericide, s. bactericida, m.

bacteriological, a. bacteriológico

bacteriologist, s. bacteriólogo, m.

bacteriology, s. bacteriología, f.

baculus, s. báculo, m.

bad, a. malo; (wicked) perverso; (ill) enfermo, malo (with estar); (naughty; undutiful) malo (with ser); (of coins) falso; (of debts) incobrable; (rotten) podrido; (harmful) nocivo; (dangerous) peligroso; (of pains, a cold) fuerte; intenso; (of a shot) errado; (mistaken) equivocado; (unfortunate) desgraciado. s. el mal, lo malo; (persons) los malos. **extremely bad,** pésimo. **from bad to worse,** de mal en peor. **It's too bad!** ¡Esto es demasiado! **to go bad,** (fruit) macarse; (food) estropearse. **bad habit,** mala costumbre, f., vicio, m. **to have the bad habit of,** tener el vicio de. **bad temper,** malhumor, mal genio, m. **bad tempered,** malhumorado. **bad turn,** flaco servicio, m., mala pasada, f.

badge, s. insignia, f.; (decoration) condecoración, f.; símbolo, emblema, m.; (mark) marca, f.

badger, s. tejón, m. v.t. cansar, molestar

badly, adv. mal. **extremely b.,** pésimamente. **to want something b.,** necesitar algo con urgencia. **b. done,** mal hecho. **b. disposed,** malintencionado

badminton, s. badminton, m.

badness, s. maldad, f.; mala calidad, f.; lo malo

baffle, v.t. desconcertar; (bewilder) tener perplejo (a); contrariar, frustrar; (obstruct) impedir; (avoid) evitar. **to b. description,** no haber palabras para describir

baffling, a. desconcertante; difícil; confuso; perturbador; (of people) enigmático

bag, s. saco, m.; talega, f.; (hand) bolsa, f., saco (de mano), m.; (for tools) capacho, m.; (for sewing) costurero, m.; (of bagpipes) fuelle, m.; (saddle) alforja, f.; (brief-case) cartera, f.; (suitcase) maleta, f.; (under the eye) ojera, f.; (game shot) caza, f. v.t. entalegar; coger, cazar; matar; tomar. v.i. (of garments) arrugarse. **to clear out bag and baggage,** liar el petate. **a bag of bones,** (person) un manojo de huesos. **bag wig,** peluquín, m.

bagasse, s. bagazo, m.

bagatelle, s. bagatela, friolera, f.; (game) billar romano, m.

bagful, s. saco, m.; bolsa, f.

baggage, s. equipaje, m.; (mil.) bagaje, m.; (madcap) pícara, f.; (jade) mujerzuela, f. **b. master,** (railway) factor, m. **b. waggon,** furgón de equipajes, m.

baggy, a. (creased, of trousers) con rodilleras, arrugado; (wide) bombacho

bagpipe, s. gaita, f.

bagpiper, s. gaitero, m.

bah, interj. ¡bah!

bail, s. (law) fianza, caución, f.; (person) fiador (-ra); (cricket) travesaño, m., barra, f. v.t. (law) poner en libertad bajo fianza; salir fiador (por); (a boat) achicar. **on b.,** en fiado. **to go b.,** dar fianza, fiar.

bailiff, s. (law) agente ejecutivo, m.; alguacil, m.; mayordomo, m.; capataz, m.

bait, s. cebo, m.; anzuelo, m.; (fodder) pienso, m. v.t. cebar; (feed) dar pienso (a); azuzar; atormentar; (attract) atraer

baiting, s. cebadura, f.; combate, m.; tormenta, f.

baize, s. bayeta, f. **green b.,** tapete verde, m.

bake, v.t. cocer; hacer (pan, etc.); (fig.) endurecer. v.i. cocerse

bakehouse, s. panadería, f.

bakelite, s. bakelita, f.

baker, s. panadero, hornero, m. **a baker's dozen,** la docena del fraile

bakery, s. panadería, f.

baking, s. cocimiento, m., cocción, f.; (batch) hornada, f.; el hacer (pan, etc.). a. (fam.) abrasador. **b.-dish,** tortera, f. **b.-powder,** levadura química, f.

balance, s. balanza, f.; equilibrio, m.; (com.) balance, saldo, m.; (in a bank) saldo (a favor del cuentacorrentista), m.; (math.) resto, m.; (ast.) Libra, f.; (pendulum) péndola, f.; (counterweight) contrapeso, m. **credit b.,** saldo acreedor, m. **debit b.,** saldo deudor, m. **net b.,** saldo líquido, m. **to lose one's b.,** perder el equilibrio. **to strike a b.,** hacer balance. **b. of power,** equilibrio político, m. **b. of trade,** balanza de comercio, f. **b.-sheet,** balance, avanzo, m. **b. wheel,** (of watches) volante, m.

balance, v.t. balancear, abalanzar; contrapesar; (accounts) saldar; equilibrar; comparar; considerar, examinar. v.i. balancearse; ser de igual peso; equilibrarse; (accounts) saldarse

balancing, s. balanceo, m.; (com.) balance, m. **b.-pole,** balancín, m.

balconied, a. con balcones, que tiene balcones

balcony, s. balcón, m.; galería, f.; (theat.) anfiteatro, m.

bald, a. calvo; (of style) seco, pobre; (fig.) desnudo, árido, pelado; sin adorno; (simple) sencillo. **to grow b.,** ponerse calvo, encalvecer

baldachin, s. baldaquín, m.

balderdash, s. galimatías, m.; jerigonza, f.; disparate, m.

baldly, adv. secamente; sencillamente

baldness, s. calvicie, f.; (of style) sequedad, pobreza, f.; (bareness) desnudez, aridez, f.

baldric, s. (belt) tahalí, m.

bale, s. (bundle) fardo, m.; (of cotton, paper, etc.) bala, f.

Balearic, a. baleárico

baleful, a. malicioso, siniestro, maligno

balefully, adv. malignamente

balk, s. obstáculo, m.; (beam) viga, f.; (billiards) cabaña, f. v.t. frustrar; impedir. v.i. resistirse, rehusar

Balkan, a. balcánico

ball, s. globo, m., esfera, f.; (plaything) pelota, f.; (as in billiards, cricket, croquet) bola, f.; (in football, basket-ball) balón, m.; (shot) bala, f.; (of wool, etc.) ovillo, m.; (of the eye) globo (del ojo), m.; (of the thumb) yema (del pulgar), f.; (of the foot) planta (del pie), f.; (dance) baile, m. v.i. apelotonarse. **red b.,** (in billiards) mingo, m. **to play b.,** jugar a la pelota. **to roll oneself into a b.,** aovillarse, hacerse un ovillo. **b.-and-socket joint,** articulación esférica, f. **b.-bearing,** cojinete de bolas, m.

ballad, s. romance, m.; (song) balada, f.

balladmonger, s. coplero (-ra)

ballast, s. (naut. and fig.) lastre, m.; (r.w.) balasto, m. v.t. lastrar; llenar de balasto

ballerina, s. bailarina, f.

ballet, s. baile ruso, ballet, m.; baile, m. **b. master,** director de ballet, m.

ballistics, s. balística, f.

balloon, s. globo aerostático, m.; (chem.) balón, m.; (toy) globo, m.;

(*arch.*) bola, *f.* **captive b.**, globo cautivo, *m.* **b. barrage**, cortina de globos de intercepción, *f.* **b.-tyre**, neumático balón, *m.*

balloonist, *s.* aeronauta, *m.* and *f.*

ballot, *s.* votación, *f.*; papeleta para votar, cédula de votación, *f. v.i.* votar, balotar. **b. box**, urna electoral, *f.*

ballroom, *s.* salón de baile, *m.*; salón de fiestas, *m.*

balm, *s.* bálsamo, *m.*; (*fig.*) ungüento, *m.*

balminess, *s.* fragancia, *f.*; aroma, *m.*; (gentleness) suavidad, *f.*

balmy, *a.* balsámico; fragante; aromático; (soft) suave; (soothing) calmante

balneal, *a.* balneario

balsam, *s.* bálsamo, *m.*

balsamic, *a.* balsámico; perfumado

Baltic, *a.* báltico

baluster, *s.* balaustre, *m.*

balustered, *a.* balaustrado

balustrade, *s.* balaustrada, barandilla, *f.*, antepecho, *m.*

bamboo, *s.* bambú, *m.*

bamboozle, *v.t.* engatusar, embaucar

bamboozler, *s.* embaucador (-ra)

bamboozling, *s.* embaucamiento, engaño, *m.*

ban, *s.* interdicción, *f.*; prohibición, *f.*; bando, *m. v.t.* prohibir; proscribir

banal, *a.* banal, vulgar, trivial

banality, *s.* banalidad, vulgaridad, trivialidad, *f.*

banana, *s.* (tree and fruit) plátano, *m.*; (fruit) banana, *f.* **b. plantation**, platanar, *m.*

band, *s.* lista, tira, *f.*; zona, *f.*; (black mourning) tira de gasa, *f.*; (sash) faja, *f.*; (ribbon) banda; cinta, *f.*; (bandage) venda, *f.*; (*mech.*) correa, *f.*; (*arch.*) listón, *m.*; (*mus.*) banda, *f.*; (group) pandilla, *f.*, grupo, *m. v.t.* congregar, reunir. *v.i.* reunirse, asociarse. **b.-saw**, sierra de cinta, *f.*

bandage, *s.* venda, *f.*, vendaje, *m. v.t.* vendar, poner un vendaje en (limbs, etc. or persons)

bandaging, *s.* vendaje, *m.*

bandbox, *s.* sombrerera de cartón, *f.*

banderol, *s.* banderola, *f.*

bandit, *s.* bandido, bandolero, *m.*

bandmaster, *s.* músico mayor, *m.*; director de orquesta, *m.*

bandsman, *s.* músico, *m.*

bandstand, *s.* quiosco de música, *m.*

bandy, *v.t.* cambiar, trocar; pasar de uno a otro

bandy-legged, *a.* estevado zanquituerto

bane, *s.* (poison) veneno, *m.*; perdición, ruina, *f.*; (nuisance) plaga, *f.*

baneful, *a.* pernicioso, funesto; dañino; maligno

banefully, *adv.* funestamente; malignamente

bang, *s.* golpe, golpazo, *m.*; (of an explosive, fire-arm) estallido, *m.*, detonación, *f.*; (of a firework) traque, *m.*; (of a door) portazo, *m.*; (with the fist) puñetazo, *m.*; (noise) ruido, *m.*; (fringe) flequillo, *m.. v.t.* golpear; (beat) sacudir; (throw) lanzar, arrojar con violencia; (a door, etc.) cerrar de golpe, cerrar con violencia. *v.i.* golpear; estallar; (thunder) retronar; (in the wind) cencerrear. *interj.* ¡pum! ¡zas!

banging, *s.* golpeadura, *f.*; sacudidura, *f.*; detonación, *f.*; ruido, *m.*

bangle, *s.* (slave b.) esclava, *f.*; pulsera, *f.*; brazalete, *m.*; (for ankles) ajorca, *f.*

banish, *v.t.* desterrar; apartar; (from the mind) despedir, ahuyentar; (suppress) suprimir

banishment, *s.* destierro, *m.*; expulsión, *f.*; relegación, *f.*; (suppression) supresión, *f.*

banister, *s.* baranda, *f.*, pasamano, *m.*

banjo, *s.* banjo, *m.*

banjoist, *s.* tocador (-ra) de banjo

bank, *s.* (of rivers, etc.) ribera, orilla, *f.*, margen, *m.*; (of clouds) banda, capa, *f.*; (of sand, fog, snow) banco, *m.*; (embankment) terraplén, *m.*; (*com.*) banco, *m.*; (gaming) banca, *f.*; (for foreign exchange) casa de cambio, *f.* **b. account**, cuenta corriente, *f.* **b. book**, libreta de banco, *f.* **b. clerk**, empleado del banco, *m.* **b. holiday**, fiesta oficial, *f.*

b.-note, billete de banco, *m.*
b. stock, acciones de un banco,
f. pl.

bank, *v.t.* estancar, represar;
amontonar; poner (dinero) en
un banco, depositar en un banco.
v.i. tener cuenta corriente en un
banco; (gaming) tener la banca;
ser banquero; (*aer.*) inclinarse al
virar

banker, *s.* banquero, *m.* (also at
cards); (money-changer) cambista, *m.* and *f.*

banking, *s.* (*com.*) banca, *f.*;
(*aer.*) vuelo inclinado, *m.* *a.*
(*com.*) bancario. **b. house,** casa
de banca, *f.*

bankrupt, *a.* insolvente, quebrado. *s.* quebrado (-da). **to go b.,**
declararse en quiebra, hacer
bancarrota

bankruptcy, *s.* bancarrota, quiebra, *f.*; (*fig.*) pobreza, decadencia, *f.* **fraudulent b.,** quiebra fraudulenta, *f.* **b. court,**
tribunal de quiebras, *m.*

banner, *s.* bandera, *f.*

banns, *s. pl.* amonestaciones,
f. pl. **to forbid the b.,** impedir
las amonestaciones. **to publish the b.,** decir las amonestaciones

banquet, *s.* banquete, *m.* *v.t.* and
v.i. banquetear

banqueting, *a.* de banquetes.
b. hall, sala de banquetes, *f.*

bantam, *s.* gallina enana, *f.*
b. weight, (*sport*) *a.* de peso
gallo. *s.* peso gallo, *m.*

banter, *v.t.* and *v.i.* tomar el pelo
(a). *s.* chistes, *m. pl.*, burlas, *f. pl.*

baptism, *s.* bautismo, *m.*; (*fig.*)
bautizo, *m.*

baptismal, *a.* bautismal

baptist, *s.* bautista, *m.* **St. John
the B.,** San Juan Bautista

baptistry, *s.* baptisterio, bautisterio, *m.*

baptize, *v.t.* bautizar

baptizing, *s.* bautizo, *m.*

bar, *s.* barra, *f.*; (of chocolate,
soap) pastilla, *f.*; (*her.*) banda, *f.*;
(on a window) reja, *f.*; (of a door)
tranca, *f.*, barrote, *m.*; (bar lever)
palanca, *f.*; (of a balance) astil,
m.; (*mus.*) barra, *f.*; (in the sea,
etc.) banco, alfaque, *m.*; (barrier)
barrera, *f.*; (barrister's profession) foro, *m.*, curia, *f.*; (*fig.*)

tribunal, *m.*; (in a court) barra,
f.; (*fig.*) impedimento, *m.*; (of
light) rayo, *m.*; (stripe) raya, *f.*;
(for refreshments) bar, *m.*; mostrador del bar, *m.* *v.t.* atrancar,
abarrotar; impedir, obstruir;
prohibir; exceptuar, excluir;
(streak) rayar. **the B.,** el cuerpo
de abogados. **to be called to
the B.,** ser recibido como abogado en los tribunales. **b.-
tender,** camarero del bar, *m.*

barb, *s.* púa, *f.*; (of an arrow,
fish-hook, etc.) lengüeta, *f.*; (of a
lance) roquete, *m.*; (of fish) barbilla, *f.*; (of a feather) barba, *f.*;
(horse) caballo berberisco, *m.*
v.t. proveer de púas; armar de
lengüetas

barbarian, *a.* bárbaro, barbárico.
s. bárbaro (-ra)

barbaric, *a.* barbárico, salvaje

barbarism, *s.* barbarismo, salvajismo, *m.*; crueldad, *f.*; (of style)
barbarismo, *m.*

barbarity, *s.* barbaridad, ferocidad, *f.*

barbarous, *a.* feroz, cruel, salvaje; inculto

barbarously, *adv.* bárbaramente,
cruelmente

barbarousness, *s.* barbaridad,
f.; crueldad, ferocidad, *f.*

barbecue, *s.* barbacoa, *f.*

barbed-wire, *s.* alambre de púas,
alambre espinoso, *m.*

barbel, *s.* (*icht.*) barbo, *m.*

barber, *s.* barbero, *m.* **barber's
shop,** barbería, *f.*

barberry, *s.* (*bot.*) bérbero, *m.*

barbican, *s.* (*mil.*) barbacana,
f.

barcarolle, *s.* barcarola, *f.*

Barcelona (of or from), *a.* and *s.*
barcelonés (-esa)

bard, *s.* bardo, vate, *m.*

bardic, *a.* de los bardos; poético

bare, *a.* desnudo; descubierto;
vacío; (mere) mero, solo; (worn)
raído; pelado, raso; (unadorned)
sencillo; (unsheathed) desnudo;
(arid) árido; (curt) seco; (unprotected) desabrigado; pobre.
v.t. desnudar; descubrir; revelar.
He bared his head, Se des-
cubrió. **to lay b.,** dejar al
desnudo; revelar

bareback, *a.* que monta en pelo.
adv. en pelo

barefaced, *a.* descarado, desvergonzado, cínico

barefoot, *a.* descalzo

bareheaded, *a.* sin sombrero, descubierto

barelegged, *a.* en pernetas, en piernas

barely, *adv.* apenas; escasamente; meramente, solamente

bareness, *s.* desnudez, *f.*; desadorno, *m.*; (aridity) aridez, *f.*; pobreza, *f.*

bargain, *s.* contrato, *m.*; pacto, acuerdo, *m.*; (purchase) ganga, *f.* *v.i.* negociar; (haggle) regatear; (expect) esperar. **into the b.,** de añadidura, también. **It is a b.,** Es una ganga; Trato hecho. **to get the best of the b.,** salir ganando. **to strike a b.,** cerrar un trato. **b. counter,** sección de saldos, *f.* **b. sale,** venta de saldos, *f.*

bargainer, *s.* negociador (-ra); regatón (-ona)

bargaining, *s.* negociación, gestión, *f.*; (haggling) regateo, *m.*

barge, *s.* (for freight) barcaza, gabarra, *f.*; falúa, *f.*; lancha, *f.* *v.i.* (into) tropezar con; dar empujones

bargee, *s.* barquero, gabarrero, *m.*

baritone, *s.* barítono, *m.*

barium, *s.* (chem.) bario, *m.*

bark, *s.* (of a tree) corteza, *f.*; (quinine) quina, *f.*; (boat, poet.) barca, *f.*; (naut.) buque de tres palos, *m.*; (of a dog) ladrido, *m.*; (of a fox) aullido, *m.*; (of a gun) ruido, *m.* *v.i.* (of a dog) ladrar; (of a fox) aullar; (of a gun) tronar

barking, *s.* ladrido, *m.*; (of stags) rebramo, *m.*; (of foxes) aullidos, *m. pl.*; (of guns) trueno, *m.*

barley, *s.* cebada, *f.* *a.* de cebada. **pearl b.,** cebada perlada, *f.* **b.-bin,** cebadera, *f.* **b. dealer,** cebadero, *m.* **b. field,** cebadal, *m.* **b.-water,** hordiate, *m.*

barm, *s.* (froth on beer) giste, *m.*; (leaven) levadura, *f.*

barmaid, *s.* moza de bar, camarera, *f.*

barn, *s.* pajar, granero, hórreo, *m.* **b.-owl,** lechuza, *f.*

barnacle, *s.* lapa, *f.*, barnacla, *m.*

barograph, *s.* barógrafo, *m.*

barometer, *s.* barómetro, *m.*

barometric, *a.* barométrico

baron, *s.* barón, *m.*

baroness, *s.* baronesa, *f.*

baronet, *s.* baronet, *m.*

baronial, *a.* de barón

barony, *s.* baronía, *f.*

baroque, *a.* barroco. **the b.,** lo barroco

barouche, *s.* birlocho, *m.*

barrack, *s.* (mil.) cuartel, *m.*, caserna, *f.* *v.t.* acuartelar

barrage, *s.* presa de contención, *f.*; (mil.) cortina de fuego, *f.*; (barrier) barrera, *f.*; (of questions) lluvia, *f.* **b. balloon,** globo de intercepción, *m.*

barrel, *s.* barril, *m.*; tonel, *m.*, cuba, *f.*; (of a gun) cañón, *m.*; (mech.) cilindro, *m.*; (of an animal) cuerpo, *m.* *v.t.* embarrilar, entonelar. **b.-organ,** organillo, órgano de manubrio, *m.*

barrelled, *a.* embarrilado; (of guns, generally in compounds) de ... cañones. **double-b. gun,** escopeta de dos cañones, *f.*

barren, *a.* estéril; (of ground) árido; (fruitless) infructuoso

barrenness, *s.* esterilidad, *f.*; aridez, sequedad, *f.*; (fruitlessness) inutilidad, *f.*

barricade, *s.* barricada, *f.*; barrera, *f.* *v.t.* cerrar con barricadas; obstruir

barricading, *s.* el cerrar con barricadas; la defensa con barricadas (de)

barrier, *s.* barrera, *f.*; impedimento, *m.*; (for customs duties) portazgo, *m.*

barring, *prep.* salvo, excepto, con la excepción de, menos

barrister, *s.* abogado (-da)

barrow, *s.* carretón, *m.*; carretilla, *f.*; (tumulus) túmulo, *m.*

barter, *s.* cambio, trueque, *m.*; tráfico, *m.* *v.t.* and *v.i.* cambiar, trocar; traficar

barterer, *s.* traficante, *m.* and *f.*

baryta, *s.* (chem.) barita, *f.*

basal, *a.* básico, fundamental

basalt, *s.* basalto, *m.*

base, *a.* bajo, vil, ruin; soez; indigno; impuro; (of metals) de mala ley. *s.* base, *f.*; fundamento, *m.*; pie, *m.*; (arch.)

pedestal, *m.*; (*mil., chem., geom.*)
base, *f.*; (of a vase) asiento, *m.*
v.t. basar; fundar. **b. action**,
bajeza, *f.* **b. line**, (*sport*) línea de
base, *f.* **b. metal**, metal común,
m.

baseball, *s.* pelota base, *f.*

baseless, *a.* sin base; sin fundamento; insostenible

basely, *adv.* bajamente, vilmente

basement, *s.* sótano, *m.*

baseness, *s.* bajeza, vileza, ruindad, *f.*

bashful, *a.* vergonzoso, ruboroso;
tímido, corto; (unsociable)
huraño, esquivo

bashfully, *adv.* vergonzosamente;
timidamente

bashfulness, *s.* vergüenza, *f.*,
rubor, *m.*; encogimiento, *m.*,
timidez, cortedad, *f.*; (unsociableness) huraña, esquivez, *f.*

basic, *a.* básico; fundamental.
b. petrol ration, ración básica
de bencina, *f.*

basil (sweet), *s.* (*bot.*) albahaca, *f.*

basilica, *s.* basílica, *f.*

basilisk, *s.* basilisco, *m.*

basin, *s.* vasija, *f.*; (for washing)
jofaina, *f.*; (barber's) bacía, *f.*;
(of a fountain) taza, *f.*; (*anat.*)
bacinete, *m.*; (of a harbour)
concha, *f.*; (of a river) cuenca,
f.; (in the earth) hoya, *f.*; (dock)
dársena, *f.*

basis, *s.* base, *f.*; fundamento; *m.*;
elemento principal, *m.*

bask, *v.i.* calentarse; (in the sun)
tomar el sol

basket, *s.* cesta, *f.*; canasta, *f.*;
(frail) espuerta, *f.* flat **b.**,
azafate, *m.* **large b.**, banasta, *f.*
b. with a lid, excusabaraja,
f. **b.-ball**, baloncesto, *m.* **b.
maker or dealer**, banastero,
cestero, *m.* **b.-work or shop or
factory**, cestería, *f.* **b.-work
chair**, sillón de mimbres, *m.*

basketful, *s.* cesta, cestada, *f.*

Basque, *a.* and *s.* vasco (-ca),
vascongado (-da). *s.* (language)
vascuence, *m.*

bas-relief, *s.* bajorrelieve, *m.*

bass, *s.* (*mus.*) bajo, *m.*; (for
tying) esparto, *m.* *a.* (*mus.*) bajo.
double b., contrabajo, *m.*
figured b., bajo cifrado, *m.*
b. clef, clave de fa, *f.* **b. string**,
bordón, *m.* **b. voice**, voz baja, *f.*

bassinet, *s.* cochecito de niño, *m.*

bassoon, *s.* (*mus.*) bajón, fagot,
m..

bassoonist, *s.* bajonista, *m.* and *f.*,
fagotista, *m.*

bastard, *s.* bastardo (-da), hijo
(-ja) natural. *a.* bastardo, ilegítimo; espurio

bastardy, *s.* bastardía, ilegitimidad, *f.*

baste, *v.t.* (*sew.*) bastear, hilvanar,
embastar; (*cul.*) enlardar, lardear

bastille, *s.* bastilla, *f.*

bastinado, *s.* bastonada, *f.*

basting, *s.* (*sew.*) embaste, *m.*;
(*cul.*) lardeamiento, *m.* **b. spoon**,
cacillo, *m.* **b. stitch**, pasillo, *m.*

bastion, *s.* bastión, baluarte, *f.*
to fortify with bastions, abastionar

bastioned, *a.* abastionado, con
bastiones

bat, *s.* (*zool.*) murciélago, *m.*; (in
cricket) paleta, *f.*; (in table
tennis) pala, *f.* *v.i.* (cricket)
golpear con la paleta

Batavian, *a.* and *s.* bátavo (-va)

batch, *s.* (of loaves, etc.) hornada,
f.; lote, *m.*; (of recruits) promoción, *f.*

bath, *s.* baño, *m.*; (room) cuarto
de baño, *m.*; (vat) bañador, *m.*;
(for swimming) piscina cubierta,
f.; (in the open air) piscina al aire
libre, *f.*; (*phot.*) baño, *m.*, solución, *f.* *v.t.* bañar, lavar. **hot
mineral baths**, termas, *f. pl.*
Order of the B., Orden del
Baño, *f.* **public baths**, casa de
baños, *f.* **reinforcing b.**, (*phot.*)
reforzador, *m.* **to take a b.**,
bañarse, tomar un baño. **b.-
chair**, cochecillo de inválido, *m.*
b.-robe, bata de baño, *f.*,
albornoz, *m.* **b.-room**, cuarto
de baño, *m.* **b.-towel**, toalla del
baño, *f.* **b.-tub**, bañera, *f.*,
baño, *m.*

bathe, *v.t.* bañar, lavar; (of light,
etc.) bañar, envolver. *v.i.*
bañarse. *s.* baño, *m.* **to go for
a b.**, ir a bañarse

bather, *s.* bañista, *m.* and *f.*;
bañador (-ra)

bathing, *a.* de baño; balneario.
s. baño, *m.* **b.-cap**, gorro de baño,
m. **b.-dress**, traje de baño, *m.*
b.-gown, albornoz, *m.*, bata de
baño, *f.* **b.-machine**, caseta de

baños, *f.* **b.-pool,** piscina, *f.*
b.-resort, estación balnearia, *f.*
b.-shoes, calzado de baño, *m.*
bathos, *s.* paso de lo sublime a lo
ridículo, *m.*; anticlímax, *m.*
batiste, *s.*; batista, *f.*
batman, *s.* (*mil.*) asistente, *m.*
baton, *s.* bastón de mando, *m.*;
(*mus.*) batuta, *f.*; (policeman's)
porra, *f.*
Batrachian, *a.* and *s.* batracio
(*m.*)
batsman, *s.* lanzador, *m.*
battalion, *s.* batallón, *m.*
batten, *v.i.* engordar (de);
medrar, prosperar. **to b. down,**
cerrar las escotillas
batter, *s.* (*cul.*) batido, *m.*; pasta,
f.; (*sport*) lanzador, *m.* *v.t.*
apalear, golpear; (demolish) derribar, demoler; (with artillery)
cañonear; batir. **to coat with
b.,** rebozar. **to b. down,** derribar
battering-ram, *s.* ariete, *m.*
battery, *s.* (*mil., nav.*) batería, *f.*;
(*elec.*) pila, batería, *f.*; (*law*)
agresión, *f.* **dry b.,** batería de
pilas, *f.* **storage b.,** acumulador, *m.* **b. cell,** pila de batería
eléctrica, *f.*
battle, *s.* batalla, *f.*; pelea, *f.*,
combate, *m.*; (struggle) lucha, *f.*
v.i. batallar, pelear; luchar.
b.-array, orden de batalla, *f.*
b.-axe, hacha de combate, *f.*
b.-cruiser, acorazado, *m.* **b.-
field,** campo de batalla, *m.*
b.-front, frente de combate, *m.*
b.-piece, (*art*) batalla, *f.* **b.-
ship,** buque de guerra, *m.*
battledore (and **shuttlecock**),
s. raqueta (y volante), *f.*
battlement, *s.* almenaje, *m.*;
muralla almenada, *f.*
battue, *s.* batida, *f.*; matanza, *f.*
bauble, *s.* (trifle) chuchería, fruslería, *f.*; (fool's) cetro de bufón,
m.
bauxite, *s.* bauxita, *f.*
Bavarian, *a.* and *s.* bávaro (-ra)
bawd, *s.* alcahueta, celestina, *f.*
bawdy, *a.* obsceno, indecente,
escabroso
bawl, *v.i.* chillar, vocear
bawling, *s.* vocerío, *m.*, chillidos,
m. pl.
bay, *s.* (*geog.*) bahía, *f.*; (small)
abra, *f.*; (*bot.*) laurel, *m.*;

(horse) bayo, *m.*; (howl) aullido,
m.; (*arch.*) abertura, *f.*; (*r.w.*)
andén, *m. a.* (of horses) bayo,
isabelino. *v.i.* aullar. **at bay,**
en jaque, acorralado. **sick-bay,**
enfermería, *f.* **to keep at bay,**
tener a distancia; tener alejado;
entretener. **bay rum,** ron de
malagueta, *m.* **bay window,**
ventana salediza, *f.*
baying, *s.* aullido, *m.*
bayonet, *s.* bayoneta, *f.* *v.t.*
herir o matar con bayoneta.
fixed b., bayoneta calada, *f.*
b. charge, carga de bayoneta, *f.*
b. thrust, bayonetazo, *m.*
bazaar, *s.* bazar, *m.*
be, *v.i.* ser; (of position, place,
state, temporariness) estar;
(exist) existir; (in impersonal
expressions) haber; (of expressions concerning the weather and
time) hacer; (remain) quedar;
(leave alone) dejar; (do) hacer;
(of one's health) estar; (of feeling
cold, hot, afraid, etc. and of
years of one's age) tener; (live)
vivir; (belong) ser (de), pertenecer (a); (matter, concern)
importar (a); (happen) ocurrir,
suceder; (find oneself) hallarse,
encontrarse, estar; (arrive) llegar
(a); (cost) costar; (be worth)
valer; (celebrate, hold) cele-
brarse, tener lugar; (forming
continuous tense with present
participle active or passive)
estar; (with past participle forming passive) ser (this construction is often replaced by reflexive form when no ambiguity
is entailed); (with infinitive expressing duty, intention) haber
de; (must) tener que. **He is a
soldier** (doctor, etc.), Él es
soldado (médico, etc.). **He is on
guard,** Él está de guardia.
They were at the door (in
the house, etc.), Estaban a
la puerta (en la casa, etc.).
I am writing a letter, Estoy
escribiendo una carta (but this
form is often replaced by a
simple tense, e.g. escribo...). **It
remains to be written,** Queda
por escribir. **What is to be
done?** ¿Qué hay que hacer?
Woe is me! ¡Ay de mí! **to be
hot** (cold), (of things) estar

caliente (frío); (of weather) hacer calor (frío); (of persons) tener calor (frío). **How is John?** He is well, ¿Cómo está Juan? Está bien de salud. It is daylight, Es de día. It is cloudy, Está nublado. She is 10, Ella tiene diez años. They are afraid, Tienen miedo. I am to go there to-morrow, He de ir allí mañana. What is to be will be, Lo que tiene que ser será. If John were to come we could go into the country, Si viniera Juan podríamos ir al campo. Be that as it may, Sea como sea. It is seven years since we saw him, Hace siete años que no le vemos. We have been here for three years, Hace tres años que estamos aquí, or Llevamos tres años aquí. There is or there are, Hay. There will be many people, Habrá mucha gente. There were many people, Había mucha gente. There are many people, Hay mucha gente. It is three miles to the next village, Estamos a tres millas del pueblo próximo. So be it! Así sea. Your pen is not to be seen, Tu pluma no se ve. It is to be hoped that . . ., Se espera que ¡ . . ; ¡Ojalá qué! The door is open, La puerta está abierta. The door was opened by Mary, La puerta fué abierta por María. to be about to, estar por; (of a more imminent action) estar para, estar a punto de. to be in, estar dentro; estar en casa. to be off, marcharse, irse. Be off! ¡Márchate! ¡Vete!; ¡Fuera! to be out, estar fuera; haber salido; no estar en casa; (of a light, etc.) estar apagado. to be up, estar levantado. to be up to, proyectar, traer entre manos; urdir, maquinar

beach, s. playa, f.; costa, f. v.t. (a boat) encallar en la costa. b. shoes, playeras, f. pl. b. suit, vestido de playa, m.

beacon, s. (lighthouse) faro, m.; (buoy) baliza, f.; (watch-tower) atalaya, f.; (fig.) guía, f. v.t. iluminar. b. fire, almenara, f.

bead, s. cuenta, f.; (of glass) abalorio, m.; (drop) gota, f.; (arch.) perla, f.; (bubble) burbuja, f.; (foam) espuma, f.; pl. beads, rosario, m. v.t. adornar con abalorios. to tell one's beads, rezar el rosario. b. work, abalorio, m.

beading, s. abalorio, m.; (arch.) friso, listón, m.

beadle, s. bedel, m.

beagle, s. perro sabueso, m.

beak, s. pico, m.; punta, f.; (naut.) espolón, m. to tap with the b., picotear

beaked, a. que tiene pico; (in compounds) de . . . pico

beaker, s. copa, f.; (chem.) vaso de precipitado, m.

beam, s. (arch.) madero, m., viga, f.; (width of a ship) manga, f.; (of a balance) palanca, f.; (of a plough) cama, f.; (of light) rayo, destello, m.; (phys.) rayo, m.; (smile) sonrisa brillante, f.; pl. beams, (of a building) envigado, m.; (of a ship) baos, m. pl. main b., (arch.) viga maestra, f. on her b.-ends, de costado; (fig.) arruinado; en la miseria. b. feather, astil, m. b. of light, rayo de luz, haz de luz, m.

beam, v.t. lanzar, emitir; difundir. v.i. brillar, fulgurar, destellar; estar radiante, estar rebosando de alegría

beaming, a. brillante; radiante

bean, s. haba, f.; judía, alubia, f.; (of coffee) grano, m. broad b., haba, f. French, haricot; kidney b., judía, f. string b., judía verde, f. b. field, habar, m.

bear, s. (zool.) oso, m.; (she-bear) osa, f.; (Stock Exchange) bajista, m. and f. Great B., (ast.) Osa Mayor, f., Septentrión, m. Little B., (ast.) Osa Menor, f. polar b., oso blanco, m. b.-cub, osezno, m. bear's den, osera, f. b.-garden, patio de osos, m.; (fam.) merienda de negros, f. b.-hunting, caza de osos, f. b.-like, osuno. b.-pit, recinto de los osos, m.

bear, v.t. and v.i. (carry) llevar; (show) ostentar; (company, etc.) hacer; (profess) profesar; (of spite, etc. and of relation) guardar; (have) tener; (fruit) dar; (give birth to) parir; (support) sostener; (endure) aguantar; (suffer) padecer, sufrir; (tolerate) tolerar, sufrir; (a strain, an operation, etc.) resistir; (lean on) apoyarse en; (experience) experimentar; (produce) producir, dar; (enjoy) disfrutar de; (use) usar; (impel) empujar; (occupy, hold) ocupar; (go) dirigirse. It was suddenly. borne in on them that ..., De pronto vieron claro que . . . I cannot b. any more, No puedo más. We cannot b. him, No podemos aguantarle, No podemos sufrirle. His language won't b. repeating, Su lenguaje no puede repetirse. to bring to b., ejercer (presión, etc.). to b. a grudge, guardar rencor (a), tener ojeriza (a). to b. arms, llevar armas; servir en el ejército o la milicia. to b. company, hacer compañía (a), acompañar (a). to b. in mind, tener en cuenta, tener presente; acordarse de. to b. oneself, conducirse, portarse. to b. to the right, ir hacia la derecha. to b. witness, atestiguar. to b. away, llevarse; ganar. to b. down, hundir; derribar; bajar. to b. down on, avanzar rápidamente hacia; correr hacia; (naut.) arribar sobre; (attack) caer sobre. to b. in, llevar adentro. to b. off, llevarse; ganar; (naut.) apartarse de la costa. to b. on, upon, apoyarse en; (refer to) referirse a. to b. out, llevar fuera; confirmar; apoyar; justificar. to b. up, llevar arriba; llevar a la cumbre (de); sostener; (recover) cobrar ánimo; (against) resistir; hacer frente a. to b. with, soportar; sufrir; aguantar; llevar con paciencia; ser indulgente con

bearable, a. soportable; aguantable; tolerable

beard, s. barba, f.; (of cereals) raspa, arista, f. v.t. desafiar. thick b., barba bien poblada, f.

bearded, a. con barba, barbudo

beardless, a. desbarbado, lampiño

bearer, s. llevador (-ra), portador (-ra); (of a bier) andero, m.; (com.) dador, portador, m. good b., (agr.) árbol fructífero, m. to b., (com.) al portador

bearing, s. porte, m.; postura, f.; presencia, f.; conducta, f.; aspecto, m.; relación, f.; (meaning) significación, f.; (naut.) demora, orientación, f.; (mech.) cojinete, soporte, m.; (endurance) tolerancia, f.; pl. bearings, (way) camino, m.; (her.) escudo de armas, m. to get one's bearings, orientarse; encontrar el camino. to lose one's bearings, desorientarse; perderse. to have a b. on, tener relación con; tener que ver con; influir en

bearish, a. osuno; rudo, áspero

bearskin, s. piel de oso, f.; birretina, f.

beast, s. animal, bruto, m.; cuadrúpedo, m.; (cattle) res, f.; bestia, f. wild b., fiera, f. b. of burden, acémila, bestia de carga, f. b. of prey, animal de rapiña, m.

beastliness, s. bestialidad, brutalidad, f.; obscenidad, f.

beastly, a. bestial, brutal; obsceno; (fam.) horrible

beat, s. latido, m., pulsación, f.; golpe, m.; (of a drum) toque (de tambor), m.; (of a clock) tictac, m.; sonido repetido, m.; vibración, f.

beat, v.t. and v.i. batir; golpear; (thrash) pegar, dar una paliza (a); (to remove dust, etc.) sacudir; (shake) agitar; (the wings) aletear; (hunting) batir; (excel) exceder, superar; ganar; (defeat) vencer; (of the rain, etc.) azotar; (a drum) tocar; (of the sun) batir, dar golpes; (throb) latir, palpitar, pulsar. to b. about the bush, andarse por las ramas. to stop beating about the bush, dejarse de historias. to b. a retreat, (mil.) emprender la retirada; huir. to b. black and blue, moler a palos. to b. hollow, vencer completamente; ganar fácilmente; aventajar con mucho. to b. it, (fam.) escaparse corriendo. to b. time, (mus.) llevar el compás; triunfar sobre la vejez. to b. to it, (*fam.*) tomar la delantera. to b. against, golpear contra; chocar contra. to b. back, rechazar; (sobs, etc.) ahogar; reprimir. to b. down, (prices) regatear; (of the sun) caer de plomo; reducir; suprimir; destruir. to b. off, rechazar; echar a un lado. to b. out, hacer salir; (metals) batir; (a tune) llevar el compás (de). to b. up, (*cul.*) batir; (a mattress) mullir; asaltar; maltratar

beaten, *a.* (of paths) trillado; (conquered) vencido; (of metals) batido; (dejected) deprimido; (trite) trivial, vulgar

beater, *s.* batidor, *m.*; (for carpets) sacudidor (de alfombras), *m.*; (*cul.*) batidor, *m.*

beatific, *a.* beatífico

beatification, *s.* beatificación, *f.*

beatify, *v.t.* beatificar

beating, *s.* batimiento, *m.*; vencimiento, *m.*; (thrashing) paliza, *f.*; (of the heart, etc.) palpitación, *f.*, latido, *m.*; (of metals) batida, *f.*; (of a drum) rataplán, toque de tambor, *m.*; (of waves) embate, *m.*; (of wings) aleteo, aletazo, *m.*

beatitude, *s.* beatitud, *f.*

beau, *s.* galán, *m.*; (fop) petimetre, *m.*

beautiful, *a.* bello, lindo, hermoso; magnífico; excelente; exquisito; elegante; encantador, delicioso

beautifully, *adv.* bellamente; (richly) ricamente; admirablemente; magníficamente; elegantemente

beautify, *v.t.* embellecer; hermosear; adornar. to b. oneself, arreglarse, ponerse elegante

beautifying, *s.* embellecimiento, *m.*; adorno, *m.*

beauty, *s.* belleza, hermosura, lindeza, *f.*; magnificencia, *f.*; excelencia, *f.*; elegancia, *f.*; encanto, *m.*; (belle) beldad, Venus, *f.* to lose one's b., desmejorarse, perder su hermosura. b. contest, concurso de belleza, *m.* b. parlour, salón de belleza, instituto de belleza, *m.* b. sleep, el primer sueño de la noche. b. spot, lunar, *m.*; lunar postizo,

m.; (place) sitio hermoso, *m.* b. treatment, másaje facial, *m.*

beaver, *s.* castor, *m.*; (hat) sombrero de copa, *m.*; (of helmet) babera, *f.*

becalmed, *a.* (of ships) encalmado, sin viento

because, *conjunc.* porque. b. of, debido a, a causa de

beckon, *v.i.* and *v.t.* hacer señas (a); llamar por señas

become, *v.i.* volverse; llegar a ser, venir a ser; convertirse en; ponerse; hacerse; (befit) convenir; (suit) ir bien (a), favorecer. He became red, Se enrojeció. The hat becomes you, El sombrero te va bien. He became king, Llegó a ser rey. What has b. of her? ¿Qué es de ella?; (Where is she?) ¿Qué se ha hecho de ella?

becoming, *a.* propio; correcto; decoroso; (suitable) conveniente; (of dress) que favorece, que va bien. This dress is b. to you, Este vestido te favorece

becomingly, *adv.* decorosamente

becomingness, *s.* propiedad, *f.*; corrección, *f.*, decoro, *m.*; (of a dress, etc.) elegancia, *f.*

bed, *s.* cama, *f.*, lecho, *m.*; (of sea) fondo, *m.*; (of river) cauce, *m.*; (*geol.*) yacimiento, *m.*; (in a garden) cuadro, macizo (de jardín), *m.*; (of a machine) asiento, *m.*; (of a building) cimiento, *m.*; (*fig.*) fundamento, *m.*, base, *f.* *v.t.* (plants) plantar; (fix) fijar, poner. double bed, cama de matrimonio, *f.* single bed, cama de monja, *f.* in bed, en cama. to be gone to bed, haber ido a la cama. to be in bed, estar acostado. to get into bed, meterse en cama. to get out of bed, levantarse de la cama. to go to bed, acostarse, ir a la cama. to make the beds, hacer las camas. to put to bed, acostar. to stay in bed, quedarse en cama, guardar cama. bed-bug, chinche, *f.* bed-clothes, ropa de cama, *f.* bed-cover, cubrecama, colcha, *f.* bed-head, cabecera, *f.* bed-pan, silleta, *f.* bed-sore, úlcera de decúbito, *f.*

bedaub, bedazzle. See daub, dazzle

bedchamber, *s.* dormitorio, *m.*, alcoba, *f.*

bedded, *a.* con . . . cama(s). **a double-b. room,** un cuarto con dos camas; un cuarto con cama de matrimonio

bedding, *s.* ropa de cama, *f.*; cama para el ganado, *f.*

bedeck, *v.t.* embellecer, adornar, engalanar

bedew, *v.t.* rociar

bedfellow, *s.* compañero (-ra) de cama

bedim, *v.t.* obscurecer, ofuscar; cegar

bedizen, *v.t.* aderezar, adornar

bedlam, *s.* belén, manicomio, *m.*; (*fig.*) babel, *m.*

bedouin, *a.* and *s.* beduino (-na)

bedraggled, *a.* mojado y sucio

bedridden, *a.* postrado en cama, inválido

bedrock, *s.* lecho de roca, *m.*; (*fig.*) principios fundamentales, fundamentos, *m. pl.*

bedroom, *s.* cuarto de dormir, dormitorio, *m.*, habitación, *f.*

bedside, *s.* lado de cama, *m.*; cabecera, *f.* **b. manner,** mano izquierda, diplomacia, *f.* **b.-table,** mesa de noche, *f.*

bedspread, *s.* sobrecama, colcha, *f.*

bedstead, *s.* cama, *f.*

bedtime, *s.* hora de acostarse, *f.*

bee, *s.* abeja, *f.*; (meeting) reunión, *f.* *a.* abejuno. **queen bee,** rey, *m.*, abeja maestra, *f.* **to have a bee in one's bonnet,** tener una manía (or idea fija). **to make a bee-line for,** ir directamente a. **bee-eater,** (*orn.*) abejaruco, *m.* **bee hive,** colmena, *f.*; abejar, *m.*; **bee-keeper,** apicultor (-ra), colmenero (-ra), abejero (-ra). **bee's wax,** cera de abeja, *f.*

beech, *s.* haya, *f.* **plantation of b. trees,** hayal, *m.* **b.-nut,** hayuco, *m.*

beechmast, *s.* hayuco, *m.*

beef, *s.* carne de vaca, *f.*; (flesh) carne, *f.*; (strength) fuerza, *f.* **roast b.,** rosbif, *m.* **b.-tea,** caldo, *m.*

beefeater, *s.* alabardero, *m.*

beefsteak, *s.* biftec, bistec, *m.*

beer, *s.* cerveza, *f.* **b. barrel,** barril de cerveza, *m.* **b.-house,** cervecería, *f.* **b. mug,** jarro para la cerveza, *m.*

beery, *a.* de cerveza; (tipsy) achispado

beet, *s.* remolacha, *f.* **b. sugar,** azúcar de remolacha, *m.*

beetle, *s.* escarabajo, *m.* **b.-browed,** cejijunto

beetling, *a.* saledizo, pendiente

beetroot, *s.* remolacha, *f.*

befall, *v.i.* acontecer, suceder, ocurrir. *v.t.* ocurrir (a), acontecer (a)

befeathered, *a.* plumado; adornado con plumas

befit, *v.t.* convenir (a), ser digno de

befitting, *a.* conveniente, apropiado; digno; oportuno

beflower, *v.t.* cubrir de flores

before, *adv.* delante; (of time), antes, anteriormente; (of order) antes; (already) ya. *prep.* delante de; en frente de; (of time, order) ante; (in the presence of) ante, en presencia de; (rather than) antes de. **b. going,** antes de marcharse. **B. I did it,** Antes de que lo hiciera; Antes de hacerlo. **as never b.,** como nunca. **b. long,** en breve, dentro de poco. **b.-mentioned,** antes citado

beforehand, *adv.* previamente, de antemano

befoul, *v.t.* ensuciar; (*fig.*) manchar, difamar

befriend, *v.t.* proteger, ayudar, favorecer, amparar

beg, *v.t.* pedir, implorar, suplicar. *v.t.* mendigar, pordiosear; vivir de limosna. **I beg to propose,** Me permito proponer; Tengo el gusto de proponer; (the health of) Brindo a la salud de. **I beg your pardon!** ¡Vd. dispense!; (when passing in front of anyone, etc.) Con permiso; (in conversation for repetition of a word) ¿Cómo? **to beg the question,** evitar, dejar a un lado

beget, *v.t.* procrear, engendrar; causar; suscitar

begetter, *s.* procreador (-ra); creador (-ra)

begetting, *s.* procreación, *f.*; origen, *m.*, causa, *f.*

beggar, *s.* mendigo (-ga), pordiosero (-ra). *v.t.* empobrecer;
arruinar. **to b. description,** no
haber palabras para describir
beggarliness, *s.* mendicidad, *f.*;
pobreza, *f.*
beggarly, *a.* miserable, pobre
beggary, *s.* miseria, pobreza, *f.*
begging, *a.* mendicante, pordiosero. *s.* mendicidad, *f.*, pordioseo, *m.* **to go b.,** andar
mendigando. **b. letter,** carta
pidiendo dinero, *f.*
begin, *v.t.* and *v.i.* empezar;
comenzar; iniciar; (a conversation) entablar; (open) abrir;
inaugurar; tener su principio;
nacer. **to b. to,** empezar a; (start
on) ponerse a; (with laughing,
etc.) romper a. **to b. with,** empezar por; para empezar, en
primer lugar
beginner, *s.* principiante (-ta);
(novice) novato (-ta); iniciador
(-ra); autor (-ra)
beginning, *s.* principio, comienzo,
m.; origen, *m.* **at the b.,** al
principio; (of the month) a
principios (de). **from the b.
to the end,** desde el principio
hasta el fin, (*fam.*) de pe a pa.
in the b., al principio. **to make
a b.,** comenzar, empezar
begone, *interj.* ¡fuera! ¡márchate!
¡vete!
begonia, *s.* begonia, *f.*
begrime, *v.t.* tiznar
begrudge, *v.t.* envidiar
beguile, *v.t.* engañar; defraudar;
(time) entretener; (charm) encantar, embelesar
beguilement, *s.* engaño, *m.*; (of
time) entretenimiento, *m.*;
(charm) encanto, *m.*
beguilingly, *adv.* encantadora-
mente
behalf, *s.* (preceded by on or
upon) por; (from) de parte (de);
a favor (de); en defensa (de)
behave, *v.i.* (oneself) conducirse,
portarse; (act) obrar, proceder.
to b. badly, portarse mal;
obrar mal. **B.!** ¡Pórtate bien!
behaviour, *s.* conducta, *f.*; comportamiento, *m.*; proceder, *m.*;
(manner) modales, *m. pl.*; (biol.)
reacción, *f.*
behaviourism, *s.* (*psy.*) behavio-
rismo, *m.*

behead, *v.t.* decapitar, descabezar
beheading, *s.* decapitación, *f.*
behest, *s.* precepto, mandato, *m.*
behind, *adv.* detrás; por detrás;
atrás; hacia atrás; en pos; (of
time and order) después; (late
and in arrears) con retraso; (old-
fashioned) atrasado. *prep.* detrás
de; por detrás de; inferior a;
menos avanzado que. *s.* (*fam.*)
trasero, *m.* **from b.,** por
detrás. **to be b. time,** retrasarse; llegar tarde. **b. the scenes,**
entre bastidores. **b. the times,**
(*fig.*) atrasado de noticias; pasado
de moda
behindhand, *a.* (out of date)
atrasado; (late) tardío; *adv.* con
retraso
behold, *v.t.* ver, mirar, contemplar; presenciar. *interj.* ¡he
aquí! ¡mira!
beholden, *a.* obligado, agradecido
beholder, *s.* espectador (-ra).
the beholders, los que lo
presenciaban
beholding, *s.* contemplación,
vista, *f.*
behoof, *s.* provecho, *m.*
behove, *v.t.* incumbir, tocar,
corresponder
beige, *s.* beige, color arena, *m.*
being, *s.* existencia, *f.*; operación,
f.; ser, *m.*; (spirit) alma, *f.*,
espíritu, *m.*; esencia, *f.* **human
b.,** ser humano, *m.*, alma viviente,
f. **for the time b.,** por ahora,
por el momento
bejewel, *v.t.* enjoyar, adornar
con joyas
belabour, *v.t.* apalear, golpear
belaced, *a.* adornado con encaje
belated, *a.* tardío
belay, *v.t.* amarrar
belch, *s.* eructo, *m.*; detonación,
f.; (of a volcano) erupción, *f.*
v.i. eructar. *v.t.* vomitar;
(curses, etc.) escupir; despedir,
arrojar
belching, *s.* eructación, *f.*; (of
smoke, etc.) vómito, *m.*, emisión,
f.
beldam, *s.* bruja, *f.*; vieja, *f.*
beleaguer, *v.t.* sitiar
beleaguerer, *s.* sitiador, *m.*
belfry, *s.* campanario, *m.*
Belgian, *a.* and *s.* belga (*m.* and *f.*)
belie, *v.t.* desmentir, contradecir;
defraudar

belief, *s.* creencia, *f.*; fe, *f.*; opinión, *f.*, parecer; *m.*; (trust) confianza, *f.* **in the b. that,** creyendo que, en la creencia de que

believable, *a.* creíble

believe, *v.t.* and *v.i.* creer; opinar, ser de la opinión, parecer (a uno); confiar, tener confianza. **I b. not,** Creo que no, Me parece que no. **I b. so,** Creo que sí, Me parece que sí. **to make (a person) b.,** hacer (a uno) creer. **to b. in,** creer en; confiar en, tener confianza en

believer, *s.* persona que cree, *f.*; creyente, *m.* and *f.*

belittle, *v.t.* achicar; conceder poca importancia a

bell, *s.* campana, *f.*; (hand-bell) campanilla, *f.*; (small, round) cascabel, *m.*; (on cows, etc.) cencerro, *m.*, esquila, *f.*; (electric, push, or bicycle) timbre, *m.*; (jester's) cascabeles, *m. pl.*; (cry of stag) bramido, *m. v.i.* poner un cascabel (a). *v.i.* (stags) bramar, roncar. **To bear away the b.,** (*fig.*) llevarse la palma. **to ring the b.,** tocar el timbre; agitar la campanilla. **to ring the bells,** tocar las campanas. **to b. the cat,** poner el cascabel al gato. **b.-boy,** botones, mozo de hotel, *m.* **b.-clapper,** badajo, *m.* **b.-flower,** campanilla, *f.* **b.-founder,** campanero, *m.* **b.-mouthed,** abocinado. **b.-pull,** tirador de campanilla, *m.* **b.-ringer,** campanero, *m.* **b.-shaped,** campanudo. **b.-tent,** pabellón, *m.* **b. tower,** campanario, *m.*

belladonna, *s.* belladona, *f.*

belle, *s.* beldad, *f.*

belles-lettres, *s. pl.* bellas letras, *f. pl.*

bellicose, *a.* belicoso, agresivo

bellicosity, *s.* belicosidad, *f.*

belligerency, *s.* beligerancia, *f.*

belligerent, *a.* beligerante; belicoso, guerrero. *s.* beligerante, *m.* and *f.*

bellow, *s.* (shout) grito, *m.*; rugido, bramido, *m.*; (of guns) trueno, *m. v.i.* gritar, vociferar; rugir, bramar; tronar.

bellowing, *s.* See **bellow**

bellows, *s.* fuelle, *m.*

belly, *s.* vientre, *m.*, barriga, *f.*; (of a jug, etc.) panza, *f.*; estómago, *m.*; (womb) seno, *m. v.t.* hinchar. *v.i.* hincharse

belong, *v.i.* pertenecer (a); tocar (a), incumbir (a); (to a place) ser de; residir en

belongings, *s. pl.* efectos, *m. pl.*; posesiones, *f. pl.*; (luggage) equipaje, *m.*

beloved, *a.* muy amado, muy querido. *s.* querido (-da)

below, *adv.* abajo; (under) debajo; (further on) más abajo; (in hell) en el infierno; (in this world) en este mundo, aquí abajo. *prep.* bajo; (underneath) debajo de; (after) después de; (unworthy of) indigno de; inferior a. **The valley lay b. us,** El valle se extendía a nuestros pies. **b. zero,** bajo cero

belt, *s.* cinturón, *m.*; (of a horse) cincha, *f.*; (corset) faja, *f.*; (geog.) zona, *f.*; (of a machine) correa (de transmisión), *f.*

bemoan, *v.t.* deplorar, lamentar

bemoaning, *s.* lamentación, *f.*

bemuse, *v.t.* confundir, desconcertar

bench, *s.* banco, *m.*; (with a back) escaño, *m.*; mesa de trabajo, *f.*; (carpenter's, shoemaker's, in a boat, in parliament) banco, *m.*; (judges) tribunal, *m.*

bend, *s.* corvadura, curva, vuelta, *f.*; (in a river, street) recodo, *m.*; (in a motor road) viraje, *m.*; (of the knee) corva, *f.*; (in a pipe) codo, *m.*; (naut.) nudo, *m.*; (her.) banda, *f.* **sheet b.,** (knot) nudo de tejedor, *m.*

bend, *v.t.* encorvar; doblegar; torcer; (the head) bajar; (the body) inclinar; (steps) dirigir, encaminar; (the mind) aplicarse, dedicarse. *v.i.* encorvarse; doblegarse; torcerse; (arch) arquear; inclinarse. **to b. the knee,** arrodillarse. **on bended knee,** de rodillas. **to b. back,** *v.t.* redoblar. *v.i.* redoblarse; inclinarse hacia atrás. **to b. down,** agacharse; inclinarse. **to b. forward,** inclinarse hacia delante. **to b. over,** inclinarse encima de

bendable, *a.* que puede doblarse; plegadizo; flexible

bending, s. doblamiento, m.; flexión, f.; inclinación, f. a. doblado; inclinado

beneath, adv. abajo; debajo; (at one's feet) a los pies de uno. prep. bajo; debajo de; al pie de; (unworthy, inferior) indigno. **He married b. him,** Se casó fuera de su clase

Benedictine, a. benedictino. s. benedictino, m.; (liqueur) benedictino, m.

benediction, s. bendición, f.; gracia divina, merced, f.

benefaction, s. beneficiación, f.; buena obra, f.; beneficio, favor, m.

benefactor, s. bienhechor, m.; protector, m.; patrono, m.; fundador, m.

benefactress, s. bienhechora, f.; protectora, f.; patrona, f.; fundadora, f.

benefice, s. beneficio eclesiástico, m., prebenda, f.

beneficence, s. beneficiencia, caridad, f., buenas obras, f. pl.

beneficent, a. benéfico, caritativo

beneficial, a. beneficioso; provechoso, útil

beneficiary, s. beneficiado (-da), beneficiario (-ia)

benefit, s. beneficio, bien, m.; provecho, m., utilidad, f.; (favour) favor, m.; (theat.) beneficio, m.; (help) ayuda, f., servicio, m. v.t. beneficiar; aprovechar; (improve) mejorar. v.i. (with by) sacar provecho de; ganar. **for the b. of,** para; en pro de, a favor de. **b. society,** sociedad benéfica, f.

benevolence, s. benevolencia, bondad, f.; liberalidad, f.; caridad, f.; favor, m.

benevolent, a. benévolo; bondadoso; caritativo. **b. society,** sociedad de beneficencia, f.

benevolently, adv. benignamente, con benevolencia

Bengali, a. and s. bengalí (m. and f.)

benighted, a. sorprendido por la noche; (fig.) ignorante

benign, benignant, a. benigno

benignity, s. benignidad, f.

benignly, adv. benignamente

bent, s. talento, m.; inclinación, afición, f. a. torcido, encorvado; resuelto

benumb. See numb

benzene, s. benceno, benzol, m.

benzine, s. bencina, f.

bequeath, v.t. legar, dejar (en el testamento); transmitir

bequest, s. legado, m.

Berber, a. and s. bereber (m. and f.)

bereave, v.t. privar (de), quitar; arrebatar; afligir. **the bereaved parents,** los afligidos padres

bereavement, s. privación, f.; (by death) pérdida, f.; aflicción, f.

bereft, a. privado (de); desamparado; indefenso. **utterly b.,** completamente solo

beret, s. boina, f.

bergamot, s. (bot.) bergamota, f.

beri-beri, s. beri-beri, m.

Berlin, a. and s. (of or from) berlinés (-esa). s. (carriage) berlina, f.

Bernard, s. Bernardo, m. **St. B. dog,** perro de San Bernardo, m.

Bernardine, a. and s. bernardo (-da)

Bernese, a. and s. bernés (-esa)

berried, a. con bayas

berry, s. baya, f.; (of coffee, etc.) fruto, m. v.i. dar bayas; coger bayas

berth, s. (bed) litera, f.; (cabin) camarote, m.; (anchorage) anclaje, fondeadero, m.; (job) empleo, m. v.t. (a ship) fondear. **to give a wide b. to,** (naut.) ponerse a resguardo de; apartarse mucho de; evitar

beryl, s. berilo, m.

beseech, v.t. suplicar, rogar, implorar; (ask for) pedir con ahínco

beseeching, a. suplicante, implorante. s. súplica, f.; ruego, m.

beseechingly, adv. suplicantemente

beset, v.t. atacar, acosar; perseguir; (block) obstruir; (surround) rodear, cercar

besetting, a. usual, frecuente; obsesionante

beside, besides, prep. al lado de; cerca de; (compared with) en comparación de, comparado con; (in addition) además de; aparte de; excepto. *adv.* además, también. to be beside oneself, estar fuera de sí

besiege, *v.t.* sitiar; (assail) asaltar, asediar; (surround) rodear; importunar

besieged, *s.* sitiado (-da)

besieger, *s.* sitiador, *m.*

besieging, *a.* sitiador. *s.* sitio, asalto, *m.*; asedio, *m.*, importunación, *f.*

besmear, *v.t.* embadurnar, ensuciar

besom, *s.* escoba, *f.*

besotted, *a.* estúpido; embrutecido; atontado

bespangled, *a.* adornado con lentejuelas; brillante (con); (studded) salpicado (de)

bespatter, *v.t.* manchar; derramar; salpicar

bespeak, *v.t.* reservar; (goods) encargar; (signify) demostrar, indicar, significar; (*poet.*) hablar

besprinkle, *v.t.* rociar

best, *a. sup.* of good and well, mejor; el (la) mejor, *m.* (*f.*), los (las) mejores, *m. pl.* (*f. pl.*). *adv.* mejor; el mejor; (most) más. As b. I can, Como mejor pueda. at the b., cuando más, en el mejor caso. He did it for the b., Lo hizo con la mejor intención. the b., lo mejor. to be at one's b., brillar; lucirse. to do one's b., hacer todo lo posible. to get the b. of, llevar la mejor parte de; triunfar de (or sobre). to make the b. of, sacar el mayor provecho de. The next b. thing to do is . . ., Lo mejor que queda ahora por hacer es . . . b. man, padrino de boda, *m.* to be b. man to, apadrinar, ser padrino de. b. seller, libro que se vende más, libro favorito, *m.*

bestial, *a.* bestial

bestiality, *s.* bestialidad, *f.*

bestir (oneself), *v.r.* menearse, moverse; preocuparse; (hurry) darse prisa

bestow, *v.t.* (place) poner; (with upon) conferir, conceder, otorgar; (a present) regalar

bestowal, *s.* puesta, *f.*; otorgamiento, *m.*, concesión, *f.*; (of a present) regalo, *m.*, dádiva, *f.*

bestower, *s.* donador (-ra)

bestride, *v.t.* montar a horcajadas en; poner una pierna en cada lado de; cruzar de un tranco

bestud, *v.t.* tachonar; salpicar

bet, *s.* apuesta, postura, *f.* *v.i.* apostar; (gamble) jugar. What do you bet? ¿Qué apuesta Vd.?

betake (oneself), *v.r.* acudir (a); darse (a); marcharse

betel, *s.* betel, *m.*

bethink (oneself), *v.r.* pensar, reflexionar; (remember) recordar, hacer memoria; ocurrirse

betimes, *adv.* pronto; de buena hora, temprano; con tiempo

betoken, *v.t.* presagiar, prometer; indicar

betray, *v.t.* traicionar; revelar, descubrir; (a woman) seducir; (show) dejar ver

betrayal, *s.* traición, *f.*; (of confidence) abuso (de confianza), *m.*; (of a woman) seducción, *f.*

betrayer, *s.* traidor (-ra)

betroth, *v.t.* desposar(se) con, prometer(se). to be betrothed to, estar desposado con

betrothal, *s.* desposorio, *m.*, esponsales, *m. pl.*; (duration) noviazgo, *m.*

betrothed, *s.* desposado (-da), futuro (-ra)

better, *a. comp.* of good, mejor; superior. *adv.* mejor; más. *v.t.* mejorar; exceder. *s.* apostador (-ra). He has bettered himself, Él ha mejorado su situación. It is b. to . . ., Es mejor . . ., Vale más . . . (followed by infin.). little b., poco mejor; algo mejor; poco más. much b., mucho mejor. our betters, nuestros superiores. so much the b., tanto mejor. the b. to, para mejor. to be b., ser mejor; (of health) estar mejor. to get b., mejorar. to get the b. of, triunfar sobre, vencer. b. half, (*fam.*) media naranja, *f.* b. off, mejor situado, más acomodado

betterment, *s.* mejora, *f.*, mejoramiento, *m.*; adelantamiento, avance, *m.*

betting, *s.* apuesta, *f.*

bettor, *s.* apostador (-ra)

between, *prep.* entre; en medio de. *adv.* en medio; entre los dos.

far b., a grandes intérvalos.
b. now and then, desde ahora
hasta entonces. b. one thing
and another, entre una cosa y
otra. b. ourselves, entre nosotros. b. whiles, de vez en cuando
bevel, s. bisel, m. v.t. abiselar
beverage, s. brebaje, m., bebida,
f.
bevy, s. grupo, m.; (of birds)
bandada, f.; (of roes) manada, f.
bewail, v.t. lamentar, llorar
bewailing, s. lamentación, f.
beware, v.i. guardarse (de);
cuidar (de); desconfiar (de).
interj. | ¡cuidado! | ¡atención! B. of
imitations! ¡Desconfiad de las
imitaciones!
bewilder, v.t. aturdir, abobar;
dejar perplejo (a); confundir
bewildered, a. aturdido, abobado;
perplejo; confuso
bewildering, a. incomprensible;
complicado
bewilderment, s. aturdimiento,
m.; perplejidad, f.; confusión, f.
bewitch, v.t. hechizar; fascinar,
encantar
bewitching, a. encantador,
hechicero, fascinante. s. em-
brujamiento, encantamiento, m.
bewitchingly, adv. de un modo
encantador
bewitchment, s. See bewitching
bey, s. bey, m.
beyond, prep. más allá de; más
lejos que; (behind) tras, detrás
de; (of time) después de; (fig.)
fuera del alcance de; (without)
fuera de; (above) encima de;
(not including) aparte. adv. más
allá; más lejos; detrás de. b. doubt,
fuera de duda. b. question,
indiscutible. b. the sea, allende
el mar. That is b. me, Eso es
demasiado para mí; Eso no está
en mi mano; Eso está fuera de
mi alcance. the back of b.,
donde Cristo dió las tres voces,
las quimbambas. the B., la
otra vida
bias, s. sesgo, bies, través, m.;
(fig.) prejuicio, m.; parcialidad, f.
v.t. influir; predisponer. to cut
on the b., cortar al sesgo
biassed, a. parcial; tendencioso
bib, s. babero, m.; pechera, f. v.i.
beber mucho, empinar el codo

Bible, s. Biblia, f.
biblical, a. bíblico. b. history,
historia sagrada, f.
bibliographer, s. bibliógrafo (-fa)
bibliographical, a. bibliográfico
bibliography, s. bibliografía, f.
bibliomania, s. bibliomanía, f.
bibliophile, s. bibliófilo, m.
bibulous, a. bebedor, borrachín
bicarbonate, s. bicarbonato, m.
bicentenary, s. segundo centenario, m.
bicephalous, a. bicéfalo
biceps, s. biceps, m.
bichloride, s. bicloruro, m.
bicker, v.i. disputar, altercar;
(of stream, etc.) murmurar,
susurrar; (of flame) bailar, centellear
bickering, s. altercado, argumento, m.
bicycle, s. bicicleta, f. v.i. andar
en bicicleta, ir de bicicleta
bicycling, s. ciclismo, m.
bicyclist, s. biciclista, m. and f.
bid, s. (at auction) postura, f.;
oferta, f. v.t. mandar, ordenar;
invitar a; (at an auction) pujar,
licitar. to make a bid for, (attempt) hacer un esfuerzo para;
procurar. to bid fair, prometer;
dar indicios de; dar esperanzas
de. to bid goodbye to, decir
adiós (a), despedirse de. to bid
welcome, dar la bienvenida (a)
biddable, a. obediente, dócil;
manso
bidder, s. postor, m., pujador
(-ra). the highest b., el mejor
postor
bidding, s. (order) orden, f.;
instrucción, f.; invitación, f.; (at
an auction) postura, licitación, f.
to do a person's b., hacer lo
que se le manda
bide, v.t. aguardar, esperar.
to b. by, (fulfil) cumplir con
bidet, s. bidé, m.
biennial, a. bianual, bienal
bier, s. andas, f. pl.; féretro,
ataúd, m.
bifocal, a. bifocal
bifurcate, v.t. and v.i. bifurcar-
(se)
bifurcation, s. bifurcación, f.
big, a. grande; grueso; (grown
up) mayor; (tall) alto; voluminoso; (vast) extenso, vasto; (full)
lleno (de); (with young) preñada;

importante. **to talk big,** echarla de importante. **big-boned,** huesudo. **big-end,** (*aut.*) biela, *f.* **big game,** caza mayor, *f.* **big gun,** (*fam.*) pájaro gordo, *m.*

bigamist, *s.* bígamo (-ma)

bigamous, *a.* bígamo

bigamy, *s.* bigamia, *f.*

bight, *s.* (in a rope) vuelta (de un cabo), *f.*; (bay)·ensenada, *f.*

bigness, *s.* grandor, *m.*; gran tamaño, *m.*; altura, *f.*; (tallness of a person) gran talle, *m.*; (vastness) extensión, *f.*; importancia, *f.*

bigot, *s.* fanático (-ca)

bigoted, *a.* fanático, intolerante

bigotry, *s.* fanatismo, *m.*, intolerancia, *f.*

bilateral, *a.* bilateral

bilberry, *s.* arándano, *m.*

bile, *s.* bilis, hiel, *f.*; mal humor, *m.*, cólera, *f.*

bilge, *s.* (*naut.*) pantoque, *m.*, sentina, *f.* **b. water,** agua de pantoque, *f.*

bilingual, *a.* bilingüe

bilious, *a.* bilioso

biliousness, *s.* biliosidad, *f.*

bill, *s.* (parliamentary) proyecto de ley, *m.*; (*law*) escrito, *m.*; (*com.*) cuenta, *f.*; (poster) cartel, *m.*; (programme) programa, *m.*; (cast) repertorio, *m.*; (bank note) billete de banco, *m.*; (of a bird) pico, *m.*; (for pruning) podadera, *f.* **due b.,** (*com.*) abonaré, *m.* **Stick no bills!** Se prohíbe fijar carteles. **b. of exchange,** letra de cambio, *f.* **b. of fare,** lista de platos, *f.*; (*fig.*) programa, *m.* **b. of health,** patente de sanidad, *f.* **b. of lading,** conocimiento de embarque, *m.* **b. of rights,** declaración de derechos, *f.* **b. of sale,** contrato de venta, *m.*, carta de venta, *f.* **b.-broker,** agente de bolsa, agente de cambio, *m.* **b.-poster,** fijador de carteles, cartelero, *m.*

bill, *v.t.* anunciar; publicar; poner en el programa; fijar carteles en. **to b. and coo,** (doves) arrullar; (*fam.*) besuquearse

billed, *a.* (in compounds) de pico

billet, *s.* alojamiento, *m.*; (of wood) pedazo (de leña), *m.*; (job)

empleo, destino, *m.* *v.t.* alojar (en or con)

billeting, *s.* alojamiento, *m.* **b. officer,** (*mil.*) aposentador, *m.*; oficial encargado de encontrar alojamiento, *m.*

billiards, *s. pl.* billar, *m.* **billiard ball,** bola de billar, *f.* **billiard cue,** taco,.*m.* **billiard cushion,** baranda de la mesa de billar, *f.* **billiard marker,** marcador, *m.* **billiard match,** partida de billar, *f.* **billiard player,** jugador (-ra) de billar. **billiard room,** sala de billar, *f.* **billiard table,** mesa de billar, *f.*

billion, *s.* billón, *m.*; (U.S.A. and France) mil millones, *m. pl.*

billionth, *a.* billonésimo; (U.S.A. and France) milmillonésimo

billow, *s.* oleada, *f.*; (*poet.*) ola, *f.*; (*fig.*) onda, *f.* *v.i.* hincharse, encresparse; ondular

billowy, *a.* ondulante, ondeante

bimetallism, *s.* bimetalismo, *m.*

bi-monthly, *a.* bimestral

bin, *s.* hucha, *f.*, arcón, *m.*; recipiente, *m.*; depósito, *m.*; cajón, *m.*; (for wine) estante, *m.*

binary, *a.* binario

bind, *v.t.* atar; unir, ligar; amarrar; (in sheaves) agavillar; (bandage) vendar; sujetar; fijar; aprisionar; (a book) encuadernar; (*sew.*) ribetear; (oblige) obligar; comprometer; (constipate) estreñir; contratar (como aprendiz). **I feel bound to,** Me siento obligado a. **to b. over,** obligar a comparecer ante el juez

binder, *s.* encuadernador (-ra); (*agr.*) agavilladora, *f.*

binding, *a.* válido, valedero; obligatorio; (*med.*) constrictivo. *s.* atadura, ligación, *f.*; (of books) encuadernación, *f.*; (*sew.*) ribete, *m.*

bindweed, *s.* (*bot.*) enredadera del campo, *f.*

binge, *s.* parranda, juerga, *f.* **to go on the b.,** ir de parranda, ir de picos pardos, ir de juerga

binnacle, *s.* (*naut.*) bitácora, *f.*

binocular, *a.* binocular. *s. pl.* **binoculars,** binóculos, gemelos, *m. pl.*

binomial, *a. and s.* binomio (*m.*)

bio-chemist, s. bioquímico, m.
bio-chemistry, s. bioquímica, f.
biogenesis, s. biogéncsis, f.
biographer, s. biógrafo (-ía)
biographical, a. biográfico
biography, s. biografía, vida, f.
biological, a. biológico
biologist, s. biólogo, m.
biology, s. biología, f.
bipartite, a. bipartido
biped, s. bípedo, m. a. bípedo, bípede
biplane, s. biplano, m.
birch, s. (bot.) abedul, m.; (rod) vara, f. a. de abedul. v.t. pegar con una vara, dar una paliza (a)
bird, s. pájaro, m.; ave, f. Birds of a feather flock together, Cada cual se arrima a su cada cual. hen b., pájara, f. b.-call, voz del pájaro, f., canto del ave, m. b. catcher or vendor, pajarero, m. bird's-eye view, vista de pájaro, perspectiva aérea, f. b.-fancier, aficionado (-da) a las aves; criador (-ra) de pájaros. b.-like, como un pájaro; de pájaro. b.-lime, liga, f. to go b.-nesting, ir a coger nidos de pájaros. b. of paradise, ave del paraíso, f. b. of passage, ave de paso, f. b. of prey, ave rapaz, f. b.-seed, alpiste, m.
biretta, s. birreta, f.
birth, s. nacimiento, m.; (act of) parto, m.; origen, m.; (childhood) infancia, f.; (family) linaje, m., familia, f.; (fig.) creación, f. from b., de nacimiento. to give b. to, dar a luz, echar al mundo, parir. b. certificate, partida de nacimiento, f. b. control, anticoncepcionismo, m. b.-mark, antojos, m. pl. b.-place, lugar de nacimiento, m. b.-rate, natalidad, f.
birthday, s. cumpleaños, m., días, m. pl.
birthright, s. derecho. de nacimiento, m.; herencia, f.
Biscayan, a. and s. vizcaíno (-na)
biscuit, s. galleta, f.; bizcocho, m. b. box or maker, galletero, m. b.-like, abizcochado
bisect, v.t. dividir en dos partes iguales; (geom.) bisecar
bisection, s. bisección, f.
bisector, s. bisectriz, f.
bisexual, a. bisexual

bishop, s. obispo, m.; (in chess) alfil, m. bishop's crozier, báculo episcopal, cayado, m.
bishopric, s. obispado, m.
bismuth, s. bismuto, m.
bison, s. bisonte, m.
bisque, s. porcelana blanca, f., bizcocho, m.
bistoury, s. bisturí, m.
bit, s. pedazo, m.; (of grass, etc.) brizna, f.; (moment) instante, m.; (quantity) cantidad, f.; (of a drill) mecha, f.; (part) parte, f.; (passage) trozo, m.; (horse's) bocado, m.; (fam.) miga, f. a bit, un tanto, algo, un poco. in bits, en pedazos. Not a bit! ¡Nada!; ¡Ni pizca!; ¡Claro que no! bit by bit, poco a poco, gradualmente. to give someone a bit of one's mind, contarle cuatro verdades. to take the bit between one's teeth, desbocarse; (fig.) rebelarse. Wait a bit! ¡Espera un momento!
bitch, s. (female dog) perra, f.; (fox) zorra, f.; (wolf) loba, f.
bite, s. mordedura, f.; mordisco, m.; (mouthful, snack) bocado, m.; (of fish and insects) picada, f.; (hold) asimiento, m.; (sting, pain) picadura, f.; (pungency) resquemor, m.; (offer) oferta, f.; (fig., mordancy) mordacidad, acritud, f. v.t. and v.i. morder; (gnaw) roer; (of fish, insects) picar; (of hot dishes) resquemar; (of acids) corroer; (deceive) engañar, defraudar; (of wheels, etc.) agarrar; (hurt, wound) herir. to b. one's tongue, morderse la lengua. to b. the dust, caer al suelo
biting, a. (stinging) picante; (mordant) mordaz, acre; (of winds, etc.) penetrante; satírico. s. mordedura, f.; roedura, f.
bitter, a. amargo (also fig.); (sour) agrio, ácido; (of winds) penetrante; (of cold) intenso; cruel. to the b. end, hasta la muerte; hasta el último extremo. b.-sweet, agridulce
bitterly, adv. amargamente; intensamente; cruelmente
bitterness, s. amargura (also fig.), f.; (sourness) acidez, f.; (of cold) intensidad, f.; crueldad, f.

bitters, *s. pl.* (drink) bíter, *m.,* angostura, *f.*

bitts, *s. pl.* (*naut.*) bitas, *f. pl.*

bitumen, *s.* betún, *m.*

bituminous, *a.* bituminoso, abetunado

bivalve, *s.* bivalvo, *m.*

bivouac, *s.* (*mil.*) vivaque, *m. v.i.* vivaquear

bizarre, *a.* raro, extravagante; grotesco

black, *a.* negro; obscuro; (sad) triste, melancólico; funesto; (wicked) malo, perverso; (sullen) malhumorado. *s.* (colour) negro, *m.*; (mourning) luto, *m.*; (negro) negro, *m.*; (negress) negra, *f.*; (stain) mancha, *f.*; (dirt) tizne, *m. v.t.* ennegrecer; tiznar. **He has a b. eye,** (*fam.*) Tiene un ojo como un tomate. **in b. and white,** por escrito. **to look on the b. side,** verlo todo negro. **b. art,** nigromancia, *f.* **b.-currant,** grosella negra, *f.* **b.-eyed,** ojinegro, con ojos negros. **b.-haired,** pelinegro, de pelo negro. **b.-lead,** plombagina, *f.* **b.-list,** lista negra, *f.* **b.-market,** estraperlo, mercado negro, *m.* **b.-marketeer,** estraperlista, *m.* and *f.* **b.-out,** oscurecimiento, apagamiento, "blackout," *m.* **b.-pudding,** morcilla, *f.* **b. sheep,** oveja negra, *f.*; (*fig.*) oveja descarriada, *f.*; (of a family) garbanzo negro, *m.* **b.-water fever,** melanuria, *f.*

blackberry, *s.* mora, zarzamora, *f.*; (bush) zarza, *f.*, moral, *m.*

blackbird, *s.* mirlo, *m.*

blackboard, *s.* encerado, *m.,* pizarra, *f.*

blacken, *v.t.* ennegrecer; tiznar; (*fig.*) manchar, desacreditar. *v.i.* ennegrecerse

blackguard, *s.* tipo de cuidado, perdido, *m.*

blackhead, *s.* espinilla, *f.*

blacking, *s.* betún, *m.*

blackish, *a.* negruzco

blackleg, *s.* (*fam.*) esquirol, *m.*

blackmail, *s.* chantaje, *m. v.t.* hacer víctima de un chantaje; arrancar dinero por chantaje (a)

blackmailer, *s.* chantajista, *m.* and *f.*

blackness, *s.* negrura, *f.*; obscuridad, *f.*; (wickedness) maldad, perversidad, *f.*

blacksmith, *s.* herrero, *m.* **blacksmith's forge,** herrería, *f.*

blackthorn, *s.* endrino, *m.*

bladder, *s.* (*anat.*) vejiga, *f.*; ampolla, *f.*; (of sea-plants) vesícula, *f.*; (of fish) vejiga natatoria, *f.*

blade, *s.* (leaf) hoja, *f.*; (of grass, etc.) brizna, *f.*; (of sharp instruments) hoja, *f.*; (of oar) pala, *f.*; (of propeller) paleta, ala, *f.*

bladed, *a.* de . . . hojas. **a two-b. knife,** un cuchillo de dos hojas

blame, *s.* culpa, *f.*; responsabilidad, *f.*; censura, *f. v.t.* culpar, echar la culpa (a); tachar, censurar, criticar; acusar. **You are to b. for this,** Vd. tiene la culpa de esto

blameless, *a.* inculpable; inocente; intachable; elegante

blamelessness, *s.* inculpabilidad, inocencia, *f.*; elegancia, *f.*

blameworthy, *a.* culpable, digno de censura, vituperable

blanch, *v.t.* (*cul.*) mondar; hacer palidecer. *v.i.* palidecer, perder el color

blanching, *s.* palidecimiento, *m.*; (*cul.*) mondadura, *f.*

blancmange, *s.* manjar blanco, *m.*

bland, *a.* afable, cortés; dulce, agradable

blandish, *v.t.* adular, halagar, acariciar

blandishment, *s.* adulación, *f.,* halago, *m.,* caricia, *f.*

blandly, *adv.* afablemente

blandness, *s.* afabilidad, urbanidad, *f.*; dulzura, *f.*

blank, *a.* en blanco; (empty) vacío; desocupado; pálido; (confused) confuso, desconcertado; (expressionless) sin expresión; (of verse) suelto; sin adorno. *s.* blanco, hueco, *m.*; papel en blanco, *m.*; laguna, *f.* **b. cartridge,** cartucho para salvas, cartucho de fogueo, *m.* **b. verse,** verso suelto, *m.*

blanket, *s.* manta, frazada, *f.*; (of a horse) sudadero, *m.*; (*fig.*) capa, *f. v.t.* cubrir con una manta. **to toss in a b.,**

mantear. wet b., aguafiestas,
m. and *f.* **b. maker** or **seller,**
mantero, *m.* **b. vote,** voto
colectivo, *m.*

blanketing, *s.* manteamiento, *m.*

blankly, *adv.* con indiferencia;
sin comprender; (flatly) categóricamente

blankness, *s.* confusión, *f.*, desconcierto, *m.*; (emptiness) vaciedad, *f.*; indiferencia, *f.*; incomprensión, *f.*

blare, *s.* sonido de la trompeta o
del clarín, (*poet.*) clangor, *m.*; (of
a motor-car horn) ruido, *m.*
v.i. sonar

blarney, *s.* labia, *f.* *v.t.* lisonjear

blaspheme, *v.i.* blasfemar. *v.t.*
renegar de, maldecir

blasphemer, *s.* blasfemador
(-ra), blasfemo (-ma)

blasphemous, *a.* blasfemo, blas-
fematorio

blasphemy, *s.* blasfemia, *f.*

blast, *s.* (of wind) ráfaga (de
viento), *f.*; (of a trumpet, etc.)
trompetazo, son, *m.*; (of a whistle)
pitido, *m.*; (draught) soplo, *m.*;
explosión, *f.*; (*fig.*) influencia
maligna, *f.* *v.t.* (rock) barrenar,
hacer saltar; (wither) marchitar,
secar; (*fig.*) destruir; (curse)
maldecir. **in full b.,** en plena
marcha. **b.-furnace,** alto horno,
horno de cuba, *m.* **b. hole,**
barreno, *m.*

blaster, *s.* barrenero, *m.*

blasting, *s.* (of rock) voladura, *f.*;
(withering) marchitamiento, *m.*;
(*fig.*) destrucción, ruina, *f.*; (cursing) maldiciones, *f. pl.* *a.*
destructor; (*fig.*) funesto. **b.
charge,** carga explosiva, *f.*

blastoderm, *s.* blastodermo, *m.*

blatant, *a.* ruidoso; agresivo;
llamativo; (boastful) fanfarrón

blaze, *s.* llama, *f.*; fuego, *m.*;
conflagración, *f.*; luz brillante, *f.*;
(of anger, etc.) acceso, *m.* *v.i.*
llamear, encenderse en llamas;
brillar, resplandecer. **a b. of
colour,** una masa de color. **Go
to blazes!** ¡Vete al infierno!

blazon, *s.* (*her.*) blasón, *m.*; (*fig.*)
proclamación, *f.* *v.t.* blasonar;
adornar; proclamar

bleach, *s.* lejía, *f.* *v.t.* blanquear;
descolorar. *v.i.* ponerse blanco;
descolorarse

bleaching, *s.* blanqueo, *m.* **b.
powder,** hipoclorito de cal, *m.*

bleak, *a.* yermo, desierto; frío;
expuesto; (sad) triste; severo

bleakness, *s.* situación expuesta,
f.; desnudez, *f.*; frío, *m.*; (sadness) tristeza, *f.*; severidad, *f.*

bleary-eyed, *a.* legañoso, cegajoso

bleat, *s.* balido, *m.* *v.t.* and *v.i.*
balar, dar balidos

bleating, *a.* balador, que bala.
s. balido, *m.*

bleed, *v.i.* sangrar, echar sangre;
sufrir. *v.t.* sangrar; arrancar
dinero a

bleeding, *s.* hemorragia, *f.*; sangría, *f.*

blemish, *s.* imperfección, *f.*,
defecto, *m.*; (on fruit) maca, *f.*;
(stain) mancha, *f.*; deshonra, *f.*

blench, *v.i.* recular, retroceder

blend, *s.* mezcla, mixtura, *f.*;
combinación, *f.*; fusión, *f.* *v.t.*
mezclar; combinar. *v.i.* mezclarse; combinarse

blende, *s.* (*min.*) blenda, *f.*

blending, *s.* mezcla, *f.*; fusión, *f.*

blenorrhœa, *s.* blenorrea, *f.*

bless, *v.t.* bendecir; consagrar;
(praise) alabar, glorificar; hacer
feliz (a). **B. me!** ¡Válgame Dios!

blessed, *a.* bendito; (*ecc.*) beato,
bienaventurado; (dear) querido;
feliz; (*fam.*) maldito

blessedness, *s.* felicidad, *f.*;
bienaventuranza, *f.*

blessing, *s.* bendición, *f.*; (grace)
bendición de la mesa, *f.*; (mercy)
merced, gracia, *f.*; favor, *m.*;
(good) bien, *m.* **He gave them
his b.,** Les echó su bendición

blight, *s.* (*agr.*) tizne, tizón, *m.*;
(of cereals) añublo, *m.*; (mould)
roña, *f.*; (greenfly) pulgón, *m.*;
(*fig.*) influencia maligna, *f.*;
(frustration) desengaño, *m.*;
(spoil-sport) aguafiestas, *m.* and
f. *v.t.* atizonar; anublar;
(wither) marchitar, secar; (*fig.*)
frustrar, destruir; malograr

blighter, *s.* bribón, *m.*

blind, *a.* ciego; (secret) secreto;
(of a door, etc.) falso; (closed)
cerrado, sin salida; (unaware)
ignorante; sin apreciación (de).
to be b., ser ciego; (*fig.*) tener
una venda en los ojos. **to be b.
in one eye,** ser tuerto. **to turn**

a b. eye, hacer la vista gorda.
b. alley, callejón sin salida, m.
b. flying, (aer.) vuelo a ciegas,
m. b. man, ciego, hombre ciego,
m. b. obedience, obediencia
ciega, f. b. side, (of persons)
lado débil, m. b. woman, ciega,
mujer ciega, f.

blind, v.t. cegar; poner una
venda en los ojos (de); (dazzle)
deslumbrar; hacer cerrar los ojos
a; hacer ignorar

blind, s. persiana, f.; (Venetian)
celosía, f.; (deception) pretexto,
m.; velo, m.

blindage, s. (mil.) blindaje, m.

blindfold, v.t. vendar los ojos (a);
(fig.) poner una venda en los ojos
(de). a. and adv. con los ojos
vendados; a ciegas; con los ojos
cerrados

blindly, adv. ciegamente; a ciegas; ignorantemente

blindman's-buff, s. gallina
ciega, f.

blindness, s. ceguedad, f.; ofuscación, f.; ignorancia, f.

blink, s. parpadeo, m., guiñada,
f.; (of light) destello, m.; reflejo,
m. v.i. parpadear, pestañear;
(of lights) destellar

blinkers, s. pl. anteojeras, f. pl.

bliss, s. felicidad, f.; deleite,
placer, m.; (ecc.) gloria, f.

blissful, a. feliz

blissfully, adv. felizmente

blissfulness, s. See bliss

blister, s. (med.) vesícula, f.;
ampolla, f.; (bubble) burbuja, f.
v.t. ampollar; (fig.) herir

blithe, a. alegre

blithely, adv. alegremente

blitheness, s. alegría, f.

blitzkrieg, s. blitzkrieg, m.,
guerra relámpago, f.

blizzard, s. ventisca, f.

bloated, a. abotagado, hinchado;
orgulloso; indecente

bloater, s. arenque ahumado,
m.

blob, s. masa, f.; mancha, f.;
gota, f.

blobber-lipped, a. bezudo, belfo

block, s. bloque, m.; (log) leño,
m.; (naut.) polea, f.;(for beheading and of a butcher) tajo, m.;
(for mounting) apeadero, m.; (of
shares, etc.) lote, m.; (of houses)
manzana, f.; (jam) atasco, m.;

(obstruction) obstrucción, f.; (for
hats) forma, f. A chip off the
old b., De tal palo tal astilla.
b. and tackle, (naut.) polea con
aparejo. b.-hook, grapa, f. b.-
house, (mil.) blocao, m.

block, v.t. bloquear; cerrar (el
paso); (stop up) atarugar, atascar; (a wheel) calzar; (a bill, etc.)
obstruir; (hats) poner en forma.
to b. the way, cerrar el paso

blockade, s. bloqueo, m. v.t.
bloquear. · to run the b., violar
el bloqueo

blockhead, s. leño, zoquete,
imbécil, m..

blond(e), a. (of hair) rubio; .(of
complexion) de tez blanca. s.
hombre rubio, m.; (woman)
rubia, mujer rubia, f. peroxide
b., rubia oxigenada, f. b. lace,
blondina, f.

blood, s. sangre, f.; (relationship)
parentesco, m.; (family) linaje,
m., prosapia, f.; (life) vida, f.;
(sap) savia, f.; jugo, m.; (horse)
caballo de pura raza, m.; (dandy)
galán, m. v.t. sangrar. bad b.,
mala sangre, f.; odio, m.; mala
leche, f. blue b., sangre azul, f.
in cold b., a sangre fría, f. My
b. is up, Se me enciende la
sangre. My b. runs cold, Se me
hiela la sangre. to be in the b.,
llevar en la sangre. b.-bank,
banco de sangre, m. b.-bath,
matanza, f. b.-coloured, de
color de sangre, sanguíneo. b.-
feud, venganza de sangre, f. .
b.-guilt, culpabilidad de homicidio, m. b.-heat, calor de sangre,
m. b.-letting, sangría, f. b.
orange, naranja dulce, f. b.-
plasma, plasma sanguíneo, m.
b.-poisoning, septicemia, f.;
infección, f. b.-pressure,
presión sanguínea, f. b. purity,
limpieza de sangre, f. b.-red,
rojo como la sangre. b.-rela-
tion, pariente (-ta) consan-
guíneo(a). b.-relationship, consanguinidad, f. b.-stain, mancha de sangre, f. b.-stained,
ensangrentado, manchado de
sangre. b.-stone, sanguinaria,
f. b.-sucker, sanguijuela, f.;
(fig.) vampiro, m.; (usurer) avaro
(-ra). b.-vessel, vaso sanguíneo,
m.

blooded, *a.* de sangre . . .; de casta . . .

bloodhound, *s.* sabueso, *m.*

bloodily, *adv.* sangrientamente; cruentamente; con ferocidad, cruelmente

bloodiness, *s.* estado sangriento, *m.*; crueldad, ferocidad, *f.*

bloodless, *a.* exangüe; pálido; incruento; anémico; indiferente

bloodshed, *s.* efusión de sangre, *f.*; matanza, carnicería, *f.*

bloodshot, *a.* (of the eye) inyectado

bloodthirstiness, *s.* sed de sangre, *f.*

bloodthirsty, *a.* sanguinario, carnicero

bloody, *a.* sangriento; (of battles) encarnizado; (cruel) sanguinario, cruel

bloom, *s.* flor, *f.*; florecimiento, *m.*; (on fruit) flor, *f.*; (prime) lozanía, *f.*; (on the cheeks) color sano, *m.* *v.i.* florecer. **in b.,** en flor

blooming, *a.* florido; en flor; fresco; lozano; brillante

blossom, *s.* flor, *f.* *v.i.* florecer. **to b. out into,** hacerse, llegar a ser; (wear) lucir; (buy) comprarse

blossomed, *a.* con flores, de flores

blossoming, *s.* floración, *f.*

blot, *s.* borrón, *m.*; mancha, *f.* (also *fig.*). *v.t.* manchar; (erase) tachar; (dry) secar. **to b. out,** borrar; destruir; secar con papel secante

blotch, *s.* (on the skin, or stain) mancha, *f.*

blotter, *s.* (*com.*) libro borrador, *m.*; teleta, *f.*

blotting-paper, *s.* papel secante, *m.*

blouse, *s.* blusa, *f.*

blow, *s.* golpe, *m.*; bofetada, *f.*; (with the fist) puñetazo, *m.*; (with the elbow) codazo, *m.*; (with a club) porrazo, *m.*; (with a whip) latigazo, *m.*; (blossoming) floración, *f.*; (disaster) desastre, *m.*, tragedia, *f.* **to come to blows,** venirse a las manos. **at a b.,** con un solo golpe; de una vez. **We are going for a b.,** Vamos a tomar el fresco. **b. below the belt,** golpe bajo, *m.*

b. in the air, golpe en vago, *m.* **b. of fate,** latigazo de la fortuna, *m.*

blow, *v.i.* (of wind) soplar (el viento), hacer viento, correr aire; (pant) jadear, echar resoplidos; (of fuses) fundirse. *v.t.* (wind instruments) tocar; soplar; (inflate) inflar; (swell) hinchar. **to b. a kiss,** tirar un beso. **to b. one's nose,** sonarse las narices. **to b. away,** disipar; ahuyentar; llevar (el viento). **to b. down,** echar por tierra, derribar (el viento). **to b. in,** llevar adentro, hacer entrar (el viento); (windows, etc.) quebrar (el viento). **to b. off,** quitar (el viento). **to b. open,** abrir (el viento). **to b. out,** hacer salir (el viento); llevar afuera (el viento); (a light) matar de un soplo, apagar soplando. **to b. over,** pasar por (el viento); soplar por; disiparse; olvidarse. **to b. up,** (inflate) inflar; (the fire) avivar (el fuego); (explode) volar; (swell) hinchar

blow-fly, *s.* moscarda, *f.*

blowing, *s.* soplo, *m.*; violencia, *f.*; (blossoming) florecimiento, *m.* **b. up,** voleo, *m.*; explosión, *f.*

blow-pipe, *s.* lámpara de soldar, *f.*, soplete, *m.*

blowzy, *a.* desaliñado

blubber, *v.i.* gimotear; berrear. *s.* (of the whale) grasa de ballena, *f.* **b.-lip,** bezo, *m.* **b.-lipped,** bezudo

bludgeon, *s.* (cachi)porra, *f.*; garrote, *m.*; estaca, *f.* *v.t.* golpear con una porra, dar garrotazos (a)

blue, *a.* azul; (with bruises) amoratado; (sad) deprimido; melancólico; (obscene) verde; (dark) sombrío; (traditionalist) conservador. *s.* azul, *m.*; (sky) cielo, *m.*; (for clothes) añil de lavandera, *m.*; *pl.* blues, melancolía, depresión, *f.*; (homesickness) morriña, *f.* *v.t.* (laundry) añilar. **to look b.,** parecer deprimido; (of prospects, etc.) ser poco halagüeño. **b. black,** azul negro, *m.*; (of hair) azabache, *m.* **b.-bottle,** (*ent.*) moscón, *m.* **b.-eyed,** con ojos azules. **b. gum,** eucalipto, *m.* **B. Peter,**

bandera de salida, *f.* **b. print,** fotocopia, *f.*; plan, *m.*

bluebell, *s.* campanilla, *f.*

blueness, *s.* color azul, *m.*

bluestocking, *s.* marisabidilla, doctora, *f.*

bluff, *a.* (of cliffs, etc.) escarpado; (of persons) franco, campechano, brusco

bluffness, *s.* franqueza, brusquedad, *f.*

bluish, *a.* azulado

bluishness, *s.* color azulado, *m.*

blunder, *s.* desacierto, desatino, *m.*; equivocación, *f.*; (in a translation, etc.) falta, *f.* *v.i.* tropezar (con); desacertar; equivocarse; (*fam.*) meter la pata. *v.t.* manejar mal; estropear

blunderbuss, *s.* trabuco, *m.*

blunderer, *s.* desatinado (-da)

blundering, *a.* desacertado; equivocado; imprudente. *s.* See **blunder**

blunt, *a.* romo, embotado; obtuso; (abrupt) brusco; franco; descortés; (plain) claro. *v.t.* enromar, embotar; (the point) despuntar; (*fig.*) hacer indiferente; (pain) mitigar

bluntly, *adv.* sin filo; sin punta; bruscamente, francamente; claramente

bluntness, *s.* embotamiento, *m.*; (*fig.*) brusquedad, franqueza, *f.*; claridad, *f.*

blur, *s.* borrón, *m.*; mancha, *f.*; imagen indistinta, *f.* *v.t.* borrar; manchar; (*phot.*) velar

blurred, *a.* borroso; indistinto; turbio

blurt (out), *v.t.* proferir bruscamente; revelar sin querer

blush, *s.* rubor, *m.*; rojo, *m.* *v.i.* enrojecerse, ruborizarse, ponerse colorado; avergonzarse (por)

blushing, *a.* ruboroso; púdico

bluster, *v.i.* (of the wind) soplar con furia; (of waves) encresparse, embravecerse; (of persons) bravear, fanfarronear. *s.* furia, violencia, *f.*; tumulto, *m.*; fanfarronería, *f.*

blustering, *a.* (of wind) violento, fuerte; (of waves) tumultuoso; (of people) fanfarrón, valentón

boa, *s.* (*zool.*) boa, *f.*; (fur) boa, *m.*

boar, *s.* verraco, *m.*; (wild) jabalí, *m.*

board, *s.* tabla, *f.*; (for notices) tablón, *m.*; (b. residence) pensión, *f.*; (table) mesa, *f.*; (food) comida, *f.*; (for chess, draughts) tablero, *m.*; (sign) letrero, *m.*; (of instruments) cuadro, *m.*; (bookbinding) cartón, *m.*; (*naut.*) bordo, *m.*; (committee) junta, dirección, *f.*; tribunal, *m.*; *pl.* **boards** (*theat.*) tablas, *f.* *pl.* **above b.,** abiertamente, sin disimulo. **free on b.,** (f.o.b.) franco a bordo. **in boards,** (of books) encartonado. **managerial b.,** junta directiva, *f.* **on b.,** a bordo. **on the boards,** (*theat.*) en las tablas. **to go on b.,** ir a bordo. **b. and lodging,** pensión completa, casa y comida, *f.* **b. of directors,** consejo de administración, *m.* **b. of examiners,** tribunal de exámenes, *m.* **B. of Trade,** junta de comercio, *f.*; Ministerio de Comercio, *m.*

board, *v.t.* (*carp.*) entablar, enmaderar; embarcar en; (*nav.*, a ship) abordar; (lodge) alojar, tomar a pensión

boarder, *s.* huésped (-da) (at school) pensionista, *m.* and *f.*, alumno (-na) interno (-na)

boarding, *s.* entablado, *m.*; (planking) tablazón, *f.*; (of a ship) abordaje, *m.*; (of a train) subida (al tren), *f.* **b.-house,** pensión, casa de huéspedes, *f.* **b.-school,** pensionado, *m.*

boast, *s.* jactancia, *f.*; ostentación, *f.*; (honour) gloria, *f.* *v.i.* jactarse, vanagloriarse; alabarse; ostentar. *v.t.* jactarse de; hacer gala de; gloriarse en

boaster, *s.* vanaglorioso (-sa), jactancioso (-sa)

boastful, *a.* vanaglorioso, jactancioso; ostentador

boastfully, *adv.* con jactancia; con ostentación

boastfulness, *s.* vanagloria, jactancia, *f.*; fanfarronería, *f.*; ostentación, *f.*

boasting, *s.* alardeo, *m.*; fanfarronería, *f.*

boat, *s.* barco, *m.*; bote, *m.*; (in a fun fair) columpio, *m.*, lancha, *f.*; (for sauce or gravy) salsera, *f.*

v.i. ir en barco; (row) remar; navegar. **to b. down,** bajar en barco. **to b. up,** subir en barco. **b. building,** construcción de barcos, *f.* **b. club,** club náutico, *m.* **b. crew,** tripulación de un barco, *f.* **b.-hook,** bichero, garabato, *m.* **b.-house,** cobertizo de las lanchas, *m.* **b.-load,** barcada, *f.* **b.-race,** regata, *f.* **b.-scoop,** achicador, *m.* **b.-shaped,** en forma de barco. **b.-train,** tren que enlaza con un vapor, *m.*

boating, *s.* pasear en bote, *m.;* manejo de un bote, *m.;* (rowing) remo, *m.* **b.-pole,** botador, *m.*

boatman, *s.* barquero, *m.*

boatswain, *s.* contramaestre, *m.* **boatswain's mate,** segundo contramaestre, *m.*

bob, *s.* (curtsey) reverencia, *f.;* (woman's hair) pelo a la romana, *m.;* (of bells) toque (de campana), *m. v.i.* saltar; moverse. *v.t.* cortar corto. **long bob,** (hair) melena, *f.* **to bob up,** ponerse de pie; surgir. **to bob up and down,** subir y bajar; bailar. **bob-tail,** rabo corto, *m.* **bob-tailed,** rabón

bobbin, *s.* carrete, huso, *m.;* (of wool, etc.) ovillo, *m.;* (cf looms, sewing-machines) bobina, *f.;* (in lace-making) bolillo, palillo, *m.*

bobsleigh, *s.* trineo doble, *m.*

bobstay, *s.* (*naut.*) barbiquejo, *m.*

bode, *v.t.* presagiar, prometer. **to b. ill,** prometer mal. **to b. well,** prometer bien

bodice, *s.* corpiño, *m.*

bodied, *a.* (in compounds) de cuerpo

bodiless, *a.* incorpóreo

bodily, *a.* del cuerpo; físico; corpóreo; real; material; (of fear) de su persona. *adv.* corporalmente; en persona, personalmente; en conjunto, enteramente; en una pieza

boding, *a.* ominoso, amenazador. *s.* presagio, *m.;* agüero, *m.*

bodkin, *s.* pasajaretas, *m.*

body, *s.* (*anat.*) cuerpo, *m.;* (trunk) tronco, *m.;* (corpse) cadáver, *m.;* (of a vehicle) caja, *f.;* (of a motor-car) carrocería, *f.;* (of a ship) casco, *m.;* (of a

church) nave, *f.;* (centre) centro, *m.;* (of a book, persons, consistency and *ast.*) cuerpo, *m.;* (person) persona, *f.;* corporación, *f.;* grupo, *m.;* (of an army) grueso (de ejército), *m.;* organismo, *m.* **in a b.,** en masa, juntos (juntas); en corporación. **to have enough to keep b. and soul together,** tener de que vivir. **b.-snatcher,** ladrón de cadáveres, *m.* **b.-snatching,** robo de cadáveres, *m.*

bodyguard, *s.* guardia de corps, *f.;* guardia, *f.;* (escort) escolta, *f.*

Boer, *a.* and *s.* bóer (*m.* and *f.*)

bog, *s.* pantano, marjal, *m.,* marisma, *f.*

bogey, *s.* duende, *m.;* (to frighten children) coco, *m.;* (nightmare) pesadilla, *f.*

boggy, *a.* pantanoso, fangoso

bogus, *a.* postizo, falso

Bohemian, *a.* and *s.* bohemio (-ia)

boil, *v.i.* bullir, hervir; (cook) cocer. *v.t.* hervir; cocer. *s.* ebullición, *f.;* (*med.*) divieso, *m.* **to b. away,** consumirse hirviendo; (*chem.*) evaporar a seco. **to b. over,** rebosar

boiler, *s.* (*cul.*) marmita, olla, *f.;* (of a furnace) caldera, *f.* **double-b.,** baño de María, *m.* **steam-b.,** caldera de vapor, *f.* **b.-maker,** calderero, *m.* **b. room,** cámara de la caldera, *f.* **b.-suit,** mono, *m.*

boiling, *s.* ebullición, *f.,* hervor, *m.;* (cooking) cocción, *f.* *a.* hirviente. **b. point,** punto de ebullición, *m.*

boisterous, *a.* (of persons) exuberante, impetuoso; (stormy) tempestuoso, borrascoso; violento

boisterously, *adv.* impetuosamente, ruidosamente; tempestuosamente; con violencia

boisterousness, *s.* exuberancia, impetuosidad, *f.;* violencia, *f.;* tempestuosidad, borrascosidad, *f.*

bold, *a.* intrépido, audaz; (determined) resuelto; (forward) atrevido; (showy) llamativo; (clear) claro. **b.-faced,** descarado, desvergonzado. **b.-faced type,** letra negra, *f.*

boldly, *adv.* intrépidamente; descaradamente; resueltamente; claramente

boldness, *s.* intrepidez, valentía, *f.*; resolución, *f.*; (forwardness) osadía, *f.*, descaro, atrevimiento, *m.*; claridad, *f.*

bole, *s.* (of a tree) tronco, *m.*

bolero, *s.* bolero, *m.*

bolide, *s.* (*ast.*) bólido, *m.*

Bolivian, *a.* and *s.* boliviano (-na)

bollard, *s.* bolardo, *m.*

Bolognese, *a.* and *s.* boloñés (-esa)

Bolshevik, *a.* and *s.* bolchevique (*m.* and *f.*)

Bolshevism, *s.* bolchevismo, *m.*

Bolshevist, *s.* bolchevista, *m.* and *f.*

bolster, *s.* travesaño, *m.* *v.t.* apuntalar; (*fig.*) apoyar

bolt, *s.* pasador, cerrojo, *m.*; (pin) perno, *m.*; (knocker) aldaba, *f.*; (roll) rollo, *m.*; (flight) huida, *f.*; (of a crossbow) flecha, *f.*; (from the blue) rayo, *m.* *adv.* (upright) recto como una flecha; enhiesto; rígido. **b. and nut,** perno y tuerca, *m.*

bolt, *v.t.* echar el cerrojo (a); empernar; (*fam.*, eat) zampar. *v.i.* huir; (horses) desbocarse, dispararse; (plants) cerner. **to b. down,** cerrar con cerrojo. **to b. in,** entrar corriendo, entrar de repente. **to b. off,** marcharse corriendo. **to b. out,** *v.i.* salir de golpe. *v.t.* cerrar fuera

bolus, *s.* bolo, *m.*

bomb, *s.* bomba, *f.* *v.t.* bombardear. **to be a b.-shell,** (*fig.*) caer como una bomba. **b.-carrier,** portabombas, *m.* **b. crater,** bombazo, *m.* **b.-release,** (*aer.*, *nav.*) lanzabombas, *m.* **b.-sight,** mira de avión de bombardeo, *f.*

bombard, *v.t.* bombardear, bombear; (*fig.*) llover (preguntas, etc.) sobre

bombardier, *s.* bombardero, *m.*

bombardment, *s.* bombardeo, *m.*

bombast, *s.* ampulosidad, pomposidad, *f.*

bombastic, *a.* bombástico, altisonante, pomposo

bomber, *s.* avión de bombardeo, bombardero, *m.* **dive b.,** bom-

bardero en picado, *m.* **heavy b.,** bombardero pesado, *m.* **light b.,** bombardero ligero, *m.* **B. Command,** Servicio de Bombardero, *m.*

bombproof, *a.* a prueba de bomba

bonafide, *a.* fidedigno

Bonapartist, *a.* and *s.* bonapartista (*m.* and *f.*)

bonbon, *s.* bombón, confite, dulce, *m.* **b. box,** bombonera, *f.*

bond, *s.* lazo, vínculo, *m.*; (*chem.*) enlace, *m.*; (financial) obligación, *f.*; (security) fianza, *f.*; (Customs) depósito, *m.*; *pl.* bonds, cadenas, *f. pl.* *a.* esclavo. **in b.,** en depósito. **bonds of interest,** intereses creados, *m. pl.* **b.-holder,** obligacionista, *m.* and *f.*

bondage, *s.* esclavitud, *f.*; servidumbre, *f.*; cautiverio, *m.*; prisión, *f.*

bone, *s.* hueso, *m.*; (of fish) espina (de pez), *f.*; (whale b.) ballena, *f.*; *pl.* bones, cuerpo, *m.* *v.t.* deshuesar; poner ballenas (a or en). **to be all skin and bones,** estar en los huesos. **to have a b. to pick with,** tener que arreglar las cuentas con. **b.-ash,** cendra, *f.*

boned, *a.* (in compounds) de huesos; deshuesado, sin hueso

bonfire, *s.* fogata, hoguera, *f.*

bonnet, *s.* capota, *f.*; (of babies) gorra, *f.*; (of men) boina, *f.*; (of chimney and of machines) sombrerete, *m.*; (of a motor-car) capó, *m.*

bonniness, *s.* aspecto sano, *m.*; hermosura, *f.*

bonny, *a.* sano; hermoso; (fat) gordo

bonus, *s.* paga extraordinaria, bonificación, *f.*; sobresueldo, *m.*; (of food, etc.) ración extraordinaria, *f.*

bon voyage, *interj.* ¡buen viaje!

bony, *a.* huesudo; (of fish-bones) lleno de espinas; óseo

booby, *s.* pazguato, bobo, *m.* **b.-prize,** último premio, *m.* **b.-trap,** trampa, *f.*; (*mil.*) mina, *f.*

book, *s.* libro, *m.*; volumen, tomo, *m.*; (of an opera) libreto, *m.* *v.t.* anotar en un libro; apuntar; (seats) tomar (localidades);

(tickets) sacar (billetes); (of the issuing clerk) dar; (reserve) reservar; inscribir; (of police officer) tomar el nombre (de); (engage) contratar; (invite) comprometer. **to turn the pages of a b.**, hojear un libro. **b.-ends**, sostén para libros, sujetalibros, m. **b.-keeper**, tenedor de libros, m. **b.-keeping**, teneduría de libros, f. **b.-maker**, apostador de profesión, m. **b. of reference**, libro de consulta, m. **b.-plate**, exlibris, m. **b.-post**, tarifa de impresos, f. **b.-shop**, librería, f. **b.-trade**, venta de libros, f.; comercio de libros, m.

bookbinder, s. encuadernador (-ra) de libros

bookbinding, s. encuadernación de libros, f.

bookcase, s. armario de libros, m.

booking, s. (of rooms, etc.) reservación, f.; (of tickets) toma, f.; (com.) asiento, m.; (engagement) contratación, f. **b.-clerk**, vendedor (-ra) de billetes. **b.-office**, despacho de billetes, m.; taquilla, f.

bookish, a. aficionado a los libros; docto, erudito

bookishness, s. afición a los libros, f.; erudición, f.

bookmark, s. marcador, m.

bookseller, s. librero, m.

bookselling, s. venta de libros, f.; comercio de libros, m.

bookshelf, s. estante para libros, m.

bookstall, s. puesto de libros, m.

bookstrap, s. portalibros, m.

bookworm, s. polilla que roe los libros, f.; (fig.) ratón de biblioteca, m.

boom, s. (naut.) botavara, f.; (of a crane) aguilón, m.; (noise) ruido, m.; (of the sea) bramido, m.; (thunder) trueno, m.; (at a harbour) cadena de puerto, f.; (com.) actividad, f.; (fig., peak) auge, m. v.i. sonar; bramar; tronar; (com.) subir; ser famoso. **b. sail**, vela de cangreja, f.

boomerang, s. bumerang, m.

boon, s. favor, m., merced, f.; bien, m., ventaja, f.; don, m.; privilegio, m. a. (of friends) íntimo

boor, s. monigote, patán, palurdo, m.

boorish, a. rudo, zafio, rústico, cerril

boorishness, s. zafiedad, patanería, tosquedad, f.

boost, v.t (elec.) aumentar la fuerza de; (fam.) empujar; subir; (advertise) dar bombo (a)

boot, s. bota, f.; (of a car) compartimiento para equipaje, m. **button-boots**, botas de botones, f. pl. **riding-boots**, botas de montar, f. pl. **to b.**, además, de añadidura. **b.-maker**, zapatero, m. **b.-tag**, tirador de bota, m. **b.-tree**, horma de bota, f.

bootblack, s. limpiabotas, m.

booted, a. con botas, calzado con botas; (in compounds) de botas . . .

bootee, s. botín, m.

booth, s. puesto, m., barraca, f.

bootjack, s. sacabotas, m.

bootlace, s. cordón para zapatos, m.

bootlegger, s. contrabandista de alcohol, m.

boots, s. mozo de hotel, botones, m.

booty, s. botín, m.; tesoro, m.

booze, v.i. emborracharse. s. alcohol, m.; borrachera, f.

boozer, s. borracho (-cha)

boracic, a. bórico. s. ácido bórico, m.

borate, s. borato, m.

borax, s. bórax, m.

Bordeaux, a. and s. (of or from) bordelés (-esa). s. (wine) vino de Burdeos, m.

border, s. borde, m.; (of a lake, etc.) orilla, f.; (edge) margen, m.; (of a diploma, etc.) orla, f.; (sew.) ribete, m., orla, f.; (fringe) franja, f.; (garden) arriate, m.; (territory) frontera, f.; límite, confín, m. v.t. (sew.) orlar, ribetear; ornar (de); (of land) lindar con. **to b. on**, (of land) tocar, lindar con; (approach) rayar en. **b. country**, región fronteriza, f.

borderer, s. habitante de una zona fronteriza; m.; escocés (-esa) de la frontera con Inglaterra

borderland, s. zona fronteriza, f.; lindes, m. pl.

borderline, *s.* frontera, *f.*; límite, *m.*; margen, *m.* *a.* fronterizo; lindero; (uncertain) dudoso, incierto

bore, *s.* taladro, barreno, *m.*; perforación, *f.*; (hole) agujero, *m.*; (of guns) calibre, *m.*; (wave) oleada, *f.*; (nuisance) fastidio, *m.*; (dullness) aburrimiento, tedio, *m.*; (person) pelmazo, *m.*, machaca, *m.* and *f.* *v.t.* taladrar, barrenar, horadar; perforar; hacer un agujero (en); (exhaust) aburrir; fastidiar. **It's a b.,** Es una lata. **to be bored,** aburrirse, fastidiarse

boreal, *a.* boreal

boreas, *s.* bóreas, *m.*

boredom, *s.* aburrimiento, *m.*; tedio, hastío, *m.*

boric, *a.* bórico

boride, *s.* (*chem.*) boruro, *m.*

boring, *a.* aburrido, pesado, tedioso; molesto, fastidioso. *s.* taladro, *m.*; horadación, *f.*; sondeo, *m.*; perforación, *f.*

born, *a.* nacido, *m.*; (by birth) de nacimiento; (b. to be) destinado a; natural (de). **He was b. in 1870,** Nació en 1870. **to be b.,** nacer, venir al mundo. **to be b. again,** renacer, volver a nacer. **well-b.,** bien nacido

borough, *s.* burgo, *m.*; villa, *f.*; ciudad, *f.* **b. surveyor,** arquitecto municipal, *m.*

borrow, *v.t.* pedir prestado; apropiarse, adoptar; copiar; (arithmetic) restar; (a book from a library) tomar prestado. **May I b. your pencil?** ¿ Quieres prestarme tu lápiz ?

borrower, *s.* el (la) que pide o toma prestado

borrowing, *s.* el pedir prestado, acto de pedir prestado, *m.*

borzoi, *s.* galgo ruso, *m.*

bosh, *s.* patrañas, tonterías, *f. pl.*; palabrería, *f.*

Bosnian, *a.* bosnio

bosom, *s.* pecho, *m.*; (heart) corazón, *m.*; (of the earth, etc.) seno, *m.* **b. friend,** amigo (-ga) del alma, amigo (-ga) íntimo (-ma)

boss, *s.* (of a shield) corcova saliente, *f.*; tachón, *m.*; (arch.) pinjante, *m.*; (fam.) amo, *m.*; jefe, *m.* *v.t.* mandar; dominar. **political b.,** cacique, *m.*

bossy, *a.* mandón, autoritario

botanical, *a.* botánico. **b. garden,** jardín botánico, *m.*

botanist, *s.* botánico (-ca)

botanize, *v.i.* herborizar

botany, *s.* botánica, *f.*

botch, *s.* (clumsy work) chapucería, *f.*; remiendo, *m.* *v.t.* chapucear, chafallar; (patch) remendar

both, *a.* and *pron.* ambos, *m. pl.*; ambas, *f. pl.*; los dos, *m. pl.*; las dos, *f. pl.* *adv.* tan(to) . . . como; (and) y; a la vez, al mismo tiempo. **It appealed both to the young and the old,** Gustó tanto a los jóvenes como a los viejos. **b. of you,** vosotros dos. **b. pretty and useful,** bonito y útil a la vez

bother, *s.* molestia, *f.*, fastidio, *m.*; (worry) preocupación, *f.*; dificultad, *f.*; (fuss) alboroto, *m.* *v.t.* molestar, fastidiar; preocupar. *v.i.* preocuparse

bottle, *s.* botella, *f.*; (smaller) frasco, *m.*; (babies) biberón, *m.*; (for water) cantimplora, *f.* *v.t.* embotellar, envasar, enfrascar. **to b. up,** (liquids, capital, armies, navies) embotellar; (feelings) refrenar. **to bring up on the b.,** criar con biberón. **b.-green,** verde botella, *m.* **b.-neck,** (in an industry) embotellado, *m.*; (in traffic) atascadero, *m.* **b.-washer,** fregaplatos, *m.* and *f.*; (machine) máquina para limpiar botellas, *f.*

bottled, *a.* en botella; (of fruit, vegetables) conservado

bottleful, *s.* botella, *f.*

bottler, *s.* embotellador (-ra)

bottling, *s.* embotellado, *m.*; envase, *m.* **b. outfit,** embotelladora, *f.*; (for fruit, etc.) aparato para conservar frutas o legumbres, *m.*

bottom, *s.* base, *f.*; (deepest part) fondo, *m.*; (last place) último lugar, *m.*; fundamento, *m.*; (of a chair) asiento, *m.*; (of a page, table, mountain, etc.) pie, *m.*; (posterior) culo, *m.*; (of a river) lecho, *m.*; (of the sea) fondo, *m.*; (of a ship) casco, *m.*; (of a skirt) orilla, *f.*; (truth) realidad, verdad, *f.*; (basis) origen, *m.*, causa, *f.* **at b.,** en

realidad. **at the b.**, en el fondo.
false b., fondo doble, fondo
secreto, *m.* **to be at the b. of,**
ocupar el último lugar en; ser el
causante de. **to get to the b.
of,** descubrir la verdad de;
profundizar en, analizar. **to
sink to the b.,** (of ships) irse a
pique
bottomed, *a.* (in compounds) de
fondo ...
bottomless, *a.* sin fondo; (of
chairs, etc.) sin asiento; (unfathomable) insondable
boudoir, *s.* tocador, gabinete de
señora, *m.*
bough, *s.* rama, *f.*, brazo (de un
árbol) *m.*
boulder, *s.* roca, peña, *f.*; canto
rodado, *m.*; bloque de roca, *m.*
boulevard, *s.* bulevar, *m.*
bounce, *s.* bote, rebote, *m.*; salto,
m.; (boasting) fanfarronería, *f.*
v.i. rebotar; saltar, brincar.
v.t. hacer botar o saltar
bouncing, *a.* (healthy) sano, robusto; vigoroso, fuerte
bound, *s.* límite, *m.*; (jump)
salto, brinco, *m.* *v.t.* limitar,
confinar. *v.i.* saltar, brincar;
(bounce) botar. **within bounds,**
dentro del límite. **b. for,** con
destino a; (of ships) con rumbo a
boundary, *s.* límite, lindero,
término, *m.*; frontera, *f.*; raya, *f.*
b. stone, mojón, *m.*
bounden, *a.* obligatorio, forzoso;
indispensable
boundless, *a.* sin límites, infinito;
inmenso
bounteous, bountiful, *a.* dadivoso, generoso; bondadoso
bountifulness, *s.* munificencia,
dadivosidad, generosidad, *f.*
bounty, *s.* generosidad, munificencia, *f.*; don, *m.*; (subsidy)
subvención, *f.*
bouquet, *s.* ramo, ramillete (de
flores), *m.*; perfume, *m.*; (of
wine) nariz, *f.*
Bourbon, *a.* borbónico. *s.* Borbón (-ona)
bourgeois, *a.* and *s.* burgués
(-esa)
bourgeoisie, *s.* burguesía, mesocracia, *f.*
bout, *s.* turno, *m.*; (in fencing,
boxing, wrestling) asalto, *m.*;
(of illness, coughing) ataque, *m.*;

(fight) lucha, *f.*, combate, *m.*;
(of drinking) borrachera, *f.*
bovine, *a.* bovino, vacuno
bow, *s.* (weapon) arco, *m.*; (of a
saddle) arzón (de silla), *m.*;
(*mus.*) arco, *m.*; (knot) lazo, *m.*;
(greeting) saludo, *m.*; reverencia,
inclinación, *f.*; (of a boat) proa, *f.*
to tie a bow, hacer un lazo.
bow and arrows, arco y flechas,
m. **bow-legged,** patizambo.
bow window, ventana saliente,
f.
bow, *v.i.* inclinarse; hacer una
reverencia, saludar; (remove the
hat) descubrirse; (*fig.*) inclinarse
(ante); (submit) someterse (a),
reconocer; agobiarse; (*mus.*)
manejar el arco. *v.t.* (usher in)
introducir en, conducir a; doblar;
inclinar. **to bow down (to),**
humillarse ante; obedecer; (worship) reverenciar, adorar. **to
bow out,** despedir con una inclinación del cuerpo
bowel, *s.* intestino, *m.*; *pl.*
bowels, (*fig.*) seno, *m.*, entrañas,
f. pl.
bower, *s.* (arbour) enramada, *f.*;
glorieta, *f.*; (boudoir) tocador
de señora, *m.*
bowing, *s.* (*mus.*) arqueada, *f.*;
saludo, *m.* *a.* (of acquaintance)
superficial
bowl, *s.* receptáculo *m.*; (of a
fountain) taza, *f.*; (of a pipe)
cazoleta, *f.*; (barber's) bacía, *f.*;
(for washing) jofaina, *f.*; (for
punch) ponchera, *f.*; (goblet)
copa, *f.*; (for soup) escudilla, *f.*;
(for fruit) frutero, *m.*; (of a
spoon) paleta, *f.*; (ball) boliche,
m. v.t. tirar; (in cricket) sacar;
(a hoop) jugar con; (in ninepins)
tumbar con una bola. **to b.
along,** recorrer; ir en coche o
carruaje (por). **to b. over,** (*fig.*)
dejar consternado (a), desconcertar
bowler, *s.* (in cricket) servidor,
m.; (hat) sombrero hongo, *m.*;
(skittle player) jugador de bolos,
m.
bowling, *s.* (in cricket) saque, *m.*;
(skittles) juego de bolos, *m.*;
juego de boliche, *m.* **b.-alley,**
(for skittles) bolera, pista de
bolos, *f.* **b.-green,** césped para
jugar al boliche, *f.*

bowls, s. juego de boliche, *m.*

bowsprit, s. bauprés, *m.*

bowstring, s. cuerda de arco, *f.*

bow-wow, s. guau, *m.*

box, s. caja, *f.*; (case) estuche, *m.*; (luggage) baúl, *m.*, maleta, *f.*; (for a hat) sombrerera, *f.*; (*bot.*) boj, *m.*; (*theat.*) palco, *m.*; (for a sentry, signalman, etc.) garita, casilla, *f.*; (on a carriage) pescante, *m.*; (blow) cachete, *m.*, bofetada, *f.*; (for a horse) vagón, *m.* **post office box,** apartado de correos, *m.* **box-kite,** cometa celular, *f.* **box-maker,** cajero, *m.* **box office,** taquilla, *f.* **box-pleat,** (*sew.*) tabla, *f.*

box, v.t. encajonar, meter en una caja. v.i. boxear. **to box the ears of,** calentar las orejas de. **to box up,** encerrar

boxer, s. (*sport*) boxeador, pugilista, *m.*

boxing, s. encajonamiento, *m.*; envase, *m.*; (*sport*) boxeo, pugilato, *m.* **B. Day,** Día de San Esteban, *m.* (A Spanish child receives its Christmas presents on the Día de Reyes (Twelfth Night).) **b.-gloves,** guantes de boxeo, *m. pl.* **b.-ring,** cuadrilátero ("ring") de boxeo, *m.*

boy, s. muchacho, niño, rapaz, *m.*; (older) chico, joven, *m.* **new boy,** nuevo alumno, *m.* **old boy,** (of a school) antiguo alumno, *m.* (*fam.*, address) chico. **small boy,** chiquillo, pequeño, crío, *m.* **b. doll,** muñeco, *m.* **boy scout,** muchacho explorador, *m.*

boycott, v.t. boicotear. s. boicot, *m.*

boyhood, s. muchachez, mocedad, *f.*; (childhood) niñez, *f.*

boyish, a. muchachil; pueril; de niñez

brace, s. (prop) puntal, barrote, *m.*; abrazadera, *f.*; (*carp.*) berbiquí, *m.*; viento, tirante, *m.*; (pair) par, *m.*; *pl.* **braces,** tirantes, *m. pl.* v.t. apuntalar; asegurar; (*carp.*) ensamblar; (*naut.*) bracear; (trousers) tirar; (*fig.*) fortalecer, refrescar

bracelet, s. pulsera, *f.*, brazalete, *m.*, ajorca, *f.*

brachial, a. braquial

brachycephalic, a. braquicéfalo

bracing, a. (of air, etc.) fortificante, tónico; estimulador

bracken, s. helecho, *m.*

bracket, s. consola, *f.*; (*arch.*) repisa, *f.*; soporte, *m.*; (on furniture, etc.) cantonera, *f.*; (*print.*) paréntesis, *m.*; (for a light) brazo (de alumbrado), *m.* v.t. (*print.*) poner entre paréntesis; juntar. **in brackets,** entre paréntesis. **They were bracketed equal,** Fueron juzgados iguales

brackish, a. salobre

bract, s. (*bot.*) bráctea, *f.*

brad, s. puntilla, *f.*

bradawl, s. lezna, *f.*

brag, v.i. jactarse, fanfarronear. s. jactancia, *f.* **to b. about,** hacer alarde de

braggart, a. baladrón, jactancioso. s. jactancioso, fanfarrón, *m.*

bragging, s. jactancia, *f.*

Brahmin, s. brahmán, *m.*

Brahminism, s. brahmanismo, *m.*

braid, s. trencilla, *f.*, cordoncillo, *m.*; (for trimming) galón, *m.*; (plait) trenza, *f.* v.t. (hair) trenzar; (trim) galonear; acordonar, trencillar

brain, s. cerebro, *m.*; entendimiento, *m.*, inteligencia, *f.*; talento, *m.*; (common sense) sentido común, *m.*; *pl.* **brains,** sesos, *m. pl.* (animal and human); cacumen, *m.* v.t. romper la crisma (a). **to blow one's brains out,** levantarse la tapa de los sesos. **to rack one's brains,** devanarse los sesos. **Brains Trust,** masa cefálica, *f.*; consorcio de inteligencias, *m.* **b.-box,** cráneo, *m.* **b.-fever,** fiebre cerebal, *f.* **b.-storm,** crisis nerviosa, *f.* **b.-wave,** idea luminosa, *f.* **b.-work,** trabajo intelectual, *m.*

brained, a. de cabeza, de cerebro

brainless, a. sin seso; tonto

brainy, a. sesudo, inteligente, talentudo

braise, v.t. (*cul.*) asar

brake, s. (of vehicles and *fig.*) freno, *m.*; (flax and hemp) caballete, *m.*; (carriage) break,

m.; (thicket) matorral, *m. v.t.*
(vehicles) frenar; (hemp, etc.)
rastrillar. **foot-b.**, freno de
pedal, *m.* **hand-b.**, freno de
mano, *m.* **to b. hard**, frenar de
repente. **to release the b.**,
quitar el freno

brakeman, *s.* guardafrenos, *m.*

bramble, *s.* zarza, *f.* **b. patch**,
breña, *f.*, zarzal, *m.*

brambly, *a.* zarzoso

bran, *s.* salvado, *m.*

branch, *s.* (of a tree, a family)
rama, *f.*; (of flowers, of learning)
ramo, *m.*; (of a river) tributario,
afluente, *m.*; (of roads, railways)
ramal, *m.*; (of a firm) sucursal,
dependencia; *f. a.* sucursal,
dependiente; (of roads, railways)
secundario. *v.i.* echar ramas;
bifurcarse, dividirse; ramificarse.
to b. off, bifurcarse, ramificarse.
to b. out, extenderse; emprender
cosas nuevas

branched, *a.* con ramas; (*bot.*)
ramoso; (of candlesticks) de . . .
brazos

branchiness, *s.* ramaje, *m.*, frondosidad, *f.*

branching, *s.* ramificación, *f.*;
división, *f.* **b. off**, bifurcación, *f.*

brand, *s.* tizón, *m.*; (torch) tea,
f.; (on cattle, etc.) hierro, *m.*;
(trade-mark) marca de fábrica,
f.; marca, *f.*; (stigma) estigma,
m. v.t. marcar con el hierro,
herrar; marcar; estigmatizar,
tildar. **b.-new**, flamante

branding, *s.* (of live-stock)
herradero, *m.*; (of slaves, criminals) estigmatización, *f.*; difamación, *f.* **b.-iron**, hierro de
marcar, *m.*

brandish, *v.t.* blandir

brandy, *s.* coñac, *m.*

brass, *s.* latón, *m.*; (*mus.*) metal,
m.; (tablet) placa conmemóra-
tiva, *f.*; (*fam.*) dinero, *m.* **the b.**,
(*mus.*) el metal. **b. band**, banda
de instrumentos de viento, *f.*
b.-neck, (*fam.*) cara dura, *f.*
b. works or shop, latonería, *f.*

brassard, *s.* brazal, *m.*

brassière, *s.* sostén, *m.*

brassy, *a.* de latón

brat, *s.* crío, *m.*

bravado, *s.* bravata, *f.*

brave, *a.* valiente, animoso, intrépido; espléndido, magnífico;

bizarro. *s.* valiente, *m.*; (Red
Indian) piel roja, *m. v.t.* desafiar,
provocar; arrostrar

bravely, *adv.* valientemente;
espléndidamente; bizarramente

bravery. *s.* valentía, *f.*, valor,
m., intrepidez, *f.*, coraje, *m.*;
esplendidez, suntuosidad, *f.*;
bizarría, *f.*

bravo, *s.* bandido, *m.*; asesino
pagado, *m. interj.* ¡bravo! ¡olé!

bravura, *s.* bravura, *f.*

brawl, *s.* camorra, reyerta, pelotera, *f. v.i.* alborotar; (of
streams) murmurar. **to start
a b.**, armar camorra

brawler, *s.* camorrista, *m.* and *f.*

brawling, *s.* alboroto, *m.*, vocinglería, *f.*; (of streams) murmullo, *m.*

brawn, *s.* (*cul.*) embutido, *m.*;
músculo, *m.*; (strength) fuerza, *f.*

brawny, *a.* membrudo, musculoso, forzudo

bray, *s.* rebuzno, *m.*; (of trumpets)
clangor, *m. v.i.* rebuznar; sonar

brazen, *a.* de latón; (of voice)
bronca; desvergonzado, descarado

brazier, *s.* (fire) brasero, *m.*;
latonero, *m.*

Brazil-nut, *s.* nuez del Brasil, *f.*

Brazilian, *a.* and *s.* brasileño (-ña)

breach, *s.* violación, contravención, *f.*; (gap) abertura, *f.*;
(*mil.*) brecha, *f. v.t.* (*mil.*) hacer
brecha (en); (in a line of defence)
hacer mella (en). **b. of confidence**, abuso de confianza, *m.*
b. of promise, incumplimiento
de la palabra de casamiento, *m.*
b. of the peace, alteración del
orden público, *f.*

bread, *s.* pan, *m.* **to earn one's
b. and butter**, ganarse el pan.
brown b., pan moreno, *m.*
unleavened b., pan ázimo, *m.*
b. and butter, pan con mantequilla, *m.*; (*fig.*) sustento diario,
m. **b.-basket**, cesta de pan, *f.*;
(*fam.*) estómago, *m.* **b.-bin**, caja
del pan, *f.* **b.-crumb**, miga, *f.*;
migaja, *f.* **b.-knife**, cuchillo
para cortar el pan, *m.* **b.
poultice**, cataplasma de miga de
pan, *f.* **b.-winner**, ganador (-ra)
de pan, trabajador (-ra)

breadfruit tree, *s.* árbol del pan,
m.

breadth, s. anchura, f.; latitud, f.; liberalidad, f.; (sew.) ancho de una tela, m.

breadthways, adv. a lo ancho

break, s. rotura, f.; (opening) abertura, f.; (geol.) rajadura, f.; (fissure) grieta, f.; solución de continuidad, f.; interrupción (also elec.), f.; (billiards) serie, f.; (change) cambio, m.; (in a boy's voice) muda (de la voz), f.; (blank) vacío, m.; (in the market) baja, f.; intervalo, m.; descanso, m.; pausa, f.; (truce) tregua, f.; (clearing) clara, f.; (mus.) quiebra (de la voz), f.; (carriage) break, m.; (fam., folly) disparate, m. **with a b. in one's voice,** con voz entrecortada. **b. of day,** aurora, alba, f. **at the b. of day,** al despuntar el alba

break, v.t. romper; quebrar; quebrantar, fracturar; (breach) abrir brecha en; (in two) partir, dividir; (into pieces) hacer pedazos, despedazar; (into small pieces) desmenuzar; (into crumbs) desmigajar; (destroy) destrozar; (a blow) parar; (a law) infringir, violar; (the bank in gambling) quebrar; (a journey, etc.) interrumpir; (of a habit) desacostumbrar, hacer perder el vicio de; (a promise) no cumplir, faltar a; (a record) superar; (plough ground) roturar; (spoil) estropear; arruinar; (com.) ir a la quiebra; (an official) degradar; (an animal) domar, amansar; (fig., crush) subyugar; (betray) traicionar; (fig., of silence, a spell, a lance, peace, the ranks) romper; (cushion) amortiguar; (lessen) mitigar; (disclose) revelar; (elec.) interrumpir. **to b. one's promise,** faltar a su palabra. **to b. the ice,** (fig.) romper el hielo. **to b. asunder,** romper en dos (partes); dividir. **to b. down,** derribar; echar abajo; destruir; (suppress) suprimir; subyugar; abolir; disolver. **to b. in,** (animals) domar, amaestrar; (persons) disciplinar; (new shoes) ahormar, romper. **to b. in two,** partir; dividir en dos; (split) hender. **to b. off,**

separar, quitar; (a branch) desgajar; (fig.) romper; interrumpir; cesar. **to b. open,** forzar, abrir a la fuerza. **to b. up,** hacer pedazos; (scatter) poner en fuga, dispersar; hacer levantar la sesión; (the ground) roturar; (parliament) disolver; (a ship) desguazar, deshacer (un buque)

break, v.i. romperse; quebrarse; quebrantarse; (of beads) desgranarse; (burst) reventar, estallar; (of abscesses) abrirse; (of a boy's voice) mudar; (fig. and of clouds, etc.) romperse; desaparecer; (of the dawn) despuntar (el alba), amanecer; (sprout) brotar; (of a ball) torcerse; (of fine weather) terminar; (change) cambiar; (of a storm) estallar. **to b. loose,** desasirse; (fig.) desencadenarse. **to b. away,** escaparse, fugarse; (from a habit) romper con; disiparse. **to b. down,** (of machinery, cars) averiarse; (fail) frustrarse, malograrse; (weep) deshacerse en lágrimas; (lose one's grip) perder la confianza en sí; (in health) sufrir una crisis de salud. **The car broke down,** El auto tuvo una avería. **to b. in,** (of burglars) forzar la entrada; irrumpir (en), penetrar (en); exclamar. **to b. in on,** sorprender; entrar de sopetón; invadir; interrumpir; caer sobre; molestar. **to b. into,** (force) forzar; (utter) romper a, prorrumpir en; empezar (a); pasar de repente a; (of time, etc.) ocupar; hacer perder. **to b. off,** (of speech) interrumpirse; cesar; (detach) desprenderse, separarse; (of branches) desgajarse. **to b. out,** huir, escaparse; (fig.) estallar; aparecer; declararse; (of fire) tomar fuego; derramarse; (of an eruption) salir. **to b. over,** derramarse por; bañar. **to b. through,** abrirse paso (por); abrirse salida (por); atravesar; (fig.) penetrar; (of the sun, etc.) romper (por). **to b. up,** (depart) separarse; (of meetings) levantarse la sesión; dispersarse; (smash) hacerse pedazos; disolverse; (of a school) cerrarse, empezar las vacaciones; (melt) fundir; desbandarse; (of a camp)

levantar (el campo); (grow old)
hacerse viejo; (be ill) estar
agotado. **to b. with,** romper
con; cesar; reñir con

breakable, a. quebradizo, frágil

breakage, s. rompimiento, quebrantamiento, m.; cosa rota, f.; fractura, f.

break-down, s. accidente, m.; (of a machine) avería, f.; (aut.) pane, f.; (failure) fracaso, m., falta de éxito, f.; deterioración, f.; (in health) crisis de salud, f. **b.-down gang,** pelotón de reparaciones, m.

breaker, s. oleada, f.

breakfast, s. desayuno, m. v.i. desayunar(se), tomar el desayuno. **to have a good b.,** desayunar bien. **b.-cup,** tazón, m. **b.-time,** hora del desayuno, f.

breaking, s. rompimiento, m.; quebrantamiento, m.; fractura, f.; ruptura, f.; (in two) división, f.; (into pieces) despedazamiento, m.; (into small pieces) desmenuzamiento, m.; (destruction) destrozo, m.; (of a blow) parada, f.; (of a law, etc.) violación, f.; (of one's word) no cumplimiento, m.; (of a journey, of sleep, etc.) interrupción, f.; (escape) escape, m., huida, f.; (of an animal) domadura, f.; (of a boy's voice) muda (de la voz), f.; (of news) revelación, f. **b. down,** demolición, f.; (of negotiations) suspensión, f. **b. in,** irrupción, f.; (of an animal) domadura, f.; (training) entrenamiento, m. **b. open,** forzamiento, m.; quebranto, m. **b. out,** huida, f., escape, m.; (fig.) estallido, m.; aparición, f.; declaración, f.; (scattering) derramamiento, m.; (of a rash) erupción, f. **b. up,** dispersión, f.; disolución, f.; fin, m.; ruina, f.; (of a school) cierre, m.; (change in weather) cambio, m.; (of a meeting) levantamiento (de una sesión), m.; (of the earth) roturación, f.

breakneck, a. rápido, veloz, precipitado

breakwater, s. malecón, rompeolas, m.

bream, s. (icht.) sargo, m. **sea-b.,** besugo, m.

breast, s. pecho, m.; (of birds) pechuga, f.; (of female animals) teta, mama, f.; (heart) corazón, m. v.i. (the waves) cortar (las olas); luchar con; (fig.) arrostrar, hacer frente a. **b.-bone,** esternón, m. **b. high,** alto hasta el pecho. **b.-pin,** alfiler de pecho, m. **b.-pocket,** bolsillo de pecho, m. **b.-stroke,** estilo pecho, m.

breasted, a. de pecho . . .; de pechuga . . .; de tetas . . . a **double-b. jacket,** una chaqueta cruzada. a **single-b. jacket,** una chaqueta

breastplate, s. peto, m.; (horses) pretal, m.

breastwork, s. (mil.) parapeto, m.

breath, s. aliento, m.; suspiro, m.; (phonetics) aspiración, f.; (breeze) soplo (de aire), m.; (of scandal, etc.) murmurio, m.; (fragrance) perfume, m., fragancia, f.; (life) vida, f. **in a b.,** de un aliento. **in the same b.,** sin respirar. **out of b.,** sin aliento. **under one's b.,** por lo bajo, entre dientes. **to draw b.,** tomar aliento. **to get one's b. back,** cobrar aliento. **to hold one's b.,** contener el aliento. **to take one's b. away.** (fig.) dejar consternado (a)

breathable, a. respirable

breathe, v.i. respirar; vivir; (of air, etc.) soplar; (take the air) tomar el fresco; (rest) tomar aliento. v.t. respirar; exhalar; dar aire (a); (whisper) murmurar; (convey) expresar, revelar; (infuse) infundir. **to b. forth fury,** echar rayos. **to b. hard,** jadear. **to b. one's last,** exhalar el último suspiro. **to b. in,** inspirar

breathing, s. respiración, f.; (of the air, etc.) soplo, m.; (phonetics) aspiración, f. a. que respira; viviente. **hard or heavy b.,** jadeo, resuello, resoplido, m. **b.-space,** (fig.) respiro, m.

breathless, a. jadeante, sin aliento; (dead) muerto; (sultry) sin un soplo de aire; intenso, profundo; (of haste) precipitado

breathlessly, *adv.* anhelosa-
mente; con expectación
breathlessness, *s.* falta de
aliento, *f.*; respiración difícil, *f.*;
(death) muerte, *f.*; (of weather)
falta de aire, *f.*
bred, *a.* criado. **ill (well) b.,** mal
(bien) criado. **pure-b.,** de raza
breech, *s.* (*anat.*) trasero, *m.*;
(of fire-arms) recámara, *f.*
breeches, *s.* calzones, *m. pl.*;
pantalones, *m. pl.* **riding-b.,**
pantalones de montar, *m. pl.*
to wear the b., (*fig.*) ponerse los
calzones
breed, *s.* casta, raza, *f.*; tipo, *m.*;
clase, *f.* *v.t.* procrear; engendrar,
crear; (bring up) educar; criar.
v.i. reproducirse; sacar cría;
multiplicarse. **to b. in-and-in,**
procrear sin mezclar razas
breeder, *s.* criador (-ra); animal
reproductor, *m.*
breeding, *s.* reproducción, *f.*;
cría, *f.*; (upbringing) crianza, *f.*;
educación, *f.*; instrucción, *f.*;
producción, *f.*; creación, *f. a.* de
cría; (of male animals) semental;
prolífico. **bad b.,** mala crianza, *f.*
good b., buena crianza, *f.*
cross b., cruzamiento de razas,
m. **B. will out,** Aunque la mona
se vista de seda, mona se queda.
b. farm, criadero, *m.*
breeze, *s.* brisa, *f.*, vientecillo,
soplo de aire, *m.*; (argument)
altercación, *f.*, argumento, *m.*;
(of coke) cisco de coque, *m.*
fresh b., brisa fresca, *f.* **light
b.,** brisa floja, *f.* **strong b.,**
viento fuerte, viento muy fresco,
m.
breezy, *a.* con brisa, fresco;
expuesto a la brisa; oreado; (of
manner) animado, jovial
brethren, *s. pl.* hermanos, *m. pl.*
Breton, *a.* and *s* bretón (-ona).
s. (language) bretón, *m.*
brevet, *s.* (*mil.*) graduación hono-
raria, *f.*; nombramiento honorario, *m.* *v.t.* (*mil.*) graduar
breviary, *s.* breviario, *m.*
brevity, *s.* brevedad, *f.*; concisión, *f.*
brew, *s.* mezcla, *f.*; brebaje, *m.*
v.t. hacer (cerveza, té, etc.);
preparar, mezclar; (*fig.*) urdir,
tramar. *v.i.* prepararse; ur-
dirse

brewer, *s.* cervecero (-ra)
brewery, *s.* cervecería, fábrica de
cerveza, *f.*
brewing, *s.* elaboración de cerveza, *f.*
briar, *s.* (wild rose) rosal silvestre, *m.*; (heather) brezo, *m.*
b. pipe, pipa de brezo, *f.*
bribable, *a.* sobornable
bribe, *s.* soborno, cohecho, *m.*
v.t. sobornar, cohechar. **to take
bribes,** dejarse sobornar
briber, *s.* cohechador (-ra)
bribery, *s.* soborno, *m.*
brick, *s.* ladrillo, *m.*; (for children)
piedra de construcción, *f.*; bloque,
m.; (*fam.*) buen chico, *m.*, joya, *f.*
a. de ladrillo. *v.t.* enladrillar.
b.-floor, ladrillado, *m.*; **b.-kiln,**
horno de ladrillo, *m.* **b.-maker,**
ladrillero, *m.* **b.-yard,** ladrillar,
m.
brickbat, *s.* tejuela, *f.*
bricklayer, *s.* albañil, *m.*
bricklaying, *s.* albañilería, *f.*
brickwork, *s.* masonería, *f.*
bridal, *a.* nupcial; de la boda; de
la novia. **b. bed,** tálamo, *m.*
b. cake, torta de la boda, *f.*
b. song, epitalamio, *m.* **b. veil,**
velo de la novia, velo nupcial, *m.*
b. wreath, corona de azahar, *f.*
bride, *s.* novia, desposada, *f.*;
(after marriage) recién casada, *f.*
bridegroom, *s.* novio, *m.*; (after
marriage) recién casado, *m.*
bridesmaid, *s.* madrina de boda,
f.; niña encargada de sostener la
cola de la novia, *f.*
bridge, *s.* (engineering, *mus.*,
naut.) puente, *m.*; lomo (de la
nariz), *m.*; (game) "bridge," *m.*
v.t. construir un puente (sobre),
pontear; (obstacles) salvar;
evitar; (fill in) ocupar, llenar.
auction b., "Bridge" por subasta, *m.* **contract b.,** "Bridge"
por contrato, *m.* **suspension-b.,**
puente colgante, *m.* **b. toll,**
pontazgo, *m.*
bridgehead, *s.* cabeza de puente,
f.
bridle, *s.* brida, *f.*; freno, *m.*
v.t. embridar, enfrenar; (*fig.*)
reprimir. *v.i.* (of horses) levantar
la cabeza; (of persons) erguirse;
hacer un gesto despreciativo.
snaffle b., bridón, *m.* **b. path,**
camino de herradura, *m.*

brief, *a.* breve, corto; conciso; lacónico, seco; rápido; fugaz, pasajero. *s.* (papal) breve, *m.*; (*law*) relación, *f.*; escrito, *m.* *v.t.* (a barrister) instruir. **to hold a b. for,** defender, abogar por. **b.-case,** portapapeles, *m.*; cartera (grande), *f.*

briefly, *adv.* brevemente; en pocas palabras; sucintamente; (tersely) secamente

brier, *s.* rosal silvestre, *m.*; zarza, *f.*

brigade, *s.* (*mil.*) brigada, *f.*; cuerpo, *m.*; asociación, *f.*

brigadier, *s.* brigadier, *m.*

brigand, *s.* bandolero, bandido, *m.*

brigandage, *s.* bandolerismo, *m.*

brigantine, *s.* bergantín, *m.*

bright, *a.* brillante, reluciente; vivo; cristalino; subido; claro; optimista; alegre; inteligente; (quick-witted) agudo; ilustre; (smiling) risueño; (of future, etc.) halagüeño. **to be as b. as a new pin,** estar como una ascua de oro. **b. blue,** azul subido, *m.* **b.-eyed,** con ojos vivos, con ojos chispeantes, ojialegre

Bright's disease, *s.* enfermedad de Bright, glomerulonefritis, *f.*

brighten, *v.t.* hacer brillar; (polish) pulir; (make happy) alegrar; (improve) mejorar. *v.i.* (of the weather) aclarar, despejarse (el cielo); sentirse más feliz; mejorar

brightly, *adv.* brillantemente; alegremente

brightness, *s.* brillo, *m.*; claridad, *f.*; esplendor, *m.*; (of colours) brillantez, *f.*; vivacidad, *f.*; inteligencia, *f.*; agudeza de ingenio, *f.*

brilliance, *s.* fulgor, brillo, *m.*, refulgencia, *f.*; esplendor, *m.*; lustre, *m.*; talento, *m.*; brillantez, gloria, *f.*

brilliant, *a.* brillante. *s.* (gem) brillante, *m.* **to be b.,** (in conversation, etc.) brillar; (be clever) ser brillante

brilliantine, *s.* brillantina, *f.*

brilliantly, *adv.* brillantemente

brim, *s.* (of a glass, etc.) borde, *m.*; (of a hat) ala, *f.*; margen, *m.*; orilla, *f.* **to be full to the b.,** estar lleno hasta los bordes;

(*fig.*) rebosar. **eyes brimming with tears,** ojos arrasados de lágrimas

brimful, *a.* hasta el borde (or los bordes); (*fig.*) rebosante

brimless, *a.* (of hats) sin ala

brimmed, *a.* (of hats) con ala

brimstone, *s.* azufre, *m.*

brindled, *a.* atigrado, abigarrado

brine, *s.* salmuera, *f.*; mar, *m.*; (*poet.*) lágrimas, *f. pl.*

bring, *v.t.* traer; llevar; transportar; (take a person or drive a vehicle) conducir; (*fig.*) acarrear, traer; causar, ocasionar; producir; crear; (induce) persuadir; hacer (ver, etc.); (be worth) valer; (sell for) vender por; (*law*) entablar (un pleito, etc.); (before a judge) hacer comparecer (ante); (present) presentar; (attract) atraer; (place) poner. **to b. home,** llevar a casa; (*fig.*) hacer ver, hacer sentir; demostrar; (a crime) probar contra. **to b. near,** acercar. **to b. about,** efectuar, poner por obra; causar, ocasionar; (achieve) lograr, conseguir. **to b. again,** traer otra vez, llevar de nuevo. **to b. away,** llevarse. **to b. back,** devolver; traer; (of memories) recordar. **to b. down,** llevar abajo, bajar; (of persons) hacer bajar; (humble) humillar; hacer caer; (of prices) hacer bajar; arruinar; destruir. **to b. down the house,** (*theat.*) hacer venirse el teatro abajo. **to b. forth,** (give birth to) dar a luz; producir; causar; sacar a luz. **to b. forward,** hacer adelantarse; empujar hacia adelante; (*fig.*) avanzar; (allege) alegar; (*com.*) llevar a nueva cuenta; presentar, producir. **brought forward,** (*com.*) suma y sigue. **to b. in,** (things) llevar adentro; (persons) hacer entrar; introducir; aparecer con, presentarse con; (meals) servir; producir; declarar; (a verdict) dictar (sentencia de), fallar. **to b. into being,** poner en práctica; dar origen (a). **to b. off,** (a ship) poner a flote; (rescue) salvar, rescatar; (carry out) efectuar, poner en práctica; (achieve) conseguir, lograr. **B. me the glass off the table,**

Tráeme el vaso que hay en la mesa. **to b. on**, causar, inducir; acarrear; iniciar. **He brought a book on to the stage**, Entró en escena llevando un libro (or con un libro). **to b. out**, sacar; poner afuera; (a person) hacer salir; publicar; (a play) poner en escena; sacar a luz; (an idea, jewels, etc.) sacar a relucir; revelar; demostrar; hacer aparecer; (a girl in society) poner de largo (a). **to b. over**, llevar al otro lado; hacer venir; traer; conducir; hacer cruzar; (convert) convertir. **to b. round**, traer; llevar; (from a swoon) sacar de un desmayo; curar; persuadir; conciliar. **to b. through**, hacer atravesar; llevar a través de; ayudar a salir (de un apuro); (an illness) curar de. **to b. to**, traer a; llevar a; (from a swoon) hacer volver en sí; (*naut.*) ponerse a la capa. **He cannot b. himself to**, No puede persuadirse a. **to b. together**, reunir; (things) juntar; amontonar; reconciliar; poner en paz. **to b. under**, someter; sojuzgar; incluir. **to b. up**, llevar arriba, subir; (a person) hacer subir; hacer avanzar; (a price) hacer subir; ir (a); andar; (breed) criar; (educate) educar, criar; (in a discussion) hacer notar; vomitar. **to b. up the rear**, ir al fin (de); (*mil.*) ir a la retaguardia. **well** (or **badly**) **brought up**, bien (o mal) educado. **to b. upon oneself**, buscarse, incurrir (en). **to b. up-to-date**, poner al día; refrescar; rejuvenecer

bringing, *s.* acción de llevar o traer, *f.*; conducción, *f.*; transporte, *m.* **b. forth**, producción, *f.* **b. in**, introducción, *f.* **b. out**, producción, *f.*; publicación, *f.*; (of a girl in society) puesta de largo, *f.* **b. under**, reducción, *f.*; subyugación, *f.* **b. up**, educación, crianza, *f.*

brink, *s.* borde, margen, *m.*; (of water) orilla, *f.*; (*fig.*) margen, *m.* **on the b.**, al margen; a la orilla. **to be on the b. of**, (doing something) estar para, estar a punto de

briny, *a.* salado

briquette, *s.* briqueta, *f.*, aglomerado de carbón, *m.*

brisk, *a.* activo; vivo; animado; rápido, acelerado; enérgico

brisket, *s.* falda, *f.*

briskly, *adv.* vivamente; enérgicamente; aprisa

briskness, *s.* actividad, *f.*; viveza, *f.*; animación, *f.*; rapidez, *f.*; energía, *f.*

bristle, *s.* cerda, seda, *f.* *v.i.* erizarse (also *fig.*)

bristling, *s.* sardina noruega

bristly, *a.* erizado, cerdoso; espinoso; hirsuto

bristol-board, *s.* cartulina, *f.*

British, *a.* británico. **the B.**, el pueblo británico; los ingleses

Briton, *s.* inglés (-esa). **Ancient B.**, britano (-na)

brittle, *a.* frágil, quebradizo, deleznable, friable

brittleness, *s.* fragilidad, friabilidad, *f.*

broach, *s.* (*cul.*) espetón, asador, *m.* *v.t.* espitar (un barril); abrir; (*fig.*) introducir

broad, *a.* ancho; grande; (extensive) vasto, extenso; (full) pleno; (of accents) marcado; (of words) lato; (clear) claro; (of the mind) liberal, tolerante; (of humour, etc.) grosero; (general) general, comprensivo. **in b. daylight**, en pleno día. **b.-brimmed**, de ala ancha. **b.-faced**, cariancho; **b.-minded**, tolerante, liberal, ancho de conciencia. **b.-mindedness**, tolerancia, liberalidad, *f.* **to be b.-minded**, ser tolerante, tener manga ancha. **b.-shouldered**, ancho de espaldas

broadcast, *s.* (*agr.*) siembra al vuelo, *f.*; (*rad.*) radiodifusión, radiotransmisión, emisión, *f.* *a.* radiado. *adv.* por todas partes; extensamente. *v.t.* (*agr.*) sembrar a vuelo; (*rad.*) radiodifundir, radiar, transmitir por radio; (news, etc.) diseminar

broadcaster, *s.* (lecturer) conferenciante, *m.* and *f.*; radiodifusor (-ra); (announcer) locutor (-ra)

broadcasting, *s.* radiación, radiodifusión, *f.*; radio, *f.* **b.-station**, estación de radio, emisora, *f.* **b.-studio**, estudio de emisión, *m.*

broadcloth, s. paño fino, m.

broaden, v.t. ensanchar. v.i. ensancharse

broadly, adv. anchamente; con marcado acento dialectal; de una manera general

broadness, s. anchura, f.; extensión, vastedad, f.; tolerancia, f.; liberalidad, f.; grosería, f.; (of accent) acento marcado, m.

broadside, s. (of a ship) costado, m.; (of guns) andanada, f.; (fig.) batería, f.; (print.) cara de un pliego, f. to be b. on, dar el costado

broadsword, s. espadón, m.

brocade, a. and s. brocado (m.). v.t. decorar con brocado. imitation b., brocatel, m.

brocaded, a. decorado con brocado; de brocado

broccoli, s. bróculi, brécol, m.

brochure, s. folleto, m.

brogue, s. acento, m.; acento irlandés, m.; (shoe) zapato grueso, m.

broil, v.t. emparrillar, asar. v.i. asarse

broken, a. roto; quebrado; (spiritless) abatido, desalentado; (infirm) agotado, debilitado; (ruined) arruinado; (of ground) desigual, escabroso; (of a language) mal pronunciado; (spoilt) estropeado; imperfecto; incompleto; (loose) suelto; (of a horse, etc.) domado; (of the weather) variable; (of sleep) interrumpido; (of the heart, of shoes, etc.) roto; (of the voice, sobs, sighs) entrecortado; (of the voice through old age, etc.) cascada; (incoherent) incoherente. b.-down, (tired) rendido, agotado; arruinado; (not working) estropeado. b.-hearted, roto el corazón, angustiado. b.-winged, aliquebrado

brokenly, adv. (of the voice) con voz entrecortada; a ratos; interrumpidamente

brokenness, s. interrupción, f.; (of the ground) desigualdad, f.; (of speech) imperfección, f.

broker, s. corredor, m.; (stock) corredor de bolsa, m.

brokerage, s. corretaje, m.

bromide, s. bromuro, m.

bromine, s. bromo, m.

bronchi, s. pl. bronquios, m. pl.

bronchial, a. bronquial

bronchitis, s. bronquitis, f.

bronco-pneumonia, s. bronconeumonía, f.

Brontosaurus, s. brontosauro, m.

bronze, s. bronce, m.; objeto de bronce, m. a. de bronce. v.t. broncear. B. Age, Edad de Bronce, f.

brooch, s. broche, m.; alfiler de pecho, m.

brood, s. (of birds) nidada, f.; (of chickens) pollada, f.; (other animals) cría, f.; prole, f. v.i. empollar. to b. over, meditar sobre, rumiar; (of mountains, etc.) dominar

broody, a. (f.) (of hens) clueca

brook, s. arroyo, riachuelo, m. v.t. tolerar, sufrir, permitir

broom, s. escoba, f.; (bot.) retama, f.; hiniesta, f. common b., retama de escobas, f. Spanish b., retama común, retama de olor, hiniesta, f. b.-handle, palo de escoba, m.

broomstick, s. palo de escoba, m.

broth, s. caldo, m.

brothel, s. burdel, lupanar, m.; casa de trato, f.

brother, s. hermano, m.; (colleague) colega, m.; (fam.) compañero, m. foster-b., hermano de leche, m. half-b., medio hermano, m. step-b., hermanastro, m. b.-in-law, hermano político, cuñado, m. b.-officer, compañero de promoción, m.

brotherhood, s. fraternidad, f.; (ecc.) cofradía, f.; hermandad, f.

brotherliness, s. fraternidad, f.

brotherly, a. fraterno

brougham, s. berlina, f.

brow, s. frente, f.; ceja, f.; (of a hill) cresta, cumbre, f.; (edge) borde, m. to knit one's b., fruncir el ceño

browbeat, v.t. intimidar, amenazar

browbeating, s. intimidación, f.

brown, a. castaño; (gallicism often used of shoes, etc.) marrón; pardo; (of complexion, eyes, hair) moreno; (dark brown) bruno; (blackish) negruzco; (toasted) tostado; (burnt) quemado. s. color moreno, m.;

color pardo, *m.*; castaño, *m.*;
(from the sun) bronce, *m. v.t.*
(toast) tostar; (a person) volver
moreno, broncear; (meat) asar.
v.i. tostarse; volverse moreno,
broncearse; asarse. **b.** **bear,**
oso pardo, *m.* **b. owl,** autillo, *m.*
b. paper, papel de estraza, *m.*
b. study, ensimismamiento, *m.,*
meditación, *f.* **b. sugar,** azúcar
moreno (or quebrado), *m.*
brownie, *s.* duende benévolo, *m.*
brownish, *a.* morenucho; que
tira a castaño o a bruno;
parduzco; trigueño
brownness, *s.* color moreno, *m.*
browse, *v.i.* pacer; (over a book)
hojear (un libro)
browsing, *s.* apacentamiento, *m.*;
hojeo (de un libro), *m.*; lectura,
f., estudio, *m.*
bruise, *s.* cardenal, *m.*; abolladura, *f.*; (in metal) bollo, *m.*; (on
fruit) maca, *f. v.t.* acardenalar,
magullar; abollar; (fruit) macar
bruising, *s.* magullamiento, *m.*;
(of metal) abolladura, *f.*; (crushing) machacadura, *f.*; (boxing)
boxeo, pugilato, *m.*
brunette, *s.* trigueña, morena, *f.*
brunt, *s.* peso, *m.*; golpe, *m.*;
choque, *m.*; esfuerzo, *m.* **to**
bear the b., soportar el peso;
sufrir el choque; (*fam.*) pagar el
pato
brush, *s.* cepillo, *m.*; (broom)
escoba, *f.*; (for whitewashing,
etc.) brocha, *f.*; (for painting)
pincel, *m.*; (of a fox) cola (de
zorro), *f.*; (undergrowth) breñal,
matorral, *m.*; (fight) escaramuza,
f.; (argument) altercación, *f.*
scrubbing-b., cepillo para fregar, *m.* **shoe-b.,** cepillo para
limpiar los zapatos, *m.* **stroke**
of the b., brochada, *f.*; pincelada,
f. **whitewash-b.,** brochón, *m.*
b. maker or seller, escobero
(-ra); pincelero (-ra)
brush, *v.t.* cepillar; (sweep)
barrer; frotar; (touch) rozar;
(touch lightly) acariciar. **to b.**
against, rozar, tocar. **to b.**
aside, echar a un lado; (*fig.*) no
hacer caso de; ignorar. **to b.**
off, sacudir(se); quitar(se);
(sweep) barrer. **to b. up,** cepillar; (wool) cardar; (tidy) asear;
(a subject) refrescar, repasar

brushing, *s.* acepilladura, *f.*;
(sweeping) barredura, *f.*; (touching) roce, rozamiento, *m.*; (of
hair) peinadura, *f.*
brushwood, *s.* enjutos, *m. pl.,*
chamarasca, *f.*; matorral, *m.*
brusque, *a.* brusco, seco
brusquely, *adv.* secamente
brusqueness, *s.* brusquedad, *f.*
Brussels, *a.* bruselense; de
Bruselas. **B.** **lace,** éncaje de
Bruselas, *m.*
brussels sprouts, *s. pl.* bretones,
m. pl.
brutal, *a.* bestial, brutal; salvaje,
inhumano
brutality, *s.* brutalidad, bestialidad, *f.*; barbaridad, ferocidad, *f.*
brutalize, *v.t.* embrutecer
brutally, *adv.* brutalmente
brute, *s.* bruto, animal, *m.*;
salvaje, bárbaro, *m.* **b. force,** la
fuerza bruta
brutish, *a.* bruto; sensual, bestial;
grosero; salvaje; estúpido; ignorante. **to become b.,** embrutecerse
bryony, *s.* brionia, *f.*
bubble, *s.* burbuja, *f.*; borbollón,
m. v.i. burbujear; borbollar,
bullir, hervir
bubbling, *s.* burbujeo, *m.*; hervidero, *m.*; (of brooks) murmullo, *m. a.* burbujeante; hirviente; (of brooks) parlero; (of
wine) espumoso, efervescente
bubonic, *a.* bubónico. **b.**
plague, peste bubónica, *f.*
buccal, *a.* bucal
buccaneer, *s.* corsario, *m.*; aventurero, *m.*
buck, *s.* (*zool.*) gamo, *m.*; (male)
macho, *m.*; (fop) galán, petimetre, *m. v.i.* (of a horse)
caracolear; fanfarronear. **to**
pass the b., (*fam.*) echarle a uno
el muerto. **b.-rabbit,** conejo, *m.*
to b. up, hacer de tripas corazón
bucket, *s.* cubo, balde, *m.,*
cubeta, *f.*
buckle, *s.* hebilla, *f. v.t.* enhe-
billar, abrochar con hebilla.
v.i. doblarse. **to b. to,** ponerse a
hacer algo con ahinco
buckled, *a.* con hebillas
buckler, *s.* broquel, *m.*, rodela,
tarjeta, *f.*
buckram, *s.* bocací, *m.*
buckshot, *s.* perdigón, *m.*

buckskin, s. ante, m.

buckwheat, s. alforfón, trigo sarraceno, m.

bucolic, a. bucólico, pastoril

bud, s. brote, m.; botón, capullo, m.; (of vines) bollón, m.; (of vegetables) gema, f. v.i. brotar, germinar. v.t. injertar de escudete

Buddhism, s. budismo, m.

Buddhist, s. budista, m. and f.

Buddhistic, a. budista, búdico

budding, s. brotadura, f.; (of roses, etc.) injerto de escudete, m.; (fig.) germen, m.

budge, v.i. moverse, menearse. v.t. mover

budgerigar, s. periquito, m.

budget, s. presupuesto, m.; (of news, etc.) colección, f. v.i. presuponer

Buenos Aires, (of or from) a. and s. bonaerense, m. and f.

buff, s. color de ante, m.; piel de ante, f. **b.-coloured**, anteado

buffalo, s. búfalo, f.

buffer, s. (railway) parachoques, m.; (of cars) amortiguador, m. **b. state**, estado tapón, m.

buffet, s. bofetón, m.; bofetada, f.; bar, m. v.t. abofetear; golpear; luchar con las olas

buffoon, s. bufón, m.

buffoonery, s. bufonería, f.

bug, s. chinche, f.

bugbear, s. pesadilla, f.

bugle, s. corneta, trompeta, f.; (bead) abalorio, m. **b. blast**, trompetazo, m.

bugler, s. trompetero, m.

build, v.t. edificar; (engines, ships, organs, etc.) construir; (a nest and fig.) hacer; (have built) hacer hacer, edificar; crear; formar; fundar. s. estructura, f.; (of the body) hechura, f.; talle, m. **to b. castles in Spain**, hacer castillos en el aire. **built-up area**, zona urbana, f. **to b. up**, construir, levantar; (block) tapar; (business, reputation) establecer, crear. **to b. upon**, (fig.) contar con, confiar en; esperar de

builder, s. constructor, m.; maestro de obras, m.; (labourer) albañil, m.; creador (-ra), fundador (-ra); arquitecto, m.

building, s. edificación, f.; construcción, f.; edificio, m.; fundación, f.; creación, f. **b. contractor**, maestro de obras, m. **b. material**, material de construcción, m. **b. site**, solar, terreno, m. **b. timber**, madera de construcción, f.

bulb, s. (bot.) bulbo, m.; (elec., phys.) bombilla, f.; (of an oil lamp) cebolla, f.

bulbous, a. bulboso

Bulgarian, a. and s. búlgaro (-ra)

bulge, s. bulto, m.; hinchazón, f.; protuberancia, f.; (mil.) bolsa (en el frente), f. v.i. hincharse; estar lleno (de)

bulging, a. lleno (de); con bultos; hinchado (de)

bulk, s. volumen, tamaño, m.; bulto, m.; (larger part) grueso, m.; mayor parte, f.; (of people) mayoría, f.; (of a ship) capacidad, f. **in b.**, (com.) en bruto, en grueso. **to b. large**, tener mucha importancia

bulkhead, s. (naut.) mamparo, m.

bulkiness, s. abultamiento, m.; volumen, tamaño, m.

bulky, a. voluminoso, grande, grueso

bull, s. toro, m.; (ast.) Tauro, m.; (of some animals) macho, m.; (Stock Exchange) alcista, m. and f.; (of the Pope) bula (del Papa), f. **a b. in a china shop**, un caballo loco en una cacharrería. **to fight bulls**, torear. **b.-calf**, ternero, m. **bull's eye**, blanco, m.; acierto, m. **b. fight**, corrida de toros, f. **b. fighter**, torero, m. **b. fighter's gala uniform**, traje de luces, m. **b.-ring**, plaza de toros, f.

bulldog, s. perro dogo, perro de presa, m.

bulldozer, s. "bulldozer," m.

bullet, s. bala, f. **spent b.**, bala fría, f. **stray b.**, bala perdida, f. **b.-proof**, a prueba de bala

bulletin, s. boletín, m.

bullfinch, s. pinzón real, m.

bullion, s. (com.) metálico, m.; oro (or plata) en barras, m. (f.)

bullock, s. becerro, m.; buey, m.

bully, s. valentón, perdonavidas, gallito, m.; rufián, m. v.t. intimidar; tratar mal. **b. beef**, vaca en lata, f.

bulrush, s. anea, f.
bulwark, s. baluarte, m.; (naut.) antepecho, m.
bumble-bee, s. abejorro, m.
bump, s. golpe, m.; ruido, m.; choque, m.; (bruise) chichón, m., roncha, f.; (aer.) sacudida, f., meneo, m. v.i. (into, against) tropezar con; (along) saltar en. v.t. chocar (contra)
bumper, s. copa llena hasta los bordes, f., vaso lleno, m.; (of a car) parachoques, m. a b. harvest, una cosecha abundante
bumpkin, s. patán, villano, m.
bumptious, a. fatuo, presuntuoso, presumido
bumptiously, adv. presuntuosamente
bumptiousness, s. fatuidad, presunción, f.
bumpy, s. (of surface) desigual, escabroso; (of a vehicle) incómodo, con mala suspensión
bun, s. buñuelo, bollo, m.; (hair) moño, m.
bunch, s. (of fruit) racimo, m.; manojo, m.; (of flowers) ramo, m.; (tuft) penacho, m.; (gang) pandilla, f. v.i. arracimarse; agruparse
bundle, s. atado, lío, m.; (of papers) legajo, m.; (of sticks) haz, m.; (sheaf) fajo, m.; (package) paquete, m.; fardo, hatillo, m.; (roll) rollo, m. v.t. atar, liar; envolver; empaquetar; (stuff) meter, introducir. to b. in, meter dentro (de). to b. out, despachar sin ceremonia, poner de patitas en la calle
bung, s. tapón, tarugo, m. v.t. atarugar
bungalow, s. casa de un solo piso, f.
bungle, v.t. estropear; hacer mal. s. equivocación, f., yerro, m.; cosa (o obra) mal hecha, f.
bungling, a. chapucero, torpe
bunion, s. juanete (del pie), m.
bunk, s. litera, f. v.i. (fam.) poner pies en polvorosa, pirarse
bunker, s. (naut.) pañol, m.; (for coal) carbonera, f.; (golf) "bunker," m., hoya de arena, f.
bunkum, s. patrañas, f. pl.
bunting, s. gallardete, m.
buoy, s. boya, baliza, f. v.t. boyar; abalizar; (fig.) sostener. light b., boya luminosa, f.

buoyancy, s. flotación, f.; (fig.) optimismo, m., alegría, f.
buoyant, a. boyante; ligero
burden, s. carga, f., peso, m.; (of a ship) tonelaje, m., capacidad, f.; (of a song) estribillo, m.; (gist) esencia, f. v.t. cargar. to be a b. on, pesar sobre
burdensome, a. pesado, oneroso, gravoso; abrumador
burdensomeness, s. pesadez, f.; agobio, m.
burdock, s. (bot.) lampillo, m.
bureau, s. buró, secreter, m.; escritorio, m.; (office) oficina, f.; departamento, m.
bureaucracy, s. burocracia, f.
bureaucrat, s. burócrata, m. and f.; (fam.) mandarín, m.
bureaucratic, a. burocrático
burgher, s. ciudadano (-na), vecino (-na)
burglar, s. ladrón de casas, escalador, m. cat b., gato, m. b. alarm, alarma contra ladrones, f. b. insurance, seguro contra robo, m.
burglary, s. robo nocturno de una casa, m.
burgle, v.i. robar una casa de noche. v.t. robar
burgomaster, s. burgomaestre, m.
Burgundian, a. and s. borgoñón (-ona)
burgundy, s. vino de Borgoña, borgoña, m.
burial, s. entierro, m. b.-ground, campo santo, cementerio, m. b. service, misa de difuntos, f. b. society, sociedad de entierros, f.
burin, s. buril, cincel, m.
burlesque, a. burlesco. s. parodia, f. v.t. parodiar
burliness, s. corpulencia, f.
burly, a. corpulento, fornido
Burmese, a. and s. birmano (-na)
burn, v.t. quemar; calcinar; (bricks) cocer; cauterizar; (the tongue) picar; (dry up) secar; (the skin by sun or wind) tostar. v.i. quemar; arder; (fig.) abrasarse (en). to b. to ashes, reducir a cenizas. to b. away, consumir(se). to b. oneself, quemarse. to b. up, quemar del todo, consumir. to b. with, (fig.) abrasarse en

burn, s. quemadura, f.; (stream) arroyo, m.

burnable, a. combustible

burner, s. quemador (-ra); mechero, m.

burning, s. quema, f.; incendio, m.; fuego, m.; (inflammation) inflamación, f.; (pain) quemazón, f.; abrasamiento, m. a. en llamas; ardiente; intenso; (notorious) notorio, escandaloso; abrasador; palpitante. **b. question,** cuestión palpitante, f.

burnish, s. bruñido, m.; lustre, brillo, m. v.t. bruñir; pulir, pulimentar, dar brillo a; (weapons) acicalar. v.i. tomar lustre

burnisher, s. bruñidor, acicalador, m.

burnishing, s. bruñido, m.; pulimento, m.; (of weapons) acicalado, m.

burnouse, s. albornoz, m.

burr, s. (bot.) cáliz de flor con espinas, m.; (mech.) rebaba, f.; sonido fuerte de la erre, m.

burrow, s. madriguera, f., vivar, m.; (for rabbits) conejera, f. v.i. amadrigar; minar

bursar, s. tesorero, m.; becario, m.

bursary, s. tesorería, f.; beca, f.

burst, s. estallido, m., explosión, f.; (in a pipe) avería, f., (fit) acceso, m.; transporte, m.; (effort) esfuerzo, m.; (expanse) extensión, f., panorama, m. **b. of applause,** salva de aplausos, f.

burst, v.i. estallar; reventar; quebrarse; romperse; (overflow) desbordar; (of seams) hacerse; derramarse (por); (into laughter) romper a; (into tears) deshacerse en. v.t. quebrar; romper; hacer estallar. **to b. upon the view,** aparecer de pronto. **to b. into,** irrumpir en; (exclamations, etc.) prorrumpir en. **to b. into tears,** romper a llorar, deshacerse en lágrimas. **to b. open,** abrir con violencia; forzar

bursting, s. estallido, m.; quebrantamiento, m.; (overflowing) desbordamiento, m.

bury, v.t. enterrar, sepultar; sumergir; (hide) esconder, ocultar; (forget) echar tierra a

bus, s. autobús, ómnibus, m. **double-decker bus,** ómnibus de dos pisos, m. **to travel by bus,** ir en autobús. **bus station,** estación de autobuses, f.

busby, s. birretina, gorra de húsar, f.

bush, s. arbusto, matojo, m.; (undergrowth) maleza, f.; tierra virgen, f.; (mech.) manguito, m.

bushel, s. medida de áridos, f. (In England 8 gallons or 36·37 litres)

bushiness, s. espesura, f.; densidad, f.

bushman, s. bosquimano, m.

bushy, a. lleno de arbustos; denso; espeso; grueso; (of eyebrows, etc.) poblado

busily, adv. diligentemente, solícitamente; afanosamente, laboriosamente. **He was b. occupied in . . . ,** Estaba muy ocupado en . . .

business, s. ocupación, f.; quehaceres, m. pl.; (matter) asunto, m., cosa, f.; empleo, oficio, m.; (com.) negocio(s), m. (pl.); casa comercial, f.; (trade) comercio, m.; (clients, connection) clientela, f.; (right) derecho, m.; (theat.) juego escénico, m., pantomima, f. **He had no b. to do that,** Él no tenía derecho a hacer eso. **Mind your own b.!** ¡No te metas donde no te llaman! **on b.,** por negocios. **to be in b. for oneself,** tener negocios por su propia cuenta. **to mean b.,** hacer algo en serio; estar resuelto. **to send about his b.,** mandar a paseo (a). **to set up in b.,** establecer un negocio. **b. affairs,** negocios, m. pl. **b. agent,** agente de negocios, m. **b. hours,** horas de trabajo, f. pl. **b.-like,** formal, práctico, sistemático. **b. man,** hombre de negocios, negociante, m.

buskin, s. borceguí, botín, coturno, m.

bust, s. (art) busto, bulto, m.; pecho, m. **b. bodice,** sostén, m.

bustard, s. avutarda, f.

bustle, s. actividad, animación, f.; confusión, f.; (of a dress) polizón, tontillo, m. v.i. menearse, darse prisa. v.t. dar prisa (a)

bustling; *a.* activo; ocupado, atareado; animado; bullicioso, ruidoso

busy, *a.* ocupado; atareado; activo, diligente; (of places) animado, bullicioso; (of streets) de gran circulación; (officious) entremetido. **to b. oneself,** ocuparse (en, con); dedicarse (a), entregarse (a); (interfere) entremeterse (con). **to be b.,** estar ocupado; estar atareado, tener mucho que hacer. **b.-body,** bullebulle, *m.* and *f.*, entremetido (-da), chismoso (-sa)

busyness, *s.* ocupación, *f.*; laboriosidad, *f.*; actividad, *f.*

but, *conjunc., prep., adv.* pero; sino; (only) solamente; (except) menos; excepto; (almost) casi; que no; si no; (that) que; (nevertheless) sin embargo, empero, no obstante; (without) sin, sin que; (of time recently passed) no más que, tan recientemente. *s.* pero, *m.* **He cannot choose but go,** No puede hacer otra cosa que marcharse. **to do nothing but . . .,** hacer únicamente . . ., no hacer más que . . . **but for,** a no ser por. **but yesterday,** solamente ayer. **but then, yet,** sin embargo

butcher, *s.* carnicero, *m.* *v.t.* matar reses; hacer una carnicería en. **butcher's boy,** mozo del carnicero, *m.* **butcher's shop,** carnicería, *f.*

butchery, *s.* carnicería, *f.*; matanza, *f.*

butler, *s.* mayordomo, *m.* **butler's pantry,** despensa, repostería, *f.*

butt, *s.* (cask) tonel, *m.*, pipa, *f.*; (for water) barril, *m.*; (of a cigarette, etc.) colilla, *f.*; (of fire-arms) culata, *f.*; (handle) mango, cabo, *m.*; (billiards) mocho, *m.*; (earthwork) terrero, *m.*; (fig., object) objeto (de), *m.*; (of bulls, etc.) topetada, *f.*; *pl.* **butts,** campo de tiro, *m.*; (target) blanco, *m.* *v.t.* (toss) topar, acornear; (meet) tropezar (con). **to b. in,** (*fam.*) entremeterse, meter baza; encajarse

butter, *s.* mantequilla, *f.* *v.t.* untar con mantequilla. **b.-dish,** mantequera, *f.* **b.-fingers,** torpe, *m.* **b.-knife,** cuchillo para mantequilla, *m.* **b.-milk,** suero de mantequilla, *m.* **b.-print,** molde para mantequilla, *m.* **b.-sauce,** mantequilla fundida, *f.*

buttercup, *s.* ranúnculo, botón de oro, *m.*

butterfly, *s.* mariposa, *f.*

butterscotch, *s.* dulce de azúcar y mantequilla, *m.*

buttery, *s.* despensa, *f.*

buttocks, *s. pl.* nalgas, posaderas, *f. pl.*

button, *s.* botón, *m.*; *pl.* **buttons,** botones, paje, *m.* *v.t.* abotonar, abrochar. *v.i.* abotonarse, abrocharse. **to press the b.,** apretar el botón. **b.-hook,** abotonador, *m.*

buttonhole, *s.* ojal, *m.*; flor que se lleva en el ojal, *f.* *v.t.* (*sew.*) hacer ojales; (embroidery) hacer el festón; (*fam.*) importunar

buttoning, *s.* abrochamiento, *m.*

buttress, *s.* estribo, macho, contrafuerte, *m.*; (*fig.*) apoyo, sostén, *m.* *v.t.* afianzar, estribar; (*fig.*) apoyar, sostener. **flying-b.,** arbotante, *m.*

buxom, *a.* (of a woman) fresca, guapetona, frescachona

buxomness, *s.* frescura, *f.*

buy, *v.t.* comprar; obtener; (achieve) lograr; (bribe) sobornar. **to buy on credit,** comprar al fiado. **to buy back,** comprar de nuevo; redimir; (ransom) rescatar. **to buy for,** (a price) comprar por; (purpose or destination) comprar para. **to buy in,** (at an auction) comprar por cuenta del dueño. **to buy off,** librarse de uno con dinero. **to buy out,** (of a business) comprar la parte de un socio. **to buy up,** comprar todo, acaparar

buyable, *a.* comprable, que se puede comprar

buyer, *s.* comprador (-ra)

buying, *s.* compra, *f.* **b. back,** rescate, *m.* **b. up,** acaparamiento, *m.*

buzz, *s.* zumbido, *m.*; (whisper) susurro, murmullo, *m.*; (of a bell) sonido (del timbre), *m.* *v.i.* zumbar; susurrar

buzzer, *s.* zumbador, *m.*; sirena, *f.*; (bell) timbre, *m.*

buzzing, *a.* zumbador, que zumba. *s.* See buzz

by, *prep.* por; de; en; a; con; (of place) cerca de, al lado de; (according to) según, de acuerdo con; (in front of, past) delante (de); (at the latest) antes de, al más tardar; (expressing agency) por; (by means of) mediante; (through, along) por; (upon) sobre; (for) para; (under) bajo. He will be here by Wednesday, Estará aquí para el miércoles; (not later than) Estará aquí antes del miércoles (or el miércoles al más tardar). How did he come by it? ¿Cómo llegó a su poder? He will come by train, Vendrá en tren. I know her by sight, La conozco de vista. There are three children by the first marriage, Hay tres niños del primer matrimonio. He goes by the name of Pérez, Se le conoce por (or bajo) el nombre de Pérez. six feet by eight, seis pies por ocho. They called her by her name, La llamaron por su nombre. The book is near by me, El libro está a mi lado. two by two, dos por dos. The picture was painted by Cézanne, El cuadro fué pintado por Cézanne. drop by drop, gota a gota. by a great deal, con mucho. by all means, naturalmente; de todos modos; cueste lo que cueste. by chance, por ventura. by day (night), de día (noche). by daylight, a la luz del día. by doing it, con hacerlo. by myself, solo; sin ayuda

by, *adv.* (near) cerca; (before) delante; al lado; a un lado; aparte; (of time) pasado. to put by, (keep) guardar; (throw away) desechar; (accumulate) acumular; (put out of the way) arrinconar. to pass by, pasar; pasar delante (de). by and by, luego; pronto; más tarde. by now, ya, antes de ahora. by the way, entre paréntesis, a propósito; de paso; al lado del camino. by-election, elección parcial, *f.* by-law, reglamento, *m.* by-pass, ruta de evitación, *f.*, desvío, *m.*; (*mech., elec.*) deri-

vación, *f. v.i.* desviarse de; (*mil.*) rebasar. by-product, derivado, *m.*; (*chem.*) producto derivado, *m.*; (*fig.*) consecuencia, *f.*; resultado, *m.*

bye, *s.* (in cricket) meta, *f.* by the bye, a propósito, entre paréntesis

bygone, *a.* pasado. Let bygones be bygones, Lo pasado pasado

bypath, *s.* senda, vereda, *f.*

byplay, *s.* pantomima, *f.*, gestos, *m. pl.*; (*theat.*) juego escénico, *m.*, escena muda, *f.*

Byronic, *a.* bironiano

bystander, *s.* espectador (-ra); *pl.* bystanders, los circunstantes

bystreet, *s.* callejuela, *f.*; calle pobre, *f.*

byway, *s.* camino desviado, *m.*; (*fig.*) senda indirecta, *f.*; *pl.* byways, andurriales, *m. pl.*

byword, *s.* proverbio, *m.*; objeto de burla o escándalo, *m.*

Byzantine, *a.* bizantino

C

c, *s.* (letter) c, *f.*; (*mus.*) do, *m.*

cab, *s.* (horse-drawn) simón, *m.*; (taxi) coche de alquiler, *m.*; (of a locomotive) cabina del conductor, *f.* cab-rank, punto de coches, *m.*

cabala, *s.* cábala, *f.*

cabalistic, *a.* cabalístico

cabaret, *s.* cabaret, *m.*; taberna, *f.*

cabbage, *s.* col, berza, *f.* red c., lombarda, *f.* c. butterfly, mariposa de col, *f.*

cabin, *s.* cabaña, choza, *f.*; (*naut.*) camarote, *m.*; (railway) garita, *f.*; (*aer.*) cabina, *f.* c. boy, grumete, *m.* c. trunk, baúl mundo, *m.*

cabinet, *s.* (piece of furniture) vitrina, *f.*; colección, exposición, *f.*; (*pol.*) gabinete, *m.*; (of a radio) cónsola, *f.* c.-maker, ebanista, *m.* c.-making, ebanistería, *f.* C. meeting, Consejo de Ministros, *m.* C. Minister, Ministro, *m.*

cable, *s.* amarra, maroma, *f.*; cable, *m.*; cable(grama), *m. v.t.* cablegrafiar. electric c., cable eléctrico, *m.* overhead c., cable aéreo, *m.*

cablegram, s. cablegrama, m.

cabman, s. cochero de punto, simón, m.

caboose, s. (naut.) cocina, f.

cabriolet, s. cabriolé, m.

cachalot, s. cachalote, m.

cache, s. escondite, escondrijo, m.

cackle, v.i. (of a hen) cacarear; (of a goose) graznar; (of humans) chacharear. s. cacareo, m.; graznido, m.; cháchara, f.

cacophony, s. cacofonía, f.

cactus, s. cacto, m.

cad, s. sinvergüenza, m.; tipo de cuidado, m.

cadaverous, a. cadavérico

caddish, a. mal educado, grosero

caddy, s. (for tea) cajita para té, f.; (golf) "caddy," m.

cadence, s. cadencia, f.

cadet, s. hermano menor, m.; (mil.) cadete, m.

cadge, v.i. sablear. v.t. dar un sablazo (a)

cadger, s. sablista, m. and f.; mendigo, m.; (loafer) golfo, m.

cadmium, s. cadmio, m.

cæcum, s. ciego, m.

Cæsarian, a. cesáreo

cæsura, s. cesura, f.

café, s. café, m.

cafeteria, s. bar automático, m.

caffeine, s. cafeína, f

cage, s. (animal's, bird's) jaula, f.; (of a lift) camarín, m.; (for transporting miners) jaula, f. v.t. enjaular; encerrar

Cain, to raise, armar lo de Dios es Cristo

cairn, s. montón de piedras, m.

cajole, v.t. lisonjear; engatusar; embromar; instar

cajolery, s. zalamerías, f. pl.; marrullería, f., engatusamiento, m.

cake, s. (cul.) pastel, m., torta, f.; (of chocolate, etc.) pastilla, f. v.t. and v.i. cuajar; formar costra; (with mud) enlodar. to sell like hot cakes, venderse como pan bendito. to take the c., llevarse la palma. c. of soap, pastilla de jabón, f. c.-shop, pastelería, f.

calamary, s. calamar, m.

calamine, s. calamina, f.

calamitous, a. calamitoso, desastroso

calamity, s. calamidad, f.; desastre, m.

calash, s. (carriage) calesa, carretela, f.; (hood) capota, f.

calcareous, a. calcáreo

calcination, s. calcinación, f.

calcine, v.t. calcinar

calcium, s. calcio, m.

calculate, v.t. calcular; adaptar. to c. on, contar con

calculated, a. premeditado. to be c. to, conducir a; ser a propósito para

calculatedly, adv. calculadamente

calculating, s. cálculo, m. a. calculador; (of persons) interesado; (shrewd) perspicaz; atento. c. machine, máquina de calcular, f., calculador, m.

calculation, s. cálculo, m.; calculación, f.

calculus, s. cálculo, m.

calendar, s. calendario, m.; almanaque, m.; (university, etc.) programa, m.

calender, s. calandria, f. v.t. calandrar, cilindrar

calends, s. pl. calendas, f. pl.

calf, s. becerro (-rra), ternero (-ra); (young of other animals) hijuelo, m.; (of the leg) pantorrilla, f.; (leather) cuero de becerro, m.; piel, f. calf's-foot, pie de ternera, m. c. love, amor de muchachos, m.

calibrate, v.t. calibrar

calibre, s. calibre (also fig.), m.

calico, s. indiana, f.; percal, m. c.-printer, fabricante de estampados, m.

Californian, a. californio. s. californio (-ia)

caliph, s. califa, m.

caliphate, s. califato, m.

calk. See caulk.

call, s. llamada, f.; (shout) grito, m.; (of a bird) canto, m.; (signal) señal, f.; (visit) visita, f.; (by a ship) escala, f.; (mil.) toque, m.; (need) necesidad, f.; (of religion, etc.) vocación, f.; invitación, f; (demand) demanda, f.; exigencia, f. They came at my c., Acudieron a mi llamada. port of c., puerto de escala, m. telephone c., llamada telefónica, f. to pay a c., hacer una visita. within c., al alcance de la voz. c.-box, cabina del teléfono, f. c.-boy, ayudante del traspunte, m.

call, *v.i.* llamar; gritar, dar voces; (visit) visitar, hacer una visita (a); venir; (stop) parar; (of a ship) hacer escala. *v.t.* llamar; (a meeting, etc.) convocar; (awaken) despertar, llamar; (say) decir; (appoint) nombrar; (at cards) declarar. **She is called Dorothy,** Ella se llama Dorotea. **Madrid calling!** ¡Aquí Radio Madrid! **Will you c. me at eight o'clock, please?** Haga el favor de despertarme (llamarme) a las ocho. **to c. at a port,** hacer escala en un puerto. **to c. a halt,** hacer alto. **to c. a strike,** declarar una huelga. **to c. names,** vituperar, injuriar. **to c. to account,** pedir cuentas (a). **to c. to arms,** tocar el arma; alarmar. **to c. to mind,** acordarse (de), recordar. **to c. to witness,** hacer testigo (de). **to c. back,** *v.t.* llamar; hacer volver; (unsay) desdecir. *v.i.* (return) volver; venir a buscar; ir a buscar. **I called back for the parcel,** Volví a buscar el paquete. **to c. for,** pedir a gritos; llamar; (demand) pedir; exigir; (collect a person) pasar a buscar; (parcels, etc.) ir (or venir) a recoger. **He called for help,** Pidió socorro a gritos. **to c. forth,** producir; provocar; inspirar; revelar; (bring together) reunir. **to c. in,** hacer entrar; invitar; (a specialist, etc.) llamar; (worn coin) retirar de la circulación; recoger. **to c. in question,** poner en duda. **to c. off,** (dogs, etc.) llamar; (a strike) cancelar; parar; terminar; (a person) disuadir (de); (postpone) aplazar; suspender; (refrain) desistir (de). **to c. on,** (visit) hacer una visita (a), ir a ver, visitar; (of a doctor) visitar; (a person to do something) recurrir (a); (for a speech) invitar (a hablar); (invoke) invocar. **I shall now c. on Mr. Martínez,** El señor Martínez tiene la palabra. **to c. out,** *v.t.* hacer salir; provocar; inspirar; (challenge) desafiar; retar. *v.i.* gritar. **to c. over,** (names) pasar lista (de). **to c. up,** hacer subir; (to the army)

llamar a filas (a); (telephone) llamar por teléfono (a); (memories) evocar. **to c. upon.** See **to c. on.**

caller, *s.* visita, *f.*
calligraphist, *s.* calígrafo, *m.*
calligraphy, *s.* caligrafía, *f.*
calling, *s.* llamamiento, *m.*; (occupation) profesión, *f.*; empleo, *m.*; vocación, *f.*; (of a meeting) convocación, *f.*
callipers, *s. pl.* compás de puntas, pie de rey, *m.*
callisthenics, *s. pl.* calistenia, *f.*
callosity, *s.* callosidad, *f.*
callous, *a.* (of skin) calloso; (*fig.*) insensible, duro, inhumano
callously, *adv.* sin piedad
callousness, *s.* falta de piedad, inhumanidad, dureza, *f.*
callow, *a.* (of birds) implume; (inexperienced) bisoño, inexperto, novato
callus, *s.* callo, *m.*
calm, *s.* calma, *f.*; paz, tranquilidad, *f.*; sosiego, *m.*; serenidad, *f. a.* (of the sea) en calma; tranquilo; sereno; sosegado. *v.t.* calmar; tranquilizar; apaciguar. *v.i.* calmarse; tranquilizarse; sosegarse. **dead c.,** calma chicha, *f.*
calming, *a.* calmante
calmly, *adv.* tranquilamente, sosegadamente; con calma
calmness, *s.* calma, tranquilidad, *f.*; ecuanimidad, serenidad, *f.*
caloric, *a.* calórico
calorie, *s.* caloría, *f.*
calorific, *a.* calorífico
calumniate, *v.t.* calumniar
calumniation, *s.* calumnia, *f.*
calumniator, *s.* calumniador (-ra)
calumny, *s.* calumnia, *f.*
calvary, *s.* calvario, *m.*
calve, *v.i.* (of a cow, etc.) parir
Calvinism, *s.* calvinismo, *m.*
Calvinist, *s.* calvinista, *m.* and *f.*
Calvinistic, *a.* calvinista
calyx, *s.* cáliz, *m.*
cam, *s.* (*mech.*) leva, *f.* **cam-shaft,** árbol de levas, *m.*
camaraderie, *s.* compañerismo, *m.*
camber, *s.* comba(dura), *f.*
cambric, *s.* batista, *f.*
camel, *s.* camello (-lla). **c.-driver,** camellero, *m.* **camel's hair,** pelo de camello, *m.*

camellia, s. camelia, f.
cameo, s. camafeo, m.
camera, s. (phot.) máquina fotográfica, f. **folding c.,** máquina
fotográfica plegable, f. **in c.,**
a puerta cerrada. **c. obscura,**
cámara obscura, f.
cami-knickers, s. camisa pantalón, f.
camisole, s. cubrecorsé, m.
camomile, s. camomila, manzanilla, f.
camouflage, s. camuflaje, m.
v.t. camuflar
camp, s. campamento, m.; campo,
m.; (fig.) vida de cuartel, f.; (for
school children, etc.) colonia, f.;
(party) partido, m. v.i. acampar,
vivir en tiendas de campaña.
to break c., levantar el campo.
c.-bed, cama de campaña, f.
c.-stool, silla de campaña, f.
campaign, s. campaña, f. v.i.
hacer una campaña
campaigner, s. veterano, m.;
propagandista, m. and f.
campaigning, s. campañas, f.
pl.
campanula, s. campánula, f.
camphor, s. alcanfor, m.
camphorated, a. alcanforado
can, v. auxil. poder; (know how to)
saber. **You can go to the village
when you like,** Puedes ir al
pueblo cuando quieras. **I cannot
allow that,** No puedo permitir
eso. **What can they mean ?** ¿Qué
quieren decir ? **If only things
could have been different!**
¡Si solamente las cosas hubiesen
sido distintas! **Can you come to
dinner on Saturday ?** ¿Puede
Vd. venir a cenar el sábado?
I can come later if you like,
Puedo (or Podría) venir más
tarde si Vd. quiere. **Mary can**
(knows how to) **play the piano,**
María sabe tocar el piano
can, s. lata, f.; (for carrying
sandwiches, etc.) fiambrera, f.
v.t. conservar en latas. **can-
opener,** abrelatas, m.
Canadian, a. canadiense. s.
canadiense, m. and f.
canaille, s. gentualla, gentuza,
f.
canal, s. canal, m.
canalization, s. canalización, f.
canalize, v.t. canalizar

canary, s. canario (-ia); color de
canario, m.; vino de Canarias, m.
roller c., canario de raza flauta.
m. **c.-seed,** alpiste, m.
cancel, v.t. cancelar; revocar;
borrar; anular. **to c. out,**
(math.) anular
cancellation, s. cancelación, f.;
revocación, f.; anulación, f.
cancer, s. (med.) cáncer, m.;
(ast.) Cáncer, m.
cancerous, a. canceroso. **to become c.,** cancerarse
candelabrum, s. candelabro, m.
candescent, a. candente
candid, a. franco; sincero. **If I
am to be c.,** Si he de decir la
verdad, Si he de ser franco
candidate, s. candidato (-ta);
aspirante, m.
candidature, s. candidatura,
f.
candidly, adv. francamente; sinceramente
candidness, s. franqueza, f.;
sinceridad, f.
candied, a. (of peel, etc.) almibarado, garapiñado
candle, s. vela, candela, f. **wax
c.,** cirio, m. **You cannot hold a
c. to him,** No llegas a la suela de
su zapato. **The game is not
worth the c.,** La cosa no vale la
pena. **to burn the c. at both
ends,** consumir la vida. **c.-
grease,** sebo, m. **c.-light,** luz de
las velas, f.; luz artificial, f. **c.-
maker,** candelero, m. **c.-power,**
(elec.) potencia luminosa, bujía, f.
c.-snuffer, apagavelas, matacandelas, m.
Candlemas, s. Candelaria, f.
candlestick, s. candelero, m.,
palmatoria, f.; (processional)
cirial, m.
candour, s. franqueza, f.; sinceridad, f.; candor, m.
candy, s. caramelo, bombón, m.
v.t. garapiñar, almibarar
candytuft, s. carraspique, m.
cane, s. (bot.) caña, f.; (for chair
seats, etc.) rejilla, f.; (walking-
stick) bastón, m.; (for punishment) vara, f. v.t. apalear,
pegar. **sugar-c.,** caña de
azúcar, f. **c.-break,** cañaveral,
m. **c. chair,** sillón de mimbres,
m. **c.-sugar,** azúcar de caña, m.
c.-syrup, miel de caña, f.

canine, *a.* canino. *s.* (tooth) diente canino, *m.*

caning, *s.* paliza, *f.*

canister, *s.* bote, *m.*, cajita, *f.*

canker, *s.* úlcera, *f.*; (in trees) cancro, *m.*; (*fig.*) cáncer, *m.* *v.t.* roer; (*fig.*) corromper

canned, *a.* en lata

cannibal, *s.* caníbal, *m.* and *f.*, antropófago (-ga). *a.* caníbal, antropófago

cannibalism, *s.* canibalismo, *m.*, antropofagia, *f.*

canning, *s.* conservación en latas, *f.* **c. factory,** fábrica de conservas alimenticias, *f.*

cannon, *s.* (fire-arm) cañón, *m.*; (billiards) carambola, *f.* *v.i.* carambolear. **to c. into,** chocar con. **c.-ball,** bala de cañón, *f.* **c.-shot,** cañonazo, *m.*

cannonade, *s.* cañoneo, *m.*

canny, *a.* cuerdo, sagaz

canoe, *s.* canoa, *f.*; piragua, *f.* *v.i.* ir en canoa

canoeist, *s.* canoero (-ra)

canon, *s.* (*ecc.*, *mus.*, *print.*) canón, *m.*; (dignitary) canónigo, *m.*; (criterion) criterio, *m.* **c. law,** derecho canónico, *m.*

canonical, *a.* canónico

canonicals, *s. pl.* vestiduras, *f. pl.*

canonization, *s.* canonización, *f.*

canonize, *v.t.* canonizar

canonry, canonship, *s.* canonjía, *f.*

canopy, *s.* dosel, toldo, *m.*; palio, *m.*; (*fig.*) capa, bóveda, *f.* **the c. of heaven,** la capa (or bóveda) del cielo

cant, *v.t.* inclinar; ladear. *v.i.* inclinarse; (be a hypocrite) camandulear. *s.* (slope) inclinación, *f.*, sesgo, desplomo, *m.*; (hypocrisy) fariseísmo, *m.*

Cantabrian, *a.* cantábrico

cantankerous, *a.* irritable, intratable, malhumorado

cantankerousness, *s.* mal humor, *m.*, irritabilidad, *f.*

cantata, *s.* cantata, *f.*

canteen, *s.* cantina, *f.*; (water bottle) cantimplora, *f.* **c. of cutlery,** juego de cubiertos, *m.*

canter, *s.* medio galope, *m.* *v.i.* andar a galope corto

canticle, *s.* cántico, *m.*

canting, *a.* hipócrita

canto, *s.* canto, *m.*

canton, *s.* (province and *her.*) cantón, *m.* *v.t.* (of soldiers) acantonar

cantonment, *s.* acantonamiento, cantón, *m.*

cantor, *s.* (*ecc.*) chantre, *m.*

canvas, *s.* lona, *f.*; (*art*) lienzo, *m.*; (*naut.*) vela, *f.*, paño, *m.* **under c.,** en tiendas de campaña; (of ships) a toda vela

canvass, *v.t.* (votes, etc.) solicitar

canvasser, *s.* solicitador (-ra) (de votos, etc.)

canvassing, *s.* solicitación (de votos, etc.), *f.*

canyon, *s.* cañón, *m.*

canzonet, *s.* chanzoneta, *f.*

caoutchouc, *s.* caucho, *m.*

cap, *s.* gorra, *f.*; (with a peak) montera, *f.*; (type of military headgear with brim at front) quépis, *m.*; (cardinal's) birrete, *m.*; (*univ.*) bonete, *m.*; (pointed) caperuza, *f.*; (woman's old-fashioned) cofia, *f.*; (jester's) gorro de bufón, *m.*; (on a bottle) cápsula, tapa, *f.* *v.t.* (*univ.*) conferir el grado (a). **cap and bells,** gorro de bufón, *m.* **cap and gown,** traje académico, *m.* **to throw one's cap over the windmill,** echar la capa al toro. **to cap it all,** ser el colmo

capability, *s.* capacidad, *f.*; aptitud, *f.*

capable, *a.* capaz; competente; (of improvement) susceptible; (full of initiative) emprendedor

capably, *adv.* competentemente

capacious, *a.* espacioso; grande; extenso

capaciousness, *s.* capacidad, *f.*; amplitud, *f.*

capacitate, *v.t.* capacitar

capacity, *s.* capacidad, *f.*; calidad, *f.*; aptitud, *f.* **in the c. of,** en calidad de. **seating c.,** número de asientos, *m.*; (in aircraft) número de plazas, *m.*

caparison, *s.* caparazón, *m.*

cape, *s.* (cloak) capa, *f.*; (short) capotillo, *m.*, capeta, *f.*; (fur) cuello, *m.*; (*geog.*) cabo, promontorio, *m.* **c. coat,** capote, *m.*

caper, *v.i.* (gambol) brincar, saltar; cabriolar, corcovear; (play) juguetear. *s.* travesura, *f.*; zapateta, *f.*; cabriola, *f.*; (whim) capricho, *m.*; (*bot.*) alcaparra, *f.*

to c. about, dar saltos, brincar; juguetear

capillarity, s. capilaridad, f.

capillary, a. capilar. s. vaso capilar, m.

capital, a. capital; mortal; de muerte; de vida; principal; (of letters) mayúscula; (very good) excelente. s. (city) capital, f.; (letter) (letra) mayúscula, f.; (com.) capital, m.; (arch.) capitel, chapitel, m. **floating c.,** capital fluctuante, m. **idle c.,** fondos inactivos, m. pl. **c. punishment,** pena de muerte, pena capital, pena de la vida, f. **C.!** ¡Estupendo! ¡Excelente! **to make c out of,** aprovecharse de, sacar ventaja de

capitalism, s. capitalismo, m.

capitalist, s. capitalista, m. and f.

capitalistic, a. capitalista

capitalization, s. capitalización, f.

capitalize, v.t. capitalizar

capitally, adv. estupendamente

capitation, s. capitación, f.

Capitol, s. Capitolio, m.

capitulate, v.i. capitular

capitulation, s. capitulación, f.

capon, s. capón, m.

caprice, s. capricho, m.

capricious, a. caprichoso

capriciously, adv. caprichosamente

capriciousness, s. carácter inconstante, m.; lo caprichoso

Capricorn, s. Capricornio, m.

capsicum, s. pimiento, m.

capsize, v.t. (naut.) hacer zozobrar; volcar. v.i. (naut.) zozobrar; volcarse

capsizing, s. (naut.) zozobra, f.; vuelco, m.

capstan, s. cabrestante, m.

capsule, s. (bot., med., chem., zool.) cápsula, f.

captain, s. (mil., nav., aer. and sport) capitán, m. v.t. capitanear. **to c. a team,** ser el capitán de un equipo. **group c.,** (aer.) capitán de aviación, m.

captaincy, s. capitanía, f.

caption, s. (arrest) arresto, m. (heading) encabezamiento, título, m.; (cinema) subtítulo, m.

captious, a. capcioso, caviloso

captivate, v.t. cautivar, seducir

captivating, a. encantador, seductor

captive, a. cautivo. s. cautivo (-va), prisionero (-ra), preso (-sa). **c. balloon,** globo cautivo, globo de observación, m.

captivity, s. cautiverio, m.

captor, s. el, m. (f. la) que hace prisionero (-ra)

capture, s. captura, f.; presa, toma, f.; (law) captura, f. v.t. prender, capturar; tomar

Capuchin, a. capuchino. s. capuchino, m. **C. nun,** capuchina, f.

car, s. (chariot) carro, m.; (tram) tranvía, m.; (motor) automóvil, coche, m.; (on a train) coche vagón, m. **sleeping car,** coche camas, m. **car park,** parque de automóviles, m.

carabineer, s. carabinero, m.

carafe, s. garrafa, f.

caramel, s. caramelo, m.; azúcar quemado, m.

carapace, s. carapacho, m.

carat, s. quilate, m.

caravan, s. caravana, f.; coche de gitanos, m.; coche habitación, m.

caravanserai, s. caravanera, f.

caravel, s. carabela, f.

caraway, s. alcaravea, f.

carbide, s. carburo, m.

carbine, s. carabina, f.

carbohydrate, s. hidrato de carbono, m.

carbolic, a. carbólico. **c. acid,** ácido fénico, m.

carbon, s. carbono, m. **c. copy,** copia en papel carbón, f. **c. dioxide,** anhídrido carbónico, m. **c. monoxide,** óxido de carbono, m. **c. paper,** papel carbón, papel de calcar, m.

carbonaceous, a. carbonoso

carbonate, s. carbonato, m.

carbonic, a. carbónico

carboniferous, a. carbonífero

carbonization, s. carbonización, f.

carbonize, v.t. carbonizar

carborundum, s. carborundo, m.

carboy, s. damajuana, garrafa, f.

carbuncle, s. (med.) carbunco, m.; (stone) carbúnculo, m.

carburettor, s. carburador, m.

carcass, s. (animal) res muerta, f.; (corpse) cadáver, m.; (body) cuerpo, m.; (of a ship) casco, m.

carcinoma, s. carcinoma, m.

card, *s.* (playing) naipe, *m.*; (pasteboard) cartulina, *f.*; (visiting, postal, etc.) tarjeta, *f.*; (index) ficha, *f.*; (for wool, etc.) carda, *f.* *v.t.* (wool, etc.) cardar. **I still have a c. up my sleeve,** Me queda todavía un recurso. **to lay one's cards on the table,** poner las cartas boca arriba. **to play one's cards well,** (*fig.*) jugar el lance. **admission c.,** billete de entrada, *m.* **post c.,** tarjeta postal, *f.* **visiting c.,** tarjeta de visita, *f.* **c.-case,** tarjetero, *m.* **c.-index,** fichero, *m.* *v.t.* poner en el fichero. **c.-sharper,** fullero, *m.* **c.-table,** mesa de juego, *f.* **c. trick,** juego de manos con cartas, *m.*

cardboard, *s.* cartón, *m.* *a.* de cartón

cardiac, *a.* cardíaco

cardigan, *s.* rebeca, chaqueta de punto, *f.*

cardinal, *a.* cardinal. *s.* cardenal, *m.* **c. number,** número cardinal, *m.* **c. points,** puntos cardinales, *m. pl.*

cardinalate, *s.* cardenalato, *m.*

carding, *s.* (of wool, etc.) cardadura, *f.* **c. machine,** carda mecánica, *f.*

cardiogram, *s.* cardiograma, *m.*

cardiograph, *s.* cardiógrafo, *m.*

care, *s.* cuidado, *m.*; atención, *f.*; inquietud, ansia, *f.*; (charge) cargo, *m.* *v.i.* preocuparse; tener interés; (suffer) sufrir. **I don't c.,** Me es igual; No me importa. **I don't c. a straw,** No se me da un bledo. **They don't c. for eggs,** No les gustan los huevos. **We don't c. what his opinion is,** Su opinión nos tiene sin cuidado (or no nos importa). **to c. for,** cuidar, mirar por; (love) querer (a); (like) gustar. **Take c.!** ¡Cuidado! ¡Ojo! **Take c. not to spoil it!** ¡Ten cuidado que no lo estropees! **Would you c. to . . . ?** ¿Le gustaría . . . ? ¿Tendría inconveniente en . . . ? **c. of,** (on a letter, etc.) en casa de. **c.-free,** *a.* libre de cuidados

careen, *v.t.* carenar. *v.i.* dar a la banda

careening, *s.* carena, *f.*

career, *s.* carrera, *f.*; curso, *m.* *v.i.* correr a carrera tendida; galopar

careful, *a.* cuidadoso (de); atento (a); prudente. **Be c.!** ¡Cuidado! **to be c.,** tener cuidado

carefully, *adv.* con cuidado; cuidadosamente; prudentemente; atentamente

carefulness, *s.* cuidado, *m.*; atención, *f.*; prudencia, *f.*

careless, *a.* sin cuidado; indiferente (a); insensible (a); negligente; (of mistakes, etc.) de (or por) negligencia

carelessly, *adv.* indiferentemente; negligentemente; descuidadamente

carelessness, *s.* indiferencia, *f.*; negligencia, *f.*; descuido, *m.*; omisión, *f.*

caress, *s.* caricia, *f.* *v.t.* acariciar

caressing, *a.* acariciador

caretaker, *s.* (of museums, etc.) guardián (-ana); (of flats, etc.) portero (-ra)

careworn, *a.* devorado de inquietud, ansioso

cargo, *s.* cargamento, *m.*, carga, *f.* **c.-boat,** barco de carga, *m.*

Caribbean, *a.* caribe

caricature, *s.* caricatura, *f.* *v.t.* caricaturizar

caricaturish, *a.* caricaturesco

caricaturist, *s.* caricaturista, *m.* and *f.*

caries, *s.* caries, *f.*

carious, *a.* cariado. **to become c.,** cariarse

Carlist, *a.* carlista. *s.* carlista, *m.* and *f.*

Carmelite, *a.* carmelita. *s.* carmelita, *m.* and *f.*

carmine, *s.* carmín, *m.* *a.* de carmín

carnage, *s.* carnicería, *f.*

carnal, *a.* carnal; sensual

carnality, *s.* carnalidad, *f.*

carnally, *adv.* carnalmente

carnation, *s.* clavel, *m.*

carnival, *s.* carnaval, *m.* *a.* de carnaval, carnavalesco

carnivore, *s.* carnívoro, *m.*

carnivorous, *a.* carnívoro

carol, *s.* villancico, *m.*; canto, *m.* *v.i.* cantar alegremente; (of birds) trinar, gorjear

Carolingian, *a.* carolingio

carotid, *s.* carótida, *f.*

carousal, s. borrachera, f.; holgorio, m., jarana, f.

carouse, v.i. emborracharse. s. borrachera, orgía, f.

carp, s. carpa, f. v.i. criticar, censurar

carpel, s. carpelo, m.

carpenter, s. carpintero, m. v.i. carpintear. **carpenter's bench,** banco de carpintero, m. **carpenter's shop,** carpintería, f.

carpentry, s. carpintería, f.

carpet, s. alfombra, f.; (fig.) tapete, m. v.t. cubrir de una alfombra, alfombrar; entapizar. **to be on the c.,** estar sobre el tapete. **c.-beater,** sacudidor de alfombras, m. **c. merchant,** alfombrista, m. **c. slippers,** zapatillas de fieltro, f.pl. **c.-sweeper,** aspirador de polvo, m.

carpeting, s. alfombrado, m.

carping, a. capcioso, criticón

carriage, s. (carrying) transporte, porte, m.; (deportment) porte, continente, m., presencia, f.; (vehicle) carruaje, m.; carroza, f.; coche, m.; (railway) departamento, m.; (chassis) chasis, bastidor, m.; (of a typewriter, etc.) carro, m. **hackney c.,** coche de plaza, m. **c. and pair,** carroza de dos caballos, f. **c. door,** portezuela, f. **c.-forward,** porte debido. **c.-free,** franco de porte. **c.-paid,** porte pagado

carrier, s. el, m. (f. la) que lleva; portador (-ra); (com.) mensajero, m.; (on a car, bicycle) porta-equipajes, m.; (of a disease) vector, m.; (aircraft) porta-aviones, m. **c.-pigeon,** paloma mensajera, f.

carrion, s. carroña, f. **c.-crow,** chova, f.

carrot, s. zanahoria, f.

carroty, a. bermejo, rojo

carry, v.t. llevar; transportar; traer; conducir; (mil., of arms) portar; (have with one) tener consigo; (an enemy position) tomar, ganar; (a motion) aprobar; (oneself) portarse; (one's point, etc.) ganar; (in the mind) retener; (conviction) convencer; (involve) implicar; (influence) influir; (send) despachar, enviar; (contain) incluir, comprender.

v.i. (of the voice, etc.) alcanzar, llegar. **The noise of the guns carried a long way,** El ruido de los cañones se oía desde muy lejos. **to fetch and c.,** traer y llevar. **to c. all before one,** vencer todos los obstáculos. **to c. into effect,** poner en efecto. **to c. one's audience with one,** captar (or cautivar) su auditorio. **to c. oneself well,** tener buena presencia. **to c. on one's back,** llevar a cuestas. **to c. the day,** quedar victorioso, quedar señor del campo. **to c. weight,** (fig.) ser de peso. **to c. along,** llevar; (drag) arrastrar; conducir; acarrear. **to c. away,** llevar; llevarse, llevar consigo; (kidnap) robar, secuestrar; (of emotions) dominar; (by enthusiasm) entusiasmar; (inspire) inspirar. **to c. forward,** llevar a cabo; avanzar; fomentar; (bookkeeping) pasar a cuenta nueva. **to c. off,** (things) llevarse; (persons) llevar consigo (a); (abduct or steal) robar; (kill) matar; (a prize) ganar. **to c. (a thing) off well,** llevar la mejor parte, salir vencedor. **to c. on,** v.t. (a discussion, etc.) seguir, continuar; mantener; (a business, etc.) tener; dirigir. v.i. ir tirando; seguir trabajando. **to c. out,** realizar, llevar a cabo; hacer, ejecutar, efectuar; (a promise) cumplir. **to c. through,** llevar a cabo

carrying, s. transporte, m.; (of a motion) adopción, f.

cart, s. carro, m. v.t. acarrear; llevar. **c.-horse,** caballo de tiro, m. **c.-load,** carretada, f., carro, m. **c.-wheel,** rueda de carro, f.; (somersault) voltereta, f.

cartage, s. carretaje, transporte, porte, m.

carte blanche, s. carta blanca, f.

cartel, s. cartel, m.

carter, s. carretero, m.

Cartesian, a. cartesiano. s. cartesiano (-na)

Carthaginian, a. cartaginés. s. cartaginés (-esa)

Carthusian, a. cartujano. **C. monk,** cartujo, m.

cartilage, s. cartílago, m.

cartilaginous, *a.* cartilaginoso

cartographer, *s.* cartógrafo, *m.*

cartography, *s.* cartografía, *f.*

cartomancy, *s.* cartomancia, *f.*

carton, *s.* caja de cartón, *f.*

cartoon, *s.* (design for tapestry, etc.) cartón, *m.*; caricatura, *f.*

cartoonist, *s.* caricaturista, *m.* and *f.*

cartridge, *s.* cartucho, *m.* **blank c.,** cartucho sin bala, *m.* **c.-belt,** cartuchera, canana, *f.* **c.-case,** cápsula de proyectil, *f.*

carve, *v.t.* tallar, labrar; grabar; cortar; (meat, etc.) trinchar; (a career, etc.) hacer, forjarse

carver, *s.* tallador, *m.*; (at table) trinchador, *m.*; (implement) trinchante, *m.*

carving, *s.* talla, *f.*; (design) tallado, *m.* **c.-knife,** trinchante, *m.*

caryatid, *s.* cariátide, *f.*

cascade, *s.* cascada, catarata, *f.*, salto de agua, *m.*; (*fig.*) chorro, *m.* *v.i.* chorrear

cascara sagrada, *s.* cáscara sagrada, *f.*

case, *s.* caso, *m.*; (*law*) proceso, *m.*, causa, *f.*; (*gram.*) caso, *m.*; (*med.*) caso, *m.*; enfermo (-ma); (box) caja, *f.*; (for scissors, etc.) vaina, *f.*; (for a cushion, etc.) funda, *f.*; (for jewels, manicure implements, etc.) estuche, *m.*; (of a piano, watch and *print.*) caja, *f.*; (for documents) carpeta, *f.*; (glass) ·vitrina, *f.*; (for a book) sobrecubierta, *f.*; (dressing) neceser, *m.* *v.t.* cubrir; forrar; resguardar. **packing-c.,** caja de embalaje, *f.* **c. of goods,** caja de mercancías, *f.*; bulto, *m.* **in any c.,** en todo caso; venga lo que venga. **in c.,** por si acaso. **in c. of emergency,** en caso de urgencia. **in such a c.,** en tal caso. **in the c. of,** en el caso de; respecto a. **lower c.,** (*print.*) caja baja, *f.* **upper c.,** (*print.*) caja alta, *f.* **c.-hardened,** (of iron) templado; (*fig.*) endurecido, indiferente

casemate, *s.* casamata, *f.*

casement window, *s.* ventana, *f.*

cash, *s.* efectivo, metálico, *m.*; dinero contante, *m.*; (*fam.*) dinero, *m.*; (*com.*) caja, *f.* *v.t.* cobrar; pagar, hacer efectivo. **hard or**

ready c., dinero contante, *m.* **to pay c.,** pagar al contado. **c. on delivery,** (C.O.D.) contra reembolso. **c. on hand,** efectivo en caja, *m.* **c.-book,** libro de caja, *m.* **c.-box,** caja, *f.* **c.-desk,** caja, *f.* **c. down,** pago al contado, *m.* **c. prize,** premio en metálico, *m.* **c.-register,** caja registradora, *f.*

cashew, *s.* anacardo, *m.*

cashier, *s.* cajero (-ra). *v.t.* ·legradar. **cashier's desk,** caja, *f.*

cashmere, *s.* cachemira, *f.*

casino, *s.* casino, *m.*

cask, *s.* pipa, barrica, *f.*, tonel, *m.*; cuba, *f.*

casket, *s.* cajita, arquilla, *f.,* cofrecito, *m.*

Caspian, *a.* caspio

cassation, *s.* (*law*) casación, *f.*

casserole, *s.* cacerola, *f.*

cassock, *s.* sotana, *f.*

cassowary, *s.* casuario, *m.*

cast, *v.t.* arrojar, tirar; (in fishing, the anchor, dice, darts, lots, a net, glances, blame, etc.) echar; (skin) mudar; (lose) perder; (a shadow, etc.) proyectar; (a vote) dar; (mould) vaciar; (accounts) echar, calcular; (a horoscope) hacer; (the parts in a play) repartir; (an actor for a part) dar el papel de; (metals) colar, fundir. **The shadow c. by the wall,** La sombra proyectada por el muro. **to c. anchor,** echar anclas, anclar. **to c. in one's lot with,** compartir la suerte de. **to c. something in a person's teeth,** echar en cara (a). **to c. lots,** echar suertes. **to c. about,** meditar, considerar; imaginar; (devise) inventar. **to c. aside,** desechar; poner a un lado; abandonar. **to c. away,** tirar lejos; desechar; (money) derrochar, malgastar. **to c. away,** (*naut.*) naufragar. **to c. down,** (overthrow) derribar, destruir; (eyes) bajar; (depress) desanimar, deprimir; (humiliate) humillar. **to be c. down,** estar deprimido. **c. iron,** *s.* hierro colado, *m.* **c.-iron,** *a.* de hierro colado; (*fig.*) inflexible. **to c. off,** quitarse; desechar; (a wife) repudiar; (desert) abandonar; (free one-**

self) librarse (de). **c.-off,** *s.*
desecho, *m.* **c.-off clothing,**
ropa de desecho, *f.* **to c. out,**
echar fuera; hacer salir; excluir.
to c. up, echar; vomitar; (a sum)
sumar; (something at a person)
reprochar

cast, *s.* (of dice, fishing-line)
echada, *f.;* (of a net) redada, *f.;*
(worm) molde, *m.;* (of a play)
reparto, *m.;* (of mind) inclinación, *f.;* (in the eye) defecto
en la mirada, *m.;* (of colour)
matiz, tinte, *m.* **c. of features,**
facciones, *f. pl.,* fisonomía, *f.*
plaster c., vaciado, *m.*

castanets, *s. pl.* castañuelas, *f. pl.*

castaway, *s.* náufrago (-ga);
(*fig.*) perdido (-da)

caste, *s.* casta, *f.;* clase social, *f.*
to lose c., desprestigiarse

castellated, *a.* almenado

castigate, *v.t.* castigar (also *fig.*)

castigation, *s.* castigo, *m.;* corrección, *f.*

Castilian, *a.* castellano. *s.* castellano (-na); (language) castellano,
m.

casting, *s.* lanzamiento, *m.;* (of
metals) fundición, colada, *f.;*
obra de fundición, *f.* **c.-net,**
esparavel, *m.* **c.-vote,** voto de
calidad, *m.*

castle, *s.* castillo, *m.;* (in chess)
torre, *f.,* roque, *m.* **to build
castles in Spain,** hacer castillos
en el aire

castor, *s.* (*zool.*) castor, *m.;* (for
sugar) azucarero, *m.;* (cruet)
convoy, *m.;* (on chairs, etc.)
ruedecilla, roldana, *f.* **c.-oil,**
aceite de ricino, *m.* **c.-sugar,**
azúcar en polvo, *m.*

castrate, *v.t.* castrar, capar

castration, *s.* castración, capadura, *f.*

casual, *a.* fortuito, accidental;
ligero, superficial; (*fam.*) despreocupado. **c. worker,** jornalero, *m.*

casually, *adv.* por casualidad; de
paso; negligentemente

casualness, *s.* (*fam.*) negligencia,
despreocupación, *f.*

casualty, *s.* víctima, *f.;* herido,
m.; (*mil.*) baja, *f.; pl.* **casualties,**
heridos, *m. pl.;* muertos, *m. pl.*
c.-list, lista de víctimas, *f.;*
(*mil.*) lista de bajas, *f.*

casuist, *s.* casuista, *m.* and *f.*

casuistic, *a.* casuista

casuistry, *s.* casuística, *f.*

cat, *s.* gato (-ta). **She is an old
cat,** Ella es una vieja chismosa. **to be like a cat on hot
bricks,** estar como en brasas.
to let the cat out of the bag,
tirar de la manta. **to lead a
cat-and-dog life,** vivir como
perros y gatos. **cat's-cradle,**
(game) cunas, *f. pl.* **cat's paw,**
(person) hombre de paja, *m.;*
(*naut.*) bocanada de viento, *f.*
cat o' nine tails, gato de siete
colas, *m.,* penca, *f.* **catwhisker,**
(*rad.*) detector, *m.*

catabolism, *s.* catabolismo, *m.*

cataclysm, *s.* cataclismo, *m.*

catacombs, *s. pl.* catacumbas,
f. pl.

catafalque, *s.* catafalco, *m.*

Catalan, *a.* catalán (-ana). *s.*
catalán; (language) catalán, *m.*

catalepsy, *s.* catalepsia, *f.*

cataleptic, *a.* cataléptico

catalogue, *s.* catálogo, *m.* *v.t.*
catalogar

catalysis, *s.* catálisis, *f.*

catalytic, *a.* catalítico

cataplasm, *s.* cataplasma, *f.*

catapult, *s.* (*mil.*) catapulta, *f.;*
(*aer.*) catapulta (para lanzar
aviones), *f.;* (toy) tirador de
gomas, *m.* *v.t.* tirar con una
catapulta (or con un tirador de
gomas); (throw) lanzar

cataract, *s.* catarata, cascada, *f.,*
salto de agua, *m.;* (of the eye)
catarata, *f.*

catarrh, *s.* catarro, *m.;* constipado, resfriado, *m.*

catarrhal, *a.* catarral

catastrophe, *s.* catástrofe, *f.,*
desastre, *m.;* (in drama) desenlace, *m.*

catastrophic, *a.* catastrófico

catcall, *s.* silbido, *m.*

catch, *v.t.* coger, agarrar, asir;
(capture) prender, haber; (a
disease) contraer; (habit) tomar;
(on a hook, etc.) enganchar;
(surprise) sorprender; (understand) comprender; (hear) oír;
(with blows, etc.) dar. *v.i.* (of a
lock) encajarse; (become entangled) engancharse; (of a fire)
encenderse. **to c. a glimpse of,**
ver por un instante (a); alcanzar

a ver, entrever. **to c. at**, asir; agarrarse (a); echar mano de; procurar asir; alargar la mano hacia; (an idea, etc.) adoptar con entusiasmo. **to c. on**, (be popular) tener éxito; (understand) .comprender: **to c.** out, coger en el acto; coger en un error; (sport) coger. **to c. up**, coger; interrumpir. **to c. up with**, (a person) alcanzar; (news) ponerse al corriente de

catch, s. presa, f.; (of fish) redada, pesca, f.; (of a window, etc.) cerradura, f.; (latch) pestillo, m.; (trick) trampa, f.; (mus.) canon, m. **a good c.**, (matrimonial) un buen partido. **to have a c. in one's voice**, hablar con voz entrecortada. **c.-as-c.-can**, lucha libre, f.

catching, a. contagioso

catchment, s. desagüe, m.

catchpenny, s. sacacuartos, m.

catchword, s. reclamo, m.; (theatre cue) pie, apunte, m.; (slogan) mote, m.

catchy, a. atractivo. **It's a c. tune**, Es una canción que se pega

catechism, s. catequismo, m.

catechist, s. catequista, m. and f.

catechize, v.t. catequizar

catechumen, s. catecúmeno (-na)

categorical, a. categórico

categorically, adv. categóricamente

category, s. categoría, f.

cater, v.i. proveer, abastecer. **to c. for all tastes**, atender a todos los gustos

caterer, s. despensero (-ra)

catering, s. provisión, f.

caterpillar, s. oruga, f. **c. tractor**, tractor de orugas, m.

caterwaul, v.i. (of a cat) maullar

caterwauler, s. (violinist, etc.) rascatripas, m.

caterwauling, s. maullidos, m. pl.; música ratonera, f.

catfish, s. siluro, m.

catgut, s. (surg.) catgut, m.; (mus.) cuerda, f.

catharsis, s. (med.) purga, f.; (fig.) catarsis, f.

cathedral, s. catedral, f.

Catherine-wheel, s. (arch.) rosa, f.; (firework) rueda de Santa Catalina, f.; (somersault) tumba, f.

catheter, s. catéter, m.

cathode, s. cátodo, m. **c. rays**, rayos catódicos, m. pl. **c. ray tube**, tubo de rayos catódicos, m.

cathodic, a. catódico

catholic, a. católico

Catholicism, s. catolicismo, m.

catkin, s. amento, m. **male c.**, amento macho, m.

catlike, a. de gato; gatuno

cattle, s. ganado vacuno, m.; ganado, m.; animales, m. pl. **c.-dealer**, ganadero, m. **c.-lifter**, hurtador de ganado, m. **c.-pen**, corral, m. **c.-raiser**, criador de ganado, m. **c.-raising**, ganadería, f. **c.-ranch**, hacienda de ganado, estancia, f. **c.-show**, exposición de ganado, f. **c.-truck**, vagón de ferrocarril para ganado, m.

catty, a. gatuno; malicioso, chismoso

Caucasian, a. and s. caucáseo (-ea).

cauldron, s. caldera, f.

cauliflower, s. coliflor, f.

caulk, v.t. calafatear

caulker, s. calafate, m.

caulking, s. calafateado, m. **c. iron**, calador, m.

causality, s. causalidad, f.

causative, a. causante

cause, s. causa, f.; (reason) motivo, m., razón, f.; (lawsuit) proceso, m. v.t. causar; ocasionar, suscitar; (oblige) hacer, obligar (a). **final c.**, (phil.) causa final, f. **to have good c. for**, tener buen motivo para

causeway, s. dique, m.; acera, f.

caustic, a. cáustico; (fig.) mordaz. **c. soda**, sosa cáustica, f.

caustically, adv. mordazmente, con sarcasmo

causticity, s. causticidad, f.

cauterization, s. cauterización, f.

cauterize, v.t. cauterizar

cautery, s. cauterio, m.

caution, s. prudencia, cautela, f.; (warning) amonestación, f.; aviso, m. v.t. amonestar. **to proceed with c.**, ir con prudencia; ir despacio

cautionary, a. (of tales) de escarmiento

cautious, *a.* cauteloso, cauto; prudente, circunspecto

cautiously, *adv.* cautamente; prudentemente. **to go c.,** (*fam.*) ir con pies de plomo

cavalcade, *s.* cabalgata, *f*

cavalier, *s.* jinete, *m.*; caballero, *m.*; galán, *m.* *a.* arrogante, altanero

cavalry, *s.* caballería, *f.* **c.-man,** jinete, soldado de a caballo, *m.*

cave, *s.* cueva, caverna, *f.* **to c. in,** hundirse; desplomarse; (*fig.*) rendirse. **c.-man,** hombre cavernícola, *m.*

cavern, *s.* caverna, *f.*

cavernous, *a.* cavernoso

caviar, *s.* caviar, *m.*

cavil, *v.i.* cavilar

cavity, *s.* cavidad, *f.*; hoyo, *m.*; hueco, *m.*; (in a lung) caverna, *f.*

cavy, *s.* cobayo (-ya), conejillo (-lla) de las Indias

caw, *s.* graznido, *m.* *v.i.* graznar, grajear

cawing, *s.* graznidos, *m. pl.*

cayenne, *s.* pimentón, *m.*

cease, *v.i.* cesar (de), dejar de; parar. *v.t.* cesar de; parar de; (payments, etc.) suspender; discontinuar. **C. fire!** ¡Cesar fuego!

ceaseless, *a.* incesante, continuo, sin cesar

ceaselessly, *adv.* sin cesar, incesantemente

ceasing, *s.* cesación, *f.* **without c.,** sin cesar

cedar, *s.* (tree and wood) cedro, *m.* **red c.,** cedro dulce, *m.*

cede, *v.t.* ceder, traspasar; (admit) conceder

cedilla, *s.* zedilla, *f.*

ceiling, *s.* techo, *m.*; (*aer.*) altura máxima, *f.* **c. price,** máximo precio, *m.*

celebrant, *s.* (*ecc.*) celebrante, *m.*

celebrate, *v.t.* celebrar; solemnizar. **Their marriage was celebrated in the autumn,** Su casamiento se solemnizó en el otoño

celebrated, *a.* célebre, famoso

celebration, *s.* celebración, *f.*; festividad, *f.*

celebrity, *s.* celebridad, *f.*

celerity, *s.* celeridad, *f.*

celery, *s.* apio, *m.*

celestial, *a.* celestial

celibacy, *s.* celibato, *m.*

celibate, *a.* célibe. *s.* célibe, *m.* and *f.*

cell, *s.* celda, *f.*; (*bot.*, *biol.*) célula, *f.*; (bees, wasps) celdilla, *f.*; (*elec.*) elemento, *m.*

cellar, *s.* sótano, *m.*; (wine) bodega, *f.*

'cellist, *s.* violoncelista, *m.* and *f.*

'cello, *s.* violoncelo, *m.*

Cellophane, *s.* (papel) Celofán, *m.*

cellular, *a.* celular, celuloso

cellule, *s.* célula, *f.*

celluloid, *s.* celuloide, *f.*

cellulose, *s.* celulosa, *f.*

Celt, *s.* celta, *m.* and *f.*

Celtiberian, *a.* celtibérico

Celtic, *a.* celta

cement, *s.* cemento, *m.* *v.t* cementar

cementation, *s.* cementación, *f.*

cemetery, *s.* cementerio, *m.*

cenacle, *s.* cenáculo, *m.*

cenotaph, *s.* cenotafio, *m.*

cense, *v.t.* incensar

censer, *s.* incensario, *m.*

censor, *s.* censor, *m.* *v.t.* censurar. **banned by the c.,** prohibido por la censura

censorious, *a.* severo; crítico

censoriousness, *s.* severidad, propensión a censurar, *f.*

censorship, *s.* censura, *f.*

censure, *v.t.* censurar, culpar, criticar

census, *s.* censo, *m.* **to take the c.,** tomar el censo, empadronar

cent, *s.* (còin) centavo, *m.* **per c.,** por ciento

centaur, *s.* centauro, *m.*

centaury, *s.* (*bot.*) centaura, *f.*

centenarian, *a.* and *s.* centenario (-ia)

centenary, *s.* centenario, *m.* *a.* centenario

centigrade, *a.* centígrado

centigramme, *s.* centigramo, *m.*

centilitre, *s.* centilitro, *m.*

centime, *s.* céntimo, *m.*

centimetre, *s.* centímetro, *m.* **cubic c.,** centímetro cúbico, *m.*

centipede, *s.* ciempiés, *m.*

central, *a.* central; céntrico. **The house is very c.,** La casa es muy céntrica. **C. American,** *a.* and *s.* centroamericano (-na). **c. depot,** central, *f.* **c. heating,** calefacción central, *f.*

centralism, *s.* centralismo, *m.*

centralist, s. centralista, m. and f.
centralistic, a. centralista
centralization, s. centralización, f.
centralize, v.t. centralizar
centrally, adv. centralmente; céntricamente
centre, s. centro, m.; medio, m. a. central; centro. v.t. centrar; concentrar (en). nervous centres, centros nerviosos, m. pl. c.-forward, (sport) delantero centro, m. c.-half, (sport) medio centro, m. c. of gravity, centro de gravedad, m. c.-piece, centro, m.
centric, a. céntrico; central
centrifugal, a. centrífugo
centripetal, a. centrípeto
centumvir, s. centunviro, m.
centuple, a. céntuplo
centuplicate, v.t. centuplicar
centurion, s. centurión, m.
century, s. siglo, m., centuria, f.
cephalalgia, s. cefalalgia, f.
cephalic, a. cefálico
ceramic, a. cerámico
ceramics, s. cerámica, f.
Cerberus, s. Cancerbero, m.
cereal, a. cereal. s. cereal, m.
cerebellum, s. cerebelo, m.
cerebral, a. cerebral
cerebro-spinal, a. cerebro-espinal
cerebrum, s. cerebro, m.
ceremonial, a. ceremonial; de ceremonia. s. ceremonial, m.
ceremonially, adv. ceremonial-mente; con ceremonia
ceremonious, a. ceremonioso
ceremoniously, adv. ceremoniosa-mente
ceremoniousness, s. ceremonia, formalidad, f.
ceremony, s. ceremonia, f. to stand on c., gastar cumplidos. without c., sin cumplidos
cerise, a. de color cereza
certain, a. (sure) seguro; cierto; (unerring) certero. a c. man, cierto hombre. I am c. that ..., Estoy seguro de que . . . to know for c., saber con toda seguridad, saber a ciencia cierta. to make c. of, asegurarse de
certainly, adv. seguramente; cier-tamente; (as a reply) sin duda; naturalmente. c. not, no, por cierto; claro que no

certainty, s. certidumbre, f.; seguridad, f.; convicción, f. of a c., seguramente
certificate, s. certificado, m.; fe, f.; partida, f.; (com.) bono, título, m.; diploma, m. v.t. certificar. birth c., partida de nacimiento, f. death c., partida de defunción, f. marriage c., partida de casamiento, f.
certificated, a. (of teachers, etc.) con título
certify, v.t. certificar; atestiguar; declarar
certitude, s. certeza, certidumbre, f.
Cerulean, a. cerúleo
Cervantine, a. cervantino
cervix, s. (anat.) cerviz, f.
cessation, s. cesación, f.
cession, s. cesión, f.
cessionary, s. cesionario (-ia)
cesspool, s. sumidero, m.
cetacean, a. cetáceo. s. cetáceo, m.
chafe, v.t. (rub) frotar; (make sore) escocer, rozar. v.i. raerse, desgastarse; escocerse; (fig.) impacientarse; (fig.) irritarse, eno-jarse
chaff, s. (of grain) ahechadura, f.; (in a general sense and fig.) paja, f.; tomadura de pelo, burla, f. v.t. (a person) tomar el pelo (a), burlarse de
chaffinch, s. pinzón, m.
chafing, s. frotación, f.; (soreness) excoriación, f.; (fig.) impaciencia, f. c.-dish, escalfador, m.
chagrin, s. mortificación, de-cepción, f., disgusto, m. v.t. mortificar
chain, s. cadena, f. v.t. encadenar. c. of mountains, cadena de montañas, cordillera, f. c.-gang, cadena de presidiarios, f. c.-mail, cota de malla, f. c.-stitch, cadeneta, f. c.-stores, tienda importante con sucursales, f.
chair, s. silla, f.; (univ.) cátedra, f.; (of a meeting) presidencia, f. v.t. llevar en hombros (a). C.! ¡Orden! easy-c., (silla) poltrona, f. to be in the c., ocupar la presidencia; presidir. to take a c., sentarse, tomar asiento. to take the c., presidir. swivel-c., silla giratoria, f. wheel-c.,

silla de ruedas, *f.* c.-back, respaldo de una silla, *m.*

chairman, *s.* presidente (-ta). to act as c., presidir

chairmanship, *s.* presidencia, *f.*

chalcedony, *s.* calcedonia, *f.*

chalcography, *s.* calcografía, *f.*

Chaldean, *a.* caldeo

chalet, *s.* chalet, *m.*

chalice, *s.* cáliz, *m.*

chalk, *s.* creta, *f.*; (for writing, etc.) tiza, *f.*, yeso, *m.* *v.t.* marcar con tiza; dibujar con tiza. to c. up, apuntar. not by a long c., no con mucho

chalky, *a.* cretáceo; cubierto de yeso; (of the complexion) pálido

challenge, *s.* provocación, *f.*; (of a sentry) quién vive, *m.*; (to a duel, etc.) desafío, reto, *m.*; (*law*) recusación, *f.*; concurso, *m.* *v.t.* (of a sentry) dar el quién vive (a); desafiar; provocar; (*law*) recusar

challenger, *s.* desafiador (-ra)

challenging, *a.* desafiador, provocador

chamber, *s.* cuarto, *m.*; sala, *f.*; (bed-) dormitorio, *m.*, alcoba, *f.*; cámara, *f.*; (*mech.*) cilindro, *m.*; (in a gun) cámara, *f.* c. concert, concierto de música de cámara, *m.* c.-maid, camarera, *f.* c. music, música de cámara, *f.* c. of commerce, cámara de comercio, *f.* c.-pot, orinal, *m.*

chamberlain, *s.* camarero, *m.* court c., chambelán, *m.* Lord C., camarero mayor, *m.*

chameleon, *s.* camaleón, *m.*

chamfer, *s.* chaflán, bisel, *m.*

chamois, *s.* gamuza, *f.*, rebeco, *m.* c. leather, piel de gamuza, *f.*

champ, *v.t.* mascar; morder. *v.i.* (*fig.*) impacientarse

champagne, *s.* (vino de) Champaña, *m.*

champion, *s.* campeón, *m.*; defensor (-ra)

championship, *s.* campeonato, *m.*; (of a cause) defensa, *f.*

chance, *s.* casualidad, *f.*; suerte, fortuna, *f.*; posibilidad, *f.*; probabilidad, *f.*; esperanza, *f.*; (opportunity) ocasión, oportunidad, *f.* *a.* fortuito; accidental. *v.i.* (*impers.*) suceder, acontecer. *v.t.* (*fam.*) arriesgar; probar. by c., por casualidad; por

ventura. if by c., si acaso. If it chances that . . ., Si sucede que; Si a mano viene que . . . The chances are that . . ., Las probabilidades son que . . . There is no c., No hay posibilidad; No hay esperanza. to let the c. slip, perder la ocasión. to take a c., aventurarse, arriesgarse. to c. to do, hacer algo por casualidad. to c. upon, encontrar por casualidad.

chancel, *s.* antealtar, entrecoro, *m.*

chancellery, *s.* cancillería, *f.*

chancellor, *s.* canciller, *m.*; (*univ.*) cancelario, *m.* C. of the Exchequer, Ministro de Hacienda, *m.*

chancellorship, *s.* cancillería, *f.*

chancery, *s.* chancillería, *f.*; (papal) cancelaría, *f.*

chandelier, *s.* araña de luces, *f.*

chandler, *s.* velero, *m.*

change, *v.t.* cambiar; transformar; modificar; (clothes) mudarse (de); (one thing for another) trocar; sustituir (por). *v.i.* cambiar; (clothes) mudarse. All c.! ¡Cambio de tren! to c. a cheque, cambiar un cheque. to c. colour, cambiar de color; (of persons) mudar de color. to c. countenance, demudarse. to c. front, (*fig.*) cambiar de frente. to c. hands, (of shops, etc.) cambiar de dueño. to c. one's clothes, cambiar de ropa, mudarse de ropa. to c. one's mind, cambiar de opinión. to c. one's tune, cambiar de tono. to c. the subject, cambiar de conversación. to c. trains, cambiar de trenes

change, *s.* cambio, *m.*; transformación, *f.*; modificación, *f.*; variedad, *f.*; (of clothes, feathers) muda, *f.*; (*theat.*, of scene) mutación, *f.*; (money) cambio, *m.*; (small coins) suelto, *m.*; (stock) bolsa, *f.*; lonja, *f.*; vicisitud, *f.*; (of bells) toque (de campanas), *m.* for a c., para cambiar, como un cambio; para variar. small c., suelto, *m.*, moneda suelta, *f.* c. of clothes, cambio de ropa, *m.*; c. of front, (*fig.*) cambio de frente, *m.* c. of heart, cambio

de frente, *m.***; conversión,** *f.* **c. of
life,** menopausia, *f.* **c.-over,**
cambio, *m.*

changeability, *s.* mutabilidad, *f.***;**
inconstancia, volubilidad, *f.*

changeable, *a.* voluble; variable;
cambiable

changeless, *a.* inmutable; constante

changeling, *s.* niño (-ña) cambiado (-da) por otro

changing, *a.* cambiante.   **c.-
room,** vestuario, *m.*

channel, *s.* (of a river, etc.) cauce,
m.; canal, *m.*; (irrigation) acequia,
f.; (strait) estrecho, *m.*; conducto, *m.*; (furrow) surco, *m.*,
estría, *f.*; (of information, etc.)
medio, *m. v.t.* acanalar; (furrow) surcar; (conduct) encauzar

chant, *s.* canto llano, *m.*; salmo,
m. v.t. salmodiar; cantar; recitar

chantey, *s.* saloma, *f.*

chaos, *s.* caos, *m.*

chaotic, *a.* caótico, desordenado

chaotically, *adv.* en desorden

chap, *v.t.* agrietar.   *v.i.* agrietarse. *s.* (*fam.*) chico, *m*:

chapel, *s.* capilla, *f.*; templo
disidente, *m.*

chapelle ardente, *s.* capilla
ardiente, *f.*

chaperon, *s.* señora de compañía,
dueña, *f. v.t.* acompañar

chaplain, *s.* capellán, *m.*

chaplaincy, *s.* capellanía, *f.*

chaplet, *s.* guirnalda, *f.*; rosario,
m.; (necklace) collar, *m.*

chapter, *s.* (in a book) capítulo,
m.; (*ecc.*) cabildo, capítulo, *m.*
a c. of accidents, una serie de
desgracias. **c. house,** sala capitular, *f.*

char, *v.t.* (a house, etc.) fregar,
hacer la limpieza de; (of fire)
carbonizar. *s.* (*fam.*) fregona,
asistenta, *f.*

charabanc, *s.* charabán, *m.*

character, *s.* carácter, *m.*; (of a
play) personaje, *m.*; (rôle) papel,
m.; (eccentric) tipo, *m.* **Gothic
characters,** caracteres góticos,
m. pl. **in c.,** característico;
apropiado. **in the c. of,** en el
papel de. **out of c.,** nada
característico; no apropiado.
principal c., protagonista, *m.*

and *f.* **c. actor,** actor de carácter, *m.* **c. actress,** característica, *f.*

characteristic, *a.* característico,
típico. *s.* característica, peculiaridad, *f.*, rasgo, *m.*

characteristically, *adv.* caracte-
rísticamente

characterization, *s.* caracterización, *f.*

characterize, *v.t.* caracterizar

characterless, *a.* sin carácter;
insípido, soso

charade, *s.* charada, *f.*

charcoal, *s.* carbón de leña, *m.*;
(for blacking the face, etc.) tizne,
m.; (art) carboncillo, *m.*   **c.
burner,** carbonera, *f.*   **c.
crayon,** carboncillo, *m.*   **c.
drawing,** dibujo al carbón, *m.*

charge, *v.t.* cargar; (enjoin)
encargar; (accuse) acusar (de);
(with price) cobrar; (with a
mission, etc.) encomendar, confiar; (*mil.*) acometer, atacar.
v.i. (*mil.*) atacar; (a price)
cobrar, pedir. **How much do
you c.?** ¿Cuánto cobra Vd.?
to c. with a crime, acusar de un
crimen

charge, *s.* (load) carga, *f.*; (price)
precio, *m.*; gasto, *m.*; (on an
estate, etc.) derechos, *m. pl.*;
(task) encargo, *m.*; (office or
responsibility) cargo, *m.*; (guardianship) tutela, *f.*; (care) cuidado,
m.; exhortación, *f.*; (*law*) acusación, *f.*; (*mil.*) ataque, *m.* **He is
in c. of . . .,** Está encargado
de . . .; **Es responsable de . . .
The diamonds are in the c.
of . . .,** Los diamantes están a
cargo de. **depth c.,** carga de
profundidad, *f.* **extra c.,** gasto
suplementario, *m.*; (on a train)
suplemento, *m.* **free of c.,**
gratis. **c. for admittance,** entrada, *f.* **to bring a c. against,**
acusar de. **to give (someone)
in c.,** entregar (una persona) a la
policía. **to take c. of,** encargarse
de

chargé d'affaires, *s.* encargado
de negocios, *m.*

charger, *s.* caballo de guerra,
corcel, *m.*

chariness, *s.* cautela, *f.*

chariot, *s.* carro, *m.*

charioteer, *s.* auriga, *m.*

charitable, a. caritativo; benéfico

charitableness, s. caridad, f.

charitably, adv. caritativamente

charity, s. caridad, f.; beneficencia, f.; (alms) limosna, f. c.
child, niño (-ña) de la doctrina

charlatan, s. charlatán (-ana);
(quack) curandero, m.

charlatanism, s. charlatanismo,
m.; curanderismo, m.

charm, s. hechizo, m.; ensalmo,
m.; (amulet) amuleto, m.; (trinket) dije, m.; (general sense)
encanto, atractivo, m. v.t. encantar, hechizar, fascinar

charming, a. encantador; atractivo, seductor, fascinador

charnel house, s. osario, m.

chart, s. (naut.) carta de marear,
f.; (graph) gráfica, f. v.t. poner
en una carta

charter, s. carta, f.; (of a city,
etc.) fuero, m.; cédula, f. v.t. (a
ship) fletar; (hire) alquilar. royal
c., cédula real, f.

chartist, s. cartista, m. and f.

charwoman, s. fregona, asistenta, f.

chary, a. cauteloso; desinclinado;
frugal

chase, s. caza, f.; seguimiento, m.
v.t. cazar; dar caza (a); perseguir; (drive off) ahuyentar; (fig.)
disipar, hacer desaparecer; (engrave) cincelar. to give c. to,
dar caza (a). to go on a wild
goose c., buscar pan de trastri-
go

chasm, s. sima, f., precipicio, m.;
(fig.) abismo, m.

chassis, s. chasis, m.

chaste, a. casto

chasten, v.t. castigar; corregir;
humillar, mortificar

chastened, a. sumiso, dócil

chastise, v.t. castigar

chastisement, s. castigo, m.

chastity, s. castidad, f.

chasuble, s. casulla, f.

chat, v.i. charlar, conversar. s.
conversación, charla, f. They
are having a c., Están char-
lando, Están de palique

chattels, s. pl. bienes muebles,
efectos, m. pl.

chatter, v.i. charlar; hablar por
los codos, chacharear; (of water)
murmurar; (of birds) piar; (of
monkeys, etc.) chillar; (of teeth)

rechinar; (of a person's teeth)
dar diente con diente. s. charla,
f.; cháchara, parla, f.; (of water)
murmurio, m.; (of birds) gorjeo,
m.; (of monkeys, etc.) chillidos,
m. pl.

chatterbox, s. badajo, m., cotorra, f.

chatterer, s. hablador (-ra)

chattering, s. charla, cháchara,
f.; (of teeth) rechinamiento, m.
a. gárrulo, chacharero, locuaz

chauffeur, s. chófer, m.

chauvinism, s. chauvinismo, m.

cheap, a. barato; (of works of art)
cursi. adv. barato. dirt c.,
baratísimo. to be dirt c.,
estar por los suelos. to hold
(something) c., tener en poco,
estimar en poco

cheapen, v.t. disminuir el valor
de; reducir el precio de

cheaply, adv. barato; a bajo
precio

cheapness, s. baratura, f.; precio
módico, m.; mal gusto, m.,
vulgaridad, f.

cheat, s. engaño, fraude, m.,
estafa, f.; (person) fullero (-ra),
trampista, m. and f., embustero
(-ra). v.t. engañar; defraudar; (at
cards) hacer trampas. He cheat-
ed me out of my property, Me
defraudó de mi propiedad

cheating, s. engaño, m.; fraude,
m.; (at cards) fullerías, f. pl.

check, s. (chess) jaque, m.; revés,
m.; impedimento, m.; contratiempo, m.; (of a bridle) cama,
f.; (control) freno, m.; control, m.; (checking) verificación, f.; (ticket) papeleta, f.;
(counterfoil) talón, m.; (square)
cuadro, m.; (bill) cuenta, f.;
(cheque) cheque, m. v.t. (chess)
jaquear; (hamper) refrenar; detener; contrarrestar; (test) verificar. v.i. detenerse. to c. off,
marcar. to c. oneself, detenerse; contenerse. to c. up,
comprobar

checked, a. (of garments, etc.) a
cuadros

checking, s. represión, f.; control,
m.; verificación, f.; comprobación, f.

checkmate, s. mate, jaque, mate,
m. v.t. dar mate (a); (plans, etc.)
frustrar

cheek, *s.* mejilla, *f.*; (*fam.*) descaro, *m.*; insolencia, *f.* **They have plenty of c.,** Tienen mucha cara dura. **c. by jowl,** cara a cara; al lado de. **c.-bone,** pómulo, *m.*

cheekiness, *s.* cara dura, insolencia, *f.*

cheeky, *a.* insolente, descarado; (pert) respondón

cheep, *s.* pío, *m.. v.i.* piar

cheer, *s.* alegría, *f.*, regocijo, *m.*; vítor, *m.*; aplauso, *m. v.t.* animar; alegrar, regocijar; vitorear, aplaudir. **to be of good c.,** estar alegre; ser feliz. **C. up!** ¡Ánimo! **to c. up,** animarse, cobrar ánimo

cheerful, *a.* alegre; jovial; de buen humor. **It is a c. room,** Es un cuarto alegre

cheerfully, *adv.* alegremente; (willingly) con mucho gusto, de buena gana

cheerfulness, *s.* alegría, *f.*; jovialidad, *f.*; buen humor, *m.*

cheering, *s.* vítores, *m. pl.*, aclamaciones, *f. pl. a.* animador

cheerless, *a.* triste; sin alegría; (dank) obscuro, lóbrego

cheese, *s.* queso, *m.* **cream c.,** queso de nata, *m.* **grated c.,** queso rallado, *m.* **c.-dish,** quesera, *f.* **c.-mite,** cresa, *f.* **c.-paring,** *s.* corteza de queso, *f. a.* (*fam.*) tacaño. **c.-vat,** quesera, *f.*

cheesemonger, *s.* vendedor (-ra) de queso

cheesy, *a.* caseoso

chemical, *a.* químico. **c. warfare,** defensa química, *f.*

chemically, *adv.* químicamente

chemicals, *s. pl.* productos químicos, *m. pl.*

chemise, *s.* camisa (de mujer), *f.*

chemist, *s.* químico, *m.* **chemist's shop,** farmacia, *f.*; droguería, *f.*

chemistry, *s.* química, *f.*

chenille, *s.* felpilla, *f.*

cheque, *s.* cheque, *m.* **crossed c.,** cheque cruzado, *m.* **c. book,** libro de cheques, *m.*

chequer, *v.t.* escaquear; (variegate) motear, salpicar; diversificar. **a chequered career,** una vida accidentada

cherish, *v.t.* amar, querer; (a hope, etc.) abrigar, acariciar

cheroot, *s.* caliqueño, *m.*

cherry, *s.* (fruit) cereza, *f.*; (tree and wood) cerezo, *m.* **c. brandy,** aguardiente de cerezas, *m.* **c. orchard,** cerezal, *m.*

cherub, *s.* querub(e), querubín, *m.*

cherubic, *a.* querúbico

chess, *s.* ajedrez, *m.* **c.-board,** tablero de ajedrez, *m.*

chessman, *s.* pieza de ajedrez, *f.*

chest, *s.* arca, *f.*, cofre, *m.*; cajón, *m.*; (*anat.*) pecho, *m.* **to throw out one's c.,** inflar el pecho. **c.-expander,** extensor, *m.* **c. of drawers,** cómoda, *f.*

chested, *a.* (in compounds) de pecho . . .

chestnut, *s.* (tree) castaño, *m.*; (fruit) castaña, *f.*; (colour) castaño, color castaño, *m.*; (horse) caballo castaño, *m.*; (joke) chiste del tiempo de Maricastaña, *m. a.* castaño. **horse-c. tree,** castaño de Indias, *m.*

chevron, *s.* (*her.*) cabrio, *m.*; (*mil.*, etc.) sardineta, *f.*

chew, *v.t.* mascar, mascullar; (ponder) masticar

chewing, *s.* masticación, *f.* **c.-gum,** chicle, *m.*

chianti, *s.* (wine) quianti, *m.*

chiaroscuro, *s.* claroscuro, *m.*

chic, *s.* chic, *m.*, elegancia, *f.*

chicanery, *s.* sofistería, *f.*

chicken, *s.* pollo, *m.* **c.-hearted,** medroso, cobarde. **c.-pox,** varicela, *f.*

chick-pea, *s.* garbanzo, *m.*

chickweed, *s.* pamplina, *f.*

chicory, *s.* achicoria, *f.*

chide, *v.t.* reprender, reñir

chidingly, *adv.* en tono de reprensión

chief, *s.* jefe, *m. a.* principal; primero; en jefe; mayor. **c.-of-staff,** jefe de Estado Mayor, *m.*

chiefly, *adv.* principalmente; sobre todo

chieftain, *s.* caudillo, *m.*; (of a clan) cabeza, jefe, *m.*

chiffon, *s.* chifón, *m.*, gasa, *f.*

chiffonier, *s.* cómoda, *f.*

chignon, *s.* moño, *m.*

chilblain, *s.* sabañón, *m.*

child, *s.* niño (-ña); hijo (-ja). **from a c.,** desde niño, desde la niñez. **with c.,** encinta, embarazada. **How many children**

have you? ¿ Cuántos hijos tiene Vd.? **child's play,** juegos infantiles, *m. pl.*; (*fig.*) niñerías, *f. pl.* **c. welfare,** puericultura, *f.*

childbirth, *s.* parto, *m.*

childhood, *s.* niñez, infancia, *f.* **from his c.,** desde su niñez, desde niño

childish, *a.* de niño; aniñado; pueril; fútil. **to grow c.,** chochear

childishly, *adv.* como un niño

childishness, *s.* puerilidad, *f.*; futilidad, *f.*

childless, *a.* sin hijos; sin niños

childlike, *a.* de niño, aniñado; pueril

children. See **child**

Chilean, *a.* and *s.* chileno (-na)

chili, *s.* chile, pimento de cornetilla, *m.*

chill, *s.* frío, *m.*; (of fear, etc.) estremecimiento, *m.*; (illness) resfriado, *m.*; (unfriendliness) frialdad, frigidez, *f. a.* frío; (unfriendly) frígido. *v.t.* enfriar; helar; (with fear, etc.) dar escalofríos (de); (discourage) desalentar. *v.i.* tener frío; tener escalofríos. **to take the c. off,** templar, calentar un poco

chilliness, *s.* frío, *m.*; (unfriendliness) frialdad, frigidez, *f.*

chilly, *a.* frío; (sensitive to cold) friolero; (of politeness, etc.) glacial, frígido

chime, *s.* juego de campanas, *m.*; repique, campaneo, *m.*; armonía, *f. v.i.* (of bells) repicar; (*fig.*) armonizar. **to c. the hour,** dar la hora

chimera, *s.* quimera, *f.*

chimerical, *a.* quimérico

chimney, *s.* chimenea, *f.*; (of a lamp) tubo (de lámpara), *m.* **c.-corner,** rincón de chimenea, *m.* **c.-pot,** sombrerete de chimenea, *m.* **c.-stack,** chimenea, *f.* **c.-sweep,** limpiador de chimeneas, deshollinador, *m.*

chimpanzee, *s.* chimpancé, *m.*

chin, *s.* barbilla, barba, *f.*, mentón, *m.* **c.-rest,** mentonera, *f.* **c.-strap,** barboquejo, *m.*; venda para la barbilla, *f.*

china, *s.* china, porcelana, *f.*; loza, *f. a.* de porcelana; de loza. **c. cabinet,** chinero, *m.*

chinchilla, *s.* (animal and fur) chinchilla, *f.*

Chinese, *a.* and *s.* chino (-na); (language) chino, *m.* **C. lantern,** farolillo de papel, *m.* **C. white,** óxido blanco de cinc, *m.*

chink, *s.* resquicio, *m.*, grieta, hendidura, *f.*; (clink) retintín, tintineo, *m. v.i.* tintinar

chintz, *s.* zaraza, *f.*

chip, *s.* astilla, *f.*; (counter) ficha, *f. v.t.* picar; cincelar. **A c. off the old block,** De tal palo tal astilla. **c. potatoes,** patatas fritas, *f. pl.*

chiromancy, *s.* quiromancia, *f.*

chiropodist, *s.* pedicuro, *m.*, callista, *m.* and *f.*

chiropody, *s.* pedicura, *f.*

chiropractor, *s.* quiropráctico, *m.*

chirp, *v.i.* piar, gorjear. *s.* pío, gorjeo, *m.*

chirping, *s.* piada, *f. a.* gárrulo, piante

chisel, *s.* escoplo, cincel, *m. v.t.* cincelar. **cold c.,** cortafrío, *m.*

chit-chat, *s.* charla, *f.*

chiton, *s.* túnica, *f.*

chitterlings, *s.* asadura, *f.*

chivalrous, *a.* caballeroso

chivalry, *s.* caballería, *f.*; caballerosidad, *f.* **novel of c.,** novela de caballería, *f.*

chive, *s.* (*bot.*) cebollana, *f.*, cebollino, *m.*

chloral, *s.* cloral, *m.*

chlorate, *s.* clorató, *m.*

chloride, *s.* cloruro, *m.*

chlorine, *s.* cloro, *m.*

chloroform, *s.* cloroformo, *m. v.t.* cloroformizar

chlorophyll, *s.* clorófila, *f.*

chlorosis, *s.* clorosis, *f.*

chock-full, *a.* lleno de bote en bote

chocolate, *s.* chocolate, *m. a.* de chocolate. **thick drinking-c.,** chocolate a la española, *m.* **thin drinking-c.,** chocolate a la francesa, *m.* **c. shop,** chocolatería, *f.*

choice, *s.* selección, *f.*; preferencia, *f.*; elección, *f.*; opción, *f.*; alternativa, *f.*; lo más escogido. *a.* escogido, selecto; excelente. **for c.,** con preferencia

choir, *s.* coro, *m.* **c.-boy,** niño del coro, *m.* **c.-master,** maestro de capilla, *m.*

choke, v.i. ahogarse; atragantarse; obstruirse. v.t. ahogar; estrangular. **to c. with laughter,** ahogarse de risa. **to c. back,** (words) tragar. **to c. off,** (a person) disuadir (de); quitarse de encima(a). **to c. up,** obstruir, cerrar, obturar; (hide) cubrir, tapar

`choking,` a. asfixiante, sofocante. s. ahogamiento, m., sofocación, f.

cholera, s. cólera, m.

choleric, a. colérico

cholesterol, s. colesterina, f.

choline, s. colina, f.

choose, v.t. escoger; elegir; optar por; (wish) querer, gustar. **They will do it when they c.,** Lo harán cuando les parezca bien. **If you c.,** Si Vd. quiere; Si Vd. gusta. **He was chosen as Mayor,** Fué elegido alcalde. **There is nothing to c. between them,** No hay diferencia entre ellos; Tanto vale el uno como el otro. **You cannot c. but love her,** No puedes menos de quererla

choosing, s. selección, f.; (for an office, etc.) elección, f.

chop, v.t. cortar; (mince) picar; (split) hender, partir. s. (meat) chuleta, f.; (jaw) quijada, f. **to c. about,** round, (of the wind) girar, virar. **to c. down,** (trees) talar. **to c. off,** separar; cortar; tajar. **to c. up,** cortar en pedazos

chopper, s. hacha, f.

choppy, a. picado, agitado

chopstick, s. palillo chino, m.

choral, a. coral

chord, s. cuerda, f.; (mus.) acorde, m.; **the right c.,** (fig.) la cuerda sensible

choreographer, s. coreógrafo, m.

choreographic, a. coreográfico

choreography, s. coreografía, f.

choriamb, s. coriambo, m.

chorister, s. corista, m.

chorus, s. coro, m.; (in revues) comparsa, f., acompañamiento, m.; (of a song) refrán, m. **to sing in c.,** cantar a coro. **c. girl,** corista, f.

chosen, a. escogido; elegido. **the c.,** los elegidos

chrestomathy, s. crestomatía, f.

chrism, s. crisma, m. or f.

Christ, s. Cristo, Jesucristo, m.

christen, v.t. bautizar

Christendom, s. cristianismo, m., cristiandad, f.

christening, s. bautizo, m. a. bautismal, de bautizo

christian, a. cristiano. s. cristiano (-na). **c. name,** nombre de pila, m.

christianity, s. cristianismo, m.

Christmas, s. Navidad, f. **A Merry C.!** ¡ Felices Pascuas (de Navidad)! **Father C.,** Padre Noël, m.; (Sp. equivalent) Los Reyes Magos. **C. box,** regalo de Navidad, m. **C. card,** felicitación de Navidad, f. **C. carol,** villancico de Navidad, m. **C. Day,** día de Navidad, m. **C. Eve,** Nochebuena, f. **C.-tide,** Navidades, f. pl. **C. tree,** árbol de Navidad, m.

chromate, s. cromato, m.

chromatic, a. cromático

chrome, s. cromo, m. **c. yellow,** amarillo de cromo, m.

chromic, a. cromico

chromium, s. cromo, m. **c.-plated,** cromado

chromosome, s. cromosoma, m.

chronic, a. crónico; inveterado

chronicle, s. crónica, f. v.t. narrar

chronicler, s. cronista, m. and f.

chronological, a. cronológico. **in c. order,** por orden cronológico

chronologically, adv. cronológicamente

chronology, s. cronología, f.

chronometer, s. cronómetro, m.

chrysalis, s. crisálida, f.

chrysanthemum, s. crisantemo, m.

chubbiness, s. gordura, f.

chubby, a. regordete, gordito. **c.-cheeked,** mofletudo

chuck, v.t. (throw) lanzar, arrojar; (discontinue) abandonar, dejar. s. (in a lathe) mandril, m. **to c. under the chin,** acariciar la barbilla (a). **to c. away,** derrochar; malgastar, perder. **to c. out,** echar, poner en la calle

chuckle, v.i. reir entre dientes. s. risa ahogada, f.; risita, f.

chum, s. compinche, camarada, m. and f. **to c. up with,** ser camarada de

chunk, s. pedazo, trozo, m.
church, s. iglesia, f.; (Protestant) templo, m. v.t. (a woman) purificar. **Poor as a c. mouse,** Más pobre que las ratas. **the C. of England,** la iglesia anglicana. **to go to c.,** ir a misa; ir al templo. **c. music,** música sagrada, f.
churching, s. misa de parida, f.
churchwarden, s. (nearest equivalent) capillero, m.
churchyard, s. cementerio, m.
churl, s. patán, m.
churlish, a. grosero, cazurro; (mean) tacaño, ruin
churn, s. mantequera, f. v.t. (cream) batir; (fig.) azotar, agitar
chute, s. (for grain, etc.) manga de tolva, f.; vertedor, m.; (in flats and fun fairs) tobogán, deslizadero, m.
ciborium, s. (chalice) copón, m.; (tabernacle) sagrario, m.; (arch.) ciborio, m.
cicada, s. cigarra, f.
cicatrice, s. cicatriz, f.
cicatrization, s. cicatrización, f.
cicatrize, v.t. cicatrizar. v.i. cicatrizarse
cider, s. sidra, f.
cigar, s. cigarro, m. **c.-box,** cigarrera, f. **c.-case,** petaca, cigarrera, f. **c.-cutter,** cortapuros, m.
cigarette, s. cigarrillo, pitillo, m. **c.-butt,** colilla, f. **c.-case,** pitillera, f. **c.-holder,** boquilla, f. **c.-lighter,** encendedor de cigarrillos, m. **c.-paper,** papel de fumar, m.
ciliary, a. ciliar
cinch, s. (of a saddle) cincha, f.; (fam.) ganga, f.; (fam.) seguridad, f. **c.-strap,** látigo, m.
cinchona, s. quina, cinchona, f.
cinder, s. ceniza, f.; carbonilla, f. **red-hot c.,** rescoldo, m. **c.-track,** pista de ceniza, f.
ciné-camera, s. máquina cinematográfica, f.
cinema, cinematograph, s. cine, cinematógrafo, m.
cinematographic, a. cinematográfico
cinematography, s. cinematografía, f.
Cingalese, a. cingalés. s. cingalés (-esa)

cinnamon, s. (spice) canela, f.; (tree) canelo, m.; color de canela, m.
cinquefoil, s. (bot.) quinquefolio, m.
cipher, s. (math.) cero, m.; (fig.) nulidad, f.; (code) cifra, f.; monograma, m. **to be a mere c.,** ser un cero
Circassian, a. circasiano. s. circasiano (-na)
circle, s. círculo, m.; (revolution) vuelta, f.; (group) grupo, m.; (club, etc.) centro, m.; (cycle) ciclo, m. v.t. dar vueltas alrededor de; rodear; ceñir. v.i. dar vueltas; (of a hawk, etc.) cernerse. **dress-c.,** (theat.) anfiteatro, m. **the family c.,** el círculo de la familia. **to come full c.,** dar la vuelta. **upper c.,** (theat.) segundo piso, m. **vicious c.,** círculo vicioso, m.
circlet, s. (of flowers, etc.) corona, f.; (ring) anillo, m.
circuit, s. circuito, m.; (tour) gira, f.; (revolution) vuelta, f.; (radius) radio, m. **short c.,** corto circuito, m. **c.-breaker,** cortacircuitos, m.
circuitous, a. indirecto; tortuoso
circuitously, adv. indirectamente
circular, a. circular; redondo. s. carta circular, f.; circular, f. **c. tour,** viaje redondo, m.
circularize, v.t. enviar circulares (a)
circulate, v.i. circular. v.t. hacer circular; poner en circulación; (news, etc.) divulgar, diseminar
circulating library, s. biblioteca por subscripción, f.
circulation, s. circulación, f.; (of a newspaper, etc.) tirada, circulación, f. **c. of the blood,** circulación de la sangre, f.
circulatory, a. circulatorio
circumcise, v.t. circuncidar
circumcised, a. circunciso
circumcision, s. circuncisión, f.
circumference, s. circunferencia, f.
circumflex, a. circunflejo. **c. accent,** acento circunflejo, m.
circumlocution, s. circunlocución, f.

circumnavigate, v.t. circunnavegar

circumnavigation, s. circunnavegación, f.

circumscribe, v.t. circunscribir;
(fig.) limitar

circumscribed, a. circunscripto;
(fig.) limitado

circumscription, s. circunscripción, f.; (fig.) limitación, restricción, f.

circumspect, a. circunspecto;
discreto, correcto; prudente

circumspection, s. circunspección, f.; prudencia, f.

circumspectly, adv. con circunspección; prudentemente

circumstance, s. circunstancia,
f.; detalle, m. aggravating c.,
circunstancia agravante, f. attenuating c., circunstancia
atenuante, f. in the circumstances, en las circunstancias.
in easy circumstances, en
buena posición, acomodado. Do
you know what his circum-
stances are ? ¿ Sabes cuál es su
situación económica ? under
the circumstances, bajo las
circunstancias

circumstantial, a. circunstancial;
detallado. c. evidence, prueba
de indicios, f.

circumvent, v.t. frustrar; impedir

circumvention, s. frustración,
f.

circumvolution, s. cirounvolu-
ción, f.

circus, s. circo, m.; plaza redonda, f.; (traffic) redondel, m.

cirrhosis, s. cirrosis, f.

cirrus, s. (all meanings) cirro, m.

cisalpine, a. cisalpino

Cistercian, a. cisterciense. C.
Order, Císter, m.

cistern, s. tanque, m.; cisterna, f.,
aljibe, m.

citadel, s. ciudadela, f.

citation, s. (law) citación, f.; cita,
f.

cite, v.t. citar

citizen, s. ciudadano (-na); vecino
(-na); natural, m. and f. fellow
c., conciudadano, m.; compatriota, m. and f.

citizenship, s. ciudadanía, f.

citrate, s. citrato, m.

citric, a. cítrico

citrine, a. cetrino

citron, s. (fruit) cidra, f.; (tree)
cidro, m.

city, s. ciudad, f. a. municipal

civet, s. algalia, f.

civic, a. cívico; municipal

civics, s. civismo, m.

civil, a. civil; doméstico; (polite)
cortés, atento; (obliging) servicial. c. defence, defensa
pasiva, f. c. engineer, ingeniero
de caminos, canales y puertos, m.
C. Service, cuerpo de emplea-
dos del Estado, m.

civilian, a. civil. s. ciudadano
(-na). c. dress, traje paisano, m.

civility, s. civilidad, cortesía, f.

civilization, s. civilización, f.

civilize, v.t. civilizar

civilized, a. civilizado

civilizing, a. civilizador

civilly, adv. civilmente, cortésmente

clack, s. golpeo, ruido sordo, m.

clad, a. vestido

claim, v.t. reclamar; pretender;
exigir; (law) demandar; (assert) afirmar. v.i. (law) pedir en
juicio. s. reclamación, f.; pretensión, f.; (law) demanda, f.;
(in a gold-field, etc.) concesión,
f.; (right) derecho, m. to lay c.
to, pretender a; exigir. to put
in a c. for, reclamar

claimant, s. (law) demandante,
m. and f.; pretendiente (-ta);
(com.) acreedor (-ra)

clairvoyance, s. doble vista, f.

clairvoyant, s. vidente, m.

clam, s. almeja, chirla, f.

clamber, v.i. trepar, encaramarse. s. subida difícil, f.

clamminess, s. viscosidad, humedad, f.

clammy, a. viscoso; húmedo,
mojado

clamorous, a. clamoroso, ruidoso,
estrepitoso

clamour, s. clamor, estruendo,
m.; gritería, vocería, f. v.i.
gritar, vociferar. to c. against,
protestar contra. to c. for, pedir
a voces

clamp, s. grapa, f.; abrazadera,
f.; (carp.) tornillo, m.; (pile)
montón, m. v.t. empalmar;
sujetar, lañar

clan, s. clan, m.; familia, f.;
partido, grupo, m.

clandestine, *a.* clandestino, furtivo

clandestinely, *adv.* en secreto, clandestinamente

clang, *v.i.* sonar; (of a gate, etc.) rechinar. *v.t.* hacer sonar. *s.* sonido metálico, *m.*; estruendo, *m.*

clank, *v.i.* dar un ruido metálico; crujir. *v.t.* hacer sonar; (glasses) hacer chocar. *s.* ruido metálico, *m.*; el crujir

clannish, *a.* exclusivista

clansman, *s.* miembro de un clan, *m.*

clap, *v.t.* (hands) batir; (spurs, etc.) poner rápidamente; (one's hat on) encasquetarse (el sombrero); (shut) cerrar apresuradamente. *v.i.* aplaudir. *s.* (of the hands) palmada, *f.*; (of thunder) trueno, *m.*; (noise) ruido, *m.* **to c. eyes on,** echar la vista encima de. **to c. someone on the back,** dar una palmada en la espalda (a). **to c. the hands,** batir las palmas

clapper, *s.* (of a bell) badajo, *m.*

clapping, *s.* aplausos, *m. pl.*

claque, *s.* claque, *f.*

claret, *s.* clarete, *m.*

clarification, *s.* clarificación, *f.*; elucidación, *f.*

clarify, *v.t.* clarificar; elucidar, aclarar

clarinet, *s.* clarinete, *m.*

clarinettist, *s.* clarinete, *m.*

clarion, *s.* clarín, *m.*

clarity, *s.* claridad, *f.*; lucidez, *f.*

clash, *v.i.* chocar; encontrarse; (of events) coincidir; (of opinions, etc.) oponerse, estar en desacuerdo; (of colours) desentonar, chocar. *s.* estruendo, fragor, *m.*; choque, *m.*; (*mil.*) encuentro, *m.*; (of opinions, etc.) desacuerdo, *m.*; disputa, *f.*

clasp, *v.t.* (a brooch, etc.) abrochar, enganchar; (embrace) abrazar; (of plants, etc.) ceñir. *s.* (brooch) broche, *m.*; (of a belt) hebilla, *f.*; (of a necklace, handbag, book) cierre, *m.*; (for the hair) pasador, *m.* **to c. someone in one's arms,** tomar en los brazos (a), abrazar. **c.-knife,** navaja, *f.*

class, *s.* clase, *f.*; (kind) especie, *f.*; (of exhibits, etc.) categoría, *f.*

v.t. clasificar. **in a c. by itself,** único en su línea. **the lower classes,** las clases bajas. **the middle classes,** la clase media. **the upper classes,** la clase alta. **c.-mate,** condiscípulo (-la). **c.-room,** sala de clase, *f.* **c. war,** lucha de clases, *f.*

classic, *a.* clásico. *s.* clásico, *m.*

classical, *a.* clásico

classicism, *s.* clasicismo, *m.*

classicist, *a.* and *s.* clasicista (*m.* and *f.*)

classics, *s. pl.* los clásicos

classifiable, *a.* clasificable

classification, *s.* clasificación, *f.*

classify, *v.t.* clasificar

clatter, *v.i.* hacer ruido; (knock) golpear; (of loose horse-shoes) chacolotear. *v.t.* hacer ruido con; chocar (una cosa contra otra). *s.* ruido, *m.*; (hammering) martilleo, *m.*; (of horse-shoes) chacoloteo, *m.*; (of a crowd) estruendo, *m.*, bulla, *f.* **John clattered along the street,** Los pasos de Juan resonaban por la calle

clause, *s.* (*gram.*) cláusula, *f.*; (*law*) condición, estipulación, cláusula, *f.*

claustrophobia, *s.* claustrofobia, *f.*

clavichord, *s.* clavicordio, *m.*

clavicle, *s.* clavícula, *f.*

claw, *s.* garra, *f.*; (of a lobster, etc.) tenaza, *f.*; (hook) garfio, gancho, *m.* *v.t.* arañar, clavar las uñas en; (tear) desgarrar. **c.-hammer,** martillo de orejas, *m.*

clay, *s.* arcilla, *f.*; barro, *m.*; (pipe) pipa de barro, *f.* **c.-pit,** barrizal, *m.*

clayey, *a.* arcilloso

clean, *a.* limpio; puro, casto. *adv.* limpio; completamente; exactamente. **to make a c. sweep (of),** no dejar títere con cabeza. **to make a c. breast of,** confesar sin tormento, no quedarse con nada en el pecho. **to show a c. pair of heels,** tomar las de Villadiego. **c. bill of health,** patente de sanidad, *m.* **c.-cut,** bien definido; claro. **c.-limbed,** bien proporcionado, gallardo. **c.-shaven,** lampiño; sin barba, bien afeitado

clean, *v.t.* limpiar; (streets) barrer; (a floor) fregar; (dry-clean) lavar al seco. **to c. one's hands** (teeth), limpiarse las manos (los dientes). **to c. up**, limpiar; (tidy) asear; poner en orden

cleaner, *s.* limpiador (-ra); (charwoman) fregona, *f.*; (stain remover) sacamanchas, *m.*; (dry-cleaner, person) tintorero (-ra)

cleaning, *s.* limpieza, *f. a.* de limpiar. **dry-c.**, lavado al seco, *m.* **c. rag**, trapo de limpiar, *m.*

cleanliness, *s.* limpieza, *f.*; aseo, *m.*

cleanness, *s.* limpieza, *f.*; aseo, *m.* pureza, *f.*

cleanse, *v.t.* limpiar; lavar; purgar; purificar

cleansing, *s.* limpieza, *f.*; lavamiento, *m.*; purgación, *f.*; purificación, *f.*

clear, *a.* claro; (of the sky) sereno, despejado; transparente; (free (from)) libre (de); (open) abierto; (of profit, etc.) neto; (of thoughts, etc.) lúcido; (apparent) evidente; explícito; (of images) distinto; absoluto; (whole) entero, completo. **c. majority**, mayoría absoluta, *f.* **c. profit**, beneficio neto, *m.* **c.-cut**, bien definido. **c.-headed**, perspicaz; inteligente. **c.-sighted**, clarividente

clear, *v.t.* aclarar; despejar; limpiar; librar (de); quitar; (one's throat) carraspear; (com., stock) liquidar; (of a charge) absolver; (one's character) vindicar; (avoid, miss) evitar; (jump) salvar, saltar; (a court, etc.) desocupar; (a debt) satisfacer; (an account) saldar; (a mortgage) cancelar; (win) ganar; hacer un beneficio de; (through customs) despachar en la aduana. *v.i.* (of sky, etc.) serenarse; escampar; (of wine, etc.) aclararse; despacharse en la aduana. **to c. the table**, levantar la mesa. **to c. the way**, abrir calle; (*fig.*) abrir paso. **to c. away**, *v.t.* quitar; disipar. *v.i.* disiparse. **to c. off**, *v.t.* (finish) terminar; (debts) pagar; (discharge) despedir. *v.i.* (of rain) despejarse, escampar; marcharse. **to c. out**, *v.i.* lim-

piar; (a drain, etc.) desatascar; vaciar; echar. *v.i.* marcharse, escabullirse. **C. out!** ¡Fuera! **to c. up**, *v.t.* poner en orden; (a mystery, etc.) aclarar, resolver. *v.i.* (of weather) serenarse, escampar, despejarse

clearance, *s.* (of trees, etc.) desmonte, *m.*; eliminación, *f.*; expulsión, *f.*; (*mech.*) espacio muerto, *m.*; despacho de aduana, *m.* **to make a c. of**, deshacerse de. **c. sale**, liquidación, venta de saldos, *f.*

clearing, *s.* (in a wood) claro, *m.*; desmonte, *m.*; (*com.*, of goods) liquidación, *f.*; (of one's character) vindicación, *f.* **c.-house**, casa de compensación, *f.*

clearly, *adv.* claramente

clearness, *s.* claridad, *f.*

cleavage, *s.* hendimiento, *m.*; (in views, etc.) escisión, *f.*

cleave, *v.t.* partir; abrir; (air, water, etc.) surcar, hender. *v.i.* partirse; (stick) pegarse, adherirse

cleaver, *s.* partidor, *m.*; hacha, *f.*

clef, *s.* clave, *f.* **treble c.**, clave de sol, *f.*

cleft, *s.* hendedura, fisura, rendija, abertura, *f.* **c.-palate**, paladar hendido, *m.*

clematis, *s.* clemátide, *f.*

clemency, *s.* (of weather) benignidad, *f.*; (of character, etc.) clemencia, *f.*

clement, *a.* (of weather) benigno; (of character, etc.) clemente, benévolo

clench, *v.t.* agarrar; (teeth, etc.) apretar; (a bargain) cerrar, concluir

clerestory, *s.* claraboya, *f.*

clergy, *s.* clero, *m.*, clérigos, *m. pl.*

clergyman, *s.* clérigo, *m.*

cleric, *s.* eclesiástico, *m.*

clerical, *a.* clerical; de oficina. **c. error**, error de oficina, *m.* **c. work**, trabajo de oficina, *m.*

clericalism, *s.* clericalismo, *m.*

clerk, *s.* (clergyman) clérigo, *m.*; (in an office) oficinista, escribiente, *m.*; oficial, *m.*; secretario, *m.*

clerkship, *s.* puesto de oficinista, *m.*; escribanía, *f.*; secretaría, *f.*

clever, *a.* listo, inteligente; ingenioso; hábil; (dexterous) diestro

cleverly, *adv.* hábilmente; diestramente, con destreza

cleverness, *s.* talento, *m.*; inteligencia, *f.*; habilidad, *f.*; (dexterity) destreza, *f.*

cliché, *s.* frase hecha, *f.*

click, *v.i.* (of the tongue) dar un chasquido; (of a bolt, etc.) cerrarse a golpe; hacer tictac. *v.t.* (one's tongue) chascar; (a bolt, etc.) cerrar a golpe. *s.* golpe seco, *m.*; tictac, *m.*; (of the tongue) chasquido, *m.* **to c. one's heels together,** hacer chocar los talones

client, *s.* cliente, *m.* and *f.*; (customer) parroquiano (-na)

clientèle, *s.* clientela, *f.*

cliff, *s.* acantilado, *m.*, roca, escarpa, *f.*

climacteric, *a.* climatérico

climate, *s.* clima, *m.*

climatic, *a.* climático

climatology, *s.* climatología, *f.*

climax, *s.* culminación, *f.*; (rhetoric) clímax, *m.*; gradación, *f.*; punto más alto, apogeo, cenit, *m.*; (of a play, etc.) desenlace, *m.*

climb, *v.t.* and *v.i.* trepar; escalar; montar; subir; ascender. **rate of c.,** (*aer.*) velocidad ascensional, *f.* **to c. down,** bajar; (*fig.*) echar el pie atrás. **to c. over,** (obstacles) salvar. **to c. up,** encaramarse por; subir por; montar

climber, *s.* alpinista, *m.* and *f.*; (plant) trepadera, enredadera, *f.*; (social) arrivista, *m.* and *f.*

clime, *s.* clima, *m.*

clinch, *v.t.* (nails, etc.) remachar, rebotar; (a bargain, etc.) cerrar; (an argument, etc.) remachar. *s.* (wrestling) cuerpo a cuerpo, "clinch," *m.*

cling, *v.i.* pegarse (a); agarrarse (a); (of scents) pegarse; (follow) seguir. **They clung together for an instant,** Quedaron abrazados un instante

clinging, *a.* tenaz; (of plants, etc.) trepador; (of persons) manso, dócil. **to be a c. vine,** (*fam.*) ser una malva

clinic, *s.* clínica, *f.*

clinical, *a.* clínico. **c. thermometer,** termómetro clínico, *m.*

clink, *v.i.* retiñir; (of glasses) chocarse. *v.t.* hacer sonar; (glasses) chocar. *s.* retintín, *m.*; (of a hammer) martilleo, *m.*; sonido metálico, *m.*; (of glasses) choque, *m.*

clip, *v.t.* (grasp) agarrar; (sheep, etc.) esquilar; (trim) recortar, cercenar; (prune) podar; (a ticket) taladrar. *s.* pinza, *f.*; (paper-clip) sujetapapeles, *m.*; (*mech.*) grapa, escarpia, *f.*; (for ornament) sujetador, *m.* **to c. a person's wings,** (*fig.*) cortar (or quebrar) las alas (a)

clipper, *s.* (person) esquilador (-ra); (*naut.* and *aer.*) clíper, *m.*; *pl.* **clippers,** tenazas de cortar, *f. pl.*; (for pruning) podaderas, *f. pl.*; (punch) taladro, *m.*

clipping, *s.* (of sheep, etc.) esquileo, *m.*; (of a newspaper, etc.) recorte, *m.*

clique, *s.* camarilla, *f.*

cliquish, *a.* exclusivista

cloak, *s.* capa, *f.*; manto, *m.*; (*fig.*) velo, *m.* *v.t.* encapotar; embozar; (conceal) ocultar, encubrir. **c. and sword play,** comedia de capa y espada, *f.* **c.-room,** guardarropa, *m.*; (ladies') tocador, *m.*; (on a station) consigna, *f.*

clock, *s.* reloj, *m.*; (of a stocking) cuadrado, *m.* **What o'clock is it?** ¿Qué hora es? **It is six o'clock,** Son las seis. **c.-face,** esfera de reloj, *f.* **c.-maker,** relojero, *m.* **c.-making,** relojería, *f.* **c.-work,** aparato de relojería, *m.* **to go like c.-work,** ir como un reloj. **c.-work train,** tren de cuerda, *m.*

clockwise, *a.* and *adv.* en el sentido de las agujas del reloj; de derecha a izquierda

clod, *s.* (of earth) terrón, *m.*; (corpse) tierra, *f.*; (person) zoquete, *m.* **c.-hopper,** patán, *m.*

clog, *s.* (shoe) zueco, zoclo, *m.*; (obstacle) estorbo, obstáculo, *m.* *v.t.* embarazar; estorbar, impedir; (block) obturar, cerrar; (*fig.*) paralizar

cloister, *s.* claustro, *m.*; convento, *m.* *v.t.* enclaustrar

cloistered, *a.* enclaustrado; retirado, aislado

close, a. estrecho; (of a prisoner) incomunicado; (reticent) reservado; (niggardly) tacaño, avaro; (scarce) escaso; (of friends) íntimo; (equal) igual; (lacking space) apretado; (dense) denso; (thick) tupido; compacto; (of a copy, etc.) fiel, exacto; (thorough) concienzudo; (careful) cuidadoso; (attentive) atento; (to the roots) a raíz; (of shaving) bueno; (of weather) pesado, sofocante; (of rooms) mal ventilado. at c. quarters, de cerca. It is c. on eight o'clock, Son casi las ocho. to press c., perseguir de cerca; fatigar c. at hand, c. by, cerca; al lado; a mano. c.-cropped, (of hair) al rape. c. fight, lucha igualada, f. c.-fisted, tacaño, apretado. c.-fitting, ajustado, ceñido al cuerpo; pequeño. c. season, veda, f. c.-up, s. (cinema) primer plano, m.

close, s. (end) fin, m., conclusión, f.; (of day) caída, f.; (mus.) cadencia, f.; (enclosure) cercado, m.; (square) plazoleta, f.; (alley) callejón, m.; (of a cathedral) patio, m. at the c. of day, a la caída de la tarde. to bring to a c., terminar; llevar a cabo. to draw to a c., tocar a su fin; estar terminando

close, v.t. cerrar; (end) concluir, terminar; poner fin a. v.i. cerrar(se); (of a wound) cicatrizarse, cerrarse; (end) terminar(se), acabar, concluir. to c. the ranks, cerrar filas. to c. about, (surround) rodear, cercar; (envelop) envolver. to c. down, v.t. cerrar. v.i. cerrar; (rad.) cerrarse. to c. in, (surround) cercar; (of night) cerrar; caer; (envelop) envolver; (of length of days) acortarse. to c. in on, cercar. to c. round, envolver; (of water) tragar. to c. up, v.t. cerrar; cerrar completamente; obstruir. v.i. (of persons) acercarse; (of a wound) cicatrizarse; cerrarse

closed, a. cerrado. Road c., Cerrado el paso. to have a c. mind, ser cerrado de mollera; sufrir de estrechez de miras

closely, adv. estrechamente; de

cerca; (carefully) cuidadosamente; (exactly) exactamente; (attentively) con atención, atentamente

closeness, s. estrechez, f.; densidad, f.; (nearness) proximidad, f.; (of a copy, etc.) fidelidad, exactitud, f.; (stuffiness) falta de aire, f.; (of friendship) intimidad, f.; (stinginess) tacañería, f.; (reserve) reserva, f.

closet, s. camarín, m.; (cupboard) alacena, f.; (water) excusado, m.

closing, s. cerramiento, m.; (of an account) saldo, m. c. time, cierre, m., hora de cerrar, f.

closure, s. conclusión, f.; (pol.) clausura, f.

clot, s. coágulo, grumo, m. v.t. coagular. v.i. coagularse, cuajarse

cloth, s. tela, f.; paño, m.; (table) mantel, m.; (clergy) clero, m. She cleaned the books with a c., Ella limpió los libros con un paño. in c., (of books) en tela

clothe, v.t. vestir; cubrir; (with authority, etc.) revestir. to c. oneself, vestirse

clothes, s. pl. vestidos, m. pl., ropa, f. a suit of c., un traje. old c. shop, ropavejería, f. c.-basket, cesta de la colada, f. c.-brush, cepillo para ropa, m. c.-hanger, percha, f. c.-horse, enjugador, m. c.-line, cuerda de la ropa, f. c.-peg, pinza de la ropa, f. c.-prop, palo para sostener la cuerda de la colada, m.

clothier, s. ropero, m. clothier's shop, ropería, f.

clothing, s. vestidos, m. pl., ropa, f. article of c., prenda de vestir, f.

clotted, a. grumoso

cloud, s. nube, f. v.t. anublar, oscurecer; empañar; (blot out) borrar. v.i. anublarse. to be under a c., estar bajo sospecha. summer c., nube de verano, f. storm-c., nubarrón, m. c.-burst, nubada, f., chaparrón, m. c.-capped, coronado de nubes

cloudiness, s. nebulosidad, f.; obscuridad, f.; (of liquids) turbiedad, f.

cloudless, a. sin nubes, despejado; sereno, claro

cloudy, *a.* nublado, nubloso; obscuro; (of liquids) turbio

clove, *s.* clavo de especia, *m.*; (of garlic) diente de ajo, *m.* **c.-tree,** clavero, *m.*

cloven, *a.* hendido. **to show the c. hoof,** enseñar la oreja. **c. hoof,** pezuña, *f.*

clover, *s.* trébol, *m.* **to be in c.,** nadar en la abundancia

clown, *s.* patán, *m.*; bufón, tonto, *m.*; (in a circus) payaso, *m.* *v.i.* hacer el tonto, hacer el payaso

clowning, *s.* payasada, *f.*

clownish, *a.* grosero; palurdo, zafio; bufón

cloy, *v.t.* empalagar

cloying, *a.* empalagoso

club, *s.* porra, cachiporra, clava, *f.*; (gymnastic) maza, *f.*; (hockey) bastón de hockey, *m.*; (golf) palo de golf, *m.*; (in cards) basto, *m.*; (social) club, *m.* *v.t.* golpear. **to c. together,** asociarse, unirse. **We clubbed together to buy him a present,** Entre todos le compramos un regalo. **c.-house,** club, *m.*

clubfoot, *s.* pie de piña, *m.*

clubman, *s.* miembro de un club, *m.*

cluck, *v.i.* cloquear. *s.* cloqueo, *m.*

clucking, *s.* cloqueo, *m.*

clue, *s.* indicio, *m.*; (to a problem) clave, *f.*; (of a cross-word) indicación, *f.*; idea, *f.*

clump, *s.* bloque, pedazo, *m.*; (of trees) grupo, *m.*; (of feet) ruido, *m.*

clumsily, *adv.* torpemente; pesadamente

clumsiness, *s.* torpeza, *f.*; falta de maña, *f.*; pesadez, *f.*

clumsy, *a.* torpe; desmañado; chapucero, sin arte; (lumbering) pesado; (in shape) disforme

cluster, *s.* (of currants, etc.) racimo, *m.*; (of flowers) ramillete, *m.*; grupo, *m.* *v.i.* arracimarse; agruparse. **They clustered round him,** Se agrupaban a su alrededor

clutch, *v.t.* agarrar; sujetar, apretar. *s.* (mech.) embrague, *m.*; (of eggs) nidada, *f.*; (fig.) garras, *f. pl.* **to fall into the clutches of,** caer en las garras de. **to make a c. at,** procurar agarrar. **to throw in the c.,**

(mech.) embragar. **to throw out the c.,** (mech.) desembragar. **c. pedal,** pedal de embrague, *m.*

clutter, *s.* desorden, *m.*, confusión, *f.* *v.t.* desordenar

clyster, *s.* lavativa, *f.*, clíster, *m.*

coach, *s.* carroza, *f.*; charabán, *m.*; (r.w.) vagón, coche, *m.*; (hackney) coche de alquiler, *m.*; (sport) entrenador, *m.*; (tutor) profesor particular, *m.* *v.t.* (sport) entrenar; (teach) preparar, dar lecciones particulares (a). **through c.,** coche directo, *m.* **c.-box,** pescante, *m.* **c.-house,** cochera, *f.*

coaching, *s.* (sport) entrenamiento, *m.*; lecciones particulares, *f. pl.*

coachman, *s.* cochero, *m.*

coachwork, *s.* carrocería, *f.*

coagulate, *v.i.* coagularse. *v.t.* coagular, cuajar

coagulation, *s.* coagulación, *f.*

coal, *s.* carbón, *m.*; pedazo de carbón, *m.*; (burning) brasa, *f.* *v.i.* carbonear, hacer carbón, *v.t.* proveer de carbón; carbonear. **to carry coals to Newcastle,** llevar leña al monte. **to haul a person over the coals,** reprender a alguien. **c.-barge,** (barco) carbonero, *m.* **c.-black,** negro como el azabache. **c.-cellar, house,** carbonera, *f.* **c.-dust,** cisco, *m.* **c.-field,** yacimiento de carbón, *m.* **c.-gas,** gas de hulla, *m.* **c.-heaver,** cargador de carbón, *m.* **c.-merchant,** carbonero, *m.* **c.-mine,** mina de carbón, *f.* **c.-miner,** minero de carbón, *m.* **c.-scuttle,** carbonera, *f.* **c.-tar,** alquitrán mineral, *m.*

coalesce, *v.i.* fundirse; unirse; incorporarse

coalescence, *s.* fusión, *f.*; unión, *f.*; incorporación, *f.*

coaling, *s.* carboneo, *m.* **c.-station,** estación de carboneo, *f.*

coalition, *s.* coalición, *f.*

coarse, *a.* (in texture) basto, burdo; tosco; (gross) grosero; vulgar. **c.-grained,** de fibra gruesa; (of persons) vulgar, poco fino

coarsen, *v.t.* (of persons) embrutecer. *v.i.* embrutecerse; (of the skin) curtirse

coarseness, s. basteza, f.; tosquedad, f.; (of persons) grosería, indelicadeza, f.; vulgaridad, f.

coast, s. costa, f.; litoral, m. v.i. costear; deslizarse en un tobogán; dejar muerto el motor. **The c. is not clear,** Hay moros en la costa. **c.-guard,** guardacostas, m. **c.-line,** litoral, m.

coastal, a. costanero, costero. **c. defences,** defensas costeras, f. pl.

coaster, s. (naut.) barco costanero, barco de cabotaje, m.

coasting, s. (naut.) cabotaje, m.

coat, s. abrigo, m.; gabán, m.; chaqueta, f.; (animal's) capa, f.; (of paint) mano, f. v.t. recubrir; (with paint, etc.) dar una mano de. **fur c.,** abrigo de pieles, m. **sports c.,** abrigo "sport," m. **c. of arms,** escudo de armas, m. **c. of mail,** cota de malla, f. **c.-hanger,** percha, f.

coatee, s. chaquetita, f.

coating, s. (of paint, etc.) capa, mano, f.

co-author, s. coautor, m.

coax, v.t. instar; halagar; persuadir (a)

coaxing, s. ruegos, m. pl.; mimos, m. pl., caricias, f. pl.; persuasión, f. a. mimoso, zalamero; persuasivo

cob, s. (horse) jaca, f.; (lump) pedazo, m.; (swan) cisne macho, m.

cobalt, s. cobalto, m. **c. blue,** azul cobalto, m.

cobble, s. (stone) guijarro, m. v.t. (with stones) empedrar con guijarros; (shoes) remendar

cobbler, s. zapatero remendón, m. **cobbler's last,** horma, f. **cobbler's wax,** cerote, m.

cobblestone, s. guijarro, m., piedra, f.

co-belligerent, s. cobeligerante, m. and f.

cobra, s. cobra, serpiente de anteojos, f.

cobweb, s. telaraña, f.

cobwebby, a. cubierto de telarañas; transparente; de gasa

cocaine, s. cocaína, f.

cochineal, s. cochinilla, f.

cochlea, s. caracol (del oído), m.

cock, s. gallo, m.; (male) macho, m.; (tap) grifo, m., espita, f.; (of a gun) martillo, m.; (weather-vane) veleta, f.; (of hay) montón, m. v.t. (a gun) amartillar; (a hat) ladear; (raise) erguir, enderezar. **a cocked hat,** un sombrero de tres picos. **at half c.,** (of a gun) desamartillada (f.). **He cocked his head,** Irguió la cabeza. **The dog cocked its ears,** El perro aguzó las orejas. **to c. one's eye at,** lanzar una mirada (a). **c.-a-doodle-doo,** quiquiriquí, m. **c.-a-hoop,** triunfante, jubiloso; arrogante. **c.-crow,** canto del gallo, m. **c.-fight,** riña de gallos, f. **c.-of-the-walk,** gallito, m. **c.-sure,** pagado de sí mismo; completamente convencido

cockade, s. escarapela, f.

cockatoo, s. cacatúa, f.

cockatrice, s. basilisco, m.

cockchafer, s. escarabajo cornudo, m.

cockerel, s. gallo joven, gallito, m.

cocker spaniel, s. sabueso, m.

cockle, s. (bivalve) bucarda, f. v.i. arrugarse; (warp) torcerse; doblarse. **c.-shell,** (pilgrims') concha, f.; (boat) cascarón de nuez, m.

Cockney, a. londinense, de Londres. s. londinense, m. and f.

cockpit, s. galería, f.; (aer.) casilla del piloto, f.; (fig.) arena, f.

cockroach, s. cucaracha, f.

cockscomb, s. cresta de gallo, f.

cocktail, s. (drink) cóctel, coctel, m. **to shake a c.,** mezclar un coctel. **a c. party,** un "cocktail." **c. shaker,** cotelera, f.

cocky, a. fatuo, presuntuoso

cocoa, s. cacao, m.

coco-nut, s. coco, m.; (fam.) cabeza, f. **c.-n. milk,** agua de coco, f. **c.-n. shy,** pim, pam, pum, m. **c.-n. tree,** cocotero, m.

cocoon, s. capullo, m.

cod, s. bacalao, m. **cod-liver oil,** aceite de hígado de bacalao, m.

coddle, v.t. criar con mimo, mimar, consentir

code, s. código, m.; clave, f.; (secret) cifra, f. v.t. poner en cifra. **signal c.,** (naut.) código de señales, m. **c. word,** palabra de clave, f.

codeine, s. codeína, f.

codex, s. códice, m.

codicil, s. codicilio, m.
codification, s. codificación, f.
codify, v.t. codificar
co-education, s. coeducación, f.
coefficient, s. coeficiente, m.
co-equality, s. coigualdad, f.
coerce, v.t. forzar, obligar; constreñir
coercion, s. coerción, coacción, f.
coercive, a. coercitivo, coactivo
coeval, a. coevo
co-exist, v.i. coexistir
co-existence, s. coexistencia, f.
coffee, s. café, m. black c., café solo, m. white c., café con leche, m. c.-bean, grano de café, m. c.-cup, taza para café, f. c.-house, café, m. c.-mill, molinillo de café, m. c.-plantation, cafetal, m. c.-pot, cafetera, f. c.-set, juego de café, m. c.-tree, cafeto, m.
coffer, s. cofre, m.; arca, caja, f.
coffin, s. ataúd, féretro, m.; caja, f.
cog, s. (mech.) diente (de rueda), m.
cogency, s. fuerza, f.
cogent, a. convincente, fuerte; urgente
cogitate, v.i. pensar, considerar, meditar
cogitation, s. reflexión, meditación, consideración, f.
cognac, s. coñac, m.
cognate, a. (of stock) consanguíneo; afín; análogo; semejante
cognition, s. cognición, f.
cognitive, a. cognoscitivo
cognizance, s. conocimiento, m.; jurisdicción, f.
cogwheel, s. rueda dentada, f.
cohabit, v.i. cohabitar
cohabitation, s. cohabitación, f.
co-heir, s. coheredero, m.
co-heiress, s. coheredera, f.
cohere, v.i. pegarse, adherirse; unirse
coherent, a. coherente; consecuente
cohesion, s. cohesión, f.; coherencia, f.
cohort, s. cohorte, f.
coif, s. cofia, f.; toca, f.
coiffure, s. peinado, m.; tocado, m.
coil, v.t. arrollar; (naut., of ropes) adujar. v.i. arrollarse; enroscarse; serpentear. s. rollo, m.;

(of a serpent and ropes) anillo, m.; (of hair) trenza, f.; (elec.) carrete, m. coils of smoke, nubes de humo, f. pl. to c. up, hacerse un ovillo
coiling, s. arrollamiento, m.; serpenteo, m.
coin, s. moneda, f.; (fam.) dinero, m. v.t. acuñar; (a new word) inventar. to pay back in the same c., pagar en la misma moneda
coinage, s. acuñación, f.; moneda, f.; sistema monetario, m.; invención, f.; (new word) neologismo, m.
coincide, v.i. coincidir (con); estar conforme, estar de acuerdo
coincidence, s. coincidencia, f.; (chance) casualidad, f.
coiner, s. acuñador de moneda, m.; monedero falso, m.; (of phrases, etc.) inventor, m.
coitus, s. coito, m.
coke, s. (carbón de) coque, m.
colander, s. colador, m.
cold, a. frío. s. frío, m.; (med.) catarro, constipado, m. I am c., Tengo frío. It is c., Está frío; (weather) hace frío. to catch a c., acatarrarse, resfriarse. to grow c., enfriarse; (of the weather) empezar a hacer frío. in c. blood, a sangre fría. c.-blooded, (fishes, etc.) de sangre fría; (chilly, of persons) friolero; (pitiless) insensible, sin piedad; (of actions) a sangre fría, premeditado. c.-chisel, cortafrío, m. c. cream, crema (para el cutis), f. c.-hearted, seco, insensible. c.-shoulder, s. frialdad, f. v.t. tratar con frialdad (a). c.-storage, conservación refrigerada, f.
coldly, adv. fríamente
coldness, s. frío, m.; (of one's reception, etc.) frialdad, f.; (of heart) inhumanidad, f.
coleopterous, a. coleóptero
colic, s. cólico, m.
coliseum, s. coliseo, m.
colitis, s. colitis, f.
collaborate, v.i. colaborar (con)
collaboration, s. colaboración, f.
collaborationist, s. colaboracionista, m. and f.
collaborator, s. colaborador (-ra)

collapse, s. derrumbamiento, m.;
desplome, m.; (med.) colapso, m.;
(of buildings and fig.) hundimiento, m.; (of plans) frustración,
f.; (failure) fracaso, m. v.i.
derrumbarse; (of buildings, etc.)
hundirse, venirse abajo; (of
persons, fall) desplomarse; (med.)
sufrir colapso; (of plans, etc.)
frustrarse, venirse abajo. **George
came to us after the c. of
France,** Jorge vino a quedarse
con nosotros después del hundimiento de Francia

collapsible, a. plegable

collar, s. (of a garment and of fur)
cuello, m.; (of a dog, etc., and
necklace) collar, m. v.t. (seize)
agarrar. **detachable c.,** cuello
suelto, m. **high c.,** alzacuello, m.
c.-bone, clavícula, f.

collate, v.t. cotejar; (to a benefice)
colacionar

collateral, a. colateral

collation, s. (all meanings) colación, f.

colleague, s. colega, m.; compañero (-ra)

collect, v.t. (assemble) reunir;
(catch) coger; acumular; (call
for) pasar a buscar, ir (or venir)
a buscar; (pick up) recoger;
(taxes, etc.) recaudar; coleccionar; (one's strength, etc. and
debts, etc.) cobrar; (letters)
recoger. v.i. reunirse, congregarse; acumularse. s. (ecc.)
colecta, f. **to c. oneself,**
reponerse

collected, a. (of persons) seguro
de si.

collecting-box, s. cepo, m.

collection, s. reunión, f.; (of data,
etc.) acumulación, f.; (of pictures, stamps, etc.) colección, f.;
(of a debt, etc.) cobranza, f.; (of
taxes, etc.) recaudación, f.; (from
a pillar-box) recogida, f.; (of laws,
etc.) compilación, f.; (ecc.) ofertorio, m.; (of donations) colecta,
f.

collective, a. colectivo. **c. bargaining,** trato colectivo, m.

collectively, adv. colectivamente

collectivism, s. colectivismo, m.

collector, s. (of pictures, etc.)
coleccionador (-ra), coleccionista,
m. and f.; cobrador, m.; (elec.)
colector, m.

college, s. colegio, m.; escuela, f.;
universidad, f. **C. of Cardinals,**
Colegio de Cardenales, m.

collegiate, a. colegial, colegiado.
c. church, iglesia colegial, f.

collide, v.i. chocar (contra),
topar (con); estar en conflicto
(con)

collie, s. perro de pastor escocés,
m.

collier, s. minero de carbón, m.;
(barco) carbonero, m.

colliery, s. mina de carbón, f.;
hullera, f.

collision, s. choque, m., colisión,
f.; (of interests, etc.) antagonismo, conflicto, m. **to come into
c. with,** chocar con

colloid, a. coloide. s. coloide, m.

colloquial, a. familiar

colloquialism, s. expresión familiar, f.

colloquially, adv. en lenguaje
familiar; familiarmente

colloquy, s. coloquio, m.

collusion, s. colusión, f. **to be
in c.,** (law) coludir; conspirar,
estar de manga

Colombian, a. colombiano. s.
colombiano (-na)

colon, s. (anat.) colon, m.;
(punctuation) dos puntos, m. pl.

colonel, s. coronel, m.

colonelcy, s. coronelía, f.

colonial, a. colonial. s. habitante
de las colonias, m. **C. Office,**
Ministerio de Asuntos Coloniales,
m.

colonist, s. colono, m.; colonizador (-ra)

colonization, s. colonización, f.

colonize, v.t. colonizar. v.i.
establecerse en una colonia

colonizer, s. colonizador (-ra)

colonizing, s. colonización, f.
a. colonizador

colonnade, s. columnata, f.

colony, s. colonia, f.

colophon, s. colofón, m.

Colorado beetle, s. escarabajo de
la patata, m.

colorimeter, s. colorímetro, m.

colossal, a. colosal, gigantesco;
enorme; (fam.) estupendo

colossus, s. coloso, m.

colour, s. color, m.; colorido, m.;
tinta, f.; materia colorante, f.;
pl. **colours,** insignia, f.; bandera,
f., estandarte, m.; (naut.) pabe-

llón, *m. v.t.* colorar; pintar; iluminar; (influence) influir, afectar. *v.i.* colorarse; ruborizarse; encenderse. **fast c.**, color estable, color sólido, *m.* **regimental colours**, bandera del regimiento, *f.* **with colours flying**, con tambor batiente, a banderas desplegadas. **to be off c.**, estar malucho, estar indispuesto. **to change c.**, (of persons) mudar de color, mudar de semblante. **to give c. to**, (a story, etc.) hacer verosímil. **to lay the colours on too thick**, recargar las tintas. **to pass with flying colours**, salir triunfante. **under c. of**, so color de, a pretexto de. **c.-blind**, daltoniano. **c.-blindness**, daltonismo, *m.*

coloured, *a.* colorado; de color
colouring, *s.* (substance) colorante, *m.*; (act of) coloración, *f.*; (art) colorido, *m.*; (of complexion) colores, *m. pl.*
colourist, *s.* colorista, *m.* and *f.*
colourless, *a.* sin color, incoloro; (fig.) insípido
colt, *s.* potro, *m.*; (boy) muchacho alegre, *m.*
colt's-foot, (bot.) fárfara, *f.*
columbine, *s.* (bot.) aguileña, *f.*; (in pantomime) Colombina, *f.*
column, *s.* columna, *f.* **Fifth c.**, quinta columna, *f.*
columned, *a.* con columnas
columnist, *s.* periodista, *m.*
coma, *s.* coma, *m.*
comatose, *a.* comatoso
comb, *s.* peine, *m.*; (for flax) carda, *f.*; (curry) almohaza, *f.*; (of cock) cresta, carúncula, *f.*; (of a wave) cima, cresta, *f.*; (honey) panal, *m. v.t.* (hair) peinar; (flax) rastrillar, cardar. **high c.**, peineta, *f.* **to c. one's hair**, peinarse
combat, *v.t.* luchar contra, combatir, resistir. *v.i.* combatir, pelear. *s.* combate, *m.*; lucha, batalla, *f.* **in single c.**, cuerpo a cuerpo
combatant, *s.* combatiente, *m. a.* combatiente
combative, *a.* belicoso, pugnaz
combination, *s.* combinación, *f*; mezcla, *f.*; unión, *f.*; asociación, *f.*; *pl.* **combinations**, camisa

pantalón, *f.* **c. lock**, cerradura de combinación, *f.*
combine, *v.t.* combinar; reunir, juntar; (chem.) combinar. *v.i.* combinarse; asociarse (con); (com.) fusionarse. *s.* asociación, *f.*; (com.) monopolio, *m.*
combings, *s. pl.* peinaduras, *f. pl.*
combustible, *a.* combustible. *s.* combustible, *m.*
combustion, *s.* combustión, *f.* **rapid c.**, combustión rápida, *f.* **spontaneous c.**, combustión espontánea, *f.*
come, *v.i.* venir; llegar; avanzar; acercarse; (happen) suceder, acontecer; (result) resultar; (find oneself) encontrarse, hallarse; (become) llegar a ser; (begin to) ponerse (a), empezar (a). **Coming!** ¡Voy! **C., c.!** ¡Vamos!; ¡No es para tanto! ¡Ánimo! **I am ready whatever comes**, Estoy preparado venga lo que venga. **He comes of a good family**, Él es (viene) de buena familia. **I came to know him well**, Llegué a conocerle bien. **I don't know what came over me**, No sé lo que me pasó. **When I came to consider it**, Cuando me puse a considerarlo. **The bill comes to sixty pesetas**, La cuenta sube a sesenta pesetas. **He comes up before the judge to-morrow**, Ha de comparecer ante el juez mañana. **What you say comes to this**, Lo que dice Vd. se reduce a esto. **What is the world coming to?** ¿Adónde va a parar el mundo? **It does not c. within my scope**, No está dentro de mi alcance. **to c. apart**, deshacerse; romperse; dividirse. **to c. home to**, (fig.) impresionar mucho, tocar en lo más íntimo; hacer comprender (a). **to c. into bloom**, empezar a tener flores, florecer. **to c. into one's head**, venir a las mientes. **to c. into the world**, venir al mundo. **to c. near**, acercarse; aproximarse, estar próximo. **to c. next**, venir después; suceder luego. **to c. to an end**, terminar, acabarse. **to c. to blows**, venir a las manos. **to c. to grief**, salir mal

parado; (of schemes, etc.) malograrse. **to c. to hand,** venir a mano; (of letters) llegar a las manos (de). **to c. to life,** despertar; animarse; resucitarse. **to c. to nothing,** frustrarse; no quedar en nada. **to c. to pass,** suceder; realizarse. **to c. to terms,** ponerse de acuerdo. **to c. true,** cumplirse, verificarse. **to c. about,** suceder, acontecer, tener lugar; (of the wind) girar. **to c. across,** dar con, encontrar por casualidad; tropezar con. **to c. after,** (a situation) solicitar; (follow) seguir (a); venir más tarde (que); (succeed) suceder. **to c. again,** volver. **to c. along,** caminar (por); andar (por); (arrive) llegar. **C. along!** ¡Ven! ¡Vamos! ¡Andando! **to c. at,** alcanzar; (attack) embestir, atacar; (gain) obtener, adquirir. **to c. away,** irse, marcharse; (break) deshacerse. **to c. back,** volver. **c.-back,** s. (*fam.*) respuesta, *f.*; contraataque, *m.* **to c. before,** llegar antes; preceder (a). **to c. between,** interponerse (entre), intervenir. **to c. by,** pasar por, pasar junto a; (acquire) obtener, adquirir; (achieve) conseguir. **to c. down,** bajar, descender; (in the world) venir a menos; (be demolished) demolerse; (collapse) derrumbarse, hundirse; (of prices) bajar; (of traditions, etc.) llegar; (fall) caer. **c.-down,** s. caída, *f.*; frustración, *f.*; desengaño, *m.*; desprestigio, *m.*; pérdida de posición, *f.* **to c. down on a person,** cantar la cartilla (a). **to c. forward,** avanzar, adelantarse; (offer) ofrecerse; presentarse. **to c. in,** entrar; (of money) ingresar; (of trains, etc.) llegar; (of the tide) crecer; (of the new year) empezar; (of fashion) ponerse de moda; (be useful) servir (para). **C. in!** ¡Adelante!; ¡Pase Vd.! **to c. into,** (a scheme) asociarse con; (property) heredar; (the mind) presentarse a la imaginación, ocurrirse (a). **to c. off,** (happen) tener lugar; realizarse, efectuarse; (be successful) tener éxito; (break off) separarse (de); romperse. **to c.**

off **well,** tener éxito; (of persons) salir bien. **to c. on,** avanzar; (of actors) salir a la escena; (progress) hacer progresos; (develop) desarrollarse; (of pain, etc.) acometer (a); (arrive) llegar; (of a lawsuit) verse. **C. on!** ¡Vamos! ¡En marcha! **to c. out,** salir; (of stars) nacer; (of buds, etc.) brotar; (of the moon, etc.) asomarse; (of stains) borrarse, salir; (of a book) ver la luz, publicarse; (of secrets) divulgarse, saberse; (of a girl, in society) ponerse de largo; (on strike) declararse en huelga; (of fashions, etc.) aparecer. **to c. out with,** (a remark) soltar; (oaths, etc.) prorrumpir (en); (disclose) revelar, hacer público. **to c. round,** (to see someone) venir a ver (a); (coax) engatusar; (after a faint, etc.) volver en sí; (after illness) reponerse; (to another's point of view) aceptar, compartir. **to c. through,** pasar por; (trials, etc.) subir; salir de; (of liquids) salirse. **to c. to,** volver en sí. **to c. together,** reunirse, juntarse; venir juntos; unirse. **to c. under,** venir (or estar) bajo la jurisdicción de; (the influence of) estar dominado por; (figure among) figurar entre, estar comprendido en. **to c. up,** subir; (of sun, moon) salir; (of plants) brotar; (of problems, etc.) surgir; (in conversation) discutirse; (before a court) comparecer. **to c. up to,** (equal) igualar, ser igual (a); rivalizar con; (in height) llegar hasta. **He came up to them in the street,** Les abordó (or se les acercó) en la calle. **We have c. up against many difficulties,** Hemos tropezado con much as dificultades. **This novel does not c. up to his last,** Esta última novela no es tan buena como la anterior. **The party did not c. up to their expectations,** La reunión no fué tan divertida como esperaban. **to c. up with,** (a person) alcanzar (a). **to c. upon,** encontrar, hallar; tropezar con; encontrar por casualidad. **to c. upon evil days,** venir a menos

comedian, s. actor cómico, comediante, m.

comedy, s. comedia, f. **c. of manners,** comedia de costumbres, f.

comeliness, s. hermosura, f.

comely, a. hermoso

comer, s. el, m. (f. la) que viene. **all comers,** todo el mundo. **first c.,** primer (-ra) venido (-da)

comet, s. cometa, m.

comfort, v.t. consolar, confortar; (encourage) animar; (reassure) alegrar. s. consuelo, m.; satisfacción, f.; comodidad, f.; bienestar, m. **He lives in great c.,** Vive con mucha comodidad. **c.-loving,** comodón

comfortable, a. cómodo; (with income) suficiente; (consoling) consolador. **to make oneself c.,** ponerse cómodo

comfortably, adv. cómodamente; suficientemente; fácilmente; con facilidad; (well) bien. **He is c. off,** Está bien de dinero

comforter, s. consolador (-ra); (baby's) chupador, m.; (scarf) bufanda, f.

comforting, a. consolador

comfortless, a. incómodo, sin comodidad; desconsolador; (of persons) inconsolable, desconsolado

comic, a. cómico; bufo; satírico. s. cómico, m.; pl. **comics,** (printed) historietas cómicas, f. pl. **c. opera,** ópera cómica, f. **c. paper,** periódico satírico, m.

comical, a. cómico; divertido, gracioso

coming, a. (with year, etc.) próximo, que viene; (promising) de porvenir; (approaching) que se acerca. s. venida, f.; llegada, f.; advenimiento, m. **c.-out party,** puesta de largo, f. **comings and goings,** entradas y salidas, f. pl.

comma, s. coma, f. **inverted commas,** comillas, f. pl.

command, v.t. mandar, ordenar; (silence, respect, etc.) imponer; (an army, fleet, etc.) comandar; capitanear; (one's emotions) dominar; (have at one's disposal) disponer de; (a military position, view) dominar; (sympathy, etc.) despertar, merecer; (of price) venderse por. v.i. mandar.

s. orden, f.; (mil., nav.) mando, m.; (of an army, etc.) comandancia, f.; (of one's emotions, etc.) dominio, m.; (of a military position, etc.) dominación, f.; disposición, f. **By Royal C., Por Real Orden;** (of shops, etc.) Proveedor de la Real Casa. **The house commands lovely views of the mountains,** La casa tiene hermosas vistas de las montañas. **word of c.,** orden, f. **Yours to c.,** A la disposición de Vd.

commandant, s. comandante, m.

commandeer, v.t. (conscript) reclutar; (mil.) requisar; expropiar

commander, s. (mil.) comandante, m.; (nav.) capitán de fragata, m.; (of order of Knighthood) comendador, m. **c.-in-chief,** generalísimo, m. **C. of the Faithful,** Comendador de los creyentes, m.

commanding, a. (mil.) comandante; imponente; (of manner) imperioso; dominante. **c. officer,** comandante en jefe, m.

commandment, s. precepto, mandamiento, m. **the Ten Commandments,** los diez mandamientos

commando, s. (mil.) comando, m.

commemorate, v.t. conmemorar

commemoration, s. conmemoración, f.

commemorative, a. conmemorativo

commence, v.t. comenzar, empezar, principiar. v.i. comenzar. **He commenced to eat,** Empezó a comer

commencement, s. principio, comienzo, m.

commend, v.t. (entrust) encomendar; recomendar; alabar

commendable, a. loable; recomendable

commendation, s. aprobación, alabanza, f., aplauso, m.

commendatory, a. (of letters) comendatorio

commensurable, a. conmensurable

commensurate, a. proporcionado (a); conforme (a)

comment, s. observación, f.; (on a work) comento, m.; explicación, nota, f. v.i. hacer una

observación (sobre); (a work)
comentar, anotar. **to c. unfavourably on,** criticar

commentary, s. comentario, m.;
(on a person, etc.) comentos,
m. pl., observaciones, f. pl.

commentator, s. comentador
(-ra); (of a work) comentarista,
m. and f.

commerce, s. comercio, m.;
negocios, m. pl.; (social) trato, m.

commercial, a. comercial; mercantil. **c. traveller,** viajante,
m. and f.

commercialism, s. mercantilismo, m.

commercialize, v.t. hacer objeto
de comercio

commercially, adv. comercial-
mente

commingle, v.t. mezclar. v.i.
mezclarse

commiserate, v.i. compadecerse
(de), apiadarse (de)

commiseration, s. conmiseración, compasión, f.

commissariat, s. comisaría, f.;
(fam.) despensa, f.

commissary, s. comisario, m.

commission, s. comisión, f.;
(mil.) graduación de oficial, f.
v.t. comisionar; (a ship) poner
en servicio activo, armar; (appoint), nombrar. **in c.,** en
servicio, activo. **out of c.,** (of
ships) inutilizado; inservible. **c.
agent,** comisionista, m. and f. **to
gain one's c.,** (mil.) graduarse
de oficial. **to put out of c.,**
retirar del servicio; poner fuera
de combate; estropear

commissionaire, s. portero, m.

commissioned, a. comisionado.
c. officer, oficial, m.

commissioner, s. comisario, m.
High C., alto comisario, m.
c. of police, jefe de policía, m.

commit, v.t. entregar (a); (a
crime) cometer; (to prison) encarcelar; (for trial) remitir. **to
c. oneself,** comprometerse. **to
c. to memory,** aprender de
memoria. **to c. to writing,**
poner por escrito

commitment, s. (financial, etc.)
obligación, responsabilidad, f.;
compromiso, m.

committal, s. (of an offence)
comisión, f.; (placing, entrusting)

entrega, f.; (to prison) encarcela-
miento, m.; (legal procedure)
auto de prisión, m.

committee, s. comité, m.; comisión, junta, f.; consejo, m. **They
decided in c.,** Tomaron la
resolución en comité. **c. of
management,** consejo de administración, m.

commodious, a. espacioso,
grande

commodiousness, s. espaciosidad, f.

commodity, s. artículo, m., mercancía, f.

commodore, s. (nav.) jefe de
escuadra, m.; comodoro, m.

common, a. común; general,
corriente; universal; vulgar; (disparaging) cursi; (elementary)
elemental. s. pastos comunes,
m. pl. **He is not a c. man,** No es
un hombre cualquiera; No es un
hombre vulgar. **in c.,** en común.
the c. man, el hombre medio.
the c. people, el pueblo. **c.
sense,** sentido común, m. **c.
soldier,** soldado raso, m. **c.
speech,** lenguaje vulgar, m. **c.
usage,** uso corriente, m.

commoner, s. plebeyo (-ya)

commonly, adv. comúnmente,
por lo general

commonness, s. frecuencia, f.;
vulgaridad, f.

commonplace, s. lugar común,
m.; trivialidad, f. a. trivial

commons, s. el pueblo; (House
of) Cámara de los Comunes, f.;
(food) provisiones, f. pl. **to be
on short c.,** comer mal, estar
mal alimentado

Commonwealth, s. estado, m.;
república, f.; comunidad (de
naciones), f.; mancomunidad, f.

commotion, s. confusión, f.;
conmoción, perturbación, f.; tumulto, m.

communal, a. comunal

commune, s. comuna, f.; comunión, f. v.i. conversar (con).
to c. with oneself, hablar consigo

communicable, a. comunicable

communicant, s. (ecc.) comul-
gante, m. and f.; (of information)
informante, m. and f.

communicate, v.t. comunicar;
(diseases) transmitir. v.i. comunicarse (con); (ecc.) comulgar

communication, *s.* comunicación, *f.* **lines of c.,** comunicaciones, *f. pl.* **to get into c. with,** ponerse en comunicación con. **c.-cord,** (in a railway carriage) timbre de alarma, *m.*

communicative, *a.* comunicativo; expansivo

communicativeness, *s.* carácter expansivo, *m.*; locuacidad, *f.*

communion, *s.* comunión, *f.* **Holy C.,** Comunión, *f.* **to take C.,** comulgar. **C. card,** cédula de Comunión, *f.* **C. cup,** cáliz, *f.* **C. table,** sagrada mesa, *f.*; altar, *m.*

communiqué, *s.* comunicación, parte, *f.* **to issue a c.,** dar parte

communism, *s.* comunismo, *m.*

communist, *s.* comunista, *m.* and *f.* *a.* comunista

community, *s.* comunidad, *f.* **the c.,** la nación; el público. **c. centre,** centro social, *m.*

commutation, *s.* conmutación, *f.*; reducción, *f.*

commutator, *s.* (*elec.*) conmutador, *m.*

commute, *v.t.* conmutar; reducir

compact, *s.* (pact) acuerdo, pacto, *m.*; (powder) polvorera, *f.* *a.* compacto; firme; sólido; apretado, cerrado; (of persons) bien hecho; (of style) conciso, sucinto

compactness, *s.* compacidad, *f.*; (of style) concisión, *f.*

companion, *s.* compañero (-ra); camarada, *m.* and *f.*; (of an Order) caballero, *m.* (or dama, *f.*). *v.t.* acompañar. **lady c.,** señora de compañía, *f.* **c.-hatch,** cubierta de escotilla, *f.* **c.-ladder,** escala de toldilla, *f.*

companionable, *a.* sociable, amistoso

companionably, *adv.* sociablemente, amistosamente

companionship, *s.* compañía, *f.*; compañerismo, *m.*

company, *s.* (*com.*, *mil.*, etc.) compañía, *f.*; (ship's) tripulación, *f.* **I shall keep you c.,** Te haré compañía. **to part c. with,** separarse de. **Present c. excepted!** ¡Mejorando lo presente! **They are not very good c.,** No son muy divertidos

comparable, *a.* comparable

comparably, *adv.* comparablemente

comparative, *a.* comparativo; relativo

comparatively, *adv.* comparativamente; relativamente

compare, *v.t.* comparar. *v.i.* compararse; poder compararse. ser comparable. **beyond c.,** sin comparación; sin igual. **to c. favourably with,** no perder por comparación con. **to c. notes,** cambiar impresiones

comparison, *s.* comparación, *f.* **in c. with,** comparado con

compartment, *s.* compartimiento, *m.*; (*r.w.*) departamento, *m.*

compass, *s.* circuito, *m.*; límites, *m. pl.*; alcance, *m.*; (of a voice) gama, *f.*; (*naut.*) brújula, *f.*; *pl.* **compasses,** compás, *m.* *v.t.* (achieve) conseguir; (plan) idear. **mariner's c.,** compás de mar, *m.*, rosa de los vientos, *f.* **pocket c.,** brújula de bolsillo, *f.* **to c. about,** cercar, rodear

compassion, *s.* compasión, *f.* **to have c. on,** apiadarse de, compadecerse de

compassionate, *a.* compasivo, piadoso. **c. leave,** permiso, *m.*

compassionately, *adv.* compasivamente, con piedad

compatibility, *s.* compatibilidad, *f.*

compatible, *a.* compatible, conciliable

compatriot, *s.* compatriota, *m.* and *f.*

compel, *v.t.* obligar (a), forzar (a); exigir; imponer. **His attitude compels respect,** Su actitud impone el respeto

compelling, *a.* compulsivo

compendious, *a.* compendioso, sucinto

compendium, *s.* compendio, *m.*; resumen, *m.*

compensate, *v.t.* compensar; (reward) recompensar; (for loss, etc.) indemnizar. **to c. for,** compensar; indemnizar contra

compensation, *s.* compensación, *f.*; (reward) recompensa, *f.*; (for loss, etc.) indemnización, *f.*

compensatory, *a.* compensatorio

compete, *v.i.* competir (con); rivalizar; ser rivales; (in a competition) concurrir

competence, *s.* aptitud, *f.*; capacidad, *f.*; competencia, *f.*

competent, *a.* competente; capaz

competently, *adv.* competentemente

competition, *s.* competencia, competición, rivalidad, *f.*; emulación, *f.*; (contest, etc.) concurso, *m.* **spirit of c.,** espíritu de competencia, *m.*

competitive, *a.* competidor; de competición. **c. examination,** oposición, *f.*

competitor, *s.* competidor (-ra)

compilation, *s.* compilación, *f.*

compile, *v.t.* compilar

compiler, *s.* compilador (-ra)

complacence, *s.* complacencia, satisfacción, *f.*; contento de sí mismo, *m.*

complacent, *a.* satisfecho; pagado de sí mismo

complacently, *adv.* con satisfacción

complain, *v.i.* quejarse; lamentarse; (*law*) querellarse. **She complains about everything,** Ella se queja de todo

complainant, *s.* (*law*) demandante, *m.* and *f.*

complaint, *s.* queja, *f.*; lamento, *m.*; (*law*) demanda, *f.*; (illness) enfermedad, *f.* **to lodge a c. (against),** quejarse (de)

complaisance, *s.* afabilidad, cortesía, *f.*

complaisant, *a.* complaciente, cortés, afable; (of husbands) consentido, sufrido

complement, *s.* complemento, *m.*; total, número completo, *m.* *v.t.* completar

complementary, *a.* complementario

complete, *a.* entero; completo; perfecto; acabado. *v.t.* completar; acabar; (happiness, etc.) coronar, poner el último toque (a); (years) cumplir; (forms) llenar

completely, *adv.* completamente, enteramente

completeness, *s.* entereza, *f.*; totalidad, *f.*

completion, *s.* terminación, *f.*, fin, *m.*

complex, *a.* complejo. *s.* complejo, *m.* **inferiority c.,** complejo de inferioridad, *m.*

complexion, *s.* tez, *f.*, cutis, *m.*; (*fig.*) carácter, *m.*

complexity, *s.* complejidad, *f.*

compliance, *s.* condescendencia, *f.*; (subservience) sumisión, *f.*; obediencia, *f.* **in c. with,** de acuerdo con, en conformidad con

compliant, *a.* condescendiente; sumiso, dócil; obediente

complicate, *v.t.* complicar

complicated, *a.* complejo; complicado; enredado

complication, *s.* complicación, *f.*

complicity, *s.* complicidad, *f.* **c. in a crime,** complicidad en un crimen

compliment, *s.* cumplido, *m.*, cortesía, *f.*; requiebro, (*fam.*) piropo, *m.*; favor, *m.*; honor, *m.*; (greeting) saludo, *m.*; (congratulation) felicitación, *f.* *v.t.* cumplimentar; requebrar; (flatter) adular, lisonjear; (congratulate) felicitar. **They did him the c. of reading his book,** Le hicieron el honor de leer su libro. **to pay compliments,** hacer cumplidos; (*fam.*) echar piropos

complimentary, *a.* lisonjero; galante. **c. ticket,** billete gratuito, *m.*

comply, *v.i.* (with) cumplir, obedecer; conformarse (con); consentir

component, *a.* componente. *s.* componente, *m.*

comport, *v.t.* (oneself), comportarse

comportment, *s.* comportamiento, *m.*, conducta, *f.*

compose, *v.t.* (all meanings) componer. **to c. oneself,** serenarse, calmarse. **to c. one's features,** componer el semblante

composed, *a.* sereno, tranquilo, sosegado

composer, *s.* compositor (-ra)

composite, *a.* compuesto; mixto. *s.* compuesto, *m.*; (*bot.*) planta compuesta, *f.*

composition, *s.* (all meanings) composición, *f.*

compositor, *s.* (*print.*) cajista, *m.* and *f.*

composure, *s.* tranquilidad, serenidad, calma, *f.*; sangre fría, *f.*, aplomo, *m.*

compôte, *s.* compota, *f.*

compound, *v.t.* mezclar, componer; concertar. *a.* compuesto. *s.* compuesto, *m.*; mixtura, *f.* **c. interest,** interés compuesto, *m.*

comprehend, *v.t.* comprender

comprehensible, *a.* comprensible

comprehensibly, *adv.* comprensiblemente

comprehension, *s.* comprensión, *f.*

comprehensive, *a.* comprensivo

comprehensiveness, *s.* alcance, *m.*, extensión, *f.*

compress, *v.t.* comprimir; condensar; reducir, abreviar. *s.* compresa, *f.*

compression, *s.* compresión, *f.*

compressor, *s.* compresor, *m.*

comprise, *v.t.* comprender, abarcar, incluir

compromise, *s.* arreglo, *m.*; componenda, *f.* *v.t.* (settle) componer, arreglar; (jeopardize) arriesgar; comprometer. *v.i.* transigir. **to c. oneself,** comprometerse

compromising, *a.* comprometedor

comptometer, *s.* calculador, *m.*

compulsion, *s.* compulsión, fuerza, *f.* **under c.,** a la fuerza

compulsory, *a.* obligatorio. **c. measures,** medidas obligatorias, *f. pl.* **c. powers,** poderes absolutos, *m. pl.*

compunction, *s.* compunción, *f.*, remordimiento, *m.*; escrúpulo, *m.* **without c.,** sin escrúpulo

computable, *a.* calculable

computation, *s.* computación, *f.*, cómputo, *m.*

compute, *v.t.* computar, calcular.

comrade, *s.* camarada, *m.* and *f.*, compañero (-ra)

comradeship, *s.* compañerismo, *m.*

con, *v.t.* estudiar; leer con atención; (*naut.*) gobernar (el buque)

concatenation, *s.* concatenación, *f.*

concave, *a.* cóncavo

concavity, *s.* concavidad, *f.*

conceal, *v.t.* esconder, ocultar; (the truth, etc.) encubrir, callar; disimular

concealed, *a.* oculto; escondido; disimulado. **c. lighting,** iluminación indirecta, *f.* **c. turning,** (on a road) viraje oculto, *m.*

concealment, *s.* ocultación, *f.*; encubrimiento, *m.*; (place of) escondite, *m.*; secreto, *m.*

concede, *v.t.* conceder

conceit, *s.* presunción, vanidad, fatuidad, *f.*, envanecimiento, *m.* **to have a good c. of oneself,** estar pagado de sí mismo

conceited, *a.* presumido, fatuo, vanidoso

conceivable, *a.* concebible, imaginable

conceivably, *adv.* posiblemente

conceive, *v.t.* concebir; (affection, etc.) tomar; (an idea, etc.) formar; (plan) formular, idear. *v.i.* concebir; (understand) comprender; (suppose) imaginar, suponer

concentrate, *v.t.* concentrar. *v.i.* concentrarse; (on, upon) dedicarse (a), entregarse (a); prestar atención (a), concentrar atención (en)

concentrated, *a.* concentrado

concentration, *s.* concentración, *f.* **c. camp,** campo de concentración, *m.*

concentric, *a.* concéntrico

concept, *s.* concepto, *m.*

conception, *s.* concepción, *f.*; conocimiento, *m.*; idea, *f.*, concepto, *m.* **to have not the remotest c. of,** no tener la menor idea de

conceptualism, *s.* conceptualismo, *m.*

concern, *v.t.* tocar, tener que ver con, importar, concernir; interesar; referirse (a); tratar (de); (trouble) preocupar, inquietar; (take part in) ocuparse (de or con). *s.* asunto, *m.*, cosa, *f.*; (share) interés, *m.*; (anxiety) inquietud, *f.*; solicitud, *f.*; (business) casa comercial, firma, *f.* **as concerns...,** en cuanto a..., respecto a... **It concerns the date of the next meeting,** Es cuestión de la fecha de la próxima reunión. **It is no c. of**

yours, No tiene nada que ver contigo. **The book is concerned with the adventures of two boys,** El libro trata de las aventuras de dos muchachos

concerned, *a.* ocupado (en); afectado: (in a crime) implicado (en); (troubled) preocupado; inquieto, agitado

concerning, *prep.* tocante a, con respecto a, referente a, sobre

concert, *s.* acuerdo, **concierto**, *m.*, armonía, *f.*; (*mus.*) **concierto**, *m.* *v.t.* concertar, acordar, **in c. with,** de acuerdo con. **c.-hall,** sala de conciertos, *f.*

concerted, *a.* concertado

concertina, *s.* concertina, *f.*

concerto, *s.* concierto, *m.*

concession, *s.* concesión, *f.*; privilegio, *m.*

concessionaire, *s.* concesionario, *m.*

concettism, *s.* (*lit.*) conceptismo, *m.*

concierge, *s.* conserje, *m.*

conciergerie, *s.* conserjería, *f.*

conciliate, *v.t.* conciliar

conciliation, *s.* conciliación, *f.*

conciliatory, *a.* conciliador

concise, *a.* conciso, breve, sucinto

concisely, *adv.* concisamente

concision, *s.* concisión, *f.*

conclave, *s.* conciliábulo, *m.*; (of cardinals) conclave, *m.*

conclude, *v.t.* concluir. *v.i.* concluirse

conclusion, *s.* conclusión, *f.* **in c.,** en conclusión, para terminar. **to come to the c. that . . .,** concluir que . . .

conclusive, *a.* conclusivo, concluyente, decisivo

conclusively, *adv.* concluyentemente

conclusiveness, *s.* carácter decisivo, *m.*, lo concluyente

concoct, *v.t.* confeccionar; inventar

concoction, *s.* confección, *f.*; mezcla, *f.*; invención, *f.*; (of a plot) maquinación, *f.*

concomitant, *a.* concomitante. *s.* concomitante, *m.*

concord, *s.* concordia, buena inteligencia, armonía, *f.*; (*mus., gram.*) concordancia, *f.*; (of sounds) armonía, *f.*

concordance, *s.* concordia, ar-

monía, *f.*; (book) concordancias, *f. pl.*

concordat, *s.* concordato, *m.*

concourse, *s.* concurrencia, muchedumbre, *f.*

concrete, *a.* concreto; de hormigón. *s.* hormigón, *m.* *v.t.* concretar; cubrir de hormigón. **reinforced c.,** hormigón armado, *m.*

concretion, *s.* concreción, *f.*

concubinage, *s.* concubinato, *m.*

concubine, *s.* concubina, manceba, *f.*

concupiscence, *s.* concupiscencia, *f.*

concupiscent, *a.* concupiscente

concur, *v.i.* coincidir, concurrir; estar de acuerdo, convenir (en)

concurrence, *s.* (agreement) acuerdo, consentimiento, *m.*, aprobación, *f.*

concurrent, *a.* concurrente; unánime; coincidente

concurrently, *adv.* concurrentemente

concussion, *s.* concusión, *f.*; (*med.*) concusión cerebral, *f.*

condemn, *v.t.* condenar; censurar, culpar; (forfeit) confiscar. **condemned cell,** celda de los condenados a muerte, *f.*

condemnation, *s.* condenación, *f.*; censura, *f.*

condensation, *s.* condensación, *f.*

condense, *v.t.* condensar. *v.i.* condensarse

condenser, *s.* (*elec., mech., chem.*) condensador, *m.*

condescend, *v.i.* dignarse; (in a bad sense) consentir (en); (with affability) condescender

condescending, *a.* condescendiente

condescendingly, *adv.* con condescendencia

condescension, *s.* condescendencia, *f.*; afabilidad, *f.*

condign, *a.* condigno

condiment, *s.* condimento, *m.*

condition, *s.* condición, *f.*; estado, *m.*; *pl.* **conditions,** condiciones, *f. pl.*; circunstancias, *f. pl.* **on c. that,** con tal que; siempre que, dado que. **to be in no c. to,** no estar en condiciones de. **to change one's c.,** cambiar de estado. **to keep oneself in c.,** mantenerse en buena forma

conditional, *a.* condicional. **to be c. on,** depender de

conditionally, *adv.* condicionalmente

conditioned, *a.* acondicionado. **c. reflex,** reflejo acondicionado, *m.*

condole, *v.i.* condolerse (de); (on a bereavement) dar el pésame

condolence, *s.* condolencia, *f.* **to present one's condolences,** dar el pésame

condonation, *s.* condonación, *f.*

condone, *v.t.* condonar, perdonar

conduce, *v.i.* contribuir, conducir

conducive, *a.* que contribuye, conducente; favorable

conduct, *s.* conducta, *f.* *v.t.* conducir; guiar; (*mus.*) dirigir; (oneself) portarse, conducirse; (*phys.*) conducir. *v.i.* (*mus.*) dirigir (una orquesta, etc.); (*phys.*) ser conductor. **conducted tour,** excursión acompañada, *f.*; viaje acompañado, *m.*

conduction, *s.* conducción, *f.*

conductive, *a.* conductivo

conductivity, *s.* conductibilidad, *f.*

conductor, *s.* (guide) guía, *m.* and *f.*; (of an orchestra) director, *m.*; (on a tram, etc.) cobrador, *m.*; (*phys.*) conductor, *m.*

conduit, *s.* conducto, *m.*; cañería, *f.*; canal, *m.*

condyle, *s.* (*anat.*) cóndilo, *m.*

cone, *s.* (*bot.,* *geom.,* etc.) cono, *m.*

confabulation, *s.* confabulación, *f.*

confection, *s.* confección, *f.* *v.t.* confeccionar

confectioner, *s.* confitero (-ra); pastelero (-ra)

confectionery, *s.* confitería, pastelería, repostería, *f.*

confederate, *a.* confederado; aliado. *s.* confederado, *m.*; (in crime) cómplice, *m.* and *f.* *v.t.* confederar. *v.i.* confederarse; aliarse

confederation, *s.* confederación, *f.*

confer, *v.t.* conceder, conferir; (an honour, etc.) otorgar, investir (con). *v.i.* consultar (con); deliberar, considerar

conference, *s.* conferencia, consulta, *f.*; conversación, *f.*

conferment, *s.* otorgamiento, *m.*; concesión, *f.*

confess, *v.t.* confesar, reconocer; (*fam.*) admitir; (of a priest) confesar; (of a penitent) confesarse. *v.i.* hacer una confesión; (one's sins) confesarse. **I c. that I was surprised,** No puedo negar que me sorprendió

confessed, *a.* confesado, declarado

confession, *s.* confesión, *f.*; reconocimiento, *m.*; declaración, *f.*; religión, *f.*; (creed) credo, *m.* **to go to c.,** confesarse. **to hear a c.,** confesar (a)

confessional, *s.* confesionario, *m.*

confessor, *s.* confesor, *m.*

confetti, *s. pl.* confeti, *m.*

confidant, *s.* confidente, *m.*

confidante, *s.* confidenta, *f.*

confide, *v.i.* confiar (a or en). *v.t.* confiar

confidence, *s.* confianza, *f.*; seguridad, *f.*; (revelation) confidencia, *f.* **in c.,** en confianza. **over-c.,** presunción, *f.* **to have c. in,** tener confianza en. **c. man,** caballero de industria, estafador, *m.* **c. trick,** timo, *m.*

confident, *a.* confiado; seguro; (conceited) presumido

confidential, *a.* confidencial; de confianza. **c. clerk,** empleado (-da) de confianza. **c. letter,** carta confidencial, *f.*

confidentially, *adv.* en confianza, confidencialmente

confidently, *adv.* confiadamente

confiding, *a.* confiado

confidingly, *adv.* con confianza

configuration, *s.* configuración, *f.*

confine, *v.t.* limitar; (imprison) encerrar. **confined space,** espacio limitado, *m.* **to be confined,** (of a woman) estar de parto, parir. **to be confined to one's room,** no poder dejar su cuarto. **to c. oneself to,** limitarse a

confinement, *s.* encierro, *m.*, prisión, *f.*; reclusión, *f.*; (of a woman) parto, *m.* **to suffer solitary c.,** estar incomunicado

confines, *s. pl.* límites, *m. pl.*; confines, *m. pl.*; fronteras, *f. pl.*

confirm, *v.t.* confirmar; corroborar; *(ecc.)* confirmar

confirmation, *s.* confirmación, *f.*; (of a treaty) **ratificación,** *f.*; *(ecc.)* confirmación, *f.*

confirmatory, *a.* confirmatorio

confirmed, *a.* inveterado

confiscate, *v.t.* confiscar

confiscation, *s.* confiscación, *f.*

conflagration, *s.* conflagración, *f.*, incendio, *m.*

conflict, *s.* conflicto, *m.*; lucha, *f.* *v.i.* estar opuesto (a), estar en contradicción (con)

conflicting, *a.* opuesto; incompatible; (of evidence) contradictorio

confluence, *s.* confluencia, *f.*

conform, *v.t.* ajustar, conformar. *v.i.* ajustarse (a), amoldarse (a); conformarse (a); adaptarse (a)

conformation, *s.* conformación, *f.*

conformity, *s.* conformidad, *f.* in c. with, en conformidad con, con arreglo a

confound, *v.t.* confundir. C. it! ¡Demonio!

confounded, *a.* perplejo; *(fam.)* maldito

confraternity, *s.* cofradía, hermandad, *f.*

confront, *v.t.* hacer frente (a), afrontar; salir al paso; confrontar

Confucianism, *s.* confucianismo, *m.*

confuse, *v.t.* turbar, aturdir; confundir (con); (the issue) obscurecer; (disconcert) desconcertar, dejar confuso (a); dejar perplejo (a). You have confused one thing with another, Has confundido una cosa con otra. My mind was confused, Mis ideas eran confusas; Tenía la cabeza trastornada

confused, *a.* confuso

confusing, *a.* turbador; desconcertante. It is all very c., Todo ello es muy difícil de comprender

confusion, *s.* confusión, *f.* covered with c., confuso, avergonzado. to be in c., estar confuso; estar en desorden

confute, *v.t.* (a person) confundir; (by evidence) refutar, confutar

congeal, *v.t.* congelar; (blood) coagular. *v.i.* congelarse, helarse; coagularse

congealment, *s.* congelación, *f.*; (of blood) coagulación, *f.*

congenial, *a.* (of persons) simpático; propicio, favorable; agradable

congenially, *adv.* agradablemente

congenital, *a.* congénito

conger, *s.* *(icht.)* congrio, *m.*

congest, *v.t.* atestar; amontonar; *(med.)* congestionar

congested, *a.* *(med.)* congestionado; (of places) atestado de gente; de mayor población; concurrido. c. area, área de mayor densidad de población, *f.*

congestion, *s.* *(med.)* congestión, *f.*; densidad del tráfico, *f.*; mayor densidad de población, *f.*

conglomerate, *a.* conglomerado. *s.* conglomerado, *m.*

conglomeration, *s.* conglomeración, *f.*

congratulate, *v.t.* felicitar, dar la enhorabuena (a); congratular

congratulation, *s.* felicitación, enhorabuena, *f.*; congratulación, *f.*

congratulatory, *a.* de felicitación, congratulatorio

congregate, *v.i.* congregarse, reunirse, juntarse

congregation, *s.* congregación, *f.*; asamblea, reunión, *f.*; (in a church) fieles, *m. pl.*; (parishioners) feligreses, *m. pl.*

congress, *s.* congreso, *m.* C.-man, miembro del Congreso, *m.*

conical, *a.* cónico

conifer, *s.* conífera, *f.*

coniferous, *a.* conífero

conjectural, *a.* conjetural

conjecturally, *adv.* conjeturalmente, por conjeturas

conjecture, *s.* conjetura, *f.* *v.t.* conjeturar

conjoint, *a.* asociado, conjunto

conjointly, *adv.* juntamente, en común

conjugal, *a.* conyugal

conjugate, *v.t.* conjugar. *v.i.* conjugarse

conjugation, *s.* conjugación, *f.*

conjunction, *s.* conjunción, *f.* in c. with, de acuerdo con

conjunctive, *a.* conjuntivo. *s.* conjunción, *f.*

conjunctivitis, *s.* conjuntivitis, *f.*

conjuncture, *s.* coyuntura, ocasión, *f.*

conjure, *v.t.* (implore) rogar, suplicar. *v.i.* (juggle) hacer juegos de manos. **a name to c. with,** un nombre todopoderoso. **to c. up,** (spirits) conjurar; (*fig.*) evocar

conjurer, conjuror, *s.* (magician) nigromante, *m.*; prestidigitador, *m.* **conjuror's wand,** varilla de virtudes, *f.*

conjuring, *s.* prestidigitación, *f.*, juegos de manos, *m. pl.* **c. trick,** juego de manos, *m.* **c. up,** evocación, *f.*

connect, *v.t.* juntar, unir; (relate) relacionar; asociar; (*elec.* and *mech.*) conectar. *v.i.* juntarse, unirse; relacionarse; asociarse; (of events) encadenarse; (of trains) enlazar. **This train connects with the Madrid express,** Este tren enlaza con el expreso de Madrid. **They are connected with the Borgia family,** Están emparentados con los Borgia, Son parientes de los Borgia

connected, *a.* conexo; (coherent) coherente; relacionado; asociado; (in a crime) implicado; (by marriage, etc.) emparentado

connectedly, *adv.* coherentemente

connecting, *a.* que une; (*mech.* and *elec.*) conectivo; (of doors, etc.) comunicante. **c.-link,** (*mech.*) varilla de conexión, *f.*; (*fig.*) lazo, *m.* **c.-rod,** biela, *f.*

connection, connexion, *s.* conexión, *f.*; unión, *f.*; (of ideas) relación, *f.*; (junction) empalme, *m.*; (of trains, boats) enlace, *m.*; (intimacy) intimidad, *f.*; (relative) pariente, *m.*; (of a firm, etc.) clientela, *f.*; (*elec.*) conexión, *f.* **in c. with,** con referencia a; en asociación con. **in this c.,** respecto a esto

conning-tower, *s.* torre de mando, *f.*

connivance, *s.* consentimiento, *m.*; complicidad, *f.*

connive (at), *v.i.* hacer la vista gorda, ser cómplice (en)

connotation, *s.* connotación, *f.*

connote, *v.t.* connotar

connubial, *a.* conyugal

conoid, *a.* conoideo. *s.* conoide, *m.*

conquer, *v.t.* conquistar; vencer. *v.i.* triunfar

conquering, *a.* conquistador, vencedor; triunfante, victorioso

conqueror, *s.* conquistador, *m.*; vencedor, *m.*

conquest, *s.* conquista, *f.* **to make a c. of,** conquistar

consanguineous, *a.* consanguíneo

consanguinity, *s.* consanguinidad, *f.*

conscience, *s.* conciencia, *f.* **in all c.,** en verdad. **with a clear c.,** con la conciencia limpia. **c.-stricken,** lleno de remordimientos

conscienceless, *a.* desalmado, falto de conciencia

conscientious, *a.* concienzudo; diligente. **c. objector,** pacifista, *m.* and *f.*; el, *m.* (*f.* la) que protesta contra

conscientiously, *adv.* concienzudamente

conscientiousness, *s.* conciencia, diligencia, *f.*; rectitud, *f.*

conscious, *a.* consciente. *s.* (*psy.*) consciente, *m.* **to become c.,** (after unconsciousness) volver en sí. **to become c. of,** darse cuenta de

consciously, *adv.* conscientemente, a sabiendas

consciousness, *s.* conciencia, *f.*; conocimiento, sentido, *m.* **to lose c.,** perder el conocimiento, perder el sentido. **to recover c.,** recobrar el sentido, volver en sí

conscript, *s.* conscripto, *m.* *a.* conscripto. *v.t.* reclutar

conscription, *s.* conscripción, *f.*

consecrate, *v.t.* consagrar; bendecir

consecration, *s.* consagración, *f.*; dedicación, *f.*

consecutive, *a.* consecutivo

consecutively, *adv.* consecutivamente

consensus, *s.* consenso, *m.*, unanimidad, *f.* **c. of opinion,** opinión general, *f.*

consent, *v.i.* consentir. *s.* consentimiento, *m.*; permiso, *m.*, aquiescencia, *f.* **by common c.,** de común acuerdo

consequence, *s.* consecuencia, *f.*; resultado, *m.*; importancia, *f.*

in c., por consiguiente. **in c. of,** de resultas de. **of no c.,** sin importancia

consequent, *a.* consecuente, consiguiente

consequential, *a.* consecuente; (of persons) fatuo, engreído

consequently, *adv.* por consiguiente, en consecuencia

conservation, *s.* conservación, *f.* **c. of energy,** conservación de energía, *f.*

conservatism, *s.* conservadurismo, *m.*

conservative, *a.* preservativo; conservador. *s.* conservador (-ra). **C. party,** partido conservador, *m.*

conservatoire, *s.* conservatorio de música, *m.*

conservatory, *s.* invernáculo, invernadero, *m.*

conserve, *v.t.* conservar

consider, *v.t.* considerar, pensar meditar; tomar en cuenta; examinar; (deem) juzgar; (believe) creer, estar convencido de (que); (of persons) considerar. **All things considered,** Considerando todos los puntos, Después de considerarlo todo

considerable, *a.* considerable

considerably, *adv.* considerablemente

considerate, *a.* considerado, solícito

considerately, *adv.* con consideración, solícitamente

consideration, *s.* consideración, *f.*; reflexión, deliberación, *f.*; remuneración, *f.* **out of c, for,** en consideración de; por consideración a. **to take into c.,** tomar en cuenta, tomar en consideración

considered, *a.* considerado

considering, *prep.* en consideración de, considerando, en vista de

consign, *v.t.* consignar; (*fig.*) enviar. **to c. to oblivion,** sepultar en el olvido

consignee, *s.* consignatorio, *m.*

consignment, *s.* consignación, *f.*; envío, *m.*

consignor, *s.* consignador, *m.*

consist, *v.i.* consistir (en); ser compatible (con). **to c. of,** componerse de, consistir de

consistence, consistency, *s.* consistencia, *f.*; compatibilidad, *f.*; lógica, *f.*; (of persons) consecuencia, *f.*

consistent, *a.* compatible; lógico; (of persons) consecuente

consistently, *adv.* conformemente (a); consecuentemente

consistory, *s.* consistorio, *m.*

consolation, *s.* consuelo, *m.,* consolación, *f.*

console, *v.t.* consolar; confortar. *s.* (arch.) cartela, *f.* **c. table,** consola, *f.*

consolidate, *v.t.* consolidar. *v.i.* consolidarse

consolidation, *s.* consolidación, *f.*

consoling, *a.* consolador; confortador

consols, *s. pl.* (títulos) consolidados, *m. pl.*

consonance, *s.* consonancia, *f.*

consonant, *a.* consonante

consort, *s.* consorte, *m.* and *f.* **to c. with,** frecuentar la compañía de; ir con; acompañar (a). **prince c.,** príncipe consorte, *m.*

conspicuous, *a.* conspicuo; prominente; notable. **to be c.,** destacarse; llamar la atención. **to make oneself c.,** ponerse en evidencia, llamar la atención

conspicuously, *adv.* visiblemente; muy en evidencia

conspiracy, *s.* conspiración, *f.*; complot, *m.*

conspirator, *s.* conspirador (-ra)

conspire, *v.i.* conspirar

constable, *s.* agente de policía, *m.*; (historical) condestable, *m.* **Chief C.,** jefe de policía, *m.*

constabulary, *s.* policía, *f.*

constancy, *s.* constancia, *f.*

constant, *a.* constante; incesante. *s.* constante, *m.*

constantly, *adv.* constantemente

constellation, *s.* constelación, *f.*

consternation, *s.* consternación, *f.*; espanto, terror, *m.*

constipate, *v.t.* estreñir

constipation, *s.* estreñimiento, *m.*

constituency, *s.* distrito electoral, *m.*

constituent, *a.* constituyente. *s.* constituyente, *m.*; componente, *m.*; elector (-ra)

constitute, *v.t.* constituir; nombrar; autorizar

constitution, s. constitución, f.

constitutional, a. constitucional

constitutionally, adv. constitucionalmente

constrain, v.t. obligar, forzar. I felt constrained to help them, Me sentí obligado a ayudarles

constrained, a. (of smiles, etc.) forzado; (of silences) violento; (of persons) avergonzado

constraint, s. fuerza, compulsión, f.; (of atmosphere) tensión, f.; (reserve) reserva, f.; vergüenza, f.

constrict, v.t. apretar, estrechar

constriction, s. constricción, f.

construct, v.t. edificar; construir

construction, s. construcción, f.; interpretación, f. to put a wrong c. on, interpretar mal

constructional, a. construccional

constructive, a. constructor

constructor, s. constructor, m.

construe, v.t. construir; (translate) traducir; (fig.) interpretar

consul, s. cónsul, m.

consular, a. consular

consulate, s. consulado, m. c. general, consulado general, m.

consult, v.t. consultar. v.i. consultar (con), aconsejarse (con)

consultant, s. (med. and other uses) especialista, m.

consultation, s. consulta, f.

consultative, a. consultativo

consulting, a. consultor. c. hours, horas de consulta, f. pl. c. rooms, consultorio, m.

consume, v.t. consumir; (eat) comerse, tragarse. v.i. consumirse. to be consumed by envy, estar consumido por la envidia. to be consumed by thirst, estar muerto de sed

consumer, s. consumidor (-ra)

consummate, a. consumido, perfecto. v.t. consumar

consummation, s. consumación, f.

consumption, s. consumo, m.; gasto, m.; (med.) tuberculosis, f. fuel c., consumo de combustible, m.

consumptive, a. destructivo; (med.) tísico, hético. s. tísico (-ca)

contact, s. contacto, m. v.t. ponerse en contacto con. to be in c. with, estar en contacto con

contagion, s. contagio, m.

contagious, a. contagioso

contagiousness, s. contagiosidad, f.

contain, v.t. contener; incluir; (geom.) encerrar; (arithmetic) ser divisible por; (oneself) dominarse. I could not c. myself, No pude dominarme

container, s. recipiente, m.; envase, m.; (box) caja, f.

contaminate, v.t. contaminar; corromper

contamination, s. contaminación, f.

contemplate, v.t. contemplar; meditar, considerar; (plan) tener intención de, pensar, proponerse.

contemplation, s. contemplación, f.; meditación, f.; expectación, esperanza, f.; (plan) proyecto, m. to have something in c., proyectar algo

contemplative, a. contemplativo

contemplatively, adv. contemplativamente; atentamente

contemporaneous, a. contemporáneo

contemporary, a. contemporáneo; (of persons) coetáneo; (of events, etc.) actual. s. contemporáneo (-ea)

contempt, s. desprecio, menosprecio, m.; desdén, m. c. of court, falta de respeto a la sala, f.

contemptible, a. menospreciable, despreciable; vil

contemptibly, adv. vilmente

contemptuous, a. desdeñoso; despectivo; de desprecio. to be c. of, desdeñar; menospreciar, tener en poco (a)

contemptuously, adv. con desprecio, desdeñosamente

contend, v.i. contender; (affirm) sostener, mantener. He contended that.., Sostuvo que...; contending parties, (law) partes litigantes, f. pl.

content, s. contenido, m.; capacidad, f.; (emotion) contento, m.; satisfacción, f. a. contento; satisfecho (de). v.t. contentar; satisfacer. to one's heart's c., a pedir de boca; a gusto de uno; cuanto quisiera

contented, a. satisfecho, contento

contentedly, adv. con satisfacción, contentamente

contention, *s.* disputa, controversia, discusión, *f.*; argumento, *m.*, opinión, *f.*

contentious, *a.* contencioso

contentment, *s.* contentamiento, *m.*; contento, *m.*

contest, *v.t.* disputar; (a suit) defender; (a match, an election, etc.) disputar. *s.* disputa, *f.*; combate, *m.*, lucha, *f.*; (competition) concurso, *m.*

contestant, *s.* contendiente, *m.* and *f.*

context, *s.* contexto, *m.*

contiguity, *s.* contigüidad, *f.*

contiguous, *a.* contiguo, lindero, adyacente

continence, *s.* continencia, *f.*

continent, *a.* continente. *s.* continente, *m.*

continental, *a.* continental

contingency, *s.* contingencia, *f.*

contingent, *a.* contingente. *s.* (*mil.*) contingente, *m.* **to be c. on,** (of events) depender de

continual, *a.* continuo

continually, *adv.* continuamente

continuance, *s.* continuación, *f.*

continuation, *s.* continuación, *f.*; prolongación, *f.*

continue, *v.i.* continuar; seguir; prolongarse; durar. *v.t.* continuar; seguir; proseguir; perpetuar; (in an office) retener. **To be continued,** Se continuará

continuer, *s.* continuador (-ra)

continuity, *s.* continuidad, *f.*

continuous, *a.* continuo. **c. performance,** sesión continua, *f.*

continuously, *adv.* de continuo, continuamente

contort, *v.t.* retorcer

contortion, *s.* contorsión, *f.*

contortionist, *s.* contorsionista, *m.*

contour, *s.* contorno, *m.*; curva de nivel, *f.* **c. map,** mapa con curvas de nivel, *m.*

contraband, *s.* contrabando, *m.*

contrabandist, *s.* contrabandista, *m.* and *f.*

contrabass, *s.* contrabajo, *m.*

contraception, *s.* anticoncepcionismo, *m.*

contraceptive, *s.* contraceptivo, *m.*

contract, *s.* pacto, *m.*; (*com.* and *law*) contrato, *m.*; (betrothal) esponsales, *m. pl.*; (marriage) capitulaciones, *f. pl.*; (cards) "Bridge," *m.* *v.t.* contraer; (acquire) adquirir, contraer; (a marriage, etc.) contraer; (be betrothed to) desposarse con; (by formal contract) contratar; pactar. *v.i.* (shrink) contraerse, encogerse; comprometerse por contrato. **breach of c.,** no cumplimiento de contrato, *m.* **c. party,** (of matrimony) contrayente, *m.* and *f.*

contractile, *a.* contráctil

contraction, *s.* contracción, *f.*

contractor, *s.* contratista, *m.* and *f.*

contradict, *v.t.* contradecir; desmentir

contradiction, *s.* contradicción, *f.*; negación, *f.*

contradictory, *a.* contradictorio; opuesto (a), contrario (a)

contralto, *s.* (voice) contralto, *m.*; (woman) contralto, *f.*

contraption, *s.* (*fam.*) artefacto, *m.*

contrapuntal, *a.* (*mus.*) de contrapunto

contrariety, *s.* contrariedad, *f.*

contrariness, *s.* (*fam.*) testarudez, terquedad, *f.*

contrariwise, *adv.* al contrario; al revés

contrary, *a.* contrario; opuesto (a); desfavorable, poco propicio; (of persons) difícil, terco. *s.* contraria, *f.*; (logic) contrario, *m.* *adv.* en contra, contrariamente. **on the c.,** al contrario. **to be c.,** (of persons) llevar la contraria

contrast, *s.* contraste, *m.* *v.t.* contrastar (con). *v.i.* contrastar (con), hacer contraste (con)

contravene, *v.t.* contravenir; atacar, oponerse (a)

contravention, *s.* contravención, *f.*

contribute, *v.t.* contribuir; (an article) escribir

contribution, *s.* contribución, *f.*; (to a review, etc.) artículo, *m.*

contributor, *s.* contribuyente, *m.* and *f.*; (to a journal) colaborador (-ra)

contributory, *a.* contribuyente *

contrite, *a.* penitente, arrepentido, contrito

contritely, *adv.* contritamente

contrition, *s.* contrición, penitencia, *f.*; arrepentimiento, *m.*

contrivance, *s.* invención, *f.*; (scheme) treta, idea, estratagema, *f.*; (machine) aparato, mecanismo, artefacto, *m.*

contrive, *v.t.* inventar; idear; proyectar. *v.i.* (succeed in) lograr, conseguir; (manage) arreglárselas

control, *s.* autoridad, *f.*; dominio, *m.*; gobierno, *m.*; dirección, *f.*; regulación, *f.*; (restraint) freno, *m.*; (*biol.* and *spirit.*) control, *m.*; (of a vehicle) conducción, *f.*; manejo, *m.*, manipulación, *f.*; *pl.* **controls,** (*mech.*) mando, *m.* *v.t.* dirigir, regir; regular; usar, manejar, manipular; controlar; (dominate) dominar; (curb) refrenar, reprimir; (command) mandar. He **lost c.** of the car, Perdió el mando (or control) del automóvil. **out of c.,** fuera de mando, fuera de control. **remote c.,** mando a distancia, *m.* **to c. oneself,** dominarse, contenerse. **to lose c.** of oneself, no lograr dominarse, perder el control. **c. stick,** (*aer.*) palanca de mando, *f.* **c. tower,** (*aer.*) torre de mando, *f.*

controller, *s.* interventor, *m.*; (device) regulador, *m.*

controlling, *s.* See **control.** *a.* regulador

controversial, *a.* debatible, discutible

controversy, *s.* controversia, *f.*; argumento, *m.*; altercación, disputa, *f.*

contumacious, *a.* contumaz, rebelde

contumacy, *s.* contumacia, rebeldía, *f.*

contumely, *s.* contumelia, *f.*

contusion, *s.* herida contusa, *f.*

conundrum, *s.* acertijo, rompecabezas, *m.*; problema, *m.*

convalesce, *v.i.* convalecer, estar convaleciente

convalescence, *s.* convalecencia, *f.*

convalescent, *a.* convaleciente. *s.* convaleciente, *m.* and *f.* **c. home,** casa de convalecencia, *f.*

convene, *v.t.* (a meeting) convocar; (person) citar. *v.i.* reunirse

convenience, *s.* conveniencia, *f.*; (comfort) comodidad, *f.*; utilidad, *f.*; (advantage) ventaja, *f.*; (public) retretes, *m.* *pl.* at one's **c.,** cuando le sea conveniente a uno. **to make a c.** of, abusar de. **with all modern conveniences,** con todo el confort moderno

convenient, *a.* conveniente; apropiado; cómodo. **I shall make it c.** to see him at 6 p.m., Arreglaré mis asúntos para verle a las seis

conveniently, *adv.* cómodamente; oportunamente; sin inconveniente

convent, *s.* convento, *m.*

conventicle, *s.* conventículo, *m.*

convention, *s.* convención, *f.*

conventional, *a.* convencional

conventionality, *s.* convencionalismo, *m.*

conventionally, *adv.* convencionalmente

conventual, *a.* conventual. *s.* conventual, *m.*

converge, *v.i.* convergir

convergence, *s.* convergencia, *f.*

convergent, *a.* convergente

conversance, *s.* familiaridad, *f.*, conocimiento, *m.*

conversant, *a.* familiar, versado, conocedor. **c. with,** versado en

conversation, *s.* conversación, *f.* **to engage in c. with,** entablar conversación con

conversational, *a.* de conversación; (talkative) locuaz

conversationally, *adv.* en tono familiar; familiarmente; en conversación

converse, *v.i.* conversar. **to c. by signs,** hablar por señas

conversely, *adv.* recíprocamente

conversion, *s.* conversión, *f.*

convert, *v.t.* convertir; transformar. *s.* converso (-sa). **to become a c.,** convertirse

convertible, *a.* convertible; transformable

convex, *a.* convexo

convexity, *s.* convexidad, *f.*

convey, *v.t.* transportar; conducir, llevar; (a meaning, etc.) comunicar, dar a entender; expresar; (*law*) traspasar

conveyance, s. transporte, m.;
conducción, f.; medio de transporte, m.; vehículo, m.; carruaje,
m.; (of property) traspaso, m.;
(document) escritura de traspaso,
f. public c., coche de alquiler, m.; ómnibus, m.

convict, s. convicto, m.; presidiario, m. v.t. (law) condenar;
culpar. c. settlement, colonia
penal, f.

conviction, s. (of a prisoner) condenación, f.; (belief) convencimiento, m., convicción, f.

convince, v.t. convencer

convincing, a. convincente

convincingly, adv. convincente-
mente

convivial, a. convivial

conviviality, s. jovialidad, f.

convocation, s. convocación, f.

convoke, v.t. convocar

convolution, s. circunvolución,
f.; espira, f.

convolvulus, s. enredadera, f.,
convólvulo, m.

convoy, v.t. convoyar, escoltar.
s. convoy, m. to sail in a c.,
navegar en convoy

convulse, v.t. agitar; sacudir;
estremecer. to be convulsed
with laughter, desternillarse de
risa, morirse de risa

convulsion, s. convulsión, f.;
conmoción, f.

convulsive, a. convulsivo

coo, v.i. arrullar; (of infants)
gorjearse. s. arrullo, m.

cooing, s. arrullo, m.

cook, s. cocinero (-ra). v.t. guisar,
cocer, cocinar; (falsify) falsear

cooker, s. cocina, f. gas c., cocina
de gas, f.

cookery, s. cocina, f. c.-book,
libro de cocina, m.

cooking, s. arte de guisar, m. or
f.; cocina, f.; (of accounts, etc.)
falsificación, f. c. range, cocina
económica, f. c.-stove, cocina, f.
c. utensils, batería de cocina, f.

cool, a. fresco; bastante frío;
(not ardent and of receptions,
etc.) frío; (calm) sereno, imperturbable. s. fresco, m. v.i.
enfriarse; (of love, etc.) resfriarse; (of the weather) refrescar;
(of persons) refrescarse. v.t.
refrescar; enfriar. to grow
cooler, (of weather) refrescarse;

(of persons) tener menos calor.
It is c., Hace fresco. to be as
c. as a cucumber, tener sangre
fría. c. drink, bebida fría, f.
c.-headed, sereno, imperturbable

coolie, s. culi, m.

cooling, s. enfriamiento, m. a.
refrescante

coolly, adv. frescamente; fríamente, con frialdad; imperturbablemente; (impudently) descaradamente

coolness, s. frescura, f.; (of a
welcome, etc.) frialdad, f.; (sang-
froid) sangre fría, serenidad, f.;
aplomo, m.

coop, s. gallinero, m.; caponera, f.
v.t. enjaular; encerrar. to keep
(someone) cooped up, tener
encerrado (a)

cooper, s. tonelero, barrilero, m.
v.t. hacer barriles

cooperage, s. cubería, tonelería, f.

co-operate, v.i. cooperar; colaborar

co-operation, s. cooperación, f.

co-operative, a. cooperativo. c.
society, cooperativa, f.

co-opt, v.t. elegir por votación

co-ordinate, v.t. coordinar. s.
(math.) coordenada, f. a. co-
ordenado

co-ordination, s. coordinación, f.

coot, s. fúlica, f.

copartner, s. copartícipe, m. and
f.; socio (-ia)

cope, s. (ecc.) capa, f.; (of heaven)
dosel, m., bóveda, f. to c. with,
contender con; (a difficulty)
hacer cara a, arrostrar

copeck, s. copec, m.

Copernican, a. copernicano

copier, s. copiador (-ra)

coping, s. (arch.) albardilla, f.
c.-stone, teja cumbrera, f.;
(fig.) coronamiento, m.

copious, a. copioso, abundante

copiously, adv. en abundancia

copiousness, s. abundancia, f.

copper, s. cobre, m.; (coin)
calderilla, f.; (vessel) caldera, f.
a. de cobre. c.-coloured, cobrizo. c.-smith, calderero, m.
c.-sulphate, sulfato de cobre, m.

copperas, s. caparrosa, f.

copperplate, s. lámina de cobre,
f.; grabado en cobre, m.

coppery, a. cobrizo

coppice, s. soto, bosquecillo, *m.*

co-proprietor, s. copropietario, *m.*

copse, s. arboleda, *f.*, bosquecillo, *m.*

Coptic, *a.* cóptico, copto. s. (language) copto, cóptico, *m.*

copulate, *v.i.* copularse

copulation, s. cópula, *f.*

copy, s. copia, *f.*; (of a book) ejemplar, *m.*; (of a paper) número, *m.*; manuscrito, *m.*; (subject-matter) material, *m.* *v.t.* copiar; imitar; tomar como modelo (a). **rough c.,** borrador, *m.* **c.-book,** cuaderno de escritura, *m.*

copying, s. imitación, *f.*; transcripción, *f.* **c. ink,** tinta de copiar, *f.*

copyist, s. copiador (-ra); (plagiarist) copiante, *m.* and *f.*

copyright, s. derechos de autor, *m. pl.*; propiedad literaria, *f.* *a.* protegido por los derechos de autor. *v.t.* registrar como propiedad literaria. **C. reserved,** Derechos reservados, Queda hecho el depósito que marca la ley

coquet, *v.i.* coquetear; (*fig.*) jugar (con)

coquetry, s. coquetería, *f.*

coquette, s. coqueta, *f.*

coquettish, *a.* coquetón; atractivo

coral, s. coral, *m.*; (polyp) coralina, *f.* *a.* de coral, coralino. **white c.,** madrépora, *f.* **c. beads,** corales, *m. pl.* **c.-island,** atalón, *m.* **c.-reef,** escollo de coral, *m.* **c. snake,** coral, *f.*

corbel, s. (*arch.*) ménsula, *f.*

cord, s. cuerda, *f.*; cordel, *m.*; cordón, *m.* *v.t.* encordelar. **spinal c.,** médula espinal, *f.* **umbilical c.,** cordón umbilical, *m.*

cordage, s. cordelería, *f.*; (*naut.*) cordaje, *m.*

cordial, *a.* cordial; sincero, fervoroso. s. cordial, *m.*

cordiality, s. cordialidad, *f.*

cordially, *adv.* cordialmente

cordon, s. cordón, *m.*; cinto, *m.* **to c. off,** acordonar

cordovan, *a.* cordobés. s. (leather) cordobán, *m.*

corduroy, s. pana de cordoncillo, *f.*

core, s. (of a fruit) corazón, *m.*; (of a rope) alma, *f.*, centro, *m.*; (of an abscess) foco, *m.*; (of a corn) ojo, *m.*; (*fig.*) núcleo, *m.*; esencia, *f.*; lo esencial

co-religionist, s. correligionario (-ia)

co-respondent, s. cómplice en un caso de divorcio, *m.* and *f.*

Corinthian, *a.* corintio. s. corintio (-ia)

cork, s. corcho, *m.*; (of a bottle) tapón, *m.* *a.* de corcho. *v.t.* tapar con corcho, taponar; (wine) encorchar; (the face) tiznar con corcho quemado. **pop of a c.,** taponazo, *m.* **to draw a c.,** descorchar. **c.-jacket,** chaleco salvavidas, *m.* **c. tree,** alcornoque, *m.*

corkscrew, s. sacacorchos, *m.*

corm, s. bulbo, *m.*

cormorant, s. cormorán, *m.*

corn, s. grano, cereal, *m.*; (wheat) trigo, *m.*; (maize) maíz, *m.*; (single seed) grano, *m.*; (on the foot, etc.) callo, *m.* **Indian c.,** maíz, *m.* **c. cure,** callicida, *m.* **c.-exchange,** bolsa de granos, *f.* **c.-field,** campo de trigo, *m.* **c.-flower,** aciano, *m.*

cornea, s. córnea, *f.*

cornelian, s. cornalina, *f.*

corneous, *a.* córneo

corner, s. ángulo, *m.*; (of a street or building) esquina, *f.*; (of a room) rincón, *m.*; (*aut.*) viraje, *m.*; (*com.*) monopolio, *m.*; (of the eye) rabo, *m.*; (Assoc. football) "corner," *m.* *v.t.* arrinconar; acorralar; (*com.*) acaparar. **the four corners of the earth,** las cinco partes del mundo. **a tight c.,** un lance apretado, un apuro. **to drive into a c.,** (*fig.*) poner entre la espada y la pared. **to look out of the c. of the eye,** mirar de reojo. **to turn the c.,** doblar la esquina; (*fig.*) pasar la crisis. **c.-cupboard,** rinconera, *f.* **c. seat,** asiento del rincón, *m.* **c.-stone,** piedra angular, *f.* (also *fig.*).

cornered, *a.* (of a person) acorralado, en aprieto; (of hats) de . . . picos. **three-c. hat,** sombrero de tres picos, *m.*

cornet, s. (musical instrument) corneta, *f.*; (*mil.*) corneta, *m.*;

(paper) cucurucho, *m.* **c. player,** cornetín, *m.*

cornflour, *s.* harina de maíz, *f.*

cornice, *s.* cornisa, *f.*

Cornish, *a.* de Cornualles

cornucopia, *s.* cornucopia, *f.*

corolla, *s.* (*bot.*) corola, *f.*

corollary, *s.* corolario, *m.*

corona, *s.* (*ast., arch.*) corona, *f.*

coronation, *s.* coronación, *f.*

coroner, *s.* (nearest equivalent) juez de primera instancia, *m.*

coronet, *s.* (of a peer, etc.) corona, *f.*; tiara, *f.*; guirnalda, *f.*

corporal, *a.* corporal. *s.* (*mil.*) cabo, *m.*; (altar-cloth) corporal *m.* **c. punishment,** castigo corporal, *m.*

corporate, *a.* corporativo

corporation, *s.* corporación, *f.*; concejo, cabildo municipal, *m.*; (*com., U.S.A.*) sociedad anónima, *f.*

corporeal, *a.* corpóreo

corps, *s.* cuerpo, *m.*

corpse, *s.* cadáver, *m.*

corpulence, *s.* gordura, obesidad, *f.*

corpulent, *a.* corpulento, grueso, gordo

corpus, *s.* cuerpo, *m.* **C. Christi,** Corpus, *m.* **c. delicti,** cuerpo del delito, *m.*

corpuscle, *s.* corpúsculo, *m.*

correct, *a.* correcto; exacto, justo. *v.t.* corregir; rectificar; amonestar, reprender

correction, *s.* corrección, *f.*; rectificación, *f.*

corrective, *a.* correctivo. *s.* correctivo, *m.*

correctly, *adv.* correctamente

correctness, *s.* corrección, *f.*; exactitud, *f.*; justicia, *f.*

correlate, *v.t.* poner en correlación. *v.i.* tener correlación

correlation, *s.* correlación, *f.*

correspond, *v.i.* corresponder (a); (by letter) escribirse, corresponderse

correspondence, *s.* correspondencia, *f.*; (*com.*) correo, *m.* **c. course,** curso por correspondencia, *m.*

correspondent, *s.* correspondiente, *m. and f.*; (*com. and journalist*) corresponsal, *m. and f.* **special c.,** corresponsal extraordinario, *m.*

corresponding, *a.* correspondiente. **c. member,** miembro correspondiente, *m.*

corridor, *s.* corredor, pasillo, *m.*; (railway) pasillo, *m.*; (*pol.*) corredor, *m.* **c. train,** tren con coches corridos, *m.*

corroborate, *v.t.* corroborar, confirmar

corroboration, *s.* corroboración, confirmación, *f.*

corroborative, *a.* corroborativo, confirmatorio

corrode, *v.t.* corroer, morder; (*fig.*) roer

corrosion, *s.* corrosión, *f.*

corrosive, *a.* corrosivo; mordaz

corrugate, *v.t.* arrugar. *v.i.* arrugarse

corrugated, *a.* arrugado; ondulado. **c. iron,** chapa canaleta, *f.*

corrugation, *s.* corrugación, *f.*, arrugamiento, *m.*

corrupt, *a.* corrompido; vicioso, desmoralizado. *v.t.* corromper. *v.i.* corromperse

corrupter, *s.* corruptor (-ra)

corruption, *s.* corrupción, *f.*

corsage, *s.* corpiño, *m.*

corsair, *s.* corsario, *m.*

corset, *s.* corsé, *m.* *v.t.* encorsetar. **c. shop,** corsetería, *f.*

Corsican, *a.* corso. *s.* corso (-sa)

cortège, *s.* séquito, acompañamiento, *m.*; desfile, *m.*

cortex, *s.* (*bot., anat.*) corteza, *f.*

cortisone, *s.* (drug) cortisona, *f.*

coruscation, *s.* brillo, *m.*

corvette, *s.* corbeta, *f.*

coryza, *s.* coriza, *f.*

co-signatory, *s.* cosignatario (-ia)

cosily, *adv.* cómodamente

cosine, *s.* coseno, *m.*

cosiness, *s.* comodidad, *f.*

cosmetic, *a.* cosmético. *s.* cosmético, *m.*

cosmic, *a.* cósmico

cosmographer, *s.* cosmógrafo, *m.*

cosmography, *s.* cosmografía, *f.*

cosmopolitan, *a.* cosmopolita. *s.* cosmopolita, *m. and f.*

cosmopolitanism, *s.* cosmopolitismo, *m.*

cosmos, *s.* cosmos, universo, *m.*

Cossack, *a.* cosaco. *s.* cosaco (-ca)

cosset, *v.t.* mimar, consentir

cost, *v.i.* costar. *s.* costa, *f.*, coste, precio, *m.*; (*fig.*) costa, *f.*; *pl.* **costs**, (*law*) costas, *f. pl.* **at all costs**, cueste lo que cueste, a toda costa. **to my c.**, a mi costa. **c. of living**, coste de la vida, *m.* **to c. a fortune**, costar un sentido

Costa-Rican, *a.* costarriqueño. *s.* costarriqueño (-ña)

coster, *s.* vendedor (-ra) ambulante

costliness, *s.* alto precio, *m.*; suntuosidad, *f.*

costly, *a.* costoso; suntuoso, magnífico

costume, *s.* traje, *m.*; (fancy-dress) disfraz, *m.*; (tailored) traje sastre, *m.*

costumier, *s.* modista, *m.* and *f.*; sastre, *m.*

cosy, *a.* cómodo; agradable; caliente. **You are very c. here**, Estás muy bien aquí

cot, *s.* (hut) choza, cabaña, *f.*; (child's) camita, *f.*

cotangent, *s.* cotangente, *f.*

coterie, *s.* círculo, grupo, *m.*; (clique) camarilla, *f.*

cotillion, *s.* cotillón, *m.*

cottage, *s.* cabaña, choza, *f.*; casita, *f.*, hotelito, *m.*; torre, villa, *f.*

cottager, *s.* aldeano (-na)

cotter, *s.* chaveta, llave, *f.*

cotton, *s.* algodón, *m.* *a.* de algodón. **I don't c. to the idea at all**, No me gusta nada la idea; La idea no me seduce. **sewing-c.**, hilo de coser, *m.* **c. goods**, géneros de algodón, *m. pl.* **c. mill**, hilandería de algodón, algodonería, *f.* **c. plantation**, algodonal, *m.* **c.-seed oil**, aceite de semilla de algodón, *m.* **c.-spinner**, hilandero (-ra) de algodón. **c.-wool**, algodón en rama, *m.* **c.-yarn**, hilo de algodón, *m.*

cottony, *a.* algodonoso

cotyledon, *s.* cotiledón, *m.*

couch, *s.* sofá, canapé, *m.*; (bed) lecho, *m.*; (lair) cama, *f.* *v.t.* (lay down) acostar, echar; (a lance) (express) expresar, redactar. *v.i.* acostarse; (crouch) agacharse; estar en acecho

couchant, *a.* (*her.*) acostado

cough, *v.i.* toser. *s.* tos, *f.* **to c. up**, escupir, expectorar. **c.-drop**, pastilla para la tos, *f.*

coughing, *s.* tos, *f.*

could. See **can**

council, *s.* consejo, *m.*; junta, *f.*; (*ecc.*) concilio, *m.* **Privy C.**, consejo privado, *m.* **to hold c.**, celebrar un consejo; aconsejarse (con); consultarse. **town c.**, ayuntamiento, *m.* **c. chamber**, sala consistorial, *f.*; sala de actos, *f.* **c. houses**, casas baratas, *f. pl.* **c. of war**, consejo de guerra, *m.*

councillor, *s.* concejal, *m.*; miembro de la junta, *m.*

counsel, *s.* consultación, *f.*; deliberación, *f.*; consejo, *m.*; (*law*) abogado, *m.* *v.t.* aconsejar. **a c. of perfection**, un ideal imposible. **to keep one's own c.**, no decir nada, callarse, guardar silencio. **to take c. with**, consultar (a), aconsejarse con

counsellor, *s.* consejero, *m.* **c. of state**, consejero de estado, *m.*

count, *v.t.* contar; calcular; (consider) creer, considerar. *v.i.* contar. *s.* cuenta, *f.*; (of votes) escrutinio, *m.*; (*law*) capítulo, *m.* **John simply doesn't c.**, Juan no cuenta para nada. **Erudition alone counts for very little**, La mera erudición sirve para muy poco. **to keep c. of**, tener cuenta de. **to lose c. of**, perder cuenta de. **to c. on**, contar con; (doing something) esperar. **to c. up**, contar

count, *s.* (title) conde, *m.*

countenance, *s.* semblante, *m.*; expresión de la cara, *f.*; aspecto, *m.*; (favour) apoyo, *m.*, ayuda, *f.* *v.t.* autorizar, aprobar; apoyar, ayudar. **to put (a person) out of c.**, desconcertar (a)

counter, *s.* (in a bank) contador, *m.*; (in a shop) mostrador, *m.*; (in games) ficha, *f.* *adv.* contra, al contrario; al revés. *a.* opuesto (a), contrario (a). *v.t.* parar; contestar. **to run c. to my inclinations**, oponerse a mis deseos. **to c. with the left**, (boxing) contestar con la izquierda. **c.-attack**, contra-ataque, *m.* **c.-attraction**, atracción contraria, *f.* **c.-offen-**

sive, contraofensiva, f. c.-reformation, contrarreforma, f. c.-revolution, contrarevolución, f.

counteract, v.t. neutralizar; frustrar

counterbalance, s. contrapeso, m. v.t. contrabalancear; compensar, igualar

counterblast, s. denunciación, f.; respuesta, f.

countercharge, s. recriminación, f. v.t. recriminar; (law) reconvenir

counterfeit, a. falso, espurio; fingido. s. falsificación, f.; imitación, f.; moneda falsa, f.; (person) impostor (-ra). v.t. imitar; (pretend) fingir; (coins, handwriting, etc.) falsificar

counterfeiter, s. falsario (-ia)

counterfoil, s. talón, m.

countermand, v.t. contramandar; (an order) revocar, cancelar. s. contraorden, f.; revocación, f.

countermarch, s. contramarcha, f.

countermeasure, s. contramedida, f.

counterpane, s. sobrecama, colcha, f.

counterpart, s. contraparte, f.; (of a document) duplicado, m.

counterplot, s. contratreta, f.

counterpoint, s. (mus.) contrapunto, m.

counterpoise, s. contrapeso, m.; equilibrio, m. v.t. contrabalancear, contrapesar

countersign, s. contraseña, f. v.t. refrendar

countess, s. condesa, f.

counting, s. cuenta, f.; numeración, f.; (of votes) escrutinio, m. c.-house, contaduría, f.

countless, a. innumerable. a c. number, un sinfín, un sinnúmero

countrified, a. rústico, campesino

country, s. país, m.; (fatherland) patria, f.; región, campiña, tierra, f.; (as opposed to town) campo, m. a. del campo; campesino, campestre, rústico. He lives in the c., Vive en el campo. c. club, club del campo, m. c. cousin, provinciano (-na). c.-dance, baile campestre, m.

c. gentleman, hacendado, m. c. girl, campesina, f.; aldeana, f. c.-house, finca., f.; casa de campo, f. c. life, vida del campo, f. c.-seat, finca, f.

countryman, s. campesino, m.; hombre del campo, m.; compatriota, m.

countryside, s. campo, m.; campiña, f.

countrywoman, s. campesina, f.; compatriota, f.

county, s. condado, m.; provincia, f. c. council, diputación provincial, f. c. town, cabeza de partido, f.; ciudad provincial, f.

coup, s. golpe, m. c. d'état, golpe de estado, m.

coupé, s. cupé, m.

couple, s. par, m.; (in a dance, etc.) pareja, f. v.t. enganchar, acoplar; (in marriage) casar; (animals) aparear; (ideas) asociar; (names) juntar. the young (married) c., el matrimonio joven

couplet, s. copla, f.

coupling, s. enganche, acoplamiento, m.; (of railway carriages) enganche, m.; (of ideas) asociación, f.

coupon, s. talón, m.; cupón, m.

courage, s. valor, m. C. ¡ ¡Ánimo! to muster up c., cobrar ánimo

courageous, a. valiente

courageously, adv. valientemente

courier, s. correo, m., estafeta, f.; (guide) guía, m.; (newspaper) estafeta, f.

course, s. curso, m.; (of time) transcurso, m.; (of events) marcha, f.; (of a river, etc.) cauce, m.; (of stars) carrera, f.; curso, m.; (of a ship) derrota, f., rumbo, m.; (way) camino, m., ruta, f.; (of conduct) línea de conducta, f.; actitud, f.; (of study) curso, m.; (of a meal) plato, m.; (of an illness) desarrollo, m.; (med.) tratamiento, m. He took it as a matter of c., Lo tomó sin darle importancia. in due c., a su tiempo debido. in the c. of time, andando el tiempo, en el transcurso de los años. of c., claro está; naturalmente. Are you coming to-morrow? Of c.! ¿Vienes mañana? ¡Ya lo creo! **the best c. to take,** lo mejor que se puede hacer

course, *v.t.* cazar, perseguir; (*poet.*) correr por, cruzar. *v.i.* (of blood, etc.) correr; cazar

court, *s.* (yard) patio, *m.*; (tennis) campo de tenis, *m.*; (fives, racquets) cancha, *f.*; (royal) corte, *f.*; (of justice) tribunal, *m.*; (following) séquito, acompañamiento, *m. v.t.* hacer la corte (a); cortejar, pretender; solicitar; (sleep) conciliar. **to pay c. to,** (a woman) galantear, pretender; (a person) hacer la rueda (a). **to respect the c.,** (*law*) guardar sala. **c. of appeal,** sala de apelación, *f.* **c. of justice,** sala de justicia, *f.*; tribunal de justicia, *m.* **supreme c.,** tribunal supremo, *m.* **c.-card,** figura, *f.* **c.-dress,** traje de corte, *m.* **c. house,** palacio de justicia, *m.* **c. jester,** bufón, *m.* **c.-martial,** tribunal militar, *m.* **c.-plaster,** tafetán inglés, tafetán de heridas, *m.* **c.-room,** sala de justicia, *f.*

courteous, *a.* cortés

courteously, *adv.* cortésmente

courteousness, *s.* cortesía, *f.*

courtesan, *s.* cortesana, *f.*

courtesy, *s.* cortesía, *f.*; favor, *m.*, merced, *f.*; permiso, *m.*

courtier, *s.* cortesano, palaciego, *m.*

courtliness, *s.* cortesía, urbanidad, *f.*; dignidad, *f.*; elegancia, *f.*

courtly, *a.* cortés, galante; digno; elegante

courtship, *s.* noviazgo, *m.*; galanteo, *m.*

courtyard, *s.* patio, *m.*

cousin, *s.* primo (-ma). **first c.,** primo (-ma) carnal. **second c.,** primo (-ma) segundo (-da)

cove, *s.* cala, abra, ensenada, *f.*

covenant, *s.* contrato, *m.*; estipulación, *f.*; pacto, *m.*; alianza, *f. v.t.* prometer; estipular

Coventry, to send to, hacer el vacío (a)

cover, *v.t.* cubrir; abrigar; (dissemble) disimular; (a distance) recorrer; (comprise) comprender; abarcar; (with confusion, etc.) llenar (de); (with a revolver, etc.)

amenazar (con); (an overdraft, etc.) garantizar; (of stallions) cubrir; (of a hen and eggs) empollar; (a story, journalism) investigar. *s.* cubierta, *f.*; (for a chair, umbrella, etc.) funda, *f.*; (of a saucepan, jar, etc.) tapa, *f.*; (dish-cover) tapadera, *f.*; (of a book) cubierta, tapa, *f.*; (of a letter) sobre, *m.*; (shelter) abrigo, *m.*; protección, *f.*; (undergrowth) maleza, *f.*; (*fig.*) velo, manto, *m.*; (pretence) pretexto, *m.*; (*com.*) garantía, *f.* **outer c.,** (of tyre) cubierta de neumático, *f.* **to c. oneself with glory,** cubrirse de gloria. **to c. up,** cubrir completamente; (with clothes) arropar; (wrap up) envolver. **to c. with a revolver,** amenazar con un revólver. **to read a book from c. to c.,** leer un libro del principio al fin. **to take c.,** refugiarse, tomar abrigo. **under c.,** bajo tejado; al abrigo

covering, *s.* cubrimiento, *m.*; cubierta, *f.*; envoltura, *f.*; capa, *f.*, abrigo, *m.* **c. letter,** carta adjunta, *f.*

coverlet, *s.* colcha, sobrecama, *f.*

covert, *s.* guarida, *f. a.* oculto; furtivo

covertly, *adv.* secretamente, furtivamente

covet, *v.t.* codiciar; ambicionar, suspirar por

covetous, *a.* codicioso; ávido; ambicioso

covetously, *adv.* codiciosamente; ávidamente

covetousness, *s.* codicia, avaricia, *f.*; avidez, *f.*; ambición, *f.*

covey, *s.* pollada, nidada, *f.*

cow, *v.t.* intimidar, acobardar

cow, *s.* vaca, *f.*; (of other animals) hembra, *f.* **c.-bell,** cencerro, *m.*, zumba, *f.* **c.-catcher,** (*aut.*) salvavidas, *m.* **c.-hide,** cuero, *m.*; penca, *f.* **c.-house,** establo, *m.*, boyera, *f.* **c.-pox,** vacuna, *f.*

coward, *s.* cobarde, *m. a.* cobarde

cowardice, *s.* cobardía, *f.*

cowardly, *a.* cobarde

cowboy, *s.* vaquero, *m.*; gaucho, "cowboy," *m.*

cower, *v.i.* no saber dónde meterse; temblar, acobardarse

cowherd, *s.* vaquero, boyero, *m.*

cowl, s. capucha, f.; (of a chimney) sombrerete, m.

cowlike, a. de vaca; bovino

co-worker, s. colaborador (-ra)

cowshed, s. establo, m.

cowslip, s. primula, f.

cox, s. timonel, m.

coxcomb, s. (of a jester) gorra de bufón, f.; mequetrefe, m.

coxswain, s. patrón, m.; (of a rowing-boat) timonel, m.

coy, a. modoso, tímido; coquetón

coyly, adv. tímidamente; con coquetería

coyness, s. timidez, modestia, f.; coquetería, f.

crab, s. (sea) cangrejo de mar, cámbaro, m.; (river) cangrejo, m.; (ast.) Cáncer, m. v.t. (thwart) frustrar. **hermit c.,** cangrejo ermitaño, m. **c.-apple,** manzana silvestre, f. **c.-louse,** ladilla, f.

crabbed, a. áspero, hosco, desabrido, arisco; (of handwriting) apretado, metido

crack, v.t. hender; quebrantar, romper; (nuts) cascar; (a whip and fingers) chasquear; (a bottle of wine) abrir. v.i. (of earth, skin, etc.) agrietarse; romperse, quebrarse; (of the voice) romper; (of the male voice) mudar. s. hendedura, rendija, f.; quebraja, f.; (of a whip) chasquido, m.; (of a rifle) estallido, m.; (blow) golpe, garrotazo, m. a. excelente, de primera categoría; estupendo. **to c. a joke,** decir un chiste. **to c. up,** v.t. dar bombo (a), alabar. v.i. (in health) quebrantarse. **c.-brained,** chiflado; estúpido, loco

cracked, a. grietado; (of a bell, etc.) hendido; (of the voice) cascada; (of a person) chiflado

cracker, s. (firework) petardo, m.; buscapiés, m.

crackle, v.i. (of burning wood, etc.) crepitar; (rustle) crujir; (of rifle fire) tirotear. s. crepitación, f.; crujido, m.; (of rifle fire) tiroteo, m.

crackling, s. See crackle; (cul.) chicharrón, m.

cracksman, s. ladrón, m.

cradle, s. cuña, f.; (fig.) niñez, infancia, f.; (for a limb) arco de protección, m.; (for winebottle)

cesta, f. v.t. mecer. **c.-song,** canción de cuna, f.

craft, s. (guile) astucia, f.; (skill) habilidad, f.; arte, m. or f.; (occupation) oficio manual, m.; profesión, f.; (guild) gremio, m.; (boat) barco, m., embarcación, f.

craftily, adv. astutamente

craftiness, s. astucia, f.

craftsman, s. artífice, m.; artesano, m.; artista, m.

craftsmanship, s. arte, m. or f.; habilidad, f.; artificio, m.

crafty, a. astuto, taimado

crag, s. peña, f., risco, despeñadero, m.

cragginess, s. escabrosidad, aspereza, fragosidad, f.

craggy, a. escabroso, escarpado, peñascoso, riscoso

cram, v.t. henchir; atestar; (one's mouth) llenar (de); (poultry) cebar; (a pupil) preparar para un examen; (a subject) empollar. v.i. (with food) atracarse. **The room was crammed with people,** La sala estaba atestada de gente

cramp, s. (med.) calambre, m.; (numbness) entumecimiento, m.; (rivet) grapa, f. v.t. dar calambre (a); (numb) entumecer; (fasten) lañar; (fig., hamper) estorbar. **to c. someone's style,** cortar los vuelos (a). **writer's c.,** calambre del escribiente, m.

cramped, a. (of space) apretado, estrecho; (of writing) menuda

cranberry, s. arándano, m.

crane, s. (orn.) grulla, f.; (machine) grúa, f. **jib c.,** grúa de pescante, f. **travelling c.,** grúa móvil, f. **to c. one's neck,** estirar el cuello. **crane's bill,** pico de cigüeña, m.

cranial, a. craneal

cranium, s. cráneo, m.

crank, s. (handle) manivela, f.; (person) maniático (-ca). v.t. poner en marcha (un motor) con la manivela

crankiness, s. (crossness) irritabilidad, f., mal humor, m.; (eccentricity) excentricidad, f.

cranky, a. (cross) irritable, malhumorado; (eccentric) chiflado, maniático, excéntrico

cranny, s. hendedura, grieta, f.

crape, s. crespón, m.
crash, v.i. caer estrepitosa-
mente; romperse; estallarse; (of
aircraft, cars) estrellarse; (fig.)
hundirse, arruinarse. s. estrépito,
estruendo, m.; estallido, m.; (of
aircraft) accidente de aviación,
m.; (car) accidente, m. (or
choque, m.) de automóviles;
(financial) ruina, f.; (fig.) hundimiento, m. to c. into,
estrellarse contra, chocar con.
c. helmet, casco, m. c.-landing,
aterrizaje violento, m.
crass, a. craso
crassness, s. estupidez, f.
crate, s. (box) caja de embalaje,
f.; (basket) canasto, m., banasta,
f.
crater, s. cráter, m.
cravat, s. corbata, f.
crave, v.t. suplicar, implorar.
to c. for, perecer por, suspirar
por, anhelar
craven, a. cobarde, pusilánime.
s. poltrón, cobarde, m.
craving, s. deseo vehemente, m.,
sed, f.
crawfish, s. cangrejo de río, m.;
cigala, f.
crawl, v.i. arrastrarse; andar a
gatas; andar a paso de tortuga;
(abase oneself) humillarse; (be
full of) abundar (en). s. paso de
tortuga, m.; (swimming) el
"crawl"
crayfish, s. cangrejo de río, m.;
cigala, f.
crayon, s. carbón, m.; pastel, m.;
(pencil) lápiz de color, m. v.t.
dibujar con pastel, etc. c.
drawing, dibujo al carbón, m.
craze, v.t. enloquecer, volver
loco (a). s. manía, f., capricho,
entusiasmo, m.; (fashion) moda,
f.
crazily, adv. locamente
craziness, s. locura, f.
crazy, a. loco; chiflado; (of
structure) dilapidado. He is c.
about music, Está loco por la
música. to be completely c., (of
persons) ser un loco de atar;
ser completamente loco. to
drive c., volver loco (a)
creak, v.i. (of shoes, chairs, etc.)
crujir; (of gates, etc.) rechinar,
chirriar. s. crujido, m.; chirrido,
m.

creaking, s. See creak
creaky, a. crujiente, que cruje;
chirriador
cream, s. crema, f.; nata, f.;
(fig.) flor, nata, f. a. de nata.
whipped c., nata batida, f. c.
cake, pastel de nata, m. c.-
cheese, queso de nata, m. c.-
coloured, de color crema. c.-
jug, jarro para crema, m. c. of
tartar, cremor, tártaro, f.
creamery, s. lechería, f.
creamy, a. cremoso
crease, s. (wrinkle) arruga, f.;
(fold) pliegue, m.; (in trousers)
raya, f.; (in cricket) línea de la
meta, f. v.t. (wrinkle) arrugar;
(fold) plegar; (trousers) poner la
raya en. v.i. arrugarse
create, v.t. crear; (appoint) nombrar; (produce) suscitar, producir
creation, s. creación, f.; establecimiento, m.; (appointment)
nombramiento, m.
creative, a. creador; de la creación
creativeness, s. facultad creativa,
inventiva, f.
creator, s. creador (-ra)
creature, s. criatura, f.; animal,
m. c. comforts, bienestar
material, m.
crèche, s. casa cuna, f.
credence, s. crédito, m., fe,
creencia, f.; (ecc.) credencia, f.
to give c. to, dar crédito (a),
creer
credentials, s. pl. credenciales,
f. pl.
credibility, s. credibilidad, verosimilitud, f.
credible, a. creíble, verosímil;
(of persons) digno de confianza
credibly, adv. creíblemente
credit, s. crédito, m.; reputación,
f.; honor, m.; (com. and banking)
crédito, m.; (in book-keeping)
data, f. v.t. dar fe (a), dar
crédito (a); creer; atribuir; (book-
keeping) acreditar. It does them
c., Les hace honor. on c., a
crédito, al fiado. open c., (com.)
letra abierta, f. to give on c.,
dar fiado. c. balance, haber, m.
creditable, a. loable, honroso,
digno de alabanza
creditably, adv. honrosamente
creditor, s. acreedor (-ra); (book-
keeping) haber, m.

credulity, *s.* credulidad, *f.*
credulous, *a.* crédulo
credulously, *adv.* con credulidad, crédulamente
creed, *s.* credo, *m.*
creek, *s.* caleta, abra, *f.*
creel, *s.* (for fish) cesta de pescador, *f.*
creep, *v.i.* arrastrarse; (of plants and birds) trepar; (of infants) andar a gatas; (totter) hacer pinitos; (slip) deslizarse; (cringe) lisonjear, rebajarse; (of one's flesh) sentir hormigueo. **to c. about on tiptoe,** andar de puntillas. **to c. into a person's favour,** insinuarse en el favor de. **to c. in,** entrar sin ser notado (en); deslizarse en. **to c. on,** (of time) avanzar lentamente; (of old age, etc.) acercarse insensiblemente. **to c. out,** salir sin hacer ruido; escurrirse. **to c. up,** trepar por; subir a gatas
creeper, *s.* (*bot.*) enredadera, *f.*; (*orn.*) trepador, *m.*; (*zool.*) reptil, *m.*
creeping, *a.* (*bot.*) trepante; (*zool.*) trepador; (servile) rastrero
cremate, *v.t.* incinerar
cremation, *s.* cremación, *f.*
crematorium, *s.* crematorio, *m.*; horno de incineración, *m.*
creole, *a.* criollo. *s.* criollo (-lla)
creosote, *s.* creosota, *f.*
crepitate, *v.i.* crepitar
crepitation, *s.* crepitación, *f.*
crescent, *s.* media luna, *f.*; (*her.*) creciente, *m.*; calle en forma de semicírculo, *f.* *a.* en forma de media luna; (*poet.*) creciente
cress, *s.* (*bot.*) berro, *m.*
cresset, *s.* farol, *m.*
crest, *s.* (of a cock, etc.) cresta, *f.*; (plume) penacho, *m.*; (of a helmet) cimera, *f.*; (of a hill) cumbre, cima, *f.*; (of a wave) cresta, *f.* **family c.,** blasón, escudo, *m.*
crestfallen, *a.* cabizbajo, cariacontecido
cretan, *a.* cretense. *s.* cretense, *m.* and *f.*
cretin, *s.* cretino (-na)
cretinism, *s.* cretinismo, *m.*
cretonne, *s.* cretona, *f.*
crevasse, *s.* grieta en un ventisquero, *f.*

crevice, *s.* intersticio, *m.*; rendija, grieta, *f.*
crew, *s.* (of ships, boats, aircraft) tripulación, *f.*; (of a gun) servidores de una ametralladora, *m. pl.*; (gang) pandilla, cuadrilla, *f.*
crib, *s.* pesebre, *m.*; (child's) camita de niño, *f.*; (plagiary) plagio, *m.* *v.t.* (plagiarize) plagiar; (steal) hurtar
crick, *s.* (in the neck) tortícolis, *m.*
cricket, *s.* (*ent.*) grillo, *m.*; (game) cricquet, *m.* **c. ball,** pelota de cricquet, *f.* **c. bat,** paleta de cricquet, *f.* **c. ground,** campo de cricquet, *m.* **c. match,** partido de cricquet, *m.*
cricketer, *s.* jugador de cricquet, *m.*
crier, *s.* (town) pregonero, *m.*
crime, *s.* crimen, *m.*; ofensa, *f.*, delito, *m.*
criminal, *a.* criminal. *s.* criminal, *m.*; reo, *m.* and *f.* **C. Investigation Department,** (nearest equivalent) policía secreta, *f.* **c. laws,** código penal, *m.*
criminally, *adv.* criminalmente
criminologist, *s.* criminalista, *m.*
criminology, *s.* criminología, *f.*
crimp, *v.t.* (hair) rizar
crimson, *s.* carmesí, *m.* *a.* de carmesí. *v.t.* teñir de carmesí. *v.i.* enrojecerse
cringe, *v.i.* temblar; asustarse, acobardarse; inclinarse (ante)
cringing, *a.* servil, humilde; adulador
crinkle, *v.i.* arrugarse; rizarse. *v.t.* arrugar. *s.* arruga, *f.*
crinoline, *s.* crinolina, *f.*, miriñaque, guardainfante, *m.*
cripple, *s.* tullido (-da); cojo (-ja). *v.t.* lisiar, tullir, estropear; (*fig.*) paralizar
crisis, *s.* crisis, *f.*
crisp, *a.* (of hair and of leaves) crespo; (fresh) fresco; (stiff) tieso; (of style) nervioso, vigoroso; (of manner) decidido; (of repartee) chispeante; (of tone) incisivo
criterion, *s.* criterio, *m.*
critic, *s.* crítico, *m.*; censor, *m.*
critical, *a.* crítico
critically, *adv.* críticamente
criticism, *s.* crítica, *f.*
criticize, *v.t.* criticar; censurar

critique, s. crítica, f.

croak, v.i. (of frogs) croar; (of ravens) graznar; (of persons) lamentarse, gruñir

croaking, s. canto de la rana, m.; graznido, m.

Croat, a. croata. s. croata, m. and f.

crochet, s. ganchillo, m. v.i. hacer ganchillo. v.t. hacer (algo) de ganchillo. **c. hook,** aguja de gancho, f., ganchillo, m. **c. work,** croché, ganchillo, m.

crockery, s. loza, f., cacharros, m. pl. **c. store,** cacharrería, f.

crocodile, s. cocodrilo, m. **c. tears,** lágrimas de cocodrilo, f. pl.

crocus, s. azafrán, m.

croft, s. campillo, m.; (farm) heredad, f.

crofter, s. colono, m.

crone, s. bruja, f.

crony, s. compinche, m. and f.

crook, s. curva, f.; (staff) cayado, m.; (swindler) caballero de industria, estafador, m. v.t. doblar, encorvar

crooked, a. curvo; encorvado; torcido; ladeado; (deformed) contrahecho; (of paths, etc.) tortuoso; (dishonest) torcido, tortuoso

crookedly, adv. torcidamente; de través

crookedness, s. encorvadura, f.; tortuosidad, f.; sinuosidad, f.

croon, v.t. and v.i. canturrear; cantar

crooner, s. cantante, m. and f.

crop, s. (of birds) buche, m.; (whip) látigo, m., fusta, f.; (handle) mango, m.; (harvest) cosecha, f.; (of the hair) cortadura, f. v.t. cortar; (nibble) rozar; (hair) rapar. **Eton c.,** pelo a la garçonne, m. **to c. up,** aparecer, surgir

croquet, s. juego de la argolla, juego de croquet, m.

croquette, s. (cul.) croqueta, f.

crosier, s. báculo, cayado del obispo, m.

cross, s. cruz, f.; (biol.) cruzamiento, m.; (sew., bias) bies, m. **in the shape of a c.,** en cruz. **the Red C.,** la Cruz Roja. **c.-bearer,** (ecc.) crucero, m.

cross, v.t. cruzar; atravesar; pasar por; (a cheque and animals)

cruzar; (thwart) contrariar. **It did not c. my mind,** No se me ocurrió. **Our letters must have crossed,** Nuestras cartas deben haberse cruzado. **to c. oneself,** (ecc.) persignarse. **to c. out,** tachar, rayar. **to c. over,** v.t. atravesar, cruzar. v.i. ir al otro lado

cross, a. transversal; cruzado; oblicuo; (contrary) opuesto (a); (bad-tempered) malhumorado. **c.-breed,** a. mestizo, atravesado. **c.-country,** a. a campo travieso. **c.-examination,** (law) repregunta, f. **c.-examine,** v.t. (law) repreguntar; interrogar. **c.-eyed,** bizco. **c.-fire,** (mil.) fuego cruzado, m.; (fig.) tiroteo m. **c.-grained,** (of wood) vetisesgado; (of persons) áspero, intratable, desabrido. **c.-legged,** con las piernas cruzadas. **c.-purpose,** despropósito, m. **at c.-purposes,** a despropósito. **c.-question,** v.t. (law) repreguntar; interrogar. **c. reference,** contrarreferencia, f. **c. section,** sección transversal, f. **c.-stitch,** punto cruzado, m. **c.-word puzzle,** crucigrama, m.

crossbar, s. travesaño, m.

crossbeam, s. viga transversal, f.

crossbow, s. ballesta, f.

crossbred, a. cruzado, mestizo; híbrido

crossbreed, s. mestizo (-za); híbrido, m.

crossing, s. cruzamiento, m.; (of the sea) travesía, f.; (intersection) cruce, m.; paso, m. **level c.,** paso a nivel, m. **pedestrian c.,** paso para peatones, m. **c.-sweeper,** barrendero, m.

crossly, adv. con mal humor, con displicencia, irritablemente

crossness, s. irritabilidad, f., mal humor, m.

crossroad, s. travesía, f.; cruce, m.; pl. **crossroads,** encrucijada, f.

crosswise, adv. en cruz; a través

crotch, s. (of a tree) bifurcación, f.; (anat.) horcajadura, f.; (of breeches) entrepiernas, f. pl.

crotchet, s. (mus.) semínima, f.; (fad) capricho, m.; extravagancia, excentricidad, f.

crotchety, *a.* caprichoso; raro, excéntrico; difícil

crouch, *v.i.* acurrucarse, agacharse, acuclillarse

croup, *s.* (disease) crup, garrotillo, *m.*; (of a horse) grupa, anca, *f.*

croupier, *s.* crupié, *m.*

crow, *s.* (*orn.*) cuervo, *m.*; (*orn.*) grajo, *m.*; (of a cock) canto del gallo, cacareo, *m.*; (of an infant) gorjeo, *m.* *v.i.* (of a cock) cantar, cacarear; (of an infant) gorjearse. **as the c.·flies,** en línea recta. **to c. over,** gallear, cantar victoria. **crow's-foot,** pata de gallo, *f.* **crow's-nest,** (*naut.*) gavias, *f. pl.*

crowbar, *s.* alzaprima, palanca, *f.*

crowd, *s.* multitud, muchedumbre, *f.*; concurso, *m.*; vulgo, *m.*; (majority) mayoría, *f.*; (*theat.*) acompañamiento, *m.* *v.i.* reunirse, congregarse; agolparse, remolinarse, apiñarse. *v.t.* (fill) llenar; atestar. **in a c.,** en tropel. **So many ideas crowded in on me,** Se me ocurrieron tantas ideas a la vez. **to follow the c.,** seguir la multitud; (*fig.*) ir con la mayoría. **to c. in,** entrar en tropel. **to c. round,** cercar, agruparse alrededor de. **to c. together,** apiñarse. **to c. up,** subir en masa, subir en tropel

crowded, *a.* lleno; atestado, apiñado; (weighed down) agobiado; (of hours, etc.) lleno

crowing, *s.* cacareo, canto del gallo, *m.*; (of an infant) gorjeos, *m. pl.*; (boasting) jactancia, *f.*

crown, *s.* corona, *f.*; (of the head) coronilla, corona, *f.*; (of a hat) copa, *f.*; (*arch.*) coronamiento, *m.* *v.t.* coronar. **c. prince,** (Sp. equiv.) Príncipe de Asturias, *m.*; príncipe heredero, *m.*

crowning, *s.* coronamiento, *m.*; (*arch.*) remate, *m.* *a.* final; supremo

crozier, *s.* See **crosier**

crucial, *a.* decisivo, crítico; difícil

crucible, *s.* crisol, *m.*

crucifix, *s.* crucifijo, *m.*

crucifixion, *s.* crucifixión, *f.*

cruciform, *a.* cruciforme

crucify, *v.t.* crucificar

crude, *a.* crudo; (of colours) chillón, llamativo; (uncivilized) cerril, inculto; (vulgar) cursi; (of truth, etc.) desnudo

crudely, *adv.* crudamente

crudity, *s.* crudeza, *f.*

cruel, *a.* cruel

cruelly, *adv.* cruelmente

cruelty, *s.* crueldad, *f.*

cruet, *s.* ánfora, vinagrera, *f.*; (stand) angarillas, *f. pl.*, convoy, *m.*

cruise, *v.i.* cruzar, navegar; (of cars) correr. *s.* viaje por mar, *m.*

cruiser, *s.* crucero, *m.*

crumb, *s.* miga, *f.*; (spongy part of bread) migaja, *f.* *v.t.* (bread) desmigajar; desmenuzar. **c. brush,** recogemigas, *m.*

crumble, *v.t.* desmigajar, desmenuzar. *v.i.* desmoronarse, desmigajarse; (*fig.*) hundirse, derrumbarse; (*fig.*) desaparecer

crumbling, *s.* (of buildings, etc.) desmoronamiento, *m.*; (*fig.*) destrucción, *f.*

crumple, *v.t.* arrugar, ajar. *v.i.* arrugarse. **to c. up,** *v.t.* (crush) estrujar; (persons) dejar aplastado. *v.i.* (collapse) hundirse, derrumbarse; (of persons) desplomarse; (despair) desalentarse

crunch, *v.t.* mascar; hacer crujir. *v.i.* crujir

crupper, *s.* baticola, *f.*

crusade, *s.* cruzada, *f.*

crusader, *s.* cruzado, *m.*

crush, *v.t.* aplastar; (to powder) moler, triturar; (grapes, etc.) exprimir; (crease) arrugar; (opposition, etc.) vencer; (annihilate) aniquilar, destruir; (abash) humillar, confundir; (hope, etc.) matar; (of sorrow, etc.) agobiar. **We all crushed into his dining-room,** Fuimos en tropel a su comedor. **to c. up,** machacar, moler; (paper, etc.) estrujar

crushing, *a.* (of defeats and replies) aplastante; (of sorrow, etc.) abrumador

crust, *s.* (of bread, pie) corteza, *f.*; (scab) costra, *f.*; (of the earth, snow) capa, *f.* *v.t.* encostrar. *v.i.* encostrarse. **c. of bread,** mendrugo de pan, *m.*

crustacean, *a.* crustáceo. *s.* crustáceo, *m.*

crustily, *adv.* irritablemente, mal-humoradamente

crustiness, *s.* mal humor, *m.*, aspereza, *f.*

crusty, *a.* costroso; (of persons) malhumorado, irritable; áspero

crutch, *s.* muleta, *f.*; (fork) horquilla, *f.*; (crotch) horcaja-dura, *f.*

crux, *s.* problema, *m.*; (knotty point) nudo, *m.*

cry, *v.i.* (weep) llorar; (shout) gritar; (exclaim) exclamar. *v.t.* (one's wares) pregonar. *s.* grito, *m.* **to cry for help,** pedir socorro a voces. **to cry to high heaven,** poner el grito en el cielo. **to cry one's eyes out,** llorar a mares. **to cry down,** desacreditar. **to cry off,** desdecirse; volverse atrás. **to cry out,** *v.t.* gritar. *v.i.* dar gritos; gritar; (*fig.*) clamar. **cry-baby,** niño (-ña) llorón (-ona)

crying, *a.* urgente; notorio. *s.* gritos, *m. pl.*; (weeping) llanto, *m.*, lamentaciones, *f. pl.*; (tears) lágrimas, *f. pl.*

crypt, *s.* cripta, *f.*

cryptic, *a.* secreto, oculto

cryptography, *s.* criptografía, *f.*

crystal, *s.* cristal, *m.* **c. set,** (*rad.*) receptor a galena, *m.*

crystalline, *a.* cristalino

crystallization, *s.* cristalización, *f.*

crystallize, *v.t.* and *v.i.* cris-talizar

crystallography, *s.* cristalo-grafía, *f.*

cub, *s.* cachorro (-rra)

Cuban, *a.* cubano. *s.* cubano (-na)

cubby-hole, *s.* refugio, *m.*; garita, *f.*; cuarto pequeño, *m.*

cube, *s.* cubo, *m.*; (of sugar) terrón, *m. v.t.* cubicar. **c. root,** raíz cúbica, *f.*

cubic, *a.* cúbico

cubicle, *s.* cubículo, *m.*

cubism, *s.* cubismo, *m.*

cubist, *s.* cubista, *m.* and *f.*

cubit, *s.* codo, *m.*

cubital, *a.* codal

cuckold, *s.* cornudo, *m.*

cuckoo, *s.* cuclillo, *m.*; (cry) cucú, *m.* **c.-clock,** reloj de cuclillo, *m.*

cucumber. *s.* cohombro *m.*

cud, *s.* rumia, *f.* **to chew the cud,** rumiar

cuddle, *v.t.* abrazar. *s.* abrazo, *m.* **to c. up together,** estar abrazados

cudgel, *s.* porra, estaca, tranca, *f. v.t.* aporrear, apalear. **to c. one's brains,** devanarse los sesos. **to take up the cudgels for,** salir en defensa de

cue, *s.* (*theat.*) pie, *m.*; (lead) táctica, *f.*; (hint) indicación, *f.*; (of hair) coleta, *f.*; (billiard) taco (de billar), *m.* **to take one's cue from,** tomar como modelo (a); seguir el ejemplo de

cuff, *v.i.* abofetear. *s.* (blow) bofetón, *m.*; (of sleeve) puño, *m.* **c.-links,** gemelos, *m. pl.*

cuirass, *s.* coraza, *f.*

cuirassier, *s.* coracero, *m.*

cuisine, *s.* cocina, *f.*

cul-de-sac, *s.* callejón sin salida, *m.*

culinary, *a.* culinario

cullender, *s.* colador, *m.*

culminate, *v.i.* culminar (en); terminar (en). **culminating point,** punto culminante, *m.*

culmination, *s.* culminación, *f.*; (*fig.*) apogeo, punto culminante, *m.*

culpability, *s.* culpabilidad, *f.*

culpable, *a.* culpable

culpably, *adv.* culpablemente

culprit, *s.* culpado (-da)

cult, *s.* culto, *m.*

cultivable, *a.* cultivable, labra-dero

cultivate, *v.t.* cultivar

cultivated, *a.* cultivado; (of persons) culto, fino

cultivation, *s.* cultivación, *f.*; (of the land) cultivo, *m.*; (of persons, etc.) cultura, *f.*

cultivator, *s.* cultivador (-ra); (machine) cultivador, *m.*

cultural, *a.* cultural

culture, *s.* cultura, *f.*; (bac-teriology) cultivo, *m. v.t.* (bac-teriology) cultivar

cultured, *a.* culto

culverin, *s.* culebrina, *f.*

culvert, *s.* alcantarilla, *f.*

cumbersome, *a.* pesado; incó-modo

cumulative, *a.* cumulativo

cumulus, *s.* cúmulo, *m.*

cuneiform, *a.* cuneiforme

cunning, *a.* astuto, taimado. *s.*
(skill) habilidad, *f.*; astucia, *f.*

cunningly, *adv.* astutamente

cup, *s.* taza, *f.*; (*ecc.* and *bot.*)
cáliz, *m.*; (*sport*) copa, *f.*; (hollow) hoyo, *m.*, hondonada, *f.*
c.-final, (*sport*) final de la copa,
m. c.-tie, (*sport*) partido eliminatorio, *m.*

cupboard, *s.* armario, *m.*; (in the
wall) alacena, *f.* c. love, amor
interesado, *m.*

cupful, *s.* taza, *f.*

cupidity, *s.* avaricia, codicia, *f.*

cupola, *s.* cúpula, *f.*

cupric, *a.* cúprico

cuprous, *a.* cuproso

cur, *s.* perro mestizo, *m.*; canalla,
m.

curable, *a.* curable

curableness, *s.* curabilidad, *f.*

curaçoa, *s.* curasao, *m.*

curare, *s.* curare *m.*

curate, *s.* vicario, *m.* c.-in-
charge, cura, *m.*

curative, *a.* curativo, terapéutico

curator, *s.* (of a museum) director,
m.; (Scots law) curador, *m.*

curb, *s.* (of a bridle) barbada, *f.*;
(*fig.*) freno, *m.*; (stone) bordillo,
m. *v.t.* (a horse) enfrenar; (*fig.*)
refrenar, reprimir; (limit) limitar

curd, *s.* requesón, *m.*; cuajada, *f.*

curdle, *v.i.* coagularse; (of blood)
helarse. *v.t.* coagular; (blood)
helar

cure, *s.* cura, *f.*; (*ecc.*) curato, *m.*
v.t. curar; (salt) salar; (*fig.*)
remediar. to take a c., tomar
una cura. c.-all, panacea, *f.*
c. of souls, cura de almas, *f.*

curer, *s.* (of fish, etc.) salador, *m.*;
(of evils, etc.) remediador, *m.*

curette, *s.* (*surg.*) cureta, *f.*

curfew, *s.* toque de queda, *m.*

curia, *s.* (*ecc.*) curia, *f.*

curing, *s.* curación, *f.*; (salting)
saladura, *f.*

curio, *s.* curiosidad, antigüedad,
f.

curiosity, *s.* curiosidad, *f.*

curious, *a.* (all meanings) curioso

curiously, *adv.* curiosamente

curl, *s.* (of hair) rizo, bucle, *m.*;
(of smoke) penacho, *m.* *v.t.*
rizar. *v.i.* rizarse; (*sport*) jugar
al "curling." in c., rizado.
to c. one's lip, hacer una

mueca de desdén. to c. up, *v t.*
arrollar; (*fig.*) dejar fuera de
combate (a). *v.i.* hacerse un
ovillo, enroscarse; (of leaves)
abarquillarse; (*fig.*) desplomarse;
desanimarse. c.-paper, papillote, *m.*

curlew, *s.* (*orn.*) zarapito, *m.*

curling, *s.* (game) "curling," *m.*
a. rizado. c.-tongs, encrespador,
m.

curly, *a.* rizado, crespo

curmudgeon, *s.* erizo, misántropo, cara de viernes, *m.*

currant, *s.* (dry) pasa de Corinto,
f.; (fresh) grosella, *f.* black c.,
grosella negra, *f.*; (bush) grosellero negro, *m.* c.-bush, grosellero, *m.*

currency, *s.* uso corriente, *m.*;
moneda corriente, *f.*, dinero, *m.*;
dinero en circulación, *m.*; valor
corriente, *m.*; estimación, *f.*

current, *a.* corriente; presente, de
actualidad; (of money) en circulación. *s.* (of water, etc., *fig.*,
elec.) corriente, *f.* alternating
c., (*elec.*) corriente alterna, *f.*
direct c., (*elec.*) corriente continua, *f.* the c. number of a
magazine, el último número de
una revista. c. events, actualidades, *f. pl.*

currently, *adv.* corrientemente,
generalmente

curricle, *s.* carriola, *f.*

curriculum, *s.* plan de estudios,
m.; curso, *m.*

curry, *v.t.* (leather) zurrar; (a
horse) almohazar; (*cul.*) condimentar con "curry." to c.
favour with, insinuarse en el
favor de. c.-comb, almohaza, *f.*

curse, *s.* maldición; blasfemia,
f.; (ruin) azote, castigo, *m.* *v.t.*
maldecir; (afflict) castigar. *v.i.*
blasfemar, echar pestes

cursed, *a.* maldito; abominable,
odioso

cursing, *s.* maldición, *f.*; blas-
femias, *f. pl.*

cursive, *a.* cursivo

cursorily, *adv.* rápidamente; de
prisa; superficialmente

cursory, *a.* rápido; apresurado;
superficial

curt, *a.* seco, brusco; corto

curtail, *v.t.* abreviar; réducir;
disminuir

curtailment, s. abreviación, f.; reducción, f.; disminución, f.

curtain, s. cortina, f.; (theat.) telón, m. v.t. poner cortinas (a) **drop c.,** telón de boca, m. **iron c.,** (pol.) telón de acero, m. **to c. off,** separar por cortinas. **c.-lecture,** reprimenda conyugal, f. **c.-raiser,** entremés. m. **c.-ring,** anilla, f.

curtly, adv. secamente, bruscamente

curtness, s. brusquedad, sequedad, f.

curtsey, s. reverencia, cortesía, f. v.i. hacer una reverencia

curvature, s. curvatura, f.

curve, s. curva, f.; (mech.) codo, m.; (aut., of a road) viraje, m. v.t. encorvar, torcer. v.i. encorvarse, torcerse; (of a road) hacer un viraje.

curved, a. curvo

curvet, s. corveta, cabriola, f., v.i. corvetear, corcovear, cabriolar

curvilinear, a. curvilíneo

cushion, s. almohada, f.; cojín, m.; (billiards) banda, f.; (of fingers, etc.) pulpejo, m. v.t. proveer de almohadas; (a shock) amortiguar; suavizar

custard, s. flan, m., natillas, f. pl.

custodian, s. custodio, m.; guardián, m.; (of a museum, etc.) director, m.

custody, s. custodia, f.; guarda, f.; prisión, f. **in safe c.,** en lugar seguro. **to take (a person) into c.,** arrestar

custom, s. costumbre, f.; uso, m.; (com.) parroquia, clientela, f.; (sales) ventas, f. pl.; pl. **Customs,** aduana, f. **to go through the Customs,** pasar por la aduana. **Customs duty,** derechos de aduana, m. pl. **Customs officer,** aduanero, m. **c.-house,** aduana, f.

customarily, adv. habitualmente, por lo general

customary, a. acostumbrado, usual, habitual

customer, s. cliente, m. and f., parroquiano (-na). **He is a queer c.,** Es un tipo raro

cut, v.t. cortar; (diamonds) tallar; (hay, etc.) segar; (carve) labrar, tallar; (engrave) grabar; (a lecture, etc.) no asistir a; (cards)

destajar, cortar; (fig., wound) herir; (reduce) reducir; abreviar; (teeth) echar; (of lines) cruzar. v.i. cortar; cortar bien; (fam., go) marcharse a prisa y corriendo. **I must get my hair cut,** He de hacerme cortar el pelo. **That cuts both ways,** Es una arma de dos filos. **His opinion cuts no ice,** Su opinión no cuenta. **Mary cut him dead,** María hizo como si no le reconociera. **to cut a caper,** dar saltos; hacer cabriolas. **to cut a person short,** echar el tablacho (a). **to cut and run,** poner los pies en polvorosa. **to cut for deal,** (cards) cortar para ver quien da las cartas. **to cut short,** (a career) terminar. **to cut to the quick,** herir en lo más vivo. **to cut across,** cortar al través; (fields, etc.) atravesar; tomar por un atajo. **to cut away,** v.t. quitar. v.i. (fam.) poner pies en polvorosa. **to cut down,** derribar; (by the sword) acuchillar; (by death, etc.) segar, malograr; (expenses, etc.) reducir; (abbreviate) cortar, abreviar. **to cut off,** cortar, separar; amputar; (on a telephone) cortar la comunicación; (gas, water, etc.) cortar; (supply of food, etc.) interrumpir; (of death) llevarse. **to cut off with a shilling,** desheredar (a). **to cut out,** (dresses, etc.) cortar; (oust) suplantar. **He is not cut out for medicine,** No tiene la disposición para la medicina. **to cut up,** trinchar, cortar en pequeños trozos; (afflict) entristecer, afligir. **to cut up rough,** (fam.) ponerse furioso

cut, a. cortado. **well-cut features,** facciones regulares, f. pl. **cut and dried opinion,** opinión hecha, idea fija, f.; ideas cerradas, f. pl. **cut glass,** cristal tallado, m.

cut, s. corte, m.; (with a whip) latigazo, m.; (with a sword) cuchillada, f.; (with a sharp instrument) tajo, m.; cortadura, f.; (in prices, etc.) reducción, f.; (engraving) grabado, m.; clisé, m.; (of cards) corte, m. **short cut,** atajo, m. **The cut of a coat,** el corte de un abrigo. **to give (someone) the cut direct,** pasar cerca de (una persona) sin saludarle. **cut-out,** s. (paper) recortado, m.; (elec.) cortacircuitos, m. **cut-throat,** s. asesino, m.

cutaneous, a. cutáneo

cute, a. cuco, listo; mono

cuteness, s. cuquería, inteligencia, f.; monería, f.

cuticle, s. cutícula, f.

cutis, s. cutis, m.

cutlass, s. alfanje, m.

cutler, s. cuchillero, m.

cutlery, s. cuchillería, f.

cutlet, s. chuleta, f.

cutter, s. cortador, m.; (naut.) cúter, m.

cutting, s. corte, m.; (of diamonds) talla, f.; (in a mountain, etc.) tajo, m.; (agr.) plantón, m.; (of cloth) retazo, m.; (newspaper) recorte, m. a. cortante; (of remarks) mordaz. **a newspaper c.,** un recorte de periódico. **c. down,** (of trees) tala, f.; reducción, f.

cuttingly, adv. mordazmente, con malicia.

cuttle-fish, s. jibia, f.

cutwater, s. tajamar, m.

cyanide, s. cianuro, m.

cyanosis, s. cianosis, f.

cyclamen, s. ciclamino, m.

cycle, s. ciclo, m.; período, m.; (bicycle) bicicleta, f. v.i. ir en bicicleta

cyclic, a. cíclico

cycling, s. ciclismo, m.

cyclist, s. ciclista, m. and f.

cycloid, s. cicloide, f.

cyclone, s. ciclón, m.

Cyclopean, a. ciclópeo

cyclostyle, s. ciclostilo, m.

cyclotrone, s. ciclotrón, m.

cygnet, s. pollo del cisne, m.

cylinder, s. cilindro, m.; (mech.) tambor, m. **c. head,** culata, f.

cylindrical, a. cilíndrico

cymbal, s. címbalo, platillo, m.

cymbalist, s. cimbalero (-ra)

cynic, s. cínico, m.

cynical, a. cínico

cynically, adv. cínicamente

cynicism, s. cinismo, m.

cynosure, s. (ast.) Osa Menor, f.; blanco, m.

cypress, s. (tree and wood) ciprés, m. **c. grove,** cipresal, m.

Cypriot, a. chipriota. s. chipriota, m. and f.

cyst, s. quiste, m.

cystic, a. cístico

cystitis, s. cistitis, f.

czar, s. zar, m.

czarevitch, s. zarevitz, m.

czarina, s. zarina, f.

Czech, a. checo. s. checo (-ca); (language) checo, m.

Czecho-Slovak, s. checoslovaco (-ca)

Czecho-Slovakian, a. checoslovaco

D

d, s. (letter) de, f.; (mus.) re, m.

dab, v.t. golpear suavemente, tocar; (sponge) esponjar; (moisten) mojar. s. golpecito, golpe blando, m.; (small piece) pedazo pequeño, m.; (blob) borrón, m.; (peck) picotazo, m.; (fam.) experto (-ta). **to dab at one's eyes,** secarse los ojos

dabble, v.t. mojar (en). v.i. chapotear; (engage in) entretenerse en; (meddle in) meterse en; (speculate in) especular en. **to d. in politics,** meterse en política

dabbler, s. aficionado (-da)

dace, s. dardo, albur, m.

dachshund, s. perro pachón, m.

dactyl, s. dáctilo, m.

dactylic, a. dactílico

dactylology, s. dactilología, f.

dactyloscopy, s. dactiloscopia, f.

daddy, s. papaíto, m. **d.-longlegs,** s. típula, f.

dado, s. (arch.) dado, neto, m.; friso, m.

daffodil, s. narciso trompón, m.

daft, a. bobo, tonto, chiflado; loco

dagger, s. daga, f., puñal, m.; (print.) cruz, f. **to be at daggers drawn,** estar a matar. **to look daggers (at),** lanzar miradas de odio (hacia), mirar echando chispas. **d. thrust,** puñalada, f.

daguerreotype, s. daguerrotipo, m.

dahlia, s. dalia, f.

daily, a. diario, de todos los días; cotidiano. adv. diariamente, cada día, todos los días; cotidianamente. s. (paper) diario, m. **d.**

bread, pan cotidiano, pan de cada día, *m*. **d. help,** (person) asistenta, *f*. **d. pay,** jornal, *m*.; (*mil*.) pre, *m*.

daintily, *adv*. delicadamente; elegantemente; con primor

daintiness, *s*. delicadeza, *f*.; elegancia, *f*.; (beauty) primor, *m*.

dainty, *a*. delicado; elegante; primoroso; exquisito; (fastidious) melindroso, difícil. *s*. bocado exquisito, *m*., golosina, *f*.

dairy, *s*. lechería, *f*. **d. cattle,** vacas lecheras, *f*. *pl*. **d.-farm,** granja, *f*. **d.-farmer,** granjero (-ra). **d.-farming,** industria lechera, *f*.

dairymaid, *s*. lechera, *f*.

dairyman, *s*. lechero, *m*.

dais, *s*. estrado, *m*.

daisy, *s*. margarita, *f*.

dale, *s*. valle, *m*.

dalliance, *s*. (delay) tardanza, *f*.; (play) jugueteo, *m*.; diversiones, *f*. *pl*.; (caresses) caricias, *f*. *pl*., abrazos, *m*. *pl*.

dally, *v.i.* tardar, perder el tiempo; entretenerse, divertirse; (make love) holgar (con); (with an idea) entretenerse con, jugar con

Dalmatian, *a*. dalmático, dálmata. *s*. dálmata, *m*. and *f*. **D. dog,** perro dálmata, *m*.

dalmatic, *s*. dalmática, *f*.

daltonism, *s*. daltonismo, *m*.

dam, *s*. (of animals) madre, *f*.; (of a river, etc.) presa, *f*., embalse, *m*.; (mole) dique, *m*.; pared de retención, *f*. *v.t.* represar, embalsar; cerrar; (restrain) contener, reprimir

damage, *s*. daño, perjuicio, *m*.; mal, *m*.; avería, *f*.; pérdida, *f*.; (*fam*., price) precio, *m*.; *pl*. **damages,** (*law*) daños y perjuicios, *m*. *pl*. *v.t.* dañar, perjudicar; estropear; deteriorar; (reputation, etc.) comprometer

damageable, *a*. que puede ser dañado; frágil

damaging, *a*. perjudicial; comprometedor

damascene, *v.t.* damasquinar

damask, *s*. (cloth) damasco, *m*.; (steel) acero damasquino, *m*. *a*. de damasco; damasquino. *v.t.* (metals) damasquinar;

(cloth) adamascar. **d.-like,** adamascado. **d. rose,** rosa de Damasco, *f*.

dame, *s*. dama, señora, *f*.; (*fam*.) madre, *f*.; (schoolmistress) amiga, *f*. **to attend a d. school,** ir a la amiga

damming, *s*. embalse, *m*., represa, *f*.; retención, *f*.; represión, *f*.

damn, *v.t.* condenar al infierno; maldecir; vituperar. **D. it!** ¡Maldito sea!

damnable, *a*. detestable, infame; (*fam*.) horrible

damnably, *adv*. abominablemente; (*fam*.) horriblemente

damnation, *s*. condenación, perdición, *f*.; maldición, *f*.; vituperación, *f*.

damned, *a*. condenado; maldito; detestable, odioso

damning, *a*. que condena; irresistible

damp, *a*. húmedo. *s*. humedad, *f*.; (mist) niebla, *f*.; exhalación, *f*.; (gas) mofeta, *f*.; (*fig*.) tristeza, depresión, *f*. *v.t.* humedecer, mojar; apagar, amortiguar; (depress) deprimir, entristecer; (stifle) ahogar; (lessen) moderar; (trouble) turbar. **d.-proof,** impermeable

damper, *s*. (of a chimney) registro de humos, *m*.; (of a piano) batiente, *m*.; (for stamps) mojador, *m*.; (gloom) depresión, tristeza, *f*.; (restraint) freno, *m*.

dampish, *a*. algo húmedo

dampness, *s*. humedad, *f*.

damsel, *s*. chica, muchacha, *f*.; damisela, *f*.

damson, *s*. ciruela damascena, *f*. **d. tree,** ciruelo damasceno, *m*.

dance, *s*. danza, *f*.; baile, *m*. *v.i.* bailar, danzar; saltar, brincar. *v.t.* bailar; hacer saltar. **to d. attendance on,** servir humildemente; hacer la rueda (a). **to lead someone a d.,** hacer bailar. **d. band,** orquesta, *f*.; orquesta de jazz, *f*. **d. floor,** pista de baile, *f*. **d. hall,** salón de baile, *m*. **d. music,** música bailable, *f*. **d.-number,** (in a theatre) bailable, *m*. **d. of death,** danza de la muerte, *f*.

dancer, s. bailarín (-ina); danzador (-ra), bailadŏr (-ra); *pl.* **dancers,** (partners) parejas de baile; *f. pl.*

dancing, s. baile, *m.,* danza, *f.* **d.-girl,** bailarina, *f.;* (Indian) bayadera, *f.* **d.-master,** maestro de baile, *m.* **d. school,** academia de baile, *f.* **d. slipper,** zapatilla de baile, *f.*

dandelion, s. diente de león, *m.*

dandle, *v.t.* mecer, hacer saltar sobre las rodillas, hacer bailar

dandruff, s. caspa, *f.*

dandy, s. dandi, petimetre, barbilindo, *m.*

dandyism, s. dandismo, *m.*

Dane, s. danés (-esa). **Great D.,** perro danés, *m.*

danger, s. peligro, *m.;* riesgo, *m.* **out of d.,** fuera de peligro. **to be in d.,** correr peligro, peligrar, estar en peligro

dangerous, *a.* peligroso; arriesgado; nocivo

dangerously, *adv.* peligrosamente

dangerousness, s. peligro, *m.*

dangle, *v.i.* colgar, pender. *v.t.* dejar colgar; oscilar; (show) mostrar

Danish, *a.* danés, de Dinamarca. s. (language) danés, *m.*

dank, *a.* húmedo

dankness, s. humedad, *f.*

Dantesque, *a.* dantesco

Danubian, *a.* danubiano

daphne, s. rododafne, *f.*

dapper, *a.* apuesto, aseado; activo, vivaz

dapple, *v.t.* motear, salpicar, manchar. **d.-grey,** *a.* rucio

dappled, *a.* (of horses) rodado, empedrado

dare, *v.i.* atreverse, osar. *v.t.* arriesgar; desafiar, provocar; hacer frente a, arrostrar. s. reto, *m.* **I d. say!** ¡Ya lo creo! ¡No lo dudo! **I d. say that ...,** No me sorprendería que ...; Supongo que ... **d.-devil,** calavera, *m.;* atrevido (-da), valeroso (-sa)

daring, *a.* intrépido, audaz; atrevido; (dangerous) arriesgado, peligroso. s. audacia, osadía, *f.,* atrevimiento, *m.;* peligro, *m.*

daringly, *adv.* atrevidamente

dark, *a.* oscuro; (of complexion, etc.) moreno; negro; lóbrego;

(of colours) oscuro; misterioso; enigmático; secreto, escondido; (sad) funesto, triste; (evil) malo, malévolo; (ignorant) ignorante, supersticioso. s. oscuridad, *f.;* (shade) sombra, *f.;* ignorancia, *f.* **after d.,** *a.* nocturno. *adv.* después del anochecer. **in the d.,** a oscuras; de noche; (*fig.*) ignorante. **to become d.,** oscurecerse; (cloud over) anublarse; (become night) anochecer. **to keep d.,** *v.t.* tener secreto. *v.i.* esconderse. **d. ages,** los siglos de la ignorancia y de la superstición. **d.-eyed,** de ojos negros, ojinegro. **d. horse,** caballo desconocido, *m.;* desconocido, hombre misterioso, *m.* **d. lantern,** linterna sorda, *f.* **d. room,** cuarto oscuro, *m.;* (*phot.*) laboratorio fotográfico, *m.;* (optics) cámara oscura, *f.*

darken, *v.t.* obscurecer; sombrear; (of colour) hacer más oscuro; (sadden) entristecer. *v.i.* obscurecerse; (of the sky) anublarse; (of the face with emotion) inmutarse.

darkening, s. oscurecimiento, *m.*

darkly, *adv.* oscuramente; misteriosamente; con malevolencia; secretamente; (archaic) indistintamente

darkness, s. oscuridad, *f.,* tinieblas, *f. pl.;* sombra, *f.;* (of colour) oscuro, *m.;* (of the complexion) color moreno, *m.;* (of eyes, hair) negrura, *f.;* (night) noche, *f.;* (ignorance) ignorancia, *f.;* (privacy) secreto, *m.* **Prince of d.,** el príncipe de las tinieblas

darling, *a.* querido, amado; (greatest) mayor. s. querido (-da); (favourite) el predilecto, la predilecta, el favorito, la favorita. **My d.!** ¡Amor mío! ¡Vida mía! ¡Pichoncito mío!

darn, *v.t.* zurcir, remendar. s. zurcido, remiendo, *m.*

darner, s. zurcidor (-ra); (implement) huevo de zurcir, *m.*

darning, s. zurcidura, *f.;* zurcido, recosido, *m.* **d.-needle,** aguja de zurcir, *f.* **d. wool,** lana de zurcir, *f.*

dart, s. dardo, *m.;* movimiento rápido, *m.;* avance rápido, *m.;* (sew.) sisa, *f.* *v.i.* lanzarse, abalanzarse (sobre); volar; correr, avanzar rápidamente. *v.t.* lanzar, arrojar; dirigir. **to make darts in,** (*sew.*) sisar

Darwinian, *a.* darviniano. *s.* darvinista, *m.* and *f.*

Darwinism, *s.* darvinismo, *m.*

dash, *s.* (spirit) fogosidad, *f.*, brío, *m.*; energía, *f.*; (impact) choque, golpe, *m.*; (mixture) mezcla, *f.*; (of a liquid) gota, *f.*; (of the pen) rasgo, *m.*; (attack) ataque, *m.*; avance rápido, *m.*; (a little) algo, un poco (de); (*gram.*) raya, *f.*; (show) ostentación, *f.* He made a d. for the door, Se precipitó a la puerta. Corrió hacia la puerta. **to cut a d.,** hacer gran papel. **d.-board,** tablero de instrumentos, *m.*

dash, *v.t.* arrojar con violencia; (break) quebrar, estrellar; (sprinkle) rociar (con), salpicar (con); (mix) mezclar; (knock) golpear; (disappoint) frustrar, destruir; (confound) confundir; (depress) desanimar. *v.i.* (rush) precipitarse; quebrarse, estrellarse; chocar (contra); (of waves) romperse. **to d. to pieces,** hacer añicos, estrellar. **to d. along,** avanzar rápidamente; correr. **to d. away,** *v.i.* marcharse apresuradamente. *v.t.* apartar bruscamente. **to d. down,** *v.i.* bajar aprisa. *v.t.* derribar; (overturn) volcar; (throw) tirar. **to d. off,** *v.i.* marcharse apresuradamente. *v.t.* hacer apresuradamente; (a letter, etc.) escribir de prisa; (sketch) bosquejar rápidamente. **to d. out,** *v.i.* salir precipitadamente; lanzarse a la calle. *v.t.* (erase) borrar; hacer saltar. **to d. through,** atravesar rápidamente; hacer de prisa. **to d. up,** llegar a prisa. (sprout) saltar

dashing, *a.* valiente; (spirited) fogoso, gallardo; majo, brillante. *s.* choque, *m.*; (breaking) quebrantamiento, *m.*; (of the waves) embate, *m.*

dastardly, *a.* cobarde

data, *s. pl.* datos, *m. pl.*

date, *s.* fecha, *f.*; (period) época, *f.*; (term) plazo, *m.*; (duration) duración, *f.*; (appointment) cita,

f.; (*bot.*) dátil, *m.* *v.t.* fechar, datar; poner fecha a; asignar. *v.i.* datar (de), remontar (a). **out of d.,** anticuado; pasado de moda; (of persons) atrasado de noticias.. **to be up to d.,** ser nuevo; ser de última moda; (of persons) estar al día. **to bring up to d.,** renovar; (of persons) poner al corriente. **to fix the d.,** señalar el día; (chronologically) ajustar los tiempos. **to d.,** hasta la fecha. **under d. (of),** con fecha (de). **up to d.,** hasta hoy, hasta ahora. **What is the d.?** ¿Qué fecha es? ¿A cómo estamos hoy? ¿A cuántos estamos hoy? **d. palm,** datilera, *f.*

dative, *a.* and *s.* dativo (*m.*)

daub, *v.t.* embadurnar; manchar, ensuciar; untar; (paint) pintorrear. *s.* embadurnamiento, *m.*; (picture) aleluya, *f.*

dauber, *s.* pintamonas, *m.* and *f.*, pintor (-ra) de brocha gorda

daughter, *s.* hija, *f.* **adopted d.,** hija adoptiva, *f.* **little d.,** hijuela, *f.* **d.-in-law,** nuera, *f.*

daughterly, *a.* de hija

daunt, *v.t.* intimidar, acobardar; dar miedo (a), espantar; (dishearten) desanimar

dauntless, *a.* impávido, intrépido

dauntlessness, *s.* impavidez, intrepidez, *f.*

dauphin, *s.* delfín, *m.*

dauphiness, *s.* delfina, *f.*

Davidic, *a.* davídico

dawdle, *v.i.* perder el tiempo; haraganear, gandulear

dawdler, *s.* gandul (-la)

dawdling, *a.* perezoso, lento

dawn, *s.* alba, madrugada, primera luz, *f.*; (*fig.*) aurora, *f.* *v.i.* amanecer, alborear, romper el día; (appear) mostrarse, asomar. **at d.,** a primera luz, al amanecer, de madrugada, al alba. **It had not dawned on me,** No me había ocurrido

day, *s.* día, *m.*; luz del día, *f.*; (day's work) jornada, *f.*; (battle) batalla, *f.*; (victory) victoria, *f.*; *pl.* days, (time) tiempos, *m. pl.*, época, *f.*; (life) vida, *f.*; (years) años, *m. pl.* *a.* diario. **all day long,** durante todo el día. **any day,** cualquier día. **by day,** de día. **by the day,** al día.. **every**

day, todos los días, cada día. **every other day,** un día sí y otro no, cada dos días. **from this day forward,** desde hoy en adelante. **from day to day,** de día en día. **Good day!** ¡Buenos días! **in these days,** en estos días. **in olden days,** en la antigüedad; (*fam.*) en tiempos de Maricastaña. **in the days of,** en los tiempos de; durante los años de; durante la vida de. **next day,** el día siguiente. **on the next day,** al día siguiente, al otro día. **one of these days,** un día de éstos. **some fine day,** el mejor día, de un día a otro. **the day after to-morrow,** pasado mañana. **the day before yesterday,** anteayer. **the day before,** la víspera. **this day week,** de hoy en ocho días; (*past*) hace ocho días. **to win the day,** ganar el día, salir victorioso. **day after day,** cada día, día tras día. **day by day,** día por día. **day in, day out,** sin cesar, día tras día. **day-book,** (*com.*) libro diario, *m.* **day's holiday,** día de asueto, *m.*; día libre, *m.* **day labourer,** jornalero, *m.* **day nursery,** guardería de niños, *f.* **day-pupil,** alumno (-na) externo (-na). **day-school,** externado, *m.* **day shift,** turno de día, *m.* **day-star,** lucero del alba, *m.* **day ticket,** billete de excursión, *m.*

daybreak, *s.* alba, *f.*, amanecer, *m.* **at d.,** al romper el día, al amanecer

daydream, *s.* ensueño, *m.*; ilusión, *f.*; fantasía, visión, *f.* *v.i.* soñar despierto; hacerse ilusiones

daydreamer, *s.* soñador (-ra); visionario (-ia)

daylight, *s.* luz del día, *f.*, día, *m.*; (contrasted with artificial light) luz natural, *f.* **in broad d.,** en plena luz del día. **It's d. robbery!** ¡Es un desuello! **d.-saving,** hora de verano, *f.*

daytime, *s.* día, *m.* **in the d.,** durante el día

daze, *v.t.* aturdir, confundir; (dazzle) deslumbrar. *s.* aturdimiento, *m.*, confusión, *f.*; perplejidad, *f.*

dazzle, *v.t.* (camouflage) dis-frazar; deslumbrar, ofuscar. *s.* deslumbramiento, *m.*; brillo, *m.* refulgencia, *f.*

dazzling, *a.* deslumbrador; brillante

deacon, *s.* diácono, *m.*

deaconess, *s.* diaconisa, *f.*

deaconship, *s.* diaconato, *m.*

dead, *a.* and *past part.* muerto; inanimado; (withered) marchito; (deep) profundo; (unconscious) inerte; inmóvil; insensible; (numb) entumecido; (complete) absoluto, completo; (sure) certero, excelente; (useless) inútil; (of colour and human character) apagado; sin espíritu; inactivo; (of eyes) mortecino; (of sound) sordo, opaco; (of villages, etc.) desierto, despoblado; (quiet) silencioso; (empty) vacío; (monotonous) monótono; (of fire) apagado; (with weight, language) muerto; (*elec.*) interrumpido; (*law*) muerto civilmente. *adv.* completamente, enteramente; del todo; directamente; exactamente; profundamente. **the d.,** los muertos. **in the d. of night,** en las altas horas de la noche. **to be d.,** estar muerto; haber muerto. **to be d. against,** estar completamente opuesto a. **to drop d.,** caer muerto; morir de repente. **to go d. slow,** ir muy lentamente. **to rise from the d.,** resucitar. **to sham d.,** hacer la mortecina, fingirse muerto. **to speak ill of the d.,** hablar mal de los muertos; (*fam.*) desenterrar los muertos. **d. ball,** pelota fuera de juego, *f.* **d.-beat,** muerto de cansancio. **d. body,** cadáver, cuerpo muerto, *m.* **d. calm,** calma profunda, *f.*; (*naut.*) calma chicha, *f.* **d. certainty,** seguridad completa, *f.* **d.-drunk,** hecho una uva. **d. end,** callejón sin salida, *m.* **d. heat,** empate, *m.* **d. language,** lengua muerta, *f.* **d.-letter,** letra muerta, *f.*; carta devuelta o no reclamada, *f.* **d.-lock,** punto muerto, *m.* **to reach a d.-lock,** llegar a un punto muerto. **d. march,** marcha fúnebre, *f.* **d. season,** temporada de calma, *f.* **d. set,** empeñado (en). **d. shot,** (person) tirador (-ra) cer-

tero (-ra) (shot) tiro certero, *m.*
d. silence, silencio profundo, *m.*
d. stop, parada en seco, *f.* **d.
tired**, rendido. **d. weight**, peso
muerto, *m.* **d. wood**, leña seca,
f.; material inútil, *m.*
deaden, *v.t.* amortiguar; (of
pain) calmar; (remove) quitar;
(of colours) apagar
deadening, *s.* amortiguamiento,
m.
deadliness, *s.* carácter mortal, *m.;*
implacabilidad, *f.*
deadly, *a.* mortal; implacable;
(*fam.*) insoportable. *adv.* mortalmente. **He was d. pale**, Él
estaba pálido como un muerto.
the seven d. sins, los siete
pecados mortales. **d. nightshade**, belladona, *f.*
deadness, *s.* falta de vida, *f.;*
inercia, *f.;* marchitez, *f.;* (numbness) entumecimiento, *m.;*
desanimación, *f.;* parálisis, *f.*
deaf, *a.* sordo. **d. people**, los
sordos. **to be d.**, ser sordo;
padecer sordera. **to be as d. as
a post**, ser más sordo que una
tapia. **to become d.**, ensordecer, volverse sordo. **to fall
on d. ears**, caer en saco roto.
to turn a d. ear, hacerse el
sordo. **d. aid**, audífono, *m.*
d.-and-dumb, sordomudo. **d.-
and-dumb alphabet**, alfabeto
manual, abecedario manual, *m.*
d.-mute, sordomudo (-da). **d.-
mutism**, sordomudez, *f.*
deafen, *v.t.* asordar, ensordecer
deafening, *a.* ensordecedor
deafly, *adv.* sordamente
deafness, *s.* sordera, *f.*
deal, *s.* (transaction) negocio,
trato, *m.;* (at cards) reparto, *m.;*
(wood) pino, *m.;* (plank) tablón
de pino, *m.* **a d., a great d.**,
mucho. **a very great d.**, muchísimo. **to conclude a d.**, cerrar
un trato
deal, *v.t.* repartir; (a blow)
asestar, dar; (cards) dar; (justice) dispensar. **to d. a blow
at**, asestar un golpe; (*fig.*) herir
(en); (*fig.*) destruir de un golpe.
to d. in, comerciar en, traficar
en; ocuparse en; meterse en.
to d. out, dispensar. **to d.
with**, (buy from) comprar de;
tener relaciones con, tratar;

entenderse con; portarse con;
(of affairs) ocuparse en, arreglar,
dirigir; (contend) luchar con;
(discuss) discutir, tratar de; (of
books) versar sobre
dealer, *s.* traficante, *m.* and *f.,*
mercader, *m.;* (at cards) el que
da las cartas
dealing, *s.* conducta, *f.;* proceder,
m.; trato, *m.;* tráfico, *m.;* *pl.*
dealings, relaciones, *f. pl.;*
transacciones, *f. pl.*
dean, *s.* (*ecc.*) deán, *m.;* (*univ.*)
decano, *m.*
deanery, *s.* deanato, deanazgo, *m.*
dear, *a.* (beloved) querido, amado; (charming) encantador,
simpático; (in letters) estimado,
querido; (favourite) predilecto;
(expensive) caro. *s.* querido
(-da); persona querida, *f.,* bien
amado (-da). *adv.* caro. **Oh d.!**
¡Dios mío! ¡Ay!
dearly, *adv.* tiernamente, entra-
ñablemente; caro
dearness, *s.* cariño, afecto, *m.,*
ternura, *f.;* (of price) precio alto, *m.*
dearth, *s.* carestía, *f.;* (of news,
etc.) escasez, *f.*
death, *s.* muerte, *f.;* (*law* and in
announcements) fallecimiento,
m., defunción, *f.* **to be at
death's door**, estar a la muerte.
to put to d., ajusticiar. **to
the d.**, a muerte. **untimely d.**,
muerte repentina, *f.;* malogro,
m. **death's head**, calavera, *f.*
d. certificate, partida de defunción, *f.* **d.-duties**, derechos
de herencia, *m. pl.* **d.-like**,
cadavérico. **d.-mask**, mascarilla, *f.* **d. penalty**, pena de
muerte, *f.* **d.-rate**, mortalidad,
f. **d.-rattle**, sarrillo, *m.* **d.-
trap**, lugar peligroso, *m.;* (*fig.*)
trampa, *f.* **d.-warrant**, sentencia de muerte, *f.* **d.-watch
beetle**, reloj de la muerte, *m.*
deathbed, *s.* lecho mortuorio,
lecho de muerte, *m.* **on one's
d.**, en su lecho de muerte
deathblow, *s.* golpe mortal, *m.*
deathless, *a.* inmortal, eterno
deathly, *a.* mortal
débâcle, *s.* (*fig.*) ruina, *f.*
debar, *v.t.* excluir, privar
debase, *v.t.* degradar, humillar,
envilecer; (the coinage) alterar
(la moneda)

debasement, *s.* degradación, humillación, *f.*, envilecimiento, *m.*; (of the coinage) alteración (de la moneda), *f.*

debasing, *a.* degradante, humillante

debatable, *a.* discutible

debate, *s.* debate, *m.*; discusión, *f.*; disputa, *f.* *v.t.* and *v.i.* debatir; discutir; disputar; considerar

debater, *s.* discutidor (-ra); orador (-ra).

debating, *s.* discusión, *f.*; argumentación, *f.*

debauch, *v.t.* corromper, pervertir; (a woman) seducir, violar; *s.* libertinaje, *m.*; borrachera, *f.*

debauched, *a.* vicioso, licencioso

debauchee, *s.* libertino, vicioso, *m.*

debauchery, *s.* libertinaje, mal vivir, *m.*, viciosidad, licencia, *f.*

debenture, *s.* obligación, *f.* **d. holder,** obligacionista, *m.* and *f.*

debilitate, *v.t.* debilitar

debilitating, *a.* debilitante

debilitation, *s.* debilitación, *f.*

debility, *s.* debilidad, *f.*

debit, *s.* débito, cargo, *m.*; saldo deudor, *m.*; "debe" de una cuenta, *m.* *v.t.* adeudar. **d. and credit,** el cargo y la data. **d. balance,** saldo deudor, *m.*

debonair, *a.* gallardo, gentil, donairoso; alegre

debonairly, *adv.* gallardamente; alegremente

debouch, *v.i.* desembocar

débris, *s.* escombros, desechos, *m. pl.*; ruinas, *f. pl.*; (geol.) despojos, *m. pl.*

debt, *s.* deuda, *f.* **a bad d.,** una deuda incobrable. **to be in the d. of,** ser en cargo a; deber dinero a; (*fig.*) sentirse bajo una obligación. **to get into d.,** adeudarse, contraer deudas

debtor, *s.* deudor (-ra); (com.) debe, *m.*

debunk, *v.t.* demoler

début, *s.* debut, *m.*; (of a play, etc.) estreno, *m.* **to make one's d.,** debutar

débutante, *s.* debutante, *f.*

decade, *s.* década, *f.*, decenio, *m.*; (of the rosary) decena, *f.*

decadence, *s.* decadencia, *f.*

decadent, *a.* decadente

decagon, *s.* decágono, *m.*

decagramme, *s.* decagramo, *m.*

decahedron, *s.* decaedro, *m.*

decalitre, *s.* decalitro, *m.*

decalogue, *s.* decálogo, *m.*

decametre, *s.* decámetro, *m.*

decamp, *v.i.* (*mil.*) decampar; escaparse, fugarse

decant, *v.t.* decantar

decantation, *s.* decantación, *f.*

decanter, *s.* garrafa, *f.*

decapitate, *v.t.* decapitar, descabezar

decapitation, *s.* decapitación, *f.*

decarbonization, *s.* descarburación, *f.*

decarbonize, *v.t.* descarbonizar

decay, *v.i.* (rot) pudrirse; degenerar; marchitarse; (of teeth) cariarse; (crumble) desmoronarse, caer en ruinas; decaer, declinar; (come down in the world) venir a menos, arruinarse. *s.* pudrición, putrefacción, *f.*; (of teeth) caries, *f.*; (withering) marchitez, *f.*; degeneración, *f.*; desmoronamiento, *m.*; ruina, *f.*; (oldness) vejez, *f.*; decadencia, declinación, *f.*; (fall) caída, *f.*

decease, *s.* fallecimiento, *m.*, defunción, *f.* *v.i.* fallecer

deceased, *s.* finado (-da), difunto (-ta). *a.* difunto

deceit, *s.* engaño, fraude, *m.*; duplicidad, *f.*

deceitful, *a.* engañoso, falso; embustero, mentiroso; ilusorio

deceitfully, *adv.* engañosamente

deceitfulness, *s.* falsedad, duplicidad, *f.*

deceivable, *a.* fácil a engañar, engañadizo

deceive, *v.t.* engañar; (disappoint) decepcionar, desilusionar; frustrar. **If my memory does not d. me,** Si la memoria no me engaña, Si mal no me acuerdo

deceiver, *s.* engañador (-ra); seductor, *m.*

deceiving, *a.* engañador

December, *s.* diciembre, *m.*

decemvirate, *s.* decenvirato, *m.*

decency, *s.* decoro, *m.*, decencia, *f.*; pudor, *m.*, modestia, *f.*; conveniencias, *f. pl.*; (*fam.*) bondad, *f.*; (manners) cortesía, *f.*, buenos modales, *m. pl.*

decennial, *a.* decenal

decent, *a.* decente; decoroso, honesto; púdico; (likable) simpático; (of things) bastante bueno; (honourable) honrado

decently, *adv.* decentemente

decentralization, *s.* descentralización, *f.*

decentralize, *v.t.* descentralizar

deception, *s.* engaño, *m.*; ilusión, *f.*

deceptive, *a.* engañoso, mentiroso, ilusorio

deceptively, *adv.* engañosamente

decide, *v.t.* decidir; (law) determinar. *v.i.* decidir, resolver; acordar, quedar en; juzgar; (law) dictar sentencia, fallar

decided, *a.* decidido; (downright) categórico, inequívoco; resuelto; positivo; definitivo

decidedly, *adv.* decididamente; categóricamente; definitivamente

deciduous, *a.* (bot.) caedizo

decigramme, *s.* decigramo, *m.*

decimal, *a.* decimal. **d. fraction,** fracción decimal, *f.* **d. point,** punto decimal, *m.* **d. system,** sistema métrico, *m.*

decimate, *v.t.* diezmar

decimation, *s.* gran mortandad, *f.*; matanza, *f.*

decimetre, *s.* decímetro, *m.*

decipher, *v.t.* descifrar; deletrear

decipherable, *a.* descifrable

decipherer, *s.* descifrador, *m.*

decipherment, *s.* el descifrar; deletreo, *m.*

decision, *s.* decisión, determinación, *f.*; (law) sentencia, *f.*, fallo, *m.*; (agreement) acuerdo, *m.*; (of character) firmeza, resolución, *f.*

decisive, *a.* decisivo; terminante, conclusivo; crítico

decisively, *adv.* decisivamente

decisiveness, *s.* carácter decisivo, *m.*; firmeza, resolución, *f.*; decisión, *f.*

deck, *s.* cubierta, *f.*; (of cards) baraja (de naipes), *f.* *v.t.* adornar, ataviar; decorar. **between decks,** entrecubiertas, *f. pl.* **lower d.,** cubierta, *f.* **promenade d.,** cubierta de paseo, *f.* **upper d.,** cubierta superior, *f.* **d.-cabin,** camarote

de cubierta, *m.* **d.-chair,** silla de tijera, *f.* **d.-hand,** marinero, estibador, *m.*

decked, *a.* ornado, ataviado; engalanado; (naut.) de . . . puentes

declaim, *v.t.* recitar. *v.i.* perorar, declamar

declamation, *s.* declamación, *f.*

declamatory, *a.* declamatorio

declaration, *s.* declaración, *f.*; manifiesto, *m.*; proclamación, *f.*

declaratory, *a.* declaratorio, declarativo

declare, *v.t.* declarar; proclamar; afirmar; manifestar; confesar. *v.i.* declarar; (law) deponer, testificar. **to d. war,** declarar la guerra

declaredly, *adv.* declaradamente, explícitamente, abiertamente

declension, *s.* declinación, *f.*

declination, *s.* declinación, *f.*

decline, *s.* declinación, decadencia, *f.*; disminución, *f.*; debilitación, *f.*; (of the day) caída, *f.*; (of stocks, shares) depresión, *f.*; (illness) consunción, *f.*; (fig., setting) ocaso, *m.* *v.i.* declinar; inclinarse; decaer; disminuir; debilitarse; (refuse) negarse (a). *v.t.* (refuse) rechazar, rehusar; (gram.) declinar; (avoid) evitar

declining, *a.* declinante. **in one's d. years,** en sus últimos años

declivity, *s.* cuesta, pendiente, *f.*, declive, *m.*

declutch, *v.i.* desembragar

decoction, *s.* decocción, *f.*

decode, *v.t.* descifrar

decoder, *s.* descifrador, *m.*

décolletée, *a.* escotado

decolouration, *s.* decoloración, *f.*

decompose, *v.t.* descomponer. *v.i.* descomponerse

decomposition, *s.* descomposición, *f.*

decompressor, *s.* decompresor, *m.*

decontaminate, *v.t.* descontaminar

decontamination, *s.* descontaminación, *f.*

decontrol, *v.t.* suprimir las restricciones sobre

decorate, *v.t.* adornar (con), embellecer; (by painting, etc.) decorar, pintar; (honour) investir (con), condecorar

decoration, *s.* decoración, *f.*; (*theat.*) decorado, *m.*; (honour) condecoración, *f.*; ornamento, *m.*

decorative, *a.* decorativo

decorator, *s.* decorador, *m.*; (interior) adornista, *m.*

decorous, *a.* decoroso, decente; correcto

decorously, *adv.* decorosamente; correctamente

decorticate, *v.t.* descortezar

decorum, *s.* decoro, *m.*; corrección, *f.*

decoy, *s.* señuelo, *m.*; añagaza, *f.*; (trap) lazo, *m.*, trampa, *f.*; (*fig.*) añagaza, *f.;* *v.t.* (birds) reclamar, atraer con señuelo; (*fig.*) tentar (con), seducir (con). **d. bird,** pájaro de reclamo, *m.*

decrease, *s.* disminución, *f.*; baja, *f.*; reducción, *f.*; (of the moon, waters) mengua, *f.* *v.i.* decrecer, disminuir; bajar; menguar. *v.t.* disminuir; reducir

decreasingly, *adv.* de menos en menos

decree, *s.* decreto, *m.*; edicto, *m.* *v.i.* and *v.t.* decretar, mandar

decrepit, *a.* decrépito

decrepitate, *v.t.* and *v.i.* decrepitar

decrepitation, *s.* decrepitación, *f.*

decrepitude, *s.* decrepitud, *f.*

decry, *v.t.* desacreditar, rebajar

decussate, *a.* decuso

dedicate, *v.t.* dedicar; consagrar; destinar; aplicar; (a book, etc.) dedicar. **to d. oneself to,** dedicarse a, consagrarse a, entregarse a

dedication, *s.* dedicación, *f.*; consagración, *f.*; (of a book, etc.) dedicatoria, *f.*

dedicatory, *a.* dedicatorio

deduce, *v.t.* derivar; deducir, inferir

deduct, *v.t.* deducir; descontar

deduction, *s.* deducción, *f.*; descuento, *m.*

deductive, *a.* deductivo

deed, *s.* acción, *f.*; hecho, acto, *m.*; hazaña, *f.*; (reality) realidad, *f.*; (*law*) escritura, *f.*; (*law*) contrato, *m.* **d. of gift,** escritura de donación, *f.*

deem, *v.t.* juzgar, creer, estimar

deep, *a.* profundo; (wide) ancho; (low) bajo; (thick) espeso; (of colours) subido; (of sounds) grave, profundo; (immersed (in)) absorto (en); (of the mind) penetrante; (secret) secreto; (intense) intenso, hondo; (cunning) astuto, artero; (dark) oscuro; (of mourning) riguroso. *s.* (*poet.*) piélago, mar, *m.*; profundidad, *f.*; abismo, *m.* *adv.* profundamente; a una gran profundidad. **to be in d. waters,** (*fig.*) estar con el agua al cuello. **to be three feet d.,** tener tres pies de profundidad. **to be d. in,** estar absorto en; (of debt) estar cargado de. **three d.,** tres de fondo. **d. into the night,** hasta las altas horas de la noche. **d.-felt,** hondamente sentido. **d.-mourning,** luto riguroso, *m.* **d.-rooted,** arraigado. **d.-sea fishing,** pesca mayor, *f.* **d.-sea lead,** escandallo, *m.* **d.-seated,** íntimo, profundo; arraigado. **d.-set,** hundido

deepen, *v.t.* profundizar, ahondar; (broaden) ensanchar; (intensify) intensificar; (increase) aumentar; (of colours) aumentar el tono de, intensificar. *v.i.* hacerse más profundo, hacerse más hondo; intensificarse; aumentarse; (of sound) hacerse más grave

deeply, *adv.* profundamente; intensamente; fuertemente

deepness, *s.* (cunning) astucia, *f.*; see **depth**

deer, *s.* ciervo (-va), venado, *m.* *a.* cervuno. **d.-hound,** galgo de cazar venados, *m.* **d.-skin,** piel de venado, *f.* **d.-stalking,** caza del ciervo, *f.*

deface, *v.t.* desfigurar, mutilar; estropear; (erase) borrar

defacement, *s.* desfiguración, mutilación, *f.*; afeamiento, *m.*; borradura, *f.*

defalcation, *s.* desfalco, *m.*

defamation, *s.* difamación, denigración, *f.*

defamatory, *a.* difamatorio, denigrante

defame, *v.t.* difamar, denigrar, calumniar

default, *s.* omisión, *f.*, descuido, *m.*; falta, *f.*; ausencia, *f.*; (*law*) rebeldía, *f.* *v.i.* dejar de cumplir; faltar; no pagar. *v.t.* (*law*) condenar en rebeldía. **in d. of,** en la ausencia de

defaulter, s. el, m. (f. la) que no cumple sus obligaciones; delincuente, m. and f.; desfalcador (-ra); (law) rebelde, m. and f.

defeat, v.t. vencer, derrotar; frustrar; (reject) rechazar; (elude) evitar; (fig.) vencer, triunfar sobre. s. derrota, f.; vencimiento, m.; frustración, f.; rechazamiento, m. **to d. one's own ends,** defraudar sus intenciones

defeatism, s. derrotismo, m.

defeatist, s. derrotista, m. and f.

defecate; v.t. defecar

defecation, s. defecación, f.

defect, s. defecto, m.; imperfección, f.; falta, f.

defection, s. defección, f.; deserción, f.; (from a religion) apostasía, f.

defective, a. defectuoso; (gram.) defectivo; falto; imperfecto; (mentally) anormal. s. persona anormal, f., anormal, m.

defectiveness, s. imperfección, f.; deficiencia, f.; defecto, m.

defence, s. defensa (also law), f.; justificación, f.; pl. **defences,** defensas, f. pl.; obras de fortificación, f. pl. **for the d.,** (of witnesses) de descargo; (of counsel) para la defensa. **in d. of,** en defensa de. **in one's own d.,** en su propia defensa. **d. in depth,** (mil.) defensa en fondo, f.

defenceless, a. indefenso, sin defensa

defencelessness, s. incapacidad de defenderse, f.; debilidad, f., desvalimiento, m.

defend, v.t. defender; proteger; preservar; sostener

defendant, s. (law) acusado (-da), procesado (-da), demandado (-da)

defender, s. defensor (-ra)

defensible, a. defendible; justificable

defensive, a. defensivo. s. defensiva, f. **to be on the d.,** estar a la defensiva

defensively, adv. defensivamente

defer, v.t. (postpone) diferir, aplazar; suspender. v.i. (yield) deferir, ceder; (delay) tardar,

aguardar. **deferred payment,** pago a plazos, m.

deference, s. deferencia, f., respeto, m.; consideración, f.

deferential, a. deferente, respetuoso

deferment, s. aplazamiento, m.; suspensión, f.

defiance, s. desafío, m.; provocación, f.; oposición, f.; insolencia, f. **in d. of,** en contra de

defiant, a. provocativo; insolente

defiantly, adv. de un aire provocativo; insolentemente

deficiency, s. falta, deficiencia, f.; imperfección, f.; defecto, m.; omisión, f.; (scarcity) carestía, f.; (in accounts) déficit, m.

deficient, a. deficiente; falto, incompleto; imperfecto; pobre; defectuoso; (not clever at) débil (en); (mentally) anormal. **to be d. in,** carecer de; ser pobre en

deficit, s. déficit, m.; descubierto, m.

defile, s. desfiladero, m. v.t. contaminar; profanar; manchar; deshonrar. v.i. (mil.) desfilar

defilement, s. contaminación, f.; corrupción, f.; profanación, f.

definable, a. definible

define, v.t. definir; (throw into relief) destacar; fijar; (law) determinar

definite, a. definido; positivo; categórico; exacto; concreto. **d. article,** artículo definido, m.

definitely, adv. positivamente; claramente

definiteness, s. carácter definido, m.; exactitud, f.; lo categórico

definition, s. definición, f.

definitive, a. definitivo

deflagration, s. deflagración, f.

deflagrator, s. deflagrador, m.

deflate, v.t. desinflar. v.i. desinflarse, deshincharse

deflation, s. desinflación, f.

deflect, v.t. desviar; apartar. v.i. desviarse; apartarse

deflection, s. desviación, f.; apartamiento, m.

defloration, s. desfloración, f.

deflower, v.t. desflorar

deform, v.t. deformar, desfigurar; afear

deformation, s. deformación, f.

deformed, a. deformado; contrahecho

deformity, s. deformidad, f.
defraud, v.t. defraudar
defrauder, s. defraudador (-ra)
defrauding, s. defraudación, f.
defray, v.t. sufragar, costear, pagar
defrayal, s. pago, m.
defrost, v.t. deshelar
deft, a. diestro; hábil
deftly, adv. con destreza; hábil-mente
deftness, s. destreza, f.; habilidad, f.
defunct, a. and s. difunto (-ta)
defy, v.t. desafiar; (face) arros-trar; (violate) contravenir
De Gaullist, a. degaullista
degeneracy, s. degeneración, f.; depravación, degradación, f.
degenerate, a. and s. degenerado (-da). v.i. degenerar
degeneration, s. degeneración, f.
deglutition, s. deglución, f.
degradation, s. degradación, f.; abyección, f.
degrade, v.t. degradar; envilecer, deshonrar
degrading, a. degradante
degree, s. grado, m.; punto, m.; clase social, f. **by degrees,** poco a poco, gradualmente. **five degrees below zero,** cinco grados bajo cero. **in the highest d.,** en sumo grado, en grado superlativo. **to a certain d.,** hasta cierto punto. **to receive a d.,** graduarse
dehiscence, s. dehiscencia, f.
dehydrate, v.t. deshidratar
dehydration, s. deshidratación, f.
dehydrator, s. deshidrator, m.
de-ice, v.t. deshelar
deicide, s. (act) deicidio, m.; (person) deicida, m. and f.
deification, s. deificación, f.
deify, v.t. deificar; endiosar
deign, v.i. dignarse. v.t. con-ceder
deism, s. deísmo, m.
deist, s. deísta, m. and f.
deistic, a. deísta
deity, s. deidad, divinidad, f.; dios, m.
dejected, a. abatido, desanimado, deprimido
dejectedly, adv. tristemente, abatidamente
dejection, s. abatimiento, de-saliento, m., melancolía, f.

delay, s. retraso, m., dilación tardanza, demora, f. v.t. re-trasar, demorar; (a person) entretener; (postpone) aplazar; (obstruct) impedir. v.i. tardar; entretenerse. **without more d.,** sin más tardar
delectable, a. deleitoso, delicioso
delectably, adv. deliciosamente
delectation, s. delectación, f., deleite, m.
delegacy, s. delegación, f.
delegate, s. delegado (-da). v.t. delegar, diputar
delegation, s. delegación, f.
delete, v.t. suprimir, borrar
deleterious, a. deletéreo
deletion, s. supresión, borradura, f.
deliberate, a. premeditado, in-tencionado; (slow) pausado, lento. v.i. and v.t. deliberar, discurrir, considerar
deliberately, adv. (intentionally) con premeditación, a sabiendas; (slowly) pausadamente, lenta-mente
deliberation, s. reflexión, deli-beración, consideración, f.; (slowness) lentitud, pausa, f.
deliberative, a. deliberativo, de liberante
delicacy, s. delicadeza, f.; fragili-dad, f.; suavidad, f.; sensibili-dad, f.; escrupulosidad, f.; (of health) debilidad, delicadez, f.; (difficulty) dificultad, f.; (food) manjar exquisito, m., golosina, f.
delicate, a. delicado; fino; frágil; suave; exquisito; delicado (de salud); (of situations) difícil
delicious, a. delicioso
deliciously, adv. deliciosamente
deliciousness, s. deleite, m., lo delicioso; excelencia, f.; delicias, f. pl.
delict, s. delito, m.
delictive, a. delictivo
delight, s. deleite, regocijo, m.; encanto, m., delicia, f.; pla cer, gozo, m. v.t. deleitar, encantar; halagar. v.i. deleitarse, com-placerse. **to be delighted with,** estar encantado con. **to d. in,** deleitarse en, complacerse en; tomar placer en
delightful, a. delicioso, precioso, encantador
delightfully, adv. deliciosamente

delimit, *v.t.* delimitar

delimitation, *s.* delimitación, *f.*

delineate, *v.t.* delinear, diseñar;
(*fig.*) pintar, describir

delineation, *s.* delineación, *f.*;
retrato, *m.*; (*fig.*) descripción, *f.*

delineator, *s.* diseñador, *m.*

delinquency, *s.* delincuencia, *f.*;
criminalidad, *f.*; culpa, *f.*; delito,
m.

delinquent, *a.* delincuente. *s.*
delincuente, *m.* and *f.*

deliquescence, *s.* delicuescencia,
f.

deliquescent, *a.* delicuescente

delirious, *a.* delirante; des-
variado; (*fam.*) loco. **to be d.,**
delirar, desvariar

delirium, *s.* delirio, desvario, *m.*
d. tremens, delirium tremens,
m.

deliver, *v.t.* librar (de); salvar
(de); (distribute) repartir; (hand
over) entregar; (recite) recitar,
decir; (a speech) pronunciar;
comunicar; (send) despachar,
expedir; (a blow) asestar; (give
dar; (bring) traer; (battle, a lecture) dar; (a woman, of a doctor)
asistir en el parto (a); (a child)
traer al mundo; (a judgment)
pronunciar. **to be delivered (of
a child),** dar a luz. **to d. oneself up,** entregarse. **delivered
free,** porte pagado.

deliverance, *s.* libramiento, rescate, *m.*; redención, salvación,
f.; (of a judgment) pronuncia,
f.

deliverer, *s.* libertador (-ra);
salvador (-ra); (distributor) repartidor (-ra); entregador (-ra)

delivery, *s.* (distribution) reparto,
m., distribución, *f.*; entrega, *f.*;
(*law*) cesión, *f.*; (of a judgment)
pronuncia, *f.*; (of a speech)
pronunciación, *f.*; (manner of
speaking) declamación, *f.*; dicción, *f.*; (of a child) parto, *m.*
on d., al entregarse. **The
letter came by the first d.,** La
carta llegó en el primer reparto.
d. man, mozo de reparto, *m.*
d. note, nota de entrega, *f.* **d.
van,** camión de reparto, *m.*

dell, *s.* hondonada, *f.*; pequeño
valle, *m.*

delouse, *v.t.* despiojar, espulgar

Delphic, *a.* délfico

Delphinium, *s.* espuela de ca
ballero, *f.*

delta, *s.* (Greek letter) delta, *f.*;
(of a river) delta, *m.*

delude, *v.t.* engañar; ilusionar.
to d. oneself, engañarse

deluded, *a.* iluso, engañado,
ciego

deluge, *s.* diluvio, *m.* *v.t.* diluviar; inundar (con)

delusion, *s.* engaño, *m.*, ceguedad,
f.; error, *m.*; ilusión, *f.*

delve, *v.t.* and *v.i.* cavar; (*fig.*)
ahondar (en), penetrar (en), investigar

demagogic, *a.* demagógico

demagogue, *s.* demagogo (-ga)

demagogy, *s.* demagogia, *f.*

demand, *s.* exigencia, *f.*; (*com.*)
demanda, *f.*; petición, *f.*; (*pol.
econ.*) consumo, *m.* *v.t.* exigir;
requerir; pedir; (claim) reclamar.
in d., en demanda. **on d.,** al
solicitarse. **to be in d.,** ser
popular. **d. note,** apremio, *m.*

demanding, *a.* exigente

demarcate, *v.t.* demarcar

demarcation, *s.* demarcación, *f.*

demean (oneself), *v.r.* degra-
darse, rebajarse

demeanour, *s.* conducta, *f.*;
continente, porte, aire, *m.*;
(manners) modales, *m. pl.*

demented, *a.* demente, loco

demerit, *s.* demérito, *m.*

demesne, *s.* dominio, *m.*, heredad,
f., tierras, *f. pl.*

demi, *prefix* semi; casi. **d.-
tasse,** taza cafetera, jícara, *f.*

demigod, *s.* semidiós, *m.*

demigoddess, *s.* semidiosa, *f.*

demijohn, *s.* damajuana, *f.*

demilitarize, *v.t.* desmilitarizar

demise, *s.* (*law*) traslación de
dominio, *f.*; sucesión de la
corona, *f.*; (death) óbito, fallecimiento, *m.*

demisemiquaver, *s.* fusa, *f.*

demobilization, *s.* desmovilización, *f.*

demobilize, *v.t.* desmovilizar

democracy, *s.* democracia, *f.*

democrat, *s.* demócrata, *m.* and
f.

democratic, *a.* democrático. **to
make d.,** democratizar

demolish, *v.t.* demoler, derribar;
(*fig.*) destruir; (eat) engullir,
devorar

demolisher, s. demoledor, m.; (fig.) destructor (-ra)

demolition, s. demolición, f.; derribo, m. a. demoledor; de demolición. **d. squad,** pelotón de demolición, m.

demon, s. demonio, diablo, m.

demonetization, s. desmonetización, f.

demonetize, v.t. desmonetizar

demoniacal, a. demoníaco

demonology, s. demonología, f.

demonstrable, a. demostrable

demonstrably, adv. demostrablemente

demonstrate, v.t. demostrar; mostrar, probar. v.i. hacer una demostración

demonstration, s. demostración, f.; manifestación, f.

demonstrative, a. demostrativo; (of persons) expresivo, mimoso. **d. pronoun,** pronombre demostrativo, m.

demonstrator, s. demostrador (-ra)

demoralization, s. desmoralización, f.

demoralize, v.t. desmoralizar

demoralizing, a. desmoralizador

demulcent, a. and s. demulcente (m.)

demur, v.i. dudar, vacilar; objetar, protestar; poner dificultades. s. objeción, prótesta, f.

demure, a. serio, modoso recatado; púdico; de una coquetería disimulada

demurely, adv. modestamente; con recato; con coquetería disimulada

demureness, s. seriedad, f., recato, m.; modestia fingida, coquetería disimulada, f.

demurrage, s. demora, f.; (naut.) sobrestadía, f.

demy, s. papel marquilla, m.; becario de Magdalen College, Oxford, m.

den, s. madriguera, guarida, f.; (of thieves) cueva, f.; (in a zoo) cercado, recinto, m.; (study) gabinete, m.; (squalid room) cuartucho, m.

denary, a. denario

denaturalization, s. desnaturalización, f.

denaturalize, v.t. desnaturalizar

denial, s. negación, f.; rechazo,

m.; contradicción, f.; negativa, f.

denizen, s. habitante, m.; ciudadano (-na)

denominate, v.t. denominar, nombrar

denomination, s. denominación, f.; secta, f.; clase, f.

denominational, a. sectario

denominator, s. (math.) denominador, m.

denote, v.t. denotar, indicar; significar

dénouement, s. desenlace, desenredo, m.; solución, f.

denounce, v.t. denunciar; delatar, acusar

denouncer, s. denunciante, m. and f., delator (-ra)

dense, a. denso; espeso, compacto; tupido; impenetrable; (fam.) estúpido

densely, adv. densamente; espesamente. **d. populated,** con gran densidad de población

density, s. densidad, f.; espesor, m.; consistencia, f.; (fam.) estupidez, f.

dent, s. mella, f.; (in metal) abolladura, f. v.t. mellar; abollar

dental, a. dental. s. letra dental, f. **d. forceps,** gatillo, m. **d. mechanic,** mecánico dentista, m. **d. surgeon,** odontólogo, m.

dentifrice, s. dentífrico, m.

dentist, s. dentista, m. and f.; odontólogo, m.

dentistry, s. odontología, f.

dentition, s. dentición, f.

denture, s. dentadura, f.

denudation, s. denudación, f.

denude, v.t. denudar, despojar, privar (de)

denunciation, s. denuncia, f.; acusación, delación, f.

denunciatory, a. denunciatorio

deny, v.t. negar; desmentir; rehusar; rechazar; renegar (de); (give up) renunciar, sacrificar. **to d. oneself,** privarse (de); sacrificar; negarse

deodorant, a. and s. desodorante (m.)

deodorize, v.t. desinfectar, destruir el olor de

depart, v.i. marcharse, irse, partir; (of trains, etc., and meaning go out) salir; (deviate) desviarse (de), apartarse (de); (go away) alejarse; (leave) dejar; (disappear) desaparecer; (alter) cambiar; (die) morir

departed, *a.* (past) pasado; desaparecido; (dead) difunto, muerto. *s.* difunto (-ta)

department, *s.* departamento, *m.*; sección, *f.*; (of learning) ramo, *m.*; (in France) distrito administrativo, *m.* **d. store,** almacén, *m.*

departmental, *a.* departamental

departure, *s.* partida, ida, *f.*; (going out, and of trains, etc.) salida, *f.*; (deviation) desviación, *f.*; (disappearance) desaparición, *f.*; (change) cambio, *m.*; (giving up) renuncia, *f.*; (death) muerte, *f.* **to take one's d.,** marcharse

depend, *v.i.* depender. **to d. on,** depender de; (rest on) apoyarse en; (count on) contar con; (trust) fiarse de; tener confianza en, estar seguro de. **That depends!** ¡Eso depende!

dependable, *a.* digno de confianza; seguro

dependence, dependency, *s.* dependencia, *f.*; subordinación, *f.*; (trust) confianza, *f.*

dependent, *a.* dependiente; subordinado; condicional. *s.* dependiente, *m.* **to be d. on,** depender de

depict, *v.t.* representar; pintar; dibujar; (fig.) describir, retratar

depiction, *s.* representación, *f.*; pintura, *f.*; dibujo, *m.*; (fig.) descripción, *f.*

depilate, *v.t.* depilar

depilation, *s.* depilación, *f.*

depilatory, *a.* and *s.* depilatorio (*m.*)

deplete, *v.t.* agotar; disipar

depletion, *s.* agotamiento, *m.*

deplorable, *a.* lamentable, deplorable

deplorably, *adv.* lamentablemente

deplore, *v.t.* deplorar, lamentar

deploy, *v.t.* desplegar. *v.i.* desplegarse. *s.* despliegue, *m.*

deployment, *s.* despliegue, *m.*

deponent, *s.* (law) declarante, deponente, *m.* and *f.* *a.* deponente. **d. verb,** verbo deponente, *m.*

depopulate, *v.t.* despoblar

depopulation, *s.* despoblación, *f.*

deport, *v.t.* deportar

deportation, *s.* deportación, *f.*

deportment, *s.* comportamiento, *m.*; porte, aire, *m.*; conducta, *f.*

depose, *v.t.* destronar; (give evidence) testificar, declarar.

deposit, *s.* depósito, *m.*; (geol.) yacimiento, filón, *m.*; sedimento, *m.* *v.t.* depositar. **to leave a d.,** dejar un depósito. **d. account,** cuenta corriente, *f.*

deposition, *s.* deposición, *f.*; (law) testimonio, *m.*, declaración, *f.*; (from the Cross) descendimiento, *m.* (de la Cruz)

depositor, *s.* depositador (-ra)

depository, *s.* depositaría, *f.*, almacén, *m.*; (of knowledge, etc.) pozo, *m.*

depôt, *s.* almacén, *m.*; (military headquarters) depósito, *m.*; (for army vehicles, etc.) parque, *m.*; (for buses, etc.) estación, *f.*

depravation, *s.* depravación, *f.*

depraved, *a.* depravado, perverso, vicioso

depravity, *s.* corrupción, maldad, perversión, *f.*

deprecate, *v.t.* desaprobar, criticar; lamentar, deplorar

deprecatingly, *adv.* con desaprobación, críticamente

deprecation, *s.* deprecación, *f.*; desaprobación, crítica, *f.*

deprecatory, *a.* deprecativo; de desaprobación, de crítica

depreciate, *v.t.* depreciar, rebajar; (fig.) tener en poco, menospreciar. *v.i.* depreciarse, deteriorarse; bajar de precio

depreciatingly, *adv.* con desprecio

depreciation, *s.* depreciación, *f.*; (fig.) desprecio, *m.*

depreciatory, *a.* (fig.) despectivo, despreciativo

depredation, *s.* depredación, *f.*

depress, *v.t.* deprimir; (weaken) debilitar; (humble) humillar; (dispirit) abatir, entristecer; (trade) desanimar, paralizar

depressed, *a.* deprimido, desalentado, melancólico, triste; (of an area) necesitado

depressing, *a.* melancólico, triste; pesimista

depressingly, *adv.* con tristeza; con pesimismo

depression, *s.* depresión, *f.*; (hollow) hoyo, *m.*; (sadness) desaliento, abatimiento, *m.*, melancolía, *f.*; (in prices) baja, *f.*; (in trade) desanimación, parálisis, *f.*; (*ast.*) depresión, *f.*

deprivation, *s.* privación, *f.*; pérdida, *f.*

deprive, *v.t.* privar (de); despojar (de); defraudar (de); (*ecc.*) destituir (de)

depth, *s.* profundidad, *f.*; (thickness) espesor, *m.*; fondo, *m.*; (of night, winter, the country) medio, *m.*; (of sound) gravedad, *f.*; (of colour, feeling) intensidad, *f.*; (abstruseness) dificultad, *f.*; (sagacity) sagacidad, *f.*; *pl.* **depths,** profundidades, *f. pl.*; abismo, *m.*; lo más hondo; lo más íntimo. **to be 4 ft. in d.,** tener cuatro pies de profundidad. **to the depths of one's being,** hasta lo más íntimo de su ser; hasta los tuétanos. **d. charge,** carga de profundidad, *f.*

depuration, *s.* depuración, *f.*

deputation, *s.* deputación, delegación, *f.*

depute, *v.t.* diputar; delegar

deputize (for), *v.i.* desempeñar las funciones de, substituir

deputy, *s.* (substitute) lugarteniente, *m.*; (agent) representante, *m.*; apoderado, *m.*; (parliamentary) diputado, *m.*; (in compounds) sub, vice. **d.-governor,** subgobernador, *m.* **d.-head,** subjefe, *m.*; (of a school) subdirector (-ra)

derail, *v.t.* (hacer) descarrilar

derailment, *s.* descarrilamiento, *m.*

derange, *v.t.* desordenar; desorganizar; turbar; (mentally) trastornar, hacer perder el juicio (a)

derangement, *s.* desorden, *m.*; turbación, *f.*; (mental) trastorno, *m.*, locura, *f.*

Derby, *s.* carrera del Derby, *f.*; (hat) sombrero hongo, *m.*

derelict, *a.* abandonado, derrelicto. *s.* derrelicto, *m.*

dereliction, *s.* abandono, *m.*; omisión, negligencia, *f.*; descuido, *m.*

deride, *v.t.* burlarse de, mofarse de; ridiculizar

derision, *s.* irrisión, *f.*, menosprecio, *m.*

derisive, *a.* irrisorio; irónico

derisively, *adv.* irrisoriamente; con ironía, irónicamente

derivation, *s.* derivación, *f.*

derivative, *a.* derivativo. *s.* derivado, *m.*

derive, *v.t.* derivar; obtener; extraer; (*fig.*) sacar, hallar. *v.i.* (from) derivar de; proceder de; remontar a

dermatitis, *s.* dermatitis, *f.*

dermatologist, *s.* dermatólogo, *m.*

dermatology, *s.* dermatología, *f.*

derogatory, *a.* despectivo, despreciativo; deshonroso

derrick, *s.* grúa, machina, *f.*; abanico, *m.*

dervish, *s.* derviche, *m.*

descant, *s.* (*mus.*) discante, *m.* *v.i.* (*mus.*) discantar; discurrir (sobre), disertar (sobre)

descend, *v.i.* descender, bajar; (be inherited) pasar a; (fall) caer; (of the sun) ponerse. *v.t.* bajar. **to d. from,** descender de. **to d. to,** (lower oneself) rebajarse; (consider) venir a, considerar. **to d. upon,** caer sobre; (arrive unexpectedly) llegar inesperadamente, invadir

descendant, *s.* descendiente, *m.* and *f.*; *pl.* **descendants,** descendencia, *f.*

descent, *s.* descenso, *m.*; bajada, *f.*; (slope) pendiente, cuesta, *f.*; (attack) invasión, *f.*, ataque, *m.*; (lineage) descendencia, alcurnia, procedencia, *f.*; (inheritance) herencia, *f.*; transmisión, *f.* **D. from the Cross,** Descendimiento de la Cruz, *m.*

describable, *a.* descriptible

describe, *v.t.* describir; pintar

description, *s.* descripción, *f.*

descriptive, *a.* descriptivo

descry, *v.t.* divisar, descubrir; (*poet.*) ver

desecrate, *v.t.* profanar

desecration, *s.* profanación, *f.*

desert, *v.t.* abandonar; dejar; (*mil.,* etc.) desertar. *v.i.* desertar. *a.* solitario; inhabitado; desierto; (*fig.*) árido. *s.* desierto, *m.*; soledad, *f.*; (merit) mérito, *m.* **to receive one's deserts,** llevar su merecido

deserted, *a.* abandonado; desierto; solitario; inhabitado. despoblado

deserter, *s.* desertor, *m.*

desertion, *s.* abandono, *m.*, deserción, *f.*; (*mil.*, etc.) deserción, *f.*

deserve, *v.t.* and *v.i.* merecer

deservedly, *adv.* merecidamente

deserving, *a.* merecedor; meritorio. **to be d. of,** merecer

desiccate, *v.t.* desecar. *v.i.* desecarse

desiccation, *s.* desecación, *f.*

design, *s.* proyecto, *m.*; plan, *m.*; intención, *f.*, propósito, *m.*; objeto, *m.*; modelo, *m.*; (pattern) diseño, dibujo, *m.*; arte del dibujo, *m.* or *f.* *v.t.* idear; proyectar; (destine) destinar; dedicar; diseñar, dibujar, delinear; planear. **by d.,** expresamente, intencionalmente

designate, *v.t.* señalar; designar; (appoint) nombrar. *a.* electo

designation, *s.* designación, *f.*; nombramiento, *m.*

designedly, *adv.* de propósito

designer, *s.* inventor (-ra), autor (-ra); delineador (-ra); dibujante, *m.* and *f.*; (of public works, etc.) proyectista, *m.* and *f.*

designing, *a.* intrigante, astuto

desirability, *s.* lo deseable; conveniencia, *f.*; ventaja, *f.*

desirable, *a.* deseable; conveniente; ventajoso; agradable; apetecible

desire, *v.t.* desear; querer; ansiar, ambicionar; (request) rogar, pedir; (order) mandar. *s.* deseo, *m.*; ansia, aspiración, *f.*; ambición, *f.*; impulso, *m.*; (will) voluntad, *f.* **to d. ardently,** perecerse por; suspirar por

desirous, *a.* deseoso (de); ambicioso (de); ansioso (de); impaciente (a); curioso (de)

desist, *v.i.* desistir; dejar (de)

desk, *s.* pupitre, *m.*; escritorio, buró, *m.*; mesa de trabajo, *f.*; (cashier's) caja, *f.*; (teacher's, lecturer's; pulpit) cátedra, *f.*

desolate, *a.* solitario; desierto; deshabitado; abandonado; arruinado; árido; (afflicted) desolado, angustiado. *v.t.* desolar; despoblar

desolation, *s.* desolación, *f.*; aflicción, angustia, *f.*, desconsuelo, *m.*

despair, *s.* desesperación, *f.* *v.i.* perder toda esperanza. **His life is despaired of,** Se ha perdido la esperanza de salvarle (la vida). **to be in d.,** estar desesperado

despairing, *a.* desesperado

despairingly, *adv.* sin esperanza

desperate, *a.* desesperado; sin esperanza; irremediable; furioso; violento; (dangerous) arriesgado, peligroso; terrible

desperately, *adv.* desesperadamente; furiosamente; terriblemente

desperation, *s.* desesperación, *f.*; furia, violencia, *f.*

despicable, *a.* vil, despreciable; insignificante

despise, *v.t.* despreciar; desdeñar

despiser, *s.* menospreciador (-ra)

despite, *prep.* a pesar de

despoil, *v.t.* despojar, desnudar

despoiler, *s.* despojador (-ra)

despoliation, *s.* despojo, *m.*

despondency, *s.* abatimiento, desaliento, *m.*, desesperación, *f.*

despondent, *a.* abatido, desanimado, deprimido

despondently, *adv.* con desaliento

despot, *s.* déspota, *m.*

despotic, *a.* despótico

despotically, *adv.* despóticamente

despotism, *s.* despotismo, *m.*

dessert, *s.* postre, *m.* *a.* de postre. **d. plate,** plato para postre, *m.* **d.-spoon,** cuchara de postre, *f.*

destination, *s.* destinación, *f.*

destine, *v.t.* destinar; dedicar; predestinar

destiny, *s.* destino, *m.*

destitute, *a.* indigente, menesteroso; desnudo (de); privado (de); desprovisto (de), falto (de); desamparado

destitution, *s.* destitución, indigencia, miseria, *f.*; privación, falta, *f.*; desamparo, *m.*

destroy, *v.t.* destruir; demoler; deshacer; (kill) matar; exterminar; (finish) acabar con

destroyer, *s.* destructor (-ra); (*nav.*) destructor, cazatorpedero, *m.*

destructible, *a.* destructible, destruible

destruction, *s.* destrucción, *f.*; demolición, *f.*; ruina, *f.*; pérdida, *f.*; muerte, *f.*; exterminio, *m.*; perdición, *f.*

destructive, *a.* destructivo, destructor; (of animals) dañino. **d. animal,** animal dañino, *m.*, alimaña, *f.*

destructiveness, *s.* destructividad, *f.*; instinto destructor, *m.*

desultory, *a.* inconexo; sin método, descosido; irregular

detach, *v.t.* separar, desprender; (unstick) despegar; (mil.) destacar

detachable, *a.* separable, de quita y pon

detached, *a.* suelto, separado; (fig., with outlook, etc.) imparcial; indiferente, despegado. **d. house,** hotelito, *m.*

detachment, *s.* separación, *f.*; (mil.) destacamento, *m.*; (fig., of mind) imparcialidad, *f.*; independencia (de espíritu, etc.), *f.*; indiferencia, *f.*

detail, *s.* detalle, *m.*; pormenor, *m.*, particularidad, *f.*; circunstancia, *f.*; (mil.) destacamento, *m. v.t.* detallar; particularizar, referir con pormenores; (mil.) destacar. **in d.,** detalladamente; al por menor; (fam.) ce por be. **to go into details,** entrar en detalles

detain, *v.t.* detener; (arrest) arrestar, prender; (withhold) retener; (prevent) impedir

detect, *v.t.* descubrir; averiguar; (discern) discernir, percibir; (elec.) detectar

detectable, *a.* perceptible

detection, *s.* descubrimiento, *m.*; averiguación, *f.*; percepción, *f.*

detective, *s.* detective, *m. a.* de detectives, policíaco. **d. novel,** novela policíaca, *f.*

detector, *s.* descubridor, *m.*; (elec.) detector, *m.*; (mech.) indicador, *m.*

detention, *s.* detención, *f.*; (arrest) arresto, *m.*; (confinement) encierro, *m.*

deter, *v.t.* desanimar, desalentar; acobardar; (dissuade) disuadir; (prevent) impedir

detergent, *a.* detersorio. *s.* detersorio, *m.*

deteriorate, *v.t.* deteriorar. *v.i.* deteriorarse; empeorar

deterioration, *s.* deterioración, *f.*; empeoramiento, *m.*

determinable, *a.* determinable

determination, *s.* determinación, *f.*; definición, *f.*; resolución, decisión, *f.*; (law) fallo, *m.*; (med.) congestión, *f.*

determine, *v.t.* determinar; definir; decidir, resolver; concluir; (fix) señalar; (law) sentenciar. *v.i.* resolverse, decidirse; (insist (on)) empeñarse en, insistir en

determined, *a.* determinado; resuelto, decidido; (of price) fijo

determining, *a.* determinante

determinism, *s.* determinismo, *m.*

determinist, *s.* determinista, *m.* and *f.*

deterministic, *a.* determinista

deterrent, *a.* disuasivo. *s.* freno, *m.* **to act as a d.,** servir como un freno

detest, *v.t.* detestar, abominar, aborrecer

detestable, *a.* detestable, aborrecible, abominable

detestation, *s.* detestación, abominación, *f.*, aborrecimiento, *m.*

dethrone, *v.t.* destronar

dethronement, *s.* destronamiento, *m.*

detonate, *v.t.* hacer detonar. *v.i.* detonar, estallar

detonation, *s.* detonación, *f.*

detonator, *s.* detonador, *m.*; señal detonante, *f.*

detour, *s.* rodeo, *m.*; desvío, *m.*

detract, *v.t.* quitar; (diminish) disminuir; (slander) detraer, denigrar

detraction, *s.* detracción, denigración, *f.*

detractor, *s.* detractor (-ra); infamador (-ra)

detriment, *s.* detrimento, *m.*; perjuicio, *m.*; daño, *m.*

detrimental, *a.* perjudicial

detruncation, *s.* destroncamiento, *m.*

deuce, *s.* (dice, cards) dos, *m.*; (tennis) "deuce," *m.* **The d.!** ¡Diantre! **to be the d. of a row,** haber moros y cristianos. **D. take it!** ¡Demonios!

Deuteronomy, *s.* Deuteronomio, *m.*

devaluation, *s.* desvalorización, *f.*

devalue, *v.t.* rebajar el valor de

devastate, *v.t.* devastar, asolar

devastation, *s.* devastación, *f.*

develop, *v.t.* desarrollar; (make progress) avanzar, fomentar; perfeccionar; (*phot.*) revelar. *v.i.* desarrollarse; crecer; avanzar, progresar; evolucionar

developer, *s.* (*phot.*) revelador, *m.*

development, *s.* desarrollo, *m.*; evolución, *f.*; progreso, avance, *m.*; (encouragement) fomento, *m.*; (event) acontecimiento, suceso, *m.*; (product) producto, *m.*; (working) explotación, *f.*; (*phot.*) revelación, *f.*

deviate, *v.i.* desviarse (de); (disagree) disentir (de)

deviation, *s.* desviación, *f.*

device, *s.* (contrivance) aparato, artefacto, mecanismo, *m.*; (invention) invento, *m.*; (trick) expediente, artificio, *m.*; (scheme) proyecto, *m.*; (design) dibujo, emblema, *m.*; (motto) divisa, leyenda, *f.*; *pl.* devices, placeres, caprichos, *m. pl.*

devil, *s.* diablo, Satanás, *m.*; demonio, *m.*; (printer's) aprendiz de impresor, *m.* **Go to the d.!** ¡Vete enhoramala! **He is a poor d.,** Es un pobre diablo. **little d.,** diablillo, *m.* **The devil's abroad,** Anda el diablo suelto. **The d. take it!** ¡Lléveselo el diablo! **to play the d. with,** arruinar por completo. **What the d.!** ¡Qué diablos! **d.-possessed,** endemoniado

devilish, *a.* diabólico, demoníaco; infernal

devilment, *s.* diablura, *f.*

devilry, *s.* diablura, *f.*; magia, *f.*; demonología, *f.*; (wickedness) maldad, *f.*; crueldad, *f.*

devious, *a.* desviado; tortuoso

deviousness, *s.* tortuosidad, *f.*

devise, *v.t.* idear, inventar; fabricar; (*law*) legar

deviser, *s.* inventor (-ra)

devitalize, *v.t.* restar vitalidad, privar de vitalidad

devoid, *a.* desprovisto (de), privado (de); libre (de), exento (de)

devolve, *v.t.* traspasar, transmitir. *v.i.* (on, upon) incumbir (a), corresponder (a), tocar (a)

devote, *v.t.* dedicar; consagrar. **to d. oneself to,** darse a, dedicarse a; consagrarse a

devoted, *a.* fervoroso, apasionado; (faithful) fiel, leal

devotedly, *adv.* con devoción

devotee, *s.* devoto (-ta), admirador (-ra); aficionado (-da)

devotion, *s.* devoción, *f.*; dedicación, *f.*; (zeal) celo, *m.*; afición, *f.*; (loyalty) lealtad, *f.*; *pl.* **devotions,** rezos, *m. pl.*, oraciones, *f. pl.*

devotional, *a.* devoto, religioso

devour, *v.t.* devorar; consumir

devourer, *s.* devorador (-ra)

devouring, *a.* devorador; absorbente

devout, *a.* devoto, piadoso

devoutly, *adv.* piadosamente

devoutness, *s.* piedad, devoción, *f.*

dew, *s.* rocío, sereno, relente, *m.*; (*fig.*) rocío, *m.* *v.t.* rociar; humedecer; (refresh) refrescar. **d.-drop,** aljófar, *m.*, gota de rocío, *f.*

dewlap, *s.* papada, *f.*, papo, *m.*

dewy, *a.* rociado, lleno de rocío; húmedo; (of eyes) lustroso

dexter, *a.* diestro

dexterity, *s.* destreza, *f.*

dextrine, *s.* dextrina, *f.*

dextrose, *s.* dextrosa, glucosa, *f.*

dextrous, *a.* diestro; hábil, listo

diabetes, *s.* diabetes, *f.*

diabetic, *a.* diabético

diabolical, *a.* diabólico

diabolo, *s.* diávolo, *m.*

diaconate, *s.* diaconato, *m.*

diacoustics, *s.* diacústica, *f.*

diadem, *s.* diadema, *f.*

diæresis, *s.* diéresis, crema, *f.*

diagnose, *v.t.* diagnosticar

diagnosis, *s.* diagnóstico, *m.*, diagnosis, *f.*

diagnostician, *s.* diagnóstico, *m.*

diagonal, *s.* diagonal, *f.*

diagonally, *adv.* diagonalmente

diagram, *s.* diagrama, *m.*; esquema, *f.*; gráfico, *m.*

diagrammatic, *a.* esquemático

dial, *s.* (sundial) reloj de sol, *m.*; (of clocks, gas-meter) esfera, *f.*; (of machines) indicador, *m.*; (of a wireless set) cuadrante graduado, *m.*; (of a telephone) marcador, disco, *m. v.t.* (a telephone number) marcar. **d. telephone,** teléfono automático, *m.*

dialect, *s.* dialecto, *m.,* habla, *f.* *a.* dialectal

dialectic, *a.* dialéctico

dialectics, *s.* dialéctica, *f.*

dialogue, *s.* diálogo, *m.* **to hold a d.,** dialogar

dialysis, *s.* diálisis, *f.*

diamantine, *a.* diamantino

diameter, *s.* diámetro, *m.*

diametrical, *a.* diametral

diametrically, *adv.* diametral-mente

diamond, *s.* diamante, *m.*; bri-llante, *m.*; (tool) cortavidrios, *m.*; (cards) oros (de baraja), *m. pl.* **rough d.,** diamante bruto, *m.* (also *fig.*). **d.-bearing,** dia-mantífero. **d. cutter,** diaman-tista, *m.* and *f.* **d. cutting,** talla de diamantes, *f.* **d. edition,** edición diamante, *f.* **d.-like,** adiamantado. **d. wedding,** bodas de diamante, *f. pl.*

diapason, *s.* diapasón, *m.*

diaper, *s.* lienzo adamascado, *m.*; (baby's) pañal, *m.*; servilleta higiénica, *f.*

diaphanous, *a.* diáfano, trans-parente

diaphragm, *s.* diafragma, *m.*

diapositive, *s.* diapositiva, *f.*

diarist, *s.* diarista, *m.* and *f.*

diarrhœa, *s.* diarrea, *f.*

diary, *s.* diario, *m.*

diastase, *s.* diastasa, *f.*

diastole, *s.* diástole, *f.*

diathermia, *s.* diatermia, *f.*

diatonic, *a.* diatónico

diatribe, *s.* diatriba, denuncia-ción violenta, *f.*

dibble, *s.* plantador, *m.* *v.t.* and *v.i.* plantar con plantador

dice, *s. pl.* dados, *m. pl.* **to load the d.,** cargar los dados

dicky, *s.* (front) pechera postiza, *f.*; (seat) trasera, *f.*; (apron) delantal, *m.* **d. seat,** (*fam.*) ahí te pudras, *m.*

dicotyledonous, *a.* dicotiledóneo

dictaphone, *s.* dictáfono, *m.*

dictate, *v.t.* dictar; mandar. *s.* (order) dictamen, *m.*; (*fig.*) dic-tado, *m.*

dictation, *s.* dictado, *m.* **to write from d.,** escribir al dictado

dictator, *s.* dictador, *m.*

dictatorial, *a.* dictatorial, dicta-torio, imperioso

dictatorship, *s.* dictadura, *f.*

diction, *s.* dicción, *f.*

dictionary, *s.* diccionario, *m.*; léxico, *m.*

dictum, *s.* dictamen, *m.*; (saying) sentencia, *f.*; (*law*) fallo, *m.*

didactic, *a.* didáctico

die, *v.i.* morir; fallecer, finar; (wither) marchitarse; (disappear) desvanecerse, desaparecer; (of light) palidecer; extinguirse; (end) cesar; (desire) ansiar, pere-cerse (por). **Never say die!** ¡Mientras hay vida, hay espe-ranza! **to die early,** morir tem-prano; malograrse. **to a die a violent death,** tener una muerte violenta, (*fam.*) morir vestido. **to die from natural causes,** morir por causas naturales; (*fam.*) morir en la cama. **to die hard,** luchar contra la muerte; tardar en morir; tardar en desaparecer. **to die of a broken heart,** morir con el corazón destrozado, morir de pena. **to die away,** desaparecer gradualmente; ex-tinguirse poco a poco; dejar de oírse poco a poco; cesar; pasar. **to die down,** extinguirse gra-dualmente; palidecer; dejar de oírse; desaparecer; (of the wind) amainar; perder su fuerza. **to die out,** desaparecer; olvidarse; dejar de existir; pasarse de moda

die, *s.* dado, *m.*; (*fig.*) suerte, *f.*; (stamp) cuño, troquel, *m.*; (*arch.*) cubo, *m.* **The die is cast,** La suerte está echada. **die-sinker,** grabador en hueco, *m.*

diehard, *s.* valiente, *m.*; tradi-cionalista empedernido, *m.*; partidario (-ia) entusiasta

Diesel, *a.* Diesel. **D. engine,** motor Diesel, *m.*

diet, *s.* dieta, *f.*, régimen dietario, *m.*; (assembly) dieta, *f.* *v.i.* estar a dieta

dietetic, *a.* dietético

dietetics, *s.* dietética, *f.*

dietician, *s.* dietista, *m.* and *f.*

differ, *v.i.* diferenciarse; (contra-dict) contradecir; (disagree) no estar de acuerdo; disentir

difference, *s.* diferencia (also *math.*), *f.*; disparidad, *f.*; con-traste, *m.*; (of opinion) disensión, *f.*; controversia, disputa, *f.* **to make no d.,** no hacer diferencia alguna; no afectar; dar lo mismo, no importar

different, *a.* distinto; diferente; vario, diverso

differential, *a.* diferencial. **d. calculus,** cálculo diferencial, *m.*

differentiate, *v.t.* diferenciar; distinguir. *v.i.* diferenciarse, distinguirse

differentiation, *s.* diferenciación, *f.*

differently, *adv.* diferentemente

difficult, *a.* difícil. **to make d.,** dificultar

difficulty, *s.* dificultad, *f.* **d. in breathing,** opresión de pecho, *f.*

diffidence, *s.* modestia, timidez, *f.*; huraña, *f.*; falta de confianza en sí mismo, *f.*

diffident, *a.* modesto, tímido; huraño; sin confianza en sí mismo

diffidently, *adv.* tímidamente; vergonzosamente

diffract, *v.t.* difractar

diffraction, *s.* difracción, *f.*

diffractive, *a.* difrangente

diffuse, *v.t.* difundir. *a.* difuso; (long-winded) prolijo

diffuseness, *s.* difusión, *f.*; prolijidad, *f.*

diffusion, *s.* difusión, *f.*; esparcimiento, *m.*; diseminación, *f.*

diffusive, *a.* difusivo

dig, *v.t.* and *v.i.* cavar; excavar; (of animals) escarbar; (mine) zapar, minar; (into a subject) ahondar (en); (with the spurs) aguijonear, dar con las espuelas; (poke) clavar. **to dig in,** enterrarse; (*mil.*) abrir trincheras; (*fam.*) arreglarse las cosas. **to dig out,** excavar; sacar cavando, sacar con azadón; extraer. **to dig up,** desenterrar; descubrir

digest, *v.t.* clasificar; codificar; (food, also *chem.* and *fig.* tolerate and think over) digerir; (of knowledge and territory) asimilar. *v.i.* digerir. *s.* compendio, resumen, *m.*; (*law*) digesto, *m.*; recopilación, *f.* **This food is easy to d.,** Este alimento es fácil de digerir; Este alimento es muy ligero

digestibility, *s.* digestibilidad, *f.*

digestible, *a.* digerible, digestible

digestion, *s.* digestión, *f.*; (of ideas) asimilación, *f.*; (*chem.*) digestión, *f.*

digestive, *a.* digestivo

digger, *s.* cavador (-ra)

digging, *s.* cavadura, *f.*; excavación, *f.*; *pl.* **diggings,** minas, *f. pl.*; excavaciones, *f. pl.*; (*fam.*) alojamiento, *m.*, posada, *f.*

digit, *s.* dígito, *m.*

digital, *a.* digital, dígito

digitalin, *s.* digitalina, *f.*

digitalis, *s.* digital, *f.*

dignified, *a.* serio, grave; majestuoso; (worthy) digno; solemne; altivo; noble

dignify, *v.t.* dignificar, honrar; exaltar; dar dignidad (a); ennoblecer

dignitary, *s.* dignatario, *m.*; dignidad, *f.*

dignity, *s.* dignidad, *f.*; (rank) rango, *m.*; (post) cargo, puesto, *m.*; (honour) honra, *f.*; (stateliness) majestad, *f.*; mesura, seriedad, *f.*; (haughtiness) altivez, *f.*; (nobility) nobleza, *f.* **to stand upon one's d.,** darse importancia

digress, *v.i.* divagar

digression, *s.* digresión, divagación, *f.*

dike, *s.* dique, *m.*; (ditch) acequia, *f.*; canal, *m.*; (embankment) zanja, *f. v.t.* represar

dilapidated, *a.* arruinado, destartalado; (of fortune) dilapidado; (of persons, families) venido a menos; (shabby) raído

dilapidation, *s.* deterioración, *f.*; ruina, *f.*, estado ruinoso, *m.*

dilatation, *s.* dilatación, *f.*; ensanche, *m.*

dilate, *v.t.* dilatar; ensanchar. *v.i.* dilatarse. **to d. upon,** extenderse sobre, dilatarse en

dilator, *s.* dilatador, *m.*

dilatoriness, *s.* tardanza, *f.*; (slowness) lentitud, *f.*

dilatory, *a.* dilatorio, tardo; (slow) lento

dilemma, *s.* dilema, *m.*

dilettante, *s.* diletante, *m.*; aficionado (-da)

dilettantism, *s.* diletantismo, *m.*

diligence, *s.* diligencia, *f.*; asiduidad, *f.*; (care) cuidado, *m.*; (coach) diligencia, *f.*

diligent, *a.* diligente, asiduo, aplicado, industrioso; (painstaking) concienzudo

diligently, *adv.* diligentemente

dilute, *v.t.* diluir; (*fig.*) adulterar. *a.* diluido

dilution, *s.* dilución, *f.*; (*fig.*) adulteración, *f.*

diluvian, *a.* diluviano

dim, *a.* (of light) tenue, débil; (of sight) turbio; (dark) sombrío, oscuro; (blurred, etc.) empañado; indistinto, confuso. *v.t.* obscurecer; empañar; (dazzle) ofuscar; (eclipse) eclipsar; reducir la intensidad (de una luz); (of memories) borrar

dimension, *s.* dimensión, *f.*; (size) tamaño, *m.*; (scope) extensión, *f.*, alcance, *m.*

dimensional, *a.* dimensional

diminish, *v.t.* disminuir; reducir; debilitar, atenuar. *v.i.* disminuir; reducirse; debilitarse, atenuarse

diminishing, *a.* menguante

diminution, *s.* disminución, *f.*; reducción, *f.*; atenuación, *f.*

diminutive, *a.* diminutivo. *s.* diminutivo, *m.*

diminutiveness, *s.* pequeñez, *f.*

dimly, *adv.* obscuramente; vagamente; indistintamente

dimness, *s.* oscuridad, *f.*; deslustre, *m.*; (of light) tenuidad (de la luz), *f.*; confusión, *f.*

dimple, *s.* hoyuelo, *m.*

dimpled, *a.* con hoyuelos, que tiene hoyuelos

din, *s.* estrépito, estruendo, ruido, *m.*; algarabía, barahúnda, *f.* *v.t.* ensordecer

dine, *v.i.* (in the evening) cenar; (at midday) comer. *v.t.* convidar a cenar or a comer. **to d. out,** cenar or comer fuera

diner, *s.* (on a train) coche comedor, coche restaurante, *m.*; cenador, *m.*; comedor, *m.*

ding-dong, *s.* tintín, *m.*

dinghy, *s.* lancha, *f.*; canoa, *f.*, bote, *m.* **rubber d.,** canoa de goma, *f.*

dinginess, *s.* deslustre, *m.*; suciedad, *f.*; oscuridad, *f.*; (of a person) desaseo, *m.*

dingy, *a.* deslucido, empañado; sucio; oscuro; (of persons) desaseado

dining-car, *s.* coche comedor, vagón restaurante, *m.*

dining-room, *s.* comedor, *m.*; refectorio, *m.*

dining-table, *s.* mesa del comedor, *f.*

dinner, *s.* (in the evening) cena, *f.*; (at midday) comida, *f.* **over the d. table,** de sobremesa. **d.-jacket,** smoking, *m.* **d. party,** cena, *f.* **d. plate,** plato, *m.* **d. roll,** panecillo, *m.* **d. service,** vajilla, *f.*

dinosaur, *s.* dinosauro, *m.*

dint, (**by d. of**) a fuerza de, a costa de

diocesan, *a.* diocesano

diocese, *s.* diócesis, *f.*

dioptric, *a.* dióptrico. *s. pl.* **dioptrics,** dióptrica, *f.*

dioxide, *s.* dióxido, *m.*

dip, *s.* inmersión, *f.*; baño, *m.*; (in the ground) declive, *m.*; (slope) pendiente, *f.*; (candle) vela de sebo, *f.*; (of the horizon) depresión (del horizonte), *f.*; (of needle) inclinación (de la aguja), *f.* *v.t.* sumergir; bañar; (put) poner. *v.i.* inclinarse hacia abajo. **to dip into a book,** hojear un libro. **to dip the colours,** saludar con la bandera. **to dip the headlights,** bajar los faros

diphtheria, *s.* difteria, *f.*

diphtheric, *a.* diftérico

diphthong, *s.* diptongo, *m.*

diplodocus, *s.* diplódoco, *m.*

diploma, *s.* diploma, *m.*

diplomacy, *s.* diplomacia, *f.*; tacto, *m.*

diplomat, *s.* diplomático, *m.*

diplomatic, *a.* diplomático. **d. bag,** valija diplomática, *f.* **d. corps,** cuerpo diplomático, *m.*

diplomatically, *adv.* diplomáticamente

dipper, *s.* (ladle) cazo, *m.*; (*ast.*) Osa Mayor, *f.*

dipsomania, *s.* dipsomanía, *f.*

dipsomaniac, *s.* dipsómano (-na)

diptych, *s.* díptica, *f.*

dire, *a.* espantoso, horrible; cruel; funesto

direct, *a.* directo; claro, inequívoco; (of descent) recto; (of electric current) continuo; exacto. *adv.* directamente. *v.t.* dirigir; (command) ordenar, encargar; dar instrucciones. **d. action,** acción directa, *f.* **d. current,** corriente continua, *f.* **d. line,** línea directa, *f.*; (of descent) línea recta, *f.* **d. object,** acusativo, *m.* **d. speech,** oración directa, *f.*

direction, *s.* dirección, *f.*; rumbo, *m.*; instrucción, *f.*; (on a letter) sobrescrito, *m.*; señas, *f. pl.* **in the d. of,** en la dirección de; hacia; (*naut.*) con rumbo a. **in all directions,** por todas partes; a los cuatro vientos. **to go in the d. of,** ir en la dirección de; tomar por. **Directions for use,** Direcciones para el uso. **d. indicator,** (on car) indicador de dirección, *m.*

directive, *a.* directivo, director

directly, *adv.* directamente; inmediatamente, en seguida

directness, *s.* derechura, *f.*

director, *s.* director (-triz, -ora), **managing d.,** director gerente, *m.*

directorate, *s.* directorio, *m.*, junta directiva, *f.*; cargo de director, *m.*

directory, *s.* directorio, *m.*, guía, *f.* **telephone d.,** guía de teléfonos, *f.*

dirge, *s.* endecha, *f.*, lamento, *m.*; canto fúnebre, *m.*

dirigible, *s.* dirigible, *m.*

dirt, *s.* mugre, suciedad, *f.*; (mud) lodo, *m.*; (earth) tierra, *f.*; (dust) polvo, *m.*; (*fig.*) inmundicia, *f.* **d.-cheap,** sumamente barato. **to be d. cheap,** (of goods) estar por los suelos. **d.-track,** pista de ceniza, *f.* **d.-track racing,** carreras en pista de ceniza, *f. pl.*

dirtiness, *s.* suciedad, *f.*; (untidiness) desaseo, *m.*; sordidez, *f.*; (meanness) bajeza, *f.*

dirty, *a.* sucio; (untidy) desaseado; (muddy) enlodado; (dusty) polvoriento; (of weather) borrascoso; (sordid) sórdido; (base, mean) vil; (indecent) indecente, verde, obsceno. *v.t.* ensuciar. **d. trick,** mala pasada, *f.*

disability, *s.* incapacidad, *f.*; impotencia, *f.*; desventaja, *f.*

disable, *v.t.* (cripple) estropear, tullir; hacer incapaz (de), incapacitar; imposibilitar; (destroy) destruir; (*law*) incapacitar legalmente

disabled, *a.* inválido; impedido, lisiado; (in the hand) manco; incapacitado; (of ships, etc.)

fuera de servicio, estropeado. **d. soldier,** inválido, *m.*

disablement, *s.* (physical) invalidez, *f.*; inhabilitación, *f.*; (*law*) impedimento, *m.*

disabuse, *v.t.* desengañar, sacar de un error

disaccustom, *v.t.* deshabituar

disadvantage, *s.* desventaja, *f.* **tó be under the d. of,** sufrir la desventaja de

disadvantageous, *a.* desventajoso

disaffected, *a.* desafecto

disaffection, *s.* desafecto, descontento, *m.*

disagree, *v.i.* no estar de acuerdo; diferir; (quarrel) reñir; (not share the opinion of) no estar de la opinión (de); (of food, etc.) sentar mal; no probar. **The meat disagreed with me,** La carne me sentó mal

disagreeable, *a.* desagradable; repugnante; (of persons) antipático, displicente

disagreeableness, *s.* lo desagradable; (of persons) displicencia, *f.*

disagreeably, *adv.* desagradablemente; con displicencia

disagreement, *s.* desacuerdo, *m.*; diferencia, *f.*; desavenencia, *f.*; discordia, *f.*; (quarrel) riña, disputa, *f.*; discrepancia, *f.*

disallow, *v.t.* negar; rechazar

disappear, *v.i.* desaparecer. **to cause to d.,** hacer desaparecer

disappearance, *s.* desaparición, *f.*

disappoint, *v.t.* desilusionar; frustrar; (hopes) defraudar; (deprive) privar de; (annoy) contrariar; (break a promise) faltar (a la palabra)

disappointedly, *adv.* con desilusión, con desengaño

disappointing, *a.* desengañador; pobre; triste; poco halagüeño

disappointment, *s.* desengaño, *m.*, decepción, *f.*; frustración, *f.*; desilusión, *f.*; (vexation) contrariedad, *f.*; contratiempo, *m.* **to suffer a d.,** sufrir un desengaño; (*fam.*) llevarse un chasco

disapproval, *s.* desaprobación, *f.*

disapprove, *v.t.* desaprobar

disapproving, *a.* de desaprobación, severo

disapprovingly, *adv.* con desaprobación

disarm, *v.t.* desarmar. *v.i.*
desarmarse; deponer las armas
disarmament, *s.* desarme, *m.*
disarrange, *v.t.* desarreglar; descomponer, desajustar; (hair)
despeinar
disarrangement, *s.* desarreglo,
m.; desajuste, *m.*; desorden, *m.*
disarray, *s.* desorden, desarreglo,
m.; confusión, *f.* *v.t.* desordenar,
desarreglar
disarticulate, *v.t.* desarticular
disarticulation, *s.* desarticulación, *f.*
disaster, *s.* desastre, *m.*; catástrofe, *m.*; infortunio, *m.*
disastrous, *a.* desastroso; funesto, trágico
disastrously, *adv.* desastrosa-
mente
disastrousness, *s.* carácter desastroso, *m.*
disavow, *v.t.* repudiar; retractar
disavowal, *s.* repudiación, *f.*
disband, *v.t.* licenciar. *v.i.*
desbandarse, dispersarse
disbelief, *s.* incredulidad, *f.*; desconfianza, *f.*
disbelieve, *v.t.* and *v.i.* descreer,
no creer; desconfiar (de)
disburse, *v.t.* desembolsar, pagar
disbursement, *s.* desembolso, *m.*
disc, *s.* disco, *m.*
discard, *v.t.* desechar, arrinconar; despedir; (at cards) descartar. *s.* (at cards) descarte, *m.*
discern, *v.t.* discernir, distinguir,
percibir
discerner, *s.* discernidor (-ra)
discernible, *a.* distinguible, perceptible
discerning, *a.* perspicaz, discernidor
discernment, *s.* discernimiento,
m.
discharge, *v.t.* descargar; (a gun)
disparar, tirar; (an arrow) lanzar; (*elec.*) descargar; emitir;
(dismiss) destituir, despedir; arrojar; (*mil.*) licenciar; (exempt)
dispensar (de); (exonerate) absolver, exonerar; (free) dar libertad (a); (from hospital) dar de
baja (a); (*law*) revocar; (perform)
cumplir, ejecutar; (pay) pagar,
saldar; (of an abscess, etc.)
supurar. **to be discharged
from the army,** ser licenciado
del ejército

discharge, *s.* (of firearms) disparo, tiro, *m.*; (of artillery)
descarga, *f.*; (of goods, cargo)
descargue, *m.*; (*elec.*) descarga,
f.; (from a wound, etc.) pus, *m.*,
supuración, *f.*; (from the intestine) flujo, *m.*; (of a debt) pago,
m.; (*com.*) descargo, *m.*; (receipt)
carta de pago, quitanza, *f.*; (*mil.*)
licencia absoluta, *f.*; (dismissal)
despedida, destitución, *f.*; (exoneration) exoneración, *f.*; (freeing)
liberación, *f.*; (from hospital)
baja, *f.*; (performance) cumplimiento, *m.*; ejecución, *f.*
disciple, *s.* discípulo (-la)
discipleship, *s.* discipulado, *m.*
disciplinarian, *s.* disciplinario
(-ia)
disciplinary, *a.* disciplinario
discipline, *s.* disciplina, *f.* *v.t.*
disciplinar
disclaim, *v.t.* renunciar (a);
(repudiate) rechazar, repudiar
disclaimer, *s.* (*law*) renunciación,
f.; repudiación, *f.*
disclose, *v.t.* descubrir, revelar
disclosure, *s.* descubrimiento,
m., revelación, *f.*
discolour, *v.t.* descolorar. *v.i.*
descolorarse
discolouration, *s.* descoloramiento, *m.*
discomfit, *v.t.* desconcertar
discomfiture, *s.* desconcierto,
m.
discomfort, *s.* falta de comodi-
dades, *f.*; incomodidad, *f.*;
malestar, *m.*; molestia, *f.*; inquietud, *f.*; dolor, *m.*
discompose, *s.* confusión, agitación, inquietud, *f.*
disconcert, *v.t.* desconcertar,
turbar; (of plans, etc.) frustrar
disconnect, *v.t.* separar; (of railway engines, etc.) desacoplar;
desconectar; (of electric plugs)
desenchufar
disconnected, *a.* inconexo; incoherente, deshilvanado
disconnectedness, *s.* inconexión,
f.; incoherencia, *f.*
disconsolate, *a.* desconsolado,
triste
disconsolately, *adv.* desconsoladamente, tristemente
disconsolateness, *s.* desconsuelo,
m.

discontent, *s.* descontento, disgusto, *m.* *v.t.* descontentar, desagradar

discontented, *a.* descontentadizo, descontento, disgustado

discontinuance, *s.* descontinuación, cesación, *f.*; interrupción, *f.*

discontinue, *v.t.* descontinuar; cesar; interrumpir; (of payments, etc.) suspender. *v.i.* cesar

discontinuous, *a.* descontinuo; interrumpido; intermitente

discord, *s.* discordia, *f.*; (*mus.*) disonancia, *f.*, desentono, *m.*

discordant, *a.* discorde, poco armonioso; incongruo; (*mus.*) disonante, desentonado. **to be d.,** discordar; ser incongruo; (*mus.*) disonar

discount, *s.* descuento, *m.*; rebaja, *f.* *v.t.* descontar; rebajar; balancear. **at a d.,** al descuento; bajo la par; fácil de obtener; superfluo; (*fig.*) en disfavor, en descrédito. **rate of d.,** tipo de descuento, *m.* **d. for cash,** descuento por venta al contado, *m.*

discourage, *v.t.* desalentar, desanimar; oponerse a; disuadir; frustrar

discouragement, *s.* desaliento, *m.*; desaprobación, oposición, *f.*; disuasión, *f.*; (obstacle) estorbo, *m.*

discouraging, *a.* poco animador, que ofrece pocas esperanzas; (with prospect, etc.) nada halagüeño

discourse, *s.* discurso, *m.*; plática, *f.*; (treatise) disertación, *f.* *v.i.* (converse) platicar, conversar; (with on, upon) disertar sobre, discurrir sobre; tratar de

discourteous, *a.* descortés, desconsiderado

discourtesy, *s.* descortesía, *f.*

discover, *v.t.* descubrir; (see) ver; (realize) darse cuenta de; (show) manifestar; revelar

discoverable, *a.* que se puede descubrir; averiguable; distinguible, perceptible ·

discoverer, *s.* descubridor (-ra); revelador (-ra)

discovery, *s.* descubrimiento, *m.*; revelación, *f.*

discredit, *s.* descrédito, *m.*; deshonra, *f.*; duda, *f.* *v.t.* dudar (de), no creer (en); desacreditar; deshonrar

discreditable, *a.* deshonroso, ignominioso, vergonzoso

discreet, *a.* discreto; prudente, circunspecto

discreetly, *adv.* discretamente; prudentemente

discrepancy, *s.* discrepancia, diferencia, *f.*; contradicción, *f.*

discrepant, *a.* discrepante; contradictorio, inconsistente

discretion, *s.* discreción, *f.*; prudencia, circunspección, *f.*; juicio, *m.*; voluntad, *f.* **at d.,** a discreción. **at one's own d.,** a voluntad (de uno). **years of d.,** edad de discreción, *f.*

discriminate, *v.i.* distinguir (entre); hacer una distinción (en favor de or en perjuicio de). *v.t.* distinguir

discriminating, *a.* discerniente, que sabe distinguir, juicioso; culto; diferencial

discrimination, *s.* discernimiento, *m.*; gusto, *m.*; distinción, *f.*; discriminación, *f.*

discursive, *a.* discursivo; digresivo

discus, *s.* disco, *m.* **d. thrower,** discóbolo, *m.*

discuss, *v.t.* discutir; hablar de; debatir; (deal with) tratar; (*fam.*, a dish) probar; (a bottle of wine) vaciar

discussion, *s.* discusión, *f.*; debate, *m.*

disdain, *s.* desdén, *m.*; altivez, *f.* *v.t.* desdeñar, desairar, despreciar. **to d. to,** desdeñarse de

disdainful, *a.* desdeñoso; altivo

disdainfully, *adv.* desdeñosamente

disease, *s.* enfermedad, *f.*; (*fig.*) mal, *m.* **infectious d.,** enfermedad contagiosa, *f.*

diseased, *a.* enfermo; (of fruit, etc.) malo

disembark, *v.t.* and *v.i.* desembarcar

disembarkation, *s.* desembarque, *m.*; (*mil.*) desembarco (de tropas), *m.*

disembarrass, *v.t.* desembarazar

disembodied, *a.* incorpóreo

disembogue, *v.t.* and *v.i.* desembocar; descargar

disembowel, *v.t.* desentrañar,
destripar

disenchant, *v.t.* desencantar;
deshechizar; desilusionar

disenchantment, *s.* desencanto,
m.; desilusión, *f.*

disengage, *v.t.* desasir; soltar;
(gears) desembragar; (uncouple)
desacoplar; (free) librar

disengaged, *a.* (free) libre

disentail, *s.* desamortización, *f.*
v.t. desamortizar

disentangle, *v.t.* (undo) desatar,
desanudar; separar; (of threads,
etc., and *fig.*) desenredar, desenmarañar. *v.i.* desenredarse

disentanglement, *s.* desatadura,
f.; separación, *f.*; desenredo, *m.*

disestablish, *v.t.* separar (la
Iglesia del Estado)

disestablishment, *s.* separación
(de la Iglesia del Estado), *f.*

disfavour, *s.* disfavor, *m.*; (disapproval) desaprobación, *f.* *v.t.*
desaprobar

disfigure, *v.t.* desfigurar, afear;
deformar; (mar) estropear

disfigurement, *s.* desfiguración,
f.; deformidad, *f.*; defecto, *m.*

disfranchise, *v.t.* privar de los
derechos civiles (a)

disfranchisement, *s.* privación
de los derechos civiles, *f.*

disgorge, *v.t.* and *v.i.* vomitar;
(of a river) desembocar (en);
hacer restitución (de lo robado)

disgrace, *s.* vergüenza, ignominia,
f.; deshonra, *f.*; (insult) afrenta,
f.; (scandal) escándalo, *m.*; disfavor, *m.* *v.t.* deshonrar; despedir con ignominia. **in d.,**
fuera de favor; desacreditado;
(of children and animals) castigado

disgraceful, *a.* deshonroso; ignominioso; escandaloso

disgracefully, *adv.* escandalosamente

disgracefulness, *s.* ignominia,
vergüenza, *f.*; deshonra, *f.*

disgruntled, *a.* refunfuñador,
enfurruñado, malhumorado

disguise, *s.* disfraz, *m.*; (mask)
máscara, *f.* *v.t.* disfrazar; cubrir,
tapar; (*fig.*, conceal) ocultar. **in
d.,** disfrazado

disgust, *s.* repugnancia, aversión,
f.; aborrecimiento, *m.*; asco, *m.*
v.t. repugnar, inspirar aversión;
disgustar; dar asco (a)

disgusted, *a.* asqueado; disgustado; furioso; (bored) aburrido

disgusting, *a.* repugnante; odioso,
horrible; asqueroso

dish, *s.* (for meat, vegetables,
fruit, etc.) fuente, *f.*; (food)
plato, *m.*; *pl.* **dishes,** platos,
m. pl., vajilla, *f.* *v.t.* servir;
(*fam.*) frustrar. **cooked d.,**
guiso, *m.* **special d. for to-day,**
plato del día, *m.* **to wash the
dishes,** fregar los platos. **d.-
cloth,** (for washing) fregador,
m.; (for drying) paño de los
platos, *m.* **d.-cover,** cubreplatos, *m.* **d.-rack,** escurreplatos, *m.* **d.-washer,** lava-
platos, *m.* **d.-water,** agua de
lavar los platos, *f.*

disharmony, *s.* falta de armonía,
f.; (disagreement) discordia, desavenencia, *f.*; incongruencia,
f.; (*mus.*) disonancia, *f.*

dishearten, *v.t.* desalentar,
desanimar; desesperar; disuadir
(de)

dishevelled, *a.* despeinado,
desgreñado; (untidy) desaseado

dishonest, *a.* falto de honradez,
tramposo; fraudulento; falso,
desleal

dishonestly, *adv.* de mala fe, sin
honradez; fraudulentamente; des-
lealmente

dishonesty, *s.* falta de honradez,
falta de integridad, *f.*; fraude,
m.; falsedad, deslealtad, *f.*

dishonour, *s.* deshonra, *f.* *v.t.*
deshonrar; (*com.*) no pagar, o no
aceptar, un giro

dishonourable, *a.* deshonroso

dishonourer, *s.* deshonrador
(-ra); profanador (-ra)

disillusion, *v.t.* desengañar, desilusionar

disillusionment, *s.* desilusión, *f.*,
desengaño, desencanto, *m.*

disinclination, *s.* aversión, *f.*

disincline, *v.t.* desinclinar

disinfect, *v.t.* desinfectar

disinfectant, *a.* and *s.* desinfectante (*m.*)

disinfection, *s.* desinfección, *f.*

disingenuous, a. tortuoso, doble, falso, insincero

disinherit, v.t. desheredar

disinheritance, s. desheredación, f.

disintegrate, v.t. despedazar, disgregar. v.i. disgregarse; desmoronarse

disintegration, s. disgregación, f.; disolución, f.; desmoronamiento m.

disinter, v.t. desenterrar

disinterested, a. desinteresado

disinterestedness, s. desinterés, m.

disinterment, s. desenterramiento, m.

disjointed, a. dislocado; desarticulado; incoherente, inconexo; (of a speech, etc.) descosido

disjointedness, s. descoyuntamiento, desencajamiento, m.; incoherencia, f.

disjunction, s. disyunción, f.

disjunctive, a. disyuntivo. **d. pronoun,** pronombre disyuntivo, m.

disk, s. disco, m.

dislike, s. aversión, f.; antipatía, f.; (hostility) animosidad, f. v.t. desagradar, no gustar; repugnar. **I d. the house,** No me gusta la casa. **I d. them,** Ellos no me gustan

dislocate, v.t. dislocar, descoyuntar; (fig.) interrumpir

dislocation, s. dislocación, f., descoyuntamiento, m.; (fig.) interrupción, f.

dislodge, v.t. desalojar

dislodgement, s. desalojamiento, m.

disloyal, a. desleal, infiel, falso

disloyalty, s. deslealtad, infidelidad, falsedad, f.

dismal, a. lóbrego, sombrío; lúgubre; funesto; triste

dismantle, v.t. (a ship or fort) desmantelar; (a machine) desmontar; (a house, etc.) desamueblar

dismantling, s. desmantelamiento, m.

dismay, s. desmayo, desaliento, m.; consternación, f.; espanto, terror, m. v.t. desanimar; consternar; espantar, horrorizar

dismember, v.t. desmembrar

dismemberment, s. desmembración, f.

dismiss, v.t. (from a job) despedir (de); (from an official position) destituir (de); (bid good-bye to) despedirse de; (after military parade) dar la orden de romper filas; (thoughts) apartar de sí; ahuyentar; (discard) desechar, descartar; (omit) pasar por alto de; (disregard) rechazar; (a parliament, etc.) disolver; (a law case) absolver de la instancia. **to d. in a few words,** tratar someramente; hablar brevemente de

dismissal, s. despedida, f.; (from an official post) destitución, f.; apartamiento, m.; (discard) descarte, m.; (of a parliament, etc.) disolución, f.

dismount, v.i. desmontar, apearse; bajar. v.t. desmontar; (dismantle) desarmar

disobedience, s. desobediencia, f.

disobedient, a. desobediente

disobediently, adv. desobedientemente

disobey, v.t. and v.i. desobedecer

disobliging, a. poco servicial

disobligingly, adv. descortésmente

disorder, s. desorden, m.; confusión, f.; (unrest) perturbación del orden público, f., motín, m.; (disease) enfermedad, f.; (mental) enajenación mental, f.; trastorno, m. v.t. desordenar, desarreglar; (of health) perjudicar; (the mind) trastornar. **in d.,** en desorden, desarreglado; (helter-skelter) atropelladamente

disordered, a. en desorden; irregular, desordenado; (of the mind and bodily organs) trastornado; (ill) enfermo; (confused) confuso

disorganization, s. desorganización, f.

disorganize, v.t. desorganizar

disorganizing, a. desorganizador

disorientate, v.t. desorientar

disorientation, s. desorientación, f.

disown, v.t. repudiar; negar; renegar de

disparage, v.t. menospreciar; desacreditar; denigrar; (spoil) perjudicar; (scorn) despreciar

disparagement, *s.* menosprecio, *m.*; denigración, *f.*; desprecio, *m.*

disparagingly, *adv.* con desprecio

disparity, *s.* disparidad, *f.*

dispassionate, *a.* desapasionado, sereno; imparcial; moderado

dispassionately, *adv.* con imparcialidad; serenamente; con moderación

dispatch, *s.* despacho, *m.*; (com.) envío, *m.*; (message) mensaje, *m.*; (communiqué) parte, *f.*; (cable) telegrama, *m.*; (promptness) prontitud, presteza, *f.*; (execution) ejecución, muerte, *f.* *v.t.* despachar; enviar, remitir; (fam., kill) despachar. **d.-case**, cartera, *f.* **d.-rider**, mensajero motociclista, *m.*

dispel, *v.t.* disipar

dispensable, *a.* dispensable

dispensary, *s.* dispensario, *m.*

dispensation, *s.* dispensación, *f.*; (of the Pope, etc.) dispensa, *f.*; (decree) ley, *f.*, decreto, *m.*; (of justice) administración, *f.*

dispense, *v.t.* dispensar; (of justice) administrar. **to d. with**, pasar sin, prescindir de

dispenser, *s.* dispensador (-ra); administrador (-ra)

dispersal, *s.* dispersión, *f.*; disipación, *f.*; esparcimiento, *m.*

disperse, *v.t.* dispersar; disipar; esparcir. *v.i.* dispersarse (also *mil.*) disiparse

dispirited, *a.* abatido, desanimado, deprimido; lánguido

dispiritedly, *adv.* desanimadamente, con desaliento; lánguidamente

displace, *v.t.* desalojar; cambiar de situación; (of liquids) desplazar; (oust) quitar el puesto (a), destituir

displacement, *s.* desalojamiento, *m.*; cambio de situación, *m.*; (of liquid) desplazamiento, *m.*; (from a post) destitución, *f.*

display, *s.* exhibición, *f.*; ostentación, *f.*; presentación, *f.*; (development) desarrollo, *m.*; manifestación, *f.*; (naval or military) maniobras, *f. pl.*; espectáculo, *m.*; (pomp) pompa, *f.*; fausto, *m.* *v.t.* exhibir; mostrar; manifestar;

ostentar; (unfold) desplegar, extender; (develop) desarrollar. **d. cabinet**, vitrina, *f.*

displease, *v.t.* desagradar; ofender; enojar

displeasing, *a.* desagradable

displeasure, *s.* desagrado, *m.*; disgusto, *m.*; disfavor, *m.*; indignación, *f.*; enojo, *m.*; (grief) angustia, *f.*

disport, *v.i.* (oneself), divertirse, entretenerse, recrearse; retozar, jugar

disposal, *s.* disposición, *f.*; (transfer) cesión, enajenación, *f.*; (sale) venta, *f.*; (gift) donación, *f.* I am at your d., Estoy a la disposición de Vd. **the d. of the troops**, la disposición de las tropas

dispose, *v.t.* disponer; inclinar. *v.i.* disponer. **to d. of**, disponer de; (finish) terminar, concluir; (get rid of) deshacerse de; (give away) regalar; (sell) vender; (transfer) ceder; (of houses, etc.) traspasar; (kill) matar; (send) enviar; (use) servirse de; (refute) refutar. **To be disposed of**, (a business, etc.) Se traspasa

disposed, *a.* (in compounds) intencionado, dispuesto. **well-d.**, bien intencionado

disposition, *s.* disposición, *f.*; (temperament) naturaleza, índole, *f.*, temperamento, carácter, *m.*; (humour) humor, *m.*

dispossess, *v.t.* desposeer (de); privar (de); desahuciar

dispossession, *s.* desposeimiento, *m.*; desahucio, *m.*

disproof, *s.* refutación, *f.*

disproportion, *s.* desproporción, *f.*

disproportionate, *a.* desproporcionado

disproportionately, *adv.* desproporcionadamente

disprovable, *a.* refutable

disprove, *v.t.* refutar

disputable, *a.* disputable; discutible

disputant, *s.* disputador (-ra)

dispute, *s.* disputa, controversia, *f.*; altercación, *f.*; discusión, *f.*; debate, *m.* *v.t.* and *v.i.* disputar. **beyond d.**, *a.* incontestable. *adv.* incontestablemente; fuera de duda

disqualification, *s.* incapacidad, *f.*; inhabilitación, *f.*; impedimento, *m.*; (*sport*) descalificación, *f.*

disqualify, *v.t.* incapacitar; inhabilitar; (*sport*) descalificar

disquiet, *s.* desasosiego, *m.*; intranquilidad, inquietud, agitación, *f.* *v.t.* desasosegar, intranquilizar, perturbar, agitar

disquieting, *a.* intranquilizador, perturbador

disquisition, *s.* disquisición, *f.*

disregard, *s.* indiferencia, *f.*; omisión, *f.*; descuido, *m.*; (scorn) desdén, *m.* *v.t.* no hacer caso de, desatender; omitir; desconocer; descuidar; despreciar

disregardful, *a.* indiferente; negligente; desatento; desdeñoso

disrepair, *s.* deterioro, mal estado, *m.*

disreputable, *a.* de mala fama; (shameful) vergonzoso, vil; (compromising) comprometedor; de mal aspecto, horrible; ruin

disreputably, *adv.* ruinmente; vergonzosamente

disrepute, *s.* disfavor, *m.*; mala fama, *f.*; deshonra, *f.*; descrédito, *m.* **to come into d.,** caer en disfavor; perder su reputación

disrespect, *s.* falta de respeto, *f.*; irreverencia, *f.*

disrespectful, *a.* irrespetuoso, irreverente

disrobe, *v.t.* desnudar. *v.i.* desnudarse

disrupt, *v.t.* quebrar; desorganizar; interrumpir; separar

disruption, *s.* quebrantamiento, *m.*; desorganización, *f.*; interrupción, *f.*; separación, *f.*

dissatisfaction, *s.* descontento, desagrado, disgusto, *m.*

dissatisfied, *a.* descontentado, malcontento, no satisfecho

dissect, *v.t.* disecar; (*fig.*) analizar

dissection, *s.* disección, *f.*; análisis, *m.*

dissector, *s.* disector, *m.*; (*fig.*) analizador (-ra)

dissemble, *v.t.* and *v.i.* disimular, fingir

dissembler, *s.* hipócrita, *m.* and *f.*; disimulador (-ra)

disseminate, *v.t.* diseminar; propagar, sembrar

dissemination, *s.* diseminación, *f.*; propagación, *f.*

dissension, *s.* disensión, *f.*; disidencia, *f.*

dissent, *s.* disentimiento, *m.* *v.i.* disentir, disidir

dissenter, *s.* disidente, *m.* and *f.*

dissentient, *a.* disidente, divergente. **without one d. voice,** unánimemente

dissertation, *s.* disertación, *f.*

disservice, *s.* deservicio, *m.*

dissimilar, *a.* disímil, desemejante, diferente

dissimilarity, *s.* desemejanza, diferencia, disparidad, *f.*

dissimulation, *s.* disimulación, *f.*, disimulo, *m.*

dissipate, *v.t.* disipar; dispersar; (waste) derrochar, desperdiciar. *v.i.* disiparse; dispersarse; (vanish) desvanecerse; (of persons) ser disoluto

dissipated, *a.* (of persons) disipado, disoluto, vicioso

dissipation, *s.* disipación, *f.*; (waste) derroche, *m.*; libertinaje, *m.*

dissociate, *v.t.* disociar

dissociation, *s.* disociación, *f.*

dissoluble, *a* disoluble

dissolute, *a.* disoluto, vicioso, licencioso

dissoluteness, *s.* disolución, inmoralidad, *f.*

dissolution, *s.* disolución, *f.*; separación, *f.*; muerte, *f.*

dissolvable, *a.* soluble

dissolve, *v.t.* disolver; derretir; (of parliament) prorrogar; (a marriage, etc.) anular; (*fig.*) disipar. *v.i.* disolverse; derretirse; (vanish) desvanecerse, disiparse, evaporarse. **to d. into tears,** deshacerse en lágrimas

dissolvent, *a.* disolutivo. *s.* disolvente, *m.*

dissonance, *s.* disonancia, *f.*; (*fig.*) discordia, falta de armonía, *f.*

dissonant, *s.* disonancia, *f.* *a.* disonante

dissuade, *v.t.* disuadir (de), apartar (de)

dissuasion, *s.* disuasión, *f.*

distaff, *s.* rueca, *f.*

distance, *s.* distancia, *f.*; lontananza, *f.*; lejanía, *f.*; trecho, *m.*; (of time) intervalo, *m.*; (difference) diferencia, *f.* **at a d.**, a alguna distancia; lejos; (from afar) desde lejos. **from a d.**, desde (or de) lejos. **in the d.**, a lo lejos, en lontananza. **to keep at a d.**, mantener lejos; guardar las distancias (con). **to keep one's d.**, mantenerse a distancia; no intimarse, guardar as distancias. **What is the d. from London to Madrid?** ¿ Qué distancia hay desde Londres a Madrid ?

distant, *a.* distante; lejano; remoto; (of manner) frío, reservado; (slight) ligero; (of references, etc.) indirecto. **He is a d. relation,** Él es un pariente lejano. **They are always rather d. with her,** La tratan siempre con bastante frialdad

distantly, *adv.* a distancia; a lo lejos; desde lejos; remotamente; (of manner) con frialdad; (slightly) ligeramente

distaste, *s.* aversión, repugnancia, *f.*; disgusto, hastío, *m.*

distasteful, *a.* desagradable

distemper, *s.* enfermedad, *f.*; (in animals) moquillo, *m.*; (*fig.*) mal, *m.*; (for walls) pintura al temple, *f.* —*v.t.* desordenar, perturbar; (walls) pintar al temple

distend, *v.t.* ensanchar; dilatar; inflar, henchir; (*med.*) distender. —*v.i.* ensancharse, etc.

distension, *s.* dilatación, *f.*; inflación, *f.*; henchimiento, *m.*; (*med.*) distensión, *f.*

distich, *s.* dístico, *m.*

distil, *v.t.* destilar; extraer. —*v.i.* destilar; exudar

distillation, *s.* destilación, *f.*; extracción, *f.*; exudación, *f.*

distiller, *s.* destilador (-ra)

distillery, *s.* destilería, *f.*, destilatorio, *m.*

distinct, *a.* distinto; diferente; cláro; notable, evidente

distinction, *s.* distinción, *f.*

distinctive, *a.* distintivo; carácterístico

distinctly, *adv.* claramente; distintamente

distinctness, *s.* claridad, *f.*; distinción, *f.*; carácter distintivo, *m.*

distinguish, *v.t.* distinguir; discernir; caracterizar; (honour)

honrar. —*v.i.* distinguir, diferenciar

distinguishable, *a.* distinguible; perceptible, discernible

distinguished, *a.* distinguido; eminente; famoso, ilustre, egregio

distinguishing, *a.* distintivo

distort, *v.t.* (twist) torcer; deformar; falsear; pervertir

distorting-mirror, *s.* (at fairs) espejo de la risa, *m.*; espejo deformador, *m.*

distortion, *s.* deformación, *f.*; torcimiento, *m.*; contorsión, *f.*; perversión, *f.*; (*rad.*) deformación, *f.*

distract, *v.t.* distraer; interrumpir; perturbar; (turn aside) desviar, apartar; (madden) enloquecer, volver loco (a)

distracted, *a.* aturdido; demente, loco

distractedly, *adv.* locamente; perdidamente

distraction, *s.* distracción, *f.*; (amusement) diversion, *f.*, pasatiempo, *m.*; (bewilderment) confusión, *f.*, aturdimiento, *m.*; (madness) locura, *f.*; frenesí, *m.* **to drive to d.**, trastornar, sacar de quicio.

distrain, *v.i.* embargar

distraint, *s.* embargo, *m.*

distraught, *a.* aturdido; desesperado; enloquecido

distress, *s.* dolor, *m.*, aflicción, *f.*; pena, *f.*; miseria, penuria, *f.*; (exhaustion) fatiga, *f.*, cansancio, *m.*; (pain) dolor, *m.*; (misfortune) desdicha, *f.*; apuro, *m.*; (danger) peligro, *m.*; (*law*) embargo, *m.* —*v.i.* afligir; dar pena (a), llenar · de angustia; cansar, fatigar; (pain) doler

distressed, *a.* afligido; necesitado, pobre

distressing, *a.* doloroso, penoso

distributable, *a.* repartible

distribute, *v.t.* (of justice, etc.) administrar; distribuir; repartir

distribution, *s.* (of justice) administración, *f.*; distribución, *f.*; reparto, *m.*

distributive, *a.* distributivo

distributor, *s.* distribuidor (-ra), repartidor (-ra). **d. of false money,** expendedor (-ra) de moneda falsa

district, *s.* distrito, *m.*; comarca, *f.*; (of a town) barrio, *m.*; (judicial) partido judicial, *m.*; jurisdicción, *f.*; región, zona, *f.*

distrust, *s.* desconfianza, *f.*; recelo, *m.*, sospecha, *f.* *v.t.* desconfiar de, sospechar

distrustful, *a.* desconfiado, receloso, suspicaz

distrustfully, *adv.* desconfiadamente, con recelo

disturb, *v.t.* perturbar; interrumpir; incomodar; (make anxious) inquietar; (alter) cambiar; (disarrange) desordenar, desarreglar. **to d. the peace**, perturbar el orden público

disturbance, *s.* perturbación, *f.*; disturbio, *m.*, conmoción, *f.*; incomodidad, *f.*; agitación, *f.*; confusión, *f.*; tumulto, *m.*; desorden, *m.*; (*rad.*) parásitos, *m. pl.*

disturber, *s.* perturbador (-ra)

disturbing, *a.* perturbador; inquietador; conmovedor, impresionante, emocionante

disunion, *s.* desunión, *f.*; discordia, *f.*

disunite, *v.t.* desunir; separar, dividir. *v.i.* separarse

disuse, *s.* desuso, *m.* *v.t.* desusar; desacostumbrar. **to fall into d.**, caer en desuso

ditch, *s.* zanja, *f.*; (for defence, etc.) foso, *m.*; (irrigation) acequia, *f.* *v.t.* zanjar; abarrancar. **to die in the last d.**, morir en la brecha

dithyramb, *s.* ditirambo, *m.*

ditto, *adv.* ídem; también

ditty, *s.* canción, cantinela, *f.*

diuretic, *a.* diurético

diurnal, *a.* diurno

divagation, *s.* divagación, *f.*

divan, *s.* diván, *m.*

dive, *s.* buceo, *m.*; (*aer.*) picada, *f.* *v.i.* bucear; sumergirse (en); (*aer.*) volar en picado; penetrar (en); (into a book) enfrascarse en. **to d. out**, salir precipitadamente. **to d.-bomb**, bombardear en picado. **d.-bomber**, avión en picado, *m.* **d.-bombing**, bombardeo en picado, *m.*

diver, *s.* buzo, *m.*; (bird) somorgujo, *m.*

diverge, *v.i.* divergir

divergence, *s.* divergencia, *f.*

divergent, *a.* divergente

diverse, *a.* diverso, vario

diversify, *v.t.* diversificar

diversion, *s.* diversión, *f.*; entretenimiento, *m.*, recreación, *f.*; pasatiempo, *m.*; placer, *m.*; (*mil.*) diversión, *f.*

diversity, *s.* diversidad, variedad, *f.*

divert, *v.t.* desviar; (amuse) divertir, entretener

diverting, *a.* divertido, entretenido

divide, *v.t.* dividir; partir; separar; (cut) cortar; (share) repartir, distribuir; (hair) hacer la raya (del pelo); (of voting) provocar una votación. *v.i.* dividirse; separarse; (of roads, etc.) bifurcarse; (of voting) votar.

divided-skirt, *s.* falda pantalón, *f.*

dividend, *s.* dividendo, *m.* **d. warrant**, cupón de dividendo, *m.*

dividers, *s. pl.* compás de puntas, *m.*

dividing, *a.* divisorio, divisor

divination, *s.* adivinación, *f.*

divine, *a.* divino; sublime; (*fam.*) estupendo. *s.* teólogo, *m.* *v.t.* (foretell) vaticinar, pronosticar; presentir; (guess) adivinar

diving, *s.* buceo, *m.*; (*aer.*) picado, *m.* **d.-bell**, campana de bucear, *f.* **d.-board**, (low) trampolín, *m.*; (high) palanca, *f.* **d.-suit**, escafandra, *f.*

divining-rod, *s.* vara divinatoria, *f.*

divinity, *s.* divinidad, *f.*; teología, *f.*

divisibility, *s.* divisibilidad, *f.*

divisible, *a.* divisible

division, *s.* división, *f.*; separación, *f.*; (distribution) repartimiento, *m.*; (*mil., math.*) división, *f.*; sección, *f.*; grupo, *m.*; (voting) votación, *f.*; (discord) discordia, desunión, *f.* **without a d.**, por unanimidad, sin votar

divisor, *s.* (*math.*) divisor, *m.*

divorce, *s.* divorcio, *m.* *v.t.* divorciarse de; (*fig.*) divorciar, separar. **to file a petition of d.**, poner una petición de divorcio

divorcee, *s.* (wife) divorciada, *f.*; (husband) divorciado, *m.*

divulge, *v.t.* divulgar, revelar

dizzily, *adv.* vertiginosamente

dizziness, *s.* vértigo, *m.;* mareo, *m.;* (bewilderment) aturdimiento, *m.,* confusión, *f.*

dizzy, *a.* vertiginoso; mareado; confuso, perplejo, aturdido

do, *v.t.* hacer; ejecutar; (one's duty, etc.) cumplir con; concluir; (cause) causar; (homage) rendir; (commit) cometer; (arrange) arreglar; (cook) cocer, guisar; (roast) asar; (*fam.,* cheat) engañar; (suit) convenir; (suffice) bastar; (act) hacer el papel (de); (*fam.,* treat) tratar (bien o mal); (learn) aprender; (exhaust) agotar; (walk) andar; (travel, journey) recorrer; (translate) traducir; (prepare) preparar. *v.i.* hacer; (behave) conducirse; (of health) estar (bien o mal); (act) obrar; (get on) ir; (be suitable, suit) convenir; (suffice) bastar; (of plants) florecer; (cook) cocerse; (last) durar. **Don't!** ¡No lo hagas!; ¡Quieto!; ¡Calla! **How do you do?** ¿Cómo está Vd?; ¡Buenos días! **Have done!** ¡Acaba de una vez! **It will do you good,** Te conviene; Te hará bien; Te sentará bien. **It will do you no harm,** No te perjudicará; No te hará daño. **I could do with one,** Me gustaría (tener) uno; (of drinks) Me bebería uno con mucho gusto. **That will do,** Eso basta; Se puede servirse de eso; Está bien así; (leave it alone) ¡Déjate de eso!; (be quiet!) ¡No digas más!; ¡Cállate! **That won't do,** Eso no es bastante; Eso no sirve; Eso no se hace así; Eso no se hace. **That will never do,** Eso no servirá; Eso no puede ser. **This will do,** (when buying an article) Me quedaré con éste; Me serviré de esto; Esto basta; Esto será suficiente; (is all right) Está bien así. **Thy will be done!** ¡Hágase tu voluntad! **to be doing,** estar haciendo; estar ocupado en (or con) hacer; (of food) estar cocinando. **to be done for,** estar perdido; estar muerto. **to do better,** hacer mejor (que); (mend one's ways) enmendarse, corregirse; (improve) mejorar, hacer progresos; (in health) encontrarse mejor. **to do nothing,** no hacer nada. **to do reverence,** rendir homenaje; inclinarse. **to do to death,** matar; asesinar; ejecutar. **to do violence to,** (*fig.*) hacer fuerza a. **to do well,** hacer bien; obrar bien; (be successful) tener éxito; hacer buena impresión; (prosperous) tener una buena posición. **to do wonders,** hacer maravillas. **to have done with,** renunciar (a); dejar de usar; dejar de hacer, cesar; concluir, terminar; no tener más que ver con; (forsake) abandonar; (a person) romper con. **to have nothing to do,** no tener nada que hacer. **to have nothing to do with,** no tener nada que ver con; (of people) no tratar; (end a friendship) romper su amistad con, dejar de ver. **well done,** bien hecho; (of food) bien guisado; (of meat) bien asado. **What is to be done?** ¿Qué hay que hacer?; ¿Qué se puede hacer? **What is to do?** ¿Qué pasa? ¿Qué hay? **When he had done speaking,** Cuando hubo terminado de hablar. **to do again,** hacer de nuevo, volver a hacer, rehacer; repetir. **He will not do it again,** No lo hará más. **to do away with,** quitar; eliminar; suprimir; hacer desaparecer; poner fin a; hacer cesar; destruir; matar. **to do by,** tratar (a), portarse con. **to do for,** arruinar; matar; (suffice) bastar para; ser a propósito para, servir para; (look after) cuidar; (as a housekeeper) dirigir la casa para. **to do out,** (a room) limpiar. **to do out of,** quitar; privar de; (steal) robar. **to do up,** (tie) atar; (fold) enrollar, plegar; envolver; (parcel) empaquetar; (arrange) arreglar; decorar; poner en orden; poner como nuevo; (iron) planchar; (launder) lavar y planchar; (tire) fatigar. **to do with,** (of people) tratar; (of things) tener que ver con; (put up with) poder con; poder sufrir. **to do without,** prescindir de; pasarse sin

do as an auxiliary verb is not translated in Spanish, e.g. **I do**

believe, creo. **Do not do that, no hagas eso. I did not know,** no sabía

When it is used for emphasis, do is translated by sí, ciertamente, claro and similar words, e.g.: **She did not know, but he did,** Ella no lo sabía pero él sí **You do paint well,** Pintas muy bien por cierto **Do come this time,** No dejes de venir esta vez

docile, *a.* dócil

docility, *s.* docilidad, *f.*

dock, *s.* dique, *m.*, dársena, *f.*; (wharf) muelle, *m.*; (in a law court) banquillo de los acusados, *m.*; (*bot.*) romaza, *f.* *v.t.* (a tail) descolar; cortar, cercenar; reducir; (money) descontar; (a ship) poner en dique. *v.i.* entrar en dique. **dry-d.,** dique seco, *m.* **floating-d.,** dique flotante, *m.* **d.-dues,** muellaje, *m.* **d. rat,** (thief) raquero, *m.*

docker, *s.* estibador, descargador del muelle, *m.*

docket, *s.* (bundle) legajo, *m.*; extracto, *m.*; minuta, *f.*; (label) etiqueta, *f.*, marbete, *m.*

dockyard, *s.* arsenal, astillero, *m.*

doctor, *s.* doctor (-ra); (medical practitioner) médico (-ca). *v.t.* visitar como médico, asistir; (repair) reparar, componer; adulterar; mezclar drogas con; falsificar. *v.i.* ejercer la medicina. **family d.,** médico de cabecera, *m.* **to graduate as a d.,** doctorarse. **d. of divinity, laws, medicine,** doctor (-ra) en teología, en derecho, en medicina, *m.*

doctoral, *a.* doctoral

doctorate, *s.* doctorado, *m.*

doctrinaire, *a.* and *s.* doctrinario (-ia)

doctrinal, *a.* doctrinal

doctrine, *s.* doctrina, *f.*

document, *s.* documento, *m.* *v.t.* documentar; probar con documentos. **d.-case,** carpeta, *f.*

documentary, *a.* documental; escrito, auténtico. **d. film,** película documental, *f.*

documentation, *s.* documentación, *f.*

dodecahedron, *s.* dodecaedro, *m.*

dodge, *s.* esguince, regate, *m.*; evasiva, *f.*; (trick) estratagema,

m., maniobra, *f.*; artefacto, *m.* *v.t.* esquivar, evadir

doe, *s.* gama, *f.* **doe rabbit,** coneja, *f.*

doer, *s.* hacedor (-ra); autor (-ra)

doeskin, *s.* ante, *m.*, piel de gama, *f.*

doff, *v.t.* quitar; (of hats, etc.) quitarse; desnudarse de

dog, *s.* perro, *m.*; (male) macho, *m.*; (andiron) morillo, *m.*; (*ast.*) Can Mayor (or Menor), Sirio, *m.* *v.t.* perseguir; seguir los pasos de; espiar. **You can't deceive an old dog,** A perro viejo no hay tus tus. **to go to the dogs,** ir a las carreras de galgos; (*fig.*) ir cuesta abajo. **mongrel dog,** perro mestizo, *m.* **thoroughbred dog,** perro de raza pura, *m.* **dog-collar,** collar de perro, *m.*; (*ecc.*) alzacuello, *m.* **dog-days,** días caniculares, *m. pl.*, canícula, *f.* **dog-eared** (of books) con las puntas de las hojas dobladas. **dog-fight,** lucha de perros, *f.*; combate aéreo, *m.* **dog-fish,** lija, *f.*, cazón, *m.* **dog in the manger,** el perro del hortelano. **dog-kennel,** perrera, *f.* **dog-latin,** bajo latín, *m.* **dog licence,** matrícula de perros, *f.* **dog-racing,** carrera de galgos, *f.* **dog-rose,** escaramujo, *m.* **dog show,** exposición canina, *f.* **dog-tooth,** (*arch.*) diente de perro, *m.* **dog-vane,** (*naut.*) cataviento, *m.*

doge, *s.* dux (de Venecia), *m.*

dogged, *a.* persistente, tenaz, pertinaz, obstinado

doggedly, *adv.* tenazmente

doggedness, *s.* pertinacia, tenacidad, terquedad, persistencia, *f.*

doggerel, *s.* malos versos, *m. pl.*; aleluyas, coplas de ciego, *f. pl.* *a.* malo, irregular

dogma, *s.* dogma, *m.*

dogmatic, *a.* dogmático

dogmatically, *adv.* dogmáticamente

dogmatize, *v.t.* and *v.i.* dogmatizar; mostrarse dogmático

doh, *s.* (*mus.*) do, *m.*

doily, *s.* pañito de adorno, *m.*

doings, *s. pl.* acciones, *f. pl.*; (deeds) hechos, *m. pl.*; (behaviour) conducta, *f.*; (happenings) acontecimientos, *m. pl.*; (works) obras, *f. pl.*; (things) cosas, *f. pl.*

doldrums, *s. pl.* calmas ecuatoriales, *f. pl.*

dole, *s.* limosna, *f.*; porción, *f.* to d. out, repartir; distribuir en porciones pequeñas; racionar; dar contra la voluntad de uno.

doleful, *a.* triste, lúgubre, melancólico; doloroso

dolefulness, *s.* tristeza, melancolía, *f.*; dolor, *m.*

doll, *s.* muñeca, *f.*

dollar, *s.* dólar, *m.*

dolly, *s.* muñeca, *f.*; (for clothes) moza, *f.* d.-tub, cubo para la colada, *m.*

dolman, *s.* dormán, *m.*

dolphin, *s.* delfín, *m.*

dolt, *s.* cabeza de alcornoque, *m.* or *f.*, zamacuco, *m.*

domain, *s.* territorio, *m.*; heredad, posesión, propiedad, *f.*; (empire) dominio, *m.*

dome, *s.* cúpula, *f.*; bóveda, *f.*; (palace) palacio, *m.*

domestic, *a.* doméstico; familiar; (home-loving) casero; (of animals) doméstico; (national) interior, nacional. *s.* doméstico, sirviente, *m.*; criada, *f.* d. economy, economía doméstica, *f.*

domesticate, *v.t.* domesticar

domesticated, *a.* (of animals) domesticado; (of persons) casero

domestication, *s.* domesticación, *f.*

domesticity, *s.* domesticidad, *f.*

domicile, *s.* domicilio, *m. v.t.* domiciliar

domiciliary, *a.* domiciliario

dominant, *a.* dominante; imperante. *s.* (*mus.*) dominante, *f.* to be d., prevalecer

dominate, *v.t.* and *v.i.* dominar

domination, *s.* dominación, *f.*

domineer, *v.i.* dominar, tiranizar. to d. over, mandar en

domineering, *a.* dominante, mandón, tiránico

Dominican, *a.* dominicano. *s.* dominicano, *m.*

dominion, *s.* dominio, *m.*; autoridad, soberanía, *f.*; imperio, *m.*; *pl.* dominions, (*ecc.*) dominaciones, *f. pl.*

domino, *s.* dominó, *m.* to go d., hacer dominó

don, *s.* (Spanish title) don, *m.*; señor, *m. v.t.* ponerse, vestirse

donation, *s.* donación, dádiva, *f.*; contribución, *f.*

done, *a.* and *past part.* hecho; (of food) cocido; (roasted) asado; (tired) rendido; (*fam.*, deceived) engañado. Well d.! ¡Bien hecho! d. for, arruinado; muerto; perdido; vencido; (spoilt) estropeado

donkey, *s.* borrico (-ca), burro (-rra). d.-engine, máquina auxiliar, *f.*

donor, *s.* donador (-ra); dador (-ra)

doom, *s.* condena, *f.*; (fate) suerte, *f.*; (judgment) destino, *m.*; ruina, *f.*; juicio, *m. v.t.* sentenciar; condenar

doomsday, *s.* día del juicio final, *m.*

door, *s.* puerta, *f.*; entrada, *f.* front d., puerta de entrada, *f.* next d., la casa vecina; la puerta de al lado, or vecina. next d. neighbour, vecino (-na) de al lado. out of doors, al aire libre; en la calle. to knock at the d., llamar a la puerta. to slam the d. in a person's face, dar con la puerta en las narices de alguien. d.-bell, timbre (non-electric, campanilla, *f.*) de llamada, *m.* d.-jamb, quicial, *m.* d. keeper, portero, *m.* d.-knob, tirador, *m.* d.-knocker, picaporte, *m.*, aldaba, *f.* d.-plate, placa, *f.* d.-shutter, cierre metálico, *m.* d.-step, peldaño de la puerta, *m.*; umbral, *m.* d.-way, portal, *m.*

dope, *s.* drogas, *f. pl.*, narcóticos, *m. pl.*; (news) información, *f.* d. fiend, morfinómano (-na)

Doric, *a.* dórico

dormant, *a.* durmiente; latente; secreto; inactivo. to go d., dormirse

dormer-window, *s.* lumbrera, *f.*

dormitory, *s.* dormitorio, *m.*

dormouse, *s.* lirón, *m.*

dorsal, *a.* dorsal

dorsum, *s.* dorso, *m.*

dory, *s.* (fish) dorado, *m.*

dose, dosage, *s.*; dosis, *f.*

dossier, *s.* documentación, *f.*

dot, *s.* punto, *m.*; (*mus.*) puntillo, *m.*; *pl.* dots, (*gram.*) puntos

suspensivos, *m. pl. v.t.* poner
punto (a una letra); (scatter)
salpicar. **on the dot,** (of time)
en punto. **to dot one's i's,**
poner los puntos sobre las íes

dotage, *s.* senectud, chochera, *f.*

dotard, *s.* viejo chocho, *m.*;
vieja chocha, *f.*; (*fam.*) carcamal,
m.

dote, *v.i.* chochear. **to d. on,**
adorar, *m.* idolatrar

doting, *a.* (both meanings) chocho

double, *a.* and *adv.* doble; dos
veces; (in a pair) en par; en dos;
doblemente; (deceitful) doble, de
dos caras, falso; ambiguo. *s.*
doble, *m.*; duplicado, *m.*; (*theat.*)
contrafigura, *f.*; *pl.* **doubles,**
(tennis) dobles, *m. pl.*, juego doble,
m. v.t. doblar; duplicar; (fold)
doblegar; (the fist) cerrar (el
puño); (*theat.* and *naut.*) doblar.
v.i. doblarse; (dodge) volverse
atrás, hacer un rodeo, dar una
vuelta; esquivarse. **to d. up,** *v.t.*
envolver; arrollar; (a person)
doblar. *v.i.* doblegarse; arrollarse; (collapse) desplomarse. **at
the d.,** corriendo. **He was
doubled up with pain,** El dolor
le hacía retorcerse. **mixed
doubles,** parejas mixtas, *f. pl.*;
dobles mixtos, *m. pl.* **double
two,** (telephone) dos dos. **with
a d. meaning,** con segunda
intención. **d.-barrelled,** de dos
cañones. **d.-bass,** contrabajo,
m. **d. bed,** cama de matrimonio,
f. **d.-bedded,** con cama de
matrimonio; con dos camas.
d.-breasted, cruzado. **d.-chin,**
papada, *f.* **d.-dealing,** duplicidad, *f.* **d.-edged,** de doble filo.
d.-entry, (*com.*) partida doble, *f.*
d.-faced, de dos caras. **d.-
jointed,** con articulaciones dobles

doublet, *s.* (garment) jubón,
justillo, *m.*; pareja, *f.*, par, *m.*

doubling, *s.* doblamiento, *m.*;
doblez, plegadura, *f.*; duplicación, *f.*; (dodging) evasiva, *f.*,
esguince, *m.*

doubloon, *s.* doblón, *m.*

doubly, *adv.* doblemente; con
duplicidad

doubt, *s.* duda, *f.*; incertidumbre,
f.; sospecha, *f. v.t.* and *v.i.*
dudar; sospechar; titubear, hesitar; temer. **beyond all d.,** fuera

de duda. **no d.,** sin duda.
There is no d. that, No hay
duda de que, No cabe duda de
que. **When in d. . . .,** En caso
de duda . . .

doubter, *s.* incrédulo (-la)

doubtful, *a.* dudoso; incierto;
perplejo; ambiguo; (of places)
sospechoso

doubtfully, *adv.* dudosamente;
inciertamente; irresolutamente;
ambiguamente

doubtfulness, *s.* duda, incertidumbre, *f.*; ambigüedad, *f.*

doubtless, *adv.* sin duda, por
supuesto; probablemente

douche, *s.* ducha, *f. v.t.* duchar

dough, *s.* pasta, masa, *f.*

dour, *a.* huraño, adusto, austero

dourly, *adv.* severamente

douse, *v.t.* zambullir; (a sail)
recoger; (*fam.*) apagar

dove, *s.* paloma, *f.* **d.-cote,**
palomar, *m.*

dovetail, *s.* (*carp.*) cola de milano,
f. v.t. (*carp.*) machihembrar,
empalmar; (*fig.*) encajar

dowager, *s.* viuda, *f.*; matrona, *f.*
d. countess, condesa viuda, *f.*

dowdiness, *s.* desaliño, deseaseo,
m.; falta de elegancia, *f.*

dowdy, *a.* desaliñado, desaseado;
poco elegante. *s.* mujer poco
elegante, *f.*

dowel, *s.* espiga, clavija, *f.*,
zoquete, *m. v.t.* enclavijar

down, *s.* (of a bird) plumón, *m.*;
(on a peach, etc.) pelusilla, *f.*;
(hair) vello, *m.*; (before the
beard) bozo, *m.*; (of a thistle,
etc.) vilano, *m.*; **ups and
downs,** vicisitudes, *f. pl.*

down, *a.* pendiente; (of trains,
etc.) descendente. *adv.* abajo;
hacia abajo; (lowered) bajado;
(of the eyes) bajos; (on the
ground) en tierra, por tierra;
(stretched out) tendido a lo
largo; (depressed) triste, abatido;
(ill) enfermo; (fallen) caído; (of
the wind) cesado; (closed) cerrado; (exhausted) agotado; (*com.*)
al contado; (of temperature) más
bajo. *prep.* abajo de; abajo; en la
dirección de; (along) a lo largo
de; por. *interj.* ¡Abajo!; ¡A
tierra! **He went d. the hill,**
Bajaba la colina. **He is d. now,**
Ha bajado ahora; Está abajo

ahora; Está derribado ahora.
The sun has gone d., Se ha
puesto el sol. **His stock has
gone d.,** (*fig., fam.*) Ha caído en
disfavor. **Prices have come d.,**
Los precios han bajado. **Their
numbers have gone d.,** Sus
números han disminuido. **to
be d. and out,** estar completamente arruinado, ser pobre de
solemnidad. **to boil d.,** reducir
hirviendo. **to come d. in the
world,** venir a menos. **While
I was going d. the river,**
Mientras iba río abajo, Mientras
bajaba al río. **d. below,** allá
abajo; abajo; en el piso de
abajo. **D. on your knees!**
¡De rodillas! **d. to,** hasta. **d.
spout,** tubo de bajada, *m.*
D. with! ¡Abajo! ¡Muera! **d.-
stream,** agua abajo. **d. train,**
tren descendente, *m.*

down, *v.t.* derribar; vencer. **to
d. tools,** declararse en huelga

downcast, *a.* bajo; cabizbajo,
deprimido, abatido

downfall, *s.* caída, *f.*; derrumbamiento, *m.*; (failure) fracaso, *m.*;
(*fig.*, ruin) decadencia, ruina, *f.*

downhearted, *a.* descorazonado,
alicaído, desalentado

downhill, *adv.* cuesta abajo,
hacia abajo. *a.* en declive, inclinado. **to go d.,** ir cuesta
abajo (also *fig.*)

downiness, *s.* vellosidad, *f.*

downpour, *s.* aguacero, chaparrón, *m.*; lluvia, *f.*

downright, *a.* franco, sincero;
categórico, terminante; absoluto.
adv. muy; completamente

downstairs, *adv.* escalera abajo;
al piso de abajo; en el piso bajo;
abajo. *a.* del piso de abajo. *s.*
planta baja, *f.*; piso de abajo, *m.*
to go d., bajar la escalera; ir al
piso de abajo

downtrodden, *a.* oprimido, es-
clavizado

downward, *a.* descendente; inclinado. *adv.* hacia abajo

downy, *a.* velloso; (*fam.*, of persons) con más conchas que un
galápago

dowry, *s.* dote, *m.* or *f.* **to give
as a d.,** dotar

dowse, *v.t.* See **douse**

doxology, *s.* doxología, *f.*

doze, *v.i.* dormitar. *s.* sueño
ligero, *m.*

dozen, *s.* docena, *f.*

drab, *a.* pardo, parduzco, grisáceo; (*fig.*) gris, monótono. *s.*
(slut) pazpuerca, *f.*; (prostitute)
ramera, *f.*

drachma, *s.* dracma, *f.*

draft, *s.* (detachment) destacamento, *m.*; (*com.*) giro, *m.*, letra
de cambio, *f.*; (for the army,
navy) conscripción, leva, *f.*;
(outline) bosquejo, *m.*; proyecto,
m.; borrador, *m.* *v.t.* (detach)
destacar; (recruit) reclutar; (outline) bosquejar, delinear; (draw
up) redactar; proyectar

drafting, *s.* (*mil., nav.*) reclutamiento, *m.*; (of a bill, etc.)
redacción, *f.*; (wording) términos, *m. pl.*

draftsman, *s.* dibujante, *m.*;
delineante, *m.*; redactor, *m.*

drag, *s.* (for dredging) draga, *f.*;
(harrow) rastrillo, *m.*; (break)
freno, *m.*; (obstacle) estorbo,
m.; (*aer.*) sonda, *f.* *v.t.* arrastrar;
(fishing nets) rastrear; (harrow)
rastrillar. *v.i.* (of the anchor)
garrar; arrastrarse por el suelo;
(of time) pasar lentamente; ir
más despacio (que); (of interest)
decaer, disminuir. **d.-hook,**
garfio, *m.* **d.-net,** brancada, *f.*

dragging, *s.* arrastre, *m.*; (of
lakes, etc.) rastreo, *m.* *a.* rastrero; cansado

draggled, *a.* mojado y sucio

dragon, *s.* dragón, *m.* **d.-fly,**
libélula, *f.*, caballito del diablo,
m.

dragoon, *s.* (*mil.*) dragón, *m.*
v.t. someter a una disciplina
rigurosa; obligar a la fuerza
(a)

drain, *s.* desaguadero, *m.*; (sewer)
cloaca, alcantarilla, *f.*; sumidero,
m.; (*agr.*) acequia, *f.* *v.t.* desaguar; sanear; (lakes, etc.) desangrar; secar; (bail) achicar;
(empty and drink) vaciar; (swallow) tragar; (*fig.*, of sorrow, etc.)
apurar; (despoil) despojar; (deprive) privar (de); (impoverish)
empobrecer; (exhaust) agotar.
v.i. desaguarse; vaciarse; (with
off) escurrirse. **to be well
drained,** tener buen drenaje.
to d. the sump, vaciar la

culata. **to d. away**, vaciar. **d.-pipe**, tubo de desagüe, *m.*

drainage, *s.* (of land) drenaje, *m.*; desagüe, *m.*; (of wounds) drenaje, *m.*; (sewage) aguas del alcantarillado, *f. pl.* **main d.**, drenaje municipal, *m.*

draining, *s.* See **drainage**. *a.* de desagüe; de drenaje. **d.-board**, escurridor, *m.*

drake, *s.* ánade macho, *m.*

dram, *s.* dracma, *f.*; (of liquor) trago, *m.*

drama, *s.* drama, *m.*

dramatic, *a.* dramático

dramatically, *adv.* dramáticamente

dramatis personæ, *s. pl.* personajes, *m. pl.*

dramatist, *s.* dramaturgo, *m.*

dramatization, *s.* versión escénica, *f.*; descripción dramática, *f.*; (of emotions) dramatización, *f.*

dramatize, *v.t.* dramatizar

drape, *v.t.* colgar, cubrir; vestir

draper, *s.* pañero (-ra)

drapery, *s.* colgaduras, *f. pl.*; ropaje, *m.*, ropas, *f. pl.*; pañería, *f.*

drastic, *a.* drástico; enérgico, fuerte

draught, *s.* (act of drawing) tiro, *m.*; (of liquid) trago, *m.*; (glass) vaso, *m.*; (of a ship) calado, *m.*; (of air) corriente de aire, *f.*; (party) destacamento, *m.*; *s. pl.* **draughts**, (game) damas, *f. pl.* *v.t.* see **draft. on d.**, (of beer, etc.) por vaso. **d. horse**, caballo de tiro, *m.* **d. screen**, cancel, *m.*

draughtboard, *s.* tablero de damas, *m.*

draughtsman, *s.* dibujante, *m.*; delineante, *m.*; redactor, *m.*; (piece in game) peón, *m.*

draughtsmanship, *s.* arte del dibujo lineal, *m.* or *f.*; redacción (de un proyecto de ley), *f.*

draughty, *a.* que tiene corriente de aire; expuesto a los vientos. **This room is d.**, Hay corriente de aire en esta habitación

draw, *v.t.* tirar; arrastrar; traer; (pluck) arrancar; (attract) atraer; (extract) extraer; sacar; hacer salir; (unsheath) desenvainar; (a bow-string) tender; (cards, dominoes) tomar, robar; (threads)

deshilar; (disembowel) destripar; (a cheque, etc.) girar, librar; (of a ship) calar; (of lines) hacer (rayas); (curtains) correr; (to draw curtains back) descorrer; (salary, money) cobrar, percibir; (obtain) obtener; (persuade) persuadir, inducir; (inhale) respirar; (a sigh) dar; (win) ganar; (a conclusion) deducir, inferir; (a distinction) hacer formular; (*sport*) empatar; (a number, etc.) sortear; (suck) chupar; (tighten) estirar; (lengthen) alargar; (comfort, etc.) tomar; (inspiration) inspirarse en; (obtain money) procurarse (recursos); (withdraw funds) retirar; (write) escribir; (draw) dibujar; (trace) trazar; (provoke) provocar. **to be drawn**, (of tickets in a lottery and cards) salir. **to d. lots**, echar suertes. **to d. water**, sacar agua. **to d. along**, arrastrar; conducir. **to d. aside**, tomar a un lado, tomar aparte; quitar de en medio, poner a un lado; (curtains) descorrer. **to d. away**, (remove) quitar; (a person) llevarse (a); apartar. **to d. back**, hacer recular; hacer retirarse; hacer volverse atrás; (curtains) descorrer. **to d. down**, hacer bajar; tirar a lo largo de (or por); bajar; (attract) atraer. **to d. forth**, hacer salir; hacer avanzar; tirar hacia adelante; conducir; (develop) desarrollar; sacar; hacer aparecer; (comment, etc.) suscitar. **to d. in**, tirar hacia adentro; sacar; acercar; atraer. **to d. off**, sacar; retirar; quitar; (water from pipes, etc.) vaciar; (*print.*) tirar; (turn aside) desviar. **to d. on, on**, (of apparel) ponerse; (boots) calzarse; (occasion) ocasionar. **to d. out**, sacar fuera; hacer salir; tirar (de); (extract) extraer; (trace) trazar; (a person) hacer hablar. **to d. over**, poner encima de; arrastrar por; hacer acercarse (a), tirar hacia; atraer; persuadir. **to d. round**, poner alrededor de. **to d. together**, reunir; acercar. **to d. up**, tirar hacia arriba; subir; sacar; extraer; (raise) levantar; alzar; (bring) traer; (bring near)

acercar; (order) ordenar; (mil.)
formar; (a document) redactar;
formular. to d. oneself up,
erguirse
draw, v.i. tirar; (shrink) encogerse; (wrinkle) arrugarse; (of
chimneys, etc.) tirar; (a picture)
dibujar; (sport) empatar; (move)
moverse; avanzar, adelantarse;
(of a ship) calar; (a sword) desnudar (la espada); (lots) echar
suertes; (attract people) atraer
gente; (com.) girar. to d. aside,
ponerse a un lado; retirarse. to
d. back, retroceder, recular; retirarse; vacilar. to d. in, retirarse; (of days) hacerse corto; (of
dusk) caer. to d. off, alejarse;
apartarse, retirarse. to d. on,
(approach) acercarse; avanzar;
(com.) girar contra; inspirarse
en. to d. out, hacerse largo; (of a
vehicle) ponerse en marcha,
empezar a andar. to d. round,
ponerse alrededor; reunirse
alrededor. to d. together, reunirse. to d. up, parar.
draw, s. tirada, f.; (of lotteries)
sorteo, m.; (sport) empate, m.;
atracción, f.; (fig., feeler) tanteo,
m. to be a big d., ser una gran
atracción
drawback, s. desventaja, f.,
inconveniente, m.
drawbridge, s. puente levadizo,
m.
drawee, s. (com.) girado, m.
drawer, s. tirador (-ra); (of
water) aguador (-ra); extractor
(-ra); (in a public-house) mozo
de taberna, m.; (designer) diseñador, m.; (sketcher) dibujante,
m. and f.; (com.) girador, m.;
(receptacle) cajón, m.; pl. drawers, (men's) calzoncillos, m. pl.;
(women's) pantalones, m. pl.
drawing, s. (pulling) tiro, m.;
atracción, f.; (extraction) extracción, f.; saca, f.; (in raffles,
etc. and of lots) sorteo, m.; (of
money) percibo, m.; (com.) giro,
m.; (sketch) dibujo, m.; (plan)
esquema, f. free-hand d.,
dibujo a pulso, m. d. from life,
dibujo del natural, m. d.-
board, tablero de dibujo, m.
d.-paper, papel para dibujar, m.
d.-pin, chinche, f. d.-room,
salón, m.

drawl, v.i. hablar arrastrando las
palabras
drawn, past part. See draw.
a. (tired) ojeroso, con ojeras, con
un aspecto de cansancio; (with
pain) desencajado. long d.
out, demasiado largo. d. sword,
espada desnuda, f. d.-thread
work, deshilados, m. pl.
dray, s carro, m. d.-horse,
caballo de tiro, m.
dread, s. pavor, temor, terror,
espanto, m.; trepidación, f.,
miedo, m. a. temible, espantoso,
terrible; augusto. v.t. temer.
v.i. tener miedo, temer. in d.
of, con miedo de, con terror
de
dreader, s. el, m. (f. la) que teme,
temedor (-ra)
dreadful, a. terrible, pavoroso,
espantoso, horroroso; formidable; augusto
dreadfully, adv. terriblemente,
horriblemente
dreadfulness, s. horror, m.
dreadnought, s. acorazado de
línea, m.
dream, s. sueño, m.; ilusión, f.;
ensueño, m.; fantasía, f. v.t.
and v.i. soñar; imaginar. He
dreamed away the hours,
Pasaba las horas soñando. I
wouldn't d. of it! ¡Ni por
sueño! in a d., en sueños;
(waking) como en sueños; mecánicamente. Sweet dreams!
¡Duerme bien! to d. of, soñar con
dreamer, s. soñador (-ra);
visionario (-ia)
dreamily, adv. como en sueños;
soñolientamente; vagamente
dreaming, s. sueños, m. pl.
dreamland, s. reino de los sueños,
m.
dreamy, a. soñador; soñoliento;
fantástico; (empty) vacío
dreariness, s. tristeza, f.; melan-
coliá, f.; lobreguez, f.
dreary, a. triste; melancólico;
lóbrego
dredge, v.t. dragar; (with sugar,
etc.) espolvorear
dredger, s. draga, f.; (for sugar)
azucarera, f.; (for flour) harinero,
m.
dredging, s. dragado, m.; (sprinkling) salpicadura, f. d. bucket,
cangilón, m.

dregs, s. pl. heces, f. pl., posos, m. pl. **to drain to the d.,** vaciar hasta las heces

drench, v.t. mojar, calar. **He is drenched to the skin,** Está calado hasta los huesos

Dresden, s. Dresde, f. **D. china,** loza de Dresde, f.

dress, v.t. (with clothes) vestir; (arrange) arreglar; (the hair) peinar(se); (a wound) curar; (hides) adobar; (cloth) aprestar; (flax) rastrillar; (stone) labrar; (wood) desbastar; (prune) podar; (a garden) cultivar; (manure) abonar; (cul.) aderezar; preparar; (season) condimentar; (a table) poner; (adorn) ataviar, adornar; revestir; (a dead body) amortajar. v.i. vestirse; ataviarse; (of troops) alinearse. **all dressed up and nowhere to go,** compuesta y sin novio. **dressed up to the nines,** vestido de veinticinco alfileres. **Left (Right) d.!** ¡A la izquierda (A la derecha) alinearse! **to d. down,** (scold) poner como un trapo (a), dar una calada (a). **to d. up,** v.t. ataviar; (disguise) disfrazar. v.i. ponerse muy elegante; disfrazarse

dress, s. (in general) el vestir; (clothes) ropa, f.; (frock) vestido, traje, m.; (uniform) uniforme, m.; (fig., covering) hábitos, m. pl.; (appearance) aspecto, m.; forma, f. **full d.,** (uniform) uniforme de gala, m.; (civilian, man's) traje de etiqueta, m.; (woman's) traje de gala, m. **morning d.,** (man's) traje de paisano, m.; (woman's) vestido de todos los días, m.; (man's formal dress) chaqué, m. **ready-made d.,** traje hecho, m. **d. allowance,** alfileres, m. pl. **d.-circle,** anfiteatro, m. **d.-coat,** frac, m. **d. protector,** sobaquera, f. **d. rehearsal,** ensayo general, m. **d. shirt,** camisa de pechera dura, f. **d. suit,** (with white tie) traje de frac, m.; (with black tie) smoking, m. **d. sword,** espada de gala, f. **d. tie,** corbata de smoking (or de frac), f.

dresser, s. el que adereza; (of wounds) practicante (de hospital), m.; (valet) ayuda de cámara,

m.; (maid) doncella, f.; (of skins) adobador de pieles, m.; (furniture) aparador, m.; (in the kitchen) armario de la cocina, m.

dressing, s. el vestir(se); aderezamiento, m.; (for cloth) apresto, m.; (of leather) adobo, m.; (of wood) desbaste, m.; (of stone) labrado, m.; (manuring) estercoladura, f.; (sauce) salsa, f.; (seasoning) condimentación, f.; (of a wound) cura, f.; (bandage) apósito, m., vendaje, m. **d.-case,** neceser, saco de noche, m. **d.-down,** (fam.) rapapolvo, m. **d.-gown,** (woman's) salto de cama, quimono, m.; (man's) batín, m. **d.-jacket,** chambra, f., peinador, m. **d.-room,** (theat.) camarín, m.; (in a house) trasalcoba, recámara, f. **d.-station,** puesto de socorro, m. **d.-table,** tocador, m., mesa de tocador, f.

dressmaker, s. modista, m. and f.

dressmaking, s. confección de vestidos, f.; arte de la modista, m. or f.

dribble, v.i. gotear; (slaver) babear. v.t. (in football) regatear. s. (in football) regate, m.

dried, a. seco; (of fruit) paso. **d. up,** (withered) marchito; (of people) enjuto. **d. fish,** cecial, m. **d. meat,** cecina, f.

drift, s. (in a ship or 'plane's course) deriva, f.; (of a current) velocidad, f.; (tendency) tendencia, f.; (meaning) significación, f.; (heap) montón, m.; (aim) objeto, propósito, fin, m.; (min.) galería, f.; (of dust, etc.) nube, f.; (shower) lluvia, f.; (impulsion) impulso, m.; violencia, f. v.i. flotar, ir arrastrado por la corriente; amontonarse; (naut.) derivar; (aer.) abatir. v.t. llevar; amontonar. **drifts of sand,** arena movediza, f. **to d. into,** (war, etc.) entrar sin querer en; (habits) dar en la flor de; (a room, etc.) deslizarse en. **d.-wood,** madera de deriva, f.

drill, s. (instrument) taladro, perforador, m., barrena, f.; ejercicio, m., educación física, f.; (mil.) instrucción militar, f.;

(cloth) dril, *m.*; (*agr.*) sembradora mecánica, *f.*; (for seeds) hilera, *f.*; (discipline) disciplina, *f.*; (teaching) instrucción, *f. v.t.* taladrar, barrenar; enseñar el ejercicio (a); enseñar la instrucción; disciplinar; (seed) sembrar en hileras. *v.i.* hacer el ejercicio; hacer la instrucción militar. **d. ground**, (in a barracks) patio de un cuartel, *m.*; (in a school) patio de recreo, *m.* **d.-sergeant**, sargento instructor, *m.*

drilling, *s.* (boring) perforación, *f.*, barrenamiento, *m.*; (of seeds) sembradura en hileras, *f.*; ejercicios, *m. pl.*; (manœuvres) maniobras, *f. pl.*

drink, *s.* bebida, *f.*; (glass of wine, etc.) copita, *f.*; (of water, etc.) vaso, *m. v.t.* beber; tomar; (empty) vaciar. *v.i.* beber. **to d. the health of**, beber a la salud de, brindar por. **to give someone a d.**, dar a beber. **Would you like a d.?** ¿Quieres beber algo? **to d. in**, absorber. **to d. off, up**, beber de un trago

drinkable, *a.* potable, bebedero

drinker, *s.* bebedor (-ra)

drinking, *s.* acción de beber, *f.*; el beber, *m.*; (alcoholism) bebida, *f. a.* que bebe; aficionado a la bebida; (of things) para beber; (drinkable) potable; (tavern) de taberna. **d.-fountain**, fuente pública para beber agua, *f.* **d. place**, bebedero, *m.*; bar, *m.* **d.-song**, canción de taberna, *f.* **d.-trough**, abrevadero, *m.*; **d.-water**, agua potable, *f.*

drip, *v.i.* and *v.t.* gotear; caer gota a gota; escurrir; destilar; chorrear. *s.* goteo, *m.*; gota, *f.*; (*arch.*) goterón, *m.*

dripping, *s.* goteo, *m.*; chorreo, *m.*; (fat) grasa, *f. a.* que gotea; mojado; que chorrea agua. **d.-pan**, grasera, *f.*

drive, *v.t.* empujar; arrojar; conducir; (grouse, etc.) batir; (a ball) golpear; (a nail, etc.) clavar; (oblige) compeler, forzar a; (a horse, plough, etc.) manejar; (*mech.* work) mover; (cause to work, of machines) hacer funcionar; (a tunnel, etc.) abrir, construir; (a bargain, etc.) hacer; (cause) impulsar, hacer; (mad,

etc.) volver. *v.i.* lanzarse; (of rain) azotar; (a vehicle) conducir; (in a vehicle) ir en (coche, etc.). **to let d. at**, (aim) asestar. **to d. a wedge**, hacer mella. **to d. home an argument**, convencer; hacer convincente. **What is he driving at?** ¿Qué se propone?; ¿Qué quiere?; ¿Qué quiere decir con sus indirectas? **to d. along**, ir en coche o carruaje por; pasearse en coche o carruaje; conducir un auto, etc., por. **to d. away**, *v.t.* echar; (chase) cazar; (flies, etc.) sacudirse, espantar; (care, etc.) ahuyentar; (of persons) apartar, alejar. *v.i.* (depart) marcharse (en coche, etc.). **to d. back**, *v.t.* rechazar; (a ball) devolver. *v.i.* volver (en auto, etc.); (arrive) llegar. **to d. down**, hacer bajar; arrojar hacia abajo; (in a vehicle) bajar (por). **to d. in, into**, *v.t.* hacer entrar; (of teeth, etc.) hincar; (nails) clavar; (*fig.*) introducir. *v.t.* entrar (en coche, carruaje); llegar (en coche, etc.). **to d. off**, See away. **to d. off the stage**, hacer dejar la escena, silbar. **to d. on**, *v.t.* empujar; hacer avanzar; (attack) atacar. *v.i.* seguir su marcha; seguir avanzando; emprender la marcha. **to d. out**, *v.t.* expulsar; hacer salir; (chase) cazar. *v.i.* salir (en coche, etc.). **to d. up**, *v.i.* llegar (en coche, etc.); parar. **to d. up to**, avanzar hasta, llegar hasta; conducir (el coche, etc.) hasta

drive, *s.* paseo (en coche, etc.), *m.*; (avenue) avenida, *f.*; (distance) trayecto, *m.*; (journey) viaje, *m.*; (*mech.*) acción, *f.*; conducción, *f.*; (*sport*) "drive," *m.*; (*mil.*) ataque, *m.*; (of a person) energía, *f.*; campaña vigorosa, *f.*; impulso, *m.* **left (right) hand d.**, conducción a la izquierda (derecha). **to take a d.**, dar un paseo en (auto, etc.). **to take for a d.**, llevar a paseo en (auto, etc.)

drivel, *s.* vaciedades, patrañas, *f. pl.*, disparates, *m. pl. v.i.* decir disparates, chochear

driver, *s.* conductor (-ra); chófer, *m.*; (of an engine) maquinista, *m.*; (of a cart) carretero, *m.*; (of a coach, carriage) cochero, *m.*; (of cattle, etc.) ganadero, *m.*; (golf) " driver," *m.*

driving, *s.* conducción, *f.*; modo de conducir, *m.*; paseo (en coche, etc.), *m.*; impulsión, *f. a.* de conducir; de chófer; para chóferes; motor; propulsor; impulsor; de transmisión; (*fig.*) impulsor; (violent) violento, impetuoso. **to go d.,** ir de paseo (en auto o carruaje). **d. licence,** carnet de chófer, *m.* **d. mirror,** espejo retrovisor, *m.* **d. seat,** asiento del conductor, *m.*; (of an old-fashioned coach, etc.) pescante, *m.* **d.-shaft,** (*mech.*) árbol motor, *m.* **d. test,** examen para choferes, *m.* **d.-wheel,** volante, *m.*; rueda motriz, *f.* **d.-whip,** látigo, *m.*

drizzle, *s.* llovizna, *f.* *v.i.* lloviznar

droll, *a.* chusco, gracioso. *s.* bufón, *m.*

dromedary, *s.* dromedario, *m.*

drone, *s.* abejón, *m.*; (*fig.*) zángano, *m.*; (hum) zumbido, *m.*; (of a song, voice) salmodia, *f.* *v.t.* and *v.i.* (hum) zumbar; (of a song, voice) salmodiar; (idle) zanganear

droning, *a.* zumbador; confuso

droop, *v.i.* inclinarse; colgar; caer; (wither) marchitarse; (fade) consumirse; (pine) desanimarse. *v.t.* bajar; dejar caer. *s.* caída, *f.*; inclinación, *f.*

drooping, *a.* caído; debilitado; lánguido; (of ears) gacho; (depressed) alicaído, deprimido

drop, *s.* gota, *f.*; (tear) lágrima, *f.*; (for the ear) pendiente, *m.*; (sweet) pastilla, *f.*; (of a chandelier) almendra, *f.*; (fall) caída, *f.*; (in price, etc.) baja, *f.*; (slope) pendiente, cuesta, *f.* **by drops,** a gotas. **d. bottle,** frasco cuentagotas, *m.* **d.-curtain,** telón de boca, *m.* **d.-hammer,** martinete, *m.* **d.-head coupé,** cupé descapotable, *m*: **d.-scene,** telón de foro, *m.*

drop, *v.t.* verter a gotas; destilar; (sprinkle) salpicar, rociar; dejar caer; soltar; (lower) bajar; (of clothes, etc.) desprenderse de, quitar; (lose) perder; (a letter in

a pillar-box) echar; (leave) dejar; (give up) renunciar (a); desistir (de); abandonar; (kill) tumbar; (a hint) soltar; (a curtsey) hacer. *v.i.* gotear, caer en gotas, destilar; (descend) bajar, descender; caer muerto; caer desmayado; (sleep) dormirse; (fall) caer; (of the wind) amainar; (of prices, temperature) bajar. **to let the matter d.,** poner fin a una cuestión. **to d. a line,** poner unas líneas. **to d. anchor,** anclar. **to d. behind,** quedarse atrás. **to d. down,** caer (a tierra). **to d. in,** entrar al pasar. **to d. off,** separarse (de); disminuir; (sleep) quedar dormido; (die) morir de repente. **to d. out,** separarse; (from a race, etc.) retirarse (de); quedarse atrás; desaparecer; ausentarse, apartarse; (decrease) disminuir; decaer. **He has dropped out of my life,** Le he perdido de vista. **to d. through,** caer por; frustrarse; no dar resultado

dropping, *s.* gotera, *f.*; gotas, *f. pl.*; (fall) caída, *f.*; *pl.* **droppings** (of a candle) moco, *m.*; (dung) cagadas, *f. pl.* **Constant d. wears away the stone,** La gotera cava la piedra

dropsical, *a.* hidrópico

dropsy, *s.* hidropesía, *f.*

dross, *s.* escoria, *f.*; (rubbish) basura, *f.*

drought, *s.* aridez, *f.*; (thirst) sed, *f.*; (dry season) sequía, *f.*

drove, *s.* manada, *f.*, hato, *m.*; (of sheep) rebaño, *m.*; (crowd) muchedumbre, *f.*

drover, *s.* ganadero, manadero, *m.*

drown, *v.i.* ahogarse. *v.t.* ahogar; sumergir; inundar; (*fig.*, of cries, sorrow, etc.) ahogar

drowning, *s.* ahogamiento, *m.*; sumersión, *f.*; inundación, *f. a.* que se ahoga

drowse, *v.i.* adormecerse

drowsily, *adv.* soñolientamente

drowsiness, *s.* somnolencia, *f.*; sueño, *m.*; (laziness) indolencia, pereza, *f.*

drowsy, *a.* soñoliento; adormecedor, soporífero; (heavy) amodorrado. **to grow d.,** adormecerse. **to make d.,** adormecer

drubbing, s. tunda, zurra, felpa, f.

drudgery, s. trabajo arduo, m., faena monótona, f.

drug, s. droga, f.; medicamento, m.; narcótico, m. v.t. mezclar con drogas; administrar drogas (a); narcotizar. v.i. tomar drogas. **d. trade,** comercio de drogas, m. **d. traffic,** contrabando de drogas, m.

druggist, s. droguero (-ra)

druid, s. druida, m.

druidical, a. druídico

drum, s. tambor, m.; (of the ear) tímpano (del oído), m.; (cylinder) cilindro, m.; (box) caja, f.; (arch.) cuerpo de columna, m. **bass d.,** bombo, m. **with drums beating,** con tambor batiente. **d.-head,** parche (del tambor), m. **d.-head service,** misa de campaña, f. **d.-major,** tambor mayor, m.

drum, v.t. and v.i. tocar el tambor; (with the fingers) tabalear, teclear; (with the heels) zapatear; (into a person's head) machacar. **to d. out,** (mil.) expulsar a tambor batiente

drummer, s. tambor, m.

drumming, s. ruido del tambor, m.; (of the heels) taconeo, m.; (of the fingers) tabaleo, tecleo, m.

drumstick, s. palillo (de tambor), m.

drunk, a. borracho, ebrio. s. borracho, m. **to be d.,** estar borracho. **to get d.,** emborracharse; (fam.) pillar un lobo. **to make d.,** emborrachar

drunkard, s. borracho (-cha)

drunken, a. borracho, ebrio

drunkenness, s. embriaguez, borrachera, ebriedad, f.

drupe, s. drupa, f.

dry, v.i. secarse. v.t. secar; desaguar; (wipe) enjugar. **to dry one's tears,** enjugarse las lágrimas; (fig.) secarse las lágrimas. **to dry up,** secarse; (of persons) acecinarse; (with old age) apergaminarse; (of ideas, etc.) agotarse; (be quiet) callarse

dry, a. seco; árido; estéril; (thirsty) sediento; (of wine) seco; (U.S.A.) prohibicionista; (squeezed) exprimido; (of toast)

sin mantequilla; (fig., chilly) aburrido; (sarcastic) sarcástico; (of humour) agudo. **on dry land,** en seco. **dry battery,** pila seca, f. **to dry-clean,** lavar al seco. **dry-cleaner,** tintorero (-ra).

dry-cleaning, lavado al seco, m.

dry-cleaning shop, tintorería, f. **dry goods,** lencería, f. **dry land,** tierra firme, f. **dry measure,** medida para áridos, f.

dry-nurse, ama seca, f. **dry-point,** punta seca, f. **dry-rot,** carcoma, f. **dry-shod,** con los pies secos

drying, s. secamiento, m.; desecación, f. a. secante; seco; para secar. **d. ground,** tendedero, m. **d. machine,** secadora, f.; (for the hair) secadora de cabello, f. **d. room,** secadero, m.

dryly, adv. secamente

dryness, s. sequedad, f.; aridez, f.; (of humour) agudeza, f.

drysalter, s. traficante en viandas saladas y secas, m.

dual, a. doble; (gram.) dual. **d. control,** mandos gemelos, m. pl. **d. personality,** conciencia doble, f.

dualism, s. dualismo, m.

duality, s. dualidad, f.

dub, v.t. (a knight) armar caballero; (call) apellidar; (nickname) motejar, apodar

dubious, a. dudoso, incierto; indeciso; problemático; ambiguo

dubiously, adv. dudosamente

dubiousness, s. carácter dudoso, m.; incertidumbre, f.; ambigüedad, f.

ducal, a. ducal

ducat, s. ducado, m.

duchess, s. duquesa, f.

duchy, s. ducado, m.

duck, s. pato (-ta), ánade, m. and f.; (sport) cero, m.; (darling) vida mía, querida, f.; (jerk) agachada, f.; (under the water) chapuz, m.; (material) dril, m.; (mil.) auto anfibio, m.; pl. **ducks,** pantalones de dril, m. pl. v.i. agacharse; (under water) chapuzarse. v.t. zabullir, sumergir; bajar, inclinar

ducking, s. chapuz, m. **d.-stool,** silla de chapuzar, f.

duckling, s. anadino (-na)

duckweed, s. lenteja acuática, f.
duct, s. conducto, canal, m.; (bot.)
tubo, m.
ductile, a. dúctil
ductility, s. ductilidad, f.
ductless, a. sin tubos
due, a. debido; (payable) pagadero; (fallen due) vencido; (fitting) propio; (expected) esperado.
·s. impuesto, m.; derecho, m. **in
due form,** en regla. **in its due
time,** a su tiempo debido. **to
fall due,** vencerse, **due bill,** (com.)
abonaré, m. **due west,** poniente
derecho, m.
duel, s. duelo, lance de honor, m.;
(fig.) lucha, f. **to fight a d.,**
batirse en duelo
duelling, s. el (batirse en) duelo
duellist, s. duelista, m.
duenna, s. dueña, f.
duet, s. dúo, m.
duettist, s. duetista, m. and f.
duffer, s. estúpido (-da); ganso,
m.; (at games, etc.) maleta, m.
dug, s. teta, f.
dug-out, s. trinchera, f.
duke, s. duque, m.
dukedom, s. ducado, m.
dulcet, a. dulce
dulcimer, s. dulcémele, m.
dull, a. (stupid) lerdo, estúpido,
obtuso; (boring, tedious) aburrido; (of pain, sounds) sordo; (of
colours and eyes) apagado; (of
light, beams, etc.) sombrío; (not
polished) mate; (pale) pálido;
(insipid) insípido, insulso; (of
people) soso, poco interesante;
(dreary, sad) triste; (grey) gris;
(of mirrors, etc.) empañado; (of
weather) anublado; (of hearing)
duro; (slow) lento, lánguido;
insensible; (blunt) romo; (com.)
encalmado, inactivo. **to find
life d.,** encontrar la vida aburrida. **d. of hearing,** duro de
oído, algo sordo. **d. pain,** dolor
sordo, m. **d. season,** temporada
de calma, f. **d.-eyed,** con ojos
apagados. **d.-witted,** lerdo
dull, v.t. (make stupid) entontecer; (lessen) mitigar; (weaken)
debilitar; (pain) calmar, aliviar;
(sadden) entristecer; (blunt) embotar; (spoil) estropear; (a
mirror, etc.) empañar; (a
polished surface) hacer mate,
deslustrar; (of enthusiasm, etc.)

enfriar; (tire) fatigar; (obstruct)
impedir
dullness, s. (stupidity) estupidez,
f.; (boredom) aburrimiento, m.;
(heaviness) pesadez, f.; (drowsiness) somnolencia, f.; (insipidity)
insipidez, insulsez, f.; (of literary
style) prosaísmo, m.; (of persons)
sosería, f.; (of a surface) deslustre, m.; (laziness) pereza,
languidez, f.; (slowness) lentitud,
f.; (tiredness) cansancio, m.;
(sadness) tristeza, f.; (bluntness)
embotamiento, m.; (of hearing)
dureza, f.; (com.) desanimación, f.
dully, adv. (stupidly) estúpidamente; sin comprender; (insipidly) insípidamente; (not
brightly) sin brillo; (slowly)
lentamente; (sadly) tristemente;
(tiredly) con cansancio; (of
sound) sordamente
duly, adv. debidamente; puntualmente
dumb, a. mudo; callado; silencioso; (fam.) tonto, estúpido.
to become d., enmudecer. **to
strike d.,** dejar sin habla. **d.-
bell,** barra con pesas, f. **d.
show,** pantomima, f. **d.
waiter,** bufete, m.
dumbfound, v.t. dejar sin habla;
confundir; pasmar
dumbness, s. mudez, f., mutismo, m.; silencio, m.
dum-dum bullet, s. bala dumdum, f.
dummy, s. (tailor's, etc.) maniquí, m.; (puppet) títere, m.;
cabeza para pelucas, f.; (figurehead) hombre de paja, testaferro,
m.; (baby's) chupador, m.; (at
cards) el muerto. a. fingido.
to be d., (at cards) ser el muerto
dump, s. depósito, m.; vaciadero,
m. v.t. depositar; (goods on a
market) inundar (con)
dumping, s. depósito, m.; vaciamiento, m.; (of goods on a
market) inundación, f. **D. prohibited,** Se prohibe arrojar la
basura
dumps, s. murria, f.
dun-coloured, a. pardo
dunce, s. asno, bobo, zoquete, m.
dunce's cap, s. coroza, f.
dunderhead, s. cabeza de alcornoque, zoquete, m.
dune, s. duna, f.

dung, s. estiércol, m.; (of rabbits, mice, deer, sheep, goats) cagarruta, f.; (of cows) boñiga, f.; (of hens) gallinaza, f. **d.-cart,** carro de basura, m.

dungarees, s. mono, m.

dungeon, s. mazmorra, f., calabozo, m.

dunghill, s. muladar, m.

duodenum, s. duodeno, m.

dupe, s. víctima, f.; tonto (-ta). v.t. embelecar, engañar. **to be a d.,** (fam.) hacer el primo

duplicate, a. duplicado, doble. s. duplicado, m.; copia, f. v.t. duplicar

duplication, s. duplicación, f.

duplicator, s. copiador, m.

duplicity, s. duplicidad, f.

durability, s. duración, f. **This is a cloth of great d.,** Este es un paño que dura mucho, Este es un paño muy duradero

durable, a. duradero

duration, s. duración, f.

duress, s. compulsión, f.; (prison) prisión, f.

during, prep. durante

dusk, s. atardecer, anochecer, m.; (twilight) crepúsculo, m.; (darkness) oscuridad, f. **at d.,** al atardecer, a la caída de la tarde

dusky, a. (swarthy) moreno; (black) negro; (dim, dark) oscuro; (of colours) sucio

dust, s. polvo, m.; (cloud of dust) polvareda, f.; (ashes) cenizas, f. pl.; (of coal) cisco, m.; (sweepings) barreduras, f. pl.; (of grain) tamo, m. v.t. desempolvar, quitar (or sacudir) el polvo de; (cover with dust) polvorear; (scatter) salpicar; (sweep) barrer; (clean) limpiar. **d.-bin,** basurero, m. **d.-cart,** carro de la basura, m. **d. cloud,** polvareda, f. **d. jacket,** (books) sobrecubierta, f. **d.-pan,** recogedor de basura, m. **d.-sheet,** guardapolvo, m. **d. storm,** vendaval de polvo, m.

duster, s. el, m. (f. la) que quita el polvo; paño (para quitar el polvo), m.; (of feathers) plumero, m.

dustiness, s. empolvoramiento, m.; estado polvoriento, m.

dusting, s. limpieza, f.; (sweeping) barredura, f.; (powder) polvos antisépticos, m. pl.

dustman, s. basurero, m.

dusty, a. polvoriento, polvoroso, empolvado; del color del polvo; (of colours) sucio. **It is very d.,** Hay mucho polvo. **to get d.,** llenarse (or cubrirse) de polvo

Dutch, a. holandés. **the D.,** los holandeses. **double D.,** griego, galimatías, m. **D. cheese,** queso de bola, m. **D. courage,** coraje falso, m. **D. woman,** holandesa, f.

Dutchman, s. holandés, m.

dutiable, a. sujeto a derechos de aduana

dutiful, a. que cumple con sus deberes; obediente, sumiso; respetuoso; excelente, muy ɓueno

dutifully, adv. obedientemente; respetuosamente

dutifulness, s. obediencia, docilidad, f.; respeto, m.

duty, s. deber, m.; obligación, f.; (greetings) respetos, m. pl.; (charge, burden) carga, f.; (tax) derecho, impuesto, m.; (mil.) servicio, m.; (guard) guardia, f. **off d.,** libre. **on d.,** de servicio. **to be on sentry d.,** estar de guardia. **to do d. as,** servir como. **to do one's d.,** hacer (or cumplir con) su deber. **to pay d. on,** pagar derechos de aduana sobre. **d.-free,** franco de derechos

dwarf, a. enano. s. enano (-na). v.t. impedir el crecimiento de; empequeñecer

dwarfish, a. enano

dwell, v.i. vivir, habitar; (with on, upon) (think about) meditar sobre, pensar en; (deal with) tratar de; hablar largamente de; (insist on) insister en; apoyarse en, hacer hincapié en; (pause over) detenerse en

dweller, s. habitante, m. and f.; (more poetic) morador (-ra)

dwelling, s. vivienda, f.; (abode) morada, habitación, f.; residencia, f.; casa, f.; (domicile) domicilio, m. **d.-house,** casa, f.

dwindle, v.i. disminuirse; consumirse; (decay) decaer; (degenerate) degenerar. **to d. to,** reducirse a

dwindling, s. disminución, f.

dye, v.t. teñir, colorar. v.i. teñirse. s. tinte, m.; (colour) color, *m.* **fast dye,** tinte estable, *m.* **dye-house,** tintorería, *f.* **dye-stuff,** materia colorante, *f.* **dye-works,** tintorería, *f.*

dyed-in-the-wool, *a.* intransigente, fanático; tradicionalista

dyeing, *s.* teñidura, tintura,. *f.*; (as a trade) tintorería, *f.* **d. and dry-cleaning shop,** tintorería, *f.*

dyer, *s.* tintorero (-ra)

dying, *a.* moribundo, agonizante; de la muerte; (of light) mortecino; (last) último; supremo; (languishing) lánguido; (deathbed) hecho en su lecho mortuorio. **to be d.,** estar agonizando; (of light) fenecer. **to be d. for,** estar muerto por

dynamic, *a.* dinámico

dynamics, *s.* dinámica, *f.*

dynamite, *s.* dinamita, *f.*

dynamo, *s.* dínamo, *f.*

dynast, *s.* dinasta, *m.*

dynastic, *a.* dinástico

dynasty, *s.* dinastía, *f.*

dysentery, *s.* disentería, *f.*

dyspepsia, *s.* dispepsia, *f.*

dyspeptic, *a.* dispéptico. *s.* dispéptico (-ca)

E

e, *s.* (letter) e, *f.*; (*mus.*) mi, *m.*

each, *a.* cada (invariable), todo. *pron.* cada uno, *m.*; cada una, *f.* **e. of them,** cada uno de ellos. **They help e. other,** Se ayudan mutuamente, Se ayudan entre sí. **to love e. other,** amarse

eager, *a.* impaciente; ansioso, deseoso; ambicioso

eagerly, *adv.* con impaciencia; con ansia;.ambiciosamente

eagerness, *s.* impaciencia, *f.*; ansia, *f.*, deseo, *m.*; (promptness) alacridad, *f.*; (zeal) fervor, *m.*

eagle, *s.* águila, *f.* **royal e.,** águila caudal, águila real, *f.* **e.-eyed,** con ojos de lince, de ojo avizor

eaglet, *s.* aguilucho, *m.*

ear, *s.* (external) oreja, *f.*; (sense of hearing) oído, *m.*; (*bot.*) espiga, panoja, *f.* **to begin to show the ear,** (grain) espigar. **to be all ears,** ser todo oídos. **to give ear,** dar oído. **to have**

a good ear, tener buen oído. **to play by ear,** tocar de oído. **to turn a deaf ear,** hacerse el sordo. **ear-ache,** dolor de oídos, *m.* **ear-drum,** tímpano (del oído), *m.* **ear-flap,** orejera, *f.* **ear-phone, ear-piece,** auricular, *m.* **ear-piercing,** penetrante, agudo. **ear-shot,** alcance del oído, *m.* **to be within ear-shot,** estar al alcance del oído. **ear-trumpet,** trompetilla, *f.* **ear wax,** cerilla, *f.*

eared, *a.* con orejas; de orejas; (*bot.*) con espigas

earl, *s.* conde, *m.*

earldom, *s.* condado, *m.*

earlier, earliest, *a. comp.* and *sup.*, más temprano; más primitivo; más antiguo; (first, of time) primero. *adv.* más temprano; más pronto; antes

earliness, *s.* lo temprano; antigüedad, *f.*, lo primitivo; (precocity) precocidad, *f.* **The e. of his arrival,** Su llegada de buena hora

early, *a.* temprano; primitivo; (of fruit, etc.) temprano, adelantado; (advanced) avanzado; (precocious) precoz; (first, of time) primero; (in the morning) matutino; (near) próximo; cercano; (premature) prematuro; (of child's age) tierno; joven. **in the e. hours,** en las primeras horas; en las altas horas (de la noche). **e. age,** edad temprana, tierna edad, *f.* **e.-fruiting,** (*agr.*) tempranal. **e. riser,** madrugador (-ra). **e.-rising,** *a.* madrugador. **e. years,** primeros años, años de la niñez, *m. pl.*

early, *adv.* temprano; al principio (de); en los primeros días (de); desde los primeros días (de); (in the month, year) a principios (de); (in time) a tiempo; (in the day) de buena hora; (soon) pronto; (among the first) entre los primeros (de). **as e. as possible,** lo más temprano posible; lo más pronto posible. **to be e.,** llegar antes de tiempo; llegar de buena hora. **to get up e.,** madrugar. **to go to bed e.,** acostarse temprano. **too e.,** demasiado temprano. **e. in the morning,** de madrugada

earmark, *v.t.* marcar; (*fig.*) destinar, reservar

earn, *v.t.* ganar; obtener, adquirir; (deserve) merecer

earnable, *a.* ganable

earnest, *a.* serio; fervoroso; diligente; sincero. **to be in e. about something,** tomarlo en serio; ser sincero (en). **e. money,** arras, *f. pl.*

earnestly, *adv.* seriamente; fervorosamente; con diligencia; sinceramente, de buena fe

earnestness, *s.* seriedad, *f.*; fervor, celo, *m.*; diligencia, *f.*; sinceridad, buena fe, *f.*

earnings, *s. pl.* (*com.*) ingresos, *m. pl.*; (salary) salario, *m.*; estipendio, *m.*; (of a workman) jornal, *m.*

earring, *s.* pendiente, arete, *m.*

earth, *s.* tierra, *f.*; (of a badger, etc.) madriguera, *f.*; (*rad.*) tierra, *f. v.t.* cubrir con tierra; (*rad.*) conectar con tierra. **clod of e.,** terrón, *m.* **half the e.,** (*fam.*) medio mundo, *m.* **on e.,** en este mundo, sobre la tierra

earthen, *a.* terrizo, terroso; (of mud) de barro

earthenware, *s.* alfar, *m.* *a.* de loza, de barro

earthiness, *s.* terrosidad, *f.*

earthly, *a.* terrestre, terrenal; de la tierra; (fleshly) carnal; (worldly) mundano; material. **There is not an e. chance,** No hay la más mínima posibilidad

earthquake, *s.* terremoto, temblor de tierra, *m.*

earthwards, *adv.* hacia la tierra

earthwork, *s.* terraplén, *m.*

earthworm, *s.* gusano de tierra, *m.*

earthy, *a.* térreo, terroso

earwig, *s.* tijereta, *f.*

ease, *s.* bienestar, *m.*; tranquilidad, *f.*; descanso, *m.*; (leisure) ocio, *m.*; (comfortableness) comodidad, *f.*; (freedom from embarrassment) naturalidad, *f.*, desembarazo, desenfado, *m.*; (from pain) alivio, *m.*; (simplicity) facilidad, *f.* *v.t.* (widen) ensanchar; aflojar; (pain) aliviar; (lighten) aligerar; (moderate) moderar; (soften) suavizar; (free) librar; (one's mind) tranquilizar. **In my moments of e.,** En mis ocios, En mis momentos de ocio. **Stand at e.!** (*mil.*) ¡En su lugar descansen! **to be at e.,** estar a sus anchas; encontrarse bien; comportarse con toda naturalidad. **with e.,** fácilmente. **to e. off,** *v.t.* (*naut.*, cables, sails) arriar. *v.i.* sentirse menos, cesar

easel, *s.* caballete de pintor, *m.*

easily, *adv.* fácilmente. **The engine runs e.,** El motor marcha bien

easiness, *s.* facilidad, *f.*; sencillez, *f.*; (of manner) desembarazo, *m.*, naturalidad, *f.*

east, *s.* este, *m.*; oriente, *m.*, (of countries) Oriente, *m.*; Levante, *m.* *a.* del este; del oriente; (of countries) de Oriente, oriental; levantino. **E.-North-E.,** estenordeste, *m.* **E.-South-E.,** estesudeste, *m.* **e. wind,** viento del este, *m.*

Easter, *s.* Pascua de Resurrección, *f.* **E. egg,** huevo de Pascua, *m.* **E. Saturday,** sábado de gloria, *m.* **E. Sunday,** domingo de Pascua, *m.*

easterly, *a.* del este; al este. *adv.* hacia el este

eastern, *a.* del este; de Oriente; oriental. *s.* oriental, *m. and f.*

easternmost, *a.* situado más al este

eastertide, *s.* tiempo de Pascua, *m.*

eastward, *adv.* hacia el este, hacia oriente

easy, *a.* fácil; sencillo; (comfortable) cómodo; (free from pain) aliviado; (*com.*) flojo; (well-off) acomodado, holgado; (calm) tranquilo; tolerante; natural; afable, condescendiente; (of virtue, women) fácil. *adv.* con calma; despacio. **I must make myself e. about,** He de tranquilizarme sobre. **Stand e.!** ¡En su lugar descansen! **to take it e.,** tomarlo con calma. **e.-chair,** silla poltrona, *f.* **e.-going,** acomodadizo; indolente; (morally) de manga ancha; (casual) descuidado

eat, *v.t.* comer; (meals, refreshments) tomar; (with a good, bad appetite) hacer; consumir; (corrode) corroer; desgastar. *v.i.*

comer; (*fam.*, of food) ser de buen (or mal) comer. **to eat one's breakfast** (lunch), tomar el desayuno, desayunar (almorzar). **to eat one's words**, retractarse. **to eat away**, comer; consumir; corroer. **to eat into**, (of chemicals) morder; (a fortune) consumir; gastar. **to eat up**, devorar (also *fig.*)

eatable, *a.* comestible, comedero. *s.pl.* **eatables**, comestibles, *m. pl.*

eater, *s.* el, *m.* (*f.*, la) que come

eating, *s.* el comer; comida, *f.* **e. and drinking**, el comer y beber. **e.-house**, casa de comidas, *f.*

eau de cologne, *s.* agua de colonia, *f.*

eaves, *s.* rafe, alero, *m.* **under the e.**, debajo del alero

eavesdrop, *v.i.* escuchar a las puertas; fisgonear, espiar

eavesdropper, *s.* fisgón (-ona)

eavesdropping, *s.* fisgoneo, *m.*

ebb, *s.* (of the tide) reflujo, *m.*; menguante, *f.*; (*fig.*) declinación, *f.*; (*fig.*) decadencia, *f.*; (of life) vejez, *f.* *v.i.* (of tide) menguar; declinar; decaer. **to ebb and flow**, fluir y refluir. **to ebb away from**, dejar; dejar aislado. **ebb-tide**, marea menguante, *f.*

ebonite, *s.* ebonita, *f.*

ebony, *s.* ébano, *m.*

ebullience, *s.* efervescencia, exuberancia, *f.*

ebullient, *a.* efervescente, exuberante

ebullition, *s.* (boiling) ebullición, *f.*, hervor, *m.*; (*fig.*) efervescencia, *f.*, estallido, *m.*

eburnine, *a.* ebúrneo

eccentric, *a.* (*geom.*) excéntrico; raro, original; extravagante, excéntrico. *s.* persona excéntrica, *f.*, original, *m.*

eccentrically, *adv.* excéntricamente

eccentricity, *s.* (*geom.*) excentricidad, *f.*; rareza, extravagancia, excentricidad, *f.*

Ecclesiastes, *s.* Eclesiastés, *m.*

ecclesiastic, *a.* eclesiástico. *s.* eclesiástico, clérigo, *m.*

ecclesiastically, *adv.* eclesiásticamente

echinus, *s.* (*arch.*) equino, *m.*; (*zool.*) erizo de mar, *m.*

echo, *s.* eco, *m.*; reverberación, resonancia, *f.* *v.t.* repercutir; (*fig.*) repetir. *v.i.* resonar, retumbar, reverberar

echoing, *a.* retumbante. *s.* eco, *m.*

eclampsia, *s.* (*med.*) eclampsia, *f.*

eclectic, *a.* and *s.* ecléctico (-ca)

eclecticism, *s.* eclecticismo, *m.*

eclipse, *s.* (*ast.*) eclipse, *m.* *v.t.* eclipsar. **to be in e.**, estar en eclipse

ecliptic, *s.* (*ast.*) eclíptica, *f.* *a.* eclíptico

eclogue, *s.* égloga, *f.*

economic, *a.* económico

economical, *a.* económico

economically, *adv.* económicamente

economics, *s.* economía política, *f.*

economist, *s.* economista, *m.* and *f.*

economize, *v.t.* economizar, ahorrar. *v.i.* hacer economías

economy, *s.* economía, *f.* **domestic e.**, economía doméstica, *f.* **political e.**, economía política, *f.*

ecstasy, *s.* éxtasis, arrebato, *m.*; transporte, *m.* **to be in e.**, estar en éxtasis

ecstatic, *a.* extático

ecstatically, *adv.* extáticamente

ectoplasm, *s.* (*biol.* and *spirit.*) ectoplasma, *m.*

Ecuadorian, *a.* and *s.* ecuatoriano (-na)

ecumenical, *a.* ecuménico

eczema, *s.* eczema, *f.*

eddy, *s.* remolino, *m.* *v.i.* remolinar; (*fig.*) remolinear

edelweiss, *s.* inmortal de las nieves, *f.*

Eden, *s.* Edén, *m.*

edge, *s.* (of sharp instruments) filo, *m.*; (of a skate) cuchilla, *f.*; margen, *m.* or *f.*; (shore) orilla, *f.*; (of two surfaces) arista, *f.*; (of books) borde, *m.*; (of a coin) canto, *m.*; (of a chair, a precipice, a forest, a kerb, etc.) borde, *m.*; (extreme) extremidad, *f.* **on e.**, de canto; (*fig.*) ansioso. **to be on e.**, (*fig.*) tener los nervios en punta. **to set on e.**, poner de canto; (of teeth) dar dentera

edge, *v.t.* (sharpen) afilar; (*sew.*) ribetear; orlar; poner un borde

(a); (cut) cortar. **to e. away,**
escurrirse. **to e. into,** *v.t.* insinuarse. *v.i.* deslizarse en. **to e.**
out, salir poco a poco
edged, *a.* afilado, cortante; (in
compounds) de . . . filos; (bor-
dered) bordeado; (of books) de
bordes . . .
edgeways, *adv.* de lado; de canto.
He couldn't get a word in e.,
No pudo meter baza en la conversación
edging, *s.* borde, *m.*; ribete, *m.*
edibility, *s.* el ser comestible
edible, *a.* comestible
edict, *s.* edicto, *m.*
edification, *s.* edificación, *f.*
edifice, *s.* edificio, *m.*
edify, *v.t.* edificar
edifying, *a.* edificante, edificador
edit, *v.t.* editar; (a newspaper,
journal) ser director de; (prepare
for press) redactar; (correct)
corregir
editing, *s.* trabajo editorial, *m.*;
redacción, *f.*; dirección, *f.*; corrección, *f.*
edition, *s.* edición, *f.*; (*print.*)
tirada, *f.* **first e.,** edición príncipe, *f.* **miniature e.,** edición
diamante, *f.*
editor, *s.* (of a book) editor, *m.*;
(of a newspaper, journal) director, *m.*
editorial, *a.* de redacción; editorial. *s.* editorial, artículo de
fondo, *m.* **e. staff,** redacción,
f.
editorship, *s.* dirección (de un
periódico, de una revista), *f.*
editress, *s.* (of a paper, journal)
directora, *f.*; editora, *f.*
educability, *s.* educabilidad, *f.*
educable, *a.* educable
educate, *v.t.* educar; formar;
(accustom) acostumbrar
educated, *a.* culto
education, *s.* educación, *f.*; enseñanza, *f.*; pedagogía, *f.* **Chair**
of e., cátedra de pedagogía, *f.*
early e., primeras letras, *f. pl.*
higher e., enseñanza superior, *f.*
educational, *a.* educativo; pedagógico; instructivo
educationalist, *s.* pedagogo, *m.*
educative, *a.* educativo
educator, *s.* educador (-ra)
educe, *v.t.* educir; deducir;
(*chem.*) extraer

eduction, *s.* educción, *f.*
Edwardian, *a.* and *s.* eduardiano
(-na)
eel, *s.* anguila, *f.* **electric eel,**
gimnoto, *m.* **eel-basket,** nasa
para anguilas, *f.*
eerily, *adv.* fantásticamente; de
modo sobrenatural
eeriness, *s.* ambiente de misterio, *m.*; efecto misterioso, *m.*
eerie, *a.* misterioso, fantástico;
sobrenatural; lúgubre
efface, *v.t.* borrar, destruir;
quitar. **to e. oneself,** retirarse;
permanecer en el fondo
effacement, *s.* borradura, *f.*
effect, *s.* efecto, *m.*; impresión, *f.*;
(result) resultado, *m.*, consecuencia, *f.*, (meaning) substancia,
f., significado, *m.*; *pl.* **effects,**
efectos, bienes, *m. pl.* *v.t.* efectuar; producir. **in e.,** en efecto,
efectivamente. **of no e.,** inútil.
striving after e., efectismo, *m.*
to feel the effects of, sentir los
efectos de; padecer las consecuencias de. **to put into e.,**
poner en práctica; hacer efectivo.
to take e., producir efecto;
ponerse en vigor
effective, *a.* eficaz; (striking) de
mucho efecto, poderoso, vistoso.
to make e., llevar a efecto
effectively, *adv.* eficazmente;
(strikingly) con gran efecto;
efectivamente, en efecto
effectiveness, *s.* eficacia, *f.*;
efecto, *m.*
effectuate, *v.t.* efectuar
effectuation, *s.* efectuación, *f.*
effeminacy, *s.* afeminación, *f.*
effeminate, *a.* afeminado, adamado. **to make e.,** afeminar
efferent, *a.* eferente
effervesce, *v.i.* estar efervescente, hervir
effervescence, *s.* efervescencia, *f.*
effervescent, *a.* efervescente
effete, *a.* gastado; estéril; decadente
effeteness, *s.* decadencia, *f.*;
esterilidad, *f.*
efficacious, *a.* eficaz
efficacy, *s.* eficacia, *f.*
efficiency, *s.* eficiencia, *f.*; buen
estado, *m.*; habilidad, *f.*; (*mech.*)
rendimiento, *m.*
efficient, *a.* eficaz; eficiente;
competente

efficiently, *adv.* eficientemente; eficazmente; competentemente

effigy, *s.* efigie, imagen, *f.*

efflorescence, *s.* (*chem.*) eflorescencia, *f.*; (*bot.*) florescencia, *f.*

effluvium, *s.* efluvio, *m.*

effort, *s.* esfuerzo, *m.* **to make an e.,** hacer un esfuerzo

effortless, *a.* sin esfuerzo

effrontery, *s.* descaro, *m.*, insolencia, *f.*

effulgence, *s.* esplendor, fulgor, *m.*

effulgent, *a.* fulgente, resplandeciente

effusion, *s.* efusión, *f.*

effusive, *a.* efusivo, expansivo

egg, *s.* huevo, *m.* **to egg on,** incitar (a). **boiled egg,** huevo cocido, *m.* **fried egg,** huevo frito, *m.* **hard egg,** huevo duro, *m.* **poached egg,** huevo escalfado, *m.* **scrambled egg,** huevos revueltos, *m. pl.* **soft egg,** huevo pasado por agua, *m.* **to lay eggs,** poner huevos. **to put all one's eggs in one basket,** (*fig.*) poner toda la carne en el asador. **egg-cup,** huevera, *f.* **egg dealer,** vendedor (-ra) de huevos. **egg flip,** huevo batido con ron, *m.* **egg plant,** berenjena, *f.* **egg-shaped,** aovado. **egg-shell,** cascarón, *m.*, cáscara de huevo, *f.* **egg-shell china,** loza muy fina, *f.* **egg-spoon,** cucharita para comer huevos, *f.* **egg-whisk,** batidor de huevos, *m.*

ego, *s.* el yo

egoism, *s.* egoísmo, *m.*

egoist, *s.* egoísta, *m.* and *f.*

egoistic, *a.* egoísta

egoistically, *adv.* egoístamente

egotism, *s.* egotismo, *m.*, egolatría, *f.*

egotist, *s.* egotista, *m.* and *f.*

egotistic, *a.* egotista

egregious, *a.* notorio

egress, *s.* salida, *f.*

Egyptian, *a.* egipcio. *s.* egipcio (-ia); cigarrillo egipcio, *m.*

Egyptologist, *s.* egiptólogo (-ga)

Egyptology, *s.* egiptología, *f.*

eh? *interj.* ¿eh? ¿qué?

eider, *s.* (*orn.*) pato de flojel, *m.*

eiderdown, edredón, *m.*

eight, *a.* and *s.* ocho (*m.*). **He is e. years old,** Tiene ocho años.

It is e. o'clock, Son las ocho. **e.-day clock,** reloj con cuerda para ocho días, *m.* **e. hundred,** *a.* and *s.* ochocientos (*m.*). **e.-syllabled,** octosilábico

eighteen, *a.* and *s.* diez y ocho (*m.*)

eighteenth, *a.* décimoctavo; (of the month) (el) diez y ocho; (of monarchs) diez y ocho. *s.* décimoctava parte, *f.* **Louis the e.,** Luis diez y ocho

eightfold, *a.* óctuple

eighth, *a.* octavo, *m.*; (of the month) (el) ocho; (of monarchs) octavo. *s.* octavo, *m.*

eighthly, *adv.* en octavo lugar

eightieth, *a.* octogésimo

eighty, *a.* and *s.* ochenta (*m.*)

either, *a.* and *pron.* uno u otro, cualquiera de los dos; ambos (-as). *.conjunc.* o (becomes u before words beginning with o or ho). *adv.* tampoco. **I do not like e.,** No me gusta ni el uno ni el otro (ni la una ni la otra). **e. . . . or,** o . . . o

ejaculate, *v.t.* exclamar, lanzar; (*med.*) eyacular

ejaculation, *s.* exclamación, *f.*; (*med.*) eyaculación, *f.*

ejaculatory, *a.* jaculatorio

eject, *v.t.* echar, expulsar; (*law*) desahuciar; (emit) despedir. emitir

ejection, *s.* echamiento, *m.*, expulsión, *f.*; (*law*) desahucio, *m.*; (emission) emisión, *f.*

eke, (out) *v.t.* aumentar, añadir a

elaborate, *a.* elaborado; primoroso; elegante; complicado; (detailed) detallado; (of meals) de muchos platos; (of courtesy, etc.) estudiado. *v.t.* elaborar; amplificar

elaborately, *adv.* primorosamente; elegantemente; complicadamente; con muchos detalles

elaborateness, *s.* primor, *m.*; elegancia, *f.*; complicación, *f.*; (care) cuidado, *m.*; minuciosidad, *f.*

elaboration, *s.* elaboración, *f.*

elapse, *v.i.* transcurrir, andar, pasar

elastic, *a.* elástico. *s.* elástico, *m.* **e. band,** anillo de goma, *m.*; cinta de goma, *f.* **e. girdle,** faja elástica, *f.*

elasticity, *s.* elasticidad, *f.*

elate, *v.t.* alegrar; **animar**

elatedly, *adv.* alegremente; triunfalmente

elation, *s.* alegría, *f.*, júbilo, *m.*; triunfo, *m.*

elbow, *s.* codo, *m.*; ángulo, *m.*; (of a chair) brazo, *m.* *v.t.* codear, dar codazos (a). **at one's e.,** a la mano. **nudge with the e.,** codazo, *m.* **to be out at e.,** enseñar los codos, tener los codos raídos: ser harapiento. **to e. one's way,** abrirse paso a codazos. **e.-chair,** silla de brazos, *f.* **e.-grease,** jugo de muñeca, *m.* **e.-piece or patch,** codera, *f.* **e. room,** libertad de movimiento, *f.*

elder, *a. comp.,* mayor. *s.* persona mayor, *f.*; señor mayor, *m.*; (among Jews and in early Christian Church) anciano, *m.*; (*bot.*) saúco. *m.*

elderly, *a.* mayor

eldest, *a. sup.* old (el, la, etc.) mayor. **e. daughter,** hija mayor, *f.* **e. son,** hijo mayor, *m.* primogénito, *m.*

elect, *v.t.* elegir. *a:* elegido; predestinado. *s.* electo, *m.*; elegido, *m.*

election, *s.* (*theol.*) predestinación, *f.*; elección, *f.* **by-e.,** elección parcial, *f.*

electioneer, *v.i.* solicitar votos; distribuir propaganda electoral

electioneering, *s.* solicitación de votos, *f.*; propaganda electoral, *f.*

elective, *a.* electivo

elector, *s.* elector (-ra); (prince) elector, *m.*

electoral, *a.* electoral. **e. register,** lista electoral, *f.*

electorate, *s.* electorado, *m.*

electric, electrical, *a.* eléctrico; (*fig.*) vivo, instantáneo. **e. arc,** arco voltaico, *m.* **e. engineer,** ingeniero electricista, *m.* **e. fire,** estufa eléctrica, *f.* **e. immersion heater,** calentador de agua eléctrico, *m.* **e. light,** luz eléctrica, *f.* **e. pad,** alfombrilla eléctrica, *f.* **e. shock,** conmoción eléctrica, *f.* **e. washing-machine,** lavadora eléctrica, *f.* **e. wire or cable,** conductor eléctrico, *m.*

electrically, *adv.* por electricidad

electrician, *s.* electricista, *m.* and *f.*

electricity, *s.* electricidad, *f.*

electrification, *s.* electrificación, *f.*

electrify, *v.t.* electrificar; (*fig.*) electrizar

electro, *prefix* (in compounds) electro. **e.-chemistry,** electroquímica, *f.* **e.-dynamics,** electrodinámica, *f.* **e.-magnet,** electroimán, *m.* **e.-magnetic,** electromagnético. **e.-plate,** *v.t.* galvanizar, platear. *s.* artículo galvanizado, *m.* **e.-therapy,** electroterapia, *f.*

electrocute, *v.t.* electrocutar

electrocution, *s.* electrocución, *f.*

electrode, *s.* electrodo, *m.*

electrolysis, *s.* electrólisis, *f.*

electrolyte, *s.* electrólito, *m.*

electrolyze, *v.t.* electrolizar

electrometer, *s.* electrómetro, *m.*

electromotive, *a.* (*f.*) electromotriz. **e. force,** fuerza electromotriz, *f.*

electron, *s.* electrón, *m.*

electroscope, *s.* electroscopio, *m.*

electrotype, *s.* electrotipia, *f.*

elegance, *s.* elegancia, *f.*

elegant, *a.* elegante; bello

elegantly, *adv.* elegantemente, con elegancia

elegiac, *a.* elegíaco

elegy, *s.* elegía, *f.*

element, *s.* elemento, *m.*; factor, *m.*; ingrediente, *m.*; (*elec.*) par, elemento, *m.*; (*chem.*, *phys.*) cuerpo simple, *m.*; *pl.* **elements,** rudimentos, *m. pl.,* nociones, *f. pl.*; (weather) intemperie, *f.*; (Eucharist) el pan y el vino. **to be in one's e.,** estar en su elemento

elemental, *a.* elemental; rudimentario

elementariness, *s.* el carácter elemental

elementary, *a.* elemental; rudimentario; primario. **e. education,** enseñanza primaria, *f.*

elephant, *s.* elefante (-ta). **e. keeper or trainer,** naire, *m.*

elephantiasis, *s.* elefantíasis, *f.*

elephantine, *a.* elefantino

elevate, *v.t.* (the Host) alzar; elevar; (the eyes, the voice) levantar; (honour) enaltecer

elevated, *a.* noble, elevado, sublime; edificante; (drunk) achispado

elevation, *s.* elevación, *f.*; enaltecimiento, *m.*; (of style, thought) nobleza, sublimidad, *f.*; (hill) eminencia, altura, *f.*

elevator, *s.* (lift) ascensor, *m.*; (for grain, etc.) montacargas, *m.*

eleven, *a.* once. *s.* once, *m.* It is e. o'clock, Son las once

eleventh, *a.* onceno, undécimo; (of month) (el) once; (of monarchs) once. *s.* onzavo, *m.*; undécima parte, *f.* at the e. hour, (*fig.*) a última hora. Louis the e., Luis once (XI)

elf, *s.* elfo, duende, *m.*; (child) trasgo, *m.*; (dwarf) enano, *m.*

elfin, *a.* de duendes; de hada

elicit, *v.t.* sacar; hacer contestar; hacer confesar; descubrir

elicitation, *s.* descubrimiento, *m.*

elide, *v.t.* elidir

eligibility, *s.* elegibilidad, *f.*

eligible, *a.* elegible; deseable

eliminate, *v.t.* eliminar; quitar

elimination, *s.* eliminación, *f.*

eliminator, *s.* eliminador, *m.*

eliminatory, *a.* eliminador

elision, *s.* elisión, *f.*

elite, *s.* nata, flor, *f.*

elixir, *s.* elixir, *m.*

Elizabethan, *a.* de la época de la Reina Isabel I de Inglaterra

elk, *s.* ante, *m.*

ell, *s.* (measure) ana, *f.*

ellipse, *s.* (*geom.*) elipse, *f.*; óvalo, *m.*

ellipsis, *s.* (*gram.*) elipsis, *f.*

elliptic, *a.* (*geom.*, *gram.*) elíptico

elm, *s.* olmo, *m.* **e. grove,** olmeda, *f.*

elocution, *s.* elocución, *f.*; (art of elocution) declamación, *f.*

elocutionist, *s.* recitador (-ra), declamador (-ra)

elongate, *v.t.* alargar; extender. *v.i.* alargarse; extenderse. *a.* alargado; (of face) perfilado

elongation, *s.* alargamiento, *m.*; prolongación, *f.*; extensión, *f.*

elope, *v.i.* evadirse, huir; fugarse (con un amante)

elopement, *s.* fuga, *f.*

eloquence, *s.* elocuencia, *f.*

eloquent, *a.* elocuente

eloquently, *adv.* elocuentemente

else, *adv.* (besides) más; (instead) otra cosa, más; (otherwise) si no, de otro modo. **anyone e.,** (cualquier) otra persona; alguien más. **Anything e.?** ¿Algo más? **everyone e.,** todos los demás. **everything e.,** todo lo demás. **nobody e.,** ningún otro, nadie más. **nothing e.,** nada más. **or e.,** o bien, de otro modo; si no. **someone e.,** otra persona, otro. **somewhere e.,** en otra parte. **There's nothing e. to do,** No hay nada más que hacer; No hay más remedio

elsewhere, *adv.* a, or en, otra parte

elucidate, *v.t.* elucidar, aclarar

elucidation, *s.* elucidación, aclaración, *f.*

elucidatory, *a.* aclaratorio

elude, *v.t.* eludir, evitar

elusive, *a.* (of persons) esquivo; fugaz; difícil de comprender

elusiveness, *s.* esquivez, *f.*; fugacidad, *f.*

elver, *s.* angula, *f.*

Elysian, *a.* elíseo. **E. fields,** campos elíseos, *m. pl.*

Elysium, *s.* elíseo, *m.*

emaciate, *v.t.* extenuar, demacrar, enflaquecer

emaciated, *a.* extenuado, demacrado. **to become e.,** demacrarse

emaciation, *s.* demacración, emaciación, *f.*; (*med.*) depauperación, *f.*

emanate, *v.i.* emanar (de), proceder (de)

emanation, *s.* emanación, *f.*; exhalación, *f.*

emancipate, *v.t.* emancipar

emancipated, *a.* emancipado

emancipation, *s.* emancipación, *f.*

emancipator, *s.* emancipador (-ra), libertador (-ra)

emancipatory, *a.* emancipador

emasculate, *a.* afeminado. *v.t.* emascular; (*fig.*) afeminar; mutilar

emasculation, *s.* emasculación, *f.*

embalm, *v.t.* embalsamar; (*fig.*) conservar el recuerdo de; perfumar

embalmer, *s.* embalsamador, *m.*

embalmment, *s.* embalsamamiento, *m.*

embankment, s. declive, m.; ribera, f.; terraplén, m.; dique, m.; (quay) muelle, m.

embargo, s. embargo, m. v.t. embargar. **to put an e. on,** embargar. **to remove an e.,** sacar de embargo

embark, v.i. embarcarse; lanzarse (a). v.t. embarcar

embarkation, s. (of persons) embarcación, f.; (of goods) embarque, m.

embarrass, v.t. impedir; (financially) apurar; (perplex) tener perplejo; (worry) preocupar; (confuse) desconcertar; turbar; (annoy) molestar

embarrassed, a. turbado

embarrassing, a. embarazoso; desconcertante; molesto

embarrassingly, adv. de un modo desconcertante; demasiado

embarrassment, s. impedimento, m.; (financial) apuro, m.; (obligation) compromiso, m.; (perplexity) perplejidad, f.; (worry) preocupación, f.; (confusion) turbación, f.

embassy, s. embajada, f.

embattled, a. en orden de batalla; (her.) almenado

embed, v.t. empotrar, enclavar; fijar

embellish, v.t. embellecer; adornar

embellishment, s. embelleçimiento, m.; adorno, m.

ember, s. rescoldo, m. **E. days,** témporas, f. pl.

embezzle, v.t. desfalcar

embezzlement, s. desfalco, m.

embezzler, s. desfalcador (-ra)

embitter, v.t. (fig.) amargar; envenenar

embittering, a. amargo

embitterment, s. amargura, f.

emblazon, v.t. blasonar; (fig.) ensalzar

emblem, s. emblema, m.

emblematic, a. emblemático

embodiment, s. incarnación, f.; expresión, f.; personificación, f.; símbolo, m.; síntesis, f.

embody, v.t. encarnar; expresar; personificar; incorporar; contener; formular; sintetizar

embog, v.t. empantanar; (fig.) sumergir, hundir

embolden, v.t. animar, dar valor (a)

embolism, s. (med.) embolia, f.

emboss, v.t. repujar, abollonar; estampar en relieve

embossment, s. abolladura, f.; relieve, m.

embower, v.t. enramar; abrigar, cubrir

embrace, s. abrazo, m. v.t. abrazar, dar un abrazo (a); (fig., seize) aprovechar; (accept) aceptar; adoptar; (engage in) dedicarse a; (comprise) incluir, abarcar; (comprehend) comprender. **They embraced,** Se abrazaron

embrasure, s. alféizar, m.; (mil.) aspillera, cañonera, f.

embrocation, s. embrocación, f

embroider, v.t. bordar; embellecer; (a tale, etc.) exagerar; v.i. hacer bordado

embroiderer, s. bordador (-ra)

embroidery, s. bordado, m.; labor, f. **e.-frame,** bastidor, m. **e. silk,** hilo de bordar, m.

embroil, v.t. enredar, embrollar; desordenar

embryo, s. embrión, m.; (fig.) germen, m. a. embrionario

embryology, s. embriología, f.

embryonic, a. embrionario

emend, v.t. enmendar; corregir

emendation, s. enmienda, f.; corrección, f.

emerald, s. esmeralda, f. a. de color de esmeralda. **e. green,** verde esmeralda, m.

emerge, v.i. emerger; surgir; (fig.) salir; aparecer

emergence, s. emergencia, f.; salida, f.; aparición, f.

emergency, s. urgencia, f.; necesidad, f.; emergencia, f.; aprieto, m. **e. exit,** salida de urgencia, f. **e. port,** (naut.) puerto de arribada, m.

emergent, a. emergente; que sale; naciente

emery, s. esmeril, m. **to polish with e.,** esmerilar. **e.-paper,** papel de lija, m.

emetic, a. and s. emético, vomitivo (m.)

emigrant, a. emigrante. s. emigrante, m. and f., emigrado, m.

emigrate, v.i. emigrar; (fam.) trasladarse

emigration, s. emigración, f. **e. officer,** oficial de emigración, m.

eminence, s. (hill) elevación, prominencia, f.; eminencia (also as title), f.; distinción, f.

eminent, a. distinguido, eminente; famoso. ilustre: notable; conspicuo

eminently, adv. eminentemente

emir, s. amir, m.

emissary, s. emisario (-ia); embajador (-ra); agente, m.

emission, s. emisión, f.

emit, v.t. despedir; exhalar; emitir

emollient, a. emoliente, lenitivo. s. emoliente, m.

emolument, s. emolumento, m.

emotion, s. emoción, f. **to cause e.,** emocionar

emotional, a. emocional, sentimental; emocionante

emotionalism, s. sentimentalismo, m.

emotionalize, v.t. considerar bajo un punto de vista sentimental

emotionally, adv. con emoción, sentimentalmente

emotionless, a. sin emoción

emotive, a. emotivo

emperor, s. emperador, m.

emphasis, s. énfasis, m. or f.; acentuación, f.

emphasize, v.t. subrayar, dar énfasis a; acentuar; insistir en

emphatic, a. enfático

emphatically, adv. con énfasis

empire, s. imperio, m.

empiric, a. empírico

empiricism, s. empirismo, m.

employ, s. empleo, m.; servicio, m. v.t. emplear; ocupar; tomar; servirse de, usar. **How do you e. yourself?** ¿ Cómo te ocupas? ¿ Cómo pasas el tiempo?

employable, a. empleable; utilizable

employee, s. empleado (-da)

employer, s. el, m. (f. la) que emplea; dueño (-ña), amo (-a); patrón (-ona)

employment, s. empleo, m.; uso, m.; ocupación, f.; aprovechamiento, m.; (post) puesto, cargo, m.; (situation) colocación, f. **E. exchange,** Bolsa de trabajo, f.

emporium, s. emporio, m.; (store) almacén, m.

empower, v.t. autorizar; permitir; ayudar (a); dar el poder (para)

empress, s. emperatriz, f.

emptiness, s. vaciedad, f.; futilidad, f.; vacuidad, f.; (verbosity) palabrería, f.

empty, a. vacío; (of a house, etc.) deshabitado, desocupado; (deserted) desierto; (vain) vano, inútil; frívolo; (hungry) hambriento. s. envase vacío, m. v.t. vaciar; descargar. v.i. vaciarse; desembocar. **e.-handed,** con las manos vacías. **e.-headed,** casquivano

emptying, s. vaciamiento, m.; abandono, m.; pl. **emptyings,** heces de la cerveza, f. pl.

empurple, v.t. empurpurar

empyrean, s. empíreo, m.

emu, s. emu, m.

emulate, v.t. emular

emulation, s. emulación, f.

emulative, a. emulador

emulsify, v.t. emulsionar

emulsion, s. emulsión, f.

emulsive, a. emulsivo

enable, v.t. (to) hacer capaz (de); ayudar (a); autorizar (para); permitir (de)

enact, v.t. (law) promulgar; decretar; (a part) hacer, desempeñar (un papel); (a play) representar; (happen) ocurrir, tener lugar

enaction, s. (law) promulgación, f.

enamel, s. esmalte, m. v.t. esmaltar

enameller, s. esmaltador (-ra)

enamelling, s. esmaltadura, f.

enamour, v.t. enamorar. **to be enamoured of,** estar enamorado de; estar aficionado a

encamp, v.t. and v.i. acampar

encampment, s. campamento, m.

encase, v.t. encajar; encerrar; (line) forrar

encasement, s. encaje, m.; encierro, m.

enceinte, a. (f.) encinta

encephalitis, s. encefalitis, f. **e. lethargica,** encefalitis letárgica, f.

enchant, v.t. encantar, hechizar; fascinar, embelesar, deleitar

enchanter, s. encantador, m.

enchanting, a. encantador, fascinador

enchantment, s. encantamiento, m.; fascinación, f., encanto, deleite, m.

enchantress, s. bruja, f.; (fig.) mujer seductora, f.

encircle, v.t. cercar; rodear; dar la vuelta (a)

enclose, v.t. cercar; meter dentro de; encerrar; (with a letter, etc.) incluir, adjuntar

enclosed, a. (of letters) adjunto

enclosure, s. cercamiento, m.; cercado, m.; recinto, m.; (wall) tapia, cerca, f.; (with a letter) contenido adjunto, m.

encomiastic, a. encomiástico

encomium, s. encomio, m.

encompass, v.t. cercar, rodear

encore, s. repetición, f. interj. ¡bis!

encounter, s. encuentro, m.; combate, m.; conflicto, m.; lucha, f. v.t. encontrar; atacar; tropezar con

encourage, v.t. animar; alentar; estimular; incitar; ayudar; (approve) aprobar; (foster) fomentar

encouragement, s. ánimos, m. pl.; estímulo, incentivo, m.; ayuda, f.; (approval) aprobación, f.; (promotion) fomento, m.

encourager, s. instigador (-ra); ayudador (-ra); aprobador (-ra); fomentador (-ra)

encouraging, a. alentador; estimulante; fomentador; (favourable) halagüeño, favorable

encouragingly, adv. de un modo alentador; con aprobación

encroach, v.i. usurpar; abusar (de); invadir; robar; (of sea, river) hurtar

encroaching, a. usurpador; invadiente

encroachment, s. usurpación, f.; abuso, m.; invasión, f.

encrust, v.t. encostrar; incrustar

encumber, v.t. impedir, estorbar; llenar; (burden) cargar; (mortgage) hipotecar; (overwhelm) agobiar

encumbrance, s. impedimento, estorbo, m.; gravamen, m.; carga, f.; (mortgage) hipoteca, f.

encyclical, s. encíclica, f.

encyclopædia, s. enciclopedia, f.

encyclopædic, a. enciclopédico

encyclopædist, s. enciclopedista, m.

end, s. fin, m.; extremidad, f.; extremo, m.; conclusión, f.; (point) punta, f.; cabo, m.; (district) barrio, m.; cabeza, f.; (death) muerte, f.; (aim) objeto, intento, m.; (purpose) propósito, m.; (issue) resultado, m.; (bit) fragmento, pedazo, m.; (of a word) terminación, f. v.i. terminar; acabar; concluir; cesar; (in) terminar en; resultar en; (with) terminar con. v.t. terminar; acabar, dar fin a. **at an end,** terminado. **at the end,** al cabo (de); al extremo (de). **from end to end,** de un extremo a otro; de un cabo a otro. **in the end,** por fin, finalmente. **on end,** de pie, de cabeza, derecho; de punta; (of hair) erizado. **no end of,** un sinnúmero de. **to make both ends meet,** pasar con lo que se tiene. **to make an end of,** acabar con. **to put an end to,** poner fin a. **to the end that,** a fin de que, para que; con objeto de. **towards the end of,** (months, years, etc.) a fines de, a últimos de; hacia el fin de. **two hours on end,** dos horas seguidas.

end-paper, s. guarda, f.

endanger, v.t. arriesgar; poner en peligro

endear, v.t. hacer querer

endearing, a. que inspira cariño; atrayente; cariñoso

endearment, s. cariño, amor, m.; caricia, terneza, f.; palabra de cariño, f.

endeavour, v.i. procurar, intentar, hacer un esfuerzo. s. esfuerzo, m., tentativa, f.

endemic, a. (med.) endémico

ending, s. fin, m.; conclusión, f.; (gram.) terminación, f.; cesación, f.; (climax) desenlace, m.

endive, s. (bot.) escarola, f.

endless, a. eterno; inacabable; infinito; sin fin; interminable; incesante

endlessly, adv. sin fin; incesantemente; sin parar

endlessness, s. eternidad, f.; infinidad, f.; continuidad, f.

endocrine, a. endocrino. s. secreción interna, f.

endocrinology, s. endocrinología, f.

endogenous, *a.* endógeno

endorse, *v.t.* (*com.*) endosar; garantizar; (uphold) apoyar; confirmar

endorsee, *s.* endosatario (-ia)

endorsement, *s.* (*com.*) endoso, *m.*; aval, *m.*, garantía, *f.*; corroboración, confirmación, *f.*

endorser, *s.* (*com.*) endosante, *m.*

endow, *v.t.* dotar; fundar; crear

endowment, *s.* dotación, *f.*; fundación, *f.*; creación, *f.*; (mental) inteligencia, *f.*; cualidad, *f.*, don, *m.* **e. policy,** póliza dotal, *f.*

endurable, *a.* sufrible, soportable; tolerable

endurance, *s.* aguante, *m.*; resistencia, *f.*; sufrimiento, *m.*; tolerancia, *f.*; paciencia, *f.*; (lastingness) duración, continuación, *f.* **beyond e.,** intolerable, inaguantable. **e test,** prueba de resistencia, *f.*

endure, *v.t.* soportar; tolerar; aguantar; sufrir; resistir. *v.i.* sufrir; (last) durar, continuar

enduring, *a.* permanente, perdurable; continuo; constante

enduringness, *s.* (lastingness) permanencia, *f.*; paciencia, *f.*; aguante, *m.*

enema, *s.* lavativa, enema, *f.*

enemy, *s.* enemigo (-ga); adversario (-ia); (in war) enemigo, *m.* *a.* del enemigo, enemigo. **to be one's own e.,** ser enemigo de sí mismo. **to become an e. of,** enemistarse con; hacerse enemigo de, volverse hostil a

energetic, *a.* enérgico

energetically, *adv.* enérgicamente

energumen, *s.* energúmeno (-na)

energy, *s.* energía, fuerza, *f.*, vigor, *m.*

enervate, *v.t.* enervar; debilitar. *a.* enervado

enervation, *s.* enervación, *f.*; debilitación, *f.*

enfeeble, *v.t.* debilitar

enfeeblement, *s.* debilitación, *f.*, desfallecimiento, *m.*

enfeoff, *v.t.* enfeudar

enfilade, *v.t.* (*mil.*) enfilar

enfold, *v.t.* envolver; abrazar

enforce, *v.t.* (a law) poner en vigor; (impose) imponer a la fuerza; hacer cumplir; conseguir por fuerza; (demonstrate) demostrar

enforcement, *s.* (of a law) ejecución (de una ley), *f.*; imposición a la fuerza, *f.*; observación forzosa, *f.*

enfranchise, *v.t.* emancipar; conceder derechos civiles (a)

enfranchisement, *s.* emancipación, *f.*; concesión de derechos civiles, *f.*

engage, *v.t.* empeñar; contratar; tomar en alquiler; tomar a su servicio; (seats, etc.) reservar; (occupy) ocupar; (attention) atraer; (in) aplicarse a, dedicarse a; (*mil.*) combatir con, librar batalla con; atacar; (of wheels) endentar con. *v.i.* obligarse; dedicarse (a); tomar parte (en); (bet) apostar; (*mil.*) librar batalla; (fight) venir a las manos. **to be engaged in,** traer entre manos, ocuparse en. **to become engaged,** prometerse. **Number engaged!** (telephone) ¡Están comunicando!

engaged, *a.* ocupado; (betrothed) prometido; reservado

engagement, *s.* obligación, *f.*; compromiso, *m.*; (date) cita, *f.*; (betrothal) palabra de casamiento, *f.*; (battle) combate, *m.*, batalla, *f.* **I have an e. at two o'clock.** Tengo una cita a las dos

engaging, *a.* simpático, atractivo

engagingly, *adv.* de un modo encantador

engender, *v.t.* (*fig.*) engendrar; excitar

engine, *s.* máquina, *f.*; motor, *m.*; (locomotive) locomotora, *f.*; (pump) bomba, *f.* **to sit with one's back to the e.,** estar sentado de espaldas a la máquina (or locomotora). **e. builder,** constructor de máquinas, *m.* **e. driver,** maquinista, *m.* **e. room,** cuarto de máquinas, *m.*; **e. works,** taller de maquinaria, *m.*

engineer, *s.* ingeniero, *m.*; mecánico, *m.* *v.t.* (*fig.*) gestionar, arreglar. **civil e.,** ingeniero de caminos, canales y puertos, *m.* **Royal Engineers,** Cuerpo de Ingenieros, *m.*

engineering, s. ingeniería, f.; (fig.) manejo, m. a. de ingeniería

English, a. inglés. s. (language) inglés, m. **in the E. fashion,** a la inglesa. **to speak E.,** hablar inglés. **to speak plain E.,** hablar sin rodeos; hablar un inglés claro. **E. Church,** iglesia anglicana, f. **E. teacher,** maestro (-ra) de inglés

Englishman, s. inglés, m.

Englishwoman, s. inglesa, f.

engrain, v.t. inculcar

engrave, v.t. grabar; esculpir, cincelar; (fig.) grabar

engraver, s. grabador (-ra); (tool) cincel, m.

engraving, s. grabadura, f.; (picture) grabado, m. **e. needle,** punta seca, f. .

engross, v.t. (a document) poner en limpio; redactar; (absorb) absorber

engrossing, a. absorbente

engulf, v.t. hundir, sumir, sumergir

engulfment, s. hundimiento, m., sumersión, f.

enhance, v.t. realzar; intensificar; aumentar; mejorar

enhancement, s. realce, m.; intensificación, f.; aumento, m.; mejoría, f.

enigma, s. enigma, m.

enigmatic, a. enigmático

enigmatically, adv. enigmáticamente

enjoin, v.t. imponer; ordenar, mandar; encargar

enjoy, v.t. disfrutar; gustar de; gozar de; poseer, tener. **to e. oneself,** recrearse, regocijarse; (amuse oneself) divertirse; entretenerse; pasarlo bien. **Did you e. yourself?** ¿Lo pasaste bien?

enjoyable, a. agradable; divertido, entretenido

enjoyableness, s. lo agradable; lo divertido

enjoyably, adv. de un modo muy agradable

enjoyer, s. el, m. (f. la) que disfruta; poseedor (-ra); (amateur) aficionado (-da)

enjoyment, s. posesión, f.; goce, disfruto, m.; (pleasure) placer, m.; aprovechamiento, m.; utilización, f.; (satisfaction) satisfacción, f.

enlarge, v.t. agrandar; aumentar; ensanchar; extender; (phot.) ampliar; dilatar; (the mind, etc.) ensanchar. v.i. agrandarse; ensancharse; aumentarse; extenderse. **an enlarged heart,** dilatación del corazón, f. **to e. upon,** tratar detalladamente, explayarse en

enlargement, s. engrandecimiento, m.; ensanchamiento, m.; (phot.) ampliación, f.; (med.) dilatación, f.; aumento, m.; amplificación, f.; (of a town, etc.) ensanche, m.

enlarger, s. (phot.) ampliadora, f.

enlighten, v.t. iluminar; aclarar; informar

enlightened, a. culto; ilustrado; inteligente

enlightening, a. instructivo

enlightenment, s. ilustración, f.; cultura, civilización, f.

enlist, v.t. (mil.) reclutar; alistar; obtener, conseguir. v.i. (mil.) sentar plaza, engancharse; alistarse

enlistment, s. (mil.) enganche, m.; reclutamiento, m.; alistamiento, m.

enliven, v.t. animar; avivar; alegrar

enmity, s. enemistad, enemiga, hostilidad, f.

ennoble, v.t. ennoblecer; ilustrar

ennoblement, s. ennoblecimiento, m.

ennui, s. tedio, m.; aburrimiento, m.

enormity, s. enormidad, f.; gravedad, f.; atrocidad, f.

enormous, a. enorme, colosal

enormously, adv. enormemente

enormousness, s. enormidad, f.

enough, a. bastante, suficiente. s. lo bastante, lo suficiente. adv. bastante; suficientemente. interj. ¡bastante! ¡basta! **to be e.,** ser suficiente; bastar

enquire. See **inquire**

enrage, v.t. enfurecer, hacer furioso; (fam.) hacer rabiar

enraged, a. furioso

enrapture, v.t. entusiasmar, extasiar; (intoxicate) embriagar; (charm) encantar, deleitar

enrich, v.t. enriquecer; (adorn) adornar, embellecer; (the land) fertilizar

enrichment, *s.* enriquecimiento,
m.; embellecimiento, *m.*; (of the
land) abono, *m.*

enrol, *v.t.* alistar; matricular;
inscribir; (perpetuate) inmortalizar

enrolment, *s.* alistamiento, *m.*;
inscripción, *f.*

ensconce, *v.t.* acomodar, colocar;
ocultar

ensemble, *s.* conjunto, *m.*

enshrine, *v.t.* poner en sagrario;
guardar con cuidado; (*fig.*) guardar como una reliquia

enshroud, *v.t.* amortajar; envolver; esconder

ensign, *s.* (badge) insignia, *f.*;
(flag) enseña, bandera, *f.*; pabellón, *m.*; bandera de popa, *f.*;
(*mil.*) alférez, *m.*; (U.S.A. navy)
subteniente, *m.*

enslave, *v.t.* esclavizar; (*fig.*).
dominar

enslavement, *s.* esclavitud, *f.*

ensue, *v.t.* conseguir. *v.i.* resultar; suceder, sobrevenir

ensuing, *a.* (next) próximo;
(resulting) resultante

ensure, *v.t.* asegurar; estar seguro de que; garantizar

entail, *v.t.* (*law*) vincular; traer
consigo, acarrear. *s.* (*law*) vinculación, *f.*; herencia, *f.*

entangle, *v.t.* enredar; coger;
(*fig.*) embrollar

entanglement, *s.* enredo, *m.*;
complicación, *f.*; intriga, *f.*;
(*mil.*, of wire) alambrada, *f.*

enter, *v.t.* entrar en; penetrar;
(of thoughts) ocurrirse; (join)
ingresar en; entrar en; (become a
member of) hacerse miembro de;
(enrol) alistarse; (a university)
matricularse; (inscribe) inscribir, poner en la lista; (note)
anotar, apuntar; (a protest)
hacer constar; (make) hacer;
formular. *v.i.* entrar; (*theat.*)
salir (a la escena); penetrar;
(*com.*) anotarse. to e. for, *v.t.*
inscribir. *v.i.* inscribirse, tomar
parte en. to e. into, entrar en;
formar parte de; (conversation)
entablar (conversación); (negotiations) iniciar; considerar;
(another's emotion) acompañar
en; (an agreement, etc.) hacer;
(sign) firmar; (bind oneself)
obligarse a, comprometerse a;

tomar parte en; (undertake)
emprender; empezar; adoptar.
to e. up, anotar; poner en la
lista; registrar. to e. upon,
comenzar, emprender; tomar
posesión de; encargarse de,
asumir; inaugurar, dar principio
a

enteric, *a.* entérico

enteritis, *s.* enteritis, *f.*

enterprise, *s.* empresa, *f.*; aventura, *f.*; (spirit) iniciativa, *f.*,
empuje, *m.*

enterprising, *a.* emprendedor,
acometedor; de mucha iniciativa

entertain, *v.t.* (an idea, etc.)
acariciar, abrigar; considerar;
(as a guest) agasajar, obsequiar;
recibir en casa; (amuse) divertir,
entretener. *v.i.* ser hospitalario;
tener invitados en casa; dar
fiestas

entertaining, *a.* entretenido,
divertido

entertainingly, *adv.* entretenidamente; (witty) graciosamente

entertainment, *s.* convite, *m.*;
fiesta, *f.*; reunión, *f.*; banquete,
m.; (hospitality) hospitalidad, *f.*;
(amusement) diversión, *f.*, entretenimiento, *m.*; espectáculo, *m.*;
función, *f.*; concierto, *m.*

enthrall, *v.t.* seducir, atraer,
encantar; absorber, captar la
atención

enthralling, *a.* absorbente; atrayente, halagüeño

enthralment, *s.* absorción, *f.*;
atracción, *f.*

enthrone, *v.t.* entronizar

enthronement, *s.* entronización,
f.

enthusiasm, *s.* entusiasmo, *m.*

enthusiast, *s.* entusiasta, *m.* and
f.

enthusiastic, *a.* entusiasta. to
make e., entusiasmar. to be e.,
entusiasmarse

enthusiastically, *adv.* con entusiasmo

entice, *v.t.* tentar, inducir; atraer,
seducir

enticement, *s.* tentación, *f.*;
atractivo, *m.*

enticing, *a.* seduciente, atrayente; halagüeño

entire, *a.* entero; completo; intacto; absoluto; perfecto; íntegro; total

entirely, *adv.* enteramente; completamente; integralmente; totalmente

entirety, *s.* totalidad, *f.*; integridad, *f.*; todo, *m.*

entitle, *v.t.* (designate) intitular; dar derecho (a); autorizar. **to be entitled to,** tener derecho a

entity, *s.* entidad, *f.*; ente, ser, *m.*

entombment, *s.* sepultura, *f.*, entierro, *m.*

entomological, *a.* entomológico

entomologist, *s.* entomólogo, *m.*

entomology, *s.* entomología, *f.*

entourage, *s.* séquito, *m.*; (environment) medio ambiente, *m.*

entr'acte, *s.* entreacto, *m.*

entrails, *s.* entrañas, tripas, *f. pl.*, intestinos, *m. pl.*

entrain, *v.i.* tomar el tren, subir al tren

entrance, *s.* entrada, *f.*; (theat.) salida (a la escena), *f.*; (into a profession, etc.) ingreso, *m.*; alistamiento, *m.*; (beginning) principio, *m.*; (door) puerta, *f.*; (porch) portal, *m.*; (of a cave) boca, *f.* **e. fee,** cuota de entrada, *f.* **e. hall,** zaguán, *m.* **e. money,** entrada, *f.*

entrance, *v.t.* (fig.) encantar, fascinar; ecstasiar

entrancing, *a.* encantador

entreat, *v.t.* suplicar, implorar, rogar

entreating, *a.* suplicante, implorante

entreatingly, *adv.* de un modo suplicante; insistentemente

entreaty, *s.* súplica, instancia, *f.*, ruego, *m.*

entrée, *s.* entrada, *f.*

entremets, *s.* entremés, *m.*

entrench, *v.t.* atrincherar

entrenchment, *s.* atrincheramiento, *m.*; (mil.) parapeto, *m.*; (encroachment) invasión, *f.*

entresol, *s.* entresuelo, *m.*

entrust, *v.t.* confiar a (or en), encomendar a; encargar

entry, *s.* entrada, *f.*; (passage) callejuela, *f.*; (note) inscripción, apuntación, *f.*; (com.) partida, *f.*; (registration) registro, *m.* **double e.,** (com.) partida doble, *f.* **single e.,** (com.) partida simple, *f.*

entwine, *v.t.* entrelazar, entretejer

enumerate, *v.t.* enumerar

enumeration, *s.* enumeración, *f.*

enumerative, *a.* enumerativo

enunciate, *v.t.* enunciar; articular

enunciation, *s.* enunciación, *f.*; articulación, *f.*

envelop, *v.t.* envolver, cubrir

envelope, *s.* sobre, *m.*

envelopment, *s.* envolvimiento, *m.*; cubierta, *f.*

enviable, *a.* envidiable

envious, *a.* envidioso. **an e. look,** una mirada de envidia

enviously, *adv.* con envidia

environment, *s.* medio ambiente, *m.*

environs, *s.* inmediaciones, *f. pl.*, alrededores, *m. pl.*

envisage, *v.t.* hacer frente a; contemplar; imaginar

envoy, *s.* enviado, *m.*; mensajero (-ra)

envy, *s.* envidia, *f.* *v.t.* envidiar

enzyme, *s.* fermento, *m.*, enzima, *f.*

epaulette, *s.* hombrera, *f.*

ephemeral, *a.* efímero; (fig.) fugaz, pasajero

Ephesian, *a.* and *s.* efesio (-ia)

epic, *a.* épico. *s.* epopeya, *f.*

epicarp, *s.* (bot.) epicarpio, *m.*

epicene, *a.* (gram.) epiceno

epicentre, *s.* epicentro, *m.*

epicure, *s.* epicúreo (-ea)

epicurean, *a.* epicúreo

Epicureanism, *s.* epicureísmo, *m.*

epidemic, *s.* epidemia, *f.*; plaga, *f.* *a.* epidémico

epidermic, *a.* epidérmico

epidermis, *s.* epidermis, *f.*

epigastric, *a.* epigástrico

epigastrium, *s.* epigastrio, *m.*

epiglottis, *s.* epiglotis, *f.*

epigram, *s.* epigrama, *m.*

epigrammatic, *a.* epigramático

epigraph, *s.* epígrafe, *m.*

epigraphy, *s.* epigrafía, *f.*

epilepsy, *s.* epilepsia, alferecía, *f.*

epileptic, *a.* and *s.* epiléptico (-ca). **e. fit,** ataque epiléptico, *m.* **e. aura,** aura epiléptica, *f.*

epilogue, *s.* epílogo, *m.*

epiphany, *s.* epifanía, *f.*

episcopacy, *s.* episcopado, *m.*

episcopal, *a.* episcopal

episcopalianism, *s.* episcopalismo, *m.*

episcopate, s. episcopado, m.
episode, s. suceso, incidente, m.;
(lit.) episodio, m.
episodic, a. episódico
epistle, s. epístola, f.
epistolary, a. epistolar
epitaph, s. epitafio, m.
epithalamium, s. epitalamio,
m.
epithet, s. epíteto, m.
epitome, s. epítome, m.
epitomize, v.t. resumir, abreviar
epoch, s. época, edad, f.
epode, s. épodo, m.
Epsom salts, s. sal de la Higuera,
f.
equability, s. igualdad (de
ánimo), ecuanimidad, f.; uniformidad, f.
equable, a. igual, ecuánime;
uniforme
equably, adv. con ecuanimidad;
igualmente; uniformemente
equal, a. igual; uniforme; imparcial; equitativo, justo. s.
igual, m. and f. v.t. ser igual a;
equivaler a; igualar; (sport)
empatar. **to be e. to,** (of persons) ser capaz de; servir para;
atreverse a; (circumstances)
estar al nivel de; sentirse con
fuerzas para. **without e.,** sin
igual; (of beauty, etc.) sin par.
e. sign, (math.) igual, m.
equality, s. igualdad, f.; uniformidad, f.
equalization, s. igualación, f.
equalize, v.t. igualar
equalizing, a. igualador; com-
pensador
equally, adv. igualmente; imparcialmente
equanimity, s. ecuanimidad, f.
equation, s. ecuación, f.
equator, s. ecuador, m.
equatorial, a. ecuatorial
equerry, s. caballerizo del rey, m.
equestrian, a. ecuestre
equiangular, a. equiángulo
equidistance, s. equidistancia, f.
equidistant, a. equidistante
equilateral, a. equilátero
equilibrist, s. equilibrista, m.
and f.
equilibrium, s. equilibrio, m.
equine, a. equino; hípico; de
caballo
equinoctial, a. equinoccial. **e.
gale,** tempestad equinoccial, f.

equinox, s. equinoccio, m.
equip, v.t. proveer; pertrechar;
equipar
equipage, s. (train) séquito, tren,
m.; (carriage) carruaje, m.
equipment, s. habilitación, f.;
equipo, m.; pertrechos, m. pl.;
material, m.; aparatos, m. pl.;
armamento, m.
equitable, a. equitativo, justo
equitableness, s. equidad, justicia, f.
equitably, adv. equitativamente,
con justicia
equity, s. equidad, f.; imparcialidad, justicia, f.
equivalence, s. equivalencia, f.
equivalent, a. and s. equivalente,
(m.) **to be e. to,** equivaler a
equivocal, a. equívoco, ambiguo
equivocally, adv. equivocadamente
equivocalness, s. ambigüedad, f.
equivocate, v.i. usar frases equí-
vocas, emplear equívocos
equivocation, s. equívoco, m.
era, s. época, era, f.
eradiation, s. irradiación, f.
eradicable, a. erradicable
eradicate, v.t. erradicar; destruir, extirpar; suprimir
eradication, s. erradicación, f.;
destrucción, f.; supresión, f.
erasable, a. borrable
erase, v.t. borrar; tachar
eraser, s. goma de borrar, f.
ink e., goma para tinta, f.
erasure, s. borradura, f.; tachón,
m.
ere, conjunc. antes de (que), antes
de. prep. antes de
erect, a. (upright) derecho; erguido; vertical; (uplifted) levantado; (standing) de pie; (firm)
firme, resuelto; (alert) vigilante.
v.t. (build) edificar, construir;
instalar; (raise) alzar; convertir
erectile, a. eréctil
erection, s. erección, f.; construcción, edificación, f.; (building) edificio, m.; (structure)
estructura, f.; instalación, f.;
(assembling) montaje, m.
erectly, adv. derecho
erectness, s. derechura, f.
erg, s. (phys.) ergio, m.
ergot, s. (med.) cornezuelo de
centeno, m.
ergotin, s. (med.) ergotina, f.

ermine, *s.* armiño, *m.* *a.* de
armiño

erode, *v.t.* corroer; comer; (*geol.*)
denudar

erosion, *s.* erosión, *f.*

erotic, *a.* erótico

err, *v.i.* desviarse; errar; desacertar; pecar

errand, *s.* mensaje, recado, *m.*;
encargo, *m.*; misión, *f.* **e.-boy,**
mensajero, mozo, *m.*

errant, *a.* errante; (of knights)
andante

erratic, *a.* (of conduct) excéntrico, irresponsable; (of thoughts,
etc.) errante; (*med.*) errático

erratum, *s.* errata, *f.*

erring, *a.* extraviado; pecaminoso

erroneous, *a.* erróneo; falso;
injusto

erroneously, *adv.* erróneamente;
falsamente; injustamente

erroneousness, *s.* falsedad, *f.*

error, *s.* error, *m.*; equivocación,
f., desacierto, *m.*; (sin) pecado,
m. **in e.,** por equivocación

eructate, *v.i.* eructar

eructation, *s.* eructo, *m.*

erudite, *a.* erudito; sabio

erudition, *s.* erudición, *f.*

erupt, *v.i.* entrar en erupción,
estar en erupción; (*fig.*) salir con
fuerza

eruption, *s.* erupción, *f.*

eruptive, *a.* eruptivo

erysipelas, *s.* erisipela, *f.*

escalade, *s.* escalada, *f.* *v.t.*
escalar

escalator, *s.* escalera móvil, escalera rodante, escalera automática, *f.*

escapable, *a.* evitable, eludible

escapade, *s.* escapada, *f.*; aventura, *f.*

escape, *s.* huida, fuga, *f.*; evasión,
evitación, *f.*; (leak) escape, *m.*;
(*fig.*) salida, *f.* *v.t.* eludir,
evitar; (of cries, groans, etc.)
dar, salir de. *v.i.* huir, fugarse,
escapar; (slip away) escurrirse;
librarse; salvarse; (leak) escaparse. **His name escapes me,** Se
me escapa (or se me olvida) su
nombre. **to e. notice,** pasar
inadvertido. **to have a narrow e.,** salvarse en una tabla.
to e. from, escaparse de; librarse de; huir de

escaping, *a.* fugitivo

escarpment, *s.* escarpa, *f.*

eschew, *v.t.* evitar

eschewal, *s.* evitación, *f.*

escort, *s.* (*mil.*) escolta, *f.*; (of
ships) convoy, *m.*; acompaña-
miento, *m.*; acompañante, *m.*
v.t. (*mil.*) escoltar; (of ships)
convoyar; acompañar

escritoire, *s.* escritorio, *m*

escudo, *s.* escudo, *m.*

escutcheon, *s.* escudo, blasón, *m.*

Eskimo, *a.* and *s.* esquimal (*m.*
and *f.*)

esoteric, *a.* esotérico

espalier, *s.* espaldera, *f.*

esparto, *s.* esparto, *m.*

especial, *a.* especial; particular

especially, *adv.* especialmente;
ante todo; en particular

Esperantist, *s.* esperantista, *m.*
and *f.*

Esperanto, *s.* esperanto, *m.*

espionage, *s.* espionaje, *m.*

esplanade, *s.* (*mil.*) explanada, *f.*;
bulevar, paseo, *m.*

espousal, *s.* desposorio, *m.*; (*fig.*)
adhesión (a una causa), *f.*

espouse, *v.t.* desposar; (a cause)
abrazar; defender

espy, *v.t.* divisar, ver, observar

esquire, *s.* escudero, *m.*; (land-
owner) hacendado, *m.*; (as a
title) don (before Christian name)

essay, *s.* tentativa, *f.*; (*lit.*)
ensayo, *m.* *v.t.* probar; procurar

essayist, *s.* ensayista, *m.* and *f.*

essence, *s.* esencia, *f.*

essential, *a.* esencial; indispensable, imprescindible; intrínseco.
s. artículo de primera necesidad,
m.; elemento necesario, *m.*

essentially, *adv.* esencialmente

establish, *v.t.* establecer; fundar;
crear; erigir; (constitute) constituir; (order) disponer; (prove)
demostrar, probar; (take root,
settle) arraigarse

established, *a.* establecido;
arraigado; (proved) demostrado:
bien conocido; (of churches)
oficial

establishment, *s.* establecimiento, *m.*; fundación, *f.*; creación, *f.*; institución, *f.*; (building)
erección, *f.*; arraigo, *m.*; (house)
casa, *f.*; (church) iglesia oficial,
f.; demostración, *f.*; reconocimiento, *m.*

estate, *s.* estado, *m.*; **clase,** *f.*; condición, *f.*; (land) propiedad, finca, *f.*; fortuna, *f.*; (inheritance) heredad, *f.*, patrimonio, *m.*; (*law*) bienes, *m. pl.* **personal e.,** bienes muebles, *m. pl.*; fortuna personal, *f.* **third e.,** estado llano, *m.* **e. agent,** agente de fincas, *m.*; agente de casas, *m.*

esteem, *s.* estima, *f.*, aprecio, *m.*; consideración, *f.* *v.t.* estimar, apreciar; creer, juzgar

ester, *s.* (*chem.*) éster, *m.*

Esthonian, *a.* and *s.* estonio (-ia). (language) estonio, *m.*

estimable, *a.* apreciable, estimable

estimableness, *s.* estimabilidad, *f.*

estimate, *s.* estimación, tasa, *f.*; cálculos, *m. pl.*; apreciación, *f.*; opinión, *f.*; *pl.* **estimates,** presupuesto, *m.* *v.t.* (value) avalorar, tasar; calcular, computar; considerar. *v.i.* hacer un presupuesto

estimation, *s.* opinión, *f.*; cálculo, cómputo, *m.*; (esteem) aprecio, *m.*, estima, *f.*

estrange, *v.t.* enajenar; ofender

estrangement, *s.* enajenación, alienación, *f.*

estuary, *s.* estuario, *m.*, ría, *f.*

etcetera, etcétera. (Used as noun, *f.*)

etch, *v.t.* grabar al agua fuerte

etcher, *s.* grabador (-ra) al agua fuerte

etching, *s.* aguafuerte, *f.*; grabado al agua fuerte, *m.* **e. needle,** punta seca, aguja de grabador, *f.*

eternal, *a.* eterno: incesante. **s.** (E.) el Eterno

eternally, *adv.* eternamente

eternity, *s.* eternidad, *f.*

eternize, *v.t.* eternizar

ether, *s.* éter, *m.*

ethereal, *a.* etéreo; vaporoso, aéreo

etheric, *a.* etéreo

etherize, *v.t.* eterizar

ethical, *a.* ético, moral

ethics, *s.* ética, *f.*; (filosofía) moral, *f.*

ethnic, *a.* étnico

ethnographic, *a.* etnográfico

ethnography, *s.* etnografía, *f.*

ethnologist, *s.* etnólogo, *m.*

ethnology, *s.* etnología, *f.*

ethyl, *s.* (*chem.*) etilo, *m.*

ethylene, *s.* (*chem.*) etileno,.*m.*

etiquette, *s.* etiqueta, *f.*

Eton coat, *s.* chaquetilla, *f.*

Eton collar, *s.* cuello de colegial, *m.*

Eton crop, *s.* pelo a la garçonne, *m.*

Etruscan, *a.* and *s.* etrusco (-ca)

etymological, *a.* etimológico

etymologist, *s.* etimólogo, *m.*, etimologista, *m.* and *f.*

etymology, *s.* etimología, *f.*

eucalyptus, *s.* encalipto, *m.*

Eucharist, *s.* Eucaristía, *f.*

eucharistic, *a.* eucarístico

Euclidean, *a.* euclídeo

eugenic, *a.* eugenésico

eugenics, *s.* eugenesia, *f.*

eulogist, *s.* elogiador (-ra), loador (-ra)

eulogistic, *a.* elogiador

eulogize, *v.t.* elogiar, alabar, encomiar

eulogy, *s.* elogio, encomio, *m.*; alabanza, *f.*; panegírico, *m.*

eunuch, *s.* eunuco, *m.*

euphemism, *s.* eufemismo, *m.*

euphonious, *a.* eufónico

euphony, *s.* eufonía, *f.*

euphuistic, *a.* alambicado, gongorino

Eurasian, *a.* and *s.* eurasio (-ia)

eurhythmic, *a.* eurítmico

eurhythmics, *s.* euritmia, *f.*

European, *a.* and *s.* europeo (-ea)

europeanize, *v.t.* europeanizar

euthanasia, *s.* eutanasia, *f.*

evacuate, *v.t.* evacuar

evacuation, *s.* evacuación, *f.*

evade, *v.t.* evadir, eludir; evitar, esquivar; rehuir

evaluate, *v.t.* evaluar, estimar; calcular

evaluation, *s.* evaluación, estimación, *f.*

evanescent, *a.* transitorio, fugaz, pasajero

evangelical, *a.* evangélico

evangelicalism, *s.* evangelismo, *m.*

evangelist, *s.* evangelista, *m.*

evangelize, *v.t.* evangelizar

evaporate, *v.i.* evaporarse; desvanecerse. *v.t.* evaporar

evaporation, *s.* evaporación, *f.*; desvanecimiento, *m.*

evaporative, *a.* evaporatorio

evasion, *s.* (escape) fuga, *f.*; evasión, *f.*; evasiva, *f.*, efugio, *m.*

evasive, *a.* evasivo, ambiguo

evasively, *adv.* evasivamente

evasiveness, *s.* carácter evasivo, *m.*

eve, *s.* víspera, *f.*; (*ecc.*) vigilia, *f.* **on the eve of,** la víspera de; (*fig.*) en vísperas de

even, *a.* (flat) llano; (smooth) liso; igual; (level with) al mismo nivel (de); uniforme; (of numbers) par; (approximate, of sums) redondo; rítmico; invariable, constante; (of temper) apacible; (just) imparcial; (monotonous) monótono, igual; (paid) pagado; (*com.*, of date) mismo. **to be e. with a person,** pagar en la misma moneda, vengarse de

even, *adv.* siquiera; aun; hasta; (also) también. **not e.,** ni siquiera. **e. as,** así como, del mismo modo que. **e. if,** aun cuando, si bien. **e. now,** aun ahora; ahora mismo. **e. so,** aun así; (nevertheless) sin embargo. **e. though,** aunque; suponiendo que

even, *v.t.* igualar; (level) allanar, nivelar; (accounts) desquitar; compensar; (accounts) hacer uniforme

evening, *s.* tarde, *f.*, atardecer, *m.*; noche, *f.*; (*fig.*) fin, *m.* *a.* vespertino, de la tarde. **Good e.!** ¡Buenas tardes! ¡Buenas noches! **in the e.,** al atardecer. **to-morrow e.,** mañana por la tarde. **yesterday e.,** ayer por la tarde. **e. class,** clase nocturna, *f.* **e. dress,** (women) traje de noche, *m.*; (men) traje de etiqueta, *m.* **e. meal,** cena, *f.* **e. paper,** periódico (or diario) de la noche, *m.* **e. star,** estrella vespertina, *f.*; (Venus) lucero de la tarde, *m.*

evenly, *adv.* igualmente; (on a level) a nivel; uniformemente; imparcialmente; (of speech) con suavidad

evenness, *s.* igualdad, *f.*; (smoothness) lisura, *f.*; uniformidad, *f.*; imparcialidad, *f.*; (of temper) ecuanimidad, serenidad, *f.*

evensong, *s.* vísperas, *f. pl.*

event, *s.* incidente, suceso, acontecimiento, *m.*; (result) consecuencia, *f.*; resultado, *m.*; caso, *m.*; (athletics) prueba, *f.*; (race) carrera, *f.* **at all events,** de todas maneras. **in such an e.,** en tal caso. **in the e. of,** en el caso de

eventful, *a.* lleno de acontecimientos; accidentado; memorable

eventual, *a.* eventual; final, último

eventuality, *s.* eventualidad, *f.*

eventually, *adv.* a la larga, al fin

ever, *adv.* siempre; (at any time) jamás; alguna vez; nunca; (even) siquiera; (very) muy; (in any way) en modo alguno. **As fast as e. he can,** Lo más aprisa que pueda. **Be it e. so big,** Por grande que sea. **Did you e.!** ¡Hábrase visto! ¡Qué cosa! **for e.,** para siempre. **for e. and e.,** para siempre jamás; (mostly ecclesiastical) por los siglos de los siglos; eternamente. **He is e. so nice,** Él es muy simpático. **Hardly e.,** casi nunca. **I don't think I have e. been there,** No creo que haya estado nunca allí. **if e.,** si alguna vez; (rarely) raramente. **nor ... e.,** ni nunca. **not ... e.,** nunca. **e. after,** desde entonces; (afterwards) después. **e. and anon,** de vez en cuando. **e. so little,** siquiera un poco; muy poco

evergreen, *a.* siempre verde. *s.* planta vivaz, *f.* **e. oak,** encina, *f.*

everlasting, *a.* eterno, perpetuo; (of colours) estable; incesante. **e. flower,** perpetua, *f.*

evermore, *adv.* eternamente

every, *a.* todo; cada (invariable); todos los, *m. pl.*; todas las, *f. pl.* **e. day,** todos los días, cada día. **e. now and then,** de cuando en cuando. **e. other day,** cada dos días

everybody, *s.* todo el mundo, *m.*; todos, *m. pl.*; todas, *f. pl.*; cada uno, *m.*; cada una, *f.*

everyday, *a.* diario, cotidiano; corriente, usual

everything, *s.* todo, *m.*; (e. that, which) todo lo (que). **e. possible,** todo lo posible

everywhere, *adv.* por todas partes

evict, *v.t.* desahuciar; expulsar

eviction, *s.* evicción, *f.*, desahucio, *m.*; expulsión, *f.*

evidence, *s.* (*law*) testimonio, *m.*, deposición, *f.*; indicios, *m. pl.*; evidencia, *f.*; prueba, *f.*; hecho, *m. v.t.* patentizar, probar. **to give e.,** dar testimonio, deponer

evident, *a.* evidente, patente, manifiesto; claro. **to be e.,** ser patente, estar a la vista

evidently, *adv.* evidentemente; claramente

evil, *a.* malo; malvado, perverso; de maldad; (*unfortunate*) aciago; de infortunio; (*of spirits*) diabólico, malo. **s.** mal, *m.*; maldad, perversidad, *f.*; (*misfortune*) desgracia, *f.* **the E. one,** el Malo. **e.-doer,** malhechor (-ra). **e. eye,** mal de ojo, aojo, *m.* **e.-minded,** mal pensado; malintencionado. **e.-speaking,** maledicencia, calumnia, *f.* **e. spirit,** demonio, espíritu malo, *m.*

evince, *v.t.* evidenciar; mostrar

eviscerate, *v.t.* destripar, desentrañar

evocation, *s.* evocación, *f.*

evocative, *a.* evocador

evoke, *v.t.* evocar

evolution, *s.* evolución, *f.*; desarrollo, *m.*; (*nav., mil.*) maniobra, *f.*; (*math.*) extracción de una raíz, *f.*; (*revolution*) revolución, vuelta, *f.*

evolutionism, *s.* evolucionismo, *m.*

evolutive, *a.* evolutivo

evolve, *v.i.* evolucionar; desarrollarse. *v.t.* producir por evolución; desarrollar; pensar

ewe, *s.* oveja, *f.* **ewe lamb,** cordera, *f.*

ewer, *s.* aguamanil, *m.*

exacerbate, *v.t.* exacerbar; agravar, empeorar

exacerbation, *s.* exacerbación, *f.*; agravación, *f.*

exact, *a.* exacto; fiel; metódico; estricto. *v.t.* exigir

exacting, *a.* exigente; severo, estricto; (*hard*) agotador, arduo

exaction, *s.* exigencia, *f.*; extorsión, exacción, *f.*

exactly, *adv.* exactamente; precisamente

exactness, *s.* exactitud, *f.*

exaggerate, *v.t.* exagerar; acentuar. *v.i.* exagerar

exaggerated, *a.* exagerado

exaggeration, *s.* exageración, *f.*

exaggerator, *s.* exagerador (-ra)

exalt, *v.t.* exaltar; enaltecer, elevar; (*praise*) glorificar, magnificar; (*intensify*) realzar; intensificar

exaltation, *s.* exaltación, elevación, *f.*; alegría, *f.*, júbilo, *m.*; (*ecstasy*) éxtasis, arrobamiento, *m.*; (*of the Cross*) exaltación, *f.*

exalted, *a.* exaltado, eminente

exaltedness, *s.* exaltación, *f.*

examination, *s.* examen, *m.*; inspección, *f.*; investigación, *f.*; (*law*) interrogatorio, *m.*; prueba, *f.* **to sit an e.,** examinarse. **written e.,** prueba escrita, *f.*

examine, *v.t.* examinar; inspeccionar; investigar; (*law*) interrogar; (*search*) reconocer; (*by touch*) tentar; observar; analizar. **to e. into,** examinar; considerar detenidamente; ahondar en

examinee, *s.* examinando (-da)

examiner, *s.* examinador (-ra); inspector (-ra)

examinership, *s.* cargo de examinador, *m.*

examining, *a.* que examina; de examen; (*law*) interrogante

example, *s.* ejemplo, *m.*; ilustración, *f.*; (*parallel*) ejemplar, *m.*; (*warning*) escarmiento, *m.* **for e.,** por ejemplo. **to set an e.,** dar ejemplo.

exasperate, *v.t.* exasperar, irritar; (*increase*) aumentar; (*worsen*) agravar

exasperating, *a.* exasperante, irritante, provocador

exasperation, *s.* exasperación, irritación, *f.*; (*worsening*) agravación, *f.*; enojo, *m.*

excavate, *v.t.* excavar; (*hollow*) vaciar

excavation, *s.* excavación, *f.*; (*arch.*) vaciado, *m.*

excavator, *s.* excavador (-ra); (*machine*) excavadora, *f.*

exceed, *v.t.* exceder; (*excel*) superar, aventajar; (*one's hopes, etc.*) sobrepujar. *v.i.* excederse. **to e. one's rights,** abusar de sus derechos, ir demasiado lejos

exceedingly, *adv.* sumamente, extremadamente; sobre manera

excel, *v.t.* aventajar, superar; vencer. *v.i.* sobresalir; distinguirse, señalarse; ser superior

excellence, *s.* excelencia, *f.*; superioridad, *f.*; perfección, *f.*; mérito, *m.*; buena calidad, *f.*

excellency, *s.* (title) Excelencia, *f.* **Your E.,** Su Excelencia

excellent, *a.* excelente; superior; perfecto; magnífico; (in examinations) sobresaliente

excellently, *adv.* excelentemente; perfectamente; magníficamente

except, *v.t.* exceptuar; omitir

except, excepting, *prep.* excepto, con excepción de; exceptuando; menos; salvo; fuera de. *conjunc.* a menos que. **except for,** si no fuese por; con excepción de; fuera de

exception, *s.* excepción, *f.*; objeción, protesta, *f.* **to make an e.,** hacer una excepción. **to take e. to,** protestar contra; tachar, criticar; desaprobar. **with the e. of.** See **excepting**

exceptional, *a.* excepcional

exceptionally, *adv.* excepcionalmente

excerpt, *s.* excerpta, *f.*, extracto, *m.* *v.t.* extraer

excess, *s.* exceso, *m.*; superabundancia, *f.*; demasía, *f.*; (com.) superávit, *m.* **in e.,** en exceso, de sobra. **in e. of,** en exceso de; arriba de. **to e.,** excesivamente, demasiado. **e. fare,** suplemento, *m.* **e. luggage,** exceso de equipaje, *m.*; (overweight) exceso de peso, *m.*

excessive, *a.* excesivo; superabundante; inmoderado, desmesurado; exagerado

excessively, *adv.* excesivamente; exageradamente

excessiveness, *s.* exceso, *m.*; superabundancia, *f.*; exageración, *f.*

exchange, *s.* cambio, trueque, *m.*; (of prisoners) canje, *m.*; (financial) cambio, *m.*; (building) bolsa, lonja, *f.*; (telephone) oficina central de teléfonos, *f.* *v.t.* cambiar (for, por); trocar; (replace) reemplazar; (prisoners) canjear; (of blows) darse; (pass from, into) pasar de ... a. *v.i.* hacer un cambio. **in e. for,** en cambio de, a trueque de; por. **to e.**

greetings, saludarse; cambiar saludos. **They exchanged looks,** Se miraron. **What is the rate of e.?** ¿Cuál es el tipo de cambio (monetario)? **e. of prisoners,** canje de prisioneros, *m.*

exchangeable, *a.* cambiable; trocable

exchequer, *s.* (public finance) Hacienda pública, *f.*; tesorería, *f.*; (funds) fondos, *m pl.* **Chancellor of the E.,** Ministro de Hacienda, *m.*

excipient, *s.* excipiente, *m.*

excise, *s.* contribución indirecta, *f.*; (customs and e.) Aduana, *f.* *v.t.* (cut) cortar, extirpar; imponer una contribución indirecta. **e. duty,** derecho de aduana, *m.*

exciseman, *s.* aduanero, *m.*

excision, *s.* excisión, *f.*; extirpación, *f.*

excitability, *s.* excitabilidad, *f.*

excitable, *a.* excitable

excitation, *s.* excitación, *f.*

excite, *v.t.* emocionar; conmover; agitar; excitar; suscitar, provocar; incitar, instigar; (attention, interest) despertar; estimular. **to become excited,** emocionarse; exaltarse; (annoyed) acalorarse; (upset) agitarse

excitedly, *adv.* con emoción; acaloradamente; agitadamente

excitement, *s.* conmoción, *f.*; agitación, *f.*; (annoyance) acaloramiento, *m.*; emoción, *f.*; estímulo, *m.*; instigación, *f.*, fomento, *m.*; (amusement) placer, *m.*

exciting, *a.* emocionante; conmovedor; agitador; muy interesante

exclaim, *v.t.* and *v.i.* exclamar. **to e. against,** clamar contra

exclamation, *s.* exclamación, *f.* **e. mark,** punto de exclamación, *m.*

exclamatory, *a.* exclamatorio

exclude, *v.t.* excluir; exceptuar; evitar; (refuse) rechazar

exclusion, *s.* exclusión, *f.*; exceptuación, *f.*; eliminación, *f.*

exclusive, *a.* exclusivo; (snobbish) exclusivista. **e. of,** no incluido; aparte de

exclusively, *adv.* exclusivamente; únicamente

exclusiveness, *s.* carácter exclusivo, *m.*

exclusivism, s. exclusivismo, m.
exclusivist, s. exclusivista, m.
and f.
excommunicate, v.t. excomulgar. a. excomulgado
excommunication, s. excomunión, f.
excrement, s. excremento, m.
excrescence, s. excrecencia, f.
excrescent, a. que forma excrecencia; superfluo
excrete, v.t. excretar
excretion, s. excreción, f.
excretory, a. excretorio
excruciating, a. atormentador,
angustioso; (of pain) agudísimo
excursion, s. excursión, f.; expedición, f.; (digression) digresión, f. e. **ticket,** billete de
excursión, m. e. **train,** tren de
excursionistas, m.
excursionist, s. excursionista,
m. and f.; turista, m. and f.
excusable, a. disculpable, excusable
excusableness, s. lo disculpable
excusably, adv. excusablemente
excuse, s. excusa, f.; disculpa, f.;
pretexto, m.; justificación, defensa, f. to **give as an e.,**
pretextar
excuse, v.t. disculpar, excusar;
dispensar (de); librar (de); (forgive) perdonar; (defend) justificar, defender; (minimize) paliar; (oneself) disculparse. **E. me!**
¡Con permiso!; ¡Perdone Vd.!
execrable, a. execrable, abominable
execrably, adv. execrablemente
execrate, v.t. execrar, abominar.
v.i. maldecir
execration, s. execración, abominación, f.; maldición, f.
executant, s. ejecutante, m. and
f.
execute, v.t. (perform) ejecutar,
poner en efecto, realizar; (art,
mus.) ejecutar; (part in a play)
hacer, desempeñar; (fulfil) cumplir; (law) otorgar (un documento); (kill) ajusticiar
execution, s. efectuación, realización, f.; (art, mus.) ejecución, f.;
(of part in a play) desempeño (de
un papel), m.; (fulfilment) cumplimiento, m.; (law) otorgamiento (de un documento), m.;
(killing) suplicio, m., ejecución

de la pena de muerte, f.; (law,
seizure) ejecución, f.
executioner, s. verdugo, m.
executive, a. ejecutivo; administrativo. s. poder ejecutivo, m.
executor, s. administrador testamentario, m.
executorship, s. ejecutoría, f.
executrix, s. administradora
testamentaria, f.
exegesis, s. exégesis, f.
exegetical, a. exegético
exemplary, a. ejemplar
exemplification, s. ejemplifi-
cación, ilustración, demostración,
f.
exemplify, v.t. ejemplificar; ilustrar, demostrar
exempt, v.t. exentar, eximir;
librar; dispensar, excusar. a.
exento; libre; excusado; inmune
exemption, s. exención, f.; libertad, f.; inmunidad, f.
exequies, s. pl. (exequy) exequias, f. pl.
exercise, s. ejercicio, m.; uso,
m.; (essay) ensayo, m.; pl.
exercises, (on land or sea)
maniobras, f. pl. v.t. ejercer;
usar, emplear; (train) ejercitar,
entrenar; adiestrar; pasear, dar
un paseo; (worry) preocupar.
v.i. hacer ejercicio; ejercitarse;
adiestrarse. **spiritual exercises,** ejercicios espirituales, m.
pl. **to take e. in the open air,**
tomar ejercicio al aire libre.
to write an e., escribir un
ejercicio. e. **book,** cuaderno de
ejercicios, m.
exert, v.t. hacer uso de, emplear,
ejercer, poner en juego; (deploy)
desplegar. to **e. oneself,** hacer un
esfuerzo (para); esforzarse (de);
trabajar mucho; tratar (de);
apurarse, tomarse mucha molestia; preocuparse
exertion, s. esfuerzo, m.; uso,
m.; (exercise) ejercicio, m.; (good
offices) diligencias, gestiones, f.
pl.; buenos oficios, m. pl.
exhalation, s. exhalación, f.;
efluvio, m.; vapor, m.; humo, m.
exhale, v.t. exhalar; emitir, despedir. v.i. evaporarse; disiparse
exhaust, v.t. agotar; (empty)
vaciar; (end) acabar; apurar;
consumir; (tire) rendir, cansar

mucho; (weaken) debilitar; (a subject) tratar detalladamente. *s.* (*mech.*) escape, *m.*; emisión de vapor, *f.*; vapor de escape, *m.* **e. pipe**, tubo de escape, *m.*

exhaustible, *a.* agotable

exhausting, *a.* cansado, agotador

exhaustion, *s.* agotamiento, *m.*; rendimiento, cansancio, *m.*; lasitud, *f.*; postración, *f.*

exhaustive, *a.* completo; minucioso

exhaustively, *adv.* detenidamente; detalladamente; minuciosamente

exhaustiveness, *s.* lo completo; minuciosidad, *f.*

exhibit, *v.t.* exhibir; manifestar, ostentar; revelar, descubrir; presentar. *v.i.* exhibir, ser expositor. *s.* objeto exhibido, *m.*; (*law*) prueba, *f.*

exhibition, *s.* exposición, *f.*; (performance) función, *f.*; espectáculo, *m.*; exhibición, *f.*; (showing) manifestación, *f.*; (grant) bolsa de estudio, beca, *f.*

exhibitionism, *s.* exhibicionismo, *m.*

exhibitionist, *s.* exhibicionista, *m.* and *f.*

exhibitor, *s.* expositor (-ra)

exhilarate, *v.t.* alegrar, alborozar

exhilarating, *a.* alegre; estimulador; vigorizador, tonificante

exhilaration, *s.* alegría, *f.*, alborozo, regocijo, *m.*

exhort, *v.t.* and *v.i.* exhortar

exhortation, *s.* exhortación, *f.*

exhumation, *s.* exhumación, *f.*

exhume, *v.t.* exhumar

exigence, *s.* exigencia, *f.*; urgencia, *f.*; (need) necesidad, *f.*

exigent, *a.* exigente; urgente

exiguous, *a.* exiguo

exiguousness, *s.* exigüidad, *f.*

exile, *s.* destierro, *m.*; (person) desterrado (-da). *v.t.* desterrar

exist, *v.i.* existir

existence, *s.* existencia, *f.*; (being) ser, *m.*; (life) vida, *f.* **to bring into e.,** causar; producir

existencialism, *s.* existencialismo, *m.*

existing, *a.* existente

exit, *s.* salida, *f.*; partida, *f.*; (death) muerte, *f.*; (*theat.*) mutis, *m.* *v.i.* (*theat.*) hacer mutis. **to**

make one's e., salir; marcharse; irse; morir; (*theat.*) hacer mutis

exodus, *s.* éxodo, *m.*; salida, *f.*; emigración, *f.*; (Old Testament) Éxodo, *m.*

exonerate, *v.t.* exonerar

exoneration, *s.* exoneración, *f.*

exorbitance, *s.* exorbitancia, *f.*

exorbitant, *a.* exorbitante

exorcism, *s.* exorcismo, *m.*

exorcist, *s.* exorcista, *m.*

exorcize, *v.t.* exorcizar, conjurar

exordium, *s.* exordio, *m.*

exoteric, *a.* exotérico

exotic, *a.* exótico. *s.* planta exótica, *f.*; (*fig.*) flor de estufa, *f.*

expand, *v.t.* extender; abrir; (wings, etc.) desplegar; (the chest, etc.) expandir; dilatar; (amplify) ampliar; (develop) desarrollar; (*fig.*) ensanchar; (increase) aumentar. *v.i.* dilatarse; hincharse; abrirse; extenderse; (*fig.*) ensancharse; (increase) aumentarse

expanse, *s.* extensión, *f.*

expansibility, *s.* (*phys.*) expansibilidad, *f.*; dilatabilidad, *f.*

expansible, *a.* (*phys.*) expansible; dilatable

expansion, *s.* expansión, *f.*; extensión, *f.*; dilatación, *f.*; (amplification) ampliación, *f.*; (development) desarrollo, *m.*; (*fig.*) ensanchamiento, *m.*; (increase) aumento, *m.*

expansionism, *s.* expansionismo, *m.*

expansive, *a.* expansivo; (of persons) efusivo, expresivo, comunicativo, afable

expansiveness, *s.* expansibilidad, *f.*; (of persons) afabilidad, *f.*

expatiate, (upon) *v.i.* extenderse en

expatiation, *s.* discurso, *m.*; digresión, *f.*

expatriation, *s.* expatriación, *f.*

expect, *v.t.* esperar; (await) aguardar; (suppose) suponer; (demand) exigir; (count on) contar con. *v.i.* creer

expectance, *s.* expectación, *f.*; esperanza, *f.*

expectant, *a.* expectante; (hopeful) esperanzado; (pregnant) embarazada

expectantly, *adv.* con expectación

expectation, *s.* expectación, *f.*; (hope) esperanza, expectativa, *f.*; probabilidad, *f.*

expectorate, *v.t.* expectorar. *v.i.* escupir

expectoration, *s.* expectoración, *f.*

expedience, *s.* conveniencia, *f.*; oportunidad, *f.*; aptitud, *f.*; (self-interest) egoísmo, *m.*

expedient, *a.* conveniente; oportuno; apto; prudente; político. *s.* expediente, recurso, medio, *m.*

expedite, *v.t.* acelerar; facilitar; (send off) despachar

expedition, *s.* expedición, *f.*; (haste) celeridad, diligencia, *f.*

expeditionary, *a.* expedicionario. **e. force,** fuerza expedicionaria, *f.*

expeditious, *a.* expedito, pronto

expeditiously, *adv.* expeditamente, prontamente

expeditiousness, *s.* prontitud, *f.*

expel, *v.t.* expeler, expulsar; echar, arrojar; despedir

expend, *v.i.* gastar, expender; (time) perder

expenditure, *s.* gasto, desembolso, *m.*; (of time) pérdida, *f.*

expense, *s.* gasto, *m.*; pérdida, *f.*; costa, *f.*; *pl.* expenses, expensas, *f. pl.*, gastos, *m. pl.* **at the e. of,** a costa de. **to be put to great e.,** tener que gastar mucho. **to pay one's expenses,** pagar sus gastos

expensive, *a.* costoso; caro

expensively, *adv.* costosamente

expensiveness, *s.* lo costoso; costa, *f.*

experience, *s.* experiencia, *f.* *v.t.* experimentar; sentir; sufrir. **by e.,** por experiencia

experienced, *a.* experimentado; experto; hábil; (lived) vivido

experiment, *s.* experimento, *m.*; prueba, *f.*; ensayo, *m.*, tentativa, *f.* *v.i.* experimentar; hacer una prueba

experimental, *a.* experimental; tentativo

experimentally, *adv.* experimentalmente; por experiencia

expert, *a.* experto; perito; hábil; (finished) acabado. *s.* experto, *m.*, especialista, *m.* and *f.*

expertly, *adv.* expertamente; hábilmente

expertness, *s.* pericia, *f.*; maestría, *f.*; habilidad, *f.*; (knowledge) conocimiento, *m.*

expiable, *a.* que se puede expiar

expiate, *v.t.* expiar; reparar

expiation, *s.* expiación, *f.*

expiatory, *a.* expiatorio

expiration, *s.* (breathing out) espiración, *f.*; (ending) expiración, *f.*; terminación, *f.*; (com.) vencimiento, *m.*; (death) muerte, *f.*

expire, *v.i.* (exhale) espirar; (die) morir, dar el último suspiro; (of fire, light) extinguirse; (end) expirar; terminar; (com.) vencer

expiry, *s.* terminación, *f.*; expiración, *f.*; (com.) vencimiento, *m.*

explain, *v.t.* explicar; aclarar; demostrar; exponer; (justify) justificar, defender. *v.i.* explicarse. **to e. away,** explicar; justificar

explainable, *a.* explicable

explanation, *s.* explicación, *f.*; aclaración, *f.*

explanatory, *a.* explicativo; aclaratorio

expletive, *a.* expletivo. *s.* interjección, *f.*

explicable, *a.* explicable

explicit, *a.* explícito

explicitly, *adv.* explícitamente

explode, *v.i.* estallar; detonar; reventar (also *fig.*). *v.t.* hacer estallar; (a mine) hacer saltar; (a belief, etc.) hacer abandonar; desechar

exploit, *s.* hazaña, proeza, *f.*; aventura, *f.* *v.t.* explotar

exploitation, *s.* explotación, *f.*

exploiter, *s.* explotador (-ra)

exploration, *s.* exploración, *f.*

exploratory, *a.* exploratorio

explore, *v.t.* explorar; examinar; averiguar; investigar; (med., surg.) explorar

explorer, *s.* explorador (-ra)

explosion, *s.* explosión, *f.*; estallido, *m.*, detonación, *f.*

explosive, *a.* and *s.* explosivo (*m.*). **high e.,** explosivo violento, *m.* **explosives chamber,** recámara, *f.*

explosiveness, *s.* propiedad explosiva, *f.*; lo explosivo; violencia, *f.*

exponent, *a.* and *s.* exponente (*m.* and *f.*)

export, s. exportación, f. v.t. exportar. **e. licence,** permiso de exportación, m. **e. trade,** comercio de exportación, m.

exportation, s. exportación, f.

exporter, s. exportador (-ra)

expose, v.t. exponer; arriesgar; (exhibit) exhibir, (unmask) desenmascarar; descubrir; revelar; (phot.) exponer; (ridicule) ridiculizar

exposed, a. descubierto; no abrigado; expuesto, peligroso

exposition, s. explicación, interpretación, f.; declaración, f.; (exhibition) exposición, f.

expostulate, v.i. protestar, **to e. with,** reprochar; reconvenir

expostulation, s. protesta, f.; reconvención, f.

exposure, s. exposición (also phot.), f.; (aspect) orientación, f.; (scandal) revelación, f., escándalo, m.; peligro, m.; exposición al frío or al calor, f.

expound, v.t. exponer, explicar; comentar

expounder, s. intérprete, m. and f.; comentador (-ra)

express, a. (clear) categórico, explícito, claro; expreso; (exact) exacto; (quick) rápido. s. (messenger, post) expreso, m.; (train) (tren) expreso, (tren) rápido, m.; (goods) exprés, m. v.t. expresar; (a letter, etc.) mandar por expreso

expressible, a. decible

expression, s. expresión, f.

expressionless, a. sin expresión

expressive, a. expresivo; que expresa

expropriate, v.t. expropiar

expropriation, s. expropiación, f.

expulsion, s. expulsión, f.

expunge, v.t. borrar; testar; omitir

expunging, s. borradura, f.; testación, f.; omisión, f.

expurgate, v.t. expurgar

expurgation, s. expurgación, f.

expurgator, s. expurgador, m.

expurgatory, a. expurgatorio

exquisite, a. exquisito, precioso, primoroso; excelente; (acute) agudo, intenso; (keen) vivo. s. elegante, petimetre, m.

exquisitely, adv. primorosamente, pulcramente; a la perfección

exquisiteness, s. primor, m., pulcritud, perfección, f.; excelencia, f.; (of pain) intensidad, f.; (keenness) viveza, f.

ex-serviceman, s. excombatiente, antiguo soldado, m.

extant, a. estante; existente; viviente

extempore, a. improvisado

extemporize, v.t. and v.i. improvisar

extend, v.t. extender; (hold out) tender, alargar; (lengthen) prolongar; (a period of time) prorrogar, diferir; (make larger) ensanchar; (increase) aumentar; dilatar; ampliar; (offer) ofrecer. v.i. extenderse; dilatarse; continuar; (give) dar de sí, estirarse; (last) prolongarse, durar; (become known) propagarse

extensible, a. extensible

extension, s. extensión, f.; expansión, f.; (increase) aumento, m.; prolongación, f.; ampliación, f.; (com.) prórroga, f.

extensive, a. extenso, ancho, vasto; grande, considerable; (comprehensive) comprensivo

extensively, adv. extensamente; generalmente

extensiveness, s. extensión, f.; amplitud, f.

extensor, s. (anat.) extensor, m.

extent, s. extensión, f.; (degree) punto, m.; (limit) límite, m. **to a great e.,** en gran parte; considerablemente. **to some e.,** hasta cierto punto. **to the full e.,** en toda su extensión; completamente. **to what e.?** ¿hasta qué punto?

extenuate, v.t. atenuar, desminuir, mitigar, paliar

extenuating, a. atenuante

extenuation, s. atenuación, mitigación, f.

exterior, a. exterior, externo; de fuera; (foreign) extranjero. s. exterior, m.; aspecto, m.; forma, f.

exterminate, v.t. exterminar

extermination, s. exterminio, m.

exterminator, s. exterminador (-ra)

exterminatory, a. exterminador

external, a. externo, exterior; (foreign) extranjero. s. pl. externals, apariencias, *f. pl.*; aspecto exterior, *m.*; comportamiento, *m.*

externally, *adv.* exteriormente

exterritorial, *a.* extraterritorial

exterritoriality, *s.* extraterritorialidad, *f.*

extinct, *a.* extinto; (of light, fire) extinguido; suprimido

extinction, *s.* extinción, *f.*

extinguish, *v.t.* extinguir; apagar; (*fig.*) eclipsar

extinguishable, *a.* apagable

extinguisher, *s.* apagador (-ra); (for fires) extintor, *m.*; (snuffer) matacandelas, *m.*

extinguishment, *s.* apagamiento, *m.*; extinción, *f.*; abolición, *f.*; (destruction) aniquilamiento, *m.*

extirpate, *v.t.* extirpar

extirpation, *s.* extirpación, *f.*

extol, *v.t.* elogiar, encomiar, alabar; cantar

extoller, *s.* alabador (-ra)

extort, *v.t.* arrancar, sacar por fuerza; exigir por amenazas

extortion, *s.* extorsión, *f.*; exacción, *f.*

extortionate, *a.* injusto; opresivo; (of price) exorbitante, excesivo

extra, *a.* and *adv.* adicional; extraordinario; suplementario; (spare) de repuesto. *prefix* (in compounds) extra. *s.* extra, *m.*; suplemento, *m.*; (of a paper) hoja extraordinaria, *f.*; (actor) supernumerario (-ia). **e. charge**, gasto suplementario, *m.*; (on the railway, etc.) suplemento, *m.* **e. mural**, *a.* de extramuros. **e. tyre**, neumático de repuesto, *m.*

extract, *v.t.* sacar; (*chem., math.*) extraer; extractar; (obtain) obtener. *s.* (*chem.*) extracto, *m.*; (excerpt) cita, *f.*

extraction, *s.* saca, *f.*; extracción, *f.*; obtención, *f.*

extradite, *v.t.* entregar por extradición

extradition, *s.* extradición, *f.*

extraneous, *a.* extraño; (irrelevant) ajeno (a)

extraordinarily, *adv.* extraordinariamente, singularmente

extraordinariness, *s.* lo extraordinario; singularidad, *f.*; (queerness) rareza, *f.*

extraordinary, *a.* extraordinario;

singular; (queer) raro, excéntrico; (incredible) increíble

extravagance, *s.* (in spending) prodigalidad, *f.*, derroche, *m.*; (of dress, speech) extravagancia, *f.*; (foolishness) disparate, *m.*; (luxury) lujo, *m.*

extravagant, *a.* extravagante; (queer) extraño, raro; (wasteful) pródigo; (of persons) gastador, manirroto; (of price) exorbitante; excesivo

extravagantly, *adv.* extravagantemente; de un modo extraño; pródigamente; profusamente; excesivamente

extreme, *a.* extremo. *s.* extremo, *m.* **in e.**, extremamente, en extremo, en sumo grado. **to carry to extremes**, llevar a extremos; llevar demasiado lejos. **E. Unction**, Extremaunción, *f.*

extremely, *adv.* sumamente; (*fam.*) muy

extremism, *s.* extremismo, *m.*

extremist, *a.* and *s.* extremista (*m.* and *f.*)

extremity, *s.* extremidad, *f.*; (point) punta, *f.*; necesidad, *f.*; *pl.* **extremities**, (*anat.*) extremidades, *f. pl.*; (measures) medidas extremas, *f. pl.*

extricate, *v.t.* desenredar; librar; sacar

extrication, *s.* liberación, *f.*

extrinsic, *a.* extrínseco

extrovert, *s.* (*psy.*) extravertido, *m.*

exuberance, *s.* exuberancia, *f.*

exuberant, *a.* exuberante

exudation, *s.* exudación, *f.*

exude, *v.t.* exudar; rezumar; sudar. *v.i.* exudar; rezumarse

exult, *v.i.* exultar; alegrarse

exultant, *a.* exultante, triunfante

exultantly, *adv.* con exultación; triunfalmente

exultation, *s.* exultación, *f.*; triunfo, *m.*

eye, *s.* ojo, *m.*; (sight) vista, *f.*; (look) mirada, *f.*; atención, *f.*; (opinion) opinión, *f.*, juicio, *m.*; (of a needle, of cheese) ojo, *m.*; (of a hook) corcheta, *f.*; (*bot.*) yema, *f.*; (of a potato) grillo, *m.* *v.t.* ojear; fijar los ojos en; examinar, mirar detenidamente.

bright eyes, ojos vivos, *m. pl.*
prominent eyes, ojos saltones,
m. pl. He couldn't keep his
eyes off Mary, Se le fueron los
ojos tras María. as far as the
eye can reach, hasta donde
alcanza la vista. before one's
eyes, a la vista de uno, ante
los ojos de uno. in my (etc.)
eyes, *(fig.)* según creo yo, en mi
opinión. in the twinkling of
an eye, en un abrir y cerrar de
ojos. with an eye to, pensando
en. with my own eyes, con
mis propios ojos. with the
naked eye, con la simple vista.
to keep an eye on, vigilar.
to make eyes at, guiñar el ojo;
mirar con ojos de enamorado.
to have one's eyes opened,
(fig.) caérsele la venda. eye-
bath, ojera, *f.* eye-opener, revelación, sorpresa, *f.* eye-pencil,
pincel para las cejas, *m.* eye-
piece, objetivo, ocular, *m.* eye-
shade, visera, *f.* eye-tooth,
colmillo, *m.* eye-witness, testigo ocular, testigo de vista, *m.*
and *f.*
eyeball, *s.* globo ocular, *m.*
eyebrow, *s.* ceja, *f.*
eyed, *a.* que tiene ojos; (in compounds) de ojos . . ., con ojos . . .;
con los ojos; (of a needle) con el
ojo . . . She is a blue-eyed
child, Ella es una niña de ojos
azules
eyeglass, *s.* lente, *m.*
eyelash, *s.* pestaña, *f.*
eyeless, *a.* sin ojos
eyelet, *s.* ojete, *m.*
eyelid, *s.* párpado, *m.*
eyesight, *s.* vista, *f.*
eyewash, *s.* loción para los ojos,
f.; (fam.) camelo, *m.* That's
all e.! ¡Eso es un camelo!
eyrie, *s.* nido (de ave de rapiña),
m.

F

f, *s.* (letter) efe, *f.; (mus.)* fa, *m.*
f sharp, fa sostenido, *m.*
fa, *s. (mus.)* fa, *m.*
fable, *s.* fábula, leyenda, historia,
f., apólogo, cuento, *m.;* (untruth)
invención, mentira, *f.*

fabled, *a.* celebrado, famoso
fabric, *s.* obra, fábrica, *f.;* estructura, construcción, *f.;* (making) manufactura, *f.;* (cloth)
tejido, paño, *m.;* textura, *f.*
fabricate, *v.t.* fabricar, construir;
(invent) fingir, inventar
fabrication, *s.* fabricación, manufactura, *f.;* construcción, *f.;* (lie)
invención, ficción, *f.*
fabulist, *s.* fabulista, *m.* and *f.*
fabulous, *a.* fabuloso
fabulousness, *s.* fabulosidad, *f.*
façade, *s.* fachada, frente, *f.*
face, *s.* superficie, *f.;* (of persons)
cara, *f.,* rostro, *m.;* (look)
semblante, aire, *m.;* (of coins)
anverso, *m.;* (grimace) mueca,
f., gesto, *m.;* (dial) esfera,
f.; (of gems) faceta, *f.;* (of
a wall) paramento, *m.;* (front)
fachada, frente, *f.;* (effrontery)
cara dura, *f.,* descaro, *m.* in the
f. of, ante; en presencia de. *(mil.)*
Left f.! ¡Izquierda! on the f. of
it, juzgando por las apariencias.
to bring f. to f., confrontar
(con). to laugh in a person's
f., reírse a la cara (de). to
make a f., hacer muecas. to
my f., en mi cara, en mis barbas.
to put a good f. on, *(fig.)* poner
(or hacer) buena cara a. to set
one's f. against, oponerse resueltamente a. to straighten
one's f., componer el semblante.
to throw in one's f., *(fig.)* dar
en rostro, dar en cara. to wash
one's f., lavarse la cara. f.
card, figura (de la baraja), *f.*
f.-cloth, paño para lavar la cara,
m. f. downwards, boca abajo.
f. lift, operación estética facial, *f.*
f. of the waters, faz de las
aguas, *f.* f. powder, polvos de
arroz, *m. pl.* f. to f., cara a
cara, de persona a persona;
frente a frente. f. value, significado literal, *m.; (com.)* valor
nominal, *m.*
face, *v.t.* mirar hacia; confrontar,
hacer cara (a); (of buildings, etc.)
mirar a, caer a (or hacia); *(fig.)*
arrostrar, enfrentarse con; (sew.)
guarnecer, aforrar. *v.i.* estar
orientado. to f. the facts, enfrentarse con la realidad. to f.
the music, *(fig.)* arrostrar las
consecuencias. to f. about

volver la espalda; (*mil.*) dar una vuelta, cambiar de frente. **to f. up to,** (*fig.*) hacer cara a

faced, *a.* con cara ..., de cara ...; (*sew.*) forrado (de). **to be two-f.,** (*fig.*) ser de dos haces

facer, *s.* puñetazo en la cara, *m.*; (*fig.*) dificultad insuperable, *f.*, problema muy grande, *m.*

facet, *s.* faceta, *f.*

facetious, *a.* chancero, chistoso, jocoso

facetiousness, *s.* jocosidad, festividad, *f.*

facial, *a.* facial. **f. expression,** expresión de la cara, *f.*, semblante, *m.*

facile, *a.* fácil

facilitate, *v.t.* facilitar

facilitation, *s.* facilitación, *f.*

facility, *s.* facilidad, *f.*; habilidad, destreza, *f.*

facing, *s.* (*sew.*) vuelta, *f.*; (of a building) paramento, *m.*; encaramiento, *m.*

facsimile, *s.* facsímile, *m.*

fact, *s.* (event) hecho, suceso, *m.*; (datum) dato, *m.*; realidad, verdad, *f.* **as a matter of f.,** en realidad. **in f.,** en efecto, en realidad. **I know as a f.,** Tengo por cierto. **The f. is ...,** La verdad es (que) ... **the f. that,** el hecho de que

faction, *s.* facción, *f.*, partido, bando, *m.*; (tumult) alboroto, *m.*

factional, *a.* partidario

factious, *a.* faccioso, sedicioso

factiousness, *s.* espíritu de facción, *m.*; rebeldía, *f.*

factitious, *a.* falso; artificial

factor, *s.* (fact) factor, elemento, *m.*; consideración, *f.*; (*math.*) factor, *m.*; (*com.*) agente, factor, *m.*

factorage, *s.* (*com.*) factoría, *f.*

factory, *s.* fábrica, manufactura, *f.*; taller, *m.* **F. Act,** ley de trabajadores industriales, *f.* **f. hand,** operario (-ia)

factotum, *s.* factótum, *m.*

factual, *a.* basado en hechos, objetivo

faculty, *s.* facultad, *f.*; (talent) habilidad, *f.*, talento, *m.*; (university) facultad, *f.*; claustro (de profesores), *m.*; (authorization) privilegio, *m.*, autoridad, *f.*

fad, *s.* capricho, *m.*, chifladura, *f.*, dengue, *m.*

faddiness, *s.* manías, *f. pl.*, excentricidad, *f.*

faddist, *s.* chiflado (-da)

faddy, *a.* caprichoso, dengoso, difícil, excéntrico

fade, *v.i.* (of plants) marchitarse, secarse; (of colour) palidecer, descolorarse; (vanish) disiparse, desaparecer; (of persons) desmejorarse; (of stains) salir. *v.t.* descolorar. **to f. away,** desvanecer; (of persons) consumirse. **f.-out,** *s.* (cinema) desaparecimiento gradual, *m.*

faded, *a.* (of plants) seco, marchito, mustio; (of colours) descolorado, pálido; (of people) desmejorado

fadeless, *a.* de colores resistentes; eterno, no olvidado; siempre joven

fading, *a.* que palidece; (of flowers) medio marchito; (of light) mortecino, pálido; decadente. *s.* desaparecimiento, *m.*, marchitez, *f.*; decadencia, *f.*

faecal, *a.* fecal

faeces, *s.* heces, *f. pl.*; excremento, *m.*

fag, *v.i.* trabajar como un negro. *v.t.* fatigar mucho; hacer trabajar. *s.* (*fam.*) pitillo, *m.* **f.-end,** fin, *m.*; restos, *m. pl.*, sobras, *f. pl.*; (of a cigarette) colilla, *f.*

faggot, *s.* haz (or gavilla) de leña, *f.*

faience, *s.* fayenza, *f.*

fail, *v.i.* faltar; fracasar, malograrse; no tener éxito, salir mal; (of strength) decaer, acabarse; (be short of) carecer (de); (*com.*) hacer bancarrota, suspender pagos. *v.t.* abandonar; (disappoint) decepcionar, engañar; (in exams.) suspender. **Do not f. to see her,** No dejes de verla. **He failed to do his duty,** Faltó a su deber

fail, *s.* **without f.,** sin falta

failing, *s.* falta, *f.*; (shortcoming) vicio, flaco, *m.*, debilidad, *f.*; malogro, fracaso, *m.*; decadencia, *f.*

failure, *s.* fracaso, *m.*; falta de éxito, *f.*; (in exams.) suspensión, *f.*; (of power) no funcionamiento, *m.*; omisión, *f.*, descuido, *m.*; (*com.*) quiebra, bancarrota, *f.*; (decay) decadencia, *f.* **on f. of,** al fracasar; bajo pena de

fain, *a.* deseoso, muy contento. He was **f. to,** Se sintió obligado a; Quería

faint, *a.* débil; (dim) indistinto, vago, borroso; (of colours) pálido, desmayado; (weak) lánguido, desfallecido; (slight) superficial, rudimentario. *v.i.* perder el sentido, desmayarse. *s.* desmayo, *m.* **to be f. with hunger,** estar muerto de hambre. **to cause to f.,** hacer desmayar. **f.-hearted,** pusilánime, medroso. **f.-heartedness,** pusilanimidad, *f.*

faintly, *adv.* débilmente; en voz débil; indistintamente

faintness, *s.* languidez, debilidad, *f.*; (swoon) desmayo, *m.*; lo indistinto; lo borroso

fair, *s.* feria, *f.*; (sale) mercado, *m.*; (exhibition) exposición, *f.*

fair, *a.* (beautiful) hermoso, lindo, bello; (of hair) rubio; (of skin) blanco; (clear, fresh) limpio, claro; (good) bueno; (favourable) favorable, propicio, próspero; (of weather) despejado, sereno; (just) imparcial; (straightforward) honrado, recto, justo; (passable) regular, mediano; (of writing) legible; (proper) conveniente. *adv.* honradamente; (politely) cortésmente; exactamente. **by f. means,** por medios honrados. **It's not f.!** ¡No hay derecho! **to become f.,** (of weather) serenarse. **to give a f. trial,** juzgar imparcialmente; dar una buena oportunidad; (*law*) procesar imparcialmente. **to make a f. copy,** poner en limpio. **f.-haired,** de pelo rubio, rubio. **f. one,** una beldad, *f.* **f. play,** (*sport*) juego limpio, *m.*; proceder leal, *m.* **f.-skinned,** de tez blanca, rubio. **f.-weather,** buen tiempo, *m.*, bonanza, *f.* **f.-weather friends,** amigos de los días prósperos, *m. pl.*

fairing, *s.* regalo de feria, *m.* **to give fairings,** feriar

fairly, *adv.* (justly) con imparcialidad; (moderately) bastante; totalmente, enteramente. **f. good,** bastante bueno; regular

fairness, *s.* belleza, hermosura, *f.*; (of skin) blancura, *f.*; (justness) imparcialidad, *f.*; (reasonableness) justicia, equidad, *f.*; (of hair) color rubio, oro, *m.*

fairway, *s.* (*naut.*) canalizo, paso, *m.*; (golf) " fairway," *m.*

fairy, *s.* hada, *f.*, duende, *m.* *a.* de hada, de duendes; (*fig.*) delicado. **f.-gold,** tesoro de duendes, *m.*; **f.-light,** lucecillo, *m.*; luminaria, *f.* **f.-like,** aduendado, como una hada. **f.-ring,** círculo mágico, *m.* **f.-tale,** cuento de hadas, *m.*; patraña, *f.*, cuento de viejas, *m.*

fairyland, *s.* país de las hadas, *m.*

faith, *s.* fe, *f.*; confianza, *f.*; (doctrine) creencia, religión, filosofía, *f.*; (honour) palabra, *f.* **in good f.,** de buena fe. **to break f.,** faltar a la palabra dada. **f.-healing,** curanderismo, *m.*

faithful, *a.* fiel, leal; (accurate) exacto; (trustworthy) veraz. **the f.,** los creyentes

faithfully, *adv.* fielmente, lealmente; (accurately) con exactitud. **Yours f.,** Queda de Vd. su att. s.s.

faithfulness, *s.* fidelidad, lealtad, *f.*; (accuracy) exactitud, *f.*

faithless, *a.* infiel, desleal, pérfido.

faithlessness, *s.* infidelidad, deslealtad, traición, *f.*

fake, *v.t.* imitar, falsificar. *s.* imitación, falsificación, *f.* **to f. up,** inventar

fakir, *s.* faquir, *m.*

Falangist, *a.* and *s.* (Spanish politics) falangista (*m.* and *f.*)

falcon, *s.* halcón, *m.* **f. gentle,** (*orn.*) neblí, *m.*

falconer, *s.* halconero, *m.*

falconry, *s.* cetrería, *f.*

faldstool, *s.* faldistorio, *m.*

Falernian, *a.* de Falernio

fall, *s.* caída, *f.*; (of temperature, mercury) baja, *f.*; (of water) salto de agua, *m.*, catarata, cascada, *f.*; (in value) depreciación, *f.*; (in price and Stock Exchange) baja, *f.*; (descent) bajada, *f.*; (autumn) otoño, *m.*; (declivity) declinación, *f.*, declive, desnivel, *m.*; (ruin) ruina, *f.*, destrucción, *f.*; (of night, etc.) caída (de la noche), *f.*; (of snow) nevada, *f.*; (of rain) golpe, *m.*; (*theat.*, of curtain) caída, bajada, *f.*; (surrender) capitulación, rendición, *f.*; (of earth) desprendimiento de tierras, *m.*; (of the tide) reflujo, *m.*

fall, *v.i.* caer; (of mercury, temperature) bajar; (collapse) desplomarse, hundirse, derrumbarse; (die) caer muerto; (descend) descender; (*theat.*, of the curtain) bajar, caer; (of a river into the sea, etc.) desembocar, desaguar; (of hair, draperies) caer; (decrease) disminuir; (of spirits) ponerse triste, sentirse deprimido; (sin) caer; (come upon) sobrevenir; (of dusk, etc.) caer, llegar; (strike, touch) tocar; (as a share) tocar en suerte; (as a duty, responsibility) tocar, corresponder; (of seasons) caer en; (of words from the lips) caer de (los labios); (say) decir, pronunciar palabras; (of exclamations) escaparse; (become) venir a ser; (happen) suceder; (be) ser. **fallen upon evil days,** venido a menos. **His face fell,** Puso una cara de desengaño. **Christmas falls on a Thursday this year,** Navidad cae en jueves este año. **to let f.,** dejar caer. **to f. a-** (followed by verb) empezar a. **He fell a-crying,** Empezó a llorar. **to f. again,** volver a caer, recaer. **to f. among,** caer entre. **to f. astern,** quedarse atrás. **to f. away,** (leave) abandonar, dejar; (grow thin) enflaquecer; marchitarse; (crumble) desmoronarse. **to f. back,** retroceder, volver hacia atrás. **to f. back upon,** recurrir a; (*mil.*) replegarse hacia. **to f. backwards,** caer de espaldas, caer hacia atrás. **to f. behind,** quedarse atrás. **to f. down,** venirse a tierra; venirse abajo, dar consigo en el suelo, caer. **to f. due,** vencer. **to f. flat,** caer de bruces; (be unsuccessful) no tener éxito. **to f. in,** caer en; (collapse) desplomarse; (*mil.*) alinearse; (expire) vencer. **to f. into,** caer en. **to f. in with,** tropezar con; reunirse con, juntarse con; (agree) convenir en; **to f. off,** caer de; (of leaves, etc.) desprenderse de, separarse de; (abandon) abandonar; (diminish) disminuir. **to f. on,** caer de (e.g. **to f. on one's back,** caer de

espaldas); (of seasons) caer en; (attack) echarse encima de, atacar. **to f. out,** (of a window, etc.) caer por; (happen) acontecer, suceder; (quarrel) pelearse, reñir; (*mil.*) romper filas. **to f. out with,** reñir con. **to f. over,** volcar, caer; (stumble) tropezar con. **to f. short,** faltar; carecer, ser deficiente; (fail) malograrse, no llegar a sus expectaciones; (of shooting) errar el tiro. **to f. through,** caer por; (fail) malograrse, fracasar. **to f. to,** empezar a, ponerse a; (be incumbent on) tocar a, corresponder a; (attack) atacar. **to f. under,** caer debajo; caer bajo; sucumbir, perecer; (incur) incurrir en, merecer. **to f. upon,** (attack) caer sobre, acometer; acaecer, tener lugar; (be incumbent) tocar a

fallacious, *a.* falaz, engañoso, ilusorio

fallaciousness, *s.* falacia, *f.,* engaño, *m.*

fallacy, *s.* error, *m.,* ilusión, *f.*

fallen, *a.* caído; arruinado; degradado. **f. angel,** ángel caído, *m.* **f. woman,** perdida, mujer caída, *f.*

fallibility, *s.* falibilidad, *f.*

fallible, *a.* falible

falling, *a.* que cae, cayente. *s.* caída, *f.*; (of mercury, temperature) baja, *f.*; (crumbling) desmoronamiento, *m.*; (collapse) hundimiento, derrumbamiento, *m.*; (of tide) reflujo, *m.*; (of water-level) bajada, *f.*; (in value) depreciación, *f.*; (of prices and Stock Exchange) baja, *f.*; (diminishment) disminución, *f.*; (in level of earth) declinación, *f.*; (*com.*, expiry) vencimiento, *m.*; (*theat.*, of curtain) bajada, caída, *f.* **f. away,** (crumbling) desmoronamiento, *m.*; desprendimiento de tierras, *m.*; (desertion) deserción, *f.*, abandono, *m.* **f. back,** retirada, *f.*, retroceso, *m.* **f. down,** caída, *f.*; derrumbamiento, *m.* **f. due,** vencimiento, *m.* **f. in,** hundimiento, *m.*; (crumbling) desmoronamiento, *m.* **f. off,** caída de, *f.*; (disappearance) desaparición, *f.*; (diminution) disminución, *f.*; (deterioration) deterioración, *f.* **f. out,**

caída por, *f.*; disensión, *f.* **f. short**, falta, *f.*; carácter inferior, *m.*; frustración, *f.* **f. star**, estrella fugaz, *f.*

fallow, *a.* (of colour) leonado; (*agr.*) barbechado; descuidado. *s.* barbecho, *m.* *v.t.* barbechar. **to leave f.**, dejar en barbecho. **f. deer**, corzo (-za)

false, *a.* incorrecto, erróneo, equivocado; falso; (unfounded) infundado; (disloyal) infiel, traidor, desleal; (not real) postizo; artificial; de imitación; (*mus.*) desafinado; (pretended) fingido; engañoso, mentiroso. **to play a person f.**, traicionar (a). **f. bottom**, fondo doble, *m.*; **f. claim**, pretensión infundada, *f.* **f. door**, surtida, *f.* **f.-hearted**, pérfido, desleal. **f. teeth**, dientes postizos, *m. pl.*; dentadura postiza, *f.*

falsehood, *s.* mentira, *f.*

falseness, *s.* falsedad, *f.*; (disloyalty) duplicidad, perfidia, traición, *f.*

falsetto, *s.* falsete, *m.*, voz de cabeza, *f.*

falsification, *s.* falsificación, *f.*; (of texts) corrupción, *f.*

falsifier, *s.* falsificador (-ra)

falsify, *v.t.* falsear, falsificar; (disappoint) defraudar, frustrar, contrariar

falter, *v.i.* (physically) titubear; (of speech) balbucir, tartamudear; (of action) vacilar. **to f. out**, balbucir; hablar con voz entrecortada; decir con vacilación

faltering, *a.* titubeante; (of speech) entrecortado; vacilante. *s.* temblor, *m.*; vacilación, *f.*

falteringly, *adv.* (of speech) balbuciente, en una voz temblorosa; con dificultad, vacilantemente

fame, *s.* fama, *f.*; reputación, *f.*; (renown) celebridad, *f.*, renombre, *m.* **of ill f.**, de mala fama

famed, *a.* reputado; renombrado, célebre, famoso

familiar, *a.* íntimo, familiar; afable, amistoso; (ill-bred) insolente, demasiado familiar; (usual) corriente, usual, común; bien conocido. *s.* amigo (-ga) íntimo (-ma); (*ecc.*) familiar, *m.*;

demonio familiar, *m.* **to be f. with**, (a subject) estar versado en, conocer muy bien; (a person) tratar con familiaridad. **to become f. with**, acostumbrarse a; familiarizarse con; (a person) hacerse íntimo de

familiarity, *s.* intimidad, familiaridad, confianza, *f.*; (friendliness) afabilidad, *f.*; (over-familiarity) insolencia, demasiada familiaridad, *f.*; (with a subject) conocimiento (de), *m.*, experiencia (de), *f.*

familiarize, *v.t.* familiarizar, acostumbrar, habituar. *v.r.* familiarizarse

familiarly, *adv.* familiarmente; amistosamente

family, *s.* familia, *f.*; (lineage) línaje, abolengo, *m.*; (*bot.*, *zool.*) familia, *f.*; (of languages) grupo, *m.* *a.* de familia; familiar; casero. **f. doctor**, médico de cabecera, *m.* **f. life**, vida de familia, *f.*; hogar, *m.* **f. man**, padre de familia, *m.* **f. name**, apellido, *m.* **f. seat**, casa solar, *f.* **f. tree**, árbol genealógico, *m.*

famine, *s.* hambre, *f.*; carestía, escasez, *f.*

famish, *v.t.* matar de hambre. *v.i.* morirse de hambre

famished, *a.* hambriento

famous, *a.* famoso, célebre, renombrado; insigne, distinguido; (*fam.*) excelente

famously, *adv.* (*fam.*) muy bien, excelentemente

fan, *s.* abanico, *m.*; (*agr.*) aventador, *m.*; (*mech.*) ventilador, *m.*; (on a windmill) volante, *m.*; (amateur) aficionado (-da); (admirer) admirador (-ra); (*arch.*) abanico, *m.* *v.t.* abanicar; (*agr.*) aventar; ventilar. **tap with a f.**, abanicazo, golpecito con el abanico, *m.* **f.-belt**, (*mech.*) correa de transmisión del ventilador, *f.* **f.-light**, tragaluz, *m.* **f. maker or seller**, abaniquero (-ra). **f.-shaped**, en abanico, abanicado, en forma de abanico

fanatic, *a.* and *s.* fanático (-ca)

fanaticism, *s.* fanatismo, *m.*

fanaticize, *v.t.* fanatizar

fancied, *a.* imaginario

fancier, *s.* aficionado (-da); (of animals) criador (-ra)

fanciful, *a.* romántico, caprichoso; fantástico

fancifulness, *s.* extravagancia, *f.*; romanticismo, *m.*

fancy, *s.* fantasía, imaginación, *f.*; (idea) idea, *f.*, ensueño, *m.*; (caprice) capricho, antojo, *m.*; (liking) afecto, cariño, *m.*; gusto, *m.*, afición, *f.*; (wish) deseo, *m.*; (fantasy) quimera, *f.* *a.* imaginario; elegante, ornado; (*com.*) de capricho, de fantasía; fantástico, extravagante. *v.t.* imaginar, figurarse; (like) gustar de; aficionarse a; antojarse. **I have a f. for . . .,** Se me antoja. . . . Just f.! ¡Toma! ¡Quia! ¡Parece mentira! **to take a f. to,** (things) tomar afición a; (people) tomar cariño (a). **f.-dress,** disfraz, *m.* **f.-dress ball,** baile de trajes, *m.*

fane, *s.* templo, *m.*

fanfare, *s.* tocata de trompetas, *f.*

fang, *s.* colmillo, *m.*; raíz de un diente, *f.*

fanged, *a.* que tiene colmillos; (of teeth) acolmillado

fangless, *a.* sin colmillos

fanner, *s.* abanicador (-ra); (*agr.*) aventador, *m.*

fanning, *s.* abaniqueo, *m.*; (*agr.*) avienta, *f.*

fantasia, *s.* (*mus.*) fantasía, *f.*

fantastic, *a.* fantástico; extravagante

fantastically, *adv.* fantásticamente; extravagantemente

fantasy, *s.* imaginación, *f.*; fantasía, quimera, visión, *f.*; creación imaginativa, *f.*

far, *adv.* lejos; a lo lejos; (much, greatly) mucho, en alto grado; (very) muy; (mostly) en gran parte. *a.* lejano, distante; (farther) ulterior. **as far as,** tan lejos como; (up to, until) hasta; en cuanto, por lo que, según que (e.g. As far as we know, Por lo que nosotros sepamos. As far as we are concerned, En cuanto a nosotros toca). **by far,** con mucho. **from far and near,** de todas partes. **from far off,** desde lejos. **He read far into the night,** Leyó hasta las altas horas de la noche. **how far?** ¿a qué distancia?; (to what extent) ¿hasta qué punto? ¿hasta dónde? **How far is it to . . .?**

¿Qué distancia hay a . . .? **in so far as,** en tanto que. **on the far side,** al lado opuesto; al otro extremo. **so far,** tan lejos; (till now) hasta ahora. **to go far,** ir lejos. **far-away,** *a.* distante, remoto, lejano; (*fig.*) abstraído, *adv.* muy lejos. **far beyond,** mucho más allá. **far-fetched,** *a.* increíble, improbable. **far-off,** *a.* distante. *adv.* a lo lejos, en lontananza. **far-reaching,** de gran alcance. **far-sighted,** sagaz, presciente, previsor. **far-sightedness,** sagacidad, previsión, *f.*

farad, *s.* (*elec.*) faradio, *m.*

farce, *s.* farsa, *f.* *v.t.* (*cul.*) embutir, rellenar

farcical, *a.* burlesco, cómico, sainetesco; absurdo, grotesco, ridículo

fare, *s.* (price) pasaje, precio del billete, *m.*; (traveller) viajero (-ra), pasajero (-ra); (food) comida, *f.* *v.i.* pasarlo (e.g. to f. well, pasarlo bien). **bill of f.,** menú, *m.* **full f.,** billete entero, *m.* **f. stage,** trayecto, *m.*

farewell, *s.* despedida, *f.*, adiós, *m.* *a.* de despedida. *interj.* ¡adiós! ¡quede Vd. con Dios! **to bid f. to,** despedirse de

farina, *s.* harina (de cereales), *f.*; (*chem.*) fécula, *f.*, almidón, *m.*; (*bot.*) polen, *m.*

farinaceous, *a.* farináceo, harinoso

farm, *s.* granja, hacienda, quintería, finca, *f.* *v.t.* cultivar, labrar (la tierra); (taxes) arrendar. *v.i.* ser granjero. **to f. out,** (taxes) dar en arriendo. **f. girl,** labradora, *f.* **f. house,** alquería, casa de labranza, granja, *f.* **f. labourer,** labriego, peón, *m.* **f. yard,** corral de una granja, *m.*

farmer, *s.* granjero, hacendado, quintero, *m.*, agrícola, *m.* and *f.*; (small) colono, labrador, *m.*; (of taxes) arrendatario, *m.*

farming, *s.* labranza, *f.*, cultivo, *m.*; agricultura, labor agrícola, *f.*; (of taxes) arriendo, *m.* *a.* de labranza, labradoril; agrícola

faro, *s.* (card game) faraón, *m.*

farouche, *a.* huraño, esquivo

farrago, *s.* fárrago, *m.*, mezcla, *f.*

farrier, *s.* herrador, *m.*

farrow, s. lechigada (de cerdos), f.
v.t. and v.i. (of a sow) parir
cerdos

farther, adv. más lejos; (beyond)
más adelante; (besides) además.
a. ulterior; más distante. **at
the f. end,** al otro extremo; en el
fondo. **f. on,** más adelante; más
allá

farthest, adv. más lejos. a. más
lejano, más distante; extremo

farthing, s. cuarto, m.; (fig.)
ardite, maravedí, m. **He hasn't
a brass f.,** No tiene dos mara-
vedís

farthingale, s. guardainfante, m.

fasces, s. pl. fasces, f. pl.

fascia, s. (arch.) faja, f.

fascicle, s. (bot.) hacecillo, m.

fascinate, v.t. fascinar; encantar,
hechizar, seducir

fascinating, a. fascinador; encantador, seduciente

fascination, s. fascinación, f.;
encanto, hechizo, m.

fascine, s. (mil.) fajina, f.

Fascism, s. fascismo, m.

Fascist, a. and s. fascista (m. and
f.).

fashion, s. (form) forma, hechura,
f.; (way) modo, m.; (custom)
costumbre, f., uso, m.; (vogue)
moda, f.; (high life) alta sociedad,
f.; (tone) buen tono, m. v.t.
hacer, labrar; inventar. **in the
Spanish f.,** a la española, al uso
de España. **the latest f.,** la
última moda. **to be in f.,** estar
de moda. **to go out of f.,** dejar
de ser de moda, perder la popularidad. **f. book,** revista de
modas, f. **f. plate,** figurín, m.

fashionable, a. de moda; elegante; de buen tono. **to be f.,**
estar en boga, ser de moda. **f.
world,** mundo elegante, mundo
de sociedad, m.

fashionableness, s. buen tono,
m.; elegancie f.

fashionably, adv. a la moda,
elegantemente

fast, a. (firm) firme; (secure)
seguro; (strong) fuerte; (fixed)
fijo; (closed) cerrado; (of boats)
amarrado; (tight) apretado; (of
colours) estable; (of trains) rápido; (of sleep) profundo; (of
friends) leal, seguro; (quick)
rápido, veloz; (of a watch)
adelantado; (dissipated) disoluto.
adv. firmemente, seguramente;
(quickly) rápidamente; (of sleep)
profundamente; (tightly) estrechamente, apretadamente; (of
rain) (llover) a cántaros; (ceaselessly) continuamente; (often)
frecuentemente; (entirely) completamente. **to be f.,** (clocks)
adelantar. **to make f.,** (naut.)
amarrar, trincar. **f. asleep,** profundamente dormido. **f. colour,**
color estable, color sólido, m.

fast, s. ayuno, m. v.i. ayunar.
to break one's f., romper el
ayuno. **f.-day,** día de ayuno, día
de vigilia, m.

fasten, v.t. (tie) atar; (fix) fijar;
sujetar; (stick) pegar; (a door)
cerrar; (bolt) echar el cerrojo;
(naut.) trincar; (together) juntar,
unir; (with buttons, hooks, etc.)
abrochar; (on, upon) fijar en;
(fig.) imputar (a). v.i. fijarse;
pegarse; (upon) agarrarse a,
asir. **to f. one's eyes on,** fijar
los ojos en. **to f. up,** cerrar;
atar; (nail) clavar

fastener, s. (bolt) pasador, m.;
(for bags, jewellery, etc.) cierre,
m.; (buckle) hebilla, f.; (of a
coat, etc.) fiador, m.; (of a book,
file) sujetador, m.; (lock) cerrojo,
m. **paper-f.,** sujetador de
papeles, m. **patent-f.,** botón
automático, m.

fastening, s. atadura, f.; sujeción,
f., afianzamiento, m.; (together)
unión, f.; (of a garment) brochadura, f.; (of a handbag) cierre, m.

fastidious, a. dengoso, melindroso, desdeñoso; (sensitive) sensitivo, delicado; (critical) discerniente, crítico

fastidiously, adv. melindrosa-
mente

fastidiousness, s. dengues, melindres, m. pl., nimiedad, f.,
desdén, m.; sensibilidad, delicadeza, f.; sentido crítico, m.

fasting, s. ayuno, m. a. and part.
de ayuno; en ayunas

fastness, s. firmeza, solidez, f.;
(stronghold) fortaleza, f.; (retreat) refugio, m.; (speed) velocidad, rapidez, f.; (dissipation)
disipación, f., libertinaje, m.

fat, a. (stout) gordo, grueso; mantecoso, graso, seboso;

(greasy) grasiento; (rich) fértil, pingüe; (productive) lucrativo. *s.* (stoutness) gordura, *f.*; (for cooking) manteca, *f.*; (lard) lardo, *m.*; (of animal or meat) grasa, *f.*; sebo, saín, *m.*; (*fig.*) riqueza, *f.*; (*fig.*) fertilidad, *f.* **to grow fat,** engordarse, ponerse grueso

fatal, *a.* fatal, mortal; funesto

fatalism, *s.* fatalismo, *m.*

fatalist, *s.* fatalista, *m.* and *f.*

fatalistic, *a.* fatalista

fatality, *s.* fatalidad, *f.*; infortunio, *m.*, calamidad, *f.*; muerte, *f.*

fatally, *adv.* mortalmente, fatalmente; inevitablemente

fate, *s.* destino, sino, hado, *m.*, providencia, *f.*; fortuna, suerte, *f.*; destrucción, ruina, *f.*; muerte, *f.* **the Three Fates,** las Parcas

fated, *a.* fatal, destinado; predestinado

fateful, *a.* decisivo, fatal; aciago, ominoso

father, *s.* padre, *m.* *v.t.* prohijar, adoptar; (on or upon) atribuir (a), imputar (a). **Eternal F.,** Padre Eterno, *m.* **Holy F.,** Padre Santo, *m.* **indulgent f.,** padre indulgente, padrazo, *m.* **Like f. like son,** De tal palo tal astilla. **F. Confessor,** (*ecc.*) director espiritual, *m.* **f.-in-law,** suegro, *m.*

fatherhood, *s.* paternidad, *f.*

fatherland, *s.* patria, madre patria, *f.*

fatherless, *a.* sin padre, huérfano de padre

fatherliness, *s.* amor paternal, *m.*; sentimiento paternal, *m.*

fatherly, *a.* paternal, de padre

fathom, *s.* (*naut.*) braza, *f.* *v.t.* sondear; (*fig.*) profundizar, tantear; (a mystery) desentrañar

fathomless, *a.* insondable; (*fig.*) incomprensible, impenetrable

fatigue, *s.* fatiga, *f.*, cansancio, *m.*; (*mil.*) faena, *f.*; (*mech.*) pérdida de resistencia, *f.* *v.t.* fatigar, cansar. **to be fatigued,** estar cansado, cansarse, fatigarse. **f. party,** (*mil.*) pelotón de castigo, *m.*

fatiguing, *a.* fatigoso

fatness, *s.* (stoutness) gordura, carnosidad, *f.*; grasa, *f.*, gordo,

m.; (richness) fertilidad, *f.*; lo lucrativo

fatten, *v.t.* engordar; (animals) cebar, sainar; (land) abonar, fertilizar. *v.i.* ponerse grueso, echar carnes

fatty, *a.* untoso, grasiento; (*chem.*) graso. **f. acid,** ácido graso, *m.* **f. degeneration,** degeneración grasienta, *f.*

fatuity, *s.* fatuidad, necedad, *f.*

fatuous, *a.* fatuo, necio, lelo

faucet, *s.* canilla, llave, *f.*, grifo, *m.*

faugh, *interj.* ¡uf! ¡bah!

fault, *s.* defecto, *m.*, imperfección, *f.*; (blame) culpa, *f.*; (mistake) falta, *f.*, error, *m.*; (in cloth) canilla, barra, *f.*; (*geol.*) falla, quiebra, *f.*; (*elec.*) avería, *f.*; (*sport*) falta, *f.* *v.i.* (*sport*) cometer una falta. **to a f.,** excesivamente. **to be at f.,** (to blame) tener la culpa; (mistaken) estar equivocado; (puzzled) estar perplejo; (of dogs) perder el rastro. **to find f.,** tachar, culpar, criticar. **Whose f. is it?** ¿Quién tiene la culpa?

faultfinder, *s.* criticón (-ona)

faultiness, *s.* defectuosidad, imperfección, *f.*

faultless, *a.* sin faltas; perfecto, sin tacha; impecable

faulty, *a.* defectuoso, imperfecto

faun, *s.* fauno, *m.*

fauna, *s.* fauna, *f.*

favour, *s.* favor, *m.*; (protection) amistad, protección, *f.*, amparo, *m.*; (permission) permiso, *m.*, licencia, *f.*; (kindness) merced, gracia, *f.*; (gift) obsequio, *m.*; (favouritism) favoritismo, *m.*, preferencia, *f.*; (benefit) beneficio, *m.*; (badge) colores, *m. pl.*; (com.) grata, atenta, *f.* *v.t.* favorecer, apoyar; mirar con favor, mostrar parcialidad (hacia); (suit) favorecer; (be advantageous) ser propicio (a); (contribute to) contribuir a, ayudar; (resemble) parecerse (a). **Circumstances f. the idea,** Las circunstancias son propicias a la idea, Las circunstancias militan en pro de la idea. **I f. the teaching of modern languages,** Soy partidario de la enseñanza de lenguas vivas. **in f. of,** a favor de, en pro de. **in**

the f. of, en el favor de. out of
f., fuera de favor; (not fashionable) fuera de moda. to count
on the f. of, tener de su parte
(a), contar con el apoyo de. to
do a f., hacer un favor. to
enjoy the f. of, gozar del favor
de. to fall out of f., caer en
desgracia; (go out of fashion)
pasar de moda. to grow in f.,
aumentar en favor

favourable, a. favorable; propicio, próspero

favourableness, s. lo favorable;
lo propicio; benignidad, benevolencia, f.

favourably, adv. favorablemente

favoured, a. favorecido; predilecto; (in compounds) parecido,
encarado

favouring, a. favorecedor, propicio

favourite, a. favorito; predilecto,
preferido. s. favorito (-ta).
court f., valido, privado, m.;
(mistress) querida (de un rey), f.;
(lover) amante (de una reina),
m. to be a f., ser favorito

favouritism, s. favoritismo, m.

fawn, s. (zool.) cervato, m.;
(colour) color de cervato, color de
ante, m. a. de color de cervato,
anteado, pardo; (of animals)
rucio, pardo. v.t. and v.i. parir
la cierva. v.i. acariciar; (on,
upon) adular, lisonjear

fawning, s. adulación, f. a.
adulador, lisonjero

fear, s. miedo, temor, m.; (apprehension) ansiedad, aprensión, f.,
recelo, m.; (respect) veneración,
f. v.i. temer; recelar; (respect)
reverenciar. v.i. tener miedo;
estar receloso, estar con cuidado.
for f. of, por miedo de. for f.
that, por temor de que, por
miedo de que. from f., por
miedo. There is no f. of . . .,
No hay miedo de (que) . . .

fearer, s. temedor (-ra), el (la) que
teme

fearful, a. miedoso, aprensivo,
receloso; (cowardly) tímido, pusilánime; (terrible) horrible, espantoso, pavoroso; (fam.) tremendo,
enorme

fearfully, adv. con miedo; tímidamente; (terribly) horriblemente; (fam.) enormemente

fearfulness, s. temor, miedo, m.;
(horribleness) lo horrible

fearless, a. sin miedo, intrépido,
audaz

fearlessness, s. intrepidez, valentía, f.

fearsome, a. temible, horrible,
espantoso

feasibility, s. practicabilidad,
posibilidad, f.

feasible, a. factible, hacedero,
practicable, ejecutable

feast, s. (ecc.) fiesta, f.; banquete,
m.; (fig.) abundancia, f. v.i.
regalarse. v.t. festejar, agasajar;
(delight) recrear, deleitar. immovable f., (ecc.), fiesta fija, f.
movable f., fiesta movible, f.
f. day, día de fiesta, m.

feasting, s. banquetes, m. pl.;
fiestas, f. pl.

feat, s. hazaña, proeza, f., hecho,
m.

feather, s. pluma, f.; (of the tail)
pena, f.; pl. feathers, plumaje,
m.; plumas, f. pl. v.i. emplumar; adornar con plumas;
(rowing) poner casi horizontal la
pala del remo. to f. one's nest,
(fam.) hacer su agosto. f.-bed,
plumón, colchón de plumas, m.
f.-brained, casquivano, alocado,
aturdido. f.-duster, plumero,
m. f.-stitch, (sew.) diente de
perro, m. f. weight, (boxing)
peso pluma, m.

feathered, a. plumado, plumoso;
adornado con plumas; (winged)
alado

feathery, a. plumoso; como plumas

feature, s. rasgo, m., característica, f.; (cinema) número de
programa, m.; pl. features (of
the face) facciones, f. pl. v.t.
dar importancia (a); (cinema)
presentar. f. film, documen-
taria, f.

febrile, a. febril

February, s. febrero, m.

fecula, s. fécula, f.

fecund, a. fecundo, fértil

fecundate, v.t. fecundar

fecundity, s. fecundidad, fertilidad, f.

federal, a. federal, federalista

federalism, s. federalismo, m.

federalist, s. federalista, federal,
m. and f.

federate, *v.t.* confederar. *v.i.*
confederarse. *a.* confederado
federation, *s.* confederación, federación, *f.*; liga, unión, asociación, *f.*
federative, *a.* federativo
fee, *s.* (feudal law) feudo, *m.*;
(homage) homenaje, *m.*; (duty)
derecho, *m.*; (professional) honorario, estipendio, *m.*; (to a servant) gratificación, *f.*; (entrance, university, etc.) cuota, *f.*; (payment) paga, *f.*
feeble, *a.* débil; lánguido; enfermizo; (of light, etc.) tenue;
(*fig.*) flojo. **to grow f.,** debilitarse; disminuir. **f.-minded,**
anormal
feebleness, *s.* debilidad, *f.*; (*fig.*)
flojedad, *f.*
feebly, *adv.* débilmente; lánguidamente
feed, *s.* alimento, *m.*; (meal)
comida, *f.*; (of animals) pienso,
forraje, *m.*; (*mech.*) alimentación,
f. *v.t.* alimentar; dar de comer
(a); (animals) cebar; (*mech.*) alimentar; mantener; (*fig.*) nutrir.
v.i. comer, alimentarse; (graze)
pastar. **to be fed up,** (*fam.*)
estar hasta la coronilla, estar
harto. **to f. on,** alimentarse de;
(*fig.*) nutrirse de. **f. pipe,** tubo de
alimentación, *f.*
feeder, *s.* el, *m.* (f. la) que da de
comer a; (eater) comedor (-ra);
(of a river) tributario, afluente,
m.; (bib) babero, *m.*; (*mech.*)
alimentador, *m.*; (cup for invalids) pistero, *m.*
feeding, *s.* alimentación, *f.* *a.*
alimenticio, de alimentación. **f.-bottle,** biberón, *m.* **f.-cup,** pistero, *m.* **f.-trough,** pesebre, *m.*
feel, *s.* (touch) tacto, *m.*; (feeling)
sensación, *f.*; (instinct) instinto,
m., percepción innata, *f.*
feel, *v.t.* (touch) tocar, tentar, palpar; (experience) sentir, experimentar; (understand) comprender; (believe) creer; (be conscious
of) estar consciente de; (the
pulse) tomar; examinar. *v.i.* sentir, ser sensible; sentirse, encontrarse; (to the touch) ser . . . al
tacto, estar. **How do you f.?**
¿ Cómo se siente Vd. ? **I f. cold,**
Tengo frío. **I f. for you,** Lo siento
en el alma; estoy muy consciente

de ello. **I f. strongly that . . .,**
Estoy convencido de que . . . **I f.
that it is a difficult question,**
Me parece una cuestión difícil.
It feels like rain, Creo que va a
llover. **to f. at home,** sentirse a
sus anchas, sentirse como en
su casa. **to f. hungry (thirsty),**
tener hambre (sed). **to f. one's
way,** andar a tientas; (*fig.*)
medir el terreno. **to f. soft,** ser
blando al tacto. **to make
itself felt,** hacerse sentir. **Your
hands f. cold,** Tus manos están
frías
feeler, *s.* (of insects) palpo, *m.*,
antena, *f.*; tentáculo, *m.*; (*fig.*)
tentativa; *f.*, balón de ensayo, *m.*
feeling, *s.* (touch) tacto, *m.*;
(sensation) sensación, *f.*; (sentiment) sentimiento, *m.*; emoción,
f.; (premonition) corazonada,
intuición, premonición, *f.*; (tenderness) ternura, *f.*; (perception)
sensibilidad, percepción, *f.*; (passion) pasión, *f.*; (belief) opinión,
f., sentir, *m.* *a.* sensible; tierno;
(compassionate) compasivo; apasionado; (moving) conmovedor
feelingly, *adv.* con emoción;
(strongly) enérgicamente, vivamente; (understandingly) comprensivamente
feign, *v.t.* fingir; (invent) inventar, imaginar; simular; (allege)
pretextar; (dissemble) disimular.
v.i. disimular
feint, *s.* artificio, engaño, *m.*; (in
fencing) treta, finta, *f.* *v.i.* hacer
finta
feldspar, *s.* (*min.*) feldespato, *m.*
felicitate, *v.t.* felicitar, congratular, dar el parabién (a)
felicitation, *s.* felicitación, *f.*,
parabién, *m.*
felicitous, *a.* feliz, dichoso, afortunado; (of phrases, etc.) feliz,
acertado; oportuno
felicity, *s.* felicidad, dicha, *f.*
feline, *a.* felino, gatuno, de gato.
s. felino, *m.*
fell, *s.* (skin) piel, *f.*; (upland)
altura, cuesta de montaña, *f.* *a.*
cruel, feroz; (unhappy) aciago,
funesto. *v.t.* talar, cortar;
(knock down) derribar; (*sew.*)
sobrecoser
feller, *s.* talador, leñador, *m.*
felling, *s.* corta, tala, *f.*

felloe, s. pina, calzadura, f.

fellow, s. compañero (-ra); (equal) igual, m. and f.; (in crime) cómplice, m. and f.; (man) hombre, m.; (boy, youth) chico, m.; (colleague) colega, m.; (of a society) miembro, m.; (of a pair of objects) pareja, f.; (fam.) tipo, chico, m. **He's a good f.,** Es un buen chico. **How are you, old f.?** ¡Hombre! ¿Cómo estás? **f.-citizen,** conciudadano (-na). **f.-countryman,** compatriota, m.; paisano (-na). **f.-creature,** semejante, m. and f. **f.-feeling,** simpatía, comprensión mutua, f. **f.-member,** compañero (-ra); colega, m. **f.-passenger,** compañero (-ra) de viaje. **f.-prisoner,** compañero (-ra) de prisión. **f.-student,** condiscípulo (-la). **f.-worker,** compañero (-ra) de trabajo; (collaborator) colaborador (-ra); (colleague) colega, m.

fellowship, s. coparticipación, f.; (companionship) compañerismo, m.; (brotherhood) comunidad, confraternidad, f.; (society) asociación, f.; (grant) beca, f.; (of a university) colegiatura, f.

felon, s. reo, criminal, m. and f.; felón (-ona); malvado (-da); (swelling) panadizo, m.

felonious, a. criminal; pérfido, traidor

felony, s. felonía, f.

felt, s. fieltro, m. **a f. hat,** un sombrero de fieltro

felucca, s. (naut.) falucho, m.

female, s. hembra, f. a. femenino. (f. is often rendered in Sp. by the feminine ending of the noun, e.g. a f. cat, una gata; a f. friend, una amiga.) **This is a f. animal,** Este animal es una hembra. **f. screw,** hembra de tornillo, tuerca, f.

feminine, a. femenino; mujeril, afeminado. **in the f. gender,** en el género femenino

feminism, s. feminismo, m.

feminist, s. feminista, m. and f.

feministic, a. feminista

femoral, a. (anat.) femoral

femur, s. (anat.) fémur, m.

fen, s. marjal, pantano, m.

fence, s. cerca, f.; (of stakes) estacada, palizada, f.; (hedge) seto, m.; (fencing) esgrima, f.; (mech.) guía, f.; (fam.) comprador (-ra) de efectos robados. v.i. esgrimir; (fig.) defenderse; (fam.) recibir efectos robados. v.t. cercar; estacar; (fig.) parar; defender; proteger. **to sit on the f.,** (fig.) estar a ver venir

fencer, s. esgrimidor, m.

fencing, s. esgrima, f.; palizada, empalizada, f. **f. mask,** careta, f. **f. master,** maestro de esgrima, maestro de armas, m. **f. match,** asalto de esgrima, m.

fend, (off) v.t. parar; defenderse de, guardarse de. v.i. (for) mantener, cuidar de. **to f. for oneself,** ganarse la vida; defenderse

fender, s. (round hearth) guardafuegos, m.; (naut.) espolón, m., defensas, f. pl.; (aut.) parachoques, m.

Fenian, a. and s. feniano (-na)

fennel, s. (bot.) hinojo, m.

ferment, s. fermento, m.; fermentación, f.; (fig.) agitación, conmoción, f. v.t. hacer fermentar; (fig.) agitar, excitar. v.i. fermentar, estar en fermentación; (fig.) hervirse, agitarse, excitarse

fermentation, s. fermentación, f.

fern, s. helecho, m.

ferny, a. cubierto de helechos

ferocious, a. feroz, bravo, salvaje

ferocity, s. ferocidad, braveza, fiereza, f.

ferreous, a. férreo

ferret, s. (zool.) hurón (-ona); **to f. out,** cazar con hurones; (discover) husmear, descubrir

ferrety, a. que se parece a un hurón, como hurón, de hurón

ferriage, s. barcaje, m.

ferric, a. férrico

ferro-concrete, s. hormigón armado, m.

ferrous, a. ferroso

ferruginous, a. ferruginoso; aherrumbrado, rojizo

ferrule, s. herrete, regatón, m., contera, f.; garrucha de tornillos, f.

ferry, s. barca de transporte, f.; barca de pasaje, f., transbordador, m. v.t. transportar de una a otra orilla, llevar en barca. v.i. cruzar un río en barca. **F.-Command,** servicio de entrega y transporte de aeroplanos, m.

ferryman, s. barquero, m.

fertile, a. fértil, fecundo; (rich) pingüe; (fig.) prolífico, abundante

fertility, s. fertilidad, fecundidad, f.

fertilization, s. (biol.) fecundación, f.; (agr.) fertilización, f., abono, m.

fertilize, v.t. (biol.) fecundar; (agr.) fertilizar, abonar

fertilizer, s. abono, m.

ferule, s. palmatoria, palmeta, férula, f.

fervent, a. ardiente; fervoroso, intenso; (enthusiastic) entusiasta, apasionado

fervently, adv. con fervor, con vehemencia

fervour, s. ardor, fervor, m., pasión, f.; (enthusiasm) entusiasmo, celo, m.; vehemencia, f.

festal, a. de fiesta; alegre, festivo, regocijado

fester, v.i. ulcerarse, enconarse; (fig.) inflamarse, amargarse. v.t. ulcerar

festival, a. de fiesta. s. festividad, f.; (ecc.) fiesta, f.; (musical, etc.) festival, m.

festive, a. de fiesta; festivo, alegre

festivity, s. festividad, fiesta, f.; (merriment) alegría, f.; júbilo, m.

festoon, s. festón, m., guirnalda, f. v.t. festonear

fetch, v.t. traer; ir a buscar; ir por; llevar; (conduct) conducir; (of tears) hacer derramar lágrimas, hacer saltársele las lágrimas; (blood) hacer correr la sangre; (produce, draw) sacar; (a blow, a sigh) dar; (acquire) conseguir; (charm) fascinar; (of price) venderse por. to go and f., ir a buscar. to f. and carry, v.i. (news) divulgar, publicar. v.i. estar ocupado en oficios humildes, trajinar. to f. away, llevarse; ir a buscar; venir a buscar. to f. back, devolver; (of persons) traer (a casa, etc.); traer otra vez. to f. down, bajar, llevar abajo; hacer bajar. to f. in, hacer entrar; (place inside) poner adentro; (persons and things) llevar adentro. to f. out, hacer salir; (bring out things) sacar; (put out) poner afuera; (an idea, etc.) sacar a relucir. to f. up, (a

parcel, etc.) subir; (a person) hacer subir; llevar arriba

fête, s. fiesta, f.

fetid, a. fétido, hediondo

fetidness, s. fetidez, f., hedor, m.

fetish, s. fetiche, m.

fetishism, s. fetichismo, m.

fetlock, s. cerneja, f

fetter, s. grillete, m.; pl. **fetters,** grillos, m. pl., cadenas, f. pl.; prisión, cárcel, f. v.t. encadenar, atar

fettle, s. condición, f., estado, m.

feud, s. enemistad, riña, f.; (feudal law) feudo, m.

feudal, a. feudal. f. lord, señor feudal, señor de horca y cuchillo, m.

feudalism, s. feudalismo, m.

feudatory, a. and s. feudatario (-ia)

fever, s. fiebre, f.; calentura, f.; (enthusiasm) pasión, afición, f. to be in a f., tener fiebre; (agitated) estar muy agitado. to be in a f. to, estar muy impaciente de. puerperal f., fiebre puerperal, f. tertian f., fiebre terciana, f. yellow f., fiebre amarilla, f.

feverish, a. febril; (fig.) ardiente, febril, vehemente. to grow f., empezar a tener fiebre, acalenturarse

feverishness, s. calentura, f.; (impatience) impaciencia, f.

few, a. and s. pocos, m. pl.; pocas, f. pl.; algunos, m. pl.; algunas, f. pl.; (few in number) número pequeño (de), m. a good f., bastantes, m. and f. pl. not a f., no pocos, m. pl. (pocas, f. pl.). the f., la minoría, f. f. and far between, raramente, en raras ocasiones; pocos y contados

fewer, a. comp. menos. The f. the better, Cuantos menos mejor

fewest, a. sup. (el) menos, m.; el menor número (de), m.; (el) menos posible de, m.

fewness, s. corto número, m.

fez, s. fez, m.

fiacre, s. coche de plaza, simón, m.

fiancé(e), s. novio (-ia); desposado (-da), prometido (-da)

fiasco, s. fiasco, mal éxito, fracaso, malogro, m.

fiat, s. fiat, mandato, m., orden, f.

fib, s. mentirilla, f. v.t. decir mentirillas, mentir

fibber, s. embustero (-ra), mentiroso (-sa)

fibre, s. fibra, f.; filamento, m., hebra, f.; (of grass, etc.) brizna, f.; (fig.) naturaleza, f.

fibrin, s. (chem.) fibrina, f.

fibroid, a. fibroso. s. fibroma, m.

fibrous, a. fibroso

fibula, s. (anat.) peroné, m.

fichu, s. pañoleta, f., fichú, m.

fickle, a. inconstante; mudable; (of persons) liviano, ligero, voluble

fickleness, s. inconstancia, f.; mudanza, f.; liviandad, ligereza, veleidad, volubilidad, f.

fictile, a. plástico; figulino

fiction, s. ficción, f.; invención, f.; literatura narrativa, f.; novelas, f. pl. **legal f.,** ficción legal, ficción de derecho, f.

fictitious, a. ficticio; imaginario; fingido

fictitiousness, s. carácter ficticio, m.; falsedad, f.

fiddle, s. violín, m. v.t. tocar ... en el violín. v.i. tocar el violín; (fidget) jugar; perder el tiempo. **to play second f.,** tocar el segundo violín; (fig.) ser plato de segunda mesa

fiddler, s. violinista, m. and f.

fiddling, a. insignificante, trivial, frívolo

fidelity, s. fidelidad, f.

fidget, v.i. estar nervioso, estar inquieto; impacientarse; trajinar; (with) jugar con. v.t. molestar; impacientar

fidgetiness, s. inquietud, nerviosidad, f.

fidgety, a. inquieto, nervioso. **to be f.,** tener hormiguillo

fiduciary, a. fiduciario. s. fideicomisario (-ia)

fief, s. feudo, m.

field, s. campo, m.; (meadow) prado, m., pradera, f.; (sown field) sembrado, m.; (phys., her.) campo, m.; (of ice) banco, m.; (min.) yacimiento, m.; (background) fondo, m.; (campaign) campaña, f.; (battle) batalla, lucha, f.; (space) espacio, m.; (of knowledge, etc.) especialidad, esfera, f.; (hunting) caza, f.; (sport) campo, m.; (competitors) todos los competidores en una carrera, etc.; (horses in a race) el campo. a. campal, pradeño; de campo; de los campos. v.t. (sport) parar y devolver la pelota. v.i. (sport) actuar como "fielder." **in the f.,** (mil.) en el campo de batalla, en campaña. **magnetic f.,** campo magnético, m. **to take the f.,** entrar en campaña. **f.-artillery,** artillería ligera, artillería montada, f. **f.-day,** (holiday) día de asueto, m.; (day out) día en el campo, m.; (mil.) día de maniobras, m. **f.-glasses,** anteojos, gemelos, m. pl. **f.-hospital,** hospital de sangre, m.; ambulancia fija, f. **f.-kitchen,** cocina de campaña, f. **f.-marshal,** capitán general de ejército, m. **f.-mouse,** ratón silvestre, m. **f. of battle,** campo de batalla, m. **f. of vision,** campo visual, m. **f.-telegraph,** telégrafo de campaña, m.

fielder, s. (sport) "fielder," m.

fiend, s. diablo, demonio, m.; malvado (-da); (addict) adicto (-ta). **morphia f.,** morfinómano (-ma)

fiendish, a. diabólico, infernal; malvado, cruel, malévolo

fiendishness, s. perversidad, crueldad, f.

fierce, a. salvaje, feroz, cruel; (of the elements) violento, furioso; (intense) intenso, vehemente

fiercely, adv. ferozmente; violentamente, con furia; intensamente, con vehemencia

fierceness, s. ferocidad, fiereza, f.; violencia, furia, f.; intensidad, vehemencia, f.

fieriness, s. ardor, m.; (flames) las llamas, f. pl.; (redness) rojez, f.; (irritability) ferocidad, irritabilidad, f.; (vehemence) pasión, vehemencia, f.; (of horses) fogosidad, f.

fiery, a. ardiente; (red) rojo; (irritable) feroz, colérico, irritable; (vehement) apasionado, vehemente; (of horses) fogoso

fife, s. (mus.) pífano, pito, m.

fifteen, a. and s. quince (m.); (of age) quince años, m. pl.

fifteenth, a. and s. décimoquinto (m.); (part) quinzavo, m., décimoquinta parte, f.; (of the month) (el) quince, *m.*; (of monarchs) quince; (*mus.*) quincena, *f.*

fifth, *a.* quinto; (of monarchs) quinto; (of the month) (el) cinco. *s.* quinto, *m.*; (part) quinto, *m.*, quinta parte, *f.*; (*mus.*) quinta, *f.* **Charles V,** Carlos quinto. **f. column,** (*pol.*) quinta columna, *f.*

fifthly, *adv.* en quinto lugar

fiftieth, *a.* quincuagésimo; (part) quincuagésima parte, *f.*, cincuentavo, *m.*

fifty, *a. and s.* cincuenta (*m.*); (of age) cincuenta años, *m. pl.*

fiftyfold, *a. and adv.* cincuenta veces

fig, *s.* higo, *m.*; (tree) higuera, *f.*; (*fig.*) bledo, ardite, *m.* **green fig,** higo, *m.*, breva, *f.* **I don't care a fig,** No se me da un higo. **to be not worth a fig,** no valer un ardite. **fig-leaf,** hoja de higuera, *f.*; (*fig.*) hoja de parra, *f.*

fight, *s.* lucha, pelea, *f.*, combate, *m.*; batalla, *f.*; (struggle) lucha, *f.*; (quarrel) riña, pelea, *f.*; (conflict) conflicto, *m.*; (valour) coraje, brío, *m.* **hand-to-hand f.,** cachetina, *f.* **in fair f.,** en buena lid. **to have a f.,** tener una pelea. **to show f.,** mostrarse agresivo

fight, *v.t.* luchar contra, batirse con; (a battle) dar (batalla); (oppose) oponer; (defend) defender, pelear por; hacer batirse. *v.i.* luchar, batirse, pelear; (with words) disputar; (struggle) luchar; (make war) hacer la guerra; (in a tournament) tornear. **to f. one's way,** abrirse paso con las armas. **to f. against,** luchar contra. **to f. off,** librarse de; sacudirse. **to f. with,** luchar con; pelear con; reñir con

fighter, *s.* luchador (-ra); combatiente, *m.*; guerrero, *m.*; duelista, *m.*; (boxer) boxeador, *m.*; (*aer.*) (avión de) caza, *m.* **night f.,** (*aer.*) (avión de) caza nocturno, *m.* **f.-bomber,** (*aer.*) caza bombardeon, *m.* **F. Command,** (*aer.*) servicio de aviones de caza, *m.*

fighting, *s.* lucha, *f.*, combate, *m.*; el pelear; (boxing) boxeo, *m.* *a.* combatiente; (bellicose) agresivo, belicoso. **f.-man,** combatiente, guerrero, *m.*

figment, *s.* ficción, invención, *f.*

figurative, *a.* figurado, metafórico; figurativo; simbólico

figuratively, *adv.* en sentido figurativo; metafóricamente

figure, *s.* figura, *f.*; forma, *f.*; (statue) estatua, figura, *f.*; (of a person) silueta, *f.*; talle, *m.*; (number) cifra, *f.*, número, *m.*; (quantity) cantidad, *f.*; (price) precio, *m.*; (*geom., gram., dance, skating*) figura, *f.*; (appearance) presencia, *f.*, aire, *m.*; (picture) imagen, *m.*; (on fabric) diseño, *m.*; (*mus.*) cifra, *f.*; *pl.* figures, aritmética, *f.*, **matemáticas**, *f. pl. v.t.* figurar; (imagine) figurarse, imaginar; (*mus.*) cifrar. *v.i.* figurar, hacer un papel; (calculate) calcular, hacer cuentas. **to f. out,** calcular; (a problem, etc.) resolver. **a fine f. of a woman,** (*fam.*) una real hembra. **lay f.,** maniquí, *m.* **to be good at figures,** estar fuerte en matemáticas. **to cut a f.,** (*fig.*) hacer figura. **to have a good f.,** tener buen talle. **f. of speech,** figura retórica, metáfora, *f.* **f. dance,** baile de figuras, *m.*, contradanza, *f.* **f.-head,** (*naut.*) mascarón, *m.* (or figura, *f.*) de proa; (*fig.*) figura decorativa, *f.*

figured, *a.* estampado, con diseños, labrado

figurine, *s.* figurilla, *f.*

filament, *s.* filamento, *m.*; hebra, *f.*

filamentous, *a.* filamentoso, fibroso

filbert, *s.* avellana, *f.*; (tree) avellano, *m.*

filch, *v.t.* sisar, ratear

filcher, *s.* sisador (-ra); ratero (-ra)

filching, *s.* sisa, *f.*

file, *s.* (line) fila, hilera, sarta, línea, *f.*; (*mil.*) fila, *f.*; (tool) lima, *f.*; (rasp) escofina, *f.*; (list) lista, *f.*, catálogo, *m.*; (for documents) carpeta, *f.*, cartapacio, *m.*; (bundle of papers) legajo, *m.*; (for bills, letters, etc.) clasificador, *m.*; archivo, *m.* **in a f.,** en fila; en cola

file, *v.t.* hacer marchar en fila; (smooth) limar; (literary work) pulir; (classify) clasificar; (note particulars) fichar; (keep guar-

dar; (a petition, etc.) presentar,
registrar. *v.i.* marchar en fila.
to f. in, entrar en fila. to f.
off, desfilar. to f. letters,
clasificar correspondencia. to f.
past, (*mil.*) desfilar

filial, *a.* filial

filiation, *s.* filiación, *f.*

filibuster, *s.* filibustero, pirata,
m.

filigree, *s.* filigrana, *f. a.* afiligranado

filing, *s.* (with a tool) limadura,
f.; clasificación, *f.*; (of a petition,
etc.) presentación, *f.*, registro,
m.; *pl.* **filings,** limaduras, *f. pl.*,
retales, *m. pl.* **f.-cabinet,** fichero,
m. **f.-card,** ficha, *f.*

fill, *v.t.* llenar; (stuff) rellenar;
(appoint to a post) proveer;
(occupy a post) desempeñar;
(imbue) henchir; (saturate) saturar; (occupy) ocupar; (a tooth)
empastar; (fulfil) cumplir;
(charge, fuel) cargar; (with food)
hartar. *v.i.* llenarse. to f. the
chair, ocupar la presidencia;
(university) ocupar la cátedra.
to f. the place of, ocupar el
lugar de; substituir; suplir. It
will be difficult to find anyone
to f. his place, Será difícil de
encontrar a alguien que haga lo
que hizo él. to f. to the brim,
llenar hasta les bordes. to f. in,
(a form) llenar (or completar)
(una hoja); (insert) insertar,
añadir; (a hollow) terraplenar.
to f. out, *v.t.* hinchar. *v.i.*
hincharse; echar carnes; (of the
face) redondearse. to f. up,
colmar, llenar hasta los bordes;
(an office) proveer; (block) macizar; (a form) completar, llenar

fillet, *s.* venda, cinta, *f.*; (of meat
or fish) filete, *m.*; (of meat)
solomillo, *m.*; (*arch.*) filete, *m.*
v.t. atar con una venda o cinta;
(*cul.*) cortar en filetes

filling, *s.* envase, *m.*; (swelling)
henchimiento, *m.*; (of a tooth)
empastadura, *f.*; (in or up, of
forms, etc.) llenar, *m.* **f. station,**
depósito de gasolina, *m.*

fillip, *s.* capirotazo, *m.*; (stimulus)
estímulo, *m.*; (trifle) bagatela, *f.*
v.t. and *v.i.* dar un capirotazo
(a); *v.t.* estimular, incitar

filly, *s.* jaca, potra, *f.*

film, *s.* (on liquids) tela, *f.*; membrana, *f.*; (coating) capa ligera,
f.; (on eyes) tela, *f.*; (cinema)
película, cinta, *f.*; (*phot.*)
película, *f.*; (*fig.*) velo, *m.*; nube,
f. *v.i.* cubrirse de un velo, etc.
v.t. cubrir de un velo, etc.; filmar,
fotografiar para el cine. roll f.,
película fotográfica, *f.* silent f.,
película muda, *f.* talking f.,
película sonora, *f.* to shoot a f.,
hacer una película. to take
part in a f., actuar, or tomar
parte, en una película. f. pack,
" film pack," *m.* f. star, estrella
de la pantalla (or del cine), *f.*

filminess, *s.* transparencia, diafanidad, *f.*

filmy, *a.* transparente, diáfano

filter, *s.* filtro, *m.* *v.t.* filtrar.
v.i. infiltrarse; (*fig.*, of news)
trascender, divulgarse. **f.-bed,**
filtro, *m.* **f.-paper,** papel filtro,
m.

filth, *s.* inmundicia, suciedad, *f.*;
(*fig.*) corrupción, *f.*; (*fig.*) obscenidad, *f.*

filthiness, *s.* suciedad, *f.*; escualidez, *f.*; (*fig.*) asquerosidad, *f.*;
(*fig.*) obscenidad, *f.*

filthy, *a.* inmundo, sucio; escuálido; (*fig.*) asqueroso; (*fig.*) obsceno

filtrate, *s.* filtrado, *m.* *v.t.* filtrar

filtration, *s.* filtración, *f.*

fin, *s.* (of fish) aleta, ala, *f.*; (of
whale) barba, *f.*; (*aer.*) aleta, *f.*

final, *a.* último, final; (conclusive) conclusivo, decisivo, terminante. *s.* (*sport*) finales, *m. pl.*;
(*univ.*) último examen, *m.* f.
blow, (*fig.*) golpe decisivo, *m.*
f. cause, (*phil.*) causa final, *f.*

finale, *s.* final, *m.*

finalist, *s.* (*sport*) finalista, *m.* and
f.

finality, *s.* finalidad, *f.*; (decision)
determinación, resolución, deci-
sión, *f.*

finally, *adv.* por fin, finalmente,
por último, a la postre; (irrevocably) irrevocablemente

finance, *s.* hacienda pública, *f.*,
asuntos económicos, *m. pl.*; finanzas, *f. pl.* *v.t.* financiar

financial, *a.* financiero, monetario. f. year, año económico, *m.*

financially, *adv.* del punto de
vista financiero

financier, s. financiero, m.

find, v.t. encontrar, hallar; (discover) descubrir, dar con; (invent) inventar, crear; (supply) facilitar, proporcionar; (provide) proveer; (instruct) instruir; (law) declarar. v.i. (law) fallar, dar sentencia. s. hallazgo, m.; descubrimiento, m. **I found him out a long time ago,** (fig.) Hace tiempo que me di cuenta de cómo era él. **I found it possible to go out,** Me fué posible salir. **The judge found them guilty,** El juez les declaró culpables. **to f. a verdict,** (law) dar sentencia, fallar. **to f. one's way,** encontrar el camino. **to f. oneself,** hallarse, verse, encontrarse. **to f. out,** averiguar, descubrir. **to f. out about,** informarse sobre (or de)

finder, s. hallador (-ra); (inventor) inventor (-ra), descubridor (-ra); (telescope, camera) buscador, m.

finding, s. hallazgo, m.; (discovery) descubrimiento, m.; (law) fallo, m., sentencia, f.

fine, s. multa, f.; (end) fin, m. **in f.,** en fin, en resumen

fine, v.t. multar, cargar una multa de

fine, a. (thin) delgado; (sharp) agudo; (delicate) fino, delicado; (minute) menudo; (refined) refinado, puro; (healthy) saludable; (of weather) bueno; magnífico; (beautiful) hermoso, lindo; excelente; (perfect) perfecto; (good) bueno; elegante; (showy) ostentoso, vistoso; (handsome) guapo; (subtle) sutil; (acute) agudo; (noble) noble; (eminent, accomplished) distinguido, eminente; (polished) pulido; (affected) afectado; (clear) claro; (transparent) transparente, diáfano. adv. muy bien. **a f. upstanding young man,** un buen mozo. **a f. upstanding young woman,** una real moza. **He's a f. fellow,** (ironically) Es una buena pieza. **That is all very f. but ...,** Todo eso está muy bien pero .... **to become f.,** (weather) mejorar

finely, adv. finamente; menudamente; elegantemente; (ironically) lindamente

fineness, s. (thinness) delgadez, f.; (excellence) excelencia, f.; delicadeza, f.; (softness) suavidad, f.; elegancia, f.; (subtlety) sutileza, f.; (acuteness) agudeza, f.; (perfection) perfección, f.; (nobility) nobleza, f.; (beauty) hermosura, f.

finery, s. galas, f. pl., atavíos magníficos, m. pl.; adornos, m. pl.; primor, m., belleza, f.

finesse, s. sutileza, diplomacia, f.; estratagema, artificio, m.; (cunning) astucia, f. v.i. valerse de estratagemas y artificios

finger, s. dedo, m.; (of a clock, etc.) manecilla, f.; (measurement) dedada, f.; (fig.) mano, f. v.t. manosear, tocar; (soil) ensuciar con los dedos; (steal) sisar; (mus., a keyed instrument) teclear, (a stringed instrument) tocar. **first f.,** dedo índice, m. **fourth f.,** dedo anular, m. **little f.,** dedo meñique, m. **second f.,** dedo de en medio, dedo del corazón, m. **to burn one's fingers,** quemarse los dedos; (fig.) cogerse los dedos. **to have at one's f.-tips,** (fig.) saber al dedillo. **f.-board,** (of piano) teclado, m.; (of stringed instruments) diapasón, m. **f.-bowl,** lavadedos, lavafrutas, m. **finger's breadth,** dedo, m. **f.-mark,** huella digital, f. **f.-nail,** uña del dedo, f. **f.-print,** impresión digital, f. **f.-stall,** dedil, m. **f.-tip,** punta (or yema) del dedo, f. **f.-wave,** peinado al agua, m.

fingered, a. (in compounds) con dedos, que tiene los dedos ....

fingering, s. (touching) manoseo, m.; (mus.) digitación, f.; (mus., the keys) tecleo, m.; (wool) estambre, m.

finial, s. pináculo, m.

finicky, a. (of persons) dengoso, remilgado; (of things) nimio

finish, s. fin, m., conclusión, terminación, f.; (final touch) última mano, f.; perfección, f.; (of an article) acabado, m.; (sport) llegada, f. v.t. terminar, acabar, concluir; llevar a cabo, poner fin a; (perfect) perfeccionar; (put finishing touch to) dar la última mano a; (kill) matar; (exhaust) agotar, rendir; (overcome)

vencer. *v.i.* acabar; concluirse.
to f. off, acabar, terminar; (kill)
matar, acabar con; (destroy)
destruir. **to f. up,** acabar; (eat)
comer; (drink) beber
finishable, *a.* acabable
finished, *a.* completo; perfecto;
(careful) cuidadoso
finisher, *s.* terminador (-ra),
acabador (-ra); pulidor (-ra);
(final blow) golpe de gracia, *m.*
finishing, *a.* concluyente. *s.*
terminación, *f.,* fin, *m.;* perfección, *f.;* (last touch) última mano,
f. **to put the f. touch,** dar la
última pincelada
finite, *a.* finito
Finn, *s.* finlandés (-esa)
finnan-haddock, *s.* (nearest
equivalent) cecial, *m.*
Finnish, *a.* finlandés. *s.* (language) finlandés, *m.*
fir, *s.* abeto, sapino, pino, *m.* **red
fir,** pino silvestre, *m.* **fir-cone,**
piña de abeto, *f.* **fir grove,**
abetal, *m.*
fire, *s.* fuego, *m.;* (conflagration)
incendio, *m.;* (on the hearth)
lumbre, *f.,* fuego, *m.;* (*fig.*)
ardor, *m.,* pasión, *f.;* (shooting)
fuego, tiro, *m.* **by f. and sword,**
a sangre y fuego. **by the f.,** cerca
del fuego; (in a house) al lado de
la chimenea. **long-range f.,** (*mil.*)
fuego de largo alcance, *m.* **short-
range f.,** (*mil.*) fuego de corto
alcance, *m.* **on f.,** en fuego,
ardiendo, en llamas; (*fig.*) impaciente; (*fig.*) lleno de pasión.
to be between two fires, (*fig.*)
estar entre dos aguas. **to make
a f.,** encender un fuego. **to miss
f.,** no dar en el blanco, errar el
tiro. **to open f.,** (*mil.*) hacer una
descarga. **to set on f.,** prender
fuego a, incendiar. **to take f.,**
encenderse. **under f.,** bajo
fuego. **f.-alarm,** alarma de
incendios, *f.* **f.-arm,** arma de
fuego, *f.* **f.-box,** hogar, *m.* **f.-
brand,** tea, *f.* **f.-brigade,** cuerpo
de bomberos, *m.* **f.-damp,**
grisú, *m.* **f.-dog,** morillo, *m.*
f.-drill, instrucción de bomberos,
f. **f.-engine,** bomba de incendios,
f. **f.-escape,** escalera de incendios, *f.* **f.-extinguisher,** extintor, matafuego, *m.* **f.-guard,**
vigilante de incendios, *m.;* alam-

brera, *f.* **f.-hose,** manguera de
incendios, *f.* **f.-insurance,** seguro
contra incendios, *m.* **f.-irons,**
badil (*m.*) y tenazas (*f. pl.*). **f.-
lighter,** encendedor, *m.* **f.-
screen,** pantalla, *f.* **f.-ship,**
brulote, *m.* **f.-shovel,** badil, *m.,*
paleta, *f.* **f.-spotter,** vigilante de
incendios, *m.* **f.-sprite,** salamandra, *f.* **f.-watching,** servicio de
vigilancia de incendios, *m.*
fire, *v.t.* incendiar, prender (or
pegar) fuego a; quemar; (bricks)
cocer; (fire-arms) disparar; (cauterize) cauterizar; (*fig.,* stimulate)
estimular, excitar; (inspire) inspirar; (*fam.,* of questions) disparar; (*fam.,* sack) despedir. *v.i.*
encenderse; (shoot) hacer fuego,
disparar (un tiro); (*fam.,* away)
disparar; (up) enojarse. **to f. a
salute,** disparar un saludo. (*mil.*)
F.! ¡Fuego!
firefly, *s.* cocuyo, *m.*
fireman, *s.* bombero, *m.;* (of an
engine, etc.) fogonero, *m.* **fireman's lift,** silleta, *f.*
fireplace, *s.* chimenea francesa,
chimenea, *f.;* (hearth) hogar, *m.*
fireproof, *a.* a prueba de incendios; incombustible
firer, *s.* disparador, *m.*
firewood, *s.* leña, *f.* **f. dealer,**
leñador (-ra), vendedor (-ra) de
leña
firework, *s.* fuego artificial,
m.
firing, *s.* (of fire-arms) disparo, *m.;*
(burning) incendio, *m.,* quema,
f.; (of bricks, etc.) cocimiento,
m.; (of pottery) cocción, *f.;* (cauterization) cauterización, *f.;* (fuel)
combustible, *m.;* (*fam.,* sacking)
despedida, *f.* **within f. range,** a
tiro. **f.-line,** línea de fuego, *f.*
f.-oven, (pottery) horno alfarero,
m. **f.-squad,** pelotón de ejecución, *m.*
firm, *a.* firme; (strong) fuerte;
(secure) seguro; sólido; (resolute)
inflexible, resoluto; severo;
(steady) constante; (persistent)
tenaz. *s.* (*com.*) casa (de comercio), empresa, *f.;* razón social, *f.*
firmament, *s.* firmamento, *m.*
firmly, *adv.* firmemente; inflexiblemente; constantemente
firmness, *s.* firmeza, *f.;* solidez, *f.;*
inflexibilidad, resolución, *f.;*

severidad, *f.*; constancia, *f.*;
tenacidad, *f.*

first, *a.* primero (primer before
m. sing. nouns); (of monarchs)
primero; (of dates) (el) primero.
s. primero, *m.*; (beginning) principio, *m. adv.* primero, en primer
lugar; (before, of time) antes;
(for the first time) por primera
vez; (at the beginning) al principio; (ahead) adelante. **at f.,** al
principio. **from the very f.,**
desde el primer momento. **to
appear for the f. time,** aparecer
(or presentarse) por primera vez;
(*theat.*) debutar. **to go f.,** ir
delante de todos, ir a la cabeza;
ir adelante. **f. and foremost,**
en primer lugar; ante todo.
f.-aid. primera cura, *f.* **f.-aid
post,** casa de socorro, *f.* **f.-
aider,** practicante, *m.* **f.-born,**
a. and *s.* primogénito (-ta).
f.-class, *a.* de primera clase;
(*fig.*) excelente. **f.-cousin,** primo
(-ma) carnal, primo (-ma) hermano (-na). **f. edition,** edición
príncipe, *f.* **f. floor,** primer piso,
m. **f. fruits,** frutos primerizos,
m. pl.; (*fig.*) primicias, *f. pl.* **f.-
hand,** *a.* original, de primera
mano. **f. letters,** primeras letras,
f. pl. **f. night,** (*theat.*) estreno,
m. **f. of all,** primero, ante todo.
f.-rate, *a.* de primera clase

firstly, *adv.* en primer lugar,
primero

firth, *s.* ría, *f.*

fiscal, *a.* and *s.,* fiscal (*m.*). **f.
year,** año económico, *m.*

fish, *s.* pez, *m.*; (out of the water)
pescado, *m.*; (*fam.*) tipo, individuo, *m. v.i.* pescar; (out) sacar.
v.i. pescar; (*fig.*) buscar. **fried f.,**
pescado frito, *m.* **He is a queer
f.,** Él es un tipo muy raro.
to be neither f. nor fowl, no
ser ni carne ni pescado. **to feel
like a f. out of water,** sentirse
fuera de su ambiente. **to f. in
troubled waters,** A río revuelto
ganancia de pescadores. **f.-eat-
ing,** *a.* ictiófago. **f.-fork,** tenedor de pescado, *m.* **f.-glue,** cola
de pescado, *f.* **f.-hook,** anzuelo,
m. **f.-knife,** cuchillo de pescado,
m. **f.-like,** de pez; como un pez,
parecido a un pez. **f. roe,** hueva,
f. **f.-server,** pala para pescado, *f.*

fishbone, *s.* espina de pescado,
raspa de pescado, *f.*

fisherman, *s.* pescador, *m.*

fishery, *s.* pesquería, *f.*

fishing, *s.* pesca, *f.* *a.* de pescar.
to go f., ir de pesca. **f.-boat,**
bote de pesca, *m.* **f.-floats,**
levas, *f. pl.* **f.-line,** sedal, *m.* **f.-
net,** red de pesca, *f.* **f.-reel,**
carretel, carrete, *m.* **f.-rod,** caña
de pescar, *f.* **f.-tackle,** aparejo
de pesca, *m.* **f. village,** pueblo
de pescadores, *m.*

fishmonger, *s.* pescadero (-ra).
fishmonger's shop, pescadería,
f.

fishpond, *s.* vivero, *m.*, piscina, *f.*

fishwife, *s.* pescadora, *f.*

fishy, *a.* de pescado; (of eyes, etc.)
de pez, como un pez; (in smell)
que huele a pescado; (*fam.*)
sospechoso; (of stories) inverosímil

fissure, *s.* grieta, hendidura,
rendija, *f.*; (*anat.,* *geol.*) fisura, *f.*

fissured, *a.* hendido

fist, *s.* puño, *m.*; (*print.*) manecilla,
f.; (handwriting) letra, *f.* **with
clenched fists,** a puño cerrado

fisticuff, *s.* puñetazo, *m.*; *pl.*
fisticuffs, agarrada, riña, *f.*

fistula, *s.* (*surg.*) fístula, *f.*

fit, *s.* espasmo, paroxismo, *m.*;
ataque, *m.*; (impulse) acceso,
arranque, *m.*; (whim) capricho,
m.; (of a garment) corte, *m.*;
(adjustment) ajuste, encaje, *m.*
by fits and starts, a tropezones,
espasmódicamente

fit, *a.* a propósito (para), bueno
(para); (opportune) oportuno;
(proper) conveniente; apto; (decent) decente; (worthy) digno;
(ready) preparado, listo; (adequate) adecuado; (capable) capaz,
en estado (de); (appropriate) apropiado; (just) justo. **It is not in a
fit state to be used,** No está en
condiciones para usarse. **to be
not fit for,** no servir para;
(through ill-health) no tener
bastante salud para. **to think
fit,** creer (or juzgar) conveniente.
fit for use, usable. **fit to eat,**
comestible

fit, *v.t.* ajustar, acomodar, encajar; adaptar (a); (furnish)
proveer (de), surtir (con); (of
tailor, dressmaker) entallar, pro-

bar; (of shoemaker) calzar; (of garments, shoes) ir (bien o mal); (prepare) preparar; (go with) ser apropiado (a); (adapt itself to) adaptarse a. *v.i.* ajustarse, acomodarse, encajarse; adaptarse; (clothes) ir (bien o mal). **to fit in,** *v.t.* encajar; incluir. *v.i.* encajarse; caber; adaptarse. **to fit out,** equipar; proveer (de); preparar. **to fit up,** montar, instalar; proveer (de). **to fit with,** proveer de

fitful, *a.* intermitente; espasmódico; caprichoso

fitfully, *adv.* por intervalos, a ratos; caprichosamente

fitly, *adv.* adecuadamente; justamente; apropiadamente

fitment, *s.* equipo, *m.*; instalación, *f.*; (of bookcase, etc.) sección, *f.*; (furniture) pieza, *f.*, mueble, *m.*

fitness, *s.* conveniencia, *f.*; aptitud, capacidad, *f.*; oportunidad, *f.*; salud, *f.*; (good health) vigor, *m.*

fitted, *a.* (of clothes) ajustado

fitter, *s.* ajustador, *m.*; (mechanic) armador, mecánico, *m.*; (tailoring) cortador, *m.*; (dressmaking) probador (-ra)

fitting, *s.* encaje, ajuste, *m.*; adaptación, *f.*; (of a garment) prueba, *f.*; (size) medida, *f.*; (installation) instalación, *f.*; *pl.* **fittings,** guarniciones, *f. pl.*; instalaciones, *f. pl.*; accesorios, *m. pl. a.* conveniente, justo; apropiado; adecuado; (worthy) digno; (of coats, etc.) ajustado. **f. room,** cuarto de pruebas, *m.* **f. in,** encaje, *m.* **f. out,** equipo, *m.* **f. up,** arreglo, *m.*; (of machines) montaje, *m.*; (of a house) mueblaje, *m.*

five, *a.* and *s.* cinco (*m.*); (of the clock) las cinco, *f. pl.*; (of age) cinco años, *m. pl.* **to be f.,** tener cinco años. **f. feet deep,** de cinco pies de profundidad. **f. feet high,** cinco pies de altura. **f.-finger exercises,** ejercicios de piano, *m. pl.* **F.-Year Plan,** Plan Quinquenal, *m.*

fivefold, *a.* quíntuplo

fiver, *s.* billete de cinco libras, *m.*

fives, *s.* (nearest equivalent) frontón a mano, *m.* **f.-court,** frontón, *m.*

fix, *s.* aprieto, apuro, *m.*; callejón sin salida, *m.* *v.t.* fijar; sujetar, afianzar; (bayonets) calar; (with nails) clavar; (*phot., chem., med.*) fijar; (decide) establecer; (a date) señalar; (eyes, attention) clavar; (on the mind) grabar, estampar; (one's hopes) poner; (base) basar, fundar; (*fam.,* put right) arreglar, componer. *v.i.* fijarse; establecerse; determinarse. **to get in a fix,** hacerse un lío. **to fix a price,** fijar un precio. **to fix on, upon,** elegir, escoger; decidir, determinar. **to fix up,** arreglar; decidir; organizar; (differences) olvidar (sus disensiones)

fixation, *s.* obsesión, idea fija, *f.*; (scientific) fijación, *f.*

fixative, *s.* (*med., phot.*) fijador, *m.*; (dyeing) mordiente, *m. a.* que fija

fixed, *a.* fijo; inmóvil; permanente; (of ideas) inflexible. **f. bayonet,** bayoneta calada, *f.* **f. price,** precio fijo, *m.* **f. star,** estrella fija, *f.*

fixedly, *adv.* fijamente; resueltamente; firmemente

fixing, *s.* fijación, *f.*; afianzamiento, *m.*; arreglo, *m.*; (of a date) señalamiento, *m.* **f. bath,** (*phot.*) baño fijador, *m.*

fixity, *s.* permanencia, *f.*; inmovilidad, *f.*; invariabilidad, *f.*; firmeza, *f.*

fixture, *s.* instalación, *f.*; accesorio fijo, *m.*; (*sport*) partido, *m.*; (*fam.*) permanencia, *f.* **f. card,** (*sport*) calendario deportivo, *m.*

fizz, *s.* espuma, *f.*; chisporroteo, *m.*; (*fam.*) champaña, *m.* *v.i.* (liquids) espumear; (sputter) chisporrotear

fizzle, *s.* (failure) fiasco, fracaso, *m.* *v.i.* chisporrotear; (out) apagarse; (fail) fracasar, no tener éxito

fjord, *s.* fiordo, *m.*

flabbergast, *v.t.* dejar con la boca abierta, dejar de una pieza

flabbiness, flaccidity, *s.* flaccidez, flojedad, *f.*; (*med.*) reblandecimiento, *m.*; (of character) debilidad, flaqueza del ánimo, *f.*

flabby, flaccid, *a.* fláccido, flojo; (*fig.*) débil

flag, *s.* bandera, *f.*; pabellón, estandarte, *m.*; (small) banderola, *f.*; (iris) (yellow) cala, *f.*, (purple) lirio cárdeno, *m.*; (stone) losa, *f.* **to dip the f.,** saludar con la bandera. **to hoist the f.,** izar la bandera. **to strike the f.,** bajar la bandera; (in defeat) rendir la bandera. **f. bearer,** portaestandarte, abanderado, *m.* **f.-day,** día de la banderita, *m.*; (in U.S.A.) día de la bandera, *m.* **f.-officer,** almirante, *m.*; vicealmirante, *m.*; jefe de escuadra, *m.* **f. of truce,** bandera blanca, bandera de paz, *f.*

flag, *v.i.* flaquear, debilitarse; languidecer; (wither) marchitarse; decaer, disminuir. *v.t.* adornar con banderas; (signal) hacer señales con una bandera; (for a race, etc.) marcar con banderas; (with stones) enlosar, embaldosar.

flagellant, *s.* flagelante, *m.*

flagellate, *v.t.* flagelar

flagellation, *s.* flagelación, *f.*

flageolet, *s.* (*mus.*) caramillo, *m.*, chirimía, *f.* **f. player,** chirimía, *m.*

flagging, *s.* pavimentación, *f.*; (floor) enlosado, *m.* *a.* lánguido, flojo

flagon, *s.* frasco, *m.*; botella, *f.*

flagrancy, *s.* escándalo, *m.*, notoriedad, *f.*

flagrant, *a.* escandaloso, notorio

flagship, *s.* capitana, *f.*

flagstaff, *s.* asta de bandera, *f.*

flagstone, *s.* losa, lancha, *f.*

flail, *s.* mayal, *m.*

flair, *s.* instinto natural, *m.*, comprensión innata, *f.*; habilidad natural, *f.*

flak, *s.* cortina (or barrera) antiaérea, *f.*

flake, *s.* escama, *f.*; laminilla, hojuela, *f.*; (of snow) copo, *m.*; (of fire) chispa, *f.* *v.t.* cubrir con escamas, etc.; exfoliar; (crumble) hacer migas de, desmigajar. *v.i.* escamarse; (off) exfoliarse; caer en copos

flaky, *a.* escamoso; en laminillas; (of pastry) hojaldrado. **f. pastry,** hojaldre, *f.*

flamboyance, *s.* extravagancia, *f.*; (*lit.*) ampulosidad, *f.*

flamboyant, *a.* (*arch.*) flamígero; extravagante, llamativo, rimbombante; (of style) ampuloso

flame, *s.* llama, *f.*; (*fig.*) fuego, *m.*; (*fam.*) amorío, *m.* *v.i.* flamear, llamear; arder, abrasarse; (shine) brillar; (up, *fig.*) inflamarse; acalorarse. **f.-coloured,** de color de llama, anaranjado. **f.-thrower,** lanzallamas, *m.*

flaming, *a.* llameante; abrasador; (of colours) llamativo, chillón; (of feelings) ardiente, fervoroso, apasionado

flamingo, *s.* (*orn.*) flamenco, *m.*

flange, *s.* (*mech.*) reborde, *m.* *v.t.* rebordear

flank, *s.* (of animal) ijada, *f.*; (human) costado, *m.*; (of hill, etc.) lado, *m.*, falda, *f.*; (*mil.*) flanco, *m.* *a.* (*mil.*, *nav.*) por el flanco. *v.t.* lindar con, estar contiguo a; (*mil.*, *nav.*) flanquear. *v.i.* estar al lado de; tocar a, lindar con.

flannel, *s.* franela, *f.* *a.* de franela

flannelette, *s.* moletón, *m.*

flap, *s.* golpe, *m.*; (of a sail) zapatazo, *m.*, sacudida, *f.*; (of a pocket) cartera, tapa, *f.*; (of skin) colgajo, *m.*; (of a shoe, etc.) oreja, *f.*; (of a shirt, etc.) falda, *f.*; (of a hat) ala, *f.*; (of trousers) bragueta, *f.*; (rever) solapa, *f.*; (of a counter) trampa, *f.*; (of a table) hoja plegadiza, *f.*; (of the wings) aletazo, *m.*; (of w.c.) tapa, *f.* *v.t.* sacudir, golpear, batir; agitar; (the tail) menear. *v.i.* agitarse; (of wings) aletear; (of sails) zapatear, sacudirse; colgar. **f.-eared,** de orejas grandes y gachas

flapjack, *s.* (*cul.*) torta de sartén, *f.*; (for powder) polvorera, *f.*

flapper, *s.* (*fam.*) polla, tobillera, chica " topolino," *f.*

flapping, *s.* batimiento, *m.*; (waving) ondulación, *f.*; (of sails) zapatazo, *m.*; (of wings) aleteo, *m.*

flare, *s.* fulgor, *m.*, llama, *f.*; hacha, *f.*; (*aer.*) cohete de señales, *m.*; (*sew.*) vuelo, *m.* *v.i.* relampaguear, fulgurar; brillar; (of a lamp) llamear; (up) encolerizarse, salirse de tino; (of epidemic) declararse; (war, etc.) desencadenarse

flash, s. relámpago, centelleo, m., ráfaga de luz, f.; brillo, m.; (from a gun) fuego, fogonazo, m.; (of wit, genius) rasgo, m.; (of joy, etc.) acceso, m. v.i. relampaguear, fulgurar, centellear; brillar; cruzar rápidamente, pasar como un relámpago. v.t. hacer relampaguear; hacer brillar; (a look, etc.) dar; lanzar; (light) encender; (powder) quemar; transmitir señales por heliógrafo; (fam.) sacar a relucir, enseñar. **shoulder-f.,** (mil.) emblema, m. **to be gone like a f.,** desaparecer como un relámpago. **to f. out,** brillar, centellear. **f. of lightning,** relámpago, rayo, m. **f. of wit,** agudeza, f., rasgo de ingenio, m.

flashily, adv. llamativamente, con mal gusto

flashing, s. centelleo, m., llamarada, f. a. centellador, relampagueante; brillante; chispeante

flashlight, s. luz de magnesio, f.; (torch) lamparilla eléctrica, f. **f. photograph,** magnesio, m.

flashy, a. llamativo, de mal gusto, charro; frívolo, superficial

flask, s. frasco, m., redoma, botella, f.; (for powder) frasco, m.; (vacuum) termos, m.

flat, a. llano; (smooth) liso; (lying) tendido, tumbado; (flattened) aplastado; (destroyed) arrasado; (stretched out) extendido; (of nose, face) chato, romo; (of tyre) desinflado; (uniform) uniforme; (depressed) desanimado; (uninteresting) monótono; (boring) aburrido; (com.) paralizado; (downright) categórico; absoluto; (nett) neto; (mus.) bemol; (of boats) de fondo plano. adv. See **flatly.** s. planicie, f.; (of a sword) hoja, f.; (of the hand) palma, f.; (land) llanura, f.; (apartment) piso, m.; (mus.) bemol, m, **to fall f.,** caer de bruces; (fig.) no tener éxito. **to make f.,** allanar. **to sing f.,** desafinar. **f. boat,** barco de fondo plano, m **f.-footed,** de pies achatados; (fig.) pedestre. **f.-iron,** plancha, f. **f. roof,** azotea, f.

flatly, adv. de plano; a nivel; (plainly) llanamente, netamente;

(dully) indiferentemente; (categorically) categóricamente

flatness, s. planicie, f.; llanura, f.; (smoothness) lisura, f.; (evenness) igualdad, f.; (uninterestingness) insulsez, insipidez, f.; abu-rrimiento, m.; (depression) desaliento, abatimiento, m.

flatten, v.t. aplanar, allanar; aplastar; (smooth) alisar; (even) igualar; (destroy) derribar, arrasar, destruir; (dismay) desconcertar; (out) extender. v.i. aplanarse, allanarse; aplastarse

flattening, s. allanamiento, m.; aplastamiento, m.; igualación, f.

flatter, v.t. adular, lisonjear, halagar; (of a dress, photograph, etc.) favorecer; (please the senses) regalar, deleitar; (oneself) felicitarse

flatterer, s. adulador (-ra), lison-jero (-ra)

flattering, a. adulador, lisonjero; (promising) halagüeño; favoreciente; deleitoso

flattery, s. adulación, f.

flatulence, s. flatulencia, f.

flatulent, a. flatulento

flaunt, v.i. (flutter) ondear; pavonearse. v.t. desplegar; ostentar, sacar a relucir; enseñar

flaunting, s. ostentación, f.; alarde, m. a. ostentoso; magnífico; (fluttering) ondeante

flautist, s. flautista, m. and f.

flavour, s. sabor, gusto, m.; (cul.) condimento, m.; (fig.) dejo, m. v.t. (cul.) sazonar, condimentar; dar un gusto (de), hacer saborear (a); (fig.) dar un dejo (de)

flavoured, a. (in compounds) de sabor . . . ; sazonado; que tiene sabor de . . .

flavouring, s. (cul.) condimento, m.; (fig.) sabor, dejo, m.

flavourless, a. insípido, soso, sin sabor

flaw, s. desperfecto, m., imperfección, f.; (crack) grieta, hendedura, f.; (in wood, metals) quebraja, f.; (in gems) pelo, m.; (in fruit) maca, f.; (in cloth) gabarro, m.; (fig.) defecto, error, m.; (wind) ráfaga de viento, f.

flawless, a. sin defecto; perfecto; impecable

flawlessness, s. perfección, f.; impecabilidad, f.

flax, s. lino, m. **to dress f.,** rastrillar lino. **f.-comb,** rastrillo, m. **f. field,** linar, m.

flaxen, a. de lino; (fair) rubio, blondo. **f.-haired,** de pelo rubio

flay, v.t. desollar; (criticize) despellejar

flaying, s. desuello, m., desolladura, f.

flea, s. pulga, f. **f. bite,** picada de pulga, f.

fleck, s. pinta, mancha, f., lunar, m.; (of sun) mota, f.; (speck) partícula, f.; (freckle) peca, f. v.t. abigarrar; manchar; (dapple) salpicar, motear

fledged, a. emplumecido, plumado; alado; (fig.) maduro

fledgeling, s. volantón, m.; (fig.) niño (-ña); (fig.) novato (-ta)

flee, v.i. huir, fugarse, escapar; (vanish) desaparecer; (avoid) evitar, huir de. v.t. abandonar

fleece, s. vellón, m.; lana, f.; toisón, m. v.t. esquilar; (fig., fam.) pelar. **Order of the Golden F.,** Orden del Toisón de Oro, f.

fleecy, a. lanudo, lanar; (white) blanquecino; (of clouds) borreguero. **f. clouds,** borregos, m. pl.

fleet, s. (navy) armada, f.; escuadra, flota, f.; (fig.) serie, f. a. alado, rápido, veloz. **F. Air Arm,** Aviación Naval, f. **f.-footed,** ligero de pies

fleeting, a. fugaz, momentáneo, efímero, pasajero

Flemish, a. flamenco. s. (language) flamenco, m.

flesh, s. carne, f.; (mankind) género humano, m., humanidad, f.; (of fruit) pulpa, f. **a man of f. and blood,** un hombre de carne y hueso. **of one's own f. and blood,** de la misma sangre de uno. **to make one's f. creep,** dar carne de gallina (a). **f.-coloured,** encarnado, de color de carne. **f.-eating,** carnívoro. **f. wound,** herida superficial, f.

fleshiness, s. carnosidad, gordura, f.

fleshpot, s. marmita, f.; (fig.) olla, f. **the fleshpots of Egypt,** las ollas de Egipto

fleshy, a. carnoso, grueso; (of fruit) pulposo; suculento

fleur-de-lis, s. flor de lis, f.

flex, s. (elec.) flexible, m. v.t. doblar. v.i. doblarse

flexibility, s. flexibilidad, f.; (of style) plasticidad, f.; docilidad, f.

flexible, a. flexible; dúctil, maleable; (of style) plástico; of) voice) quebradizo; adaptable; dócil

flexion, s. flexión, f.; (gram.) inflexión, f.; (gram.) flexión, f.

flexor, s. (anat.) músculo flexor, m.

flick, s. golpecito, toque, m.; (of the finger) capirotazo, m.; (fam.) cine, m. v.t. dar un golpecito a; dar ligeramente con un látigo; sacudir. **to f. over the pages of,** hojear

flicker, s. estremecimiento, temblor, m.; fluctuación, f.; (of bird) aleteo, m.; (of flame) onda (de una llama), f.; (of eyelashes) pestañeo, m.; (of a smile) indicio, f. v.i. agitarse; (of flags) ondear; vacilar

flickering, a. tenue; vacilante

flier, s. volador (-ra); aviador (-ra); piloto, m.; fugitivo (-va)

flight, s. vuelo, m.; (of bird of prey) colada, f.; (flock of birds) bandada, f.; (migration) migración, f.; (of time) transcurso, m.; (of imagination, etc.) arranque, m.; (volley) lluvia, f.; (of aeroplanes) escuadrilla (de aviones), f.; (of stairs) tramo, tiro, m.; (staircase) escalera, f.; (of locks on canal, etc.) ramal, m.; (escape) huida, fuga, f. **long-distance f.,** (aer.) vuelo de distancia, m. **non-stop f.,** (aer.) vuelo sin parar, m. **reconnaissance f.,** (aer.) vuelo de reconocimiento, vuelo de patrulla, m. **test f.,** (aer.) vuelo de pruebas, m. **to put to f.,** ahuyentar, poner en fuga. **to take f.,** alzar el vuelo. **f.-lieutenant,** teniente aviador, m. **f.-sergeant,** sargento aviador, m.

flightiness, s. frivolidad, veleidad, ligereza, f.

flighty, a. frívolo, inconstante, veleidoso

flimsiness, s. falta de solidez, endeblez, f.; fragilidad, f.; (of arguments) futilidad, f.

flimsy, a. endeble; frágil; fútil, insubstancial

flinch, *v.i.* echarse atrás, retirarse (ante); vacilar, titubear. **without flinching**, sin vacilar; sin quejarse

fling, *v.t.* arrojar, echar, tirar; lanzar; (scatter) derramar; (oneself) echarse; (oneself upon) echarse encima; (*fig.*) confiar en. *v.i.* lanzarse; marcharse precipitadamente; saltar. *s.* tiro, *m.*; (of dice, etc.) echada, *f.*; (gibe) sarcasmo, *m.*, burla, chufleta, *f.*; (of horse) respingo, brinco, *m.*; baile escocés, *m.* **in full f.**, en plena operación; en progreso. **to have one's f.**, darse un verde, correrla. **to f. away**, *v.t.* desechar; (waste) desperdiciar, malgastar, perder. *v.i.* marcharse enfadado; marcharse rápidamente. **to f. back**, (a ball) devolver; (the head) echar atrás. **to f. down**, tirar al suelo; arrojar; derribar. **to f. off**, *v.t.* rechazar; apartar; (a garment, etc.) quitar. *v.i.* marcharse sin más ni más. **to f. oneself down**, tumbarse, echarse; despeñarse (por). **to f. oneself headlong**, despeñarse. **to f. open**, abrir violentamente, abrir de repente. **to f. out**, *v.t.* echar a la fuerza; (a hand) alargar, extender. *v.i.* salir apresuradamente. **to f. over**, (upset) volcar; arrojar por; abandonar. **to f. up**, lanzar al aire; levantar, erguir; renunciar (a), abandonar; dejar

flint, *s.* pedernal, *m.*; (for producing fire) piedra de encendedor, *f.*

flinty, *a.* pedernalino; (*fig.*) endurecido

flippancy, *s.* levedad, ligereza, *f.*; frivolidad, *f.*; impertinencia, *f.*

flippant, *a.* poco serio, ligero; frívolo; impertinente

flipper, *s.* aleta, *f.*

flirt, *s.* (man) coquetón, castigador, *m.*; (woman) coqueta, castigadora, *f.* *v.t.* (shake) sacudir; (move) agitar; (wave) menear. *v.i.* flirtear, coquetear; (toy with) jugar con; divertirse con

flirtation, *s.* flirteo, amorío, *m.*

flirtatious, *a.* (of men) galanteador, castigador; (of women) coqueta

flit, *v.i.* revolotear, mariposear; (move silently) deslizarse, pasar silenciosamente; (depart) irse, marcharse; mudarse por los aires. **to f. about**, ir y venir silenciosamente. **to f. past**, pasar como una sombra

flitch, *s.* (of bacon) hoja de tocino, *f.*

float, *s.* masa flotante, *f.*; (raft) balsa, *f.*; (mech.) flotador, *m.*; (of fishing rod or net) corcho, *m.*; (of fish) vejiga natatoria, *f.*; (for swimming) nadadera, calabaza, *f.*; (for tableaux) carroza, *f.*; *pl.* **floats**, (*theat.*) candilejas, *f.* *v.i.* flotar; (flags, hair, etc.) ondear; (wander) vagar; (*naut.*) boyar. *v.t.* poner a flote; hacer flotar; (a grounded ship) desencallar; (*com.*, a company) fundar; (a loan, etc.) emitir, poner en circulación; (launch a ship) botar; (flood) inundar

floating, *s.* flotación, *f.*, flote, *m.*; (*com.*) fundación (de una compañía), *f.*; (of a loan) emisión, *f.*; (of a ship) botadura, *f.* *a.* flotante; boyante; (*com.*) en circulación, flotante; fluctuante, variable. **f. capital**, capital fluctuante, *m.* **f. debt**, deuda flotante, *f.* **f. dock**, dique flotante, *m.* **f. light**, buque faro, *m.* **f. population**, población flotante, *f.* **f. rib**, costilla flotante, *f.*

flock, *s.* rebaño, *m.*, manada, *f.*; (of birds) bandada, *f.*; (*fig.*) grey, *f.*; (crowd) multitud, muchedumbre, *f.*; (parishioners) congregación, *f.*; (of wool or cotton) vedija (de lana o de algodón), *f.*; *pl.* **flocks**, (for stuffing) borra, *f.* *v.i.* concurrirse, reunirse, congregarse; ir en tropel, acudir; (birds) volar en bandada. **f.-bed**, colchón de borra, *m.*

floe, *s.* banco de hielo, *m.*

flog, *v.t.* azotar; castigar

flogging, *s.* azotamiento, vapuleo, *m.*

flood, *s.* inundación, *f.*; (Bible) diluvio, *m.*; (of the tide) flujo, *m.*; (*fig.*) torrente, *m.*; (abundance) copia, abundancia, *f.*; (fit) paroxismo, *m.* *v.t.* inundar; sumergir; (of tears) mojar. *v.i.* desbordar. **f. lighting**, iluminación intensiva, *f.*

floodgate, *s.* compuerta (de esclusa), *f.*

flooding, *s.* inundación, *f.*; desbordamiento, *m.*; (*med.*) hemorragia uterina, *f.*

floodtide, *s.* marea creciente, *f.*

floor, *s.* suelo, piso, *m.*; (wooden) entarimado, *m.*; (storey) piso, *m.*; (of a cart) cama, *f.*; (*agr.*) era, *f. v.t.* entablar; echar al suelo, derribar; (*fig.*) desconcertar, confundir. **on the f.,** en el suelo. **on the ground f.,** en el piso bajo. **to take the f.,** (*fig.*) tener la palabra. **f.-polisher,** lustrador de piso, *m.*

flooring, *s.* tablado, *m.*, tablazón, *f.*; piso, *m.*

flop, *s.* golpe, *m.*; ruido sordo, *m.*; (splash) chapoteo, *m.*; (*fam.*) fiasco, *m. v.i.* dejarse caer

flora, *s.* flora, *f.*

floral, *a.* floral. **f. games,** juegos florales, *m. pl.*

Florentine, *a.* and *s.* florentino (-na)

florescence, *s.* florescencia, *f.*

floret, *s.* flósculo, *m.*, florecilla, *f.*

floriculture, *s.* floricultura, *f.*

floriculturist, *s.* floricultor (-ra)

florid, *a.* florido; demasiado ornado, cursi, llamativo; (of complexion) rubicundo

floridness, *s.* floridez, *f.*, estilo florido, *m.*; demasiada ornamentación, vulgaridad, *f.*, mal gusto, *m.*; (of complexion) rubicundez, *f.*

florin, *s.* florín, *m.*

florist, *s.* florista, *m.* and *f.*

floss, *s.* seda floja, filoseda, *f.*; (of maize) penacho, *m.*; (of a cocoon) cadarzo, *m.* **f. silk,** seda floja, *f.*

flotilla, *s.* flotilla, *f.*

flotsam, *s.* pecio, *m.*

flounce, *s.* volante, *m. v.i.* saltar de impaciencia. **to f. out,** salir airadamente

flounder, *s.* (nearest equivalent) (*icht.*) platija, *f.*; tumbo, *m. v.i.* tropezar; revolcarse; andar dificultosamente

flour, *s.* harina, *f. v.t.* enharinar. **f.-bin,** tina, *f.*, harinero, *m.* **f. merchant,** harinero, *m.*

flourish, *s.* movimiento, *m.*; gesto, saludo, *m.*; (of a pen) plumada, *f.*; (on the guitar, in fencing) floreo, *m.*; preludio, *m.*; (fanfare) tocata (de trompetas), *f.*; (of a signature) rúbrica, *f.*; (in rhetoric) floreo, *m. v.i.* (of plants) vegetar; (prosper) prosperar, medrar; florecer; (of the guitar, in fencing) florear; (*mus.*) preludiar; (with a pen) hacer plumadas (or rasgos de pluma); (of a signature) firmar con rúbrica; (sound a fanfare) hacer una tocata (de trompetas). *v.t.* agitar en el aire, blandir

flourishing, *a.* (of plants) lozano; floreciente; (prosperous) próspero; (happy) feliz

flourmill, *s.* molino de harina, *m.*, fábrica de harina, *f.*

floury, *a.* harinoso

flout, *v.t.* burlarse de; despreciar, no hacer caso de

flow, *s.* flujo, *m.*; corriente, *f.*; chorro, *m.*; (of water) caudal, *m.*; (output) producción total, cantidad, *f.*; (of the tide) flujo (de la marea), *m.*; (of words) facilidad, *f. v.i.* fluir, manar; correr; (of the tide) crecer (la marea); (pass) pasar, correr; (result) resultar (de), provenir (de); (of hair, drapery) caer, ondular; (abound) abundar (en). **to f. away,** escaparse, salir. **to f. back,** refluir. **to f. down,** descender, fluir hacia abajo; (of tears) correr por. **to f. from,** dimanar de; manar de; (*fig.*) provenir de. **to f. in,** llegar en abundancia. **to f. into,** (rivers) desaguar en, desembocar en. **to f. over,** derramarse por. **to f. through,** fluir por; atravesar; (water) regar. **to f. together,** (rivers) confluir

flower, *s.* flor, *f.*; (best) flor y nata, crema, *f. v.i.* florecer. **in f.,** en flor. **No flowers by request,** (for a funeral) No flores por deseo del finado. **f.-bud,** capullo, *m.* **f.-garden,** jardín, *m.* **f. girl,** florista, vendedora de flores, *f.* **f. market,** mercado de flores, *m.* **f.-piece,** florero, *m.* **f. pot,** tiesto, *m.*, maceta, *f.* **f. show,** exposición de flores, *f.* **f. vase,** florero, *m.*

flowerbed, *s.* cuadro, macizo, *m.*

flowered, *a.* (in compounds) con flores; con dibujos de flores

floweriness, s. abundancia de flores, f.; (of style) floridez, f., estilo florido, m.

flowering, s. florecimiento, m. a. floreciente; con flores; (of shrubs) de adorno. **f. season,** época de la floración, f.

flowerless, a. sin flores

flowery, a. florido

flowing, s. flujo, m.; derrame, m. a. fluente, corriente; (of tide) creciente; (waving) ondeante; suelto; (of style) flúido

fluctuate, v.i. fluctuar, vacilar; variar

fluctuating, a. fluctuante, vacilante; variable; (hesitating) irresoluto, dudoso

fluctuation, s. fluctuación, f.; cambio, m., variación, f.; (hesitancy) indecisión, vacilación, f.

flue, s. (of a chimney) cañón, m.; (of a boiler) tubo, m.

fluency, s. fluidez, f.

fluent, a. flúido; fácil

fluently, adv. corrientemente, con facilidad

fluff, s. borra, pelusa, f., tamo, m.

fluffy, a. velloso; (feathered) plumoso; (woolly) lanudo; (of hair) encrespado

fluid, s. flúido, líquido, m. a. flúido

fluidity, s. fluidez, f.

fluke, s. (in billiards) chiripa, f.; (naut.) uña, f.; (fam.) carambola, chiripa, chambonada, f. **by a f.,** de carambola, por suerte. **f.-worm,** duela del hígado, f.

flunkey, s. lacayo, m.; (fig.) adulador, m.

fluorescence, s. fluorescencia, f.

fluorescent, a. fluorescente

fluorine, s. (chem.) flúor, m.

fluorite, s. fluorita, f.

flurry, s. (of wind) ráfaga, f.; (squall) chubasco, m.; agitación, f.; conmoción, f. v.t. agitar

flush, s. rubor, m.; (in the sky) arrebol, rojo, color de rosa, m.; emoción, f., acceso, m.; sensación, f.; (at cards) flux, m.; vigor, m.; (flowering) floración, f.; abundancia, f.; (of youth, etc.) frescura, f. a. (level) igual, parejo; abundante; (generous) pródigo, liberal; (rich) adinerado. v.i. ruborizarse, enrojecerse, ponerse colorado; (flood) inundarse,

llenarse (de agua, etc.); (of sky) arrebolarse. v.t. inundar, limpiar con un chorro de agua, etc., lavar; (of blood) circular por; (redden) enrojecer; (make blush) hacer ruborizarse; (exhilarate) excitar, animar; (inflame) inflamar, encender; (make level) igualar, nivelar. **f. with,** a ras de

flushing, s. rojez, f.; (cleansing) limpieza, lavadura, f.; (flooding) inundación, f.

fluster, s. agitación, confusión, f., aturdimiento, m. v.t. agitar, poner nervioso (a), aturdir; (oneself) preocuparse. v.i. agitarse; estar nervioso, estar perplejo; (with drink) estar entre dos velas

flute, s. flauta, f.; (arch.) estría, f.; (organ-stop) flautado, m. v.i. tocar la flauta, flautear; tener la voz flauteada. v.t. tocar (una pieza) en la flauta; (groove) encanutar, acanalar, estriar. **f. player,** flautista, m. and f.

fluted, a. (grooved) acanalado

fluting, s. (mus.) son de la flauta, m.; (of birds) trinado, m.; (arch.) estría, f.; (sew.) rizado, m.

flutter, s. (of wings) aleteo, m.; (of leaves, etc.) murmurio, m.; (of eyelashes) pestañeo, m.; (of flags, etc.) ondeo, m., ondulación, f.; (excitement) agitación, f.; (stir) sensación, f.; (gamble) jugada, f. v.i. (of birds) aletear; revolotear; (of butterflies) mariposear; (of flags) ondear; palpitar; (of persons) estar agitado. v.t. agitar; (the eyelashes) pestañear; (agitate) agitar, alarmar

fluttering, s. mariposeo, m.; revoloteo, m.; (of birds) aleteo, m.; (of leaves, etc.) murmurio, m.; (of flags, etc.) ondeo, m., ondulación, f.; (of eyelashes) pestañeo, m.

fluvial, a. fluvial

flux, s. flujo, m.

fly, s. (insect) mosca, f.; (on a fish-hook) mosca artificial, f.; (carriage) calesín, m.; (of breeches) bragueta, f.; (theat.) bambalina, f.; (of a tent) toldo, m.; (flight) vuelo, m.; (of a flag) vuelo, m. **fly-blown,** manchado por las moscas. **fly-by-night,** trasnochador (-ra). **fly-catcher,** (orn.) papamoscas, m.; matamoscas, m. **fly-fishing,**

pesca con moscas artificiales, *f.*
fly-leaf, guarda (de un libro), *f.*
fly-paper, papel matamoscas,
m. **fly-swatter,** matamoscas, *m.*
fly-wheel, (*mech.*) volante, *m.*
fly, *v.i.* volar; (flutter) ondear;
(jump) saltar; (rush) lanzarse,
precipitarse; (pass away) pasar
volando, volar; (run off) marcharse a todo correr; (escape)
huir, escapar; (seek refuge)
refugiarse; (to the head, of
intoxicants) subirse; (vanish)
desaparecer. *v.t.* hacer volar;
hacer ondear, enarbolar; (an
aeroplane) pilotar, dirigir; (flee
from) huir de; evitar. **to let fly**
(at), descargar, tirar; (*fig.*) saltar
la sinhueso. **to fly about,** volar
en torno de; revolotear. **to fly
at,** lanzarse sobre; acometer,
asaltar. **to fly away,** emprender
el vuelo. **to fly back,** volar hacia
el punto de partida; (of doors,
etc.) abrir, or cerrar, de repente.
to fly down, volar abajo. **to
fly in,** volar dentro de; volar
adentro; (of aeroplanes) llegar
(el avión). **to fly in pieces,**
hacerse pedazos. **to fly into a
rage,** montarse en cólera. **to fly
low,** rastrear; (*aer.*) volar a poca
altura. **to fly off,** emprender el
vuelo; (hasten) marcharse volando; (of buttons, etc.) saltar (de),
separarse (de). **to fly open,**
abrirse de repente. **to fly over,**
volar por, volar por encima de.
to fly upwards, volar hacia
arriba; subir
flying, *s.* vuelo, *m.* *a.* volante,
volador; que vuela; de volar;
volátil; (hasty) rápido; (flowing)
ondeante, ondulante. **to shoot
f.,** tirar al vuelo. **with f. colours,**
con banderas desplegadas, triunfante. **f.-boat,** hidroavión, *m.*
f.-bomb, bomba volante, *f.* **f.-
bomb attack,** fuego de repre-
salías del arma V., *m.* **f.-
buttress,** botarel, arbotante, *m.*
f.-column, (*mil.*) cuerpo volante,
m. **f.-fish,** (pez) volador, *m.* **f.-
fortress,** (*aer.*) fortaleza volante,
f. **f.-officer,** oficial de aviación,
m. **f.-sickness,** mal de altura,
m. **f.-squad,** escuadra ligera, *f.*
f.-test, (*aer.*) examen de pilotaje,
m.

foal, *s.* potro (-ra). *v.i.* and *v.t.*
parir una yegua
foam, *s.* espuma, *f.* *v.i.* espumar;
(of horses, etc.) echar espuma-
rajos. **to f. and froth,** (of the
sea) hervir
foamy, *a.* espumoso
fob, *s.* bolsillo del reloj, *m.*; faltriquera pequeña, *f.* *v.t.* (off)
engañar con
focal, *a.* focal
focus, *s.* foco, *m.*; centro, *m.* *v.t.*
enfocar; concentrar. *v.i.* conver-
gir. **in f.,** en foco
fodder, *s.* (*agr.*) pienso, forraje,
m. *v.t.* dar forraje (a)
foe, *s.* enemigo, *m.*
foetal, *a.* fetal
foetus, *s.* feto, *m.*
fog, *s.* neblina, niebla, *f.*; (*fig.*)
confusión, *f.*; (*fig.*) perplejidad, *f.*
v.t. obscurecer; (*phot.*) velar;
(*fig.*) ofuscar. *v.i.* hacerse nebuloso; (*phot.*) velarse. **fog-signal,** señal de niebla, *f.*
fogbound, *a.* rodeado de niebla;
detenido por la niebla
fogey, *s.* obscurantista, *m.* **He is
an old f.,** Él es un señor chapado
a la antigua
fogginess, *s.* oscuridad, neblina,
f.
foggy, *a.* nebuloso; (*phot.*) velado. **It is f.,** Hay niebla
foghorn, *s.* sirena, *f.*; bocina, *f.*
foible, *s.* flaco, *m.*, debilidad,
f.
foil, *s.* (sword) florete, *m.*; (coat)
hoja, *f.*; (of a mirror) azogado,
m. *v.t.* frustrar. **She makes a
good f. for her sister's beauty,**
Ella hace resaltar la belleza de
su hermana
foiling, *s.* frustración, *f.*
foist, *v.t.* imponer; insertar,
incluir; engañar (con)
fold, *s.* doblez, *f.*, pliegue, *m.*;
arruga, *f.*; (*sew.*) cogido, *m.*; (for
sheep) redil, aprisco, *m.*; (*fig.*)
iglesia, congregación de los fieles,
f.; (in compounds) vez, *f.* *v.t.*
doblar, plegar, doblegar; (the
arms) cruzar (los brazos); (embrace) abrazar; (wrap) envolver;
(clasp) entrelazar; (sheep) meter
en redil, encerrar. *v.i.* doblarse,
plegarse; cerrarse
folder, *s.* doblador (-ra); plegadera, *f.*

folding, s. plegadura, f., dobla-miento, m.; (of sheep) encerra-miento, m. a. plegadizo. f.-door, puerta plegadiza, f. f.-machine, plegador, m. f.-seat, (aut.) traspuntín, m. f.-table, mesa de tijeras, f.; mesa plega-diza, f.

foliage, s. follaje; m., frondas, f. pl. thick f., frondosidad, f.

folio, s. folio, m.; (a volume) in-folio, m. a. de infolio. v.t. foliar

folk, s. (nation) pueblo, m., nación, f.; gente, f.; pl. folks, (fam.) familia, f.; parientes, m. pl. f.-dance, danza popular, f.

folklore, s. folklore. m., tradi-ciones folklóricas, f. pl.

folklorist, s. folklorista, m. and f.

folksong, s. canción popular, f.; romance, m.; copla, f.

folktale, s. conseja, f., cuento popular, m.

follicle, s. (anat., bot.) folículo, m.

follow, v.t. seguir; (pursue) perse-guir; (hunt) cazar; (adopt) adop-tar; (understand) comprender; (notice) observar. v.i. ir, or venir, detrás; (of time) venir después; (gen. impers.) seguir, resultar; seguirse. as follows, como sigue. I shall f. your advice, Seguiré tus consejos. to f. on the heels of, (fig.) pisar los talones (a). to f. suit, (at cards) asistir, jugar el mismo palo; (fig.) imitar. to f. up, proseguir; continuar; (pursue) perseguir; (enhance) reforzar. f.-me-lads, (fam.) síguemepollo, m.

follower, s. seguidor (-ra); ad-herente, secuaz, m. and f.; (imitator) imitador (-ra); (lover) novio, m.; pl. followers, acom-pañamiento, séquito, m.

following, s. séquito, acompaña-miento, m., comitiva, f.; parti-darios, m. pl., adherentes, m. and f. pl. a. siguiente; próximo. f. wind, viento en popa, m.

folly, s. locura, extravagancia, absurdidad, tontería, f., dispa-rate, m.

foment, v.t. (poultice) fomentar; provocar, incitar, instigar; (as-sist) fomentar, proteger, pro-mover

fomentation, s. (med.) fomenta-ción, f.; provocación, instiga-ción, f.; fomento, m., protección, f.

fomenter, s. fomentador (ra-), instigador (-ra)

fond, a. (credulous) vano, cré-dulo, vacío; (doting) demasiado indulgente; (loving) cariñoso, tierno, afectuoso; (addicted to) aficionado a, adicto a, amigo de. to be f. of, (things) tener afición a, estar aficionado de; (people) tener cariño (a). to grow f. of, (things) aficionarse a; (people) tomar cariño (a)

fondle, v.t. mimar, acariciar; jugar (con.)

fondly, adv. (vainly) vanamente, sin razón; cariñosamente, tierna-mente

fondness, s. cariño, afecto, m.; (for things) afición, inclinación, f.; gusto, m.

font, s. pila bautismal, f.; (poet.) fuente, f.; (print.) fundición, f.

food, s. alimento, m.; comida, f., el comer; (of animals) pasto, m.; (fig.) pábulo, m.; materia, f. She gave him f., Ella le dió de comer. You have given me f. for thought, Me has dado en qué pensar. f.-card, cartilla de racionamiento, f. F. Ministry, Ministerio de Alimentación, m. f. value, valor nutritivo, m.

foodstuffs, s. pl. comestibles, víveres, m. pl.

fool, s. tonto (-ta), mentecato (-ta), majadero (ra) necio (-ia); (jester) bufón, m.; (butt of jest) hazmerreír, m.; víctima, f.; (cul.) compota de frutas con crema, f. v.i. tontear, hacer tonterías. v.t. poner en ridículo (a); (de-ceive) engañar, embaucar; (with) jugar con. to make a f. of one-self, ponerse en ridículo. to f. about, v.i. perder el tiempo, vagabundear. to f. away, mal-gastar, malbaratar. fool's bauble, cetro de bufón, m. fool's cap, gorro de bufón, m.

foolhardiness, s. temeridad, f.

foolhardy, a. temerario, atrevido

fooling, s. payasada, bufonada, f.; (deceiving) engaño, m., burla, f.

foolish, a. imprudente; estúpido, tonto; ridículo, absurdo; imbécil

foolishly, adv. imprudentemente; tontamente; imbécilmente

foolishness, s. imprudencia, f.; estupidez, tontería, f., disparate, m.; ridiculez, f.; imbecilidad, f.

foolproof, a. (of utensils, etc.) con garantía absoluta

foolscap, s. (nearest equivalent) papel de barba, m.

foot, s. pie, m.; (of animals, furniture) pata, f.; (of bed, sofa, grave, ladder, page, etc.) pie, m.; (hoof) pezuña, f.; (metric unit and measure) pie, m.; (mil.) infantería, f.; (base) base, f.; (step) paso, m. a. (mil.) de a pie; a pie. v.i. ir a pie; venir a pie; bailar. v.t. hollar; (account) pagar (una cuenta); (stockings) poner pie (a). on f., a pie; (of soldiers) de a pie; (in progress) en marcha. to go on f., ir a pie, andar. to put one's best f. forward, apretar el paso; (fig.) hacer de su mejor. to put one's f. down, poner pies en pared. to put one's f. in it, meter la pata. to rise to one's feet, ponerse de pie. to set f. on, pisar, hollar. to set on f., poner en pie; (fig.) poner en marcha. to trample under f., pisotear. f.-and-mouth disease, glosopeda, f. f.-brake, freno de pedal, m. f.-pump, fuelle de pie, m. f.-rule, (nearest equivalent) doble decímetro, m. f.-soldier, soldado de a pie, infante, m.

football, s. (game) fútbol, m.; (ball) pelota de fútbol, f. f. field, campo de fútbol, m. f. match, partida de fútbol, f. f. pools, apuestas de fútbol, f. pl.; (in Spain) apuestas benéficas de fútbol, f. pl.

footballer, s. futbolista, m.

footbath, s. baño de pies, m.

footboard, s. estribo, m.

footbridge, s. puente para peatones, m.

footed, a. con pies; de pies ...; de patas ...

footfall, s. pisada, f., paso, m.

foothills, s. pl. faldas de la montaña, f. pl.

foothold, s. hincapié, m.; posición establecida, f.

footing, s. hincapié, m.; posición firme, f.; condiciones, f. pl.; relaciones, f. pl. on a peacetime f., en pie de paz. to be on an equal f., estar en pie de igualdad, estar en iguales condiciones. to miss one's f., resbalar

footlights, s. pl. canilejas, candilejas, f. pl. to get across the f., hacer contacto con el público

footman, s. lacayo, m.

footmuff, s. fólgo, m., bolsa de pieles, f.

footnote, s. nota al pie de una página, f.

footpad, s. salteador de caminos, m.

footpath, s. senda, vereda, f.; sendero, m.

footprint, s. huella, pisada, f., vestigio, m.

footsore, a. con los pies lastimados

footstep, s. paso, m.; (trace) pisada, huella, f. to follow in the footsteps of, (fig.) seguir las pisadas de

footstool, s. escabel, banquito, m.

footwarmer, s. calientapiés, m.

footwear, s. calzado, m.

fop, s. petimetre, m.

foppery, s. afectación en el vestir, f.; vanidad, f.

foppish, a. presumido, afectado; elegante

for, prep. (expressing exchange, price or penalty of, instead of, in support or favour of, on account of) por; (expressing destination, purpose, result) para; (during) durante, por; (for the sake of) para; (because of) a causa de; (in spite of) a pesar de; (as) como; (with) de; (in favour of) en favor de; (towards) hacia; (that) que, para que (with subjunc.); a; (before) antes de; (searching for) en busca de; (bound for) con rumbo a; (regarding) en cuanto a; (until) hasta. He is in business for himself, Tiene negocios por su propia cuenta. It is raining too hard for you to go there, Llueve demasiado para que vayas allí. It is not for him to decide, No le toca a él decidirlo. Were it not for ..., Si no fuese por ... She has not been to see me for a week, Hace una semana que no viene a verme. It is impossible for them to go out, Les es imposible salir. but for all that, pero con todo. **for ever**, por (or para) siempre. **for fear that**, por miedo de que. **for myself**, en cuanto a mí, personalmente. **for the present**, por ahora. **for what reason ?** ¿ para qué ? ¿ por cuál motivo ?

for, *conjunc.* porque; visto que, pues, puesto que, en efecto, ya que

forage, *s.* forraje, *m.* *v.t.* and *v.i.* forrajear. **to f. for**, buscar. **f. cap**, gorra de cuartel, *f.*

forager, *s.* forrajeador, *m.*

foraging, *s.* forraje, *m.*

forasmuch as, *conjunc.* puesto que, como que, ya que

foray, *s.* correría, cabalgada, *f.*; saqueo, *m.*

forbear, *v.t.* and *v.i.* dejar (de), guardarse (de); abstenerse de; evitar; reprimirse (de); rehusarse (de); (cease) cesar (de); (be patient) ser paciente; ser tolerante

forbear, *s.* antecesor, *m.*, ascendiente, *m.* and *f.*

forbearance, *s.* abstención, *f.*; tolerancia, transigencia, *f.*; indulgencia, *f.*; paciencia, *f.*

forbearing, *a.* tolerante, transigente; generoso, magnánimo; paciente

forbid, *v.t.* prohibir, defender (de); impedir. **I f. you to do it**, Te prohíbo hacerlo. **The game is forbidden**, El juego está prohibido. **They have forbidden me to . . .**, Me han defendido de . . ., **Heaven f.!** ¡Dios no lo quiera!

forbidden, *a.* prohibido; ilícito. **f. fruit**, fruto prohibido; *m.*

forbidding, *a.* repugnante, horrible; antipático, desagradable; (dismal) lúgubre; (threatening) amenazador. *s.* prohibición, *f.*

force, *s.* fuerza, *f.*; violencia, *f.*; vigor, *m.*; (efficacy) eficacia, *f.*; (validity) validez, *f.*; (power) poder, *m.*; (motive) motivo, *m.*, razón, *f.*; (weight) peso, *m.*, importancia, *f.*; (police) policía, *f.*; *pl.* **forces**, (*mil.*) fuerzas, tropas, *f. pl.* **by main f.**, por fuerza mayor. **in f.**, vigente, en vigor. **to be in f.**, estar vigente

force, *v.t.* forzar; (compel) obligar, constreñir, precisar; (ravish) violar; (*cul.*) rellenar; (impose) imponer; (plants) forzar; (the pace) apresurar; (cause) hacer; (a lock, etc.) forzar. **to f. oneself into**, entrar a la fuerza en; (a garment) ponerse con dificultad; imponerse a la fuerza. **to f. oneself to**, esforzarse a. **to f. the pace** forzar el paso. **to f. away**, ahuyentar. **to f. back**, hacer retroceder; rechazar; (a. sigh, etc.) ahogar. **to f. down**, hacer bajar, obligar a bajar; (make swallow) hacer tragar; (of aeroplanes) hacer tomar tierra. **to f. in**, introducir a la fuerza; obligar a entrar. **to f. into**, meter a la fuerza; obligar a entrar (en). **to f. on**, upon, imponer. **to f. open**, abrir a la fuerza; (a lock) romper, forzar. **to f. out**, hacer salir; empujar hacia fuera; (words) pronunciar con dificultad. **to f. up**, obligar a subir; hacer subir; hacer vomitar

forced, *a.* forzado; forzoso; afectado. **f. landing**, (*aer.*) aterrizaje forzoso, *m.* **f. march**, (*mil.*) marcha forzada, *f.*

forceful, *a.* See **forcible**

forcemeat, *s.* picadillo, *m.*; relleno, *m.* **f. ball**, albóndiga, *f*

forceps, *s. pl.* fórceps, *m. pl.*; pinzas, *f. pl.* **arterial f.**, pinzas hemostáticas, *f. pl.*

forcible, *a.* fuerte; a la fuerza; violento; enérgico, vigoroso; poderoso; (*lit.*) vívido, gráfico, vehemente. **f. feeding**, alimentación forzosa, *f.*

forcibleness, *s.* fuerza, *f.*; vigor, *m.*, energía, *f.*; vehemencia, *f.*

forcibly, *adv.* a la fuerza

forcing, *s.* forzamiento, *m.*; compulsión, *f.* **f. frame**, semillero, *m.*, especie de invernadero, *f.*

ford, *s.* vado, *m.* *v.t.* vadear

fordable, *a.* vadeable

fore, *a.* delantero; (*naut.*) de proa. *adv.* delante; (*naut.*) de proa. **f.-and-aft**, (*naut.*) de popa a proa.

forearm, *s.* antebrazo, *m.* *v.t.* armar de antemano; preparar

forebode, *v.t.* presagiar, augurar, anunciar; presentir

foreboding, *s.* presagio, augurio, *m.*; presentimiento, *m.*, corazonada, *f.*

forecast, *s.* pronóstico, *m.*; proyecto, plan, *m.* *v.t.* pronosticar;

proyectar. **weather f.,** pronóstico del tiempo, *m.*

forecastle, *s.* (*naut.*) castillo de proa, *m.*

foreclose, *v.t.* excluir; impedir; vender por orden judicial; anticipar el resultado de; decidir de antemano

foreclosure, *s.* venta por orden judicial, *f.*; juicio hipotecario, *m.*

foredoom, *v.t.* predestinar

forefather, *s.* antepasado, antecesor, *m.*

forefinger, *s.* índice, dedo índice, *m.*

forefoot, *s.* pata delantera, *f.*

forefront, *s.* delantera, primera línea, *f.*; frente, *m.*; vanguardia, *f.* **in the f.,** en la vanguardia; en el frente

foregoing, *a.* precedente, anterior

foregone, *a.* decidido de antemano; previsto

foreground, *s.* primer plano, primer término, frente, *m.* **in the f.,** (*art*) en primer término

forehand, *a.* derecho. **f. stroke,** golpe derecho, *m.*

forehead, *s.* frente, *f.*

foreign, *a.* extranjero; extraño; exótico; exterior; (alien) ajeno. **f. affairs,** asuntos extranjeros, *m. pl.* **f. body,** cuerpo extraño, *m.* **f. debt,** deuda exterior, *f.* **F. Legion,** tercio extranjero, *m.* **F. Office,** Ministerio de Relaciones Extranjeras, *m.* **f. parts,** extranjero, *m.* **f. policy,** política internacional, *f.* **F. Secretary,** Secretario de Asuntos Extranjeros, Secretario de Asuntos Exteriores, Ministro de Relaciones Extranjeras, *m.* **f. trade,** comercio con el extranjero, *m.*

foreigner, *s.* extranjero (-ra)

foreignness, *s.* extranjerismo, *m.*; (strangeness) extrañeza, *f.*; lo exótico

foreknowledge, *s.* presciencia, precognición, *f.*

foreland, *s.* promontorio, cabo, *m.*

foreleg, *s.* pata delantera, *f.*

forelock, *s.* guedeja, vedeja, *f.*; (of a horse) copete, tupé, *m.* **to take time by the f.,** asir la ocasión por la melena

foreman, *s.* (of jury) presidente (del jurado), *m.*; (of a farm)

mayoral, *m.*; (in a works) capataz, *m.*

foremost, *a.* delantero; de primera fila; más importante. *adv.* en primer lugar; en primera fila

forensic, *a.* forense, legal. **f. medicine,** medicina legal, *f.*

foreordained, *a.* predestinado

forerunner, *s.* precursor (-ra), predecesor (-ra); (presage) anuncio, presagio, *m.*

foresail, *s.* vela de trinquete, *f.*

foresee, *v.t.* prever, anticipar

foreseeing, *a.* presciente, sagaz

foreseer, *s.* previsor (-ra)

foreshadow, *v.t.* anunciar, prefigurar; simbolizar; hacer sentir.

foreshore, *s.* playa, *f.*

foreshorten, *v.t.* (*art*) escorzar

foreshortening, *s.* (*art*) escorzo, *m.*

foresight, *s.* presciencia, *f.*; previsión, prudencia, *f.*; (of gun) punto de mira, *m.*; (optical) croquis de nivel, *m.*

forest, *s.* bosque, *m.*, selva, *f.* *v.t.* arbolar

forestal, *a.* selvático, forestal

forestall, *v.t.* anticipar, saltear; prevenir; (*com.*) acaparar

forestalling, *s.* anticipación, *f.*

forestation, *s.* repoblación forestal, *f.*

forester, *s.* silvicultor, guardamonte, ingeniero forestal, *m.*; habitante de los bosques, *m.*

forestry, *s.* silvicultura, *f.*

foresworn, *a.* perjuro

foretaste, *s.* muestra, *f.*; presagio, *m.* *v.t.* gustar con anticipación

foretell, *v.t.* predecir, profetizar; anunciar, presagiar

foreteller, *s.* profeta, *m.*; presagio, *m.*

foretelling, *s.* profecía, predicción, *f.*

forethought, *s.* presciencia, previsión, *f.*; prevención, *f.*

foretop, *s.* (*naut.*) cofa de trinquete, *f.*

forewarn, *v.t.* prevenir

forewarning, *s.* presagio, *m.*

forewoman, *s.* encargada, *f.*; primera oficiala, *f.*

foreword, *s.* prefacio, *m.*, introducción, *f.*

forfeit, *s.* pérdida, *f.*; (fine) multa, *f.*; (in games) prenda, *f.*; (of rights, goods, etc.) confiscación, *f. a.* confiscado. *v.t.* perder; perder el derecho o el título de

forfeiture, *s.* pérdida, *f.*; confiscación, *f.*; secuestro, *m.*

forgather, *v.i.* reunirse

forge, *s.* fragua, *f.*; (smithy) herrería, *f. v.t.* and *v.i.* fraguar, forjar; (fabricate) inventar, fabricar; falsificar; (advance) avanzar lentamente. **to f. ahead,** abrirse camino; avanzar

forged, *a.* (of iron) forjado; (of cheques, etc.) falso, falsificado

forger, *s.* falsificador (-ra), falsario (-ia); (creator) artífice, *m.* and *f.*

forgery, *s.* falsificación, *f.*

forget, *v.t.* olvidar; descuidar. *v.i.* olvidarse. **to f. about,** olvidarse de, desacordarse de. **to f. oneself,** olvidarse de sí mismo; propasarse; (in anger) perder los estribos

forgetful, *a.* olvidadizo; descuidado, negligente

forgetfulness, *s.* olvido, *m.*; descuido, *m.*; falta de memoria, *f.*

forget-me-not, *s.* (*bot.*) miosota nomeolvides, *f.*

forging, *s.* fraguado, *m.*; falsificación, *f.*

forgivable, *a.* perdonable, excusable

forgive, *v.t.* perdonar, disculpar, condonar; (debts) remitir

forgiveness, *s.* perdón, *m.*; condonación, *f.*; (remission) remisión, *f.*

forgiving, *a.* misericordioso, clemente, dispuesto a perdonar

forgo, *v.t.* renunciar, sacrificar, privarse de; abandonar, ceder

forgoing, *s.* renunciación, *f.*, sacrificio, *m.*; cesión, *f.*

fork, *s.* (*agr.*) horca, horquilla, *f.*; (table-fork) tenedor, *m.*; bifurcación, *f.*; (of rivers) confluencia, *f.*; (of branches) horcadura, *f.*; (of legs) horcajadura, *f.*; (for supporting trees, etc.) horca, *f.*; (*mus.*) diapasón normal, *m. v.t.* hacinar con horca. *v.i.* bifurcarse; ramificarse

forked, *a.* bifurcado, hendido, ahorquillado. **f. lightning,** relámpago, *m.* **f. tail,** cola hendida, *f.*

forlorn, *a.* abandonado, desamparado, desesperado. **f. hope,** aventura desesperada, *f.*

forlornness, *s.* desamparo, *m.*, miseria, *f.*; desolación, *f.*, desconsuelo, *m.*

form, *s.* forma, *f.*; figura, *f.*; (shadowy) bulto, *m.*; (formality) formalidad, *f.*; ceremonia, *f.*; (*ecc.*) rito, *m.*; método, *m.*; regla, *f.*; (in a school) clase, *f.*; (lair) cama, *f.*; (seat) banco, *m.*; (system) sistema, *m.* (ghost) espectro, *m.*; aparición, *f.*; (to fill up) documento, *m.*; hoja, *f.*; (state) condición, *f.*; (*lit.*) construcción, forma, *f.* **It is a matter of f.,** Es una pura formalidad. **in due f.,** en debida forma, en regla. **in the usual f.,** (*com.*) al usado. **It is not good f.,** No es de buena educación

form, *v.t.* formar; (a habit) contraer; (an idea) hacerse (una idea). *v.i.* formarse. **to f. fours,** (*mil.*) formar a cuatro

formal, *a.* esencial; formal; ceremonioso, solemne; (of person) etiquetero, formalista. **f. call,** visita de cumplido, *f.*

formaldehyde, *s.* formaldehido, *m.*

formalin, *s.* formalina, *f.*

formalism, *s.* formalismo, *m.*

formality, *s.* formalidad, *f.*; ceremonia, solemnidad, *f.*

formally, *adv.* formalmente

format, *s.* formato, *m.*

formation, *s.* formación, *f.*; disposición, *f.*, arreglo, *m.*; organización, *f.*; (*mil.*, *geol.*) formación, *f.*

formative, *a.* formativo

forme, *s.* (*print.*) forma, *f.*, molde, *m.*

former, *a.* primero; antiguo; anterior; pasado. **in f. times,** antes, antiguamente. **the f.,** ése, aquél, *m.*; ésa, aquélla, *f.*; aquéllos, *m. pl.*; aquéllas, *f. pl.*

former, *s.* formador (-ra); creador (-ra), autor (-ra)

formerly, *adv.* antiguamente, antes

formidable, *a.* formidable; terrible, espantoso

formidableness, *s.* lo formidable; carácter formidable, *m.*

formless, *a.* informe

formlessness, *s.* falta de forma, *f.*

formula, *s.* fórmula, *f.* **standard f.,** (*math., chem.*) fórmula clásica, *f.*

formulate, *v.t.* formular

formulism, *s.* formalismo, *m.*

fornicate, *v.i.* fornicar

fornication, *s.* fornicación, *f.*

fornicator, *s.* fornicador (-ra)

forsake, *v.t.* dejar; desertar; abandonar, desamparar; separarse de; (of birds, the nest) aborrecer; (one's faith) renegar de

forsaker, *s.* el, *m.* (*f.* la) que abandona; desertor, *m.*; renegado (-da)

forsooth, *adv.* ciertamente, claro está

forswear, *v.t.* abjurar; renunciar a. **to f. oneself,** perjurarse

forswearing, *s.* abjuración, *f.*; renuncia, *f.*; perjurio, *m.*

fort, *s.* fortaleza, *f.*, fuerte, *m.*

forte, *s.* fuerte, *m.* *a.* (*mus.*) fuerte

forth, *adv.* (on) adelante, hacia adelante; (out) fuera; (in time) en adelante, en lo consecutivo; (show) a la vista. **and so f.,** y así en lo sucesivo; etcetera

forthcoming, *a.* próximo; futuro; en preparación

forthwith, *adv.* en seguida, sin tardanza

fortieth, *a.* cuadragésimo; cuarenta. *s.* cuarentavo, *m.*

fortifiable, *a.* fortificable

fortification, *s.* fortificación, *f.*

fortify, *v.t.* fortificar; fortalecer; confirmar; (*fig.*) proveer (de)

fortitude, *s.* aguante, *m.*, fortaleza, *f.*, estoicismo, *m.*

fortnight, *s.* quince días, *m. pl.*, dos semanas, *f. pl.*; quincena, *f.* **a f. ago,** hace quince días. **a f. to-morrow,** mañana en quince. **in a f.,** dentro de quince días; al cabo de quince días. **once a f.,** cada quince días

fortnightly, *a.* quincenal. *adv.* cada dos semanas, dos veces al mes. *s.* revista quincenal, *f.*

fortress, *s.* fortaleza, plaza fuerte, *f.*

fortuitous, *a.* fortuito, accidental

fortuitously, *adv.* accidentalmente

fortuity, *s.* casualidad, *f.*; accidente, *m.*

fortunate, *a.* dichoso, feliz; afortunado; próspero. **to be f.,** (of persons) tener suerte

fortunately, *adv.* afortunadamente, por dicha, felizmente

fortune, *s.* suerte, fortuna, *f.*, destino, *m.*; (money) caudal, *m.*, fortuna, *f.*; bienes, *m. pl.*; buenaventura, *f.* **good f.,** buena fortuna, dicha, *f.* **ill f.,** mala suerte, *f.* **to cost a f.,** costar un sentido. **to make one's f.,** enriquecerse; (*fam.*) hacer su pacotilla. **to tell fortunes,** echar las cartas. **f.-hunter,** buscador de dotes, aventurero, *m.* **f.-teller,** adivinadora, *f.*; echadora de cartas, *f.* **f.-telling,** buenaventura, *f.*

forty, *a. and s.* cuarenta (*m.*). **He is turned f.,** Él ha cumplido los cuarenta. **person of f.,** cuarentón (-ona). **She is f.,** Ella tiene cuarenta años

forum, *s.* foro, *m.*

forward, *a.* avanzado; adelantado; (of position) delantero; (ready) preparado; (eager) pronto, listo, impaciente; activo, emprendedor; (of persons, fruit, etc.) precoz; (pert) insolente, desenvuelto, atrevido. *adv.* adelante; hacia adelante; (of time) en adelante; (farther on) más allá; hacia el frente; en primera linea. *v.t.* ayudar, promover; adelantar; (letters) hacer seguir; (*com.*) expedir, remitir; (a parcel) despachar; (hasten) apresurar; (plants) hacer crecer. *s.* (*sport*) delantero, *m.* **centre-f.,** (*sport*) delantero centro, *m.* **from this time f.,** de hoy en adelante. **Please f.,** ¡Haga seguir! **putting f. of the clock,** el adelanto de la hora. **to carry f.,** (*com.*) pasar a cuenta nueva. **to go f.,** adelantarse; estar en marcha, estar en preparación. **f. line,** (*sport*) delantera, *f.* **F.!** ¡Adelante!

forwarder, *s.* promotor (-ra); (*com.*) remitente, *m.*

forwarding, *s.* fomento, *m.*, promoción, *f.*; (*com.*) expedición, *f.*, envío, *m.*

forwardness, *s.* progreso, adelantamiento, *m.*; (haste) apresuramiento, *m.*; (of persons, fruit, etc.) precocidad, *f.*; (pertness) desenvoltura, insolencia, frescura, *f.*, descaro, *m.*; (eagerness) impaciencia, *f.*

fosse, *s.* foso, *m.*

fossil, *a.* and *s.* fósil (*m.*)

fossilization, *s.* fosilización, *f.*

fossilize, *v.t.* fosilizar; petrificar. *v.i.* fosilizarse

foster, *v.t.* provocar, promover, suscitar; (favour) favorecer, ser propicio a. **f.-brother,** hermano de leche, *m.* **f.-child,** hijo (-ja) de leche. **f.-father,** padre adoptivo, *m.* **f.-mother,** ama de leche, *f.* **f.-sister,** hermana de leche, *f.*

foul, *a.* sucio, asqueroso, puerco; (evil-smelling) hediondo, fétido; (of air) viciado; impuro; (language) ofensivo; (coarse) indecente, obsceno; (harmful) nocivo, dañino; (wicked) malvado; infame; vil; (unfair) injusto; (*sport*) sucio; (ugly) feo; (entangled) enredado; (with corrections) lleno de erratas; (choked) atascado; (of weather) borrascoso, tempestuoso; malo, desagradable; (repulsive) repugnante. *s.* (*sport*) juego sucio, *m.* *v.t.* ensuciar; (*naut.*) chocar, abordar; (block) atascar; (the anchor) enredar; (dishonour) deshonrar. *v.i.* atascarse; (anchor) enredarse; (*naut.*) chocar. **to fall f. of,** (*naut.*) abordar (un buque); (*fig.*) habérselas con. **by fair means or f.,** a las buenas o a las malas. **f. breath,** aliento fétido, aliento corrompido, *m.* **f. brood,** peste de las abejas, *f.* **f. language,** palabras ofensivas, *f. pl.*; lenguaje obsceno, *m.* **f. play,** juego sucio, *m.* **f. weather,** mal tiempo, tiempo borrascoso, *m.*

found, *v.t.* fundar; (metal, glass) fundir; (create, etc.) establecer

foundation, *s.* fundación, *f.*; establecimiento, *m.*; creación, *f.*; (*arch.*) cimiento, embasamiento, *m.*; (basis) base, *f.*; (cause) causa, *f.*, origen, principio, *m.*; (endowment) dotación, *f.*; refuerzo, *m.* **to lay the f.,** poner las fundaciones. **f. stone,** piedra angular, *f.*; (*fig.*) primera piedra, *f.* **to lay the f. stone,** poner la piedra angular

founder, *s.* fundador (-ra); (of metals) fundidor, *m.* *v.t.* (a ship)

hacer zozobrar. *v.i.* zozobrar, irse a pique; (*fig.*) fracasar

foundering, *s.* (*naut.*) zozobra, *f.*

founding, *s.* fundación, *f.*; establecimiento, *m.*; (of metals) fundición, *f.*

foundling, *s.* hijo (-ja) de la cuna, expósito (-ta). **f. hospital or home,** casa cuna, inclusa, *f.*

foundress, *s.* fundadora, *f.*

foundry, *s.* fundición, *f.*

fountain, *s.* fuente, *f.*; (spring) manantial, *m.*; (jet) chorro, *m.*; (artificial) fuente, *f.*, surtidero, *m.*; (source) origen, principio, *m.* **f. head,** fuente, *f.* **f. pen,** pluma estilográfica, *f.*

four, *a.* and *s.* cuatro (*m.*). **It is f. o'clock,** Son las cuatro. **She is f.,** Ella tiene cuatro años. **on all fours,** a gatas. **f.-course,** (of meals) de cuatro platos. **f.-engined,** cuadrimotor. **f.-engined 'plane,** cuadrimotor, *m.* **f.-footed,** cuadrúpedo. **f.-horse,** de cuatro caballos. **f. hundred,** cuatrocientos. **f.-in-hand,** tiro par, *m.* **f.-part,** (of a song) a cuatro voces. **f.-wheel brakes,** freno en las cuatro ruedas, *m.*

fourfold, *a.* cuádruple

fourpence, *s.* cuatro peniques, *m. pl.*

fourpenny, *a.* que cuesta cuatro peniques, de cuatro peniques

fourposter, *s.* cama de matrimonio, *f.*

fourscore, *a.* and *s.* ochenta (*m.*)

foursome, *s.* partido de cuatro personas, *m.*

fourteen, *a.* and *s.* catorce (*m.*). **He is f.,** Tiene catorce años

fourteenth, *a.* and *s.* décimocuarto (*m.*); (of the month) (el) catorce, *m.*; (of monarchs) catorce. **April f.,** El 14 (catorce) de abril

fourth, *a.* cuarto; (of the month) el cuatro; (of monarchs) cuarto. *s.* (fourth part) cuarta parte, *f.*; (*mus.*) cuarta, *f.* **f. dimension,** cuarta dimensión, *f.* **f. term,** (U.S.A. *pol.*) cuarto mandato, *m.*

fourthly, *adv.* en cuarto lugar

fowl, *s.* gallo, *m.*; gallina, *f.*; (chicken) pollo, *m.*; (bird) ave, *f.*; (barndoor f.) ave de corral, *f.*

v.i. cazar aves. **f.-house** or **run**, gallinero, *m.*

fox, *s.* zorro, *m.*; (vixen) zorra, raposa, *f.*; (*fig.*) zorro, taimado, *m. v.i.* disimular. *v.t.* (books) descolorar. **f.-brush**, cola de raposa, *f.* **f.-earth**, zorrera, *f.* **f.-hunting**, caza de zorras, *f.* **f. terrier**, "fox terrier," *m.*

foxglove, *s.* digital, dedalera; *f.*

foxhound, *s.* perro zorrero, *m.*

foxiness, *s.* zorrería, astucia, *f.*

foxtrot, *s.* "foxtrot," *m.*

foxy, *a.* de zorro; zorrero, astuto

foyer, *s.* foyer. salón de descanso, *m.*

fraction, *s.* (*math.*) fracción, *f.*, número quebrado, *m.*; pequeña parte, *f.*; fragmento, *m.* **improper f.**, (*math.*) fracción impropia, *f.* **proper f.**, (*math.*) fracción propia, *f.*

fractional, *a.* fraccionario

fractious, *a.* malhumorado, enojadizo

fractiousness, *s.* mal humor, *m.*

fracture, *s.* (*surg.*) fractura, *f. v.t.* fracturar. **compound f.**, fractura conminuta, *f.*

fragile, *a.* frágil, quebradizo; (of persons) delicado

fragility, *s.* fragilidad, *f.*

fragment, *s.* fragmento, *m.*; trozo, pedazo, *m.* **to break into fragments**, hacer pedazos, hacer añicos

fragmentary, *a.* fragmentario

fragrance, *s.* fragancia, *f.*, buen olor, perfume, aroma, *m.*

fragrant, *a.* fragante, oloroso. **to make f.**, perfumar

frail, *a.* frágil, quebradizo; débil, endeble. *s.* capacho, *m.*, espuerta, *f.*

frailty, *s.* fragilidad, *f.*; debilidad, *f.*

frame, *s.* constitución, *f.*; sistema, *m.*; organización, *f.*; (of the body) figura, *f.*, talle, *m.*; (of window, picture) marco, *m.*; (of machine, building) armadura, *f.*; (of a bicycle) cuadro (de bicicleta), *m.*; (*agr.*) cajonera, *f.*; (embroidery) bastidor (para bordar), *m.*; (skeleton) esqueleto, *m.*; (*lit.*) composición, construcción, *f.*; (of spectacles) armadura, *f.*; (of mind) disposición (de ánimo), ; humor, *m. v.t.* formar; construir; arreglar; ajustar; (a picture) enmarcar; componer, hacer; (draw up) redactar; (think up) idear, inventar; (words) articular, pronunciar

framer, *s.* fabricante de marcos, *m.*; autor (-ra), creador (-ra), inventor (-ra)

framework, *s.* armadura, armazón, *f.*, esqueleto, *m.*; organización, *f.*; (basis) base, *f.*

franc, *s.* (coin) franco, *m.*

franc-tireur, *s.* francotirador, *m.*

franchise, *s.* (exemption) franquicia, *f.*; privilegio, *m.*; (vote) derecho de sufragio, *m.*; (citizenship) derecho político, *m.*

Franciscan, *a.* and *s.* franciscano (-na)

Franco-, (in compounds) franco- . . . *a.* (Spanish *pol.*—referring to General Franco) franquista

Francophile, *a.* and *s.* afrancesado (-da)

Frank, *s.* franco (-ca), galo (-la)

frank, *a.* franco, cándido, sincero; abierto. *v.t.* franquear

frankincense, *s.* incienso, *m.*

frankly, *adv.* francamente; sinceramente; cara a cara; sin rodeos, claramente; abiertamente. **to speak f.**, hablar claro, hablar sin rodeos

frankness, *s.* franqueza, *f.*; sinceridad, *f.*, candor, *m.*

frantic, *a.* frenético, furioso, loco. **He drives me f.**, Me vuelve loco

fraternal, *a.* fraterno, fraternal

fraternity, *s.* fraternidad, hermandad, *f.*

fraternization, *s.* fraternización, *f.*

fraternize, *v.i.* fraternizar

fratricidal, *a.* fratricida

fratricide, *s.* (person) fratricida, *m.* and *f.*; (action) fratricidio, *m.*

fraud, *s.* fraude, *m.*; engaño, embuste, *m.*; (person) farsante, *m.*, embustero (-ra)

fraudulence, *s.* fraudulencia, fraude, *f.*

fraudulent, *a.* fraudulento

fraught, *a.* (with) cargado de; lleno de, preñado de

fray, *s.* refriega, riña, *f.*; combate, *m.*, batalla, *f.*; (rubbing) raedura, *f. v.t.* raer, tazar. *v.i.* tazarse, deshilarse

frayed, *a.* raído

fraying, *s.* raedura, deshiladura, *f.*

freak, *s.* monstruo, *m.*; fenómeno, *m.*; (whim) capricho, *m.*

freakish, *a.* monstruoso; caprichoso; extravagante; raro, singular

freakishness, *s.* carácter caprichoso, *m.*; extravagancia, *f.*; rareza, extrañeza, *f.*

freckle, *s.* peca, *f.* *v.i.* tener pecas; salir pecas (a la cara, etc.)

freckled, *a.* pecoso, con pecas

free, *a.* (in most senses) libre; independiente; emancipado; desembarazado; abierto; limpio (de); franco; (voluntary) voluntario; (self-governing) autónomo, independiente; accesible; (disengaged) desocupado; (vacant) vacío; (exempt) exento (de); (immune) inmune (de); ajeno; gratuito; (loose) suelto; (generous) generoso, liberal; (vicious) disoluto, licencioso; (bold) atrevido; (impudent) insolente, demasiado familiar. *adv.* gratis, gratuitamente. **There are two f. seats in the train,** Hay dos asientos libres en el tren. **to get f.,** libertarse. **to make f. with,** tomarse libertades con; usar como si fuera suyo. **to set f.,** poner en libertad. **f. agent,** libre albedrío, *m.* **f. and easy,** familiar, sin ceremonia. **f. gifts,** (*com.*) objetos de reclamo, *m. pl.* **f.-hand drawing,** dibujo a pulso, *m.* **f. kick,** (*sport*) golpe franco, *m.* **f. love,** amor libre, *m.* **f. play,** rienda suelta, *f.*; (*mech.*) holgura, *f.* **f. port,** puerto franco, *m.* **f. speech,** libertad de palabra, *f.* **f. thought,** libre pensamiento, *m.* **f. ticket,** (*theat.*) billete de favor, *m.* **f. trade,** *a.* librecambista. *s.* librecambio, *m.* **f. trader,** librecambista, *m.* and *f.* **f. verse,** verso libre, verso suelto, *m.* **f. wheeling,** rueda libre, *f.* **f. will,** propia voluntad, *f.*; (theology) libre albedrío, *m.*

free, *v.t.* libertar, poner en libertad (a); librar (de); (save) salvar; emancipar; exentar; (of obstacles, difficulties) desembarazar; **to f. from,** libertar de; librar de; (clean) limpiar de

freebooter, *s.* pirata, filibustero, *m.*

freeborn, *a.* nacido libre, libre por herencia

freedman, *s.* liberto, *m.*

freedom, *s.* libertad, *f.*; independencia, *f.*; exención, *f.*; inmunidad, *f.*; soltura, facilidad, *f.*; franqueza, *f.*; (over-familiarity) insolencia, *f.*; (boldness) audacia, intrepidez, *f.*; (of customs) licencia, *f.* **to receive the f. of a city,** ser recibido como ciudadano de honor. **f. of speech,** libertad de palabra, *f.* **f. of the press,** libertad de la prensa, *f.* **f. of worship,** libertad de cultos, *f.*

freehold, *s.* feudo franco, *m.*

freeing, *s.* liberación, *f.*; emancipación, *f.*; salvación, *f.*; (from obstruction) desembarazo, *m.*; limpieza, *f.*

freelance, *s.* (*mil.*) soldado libre, *m.*; (*pol.*) independiente, *m.*; aventurero (-ra). **f. journalist,** periodista libre, *m.*

freely, *adv.* libremente; francamente; generosamente; sin reserva

freeman, *s.* hombre libre, *m.*; (of a city) ciudadano de honor, *m.*

freemason, *s.* francmasón, *m.* **freemason's lodge,** logia masónica, *f.*

freemasonry, *s.* francmasonería, masonería, *f.*

freethinker, *s.* librepensador (-ra)

freeze, *v.t.* helar; (meat, etc.) congelar; (*fig.*) helar. *v.i.* helarse; congelarse; (*impers.,* of the weather) helar. **to f. to death,** morir de frío

freezing, *s.* hielo, *m.*; congelación, *f. a.* glacial; congelante, frigorífico. **f. mixture,** mezcla frigorífica, *f.* **f. of assets,** bloqueo de los depósitos bancarios, *m.* **f.-point,** punto de congelación, *m.* **above f.-point,** sobre cero. **below f.-point,** bajo cero

freight, *s.* flete, *m.*; porte, *m.* *v.t.* fletar

freightage, *s.* flete, *m.*; carga, *f.*; transporte, *m.*

freighter, *s.* fletador, *m.*; (ship) buque de carga, *m.*

French, *a.* francés. *s.* (language) francés, *m.*; (people) los franceses, *m. pl.* **in the F. fashion,** a la francesa. **to take F. leave,**

despedirse a la inglesa. **What is the F. for hat?** ¿Cómo se dice sombrero en francés? **F. spoken**, Se habla francés. **F. bean**, judía, *f.* **F. chalk**, jabón de sastre, *m.* **F. horn**, trompa, *f.* **F. lesson**, lección de francés, *f.* **F. marigold**, flor del estudiante, *f.* **F. polish**, barniz de muebles, *m.* **F. poodle**, perro (-rra) de aguas. **F. roll**, panecillo, *m.* **F. window**, puerta, ventana, *f.*

Frenchify, *v.t.* afrancesar

Frenchman, *s.* francés, *m.* **a young F.**, un joven francés

Frenchwoman, *s.* francesa, mujer francesa, *f.* **a young F.**, una joven francesa, una muchacha francesa, *f.*

frenzied, *a.* frenético

frenzy, *s.* frenesí, delirio, paroxismo, *m.*

frequency, *s.* frecuencia, *f.* **high f.**, alta frecuencia, *f.* **low f.**, baja frecuencia, *f.*

frequent, *a.* frecuente; (usual) común, corriente. *v.t.* frecuentar

frequentation, *s.* frecuentación, *f.*

frequenter, *s.* frecuentador (-ra)

frequently, *adv.* frecuentemente, con frecuencia, muchas veces; comúnmente

fresco, *s.* (*art*) fresco, *m.*, pintura al fresco, *f.* *v.t.* pintar al fresco

fresh, *a.* fresco; nuevo; reciente; (newly arrived) recién llegado; (inexperienced) inexperto, bisoño; (of water, not salt) dulce; puro; (healthy) sano; (brisk) vigoroso, enérgico; (vivid) vivo, vívido; (bright) brillante; (cheeky) fresco. *adv.* nuevamente, recién (with past participle). **He came to us f. from school**, Vino a nosotros recién salido de su colegio. **We are going to take the f. air**, Vamos a tomar el fresco. **The milk is not f.**, La leche no está fresca. **f.-complexioned**, de buenos colores. **f. news**, noticias nuevas, *f. pl.* **f. troops**, tropas nuevas, *f. pl.*; (reinforcements) tropas de refuerzo, *f. pl.* **f. water**, agua fresca, *f.*; (not salt) agua dulce, *f.* **f. wind**, viento fresco, *m.*

freshen, *v.t.* refrescar; (remove salt) desalar. *v.i.* (wind) refrescar. **to f. up**, renovar; refrescar; (of dress, etc.) arreglar

freshly, *adv.* nuevamente; recientemente

freshness, *s.* frescura, *f.*; (newness) novedad, *f.*; (vividness, brightness) intensidad, *f.*; pureza, *f.*; (beauty) lozanía, hermosura, *f.*; (cheek) frescura, *f.*, descaro, *m.*

freshwater, *s.* agua dulce, *f.* **f. sailor**, marinero de agua dulce, *m.*

fret, *s.* agitación, *f.*; ansiedad, preocupación, *f.*; (*arch.*) greca, *f.*; (of stringed instrument) traste, *m.* *v.t.* roer; (of a horse) bocezar; (corrode) desgastar, corroer; (of the wind, etc.) rizar; (worry) tener preocupado (a); irritar, enojar; (lose) perder; (oneself) apurarse, consumirse; (*arch.*) calar. *v.i.* torturarse, preocuparse, inquietarse; (complain) quejarse; (mourn) lamentarse, estar triste

fretful, *a.* mal humorado, mohino, quejoso, irritable

fretfully, *adv.* irritablemente, con mal humor

fretfulness, *s.* mal humor, *m.*, irritación, *f.*

fretsaw, *s.* serrucho de calar, *m.*, sierra de marquetería, *f.*

fretwork, *s.* calado, *m.*

Freudian, *a.* Freudiano

friar, *s.* fraile, *m.* **Black f.**, dominicano, *m.* **Grey f.**, franciscano, *m.* **White f.**, carmelita, *m.* **f.-like**, frailesco

friary, *s.* convento de frailes, *m.*

fricative, *a. and s.* fricativo (*m.*)

friction, *s.* frote, frotamiento, roce, *m.*; (*phys.*) rozamiento, *m.*; fricción, *f.* **to give a f.**, friccionar, dar fricciones (a). **f. gearing**, engranaje de fricción, *m.* **f. gloves**, guantes de fricciones, *m. pl.*

Friday, *s.* viernes, *m.* **Good F.**, Viernes Santo, *m.*

fried, *a.* frito. **f. egg**, huevo frito, *m.*

friend, *s.* amigo (-ga); (acquaintance) conocido (-da); (Quaker) cuáquero (-ra); (follower) adherente, *m.*; partidario (-ia);

(ally) aliado (-da); *pl.* **friends,**
amistades, *f. pl.*; amigos, *m. pl.*
a f. of yours, un amigo tuyo,
uno de tus amigos. **to make
friends,** hacer amigos; (become
friends) hacerse amigos; (after
a quarrel) hacer las paces.
Friends! (to sentinel) ¡Gente de
paz!

friendless, *a.* sin amigos; desamparado

friendliness, *s.* amabilidad, afabilidad, cordialidad, amigabilidad, *f.*

friendly, *a.* amistoso, amigable,
amigo; afable, acogedor, simpático; propicio, favorable. **to
be f. with,** ser amigo de. **f.
society,** sociedad de socorros, *f.*

friendship, *s.* amistad, intimidad,
f.

frieze, *s.* friso, *m.*; (cloth) frisa,
jerga, *f.*

frigate, *s.* (*nav.*) fragata, *f.*

fright, *s.* terror, susto, *m.*; (guy)
espantajo, *m.* *v.t.* asustar. **to
have a f.,** tener un susto. **to
take f.,** asustarse

frighten, *v.t.* espantar, dar un
susto (a), alarmar, asustar;
horrorizar; (overawe) acobardar.
**to be frightened out of one's
wits,** estar muerto de miedo.
to f. away, ahuyentar, espantar

frightened, *a.* miedoso, tímido,
medroso, nervioso

frightening, *a.* que da miedo;
alarmante, amedrentador; horrible

frightful, *a.* horrible, espantoso,
horroroso; (*fam.*) tremendo,
enorme

frightfully, *adv.* horrorosamente;
(*fam.*) enormemente

frightfulness, *s.* horror, *m.*

frigid, *a.* frío; helado; (*med.*) impotente

frigidity, *s.* frialdad, frigidez, *f.*;
(*med.*) impotencia, *f.*

frigidly, *adv.* fríamente

frill, *s.* (*sew.*) volante, *m.*; (jabot)
chorrera, *f.*; (round a bird's neck)
collarín de plumas, *m.*; (of
paper) frunce, *m.* *v.t.* alechugar;
fruncir

frilling, *s.* fruncido, *m.*

fringe, *s.* fleco, *m.*, franja, *f.*; (of
hair) flequillo, *m.*; (edge) borde,
m., margen, *m.* or *f.* *v.t.* guar-

necer con fleco, franjar; adornar;
(grow by) crecer al margen (de)

Frisian, *a.* and *s.* frisón (-ona);
(language) frisón, *m.*

frisk, *v.i.* retozar, brincar

friskiness, *s.* viveza, agilidad, *f.*

frisky, *a.* retozón, juguetón

fritillary, *s.* (*bot.*) fritilaria, *f.*

fritter, *s.* (*cul.*) fruta de sartén, *f.*
v.t. (away) malgastar, desperdiciar; perder

frivolity, *s.* frivolidad, ligereza,
f.; futilidad, *f.*

frivolous, *a.* frívolo, ligero, liviano; (futile) trivial, fútil

frizz, *v.t.* (cloth) frisar; (hair)
rizar

frizzy, *a.* (of hair) crespo, rizado

fro, *adv.* hacia atrás. **movement
to and fro,** vaivén, *m.* **to and
fro,** de un lado a otro. **to go to
and fro,** ir y venir

frock, *s.* vestido, *m.*; (of a monk)
hábito, *m.*; (of priest) sotana, *f.*
f.-coat, levita, *f.*

frog, *s.* rana, *f.* **to have a f. in
the throat,** padecer carraspera

frolic, *s.* (play) juego, *m.*; (mischief) travesura, *f.*; (folly) locura,
extravagancia, *f.*; (joke) chanza,
f.; (amusement) diversión, *f.*;
(wild party) holgorio, *m.*, parranda, *f.* *v.i.* retozar, juguetear;
divertirse

frolicsome, *a.* retozón, juguetón

from, *prep.* de; desde; (according
to) según; (in the name of, on
behalf of) de parte de; (through,
by) por; (beginning on) a contar
de; (with) con. **He is coming
here f. the dentist's,** Vendrá
aquí desde casa del dentista.
Give him this message f. me,
Dale este recado de mi parte.
Judging f. his appearance,
Juzgando por su apariencia.
prices f. fifty pesetas upwards, precios desde cincuenta
pesetas en adelante. **F. what I
hear,** Según mi información,
Según lo que oigo. **f. above,**
desde arriba. **f. among,** de
entre. **f. afar,** de lejos, desde
lejos. **f. time to time,** de
cuando en cuando, de vez en
cuando

frond, *s.* (*bot.*) fronda, *f.*

front, *s.* frente, *f.*; cara, *f.*; (*mil.*)
frente, *m.*; (battle line) línea de

combate, *f.*; (of a building) fachada, *f.*; (of shirt) pechera, *f.*; (at
the seaside) playa, *f.*; (promenade) paseo de la playa, *m.*;
(forefront) primera línea, *f.*;
(forepart) parte delantera, *f.*;
(*theat.*) auditorio, *m.*; (impudence) descaro, *m. a.* delantero;
anterior; de frente; primero. *adv.*
hacia delante. *v.i.* mirar a, dar a;
hacer frente a. **in f.**, en frente.
in f. of, en frente de; (in the
presence of) delante de, en la
presencia de. **to face f.**, hacer
frente. **to put on a bold f.**, hacer
de tripas corazón. **f. door**,
puerta de entrada, puerta principal, *f.* **f. line**, (*mil.*) línea del
frente, *f.*; primera línea, *f.* **f.
seat**, (at an entertainment, etc.)
delantera, *f.* **f. tooth**, diente incisivo, *m.* **f. view**, vista de
frente, *f.*; vista de cerca, *f.*
frontage, *s.* (of a building) fachada, *f.*; (site) terreno de . . .
metros de fachada, *m.*
frontal, *a.* (*mil.*) de frente; (*anat.*)
frontal
frontier, *s.* frontera, *f.*; (*fig.*)
límite, *m. a.* fronterizo
frontispiece, *s.* (of a building)
frontispicio, *m.*, fachada, *f.*; (of a
book) portada, *f.*
frontless, *a.* sin frente
frost, *s.* escarcha, *f.*; helada, *f.*
v.t. helar; (*cul.*) escarchar; (glass)
deslustrar; (*fig.*) escarchar. *v.i.*
helar. **f.-bitten**, helado
frostbite, *s.* efectos del frío, *m.*
pl.
frosted, *a.* escarchado; helado;
(of glass) deslustrado, opaco;
(*cul.*) escarchado
frostily, *adv.* (*fig.*) glacialmente,
con frialdad.
frostiness, *s.*; frío glacial, *m.*
frosting, *s.* escarcha, *f.*; (of glass)
deslustre, *m.*; (*cul.*) escarcha, *f.*
frosty, *a.* helado; de hielo; (of
hair) canoso; (*fig.*) glacial, frío.
It was f. last night, Anoche heló
froth, *s.* espuma, *f.*; (*fig.*) frivolidad, vanidad, *f. v.i.* espumar,
hacer espuma; echar espuma.
v.t. hacer espumar; hacer echar
espuma
frothiness, *s.* espumosidad, *f.*;
(*fig.*) frivolidad, superficialidad,
vaciedad, *f.*

frothy, *a.* espumoso, espumajoso;
(*fig.*) frívolo, superficial
frown, *s.* ceño, *m.*; cara de juez,
expresión severa, *f.*; desaprobación, *f.*; (of fortune) revés,
golpe, *m. v.i.* fruncir el ceño.
to f. at, upon, mirar con desaprobación; ser enemigo de; desaprobar
frowning, *a.* ceñudo; severo;
amenazador
frowningly, *adv.* severamente
frowsiness, *s.* mal olor, *m.*;
(dirtiness) suciedad, *f.*; (untidiness) desaliño, desaseo, *m.*
frowsy, *a.* fétido, mal oliente; mal
ventilado; (dirty) sucio; (untidy) desaliñado, desaseado
frozen, *a.* helado; cubierto de
hielo; congelado; (*geog.* and *fig.*)
glacial. **to be f. up**, estar helado.
f. meat, carne congelada, *f.*
fructiferous, *a.* fructífero
fructification, *s.* fructificación, *f.*
fructify, *v.i.* fructificar. *v.t.*
fecundar
frugal, *a.* económico; frugal;
sobrio
frugality, *s.* economía, *f.*; frugalidad, sobriedad, *f.*
frugivorous, *a.* frugívoro
fruit, *s.* (in general sense) fruto,
m.; (off a tree or bush) fruta, *f.*;
(*fig.*) fruto, *m.*; resultado, *m.*,
consecuencia, *f. v.i.* frutar, dar
fruto. **bottled f.**, fruta en
almíbar, *f.* **candied f.**, fruta
azucarada, *f.* **dried f.**, fruta
seca, *f.* **first fruits**, primicias,
f. pl. **soft f.**, frutas blandas, *f.
pl.* **stone f.**, fruta de hueso,
f. **f.-bearing**, frutal. **f.-cake**,
pastel de fruta, *m.* **f.-dish**,
frutero, *m.* **f. farming**, fruticultura, *f.* **f.-knife**, cuchillo de
postres, *m.* **f. shop**, frutería, *f.*
f. tree, frutal, *m.*
fruiterer, *s.* frutero (-ra)
fruitful, *a.* fructuoso, fértil; prolífico, fecundo; provechoso
fruitfulness, *s.* fertilidad, *f.*;
fecundidad, *f.*; provecho, *m.*
fruition, *s.* fruición, *f.*
fruitless, *a.* infructuoso, estéril;
inútil
fruitlessness, *s.* infructuosidad,
esterilidad, *f.*; inutilidad, *f.*
fruity, *a.* de fruta; (wines) vinoso;
(of voice) melodioso

frump, s. estantigua, f.

frumpish, a. estrafalario; fuera de moda

frustrate, v.t. frustrar; defraudar; malograr; destruir; anular

frustration, s. frustración, f.; defraudación, f.; malogro, m.; destrucción, f.; desengaño, m.

fry, s. (cul.) fritada, f. v.t. freír. v.i. freírse. **small fry,** (fam.) gente menuda, f.

frying, s. fritura, f., el freír. **to fall out of the f.-pan into the fire,** ir de mal en peor, andar de zocos en colodros. **f.-pan,** sartén, f.

fuchsia, s. (bot.) fuscia, f.

fuchsine, s. (chem.) fucsina, f.

fuddle, v.t. atontar, aturdir; embriagar, emborrachar

fudge, s. patraña, tontería, f., disparate, m. interj. ¡qué disparate! ¡qué va!

fuel, s. combustible, m.; (fig.) cebo, pábulo, m. v.t. cebar, echar combustible en. v.i. tomar combustible. **to add f. to the flame,** echar leña al fuego. **f. consumption,** consumo de combustible, m. **f.-oil,** aceite combustible, aceite de quemar, m. **f.-tank,** depósito de combustible, m.

fuelling, s. aprovisionamiento de combustible, m.

fugitive, a. fugitivo; pasajero, perecedero; transitorio, efímero, fugaz. s. fugitivo (-va); (from justice) prófugo (-ga); (mil.) desertor, m.; (refugee) refugiado (-da)

fugue, s. (mus.) fuga, f.

fulcrum, s. (mech.) fulcro, m.

fulfil, v.t. cumplir; (satisfy) satisfacer; (observe) observar; guardar. **to be fulfilled,** cumplirse, realizarse

fulfilment, s. cumplimiento, m.; desempeño, ejercicio, m.; (satisfaction) satisfacción, realización, f.; (observance) observancia, f.

full, a. lleno; colmado; todo; pleno; (crowded) atestado; (replete) harto; abundante; (intent on) preocupado con, pensando en; (loose) amplio; (plentiful) copioso; (occupied) ocupado; completo; (resonant) sonoro; (mature) maduro; puro; per-

fecto; (satiated) saciado (de); (of the moon, sails) lleno; (weighed down) agobiado, abrumado; (detailed) detallado; (with uniform, etc.) de gala; (with years, etc.) cumplido. s. colmo, m.; totalidad, f. adv. muy; completamente, totalmente. **f. many a flower,** muchas flores. **at f. gallop,** a galope tendido. **at f. speed,** a todo correr; a toda velocidad. **His hands are f.,** Sus manos están llenas. **The moon was at the f.,** La luna estaba llena. **In f.,** por completo; sin abreviaciones; integralmente. **in f. swing,** en plena actividad. **in f. vigour,** en pleno vigor. **to the f.,** completamente; hasta la última gota; a la perfección. **to be f. to the brim,** estar lleno hasta el tope. **f.-blooded,** sanguíneo; de pura raza; (fig.) viril, vigoroso; (fig.) apasionado. **f.-blown,** en plena flor, abierto. **f. dress,** a. de gala. s. traje de etiqueta, traje de ceremonia, m. **f.-face,** de cara. **f.-flavoured,** (wine) abocado. **f.-grown,** adulto; completamente desarrollado. **f.-length,** de cuerpo entero. **f. moon,** luna llena, f.; plenilunio, m. **f. name,** nombre y apellidos, m. **f. powers,** plenos poderes, m. pl. **f. scale,** tamaño natural, m. **f. scope,** carta blanca, f.; toda clase de facilidades. **f. steam ahead,** a todo vapor. **f. stop,** (gram.) punto final, m.

full, v.t. (cloth) abatanar

fuller, s. batanero, m. **fuller's earth,** tierra de batán, galactita, f.

fulling, s. abatanadura, f. **f.-mill,** batán, m.

fullness, s. abundancia, f.; plenitud, f.; (repletion) hartura, f.; (of clothes) amplitud, f.; (stoutness) gordura, f.; (swelling) hinchazón, f. **She wrote with great f. of all that she had seen,** Ella describía muy detalladamente todo lo que había visto. **in the f. of time,** andando el tiempo

fully, adv. plenamente; enteramente. **It is f. six years since**

. . ., Hace seis años bien cumplidos que . . . **It is f. 9 o'clock,**
Son las nueve bien sonadas. **f.
dressed,** completamente vestido

fulminant, *a.* (*med.*) fulminante

fulminate, *s.* (*chem.*) fulminato, *m.*
v.i. estallar; **fulminar.** *v.t.*
volar; fulminar

fulminous, *a.* fulmíneo, fulminoso

fulsome, *a.* servil; insincero,
hipócrita; asqueroso, repugnante

fumarole, *s.* fumarola, *f.*

fumble, *v.i.* (grope) ir a tientas;
procurar hacer algo; chapucear
(con); (for a word) titubear

fumbling, *s.* hesitación, *f.*; tacto
incierto, *m. a.* incierto; vacilante

fumblingly, *adv.* de manera in-
cierta; a tientas

fume, *s.* vaho, humo, gas, *m.*;
emanación, *f.*; mal olor, *m.*,
fetidez, *f.*; (*fig.*) vapor, *m.*; (state
of mind) agitación, *f.*; frenesí, *m.*
v.i. humear; refunfuñar, echar
pestes

fumigate, *v.t.* fumigar; sahumar,
perfumar; desinfectar

fumigation, *s.* fumigación, *f.*;
sahumerio, *m.*

fumigator, *s.* fumigador (-ra);
(apparatus) fumigador, *m.*

fumigatory, *a.* fumigatorio

fuming, *s.* refunfuño, *m. a.*
refunfuñador

fumy, *a.* humoso

fun, *s.* diversión, *f.*, entretenimiento, *m.*; (joke) chanza, broma,
f. **for fun,** para divertirse; en
chanza. **in fun,** de burlas. **to
have fun,** divertirse. **to poke fun
at,** burlarse de, mofarse de, ridiculizar

funambulist, *s.* funámbulo (-la)

function, *s.* función, *f. v.i.* funcionar

functional, *a.* funcional

functionary, *s.* funcionario, *m.
a.* funcional

functioning, *s.* funcionamiento,
m.

fund, *s.* fondo, *m.*; *pl.* **funds,**
fondos, *m. pl.*; (*fam.*) dinero, *m.*
public funds, fondos públicos,
m. pl. **sinking f.,** fondo de
amortización, *m.*

fundamental, *a.* fundamental,
básico; esencial. *s.* fundamento,
m.

fundamentally, *adv.* fundamen-
talmente, básicamente; esencialmente

funeral, *a.* funeral, fúnebre,
funerario. *s.* funerales, *m. pl.*;
entierro, *m.* **to attend the f.
(of),** asistir a los funerales (de).
f. furnisher, director de pompas
fúnebres, *m.* **f. procession,**
cortejo fúnebre, *m.* **f. pyre,** pira
funeraria, *f.* **f. service,** misa de
difuntos, *f.*

funereal, *a.* fúnebre, lúgubre

fungicide, *s.* anticriptógamo, *m.*

fungous, *a.* fungoso

fungus, *s.* hongo, *m.*

funicular, *a.* funicular. **f. railway,** ferrocarril funicular, *m.*

funnel, *s.* (*chem.*) embudo, *m.*;
(*naut.*) chimenea, *f.*; (of a chimney) cañón (de chimenea), *m.*
f.-shaped, en forma de embudo

funnily, *adv.* de un modo raro

funniness, *s.* lo divertido; rareza.
extrañeza, *f.*

funny, *a.* cómico, gracioso; divertido; (strange) extraño, raro;
(mysterious) misterioso. **It
struck me as f.,** (amused me)
Me hizo gracia; (seemed strange)
Me pareció raro. **f.-bone,**
hueso de la alegría, *m.*

fur, *s.* piel, *f.*; depósito, sarro, *m.*;
(on tongue) saburra, *f. a.* hecho
de pieles. *v.t.* forrar, o adornar,
or cubrir, con pieles; depositar
sarro sobre; (the tongue) ensu-
ciarse la lengua. *v.i.* estar forrado, or adornado, or cubierto, con
pieles; formarse incrustaciones;
(of the tongue) tener la lengua
sucia. **fur cap,** gorra de pieles, *f.*
fur cape, cuello de piel, *m.*; capa
de pieles, *f.* **fur trade,** peletería,
f.

furbelow, *s.* faralá, volante, *m.*

furbish, *v.t.* pulir; renovar:
limpiar

furious, *a.* furioso. **to become
f.,** ponerse furioso, enfurecerse

furiously, *adv.* furiosamente, con
furia

furiousness, *s.* furia, *f.*

furl, *v.t.* plegar; enrollar; (*naut.*)
aferrar

furling, *s.* plegado, *m.*; (*naut.*)
aferramiento, *m.*

furlong, *s.* estadio, *m.*

furlough, *s.* (*mil.*) permiso, *m.*

v.t. conceder un permiso (a). **on f.**, de permiso

furnace, s. horno, m.; (of steam boiler) fogón, m.; (for central heating) caldera de calefacción central, f.; (for smelting) cubilote, m.

furnish, v.t. proveer (de), equipar (de), suplir (de); amueblar; (an opportunity) proporcionar; producir

furnished, a. amueblado, con muebles. **f. house**, casa amueblada, f.

furnisher, s. decorador, m.; proveedor (-ra)

furnishing, s. provisión, f., equipo, m.; pl. **furnishings**, accesorios, m. pl.; mobiliario, mueblaje, m.

furniture, s. mobiliario, mueblaje, m.; ajuar, equipo, m.; avíos, m. pl.; (naut.) aparejo, m. **a piece of f.**, un mueble. **to empty of f.**, desamueblar, quitar los muebles (de). **f. dealer or maker**, mueblista, m. and f. **f. factory**, mueblería, f. **f. polish**, crema para muebles, f. **f. remover**, transportador de muebles, m.; (packer) embalador, m. **f. repository**, guardamuebles, m. **f. van**, carro de mudanzas, m.

furore, s. furor, m.

furred, a. forrado or cubierto or adornado de piel; (of the tongue) sucia

furrier, s. peletero, m. **furrier's shop**, peletería, f.

furrow, s. surco, m.; (carp.) muesca, f.; (arch.) estría, f.; (wrinkle) arruga, f. v.t. surcar

furry, a. cubierto de piel; parecido a una piel; hecho de pieles

further, a. ulterior, más distante; (other) otro; opuesto; adicional, más. adv. más lejos; más allá; además; también; por añadidura. v.t. promover, fomentar; ayudar. **on the f. side**, al otro lado. **till f. orders**, hasta nueva orden. **f. on**, más adelante; más allá

furtherance, s. fomento, m., promoción, f.; progreso, avance, m.

furthermore, adv. además, por añadidura

furthest, a. (el, la, lo) más lejano or más distante; extremo. adv. más lejos

furtive, a. furtivo

furtively, adv. furtivamente, a hurtadillas. **to look at f.**, mirar de reojo

fury, s. furor, enfurecimiento, m., rabia, f.; violencia, f.; frenesí, arrebato, m.; furia, f. (also myth.). **like a f.**, hecho una furia. **to breathe forth f.**, echar rayos

furze, s. (bot.) tojo, m.

fuse, s. (of explosives) espoleta, mecha, f.; (elec.) fusible, m. v.t. (metals) fundir; fusionar, mezclar. v.i. (metals) fundirse; mezclarse. **safety-f.**, espoleta de seguridad, f. **time-f.**, espoleta de tiempo, f. **to blow a f.**, fundir un fusible. **f. box**, caja de fusibles, f. **f. wire**, fusible, m.

fuselage, s. (aer.) fuselaje, m.

fusible, a. fusible

fusilier, s. fusilero, m.

fusillade, s. descarga cerrada, f.

fusion, s. fusión, f.; unión, f.; (melting) fundición, f.

fuss, s. agitación, f.; (bustle) conmoción, bulla, f.; bullicio, m. v.i. agitarse. preocuparse. v.t. poner nervioso. **There's no need to make such a f.**, No es para tanto. **to make a f. of**, (a person) hacer la rueda (a), ser muy atento (a); (spoil) mimar mucho (a). **to f. about**, andar de acá para allá

fussily, adv. nerviosamente; de un aire importante

fussy, a. meticuloso, nimio; nervioso; (of style) florido, hinchado; (of dress) demasiado adornado

fustigate, v.t. fustigar

fusty, a. (mouldy) mohoso; mal ventilado; mal oliente; (of views, etc.) pasado de moda

futile, a. fútil, superficial, frívolo; inútil

futility, s. futilidad, superficialidad, frivolidad, f.; (action) tontería, estupidez, f.

future, a. futuro, venidero. s. futuro, porvenir, m. **in the f.**, en adelante, en lo venidero, en lo sucesivo. **for f. reference**, para información futura. **f. perfect tense**, (gram.) futuro perfecto, m. **f. tense**, (gram.) futuro, m.

futurism, s. futurismo, m.

futurist, s. futurista, m. and f.

futuristic, *a.* futurístico

uzz, *s.* tamo, *m.*, pelusa, *f.* **f.-ball,** (*bot.*) bejín, *m.*

fuzzy, *a.* crespo rizado; velloso

G

g, *s.* (letter) ge, *f.*; (*mus.*) sol, *m.* **G clef,** clave de sol, *f.*

gab, *s.* (*fam.*) labia, *f.* **to have the gift of the gab,** tener mucha labia

gabardine, *s.* gabardina, *f.*

gabble, *v.i.* chacharear, garlar; hablar indistintamente; (of goose and some birds) graznar. *v.t.* decir indistintamente; decir rápidamente; (a language) chapurrear; mascullar. *s.* cháchara, *f.*; vocerío, *m.*; (of goose and some birds) graznido, *m.*

gabbler, *s.* charlatán (-ana), chacharero (-ra)

gabbling, *s.* See **gabble**

gable, *s.* (*arch.*) gablete, hastial, *m.* **g.-end,** alero, *m.*

gad, *v.i.* corretear, callejear. **to gad about,** correr por todos lados; divertirse.

gadabout, *s.* azotacalles, *m.* and *f.* gandul (-la), vagabundo (-da)

gadding, *a.* callejero; vagabundo. *s.* vagancia, *f.*; vida errante, *f.*; gandulería, *f.*

gad-fly, *s.* (*ent.*) tábano, *m.*; (*fam.*) moscardón, *m.*

gadget, *s.* accesorio, *m.*; aparato, *m.*; chuchería, *f.*

Gael, *s.* escocés (-esa) del norte; celta, *m.* and *f.*

Gaelic, *a.* gaélico. *s.* gaélico, *m.*

gaff, *s.* (hook) garfio, *m.*; (*naut.*) pico de cangrejo, *m.*; (theatre) teatrucho, *m.*

gaffer, *s.* viejo, tío, abuelo, *m.*

gag, *s.* mordaza, *f.*; (*theat.*) morcilla, *f.* *v.t.* amordazar; (*fig.*) hacer callar. *v.i.* (*theat.*) meter morcillas

gage, *s.* prenda, fianza, *f.*; (symbol of challenge) guante, *m.*; (challenge) desafío, *m.* See **gauge**

gagging, *s.* amordazamiento, *m.*

gaggle, *s.* (cry) graznido, *m.*; (of geese) manada (de ocas), *f.* *v.i.* graznar; cacarear

gaiety, *s.* alegría, *f.*; animación, vivacidad, *f.*; (entertainment) diversión, festividad, *f.*

gaily, *adv.* alegremente

gain, *s.* ganancia, *f.*; provecho, beneficio, *m.*; (increase) aumento, *m.*; (riches) riqueza, *f.* *v.t.* ganar; (acquire) conseguir; adquirir; obtener; conquistar, captar; (friends) hacerse; (reach) llegar a, alcanzar. *v.i.* ganar; (improve) mejorar; (of a watch) adelantarse. **What have they gained by going to Canada?** ¿Qué han logrado con marcharse al Canadá? **to g. ground,** (*fig.*) ganar terreno. **to g. time,** ganar tiempo. **to g. on, upon,** acercarse a; (overtake) alcanzar; (outstrip) dejar atrás, pasar; (of sea) invadir; (of habits) imponerse

gainful, *a.* ganancioso, lucrativo; ventajoso

gainfully, *adv.* ventajosamente; lucrativamente

gainings, *s.* ganancias, *f. pl.*; emolumentos, *m. pl.*

gainsay, *v.t.* contradecir; oponer; negar

gainsaying, *s.* contradicción, *f.*; oposición, *f.*; negación, *f.*

gait, *s.* porte, andar, *m.*; paso, *m.*, andadura, *f.*

gaiter, *s.* polaina, *f.*; (spat) botín, *m.*

gala, *s.* gala, fiesta, *f.* **g.-day,** día de fiesta, *m.* **g.-dress,** traje de gala, *m.*

galantine, *s.* galantina, *f.*

Galatian, *a.* and *s.* gálata (*m.* and *f.*)

galaxy, *s.* (*ast.*) vía láctea, *f.*; (*fig.*) constelación, *f.*; grupo brillante, *m.*

gale, *s.* vendaval, ventarrón, *m.*; (storm) temporal, *m.*; tempestad, *f.*

galenic, *a.* galénico

Galenism, *s.* galenismo, *m.*

Galician, *a.* and *s.* gallego (-ga). **G. dialect,** gallego, *m.*

Galilean, *a.* and *s.* galileo (-ea)

gall, *s.* (on horses) matadura, *f.*; (abrasion) rozadura, *f.*; hiel, bilis, *f.*; (*fig.*) hiel, amargura, *f.*; rencor, *m.*; (American slang) descaro, *m.*, impertinencia, *f.*; (*bot.*) agalla, *f.* *v.t.* rozar;

(*fig.*) mortificar, herir. **g.-apple,** agalla, *f.* **g.-bladder,** vejiga de la hiel, *f.* **g.-stone,** cálculo hepático, *m.*

gallant, *a.* hermoso; (imposing) imponente, majestuoso; (brave) valiente, gallardo, valeroso, intrépido; (chivalrous) caballeroso; noble; (attentive to ladies, or amorous) galante. *s.* galán, *m.* *v.t.* galantear, cortejar

gallantly, *adv.* (bravely) valientemente; caballerosamente; cortésmente; galantemente

gallantry, *s.* (bravery) valentía, *f.,* valor, *m.;* heroísmo, *m.,* proeza, *f.;* (chivalry) caballerosidad, *f.;* (towards women, or amorousness) galantería, *f.*

galleon, *s.* galeón, *m.*

gallery, *s.* galería, *f.;* pasillo, *m.;* (of a cloister) tránsito, *m.;* (cloister) claustro, *m.;* (for spectators) tribuna, *f.;* (*theat.*) paraíso, gallinero, *m.;* (theatre audience) galería, *f.;* (of portraits, etc.) galería, colección, *f.;* (*min., mil.*) galería, *f.;* (building) museo, *m.* **art g.,** museo de pinturas, *m.*

galley, *s.* (*naut., print.*) galera, *f.;* (kitchen) cocina, *f.;* (rowing-boat) falúa de capitán, *f.* **to condemn to the galleys,** echar a galeras. **wooden g.,** (*print.*) galerín, *m.* **g.-proof,** galerada, *f.* **g.-slave,** galeote, *m.*

galliard, *s.* gallarda, *f.*

Gallic, *a.* gálico, galicano; francés

gallicism, *s.* galicismo, *m.*

Gallicize, *v.t.* afrancesar

galling, *a.* (*fig.*) irritante; mortificante

galliot, *s.* (*naut.*) galeota, *f.*

gallivant, *v.i.* callejear, corretear; divertirse; ir de parranda

gallon, *s.* galón, *m.*

galloon, *s.* galón, *m.,* trencilla, *f.*

gallop, *s.* galope, *m.* *v.i.* galopar; ir aprisa. *v.t.* hacer galopar, **at full g.,** a rienda suelta, a galope tendido. **to g. back,** volver a galope. **to g. down,** bajar a galope. **to go off,** marcharse galopando; alejarse corriendo. **to g. past,** desfilar a galope ante. **to g. through,** cruzar a galope. **to g. up,** *v.t.* subir a galope. *v.i.* llegar a galope

gallopade, *s.* (dance) galop, *m.*

galloping, *s.* galope, *m.;* galopada, *f.* *a.* que va a galope; (*med.*) galopante. **g. consumption,** tisis galopante, *f.*

gallows, *s.* patíbulo, *m.,* horca, *f.;* (framework) montante, *m.* **g.-bird,** criminal digno de la horca, *m.*

galop, *s.* galop, *m.*

galore, *adv.* en abundancia

galvanic, *a.* (*elec.*) galvánico; espasmódico

galvanism, *s.* (*elec.*) galvanismo, *m.*

galvanization, *s.* galvanización, *f.*

galvanize, *v.t.* galvanizar

galvanometer, *s.* galvanómetro, *m.*

gambit, *s.* (chess) gambito, *m.;* (*fig.*) táctica, *f,*

gamble, *s.* juego de azar, *m.;* jugada, *f.;* aventura, *f.;* (*com.*) especulación, *f.* *v.i.* jugar por dinero; especular; (with) (*fig.*) aventurar, arriesgar. **to g. on the Stock Exchange,** jugar en la bolsa. **to g. away,** perder al juego

gambler, *s.* jugador (-ra)

gambling, *s.* juego, *m.* *a.* jugador; de juego. **g.-den,** casa de juego, *f.,* garito, *m.*

gamboge, *s.* gutagamba, *f.*

gambol, *s.* salto, brinco, retozo, *m.;* cabriola, *f.;* juego, *m.* *v.i.* saltar, brincar, retozar; juguetear

game, *s.* juego, *m.;* (match) partido, *m.;* (jest) chanza, *f.;* (trick) trampa, *f.;* (birds, hares, etc.) caza menor, *f.;* (tigers, lions, etc.) caza mayor, *f.;* (flesh of game) caza, *f.;* *pl.* **games,** deportes, *m. pl. a.* de caza; (courageous) valiente, animoso, brioso; resuelto. *v.i.* jugar por dinero. **He is g. for anything,** Se atreve a todo. **big g. hunting,** caza mayor, *f.* **head of g.,** pieza de caza, *f.* **It is a g. at which two can play,** Donde las dan las toman. **The g. is not worth the candle,** La cosa no vale la pena. **The g. is up,** (*fig.*) El proyecto se ha frustrado. **to make g. of,** (things) burlarse de; (persons) tomar el pelo a;

mofarse de. **to play the g.,** (*fig.*) jugar limpio. **to g. away.** perder al juego. **g. of cards,** juego de naipes, *m.* **g. of chance,** juego de azar, *m.* **g.-bag,** morral, *m.* **g. drive,** batida de caza, *f.* **g.-laws,** leyes de caza, *f. pl.* **g.-licence,** licencia de caza, *f.* **g.-pie,** tortada, *f.* **g. preserve,** coto de caza, *m.*

gamekeeper, *s.* guardabosque, *m.*

gamely, *adv.* valientemente

gameness, *s.* valentía, resolución, fortaleza, *f.*

gamete, *s.* gameto, *m.*

gaming, *s.* juego, *m. a.* de juego. **g.-house,** garito, *m.* **g.-table,** mesa de juego, *f.*; (*fig.*) juego, *m.*

gammon, *s.* (of bacon) jamón, *m. v.t.* curar (jamón)

gamut, *s.* gama, *f.*

gander, *s.* ganso, *m.*

gang, *s.* cuadrilla, pandilla, *f.*; (squad) pelotón, *m.*; (of workers) brigada, cuadrilla, *f.*; grupo, *m.* **g.-plank,** plancha, *f.*

ganglion, *s.* ganglio, *m.*; (*fig.*) centro, *m.*

gangrene, *s.* gangrena, *f. v.t.* gangrenar. *v.i.* gangrenarse

gangrenous, *a.* gangrenoso

gangster, *s.* pistolero, gángster, *m.*

gangue, *s.* (*min.*) ganga, *f.*

gangway, *s.* pasillo, *m.*; (*naut.*) plancha, *f.*, pasamano, *m.*; (opening in ship's side) portalón, *m.* **midship g.,** crujía, *f.*

gaol, *s.* cárcel, prisión, *f.*; encierro, *m. v.t.* encarcelar. *a.* carcelario, carcelero. **g.-bird,** malhechor; presidiario, *m.*

gaoler, *s.* carcelero (-ra)

gap, *s.* brecha, *f.*; abertura, *f.*; (hole) boquete, *m.*; (pass) desfiladero, paso, *m.*; (ravine) hondonada, barranca, *f.*; (blank) laguna, *f.*, vacío, *m.*; (crack) intersticio, *m.*, hendedura, *f.*, resquicio, *m.* **to fill a gap,** llenar un boquete; llenar un vacío

gape, *v.i.* estar con la boca abierta, papar moscas. **to g. at,** mirar con la boca abierta

gaping, *s.* huelgo, *m.*; abertura, *f. a.* que bosteza; boquiabierto; abierto

garage, *s.* garaje, *m. v.t.* poner (un coche, etc.) en un garaje. **g. proprietor,** garajista, *m.*

garb, *s.* traje, vestido, *m.*; uniforme, *m.*; (*her.*) espiga, *f. v.t.* vestir, ataviar

garbage, *s.* basura, inmundicia, *f.*

garble, *v.t.* falsear, mutilar, pervertir

garden, *s.* jardín, *m.*; huerto, *m.*; (fertile region) huerta, *f. a.* de jardín. *v.i.* trabajar en el jardín, cultivar un huerto. **g. city,** ciudad jardín, *f.* **g.-frame,** semillero, *m.* **g. mould,** tierra vegetal, *f.* **g.-party,** fiesta de jardín, *f.* **g.-plot,** parterre, *m.* **g. produce,** hortalizas, legumbres, *f. pl.* **g. roller,** rodillo, *m.* **g.-seat,** banco de jardín, *m.* **g. urn,** jarrón, *m.*

gardener, *s.* jardinero, *m.*

gardenia, *s.* gardenia, *f.*, jazmín de la India, *m.*

gardening, *s.* jardinería, *f.*; horticultura, *f. a.* de jardinería

gargantuan, *a.* gargantuesco; tremendo, enorme

gargle, *s.* (liquid) gargarismo, *m.*; gárgaras, *f. pl. v.i.* hacer gárgaras, gargarizar

gargling, *s.* gargarismo, *m.*

gargoyle, *s.* gárgola, *f.*

garish, *a.* cursi, llamativo, charro, chillón

garishness, *s.* cursería, ostentación, *f.*, lo llamativo

garland, *s.* guirnalda, *f.*; corona, *f.*; (anthology) florilegio, *m.*; (*arch.*) festón, *m. v.t.* enguirnaldar

garlic, *s.* ajo, *m.*

garment, *s.* prenda de vestir, *f.*; traje, vestido, *m.*; (*fig.*) vestidura, *f.*; (*fig.* cloak) capa, *f.*

garner, *s.* granero, *f.*; tesoro, *m.*; colección, *f. v.t.* atesorar, guardar

garnet, *s.* granate, *m.*

garnish, *s.* (*cul.*) aderezo, *m.*; adorno, *m. v.t.* (*cul.*) aderezar; embellecer, adornar

garnishing, *s.* See **garnish**

garret, *s.* guardilla, buhardilla, *f.*, desván, *m.*

garrison, *s.* guarnición, *f.*, presidio, *m. v.t.* guarnecer, presidiar. **g. town,** plaza de armas, *f.*

garrotte, s. garrote, m. v.t.
agarrotar, dar garrote (a)

garrulity, s. garrulidad, locuacidad, charlatanería, f.

garrulous, a. gárrulo, locuaz,
charlatán

garter, s. liga, f.; (G.) Jarretera, f.
v.t. atar con liga; investir con la
Jarretera. **Order of the G.,**
Orden de la Jarretera, f.

gas, s. gas, m.; (fig., fam.) palabrería, f.; (petrol) bencina, f.
a. de gas; con gas; para gases.
v.t. asfixiar con gas; (mil.)
atacar con gas; saturar de gas.
gas attack, ataque con gases
asfixiantes, m. **gas-bag,** bolsa
de gas, f.; (fam.) charlatán
(-ana). **gas-burner,** mechero
de gas, m. **gas-chamber,**
cámara de gas, f. **gas de-**
tector, detector de gases, m.
gas-fire, estufa de gas, f.
gas-fitter, gasista, m. **gas-**
fittings, lámparas de gas, f. pl.
gas-light, luz de gas, f.; mechero de gas, m. **gas-main,**
cañería maestra de gas, f. **gas-**
man, gasista, m. **gas-mantle,**
camiseta incandescente, f. **gas-**
mask, máscara para gases, f.
gas-meter, contador de gas, m.
gas-pipes, cañerías (or tuberías)
de gas, f. pl. **gas-ring,** fogón
de gas, m. **gas-shell,** obús de
gases asfixiantes, m. **gas-stove,**
cocina de gas, f. **gas warfare,**
guerra química, f. **gas-works,**
fábrica de gas, f.

Gascon, a. and s. gascón (-ona)

gaseous, a. gaseoso

gash, s. cuchillada, f.; herida
extensa, f. v.t. acuchillar; herir
extensamente

gasket, s. aro de empaquedura,
m.

gasolene, s. gasolina, f.

gasometer, s. gasómetro, m.

gasp, s. boqueada, f. v.i. boquear. **to be at the last g.,**
estar agonizando. **to g. for**
breath, luchar por respirar.
to g. out, decir anhelante, decir
con voz entrecortada

gastric, a. gástrico

gastritis, s. gastritis, f.

gastronome, s. gastrónomo (-ma)

gastronomic, a. gastronómico

gastronomy, s. gastronomía, f.

gate, s. puerta, f.; cancela, verja,
f.; entrada, f.; (of a lock, etc.)
compuerta, f.; (across a road,
etc.) barrera, f.; (money) entrada, f.; (fig.) puerta, f. **auto-**
matic g., (at level crossings, etc.)
barrera de golpe, f. **to g.-**
crash, asistir sin invitación.
g.-keeper, portero, m.; guardabarrera, m. and f. **g.-money,**
entrada, f. **g.-post,** soporte de
la puerta, m.

gateway, s. entrada, f.; puerta,
f.; paso, m.; vestíbulo, m.; (fig.)
puerta, f.

gather, v.t. (assemble) reunir;
(amass) acumular, amontonar;
(acquire) obtener, adquirir; hacer
una colección (de); cobrar; (harvest) cosechar, recolectar; (pick
up) recoger; (pluck) coger; (infer)
sacar en limpio, aprender; (sew.)
fruncir; (the brows) fruncir (el
ceño). v.i. reunirse, congregarse; amontonarse; (threaten)
amenazar; (sadden) amargar;
(fig., hover over) cernerse (sobre);
(increase) aumentar, crecer; (be
covered) cubrirse; (fester) supurar. s. (sew.) frunce, pliegue,
m. **to g. breath,** tomar aliento.
to g. speed, ganar velocidad.
to g. strength, cobrar fuerzas.
I g. from Mary that they are
going abroad, Según lo que
me ha dicho María, ellos van
al extranjero. **to g. in,** juntar;
reunir; (harvest) cosechar; coger.
to g. together, v.t. reunir. v.i.
reunirse. **to g. up,** recoger;
coger; tomar; (one's limbs) encoger. **to g. up the threads,**
(fig.) recoger los hilos.

gatherer, s. cogedor, colector, m.;
(harvester) segador, m.; (of
grapes) vendimiador (-ra); (of
taxes) recaudador, m.

gathering, s. cogedura, f.; (fruit,
etc.) recolección, f.; (of taxes)
recaudación, f.; amontonamiento, m.; colección, f.; (med.)
absceso, m.; (sew.) fruncimiento,
m.; (assembly) reunión, asamblea, f.; (crowd) concurrencia,
muchedumbre, f.

gathers, s. (sew.) fruncidos,
pliegues, m. pl.

gauche, a. torpe, huraño

gaudily, *adv.* ostentosamente; brillantemente

gaudiness, *s.* ostentación, *f.*; brillantez, *f.*

gaudy, *a.* llamativo, vistoso, brillante, ostentoso

gauge, *s.* (of gun) calibre, *m.*; (railway) entrevía, *f.*; (for measuring) indicador, *m.*; regla de medir, *f.*; (*naut.*) calado, *m.*; (*fig.*) medida, *f.*; (test) indicación, *f.*; (model) norma, *f.* *v.t.* calibrar; medir; estimar; (ship's capacity) arquear; (judge) juzgar; (size up) tomar la medida (de); (*fig.*) interpretar; (*sew.*) fruncir; (liquor) aforar. **broad (narrow) g. railway,** ferrocarril de vía ancha (estrecha), *m.* **pressure g.,** manómetro, *m.* **water g.,** indicador del nivel de agua, *m.*

gauging, *s.* medida, *f.*; (of ship's capacity) arqueo, *m.*; (of liquor) aforamiento, *m.*; (*fig.*) apreciación, *f.*; interpretación, *f.*

gaunt, *a.* anguloso, huesudo, desvaído; (of houses, etc.) lúgubre

gauntlet, *s.* guante de manopla, *m.*; (part of armour) manopla, *f.*, guantelete, *m.* **to throw down the g.,** echar el guante, desafiar

gauntness, *s.* angulosidad, flaqueza, *f.*

gauze, *s.* gasa, *f.*; (mist) bruma, *f.* **wire-g.,** tela metálica, *f.*

gauziness, *s.* diafanidad, *f.*

gauzy, *a.* diáfano; de gasa

gavotte, *s.* gavota, *f.*

gawkiness, *s.* torpeza, desmaña, *f.*

gawky, *a.* anguloso, desgarbado, torpe

gay, *a.* alegre; festivo, animado; ligero de cascos, disipado; vicioso; inmoral; (of colours) brillante, llamativo. **to lead a gay life,** llevar una vida de placeres. **to make gay,** alegrar; animar

gaze, *s.* mirada, *f.*; mirada fija, *f.* *v.i.* mirar; mirar fijamente, contemplar

gazelle, *s.* gacel (-la)

gazer, *s.* espectador (-ra)

gazette, *s.* gaceta, *f.* *v.t.* publicar en la gaceta. **Pathé G.,** (cinema) Actualidades, *f. pl.*

gazing, *s.* contemplación, *f.* *a.* contemplador; que presencia, que asiste a

gear, *s.* (apparel) atavíos, *m. pl.*; (harness) guarniciones, *f. pl.*, arneses, *m. pl.*; (tackle) utensilios, *m. pl.*, herramientas, *f. pl.*; (*naut.*) aparejo, *m.*; (*mech.*) engranaje, *m.*; juego, *m.*, marcha, *f.* *v.t.* aparejar, enjaezar; (*mech.*) poner en marcha, hacer funcionar. *v.i.* (*mech.*) engranar, endentar. **low g.,** primera velocidad, *f.* **neutral g.,** punto muerto, *m.* **reverse g.,** marcha atrás, *f.* **second g.,** segunda velocidad, *f.* **three-speed g.,** cambio de marchas de tres velocidades, *m.* **top g.,** tercera (or cuarta— according to gear-box) velocidad, *f.* **to change g.,** cambiar de marcha, cambiar de velocidad. **to throw out of g.,** (*fig.*) desquiciar. **g.-box,** caja de velocidades, *f.* **g.-changing,** cambio de velocidad, *m.* **g.-changing lever,** palanca de cambio de velocidad, palanca de cambio de marchas, *f.*

gearing, *s.* engranaje, *m.*

gee up, *interj.* ¡arre!

gehenna, *s.* gehena, *m.*

geisha, *s.* geisha, *f.*

gelatine, *s.* gelatina, *f.* **cooking g.,** gelatina seca, *f.*

gelatinous, *a.* gelatinoso

geld, *v.t.* capar, castrar

gelder, *s.* castrador, *m.*

gelding, *s.* castración, capadura, *f.*; caballo castrado, *m.*; animal castrado, *m.*

gelid, *a.* gélido, helado; (*fig.*) frío, frígido

gelignite, *s.* gelignita, *f.*

gem, *s.* piedra preciosa, *f.*; joya, alhaja, *f.*; (*fig.*) joya, *f.* *v.t.* adornar con piedras preciosos; enjoyar

Gemini, *s.* (los) Gemelos

gender, *s.* (*gram.*) género, *m.*; sexo, *m.*

gene, *s.* (*biol.*) gene, *m.*

genealogical, *a.* genealógico. **g. tree,** árbol genealógico, *m.*

genealogist, *s.* genealogista, *m.* and *f.*

genealogy, *s.* genealogía, *f.*

general, *a.* general; universal; común; corriente; (usual) acos-

tumbrado, usual; del público,
público. s. lo general; (mil., ecc.)
general, m.; (fam.) criada para
todo, f. **in g.**, por lo general, en
general, generalmente. **to become g.**, generalizarse. **to
make g.**, generalizar, hacer
general. **g. average**, (marine
insurance) avería gruesa, f. **g.
election**, elección general, f.
g. meeting, pleno, mitin general,
m. **g. opinion**, voz común,
opinión general, f. **G. Post
Office**, Oficina Central de Correos, f. **g. practitioner**, médico
(-ca) general. **g. public**, público, m.

generalissimo, s. (mil.) generalísimo, m.

generality, s. generalidad, f.

generalization, s. generalización,
f.

generalize, v.t. and v.i. generalizar

generally, adv. en general, por
regla general, por lo general,
generalmente; comúnmente, por
lo común

generalship, s. (mil.) generalato,
m.; (strategy) táctica, estrategia,
f.; dirección, jefatura, f.

generate, v.t. (beget) engendrar,
procrear; (phys., chem.) generar;
(fig.) producir, crear

generation, s. procreación, f.;
generación, f.; (fig.) producción,
creación, f. **the younger g.**,
los jóvenes

generative, a. generador

generator, s. (mech.) generador,
m.; dínamo, f.

generic, a. genérico

generosity, s. generosidad, f.;
liberalidad, f.

generous, a. generoso; liberal,
dadivoso; magnánimo; (plentiful) abundante; (of wines) generoso

generously, adv. generosamente;
abundantemente

genesis, s. principio, origen, m.;
(G) Génesis, m.

genetic, a. genésico

genetics, s. genética, f.

Genevan, a. and s. ginebrés
(-esa), ginebrino (-na)

genial, a. (of climate) agradable,
bueno; (of persons) afable, bondadoso; de buen humor, bonachón

geniality, s. afabilidad, bondad,
f.; buen humor, m.

genially, adv. afablemente

genie, s. genio, m.

genital, a. genital, sexual. s. pl.
genitals, genitales, m. pl.

genitive, a. and s. (gram.) genitivo (m.)

genius, s. genio, m.; carácter, m.
índole, f.; ingenio, m.; (fam.)
talento, m.

Genoese, a. and s. genovés (-esa)

genre, s. género, m. **g. painting**,
cuadro de género, m.

genteel, a. fino; (affected) remilgado, melindroso; de buen
tono; de buena educación

gentian, s. genciana, f.

gentile, a. and s. gentil (m. and f.)

gentility, s. aristocracia, f.;
respetabilidad, f.

gentle, a. noble, bien nacido, de
buena familia; amable; suave;
ligero; dulce; (docile) manso,
dócil; (affectionate) cariñoso;
bondadoso; sufrido, paciente;
cortés; pacífico, tolerante. He
was a man of **g. birth**, Era un
hombre bien nacido. " **G.
reader**," "Querido lector"

gentlefolk, s. pl. gente de bien,
gente fina, f.; gente de buena
familia, f.

gentleman, s. caballero, señor,
m.; gentilhombre, m. **Ladies
and gentlemen**, Señoras y
caballeros, Señores. **young g.**,
señorito, m. **to be a perfect g.**,
ser un caballero perfecto. **g.-in-
waiting**, gentilhombre de la
cámara, m.

gentlemanliness, s. caballerosidad, f.

gentlemanly, a. caballeroso

gentleness, s. amabilidad, f.;
suavidad, f.; dulzura, f.; mansedumbre, docilidad, f.; bondad, f.;
paciencia, f.; cortesía, f.; tolerancia, f.

gentlewoman, s. dama, f.; dama
de servicio, f.

gently, adv. suavemente; dulcemente; silenciosamente, sin
ruido; (slowly) despacio, poco a
poco. **g. born**, bien nacido

gentry, s. pequeña aristocracia,
alta clase media, f.; (disparaging)
gente, f.

genuflect, v.i. doblar la rodilla

genuflexion, *s.* genuflexión, *f.*

genuine, *a.* puro; genuino; verdadero; real; sincero; auténtico

genuinely, *adv.* genuinamente; verdaderamente; realmente; sinceramente

genuineness, *s.* pureza, *f.*; autenticidad, *f.*; verdad, *f.*; sinceridad, *f.*

genus, *s.* género, *m.*

geocentric, *a.* geocéntrico

geodesic, *a.* geodésico

geodesy, *s.* geodesia, *f.*

geographer, *s.* geógrafo, *m.*

geographical, *a.* geográfico

geographically, *adv.* geográficamente; desde el punto de vista geográfico

geography, *s.* geografía, *f.*

geological, *a.* geológico

geologically, *adv.* geológicamente; desde el punto de vista geológico

geologist, *s.* geólogo, *m.*

geologize, *v.i.* estudiar la geología. *v.t.* estudiar desde un punto de vista geológico

geology, *s.* geología, *f.*

geomancy, *s.* geomancia, *f.*

geometric, *a.* geométrico

geometrician, *s.* geómetra, *m.*

geometry, *s.* geometría, *f.*

geophysics, *s.* geofísica, *f.*

Georgian, *a.* (*geog.*) georgiano; del principio del siglo diez y nueve

georgic, *s.* geórgica, *f.*

geotropism, *s.* geotropismo, *m.*

geranium, *s.* geranio, *m.*

gerb, *s.* (*her.*) espiga, *f.*

gerfalcon, *s.* gerifalte, *m.*

germ, *s.* embrión, germen, *m.*; microbio, bacilo, *m.*; (*fig.*) germen, *m.* **g.-cell,** célula germinal, *f.*

German, *a.* alemán; germánico. *s.* alemán (-ana); (language) alemán, *m.*; germano (-na), germánico (-ca). **Sudeten G.,** alemán (-ana) sudete. **G. measles,** rubeola, *f.*

germander, *s.* (*bot.*) camedrio, *m.*

germane, *a.* pertinente (a), a propósito (a)

Germanic, *a.* germánico. *s.* (language) germánico, *m.*

Germanization, *s.* germanización, *f.*

Germanize, *v.t.* germanizar. *v.i.* germanizarse

Germanophil, *s.* germanófilo (-la)

germicidal, *a.* bactericida

germicide, *s.* desinfectante, *m.*

germinal, *a.* germinal. *s.* (G) germinal, *m.*

germinate, *v.i.* germinar, brotar. *v.t.* hacer germinar

germination, *s.* germinación, *f.*

germinative, *a.* germinativo

gerund, *s.* gerundio, *m.*

gerundive, *s.* gerundio adjetivado, *m.*

Gestapo, *s.* Gestapo, *f.*

gestation, *s.* gestación, *f.*

gesticulate, *v.i.* gesticular, hacer gestos; accionar. *v.t.* expresar por gestos

gesticulation, *s.* gesticulación, *f.*

gesticulatory, *a.* gesticular

gesture, *s.* movimiento, *m.*; gesticulación, *f.*; (of the face) gesto, *m.*, mueca, *f.*; ademán, *m.*, acción, *f.* *v.i.* gesticular. *v.t.* decir por gestos; acompañar con gestos

get, *v.t.* (obtain) obtener; (acquire) adquirir; (buy) comprar; (take) tomar; (receive) recibir; (gain, win) ganar; (hit) acertar, dar; (place) poner; (achieve) alcanzar, lograr; (make) hacer; (call) llamar; (understand) comprender; (catch) coger; (procreate) procrear, engendrar; (induce) persuadir; (invite) convidar, invitar; (cause) hacer; (with have and past part.) tener; (with have and past part. followed by infin.) tener que; (followed by noun and past part.) hacer; (fetch) buscar, ir a buscar; (order) mandar, disponer; (procure) procurar; (bring) traer; (money) hacer; (a reputation, etc.) hacerse; (a prize, an advantage) llevar; (learn) aprender; (be) ser. *v.i.* (become) hacerse; ponerse; venir a ser; (old) envejecerse; (angry) montar (en cólera), enojarse; (arrive) llegar a; (attain) alcanzar; (accomplish) conseguir, lograr; (drunk) emborracharse; (hurt) hacerse daño; (wet) mojarse; (cool) enfriarse; (money) hacer (dinero); (of health) ponerse; (find oneself) hallarse, encon-

trarse; (late) hacerse (tarde);
(dark) empezar a caer (la noche),
empezar a oscurecer; (put oneself) meterse; (grow, be) estar;
(on to or on top of) montar
sobre, subir a. **He has got
run over,** Ha sido atropellado.
It gets on my nerves, Se
me pone los nervios en punta.
Let's get it over! ¡Vamos
a concluir de una vez! **How
do you get on with her?**
¿Cómo te va con ella? **She
must be getting on for twenty,**
Ella tendrá alrededor de veinte
años. **to get a suit made,**
mandar hacerse un traje. **to
get better,** (in health) mejorar
de salud; hacer progresos adelantar. **to get dark,** obscurecer.
to get into conversation with,
trabar conversación con. **to get
into bad company,** frecuentar
malas compañías. **to get into
the habit of,** acostumbrarse a.
to get married, casarse. **to
get near,** acercarse. **to get
one's own way,** salir con la
suya. **to get oneself up as,**
disfrazarse de. **to get out in a
hurry,** salir apresuradamente;
marcharse rápidamente, (fam.)
salir pitando. **to get out of the
way,** quitarse de en medio,
apartarse. **to get rid of,**
desembarazarse de, librarse de;
salir de; perder. **to have got,**
poseer; tener; padecer. **Get on!**
¡Adelante!; (to a horse) ¡Arre!;
(continue) ¡Sigue! **Get out!**
¡Fuera! ¡Largo de aquí! ¡Sal!
Get up! ¡Levántate!; (to a
horse) ¡Arre! **to get about,**
moverse mucho; andar mucho;
(attend to business affairs) ir
a sus negocios; (travel) viajar;
(get up from sick bed) levantarse;
(go out) salir; (be known) saberse,
divulgarse, hacerse público. **to
get above,** subir a un nivel más
alto (de). **to get across,** v.i.
cruzar, atravesar. v.t. hacer
cruzar. **to get along,** v.i. (depart) marcharse; (continue) seguir, vivir; (manage) ir, ir
tirando. v.t. llevar; traer; hacer
andar por. **How are you getting along?** ¿Cómo te va? **I
am getting along all right,**

thank you, Voy tirando, gracias.
to get along without, pasarse
sin. **to get at,** (remove) sacar;
(find) encontrar; (reach) llegar a;
alcanzar; (discover) descubrir;
(allude to) aludir a; (understand)
comprender. **to get away,** v.i.
dejar (un lugar); marcharse,
irse; (escape) escaparse. v.t.
ayudar a marcharse; ayudar a
escaparse. **to get away with,**
llevarse, marcharse con; (fam.)
salir con la suya. **to get back,**
v.i. regresar, volver; (get home)
volver a casa; (be back) estar de
vuelta. v.t. (recover) recobrar;
(receive) recibir; (find again)
hallar de nuevo. **to get down,**
v.i. bajar, descender. v.t. bajar;
(take off a hook) descolgar;
(swallow) tragar; (note) anotar;
escribir. **to get down to,**
ponerse a (estudiar, trabajar,
etc.). **to get in,** v.i. entrar en;
lograr entrar en; (slip in) colarse
en; (of political party) entrar en
el poder; (of a club) hacerse
socio de; (return) regresar;
(home) volver a casa; (find oneself) hallarse, estar; (a habit)
adquirir. v.t. hacer entrar en;
(a club, etc.) hacer socio de; (a
word) decir. **to get into.** See **to
get in. to get off,** v.t. apearse de;
bajar de; (send) enviar; (from
punishment) librar; (bid good-
bye) despedirse de; (remove)
quitar, sacar. v.i. apearse; bajar;
(from punishment) librarse;
(leave) ponerse en camino, marcharse. **to get on,** v.i. (wear)
tener puesto; (progress) hacer
progresos, adelantar; (prosper)
medrar, prosperar; (succeed)
tener éxito; avanzar; seguir el
camino; (agree) avenirse. v.t.
(push) empujar; (place) poner;
(cause) hacer; (clothes) ponerse;
(mount) subir a. **to get open,**
abrir. **to get out,** v.t. hacer salir;
sacar; (publish) publicar; divulgar. v.i. salir; escapar; (descend)
bajar (de). **to get over,** (cross)
atravesar, cruzar; (an illness,
grief, etc.) reponerse; (excuse)
perdonar; (surmount) superar;
(ground) recorrer. **to get round,**
(a person) persuadir; (surround)
rodear; (avoid) evitar; (diffi-

culties) superar, vencer. **to get through**, pasar por; (time) pasar, entretener; (money) gastar; (finish) terminar, acabar; (pierce or enter) penetrar; (communicate) comunicar (con); (difficulties) vencer; (an exam) aprobar. **to get to**, llegar a; encontrar; (begin) empezar. **to get together**, *v.t.* reunir, juntar. *v.i.* reunirse, juntarse. **to get under**, ponerse debajo de; (control) dominar. **to get up**, *v.t.* (raise) alzar, levantar; (carry up things) subir; hacer subir; organizar; preparar; (learn) aprender; (linen) blanquear, colar; (ascend) subir; hacer; (dress) ataviar; (steam) generar; (a play) ensayar, poner en escena. *v.i.* levantarse; (on a horse) montar a caballo; (of the wind) refrescarse; (of the fire) avivarse; (of the sea) embravecerse. **to get up to**, llegar a; alcanzar

get-at-able, *a.* accesible

getting, *s.* adquisición, *f.*; (of money) ganancia, *f.* **g. up**, preparación, *f.*; organización, *f.*; (of a play) representación (de una comedia), puesta en escena, *f.*

get-up, *s.* atavío, *m.*; (of a book, etc.) aspecto, *m.*

gewgaw, *s.* chuchería, *f.*

geyser, *s.* geiser, *m.*; (for heating water) calentador (de agua), *m.*

ghastliness, *s.* horror, *m.*; palidez mortal, *f.*; aspecto miserable, *m.*; (boringness) tedio, aburrimiento, *m.*; lo desagradable

ghastly, *a.* horrible; de una palidez mortal; cadavérico; (boring) aburrido; muy desagradable

gherkin, *s.* cohombrillo, *m.*

ghetto, *s.* judería, *f.*

Ghibelline, *a.* and *s.* gibelino (-na)

ghost, *s.* fantasma, espectro, aparecido, *m.*; (spirit) alma, *f.*, espíritu, *m.*; (shadow) sombra *f.*; (writer) mercenario, *m.* **Holy G.**, Espíritu Santo, *m.* **to give up the g.**, entregar el alma; perder la esperanza, desesperarse. **to look like a g.**, parecer un fantasma

ghostliness, *s.* espiritualidad, *f.*; lo misterioso; palidez, *f.*; tenuidad, *f.*

ghostly, *a.* espiritual; espectral; misterioso; pálido; vaporoso, tenue; indistinto

ghoul, *s.* vampiro, *m.*

ghoulish, *a.* insano; cruel; sádico

giant, *s.* gigante, *m.*; (*fig.*) coloso, *m. a.* gigantesco; de gigantes; de los gigantes. **g.-killer**, matador de gigantes; *m.* **g.-stride**, (gymnastics) paso volante, *m.*

giantess, *s.* giganta, *f.*

giantism, *s.* gigantismo, *m.*

gibber, *v.i.* hablar incoherentemente, hablar entre dientes; farfullar, hablar atropelladamente; decir disparates

gibberish, *s.* galimatías, *m.*; jerigonza, *f.*, griego, *m.*

gibbet, *s.* horca, *f.*, patíbulo, *m.* **to die on the g.**, morir ahorcado

gibbon, *s.* (*zool.*) gibón, *m.*

gibe, *s.* improperio, escarnio, *m.*, burla, mofa, *f. v.i.* criticar. **to g. at**, burlarse de, ridiculizar, mofarse de

gibing, *a.* burlón, mofador. *s.* mofas, burlas, *f. pl.*

gibingly, *adv.* burlonamente, con sorna

giblets, *s.* menudillos, *m. pl.*

giddily, *adv.* vertiginosamente; frívolamente, atolondradamente

giddiness, *s.* vértigo, *m.*; atolondramiento, *m.*; inconstancia, *f.*; frivolidad, ligereza de cascos, *f.*

giddy, *a.* vertiginoso; mareado; atolondrado, casquivano, frívolo; inconstante. **She felt very g.**, Se sintió muy mareada. **to make g.**, dar vértigo (a), marear

gift, *s.* regalo, *m.*, dádiva, *f.*; (quality) don, talento, *m.*; prenda, *f.*; poder, *m.*; (*law*) donación, *f.*; (offering) ofrenda, oblación, *f.* **deed of g.**, (*law*) escritura de donación, *f.* **in the g. of**, en el poder de, en las manos de. **I wouldn't have it as a g.**, No lo tomaría ni regalado. **You must not look a g. horse in the mouth**, A caballo regalado no le mires el diente. **g. of tongues**, don de las lenguas, *m.*

gifted, *a.* talentoso

gig, *s.* (carriage) carrocín, *m.*; (boat) falúa, lancha, *f.*; (for

wool) máquina de cardar paño,
f.; (harpoon) arpón, *m.*

gigantic, *a.* gigantesco; colosal, enorme

giggle, *v.i.* reírse sin motivo; reírse disimuladamente. *s.* risa disimulada, *f.*

giggling, *s.* risa estúpida, *f.*; risa nerviosa, *f.*

gild, *v.t.* dorar; (metals) sobredorar; embellecer. **to g. the pill**, dorar la píldora

gilder, *s.* dorador, *m.*

gilding, *s.* dorado, *m.*, doradura, *f.*; embellecimiento, *m.*

gill, *s.* (of fish) agalla, branquia, *f.*; (ravine) barranco, *m.*; (measure) medida de líquidos, *f.* (¼ litro)

gilt, *s.* dorado, *m.*; pan de oro, *m.*; relumbrón, *m.*; (*fig.*) encanto, *m.* *a.* dorado, áureo. **g.-edged**, (of books) con los bordes dorados. **g.-edged security**, papel del Estado, *m.*; valores de toda confianza, *m. pl.*

gimcrack, *s.* chuchería, *f.* *a.* de baratillo, cursi; mal hecho

gimlet, *s.* barrena, *f.*, taladro, *m.*

gin, *s.* (drink) ginebra, *f.*; (snare) trampa, *f.* *v.t.* (snare) coger con trampa. **g. block**, (*mech.*) garrucha, *f.*

ginger, *s.* jengibre, *m.*; (*fam.*) energía, *f.*, brío, *m.* *a.* rojo. *v.t.* sazonar con jengibre; (*fam.*) animar, estimular. **g.-beer**, gaseosa, *f.*

gingerly, *adv.* con gran cuidado; delicadamente

gingham, *s.* guinga, *f.*

gingivitis, *s.* gingivitis, *f.*

gipsy, *s.* gitano (-na). *a.* gitano, gitanesco; (music) flamenco

gipsydom, *s.* gitanería, *f.*

giraffe, *s.* jirafa, *f.*

gird, *v.t.* ceñir; (invest) investir; (surround) cercar, rodear; (put on) revestir. **to g. oneself for the fray**, prepararse para la lucha

girder, *s.* viga, jácena, *f.* **main g.**, viga maestra, *f.*

girdle, *s.* (belt) cinturón, *m.*; (corset) faja, *f.*; circunferencia, *f.*; zona, *f.* *v.t.* ceñir; (*fig.*) cercar, rodear

girl, *s.* niña, *f.*; chica, muchacha, *f.*; (maidservant) criada, mucha-

cha, *f.*; (young lady) señorita, *f.*; a .young g., una jovencita; (little older) una joven. **old g.**, (of a school) antigua alumna, *f.*; (*fam.*) vieja, *f.*; (*fam.*, affectionate) chica, *f.* **g. friend**, amiguita, *f.* **g. guide**, exploradora, *f.* **girls' school**, colegio de niñas, colegio de señoritas, *m.*

girlhood, *s.* niñez, *f.*; juventud, *f.*

girlish, *a.* de niña, de muchacha; (of boys) afeminado; joven

girth, *s.* (of horse, etc.) cincha, *f.*; circunferencia, *f.*; (of person) talle, *m.*; (obesity) corpulencia, obesidad, *f.*

gist, *s.* esencia, substancia, *f.*, importe, *m.*

give, *v.t.* dar; (a present) regalar; (infect) contagiar; (impart) comunicar; (grant) otorgar; (allow, concede) conceder; (assign) asignar, señalar; (appoint) nombrar; (a toast) brindar (a la salud de); (a party, ball, etc.) dar; (a bill) presentar; (wish) desear; (punish) castigar; (pay) pagar; (hand over) entregar; (names at baptism) imponer; (produce) producir; dar; (cause) causar; (of judicial sentences) condenar a; (evoke) proporcionar; (provoke) provocar; (devote) dedicar, consagrar; (sacrifice) sacrificar; (evidence, an account, orders, a lesson, a performance, a concert) dar; (a cry, shout) lanzar, proferir; (a laugh) soltar; (describe) describir; (paint) pintar; (write) escribir; (offer) ofrecer; (show) mostrar; (transmit) transmitir; (heed, pain) hacer; (a speech) pronunciar, hacer; (award, adjudge) adjudicar; (ear) prestar (oído (a)). *v.i.* dar; ser dadivoso, mostrarse generoso; (give in) ceder; (be elastic) dar de sí; ablandarse; (collapse) hundirse. **G. them my best wishes!** ¡Dales mis mejores recuerdos! **G. us a song!** ¡Cántanos algo! **I can g. him a lift in my car**, Puedo ofrecerle un asiento en mi auto. **I g. you my word**, Os doy mi palabra. **to g. a good account of oneself**, defenderse bien; hacer bien; salir bien. **to g. a person a piece of one's**

mind, contarle cuatro verdades.
to g. chase, dar caza (a). **to
g. it to a person,** poner a uno
como nuevo; reprender; (beat)
pegar, dar de palos. **to g. of
itself,** dar de sí. **to g. rise to,**
dar lugar a, ocasionar, causar.
to g. way, no poder resistir;
(break) romperse; (yield) ceder;
(collapse) hundirse; (retreat) retroceder. **to g. way to,** (retreat
before) retirarse ante; (abandon
oneself to) entregarse a, abandonarse a. **to g. away,** enajenar;
dar; regalar; (sell cheaply) vender a un precio muy bajo; (get
rid of) deshacerse de; (sacrifice)
sacrificar; (a secret) revelar;
(betray) traicionar; (expose)
descubrir; (tell) contar; (a bride)
conducir al altar. **He gave himself away,** Reveló su pensamiento sin querer. **to g. back,**
v.t. devolver; restituir. *v.i.* retirarse, cejar. **to g. forth,**
divulgar, publicar; (scatter) derramar; (emit) emitir, despedir;
(smoke, rays) echar. **to g. in,**
v.t. entregar; presentar. *v.i.*
darse por vencido. **to g. in to,**
(agree with) asentir en, consentir
en; rendirse ante. **Mary always
gives in to George,** María hace
siempre lo que Jorge quiere.
to g. off, (of odours, etc.) emitir,
exhalar, despedir. **to g. out,** *v.t.*
(distribute) distribuir, repartir;
(allocate) asignar; (publish) publicar; (announce) anunciar; (reveal) divulgar; (allege) afirmar,
hacer saber; (emit) emitir. *v.i.*
(be exhausted) agotarse; (end)
acabarse; (be lacking) faltar.
to g. over, *v.t.* entregar; (transfer) traspasar; cesar de. *v.i.*
cesar. **to g. up,** entregar; ceder;
(renounce) renunciar (a); (sacrifice) sacrificar; (abandon) abandonar; (cease) dejar de; (as lost)
dar por perdido; (of a patient)
desahuciar; (a post) dimitir de;
(return) devolver, restituir; (a
problem) renunciar (a resolver un
problema); (lose hope) perder la
esperanza; (give in) darse por
vencido. **I had given you up,**
(didn't expect you), Creí que no
ibas a venir. **to g. oneself up
to,** entregarse a; dedicarse a;

(*mil.*) rendirse a. **to g. up one's
seat,** ceder su sitio (or asiento).
to g. upon, (overlook) dar sobre
give, *s.* elasticidad, *f.*; el dar de
sí; (concession) concesión, *f.*
g. and take, concesiones mutuas,
f. pl. **g. away,** (*fam.*) revelación
indiscreta, *f.*
given, *a.* dado; especificado;
convenido; (with to) dado a,
adicto a. **in a g. time,** en un
tiempo dado. **g. that,** dado que
giver, *s.* dador (-ra); donador
(-ra)
gizzard, *s.* molleja, *f.* **It sticks
in my g.,** (*fam.*) No lo puedo
tragar
glabrous, *a.* glabro, lampiño
glacial, *a.* glacial
glacier, *s.* glaciar, *m.*
glacis, *s.* (*mil.*) glacis, *m.*, explanada, *f.*
glad, *a.* feliz, alegre; contento,
satisfecho; (*fam.*) elegante. **to
be g.,** alegrarse, estar contento;
estar satisfecho. **to give the g.
eye,** hacer ojos
gladden, *v.t.* alegrar, regocijar
glade, *s.* claro, *m.*; rasa, *f.*
gladiator, *s.* gladiador, *m.*
gladiatorial, *a.* gladiatorio
gladiolus, *s.* (*bot.*) gladiolo, gla-
dío, *m.*; espadaña, *f.*
gladly, *adv.* alegremente; con
mucho gusto, gustoso, de buena
gana
gladness, *s.* alegría, felicidad, *f.*,
contento, *m.*; placer, *m.*
glamorous, *a.* exótico; garboso
glamour, *s.* encanto, *m.*, fascinación, *f.*; garbo, *m.* **g. girl,**
belleza exótica, *f.*
glance, *s.* (of a projectile) desviación, *f.*; (of light) vislumbre, *f.*;
relumbrón, centelleo, *m.*; (look)
vistazo, *m.*, ojeada, *f.*; mirada, *f.*
v.i. desviarse; relumbrar, centellear, brillar; (with at) ojear,
echar un vistazo a, lanzar miradas a; (a book) hojear; mirar;
mirar de reojo; (*fig.*) indicar
brevemente. **at a g.,** con un
vistazo; en seguida. **at the
first g.,** a primera vista. **to g.
off,** desviarse (al chocar). **to g.
over,** repasar, echar un vistazo
a; (a book) hojear
glancing, *a.* (of a blow) que roza

gland, s. (anat., bot.) glándula, f.; (in the neck) ganglio, m. **to have swollen glands,** tener una inflamación de los ganglios

glanders, s. (in horses, etc.) muermo, m.

glandular, a. glandular

glare, s. brillo, fulgor, m.; luminosidad, f.; reflejo, m.; (look) mirada feroz, f. v.i. relumbrar, centellear; (stare) mirar con ferocidad, mirar fijamente

glaring, a. deslumbrante, brillante; (of colours) chillón, llamativo; (of looks) de mirada feroz; (flagrant) notorio, evidente

glaringly, adv. brillantemente; con mirada feroz; notoriamente

glass, s. vidrio, m.; cristal, m.; (glassware) artículos de vidrio, m. pl.; cristalería, f.; (for drinking) vaso, m., copa, f.; (pane) cristal, m.; (mirror) espejo, m.; (telescope) telescopio, m.; cataleja, m.; (barometer) barómetro, m.; (hour-glass) reloj de arena, m.; (of a watch) vidrio (de reloj), m.; pl. **glasses,** (binoculars) anteojos, m. pl.; (spectacles) lentes, m. pl.; (opera glasses) gemelos de teatro, m. pl. a. de vidrio; de cristal. v.t. vidriar. **John wears glasses,** Juan lleva gafas. **The g. is falling (rising),** El barómetro baja (sube). **to clink glasses,** trincar las copas. **to look in the g.,** mirarse en el espejo. **clear g.,** vidrio trasparente, m. **cut g.,** cristal tallado, m. **frosted g.,** vidrio jaspeado, m. **plate-g.,** vidrio plano, m.; **safety g.,** vidrio inastillable, m. **stained g.,** vidrio de color, vidrio pintado, m. **under g.,** bajo vidrio; en invernáculo. **g. bead,** abalorio, m.; cuenta de vidrio, f. **g.-blower,** soplador de vidrio, m. **g.-blowing,** el soplar de vidrio. **g. case,** escaparate, m. **g.-cloth,** paño para vasos, m. **g. eye,** ojo de cristal, m. **g. paper,** papel de vidrio, m. **g. roof,** techo de cristal, m. **g. window,** vidriera, f.

glasscutter, s. cortador de vidrio, m.

glassful, s. contenido de un vaso, m.; vaso, vaso lleno, m., copa, f.

glasshouse, s. fábrica de vidrio, f.; vidriería, f.; invernáculo, invernadero, m., estufa, f.

glassware, s. cristalería, f.

glassy, a. vitreo; (of eyes) vidrioso; (fig.) cristalino; (smooth) liso, raso

glaucous, a. de color verdemar; (bot.) glauco

glaze, s. barniz, m.; lustre, brillo, m. v.t. poner vidrios (a); vidriar; barnizar; (paper, leather, etc.) satinar. v.i. (of eyes) vidriarse, ponerse vidrioso

glazier, s. vidriero, m.

glazing, s. vidriado, m.; barnizado, m.; satinado, m.; (material) barniz, m.

gleam, s. rayo, destello, m.; (of colour) viso, m., mancha, f.; (fig.) rayo, m.; (in the eye) chispa, f. v.i. relucir, centellear, resplandecer; brillar; reflejar la luz; (fig.) brillar. **g. of hope,** rayo de esperanza, m.

gleaming, a. reluciente, centelleante; brillante. s. see **gleam**

glean, v.t. espigar, rebuscar; recoger. v.i. espigar

gleaner, s. espigador, m.; recogedor (-ra)

gleaning, s. espigueo, m.; rebusca, recolección, f.; pl. **gleanings,** fragmentos, m. pl.

glee, s. alegría, f., júbilo, alborozo, m.; (mus.) canción para voces solas, f.

gleeful, a. alegre, jubiloso, gozoso

gleefully, adv. alegremente, con júbilo

glen, s. cañada, f.; cañón, m., hondonada, f.

glib, a. locuaz, voluble; (easy) fácil

glibness, s. locuacidad, volubilidad, f.; (easiness) facilidad, f.

glide, s. deslizamiento, m.; (aer.) planeo, m. v.i. deslizarse; resbalar; (aer.) planear. **to g. away,** escurrirse; desaparecer silenciosamente

glider, s. (aer.) avión sin motor, m.

gliding, s. (aer.) vuelo sin motor, m.

glimmer, s. luz trémula, luz débil, f., tenue resplandor, m.; vislumbre, f. v.i. brillar con luz trémula, rielar (fig.); tener vislumbres (de)

glimpse, s. vistazo, m.; vislumbre, f.; indicio, m.; impresión, f.; vista, f. v.t. entrever, divisar; tener una vista (de); ver por un instante; vislumbrar

glint, s. tenue resplandor, m.; lustre, m.; centelleo, m.; reflejo, m.; (in the eye) chispa, f. v.i. relucir, destellar, rutilar; reflejar

glisten, v.i. brillar, relucir

glistening, a. coruscante; brillante, reluciente

glitter, s. brillo, resplandor, m. rutilación, f. v.i. brillar, resplandecer, relucir; rutilar. **All that glitters is not gold,** Todo lo que reluce no es oro

glittering, a. reluciente, resplandeciente; (fig.) brillante

gloat (over), v.i. recrearse en, gozarse en, deleitarse en

globe, s. globo, m.; esfera, f.; (for fish) pecera, f.; (for gas, electric light) globo, m. **geographical g.,** globo terrestre, m. **g.-trotter,** trotamundos, m.

globular, a. globular, esférico

globule, s. glóbulo, m.

globulous, a. globuloso

gloom, s. obscuridad, f.; lobreguez, f., tinieblas, f. pl.; (fig.) melancolía, tristeza, f.; taciturnidad, f. v.i. (fig.) ponerse melancólico; ser taciturno

gloomily, adv. obscuramente; (fig.) tristemente; taciturnamente

gloomy, a. obscuro; sombrío, lóbrego; melancólico, triste; taciturno; (of prospects, etc.) poco halagüeño, nada atrayente

glorification, s. glorificación, f.

glorify, v.t. glorificar; exaltar; alabar

glorious, a. glorioso; espléndido, magnífico; insigne; (fam.) estupendo

glory, s. gloria, f.; esplendor, m., magnificencia, f.; (art) gloria, f. v.i. recrearse, gozarse; glorificarse, jactarse. **to be in one's g.,** estar en la gloria. **to g. in,** hacer gala de, glorificarse en

gloss, s. (sheen) lustre, brillo, m.; (fig.) apariencia, f.; (note) glose, m.; (excuse) disculpa, f. v.t. pulir; glosar. **to g. over,** (faults) disculpar, excusar

glossary, s. glosario, m.

glossator, s. glosador (-ra)

glossiness, s. lustre, m., tersura, f.; brillo, m.

glossy, a. lustroso, terso; brillante; (of hair) liso

glottis, s. (anat.) glotis, f.

glove, s. guante. **evening gloves,** guantes largos, m. pl. **to be hand in g. with,** juntar diestra con diestra. **to fit like a g.,** sentar como un guante. **to put on one's gloves,** ponerse los guantes. **g. shop,** guantería, f. **g.-stretcher,** ensanchador (or abridor) de guantes, m.

glover, s. guantero (-ra)

glow, s. incandescencia, f.; claridad, f.; luz difusa, f.; (heat) calor, m.; (of colour) intensidad, f.; color vivo, m.; (enthusiasm) ardor, entusiasmo, m.; (redness) rojez, f.; (in the sky) arrebol, m.; (of pleasure, etc.) sentimiento de placer, m.; sensación de bienestar, f. v.i. estar incandescente; arder; abrasarse; sentir entusiasmo; mostrarse rojo; experimentar un sentimiento de placer o una sensación de bienestar. **to g. with health,** estar rebosando de salud. **g.-worm,** luciérnaga, f.

glower, s. ceño, m.; mirada amenazadora, f. v.i. poner cara de pocos amigos, mirar airadamente; tener los ojos puestos (en)

glowing, a. candente, incandescente; ardiente; entusiasta; satisfecho; intenso; (bright) vivo; (red) encendido; (with health) rebosante de salud. s. see glow

glowingly, adv. encendidamente; (fig.) con entusiasmo

gloy, s. engrudo, m.

glucose, s. glucosa, f.

glue, s. engrudo, m., cola, f. v.t. encolar, engrudar; pegar; (fig.) fijar, poner. **He kept his eyes glued on them,** Tenía los ojos fijados (or pegados) en ellos. **g.-pot,** pote de cola, m.

gluey, a. gomoso; pegajoso, viscoso

glueyness, s. viscosidad, f.

gluing, s. encoladura, f.

glum, *a.* deprimido, taciturno, sombrío

glumly, *adv.* taciturnamente

glumness, *s.* taciturnidad, *f.*; desaliento, *m.*

glut, *s.* superabundancia, *f.*, exceso, *m.* *v.t.* (satiate) hartar; (*fig.*) saciar; (the market) inundar

gluteal, *a.* glúteo

glutinous, *a.* glutinoso, pegajoso, viscoso

glutton, *s.* glotón (-ona); (*fig.*) ávido (-da)

gluttonous, *a.* glotón, comilón

gluttony, *s.* glotonería, gula, *f.*

glycerine, *s.* glicerina, *f.*

glycine, *s.* (*chem.*) glicocola, *f.*

gnarled, *a.* nudoso; (of human beings) curtido

gnash, *v.t.* rechinar, crujir (los dientes)

gnashing, *s.* rechinamiento (de dientes), *m.*

gnat, *s.* mosquito, *m.*

gnaw, *v.t.* roer; morder; (of wood by worms) carcomer; (*fig.*) roer

gnawing, *s.* roedura, *f.*; mordedura, *f.* *a.* roedor; mordedor

gnome, *s.* gnomo, *m.*

gnomon, *s.* gnomon, *m.*

gnostic, *a.* and *s.* gnóstico (-ca)

gnosticism, *s.* gnosticismo, *m.*

go, *v.i.* ir; (depart) irse, marcharse; (go towards) dirigirse a, encaminarse a; (lead to, of roads, etc.) conducir a, ir a; (vanish) desaparecer; (leave) dejar, salir de; (lose) perder; (pass) pasar; (of time) transcurrir, pasar; (be removed) quitarse; (be prohibited) prohibirse; (fall) caer; (collapse) hundirse; (be torn off) desprenderse; desgajarse; (*mech.*) funcionar, trabajar, andar; (sound) sonar; (of the heart) palpitar, latir; (follow) seguir; (gesture) hacer un gesto; (be stated) decirse, afirmarse; (live) vivir; (wear) llevar; (turn out) salir, resultar; (improve) mejorar; (prosper) prosperar; (turn, become) ponerse; volverse; (to sleep) dormirse; (into a faint) desmayarse; (decay) echarse a perder, estropearse; (turn sour) agriarse; (become, adopt views, etc.) hacerse; (be sold) venderse; (be decided);

decidirse, ser decidido; (have) tener; (by will) pasar; (belong) pertenecer; (receive) recibir; (have its place) estar; (put) ponerse; (going plus infin.) ir a; (die) morir, irse; (do a journey, a given distance) hacer; (a pace, step) dar; (take) tomar; (escape) escaparse, (contribute). contribuir (a); (harmonize) armonizar (con); (be current) ser válido; (be) ser; (of a document, etc., run) rezar, decir; (attend) asistir a; (be broken) estar roto; (be worn) estar raído; (be granted) darse, otorgarse. It's gone five, Ya dieron las cinco. It's time to be going, Es hora de marcharse. Let's go! ¡Vamos! These two colours go well together, Estos colores armonizan bien. Well, how goes it? ¿Bueno, qué tal? ¿Cómo te va? Who goes there? (*mil.*) ¿Quién va? to go and fetch, ir a buscar. to let go, soltar; dejar ir. to go one's way, seguir su camino. to go wrong, salir mal, fracasar; (sin) descarriarse. Go on! ¡Adelante! (continue) ¡Siga!; (*fam.*) ¡Qué va! to go about, dar la vuelta a; rodear; recorrer; (undertake) emprender, hacer; intentar; (of news, etc.) circular; (*naut.*) virar de bordo. Go about your business! ¡Métete en lo que to importa! to go abroad, ir al extranjero; salir a la calle; publicarse, divulgarse. to go across, cruzar, atravesar; pasar. to go after, andar tras; seguir; (seek) ir a buscar; (persecute) perseguir. to go again, ir de nuevo; (be present) asistir otra vez; volver. to go against, ir contra; militar contra; oponerse a; ser desfavorable a. to go ahead, adelantar, avanzar; progresar; prosperar; (lead) ir a la cabeza (de), conducir; (*naut.*) marchar hacia adelante. to go along, andar por; recorrer; (depart) irse, marcharse. to go along with, acompañar (a). to go aside, quitarse de en medio; apartarse, retirarse. to go astray, perderse; extraviarse, descarriarse. to go at, atacar, acometer; (undertake) empren-

der; empezar a. **to go at it
again,** (*fam.*) volver a la carga.
to go away, irse, marcharse;
ausentarse; alejarse; desaparecer. **to go away with,** marcharse con; (an object) llevarse.
to go back, volver; (retreat)
retroceder, volverse atrás; (in
history) remontarse a. **to go
back on,** (a promise, etc.) faltar
a; (retract) retractarse; (betray)
traicionar. **to go backwards,**
retroceder, cejar; desandar lo
andado; (*fig.*) deteriorar, empeorar. **to go backwards and
forwards,** ir y venir; oscilar. **to
go before,** (lead) ir a la cabeza de,
conducir; anteceder; proceder;
(a judge, etc.) comparecer ante.
to go behind, ir detrás de;
esconderse detrás de; seguir;
(evidence, etc.) mirar más allá
de. **to go between,** ponerse
entre; interponerse; (as a mediator) mediar; (insert) intercalarse; (travel) ir entre; llevar
cartas entre, serm ensajero de.
to go beyond, ir más allá;
exceder. **to go by,** pasar
por; pasar cerca de, pasar junto
a; ir por; (of time) transcurrir,
pasar; (follow) seguir; guiarse
por, atenerse a; (judge by)
juzgar por; (a name) pasar por;
tomar el nombre de. **to go
down,** bajar, descender; (of the
sun) ponerse; (sink) hundirse;
sumergirse; (fall) caer; (be remembered) ser recordado; (believe) tragar; ser creído. **to go
down again,** bajar de nuevo;
volver a caer. **to go far,** ir lejos;
influir mucho (en); impresionar
mucho; (contribute) contribuir
(a). **to go for,** (seek) ir en busca
de; procurar tener; (attack)
echarse encima de, atacar. **to
go for a ride (by car, bicycle,
on horseback),** dar un paseo (en
coche, en bicicleta, a caballo). **to
go forth,** salir; publicarse. **to go
forward,** adelantar, avanzar;
progresar; continuar; (happen)
tener lugar. **to go from,** dejar,
abandonar; separarse de, apartarse de; marcharse de. **to go in,**
entrar en; (a railway carriage,
etc.) subir a; (compete) concurrir. **to go in again,** volver a

entrar en, entrar de nuevo en.
to go in and out, entrar y salir;
ir y venir. **to go in for,** entrar a
buscar; dedicarse a, entregarse a;
(buy) comprarse; tomar parte en;
(an examination) tomar (un
examen); (for a competition)
entrar en (un concurso); (try)
ensayar; arriesgar. **to go into,**
entrar en; examinar; investigar;
ocuparse con. **to go near,** acercarse a. **to go off,** marcharse; (explode) estallar; (of fire-arms) dispararse; (of the voice, etc.)
perder (la voz, etc.); (run away)
huir, fugarse. **to go off badly,**
salir mal, fracasar, no tener
éxito. **to go off well,** salir bien,
tener éxito. **to go on,** subirse a;
continuar; durar; avanzar; proseguir su marcha; progresar;
prosperar; (*theat.*) entrar en
escena; (of clothes) ponerse;
(rely on) apoyarse en. **Don't go
on like that,** No seas así, No te
pongas así. **This glove will not
go on me,** No puedo ponerme
este guante. **to be gone on a
person,** (*fam.*) estar loco por.
I went on to say . . . , Después
dije; Continuando mi discurso
dije . . . **It was going on for
six o'clock when . . .** Serían
alrededor de las seis cuando . . .
He is going on for fifty, Raya
en los cincuenta años. **to go on
foot,** ir a pie. **to go on with,**
continuar con; empezar. **to go
out,** salir; (descend) bajar; (of
fires, lights) extinguirse, apagarse; (of fashion, etc.) pasar
(de); (the tide) menguar; (retire)
retirarse; (in society) frecuentar
la alta sociedad; (die) morir;
(arouse) excitar. **to go out of
fashion,** pasar de moda. **to go
out of one's way (to),** dejar su
camino (para); (lose oneself) perder el camino, extraviarse; (take
trouble) desvivirse (por), tomarse
molestia (para). **to go over,**
cruzar; pasar por encima; (to
another party or to the other
side) pasarse a; (read) repasar;
examinar. **to go past,** pasar;
pasar en frente de. **to go round,**
dar la vuelta a; (revolve) girar;
(surround) rodear; (of news, etc.)
divulgarse; (be enough) ser sufi-

ciente para todos. **to go through**, ir por, pasar por; re-correr; (pierce) penetrar, atra-vesar; (examine) examinar; (suffer) padecer, sufrir; (experi-ence) experimentar; (live) vivir; (of time) pasar; (of money) malgastar, derrochar. **to go through with**, llevar a cabo; terminar. **to go to**, ir a, en-caminarse a; (a person) acer-carse a, dirigirse a; (help, be useful) servir para; (be meant for) destinarse a; (rise of price) subir a; (find) encontrar; (of a bid) subir una apuesta hasta. **to go to war**, declarar la guerra. **to go together**, ir juntos (juntas). **to go towards**, encaminarse hacia, ir hacia; (help) ayudar a. **to go under**, pasar por debajo de; (sink) hundirse; (fail) fracasar; (be bankrupt) arruinarse, de-clararse en quiebra; (the name of) hacerse pasar por. **to go up**, subir; ir arriba; (a tree) trepar; (a ladder, etc.) subir; (a river) ir río arriba; (to town) ir a; (ex-plode) estallar. **to go up and down**, subir y bajar; oscilar; ir de una parte a otra. **to go upon**, subirse a; (rely on) apoyarse en; obrar según; em-prender. **to go upstairs**, ir arriba; (to another storey, as in a flat) subir al otro piso; subir la escalera. **to go up to**, acercarse a; (of a bid) subir una apuesta hasta. **to go with**, acompañar; (agree with) estar de acuerdo con; (of principles) seguir, ser fiel a; (harmonize) armonizar con; (be suitable to) ir bien con; convenir a; (fam. get along) ir. **to go without**, marcharse sin, (lack) pasarse sin. **It goes with-out saying that . . .**, No hay que decir que . . . .

go, s. (fashion) moda, boga, f.; (happening) suceso, m.; (fix) apuro, m.; (energy) energía, f., empuje, brío, m.; (turn) turno, m.; (attempt) tentativa, f.; (action) movimiento, m., acción, f.; (bargain) acuerdo, m. **It's a go!** (agreed) ¡Trato hecho! ¡Acordado! ¡Entendidos! **It is all the go**, Hace furor, Es la gran moda. **It is no go**, No puede ser,

Es imposible. **Now it's my go**, Ahora me toca a mí, Ahora es mi turno. **on the go**, en movi-miento; entre manos; ocupado. **to have a go**, probar suerte; procurar, tratar de; tener un turno

goad, s. garrocha, aguijada, f., aguijón, m.; (fig.) acicate, estí-mulo, m. v.t. aguijar, picar; (fig.) incitar, estimular, empujar. **prick with a g.**, aguijonazo, m.

go-ahead, a. emprendedor: pro-gresivo

goal, s. (posts in football, etc.) meta, portería, f.; (score) gol, m.; (in racing) meta, f.; (destination) destinación, f.; (fig.) ambición, f.; (purpose, objective) fin, ob-jeto, m. **to score a g.**, marcar un gol. **g.-keeper**, guardameta, m. portero (-ra). **g.-post**, palo de la portería, m.

goat, s. cabra, f.; (ast.) capri-cornio, m. **he-g.**, cabrón, m. **young g.**, cabrito, m, chivo (-va). **g.-herd**, cabrero, m. **g. skin**, piel de cabra, f.; (wineskin) odre, m.

goatee, s. pera, perilla, f.

goatish, a. cabruno; de cabra; lascivo

goatsucker, s. (orn.) chota-cabras, f.

gobble, v.t. and v.i. engullir, tragar. v.i. (of turkey) gluglu-tear. s. glugluteo, m., voz del pavo, f.

gobbler, s. engullidor (-ra), tragón (-ona); (fam.) pavo, m.

go-between, s. trotaconventos, f.; alcahuete, m.; (mediator) media-nero (-ra)

goblet, s. copa, f.

goblin, s. trasgo, duende, m.

go-by, to give the, evitar; pasar por alto de; omitir

go-cart, s. andaderas, f. pl.; pollera, f.; cochecito de nino, m.

god, s. dios, m.; pl. **gods**, dioses, m. pl.; (in a theatre) público del paraíso, m.; paraíso, m. **By God!** ¡Vive Dios! **For God's sake**, ¡Por el amor de Dios!; ¡Por Dios! **Please God**, ¡Plegue a Dios! **Thank God!** ¡Gracias a Dios! **God forbid!** ¡No lo quiera Dios! **God grant it!** ¡Dios lo quiera! **God keep you!** ¡Dios le guarde!

¡Vaya Vd. con Dios! **God willing** (D.V.), Dios mediante

godchild, *s.* ahijado (-da)

goddaughter, *s.* ahijada, *f.*

goddess, *s.* diosa, *f.*; (*poet.*) dea, *f.*

godfather, *s.* padrino, *m.* **to be a g. to**, ser padrino de, sacar de pila (a)

godfearing, *a.* timorato, temeroso de Dios; religioso

godforsaken, *a.* dejado de la mano de Dios; (of places) remoto, solitario

Godhead, *s.* divinidad, *f.*

godless, *a.* impío, irreligioso; sin Dios

godlessness, *s.* impiedad, irreligiosidad, *f.*

godlike, *a.* divino

godliness, *s.* piedad, *f.*; santidad, *f.*

godly, *a.* devoto, piadoso, religioso

godmother, *s.* madrina, *f.* **fairy g.**, hada madrina, *f.* **to be a g. to**, ser madrina de

godparent, *s.* padrino, *m.*; madrina, *f. pl.* **godparents**, padrinos, *m. pl.*

godsend, *s.* bien, *m.*; buena suerte, *f.*; fortuna, *f.*

go-getter, *s.* buscavidas, *m.* and *f.*

goggle, *s.* mirada fija, *f.*; *pl.* **goggles**, anteojos, *m. pl.*, gafas, *f. pl.*; (of a horse) anteojeras, *f. pl. v.i.* mirar fijamente; salirse a uno los ojos de la cabeza. **g.-eyed**, de ojos saltones. **g.-eyes**, ojos saltones, *m. pl.*

going, *s.* ida, *f.*; (departure) partida, marcha, *f.*; salida, *f.*; (pace) paso, *m.*; (speed) velocidad, *f.* **It was heavy g.**, El avance era lento; El progreso era lento; (of parties, etc.) Era aburrido. **The g. was difficult on those mountainous roads**, El conducir (or el ir or el andar) era difícil en aquellos caminos de montaña. **g. back**, vuelta, *f.*, regreso; *m.* **g. down**, bajada, *f.*, descenso, *m.*; (of the sun, etc.) puesta, *f.* **g. forward**, avance, *m.*; progreso, *m.* **g. in**, entrada, *f.* **g. in and out**, idas y venidas, *f. pl.* **g. out**, salida, *f.*; (of a fire, light) apagamiento, *m.*

going, *a. pres. part.* que va, yendo; que funciona. **G.**, **g.**, **gone** (at an auction) A la una, a las dos, a las tres. **goings-on**, (tricks) trapujos, *m. pl.*; (conduct) conducta, *f.* **g. concern**, empresa próspera, *f.* **g. to**, con destino a

goitre, *s.* bocio, *m.*

gold, *s.* oro, *m.*; color de oro, *m. a:* de oro; áureo. **All that glitters is not g.**, No es oro todo lo que reluce. **cloth of g.**, tela de oro, *f.* **dull g.**, oro mate, *m.* **light g.**, oro pálido, *m.* **old g.**, oro viejo, *m.* **g.-beater**, batidor de oro, *m.* **g.-digger**, minero de oro, *m.*; (woman) aventurera, *f.* **g. dust**, oro en polvo, *m.* **g.-fever**, fiebre de oro, *f.* **g. lace**, galón de oro, *m.* **g. lacquer**, sisa dorada, *f.* **g. leaf**, pan de oro, oro batido, *m.* **g.-mine**, mina de oro, *f.* **g. piece**, moneda de oro, *f.* **g. plate**, vajilla de oro, *f.* **g. standard**, patrón oro, *m.* **g.-thread**, hilo de oro, *m.* **g.-yielding**, *a.* aurífero

golden, *a.* de oro; dorado; áureo; amarillo; (*fig.*) feliz; excelente. **to become g.**, dorarse. **g. age**, edad de oro, *f.* **g.-crested wren**, abadejo, *m.* **g. hair**, cabellos dorados (or de oro), *m. pl.* **G. Legend**, leyenda áurea, *f.* **g. mean**, justo medio, *m.* **g. rose**, rosa de oro, *f.* **g. rule**, regla áurea, *f.* **g. syrup**, jarabe de arce, *m.* **g. voice**, voz de oro, *f.* **g. wedding**, bodas de oro, *f. pl.*

goldfinch, *s.* jilguero, *m.*

goldfish, *s.* carpa dorada, *f.* **g. bowl**, pecera, *f.*

goldsmith, *s.* orfebre, *m.*

golf, *s.* golf, *m.* **g.-club**, palo de golf, *m.*; club de golf, *m.* **g.-course**, campo de golf, *m.*

golfer, *s.* jugador (-ra) de golf

golliwog, *s.* negrito, *m.*, muñeca negra de trapo, *f.*

golosh, *s.* chanclo, *m.*

gonad, *s.* gónada, *f.*

gondola, *s.* góndola, *f.*

gondolier, *s.* gondolero, *m.*

gone, *a.* and *past part.* ido; (lost) perdido; (ruined) arruinado; (dead) muerto; (past) pasado;

(disappeared) desaparecido; (fainted) desmayado; (suppressed) suprimido; (pregnant) encinta; (drunk) borracho; (ended) terminado; (exhausted) agotado; (ill) enfermo. **far g.,** avanzado; (in years) de edad avanzada; (of illness) cerca de la muerte, muy enfermo; (in love) loco de amor; (drunk) muy borracho. **It is all g.,** No hay más. **It is g. seven o'clock,** Son las siete y pico, Son las siete ya

gong, s. gong, m.; (Chinese) batintín, m.

gonorrhœa, s. gonorrea, f.

good, a. bueno (before m. sing. nouns) buen; agradable; afortunado; (appropriate) apropiado, oportuno; (beneficial) provechoso, ventajoso; (wholesome) sano, saludable; (suitable) apto; (useful) útil; (kind) bondadoso; (much) mucho; (obliging) amable; (virtuous) virtuoso; (skilled) experto; (fresh) fresco; (genuine) genuino, legítimo; verdadero. adv. bien. interj. ¡bueno! ¡bien! **a g. deal,** mucho. **a g. many,** bastantes. **a g. turn,** un favor. **a g. way,** (distance) un buen trecho; mucho. **a g. while,** un buen rato. **as g. as,** tan bueno como. **Be so g. as to . . . !** Haga el favor de, Tenga Vd. la bondad de (followed by infin.). **fairly g.,** a. bastante bueno. adv. bastante bien. **I'm g. for another five miles,** Tengo fuerzas para cinco millas más. **It was g. of you to do it,** Vd. fué muy amable de hacerlo, Vd. tuvo mucha bondad de hacerlo. **to be no g. at this sort of thing,** no servir para tales cosas. **to have a g. time,** pasarlo bien. **to make g.,** reparar; indemnizar; (accomplish) llevar a cabo, poner en práctica; justificar; (a promise) cumplir. **very g.,** a. muy bueno. adv. muy bien. **g.-feeling,** buena voluntad, f. **g.-fellowship,** compañerismo, m.; buena compañía, f. **g.-for-nothing,** s. papanatas, badulaque, m. **to be g.-for-nothing,** no servir para nada. **g. luck,** buena suerte, f. **g. manners,** buenos modales, m.

pl.; buena crianza, educación, f. **g. nature,** buen natural, m.; buen humor, m. **g.-natured,** de buen natural; de buen humor, bonachón. **g. offices,** buenos oficios, m. pl. **g.-tempered,** de buen humor

good, s. bien, m.; provecho, m.; utilidad, f.; pl. **goods.** See separate entry. **I am saying this for your g.,** Lo digo para tu bien. **Much g. may it do you!** ¡Buen provecho te haga! **for g. and all,** para siempre jamás. **It is no g.,** Es inútil; No vale la pena. **the g.,** el bien; (people) los buenos. **They have gone for g.,** Se han marchado para no volver. **to do one g.,** hacer bien a uno; mejorar; ser provechoso (a uno); (suit) sentar bien (a uno). **What is the g. of . . . ?** ¿Para qué sirve . . . ?; ¿Qué vale . . . ? **g. and evil,** el bien y el mal

good-bye, interj. ¡adiós! s. adiós, m., despedida, f. **to bid g.-b.,** decir adiós. **G.-b. for the present!** ¡Hasta la vista! ¡Hasta luego! **G.-b. until to-morrow, then,** Hasta mañana pues, adiós, Hasta mañana entances.

goodness, s. bondad, f.; (of quality) buena calidad, f.; (of persons) amabilidad, benevolencia, f.; (essence) esencia, substancia, f.; bien, m.; excelencia, f.; interj. ¡Jesús! ¡Dios mío! **For g. sake!** ¡Por Dios! **I wish to g. that,** ¡Ojalá que . . . !

goods, s. pl. bienes, efectos, m. pl.; artículos, m. pl.; (com.) mercancías, f. pl., géneros, m. pl. **by g.-train,** en pequeña velocidad. **stolen g.,** objetos robados, m. pl. **g. lift,** montacargas, m. **g. office,** depósito de mercancías, m. **g. station,** estación de carga, f. **g.-train,** tren de mercancías, m. **g. van,** furgón, m. **g. waggon,** vagon de mercancías, m.

goodwill, s. benevolencia, f.; buena voluntad, f.; (of a business) clientela, f.

goose, s. oca, f., ganso (-sa); plancha de sastre, f. a. de oca. **g. flesh,** (fig.) carne de gallina, f. **g. girl,** ansarera, f. **g.-step,** paso de oca, m.

gooseberry, s. uva espina, f.

Gordian, a. gordiano. **G. knot,** nudo gordiano, m.

gore, s. sangre, f.; (sew.) sesga, nesga, f. v.t. acornear; desgarrar; herir (con arma blanca)

gorge, s. (valley) cañón, barranco, m.; (heavy meal) comilona, f., atracón, m. v.t. engullir, tragar. v.i. hartarse, atracarse

gorgeous, a. magnífico; espléndido, suntuoso; (fam.) maravilloso, estupendo

gorgeously, adv. magníficamente

gorgeousness, s. magnificencia, f.; suntuosidad, f., esplendor, m.

gorilla, s. gorila, m.

gormandize, v.i. glotonear

gormandizer, s. glotón (-ona)

gorse, s. tojo, m., aulaga, f.

gory, a. ensangrentado; sangriento

gosh, interj. ¡caray! ¡caramba!

goshawk, s. (orn.) azor, m.

gosling, s. ansarino, m.

gospel, s. evangelio, m.; doctrina, f. **The G. according to St. Mark,** El Evangelio según San Marcos. **to believe as g. truth,** creer como si fuese el evangelio. **to preach the G.,** predicar el evangelio

gospeller, s. evangelista, m.; misionero, m.

gossamer, s. hilo de araña, m., red de araña, telaraña, f.; (filmy material) gasa, f.; hilo finísimo, m. a. de gasa; sutil, delgado, fino

gossip, s. murmurador (-ra), chismoso (-sa), hablador (-ra); (scandal) chisme, m.; habladuría, murmuración, f.; (obsolete, of a woman) comadre, f.; (talk) charla, f. v.i. charlar, conversar; (in bad sense) murmurar, chismear; criticar. **to g. about,** charlar de; poner lenguas en, cortar un sayo (a); hablar mal de. **g. column,** gacetilla, f.

gossiping, a. charlatán, hablador; chismoso, murmurador. s. See **gossip**

Goth, s. godo (-da); bárbaro (-ra)

Gothic, a. (art) gótico; (of race) godo; bárbaro. s. lengua goda,

f.; arquitectura gótica, f. **G. characters,** letra gótica, f.

gouge, s. gubia, f. v.t. escoplear. **to g. out,** vaciar; sacar

gourd, s. calabaza, f.

gourmand, s. glotón, m.

gourmet, s. gastrónomo, m.

gout, s. (med.) gota, f.

gouty, a. gotoso

govern, v.t. gobernar; regir; (guide) guiar; dominar; domar, refrenar; (gram.) regir; (regulate) regular

governable, a. gobernable; manejable; dócil

governess, s. institutriz, f.; (in a school) maestra, f.

governing, a. gubernante; director; (with principle, etc.) directivo. s. See **government**

government, s. gobierno, m.; dirección, f.; autoridad, f. **g. bond,** bono del gobierno, m. **g. house,** palacio del gobernador, m. **g. office,** oficina del gobierno, f. **g. stock,** papel del Estado, m.

governmental, a. gubernamental, gubernativo

governor, s. gobernador (-ra); vocal de la junta de gobierno, m. and f.; (of a prison) director (-ra) (de una prisión); (mech.) regulador, m. **g.-general,** gobernador general, virrey, m.

governorship, s. gobierno, m.; dirección, f.

gown, s. toga, f.; (cassock) sotana, f.; (dressing-g.) bata, f.; (for sleeping) camisa de noche, f.; (bathing-wrap) albornoz, m.; (dress) vestido, traje, m.

Goyesque, a. goyesco

grab, s. asimiento, m., presa, f.; (mech.) gancho, m. v.t. arrebatar, asir, agarrar; (fig.) alzarse con, tomar

grabber, s. cogedor (-ra); codicioso (-sa)

grace, s. elegancia, f.; simetría, armonía, f.; gracia, gentileza, f., donaire, m.; encanto, m.; (goodness) bondad, f.; gracia, f.; merced, f., favor, m.; (period of time) plazo, m.; (privilege) privilegio, m.; (theol.) gracia divina, f.; (at table) bendición de la mesa, f.; (as a title) excelentísimo, (to an archbishop) ilus-

trísimo. *v.t.* adornar; favorecer;
honrar. **airs and graces,**
humos, *m. pl.* **The Three
Graces,** Las Gracias. **three
days' g.,** plazo de tres días, *m.*
**to get into a person's good
graces,** congraciarse con; caer
en gracia con. **to say g.,**
bendecir la mesa. **with a bad
g.,** a regañadientes. **with a
good g.,** de buena gana. **g.-
note,** (*mus.*) nota de adorno,
f.

graceful, *a.* airoso, gentil, gracioso; elegante; bonito

gracefully, *adv.* airosamente,
gentilmente; con gracia; elegantemente

gracefulness. See **grace**

graceless, *a.* réprobo; dejado de
la mano de Dios; sin gracia

gracious, *a.* (merciful) piadoso,
clemente; (urbane) afable, condescendiente, agradable. **Good
g.!** ¡Vamos! ¡Dios mío!

graciously, *adv.* afablemente;
con benevolencia. **to be g.
pleased,** tener a bien

graciousness, *s.* amabilidad,
afabilidad, condescendencia, *f.*

gradate, *v.t.* graduar; (*art*) degradar

gradation, *s.* graduación, *f.*;
(*mus.*) gradación, *f.*; paso gradual, *m.*; serie, *f.*

grade, *s.* grado, *m.*; (quality)
calidad, clase, *f.*; (gradient)
pendiente, *f.*, declive, *m. v.t.*
graduar, clasificar; (cattle breeding) cruzar. **down g.,** cuesta
abajo. **up g.,** cuesta arriba.
highest g., *s.* primera clase, *f.*
a. de primera clase; de calidad
excelente

gradient, *s.*, declive, *m.*, cuesta,
pendiente, *f.*

gradin, *s.* grada, *f.*, peldaño,
m.

gradual, *a.* gradual. *s.* (*ecc.*)
gradual, *m.*

gradually, *adv.* gradualmente;
poco a poco

graduate, *s.* licenciado (-da). *a.*
graduado. *v.t.* graduar. *v.i.*
graduarse; (as a doctor) doctorarse. **to g. as,** recibirse de

graduation, *s.* graduación, *f.*

Græco-, *prefix* (in compounds)
greco-

graft, *s.* (*bot.*) injerto, *m.*; (*surg.*)
injerto de piel, *m.*; (swindle)
estafa, *f.*; (bribery) soborno, *m.*
v.t. (*bot.*) injertar; (*surg.*) injertar
un trozo de piel; (*fig.*) inje-
rir

grafting, *s.* (*bot.*) injerto, *m.*;
(*surg.*) injerto de piel, *m.*; (*fig.*)
inserción, *f.*

grail, *s.* grial, *m.*

grain, *s.* (corn) grano, *m.*; (cereal)
cereal, *m.* or *f.*; (seed, weight)
grano, *m.*; (trace) pizca, *f.*; (of
wood, etc.) fibra, hebra, veta, *f.*;
(of leather) flor, *f.*; (texture)
textura, *f. v.t.* granear; granu-
lar; (wood, marble, etc.) vetear.
against the g., a contrapelo.
g. lands, mieses, *f. pl.*

grammar, *s.* gramática, *f.* **g.-
school,** instituto de segunda
enseñanza, *m.*

grammarian, *s.* gramático, *m.*

grammatical, *a.* gramático

grammatically, *adv.* gramati-
calmente

grammaticalness, *s.* corrección
gramatical, *f.*

gramme, *s.* gramo, *m.*

gramophone, *s.* gramófono, *m.*
cabinet g., gramófono de tipo
consola, *m.* **portable g.,** gramófono portable, *m.* **g. needle,**
aguja de gramófono, *f.* **g.-
record,** disco de gramófono, *m.*

granary, *s.* granero, hórreo, *m.*,
troj, *f.* **g. keeper,** trojero, *
m.*

grand, *a.* magnífico, soberbio;
imponente; (of dress) espléndido,
vistoso; (of people) distinguido, importante; aristocrático;
(proud) orgulloso; (of style)
elevado, sublime; (morally)
noble; augusto; (main) principal;
(full) completo; (*fam.*) estupendo,
magnífico; (with duke, etc.) gran.
s. piano de cola, *m.* **g.-aunt,** tía
abuela, *f.* **G. Cross,** gran cruz, *f.*
G. Duchess, gran duquesa, *f.*
G. Duke, gran duque, *m.* **G.
Lodge,** (of freemasons) Gran
Oriente, *m.* **G. Master,** gran
maestre, *m.* **g.-nephew,** sobrino,
m. **g.-niece,** sobrina, *f.* **g.
opera,** ópera, *f.* **g. piano,** piano
de cola, *m.* **g.-stand,** tribuna, *f.*
g.-uncle, tío abuelo, *m.* **g.
vizier,** gran visir, *m.*

grandchild, s. nieto (-ta). **great-g.,** bisnieto (-ta). **great-great-g.,** tataranieto (-ta)

granddaughter, s. nieta, f. **great-g.,** bisnieta, f. **great-great-g.,** tataranieta, f.

grandee, s. grande de España o Portugal, m.

grandeur, s. magnificencia, f.; grandiosidad, f.; magnitud, grandeza, f.; (pomp) pompa, f., fausto, m.

grandfather, s. abuelo, m. **great-g.,** bisabuelo, m. **great-great-g.,** tatarabuelo, m.

grandfather's clock, reloj de péndulo, m.

grandfatherly, a. de abuelo

grandiloquence, s. grandilocuencia, f.

grandiloquent, a. grandílocuo

grandiose, a. grandioso, sublime; impresionante; imponente; (in a bad sense) extravagante: (of style) bombástico, hinchado

grandmother, s. abuela, f. **great-g.,** bisabuela, f. **great-great-g.,** tatarabuela, f.

grandness, s. magnificencia, f.; aristocracia, f.; (pride) orgullo, m.; grandiosidad, f.; (of style) sublimidad, f.; (of character) nobleza, f.

grandparent, s. abuelo, m.; abuela, f.; pl. **grandparents,** abuelos, m. pl. **great-grandparents,** bisabuelos, m. pl. **great-great-grandparents,** tatarabuelos, m. pl.

grandson, s. nieto, m. **great-g.,** bisnieto, m. **great-great-g.,** tataranieto, m.

grange, s. granja, f.; casa de campo, f.

granite, s. granito, m.

granny, s. abuelita, nana, f.; abuela, f. **g. knot,** nudo al revés, m.

grant, s. concesión, f.; otorgamiento, m.; donación, f.; privilegio, m.; (for study) beca, bolsa de estudio, f.; (transfer) traspaso, m., cesión, f. v.t. conceder; (bestow) otorgar, dar; donar; (agree to) acceder a, asentir en; permitir; (transfer) traspasar; (assume) suponer. **to take for granted,** descontar; dar por hecho. **God g. it!** ¡Dios lo

quiera! **granted that,** dado que

grantee, s. cesionario (-ia), adjudicatorio (-ia)

grantor, s. cesionista, m. and f.; otorgador (-ra)

granulated, a. granulado

granulation, s. granulación, f.

granule, s. gránulo, m.

granulous, a. granuloso

grape, s. uva, f. **bunch of grapes,** racimo de uvas, m. **muscatel g.,** uva moscatel, f. **sour grapes,** uvas agrias, f. pl.; (phrase) ¡están verdes! **g.-fruit,** toronja, f. **g. gatherer,** vendimiador (-ra). **g. harvest,** vendimia, f. **g. juice,** mosto, m. **g.-shot,** metralla, f. **g. stone,** granuja, f. **g.-sugar,** glucosa, f. **g.-vine,** vid, parra, f.

graph, s. gráfica, f.; diagrama, m.

graphic, a. gráfico

graphite, s. grafito, m.

graphology, s. grafología, f.

grapple, s. (naut.) rezón, arpeo, m.; lucha a brazo partido, f. v.t. (naut.) aferrar; asir, agarrar. v.i. (naut.) aferrarse. **to g. with,** luchar a brazo partido (con); (fig.) luchar con

grappling, s. (naut.) aferramiento, m.; lucha cuerpo a cuerpo, f.; (with a problem) lucha con, f.

grasp, s. agarro, m.; (reach) alcance, m.; (of a hand) apretón, m.; (power) garras, f. pl., poder, m.; (understanding) comprensión, f.; inteligencia, capacidad intelectual, f. v.t. agarrar, asir; empuñar; abrazar; (fig.) comprender, alcanzar; (a hand) estrechar. v.i. agarrarse. **within one's g.,** al alcance de uno. **to g. at,** asirse de

grasping, s. asimiento, m.; (understanding) comprensión, f. a. codicioso, tacaño; mezquino

graspingness, s. codicia, f.

grass, s. hierba, f.; (pasture) pasto, herbaje, m.; (sward) césped, m. v.t. cubrir de hierba; sembrar de hierba; apacentar. **to hear the g. grow,** sentir crecer la hierba. **to let the g. grow,** (fig.) dejar crecer la hierba. **to turn out to g.,** echar al pasto. **g.-blade,** brizna de hierba, f. **g.-green,** a. and s.

verde como la hierba (*m.*). **g.-
grown**, cubierto de hierba.
g.-land, pradera, *f.* **g.-snake**,
culebra, *f.* **g. widow**, mujer
cuyo marido está ausente, *f.* **to
be a g. widow**, estar viuda.

grasshopper, *s.* saltamontes, *m.*
grasshopper's chirp, chirrido
(del saltamontes), *m.*

grassy, *a.* parecido a la hierba,
como la hierba; cubierto de
hierba; de hierba

grate, *s.* parrilla, *f.*; (grating) reja,
f. v.t. raspar, raer; (*cul.*) rallar;
(make a noise) hacer rechinar.
v.i. rozar; rechinar, chirriar.
to g. on, **upon**, (of sounds)
irritar, molestar; chocar con.
to g. on the ear, herir el oído

grateful, *a.* agradecido, reconocido; (pleasant) agradable, grato

gratefully, *adv.* agradecidamente;
gratamente

gratefulness, *s.* agradecimiento,
m., gratitud, *f.*; (pleasantness)
agrado, *m.*

grater, *s.* (*cul.*) rallador, *m.*

gratification, *s.* satisfacción, *f.*;
(pleasure) placer, gusto, *m.*

gratified, *a.* satisfecho, contento

gratify, *v.t.* satisfacer; (please)
gratificar, agradar

gratifying, *a.* satisfactorio, agradable

grating, *s.* reja, *f.*; rejilla, *f.*;
(*naut.*) jareta, *f.*; (optics) retículo,
m.; (sound) rechinamiento, chirrido, *m. a.* rechinante, chirriador; áspero

gratis, *a.* and *adv.* gratis

gratitude, *s.* agradecimiento, *m.*,
gratitud, *f.*

gratuitous, *a.* gratuito

gratuitously, *adv.* gratuitamente

gratuitousness, *s.* gratuidad, *f.*

gratuity, *s.* gratificación, propina, *f.*

grave, *s.* (hole) sepultura, fosa,
f.; (monument) tumba, *f.*, sepulcro, *m.*; (*fig.*) muerte, *f.* **g.-
digger**, enterrador, sepulturero,
m.

grave, *a.* grave; importante;
serio; sobrio; (anxious) preocupado; (of accent) grave. *s.* (grave
accent) acento grave, *m.*

gravel, *s.* grava, *f.*; cascajo,
casquijo, *m.*; (*med.*) arenillas,
f. pl., cálculo, *m.*

gravely, *adv.* gravemente; seriamente

Graves' disease, *s.* bocio exof-
tálmico, *m.*

gravestone, *s.* lápida mortuoria,
f.

graveyard, *s.* campo santo,
cementerio, *m.*

gravitate, *v.i.* gravitar; tender

gravitation, *s.* gravitación, *f.*;
tendencia, *f.*

gravity, *s.* (*phys.*) gravedad, *f.*;
seriedad, *f.*; solemnidad, *f.*;
gravedad, *f.*; (weight) peso, *m.*;
importancia, *f.*; (enormity) enormidad, *f.*; (danger) peligro, *m.*
centre of g., centro de gravedad,
m. **law of g.**, ley de la gravedad,
f. **specific g.**, peso específico, *m.*

gravy, *s.* salsa, *f.*; jugo (de la
carne), *m.* **g.-boat**, salsera, *f.*

gray. See **grey**

grayling, *s.* (*icht.*) tímalo, *m.*

graze, *s.* abrasión, *f.*; (brush)
roce, *m. v.i.* pacer, apacentarse.
v.t. pastorear, apacentar;
(brush) rozar

grazing, *s.* (*agr.*) apacentamiento,
pastoreo, *m.*; (brushing) rozadura, *f. a.* que pace, herbívoro;
(of land) pacedero. **g. land**,
pasto, *m.*

grease, *s.* grasa, *f.*; (dirt) mugre,
f.; (of a candle) sebo, *m.*, cera, *f.
v.t.* engrasar; manchar con grasa;
(*fig.*, *fam.*) untar. **to g. the
wheels**, (*fig.*) untar el carro.
g.-box, (*mech.*) caja de sebo, *f.*
g.-gun, engrasador de compresión, *m.* **g.-paint**, afeites de
actor (or de actriz), *m. pl.*
g.-proof paper, papel impermeable, *m.* **g. spot**, lámpara,
mancha de grasa, *f.*, saín, *m.*

greaser, *s.* engrasador, *m.*

greasiness, *s.* graseza, *f.*; lo
aceitoso; untuosidad, *f.*

greasing, *s.* engrasado, *m.*

greasy, *a.* grasiento; (oily)
aceitoso; (grubby) mugriento,
bisunto; (*fig.*) lisonjero. **g. pole**,
cucaña, *f.*

great, *a.* gran; grande; enorme;
vasto; (much) mucho; (famous)
famoso, ilustre; noble, sublime;
(intimate) íntimo; importante;
principal; poderoso; magnífico,
impresionante; (*fam.*) famoso,
estupendo; (of time) largo;

(clever) fuerte. **Alexander the G.**, Alejandro magno. **the G. Mogul**, el Gran Mogul. **a g. deal**, mucho. **a g. man**, un grande hombre, un hombre famoso. **a g. many**, muchos (muchas). **He lived to a g. age**, Vivió hasta una edad avanzada. **so g.**, tan grande, tamaño. **the g.**, los grandes hombres. **g. on**, aficionado a. **g.-aunt**, tía abuela, *f.* **g.-grandchild**, etc. See **grandchild**, etc. **g.-hearted**, valeroso; magnánimo, generoso. **G. Power**, gran poder, *m.* **G. War**, gran guerra, *f.*

greatcoat, *s.* sobretodo, *m.*

greater, *a.* comp. of **great**, mayor; más grande. **to make g.**, agrandar. **G. London**, Londres con sus suburbios.

greatest, *a.* sup. of **great**, más grande; mayor; máximo; más famoso; sumo

greatly, *adv.* mucho; con mucho; (very) muy; noblemente

greatness, *s.* grandeza, *f.*; grandiosidad, *f.*; extensión, vastedad, *f.*; importancia, *f.*; poder, *m.*; majestad, *f.*; esplendor, *m.*; (intensity) intensidad, *f.*; (enormity) enormidad, *f.*

Grecian, *a.* griego

greed, *s.* (cupidity) codicia, rapacidad, avaricia, *f.*; avidez, ansia, *f.*; (of food) gula, glotonería, *f.*

greedily, *adv.* codiciosamente; con avidez; (of eating) vorazmente

greedy, *a.* (for food) glotón; codicioso; ambicioso; ávido; deseoso

Greek, *a.* and *s.* griego (-ga); (language) griego, *m.* **It's all G. to me**, Para mí es como si fuese en latín. **G. key**, greca, *f.* **G. tunic**, peplo, *m.*

green, *a.* verde; (inexpert) inexperto, bisoño; (recent) nuevo, reciente; (fresh) fresco; (of complexion) pálido, descolorido; (flowery) floreciente; (vigorous) lozano; (young) joven; (unripe) verde; (credulous) crédulo; (raw) crudo; (of wood, vegetables) verde. *s.* verde, color verde, *m.*; (vegetables) verdura, *f.*; (meadow) prado, *m.*; (turf)

césped, *m.*; (grass) hierba, *f.*; (bowling) campo de juego, *m.* *v.t.* teñir (or pintar) de verde. **bright g.**, *s.* verdegay, verde claro, *m.* **dark g.**, *s.* verdinegro, *m.* **light g.**, *s.* verde pálido, *m.* **to grow or look g.**, verdear. **g.-eyed**, de ojos verdes. **g. peas**, guisantes, *m. pl.* **g. table**, tapete verde, *m.*

greenery, *s.* follaje, *m.*; verdura, *f.*

greenfly, *s.* pulgón, *m.*

greengage, *s.* (*bot.*) claudia, ciruela verdal, *f.*

greengrocer, *s.* verdulero (-ra)

greengrocery, *s.* verdulería, *f.*

greenhorn, *s.* bisoño (-ña); papanatas, *m.*

greenhouse, *s.* invernáculo, invernadero, *m.*

greenish, *a.* verdoso. **g.-yellow**, cetrino

Greenlander, *s.* groelandés (-esa)

greenness, *a.* lo verde; verdor, *m.*, verdura, *f.*; (inexperience) falta de experiencia, *f.*; (vigour) vigor, *m.*, lozanía, *f.*; (newness) novedad, *f.*; (of wood, fruit) falta de madurez, *f.*

greenroom, *s.* (*theat.*) saloncillo, *m.*

greenstuff, *s.* hortalizas, legumbres, *f. pl.*

greet, *v.t.* saludar; recibir; (express pleasure) dar la bienvenida (a)

greeting, *s.* salutación, *f.*, saludo, *m.*; recepción, *f.*; (welcome) bienvenida, *f.*; *pl.* **greetings**, recuerdos, *m. pl.*

gregarious, *a.* gregario

gregariousness, *s.* gregarismo, *m.*

Gregorian, *a.* gregoriano

grenade, *s.* granada, bomba, *f.* **hand-g.**, bomba de mano, *f.*

grenadier, *s.* granadero, *m.*

grenadine, *s.* granadina, *f.*

grey, *a.* gris; (of animals) rucio. *s.* color gris, gris, *m.*; caballo gris, *m.* **His hair is turning g.**, El pelo se le vuelve gris. **g.-haired**, de pelo gris. **g. matter**, materia gris, *f.*; cacumen, *m.* **g. mullet**, (*icht.*) mújol, *m.* **g. squirrel**, gris, *m.* **g. wolf**, lobo gris, *m.*

greyhound, *s.* galgo, lebrel, *m.* **g. bitch**, galga, *f.*; **g. racing**, carreras de galgos, *f. pl.*

greyish, *a.* grisáceo, agrisado; (of hair) entrecano

greyness, *s.* color gris, gris, *m.*; (*fig.*) monotonía, *f.*

grid, *s.* (of electric power) red, *f.*; rejilla, *f.*; (for water, etc.) alcantarilla, *f.*

gridiron, *s.* (*cul.*) parrilla, *f.*; (of electric power) red, *f.*; (*theat.*) telar, *m.*

grief, *s.* angustia, pena, aflicción, *f.*; dolor, suplicio, *m.* **to come to g.,** pasarlo mal, tener un desastre

grievance, *s.* injusticia, *f.*; motivo de queja, *m.*

grieve, *v.t.* entristecer, afligir, angustiar; atormentar. *v.i.* entristecerse, afligirse, acongojarse. **to g. for,** lamentar: echar de menos

grievous, *a.* (heavy) oneroso, gravoso; opresivo; doloroso, penoso; lamentable; cruel. **a g. error,** un error lamentable

grievousness, *s.* (weight) peso, *m.*; carácter opresivo, *m.*; dolor, *m.*, aflicción, *f.*; enormidad, *f.*; crueldad, *f.*

griffin, *s.* grifo, *m.*; (*fig.*) chaperon) carabina, *f.*; (dog) grifón, *m.*

grill, *s.* (*cul.*) parrilla, *f.*; (grating) rejilla, *f.*; (before a window) reja, *f.*; (food) asado a la parrilla, *m.* *v.t.* (*cul.*) asar a la parrilla; (burn) quemar; (question) interrogar; (torture) torturar. *v.i.* (*cul.*) asarse a la parrilla; (be burnt) quemarse. **g.-room,** "grill-room," *m.*, parrilla, *f.*

grille, *s.* reja, *f.*; rejilla, *f.*; (screen) verja, *f.*

grilled, *a.* (*cul.*) a la parrilla; con rejilla

griller, *s.* (*cul.*) parrilla, *f.*

grim, *a.* (fierce) feroz, salvaje; (severe) severo, ceñudo, adusto; inflexible; (frightful) horrible

grimace, *s.* mueca, *f.*, gesto, mohín, visaje, *m.* *v.i.* hacer muecas

grime, *s.* mugre, *f.*; suciedad, *f.* **to cover with g.,** enmugrecer

grimly, *adv.* severamente; sin sonreír; inflexiblemente; (without retreating) sin cejar; (frightfully) horriblemente; de un modo espantoso

grimness, *s.* (ferocity) ferocidad, *f.*; (severity) severidad, *f.*; inflexibilidad, *f.*; (frightfulness) horror, *m.*, lo espantoso

grimy, *a.* mugriento, sucio

grin, *s.* sonrisa grande, *f.*; sonrisa burlona, *f.*; (grimace) mueca, *f.* *v.i.* sonreír mostrando los dientes; sonreír sarcásticamente; sonreír de un modo burlón

grind, *v.t.* (to powder) pulverizar; moler; (break up) quebrantar; (oppress) agobiar, oprimir; (sharpen) afilar, amolar; (a barrel-organ) tocar (un manubrio); (the teeth) crujir, rechinar (los dientes); (into) reducir a; (*fam.*, teach) empollar. *v.i.* moler; (*fig.*, *fam.*) trabajar laboriosamente. *s.* (*fig.*, *fam.*) trabajo pesado, *m.*

grinder, *s.* (of scissors, etc.) afilador, *m.*; (of an organ) organillero; (mill-stone) piedra de moler, *f.*; (molar) muela, *f.*; (swot) estudiantón, *m.*

grinding, *a.* (tedious) cansado, aburrido; opresivo; (of pain) incesante. *s.* pulverización, *f.*; amoladura, *f.*; (of grain) molienda, *f.*; (polishing) pulimento, bruñido, *m.*; (oppression) opresión, *f.*; (of teeth) rechinamiento, *m.*

grindstone, *s.* amoladera, afiladera, piedra de amolar, *f.* **to have one's nose to the g.,** batir el yunque

grinning, *a.* sonriente; riente; (mocking) burlón

grip, *s.* asimiento, agarro, *m.*; (claws, clutches) garras, *f. pl.*; (hand) mano, *f.*; (of shaking hands) apretón de manos, *m.*; (of a weapon, etc.) empuñadura, *f.*; (reach) alcance, *m.*; (understanding) comprensión, *f.*; (control) dominio, *m.*; (bag) portamanteo, *m.*; maleta, *f.* *v.t.* asir, agarrar; agarrarse; (of wheels) agarrarse; (*mech.*) morder; (a sword, etc.) empuñar; (pinch) pellizcar; (surround) cercar; (understand) comprender; (press; to grip the hand and (*fig.*) the heart) apretar; (fill) llenar; (the attention) atraer, llamar; (sway, hold) dominar

gripe, *s.* (*fam.*, pain) retortijón (de tripas), *m.*

grisly, *a.* espantoso; repugnante

grist, *s.* molienda, *f.* **Everything is g. to their mill,** Ellos sacan partido de todo

gristle, *s.* cartílago, *m.*, ternilla, *f.*

gristly, *a.* cartilaginoso

grit, *s.* cascajo, *m.*; polvo, *m.*; (*fig.*) firmeza (de carácter), *f.*; (courage) valor, *m.*; (endurance) aguante, *m.*

gritty, *a.* arenoso, arenisco

grizzled, *a.* (of hair, etc.) gris; canoso; grisáceo

grizzly bear, *s.* oso (-sa) pardo (-da)

groan, *s.* gemido, *m.* *v.i.* gemir; (creak) crujir. **to g. out,** decir (or contar) entre gemidos. **to g. under,** sufrir bajo, gemir bajo; (of weight) crujir bajo

groaning, *s.* gemidos, *m.* *pl.* *a.* que gime, gemidor; (under a weight) crujiente

grocer, *s.* abacero (-ra) vendedor (-ra) de comestibles. **grocer's shop,** tienda de comestibles, *f.*

grocery, *s.* negocio de comestibles, *m.*; *pl.* **groceries,** provisiones, *f.* *pl.*, comestibles, *m.* *pl.*

grog, *s.* grog, *m.*

groin, *s.* (*anat.*) ingle, *f.*

groom, *s.* (in a royal household) gentilhombre, *m.*; lacayo, *m.*; mozo de caballos, *m.*; (of a bride) novio, *m.* *v.t.* (a horse) cuidar; (oneself) arreglarse. **She is always well groomed,** Ella está siempre muy bien arreglada

groomsman, *s.* padrino de boda, *m.*

groove, *s.* ranura, muesca, *f.*; estría, *f.*; surco, *m.*; (*fig.*) rutina, *f.* *v.t.* entallar; estriar

grooved, *a.* con ranura; estriado

grope, *v.i.* andar a tientas; (with for) buscar a tientas; procurar encontrar, buscar. **to g. one's way towards,** avanzar a tientas hacia; (*fig.*) avanzar poco a poco hacia

gropingly, *adv.* a tientas; irresolutamente

gross, *s.* (*com.*) gruesa, *f.*; totalidad, *f.* *a.* grueso; denso, espeso; (unrefined) grosero; (great) grande; (crass) craso; total; (*com.*) bruto; (tremendous) enorme. **in g.,** en grueso. **g.**

amount, total, *m.*; (*com.*) importe bruto, *m.* **g. weight,** peso bruto, *m.*

grossly, *adv.* groseramente; (much) enormemente

grossness, *s.* gordura, *f.*; (vulgarity) grosería, *f.*; obscenidad, *f.*; (enormity) enormidad, *f.*

grotesque, *a.* grotesco; extravagante, estrambótico; ridículo. *s.* grotesco, *m.*

grotesquely, *adv.* grotescamente

grotesqueness, *s.* lo grotesco; ridiculez, *f.*

grotto, *s.* gruta, *f.*

ground, *s.* suelo, *m.*; (of water and *naut.*) fondo, *m.*; (earth) tierra, *f.*; (*fig.*) terreno, *m.*; (strata) capa, *f.*; (*sport*) campo, *m.*; (parade) plaza (de armas), *f.*; (background) fondo, *m.*; (basis) base, *f.*, fundamento, *m.*; (reason) causa, *f.*; motivo, *m.*; (excuse) pretexto, *m.*; *pl.* **grounds,** jardines, *m.* *pl.*, parque, *m.*; (sediment) sedimento, *m.*, heces, *f.* *pl.*; (reason) causa, *f.* *v.i.* (*naut.*) varar, encallar. *v.t.* poner en tierra; (*naut.*) hacer varar; (*elec.*) conectar con tierra; (base) fundar (en), basar (en); (teach) enseñar los rudimentos (de). *a.* molido; en polvo; (of floors, storeys) bajo; (of glass) deslustrado; (*bot.*) terrestre. **common g.,** tierra comunal, *f.*; (*fig.*) tierra común, *f.* **He is on his own g.,** Está en terreno propio. **It fell to the g.,** Cayó al suelo; (*fig.*) Fracasó. **It is on the g.,** Está en el suelo. **It suits me to the g.,** Me viene de perilla. **to break fresh g.,** (*fig.*) tratar problemas nuevos. **to be well grounded in,** conocer bien los elementos (or rudimentos) de. **to cover g.,** cubrir terreno; recorrer; (in discussion) tocar muchos puntos. **to cut the g. from beneath one's feet,** hacer perder la iniciativa (a). **to give g.,** retroceder; perder terreno. **to raze to the g.,** echar por tierra, arrasar. **to stand one's g.,** resistir el ataque; no darse por vencido; (*fig.*) mantenerse firme, mantenerse en sus trece. **to win g.,** ganar terreno. **g. coffee,** café molido, *m.* g.-colour, (of paint) primera capa, *f.*; (color de) fondo, *m.*; g.-floor, piso bajo, *m.* g. glass, vidrio deslustrado, *m.* g.-ivy, hiedra terrestre, *f.* g. nut, cacahuete, *m.* g.-plan, (*arch.*) planta, *f.* g.-rent, censo, *m.* g.-sheet, tela impermeable, *f.*; g. staff, (*aer.*) personal del aeropuerto, *m.* g.-swell, mar de fondo, *m.*

grounded, *a.* fundado. The aeroplanes are g., Los aviones no pueden despegar. His suspicions are well g., Tiene motivos para sus sospechas

grounding, *s.* (*naut.*) encalladura, *f.*; (teaching) instrucción en los rudimentos, *f.*

groundless, *a.* sin fundamento, inmotivado, sin causa, sin motivo

groundsel, *s.* (*bot.*) hierba cana, *f.*

groundwork, *s.* fundamento, *m.*; base, *f.*; principio, *m.*

group, *s.* grupo, *m.* *v.t.* agrupar. *v.i.* agruparse. g. captain, coronel de aviación, *m.*

grouping, *s.* agrupación, *f.*

grouse, *s.* (*orn.*) ortega, *f.* *v.i.* rezongar, refunfuñar

grove, *s.* soto, boscaje, *m.*; arboleda, *f.*

grovel, *v.i.* arrastrarse; (*fig.*) humillarse

grovelling, *a.* (*fig.*) servil; ruin

grow, *v.i.* crecer; (increase) aumentar; (become) hacerse; empezar a; llegar a; (turn) volverse, ponerse; (flourish) progresar, adelantar; (develop) desarrollarse; (extend) extenderse. *v.t.* cultivar; dejar crecer. I grew to fear it, Llegué a temerlo. to g. cold, ponerse frío; enfriarse; (of weather) empezar a hacer frío. to g. fat, engordar. to g. hard, ponerse duro; (*fig.*) endurecerse. to g. hot, ponerse caliente; calentarse; (of weather) empezar a hacer calor. to g. old, envejecer. to g. tall, crecer mucho; ser alto. to g. again, crecer de nuevo. to g. into, hacerse, llegar a ser; venir a ser. to g. out of, brotar de; originarse en; (a habit) desacostumbrarse poco a poco. He

is growing out of his clothes, La ropa se le hace pequeña. to g. up, (of persons) hacerse hombre (mujer); desarrollarse; (of a custom, etc.) imponerse. to g. upon, crecer sobre; llegar a dominar; (make think) hacer creer, empezar a pensar; (of a habit) arraigar en

grower, *s.* cultivador (-ra)

growing, *s.* crecimiento, *m.*; desarrollo, *m.*; (increase) aumento, *m.*; (of flowers, etc.) cultivación, *f.* *a.* creciente

growl, *s.* gruñido, *m.*; reverberación, *f.*; trueno, *m.* *v.i.* gruñir; (of guns) tronar; (of thunder) reverberar. to g. out, decir gruñendo

grown, *a.* crecido; maduro; adulto. a g. up, una persona mayor. to be full-g., estar completamente desarrollado; haber llegado a la madurez. g. over with, cubierto de

growth, *s.* crecimiento, *m.*; (development) desarrollo, *m.*; (progress) progreso, adelanto, *m.*; (increase) aumento, *m.*; (cultivation) cultivo, *m.*; (vegetation) vegetación, *f.*; (*med.*) tumor, *m.* He has a week's g. on his chin, Tiene una barba de una semana

grub, *s.* larva, *f.*, gusano, *m.* *v.t.* (with up, out) desarraigar; cavar; desmalezar; (*fig.*, *fam.*) buscar

grubbiness, *s.* suciedad, *f.*; (untidiness) desaliño, *m.*

grubby, *a.* lleno de gusanos; sucio; bisunto; desaliñado

grudge, *s.* motivo de rencor, *m.*; rencor, resentimiento, *m.*, ojeriza, *f.*; mala voluntad, *f.*; aversión, *f.* *v.t.* envidiar. to bear a g., tener ojeriza

grudging, *a.* (niggardly) mezquino; envidioso; poco generoso; de mala gana; nada afable

grudgingly, *adv.* de mala gana, contra su voluntad; con rencor; a regañadientes

gruel, *s.* gachas, *f. pl.*

gruesome, *a.* pavoroso, horrible; macabro

gruff, *a.* (of the voice) bronco, grave, áspero; (of manner) brusco, malhumorado

gruffly, *adv.* en una voz bronca (or áspera); bruscamente, con impaciencia, malhumoradamente

gruffness, *s.* aspereza, bronquedad, *f.*; brusquedad, sequedad, impaciencia, *f.*, mal humor, *m.*

grumble, *s.* ruido sordo, trueno, *m.*; estruendo, *m.*; (complaint) refunfuño, rezongo, *m.* *v.i.* tronar; refunfuñar, rezongar; hablar entre dientes; quejarse; protestar (contra). *v.t.* decir refunfuñando

grumbler, *s.* murmurador (-ra), refunfuñador (-ra)

grumbling, *a.* gruñón, refunfuñador; regañón; descontento. *s.* See **grumble**

grumblingly, *adv.* a regañadientes, refunfuñando

grumpiness, *s.* mal humor, *m.*, irritabilidad, *f.*

grumpy, *a.* malhumorado, irritable

grunt, *s.* gruñido, *m.* *v.i.* gruñir

grunting, *a.* gruñidor

guarantee, *s.* (*law*) persona de quien otra sale fiadora, *f.*; garantía, *f.*; abono, *m.* *v.t.* garantizar; responder de; abonar; (assure) asegurar, acreditar

guarantor, *s.* garante, *m.* and *f.*

guard, *s.* (watchfulness) vigilancia, *f.*; (in fencing) guardia, *f.*; (of a sword) guarnición, *f.*; (sentry) centinela, *m.*; (soldier) guardia, *m.*; (body of soldiers) guardia, *f.*; (escort) escolta, *f.*; (keeper) guardián, *m.*; (protection) protección, defensa, *f.*; (of a train) jefe de tren, *m.* *v.t.* guardar; proteger, defender; vigilar; (escort) escoltar. **to g. against,** guardarse de. **the changing of the g.,** el relevo de la guardia. **to be on g.,** (*mil.*) estar de guardia; (in fencing) estar en guardia. **to be on one's g.,** estar prevenido, estar alerta. **to be off one's g.,** estar desprevenido. **to mount g.,** (*mil.*) montar la guardia; vigilar. **guard's van,** furgón de equipajes, *m.* **g.-house,** cuerpo de guardia, *m.*; prisión militar, *f.*

guarded, *a.* (reticent) reservado, circunspecto, prudente, discreto

guardedly, *adv.* prudentemente, con circunspección, discretamente

guardian, *s.* protector (-ra); guardián (-ana); (*law*) tutor, *m.* *a.* que guarda; tutelar. **g. angel,** ángel de la guarda, ángel custodio, *m.*; deidad tutelar, *f.*

guardianship, *s.* protección, *f.*; patronato, *m.*; (*law*) curaduría, tutela, *f.*

guardsman, *s.* guardia, *m.*

Guatemalan, *a.* and *s.* guatemalteco (-ca)

guava, *s.* (*bot.*) guayaba, *f.*

gudgeon, *s.* (*mech.*) gorrón, *m.*; cuello de eje, *m.*

Guelph, *a.* and *s.* güelfo (-fa)

guerrilla, *s.* guerrilla, *f.*; (soldier) guerrillero, *m.* *a.* de guerrilla. **g. warfare,** guerra de guerrilla, *f.*

guess, *s.* adivinación, *f.*; estimación, *f.*; conjetura, *f.*; sospecha, *f.* *v.t.* and *v.i.* adivinar; conjeturar; sospechar; imaginar; (suppose) suponer, creer; calcular. **to g.** at, formar una opinión sobre; imaginar. **a rough g.,** estimación aproximada, *f.* **at a g.,** a poco más o menos, a ojo de buen cubero. **g.-work,** conjeturas, suposiciones, *f. pl.*

guest, *s.* (at a meal) convidado (-da), invitado (-da); (at a hotel, etc.) huésped (-da); (*biol.*) parásito, *m.* **g.-room,** cuarto de amigos, *m.*

guffaw, *s.* carcajada, *f.* *v.i.* reírse a carcajadas, soltar el trapo

guidance, *s.* dirección, *f.*; gobierno, *m.*; (advice) consejos, *m. pl.*; inspiración, *f.*

guide, *s.* (person) guía, *m.* and *f.*; (girl g.) exploradora, *f.*; (book and *fig.*) guía, *f.*; mentor, *m.*; modelo, *m.*; (inspiration) norte, *m.*; (*mech.*) guía, *f.* *v.t.* guiar; conducir; encaminar; dirigir; (govern) gobernar. **g.-book,** guía (de turistas), *f.* **g.-post,** poste indicador, *m.*

guiding, *a.* que guía; directivo; decisivo. *s.* See **guidance**

guild, *s.* gremio, *m.* *a.* gremial. **g. member,** gremial, *m.*

guilder, *s.* (coin) florín holandés, *m.*

guile, *s.* astucia, superchería, maña, *f.*

guileful, *a.* astuto

guileless, *a.* cándido, sin malicia, inocente

guilelessly, *adv.* inocentemente

guilelessness, *s.* inocencia, candidez, *f.*

guillotine, *s.* guillotina, *f.* *v.t.* guillotinar

guilt, *s.* culpabilidad, *f.;* crimen, *m.;* (sin) pecado, *m.*

guiltily, *adv.* culpablemente; como si fuese culpable

guiltless, *a.* libre de culpa, inocente; puro; ignorante

guilty, *a.* culpable; delincuente; criminal. **to find g.,** encontrar culpable. **to plead g.,** confesarse culpable. **g. party,** culpable, *m.*

guinea, *s.* guinea, *f.* **g.-fowl,** gallina de Guinea, *f.* **g.-pig,** conejillo de las Indias, cobayo, *m.*

guise, *s.* manera, guisa, *f.;* (garb) traje, *m.;* (mask) máscara, *f.;* (fig.) pretexto, *m.* **under the g. of,** bajo el pretexto de; bajo la apariencia de

guitar, *s.* guitarra, *f.*

guitarist, *s.* guitarrista, *m. and f.*

gules, *s.* (her.) gules, *m. pl.*

gulf, *s.* golfo, *m.;* abismo, *m.*

gull, *s.* (orn.) gaviota, *f.;* (dupe) primo, *m.* *v.t.* engañar, timar, defraudar

gullet, *s.* esófago, *m.;* garganta, *f.*

gullibility, *s.* credulidad, *f.*

gullible, *a.* crédulo

gully, *s.* hondonada, barranca, *f.;* (gutter) arroyo, *m.*

gulp, *s.* trago, sorbo, *m.* *v.t.* engullir, tragar; (repress) ahogar; (believe) tragar. **to g. up,** vomitar

gum, *s.* (of the mouth) encía, *f.;* goma, *f.* *v.t.* engomar; pegar con goma. **gum arabic,** goma arábiga, *f.* **gum boots,** botas de goma, *f. pl.* **gum-resin,** gomorresina, *f.* **gum starch,** aderezo, *m.* **gum tree,** eucalipto, *m.*

gumboil, *s.* flemón, *m.*

gumminess, *s.* gomosidad, *f.*

gummy, *a.* gomoso

gumption, *s.* sentido común, *m.*

gun, *s.* arma de fuego, *f.;* (handgun) fusil, *m.;* (sporting g.) esco-

peta, *f.;* (pistol) pistola, *f.,* revólver, *m.;* (cannon) cañón, *m.;* (firing) cañonazo, *m.* **big gun,** (fam.) pájaro gordo, *m.* **heavy gun,** cañón de grueso calibre, *m.* **gun-barrel,** cañón de escopeta, *m.* **gun-carriage,** cureña, *f.* **gun-cotton,** pólvora de algodón, *f.* **gun-fire,** cañonazos, *m. pl.,* fuego, *m.* **gun-metal,** bronce de cañón, *m.;* pavón, *m.* **gun-room,** armería, *f.;* (on a ship) polvorín, *m.* **gun-running,** contrabanda de armas, *f.* **gun-turret,** torre, *f.* **gun wound,** balazo, *m.*

gunboat, *s.* cañonero, *m.,* lancha bombardera, *f.*

gunman, *s.* escopetero, armero *m.;* bandido armado, *m.;* gángster, apache, *m.*

gunner, *s.* artillero, *m.;* escopetero, *m.*

gunpowder, *s.* pólvora, *f.*

gunshot, *s.* escopetazo, *m.;* tiro de fusil, *m.*

gunsmith, *s.* escopetero, armero, *m.*

gunwale, *s.* (naut.) regala, borda, *f.*

gurgle, *s.* murmullo, murmurio, gorgoteo, *m.;* gluglu, *m.;* (of a baby) gorjeo, *m.* *v.i.* murmurar; hacer gluglu; (of babies) gorjear

gurgling, *a.* murmurante; (of babies) gorjeador. *s.* See **gurgle**

gush, *s.* chorro, *m.;* (of words) torrente, *m.;* (of emotion) efusión, *f.* *v.i.* chorrear, borbotar; surtir, surgir. **to g. out,** saltar, brotar a borbotones. **to g. over,** (fig.) hablar con efusión de

gushing, *a.* hirviente; (of people) efusivo, extremoso, empalagoso

gusset, *s.* (sew.) escudete, *m.*

gust, *s.* (of wind) ráfaga, bocanada (de aire), *f.;* (fig.) arrebato, acceso, *m.*

gustatory, *a.* gustatorio

gusto, *s.* brío, *m.;* entusiasmo, *m.*

gusty, *a.* borrascoso

gut, *s.* intestino, *m.,* tripa, *f.;* (catgut) cuerda de tripa, *f.;* (naut.) estrecho, *m.;* *pl.* **guts,** tripas, *f. pl.;* (content) meollo, *m.,* substancia, *f.;* (stamina) aguante, espíritu, *m.* *v.t.* (of fish, etc.) destripar; (plunder)

saquear; destruir por completo;
quemar completamente ·

gutta-percha, s. gutapercha, f.

gutter, s. canal, m.; (of a street)
arroyo (de la calle), m.; (ditch)
zanja, f.; (fig.) hampa, f. v.i.
surcar. v.i. gotear; (of a candle)
cerotear, gotear la cera. **g.
spout,** canalón, m.

guttersnipe, s. golfillo, m., niño
(-ña) del hampa

guttural, a. gutural. s. letra
gutural, f.

gutturally, adv. guturalmente

guy, s. (rope) viento, m.; (naut.)
guía, f.; (effigy) mamarracho, m.;
(scarecrow) espantajo, m. v.t.
sujetar con vientos o guías;
burlarse de

guzzle, v.t. tragar, engullir. v.i.
atracarse, engullir; emborracharse. s. comilón, m.; borrachera, f.

guzzler, s. tragador (-ra); borracho (-cha)

gymnasium, s. gimnasio, m.

gymnast, s. gimnasta, m.

gymnastic, a. gimnástico. **g.
rings,** anillas, f. pl.

gymnastics, s. gimnasia, f.

gynæcological, a. ginecológico

gynæcologist, s. ginecólogo (-ga)

gynæcology, s. ginecología, f.

gynœcium, s. (bot.) gineceo, m.

gypsum, s. yeso, m.

gypsy, s. See **gipsy**

gyrate, v.i. girar, rodar

gyration, s. giro, m., vuelta, f.

gyratory, a. giratorio

gyro-compass, s. brújula giroscópica, f.

gyroscope, s. (phys.) giroscopio,
m.

gyves, s. grillos, m. pl.; esposas,
f. pl.

H

h, s. (letter) hache, f.

ha, interj., ¡ah!

haberdasher, s. mercero, r.t.

haberdashery, s. mercería, f.

habiliment, s. vestidura, f.; pl.
habiliments, indumentaria, f.

habilitate, v.t. habilitar

habilitation, s. habilitación, f.

habit, s. costumbre, f., hábito, m.;
(temperament) temperamento,

carácter, m.; (use) uso, m.;
(of body) complexión, constitución, f.; (ecc.) hábito, m. **to be
in the h. of,** soler, acostumbrar,
estar acostumbrado a. **to have
bad habits,** estar malacostumbrado. **to have the bad h. of,**
tener el vicio (or la mala costumbre) de. **to contract the
h. of,** contraer la costumbre de.
h. maker, sastre de·trajes de
montar, m.

habitability, s. habitabilidad, f.

habitable, a. habitable, vividero

habitat, s. (bot., zool.) medio, m.,
habitación, f.

habitation, s. habitación, f.

habitual, a. habitual, acostumbrado, usual; constante; común

habitually, adv. habitualmente;
constantemente; comúnmente

habituate, v.t. habituar, acostumbrar

habituation, s. habituación, f.

habitué, s. parroquiano (-na);
veterano (-na)

hack, s. caballo de alquiler, m.;
rocín, jaco, m.; (writer) escritor
mercenario, m. v.t. acuchillar;
tajar, cortar. v.i. cortar. **to h.
to pieces,** cortar en pedazos;
pasar a cuchillo

hacking, a. (of coughs) seco

hackle, s. (for flax, hemp) rastrillo,
m.

hackney carriage, s. coche de
plaza, coche de alquiler, m.

hackneyed, a. trillado, usado,
repetido

hacksaw, s. sierra de cerrajero,
sierra para metal, f.

hackwork, s. trabajo de rutina,
m.

· **haddock,** s. merlango, m., pescadilla, f.

Hades, s. infierno, m.

hæmoglobin, s. (chem.) hemoglobina, f.

hæmophilia, s. (med.) hemofilia,
f.

hæmorrhage, s. hemorragia, f.,
flujo de sangre, m.

hæmorrhoids, s. pl. (med.) hemorroides, f.

haft, s. mango, tomadero, m.,
manija, f.; puño, m.

hag, s. bruja, f.

haggard, a. ojeroso, trasnochado,
trasojado

haggardly, *adv.* ansiosamente

haggardness, *s.* aspecto ojeroso, *m.*

haggle, *v.i.* regatear; vacilar

haggling, *s.* regateo, *m.* *a.* regatón

hagiographer, *s.* hagiógrafo, *m.*

hagiography, *s.* hagiografía, *f.*

ha, ha! *interj.* ¡ja, ja!

hail, *s.* (salutation) saludo, *m.*; (shout) grito, *m.*; aclamación, *f.*; (frozen rain) granizo, *m.*; (of blows) lluvia, *f.* *interj.* ¡salve! *v.t.* saludar; llamar; aclamar; (*fig.*) lanzar, echar. *v.i.* (hailstones) granizar; (blows, etc.) llover. **to h. from,** proceder de, ser natural de. **within h.,** al habla. **H. Mary,** Salve Regina, Avemaría, *f.*

hailshot, *s.* perdigón, *m.*

hailstone, *s.* granizo, pedrisco, *m.*

hailstorm, *s.* granizada, *f.*

hair, *s.* (single h.) cabello, *m.*; (*zool.*, *bot.*) pelo, *m.*; (of horse's mane) crin, *f.*; (head of h.) cabellera, mata de pelo, *f.*, pelo, *m.*; (superfluous) vello, *m.*; (fibre) fibra, *f.*, filamento, *m.*; (on the pen) raspa, *f.*, pelo, *m.*; (*fig.*) pelo, *m.* **lock of h.,** bucle, rizo, *m.*; mecha, *f.* **to dress one's h.,** peinarse. **to have one's h. cut,** hacerse cortar el pelo. **to part the h.,** hacer(se) la raya del pelo. **to put up the h.,** hacerse el moño; (to "come out") ponerse de largo. **to tear one's h.,** mesarse los cabellos. **h. combings,** peinaduras, *f. pl.* **h.-curler,** tirabuzón, *m.* **h. dryer,** secadora de cabello, *f.* **h. dye,** tinte para el pelo, *m.* **h.-net,** redecilla, *f.* **h.-oil,** brillantina, *f.* **h.-raising,** horripilante, espeluznante. **h.-ribbon,** cinta para el pelo, *f.* **h.-shirt,** cilicio, *m.* **h. slide,** pasador, *m.* **h.-splitting,** sofistería, argucia, *f.* **h.-spring,** muelle del volante, *m.* **h.-switch,** añadido, *m.* **h.-trigger,** pelo de una pistola, *m.*

hairbreadth, *s.* pelo, *m.* **to have a h. escape,** escapar por un pelo.

hairbrush, *s.* cepillo para el cabello, *m.*

hairdresser, *s.* peluquero (-ra), peinadora, *f.*

hairdressing, *s.* peinado, *m.* **h. establishment or trade,** peluquería, *f.*

haired, *a.* peludo, con pelo; (in compounds) de pelo . . .

hairiness, *s.* vellosidad, *f.*

hairless, *a.* sin pelo; calvo

hairlike, *a.* filiforme

hairpin, *s.* horquilla, *f.* **h. bend,** viraje en horquilla, *m.*

hairy, *a.* peludo; velloso; (*bot.*) hirsuto

Haiti, *a.* and *s.* (of, or from) haitiano (-na)

hake, *s.* merluza, *f.*

halberd, *s.* alabarda, *f.*

halberdier, *s.* alabardero, *m.*

halcyon, *s.* alción, martín pescador, *m.* *a.* (*fig.*) feliz, sereno, tranquilo

hale, *a.* fuerte, sano, robusto. *v.t.* hacer comparecer

half, *s.* mitad, *f.*; (school term) trimestre, *m.* *a.* medio; semi. *adv.* a medias; mitad; (almost) casi; insuficientemente; imperfectamente. **I don't h. like it,** No me gusta nada. **It is h.-past two,** Son las dos y media. **an hour and a h.,** una hora y media. **better h.,** (*fam.*) media naranja, cara mitad, *f.* **by halves, a medias,** en dos mitades. **one h.,** la mitad. **to go halves,** ir a medias. **to h. close,** entornar. **to h. open,** entreabrir. **h. a bottle,** media botella, *f.* **h. a crown,** media corona, *f.* **h.-alive,** semivivo. **h. an hour,** media hora, *f.* **h.-and-h.,** mitad y mitad; en partes iguales. **h.-asleep,** semidormido, medio dormido. **h.-awake,** medio despierto, entre duerme y vela. **h.-back,** (*sport*) medio, *m.* **h.-baked,** medio cocido, crudo; (*fig.*) poco maduro. **h.-binding,** encuadernación en media pasta, *f.* **h.-breed,** *a.* mestizo. *s.* cruce, *m.* **h.-brother,** hermanastro, hermano de padre o de madre, *m.* **h.-caste,** mestizo. **h. circle,** semicírculo, *m.* **h.-closed,** entreabierto; medio cerrado. **h.-dead,** medio muerto; más muerto que vivo. **h.-done,** hecho a medias, sin acabar. **h.-dozen,** media docena, *f.* **h.-dressed,** medio desnudo. **h.**

fare, medio billete, *m.* **h.-full,** medio lleno. **h.-hearted,** débil, poco eficaz, lánguido; indiferente, sin entusiasmo. **h.-heartedness,** debilidad, *f.;* indiferencia, *f.* **h.-holiday,** media fiesta, *f.* **h.-hourly,** cada media hora. **h.-length,** (portrait) de medio cuerpo. **h.-length coat,** abrigo de tres cuartos, *m.* **h.-light,** media luz, *f.* **h.-mast,** a media asta. **h.-measure,** medida poco eficaz, *f.* **h.-moon,** *s.* media luna, *f.;* (*ast.*) semilunio, *m.;* ·(of a nail) blanco (de la uña), *m.* **h.-mourning,** medio luto, *m.* **h.-pay,** media paga, *f.* **h.-price,** a mitad de precio. **h.-seas-over** (*fam.*) entre dos velas. **h.-sister,** hermanastra, hermana de padre o de madre, *f.* **h.-time,** (*sport*) media parte, *f.,* medio tiempo, *m.* **h.-tone,** de medio tono. **h.-tone illustration,** fotograbado a media tinta, *m.* **h.-truth,** verdad a medias, *f.* **h.-turn,** media vuelta, *f.* **h.-way,** a medio camino; medio. **h.-witted,** medio loco, tonto, imbécil. **h.-year,** medio año, *m.* **h.-yearly,** semestral

halfpenny, *s.* medio penique, *m.;* (*fam.*) perra gorda, *f.*

halibut, *s.* halibut, *m.;* (genus) hipogloso, *m.*

halitosis, *s.* halitosis, *f.*

hall, *s.* (mansion) mansión, casa de campo, *f.,* caserón, *m.;* (public building) edificio *m.,* casa (de); (town h.) casa del ayuntamiento, *f.;* (room) sala, *f.;* (entrance) vestíbulo, *m.;* (dining room) comedor, *m.;* (of residence for students) residencia, *f.* **h. door,** portón, *m.,* puerta del vestíbulo, *f.;* **h. porter,** conserje, *m.* **h.-stand,** perchero, *m.*

hallelujah, *s.* aleluya, *f.*

hallmark, *s.* marca de ley, *f.;* (*fig.*) señal, *f.;* indicio, *m.* *v.t.* poner la marca de ley sobre; (*fig.*) sellar

hallo, *interj.* ¡hola!; (on telephoning someone) ¡oiga! ¡aló!; (answering telephone) ¡diga! ¡aló!

halloo, *v.t.* (hounds) azuzar; perseguir dando voces; (call) llamar

hallow, *v.t.* santificar; reverenciar; (consecrate) consagrar

Hallowe'en, *s.* víspera del día de difuntos, *f.*

hallucination, *s.* alucinación, ilusión, *f.;* visión, *f.;* fantasma, *m.*

hallucinatory, *a.*·alucinador

halo, *s.* halo, nimbo, *m.*

halogen, *s.* (*chem.*) halógeno, *m.*

haloid, *a.* (*chem.*) haloideo

halt, *s.* (*mil.*) alto, *m.;* cesación, *f.;* interrupción, *f.;* (on a railway) apeadero, *m.;* (for trams, buses) parada, *f.* *v.t.* parar, detener. *v.i.*· pararse, detenerse; ·(*mil.*) hacer alto; cesar; interrumpirse; (in speech) titubear; (of verse) estar cojo; (doubt) dudar; (limp) cojear. **H.!** (*mil.*) ¡Alto!

halter, *s.* ronzal, cabestro, *m.;* (for hanging) dogal, *m.* *v.t.* encabestrar, cabestrar

halting, *s.* parada, *f.;* interrupción, *f.* *a.* (of gait) cojo; incierto; vacilante; (of speech) titubeante

halve, *v.t.* partir (or dividir) en dos mitades

halyard, *s.* (*naut.*) driza, *f.*

ham, *s.* jamón, *m.;* (*anat.*) pernil, *m.*

hamadryad, *s.* hamadríade, *f.*

hamlet, *s.* aldea, *f.,* pueblecito, *m.*

hammer, *s.* martillo, *m.;* (stone cutter's) maceta, *f.;* (mason's) piqueta, *f.;* (of fire-arms) percusor, *m.;* (of piano) macillo, *m.* *v.t.* amartillar, martillar, batir. **to throw the h.,** lanzar el martillo. **under the h.,** en subasta, al remate: **h. blow,** martillazo, *m.*

hammering, *s.* martilleo, martillazo, *m.* **by h.,** a martillo

hammock, *s.* hamaca, *f.;* (*naut.*) coy, *m.*

hamper, *s.* banasta, canasta, *f.,* cesto grande, *m.* *v.t.* estorbar, dificultar, impedir; (*fig.*) embarazar

hamster, *s.* (*zool.*) hámster, *m.*

hand, *s.* mano, *f.;* (of animal) pata, mano, *f.;* (worker) operario (-ia); obrero (-ra); (skill) habilidad, *f.;* (side) mano, *f.,* lado, *m.;* (measure) palmo, *m.;* (of a clock) manecilla, *f.;* (of instruments) aguja, *f.;* (applause) aplauso, *m.*; (power) poder, *m.*; las manos; (at cards) mano, *f.*; (card player) jugador, *m.*; (signature) firma, *f.*; (handwriting) letra, escritura, *f.*; (influence) influencia, parte, mano, *f.* an old h., un veterano; un perro viejo. at h., a mano, al lado, cerca. at the hands of, de manos de. by h., a mano; (on the bottle) con biberón. from h. to h., de mano a mano. in h., entre manos; (of money) de contado. in the hands of, (*fig.*) en el poder de. Hands wanted, Se desean trabajadores. h. over h., mano sobre mano. hand's breadth, palmo, *m.* Hands off! ¡Fuera las manos! Hands up! ¡Manos arriba! lost with all hands, (of a ship) perdido con toda su tripulación. off one's hands, despachado; (of a daughter) casada. on all hands, por todas partes. on h., entre manos; (of goods) existente; (present) presente. on one's hands, a cargo de uno. on the one h., por un lado; a un lado. on the other h., por otra parte; en cambio. out of h., luego, inmediatamente; revoltoso. to come to h., venir a mano; (of letters) llegar a las manos (de). to get one's h. in, ejercitarse. to have a h. in, tener parte en; intervenir en. to have no h. in, no tener arte ni parte en. to have on h., traer entre manos. to have the upper h., tener la sartén por el mango; llevar la ventaja. to hold one's h., abstenerse; detenerse. to hold hands, cogerse de las manos. to lay hands on, tocar; poner mano en; echar manos a. to set one's h. to, emprender; (sign) firmar. to shake hands, estrechar la mano. to stretch out one's hands, tender las manos. to take one's hands off, no tocar. with folded hands, mano sobre mano. with his hands behind his back, con las manos en la espalda. h.-in-h., cogidos (cogidas) de las manos. h.-lever, manija, *f.* h.-loom, telar de

mano, *m.* h. luggage, equipaje de mano, *m.* h.-made, hecho a mano. h.-mill, molinillo, *m.* h.-pump, *s.* (*naut.*) sacabuche, *m.* h. rail, pasamano, *m.*, baranda, balustrada, *f.* h.-sewn, cosido a mano. h.-to-h., de mano en mano; (of a fight) a brazo partido, cuerpo a cuerpo. h.-to-h. fight, cachetina, *f.* h.-to-mouth, precario. to live from h.-to-mouth, vivir de día en día

hand, *v.t.* dar; entregar; alargar. to h. down, bajar; (a person) ayudar a bajar; transmitir. to h. in, entregar; (a person) ayudar a entrar; (one's resignation) dimitir; (send) mandar, enviar. to h. on, transmitir. to h. out, *v.t.* distribuir; (a person) ayudar a salir; (from a vehicle) ayudar a bajar. *v.i.* (*fam.*) pagar. to h. over, *v.t.* entregar. *v.i.* (*mil.*) traspasar los poderes (a). to h. round, pasar de mano en mano; pasar; ofrecer, to h. up, subir; (a person) ayudar a subir

handbag, *s.* bolso, saco, monedero, *m.*

handbarrow, *s.* carretilla, *f.*, angarillas, *f. pl.*

handbell, *s.* campanilla, *f.*

handbill, *s.* anuncio, *m.*

handbook, *s.* manual, compendio, tratado, *m.*; anuario, *m.*; (guide) guía, *f.*

handbreadth, *s.* palmo, *m.*

handcart, *s.* carretilla de mano, *f.*, carretón, *m.*

handcuff, *s.* esposa, *f.*, grillo, *m.* (gen. *pl.*). *v.t.* poner las esposas (a), maniatar

handed, *a.* (in compounds) que tiene manos; de manos . . .; con las manos . . . four-h., (*sport*) de cuatro personas. one-h., manco

handful, *s.* puño, puñado, manojo, *m.* to be a h., (*fam.*) tener el diablo en el cuerpo. in handfuls, a manojos

handgrip, *s.* apretón de manos, *m.*

handicap, *s.* desventaja, *f.*; obstáculo, *m.*; (*sport*) handicap, *m.*; ventaja, *f.* *v.t.* (*fig.*) perjudicar, impedir, dificultar

handicraft, *s.* mano de obra, *f.*; (skill) destreza manual, *f.*

handiwork, *s.* mano de obra, *f.*; trabajo manual, *m.*; obra, *f.*; (deed) acción, *f.*, hecho, *m.*

handkerchief, *s.* pañuelo, *m.*

handle, *s.* mango, puño, *m.*; (lever) palanca, *f.*; (of baskets, dishes, jugs) asa, *f.*; (of doors, windows, drawers) pomo, *m.*; (to one's name) designación, *f.*; título, *m.*; (excuse) pretexto, *m.* *v.t.* (touch) tocar; manejar, manipular; (treat) tratar; (deal in) comerciar en; tomar; (paw) manosear; (direct) dirigir; (control) gobernar; (pilot) pilotar; (a theme) explicar, tratar de. **h.-bar,** manillar, *m.* **h.-bar grip,** puño de un manillar, *m.*

handless, *a.* sin manos; manco; (*fig.*) torpe

handling, *s.* manejo, *m.*; manipulación, *f.*; (treatment) trato, *m.*, relaciones (con), *f. pl.*; (thumbing) manosco, *m.*; interpretación, *f.*; (*art*) tratamiento, *m.*, técnica, *f.*

handmaid, *s.* sirvienta, criada, *f.*; (*fig.*) mayordomo, *m.*

handsaw, *s.* sierra de mano, *f.*, serrucho, *m.*

handshake, *s.* apretón de manos, *m.*

handsome, *a.* (generous) generoso; magnánimo; considerable; hermoso, bello; elegante; (of people) guapo, distinguido; excelente; (flattering) halagüeño. **He was a very h. man,** Era un hombre muy guapo

handsomely, *adv.* generosamente; con magnanimidad; elegantemente; bien

handsomeness, *s.* generosidad, *f.*; magnanimidad, *f.*; hermosura, *f.*; elegancia, *f.*; distinción, *f.*

handspring, *s.* voltereta sobre las manos, *f.*

handwork, *s.* obra hecha a mano, *f.*, trabajo a mano, *m.*; (needlework) labor de aguja, *f.*

handworked, *a.* hecho a mano; (embroidered) bordado

handwriting, *s.* caligrafía, letra, escritura, *f.*

handy, *a.* (of persons) diestro, mañoso, hábil; (of things) conveniente; útil; (near) cercano, a mano. *adv.* cerca. **h.-man,**

hombre de muchos oficios, *m.*; factótum, *m.*

hang, *v.t.* colgar; suspender; (execute) ahorcar; (the head) bajar; dejar caer; (upholster) entapizar; (with wallpaper) empapelar; (drape) poner colgaduras en; (place) poner; (cover) cubrir. *v.i.* colgar, pender; estar suspendido; (be executed) ser ahorcado; (of garments) caer. *s.* (of garments) caída, *f.*; (of a machine) mecanismo, *m.*; (meaning) sentido, *m.*, significación, *f.* **to h. by a thread,** pender de un hilo. **to h. in the balance,** estar en la balanza. **to h. fire,** estar (una cosa) en suspenso. **to h. loose,** caer suelto; (clothes) venir ancho. **to h. about,** (surround) rodear, pegarse a; (frequent) frecuentar; (haunt) rondar; (be imminent) ser inminente, amenazar; (embrace) abrazar. **to h. back,** retroceder; quedarse atrás; (*fig.*) vacilar, titubear. **to h. down,** colgar, pender; estar caído; caerse. **to h. on,** seguir agarrado (a); apoyarse en; (*fig.*) persistir; (a person's words) estar pendiente de, beber; (remain) quedarse. **to h. out,** *v.t.* tender. *v.i.* (lean out) asomarse (por); (*fam.*, live) habitar. **to h. over,** colgar por encima; (brood) cernerse sobre; (lean over) inclinarse sobre; quedarse cerca de; (overhang) sobresalir; (overarch) abovedar; (threaten) amenazar. **to h. together,** (of persons) permanecer unidos; (of things) tener cohesión; (be consistent) ser lógico, ser consistente. **to h. up,** colgar; suspender; (*fig.*) dejar pendiente, interrumpir. **to h. upon,** apoyarse en; (a person's words) beber las palabras de uno

hangar, *s.* cobertizo de aeroplanos, *m.*

hanger, *s.* colgadero, *m.*; percha *f.* **h.-on,** parásito, *m.*; dependiente, *m.*

hanging, *s.* colgamiento, *m.*; (killing) ahorcamiento, *m.*; *pl.* **hangings,** colgaduras, *f. pl.*, cortinajes, *m. pl.* *a.* pendiente colgante; péndulo; (of gardens) pensil. **It's not a h. matter,** No

es una cuestión de vida y muerte.
h. bridge, puente colgante, *m.*
h. committee, junta de una
exposición; *f.* **h. lamp,** lámpara
de techo, *f.*
hangman, *s.* verdugo, *m.*
hangnail, *s.* padrastro, *m.*
hangover, *s.* hangover, *m.*
hank, *s.* madeja, *f.*
hanker, *v.i.* (with after) ansiar,
ambicionar; (with for) anhelar,
suspirar por, desear con vehemencia
hankering, *s.* ambición, *f.*; deseo
vehemente, *m.*
hanky-panky, *s.* superchería, *f.*;
engaño, *m.*
Hanoverian, *a.* and *s.* hannove-
riano (-na)
Hanseatic, *a.* anseático
hansom cab, *s.* simón, *m.*
hap, *s.* casualidad, suerte, *f.*;
suceso fortuito, *m.*
haphazard, *s.* casualidad, *f.* *a.*
fortuito, casual
hapless, *a.* desgraciado, desdichado
haplessness, *s.* desgracia, desdicha, *f.*
happen, *v.i.* suceder, acontecer,
ocurrir, pasar; (to be found, be)
hallarse por casualidad; (take
place) tener lugar, verificarse;
(arise) sobrevenir. **Do you know
what has happened to . . . ?**
¿ Sabes qué se ha hecho de . . . ?
as if nothing had happened,
como si no hubiese pasado nada.
**He turned up as if nothing
had happened,** Se presentó
como si tal cosa. **How did it h. ?**
¿ Cómo fué esto ? **If they h. to
see you,** Si acaso te vean. **I
happened to be in London,** Me
hallaba por casualidad en Londres. **It won't h. again,** Esto no
volverá a suceder. **whatever
happens,** venga lo que venga
happening, *s.* suceso, acontecimiento, hecho, *m.*, ocurrencia, *f.*
happily, *adv.* felizmente; por
suerte
happiness, *s.* felicidad, dicha, *f.*;
alegría, *f.*, regocijo, *m.*
happy, *a.* (lucky) afortunado;
(felicitous) feliz, oportuno;
feliz, dichoso; alegre, regocijado.
to be h., estar contento, ser
feliz. **to be h. about,** alegrarse

de. **to make h.,** hacer feliz,
alegrar. **h.-go-lucky,** irresponsable, descuidado
harangue, *s.* arenga, *f.* *v.t.*
arengar. *v.i.* pronunciar una
arenga
harass, *v.t.* hostigar, acosar;
atormentar; preocupar; (mil.)
picar. **to h. the rear-guard,**
picar la retaguardia
harbinger, *s.* (*fig.*) precursor,
heraldo, *m.*; presagio, anuncio,
m. *v.t.* anunciar, presagiar
harbour, *s.* puerto, *m.*; (bay)
bahía, *f.*; (haven) asilo, refugio,
m. *v.t.* dar refugio (a), albergar,
acoger; (cherish) abrigar, acariciar; (conceal) esconder. **inner
h.,** puerto, *m.* outer h., rada
del puerto, *f.* **to put into h.,**
entrar en el puerto. **h. bar,**
barra del puerto, *f.* **h.-dues,**
derechos de puerto, *m.* *pl.* **h.-
master,** capitán de puerto,
contramaestre de puerto, *m.*
harbourer, *s.* amparador (-ra),
protector (-ra); (criminal) encubridor (-ra)
hard, *a.* duro; (firm) firme; difícil;
laborioso, agotador; violento;
poderoso; arduo; fuerte, recio;
vigoroso, robusto; insensible,
inflexible; cruel; (of weather) inclemente, severo; (unjust) injusto, opresivo; (stiff) tieso; (of
water) cruda; (of wood) brava.
adv. duro; duramente; con ahinco; con fuerza; de firme; difícilmente; (of gazing) fijamente;
severamente; (firmly) firmemente; vigorosamente; (of raining) a cántaros, mucho; (quickly)
rápidamente; excesivamente;
(much) mucho; (of bearing misfortune) a pechos; (attentively)
atentamente; (heavily) pesadamente; (badly) mal; (closely) de
cerca, inmediatamente. **It was
a h. blow,** Fué un golpe recio. **to
be h. put to,** encontrar difícil. **to
go h.,** endurecerse. **to go h.
with,** irle mal a uno. **to have a
h. time,** pasar apuros, pasarlo
mal. **to look h. at,** mirar
atentamente, examinar detenidamente; mirar fijamente. **to
be a h. drinker,** ser un bebedor
empedernido. **h. and fast rule,**
regla inalterable, *f.* **h.-bitten,** de

carácter duro. a. **h.-boiled egg,** un huevo duro. **h. breathing,** resuello, *m.* **h. by,** muy cerca. **h. cash,** efectivo, *m.* **h.-earned,** difícilmente conseguido; ganado con el sudor de la frente. **h.-featured,** de facciones duras. **h.-fisted,** tacaño. **h.-fought,** arduo, reñido. **h.-headed,** práctico, perspicaz. **h.-hearted,** duro de corazón, insensible. **h.-heartedness,** insensibilidad, *f.* **h. labour,** (*law*) trabajos forzados, *m. pl.,* presidio, *m.* **h-mouthed,** (of horses) boquiduro. **h. of hearing,** duro de oído. **h.-up,** apurado. **to be very h.-up,** ser muy pobre; (*fam.*) estar a la cuarta pregunta. **h.-wearing,** duradero; sufrido. **h.-won,** See **h.-earned. h.-working,** trabajador, hacendoso, diligente

harden, *v.t.* endurecer; (metal) templar; robustecer; (to war) aguerrir; (make callous) hacer insensible. *v.i.* endurecerse; hacerse duro; templarse; robustecerse; (of shares) entonarse

hardening, *s.* endurecimiento, *m.*; (of metal) temple, *m.* **h. of the arteries,** arteriosclerosis, *f.*

hardiness, *s.* vigor, *m.,* fuerza, robustez, *f.*; audacia, *f.*

hardly, *adv.* duramente; difícilmente; (badly) mal; severamente; (scarcely) apenas, casi. **h. ever,** casi nunca

hardness, *s.* dureza, *f.*; severidad, *f.*; inhumanidad, insensibilidad, *f.*; (stiffness) tiesura, *f.*; (difficulty) dificultad, *f.*; (of water) crudeza, *f.*; (of hearing) dureza de oído, *f.*

hardship, *s.* penas, *f. pl.,* trabajos, *m. pl.*; infortunio, *m.,* desdicha, *f.*; (suffering) sufrimiento, *m.*; (affliction) aflicción, *f.*; (privation) privación, *f.* **to undergo h.,** pasar trabajos

hardware, *s.* ferretería, *f.*

hardwood, *s.* madera brava, *f.*

hardy, *a.* audaz, intrépido; (strong) fuerte, robusto; (*bot.*) resistente

hare, *s.* liebre, *f.* **young h.,** lebrato, *m.* **h. and hounds,** rally paper, *m.,* caza de papelitos, *f.* **h.-brained,** casquivano, atronado,

con cabeza de chorlito. **hare's foot,** mano de gato, *f.* **h.-lip,** labio leporino, *m.* **h.-lipped,** labihendido

harebell, *s.* campanilla, campánula, *f.*

harem, *s.* harén, serrallo, *m.*

haricot, *s.* (green bean) judía, *f.*; (dried bean) alubia, *f.*

hark, *v.t.* escuchar; oír. **to h. back,** volver al punto de partida; volver a la misma canción

harlequin, *s.* arlequín, *f.*

harlequinade, *s.* arlequinada, *f.*

harlot, *s.* ramera, prostituta, meretriz, *f.*

harlotry, *s.* prostitución, *f.*

harm, *s.* mal, *m.*; daño, *m.*; perjuicio, *m.*; (danger) peligro, *m.*; (detriment) menoscabo, *m.*; (misfortune) desgracia, *f.* *v.t.* hacer mal (a); dañar, hacer daño (a); perjudicar. **And there's no h. in that,** Y en eso no hay mal. **to keep out of harm's way,** evitar el peligro; guardarse del mal

harmful, *a.* malo; dañino, perjudicial, nocivo; (dangerous) peligroso. **to be h.,** (of food, etc.) hacer mal (a); (of pests) ser dañino; (of behaviour, etc.) perjudicar

harmfulness, *s.* lo malo; perniciosidad, *f.*; daño, *m.*; peligro, *m.*

harmless, *a.* innocuo; inofensivo; inocente

harmlessness, *s.* innocuidad, *f.*; inocencia, *f.*

harmonic, *s.* (*phys., math.*) harmónica, *f.*; (*mus.*) armónico, *m.* *a.* (*mus.*) armónico

harmonica, *s.* armónica, *f.*

harmonics, *s.* armonía, *f.*; (tones) armónicos, *m. pl.*

harmonious, *a.* armonioso

harmoniously, *adv.* armoniosamente; (*fig.*) en armonía

harmoniousness, *s.* armonía, *f.*

harmonium, *s.* armonio, *m.*

harmonization, *s.* armonización, *f.*

harmonize, *v.t.* armonizar. *v.i.* armonizarse, estar en armonía

harmony, *s.* armonía, *f.*; (*fig.*) paz, *f.,* buenas relaciones, *f. pl.*; música, *f.* **to live in h.,** vivir en paz

harness, s. guarniciones, f. pl.,
jaeces, m. pl.; (armour) arnés, m.
v.t. enjaezar; (yoke) enganchar;
(water) represar. to die in h.,
(fig.) morir en la brecha. h.
maker, guarnicionero, m. h.
room, guadarnés, m.

harp, s. arpa, f. to h. on, volver
a la misma canción, volver a
repetir

harpist, s. arpista, m. and f.

harpoon, s. arpón, m. v.t. arponear

harpooner, s. arponero, m.

harpsichord, s. arpicordio, m.

harpy, s. arpía, f.

harridan, s. bruja, f.

harrow, s. (agr.) rastra, f.,
escarificador, m. v.t. (agr.) es-
carificar; (fig.) lastimar, atormentar

harrowing, a. patibulario, conmovedor, atormentador, angustioso

harry, v.t. devastar, asolar; (persons) robar; perseguir; (worry)
atormentar; (annoy) molestar

harsh, a. áspero; (of voice)
ronco; (of sound) discordante;
(of colours) áspero; duro; chillón;
severo, duro; (of features) duro;
(of taste) ácido, acerbo

harshly, adv. severamente

harshness, s. (roughness) aspereza, f.; (of voice) ronquedad,
aspereza, f.; (of sound) disonancia, f.; (of colours) aspereza, f.;
severidad, f.; dureza, f.; (of
taste) acidez, f.

hart, s. ciervo, m.

harum-scarum, s. tronera, saltabarrancos, m. and f., molino, m.
a. irresponsable

harvest, s. cosecha, siega, f.;
recolección, f.; (fig.) producto,
fruto, m. v.t. cosechar; recoger.
h. festival, fiesta de la cosecha,
f.

harvester, s. segador, m., cose-
chero (-ra); (machine) segadora,
f.

hash, s. (cul.) picado, m. v.t.
(cul.) picar

hashish, s. quif, m.

hasp, s. pasador, m.; sujetador,
m.

hassock, s. cojín, m.

haste, s. prisa, rapidez, f.; precipitación, f.; urgencia, f. v.t.

dar prisa (a); acelerar; precipitar.
v.i. darse prisa; acelerarse;
precipitarse. in h., de prisa,
aprisa. to be in h., estar de
prisa, llevar prisa. in great h.,
muy aprisa, aprisa y corriendo,
precipitadamente; con mucha
prisa. More h. less speed,
(Spanish equivalent. Words said
by Charles III of Spain to his
valet) ¡Vísteme despacio que voy
de prisa!

hasten, v.t. acelerar, apresurar;
precipitar. v.i. darse prisa,
apresurarse; moverse con rapidez; correr. to h. one's steps,
apretar el paso. to h. away,
marcharse rápidamente. to h.
back, regresar apresuradamente.
to h. down, bajar rápidamente.
to h. on, seguir el camino sin
descansar; seguir rápidamente.
to h. out, salir rápidamente.
to h. towards, ir rápidamente
hacia; correr hacia. to h. up,
subir aprisa, correr hacia arriba;
darse prisa

hastily, adv. de prisa, rápidamente; con precipitación, precipitadamente; (angrily) impacientemente; airadamente;
(thoughtlessly) sin reflexión

hastiness, s. rapidez, f.; precipitación, f.; (anger) impaciencia,
irritación, f.

hasty, a. rápido, apresurado;
precipitado; (superficial) superficial, ligero; (ill-considered)
desconsiderado, imprudente;
(angry) impaciente, irritable;
violento, apasionado

hat, s. sombrero, m. to pass
round the h., pasar el platillo.
Andalusian h., sombrero calañés, m. bowler h., sombrero
hongo, m. broad-brimmed h.,
sombrero chambergo, m. Panama h., sombrero de jipijapa, m.
picture h., pamela, f. shovel h.,
sombrero de teja, m. soft felt h.,
sombrero flexible, m. straw h.,
sombrero de paja, m. three-
cornered h., sombrero de tres
picos, m. top-h., sombrero de
copa, m. h. shop or trade,
sombrerería, f.

hatband, s. cinta de sombrero, f.,
cintillo, m.

hatblock, s. formillón, f.

hatbox, *s.* sombrerera, *f.*

hatbrush, *s.* cepillo para sombreros, *m.*

hatch, *s.* (wicket) compuerta, *f.*; (trap-door) puerta caediza, *f.*; (*naut.*) escotilla, *f.*; compuerta de esclusa, *f.*; (of chickens) pollada, *f.*; (of birds) nidada, *f. v.t.* (birds) empollar; incubar, encobar; (*fig.*) tramar, urdir. *v.i.* empollarse, salir del cascarón; incubarse; (*fig.*) madurarse. **to h. a plot,** urdir un complot, conspirar. **to h. chickens,** sacar pollos

hatchet, *s.* hacha pequeña, *f.*, machado, *m.* **to bury the h.,** hacer la paz. **h.-faced,** de cara de cuchillo

hatching, *s.* incubación, *f.*; (of a plot) maquinación, *f.*

hatchway, *s.* (*naut.*) escotilla, *f.*

hate, *s.* odio, aborrecimiento, *m.*, aversión, *f.*; abominación, *f.* *v.t.* odiar, aborrecer, detestar; repugnar; saber mal, sentir. **I h. to trouble you,** Me sabe mal molestarle, Siento mucho molestarle. **to h. the sight of,** (*fam.*) no poder ver (a)

hateful, *a.* odioso, aborrecible; repugnante

hatefulness, *s.* odiosidad, *f.*, lo odioso; maldad, *f.*

hater, *s.* aborrecedor (-ra). **to be a good h.,** saber odiar

hatful, *s.* un sombrero lleno (de)

hatless, *a.* sin sombrero, descubierto

hatpin, *s.* horquilla de sombrero, *f.*

hatred, *s.* odio, aborrecimiento, *m.*, detestación, *f.*; aversión, enemistad, *f.*

hatstand, *s.* perchera, *f.*

hatter, *s.* sombrerero, *m.* **as mad as a h.,** loco como una cabra

hauberk, *s.* cota de mallas, *f.*

haughtiness, *s.* altanería, arrogancia, altivez, soberbia, *f.*, orgullo, *m.*

haughty, *a.* altanero, arrogante, altivo, orgulloso

haul, *s.* (pull) tirón, *m.*; (of fish) redada, *f.*; (booty) botín, *m.* *v.t.* arrastrar, tirar de; (*naut.*) halar. **to h. at, upon,** (ropes, etc.) aflojar, soltar, arriar. **to h. down,** (flags, sails) arriar

haulage, *s.* transporte, acarreo, *m.*; coste de transporte, *m.* **h. contractor,** contratista de transporte, *m.*

haunch, *s.* anca, culata, *f.*; (of meat) pierna, *f.* **h.-bone,** hueso ilíaco, *m.*

haunt, *s.* punto de reunión, lugar frecuentado (por), *m.*; (lair) cubil, nido, *m.*, guarida, *f. v.t.* frecuentar; rondar; (of ideas) perseguir; (of ghosts) aparecer, visitar. **It is a h. of thieves,** Es una cueva de ladrones

haunted, *a.* (by spirits) encantado

haunter, *s.* frecuentador (-ra); (ghost) fantasma, espectro, *m.*

haunting, *s.* frecuentación, *f.*; aparición de un espectro, *f. a.* persistente

hautboy, *s.* oboe, *m.*

hauteur, *s.* altivez, *f.*

Havana, Havanese, *s.* (cigar) habano, *m.*; (native) habanero (-ra), habano (-na)

have, *v.t.* tener; poseer; (suffer) padecer; (spend) pasar; (eat or drink) tomar; (eat) comer; (a cigarette) fumar; (a bath, etc.) tomar; (a walk, a ride) dar; (cause to be done) mandar (hacer), hacer (hacer); (deceive) engañar; (defeat) vencer; (catch) coger; (say) decir; (allow) permitir; (tolerate) tolerar, sufrir; (obtain) lograr, conseguir; (wish) querer; (know) saber; (realize) realizar; (buy) comprar; (acquire) adquirir. As an auxiliary verb, haber (e.g. **I h. done it,** Lo he hecho, etc.). **As fate would h. it,** Según quiso la suerte. **Do you h. to go?** ¿Tiene Vd. que marcharse? **H. him come here,** Hazle venir aquí. **I h. been had,** Me han engañado. **I h. a good mind to . . . ,** Tengo ganas de . . . **I had all my books stolen,** Me robaron todos mis libros. **You had better go,** Es mejor que te vayas. **I had rather,** Preferiría, Me gustaría más bien. **I h. had a suit made,** Mandé hacerme un traje, Hice hacerme un traje. **I would not h. had it otherwise,** No lo hubiese querido de otra manera. **I will not h. it,** No lo quiero; No quiero tomarlo; (object) No lo permitiré. **If we**

had known, Si lo hubiésemos
sabido. It has to do with the
sun, Está relacionado con el sol,
Tiene que ver con el sol. What
are you going to h.? ¿Qué va
Vd. a tomar? Will you h. some
jam? ¿Quiere Vd. mermelada?
to h. breakfast, desayunar.
to h. dinner, supper, cenar.
to h. lunch, almorzar. to h.
for tea, invitar a tomar el té;
(of food) merendar. to h. tea,
tomar el té. to h. it out with,
habérselas con. to h. just,
acabar de. I h. just done it,
Acabo de hacerlo. to h. on
hand, traer entre manos. to h.
one's eye on, no perder de vista
(a), vigilar. to h. one's tail
between one's legs, ir rabo
entre piernas. to h. to, tener
que; deber. It has to be so,
Tiene que ser así. to h. too
much of, sobrar, tener demasiado de. He has too much
time, Le sobra tiempo. • to h.
about one, tener (or llevar) consigo. to h. back, aceptar;
recibir. to h. down, hacer
bajar. She had her hair
down, El pelo le caía por las
espaldas. to h. in, hacer entrar.
to h. on, vestir, llevar puesto;
(engagements) tener (compro-
misos). to h. out, hacer salir;
llevar a paseo; llevar fuera;
(have removed) hacerse sacar;
quitar. to h. up, (persons) hacer
subir; (things) subir; (law) llevar
a (ante) los tribunales. to h.
with one, tener consigo. I h.
her with me, La tengo conmigo,
Ella me acompaña.

haven, s. puerto, m., abra, f.;
(fig.) oasis, abrigo, refugio, m.

haversack, s. mochila, f., morral,
m.

havoc, s. destrucción, ruina, f.;
(fig.) estrago, m. to wreak h.
among, destruir; (fig.) hacer
estragos entre (or en)

haw, s. (bot.) acerola, f.

Hawaiian, a. de Hawai

hawk, s. halcón, m.; gavilán,
milano, m. v.i. cazar con halcón.
v.t. vender mercancías por las
calles; (fig.) difundir. **h.-eyed,**
de ojos de lince. **h.-nosed,** de
nariz aguileña

hawker, s. halconero, m.; (vendor) buhonero, m., vendedor
(-ra) ambulante

hawking, s. caza con halcones,
cetrería, f.; (expectorating) gar-
gajeo, m.; (selling) buhonería, f.

hawser, s. maroma, f., calabrote,
m.

hawthorn, s. espino, m. **white
h.,** espino blanco, m.

hay, s. heno, m. to make hay
while the sun shines, hacer su
agosto. hay fever, fiebre del
heno, f. **hay-fork,** horca, f.

hayloft, s. henil, m.

haymaker, s. segador (-ra);
(machine) segadora, f.

haymaking, s. recolección del
heno, f.

haystack, s. almiar, m., niara, f.

hazard, s. azar, m., suerte, f.;
riesgo, peligro, m.; (game) juego
de azar, m. v.t. arriesgar, aventurar. at all hazards, a todo
riesgo

hazardous, a. azaroso, arriesgado, peligroso

haze, s. bruma, f.; confusión, f.

hazel, s. avellano, m. **h.-nut,**
avellana, f.

hazy, a. brumoso, calinoso; confuso

he, pers. pron. él. s. (of humans)
varón, m.; (of animals) macho,
m. **he who,** el que, quien. **he-
goat,** macho cabrío, m. **he-man,**
todo un hombre, hombre cabal, m.

head, v.t. golpear con la cabeza;
encabezar; (lead) capitanear;
(direct) dirigir, guiar; (wine)
cabecear. v.i. estar a la cabeza
de; dirigirse a. **headed for,** con
rumbo a, en dirección a. to
h. off, interceptar; desviar; (fig.)
distraer

head, s. (anat.) cabeza, f.; (upper
portion) parte superior, f.; (of a
coin) cara, f.; (hair) cabellera, f.;
(individual) persona, f.; (of
cattle) res, f.; (of a mountain)
cumbre, f.; (of a ladder) último
peldaño, m.; (of toadstools)
sombrero, m.; (of trees) copa, f.;
(of a stick) puño, m.; (of a cylinder) culata, f.; (of a river, etc.)
manantial, origen, m.; (of a bed)
cabecera, f.; (of nails, pins) cabeza, f.; (froth) espuma, f.; (flower)
flor, f.; (leaves) hojas, f. pl.;

(first place) primer puesto, *m.*; (of game, fish) pieza, *f.*; (of a page, column) cabeza, *f.*; (cape) cabo, *m.*; (of an arrow, dart, lance) punta, *f.*; (front) frente, *m.*; (leader) jefe, cabeza, *m.*; (chief) director (-ra), superior (-ra); presidente (-ta); (of a school) director (-ra); (of a cask) fondo, *m.*; (*mech.*) cabezal, *m.*; (of an axe) filo, *m.*; (of a bridge) cabeza, *f.*; (of a jetty, pier) punta, *f.*; (of a ship) proa, *f.*; (of a flower) cabezuela, *f.*; (of asparagus) punta, *f.*; (of a table) cabeza, *f.*; (of the family) jefe, cabeza, *m.*; (seat of honour) cabecera, *f.*; (title) título, *m.*; (aspect) punto de vista, *m.*; (division) capítulo, *m.*; (management, direction) dirección, *f.*; (talent) talento, *m.*, cabeza, *f.*; (intelligence) inteligencia, *f.* *a.* principal; primero; en jefe. at the h. of, a la cabeza de. crowned h., testa coronada, *f.* from h. to foot, de pies a cabeza; de hito en hito; de arriba abajo. He took it into his h. to ..., Se le ocurrió de ... This story has neither h. nor tail, Este cuento no tiene pies ni cabeza. with h. held high, con la frente levantada. to come to a h., llegar a la crisis; llegar al punto decisivo. to get an idea out of a person's h., quitar una idea a uno de la cabeza. to keep one's h., (*fig.*) conservar la sangre fría, no perder la cabeza. to lose one's h., (*fig.*) perder la cabeza. to put into a person's h., (*fig.*) meter (a uno) en la cabeza. to run one's h. against, golpear la cabeza contra. h. first, de cabeza. h. of cattle, res, *f.* h. office, central, *f.* h. of hair, cabellera, *f.*; mata de pelo, *f.* h.-on, de cabeza. h.-on collision, choque de frente, *m.* h. opening, (of a garment) cabezón, *m.* heads or tails, cara o cruz. h. over heels, de patas arriba. h. over heels in love, calado hasta los huesos. h.-dress, tocado, *m.*; peinado, *m.*; sombrero, *m.* h. voice, voz de cabeza, *f.* h. waiter, maître d'hôtel, *m.*

headache, *s.* dolor de cabeza, *m.*; (*fig.*) quebradero de cabeza, *m.*

headboard, *s.* cabecera de una cama, *f.*

headed, *a.* con cabeza ...; que tiene la cabeza...; de cabeza...; (of an article) intitulado. **large** h., cabezudo

header, *s.* caída de cabeza, *f.*; salto de cabeza, *m.*

headgear, *s.* tocado, *m.*; sombrero, gorro, *m.*

heading, *s.* (*naut.*) el poner la proa en dirección (a); el guiar en dirección (a); (of a book, etc.) título, encabezamiento, *m.*; (Association football) golpe de cabeza, *m.* **to come under the h. of,** estar incluido entre; clasificarse bajo

headland, *s.* cabo, promontorio, *m.*

headless, *a.* sin cabeza

headlight, *s.* (*aut.*) faro, *m.*; (*r.w.*, *naut.*) farol, *m.* **to dip the headlights,** bajar los faros. **to switch on the headlights,** encender los faros (or los faroles)

headline, *s.* (of a newspaper) titular, *m.*; (to a chapter) título de la columna, *m.*

headlong, *a.* precipitado; despeñado. *adv.* de cabeza; precipitadamente. **to fall h.,** caer de cabeza

headman, *s.* cacique, cabecilla, *m.*; (foreman) capataz, contramaestre, *m.*

headmaster, *s.* director de colegio, rector, *m.*

headmistress, *s.* directora de colegio, rectora, *f.*

headphones, *s. pl.* auriculares, *m. pl.*

headquarters, *s.* (*mil.*) cuartel general, *m.*; oficina central, *f.*; jefatura, *f.*; centro, *m.*

headrace, *s.* (of a mill-race) saetín, *m.*

headrest, *s.* respaldo, *m.*; apoyo para la cabeza, *m.*

headship, *s.* autoridad suprema, *f.*; jefatura, *f.*; dirección, *f.*

headstall, *s.* bozo, *m.*

headstone, *s.* piedra mortuoria, *f.*

headstrong, *a.* impetuoso, terco, testarudo

headway, *s.* marcha, *f.*; (*fig.*) progreso, avance, *m.* **to make**

h., avanzar; (*fig.*) hacer progresos; (*fig.*) prosperar

headwind, *s.* viento en contra, *m.*

heady, *a.* apasionado, violento; impetuoso, precipitado; (obstinate) terco; (of alcohol) encabezado; (*fig.*) embriagador

heal, *v.t.* curar, sanar; (flesh) cicatrizar. *v.i.* curar, sanar; cicatrizarse; (superficially) sobresanar

healable, *a.* curable

healer, *s.* sanador (-ra), curador (-ra); curandero, *m.*

healing, *a.* curador, sanador; médico. *s.* curación, *f.*; cura, *f.*, remedio, *m.*

health, *s.* salud, *f.*; higiene, sanidad, *f.* Here's to your very good h.! ¡Salud y pesetas! He is in good h., Disfruta de buena salud. to drink a person's h., beber a la salud de. to enjoy good h., gozar de buena salud. to look full of h., vender salud. h.-giving, saludable. h. inspection, visita de sanidad, *f.* h. officer, inspector de sanidad, *m.* h. resort, balneario, *m.*

healthiness, *s.* buena salud, *f.*; sanidad, salubridad, *f.*

healthy, *a.* sano; con buena salud; (healthful) saludable. to be h., tener buena salud

heap, *s.* montón, *m.*; rima, pila, *f.*, acervo, *m.*; (of people) muchedumbre, *f.*, tropel, *m.* *v.t.* amontonar; apilar; colmar. in heaps, a montones. We have heaps of time, Nos sobra tiempo, Tenemos tiempo de sobra. to h. together, juntar, mezclar. to h. up, upon, colmar; amontonar; (*agr.*) hacinar; (*fig.*) acumular

hear, *v.t.* oír; (listen) escuchar; (attend) asistir a; (give audience) dar audiencia (a); (a lawsuit) ver (un pleito); (speak) hablar; (be aware of, feel) sentir. *v.i.* oír; tener noticias; (learn) enterarse de; (allow) permitir. H.! H.! ¡Muy bien! ¡Bravo! I have heard it said that ... He oído decir que ... Let me h. from you! ¡Mándame noticias tuyas! They were never heard of again, No se volvió a saber de ellos, No se supo más de ellos. to h. about, oír de; (know) saber

de, tener noticias de; recibir información sobre. to h. from, ser informado por; tener noticias de; recibir carta de. to h. of, enterarse de, saber; recibir información sobre; (allow) permitir

hearer, *s.* oyente, *m.* and *f.*

hearing, *s.* (sense of) oído, *m.*; alcance del oído, *m.*; presencia, *f.*; audición, *f.*; (*law*) vista (de una causa) *f.* It was said in my h., Fué dicho en mi presencia. out of h., fuera del alcance del oído. within h., al alcance del oído

hearsay, *s.* fama, *f.*, rumor, *m.* by h., de oídas

hearse, *s.* coche fúnebre, *m.*

heart, *s.* corazón, *m.*; (feelings) entrañas, *f. pl.*; (of the earth, etc.) seno, corazón, *m.*; (of lettuce, etc.) cogollo, repollo, *m.*; (suit in cards) copas, *f. pl.*; (*bot.*) médula, *f.*; (soul) alma, *f.*; (courage) valor, *m.*; ánimo, *m.* at h., en el fondo, esencialmente. by h., de memoria. from the h., con toda sinceridad, de todo corazón. He is a man after my own h., Él es un hombre de los que me gustan. I have no h. to do it, No tengo valor de hacerlo. in the h. of the country, en medio del campo. to break one's h., partirse el corazón. to have one's h. in one's mouth, tener el alma en un hilo, estar muerto de miedo. to have no h., (*fig.*) no tener entrañas. to lose h., desanimarse, descorazonarse. to set one's h. on, poner el corazón en. to take h., cobrar ánimo; (*fam.*) hacer de tripas corazón. to take to h., tomar a pechos. to wear one's h. on one's sleeve, tener el corazón en la mano. with all my h., con toda el alma. h.-ache, angustia, pena, *f.*; h.-beat, latido del corazón, *m.* h.-breaker, (woman) coqueta, *f.*; (man) ladrón de corazones, *m.* h. disease, enfermedad del corazón, enfermedad cardíaca, *f.* h. failure, colapso cardíaco, *m.* h.-rending, desgarrador, angustioso. h.-searching, examen de conciencia, *m.* h.-shaped, acorazonado, en forma de corazón. **h.-strings**, fibras del corazón, *f. pl.* **h.-to-h. talk**, conversación íntima, *f.* **h.-whole**, libre de afectos

heartbreaking, *a.* desgarrador, angustioso, doloroso, lastimoso

heartbroken, *a.* acongojado, afligido, transido de dolor

heartburn, *s.* acidez del estómago, acedía, *f.*

heartburning, *s.* rencor, *m.*, animosidad, envidia, *f.*

hearted, *a.* de corazón . . . que tiene el corazón . . . **kind-h.**, de buen corazón, bondadoso

hearten, *v.t.* alentar, animar

heartfelt, *a.* hondo; de todo corazón, sincero; más expresivo

hearth, *s.* hogar, *m.*; chimenea, *f.*; (*fig.*) hogar, *m.*

heartily, *adv.* cordialmente; sinceramente; enérgicamente; con entusiasmo; (of eating) con buen apetito; (very) muy, completamente. **I am h. sick of it all,** (*fam.*) Estoy harto hasta los dientes

heartiness, *s.* cordialidad, *f.*; sinceridad, *f.*; energía, *f.*, vigor, *m.*; vehemencia, *f.*; entusiasmo, *m.*; (of appetite) buen diente, buen apetito, *m.*

heartless, *a.* sin corazón, sin piedad, despiadado, inhumano, cruel

heartlessness, *s.* falta de corazón, inhumanidad, crueldad, *f.*

heartsease, *s.* (*bot.*) trinitaria, *f.*, pensamiento, *m.*

hearty, *a.* cordial; sincéro; enérgico; vigoroso; robusto; (frank) campechano; (of appetite) voraz; bueno; (big) grande

heat, *s.* calor, *m.*; (in animals) celo, *m.*; (of an action) calor, *m.*; (*fig.*) vehemencia, fogosidad, *f.*; (*fig.*) fuego, *m.*; (passion) ardor, *m.*, pasión, *f.*; (of a race) carrera eliminatoria, *f.* *v.t.* calentar; (excite) conmover, acalorar, excitar; (annoy) irritar. *v.i.* calentarse. **dead h.**, empate, *m.* **in h.**, en celo. **in the h. of the moment**, en el calor del momento. **to become heated**, (*fig.*) acalorarse, exaltarse. **white h.**, candencia, incandescencia, *f.* **h. lightning**, fucilazo, *m.* **h.**

spot, pápula, *f.*; terminación sensible, *f.* **h. stroke**, insolación, *f.* **h. wave**, onda de calor, *f.*

heated, *a.* calentado; caliente; excitado; apasionado

heatedly, *adv.* con vehemencia, con pasión

heater, *s.* calentador, *m.*; calorífero, *m.*; (stove) estufa, *f.*; (for plates) calientaplatos, *m.* **water-h.**, calentador de agua, *m.*

heath, *s.* brezal, *m.*; yermo, páramo, *m.*; (*bot.*) brezo, *m.*

heathen, *s.* pagano (-na); idólatra, *m.* and *f.*; ateo (-ea), descreído (-da). *a.* pagano; ateo; bárbaro

heathenism, *s.* paganismo, *m.*; idolatría, *f.*; ateísmo, *m.*

heather, *s.* brezo, *m.*

heathery, *a.* cubierto de brezo

heating, *s.* calefacción, *f.* *a.* calentador; (of drinks) fortificante. **central h.**, calefacción central, *f.*

heave, *v.t.* alzar, levantar; (*naut.*) izar; (the anchor, etc.) virar; (throw) arrojar, lanzar; elevar; (extract) extraer; (emit) dar, exhalar. *v.i.* subir y bajar; palpitar; agitarse. *s.* tirón, *m.*; (of the sea) vaivén, *m.* **to h. in sight**, aparecer, surgir. **to h. out sail**, (*naut.*) desenvergar. **to h. the lead**, (*naut.*) escandallar. **to h. to**, (*naut.*) estarse a la capa

heaven, *s.* cielo, *m.*; firmamento, *m.*; paraíso, *m.* **Heavens!** ¡Cielos! ¡Por Dios! **Thank H.!** ¡Gracias a Dios! **h.-born**, celeste. **h.-sent**, (*fig.*) providencial

heavenliness, *s.* carácter celestial, *m.*; delicia, *f.*

heavenly, *a.* celeste, celestial; divino; (*fig.*) delicioso. **h. body**, astro, *m.*

heaver, *s.* cargador, *m.*

heavily, *adv.* pesadamente; torpemente; penosamente; (slowly) lentamente; severamente; excesivamente; (of sighing) hondamente; (sadly) tristemente; (of rain, etc.) reciamente, fuertemente; (of wind) con violencia. **He fell h.,** Cayó de plomo. **to lie h. upon,** pesar mucho sobre. **to rain h.,** llover mucho, diluviar

heaviness, s. peso, m.; (lethargy) torpor, letargo, m.; sueño, m., languidez, f.; (clumsiness) torpeza, f.; (severity) severidad, f.; importancia, responsabilidad, f.; dificultad, f.; (gravity) gravedad, f.; tristeza, melancolía, f.; (boredom) sosería, insulsez, f.; (of style) monotonía, ponderosidad, f.

heaving, s. levantamiento, m.; (of the anchor, etc.) virada, f.; (of the sea) vaivén, m.; (of the breast) palpitación, f.

heavy, a. pesado; torpe; sin gracia; (slow) lento; (thick) grueso; (strong) fuerte; (hard) duro; grave; difícil; oneroso; responsable, importante; (oppressive) opresivo; penoso; grande; (sad) triste, melancólico; (of the sky) anublado; (of food) indigesto; (tedious) aburrido, soso; (pompous) pomposo; (of roads) malo; (of scents) fuerte, penetrante; (of sleep, weather) pesado; (weary) rendido; (charged with) cargado de; (of a meal) grande, abundante; (violent) violento; (of a cold, etc.) malo; (drowsy) soñoliento; (torpid) tórpido; (of rain, snow, hail) fuerte, recio; (of firing) intenso; (of sighs) profundo; (of soil) recio, de mucha miga; (phys., chem.) pesado. **to be h.,** pesar mucho. **How h. are you?** ¿Cuánto pesa Vd.? **h.-armed,** pesado; armado hasta los dientes. **h.-eyed,** con ojeras. **h.-guns,** artillería pesada, f. **h.-handed,** de manos torpes; (fig.) tiránico, opresivo. **h.-hearted,** triste, apesadumbrado. **h. industry,** industria pesada, f. **h.-laden,** muy cargado. **h. losses,** (mil.) pérdidas cuantiosas, f. pl. **h.-weight,** (sport) peso pesado, m.

Hebraic, a. hebreo, judaico

Hebraism, s. Judaísmo, hebraísmo, m.

Hebraist, s. hebraísta, m.

Hebrew, s. hebreo (-ea), judío (-ía): (language) hebreo, m.

hecatomb, s. hecatombe, f.

heckle, v.t. (fig.) interrumpir, importunar con preguntas

heckler, s. perturbador (-ra)

heckling, s. interrupción, f.

hectare, s. hectárea, f.

hectic, a. (consumptive) hético; (feverish) febril; (fig., fam.) agitado

hectogramme, s. hectogramo, m.

hectograph, s. hectógrafo, m.

hectolitre, s. hectolitro, m.

hector, v.t. intimidar, amenazar

hectoring, a. imperioso; amenazador

hectowatt, s. (elec.) hectovatio, m.

hedge, s. seto, m.; barrera, f. v.t. cercar con un seto; rodear. v.i. (fig.) titubear, vacilar. **h.-hopping,** (aer.) vuelo a ras de tierra, m. **h.-sparrow,** acentor de bosque, m.

hedgehog, s. erizo, m. **h. position,** (mil.) puesto fuerte, m.

hedgerow, s. borde, seto, m.

hedonism, s. hedonismo, m.

hedonist, s. hedonista, m. and f.

heed, s. atención, f., cuidado, m. v.t. atender; observar, considerar; escuchar. v.i. hacer caso.

heedful, a. atento; cuidadoso

heedless, a. desatento; descuidado, negligente; distraído

heedlessly, adv. sin hacer caso; negligentemente; distraídamente

heedlessness, s. desatención, distracción, f.; descuido, m.; negligencia, f.; inconsideración, f.

heel, s. (anat.) talón, calcañar, m.; (of shoe) tacón, m.; (of a violin, etc., bow) talón, m.; (remains) restos, m. pl. v.t. poner tacón a; poner talón a; (naut.) hacer zozobrar. v.i. (naut.) zozobrar. **rubber h.,** tacón de goma, m. **She let him cool his heels for half an hour,** Ella le dió un plantón de media hora. **to follow on a person's heels,** pisarle (a uno) los talones. **to be down at h.,** (of shoes) estar gastados los tacones; estar desaseado. **to take to one's heels,** apretar a correr, poner pies en polvorosa. **to turn on one's h.,** dar media vuelta. **h.-bone,** zancajo, m. **h.-piece,** talón, m.

heeltap, s. tapa de tacón, f.; escurridura, f.

heft. See haft.

Hegelian, a. hegeliano

Hegelianism, *s.* hegelianismo, *m.*

hegemony, *s.* hegemonía, *f.*

hegira, *s.* Hégira, *f.*

heifer, *s.* ternera, vaquilla, *f.*

heigh, *interj.* (calling attention) ¡oye! ¡oiga! **h.-ho!** ¡ay!

height, *s.* altura, *f.*; elevación, *f.*; altitud, *f.*; (stature) estatura, *f.*; (high ground) cerro, *m.*, colina, *f.*; (sublimity) sublimidad, excelencia, *f.*; colmo, *m.*; (zenith) auge, *m.*, cumbre, *f.*

heighten, *v.t.* hacer más alto; (enhance) realzar; (exaggerate) exagerar; (perfect) perfeccionar; (intensify) intensificar

heightening, *s.* elevación, *f.*; (enhancement) realce, *m.*; (exaggeration) exageración, *f.*; (perfection) perfección, *f.*; (intensification) intensificación, *f.*

heinous, *a.* atroz, nefando, horrible.

heinousness, *s.* atrocidad, enormidad, *f.*

heir, *s.* heredero, *m.* **h. apparent,** heredero aparente, *m.* **h.-at-law,** heredero forzoso, *m.* **h. presumptive,** presunto heredero, *m.*

heiress, *s.* heredera, *f.*

heirloom, *s.* reliquia de familia, *f.*; (fig.) herencia, *f.*

helical, *a.* espiral

helicon, *s.* helicón, *m.*

helicopter, *s.* helicóptero, *m.*

heliocentric, *a.* heliocéntrico

heliograph, *s.* heliógrafo, *m.*

helioscope, *s.* helioscopio, *m.*

heliostat, *s.* helióstato, *m.*

heliotherapy, *s.* (*med.*) helioterapia, *f.*

heliotrope, *s.* (*bot.*) heliotropo, *m.*

heliotropism, *s.* (*bot.*) heliotropismo, *m.*

helium, *s.* (*chem.*) helio, *m.*

helix, *s.* (*geom.*) hélice, *m.*; (*arch.*, *geom.*) espira, *f.*

hell, *s.* infierno, *m.* **h.-fire,** fuego del infierno, *m.*, llamas del infierno *f. pl.*

hellebore, *s.* (*bot.*) eleboro, *m.*

Hellenic, *a.* helénico

Hellenism, *s.* helenismo, *m.*

Hellenist, *s.* helenista, *m.* and *f.*

Hellenistic, *a.* helenístico

Hellenize, *v.t.* helenizar

hellish, *a.* infernal; (*fam.*) horrible, detestable

hello, *interj.* See **hallo**

helm, *s.* caña del timón, *f.*; timón, gobernalle, *m.* **to obey the h.,** obedecer el timón. **to take the h.,** gobernar el timón; ponerse a pilotar

helmet, *s.* casco, *m.*; (in olden days) yelmo, capacete, *m.*; (sun) casco colonial, *m.*

helminthic, *a.* helmíntico, vermífugo

helmsman, *s.* timonero, *m.*

helot, *s.* ilota, *m.* and *f.*

help, *s.* ayuda, *f.*; auxilio, socorro, *m.*; (protection) favor, *m.*, protección, *f.*; (remedy) remedio, *m.*; (co-operation) cooperación, *f.*, concurso, *m.*; (domestic) criada, *f.* **A little h. is worth a lot of sympathy,** Más vale un toma que dos te daré. **There's no h. for it,** No hay más remedio. **to call for h.,** pedir socorro a gritos. **without h.,** a solas, sin la ayuda de nadie

help, *v.t.* ayudar; socorrer, auxiliar; (favour) favorecer; (mitigate) aliviar; (contribute to) contribuir a, facilitar; (avoid) evitar. *v.i.* ayudar. **He cannot h. worrying,** No puede menos de preocuparse. **God h. you!** ¡Dios te ampare! **So h. me God!** ¡Así Dios me salve! **to h. one another,** ayudarse mutuamente. **to h. oneself,** (to food) servirse. **to h. down, off,** ayudar a bajar; ayudar a apearse. **to h. in,** ayudar a entrar. **to h. along, forward, on,** avanzar, fomentar; promover; contribuir a. **Shall I h. you on with the dress?** ¿Quieres que te ayude a ponerte el vestido? **to h. out,** ayudar a salir; (from a vehicle) ayudar a bajar; (of a difficulty, etc.) sacar; suplir la falta de; ayudar. **to h. over,** ayudar a cruzar; (a difficulty) ayudar a salir (de un apuro); ayudar a vencer (un obstáculo, etc.); (a period) ayudar a pasar. **to h. to,** contribuir a, ayudar en; (food) servir. **to h. up,** ayudar a subir; ayudar a levantarse, levantar

helper, *s.* auxiliador (-ra); asistente (-ta); (protector) favore-

cedor (-ra); bienhechor (-ra);
(colleague) colega, m.; (co-
worker) colaborador (-ra). **He
thanked all his helpers,** Dió las
gracias a todos los que le habían
ayudado

helpful, a. útil, provechoso;
(obliging) servicial, atento; (favourable) favorable; (healthy)
saludable

helpfulness, s. utilidad, ƒ.; bondad, ƒ.

helping, s. ayuda, ƒ.; (of food)
porción, ración, ƒ., plato, m.
Won't you have a second h.?
¿No quiere usted servirse más
(or otra vez)? ¿No quiere usted
repetir? **to lend a h. hand (to),**
prestar ayuda (a)

helpless, a. desamparado, abandonado; (through infirmity) imposibilitado; impotente, sin fuerzas (para); (shiftless) incompetente, inútil

helplessness, s. desamparo, m.;
invalidez, debilidad, ƒ.; impotencia, ƒ.; incompetencia, ƒ.

helpmeet, s. compañero (-ra)
perfecto (-ta); esposa, ƒ.

helter-skelter, adv. atropelladamente; en desorden. s. barahunda, ƒ.

Helvetian, a. and s. helvecio (-ia)

hem, s. (sew.) dobladillo, filete, m.,
bastilla, ƒ.; (edge) orilla, ƒ.
interj. ¡ejem! v.t. hacer dobladillo en, dobladillar. v.i. (cough)
fingir toser. **false hem,** (sew.)
dobladillo falso, m. **running
hem,** (sew.) jareta, ƒ. **to hem
and haw,** tartamudear; vacilar.
to hem in, cercar, sitiar

hemicycle, s. hemiciclo, m.

hemisphere, s. hemisferio, m.

hemispherical, a. hemisférico,
semiesférico

hemistitch, s. hemistiquio, m.

hemlock, s. (bot.) cicuta, ƒ.

hemp, s. cáñamo, m. **h. cloth,**
lienzo, m. **h.-seed,** cañamón, m.

hemstitch, s. vainica, ƒ. v.t.
hacer vainica en

hen, s. gallina, ƒ.; (female bird)
hembra, ƒ. **the hen pheasant,**
la hembra del faisán. **hen bird,**
pájara, ƒ. **hen-coop or house,**
gallinero, m. **hen party,** (fam.)
reunión de mujeres, ƒ. **hen-
roost,** nidal, ponedero, m.

henbane, s. (bot.) beleño, m.

hence; adv. (of place) de aquí; (of
time) de ahora, de aquí a, al cabo
de, en; (therefore) por eso, por lo
tanto, por consiguiente. interj.
¡fuera! ¡fuera de aquí! **I shall
come to see you a month h.,**
Vendré a verte en un mes (or al
cabo de un mes). **ten years h.,**
de aquí a diez años. **h. the fact
that . . .,** de aquí que. . . . **H. it
happens that . . .,** Por eso
sucede que . . .

henceforth, adv. desde aquí en
adelante, de hoy en adelante

henchman, s. escudero, m.; satélite, secuaz, m.

hendecagon, s. endecágono, m.

hendecasyllabic, a. hendecasílabo

henna, s. alheña, ƒ.

henpecked, a. gobernado por su
mujer, que se deja mandar por
su mujer

hepatic, a. hepático

heptachord, s. (mus.) hepta-
cordo, m.

heptad, s. septenario, m., septena,
ƒ.

heptagon, s. (geom.) heptágono,
m.

heptagonal, a. heptagónico

heptahedron, s. heptaedro, m.

heptarchy, s. heptarquía, ƒ.

heptateuch, s. heptateuco, m.

her, pers. pron. direct object, la;
(with prepositions) ella. pers.
pron. indirect object, le, a ella.
poss. a., su, m. and ƒ.; sus, m. and
ƒ. pl., de ella. **I saw her on
Wednesday,** La vi el miércoles.
The message is for her, El
recado es para ella. **It is her
book,** Es su libro, Es el libro de
ella

herald, s. heraldo, m.; presagio,
anuncio, m. v.t. proclamar;
anunciar, presagiar

heraldic, a. heráldico

heraldry, s. heráldica, ƒ.

herb, s. hierba, ƒ.

herbaceous, a. herbáceo

herbage, s. herbaje, m.; pasto, m.

herbal, a. herbario. s. herbolaria,
ƒ.

herbalist, s. herbario, m., simplista, m. and ƒ.

herbarium, s. herbario, m.

herbivorous, a. herbívoro

herby, *a.* herbáceo

Herculean, *a.* hercúleo

herd, *s.* manada, *f.*; (of cattle) hato, *m.*; (race) raza, *f.*; (*fig.*, contemptuous) populacho, *m.*, masa, *f.* *v.t.* reunir en manadas; reunir en hatos; (sheep) reunir en rebaños; guiar las manadas, etc. *v.i.* ir en manadas, hatos o rebaños; asociarse, reunirse. **h.-instinct,** instinto gregario, *m.*; instinto de las masas, *m.*

herdsman, *s.* ganadero, pastor, manadero, *m.*; (head herdsman) rabadán, *m.*

here, *adv.* aquí; (at roll-call) ¡presente!; acá; an este punto; ahora. *s.* presente, *m.* **And h. he looked at me,** Y a este punto me miró. **Come h.!** ¡Ven acá! **in h.,** aquí dentro. **h. below,** aquí abajo, en la tierra. **h. and there,** aquí y allá. **h., there and everywhere,** en todas partes. **H. I am,** Heme aquí. **h. is . . .,** he aquí . . . . **H. they are,** Aquí los tienes, Aquí están. **Here's to you!** (on drinking) ¡Salud y pesetas! ¡A tu salud!

hereabouts, *adv.* por aquí cerca

hereafter, *adv.* en lo futuro; desde ahora; en adelante. *s.* futuro, *m.* **the H.,** la otra vida

hereat, *adv.* en esto

hereby, *adv.* por esto, por las presentes

hereditarily, *adv.* hereditariamente, por herencia

hereditary, *a.* hereditario

heredity, *s.* herencia, *f.*

herein, *adv.* en esto; aquí dentro; incluso

hereinafter, *adv.* después, más adelante

hereof, *adv.* de esto

heresiarch, *s.* heresiarca, *m.*

heresy, *s.* herejía, *f.*

heretic, *s.* hereje, *m.* and *f.*

heretical, *a.* herético

hereunder, *adv.* abajo

hereupon, *adv.* en esto, en seguida

herewith, *adv.* junto con esto, con esto; ahora, en esta ocasión

heritage, *s.* herencia, *f.*

hermaphrodite, *a.* and *s.* hermafrodita (*m.* and *f.*)

hermaphroditism, *s.* hermafroditismo, *m.*

hermetic, *a.* hermético

hermit, *s.* ermitañ. *m.* **h. crab,** paguro, cangrejo ermitaño, *m.*

hermitage, *s.* ermita, *f.*

hernia, *s.* hernia, *f.*

hero, *s.* héroe, *m.* **h.-worship,** culto a los héroes, *m.*

heroic, *a.* heroico, épico

heroin, *s.* (*chem.*) heroína, *f.*

heroine, *s.* heroína, *f.*

heroism, *s.* heroísmo, *m.*

heron, *s.* garza, *f.*

herpes, *s.* *pl.* herpes, *m.* or *f.* *pl.*

herring, *s.* arenque, *m.*

hers, *poss. pron.* 3*rd sing.* (el) suyo, *m.*; (lá) suya, *f.*; (los) suyos, *m. pl.*; (las) suyas, *f. pl.*; de ella. **This book is h.,** Este libro es suyo, Este libro es de ella. **This book is h.,** not mine, Este libro es el suyo no el mío. **A sister of h.,** Una de sus hermanas

herself, *pron.* sí misma, sí; ella misma; (with reflexive verb) se. **She has done it by h.,** Ella lo ha hecho por sí misma. **She h. told me so,** Ella misma me lo dijo. **She is by h.,** Ella está a solas, Ella está sola

Hertzian, *a.* hertziano

hesitancy. See **hesitation**

hesitant, *a.* indeciso, vacilante, irresoluto. **to be h.,** mostrarse irresoluto

hesitate, *v.i.* vacilar, dudar; titubear. **I do not h. to say . . .,** No vacilo en decir . . . **He hesitated over his reply,** Tardaba en dar su respuesta

hesitatingly, *adv.* irresolutamente; titubeando

hesitation, *s.* vacilación, hesitación, *f.*; irresolución, indecisión, *f.*; (reluctance) aversión, repugnancia, *f.*; titubeo, *m.*

Hesperian, *a.* hesperio

Hesperus, *s.* (*ast.*) héspero, *m.*

hetaira, *s.* hetaira, *f.*

heterodox, *a.* heterodoxo

heterodoxy, *s.* heterodoxia, *f.*

heterodyne, *a.* (*f.*) (*rad.*) heterodina

heterogeneity, *s.* heterogeneidad, *f.*

heterogeneous, *a.* heterogéneo

hew, *v.t.* cortar, tajar; (trees) talar; (a career, etc.) hacerse

hewer, *s.* partidor, talador, *m.*

hexagon, *s.* hexágono, *m.*

hexagonal, *a.* hexagonal

hexahedron, s. (*geom.*) hexaedro, m.

hexameter, s. hexámetro, m.

hey, *interj.* ¡he! ¡oye!

heyday, s. apogeo, colmo, m.; buenos tiempos, m. pl.; reinado, m.; pleno vigor, m.

hi, *interj.* ¡oye! ¡hola!

hiatus, s. hiato, m.; laguna, f., vacío, m.

hibernate, v.i. invernar

hibernation, s. invernada, f.

Hibernian, a. hibernés

hibiscus, s. (*bot.*) hibisco, m.

hiccough, s. hipo, m. v.i. hipar. v.t. decir con hipo

hidden, a. escondido, secreto, oculto

hide, s. piel, f.; pellejo, cuero, m.

hide, v.t. esconder, ocultar; (cover) cubrir, tapar; (dissemble) disimular; (meaning) obscurecer. v.i. esconderse; ocultarse; refugiarse. **to h. from each other,** esconderse el uno del otro. **to play h.-and-seek,** jugar al escondite

hidebound, a. (*fig.*) muy conservador, reaccionario, de ideas muy tradicionales

hideous, a. horrible, repulsivo, horroroso; repugnante, odioso

hideously, adv. horriblemente. **to be h. ugly,** (of people) ser más feo que Picio

hideousness, s. fealdad, horribilidad, f.; repugnancia, f.

hiding, s. ocultación, f.; encubrimiento, m.; refugio, m.; (fam.) paliza, tunda, f. **h.-place,** escondite, escondrijo, m.

hie, v.i. apresurarse, ir a prisa

hierarch, s. jerarca, m.

hierarchical, a. jerárquico

hierarchy, s. jerarquía, f.

hieratical, a. hierático

hieroglyph, s. jeroglífico, m.

hierophant, s. hierofante, m.

higgledy-piggledy, adv. revueltamente, en confusión; en montón, en desorden

high, a. alto; elevado; (with altar, Mass, street, festival) mayor; grande; eminente; aristocrático; (of shooting) fijante; (of quality) superior; excelente; (haughty) orgulloso; (solemn) solemne; (good) bueno; noble; supremo; sumo; (of price) subido;

(*mus.*) agudo; (of the sea) tempestuoso, borrascoso; (of wind and explosives) violento, fuerte; (of polish) brillante; (with speed) grande; (with tension, frequency) alto; (with number, etc.) importante, grande; (with colours) subido; (of food) pasado; (angry) enojado, airado; (of cheek bones) saliente, prominente; (well-seasoned) picante; (flattering) lisonjero. adv. alto; hacia arriba; arriba; (deeply) profundamente; fuertemente; con violencia; (of price) a un precio elevado; (luxuriously) lujosamente; (*mus.*) agudo. **a room 12 ft. h.,** un cuarto de doce pies de altura. **I knew her when she was so h.,** La conocí tamaña. **It is h. time he came,** Ya es hora de que viniese. **on h.,** en alto, arriba; en los cielos. **h. altar,** altar mayor, m. **h. and dry,** en la playa, varado; (*fig.*) en seco. **h. and low,** de arriba abajo; por todas partes. **h.-born,** aristocrático, de alta alcurnia. **h.-bred,** (of people) de buena familia; (of animals) de buena raza. **h.-class,** de buena clase; de alta calidad. **h. collar,** alzacuello, m. **h. coloured,** de colores vivos; (*fig.*) exagerado. **H. Command,** (*mil.*, *nav.*) Alto Mando, m. **H. Court,** tribunal supremo, m. **h. day,** día festivo, m. **h. explosive,** explosivo violento, m. **h.-flown,** hinchado, retumbante, altisonante. **h. frequency,** alta frecuencia, f. **h.-handed,** arbitrario, dominador, despótico. **h.-heeled,** a. de tacón alto. **h. jump,** salto de altura, m. **h. land,** tierras altas, f. pl.; eminencia, f. **h. light,** (*art*) realce, m.; acontecimiento de más interés, m.; momento culminante, m. **h. mass,** misa mayor, f. **h.-minded,** de nobles pensamientos; arrogante. **h.-necked,** con cuello alto. **h.-pitched,** de tono alto, agudo. **h.-powered,** de alta potencia. **h.-powered car,** coche de muchos caballos, m. **h. precision,** suma precisión, f. **h. pressure,** s. alta presión, f.; (*fig.*) urgencia, f.;

a. de alta presión; (*fig.*) urgente: **h.-priced**, caro. **h. priest**, sumo sacerdote, alto sacerdote, *m.* **h. relief**, alto relieve, *m.* **h. road**, carretera mayor, *f.* **h. school**, instituto de segunda enseñanza, *m.*; colegio particular, *m.* **h. sea**, marejada, *f.* **h. seas**, alta mar, *f.* **h.-seasoned**, picante. **h. society**, alta sociedad, *f.* **h.-sounding**, altisonante, bombástico. **h.-speed**, de alta velocidad. **h.-spirited**, brioso; alegre. **h.-strung**, nervioso, excitable, sensitivo. **h. ténsion**, alta tensión, *f.* **h. tide**, marea alta, *f.* **h.-toned**, (*mus.*) agudo; (*fam.*) de alto copete; aristocrático. **h. treason**, alta traición, *f.* **h. water**, marea alta, pleamar, *f.* **h.-water mark**, límite de la marea, *m.*; (*fig.*) colmo, *m.*; apogeo, *m.*

highbrow, *a.* and *s.* intelectual, (*m.* and *f.*)

higher, *a. comp.* of **high**, más alto; más elevado; superior. **on a h. plane**, en un nivel más alto. **h. education**, enseñanza superior, *f.* **h. mathematics**, matemáticas superiores, *f. pl.* **the h. criticism**, la alta crítica. **h. up**, más arriba. **h. up the river**, rió arriba

highest, *a. superl.* of **high**, el más alto; la más alta; los más altos; las más altas; sumo; supremo; excelente. **h. common factor**, (*math.*) máximo común divisor, *m.* **h. references**, (of cook, gardener, etc.) informes inmejorables, *m. pl.*; (*com.*) referencias excelentes, *f. pl.*

highland, *s.* altiplanicie, *f.*; montañas, *f. pl.*, distrito montañoso, *m. a.* montañoso

highlander, *s.* montañés (-esa); esocés (-esa) del norte

highly, *adv.* altamente; mucho; muy; extremadamente; grandemente; bien; favorablemente; con lisonja, lisonjeramente. **h. seasoned**, picante. **h. strung**, nervioso, excitable

highness, *s.* altura, *f.*; elevación, *f.*; excelencia, *f.*; nobleza, *f.*; (title) Alteza, *f.* **His (Her) Royal H.**, Su Alteza Real

highway, *s.* camino real, *m.*, carretera, *f.* **h. code**, código de la via pública (or de la circulación), *m.* **h. robbery**, salteamiento de caminos, atraco, *m.*

highwayman, *s.* salteador de caminos, *m.*

hike, *v.i.* ir de excursión. *s.* marcha con equipo, *f.*

hiker, *s.* excursionista, *m.* and *f.*

hiking, *s.* excursionismo, *m.*; marcha con equipo, *f.*

hilarious, *a.* alegre

hilarity, *s.* hilaridad, *f.*

hill, *s.* colina, *f.*, cerro, otero, *m.*; monte, *m.*, montaña, *f.*; (pile) montón, *m.* **h.-side**, falda de montaña, ladera de una colina, *f.* **h.-top**, cumbre de una colina, *f.*

hilliness, *s.* montuosidad, *f.*, lo montañoso

hillman, *s.* montañés, *m.*

hillock, *s.* altozano, montículo, collado, *m.*

hilly, *a.* montañoso

hilt, *s.* puño, *m.*, empuñadura, *f.*

him, *pers. pron., 3rd sing., direct object* le, lo; (with prep.) él; *indirect object* le, a él; (with a direct obj. in 3rd person) se. **I gave him the magazine**, Le dí la revista. **I gave it to him**, Se lo dí a él. **This is for him**, Esto es para él

Himalayan, *a.* himalayo

himself, *pron.* sí, sí mismo; él mismo; (reflexive) se. **He did it by h.**, Lo hizo por sí mismo. For other examples see **herself**

hind, *s.* corza, cierva, *f. a.* trasero, posterior. **h.-quarters**, cuarto trasero, *m.*; (of a horse) ancas, *f. pl.*

hinder, *a.* trasero, posterior

hinder, *v.t.* impedir, estorbar; embarazar, dificultar; interrumpir. *v.i.* ser un obstáculo; formar un obstáculo

hinderer, *s.* estorbador (-ra); interruptor (-ra)

hindmost, *a.* posterior, postrero, último

hindrance, *s.* obstáculo, estorbo, impedimento, *m.*; perjuicio, *m.*; interrupción, *f.*

Hinduism, *s.* indoísmo, *m.*

Hindustani, *a.* indostanés. *s.* (language) indostani, *m.*

hinge, *s.* gozne, pernio, *m.*, bisagra, *f.*; articulación, *f.*; (*fig.*)

eje, *m.* *v.i.* moverse (or abrirse)
sobre goznes; (*fig.*) depender (de).
v.t. engoznar

hinged, *a.* con goznes

hint, *s.* indirecta, insinuación,
sugestión, *f.*; (advice) consejo,
m. *v.t.* dar a entender, decir con
medias palabras, insinuar, sugerir. *v.i.* insinuar. to take
the h., darse por aludido

hinterland, *s.* interior (de un
país), *m.*

hip, *s.* (*anat.*) cadera, *f.*; (*bot.*)
fruto del rosal silvestre, *m.* h.-
bath, baño de asiento, *m.* h.-
bone, hueso ilíaco, *m.* h.-joint,
articulación de la cadera, *f.* h.-
pocket, faltriquera, *f.*

hipped, *a.* de caderas

hippodrome, *s.* hipódromo, *m.*

hippogryph, *s.* (*myth.*) hipógrifo,
m.

hippophagous, *a.* hipófago

hippopotamus, *s.* hipopótamo,
m.

hire, *s.* alquiler, arriendo, *m.*;
salario, *m.* *v.t.* alquilar, arrendar; tomar en arriendo; (person)
contratar; tomar a su servicio.
to h. out, alquilar. for or on h.,
de alquiler. h.-purchase, compra a plazos, *f.*

hireling, *s.* mercenario, *m.*

hirer, *s.* alquilador (-ra), arrendador (-ra)

hirsute, *a.* hirsuto. non-h. (*bot.*)
lampiño

his, *poss. pron.*, *3rd sing.* (el) suyo,
m.; (la) suya, *f.*; (los) suyos, *m.*
pl.; (las) suyas, *f. pl.*; de él. *poss.*
a. su, *m.* and *f.*; sus, *m.* and *f. pl.*;
de él. his handkerchiefs, sus
pañuelos. his mother, su madre,
la madre de él. a sister of his,
una de sus hermanas, una hermana suya

Hispanism, *s.* hispanismo, *m.*

Hispanist, *s.* hispanista, *m.* and *f.*

hispanize, *v.t.* españolizar

Hispano-American, *a.* hispanoamericano

hiss, *s.* silbido, *m.*; (sputter)
chisporroteo, *m.* *v.i.* silbar

hissing, *s.* silbido, *m.*; chisporroteo, *m.* *a.* silbante

hist, *interj.* ¡chist!

histologist, *s.* histólogo, *m.*

histology, *s.* histología, *f.*

historian, *s.* historiador (-ra)

historic, *a.* histórico

historical, *a.* histórico. h. truth,
verdad histórica, *f.*

historically, *adv.* históricamente

historiographer, *s.* historiógrafo,
m.

historiography, *s.* historiografía,
f.

history, *s.* historia, *f.* Biblical
h., historia sagrada, *f.* natural
h., historia natural, *f.*

histrionic, *a.* histriónico

hit, *s.* golpe, *m.*; (*aer.*) impacto,
m.; (success) éxito, *m.*; (piece of
luck) buena suerte, *f.*; (satire)
sátira, *f.* *v.t.* golpear; (buffet)
abofetear, pegar; (find) dar con,
tropezar con; (attain) acertar;
(guess) adivinar; (attract) atraer;
(deal) lanzar, dar; (wound) herir,
hacer daño (a). direct hit, (*aer.*)
impacto de lleno, *m.* lucky hit,
acierto, *m.* to hit a straight
left, (boxing) lanzar un directo
con la izquierda. to hit the
mark, dar en el blanco; (*fig.*) dar
en el clavo. hit or miss,
acierto o error. to hit against,
dar contra, estrellar contra. to
hit back, defenderse; devolver
golpe por golpe. to hit off,
imitar; (a likeness) coger. to hit
out, abofetear; (*fig.*) atacar;
golpear (la pelota) fuera. to
hit upon, dar con; tropezar con;
encontrar por casualidad; (remember) acordarse de

hitch, *s.* (jerk) sacudida, *f.*; nudo
fácil de soltar, *m.*; (*fig.*) obstáculo, *m.*; (*fig.*) dificultad, *f.* *v.t.*
sacudir; (a chair, etc.) arrastrar,
empujar; amarrar, enganchar;
atar. *v.i.* (along a seat, etc.)
correrse (en); (get entangled)
enredarse, cogerse; (rub) rascarse.
without a h., sin dificultad alguna, viento en popa; (smoothly)
a pedir de boca. to h. up,
sacudir, dar una sacudida (a)

hither, *adv.* hacia aquí; hacia
acá; aquí. *a.* citerior, más
cercano. h. and thither, acá y
acullá

hitherto, *adv.* hasta ahora, hasta
el presente

Hitlerian, *a.* hitleriano, nacista

Hitlerism, *s.* hitlerismo, nacismo,
m.

Hittite, *a.* and *s.* heteo (-ea)

hive, *s.* (for bees) colmena, *f.*; (swarm) enjambre, *m.*; (*fig.*) centro, *m.* *v.t.* (bees) enjambrar. **a h. of industry**, un centro de industria

hoard, *s.* acumulación, *f.*; provisión, *f.*; tesoro, *m.* *v.t.* acumular, amasar, amontonar; guardar

hoarder, *s.* acaparador (-ra)

hoarding, *s.* amontonamiento, *m.*; acaparamiento, *m.*; (fence) empalizada, cerca, *f.*; palizada de tablas, *f.*

hoar-frost, *s.* escarcha, helada blanca, *f.*

hoariness, *s.* (of the hair) canicie, *f.*; blancura, *f.*; (antiquity) vejez, vetustez, *f.*

hoarse, *a.* ronco; discordante. **to be h.**, tener la voz ronca. **to grow h.**, enronquecerse

hoarsely, *adv.* roncamente

hoarseness, *s.* ronquera, *f.*; (*fam.*) carraspera, *f.*

hoary, *a.* (of the hair) canoso; blanco; (old) vetusto, antiguo, viejo

hoax, *s.* estafa, *f.*, engaño, *m.*; broma pesada, *f.*; burla, *f.* *v.t.* estafar, engañar; burlar

hoaxer, *s.* burlador (-ra); estafador (-ra)

hob, *s.* repisa interior del hogar, *f.*

hobble, *s.* (gait) cojera, *f.*; traba, maniota, *f.* *v.i.* cojear. *v.t.* manear. **h.-skirt**, falda muy estrecha, *f.*

hobby, *s.* pasatiempo, *m.*, recreación, *f.*; manía, afición, *f.*; **h.-horse**, caballo de cartón, *m.*; (*fig.*) caballo de batalla, *m.*

hobgoblin, *s.* trasgo, duende, *m.*

hobnail, *s.* clavo de herradura, clavo de botas, *m.*

hobnailed, *a.* (of boots) con clavos

hobnob, *v.i.* codearse, tratar con familiaridad

hock, *s.* (*anat.*) pernil, *m.*; (wine) vino del Rin, *m.*

hockey, *s.* hockey, *m.* **h. ball**, bola, pelota de hockey, *f.* **h. stick**, bastón de hockey, *m.*

hocus-pocus, *s.* juego de pasa pasa, *m.*; engaño, *m.*, treta, *f.*

hod, *s.* cuezo, *m.*

hoe, *s.* azadón, *m.* *v.t.* azadonar; sachar

hoeing, *s.* cavadura con azadón, *f.*; sachadura, *f.*

hoer, *s.* azadonero, *m.*

hog, *s.* cerdo, puerco, *m.* **to go the whole hog**, ir al extremo. **hog-skin**, piel de cerdo, *f.*

hoggish, *a.* porcuno; (greedy) comilón, tragón; (selfish) egoísta

Hogmanay, *s.* Año Nuevo, *m.*

hogshead, *s.* bocoy, *m.*

hoist, *s.* levantamiento, *m.*; (lift) montacargas, *m.*; (winch) cabria, *f.*; (crane) grúa, *f.* *v.t.* levantar, alzar; (flags) enarbolar; suspender; (*naut.*) izar

hoity-toity, *a.* picajoso, quisquilloso; presuntuoso

hold, *s.* asimiento, agarro, *m.*, presa, *f.*; asidero, *m.*; (*fig.*) autoridad, *f.*, poder, *m.*; (*fig.*) comprensión, *f.*; (of a ship) cala, bodega, *f.* **to loose one's h.**, aflojar su presa. **to lose one's h.**, perder su presa. **to seize h. of**, asirse de, echar mano de. **h.-all**, funda, *f.* **h.-up**, (robbery) atraco, robo a mano armada, *m.*; (in traffic) atasco (or obstáculo) en el tráfico, *m.*; (in work) parada, cesación (de trabajo), *f.*

hold, *v.t.* tener; asir, agarrar; coger; retener; (embrace) abrazar; (a post) ocupar; (a meeting, etc.) celebrar; (bear weight of) aguantar, soportar; (own) poseer; (*mil.*) ocupar, defender; (contain) contener; (have in store) reservar; tener capacidad para; (retain) retener; (believe) creer, sostener; (consider) opinar, tener para (mí, etc.); juzgar; (restrain) detener; contener; (of attention, etc.) mantener; (manœuvres) hacer; (observe) guardar. *v.i.* resistir, aguantar; (be valid) ser válido; regir; (apply) aplicarse; (last) continuar, seguir. *interj.* ¡tente! ¡para! **The room won't h. more**, En este cuarto no caben más. **They h. him in great respect**, Le tienen mucho respeto. **The theory does not h. water**, La teoría es falsa, La teoría no es lógica. **to h. one's own**, defenderse, mantenerse en sus trece. **to h. one's tongue**, callarse. **to h. sway**, mandar; reinar. **to h. tightly**, agarrar fuertemente; (clasp) estrechar. **H. the line!** (telephone) ¡Aguarde un momento! **to h. back,** *v.t.* detener; contener; retener; esconder; abstenerse de entregar. *v.i.* quedarse atrás; vacilar, dudar; tardar en. **to h. by,** seguir; basarse en, apoyarse en. **to h. down,** sujetar; (oppress) oprimir. **to h. fast,** *v.t.* sujetar fuertemente. *v.i.* mantenerse firme; (*fig.*) estar agarrado (a). **to h. forth,** *v.t.* ofrecer; expresar. *v.i.* hacer un discurso, perorar. **to h. in,** *v.t.* contener; retener. *v.i.* contenerse. **to h. off,** *v.t.* apartar, alejar. *v.i.* apartarse, alejarse, mantenerse alejado. **to h. on,** seguir, persistir en; aguantar. **to h. out,** *v.t.* alargar, extender; ofrecer. *v.i.* aguantar; durar, resistir. **to h. over,** tener suspendido sobre; (postpone) aplazar; (*fig.*) amenazar con. **to h. to,** agarrarse a; atenerse a. **to h. together,** *v.t.* unir; juntar. *v.i.* mantenerse juntos.. **to h. up,** *v.t.* (display) mostrar, enseñar; levantar; sostener, soportar; (rob) atracar, saltear; (delay) atrasar; (stop) interrumpir, parar. *v.i.* mantenerse en pie; (of weather) seguir bueno. **The train has been held up by fog,** El tren viene con retraso a causa de la niebla.

holder, *s.* el *m.* (*f.* la) que tiene; poseedor (-ra); (*com.*) tenedor (-ra); inquilino (-na); propietario (-ia); (support) soporte, *m.*; mango, *m.*; asa, *f.*; (in compounds) porta . . .

holding, *s.* tención, *f.*; posesión, *f.*; propiedad, *f.*; (leasing) arrendamiento, *m.*; (celebration) solemnización, *f.*; (of a meeting) el celebrar, el tener; *pl.* **holdings,** (*com.*) valores habidos, *m. pl.*

hole, *s.* hoyo, *m.*; boquete, *m.*; agujero, *m.*; cavidad, *f.*; (hollow) depresión, *f.*, hueco, *m.*; orificio, *m.*; (tear) roto, desgarro, *m.*; (eyelet) punto, *m.*; (in cheese) ojo, *m.*; (in stocking) rotura, *f.*, punto, *m.*; (lair) madriguera, *f.*; (nest) nido, *m.*; (golf) hoyo, *m.*; (fix) aprieto, *m.* *v.t.* agujerear; excavar; (bore) taladrar; (sport)

meter la pelota (en). **to h. out,** (golf) meter la pelota en el hoyo. **h.-and-corner,** *a.* (*fam.*) bajo mano, secreto

holiday, *s.* día feriado, *m.*; día de fiesta, día festivo, *m.*; vacación, *f.* *a.* festivo, alegre; de vacación; de vacaciones; de excursión; (summer) veraniego. **day's h.,** día de asueto, *m.* **to take a h.,** tomar una vacación; hacer fiesta. **h. camp,** colonia veraniega, *f.* **h.-maker,** excursionista, turista, *m.* and *f.*; (in the summer) veraneante, *m.* and *f.* **holidays with pay,** vacaciones retribuidas, *f. pl.*

holiness, *s.* santidad, *f.*

holland, *s.* lienzo crudo, *m.* *a.* de Holanda, holandés. **H. gin,** ginebra holandesa, *f.*

hollow, *a.* hueco; cóncavo; (empty) vacío; (of eyes, etc.) hundido; (of sound) sordo; (of a cough) cavernoso; (echoing) retumbante; (*fig.*, unreal) vacío, falso; insincero. *adv.* vacío; (*fam.*) completamente. *s.* hueco, *m.*; concavidad, *f.*; (hole) hoyo, *m.*; cavidad, *f.*; (valley) hondanada, *f.*, barranco, *m.*; (groove) ranura, *f.*; (depression) depresión, *f.*; (in the back) curvadura, *f.* *v.t.* excavar, ahuecar; vaciar. **h.-cheeked,** con las mejillas hundidas. **h.-eyed,** con los ojos hundidos, de ojos hundidos

hollowness, *s.* concavidad, *f.*; (falseness) falsedad, *f.*; insinceridad, *f.*

holly, *s.* acebo, agrifolio, *m.*

hollyhock, *s.* malva loca, malva real, *f.*

holm, *s.* ribera del río, *f.*; isleta de río, *f.* **h.-oak,** encina, *f.*

holocaust, *s.* holocausto, *m.*

holograph, *s.* hológrafo, *m.*

holster, *s.* pistolera, *f.*

holy, *a.* santo; sagrado; (blessed) bendito. **most h.,** *a.* santísimo. **to make h.,** santificar. **H. Father,** Padre Santo, El Papa, *m.* **H. Ghost,** Espíritu Santo, *m.* **H. Land,** Tierra Santa, *f.* **H. Office,** Santo Oficio, *m.*, Inquisición, *f.* **H. Orders,** órdenes sagradas, *f. pl.* **h. places,** santos lugares, *m. pl.* **H. Scripture,** Sagrada Escritura, *f.* **H.**

See, Cátedra de San Pedro, *f.*
h. water, agua bendita, *f.* **H.
Souls**, las Ánimas Benditas.
h. water stoup, acetre, *m.* **H.
Week**, Semana Santa, *f.*

homage, *s.* homenaje, *m.*; culto,
m.; reverencia, *f.* **To pay h.**,
rendir homenaje

home, *s.* casa, *f.*; hogar, *m.*;
domicilio, *m.*, residencia, *f.*;
(institution) asilo, *m.*; (haven)
refugio, *m.*; (habitation) morada,
f.; (country of origin) país de
origen, *m.*; (native land) patria,
f.; (environment) ambiente natural, *m.*; (sport) meta, *f.* *a.*
casero, doméstico; nativo; nacional, del país; indígena. *adv.*
a casa, hacia casa; (in one's
country) en su patria; (returned)
de vuelta; (of the feelings) al
corazón, al alma; (to the limit)
al límite. **at h.**, en casa; (*fig.*) en
su elemento; (of games) en
campo propio; de recibo. **at
h. day**, día de recibo, *m.* **He
shot the bolt h.**, Echó el
cerrojo. **one's long h.**, su
última morada. **to be at h.**,
estar en casa; estar de recibo.
to be away from h., estar
fuera de casa; estar ausente. **to
bring h.**, traer (or llevar) a casa;
hacer ver; convencer; llegar al
alma; (a crime) probar (contra).
to go h., volver a casa; volver a
la patria; (be effective) hacer su
efecto; (move) herir en lo más
vivo. **to make oneself at h.**,
ponerse a sus anchas, sentirse
como en casa de uno. **to strike
h.**, dar en el blanco; herir; (hit)
golpear; herir en lo más vivo;
hacerse sentir. **h. affairs**, asuntos
domésticos, *m. pl.* (Ministry of)
Gobernación, *f.* **h.-bred**, criado
en el país. **h.-brewed**, fermentado en el país; fermentado en
casa. **h.-coming**, regreso al
hogar, *m.* **h. counties**, condados
alrededor de Londres, *m. pl.* **H.
Defence**, defensa nacional, *f.* **h.
farm**, residencia del propietario
de una finca, *f.* **h. front**, frente
doméstico, *m.* **H. Guard**, milicia
nacional, *f.* **h. life**, vida de
familia, *f.* **h.-made**, hecho en
casa. **H. Office**, Ministerio de
Gobernación, *m.* **H. Rule**, auto-

nomía, *f.* **H. Secretary**, Ministro de Gobernación, *m.* **h.
stretch**, último trecho de una
carrera, *m.* **h. truth**, verdad,
(*fam.*) fresca, *f.* **to tell someone
a few h. truths**, contarle cuatro
verdades

homeless, *a.* sin casa; sin
hogar

homeliness, *s.* comodidad, *f.*;
sencillez, *f.*; (ugliness) fealdad,
f.

homely, *a.* doméstico; familiar;
(unpretentious) sencillo; llano;
(ugly) feo

Homeric, *a.* homérico

homesick, *a.* nostálgico. **to be
h.**, tener morriña

homesickness, *s.* nostalgia, añoranza, morriña, *f.*

homespun, *a.* tejido en casa;
hecho en casa; basto, grueso

homestead, *s.* hacienda, *f.*; casa
solariega, *f.*; casa, *f.*

homeward, *adv.* hacia casa, en
dirección al hogar; de vuelta;
hacia la patria. **h.-bound**, en
dirección a casa; (of ships) con
rumbo al puerto de origen; (of
other traffic) de vuelta

homicidal, *a.* homicida

homicide, *s.* (act) homicidio, *m.*;
(person) homicida, *m.* and *f.*

homily, *s.* (*ecc.*) homilía, *f.*;
sermón, *m.*

homing pigeon, *s.* palomo (-ma)
mensajero (-ra)

homœopath, *s.* homeópata, *m.*
and *f.*

homœopathic, *a.* homeópata

homœopathy, *s.* homeopatía, *f.*

homogeneity, *s.* homogeneidad,
f.

homogeneous, *a.* homogéneo

homologous, *a.* homólogo

homonym, *s.* homónimo, *m.*

homonymous, *a.* homónimo

homosexual, *a.* and *s.* homosexual (*m.* and *f.*)

Honduran, *a.* and *s.* hondureño
(-ña)

hone, *s.* piedra de afilar, *f.* *v.t.*
afilar, vaciar

honest, *a.* honrado; decente,
honesto; (chaste) casto; (loyal)
sincero, leal; (frank) franco;
imparcial. **an h. man**, un
hombre de buena fe, un hombre
honrado, un hombre decente

honesty, s. honradez, f.; honestidad, f.; (chastity) castidad, f.;
sinceridad, f.; rectitud, imparcialidad, f.

honey, s. miel, f. **h.-bee,** abeja
obrera, f. **h.-coloured,** melado.
h.-pot, jarro de miel, m. **h.-
tongued,** melifluo; de pico de
oro

honeycomb, s. panal, m.

honeycombed, a. apanalado

honeydew, s. mielada, f.; (fig.)
ambrosia, f.

honeyed, a. de miel; (fig.) meloso,
adulador

honeymoon, s. luna de miel, f.;
viaje de novios, m.

honeysuckle, s. madreselva, f.

honorarium, s. honorario, m.

honorary, a. honorario, honorífico. **h. member,** socio (-ia)
honorario (-ia). **h. mention,**
mención honorífica, f.

honour, s. honor, m.; honra, f.;
honradez, rectitud, integridad,
f.; pl. **honours,** honores, m. pl.;
condecoraciones, f. pl.; (last
h.) honras, pompas fúnebres,
f. pl. v.t. honrar; (God)
glorificar; (decorate) condecorar,
laurear; (respect) respetar; reverenciar; (com.) aceptar; (a
toast) beber. **On my h.,** A fe
mía. **point of h.,** punto de
honor, pundonor, m. **word of
h.,** palabra de honor, f. **Your
H.,** (to a judge) Excelentísimo
Señor Juez

honourable, a. honorable; glorioso; digno; ilustre; (sensitive
of honour) pundonoroso

honourableness, s. honradez, f.

honourably, adv. honorable-
mente; dignamente

hood, s. capucha, caperuza, f.;
(folding, of vehicles) capota, f.;
(of a carriage) caparazón, fuelle,
m.; (university) muceta, f.; (of a
fireplace) campana (de hogar),
f.; (cowl of chimney) sombrerete
(de chimenea), m. v.t. cubrir con
capucha; cubrir; (the eyes) ocultar, cubrir, velar

hooded, a. con capucha

hoodwink, v.t. vendar (los ojos);
(fig.) engañar, embaucar, burlar

hoof, s. casco, m.; (cloven)
pezuña, f.

hoofed, a. ungulado

hook, s. gancho, garfio, m.;
(boat-) bichero, m.; (fish-) anzuelo, m.; (on a dress) corchete,
m.; (hanger) colgadero, m.; (claw)
garra, f. v.t. enganchar; (a dress)
abrochar; (fish) pescar, coger;
(nab) atrapar, pescar. **by h. or
by crook,** a tuertas o a derechas.
left h., (boxing) izquierdo, m.
right h., (boxing) derecho, m.
to catch oneself on a h.,
engancharse. **h. and eye,** los
corchetes. **h.-nosed,** con nariz
de gancho, con nariz aguileña.
h.-up, (rad.) circuito, m.; transmisión en circuito, f.

hookah, s. narguile, m.

hooked, a. con ganchos; corvo,
ganchoso

hooking, s. enganche, m.; (of a
dress) abrochamiento, m.; (of
fish and fam.) pesca, f.

hookworm, s. anquilostoma, m.

hooligan, s. rufián, m.

hooliganism, s. rufianería, f.

hoop, s. aro, arco, m.; (of a skirt)
miriñaque, m.; (croquet) argolla,
f.; (toy) aro, m.; círculo, m. v.t.
poner aros a; (fig.) rodear

hoot, s. (of owls) ululación, f.,
grito, m.; (whistle) silbido, m.;
ruido, clamor, m. v.i. (of owls)
ulular, gritar; silbar; (aut.) avisar
con la bocina. **to h. off the
stage,** hacer abandonar la escena. **to h. down,** silbar

hooter, s. sirena, f.; (aut.) bocina,
f.; (whistle) pito, m.

hooting, s. See **hoot**

hop, s. salto, brinco, m.; (bot.)
lúpulo, m.; (bot.) flores de oblón,
f. pl.; (dance) baile, m. v.i.
saltar con un pie; andar dando
brincos; saltar; (limp) cojear;
recoger lúpulo; (of plant) dar
lúpulo. v.t. saltar. **hop-garden,**
huerto de lúpulo, m. **hop-kiln,**
horno para secar lúpulo, m.
hop-picker, recolector (-ra) de
lúpulo. **hop-picking,** recolección de lúpulos, f.

hope, s. esperanza, f.; (faith) confianza, f.; (expectation) anticipación, expectación, f.; (probability) probabilidad, f.; (illusion)
ilusión, f.; sueño, m. v.i. esperar.
to live in h. that, vivir con la
esperanza de que. **to lose h.,**
desesperarse. **to h. against h.,**

esperar sin motivo, esperar lo imposible. **to h. for,** desear. **to h. in,** confiar en

hopeful, *a.* lleno de esperanzas, confiado; optimista; (*fig.*) risueño. *s.* (*fam.*) la esperanza de la casa. **to look h.,** (*fig.*) prometer bien

hopefully, *adv.* con esperanza

hopefulness, *s.* optimismo, *m.*; (*fig.*) aspecto prometedor, *m.*

hopeless, *a.* desesperado, sin esperanza; irremediable; (of situations) imposible; (of disease) incurable. **to be h.,** (lose hope) desesperarse; (have no remedy) ser irremediable; (of disease) no tener cura. **to make h.,** hacer perder la esperanza, desesperar; dejar sin remedio; (a situation) hacer imposible; (an illness) hacer imposible de curar

hopelessly, *adv.* sin esperanza; sin remedio; imposiblemente; incurablemente

hopelessness, *s.* desesperación, *f.*; (of an illness) imposibilidad de curar, *f.*; lo irremediable; imposibilidad, *f.*

hopscotch, *s.* infernáculo, *m.*

horal, horary, *a.* horario

Horatian, *a.* horaciano

horde, *s.* horda, *f.*

horizon, *s.* horizonte, *m.*

horizontal, *a.* horizontal. **h. suspension,** (gymnastics) plancha, *f.*

horizontality, *s.* horizontalidad, *f.*

horizontally, *adv.* horizontalmente

hormone, *s.* hormona, *f.*

horn, *s.* (of bull, etc.) cuerno, *m.*; (antler) asta, *f.*; (of an insect) antena, *f.*; (of a snail) tentáculo, *m.*; (*mus.*) cuerno, *m.*; trompa, *f.*; (of motor and gramophone) bocina, *f.*; (of moon) cuerno (de la luna), *m.* **articles made of h.,** objetos de cuerno, *m. pl.* **on the horns of a dilemma,** entre la espada y la pared. **h. of plenty,** cuerno de abundancia, *m.*; cornucopia, *f.* **h.-rimmed spectacles,** anteojos de concha, *m. pl.* **h. thrust,** cornada, *f.*

hornbook, *s.* cartilla, *f.*

horned, *a.* cornudo; (antlered) enastado

hornet, *s.* avispón, abejón, *m.*

horniness, *s.* dureza, *f.*; callosidad, *f.*

horny, *a.* córneo; calloso; duro. **h.-handed,** con manos callosas

horoscope, *s.* horóscopo, *m.*

horrible, *a.* horrible, repugnante, espantoso; (of price) enorme; (*fam.*) horrible

horribleness, *s.* horribilidad, *f.*, horror, *m.*, lo espantoso

horribly, *adv.* horriblemente

horrid, *a.* horroroso; desagradable

horridness, *s.* horror, *m.*; lo desagradable

horrific, *a.* horrífico, horrendo

horrify, *v.t.* horrorizar; escandalizar

horrifying, *a.* horroroso, horripilante

horror, *s.* horror, *m.* **h.-stricken,** horrorizado

hors d'œuvres, *s. pl.* entremeses, *m. pl.*

horse, *s.* caballo, *m.*; (cavalry) caballería, *f.*; (frame) caballete, *m.*; (gymnastics and as punishment) potro, *m.* *a.* caballar, caballuno. *v.t.* montar a caballo. **pack of horses,** caballada, *f.* **to ride a h.,** cabalgar, montar a caballo. **H. Artillery,** artillería montada, *f.* **h. blanket,** manta para caballos, *f.*; sudadero, *m.* **h.-block,** montador, *m.* **h.-box,** vagón para caballos, *m.* **h.-breaker,** domador de caballos, *m.* **h.-cab,** simón, *m.* **h.-chestnut,** castaña pilonga, *f.* **h.-chestnut flower,** candela, *f.* **h.-collar,** collera, *f.* **h.-dealer,** chalán, *m.* **h.-doctor,** veterinario, *m.* **h.-flesh,** carne de caballo, *f.* **h.-fly,** tábano, *m.* **H. Guards,** guardias montadas, *f. pl.* **h.-latitudes,** calmas de Cáncer, *f. pl.* **h.-laugh,** carcajada, *f.* **h.-master,** maestro de equitación, *m.* **h. meat,** carne de caballo, *f.* **h. pistol,** pistola de arzón, *f.* **h.-play,** payasada, *f.* **h.-power,** caballo de vapor, *m.*; potencia, *f.* **a twelve-h.p. car,** un coche de doce caballos. **h.-race,** carrera de caballos, *f.* **h.-radish,** rábano picante, *m.* **h.-sense,** sentido común, *m.*, gramática parda, *f.* **h. show,**

exposición de caballos, *f.*; concurso de caballos, *m.* **h.-trainer,** entrenador de caballos, *m.* **h. tram,** tranvía de sangre, *m.* **h. trappings,** monturas, *f. pl.*

horseback, *s.* lomo de caballo, *m.* **on h.,** a caballo. **to ride on h.,** ir a caballo

horsehair, *s.* crin, *f.*

horseman, *s.* jinete, cabalgador, *m.*

horsemanship, *s.* equitación, *f.*, manejo del caballo, *m.*

horseshoe, *s.* herradura, *f.* **h. arch,** arco de herradura, arco morisco, *m.*

horsewhip, *s.* látigo, *m.* *v.t.* zurriagar, pegar con látigo

horsewoman, *s.* amazona, *f.*

horsy, *a.* de caballo; aficionado a caballos; grosero

hortative, *a.* exhortatorio

horticultural, *a.* horticultural. **h. show,** exposición de flores, *f.*

horticulturalist, *s.* horticultor (-ra)

horticulture, *s.* horticultura, *f.*

hosanna, *s.* hosanna, *m.*

hose, *s.* (tube) manga, *f.*; (breeches) calzón, *m.*; (stockings) medias, *f. pl.*; (socks) calcetines, *m. pl.* **h. man,** manguero, *m.* **h.-pipe,** manga de riego, manguera, *f.*

hosier, *s.* calcetero (-ra)

hosiery, *s.* calcetería, *f.* **h. trade,** calcetería, *f.*

hospice, *s.* hospicio, *m.*; asilo, refugio, *m.*

hospitable, *a.* hospitalario

hospitableness, *s.* hospitalidad, *f.*

hospitably, *adv.* hospitalariamente

hospital, *s.* hospital, *m.*; (school) colegio, *m.* **h. nurse,** enfermera, *f.* **h. ship,** buque hospital, *m.* **h. ward,** sala de hospital, *f.*

hospitality, *s.* hospitalidad, *f.*

host, *s.* huésped, convidador, *m.*; (at an inn) patrón, mesonero, *m.*; (army) ejército, *m.*; (crowd) multitud, muchedumbre, *f.*; (ecc.) hostia, *f.*; *pl.* **hosts,** huestes, *f. pl.* **h.-plant,** planta huésped, *f.*

hostage, *s.* rehén, *m.*; (fig.) prenda, *f.*

hostel, *s.* hostería, *f.*; club, *m.*; residencia de estudiantes, *f.*

hostelry, *s.* hospedería, *f.*; parador, mesón, *m.*

hostess, *s.* ama de la casa, *f.*; la que recibe a los invitados; la que convida; (of an inn) patrona, mesonera, *f.*

hostile, *a.* enemigo; hostil, contrario (a); (of circumstances, etc.) desfavorable

hostility, *s.* enemistad, *f.*, antagonismo, *m.*, mala voluntad, *f.*; hostilidad, guerra, *f* **suspension of hostilities,** suspensión de hostilidades, *f.*

hot, *a.* caliente; (of a day, etc.) caluroso; (piquant) picante; ardiente; vehemente, impetuoso; violento; impaciente; colérico; entusiasta; lleno de deseo; (art) intenso; (great) grande, mucho; (vigorous) enérgico. **You are getting very hot now,** (fam.) (in a game, etc.) Te estás quemando. **It is hot,** Está caliente; (of weather) Hace calor. **to grow hot,** calentarse; (fig.) acalorarse; (of weather) empezar a hacer calor. **to make hot,** calentar; dar calor (a); (fam.) dar vergüenza. **hot-blooded,** de sangre caliente; apasionado; colérico. **hot-foot,** aprisa, apresuradamente. **hot-headed,** impetuoso. **hot-plate,** (elec.) calientaplatos, *m.* **hot springs,** termas, *f. pl.* **hot-tempered,** colérico, irascible. **hot water,** agua caliente, *f.* **hot-water bottle,** bolsa de goma, *f.* **hot-water pipes,** las cañerías del agua caliente

hotbed, *s.* semillero, vivero, *m.*; (fig.) semillero, foco, *m.*

hotchpotch, *s.* potaje, *m.*; (fig.) mezcolanza, *f.*, fárrago, *m.*

hotel, *s.* hotel, *m.* **h.-keeper,** hotelero (-ra)

hothead, *s.* exaltado (-da), fanático (-ca)

hothouse, *s.* invernáculo, *m.*, estufa, *f.* **h. plant,** (fig.) planta de estufa, *f.*

hotly, *adv.* calurosamente; con vehemencia; coléricamente

hotpot, *s.* estofado, *m.*

Hottentot, *a.* and *s.* hotentote (-ta)

hough, s. (zool.) pernil, m.; (in man) corva, f.

hound, s. perro de caza, sabueso de artois, m.; perro, m.; (fam.) canalla, m. v.t. cazar con perros; (fig.) perseguir; (fig.) incitar. **master of hounds,** montero, m. **pack of hounds,** jauría, f.

hour, s. hora, f.; momento, m.; ocasión, oportunidad, f. pl. **hours,** horas, f. pl. **after hours,** después de las horas del trabajo. **at the eleventh h.,** al último momento. **by the h.,** por horas; horas enteras. **small hours,** altas horas de la noche, (fam.) las tantas, f. pl. **to keep late hours,** acostarse tarde. **to strike the h.,** dar la hora. **h.-glass,** reloj de arena, m. **h.-hand,** horario, m. **h. of death,** hora suprema, hora de la muerte, f.

houri, s. hurí, f.

hourly, a. cada hora; por hora; continuo. adv. a cada hora; de un momento a otro

house, s. casa, f.; (home) hogar, m.; (lineage) familia, f., abolengo, m.; (theat.) sala, f., teatro, m.; (com.) casa comercial, f.; (takings) entrada, f.; (audience) público, m.; (of Lords, Commons) cámara, f.; (college) colegio, m.; (parliament) parlamento, m.; (building) edificio, m. a. de casa; de la casa; doméstico. v.t. dar vivienda (a); alojar, recibir (or tener) en casa de uno; (store) poner, guardar. **The cottage will not h. them all,** No habrá bastante sitio para todos ellos en la cabaña, No cabrán todos en la cabaña. **country-h.,** finca, f.; casa de campo, f. **full h.,** casa llena, f.; (theat.) lleno, m. **to bring down the h.,** (theat.) hacer venirse el teatro abajo. **to keep h.,** llevar la casa; ser ama de casa. **to keep open h.,** tener mesa puesta, ser hospitalario. **to set up h.,** poner casa. **h. of cards,** castillo de naipes, m. **H. of Commons,** Cámara de los Comunes, f. **H. of Lords,** Cámara de los Lores, f. **h.-agent,** agente de casas, m. **h.-boat,** barco-habitación, m., casa flotante, f. **h.-dog,** perro de guardia, m.; perro de casa, m. **h.-fly,** mosca doméstica, f. **h. furnisher,** mueblista, m. and f. **h. painter,** pintor de brocha gorda, m. **h. party,** reunión en una casa de campo, f. **h.-physician,** médico (-ca) interno (-na). m. **h. porter,** portero, m. **h. property,** propiedad inmueble, f. **h.-room,** capacidad de una casa, f. **h. slipper,** zapatilla, f., pantuflo, m. **h.-surgeon,** cirujano interno, m. **h.-to-h.,** de casa en casa. **h.-warming,** reunión para colgar la cremallera, f.

housebreaker, s. ladrón de casas, m.

housebreaking, s. robo de una casa, m.

houseful, s. casa, f.

household, s. casa, f.; familia, f.; hogar, m. a. de la casa; doméstico; del hogar. **to be a h. word,** andar en lenguas. **h. accounts,** cuentas de la casa, f. pl. **h. duties,** labores de la casa, f. pl. **h. gods,** penates, m. pl. **h. goods,** ajuar, mobiliario, m. **h. management,** gobierno de la casa, m.

householder, s. padre de familia, m.; dueño (-ña) (or inquilino (-na)) de una casa

housekeeper, s. ama de llaves, f.; mujer de su casa, f.

housekeeping, s. gobierno de la casa, m.; economía doméstica, f. a. doméstico. **to set up h.,** poner casa

houseleek, s. (bot.) siempreviva, f.

housemaid, s. camarera, sirvienta, f. **housemaid's knee,** rodilla de fregona, f.

housetops, s. tejado, m.; (flat roof) azotea, f. **to shout from the h.,** pregonar a los cuatro vientos

housewife, s. madre de familia, mujer de su casa, f.; (sewing-bag) neceser de costura, m.

housewifely, a. propio de una mujer de su casa; doméstico; (of a woman) hacendosa

housewifery, s. economía doméstica, f.

housing, s. provisión de vivienda, f.; (storage) almacenaje, m.; alojamiento, m.; (fam.) casa, vivienda, *f.* **h. scheme**, urbanización, *f.* **h. shortage**, crisis de vivienda, *f.*

hovel, *s.* casucha, *f.*

hover, *v.i.* revolotear; (of hawks, etc.) cernerse; estar suspendido; rondar; seguir de cerca, estar al lado (de); (*fig.*) vacilar, dudar

hovering, *s.* revoloteo, *m.*; (of birds of prey) calada, *f.*; (*fig.*) vacilación, *f.* *a.* revolante, que revolotea; que se cierne (sobre); (menacing) que amenaza, inminente

how, *adv.* cómo; (by what means, in what manner) de qué modo; (at what price) a qué precio; qué; cuánto. *s.* el cómo. **to know how**, saber. **For how long**? ¿ Por cuánto tiempo ? **How are you** ? ¿ Cómo está Vd. ? (*fam.*) ¿ Qué tal ? **How old are you** ? ¿ Qué edad tiene Vd. ? **How beautiful** ! ¡ Qué hermoso ! **How big** ! ¡ Cuán grande ! **How early** ? ¿ Cuán temprano ?; ¿ Cuándo a más tardar ? **How far** ? ¿ A qué distancia ? ¿ Hasta qué punto ? ¿ Hasta dónde ? **How fast** ? ¿ A qué velocidad ? **How few** ! ¡ Qué pocos ! **How little** ! ¡ Qué pequeño ! ; ¡ Qué poco ! **How long** ? ¿ Cuánto tiempo ? **How many** ? ¿ Cuántos ? *m. pl.*; ¿ Cuántas ? *f. pl.* **How much is it** ? ¿ Cuánto vale ? **How much cloth do you want** ? ¿ Cuánta tela quieres ? **How often** ? ¿ Cuán a menudo ? ¿ Cuántas veces ?

howbeit, *conjunc.* no obstante, sin embargo

howdah, *s.* castillo, *m.*

however, *adv.* como quiera (que) (followed by subjunctive); por más que (followed by subjunctive); por . . . que (followed by subjunctive). *conjunc.* (nevertheless) sin embargo, no obstante. **h. good it is**, por bueno que sea. **h. he does it**, como quiera que lo haga. **h. it may be**, sea como sea. **h. much**, por mucho que

howitzer, *s.* obús, *m.*

howl, *s.* aullido, *m.*; (groan) gemido, *m.*; (cry) grito, *m.*; (roar) rugido, bramido, *m.*; lamento, *m.* *v.i.* aullar; gemir; gritar; rugir, bramar. *v.t.* chillar. **Each time he opened his mouth he was howled down**, Cada vez que abrió la boca se armó una bronca

howler, *s.* aullador (-ra); (*zool.*) mono (-na) chillón (-ona); (blunder) coladura, plancha, *f.*

howling, *a.* aullante; gemidor (crying) que llora; bramante, rugiente. *s.* los aullidos; (groaning) el gemir, los gemidos; (crying) los gritos; (weeping) el lloro; (roaring) los bramidos, el rugir; los lamentos

hoyden, *s.* muchacha traviesa, locuela, *f.*

hub, *s.* (of a wheel) cubo (de rueda) *m.*; (*fig.*) centro, *m.* **hub cap**, tapa de cubo, *f.*

hubble-bubble, *s.* narguile, *m.*

hubbub, *s.* algarada, barahunda, *f.*

huckster, *s.* revendedor (-ra). *v.i.* revender; (haggle) regatear

huddle, *s.* (heap) montón, *m.*; colección, *f.*; (group) corrillo, grupo, *m.*; (mixture) mezcla, *f.* *v.t.* arrebujar, amontonar; acurrucar, arrebujar; (throw on) echarse. *v.i.* amontonarse; apiñarse; acurrucarse, arrebujarse

hue, *s.* color, *m.*; matiz, tono, *m.*; (of opinion) matiz, *m.*; (clamour) clamor, *m.*, gritería, *f.* **hue and cry**, alarma, *f.*

huff, *s.* acceso de cólera, *m.*

huffily, *adv.* malhumoradamente; petulantemente

huffiness, *s.* mal humor, *m.*; petulancia, *f.*; arrogancia, *f.*

hug, *s.* abrazo, *m.* *v.t.* abrazar, apretujar; (*fig.*) acariciar; (*naut.*) navegar muy cerca de. **to hug oneself**, (*fig.*) congratularse

huge, *a.* enorme, inmenso; gigante; vasto

hugely, *adv.* inmensamente, enormemente

hugeness, *s.* inmensidad, enormidad, *f.*; vastedad, *f.*

Huguenot, *a.* and *s.* hugonote (-ta)

hulk, *s.* barco viejo, *m.*; pontón, *m.*

hulking, *a.* pesado, desgarbado

hull, *s.* (*naut.*) casco (de un buque), *m.*; (shell) cáscara, *f.*; (pod) vaina, *f.* *v.t.* mondar

hullabaloo, *s.* alboroto, tumulto, *m.*; vocerío, *m.*

hullo, *interj.* See **hallo**

hum, *s.* zumbido, *m.*; ruido confuso, *m.* *v.i.* (sing) canturrear; zumbar; (confused sound) zurrir; (hesitate) vacilar. *v.t.* (a tune) tararear

human, *a.* humano. **the h. touch,** el don de gentes. **h. being,** ser humano, hombre, *m.*

humane, *a.* humanitario, humano

humanely, *adv.* humanitariamente

humaneness, *s.* humanidad, *f.*

humanism, *s.* humanismo, *m.*

humanist, *s.* humanista, *m.* and *f.*

humanistic, *a.* humanista

humanitarian, *a.* humanitario

humanitarianism, *s.* humanitarismo, *m.*

humanity, *s.* humanidad, *f.*; raza humana, *f.* **the Humanities,** las Humanidades

humanize, *v.t.* humanizar; (milk) maternizar. *v.i.* humanizarse

humanly, *adv.* humanamente

humble, *a.* humilde; modesto; (cringing) servil; sumiso; pobre. *v.t.* humillar; mortificar. **to h. oneself,** humillarse

humbleness, *s.* humildad, *f.*; modestia, *f.*; (abjectness) servilismo, *m.*; sumisión, *f.*; pobreza, *f.*; (of birth, etc.) obscuridad, *f.*

humbling, *s.* humillación, *f.*; mortificación, *f.*

humbly, *adv.* humildemente; modestamente; servilmente

humbug, *s.* (fraud) embuste, engaño, *m.*; (nonsense) disparate, *m.*, tontería, *f.*; mentira, *f.*; (person) farsante, charlatán, *m.*; (sweetmeat) caramelo de menta, *m.* *v.t.* engañar, embaucar; burlarse de

humdrum, *a.* monótono; aburrido

humeral, *a.* humeral. *s.* (ecc.) velo humeral, *m.*

humerus, *s.* (anat.) húmero, *m.*

humid, *a.* húmedo

humidity, *s.* humedad, *f.*

humiliate, *v.t.* humillar, mortificar. **to h. oneself,** humillarse

humiliating, *a.* humillante; degradante

humiliation, *s.* humillación, mortificación, *f.*; degradación, *f.*

humility, *s.* humildad, *f.*; modestia, *f.*

humming, *s.* zumbido, *m.*; (of a tune) tarareo, *m.* *a.* zumbador. **h.-bird,** pájaro mosca, colibrí, *m.* **h.-top,** trompa, *f.*

hummock, *s.* montecillo, *m.*, mota, *f.*

humoresque, *s.* (mus.) capricho musical, *m.*

humorist, *s.* humorista, *m.* and *f.*

humorous, *a.* humorístico; cómico, risible

humorously, *adv.* humorísticamente; cómicamente

humorousness, *s.* humorismo, *m.*; lo cómico

humour, *s.* humor, *m.*; humorismo, *m.*; (temperament) disposición, *f.*, carácter, *m.*; (whim) capricho, *m.* *v.t.* seguir el humor (a), complacer; satisfacer, consentir en; (a lock, etc.) manejar. **in a good (bad) h.,** de buen (mal) humor. **I am not in the h. to . . .** No estoy de humor para . . . **sense of h.,** sentido de humor, *m.*

humoured, *a.* (in compounds) de humor . . . **good-h.,** de buen humor. **ill-h.,** malhumorado, de mal humor

humourless, *a.* sin sentido humorístico, sin sentido de humor

hump, *s.* joroba, giba, *f.*; (hillock) montecillo, *m.*; (fam.) depresión, *f.*

humpback, *s.* giba, joroba, *f.*; (person) jorobado (-da), giboso (-sa)

humpbacked, *a.* jorobado, giboso, corcovado

humph, *interj.* ¡qué va!; ¡patrañas!

humus, *s.* humus, mantillo, *m.*

Hun, *s.* huno (-na); (fam.) alemán (-ana)

hunchback, *s.* joroba, giba, *f.*; (person) jorobado (-da), corcovado (-da), giboso (-sa)

hunchbacked, *a.* jorobado, giboso, corcovado

hundred, *s.* ciento, *m.*; centenar, *m.*, centena, *f.* *a.* ciento; (before nouns and adjectives, excluding numerals, with the exception of mil and millón) cien. **a h. thousand,** cien mil. **one h. and one,** ciento uno. **by the h.,** a centenares. **hundreds of**

people, centenares de personas, *m. pl.* **h.-millionth,** *a.* and *s.* cienmillonésimo (*m.*). **h.-thousandth,** *a.* and *s.* cienmilésimo (*m.*)

hundredfold, *adv.* cien veces. *s.* céntuplo, *m.*

hundredth, *a.* centésimo, céntimo. *s.* centésimo, *m.*, centésima parte, *f.*

hundredweight, *s.* quintal, *m.*

Hungarian, *a.* and *s.* húngaro (-ra); (language) húngaro, *m.*

hunger, *s.* hambre, *f.*; apetito, *m.*; (craving) deseo, *m.*, ansia, *f.* *v.i.* estar hambriento, tener hambre. **to h. for,** desear, ansiar. **h.-strike,** huelga de hambre, *f.*

hungrily, *adv.* hambrientamente, con hambre; ansiosamente

hungry, *a.* hambriento; (of land) pobre; (anxious) deseoso. **to be h.,** tener hambre. **to make h.,** dar hambre

hunk, *s.* rebanada, *f.*, pedazo, *m.*

hunt, *s.* caza, cacería, montería, *f.*; grupo de cazadores, *m.*; (search) busca, *f.*; (pursuit) persecución, *f.* *v.t.* cazar; cazar a caballo; (search) buscar; rebuscar, explorar; (pursue) perseguir. **to h. down,** perseguir. **to h. for,** buscar. **to h. out,** buscar; descubrir, desenterrar

hunter, *s.* cazador, *m.*; caballo de caza, *m.*; (watch) saboneta, *f.*

hunting, *s.* caza, *f.*; caza a caballo, *f.*; persecución, *f.* *a.* cazador, de caza. **to go h.,** ir a cazar. **h.-box,** pabellón de caza, *m.* **h.-cap,** gorra de montar, *f.* **h.-crop,** látigo para cazar, *m.* **h.-ground,** terreno de caza, *m.* **h.-horn,** cuerno de caza, *m.*, corneta de monte, *f.* **h. party,** partido de caza, *m.*, cacería, *f.*

huntress, *s.* cazadora, *f.*

huntsman, *s.* cazador, montero, *m.*

huntsmanship, *s.* montería, arte de cazar, *f.*

hurdle, *s.* valla, *f.*; zarzo, *m.* **h.-race,** carrera de obstáculos, *f.*; carrera de vallas, *f.*

hurdy-gurdy, *s.* organillo, *m.*

hurl, *v.t.* lanzar, tirar, arrojar, echar. **to h. oneself,** lanzarse. **to h. oneself against,** arrojarse

a (or contra). **to h. oneself upon,** abalanzarse sobre

hurly-burly, *s.* alboroto, tumulto, *m.*

hurrah, *interj.* ¡hurra! ¡viva! *s.* vítor, *m.* **to shout h.,** vitorear

hurricane, *s.* huracán, *m.* **h.-lamp,** lámpara sorda, *f.*

hurried, *a.* apresurado, precipitado; hecho a prisa; superficial

hurriedly, *adv.* apresuradamente, precipitadamente, con prisa; superficialmente; (of writing) a vuela pluma

hurry, *s.* prisa, *f.*; precipitación, *f.*; urgencia, *f.*; confusión, *f.*; alboroto, *m.* **in a h.,** aprisa. **in a great h.,** aprisa y corriendo. **to be in a h.,** llevar prisa, estar de prisa. **There is no h.,** No corre prisa, No hay prisa

hurry, *v.t.* apresurar, dar prisa (a); llevar aprisa; hacer andar aprisa; enviar apresuradamente; precipitar; acelerar. *v.i.* darse prisa; apresurarse. **to h. after,** correr detrás de, seguir apresuradamente. **to h. away,** *v.i.* marcharse aprisa, marcharse corriendo; huir; salir precipitadamente. *v.t.* hacer marcharse aprisa; llevar con prisa. **to h. back,** *v.i.* volver aprisa, apresurarse a volver. *v.t.* hacer volver aprisa. **to h. in,** *v.i.* entrar aprisa, entrar corriendo. *v.t.* hacer entrar aprisa. **to h. off.** See **to h. away.** **to h. on,** *v.i.* apresurarse. *v.t.* apresurar, precipitar. **to h. out,** salir rápidamente. **to h. over,** hacer rápidamente; concluir aprisa; despachar rápidamente; (travel over) atravesar aprisa; pasar rápidamente por. **to h. towards,** llevar rápidamente hacia; arrastrar hacia; impeler hacia. **to h. up,** *v.i.* darse prisa. *v.t.* apresurar, precipitar; estimular

hurt, *s.* herida, *f.*; (harm) daño, mal, *m.*; perjuicio, *m.* *v.t.* (wound) herir; (cause pain) doler; hacer daño (a); hacer mal (a); (damage) perjudicar, estropear; (offend) ofender; (the feelings) mortificar, lastimar, herir. *v.i.* doler; hacer mal; perjudicarse, estropearse. **I haven't h. myself,** No me he

hecho daño. Does it still h. you? ¿Te duele todavía? **to h. deeply,** (*fig.*) herir en el alma. **to h. a person's feelings,** herirle (a uno) el amor propio, lastimar, ofender

hurtful, *a.* nocivo, dañino; injurioso, pernicioso

hurtfulness, *s.* nocividad, *f.*; perniciosidad, *f.*

hurtle, *v.t.* lanzar. *v.i.* lanzarse; volar; caer

husband, *s.* esposo, marido, *m.* *v.t.* economizar, ahorrar. **h. and wife,** los esposos, los cónyuges

husbandry, *s.* labor de los campos, agricultura, *f.*; (thrift) frugalidad, parsimonia, *f.*

hush, *s.* silencio, *m.*, tranquilidad, *f.* *interj.* ¡chitón! ¡calla! ¡silencio! *v.t.* silenciar, hacer callar, imponer silencio (a); (a baby) adormecer; (*fig.*) sosegar, calmar. *v.i.* callarse, enmudecer. **to h. up,** mantener secreto, ocultar. **h.-h.,** secreto. **h. money,** soborno, chantaje, *m.*

hushaby, *interj.* ¡duerme!

husk, *s.* (of grain) cascabillo, *m.*; zurrón, *m.*; cáscara, *f.*; (of chestnut) erizo, *m.*

huskily, *adv.* roncamente

huskiness, *s.* ronquera, *f.*; (*fam.*) robustez, *f.*

husky, *a.* (of voice) ronco; (*bot.*) cascarudo; (Eskimo) esquimal; (*fam.*) robusto, fuerte. *s.* perro esquimal, *m.*

hussar, *s.* húsar, *m.*

hussy, *s.* pícara, bribona, *f.*

hustle, *v.t.* empujar, codear; (*fig.*) precipitar; (*fam.*) acelerar. *v.i.* codearse; andarse de prisa

hut, *s.* choza, cabaña, barraca, *f.*

hutch, *s.* (chest) arca, *f.*, cofre, *m.*; (cage) jaula, *f.*; (for rabbits) conejera, *f.*; (for rats) ratonera, *f.*; (*fam.*) choza, *f.*

hutment, *s* campamento de chozas, *m.*

hyacinth, *s.* jacinto, *m.*

hybrid, *a.* híbrido; mestizo, mixto. *s.* híbrido, *m.*

hybridism, *s.* hibridismo, *m.*

hybridization, *s.* hibridación, *f.*

hybridize, *v.t.* cruzar. *v.i.* producir (or generar) híbridos

hydra, *s.* (*zool., ast.*) hidra, *f.*

hydrangea, *s.* (*bot.*) hortensia, *f.*

hydrant, *s.* boca de riego, *f.*

hydrate, *s.* (*chem.*) hidrato, *m.* *v.t.* hidratar

hydration, *s.* hidratación, *f.*

hydraulic, *a.* hidráulico. **h. engineering,** hidrotecnia, *f.*

hydraulics, *s.* hidráulica, *f.*

hydro, *s.* (hotel) balneario, *m.*

hydrocarbon, *s.* (*chem.*) hidrocarburo, *m.*

hydrocephalic, *a.* (*med.*) hidrocéfalo

hydrochloric, *a.* clorhídrico. **h. acid,** ácido clorhídrico, *m.*

hydrochloride, *s.* (*chem.*) clorhidrato, *m.*

hydrodynamic, *a.* hidrodinámico

hydrodynamics, *s.* hidrodinámica, *f.*

hydrogen, *s.* hidrógeno, *m.* **h. peroxide,** agua oxigenada, *f.*

hydrogenation, *s.* hidrogenación, *f.*

hydrogenize, *v.t.* hidrogenizar

hydrography, *s.* hidrografía, *f.*

hydrology, *s.* hidrología, *f.*

hydrolysis, *s.* hidrólisis, *f.*

hydromancy, *s.* hidromancia, *f.*

hydromel, *s.* aguamiel, *f.*, hidromel, *m.*

hydrometer, *s.* hidrómetro, *m.*

hydropathic, *a.* hidropático. **h. establishment,** balneario, *m.*

hydrophobia, *s.* hidrofobia, rabia, *f.*

hydrophobic, *a.* hidrofóbico, rabioso

hydroplane, *s.* hidroplano, *m.*

hydroquinone, *s.* (*chem.*) hidroquinona, *f.*

hydroscope, *s.* hidroscopio, *m.*

hydrostatics, *s. pl.* hidrostática, *f.*

hydrotherapic, *a.* hidroterápico

hydrotherapy, *s.* hidroterapia, *f.*

hyena, *s.* hiena, *f.*

hygiene, *s.* higiene, *f.* **personal h.,** higiene privada, *f.*

hygienic, *a.* higiénico

hygrometer, *s.* higrómetro, *m.*

hymen, *s.* (*anat.*) himen, *m.*; himeneo, *m.*

hymeneal, *a.* nupcial

hymn, *s.* himno, *m.* **h.-book,** himnario, *m.*

hyperbola, *s.* (*geom.*) hipérbola, *f.*

hyperbole, *s.* hipérbole, *f.*

hyperbolical, *a.* hiperbólico

hypercritic, s. hipercrítico, m.
hypercritical, a. hipercrítico, criticón
hypersensitive, a. vidrioso, quisquilloso
hypertrophy, s. hipertrofia, f. v.i. hipertrofiarse
hyphen, s. guión, m.
hypnosis, s. hipnosis, f.
hypnotic, a. hipnótico. s. (person) hipnótico (-ca); (drug) hipnótico, narcótico, m.
hypnotism, s. hipnotismo, m.
hypnotist, s. hipnotizador (-ra)
hypnotization, s. hipnotización, f.
hypnotize, v.t. hipnotizar
hypo, s. (sodium hyposulphite) hiposulfito sólido, m.
hypochondria, s. hipocondria, f.
hypochondriac, s. hipocondríaco (-ca)
hypochondriacal, a. hipocondríaco
hypocrisy, s. hipocresía, f.; mojigatería, gazmoñería, f.
hypocrite, s. hipócrita, m. and f.; mojigato (-ta). to be a h., ser hipócrita
hypocritical, a. hipócrita; mojigato, gazmoño
hypocritically, adv. hipócritamente, con hipocresía
hypodermic, a. hipodérmico. h. syringe, jeringa de inyecciones, f.
hypophosphate, s. hipofosfato, m.
hypostatic, a. hipostático
hypotenuse, s. (geom.) hipotenusa, f.
hypothesis, s. hipótesis, f.
hypothetical, a. hipotético
hyssop, s. (bot., ecc.) hisopo, m.
hysterectomy, s. (surg.) histerectomía, f.
hysteria, s. (med.) histerismo, m.; histeria, f., ataque de nervios, m.
hysterical, a. histérico. to become h., tener un ataque de nervios. hysterics, s. pl. ataque de nervios, m.

I

i, s. (letter) i, f. pers. pron yo. It is I, Soy yo. Normally omitted, the verb alone being used except when yo is needed for emphasis, e.g. Hablo a María, I speak to Mary, but Yo sé tocar el violín, pero Juan toca el piano, I can play the violin, but John plays the piano
iambic, a. yámbico. s. verso yámbico, m.
iambus, s. yambo, m.
Iberian, a. ibero, ibérico. s. íbero (-ra)
ibex, s. (zool.) íbice, m.
ibis, s. (orn.) íbis, f.
ice, s. hielo, m.; (ice cream) helado, m. v.t. helar; cubrir de hielo; congelar, cuajar; (a cake, etc.) garapiñar, escarchar, alcorzar. to ice up, (aer., aut.) helarse. to be as cold as ice, (fam.) estar hecho un hielo. His words cut no ice, Sus palabras ni pinchan ni cortan. ice-age, edad del hielo, f. ice-axe, piolet, m. ice-box, nevera, f. ice-cream, helado, mantecado, m. ice-cream cone, cucurucho de helado, m. ice-cream freezer, heladora, f. ice-cream vendor, mantequero (-ra). ice-field, campo de hielo, m. ice-floe, témpano de hielo flotante, m. ice hockey, hockey sobre patines, m. ice-pack, bolsa para hielo, f. ice-skates, patines de cuchilla, m. pl. ice water, agua helada, f.
iceberg, s. iceberg, témpano de hielo, banco de hielo, m.
icebound, a. aprisionado por el hielo; atascado en el hielo; (of roads, etc.) helado
iced, a. helado; congelado, cuajado; (cakes) garapiñado, escarchado; (of drinks) con hielo. i. drink, sorbete, m.
Icelander, s. islandés (-esa)
icelandic, a. islandés, islándico. s. (language) islandés, m.
iceman, s. nevero, m.
ichnographical, a. icnográfico
ichnography, s. icnografía, f.
ichthyol, s. (pharm.) ictiol, m.
ichthyologist, s. ictiólogo, m.
ichthyology, s. ictiología, f
ichthyophagous, a. ictiófago
ichthyosaurus, s. (zool.) ictiosauro, m.
ichthyosis, s. (med.) ictiosis, f.
icicle, s. carámbano, canelón, cerrión, m.

icily, *adv.* fríamente; (*fig.*) frígidamente, con indiferencia, con frialdad

iciness, *s.* frialdad, frigidez, *f.*; (*fig.*) indiferencia, frigidez, *f.*

icing, *s.* helada, *f.*, hielo, *m.*; (on a cake, etc.) alcorza, capa de azúcar, *f.*

icon, *s.* icono, *m.*

iconoclast, *s.* iconoclasta, *m.* and *f.*

iconoclastic, *a.* iconoclasta

iconography, *s.* iconografía, *f.*

iconology, *s.* iconología, *f.*

icosahedron, *s.* (*geom.*) icosaedro, *m.*

icy, *a.* helado; glacial, frío; (*med.*) álgido; (*fig.*) indiferente, desabrido; (*poet.*) frígido, gélido

idea, *s.* idea, *f.*, concepto, *m.*; (opinion) juicio, *m.*, opinión, *f.*; (notion) impresión, noción, *f.*; (plan) proyecto, plan, designio, *m.* **to form an i. of,** hacerse una idea de, formar un concepto de. **to have an i. of,** tener una idea de; tener nociones de. **An i. struck me,** Se me ocurrió una idea. **full of ideas,** preñado (o lleno) de ideas. **I had no i. that . . .** No tenía la menor idea de que . . . No sabía que . . . **What an i.!** ¡Qué idea!

ideal, *a.* ideal; excelente, perfecto; (utopian) utópico; (imaginary) imaginario, irreal, ficticio. *s.* ideal, *m.*; modelo, prototipo, *m.*

idealism, *s.* idealismo, *m.*

idealist, *s.* idealista, *m.* and *f.*

idealistic, *a.* idealista

idealization, *s.* idealización, *f.*

idealize, *v.t.* idealizar

ideally, *adv.* idealmente

ideation, *s.* (*phil.*) ideación, *f.*

idem, *adv.* ídem

identical, *a.* idéntico, mismo, igual; muy parecido, semejante

identically, *adv.* idénticamente

identifiable, *a.* identificable

identification, *s.* identificación, *f.* **i. number,** placa de identidad, *f.*

identify, *v.t.* identificar. **to i. oneself with,** identificarse con

identity, *s.* identidad, *f.* **i. card,** cédula personal, *f.*; carnet de identidad, *m.* **i. disc,** disco de identidad, *m.*

ideogram, ideograph, *s.* ideograma, *m.*

ideography, *s.* ideografía, *f.*

ideological, *a.* ideológico

ideologist, *s.* ideólogo (-ga)

ideology, *s.* ideología, *f.*

Ides, *s. pl.* idus, *m. pl.*

idiocy, *s.* idiotez, imbecilidad, *f.*; (foolishness) necedad, tontería, sandez, *f.*

idiom, *s.* idiotismo, *m.*; modismo, *m.*, locución, *f.*; (language) habla, *f.*; lenguaje, *m.*

idiomatic, *a.* idiomático

idiopathy, *s.* (*med.*) idiopatía, *f.*

idiosyncrasy, *s.* idiosincrasia, *f.*

idiosyncratic, *a.* idiosincrásico

idiot, *s.* idiota, imbécil, *m.* and *f.*; (fool) necio (-ia), tonto (-ta), mentecato (-ta)

idiotic, *a.* idiota, imbécil; (foolish) necio, tonto, sandío

idle, *a.* desocupado; indolente, ocioso; (unemployed) cesante, sin empleo; (lazy) perezoso, holgazán; (of machines) parado, inactivo; (useless) vano, inútil, sin efecto; (false) falso, mentiroso, infundado; (stupid) fútil, frívolo. *v.i.* holgar, estar ocioso; holgazanear, haraganear, gandulear. **to i. away,** malgastar, perder. **to i. away the time,** pasar el rato, matar el tiempo. **i. efforts,** vanos esfuerzos, *m. pl.* **i. fancies,** ilusiones, fantasías, *f. pl.*, sueños, *m. pl.* **i. hours,** horas desocupadas, *f. pl.* **i. question,** pregunta ociosa, *f.* **i. tale,** cuento de viejas, *m.*

idleness, *s.* ociosidad, indolencia, inacción, *f.*; pereza, holgazanería, gandulería, *f.*; (uselessness) inutilidad, futilidad, *f.*

idler, *s.* ocioso (-sa); haragán (-ana); perezoso (-sa), holgazán (-ana), gandul (-la)

idly, *adv.* ociosamente, perezosamente; (uselessly) vanamente

idol, *s.* ídolo, *m.* **a popular i.,** el ídolo de las masas, *m.*

idolater, *s.* idólatra, *m.* and *f.*; (admirer) amante, *m.* and *f.*, esclavo (-va), admirador (-ra)

idolatrous, *a.* idólatra, idolátrico

idolatrously, *adv.* idolatradamente, con idolatría

idolatry, *s.* idolatría, *f.*; (devotion) adoración, pasión, *f.*

ileac, *a.* (*anat.*) ilíaco

idolization, *s.* idolatría, *f.*

idolize, *v.t.* idolatrar, adorar

idyll, *s.* idilio, *m.*

idyllic, *a.* idílico

if, *conjunc.* si; (even if) aunque, aun cuando; (whenever) cuando, en caso de que; (whether) si. as if, como si (foll. by subjunc.). **If he comes, we shall tell him,** Si viene se lo diremos. **If he had not killed the tiger she would be dead,** Si él no hubiera matado al tigre ella estaría muerta. **If ever there was one,** Si alguna vez lo hubiera. **if necessary,** si fuese necesario. **if not,** si no. **If only!** ¡Ojalá que! (foll. by subjunc.)

igloo, *s.* choza de hielo, *f.*

igneous, *a.* ígneo

ignite, *v.t.* encender, pegar fuego (a), incendiar. *v.i.* prender fuego, incendiarse; arder

ignition, *s.* ignición, *f.*; (*aut.*) encendido, *m.* **i. coil,** (*aut.*) carrete de inducción del encendido, *m.* **i. key,** (*aut.*) llave del contacto, *f.*

ignoble, *a.* innoble, vil, indigno

ignobleness, *s.* bajeza, vileza, *f.*

ignobly, *adv.* bajamente, vilmente

ignominious, *a.* ignominioso

ignominiously, *adv.* ignominiosamente

ignominy, *s.* ignominia, deshonra, afrenta, *f.*

ignoramus, *s.* ignorante, *m.* and *f.*

ignorance, *s.* ignorancia, *f.*; (unawareness) desconocimiento, *m.* **to plead i.,** pretender ignorancia

ignorant, *a.* ignorante; inculto. **He is an i. fellow,** Él es un ignorante. **to be i. of,** no saber, ignorar. **to be very i.,** ser muy ignorante, (*fam.*) ser muy burro

ignorantly, *adv.* ignorantemente, por ignorancia; neciamente

ignore, *v.t.* no hacer caso de, desatender; (omit) pasar por alto de; (*law*) rechazar; (pretend not to recognize) hacer semblante de no reconocer; (not recognize) no reconocer

iguana, *s.* (*zool.*) iguana, *f.*

ileum, *s.* (*anat.*) íleon, *m.*

Iliad, *s.* Ilíada, *f.*

ilium, *s.* (*anat.*) ilion, *m.*

ill, *s.* mal, *m.* *a.* (sick) enfermo, malo; (bad) malo; (unfortunate) desdichado, funesto. *adv.* mal. **to be ill,** estar malo. **to be taken ill,** caer enfermo. **ill-advised,** mal aconsejado; desacertado, imprudente. **ill-advisedly,** imprudentemente. **ill at ease,** incómodo. **ill-bred,** mal criado, mal educado, mal nacido. **ill-breeding,** mala crianza, mala educación, *f.* **ill-disposed,** malintencionado. **ill fame,** mala fama, *f.* **ill-fated,** malhadado, malaventurado, aciago, fatal. **ill-favoured,** mal parecido, feúcho. **ill-feeling,** hostilidad, *f.*, rencor, *m.* **ill-gotten,** mal adquirido. **ill-humour,** mal humor, *m.* **ill-humoured,** de mal humor, malhumorado. **ill-luck,** desdicha, mala suerte, malaventura, *f.*; infortunio, *m.* **ill-mannered,** mal educado. **ill-natured,** malévolo, perverso. **ill-naturedly,** malignamente. **ill-omened,** nefasto. **ill-spent,** malgastado, perdido. **ill-spoken,** mal hablado. **ill-suited,** malavenido. **ill-timed,** inoportuno, intempestivo. **ill-treat,** maltratar, malparar, tratar mal. **ill-treated,** que ha sido tratado mal; maltrecho. **ill-treatment,** maltratamiento, *m.*, crueldad, *f.* **ill-turn,** mala jugada, *f.* **to do an ill-turn,** hacer un flaco servicio. **ill will,** mala voluntad, *f.*; rencor, *m.*, ojeriza, *f.* **to bear a person ill will,** guardarle rencor

illegal, *a.* ilegal; indebido, ilícito

illegality, *s.* ilegalidad, *f.*

illegally, *adv.* ilegalmente

illegibility, *s.* ilegibilidad, *f.*

illegible, *a.* ilegible, indescifrable

illegibly, *adv.* de un modo ilegible

illegitimacy, *s.* ilegitimidad, *f.*; falsedad, *f.*

illegitimate, *a.* ilegítimo, bastardo; falso; ilícito, desautorizado

illegitimately, *adv.* ilegítimamente

illiberal, *a.* iliberal; intolerante, estrecho de miras; (mean) avaro, tacaño, ruin

illiberality, *s.* iliberalidad, *f.*; intolerancia, *f.*; (avarice) tacañería, avaricia, ruindad, *f.*

illiberally, *adv.* avariciosamente, ruinmente

illicit, *a.* ilícito, indebido, ilegal

illicitly, *adv.* ilícitamente, ilegalmente

illicitness, *s.* ilicitud, ilegalidad, *f.*

illimitable, *a.* ilimitado, sin límites, infinito

illiteracy, *s.* analfabetismo, *m.*

illiterate, *a.* and *s.* analfabeto (-ta), iliterato (-ta)

illness, *s.* enfermedad, dolencia, *f.*, mal, *m.*

illogical, *a.* ilógico; absurdo, irracional

illogicality, *s.* falta de lógica, *f.*; absurdo, *m.*, irracionalidad, *f.*

illuminant, *a.* iluminador, alumbrador

illuminate, *v.t.* iluminar, alumbrar; (art) iluminar; (explain) aclarar, ilustrar

illuminated, *a.* iluminado, encendido; (art) iluminado. **i. sign**, letrero luminoso, *m.*

illuminati, *s. pl.* secta de los alumbrados, *f.*

illuminating, *a.* iluminador; (explanatory) aclaratorio. *s.* (art) iluminación, *f.*

illumination, *s.* iluminación, *f.*, alumbrado, *m.*; (for decoration) luminaria, *f.*; (art) iluminación, *f.*; (fig.) inspiración, *f.*

illuminator, *s.* (art) iluminador (-ra)

illumine, *v.t.* encender, alumbrar; .(fig.) inspirar

illusion, *s.* ilusión, *f.*, engaño, *m.*; (dream) esperanza, ilusión, *f.*, ensueño, *m.* **to harbour illusions**, tener ilusiones

illusive, *a.* ilusivo, engañoso, falso

illusively, *adv.* falsamente, aparentemente

illusoriness, *s.* ilusión, falsedad, *f.*, engaño, *m.*

illusory, *a.* ilusorio, deceptivo, falso, irreal

illustrate, *v.t.* ilustrar, aclarar, explicar, elucidar; (art) ilustrar; (prove) probar, demostrar

illustration, *s.* ejemplo, *m.*; ilustración, *f.*; (art) grabado, *m.*; estampa, *f.*; (explanation) elucidación, aclaración, *f.*

illustrative, *a.* ilustrativo, ilustrador, explicativo, aclaratorio

illustrator, *s.* ilustrador (-ra), grabador (-ra)

illustrious, *a.* ilustre, famoso, renombrado, distinguido

illustriously, *adv.* ilustremente, noblemente

illustriousness, *s.* eminencia, *f.*, renombre, *m.*, grandeza, *f.*

Illyrian, *a.* and *s.* ilirio (-ia)

image, *s.* (optics) imagen, *f.*; efigie, imagen, *f.*; (religious) imagen, estatua, *f.*; (art) figura, *f.*; (metaphor) metáfora, expresión, *f.*; (of a person) retrato, *m.* **to be the i. of**, ser el retrato de. **sharp i.**, imagen nítida, *f.* **i. breaker**, iconoclasta, *m.* and *f.* **i. vendor**, vendedor (-ra) de imágenes

imagery, *s.* (art) imaginería, *f.*; (style) metáforas, *f. pl.*

imaginable, *a.* imaginable

imaginary, *a.* imaginario; fantástico, de ensueño

imagination, *s.* imaginación, *f.*; imaginativa, fantasía, inventiva, *f.*, ingenio, *m.*

imaginative, *a.* imaginativo; fantástico

imagine, *v.t.* imaginar, concebir; idear, proyectar, inventar; figurarse, suponer. **Just i.!** ¡Imagínese usted!

imaum, *s.* imán, *m.*

imbecile, *a.* imbécil; (foolish) necio, estúpido, tonto. *s.* imbécil, *m.* and *f.*; (fool) necio (-ia), tonto (-ta), estúpido (-da)

imbecility, *s.* imbecilidad, *f.*; (folly) necedad, sandez, *f.*

imbibe, *v.t.* embeber, absorber; (drink) sorber, chupar; empaparse de

imbibing, *s.* imbibición, absorción, *f.*

imbrex tile, cobija, *f.*

imbricate, *a.* (zool., bot.) imbricado

imbroglio, *s.* embrollo, lío, *m.*

imbue, *v.t.* imbuir, calar, empapar; teñir. **to i. with**, infundir de

imitable, *a.* imitable

imitate, *v.t.* imitar; copiar, reproducir; *(counterfeit)* contrahacer

imitation, *s.* imitación, *f.*; copia, *f.*; remedo, traslado, *m. a.* imitado; falso, artificial

imitative, *a.* imitativo; imitador

imitativeness, *s.* facultad imitativa (or de imitacion), *f.*

imitator, *s.* imitador (-ra); contrahacedor (-ra), falsificador (-ra)

immaculate, *a.* inmaculado, puro; *(of dress)* elegante. **I. Conception,** La Purísima Concepción

immaculately, *adv.* inmaculadamente; elegantemente

immaculateness, *s.* pureza, *f.*; *(of dress)* elegancia, *f.*

immanence, *s.* inmanencia, inherencia, *f.*

immanent, *a.* inmanente; inherente

immaterial, *a.* inmaterial, incorpóreo; sin importancia. **It is i. to me,** Me es indiferente, No me importa

immateriality, *s.* inmaterialidad, *f.*

immature, *a.* inmaturo; precoz; *(of fruit)* verde

immaturity, *s.* falta de madurez, *f.*; precocidad, *f.*

immeasurability, *s.* inmensurabilidad, inmensidad, *f.*

immeasurable, *a.* inmensurable, inmenso, imponderable

immeasurably, *adv.* inmensamente, enormemente

immediate, *a.* *(of place)* inmediato, cercano, contiguo; *(of time)* próximo, inmediato, directo; *(of action)* inmediato, perentorio; *(on letters)* urgente. **to take i. action,** tomar acción inmediata

immediately, *adv.* *(of place)* próximamente, contiguamente; *(of time)* luego, seguidamente, en el acto, ahora mismo, enseguida; directamente; *(as soon as)* así que

immemorial, *a.* inmemorial, inmemorable

immemorially, *adv.* desde tiempo inmemorial

immense, *a.* inmenso, enorme; vasto, extenso; infinito

immensely, *adv.* inmensamente, enormemente

immensity, *s.* inmensidad, *f.*; extensión, vastedad, *f.*

immerse, *v.t.* sumergir, hundir en, zambullir; bautizar por sumersión. *(fig.)* **to be immersed in,** estar absorto en

immersion, *s.* sumersion, *f.*, hundimiento, *m.*; *(ast.)* inmersión, *f.*

immigrant, *a.* and *s.* inmigrante *(m.* and *f.)*

immigrate, *v.i.* inmigrar

immigration, *s.* inmigración, *f.*

imminence, *s.* inminencia, *f.*

imminent, *a.* inminente

immobile, *a.* inmóvil, inmoble; impasible, imperturbable

immobility, *s.* inmovilidad, *f.*; impasibilidad, imperturbabilidad, *f.*

immobilization, *s.* inmovilización, *f.*

immobilize, *v.t.* inmovilizar

immoderate, *a.* inmoderado, excesivo, indebido

immoderately, *adv.* inmoderadamente, excesivamente

immoderateness, *s.* inmoderación, *f.*, exceso, *m.*

immodest, *a.* inmodesto; indecente, deshonesto; *(pert)* atrevido, descarado

immodestly, *adv.* impúdicamente, inmodestamente

immodesty, *s.* inmodestia, impudicia, *f.*; deshonestidad, licencia, *f.*; *(forwardness)* descaro, atrevimiento, *m.*

immolate, *v.t.* inmolar, sacrificar

immolation, *s.* inmolación, *f.*, sacrificio, *m.*

immolator, *s.* inmolador (-ra)

immoral, *a.* inmoral; licencioso, vicioso; incontinente

immorality, *s.* inmoralidad, *f.*

immortal, *a.* inmortal; perenne, eterno, imperecedero. *s.* inmortal, *m.* and *f.*

immortality, *s.* inmortalidad, *f.*; fama inmortal, *f.*

immortalize, *v.t.* inmortalizar, perpetuar

immortally, *adv.* inmortalmente, eternamente, para siempre

immortelle, *s.* *(bot.)* siempreviva, perpetua, *f.*

immovability, *s.* inamovibilidad, inmovilidad, *f.*; (of purpose) inflexibilidad, tenacidad, constancia, *f.*

immovable, *a.* inmoble, fijo, inmóvil; (of purpose) inconmovible, inalterable, constante. *s. pl.* **immovables** (*law*) bienes inmuebles, *m. pl.* (*ecc.*) **i. feast,** fiesta fija, *f.*

immovably, *adv.* inmóvilmente, fijamente

immune, *a.* inmune, libre; (*med.*) inmune. **i. from,** exento de; libre de

immunity, *s.* inmunidad, libertad, *f.*; exención, *f.*; (*med.*) inmunidad, *f.*

immunization, *s.* (*med.*) inmunización, *f.*

immunize, *v.t.* inmunizar

immure, *v.t.* emparedar, recluir, encerrar

immutability, *s.* inmutabilidad, inalterabilidad, *f*

immutable, *a.* inmutable, inalterable, constante

immutably, *adv.* inmutablemente

imp, *s.* trasgo, diablillo, duende, *m.*; (child) picaruelo (-la)

impact, *s.* impacto, *m.*, impacción, *f.*; choque, *m.*, colisión, *f.*

impair, *v.t.* perjudicar, echar a perder, deteriorar, empeorar, desmejorar. **to be impaired,** deteriorarse, perjudicarse

impairment, *s.* deterioración, *f.*, perjuicio, empeoramiento, *m.*

impale, *v.t.* (punishment) empalar; (with a sword) atravesar, espetar

impalement, *s.* (punishment) empalamiento, *m.*; atravesamiento, *m.*, transfixión, *f.*

impalpability, *s.* impalpabilidad, intangibilidad, *f.*

impalpable, *a.* impalpable, intangible; incorpóreo

imparisyllabic, *a.* imparisilábico

impart, *v.t.* comunicar, dar parte (de); conferir

impartial, *a.* imparcial, ecuánime

impartiality, *s.* imparcialidad, ecuanimidad, entereza, *f.*, desinterés, *m.*

impartially, *adv.* imparcialmente, con desinterés

impassability, *s.* impracticabilidad, *f.*

impassable, *a.* intransitable, impracticable; (of water) invadeable

impasse, *s.* (also *fig.*) callejón sin salida, *m.*

impassibility, *s.* impasibilidad, imperturbabilidad, indiferencia, *f.*

impassible, *a.* impasible, insensible; indiferente, imperturbable

impassion, *v.t.* apasionar, conmover

impassioned, *a.* apasionado, vehemente, ardiente

impassive, *a.* impassible, insensible; indiferente, imperturbable; apático

impassively, *adv.* indiferentemente

impassivity, *s.* impasibilidad, *f.*; indiferencia, *f.*; apatía, *f.*

impatience, *s.* impaciencia, *f.*

impatient, *a.* impaciente; intolerante. **to make i.,** impacientar. **to grow i.,** impacientarse, perder la paciencia. **to grow i. at,** impacientarse ante. **to grow i. to,** impacientarse a or por. **to grow i. under,** impacientarse bajo

impatiently, *adv.* con impaciencia, impacientemente

impeach, *v.t.* (*law*) denunciar, delatar, acusar; censurar, criticar, tachar

impeachable, *a.* (*law*) delatable, denunciable, acusable; censurable

impeacher, *s.* acusador (-ra), denunciador (-ra), delator (-ra)

impeachment, *s.* (*law*) acusación, denuncia, *f.*; reproche, *m.*, queja, *f.*

impeccability, *s.* (perfection) impecabilidad, perfección, *f.*; elegancia, *f.*

impeccable, *a.* impecable, intachable, perfecto; elegante

impeccably, *adv.* perfectamente; elegantemente

impecuniosity, *s.* indigencia, pobreza, *f.*

impecunious, *a.* indigente, pobre

impede, *v.t.* impedir, obstruir, estorbar; (*fig.*) dificultar, embarazar

impediment, *s.* obstáculo, estorbo, *m.*; (*fig.*) dificultad, *f.*;

(*law*) impedimento, *m.* **to have
an i. in one's speech,** tener una
dificultad en el hablar

impel, *v.t.* impulsar, impeler;
(*fig.*) estimular, obligar, mover,
constreñir. **I felt impelled (to),**
Me sentí obligado (a)

impellent, *a.* impulsor

impend, *v.i.* ser inminente,
amenazar

impending, *a.* inminente, pendiente

impenetrability, *s.* impenetrabilidad, *f.*; (*fig.*) enigma, secreto,
misterio, *m.*

impenetrable, *a.* impenetrable;
intransitable; denso, espeso;
(*fig.*) enigmático, insondable,
secreto

impenetrably, *adv.* impenetrable-
mente, densamente

impenitence, *s.* impenitencia, *f.*

impenitent, *a.* impenitente, incorregible

impenitently, *adv.* sin penitencia

imperative, *a.* imperioso, perentorio; (*gram.*) imperativo; (*necessary*) esencial, urgente. *s.* mandato, *m.*, orden, *f.*; (*gram.*)
imperativo, *m.* **in the i.,** en el
imperativo

imperatively, *adv.* imperativa-
mente

imperativeness, *s.* perentoriedad, *f.*; urgencia, importancia,
f.

imperatorial, *a.* imperatorio

imperceptible, *a.* imperceptible,
insensible

imperceptibly, *adv.* imperceptiblemente

imperceptive, *a.* insensible

imperfect, *a.* imperfecto; incompleto, defectuoso. *a. and s.*
(*gram.*) imperfecto (*m.*)

imperfection, *s.* imperfección,
f.; defecto, desperfecto, *m.*;
falta, tacha, *f.*

imperfectly, *adv.* imperfectamente

imperial, *a.* imperial, imperatorio. *s.* (beard) pera, *f.* **i.
preference,** preferencia dentro
del Imperio, *f.*

imperialism, *s.* imperialismo, *m.*

imperialist, *s.* imperialista, *m.*
and *f.*

imperialistic, *a.* imperialista

imperially, *adv.* imperialmente

imperil, *v.t.* arriesgar, poner en
peligro, aventurar

imperious, *a.* imperioso, altivo,
arrogante; (*pressing*) urgente,
apremiante

imperiously, *adv.* imperiosa-
mente, con arrogancia

imperiousness, *s.* autoridad,
arrogancia, altivez, *f.*; necesidad,
urgencia, *f.*, apremio, *m.*

imperishability, *s.* (immortality)
inmortalidad, perennidad, *f.*

imperishable, *a.* imperecedero,
inmarchitable, perenne, eterno

impermanence, *s.* inestabilidad,
interinidad, *f.*; brevedad, fugacidad, *f.*

impermanent, *a.* interino, no
permanente

impermeability, *s.* impermeabilidad, *f.*

impermeable, *a.* impermeable

impersonal, *a.* impersonal, objetivo; (*gram.*) impersonal

impersonality, *s.* objetividad, *f.*

impersonally, *adv.* impersonal-
mente

impersonate, *v.t.* personificar,
simbolizar; (*theat.*) representar

impersonation, *s.* personificación, simbolización, *f.*; (*theat.*)
representación, *f.*

impertinence, *s.* impertinencia,
majadería, insolencia, *f.*; inoportunidad, *f.*; despropósito, *m.*

impertinent, *a.* impertinente,
insolente; (*unseasonable*) intempestivo, inoportuno; (*irrelevant*)
fuera de proposito

impertinently, *adv.* con insolencia, impertinentemente

imperturbability, *s.* imperturbabilidad, serenidad, impasibilidad, *f.*; impavidez, *f.*

imperturbable, *a.* imperturbable, impasible, sereno; impávido

imperturbably, *adv.* con serenidad, imperturbablemente

impervious, *a.* impermeable, impenetrable; (*fig.*) insensible. **He
is i. to arguments,** Él no hace
caso de argumentos

imperviousness, *s.* impermeabilidad, impenetrabilidad, *f.*;
(*fig.*) insensibilidad, *f.*

impetigo, *s.* (*med.*) impétigo, *m.*

impetuosity, *s.* impetuosidad,
temeridad, irreflexión, *f.*

impetuous, *a.* impetuoso, temerario, irreflexivo; violento, vehemente

impetuously, *adv.* impetuosamente; con vehemencia

impetus, *s.* (*mech.*) ímpetu, *m.*, impulsión, *f.*; (*fig.*) incentivo, estímulo, impulso, *m.*

impiety, *s.* impiedad, irreligión, irreligiosidad, *f.*

impinge (upon), *v.i.* chocar con, tropezar con

impious, *a.* impío, irreligioso, sacrílego; (wicked) malvado, perverso, malo

impiously, *adv.* impíamente

impish, *a.* travieso, revoltoso, enredador

implacability, *s.* implacabilidad, *f.*

implacable, *a.* implacable, inexorable, inflexible, riguroso

implacably, *adv.* implacablemente

implant, *v.t.* (*fig.*) implantar, inculcar, instilar

implantation, *s.* (*fig.*) implantación, instilación, inculcación, *f.*

implement, *s.* instrumento, utensilio, *m.*, herramienta, *f.*; (of war) elemento, *m.* *v.t.* cumplir, hacer efectivo; llevar a cabo

implicate, *v.t.* enredar, envolver; (imply) implicar, contener, llevar en sí; (in a crime) comprometer. **to be implicated in a crime,** estar implicado en un crimen.

implication, *s.* implicación, inferencia, sugestión, *f.*; (in a crime) complicidad, *f.*

implicit, *a.* implícito, virtual, tácito; (absolute) ciego, absoluto, implícito. **with i. faith,** con fe ciega

implicitly, *adv.* implícitamente

implicitness, *s.* carácter implícito, *m.*, lo implícito

implied, *a.* tácito, implícito

implore, *v.t.* implorar, suplicar

imploring, *a.* suplicante, implorante

imploringly, *adv.* con encarecimiento, a súplica, de un modo suplicante

imply, *v.t.* implicar, indicar, presuponer; (mean) querer decir, significar; (hint) insinuar, sugerir

impolicy, *s.* indiscreción, imprudencia, impolítica, *f.*

impolite, *a.* descortés, mal educado

impolitely, *adv.* con descortesía

impoliteness, *s.* descortesía, falta de urbanidad, *f.*

impolitic, *a.* impolítico

imponderability, *s.* imponderabilidad, *f.*

imponderable, *a.* imponderable

import, *v.t.* (*com.*) importar; (mean) significar, querer decir. *a.* (*com.*) importado, de importación. *s.* (*com.*) importación, *f.*; (meaning) significado, sentido, *m.*; (value) importe, valor, *m.*; (contents) contenido, tenor, *m.*; importancia, *f.* **i. duty,** derechos de importación (or de entrada), *m. pl.* **i. licence,** permiso de importación, *m.* **i. trade,** negocios de importación, *m. pl.*

importable, *a.* importable, que se puede importar

importance, *s.* importancia, *f.*; valor, alcance, *m.*, magnitud, *f.*; consideración, eminencia, *f.* **to be fully conscious of one's i.,** tener plena conciencia de su importancia

important, *a.* importante; distinguido; presuntuoso, vanidoso. **to be i.,** importar, ser importante. **i. person,** personaje, *m.*, persona importante, *f.*

importantly, *adv.* importantemente, con importancia

importation, *s.* importación, *f.*; (*com.*) introducción (or importación) de géneros extranjeros, *f.*

importer, *s.* importador (-ra)

importunate, *a.* (of a demand) insistente, importuno; (of persons) impertinente, pesado

importunately, *adv.* importunadamente

importune, *v.t.* importunar, asediar, perseguir

importuning, *s.* persecución, importunación, *f.*

importunity, *s.* importunidad, insistencia, impertinencia, *f.*

impose, *v.t.* (on, upon) imponer, infligir, cargar; (*print.*) imponer. *v.i.* (on, upon) (deceive) engañar, embaucar

imposing, *a.* imponente, impresionante; (of persons) majestuoso, importante

imposition, s. imposición, f.;
(burden) impuesto, tributo, m.,
carga, f.; (print., etc.) imposición,
f.; (trick) fraude, engaño, m.,
decepción, f.

impossibility, s. imposibilidad, f.

impossible, a. imposible. Nothing is i., No. hay nada imposible. (fam.) De menos nos
hizo Dios. to do the i., hacer lo
imposible

impossibly, adv. imposiblemente

impost, s. impuesto, m., contribución, gabela, f.

impostor, s. impostor (-ra),
bribón (-ona), embustero (-ra)

imposture, s. impostura, f.,
engaño, fraude, m.

impotence, s. impotencia, f.

impotent, a. impotente

impotently, adv. impotentemente

impound, v.t. acorralar; (water)
embalsar; (goods) confiscar

impoverish, v.t. empobrecer,
depauperar, arruinar; (health)
debilitar; (land) agotar

impoverished, a. indigente, necesitado; (of land) agotado

impoverishment, s. empobrecimiento, m., ruina, f.; (of land)
agotamiento, m.

impracticability, s. impracticabilidad, imposibilidad, f.

impracticable, a. impracticable,
no factible, imposible

imprecation, s. imprecación,
maldición, f.

imprecatory, a. imprecatorio,
maldiciente

impregnable, a. inexpugnable,
inconquistable

impregnate, v.t. impregnar,
empapar; (biol.) fecundar. to
become impregnated, impreg-
narse

impregnation, s. impregnación,
f.; (biol.) fecundación, fertilización, f.; (fig.) inculcación, f.

impresario, s. empresario, m.

imprescriptible, a. imprescriptible, inalienable

impress, v.t. imprimir; (on the
mind) impresionar; inculcar, imbuir; (with respect) imponer;
(mil.) reclutar; (of goods) confiscar. s. impresión, marca,
señal, huella, f.

impression, s. impresión, f.;
marca, señal, huella, f.; (print.)

impresión, f.; efecto, m.; idea,
noción, f. He has the i. that
they do not like him, Sospecha
que no les es simpático. to be
under the i., tener la impresión

impressionability, s. susceptibilidad, sensibilidad, f.

impressionable, a. susceptible,
impresionable, sensitivo

impressionism, s. impresionismo, m.

impressionist, s. impresionista,
m. and f.

impressionistic, a. impresionista

impressive, a. impresionante;
emocionante; imponente, majestuoso; enfático

impressively, adv. solemnemente, de modo impresionante;
enfáticamente

impressiveness, s. efecto impresionante, m.; grandiosidad,
pompa, f.; majestuosidad, f.;
fuerza, f.

imprint, s. impresión, señal,
marca, huella, f.; (print.) pie de
imprenta, m. v.t. imprimir; (on
the mind) grabar, fijar

imprison, v.t. encerrar, encarcelar, aprisionar

imprisonment, s. encarcelación,
prisión, f., encierro, m.

improbability, s. improbabilidad, f.; inverosimilitud, f.

improbable, a. improbable; inverosímil

improbity, s. improbidad, f.

impromptu, a. indeliberado,
impremeditado, espontáneo.
adv. de improviso, in promptu.
s. improvisación, f.

improper, a. impropio, inadecuado; incorrecto; indebido; indecente, índecoroso. i. fraction,
(math.) quebrado impropio, m.

improperly, adv. impropiamente,
incorrectamente; indecorosa-
mente

impropriety, s. inconveniencia,
f.; incorrección, f.; (style) impropiedad, f.; falta de decoro, f.

improvable, a. mejorable, perfectible

improve, v.t. mejorar; perfeccionar; (beautify) embellecer,
hermosear; (land) bonificar; (lit.)
corregir, enmendar; (cultivate)
cultivar; (increase) aumentar;

(an opportunity) aprovechar; (strengthen) fortificar; (business) sacar provecho de, explotar. *v.i.* mejorar; perfeccionarse; (progress) hacer progresos, progresar, adelantarse; (*com.*) subir; (become beautiful) hacerse hermoso, embellecerse; (increase) aumentarse. **to i. upon,** mejorar, perfeccionar; pulir

improvement, *s.* mejora, *f.*; perfeccionamiento, *m.*; aumento, *m.*; adelantamiento, progreso, *m.*; (in health) mejoría, *f.*; embellecimiento, *m.*; cultivación, *f.*; (of land) abono, *m.*

improver, *s.* aprendiz (-za)

improvidence, *s.* imprevisión, *f.*; improvidencia, *f.*

improvident, *a.* impróvido, desprevenido

improvidently, *adv.* impróvidamente

improvisation, *s.* improvisación, *f.*

improvise, *v.t.* improvisar

improviser, *s.* improvisador (-ra)

imprudence, *s.* imprudencia, *f.*; desacierto, *m.*, indiscreción, *f.*

imprudent, *a.* imprudente; desacertado, indiscreto, mal avisado, irreflexivo

imprudently, *adv.* imprudentemente; sin pensar

impudence, *s.* impudencia, *f.*, descaro, *m.*, insolencia, desvergüenza, *f.*, atrevimiento, *m.*

impudent, *a.* impudente, descarado, insolente, desvergonzado, atrevido

impudently, *adv.* descaradamente, con insolencia

impugn, *v.t.* impugnar, contradecir, atacar

impugnable, *a.* impugnable, atacable

impugnment, *s.* impugnación, *f.*

impulse, *s.* ímpetu, *m.*, impulsión, *f.*; impulso, estímulo, *m.*; incitación, instigación, *f.*; motivo, *m.*; (fit) arranque, arrebato, acceso, *m.*

impulsion, *s.* ímpetu, *m.*, impulsión, *f.*; empuje, *m.*, arranque, *m.*

impulsive, *a.* impelente; irreflexivo, impulsivo

impulsively, *adv.* por impulso

impulsiveness, *s.* irreflexión, *f.*; carácter impulsivo, *m.*

impunity, *s.* impunidad, *f.* **with i.,** impunemente

impure, *a.* impuro; adulterado, mezclado; (indecent) deshonesto, indecente; (dirty) turbio, sucio

impurely, *adv.* impuramente

impurity, *s.* impureza, *f.*; adulteración, mezcla, *f.*; deshonestidad, liviandad, *f.*; suciedad, turbiedad, *f.*

imputable, *a.* imputable, atribuible

imputation, *s.* imputación, atribución, *f.*; (in a bad sense) acusación, *f.*, reproche, *m.*

impute, *v.t.* imputar, achacar, atribuir; acusar, reprochar

imputer, *s.* imputador (-ra); recriminador (-ra), acusador (-ra)

in, *prep.* en; a; (of duration) durante, mientras; (with) con; (through) por; dentro de; (under) bajo; (following a superlative) de; (of specified time) dentro de, de aquí a; (with afternoon, etc.) por; (out of) sobre. **dressed in black,** vestido de negro. **in London,** en Londres. **in the morning,** por la mañana; (in the course of) durante la mañana. **in time,** a tiempo; dentro de algún tiempo. **in a week,** dentro de una semana. **in the best way,** del mejor modo. **in writing,** por escrito. **in anger,** con enojo. **in the hand,** en la mano. **in addition to,** además de, a más de. **in case,** por si acaso, en caso de que. **in order to,** a fin de, **para** (foll. by infin.). **in order that,** para que (foll. by subjunc.). **in so far as,** en cuanto. **in spite of,** a pesar de. **in the distance,** a lo lejos, en lontananza. **in the meantime,** entre tanto. **in the middle of,** en el medio de; a la mitad de. **in the style of,** al modo de; a la manera de, a la (francesa, etc.)

in, *adv.* adentro, dentro; (at home) en casa; (of sun) escondido; (of fire) alumbrado; (in power) en el poder; (of harvest) cosechado; (of boats) entrado (with haber); (of trains) llegado (with haber). **to be in,** estar dentro; haber llegado; estar en casa. **to be in for,** estar expuesto a, correr el riesgo de. **to be in with a person,** ser muy amigo de, estar muy metido con. **Come in!** ¡Adelante!; ¡Pase usted! **ins and outs,** sinuosidades, *f. pl.*; (of river) meandros, *m. pl.*; (of an affair) pormenores, detalles, *m. pl.*

in, *a.* interno. **in-law** (of relations) político. **in-patient,** enfermo (-ma) de hospital

inability, *s.* incapacidad, inhabilidad, ineptitud, incompetencia, *f.*; impotencia, *f.*

inaccessibility, *s.* inaccesibilidad, *f.*

inaccessible, *a.* inaccesible

inaccuracy, *s.* inexactitud, incorrección, *f.*

inaccurate, *a.* inexacto, incorrecto

inaccurately, *adv.* inexactamente, erróneamente

inaction, *s.* inacción, *f.*

inactive, *a.* inactivo, pasivo; (of things) inerte; (lazy) perezoso, indolente; (machinery) parado; (motionless) inmóvil; (at leisure) desocupado, sin empleo

inactivity, *s.* inactividad, pasividad, *f.*; (of things) inercia, *f.*; pereza, indolencia, *f.*; (of machinery) paro, *m.*; inmovilidad, *f.*; (leisure) desocupación, *f.*

inadaptable, *a.* inadaptable, no adaptable

inadequacy, *s.* insuficiencia, escasez, *f.*; imperfección, *f.*, defecto, *m.*

inadequate, *a.* inadecuado, insuficiente, escaso; imperfecto, defectuoso

inadequately, *adv.* inadecuadamente

inadmissible, *a.* inadmisible, no admisible

inadvertence, *s.* inadvertencia, *f.*; equivocación, *f.*, descuido, *m.*

inadvertent, *a.* inadvertido, accidental, casual; negligente

inadvertently, *adv.* inadvertidamente, sin querer

inalienability, *s.* inalienabilidad, *f.*

inalienable, *a.* inajenable, inalienable

inalterability, *s.* inalterabilidad, *f.*

inalterable, *a.* inalterable

inalterably, *adv.* inalterablemente, sin alteración

inamorata, *s.* dulce amiga, amada, querida, *f.*

inane, *a.* lelo, fatuo, vacío, necio

inanimate, *a.* (of matter) inanimado; sin vida, exánime, muerto

inanition, *s.* inanición, *f.*

inanity, *s.* vacuidad, fatuidad, necedad, *f.*

inappeasable, *a.* implacable, riguroso

inapplicability, *s.* no aplicabilidad, *f.*

inapplicable, *a.* inaplicable

inapposite, *a.* fuera de propósito, no pertinente, inoportuno

inappreciable, *a.* inapreciable, imperceptible

inappreciation, *s.* falta de apreciación, *f.*

inappreciative, *a.* desagradecido, ingrato. **i. of,** insensible a, indiferente a

inapproachable, *a.* inaccesible, huraño, adusto

inappropriate, *a.* impropio, inconveniente, inadecuado, incongruente; inoportuno

inappropriately, *adv.* impropiamente; inoportunamente

inappropriateness, *s.* impropiedad, inconveniencia, incongruencia, *f.*; inoportunidad, *f.*

inapt, *a.* inepto, inhábil; impropio

inaptitude, *s.* ineptitud, inhabilidad, *f.*; impropiedad, *f.*

inarticulate, *a.* (of speech) inarticulado; (reticent) inexpresivo, reservado; indistinto; (*anat.*) inarticulado

inarticulately, *adv.* indistintamente, de un modo inarticulado

inarticulateness, *s.* tartamudez, *f.*; inexpresión, reserva, *f.*; silencio, *m.*

inartistic, *a.* antiartístico, antiestético

inartistically, *adv.* sin gusto (estético)

inasmuch (as), *adv.* puesto que, visto que, dado que

inattention, *s.* desatención, inaplicación, abstracción, *f.*; falta
de solicitud, *f.*

inattentive, *a.* desatento, distraído; poco solicito, no
atento

inattentively, *adv.* sin atención,
distraídamente

inaudibility, *s.* imposibilidad de
oír, *f.*

inaudible, *a.* inaudible, no audible, ininteligible

inaudibly, *adv.* indistintamente,
de modo inaudible

inaugural, *a.* inaugural

inaugurate, *v.t.* inaugurar;
(open) estrenar, abrir, dedicar;
(install) investir, instalar; (initiate) originar, iniciar, dar
lugar (a)

inauguration, *s.* inauguración,
f.; (opening) estreno, *m.*, apertura, *f.*; (investiture) instalación,
investidura, *f.*

inauspicious, *a.* poco propicio,
desfavorable; ominoso, triste,
infeliz

inauspiciously, *adv.* en condiciones desfavorables, desfavorablemente; infelizmente, bajo
malos auspicios

inauspiciousness, *s.* condiciones
desfavorables, *f. pl.*; infelicidad,
f.; malos auspicios, *m. pl.*

inborn, *a.* innato, instintivo,
inherente

inbred, *a.* innato, inherente,
instintivo

Inca, *a.* incaico, de los incas.
s. inca, *m.*

incalculability, *s.* imposibilidad
de calcular, *f.*; (of persons)
volubilidad, veleidad, *f.*; infinidad, inmensidad, *f.*

incalculable, *a.* incalculable, innumerable; (of persons) voluble,
veleidoso, caprichoso; infinito,
inmenso

incalculably, *adv.* enormemente,
infinitamente; caprichosamente

incandescence, *s.* incandescencia,
candencia, *f.*

incandescent, *a.* incandescente,
candente. **i. light,** luz incandescente, *f.* **to make i.,** encandecer

incantation, *s.* hechizo, *m.*, en-
cantación, *f.*, ensalmo, *m.*

incapability, *s.* incapacidad, *f.*;
inhabilidad, ineptitud, incompetencia, *f.*

incapable, *a.* incapaz; inhábil,
incompetente; (physically) imposibilitado

incapacitate, *v.t.* imposibilitar,
incapacitar, inutilizar; (disqualify) inhabilitar, incapacitar

incapacitation, *s.* inhabilitación,
f.

incapacity, *s.* incapacidad, inhabilidad, *f.*

incarcerate, *v.t.* encarcelar

incarceration, *s.* encarcelación,
prisión, *f.*

incarnadine, *a.* (*poet.*) encarnado; encarnadino, colorado

incarnate, *a.* encarnado. *v.t.*
encarnar

incarnation, *s.* encarnación, *f.*

incautious, *a.* incauto, imprudente

incautiously, *adv.* incautamente

incautiousness, *s.* imprudencia,
negligencia, falta de cautela, *f.*

incendiarism, *s.* incendiarismo,
m.

incendiary, *a.* incendiario. **i.
bomb,** incendiaria, *f.*

incense, *s.* incienso, *m.*; (*fig.*)
adulación, *f.* *v.t.* (*ecc.*) incensar;
(annoy) irritar, exasperar, enojar.
i. burner, incensario, *m.*

incentive, *s.* incentivo, estímulo,
motivo, *m.* *a.* estimulador, in-
citativo

inception, *s.* comienzo, principio,
m.; inauguración, *f.*

incertitude, *s.* incertidumbre,
f.

incessant, *a.* incesante, continuo,
constante

incessantly, *adv.* incesantemente,
sin cesar

incest, *s.* incesto, *m.*

incestuous, *a.* incestuoso

inch, *s.* pulgada, *f.* **every i. a
man,** hombre hecho y derecho.
Not an i.! ¡Ni pizca! **within an
i. of,** a dos dedos de. **i. by i.,**
palmo a palmo, paso a paso.
i. tape, cinta métrica, *f.*

inchoate, *a.* rudimentario; imperfecto, incompleto

incidence, *s.* incidencia, *f.*

incident, *a.* propio, característico,
incidental. *s.* incidente, acontecimiento, *m.*, ocurrencia, *f.*

incidental, *a.* incidente, incidental; accidental, accesorio, no esencial. **i. expenses,** gastos imprevistos, *m. pl.*

incidentally, *adv.* incidentalmente; a propósito

incinerate, *v.t.* incinerar

incineration, *s.* incineración, cremación, *f.*

incinerator, *s.* incinerador, *m.*

incipient, *a.* incipiente, naciente, rudimentario

incise, *v.t.* cortar; (*art*) grabar, tajar

incised, *a.* (*bot.*) recortado

incision, *s.* incisión, *f.*; corte, tajo, *m.*; (*med.*) abscisión, *f.*

incisive, *a.* (of mind) agudo, penetrante; (of words) mordaz, incisivo, punzante

incisively, *adv.* en pocas palabras; mordazmente, incisivamente

incisiveness, *s.* (of mind) agudeza, penetración, *f.*; (of words) mordacidad, *f.*, sarcasmo, *m.*

incisor, *s.* diente incisivo, *m.*

incite, *v.t.* incitar, estimular, animar; provocar, tentar. **to i. to,** mover a, incitar a

incitement, *s.* incitación, instigación, *f.*; estímulo, *m.*; tentación, *f.*; aliciente, *m.*

incivility, *s.* incivilidad, descortesía, *f.*

inclemency, *s.* inclemencia, *f.*, rigor, *m.*

inclement, *a.* inclemente, riguroso, borrascoso

inclination, *s.* inclinación, *f.*; (slope) declive, *m.*, pendiente, cuesta, *f.*; (tendency) propensión, tendencia, *f.*; (liking) afición, *f.*; amor, *m.*; (bow) reverencia, *f.*; (*geom.*) inclinación, *f*

incline, *v.t.* inclinar, torcer; doblar; (cause) inclinar (a), hacer. *v.i.* inclinarse, torcerse; (tend) tender, propender, inclinarse; (colours) tirar (a). *s.* declive, *m.*, pendiente, cuesta, inclinación, *f.* **I am inclined to believe it,** Me inclino a creerlo. **I am inclined to do it,** Estoy por hacerlo, Creo que lo haré

inclined, *a.* torcido, inclinado, doblado; (*fig.*) propenso, adicto. **i. plane,** plano inclinado, *m.*

include, *v.t.* incluir, contener, encerrar; comprender, abrazar

including, *present part.,* incluso, inclusive. **not i.,** no comprendido

inclusion, *s.* inclusión, *f.*

inclusive, *a.* inclusivo. **January 2nd to January 12th i.,** Del 2 al 12 de enero, ambos inclusivos. **not i. of,** sin contar, exclusivo de. **i. of,** que incluye. **i. terms,** todo incluido, todos los gastos incluidos

incognito, *a.* and *adv.* and *s.* incógnito (*m.*)

incoherence, *s.* incoherencia, inconsecuencia, *f.*

incoherent, *a.* incoherente, inconexo, inconsecuente. **an i. piece of writing,** un escrito sin pies ni cabeza

incoherently, *adv.* con incoherencia

incombustibility, *s.* incombustibilidad, *f.*

incombustible, *a.* incombustible

income, *s.* renta, *f.*, ingreso, *m.*; (*com.*) rédito, *m.* **i.-tax,** impuesto de utilidades, *m.* **i.-tax commissioners,** inspectores de impuestos de utilidades, *m. pl.* **i.-tax return;** declaración de utilidades, *f.*

incomer, *s.* recién llegado (-da); nuevo (-va) ocupante

incoming, *a.* entrante; nuevo. *s.* entrada, llegada, *f.* *s. pl.,* incomings, ingresos, *m. pl.*

incommensurability, *s.* inconmensurabilidad, *f.*

incommensurable, *a.* inconmensurable, no conmensurable

incommensurate, *a.* desproporcionado, desmedido

incommode, *v.t.* incomodar, molestar, fastidiar

incommodious, *a.* estrecho; incómodo, inconveniente

incommodiousness, *s.* estrechez, *f.*; incomodidad, *f.*

incommunicable, *a.* incomunicable, indecible, inexplicable

incommunicative, *a.* insociable, intratable, adusto, huraño

incomparable, *a.* incomparable; sin par, sin igual, excelente

incomparableness, *s.* excelencia, perfección, *f.*

incomparably, *adv.* incomparablemente, con mucho

incompatibility, *s.* incompatibilidad, *f.*

incompatible, *a.* incompatible

incompetence, *s.* incompetencia, ineptitud, inhabilidad, *f.*; (*law*) incapacidad, *f.*

incompetent, *a.* incompetente, incapaz, inepto, inhábil; (*law*) incapaz

incompetently, *adv.* inhábilmente

incomplete, *a.* incompleto; imperfecto, defectuoso; (unfinished) sin terminar, inacabado, inconcluso

incompletely, *adv.* incompletamente; imperfectamente

incompleteness, *s.* estado incompleto, *m.*; imperfección, *f.*; inconclusión, *f.*

incomprehensibility, *s.* incomprensibilidad, *f.*

incomprehensible, *a.* incomprensible

incomprehension, *s.* incomprensión, falta de comprensión, *f.*

inconceivable, *a.* inconcebible, inimaginable

inconclusive, *a.* inconcluyente, cuestionable, dudoso, no convincente

inconclusiveness, *s.* carácter inconcluso, *m.*, falta de conclusiones, *f.*

incongruity, *s.* incongruencia, desproporción, disonancia, *f.*

incongruous, *a.* incongruente, incongruo; chocante, desproporcionado, disonante

incongruously, *adv.* incongruentemente, incongruamente

inconsequence, *s.* inconsecuencia, *f.*

inconsequent, inconsequential, *a.* inconsecuente, ilógico; inconsistente

inconsiderable, *a.* insignificante

inconsiderate, *a.* desconsiderado, irreflexivo, irrespetuoso

inconsiderately, *adv.* sin consideración, desconsideradamente

inconsiderateness, *s.* desconsideración, falta de respeto, *f.*

inconsistency, *s.* inconsistencia, inconsecuencia, incompatibilidad, contradicción, anomalía, *f.*

inconsistent, *a.* inconsistente, inconsiguiente, incompatible, contradictorio, anómalo

inconsistently, *adv.* contradictoriamente

inconsolable, *a.* inconsolable, desconsolado. **to be i.,** estar inconsolable, (*fam.,* of a woman) estar hecha una Magdalena

inconsolably, *adv.* desconsoladamente

inconspicuous, *a.* que no llama la atención; insignificante, humilde, modesto

inconspicuously, *adv.* humildemente, modestamente

inconspicuousness, *s.* modestia, humildad, *f.*

inconstancy, *s.* inconstancia, movilidad, *f.*; mudanza, veleidad, *f.*

inconstant, *a.* inconstante, mudable, variable; veleidoso, volátil, voluble

incontestable, *a.* incontestable, evidente, indisputable

incontinence, *s.* incontinencia, *f.*

incontinent, *a.* incontinente

incontrollable, *a.* ingobernable, indomable

incontrovertible, *a.* incontrovertible, incontrastable

inconvenience, *s.* incomodidad, inconveniencia, *f.*; (of time) inoportunidad, *f.* *v.t.* incomodar, causar inconvenientes (a)

inconvenient, *a.* incómodo, inconveniente, molesto, embarazoso; (of time) inoportuno. **at an i. time,** a deshora

inconveniently, *adv.* incómodamente; (of time) inoportunamente

inconvertible, *a.* inconvertible

inconvincible, *a.* inconvencible

inco-ordination, *s.* falta de coordinación, *f.*

incorporate, *v.t.* incorporar, agregar; comprender, incluir, encerrar. *v.i.* asociarse, incorporarse. *a.* incorpóreo, inmaterial; incorporado, asociado

incorporation, *s.* incorporación, agregación, *f.*; asociación, *f.*

incorporeal, *a.* incorpóreo, inmaterial

incorporeity, *s.* incorporeidad, inmaterialidad, *f.*

incorrect, *a.* incorrecto; inexacto, erróneo, falso

incorrectly, *adv.* incorrectamente

incorrectness, *s.* incorrección, *f.*

incorrigibility, *s:* incorregibili-
dad, *f.*
incorrigible, *a.* incorregible,
empecatado
incorrigibly, *adv.* incorregible-
mente, obstinadamente
incorrupt, *a.* incorrupto; recto,
honrado
incorruptibility, *s.* incorrupti-
bilidad, *f.*; honradez, probidad, *f.*
incorruptible, *a.* incorrupto;
honrado, incorruptible
incorruption, *s.* incorrupción, *f.*
increase, *v.t.* aumentar, acrecentar; (in numbers) multiplicar;
(extend) ampliar, extender; (of
price) encarecer, aumentar. *v.i.*
aumentar, crecer; multiplicarse;
extenderse; encarecerse, aumentar. *s.* aumento, crecimiento, *m.*;
multiplicación, *f.*; (in price)
encarecimiento, *m.*, alza, *f.*; (of
water) crecida, *f.*; (of moon)
creciente, *f.* **It is on the i.**,
Va en aumento. **to i. and
multiply**, crecer y multiplicar
increasingly, *adv.* más y más;
en creciente, en aumento
incredibility, *s.* incredibilidad, *f.*
incredible, *a.* increíble; fabuloso,
extraordinario. **It seems i.**, Es
increíble. (*fam.*) Parece mentira
incredibly, *adv.* increíblemente
incredulity, *s.* incredulidad, *f.*,
escepticismo, *m.*
incredulous, *a.* incrédulo, escéptico
incredulously, *adv.* con incredulidad, escépticamente
increment, *s.* aumento, incremento, *m.*; adición, añadidura,
f.; (*math.*) incremento, *m.* **unearned i.**, plusvalía, mayor valía,
f.
incriminate, *v.t.* incriminar
incriminating, *a.* incriminante,
acriminador :
incrust, *v.t.* incrustar, encostrar
incrustation, *s.* incrustación, *f.*;
(scab) costra, *f.*
incubate, *v.t.* empollar; (*med.*)
incubar
incubation, *s.* empolladura, incubación, *f.*; (*med.*) incubación, *f.*
incubator, *s.* incubadora, *f.*
incubus, *s.* íncubo, *m.*; (burden)
carga, *f.*
inculcate, *v.t.* inculcar, implantar, instilar

inculcation, *s.* inculcación, implantación, instilación, *f.*
incumbency, *s.* posesión o duración de un beneficio eclesiástico, *f.*
incumbent, *a.* obligatorio. *s.*
(*ecc.*) beneficiado, *m.* **to be i.
on**, incumbir a, ser de su
obligación
incur, *v.i.* incurrir (en), incidir
(en). **to i. an obligation**,
contraer una obligación
incurability, *s.* incurabilidad, *f.*
incurable, *a.* incurable, insanable; (*fig.*) sin solución, irremediable. *s.* incurable, *m.* and *f.*
incurably, *adv.* incurablemente,
irremediablemente
incurious, *a.* indiferente, sin
interés; incurioso, negligente,
descuidado
incursion, *s.* incursión, invasión,
irrupción, *f.*, acometimiento, *m.*
incus, *s.* (*anat.*) yunque, *m.*
indebted, *a.* empeñado, adeu-
dado; (obliged) reconocido
indebtedness, *s.* deuda, *f.*; (gratitude) obligación, *f.*; agradecimiento, *m.*
indecency, *s.* indecencia, *f.*
indecent, *a.* indecente; obsceno,
deshonesto
indecently, *adv.* torpemente, in-
decentemente
indecision, *s.* indecisión, vacilación, irresolución, *f.*
indecisive, *a.* indeciso, irresoluto,
vacilante
indeclinable, *a.* indeclinable
indecorous, *a.* indecoroso, indecente, indigno
indecorum, *s.* indecoro, *m.*,
indecencia, *f.*; incorrección, *f.*
indeed, *adv.* en efecto, de veras,
a la verdad, realmente, por
cierto, claro está. *interr.* ¿ de
veras ? ¿ es posible ? **I shall be
very glad i.**, Estaré contento de
veras. **It is i. an excellent
book**, Es en efecto un libro
excelente. **There are differences i. between this house
and the other**, Hay diferencias,
claro está, entre esta casa y la
otra
indefatigability, *s.* resistencia,
f., aguante, *m.*, tenacidad, *f.*
indefatigable, *a.* incansable, infatigable, resistente

indefatigably, *adv.* infatigable-
mente
indefensible, *a.* indefendible,
insostenible
indefinable, *a.* indefinible
indefinite, *a.* indefinido, incierto;
(delicate) sutil, delicado; (*gram.*)
indefinido; (vague) vago. (*gram.*)
i. article, artículo indefinido, *m.*
indefinitely, *adv.* indefinida-
mente
indefiniteness, *s.* el carácter
indefinido, *m.*; vaguedad, *f.*
indelibility, *s.* resistencia, *f.*, lo
indeleble; (*fig.*) duración, tenacidad, *f.*
indelible, *a.* indeleble, imborrable; (*fig.*) inolvidable
indelibly, *adv.* indeleblemente
indelicacy, *s.* falta de buen gusto,
grosería, *f.*; (tactlessness) indiscreción, falta de tacto, *f.*
indelicate, *a.* grosero, descortés;
indecoroso, inmodesto; (tactless)
inoportuno, indiscreto
indemnification, *s.* indemnización, compensación, *f.*
indemnify, *v.t.* indemnizar,
compensar
indemnity, *s.* indemnización,
reparación, *f.*
indent, *v.t.* endentar, mellar;
(*print.*) sangrar
indentation, *s.* impresión, depresión, *f.*; corte, *m.*, mella, *f.*;
línea quebrada, *f.*, zigzag, *m.*
indenture, *s.* escritura, *f.*, instrumento, *m. v.t.* escriturar
independence, *s.* independencia,
libertad, *f.*; (autonomy) autonomía, *f.* **I. Day,** Fiesta de la
Independencia, *f.*
independent, *a.* independiente;
libre; (autonomous) autónomo;
i. of, libre de; aparte de. **a person of i. means,** una persona
acomodada
independently, *adv.* inde-
pendientemente
indescribability, *s.* imposibilidad
de describir, *f.*, lo indescriptible
indescribable, *a.* indescriptible;
indefinible, indecible, inexplicable; incalificable
indestructibility, *s.* indestructibilidad, *f.*
indestructible, *a.* indestructible
indeterminable, *a.* indeterminable

indeterminate, *a.* indeterminado,
indefinido, vago; (*math.*) indeterminado
indetermination, *s.* irresolución,
indecisión, duda, vacilación, *f.*
index, *s.* (forefinger) dedo índice,
m.; (of book) tabla de materias,
f., índice, *m.*; (on instruments)
manecilla, aguja, *f.*; (*math.*)
índice, *m.*; (sign) señal, indicación, *f. v.t.* poner índice (a);
poner en el índice. **i. card,** ficha,
f. **I. expurgatorius,** Índice expurgatorio, *m.*
India, *s.* India, *f.* **I. paper,** papel
de China, *m.* **i.-rubber,** (*bot.*)
caucho, *m.*; (eraser) goma de
borrar, *f.* **i.-rubber tree,** yacio,
m.
Indian, *a.* and *s.* indio (-ia). **I.
chief,** cacique, *m.* **I. club,** maza,
f. **I. corn,** maíz, *m.* **I. ink,**
tinta china, *f.* **I. summer,**
veranillo de San Martín, *m.*
indicate, *v.t.* indicar, señalar;
(show) denotar, mostrar, anunciar
indication, *s.* indicación, *f.*;
señal, *f.*, indicio, síntoma, *m.*;
prueba, *f.*
indicative, *a.* indicador, indicativo, demostrativo; (*gram.*)
indicativo. *s.* (*gram.*) indicativo,
m. **to be i. of,** indicar, señalar
indicator, *s.* indicador, señalador,
m.
indict, *v.t.* acusar; (*law*) demandar, enjuiciar
indictable, *a.* procesable, denunciable, enjuiciable
indictment, *s.* acusación, *f.*;
(*law*) procesamiento, *m.*
indifference, *s.* indiferencia,
apatía, *f.*, desinterés, desapego,
m.; imparcialidad, neutralidad,
f.; (coldness) frialdad, tibieza, *f.*
indifferent, *a.* indiferente,
apático; imparcial, neutral;
frío; (ordinary) regular, ordinario, ni bien ni mal
indifferently, *adv.* con indiferencia; imparcialmente; fria-
mente
indigence, *s.* indigencia, necesidad, penuria, *f.*
indigenous, *a.* indígena nativo,
natural
indigent, *a.* indigente, necesitado,
menesteroso

indigestible, *a.* indigesto

indigestion, *s.* indigestión, *f.*; (*fig.*) empacho, ahito, *m.*

indignant, *a.* indignado. **to make i.,** indignar

indignantly, *adv.* con indignación

indignation, *s.* indignación, cólera, *f.*

indignity, *s.* indignidad, *f.*; ultraje, *m.*

indigo, *s.* añil, índigo, *m.*

indirect, *a.* indirecto; oblicuo; tortuoso; (*gram.*) **i. case,** caso oblicuo, *m.*

indirectly, *adv.* indirectamente

indirectness, *s.* (of route) rodeo, *m.*, desviación, *f.*; oblicuidad, *f.*; (falsity) tortuosidad, *f.*

indiscernible, *a.* imperceptible

indiscipline, *s.* indisciplina, falta de disciplina, *f.*

indiscreet, *a.* indiscreto, imprudente, impolítico

indiscreetly, *adv.* indiscretamente

indiscretion, *s.* indiscreción, imprudencia, *f.*; (slip) desliz, *m.*

indiscriminate, *a.* general, universal; indistinto, promiscuo

indiscriminately, *adv.* promiscuamente

indiscrimination, *s.* universalidad, indistinción, *f.*

indispensability, *s.* indispensabilidad, precisión, necesidad, *f.*

indispensable, *a.* imprescindible, indispensable, insustituible

indispensably, *adv.* forzosamente, indispensablemente

indispose, *v.t.* indisponer. **to be indisposed,** estar indispuesto, indisponerse

indisposed, *a.* indispuesto, enfermo, destemplado; (reluctant) maldispuesto

indisposition, *s.* indisposición, enfermedad, *f.*

indisputability, *s.* verdad manifiesta, certeza, evidencia, *f.*

indisputable, *a.* innegable, incontestable; irrefutable, evidente

indisputably, *adv.* indisputablemente

indissolubility, *s.* indisolubilidad, *f.*

indissoluble, *a.* indisoluble

indissolubly, *adv.* indisolublemente

indistinct, *a.* indistinto; indeterminado, confuso, vago

indistinctly, *adv.* indistintamente; confusamente, vagamente

indistinctness, *s.* incertidumbre, vaguedad, indistinción, indeterminación, *f.*

indistinguishable, *a.* indistinguible

indite, *v.t.* escribir, componer; dictar

indium, *s.* (*chem.*) indio, *m.*

individual, *a.* (single) solo, único; individual, individuo, particular, propio; personal. *s.* individuo, *m.*, particular, *m.* and *f.*

individualism, *s.* individualismo, *m.*

individualist, *s.* individualist, *m.* and *f.*

individualistic, *a.* individualista

individuality, *s* individualidad, personalidad, *f.*; carácter, *m.*, naturaleza, *f.*

individualize, *v.t.* particularizar, individuar

individually, *adv.* individualmente, particularmente

indivisibility, *s.* indivisibilidad, *f.*

indivisible, *a.* incompartible, impartible, indivisible

indivisibly, *adv.* indivisiblemente

Indo, (in compounds) indo. **I.-Chinese,** *a.* and *s.* indochino (-na). **I.-European,** indoeuropeo. **I.-Germanic,** indogermánico

indocile, *a.* indócil, desobediente, rebelde

indocility, *s.* indocilidad, desobediencia, falta de docilidad, *f.*

indolence, *s.* indolencia, pereza, desidia, *f.*

indolent, *a.* indolente, perezoso, holgazán; (*med.*) indoloro

indolently, *adv.* perezosamente

indomitable, *a.* indomable, indómito

indoor, *a.* de casa; de puertas adentro, interno. **i. tennis,** tenis en pistas cubiertas, *m.*

indoors, *adv.* en casa; adentro, bajo techo

indorsee, *s.* endosatario (-ia)

indubitable, *a.* indudable

indubitably, *adv.* indudablemente, sin duda

induce, *v.t.* inducir, mover; instigar, incitar; producir, oca-

sionar; (*elec.*) inducir. **Nothing
would i. me to do it,** Nada me
induciría a hacerlo

inducement, *s.* incitamento, *m.*;
estímulo, *m.*; aliciente, atractivo,
m.; tentación, *f.*

induct, *v.t.* instalar; introducir,
iniciar

induction, *s.* instalación, *f.*;
iniciación, introducción, *f.*;
(*phys.*) inducción, *f.* **i. coil,**
carrete de inducción, *m.*

inductive, *a.* (of reasoning) inductivo; (*phys.*) inductor

inductor, *s.* (*phys.*) inductor, *m.*

indulge, *v.t.* (children) consentir,
mimar; (a desire) satisfacer, dar
rienda suelta a; (with a gift)
agasajar (con), dar gusto (con).
to i. in, *v.t.* consentir en.
v.i. entregarse a, permitirse,
gustar de

indulgence, *s.* (of children) mimo,
cariño excesivo, *m.*; (of a desire)
propension (a), afición (a), *f.*; (towards others) tolerancia, transigencia, *f.*; (*ecc.*) indulgencia, *f.*

indulgent, *a.* indulgente; tolerante, transigente

indulgently, *adv.* indulgente-
mente

indult, *s.* (*ecc.*) indulto, *m.*

industrial, *a.* industrial. **i.
alcohol,** alcohol desnaturalizado,
m. **i. school,** escuela de artes y
oficios, *f.* (*com.*) **i. shares,**
valores industriales, *m. pl.*

industrialism, *s.* industrialismo,
m.

industrialist, *s.* industrial, *m.*

industrialization, *s.* industrialización, *f.*

industrialize, *v.t.* industrializar

industrious, *a.* industrioso, aplicado, diligente

industriously, *adv.* industriosa-
mente, diligentemente

industriousness, *s.* industria,
laboriosidad, *f.*

industry, *s.* diligencia, aplicación,
f.; (work) trabajo, *m.*, labor, *f.*;
(*com.*) industria, *f.*

inebriate, *a.* borracho, ebrio.
s. borracho (-cha). *v.t.* embriagar,
emborrachar

inebriation, *s.* embriaguez, borrachera, *f.*

inedible, *a.* incomible, no comestible

inedited, *a.* inédito

ineffable, *a.* indecible, inefable

ineffaceable, *a.* imborrable, indeleble

ineffective, *a.* ineficaz; vano,
fútil. **to be i.,** (of persons) no
pinchar ni cortar. **to prove i.,**
quedar sin efecto; no tener
influencia

ineffectiveness, *s.* ineficacia, *f.*;
futilidad, *f.*

inefficiency, *s.* ineficacia, incompetencia, ineptitud, *f.*

inefficient, *a.* ineficaz, incapaz

inefficiently, *adv.* ineficazmente

inelastic, *a.* inelástico

inelasticity, *s.* falta de elasticidad,
f.

inelegance, *s.* inelegancia, fealdad, vulgaridad, *f.*

inelegant, *a.* inelegante, ordinario, de mal gusto

inelegantly, *adv.* sin elegancia

ineligibility, *s.* ineligibilidad, *f.*

ineligible, *a.* inelegible

inept, *a.* inepto, inoportuno;
absurdo, ridículo; (of persons)
incompetente, ineficaz

ineptitude, *s.* ineptitud, *f.*; necedad, *f.*; (of persons) incapacidad,
incompetencia, *f.*

ineptly, *adv.* ineptamente, neciamente

inequality, *s.* desigualdad, desemejanza, disparidad, *f.*; (of
surface) escabrosidad, aspereza,
f.; (*fig.*) injusticia, *f.*; (of opportunity) diferencia, *f.*

inequitable, *a.* desigual, injusto

inequity, *s.* injusticia, desigualdad, *f.*

ineradicable, *a.* indeleble, imborrable

ineradicably, *adv.* indeleblemente

inert, *a.* inerte, inactivo, pasivo;
ocioso, flojo, perezoso

inertia, *s.* inercia, inacción, *f.*;
abulia, pereza, *f.*; (*phys.*) inercia,
f.

inertly, *adv.* indolentemente, sin
mover, pasivamente

inescapable, *a.* ineludible, inevitable

inessential, *a.* no esencial

inestimable, *a.* inestimable

inevitability, *s.* fatalidad, necesidad, *f.*; lo inevitable

inevitable, *a.* inevitable, necesario, fatal, forzoso, ineludible

inevitably, *adv.* inevitablemente, necesariamente, forzosamente

inexact, *a.* inexacto, incorrecto

inexactitude, *s.* inexactitud, *f.*

inexactly, *adv.* inexactamente

inexcusable, *a.* imperdonable, inexcusable, irremisible

inexcusableness, *s.* enormidad, *f.*; lo inexcusable

inexcusably, *adv.* inexcusablemente

inexhaustible, *a.* inagotable, inexhausto

inexorability, *s.* inflexibilidad, inexorabilidad, *f.*

inexorable, *a.* inexorable, inflexible, duro

inexorably, *adv.* inexorablemente, implacablemente

inexpediency, *s.* inoportunidad, inconveniencia, imprudencia, *f.*

inexpedient, *a.* inoportuno; inconveniente; impolítico, imprudente. **to deem i.,** creer inoportuno

inexpensive, *a.* poco costoso, barato

inexpensiveness, *s.* baratura, *f.*, bajo precio, *m.*

inexperience, *s.* inexperiencia, falta de experiencia, *f.*

inexperienced, *a.* inexperto, novato

inexpert, *a.* inexperto, imperito

inexpertly, *adv.* sin habilidad

inexpertness, *s.* impericia, torpeza, *f.*

inexpiable, *a.* inexpiable

inexplicable, *a.* inexplicable

inexplicably, *adv.* inexplicablemente

inexplicit, *a.* no explícito

inexplosive, *a.* inexplosible

inexpressible, *a.* inexplicable, indecible, inefable

inexpressive, *a.* inexpresivo; (of persons) reservado, callado, poco expresivo, retraído

inexpressiveness, *s.* falta de expresión, *f.*; (of persons) reserva, *f.*, silencio, retraimiento, *m.*

inexpugnable, *a.* inexpugnable

inextinguishable, *a.* inapagable, inextinguible

inextricable, *a.* inextricable, intrincado, enmarañado

inextricably, *adv.* intrincadamente

infallibility, *s.* infalibilidad, *f.*

infallible, *a.* infalible

infallibly, *adv.* infaliblemente

infamous, *a.* infame, torpe, vil, ignominioso; odioso, repugnante

infamously, *adv.* infamemente

infamy, *s.* infamia, torpeza, vileza, ignominia, *f.*; deshonra, *f.*

infancy, *s.* infancia, niñez, *f.*; (*law*) minoridad, *f.*

infant, *s.* criatura, *f.*; crío (-ía), niño (-ña); (*law*) menor, *m.* and *f.* **i. school,** escuela de párvulos, *f.*

infanticidal, *a.* infanticida

infanticide, *s.* (act) infanticidio, *m.*; (person) infanticida, *m.* and *f.*

infantile, *a.* infantil. **i. paralysis,** parálisis infantil, *f.*

infantry, *s.* (*mil.*) infantería, *f.*

infantryman, *s.* (*mil.*) infante, peón, *m.*

infatuate, *v.t.* infatuar, embobar

infatuation, *s.* infatuación, *f.*, encaprichamiento, *m.*

infect, *v.t.* infectar, contagiar; (*fig.*) pegar, influir; (*fig. in a bad sense*) corromper, pervertir, inficionar. **to become infected,** infectarse

infected, *a.* infecto

infection, *s.* infección, *f.*, contagio, *m.*; (*fig.*) influencia, *f.*; (*fig. in a bad sense*) corrupción, perversión, *f.*

infectious, *a.* infeccioso, contagioso; (*fig. in a bad sense*) corruptor; (*fig.*) contagioso

infectiousness, *s.* contagiosidad, *f.*

infelicitous, *a.* poco apropiado, desacertado

infelicity, *s.* infelicidad, desdicha, *f.*, infortunio, *m.*; desacierto, *m.*, inoportunidad, *f.*

infer, *v.t.* inferir, concluir, educir, deducir, implicar

inferable, *a.* deducible, demostrable

inference, *s.* inferencia, deducción, conclusión, *f.*

inferential, *a.* ilativo, deductivo

inferior, *a.* inferior; (in rank) subordinado, subalterno; (of position) secundario. *s.* inferior, *m.* and *f.*, subordinado (-da). **to be not i.,** no ser inferior, (*fam.*) no quedarse en zaga

inferiority, *s.* inferioridad, *f.* **i. complex,** complejo de inferioridad, *m.*

infernal, *a.* infernal; (*poet.*) inferno, tartáreo

infernally, *adv.* infernalmente

inferno, *s.* infierno, *m.*

infertile, *a.* infértil, infecundo, estéril

infertility, *s.* infertilidad, infecundidad, esterilidad, *f.*

infest, *v.t.* infestar. **to be infested with,** plagarse de

infestation, *s.* infestación, *f.*

infidel, *s.* infiel, gentil, *m.* and *f.*, pagano (-na); (atheist) descreído (-da), ateo (-ea). *a.* pagano; infiel, descreído, ateo

infidelity, *s.* infidelidad, alevosía, perfidia, *f.*

infiltrate, *v.t.* infiltrar. *v.i.* infiltrarse

infiltration, *s.* infiltración, *f.*

infinite, *a.* infinito, ilimitado; inmenso, enorme; (of number) innumerable, infinito. *s.* infinito, *m.*

infinitely, *adv.* infinitamente

infinitesimal, *a.* infinitesimal. **i. calculus,** cálculo infinitesimal, *m.*

infinitive, *a.* and *s.* (*gram.*) infinitivo (*m.*)

infinitude, infinity, *s.* infinidad, infinitud, *f.*; (extent) inmensidad, *f.*; (of number) sinfin, *m.*; (*math.*) infinito, *m.*

infirm, *a.* achacoso, enfermizo, enclenque; (shaky) inestable, inseguro; (of purpose) irresoluto, vacilante

infirmary, *s.* enfermería, *f.*, hospital, *m.*

infirmity, *s.* achaque, *m.*, enfermedad, dolencia, *f.*; (fault) flaqueza, falta, *f.*

inflame, *v.t.* encender; (excite) acalorar, irritar, provocar; (*med.*) inflamar. *v.i.* encenderse, arder; acalorarse, irritarse; (*med.*) inflamarse

inflammability, *s.* inflamabilidad, *f.*

inflammable, *a.* inflamable

inflammation, *s.* inflamación, *f.*

inflammatory, *a.* inflamador; (*med.*) inflamatorio

inflate, *v.t.* inflar, hinchar; (with pride) engreír, ensoberbecer

inflation, *s.* inflación, hinchazón, *f.*; (*com.*) inflación, *f.*

inflationism, *s.* inflacionismo, *m.*

inflationist, *s.* inflacionista, *m.* and *f.*

inflator, *s.* (*mech.*) bomba para inflar, *f.*

inflect, *v.t.* torcer; (voice) modular; (*gram.*) conjugar, declinar

inflection, *s.* dobladura, *f.*; (of voice) tono, acento, *m.*, modulación, *f.*; (*gram.*) conjugación, declinación, *f.*

inflexibility, *s.* inflexibilidad, dureza, rigidez, *f.*

inflexible, *a.* inflexible, rígido; (*fig.*) inexorable, inalterable

inflexibly, *adv.* inflexiblemente

inflict, *v.t.* infligir, imponer

infliction, *s.* imposición, *f.*; castigo, *m.*

inflorescence, *s.* (*bot.*) inflorescencia, *f.*

inflow, *s.* afluencia, *f.*, flujo, *m.*

influence, *s.* influencia, *f.*, influjo, *m.*; ascendiente, *m.*; (importance) influencia, importancia, *f.* *v.t.* influir, afectar; persuadir, inducir. **to have i. over,** (a person) tener ascendiente sobre. (*law*) **undue i.,** influencia indebida, *f.*

influential, *a.* influyente; (of person) prestigioso, importante

influenza, *s.* (*med.*) gripe, *f.*, trancazo, *m.*

influx, *s.* influjo, *m.*; (of rivers) desembocadura, afluencia, *f.*

inform, *v.t.* (fill) infundir, llenar; (tell) informar, enterar, advertir; instruir; (about) poner al corriente de, participar. *v.i.* (with against) delatar (a), denunciar. **to i. oneself,** informarse, enterarse. **to be informed about,** estar al corriente de

informal, *a.* irregular; sin ceremonia, de confianza

informality, *s.* irregularidad, *f.*; falta de ceremonia, sencillez, *f.*; intimidad, *f.*

informally, *adv.* sin ceremonia

informant, *s.* informante, *m.* and *f.*; informador (-ra)

information, *s.* información, instrucción, *f.*; noticia, *f.*, aviso, *m.*; (*law*) denuncia, delación, *f.* **piece of i.,** información, *f.* **i. bureau,** oficina de información, *f.*

informative, *a.* informativo.

informer, *s.* delator (-ra), denunciador (-ra)

infra-red, *a.* (*phys.*) infrarrojo, ultrarrojo

infraction, *s.* contravención, infracción, transgresión, *f.*

infrequency, *s.* infrecuencia, rareza, irregularidad, *f.*

infrequent, *a.* infrecuente, raro, irregular

infrequently, *adv.* rara vez, infrecuentemente

infringe, *v.t.* infringir, violar, contravenir, quebrantar

infringement, *s.* contravención, violación, infracción, *f.*

infringer, *s.* infractor (-ra), contraventor (-ra), violador (-ra), transgresor (-ra)

infuriate, *v.t.* enfurecer, enloquecer, enojar. **to be infuriated,** estar furioso

infuse, *v.t.* vaciar, infiltrar; (*fig.*) infundir, inculcar, instilar

infusible, *a.* infundible

infusion, *s.* infusión, *f.*; (*fig.*) instilación, inculcación, *f.*

ingathering, *s.* cosecha, recolección, *f.*

ingenious, *a.* ingenioso; mañoso, hábil

ingeniously, *adv.* ingeniosamente, hábilmente

ingenuity, *s.* ingeniosidad, inventiva, listeza, habilidad, *f.*

ingenuous, *a.* ingenuo, franco, sincero, cándido, sencillo, inocente

ingenuousness, *s.* ingenuidad, franqueza, sinceridad, *f.*; candor, *m.*

ingest, *v.t.* ingerir

ingestion, *s.* ingestión, *f.*

ingle-nook, *s.* rincón del fuego, *m.*

inglorious, *a.* vergonzoso, ignominioso, deshonroso; desconocido, obscuro

ingloriously, *adv.* vergonzosamente, ignominiosamente; obscuramente

ingloriousness, *s.* deshonra, ignominia, *f.*; obscuridad, *f.*

ingoing, *a.* entrante, que entra. *s.* ingreso, *m.*, entrada, *f.*; (*com.*) **i. and outgoing,** entradas y salidas, *f. pl.*

ingot, *s.* pepita, *f.*, lingote, *m.*; (of any metal) barra, *f.*

ingrained, *a.* innato, natural

ingratiate, *v.t.* (oneself with) congraciarse con, captarse la buena voluntad de, insinuarse en el favor de

ingratiating, *a.* obsequioso

ingratitude, *s.* ingratitud, *f.*, desagradecimiento, *m.*

ingredient, *s.* ingrediente, *m.*

ingress, *s.* ingreso, *m.*; derecho de entrada, *m.*

ingrowing, *a.* que crece hacia adentro. **i. nail,** uñero, *m.*

ingurgitate, *v.t.* ingurgitar

ingurgitation, *s.* (*med.*) ingurgitación, *f.*

inhabit, *v.t.* habitar, ocupar, vivir en, residir en

inhabitable, *a.* habitable, vividero

inhabitant, *s.* habitante, residente, *m.*; vecino (-na)

inhabited, *a.* habitado, poblado

inhalation, *s.* inspiración, *f.*; (*med.*) inhalación, *f.*

inhale, *v.t.* aspirar; (*med.*) inhalar

inhaler, *s.* inhalador, *m.*

inharmonious, *a.* (*mus.*) disonante, inarmónico; desavenido, discorde, desconforme. **to be i.,** disonar; (of people) llevarse mal

inhere, *v.i.* ser inherente; pertenecer (a), residir (en)

inherence, *s.* inherencia, *f.*

inherent, *a.* inherente; innato, intrínseco, natural

inherently, *adv.* intrínsecamente

inherit, *v.t.* heredar

inheritance, *s.* herencia, *f.*; patrimonio, abolengo, *m.*

inheritor, *s.* heredero, *m.*

inheritress, *s.* heredera, *f.*

inhibit, *v.t.* inhibir, impedir; (*ecc.*) prohibir

inhibition, *s.* inhibición, *f.*

inhibitory, *a.* inhibitorio

inhospitable, *a.* inhospitalario

inhospitably, *adv.* desabridamente

inhospitality, *s.* inhospitalidad, *f.*

inhuman, *a.* inhumano; cruel, bárbaro

inhumanity, *s.* inhumanidad, crueldad, *f.*

inhumanly, *adv.* inhumanamente, cruelmente

inhume, *v.t.* inhumar, sepultar

inimical, *a.* enemigo, hostil, opuesto, contrario

inimically, *adv.* hostilmente

inimitable, *a.* inimitable

inimitably, *adv.* inimitablemente

iniquitous, *a.* inicuo, malvado, perverso, nefando; (*fam.*) diabólico

iniquity, *s.* iniquidad, maldad, injusticia, *f.*

initial, *a.* inicial. *s.* inicial, letra inicial, *f.* *v.t.* firmar con las iniciales

initially, *adv.* al principio, en primer lugar

initiate, *a.* iniciado. *v.t.* iniciar, poner en pie, empezar, entablar; (a person) admitir

initiation, *s.* principio, *m.*; (of a person) iniciación, admisión, *f.*

initiative, *s.* iniciativa, *f.* to take the i., tomar la iniciativa

initiator, *s.* iniciador (-ra)

inject, *v.t.* inyectar

injection, *s.* inyección, *f.* i. syringe, jeringa de inyecciones, *f.*

injudicious, *a.* imprudente, indiscreto

injudiciously, *adv.* imprudentemente

injudiciousness, *s.* imprudencia, indiscreción, *f.*

injunction, *s.* precepto, mandato, *m.*; (*law*) embargo, *m.*

injure, *v.t.* perjudicar, dañar; menoscabar, deteriorar; (hurt) lastimar, lisiar. to i. oneself, hacerse daño

injured, *a.* (physically) lisiado; (morally) ofendido

injurer, *s.* perjudicador (-ra)

injurious, *a.* dañoso, perjudicial, malo; ofensivo, injurioso

injuriously, *adv.* perjudicialmente

injury, *s.* perjuicio, daño, *m.*; (physical) lesión, *f.*; (insult) agravio, insulto, *m.*

injustice, *s.* injusticia, desigualdad, *f.* You do him an i., Le juzgas mal

ink, *s.* tinta, *f.* *v.t.* entintar. copying-ink, tinta de copiar, *f.* marking-ink, tinta indeleble, *f.* printer's ink, tinta de imprenta, *f.* ink-stand or ink-well, tintero, *m.*

inker, *s.* (*print.*) rodillo, *m.*

inkling, *s.* sospecha, noción, *f.*

inky, *a.* manchado de tinta. i. black, negro como el betún

inland, *s.* el interior de un país. *a.* interior; del país, regional. *adv.* tierra adentro. to go i., internarse en un país. I. Revenue, delegación de contribuciones, *f.* i. town, ciudad del interior, *f.*

inlay, *v.t.* taracear, ataracear, embutir; incrustar. *s.* taracea, *f.*, embutido, *m.*

inlayer, *s.* incrustador, *m.*

inlet, *s.* entrada, admisión, *f.*; (*geog.*) ensenada, *f.* i. valve, válvula de admisión, *f.*

inmate, *s.* residente, habitante, *m.*; (of hospital) paciente, *m.* and *f.*; enfermo (-ma)

inmost. See **innermost**

inn, *s.* posada, fonda, venta, *f.*, mesón, *m.* Inns of Court, Colegio de Abogados, *m.*

innate, *a.* innato, inherente, instintivo, nativo

innately, *adv.* naturalmente, instintivamente

innavigable, *a.* innavegable

inner, *a.* interior, interno. i. tube (*aut.*) cámara de neumatico, cámara de aire, *f.*

innermost, *a.* más adentro; (*fig.*) más íntimo, más hondo

innings, *s.* (sport) turno, *m.*

innkeeper, *s.* fondista, *m.* and *f.*; tabernero (-ra), mesonero (-ra), posadero (-ra)

innocence, *s.* inocencia, *f.*; pureza, *f.*; (guilelessness) simplicidad, *f.*, candor, *m.*

innocent, *a.* inocente, puro; (guiltless) inocente, inculpable; (foolish) simple, tonto, candoroso, inocentón; (harmless) innocuo. *s.* inocente, *m.* and *f.* Holy Innocents, Santos Inocentes, *m. pl.*

innocently, *adv.* inocentemente

innoculator, *s.* inoculador, *m.*

innocuous, *a.* innocuo, inofensivo

innocuousness, *s.* inocuidad, *f.*

innovate, *v.t.* innovar

innovation, *s.* innovación, *f.*

innovator, *s.* innovador (-ra)

innovatory, *a.* innovador

innuendo, *s.* indirecta, insinuación, *f.*

innumerable, *a.* innumerable, incalculable. i. things, un sinfín de cosas

inobservance, s. inobservancia, f., incumplimiento, m.

inoculate, v.t. inocular

inoculation, s. inoculación, f.

inodorous, a. inodoro

inoffensive, a. inofensivo, innocuo; (of people) pacífico, apacible, manso

inoffensively, adv. inofensivamente

inoffensiveness, s. inocuidad, f.; (of people) mansedumbre, f.

inoperable, a. inoperable

inoperative, a. ineficaz, impracticable, inútil

inopportune, a. inoportuno; intempestivo, inconveniente

inopportunely, adv. inoportunamente, a destiempo

inopportuneness, s. inoportunidad, inconveniencia, f.

inordinate, a. desordenado, excesivo

inordinately, adv. desmedidamente

inorganic, a. inorgánico

inoxidizable, a. inoxidable

inquest, s. (law) indagación, investigación, f.

inquietude, s. inquietud, f., desasosiego, m., agitación, preocupación, f.

inquire, v.t. and v.i. preguntar, averiguar, indagar. **to i. about,** (persons) preguntar por; (things) hacer preguntas sobre. **to i. into,** investigar, examinar, averiguar. **to i. of,** preguntar a. **I. within!** Se dan informaciones.

inquirer, s. indagador (-ra), inquiridor (-ra)

inquiring, a. indagador, inquiridor

inquiringly, adv. interrogativamente

inquiry, s. interrogación, pregunta, f.; indagación, pesquisa, investigación, f.; examen, m. **i. office,** oficina de informaciones, f. **on i.,** al preguntar

inquisition, s. investigación, indagación, f.; inquisición, f. **Holy I.,** Santo Oficio, m., Inquisición, f.

inquisitive, a. curioso, inquiridor; preguntador, impertinente, mirón

inquisitively, adv. con curiosidad. impertinentemente

inquisitiveness, s. curiosidad, f.; impertinencia, f.

Inquisitor, s. (ecc.) inquisidor, m.

inquisitorial, a. inquisitorial, inquisidor

inroad, s. incursión, f.

insalivate, v.t. insalivar

insalivation, s. insalivación, f.

insalubrious, a. malsano, insalubre

insane, a. loco, demente, insano; (senseless) insensato, ridículo. **to become i.,** enloquecer, volverse loco, perder la razón. **to drive i.,** volver a uno el juicio, enloquecer, trastornar. **i. person,** demente, m. and f., loco (-ca)

insanely, adv. locamente

insanitary, a. antihigiénico, malsano

insanity, s. demencia, locura, f.; enloquecimiento, m.; (folly) insensatez, ridiculez, f.

insatiability, s. insaciabilidad, f.

insatiable, a. insaciable

insatiably, adv. insaciablemente

inscribe, v.t. (all meanings) inscribir

inscription, s. inscripción, f.; letrero, m.; (of a book) dedicatoria, f.; (com.) inscripción, anotación, f., asiento, m.

inscrutability, s. enigma, misterio, m.; incomprensibilidad, f.

inscrutable, a. enigmático, insondable, incomprensible, inescrutable

inscrutably, adv. incomprensiblemente, enigmáticamente

insect, s. insecto, m. **i. powder,** polvos insecticidas, m. pl.

insecticide, a. and s. insecticida (m.)

insectivorous, a. insectívoro

insecure, a. inseguro, precario

insecurely, adv. inseguramente

insecurity, s. inseguridad, f.; incertidumbre, inestabilidad, f.

inseminate, v.t. (fig.) implantar; (med.) fecundar

insemination, s. (fig.) implantación, f.; (med.) fecundación, f.

insensate, a. (unfeeling) insensible, insensitivo; (stupid) insensato, sin sentido, necio

insensibility, s. insensibilidad, inconsciencia, f.; (stupor) sopor, letargo, *m.*; impasibilidad, ·indiferencia, *f.*

insensible, *a.* insensible,· inconsciente; indiferente, impasible, duro de corazón; (scarcely noticeable)· imperceptible. **to make i.,** (to sensations) hacer indiferente (a); insensibilizar

insensibly, *adv.* insensiblemente, imperceptiblemente

insensitive, *a.* insensible, insensitivo

insensitiveness, *s.* insensibilidad, *f.*

insentient, *a.* insensible

inseparability, *s.* inseparabilidad, *f.*

inseparable, *a.* inseparable

inseparably, *adv.* inseparablemente

insert, *v.t.* insertar, intercalar; (introduce) meter dentro, introducir, encajar; (in a newspaper) publicar

insertion, *s.* inserción, intercalación, *f.*; (introduction) introducción, *f.*; metimiento, encaje, *m.*; (sew.) entredós, *m.*; (in a newspaper) publicación, *f.*

inshore, *a.* cercano a la orilla. *adv.* cerca de la orilla. **i. fishing,** pesca de arrastre, *f.*

inside, *a.* interior, interno. *adv.* adentro, dentro. *s.* interior, *m.*; (contents) contenido, *m.*; (lining) forro, *m.*; (fam., stomach) entrañas, ·*f. pl.* **to turn i. out,** volver al revés. **to walk on the i. of the pavement,** andar a la derecha de la acera. **from the i.,** desde el interior; por dentro. **on the i.,** por dentro, en el interior. **i. information,** información confidencial, *f.* **i. out,** al revés, de dentro afuera

insidious, *a.* insidioso, engañoso, traidor

insidiously, *adv.* insidiosamente

insidiousness, *s.* insidia, *f.*; engaño, *m.*, traición, *f.*

insight, *s.* percepción, perspicacia, intuición, *f.*

insignia, *s. pl.* insignias, *f. pl.*

insignificance, *s.* insignificancia, futilidad, pequeñez, *f.*

insignificant, *a.* insignificante, fútil, trivial

insincere, *a.* insincero, hipócrita, falso

insincerely, *adv.* falsamente, hipócritamente

insincerity, *s.* insinceridad, hipocresía, falsedad, falta de sinceridad, doblez, *f.*

insinuate, *v.t.* insinuar, introducir; (hint) soltar una indirecta, sugerir; (oneself) insinuarse, introducirse con habilidad

insinuation, *s.* insinuación, introducción, *f.*; (hint) indirecta, *f.*

insipid, *a.* insípido, insulso; (dull) soso

insipidity, *s.* insipidez, insulsez, *f.*, desabor, *m.*; (dullness) sosería, *f.*

insist, *v.i.* insistir; persistir, obstinarse. **to i. on,** insistir en; obstinarse en, hacer hincapié en, aferrarse en (or a)

insistence, *s.* insistencia, *f.*; obstinación, pertinacia, *f.*

insistent, *a.* insistente; porfiado, obstinaz

insistently, *adv.* con insistencia; porfiadamente

insobriety, *s.* falta de sobriedad, *f.*; embriaguez, ebriedad, *f.*

insole, *s.* (of shoes) plantilla, *f.*

insolence, *s.* insolencia, altanería, majadería, frescura, *f.*, atrevimiento, descaro, *m.*

insolent, *a.* insolente, arrogante, atrevido, descarado, desmesurado, fresco

insolently, *adv.* insolentemente, con descaro

insolubility, *s.* insolubilidad, *f.*

insoluble, *a.* insoluble

insolvency, *s.* insolvencia, *f.*

insolvent, *a.* insolvente

insomnia, *s.* insomnio, *m.*

insomuch, *adv.* (gen. with as or that) de modo (que), así (que), de suerte (que)

inspect, *v.t.* examinar, investigar, inspeccionar; (officially) registrar, reconocer

inspection, *s.* inspección, investigación, *f.*; examen, *m.*; (official) reconocimiento, registro, *m.*

inspector, *s.* inspector, *m.*, veedor, interventor, *m.*

inspectorate, *s.* inspectorado, *m.*; cargo de inspector, *m.*

inspiration, s. (of breath) inspiración, aspiración, f.; numen, m., inspiración, vena, f. to find i. in, inspirarse en.

inspire, v.t. (inhale) aspirar, inspirar; (stimulate) animar, alentar, iluminar; (suggest) sugerir, inspirar; infundir. to i. enthusiasm, entusiasmar. to i. hope, dar esperanza, esperanzar

inspired, a. inspirado, intuitivo, iluminado; (of genius) genial

inspirer, s. inspirador (-ra)

inspiring, a. alentador, animador; inspirador

inspirit, v.t. alentar, inspirar, estimular, animar

inspiriting, a. alentador, estimulador

inspissate, v.t. espesar, condensar; (lime, mortar, etc.) encerar

inspissation, s. condensación, f.; (of lime, mortar, etc.) enceramiento, m.

instability, s. inestabilidad, mutabilidad, inconstancia, f.

install, v.t. (all meanings) instalar. to i. oneself, instalarse, establecerse

installation, s. (all meanings) instalación, f.

instalment, s. (of a story) entrega, f.; (com.) plazo, m., cuota, f. by instalments, (com.) a plazos. i. plan, pago a plazos, pago por cuotas, m.

instance, s. ejemplo, caso, m.; (request) solicitación, f., ruego, m.; (law) instancia, f. v.t. citar como ejemplo, mencionar; demostrar, probar. for i., por ejemplo, verbigracia. in that i. . . ., en el caso . . . in the first i., en primer lugar, primero

instant, a. inmediato, urgente; (com.) corriente, actual. s. instante, momento, m.; (fam.) tris, santiamén, m. (com.) the 2nd i., el 2º (segundo) del corriente. this i., (immediately) en seguida

instantaneous, a. instantáneo. (phot.) i. exposure, instantánea, f.

instantaneously, adv. instantáneamente

instantaneousness, s. instantaneidad, f.

instantly, adv. en seguida, al instante, inmediatamente

instead, adv. en cambio; (with of) en vez de, en lugar de

instep, s. empeine, m.

instigate, v.t. instigar, incitar, aguijar, animar, provocar; fomentar

instigating, a. instigador, provocador, fomentador

instigation, s. instigación, incitación, f.; estímulo, m.

instigator, s. instigador (-ra), provocador (-ra), fomentador (-ra)

instil, v.t. instilar; (ideas) inculcar, infundir

instilment, s. inculcación, implantación, insinuación, f.

instinct, s. instinto, m. i. with, imbuido de, lleno de. by i., por instinto, movido por instinto

instinctive, a. instintivo, espontáneo

instinctively, adv. por instinto

institute, v.t. instituir, fundar, establecer; (an inquiry) iniciar, empezar. s. instituto, m.; pl. institutes, (law) instituta, f.

institution, s. (creation) fundación, creación, f.; institución, f., instituto, m.; (beginning) comienzo, m., iniciación, f.; (charitable) asilo, m.; (custom) uso, m., costumbre, tradición, f.

institutional, a. institucional

instruct, v.t. (teach) instruir, enseñar; (order) mandar, dar orden (a)

instruction, s. (teaching) instrucción, enseñanza, f.; pl. instructions, (orders) instrucciones, f. pl., orden, f., mandato, m.

instructive, a. instructivo, instructor, informativo

instructively, adv. instructivamente

instructiveness, s. el carácter informativo, lo instructivo

instructor, s. instructor, preceptor, m.

instrument, s. instrumento, m.; (tool) herramienta, f., utensilio, aparato, m.; (agent) órgano, agente, medio, m.; (law) instrumento, m., escritura, f.; v.t. (mus.) instrumentar. percussion i., instrumento de percusión, m. scientific instruments, instrumentos científicos, *m. pl.* **stringed i.,** instrumento de cuerda, *m.* **wind i.,** instrumento de viento, *m.*

instrumental, *a.* instrumental; influyente. **to be i. in,** contribuir a

instrumentalist, *s.* (*mus.*) instrumentista, *m.*

instrumentality, *s.* mediación, intervención, agencia, *f.,* buenos oficios, *m. pl.*

instrumentation, *s.* (*mus.*) instrumentación, *f.;* mediación, *f.*

insubordinate, *a.* insubordinado, rebelde, desobediente, refractario

insubordination, *s.* insubordinación, rebeldía, desobediencia, *f.*

insubstantial, *a.* irreal; insubstancial

insubstantiality, *s.* irrealidad, *f.;* insubstancialidad, *f.*

insufferable. See **intolerable**

insufficiency, *s.* insuficiencia, falta, carestía, *f.*

insufficient, *a.* insuficiente, falto

insufficiently, *adv.* insuficientemente

insufflate, *v.t.* insuflar

insular, *a.* isleño, insular; (narrowminded) intolerante, iliberal

insularity, *s.* carácter isleño, *m.;* (narrow-mindedness) iliberalidad, intolerancia, *f.*

insulate, *v.t.* aislar

insulating, *a.* aislador. **i. tape,** (*elec.*) cinta aisladora, *f.*

insulation, *s.* aislamiento, *m.*

insulator, *s.* (*elec.*) aislador, *m.*

insulin, *s.* (*med.*) insulina, *f.*

insult, *s.* insulto, agravio, ultraje, *m.,* afrenta, ofensa, *f.* *v.t.* insultar, ofender, afrentar. **He was insulted,** Fué insultado; Se mostró ofendido

insulter, *s.* insultador (-ra)

insulting, *a.* insultante, injurioso, ofensivo. **He was very i. to them,** Les insultó, Les trató con menosprecio

insultingly, *adv.* con insolencia, ofensivamente

insuperability, *s.* dificultades insuperables, *f. pl.,* imposibilidad, *f.,* lo insuperable

insuperable, *a.* insuperable, invencible

insuperably, *adv.* invenciblemente

insupportable, *a.* insoportable, inaguantable, intolerable, insufrible

insupportably, *adv.* insufriblemente, insoportablemente

insurable, *a.* asegurable

insurance, *s.* aseguramiento, *m.;* (*com.*) seguro, *m.;* aseguración, *f.* **accident i.,** seguro contra accidentes, *m.* **fire-i.,** seguro contra incendio, *m.* **life i.,** seguro sobre la vida, *m.* **maritime i.,** seguro marítimo, *m.* **National I. Act,** Ley del Seguro Nacional Obligatorio, *f.* **i. broker,** corredor de seguros, *m.* **i. company,** compañía de seguros, *f.* **i. policy,** póliza de seguros, *f.* **i. premium,** prima de seguros, *f.*

insurant, *s.* asegurado (-da)

insure, *v.t.* (*com.*) asegurar. **to i. oneself,** asegurarse. **the insured,** (person) el asegurado

insurer, *s.* asegurador (-ra)

insurgent, *a.* insurgente, rebelde; (of sea) invasor. *s.* rebelde, *m.* and *f.,* insurrecto (-ta)

insurmountable, *a.* insuperable, invencible, intransitable

insurrection, *s.* insurrección, sublevación, *f.,* levantamiento, *m.*

insurrectionary, *a.* rebelde, amotinado, insurgente

insusceptible, *a.* no susceptible, indiferente, insensible

intact, *a.* intacto, íntegro, indemne

intake, *s.* (of a stocking) menguado, *m.;* (*mech.*) aspiración, *f.;* válvula de admisión, *f.;* (*aer.*) admisión, toma, *f.;* orificio de entrada, *m.*

intangibility, *s.* intangibilidad, *f.*

intangible, *a.* intangible; incomprensible

integer, *s.* (*math.*) número entero, *m.*

integral, *a.* íntegro, intrínseco, inherente; (*math.*) entero. *s.* (*math.*) integral, *f.* **i. calculus,** cálculo integral, *m.*

integrate, *v.t.* integrar, completar; formar en un todo; (*math.*) integrar

integrity, *s.* integridad, honradez, rectitud, entereza, *f.*

integument, s. integumento, tegumento, m.

intellect, s. intelecto, entendimiento, m.

intellectual, a. intelectual, mental. s. pl. **intellectuals,** los intelectuales

intellectualism, s. intelectualismo, m., intelectualidad, f.

intellectually, adv. intelectualmente, mentalmente

intelligence, s. inteligencia, comprensión, mente, f.; (quickness of mind) agudeza, perspicacia, f.; (news) noticia, f., conocimiento, informe, m. **the latest i.,** las últimas noticias. **i. quotient,** cociente de inteligencia, m. **I. Service,** Inteligencia, f.; policía secreta, f. **i. test,** prueba de inteligencia, f.

intelligent, a. inteligente

intelligentsia, s. clase intelectual, intelectualidad, f., (fam.) masa cefálica, f.

intelligibility, s. comprensibilidad, inteligibilidad, f.

intelligible, a. inteligible, comprensible

intelligibly, adv. inteligiblemente

intemperance, s. intemperancia, inmoderación, f.; exceso en la bebida, m.

intemperate, a. intemperante, destemplado, descomedido; inmoderado; bebedor en exceso

intemperately, adv. inmoderadamente

intend, v.t. intentar, proponerse, pensar; destinar, dedicar; (mean) querer decir. **to be intended,** estar destinado; tener por fin; querer decir

intendant, s. intendente, m.

intended, a. pensado, deseado. s. (fam.) novio (-ia), futuro (-ra), prometido (-da)

intense, a. intenso, vivo, fuerte; (of emotions) profundo, hondo, vehemente; (of colours) subido, intenso; (great) extremado, sumo, muy grande

intensely, adv. intensamente

intensification, s. intensificación, f.; aumento, m.

intensify, v.t. intensar, intensificar; aumentar

intensity, s. intensidad, fuerza, f.; (of emotions) profundidad,

vehemencia, violencia, f.; (of colours) intensidad, f.

intensive, a. intensivo

intent, s. intento, propósito, deseo, m. a. atento; (absorbed) absorto, interesado; (on doing) resuelto a, decidido a. **to all intents and purposes,** en efecto, en realidad. **to be i. on,** (reading, etc.) estar absorto en, entregarse a. **with i. to defraud,** con el propósito deliberado de defraudar

intention, s. intención, voluntad, f., propósito, pensamiento, proyecto, m.

intentional, a. intencional, deliberado, premeditado

intentionally, adv. a propósito, intencionalmente, de pensado

intentioned, a. intencionado

intently, adv. atentamente

intentness, s. atención, f.

inter, v.t. enterrar, sepultar

inter, pref. inter, entre. **i.-allied,** interaliado, de los aliados. **i.-denominational,** intersectario. **i.-university,** interuniversitario. **i.-urban,** interurbano

interaction, s. interacción, acción recíproca, acción mutua, f.

intercalate, v.t. intercalar, interpolar

intercede, v.i. interceder, mediar. **to i. for,** hablar por

intercept, v.t. interceptar, detener; entrecoger, atajar

interception, s. interceptación, detención, f.

intercession, s. mediación, intercesión, f.

intercessor, s. intercesor (-ra), mediador (-ra)

interchange, s. intercambio, m.; (of goods) comercio, tráfico, m. v.t. cambiar, trocar; alternar

interchangeable, a. intercambiable

intercolumniation, s. (arch.) intercolumnio, m.

intercommunicate, v.i. comunicarse

intercommunication, s. comunicación mutua, f.; comercio, m.

intercostal, a. (anat.) intercostal

intercourse, s. (social) trato, m., relaciones, f. pl.; (com.) comercio, tráfico, *m.*; (of ideas) inter-cámbio, *m.*; (sexual) coito, trato sexual, *m.*

intercutaneous, *a.* intercutáneo

interdependence, *s.* dependencia mutua, mutualidad, *f.*

interdependent, *a.* mutuo

interdict, *s.* interdicto, veto, *m.*, prohibición, *f.*; (*ecc.*) entredicho, *m. v.t.* interdecir, prohibir, privar; *(ecc.)* poner entredicho

interdiction, *s.* interdicción, prohibición, *f.*

interest, *s.* interés, *m.*; provecho, *m.*; (*com.*) premio, rédito, interés, *m.*; (in a firm) participación, *f.*; (curiosity) interés, *m.*; curiosidad, *f.*; simpatía, *f.*; (influence) influencia, *f. s. pl.* **interests**, (commercial undertakings) empresas, *f. pl.*, intereses, negocios, *m. pl. v.t.* interesar. **to be interested in**, interesarse en, (on behalf of) por. **to be in one's own i.**, ser en provecho de uno, ser en su propio interés. **to bear eight per cent. i.**, dar interés del ocho por ciento. **to pay with i.**, pagar con creces. **to put out at i.**, dar a interés. **in the interests of**, en interés de. **compound i.**, interés compuesto, *m.* **simple i.**, interés sencillo, *m.* **vested interests**, intereses creados, *m. pl.*

interesting, *a.* interesante, curioso, atractivo

interestingly, *adv.* amenamente, de modo interesante

interfere, *v.i.* intervenir, meterse, entremeterse; mezclarse; (*fam.*) mangonear, meter las narices; (with) meterse con; (impede) estorbar, impedir

interference, *s.* intervención, *f.*, entrometimiento, *m.*; (obstacle) estorbo, obstáculo, *m.*; (*phys.*) interferencia, *f.*; (*rad.*) parásitos, *m. pl.*

interfering, *a.* entremetido, oficioso; (*fam.*) mangoneador

interim, *s.* ínterin, intermedio, *m. a.* interino, provisional. **in the i.**, entre tanto, en el ínterin. (*com.*) **i. dividend**, dividendo interino, *m.*

interior, *a.* interior, interno; doméstico. *s.* interior, *m.*

interject, *v.t.* interponer

interjection, *s.* exclamación, interjección, *f.*; interposición, *f.*

interlace, *v.t.* entrelazar, entretejer

interleave, *v.t.* interfoliar, interpaginar

interline, *v.t.* entrerrenglonar, interlinear

interlinear, *a.* interlineal

interlineation, *s.* interlineación, *f.*

interlining, *s.* entretela, *f.*

interlock, *v.t.* (of wheels, etc.) endentar; trabar; cerrar. *v.i.* endentarse; entrelazarse, unirse; cerrar

interlocutor, *s.* interlocutor (-ra)

interloper, *s.* intruso (-sa); (*com.*) intérlope, *m.*

interloping, *a.* intérlope

interlude, *s.* intervalo, intermedio, *m.*; (*mus.*) interludio, *m.*; (*theat.*) entremés, *m.*

intermarriage, *s.* casamiento entre parientes próximos o entre razas distintas, *m.*

intermarry, *v.i.* contraer matrimonio parientes próximos o personas de razas distintas

intermediary, *a. and s.* intermediario (-ia)

intermediate, *a.* intermedio, medio, medianero. *s.* sustancia intermedia, *f. v.i.* intervenir, mediar

interment, *s.* entierro, funeral, *m.*

intermezzo, *s.* (*theat.*) intermedio, *m.*; (*mus.*) intermezzo, *m.*

interminable, *a.* interminable, inacabable

interminably, *adv.* interminablemente, sin fin, sin cesar

intermingle, *v.t.* entremezclar, entreverar. *v.i.* mezclarse

intermission, *s.* intermisión, interrupción, pausa, *f.*; (*theat.*) entreacto, *m.* **without i.**, sin pausa, sin tregua

intermittence, *s.* intermitencia, alternación, *f.*

intermittent, *a.* intermitente, discontinuo; (of fever) intermitente

intermittently, *adv.* a intervalos, a ratos, a pausas

intern, *s.* (*med.*) practicante de hospital, *m.*, interno (-na). *v.t.* confinar, encerrar

internal, *a.* interno, interior; (of affairs) doméstico, civil; intrínseco; íntimo. **i.-combustion engine,** motor de combustión interna, *m.*

internally, *adv.* interiormente

international, *a.* internacional. *s.* (*sport*) un partido internacional. **i. law,** derecho internacional, *m.*

internationalism, *s.* internacionalismo, *m.*

internationalist, *s.* internacionalista, *m.* and *f.*

internationalization, *s.* internacionalización, *f.*

internationalize, *v.t.* hacer internacional, poner bajo un control internacional

internecine, *a.* sanguinario, feroz

internee, *s.* internado (-da)

internment, *s.* internamiento, *m.* **i. camp,** campo de internamiento, *m.*

internode, *s.* internodio, cañuto, *m.*

interoceanic, *a.* interoceánico

interpolate, *v.t.* interpolar, intercalar, interponer

interpolation, *s.* interpolación, inserción, añadidura, *f.*

interpolator, *s.* interpolador (-ra)

interpose, *v.t.* interponer; (a remark) interpolar. *v.i.* interponerse, intervenir; (interfere) entrometerse; interrumpir

interposition, *s.* interposición, *f.*; entrometimiento, *m.*

interpret, *v.t.* interpretar; (translate) traducir; (explain) explicar, descifrar. *v.i.* interpretar.

interpretation, *s.* interpretación, *f.*; (translation) traducción, *f.*; (explanation) explicación, *f.*

interpretative, *a.* interpretativo, interpretador

interpreter, *s.* intérprete, *m.* and *f.*

interregnum, *s.* interregno, *m.*

interrelation, *s.* relación mutua, *f.*

interrogate, *v.t.* interrogar, examinar, preguntar

interrogating, *a.* interrogante

interrogation, *s.* interrogación, *f.*, examen, *m.*; pregunta, *f.* **mark of i.,** punto de interrogación, *m.*

interrogative, *a.* interrogativo. *s.* palabra interrogativa, *f.*

interrogatively, *adv.* interrogativamente

interrogator, *s.* examinador (-ra), interrogador (-ra)

interrogatory, *a.* interrogativo. *s.* interrogatorio, *m.*

interrupt, *v.t.* interrumpir

interruptedly, *adv.* interrumpidamente

interrupter, *s.* interruptor (-ra); (*elec.*) interruptor, *m.*

interruption, *s.* interrupción, *f.*

intersect, *v.t.* cruzar. *v.i.* cruzarse, intersecarse

intersection, *s.* intersección, *f.*; cruce, *m.*

intersperse, *v.t.* diseminar, esparcir; interpolar, entremezclar

interstice, *s.* intervalo, intermedio, *m.*; (chink) intersticio, *m.*, hendedura, *f.*

intertropical, *a.* intertropical

intertwine, *v.t.* entretejer, entrelazar. *v.i.* entrelazarse

interval, *s.* intervalo, intermedio, *m.*, pausa, *f.*; (*theat.*) entreacto, *m.*, intermisión, *f.*; (in schools) recreo, *m.* **at intervals,** a trechos, de vez en cuando. **lucid i.,** intervalo lúcido, *m.*

intervene, *v.i.* intervenir, tomar parte (en); mediar; (occur) sobrevenir, acaecer; (law) interponerse

intervening, *a.* intermedio; interventor

intervention, *s.* intervención, mediación, *f.*

interventionist, *s.* (*pol.*) partidario (-ia) de la intervención

interview, *s.* entrevista, *f.*, interviev, *m.* *v.t.* entrevistarse con

interviewer, *s.* interrogador (-ra); (reporter) reportero, periodista, *m.*

intervocalic, *a.* intervocálico

interweave, *v.t.* entretejer, entrelazar

interweaving, *s.* entretejimiento, *m.*

intestacy, *s.* ausencia de un testamento, *f.*

intestate, *a.* and *s.* intestado (-da)

intestinal, *a.* intestinal, intestino. **i. worm,** lombriz intestinal, *f.*

intestine, *s.* intestino, *m.* **large i.,** intestino grueso, *m.* **small i.,** intestino delgado, *m.*

intimacy, *s.* intimidad, *f.*, familiaridad, *f.*; (of princes) privanza, *f.*

intimate, *a.* íntimo; (of relations) entrañable, estrecho; intrínseco, esencial; (of knowledge) profundo, completo, detallado. *s.* amigo (-ga) de confianza. *v.t.* intimar, dar a entender, indicar. **to become i.**, intimarse. **to be on i. terms with**, tratar de tú (a), ser amigo íntimo de

intimately, *adv.* íntimamente, al fondo

intimation, *s.* intimación, indicación, *f.*; (hint) insinuación, indirecta, *f.*

intimidate, *v.t.* intimidar, aterrar, infundir miedo (a), espantar, acobardar, amedrentar

intimidation, *s.* intimidación, *f.*

intimidatory, *a.* aterrador, amenazador

into, *prep.* en; a, al, a la; dentro, adentro; (of transforming, forming, etc.) en. **Come i. the park (the town)**, Venga usted al parque (a la ciudad). **Throw it i. the fire**, Échalo al (or en el) fuego. **She went i. the house**, Ella entró dentro de la casa. **to look i.**, mirar dentro de; mirar hacia el interior (de); investigar

intolerable, *a.* intolerable, insufrible, inaguantable, insoportable, inllevable

intolerableness, *s.* intolerabilidad, *f.*

intolerably, *adv.* intolerablemente, insufriblemente

intolerance, *s.* intolerancia, intransigencia, *f.*

intolerant, *a.* intolerante, intransigente; (med.) intolerante

intonation, *s.* entonación, *f.*

intone, *v.t.* entonar; (ecc.) salmodiar

intoxicant, *a.* embriagador. *s.* bebida alcohólica, *f.*

intoxicate, *v.t.* emborrachar, embriagar; (med.) intoxicar, envenenar; (excite) embriagar, embelesar

intoxicated, *a.* borracho; (excited) ebrio, embriagado; (med.) intoxicado

intoxicating, *a.* embriagador

intoxication, *s.* borrachera, embriaguez, *f.*; (med.) intoxicación, *f.*, envenenamiento, *m.*; (excitement) entusiasmo, *m.*, ebriedad, *f.*

intractability, *s.* insociabilidad, hurañería, *f.*

intractable, *a.* intratable, insociable, huraño

intrados, *s.* (arch.) intradós, *m.*

intramural, *adv.* intramuros

intransigence, *s.* intransigencia, intolerancia, *f.*

intransigent, *a.* intransigente, intolerante

intransitive, *a.* intransitivo, neutro

intra-uterine, *a.* (med.) intrauterino

intravenous, *a.* (med.) intravenoso

intrepid, *a.* intrépido, osado, audaz

intrepidity, *s.* intrepidez, osadía, audacia, *f.*

intrepidly, *adv.* intrépidamente, audazmente

intricacy, *s.* intrincación, complejidad, *f.*

intricate, *a.* intrincado, complejo

intricately, *adv.* intrincadamente

intrigue, *s.* intriga, maquinación, *f.*, enredo, *m.*; (amorous) lío, *m. v.i.* intrigar, enredar; (amorous) tener un lío. *v.t.* (interest) atraer, interesar; (with) intrigar con

intriguer, *s.* intrigante, *m.* and *f.*, urdemalas, *m.*, enredador (-ra)

intriguing, *a.* enredador; (attractive) atrayente, interesante, seductor

intrinsic, *a.* intrínseco, innato, inherente, esencial

intrinsically, *adv.* intrínsecamente, esencialmente

introduce, *v.t.* introducir; hacer entrar; insertar, injerir; (a person) presentar; poner de moda, introducir; (a bill) presentar; (a person to a thing) llamar la atención sobre. **Permit me to i. my friend**, Permítame que le presente mi amigo

introducer, *s.* introductor (-ra)

introduction, *s.* introducción, *f.*; (of a book) prefacio, prólogo, *m.*, advertencia, *f.*; (of a person) presentación, *f.*; inserción, *f.*

introductory, *a.* introductor, preliminar, preparatorio

introit, *s.* introito, *m.*

intromission, *s.* intromisión, *f.*

introspection, *s.* introspección, *f.*

introspective, *a.* introspectivo·

introversion, *s.* (*psy.*) introversión, *f.*

introvert, *a.* and *s.* (*psy.*) introverso (-sa)

intrude, *v.t.* introducir, imponer. *v.i.* entremeterse, inmiscuirse. Do I i. ? ¿ Estorbo ?

intruder, *s.* intruso (-sa)

intrusion, *s.* intrusión, *f.*; (*geol.*) intromisión, *f.*

intrusive, *a.* intruso

intubate, *v.t.* (*surg.*) intubar

intubation, *s.* (*surg.*) intubación, *f.*

intuition, *s.* intuición, *f.* to know by i., intuir, saber por intuición

intuitive, *a.* intuitivo

intumescence, *s.* intumescencia, *f.*

intumescent, *a.* intumescente

inulin, *s.* (*chem.*) inulina, *f.*

inundate, *v.t.* inundar, anegar; (*fig.*) abrumar

inundation, *s.* inundación, anegación, *f.*; (*fig.*) diluvio, *m.*, abundancia, *f.*

inure, *v.t.* endurecer, habituar

inurement, *s.* habituación, *f.*

invade, *v.t.* invadir, irrumpir, asaltar; (*med.*) invadir

invader, *s.* invasor (-ra), acometedor (-ra), agresor (-ra)

invading, *a.* invasor, irruptor

invagination, *s.* invaginación, *f.*

invalid, *a.* inválido, nulo. to become i., caducar

invalid, *s.* inválido (-da), enfermo (-ma). to become an i., quedarse inválido. to i. out of the army, licenciar por invalidez. i. carriage, cochecillo de inválido, *m.*

invalidate, *v.t.* invalidar, anular

invalidation, *s.* invalidación, *f.*

invalidity, *s.* invalidez, nulidad, *f.*

invaluable, *s.* inestimable

invariability, *s.* invariabilidad, invariación, inalterabilidad, inmutabilidad, *f.*

invariable, *a.* invariable, inmutable, inalterable

invariably, *adv.* invariablemente, inmutablemente

invariant, *s.* (*math.*) invariante, *m.*

invasion, *s.* invasión, irrupción, *f.*; (*med.*) invasión, *f.*

invective, *s.* invectiva, diatriba, *f.*

inveigh (against), *v.i.* desencadenarse (contra), prorrumpir en invectivas (contra)

inveigle, *v.t.* seducir, engatusar, persuadir

inveiglement, *s.* seducción, persuasión, *f.*

invent, *v.t.* inventar, descubrir, originar; (a falsehood) fingir; (create) idear, componer

invention, *s.* invención, *f.*, invento, descubrimiento, *m.*; (imagination) ingeniosidad, inventiva, *f.*; (falsehood) ficción, mentira, *f.*; (finding) invención, *f.*, hallazgo, *m.*

inventive, *a.* inventor, inventivo; ingenioso, despejado

inventiveness, *s.* inventiva, *f.*

inventor, *s.* inventor (-ra), autor (-ra)

inventory, *s.* inventario, *m.*; descripción, *f.* *v.t.* inventariar

inverse, *a.* inverso. i. proportion, razón inversa, *f.*

inversely, *adv.* inversamente, a la inversa

inversion, *s.* inversión, *f.*, trastrocamiento, *m.*; (*gram.*) hipérbaton, *m.*

invert, *v.t.* invertir, trastornar, trastrocar. inverted commas, comillas, *f. pl.*

invertebrate, *a.* and *s.* invertebrado (*m.*)

invest, *v.t.* (*com.*) invertir; (*mil.*) sitiar, cercar; (foll. by with) poner, cubrir con; (of qualities) conferir, otorgar, dar. *v.i.* (with in) poner dinero en, echar caudal en; (*fam.*) comprar

investigable, *a.* averiguable

investigate, *v.t.* investigar, estudiar; examinar, averiguar; explorar

investigation, *s.* investigación, *f.*, estudio, *m.*; examen, *m.*, averiguación, *f.*; encuesta, pesquisa, *f.*

investigator, *s.* investigador (-ra) averiguador (-ra)

investigatory, *a.* investigador

investiture, *s.* investidura, instalación, *f.*

investment, *s.* (*com.*, of money)
inversión, *f.*, empleo, *m.*; (*mil.*)
cerco, *m.*; (investiture) instalación, *f.*; *pl.* investments, (*com.*)
acciones, *f. pl.*, fondos, *m. pl.*

investor, *s.* inversionista, *m.*;
accionista, *m.* and *f.*

inveteracy, *s.* antigüedad, *f.*, lo
arraigado

inveterate, *a.* inveterado, antiguo,
arraigado, incurable

invidious, *a.* odioso, repugnante,
injusto

invidiousness, *s.* injusticia, *f.*,
lo odioso

invigorate, *v.t.* vigorizar, dar
fuerza (a), avivar

invigorating, *a.* fortaleciente,
fortificador, vigorizador

invincibility, *s.* invencibilidad, *f.*

invincible, *a.* invencible, indomable; (*fig.*) insuperable

invincibly, *adv.* invenciblemente

inviolability, *s.* inviolabilidad, *f.*

inviolable, *a.* inviolable

inviolate, *a.* inviolado

invisibility, *s.* invisibilidad, *f.*

invisible, *a.* invisible. i. ink,
tinta simpática, *f.* i. mending,
zurcido invisible, *m.*

invisibly, *adv.* invisiblemente

invitation, *s.* invitación, *f.*; convite, *m.*; (card) tarjeta de invitación, *f.*

invite, *v.t.* invitar, convidar;
(request) pedir, rogar; (of things)
incitar, tentar. to i. to dance,
sacar a bailar

inviting, *a.* atrayente, incitante;
(of food) apetitoso; (of looks)
provocativo

invocation, *s.* invocación, *f.*

invocatory, *a.* invocatorio, invocador

invoice, *s.* (*com.*) factura, *f.*
v.t. facturar. proforma i.,
factura simulada, *f.* shipping
i., factura de expedición, *f.*
i. book, libro de facturas, *m.*

invoke, *v.t.* invocar; suplicar,
implorar; (*laws*) acogerse (a)

involucre, *s.* (*bot.*) involucro,
m.

involuntarily, *adv.* sin querer,
involuntariamente

involuntariness, *s.* involuntariedad, *f.*

involuntary, *a.* involuntario; instintivo, inconsciente

involve, *v.t.* (entangle) enredar,
embrollar, enmarañar; (implicate) comprometer; (imply) implicar, ocasionar, traer consigo

involved, *a.* complejo, intrincado; (of style) confuso, obscuro

invulnerability, *s.* invulnerabilidad, *f.*

invulnerable, *a.* invulnerable

inward, *a.* interior, interno;
íntimo, espiritual

inwardly, *adv.* interiormente;
para sí, entre sí

inwards, *adv.* hacia dentro;
adentro

iodide, *s.* (*chem.*) yoduro, *m.*

iodine, *s.* yodo, *m.* i. poisoning,
yodismo, *m.*

iodoform, *s.* yodoformo, *m.*

ion, *s.* (*chem.*) ion, *m.*

Ionian, *a.* and *s.* jónico (-ca)

Ionic, *a.* jónico. i. foot (*poet.*)
jónico, *m.*

iota, *s.* (letter) iota, *f.*; jota,
pizca, *f.*, ápice, *m.* not an i.,
ni pizca

I.O.U. *s.* (*com.*) abonaré, *m.*

ipecacuanha, *s.* ipecacuana, *f.*

Iranian, *a.* and *s.* iranio (-ia)
(Asia)

irascibility, *s.* irascibilidad,
iracundia, irritabilidad, *f.*

irascible, *a.* irascible, iracundo,
irritable

irate, *a.* airado, colérico, enojado

ire, *s.* ira, cólera, furia, *f.*

iridescence, *s.* iridiscencia, *f.*

iridescent, *a.* iridiscente. to
look i., irisar, tornasolarse

iridium, *s.* (*chem.*) iridio, *m.*

iris, *s.* (*anat.*) iris, *m.*; (*bot.*)
irídea, *f.*

Irish, *a.* and *s.* irlandés (-esa).
the I., los irlandeses

irksome, *a.* fastidioso, tedioso,
aburrido

irksomeness, *s.* tedio, fastidio,
aburrimiento, *m.*

iron, *s.* hierro, *m.*; (for clothes)
plancha, *f.*; (tool) utensilio, *m.*,
herramienta, *f.*; (golf) hierro,
m.; *pl.* irons, grillos, *m. pl.*,
cadenas, *f. pl.* *a.* de hierro,
férreo; (*fig.*) duro, severo. *v.t.*
(linen) planchar; (with out)
allanar. to have too many
irons in the fire, tener demasia-

dos asuntos entre manos. **to put in irons,** echar grillos (a). **to strike while the i. is hot,** A hierro caliente batir de repente. **cast-i.,** hierro colado, *m.* **scrap i.,** hierro viejo, *m.* **sheet i.,** hierro en planchas, *m.* **wrought i.,** hierro dulce, *m.* **i. age,** edad de hierro, *f.* **i.-foundry,** fundición de hierro, *f.* **i. lung,** (*med.*) pulmón de hierro, *m.* **i.-mould,** mancha de orín, *f.* **i. smelting furnace,** alto horno, *m.* **i. tonic,** (*med.*) reconstituyente ferruginoso, *m.* **i. will,** voluntad de hierro, *f.*

ironclad, *a.* blindado, acorazado. *s.* buque de guerra blindado, acorazado, *m.*

ironer, *s.* planchador·(-ra)

ironical, *a.* irónico

ironically, *adv.* con ironía, irónicamente

ironing, *s.* planchado, *m.*; ropa por planchar, *f.* *a.* de planchar. **i. board,** tabla de planchar, *f.*

ironist, *s.* ironista, *m.* and *f.*

ironmonger, *s.* ferretero (-ra). **ironmonger's shop,** ferretería, *f.*

ironmongery, *s.* ferretería, quincallería, *f.*

ironwork, *s.* herraje, *m.*; obra de hierro, *f.*

ironworks, *s.* herrería, *f.*

irony, *s.* ironía, *f.* *a.* (like iron) ferrugiento

Iroquois, *a.* and *s.* iroqués (-esa) (Indians)

irradiate, *v.t.* irradiar; (*fig.*) iluminar, aclarar

irradiation, *s.* irradiación, *f.*; (*fig.*) iluminación, *f.*

irrational, *a.* ilógico, ridículo, irracional

irrationality, *s.* irracionalidad, *f.*

irreclaimable, *a.* irrecuperable, irredimible; (of land) inservible, improductivo; irreformable

irreconcilable, *a.* irreconciliable

irreconcilably, *adv.* irremediablemente

irrecoverable, *a.* irrecuperable, incobrable

irredeemable, *a.* irredimible, perdido. **i. government loan,** deuda perpetua, *f.*

irredeemably, *adv.* perdidamente

irreducible, *a.* irreducible

irrefutability, *s.* verdad, *f.*

irrefutable, *a.* irrefutable, indisputable, innegable, irrebatible

irrefutably, *adv.* irrefutablemente

irregular, *a.* irregular; anormal; (of shape) disforme; desordenado; (*gram.*) irregular; (of surface) desigual, escabroso

irregularity, *s.* irregularidad,·*f.*; anormalidad, *f.*; (of shape) desproporción, irregularidad, *f.*; (of surface) escabrosidad, desigualdad, *f.*; exceso, *m.*, demasía, *f.*

irregularly, *adv.* irregularmente

irrelevance, *s.* inconexión, *f.*; inoportunidad, *f.*; futilidad, poca importancia, *f.*; (stupidity) desatino, *m.*, impertinencia, *f.*

irrelevant, *a.* inaplicable, fuera de propósito; inoportuno; sin importancia, fútil; (stupid) impertinente

irreligion, *s.* irreligión, impiedad, *f.*

irreligious, *a.* irreligioso, impío

irremediable, *a.* irremediable, irreparable

irremediably, *adv.* sin remedio, irremediablemente

irreparable, *a.* irreparable

irreparably, *adv.* irreparablemente

irreplaceable, *a.* irreemplazable

irrepressible, *a.* incontrolable, indomable

irreproachable, *a.* irreprochable, intachable

irreproachably, *adv.* irreprochablemente

irresistible, *a.* irresistible

irresistibleness, *s.* superioridad, *f.*

irresistibly, *adv.* irresistiblemente

irresolute, *a.* irresoluto, indeciso, vacilante

irresoluteness, *s.* irresolución, indecisión, *f.*

irrespective, *a.* (with of) independiente de, aparte de, sin distinción de

irresponsibility, *s.* irresponsabilidad, *f.*

irresponsible, *a.* irresponsable

irretrievable, *a.* irrecuperable

irretrievably, *adv.* irreparablemente, sin remedio

irreverence, s. irreverencia, f.
irreverent, a. irreverente, irrespetuoso
irrevocability, s. irrevocabilidad, f.
irrevocable, a. irrevocable; inquebrantable
irrevocably, adv. irrevocablemente
irrigable, a. regadío
irrigate, v.t. (agr.) regar; (med.) irrigar
irrigation, s. (agr.) riego, m.; (med.) irrigación, f. **i. channel,** cacera, acequia, f., canal de riego, m.
irritability, s. irritabilidad, iracundia, f.
irritable, a. irritable, irascible, iracundo
irritably, adv. con irritación; airadamente
irritant, a. irritante, irritador. s. irritador, m.; (med.) medicamento irritante, m.
irritate, v.t. provocar, estimular; irritar, molestar, exasperar; (med.) irritar
irritating, a. irritador, irritante
irritatingly, adv. de un modo irritante
irritation, s. irritación, f., enojo, m.; (physiol.) picazón, f., picor, m.
irruption, s. irrupción, invasión, f.
Ishmaelite, q. and s. ismaelita (m. and f.)
isinglass, s. cola de pescado, f.
Islamic, a. islámico
Islamism, s. islamismo, m.
Islamite, a. and s. islamita (m. and f.)
island, s. isla, f. a. isleño
islander, s. isleño (-ña)
islet, s. isleta, f.; islote, m.
isobaric, a. isobárico
isochromatic, a. isocromático
isochronism, s. isocronismo, m.
isolate, v.t. aislar, apartar
isolated, a. aislado, apartado, solitario; único, solo
isolation, s. aislamiento, apartamiento, m., soledad, f.
isolationism, s. (pol.) islacionismo, m.
isolationist, a. and s. (pol.) islacionista, aislacionista (m. and f.)
isomeric, a. (chem.) isomero

isomerism, s. (chem.) isomería, f.
isometric, a. isométrico
isomorphic, a. isomorfo
isosceles, a. isósceles
isothermal, a. isotermo
isotope, s. isotope, isotopo, m.
Israelite, a. and s. israelita (m. and f.)
issue, s. salida, f.; (result) resultado, m., consecuencia, f.; (of a periodical) número, m.; (print.) edición, tirada, f.; (offspring) prole, sucesión, f.; (of notes, bonds) emisión, f.; (med.) flujo, m.; cuestión, f., problema, m. v.i. salir, fluir, manar; nacer, originarse; resultar, terminarse. v.t. (an order) expedir, emitir, dictar; publicar, dar a luz; (of notes, bonds) poner en circulación, librar. **at i.,** en disputa, en cuestión. **to join i.,** llevar la contraria, oponer
isthmian, a. ístmico
isthmus, s. istmo, m.
it, pron. (as subject) él, m.; ella, f.; (gen. omitted with all verbs in Sp.); (as object) lo, m.; la, f.; (as indirect object) le (se with an object in 3rd pers.); (meaning that thing, that affair) eso, ello. Sometimes omitted in other cases, e.g. **He has thought it necessary to stay at home,** Ha creído necesario de quedarse en casa. **We heard it said that . . . ,** Oímos decir que . . . , s. (slang) garbo, aquél, m.; atractivos, m. pl. **Is it not so?** ¿No es así? **That is it,** Eso es. **It is I,** Soy yo
Italian, a. and s. italiano (-na) (language) italiano, m. (art) I. **School,** escuela italiana, f.
Italianism, s. italianismo, m.
Italianize, v.t. italianizar
italic, a. (of Italy) itálico; (print.) itálico, bastardillo. s. letra bastardilla, bastardilla, letra itálica, f.
italicize, v.t. imprimir en bastardilla; dar énfasis (a)
itch, s. sarna, f.; (fig.) picazón, f.; prurito, capricho, m. v.i. picar; (fig.) sentir picazón; (with to) rabiar por, suspirar por.
itching, s. picazón, f., picor, m. a. sarnoso, picante; (med.) pru-

riginoso. **to have an i. palm**, (*fig.*) ser de la virgen del puño

item, *s.* ítem, artículo, *m.*; (*com.*) partida, *f.*; punto, detalle, *m.*; (of a programme) número, *m.*; asunto, *m.* *adv.* ítem

iterate, *v.t.* iterar, repetir

iteration, *s.* iteración, repetición, *f.*

iterative, *a.* iterativo

itinerant, *a.* nómada, errante

itinerary, *s.* itinerario, *m.*, ruta, *f.*

its, *poss. a.* su (with pl. obj.) sus. **a book and its pages**, un libro y sus páginas.

itself, *pron.* él mismo, *m.*; ella misma, *f.*; (with prep.) sí; (with reflex. verb) se; (with noun) el mismo, la misma; (meaning alone) solo. **in i.**, en sí

ivied, *a.* cubierto de hiedra

ivory, *s.* marfil, *m.* *a.* ebúrneo, de marfil, marfileño. **vegetable i.**, marfil vegetal, *m.* **i. carving**, talla de marfil, *f.*

ivy, *s.* hiedra, *f.*

J

J, *s.* (letter) jota, *f.*

jab, *v.t.* (with a hypodermic needle, etc.) pinchar; introducir (en); clavar (con); (scrape) hurgar; (place) poner. *s.* pinchazo, *m.*; golpe, *m.* **He jabbed his pistol in my ribs**, Me puso la pistola en las costillas

jabber, *v.t. and v.i.* chapurrear; (of monkeys) chillar

jabbering, *s.* chapurreo, *m.*; (of monkeys) chillidos, *m. pl.*

jabot, *s.* chorrera, *f.*

jacinth, *s.* jacinto, *m.*

Jack, *s.* Juan, *m.*; (man) hombre, *m.*; (sailor) marinero, *m.*; (in cards) sota, *f.*; (for raising weights) gato, *m.*; (of a spit) torno, *m.*; (of some animals) macho, *m.*; (bowls) boliche, *m.* *v.t.* (with up) solevantar con gatos. **Union J.**, pabellón británico, *m.* **j.-boot**, bota de montar, *f.* **J.-in-office**, mandarín, funcionario impertinente, *m.* **J.-in-the-box**, faca, *f.* **j.-knife**, navaja, *f.* **J. of all trades**, hombre de muchos oficios, *m.*

j.-rabbit, liebre americana, *f.* **J.-tar**, marinero, *m.*

jackal, *s.* chacal, adive, *m.*

jackanapes, *s.* impertinente, *m.*; mequetrefe, *m.*

jackass, *s.* asno, *m.*; (fool) tonto, asno, *m.* **laughing j.**, martín pescador, *m.*

jackdaw, *s.* chova, *f.*

jacket, *s.* chaqueta, *f.*; americana, *f.*; (for boilers, etc.) camisa, *f.*; (of a book) sobrecubierta, *f.* **strait j.**, camisa de fuerza, *f.*

Jacobin, *s.* jacobino (-na)

Jacobinism, *s.* jacobinismo, *m.*

jade, *s.* (*min.*) jade, *m.*; (horse) rocín, *m.*; (woman) mala pécora, *f.*; (saucy wench) mozuela, picaruela, *f.*

jaded, *a.* fatigado, agotado, rendido; (of the palate) saciado

jagged, *a.* dentado

jaguar, *s.* jaguar, *m.*

jail. See **gaol**

jalousie, *s.* celosía, *f.*

jam, *v.t.* (ram) apretar; apiñar; estrujar; (a machine) atascar; (radio) causar interferencia (a); (preserve) hacer confitura de. *v.i.* atascarse. *s.* (of people) agolpamiento, *m.*; (traffic) atasco, *m.*; (preserve) confitura, mermelada, compota, *f.* **He jammed his hat on**, Se encasquetó el sombrero. **He jammed the brakes on suddenly**, Frenó de repente. **jam-dish**, compotera, *f.* **jam-jar**, pote para confitura, *m.*

Jamaican, *a.* jamaicano, de Jamaica. *s.* jamaicano (-na)

jamb, *s.* jamba, *f.*

jamming, *s.* (*rad.*) interferencias, *f. pl.*

jangle, *v.i.* cencerrear; chocar; rechinar. *s.* cencerreo, *m.*; choque, *m.*; rechinamiento, *m.*

janissary, *s.* jenízaro, *m.*

janitor, *s.* portero, *m.*; (in a university, etc.) bedel, *m.*

Jansenism, *s.* jansenismo, *m.*

Jansenist, *a. and s.* jansenista (*m. and f.*)

January, *s.* enero, *m.*

japan, *s.* charol, *m.* *v.t.* charolar

Japanese, *a.* japonés. *s.* japonés (-esa); (language) japonés, *m.*

japonica, *s.* camelia japonesa, *f.*

jar, s. chirrido, m.; choque, m.;. sacudida, f.; vibración, trepidación, f.; (quarrel) riña, f.; (receptacle) jarra, f.; (for tobacco, honey, cosmetics, etc.) pote, m.; (Leyden) botella (de Leyden), f. v.i. chirriar; vibrar, trepidar; chocar; (of sounds) ser discorde; (of colours) chillar. v.t. sacudir; hacer vibrar. It jarred on my nerves, Me atacaba los nervios. It gave me a nasty jar, (fig.) Me hizo una impresión desagradable. on the jar, entreabierto

jardinière, s. jardinera, f.

jargon, s. jerga, jerigonza, f.; monserga, f.; (technical) lenguaje especial, m.

jarring, a. discorde, disonante; en conflicto, opuesto; (to the nerves) que ataca a los nervios

jasmine, s. jazmín, m. yellow j., jazmín amarillo, m.

jasper, s. (min.) jaspe, m.

jaundice, s. ictericia, f.

jaundiced, a. envidioso; desengañado, desilusionado

jaunt, s. excursión, f. v.i. ir de excursión

jauntily, adv. airosamente, con garbo

jauntiness, s. garbo, m., gentileza, ligereza, f.

jaunty, a. garboso, airoso

Javanese, a. javanés. s. javanés (-esa)

javelin, s. jabalina, f. j. throwing, lanzamiento de la jabalina, m.

jaw, s. quijada, f.; maxilar, m.; pl., jaws, boca, f.; (of death, etc.) garras, f. pl.; (mech.) quijada, f.; (narrow entrance) boca, abertura, f. jaw-bone, mandíbula, f.; (anat.) hueso maxilar, m.

jay, s. arrendajo, m.

jazz, s. jazz, m. v.i. bailar el jazz. j. band, orquesta de jazz, f.

jealous, a. celoso; envidioso. to be j. of, tener celos de. to make j., dar celos (a)

jealously, adv. celosamente

jealousy, s. celos, m. pl.

jeep, s. (mil.) jip, m.

jeer, s. burla, mofa, f.; insulto, m. v.i. burlarse; (with at) mofarse de

jeerer, s. mofador (-ra)

jeering, a. mofador. s. burlas, f. pl.; insultos, m. pl.

jeeringly, adv. burlonamente

jellied, a. en gelatina

jelly, s. jalea, f.; gelatina, f. v.i. solidificarse. j.-bag, manga, f. j.-fish, medusa, f.

jemmy, s. palanqueta, f., pie de cabra, m.

jennet, s. jinete, m., jaca española, f.

jenny, s. (crane) grúa locomóvil, f.; (weaving) torno, m. j.-wren, (orn.) reyezuelo, m.

jeopardize, v.t. arriesgar; comprometer

jeopardy, s. peligro, m.

jeremiad, s. jeremiada, f.

jerk, s. sacudida, f. v.t. sacudir, dar una sacudida (a); lanzar bruscamente; (pull) tirar de; (push) empujar. v.i. moverse a sacudidas. I jerked myself free, Me libré de una sacudida

jerkily, adv. con sacudidas; espasmódicamente; nerviosamente

jerkin, s. justillo, m.

jerky, a. espasmódico; nervioso (also of style)

jerry-builder, s. mal constructor, m.

jerry-building, s. mala construcción, f.

jerry-built, a. mal construido, de pacotilla

jersey, s. jersey, m. a. de jersey; de Jersey. football j., camiseta de fútbol, f., jersey de fútbol, m. J. cow, vaca de Jersey, f.

jest, s. broma, chanza, f.; (joke) chiste, m.; (laughing-stock) hazmerreír, m. v.i. bromear; burlarse (de). in j., en broma, de guasa

jester, s. burlón (-ona); (practical joker, etc.) bromista, m. and f.; (at a royal court) bufón, m.

jesting, s. bromas, f. pl.; chistes, m. pl.; burlas, f. pl. a. de broma; burlón

jestingly, adv. en broma

Jesuit, s. Jesuita, m. the Jesuits, los Jesuitas, la Compañía de Jesús

Jesuitical, a. jesuítico

jet, s. (min.) azabache, m.; (stream) chorro, m.; (pipe) surtidero, m.; (burner) mechero, m. v.i. chorrear. jet-black, negro como el azabache, de azabache. **jet-propelled engine,** motor de retroacción, *m.* **jet-propelled 'plane,** aeroplano de reacción, *m.*

jetsam, *s.* echazón, *f.*; *(fig.)* víctima, *f.*

jettison, *s.* echazón, *f.* *v.t.* echar (mercancías) al mar; *(fig.)* librarse de, abandonar

jetty, *s.* dique, malecón, *m.*; (landing-pier) embarcadero, muelle, *m.*

Jew, *s.* judío, *m.* **Jew's harp,** birimbao, *m.*

jewel, *s.* joya, alhaja, *f.*; (of a watch) rubí, *m.*; *(fig.)* alhaja, *f.* *v.t.* enjoyar, adornar con piedras preciosas. **j.-box, -case,** joyero, *m.*

jewelled, *a.* adornado con piedras preciosas, enjoyado; (of a watch) con rubíes

jeweller, *s.* joyero (-ra). **jeweller's shop,** joyería, *f.*

jewellery, *s.* joyas, *f. pl.*; artículos de joyería, *m. pl.*

Jewess, *s.* judía, *f.*

Jewish, *a.* judío

Jewry, *s.* judería, *f.*

jib, *s.* *(naut.)* foque, *m.* *v.i.* (of a horse) plantarse; (refuse) rehusar. **to jib at,** vacilar en; mostrarse desinclinado. **jib-boom,** *(naut.)* botalón de foque, *m.*

jiffy, *s.* instante, credo, *m.* **in a j.,** en un decir Jesús, en un credo

jig, *s.* (dance) jiga, *f.* *v.i.* bailar una jiga; bailar, agitarse sacudirse. *v.t.* agitar, sacudir; (sieve) cribar

jigger, *s.* *(naut.)* cangreja de mesana, *f.*; aparejo de mano, *m.*; jigger, *m.*

jigsaw puzzle, *s.* rompecabezas, *m.*

jilt, *v.t.* dar calabazas (a)

jingle, *s.* tintineo, *m.*; ruido, *m.*; verso, *m.*; estribillo, *m.* *v.i.* tintinar; sonar; rimar

jingoism, *s.* jingoísmo, *m.*

jitters, to have the, no tenerlas todas consigo, no saber dónde meterse

job, *s.* tarea, *f.*; trabajo, *m.*; empleo, *m.*; (affair) asunto, *m.*; (thing) cosa, *f.*; (unscrupulous transaction) intriga, *f.* **It is a**

good (bad) job that ..., Es una buena (mala) cosa que ... **He has done a good job,** Ha hecho un buen trabajo. **He has lost his job,** Ha perdido su empleo, Le han declarado cesante. **odd-job man,** factótum, *m.* **job-lot,** colección miscelánea, *f.*; *(com.)* saldo de mercancías, *m.*

jobber, *s.* (workman) destajista, *m.*; (in stocks) agiotista, *m.*; *(com.)* corredor, *m.*

jobbery, *s.* intrigas, *f. pl.*

jobless, *a.* sin trabajo

jockey, *s.* jockey, *m.* *v.t.* engañar; (with into) persuadir, hacer; (with out of) quitar, robar. **j. cap,** gorra de jockey, *f.* **J. Club,** jockey-club, *m.*

jocose, *a.* jocoso, gracioso, guasón

jocosity, *s.* jocosidad, *f.*

jocular, *a.* gracioso, alegre; chistoso, zumbón

jocularity, *s.* alegría, jocosidad, *f.*

jocularly, *adv.* en broma; alegremente

jocund, *a.* alegre, jovial; jocundo

jocundity, *s.* alegría, *f.*; jocundidad, *f.*

jog, *v.t.* empujar; (the memory) refrescar. *v.i.* ir despacio; andar a trote corto. *s.* empujón, *m.* **He jogged me with his elbow,** Me dió con el codo. **jog-trot,** trote corto, *m.*

join, *v.t.* juntar; unir; añadir; (railway lines) empalmar; juntarse con; (meet) encontrarse (con); reunirse (con); (a club, etc.) hacerse miembro (de); (share) acompañar; (regiments, ships) volver (a). *v.i.* juntarse; unirse; asociarse. *s.* unión, *f.*; (railway) empalme, *m.*; (roads) bifurcación, *f.* **At what time will you j. me?** ¿A qué hora me vendrás a buscar? **He has joined his ship,** Ha vuelto a su buque. **Will you j. me in a drink?** ¿Me quieres acompañar en una bebida? **to j. battle,** librar batalla. **to j. forces,** combinar; *(fam.)* juntar meriendas. **to j. in,** tomar parte en, participar en. **to j. together,** *v.t.* unir, juntar. *v.i.* juntarse; asociarse. **to j. up,** alistarse

joiner, *s.* carpintero, ensamblador, *m.*

joinery, *s.* ensambladuría, *f.*; carpintería, *f.*

joining, *s.* juntura, conjunción, *f.*; (*carp.*) etc.) ensambladura, *f.*; (*fig.*) unión, *f.*

joint, *s.* juntura, junta, *f.*; (*anat.*) coyuntura, articulación, *f.*; (knuckle) nudillo, *m.*; (of meat) cuarto, *m.*; (hinge) bisagra, *f.*; (*bot.*) nudo, *m.* *a.* unido; combinado; colectivo; mixto; mutuo; (in compounds) co. *v.t.* juntar; (meat) descuartizar. **out of j.**, dislocado; (of the times) fuera de compás. **j. account**, cuenta corriente mutua, *f.* **j.-heir**, coheredero, *m.* **j. stock company**, compañía por acciones, sociedad anónima, *f.*

jointed, *a.* articulado; (foldable) plegadizo

jointly, *adv.* juntamente, en común, colectivamente

joist, *s.* sopanda, viga, *f.*

joke, *s.* chiste, *m.*; burla, broma, *f.* *v.i.* bromear, chancearse. *v.t.* burlarse (de). **Can he take a j.?** ¿Sabe aguantar una broma? **practical j.**, broma pesada, *f.* **to play a j.**, gastar una broma, hacer una burla

joker, *s.* bromista, *m.* and *f.*; (in cards) comodín, *m.*

joking, *s.* chistes, *m. pl.*, bromas, *f. pl. a.* chistoso; cómico

jokingly, *adv.* en broma, de guasa

jollification, *s.* regocijo, *m.*; festividades, fiestas, *f. pl.*

jollity, *s.* alegría, *f.*, regocijo, *m.*

jolly, *a.* alegre, jovial; (tipsy) achispado; (amusing) divertido; (nice) agradable. *adv.* muy. **He is a j. good fellow**, Es un hombre estupendo. **I am j. glad**, Estoy contentísimo, Me alegro mucho

jolt, *s.* sacudida, *f.* *v.t.* sacudir. *v.i.* (of a vehicle) traquetear

jolting, *s.* sacudidas, *f. pl.*, sacudimiento, *m.*; (of a vehicle) traqueteo, *m.*

jongleur, *s.* juglar, *m.*

jonquil, *s.* (*bot.*) junquillo, *m.*

joss, *s.* ídolo chino, *m.* **j.-stick**, pebete, *m.*

jostle, *v.t.* empujar, empellar. *v.i.* dar empujones, codear

jot, *s.* jota, pizca, *f.* *v.t.* (down) apuntar. **not a jot**, ni jota, ni

pizca. **to be not worth a jot**, no valer un comino

jotter, *s.* taco para notas, *m.*; (exercise book) cuaderno, *m.*

jotting, *s.* apunte, *m.*; observación, *f.*

joule, *s.* (*elec.*) julio, *m.*

journal, *s.* (diary) diario, *m.*; (ship's) diario de navegación, *m.*; (newspaper) periódico, *m.*; (review) revista, *f.*

journalese, *s.* lenguaje periodístico, *m.*

journalism, *s.* periodismo, *m.*

journalist, *s.* periodista, *m.* and *f.*

journalistic, *a.* periodístico

journey, *s.* viaje, *m.*; expedición, *f.*; trayecto, *m.*; camino, *m.* *v.i.* viajar. **a j. by sea**, un viaje por mar. **Pleasant j.!** ¡Buen viaje! **outward j.**, viaje de ida, *m.* **return j.**, viaje de regreso, *m.*

joust, *s.* justa, *f.*, torneo, *m.* *v.i.* justar, correr lanzas

Jove, *s.* Júpiter, *m.* **By J.!** ¡Pardiez! ¡Caramba!

jovial, *a.* jovial

joviality, *s.* jovialidad, *f.*

jovially, *adv.* jovialmente

jowl, *s.* (cheek) carrillo, *m.*; (of cattle, etc.) papada, *f.*; (jaw) quijada, *f.*

joy, *s.* alegría, *f.*; felicidad, *f.*; deleite, placer, *m.* *v.i.* alegrarse. **I wish you joy**, Te deseo la felicidad. **joy-ride**, excursión en coche, *f.*; vuelo en avión, *m.* **joy-stick**, (of an aeroplane) palanca de gobierno, *f.*

joyful, *a.* alegre

joyfully, *adv.* alegremente

joyfulness, *s.* alegría, *f.*

joyless, *a.* sin alegría, triste

joylessly, *adv.* tristemente

joylessness, *s.* falta de alegría, tristeza, *f.*

joyous. See **joyful**

jubilant, *a.* jubiloso; triunfante

jubilantly, *adv.* con júbilo, alegremente; triunfalmente

jubilation, *s.* júbilo, *m.*, alegría, *f.*; ruido triunfal, *m.*

jubilee, *s.* jubileo, *m.*

Judaic, *a.* judaico

Judaism, *s.* hebraísmo, judaísmo, *m.*

Judas, *s.* (traitor and hole) judas, *m.*

judge, *s.* juez, *m.*; (connoisseur) conocedor (-ra) (de); (umpire) arbitrio, *m. v.t.* juzgar; considerar, tener por. *v.i.* servir como juez; juzgar. **judging by**, a juzgar por. **to be a good j. of**, ser buen juez de. **to j. for oneself**, formar su propia opinión

judg(e)ment, *s.* (law) fallo, *m.*; sentencia, *f.*; juicio, *m.*; (understanding) entendimiento, discernimiento, *m.*; (opinion) opinión, *f.*, parecer, *m.* **In my j....**, Según mi parecer, . . . **Según creo yo** . . . **Last J.**, Juicio Final, *m.* **to pass j. on**, (law) pronunciar sentencia (en or sobre); dictaminar sobre; juzgar. **to sit in j. on**, ser juez de; juzgar. **J.-day**, Día del Juicio, *m.* **j.-seat**, tribunal, *m.*

judgeship, *s.* judicatura, *f.*

judicature, *s.* judicatura, *f.*; (court) juzgado, *m.*

judicial, *a.* judicial; legal; (of the mind) juicioso. **j. inquiry**, investigación judicial, *f.* **j. separation**, separación legal, *f.*

judicially, *adv.* judicialmente

judiciary, *a.* judicial. *s.* judicatura, *f.*

judicious, *a.* juicioso, prudente.

judiciously, *adv.* prudentemente, juiciosamente

judiciousness, *s.* juicio, *m.*, prudencia, sensatez, *f.*

jug, *s.* jarro, *m.*; cántaro, *m.*; pote, *m. v.t.* (cul.) estofar. *v.i.* (of nightingale) trinar, cantar. **jugged hare**, *s.* liebre en estofado, *f.*

juggle, *v.i.* hacer juegos malabares. **to j. out of**, (money, etc.) quitar con engaño, estafar. **to j. with**, (fig.) (facts, etc.) tergiversar, falsificar; (person) engañar

juggler, *s.* malabarista, *m.* and *f.*; (deceiver) estafador (-ra)

jugglery, *s.* prestidigitación, *f.*; juegos malabares, *m. pl.*; (imposture) engaño, *m.*, estafa, *f.*, trampas, *f. pl.*

Jugo-Slav, *s.* yugoeslavo (-va). *a.* yugoeslavo, de los yugoeslavos

jugular, *a.* (anat.) yugular. **j. vein**, yugular, *m.*

juice, *s.* jugo, *m.*; (fig.) zumo, *m.* **digestive juices**, jugos digestivos, *m. pl.*

juiciness, *s.* jugosidad, *f.*; suculencia, *f.*

juicy, *a.* jugoso; suculento

jujube, *s.* pastilla, *f.*

ju-jitsu, *s.* jiujitsu, *m.*

July, *s.* julio, *m.*

jumble, *v.t.* mezclar, confundir. *s.* mezcla confusa, colección miscelánea, confusión, *f.* **j. sale**, tómbola, *f.*

jump, *s.* salto, *m.*; (in prices, etc.) aumento, *m.* **at one j.**, de un salto. **high j.**, salto de altura, *m.* **long j.**, salto de longitud, *m.* **to be on the j.**, (fam.) estar nervioso, tener los nervios en punta

jump, *v.i.* saltar; dar un salto; brincar; (of tea-cups, etc.) bailar; (throb) pulsar. *v.t.* saltar; hacer saltar; (a child) brincar; (omit) pasar por alto de, omitir. **The train jumped the rails**, El tren se descarriló. **to j. out of bed**, saltar de la cama. **to j. to the conclusion that...**, darse prisa a concluir que . . . **to j. about**, dar saltos, brincar; revolverse, moverse de un lado para otro. **to j. at**, saltar sobre; precipitarse sobre, abalanzarse hacia; (an offer) apresurarse a aceptar; (seize) coger con entusiasmo. **to j. down**, bajar de un salto. **to j. over**, saltar; saltar por encima de. **to j. up**, saltar; (on to a horse, etc.) montar rápidamente; levantarse apresuradamente. **to j. with**, (agree) convenir en, estar conforme con

jumper, *s.* saltador (-ra); (sailor's) blusa, *f.*; jersey, sweater, *m.*

jumping, *s.* saltos, *m. pl. a.* saltador. **j.-off place**, base avanzada, *f.*; (fig.) trampolín, *m.* **j.-pole**, pértiga, *f.*

jumpiness, *s.* nerviosidad, *f.*

jumpy, *a.* nervioso, agitado

junction, *s.* unión, *f.*; (of roads) bifurcación, *f.*; (railway) empalme, *m.*; (connection) conexión, *f.*

juncture, *s.* coyuntura, *f.*; momento, *m.*; crisis, *f.*, momento crítico, *m.*; (joint) junta, *f.*

June, *s.* junio, *m.*

jungle, *s.* selva, *f.* **j.-fever,** fiebre palúdica, *f.*

junior, *a.* joven; hijo; más joven; menos antiguo; subordinado, segundo. *s.* joven, *m.* and *f.* **Carmen is my j. by three years,** Carmen es tres años más joven que yo. **James Thomson, Jnr.,** James Thómson, hijo. **the j. school,** los pequeños. **j. partner,** socio más joven, *m.*

juniper, *s.* (*bot.*) enebro, *m.*

junk, *s.* trastos viejos, *m. pl.*; (nonsense) patrañas, *f. pl.*; (*naut.*) junco, *m.*; (salt meat) tasajo, *m.* **j.-shop,** tienda de trastos viejos, *f.*

junketing, *s.* festividades, *f. pl.*

juridical, *a.* jurídico

jurisconsult, *s.* jurisconsulto, *m.*

jurisdiction, *s.* jurisdicción, *f.*; competencia, *f.*

jurisprudence, *s.* jurisprudencia, *f.*

jurist, *s.* jurista, legista, *m.*

juror, *s.* (miembro del) jurado, *m.*

jury, *s.* jurado, *m.* **to be on the j.,** formar parte del jurado. **j.-box,** tribuna del jurado, *f.*

juryman, *s.* miembro del jurado, *m.*

just, *a.* justo; justiciero; exacto; fiel. **Peter the J.,** Pedro el justiciero

just, *adv.* justamente, exactamente; precisamente; (scarcely) apenas; (almost) casi; (entirely) completamente; (simply) meramente, solamente, tan sólo; (newly) recién (followed by past part.), recientemente. **He only j. missed being run over,** Por poco le atropellaron. **It is j. near,** Está muy cerca. **It is j. the same to me,** Me es completamente igual. **J. as he was leaving,** Cuando estaba a punto de marcharse, En el momento de marcharse. **That's j. it!** ¡Eso es! ¡Exactamente! **to have j.,** acabar de. **They have j. dined,** Acaban de cenar. **J. as you wish,** Como Vd. quiera. **j. at that moment,** precisamente en aquel momento. **j. by,** muy cerca; al lado. **j. now,** ahora mismo; hace poco; pronto, dentro de poco. **j. yet,** todavía.

They will not come j. yet, No vendrán todavía

justice, *s.* justicia, *f.*; (judge) juez, *m.*; (magistrate) juez municipal, *m.* **to bring to j.,** llevar ante el juez (a). **to do j. to,** (a person) hacer justicia (a); (a meal) hacer honor (a). **to do oneself j.,** quedar bien

justifiable, *a.* justificable

justifiably, *adv.* con justicia, justificadamente

justification, *s.* justificación, *f.*

justify, *v.t.* justificar, vindicar; (excuse) disculpar; (*print.*) justificar. **to be justified in,** tener derecho (a), tener motivo para, tener razón (en)

justly, *adv.* justamente; con justicia; con derecho; con razón; exactamente; debidamente

justness, *s.* justicia, *f.*; exactitud, *f.*

jut, *v.i.* salir, proyectar; sobresalir

jute, *s.* yute, *m.*

juvenile, *a.* juvenil; de la juventud; para la juventud; joven; de niños; para niños. *s.* joven, *m.* and *f.* **j. court,** tribunal de menores, *m.* **j. lead,** (*theat.*) galancete, galán joven, *m.* **j. offender,** delincuente infantil, *m.*

juxtapose, *v.t.* yuxtaponer

juxtaposition, *s.* yuxtaposición, *f.*

K

k, *s.* (letter) ka, *f.*

Kaffir, *a.* cafre. *s.* cafre, *m.*

Kaiser, *s.* káiser, emperador, *m.*

kaleidoscope, *s.* calidoscopio, *m.*

kaleidoscopic, *a.* calidoscópico

kangaroo, *s.* canguro, *m.*

Kantian, *a.* kantiano

Kantianism, *s.* kantismo, *m.*

kaolin, *s.* caolín, *m.*

kapok, *s.* miraguano, *m.*

katabolism, *s.* catabolismo, *m.*

keel, *s.* quilla, *f.* *v.t.* carenar. **to k. over,** volcar; caer; (*naut.*) zozobrar

keelson, *s.* sobrequilla, *f.*

keen, *a.* (of edges) afilado; agudo; penetrante; vivo; sutil; ardiente; celoso, entusiasta; mordaz; (desirous) ansioso; (of appetite) grande, bueno. **He is a k. tennis player,** Es muy aficionado a jugar al tenis. **Joan has a very k. ear,** Juana tiene un oído muy agudo. **I'm not very k. on apples,** No me gustan mucho las manzanas

keenly, *adv.* agudamente; vivamente; (of feeling) hondamente; (of looking) atentamente

keenness, *s.* (of a blade) afiladura, *f.*; agudeza, *f.*; viveza, *f.*; sutileza, *f.*; perspicacia, *f.*; (enthusiasm) entusiasmo, *m.*, afición, *f.*; (desire) ansia, *f.*

keep, *v.t.* guardar; tener; quedarse con; retener; conservar; mantener; (a shop, hotel, etc.) dirigir, tener; (a school) ser director de; (a promise, etc.) cumplir; (the law, etc.) observar, guardar; (celebrate) solemnizar; (a secret) guardar; (books, accounts, a house, in step) llevar; (sheep, etc., one's bed) guardar; (a city, etc.) defender; (domestic animals, cars, etc.) tener; (lodge) alojar; (detain) detener; (reserve) reservar; (cause) hacer. **They had kept this room for me,** Me habían reservado este cuarto. **Dorothy has kept the blue dress,** Dorotea se ha quedado con el vestido azul. **The government could not k. order,** El gobierno no sabía mantener el orden. **I did not know how to k. their attention,** No sabía retener su atención. **Carmen kept quiet,** Carmen guardó silencio, Carmen se calló. **Can you k. a secret?** ¿Sabes guardar un secreto? **to k. an appointment,** acudir a una cita. **to k. in repair,** conservar en buen estado. **to k. a person from doing something,** evitar que una persona haga algo. **to k. someone waiting,** hacer que espere alguien. **to k. something from someone,** ocultar algo de alguien. **We were kept at it night and day,** Nos hacían trabajar día y noche. **I always k. it by me,** Lo tengo siempre a mi lado (or conmigo). **to k. away,** alejar; mantener a distancia; no dejar venir. **to k. back,** (a crowd,

etc.) detener; cortar el paso (a); no dejar avanzar; (retain) guardar, retener; reservar; (tears, words) reprimir, contener; (evidence, etc.) callar, suprimir. **to k. down,** no dejar subir (a); sujetar; (a nation, etc.) oprimir, subyugar; (emotions) dominar; (prices, expenses) mantener bajo; (check) moderar, reprimir. **to k. in,** (feelings) contener; reprimir; (the house) hacer quedarse en casa, no dejar salir; (imprison) encerrar; (school) hacer quedar en la escuela (a). **to k. off,** alejar; tener a distancia (a); cerrar el paso (a), no dejar avanzar; no andar sobre; no tocar; (a subject) no tratar de, no discutir, no tocar. **K. your hands off!** ¡No toques! **to k. on,** guardar; retener; (eyes) fijar en, poner en. **to k. out,** no dejar entrar; excluir. **It is difficult to k. him out of trouble,** Es difícil de evitar que se meta en líos. **to k. to,** seguir; limitarse a; adherirse a; (a path, etc.) seguir por; (one's bed) guardar; (fulfil) cumplir; (oblige) hacer, obligar. **to k. under,** subyugar, oprimir; dominar; controlar. **to k. up,** mantener; (appearances) guardar; conservar; persistir en; (prices) sostener; (in good repair) conservar en buen estado; (go on doing) continuar. **He kept me up late last night,** Me entretuvo hasta muy tarde anoche; Me hizo trasnochar ayer; Me hizo velar anoche. **to k. one's end up,** volver por sí, hacerse fuerte. **to k. up one's spirits,** no desanimarse

keep, *v.i.* quedar; (be) estar; (continue) seguir, continuar; mantenerse; (at home, etc.) quedarse, permanecer; (be accustomed) acostumbrar, soler; (persist) perseverar; (of food) conservarse fresco. **How is he keeping?** ¿Cómo está él? **to k. in with someone,** cultivar a alguien. **to k. up with the times,** mantenerse al corriente. **to k. at,** seguir; persistir; perseverar; (pester) importunar. **John keeps at it,** Juan trabaja sin descansar. **to k. away,** mantenerse apartado; mantenerse a distancia; no acudir. **to k. back,** hacerse a un lado, apartarse, alejarse. **to k. down,** quedarse tumbado; seguir acurrucado; no levantarse; esconderse. **to k. from,** (doing something) guardarse de. **to k. off,** mantenerse a distancia. **If the storm keeps off,** Si no estalla una tempestad. **If the rain keeps off,** Si no empieza a llover, Si no hay lluvia. **to k. on,** continuar; seguir. **to k. straight on,** seguir derecho. **I'm tired, but I still k. on,** Estoy cansado, pero sigo trabajando. **to k. out,** quedarse fuera **to k. out of,** (quarrels, trouble, etc.) no meterse en, evitar. **to k. out of sight,** no dejarse ver, no mostrarse, mantenerse oculto. **to k. together,** quedarse juntos; reunirse

keep, s. (of a castle) mazmorra, f.; (maintenance) subsistencia, f.; comida, f. **for keeps,** para siempre jamás

keeper, s. guarda, m. and f.; (in a park, zoo, of a lunatic) guardián, m.; (of a museum, etc.) director, m.; (of animals) criador (-ra) (gamekeeper) guardabosque, m.; (of a boarding-house, shop, etc.) dueño (-ña); (of accounts, books) tenedor, m. **Am I my brother's k.?** ¿Soy yo responsable por mi hermano?

keeping, s. guarda, f.; conservación, f.; protección, f.; (of a rule) observación, f.; (of an anniversary, etc.) celebración, f.; (of a person) mantenimiento, m. **in k. with,** en armonía con; de acuerdo con. **out of k. with,** en desacuerdo con. **to be in safe k.,** estar en buenas manos; estar en un lugar seguro. **k. back,** retención, f.

keepsake, s. recuerdo, m.

keg, s. barrilete, m.

ken, s. alcance de la vista, m.; vista, f.; comprensión, f.

kennel, s. (of a dog) perrera, f.; (of hounds) jauría, f.; (dwelling) cuchitril, m.; (gutter) arroyo, m. **k. man,** perrero, m.

kepi, s. quepis, m.

kerb, kerb-stone, s. bordillo, m.

kerchief, s. pañuelo, m.; pañoleta, f. **brightly-coloured k.,** pañuelo de hierbas, m.

kermes, s. quermes, m.; quermes mineral, m.

kermess, s. kermese, f.

kernel, s. almendra, semilla, f.; (fig.) meollo, m., esencia, f.

kerosene, s. petróleo de lámpara, m.; kerosén, m.

kestrel, s. cernícalo, m.

ketch, s. queche, m.

ketchup, s. salsa de tomate y setas, f.

kettle, s. caldero, m. **a pretty k. of fish,** una olla de grillos. **k.-drum,** timbal, m. **k.-drum player,** timbalero, m.

key, s. llave, f.; (fig., arch., mus.) clave, f.; (tone) tono, m.; (of a piano, typewriter, etc.) tecla, f.; (mech.) chaveta, f.; (of a wind instrument) pistón, m.; (winged fruit) sámara, f.; (elec.) conmutador, m. **major (minor) key,** tono mayor (menor), m. **latch-key,** llave de la puerta, f.; (Yale) llavín, m. **master key, skeleton key,** llave maestra, f. **skeleton key,** ganzúa, f. **He is all keyed up,** Tiene los nervios en punta. **key industry,** industria clave, f. **key man,** hombre indispensable, m. **key point,** punto estratégico, m. **key-ring,** llavero, m. **key signature,** (mus.) clave, f. **key word,** palabra clave, f.

keyboard, s. teclado, m.

keyhole, s. ojo de la cerradura, m. **through the k.,** por el ojo de la cerradura

keynote, s. (mus.) tónica, f.; (fig.) piedra clave, idea fundamental, f.

keystone, s. piedra clave, f.

khaki, s. caqui, m.

khan, s. kan, m.

Khedive, s. jedive, m.

kick, v.t. dar un puntapié (a); golpear; (a goal) chutar. v.i. (of horses, etc.) dar coces, cocear; (of guns) recular. **to k. one's heels,** hacer tiempo. **to k. up a row,** hacer un ruido de mil diablos; (quarrel) armar camorra. **to k. about,** dar patadas (a). **to k. away,** quitar con el pie; lanzar con el pie. **to k. off,**

quitar con el pie; lanzar; sacudirse. **k.-off**, *s.* "kick-off," *m.*
to k. out, echar a puntapiés

kick, *s.* puntapié, *m.*; golpe, *m.*; coz, *f.*; (of guns) culatazo, *m.* free k., golpe franco, *m.*

kicking, *s.* coces, *f. pl.*; acoceamiento, *m.*; pataleo, *m.*; golpeamiento, *m.*

kid, *s.* cabrito, *m.*, chivo (-va); carne de cabrito, *f.*; (leather) cabritilla, *f.*; (*fam.*) crío, *m.* kid gloves, guantes de cabritilla, *m. pl.*

kidnap, *v.t.* secuestrar

kidnapper, *s.* secuestrador (-ra); ladrón (-ona) de niños

kidnapping, *s.* secuestro, *m.*

kidney, *s.* riñón, *m.*; (*fig.*) especie; índole, *f.* k.-bean, (plant) judía, *f.*; (fruit) habichuela, judía, *f.* fréjol, *m.*

kief, *s.* marihuana, *f.*

kill, *v.t.* matar; destruir; suprimir. to k. off, exterminar. to k. time, entretener el tiempo. to k. two birds with one stone, matar dos pájaros de un tiro. k.-joy, aguafiestas, *m.* and *f.*

killer, *s.* matador (-ra); (murderer) asesino, *m.* and *f.*

killing, *s.* matanza, *f.*; (murder) asesinato, *m.* *a.* matador; destructivo; (comic) cómico; ridículo, absurdo; (ravishing) irresistible

kiln, *s.* horno, *m.*

kilo, *s.* kilo, *m.*

kilocycle, *s.* (*elec.*) kilociclo, *m.*

kilogramme, *s.* kilo(gramo), *m.*

kilolitre, *s.* kilolitro, *m.*

kilometre, *s.* kilómetro, *m.*

kilometric, *a.* kilométrico

kilowatt, *s.* (*elec.*) kilovatio, *m.*

kilt, *s.* falda escocesa, *f.*

kimono, *s.* quimono, *m.*

kin, *s.* parientes, *m. pl.*; familia, *f.*; clase, especie, *f.* the next of kin, los parientes próximos, la familia

kind, *s.* género, *m.*, clase, *f.*; especie, *f.*; (*fam.*) tipo, *m.* He is a queer k. of person, Él es un tipo muy raro. What k. of cloth is it? ¿Qué clase de tela es? Nothing of the k! ¡Nada de eso! payment in k., pago en especie, *m.*

kind, *a.* bondadoso, bueno; cariñoso, tierno; amable; favorable,

propicio. Will you be so k. as to... Tenga Vd. la bondad de... With k. regards, Con un saludo afectuoso. You have been very k. to her, Vd. ha sido muy bueno para ella. k.-hearted, bondadoso. k.-heartedness, bondad, benevolencia, *f.*

kindergarten, *s.* jardín de la infancia, kindergarten, *m.*

kindle, *v.t.* encender; hacer arder; (*fig.*) avivar. *v.i.* prender, empezar a arder; encenderse; (*fig.*) inflamarse

kindliness, *s.* bondad, *f.*

kindling, *s.* encendimiento (del fuego), *m.*; (wood) leña menuda, *f.*

kindly, *a.* bondadoso; bueno; benévolo; propicio, favorable; (of climate) bénigno. *adv.* con bondad, bondadosamente; fácilmente. K. sit down, Haga el favor de sentarse

kindness, *s.* bondad, *f.*; benevolencia, *f.*; amabilidad, *f.*; cariño, *m.*; favor, *m.*, atención, *f.*

kindred, *s.* parentesco, *m.*; parientes, *m. pl.*; familia, *f.*; afinidad, *f.* *a.* emparentado; hermano

kinematics, *s.* cinemática, *f.*

king, *s.* (ruler, important person, chess, cards) rey, *m.*; (in draughts) dama, *f.* king's evil, escrófula, *f.* k.-bolt, perno real, *m.* k.-craft, arte de reinar, *m.* or *f.* k.-cup, (*bot.*) botón de oro, *m.* K.-of-Arms, rey de armas, *m.* k.-post, pendolón, *m.*

kingdom, *s.* reino, *m.* animal k., reino animal, *m.*

kingfisher, *s.* martín pescador, alción, *m.*

kingless, *a.* sin rey

kingly, *a.* de rey, real

kink, *s.* nudo, *m.*; pliegue, *m.*; (curl) rizo, *m.*; (*fig.*) peculiaridad, *f.*

kinsfolk, *s.* parientes, *m. pl.*, familia, *f.*

kinship, *s.* parentesco, *m.*; afinidad, *f.*

kinsman, *s.* pariente, deudo, *m.*

kinswoman, *s.* parienta, *f.*

kiosk, *s.* quiosco, *m.*

kipper, *s.* arenque ahumado, *m.* *v.t.* ahumar

kiss, *s.* beso, *m.*; (in billiards) pelo, *m.* *v.t.* besar; dar un beso (a); (of billiard balls) tocar. **to k. each other**, besarse. **k.-curl**, rizo de la sien, *m.*, sortijilla, *f.*

kit, *s.* (tub) cubo, *m.*; (for tools, etc.) cajita, caja, *f.*; (soldier's) equipo, *m.* **kit-bag**, mochila, *f.*

kitchen, *s.* cocina, *f.* **k.-boy**, pinche (de cocina), *m.* **k.-garden**, huerta, *f.* **k.-maid**, fregona, *f.* **k.-range**, cocina económica, *f.* **k.-sink**, fregadero, *m.* **k.-stove**, horno de cocina, *m.* **k. utensils**, batería de cocina, *f.*

kitchenette, *s.* cocinilla, *f.*

kite, *s.* (orn.) milano, *m.*; cometa, pájara, *f.* **to fly a k.**, hacer volar una cometa. **box-k.**, cometa celular, *f.*

kith and kin, *s. pl.* parientes y amigos, *m. pl.*

kitten, *s.* gatito (-ta). *v.i.* (of a cat) parir

kittenish, *a.* de gatito; juguetón

kitty, *s.* michito, *m.*; (in card games) platillo, *m.*

kleptomania, *s.* cleptomanía, *f.*

kleptomaniac, *a.* cleptómano. *s.* cleptómano (-na)

knack, *s.* destreza, *f.*; talento, *m.*; (trick) truco, *m.*

knapsack, *s.* mochila, *f.*; (mil.) alforja, *f.*

knave, *s.* bellaco, truhán, tunante, *m.*; (at cards) sota, *f.*

knavery, *s.* bellaquería, truhanería, *f.*

knavish, *a.* de bribón; taimado, truhanesco

knead, *v.t.* amasar; (massage) sobar; (fig.) formar

kneading, *s.* amasijo, *m.*; (massaging) soba, *f.* **k.-trough**, amasadera, *f.*

knee, *s.* rodilla, *f.*; (fig.) ángulo, codillo, *m.* **on bended k.**, de hinojos. **on one's knees**, de rodillas, arrodillado. **to go down on one's knees**, arrodillarse, ponerse de rodillas. **k.-breeches**, calzón corto, *m.*; calzón ceñido, *m.*; (Elizabethan) gregüescos, *m. pl.* **k.-cap**, rótula, *f.* **k.-deep**, hasta las rodillas. **k.-joint**, articulación de la rodilla, *f.*; (mech.) junta de codillo, *f.* **k.-pad**, rodillera, *f.*

kneel (down), *v.i.* arrodillarse, hincarse de rodillas, ponerse de rodillas

kneeling, *a.* arrodillado, de rodillas

knell, *s.* toque de difuntos, tañido fúnebre, *m.*; toque de campañas, *m.*; (fig.) muerte, *f.* *v.i.* tocar a muerto. *v.t.* (fig.) anunciar, presagiar

knickerbockers, *s. pl.* bragas, *f. pl.*; calzón corto, *m.*; (women's) pantalones, *m. pl.*

knick-knack, *s.* chuchería, *f.*

knife, *s.* cuchillo, *m.* **to have one's k. in someone**, tener enemiga (a), querer mal (a). **war to the k.**, guerra a muerte, *f.* **k.-edge**, filo de cuchillo, *m.*; fiel de soporte, *m.* **k. grinder**, amolador, *m.* **k.-handle**, mango de cuchillo, *m.* **k. thrust**, cuchillada, *f.*

knight, *s.* caballero, *m.*; (at chess) caballo, *m.* *v.t.* armar caballero; (in modern usage) dar el título de caballero (a). **untried k.**, caballero novel, *m.* **k. commander**, comendador, *m.* **k.-errant**, caballero andante, *m.* **k.-errantry**, caballería andante, *f.* **k. of the rueful countenance**, el caballero de la triste figura

knighthood, *s.* caballería, *f.*; (in modern usage) título de caballero, *m.*

knightly, *a.* caballeresco; de caballero; de caballería

knit, *v.t.* and *v.i.* hacer calceta, hacer media; juntar, ligar; unir. **Isabel is knitting me a jumper**, Isabel me hace un jersey de punto de media. **to k. one's brows**, fruncir el ceño

knitted, *a.* de punto. **k. goods**, géneros de punto, *m. pl.*

knitter, *s.* calcetero (-ra); (machine) máquina de hacer calceta, *f.*

knitting, *s.* acción de hacer calceta, *f.*; trabajo de punto, *m.*, labor de calceta, *f.*; unión, *f.* **k.-machine**, máquina de hacer calceta, *f.* **k.-needle**, aguja de media, aguja de hacer calceta, *f.*

knob, *s.* protuberancia, *f.*; (of a door, etc.) perilla, borlita, *f.*; (ornamental) bellota, *f.*; (of sugar) terrón, *m.*; (of a stick) puño, *m.*

knock, s. golpe, m.; choque, m.; (with a knocker) aldabada, f.

knock, v.t. golpear; chocar (contra). v.i. llamar a la puerta; (of an engine) picar. **to k. one's head against,** chocar con la cabeza contra, dar con la cabeza contra. **to k. about,** v.t. pegar; aporrear. v.i. viajar; vagar, rodar; callejear. **to k. against,** golpear contra; chocar contra. **to k. down,** derribar; (of vehicles) atropellar; (houses, etc.) demoler; (an argument, etc.) destruir; (a tender, etc.) rebajar; (of an auctioneer) rematar al mejor postor. **to k. in,** (nails, etc.) clavar. **to k. into one another,** toparse. **to k. off,** hacer caer; sacudir; quitar; (from price) descontar; (from speed, etc.) reducir; (finish) terminar pronto; (runs in cricket) hacer. **to k. out,** (remove) quitar; (boxing) dejar fuera de combate, noquear; (fig., stun) atontar; (an idea, etc.) bosquejar. **to k. over,** volcar. **to k. up,** hacer saltar; (call) llamar; (runs at cricket) hacer; (tire) agotar, rendir; (building) construir toscamente. **to k. up against,** chocar contra; tropezar con. **k.-kneed,** a. patiabierto. **k.-out,** "knock-out," m.

knocker, s. (on a door) aldaba, f. **k.-up,** despertador, m.

knocking, s. golpes, m. pl., golpeo, m.; (with a knocker) aldabeo, m. **k. over,** vuelco, m.; (by a vehicle) atropello, m.

knoll, s. altillo, otero, m.

knot, s. nudo, m.; (bow) lazo, m.; (of hair) moño, m.; (naut.) nudo, m., milla náutica, f.; (of people) corrillo, grupo, m.; (on timber) nudo, m. v.t. anudar. v.i. hacer nudos; enmarañarse. **to tie a k.,** hacer un nudo.

knotted, a. nudoso.

knotty, a. nudoso; (fig.) intrincado, difícil, complicado. **a k. problem,** un problema difícil.

knout, s. knut, m.

know, v.t. conocer; saber; (understand) comprender; (recognize) reconocer. **I k. her very well by sight,** La conozco muy bien de vista. **John knows Latin,** Juan sabe latín. **How can I k.?** ¿Cómo lo voy a saber yo? **I knew you at once,** Te reconocí en seguida. **They always k. best,** Ellos tienen siempre razón. **Did you k. about Philip?** ¿Has oído lo de Felipe? **to be in the k.,** estar bien informado, saber de buena tinta. **to get to k.,** (a person) llegar a conocer, trabar amistad con. **to make known,** dar a conocer; manifestar. **Who knows?** ¿Quién sabe? **to k. by heart,** saber de coro. **to k. how,** (to do something) saber. **to k. oneself,** conocerse a sí mismo. **k.-all,** sábelotodo, m. and f., marisabidilla, f.

knowing, a. inteligente; malicioso; (of animals) sabio. **There is no k.,** No hay modo de saberlo. **worth k.,** digno de saberse

knowingly, adv. a sabiendas, de intento; conscientemente; (cleverly) hábilmente; (with look, etc.) de un aire malicioso

knowledge, s. conocimiento, m. **To the best of my k. the book does not exist,** El libro no existe que yo sepa. **He has a thorough k. of ...,** Conoce a fondo ... **lack of k.,** ignorancia, f. **He did it without my k.,** Lo hizo sin que lo supiera yo. **It is a matter of common k. that ...,** Es notorio que ...

knowledgeable, a. sabedor

known, a. conocido

knuckle, s. (of a finger) nudillo, m., articulación del dedo, f.; (of meat) jarrete, m. **He knuckled down to his work,** Se puso a trabajar con ahinco. **to k. under,** someterse. **k.-duster,** rompecabezas, m.

kopeck, s. copec, f.

Koran, s. Corán, Alcorán, m.

kosher, a. autorizado por la ley judía

kowtow, v.i. saludar humildemente; (fig.) bajar la cerviz

kraal, s. kraal, m.

Krausist, a. and s. krausista (m. and f.)

Kremlin, s. Kremlín, m.

kudos, s. prestigio, m., gloria, f.

Kurdish, a. curdo

kursaal, s. casino, m.
kyle, s. estrecho, m.
kyrie eleison, s. kirieleisón, m.

L

l, s. (letter) ele, f.
la, s. (mus.) la, m.
labarum, s. lábaro, m.
label, s. etiqueta, f.; (on a museum specimen, etc.) letrero, m.; (fig.) calificación, f. v.t. poner etiqueta en; marcar, rotular; (fig.) calificar, designar, clasificar
labial, a. labial. s. letra labial, f.
laboratory, s. laboratorio, m.
laborious, a. laborioso; arduo, difícil, penoso
laboriously, adv. laboriosamente; con dificultad, penosamente
laboriousness, s. laboriosidad, f.; dificultad, f.
labour, s. trabajo, m.; labor, f.; fatiga, pena, f.; clase obrera, f.; (manual workers) mano de obra, f.; (effort) esfuerzo, m.; (of childbirth) dolores de parto, m. pl. v.i. trabajar; (strive) esforzarse, afanarse; (struggle) forcejear, luchar; (try) procurar, tratar de; avanzar con dificultad; (in childbirth) estar de parto. v.t. elaborar; pulir, perfeccionar. to l. under, sufrir; tener que luchar contra. hard l., trabajo arduo, m.; (law) trabajos forzosos, m. pl., presidio, m. Ministry of L., Ministerio de Trabajo, m. to be in l., estar de parto. to l. in vain, trabajar en balde, arar en el mar. to l. under a delusion, estar en el error, estar equivocado. L. Exchange, Bolsa de Trabajo, f. L. party, partido laborista, partido obrero, m. l. question, cuestión obrera, f.; (domestic) problema del servicio, m. l.-saving, a. que ahorra trabajo
laboured, a. (of style) premioso, artificial; forzado; (of breathing) fatigoso; (slow) torpe, lento
labourer, s. obrero, m.; (on the land) labrador, labriego, m.; (on the roads, etc.) peón, m.; (by the day) jornalero, m.
Labrador dog, s. perro de Labrador, m.

laburnum, s. codeso, m.
labyrinth, s. laberinto, m.
labyrinthine, a. laberíntico; intrincado
lac, s. laca, f.
lace, s. (of shoes, corsets, etc.) cordón, m.; (tape) cinta, f.; encaje, m.; (narrow, for trimming) puntilla, f.; (of gold or silver) galón, m. v.t. and v.i. (shoes, etc.) atarse los cordones; (trim) guarnecer con encajes, etc.; (fig.) ornar; (a drink) echar (coñac, etc.) en. blond l., blonda, f. gold l., galón de oro, m. point l., encaje de aguja, m. l. curtain, cortina de encaje, f.; (of net) visillo, m. l. maker or seller, encajera, f. l. making, obra de encaje, f. l.-pillow, almohadilla para encajes, f. l. shoes, zapatos con cordones, m. pl.
Lacedemonian, a. lacedemonio. s. lacedemonio (-ia)
lacerate, v.t. lacerar
laceration, s. laceración, f.
lachrymal, a. lagrimal, lacrimal
lachrymose, a. lacrimoso
lack, s. falta, f.; carestía, escasez, f.; (absence) ausencia, f.; (need) necesidad, f. v.t. carecer de; no tener; necesitar. v.i. hacer falta; necesitarse. to l. confidence in oneself, no tener confianza en sí mismo, carecer de confianza en sí mismo. l.-lustre, (of eyes) apagado, mortecino
lackadaisical, a. lánguido; indiferente; (dreamy) ensimismado, distraído
lackey, s. lacayo, m.
laconic, a. lacónico
laconically, adv. lacónicamente
laconicism, s. laconismo, m.
lacquer, s. laca, f. v.t. dar laca (a), barnizar con laca. gold l., sisa dorada, f. l. work, laca, f.
lacquering, s. barnizado de laca, m.; laca, capa de barniz de laca, f.
lacrosse, s. (sport) "lacrosse," f.
lactate, s. lactato, m. v.i. lactar
lactation, s. lactancia, f.
lacteal, a. lácteo
lactic, a. láctico
lactose, s. lactosa, f.
lacuna, s. laguna, f.
lacustrine, a. lacustre

lacy, *a.* de encaje; parecido a encaje; (*fig.*) transparente, etéreo

lad, *s.* muchacho, joven, mozalbete, *m.*; zagal, *m.*; (stable, etc.) mozo, *m.* **He's some l.!** ¡Qué tío que es! **l. of the village,** chulo, *m.*

ladder, *s.* escalera de mano, *f.*; (*naut.*) escala, *f.*; (in a stocking, etc.) carrera, *f.* **companion l.,** escala de toldilla, *f.* **to l. one's stocking,** escurrirse un punto de las medias

Ladies and gentlemen, Señoras y señores, Señores. **ladies' man,** hombre de salón, Perico entre ellas, *m.*

lading, *s.* flete, *m.*, carga, *f.*

ladle, *s.* cucharón, cazo, *m.* *v.t.* servir con cucharón; (a boat) achicar; (*fam.*) distribuir, repartir

ladleful, *s.* cucharada, *f.*

lady, *s.* dama, *f.*; señora, *f.*; (English title) milady, *f.*; (woman) mujer, *f.* **to be a l.,** ser una señora. **leading l.,** (*theat.*) dama primera, *f.* **Our L.,** Nuestra Señora. **young l.,** señorita, *f.*; (*fam.*) novia, *f.* **lady's maid,** doncella, *f.* **l. of the house,** señora de la casa, *f.* **l.-bird,** (*ent.*) mariquita, vaca de San Antón, *f.* **L. Chapel,** capilla de la Virgen, *f.* **L. Day,** día de la Anunciación (de Nuestra Señora), *m.* **l.-help,** asistenta, *f.* **l.-in-waiting,** dama de servicio, *f.* **l.-killer,** ladrón de corazones, castigador, Tenorio, *m.* **l.-love,** querida, amada, *f.* **l. mayoress,** alcaldesa, *f.*

ladylike, *a.* de dama; elegante; distinguido; bien educado; delicado; (of men) afeminado

ladyship, *s.* señoría, *f.* **Your L.,** Su Señoría

lag, *v.t.* recubrir; aislar. *v.i.* retrasarse; quedarse atrás; ir (or andar) despacio; rezagarse; (*naut.*) roncear. *s.* retraso, *m.*; (*mech.*) retardación de movimiento, *f.*

laggard, *s.* holgazán (-ana), haragán (-ana)

lagoon, *s.* laguna, *f.*

laid, *past part.* of verb **to lay. l. up,** (ill) enfermo; (*naut.*) inactivo; (of cars, etc.) fuera de circulación

lair, *s.* cubil, *m.*; guarida, madriguera, *f.*

laird, *s.* hacendado escocés, *m.*

laity, *s.* legos, *m. pl.*

lake, *s.* lago, *m.*; (pigment) laca, *f.* **small l.,** laguna, *f.* **l. dwelling,** vivienda palustre, *f.*

lama, *s.* lama, *m.*

lamaism, *s.* lamaísmo, *m.*

lamb, *s.* cordero (-ra). *v.i.* parir corderos. **lamb's wool,** lana de cordero, *f.*

lambent, *a.* ondulante, vacilante; centelleante

lamblike, *a.* manso como un cordero; inocente

lambskin, *s.* corderina, piel de cordero, *f.*

lame, *a.* estropeado, lisiado; (in the feet) cojo; (of metre) que cojea, malo; (of arguments) poco convincente; frívolo, flojo. *v.t.* lisiar; hacer cojo. **a l. excuse,** un pretexto frívolo. **to be l.,** (in the feet) (permanently) ser cojo; (temporarily) estar cojo

lamely, *adv.* cojeando, con cojera; (*fig.*) sin convicción; mal

lameness, *s.* cojera, *f.*; falta de convicción, *f.*

lament, *s.* lamento, *m.*; queja, lamentación, *f.* *v.i.* lamentarse; quejarse. *v.t.* lamentar, deplorar, llorar

lamentable, *a.* lamentable, deplorable; lastimero

lamentably, *adv.* lamentablemente

lamentation, *s.* lamentación, *f.*, lamento, *m.* **Book of Lamentations,** Libro de los lamentos, *m.*

lamenting, *s.* lamentación, *f.*

lamina, *s.* lámina, *f.*

laminate, *a.* laminado, laminar. *v.t.* laminar

lamp, *s.* lámpara, *f.*; (on vehicles, trains, ships and in the street) farol, *m.*; luz, *f.*; (oil) candil, *m.*, lámpara de aceite, *f.* **safety-l.,** lámpara de seguridad, lámpara de los mineros, *f.* **street l.,** farol (de las calles), *m.* **l.-black,** negro de humo, *m.* **l.-chimney,** tubo de una lámpara, *m.* **l. factory or shop,** lamparería, *f.* **l.-holder,** portalámpara, *f.* **l.-lighter,** farolero, lamparero, *m.* **l.-post,** farola, *f.* **l.-shade,**

pantalla de una lámpara, *f.* **l. stand,** pie de lámpara, *m.*

lamplight, *s.* luz de la lámpara, *f.*; luz artificial, *f.* **in the l.,** a la luz de la lámpara; en luz artificial

lampoon, *s.* pasquinada, *f.,* pasquín, *m.* *v.t.* pasquinar, satirizar

lampooner, *s.* escritor (-ra) de pasquinadas, libelista, *m.*

lamprey, *s.* lamprea, *f.*

Lancastrian, *a.* lancastriano

lance, *s.* lanza, *f.*; (soldier) lancero, *m.* *v.t.* alancear; (med.) lancinar. **l. in rest,** lanza en ristre, *f.* **l. thrust,** lanzada, *f.* **l.-corporal,** soldado de primera clase, *m.*

lancer, *s.* (mil.) lancero, *m.*; *pl.* **lancers,** (dance and music) lanceros, *m. pl.*

lancet, *s.* lanceta, *f.* **l. arch,** arco puntiagudo, *m.*

lancing, *s.* lancetada, *f.*

land, *s.* tierra, *f.*; terreno, *m.*; (country) país, *m.*; (region) región, *f.*; territorio, *m.*; (estate) bienes raíces, *m. pl.,* tierras, fincas, *f. pl.* *v.t.* desembarcar; echar en tierra; (fig., place) poner; (fam.) dejar plantado (con); (obtain) obtener; (a fish) sacar del agua; (a blow) dar (un golpe); (leave) dejar. *v.i.* desembarcar; saltar en tierra; (of a plane) aterrizar; (arrive) llegar; (fall) caer. **cultivated l.,** tierras cultivadas, *f. pl.* **dry l.,** (not sea) tierra firme, *f.* **native l.,** patria, *f.*; suelo natal, *m.* **on l.,** en tierra. **to see how the l. lies,** (fig.) tantear el terreno. **l. of milk and honey,** jauja, *f.,* paraíso, *m.* **l. of promise,** tierra de promisión, *f.* **l. agent,** procurador de fincas, *m.* **l. breeze,** brisa de tierra, *f.* **l. forces,** fuerzas terrestres, *f. pl.* **l. law,** leyes agrarias, *f. pl.* **l.-locked,** cercado de tierra. **l.-lubber,** marinero de agua dulce, *m.* **l. mine,** mina terrestre, *f.* **l. surveying,** agrimensura, *f.* **l. surveyor,** agrimensor, *m.* **l. tax,** contribución territorial, *f.*

landau, *s.* landó, *m.*

landed, *a.* hacendado. **l. gentry,** hacendados, terratenientes, *m.*

pl. **l. property,** bienes raíces, *m. pl.*

landfall, *s.* derrumbamiento de tierras, *m.*

landing, *s.* desembarque, desembarco, *m.*; (landing-place) desembarcadero, *m.*; (aer.) aterrizaje, *m.*; (of a stair) descanso, rellano, *m.,* mesilla, *f.* **forced l.,** aterrizaje forzoso, *m.* **l. certificate,** (com.) tornaguía, *f.* **l. craft,** barcaza de desembarco, *f.* **l. field,** campo de aterrizaje, *m.,* pista de vuelo, *f.* **l.-net,** salabardo, *m.* **l. party,** trozo de abordaje, *m.* **l. signal,** (aer.) señal de aterrizaje, *f.* **l.-stage,** desembarcadero, *m.*; (jetty) atracadero, *m.*

landlady, *s.* patrona, huéspeda, *f.*

landlord, *s.* (of houses, land) propietario, *m.*; hotelero, patrón, *m.*

landmark, *s.* (of a hill or mountain) punto destacado, *m.*; lugar conocido, *m.*; característica, *f.*; (fig.) monumento, *m.*

landowner, *s.* hacendado, terrateniente, *m.*

landscape, *s.* paisaje, *m.*; perspectiva, *f.* **l. gardener,** arquitecto de jardines, *m.* **l. painter,** paisajista, *m. and f.*

landslide, *s.* desprendimiento de tierras, *m.*; (fig.) cambio brusco de la opinión pública, *m.*

landward, *adv.* hacia tierra

lane, *s.* vereda, senda, *f.*; (of traffic) línea, *f.*

language, *s.* lenguaje, *m.*; lengua, *f.,* idioma, *m.* **modern l.,** lengua viva, *f.* **strong l.,** palabras mayores, *f. pl.*

langue d'oc, *s.* lengua de oc, *f.*

langue d'oïl, *s.* lengua de oïl, *f.*

languid, *a.* lánguido

languidly, *adv.* lánguidamente

languidness, *s.* languidez, *f.*

languish, *v.i.* languidecer

languishing, *a.* lánguido; amoroso, sentimental

languishingly, *adv.* lánguidamente; amorosamente

languor, *s.* languidez, *f.*

languorous, *a.* lánguido

languorously, *adv.* con langor

lank, *a.* flaco, descarnado, alto y delgado; (of hair) lacio

lankiness, s. flaqueza, f., gran talle, m.

lanky, a. talludo, alto y delgado, descarnado

lanoline, s. lanolina, f.

lansquenet, s. sacanete, m.

lantern, s. linterna, f.; (naut. and of a lighthouse) farol, m.; (arch.) linterna, f.; (small) farolillo, m. dark l., linterna sorda, f. **magic l.,** linterna mágica, f. **l.-jawed,** carilargo. **l. maker,** farolero, m. **l. slide,** diapositiva, f.

lanyard, s. (naut.) acollador, m.

lap, s. regazo, m.; falda, f.; (knees) rodillas, f. pl.; (lick) lamedura, f.; (of water) murmurio, susurro, m.; (in a race) vuelta completa a una pista, f.; (stage) etapa, f. v.t. (wrap) envolver; (cover) cubrir; (fold) plegar; (lick) lamer; (swallow) tragar. v.i. (overlap) traslaparse; estar replegado; (lick) lamer; (of water) murmurar, susurrar, besar. **l.-dog,** perro de faldas, perro faldero, m.

lapel, s. solapa, f.

lapidary, a. lapidario

lapidate, v.t. lapidar

lapidation, s. lapidación, f.

lapis lazuli, s. lapislázuli, m.

Laplander, s. lapón (-ona)

lapping, s. (licking) lamedura, f.; (of water) murmurio, susurro, chapaleteo, m.

Lappish, a. lapón. s. (language) lapón, m.

lapse, s. lapso, m.; (fault) desliz, m., falta, f.; (of time) transcurso, intervalo, m.; (fall) caída, f.; (law, termination) caducidad, f. v.i. recaer (en), reincidir (en); volver a, caer de nuevo (en); (law, cease) caducar; (law, pass to) pasar (a); dejar de existir, desaparecer. **after the l. of three days,** después de tres días, al cabo de tres días. **with the l. of years,** en el transcurso de los años

lapwing, s. ave fría, f.

larboard, s. babor, m. a. de babor

larceny, s. latrocinio, m.

larch, s. (tree and wood) alerce, lárice, m.

lard, s. manteca, f.; lardo, m. v.t. (cul.) lardear, mechar; (fig.) sembrar (con), adornar (con)

larder, s. despensa, f.

large, a. grande; grueso; amplio; vasto, extenso; (wide) ancho; considerable; (in number) numeroso; (main, chief) principal; liberal; magnánimo. **at l.,** en libertad, suelto. **on the l. side,** algo grande. **l.-headed,** cabezudo. **l.-hearted,** que tiene un gran corazón, magnánimo. **l. mouth,** boca grande, boca rasgada, f. **l.-nosed,** narigudo. **l. scale,** en gran escala. **l.-sized,** de gran tamaño. **l.-toothed,** dentudo, que tiene dientes grandes. **l. type,** letras grandes, f. pl.

largely, adv. grandemente; en gran manera; considerablemente; muy; ampliamente; liberalmente; extensamente

largeness, s. gran tamaño, m.; (of persons) gran talle, m.; amplitud, f.; vastedad, extensión, f.; (width) anchura, f.; liberalidad, f.; (generosity) magnanimidad, f.; grandeza de ánimo, f.

larger, a. comp. más grande, etc. See **large. to grow l.,** crecer, aumentarse. **to make l.,** hacer más grande; aumentar

largesse, s. liberalidad, f.

largo, s. and adv. (mus.) largo (m.)

lariat, s. lazo, m.

lark, s. alondra, f.; (spree) juerga, f.; (joke) risa, f. **to rise with the l.,** levantarse con las gallinas

larkspur, s. (bot.) espuela de caballero, f.

larva, s. larva, f.

laryngeal, a. laríngeo

laryngitis, s. laringitis, f.

larynx, s. laringe, f.

Lascar, s. láscar, m.

lascivious, a. lascivo, lujurioso

lasciviously, adv. lascivamente

lasciviousness, s. lujuria, lascivia, f.

lash, s. (thong) tralla, f.; (whip) látigo, m.; (blow) latigazo, m.; azote, m.; (of the eye) pestaña, f. v.t. dar latigazos (a); azotar; (of waves) romper contra; (of hail, rain) azotar; (excite) provocar; (the tail) agitar (la cola); (scold) fustigar; (fasten) sujetar, atar;

(*naut.*) trincar. **to l. out,** (of horses, etc.) dar coces; (in words) prorrumpir (en)

lashing, *s.* (whipping) azotamiento, *m.*; (tying) ligadura, atadura, *f.*; amarradura, *f.*

lass, *s.* muchacha, chica, mozuela, *f.*; zagala, *f.*; niña, *f.*

lassitude, *s.* lasitud, *f.*

lasso, *s.* lazo, *m.*, mangana, *f.* *v.t.* lazar, manganear

last, *v.i.* durar; subsistir, conservarse; continuar

last, *a.* último; (with month, week, etc.) pasado; (supreme) extremo, (el) mayor. *adv.* al fin; finalmente; por último; después de todos; por última vez; la última vez. *s.* el, *m.* (*f.* la) último (-ma); los últimos, *m. pl.* (*f. pl.* las últimas); (end) fin, *m.*; (for shoes) horma, *f.* **at l.,** en fin; por fin, a la postre. **at the l. moment,** a última hora. **I have not been there these l. five years,** Hace cinco años que no voy allí. **John spoke l.,** Juan habló el ultimo. **She came at l.,** Por fin ella llegó. **to the l.,** hasta el fin. **l. but one,** penúltimo (-ma). **l. hope,** última esperanza, *f.*; último recurso, *m.* **l. kick,** (*fam.*) último suspiro, *m.* **l. night,** anoche. **l. week,** la última semana; la semana pasada

lasting, *a.* permanente, perdurable; duradero; constante; (of colours) sólido

lastingness, *s.* permanencia, *f.*; duración, *f.*

lastly, *adv.* en conclusión, por fin, finalmente, por último

latch, *s.* pestillo, *m.* *v.t.* cerrar con pestillo. **l.-key,** llave de la puerta, *f.*; (Yale) llavín, *m.*

late, *a.* tarde; tardío; (advanced) avanzado; (last) último; reciente; (dead) difunto; (former) antiguo, ex . . .; (new) nuevo. *adv.* tarde. **Better l. than never,** Más vale tarde que nunca. **Helen arrived l.,** Elena llegó tarde. **The train arrived five minutes l.,** El tren llegó con cinco minutos de retraso. **He keeps l. hours,** Se acuesta muy tarde, Se acuesta a las altas horas de la noche (*fam.*, a las tantas).

of l., últimamente. **to grow l.,** hacerse tarde. **l. eighteenth-century poetry,** la poesía de fines del siglo diez y ocho

lateen, *a.* latino. **l. sail,** vela latina, *f.*

lately, *adv.* recientemente; últimamente, poco ha

latency, *s.* estado latente, *m.*

lateness, *s.* lo tarde; lo avanzado; retraso, *m.* **the l. of the hour,** la hora avanzada

latent, *a.* latente

later, *a.* más tarde; posterior; más reciente. *adv.* más tarde; (afterwards) luego, después; posteriormente. **sooner or l.,** tarde o temprano. **l. on,** más tarde

lateral, *a.* lateral, ladero

laterally, *adv.* lateralmente

Lateran, *a.* lateranense

latest, *a.* and *adv. sup.* último; más reciente, etc, See **late.** **at the l.,** a lo más tarde, a más tardar. **l. fashion,** última moda, *f.* **l. news,** últimas noticias, *f. pl.*; novedad, *f.*

latex, *s.* (*bot., chem.*) látex, *m.*

lath, *s.* listón, *m.* **to be as thin as a l.,** no tener más que el pellejo, estar en los huesos

lathe, *s.* torno, *m.*

lather, *s.* espuma de jabón, *f.*, jabonaduras, *f. pl.*; (of sweat) espuma, *f.* *v.t.* enjabonar; (*fam.*) zurrar. *v.i.* hacer espuma

lathering, *s.* jabonadura, *f.*; (*fam.*) tunda, zurra, *f.*

latifundia, *s. pl.* latifundios, *m. pl.*

Latin, *s.* latín, *m.* *a.* latino. **Low L.,** bajo latín, *m.* **L.-American,** *a.* latinoamericano. *s.* latinoamericano (-na)

Latinism, *s.* latinismo, *m.*

Latinist, *s.* latinista, *m.* and *f.*

latinize, *v.t.* latinizar

latitude, *s.* latitud, *f.*; libertad, *f.*

latitudinal, *a.* latitudinal

latitudinarian, *a.* latitudinario

latrine, *s.* letrina, *f.*

latter, *a.* más reciente; último, posterioro; moderno. **the l.,** éste, *m.*; ésta, *f.*; esto, *neut.*; éstos, *m. pl.*; éstas, *f. pl.* **the l. half,** la segunda mitad. **towards the l. end of the year,** hacia fines del año. **L. Day Saints,** mormones, *m. pl.*

latterly, *adv.* recientemente, últimamente; en los últimos tiempos; hacia el fin

lattice, *s.* rejilla, *f.*; celosía, reja, *f. v.t.* poner celosías (a); entrelazar. **l.-work,** enrejado, *m.*

latticed, *a.* (of windows, etc.) con reja

Latvian, *a.* latvio. *s.* latvio (-ia)

laud, *s.* alabanza, *f.*; *pl.* **lauds,** (*ecc.*) laudes, *f. pl. v.t.* alabar, elogiar

laudability, *s.* mérito, *m.*, lo meritorio

laudable, *a.* loable, meritorio

laudably, *adv.* landablemente

laudanum, *s.* láudano, *m.*

laudatory, *a.* laudatorio

laugh, *s.* risa, *f.*; carcajada, *f. v.t.* reír; (smile) sonreír; reírse. **loud l.,** risa estrepitosa, *f.* to **l. in a person's face,** reírsele a uno en las barbas. **to l. loudly,** reírse a carcajadas. **to l. to oneself,** reírse interiormente. **to l. to scorn,** poner en ridículo. **to l. at,** reírse de; burlarse de; ridiculizar

laughable, *a.* risible, irrisible, ridículo, absurdo

laughing, *a.* risueño, alegre; (absurd) risible. *s.* risa, *f.* to **burst out l.,** reírse a carcajadas. **l.-gas,** gas hilarante, *m.* **l.-stock,** hazmerreír, *m.*

laughingly, *adv.* riendo

laughter, *s.* risa, *f.*; (in a report) risas, *f. pl.* **burst of l.,** carcajada, *f.* to **burst into l.,** soltar el trapo, reírse a carcajadas, desternillarse de risa

launch, *s.* botadura (de un buque), *f.*; lancha, *f.*; bote, *m.*; canoa, *f. v.t.* (throw) lanzar; (a blow) asestar; (a vessel) botar, echar al agua; (begin) iniciar, dar principio a; (make) hacer. **to l. an offensive,** (*mil.*) emprender nna ofensiva. **to l. into,** arrojarse en; entregarse a. **motor l.,** canoa automóvil, *f.* **steam l.,** bote de vapor, *m.*

launching, *s.* botadura (de un buque), *f.*; (throwing) lanzamiento, *m.*; (beginning) iniciación, *f.*; inauguración, *f.*; (of a

loan, etc.) emisión, *f.* **l. site,** rampa, *f.*

launder, *v.t.* lavar y planchar (ropa)

laundress, *s.* lavandera, *f.*

laundry, *s.* lavadero, *m.*, lavandería, *f.*; (washing) colada, *f.*; (*fam.*) ropa lavada or ropa para lavar, *f.* **l.-man,** lavandero, *m.*

laureate, *a.* laureado. *s.* poeta laureado, *m.*

laurel, *s.* laurel, cerezo, *m. a.* láureo. **to crown with l.,** laurear. **l. wreath,** lauréola, *f.*

lava, *s.* lava, *f.*

lavabo, *s.* lavabo, *m.*; (*ecc.*) lavatorio, *m.*

lavatory, *s.* lavabo, *m.*; retrete, excusado, *m.*

lave, *v.t.* bañar

lavender, *s.* espliego, *m.*, lavanda, *f.* **l.-water,** agua de lavanda, *f.*

lavish, *a.* pródigo; profuso, abundante. *v.t.* prodigar

lavishly, *adv.* pródigamente; en profusión

lavishness, *s.* prodigalidad, *f.*; profusión, abundancia, *f.*

law, *s.* ley, *f.*; derecho, *m.*; jurisprudencia, *f.*; código de leyes, *m.* **according to law,** según derecho. **canon law,** derecho canónico, *m.* **civil law,** derecho civil, *m.* **constitutional law,** derecho político, *m.* **criminal law,** derecho penal, *m.* **in law,** por derecho, de acuerdo con la ley; desde el punto de vista legal. **international law,** derecho internacional, *m.* **maritime law,** código marítimo, *m.* **sumptuary laws,** leyes suntuarias, *f. pl.* **to be the law,** ser la ley. **to go to law,** pleitear (sobre). **to sue at law,** pedir en juicio, poner pleito. **to take the law into one's own hands,** tomar la ley por su propia mano. **law-abiding,** observante de la ley; amigo del orden. **law-breaker,** transgresor (-ra). **law court,** tribunal de justicia, *m.*; palacio de justicia, *m.* **law of nature,** ley natural, *f.* **law report,** revista de tribunales, *f.* **law school,** escuela de derecho, *f.* **law student,** estudiante de derecho, *m.* and *f.*

lawful, *a.* legítimo; legal; lícito; válido

lawfully, *adv.* legalmente; legítimamente, lícitamente

lawfulness, *s.* legalidad, *f.*; legitimidad, *f.*

lawgiver, *s.* legislador (-ra)

lawless, *a.* ilegal; desordenado; ingobernable, rebelde

lawlessness, *s.* ilegalidad, *f.*; desorden, *m.*; rebeldía, *f.*

lawn, *s.* césped, prado, *m.*; (cloth) estopilla, *f.* **l.-mower,** máquina segadora del césped, *f.* **l.-tennis,** tenis (en pista de hierba), *m.*

lawsuit, *s.* pleito, litigio, *m.*, causa, acción, *f.*

lawyer, *s.* abogado (-da). **lawyer's office or practice,** bufete, *m.*

lax, *a.* laxo; indisciplinado; vago; descuidado

laxative, *s.* laxante, *m.*, purga, *f.* *a.* laxativo

laxity, *s.* laxitud, *f.*; descuido, *m.*; indiferencia, *f.*

lay, *a.* laico, seglar, lego; profano. *s.* poema, *m.*, trova, *f.*; romance, *m.*; (song) canción, *f.* **the lay of the land,** la configuración del terreno. **lay brother,** confeso, monigote, *m.* **lay figure,** maniquí, *m.* **lay sister,** (hermana) lega, *f.*

lay, *v.t.* and *v.i.* poner; colocar; dejar; (strike) tumbar; (demolish) derribar; (the dust) matar; (pipes, etc.) instalar; (hands on) asentar (la mano en); (deposit) depositar; (beat down corn, etc.) encamar, abatir; (eggs) poner; (the table) cubrir, poner; (stretch) extender(se); (bury) depositar en el sepulcro; (a bet) hacer; (wager) apostar; (an accusation) acusar; (the wind, etc.) sosegar, amainar; (a ghost) exorcizar; (impute) atribuir, imputar; (impose) imponer; (prepare) preparar; (make) hacer; (open) abrir; (blame, etc.) echar; (claim) reclamar; (reveal) revelar. **Don't lay the blame on me!** ¡No me eches la culpa! **We laid our plans,** Hicimos nuestros planes; Hicimos nuestros preparativos. **to lay siege to,** asediar. **to lay the colours on too thick,** (*fig.*)

recargar las tintas. **to lay the foundations,** abrir los cimientos; (*fig.*) crear, establecer; fundar. **to lay about one,** dar garrotazos de ciego. **to lay aside,** poner a un lado; arrinconar; (save) ahorrar; (cast away) desechar; abandonar; (reserve) reservar; (a person) apartar de sí; (incapacitate) incapacitar. **to lay before,** mostrar; presentar; poner a la vista; revelar. **to lay by,** See **to lay aside**. **to lay down,** acostar; depositar; (a burden) posar; (arms) rendir; (one's life); entregar; (give up) renunciar (a); (sketch out) trazar, dibujar; (plan) proyectar; (keep) guardar; (as a principle) establecer, sentar; (the law) dictar. **to lay oneself down,** echarse, tumbarse. **to lay in,** (a stock) proveerse de, hacer provisión de; (hoard) ahorrar; (buy) comprar. **to lay off,** (*naut.*) virar de bordo; (*fam.*) quitarse de encima. **to lay on,** *v.t.* colocar sobre; (thrash) pegar; (blows) descargar; (paint, etc.) dar; (water, etc.) instalar; (impose) imponer; (exaggerate) exagerar. *v.i.* atacar. **to lay open,** abrir; descubrir, revelar; manifestar; exponer. **to lay oneself open to attack,** exponerse a ser atacado. **to lay out,** poner; arreglar; (the dead) amortajar; (one's money) invertir, emplear; (at interest) poner a rédito; (plan) planear; (knock down) derribar. **to lay oneself out to,** esforzarse a; tomarse la molestia de. **to lay over,** cubrir; sobreponer; extender sobre. **to lay to,** *v.i.* (*naut.*) estar a la capa. **to lay up,** guardar, acumular, atesorar; poner a un lado; (a ship) desarmar; (a car) poner fuera de circulación; (a person) obligar a guardar cama, incapacitar

layer, *s.* capa, *f.*; (*geol.*) estrato, *m.*; (*min.*) manto, *m.*; (bird) gallina (pata, etc.) ponedera, *f.*; (one who bets) apostador (-ra); (*agr.*) acodo, *m.* *v.t.* (of plants) acodar

layering, *s.* (*agr.*) acodadura, *f.*

layette, *s.* canastilla, *f.*

laying, *s.* colocación, *f.*; puesta,

f.; (of an egg) postura, *f.* **l. down**, depósito, *m.*; conservación, *f.*; (explanation) exposición, *f.* **l. on of hands**, imposición de manos, *f.* **l. out**, tendedura, *f.*; (of money) empleo, *m.*; inversión, *f.*; (arrangement) arreglo, *m.*

layman, *s.* seglar, *m.* and *f.*; profano (-na)

layout, *s.* plan, *m.*; disposición, *f.*; distribución, *f.*; esquema, *m.*

lazar, *s.* lázaro, *m.*

lazaretto, *s.* lazareto, *m.*

laze, *v.i.* holgazanear, gandulear, no hacer nada; encontrarse a sus anchas

lazily, *adv.* perezosamente; indolentemente; lentamente

laziness, *s.* pereza, holgazanería, *f.*; indolencia, *f.*; lentitud, *f.*

lazy, *a.* perezoso, holgazán; indolente. **l.-bones**, gandul (-la)

lead, *s.* (metal) plomo, *m.*; (in a pencil) mina, *f.*; (plummet) sonda, *f.*; (*print.*) interlínea, *f.*; *pl.* **leads**, (roofs) tejados, *m. pl.* *v.t.* emplomar; guarnecer con plomo; (*print.*) interlinear. **black-l.**, grafito, *m.* **deep-sea l.**, (*naut.*) escandallo, *m.* **white l.**, albayalde, *m.* **to heave the l.**, echar el escandallo, sondar. **l.-coloured**, de color de plomo, plomizo. **l. mine**, mina de plomo, *f.* **l. poisoning**, saturnismo, *m.*

lead, *s.* delantera, *f.*; primer lugar, *m.*; dirección, *f.*, mando, *m.*; (suggestion) indicación, *f.*; (influence) influencia, *f.*; (dog's) traílla, *f.*; (*theat.*) protagonista, *m.* and *f.*; (*theat.*) papel principal, *m.*; (at cards) mano, *f.*

lead, *v.t.* and *v.i.* (conduct) conducir, llevar; guiar; (induce) mover, persuadir, inducir; inclinar; (cause) hacer, causar; (captain) capitanear, encabezar; dirigir; (channel) encauzar; (with life) llevar; (give) dar; (head) ir a la cabeza de; (*mil.*) mandar; (at cards) salir; (at games) jugar en primer lugar; tomar la delantera; (*fig.*) superar a los demás; (of roads) conducir. **to take the l.**, ir delante; ir a la cabeza, tomar la delantera; tomar la iniciativa. **to l. one to think**, hacer pensar.

to l. the way, mostrar el camino; ir adelante. **to l. along**, llevar (por la mano, etc.), conducir; conducir por; guiar. **to l. astray**, descarriar; desviar (de), seducir (de). **to l. away**, conducir (a otra parte); llevarse (a). **to l. back**, conducir de nuevo; hacer volver. **This path leads back to the village**, Por esta senda se vuelve al pueblo. **to l. in, into**, conducir a (or ante); introducir en, hacer entrar en; invitar a entrar en; (of rooms) comunicarse con; (sin, etc.) inducir a. **to l. off**, *v.i.* ir adelante; (begin) empezar; (of rooms) comunicarse con. *v.t.* hacer marcharse, llevarse (a). **to l. on**, *v.t.* conducir; guiar; hacer pensar en; (make talk) dar cuerda (a). *v.i.* ir a la cabeza; tomar la delantera. **to l. out**, conducir afuera; (to dance) sacar. **to l. to**, conducir a; desembocar en, salir a; (cause) dar lugar a, causar; (make) hacer; (incline) inclinar. **This street leads to the square**, Por esta calle se va a la plaza, Esta calle conduce a la plaza. **to l. up to**, conducir a; (in conversation, etc.) preparar el terreno para; preparar; tener lugar antes de, ocurrir antes de

leaden, *a.* hecho de plomo, plúmbeo; (of skies, etc.) plomizo, de color de plomo, aplomado. **l.-footed**, pesado; lento

leader, *s.* conductor (-ra); guía, *m.* and *f.*; jefe (-fa); general, *m.*; director (-ra); (in a journal) artículo de fondo, *m.*; (of an orchestra) primer violín, *m.* **follow-my-l.**, (game) juego de seguir la fila, *m.*

leadership, *s.* dirección, *f.*; jefatura, *f.*; (*mil.*) mando, *m.*

lead-in, *a.* (*rad.*) de entrada. *s.* (*rad.*) conductor de entrada, *m.*

leading, *s.* (leadwork) emplomadura, *f.*

leading, *s.* (guidance) dirección, *f.* *a.* principal; primero; importante; eminente. **l. article**, artículo de fondo, *m.*; editorial, *m.* **l. card**, primer naipe, *m.* **l. counsel**, abogado (-da) principal. **l. lady**, (*theat.*) dama primera, primera actriz, *f.*; (cinema) estrella (de la pantalla), *f.* **l. man,** (*theat.*) primer galán, *m.* **l. question,** pregunta que sugiere la respuesta, *f.*; cuestión importante, *f.* **l. strings,** andadores, *m. pl.*; (*fig.*) tutelaje, *m.*

leaf, *s.* (*bot.* and of a page, door, window, table, screen, etc.) hoja, *f.*; (petal) pétalo, *m. v.i.* echar hojas. **gold l..** pan de oro, *m.* **to turn over a new l.,** volver la hoja, hacer libro nuevo, hacer vida nueva. **to turn over the leaves of a book,** hojear (un libro). **l.-bud,** yema, *f.* **l.-mould,** . abono verde, *m.* **l. tobacco,** tabaco en hoja, *m.*

leafiness, *s.* frondosidad, *f.*

leafless, *a.* sin hojas

leaflet, *s.* hojuela, *f.*; (pamphlet) folleto, *m.*

leafy, *a.* frondoso

league, *s.* (measure) legua, *f.*; liga, federación, sociedad, *f.*; (football) liga, *f. v.t.* aliar; asociar. *v.i.* aliarse; asociarse, confederarse. **to be in l.,** (*fam.*) estar de manga. **L. of Nations,** Sociedad de las Naciones, *f.*

leak, *s.* (hole) agujero, *m.*, grieta, *f.*; (*naut.*) vía de agua, *f.*; (of gas, liquids, etc.) escape, *m.*; (in a roof, etc.) gotera, *f.*; (*elec.*) resistencia de escape, *f. v.i.* (*naut.*) hacer agua; (gas, liquids, etc.) escaparse, salirse; (drip) gotear. **to l. out,** (of news, etc.) trascender, saberse. **to spring a l.,**. aparecer una vía de agua, hacer agua

leakage, *s.* (of gas, liquids) escape, *m.*, fuga, *f.*; derrame, *m.*; pérdida, *f.*; (of information) revelación, *f.*

leaky, *a.* (*naut.*) que hace agua; agujereado; poroso; que tiene goteras

lean, *a.* magro, seco, enjuto, delgado; (of meat) magro; (*fig.*) pobre, estéril. *s.* carne magra, *f.*, magro, *m.* **to grow l.,** enflaquecer

lean, *v.i.* inclinarse; apoyarse (en). *v.t.* apoyar (en); dejar arrimado (en). **to l. out of the window,** asomarse a la ventana. **to l. against,** apoyarse en, recostarse en (or contra). **to l. back,** echarse hacia atrás; recos-

tarse. **to l. over,** inclinarse. **to l. upon,** apoyarse en (also *fig.*); descansar sobre

leaning, *s.* inclinación, tendencia, *f.*; predilección, afición, *f.*

leanness, *s.* magrura, flaqueza, *f.*; (of meat) magrez, *f.*; (*fig.*) pobreza, *f.*

leap, *s.* salto, *m.*; brinco, *m.*; (caper) zapateta, *f.*; (*fig.*) salto, *m. v.i.* saltar, dar un salto; brincar. *v.t.* saltar; hacer saltar. **at one l.,** en un salto. **by leaps and bounds,** en saltos. **My heart leaped,** Mi corazón dió un salto. **to l. to the conclusion that . . .,** saltar a la conclusión de que . . . **to l. to the eye,** saltar a la vista. **l.-frog,** salto, *m.* **l. year,** año bisiesto, *m.*

leaper, *s.* saltador (-ra)

leaping, *a.* saltador. *s.* saltos, *m. pl.*

learn, *v.t.* and *v.i.* aprender; instruirse; enterarse de. **to l. by heart,** aprender de memoria. **to l. from a reliable source,** saber de buena tinta. **to l. from experience,** aprender/ por experiencia

learned, *a.* sabio, docto; erudito; (of professions) liberal; versado (en), entendido (en); **a l. society,** una sociedad erudita

learner, *s.* aprendedor (-ra)

learning, *s.* saber, *m.*; conocimientos, *m. pl.*; erudición, *f.*; estudio, *m.*; (literature) literatura, *f.*

lease, *s.* arrendamiento, arriendo, *m.*; contrato de arrendamiento, *m. v.t.* dar en arriendo, arrendar. **on l.,** en arriendo. **to take a new l. of life,** recobrar su vigor. **L.-lend bill,** ley de préstamo y arriendo, *f.*

leasehold, *s.* censo, *m. a.* censatario

leaseholder, *s.* concesionario, *m.*; arrendatario (-ia)

leash, *s.* (of a dog) traílla, *f.*

least, *a. sup.* little, mínimo; el (la, etc.) menor; más pequeño. *adv.* menos. *s.* lo menos. **at l.,** siquiera; por lo menos, al menos. **at the very l.,** a lo menos. **not in the l.,** de ninguna manera, nada. **to say the l. of,** sin exagerar, para no decir más

leather, s. cuero, m.; piel, f. a. de cuero; de piel. **patent l.,** charol, m. **Spanish l.,** cordobán, m. **tanned l.,** curtido, m. **l. apron,** mandil, m. **l. bag,** saco de cuero, m. **l. bottle,** bota, f. **l. breeches,** pantalón de montar, m. **l. jerkin,** coleto, m. **l. shield,** adarga, f. **l. strap,** correa, f. **l. trade,** comercio en cueros, m.

leatherette, s. cartón cuero, m.

leathery, a. de cuero; (of the skin) curtido por la intemperie; (tough) correoso

leave, s. (permission) permiso, m.; (mil., etc.) licencia, f.; (farewell) despedida, f. v.t. and v.i. dejar; abandonar; salir (de), quitar, marcharse (de); (as surety) empeñar; (by will) legar, mandar; (an employment) darse de baja (de), dejar; (give into the keeping of) entregar; (bid farewell) despedirse (de). **By your l.,** Con permiso de Vd. (Vds.). **on l.,** de permiso. **l.-taking,** despedida,, f. pl. **to be left,** quedar. **to be left over,** quedar; sobrar. **Two from four leaves two,** De cuatro a dos van dos. **to take French l.,** despedirse a la inglesa. **to take l. of,** despedirse de. **to take one's l.,** marcharse; despedirse. **to l. a deep impression,** (fig.) impresionar mucho; quedar grabado (en). **to l. undone,** dejar de hacer, no hacer; dejar sin terminar. **to l. about,** v.t. dejar por todas partes. v.i. (of time) marcharse a eso de ... **to l. ajar,** entreabrir, entornar. **to l. alone,** dejar a solas; dejar en paz; no molestar, no meterse con. **to l. aside,** omitir; prescindir de; olvidar. **to l. behind,** dejar atrás; olvidar. **to l. off,** v.t. dejar de; abandonar; (garments) no ponerse, quitarse. v.i. terminar. **to l. out,** dejar fuera; dejar a un lado, descontar; omitir; pasar por; (be silent about) callar; suprimir. **to l. to,** dejar para; dejar hacer

leaved, a. con hojas; de ... hojas

leaven, s. levadura, f., fermento, m. v.t. fermentar; (fig., permeate) penetrar (en), infiltrar en, imbuir; (a speech) salpimentar (con)

leaving, s. salida, partida, marcha, f.; pl. **leavings,** sobras, f. pl.; desechos, m. pl.

lecherous, a. lascivo, lujurioso

lechery, s. lascivia, lujuria, f.

lectern, s. atril, m.; (in a church) facistol, m.

lecture, s. conferencia, f.; (in a university) lección, clase, f.; discurso, m.; (fam., scolding) sermoneo, m. v.i. dar una conferencia; (in a university) dar clase. v.t. (fam., scold) predicar, sermonear. **l. room,** sala de conferencias, f.; (in a university) sala de clase, aula, f.

lecturer, s. conferenciante, m. and f.; (in a university) auxiliar, m.; (professor) catedrático (-ca), profesor (-ra)

lectureship, s. auxiliaría, f.

ledge, s. borde, m.; capa, f.; (of a window) alféizar, m.; (shelf) anaquel, m.

ledger, s. libro mayor, m.

lee, s. (naut.) sotavento, m. a. a sotavento

leech, s. sanguijuela, f.

leek, s. puerro, m.

leer, v.i. mirar de soslayo; guiñar el ojo; mirar con los ojos llenos de deseo. s. mirada de soslayo, f.; mirada de lascivia, f.

lees, s. pl. heces, f. pl.; sedimento, m.

leeward, s. sotavento, m. **on the l. side,** a sotavento

leeway, s. deriva, f.

left, past part. dejado, etc. See **leave.** a. izquierdo. adv. a la izquierda; hacia la izquierda. s. izquierda, f. **on the l.,** a la izquierda. **the L.,** (pol.) las izquierdas. **L. face!** ¡Izquierda! **l.-hand,** mano izquierda, f.; izquierda, f. **l.-hand drive,** conducción a la izquierda, f. **l.-handed,** zurdo. **l. luggage office,** consigna, f. **l.-overs,** sobras, f. pl., desperdicios, m. pl.

leg, s. pierna, f.; (of animals, birds, furniture) pata, f.; (of a triangle) cateto, m.; (of a pair of compasses, trousers, lamb, veal) pierna, f.; (of boots, stockings) caña, f.; (of pork) pernil, m.; (support) pie, m.; (stage) etapa, f. **to be on one's last legs,** estar en las últimas; estar aca-

bándose; estar sin recursos. **to
pull a person's leg,** tomar el
pelo (a). **leg-pull,** tomadura de
pelo, *f*. **leg-of-mutton sleeve,**
manga de pernil, *f*.

legacy, *s*. legado, *m*., manda, *f*.;
herencia, *f*.

legal, *a*. legal; de derecho;
jurídico; (lawful, permissible)
legítimo, lícito; (of a lawyer) de
abogado. **l. expenses,** litisexpensas, *f. pl*. **l. inquiry,**
investigación jurídica, *f*.

legality, *s*. legalidad, *f*.

legalization, *s*. legalización, *f*.

legalize, *v.t*. legalizar; autorizar,
legitimar

legally, *adv*. según la ley; según
derecho; legalmente

legate, *s*. legado, *m*. **Papal l.,**
legado papal, *m*.

legatee, *s*. legatario (-ia)

legateship, *s*. legacía, legación, *f*.

legation, *s*. legación, *f*.

legend, *s*. leyenda, *f*.

legendary, *a*. legendario

legerdemain, *s*. juegos de manos,
m. pl.

legged, *a*. con piernas; de piernas
. . .; de patas . . . **a three-l.
stool,** un taburete de tres patas.
long l., zancudo

leggings, *s. pl*. polainas, *f. pl*.

leghorn, *s*. paja italiana, *f*.;
sombrero de paja italiana, *m*.

legibility, *s*. legibilidad, *f*.

legible, *a*. legible

legibly, *adv*. legiblemente

legion, *s*. legión, *f*. **L. of Honour,**
Legión de Honor, *f*.

legionary, *a*. legionario. *s*. legionario, *m*.

legislate, *v.t*. legislar

legislation, *s*. legislación, *f*.

legislative, *a*. legislativo, legislador

legislator, *s*. legislador (-ra)

legislature, *s*. legislatura, *f*.

legist, *s*. legista, *m*.

legitimacy, *s*. legitimidad, *f*.;
justicia, *f*.

legitimate, *a*. legítimo; justo

legitimately, *adv*. legitimamente

legitimation, *s*. legitimación, *f*.

leguminous, *a*. leguminoso

leisure, *s*. ocio, *m*., desocupación,
f.; tiempo libre, *m*. **at one's l.,**
con sosiego, despacio. **You can
do it at your l.,** Puedes hacerlo·

cuando tengas tiempo. **to be at
l.,** estar desocupado, no tener
nada que hacer. **l. moments,**
ratos perdidos, momentos de ocio,
m. pl.

leisured, *a*. desocupado, libre; sin
ocupación; (wealthy) acomoda-
do

leisureliness, *s*. (slowness) lentitud, deliberación, *f*.; tardanza, *f*.

leisurely, *a*. pausado, lento,
deliberado; tardo

lemon, *s*. limón, *m*.; (tree)
limonero, *m*. *a*. limonado, de
color de limón; hecho o sazonado
con limón. **l. drop,** pastilla de
limón, *f*. **l.-grove,** limonar, *m*.
l.-squash, limonada natural, *f*.
l.-squeezer, exprime limones,
m., exprimidera, *f*.

lemonade, *s*. limonada, *f*. **l.
powder,** limonada seca, *f*.

lemur, *s*. lemur, *m*.

lend, *v.t*. prestar. **to l. an ear to,**
prestar atención a. **It does not
l. itself to . . .,** No se presta
a . . . **to l. a hand,** echar una
mano, dar una mano, ayudar.

lender, *s*. el, *m*. (*f*. la) que presta;
prestador (-ra); (of money) prestamista, *m*. and *f*.; (com.) mutuante, *m*. and *f*.

lending, *s*. prestación, *f*., préstamo, *m*. **l.-library,** biblioteca
circulante, *f*.

length, *s*. largo, *m*.; longitud, *f*.;
(of fabric) corte, *m*.; (of a ship)
eslora, *f*.; (in racing) largo, *m*.;
distancia, *f*.; (in time) duración,
f.; alcance, *m*. **at l.,** por fin,
finalmente; (in full) extensamente, largamente. **by a l.,** por
un largo. **full-l.,** de cuerpo
entero. **three feet in l.,** tres pies
de largo. **to go the l. of . . .,**
llegar al extremo de . . .

lengthen, *v.t*. alargar; prolongar;
extender. *v.i*. alargarse; prolongarse; extenderse; (of days)
crecer

lengthening, *s*. alargamiento,
m.; prolongación, *f*.; crecimiento,
m.

lengthily, *adv*. largamente

lengthiness, *s*. largueza, *f*.; prolijidad, *f*.

lengthy, *a*. largo; demasiado
largo, larguísimo; (of speech)
prolijo; verboso

lenience, leniency, s. lenidad, f.; indulgencia, f.
lenient, a. indulgente; poco severo
leniently, adv. con indulgencia
lenitive, a. lenitivo. s. lenitivo, m.
lens, s. lente, m.; (of the eye) cristalino, m.
Lent, s. Cuaresma, f.
Lenten, a. de Cuaresma, cuaresmal
lentil, s. lenteja, f.
lentitude, s. lentitud, f.
Leo, s. León, m.
leonine, a. leonino
leopard, s. leopardo, m.
leper, s. leproso (-sa). **l. colony,** colonia de leprosos, f.
lepidoptera, s. pl. lepidópteros, m. pl
leprosy, s. lepra, f.
leprous, a. leproso
Lesbian, a. lesbio. s. lesbio (-ia)
lese-majesty, s. crimen de lesa majestad, m.
lesion, s. lesión, f.
less, a. menor; más pequeño; menos; inferior. adv. menos; sin. **l. than,** menos de (que). **more or l.,** poco más o menos. **no l.,** nada menos. **none the l.,** sin embargo. **to grow l.,** disminuir. **l. and l.,** cada vez menos
lessee, s. arrendatario (-ia); inquilino (-na)
lessen, v.i. disminuir; reducirse. v.t. disminuir; reducir; (lower) rebajar; (disparage) menospreciar
lessening, s. disminución, f.; reducción, f.
lesser, a. comp. menor; más pequeño. See **little**
lesson, s. lección, f. **to give a l.,** dar lección, dar clase; (fig.) dar una lección (a). **to hear a l.,** tomar la lección
lessor, s. arrendador (-ra)
lest, conjunc. para que no; por miedo de (que), no sea que. **I did not do it l. they should not like it,** No lo hice por miedo de que no les gustase
let, v.t. dejar, permitir; (lease) arrendar. v.i. alquilarse, ser alquilado. Let as an expression of the imperative is rendered in Spanish by the subjunctive or the imperative, e.g. Let them go!

¡Que vayan! ¡Déjalos marchar! He let them go, Les dejó marchar. **to let fall,** dejar caer. **to let go,** dejar marchar; soltar; poner en libertad (a). **to let loose,** dar suelta a; (fig.) desencadenar. **to let one know,** hacer saber, comunicar. **to let the cat out of the bag,** tirar de la manta. **to let the chance slip,** perder la ocasión. **to let alone,** (a thing) no tocar; (a person) dejar en paz, dejar tranquilo; (an affair) no meterse (en or con); (omit) no mencionar, omitir toda mención de. **to let down,** bajar; (by a rope) descolgar; (hair, etc.) dejar caer; (a dress, etc.) alargar; (naut.) calar; (disappoint) dejar plantado. **to let in,** dejar entrar; hacer entrar; invitar a entrar; recibir; (insert) insertar. **to let into,** (initiate) iniciar en, admitir en; (a secret) revelar. Other meanings, see **to let in. to let off,** dejar salir; dejar en libertad; exonerar; perdonar; (a gun) disparar; (fireworks, etc.) hacer estallar. **to let out,** dejar salir; poner en libertad; (from a house) acompañar a la puerta; abrir la puerta; (sew.) ensanchar; (hire) alquilar; (the fire, etc.) dejar extinguirse. **to let up,** dejar subir; (decrease) disminuir; (end) terminar
let, s. estorbo, impedimento, obstáculo, m. **without let or hindrance,** sin estorbo ni obstáculo
lethal, a. letal. **l. weapon,** instrumento de muerte, m.
lethargic, a. aletargado; letárgico
lethargy, s. letargo, m.; (med.) letargía, f.
letter, s. (of the alphabet) letra, f.; (epistle) carta, f.; (print.) carácter, m.; (lessor) arrendador (-ra); pl. letters, letras, f. pl.; (correspondence) correo, m.; correspondencia, f. v.t. inscribir; imprimir. **capital l.,** letra mayúscula, f. **first letters,** (fig.) primeras letras, f. pl. **registered l.,** carta certificada, f., certificado, m. **small l.,** letra minúscula, f. **the l. of the law,** la ley escrita. **to be l.-perfect,** saber

de memoria. **to the l.**, (*fig.*) a la letra. **letters patent**, patente, *f.*; título de privilegio, *m.* **l.-balance**, pesacartas, *m.* **l.-book**, (*com.*) libro copiador, *m.* **l.-box**, buzón de correos, *m.* **l.-card**, tarjeta postal del gobierno, *f.* **l. of credit**, carta de crédito, *f.* **l. of introduction**, carta de presentación, *f.* **l.-writer**, escritor (-ra) de cartas

lettered, *a.* culto, instruido; (printed) impreso

lettering, *s.* inscripción, *f.*; letrero, rótulo, *m.*

letterpress, *s.* imprenta, *f.*; (not illustrations) texto, *m.*

letting, *s.* (hiring) arrendamiento, *m.*

lettuce, *s.* lechuga, *f.* **l. plant**, lechuguino, *m.* **l. seller**, lechuguero (-ra)

leucocyte, *s.* leucocito, *m.*

Levantine, *a.* and *s.* levantino (-na)

levee, *s.* besamanos, *m.*, recepción, *f.*

level, *s.* nivel, *m.*; ras, *m.*, flor, *f.*; llano, *m.*; (plain) llanura, *f.*; (instrument) nivel, *m.* *a.* llano; igual; al nivel (de); uniforme; imparcial. *adv.* a nivel; igualmente. *v.t.* nivelar; igualar; allanar; (a blow) asestar; (a gun) apuntar; (raze) arrasar, derribar; adaptar; hacer uniforme. **on the l.**, a nivel; (*fig.*) de buena fe. **spirit l.**, nivel de burbuja, *m.* **to make l. again**, reilanar. **l. country**, campaña, llanura, *f.* **l. with the ground**, a ras de la tierra. **l. with the water**, a flor de agua. **l. crossing**, paso a nivel, *m.* **l.-headed**, sensato, cuerdo. **l. stretch**, rellano, *m.*; llanura, *f.*

leveller, *s.* nivelador (-ra)

levelling, *a.* nivelador; de nivelación; igualador. *s.* nivelación, *f.*; allanamiento, *m.*; (to the ground) arrasamiento, *m.*; igualación, *f.*

levelness, *s.* nivel, *m.*; planicie, *f.*; igualdad, *f.*

lever, *s.* palanca, *f.*; (handle) manivela, *f.*; escape de reloj, *m.*; (excuse) pretexto, *m.*; (means) modo, *m.* *v.t.* sopalancar. **control l.**, (*aer.*) palanca de mando, *f.* **hand-l.**, palanca de mano, *f.*

leverage, *s.* sistema de palancas, *m.*; acción de palanca, *f.*; (*fig.*) influencia, fuerza, *f.*, poder, *m.*

Leviathan, *s.* leviatán, *m.*

levitation, *s.* levitación, *f.*

Levite, *s.* levita, *m.*

Levitical, *a.* levítico

Leviticus, *s.* Levítico, *m.*

levity, *s.* levedad, frivolidad, ligereza, *f.*

levy, *s.* exacción (de tributos), *f.*; impuesto, *m.*; (of a fine) imposición, *f.*; (*mil.*) leva, *f.* *v.t.* (taxes) exigir; (a fine) imponer; (troops) reclutar, enganchar

levying, *s.* (of a tax) exacción (de tributos), *f.*; (of a fine) imposición, *f.*; (of troops) leva, *f.*

lewd, *a.* lascivo, lujurioso, impúdico

lewdness, *s.* lascivia, lujuria, impudicia, *f.*

lexicographer, *s.* lexicógrafo, *m.*

lexicography, *s.* lexicografía, *f.*

lexicon, *s.* léxico, *m.*; diccionario, *m.*

liability, *s.* responsabilidad, obligación, *f.*; tendencia, *f.*; riesgo, *m.*; *pl.* **liabilities**, obligaciones, *f. pl.*; (com.) pasivo, *m.*

liable, *a.* responsable; propenso (a); expuesto (a); sujeto (a)

liaison, *s.* lío, *m.*; coordinación, *f.* **l. officer**, oficial de coordinación, *m.*

liar, *s.* mentiroso (-sa)

libation, *s.* libación, *f.*

libel, *s.* libelo, *m.*; difamación, *f.* *v.t.* difamar, calumniar

libeller, *s.* libelista, *m.*, difamador (-ra)

libellous, *a.* difamatorio

liberal, *a.* liberal; generoso; abundante. *s.* liberal, *m.* and *f.* **l. profession**, carrera liberal, *f.* **l.-minded**, tolerante. **l.-mindedness**, tolerancia, *f.*

liberalism, *s.* liberalismo, *m.*

liberality, *s.* liberalidad, *f.*; generosidad, *f.*

liberalize, *v.t.* liberalizar

liberate, *v.t.* (a prisoner) poner en libertad; librar (de); (a gas, etc.) dejar escapar

liberation, *s.* liberación, *f.*; (of a captive) redención, *f.*; (of a slave) manumisión, *f.*

liberator, *s.* libertador (-ra)

libertinage, s. libertinaje, m.

libertine, s. libertino, m.

libertinism, s. libertinaje, m.

liberty, s. libertad, f.; (familiarity) familiaridad, f.; (right) privilegio, m., prerrogativa, f.; (leave) permiso, m. **at l.,** en libertad; desocupado, libre. **I have taken the l. of giving them your name,** Me he tomado la libertad de darles su nombre. **to set at l.,** poner en libertad (a). **to take liberties with,** tratar con familiaridad; (a text) tergiversar. **l. of speech,** libertad de palabra, libertad de expresión, f. **l. of thought,** libertad de pensamiento, f.

libidinous, a. libidinoso

Libra, s. Libra, f.

librarian, s. bibliotecario (-ia)

librarianship, s. carrera (f.) or empleo (m.) de bibliotecario

library, s. biblioteca, f.; (book shop) librería, f. **l. catalogue,** catálogo de la biblioteca, m.

librettist, s. libretista, m. and f.

libretto, s. libreto, m.

Libyan, a. and s. libio (-ia)

licence, s. licencia, f., permiso, m.; autorización, f.; (driving) carnet de chófer, permiso de conducción, m.; (of a car) permiso de circulación, m.; (for a wireless, etc.) licencia, f.; (marriage) licencia de casamiento, f.; (excess) libertinaje, desenfreno, m. **import l.,** permiso de importación, m. **poetic l.,** licencia poética, f. **l. number,** (of a car) número de matriculación, m.

license, v.t. licenciar; autorizar; (a car) sacar la licencia del automóvil

licensee, s. concesionario (-ia)

licentiate, s. licenciado (-da)

licentious, a. licencioso, disoluto

licentiousness, s. libertinaje, m., disipación, f.

lichen, s. liquen, m.

licit, a. lícito

lick, v.t. lamer; (of waves) besar; (of flames) bailar; (thrash) azotar; (defeat) vencer. **to l. one's lips,** relamerse los labios, chuparse los dedos. **to l. the dust,** morder el polvo

licking, s. lamedura, f.; (beating) paliza, tunda, f.; (defeat) derrota, f.

lictor, s. lictor, m.

lid, s. cobertera, f.; tapa, f.; (of the eye) párpado, m.

lie, s. mentira, f.; invención, falsedad, f.; mentís, m. v.i. mentir. **to give the lie to,** desmentir, dar el mentís. **to lie barefacedly,** mentir por la mitad de la barba. **white lie,** mentira oficiosa, f.

lie, v.i. estar tumbado, estar echado; estar recostado; descansar, reposar; (in the grave) yacer; (be) estar; (be situated) hallarse, estar situado; (stretch) extenderse; (sleep) dormir; (depend) depender; (consist) consistir, estribar; (as an obligation) incumbir. **Here lies . . .,** Aquí descansa . . . **It does not lie in my power,** No depende de mí. **to let lie,** dejar; dejar en paz. **to lie at anchor,** estar anclado. **to lie fallow,** estar en barbecho; (fig.) descansar. **to lie about,** estar esparcido por todas partes; estar en desorden. **to lie along,** estar tendido a lo largo de; (naut.) dar a la banda. **to lie back,** recostarse; apoyarse (en). **to lie by,** estar acostado al lado de; (of things, places) estar cerca (de); descansar. **to lie down,** tenderse, tumbarse, echarse, acostarse; reposar. **Lie down!** (to a dog) ¡Échate! **to lie down under,** tenderse bajo; (an insult) tragar, sufrir. **to lie in,** consistir en; depender de; (of childbirth) estar de parto. **to lie open,** estar abierto; estar expuesto (a); estar al descubierto, estar a la vista. **to lie over,** (be postponed) quedar aplazado. **to lie to,** (naut.) estarse a la capa, ponerse en facha. **to lie under,** estar bajo, hallarse bajo; estar bajo el peso de; (be exposed to) estar expuesto a. **to lie with,** dormir con; (concern) tocar (a); corresponder (a)

lie, s. configuración, f.; disposición, f.; posición, f. **the lie of the land,** la configuración del terreno

liege, *a.* feudatario. *s.* señor feudal, *m.*; vasallo, *m.*

lieu, *s.* lugar, *m.* **in l. of,** en lugar de, en vez de .

lieutenancy, *s.* lugartenencia, tenencia, *f.*

lieutenant, *s.* teniente, lugarteniente, *m.*; (naval) alférez, *m.* **first l.,** (in the army) primer teniente, teniente, *m.*; (in the navy) alférez de navío, *m.* **naval l.,** teniente de navío, *m.* **second l.,** (in the army) segundo teniente, *m.*; (in the navy) alférez de fragata, *m.* **l.-colonel,** teniente coronel, *m.* **l.-commander,** capitán de fragata, *m.* **l.-general,** teniente general, *m.* **l.-governor,** subgobernador, *m.*

life, *s.* vida, *f.*; (being) ser, *m.*; (society) mundo, *m.*, sociedad, *f.*; (vitality) vitalidad, *f.*; vigor, *m.* *a.* de vida; (of annuities, etc.) vitalicio; (life-saving) de salvamento. **for l.,** de por vida. **from l.,** del natural. **high l.,** gran mundo, *m.*, alta sociedad, *f.* **low l.,** vida del hampa, vida de los barrios bajos, *f.* **to the l.,** al vivo. **to lay down one's l.,** entregar la vida. **to take one's l. in one's hands,** jugarse la vida. **l. annuity,** fondo vitalicio, *m.* **l.-belt,** (cinturón) salvavidas, *m.* **l.-blood,** sangre vital, *f.*; (fig.) nervio, *m.*; vigor, *m.* **l.-boat,** (on a ship) bote salvavidas, *m.*; (on the coast) lancha de salvamento, *f.* **l.-boat station,** estación de salvamento, *f.* **l.-giving,** vivificante, que da vida; tonificante. **l.-guard,** guardia militar, *f.*; Guardia de Corps, *f.* **l.-insurance,** seguro sobre la vida, *m.* **l.-interest,** usufructo, *m.* **l.-jacket,** chaleco salvavidas, *m.* **l.-like,** natural. **l.-line,** cable de salvamento, *m.* **l.-saving,** *a.* de salvamento; curativo. **l.-saving apparatus,** aparato salvavidas, *m.* **l.-sized,** de tamaño natural.

lifeless, *a.* sin vida, muerto; inanimado; (fig.) desanimado

lifelong, *a.* de toda la vida

lifetime, *s.* vida, *f.*

lift, *s.* esfuerzo para levantar, *m.*; acción de levantar, *f.*; alza, *f.*; (blow) golpe, *m.*; (help) ayuda, *f.*; (for passengers) ascensor, *m.*; (for goods) montacargas, *m.*; *pl.* **lifts,** (naut.) balancines, *m. pl.* **to give a l. to,** ayudar; llevar en auto, etc. **l. attendant,** ascensorista, *m.* and *f.*

lift, *v.t.* levantar; alzar, elevar; (pick up) coger; (one's hat) quitarse; (steal) hurtar; exaltar. *v.i.* (of mist) disiparse; desaparecer. **to l. the elbow,** empinar el codo. **to l. down,** quitar (de); (a person) bajar en brazos. **to l. up,** alzar; erguir, levantar; levantar en brazos

lifting, *s.* acción de levantar, *f.*; levantamiento, alzamiento, *m.*

ligament, *s.* ligamento, *m.*

ligature, *s.* (surg., mus.) ligadura, *f.*

light, *a.* (not dark) claro, con mucha luz, bañado de luz; (of colours) claro; (not heavy, and of sleep, food, troops, movements) ligero; (of reading) de entretenimiento; (irresponsible) frívolo; (easy) fácil; (slight) leve; (of hair) rubio; (happy) alegre; (fickle) inconstante, liviano; (of complexion) blanco. *adv.* ligero. **to be l.,** no pesar mucho; estar de día. **to grow l.,** (dawn) clarear; iluminarse. **to make l. of,** no tomar en serio; no preocuparse de; (suffering) sufrir sin quejarse. **l.-coloured,** (de color) claro. **l.-fingeredness,** sutileza de manos, *f.* **l.-footed,** ligero de pies. **l.-haired,** de pelo rubio. **l.-headed,** casquivano, ligero de cascos; delirante. **l.-headedness,** ligereza de cascos, frivolidad, *f.*; delirio, *m.* **l.-hearted,** alegre (de corazón). **l.-heartedness,** alegría, *f.* **l. horse,** (mil.) caballería ligera, *f.* **l. troops,** tropas ligeras, *f. pl.* **l.-weight,** *s.* (boxing) peso ligero, *m.* *a.* de peso ligero

light, *s.* luz, *f.*; (day) día, *m.*; (match) cerilla, *f.*; (of a cigarette, etc.) fuego, *m.*; (of a window) cristal, vidrio, *m.*; (point of view) punto de vista, *m.*; (in a picture) toque de luz, *m.*; *pl.* **lights,** (offal) bofes, *m. pl.* **against the l.,** al trasluz. **by the l. of,** a la luz de; según. **half-l.,** media luz, *f.* **high light(s),** (art) claros, *m. pl.;* *(fig.)* momento ·culminante, *m.;* acontecimiento de más interés, *m.* to come to l., descubrirse. to put a l. to the fire, encender el fuego. ¯l.-year, año de luz, *m.*

light, *v.t.* (a lamp, fire, etc.) encender; iluminar. *v.i.* encenderse; iluminarse; *(fig.)* animarse; brillar. to l. upon, encontrar por casualidad; tropezar con

lighten, *v.t.* (illuminate) iluminar; (of weight) aligerar; (cheer) alegrar; (mitigate) aliviar. *v.i.* (grow light) clarear; (of lightning) relampaguear; (become less heavy) disminuir de peso, aligerarse; volverse ·más alegre

lightening, *s.* aligeramiento, *m.;* (easing) alivio, *m.;* luz, *f.*

lighter, *s.* (boat) lancha, barcaza, gabarra, *f.;* (device) encendedor, *m.* pocket l., encendedor de bolsillo, *m.* l. man, gabarrero, *m.*

lighthouse, *s.* faro, *m.* l.-keeper, guardafaro, *m.*

lighting, *s.* iluminación, *f.;* alumbrado, *m.* flood l., iluminación intensiva, *f.* l.-up time, hora de encender los faros, *f.*

lightly, *adv.* ligeramente; fácilmente; (slightly) levemente; ágilmente; sin seriedad. l. wounded, levemente herido

lightness, *s.* ligereza, *f.;* poco peso, *m.;* agilidad, *f.;* (brightness) claridad, *f.;* (inconstancy) liviandad, inconstancia, *f.;* frivolidad, *f.*

lightning, *s.* relámpago, rayo, *m.* as quick as l., como un relámpago. to be struck by l., ser herido por un relámpago. l.-conductor, pararrayos, *m.*

lightship, *s.* buque faro, *m.*

lightsome, *a.* ágil; alegre

ligneous, *a.* leñoso

lignite, *s.* lignito, *m.*

Ligurian, *a.* ligurino. *s.* ligurino (-na)

likable, *a.* simpático

like, *a.* semejante; parecido; igual, mismo; (characteristic) típico, característico; (likely) probable; (equivalent) equivalente. *adv.* como; igual (que); del ·mismo modo (que). ·*s.* semejante, igual, *m.* and *f.;* tal

cosa, *f.;* cosas semejantes, *f. pl.* Don't speak to me l. that, No me hables así. He was l. a fury, Estaba hecho una furia. They are very l. each other, Se parecen mucho. .to ·be l., parecerse (a), semejar. to look l., parecer ser .(que); tener el aspecto de; (of persons) parecerse (a). to return l. for l., pagar en la misma moneda

like, *v.t.* gustar, agradar; estar aficionado (a), gustar de; (wish) querer. As you l., Como. te parezca bien, Como quieras. If you l., Si quieres. James likes painting, Jaime está aficionado a la pintura. Judith does not l. the north of England, A Judit no le gusta el norte de Inglaterra. I don't l. to do it, No me gusta hacerlo. I should l. him to go to Madrid, Me gustaría que fuese a Madrid

likelihood, *s.* posibilidad, *f.;* probabilidad, *f.*

likely, *a.* probable; verosímil, creíble, plausible; posible; (suitable) satisfactorio, apropiado; (handsome) bien ·parecido. *adv.* probablemente. They are not l. to come, No es probable que vengan

liken, *v.t.* comparar

likeness, *s.* parecido, *m.,* ·semejanza, *f.;* (portrait) retrato, *m.*

likewise, *adv.* igualmente, asimismo, también. *conjunc.* además

liking, *s.* (for persons) simpatía, *f.,* cariño, *m.;* (for things) gusto, *m.,* afición, *f.;* (appreciation) aprecio, *m.* I have a l. for old cities, Me gustan (or me atraen) las viejas ciudades. to take a l. to, (things) aficionarse a; (persons) prendarse de, tomar cariño (a)

lilac, *s.* lila, *f.* l. colour, color de lila, *m.*

Lilliputian, .*a.* liliputiense. *s.* liliputiense, *m.* and *f.*

lilt, *s.* canción, *f.;* ritmo, *m.;* ·armonía, *f.*

lily, *s.* lirio, *m.,* azucena, *f.;* (of France) flor de lis, *f.* l. of the valley, lirio de los valles, muguete, *m.* l.-white, ·blanco como la azucena

limb, s. (*anat.*) miembro, m:; (of a tree) rama, f.

limbless, a. mutilado

limbo, s. limbo, m.

lime, s. (*chem.*) cal, f.; (for catching birds) liga, hisca, f.; (linden tree) tilo, m.; (tree like a lemon) limero, m.; (fruit) lima, f. v.t. (whiten) encalar; (*agr.*) abonar con cal. **slaked l.,** cal muerta, f. **l.-flower,** flor del tilo, tila, f.; flor del limero, f. **l.-juice,** jugo de lima, m. **l.-kiln,** calera, f. **l.-pit,** pozo de cal, m.

limelight, s. luz de calcio, f.; (*fig.*) centro de atención, m.; publicidad, f. **to be in the l.,** ser el centro de atención

limen, s. (*psy.*) limen, m.

limestone, s. piedra caliza, f. **l. deposit,** calar, m.

limit, s. límite, m.; confín, m.; linde, m. or f.; limitación, f. v.t. limitar; fijar; (restrict) restringir. **This is the l.!** ¡Este es el colmo! ¡No faltaba más!

limitation, s. limitación, f.; restricción, f.

limitative, a. restrictivo, limitativo

limited, a. limitado; restringido; escaso; (of persons) de cortos alcances; (*com.*) anónimo. **l. company,** sociedad anónima, f.

limitless, a. sin límites; ilimitado, inmenso

limousine, s. limousine, f., coche cerrado, m.

limp, a. flojo; débil; fláccido; lánguido. s. cojera, f. v.i. cojear. **to l. off,** marcharse cojeando. **to l. up,** acercarse cojeando; subir cojeando

limpet, s. lapa, f.

limpid, a. límpido, cristalino, puro

limpidity, s. limpidez, f.

limping, a. cojo

limply, adv. flojamente; débilmente; lánguidamente

limpness, s. flojedad, f.; debilidad, f.; languidez, f.

linchpin, s. pezonera, f.

linden, s. tilo, m.

line, v.t. (furrow) surcar; (troops, etc.) poner en fila; alinear; (clothes, nests, etc.) forrar; (building) revestir; (one's pocket) llenar. v.i. estar en línea, alinearse

line, s. (most meanings) línea, f.; (cord) cuerda, f.; (*naut.*) cordel, m.; (fishing) sedal, m.; (railway) vía, f.; (wrinkle) surco, m.; arruga, f.; (row) hilera, ringlera, fila, f.; (of verse) verso, m.; (*print.*) renglón, m.; (of business) ramo, m.; profesión, f.; (interest) especialidad, f. **bowling or serving l.,** línea de saque, f. **hard lines,** mala suerte, f.; apuro, m., situación difícil, f. **in a l.,** en fila; en cola. **in direct l.,** (of descent) en línea recta. **It is not in my l.,** No es una especialidad mía; No es uno de mis intereses. **on the lines of,** conforme a; parecido a. **to cross the l.,** (equator) pasar la línea; (railway) cruzar la vía. **to drop a l.,** escribir unas líneas; poner unas líneas. **to read between the lines,** leer entre líneas. **l.-drawing,** dibujo de líneas, m. **l. of battle,** línea de batalla, f.

lineage, s. linaje, m., familia, raza, f.

lineal, a. lineal

lineament, s. lineamento, m.; (of the face) facciones, f. pl.

linear, a. lineal. **l. equation,** ecuación de primer grado, f.

lined, a. rayado, con líneas; (of the face) surcado, arrugado; (of gloves, etc.) forrado

linen, s. lino, m.; (*fam.*) ropa blanca, f.; a. de lino. **clean l.,** ropa limpia, f. **dirty l.,** ropa sucia, f.; ropa para lavar, f. **table-l.,** mantelería, f. **l. cupboard,** armario para ropa blanca, m. **l. draper,** lencero (-ra). **l.-draper's shop,** lencería, f. **l. room,** lencería, f. **l. tape,** trenzadera, f. **l. thread,** hilo de lino, m.

liner, s. (ship) transatlántico, m.; buque de vapor, m.; (*aer.*) avión de pasaje, m.

linesman, s. soldado de línea, m.; (*sport*) juez de línea, m.

ling, s. (*bot.*) brezo, m.; (*icht.*) especie de abadejo, f.

linger, v.i. (remain) quedarse; tardar en marcharse; ir lentamente; hacer algo despacio

lingerie, s. ropa blanca, f.

lingering, a. lento; largo, prolongado; melancólico, triste

lingeringly, *adv.* lentamente; largamente; melancólicamente

linguist, *s.* lingüista, *m.* and *f.*

linguistic, *a.* lingüístico

linguistics, *s.* lingüística, *f.*

liniment, *s.* linimento, *m.*

lining, *s.* (of a garment, etc.) forro, *m.*; (building) revestimiento, *m.*

link, *s.* (in a chain) eslabón, *m.*; (of beads) sarta, *f.*; (*fig.*) enlace, *m.*, cadena, *f.*; conexión, *f.*; (*mech.*) corredera, *f.*; (torch) hacha de viento, *f.* *v.t.* enlazar, unir; (*fig.*) encadenar. **missing l.,** (*fig.*) eslabón perdido, *m.* **to l. arms,** cogerse del brazo

linking, *s.* encadenamiento, *m.*; (*fig.*) conexión, *f.*

links, *s. pl.* campo de golf, *m.*

linnet, *s.* verderón, *m.*

linoleum, *s.* linóleo, *m.*

linotype, *s.* linotipia, *f.*

linseed, *s.* linaza, *f.* **l. cake,** bagazo, *m.* **l.-oil,** aceite de linaza, *m.*

linstock, *s.* (*mil.*) botafuego, *m.*

lint, *s.* (*med.*) hilas, *f. pl.*; (fluff) borra, *f.*

lintel, *s.* dintel, *m.*; (threshold) umbral, *m.*

lion, *s.* león, *m.*; (*fig.*) celebridad, *f.* **l. cage or den,** leonera, *f.* **l.-hearted,** valeroso. **l.-hunter,** cazador (-ra) de leones. **l.-keeper,** leonero (-ra). **lion's mane,** melena, *f.* **l.-tamer,** domador (-ra) de leones

lioness, *s.* leona, *f.*

lionize, *v.t.* dar bombo (a), hacer la rueda (a), tratar como una celebridad (a)

lip, *s.* labio, *m.*; (of a vessel) pico, *m.*; (of a crater) borde, *m.*; (*fig.*) boca, *f.* **to open one's lips,** abrir la boca. **to smack one's lips,** (also *fig.*) chuparse los dedos. **lip-reading,** interpretación del movimiento de los labios, *f.* **lip-service,** amor fingido, *m.*; promesas hipócritas, *f. pl.* **lip-stick,** lápiz para los labios, *m.*

lipped, *a.* (in compounds) con labios . . ., que tiene labios; (of vessels in compounds) con . . . picos

liquefaction, *s.* licuefacción, *f.*

liquefiable, *a.* liquidable

liquefy, *v.t.* liquidar. *v.i.* liquidarse

liqueur, *s.* licor, *m.* **l.-glass,** copita de licor, *f.* **l.-set,** licorera, *f.*

liquid, *s.* líquido, *m.* *a.* líquido; límpido. **l. air,** aire líquido, *m.* **l. measure,** medida para líquidos, *f.*

liquidate, *v.t.* liquidar; saldar (cuentas); (*mil.*) soldar

liquidation, *s.* liquidación, *f.*

liquidness, *s.* liquidez, *f.*; fluidez, *f.*

liquor, *s.* licor, *m.* **l. shop,** aguardentería, *f.* **l. traffic,** negocio de vinos y licores, *m.*; contrabando, *m.*

liquorice, *s.* regaliz, *m.*

lira, *s.* lira, *f.*

lisle thread, *s.* hilo, *m.*

lisp, *s.* ceceo, *m.*; balbuceo, *m.* *v.i.* cecear; balbucir

lisping, *a.* ceceoso; balbuciente. *s.* ceceo, *m.*; (of a child, etc.) balbuceo, *m.*

lissom, *a.* flexible; ágil

list, *s.* lista, *f.*; catálogo, *m.*; matrícula, *f.*; (*naut.*) recalcada, *f.*; inclinación, *f.*; (tournament) liza, *f.* *v.t.* hacer una lista de; catalogar; matricular, inscribir. *v.i.* (*naut.*) recalcar; inclinarse a un lado. **to enter the lists,** entrar en liza. **l. of wines,** lista de vinos, *f.*

listen, *v.i.* escuchar; (attend) atender. **Don't you want to l. to the music?** ¿No quieres escuchar la música? **to l. in,** (to the radio) escuchar la radio; (eavesdrop) escuchar a hurtadillas

listener, *s.* oyente, *m.* and *f.*; (to radio) radiooyente, *m.* and *f.*

listless, *a.* lánguido, apático, indiferente

listlessly, *adv.* lánguidamente, indiferentemente

listlessness, *s.* apatía, languidez, indiferencia, inercia, *f.*

litany, *s.* letanía, *f.*

literal, *a.* literal. **l.-minded,** sin imaginación

literally, *adv.* literalmente

literalness, *s.* literalidad, *f.*

literarily, *adv.* literariamente

literary, *a.* literario

literate, *a.* and *s.* literato (-ta)

literature, s. literatura, f.

lithe, a. flexible; sinuoso y delgado; ágil

litheness, s. flexibilidad, f.; sinuosidad, f.; delgadez, f.; agilidad, f.

lithiasis, s. litiasis, f., mal de piedra, m.

lithograph, s. litografía, f. v.t. litografiar

lithographer, s. litógrafo, m.

lithographic, a. litográfico

lithography, s. litografía, f.

Lithuanian, a. lituano. s. lituano (-na); (language) lituano, m.

litigant, s. litigante, m. and f.

litigate, v.i. and v.t. litigar, pleitear

litigation, s. litigación, f.

litigious, a. litigioso

litmus, s. tornasol, m. l. paper, papel de tornasol, m.

litre, s. litro, m.

litter, s. litera, f.; (stretcher) camilla, f.; (bed) lecho, m.; cama de paja, f.; (brood) camada, cría, f.; (rubbish) cosas en desorden, f. pl.; (papers) papeletas, f. pl.; (untidiness) desarreglo, desorden, m., confusión, f. v.t. poner en desorden

little, a. pequeño; poco; (scanty) escaso; insignificante; bajo, mezquino. adv. poco. a l., un poco (de); un tanto. in l., en pequeño. not a l., no poco; bastante. l. by l., poco a poco. l. or no, poco o nada. however l., por pequeño que. as l. as possible, lo menos posible. to make l. of, no dar importancia a; sacar poco en claro de, no comprender bien; no hacer caso de; (persons) acoger mal. l. by l., poco a poco. l. finger, dedo meñique, m. l. one, pequeñuela, f., pequeñito, m.

littleness, s. pequeñez, f.; poquedad, f.; mezquindad, f.; trivialidad, f.

littoral, a. and s. litoral (m.)

liturgical, a. litúrgico. l. calendar, calendario litúrgico, m.

liturgy, s. liturgia, f.

live, a. vivo, viviente; (alight) encendido; (of a wire, etc.) cargado de electricidad. l. cartridge, cartucho con bala, m. l. coal, ascua, f. l.-stock,

ganadería, f. l. wire, conductor eléctrico, m.; (fig.) fuerza viva, f.

live, v.i. vivir; residir, habitar; (of ships) mantenerse a flote; salvarse; subsistir. v.t. (one's life) llevar, pasar. Long l.! ¡Viva! to have enough to l. on, tener de qué vivir. to l. together, convivir. to l. again, volver a vivir. to l. at, vivir en, habitar. to l. down, sobrevivir a; (a fault) lograr borrar. to l. on, vivir de. to l. up to, vivir con arreglo a, vivir en conformidad con; estar al nivel de, merecer. to l. up to one's income, vivir al día, gastarse toda la renta

livelihood, s. vida, subsistencia, f. to make a l., ganar la vida

liveliness, s. vivacidad, vida, f.; animación, f.; alegría, f.

livelong, a. entero, todo; eterno. all the l. day, todo el santo día

lively, a. vivo; vivaracho; brioso, enérgico; alegre; bullicioso; animado; (fresh) fresco; (of colours) brillante; intenso

liver, s. vividor (-ra), el, m. (f. la) que vive; habitante, m.; (anat.) hígado, m. l. complaint, mal de hígado, m. l. extract, extracto de hígado, m.

livery, s. librea, f.; uniforme, m.; (poet.) vestiduras, f. pl. l. stables, pensión de caballos, f.; cochería de alquiler, f.

livid, a. lívido; cárdeno, amoratado

lividness, s. lividez, f.

living, a. viviente; vivo, vital. s. vida, f.; modo de vivir, m.; beneficio eclesiástico, m. the l., los vivos. to make one's l., ganarse la vida. l. memory, memoria de personas vivientes, memoria de los que aún viven, f. l.-room, sala de estar, f. l. soul, ser viviente; (fam.) bicho viviente, m. l. wage, jornal básico, m.

lizard, s. lagarto (-ta). giant l., dragón, m. wall l., lagartija, f. l. hole, lagartera, f.

llama, s. llama, f.

load, s. carga, f.; peso, m.; (cart) carretada, f.; (elec.) carga, f.; (quantity) cantidad, f. v.t. cargar (con); (with honours)

llenar (de); (*fig.*, weigh down)
agobiar (con); (a stick with lead)
emplomar; (*elec.*, and of dice)
cargar; (wine) mezclar vino con
un narcótico. **to be loaded with
fruit**, estar cargado de fruta. **to
l. oneself with**, cargarse de. **to
l. the dice**, cargar los dados. **to
l. again**, recargar

loader, *s.* cargador, *m.*

loading, *s.* carga, *f.* **l. depot**,
cargadero, *m.*

loaf, *s.* pan, *m.*; (French) barra de
pan, *f.* *v.i.* golfear, vagabundear, gandulear. **l. sugar**, azúcar de pilón, *m.*

loafer, *s.* vago (-ga); azotacalles,
m. and *f.*; gandul (-la); golfo (-fa)

loafing, *s.* gandulería, *f.*, vagabundeo, *m.*

loam, *s.* marga, *f.*

loamy, *a.* margoso

loan, *s.* empréstito, *m.*; (lending)
prestación, *f.*; préstamo, *m.* *v.t.*
prestar. **l. fund**, caja de em-
préstitos, *f.* **l. office**, casa de
préstamos, *f.*

loath, *a.* desinclinado, poco dispuesto

loathe, *v.t.* abominar, detestar,
odiar, aborrecer; repugnar

loather, *s.* el, *m.* (*f.* la) que odia;
aborrecedor (-ra)

loathing, *s.* aborrecimiento, odio,
m.; repugnancia, aversión, *f.*

loathsome, *a.* odioso, aborrecible;
asqueroso; repugnante

loathsomeness, *s.* carácter repugnante, *m.*; asquerosidad, *f.*

lobby, *s.* pasillo, *m.*; antecámara,
f.; (in a hotel, house) vestíbulo,
recibidor, *m.*; (waiting-room)
sala de espera, *f.*; (in Parliament)
sala de los pasos perdidos, *f.*
v.t. and *v.i.* cabildear

lobe, *s.* (*bot.*) lobo, *m.*; (*anat.*,
arch.) lóbulo, *m.*

lobed, *a.* lobulado

lobelia, *s.* lobelia, *f.*

lobster, *s.* langosta, *f.*; bogavante,
m. **l.-pot**, cambín, *m.*, nasa, *f.*

lobule, *s.* lóbulo, *m.*

local, *a.* local; de la localidad. **l.
anæsthetic**, anestésico local,
m. **l. colour**, color local, *m.*

locale, *s.* local, *m.*

locality, *s.* localidad, *f.*; situación, *f.*

localization, *s.* localización, *f.*

localize, *v.t.* localizar

locally, *adv.* localmente

locate, *v.t.* situar; colocar; localizar. **to be located**, situarse;
hallarse

location, *s.* colocación, *f.*; emplazamiento, *m.*; localidad, *f.*;
situación, posición, *f.*

locative, *a.* and *s.* (*gram.*) locativo
(*m.*)

loch, *s.* lago, *m.*

lock, *s.* cerradura, *f.*; (of a gun)
cerrojo, *m.*; (in wrestling) llave,
f.; (on rivers, canals) presa, *f.*;
(at a dock) esclusa, *f.*; (of hair)
mechón, *m.*, guedeja, *f.*; (ringlet)
bucle, *m.*; *pl.* **locks**, (hair) cabellos, *m. pl.*, pelo, *m.* **spring l.**,
cerradura de golpe, *f.* **to put a
l. on**, poner cerradura a. **under
l. and key**, bajo cuatro llaves.
l.-jaw, trismo, *m.* **l. keeper**,
esclusero, *m.* **l.-out strike**,
huelga patronal, *f.*

lock, *v.t.* cerrar con llave; (*fig.*)
encerrar; (embrace) abrazar estrechamente; (of wheels, etc.)
trabar; (twine) entrelazar. *v.i.*
cerrarse con llave. **to l. in**, cerrar
con llave; encerrar. **to l. out**,
cerrar la puerta (a); dejar en la
calle (a). **to l. up**, encerrar; (imprison) encarcelar

locker, *s.* (drawer) cajón, *m.*;
(cupboard) armario, *m.*; (*naut.*)
cajonada, *f.*

locket, *s.* guardapelo, *m.*; medallón, *m.*

locksmith, *s.* cerrajero, *m.* **locksmith's trade**, cerrajería, *f.*

locomotion, *s.* locomoción, *f.*

locomotive, *a.* locomotor. *s.*
locomotora, *f.*

locum tenens, *s.* interino (-na)

locust, *s.* langosta migratoria, *f.*

locution, *s.* locución, *f.*

locutory, *s.* locutorio, *m.*

lode, *s.* filón, *m.*

lodestar, *s.* estrella polar, *f.*;
(*fig.*) norte, *m.*

lodge, *s.* casita, garita, *f.*; casa de
guarda, *f.*; (freemason's) logia,
f.; (porter's) portería, *f.* *v.i.*
hospedarse, alojarse, vivir, parar;
penetrar; entrar (en); fijarse (en).
v.t. hospedar, alojar; albergar;
(a blow) asestar; (a complaint)
hacer, dar; (money, etc.) depositar. **to l. an accusation**

against, querellarse contra, quejarse de. **l.-keeper,** conserje, *m.*

lodger, *s.* huésped (-eda)

lodging, *s.* hospedaje, alojamiento, *m.*; (inn) posada, *f.*; residencia, *f.*; casa, *f.* **l.-house,** casa de huéspedes, *f.*

loft, *s.* desván, sotabanco, *m.*; pajar, *m.*

loftily, *adv.* en alto; (proudly) con arrogancia, con altanería

loftiness, *s.* altura, *f.*; sublimidad, *f.*; nobleza, *f.*; dignidad, *f.*; (haughtiness) altanería, soberbia, *f.*

lofty, *a.* alto; sublime; noble; eminente; (haughty) altanero, soberbio

log, *s.* madero, tronco, *m.*; palo, *m.*; leño, *m.*; (*naut.*) barquilla, *f.* **to lie like a log,** estar hecho un tronco. **log-book,** (*naut.*) cuaderno de bitácora, *m.* **log-cabin,** caney, *m.* **log-wood,** palo campeche, *m.*

logarithm, *s.* logaritmo, *m.*

logarithmic, *a.* logarítmico

logic, *s.* lógica, *f.*

logical, *a.* lógico

logically, *adv.* lógicamente

logician, *s.* lógico (-ca)

loin, *s.* ijar, *m.*; (of meat) falda, *f.*; *pl.* loins, lomos, *m. pl.* **to gird up one's loins,** (*fig.*) arremangarse los faldones. **l.-cloth,** taparrabo, *m.*

loiter, *v.i.* vagabundear, vagar, errar; haraganear; rezagarse

loiterer, *s.* haragán (-ana); vago (-ga); rezagado (-da)

loll, *v.i.* recostarse (en), apoyarse (en). *v.t.* (the tongue) sacar

Londoner, *s.* londinense, *m.* and *f.*

lone. See **lonely**

loneliness, *s.* soledad, *f.*; aislamiento, *m.*

lonely, *a.* solitario; solo; aislado, remoto; desierto

lonesome, *a.* solo, solitario

long, *a.* largo; prolongado; de largo; (extensive) extenso; (big) grande; (much) mucho. **a l. time,** mucho tiempo. **It is five feet l.,** Tiene cinco pies de largo. **l.-armed,** que tiene los brazos largos. **l.-boat,** falúa, *f.* **l. clothes,** (infant's) mantillas, *f. pl.* **l.-distance call,** conferencia telefónica, *f.* **l.-distance race,**

carrera de fondo, *f.* **l.-eared,** de orejas largas. **l.-faced,** de cara larga, carilargo. **l.-forgotten,** olvidado hace mucho tiempo. **l.-haired,** que tiene el pelo largo. **l.-headed,** dolicocéfalo; (*fig.*) astuto, sagaz. **l.-legged,** zanquilargo, zancudo. **l.-lived,** que vive hasta una edad avanzada; longevo; duradero. **l.-lost,** perdido hace mucho tiempo. **l.-sighted,** présbita; previsor; sagaz. **l.-standing,** viejo, de muchos años. **l.-suffering,** sufrido, paciente. **l.-tailed,** de cola larga. **l.-waisted,** de talle largo. **l.-winded,** prolijo

long, *adv.* mucho tiempo; mucho; durante mucho tiempo. **as l. as,** mientras (que). **before l.,** dentro de poco. **the l. and the short of it,** en resumidas cuentas. **How l. has she been here?** ¿Cuánto tiempo hace que ella está aquí? **not l. before,** poco tiempo antes. **l. ago,** tiempo ha, muchos años ha

long, *v.i.* anhelar, suspirar (por), desear con vehemencia

longanimity, *s.* longanimidad, *f.*

longer, *a. comp.* más largo. *adv. comp.* más tiempo. **How much l. must we wait?** ¿Cuánto tiempo más hemos de esperar? **He can no l. walk as he used,** Ya no puede andar como antes

longevity, *s.* longevidad, *f.*

longing, *a.* anheloso, ansioso; de envidia. *s.* anhelo, *m.*, ansia, *f.*; deseo vehemente, *m.*; envidia, *f.*

longingly, *adv.* con ansia; impacientemente; con envidia

longish, *a.* algo largo

longitude, *s.* longitud, *f.*

longitudinal, *a.* longitudinal

loofah, *s.* esponja vegetal, *f.*

look, *s.* mirada, *f.*; (glance) vistazo, *m.*, ojeada, *f.*; (air) semblante, aire, porte, *m.*; (appearance) aspecto, *m.*; apariencia, *f.* **good looks,** buen parecer, *m.*; guapeza, *f.* **the new l.,** la nueva línea, la nueva silueta, la nueva moda. **to be on the l.-out,** andar a la mira

look, *v.i.* and *v.t.* mirar; considerar; contemplar; (appear, seem) parecer; tener aire (de); tener aspecto (de); hacer el efecto (de); (show oneself) mostrarse; (of buildings, etc.) caer (a), dar (a); mirar (a). **to l. alike,** parecerse. **to l. hopeful,** (*fig.*) prometer bien. **to l. out of the corner of the eye,** mirar de reojo. **to l. (a person) up and down,** mirar de hito en hito. **to l. about one,** mirar a su alrededor; observar. **to l. after,** tener la mirada puesta en, mirar; (care for) cuidar; (watch) vigilar; mirar por. **to l. at,** mirar; considerar; examinar. He looked at his watch, Miró su reloj. He looked at her, La miró. **to l. away,** desviar los ojos, apartar la mirada. **to l. back,** mirar hacia atrás, volver la cabeza; (in thought) pensar en el pasado. **to l. down,** bajar los ojos; mirar el suelo; mirar hacia abajo. **to l. down upon,** dominar, mirar a; (scorn) despreciar. **to l. for,** buscar; buscar con los ojos; (await) aguardar; (expect) esperar. **to l. forward,** mirar hacia el porvenir; pensar en el futuro; esperar con ilusión. **to l. in,** entrar por un instante, hacer una visita corta. **to l. into,** mirar dentro de; mirar hacia el interior de; estudiar, investigar. **to l. on,** *v.t.* mirar; considerar; (of buildings, etc.) dar a. *v.i.* ser espectador. **to l. on to,** dar a, mirar a. **to l. out,** *v.i.* (be careful) tener cuidado; (look through) mirar por; asomarse a. *v.t.* (search) buscar; (find) hallar; (choose) escoger, elegir. **L. out!** ¡Atención! ¡Ojo! **to l. out for,** buscar; (await) aguardar, esperar; (be careful) tener cuidado con. **to l. out of,** mirar por; asomarse a. **to l. over,** mirar bien; (persons) mirar de hito en hito; examinar; visitar; (a house) inspeccionar; (a book) hojear; mirar superficialmente. **to l. round,** *v.t.* (a place) visitar. *v.i.* volver la cabeza, volverse; mirar hacia atrás. **to l. round for,** buscar con los ojos; buscar por todas partes. **to l. through,** mirar por; mirar a través de; examinar; (search) registrar; (understand) registrar. **to l. to,** (be careful of)

tener cuidado de; (attend to) atender a; (care for) cuidar de; (count on) contar con; (resort to) acudir a; (await) esperar. **to l. towards,** mirar hacia, mirar en la dirección de; caer a. **to l. up,** *v.i.* mirar hacia arriba; (aspire) aspirar; (improve) mejorar. *v.t.* visitar, ir (or venir) a ver; (turn up) buscar; averiguar. **to l. upon,** mirar. Other meanings see **to l. on.** They l. upon her as their daughter, La miran como una hija suya. **to l. up to,** (*fig.*) respetar

look-out, *s.* vigilancia, observación, *f.*; (view) vista, *f.*, panorama, *m.*; (view-point) miradero, *m.*; (*mil.*) atalaya, *m.*; (*naut.*) gaviero, *m.*; (*fig.*, prospect) perspectiva, *f.*

looked-for, *a.* esperado; deseado

looker-on, *s.* espectador (-ra)

looking, *a.* (in compounds) de . . . aspecto, de . . . apariencia. **dirty-l.,** de aspecto sucio. **l.-glass,** espejo, *m.*

loom, *s.* telar, *m.* *v.i.* asomar, aparecer

loop, *s.* (turn) vuelta, *f.*; (in rivers, etc.) recodo, *m.*, curva, *f.*; (fold) pliegue, *m.*; bucle, *m.*; (fastening) fiador, *m.*, presilla, *f.*; (aer.) rizo, *m.*; (knot) nudo corredizo, *m.* **to l. the l.,** (*aer.*) hacer el rizo, hacer rizos. **l.-line,** ferrocarril de empalme, *m.*

loophole, *s.* saetera, aspillera, *f.*; (*fig.*) escapatoria, *f.*; pretexto, *m.*, excusa, *f.*

loose, *a.* suelto; (free) libre; (slack) flojo; (of garments) holgado; (untied) desatado; (unfastened) desprendido; movible; (unchained) desencadenado; en libertad; (of the bowels) suelto (de vientre); (pendulous) colgante; (of a nail, tooth, etc.) inseguro; poco firme; que se mueve; (of knots, etc.) flojo; (of the mind, etc.) incoherente, ilógico; poco exacto; (of style, etc.) vago, impreciso; (of conduct) disoluto, vicioso; (careless) negligente, descuidado. *v.t.* (untie) desatar; desprender; soltar; aflojar; (of a priest) absolver; (*fig.*) desencadenar. **to break l.,** desprenderse; soltarse; liber-

tarse; escapar; (fig.) desencadenarse. to let l., desatar;
aflojar; poner en libertad; soltar;
(fig.) desencadenar; (interject)
lanzar. to turn l., poner en
libertad; dar salida (a); echar de
casa, poner en la calle. to work
l., desprenderse; aflojarse; des-
vencijarse. l.-box, caballeriza, f.
l. change, suelto, m. l.-leaf
notebook, libreta de hojas suel-
tas, f.

loosely, adv. flojamente; sueltamente; (vaguely) vagamente;
incorrectamente; incoherentemente; (carelessly) negligentemente; (viciously) disolutamente

loosen, v.t. (untie) desatar; aflojar; soltar; desasir; (the tongue)
desatar; (fig.) hacer menos riguroso, ablandar

looseness, s. flojedad, f.; (of
clothing) holgura, f.; soltura, f.;
relajación, f.; (of the bowels)
diarrea, f.; (viciousness) licencia,
f., libertinaje, m.; (vagueness)
vaguedad, f.; incoherencia, f.

loosening, s. desprendimiento,
m.; desasimiento, m.; aflojamiento, m.

loot, s. botín, m. v.t. saquear

looter, s. saqueador (-ra)

looting, s. saqueo, pillaje, m. a.
saqueador

lop, v.t. mochar; podar; destroncar; cortar de un golpe. a. (of
ears) gacho. to lop off the ends,
cercenar. to lop off the top,
desmochar. lop-sided, desproporcionado; desequilibrado

lopping, s. desmoche, m.; poda,
f.

loquacious, a. locuaz, gárrulo

loquacity, s. locuacidad, garrulidad, f.

lord, s. señor, m.; (husband)
esposo, m.; (English title) lord,
m. (pl. lores); (Christ) Señor, m.
feudal l., señor de horca y
cuchillo, m. my l., milord. my
lords, milores. Our L., Nuestro
Señor. the Lord's Prayer, el
Padre nuestro. to l. it over,
mandar como señor, mandar a
la baqueta. L. Chamberlain,
camarero mayor, m. L. Chancellor, gran canciller, m. L. Chief
Justice, presidente del tribunal

supremo, m. L.-Lieutenant, virrey, m. L. Mayor, alcalde, m.
L. Privy Seal, guardasellos del
rey, m.

lordliness, s. suntuosidad, f.;
liberalidad, munificencia, f.;
dignidad, f.; (haughtiness) altivez,
arrogancia, f.

lordly, a. señorial, señoril; altivo,
arrogante

lordship, s. señoría, f.; señorío,
poder, m. his l., su señoría

lore, s. saber, m.; erudición, f.;
tradiciones, f. pl.

lorgnette, s. impertinentes, m.
pl.

lorry, s. camión, m.; carro, m.

lose, v.t. perder; hacer perder,
quitar; (forget) olvidar. v.i.
perder; (of clocks) atrasar. to be
lost in thought, estar ensimismado, estar absorto. to l. oneself, perderse; entregarse (a).
to l. one's footing, resbalar.
to l. one's way, extraviarse,
perder el camino. to l. one's
self-control, perder el tino.
to l. one's head, perder la
cabeza. to l. ground, perder
terreno. to l. one's voice,
perder la voz. to l. patience,
perder la paciencia, perder los
estribos

loser, s. perdedor (-ra)

losing, a. perdedor. s. pérdida,
f.

loss, s. pérdida, f. at a l., (com.)
con pérdida; perplejo, dudoso.
heavy losses, (mil.) pérdidas
cuantiosas, f. pl. We are at a l.
for words ..., No tenemos palabras para ...

lot, s. suerte, f.; fortuna, f.; lote,
m.; parte, porción, cuota, f.; (for
building) solar, m. a lot of
people, muchas personas. Our
lot would have been very
different, Nuestra suerte hubiera sido muy distinta, Otro
gallo nos cantara. to draw lots,
echar suertes, sortear. to take
the lot, (fam.) alzarse con el
santo y la limosna

lotion, s. loción, f.

lottery, s. lotería, f. l. ticket,
billete de la lotería, m.

lotus, s. loto, m. l.-eating, loto-
fagia, f.; (fig.) indolencia, pereza,
f.

loud, *a.* fuerte; (noisy) ruidoso, estrepitoso; alto; (gaudy) chillón, llamativo, cursi. *adv.* ruidosamente. **l.-speaker,** (*rad.*) altavoz, altoparlante, *m.*

loudly, *adv.* en alta voz; fuertemente; ruidosamente, con estrépito

loudness, *s.* (noise) ruido, *m.*; sonoridad, *f.*; (force) fuerza, *f.*; (of colours, etc.) mal gusto, *m.*, vulgaridad, *f.*

louis, *s.* (coin) luis, *m.*

lounge, *s.* sala de estar, *f.*; salón, *m.* *v.i.* reclinarse, ponerse a sus anchas; apoyarse (en); gandulear; vagar. **l. chair,** poltrona, *f.* **l.-lizard,** (*fam.*) pollo pera, *m.* **l.-suit,** traje de americana, *m.*

lounger, *s.* holgazán (-ana); golfo (-fa), azotacalles, *m.* and *f.*

lour. See **lower**

louse, *s.* piojo, *m.*

lousy, *a.* piojoso

lout, *s.* patán, zamacuco, *m.*

loutish, *a.* rústico

lovable, *a.* amable; simpático

lovableness, *s.* amabilidad, *f.*

love, *s.* amor, *m.*; (friendship) amistad, *f.*; (enthusiasm, liking) afición, *f.*; (in tennis) cero, *m.* *v.t.* querer, amar; gustar mucho; tener afición (a). *v.i.* estar enamorado. **I should l. to dine with you,** Me gustaría mucho cenar con Vds. **to be in l. with,** estar enamorado de. **to fall in l. with,** enamorarse de. **They l. each other,** Se quieren. **to make l. to,** hacer el amor (a), galantear. **l.-affair,** amorío, *m.* **l.-bird,** periquito, *m.* **l.-letter,** carta de amor, *f.* **l.-making,** galanteo, *m.* **l.-philtre,** filtro, *m.* **l.-song,** canción de amor, *f.* **l.-story,** historia de amor, *f.* **l.-token,** prenda de amor, *f.*

loveless, *a.* sin amor

loveliness, *s.* hermosura, belleza, *f.*; encanto, *m.*; amabilidad, *f.*

lovely, *a.* hermoso, bello; delicioso; amable; (*fam.*) estupendo

lover, *s.* amante, *m.* and *f.*; aficionado (-da)

lovesick, *a.* enfermo de amor, enamorado

loving, *a.* amoroso; cariñoso; (friendly) amistoso; de amor

low, *a.* bajo; de poca altura; (of dresses, etc.) escotado; (of musical notes) grave; (soft) suave; (feeble) débil; (depressed) deprimido, triste, abatido; (plain) sencillo; (of a fever) lento; (of a bow) profundo; pequeño; inferior; humilde; (ill) enfermo; (vile) vil, ruin; obsceno, escabroso. *adv.* bajo; cerca de la tierra; en voz baja; (cheaply) barato, a bajo precio. **in a low voice,** en voz baja, paso. **to lay low,** (kill) tumbar; (knock down) derribar; incapacitar. **to lie low,** descansar; estar muerto; esconderse, agacharse; callar. **to run low,** escasear. **low-born,** de humilde cuna. **low-brow,** nada intelectual. **low comedy,** farsa, *f.* **low flying,** *s.* bajo vuelo, *m.* *a.* que vuela bajo; terrero, rastrero; que vuela a ras de tierra. **low frequency,** baja frecuencia, *f.* **low Latin,** bajo latín, *m.* **Low Mass,** misa rezada, *f.* **low neck,** escote, *m.* **low-necked,** escotado. **low-pitched,** grave. **low-spirited,** deprimido. **Low Sunday,** domingo de Cuasimodo, *m.* **low tension,** baja tensión, *f.* **low trick,** mala pasada, *f.* **low water,** marea baja, bajamar, *f.*; (of rivers) estiaje, *m.*

low, *v.i.* berrear, mugir. *s.* berrido, mugido, *m.*

lower, *v.t.* bajar; descolgar; disminuir; (price) rebajar; (a boat, sails) arriar. *v.i.* (of persons) fruncir el ceño, mostrarse malhumorado; (of the sky) encapotarse, cargarse; (menace) amenazar. **to l. a boat,** arriar un bote. **to l. oneself,** (by a rope, etc.) descolgarse. **to l. the flag,** abatir la bandera

lower, *a. comp.* más bajo; menos alto; bajo; inferior. **l. classes,** clase obrera, *f.*, clases bajas, *f. pl.* **l. down,** más abajo. **L. House,** Cámara de los Comunes, *f.*; cámara baja, *f.* **l. jaw,** mandíbula inferior, *f.* **l. storey,** piso bajo, *m.*; piso de abajo, *m.*

lowering, *s.* abajamiento, *m.*; descenso, *m.*; (of prices) baja, *f.*; (of a boat) arriada, *f.*; (of the flag) abatimiento, *m.* *a.* (of

persons) ceñudo; (of the sky)
anublado, encapotado; (threatening) amenazador

lowest, *a. sup.* el (la, etc.) más
bajo; el (la, etc.) más profundo;
ínfimo

lowing, *s.* berrido, mugido, *m.*

lowland, *s.* tierra baja, *f.* **The
Lowlands,** las tierras bajas de
Escocia

lowliness, *s.* humildad, *f.;* modestia, *f.*

lowly, *a.* humilde

lowness, *s.* poca altura, *f.;* situación poco elevada, *f.;* pequeñez,
f.; (of musical notes) gravedad,
f.; (softness) suavidad, *f.;*
(feebleness) debilidad, *f.;* (sadness) tristeza, *f.,* abatimiento
m.; (of price) baratura, *f.;*
inferioridad, *f.;* humildad, *f.;*
(vileness) bajeza, *f.;* obscenidad,
f.

loyal, *a.* leal, fiel

loyalist, *s.* realista, *m.* and *f.;*
defensor (-ra) del gobierno legítimo

loyally, *adv.* lealmente

loyalty, *s.* lealtad, fidelidad, *f.*

lozenge, *s.* pastilla, *f.*

lubricant, *a.* and *s.* lubricante
(*m.*)

lubricate, *v.t.* lubricar, engrasar

lubricating-oil, *s.* aceite lubricante, *m.*

lubrication, *s.* lubricación, *f.,*
engrasado, *m.*

lubricator, *s.* lubricador, *m.;*
engrasador, *m.*

lucerne, *s.* alfalfa, *f.*

lucid, *a.* lúcido; claro

lucidity, *s.* lucidez, *f.;* claridad, *f.*

lucidly, *adv.* claramente

luck, *s.* destino, azar, *m.;* (good)
buenaventura, suerte, *f.* **to bring
bad l.,** traer mala suerte. **to try
one's l.,** probar fortuna

luckily, *adv.* por fortuna, afortunadamente, felizmente

luckless, *a.* desdichado

lucky, *a.* afortunado; dichoso,
venturoso; feliz. **to be l.,** tener
buena suerte

lucrative, *a.* lucrativo

lucre, *s.* lucro, *m.*

lucubration, *s.* lucubración, *f.*

ludicrous, *a.* absurdo, risible,
ridículo

ludicrousness, *s.* ridiculez, *f.*

luft, *v.i.* (*naut.*) orzar

lug, *s.* tirón, *m.;* (ear and projection) oreja, *f.* *v.t.* tirar (de);
arrastrar. **to lug about,** arrastrar (por); llevar con dificultad.
to lug in, arrastrar adentro;
introducir; hacer entrar. **to lug
out,** arrastrar afuera; hacer
salir

luggage, *s.* equipaje, *m.* **excess
l.,** exceso de peso, *m.* **piece of
l.,** bulto, *m.* **to register one's
l.,** facturar el equipaje. **l.
carrier,** (on 'buses, etc.) baca,
f.; (on a car) portaequipajes, *m.*
l. porter, mozo de equipaje, *m.*
l. rack, (on a car) portaequipajes, *m.;* (in a train) rejilla para
el equipaje, *f.* **l. receipt,** talón
de equipaje, *m.* **l. room,** consigna, *f.* **l. van,** furgón de equipajes, *m.*

lugubrious, *a.* lúgubre

lugubriously, *adv.* lúgubremente

lukewarm, *a.* tibio, templado;
(*fig.*) indiferente, frío

lukewarmness, *s.* tibieza, *f.;*
(*fig.*) indiferencia, frialdad, *f.*

lull, *s.* momento de calma, *m.;*
tregua, *f.;* silencio, *m.* *v.t.* (a
child) arrullar, adormecer;
(soothe) sosegar, calmar; disminuir, mitigar

lullaby, *s.* canción de cuna, *f.*

Lullian, *a.* luliano

lumbago, *s.* lumbago, *m.*

lumbar, *a.* lumbar

lumber, *s.* (wood) maderas de
sierra, *f. pl.;* (rubbish) trastos
viejos, *m. pl.* *v.t.* amontonar
trastos viejos; obstruir. *v.i.*
andar pesadamente; avanzar
ruidosamente, avanzar con ruido
sordo. **l.-jack,** maderero, ganchero, *m.* **l.-room,** leonera, *f.*
l.-yard, maderería, *f.,* depósito
de maderas, *m.*

lumbering, *a.* pesado

luminary, *s.* lumbrera, *f.*

luminosity, *s.* luminosidad, *f.*

luminous, *a.* luminoso

lump, *s.* masa, *f.;* bulto, *m.;*
pedazo, *m.;* (swelling) hinchazón,
f.; protuberancia, *f.* *v.t.* amontonar. **to l. together,** mezclar;
incluir. **in the l.,** en la masa; en
grueso. **Let him l. it!** ¡Qué se
rasque! **l. in one's throat,**
nudo en la garganta, *m.* **l. of**

sugar, terrón de azúcar, *m.* **l. sum,** cantidad gruesa, *f.*

lunacy, *s.* locura, *f.*

lunar, *a.* lunar

lunatic, *s.* loco (-ca); demente, *m.* and *f. a.* de locos; loco. **l. asylum,** manicomio, *m.*

lunch, luncheon, *s.* almuerzo, *m.*; (snack) merienda, *f. v.i.* almorzar. **l. basket or pail,** fiambrera, *f.*

lunette, *s.* (*arch., mil.*) luneta, *f.*

lung, *s.* pulmón, *m.*

lunge, *s.* (fencing) estocada, *f.*; embestida, *f. v.i.* dar una estocada; abalanzarse sobre

lupin, *s.* lupino, altramuz, *m.*

lurch, *s.* sacudida, *f.*; (*naut.*) guiñada, *f.*; tambaleo, *m.*; movimiento brusco, *m. v.i.* (*naut.*) guiñar; tambalearse; andar haciendo eses. **to leave in the l.,** dejar plantado

lure, *s.* añagaza, *f.*; reclamo, *m.*; aliciente, atractivo, *m.*; seducción, *f. v.t.* atraer, tentar

lurid, *a.* misterioso, fantástico; cárdeno; ominoso; funesto; triste; (orange) anaranjado; (vicissitudinous) accidentado

lurk, *v.i.* acechar, espiar; esconderse

lurking, *a.* (in ambush) en acecho; (of fear, etc.) vago

luscious, *a.* delicioso; suculento; meloso; atractivo, apetitoso; sensual

lusciousness, *s.* suculencia, *f.*; melosidad, *f.*; atractivo, *m.*; sensualidad, *f.*

lush, *a.* jugoso; fresco y lozano; maduro

lust, *s.* lujuria, lascivia, *f.*; codicia, *f.*; deseo, *m.* **l. for revenge,** deseo de venganza, *m.*

lustful, *a.* lujurioso, lúbrico; lascivo

lustre, *s.* lustre, brillo, *m.*; brillantez, *f.*

lustreless, *a.* sin brillo; mate, deslustrado; (of eyes) apagado

lustrous, *a.* lustroso

lustrum, *s.* lustro, quinquenio, *m.*

lusty, *a.* vigoroso, fuerte, lozano

lute, *s.* laúd, *m.*, vihuela, *f.* **l.-player,** vihuelista, *m.* and *f.*

Lutheran, *a.* luterano. *s.* luterano (-na)

Lutheranism, *s.* luteranismo, *m.*

luxation, *s.* luxación, *f.*

luxuriance, *s.* lozanía, *f.*; exuberancia, superabundancia, *f.*

luxuriant, *a.* lozano; fértil; exuberante

luxuriate, *v.i.* crecer con exuberancia; complacerse (en); disfrutar (de), gozar (de)

luxurious, *a.* lujoso

luxuriously, *adv.* lujosamente, con lujo

luxury, *s.* lujo, *m.* **l. goods,** artículos de lujo, *m. pl.*

lycanthropy, *s.* licantropía, *f.*

lyceum, *s.* liceo, *m.*

Lydian, *a.* lidio. *s.* lidio (-ia)

lye, *s.* lejía, *f.*

lying, *a.* (recumbent) recostado; (untrue) mentiroso, falso. *s.* mentiras, *f. pl.* **l.-in,** parto, *m.*

lymph, *s.* linfa, *f.*; vacuna, *f.*

lymphatic, *a.* linfático; flemático

lynch, *v.t.* linchar

lynching, *s.* linchamiento, *m.*

lynx, *s.* lince, *m.* **l.-eyed,** de ojos de lince

lyre, *s.* lira, *f.* **l.-bird,** pájaro lira, *m.*

lyric, *s.* poesía lírica, *f.*; poema lírico, *m.*; letra de una canción, *f.*

lyrical, *a.* lírico

lyricism, *s.* lirismo, *m.*

M

m, *s.* (letter) eme, *f.*

ma'am, *s.* señora, *f.*

macabre, *a.* macabro

macadam, *s.* macadán, *m. a.* de macadán

macadamize, *v.t.* macadanizar

macaroni, *s.* macarrones, *m. pl.*

macaronic, *a.* macarrónico

macaroon, *s.* macarrón de almendras, *m.*

Macassar oil, *s.* aceite de Macasar, *m.*

macaw, *s.* macagua, *f.*, guacamayo, *m.*

mace, *s.* maza, *f.*; (*cul.*) macis, *f. m.-bearer,** macero, *m.*

Macedonian, *a.* macedón, macedonio. *s.* macedonio (-ia)

macerate, *v.t.* macerar. *v.i.* macerarse

maceration, *s.* maceración, *f.*
Machiavellian, *a.* maquiavélico
Machiavellism, *s.* maquiavelismo, *m.*
machination, *s.* maquinación, *f.*
machine, *s.* máquina, *f.*; mecanismo, *m.*; aparato, *m.*; instrumento, *m.*; organización, *f.* *v.t.* trabajar a máquina; (*sew.*) coser a máquina. **m.-gun**, *s.* ametralladora, *f.* *v.t.* ametrallar. **m.-gun carrier**, portametralladoras, *m.* **m.-gunner**, ametrallador, *m.* **m.-made**, hecho a máquina. **m.-oil**, aceite de motores, *m.* **m.-shop**, taller de maquinaria, *m.* **m.-tool**, máquina herramienta, *f.*
machinery, *s.* maquinaria, *f.*; mecanismo, *m.*; organización, *f.*; sistema, *m.*
machinist, *s.* maquinista, *m.* and *f.*; (*sew.*) costurera a máquina, *f.*
mackerel, *s.* caballa, *f.* **m. sky**, cielo aborregado, *m.*
mackintosh, *s.* impermeable, *m.*
macrocephalous, *a.* macrocéfalo
macrocosm, *s.* macrocosmo, *m.*
mad, *a.* loco; fuera de sí; (of a dog, etc.) rabioso; furioso. **as mad as a hatter**, loco como una cabra. **to drive mad**, volver loco (a). **to go mad**, volverse loco, enloquecer, perder el seso. **mad with joy** (pain), loco de alegría (dolor). **mad dog**, perro rabioso, *m.*
madam, *s.* señora, *f.*; (French form) madama, *f.* **Yes, m.**, Sí señora
madcap, *s.* locuelo (-la), *f.*, botarate, *m.*; tarambana, *m.* and *f.*
madden, *v.t.* enloquecer; enfurecer, exasperar
maddening, *a.* exasperante, irritador
madder, *s.* (*bot.*) rubia, *f.*
made, *past part.* and *a.* hecho; formado. **a m. man**, un hombre que tiene su posición ya hecha. **m.-to-measure**, hecho a la medida. **m.-up**, compuesto; (of clothes) confeccionado, ya hecho; (of the face) pintado; (fictitious) inventado, ficticio; artificial
Madeira, *s.* vino de Madeira, *m.* *a.* de Madeira
madhouse, *s.* casa de locos. *f.*, manicomio, *m.*

madly, *adv.* locamente; furiosamente
madman, *s.* loco, *m.*
madness, *s.* locura, *f.*; (of a dog, etc.) rabia, *f.*; furia, *f.*
Madonna, *s.* Virgen, Madona, *f.*
madrepore, *s.* madrépora, *f.*
madrigal, *s.* madrigal, *m.*
Madrilenian, *a.* madrileño, matritense. *s.* madrileño (-ña)
madwoman, *s.* loca, *f.*
Maecenas, *s.* mecenas, *m.*
maelstrom, *s.* remolino, vórtice, *m.*
maenad, *s.* ménade, *f.*
magazine, *s.* (store) almacén, *m.*; (for explosives) polvorín, *m.*, santabárbara, *f.*; (periodical) revista, *f.* **m. rifle**, rifle de repetición, *m.*
Magdalen, *s.* magdalena, *f.*
magenta, *s.* color magenta, *m.*
maggot, *s.* gusano, *m.*, cresa, *f.*; (*fig.*) manía, *f.*, capricho, *m.*
maggoty, *a.* gusanoso
Magi, *s. pl.* (the), los reyes magos
magic, *s.* magia, *f.*; mágica, *f.*; (*fig.*) encanto, *m.* *a.* mágico. **as if by m.**, por ensalmo. **m. lantern**, linterna mágica, *f.*
magically, *adv.* por encanto
magician, *s.* mago, mágico, brujo, *m.*; (conjurer) jugador de manos, *m.*
magisterial, *a.* magistral
magisterially, *adv.* magistralmente
magistracy, *s.* magistratura, *f.*
magistrate, *s.* magistrado, *m.*; juez municipal, *m.*
Magna Charta, *s.* Carta Magna, *f.*
magnanimity, *s.* magnanimidad, generosidad, *f.*
magnanimous, *a.* magnánimo, generoso
magnanimously, *adv.* magnánimamente
magnate, *s.* magnate, *m.*
magnesia, *s.* magnesia, *f.*
magnesium, *s.* magnesio, *m.* **m. light**, luz de magnesio, *f.*
magnet, *s.* imán, *m.*
magnetic, *a.* magnético; (*fig.*) atractivo. **m. field**, campo magnético, *m.* **m. needle**, brújula, *f.*
magnetically, *adv.* magnéticamente

magnetics, s. ciencia del magnetismo, f.

magnetism, s. magnetismo, m.

magnetization, s. imanación, magnetización, f.

magnetize, v.t. magnetizar, imanar; (hypnotize) magnetizar; (fig.) atraer

magneto, s. magneto, m.

Magnificat, s. Magnificat, m.

magnification, s. (by a lens, etc.) aumento, m.; exageración, f.

magnificence, s. magnificencia, f.

magnificent, a. magnífico

magnificently, adv. magníficamente

magnify, v.t. (by lens) aumentar; exagerar; (praise) magnificar

magnifying, a. de aumento. m. glass, lente de aumento, m.

magniloquence, s. grandilocuencia, f.

magniloquent, a. grandílocuo

magnitude, s. magnitud (also ast.), f.

magnolia, s. magnolia, f.

magnum, s. botella de dos litros, f.

magpie, s. marica, picaza, f.

Magyar, s. magiar, m. and f.; (language) magiar, m.

maharaja, s. maharajá, m.

mahogany, s. caoba, f. a. de caoba

Mahomedan. See Mohammedan

maid, s. doncella, muchacha, f.; virgen, f.; soltera, f.; (servant) criada, f.; (daily) asistenta, f. old m., solterona, f. to remain an old m., quedarse soltera, quedarse para tía. m.-of-all-work, criada para todo, f. m.-of-honour, dama de honor, f.

maiden, s. doncella, joven, soltera, f.; virgen, f.; zagala, f. a. de soltera; soltera (f.); virginal; (of speeches, voyages, etc.) primero. m. lady, dama soltera, f. m.-name, apellido de soltera, m. m. speech, primer discurso, m.

maidenhair, s. adianto, m.

maidenhead, s. himen, m.

maidenhood, s. doncellez, virginidad, f.

maidenly, a. virginal; modesto, modoso; tímido

maidservant; s. criada, sirvienta, f.

mail, s. mala, f.; (bag) valija, f.; correo, m.; correspondencia, f.; (armour) cota de malla, f. v.t. mandar por correo; armar con cota de malla, f. **royal m.,** mala real, f. **m.-bag,** valija de correo, f.; portacartas, m. **m.-boat,** buque correo, m. **m.-cart,** ambulancia de correos, f. **m.-clad,** vestido de cota de malla; armado. **m.-coach,** coche correo, m., diligencia, f. **m.-order,** pedido postal, m. **m.-order business,** negocio de ventas por correo, m. **m.-'plane,** avión postal, m. **m. service,** servicio de correos, m. **m. steamer,** vapor correo, m. **m. train,** tren correo, m. **m. van,** (on a train) furgón postal, m.

mailed, a. de malla; armado. **m. fist,** (fig.) puño de hierro, m.

maim, v.t. mancar; mutilar, tullir; estropear

maimed, a. manco; tullido, mutilado

main, a. mayor; principal; más importante, esencial; maestro. s. (mainland) continente, m.; (sea) océano, m.; (pipe) cañería maestra, f. **by m. force,** por fuerza mayor. **in the m.,** en general, generalmente; en su mayoría. **m. beam,** viga maestra, f. **m. body,** (of a building) ala principal, f.; (of a church) cuerpo (de iglesia), m.; (of an army) cuerpo (del ejército), m.; mayor parte, mayoría, f. **m. line,** línea principal, f. **m. mast,** palo mayor, m. **m. thing,** cosa principal, f., lo más importante. **m. wall,** pared maestra, f.

mainland, s. continente, m.; tierra firme, f.

mainly, adv. principalmente; en su mayoría; generalmente

mainsail, s. vela mayor, f.

mainspring, s. (of a watch) muelle real, m.; motivo principal, m.; origen, m.

mainstay, s. estay mayor, m.; (fig.) sostén principal, m.

maintain, v.t. mantener; sostener; tener; guardar; afirmar

maintainable, *a.* sostenible; de-fendible

maintenance, *s.* mantenimiento, *m.*; manutención, *f.*; sustento, *m.*; conservación, *f.*, subsistencia, *f.*

maize, *s.* maíz, *m.* **m. field,** maizal, *m.*

majestic, *a.* majestuoso

majestically, *adv.* majestuosa-mente

majesty, *s.* majestad, *f.*; majes-tuosidad, *f.* **His** or **Her M.,** Su Majestad

majolica, *s.* mayólica, *f.*

major, *a.* mayor; principal. *s.* mayor de edad, *m.*; (*mil.*) comandante, *m.* **m.-domo,** mayordomo, *m.* **m.-general,** general de división, *m.* **m. road,** carretera, *f.*; ruta de prioridad, *f.* **m. scale,** escala mayor, *f.*

majority, *s.* mayoría, *f.*; mayor número, *m.*; generalidad, *f.* **to have attained one's m.,** ser mayor de edad

make, *v.t.* hacer; crear, formar; (manufacture) fabricar, confec-cionar; construir; (produce) pro-ducir; causar; (prepare) pre-parar; (a bed, a fire, a remark, poetry, friends, enemies, war, a curtsey) hacer; (earn, win) ganar; (a speech) pronunciar; (compel) obligar (a), forzar (a); inclinar (a); (arrive at) alcanzar, llegar (a); (calculate) calcular; (ar-range) arreglar; deducir; (be) ser; (equal) ser igual a; (think) creer; (appoint as) constituir (en), hacer; (behave) portarse (como). *v.i.* (begin) ir (a), empe-zar (a); (make as though) hacer (como si); (of the tide) crecer; contribuir (a); tender (a). **He made as if to go,** Hizo como si se marchara. **to m. as though . . .,** aparentar, fingir. **It made me ill,** Me sentó mal. **They have made it up,** Han hecho las paces. **They m. a great deal of money,** Hacen (or ganan) mucho dinero. **You cannot m. me believe it,** No puedes hacerme creerlo. **He is making himself ridiculous,** Se está poniendo en ridículo. **to m. ready,** preparar. **to m. the tea,** hacer el té; preparar el té. **Two and two m. four,** Dos y

dos son cuatro. **to m. oneself known,** darse a conocer. **to m. one of . . .,** ser uno de . . . **to m. after,** seguir; correr detrás de. **to m. again,** hacer de nuevo, rehacer. **to m. away with,** quitar; suprimir; destruir; (kill) matar; (squander) derrochar; (steal) llevarse; hurtar. **to m. away with oneself,** quitarse la vida, suicidarse. **to m. for,** en-caminarse a, dirigirse a; (attack) abalanzarse sobre, atacar; (tend to) contribuir a, tender a. **to m. off,** marcharse corriendo, lar-garse; huir, escaparse. **to m. out,** (discern) distinguir; desci-frar; (understand) comprender; (prove) probar, justificar; (draw up) redactar; (fill in a form) completar, llenar; (a cheque, etc.) extender; (an account) hacer; (get on, succeed or otherwise) ir (with bien or mal); (convey) dar la impresión de que; sugerir. **I cannot m. it out,** No lo puedo comprender. **How did you m. out (get on)?** ¿Cómo te fué? **to m. over,** hacer de nuevo, rehacer; (transfer) ceder, tras-pasar. **to m. up,** hacer; acabar; concluir; (clothes) confeccionar; fabricar; (the face) pintarse, maquillarse; (the fire) echar carbón, etc. a; (*print.*) com-paginar; (invent) inventar; (lies) fabricar; (compose) formar; (package) empaquetar; reparar; indemnizar; compensar; (an ac-count) ajustar; preparar; arre-glar; (conciliate) conciliar; enu-merar; (*theat.*) caracterizarse. **to m. up for,** reemplazar; com-pensar; (lost time, etc.) recobrar. **to m. up to,** compensar; in-demnizar; (flatter) adular, hala-gar; procurar congraciarse con, procurar obtener el favor de; (court) galantear (con)

make, *s.* forma, *f.*; hechura, *f.*; estructura, *f.*; confección, *f.*; manufactura, *f.*; producto, *m.*; (trade name) marca, *f.*; (charac-ter) carácter, temperamento, *m.* **m.-believe,** *s.* artificio, pretexto, *m. a.* fingido. *v.i.* fingir. **land of m.-believe,** reino de los sueños, *m.* **m.-up,** (for the face, etc.) maquillaje, *m.*; (*theat.*)

caracterización, *f.*; (*print.*) imposición,*f.*; (whole) conjunto,*m.*; (character) carácter, modo de ser,*m.*

maker, *s.* creador, *m.*; autor (-ra); artífice, *m.* and *f.*; (manufacturer) fabricante, *m.*; constructor, *m.*; (of clothes, etc.) confeccionador (-ra); (worker) obrero (-ra)

makeshift, . *s:* expediente, *m.* *a.* provisional

makeweight, *s.* añadidura (de peso), *f.*, contrapeso, *m.*; (*fig.*) suplente, *m.*

making, *s.* creación; *f.*; hechura, *f.*; (manufacture) fabricación, *f.*; construcción, *f.*; (of clothes, etc.) confección, *f.*; formación, *f.*; preparación, *f.*; estructura, *f.*; composición, *f.*; *pl.* makings, (profits) ganancias, *f. pl.*; (elements) elementos, *m. pl.*; germen, *m.*; rasgos esenciales, *m. pl.*, características, *f. pl.* m.-up, (of clothes) confección,*f.*; (*print.*) ajuste, *m.*; (of the face) maquillaje, *m.*; (invention) invención, *f.*; fabricación,*f.*

Malacca cane, *s.* bastón de junquillo, *m.*

Malachite, *s.* malaquita, *f.*

maladjustment, *s.* mal ajuste, *m.*; inadaptación, *f.*

maladministration, *s.* desgobierno, *m.*, mala administración, *f.*; (of funds) malversación, *f.*

maladroit, *a.* torpe

maladroitly, *adv.* torpemente

maladroitness, *s.* torpeza, *f.*

malady, *s.* enfermedad, *f.*; mal, *m.*

Malaga, *s.* vino de Málaga, *m.*

malaria, *s.* paludismo, *m.*

malarial, *a.* palúdico. m. fever, fiebre palúdica, *f.*

Malayan, *a.* malayo. *s.* malayo (-ya)

malcontent, *s.* malcontento (-ta). *a.* descontento

male, *a.* macho; masculino. *s.* macho, *m.*; varón, *m.* m. child, niño, *m.*; niño varón, *m.*; (son) hijo varón, *m.* m. flower, flor masculina,*f.* m. issue, sucesión masculina, *f.* m. nurse, enfermero, *m.* m. sex, sexo masculino, *m.*

malediction, *s.* maldición, *f.*

malefactor, *s.* malhechor (-ra)

malefic, *a.* maléfico

malevolence, *s.* malevolencia, *f.*

malevolent, *a.* malévolo, maligno

malevolently, *adv.* malignamente

malformation, *s.* formación anormal, deformidad, *f.*

malice, *s.* malicia, *f.*; (law) alevosía, *f.* to bear m., guardar rencor

malicious, *a.* malicioso; maligno, rencoroso

maliciously, *adv.* maliciosamente

maliciousness, *s.* malicia, mala intención, *f.*

malign, *v.t.* calumniar, difamar. *a.* maligno; malévolo

malignancy, *s.* malignidad, *f.*; malevolencia, *f.*

malignant, *a.* maligno; malévolo; (*med.*) maligno

malinger, *v.i.* fingirse enfermo

malingerer, *s.* enfermo (-ma) fingido (-da)

malingering, *s.* enfermedad fingida, *f.*

mallard, *s.* pato (-ta), silvestre

malleability, *s.* maleabilidad, *f.*

malleable, *a.* maleable

mallet, *s.* mazo, *m.*; (in croquet) pala, *f.*, mazo, *m.*; (in polo) maza (de polo), *f.*

mallow, *s.* malva, *f.*

malmsey, *s.* (wine) malvasía, *f.*

malnutrition, *s.* desnutrición, alimentación deficiente, *f.*

malodorous, *a.* de mal olor, hediondo, fétido

malpractice, *s.* (wrongdoing) maleficencia, *f.*; (by a doctor) tratamiento equivocado, perjudicial o ilegal, *m.*; (malversation) malversación, *f.*; inmoralidad, *f.*

malt, *s.* malta, *m.* *v.t.* preparar el malta. m.-house, fábrica de malta, *f.* m. vinegar, vinagre de malta, *m.*.

Maltese, *a.* maltés. *s.* maltés (-esa). M. cat, gato maltés, *m.* M. cross, cruz de Malta, *f.* M. dog, perro maltés, *m.*

Malthusian, *a.* maltusiano

Malthusianism, *s.* maltusianismo, *m.*

maltose, *s.* maltosa, *f.*

maltreat, *v.t.* maltratar

maltreatment, *s.* maltrato, *m.*

malversation, s. malversación, f.

mameluke, s. mameluco, m.

mamma, s. (anat.) mama, f.; (mother) mamá, f.

mammal, s. mamífero, m.

mammalian, a. mamífero

mammary, a. mamario. m. gland, mama, teta, f.

mammon, s. becerro de oro, m.

mammoth, s. mamut, m. a. gigantesco, enorme

man, s. hombre, m.; varón, m.; persona, f.; (servant) criado, m.; (workman) obrero, m.; (soldier) soldado, m.; (sailor) marinero, m.; (humanity) raza humana, m.; (husband) marido, m.; (at chess) peón, m.; (at draughts) dama, f.; (a ship) buque, m. no man, nadie; ningún hombre. young man, joven, m. to a man, como un solo hombre. to come to man's estate, llegar a la edad viril. Man overboard! ¡Hombre al agua! man and wife, marido y mujer, m., cónyuges, m. pl. man about town, hombre de mundo, señorito, m. man-at-arms, hombre de armas, m. man-eater, caníbal, m. and f.; tigre, m. man-eating, a. antropófago. man hater, misántropo, m.; mujer que odia a los hombres, f. man-hole, pozo, m. man-hunter, caníbal, m. and f.; (woman) castigadora, f. man in charge, encargado, m. man in the moon, mujer de la luna, f. man in the street, hombre de la calle, hombre medio, m. man of letters, hombre de letras, literato, m.; man of straw, bausán, m.; (figure-head) testaferro, m. man of the world, hombre de mundo, m. man of war, buque de guerra, m. man-power, mano de obra, f. man servant, criado, m.

man, v.t. armar; (mil.) poner guarnición (a); ocupar; (naut.) tripular; dirigir; (fig.) fortificar

manacle, s. manilla, f.; pl. manacles, esposas, f. pl.; grillos, m. pl. v.t. poner esposas (a)

manage, v.t. manejar; (animals) domar; dirigir; gobernar; administrar; (arrange) agenciar, arreglar; (work) explotar; (do) hacer; (eat) comer. v.i. arre-

glárselas (para); (get along) ir tirando; (know how) saber hacer; (succeed in) lograr; (do) hacer

manageability, s. lo manejable; flexibilidad, f.; (of animals, persons) docilidad, mansedumbre, f.

manageable, a. manejable; flexible; (of persons, animals) dócil

management, s. manejo, m.; dirección, f.; gobierno, m.; administración, f.; arreglo, m.; (working) explotación, f.; (com.) gerencia, f.; (theat.) empresa, f.; conducta, f.; (economy) economía, f.; (skill) habilidad, f.; prudencia, f. the m., la dirección, el cuerpo de directores. domestic m., economía doméstica, f.

manager, s. director, m.; administrador, m.; jefe, m.; (theat.) empresario, m.; (com.) gerente, m.; regente, m. She is not much of a m., Ella no es muy mujer de su casa. manager's office, dirección, f.

manageress, s. directora, f.; administradora, f.; jefa, f.

managerial, a. directivo; administrativo. m. board, junta directiva, f.

managership, s. puesto de director, m.; jefatura, f.

managing, a. directivo; (officious) mandón, dominante; (niggardly) tacaño

manatee, s. manatí, m.

Manchurian, a. manchuriano. s. manchuriano (-na)

mandarin, s. mandarín, m.; (language) mandarina, f. m. orange, mandarina, f.

mandatary, s. mandatario, m.

mandate, s. mandato, m. mandated territory, territorios bajo mandato, m. pl.

mandible, s. mandíbula, f.

mandolin, s. bandolín, m., bandurria, f.

mandrake, s. mandrágora, f.

mandrill, s. mandril, m.

mane, s. melena, f.; (of a horse) crines, f. pl.

maned, a. (in compounds) con melena...; con crines...

manfully, adv. valientemente; vigorosamente

manganate, s. manganato, m.

manganese, s. manganeso, m.

mange, s. sarna, *f.*; (in sheep) roña, *f.*

manger, s. pesebre, *m.*

manginess, s. estado sarnoso, *m.*

mangle, s. (for clothes) exprimidor de la ropa, *m.* *v.t.* pasar por el exprimidor; (mutilate) mutilar, lacerar, magullar; (a text) mutilar

mangling, s. (mutilation) mutilación, laceración, *f.*

mango, s. mango, *m.*

mangy, *a.* sarnoso

manhandle, *v.t.* maltratar

manhood, s. virilidad, *f.*; edad viril, *f.*; masculinidad, *f.*; los hombres; (manliness) hombradía, *f.*, valor, *m.*

mania, s. manía, *f.*; obsesión, *f.*; capricho, *m.*, chifladura, *f.*

maniac, s. maníaco (-ca). *a.* maníaco, maniático

Manichaean, *a.* maniqueo

Manichee, s. maniqueo (-ea)

manicure, s. manicura, *f.* *v.t.* arreglar las uñas. **m.-set,** estuche de manicura, *m.*

manicurist, s. manicuro (-ra)

manifest, s. (*naut.*) manifiesto, *m.* *v.t.* mostrar; hacer patente, probar; manifestarse. *v.i.* manifestarse. *a.* manifiesto, evidente, claro, patente. **to make m.,** poner de manifiesto

manifestation, s. manifestación, *f.*

manifestly, *adv.* evidentemente, manifiestamente

manifesto, s. manifiesto, *m.*

manifold, *a.* múltiple; numeroso; diverso, vario

manikin, s. enano, *m.*; muñeco, *m.*; (*art*) maniquí, *m.*

Manilla, s. Manila, *f.*; cigarro filipino, *m.* **M. hemp,** cáñamo de Manila, *m.*

maniple, s. manípulo, *m.*

manipulate, *v.t.* manipular

manipulation, s. manipulación, *f.*

manipulative, *a.* manipulador

mankind, s. humanidad, raza humana, *f.*, género humano, *m.*

manlike, *a.* de hombre, masculino; varonil; (of a woman) hombruno

manliness, s. masculinidad, hombradía, *f.*; virilidad, *f.*; valor, *m.*; (of a woman) aire hombruno, *m.*

manly, *a.* masculino, de hombre; varonil, viril; valiente; fuerte. **to be very m.,** ser muy hombre, ser todo un hombre

manna, s. maná, *m.*

mannequin, s. manequín, modelo, *f.* **m. parade,** exposición de modelos, *f.*

manner, s. manera, *f.*, modo, *m.*; aire, porte, *m.*; conducta, *f.*; (style) estilo, *m.*; (sort) clase, *f.*; (*gram.*) modo, *m.*; *pl.* **manners,** modales, *m. pl.* crianza, educación, *f.*; (customs) costumbres, *f. pl.* **after the m. of,** en (or según) el estilo de. **in a m. of speaking,** en cierto modo, para decirlo así. **in this m.,** de este modo. **to have bad (good) manners,** tener malos (buenos) modales, ser mal (bien) criado. **the novel of manners,** la novela de costumbres

mannered, *a.* amanerado; (in compounds) ... educado, de ... modales; de costumbres ... **well-m.,** bien educado, de buenos modales

mannerism, s. amaneramiento, *m.*; afectación, *f.*; (*theat.*) latiguillo, *m.* **to acquire mannerisms,** amanerarse

manneriness, s. cortesía, buena educación, urbanidad, *f.*

mannerly, *a.* cortés, bien educado, atento

mannish, *a.* (of a woman) hombruno; de hombre, masculino

manœuvre, s. maniobra, *f.* *v.i.* maniobrar, hacer maniobras. *v.t.* hacer maniobrar; manipular

manœuvring, s. maniobras, *f. pl.*; maquinaciones, intrigas, *f. pl.*

manometer, s. manómetro, *m.*

manor, s. feudo, *m.*; finca, hacienda, *f.*; casa solariega, *f.*; señorío, *m.*

manorial, *a.* señorial

manse, s. rectoría, *f.*

mansion, s. mansión, *f.*; casa solariega, *f.*; hotel, *m.* **m.-house,** casa solariega, *f.*; residencia del alcalde de Londres, *f.*

manslaughter, s. homicidio, *m.*; (*law*) homicidio sin premeditación, *m.*

mantelpiece, s. repisa de chimenea, *f.*

mantilla, s. mantilla, f.
mantle, s. capa, f., manto, m.; (fig.)cobertura, f.; (gas)camisa, f.; (zool.) manto, m. v.t. cubrir; envolver; ocultar. v.i. extenderse; (of blushes) inundar, subirse (a las mejillas)
mantlet, s. mantelete, m.
Mantuan, a. mantuano
manual, a. manual. s. manual, m.; (mus.) teclado de órgano, m. **m. work,** trabajo manual, m.
manufactory, s. fábrica, f., taller, m.
manufacture, s. fabricación, f.; manufactura, f. v.t. manufacturar, fabricar
manufacturer, s. fabricante, industrial, m. **manufacturer's price,** precio de fábrica, m.
manufacturing, a. manufacturero, fabril. s. fabricación, f.
manure, s. estiércol, abono, m. v.t. estercolar, abonar. **m. heap,** estercolero, m.
manuring, s. estercoladura, f.
manuscript, s. manuscrito, m. a. manuscrito
Manx, a. de la Isla de Man
many, a. muchos (-as); numeroso; diversos (-as); varios (-as). s. muchos (-as); la mayoría; las masas; muchedumbre, multitud, f. **a great m.,** muchísimos, m. pl., muchísimas, f. pl.; un gran número. **as m. as . . .,** tantos como . . . **How m. are there?** ¿Cuántos hay? ¿Cuántas hay? **m. a time,** muchas veces. **three too m.,** tres de más. **for m. long years,** por largos años. **m.-coloured,** multicolor. **m.-headed,** con muchas cabezas. **m.-sided,** multilátero; polifacético; complicado
Maori, s. maorí, m. (pl. maoríes)
map, s. mapa, m.; plano, m.; (chart) carta, f. v.t. hacer un mapa (or plano) de. **to map out,** (surv.) apear; trazar; (plan) proyectar. **ordnance map,** mapa del estado mayor, m. **map of the world,** mapamundi, mapa del mundo, m. **map-making,** cartografía, f.
maple, s. (tree) arce, m.; (wood)

madera de arce, f. **m.-syrup,** jarabe de arce, m.
mapping, s. cartografía, f.
mar, v.t. estropear; desfigurar; (happiness) destruir, aguar; frustrar
marabou, s. marabú, m.
maraschino, s. marrasquino, m. **m. cherries,** cerezas en marrasquino, f. pl.
maraud, v.i. merodear
marauder, s. merodeador, m.
marauding, a. merodeador. s. merodeo, m.
marble, s. mármol, m.; (for playing with) canica, f. a. de marmol, marmóreo; (fig.) insensible; (of paper, etc.) jaspeado. v.t. jaspear. **m. cutter,** marmolista, m. **m. works,** marmolería, f.
marbled, a. jaspeado
marcasite, s. marcasita, f.
marcel wave, s. ondulado marcel, m.
March, s. marzo, m. **as mad as a M. hare,** loco como una cabra, loco de atar
march, s. marcha, f.; (step) paso, m.; (fig.) marcha, f., progreso, m. **forced m.,** marcha forzada, f. **quick m.,** paso doble, m. **to steal a m. on,** tomar la delantera (a), ganar por la mano (a). **to strike up a m.,** batir la marcha. **m.-past,** desfile, m.
march, v.i. marchar; (of properties) lindar (con). v.t. hacer marchar, poner en marcha (a). **to m. back,** v.i. regresar (or volver) a pie. v.t. hacer volver a pie. **to m. in,** entrar (a pie) en. **to m. off,** marcharse. **to m. on,** seguir marchando; seguir adelante; avanzar. **to m. past,** desfilar ante
marching, s. marcha, f. a. en marcha; de marcha. **to receive one's m. orders,** recibir la orden de marchar; (fam.) ser despedido. **m. order,** orden de marcha, m. **m. song,** canción de marcha, f.
marchioness, s. marquesa, f.
marchpane, s. mazapán, m.
marconigram, s. (message) radiograma, m.
mardi gras, s. martes de carnaval, m.
mare, s. yegua, f.

margarine, *s.* margarina, *f.*

margin, *s.* borde, lado, *m.*, orilla, *f.*; (of a page) margen, *m.* or *f.*; reserva, *f.*; sobrante, *m.* **in the m.,** al margen

marginal, *a.* marginal. **m. note,** acotación, *f.*

marguerite, *s.* margarita, *f.*

Marian, *a.* mariano

marigold, *s.* caléndula, maravilla, *f.*

marine, *a.* marino, de mar; marítimo; naval. *s.* (fleet) marina, *f.*; (soldier) soldado de marina, *m.* **Tell that to the marines!** ¡Cuéntaselo a tu tía! **mercantile m.,** marina mercante, *f.* **m. forces,** infantería de marina, *f.* **m. insurance,** seguro marítimo, *m.*

mariner, *s.* marinero, marino, *m.* **mariner's compass,** aguja de marear, brújula, *f.*

Marinism, *s.* marinismo, *m.*

Mariolatry, *s.* mariolatría, *f.*

marionette, *s.* marioneta, *f.*, títere, *m.*

marital, *a.* marital

maritime, *a.* marítimo

marjoram, *s.* mejorana, *f.*, orégano, *m.*

mark, *s.* marca, *f.*; señal, *f.*; mancha, *f.*; impresión, *f.*; (target) blanco, *m.*; (standard) norma, *f.*; (level) nivel, *m.*; (distinction) importancia, distinción, *f.*; (in examinations) nota, *f.*; calificación, *f.*; (signature) cruz, *f.*; (coin) marco, *m.* *v.t.* marcar; señalar; (price) poner precio (a); (notice) observar, darse cuenta (de); (characterize) caracterizar. **trade-m.,** marca de fábrica, *f.* **to be beside the m.,** no dar en el blanco; errar el tiro; (*fig.*) no tener nada que ver con; equivocarse. **to hit the m.,** dar en el blanco; (*fig.*) dar en el clavo. **to make one's m.,** firmar con una cruz; distinguirse. **to m. time,** marcar el paso; (*fig.*) hacer tiempo. **to m. down,** (a person) señalar; escoger; (in price) rebajar. **to m. out,** marcar; trazar; definir; (erase) borrar; (a person) escoger; destinar

Mark, *s.* Marcos. **The Gospel according to St. M.,** El Evangelio de San Marcos

marked, *a.* marcado; señalado; notable; acentuado; particular, especial. **He speaks with a m. Galician accent,** Habla con marcado acento gallego

markedly, *adv.* marcadamente; notablemente; especialmente, particularmente

marker, *s.* (billiards) marcador, *m.*; (football, etc.) tanteador, *m.*

market, *s.* mercado, *m.*; tráfico, *m.*; venta, *f.*; (price) precio, *m.*; (shop) bazar, emporio, *m.* *v.t.* and *v.i.* comprar en un mercado; vender en un mercado. **black m.,** mercado negro, estraperlo, *m.* **open m.,** mercado al aire libre, *m.*; (*fig.*) mercado libre, *m.* **m.-day,** día de mercado, *m.* **m.-garden,** huerto, *m.*, huerta, *f.* **m.-gardener,** hortelano, *m.* **m.-place,** plaza de mercado, *f.*; (*fig.*) mercado, *m.* **m. price,** precio corriente, *m.* **m.-stall,** tabanco, puesto de mercado, *m.* **m.-woman,** verdulera, *f.*

marketable, *a.* comerciable, vendible; corriente

marketing, *s.* venta, *f.*; compra en un mercado, *f.*; mercado, *m.* **to go m.,** ir al mercado

marking, *s.* marca, *f.*; (spot on animals, etc.) pinta, *f.* **m.-ink,** tinta de marcar, *f.* **m.-iron,** ferrete, hierro de marcar, *m.*

marksman, *s.* tirador (-ra)

marksmanship, *s.* puntería, *f.*

marl, *s.* marga, *f.*

marlinespike, *s.* pasador, *m.*

marly, *a.* margoso

marmalade, *s.* mermelada de naranjas amargas, *f.*

marmoreal, *a.* marmóreo

marmoset, *s.* tití, *m.*

marmot, *s.* (*zool.*) marmota, *f.*

maroon, *s.* (colour) marrón, *m.*; (slave) cimarrón (-ona); (firework) petardo, *m.* *a.* de marrón. *v.t.* abandonar, dejar

marquee, *s.* marquesina, *f.*

marqueterie, *s.* marquetería, *f.*

marquis, *s.* marqués, *m.*

marquisate, *s.* marquesado, *m.*

marquise, *s.* marquesa, *f.*

marriage, *s.* matrimonio, *m.*; unión, *f.*; (wedding) boda, *f.*, casamiento, *m.* **by m.,** (of relationship) político. **She is an**

aunt by m., Ella es una tía
política. m. articles, capitulaciones (matrimoniales), f. pl. m.
contract, contrato matrimonial,
m. m. licence, licencia de casamiento, f. m. portion, dote,
m. or f. m. rate, nupcialidad, f.
m. register, acta matrimonial,
f. m. song, epitalamio, m.
marriageable, a. casadero
married, past part. and a. casado;
matrimonial, conyugal. newly-
m. couple, los recién casados.
to get m. to, casarse con. m.
couple, matrimonio, m., cónyuges, m. pl. m. life, vida
conyugal, f.
marrow, s. tuétano, m., médula,
f.; (fig.) meollo, m. to the m. of
one's bones, hasta los tuétanos.
marrowbone, s. hueso medular,
m. on one's marrowbones, de
rodillas
marry, v.t. casarse con, contraer
matrimonio con; casar; (of a
priest) unir en matrimonio; (fig.)
juntar, unir. v.i. casarse. to m.
again, volver a casarse
Marseillaise, s. marsellesa, f.
marsh, s. marjal, pantano, m.
m.-mallow, (bot.) malvavisco,
m. m. marigold, calta, f.
marshal, s. mariscal, m. v.t.
poner en orden, arreglar; dirigir.
field-m., capitán general de
ejército, m.
marshalling, s. ordenación, f.;
dirección, f. m.-yard, (railway)
apartadero ferroviario, m.
marshalship, s. mariscalía, f.
marshiness, s. estado pantanoso,
m.
marshy, a. pantanoso
mart, s. (poet.) plaza de mercado,
f.; mercado, m.; emporio, m.;
(auction rooms) martillo, m.
marten, s. marta, f.
martial, a. militar; marcial,
belicoso. m. array, orden de
batalla, m. m. law, derecho
militar, m.; estado de guerra, m.
m. spirit, marcialidad, f., espíritu belicoso, m.
martially, adv. militarmente;
marcialmente
Martian, a. marciano
martin, s. vencejo, m.
martinet, s. (mil.) ordenancista,
m.; rigorista, m. and f.

Martinmas, s. día de San Martín,
m.
martyr, s. mártir, m. and f. v.t.
martirizar
martyrdom, s. martirio, m.
martyrize, v.t. martirizar
marvel, s. maravilla, f. to m. at,
maravillarse de, admirarse de
marvellous, a. maravilloso
marvellously, adv. maravillosamente
marvellousness, s. maravilla, f.,
carácter maravilloso, m., lo
maravilloso
Marxism, s. marxismo, m.
Marxist, a. and s. marxista (m.
and f.)
marzipan, s. mazapán, m.
mascot, s. mascota, f.
masculine, a. masculino; varonil,
macho; de hombre; (of a woman)
hombruno. s. masculino, m.
masculinity, s. masculinidad,
f.
mash, s. mezcla, f.; amasijo, m.;
pasta, f., puré, m. v.t. mezclar;
amasar. mashed potatoes, puré
de patatas, m.
mashie, s. (golf) " mashie," m.
mask, s. máscara, f.; antifaz, m.;
(death) mascarilla, f.; (person)
máscara, m. and f. v.t. enmascarar; (fig.) encubrir, disimular.
v.i. ponerse una máscara; disfrazarse. masked ball, s. baile
de máscaras, m.
masker, s. máscara, m. and f.
masochism, s. masoquismo, m.
mason, s. albañil, m.; (freemason)
francmasón, masón, m.
masonic, a. masónico. m. lodge,
logia de francmasones, f.
masonry, s. (trade) albañilería,
f.; mampostería, f.
masque, s. mascarada, f.
masquerade, s. mascarada, f.
masquerader, s. máscara, m. and
f.
Mass, s. misa, f. to hear M., oír
misa. to say M., celebrar misa.
High M., Misa mayor, f. Low
M., Misa rezada, f. M. book,
libro de misa, m.
mass, s. masa, f.; (shape) bulto,
m.; (heap) montón, m.; (great
number) muchedumbre, f.;
(cloud of steam, etc.) nube, f.
v.t. amasar; (mil.) concentrar.
v.i. congregarse en masa. in a

m., en masa; en conjunto. **the m.** (of) ..., la mayoría (de) ... **the masses,** las masas, el vulgo, el pueblo. **m. formation,** columna cerrada, f. **m.-meeting,** mitín popular, m. **m.-production,** fabricación en serie, f.

massacre, s. matanza, carnicería, f. v.t. hacer una carnicería (de)

massage, s. masaje, m.; (friction) fricción, f. v.t. dar un masaje (a)

masseur, masseuse, s. masajista, m. and f.

massive, a. macizo; sólido

massively, adv. macizamente; sólidamente

massiveness, s. macicez, f.; solidez, f.

mast, s. (naut.) palo, árbol, m.; (for wireless) mástil, m.; poste, m.; (beech) hayuco, m.; (oak) bellota, f. v.t. (naut.) arbolar. **at half-m.,** a media asta. **m.-head,** calcés, tope, m.

masted, a. arbolado; (in compounds) de ... palos

master, s. (of the house, etc.) señor, amo, m.; maestro, m.; (naut.) patrón, m.; (owner) dueño, m.; (teacher) profesor, maestro, m.; (young master and as address) señorito, m.; director, m.; jefe, m.; (expert) perito, m.; (of a military order) maestre, m. a. maestro; superior. v.t. dominar; ser maestro en; dominar, conocer a fondo. **This picture is by an old m.,** Este cuadro es de un antiguo pintor famoso. **to be m. of oneself,** ser dueño de sí. **to be one's own m.,** ser dueño de sí mismo; trabajar por su propia cuenta; ser independiente; estar libre. **m. builder,** maestro de obras, m. **m. hand,** mano maestra, f. **M. of Arts,** maestro (-tra) en artes. **M. of Ceremonies,** maestro de ceremonias, m. **M. of Foxhounds,** cazador mayor, m. **M. of the Horse,** caballerizo mayor del rey, m. **M. of the Rolls,** archivero mayor, m. **m.-key,** llave maestra, f. **m. mind,** águila, f., ingenio, m. **m. stroke,** golpe maestro, m.

masterful, a. imperioso, dominante; autoritario, arbitrario

masterfulness, s. imperiosidad, f.; arbitrariedad, f.

masterless, a. sin amo

masterliness, s. maestría, f.; excelencia, f.; perfección, f.

masterly, a. maestro; excelente; perfecto. **m. performance,** obra maestra, f.; (theat.) representación perfecta, f.; ejecución excelente, f.

masterpiece, s. obra maestra, f.

masterstroke, s. golpe magistral, golpe de maestro, m.

mastery, s. dominio, m.; autoridad, f.; poder, m.; ventaja, f.; superioridad, maestría, f.; conocimiento profundo, m. **to gain the m. of,** hacerse el señor de; llegar a dominar

mastic, s. masilla, almáciga, f.

masticate, v.t. masticar, mascar

mastication, s. masticación, f.

masticatory, a. masticatorio

mastiff, s. mastín, alano, m.

mastodon, s. mastodonte, m.

mastoid, a. mastoides. s. apófisis mastoides, f.

masturbate, v.i. masturbarse

masturbation, s. masturbación, f.

mat, s. esterilla, f.; alfombrilla, f.; (on the table) tapete individual, m. v.t. (tangle) enmarañar, desgreñar. v.i. enmarañarse

match, s. (sport.) partido, m.; (wrestling, boxing) lucha, f.; (fencing) asalto, m.; (race) carrera, f.; (contest) concurso, m.; (equal) igual, m. and f.; (pair) pareja, f.; compañero (-ra) (marriage) boda, f., casamiento, m.; (for lighting) cerilla, f., fósforo, m.; (for guns) mecha, f. v.t. competir con; (equal) igualar; ser igual (a); hacer juego con; emparejar, aparear; armonizar. v.i. ser igual; hacer juego; armonizarse. **good m.,** (fam.) buen partido, m. **as thin as a m.,** más delgado que una cerilla. **to meet one's m.,** dar con la horma de su zapato. **to play a m.,** jugar un partido. **m.-box,** cajita de cerillas, fosforera, f. **m.-seller,** fosforero (-ra)

matchless, a. incomparable, sin igual, sin par

matchwood, s. madera para cerillas, f.

mate, *s.* compañero, camarada, *m.*; (spouse) compañero (-ra); pareja, *f.*; (on merchant ships) piloto, *m.*; (assistant) ayudante, *m.*; (at chess) mate, *m.* *v.t.* (marry) casar, desposar; (animals, birds) aparear, acoplar; (at chess) dar jaque mate (a). *v.i.* casarse; aparearse, acoplarse

maté, *s.* maté, té del Paraguay, *m.*

materfamilias, *s.* madre de familia, *f.*

material, *a.* material; importante, esencial; considerable; sensible, notable; grave. *s.* material, *m.*; materia, *f.*; (fabric) tela, *f.*; tejido, *m.* raw materials, materias primas, *f. pl.* writing materials, utensilios de escritorio, *m. pl.*; papel de escribir, *m.*

materialism, *s.* materialismo, *m.*

materialist, *s.* materialista, *m.* and *f.*

materialistic, *a.* materialista

materiality, *s.* materialidad, *f.*; importancia, *f.*

materialization, *s.* materialización, *f.*

materialize, *v.t.* materializar

materially, *adv.* materialmente

maternal, *a.* materno, maternal. m. grandparents, abuelos maternos, *m. pl.*

maternity, *s.* maternidad, *f.* m. centre, centro de maternidad, *m.* m. hospital, casa de maternidad, *f.*

mathematical, *a.* matemático

mathematician, *s.* matemático, *m.*

mathematics, *s. pl.*; matemáticas, *f. pl.* applied m., matemáticas prácticas, *f. pl.* higher m., matemáticas superiores, *f. pl.* pure m., matemáticas teóricas, *f. pl.*

matinee, *s.* matinée, función de tarde, *f.*

mating, *s.* (of animals) apareamiento, acoplamiento, *m.*; unión, *f.*; casamiento, *m.*

matins, *s. pl.* (ecc.) maitines, *m. pl.*

matrass, *s.* matraz, *m.*

matriarch, *s.* matriarca, *f.*

matriarchal, *a.* matriarcal

matriarchy, *s.* matriarcado, *m.*

matricide, *s.* (crime) matricidio, *m.*; (person) matricida, *m.* and *f.*

matriculate, *v.t.* matricular. *v.i.* matricularse

matriculation, *s.* matriculación, *f.*

matrimonial, *a.* matrimonial, de matrimonio; marital. m. agency, agencia de matrimonios, *f.*

matrimony, *s.* matrimonio, *m.*

matrix, *s.* matriz, *f.*

matron, *s.* matrona, mujer casada, madre de familia, *f.*; (of a hospital) matrona, *f.*; (of a school) ama de llaves, *f.*; directora, *f.* m. of honour, (at a wedding) madrina, *f.*

matronly, *a.* de matrona, matronal; respetable; serio

matt, *a.* mate

matted, *a.* enmarañado, enredado

matter, *s.* materia, *f.*; substancia, *f.*; caso, *m.*; cuestión, *f.*; asunto, *m.*; causa, *f.*; (distance) distancia, *f.*; (amount) cantidad, *f.*; (duration) espacio de tiempo, *m.*; (importance) importancia, *f.*; (*med.*) pus, *m.*; *pl.* matters, asuntos, *m. pl.*, etc.; situación, *f.* as if nothing were the m., como si no hubiese pasado nada. for that m., en cuanto a eso. grey m., substancia gris, *f.* in the m. of, en el caso de. It is a m. of taste, Es cuestión de gusto. printed m., impresos, *m. pl.* What is the m.? ¿Qué pasa? ¿Qué hay? What is the m. with him? ¿Qué tiene él? ¿Qué le pasa? m.-of-course, cosa natural, *f.* m.-of-fact, práctico; sin imaginación; positivista. m. of fact, *s.* hecho positivo, *m.*, realidad, *f.* As a m. of fact . . ., En realidad . . ., El caso es que . . . m. of form, cuestión de fórmula, *f.*; pura formalidad, *f.*

matter, *v.i.* importar; (discharge) supurar. What does it m.? ¿Qué importa? It doesn't m., Es igual, No importa, Da lo mismo

matting, *s.* estera, *f.*

mattock, *s.* zapapico, *m.*, piqueta, *f.*

mattress, *s.* colchón, *m.* spring-m., colchón de muelles, *m.* m.-maker, colchonero, *m.*

mature, *a.* maduro; (*com.*) vencido. *v.t.* madurar. *v.i.* madurarse; (*com.*) vencer maturely, *adv.* maduramente

maturity, *s.* madurez, *f.*; edad madura, *f.*; (*com.*, of a bill) vencimiento, *m.*

matutinal, *a.* matutino

maudlin, *a.* sensiblero; lacrimoso; (tipsy) calamocano

maul, *v.t.* maltratar; herir

maundy, *s.* lavatorio, *m.* M. Thursday, Jueves Santo, *m.*

mausoleum, *s.* mausoleo, *m.*

mauve, *s.* color purpúreo delicado, color de malva, *m.* *a.* de color de malva

mavis, *s.* (*orn.*) malvís, *m.*

maw, *s.* (of a ruminant) cuajar, *m.*; (of a bird) buche, *m.*; (*fig.*) abismo, *m.*

mawkish, *a.* insípido, insulso; sensiblero; asqueroso

mawkishness, *s.* insipidez, insulsez, *f.*; sensiblería, *f.*; asquerosidad, *f.*

maxilla. *s.* hueso maxilar, maxilar, *m.*

maxillary, *a.* maxilar

maxim, *s.* máxima, *f.*

maximum, *a.* máximo. *s.* máximo, *m.*

may, *v. aux.*, poder; ser posible; (expressing wish, hope) ojalá que . . ., Dios quiera que . . ., or the present subjunctive may be used, e.g. May you live many years! ¡ (qué) Viva Vd. muchos años! (to denote uncertainty, the future tense of the verb is often used, e.g. You may perhaps remember the date, Vd. quizás se acordará de la fecha. Who may he be? ¿Quién será el?) May God grant it! ¡ (que) Dios lo quiera! It may be that . . ., Puede ser que . . ., Es posible que . . ., Quizás . . . He may come on Saturday, Es posible que venga el sábado; Puede venir el sábado. May I come in? ¿Puedo entrar? ¿Se puede entrar?. May I come and see you? ¿Me das permiso para hacerte una visita? ¿Me dejas venir a verte? May I go then? ¿ Puedo irme pues? ¿Tengo permiso para marcharme entonces?

May, *s.* mayo, *m.*; (*fig.*) abril, *m.*; (*bot.*) espina blanca, *f.* May Day, primero de mayo, *m.* may-flower, flor del cuclillo, *f.* may-fly, cachipolla, *f.* May queen, maya, *f.*

maybe, *adv.* quizás, tal vez

mayonnaise, *s.* mayonesa, *f.* m. sauce, salsa mayonesa, *f.*

mayor, *s.* alcalde, *m.*

mayoral, *a.* de alcalde

mayoress, *s.* alcaldesa, *f.*

maypole, *s.* mayo, *m.* m. dance, danza de cintas, *f.*

maze, *s.* laberinto, *m.*; (*fig.*) perplejidad, *f.* *v.t.* dejar perplejo, aturdir

mazurka, *s.* mazurca, *f.*

me, *pron.* me; (after a preposition only) mí. They sent it for me, Lo mandaron para mí. Dear me! ¡Ay de mí!

meadow, *s.* prado, *m.*, pradera, *f.* m.-sweet, reina de los prados, *f.*

meagre, *a.* magro, enjuto, flaco; (scanty) exiguo, escaso, insuficiente; pobre; (*fig.*) árido

meagrely, *adv.* pobremente

meagreness, *s.* exigüidad, escasez, *f.*; pobreza, *f.*; (*fig.*) aridez, *f.*

meal, *s.* comida, *f.*; (flour) harina, *f.* to have a good m., tener una buena comida, comer bien. test m., (*med.*) comida de prueba, *f.* m.-time, hora de comida, *f.*

mealy, *a.* harinoso; (of the complexion) pastoso

mean, *a.* (middle) medianero; (average) mediano; (humble) humilde; pobre; inferior; bajo, vil, ruin; (avaricious) tacaño, mezquino. m.-spirited, vil, de alma ruin

mean, *s.* medio, *m.*; medianía, *f.*; *pl.* means, medio, *m.*; expediente, *m.*; medios, *m. pl.*; (financial) recursos, *m. pl.*; modo, *m.*, manera, *f.* by all means, por todos los medios; (certainly) ¡ya lo creo! ¡no faltaba más! ¡naturalmente! by means of, mediante, por medio de; con la ayuda de. by no means, de ningún modo; nada. by some means, de algún modo, de alguna manera

mean, *v.t.* destinar (para); pretender, proponerse; intentar, pensar; querer decir, significar; importar; (wish) querer; (concern, speak about) tratarse (de).

v.i. tener el propósito, tener la intención. **I did not m. to do it,** Lo hice sin querer. **What does this word m.?** ¿Qué significa esta palabra? **What do you m. by that?** ¿Qué quieres decir con eso? **This portrait is meant to be Joan,** Este retrato quiere ser Juana. **What do they m. to do?** ¿Qué piensan (or se proponen) hacer? **Do you really m. it?** ¿Lo dices en serio? **Charles always means well,** Carlos siempre tiene buenas intenciones

meander, *s.* meandro, serpenteo, *m.;* camino tortuoso, *m. v.i.* serpentear; errar, vagar; (in talk) divagar

meandering, *s.* meandros, *m. pl.,* serpenteo, *m.;* (in talk) divagaciones, *f. pl. a.* serpentino, tortuoso

meaning, *s.* intención, voluntad, *f.;* significación, *f.,* significado, *m.;* (of words) acepción, *f.;* (sense) sentido, *m.;* (thought) pensamiento, *m. a.* significante. **double m.,** doble intención, *f.* **He gave me a m. look,** Me miró con intención. **What is the m. of it?** ¿Qué significa? ¿Qué quiere decir?

meaningless, *a.* sin sentido; insensato; insignificante

meaningly, *adv.* significativamente; con intención

meanness, *s.* pobreza, *f.;* inferioridad, *f.;* mediocridad, *f.;* bajeza, ruindad, *f.;* (stinginess) mezquindad, tacañería, *f.*

meantime, meanwhile, *s.* ínterin, *m. adv.* entre tanto, mientras tanto, a todo esto. **in the m.,** mientras tanto, en el ínterin

measles, *s.* sarampión, *m.* **German m.,** rubéola, *f.*

measurable, *a.* mensurable

measure, *s.* medida, *f.;* capacidad, *f.;* (for measuring) regla, *f.;* número, *m.;* proporción, *f.;* (limit) límite, *m.;* (fig., step) medida, *f.;* (metre) metro, *m.;* (mus.) compás, *m.;* (degree) grado, *m.;* manera, *f.;* (parliamentary) proyecto (de ley), *m. v.t.* medir; proporcionar, distribuir; (water) aforar; (land) apear;

(height of persons) tallar; (for clothes) tomar las medidas (a); (judge) juzgar; (test) probar; (*poet.,* traverse) recorrer. **a suit made to m.,** un traje hecho a medida. **in great m.,** en gran manera, en alto grado. **in some m.,** hasta cierto punto. **to m. one's length,** caer tendido. **to take a person's m.,** (*fig.*) tomar las medidas (a). **to m. up to,** (*fig.*) estar al nivel de, ser igual a

measured, *a.* mesurado, moderado; uniforme; limitado. **to walk with m. tread,** andar a pasos contados

measurement, *s.* medición, *f.;* medida, *f.;* dimensión, *f.*

meat, *s.* carne, *f.;* (food) alimento, *m.;* (meal) comida, *f.;* (fig.) substancia, *f.* **to sit at m.,** estar a la mesa. **cold meats,** fiambres, *m. pl.* **m.-ball,** albóndiga, *f.* **m.-chopper,** picador, *m.* **m.-dish,** fuente, *f.* **m.-eater,** comedor (-ra) de carne. **m. extract,** carne concentrada, *f.* **m.-market,** carnicería, *f.* **m.-pie,** pastel de carne, *m.* **m.-safe,** fresquera, *f.*

meatus, *s.* meato, *m.*

meaty, *a.* carnoso; (*fig.*) substancial

mechanic, *s.* mecánico, *m.*

mechanical, *a.* mecánico; maquinal

mechanically, *adv.* mecánicamente; maquinalmente

mechanics, *s.* mecánica, *f.*

mechanism, *s.* mecanismo, *m.;* (philosophy) mecanicismo, *m.*

mechanize, *v.t.* convertir en máquina; (gen. *mil.*) mecanizar; motorizar

medal, *s.* medalla, *f.*

medallion, *s.* medallón, *m.*

medallist, *s.* grabador de medallas, *m.;* el, *m.* (*f.* la) que recibe una medalla

meddle, *v.i.* tocar; meterse (con or en); entremeterse, inmiscuirse; intrigar

meddler, *s.* entremetido (-da); intrigante, *m.* and *f.*

meddlesome, *a.* entremetido; oficioso; impertinente; enredador, intrigante. **to be very m.,** meterse en todo

meddlesomeness, s. entremetimiento, m.; oficiosidad, f.; impertinencia, f.; intrigas, f. pl.

mediæval, a. medieval

mediævalism, s. afición a la edad media, f.; espíritu medieval, m.

median, a. del medio

mediate, v.i. intervenir, mediar, arbitrar; abogar (por). a. medio; interpuesto

mediation, s. mediación, intervención, f.; intercesión, f.; interposición, f.

mediator, s. mediador (-ra); arbitrador, m.; intercesor (-ra)

mediatory, a. de mediador; intercesor

medical, a. médico; de medicina; de médico. s. (fam.) estudiante de medicina, m. **Army M. Service,** Servicio de Sanidad Militar, m. **m. books,** libros de medicina, m. pl. **m. examination,** exan.en médico, m., exploración médica, f. **m. jurisprudence,** medicina legal, f. **m. knowledge,** conocimientos médicos, m. pl. **m. practitioner,** médico (-ca). m. **school,** escuela de medicina, f.

medically, adv. médicamente

medicament, s. medicamento, m.

medicate, v.t. medicar; medicinar

medicated, a. medicado

medication, s. medicación, f.

medicinal, a. medicinal

medicine, s. medicina, f.; medicamento, m.; (charm) ensalmo, hechizo, m. **patent m.,** específico farmacéutico, m. **m. ball,** balón medical, m. **m. chest,** botiquín, m. **m. man,** hechizador, m.

medico-, prefix, médico-. **m.-legal,** médicolegal

mediocre, a. mediocre

mediocrity, s. mediocridad, f.; medianía, f.

meditate, v.t. idear, proyectar, meditar. v.i. meditar, reflexionar; pensar, intentar

meditation, s. meditación, f.

meditative, a. meditabundo, contemplativo; de meditación

meditatively, adv. reflexivamente

Mediterranean, a. mediterráneo. s. mar mediterráneo, m.

medium, s. medio, m.; término medio, m.; (environment) medio ambiente, m.; (agency) intermediario, m.; (spiritualism) médium, m.; (art) medio, m. a. mediano; regular; mediocre. **through the m. of,** por medio de. **m.-sized,** de tamaño regular

medlar, s. (fruit) níspola, f.; (tree) níspero, m.

medley, s. mezcla, f.; miscelánea, f. a. mezclado, mixto

medulla, s. medula, f.

meek, a. dulce, manso; humilde; modesto; pacífico

meekly, adv. mansamente; humildemente; modestamente

meekness, s. mansedumbre, f.; humildad, f.; modestia, f.

meet, v.t. encontrar; encontrarse con; tropezar con; (by arrangement) reunirse con; (make the acquaintance of) conocer (a); (satisfy) satisfacer; cumplir (con); (a bill) pagar, saldar; (refute) refutar; (fight) batirse (con); (confront) hacer frente (a). v.i. juntarse; encontrarse; reunirse; verse; (of rivers) confluir. s. montería, f. a. conveniente. **I shall m. you at the station,** Te esperaré en la estación. **Until we m. again!** ¡Hasta la vista! **to go to m.,** ir al encuentro de. **to m. half-way,** encontrar a la mitad del camino; partir la diferencia con; hacer concesiones (a). **to m. the eye,** saltar a la vista. **to m. with,** encontrar; experimentar; sufrir

meeting, s. encuentro, m.; reunión, f.; (interview) entrevista, f.; (of rivers, etc.) confluencia, f.; (public, etc.) mitin, m.; (council) concilio, m.; concurso, m.; (race) concurso de carreras de caballos, m. **creditors' m.,** concurso de acreedores, m. **m.-house,** templo de los Cuáqueros, m. **m.-place,** lugar de reunión, m.; lugar de cita, m.; centro, m. **to adjourn the m.,** levantar la sesión. **to call a m.,** convocar un mitin. **to open the m.,** abrir la sesión

megalith, s. megalito, m.

megalithic, a. megalítico

megalomania, s. megalomanía, f.

megalomaniac, s. megalómano (-na)

megaphone, s. megáfono, porta-voz, m.

melancholia, s. melancolía, f.

melancholy, a. melancólico. s. melancolía, f.

melinite, s. melinita, f.

mellifluence, s. melifluidad, f.

mellifluous, a. melifluo; dulce

mellow, a. maduro; dulce; (of wine) rancio; blando; suave; (of sound) melodioso; (slang) alegre; (tipsy) entre dos luces. v.t. madurar; ablandar; suavizar. v.i. madurarse

mellowing, s. maduración, f.

mellowness, s. madurez, f.; dulzura, f.; (of wine) ranciedad, f.; blandura, f.; suavidad, f.; melodía, f.

melodic, a. melódico

melodious, a. melodioso

melodiously, adv. melodiosamente

melodiousness, s. melodía, f.

melodrama, s. melodrama, m.

melodramatic, a. melodramático

melodramatically, adv. melodramáticamente

melody, s. melodía, f.

melon, s. melón, m.; sandía, f. **slice of m.,** raja de melón, f. **m. bed,** sandiar, m. **m.-shaped,** amelonado

melt, v.i. derretirse; deshacerse; disolverse; evaporarse; desaparecer; (of money, etc.) hacerse sal y agua; (relent) enternecerse, ablandarse. v.t. fundir; (snow, etc.) derretir; (fig., soften) ablandar. **He melted away,** (fam.) Se escurrió. **to m. into tears,** deshacerse en lágrimas. **to m. down,** fundir

melting, a. fundente; (forgiving) indulgente; (tender) de ternura; lánguido; dulce. s. fusión, f.; derretimiento, m. **m. point,** punto de fusión, m. **m.-pot,** crisol, m.

member, s. miembro, m.; (of a club, etc.) socio (-ia). **M. of Parliament,** diputado a Cortes, m.

membership, s. calidad de miembro or socio, f.; número de miembros (or socios), m.

membrane, s. membrana, f.

membranous, a. membranoso

memento, s. recuerdo, m.

memoir, s. memoria, f.

memorable, a. memorable

memorably, adv. memorablemente

memorandum, s. memorándum, m.

memorial, a. conmemorativo. s. monumento conmemorativo, m.; memorial (also law), m.

memorize, v.t. aprender de memoria

memory, s. memoria, f.; recuerdo, m. **from m.,** de memoria. **If my m. does not deceive me,** Si mal no me acuerdo. **in m. of,** en conmemoración de; en recuerdo de

menace, s. amenaza, f. v.t. amenazar

menacing, a. amenazador

menacingly, adv. con amenazas

menagerie, s. colección de fieras, f.; casa de fieras, f.

mend, v.t. remendar; componer; reparar; (darn) zurcir; (rectify) remediar; reformar; enmendar; (a fire) echar carbón (or leña, etc.) a; (one's pace) avivar. v.i. (in health and of the weather) mejorar. s. remiendo, m.; (darn) zurcido, m. **to be on the m.,** estar mejor. **to m. one's ways,** reformarse, enmendarse

mendacious, a. mendaz

mendacity, s. mendacidad, f.

Mendelism, s. mendelismo, m.

mender, s. componedor (-ra); (darner) zurcidor (-ra); reparador (-ra); (cobbler and tailor) remendón, m.

mendicancy, s. mendicidad, f.

mendicant, a. mendicante. s. mendicante, m. and f. **m. friar,** fraile mendicante, m.

mending, s. compostura, f.; reparación, f.; (darning) zurcidura, f.; ropa por zurcir, f.

menial, a. doméstico; servil; bajo, ruin. s. criado (-da); lacayo, m.

meningeal, a. meníngeo

meningitis, s. meningitis, f.

menopause, s. menopausia, f.

menses, s. menstruación, f.

menstrual, a. menstrual

menstruate, v.i. menstruar

menstruation, s. menstruación, f.

mental, *a.* mental; intelectual. **m.** derangement, enajenación mental, *f.* **m.** hospital, manicomio, *m.*

mentality, *s.* mentalidad, *f.*

mentally, *adv.* mentalmente. **m.** deficient, anormal

menthol, *s.* mentol, *m.*

mention, *s.* mención, *f.*; alusión, *f.* *v.t.* hacer mención (de), mencionar, mentar, hablar (de); aludir (a); (quote) citar; (in dispatches) nombrar. **Don't m. it!** ¡No digas nada!; ¡No hay de qué!

mentor, *s.* mentor, *m.*

menu, *s.* menú, *m.*; lista de platos, *f.*

meow, *v.i.* maullar. *s.* maullido, *m.*

Mephistophelean, *a.* mefistofélico

mephitic, *a.* mefítico

mercantile, *a.* mercantil; mercante. **m.** law, derecho mercantil, *m.* **m.** marine, marina mercante, *f.*

mercantilism, *s.* mercantilismo, *m.*

mercenariness, *s.* lo mercenario

mercenary, *a.* mercenario. *s.* (soldier) mercenario, *m.*

mercer, *s.* mercero, *m.*

mercerize, *v.t.* mercerizar

mercery, *s.* mercería, *f.*

merchandise, *s.* mercancía, *f.*

merchant, *s.* traficante (en), *m.* and *f.*; negociante (en), *m.*; comerciante, *m.* and *f.*, mercader, *m.* *a.* mercante. **The M. of Venice,** El Mercader de Venecia. **m.** navy, service, marina mercante, *f.* **m.** ship, buque mercante, *m.*

merchantman, *s.* buque mercante, *m.*

merciful, *a.* misericordioso, piadoso; compasivo; clemente; indulgente

mercifully, *adv.* misericordiosamente; compasivamente; con indulgencia

mercifulness, *s.* misericordia, *f.*; compasión, *f.*; indulgencia, *f.*

merciless, *a.* despiadado, inhumano

mercilessly, *adv.* sin piedad

mercilessness, *s.* inhumanidad, *f.*; falta de compasión, *f.*

mercurial, *a.* mercurial; (changeable) volátil; (lively) vivo

mercury, *s.* mercurio, *m.*; (*ast.* and *myth.*) Mercurio, *m.* **Mercury's wand,** caduceo, *m.*

mercy, *s.* misericordia, *f.*; compasión, *f.*; clemencia, *f.*; indulgencia, *f.*; merced, *f.* **at the m. of the elements,** a la intemperie. **to be at the m. of,** estar a la merced de

mere, *a.* mero; simple; no más que, solo. *s.* lago, *m.*

merely, *adv.* meramente, solamente; simplemente, sencillamente

meretricious, *a.* (archaic) meretricio; (flashy) de oropel; llamativo, charro

meretriciousness, *s.* mal gusto, *m.*

merge, *v.t.* fundir; (*com.*) fusionar; mezclar. *v.i.* fundirse; (*com.*) fusionarse; mezclarse

merger, *s.* combinación, *f.*; (*com.*) fusión, *f.*

meridian, *s.* (*geog.*, *ast.*) meridiano, *m.*; (noon) mediodía, *m.*; (peak) apogeo, *m.*

meridional, *a.* meridional

meringue, *s.* merengue, *m.*

merino, *a.* de merino; merino. *s.* (fabric and sheep) merino, *m.*

merit, *s.* mérito, *m.* *v.t.* merecer, ser digno de

meritorious, *a.* meritorio

meritoriously, *adv.* merecidamente

meritoriousness, *s.* mérito, *m.*

merlon, *s.* merlón, *m.*, almena, *f.*

mermaid, *s.* sirena, *f.*

merman, *s.* tritón, *m.*

Merovingian, *a.* merovingio. *s.* merovingio, *m.*

merrily, *adv.* alegremente

merriment, *s.* alegría, *f.*; júbilo, *m.*; regocijo, *m.*; diversión, *f.*; juego, *m.*

merriness, *s.* alegría, *f.*; regocijo, *m.*; (*fam.*) ebriedad, *f.*

merry, *a.* alegre; jovial; feliz; regocijado, divertido; (tipsy) calamocano. **to make m.,** divertirse. **to make m. over,** reírse de. **M. Christmas!** ¡Felices Navidades! **m.-andrew,** bufón, *m.* **m.-go-round,** caballitos, *m.* *pl.*, tiovivo, *m.* **m.-making,** festividades, fiestas, *f. pl.*

meseems, *v.i.* tengo para mí; me parece

meseta, *s.* meseta, *f.*

mesh, *s.* malla, *f.;* (*mech.*) engranaje, *m.;* (network) red, *f.;* (snare) lazo, *m.* *v.t.* coger con red; (*mech.*) endentar

mesmerism, *s.* mesmerismo, *m.*

mesmerize, *v.t.* hipnotizar

mesocarp, *s.* mesocarpio, *m.*

mess, *s.* (of food) plato de comida, *m.;* porción, ración, *f.;* rancho, *m.;* (mixture) mezcla, *f.;* (disorder) desorden, *m.;* suciedad, *f.;* (failure) fracaso, *m.* *v.t.* (dirty) ensuciar; desordenar; (mismanage) echar a perder. **to be in a m.,** (*fam.*) estar aviado. **to get in a m.,** (*fam.*) hacerse un lío. **to make a m. of,** ensuciar; desordenar; (spoil) echarlo todo a rodar

message, *s.* mensaje, *m.;* recado, *m.;* (telegraphic) parte, *m.* **I have to take a m.,** Tengo que hacer un recado

messenger, *s.* mensajero (-ra); (of telegrams) repartidor, *m.;* heraldo, *m.;* anuncio, *m.*

Messiah, *s.* Mesías, *m.*

Messianic, *a.* mesiánico

messrs., *s. pl.* (abbreviation) sres (from señores), *m. pl.*

metabolism, *s.* metabolismo, *m.*

metabolize, *v.a.* metabolizar

metacarpal, *a.* metacarpiano

metacarpus, *s.* metacarpo, *m.*

metal, *s.* metal, *m.;* vidrio en fusión, *m.;* (road) grava, *f.;* (*her.*) metal, *m.;* (mettle) temple, temperamento, *m.;* brío, fuego, *m.;* *pl.* metals, (of a railway) rieles, *m. pl.* **m. engraver,** grabador en metal, *m.* **m. polish,** limpiametales, *m.* **m. shavings,** cizallas, *f. pl.* **m. work,** metalistería, *f.* **m. worker,** metalario, *m.*

metallic, *a.* metálico

metalliferous, *a.* metalífero

metalloid, *s.* metaloide, *m.*

metallurgic, *a.* metalúrgico

metallurgist, *s.* metalúrgico, *m.*

metallurgy, *s.* metalurgia, *f.*

metamorphosis, *s.* metamorfosis, *f.*

metaphor, *s.* metáfora, *f.*

metaphorical, *a.* metafórico

metaphysical, *a.* metafísico

metaphysician, *s.* metafísico, *m.*

metaphysics, *s.* metafísica, *f.*

metatarsus, *s.* metatarso, *m.*

metathesis, *s.* metátesis, *f.*

mete (out), *v.t.* repartir, distribuir

metempsychosis, *s.* metempsicosis, *f.*

meteor, *s.* meteoro, *m.*

meteoric, *a.* meteórico

meteorite, *s.* meteorito, *m.*

meteorological, *a.* meteorológico

meteorologist, *s.* meteorologista, *m.* and *f.*

meteorology, *s.* meteorología, *f.*

meter, *s.* (for gas, etc.) contador, *m.;* see metre

methane, *s.* metano, *m.*

methinks, *v.i.* me parece; creo

method, *s.* método, *m.;* técnica, *f.;* táctica, *f.*

methodical, *a.* metódico; ordenado, sistemático

Methodism, *s.* metodismo, *m.*

Methodist, *s.* metodista, *m.* and *f.*

methyl, *s.* metilo, *m.* **m. alcohol,** alcohol metílico, *m.*

methylated spirit, *s.* alcohol desnaturalizado, *m.*

methylic, *a.* metílico

meticulous, *a.* meticuloso; minucioso

meticulously, *adv.* con meticulosidad

meticulousness, *s.* meticulosidad, *f.;* minuciosidad, *f.*

metre, *s.* (verse and measure) metro, *m.*

metric, *a.* métrico. **m. system,** sistema métrico, sistema decimal, *m.*

metrics, *s.* métrica, *f.*

metrology, *s.* metrología, *f.*

metronome, *s.* metrónomo, *m.*

metropolis, *s.* metrópoli, *f.;* capital, *f.*

metropolitan, *a.* metropolitano; de la capital. *s.* (*ecc.*) metropolitano, *m.*

mettle, *s.* temple, temperamento, *m.;* fuego, brío, *m.;* valor, *m.* **You have put him on his m.,** Le has picado en el amor propio

mew, *s.* (gull) gaviota, *f.;* (of a cat) maullido, *m.;* (of sea-birds) alarido, *m.* *v.i.* (of a cat) maullar; (of sea-birds) dar alaridos. **to mew up,** encerrar

mewing, s. maullido, m. a. que
maúlla

mews, s. establos, m. pl., caballeriza, f.

Mexican, a. mejicano. s. mejicano (-na)

mezzanine, s. entresuelo, m.

mezzo-soprano, s. (no exact
equivalent) voz de tiple, f.;
(person) tiple, soprano, f.; (part)
tiple, soprano, m.

mezzotint, s. grabado a la media
tinta, m. v.t. grabar a la media
tinta

mi, s. (mus.) mi, m.

miaow, s. miau, m. v.i. maullar

miasma, s. miasma, m.

miasmatic, a. miasmático

mica, s. mica, f.

Michaelmas, s. fiesta de San
Miguel, f.

microbe, s. microbio, m.

microbial, a. microbiano

microbiologist, s. microbiólogo,
m.

microbiology, s. microbiología, f.

microcephalous, a. microcéfalo

microcosm, s. microcosmo, m.

micron, s. micra, f.

microphone, s. micrófono, m.

micro-photograph, s. microfoto-
grafía, f.

microscope, s. microscopio, m.

microscopic, a. microscópico

micturition, s. micción, f.

mid, a. medio. prep. entre; en
medio de; a mediados de. from
mid May to August, desde
mediados de mayo hasta agosto.
in mid air, en medio del aire.
in mid channel, en medio del
canal. in mid winter, en medio
del invierno

midday, s. mediodía, m. a. del
mediodía, meridional. at m., a
mediodía

midden, s. muladar, m.

middle, a. medio; de en medio;
del centro; intermedio; (average)
mediano. s. medio, m.; mitad,
f.; centro, m.; (waist) cintura, f.
in the m. of, en medio de. in
the m. of nowhere, donde
Cristo dió las tres voces. towards the m. of the month, a
mediados del mes. m. age, edad
madura, f. m.-aged, de edad
madura, de cierta edad. M.
Ages, edad media, f. m. class,

clase media, burguesía, f. a. de
la clase media, burgués. m.
distance, término medio, m. m.
ear, oído medio, m. m. finger,
dedo de en medio (or del
corazón), m. m. way, (fig.)
término medio, m. m. weight,
peso medio, m.

middleman, s. agente de negocios, m.; (retailer) revendedor,
m.; intermediario, m.

middling, a. mediano; mediocre;
regular, así, así

midge, s. mosquito, m.; mosca de
agua, f.

midget, s. enano (-na). m. submarine, submarino de bolsillo,
m.

midnight, s. medianoche, f. a.
de medianoche; nocturno. at m.,
a medianoche. to burn the m.
oil, quemarse las cejas. M.
Mass, misa del gallo, f.

midriff, s. diafragma, m.

midship, a. maestro. s. medio
del buque, m. m. beam, bao
maestro, m. m. gangway,
crujía, f.

midshipman, s. guardiamarina,
m.

midst, s. medio, m.; seno, m.
prep. entre. in the m. of, en
medio de. There is a traitor
in our m., Hay un traidor entre
nosotros (or en nuestra compañía)

midstream, in, en medio de la
corriente

midsummer, s. pleno verano,
m.; solsticio estival, m.; fiesta de
San Juan, f. A M. Night's
Dream, El Sueño de la Noche
de San Juan

midway, a. and adv. situado a
medio camino; a medio camino, a
la mitad del camino; entre. s.
mitad del camino, f.; medio, m.
m. between . . ., equidistante
de . . ., entre

midwife, s. comadrona, partera,
f.

midwifery, s. obstetricia, f.

midwinter, s. medio del invierno,
m.

mien, s. aire, m.; porte, semblante, m.

might, v.i. poder. It m. or m.
not be true, Podría o no podría
ser verdad. How happy Mary

m. have been! ¡Qué feliz pudo haber sido María! **I thought that you m. have seen him in the theatre,** Creí que pudieras haberle visto en el teatro. **That I m. . . .!** ¡Qué yo pudiese . . .¡ **This m. have been avoided if . . .** Esto podía haberse evitado si . . .

might, s. fuerza, f.; poder, m. **with m. and main,** con todas sus fuerzas

mightily, adv. fuertemente; poderosamente; (fam.) muchísimo, sumamente

mightiness, s. fuerza, f.; poder, m.; grandeza, f.

mighty, a. fuerte, vigoroso; poderoso; grande; (fam.) enorme; (proud) arrogante. adv. (fam.) enormemente, muy

mignonette, s. reseda, f.

migraine, s. migraña, jaqueca, f.

migrant, a. migratorio, de paso. s. ave migratoria, ave de paso, f.

migrate, v.i. emigrar

migration, s. migración, f.

migratory, a. migratorio, de paso; (of people) nómada, pasajero

Mikado, s. micado, m.

Milanese, a. milanés. s. milanés (-esa)

milch, a. (f.) (of cows) lechera

mild, a. apacible, pacífico; manso; dulce; suave; (of the weather) blando; (med.) benigno; (light) leve; (of drinks) ligero; (weak) débil

mildew, s. mildeu, añublo, m.; moho, m. v.t. anublar; enmohecer. v.i. anublarse; enmohecerse

mildly, adv. suavemente; dulcemente; con indulgencia

mildness, s. apacibilidad, f.; mansedumbre, f.; suavidad, f.; (of weather) blandura, f.; dulzura, f.; indulgencia, f.; (weakness) debilidad, f.

mile, s. milla, f.

mileage, s. distancia en millas, f.; kilometraje, m.

milestone, s. hito, m., piedra miliaria, f.; mojón kilométrico, m.

milfoil, s. milenrama, f.

militancy, s. carácter militante, m.; belicosidad, f.

militant, a. militante, combatiente; belicoso; agresivo. s. combatiente, m. and f.

militarily, adv. militarmente

militariness, s. lo militar, el carácter militar

militarism, s. militarismo, m.

militarist, s. militarista, m. and f.

militaristic, a. militarista

militarization, s. militarización, f.

militarize, v.t. militarizar

military, a. militar; de guerra. **the m.,** los militares. **m. academy,** colegio militar, m. **m. camp,** campo militar, m. **m. law,** código militar, m. **m. man,** militar, m. **m. police,** policía militar, f. **m. service,** servicio militar, m.

militate (against), v.i. militar contra

militia, s. milicia, f.

militiaman, s. miliciano, m.

milk, s. leche, f. a. de leche; lácteo. v.t. ordeñar. v.i. dar leche. **to have m. and water in one's veins,** tener sangre de horchata. **condensed m.,** leche condensada, leche en lata, f. **m.-can,** lechera, f. **m.-cart,** carro de la leche, m. **m. chocolate,** chocolate con leche, m. **m. of magnesia,** leche de magnesia, f. **m.-pail,** ordeñadero, m. **m.-tooth,** diente de leche, m. **m.-white,** blanco como la leche

milkiness, s. lactescencia, f.; carácter lechoso, m.; (whiteness) blancura, f.

milking, s. ordeño, m. **m.-machine,** máquina ordeñadora, f. **m.-stool,** taburete, banquillo, m.

milkmaid, s. lechera, f.

milkman, s. lechero, m.

milksop, s. marica, m.

milky, a. lechero; de leche; lechoso, como leche; (ast.) lácteo. **M. Way,** vía láctea, f.

mill, s. molino, m.; (for coffee, etc.) molinillo, m.; (factory) fábrica, f.; taller, m.; (textile) hilandería, f.; fábrica de tejidos, f.; (fight) riña a puñetazos, f.; pugilato, m. v.t. (grind) moler; (coins) acordonar; (cloth) abatanar; (chocolate) batir. **cotton**

m., hilandería de algodón, *f.*
hand-m., molinillo, *m.* **paper-
m.,** fábrica de papel, *f.* **saw-m.,**
serrería, *f.* **spinning m.,** hilandería, *f.* **water m.,** molino de
agua, *m.* **m.-course,** saetín,
canal de molino, *m.* **m.-dam,**
esclusa de molino, *f.* **m.-hand,**
obrero (-ra). **m.-pond,** cubo, *m.*
m.-race, caz, *m.* **m.-wheel,**
rueda de molino, *f.*
millenary, *a.* milenario. *s.* milenario, *m.*
millennial, *a.* milenario
millennium, *s.* milenario, *m.*
miller, *s.* molinero, *m.* **the
miller's wife,** la molinera
millet, *s.* mijo, *m.*
milliard, *s.* mil millones, *m. pl.*
milligramme, *s.* miligramo, *m.*
millilitre, *s.* mililitro, *m.*
millimetre, *s.* milímetro, *m.*
milliner, *s.* sombrerero (-ra),
modista, *m.* and *f.* **milliner's
shop,** sombrerería, tienda de
modista, *f.*
millinery, *s.* sombreros, *m. pl.*;
modas, *f. pl.*; tienda de modista, *f.*
milling, *s.* molienda, *f.*; acuñación,
f.; (edge of coin) cordoncillo, *m.*
m. machine, fresadora, *f.*
million, *s.* millón, *m.* **the m.,** las
masas
millionaire, *a.* millonario. *s.*
millonario, *m.*
millionairess, *s.* millonaria, *f.*
millionth, *a.* millonésimo
millstone, *s.* piedra de moler,
muela, *f.*
mime, *s.* (Greek·farce and actor)
mimo, *m.*; (mimicry) mímica, *f.*;
pantomima, *f.* *v.i.* hacer en
pantomima
mimesis, *s.* mimetismo, *m.*
mimetic, *a.* mímico, imitativo
mimic, *a.* mímico; (pretended)
fingido. *s.* imitador (-ra). *v.t.*
imitar, contrahacer; (*biol.*) imitar,
adaptarse a
mimicry, *s.* mímica, imitación,
f.; (*biol.*) mimetismo, *m.*
mimosa, *s.* mimosa, *f.*
mimulus, *s.* mímulo, *m.*
minaret, *s.* minarete, *m.*; (of a
mosque) alminar, *m.*
minatory, *a.* amenazador
mince, *v.t.* desmenuzar; (meat)
picar; (words) medir (las palabras). *v.i.* andar con pasos

menuditos; andar o moverse con
afectación; hacer remilgos. **m.-
meat,** carne picada, *f.*; (sweet)
conserva de fruta y especias, *f.*
mincing, *a.* afectado. *s.* acción
de picar carne, *f.* **m. machine,**
máquina de picar carne, *f.*
mincingly, *adv.* con afectación;
con pasos menuditos
mind, *s.* inteligencia, *f.*; espíritu
ánimo, *m.*; imaginación, *f.*; alma,
f.; (memory) memoria, *f.*, recuerdo, *m.*; (understanding) entendimiento, *m.*; (genius) ingenio,
m.; (cast of mind) mentalidad,
f.; (opinion) opinión, *f.*; (liking)
gusto, *m.*; (thoughts) pensamiento, *m.*; (intention) propósito, *m.*, intención, *f.*; (tendency) propensión, inclinación,
f. **I have a good m. to go
away,** Por poco me marcho;
Tengo gana de marcharme. **I
have changed my m.,** He
cambiado de opinión. **out of m.,**
olvidado. **I shall give him a
piece of my m.,** Le diré cuatro
verdades. **It had quite gone
out of my m.,** Lo había olvidado
completamente. **I can see it in
my mind's eye,** Está presente
a mi imaginación. **I shall bear
it in m.,** Lo tendré en cuenta.
**I thought in my own m.
that ...,** Pensé por mis adentros
que ... **We are both of the
same m.,** Ambos nosotros somos
de la misma opinión. **to be out
of one's m.,** estar fuera de
juicio. **to call to m.,** acordarse
de. **to have something on
one's m.,** estar preocupado. **to
make up one's m. (to),** resolverse (a), decidirse (a), determinar; animarse (a). **m.-
reader,** adivinador (-ra) del
pensamiento
mind, *v.t.* (remember) recordar,
no olvidar; (heed) atender a;
hacer caso de; tener cuidado de;
(fear) tener miedo de; (obey)
obedecer; preocuparse de; (object to) molestar; importar; (care
for) cuidar. *v.i.* tener cuidado;
molestar; (feel) sentir; (fear)
tener miedo; (be the same thing)
ser igual. **Do you m. being
quiet a moment?** ¿Quieres
hacer el favor de callarte un

momento? **Do you m. if I
smoke?** ¿ Le molesta si fumo?
They don't m., No les importa,
Les es igual. **Never m.!** ¡No se
moleste!; ¡No se preocupe!; ¡No
importa! ¡Vaya! **M. what you
are doing!** ¡Cuidado con lo que
haces! **M. your own business!**
¡No te metas donde no te
llaman!

minded, *a.* dispuesto, inclinado;
de . . . pensamientos; de . . .
disposición

mindful, *a.* atento (a), cuidadoso
(de); que se acuerda (de)

mine, *a. poss.* mío, *m.* (mía, *f.*;
míos, *m. pl.*; mías, *f. pl.*); el mío,
m. (la mía, *f.*; lo mío, *neut.*; los
míos, *m. pl.*; las mías, *f. pl.*); mi
(*pl.* mis). **a dog of m.,** un perro
mío; uno de mis perros

mine, *s.* mina, *f. v.t.* minar;
extraer; sembrar minas en, colocar minas en. *v.i.* minar; hacer
una mina; dedicarse a la minería.
drifting m., mina a la deriva, *f.*
land m., mina terrestre, *f.*
magnetic m., mina magnética,
f. **to lay mines,** colocar (or
sembrar) minas. **m.-sweeper,**
dragaminas, buque barreminas,
m.

minefield, *s.* campo de minas, *m.*;
barrera de minas, *f.*

minelayer, *s.* barco siembra-
minas, lanzaminas, *m.*

miner, *s.* minero, *m.*; (*mil.*) zapador minador, *m.*

mineral, *s.* mineral, *m.* *a.*
mineral. **m. baths,** baños, *m.*
pl. **m. water,** agua mineral, *f.*;
gaseosa, *f.*

mineralogical, *a.* mineralógico

mineralogist, *s.* mineralogistá,
m.

mineralogy, *s.* mineralogía, *f.*

mingle, *v.t.* mezclar; confundir.
v.i. mezclarse; confundirse

mingling, *s.* mezcla, *f.*

miniature, *s.* miniatura, *f.* *a.* en
miniatura. **m. edition,** edición
diamante, *f.*

miniaturist, *s.* miniaturista, *m.*
and *f.*

minim, *s.* (*mus.*) mínima, *f.*; (*ecc.*)
mínimo, *m.*

minimize, *v.t.* reducir al mínimo; mitigar; (underrate) tener
en menos, despreciar

minimum, *s.* mínimo, *m.* *a.*
mínimo

mining, *s.* minería, *f.* *a.* minero;
de mina; de minas; de minero.
m. engineer, ingeniero de
minas, *m.*

minion, *s.* favorito (-ta); satélite,
m.; (*print.*) miñona, *f.*

minister, *s.* ministro, *m.* *v.i.*
servir; suministrar, proveer de;
(contribute) contribuir (a). **M.
of Health,** Ministro de Sanidad,
m. **M. of War,** Ministro de la
Guerra, *m.*

ministerial, *a.* ministerial

ministration, *s.* (*ecc.*) ministerio,
m.; servicio, *m.*; agencia, *f.*

ministry, *s.* ministerio, *m.* **M. of
Food,** Ministerio de Abastecimientos, *m.*

miniver, *s.* gris, *m.*

mink, *s.* visón, *m.*

minnow, *s.* pez pequeño de agua
dulce, *m.*

minor, *a.* menor. *s.* menor de
edad, *m.*; (logic) menor, *f.*;
(*mus.*) tono menor, *m.*; (*ecc.*)
menor, *m.* **to be a m.,** ser menor
de edad. **m. key,** tono menor,
m. **m. orders,** (*ecc.*) órdenes
menores, *f. pl.* **m. scale,** escala
menor, *f.*

minority, *s.* minoría, *f.*; (of age)
minoridad, *f.* **in the m.,** en la
minoría

minster, *s.* catedral, *f.*; monasterio, *m.*

minstrel, *s.* trovador, juglar, *m.*;
músico, *m.*; cantante, *m.*

minstrelsy, *s.* música, *f.*; canto,
m.; arte del trovador, *m.* or *f.*;
gaya ciencia, *f.*

mint, *s.* (*bot.*) menta, hierbabuena, *f.*; casa de moneda, *f.*;
(*fig.*) mina, *f.*; (source) origen, *m.*
v.t. (money) acuñar; (*fig.*) inventar

minter, *s.* acuñador, *m.*; (*fig.*)
inventor (-ra)

minting, *s.* (of coins) acuñación,
f.; (*fig.*) invención, *f.*

minuet, *s.* minué, *m.*

minus, *a.* menos; negativo; desprovisto de; sin. *s.* signo menos,
m.; cantidad negativa, *f.*

minute, *a.* menudo, diminuto;
insignificante; minucioso

minute, *s.* momento, *m.*; instante,
m.; (note) minuta, *f.*; *pl.* **min-**

utes, actas, *f. pl.* **in a m.,** en un
instante. **m.-book,** libro de
actas, minutario, *m.* **m.-hand,**
minutero, *m.*

minutely, *adv.* minuciosamente;
en detalle; exactamente

minuteness, *s.* suma pequeñez,
f.; minuciosidad, *f.*

minx, *s.* picaruela, *f.*; coqueta, *f.*

miracle, *s.* milagro, *m.* **m.-
monger,** milagrero (-ra). **m.
play,** milagro, *m.*

miraculous, *a.* milagroso

miraculously, *adv.* milagrosa-
mente, por milagro

miraculousness, *s.* carácter milagroso, *m.*, lo milagroso

mirage, *s.* espejismo, *m.*

mire, *s.* fango, lodo, *m.*; (miry
place) lodazal, *m.*

mirror, *s.* espejo, *m.* *v.t.* reflejar.
to look in the m., mirarse al
espejo. **full-length m.,** espejo
de cuerpo entero, *m.* **small m.,**
espejuelo, *m.*

mirth, *s.* alegría, *f.*, júbilo, *m.*;
risa, *f.*; hilaridad, *f.*

mirthful, *a.* alegre

mirthless, *a.* sin alegría, triste

miry, *a.* lodoso, fangoso, cenagoso

misadventure, *s.* desgracia, *f.*;
accidente, *m.*

misanthrope, *s.* misántropo, *m.*

misanthropic, *a.* misantrópico

misanthropy, *s.* misantropía,
f.

misapplication, *s.* mala aplicación, *f.*; mal uso, *m.*; abuso, *m.*

misapply, *v.t.* aplicar mal; hacer
mal uso de; abusar de

misapprehend, *v.t.* comprender
mal; equivocarse sobre

misapprehension, *s.* concepto
erróneo, *m.*; equivocación, *f.*,
error, *m.*

misappropriate, *v.t.* malversar

misappropriation, *s.* malversación, *f.*

misbehave, *v.i.* portarse mal; (of
a child) ser malo

misbehaviour, *s.* mala conducta,
f.

miscalculate, *v.t.* calcular mal;
engañarse (sobre)

miscalculation, *s.* mal cálculo,
error, *m.*; desacierto, *m.*

miscall, *v.t.* mal nombrar; llamar
equivocadamente; (abuse) insultar

miscarriage, *s.* (*med.*) aborto, *m.*;
(failure) malogro, fracaso, *m.*;
(of goods) extravío, *m.*

miscarry, *v.i.* (*med.*) abortar,
malparir; (fail) malograrse, frustrarse; (of goods) extraviarse

miscellaneous, *a.* misceláneo;
vario, diverso

miscellany, *s.* miscelánea, *f.*

mischance, *s.* mala suerte, *f.*;
infortunio, *m.* desgracia, *f.*;
accidente, *m.*

mischief, *s.* daño, *m.*; mal, *m.*;
(wilfulness) travesura, *f.*; (person) diablillo, *m.* **m.-maker,**
enredador (-ra), chismoso (-sa);
alborotador, *m.*; malicioso (-sa).
m.-making, *a.* enredador; chismoso; malicioso; alborotador

mischievous, *a.* dañino, perjudicial, malo; malicioso; chismoso; (wilful) travieso; juguetón;
(of glances, etc.) malicioso

mischievously, *adv.* maliciosamente; con (or por) travesura

mischievousness, *s.* mal, *m.*;
malicia, *f.*; maleficencia, *f.*;
travesura, *f.*

misconceive, *v.t.* formar un
concepto erróneo de; concebir
mal, juzgar mal

misconception, *s.* concepto erróneo, *m.*, idea falsa, *f.*; error,
m., equivocación, *f.*; engaño, *m.*

misconduct, *s.* mala conducta, *f.*
to m. oneself, portarse mal

misconstruction, *s.* mala interpretación, *f.*; falsa interpretación, *f.*; tergiversación, *f.*; mala
traducción, *f.*

misconstrue, *v.t.* interpretar
mal; entender mal; tergiversar;
traducir mal

miscount, *v.t.* contar mal, equivocarse en la cuenta de; calcular
mal. *s.* error, *m.*; yerro de
cuenta, *m.*

miscreant, *s.* malandrín, *m.*;
bribón, *m.* *a.* vil, malandrín

misdeed, *s.* delito, malhecho,
crimen, *m.*

misdemeanour, *s.* mala conducta, *f.*; (*law*) delito, *m.*; ofensa,
f., malhecho, *m.*

misdirect, *v.t.* informar mal
(acerca del camino); (a letter)
dirigir mal, poner unas señas
incorrectas en

miser, *s.* avaro (-ra)

miserable, *a.* infeliz, desgraciado; miserable; despreciable; sin valor

miserably, *adv.* miserablemente

miserliness, *s.* avaricia, tacañería, *f.*

miserly, *a.* avaro, tacaño

misery, *s.* miseria, *f.*; sufrimiento, *m.*; dolor, tormento, *m.*

misfire, *v.i.* no dar fuego; (of a motor-car, etc.) hacer falsas explosiones, errar el encendido

misfit, *s.* traje que no cae bien, *m.*; zapato que no va bien, *m.*; (person) inadaptado, *m.*

misfortune, *s.* infortunio, *m.*, mala suerte, adversidad, *f.*; desdicha, desgracia, *f.*; mal, *m.*

misgive, *v.t.* hacer temer; llenar de duda; hacer recelar; hacer presentir

misgiving, *s.* temor, *m.*; duda, *f.*; recelo, *m.*; presentimiento, *m.*

misgovern, *v.t.* gobernar mal; administrar mal; dirigir mal

misgovernment, *s.* desgobierno, *m.*; mala administración, *f.*

misguided, *a.* mal dirigido; extraviado; engañado; (blind) ciego

misguidedly, *adv.* equivocadamente

mishap, *s.* desgracia, *f.*; contratiempo, accidente, *m.* **to have a m.,** sufrir una desgracia; tener un accidente

misinform, *v.t.* informar mal; dar informes erróneos (a)

misinformation, *s.* noticia falsa, *f.*; información errónea, *f.*

misinterpret, *v.t.* interpretar mal; entender mal; torcer; tergiversar; traducir mal

misinterpretation, *s.* mala interpretación, *f.*; interpretación falsa, *f.*; tergiversación, *f.*; mala traducción, *f.*

misjudge, *v.t.* juzgar mal; equivocarse (en or sobre); tener una idea falsa de

misjudgment, *s.* juicio errado, *m.*; idea falsa, *f.*; juicio injusto, *m.*

mislay, *v.t.* extraviar, perder

mislead, *v.t.* extraviar; llevar a conclusiones erróneas, despistar; engañar

misleading, *a.* de falsas apariencias; erróneo, falso; engañoso

mismanage, *v.t.* administrar mal; dirigir mal; echar a perder

mismanagement, *s.* mala administración, *f.*; desgobierno, *m.*

misname, *v.t.* mal nombrar; llamar equivocadamente

misnomer, *s.* nombre equivocado *m.*; nombre inapropiado, *m.*

misogamist, *s.* misógamo (-ma)

misogamy, *s.* misogamia, *f.*

misogynist, *s.* misógino, *m.*

misogyny, *s.* misoginia, *f.*

misplace, *v.t.* colocar mal; poner fuera de lugar

misplaced, *a.* mal puesto; inoportuno; equivocado

misprint, *s.* error de imprenta, *m.*, errata, *f.* *v.t.* imprimir con erratas

mispronounce, *v.t.* pronunciar mal

mispronunciation, *s.* mala pronunciación, *f.*

misquotation, *s.* cita errónea, *f.*

misquote, *v.t.* citar mal, citar erróneamente

misrepresent, *v.t.* desfigurar; tergiversar; falsificar

misrepresentation, *s.* desfiguración, *f.*; tergiversación, *f.*; falsificación, *f.*

misrule, *v.t.* gobernar mal. *s.* mal gobierno, desgobierno, *m.*; confusión, *f.*

miss, *s.* señorita, *f.*

miss, *v.t.* (one's aim) errar (el tiro, etc.); no acertar (a); (let fall) dejar caer; (lose a train, the post, etc., one's footing, an opportunity, etc.) perder; (fall short of) dejar de; no ver; no notar; pasar por alto de; omitir; echar de menos; notar la falta de; no encontrar. *v.i.* errar; (fail) salir mal, fracasar. **I m. you very much,** Te echo mucho de menos. **to be missing,** faltar; estar ausente; haberse marchado; haber desaparecido. **to m. one's mark,** errar el blanco. **to m. out,** omitir, pasar por alto de

missal, *s.* misal, *m.*

missel thrush, *s.* cagaaceite, *m.*

misshapen, *a.* deforme

missile, *s.* arma arrojadiza, *f.*; proyectil, *m.*

missing, *a.* que falta; perdido; ausente; (*mil.*) desaparecido

mission, *s.* misión, *f.*

missionary, *s.* misionero, *m.*

missionize, *v.i.* misionar

missis, s. señora, f.; (fam.) mujer, f.

missive, s. misiva, f.

misspend, v.t. malgastar; desperdiciar; perder

mist, s. bruma, neblina, f.; vapor, m; (drizzle) llovizna, f.; (fig.) nube, f. v.t. anublar, empañar. v.i. lloviznar

mistakable, a. confundible

mistake, v.t. comprender mal; equivocarse sobre; errar; (with for) confundir con, equivocarse con. s. equivocación, f.; error, m.; inadvertencia, f.; (in an exercise, etc.) falta, f. **And no m.!** (fam.) Sin duda alguna. **by m.**, por equivocación; (involuntarily) sin querer. **If I am not mistaken**, Si no me engaño, Si no estoy equivocado. **to make a m.**, equivocarse

mistaken, a. (of persons and things) equivocado; (of things) erróneo; incorrecto

mistakenly, adv. equivocadamente; injustamente, falsamente

mister, s. señor, m.

mistily, adv. a través de la neblina; obscuramente; indistintamente, vagamente

mistimed, a. intempestivo; inoportuno

mistiness, s. neblina, bruma, f.; vaporosidad, f.; obscuridad, f.

mistletoe, s. muérdago, m.

mistral, s. (wind) maestral, m.

mistranslate, v.t. traducir mal; interpretar mal

mistranslation, s. mala traducción, f.; traducción inexacta, f.

mistress, s. señora, f.; maestra, f.; (fiancée) prometida, f.; (beloved) amada, dulce dueña, f.; (concubine) amiga, querida, f. **M. (Mrs.)** Gómez, Sra Gómez. **M. of the Robes**, camarera mayor, f.

mistrust, v.t. desconfiar de, no tener confianza en; dudar de. s. desconfianza, f.; recelo, m., suspicacia, f.; aprensión, f.

mistrustful, a. desconfiado; receloso, suspicaz. **to be m. of**, recelarse de

misty, a. brumoso, nebuloso; vaporoso; (of the eyes) anublado; (of windows, etc.) empañado

misunderstand, v.t. comprender mal; tomar en sentido erróneo; interpretar mal

misunderstanding, s. concepto erróneo, error, m.; equivocación, f.; (disagreement) desavenencia, f.

misuse, v.t. emplear mal; abusar de; (funds) malversar; (ill-treat) tratar mal. s. abuso, m.; (of funds) malversación, f.

mite, s. (coin) ardite, m.; (trifle) pizca, f.; óbolo, m.; (ent.) ácaro, m.

mitigate, v.t. (pain) aliviar; mitigar; suavizar

mitigation, s. (of pain) alivio, m.; mitigación, f.

mitre, s. mitra, f.; (carp.) inglete, m. v.t. (carp.) cortar ingletes en

mitred, a. mitrado

mitten, s. mitón, m.

mix, v.t. mezclar; (salad) aderezar; (concrete, etc.) amasar; combinar, unir; (sociably) alternar (con); (confuse) confundir. v.i. mezclarse; frecuentar la compañía (de); frecuentar; (get on well) llevarse bien

mixed, a. mezclado; vario, surtido; mixto; (confused) confuso. **m. doubles**, parejas mixtas, f. pl. **m. up**, (in disorder) revuelto; confuso. **m. up with**, implicado en; asociado con

mixer, s. mezclador, m.; (person) mezclador (-ra); (fam.) persona sociable, f. **electric m.**, mezclador eléctrico, m.

mixture, s. mezcla, f.; (medicine) poción, medicina, f.

mizzen, s. mesana, f. **m.-mast**, palo de mesana, m. **m.-sail**, vela de mesana, f. **m.-topsail**, sobremesana, f.

mnemonics, s. mnemotecnia, f.

Moabite, s. moabita, m. and f.

moan, v.t. lamentar; llorar. v.i. gemir; quejarse, lamentarse. s. gemido, m.; lamento, m.; quejido, m.

moaning, s. gemidos, m. pl.

moat, s. foso, m.

mob, s. (crowd) muchedumbre, multitud, f.; (rabble) populacho, m., gentuza, f. v.t. atropellar; atacar. **mob-cap**, cofia, f.

mobile, a. móvil; ambulante; (fickle) voluble. **m. canteen**, cantina ambulante, f.

mobility, s. movilidad, f.

mobilization, s. movilización, f.

mobilize, v.t. movilizar.   v.i. movilizarse

moccasin, s. mocasín, m.

Mocha, s. café de Moca, m.

mock, v.t. ridiculizar; burlarse (de), mofarse (de); (cause to fail) frustrar; (mimic) imitar; (delude) engañar. v.i. mofarse, burlarse, reírse. a. cómico, burlesco; falso; fingido; imitado. **to make a m. of,** poner en ridículo; hacer absurdo; burlarse de. **m.-heroic,** heroico-cómico. **m.-orange,** (bot.) jeringuilla, f. **m.-turtle soup,** sopa hecha con cabeza de ternera a imitacion de tortuga, f.

mocker, s. mofador (-ra); el, m. (f. la) que se burla de

mockery, s. mofa, burla, f.; ridículo, m.; ilusión, apariencia, f. **to make a m. of,** mofarse de; hacer ridículo

mocking, a. burlón. **m. bird,** pájaro burlón, m.

mockingly, adv. burlonamente

modal, a. modal

modality, s. modalidad, f.

mode, s. modo, m.; manera, f.; (fashion) moda, f.; uso, m., costumbre, f.

model, s. modelo, m.; (artist's) modelo vivo, m. a. modelo; en miniatura. v.t. modelar; moldear; formar; hacer; planear. **m. display,** (hats, etc.) exposición de modelos, f. **m. railway,** ferrocarril en miniatura, m.

modeller, s. modelador (-ra); disenador, m.

modelling, s. modelado, m.; modelo, m. **m. wax,** cera para moldear, f.

moderate, a. moderado; (of prices, etc.) módico; (fair, medium) regular, mediano; razonable; mediocre. s. moderado, m. v.t. moderar; modificar; calmar. v.i. moderarse; calmarse

moderately, adv. moderadamente; módicamente; medianamente; bastante; razonablemente; mediocremente

moderation, s. moderación, f. **in m.,** en moderación

moderator, s. moderador, m.; (Church of Scotland) presidente,

m.; (univ.) examinador, m.; (univ.) inspector de exámenes, m. **m. lamp,** lámpara de regulador, f.

modern, a. moderno. s. modernista, m. and f. **in the m. way,** a la moderna. **m. languages,** lenguas vivas, m. pl.

modernism, s. modernismo, m.

modernist, s. modernista, m. and f.

modernistic, a. modernista

modernity, s. modernidad, f.

modernization, s. modernización, f.

modernize, v.t. modernizar

modernness, s. modernidad, f.

modest, a. modesto; (of a woman) púdico

modestly, adv. modestamente

modesty, s. modestia, f.; (of a woman) pudor, m.

modicum, s. porción pequeña, f.; poco, m.

modifiable, a. modificable

modification, s. modificación, f.

modify, v.t. modificar. **It has been much modified,** Se ha modificado mucho; Se ha hecho muchas modificaciones

modifying, a. modificante, modificador

modillion, s. (arch.) modillón, m.

modish, a. (que está) a la moda; en boga; elegante

modishness, s. elegancia, f.

modiste, s. modista, m. and f.

modulate, v.t. and v.i. modular

modulation, s. modulación, f.

Mogul, a. mogol. s. mogol (-la). **the Great M.,** el Gran Mogol

Mohammedan, a. mahometano. s. mahometano (-na)

Mohammedanism, s. mahometismo, m.

Mohicans, s. pl. mohicanos, m. pl.

moiety, s. mitad, f.

moiré, s. muaré, m.

moist, a. húmedo

moisten, v.t. humedecer, mojar

moisture, s. humedad, f.

molar, s. muela, f. a. molar

molasses, s. pl. melaza, f.

Moldavian, a. moldavo. s. moldavo (-va)

mole, s. (animal) topo, m.; (spot) lunar, m.; (breakwater) dique, malecón, m.; muelle, m.

molecular, a. molecular

molecule, s. molécula, f.
molehill, s. topera, f.
moleskin, s. piel de topo, f.
molest, v.t. molestar; perseguir, importunar; faltar al respeto (a)
molestation, s. importunidad, persecución, f.; molestia, incomodidad, f.
mollification, s. apaciguamiento, m.; mitigación, f.
mollify, v.t. apaciguar, **calmar;** mitigar
mollusc, s. molusco, m.
molly-coddle, s. alfeñique, mírame y no me toques, m.; niño (-ña), mimado (-da)
Moloch, s. Moloc, m.
molten, a. fundido; derretido
moment, s. momento, m.; instante m.; (importance) importancia, f. **at this m.,** en este momento. **Do it this m.!** ¡Hazlo al instante (or en seguida)!
momentarily, adv. momentáneamente; cada momento
momentariness, s. momentaneidad, f.
momentary, a. momentáneo
momentous, a. de suma importancia; crítico; grave
momentousness, s. importancia, f.; gravedad, f.
momentum, s. momento, m.; (fig.) ímpetu, m. **to gather m.,** cobrar velocidad, acelerar
monarch, s. monarca, m.
monarchic, a. monárquico
monarchism, s. monarquismo, m.
monarchist, s. monárquico (-ca)
monarchy, s. monarquía, f.
monastery, s. monasterio, m.
monastic, a. monástico. **m. life,** vida de clausura, f.
monasticism, s. vida monástica, f.
Monday, s. lunes, m.
monetary, a. monetario
monetization, s. monetización, f.
money, s. dinero, m.; (coin) moneda, f.; sistema monetario, m. **paper m.,** papel moneda, m. **ready m.,** dinero contante, m. **to make m.,** ganar (or hacer) dinero; enriquecerse. **M. talks,** Poderoso caballero es Don Dinero. **m.-bag,** talega, f.; (person) ricacho (-cha). **m.-bags,** riqueza, f. **m.-box,** alcancía,

hucha, f. **m.-changer,** cambista, m. and f. **m.-lender,** prestamista, m. and f. **m.-making,** s. el hacer dinero; prosperidad, ganancia, f. a. lucrativo. **m.-order,** giro postal, m.
moneyed, a. adinerado; acomodado
Mongolian, a. mogol. s. mogol (-la); (language) mogol, m.
mongoose, s. mangosta, f.
mongrel, a. mestizo, atravesado. s. perro mestizo, m.; (in contempt) mestizo, m.
monitor, s. monitor, m.
monitory, a. monitorio. s. (ecc.) monitorio, m.
monk, s. monje, m. **to become a m.,** hacerse monje, tomar el hábito. **monk's-hood,** acónito, m.
monkey, s. mono (-na); (imp) diablillo, m.; (of a pile-driver) pilón de martinete, m.; (in glass-making) crisol, m. **to m. with,** meterse con; entremeterse. **m. nut,** cacahuete, m. **m.-puzzle,** (tree) araucaria, f. **m. tricks,** monadas, travesuras, diabluras, f. pl. **m.-wrench,** llave inglesa, f.
monkish, a. monacal, de monje; monástico
monochord, s. monocordio, m.
monochromatic, a. monocromo
monochrome, s. monocromo, m.
monocle, s. monóculo, m.
monocotyledonous, a. monocotiledóneo
monogamist, s. monógamo (-ma)
monogamous, a. monógamo
monogamy, s. monogamia, f.
monogram, s. monograma, m.
monograph, s. monografía, f., opúsculo, m.
monolith, s. monolito, m.
monolithic, a. monolítico
monologue, s. monólogo, m.
monomania, s. monomanía, f.
monomaniac, s. monomaníaco (-ca)
monomial, s. monomio, m. a. de un solo término
monoplane, s. monóplano, m.
monopolist, s. monopolista, m. and f.; acaparador (-ra)
monopolization, s. monopolio, m.

monopolize, *v.t.* monopolizar

monopoly, *s.* monopolio, *m.*

monosyllabic, *a.* monosilábico

monosyllable, *s.* monosílabo, *m.*

monotheism, *s.* monoteísmo, *m.*

monotheist, *s.* monoteísta, *m.* and *f.*

monotone, *s.* monotonía, *f.*

monotonous, *a.* monótono

monotony, *s.* monotonía, *f.*

monotype, *s.* monotipia, *f.*

monoxide, *s.* monóxido, *m.*

monseigneur, *s.* monseñor, *m.*

monsoon, *s.* monzón, *m.* or *f.*

monster, *s.* monstruo, *m.*

monstrance, *s.* custodia, *f.*

monstrosity, *s.* monstruosidad, *f.*

monstrous, *a.* monstruoso; horrible, atroz; enorme

montage, *s.* montaje, *m.*

Montenegran, *a.* montenegrino. *s.* montenegrino (-na)

Montevidean, *a.* montevideano. *s.* montevideano (-na)

month, *s.* mes, *m.* **He arrived a m. ago,** Llegó hace un mes

monthly, *a.* mensual. *adv.* mensualmente, cada mes. *s.* revista (or publicación) mensual, *f.*; *pl.* **monthlies,** menstruación, regla, *f.* **m. salary or payment,** mensualidad, *f.*

monticule, *s.* montículo, *m.*

monument, *s.* monumento, *m.*

monumental, *a.* monumental

moo, *v.i.* (of cattle) mugir. *s.* mugido, *m.*

mood, *s.* humor, *m.*; espíritu, *m.*; (*gram.*) modo, *m.*

moodily, *adv.* taciturnamente; tristemente, pensativamente

moodiness, *s.* mal humor, *m.*, taciturnidad, *f.*; melancolía, tristeza, *f.*

moody, *a.* taciturno, de mal humor; triste, melancólico, pensativo

mooing, *s.* (of cattle) mugido, *m.*

moon, *s.* luna, *f.*; satélite, *m.*; mes lunar, *m.*; luz de la luna, *f.* **full m.,** plenilunio, *m.*; luna llena, *f.* **new m.,** novilunio, *m.*, luna nueva, *f.*

moonbeam, *s.* rayo de luna, *m.*

moonless, *a.* sin luna

moonlight, *s.* luz de la luna, *f.* **in the m.,** a la luz de la luna. **to do a m. flit,** (*fam.*) mudarse por el aire

moonlit, *a.* iluminado por la luna.

moonshine, *s.* claridad de la luna, *f.*; (*fig.*) música celestial, ilusión, *f.*

moonstone, *s.* adularia, *f.*

moonstruck, *a.* lunático

Moor, *s.* moro (-ra)

moor, *s.* páramo, brezal, *m.*; (marsh) pantano, *m.*; (for game) coto, *m.* *v.t.* amarrar, aferrar; afirmar con anclas o cables. **m.-hen,** polla de agua, *f.*

mooring, *s.* amarre, *m.* **m.-mast,** (*aer.*) poste de amarre, *m.*

moorings, *s. pl.* amarradero, *m.*

Moorish, *a.* moro; árabe. **M. architecture,** arquitectura árabe, *f.* **M. girl,** mora, *f.*

moorland, *s.* páramo, brezal, *m.*

moose, *s.* anta, *f.*

moot, *s.* junta, *f.*; ayuntamiento, *m.* *a.* discutible. *v.t.* (bring up) suscitar; (discuss) discutir, debatir

mop, *s.* (implement) "mop," *m.*, escoba con fleco, *f.*; (of hair) mata (de pelo), *f.* *v.t.* limpiar con un "mop"; (dry) enjugar, secar. **to mop up,** (*fam.*) limpiar; (*mil.*) acabar (con el enemigo)

mope, *v.i.* estar melancólico, estar deprimido; estar aburrido. **to m. about,** vagar tristemente

moquette, *s.* moqueta, *f.*

moraine, *s.* morena, *f.*

moral, *a.* moral; (chaste) casto, virtuoso; honrado. *s.* (maxim) moraleja, *f.*; *pl.* **morals,** moralidad, *f.*; ética, *f.*; moral, *f.*; (conduct) costumbres, *f. pl.*, *m.* **philosophy,** filosofía moral, *f.* **m. support,** apoyo moral, *m.* **m. tale,** apólogo, *m.*

morale, *s.* moral, *f.*

moralist, *s.* moralista, *m.*

morality, *s.* moralidad, *f.*; virtud, *f.*; castidad, *f.* **m. play,** moralidad, *f.*, drama alegórico, *m.*

moralization, *s.* moralización, *f.*

moralize, *v.t.* and *v.i.* moralizar

moralizer, *s.* moralizador (-ra)

moralizing, *a.* moralizador

morally, *adv.* moralmente

morals. See **moral**

morass, *s.* marisma, ciénaga, *f.*

moratorium, *s.* moratoria, *f.*

Moravian, *a.* moravo. *s.* moravo (-va)

morbid, *a.* mórbido, mórboso; (of the mind, etc.) insano

morbidezza, *s.* (*art* and *lit.*) morbidez, *f.*

morbidity, *s.* morbidez, *f.*

mordacity, *s.* mordacidad, *f.*

mordant, *a.* mordaz; (of acid) mordiente. *s.* mordiente, *m.*

more, *a.* and *adv.* más. The m. he earns, the less he saves, Cuanto más gana, menos ahorra. the m. the better, cuanto más, tanto mejor. without m. ado, sin más ni más; sin decir nada. Would you like some m.? ¿ Quiere Vd. más? (of food) ¿ Quiere Vd. repetir? no m., no más; (never) nunca más; (finished) se acabó. once m., otra vez, una vez más. m. and m., cada vez más, más y más. m. or less, más o menos; (about) poco más o menos

moreover, *adv.* además, también; por otra parte

morganatic, *a.* morganático

morgue, *s.* depósito de cadáveres, *m.*

moribund, *a.* moribundo

Mormon, *a.* mormónico. *s.* mormón (-ona)

Mormonism, *s.* mormonismo, *m.*

morning, *s.* mañana, *f.* *a.* matutino, de la mañana. Good m.! ¡Buenos días! the next m., la mañana siguiente. very early in the m., muy de mañana. m. coat, chaqué, *m.* m. dew, rocío de la mañana, *m.* m. paper, periódico de la mañana, *m.* m. star, lucero del alba, *m.* m. suit, chaqué, *m.*

Moroccan, *a.* marroquí, marrueco. *s.* marrueco (-ca), marroquí, *m.* and *f.*

morocco, *s.* (leather) marroquí, tafilete, *m.*

morose, *a.* sombrío, taciturno, malhumorado

morosely, *adv.* taciturnamente

moroseness, *s.* taciturnidad, *f.*; mal humor, *m.*

morphia, morphine, *s.* morfina, *f.* m. addict, morfinómano (-na)

Morphinism, *s.* morfinismo, *m.*

morphological, *a.* morfológico

morphology, *s.* morfología, *f.*

morrow, *s.* mañana, *f.*; día siguiente, *m.*

Morse code, *s.* clave telegráfica de Morse, *f.*

morsel, *s.* pedazo, *m.*; (mouthful) bocado, *m.*

mortal, *a.* mortal. *s.* mortal, *m.* and *f.* m. sin, pecado mortal, pecado capital, *m.*

mortality, *s.* mortalidad, *f.*

mortally, *adv.* mortalmente

mortar, *s.* (for building) argamasa, *f.*; (for mixing and *mil.*) mortero, *m.* m. and pestle, mortero y majador, *m.* m.-board, (in building) cuezo, *m.*; (academic cap) birrete, *m.*

mortgage, *s.* hipoteca, *f.* *v.t.* hipotecar. *a.* hipotecario. to pay off a m., redimir una hipoteca

mortgageable, *a.* hipotecable

mortgagee, *s.* acreedor (-ra) hipotecario (-ia)

mortgagor, *s.* deudor (-ra) hipotecario (-ia)

mortification, *s.* mortificación, *f.*; humillación, *f.*; (*med.*) gangrena, *f.*

mortify, *v.t.* mortificar; humillar. *v.i.* (*med.*) gangrenarse

mortifying, *a.* humillante

mortise, *s.* muesca. *f.* *v.t.* hacer muescas (en); ensamblar

mortmain, *s.* manos muertas, *f.* *pl.*

mortuary, *a.* mortuorio. *s.* depósito de cadáveres, *m.*

Mosaic, *a.* mosaico

mosaic, *s.* mosaico, *m.*

Moslem, *a.* musulmán, mahometano. *s.* musulmán (-ana)

mosque, *s.* mezquita, *f.*

mosquito, *s.* mosquito, *m.* m. net, mosquitero, *m.*

moss, *s.* musgo, *m.*; moho, *m.*; (swamp) marjal, *m.*

mossgrown, *a.* musgoso, cubierto de musgo; (*fig.*) anticuado

mossiness, *s.* estado musgoso, *m.*

mossy, *a.* musgoso

most, *a.* el (la, los, etc.) más; la mayor parte de; la mayoría de; (el, etc.) mayor. *adv.* más; el (la, etc.) más; (extremely) sumamente; (very) muy; (before adjectives sometimes expressed by superlative, e.g. m. reverend, reverendísimo, m. holy, santísimo, etc.). *s.* (highest price) el mayor precio; la mayor parte;

el mayor número; lo más. **m. of all**, sobre todo. **m. people**, la mayoría de la gente. **at the m.**, a lo más, a lo sumo. **for the m. part**, en su mayor parte; casi todos; generalmente, casi siempre. **to make the m. of**, sacar el mayor partido posible de; aprovechar bien; exagerar

mostly, *adv.* principalmente; en su mayoría; en su mayor parte; casi siempre; en general, generalmente

mote, *s.* átomo, *m.*; mota, *f.* **to see the m. in our neighbour's eye and not the beam in our own**, ver la paja en el ojo del vecino y no la viga en el nuestro

motet, *s.* motete, *m.*

moth, *s.* mariposa nocturna, *f.*; polilla, *f.*; (aircraft) "moth," *m.* **m.-ball**, bola de naftalina, *f.* **m.-eaten**, apolillado

mother, *s.* madre, *f.*; madre de familia, *f.*; (of alcoholic liquors) madre, *f.* *v.t.* cuidar como una madre (a); servir de madre (a); (animals) ahijar. **M. Church**, madre iglesia, *f.*; iglesia metropolitana, *f.* **m.-in-law**, suegra, *f.* **m. land**, (madre) patria, *f.* **m.-of-pearl**, *s.* madreperla, *f.*, nácar, *m. a.* nacarado, nacáreo. **M. Superior**, (madre) superiora, *f.* **m. tongue**, lengua materna, *f.*

motherhood, *s.* maternidad, *f.*

motherless, *a.* huérfano de madre, sin madre

motherlike, *a.* de madre, como una madre

motherliness, *s.* cariño maternal, *m.*

motherly, *a.* maternal

motif, *s.* motivo, *m.*; tema, *m.*; (sew.) adorno, *m.*

motion, *s.* movimiento, *m.*; (mech.) marcha, operación, *f.*; mecanismo, *m.*; (sign) seña, señal, *f.*; (gesture) ademán, gesto, *m.*; (carriage) aire, porte, *m.*; (of the bowels) movimiento del vientre, *m.*, deyección, *f.*; (will) voluntad, *f.*, deseo, *m.*; (proposal in an assembly or debate) proposición, moción, *f.*; (law) pedimento, *m. v.t.* hacer una señal (a). *v.i.* hacer señas. **to set in m.**, poner en marcha. **m. picture**, foto-

grafía cinematográfica, película, *f.* **m. picture theatre**, cine, *m.*

motionless, *a.* inmóvil

motivate, *v.t.* motivar

motive, *s.* motivo, *m. a.* motor; motivo. **with no m.**, sin motivo. **m. power**, fuerza motriz, *f.*

motley, *a.* abigarrado, multicolor; (mixed) diverso, vario. *s.* traje de colores, *m.*, botarga, *f.*

motor, *s.* motor, *m.*; automóvil, *m. a.* motor; movido por motor; con motor; (travelling) de viaje. *v.i.* ir en automóvil. *v.t.* llevar en automóvil (a). **m.-boat**, lancha automóvil, *f.* **m.-bus**, autobús, ómnibus, *m.* **m.-car**, automóvil, *m.* **m.-coach**, autobús, *m.* **m.-cycle**, motocicleta, *f.* **m.-cyclist**, motociclista, *m.* and *f.* **m.-launch**, canoa automóvil, *f.* **m.-oil**, aceite para motores, *m.* **m.-road**, autopista, *f.* **m.-rug**, manta de viaje, *f.* **m.-scooter**, bicicleta con motor, *f.* **m.-spirit**, bencina, *f.*

motoring, *s.* automovilismo, *m.*

motorist, *s.* automovilista, motorista, *m.* and *f.*

mottled, *a.* abigarrado; (of marble, etc.) jaspeado, esquizado; manchado (con), con manchas (de); pintado (con)

motto, *s.* (her.) divisa, *f.*; mote, *m.*; (in a book, etc.) lema, *m.*

mould, *s.* (fungus) moho, *m.*; (humus) mantillo, *m.*; (iron-mould) mancha de orín, *f.*; (matrix) molde, *m.*, matriz, *f.*; (cul.) cubilete, *m.*; (naut.) gálibo, *m.*; (for jelly, etc.) molde, *m.*; (arch.) moldura, *f.*; (temperament) temple, *m.*, disposición, *f. v.t.* moldear; (cast) vaciar; (carp.) moldurar; (naut.) galibar; (fig.) amoldar, formar; (agr.) cubrir con mantillo. **to m. oneself on**, modelarse sobre. **m.-board**, (of a plough) orejera, *f.*

moulder, *s.* moldeador, *m.*; (fig.) amoldador (-ra); creador (-ra). *v.i.* desmoronarse, convertirse en polvo; (fig.) decaer, desmoronarse; vegetar

mouldiness, *s.* moho, *m.*

moulding, *s.* amoldamiento, *m.*; vaciado, *m.*; (arch.) moldura, *f.*; (fig.) formación, *f.*

mouldy, *a.* mohoso, enmohecido; (*fig.*) anticuado.

moult, *v.i.* mudar. *s.* muda, *f.*

mound, *s.* montón, *m.*; (knoll) altozano, *m.*; (for defence) baluarte, *m.*; (for burial) túmulo, *m.*

mount, *s.* (hill, and in palmistry) monte, *m.*; (for riding) caballería, *f.*; montadura, *f.*; (for a picture) borde, *m.* *v.t.* subir; (machines, etc.) montar; (jewels) engastar; (a picture) poner un borde a; (a play) poner en escena; poner a caballo; proveer de caballo. *v.i.* montar; subir; (increase) aumentar. **to m. a horse,** subir a caballo, montar. **to m. guard,** (*mil.*) montar la guardia. **to m. the throne,** subir al trono

mountain, *s.* montaña, *f.*; (mound) montón, *m.* *a.* de montaña(s); montañés; alpino, alpestre. **to make a m. out of a molehill,** convertir un grano de arena en una montaña. **m.-chain,** cadena de montañas, *f.* **m. dweller,** montañés (-esa). **m. railway,** ferrocarril de cremallera, *m.* **m.-side,** falda de una montaña, *f.*

mountaineer, *s.* (inhabitant) montañés (-esa); (climber) alpinista, *m.* and *f.* *v.i.* hacer alpinismo

mountaineering, *s.* alpinismo, *m.*

mountainous, *a.* montañoso; (huge) enorme

mountebank, *s.* saltabanco, *m.*; charlatán, *m.*

mounting, *s.* (ascent) subida, *f.*; ascensión, *f.*; (of machinery, etc.) armadura, *f.*; montadura, *f.*; (of a precious stone) engaste, *m.* **m.-block,** subidero, *m.*

mourn, *v.i.* afligirse, lamentarse; (wear mourning) estar de luto. *v.t.* llorar; lamentar; llevar luto por

mourner, *s.* lamentador (-ra); (paid) plañidera, *f.*; el, *m.* (*f.* la) que acompaña al féretro

mournful, *a.* triste, acongojado; funesto, lúgubre; fúnebre; lamentable

mournfully, *adv.* tristemente

mournfulness, *s.* tristeza, *f.*; melancolía, aflicción, *f.*, pesar, *m.*

mourning, *s.* aflicción, *f.*; lamentación, *f.*; luto, *m.* **deep m.,** luto riguroso, *m.* **half m.,** medio luto, *m.* **to be in m.,** estar de luto. **to be in m. for,** llevar luto por. **to come out of m.,** dejar el luto. **m.-band,** (on the hat) tira de gasa, *f.*; (on the arm) brazal de luto, *m.* **m.-coach,** coche fúnebre, *m.*

mouse, *s.* ratón (-na); (*naut.*) barrilete, *m.* *v.i.* cazar ratones. **m.-coloured,** de color de rata. **m.-hole, m.-trap,** ratonera, *f.*

mouser, *s.* gato ratonero, *m.*

mousing, *s.* caza de ratones, *f.*

moustache, *s.* bigote, mostacho, *m.*

mousy, *a.* ratonesco, ratonil

mouth, *s.* (*anat.,* human being, of a bottle, cave) boca, *f.*; entrada, *f.*; (of a river) desembocadura, *f.*; (of a channel) embocadero, *m.*; (of a wind-instrument) boquilla, *f.* *v.t.* pronunciar con afectación; (chew) mascar. *v.i.* clamar a gritos, vociferar. **down in the m.,** (*fam.*) con las orejas caídas. **It makes my m. water,** Se me hace la boca agua. **large m.,** boca rasgada, *f.* **m.-gag,** abrebocas, *m.* **m.-organ,** armónica, *f.* **m.-wash,** enjuague, *m.*

mouthed, *a.* que tiene boca . . .; de boca . . . **open-m.,** boquiabierto

mouthful, *s.* bocado, *m.*; (of smoke, air) bocanada, *f.*

mouthpiece, *s.* (of wind-instruments, tobacco-pipe, waterpipe) boquilla, *f.*; (of a wineskin) brocal, *m.*; (spokesman) portavoz, *m.*; intérprete, *m.* and *f.*

movable, *a.* movible; (of goods) mobiliario. **m. feast,** fiesta movible, *f.*

movables, *s. pl.* bienes muebles, efectos, *m. pl.*

move, *s.* movimiento, *m.*; (of household effects) mudanza, *f.*; (motion) marcha, *f.*; (in a game) jugada, *f.*; (*fig.,* step) paso, *m.*; (device) maniobra, *f.* **Whose m. is it?** ¿A quién le toca jugar? **to be on the m.,** estar en movimiento; estar de viaje. **to be always on the m.,** (*fam.*) parecer una lanzadera

move, v.t. mover; poner en marcha; (furniture) trasladar; cambiar de lugar; (stir) remover; (shake) agitar, hacer temblar; (transport) transportar; (a piece in chess, etc.) jugar; (pull) arrancar; (impel) impulsar; (incline) inclinar, disponer; (affect emotionally) conmover, emocionar, enternecer; impresionar. v.i. moverse; ponerse en marcha; (walk) andar; ir; avanzar; (a step forward, etc.) dar; (move house) trasladarse; (act) entrar en acción; (in games) hacer una jugada; (progress) progresar; (shake) agitarse, temblar; removerse; (propose in an assembly) hacer una proposición; (in a court of law) hacer un pedimento; (grow) crecer. to m. about, pasearse; ir y venir; (of traffic) circular; (remove) trasladarse; (stir, tremble) agitarse. to m. along, caminar por; avanzar por. to m. aside, v.t. apartar; poner a un lado; (curtains) descorrer. v.i. ponerse a un lado; quitarse de en medio. to m. away, v.t. alejar. v.i. alejarse; marcharse; trasladarse; mudar de casa. to m. back, retroceder, volver hacia atrás. to m. down, bajar, descender. to m. forward, adelantarse; avanzar; progresar. to m. in, entrar (en); tomar posesión de una casa. to m. off, v.t. quitar. v.i. marcharse; ponerse en marcha; alejarse, apartarse. to m. on, avanzar; ponerse en marcha; circular; (of time) pasar, correr. to m. out, v.t. sacar, quitar. v.i. salir; (from a house) mudarse, abandonar (una casa, etc.). to m. round, dar vueltas; girar; (turn round) volverse. to m. to, (make) hacer, animar (a); causar. to m. up, v.t. montar, subir. v.i. montar; avanzar

movement, s. movimiento, m.; (mech.) mecanismo, m.; (Stock Exchange) actividad, f. encircling m., (mil.) movimiento envolvente, m.

mover, s. motor, m.; móvil, m.; promotor (-ra); (of a motion, proposer) autor (-ra) de una moción

movie, s. (fam.) cine, m. m. camera, máquina de impresionar, f. m. star, estrella de la pantalla, f.

moving, a. móvil; motor; (affecting) emocionante, conmovedor; impresionante; patético. s. movimiento, m.; traslado, m.; cambio de domicilio, m. m. picture, fotografía cinematográfica, f. m. staircase, escalera móvil, f.

movingly, adv. con emoción; patéticamente

mow, v.t. segar. v.i. (grimace) hacer muecas

mowing, s. siega, f. m.-machine, segadora, f.

Mozarab, s. mozárabe, m. and f.

Mozarabic, a. mozárabe

Mr. See mister

Mrs. See mistress

much, a. mucho. adv. mucho; (by far) con mucho; (with past part.) muy; (pretty nearly), casi, más o menos. m. of a size, más o menos del mismo tamaño. I was m. angered, Estuve muy enfadado. as m. as, tanto como. as m. more, otro tanto. How m. is it? ¿Cuánto es? ¿Cuánto cuesta? however m. . . ., por mucho que . . . not m., no mucho. not to think m. of, tener en poco (a). so m. so that, tanto que. too m., demasiado. to make m. of, dar grande importancia a; (a person) apreciar, querer; agasajar; (a child) mimar, acariciar

mucilage, s. mucílago, m.

mucilaginous, a. mucilaginoso

muck, s. (dung) estiércol, m.; (filth) porquería, inmundicia, f.; suciedad, f.; (rubbish, of a literary work, etc.) porquería, f. to m. up, ensuciar; (spoil) estropear por completo

mucky, a. muy sucio; puerco; asqueroso, repugnante

mucosity, s. mucosidad, f.

mucous, a. mucoso. m. membrane, mucosa, f.

mucus, s. mucosidad, f.; (from the nose) moco, m.

mud, s. lodo, barro, fango, m. to stick in the mud, (of a ship, etc.) embarrancarse. mud-bath, baño de barro, m. mud wall, tapia, f.

muddiness, s. estado fangoso, *m.*; (of liquids) turbiedad, *f.*; suciedad, *f.*

muddle, v.t. (bewilder) dejar perplejo, aturdir; (intoxicate) emborrachar; (stupefy) entontecer; (spoil) estropear; embarullar, dejar en desorden; hacer un lío de. s. desorden, *m.*; confusión, *f.*; lío, embrollo, *m.* **in a m.,** en desorden; en confusión. **to make a m.,** armar un lío. **to m. away,** derrochar sin ton ni son

muddled, a. desordenado; confuso; estúpido; torpe; (drunk) borracho

muddy, a. fangoso, lodoso, barroso; cubierto de lodo; (of liquids, etc.) turbio; (of the complexion) cetrino. v.t. enlodar, cubrir de lodo; ensuciar; (liquids) enturbiar

mudguard, s. guardabarro, *m.*

muezzin, s. almuecín, almuédano, *m.*

muff, s. manguito, *m.*; (for a car radiator) cubierta para radiador, *f.*; (fam., at games, etc.) maleta, *m.* v.t. dejar escapar (una pelota); (an opportunity) perder

muffin, s. mollete, *m.*

muffle, v.t. embozar, arrebozar; envolver; encubrir, ocultar, tapar; (stifle sound of) apagar; (oars, bells) envolver con tela para no hacer ruido; (fig.) ahogar. **to m. oneself up,** embozarse

muffled, a. (of sound) sordo; confuso; apagado. **m. drum,** tambor enlutado, *m.*

muffler, s. bufanda, tapaboca, *f.*; (furnace) mufla, *f.*; (of a car radiator) cubierta para radiador, *f.*; (silencer) silencioso, *m.*

mufti, s. mufti, *m.*

mug, s. vaso, *m.*; (tankard) pichel, *m.*; (face) jeta, *f.*; (dupe) primo, *m.*; (at games, etc.) maleta, *m.*

mulatto, a. mulato. s. mulato (-ta). **m.-like,** amulatado

mulberry, s. (fruit) mora, *f.*; (bush) morera, *f.* **m. plantation,** moreral, *m.*

mule, s. mulo (-la); (slipper) mula, chinela, *f.*; (spinningjenny) huso mecánico, *m.*

muleteer, s. mulatero, *m.*

mulish, a. mular; terco como una mula

mulishness, s. terquedad de mula, *f.*

mullet, s. (red) salmonete, *m.*, trilla, *f.*; (grey) mújol, *m.*

multicoloured, a. multicolor

multifarious, a. numeroso, mucho; diverso, vario

multiform, a. multiforme

multilateral, a. multilátero

multi-millionaire, a. multimillonario, archimillonario. s. multimillonario, *m.*

multiple, a. múltiplo. s. múltiplo, *m.*

multiplicand, s. multiplicando, *m.*

multiplication, s. multiplicación, *f.* **m. table,** tabla de multiplicación, *f.*

multiplicity, s. multiplicidad, *f.*

multiplier, s. (math.) multiplicador, *m.*; máquina de multiplicar, *f.*

multiply, v.t. multiplicar. v.i. multiplicarse

multitude, s. multitud, *f.* **the m.,** las masas

multitudinous, a. muy numeroso

mumble, v.i. and v.t. musitar, hablar entre dientes; refunfuñar; (chew) mascullar

mummer, s. momero (-ra); máscara, *m.* and *f.*

mummery, s. momería, *f.*; mascarada, *f.*

mummification, s. momificación, *f.*

mummify, v.t. momificar. v.i. momificarse

mummy, s. momia, *f.*; carne de momia, *f.*; (fam., mother) mama, *f.* **m. case,** sarcófago, *m.*

mumps, s. pl. parotiditis, papera, *f.*

munch, v.t. masticar, mascullar, mascar

mundane, a. mundano

municipal, a. municipal. **m. charter,** fuero municipal, *m.* **m. government,** gobierno municipal, *m.*

municipality, s. municipio, *m.*

munificence, s. munificencia, *f.*

munificent, a. munífico, generoso

munition, s. munición, *f.* v.t. municionar. **m. dump,** depósito de municiones, *m.* **m. factory,** fábrica de municiones, *f.* **m. worker,** obrero (-ra) de una fábrica de municiones

Munroe doctrine, *s.* monroísmo, *m.*

mural, *a.* mural. *s.* pintura mural, *f.*

murder, *s.* asesinato, *m.* *v.t.* asesinar; dar muerte (a), matar; (a work, etc.) degollar. **He was murdered,** Murió asesinado. **wilful m.,** homicidio premeditado, *m.*

murderer, *s.* asesino, *m.*

murderess, *s.* asesino, *f.*

murderous, *a.* homicida; cruel, sanguinario; fatal; imposible, intolerable

murderously, *adv.* con intento de asesinar; (with look) con ojos asesinos; cruelmente

murkiness, *s.* obscuridad, lobreguez, *f.*, tinieblas, *f. pl.*

murky, *a.* lóbrego, negro, obscuro; (of one's past, etc.) negro, accidentado

murmur, *s.* murmullo, *m.*; rumor, *m.*; susurro, *m.*; (grumble) murmurio, *m.* *v.i.* murmurar, susurrar; (complain) murmurar, quejarse. *v.t.* murmurar, decir en voz baja

murmuring, *s.* murmurio, *m.* *a.* que murmura, susurrante

muscatel, *a.* moscatel. *s.* moscatel, *m.* **m. grape,** uva moscatel, *f.*

muscle, *s.* músculo, *m.*

Muscovite, *a.* moscovita. *s.* moscovita, *m.* and *f.*

muscular, *a.* muscular, musculoso; (brawny) membrudo, fornido. **m. pains,** (in the legs, etc.) agujetas, *f. pl.*

muscularity, *s.* fuerza muscular, *f.*

musculature, *s.* musculatura, *f.*

Muse, *s.* musa, *f.*

muse, *s.* meditación, *f.* *v.i.* meditar, reflexionar, rumiar; mirar las musarañas, estar distraído. **to m. on,** meditar en (or sobre)

museum, *s.* museo, *m.*

mushroom, *s.* seta, *f.* *a.* de setas; de forma de seta; (upstart) advenedizo; (ephemeral) efímero, de un día. **m.-bed,**

setal, *m.* **m.-spawn,** esporas de setas, *f. pl.*

music, *s.* música, *f.*; armonía, *f.*; melodía, *f.* *a.* de música. **to set to m.,** poner en música. **m.-hall,** teatro de variedades, *m.*; salón de conciertos, *m.* **m. master,** profesor de música, *m.* **m. publisher,** editor de obras musicales, *m.* **m. stand,** atril, *m.*; tablado para una orquesta, *m.* **m. stool,** taburete de piano, *m.*

musical, *a.* musical; de música; armonioso, melodioso. **She is very m.,** Ella está muy aficionada a la música; Ella tiene mucho talento para la música. **m.-box,** caja de música, *f.* **m. comedy,** zarzuela, *f.* **m. instrument,** instrumento de música, *m.*

musically, *adv.* musicalmente; melodiosamente

musician, *s.* músico (-ca)

musing, *s.* meditación, *f.*; ensueños, *m. pl.* *a.* pensativo, meditabundo

musingly, *adv.* reflexivamente

musk, *s.* (substance) almizcle, *m.*; perfume de almizcle, *m.* *a.* de almizcle; almizclero; (of scents) almizcleño. **m.-deer,** almizclero, *m.* **m.-rat,** rata almizclera, *f.*

musket, *s.* mosquete, *m.*

musketeer, *s.* mosquetero, *m.*

musketry, *s.* mosquetería, *f.*

muslin, *s.* muselina, *f.* *a.* de muselina

musquash, *s.* rata almizclera, *f.*

mussel, *s.* mejillón, *m.* **m.-bed,** criadero de mejillones, *m.*

Mussulman, *a.* musulmán. *s.* musulmán (-ana)

must, *v.i.* haber de; tener que; deber; (expressing probability) deber de ser. **This question m. be settled without delay,** Esta cuestión debe ser resuelta sin demora. **You m. do it at once,** Tienes que hacerlo en seguida. **I m. have seen him in the street sometime,** Debo haberle visto en la calle alguna vez. **One m. eat to live,** Se ha de comer para vivir. **Well, go if you m.,** Bueno, vete si no hay más remedio. **It m. be a difficult decision for him,** Debe ser una decisión difícil para él. **It m. have been about twelve o'clock when . . .**, Serían las doce cuando ...

must, s. mosto, zumo de la uva, m.; (mould) moho, m.

mustang, s. potro mesteño, m.

mustard, s. mostaza, f. **m. gas**, iperita, f. **m. plaster**, sinapismo, m. **m. pot**, mostacera, f. **m. spoon**, cucharita para la mostaza, f.

muster, s. lista, f., rol, m.; revista, f.; reunión, f. v.t. pasar lista (de); pasar revista (a); reunir. v.i. juntarse, reunirse. **to m. out**, (from the army) dar de baja (a). **to m. up sufficient courage**, cobrar ánimos suficientes. **to pass m.**, pasar revista; ser aceptado. **m.-roll**, (mil.) muestra, f.; (naut.) rol de la tripulación, m.

mustiness, s. moho, m.; ranciedad, f.; (of a room, etc.) olor de humedad, m.

musty, a. mohoso; rancio; que huele a humedad. **to go m.**, enmohecerse

mutability, s. mutabilidad, f.; inconstancia, inestabilidad, f.

mutable, a. mudable; inconstante, inestable

mutation, s. mutación, f.

mute, a. mudo; silencioso. s. mudo (-da); (mus.) sordina, f.; (phonetics) letra muda, f. **deaf m.**, sordomudo (-da)

muted, a. (of sounds) sordo, apagado

mutely, adv. mudamente; en silencio

muteness, s. mudez, f.; silencio, m.

mutilate, v.t. mutilar; estropear.

mutilation, s. mutilación, f.

mutineer, s. amotinador, rebelde, m.

mutinous, a. amotinado; rebelde, sedicioso; turbulento

mutiny, s. motín, m.; sublevación, insurrección, f. v.i. amotinarse, sublevarse

mutter, v.t. and v.i. murmurar, musitar; mascullar, decir (or hablar) entre dientes; gruñir, refunfuñar; (of thunder, etc.) tronar, retumbar. s. murmurio, m.; rumor, m.; retumbo, m.

mutton, s. carnero, m. a. de carnero. **m.-chop**, chuleta, f.

mutual, a. mutuo, recíproco; común. **by m. consent**, de común acuerdo. **m. aid society**, sociedad de socorros mutuos, f. **m. insurance company**, sociedad de seguros mutuos, f.

mutualism, s. mutualismo, m.

mutuality, s. mutualidad, f.

mutually, adv. mutuamente, recíprocamente

muzzle, s. (snout) hocico, m.; (for a dog) bozal, m.; (of a gun) boca, f. v.t. abozalar, poner un bozal (a); (fig., gag) amordazar, imponer silencio (a)

muzzling, s. acción de abozalar, f.; (fig., gagging) amordazamiento, m.

my, a. poss. mi, m. and f.; mis, m. and f. pl. **my relatives**, mis parientes. **My goodness!** ¡ Dios mío!

mycology, s. micología, f.

myelitis, s. mielitis, f.

myope, s. miope, m. and f.

myopia, miopía, f.

myopic, a. miope

myosotis, s. miosota, f.

myriad, s. miríada, f.

myrmidon, s. rufián, m.; asesino, m.; secuaz, m.

myrrh, s. mirra, f.

myrtle, s. mirto, arrayán, m.

myself, pron. yo mismo; (as a reflexive with a preposition) mí; (with a reflexive verb) me. **I m. sent it**, yo mismo (-ma) lo mandé

mysterious, a. misterioso

mysteriously, adv. misteriosamente

mysteriousness, s. misterio, m., lo misterioso

mystery, s. misterio, m. **m. play**, (religious) misterio, drama litúrgico, m.; (thriller) comedia de detectives, f. **m. story**, novela policíaca, f.; novela de aventuras, f.

mystic, a. místico

mysticism, s. misticismo, m.

mystification, s. mistificación, f.

mystify, v.t. mistificar

myth, s. mito, m.

mythical, a. mítico

mythologist, s. mitólogo, m.

mythology, s. mitología, f.

myxœdema, s. mixedema, m.

N

n, *s.* (letter) ene, *f.*

nab, *v.t.* (*fam.*) atrapar, apresar, agazapar

nabob, *s.* nabab, *m.*; ricacho, *m.*

nacelle, *s.* (*aer.*) barquilla, *f.*

nacre, *s.* nácar, *m.*, madreperla, *f.*

nacreous, *a.* nacarino

nadir, *s.* nadir, *m.*

nag, *s.* jaca, *f.*; (wretched hack) rocín, jamelgo, penco, *m.*; *v.t.* zaherir, echar en cara, regañar; (of one's conscience) remorder. *v.i.* criticar, regañar

nagging, *s.* zaherimiento, *m.* *a.* zaheridor, criticón; (pain) continuo, incesante, constante

naiad, *s.* (*myth.*) náyade, *f.*

nail, *v.t.* clavar, enclavar; (for ornament) clavetear, tachornar, adornar con clavos. *s.* uña, *f.*; (*mech.*) clavo, *m.*; (animal's) garra, *f.* **to n. down,** sujetar (or cerrar) con clavos. **to n. to** (on to), clavar en. **to n. together,** fijar con clavos. (*fam.*) **on the n.,** en el acto, en seguida. (*fam.*) **to hit the n. on the head,** dar en el clavo. **brass-headed n.,** tachón, *m.* **French n.,** punta de París, *f.* **headless n.,** puntilla, *f.* **hob-n.,** clavo de herradura, *m.* **hook n.,** gancho, *m.* **round-headed n.,** bellota, *f.* **n.-brush,** cepillo para las (or de) uñas, *m.* **n.-file,** lima para las uñas, *f.* **n. head,** cabeza de un clavo, *f.* **n.-puller,** sacaclavos, arrancaclavos, botador, *m.* **n.-scissors,** tijeras para las uñas, *f. pl.* **n. trade,** ferretería, *f.* **n. varnish,** barniz para las uñas, *m.*

nailed, *a.* adornado con clavos, claveteado

nailer, *s.* fabricante de clavos, chapucero, *m.*

nailing, *s.* enclavación, *f.*

nainsook, *s.* nanzú, *m.*

naïve, *a.* ingenuo, candoroso, espontáneo

naïvely, *adv.* ingenuamente, espontáneamente

naïveté, *s.* ingenuidad, naturalidad, franqueza, *f.*; candor, *m.*

naked, *a.* desnudo, nudo; desabrigado, indefenso, desampa-rado; (birds) implume; calvo; (truth) simple, sencillo, puro; evidente, patente. **stark n.,** en cueros vivos, tal como le parió su madre. **with the n. sword,** con la espada desnuda. **n. eye,** simple vista, *f.* **n. light,** llama descubierta, *f.*

nakedly, *adv.* nudamente; desabrigadamente; abiertamente, claramente

nakedness, *s.* desnudez, *f.*; (*fig.*) desabrigo, *m.*, aridez, *f.*; (*fig.*) claridad, *f.* **the truth in all its n.,** la verdad desnuda

namby-pamby, *a.* soso, insípido, ñoño

name, *s.* nombre, *m.*; título, *m.*; fama, opinión, *f.*; renombre, crédito, *m.*; autoridad, *f.*; apodo, mal nombre, *m.* *v.t.* nombrar, llamar, imponer el nombre de, apellidar; mencionar, señalar; (appoint) designar, elegir; (ships) bautizar. **by n.,** por nombre. **Christian n.,** nombre de pila, *m.* **in his n.,** en nombre de él, en nombre suyo; de parte de él. **in n. only,** nada más que en nombre. **to be named,** llamarse. **to call** (a person) **names,** poner como un trapo (a). **to go under the n. of,** vivir bajo el nombre de. **to have a good n.,** tener buena fama. **What is her n.?** ¿Como se llama ella? **n. day,** santo, *m.* **n. plate,** (machinery) placa de fábrica, *f.*; (streets) rótulo, *m.*; (professional) placa profesional, *f.*

nameless, *a.* anónimo; desconocido; (inexpressible) vago, indecible

namely, *adv.* a saber, es decir

namesake, *s.* tocayo (-ya)

naming, *s.* bautizo, *m.*; nombramiento, *m.*; designación, *f.*

nanny-goat, *s.* cabra, *f.*

nap, *s.* (cloth) pelusa, *f.*, pelo, tamo, *m.*; (plants) vello, *m.*, pelusilla, *f.*; (sleep) siesta, *f.*, sueño, *m.*; (cards) napolitana, *f.* **to take a nap,** *v.i.* dormitar, echar un sueño. **to take an afternoon nap,** dormir la siesta. **to be caught napping,** estar desprevenido

nape, *s.* nuca, *f.*, cogote, *m.*; (animal's) testuz, *m.*

naphtha, · *s.* (*chem.*) nafta, *f.* **wood n.,** alcohol metílico, *m.*

naphthalene, *s.* (*chem.*) naftalina, *f.*

naphthol, *s.* (*chem.*) naftol, *m.*

napkin, *s.* (table) servilleta, *f.*; (babies') pañal, *m.* **n.-ring,** servilletero, *m.*

Napoleonic, *a.* napoleónico

narcissism, *s.* narcisismo, *m.*

narcissus, *s.* narciso, *m.*

narcosis, *s.* (*med.*) narcosis, *f.*

narcotic, *a.* (*med.*) narcótico, calmante, soporífero. *s.* (*med.*) narcótico, *m.*, opiata, *f.*

nard, *s.* (*bot.*) nardo, *m.*, tuberosa, *f.*

narghile, *s.* narguile, *m.*

narrate, *v.t.* narrar, contar; referir, relatar

narration, *s.* narración, narrativa; relación, descripción, *f.*, relato, *m.*

narrative, *a.* narrador, narrativo, narratorio. *s.* narrativa, *f.*; descripción, *f.*

narrator, *s.* narrador (-ra), relator (-ra), descriptor (-ra)

narrow, *v.t.* estrechar, angostar; reducir, limitar. *v.i.* reducirse, hacerse más estrecho; (eyes) entornarse; (knitting) menguar. *a.* estrecho, angosto; limitado, restringido, reducido, corto; (avaricious) ruin, avaro, mezquino; (ideas) intolerante, intransigente. *s. pl.* **narrows,** (*naut.*) estrecho, *m.*; desfiladero, paso estrecho, *m.* **to have a n. escape,** escapar en una tabla. **n.-brimmed** (hats), de ala estrecha. **n. circumstances,** estrechez, escasez de medios, *f.* **n.-gauge railway,** ferrocarril de vía estrecha (or de vía angosta), *m.* **n. life,** vida de horizontes estrechos, *f.* **n. majority,** escasa mayoría, *f.* **n.-minded,** intolerante, intransigente. **n.-mindedness,** intolerancia, intransigencia, estrechez de miras, *f.*

narrowing, *s.* estrechez, *f.*, estrechamiento, *m.*; reducción, limitación, *f.*; (in knitting) menguado, *m.*

narrowly, *adv.* estrechamente; por poco, con dificultad; atentamente, cuidadosamente. **I n.**

escaped being run over, Por poco me atropellan

narrowness, *s.* estrechez, angostura, *f.*; (of means) pobreza, miseria, *f.*; (of ideas) intolerancia, intransigencia, *f.*

nasal, *a.* nasal, gangoso. *s.* letra nasal, *f.*

nasalize, *v.t.* nasalizar

nasally, *adv.* nasalmente. **to speak n.,** hablar por las narices, ganguear

nascent, *a.* naciente

nastily, *adv.* suciamente; ofensivamente, de un modo insultante; maliciosamente, con malignidad

nastiness, *s.* suciedad, inmundicia, porquería, *f.*; (indecency) obscenidad, indecencia, *f.*; (rudeness) insolencia, impertinencia, grosería, *f.*; (difficulty) dificultad, *f.*, lo malo

nasturtium, *s.* mastuerzo, *m.*, capuchina, *f.*

nasty, *a.* nauseabundo, repugnante; asqueroso, inmundo, sucio; (obscene) indecente, obsceno; desagradable, malo; (malicious) rencoroso, malicioso; violento; malévolo, amenazador; peligroso; difícil. (*fig.*) **to be in a n. mess,** tener el agua al cuello. **to turn n.,** (*fam.*) ponerse desagradable

natal, *a.* natal, natalicio, de nacimiento, nativo

natation, *s.* natación, *f.*

natatory, *a.* natatorio

nation, *s.* nación, *f.*, estado, país, *m.*; (people) pueblo, *m.*

national, *a.* nacional; público; patriótico. *s.* nacional, *m.* and *f.* **n. anthem,** himno nacional, *m.* **n. debt,** deuda pública, *f.* **n. schools,** escuelas públicas, *f. pl.* **n. socialism,** nacionalsocialismo, *m.* **n. socialist,** *a.* and *s.* nacionalsocialista (*m.* and *f.*). **n. syndicalism,** (*pol.*) nacionalsindicalismo, *m.* **n. syndicalist,** *a.* and *s.* (*pol.*) nacionalsindicalista (*m.* and *f.*)

nationalism, *s.* nacionalismo, patriotismo, *m.*

nationalist, *a.* and *s.* nacionalista (*m.* and *f.*)

nationality, · *s.* nacionalidad, *f.*; nación, *f.*

nationalization, s. nacionalización, f.

nationalize, v.t. nacionalizar

nationally, adv. nacionalmente, como nación; del punto de vista nacional

native, a. (of a place) nativo, natal, oriundo; indígena; nacional, típico, del país; (of genius) natural, innato, instintivo; (min.) nativo; (language) vernáculo. s. nacional, m. and f.; natural, m. and f.; ciudadano (-na) indígena, aborigen (gen. pl.), m. and f.; producto nacional, m. **He is a n. of Madrid,** Nació en Madrid, Es natural de Madrid, Él es madrileño. **n. land,** patria, tierra, f. **n. place,** lugar natal, m. **n. region,** patria chica, f. **n. soil,** terruño, m. **n. tongue,** lengua materna, f.

nativity, s. navidad, natividad, f.; (manger) nacimiento, m.

natty, a. (fam.) chulo, majo; coquetón

natural, a. natural; (wild) virgen, salvaje; nativo; (of products) crudo; normal; (usual) acostumbrado, corriente, natural; (of likeness) fiel, verdadero; (illegitimate) ilegítimo, bastardo; (of qualities) innato, instintivo; físico, característico, propio; (of people) inafectado, sencillo, genuino; (mus.) natural. s. (mus.) becuadro, m.; (mus.) nota natural, f.; imbécil, m. and f. **n. features,** geografía física, f. **n. history,** historia natural, f. **n. philosophy,** filosofía natural, f. **n. science,** ciencias naturales, f. pl. **n. selection,** selección natural, f. **n. state,** estado virgen, m.

naturalism, s. naturalismo, m.

naturalist, s. (lit. and science) naturalista, m. and f.

naturalistic, a. naturalista

naturalization, s. naturalización, f.; aclimatación, f. **n. papers,** carta de naturaleza, f.

naturalize, v.t. naturalizar; aclimatar. **to become naturalized,** naturalizarse

naturally, adv. naturalmente, por naturaleza; normalmente; sin afectación; instintivamente, por instinto; (without art) al natural

naturalness, s. naturalidad, f.; sencillez, desenvoltura, f.; desembarazo, m.

nature, s. naturaleza, f.; (of people) carácter, fondo, temperamento, genio, natural, modo de ser, m.; (kind) género, m., especie, f.; (essence) condición, esencia, cualidad, f. (art) **from n.,** del natural. **good n.,** bondad natural, afabilidad, f. **ill n.,** mala índole, f. **nature cure,** naturismo, m. **n. curist,** naturista, m. and f. **n. study,** historia natural, f. **n. worship,** panteísmo, culto de la naturaleza, m.

natured, a. de carácter, de índole, con un modo de ser, de condición

naught, s. nada, f.; cero, m. a. inútil, sin valor. **all for n.,** todo en balde. **to come to n.,** malograrse. **to set at n.,** tener en menos; despreciar

naughtily, adv. traviesamente; con picardía, con malicia

naughtiness, s. travesura, picardía, mala conducta, f.; malicia, f.

naughty, a. travieso, pícaro, revoltoso, malo; salado, escabroso, verde (stories, etc.). **to be n.,** (children) ser malo

nausea, s. náusea, f., bascas, f. pl., mareo, m.; (fig.) asco, m.; repugnancia, f.

nauseate, v.t. dar náuseas; (fig.) repugnar, dar asco

nauseating, a. repugnante, horrible; asqueroso

nauseous, a. nauseabundo, asqueroso; (fig.) repugnante

nauseousness, s. náusea, asquerosidad, f.; (fig.) repugnancia, f., asco, m.

nautical, a. náutico, marítimo. **n. twenty-four hours,** singladura, f.

nautilus, s. (zool.) argonauta, nautilo, m.

naval, a. naval; de marina, marítimo. **n. base,** base naval, f. **n. engagement,** batalla naval, f. **n. hospital,** hospital de marina, m. **n. law,** código naval, m. **n. officer,** oficial de marina, m. **n. power,** poder marítimo, m. **n. reservist,** marinero de reserva, m. **n. yard,** arsenal, m.

Navarrese, *a.* and *s.* navarro (-rra)

nave, *s.* (*arch.*) nave, *f.*; (of wheels) cubo, *m.*

navel, *s.* ombligo, *m.* **n. string,** cordón umbilical, *m.*

navicert, *s.* pasavante, *m.*

navigability, *s.* navegación, practicabilidad de navegar, *f.*

navigable, *a.* navegable, practicable

navigate, *v.t.* navegar, marear, dirigir (un buque); (*fig.*) conducir, guiar. *v.i.* navegar

navigation, *s.* navegación, *f.*; (science of) náutica, marina, *f.* **n. company,** empresa naviera, *f.* **n. laws,** derecho marítimo, *m.* **n. lights,** luces de navegación, *f. pl.*

navigator, *s.* navegador, navegante, *m.*; piloto, *m.*

navvy, *s.* peón, bracero, jornalero, *m.*; (*mech.*) máquina, excavadora, *f.* **road n.,** peón caminero, *m.* **to work like a n.,** estar hecho un azacán, sudar la gota gorda

navy, *s.* marina, *f.*; armada, *f.*; (colour) azul marino, *m.* **n. board,** consejo de la armada, *m.* **N. Department** (U.S.A.) ministerio de Marina, *m.* **n. estimates,** presupuesto de marina, *m.* **n. list,** escalafón de marina, *m.*

nay, *adv.* no; al contrario, más bien, mejor dicho. *s.* negativa, *f.*, voto contrario, *m.*

Nazarene, *a.* and *s.* nazareno (-na)

Nazi, *a.* and *s.* nacionalsocialista, naci (*m.* and *f.*)

Nazism, *s.* nacismo, *m.*

Neapolitan, *a.* and *s.* neapolitano (-na)

near, *v.i.* acercarse, aproximarse. *a.* cercano, inmediato, contiguo; (of time) inminente, próximo; (relationship) cercano, consanguíneo; (of friends) íntimo, entrañable; (mean) tacaño, avariento

near, *prep.* cerca de, junto a; hacia, en la dirección de; (of time) cerca de, casi. *adv.* cerca; (time) cerca, próximamente. **to be n. to,** estar cerca de. **to bring n.,** acercar, aproximar.

It was a n. thing, Escapamos por un pelo. **n. at hand,** a la mano; (time) cerca, inminente. **n.-by,** *a.* cercano, inmediato. *adv.* cerca. **n. side,** (of vehicles) lado de la acera, *m.* **n.-sighted,** corto de vista, miope. **n.-sightedness,** miopía, *f.*

nearest, *a. comp.* and *sup.* más cercano, más cerca; más corto. **the n. way,** el camino más corto, el camino directo

nearly, *adv.* casi; cerca de, aproximadamente; estrechamente; íntimamente. **not n.,** no lo bastante, no lo suficientemente. **It touches me n.,** Me toca de cerca, Es de sumo interés para mí. **They n. killed me,** Por poco me mataron. **to be n.,** (of age) frisar en, rayar en

nearness, *s.* (of place) cercanía, proximidad, contigüidad, *f.*; (of time) inminencia, proximidad, *f.*; (relationship) consanguinidad, *f.*; (avarice) avaricia, tacañería, *f.*; (dearness) intimidad, amistad estrecha, *f.*

neat, *a.* (*zool.*) vacuno; elegante, sencillo, de buen gusto; (of the body) bien hecho, airoso, esbelto; (clean) limpio, aseado; (of handwriting) legible, bien proporcionado; pulido, esmerado, acabado; hábil, astuto, diestro; (of liquor, spirits) puro, solo. **to make a n. job of,** hacer (algo) bien

neatly, *adv.* sencillamente, con elegancia, con primor; con aseo, limpiamente; bien (proporcionado); diestramente, hábilmente

neatness, *s.* aseo, *m.*, limpieza, *f.*; elegancia, sencillez, *f.*; buen gusto, *m.*; destreza, habilidad, *f.*; (aptness) pertinencia, *f.*

nebula, *s.* (*ast.*) nebulosa, *f.*

nebulosity, *s.* nebulosidad, *f.*; (*ast.*) nebulosa, *f.*; vaguedad, imprecisión, *f.*

nebulous, *a.* nebuloso; vago, impreciso, confuso

necessarily, *adv.* necesariamente; inevitablemente, sin duda

necessary, *a.* necesario, inevitable; imprescindible, preciso, indispensable, esencial; obligatorio, debido, forzoso. *s.* re-

quisito esencial, *m.* **if n.,** en caso
de necesidad; si fuera necesario.
to be n., hacer falta; necesitarse
necessitate, *v.t.* necesitar, exigir,
requerir, obligar
necessitous, *a.* pobre, indigente,
miserable, necesitado
necessity, *s.* necesidad, *f.*; consecuencia, *f.*, resultado, efecto,
m.; inevitabilidad, fatalidad, *f.*;
(poverty) indigencia, pobreza, *f.*
**Fire and clothing are neces-
sities,** El fuego y el vestir son
cosas necesarias. **from n.,** por
necesidad. **in case of n.,** si
fuese necesario, en caso de
necesidad. **of n.,** de necesidad,
sin remedio. **physical necessities,** menesteres físicos, *m. pl.*
prime n., artículo de primera
necesidad, *m.* **to be under the
n. of,** tener que, tener la necesidad de
neck, *s.* cuello, *m.*, garganta, *f.*;
(of bottles) gollete, cuello, *m.*;
(of animals) pescuezo, *m.*; (geog.)
istmo, *m.*, lengua de tierra, *f.*;
(of musical instruments) clavi-
jero, mástil, *m.*; (sew.) escote, *m.*
low-necked, (of dresses) escotado. **She fell on his n.,** Ella se
colgó de su cuello. **He won by a
n.,** Ganó por un cuello; (*fig.*)Ganó
por un tris. **to break anyone's
n.,** romperle el pescuezo. **to
wring the n. of,** torcer el pescuezo (a). **n. and n.,** parejos.
n. or nothing, todo o nada,
perdiz o no comerla. **n. stock,**
alzacuello, *m.*
neckband, *s.* tirilla de camisa, *f.*
necklace, *s.* collar, *m.*
necklet, *s.* collar, *m.*; (of fur)
cuello, *m.*
necktie, *s.* corbata, *f.*
necrological, *a.* necrológico
necrology, *s.* necrología, *f.*
necromancer, *s.* nigromante, *m.*
necromancy, *s.* nigromancia, *f.*
necropolis, *s.* necrópolis, *f.*
nectar, *s.* néctar, *m.*
nectarine, *s.* (bot.) variedad de
melocotón, *f.*
nectary, *s.* (bot.) nectario, *m.*
need, *v.t.* necesitar, haber menester, requerir, exigir. *v.i.* ser
necesario, hacer falta, carecer;
haber (de). **N. I obey?** ¿He de
obedecer? **One needs to go**

carefully, Hay que ir con
cuidado. **The work n. not be.
done for tomorrow,** No es
preciso hacer el trabajo para
mañana
need, *s.* necesidad, *f.*; cosa
necesaria, *f.*; falta; (poverty)
indigencia, pobreza, *f.*; urgencia,
f.; (shortage) escasez, carestía, *f.*
in case of n., en caso de
necesidad, en caso de urgencia.
I have n. of two more books,
Me hacen falta dos libros más
needful, *a.* necesario, preciso;
indispensable, esencial. **the n.,**
lo necesario
needfulness, *s.* necesidad, falta, *f.*
neediness, *s.* pobreza, penuria,
miseria, estrechez, *f.*
needle, *s.* (sew.) aguja, *f.*; (of
compass) brújula, aguja ima-
nada, *f.*; (monument) obelisco,
m.; (of scales) fiel, *m.*, lengüeta,
f.; (of instruments) índice, *m.*;
(*med.*) aguja de inyecciones, *f.*
(*fam.*) **to be as sharp as a n.,**
no tener pelo de tonto. **pack n.,**
aguja espartera, *f.* **n.-case,**
alfiletero, agujero, *m.* **n. maker,**
fabricante de agujas, *m.* **n.-
shaped,** en forma de aguja,
acicular
needless, *a.* innecesario, supér-
fluo. **n. to say,** claro está
needlessly, *adv.* innecesariamente, inútilmente; en vano, de
balde
needlessness, *s.* superfluidad, *f.*,
lo innecesario
needlewoman, *s.* (professional)
cosedora, *f.*; costurera, *f.* **She is
a good n.,** Ella cose bien (or
es una buena cosedora)
needlework, *s.* labor de aguja,
labor blanca, costura, *f.*; bordado, *m.* **to do n.,** hacer
costura
needs, *adv.* necesariamente, sin
remedio. *s. pl.* necesidades, *f. pl.*
if n. must, si hace falta. **N. must
when the devil drives,** A la
fuerza ahorcan
needy, *a.* necesitado, menesteroso,
corto de medios, pobre, apurado
ne'er do well, *s.* calavera, perdido, *m.* **to be a n.,** ser de mala
madera
nefarious, *a.* nefario, vil, nefando

nefariously, *adv.* vilmente, nefariamente

negation, *s.* negación, *f.*

negative, *v.t.* negar, denegar; votar en contra (de), oponerse (a); (prevent) impedir, imposibilitar. *a.* negativo. *s.* negativa, negación, *f.*; repulsa, denegación, *f.*; (*phot.*) negativo, *m.*, prueba negativa, *f.*; (*elec.*) electricidad negativa, *f.* **to reply in the n.,** dar una respuesta negativa

negatively, *adv.* negativamente

negativeness, *s.* el carácter negativo

neglect, *v.t.* descuidar, desatender; abandonar, dejar; (ignore) despreciar, no hacer caso (de); omitir, olvidar. *s.* descuido, *m.*, desatención, *f.*; inobservancia, *f.*; abandono, olvido, *m.*; desdén, *m.*, frialdad, *f.* **to fall into n.,** caer en desuso. **to n. one's obligations,** descuidar sus obligaciones

neglectful, *a.* negligente, descuidado, omiso

negligee, *s.* salto de cama, quimono, *m.*, bata, *f.*

negligence, *s.* negligencia, *f.*, descuido, *m.*; flojedad, pereza, *f.*; (of dress) desaliño, *m.*

negligent, *a.* negligente, descuidado; remiso, flojo, perezoso

negligently, *adv.* negligentemente; con indiferencia

negligible, *a.* insignificante, escaso, insuficiente; sin importancia, desdeñable

negotiable, *a.* negociable; (of a road) practicable, transitable

negotiate, *v.t.* gestionar, agenciar, tratar; (a bend) tomar; (an obstacle) salvar, franquear; *v.i.* negociar. **to n. a bill of exchange,** descontar una letra de cambio. **to n. for a contract,** tratar un contrato

negotiation, *s.* negociación, *f.*; (*com.*) gestión, transacción, *f.*; (of a bend) toma, *f.*; (of an obstacle) salto, *m.*

negotiator, *s.* negociador (-ra)

negress, *s.* negra, *f.*

negro, *a.* and *s.* negro (*m.*)

negroid, *a.* negroide, de los negros

Negus, *s.* negus, emperador de Etiopía, *m.*

neigh, *v.i.* relinchar. *s.* relincho, relinchido, *m.*

neighbour, *s.* vecino (-na); (biblical) prójimo (-ma)

neighbourhood, *s.* vecindad, *f.*, vecindario, *m.*; cercanía, *f.*, afueras, *f. pl.*, alrededores, *m. pl.*

neighbouring, *a.* vecino; cercano, inmediato, adyacente

neighbourliness, *s.* buena vecindad, *f.*

neighbourly, *a.* amistoso, sociable, bondadoso. **to be n.,** ser de buena vecindad.

neither, *a.* ningún; ninguno de los dos, e.g. N. explanation is right, Ninguna de las dos explicaciones es correcta. *conjunc.* ni, tampoco, e.g. N. Mary nor John, Ni María ni Juan. N. will he give it to her, Él tampoco se lo dará. *pron.* ni uno ni otro, ninguno, e.g. N. of them heard it, Ni uno ni otro lo oyó.

Nemesis, *s.* némesis, *f.*; justicia, *f.*

nenuphar, *s.* (*bot.*) nenúfar, *m.*

neo-, *prefix* neo. **neo-Catholic,** *a.* and *s.* neo-católico (-ca). **neo-Platonic,** neoplatónico. **neo-Platonism,** neoplatonismo, *m.*

neolithic, *a.* neolítico

neologism, *s.* neologismo, *m.*

neon, *s.* (*chem.*) neón, *m.*

neophyte, *s.* neófito (-ta); aspirante, *m.* and *f.*

neoplasm, *s.* (*med.*) neoplasma, tumor, *m.*

nephew, *s.* sobrino, *m.*

nephritic, *a.* (*med.*) nefrítico

nephritis, *s.* (*med.*) nefritis, *f.*

nepotism, *s.* nepotismo, *m.*

Nereid, *s.* nereida, *f.*

nerve, *s.* (*anat.*, *bot.*) nervio, *m.*; valor, ánimo, *m.*; vitalidad, *f.*; (*fam.*) descaro, *m.*, desvergüenza, frescura, *f.* *v.t.* animar, alentar, envalentonar; esforzar; dar fuerza (a). *v.i.* animarse, esforzarse (a). **My nerves are all on edge,** Se me crispan los nervios. **n.-cell,** neurona, *f.* **to lose one's n.,** perder la cabeza; perder los nervios. **to strain every n.,** hacer un esfuerzo supremo. **n. centre,** centro nervioso, *m.* **n.-racking,** espantoso, horripi-

lante. **n. strain,** tensión nerviosa, *f.*
nerveless, *a.* sin nervio; enervado
nerviness, *s.* nervosidad, *f.*
nervous, *a.* nervioso, asustadizo, tímido; agitado, excitado; (of style) vigoroso. **n. breakdown,** crisis nerviosa, *f.* **n. system,** sistema nervioso, *m.*
nervously, *adv.* nerviosamente; timidamente
nervousness, *s.* nervosidad, timidez, *f.*; agitación, *f.*; (of style) vigor, *m.*; energía, *f.*
nervy, *a.* nervioso
nest, *v.i.* anidar, hacerse un nido. *s.* (bird's) nido, *m.*; (animal's) madriguera, *f.*; (of drawers) juego, *m.*, serie, *f.*; (of thieves) cueva, guarida, *f.*; (*fam.*) casita, *f.*, hogar, *m.* **to feather one's n.,** hacer su agosto. **n.-egg,** (*fig.*) nidal, *m.* **n. of eggs,** nidada de huevos, *f.*
nestle, *v.t.* apoyar. *v.i.* apiñarse, hacerse un ovillo. **to n. up to a person,** apretarse contra
nestling, *s.* pichón, pollo, *m.*; pajarito, *m.*
net, *v.t.* coger con redes; obtener, coger; cubrir con redes. *v.i.* hacer redes. *s.* red, *f.*; (mesh) malla, *f.*; (fabric) tul, *m.* **net making,** manufactura de redes, *f.*
net, *a.* (*com.*) líquido, neto, limpio; (of fabric) de tul. **net amount,** importe líquido, importe neto, *m.* **net balance,** saldo líquido, *m.* **net cost,** precio neto, *m.* **net profit,** beneficio neto (or líquido), *m.*
nether, *a.* inferior, bajero, más bajo. **n. regions,** infierno, *m.*
Netherland, *a.* neerlandés, holandés
Netherlander, *s.* neerlandés (-esa), holandés (-esa)
nethermost, *a.* lo más bajo, ínfimo, más hondo
netting, *s.* red, (obra de) malla, *f.*; (*naut.*) jareta, *f.*; manufactura de redes, *f.*; pesca con redes, *f.* **wire-n.,** tela metálica, malla de alambre, *f.*
nettle, *v.t.* picar; (*fig.*) irritar, picar, fastidiar, disgustar. *s.* ortiga, *f.* **n.-rash,** urticaria, *f.*
network, *s.* red, malla, randa, *f.*;

(of communications) sistema, *m.*, red, *f.*
neuralgia, *s.* neuralgia, *f.*
neuralgic, *a.* neurálgico
neurasthenia, *s.* neurastenia, *f.*
neurasthenic, *a.* and *s.* neurasténico (-ca)
neurectomy, *s.* (*surg.*) neurectomía, *f.*
neuritis, *s.* neuritis, *f.*
neurologist, *s.* neurólogo, *m.*
neurology, *s.* neurología, *f.*
neurone, *s.* (*anat.*) neurona, *f.*
neuropath, *s.* neurópata, *m.*
neuropathic, *a.* neuropático
neurosis, *s.* neurosis, *f.*
neurotic, *a.* and *s.* neurótico (-ca)
neuter, *a.* neutro; (of verbs) intransitivo; (*zool.*, *bot.*) sin sexo
neutral, *a.* neutral; (*chem.*, *mech.*) neutro; (of colours) indeciso, indeterminado; (of persons) imparcial, indiferente. *s.* neutral, *m.* and *f.* (*mech.*) **to go into n.,** pasar a marcha neutra
neutrality, *s.* neutralidad, *f.*; indiferencia, *f.*; imparcialidad, *f.*
neutralization, *s.* neutralización, *f.*
neutralize, *v.t.* neutralizar
never, *adv.* nunca, jamás; de ningún modo, no; ni aun, ni siquiera. **Better late than n.,** Más vale tarde que nunca. **Were the hour n. so late,** Por más tarde que fuese la hora. **n. again,** nunca jamás. **n. a one,** ni siquiera uno. **n. a whit,** ni pizca. **N. mind!** ¡No importa! ¡No te preocupes! ¡No hagas caso! **n.-ceasing,** continuo, incesante. **n.-ending,** inacabable, eterno, sin fin. **n.-failing,** infalible. **n.-to-be-forgotten,** inolvidable
nevermore, *adv.* nunca jamás
nevertheless, *adv.* sin embargo, no obstante, con todo
new, *a.* nuevo; novel, fresco; distinto, diferente; moderno; (inexperienced) novato, no habituado; reciente. *adv.* (in compounds) recién. **as good as new,** como nuevo. **brand-new,** flamante, nuevecito. **new-born,** recién nacido. **new-comer,** recién llegado (-da). **new-fashioned,** de última moda. **new-found,** recién hallado. **new-**

laid egg, huevo fresco, *m.*
new moon, luna nueva, *f.*,
novilunio, *m.* new rich, ricacho
(-cha); indio, *m.* New Testament, Nuevo Testamento, *m.*
New World, Nuevo Mundo, *m.*
New York(er), *a.* and *s.* neoyorquino (-na). New Zealand-
(er), *a.* and *s.* neozelandés
(-esa)

newel, *s.* (of stair) alma, *f.*,
árbol, nabo, *m.* n.-post, pilarote
(de escalera), *m.*

newest, *a. sup.* novísimo; más
reciente

Newfoundland, *a.* de Terranova.
N. dog, perro de Terranova, *m.*

newish, *a.* bastante nuevo

newly, *adv.* nuevamente; hace
poco, recientemente. The abb.
form recién is used only with
past part., e.g. the n. painted
door, la puerta recién pintada.
the n.-weds, los desposados,
los recién casados

newness, *s.* novedad, *f.*; inexperiencia, falta de práctica, *f.*;
innovación, *f.*

news, *s. pl.* noticias, *f. pl.*; nueva,
f.; reporte, aviso, *m.*; novedad,
f. No n. is good n., Falta de
noticias, buena señal. piece of
n., noticia, *f.* What's the n.?
¿Qué hay de nuevo? n. agency,
agencia de noticias, agencia
periodística, *f.* n.-agent, agente
de la prensa, *m.*; vendedor (-ra)
de periódicos, *m.* n. bulletin, (*rad.*)
boletín de noticias, *m.* (*fam.*)
n.-hound, gacetillero (-ra). n.
items, noticias de actualidad, *f.
pl.* n.-print, papel para periódicos, *m.* n.-room, gabinete de
lectura, *m.* n. reel, revista
cinematográfica, *f.*, actualidades,
f. pl. n.-stand, quiosco de periódicos, *m.* n. theatre, cine de
actualidades, *m.*

newspaper, *s.* periódico, diario,
m. n. cutting, recorte de
periódico, *m.* n. paragraph,
suelto, *m.* n. reporter, reportero
(-ra); periodista, *m.* and *f.* n.
reporting, reporterismo, *m.* n.
serial, folletín, *m.*, novela por
entregas, *f.* n. vendor, vendedor
(-ra) de periódicos, *s.*

newsy, *a.* (*fam.*) lleno de noticias,
noticioso

newt, *s.* tritón, *m.*

Newtonian, *a.* neutoniano

next, *a.* (of place) siguiente,
vecino, contiguo; (of time)
próximo, siguiente. on the n.
page, a la página siguiente.
the n. day, el día siguiente.
the n.-door house, la casa
vecina. the n. life, la otra
vida. n. month (year), el mes
(año) próximo (or que viene).
n. time, otra vez, la próxima
vez

next, *adv.* (of time) luego, en
seguida; (of place) inmediatamente después. I come n.,
Ahora me toca a mí. It is n. to a
certainty that . . ., Es casi
seguro que . . . the n. best, el
segundo. the n. of kin, los
parientes cercanos. to wear n.
to the skin, llevar sobre la piel.
n. to, al lado de, junto a;
primero después de; casi. n. to
nothing, casi nada, muy poco.
What n.? ¿Qué más?; ¿Y
ahora qué?

nib, *s.* punto, tajo (de una
pluma), *m.*

nibble, *v.t.* mordiscar, mordis-
quear, roer; (horses) rozar;
(fish) picar; (*fig.*) considerar,
tantear; *v.i.* picar. *s.* mordisco,
m.; roedura, *f.*

niblick, *s.* (golf) niblick, *m.*

Nicaraguan, *a.* and *s.* nicaragüeño (-ña)

nice, *a.* escrupuloso, minucioso,
exacto; (of persons) simpático,
afable, amable; fino; (of things)
agradable, bonito; bueno; sutil,
delicado; (*fam., iron.*) bonito. a
n. point, un punto delicado.
a n. view, una vista agradable
(or bonita). n.-looking, guapo.
n. people, gente fina, *f.*; gente
simpática, *f.*

nicely, *adv.* muy bien; con
elegancia; primorosamente; con
amabilidad, gentilmente; agradablemente

Nicene, *a.* niceno, de Nicea

niceness, *s.* exactitud, minuciosidad, *f.*; (of persons) bondad,
amabilidad, *f.*; amenidad, hermosura, *f.*; lo bonito; sutileza, *f.*;
refinamiento, *m.*

nicety, *s.* exactitud, *f.*; sutileza,
f., refinamiento, *m.* niceties,

s. pl. detalles, *m. pl.* **to a n.**, con la mayor precisión; **a la perfección**

niche, *s.* nicho, templete, *m.*; (vaulted) hornacina, *f.* (*fig.*) **to find a n. for oneself,** encontrarse una buena posición; situarse

nick, *v.t.* cortar en muescas, mellar, tarjar. *s.* mella, muesca, *f.* **in the n. of time,** en el momento oportuno, a tiempo

nickel, *s.* níquel, *m.*; (*com.*) moneda de níquel, *f.* **n.-plated,** niquelado

nickname, *v.t.* apodar, motejar, apellidar. *s.* apodo, sobrenombre, mote, *m.*

nicotine, *s.* nicotina, *f.*

nicotinism, *s.* nicotismo, *m.*

nictitating membrane, *s.* (*anat.*) membrana nictitante, *f.*

niece, *s.* sobrina, *f.*

niggardliness, *s.* tacañería, avaricia, parsimonia, mezquindad, *f.*

niggardly, *a.* tacaño, avaricioso, mezquino, ruin, miserable

nigger, *s.* negro (-ra). **to work like a n.,** trabajar como un negro. **n. in the wood pile,** gato encerrado, *m.*

niggling, *a.* nimio, meticuloso; escrupuloso, minucioso

nigh. See **near**

night, *s.* noche, *f.*; (*fig.*) oscuridad, *f.*, tinieblas, *f. pl.* **all n.,** toda la noche, la noche entera. **all n. service,** servicio nocturno permanente, *m.* **at or by n.,** de noche. **every n.,** todas las noches, cada noche. **Good n.!** ¡Buenas noches! **last n.,** ayer por la noche, anoche, la noche pasada. **restless n.,** noche mala, noche toledana, *f.* **the n. before last,** anteayer por la noche, *m.* **to-n.,** esta noche. **to-morrow n.,** mañana por la noche. **to be n.,** ser de noche. **to spend the n.,** pernoctar, pasar la noche. **n.-bird,** pájaro nocturno, *m.*; (*fam.*) trasnochador (-ra). **n.-blindness,** nictalopia, *f.* **n.-cap,** gorro de dormir, *m.* **n. clothes,** traje de dormir, *m.* **n. club,** cabaret, *m.* **n. dew,** relente, sereno, *m.* **n. flying,** vuelo nocturno, *m.* **n.-jar,** (*orn.*)

chotacabras, *m.* **n.-light,** mariposa, lamparilla, *f.* **n. mail,** último correo, *m.*; tren correo de la noche, *m.* **n. school,** escuela nocturna, *f.* **n. shift,** turno de noche, *m.* **n. watch,** ronda de noche, *f.*; (*naut.*) sonochada, *f.* **n. watchman,** (in the street) sereno, *m.*; (of a building) vigilante, *m.*

nightfall, *s.* anochecer, crepúsculo, atardecer, *m.*

nightgown, *s.* camisa de noche, *f.*

nightingale, *s.* ruiseñor, *m.*

nightly, *a.* de noche; nocturno, nocturnal. *adv.* todas las noches, cada noche

nightmare, *s.* pesadilla, *f.*

nightmarish, *a.* de pesadilla, horrible

nightshade, *s.* (*bot.*) hierba mora, *f.*, solano, *m.*

Nihilism, *s.* nihilismo, *m.*

nihilist, *s.* nihilista, *m.* and *f.*.

nimble, *a.* ágil, activo; vivo, listo. **n.-fingered,** ligero de dedos. **n.-witted,** despierto, vivo

nimbleness, *s.* agilidad, actividad, *f.*; viveza, habilidad, *f.*

nimbly, *adv.* ágilmente, ligeramente

nimbus, *s.* nimbo, *m.*, aureola, *f.*

nincompoop, *s.* papirote, *m.*, papanatas, *m.* and *f.*, tonto (-ta)

nine, *a.* and *s.* nueve (*m.*). **He is n.,** Tiene nueve años. **The N.,** las nueve Musas. **n. o'clock,** las nueve. **to be dressed up to the nines,** estar hecho un brazo de mar

ninefold, *a.* and *adv.* nueve veces

ninepins, *s.* juego de bolos, *m.*

nineteen, *a.* and *s.* diez y nueve, diecinueve (*m.*)

nineteenth, *a.* décimonono. *s.* (of month) el diez y nueve; (of monarchs) diez y nueve. **the n. century,** el siglo diez y nueve

ninetieth, *a.* nonagésimo, noventa

ninety, *a.* and *s.* noventa (*m.*). **n.-one,** noventa y uno. **n.-two,** noventa dos. **the n.-first chapter,** el capítulo noventa y uno

ninny, *s.* parapoco, chancleta, *m.* and *f.*; mentecato (-ta)

ninth, *a.* noveno, nono. *s.* nueve, *m.*; (of the month) el nueve (of sovereigns) nono. **one n.,** un noveno

ninthly, *adv.* en noveno (or nono) lugar

nip, *v.t.* pellizcar, pinchar; mordiscar, morder; (wither) marchitar; (freeze) helar; (run) correr. *v.i.* pinchar; picar (el viento). *s.* pellizco, pinchazo, *m.*; mordisco, *m.*; (of spirits) trago, *m.*; copita, *f.*; (in the air) viento frío, hielo, *m.* **to nip in,** colarse dentro, deslizarse en. **to nip off,** pirarse, mudarse. (*fig.*) **to nip in the bud,** cortar en flor

nippers, *s. pl.* alicates, *m. pl.*; tenacillas, pinzas, *f. pl.*

nipping, *s.* pinchadura, *f.*; mordedura, *f. a.* punzante; helado, glacial, mordiente. **n.** off, (of a point) despuntadura, *f.*

nipple, *s.* pezón, *m.*; pezón artificial, *m.*

nit, *s.* (*ent.*) liendre, *f.*

nitrate, *s.* (*chem.*) nitrato, *m.*

nitre, *s.* salitre, *m.*

nitric, *a.* nítrico

nitrite, *s.* (*chem.*) nitrito, *m.*

nitro-, *prefix* (*chem.*) nitro. **n.-cellulose,** algodón pólvora, *m.* **n.-glycerine,** nitroglicerina, *f.*

nitrobenzol, *s.* (*chem.*) nitrobenzol, *m.*

nitrogen, *s.* (*chem.*) nitrógeno, *m.*

nitrous, *a.* nitroso, salitral

no, *a.* ningún, ninguno, ninguna, e.g. **by no means,** de ningún modo. No is often not translated in Sp., e.g. **I have no time,** No tengo tiempo. *adv.* no. *s.* voto negativo, no, *m.* **to be of no account,** no tener importancia; no significar nada. **to be no good for,** no servir para. **to be of no use,** ser inútil. **to have no connection with,** no tener nada que ver con. **for no reason,** sin motivo alguno. **No Admittance,** Entrada Prohibida. **no, indeed,** no, por cierto. **no-man's land,** tierra de nadie, *f.* **no more,** no más. **No more of this!** ¡No hablemos más de eso! **no one,** nadie, ninguno. **no sooner,** no bien, tan pronto (como). **no such thing,** no tal. **No Thoroughfare,** Prohibido el Paso. **whether or no,** sea o no sea

Noah's Ark, *s.* arca de Noé, *f.*

nobility, *s.* nobleza, *f.*; (of rank) aristocracia, nobleza, *f.*; (of conduct) caballerosidad, hidalguía, generosidad, bondad, *f.*; (grandeur) grandeza, sublimidad, *f.* **the higher n.,** los nobles de primera clase

noble, *a.* noble; (in rank) aristocrático, noble, linajudo; (of conduct) caballeroso, generoso; (of buildings) sublime, magnífico. *s.* noble, *m.*, aristócrata, *m.* and *f.* **to make n.,** ennoblecer. **n.-mindedness,** generosidad, grandeza de alma, *f.* **n. title,** título de nobleza, título del reino, *m.*

noblewoman, *s.* dama noble, mujer noble, aristócrata, *f.*

nobly, *adv.* noblemente, generosamente. **n. born,** noble de nacimiento

nobody, *s.* nadie, ninguno. **There was n. there,** No había nadie allí. (*fam.*) **a n.,** un (una) cualquiera, una persona insignificante. **n. else,** nadie más, ningún otro

nocturnal, *a.* nocturno, nocherniego, nocturnal

nocturne, *s.* (*mus.*) nocturno, *m.*

nod, *v.t.* inclinar la cabeza; hacer una señal (or señas) con la cabeza; *v.i.* dar cabezadas; cabecear; (of trees) mecerse, inclinarse; inclinar la cabeza. *s.* señal (or seña) con la cabeza, *f.*; inclinación de la cabeza, *f.*; cabeceo, *m.*, cabezada, *f.* **A nod is as good as a wink,** A buen entendedor pocas palabras. **He nodded to me as he passed,** Me saludó con la cabeza al pasar. **He signed to me with a nod,** Me hizo una señal con la cabeza

nodding, *a.* que cabecea; (*bot.*) colgante, inclinado; temblante. *s.* cabeceo, *m.*; saludo con la cabeza, *m.*

noddle, *s.* mollera, *f.*

node, *s.* (*bot.*, *med.*) nudo, *m.*

nodule, *s.* nódulo, *m.*; nudillo, *m.*

noise, *s.* ruido, son, *m.*; tumulto, clamor, estruendo, alboroto, *m.* **to make a n.,** hacer ruido. **to n. abroad,** divulgar, publicar

noiseless, *a.* silencioso, callado, sin ruido

noiselessness, *s.* silencio, *m.*, falta de ruido, *f.*

noisily, *adv.* ruidosamente

noisiness, *s.* ruido, estrépito, tumulto, clamor, *m.*; (of voices) gritería, *f.*

noisome, *a.* ofensivo; fétido, apestoso

noisy, *a.* ruidoso; estruendoso; estrepitoso, clamoroso

nomad, *a.* nómada, errante; (of flocks) trashumante. *s.* nómada, *m.* and *f.*

nomadism, *s.* nomadismo, *m.*

nomenclature, *s.* nomenclatura, *f.*

nominal, *a.* nominal; titular; insignificante, de poca importancia. **the n. head,** el director en nombre

nominalism, *s.* nominalismo, *m.*

nominalist, *a.* and *s.* nominalista (*m.* and *f.*)

nominally, *adv.* nominalmente, en nombre

nominate, *v.t.* nombrar, designar, elegir; fijar, señalar

nominating, *a.* nominador

nomination, *s.* nombramiento, *m.*, nominación, *f.*; señalamiento, *m.*

nominative, *a.* and *s.* (*gram.*) nominativo (*m.*)

nominator, *s.* nominador (-ra)

nominee, *s.* candidato favorito, *m.*

non, *adv.* non; des-; in-; falta de. **non-acceptance,** rechazo, *m.* **non-acquaintance,** ignorancia, *f.* **non-admission,** no admisión, *f.*; denegación, *f.*, rechazo, *m.* **non-aggression,** no agresión, *f.* **non-alcoholic,** no alcohólico. **non-appearance,** ausencia, *f.*; (*law*) no comparecencia, contumacia, *f.* **non-arrival,** ausencia, *f.*; falta de recibo, *f.* **non-attendance,** falta de asistencia, ausencia, *f.* **non-combatant,** no combatiente. **non-commissioned officer,** oficial subalterno, *m.* **non-committal,** evasivo, equívoco, ambiguo. **non-compliance,** falta de obediencia, *f.* **non-concurrence,** falta de acuerdo, *f.* **non-conducting,** no conductivo. **non-conductor,** mal conductor, *m.*; (*elec.*) aislador,

m. **non-contagious,** no contagioso. **non-co-operation,** (*pol.*) resistencia pasiva, *f.*; no cooperación, *f.* **non-delivery,** falta de entrega, *f.* **non-essential,** no esencial, prescindible. **non-execution,** no cumplimiento, *m.* **non-existence,** no existencia, *f.* **non-existent,** inexistente, no existente. **non-intervention,** no intervención, *f.* **non-manufacturing,** no industrial. **non-member,** visitante, *m.* and *f.* **non-observance,** incumplimiento, *m.*; violación, *f.* **non-payment,** falta de pago, *f.* **non-performance,** falta de ejecución, *f.* **non-poisonous,** no venenoso, innocuo. **non-resistance,** falta de resistencia, *f.*; obediencia pasiva, *f.* **non-skid,** antideslizante, antirresbaladizo. **non-smoking,** que no fuma; (of a railway compartment, etc.) para no fumadores. **non-stop,** continuo, incesante; directo, sin parar; (*aer.*) sin escalas

nonagenarian, *a.* and *s.* nonagenario (-ia)

nonchalance, *s.* aplomo, *m.*, indiferencia, frialdad, calma, *f.*

nonchalant, *a.* indiferente, frío, impasible

nonchalantly, *adv.* con indiferencia

nonconformist, *a.* and *s.* disidente (*m.* and *f.*)

nonconformity, *s.* disidencia, *f.*

nondescript, *a.* indeterminado, indefinido, indeciso, mediocre

none, *pron.* nadie, ninguno; nada. *a.* and *s.* ninguno (-na). *adv.* no; de ningún modo, de ninguna manera. **I have n.,** No lo tengo, No tengo ninguno. **We have n. of your things,** No tenemos ninguna de tus cosas. **I was n. the worse,** No me hallaba peor. **N. can read his account with pleasure,** Nadie puede leer su narración con gusto. **n. the less,** no menos; sin embargo

nonentity, *s.* persona sin importancia, medianía, *f.*, cero, *m.*

nones, *s. pl.* (*ecc.*) nona, *f.*; (Roman Calendar) nonas, *f. pl.*

nonplussed, *a.* cortado, perplejo, confuso

nonsense, *s.* disparate, despropósito, desatino, *m.*, absurdidad, *f.*; (*fam.*) galimatías, *m.*; pamplina, patraña, *f.* **to talk n.,** hablar sin ton ni son. **N.!** ¡A otro perro con este hueso! ¡Patrañas!

nonsensical, *a.* absurdo, ridículo, disparatado

noodle, *s.* (*cul.*) tallarín, *m.*; (*fam.*) mentecato (-ta), bobo (-ba)

nook, *s.* escondrijo, lugar retirado, rincón, *m.*

noon, *s.* mediodía, *m.*; (*fig.*) punto culminante, apogeo, *m.* *a.* de mediodía, meridional. **at n.,** a mediodía

noose, *v.t.* coger con lazos. *s.* lazo corredizo, dogal, *m.*

nopal, *s.* (*bot.*) nopal, *m.*

nor, *conjunc.* ni, no, tampoco. **He removed neither his coat nor his hat,** No se quitó ni el gabán ni el sombrero. **Nor was this the first time,** Y no fué ésta la primera vez. **Nor I,** Ni yo tampoco

Nordic, *a.* and *s.* nórdico (-ca)

norm, *s.* modelo, *m.*, norma, regla, pauta, *f.*; (of size) marca, *f.*; (*bot., zool.*) tipo, *m.*

normal, *a.* normal; común, natural, corriente, regular; (*math.*) perpendicular, normal. *s.* condición normal, *f.*, estado normal, *m.*; (*math.*) normal, *f.* **to become n.,** normalizarse, hacerse normal. **to make n.,** normalizar. **N. School,** Escuela Normal, *f.*

normality, *s.* normalidad, *f.*

normalization, *s.* normalización, *f.*

normalize, *v.t.* normalizar

normally, *adv.* normalmente

Norman, *a.* and *s.* normando (-da)

Norse, *s.* noruego (language), *m.* *a.* escandinavo

Norseman, *s.* normando, viking (*pl.* -os), hombre del norte, *m.*

north, *s.* norte, *m.* *a.* del norte, septentrional. **n. by west,** norte, cuarta noroeste. **n. of the city,** al norte de la ciudad. **N.-American,** *a.* and *s.* norteamericano (-na). **n.-east,** *a.* and

s. nordeste (*m.*). **n.-easter,** viento del nordeste, *m.* **n.-easterly,** del nordeste (winds). **n.-eastern,** del nordeste (places). **n.-eastward,** hacia el nordeste. **n.-n.-east,** nornordeste, *m.* **n.-n.-west,** nornorueste, *m.* **n.-polar,** ártico. **N. Star,** estrella del norte, estrella polar, *f.* **n.-west,** noroeste, *m.* **n.-wester,** viento del noroeste, *m.* **n.-westerly,** del noroeste (winds). **n.-westerly gale,** temporal del noroeste, *m.* **n.-western,** del noroeste; situado al noroeste. **n.-westwards,** hacia el noroeste. **n. wind,** el viento del norte, el cierzo

northern, *a.* del norte, septentrional, norteño; (of races) nórdico. **N. Cross,** crucero, *m.* **n. lights,** aurora boreal, *f.*

northerner, *s.* hombre del norte, *m.*, habitante del norte, *m.* and *f.*

northernmost, *a. sup.* al extremo norte, más septentrional

northwards, *adv.* hacia el norte

Norwegian, *a.* and *s.* noruego (-ga); (language) noruego, *m.*

nose, *s.* nariz, *f.*; (of animals) hocico, *m.*; (sense of smell) olfato, *m.*; (of ships) proa, *f.*; (of jug) pico, *m.*, boca, *f.*; (projecting piece) cuerno, *m.*, nariz, *f.*; (of aeroplane) cabeza, *f.* *v.t.* acariciar con la nariz; avanzar lentamente. *v.i.* husmear, olfatear. **to n. into,** (*fam.*) meter las narices, poner baza. **to n. out,** descubrir, averiguar. **to bleed at the n.,** echar sangre por las narices. **to blow one's n.,** sonar (or limpiarse) las narices. **to keep one's n. to the grindstone,** estar sobre el yunque, batir el cobre. (*fig.*) **to lead by the n.,** tener a uno agarrado por las narices. **to pay through the n.,** costar un ojo de la cara. **to speak through the n.,** ganguear. **to turn up one's n.,** (*fig.*) hacer gestos (a), volver la cara. **flat n.,** nariz chata, *f.* **snub n.,** nariz respingona, *f.* **well-shaped n.,** nariz perfilada, *f.* **under one's n.,** bajo las narices de uno. **n.-bag,** cebadera, mochila, *f.*; morral, *m.* **n.-bleeding,** (*med.*)

epistaxis, f.; hemorragia de las narices, f. **n.-dive**, (*aer.*) descenso de cabeza, picado, *m.* *v.i.* picar. **n.-piece**, (of microscope) ocular, *m.* **n.-ring**, (of a bull, etc.) narigón, *m.*

-nosed, *a.* de nariz . . ., con la nariz . . .

nosegay, *s.* ramillete, *m.*

nosey-Parker, *s.* (*fam.*) mequetrefe, *m.*; cócora, *m.* and *f.*

nostalgia, *s.* nostalgia, añoranza, *f.*

nostalgic, *a.* nostálgico

nostril, *s.* ventana de la nariz, *f.* *s.* *pl.* nostrils, narices, *f.* *pl.*

nostrum, *s.* panacea, *f.*, cúralotodo, *m.*; medicina patentada, *f.*

not, *adv.* no; sin; ni, ni siquiera. Is it not true? We think not, ¿No es verdad? No lo creemos. You have seen Mary, have you not? ¿Vd. ha visto a María, verdad? not caring whether he came or not, sin preocuparse de que viniese o no. not that he will come, no es decir que venga. not at all, de ningún modo; (courtesy) ¡de nada! not even, ni siquiera. not guilty, no culpable. not one, ni uno. not so much as, no tanto como; ni siquiera. not to say, por no decir

notability, *s.* notabilidad, *f.*; (person) notable, *m.* and *f.*, persona de importancia, *f.*

notable, *a.* notable, señalado, memorable; digno de atención. *s.* persona eminente, *f.*, notable, *m.* and *f.*

notably, *adv.* notablemente, señaladamente

notarial, *a.* notarial, de notario

notary, *s.* notario, escribano, *m.*

notation, *s.* notación, *f.*

notch, *v.t.* cortar muescas (en); mellar, ranurar, entallar. *s.* muesca, mella, ranura, entalladura, *f.*

note, *v.t.* notar, observar; anotar, apuntar; advertir, hacerse cuenta de. *s.* (*mus.*) nota, *f.*; son, acento, *m.*; (letter) recado, billete, *m.*; anotación, glosa, *f.*; apuntación, *f.*, apunte, *m.*, nota, *f.*; (importance) importancia, distinción, *f.*; (*com.*) vale, abo-

naré, *m.*; (sign) marca, señal, *f.* to n. down, anotar. worthy of note, digno de atención. **n.-book**, libro de apuntes, cuaderno, *m.*, libreta, *f.* **n.-case**, cartera, *f.* (*com.*) **n.** of hand, pagaré, *m.* **n.-paper**, papel de escribir, *m.* **n.-taker**, apuntador (-ra)

noted, *a.* célebre, famoso, ilustre, eminente, insigne

noteworthy, *a.* digno de nota, notable, digno de atención

nothing, *s.* nada, *f.*; la nada; cero, *m.* *adv.* en nada. to come to n., anonadarse, fracasar. to do n., no hacer nada. to do n. but, no hacer más que. to have n. to do with, no tener nada que ver con; (*fam.*) no tener arte ni párte en. There is n. else to do, No hay nada más que hacer; No hay más remedio. There is n. to fear, No hay de qué tener miedo. We could make n. of the book, No llegamos a comprender el libro. for n., de balde, en vano; gratis. next to n., casi nada. n. else or more, nada más. n. like, ni con mucho. n. much, poca cosa. n. new, nada nuevo. n. similar, nada semejante. n. to speak of, poca cosa

nothingness, *s.* nada, *f.*

notice, *v.t.* observar, reparar en, darse cuenta (de); marcar, caer en la cuenta (de); fijarse (en). *s.* observación, atención, *f.*; aviso, *m.*, notificación, *f.*; anuncio, *m.*; (term) plazo, *m.*; (review) crítica, *f.* at short n., a corto aviso. until further n., hasta nuevo aviso (or orden). to attract n., atraer la atención. I hadn't noticed, No me había fijado. to be beneath one's n., no merecer su atención. to be under n., estar dimitido. to bring to the notice of, dar noticia de. to escape n., pasar desapercibido. to give n., hacer saber, informar; (of employer) despedir (a); (of employee) dimitir, dar la dimisión. to take n. of, notar, darse cuenta de; hacer caso, atender (a). **n. board**, letrero, tablero de anuncios, *m.* **n. to quit,** desahucio, *m.*

noticeable, *a.* perceptible, evidente; digno de observación, notable

noticeably, *adv.* perceptiblemente; notablemente

notifiable, *a.* declarable, notificable

notification, *s.* notificación, intimación, advertencia, *f.,* aviso, *m.*

notify, *v.t.* notificar, comunicar, avisar, intimar, hacer saber

notion, *s.* noción, idea, *f.,* concepto, *m.;* (view) opinión, *f.,* parecer, *m.;* (novelty) novedad, *f.;* artículo de fantasía, *m.* **I have a n. that . . .,** Tengo la idea de que . . ., Sospecho que . . . **I haven't a n.,** No tengo idea

notoriety, *s.* notoriedad, publicidad, *f.;* escándalo, *m.;* persona notoria, *f.*

notorious, *a.* notorio, famoso, conocido; escandaloso, sensacional

notoriously, *adv.* notoriamente

notwithstanding, *prep.* a pesar de. *adv.* sin embargo, no obstante. *conjunc.* aunque, bien que, por más que

nougat, *s.* turrón, *m.*

nought, *s.* (*math.*) cero, *m.;* nada, *f.*

noun, *s.* substantivo, nombre, *m.*

nourish, *v.t.* sustentar, alimentar, nutrir; (*fig.*) fomentar, favorecer

nourishing, *a.* nutritivo, alimenticio, nutricio

nourishment, *s.* nutrición, *f.;* sustento, *m.;* alimento, *m.;* (*fig.*) fomento, pasto, *m.*

novel, *a.* nuevo, original, inacostumbrado. *s.* novela, *f.* **n. of** roguery, novela picaresca, *f.*

novelette, *s.* novela corta, *f.*

novelist, *s.* novelista, *m.* and *f.*

novelty, *s.* novedad, *f.;* innovación, *f.;* cambio, *m.*

November, *s.* noviembre, *m.*

novena, *s.* (*ecc.*) novena, *f.*

novice, *s* (*ecc.*) novicio (-ia); comenzante, principiante, *m.* and *f.*, aspirante, *m.*

novitiate, *s.* (*ecc.*) noviciado, *m.*

novocain, *s.* (*med.*) novocaína, *f.*

now, *adv.* ahora, actualmente, al presente, a la fecha; en seguida, ahora, inmediatamente; poco ha, hace poco; pues bien. *interj.* ¡A ver! ¡Vamos! *conjunc.* pero, mas. *s.* presente, *m.,* actualidad, *f.* **before now,** antes, en otras ocasiones, ya, previamente. **just now,** ahora mismo, hace poco. **now . . . now,** ya . . . ya; sucesivamente, en turno. **now and then,** de vez en cuando, de tarde en tarde. **now that,** ya que, ahora que, dado que. **until now,** hasta el presente, hasta aquí, hasta ahora

nowadays, *adv.* hoy en día, actualmente, en nuestros días

nowhere, *adv.* en ninguna parte. **in the middle of n.,** donde Cristo dió las tres voces. **n. else,** en ninguna otra parte. (*fam.*) **n. near,** ni con mucho; muy lejos (de)

nowise, *adv.* de ningún modo, en modo alguno, de ninguna manera

noxious, *a.* dañoso, nocivo; pestífero

noxiousness, *s.* nocividad, *f.*

nozzle, *s.* (of a hose-pipe) boquilla, *f.;* (*mech.*) gollete, *m.;* tubo de salida, *m.,* tobera, *f.;* inyector, *m.*

nuance, *s.* matiz, *m.,* gradación, sombra, *f.*

Nubian, *a.* and *s.* nubio (-ia)

nubile, *a.* núbil

nuclear, *a.* nuclear

nucleus, *s.* núcleo, *m.;* centro, foco, *m.*

nude, *a.* desnudo, nudo

nudge, *v.t.* dar un codazo (a). *s.* codazo, *m.*

nudism, *s.* nudismo, *m.*

nudist, *s.* nudista, *m.* and *f.*

nudity, *s.* desnudez, *f.*

nugget, *s.* (*min.*) pepita, *f.*

nuisance, *s.* molestia, incomodidad, *f.,* fastidio, *m.;* (*fam.*) tostón, *m.,* lata, *f.* **to make a n. of oneself,** meterse donde no le llaman, ser un pelmazo. **What a n.!** ¡Qué lata! ¡Qué fastidio!

null, *a.* nulo, inválido, sin fuerza legal. **n. and void,** nulo y sin efecto

nullification, *s.* anulación, invalidación, *f.*

nullity, *s.* nulidad, *f.*

numb, *v.t.* entumecer, entorpecer, *a.* entumecido; torpe, dormido; paralizado; (*fig.*) insensible, pasmado. **n. with cold,** entumecido de frío

number, *v.t.* numerar, contar; poner número (a); (pages of a book) foliar; ascender a. *s.* número, *m.*; (figure) cifra, *f.*; (crowd) multitud, muchedumbre, *f.*; cantidad, *f.*; (of a periodical) ejemplar, *m.*; (*gram.*) número, *m.*; *pl.* versos, *m. pl.* **Numbers,** (Bible) Números, *m. pl.*; **to be numbered among,** figurar entre. **among the n. of,** entre la muchedumbre de. **a n. of,** varios, muchos, una cantidad de. **in great n.,** en gran número; en su mayoría. **Nº 6 Peace Street,** Calle de la Paz nº 6 (número) 6. **one of their n.,** uno entre ellos. **n. board,** (racing) indicador, *m.* **n. plate,** (*aut.*) chapa de identidad, placa de número, *f.*

numbering, *s.* numeración, *f.*

numberless, *a.* innumerable, sin número, sin fin, infinito

numbness, *s.* entumecimiento, entorpecimiento, *m.*; (*fig.*) insensibilidad, *f.*

numeral, *a.* numeral. *s.* número, *m.*, cifra, *f.*; (*gram.*) nombre o adjetivo numeral, *m.*

numerator, *s.* numerador

numerical, *a.* numérico

numerically, *adv.* numéricamente

numerous, *a.* numeroso; nutrido, grande; muchos (-as)

numerousness, *s.* numerosidad, multitud, muchedumbre, *f.*

numismatic, *a.* numismático. *s. pl.* **numismatics,** numismática, *f.*

numismatist, *s.* numismático, *m.*

numskull, *s.* zote, topo, *m.*

nun, *s.* monja, religiosa, *f.* **to become a nun,** profesar, tomar el hábito, meterse monja

nunciature, *s.* nunciatura, *f.*

nuncio, *s.* nuncio, *m.* **acting n.,** pronuncio, *m.*

nunnery, *s.* convento de monjas, *m.*

nuptial, *a.* nupcial. *s. pl.* **nuptials,** nupcias, *f. pl.*, enlace, *m.*

N. Mass, (*ecc.*) misa de velaciones, *f.* **n. song,** epitalamio, *m.*

nurse, *v.t.* criar; dar de mamar (a), amamantar; (the sick) cuidar, asistir; (fondle) acariciar, mecer; (*fig.*) fomentar, promover. *v.i.* trabajar como enfermera. *s.* (of the sick) enfermera, *f.*; (wet) nodriza, ama de leche, *f.*; (children's) niñera, *f.*; (*fig.*) fomentador, *m.* **male n.,** enfermero, *m.*

nursery, *s.* (*agr.*) plantel, semillero, criadero, *m.*; cuarto de los niños, *m.*; (*fig.*) sementera, *f.*; semillero, *m.* **n. governess,** aya, *f.* **n. rhyme,** canción infantil, *f.*

nurseryman, *s.* horticultor, *m.*; jardinero, *m.*

nursing, *s.* lactancia, crianza, *f.*; (of the sick) asistencia, *f.*, cuido, *m.* **n. home,** clínica, *f.* **n. mother,** madre lactante, *f.*

nurture, *v.t.* alimentar; criar, educar. *s.* nutrición, alimentación, *f.*; crianza, educación, *f.*

nut, *v.i.* coger nueces. *s.* (*bot.*) nuez, *f.*; (*mech.*) tuerca, hembra de tornillo, *f.* (*fam.*) **to be a tough nut to crack,** ser un tío de cuidado. **to crack nuts,** cascar nueces. **to go nutting,** ir a coger nueces. **cashew nut,** anacardo, *m.* **loose nut,** (*mech.*) tuerca aflojada, *f.* **nut-brown,** castaño. **nut tree,** nogal, *m.*

nutcrackers, *s. pl.* cascanueces, quebrantanueces, *m.*

nutmeg, *s.* nuez moscada, nuez de especia, *f.*

nutria, *s.* (*zool.*) nutria, *f.*

nutriment, *s.* nutrimento, alimento, *m.*

nutrition, *s.* nutrición, alimentación, *f.*

nutritious, nutritive, *a.* nutritivo, alimenticio, alible

nutshell, *s.* cáscara de nuez, *f.* **to put in a n.,** decir en resumidas cuentas

nutty, *a.* de nuez

nux vomica, *s.* nuez vómica, *f.*

nuzzle, *v.t.* acariciar con la nariz

nylon, *s.* nilón, nylon, *m.* **n. stockings,** medias de cristal (or de nilón), *f. pl.*

nymph, s. ninfa, f.; (ent.) crisálida, f. **n.-like,** como una ninfa; de ninfa

nymphomania, s. ninfomanía, f., furor uterino, m.

O

o, s. (letter) o, f. interj. ¡o! **O that ...!** ¡Ojalá que!

oaf, s. zoquete, zamacuco, m.

oafish, a. lerdo, torpe

oafishness, s. torpeza, estupidez, f.

oak, s. (tree and wood) roble, m. **a.** de roble. **carved oak,** roble tallado, m. **holm-oak,** encina, f. **oak-apple,** agalla, f. **oak grove,** robledo, m.

oakum, s. estopa, f.

oar, s. remo, m. **to lie on the oars,** cesar de remar. **to pull at the oars,** bogar, remar. **to put in one's oar,** (fam.) meter baza. **to ship the oars,** armar los remos. **to unship the oars,** desarmar los remos. **oar-stroke,** palada, f.

oared, a. provisto de remos, de ... remos

oarsman, s. remero, bogador, m.

oarsmanship, s. arte de remar, m. or f.

oasis, s. oasis, m.

oast, s. horno para secar el lúpulo, m.

oat, s. (bot.) avena, f. **wild oat,** avena silvestre, f. **to sow one's wild oats,** correrla, andarse a la flor del berro. **oat field,** avenal, m.

oatcake, s. torta de avena, f.

oath, s. juramento, m.; (curse) blasfemia, f., reniego, m. **on o.,** bajo juramento. **to break an o.,** violar el juramento. **to put on o.,** tomar juramento, hacer prestar juramento. **to take an o.,** prestar (or hacer) juramento. **to take the o. of allegiance,** jurar la bandera

oatmeal, s. harina de avena, f.

obbligato, s. (mus.) obligado, m.

obduracy, s. obduración, obstinación, terquedad, f.

obdurate, a. obstinado, terco, porfiado. **He is o. to our**

requests, Es sordo a nuestros ruegos

obedience, s. obediencia, sumisión, docilidad, f. **blind o.,** obediencia ciega, f. **in o. to,** conforme a, de acuerdo con

obedient, a. obediente, sumiso, dócil. **to be o. to,** ser obediente (a), obedecer (a)

obediently, adv. obedientemente, dócilmente. **Yours o.,** su atento servidor (su att. s.)

obeisance, s. reverencia, cortesía, f., saludo, m.; (homage) homenaje, m.

obelisk, s. obelisco, m.

obese, a. obeso, corpulento, grueso, gordo

obesity, s. obesidad, gordura, corpulencia, f.

obey, v.t. and v.i. obedecer. v.t. (carry out) cumplir, observar. **to be obeyed,** ser obedecido.

obfuscate, v.t. ofuscar, cegar

obfuscation, s. ofuscamiento, m., confusión, f.

obituary, a. mortuorio, necrológico. s. obituario, m., necrología, f. **o. column,** (in newspaper) sección necrológica, f. **o. notice,** esquela de defunción, f.

object, s. objeto, artículo, m., cosa, f.; (purpose) propósito, intento, m.; (aim) fin, término, m.; (gram.) complemento, m.; (fam.) individuo, m. v.t. objetar, poner reparos (a). v.i. oponerse, poner objeciones. **I o. to that remark,** Protesto contra esa observación. **If you don't o.,** Si Vd. no tiene inconveniente. **o. finder,** objetivo, m. **o. lesson,** lección de cosas, f.; lección práctica, f.

objection, s. objeción, protesta, f., reparo, m.; (obstacle) dificultad, f., inconveniente, m. **to have no o.,** no tener inconveniente. **to raise an o.,** hacer constar una protesta, poner una objeción.

objectionable, a. censurable, reprensible; desagradable, molesto

objective, a. objetivo; (gram.) acusativo. s. objeto, propósito, m.; destinación, f.; (mil.) objetivo, m. (gram.) **o. case,** caso acusativo, m.

objectively, *adv.* objetivamente

objectivism, *s.* (*phil.*) objetivismo, *m.*

objectivity, *s.* objetividad, *f.*

objector, *s.* objetante, *m.* and *f.*, impugnador (-ra). **conscientious o.,** (dissident) el, *m.* (*f.* la) que protesta contra; (pacifist) pacifista, *m.* and *f.*

oblation, *s.* oblación, ofrenda, *f.*

obligation, *s.* obligación, *f.*; deber; *m.* precisión, *f.*; compromiso, *m.* **of o.,** de deber; de precepto. **to be under an o.,** estar bajo una obligación; deber un favor. **to place under an o.,** poner bajo una obligación

obligatory, *a.* obligatorio, forzoso

oblige, *v.t.* (insist on) obligar, hacer, forzar; (gratify) hacer un favor (a), complacer. **He obliged me with a match,** Me hizo el favor de una cerilla. **They are much obliged to you,** Le están muy reconocidos. **Much obliged!** ¡Se agradece!

obliging, *a.* atento, condescendiente, complaciente, servicial

obligingly, *adv.* cortésmente

obligingness, *s.* cortesía, amabilidad, bondad, *f.*

oblique, *a.* oblicuo, sesgado; (indirect) indirecto, evasivo; (*gram.*) oblicuo

obliquely, *adv.* oblicuamente, al sesgo, sesgadamente; indirectamente. **to place o.,** poner al sesgo

obliquity, *s.* oblicuidad, *f.*, sesgo, *m.*; (of conduct, etc.) tortuosidad, *f.*

obliterate, *v.t.* borrar; destruir, aniquilar. **to be obliterated,** borrarse; quedar destruido

obliteration, *s.* testación, *f.*; destrucción, *f.* **o. raid,** bombardeo de saturación, *m.*

oblivion, *s.* olvido, *m.* **to cast into o.,** echar al olvido

oblivious, *a.* olvidadizo, descuidado

oblong, *a.* oblongo, cuadrilongo, rectangular. *s.* rectángulo, cuadrilongo, *m.*

obloquy, *s.* infamia, maledicencia, deshonra, *f.*

obnoxious, *a.* odioso, ofensivo, aborrecible

obnoxiously, *adv.* odiosamente

obnoxiousness, *s.* odiosidad, *f.*

oboe, *s.* (*mus.*) oboe, *m.* **o. player,** oboe, *m.*

obol, *s.* óbolo, *m.*

obscene, *a.* indecente, obsceno, escabroso

obscenely, *adv.* obscenamente, escabrosamente

obscenity, *s.* indecencia, obscenidad, *f.*

obscurantism, *s.* obscurantismo, *m.*

obscurantist, *a.* and *s.* obscurantista (*m.* and *f.*)

obscuration, *s.* (*ast.*) obscurecimiento, *m.*

obscure, *a.* (indistinct) ·obscuro, indistinto; (dark) lóbrego, tenebroso; (remote) retirado, apartado; (puzzling) confuso; (unknown) desconocido; humilde; (difficult to understand) abstruso, obscuro; (vague) vago. *v.t.* obscurecer; (hide) esconder; (eclipse) eclipsar. **to o. the issue,** hacer perder de vista el problema

obscurely, *adv.* obscuramente; humildemente, retiradamente; confusamente; vagamente

obscurity, *s.* (darkness) obscuridad, lobreguez, *f.*; (difficulty of meaning) ambigüedad, confusión, vaguedad, *f.*; humildad, *f.*

obsequies, *s. pl.* exequias; *f. pl.*, ritos fúnebres, *m. pl.*

obsequious, *a.* servil, empalagoso, zalamero

obsequiously, *adv.* servilmente

obsequiousness, *s.* servilismo, *m.*, sumisión, *f.*

observable, *a.* observable, perceptible, visible; notable ·

observably, *adv.* notablemente

observance, *s.* observancia, *f.*, cumplimiento, *m.*; práctica, costumbre, *f.*; (religious) rito, *m.*

observant, *a.* observador; obediente, atento. **o. of,** observador de; atento a

observation, *s.* observación, *f.*, examen, escrutinio, *m.*; (experience) experiencia, *f.*; (remark) advertencia, *f.*, comento, *m.* **to escape o.,** no ser advertido. **o. car.,** vagón Pullman, *m.*

o. post, puesto de observación, *m.*

observatory, *s.* observatorio, *m.*

observe, *v.t.* (laws) cumplir; (holy days, etc.) guardar; (notice) observar, mirar, notar, ver, reparar en; (remark) decir, advertir; (examine) vigilar, atisbar, examinar; (ast.) observar. *v.i.* ser observador. **to o. silence,** guardar silencio

observer, *s.* observador (-ra)

obsess, *v.t.* obsesionar, obcecar

obsessed, *a.* obseso

obsession, *s.* obsesión, obcecación, idea fija, manía, *f.*

obsidian, *s.* (min.) obsidiana, *f.*

obsolescent, *a.* que se hace antiguo or que cae en desuso

obsolete, *a.* obsoleto, anticuado; (biol.) rudimentario or atrofiado

obstacle, *s.* obstáculo, impedimento, *m.*; dificultad, *f.*, inconveniente, *m.* **to put obstacles in the way of,** (fig.) dificultar, hacer difícil. **o. race,** carrera de obstáculos, *f.*

obstetric, *a.* obstétrico

obstetrician, *s.* ginecólogo, *m.*, especialista en obstetricia, *m.* and *f.*

obstetrics, *s.* obstetricia, tocología, *f.*

obstinacy, *s.* obstinación, terquedad, tenacidad, porfía, *f.*, tesón, *m.*; persistencia, *f.*

obstinate, *a.* terco, porfiado, obstinado, tenaz; refractario; persistente, pertinaz. **to be o.,** ser terco; porfiar. **to be o. about,** obstinarse en.

obstinately, *adv.* tercamente

obstreperous, *a.* trubulento, ruidoso

obstruct, *v.t.* obstruir; impedir; cerrar; (thwart) estorbar; (hinder) dificultar, embarazar; (the traffic) obstruir, atascar. *v.i.* estorbar. **to become obstructed,** obstruirse, cerrarse

obstruction, *s.* obstrucción, *f.*; estorbo, obstáculo, *m.* **to cause a street o.,** obstruir el tráfico

obstructionism, *s.* obstruccionismo, *m.*

obstructionist, *s.* obstruccionista, *m.* and *f.*

obstructive, *a.* estorbador, obstructor

obtain, *v.t.* obtener, conseguir, lograr; recibir; (by threats) arrancar. *v.i.* estar en boga, estar en vigor, predominar. **to o. on false pretences,** conseguir por engaño

obtainable, *a.* asequible, alcanzable. **easily o.,** fácil a obtener

obtainer, *s.* conseguidor (-ra), adquisidor (-ra)

obtainment, *s.* obtención, *f.*, logro, *m.*

obtrude, *v.t.* imponer

obtrusion, *s.* imposición, *f.*; importunidad, *f.*

obtrusive, *a.* importuno; entremetido; pretencioso

obtrusiveness, *s.* importunidad, *f.*; entremetimiento, *m.*

obtuse, *a.* (blunt) obtuso, romo; (stupid) estúpido, torpe, lerdo. **o. angle,** obtusángulo, *m.*

obtuseness, *s.* (bluntness) embotamiento, *m.*; (stupidity) estupidez, torpeza, *f.*

obverse, *a.* del anverso. *s.* anverso, *m.*

obviate, *v.t.* obviar, evitar

obvious, *a.* evidente, manifiesto, patente, obvio, aparente, transparente; poco sutil

obviously, *adv.* evidentemente, patentemente

obviousness, *s.* evidencia, transparencia, *f.*

ocarina, *s.* (mus.) ocarina, *f.*

occasion, *s.* ocasión, *f.*; oportunidad, *f.*, momento oportuno, tiempo propicio, *m.*; (reason) motivo, origen, *m.*, causa, razón, *f.*; (need) necesidad, *f.* *v.t.* ocasionar, causar, producir. **As o. demands,** Cuando las circunstancias lo exigen, En caso necesario. **for the o.,** para la ocasión. **on one o.,** una vez. **on the o. of,** en la ocasión de. **on that o.,** en tal ocasión, en aquella ocasión. **He has given me no o. to say so,** No me ha dado motivos de decirlo. **There is no o. for it,** No hay necesidad para ello. **to have o. to,** haber de, tener que, necesitar. **to lose no o.,** no perder ripio (or oportunidad). **to rise to the o.,** estar al nivel de las circunstancias. **to take this o.,** aprovechar esta oportunidad

occasional, *a.* (occurring at times) de vez en cuando, intermitente; poco frecuente, infrecuente; (of verse) de ocasión. **o. table,** mesilla, *f.*

occasionally, *adv.* de vez en cuando

occident, *s.* occidente, *m.*

occidental, *a.* occidental

occipital, *a.* (*anat.*) occipital

occiput, *s.* (*anat.*) occipucio, *m.*

occlude, *v.t.* obstruir, cerrar; (*med.*) ocluir; (*chem.*) absorber

occlusion, *s.* cerramiento, *m.*; (*med.*) oclusión, *f.*; (*chem.*) absorción de gases, *f.*

occlusive, *a.* oclusivo

occult, *a.* oculto, escondido, misterioso; mágico. **o. sciences,** creencias ocultas, *f. pl.*

occultation, *s.* (*ast.*) ocultación, *f.*, eclipse, *m.*

occultism, *s.* ocultismo, *m.*

occultist, *s.* ocultista, *m.* and *f.*

occupancy, *s.* ocupación, posesión, *f.*; (tenancy) tenencia, *f.*

occupant, *s.* habitante, *m.* and *f.*; ocupante, *m.* and *f.*; (tenant) inquilino (-na)

occupation, *s.* ocupación *f.*; (tenure) inquilinato, *m.*, tenencia, *f.*; (work) trabajo, quehacer, *m.*, labor, *f.*; (employment) empleo, oficio, *m.*; profesión, *f.*

occupational, *a.* de oficio. **o. disease,** enfermedad profesional, *f.*

occupier, *s.* ocupante, *m.* and *f.*, inquilino (-na)

occupy, *v.t.* ocupar; (live in) vivir en, habitar; (time) emplear, pasar; (take over) apoderarse de, ocupar. **to o. oneself in** or **with,** ocuparse en. **to be occupied in** or **with,** estar ocupado con, ocuparse en

occur, *v.i.* (happen) suceder, tener lugar, acaecer; (exist) encontrarse, existir; (of ideas) ocurrirse, venirse. **to o. to one's mind,** venírsele a las mientes. **to o. again,** volver a suceder, ocurrir de nuevo. **An idea occurred to her,** Se le ocurrió una idea

occurrence, *s.* ocurrencia, *f.*; incidente, suceso, acontecimiento, *m.* **to be of frequent o.,** ocurrir con frecuencia, acontecer a menudo

ocean, *s.* océano, *m.*; (*fig.*) mar, abundancia, *f.* **o.-going vessel,** buque de alta mar, *m.*

oceanic, *a.* oceánico

oceanography, *s.* oceanografía, *f.*

ocelot, *s.* (*zool.*) ocelote, *m.*

ochre, *s.* ocre, *m.*

ochreous, *a.* de ocre, ocroso

octagon, *s.* octágono, *m.*

octagonal, *a.* octagonal

octahedron, *s.* (*geom.*) octaedro, *m.*

octant, *s.* (*ast., phys.*) octante, *m.*

octave, *s.* (*ecc.,* metrics, *mus.*) octava, *f.*

octavo, *s.* (*print.*) libro, etc. en octavo (8°), *m.* **in o.,** en octavo. **large o.,** octavo mayor, *m.* **small o.,** octavo menor, *m.*

octet, *s.* (*mus.*) octeto, *m.*

October, *s.* octubre, *m.* **the 2nd of O.,** 1906, el segundo (2°) de octubre de mil novecientos seis (1906)

octogenarian, *a.* and *s.* octogenario (-ia)

octopus, *s.* pulpo, *m.*

octoroon, *s.* ochavón (-ona)

octosyllabic, *a.* octosilábico, de ocho sílabas

octroi, *s.* fielato, *m.* **o. officer,** portalero, *m.*

octuple, *a.* óctuple

ocular, *a.* ocular, visual. *s.* ocular, *m.*

oculist, *s.* oculista, *m.* and *f.*

odalisque, *s.* odalisca, *f.*

odd, *a.* (of numbers) impar; (of volumes, etc.) suelto; (strange) raro, curioso, extraño, extravagante; (casual) casual, accidental; (extra) y pico, y tantos, sobrante; (of gloves, etc.) sin pareja. **at odd moments,** en momentos de ocio. **at odd times,** de vez en cuando. **thirty odd,** treinta y pico. **odd numbers,** números impares, *m. pl.* **odd or even,** pares o impares. **odd trick,** (at cards) una baza más

oddity, *s.* excentricidad, rareza, extravagancia, *f.*; (person) ente singular, *m.*; (curio) objeto curioso, *m.*, antigüedad, *f.*

oddly, *adv.* singularmente

oddment, *s.* bagatela, baratija, *f.*

oddness, *s.* singularidad, rareza, extravagancia, *f.*

odds, *s. pl.* diferencia, desigualdad, *f.*; (superiority) ventaja,
superioridad, *f.*; (quarrel) disputa, riña, *f.* **The o. are that
. . .,** Lo más probable es que . . .
to fight against dreadful o.,
luchar contra fuerzas muy superiores. **o. and ends,** (remains) sobras y picos, *f. pl.*;
(trifles) ñaques, *m. pl.*, chucherías,
f. pl.

odious, *a.* odioso, detestable,
aborrecible, repugnante

odiousness, *s.* odiosidad, *f.*

odium, *s.* odio, *m.*

odontologist, *s.* odontólogo, *m.*

odontology, *s.* odontología, *f.*

odoriferous, *a.* odorífero; (perfumed) oloroso, perfumado

odorous, *a.* fragante, oloroso

odour, *s.* olor, *m.*, (fragrance)
perfume, aroma, *m.*, fragancia,
f.; (*fig.*) sospecha, *f.* **in bad o.,**
(*fig.*) en disfavor. **o. of sanctity,**
olor de santidad, *m.*

odourless, *a.* inodoro

odyssey, *s.* odisea, *f.*

œdema, *s.* (*med.*) edema, *m.*

Œdipus complex, *s.* complejo
de Edipo, *m.*

œsophagus, *s.* (*anat.*) esófago,
m.

of, *prep.* de. **of** has many idiomatic translations which are
given as far as possible under the
heading of the word concerned.
It is also often omitted. **I
robbed him of his reward,**
Le robé su recompensa. **I
was thinking of you,** Pensaba
en ti. **It was very good of
you to . . .,** Vd. ha tenido mucha
bondad de . . . **Your naming of
the child Mary,** El que (the
fact that) Vd. haya dado el
nombre de María al niño. **29th
of Sept., 1936,** el 29 de Septiembre de 1936. **Of course!** ¡Claro
está! ¡Ya lo creo! ¡Naturalmente! **of late,** últimamente.
of the (before *m. sing.*) del;
(before *f. sing.*) de la; (before *m.
pl.*) de los; (before *f. pl.*) de las.
to dream of, soñar con. **to
smell of,** oler a, tener olor de.
to taste of, etc., saber a, tener
gusto de. See individual verbs

off, *prep.* de; fuera de; cerca de;
desde; (*naut.*) a la altura de.

from off, de. **Take your
gloves off the table !** ¡Quítate
los guantes de la mesa! **The
wheel was off the car,** La rueda
se había desprendido del coche.
to be off duty, no estar de
servicio; (*mil.*) no estar de guardia.
to lunch off cold meat,
almorzar de carne fría. **off
one's head,** chiflado

off, *a.* (contrasted with near) de la
derecha, derecho; (unlikely)
improbable, remoto. *adv.* (with
intransitive verbs of motion) se
(e.g. **He has gone off,** Se ha
marchado); (contrasted with on)
de (e.g. **He has fallen off the
horse,** Ha caído del caballo);
(of place at a distance) lejos, a
distancia de; (of time) generally
a verb is used (e.g. **The wedding
is three months off,** Faltan tres
meses para la boda); (completely) enteramente. **Off** is
often not translated in Sp.
(e.g. **to put off,** aplazar, **to cut
off,** cortar, etc.). **a day off,**
un día libre, un día de asueto, *m.*
**How far off is the house from
here ? The house is five miles
off.** ¿Cuántas millas hay desde
la casa hasta aquí? La casa
está a cinco millas de aquí. **His
hat is off,** Está sin sombrero, Se
ha quitado el sombrero. **The
cover is off,** La cubierta está
quitada. **The party is off,** Se
ha cancelado la reunión. **6% off,**
un descuento de seis por ciento.
interj. **Off with you!** ¡Márchate! ¡Fuera! **off and on,** de vez
en cuando, espasmódicamente.
off colour, (ill) malucho; (of
jokes) verde. **off season,** estación muerta, *f.* **off-shore,** a
vista de tierra. **off-stage,** entre
bastidores

offal, *s.* (butchers') menudencias,
f. pl., asadura, *f.*, menudos, despojos, *m. pl.*; desperdicio, *m.*

offence, *s.* ofensa, transgresión,
violación, *f.*; pecado, *m.*; (*law*)
delito, crimen, *m.*; (insult) agravio, *m.*, afrenta, *f.* **the first o.,**
el primer delito, *m.* **fresh o.,**
nuevo delito, *m.* **political o.,**
crimen político, *m.* **technical
o.,** (*law*) cuasidelito, *m.* **to
commit an o. against,** ofender

contra. **to take o.,** resentirse, darse por ofendido

offend, *v.t.* ofender; agraviar; insultar; herir; desagradar, disgustar; *v.i.* ofender, pecar. **to be offended,** resentirse, insultarse. **This offends my sense of justice,** Esto ofende mi sentimiento de justicia. **to o. against,** pecar contra; violar

offender, *s.* delincuente, *m.* and *f.*; agraviador (-ra), pecador (-ra), transgresor (-ra). **old o.,** *(law)* criminal inveterado, *m.*

offensive, *a.* ofensivo, desagradable, repugnante; (insulting) injurioso, agraviador, agresivo. *s. (mil.)* ofensiva, *f.* **to take the o.,** tomar la ofensiva

offensiveness, *s.* lo desagradable; (insult) ofensa, *f.*; lo injurioso

offer, *s.* oferta, *f.*; ofrecimiento, *m.*; (of help) promesa, *f.*; proposición, *f.*; *(com.)* oferta, *f.* *v.t.* ofrecer; prometer; (opportunities, etc.) deparar, brindar; tributar. *v.i.* ofrecerse, ocurrir, surgir. **to o. up,** ofrecer; inmolar, sacrificar. **He did not offer to go,** No hizo ademan de marcharse. **to o. resistance,** oponer resistencia. **o. of marriage,** oferta de matrimonio, *f.*

offerer, *s.* ofrecedor (-ra)

offering, *s.* ofrecimiento, *m.*; *(ecc.)* ofrenda, oblación, *f.*, sacrificio, *m.*; regalo, don, *m.*, dádiva, *f.*

offertory, *s. (ecc.)* ofertorio, *m.* **o. box,** cepillo, *m.*

offhand, *a.* sin preparación, de repente; (casual) casual, despreocupado; (discourteous) brusco, descortés

offhandedly, *adv.* sin preparación, espontáneamente; negligentemente; bruscamente

office, *s.* oficio, *m.*; (post) cargo, puesto, destino, *m.*; (state department) ministerio, *m.*; (of a Cabinet minister) cartera, *f.*; (room) oficina, *f.*; despacho, escritorio, *m.*; (of a newspaper) redacción, *f.*; (lawyer's) bufete, *m.*; departamento, *m.*; *(ecc.)* oficio, *m. pl.* offices, negocio, *m.*; oficinas, *f. pl.*; (prayers) rezos, *m. pl.*; *(ecc.)* oficios, *m. pl.*

domestic offices, dependencias, *f. pl.* **good offices,** *(fig.)* buenos oficios, *m. pl.* **head o.,** casa central, oficina principal, *f.* **private o.,** despacho particular, *m.* **to be in o.,** estar en el poder. **o.-bearer,** miembro de la junta, *m.*; funcionario, *m.* **o.-boy,** mozo de oficina, *m.* **o. employee,** oficinista, *m.* **o. hours,** horas de oficina, *f. pl.*; (professions) horas de consulta, *f. pl.* **o.-seeker,** aspirante, *m.*; pretendiente, *m.* **o. work,** trabajo de oficina, *m.*

officer, *s.* oficial, funcionario, *m.*; (police) agente de policía, *m.*; (of the Church) dignatario, *m.*; *(mil., nav., aer.)* oficial, *m.* *v.t.* mandar. **commissioned o.,** oficial, *m.* **non-commissioned o.,** oficial subalterno, *m.* **to be well officered,** tener buena oficialidad. **Officers' Training Corps,** Escuela de Oficiales, *f.*

official, *a.* oficial; autorizado; ceremonioso, grave. *s.* funcionario, *m.*; oficial público, *m.* **high o.,** funcionario importante, *m.* **o. mourning,** duelo oficial, *m.* **o. receiver,** fiscal de quiebras, *m.*

officialdom, *s.* funcionarismo, *m.*; círculos oficiales, *m. pl.*

officially, *adv.* oficialmente

officiant, *s.* oficiante, *m.*

officiate, *v.i.* celebrar; oficiar; funcionar

officiating, *a.* oficiante; celebrante. **o. priest,** sacerdote oficiante, celebrante, *m.*

officious, *a.* oficioso, entremetido

officiously, *adv.* oficiosamente

officiousness, *s.* oficiosidad, *f.*

offing, *s. (naut.)* mar afuera, *m.* **in the o.,** cerca

offset, *s.* compensación, *f.* *v.t.* compensar, neutralizar

offshoot, *s.* renuevo, vástago, *m.*

offside, *a.* (of a car) del lado derecho (or izquierda); *(sport)* fuera de juego

offspring, *s.* vástago, *m.*; descendiente, *m.* and *f.*; prole, *f.*; hijos, *m. pl.*

often, *adv.* a menudo, mucho, con frecuencia, frecuentemente, muchas veces. **as o. as,** tan a menudo como, siempre que.

as o. as not, no pocas veces. How o. ? ¿Cuántas veces? It is not o. that ..., No ocurre con frecuencia que ... so o., tantas veces, con frecuencia. Do you go there o. ? ¿Va Vd. allí con frecuencia (or frecuentemente) ? Not o., Voy rara vez allí

ogival, a. (arch.) ojival

ogive, s. (arch.) ojiva, f.

ogle, v.t. and v.i. comer(se) con los ojos (a), ojear, guiñar el ojo (a). s. ojeada, f., guiño, m.

ogling, s. guiño, m., ojeada, f.

ogre, s. ogro, m.

oh! interj. ¡o! O no! ¡Cal ¡Claro que no!

ohm, s. (elec.) ohmio, m.

ohmic, a. (elec.) óhmico

oil, s. aceite, m.; petróleo, m.; óleo, m. v.t. aceitar, engrasar; olear, ungir, untar; (bribe) sobornar, untar la mano; (fig.) suavizar. a. aceitero; petrolero. to pour oil on troubled waters, echar aceite sobre aguas turbulentas. to strike oil, encontrar un pozo de petróleo; (fig.) encontrar un filón. crude oil, petróleo bruto, m. heavy oil, aceite pesado, m. thin oil, aceite ligero, m. (art) in oils, al óleo. oil-bearing, petrolífero. oil-box, engrasador, m. oil-burner, quemador de petróleo, m. oil-can, aceitera, f. oil-colours, pinturas al óleo, f. pl. oil-field, yacimiento petrolífero, m. oil-filter, separador de aceite, m. oil-gauge, nivel de aceite, m. oil lamp, velón, candil, quinqué, m. oil of turpentine, aceite de trementina, aguarrás, m. oil-painting, pintura al óleo, f. oil pipe-line, oleoducto, m. oil shop, aceitería, f. oil-silk, encerado, m. oil stove, estufa de petróleo, f. oil tanker, (naut.) petrolero, m. oil-well, pozo de petróleo, m.

oilcake, s. bagazo, m.

oilcloth, s. hule, m.; linóleo, m.

oiler, s. (can) aceitera, f.; (naut.) petrolero, m.; lubricador, m.

oiliness, s. oleaginosidad, untuosidad, f.

oiling, s. engrasado, m.

oilskin, s. encerado, m.

oily, a. aceitoso, grasiento

ointment, s. ungüento, m., pomada, f.

old, a. viejo; antiguo, anciano; (of wines, etc.) añejo; (worn out) usado, gastado; (inveterate) arraigado, inveterado. How old are you? ¿Cuántos años tiene usted? to be sixteen years old, tener dieciséis años. He is old enough to know his own mind, Tiene bastante edad para saber lo que quiere. to grow old, envejecer. to remain an old maid, quedar soltera; (fam.) quedarse para vestir imágenes. of old, antiguamente. prematurely old, revejido averiado. old age, vejez, senectud, f. old bachelor, solterón, m. old clothes, ropa vieja (or usada), ropa de segunda mano, f. old-clothes dealer, ropavejero-(-ra). old-clothes shop, ropavejería, f. old-established, viejo. old-fashioned, pasado de moda, viejo; (of people) chapado a la antigua. old lady, anciana, dama vieja, f. old-looking, de aspecto viejo, avejentado. old maid, solterona, f. old-maidish, remilgado. old man, viejo, m.; (theat.) barba, m. old salt, lobo de mar, m. Old Testament, Antiguo Testamento, m. old wives' tale, cuento de viejas, m. old woman, vieja, f. Old World, Viejo Mundo, m.

olden, a. antiguo. o. days, días pasados, m. pl.

older, a. comp. más viejo, mayor. The older the madder, A la vejez viruelas

oldish, a. bastante viejo, de cierta edad

oldness, s. antigüedad, ancianidad, edad, f.

oleaginous, a. oleaginoso

oleander, s. (bot.) adelfa, f. baladre, m.

oleograph, s. oleografía, f.

olfactory, a. olfatorio, olfativo

oligarchic, a. oligárquico

oligarchy, s. oligarquía, f.

olivaceous, a. oliváceo

olive, s. (tree) olivo, m.; (fruit) aceituna, oliva, f. a. aceitunado. wild o. tree, acebuche, m. o.-complexioned, con tez acei-

túnada. **o. green,** verde oliva, *m.*
o. grove, olivar, *m.* **o. oil,**
aceite de oliva, *m.*

olympiad, *s.* olimpíada, *f.*

olympian, *a.* olímpico

olympic, *a.* olímpico. **o. games,**
juegos olímpicos, *m. pl.*

olympus, *s.* olimpo, *m.*

omasum, *s.* (*zool.*) librillo, libro,
m.

ombre, *s.* tresillo, hombre, *m.*

omega, *s.* omega, *f.*

omelette, *s.* tortilla, *f.* **sweet o.,**
tortilla dulce, *f.*

omen, *s.* pronóstico, presagio,
agüero, *m.* *v.t.* agorar, anunciar

ominous, *a.* ominoso, azaroso,
siniestro, amenazante

ominously, *adv.* ominosamente,
con amenazas

omission, *s.* omisión, *f.*; olvido,
descuido, *m.*; supresión, *f.*

omit, *v.t.* omitir; olvidar, descuidar; (suppress) suprimir, excluir, callar, dejar a un lado

omitting, *pres. part.* salvo, excepto

omnibus, *s.* ómnibus, autobús,
m. **o. conductor,** cobrador de
autobús, *m.* **o. driver,** conductor de autobús, *m.* **o. route,**
trayecto de autobús, *m.* **o. service,** servicio de autobuses, *m.*
o. volume, volumen de obras
coleccionadas, *m.*

omnipotence, *s.* omnipotencia, *f.*

omnipotent, *a.* omnipotente,
todopoderoso

omnipresence, *s.* omnipresencia,
ubicuidad, *f.*

omnipresent, *a.* ubicuo

omniscience, *s.* omnisciencia, *f.*

omniscient, *a.* omnisio, omnis-
ciente

omnivorous, *a.* omnívoro

omoplate, *s.* (*anat.*) omoplato, *m.*

on, *prep.* (upon) sobre, en,
encima de; (concerning) de,
acerca de, sobre; (against) contra; (after) después; (according
to) según; (with gerund) en;
(with infin.) al; (at) a; (connected with, employed in) de;
(by means of) por, mediante;
(near to) cerca de, sobre; (into)
en. Untranslated before days of
week, dates of month or time of
day (e.g. **on Monday,** el lunes.
on Friday afternoons, los

viernes por la tarde). **She has a
bracelet on her wrist,** Ella
tiene un brazalete en la muñeca.
**He will retire on a good
income,** Se retirará con una
buena renta. **On my uncle's
death,** Después de la muerte (or
A la muerte) de mi tío, En
muriendo mi tío. **On seeing
them, he stopped,** Al verles
se paró. **on the next page,**
a la página siguiente. **on this
occasion,** en esta ocasión. **on
the other hand,** en cambio.
on second thoughts, luego
de pensarlo bien. **on the way,**
en camino. **on one side,** a
un lado. **on the left,** a la
izquierda. **on time,** puntualmente. **On my honour,** Bajo
palabra de honor. **on pain
of death,** so (bajo) pena de
muerte. **on an average,** por
término medio. **on his part,**
por su parte. **on and after,**
desde, a partir de. **on credit,** de
fiado. **on fire,** ardiendo, en
llamas. **on foot,** a pie. **on
purpose,** a propósito; con intención. **on,** *adv.* puesto (e.g.
She has her gloves on, Ella
tiene los guantes puestos); (forward) adelante, hacia adelante;
(continue, with a verb) seguir,
continuar (e.g. **He went on
talking,** Siguió hablando). Often
on is included in Sp. verb (e.g.
The new play is on, Se ha
estrenado la nueva comedia.
The fight is on, Ya ha empezado la lucha). **On!** *interj.*
¡Adelante! **and so on,** y así
sucesivamente. **to have on,**
llevar puesto. **on and off,** de
vez en cuando. **on and on,** sin
cesar

onanism, *s.* onanismo, *m.*

once, *adv.* una vez; (formerly) en
otro tiempo, antiguamente; *conjunc.* si (e.g. **O. you give him
the opportunity,** Si le das la
oportunidad). **all at o.,** todo
junto, a un mismo tiempo;
simultáneamente; (suddenly) súbitamente, de repente. **at o.,**
en seguida, inmediatamente.
for o., por una vez. **more than
o.,** más de una vez. **not o.,** ni
siquiera una vez. **o. before,** una

vez antes. **o. for all,** una vez para siempre; por última vez. **o. in a way,** de vez en cuando. **o. more,** otra vez. **o. or twice,** una vez o dos, algunas veces. **o. too often,** una vez demasiado. **O. upon a time,** En tiempos pasados, En tiempos de Maricastaña; (as beginning of a story) Érase una vez, Hubo una vez

one, *a.* un, uno, una; (first) primero; (single) único, solo; (indifferent) igual, indiferente; (some, certain) algún, cierto, un (e.g. **one day,** cierto día). *s.* uno; (hour) la una; (of age) un año. Often untranslated in Sp. (e.g. **I shall take the blue one,** Tomaré el azul). *pron.* se; uno. **one's,** su, de uno (e.g. **one's work,** el trabajo de uno). **I for one do not think so,** Yo por uno no lo creo. **It is all one,** Es igual, No hace diferencia alguna. **only one,** un solo. **that one,** ése, *m.*, ésa, *f.*, eso, *neut.* **this one,** éste, *m.*, ésta, *f.*, esto, *neut.* **these ones,** éstos, etc. **those ones,** ésos, etc. **the one,** el (que), *m.*, la (que), *f.* **with one accord,** unánimemente. **one and all,** todos. **one another,** se, uno a otro, mutuamente. **one by one,** uno a uno. **one day,** un día; un día de éstos, algún día. **one-eyed,** tuerto. **one-handed,** manco. **one-sided,** parcial. **one-way street,** calle de dirección única, *f.* **one-way traffic,** tráfico en una sola dirección, *m.*

oneness, *s.* unidad, *f.*

onerous, *a.* oneroso, pesado, molesto, gravoso

onerousness, *s.* pesadez, molestia, dificultad, inconveniencia, *f.*

oneself, *pron.* se, uno mismo (una misma); (after prep.) sí mismo, sí. **It must be done by o.,** Uno mismo ha de hacerlo

onion, *s.* cebolla, *f.* **string of onions,** ristra de cebollas, *f.* **young o.,** babosa, *f.* **o. bed,** cebollar, *m.* **o. seed,** cebollino, *m.* **o. seller,** cebollero (-ra)

onlooker, *s.* espectado (-ra), observador (-ra); testigo, *m.* and *f.*

only, *a.* único, solo. *adv.* única-

mente, sólo; no...más (que), tan sólo; con la excepción de, salvo. *conjunc.* pero, salvo (que), si no fuera (que). **I shall o. give you three,** No te daré más de tres. **The o. thing one can do,** Lo único que se puede hacer. **I o. wished to see her,** Quería verla nada más. **if o.,** ¡ojalá (que)! **not o. ..., no sólo ... o.-begotten,** *a.* unigénito. **o. child,** hijo (-ja) único (-ca)

onomatopœia, *s.* onomatopeya, *f.*

onomatopœic, *a.* onomatopéyico

onrush, *s.* asalto, ataque, acometimiento, *m.*, acometida, embestida, *f.*; (of water, etc.) acceso, *m.*; torrente, *m.*, corriente, *f.*

onset, *s.* ataque, *m.*, acometida, *f.*; (beginning) principio, *m.* **at the first o.,** al primer ímpetu

onslaught, *s.* asalto, ataque, *m.*

ontogenesis, *s.* (*biol.*) ontogenia, *f.*

ontology, *s.* (*phil.*) ontología, *f.*

onus, *s.* responsabilidad, *f.* **o. of proof,** obligación de probar, *f.*

onward, *a.* progresivo. *adv.* adelante, hacia adelante; (as a command) ¡Adelante!

onyx, *s.* (*min.*) ónice, *m.*

ooze, *s.* légamo, limo, fango, *m.*, lama, *f.* *v.i.* exudar, rezumarse; manar; *v.t.* sudar. **to o. satisfaction,** caérsele (a uno) la baba. **to o. away,** (of money, etc.) desaparecer, volar. **to o. out,** (news) divulgarse

oozing, *a.* fangoso, legamoso, lamoso

opacity, *s.* opacidad, *f.*

opal, *s.* ópalo, *m.*

opalescence, *s.* opalescencia, *f.*

opalescent, *a.* opalescente, iridiscente

opaline, *a.* opalino

opaque, *a.* opaco

opaqueness, *s.* opacidad, *f.*

open, *v.t.* abrir; (a package) desempaquetar, desenvolver; (remove lid) destapar; (unfold) desplegar; (inaugurate) inaugurar; iniciar, empezar; establecer; (an abscess) cortar; (with arms, heart, eyes) abrir; (with mind, thought) descubrir, revelar; (make accessible) franquear, hacer accesible; (tear) romper; *v.i.* abrirse; empezar, comenzar; (of a view, etc.) aparecer, extenderse; inaugurarse; (of a career, etc.) prepararse. **to o. fire against,** abrir el fuego contra. **to o. into,** comunicar con, salir a. **to o. into each other,** (of rooms) comunicarse. **to o. on,** mirar a, dar a, caer a. **to o. out,** *v.i.* abrir; desplegar; revelar. *v.i.* extenderse; revelarse. **to o. the eyes of,** (*fig.*) desengañar, desilusionar. **to o. up,** abrir; explorar, hacer accesible; revelar; (*fig., fam.*) desabrocharse. **to o. with** or **by,** empezar con

open, *a.* abierto; descubierto; expuesto; (unfenced) descercado; (not private) público; libre; (unfolded) desplegado, extendido; (persuasible) receptivo; no resuelto, pendiente; (frank) franco, candoroso; (with sea) alto; (liberal) generoso, hospitalario; sin prejuicios; (*com.*) abierto, pendiente; sin defensa; (of weather) despejado; (of a letter) sin sellar; (without a lid) destapado; (well-known) manifiesto, bien conocido. *s.* aire libre, *m.* **in the o.,** al descubierto. **in the o. air,** al aire libre, al raso, a cielo abierto. **to break o.,** forzar. **to cut o.,** abrir de un tajo, cortar. **to leave o.,** dejar abierto. **wide o.,** muy abierto; (of doors) de par en par. **o. boat,** barco descubierto, *m.* **o. car,** coche abierto, *m.* **o. carriage,** carruaje descubierto, *m.* **o. cast,** (*min.*) roza abierta, *f.* **o.-eyed,** con los ojos abiertos. **o.-handed,** generoso, dadivoso. **o. letter,** carta abierta, *f.* **o.-minded,** imparcial. **o.-mouthed,** con la boca abierta, boquiabierto. **o. question,** cuestión por decidir, cuestión discutible, *f.* **o. secret,** secreto a voces, *m.* **o. sea,** alta mar, *f.* **o. town,** ciudad abierta, *f.* **o. tramcar,** jardinera, *f.* **o. truck,** vagoneta, *f.* **o.-work,** (*sew.*) calado, enrejado, *m.*

opener, *s.* abridor, *m.*

opening, *s.* abertura, brecha, *f.*; orificio, *m.*; inauguración, apertura, *f.*; principio, *m.*; (chance)

oportunidad, *f.*; (employment) puesto, *m.* **o. price,** (*com.*) (on Exchange) precio de apertura, *m.*

openly, *adv.* abiertamente, francamente; públicamente

openness, *s.* situación expuesta, *f.*; espaciosidad, *f.*; franqueza, *f.*, candor, *m.*; imparcialidad, *f.*

opera, *s.* ópera, *f.* **comic o.,** zarzuela, *f.* **o.-cloak,** abrigo de noche, *m.* **o.-glasses,** gemelos de teatro, *m. pl.* **o.-hat,** clac, *m.* **o.-house,** teatro de la ópera, *m.* **o. singer,** cantante de ópera, operista, *m.* and *f.*

operate, *v.i.* funcionar, trabajar; obrar; (with on, upon) producir efecto sobre; influir; (*surg.*) operar; (on Exchange) especular, jugar a la bolsa; *v.t.* hacer funcionar, manejar; mover, impulsar; dirigir

operatic, *a.* de ópera

operating, *a.* (of surgeons) operante; de operación. **o. table,** mesa de operaciones, *f.* **o. theatre,** anfiteatro, *m.*; sala de operaciones, *f.*

operation, *s.* funcionamiento, *m.*, acción, *f.*; (*surg.*) intervención quirúrgica, operación, *f.*; (*mil., naut.*) maniobra, *f.*; manipulación, *f.* **to come into o.,** ponerse en práctica; hacerse efectivo. **to continue in o.,** (*laws*) seguir en vigor. **to perform an o.,** (*surg.*) operar, praticar una intervención quirúrgica; hacer una maniobra. **to put into o.,** poner en práctica

operative, *a.* operativo, activo. *s.* operario (-ia), obrero (-ra). **to become o.,** tener efecto

operator, *s.* operario (-ia); (telephone) telefonista, *m.* and *f.*; (machines, engines) maquinista, *m.* and *f.*; (*surg.*) operador, *m.*

operetta, *s.* opereta, *f.*

ophthalmia, *s.* oftalmía, *f.*

ophthalmic, *a.* oftálmico

ophthalmologist, *s.* oftalmólogo, *m.*

ophthalmology, *s.* oftalmología, *f.*

opiate, *s.* opiata, *f.*, narcótico, *m.* *a.* opiado

opine, *v.i.* and *v.t.* opinar, creer

opinion, s. opinión, f., parecer, juicio, m.; concepto, m., idea, f. **in my o.,** según mi parecer. **to be of the o. that,** ser de la opinión que, opinar que. **to be of the same o.,** estar de acuerdo, concurrir. **public o.,** opinión (or voz) pública, f.

opinionated, a. terco, obstinado

opium, s. opio, m. **o. addict,** opiónamo (-ma). **o. den,** fumadero de opio, m. **o. eater,** mascador de opio, opiófago, m. **o. smoker,** fumador (-ra) de opio

opponent, s. antagonista, m. and f., enemigo (-ga); contrario (-ia), adversario (-ia), competidor (-ra)

opportune, a. oportuno, tempestivo, conveniente, a propósito. **to be o.,** venir al caso. **o. moment,** momento oportuno, m.; hora propicia, f.

opportunely, adv. oportunamente. **to come o.,** venir a pelo

opportuneness, s. oportunidad, tempestividad, conveniencia, f.

opportunism, s. oportunismo, m.

opportunist, s. oportunista, m. and f.

opportunity, s. oportunidad, ocasión, posibilidad, f. **to give an o. for,** dar margen para. **to open new opportunities,** abrir nuevos horizontes. **to take the o.,** tomar la oportunidad

opposable, a. oponible

oppose, v.t. (counterbalance) oponer, contrarrestar; combatir; hacer frente (a), contrariar, pugnar contra, oponerse (a)

opposed (to), a. opuesto a, enemigo de, contra

opposing, a. opuesto; enemigo, contrario

opposite, a. (facing) de cara a, frente a, del otro lado de; opuesto; (antagonistic) contrario, antagónico; otro, diferente. s. contraria, f., lo opuesto; antagonista, m. and f.; adversario (-ia). **the o. sex,** el otro sexo. **o. leaves,** (bot.) hojas opuestas, f. pl. **o. to,** frente a; distinto de

opposition, s. oposición, f.; (obstacle) estorbo, impedimento, m., dificultad, f.; resistencia, hostili-

dad, f.; (ast., pol.) oposición, f.; (difference) contraste, m., diferencia, f. a. de la oposición. **in o.,** en oposición; (pol.) en la oposición. **to be in o.,** estar en oposición; (pol.) ser de la oposición, estar en la oposición

oppress, v.t. oprimir, tiranizar, sojuzgar, apremiar; (of moral causes) abrumar, agobiar, desanimar; (of heat, etc.) ahogar

oppression, s. opresión, tiranía, crueldad, f.; (moral) agobio, sufrimiento, m., ansia, f.; (difficulty in breathing) sofocación, f., ahogo, m.

oppressive, a. opresivo, tiránico, cruel; (taxes, etc.) gravoso; (of heat) sofocante, asfixiante; agobiador, abrumador

oppressor, s. opresor (-ra), sojuzgador (-ra), tirano (-na)

opprobrious, a. oprobioso, vituperioso; infame

opprobrium, s. oprobio, m., ignominia, f.

opt, v.i. optar, escoger, elegir

optative, a. (gram.) optativo. s. modo optativo, m.

optic, optical, a. óptico. **o. illusion,** ilusión óptica, f; engaño a la vista, trampantojo, m. **o. nerve,** nervio óptico, m.

optician, s. óptico, m.

optics, s. óptica, f.

optimism, s. optimismo, m.

optimist, s. optimista, m. and f.

optimistic, a. optimista

optimum, s. lo óptimo; (used as adjective) óptimo

option, s. opción, f. (all meanings)

optional, a. discrecional, facultativo

opulence, s. opulencia, riqueza, magnificencia, f.; (abundance) abundancia, copia, f.

opulent, a. opulento, rico, acaudalado; abundante

opus, s. obra, composición, f.

opuscule, s. opúsculo, m.

or, conjunc. o; (before a word beginning with o or ho) u; (negative) ni. s. (her.) oro, m. **an hour or so,** una hora más o menos, alrededor de una hora. **either ... or, o ... o. or else,** o bien. **whether ... or, que ... que, siquiera ... siquiera, ya ... ya, without ... or,** sin ... ni

oracle, *s.* oráculo, *m.*

oracular, *a.* profético, vatídico; ambiguo, misterioso, sibilino; dogmático, magistral.

oral, *a.* verbal, hablado; (*anat.*) oral, bucal

orange, *s.* (tree) naranjo, *m.*; (fruit) naranja, *f.*; **bitter o.,** naranja amarga, *f.* **blood o.,** naranja dulce, *f.* **tangerine o.,** naranja mandarina, *f.* **o. blossom,** azahar, *m.* **o. colour,** color de naranja, *m.* **o.-coloured,** de color de naranja, anaranjado. **o.-flower water,** agua de azahar, *f.* **o. grove,** naranjal, *m.* **o. grower** (or seller), naranjero (-ra). **o. peel,** piel de naranja, *f.* **o.-stick,** (for nails) limpiauñas, *m.*

orangeade, *s.* naranjada, *f.*; (mineral water) gaseosa, *f.*

orangery, *s.* naranjal, *m.*

orang-outang, *s.* (*zool.*) orangután, *m.*

oration, *s.* oración, declamación, *f.*, discurso, *m.*

orator, *s.* orador (-ra), declamador (-ra)

oratorical, *a.* oratorio, declamatorio, retórico

oratorio, *s.* (*mus.*) oratorio, *m.*

oratory, *s.* oratoria, elocuencia, *f.*; (*ecc.*) oratorio, *m.*, capilla, *f.*

orb, *s.* orbe, *m.*; esfera, *f.*, globo, *m.*; astro, *m.* (*poet.*) ojo, *m.*

orbit, *s.* (*ast.*) órbita, *f.*; (*anat.*) órbita, cuenca del ojo, *f.*

orbital, *a.* (*anat.*) orbital

orchard, *s.* huerto, vergel, *m.*; (especially of apples) pomar, *m.*

orchestra, *s.* orquesta, *f.* **with full o.,** con gran orquesta. (*theat.*) **o. stall,** butaca de platea, *f.*

orchestral, *a.* orquestal, instrumental

orchestrate, *v.t.* orquestar, instrumentar

orchestration, *s.* orquestración, instrumentación, *f.*

orchid, *s.* orquídea, *f.*

orchitis, *s.* (*med.*) orquitis, *f.*

ordain, *v.t.* mandar, disponer, decretar; (*ecc.*) ordenar. **to be ordained as,** (*ecc.*) ordenarse de

ordeal, *s.* (*hist.*) ordalías, *f. pl.*; prueba severa, *f.*

order, *s.* (most meanings) orden, *m.*; (command) precepto, mandamiento, decreto, *m.*; orden, *f.*; (rule) regla, *f.*; (for money) libranza postal, *f.*; (for goods) pedido, encargo, *m.*; (arrangement) método, arreglo, *m.*, clasificación, *f.*; (condition) estado, *m.*; (*arch.*) estilo, *m.*; (*zool.*, *bot.*) orden, *m.*; (sort) clase, especie, *f.*; (rank) clase social, *f.*; (*ecc.*) orden, *f.*; (badge) condecoración, insignia, *f.*; (association) sociedad, asociación, compañía, *f.*; (to view a house, etc.) permiso, *m.*; (series) serie, *f.* **His liver is out of o.,** No está bién del hígado. **in good o.,** en buen estado; arreglado. **in o.,** (alphabetical, etc.) en orden; arreglado; (parliamentary) en regla. **in o. that,** para que, a fin de que. **in o. to,** a fin de, para. **out of o.,** estropeado, descompuesto; (on a notice) No funciona; (parliamentary) fuera del orden del día. **till further o.,** hasta nueva orden. **to o.,** (*com.*) por encargo especial. **to give an o.,** dar una orden; (*com.*) poner un pedido. **to go out of o.,** descomponerse. **to keep in o.,** mantener en orden. **to put in o.,** poner en orden, ordenar. **to take holy orders,** tomar órdenes sagradas. **O! ¡Orden! O. in Council,** orden real, *f.* **o. of knighthood,** orden de caballería, *f.* **o. of the day,** orden del día, *f.* **o. paper,** orden del día, *f.*; reglamento, *m.*

order, *v.t.* disponer; arreglar; (command) mandar, ordenar; (request) rogar, pedir; (direct) dirigir, gobernar; (*com.*) encargar, cometer; (a meal, a taxi) encargar. **I ordered them to do it,** Les mandé hacerlo. **to o. about,** mandar. **to o. back,** hacer volver, mandar que vuelva. **to o. down,** hacer bajar, pedir (a uno) que baje. **to o. in,** mandar entrar. **to o. off,** despedir, decir (a uno) que vaya. **to o. out,** mandar salir; (the troops) hacer salir la tropa; echar. **to o. up,** mandar subir, hacer subir

orderliness, *s.* orden, aseo, método, *m.*; limpieza, *f.*; buena conducta, formalidad, *f.*; buena administración, *f.*

orderly, *a.* bien arreglado, metódico; aseado, en orden; (of behaviour) formal, bien disciplinado. *s.* (*mil.*) ordenanza, *m.*; ayudante de hospital *m.*

ordinal, *a.* and *s.* ordinal (*m.*)

ordinance, *s.* ordenanza, *f.*, reglamento, *m.*; (*arch.*) ordenación, *f.*; (*ecc.*) rito, *m.*

ordinand, *s.* (*ecc.*) ordenando, *m.*

ordinarily, *adv.* de ordinario, ordinariamente, comúnmente

ordinary, *a.* (usual) corriente, común, usual, ordinario, normal; (average) mediano, mediocre; (somewhat vulgar) ordinario, vulgar. *s.* (*ecc.*) ordinario, *m.* out of the o., excepcional; poco común. o. seaman, marinero, *m.* o. share, (*com.*) acción ordinaria, *f.*

ordination, *s.* (*ecc.*) ordenación, *f.*

ordnance, *s.* artillería, *f.*, cañones, *m. pl.*; pertrechos de guerra, *m. pl.* o. survey map, mapa del estado mayor, *m.* o. survey number, acotación, *f.*

ore, *s.* (*min.*) mena, *f.*, quijo, *m.*

Oread, *s.* (*myth.*) oréade, *f.*

organ, *s.* (all meanings) órgano, *m.* barrel-o., organillo, órgano de manubrio, *m.* o.-blower, entonador (-ra). o.-grinder, organillero (-ra). o.-loft, tribuna del órgano, *f.* o.-pipe, cañón de órgano, *m.* o.-stop, registro de órgano, *m.*

organdie, *s.* organdí, *m.*

organic, *a.* orgánico. o. chemistry, química orgánica, *f.*

organically, *adv.* orgánicamente

organism, *s.* organismo, *m.*

organist, *s.* organista, *m.* and *f.*

organization, *s.* organización, *f.*; grupo, *m.*, asociación, sociedad, *f.*; organismo, *m.*

organize, *v.t.* organizar; arreglar. *v.i.* organizarse; asociarse, constituirse

organizer, *s.* organizador (-ra)

organizing, *a.* organizador

orgasm, *s.* (*med.*) orgasmo, *m.*

orgiastic, *a.* orgiástico

orgy, *s.* orgía, *f.*

oriel, *s.* (*arch.*) mirador, *m.*

orient, *a.* (*poet.*) naciente, oriental. *s.* Oriente, Este, *m.* pearl of fine o., perla de hermoso oriente, *f.*

oriental, *a.* and *s.* oriental (*m.* and *f.*)

orientalism, *s.* orientalismo, *m.*

orientalist, *s.* orientalista, *m.* and *f.*

orientate, *v.t.* orientar; dirigir, guiar. *v.i.* mirar (or caer) hacia el este; orientarse

orientation, *s.* orientación, *f.*

orifice, *s.* orificio, *m.*; abertura, boca, *f.*

oriflamme, *s.* oriflama, *f.*

origin, *s.* origen, génesis, *m.*; raíz, causa, *f.*; principio, comienzo, *m.*; (extraction) descendencia, procedencia, familia, *f.*, nacimiento, *m.*

original, *a.* original; primitivo, primero; ingenioso. *s.* original, *m.*; prototipo, modelo, *m.* o. sin, pecado original, *m.*

originality, *s.* originalidad, *f.*

originally, *adv.* originalmente; al principio; antiguamente

originate, *v.t.* (produce) ocasionar, producir, suscitar, iniciar, engendrar; (create) inventar, crear. *v.i.* originarse, surgir, nacer. to o. in, tener su origen en, surgir de, emanar de, venir de

origination, *s.* origen, principio, génesis, *m.*

originator, *s.* iniciador (-ra), fundador (-ra); autor (-ra), creador (-ra)

oriole, *s.* (*orn.*) oropéndola, *f.*

Orion, *s.* (*ast.*) Orión, *m.*

orlop, *s.* (*naut.*) sollado, *m.*

ornament, *s.* adorno, *m.*; decoración, *f.*; (*fig.*) ornamento, *m.*; (trinket) chuchería, *f.* *s. pl.* **ornaments,** (*ecc.*) ornamentos, *m. pl.* *v.t.* ornar, adornar, decorar, embellecer

ornamental, *a.* ornamental, decorativo

ornamentation, *s.* ornamentación, decoración, *f.*

ornate, *a.* vistoso, ornado en demasía, barroco

ornateness, *s.* elegancia, vistosidad, magnificencia, *f.*

ornithological, *a.* ornitológico

ornithologist, *s.* ornitólogo, *m.*

ornithology, *s.* ornitología, *f.*

orphan, *a.* and *s.* huérfano (-na)

orphanage, *s.* orfanato, hospicio, *m.*

orphanhood, *s.* orfandad, *f.*

Orphean, *a.* órfico

orris, *s.* galón, *m.*, trencilla, *f.*; (*bot.*) iris florentina, *f.*

orthochromatic, *a.* (*phot.*) ortocromático

orthodox, *a.* ortodoxo

orthodoxy, *s.* ortodoxia, *f.*

orthographic, *a.* ortográfico

orthography, *s.* ortografía, *f.*

orthopædic, *a.* ortopédico

orthopædics, *s.* ortopedia, *f.*

orthopædist, *s.* ortopedista, *m.* and *f.*, ortopédico (-ca)

ortolan, *s.* (*orn.*) hortelano, *m.*

oscillate, *v.i.* oscilar, fluctuar; (hesitate) dudar, vacilar. *v.t.* hacer oscilar

oscillation, *s.* oscilación, fluctuación, vibración, *f.*; (*elec.*) oscilación, *f.*

oscillator, *s.* oscilador, *m.*

oscillatory, *a.* oscilante

osculation, *s.* ósculo, *m.*

osier, *s.* (*bot.*) mimbre, *m.* or *f.* **o. bed,** mimbrera, *f.*

osmic, *a.* (*chem.*) ósmico

osmium, *s.* (*chem.*) osmio, *m.*

osmosis, *s.* (*phys., chem.*) ósmosis, *f.*

osprey, *s.* (*orn.*) quebrantahuesos, *m.*

osseous, *a.* óseo

ossification, *s.* osificación, *f.*

ossify, *v.t.* osificar; *v.i.* osificarse

ossuary, *s.* osario, *m.*

osteitis, *s.* (*med.*) osteítis, *f.*

ostensible, *a.* ostensible; aparente, engañoso, ilusorio

ostensibly, *adv.* en apariencia, ostensiblemente

ostentation, *s.* ostentación, *f.*; aparato, fausto, boato, alarde, *m.*, soberbia, *f.*

ostentatious, *a.* ostentoso; aparatoso, fastuoso, rumboso

ostentatiously, *adv.* con ostentación

osteology, *s.* osteología, *f.*

osteomyelitis, *s.* (*med.*) osteomielitis, *f.*

osteopath, *s.* osteópata, *m.*

osteopathy, *s.* osteopatía, *f.*

osteoplasty, *s.* (*surg.*) osteoplastia, *f.*

ostler, *s.* mozo de cuadras, establero, *m.*

ostracism, *s.* ostracismo, *m.*

ostracize, *v.t.* desterrar; excluir del trato, echar de la sociedad

ostreiculture, *s.* ostricultura, *f.*

ostrich, *s.* avestruz, *m.* **o. farm,** criadero de avestruces, *m.*

otalgia, *s.* (*med.*) otalgia, *f.*, dolor de oídos, *m.*

other, *a.* otro. *pron.* el otro, *m.*; la otra, *f.*; lo otro, *neut. adv.* (with than) de otra manera que, de otro modo que; otra cosa que. **this hand, not the o.,** esta mano, no la otra. **every o. day,** un día sí y otro no, cada dos días. **no o.,** ningún otro, *m.*; otra ninguna, *f.* **someone or o.,** alguien. **the others,** los (las) demás, *m.* (*f.*) *pl.*; los otros, *m. pl.*; las otras, *f. pl.* **o. people,** otros, *m. pl.*, los demás

otherwise, *adv.* de otra manera, de otro modo, otramente; (in other respects) por lo demás, por otra parte; (if not) si no

otitis, *s.* (*med.*) otitis, *f.*

otologist, *s.* otólogo, *m.*

otology, *s.* otología, *f.*

otter, *s.* (*zool.*) nutria, *f.* **o. hound,** perro para cazar la nutria

ottoman, *a.* otomano, turco. *s.* otomana, *f.*

ought, *v. aux.*, deber, tener la obligación (de); ser conveniente, convenir; ser necesario (que), tener que. **I o. to have done it yesterday,** Debí haberlo hecho ayer. **She o. not to come,** Ella no debe (debiera, debería) venir. **He o. to see them to-morrow,** (should) Conviene que les vea mañana; Tiene la obligación de verles mañana; (must) Es necesario que les vea mañana, Tiene que verles mañana.

ounce, *s.* (animal and weight) onza, *f.* **He hasn't an o. of common sense,** No tiene pizca de sentido común

our, *a.* nuestro

ours, *pron.* nuestro, *m.*; nuestra, *f.*; nuestros, *m. pl.*; nuestras, *f. pl.*; de nosotros, *m. pl.*; de nosotras, *f. pl.*; el nuestro, *m.*; la nuestra, *f.*; lo nuestro, *neut.*; los nuestros, *m. pl.*; las nuestras, *f. pl.* **This**

hat is ours, Este sombrero es nuestro (or el nuestro)

ourselves, *pron. pl.* nosotros mismos, *m. pl.*; nosotras mismas, *f. pl.*

oust, *v.t.* despedir, desahuciar, expulsar, echar

out, *adv.* afuera; hacia fuera;. (gone out) fuera, salido, ausente; (invested) puesto; (published) publicado, salido; (discovered) conocido, descubierto; (on strike) en huelga; (mistaken) en error, equivocado; (of journeys) de ida; (of fire, etc.) extinguido; (at sea) en el mar; (of girls in society) puesta de largo, que ha entrado en sociedad; (of fáshion) fuera de moda; (of office) fuera del poder; (in holes) roto, agujereado, andrajoso; (exhausted) agotado; (expired) vencido; (of a watch) llevar . . . minutos (horas) de atraso or de adelanto; (unfriendly) reñido; (way out) salida, *f.*; (sport) fuera de' juego; (of flowers) abierto; (of chickens) empollado. **a scene out of one of Shakespeare's plays**, una escena de una de las comedias de Shakespeare. **I am out £6,** He perdido seis libras. **I am out of tea,** Se me ha acabado el té. **to drink out of a glass,** beber de un vaso. **to read out of a book,** leer en un libro. **to speak out,** hablar claro. **Murder will out,** El asesinato se descubrirá. **out-and-out,** completo; (with rogue, etc.) redomado. **out of,** fuera de; (beyond) más allá de; (through, by) por; (with) con; (without) sin; (from among) entre; (in) en; (with a negative sense) no. **out of breath,** jadeante, sin aliento. **out of character,** impropio. **out of commission,** fuera de servicio. **out of danger,** fuera de peligro. **out of date,** anticuado. **out of hand,** en seguida; indisciplinado. **out of money,** sin dinero. **out of necessity,** por necesidad. **out of one's mind,** loco, demente. **out of order.** See order. **out of print,** agotado. **out of reach,** fuera de alcance,

inasequible. **out of season,** fuera de temporada. **out of sight,** fuera del alcance de la vista; invisible. **Out of sight, out of mind,** Ojos que no ven, corazón que no siente. **out of sorts,** indispuesto. **out of temper,** de mal genio. **out of the question,** imposible. **out of the way,** *adv.* (of work) terminado, hecho; (remote) fuera del camino; (put aside) arrinconado; donde no estorbe. **out-of-the-way,** *a.* remoto, aislado; (unusual) extraordinario, singular. **out of touch with,** alejado de; sin relaciones con; sin simpatía con. **out of work,** sin empleo, sin trabajo, en paro forzoso. **out-patient,** enfermo (-ma) de un dispensario. **Out!** *interj.* ¡Fuera! ¡Fuera de aquí! ¡Márchate! **Out with it!** ¡Hable Vd.! sin rodeos! ¡Hablen claro!

outbalance, *v.t.* exceder, sobrepujar

outbid, *v.t.* pujar, mejorar

outbidding, *s.* puja, mejora, *f.*

outbreak, *s.* (of war) declaración, *f.*; comienzo, *m.*; (of disease) epidemia, *f.*; (of crimes, etc.) serie, *f.*

outbuilding, *s.* dependencia, *f.*, edificio accesorio, anexo, *m.*

outburst, *s.* acceso, arranque, *m.*, explosión, *f.*

outcast, *s.* paria, *m.* and *f.*; desterrado (-da), proscripto (-ta)

outclass, *v.t.* aventajar, ser superior (a), exceder

outcome, *s.* consecuencia, *f.*, resultado, *m.*

outcry, *s.* clamor, grito, *m.*; protesta, *f.*

outdistance, *v.t.* dejar atrás

outdo, *v.t.* eclipsar, aventajar, sobrepujar

outdoor, *a.* externo; (of activities) al aire libre; fuera de casa

outdoors, *adv.* fuera.de casa; al aire libre

outer, *a.* externo, exterior

outermost, *a. sup.* (el, etc.) más externo, más exterior; extremo, de más allá

outfit, *s.* equipo, *m.*; (of clothes) traje, *m.*; (of furniture or trousseau) ajuar, *m.*; (gear) pertrechos, avíos, *m. pl.* *v.t.* aviar, equipar

outfitter, *s.* proveedor (-ra), abastecedor (-ra)

outflank, *v.t.* (*mil.*) flanquear; ser más listo (que)

outgeneral, *v.t.* superar en estrategia

outgoing, *a.* saliente, que sale; cesante. **outgoings,** *s. pl.* gastos, *m. pl.*

outgrow, *v.t.* hacerse demasiado grande para; crecer más que; (ideas) perder; (illness) curarse de con la edad; pasar de la edad de, ser ya viejo para. **to o. one's clothes,** quedársele a uno chica la ropa. **to o. one's strength,** estar demasiado crecido para su edad

outgrowth, *s.* excrecencia, *f.*; resultado, fruto, *m.*, consecuencia, *f.*

outhouse, *s.* edificio accesorio, *m.*

outing, *s.* excursión, vuelta, *f.*, paseo, *m.*

outlandish, *a.* extraño, singular, raro; absurdo, ridículo

outlast, *v.t.* durar más que; (outlive) sobrevivir a

outlaw, *s.* bandido, proscrito, *m. v.t.* proscribir

outlay, *s.* gasto, desembolso, *m.*

outlet, *s.* salida, *f.*; orificio de salida, *m.*; (of drains, etc.) desagüe, *m.*; (of streets, rivers) desembocadura, *f.*; (*fig.*) escape, *m.*, válvula de seguridad, *f.*

outline, *s.* perfil, contorno, *m.*; (drawing) esbozo, bosquejo, *m.*; idea general, *f.*; plan general, *m. v.t.* esbozar, bosquejar. **in o.,** en esbozo; en perfil. **to be outlined** (against), dibujarse (contra), destacarse (contra)

outlive, *v.t.* sobrevivir (a); (live down) hacer olvidar

outlook, *s.* (view) perspectiva, vista, *f.*; (opinion) actitud, *f.*, punto de vista, *m.*; aspecto, *m.*, apariencia, *f.*; (for trade, etc.) perspectiva, *f.*, posibilidades, *f. pl.* **o. tower,** atalaya, *f.*

outlying, *a.* remoto, lejano, distante

outmanœuvre, *v.t.* superar en estrategia

outmatch, *v.t.* aventajar, superar

outmoded, *a.* anticuado, pasado de moda

outnumber, *v.t.* ser más numerosos que, exceder en número

outpost, *s.* (*mil.*) avanzada, *f.*, puesto avanzado, *m.*

outpouring, *s.* derramamiento, *m.*; efusión, *f.*

output, *s.* producción, *f.* **o. capacity,** capacidad de producción, *f.*

outrage, *s.* barbaridad infamia, atrocidad, *f.*; rapto, *m.*, violación, *f. v.t.* ultrajar; violar; violentar

outrageous, *a.* atroz, terrible; desaforado, monstruoso; injurioso; ridículo

outrageousness, *s.* lo atroz; violencia, furia, *f.*; escándalo, *m.*; enormidad, *f.*; lo excesivo; lo horrible

outré, *a.* cursi, extravagante

outride, *v.t.* cabalgar más a prisa que

outrider, *s.* batidor, *m.*

outright, *adv.* (frankly) francamente, sin reserva; (immediately) en seguida, inmediatamente. *a.* categórico; completo; franco

outrival, *v.t.* vencer, superar

outrun, *v.t.* correr más que

outset, *s.* principio, comienzo, *m.*

outshine, *v.t.* brillar más que, eclipsar en brillantez; superar, eclipsar

outside, *adv.* afuera, fuera. *prep.* fuera de, al otro lado de, al exterior de; (besides) aparte de, fuera de. *a.* externo, exterior; (of labour, etc.) desde fuera; máximo; ajeno. *s.* exterior, *m.*; superficie, *f.*; aspecto, *m.*, apariencia, *f.* **at the o.,** a lo sumo, cuando más. **from the o.,** de (or desde) fuera. **on the o.,** (externally) por fuera. **o. the door,** a la puerta

outsider, *s.* forastero (-ra); desconocido (-da); caballo desconocido, *m.*; persona poco deseable, *f.*

outsize, *s.* artículo de talla mayor que las corrientes, *m.*

outskirts, *s. pl.* alrededores, *m. pl.* afueras, inmediaciones, cercanías, *f. pl.*

outspoken, *a.* franco. **to be o.,** decir lo que se piensa, no tener pelos en la lengua

outspokenness, *s.* franqueza, *f.*

outspread, *a.* extendido; (of wings) desplegadas

outstanding, *a.* excelente; sobresaliente, conspicuo; (*com.*) pendiente, sin pagar. **to be o.,** (*com.*) estar pendiente; (*fig.*) sobresalir. **o. account,** (*com.*) cuenta pendiente, *f.*

outstay, *v.t.* quedarse más tiempo que. **to o. one's welcome,** pegársele la silla

outstretched, *a.* extendido

outstrip, *v.t.* dejar atrás, pasar; aventajar, superar

outvote, *v.t.* emitir más votos que; rechazar por votación

outward, *a.* exterior, externo; aparente, visible. *adv.* exteriormente; hacia fuera; superficialmente. **o. bound,** con rumbo a . . . **o. voyage,** el viaje de ida

outwardly, *adv.* exteriormente; hacia fuera; en apariencia

outwear, *v.t.* durar más que; gastar

outweigh, *v.t.* exceder, valer más que

outwit, *v.t.* ser más listo que; vencer

outworn, *a.* anticuado, ya viejo

oval, *s.* óvalo, *m.* *a.* oval, ovalado, aovado

ovarian, *a.* (*bot.*, *zool.*) ovárico

ovariotomy, *s.* (*surg.*) ovariotomía, *f.*

ovary, *s.* ovario, *m.*

ovation, *s.* ovación, recepción entusiasta, *f.*

oven, *s.* horno, *m.* **o. peel,** pala de horno, *f.* **o. rake,** hurgón, *m.*

over, *prep.* (above, upon, over) sobre, encima de; (on the other side) al otro lado de; (across) allende, a través de; (more than) más de; (beyond) más allá de; (of rank) superior a; (during) durante; (in addition) además de; (through) por. *s.* (cricket) serie de saques, *f.* *adv.* encima; en; por encima; al otro lado; de un lado a otro; enfrente; al lado contrario; de un extremo a otro; (finished) terminado; (ruined) arruinado, perdido; (more) más; (excessively) demasiado, excesivamente; (covered) cubierto (de); (extra) en exceso; (completely) enteramente; (from head to foot) de pies a cabeza, de hito

en hito; (of time) pasado. **over** is also used as a prefix. Indicating excess, it is generally translated by demasiado or excesivamente. In other meanings, it is either omitted or may form part of the verb, being translated as re-, super-, trans-, ultra. Very often a less literal translation is more successful than the employment of the above prefixes. **all o.,** (everywhere) en todas partes; (finished) todo acabado; (covered) cubierto (de); (up and down) de pies a cabeza. **all the world o.,** en todo el mundo. **embroidered all o.,** todo bordado. **He is o. in Germany,** Está en Alemania. **He trembled all o.,** Estaba todo tembloroso. **that which is o.,** el exceso, lo que queda. **to read o.,** leer, repasar. **o. again,** de nuevo. **o. and above,** por encima de, fuera de, en exceso de. **o. and o.,** repetidamente, muchas veces. **o. my signature,** bajo mi firma. **o. six months since . . .,** Más de seis meses desde que . . .

overabundance, *s.* sobreabundancia, *f.*

overabundant, *a.* sobreabundante

overact, *v.t.* exagerar (un papel)

overall, *s.* bata, *f.*; guardapolvo, *m.*; *pl.* overalls, mono, *m.*

over-anxious, *a.* demasiado ansioso; demasiado inquieto. **to be o.-a.,** preocuparse demasiado

overarch, *v.t.* abovedar

overawe, *v.t.* intimidar, acobardar

overbalance, *v.t.* hacer perder el equilibrio. hacer caer; preponderar. *v.i.* perder el equilibrio, caer

overbalancing, *s.* pérdida del equilibrio, caída, *f.*; preponderancia, *f.*

overbearing, *a.* dominante, autoritario, imperioso

overboard, *adv.* al agua, al mar.

overbold, *a.* temerario, intrépido; atrevido

overburden, *v.t.* sobrecargar, agobiar

overcast, *a.* anublado, cerrado, encapotado. *v.t.* (sew) sobrehilar **to become o.,** anublarse

overcharge, s. recargo, m.; (price) recargo de precio, precio excesivo, m. v.t. recargar, cobrar un precio excesivo; (elec.) sobrecargar. v.i. cobrar demasiado

overcloud, v.t. anublar; (fig.) entristecer

overcoat, s. abrigo, sobretodo, gabán, m.

overcome, v.t. vencer, rendir, subyugar; (difficulties) triunfar de, allanar, dominar. v.i. saber vencer. a. (by sleep, etc.) rendido; (at a loss) turbado, confundido; (by kindness) agradecidísimo

over-confidence, s. confianza excesiva, f.

over-cooked, a. recocido, demasiado cocido

overcrowd, v.t. atestar, llenar de bote en bote; (over-populate) sobrepoblar

overcrowding, s. sobrepoblación, f.

overdo, v.t. exagerar; ir demasiado lejos, hacer demasiado; (cul.) recocer; (overtire) fatigarse demasiado

overdose, s. dosis excesiva, f.

overdraft, s. (com.) giro en descubierto, m.

overdraw, v.t. and v.i. (com.) girar en descubierto

over-dressed, a. que viste demasiado; cursi

overdue, a. atrasado; (com.) vencido y no pagado

overeat, v.i. comer demasiado, atracarse

over-estimate, v.t. estimar en valor excesivo; exagerar. s. presupuesto excesivo, m.; estimación excesiva, f.

over-excite, v.t. sobreexcitar

over-exposure, s. (phot.) exceso de exposición, m.

over-fatigue, v.t. fatigar demasiado. s. cansancio excesivo, m.

over-feeding, s. sobrealimentación, f.

overflow, v.t. inundar, derramarse por; (fig.) cubrir, llenar; desbordarse. v.i. (with) rebosar de. s. inundación, f., desbordamiento, derrame, m.; (fig.) residuo, resto, exceso, m.; (plumbing) sumidero, vertedero, m., descarga, f. The river over-

flowed its banks, El río se desbordó

overflowing, a. rebosante; superabundante. filled to o., lleno hasta los bordes. o. with health, rebosante de salud, vendiendo salud

overgrown, a. (gawky) talludo; (plants) exuberante, vicioso; frondoso, cubierto de verdura

overhang, v.t. caer a, mirar a; colgar; (fig.) amenazar. v.i. colgar, sobresalir; (fig.) amenazar

overhanging, a. saledizo, sobresaliente; colgante, pendiente

overhaul, v.t. examinar, investigar; componer, hacer una inspección general de; (of boats overtaking) alcanzar. s. examen, m., investigación, f.; (med.) exploración general, f.

overhead, adv. arriba, en lo alto, encima de la cabeza. a. aéreo, elevado; general, fijo. o. cable, cable eléctrico, m. o. expenses, gastos generales, m. pl. o. railway, ferrocarril aéreo (or elevado), m.

overhear, v.t. (accidentally) oír por casualidad, oír sin querer; (on purpose) alcanzar a oír, lograr oír

overheat, v.t. acalorar, hacer demasiado caliente, recalentar. v.i. (in argument) acalorarse; hacerse demasiado caliente

overheating, s. calor excesivo, m.

over-indulge, v.t. mimar demasiado; dedicarse a algo con exceso; tomar algo con exceso. v.i. darse demasiada buena vida

overjoyed, a. contentísimo, lleno de alegría, encantado

overland, adv. por tierra. a. terrestre, trascontinental

overlap, v.i. traslaparse; coincidir. s. traslapo, m.

overlay, v.t. cubrir, dar una capa; (with silver) platear; (with gold) dorar. s. capa, f.; cubierta, f.

overleaf, adv. a la vuelta

overload, v.t. sobrecargar, recargar. s. sobrecarga, f.

overlook, v.t. (face) dar a, mirar a, dominar; (supervise) vigilar, examinar, inspeccionar; (not

notice) no notar, no fijarse en;
(neglect) desdeñar; (ignore) no
darse cuenta de, ignorar; (excuse) perdonar, tolerar, hacer la
vista gorda

overlord, *s.* señor de horca y
cuchillo, señor, jefe, *m.*

overlordship, *s.* señoría, *f.*

overmaster, *v.t.* dominar, vencer

overmastering, *a.* dominante;
irresistible

overmuch, *adv.* demasiado, en
exceso

overnight, *adv.* la noche pasada,
durante la noche; toda la noche.
a. de la víspera, nocturno. **to
stay o. with,** pasar la noche
con

over-paint, *v.t.* pintar demasiado; (*fig.*) recargar las tintas

overpay, *v.t.* pagar demasiado

overpayment, *s.* pago excesivo,
m.

over-populate, *v.t.* sobrepoblar

overpower, *v.t.* vencer, subyugar; (of scents, etc.) trastornar; rendir, dominar

overpowering, *a.* irresistible

overpraise, *v.t.* encarecer, alabar mucho

over-produce, *v.t.* and *v.i.*
sobreproducir

over-production, *s.* sobreproducción, *f.*

overrate, *v.t.* exagerar el valor
de; (of property) sobrevalorar

overreach, *v.t.* sobrealcanzar.
to o. oneself, sobrepasarse, ir
demasiado lejos

override, *v.t.* (trample) pasar
por encima (de); (*fig.*) rechazar,
poner a un lado; (bully) dominar;
(a horse) fatigar, reventar

overripe, *a.* demasiado maduro

overrule, *v.t.* (law) denegar, no
admitir; vencer

overrun, *v.t.* (flood) inundar;
(ravage) invadir; (infest) plagar,
infestar; desbordarse, derramarse

oversea, *a.* ultramarino, de ultramar. *adv.* en ultramar, allende
los mares

oversee, *v.t.* vigilar, inspeccionar

overseer, *s.* capataz, mayoral,
sobrestante, contramaestre, *m.*;
inspector (-ra), veedor (-ra)

oversell, *v.t.* and *v.i.* vender en
exceso

over-sensitive, *a.* demasiado
sensitivo; vidrioso; susceptible

oversew, *v.t.* sobrecoser

overshadow, *v.t.* sombrear; (*fig.*)
eclipsar, obscurecer; (sadden)
entristecer

overshoe, *s.* chanclo, *m.*; (for
snow) galocha, *f.*

overshoot, *v.t.* tirar más allá
del blanco; (*fig.*) exceder, rebasar
el límite conveniente, ir más allá
de lo razonable. **to o. oneself,**
exagerar; propasarse, descomedirse

oversight, *s.* inadvertencia,
omisión, equivocación, *f.*; descuido, *m.*

oversleep, *v.i.* dormir demasiado;
(*fam.*) pegársele a uno las sábanas,
levantarse demasiado tarde

overspend, *v.t.* and *v.i.* gastar
demasiado

overspread, *v.t.* desparramar,
salpicar, esparcir, sembrar;
cubrir

overstate, *v.t.* exagerar, encarecer, ponderar

overstatement, *s.* exageración,
ponderación, *f.*

overstep, *v.t.* exceder, pasar,
violar; rebasar, pasar más allá
(de)

overstrain, *v.t.* fatigar demasiado, agotar. *s.* fatiga, *f.* **to o.
oneself,** esforzarse demasiado,
cansarse demasiado

overstrung, *a.* nervioso, excitable; (piano) de cuerdas cruzadas

over-subscribe, *v.t.* subscribir
en exceso

overt, *a.* abierto, público; manifiesto, evidente

overtake, *v.t.* alcanzar, pasar,
dejar atrás; adelantarse (a);
(surprise) coger, sorprender;
(overwhelm) vencer, dominar

overtax, *v.t.* oprimir de tributos;
agobiar, cansar demasiado

overthrow, *v.t.* volcar, echar por
tierra, derribar; (*fig.*) vencer,
destruir, destronar. *s.* vuelco,
derribo, *m.*; (*fig.*) destrucción,
ruina, *f.*

overtime, *adv.* fuera de las horas
estipuladas. *s.* horas extraordinarias de trabajo, *f. pl.* **to
work o.,** trabajar horas extraordinarias

overtone, *s.* (*mus.*) armónico, *m.*

overtop, *v.t.* dominar, sobresalir, elevarse encima de

overture, *s.* (*mus.*) obertura, *f.*

overturn, *v.t.* volcar, derribar, echar a rodar, echar abajo; (upset) revolver, desordenar. *v.i.* volcar, venirse abajo, allanarse; estar revuelto

overturning, *s.* vuelco, salto de campana, *m.*

overweening, *a.* arrogante, insolente, altivo

overweight, *s.* sobrepeso, exceso en el peso, *m.* **to be o.,** pesar más de lo debido

overwhelm, *v.t.* (conquer) vencer, aplastar, derrotar; (of waves, etc.) sumergir, hundir, inundar, engolfar; (in argument) confundir, dejar confuso, avergonzar; (of grief, etc.) vencer, postrar, dominar; (of work) inundar

overwhelming, *a.* irresistible, invencible, abrumador

overwind, *v.t.* (a watch) dar demasiada cuerda a; romper la cuerda de

overwork, *v.t.* hacer trabajar demasiado (or con exceso); esclavizar. *v.i.* trabajar demasiado. *s.* exceso de trabajo, demasiado trabajo, *m.*

overwrought, *a.* (overworked) agotado por el trabajo, rendido, muy cansado; nerviosísimo, sobreexcitado, exaltado, muy agitado

oviduct, *s.* (*zool.*) oviducto, *m.*

ovine, *a.* ovejuno

oviparous, *a.* ovíparo

ovoid, *a.* ovoide

ovo-viviparous, *a.* ovovivíparo

ovulation, *s.* (*med.*) ovulación, *f.*

ovule, *s.* (*bot.*) óvulo, *m.*

ovum, *s.* (*biol.*) óvulo, *m.*

owe, *v.t.* deber, tener deudas (de); deber, estar agradecido (por), estar obligado (a). *v.i.* estar en deuda, estar endeudado, tener deudas. **He owes his tailor £30,** Le debe treinta libras a su sastre. **I owe him thanks for his help,** Le estoy agradecido por su ayuda (or Le debo las gracias por . . .). **He owes his success to good fortune,** Su éxito se debe a la suerte

owing, *a.* sin pagar. **o. to,** debido a, a causa de, por. **We had to stay in o. to the rain,** Tuvimos que quedarnos en casa a causa de la lluvia. **What is o. to you now?** ¿Cuánto se le debe ahora?

owl, *s.* buho, mochuelo, *m.* **barn** or **screech owl,** lechuza, *f.* **brown owl,** autillo, *m.*

owlish, *a.* parecido a un buho, de buho

own, *a.* propio. *s.* (dearest) bien, *m.* *v.t.* poseer, tener, ser dueño de; (recognize) reconocer; (admit) confesar. *v.i.* confesar. **my (thy, his, our, your) own,** mi (tu, su, nuestro, vuestro) propio, *m.* (*f.* propia); mis (tus, sus, nuestros, vuestros) propios, *m. pl.* (*f. pl.* propias); (when not placed before a noun) el mío (tuyo, suyo, nuestro, vuestro), la mía (tuya, etc.), los míos (tuyos, etc.), las mías (tuyas, etc.); (relations) los suyos. **in his own house,** en su propia casa. **my (thy, his, etc.) own self,** yo (tú, él) mismo, *m.* (*f.* misma, *m. pl.* mismos, *f. pl.* mismas). **a room of one's own,** un cuarto para sí (or para uno mismo). **to be on one's own,** ser independiente; estar a solas. **to hold one's own,** mantenerse en sus trece. **to own up,** confesar

owner, *s.* dueño (-ña), propietario (-ia), posesor (-ra)

ownerless, *a.* sin dueño, sin amo

ownership, *s.* posesión, *f.*, dominio, *m.*; propiedad, *f.*

ox, *s.* buey (*pl.* bueyes), *m.* **ox-eye daisy,** margarita, *f.* **ox-stall,** boyera, *f.*

oxalic, *a.* (*chem.*) oxálico. **o. acid,** ácido oxálico, *m.*

oxidation, *s.* (*chem.*) oxidación, *f.*

oxide, *s.* (*chem.*) óxido, *m.*

oxidization, *s.* oxidación, *f.*

oxidize, *v.t.* (*chem.*) oxidar; *v.i.* oxidarse

oxlip, *s.* (*bot.*) prímula, *f.*

oxy-acetylene, *s.* oxiacetileno, *m.* *a.* oxiacetilénico. **o.-a. welder,** soldador oxiacetilénico, *m.*

oxygen, *s.* oxígeno, *m.* **o. mask,** máscara de oxígeno, *f.* **o. tent,** tienda de oxígeno, *f.*

oxygenate, *v.t.* (*chem.*) oxigenar

oxygenation, *s.* (*chem.*) oxigenación, *f.*

oyez, oyez! *interj.* ¡oíd!

oyster, *s.* ostra, *f.* **o. bed,** pescadero (or criadero) de ostras, *m.* **o. culture,** ostricultura, *f.*

ozone, *s.* ozono, *m.*

P

p, *s.* (letter) pe, *f.* **to mind one's p's and q's,** poner los puntos sobre las íes; ir con pies de plomo

pabulum, *s.* pábulo, *m.*; sustento, *m.*

pace, *s.* paso, *m.*; (gait) andar, *m.*, marcha, *f.*; (of a horse) andadura, *f.*; (speed) velocidad, *f.* *v.i.* pasear(se), andar; (of a horse) amblar. *v.t.* recorrer, andar por; marcar el paso para; (with out) medir a pasos. **at a good p.,** a un buen paso. **to keep p. with,** ajustarse al paso de, ir al mismo paso que; andar al paso de; (events) mantenerse al, corriente de. **to p. up and down,** pasearse, dar vueltas. **p.-maker,** el que marca el paso

paced, *a.* de andar . . .; (of a horse) de andadura . . .; de paso . . .

pachyderm, *s.* paquidermo, *m.*

pacific, *a.* (*geog.*) pacífico; sosegado, tranquilo, pacífico. **He is of a p. disposition,** Él es amigo de la paz

pacifically, *adv.* pacíficamente

pacification, *s.* pacificación, *f.*

pacificatory, *a.* pacificador

pacifier, *s.* pacificador (-ra)

pacifism, *s.* pacifismo, *m.*

pacifist, *a.* pacifista. *s.* pacifista, *m.* and *f.*

pacify, *v.t.* pacificar; calmar, tranquilizar; aplacar, conciliar

pack, *s.* (bundle) fardo, lío, *m.*; paquete, *m.*; (load) carga, *f.*; (of hounds) jauría, *f.*; (herd) hato, *m.*; (of seals) manada, *f.*; (of cards) baraja (de naipes), *f.*; (of rogues) cuadrilla, *f.*; (of lies, etc.) colección, *f.*; masa, *f.*; (of ice) témpanos flotantes, *m. pl.*; (Rugby football) delanteros,

m. pl.; (for the face) compresa, *f.* **p.-horse,** caballo de carga, *m.* **p.-needle,** aguja espartera, *f.* **p.-saddle,** albarda, *f.* **p.-thread,** bramante, *m.*

pack, *v.t.* embalar; empaquetar; envasar; encajonar; (a suit-case, etc.) hacer; (cram) apretar; (crowd) atestar, llenar; (a pipe joint, etc.) empaquetar; (an animal) cargar. *v.i.* llenar; (one's luggage) hacer el equipaje, hacer el baúl, arreglar el equipaje. **packed like sardines,** como sardinas en banasta. **The train was packed,** El tren estababa lleno de bote en bote. **to p. off,** (a person) despachar; poner de partitas en la calle. **to p. up,** hacer el equipaje; empaquetar; embalar; (*fam.*) liar el hato

package, *s.* paquete, *m.*; bulto, *m.*; (bundle) fardo, *m.*

packer, *s.* embalador, *m.*; envasador (-ra)

packet, *s.* paquete, *m.*; (of cigarettes, etc.) cajetilla, *f.*; (boat) paquebote, *m.* **to make one's p.,** (*fam.*) hacer su pacotilla

packing, *s.* embalaje, *m.*; envoltura, *f.*; envase, *m.*; (on a pipe, etc.) guarnición, *f.* **I must do my p.,** Tengo que arreglar el equipaje. **p.-case,** caja de embalaje, *f.* **p.-needle,** aguja espartera, *f.*

pact, *s.* pacto, convenio, *m.* **to make a p.,** pactar

pad, *s.* almohadilla, *f.*, cojinete, *m.*; (on a bed, chair) colchoneta, *f.*; (on a wound) cabezal, *m.*; (for polishing) muñeca, *f.*; (hockey) defensa, *f.*; (cricket) espinillera, *f.*; (writing) bloque, *m.*; (of a calendar) ·taco, *m.*; (blotting) secafirmas, *m.*; (of a quadruped's foot) pulpejo, *m.*; (of fox, hare) pata, *f.*; (leaf) hoja grande, *f.* *v.t.* almohadillar; acolchar; rellenar, forrar; (out, a book, etc.) meter paja en. **inking-pad,** almohadilla de entintar, *f.* **padded cell,** celda acolchonada, *f.* **shoulder-pad,** (in a garment) hombrera, *f.*

padding, *s.* relleno, *m.*, almohadilla, *f.*; (material) borra, *f.*, algodón, *m.*; (*fig.*) paja, *f.*, ripio, *m.*

paddle, *s.* (oar) canalete, zagual, *m.*; paleta, *f.*; (flipper) aleta, *f.* *v.t.* and *v.i.* remar con canalete; (dabble) chapotear. **double p.,** remo doble, *m.* **p.-steamer,** vapor de ruedas, vapor de paleta, *m.* **p.-wheel,** rueda de paletas, *f.*

paddler, *s.* remero (-ra); el, *m.* (*f.* la) que chapotea

paddling, *s.* chapoteo, chapaleo, *m.*

paddock, *s.* prado, *m.*, dehesa, *f.*; parque, *m.*; (near a racecourse) picadero, *m.*; (toad) sapo, *m.*

padlock, *s.* candado, *m.* *v.t.* cerrar con candado, acerrojar

Paduan, *a.* and *s.* paduano (-na)

pæan, *s.* himno de alegría, *m.*

pagan, *a.* and *s.* pagano (-na)

paganism, *s.* paganismo, *m.*

page, *s.* (boy) paje, *m.*; (squire) escudero, *m.*; (of a book, etc.) página, *f.*; (*fig.*) hoja, *f.* *v.t.* compaginar; (a person) hacer llamar por un paje. **on p. nine,** a la página nueve. **to turn the p.,** (*fig.*) volver la hoja

pageant, *s.* espectáculo, *m.*; (procession) desfile, *m.*; representación teatral, *f.*; fiesta, *f.*; (*fig.*) pompa, *f.*, aparato, *m.*

pageantry, *s.* pompa, *f.*, aparato, *m.*, magnificencia, *f.*

paginate, *v.t.* paginar

pagination, *s.* paginación, *f.*

pagoda, *s.* pagoda, *f.*

paid, *a.* pagado; (on a parcel) porte pagado. **p. mourner,** plañidera, *f.* **p.-up share,** acción liberada, *f.*

pail, *s.* cubo, pozal, *m.*, cubeta, *f.*

pailful, *s.* cubo (de agua, etc.), *m.*

pain, *s.* dolor, *m.*; sufrimiento, *m.*; (mental) tormento, *m.*, angustia, *f.*; (*law*) pena, *f.*; *pl.* **pains,** (effort) trabajo, esfuerzo, *m.* *v.t.* doler; atormentar, afligir. **dull p.,** dolor sordo, *m.* **I have a p. in my head,** Me duele la cabeza. **on p. of death,** so pena de muerte. **to be in great p.,** sufrir mucho. **to take pains,** tomarse trabajo, esforzarse, esmerarse

pained, *a.* dolorido; afligido; de angustia

painful, *a.* doloroso; angustioso; fatigoso; (troublesome) molesto; (embarrassing) embarazoso; difícil; (laborious) arduo

painfully, *adv.* dolorosamente; penosamente; fatigosamente; con angustia; laboriosamente

painfulness, *s.* dolor, *m.*; angustia, aflicción, *f.*; tormento, *m.*; dificultad, *f.*

painless, *a.* sin dolor, indoloro

painlessly, *adv.* sin dolor; sin sufrir

painlessness, *s.* falta de dolor, *f.*

painstaking, *a.* concienzudo; diligente, industrioso; cuidadoso. *s.* trabajo, *m.*; diligencia, industria, *f.*; cuidado, *m.*

paint, *s.* pintura, *f.*; (for preserving metal) pavón, *m.*; (rouge) colorete, *m.* *v.t.* pintar. *v.i.* pintar; pintarse. **The door is painted blue,** La puerta está pintada de azul. **p.-box,** caja de pinturas, *f.* **p.-brush,** pincel, *m.*; (for house painting) brocha, *f.*

painter, *s.* pintor (-ra); (house) pintor de brocha gorda, pintor de casas, *m.*; (of a boat) boza, *f.* **sign-p.,** pintor de muestras, *m.*

painting, *s.* pintura, *f.*; (picture) cuadro, *m.*, pintura, *f.*

pair, *s.* par, *m.*; (of people) pareja, *f.*; (of oxen) yunta, *f.* *v.t.* parear, emparejar; (persons) unir, casar; (animals) aparear. *v.i.* parearse; casarse; aparearse. **a carriage and p.,** un landó con dos caballos. **a p. of steps,** una escalera de mano. **a p. of trousers,** unos pantalones. **in pairs,** de dos en dos; por parejas. **to p. off,** *v.i.* formar pareja; (*fam.*) casarse

pal, *s.* camarada, compinche, *m.* and *f.*; amigote, *m.*

palace, *s.* palacio, *m.*

paladin, *s.* paladín, *m.*

palæographer, *s.* paleógrafo, *m.*

palæography, *s.* paleografía, *f.*

palæolithic, *a.* paleolítico

palæology, *s.* paleología, *f.*

palæontology, *s.* paleontología, *f.*

palanquin, *s.* palanquín, *m.*

palatable, *a.* sabroso, apetitoso; (*fig.*) agradable, aceptable

palatableness, s. buen sabor, gusto agradable, m.; (*fig.*) lo agradable

palatably, adv. agradablemente

palatal, a. paladial. s. letra paladial, f.

palatalize, v.t. palatizar

palate, s. paladar, m. **hard p.,** paladar, m. **soft p.,** velo del paladar, m.

palatial, a. (of a palace) palaciego; (sumptuous) magnífico, suntuoso

Palatinate, s. palatinado, m.

Palatine, a. palatino

pale, s. (stake) estaca, f.; límite, m.; (her.) palo, m. a. pálido; (wan) descolorido; (of colours) claro, desmayado; (of light) tenue, mortecino; (lustreless) sin brillo, muerto. v.i. palidecer, perder el color; (*fig.*) eclipsarse

palely, adv. pálidamente; vagamente, indistintamente

paleness, s. palidez, f.; (wanness) descoloramiento, m., amarillez, f.; (of light) tenuidad, f.

palette, s. paleta, f. **p.-knife,** espátula, f.

palfrey, s. palafrén, m.

Pali, s. pali, m.

palimpsest, s. palimpsesto, m.

paling, s. palizada, estacada, valla, f.

palinode, s. palinodia, f.

palisade, s. palenque, m., tranquera, palizada, f.; (mil.) estacada, f.

palish, a. algo pálido; paliducho

pall, s. (on a coffin) paño mortuorio, m.; (*fig.*, covering) manto, m., capa, f.; (ecc.) palio, m.; (over a chalice) palia, f. v.i. perder el sabor, hacerse insípido; saciarse (de); aburrirse (de), cansarse (de). **The music of Bach never palls on me,** No me canso nunca de la música de Bach

palladium, s. (min.) paladio, m.; (safeguard) paladión, m.

pallet, s. jergón, m.; camilla, f.; (mech.) fiador de rueda, m.; torno de alfarero, m.

palliasse, s. jergón, m.

palliate, v.t. (pain) paliar, aliviar; mitigar; (excuse) disculpar, excusar

palliation, s. paliación, f.; mitigación, f.; disculpa, f.

palliative, a. paliativo; (extenuating) atenuante. s. paliativo, m.

pallid, a. pálido

pallidness, s. palidez, f.

pallium, s. palio, m.

pallor, s. palidez, f.

palm, s. (of the hand, and *fig.*, victory) palma, f.; (measurement) ancho de la mano, m.; (tree) palmera, f. v.t. (a card, etc.) empalmar; (with off) defraudar (con); dar gato por liebre (a). **to bear away the p.,** llevar la palma. **p. branch,** palma, f. **p. grove,** palmar, m. **p.-oil,** aceite de palma, m.; (bribe) soborno, m. **P. Sunday,** Domingo de Ramos, m. **p. tree,** palmera, f.

palmate, a. palmeado (also *bot.*)

palmer, s. peregrino, m.; (caterpillar) oruga velluda, f.

palming, s. (in conjuring, etc.) empalme, m.

palmist, s. quiromántico (-ca)

palmistry, s. quiromancía, f.

palmy, a. palmar; (flourishing) floreciente; (happy) dichoso, feliz; (prosperous) próspero; triunfante

palp, s. palpo, m.

palpability, s. palpabilidad, f.

palpable, a. palpable

palpably, adv. palpablemente

palpate, v.t. palpar

palpation, s. palpación, f.

palpitate, v.i. palpitar

palpitating, a. palpitante

palpitation, s. palpitación, f.

palsied, a. paralítico

palsy, s. parálisis, f. v.t. paralizar

paltriness, s. mezquindad, pequeñez, f.

paltry, a. mezquino, insignificante, pobre

paludism, s. (med.) paludismo, m.

pampas, s. pampa, f.

pamper, v.t. mimar, consentir demasiado; criar con mimos, regalar; alimentar demasiado bien

pampered, a. mimado, consentido; demasiado bien alimentado

pamphlet, s. folleto, m.

pamphleteer, s. folletinista, m. and f.

pan, s. (vessel) cazuela, f.; cacerola, f.; (brain) cráneo, m.; (of a balance) platillo, m.; (of a firelock) cazoleta, *f.* *prefix*, pan-. **to pan off,** separar el oro en una gamella. **to pan out,** dar oro; (*fig.*) suceder. **Pan-American- ism,** panamericanismo, *m.*

Pan, *s.* Pan, *m.* **pipes of Pan,** flauta de Pan, *f.*

panacea, *s.* panacea, *f.*

panache, *s.* penacho, *m.*

panada, *s.* (*cul.*) panetela, *f.*

Panama, *a.* panameño. **native of** P., panameño (-ña). **P. hat,** sombrero de jipijapa, *m.*

pancake, *s.* fruta de sartén, hojuela, *f.* **p. landing,** (*aer.*) aterrizaje brusco, *m.* **P. Tues- day,** Martes de Carnaval, *m.*

panchromatic, *a.* pancromático

pancreas, *s.* páncreas, *m.*

pancreatic, *a.* pancreático

panda, *s.* (*zool.*) panda, *m.* and *f.*

pandemic, *a.* pandémico

pandemonium, *s.* pandemónium, *m.*

pander, *s.* alcahuete, *m.* *v.i.* alcahuetear. **to p. to,** prestarse a; favorecer, ayudar

pandore, *s.* (*mus.*) bandola, *f.*

pane, *s.* hoja de vidrio o cristal, *f.*; cuadro, *m.*

panegyric, *a.* panegírico. *s.* panegírico, *m.*

panegyrist, *s.* panegirista, *m.*

panel, *s.* panel, entrepaño, *m.*; (*art*) tabla, *f.*; (in a dress) paño, *m.*; (list) lista, *f.*, registro, *m.*; (jury) jurado, *m.*; lista de jurados, *f.* *v.t.* labrar a entre- paños; artesonar. **p. doctor,** médico (-ca) de seguros

panelled, *a.* entrepañado; (of ceilings) artesonado. **p. ceiling,** artesonado, *m.*

panelling, *s.* entrepaños, *m. pl.*; artesonado, *m.*

panful, *s.* cazolada, *f.*

pang, *s.* punzada (de dolor), *f.*, dolor agudo, *m.*; dolor, *m.*; (an- guish of mind) angustia, *f.*, tor- mento, *m.*; (of conscience) re- mordimiento, *m.*

panic, *s.* pánico, *m.*; pavor, espanto, *m.*; terror súbito, *m.* *a.* pánico. *v.i.* espantarse. **p.- monger,** alarmista, *m.* and *f.* **p.-stricken,** aterrorizado, des- pavorido

panicky, *a.* (*fam.*) lleno de pánico; nervioso

panicle, *s.* (*bot.*) panoja, *f.*

pannier, *s.* (basket) alforja, *f.*; cesto, *m.*; (bustle) caderillas, *f. pl.*

panoply, *s.* panoplia, *f.*

panorama, *s.* panorama, *m.*

panoramic, *a.* panorámico

pansy, *s.* pensamiento, *m.*, trini- taria, *f.*; (*fam.*) marica, maricón, *m.*

pant, *v.i.* jadear; (of dogs) hipar; resollar; (of the heart) palpitar. *s.* jadeo, *m.*; palpitación, *f.* **to p. after,** suspirar por

pantaloon, *s.* (trouser) pantalón, *m.*; (Pantaloon) Pantalón, *m.*

pantechnicon, *s.* almacén de muebles, *m.*; (van) carro de mu- danzas, *m.*

pantheism, *s.* panteísmo, *m.*

pantheist, *s.* panteísta, *m.* and

pantheistic, *a.* panteísta

pantheon, *s.* panteón, *m.*

panther, *s.* pantera, *f.*

panties, *s. pl.* pantalones, *m. pl.*

pantile, *s.* canalón, *m.*

panting, *a.* jadeante, sin aliento. *s.* jadeo, *m.*; resuello, *m.*, res- piración difícil, *f.*; palpitación, *f.*

pantograph, *s.* pantógrafo, *m.*

pantomime, *s.* pantomima, *f.*; revista, *f.* **in p.,** en pantomima; por gestos

pantry, *s.* despensa, *f.*

pants, *s. pl.* calzoncillos, *m. pl.*; (trousers) pantalones, *m. pl.*

Panzer division, *s.* división motorizada, *f.*

pap, *s.* (nipple) pezón, *m.*; (soft food) papilla, *f.*

papa, *s.* papá, *m.*

Papacy, *s.* papado, pontificado, *m.*

Papal, *a.* papal, pontificio. **P. bull,** bula pontificia, *f.* **P. nuncio,** nuncio del Papa, nuncio apostólico, *m.* **P. See,** sede apostólica, *f.*

papaverous, *a.* (*bot.*) papaverá- ceo

paper, *s.* papel, *m.*; hoja de papel, *f.*; documento, *m.*; (lecture) comunicación, conferencia, *f.*; (newspaper) periódico, *m.*; (journal) revista, *f.*; (exám.) examen escrito, *m.*; ejercicio, *m.*; *pl.* papers, (credentials) docu- mentación, *f.*, credenciales, *f. pl.*;

(com.) valores negociables, *m. pl.*;
(packet) paquete, *m. a.* de
papel; para papeles; parecido al
papel. *v.t.* (a room) empapelar;
(a parcel) envolver. **daily p.**,
diario, *m.* **in p. covers**, (of
books) en rústica. **a slip of p.**,
una papeleta. **to send in one's
papers**, entregar su dimisión.
p. bag, saco de papel, *m.* **p.-
chase**, rally-paper, *m.* **p. clip**,
prendedero de oficina, "clip,"
m. **p.-cutting machine**, guillotina, *f.* **p. folder**, plegadera, *f.*
p.-hanger, empapelador, *m.* **p.-
hanging**, empapelado, *m.* **p.-
knife**, cortapapel, *m.* **p.-maker**,
fabricante de papel, *m.* **p.-
making**, manufactura de papel,
f. **p.-mill**, fábrica de papel, *f.*
p.-money, papel moneda, *m.*
p.-pulp, pasta, *f.* **p.-streamer**,
serpentina, *f.* **p.-weight**, pisapapeles, *m.*

papering, *s.* (of a room) empapelado, *m.*

papery, *a.* semejante al papel

papier mâché, *s.* cartón piedra,
m.

papillary, *a.* papilar

papist, *s.* papista, *m.* and *f.*;
católico (-ca)

papistic, *a.* papista

papoose, *s* niño indio, *m.*

paprika, *s.* pimienta húngara, *f.*

papyrus, *s.* papiro, *m.*

par, *s.* par, *f.* **at par**, (com.) a la
par. **above (below) par**, (com.)
por encima (or debajo) de la par.
He is a little below par, No
está muy bien de salud. **to be
on a par with**, ser el equivalente
de; ser igual a. **par excellence**,
por excelencia

parable, *s.* parábola, *f.*

parabola, *s.* (geom.) parábola, *f.*

parachute, *s.* paracaídas, *m.*;
(bot.) vilano, *m.* **to p. down**,
lanzarse en paracaídas. **p.
troops**, cuerpo de paracaidistas,
m.

parachutist, *s.* paracaidista, *m.*

Paraclete, *s.* paráclito, *m.*

parade, *s.* alarde, *m.*; (mil.)
parada, revista, *f.*; (procession)
desfile, *m.*, procesión, *f.*; (promenade) paseo, *m.* *v.t.* (display)
hacer alarde de, hacer gala de,
ostentar; (troops) formar en

parada; pasar revista (a); (patrol)
recorrer. *v.i.* (mil.) tomar parte
en una parada; desfilar. **to p.
up and down**, pasearse. **p.-
ground**, campo de instrucción,
m.; plaza de armas, *f.*

paradigm, *s.* paradigma, *m.*

paradise, *s.* paraíso, edén, *m.*;
(fig.) jauja, *f.* **bird of p.**, ave del
paraíso, *f.*

paradisiac, *a.* paradisíaco

paradox, *s.* paradoja, *f.*

paradoxical, *a.* paradójico

paradoxicality, *s.* lo paradójico

paradoxically, *adv.* paradójica-
mente

paraffin, *s.* parafina, *f.* *v.t.*
parafinar. **p.-oil**, parafina lí-
quida, *f.*

paragon, *s.* modelo perfecto, dechado, *m.*

paragraph, *s.* párrafo, *m.*; (in a
newspaper) suelto, *m.* *v.t.* dividir
en párrafos; escribir un suelto
sobre. **new p.**, párrafo aparte,
m.

paragrapher, *s.* gacetillero, *m.*

Paraguayan, *a.* and *s.* paraguayo
(-ya)

parakeet, *s.* (orn.) perico, *m.*

parallel, *a.* paralelo; igual; semejante, análogo. *s.* línea paralela,
f.; paralelo, *m.*; (mil.) paralela,
f.; (geog.) paralelo, *m.*; (print.)
pleca, *f.* *v.t.* poner en paralelo;
cotejar, comparar; igualar. **to
run p. to**, ser paralelo a; ser
conforme a. **p. bars**, paralelas,
f. pl.

parallelism, *s.* paralelismo, *m.*

parallelogram, *s.* paralelogramo,
m.

paralysation, *s.* paralización, *f.*

paralyse, *v.t.* paralizar

paralysis, *s.* parálisis, *f.*

paralytic, *a.* and *s.* paralítico (-ca)

paramount, *a.* supremo, sumo

paramour, *s.* amante, querido,
m.; querida, amiga, *f.*

paranoia, *s.* paranoia, *f.*

paranoiac, *s.* paranoico, *m.*

parapet, *s.* (arch. and mil.) parapeto, *m.*

parapeted, *a.* con parapeto

paraphernalia, *s.* (law) bienes
parafernales, *m. pl.*; (finery)
atavíos, adornos, *m. pl.*; equipo,
m.; arreos, *m. pl.*; insignias,
f. pl.

paraphrase, s. paráfrasis, f. v.t. parafrasear

parasite, s. parásito, m.; (fam.) zángano, m., gorrista, m. and f.

parasitic, a. parásito, parasitario; (med.) parasítico

parasitology, s. parasitología, f.

parasol, s. parasol, quitasol, m.

parathyroid, a. paratiroides. s. paratiroides, f. pl.

paratroops, s. pl. paracaidistas, m. pl.

paratyphoid, s. paratifoidea, f.

parboil, v.t. sancochar

parcel, s. paquete, m.; fardo, m.; (of land) parcela, f. **to p. out,** repartir, distribuir; dividir. **to p. up,** envolver, empaquetar. **p. post,** servicio de paquetes, m.

parcelling, s. empaque, m.; (out) reparto, m., distribución, f.; división, f.

parch, v.t. secar; abrasar, quemar; (roast) tostar. v.i. secarse; quemarse, abrasarse

parched, a. seco, sediento. **p. with thirst,** muerto de sed

parchedness, s. sequedad, aridez, f.

parchment, s. pergamino, m.; (of a drum) parche, m. **p.-like,** apergaminado

pardon, s. perdón, m.; (ecc.) indulgencia, f. v.t. perdonar; indultar, amnistiar. **a general p.,** una amnistía. **I beg your p.!** ¡Vd. dispense!; ¡Perdone Vd.! **to beg p.,** pedir perdón; disculparse. **P.?** ¿Cómo?

pardonable, a. perdonable, disculpable, excusable

pardonableness, s. disculpabilidad, f.

pardonably, adv. disculpablemente, excusablemente

pardoner, s. vendedor de indulgencias, m.; perdonador (-ra)

pardoning, s. perdón, m.; remisión, f.

pare, v.t. (one's nails) cortar; (fruit) mondar; (potatoes, etc.) pelar; (remove) quitar; (reduce) reducir

parenchyma, s. (bot., anat.) parénquima, m.

parent, s. padre, m.; madre, f.; (ancestor) antepasado, m.; (origin) origen, m., fuente, f.; (cause) causa, f.; (author) autor,

m.; autora, f.; pl. **parents,** padres, m. pl. a. madre, materno; principal

parentage, s. parentela, f.; linaje, m., familia, alcurnia, f.; procedencia, f., nacimiento, origen, m.

parental, a. paternal; maternal, de madre

parentally, adv. como un padre; como una madre

parenthesis, s. paréntesis, m.

parenthetical, a. entre paréntesis; de paréntesis

parenthood, s. paternidad, f.; maternidad, f.

pariah, s. paria, m. and f.

parietal, a. parietal

paring, s. (act) raedura, f.; peladura, mondadura, f.; (shred) brizna, f.; (refuse) desecho, desperdicio, m. **p.-knife,** trinchete, m.

parish, s. parroquia, f.; feligresía, f. a. parroquial. **p. church,** parroquia, f. **p. clerk,** sacristán de parroquia, m. **p. priest,** párroco, m. **p. register,** registro de la parroquia, m.

parishioner, s. parroquiano (-na); feligrés (-esa)

Parisian, a. parisiense. s. parisiense, m. and f.

parisyllabic, a. parisílabo

parity, s. paridad, f.

park, s. parque, m.; jardín, m. v.t. (vehicles) estacionar; (dump) depositar. **car p.,** parque de automóviles, m. **p.-keeper,** guardián del parque, m.

parking, s. (of vehicles) estacionamiento, m.; (dumping) depósito, m. **No p.!** ¡Prohibido estacionarse! **p. lights,** (aut.) luces de estacionamiento, f. pl. **p. place,** parque de estacionamiento, m.

parlance, s. lenguaje, m. **in common p.,** en lenguaje vulgar

parley, s. plática, conversación, f.; discusión, f.; (mil.) parlamento, m. v.i. (mil.) parlamentar; discutir; conversar. v.t. hablar

Parliament, s. parlamento, m.; cortes, f. pl.; cuerpo legislativo, m.

parliamentarian, a. and s. parlamentario (m.)

parliamentarianism, s. parlamentarismo, m.

parliamentary, *a.* parlamentario.
p. immunity, inviolabilidad parlamentaria, *f.*

parlour, *s.* salón, gabinete, *m.*; sala de recibo, *f.*; (in a convent) locutorio, *m.* p. games, juegos de prendas, *m. pl.* p.-maid, camarera, *f.*

parlous, *a.* crítico, malo. *adv.* sumamente, muy

Parmesan, *a.* parmesano, de Parma. *s.* parmesano (-na). P. cheese, queso de Parma, *m.*

Parnassian, *a.* del parnaso; parnasiano. *s.* parnasiano, *m.*

Parnassus, *s.* Parnaso, *m.*

parochial, *a.* parroquial, parroquiano; provincial

parochialism, *s.* provincialismo, *m.*

parochially, *adv.* por parroquias

parodist, *s.* parodista, *m.* and *f.*

parody, *s.* parodia, *f. v.t.* parodiar

parole, *s.* (of a prisoner) palabra de honor, *f.*

parotid, *s.* (*anat.*) parótida, *f.*

paroxysm, *s.* paroxismo, *m.*; ataque, acceso, *m.*

parquet, *s.* parquet, *m.*

parricide, *s.* (act) parricidio, *m.*; (person) parricida, *m.* and *f.*

parrot, *s.* papagayo, loro, *m.*

parry, *v.t.* (a blow, and in fencing) parar; rechazar; evitar. *s.* parada, *f.*; (in fencing) quite, *m.*, parada, *f.*

parse, *v.t.* analizar

Parsee, *s.* parsi, *m.*

parsimonious, *a.* parsimonioso

parsimoniously, *adv.* con parsimonia

parsimony, *s.* parsimonia, *f.*

parsing, *s.* análisis, *m.* or *f.*

parsley, *s.* perejil, *m.*

parsnip, *s.* chirivía, *f.*

parson, *s.* párroco, cura, *m.*; (clergyman) clérigo, *m.*

parsonage, *s.* rectoría, *f.*

part, *s.* parte, *f.*; porción, *f.*; trozo, *m.*; (*mech.*) pieza, *f.*; (*gram.* and of a literary work) parte, *f.*; (of a living organism) miembro, *m.*; (duty) deber, *m.*, obligación, *f.*; (*theat.*) papel, *m.*; (*mus.*) voz, *m.*; *pl.* parts, (region) partes, *f. pl.*, lugar, *m.*; (talents) partes, dotes, *f. pl.* foreign parts, países extranjeros, *m. pl.*, el extranjero. For my p. . . ., Por lo que a mí toca, Por mi parte. for the most p., en su mayoría. from all parts, de todas partes. in p., en parte; parcialmente. spare p., pieza de recambio, *f.* The funny p. of it is . . ., Lo cómico del asunto es . . . the latter p. of the month, los últimos días del mes, la segunda quincena del mes. to form p. of, formar parte de. to play a p., hacer un papel. to take a person's p., apoyar a alguien, ser partidario de alguien. to take in good p., tomar bien. to take p. in, tomar parte en, participar en. p. of speech, parte de la oración, *f.* p.-owner, copropietario (-ia). p.-time job, trabajo de unas cuantas horas, *m.*

part, *v.t.* distribuir, repartir; dividir; separar (de); (open) abrir. *v.i.* partir, marcharse; despedirse; (of roads, etc.) bifurcarse; dividirse; (open) abrirse. to p. one's hair, hacerse la raya. to p. from, (things) separarse de; (people) despedirse de. to p. with, separarse de; deshacerse de; perder; (dismiss) despedir (a)

partake, *v.i.* participar de, compartir; tomar parte en. *v.i.* tomar algo (de comer, de beber). to p. of, comer (beber) de; tener rasgos de

partaker, *s.* partícipe, *m.* and *f.*

parthenogenesis, *s.* partenogénesis, *f.*

Parthian, *a.* parto. *s.* parto (-ta). P. shot, la flecha del parto

partial, *a.* parcial; (fond of) aficionado (a). p. eclipse, eclipse parcial, *m.*

partiality, *s.* parcialidad, *f.*; preferencia, predilección, *f.*

partially, *adv.* en parte, parcialmente; (with bias) con parcialidad

participant, *a.* participante. *s.* partícipe, *m.* and *f.*

participate, *v.i.* participar (de), compartir; tomar parte (en)

participation, *s.* participación, *f.*

participator, *s.* partícipe, *m.* and *f.*

participial, *a.* (*gram.*) participial
participle, *s.* (*gram.*) participio,
m. **past p.,** participio pasado
(or pretérito or pasivo) (or
present p., participio activo (or
presente), *m.*
particle, *s.* partícula, *f.*; (*fig.*)
átomo, grano, *m.*, pizca, *f.*;
(*gram.*) partícula, *f.*
parti-coloured, *a.* bicolor
particular, *a.* particular; especial; individual; singular; cierto;
exacto; escrupuloso; difícil, exigente. *s.* detalle, pormenor, *m.*;
circunstancia, *f.*; caso particular,
m.; *pl.* **particulars,** informes,
detalles, *m.* *pl.* **further particulars,** más detalles. **in p.,** en
particular; sobre todo. **He is
very p. about . . .,** Es muy
exigente en cuanto a . . .; Le es
muy importante . . ., Le importa mucho . . .
particularize, *v.t.* particularizar,
detallar; especificar
particularly, *adv.* en particular;
particularmente; sobre todo
parting, *s.* despedida, *f.*; partida,
f.; separación, *f.*; (of the hair)
raya, crencha, *f.*; (cross roads)
bifurcación, *f.* *a.* de despedida.
at p., al despedirse. **to reach
the p. of the ways,** (*fig.*) llegar
al punto decisivo
partisan, *s.* partidario (-ia);
(fighter) guerrillero, *m.* *a.* partidario; de guerrilleros
partisanship, *s.* partidarismo, *m.*
partition, *s.* partición, *f.*; división, *f.*; (wall) pared, *f.*, tabique,
m. **the p. of Ireland,** la división de Irlanda
partitive, *a.* partitivo. *s.* palabra
partitiva, *f.*
partly, *adv.* en parte
partner, *s.* asociado (-da); (*com.*)
socio (-ia); (dancing) pareja, *f.*;
(in games, and companion) compañero (-ra); (spouse) consorte,
m. and *f.*; (in crime) codelincuente, *m.* and *f.* **sleeping p.,**
socio comanditario, *m.* **working p.,** socio industrial, *m.*
partnership, *s.* asociación, *f.*;
(*com.*) sociedad, compañía, *f.*
deed of p., artículos de sociedad,
m. *pl.* **to take into p.,** tomar
como socio (a). **to form a p.,**
asociarse

partridge, *s.* (*orn.*) perdiz, *f.*
young p., perdigón, *m.*
parturient, *a.* (*f.*) parturienta. *s.*
parturienta, *f.*
parturition, *s.* parto, *m.*
party, *s.* partido, *m.*; grupo, *m.*;
(of pleasure, etc.) partida, *f.*;
reunión, fiesta, *f.*; (*mil.*) pelotón,
destacamento, *m.*; (*law*) parte,
f.; (person) interesado (-da);
(accessory) cómplice, *m.* and *f.*
rescue p., pelotón de salvamento, *m.* **to be a p. to,**
prestarse a; ser cómplice en.
to give a p., dar una fiesta, dar
una reunión. **p.-spirit,** espíritu
del partido, *m.* **p.-wall,** pared
medianera, *f.*
parvenu, *s.* advenedizo (-za)
parvis, *s.* (*arch.*) atrio, *m.*
Paschal, *a.* pascual
pasha, *s.* bajá, *m.*
pasquinade, *s.* pasquinada, *f.*
pass, *s.* (in an exam.) aprobación,
f.; (crisis) crisis, situación crítica,
f.; estado, *m.*; (with the hands)
pase, *m.*; (permit) permiso, *m.*;
(*mil.*) licencia, *f.*; (safe-conduct)
salvoconducto, *m.*; (in football,
etc.) pase, *m.*; (membership card)
carnet, *m.*; (defile) desfiladero,
paso, *m.*; (*naut.*) rebasadero, *m.*;
(fencing) estocada, *f.* **free p.,**
billete de favor, *m.* **p.-book,**
libreta de banco, *f.* **p. certificate,** (in exams.) aprobado, *m.*
p.-key, llave maestra, *f.*
pass, *v.i.* pasar; (of time) correr,
pasar, transcurrir; (happen)
ocurrir, tomar lugar; (end) cesar,
desaparecer; (die) morir. *v.t.*
pasar; hacer pasar; (the butter,
etc.) dar, alargar; (in football,
hockey) pasar; (excel) aventajar,
exceder; (a Bill, an examination)
aprobar; (sentence) fallar, pronunciar; (a remark) hacer;
(transfer) traspasar; (tolerate)
sufrir, tolerar; evacuar. **He
passed in Psychology,** Aprobó
la psicología. **to allow to p.,**
ceder el paso (a). **to bring
to p.,** ocasionar. **to come to p.,**
suceder. **to let p.,** (put up with)
dejar pasar; no hacer caso de;
(forgive) perdonar. **to p. a vote
of confidence,** votar una proposición de confianza. **to p. the
buck,** (*fam.*) echarle a uno el

muerto. **to p. along,** pasar por;
pasar. **to p. away,** pasar; desaparecer; (die) morir, fallecer;
(of time) transcurrir. **to p. by,**
pasar por, pasar delante de,
pasar al lado de; (omit) pasar por
alto de, omitir; (ignore) pasar
sin hacer caso de. **to p. for,**
pasar por. **to p. in,** entrar. **to
p. in and out,** entrar y salir.
to p. off, v.i. pasar; cesar,
acabarse; desaparecer; (evaporarse, disiparse; (of events) tener
lugar. v.t. (oneself) darse por;
dar por, hacer pasar por. **to p. a
cat off as hare,** dar gato por
liebre. **to p. on,** v.i. pasar;
seguir su camino, continuar su
marcha. v.t. pasar algo de uno
a otro. **to p. out,** salir. **to p.
over,** pasar por encima de;
pasar; cruzar, atravesar; (transfer) traspasar; (disregard) pasar
por alto de, dejar a un lado;
omitir. **to p. over in silence,**
pasar en silencio (por). **to p.
round,** circular. **to p. through,**
cruzar, atravesar, pasar por;
(pierce) traspasar; (fig.) experimentar
passable, a. transitable, pasadero; (fairly good) regular, mediano; tolerable
passably, adv. medianamente,
pasaderamente, tolerablemente
passage, s. pasaje, m.; paso,
tránsito, m.; (voyage) viaje, m.,
travesía, f.; (corridor) pasillo,
m.; (entrance) entrada, f.; (way)
camino, m.; (alley) callejón, m.;
(in a mine) galería, f.; (of time)
transcurso, m.; (of birds) pasa,
f.; (in a book, and mus.) pasaje,
m.; (occurrence) episodio, incidente, m.; (of a Bill) aprobación,
f. **p. money,** pasaje, m. **p. of
arms,** lucha, f., combate, m.;
disputa, f.
passementerie, s. pasamanería, f.
passenger, s. viajero (-ra); (on
foot) peatón, m. **by p. train,** en
gran velocidad
passer-by, s. transeúnte, paseante, m. and f.
passing, a. pasajero; fugitivo;
momentáneo. adv. sumamente
extremadamente. s. pasada, f.;
paso, m.; (death) muerte, f.;
(disappearance) desaparición, f.;

(of a law) aprobación, f. **in p.,** de
paso. **p.-bell,** toque de difuntos, m.
passion, s. pasión, f.; (Christ's)
Pasión, f.; (anger) cólera, f. **to
fly into a p.,** montar en cólera.
p.-flower, pasionaria, granadilla, f. **P. play,** drama de la
Pasión, m. **P. Sunday,** Domingo
de Pasión, m. **P. Week,** Semana
Santa, f.
passionate, a. apasionado;
(quick-tempered) irascible, colérico; (fervid) vehemente, intenso,
ardiente
passionately, adv. con pasión,
apasionadamente; (irascibly)
coléricamente; (fervidly) con vehemencia, ardientemente
passionless, a. sin pasión, frío;
impasible; imparcial
passive, a. pasivo. s. (gram.)
pasiva, f. **p. resistance,** resistencia pasiva, f.
passively, adv. pasivamente
passiveness, passivity, s. pasividad, f.
Passover, s. Pascua, f.
passport, s. pasaporte, m.
password, s. contraseña, f.
past, a. pasado; último; (expert)
consumado; (former) antiguo,
ex-. s. pasado, m.; historia, f.,
antecedentes, m. pl. prep. después de; (in front of) delante de;
(next to) al lado de; (beyond)
más allá de; (without) sin; fuera
de; (of age) más de; (no longer
able to) incapaz de. adv. más
allá. (The translation of past as
an adverb is often either omitted,
or included in the verb, e.g. **The
years flew p.,** Los años trans-
currieron. **for centuries p.,**
durante siglos.) **I am p. caring,**
Nada me importa ya. **It is a
quarter p. ten,** Son las diez y
cuarto. **It is p. four o'clock,**
Son después de las cuatro.
what's p. is p., lo pasado,
pasado. **p. doubt,** fuera de duda.
p. endurance, insoportable. **p.
help,** sin remedio, irremediable.
p. hope, sin esperanza. **p.-
master,** maestro, consumado,
experto, m. **p. participle,** participio pasado, m. **p. president,**
ex-presidente, m. **p. tense,**
(tiempo) pretérito, m.

paste, s. pasta, f.; (gloy) engrudo, m. v.t. (affix) pegar; (glue) engomar, engrudar

pasteboard, s. cartón, m., cartulina, f. a. de cartón, de cartulina

pastel, s. (art) pastel, m. **p. drawing,** pintura al pastel, f.

pastelist, s. pastelista, m. and f.

pastern, s. (of a horse) cuartilla, f.

pasteurization, s. pasteurización, f.

pasteurize, v.t. pasteurizar

pastille, s. pastilla, f.

pastime, s. pasatiempo, entretenimiento, m., diversión, recreación, f.

pastor, s. pastor, m.

pastoral, a. pastoril; (ecc.) pastoral. s. (ecc.) pastoral, f.; (poet., mus.) pastorela, f.

pastorate, s. pastoría, f.

pastry, s. (dough) pasta, f.; pastel, m., torta, f.; pastelería, f. **p.-cook,** repostero, m., pastelero (-ra)

pasturage, s. (grass, etc.) pasto, m.; pasturaje, m.; pastoreo, m.

pasture, s. (grass, etc.) pasto, herbaje, m.; pasturaje, m.; (field) prado, m., pradera, dehesa, f. v.i. pacer; pastar. v.t. apacentar, pastar

pasty, a. pastoso; (pale) pálido. s. empanada, f.

pat, s. toque, m.; caricia, f.; (for butter) molde (de mantequilla), m. v.t. tocar; acariciar, pasar la mano (sobre). adv. a propósito; oportunamente; fácilmente. **pat of butter,** pedacito de mantequilla, m. **pat on the back,** golpe en la espalda, m.; (fig.) elogio, m.

Patagonian, a. and s. patagón (-ona)

patch, s. (mend) remiendo, m.; (piece) pedazo, m.; (plaster and aut., etc.) parche, m.; (beauty spot) lunar postizo, m.; (of ground) parcela, f.; (of flowers, etc.) masa, f.; (stain, and fig.) mancha, f. v.t. (mend) remendar; poner remiendo (a); pegar; (roughly) chafallar; (the face) ponerse lunares postizos. **a p. of blue sky,** un pedazo de cielo azul. **the patches of green grass,** las manchas de hierba verde. **to be not a p. on,** no ser

de la misma clase que; (of persons) no llegarle a los zancajos de. **to p. up a quarrel,** hacer las paces

patchwork, s. labor de retazos, obra de retacitos, f.; (fig.) mezcla, mezcolanza, f. **p. quilt,** centón, m.

patchy, a. desigual; manchado

patella, s. (anat.) rótula, f.

paten, s. (ecc.) patena, f.

patency, s. evidencia, claridad, f.

patent, a. evidente, patente; patentado. s. patente, f. v.t. patentar. **p. of nobility,** carta de hidalguía, ejecutoria, f. **P. applied for,** Patente solicitada. **p. leather,** s. charol, m. a. de charol. **p. medicine,** específico farmacéutico, m.

patentee, s. el, m. (f. la) que obtiene una patente; inventor (-ra)

patently, adv. evidentemente, claramente

paterfamilias, s. padre de familia, m.

paternal, a. paterno, paternal

paternally, adv. paternalmente

paternity, s. paternidad, f.

path, s. senda, vereda, f., sendero, m.; camino, m.; (track) pista, f.; (traject) trayectoria, f. **the beaten p.,** el camino trillado

pathetic, a. patético

pathetically, adv. patéticamente

pathless, a. sin senda

pathogenic, a. (med.) patógeno

pathological, a. patológico

pathologist, s. patólogo, m.

pathology, s. patología, f.

pathos, s. lo patético

patience, s. paciencia, f. **He tries my p. very much,** Me cuesta mucho no impacientarme con él. **to lose p.,** perder la paciencia; (grow angry) perder los estribos. **to play p.,** hacer solitarios

patient, a. paciente. s. paciente, m. and f.; (ill person) enfermo (-ma)

patiently, adv. con paciencia, pacientemente

patina, s. pátina, f.

patois, s. dialecto, m.

patriarch, s. patriarca, m.

patriarchal, a. patriarcal

patriarchy, s. patriarcado, m.

patrician, *a.* and *s.* patricio (-ia)

patrimonial, *a.* patrimonial

patrimony, *s.* patrimonio, *m.*

patriot, *s.* patriota, *m.* and *f.*

patriotic, *a.* patriótico

patriotically, *adv.* patrióticamente

patriotism, *s.* patriotismo, *m.*

patrol, *s.* patrulla, *f.*; ronda, *f.* *v.i.* and *v.t.* patrullar; rondar; recorrer. **p. boat,** lancha escampavía, *f.* **p. flight,** vuelo de patrulla, *m.*

patron, *s.* (of a freed slave) patrono, *m.*; (of the arts, etc.) mecenas, protector, *m.*; (customer) parroquiano (-na), cliente, *m.* and *f.* **p. saint,** santo (-ta), patrón (-ona)

patronage, *s.* (protection) patrocinio, *m.*; protección, *f.*; (ecc.) patronato, *m.*; (regular custom) clientela, *f.*; (of manner) superioridad, *f.*

patronal, *a.* patronal

patroness, *s.* patrona, *f.*; protectora, *f.*; (of a charity, etc.) patrocinadora, *f.*; (of a regiment, etc.) madrina, *f.*

patronize, *v.t.* patrocinar; proteger, favorecer; (a shop) ser parroquiano de; (treat arrogantly) tratar con superioridad

patronizing, *a.* (with air, behaviour, etc.) de superioridad, de altivez

patronymic, *a.* and *s.* patronímico (*m.*)

patten, *s.* zueco, chanclo, *m.*

patter, *s.* (jargon) jerga, *f.*; charla, *f.*; (of rain) azotes, *m. pl.*; (of feet) son, *m.*; golpecitos, *m. pl.* *v.t.* (repeat) decir mecánicamente. *v.i.* (chatter) charlar; (of rain) azotar, bailar; correr ligeramente

pattern, *s.* modelo, *m.*; (sew. and dressmaking) patrón, *m.*; (in founding) molde, *m.*; (templet) escantillón, *m.*; (of cloth, etc.) muestra, *f.*; (design) dibujo, diseño, *m.*; (example) ejemplar, *m.* *v.t.* diseñar; estampar. **p. book,** libro de muestras, *m.*

patty, *s.* empanada, *f.*, pastelillo, *m.*

paucity, *s.* poquedad, *f.*; corto número, *m.*; insuficiencia, escasez, *f.*

Pauline, *a.* de San Pablo

paunch, *s.* panza, barriga, *f.*

pauper, *s.* pobre, *m.* and *f.*

pauperism, *s.* pauperismo, *m.*

pauperization, *s.* empobrecimiento, *m.*

pauperize, *v.t.* empobrecer, reducir a la miseria

pause, *s.* pausa, *f.*; intervalo, *m.*; silencio, *m.*; interrupción, *f.*; (mus.) pausa, *f.* *v.i.* pausar, hacer una pausa; detenerse, interrumpirse; vacilar. **to give p. to,** hacer vacilar (a)

pavan, *s.* (dance) pavana, *f.*

pave, *v.t.* empedrar, enlosar. **to p. the way for,** facilitar el paso de, preparar el terreno para, abrir el camino de

pavement, *s.* pavimento, *m.*; (sidewalk) acera, *f.* **p.-artist,** pintor callejero, *m.*

pavilion, *s.* pabellón, *m.*; (for a band, etc.) quiosco, *m.*; (tent) tienda de campaña, *f.*

paving, *s.* pavimentación, *f.*; empedrado, *m.*; see **pavement.** **p.-stone,** losa, *f.*

paw, *s.* pata, *f.*; (with claws) garra, *f.*; (fam.) manaza, *f.* *v.t.* tocar con la pata; (scratch) arañar; (handle) manosear. *v.i.* (of a horse) piafar

pawing, *s.* (of a horse) el piafar; (handling) manoseo, *m.*

pawn, *s.* (in chess) peón (de ajedrez), *m.*; empeño, *m.*; (fig.) prenda, *f.* *v.t.* empeñar, pignorar; dar en prenda. **p.-ticket,** papeleta de empeño, *f.*

pawnbroker, *s.* prestamista, *m.* and *f.*

pawning, *s.* empeño, *m.*, pignoración, *f.*

pawnshop, *s.* casa de préstamos, casa de empeño, *f.*, monte de piedad, *m.*

pay, *s.* paga, *f.*; (mil., nav.) soldada, *f.*; salario, *m.*; (of a workman) jornal, *m.*; (reward) recompensa, compensación, *f.*; (profit) beneficio, provecho, *m.* **pay-day,** día de paga, *m.* **pay-office,** pagaduría, *f.* **pay-sheet,** nómina, *f.*

pay, *v.t.* pagar; (a debt) satisfacer; (spend) gastar; (recompense) remunerar, recompensar; (hand over) entregar; (yield) producir; (a visit) hacer; (attention) prestar; (homage) rendir; (one's respects) presentar. *v.i.* pagar; producir ganancia; sacar provecho; ser una ventaja, ser provechoso. **It would not pay him to do it,** El hacerlo no le saldría a cuenta. **to pay a compliment** (to), cumplimentar, decir alabanzas (a), echár una flor (a). **to pay attention,** prestar atención; hacer caso. **to pay cash,** pagar al contado. **to pay in advance,** pagar adelantado. **to pay in full,** saldar. **to pay off old scores,** ajustar cuentas viejas. **to pay one's addresses to,** hacer la corte (a), pretender en matrimonio (a). **to pay the penalty,** sufrir el castigo. **to pay with interest,** (*fig.*) pagar con creces. **to pay again,** volver a pagar, pagar de nuevo. **to pay back,** devolver, restituir; (money only) reembolsar; (*fig.*) pagar en la misma moneda, vengarse (de). **to pay down,** pagar al contado. **to pay for,** pagar, costear; satisfacer. **to pay in,** ingresar. **to pay off,** (persons) despedir; (a debt) saldar; (a mortgage) cancelar, redimir. **to pay out,** (persons) vengarse de; (money) pagar; (ropes, etc.) arriar. **to pay up,** pagar; pagar por completo; (shares, etc.) redimir

payable, *a.* pagadero; a pagar; que puede ser pagado

payee, *s.* tenedor, *m.*

payer, *s.* pagador (-ra)

paying, *s.* See **payment**

paymaster, *s.* pagador, *m.*; tesorero, *m.* **P.-General,** ordenador general de pagos, *m.*

payment, *s.* pago, *m.*, paga, *f.*; remuneración, *f.*; (*fig.*) recompensa, satisfacción, *f.*; (*fig.*) premio, *m.* **in p. of,** en pago de. **on. p. of,** mediante el pago de. **p. in advance,** pago adelantado, anticipo, *m.*

pea, *s.* guisante, *m.* **dry or split peas,** guisantes secos, *m. pl.* **sweet pea,** guisante de olor, *m.* **pea-flour,** harina de guisantes, *f.* **pea-green,** verde claro, *m.* **pea-jacket,** chaquetón de piloto, *m.* **pea-shooter,** cerbatana, *f.*

peace, *s.* paz, *f.*; tranquilidad, quietud, *f.*, sosiego, *m.*; (*law*) orden público, *m.* **P.!** ¡Silencio! **to hold one's p.,** callarse, guardar silencio. **to make p.,** hacer las paces. **P. be upon this house!** ¡Paz sea en esta casa! **p.-footing,** pie de paz, *m.* **p.-loving,** pacífico. **p.-offering,** sacrificio propiciatorio, *m.*; satisfacción, oferta de paz, *f.*

peaceable, *a.* pacífico; apacible; tranquilo, sosegado

peaceableness, *s.* paz, *f.*; apacibilidad, *f.*; tranquilidad, quietud, *f.*, sosiego, *m.*

peaceably, *adv.* pacíficamente; tranquilamente

peaceful, *a.* pacífico; tranquilo; silencioso. **to come with p. intentions,** venir de paz

peacefully, *adv.* en paz; pacíficamente; tranquilamente

peacefulness, *s.* paz, *f.*; tranquilidad, calma, quietud, *f.*; silencio, *m.*; carácter pacífico, *m.*

peacemaker, *s.* pacificador (-ra); conciliador (-ra)

peach, *s.* (fruit) melocotón, *m.*; (tree) melocotonero, melocotón, *m.*; (girl) breva, *f.* **p.-colour,** color de melocotón, *m.*

peacock, *s.* pavo real, pavón, *m.* *v.i.* pavonearse; darse humos. **The p. spread its tail,** El pavo real hizo la rueda

peahen, *s.* pava real, *f.*

peak, *s.* punta, *f.*; (of a cap) visera, *f.*; (of a mountain) peñasco, *m.*, cumbre, cima, *f.*; (mountain itself) pico, *m.*; (*naut.*, of a hull) pico, *m.*; (*fig.*) auge, apogeo, *m.*; punto más alto, *m.* *v.i.* consumirse, enflaquecer. **p. hours,** horas de mayor tráfico, *f.pl.*

peaked, *a.* en punta; puntiagudo; picudo; (of a cap) con visera; (wan) ojeroso; (thin) delgaducho, macilento, consumido

peal, *s.* toque (or repique) de campanas, *m.*; campanillazo, *m.*; carillón, *m.*; (noise) estruendo, ruido, *m.*; (of thunder) trueno, *m.*; (of an organ) sonido, *m.* *v.i.* repicar; sonar. *v.t.* tañer, echar a vuelo (las campanas); (of a bell that one presses) hacer sonar, tocar. **a p. of laughter,** una carcajada

peanut, *s.* cacahuete, *m.* **p.-butter,** mantequilla de cacahuete, *f.*

pear, *s.* pera, *f.* **p.-shaped,** piriforme, de figura de pera. **p.-tree,** peral, *m.*

pearl, *s.* (all meanings) perla, *f.*; (mother-of-pearl) nácar, *m.* *a.* de perla; perlero. *v.t.* (dew) rociar, aljofarar. *v.i.* pescar perlas; formar perlas. **seed p.,** aljófar, *m.* **p.-ash,** carbonato potásico, *m.* **p.-barley,** cebada perlada, *f.* **p.-button,** botón de nácar, *m.* **p.-fisher,** pescador de perlas, *m.* **p.-fishery,** pescaduría de perlas, *f.* **p.-grey,** gris de perla, *m.*

pearly, *a.* perlino; de perla; nacarado; (dewy) aljofarado

peasant, *s.* campesino (-na), labrador (-ra). *a.* campesino

peasantry, *s.* campesinos, *m. pl.*, gente del campo, *f.*

peat, *s.* turba, *f.* **p.-bog,** turbera, *f.*

peaty, *a.* turboso

pebble, *s.* guijarro, *m.*, pedrezuela, guija, *f.*; (gravel) guijo, *m.*; cristal de roca, *m.*; lente de cristal de roca, *m.*

pebbled, pebbly, *a.* guijarroso, enguijarrado

peccadillo, *s.* pecadillo, *m.*

peck, *s.* (of a bird) picotazo, *m.*, picada, *f.*; (kiss) besito, *m.*; (large amount) montón, *m.*; multitud, *f.* *v.t.* (of a bird) picotear; sacar (or coger) con el pico; (kiss) besar rápidamente. *v.i.* (with at) picotear; picar

pectin, *s.* (*chem.*) pectina, *f.*

pectoral, *a.* pectoral

peculiar, *a.* particular, peculiar, individual; propio, característico; (marked) especial; (unusual) extraño, raro, extraordinario

peculiarity, *s.* peculiaridad, particularidad, *f.*; singularidad, *f.*; (eccentricity) excentricidad, rareza, *f.*

peculiarly, *adv.* particularmente, peculiarmente; especialmente; extrañamente

pecuniarily, *adv.* pecuniariamente

pecuniary, *a.* pecuniario

pedagogic, *a.* pedagógico

pedagogue, *s.* pedagogo, *m.*

pedagogy, *s.* pedagogía, *f.*

pedal, *a.* (*zool.*) del pie. *s.* pedal, *m.* *v.i.* pedalear

pedant, *s.* pedante, *m.* and *f.*

pedantic, *a.* pedante

pedantically, *adv.* con pedantería, pedantescamente

pedantry, *s.* pedantería, *f.*

peddle, *v.i.* ser buhonero. *v.t.* revender

peddling, *s.* buhonería, *f.* *a.* trivial, insignificante; mezquino

pedestal, *s.* pedestal, *m.*; (*fig.*) fundamento, *m.*, base, *f.* **to put on a p.,** (*fig.*) poner sobre un pedestal

pedestrian, *s.* peatón, peón, *m.* *a.* pedestre; (*fig.*) patoso. **p.-crossing,** cruce de peatones, *m.* **p. traffic,** circulación de los peatones, *f.*

pediatrician, *s.* pediatra, *m.* and *f.*

pedicel, *s.* (*bot.*) pedículo, *m.*

pedigree, *s.* genealogía, *f.*; raza, *f.*; (of words) etimología, *f.* *a.* (of animals) de raza, de casta. **p. dog,** perro de casta, *m.*

pediment, *s.* (*arch.*) frontón, *m.*

pedlar, *s.* buhonero, *m.*

pedometer, *s.* pedómetro, cuentapasos, *m.*

peduncle, *s.* (*bot.*) pedúnculo, *m.*

peel, *s.* (baker's) pala, *f.*; (of fruit, etc.) piel, *f.*, hollejo, *m.* *v.t.* pelar, mondar; (bark) descortezar. *v.i.* descascararse, desconcharse; (of the bark of a tree) descortezarse

peeling, *s.* (of fruit, etc.) peladura, monda, *f.*; (of bark) descortezadura, *f.*; (of paint, etc.) desconchadura, *f.*

peep, *v.i.* (of birds) piar; (of mice) chillar; (peer) atisbar, mirar a hurtadillas; (appear) asomar; mostrarse; (of the dawn) despuntar. *s.* (of birds) pío, *m.*; (of mice) chillido, *m.*; (glimpse) vista, *f.*; (glance) ojeada, mirada furtiva, *f.*; **at the p. of day,** al despuntar el día. **p.-hole,** mirilla, *f.*, atisbadero, *m.*; escucha, *f.* **p.-show,** óptica, *f.*

peer, *s.* par, *m.*; igual, *m.* and *f.* *v.i.* atisbar; escudriñar; (*fig.*) asomar, aparecer

peerage, *s.* nobleza, aristocracia, *f.*; dignidad de par, *f.*

peeress, *s.* paresa, *f.*

peerless, *a.* sin par, incomparable, sin igual

peevish, *a.* displicente, malhumorado; picajoso, vidrioso, enojadizo

peevishness, *s.* displicencia, *f.*, mal humor, *m.*; impaciencia, *f.*

peg, *s.* clavija, *f.*; (of a tent) estaca, *f.*; (of a barrel) estaquilla, *f.*; (of a violin, etc.) clavija, *f.*; (for coats, etc.) colgadero, *m.*; (of whisky, etc.) trago, *m.*; (*fig.*) pretexto, *m.* *v.t.* clavar, enclavijar, empernar. **to take down a peg,** bajar los humos (a). **to peg away,** batirse el cobre. **to peg down,** fijar con clavijas; (a tent) sujetar con estacas; (prices) fijar

Pegasus, *s.* Pegaso, *m.*

peignoir, *s.* peinador, salto de cama, *m.*, bata, *f.*

pekinese, *s.* perro (-rra) pequinés (-esa)

Pelagian, *a.* pelágico

pelican, *s.* pelícano, *m.*

pellagra, *s.* (*med.*) pelagra, *f.*

pellet, *s.* bolita, *f.*; (pill) píldora, *f.*; (shot) perdigón, *m.*

pell-mell, *adv.* a trochemoche; atropelladamente

pellucid, *a.* diáfano

Peloponesian, *a.* and *s.* peloponense (*m.* and *f.*)

pelota, *s.* pelota vasca, *f.* **p. player,** pelotari, *m.*

pelt, *s.* pellejo, *m.*; cuero, *m.*; (fur) piel, *f.*; (blow) golpe, *m.* *v.t.* llover (piedras, etc.) sobre, arrojar . . . sobre; (questions) disparar; (throw) tirar. *v.i.* (of rain) azotar, diluviar

pelvic, *a.* pélvico, pelviano

pelvis, *s.* pelvis, *f.*

pen, *s.* (for sheep, etc.) aprisco, *m.*; corral, *m.*; (paddock) parque, *m.*; (for hens) pollera, *f.*; (for writing and *fig.*, author, etc.) pluma, *f.* *v.t.* (shut up) acorralar; encerrar; (write) escribir (con pluma). **pen-and-ink drawing,** dibujo a la pluma, *m.* **pen-holder,** portaplumas, *m.* **pen-name,** seudónimo, *m.* **pen-wiper,** limpiaplumas, *m.*

penal, *a.* penal. **p. code,** código penal, *m.* **p. colony,** colonia penal, *f.* **p. servitude,** trabajos forzados (or forzosos), *m. pl.* **p.**

servitude for life, cadena perpetua, *f.*

penalization, *s.* castigo, *m.*

penalize, *v.t.* penar, imponer pena (a); castigar

penalty, *s.* (*law*) penalidad, *f.*; castigo, *m.*; (fine) multa, *f.*; (risk) riesgo, *m.*; (*sport*) "penalty," *m.* **the p. of,** la desventaja de. **under p. of,** so pena de. **p. kick,** (football) "penalty," *m.*

penance, *s.* penitencia, *f.* **to do p.,** hacer penitencia

penchant, *s.* tendencia, *f.*; inclinación, *f.*

pencil, *s.* lápiz, *m.*; (automatic) lapicero, *m.* *v.t.* escribir (or dibujar or marcar) con lápiz. **p.-case,** estuche para lápices, *m.* **p.-holder,** lapicero, *m.* **p.-sharpener,** cortalápices, afilalápices, *m.*

pendant, *s.* (jewel) pendiente, *m.*; (*arch.*) culo de lámpara, *m.*; (*naut.*, rope) amantillo, *m.*; (flag) gallardete, *m.*

pending, *a.* pendiente. *prep.* durante. **to be p.,** pender; amenazar

pendulous, *a.* péndulo; colgante; oscilante

pendulum, *s.* péndola, *f.*, péndulo, *m.*

penetrability, *s.* penetrabilidad, *f.*

penetrable, *a.* penetrable

penetrate, *v.t.* and *v.i.* penetrar

penetrating, *a.* penetrante

penetratingly, *adv.* penetrantemente

penetration, *s.* penetración, *f.*

penguin, *s.* pingüino, pájaro bobo, *m.*

penicillin, *s.* penicilina, *f.*

peninsula, *s.* península, *f.*

peninsular, *a.* peninsular. **P. War,** Guerra de la Independencia, *f.*

penis, *s.* pene, *m.*

penitence, *s.* penitencia, *f.*

penitent, *a.* penitente. *s.* penitente, *m.* and *f.*

penitential, *a.* penitencial

penitentiary, *s.* (*ecc.*) penitenciaria, *f.*; casa de corrección, *f.*; penitenciaría, *f.*; presidio, *m.*; cárcel modelo, *f.* *a.* penitenciario

penitently, *adv.* penitentemente

penknife, *s.* cortaplumas, *m.*

penmanship, s. caligrafía, f.

pennant, s. (naut.) gallardete, m.; banderola, f.; (ensign) insignia, bandera, f.

penniless, a. sin un penique, sin blanca; indigente, pobre de solemnidad. to leave p., dejar en la miseria; (fam.) dejar sin camisa

pennilessness, s. falta de dineros, extrema pobreza, f.

penning, s. escritura, f.; (drawing up) redacción, f.; (of bulls, etc.) acorralamiento, m.

pennon, s. pendón, m., banderola, f.; (ensign) bandera, insignia, f.

Pennsylvanian, a. and s. pensilvano (-na)

penny, s. penique, m.; (nearest Spanish equivalent) perra gorda, f. a. de un penique. p.-a-liner, gacetillero, m. p. dreadful, folletín, m., novela por entregas, f. p.-in-the-slot machine, tragaperras, m.

pennyworth, s. penique, valor de un penique, m.

pension, s. pensión, f.; (mil.) retiro, m.; (grant) beca, f.; (boarding-house) pensión de familia, f. v.t. pensionar, dar una pensión (a); (with off) jubilar. old age p., pensión para la vejez, f. retirement p., pensión vitalicia, f.

pensioner, s. pensionista, m. and f.; (mil. and nav.) inválido, m.

pensive, a. pensativo, meditabundo; cabizbajo, triste

pensively, adv. pensativamente; tristemente

pensiveness, s. reflexión, meditación profunda, f.; tristeza, melancolía, f.

pentagon, s. pentágono, m.

pentagonal, a. pentágono

pentagram, s. (mus.) pentagrama, m.

pentahedron, s. (geom.) pentaedro, m.

pentameter, s. pentámetro, m.

pentane, s. (chem.) pentano, m.

Pentateuch, s. pentateuco, m.

Pentecost, s. Pentecostés, m., Pascua, f.

pentecostal, a. de Pentecostés, pascual

penthouse, s. cobertizo, tinglado, m., tejavana, f.

pent-up, a. encerrado; enjaulado; (of emotion) reprimido

penultimate, a. penúltimo. s. penúltimo, m.

penurious, a. pobre; escaso; (stingy) tacaño, avaro

penury, s. penuria, f.

peony, s. peonía, f., saltaojos, m.

people, s. pueblo, m.; nación, f.; gente, f.; personas, f. pl.; (used disparagingly, mob) populacho, vulgo, m.; (inhabitants) habitantes, m. pl.; (subjects) súbditos, m. pl.; (relations) parientes, m. pl.; familia, f. v.t. poblar. little p., (children) gente menuda, f. respectable p., gente de bien, f. the p. of Burgos, los habitantes de Burgos. P. say, Se dice, La gente dice. Very few p. think as you do, Hay muy pocas personas que piensen como Vd. How are your p. (family)? ¿Cómo están los de tu casa? ¿Cómo está tu familia?

peopling, s. población, f.; colonización, f.

peplum, s. peplo, m.

pepper, s. pimienta, f.; (plant) pimentero, pimiento, m. v.t. sazonar con pimienta; (pelt) acribillar; (with questions) disparar; (a literary work with quotations, etc.) salpimentar. black p., pimienta negra, f. red p., pimiento, m.; (cayenne) pimentón, m. p.-castor, pimentero, m.

peppercorn, s. grano de pimienta, m.

peppermint, s. menta, f. p.-drop, pastilla de menta, f.

peppery, a. picante; (irascible) colérico, irascible

pepsin, s. (chem.) pepsina, f.

peptic, a. péptico

peptone, s. peptona, f.

per, prep. por. ninety miles per hour, noventa millas por hora. ten pesetas per dozen, diez pesetas la docena. £60 per annum, sesenta libras al año. per cent, por ciento

perambulate, v.t. recorrer

perambulator, s. cochecito para niños, m.

percale, s. percal, m.

percaline, s. percalina, f.

perceive, *v.t.* percibir, comprender, darse cuenta de; percibir, discernir

percentage, *s.* tanto por ciento, *m.*; porcentaje, *m.*

perceptible, *a.* perceptible, visible; sensible

perceptibly, *adv.* visiblemente; sensiblemente

perception, *s.* percepción, *f.*; sensibilidad, *f.*

perceptive, *a.* perceptivo

perch, *s.* (*icht.*) perca, *f.*; (for birds) percha, *f.*; (measure) pértica, *f.* *v.i.* posarse (en or sobre). *v.t.* posar (en or sobre)

percolate, *v.i.* filtrar; (*fig.*) penetrar. *v.t.* filtrar, colar

percolation, *s.* filtración, *f.*

percolator, *s.* filtro, *m.* coffee p., colador de café, *m.*

percussion, *s.* percusión, *f.*; choque, *m.* p. cap, fulminante, *m.* p. instrument, instrumento de percusión, *m.*

perdition, *s.* perdición, *f.*; ruina, *f.*

peregrination, *s.* peregrinación, *f.*

peremptorily, *adv.* perentoriamente

peremptoriness, *s.* perentoriedad, *f.*

peremptory, *a.* perentorio; (of manner, etc.) imperioso, autoritario

perennial, *a.* (*bot.*) vivaz; perenne; eterno, perpetuo. *s.* planta vivaz, *f.*

perennially, *adv.* perennemente

perfect, *a.* perfecto; (of a work) acabado; completo. *s.* (*gram.*) (tiempo) perfecto, *m.* *v.t.* perfeccionar; (oneself) perfeccionarse. to have a p. knowledge of . . ., conocer a fondo . . . They are p. strangers to me, Me son completamente desconocidos

perfectible, *a.* perfectible

perfecting, *s.* perfeccionamiento, *m.*; terminación, *f.*

perfection, *s.* perfección, *f.*; excelencia, *f.* to p., a la perfección, a las mil maravillas

perfectionist, *s.* perfeccionista, *m.* and *f.*

perfectly, *adv.* perfectamente

perfidious, *a.* pérfido

perfidy, *s.* perfidia, *f.*

perforate, *v.t.* perforar, agujerear

perforating, *a.* perforador

perforation, *s.* perforación, *f.*; agujero, *m.*

perforce, *adv.* a la fuerza, forzosamente

perform, *v.t.* hacer; poner por obra, llevar a cabo; desempeñar, cumplir; ejercer; (a piece of music, etc.) ejecutar; realizar; (a play) representar, dar; (a part in a play) desempeñar (el papel de . . .); (Divine Service) oficiar. *v.i.* (*theat.*) trabajar, representar un papel; (a musical instrument) tocar; (sing) cantar; (of animals) hacer trucos

performable, *a.* hacedero, practicable, ejecutable; (*theat.*) que puede representarse; (*mus.*) tocable

performance, *s.* ejecución, realización, *f.*; desempeño, ejercicio, *m.*; cumplimiento, *m.*; acción, *f.*; hazaña, *f.*; (work) obra, *f.*; (*theat.*) función, representación, *f.*; (*theat.*, acting of a part) interpretación, *f.*; (*mus.*) ejecución, *f.*; (*mech.*) potencia, *f.* first p., (*theat.*) estreno, *m.*

performer, *s.* (*mus.*) ejecutante, *m.* and *f.*, músico, *m.*; (*theat.*) actor (-triz), representante, *m.* and *f.*; artista, *m.* and *f.*

performing, *a.* (of animals) sabio. p. dog, perro sabio, *m.*

perfume, *s.* perfume, *m.*; fragancia, *f.*; aroma, *m.* *v.t.* perfumar; embalsamar, aromatizar, llenar con fragancia. p. burner, perfumador, *m.*

perfumer, *s.* perfumista, *m.* and *f.*

perfumery, *s.* perfumería, *f.*

perfuming, *s.* acción de perfumar, *f.* *a.* que perfuma

perfunctorily, *adv.* perfunctoriamente, sin cuidado; superficialmente

perfunctoriness, *s.* descuido, *m.*, negligencia, *f.*; superficialidad, *f.*

perfunctory, *a.* perfunctorio, negligente; superficial; ligero, de cumplido

pergola, *s.* emparrado, cenador, *m.*

perhaps, *adv.* quizá(s), tal vez

perianth, *s.* (*bot.*) perigonio, periantio, *m.*

pericardium, s. (anat.) pericardio, m.

pericarp, s. (bot.) pericarpio, m.

peril, s. peligro, m.; riesgo, m. v.t. poner en peligro; arriesgar. **at one's p.,** a su riesgo. **in p.,** en peligro

perilous, a. peligroso, arriesgado

perimeter, s. perímetro, m.

perineum, s. (anat.) perineo, m.

period, s. período, m.; época, f.; edad, f., tiempo, m.; duración, f.; término, plazo, m.; (gram.) período, m.; (full stop) punto final, m.; (med.) menstruación, regla, f. **p. furniture,** muebles de época, m. pl.

periodic, a. periódico

periodical, a. periódico. s. publicación periódica, revista, f.

periodically, adv. periódicamente

periodicity, s. periodicidad, f.

periosteum, s. (anat.) periostio, m.

peripatetic, a. peripatético

peripheral, a. periférico

periphery, s. periferia, f.

periphrastic, a. perifrástico

periscope, s. periscopio, m.

perish, v.i. perecer; marchitarse; desaparecer, acabar. **to be perished with cold,** estar muerto de frío

perishable, a. perecedero, frágil

peristyle, s. (arch.) peristilo, m.

peritoneum, s. peritoneo, m.

peritonitis, s. peritonitis, f.

periwig, s. peluca, f.

periwinkle, s. (zool.) caracol marino, m.; (bot.) vincapervinca, f.

perjure, v.t. perjurar. **to p. oneself,** perjurarse

perjurer, s. perjuro (-ra); perjurador (-ra)

perjury, s. perjurio, m. **to commit p.,** jurar en falso, perjurar

perk (up), v.i. levantar la cabeza; recobrar sus bríos, alzar la cabeza; sacar la cabeza

perkiness, s. desenvoltura, gallardía, f., despejo, m.

perky, a. desenvuelto, gallardo; coquetón; atrevido; (gay) alegre

permanence, s. permanencia, f.; estabilidad, f.

permanent, a. permanente; estable; (of posts, etc.) fijo. **p. wave,** ondulación permanente, f. **p. way,** (r.w.) vía, f.

permanganate, s. permanganato, m.

permeability, s. permeabilidad, f.

permeable, a. permeable

permeate, v.t. penetrar; impregnar; (fig.) infiltrar (en)

permeation, s. penetración, f.; impregnación, f.; (fig.) infiltración, f.

permissible, a. permisible, admisible; lícito

permission, s. permiso, m., licencia, f.

permissive, a. permisivo, tolerado; (optional) facultativo

permit, v.t. permitir; dar permiso (a), dejar; tolerar, sufrir; admitir. s. permiso, m.; licencia, f.; pase, m. **Will you p. me to smoke?** ¿Me permites fumar?

permutation, s. permutación, f.

permute, v.t. permutar

pernicious, a. pernicioso. **p. anæmia,** anemia perniciosa, f.

perniciousness, s. perniciosidad, f.

pernickety, a. tiquismiquis

peroration, s. peroración, f.

peroxide, s. peróxido, m.

perpendicular, a. perpendicular. s. perpendicular, f.

perpendicularity, s. perpendicularidad, f.

perpendicularly, adv. perpendicularmente

perpetrate, v.t. (law) perpetrar; cometer

perpetration, s. (law) perpetración, f.; comisión, f.

perpetrator, s. el, m. (f. la) que comete; (law) autor (-ra); perpetrador (-ra)

perpetual, a. perpetuo, perdurable, eterno; incesante, constante; (life-long) perpetuo

perpetually, adv. perpetuamente; sin cesar; continuamente; constantemente

perpetuate, v.t. perpetuar, eternizar; inmortalizar

perpetuation, s. perpetuación, f.

perpetuity, s. perpetuidad, f. **in p.,** para siempre

perplex, v.t. dejar perplejo, aturdir, confundir; embrollar

perplexed, *a.* perplejo, irresoluto; confuso; (of questions, etc.) complicado, intrincado

perplexedly, *adv.* perplejamente

perplexing, *a.* difícil; complicado; confuso

perplexity, *s.* perplejidad, *f.*; confusión, *f.*

perquisites, *s. pl.* emolumentos, *m. pl.*; gajes, percances, *m. pl.*; (tips) propinas, *f. pl.*

persecute, *v.t.* perseguir; importunar, molestar

persecution, *s.* persecución, *f.*

persecutor, *s.* perseguidor (-ra)

perseverance, *s.* perseverancia, *f.*

persevere, *v.i.* perseverar

persevering, *a.* perseverante

perseveringly, *adv.* con perseverancia, perseverantemente

Persian, *a.* persa; de Persia; pérsico. *s.* persa, *m.* and *f.*; (language) persa, *m.* **P. blinds,** persianas, *f. pl.* **P. cat,** gato (-ta) de Angora

persiennes, *s. pl.* persianas, *f. pl.*

persist, *v.i.* persistir; persistir (en), empeñarse (en), obstinarse (en)

persistence, *s.* persistencia, *f.*

persistent, *a.* persistente

persistently, *adv.* con persistencia, persistentemente

person, *s.* persona, *f.* **first p.,** (*gram.*) primera persona, *f.* **in p.,** en persona. **no p.,** nadie

personable, *a.* bien parecido

personage, *s.* personaje, *m.*

personal, *a.* personal; íntimo; particular; en persona; (movable) mueble. **He is to make a p. appearance,** Va a estar presente en persona. **p. column,** (in a newspaper) columna de los suspiros, *f.* **p. equation,** ecuación personal, *f.* **p. estate,** (goods) bienes muebles, *m. pl.*

personality, *s.* personalidad, *f.*; (insult) personalismo, *m.* **dual p.,** conciencia doble, *f.*

personally, *adv.* personalmente

personate *v.t.* (in a play) hacer el papel de; (impersonate) hacerse pasar por

personification, *s.* personificación, *f.*

personify, *v.t.* personificar

personnel, *s.* personal, *m.*

perspective, *s.* perspectiva, *f. a.* en perspectiva

perspicacious, *a.* perspicaz, clarividente, sagaz

perspicacity, *s.* perspicacia, clarividencia, sagacidad, *f.*

perspicuity, *s.* perspicuidad, claridad, lucidez, *f.*

perspicuous, *a.* perspicuo, claro

perspiration, *s.* sudor, *m.*

perspire, *v.i.* sudar, transpirar

persuadable, *a.* persuasible

persuade, *v.t.* persuadir; inducir (a), instar (a), mover (a), inclinar (a)

persuasion, *s.* persuasión, *f.*; persuasiva, *f.*; opinión, *f.*; creencia, *f.*; religión, *f.*; secta, *f.*

persuasive, *a.* persuasivo. *s.* persuasión, *f.*; aliciente, atractivo, *m.*

persuasively, *adv.* de un modo persuasivo, persuasivamente

persuasiveness, *s.* persuasiva, *f.*

pert, *a.* petulante; respondón, desparpajado

pertain, *v.i.* pertenecer (a); tocar (a), incumbir (a), convenir (a); estar relacionado (con)

pertinacious, *a.* pertinaz

pertinaciously, *adv.* con pertinacia

pertinacity, *s.* pertinacia, *f.*

pertinence, *s.* pertinencia, *f.*

pertinent, *a.* pertinente, atinado

pertinently, *adv.* atinadamente

pertly, *adv.* con petulancia; con descaro

pertness, *s.* petulancia, *f.*; desparpajo, descaro, *m.*

perturb, *v.t.* perturbar, agitar, turbar, inquietar

perturbation, *s.* perturbación, agitación, inquietud, *f.*; confusión, *f.*; desorden, *m.*

perturbed, *a.* perturbado, agitado, ansioso, intranquilo

perturbing, *a.* perturbador, inquietador

peruke, *s.* peluca, *f.*

perusal, *s.* lectura, *f.*; examen, *m.*

peruse, *v.t.* leer con cuidado, estudiar, examinar

Peruvian, *a.* and *s.* peruano (-na)

pervade, *v.t.* penetrar; llenar; saturar; difundirse por; reinar en

pervasion, s. penetración, f.

pervasive, a. penetrante

perverse, a. (wicked) perverso, depravado; obstinado; travieso; intratable

perversion, s. perversión, f.

perversity, s. (wickedness) perversidad, f.; obstinacia, f.; travesura, f.

perversive, a. perversivo

pervert, v.t. pervertir; (words, etc.) torcer, tergiversar

pervious, a. penetrable; permeable

pessary, s. (surg.) pesario, m.

pessimism, s. pesimismo, m.

pessimist, s. pesimista, m. and f.

pessimistic, a. pesimista

pessimistically, adv. con pesimismo

pest, s. insecto nocivo, m.; animal dañino, m.; parásito, m.; (pestilence) peste, f.; (fig.) plaga, f.; (person) mosca, f.

pester, v.t. importunar, molestar, incomodar. **to p. constantly,** (fam.) no dejar a sol ni a sombra

pestering, s. importunaciones, f. pl.

pestilence, s. pestilencia, peste, f.; plaga, f.

pestilential, a. pestilente, pestiferd; pernicioso

pestle, s. mano de mortero, f. v.t. pistar, machacar, majar

pet, s. animal doméstico, m.; niño (-ña) mimado (-da); favorito (-ta); (dear) querido (-da); (peevishness) despecho, malhumor, m. v.t. acariciar; (spoil) mimar. **to be a great pet,** ser un gran favorito

petal, s. pétalo, m., hoja, f.

Peter, s. Pedro, m. **blue P.,** bandera de salida, f. **Peter's pence,** los diezmos de San Pedro

peter (out), v.i. desaparecer; agotarse

petition, s. petición, f.; súplica, f.; instancia, solicitud, f.; memorial, m. v.t. suplicar; pedir, demandar; dirigir un memorial (a). **to file a p.,** elevar una instancia

petitioner, s. peticionario (-ia)

Petrarchan, a. petrarquista

petrel, s. petrel, m.

petrifaction, s. petrificación, f.

petrify, v.t. petrificar; (fam.)

dejar seco. **to become petrified,** petrificarse

petrol, s. bencina, gasolina, f. a. de gasolina, de bencina. **to run out of p.,** tener una pana de bencina. **p. gauge,** indicador del nivel de gasolina, m. **p. pump,** surtidor de gasolina, m. **p. station,** puesto de bencina, m.. estación de servicio, f. **p. tank,** depósito de bencina, m.

petroleum, s. petróleo, m. a. petrolero; de petróleo. **p. works,** refinería de petróleo, f.

petrology, s. petrografía, f.

petrous, a. pétreo

petticoat, s. enagua, f.; pl. petticoats, (slang) faldas, f. pl. a. de faldas, de mujeres; de mujer

pettifogger, s. (lawyer) picapleitos, m.; (quibbler) sofista, m.

pettifogging, a. charlatán, mezquino, trivial

pettiness, s. trivialidad, insignificancia, f.; pequeñez, f.; mezquindad, f.; ruindad, bajeza, f.

petty, a. trivial, sin importancia, insignificante; inferior; pequeño; mezquino; ruin; bajo. **p. cash,** gastos menores de caja, m. pl. **p. expenses,** gastos menudos, m. pl. **p. officer,** suboficial, m. **p. thief,** ratero (-ra)

petulance, s. mal humor, m., displicencia, irritabilidad, f.

petulant, a. malhumorado, displicente, enojadizo, irritable

petulantly, adv. displicentemente, con mal humor

petunia, s. petunia, f.

pew, s. banco de iglesia, m. **p. opener,** sacristán, m.

pewter, s. peltre, m. a. de peltre

phaeton, s. faetón, m.

phagocyte, s. fagocito, m.

phalange, s. falange, f.

phalanx, s. falange, f.

phallic, a. fálico

phallus, s. falo, m.

phanerogam, s. fanerógama, f.

phanerogamous, a. fanerógamo

phantasmagoria, s. fantasmagoria, f.

phantasmagoric, a. fantasmagórico

phantom, s. fantasma, espectro, m.; sombra, ficción, f.; visión, f.

Pharisaical, a. farisaico

Pharisee, s. fariseo, m.
pharmaceutical, a. farmacéutico
pharmacist, s. farmacéutico, m.
pharmacological, a. farmacológico
pharmacologist, s. farmacólogo, m.
pharmacology, s. farmacología, f.
pharmacopœia, s. farmacopea, f.
pharmacy, s. farmacia, f.
pharyngeal, a. faringeo
pharyngitis, s. faringitis, f.
pharynx, s. faringe, f.
phase, s. fase, f.; aspecto, m.; (ast.) fase, f.
pheasant, s. faisán, m. hen p., faisana, f. p. shooting, caza de faisanes, f.
pheasantry, s. faisanera, f.
phenacetin, s. fenacetina, f.
phenic, a. fénico
phenol, s. fenol, m.
phenomenal, a. fenomenal
phenomenally, adv. fenomenalmente
phenomenon, s. fenómeno, m.
phial, s. redoma, f.
philander, v.i. galantear
philanderer, s. Tenorio, galanteador, m.
philandering, s. galanteo, m.
philanthropic, a. filantrópico
philanthropist, s. filántropo, m.
philanthropy, s. filantropía, f.
philatelic, a. filatélico
philatelist, s. filatelista, m. and f.
philately, s. filatelia, f.
philharmonic, a. filarmónico
philippic, s. filípica, f.
Philippine, a. and s. filipino (-na)
Philistine, a. and s. filisteo (-ea)
philological, a. filológico
philologist, s. filólogo, m.
philology, s. filología, f.
philosopher, s. filósofo, m. philosopher's stone, piedra filosofal, f.
philosophic(al), a. filosófico
philosophize, v.i. filosofar
philosophy, s. filosofía, f. moral p., filosofía moral, f. natural p., filosofía natural, f.
philtre, s. filtro, m.
phlebitis, s. flebitis, f.
phlebotomist, s. sangrador, flebotómiano, m.
phlebotomy, s. flebotomía, f.

phlegm, s. flema, f.
phlegmatic, a. flemático
phlogistic, a. flogístico
phlogiston, s. flogisto, m.
phlox, s. flox, m.
Phœnician, a. and s. fenicio (-ia)
phœnix, s. fénix, f.
phonetic, a. fonético
phonetically, adv. fonéticamente
phoneticist, s. fonetista, m. and f.
phonetics, s. fonética, f.
phoney, a. falso; espurio. p. war, guerra tonta, f.
phonograph, s. fonógrafo, m.
phonological, a. fonológico
phonology, s. fonología, f.
phosgene, s. fosgeno, m.
phosphate, s. fosfato, m.
phosphoresce, v.i. fosforecer, ser fosforescente
phosphorescence, s. fosforescencia, f.
phosphorescent, a. fosforescente
phosphoric, a. fosfórico
phosphorite, s. fosforita, f.
phosphorus, s. fósforo, m.
photochemistry, s. fotoquímica, f.
photogenic, a. fotogénico
photo(graph), s. foto(grafía), f. v.i. fotografiar, retratar. to have one's p. taken, hacerse retratar
photographer, s. fotógrafo, m.
photographic, a. fotográfico
photography, s. fotografía, f.
photogravure, s. fotograbado, m.
photostat, s. fotostato, m.
photosynthesis, s. fotosíntesis, f.
phrase, s. frase, f.; (mus.) frase musical, f. v.i. expresar, frasear; redactar. p.-book, libro de frases, m.
phraseology, s. fraseología, f.
phrasing, s. (drawing up) redacción, f.; (style) estilo, m.; (mus.) frases, f. pl.
phrenetic, a. frenético
phrenologist, s. frenólogo, m.
phrenology, s. frenología, f.
phrenopathist, s. frenópata, m.
phrenopathy, s. frenopatía, f.
Phrygian, a. and s. frigio (-ia)
phthisis, s. tisis, f.
phylactery, s. filacteria, f.
phylloxera, s. filoxera, f.
physical, a. físico. p. fitness, buen estado físico, m. p. geo-

graphy, geografía física, *f.* **p. jerks,** ejercicios físicos, *m. pl.* **p. sciences,** ciencias físicas, *f. pl.* **p. training,** educación física, *f.*

physically, *adv.* físicamente
physician, *s.* médico (-ca)
physicist, *s.* físico, *m.*
physics, *s.* física, *f.*
physiognomist, *s.* fisonomista, *m.* and *f.*
physiognomy, *s.* fisonomía, *f.*
physiological, *a.* fisiológico
physiologically, *adv.* fisiológicamente
physiologist, *s.* fisiólogo, *m.*
physiology, *s.* fisiología, *f.*
physiotherapy, *s.* fisioterapia, *f.*
physique, *s.* físico, *m.*
pianist, *s.* pianista, *m.* and *f.*
piano, pianoforte, *s.* piano, *m.* **baby grand p.,** piano de media cola, *m.* **grand p.,** piano de cola, *m.* **upright p.,** piano vertical, *m.* **p. maker,** fabricante de pianos, *m.* **p. stool,** taburete de piano, *m.* **p. tuner,** afinador de pianos, *m.*
pianola, *s.* piano mecánico, *m.*
picaresque, *a.* picaresco
piccolo, *s.* flautín, *m.*
pick, *s.* (tool) pico, zapapico, *m.*; (mattock) piqueta, *f.*; (choice) selección, *f.*; derecho de elección, *m.*; (best) lo mejor, lo más escogido; (*fig.,* cream) flor, nata, *f.* **tooth-p.,** mondadientes, *m.* **p.-a-back,** sobre los hombros, a cuestas. **p.-axe,** zapapico, *m.* alcotana, *f.* **p.-me-up,** tónico, *m.*; trago, *m.*
pick, *v.t.* (with a pick-axe, make a hole) picar; (pluck, pick up) coger; (remove) sacar; (clean) limpiar; (one's teeth) mondarse (los dientes); (one's nose) hurgarse (las narices); (a bone) roer; (a lock) abrir con ganzúa; (a pocket) bolsear, robar del bolsillo; (peck) picotear; (choose) escoger; (a quarrel) buscar. *v.i.* (steal) hurtar, robar; (nibble) picar. **I have a bone to p. with you,** Tengo que ajustar unas cuentas contigo. **Take your p.!** ¡Escoja! **to p. and choose,** mostrarse difícil. **to p. to pieces,** (*fig.*) criticar severa-

mente. **to p. one's way through,** abrirse camino entre; andar con precaución por; andar a tientas por. **to p. off,** coger; arrancar; quitar; (shoot) disparar; fusilar. **to p. out,** entresacar; escoger; (recognize) reconocer; (understand) llegar a comprender; (a tune) tocar de oídas; (a song) cantar de oídas; (of colours) contrastar, resaltar. **to p. up,** *v.t.* (ground, etc.) romper con pico; coger; tomar; recoger; (raise) levantar, alzar; (information, etc.) cobrar, adquirir; (a living) ganar; (make friends with) trabar amistad con; (recover) recobrar; (find) encontrar, hallar; (buy) comprar; (learn) aprender; (a wireless message) interceptar; (a radio station) oír, tener. *v.i.* recobrar la salud; reponerse; mejorar. *s.* (*mech.*) recobro, *m.*
picket, *s.* estaca, *f.*; (*mil.,* and during strikes) piquete, *m.* *v.t.* cercar con estacas; poner piquetes ante (or alrededor de); poner de guardia; estacionar
picking, *s.* (gathering) recolección, *f.*; (choosing) selección, *f.*; (pilfering) robo, *m.*; *pl.* **pickings,** desperdicios, *m. pl.*; (perquisites) gajes, *m. pl.*; ganancias, *f. pl.*
pickle, *s.* (solution) escabeche, *m.*; (vegetable, etc.) encurtido, *m.*; (plight) apuro, *m.*; (child) diablillo, *m.* *v.t.* encurtir, escabechar
picklock, *s.* (thief and instrument) ganzúa, *f.*
pickpocket, *s.* carterista, *m.*, ratero (-ra)
picnic, *s.* partida de campo, jira, *f.*; picnic, *m.* *v.i.* llevar la merienda al campo, hacer un picnic
picnicker, *s.* excursionista, *m.* and *f.*
picrate, *s.* picrato, *m.*
picric, *a.* pícrico
pictorial, *a.* pictórico; ilustrado. *s.* revista ilustrada, *f.*
pictorially, *adv.* pictóricamente; en grabados; por imágenes
picture, *s.* cuadro, *m.*; (of a person) retrato, *m.*; imagen, *f.*; (illustration) grabado, *m.*, lá-

mina, *f.*; fotografía, *f.*; (outlook) perspectiva, *f.*; idea, *f.* *v.t.* pintar; describir; imaginar. **to go to the pictures,** ir al cine. **motion p.,** película, *f.* **talking p.,** película sonora, *f.* **p. book,** libro con láminas, *m.* **p. frame,** marco, *m.* **p. gallery,** museo de pinturas, *m.*; galería de pinturas, *f.* **p. hat,** pamela, *f.* **p. palace,** cine, *m.* **p. postcard,** tarjeta postal, *f.* **p. restorer,** restaurador de cuadros, *m.* **p. writing,** pictografía, *f.*

picturesque, *a.* pintoresco

picturesqueness, *s.* carácter pintoresco, *m.*, lo pintoresco; pintoresquismo, *m.*

pie, *s.* (savoury) empanada, *f.*; (sweet) pastel, *m.*, torta, *f.*; (of meat) pastelón, *m.*; (*print.*) pastel, *m.* **apple pie,** torta de manzanas, *f.* **to eat humble pie,** bajar las orejas. **to have a finger in the pie,** meter baza

piebald, *a.* pío; tordo

piece, *s.* pedazo, *m.*; trozo, *m.*; parte, porción, *f.*; (literary, artistic work, coin, of fabric, at chess, etc. and slang) pieza, *f.*; (of luggage) bulto, *m.*; (of paper) hoja, *f.*; (of ground) parcela, *f.*; (of money) moneda, *f.* *v.t.* remendar; unir, juntar. **a p. of advice,** un consejo. **a p. of bread,** un pedazo de pan; una rebanada de pan. **a p. of folly,** un acto de locura. **a p. of furniture,** un mueble. **a p. of insolence,** una insolencia. **a p. of news,** una noticia. **a p. of paper,** un papel, una hoja de papel. **a p. of poetry,** una poesía. **Peter has a five-shilling p.,** Pedro tiene una moneda de cinco chelines. **to break in pieces,** *v.t.* hacer pedazos, romper. *v.i.* hacerse pedazos, romperse. **to come or fall to pieces,** deshacerse; (of machines) desarmarse. **to cut in pieces,** cortar en pedazos; (an army) destrozar. **to give a p. of one's mind (to),** decir cuatro verdades (a), decir cuántas son cinco (a). **to go to pieces,** (of persons) hacerse pedazos. **to take to pieces,** (a machine) desmontar; deshacer. **to tear**

or pull to pieces, hacer pedazos, despedazar; desgarrar. **p. goods,** géneros en piezas, *m.* *pl.* **p.-work,** trabajo a destajo, *m.* **to do p.-work,** trabajar a destajo. **p.-worker,** destajista, *m.* and *f.*

piecemeal, *adv.* en pedazos; a remiendos; en detalle; poco a poco

piecrust, *s.* pasta, *f.*

pied, *a.* bicolor; abigarrado, de varios colores

pier, *s.* (jetty) dique, *m.*; embarcadero, *m.*; malecón, *m.*; (of a bridge) pila, *f.*; (pillar) columna, *f.*; (between windows, etc.) entrepaño, *m.* **p.-glass,** espejo de cuerpo entero, *m.* **p. head,** punta del dique, *f.* **p. table,** consola, *f.*

pierce, *v.t.* penetrar; (of sorrow, etc.) traspasar, herir; (bore) agujerear, taladrar. *v.i.* penetrar

piercing, *a.* penetrante; (of the wind, etc.) cortante; (of the voice, etc.) agudo. *s.* penetración, *f.*

piercingly, *adv.* de un modo penetrante, agudamente

pietism, *s.* pietismo, *m.*

pietist, *s.* pietista, *m.* and *f.*

pietistic, *a.* pietista

piety, *s.* piedad, devoción, *f.*

piezometer, *s.* (*phys.*) piezómetro, *m.*

piffle, *s.* patrañas, tonterías, *f.* *pl.*

pig, *s.* puerco, cerdo, *m.*; (*fam.*) cochino, *m.*; (metal) lingote, *m.* **to buy a pig in a poke,** cerrar un trato a ciegas. **pig-eyed,** de ojos de cerdo. **p.-iron,** lingote de fundición, *m.*

pigeon, *s.* paloma, *f.*, palomo, *m.*; (*fam.*) primo, *m.* *v.t.* embaucar, engañar. **carrier p.,** paloma mensajera, *f.* **clay p.,** pichón de barro, platillo de arcilla, *m.* **male p.,** pichón, *m.* **pouter p.,** paloma buchona, *f.* **young p.,** palomino, *m.* **p. fancier,** palomero, *m.* **p.-hole,** casilla, *f.* *v.t.* encasillar. **set of p.-holes,** encasillado, *m.* **p.-shooting,** tiro de pichón, *m.* **p.-toed,** patituerto

piggery, *s.* pocilga, *f.*

pigheaded, *a.* terco, testarudo

pigheadedness, *s.* terquedad, testarudez, *f.*

piglet, *s.* cerdito, *m.*

pigment, *s.* pigmento, *m.*

pigmentary, *a.* pigmentario

pigmentation, *s.* pigmentación, *f.*

pigskin, *s.* piel de cerdo, *f.*

pigsty, *s.* pocilga, *f.*

pigtail, *s.* coleta, *f.*

pike, *s.* (*mil.*) pica, *f.*, chuzo, *m.*; (peak) pico, *m.*

pikeman, *s.* piquero, *m.*

pikestaff, *s.* mango de pica, *m.*; (staff) bordón, *m.* to be as plain as a p., saltar a los ojos

pilaster, *s.* pilastra, *f.*

pile, *s.* estaca, *f.*; poste, *m.*; (engineering) pilote, *m.*; (heap) pila, *f.*, montón, *m.*; (pyre) pira, *f.*; (building) edificio grande, *m.*; (*elec.*) pila, *f.*; (hair) pelo, *m.*; (nap) pelusa, *f.*; *pl.* piles, (*med.*) hemorroides, almorranas, *f. pl.* *v.t.* clavar pilotes en; apoyar con pilotes; (heap) amontonar; (load) cargar. to make one's p., (*fam.*) hacer su pacotilla. to p. arms, poner los fusiles en pabellón. to p. on, (coal, etc.) echar; (increase) aumentar. to p. it on, exagerar, intensificar; (a table) cargar. to p. up, amontonarse; acumularse; (of a ship) encallar. p.-driver, machina, *f.*; martinete, *m.* p.-dwelling, vivienda palustre, *f.*

pilfer, *v.t.* sisar, sonsacar, hurtar, ratear

pilferer, *s.* sisador (-ra), ratero (-ra)

pilfering, *s.* sisa, ratería, *f.*

pilgrim, *s.* peregrino (-na). pilgrim's staff, bordón, *m.*

pilgrimage, *s.* peregrinación, *f.*; romería, *f.* to make a p., hacer una peregrinación, peregrinar; ir en romería

piling, *s.* amontonamiento, *m.*; (of buildings) pilotaje, *m.*

pill, *s.* píldora, *f.* to gild the p., (*fig.*) dorar la píldora. p.-box, caja de píldoras, *f.*; (*mil.*) nido de ametralladoras, *m.*

pillage, *v.t.* pillar, saquear. *s.* saqueo, *m.*

pillager, *s.* saqueador (-ra)

pillaging, *s.* pillaje, *m.* *a.* pillador, saqueador

pillar, *s.* pilar, *m.*, columna, *f.*; (person) sostén, soporte, *m.* from p. to post, de Ceca en Meca. p. of salt, estatua de sal, *f.* the Pillars of Hercules, las Columnas de Hércules. to be a p. of strength, (*fam.*) ser una roca. p.-box, buzón, *m.*

pillared, *a.* con columnas, sostenido por columnas; en columnas

pillion, *s.* (on a horse, etc.) grupera, *f.*; (on a motor-cycle) grupa, *f.* to ride p., ir a la grupa

pillory, *s.* picota, argolla, *f.* *v.t.* empicotar; (*fig.*) poner en ridículo; censurar duramente

pillow, *s.* almohada, *f.*; (for lacemaking) cojín, *m.*; (of a machine) cojinete, *m.* *v.t.* apoyar; reposar; servir como almohada. to take counsel of one's p., consultar con la almohada. p.-case, funda de almohada, *f.*

pilot, *s.* piloto, *m.*; (*naut.*) práctico, piloto (de puerto), *m.* *v.t.* guiar, conducir; (*naut.*, *aer.*) pilotar, pilotear. p. boat, vaporcito del práctico, *m.* p. jacket, chaquetón de piloto, *m.* p. officer, oficial de aviación, *m.*

pilotage, *s.* pilotaje, *m.*; (*naut.* practicaje, *m.*

pilotless, *a.* sin piloto

pimento, *s.* pimiento, *m.*

pimp, *s.* rufián, alcahuete, *m.* *v.i.* alcahuetear

pimpernel, *s.* (*bot.*) pimpinela, *f.*

pimple, *s.* grano, *m.*

pimply, *a.* con granos

pin, *s.* alfiler, *m.*; prendedor, *m.*; clavija, *f.*; clavo, *m.*, chaveta, *f.*; (bolt) perno, *m.* *v.t.* prender con alfileres; (with a peg) enclavijar; fijar; sujetar. to pin up, sujetar con alfileres; (the hair) sujetar con horquillas. drawing-pin, hat-pin, etc. See under D, H, etc. I don't care a pin, No me importa un bledo. to be on pins, estar en ascuas. to suffer from pins and needles, tener agujones. pin-head, cabeza de alfiler, *f.* pin-money, alfileres, *m. pl.* pin-oak, (*bot.*) pincarrasco, *m.*, carrasca, *f.* pin point, punta de alfiler, *f.* pin-prick, alfilerazo, *m.*

pinafore, s. delantal de niño, m.

pince-nez, s. quevedos, m. pl.

pincers, s. pl. pinzas, tenazas, f. pl., alicates, m. pl.; (of crustaceans) pinzas, f. pl. **p. movement,** movimiento de pinzas, m.

pinch, v.t. pellizcar; (crush) estrujar; aplastar; apretar; (of the cold) helar; (steal) hurtar, birlar; (arrest) coger, prender. s. pellizco, tornisçón, m.; pulgarada, f.; (of snuff) polvo, m.; (distress) miseria, f.; (pain) dolor, m., angustia, f. **at a p.,** en caso de apuro. **to know where the shoe pinches,** saber (uno) dónde le aprieta el zapato

pinched, a. (by the cold) helado; (wan) marchito, descolorido

pincushion, s. acerico, m.

Pindaric, a. pindárico

pine, s. (bot.) pino, m. v.i. languidecer, marchitarse, consumirse. **to p. for,** anhelar, suspirar por, perecer por. **pitch-p.,** pino de tea, m. **p.-apple,** piña de las Indias, f., ananás, m. **p. cone,** piña, f. **p. kernel,** piñón, m. **p. needle,** pinocha, f. **p. wood,** pinar, m., pineda, f.

pineal, a. en figura de piña; (anat.) pineal

ping, s. silbido de una bala, m.; zumbido, m. **p.-pong,** tenis de mesa, "ping-pong," m.

pinion, s. (wing) ala, f.; (small feather) piñón, m.; (in carving) alón, m.; (wheel) piñón, m. v.t. atar las alas de; cortar un piñón de; (a person) atar; (the arms of) trincar, asegurar

pink, s. (bot.) clavel, m.; color de rosa, m.; (perfection) modelo, m.; colmo, m.; (hunting) color rojo, m.; levitón rojo de caza, m. a. de color de rosa, rosado. v.t. (sew.) picar; (pierce) penetrar, atravesar. v.i. (of an engine) picar

pinking, s. (sew.) picadura, f.

pinkish, a. rosáceo

pinkness, s. color de rosa, m.

pinnace, s. (naut.) pinaza, f.

pinnacle, s. pináculo, m.

pinnate, a. pinado

pint, s. (measure) pinta, f.

pintle, s. (pin) perno, m.

piolet, s. piolet, m.

pioneer, s. pionero, explorador, m.; introductor, m. **to be a p. in . . .,** ser el primero en (or a) . . .

pious, a. pío, devoto, piadoso

piously, adv. piadosamente, devotamente

pip, s. (of fruit) pepita, f.; (on cards, dice) punto, m.; (disease) moquillo, m.; (of an army, etc., officer) insignia, f.

pipe, s. (for tobacco) pipa de fumar, f.; (mus.) caramillo, m.; (boatswain's) pito, m.; (of a bird) trino, m.; (voice) voz aguda, f.; tubo, m.; (for water, etc.) cañería, f.; (of a hose) manga, f.; (of an organ) cañón, m.; (of wine) pipa, f.; pl. pipes, (mus.) gaita, f. v.i. tocar el caramillo (or la gaita); empezar a cantar; silbar; (of birds) trinar. v.t. (a tune) tocar; (sing) cantar; (whistle) llamar con pito; conducir con cañerías; instalar cañerías en. **He smokes a p.,** Fuma en pipa. **I smoked a p.** (of tobacco) **before I went to bed,** Fumé una pipa antes de acostarme. **Put that in your p. and smoke it!** ¡Chúpate eso! **p. clay,** blanquizal, m. **p. cleaner,** limpiapipas, m. **p. layer,** cañero, fontanero, m. **p. laying,** instalación de cañerías, f. **p.-line,** cañería, f.; (oil) oleoducto, m. **p. tobacco,** tabaco de pipa, m.

pipeful, s. pipa, f.

piper, s. (bagpiper) gaitero, m.; flautista, m. and f.

pipette, s. (chem.) pipeta, f.

piping, s. sonido del caramillo, m.; música de la flauta, etc., f.; (of birds) trinos, m. pl.; voz aguda, f.; (for water, etc.) cañería, tubería, f.; (sew.) cordoncillo, m. **p.-hot,** hirviente

pipkin, s. ollita de barro, f.

pippin, s. (apple) camuesa, f.

piquancy, s. picante, m.

piquant, a. picante

pique, s. (resentment, and score in game) pique, m. **to p. oneself upon,** preciarse de, jactarse de. **to be piqued,** estar enojado; (fam.) amoscarse

piquet, s. juego de los cientos, m.

piracy, s. piratería, f.

pirate, s. pirata, m. v.i. piratear.
v.t. publicar una edición furtiva
de. **p. edition,** edición furtiva,
f.
piratical, a. pirata, pirático; de
pirata, de piratas
pirouette, s. pirueta, f.
piscatorial, a. piscatorio
Pisces, s. pl. peces, m. pl.
pisciculture, s. piscicultura, f.
piscina, s. piscina, f.
piscine, a. píceo
pistachio, s. pistacho, m.
pistil, s. (bot.) pistilo, m.
pistol, s. pistola, f. **p. belt,**
charpa, f., cinto de pistolas, m.
p. case, pistolera, f. **p. shot,**
pistoletazo, m.
piston, s. (mech.) émbolo, pistón,
m.; (mus.) pistón, m., llave, f.
p. ring, anillo de émbolo,
segmento de émbolo, m. **p. rod,**
biela, f. **p. stroke,** carrera del
émbolo, f.
pit, s. hoyo, m.; foso, m.; (in a
garage) foso de reparación, m.;
(theat.) platea, f.; (trap) trampa,
f.; (scar) hoyo, m.; precipicio,
m.; (hell) infierno, m. v.t. (with
smallpox) marcar con viruelas;
(against) competir con. **pit-**
head, boca de mina, f. **pit of the**
stomach, boca del estómago, f.
pit stall, butaca de platea, f.
pitch, s. (chem.) pez, brea, f.,
alquitrán, m.; (place) puesto,
m.; (throwing) lanzamiento, m.;
(distance thrown) alcance, m.;
(for cricket) cancha, f.; (bowling)
saque, m.; (slope) pendiente,
inclinación, f.; (height) elevación, f.; (mus.) tono, m.; (fig.,
degree) grado, extremo, m.;
(naut., aer.) cabeceo, m.; (of
threads of a screw, etc.) paso,
m. v.t. (camp) asentar; (a tent,
etc.) colocar, poner; (throw)
lanzar, arrojar, tirar; (cricket,
etc.) lanzar; (fix in) clavar; (mus.)
graduar el tono de; (tell) narrar.
v.i. (fall) caer; (naut.) cabecear,
zozobrar; (aer.) cabecear. **to**
paint with p., embrear. **to p.**
into, (attack) acometer, atacar;
(scold) desatarse contra; (food)
engullir. **p.-black,** negro como
la pez; oscuro como boca de
lobo. **p.-pine,** pino de tea, m.
p.-pipe, diapasón vocal, m.

pitched battle, s. batalla campal, f.
pitcher, s. jarro, cántaro, m.; (in
baseball) lanzador de pelota, m.
pitcherful, s. jarro (de), m.
pitchfork, s. horquilla, f., aventador, m. v.t. levantar con horquilla; (fig.) lanzar
pitching, s. (pavement) adoquinado, m.; (of a ship) socollada,
f.; cabeceo, m.
piteous, a. lastimero; triste;
plañidero; compasivo, tierno
piteousness, s. estado lastimero,
m.; tristeza, f.; compasión, ternura, f.
pitfall, s. trampa, f.; (fig.) añagaza, f., lazo, peligro, m.
pith, s. (bot.) médula, f.; médula
espinal, f.; (fig.) meollo, m.;
fuerza, f., vigor, m.; substancia,
f.; quinta esencia, f.; importancia, f.
pithiness, s. jugosidad, f.; fuerza,
f., vigor, m.
pithy, a. meduloso; (fig.) jugoso;
enérgico, vigoroso
pitiable, a. lastimoso, digno de
compasión; (paltry) despreciable
pitiful, a. piadoso, compasivo;
conmovedor, doloroso, lastimero;
(contemptible) miserable
pitifully, adv. lastimosamente
pitiless, a. sin piedad, despiadado
pitilessness, s. crueldad, inhumanidad, f.
pitman, s. minero, m.; aserrador
de foso, m.
pittance, s. pitanza, f.; pequeña
porción, f.; ración de hambre, f.
pitted, a. picoso
pituitary, a. pituitario
pity, s. piedad, compasión, f.;
lástima, f. v.t. compadecerse de,
tener lástima (a); compadecer.
It is a p. that . . ., Es lástima
que . . . **Have p.!** ¡Ten piedad!
to take p. on, tener lástima (de).
to move to p., dar lástima (a),
enternecer
pityingly, adv. con lástima
pivot, s. pivote, m.; eje, m.; (fig.)
punto de partida, m. v.i. girar
sobre un pivote o eje
pivotal, a. (fig.) cardinal, principal, fundamental
pixy, s. duende, m. **p. hood,**
caperuza, f.

placability, s. placabilidad, f.
placable, a. aplacable, placable
placard, s. cartel, m. v.t. fijar
carteles (en); publicar por carteles
placate, v.t. aplacar, ablandar,
apaciguar
placatory, a. placativo
place, s. lugar, m.; sitio, m.; (position) puesto, m.; (seat) asiento,
m.; (laid at table) cubierto, m.;
(square) plaza, f.; (house) residencia, f.; (in the country) casa
de campo, finca, f.; (in a book)
pasaje, m.; (in an examination)
calificación, f.; (rank) posición,
f., rango, m.; situación, f.;
(employment) empleo, m., colocación, f. v.t. poner; colocar; (in
employment) dar empleo (a);
(appoint) nombrar; (an order)
dar; (money) invertir; (remember) recordar, traer a la memoria; (size up) fijar; (confidence)
poner. in p., en su lugar; apropiado. in p. of, en vez de, en
lugar de. in the first p., en
primer lugar, primero. in the
next p., luego, después. out of
p., fuera de lugar; inoportuno.
It is not my p. to . . ., No me
toca á mi de . . . to give p. to,
ceder el paso (a); ceder (a). to
take p., verificarse, tener lugar,
ocurrir. p. of business, oficina,
f. p. of worship, edificio de
culto, m.
placenta, s. placenta, f.
placental, a. placentario
placid, a. plácido, apacible; calmoso; sereno, sosegado; dulce
placidity, s. placidez, f.; serenidad, tranquilidad, f., sosiego, m.
placidly, adv. plácidamente
placing, s. colocación, f.; posición, f.; localización, f.
placket, s. abertura (en una falda),
f.
plagiarism, s. plagio, m.
plagiarist, s. plagiario (-ia)
plagiarize, v.t. plagiar, hurtar
plague, s. plaga, f.; peste, pestilencia, f. v.t. importunar, atormentar; plagar
plaice, s. (nearest equivalent)
platija, f.
plaid, s. manta escocesa, f.;
género de cuadros, m. a. a
cuadros

plain, a. claro; evidente; (simple)
sencillo; llano; sin adorno; (flat)
liso, igual; (candid) franco; (with
truth, etc.) desnudo; mero; puro,
sin mezcla; (of words) redondo;
(ugly) feo. adv. claramente;
llanamente; sencillamente; francamente. s. llanura, f., llano, m.
the p. truth, la pura verdad. p.
clothes, traje de paisano, m. p.
clothes man, detective, m. p.
cooking, cocina sencilla, cocina
casera, f. p. dealing, buena fe,
sinceridad, f. p. dweller, llanero
(-ra). p. living, vida sencilla, f.
p. people, gente sencilla, f.
p. sailing, (fig.) camino fácil, m.
p. sewing, costura, f. p.-song,
canto llano, m. p. speaking,
franqueza, f. p.-spoken, franco
plainly, adv. claramente; sencillamente; llanamente; francamente;
rotundamente
plainness, s. claridad, f.; sencillez, f.; llaneza, f.; franqueza,
f.; (ugliness) fealdad, f.
plainsman, s. hombre de las
llanuras, m.
plaint, s. queja, f., lamento, m.;
(law) demanda, querella, f.
plaintiff, s. demandante, m. and
f., actor, m.
plaintive, a. quejumbroso, dolorido; patético
plaintively, adv. quejumbrosamente
plaintiveness, s. melancolía,
tristeza, f.; voz quejumbrosa,
f.
plait, s. trenza, f. v.t. trenzar;
tejer. in plaits, (of hair) en
trenzas
plan, s. plan, m.; (map) plano, m.;
proyecto, m. v.t. planear; proyectar; proponerse. The Marshall P., El Plan Marshall. to
make a p. of, trazar un plano de.
to make plans, hacer proyectos
planchette, s. mesa giratoria, f.
plane, s. (tree) plátano, m.; (tool)
cepillo, m.; (geom.) plano, m.;
(level) nivel, m.; (aer.) avión, m.
a. plano. v.t. (carp.) acepillar,
alisar. v.i. (aer.) planear
planet, s. planeta, m.
planetarium, s. planetario, m.
planetary, a. planetario
planing, s. acepilladura, alisa-
dura, f.

plank, s. tabla, f.; (fig.) fundamento, principio, m.; pl. **planks,**
tablazón, f. v.t. entablar, enmaderar

planking, s. entablado, m., tablazón, f.

plankton, s. plankton, m.

planned, a. proyectado, planeado; dirigido. p. **economy,**
economía dirigida, f.

planner, s. proyectista, m. and f.;
autor (-ra) de un plan

planning, s. proyecto, m.; concepción, f.

plant, s. (bot.) planta, f.; instalación, f., material, m. v.t.
plantar; (place) colocar; fijar;
(a blow) asestar; (people) establecer; (instil) inculcar, imbuir
(con); (conceal) esconder. p.
pot, florero, m. p. **stand,** jardinera, f.

plantain, s. (bot.) llantén, m.

plantation, s. plantación, f.;
plantío, m.; (fig.) colonia, f.;
introducción, f., establecimiento,
m.

planter, s. plantador, cultivador,
m.

planting, s. plantación, f.; (fig.)
colonia, f.; introducción, f. p.
out, trasplante, m.

plantlike, a. como una planta; de
planta

plaque, s. placa, f.; medalla,
f.

plash, s. (puddle) charco, m.;
(sound) chapaleteo, m. v.t. and
v.i. chapotear, chapalear

plasma, s. plasma, m.

plasmic, a. plasmático

plaster, s. (for walls, etc.) argamasa, f.; yeso, m.; (med.)
parche, emplasto, m. v.t. (walls,
etc.) enlucir, enyesar; poner
emplastos (a or en); (daub)
embadurnar, manchar; (cover)
cubrir. p. **cast,** vaciado, yeso,
m. p. of Paris, escayola, f.

plasterer, s. yesero, m.

plastering, s. revoque, enyesado,
guarnecido, m. p. **trowel,** fratás,
m.

plastic, a. plástico. s. plástica, f.;
pl. **plastics,** materias plásticas,
f. pl. p. **surgery,** cirugía
plástica, f.

plasticine, s. plasticina, f.

plasticity, s. plasticidad, f.

plate, s. plancha, chapa, f.; (engraving and phot.) of a doctor,
etc.) placa, f.; (illustration)
lámina, f.; (cutlery, etc.) vajilla,
f.; (for eating) plato, m.; (for
money) platillo, m.; electrotipo,
m.; (dental) dentadura postiza, f.
v.t. (with armour) blindar; (with
metal) planchear; (silver) platear; (electro-plate) niquelar.
silver p., vajilla de plata, plata,
f. p.-armour, armadura, f.; (of
a ship) blindaje, m. p.-draining
rack, escurreplatos, m. p.-
glass, vidrio plano, m. p.-
rack, escurridero para platos,
m. p. warmer, calientaplatos,
m.

plateau, s. meseta, altiplanicie, f.

plateful, s. plato (de), m.

plater, s. plateador, m.; platero,
m.

plateresque, a. (arch.) plateresco

platform, s. plataforma, f.; (railway) andén, m. p. ticket, billete
de andén, m.

plating, s. niquelado, m.; electro-
galvanización, f.; (with armour)
blindaje, m.

platinum, s. platino, m. p.
blonde, rubia platino, f.

platitude, s. perogrullada, f.,
lugar común, m.; trivialidad,
vulgaridad, f.

platitudinous, a. lleno de pero-
grulladas; trivial

platonic, a. platónico

Platonism, s. platonismo, m.

Platonist, s. platonista, m. and f.

platoon, s. (mil.) pelotón, m.

platter, s. fuente, f., trinchero, m.;
plato, m.

plaudit, s. aplauso, m., aclamación, f.; (praise) elogio, m., alabanza, f.

plausibility, s. plausibilidad, f.

plausible, a. plausible

plausibly, adv. plausiblemente

play, v.i. jugar; (frolic) juguetear,
retozar; recrearse, divertirse;
(mech.) moverse; (on a musical
instrument) tocar; (wave) ondear, flotar; (theat.) representar;
(behave) conducirse. v.t. jugar;
(of a searchlight, etc.) enfocar;
(direct) dirigir; (a fish) agotar;
(a joke, etc.) hacer; (a piece in a
game) mover; (a musical instrument or music) tocar; (a string

instrument) tañer; (a character in a play) hacer el papel de; (a drama, etc.) representar, poner en escena. **to p. a joke**, gastar una broma, hacer una burla. **to p. fair**, jugar limpio. **to p. false**, jugar sucio, engañar. **to p. the fool**, hacèrse el tonto, hacerse el payaso. **to p. at**, jugar a; (pretend) fingir; hacer sin entusiasmo. **to p. off**, confrontar, contraponer. **to p. on**. See **to p. upon. to p. on the . . .**, (of musical instruments) tocar. **to p. to**, (a person) tocar para. **to p. upon**, tocar; (a person's fears, etc.) explotar. **to p. up to**, (a person) adular, hacer la rueda (a). **to p. with**, jugar con; burlarse de; (an idea) acariciar

play, s. juego, m.; diversión, f., recreo, m.; (reflection) reflejo, m.; movimiento libre, m.; (to the imagination, etc.) rienda suelta, f.; (mech.) holgura, f.; (lit.) pieza dramática, comedia, f.; (performance) función, representación, f.; (theatre) teatro, m. **fair p.**, juego limpio, m. **foul p.**, juego sucio, m.; traición, perfidia, f. **to bring into p.**, poner en juego. **to come into p.**, entrar en juego. **to give p. to**, dar rienda a. **p. on words**, juego de palabras, m. **p.-pen**, cuadro enrejado, m.

playact, v.i. hacer la comedia

playbill, s. cartel, m.; programa, m.

played-out, a. agotado; viejo

player, s. jugador (-ra); (theat.) actor (-triz), representante, m. and f.; (mus.) músico (-ca), tocador (-ra)

playfellow, s. camarada, m. and f.; compañero (-ra) de juego

playful, a. juguetón; travieso; alegre

playfully, adv. en juego, de broma; alegremente

playfulness, s. carácter juguetón, m.; travesuras, f. pl.; alegría, f.

playgoer, s. persona que frecuenta los teatros, f.; espectador de comedias, m.

playground, s. patio de recreo, m.

playing, s. juego, m. **p.-cards**, naipes, m. pl., cartas, f. pl. p

field, campo de deportes, m.

playlet, s. comedia corta, f.

playmate. See **playfellow**

plaything, s. juguete, m.

playtime, s. recreación, f.; (in schools) hora de recreo, f., recreo, m.

playwright, s. dramaturgo, m., autor (-ra) de comedias

plea, s. (law) informe, m.; declaración, f.; (law) acción, f., proceso, m.; (excuse) pretexto, m., excusa, f.; (entreaty) súplica, f. **under p. of**, bajo pretexto de, con excusa de

plead, v.i. (law) pleitear; (law) declarar; suplicar; (of counsel, etc.) abogar (por); interceder (por). v.t. defender en juicio; aducir, alegar; pretender. **to p. guilty**, confesarse culpable. **to p. not guilty**, negar la acusación. **to p. ignorance**, pretender ignorancia

pleading, s. súplicas, f. pl.; (law) defensa, f.; pl. **pleadings**, alegatos, m. pl. a. implorante

pleasant, a. agradable; placentero; ameno; encantador; dulce; alegre; (of persons) simpático, amable; bueno; divertido

pleasantly, adv. agradablemente; de un modo muy amable; alegremente

pleasantness, s. agrado, m.; placer, m.; amabilidad, f.; alegría, f.

pleasantry, s. jocosidad, f.; broma, chanza, f.

please, v.i. dar placer, gustar, dar gusto, agradar; parecer bien, querer, servirse; tener a bien, placer. v.t. deleitar, agradar, gustar; halagar; contentar, satisfacer. **I shall do what I p.**, Haré lo que me parezca bien. **If you p.**, Si te parece bien; Con tu permiso. **She is very easy to p.**, Es muy fácil de darle placer a ella. **When you p.**, Cuando Vd. quiera, Cuando a Vd. le venga bien. **P. sit down!** ¡Haga el favor de sentarse! ¡Sírvase de sentarse! **P. God!** ¡Plegue a Dios!

pleased, a. contento (de or con); encantado (de); alegre (de); satisfecho (de or con). **I am p. with my new house**, Estoy contento

con mi nueva casa. **I am p. to
meet you,** Me alegro de conocer
a Vd. **to be p.,** estar contento;
complacerse en
pleasing, *a.* agradable, grato;
placentero; halagüeño
pleasurable, *a.* agradable; divertido, entretenido
pleasure, *s.* placer, *m.*; gusto,
m.; satisfacción, *f.*; (will) voluntad, *f.*; recreo, *m.*; diversión, distracción, *f.* **to give p.** (to), dar
placer (a); deleitar, agradar;
complacer. **to take p. in,**
gustar de, disfrutar de; complacerse en. **I shall do it with
great p.,** Lo haré con mucho
gusto, Lo haré gustoso. **p.-
boat,** barco de recreo, *m.* **p.-
ground,** parque de atracciones,
m. **p.-seeking,** amigo de placeres, frívolo. **p. trip,** viaje de
recreo, *m.*; excursión, *f.*
pleat, *s.* pliegue, *m.* *v.t.* plegar,
hacer pliegues en
pleating, *s.* plegado, *m.*
plebeian, *a.* plebeyo. *s.* plebeyo
(-ya)
plebiscite, *s.* plebiscito, *m.* **to
take a p.,** hacer un plebiscito
plectrum, *s.* plectro, *m.*
pledge, *s.* prenda, *f.*; empeño,
m.; garantía, *f.*; (hostage) rehén,
m.; (toast) brindis, *m.* *v.t.*
empeñar, dar en prenda; garantizar; brindar por; prometer.
to p. oneself, comprometerse.
to p. support for, prometer
apoyo para
pledgor, *s.* prendador (-ra)
Pleiades, *s. pl.* pléyades, *f.
pl.*
plenary, *a.* pleno; plenario. **p.
indulgence,** indulgencia plenaria, *f.* **p. session,** sesión plenaria, *f.*
plenipotentiary, *a.* plenipotenciario. *s.* plenipotenciario, *m.*
plenitude, *s.* plenitud, *f.*
plenteous, plentiful, *a.* copioso,
abundante. **to be p.,** abundar
plentifully, *adv.* en abundancia
plenty, *s.* abundancia, *f.*; en
abundancia; de sobra; mucho.
adv. (*fam.*) bastante. **There is
p. of food,** Hay comida en
abundancia. **We have p. of
time,** Tenemos tiempo de sobra
pleonasm, *s.* pleonasmo, *m.*

pleonastic, *a.* pleonástico
plethora, *s.* plétora, *f.*
pleurisy, *s.* pleuresía, *f.*
plexus, *s.* plexo, *m.*
pliability, *s.* flexibilidad, *f.*;
docilidad, *f.*
pliable, pliant, *a.* flexible; dócil
pliers, *s. pl.* pinzas, *f. pl.*, alicates,
m. pl., tenazas, *f. pl.*
plight, *v.t.* (one's word) empeñar;
dar; prometer en matrimonio.
s. (fix) aprieto, apuro, *m.* **to p.
one's troth,** dar palabra de
matrimonio
plinth, *s.* (*arch.*) plinto, *m.*
plod, *v.i.* andar despacio, caminar con trabajo; (*fig.*) trabajar
con ahínco
plodder, *s.* trabajador lento y
concienzudo, *m.*; (student) empollón (-ona)
plot, *s.* (of land) parcela, *f.*;
terreno, solar, *m.*; (plan) proyecto, *m.*; estratagema, *m.*;
(literary) intriga, trama, *f.*;
(story) argumento, *m.*; (conspiracy) conjuración, *f.*, complot, *m.* *v.t.* trazar (un plano,
etc.); urdir, tramar. *v.i.* conspirar, intrigar
plotter, *s.* conspirador (-ra),
conjurado (-da)
plotting, *s.* trazado (de un plano,
una gráfica), *m.*; (conspiracy)
conspiración, *f.*; maquinaciones,
f. pl.; (hatching) trama, *f.*
plough, *s.* arado, *m.*; (*ast.*) el
Carro, la Osa Mayor; (in an
examination) escabechina, *f.*
v.t. and *v.i.* arar; (*fig.*) surcar;
(in examinations) escabechar,
dar calabazas (a), suspender.
p. handle, esteva, *f.* **to p. up,**
roturar
ploughman, *s.* arador, surcador,
m.; (peasant) labrador, *m.*
ploughshare, *s.* reja de arado, *f.*
plover, *s.* ave fría, *f.*, chorlito, *m.*
pluck, *v.t.* (pick) coger; (a bird)
desplumar; (*mus.*) puntear; (in
an examination) calabacear, escabechar. *v.i.* tirar (de). *s.* (tug)
tirón, *m.*; (of an animal) asadura,
f.; (courage) coraje, *m.* **to p. up
courage,** tomar coraje, sacar
ánimos. **to p. off,** quitar. **to p.
out,** arrancar; quitar
pluckily, *adv.* valientemente
pluckiness, *s.* coraje, valor, *m.*

plucky, *a.* valiente, esforzado, resuelto, animoso

plug, *s.* tapón, tarugo, *m.*; (in building) nudillo, *m.*; (of a switchboard) clave, *f.*; (*elec.*) enchufe, *m.*; (of a w.c.) tirador, *m.*; (of a bath, etc.) tapón, *m.*; (of tobacco) rollo, *m.* *v.t.* atarugar, taponar, obturar; (in building) rellenar. *v.i.* (with away) batirse el cobre, sudar la gota gorda. **to p. in,** enchufar

plum, *s.* (tree) ciruelo, *m.*; (fruit) ciruela, *f.*; (raisin) pasa, *f.*; (*fam.*, prize) breva, golosina, *f.* **p. cake,** pastel de fruta, *m.*

plumage, *s.* plumaje, *m.*

plumb, *s.* plomada, *f.*; (sounding-lead) escandallo, *m.* *a.* perpendículo; recto; completo. *adv.* a plomo, verticalmente; exactamente. *v.t.* aplomar; (*naut.*) sondar; (*fig.*, pierce) penetrar; (understand) comprender. *v.i.* trabajar como plomero. **p.-line,** plomada, *f.*

plumbago, *s.* plombagina, *f.*

plumber, *s.* plomero, fontanero, *m.*; instalador de cañerías, *m.*

plumbic, *a.* (*chem.*) plúmbico

plumbing, *s.* plomería, fontanería, *f.*; instalación de cañerías, *f.*

plumbless, *a.* (*poet.*) insondable

plume, *s.* pluma, *f.*; penacho, *m.* *v.t.* adornar con plumas; desplumar; **to p. itself,** (of a bird) limpiarse las plumas. **to p. oneself on,** echárselas de, hacer alarde de; jactarse de

plumed, *a.* plumado; con plumas; empenachado

plumelet, *s.* agujas, *f. pl.*

plummet, *s.* plomada, *f.*; (weight) plomo, *m.*; (sounding-lead) sonda, *f.*

plump, *a.* gordito, grueso; rollizo; hinchado. *adv.* de golpe; claramente. *v.t.* (swell) hinchar, rellenar; (make fall) hacer (or dejar) caer. *v.i.* (swell) hincharse; engordar; (fall) caer a plomo; dejarse caer. **to p. for,** escoger, dar apoyo (a); votar por. **p.-cheeked,** mofletudo

plumpness, *s.* gordura, *f.*; lo rollizo

plumy, *a.* como una pluma; plumado

plunder, *v.t.* saquear; pillar; despojar. *s.* saqueo, pillaje, *m.*; (booty) botín, despojo, *m.*

plunderer, *s.* saqueador (-ra); ladrón (-ona)

plundering, *s.* saqueo, *m.*; despojo, *m.* *a.* saqueador

plunge, *v.t.* chapuzar; sumergir; hundir; meter. *v.i.* sumergirse; (into water) zambullirse; (rush) precipitarse, lanzarse; (*naut.*) zozobrar; (of a horse) encabritarse; (gamble) jugarse el todo. *s.* sumersión, *f.*; zambullida, *f.*; chapuz, *m.*; (rush) salto, *m.*; (*fig.*, step) paso, *m.*

plunger, *s.* (*mech.*) émbolo, *m.*

plunging, *a.* (of a ship) zozobra, *f.*; (of a horse) cabriolas, *f. pl.*; saltos, *m. pl.* Other meanings see **plunge**

pluperfect, *s.* pluscuamperfecto, *m.*

plural, *a.* plural. *s.* plural, *m.* **in the p.,** en el plural. **to make p.,** poner en plural

plurality, *s.* pluralidad, *f.*

pluralize, *v.t.* pluralizar

plus, *prep.* and *a.* más; (*math.*, *elec.*) positivo. *s.* signo más, *m.*; (*math.*) cantidad positiva, *f.* **p. fours,** pantalones de golf, *m. pl.*

plush, *s.* felpa, *f.*; velludo, *m.*

plushy, *a.* felpudo; de felpa

Pluto, *s.* Plutón, *m.*; (pipe-line) oleoducto, *m.*

plutocracy, *s.* plutocracia, *f.*

plutocrat, *s.* plutócrata, *m.* and *f.*

plutocratic, *a.* plutocrático

Plutonic, *a.* (*geol.*) plutónico

pluvial, *a.* pluvial. *s.* capa pluvial, *f.*

pluviometer, *s.* pluviómetro, *m.*

ply, *s.* cabo, *m.* *v.t.* emplear, usar; manejar; ejercer; ofrecer, servir (con); importunar (con). *v.i.* hacer el trayecto; hacer el servicio; ir y venir; hacer viajes. **to ply for hire,** tomar viajeros; ofrecerse para ser alquilado

plywood, *s.* madera contrachapada, *f.*

pneumatic, *a.* neumático. *s.* (tyre) neumático, *m.* **p. drill,** barreno neumático, *m.*

pneumococcus, *s.* neumococo, *m.*

pneumonia, *s.* pulmonía, *f.* **double p.,** pulmonía doble, *f.*

poach, *v.i.* cazar (or pescar) en
vedado. *v.t.* robar caza de un
vedado; (*fig.*) invadir; (*fig.*, steal)
hurtar; (eggs) escalfar. to p.
upon another's preserves, meterse en los asuntos de otro
poacher, *s.* cazador furtivo,
m.
poaching, *s.* caza (or pesca)
furtiva, *f.*
pock, *s.* pústula, *f.* p.-mark,
hoyo, *m.* p.-marked, picado de
viruelas
pocket, *s.* bolsillo, *m.*; bolsillo del
reloj, *m.*; faltriquera, *f.*; (*min.*)
bolsa, *f.*, depósito, *m.*; (*fig.*)
bolsa, *f.*; (in billiards) tronera, *f.*
v.t. meter (or poner) en el bolsillo; (an insult) tragarse; (in
billiards) entronerar; (a profit)
ganar; apropiarse. air-p., bolsa
de aire, *f.* to be out of p., haber
perdido, tener una pérdida. to
have a person in one's p.,
calzarse a una persona. to p.
one's pride, olvidarse de su
orgullo. p. battleship, acorazado de bolsillo, *m.* p.-book,
cartera, *f.* p. dictionary, diccionario de bolsillo, *m.* p.-flap,
portezuela, *f.* p.-handkerchief,
pañuelo (de bolsillo), *m.* p.-
knife, cortaplumas, *m.* p.-
lighter, encendedor de bolsillo,
m. p.-money, dinero para gastos
particulares, *m.* p. picking,
ratería de carterista, *f.*
pocketful, *s.* bolsillo lleno (de),
m.; lo que cabe en un bolsillo
pod, *s.* (*bot.*) vaina, *f.*; (of a silkworm) capullo, *m.* *v.t.* des-
vainar; mondar. *v.i.* hincharse,
llenarse
podgy, *a.* gordo, grueso
poem, *s.* poema, *m.*; *pl.* poems,
poesías, *f. pl.*, versos, *m. pl.*
poet, *s.* poeta, *m.* P. Laureate,
poeta laureado, *m.*
poetaster, *s.* poetastro, *m.*
poetess, *s.* poetisa, *f.*
poetic, *a.* poético. p. licence,
licencia poética, *f.*
poetically, *adv.* poéticamente
poeticize, *v.t.* poetizar; hacer un
poema (de)
poetics, *s.* poética, *f.*
poetry, *s.* poesía, *f.*; versos,
poemas, *m. pl.*
pogrom, *s.* pogrom, *m.*

poignancy, *s.* (of emotions) profundidad, violencia, *f.*, lo patético; (of a retort, etc.) mordacidad, acerbidad, *f.*
poignant, *a.* (moving) conmovedor, hondo, agudo; patético;
(mordant) mordaz, agudo
poignantly, *adv.* de un modo
conmovedor, patéticamente;
mordazmente
point, *s.* (usual meanings and *ast.*,
math., in cards, in a speech, etc.)
punto, *m.*; característica, *f.*;
cualidad, *f.*; (purpose) motivo,
fin, *m.*; (question) cuestión, *f.*;
asunto, *m.*; (wit) agudeza, *f.*;
(significance) significación, *f.*;
(detail) detalle, *m.*; (in rationing)
cupón, *m.*; (sharp end) punta, *f.*;
(of a shawl, etc.) pico, *m.*; (of
land) promontorio, cabo, *m.*;
(engraving) buril, *m.*; (railway)
aguja, *f.*; (of horses) cabo, *m.*
Mary has many good points,
María tiene muchas cualidades
buenas. There is no p. in
being angry, No hay para qué
enfadarse. in p., en cuestión; a
propósito. in p. of fact, en
efecto, en verdad. on the p. of,
a punto de. to be to the p.,
venir al caso; ser apropiado. to
carry one's p., salir con la
suya. to come to the p., ir al
grano, ir al caso. to make a p.
of, insistir en; tener por principio.
to win on points, (boxing)
ganar por puntos. p. at issue,
cuestión bajo consideración, *f.*,
punto en cuestión. p.-blank, a
boca de jarro. p.-duty, regulación de tráfico, *f.* p. lace, encaje
de aguja, *m.* p. of honour,
punto de honor, *m.*; cuestión de
honor, *f.* p. of order, cuestión
de orden, *f.* p. of view, punto de
vista, *m.*
point, *v.t.* sacar punta (a), afilar;
(a moral, etc.) inculcar; (in
building) rejuntar; (*gram.*) puntuar; (of dogs) mostrar la caza.
He pointed his gun at them,
Les apuntó con su fusil. The
hands of the clock pointed to
seven o'clock, Las agujas del
reloj marcaban las siete. to p.
with the finger, señalar con el
dedo. to p. at, señalar, indicar;
(with a gun) apuntar; dirigir.

to p. out, señalar, indicar; enseñar, mostrar; advertir

pointed, *a.* (sharpened) afilado; (in shape) puntiagudo; picudo; (*arch.*) ojival; (*fig.*) mordaz; satírico; (of a remark, etc.) directo; personal; aparente, evidente

pointedly, *adv.* explícitamente, categóricamente; mordazmente; directamente; satíricamente

pointedness, *s.* forma puntiaguda, *f.*; (incisiveness) mordacidad, aspereza, *f.*; claridad, *f.*

pointer, *s.* (of a clock, weighing-machine, etc.) aguja, *f.*; (of a balance) fiel, *m.*; (wand) puntero, *m.*; (*fig.*) índice, *m.*; (dog) perro de muestra, *m.*

pointillisme, *s.* (*art*) puntillismo, *m.*

pointing, *s.* (in building) rejuntado, *m.*; (of a gun) puntería, *f.*

pointless, *a.* sin motivo, innecesario; fútil; sin importancia

pointlessly, *adv.* sin motivo, sin necesidad; fútilmente

pointsman, *s.* (railway) guardagujas, *m.*; (policeman) guardia del tráfico, *m.*

poise, *v.t.* balancear; pesar. *v.i.* balancearse; posar, estar suspendido. *s.* equilibrio, *m.*; (of mind) serenidad de ánimo, sangre fría, *f.*; aplomo, *m.*; (bearing) porte, aire, *m.*

poison, *s.* veneno, *m.*; (*fig.*) ponzoña, *f.*, veneno, *m.* *v.t.* envenenar; intoxicar; (*fig.*) emponzoñar. **p. gas,** gas asfixiante, *m.*

poisoner, *s.* envenenador (-ra); (*fig.*) corruptor (-ra)

poisoning, *s.* envenenamiento, *m.*; intoxicación, *f.*

poisonous, *a.* venenoso; tóxico; (*fig.*) ponzoñoso, pernicioso. **a p. snake,** una serpiente venenosa

poisonousness, *s.* venenosidad, *f.*; toxicidad, *f.*; (*fig.*) veneno, *m.*, ponzoña, *f.*

poke, *v.t.* (thrust) clavar; (make) hacer; (the fire) atizar; hurgar; (push) empujar; (put away) arrinconar. *v.i.* andar a tientas; meterse. **Don't p. your nose into other people's business!** ¡No te metas donde no te llaman! **They poked his eyes**

out, Le saltaron los ojos. **to p. fun at,** burlarse de, mofarse de. **to p. the fire,** atizar la lumbre (or el fuego). **to p. about for,** buscar a tientas. **p.-bonnet,** capelina, *f.*

poker, *s.* (game) póker, *m.*; (for the fire) hurgón, atizador, *m.* **p. work,** pirograbado, *m.*

poky, *a.* estrecho, ahogado, pequeño; miserable

polar, *a.* polar. **p. bear,** oso (-sa) blanco (-ca). **p. lights,** aurora boreal, *f.*

polarimeter, *s.* polarímetro, *m.*

polarity, *s.* polaridad, *f.*

polarization, *s.* polarización, *f.*

polarize, *v.t.* polarizar

pole, *s.* palo largo, *m.*; poste, *m.*; (of a tent) mástil, *m.*; (of a cart) pértiga, *f.*; (*sport*) pértiga, garrocha, *f.*; (measurement) percha, *f.*; (*ast., geog., biol., math., elec.*) polo, *m.* *v.t.* (a punt) impeler con pértiga. **from p. to p.,** de polo a polo. **greasy p.,** cucaña, *f.* **under bare poles,** (*naut.*) a palo seco. **p.-axe,** hachuela de mano, *f.*; hacha de marinero, *f.*; (butcher's) mazo, *m.* **p. jumping,** salto de pértiga, salto a la garrocha, *m.* **p.-star,** estrella polar, *f.*

Pole, *s.* polaco (-ca)

polemic, *s.* polémica, *f.*

polemical, *a.* polémico

police, *s.* policía, *f.* *v.t.* mantener servicio de policía en; mantener el orden público en; administrar, regular. **mounted p.,** policía montada, *f.* **p. constable,** (agente de) policía, guardia urbano, *m.* **p. court,** tribunal de la policía, *m.* **p. dog,** perro de policía, *m.* **p. force,** cuerpo de policía, *m.*, policía, *f.* **p. magistrate,** juez municipal, *m.* **p. station,** comisaría de policía, *f.* **p. trap,** puesto oculto de la policía del tráfico, *m.* **p. woman,** agente femenino de policía, *m.*

policeman, *s.* policía, guardia, *m.*

polichinelle, *s.* polichinela, *m.*

policy, *s.* política, *f.*; táctica, *f.*; sistema, *m.*; norma de conducta, *f.*; ideas, *f. pl.*; principios, *m. pl.*; prudencia, *f.*; (insurance) póliza, *f.* **fixed premium p.,** póliza a prima fija, *f.* **p.-holder,** asegurado (-da), tenedor de una póliza, m.

poliomyelitis, s. poliomielitis, f.

polish, v.t. (metals and wood) pulir; (furniture and shoes) dar brillo (a); (*lit.* works) pulir, limar; (persons) descortezar, civilizar. s. (shine) brillo, m.; (furniture) cera para los muebles, f.; (metal, silver) líquido para limpiar metales, m.; (for shoes) betún para zapatos, m.; (varnish) barniz, m.; (of *lit.* works) pulidez, elegancia, f.; (of persons) urbanidad, cultura, f. **to p. off,** terminar a prisa; (a person) acabar con; (food) engullir

Polish, a. polaco, polonés. s. (language) polaco, m.

polished, a. (of verses, etc.) pulido, elegante; (of person) culto, distinguido; (of manners) fino, cortés

polisher, s. (machine) pulidor, m.; lustrador, m. **floor-p.,** lustrador de piso, m. **French p.,** barnizador, m.

polite, a. cortés, bien educado; atento; elegante

politely, adv. cortésmente; atentamente

politeness, s. cortesía, f. **for p. sake,** por cortesía

politic, a. político

political, a. político. **p. agent,** agente político, m. **p. economist,** hacendista, m. **p. economy,** economía política, f.

politically, adv. políticamente

politician, s. político (-ca)

politics, s. política, f. **to dabble in p.,** meterse en política

polity, s. forma de gobierno, constitución política, f.

polka, s. polca, f.

poll, s. (head of person) cabeza, f.; (voters' register) lista electoral, f.; (voting) votación, f.; (polling booth) colegio electoral, m.; (counting of votes) escrutinio, m. v.t. (trees) desmochar; (vote) votar, dar su voto (a); (obtain votes) obtener, recibir; (count votes) escrutar. **p.-tax,** capitación, f.

pollard, v.t. desmochar. s. (tree) árbol desmochado, m.

pollen, s. polen, m.

pollinate, v.t. fecundar con polen

pollination, s. polinización, f.

polling, s. votación, f. **p. booth,** colegio electoral, m.

pollute, v.t. contaminar; ensuciar; profanar; (corrupt morally) corromper

polluter, s. profanador (-ra), corruptor (-ra)

pollution, s. contaminación, f.; profanación, f.; corrupción, f.

Pollux, s. (*ast.*) Pólux, m.

polo, s. polo, m. **p. mallet,** maza de polo, f. **p. player,** jugador de polo, polista, m.

polonaise, s. polonesa, f.

poltroon, s. cobarde, m.

polyandry, s. poliandria, f.

polyanthus, s. primavera, f.

polychrome, a. policromo

polygamist, s. polígamo (-ma)

polygamous, a. polígamo

polygamy, s. poligamia, f.

polygenesis, s. poligenismo, m.

polyglot, s. poligloto (-ta). **p. Bible,** poliglota, f.

polygon, s. polígono, m.

polygonal, a. polígono

polyhedron, s. poliedro, m.

polymorphous, a. polimorfo

Polynesian, s. polinesio (-ia)

polynome, s. polinomio, m.

polyp, s. pólipo, m.

polyphonic, a. polifónico

polyphony, s. polifonía, f.

polypus, s. pólipo, m.

polystyle, a. polistilo

polysyllabic, a. polisílabo

polytechnic, a. politécnico

polytheism, s. politeísmo, m.

polytheistic, a. politeísta

pomade, s. pomada, f.

pomegranate, s. granada, f.

Pomeranian, a. pomerano. **P. dog,** perro pomerano, m.

pommel, s. pomo, m. v.t. aporrear

pomology, s. pomología, f.

pomp, s. pompa, magnificencia, f., fausto, aparato, m.; ostentación, f.

Pompeian, a. pompeyano

pompom, s. pompón, m.

pomposity, s. pomposidad, presunción, f.; (of language) ampulosidad, f.

pompous, a. pomposo, ostentoso; (of style) ampuloso, hinchado; importante. **to be p.,** (of persons) darse tono

pompously, *adv.* pomposamente
pond, *s.* charca, *f.*, estanque, *m.*
ponder, *v.t.* ponderar, estudiar, considerar. *v.i.* meditar (sobre), reflexionar (sobre)
ponderable, *a.* ponderable
ponderous, *a.* pesado; macizo; abultado; grave; (dull) pesado, aburrido
ponderously, *adv.* pesadamente; gravemente
ponderousness, *s.* pesadez, *f.*; gravedad, importancia, *f.*
poniard, *s.* puñal, *m.* *v.t.* apuñalar
pontiff, *s.* pontífice, *m.*
pontifical, *a.* pontificio
pontificate, *s.* pontificado, *m.*
pontoneer, *s.* pontonero, *m.*
pontoon, *s.* pontón, *m.* **p. bridge**, puente de pontones, *m.*
pony, *s.* jaca, *f.*
poodle, *s.* perro (-rra) de aguas (or de lanas)
pooh-pooh, *v.t.* despreciar, desdeñar. **Pooh!** ¡Bah!
pool, *s.* (in a river) rebalsa, *f.*; charca, *f.*, estanque, *m.*; (of blood, etc.) charco, *m.*; (in cards) baceta, *f.*; (*com.*) asociación, *f.*; (*fig.*) fuente, *f.*; *pl.* **pools**, (football) apuestas benéficas de fútbol, *f. pl.* *v.t.* (resources, etc.) combinar; juntar
poop, *s.* popa, *f.* **p. lantern**, fanal, *m.*
poor, *a.* pobre; malo; (insignificant or unfortunate) infeliz, desgraciado. **the p.**, los pobres. **to be in p. health**, estar mal de salud. **to be p. stuff**, ser de pacotilla. **to be poorer than a church mouse**, ser más pobre que las ratas. **to have a p. opinion of**, tener en poco (a). **P. me!** ¡Ay de mí! ¡Pecador de mí! **p.-box**, cepillo, *m.* **p.-law**, ley de asistencia pública, *f.* **p.-spirited**, apocado
poorhouse, *s.* asilo, *m.*
poorly, *adv.* pobremente; mal. *a.* indispuesto, malo
poorness, *s.* pobreza, *f.*; mala calidad, *f.*; (lack) carestía, *f.*; (of soil) infertilidad, *f.*; (of character) mezquindad, *f.*
pop, *s.* (of a cork) taponazo, *m.*;

(of a gun) detonación, *f.*; (drink) gaseosa, *f.* *adv.* ¡pum! *v.i.* (of a cork) saltar; (of guns) detonar. *v.t.* (corks) hacer saltar; (a gun, a question, etc.) disparar. **popgun**, escopeta de aire comprimido, *f.* **to pop down**, bajar apresuradamente. **to pop in**, (visit) dejarse caer; entrar rápidamente. **to pop off**, marcharse a prisa; (die) estirar la pata. **to pop up**, subir corriendo; aparecer de pronto
pope, *s.* Papa, *m.*
popery, *s.* papismo, *m.*
popinjay, *s.* (fop) pisaverde, *m.*
popish, *a.* papista
poplar, *s.* (black) chopo, álamo, *m.*; (white) álamo blanco, *m.* **p. grove**, alameda, *f.*
poplin, *s.* popelina, *f.*
poppy, *s.* amapola, adormidera, *f.*
populace, *s.* pueblo, *m.*; (scornful) populacho, *m.*
popular, *a.* popular; en boga, de moda; común. **He is a p. hero**, Él es un héroe popular
popularity, *s.* popularidad, *f.*
popularization, *s.* vulgarización, *f.*
popularize, *v.t.* popularizar, vulgarizar
popularly, *adv.* popularmente
populate, *v.t.* poblar
population, *s.* población, *f.*
populous, *a.* populoso; muy poblado
porcelain, *s.* porcelana, *f.*
porch, *s.* pórtico, *m.*; (of a house) portal, *m.*
porcine, *a.* porcino, porcuno
porcupine, *s.* puerco espín, *m.*
pore, *s.* poro, *m.* **to p. over**, estar absorto en; examinar cuidadosamente
pork, *s.* carne de cerdo, *f.* **salt p.**, tocino, *m.* **p. butcher**, tocinero, *m.* **p. pie**, pastel de carne de tocino, *m.*
pornographic, *a.* pornográfico
pornography, *s.* pornografía, *f.*
porosity, *s.* porosidad, *f.*
porous, *a.* poroso
porphyry, *s.* pórfido, *m.*
porpoise, *s.* marsopa, *f.*, puerco marino, *m.*
porridge, *s.* "Quaker oats," *m.*

port, *s.* puerto, *m.*; (in a ship)
porta, *f.*; (larboard) bábor, *m.*;
(wine) vino de Oporto, *m.*; (mien)
porte, *m.*, presencia, *f.* *v.t.* (the
helm) poner a babor; (*mil.*) llevar
un fusil terciado. **to put into p.**,
tomar puerto. **to stop at a p.**,
hacer escala en un puerto. **p.
dues,** derechos de puerto, *m.*
pl.

portable, *a.* portátil; móvil. **p.
typewriter,** máquina de escribir
portátil (or de viaje), *f.* **p.
wireless,** radio portátil, *f.*

portal, *s.* portal, *m.*

portcullis, *s.* rastrillo, *m.*

portend, *v.t.* presagiar, anunciar

portent, *s.* augurio, presagio, *m.*;
portento, *m.*

portentous, *a.* ominoso; portentoso; importante

porter, *s.* (messenger) mozo de
cordel, *m.*; (of a university,
hotel) portero, *m.*; (of a block of
flats) conserje, *m.*; (railway)
mozo de estación, *m.*; (drink)
cerveza negra, *f.* **porter's
lodge,** portería, *f.*; conserjería, *f.*

porterage, *s.* porte, *m.*

portfolio, *s.* carpeta, *f.*; (*pol.*, of a
minister) cartera, *f.*; (*pol.*, ministry) ministerio, *m.*

porthole, *s.* tronera, *f.*

portico, *s.* pórtico, *m.*

portière, *s.* antepuerta, *f.*

portion, *s.* porción, *f.*; parte, *f.*;
(marriage) dote, *m.* or *f.*; (piece)
pedazo, *m.*; (in a restaurant)
ración, *f.*; (in life) fortuna, *f.*
v.t. dividir; repartir; (dower)
dotar

portliness, *s.* corpulencia, *f.*

portly, *a.* corpulento, grueso

portmanteau, *s.* maleta, *f.*

Porto-Rican, *a.* and *s.* portorriqueño (-ña)

portrait, *s.* retrato, *m.* **p.
painter,** pintor (-ra) de retratos

portraiture, *s.* retratos, *m.* *pl.*;
descripción, pintura, *f.*

portray, *v.t.* retratar; pintar;
representar; (in words) describir,
pintar

portrayal, *s.* pintura, *f.*; retrato,
m.; (in words) descripción, *f.*

portrayer, *s.* retratista, *m.* and *f.*,
pintor (-ra)

portress, *s.* portera, *f.*; (in a
convent) tornera, *f.*

Portuguese, *a.* portugués. *s.*
portugués (-esa); (language) portugués, *m.*

pose, *v.t.* colocar; (a problem, etc.)
plantear; (a question) hacer; *v.i.*
colocarse; (with as) echárselas
de, dárselas de, fingir ser;
hacerse pasar por. *s.* actitud,
postura, *f.*; (affected) pose, *f.*;
(deception) engaño, *m.*

poser, *s.* problema difícil, *m.*; (in
an examination) pega, *f.*; pregunta embarazosa, *f.*

position, *s.* posición, *f.*; situación,
f.; actitud, postura, *f.*; condición,
f., estado, *m.*; (post) puesto,
empleo, *m.* **He is not in a p.
to . . .**, No está en condiciones
de . . ., No está para . . . **to
place in p.**, poner en posición,
colocar

positive, *a.* positivo. (also *math.*,
elec.); absoluto; (convinced) convencido, seguro; (downright)
categórico; (*fam.*) completo. *s.*
realidad, *f.*; (*phot.*) prueba positiva, *f.*

positively, *adv.* positivamente;
categóricamente

positiveness, *s.* certitud, seguridad, *f.*; terquedad, obstinacia,
f.

positivism, *s.* positivismo, *m.*

positivist, *s.* positivista, *m.* and
f.

positivistic, *a.* positivista

posse, *s.* pelotón, *m.*; multitud,
muchedumbre, *f.*

possess, *v.t.* poseer; gozar (de);
(of ideas, etc.) dominar. **to p.
oneself of,** apoderarse de, apropiarse. **What possessed you to
do it?** ¿Qué te hizo hacerlo?

possession, *s.* posesión, *f.* **to
take p. of,** tomar posesión de;
hacerse dueño de, apoderarse de;
(a house, etc.) entrar en, ocupar

possessive, *a.* posesivo. *s.* posesivo, *m.*

possessor, *s.* poseedor (-ra);
dueño (-ña); propietario (-ia)

possibility, *s.* posibilidad, *f.*

possible, *a.* posible. **as soon as
p.**, cuanto antes. **to make p.**,
hacer posible, posibilitar

possibly, *adv.* posiblemente; (perhaps) quizás. **I shall come as
soon as I p. can,** Vendré lo más
pronto posible

post, s. (pole) poste, *m.*; (of a
sentry, etc.) puesto, *m.*; (employment) empleo, *m.*; (mail) correo,
m.; (mil.) toque, *m.* *v.t.* (a
notice) fijar; anunciar; (to an
appointment) destinar; (letters,
etc.) echar al correo; (com.)
pasar al libro mayor; (inform)
tener al corriente. *v.i.* viajar en
posta. by return of p., a
vuelta de correo. P. no bills!
Se prohibe fijar carteles. registered p., correo certificado, *m.*
p. card, postal, *f.* p.-chaise,
silla de posta, *f.* p.-date,
posfecha, *f.* p.-free, franco de
porte. p.-haste, con gran celeridad. p.-horse, caballo de posta,
m. p.-impressionism, post-
impresionismo, *m.* p.-mortem,
s. autopsia, *f.* p.-natal, post-
natal. p.-nuptial, postnupcial.
p. office, correo, *m.*; (on a train)
ambulancia de correos, *f.* p.
office box, apartado de correos,
m. p. office savings bank,
caja postal de ahorros, *f.* p.-
paid, porte pagado; franco. p.-
war, *s.* postguerra, *f.* *a.* de la
postguerra

postage, *s.* porte de correos,
franqueo, *m.* p. stamp, sello
postal, *m.*

postal, *a.* postal. p. order, orden
postal de pago, *f.* p. packet,
paquete postal, *m.*

poster, *s.* cartel, *m.* *v.t.* fijar
carteles (a or en); anunciar por
carteles. bill-p., fijador de
carteles, *m.*

poste restante, *s.* lista de correos,
f.

posterior, *a.* posterior. *s.* trasero,
m., asentaderas, *f. pl.*

posteriority, *s.* posterioridad, *f.*

posterity, *s.* posteridad, *f.*

postern, *s.* postigo, *m.*; (mil.)
poterna, *f.*

postgraduate, *s.* estudiante graduado que hace estudios avanza-
dos, *m.* *a.* avanzado; para
estudiantes graduados

posthumous, *a.* póstumo

posthumously, *adv.* después de
la muerte

postilion, *s.* postillón, *m.*

postman, *s.* cartero, *m.*

postmark, *s.* matasellos, *m.* *v.t.*
poner matasellos (a)

postmaster, *s.* administrador de
correos, *m.*

postmeridian, *a.* postmeridiano

postmistress, *s.* administradora
de correos, *f.*

postpone, *v.t.* aplazar, diferir;
retrasar; (subordinate) postergar

postponement, *s.* aplazamiento,
m.; tardanza, *f.*

postscript, *s.* posdata, *f.*

postulant, *s.* postulante, *m.* and
f.; (ecc.) postulante (-ta)

postulate, *s.* postulado, *m.* *v.t.*
postular

posture, *s.* postura, actitud, *f.*;
(of affairs) estado, *m.*, situación, *f.*
v.i. tomar una postura

posy, *s.* (nosegay) ramillete de
flores, *m.*; flor, *f.*; (motto) mote,
m.

pot, *s.* pote, *m.*; tarro, *m.*; (flower-)
tiesto, *m.*; (for cooking) olla
marmita, *f.*; jarro, *m.* *v.t.* plantar en tiestos; conservar en potes.
pot-bellied, panzudo. pot-
boiler, obra literaria escrita
para ganar dinero, *f.* pot-herb,
hierba que se emplea para
sazonar, hortaliza, *f.* pot-hole,
bache, *m.*; agujero grande, *m.*
pot-luck, comida ordinaria, *f.*
pot-shot, tiro fácil, *m.*; tiro al
azar, *m.*

potable, *a.* potable

potage, *s.* potaje, *m.*

potash, *s.* potasa, *f.* caustic p.,
potasa cáustica, *f.*

potassium, *s.* potasio, *m.*

potation, *s.* potación, *f.*

potato, *s.* patata, *f.* sweet p.,
batata, *f.* p. beetle, coleóptero
de la patata, *m.* p. omelette,
tortilla a la española, *f.* p.
patch, patatal, *m.* p. peeler,
pelapatatas, *m.*

potency, *s.* potencia, *f.*; fuerza,
eficacia, *f.*

potent, *a.* potente, fuerte; eficaz

potentate, *s.* potentado, *m.*

potential, *a.* potencial; virtual;
(phys., gram.) potencial. *s.* poder,
m.; (gram.) modo potencial, *m.*;
(phys.) energía potencial, *f.*;
(elec.) tensión potencial, *f.*

potentiality, *s.* potencialidad, *f.*

pothook, *s.* garabato de cocina,
m.; palote, *m.*; (scrawl) garabato,
m.

potion, *s.* poción, *f.*

potpourri, s. popurrí, m.

potter, s. alfarero, m. v.i. gandulear. v.t. perder. **potter's clay,** barro de alfarero, m. **potter's wheel,** tabanque, m. **potter's workshop,** alfar, m.

pottery, s. alfarería, f.; (china) loza, porcelana, f.

pouch, s. bolsa, f.; (zool.) bolsa marsupial, f.; (for tobacco) tabaquera, f.; (for cartridges) cartuchera, f. v.t. embolsar. v.i. bolsear

poulterer, s. pollero (-ra)

poultice, s. apósito, emplasto, m. v.t. poner emplastos (a or en)

poultry, s. volatería, f. **p. dealer,** gallinero (-ra), vendedor (-ra) de volatería. **p. yard,** gallinero, m.

pounce, s. (swoop) calada, f. v.i. (swoop) calarse; saltar (sobre); agarrar, hacer presa (en); (fig.) atacar; descubrir, hacer patente

pound, s. (weight and currency) libra, f.; (for cattle) corral de concejo, m.; (thump) golpe, m. v.t. (break up) machacar, pistar; (beat) batir; (thump) golpear, aporrear. **p. sterling,** libra esterlina, f. **p. troy,** libra medicinal, f.

pounding, s. machucamiento, m.; batimiento, m.

pour, v.t. vaciar, verter; derramar. v.i. correr; (of rain) diluviar, llover a cántaros; (fill) llenar; (of crowds, words, etc.) derramarse. **to p. out the tea,** servir el té. **The crowd poured in,** La multitud entró en tropel

pouring, a. (of rain) torrencial

pout, v.i. torcer el gesto; hacer pucheritos

poverty, s. pobreza, f. **p.-stricken,** menesteroso, indigente, necesitado

powder, s. polvo, m.; (face) polvos de arroz, m. pl.; (gun) pólvora, f. v.i. polvorear; (crush) reducir a polvo, pulverizar. v.i. ponerse polvos. **p.-flash,** fogonazo, m. **p.-flask,** polvorín, m. **p.-magazine,** santabárbara, f. **p.-mill,** fábrica de pólvora, f. **p.-puff,** polvera, borla de empolvarse, f.

powdered, a. en polvo

powdery, a. polvoriento; friable

power, s. poder, m.; facultad, capacidad, f.; vigor, m., fuerza, f.; (pol. and math.) potencia, f.; (mech.) fuerza, f.; influencia, f. **As far as lies within my p.,** En cuanto me sea posible. **It does not lie within my p.,** No está dentro de mis posibilidades, No está en mi poder. **the Great Powers,** las grandes potencias. **the powers that be,** los que mandan. **to be in p.,** estar en el poder. **p.-house,** p.-station, central eléctrica, f. **p. of attorney,** poderes, m. pl., procuración, f. **to grant p. of attorney (to),** dar poderes (a)

powerful, a. poderoso; fuerte; eficaz; potente; (of arguments, etc.) convincente

powerfully, adv. poderosamente; fuertemente

powerless, a. impotente

pow-wow, s. conferencia, f.; conversación, f.

pox, s. sífilis, f.; (small-pox) viruelas, f. pl.; (chicken-pox) viruelas falsas, f. pl.

practicability, s. factibilidad, f.

practicable, a. practicable, factible, posible; viable, transitable

practical, a. práctico; virtual. **p. joke,** broma pesada, f.

practically, adv. prácticamente; en práctica; virtualmente; (in fact) en efecto. **p. nothing,** casi nada

practicalness, s. carácter práctico, m.

practice, s. (custom) costumbre, f.; práctica, f.; ejercicio, m.; (of a doctor, etc.) clientela, f.; profesión, f.; (religious) rito, m., ceremonias, f. pl.; (experience) experiencia, f. **It is not his p. to . . .,** No es su costumbre de . . . **to be out of p.,** estar desentrenado. **to put into p.,** poner en práctica. **P. makes perfect,** El ejercicio hace maestro

practise, v.t. tener la costumbre de; practicar; (a profession) ejercer; (a game) entrenarse en; (work at) estudiar; (a musical instrument) tocar; (accustom) acostumbrar. **to p. what one preaches,** predicar con el ejemplo

practised, *a.* experimentado; experto

practitioner, *s.* médico (-ca). **general p.,** médico (-ca) general

pragmatic, *a.* pragmatista; (historical) pragmático; práctico

pragmatism, *s.* pragmatismo, *m.*

pragmatist, *s.* pragmatista, *m.* and *f.*

prairie, *s.* pradera, sabana, pampa, *f.* *a.* de la pradera, etc.

praise, *v.t.* alabar; ensalzar, glorificar; elogiar. *s.* alabanza, *f.*; elogio, *m.*; glorificación, *f.*, ensalzamiento, *m.* **to p. to the skies,** poner en los cuernos de la luna, hacerse lenguas de

praiseworthiness, *s.* mérito, *m.*

praiseworthy, *a.* digno de alabanza, laudable

prance, *v.i.* (of a horse) caracolear, encabritarse, cabriolar; saltar; andar airosamente. *s.* corveta, cabriola, *f.*; salto, *m.*

prank, *s.* travesura, diablura, *f.* **to play pranks,** hacer diabluras

prate, prattle, *v.i.* charlar, chacharear; (lisp) balbucir; (of brooks, etc.) murmurar, susurrar. *v.t.* divulgar. *s.* charla, cháchara, *f.*; balbuceo, *m.*

prattler, *s.* parlanchín (-ina); (gossip) chismoso (-sa); (child) niño (-ña)

prattling, *s.* charla, *f.*; (lisping) balbuceo, *m.*; (of brooks, etc.) murmullo, susurro, ruido armonioso, *m.* *a.* charlatán, gárrulo; balbuciente; (of brooks, etc.) parlero

prawn, *s.* camarón, *m.*

pray, *v.t.* and *v.i.* suplicar; implorar; rezar, orar. **P. be seated,** Haga el favor de sentarse

prayer, *s.* rezo, *m.*, plegaria, oración, *f.*; súplica, *f.*; (*law*) petición, *f.* **p. book,** libro de devociones, devocionario, *m.* **p.-meeting,** reunión para rezar, *f.* **p.-rug,** alfombra de rezo, *f.*

praying, *s.* rezo, *m.*; suplicación, *f.*

preach, *v.t.* and *v.i.* predicar

preacher, *s.* predicador (-ra). **to turn p.,** meterse a predicar

preaching, *s.* predicación, *f.* *a.* predicador

preamble, *s.* preámbulo, *m.*

prearrange, *v.t.* preparar de antemano, predisponer

prebend, *s.* prebenda, *f.*; prebendado, *m.*

prebendary, *s.* prebendado, *m.*

precarious, *a.* precario; inseguro; incierto, arriesgado

precariously, *adv.* precariamente

precariousness, *s.* condición precaria, *f.*; inseguridad, *f.*; incertidumbre, *f.*

precaution, *s.* precaución, *f.* **to take precautions,** tomar precauciones

precautionary, *a.* de precaución; preventivo

precede, *v.t.* preceder (a), anteceder (a); tomar precedencia (a), exceder en importancia (a). *v.i.* ir delante; tener la precedencia

precedence, *s.* precedencia, *f.*; prioridad, *f.*; superioridad, *f.* **to take p. over,** tomar precedencia (a), preceder (a)

precedent, *s.* precedente, *m.* *a.* precedente. **without p.,** sin precedente

preceding, *a.* anterior, precedente

precentor, *s.* chantre, *m.*

precept, *s.* precepto, *m.*

preceptor, *s.* preceptor, *m.*

precincts, *s. pl.* recinto, *m.*; ámbito, *m.*; distrito, barrio, *m.*

preciosity, *s.* afectación, *f.*

precious, *a.* precioso; de gran valor; hermoso; amado; muy querido; (with rogue, etc.) redomado; completo. **p. little,** muy poco. **p. nearly,** casi, por poco . . . **p. stone,** piedra preciosa, *f.*

preciousness, *s.* preciosidad, *f.*; gran valor, *m.*

precipice, *s.* precipicio, *m.*

precipitancy, *s.* precipitación, *f.*

precipitant, *a.* precipitado

precipitate, *v.t.* precipitar, despeñar, arrojar; acelerar; (*chem.*) precipitar. *v.i.* precipitarse. *s.* precipitado, *m.* *a.* precipitado, súbito. **to p. oneself,** tirarse, lanzarse

precipitately, *adv.* precipitadamente

precipitation, *s.* precipitación (also *chem.*), *f.*; (*chem.*) precipitado, *m.*

precipitous, *a.* precipitoso, escarpado, acantilado

precipitously, *adv.* en precipicio

precise, *a.* preciso; exacto; justo; puntual; escrupuloso; formal; claro; pedante, afectado; ceremonioso

precisely, *adv.* precisamente; exactamente; puntualmente; escrupulosamente; claramente; con afectación; ceremoniosamente. **at six o'clock p.,** a las seis en punto

precision, *s.* precisión, *f.*; exactitud, *f.*; puntualidad, *f.*; escrupulosidad, *f.*; claridad, *f.*; afectación, *f.*; ceremonia, *f.*

preclude, *v.t.* excluir; impedir, hacer imposible

preclusion, *s.* exclusión, *f.*; imposibilidad, *f.*

precocious, *a.* precoz

precocity, *s.* precocidad, *f.*

preconceived, *a.* preconcebido

preconception, *s.* idea preconcebida, *f.*; (prejudice) prejuicio, *m.*

preconcerted, *a.* concertado de antemano

precursor, *s.* precursor (-ra)

precursory, *a.* precursor

predatory, *a.* rapaz; de rapiña; voraz

predecease, *v.t.* morir antes (de or que); (*law*) premorir, *s.* (*law*) premuerto, *m.*

predecessor, *s.* predecesor (-ra); (ancestor) antepasado, *m.*

predestination, *s.* predestinación, *f.*

predestine, *v.t.* predestinar

predetermination, *s.* predeterminación, *f.*

predetermine, *v.t.* predeterminar

predicament, *s.* (logic) predicamento, *m.*; situación, *f.*; (fix) apuro, *m.*; *pl.* **predicaments,** categorías, *f. pl.*

predicate, *v.t.* afirmar. *s.* (logic, *gram.*) predicado, *m.*

predict, *v.t.* predecir, pronosticar, profetizar

prediction, *s.* predicción, *f.*; pronóstico, vaticinio, *m.*, profecía, *f.*

predictor, *s.* pronosticador (-ra), profeta (-isa)

predilection, *s.* predilección, *f.*

predispose, *v.t.* predisponer

predisposition, *s.* predisposición, *f.*

predominance, *s.* predominio, *m.*

predominant, *a.* predominante

predominantly, *adv.* predominantemente

predominate, *v.i.* predominar

pre-eminence, *s.* preeminencia, *f.*; primacia, superioridad, *f.*

pre-eminent, *a.* preeminente; superior; extraordinario

pre-eminently, *adv.* preeminentemente; extraordinariamente; por excelencia; entre todos

preen, *v.t.* (of birds) limpiarse; (of people) darse humos, jactarse

pre-exist, *v.i.* preexistir

pre-existence, *s.* preexistencia, *f.*

prefabricated, *a.* prefabricado

preface, *s.* prólogo, *m.*; (*ecc.*) prefacio, *m.*; introducción, *f.* *v.t.* dar principio (a), empezar. **He prefaced his remarks by . . .,** Dijo como introducción a sus observaciones . . .

prefatory, *a.* preliminar, introductorio; a manera de prólogo

prefect, *s.* prefecto, *m.*

prefecture, *s.* prefectura, *f.*

prefer, *v.t.* preferir, gustar más (a); (promote) ascender, elevar; (a charge, etc.) presentar. **to p. a charge against,** pedir en juicio (a). **I p. oranges to apples,** Me gustan más las naranjas que las manzanas (or Prefiero las naranjas a las manzanas)

preferability, *s.* preferencia, ventaja, *f.*

preferable, *a.* preferible

preferably, *adv.* preferiblemente, con preferencia

preference, *s.* preferencia, *f.*; privilegio, *m.* **p. share,** acción privilegiada, acción preferente, *f.*

preferential, *a.* preferente

preferment, *s.* promoción, *f.*, ascenso, *m.*; puesto eminente, *m.*

preferred, *a.* preferente; favorito, predilecto. **p. share,** acción preferente, *f.*

prefix, *v.t.* anteponer, prefijar; (to a word) poner prefijo (a). *s.* prefijo, *m.*

pregnancy, *s.* embarazo, *m.*, preñez, *f.*

pregnant, *a.* embarazada, encinta, preñada (*f.*); *(fig.)* fértil; *(fig.)* preñado

prehensile, *a.* prensil

prehistoric, *a,* prehistórico

prehistory, *s.* prehistoria, *f.*

prejudge, *v.t.* prejuzgar

prejudice, *s.* prejuicio, *m.*; *(law)* perjuicio, *m.* *v.t.* influir, predisponer; *(damage)* perjudicar. **without p.,** sin perjuicio

prejudiced, *a.* parcial; con prejuicios

prejudicial, *a.* perjudicial

prelacy, *s.* prelacía, *f.*; episcopado, *m.*

prelate, *s.* prelado, *m.*

preliminarily, *adv.* preliminarmente

preliminary, *a.* preliminar. *s.* preliminar, *m.*

prelude, *s.* preludio, *m.*; presagio, *m.* *v.t.* and *v.i.* preludiar

premature, *a.* prematuro

prematurely, *adv.* prematuramente

prematureness, *s.* lo prematuro

premeditate, *v.t.* premeditar

premeditatedly, *adv.* premeditadamente, con premeditación

premeditation, *s.* premeditación, *f.*

premier, *a.* primero, principal. *s.* primer ministro, *m.*; *(in Spain)* presidente del Consejo de Ministros, *m.*

première, *s.* estreno, *m.*

premiership, *s.* puesto de primer ministro, *m.*; *(in Spain)* presidencia del Consejo de Ministros, *f.*

premise, *s.* *(logic)* premisa, *f.*; *pl.* premises, local, *m.*; recinto, *m.*; establecimiento, *m.*; propiedad, *f.*; tierras, *f.* *pl.* **on the premises,** en el local; en el establecimiento

premium, *s.* *(prize)* premio, *m.*, recompensa, *f.*; *(com.)* prima, *f.*; precio, *m.* **at a p.,** a premio; a una prima; *(of shares)* sobre la par; *(fig.)* en boga, muy solicitado, en gran demanda

premonition, *s.* presentimiento, presagio, *m.*

premonitory, *a.* premonitorio

prenatal, *a.* prenatal, antenatal

preoccupation, *s.* preocupación, *f.*

preoccupied, *a.* preocupado; abstraído, absorto

preoccupy, *v.t.* preocupar

prepaid, *a.* porte pagado, franco de porte

preparation, *s.* preparación, *f.*; preparativo, *m.*, disposición, *f.*; *(patent food)* preparado, *m.* **I have made all my preparations,** He hecho todos mis preparativos. **The book is in p.,** El libro está en preparación

preparative, *a.* preparativo. *s.* preparativo, *m.*

preparatory, *a.* preparatorio, preparativo; preliminar. **p. school,** colegio particular, *m.* **p. to,** como preparación para; antes de

prepare, *v.t.* preparar; aparejar, aviar; equipar; *(cloth)* aprestar. *v.i.* prepararse; hacer preparativos

preparedness, *s.* estado de preparación, *m.*; preparación, *f.*, apercibimiento, *m.*

prepay, *v.t.* pagar adelantado; *(a letter, etc.)* franquear

prepayment, *s.* pago adelantado, *m.*; *(of a letter, etc.)* franqueo, *m.*

preponderance, *s.* preponderancia, *f.*

preponderant, *a.* preponderante, predominante

preponderantly, *adv.* predominantemente; en su mayoría

preponderate, *v.i.* preponderar; prevalecer (sobre), predominar (sobre)

preposition, *s.* preposición, *f.*

prepositional, *a.* preposicional

prepossess, *v.t.* predisponer; causar buena impresión (a)

prepossessing, *a.* atractivo

preposterous, *a.* ridículo, absurdo

preposterously, *adv.* absurdamente

preposterousness, *s.* ridiculez, *f.*

prepuce, *s.* prepucio, *m.*

Pre-Raphaelite, *a.* and *s.* prerrafaelista (*m.* and *f.*)

prerequisite, *s.* requisito necesario, esencial, *m.* *a.* previamente necesario, esencial

prerogative, *s.* prerrogativa, *f.*

presage, *s.* presagio, *m.*; anuncio, *m.* *v.t.* presagiar; anunciar

Presbyterian, *a.* and *s.* presbiteriano (-na)

Presbyterianism, *s.* Presbiterianismo, *m.*

presbytery, *s.* presbiterio, *m.*

prescience, *s.* presciencia, previsión, *f.*

prescient, *a.* presciente

prescind, *v.i.* prescindir (de); separar (de). *v.i.* separarse

prescribe, *v.t.* and *v.i.* prescribir; (*med.*) recetar; dar leyes; (*law*) prescribir

prescription, *s.* prescripción (also *law*), *f.*; (*med.*) receta, *f.*

presence, *s.* presencia, *f.*; (ghost) aparición, *f.* in the p. of, en presencia de, delante; a vista de. p. of mind, presencia de ánimo, serenidad de ánimo, *f.*

present, *a.* presente; actual; (with month) corriente; (*gram.*) presente. at p., al presente, actualmente. at the p. day, a la fecha, en la actualidad, hoy día. P. company excepted! ¡Mejorando lo presente! to be p. at, presenciar, ser testigo de; asistir a, acudir a; hallarse en. p.-day, de hoy, actual. p. tense, (*gram.*) tiempo presente, *m.*

present, *s.* (time) presente, *m.*; actualidad, *f.*; (*gram.*) tiempo presente, *m.*; (gift) regalo, *m.*, dádiva, *f.* By these presents . . ., (*law*) Por estas presentes . . . to make a p. of, regalar. Jane made me a p. of a watch, Juana me regaló un reloj

present, *v.t.* presentar; ofrecer; manifestar; (a gift) regalar, dar; (*ecc., mil.*) presentar. New problems presented themselves, Nuevos problemas surgieron. to p. arms, presentar las armas. He presented himself in the office, Se presentó en la oficina. He presented his friend Mr. Moreno to me, Me presentó su amigo el Sr. Moreno

presentable, *a.* presentable

presentation, *s.* presentación, *f.*; homenaje, *m.*; (exhibition) exposición, *f.* on p., (*com.*) a presentación

presentiment, *s.* presentimiento, *m.*, corazonada, *f.* I had a p. that . . ., Tuve el presentimiento

de que . . ., Tuve una corazonada . . . to have a p. about, presentir

presently, *adv.* pronto; en seguida; dentro de poco

preservation, *s.* conservación, *f.*; (from harm) preservación, *f.*

preservative, *a.* preservativo. *s.* preservativo, *m.*

preserve, *v.t.* preservar (de); guardar; proteger; conservar; (*cul.*) hacer conservas de; (in syrup) almíbarar. *s.* (*cul.*) conserva, *f.*; (of fruit) compota, confitura, *f.*; (covert) coto, *m.* preserved fruit, dulce de almíbar, *m.* p. dish, compotera, *f.*

preserver, *s.* conservador (-ra); (saviour) salvador (-ra); (benefactor) bienhechor (-ra)

preserving, *s.* (from harm) preservación, *f.*; conservación, *f.* p. pan, cazuela para conservas, *f.*

preside, *v.i.* (over) presidir; dirigir, gobernar. He presided at the meeting, Él presidió la reunión

presidency, *s.* presidencia, *f.*

president, *s.* presidente, *m.*; (of a college) rector, *m.* lady p., presidenta, *f.*

presidential, *a.* presidencial

presidentship, *s.* presidencia, *f.*

press, *v.t.* prensar; (juice out of) exprimir; (clothes) planchar; (a bell, a hand, and of a shoe, etc.) apretar; (embrace) dar un abrazo (a); (a stamp, a kiss, etc.) imprimir; (an enemy) hostigar, acosar; (in a game) apretar; (crowd upon) oprimir; (emphasize) insistir en; (urge) instar, instigar; (compel) obligar; apremiar; (oppress) abrumar, agobiar; (paper) satinar; (an advantage) aprovecharse de. Lola pressed his hand, Lola le apretó la mano. Time presses, El tiempo es breve. I did not p. the point, No insistí en la cuestión. to p. against, pegar(se) contra. to p. down, comprimir; (*fig.*) agobiar. to p. for, exigir, reclamar. to p. forward, on, avanzar; seguir el camino, continuar la marcha; (hurry) apretar el paso

press, s. (pressure) apretón, *m.*; (push) golpe, *m.*; (throng) muchedumbre, *f.*; (of business, etc.) urgencia, *f.*; (apparatus) prensa, *f.*; (printing press and publishing firm) imprenta, *f.*; (cupboard) armario, *m.* **Associated P.,** Prensa Asociada, *f.* **freedom of the p.,** libertad de la prensa, *f.* **in the p.,** en prensa. **in the p. of battle,** en lo más reñido de la batalla. **to go to p.,** entrar en prensa. **p.-agent,** agente de publicidad, *m.* **p.-box,** tribuna de la prensa, *f.* **p.-cutting,** recorte de prensa, *m.* **p.-gallery,** tribuna de la prensa, *f.* **p.-gang,** ronda de enganche, *f.* **p.-mark,** número de catálogo, *m.* **p. proof,** prueba de imprenta, *f.* **p.-room,** taller de imprenta, *m.* **p.-stud,** botón automático, *m.*

pressing, *a.* urgente, apremiante; importuno. *s.* prensado, *m.*, prensadura, *f.*; expresión, *f.*; (of a garment) planchado, *m.*

pressingly, *adv.* urgentemente, con urgencia; importunamente

pressman, s. tirador, *m.*; (journalist) periodista, *m.*

pressure, s. presión, *f.*; (of the hand) apretón, *m.*; apremio, *m.*; opresión, *f.*; (weight) peso, *m.*; (force) fuerza, *f.*; urgencia, *f.* **p.-cooker,** autoclave, *m.* **p.-gauge,** manómetro, *m.*

prestidigitation, s. prestidigitación, *f.*, juegos de manos, *m. pl.*

prestige, s. prestigio, *m.*

presumable, *a.* presumible

presumably, *adv.* presumiblemente

presume, *v.t.* presumir; suponer; sospechar; (attempt) pretender. *v.i.* presumir; tomarse libertades; abusar (de)

presumption, s. presunción, *f.*; suposición, *f.*; (effrontery) atrevimiento, *m.*; insolencia, *f.*

presumptive, *a.* presuntivo; (with heir, etc.) presunto

presumptuous, *a.* presumido, insolente, presuntuoso; atrevido

presumptuously, *adv.* presuntuosamente

presumptuousness, s. presunción, presuntuosidad, *f.*; atrevimiento, *m.*

presuppose, *v.t.* presuponer

presupposition, s. presuposición, *f.*

pretence, s. (claim) pretensión, *f.*; afectación, *f.*; (simulation) fingimiento, *m.*; pretexto, *m.* **false pretences,** apariencias fingidas, *f. pl.*; engaño, *m.*, estafa, *f.* **to make a p. of,** fingir. **under p. of, bajo pretexto de**

pretend, *v.t.* dar como pretexto de; aparentar, fingir, simular, hacer el papel (de). *v.i.* pretender (a); tener pretensiones (de); ser pretendiente (a); fingir

pretended, *a.* supuesto, fingido; falso

pretender, s. pretendiente, *m.*; hipócrita, *m.* and *f.*

pretension, s. pretensión, *f.*; afectación, simulación, *f.*

pretentious, *a.* pretencioso; (of persons) presumido

pretentiousness, s. pretensiones, *f. pl.*, lo pretencioso

preterite, s. (tiempo) pretérito, *m.* *a.* pretérito, pasado

pretext, s. pretexto, *m.* *v.t.* pretextar. **under p. of,** bajo pretexto de, so color de

prettily, *adv.* lindamente; con gracia; agradablemente

prettiness, s. lo bonito; elegancia, *f.*; gracia, *f.*

pretty, *a.* bonito; (of women, children) guapo, mono; (of men) lindo; elegante; excelente; (*iron.*) bueno. *adv.* bastante; medianamente; (very) muy; (almost) casi. **p. good,** bastante bueno. **p.-p.,** de muñeca; mono. *s.* chuchería, *f.*, guapos, *m. pl.* **p. ways,** monerías, *f. pl.*

prevail, *v.i.* prevalecer, predominar; ser la costumbre. **to p. against or over,** triunfar de, vencer (a). **to p. on, upon,** inducir, convencer, persuadir. **to be prevailed upon to,** dejarse persuadir a

prevailing, *a.* prevaleciente; dominante; predominante, reinante; general; común; (fashionable) en boga

prevalence, s. predominio, *m.*; existencia, *f.*; (habit) costumbre, *f.*; (fashion) boga, *f.*

prevalent, *a.* prevaleciente; predominante; general; común; corriente; (fashionable) en boga

prevaricate, *v.i.* tergiversar; (*law*) prevaricar

prevarication, *s.* tergiversación, *f.*, equívoco, *m.*

prevaricator, *s.* tergiversador (-ra)

prevent, *v.t.* evitar; (hinder) impedir (a)

preventable, *a.* evitable

prevention, *s.* prevención, *f.*; (preventive) estorbo, obstáculo, *m.*

preventive, *a.* preventivo. *s.* preservativo, *m.*

preview, *s.* vista de antemano, *f.*; (of a film) función privada, *f.*

previous, *a.* previo, anterior. **p. to**, antes de

previously, *adv.* anteriormente, antes, previamente

previousness, *s.* anterioridad, *f.*; inoportunidad, *f.*

prevision, *s.* previsión, *f.*

pre-war, *a.* de antes de la guerra

prey, *s.* presa, *f.*; (*fig.*) víctima, *f.*; (booty) botín, *m.* *v.i.* (of animals) devorar; (plunder) robar, pillar; (of sorrow, etc.) hacer presa (de); agobiar, consumir; (sponge on) vivir a costa de. **to fall a p. to**, ser víctima de

price, *s.* precio, *m.*; valor, *m.*; costa, *f.* *v.t.* evaluar, tasar; poner precio a; preguntar el precio de; fijar el precio de. **at any p.**, a cualquier precio; (whatever the cost) cueste lo que cueste. **at a reduced p.**, a precio reducido. **fixed p.**, precio fijo, *m.* **price ceiling**, precio máximo, *m.* **p. control**, control de precios, *m.* **price list**, lista de precios, *f.*; tarifa, *f.*; (of shares, etc.) boletín de cotización, *m.*

priceless, *a.* sin precio; (amusing) divertidísimo. **These jewels are p.**, Estas joyas no tienen precio

prick, *s.* pinchazo, *m.*; picadura, *f.*; punzada, *f.*; (prickle) espina, *f.*; (with a goad) aguijonazo, *m.*; (with a pin) alfilerazo, *m.*; (with a spur) espolada, *f.*; (of conscience) remordimiento, escrú-

pulo, *m.* *v.t.* pinchar, punzar; picar; (with remorse) atormentar, causar remordimiento (a); (urge on) incitar. **to p. the ears**, aguzar las orejas

pricking, *s.* picadura, *f.*; punzada, *f.* **prickings of conscience**, remordimientos, *m. pl.*

prickle, *s.* espina, *f.*; (irritation) escozor, *m.*

prickly, *a.* espinoso; erizado. **p. heat**, salpullido causado por el calor, *m.* **p. pear**, higo chumbo, *m.*, chumbera, *f.*

pride, *s.* orgullo, *m.*; arrogancia, *f.*; (splendour) pompa, *f.*, fausto, aparato, *m.*; belleza, *f.*; vigor, *m.*; (of lions) manada, *f.* **to take p. in**, estar orgulloso de. **to p. oneself**, sentirse orgulloso, ufanarse. **to p. oneself upon**, jactarse de, preciarse de

prie-dieu, *s.* reclinatorio, *m.*

prier, *s.* espía, *m.* and *f.*; curioso (-sa)

priest, *s.* sacerdote, *m.*; cura, *m.* **high-p.**, sumo sacerdote, *m.* **p.-ridden**, dominado por el clero

priestcraft, *s.* intrigas eclesiásticas, *f. pl.*, clericalismo, *m.*

priestess, *s.* sacerdotisa, *f.*

priesthood, *s.* sacerdocio, *m.*

priestly, *a.* sacerdotal

prig, *s.* fatuo (-ua), mojigato (-ta)

priggish, *a.* fatuo, gazmoño

priggishness, *s.* gazmoñería, fatuidad, *f.*

prim, *a.* almidonado, etiquetero; peripuesto; afectado

primacy, *s.* primacía, *f.*

prima donna, *s.* cantatriz, *f.*

primæval, *a.* primevo, primitivo

primarily, *adv.* en primer lugar, principalmente

primary, *a.* primario; primitivo; principal. **p. education**, enseñanza primaria, *f.* **p. colours**, colores primarios, *m. pl.* **p. school**, escuela primaria, *f.*

primate, *s.* primado, *m.*

primateship, *s.* primacía, *f.*

prime, *a.* primero; principal; excelente; de primera calidad; de primera clase. *s.* (spring) primavera, *f.*; (of life, etc.) flor, *f.*; vigor, *m.*; (best) nata, crema, *f.*; (*ecc.*) prima, *f.*; (number) número primo. *m.* *v.t.* preparar, aprestar; (fire-arms) cebar; (with paint, etc.) imprimar; (instruct) dar instrucciones (a), informar. **in his p.**, en la flor de su edad. **of p. quality**, de primera calidad. **P. Minister**, Primer Ministro, *m.* **p. necessity**, artículo de primera necesidad, *m.*

primer, *s.* cartilla, *f.*, abecedario, *m.*; libro de lectura, *m.*; (prayer book) devocionario, *m.*

priming, *s.* preparación, *f.*; (of fire-arms) cebo, *m.*; (of paint, etc.) imprimación, *f.*; instrucción, *f.*

primitive, *a.* primitivo; anticuado. *s.* primitivo, *m.*

primitiveness, *s.* lo primitivo; carácter primitivo, *m.*

primly, *adv.* afectadamente, con afectación; gravemente

primness, *s.* afectación, *f.*; gravedad, *f.*

primogeniture, *s.* primogenitura, *f.*

primordial, *a.* primordial

primrose, *s.* primavera, *f.*; color amarillo pálido, *m.*

primula, *s.* oreja de oso, *f.*

prince, *s.* príncipe, *m.* **P. Consort**, príncipe consorte, *m.* **P. of Wales**, príncipe heredero, *m.*; (Spanish equivalent) Príncipe de Asturias, *m.* **P. Regent**, príncipe regente, *m.*

princeliness, *s.* magnificencia, *f.*; nobleza, *f.*

princely, *a.* principesco; magnífico; noble

princess, *s.* princesa, *f.*

principal, *a.* principal; fundamental; mayor. *s.* principal, jefe, *m.*; (of a university) rector, *m.*; (of a school) director (-ra), *m.*; (law) causante, *m.*; (com.) capital, *m.*

principality, *s.* principado, *m.*

principally, *adv.* principalmente

principle, *s.* principio, *m.* **in p.**, en principio

principled, *a.* de principios . . .

print, *s.* (mark) impresión, marca, *f.*; (type) letra de molde, *f.*, tipo, *m.*; (of books) imprenta, *f.*; (fabric) estampado, *m.*; (picture) grabado, *m.*; (photograph) positiva impresa, *f.*; (mould) molde, *m.* *v.t.* marcar; imprimir; (on the mind) grabar; (print.) tirar, hacer una tirada (de); (in photo-

graphy) tirar una prueba (de); (publish) sacar a luz, publicar; (fabrics) estampar. **in p.**, impreso; publicado; (available) existente. **to be out of p.**, estar agotado. **p. dress**, vestido estampado, *m.*

printed, *a.* impreso. **p. fabric**, estampado, *m.* **p. matter**, impresos, *m. pl.*

printer, *s.* impresor, *m.*; tipógrafo, *m.* **printer's devil**, aprendiz de impresor, *m.* **printer's ink**, tinta de imprenta, *f.* **printer's mark**, pie de imprenta, *m.*

printing, *s.* imprenta, *f.*; impresión, *f.*; (of fabrics) estampación, *f.*; (art of) tipografía, *f.* **p. house**, imprenta, *f.* **p. machine**, máquina de imprimir, *f.* **p. press**, prensa tipográfica, *f.* **p. types**, caracteres de imprenta, *m. pl.*

prior, *s.* prior, *m.* *a.* anterior, previo. **p. to**, anterior a, antes de

prioress, *s.* priora, *f.*

priority, *s.* prioridad, *f.*

priorship, *s.* priorato, *m.*

priory, *s.* priorato, *m.*

prise. See **prize**

prism, *s.* prisma, *m.*; espectro solar, *m.*

prismatic, *a.* prismático

prison, *s.* prisión, cárcel, *f.* **p. breaking**, huida de la prisión, *f.* **p. camp**, campo de prisioneros, *m.* **p. van**, coche celular, *m.* **p. yard**, patio de la prisión, *m.*

prisoner, *s.* prisionero (-ra), preso (-sa). **to take p.**, prender, hacer prisionero (a)

pristine, *a.* pristino, original

privacy, *s.* soledad, *f.*, aislamiento, retiro, *m.*; intimidad, *f.*; secreto, *m.*

private, *a.* particular; privado; secreto; confidencial; reservado; íntimo; personal; doméstico; (of hearings, etc.) a puertas cerradas, secreto; (own) propio. *s.* (soldier) soldado raso, *m.* **in p.**, en secreto; confidencialmente, de persona a persona. **They wish to be p.**, Quieren estar a solas. **p. company**, sociedad en comandita, *f.* **p. hotel**, pensión, *f.* **p. house**, casa particular, *f.* **p. individual**, particular, *m.* and *f.* **p. inter-**

view, entrevista privada, *f.* **p. life,** vida privada, *f.* **p. office,** despacho particular, *m.* **p. secretary,** secretario (-ia) particular. **p. view,** (of a film) función privada, *f.*; (of an exhibition) día de inauguración, *m.*

privateer, *s.* corsario, *m.*

privately, *adv.* privadamente; en secreto; personalmente; confidencialmente; (of hearings) a puertas cerradas

privation, *s.* privación, *f.*; carencia, escasez, *f.*

privet, *s.* alheña, *f.*

privilege, *s.* privilegio, *m.*; derecho, *m.*; inmunidad, *f.* *v.t.* privilegiar

privileged, *a.* privilegiado; confidencial

privy, *a.* privado; cómplice; enterado; personal, particular. *s.* (latrine) retrete, *m.* **P. Council,** Consejo Privado, *m.*

prize, *s.* premio, *m.*; recompensa, *f.*, galardón, *m.*; (capture) presa, *f. a.* que ha ganado un premio; premiado; (huge) enorme; (complete) de primer orden. *v.t.* estimar, apreciar. **to p. open,** abrir con una palanca. **to carry off the p.,** ganar el premio. **cash p.,** premio en metálico, *m.* **first p.,** primer premio, *m.*; (in a lottery) premio gordo, *m.* **P. Court,** tribunal de presas, *m.* **p. fight,** partido de boxeo, *m.* **p. fighter,** boxeador, *m.* **p. giving,** distribución de premios, *f.* **p. money,** premio en metálico, *m.*; (boxing) bolsa, *f.*

pro, *prep.* .pro. **pro forma invoice,** factura simulada, *f.*

probability, *s.* probabilidad, *f.*

probable, *a.* probable

probably, *adv.* probablemente

probate, *s.* verificación de un testamento, *f.*

probation, *s.* probación, *f.*; (law) libertad vigilada, *f.*

probationary, *a.* de probación; de prueba

probationer, *s.* novicio, *m.*; estudiante de enfermera, *f.*; candidato, *m.*; aspirante, *m.*

probe, *s.* (surg.) sonda, cala, tienta, *f. v.t.* (surg.) tentar; escudriñar

probing, *s.* sondeo, *m.*

probity, *s.* probidad, integridad, *f.*

problem, *s.* problema, *m.*; cuestión, *f.* **p. play,** drama de tesis, *m.*

problematic, *a.* problemático

proboscis, *s.* (of an elephant) trompa, *f.*; (of an insect) trompetilla, *f.*

procedure, *s.* procedimiento, *m.*

proceed, *v.i.* seguir el camino, continuar la marcha; avanzar, seguir adelante; ir; proceder; ponerse (a); empezar (a); (say) proseguir; (come to) llegar a, ir a; (of a play, etc.) desarrollarse. **Before we p. any further . . .,** Antes de ir más lejos... **to p. to blows,** llegar a las manos. **to p. against,** proceder contra, procesar. **to p. from,** venir de. **to p. with,** proseguir; poner por obra; usar

proceeding, *s.* modo de obrar, *m.*; conducta, *f.*; procedimiento, *m.*; transacción, *f.*; *pl.* **proceedings,** (measures) medidas, *f. pl.*, actos, *m. pl.*; (of a learned society) actas, *f. pl.* **to take proceedings against.** (law) procesar

proceeds, *s. pl.* producto, *m.*; ganancias, *f. pl.*; beneficios, *m. pl.* **net p.,** producto neto, *m.*

process, *s.* proceso, *m.*; (method) procedimiento, *m.*; (course) curso, *m.*; marcha, *f.*; (law, zool.) proceso, *m.* **in p. of,** en curso de. **in the p. of time,** con el tiempo, marchando el tiempo

procession, *s.* desfile, *m.*; cortejo, *m.*; (religious) procesión, *f.* **funeral p.,** cortejo fúnebre, *m.* **to walk in p.,** desfilar

processional, *a.* procesional

proclaim, *v.t.* proclamar; publicar, pregonar; anunciar; (reveal) revelar; (outlaw) denunciar

proclamation, *s.* proclamación, *f.*; proclama, *f.*, anuncio, *m.*; declaración, *f.*

proclivity, *s.* proclividad, propensión, *f.*

procrastinate, *v.i.* tardar (en decidirse), aplazar su decisión; vacilar; perder el tiempo

procrastination, *s.* dilación, tardanza, *f.*; vacilación, *f.*; pereza, *f.*

procrastinator, s. perezoso (-sa)

procreate, v.t. procrear

procreation, s. procreación, f.

procreator, s. procreador (-ra)

proctor, s. procurador, m.; (univ.) censor, m.

procurable, a. procurable; asequible

procure, v.t. obtener, conseguir, lograr

procurement, s. obtención, f., logro, m.

procurer, s. alcahuete, m.

procuress, s. alcahueta, celestina, trotaconventos, f.

prod, s. (with a bayonet, etc.) punzada, f.; (fig.) pinchazo, m. v.t. punzar; (in the ribs, etc.) clavar; (fig.) pinchar

prodigal, a. and s. pródigo (-ga)

prodigality, s. prodigalidad, f.

prodigally, adv. pródigamente

prodigious, a. prodigioso

prodigiousness, s. prodigiosidad, f.; enormidad, f.

prodigy, s. prodigio, m.; portento, m. an infant p., un niño prodigio

produce, v.t. producir; dar frutos; (show) mostrar, presentar; (take out) sacar; (occasion) causar, traer consigo, ocasionar; (goods) fabricar, manufacturar; (of shares, etc.) rendir; (geom.) prolongar; (a play) poner en escena. s. producto, m.; víveres, comestibles, m. pl.

producer, s. productor (-ra); (theat.) director de escena, m.

product, s. producto, m.; (result) fruto, resultado, m., consecuencia, f.; (math.) producto, m.

production, s. producción, f.; producto, m.; (geom.) prolongación, f.; (of a play) dirección escénica, f.; (performance) producción, f. p. cost, coste de producción, m.

productive, a. productivo

productivity, s. productividad, f.

profanation, s. profanación, f.

profane, a. profano; sacrílego, blasfemo. v.t. profanar

profaner, s. profanador (-ra)

profanity, s. profanidad, f.; blasfemia, f.

profess, v.t. (assert) afirmar, manifestar; declarar; (a faith, a profession, teach) profesar;

(feign) fingir; (pretend) tener pretensiones de. v.i. (as a monk or nun) tomar estado, entrar en religión. He professed himself surprised, Se declaró sorprendido

professed, a. declarado; (ecc.) profeso; ostensible, fingido

profession, s. profesión, f.; carrera, f.; declaración, f. p. of faith, profesión de fe, f. the learned professions, las carreras liberales

professional, a. profesional; de la profesión; de profesión; de carrera. p. diplomat, diplomático (-ca) de carrera. p. etiquette, etiqueta profesional, f. p. man, hombre profesional, m.; hombre de carrera liberal, m.

professionally, adv. profesionalmente

professor, s. catedrático (-ca), profesor (-ra)

professorate, s. profesorado, m.

professorial, a. de catedrático; de profesor

professorship, s. cátedra, f.

proffer, v.t. proponer; ofrecer. s. oferta, f.

proficiency, s. pericia, habilidad, f.

proficient, a. proficiente, experto, adepto, perito

profile, s. perfil, m. v.t. perfilar. in p., de perfil

profit, s. provecho, m.; utilidad, f.; ventaja, f.; (com.) ganancia, f. v.t. aprovechar. v.i. ganar; (com.) sacar ganancia. to p. by, aprovechar. gross p., ganancia total, f. p. and loss, ganancias y pérdidas, f. pl. p. sharing, participación en las ganancias, f.

profitable, a. provechoso, útil, ventajoso; lucrativo. p. use, aprovechamiento, m.

profitably, adv. con provecho, provechosamente; lucrativamente

profiteer, s. estraperlista, m. and f.

profitless, a. sin provecho, infructuoso, inútil

profligacy, s. libertinaje, m.

profligate, a. licencioso, disoluto. s. libertino, m.

profound, a. profundo

profoundly, *adv.* profundamente

profundity, *s.* profundidad, *f.*

profuse, *a.* profuso; pródigo; lujoso

profusely, *adv.* profusamente; pródigamente; lujosamente

profusion, *s.* profusión, abundancia, *f.*; prodigalidad, *f.*; exceso, *m.*

progenitor, *s.* progenitor, *m.*; (ancestor) antepasado, *m.*

progeny, *s.* prole, *f.*

prognosis, *s.* prognosis, *f.*; presagio, *m.*; (*med.*) pronóstico, *m.*

prognosticate, *v.t.* pronosticar, presagiar

prognostication, *s.* pronosticación, *f.*; pronóstico, presagio, augurio, *m.*

programme, *s.* programa, *m.*

progress, *s.* progreso, *m.*; avance, *m.*; (betterment) mejora, *f.*; (of events) marcha, *f.* *v.i.* avanzar, marchar; (improve) progresar, adelantar; mejorar. **to make p.,** adelantarse; hacer progresos

progression, *s.* progresión, *f.*

progressive, *a.* progresivo; avanzado; (*pol.*) progresista. *s.* (*pol.*) progresista, *m.* and *f.*

progressively, *adv.* progresivamente

progressiveness, *s.* carácter progresivo, *m.*

prohibit, *v.t.* prohibir; defender; (prevent) impedir, privar. **His health prohibited him from doing it,** Su salud le impidió hacerlo

prohibition, *s.* prohibición, *f.*; interdicción, *f.*; (of alcohol) prohibicionismo, *m.*

prohibitionist, *s.* prohibicionista, *m.* and *f.*

prohibitive, *a.* prohibitivo, prohibitorio

project, *v.t.* (all meanings) proyectar. *v.i.* sobresalir; destacarse. *s.* proyectil, plan, *m.*

projectile, *s.* proyectil, *m.* *a.* arrojadizo

projecting, *a.* saliente; (of teeth) saltón

projection, *s.* (hurling) lanzamiento, *m.*; prominencia, protuberancia, *f.*; (other meanings) proyección, *f.*

projector, *s.* proyectista, *m.* and *f.*; proyector, *m.*

proletarian, *a.* proletario

proletariate, *s.* proletariado, *m.*

prolific, *a.* prolífico; fecundo, fértil

prolix, *a.* prolijo

prolixity, *s.* prolijidad, *f.*

prologue, *s.* prólogo, *m.* *v.t.* prologar

prolong, *v.t.* prolongar

prolongation, *s.* prolongación, *f.*

promenade, *s.* paseo, *m.*; bulevar, *m.*; avenida, *f.* *v.i.* pasearse. *v.t.* recorrer, andar por, pasearse por. **p. deck,** cubierta de paseo, *f.*

Promethean, *a.* de Prometeo

prominence, *s.* prominencia, *f.*; protuberancia, *f.*; eminencia, *f.*; importancia, *f.*

prominent, *a.* prominente, saliente; (of eyes, teeth) saltón; (distinguished) eminente, distinguido. **They placed the vase in a p. position,** Pusieron el florero muy a la vista. **to play a p. part,** desempeñar un papel importante. **p. eyes,** ojos saltones, *m. pl.*

promiscuous, *a.* promiscuo

promiscuousness, *s.* promiscuidad, *f.*

promise, *s.* promesa, *f.*; (hope) esperanza, *f.*; (word) palabra, *f.*; (future) porvenir, *m.* *v.t.* and *v.i.* prometer. **a young man of p.,** un joven de porvenir. **to break one's p.,** faltar a su palabra; no cumplir una promesa. **to keep one's p.,** guardar su palabra; cumplir su promesa. **to p. and do nothing,** apuntar y no dar. **under p. of,** bajo palabra de. **p. of marriage,** palabra de matrimonio, *f.*

promised, *a.* prometido. **P. Land,** Tierra de Promisión, *f.*

promising, *a.* que promete bien; prometedor; (of the future, etc.) halagüeño; (of persons) inteligente

promissory, *a.* promisorio. **p. note,** pagaré, abonaré, *m.*

promontory, *s.* promontorio, *m.*

promote, *v.t.* fomentar, promover; provocar; (aid) favorecer, proteger; avanzar; estimular; (to a post) ascender; (an act, bill) promover; (*com.*) negociar

promoter, s. promotor (-ra); instigador (-ra); (*theat.*, etc.) empresario, *m.*

promotion, s. (encouragement) fomento, *m.*; (furtherance) adelanto, *m.*; protección, *f.*, favorecimiento, *m.*; (in employment, etc.) promoción, *f.*, ascenso, *m.*; (of a company, etc.) creación, *f.*

prompt, *a.* pronto; diligente; presuroso; puntual; rápido; (*com.*) inmediato. *v.t.* impulsar, incitar, mover; dictar; insinuar; (*theat.*) apuntar; (remind) recordar. **He came at five o'clock p.**, Vino a las cinco en punto. **p. book**, libro del traspunte, *m.* **p. box**, concha (del apuntador), *f.*

prompter, s. (*theat.*) apuntador, *m.*

prompting, s. sugestión, *f.*; instigación, *f.*; *pl.* **promptings**, impulso, *m.*; (of the heart, etc.) dictados, *m. pl.*

promptitude, s. prontitud, presteza, *f.*; prisa, expedición, *f.*; puntualidad, *f.*

promptly, *adv.* inmediatamente, en seguida; con prontitud, con celeridad; puntualmente

promptness, s. See **promptitude**

promulgate, *v.t.* promulgar; divulgar, diseminar

promulgation, s. promulgación, *f.*; divulgación, diseminación, *f.*

prone, *a.* postrado; inclinado, propenso

proneness, s. postración, *f.*; inclinación, tendencia, propensión, *f.*

prong, s. (pitchfork) horquilla, *f.*; (of a fork) diente, *m.*, púa, *f.*

pronged, *a.* dentado, con púas

pronominal, *a.* pronominal

pronoun, s. pronombre, *m.*

pronounce, *v.t.* pronunciar; declarar; articular

pronounced, *a.* marcado; perceptible; bien definido

pronouncement, s. pronunciamiento, *m.*

pronunciation, s. pronunciación, *f.*; articulación, *f.*

proof, s. prueba, *f.*; demostración, *f.*; ensayo, *m.*; (law) testimonio, *m.*; (*phot.*, *print.*) prueba, *f.*; (*math.*) comprobación, *f. a.*

hecho a prueba (de); impenetrable (a); (*fig.*) insensible (a). *v.t.* (raincoats, etc.) impermeabilizar. **in p. whereof**, en fe de lo cual. **p. against bombs**, a prueba de bombas. **p.-reading**, corrección de pruebas, *f.*

prop, s. apoyo, puntal, estribadero, *m.*; (for a tree) horca, *f.*, rodrigón, *m.*; (*naut.*) escora, *f.*; (*fig.*) báculo, *m.*, columna, *f.*, apoyo, *m.* *v.t.* apoyar; apuntalar; (a tree) ahorquillar; (a building) acodalar; (*naut.*) escorar; (*fig.*) sostener. **He propped himself against the wall**, Se apoyó en el muro, Se arrimó al muro

propaganda, s. propaganda, *f.*

propagandist, s. propagandista, *m.* and *f.*

propagate, *v.t.* propagar. *v.i.* propagarse

propagation, s. propagación, *f.*

propagator, s. propagador (-ra)

propel, *v.t.* propulsar, empujar, mover

propeller, s. propulsor, *m.*; (*mech.*) hélice, *f.*

propelling, s. propulsión, *f.* **p. pencil**, lapicero, *m.*

propensity, s. propensión, tendencia, inclinación, *f.*

proper, *a.* propio; apropiado; correcto; decente; (prim) afectado; serio, formal; (exact) justo, exacto; (suitable (for)) bueno (para), apto (para); (true) verdadero; (characteristic) peculiar; (*her.*) natural; (with rascal, etc.) redomado; (handsome) guapo. **If you think p.**, Si te parece bien. **p. noun**, nombre propio, *m.*

properly, *adv.* decentemente; correctamente; propiamente; bien. **to do (a thing) p.**, hacer algo bien. **p. speaking**, propiamente dicho

propertied, *a.* propietario, hacendado; (rich) pudiente, adinerado

property, s. propiedad, *f.*; (belongings) bienes, *m. pl.*; posesiones, *f. pl.*; (estate) hacienda, *f.*; (quality) cualidad, *f.*; *pl.* **properties**, (*theat.*) accesorios, *m. pl.* **personal p.**, bienes muebles, *m. pl.*; cosas personales, *f. pl.* **real p.**, bienes raíces, *m. pl.* **p. man**, (*theat.*) encargado

de los accesorios, *m.* **p. owner,**
propietario (-ia). **p. tax,** contribución sobre la propiedad, *f.*
prophecy, *s.* profecía, *f.*; predicción, *f.*
prophesier. See **prophet**
prophesy, *v.t.* profetizar; presagiar, predecir. *v.i.* hacer profecías
prophet, *s.* profeta, *m.*
prophetess, *s.* profetisa, *f.*
prophetic, *a.* profético
prophetically, *adv.* proféticamente
prophylactic, *a.* and *s.* profiláctico (*m.*)
propinquity, *s.* propincuidad, proximidad, *f.*; (relationship) parentesco, *m.*
propitiate, *v.t.* propiciar; apaciguar, conciliar
propitiation, *s.* propiciación, *f.*
propitiator, *s.* propiciador (-ra)
propitiatory, *a.* propiciador
propitious, *a.* propicio, favorable
propitiousness, *s.* lo propicio
proportion, *s.* proporción, *f.*; parte, *f.*; porción, *f.*; *pl.* **proportions,** proporciones, *f. pl.*; dimensiones, *f. pl. v.t.* proporcionar; repartir, distribuir. **in p.,** en proporción; conforme (a), según; (*com.*) a prorata. **in p. as,** a medida que. **out of p.,** desproporcionado. **He has lost all sense of p.,** Ha perdido su equilibrio (mental)
proportional, *a.* proporcional; en proporción (a); proporcionado (a). **p. representation,** representación proporcional, *f.*
proportionally, *adv.* proporcionalmente, en proporción
proportionate, *a.* proporcionado; proporcional. *v.t.* proporcionar
proportionately, *adv.* See **proportionally**
proposal, *s.* proposición, *f.*; oferta, *f.*; (plan) propósito, proyecto, *m.* **p. of marriage,** oferta de matrimonio, *f.*
propose, *v.t.* proponer; ofrecer; (a toast) dar, brindar. *v.i.* pretender, intentar, tener la intención de; pensar; (marriage) declararse
proposer, *s.* proponente, *m.*; (of a motion) autor (-ra) de una proposición
proposition, *s.* proposición, *f.*; (plan) proyecto, propósito, *m.*

propound, *v.t.* proponer; plantear, presentar
proprietary, *a.* propietario; de propiedad
proprietor, *s.* propietario, *m.*; dueño, *m.*
proprietorship, *s.* propiedad, pertenencia, *f.*
proprietress, *s.* propietaria, *f.*; dueña, *f.*
propriety, *s.* decoro, *m.*; conveniencia, *f.*; corrección, *f.*
propulsion, *s.* propulsión, *f.*
propulsive, *a.* propulsor
prorogation, *s.* prorrogación, *f.*
prorogue, *v.t.* prorrogar, suspender (la sesión de una asamblea legislativa)
pros and cons, el pro y el contra
prosaic, *a.* prosaico
prosaically, *adv.* prosaicamente
proscenium, *s.* proscenio, *m.*
proscribe, *v.t.* proscribir
proscription, *s.* proscripción, *f.*
prose, *s.* prosa, *f.* **p. writer,** prosista, *m.* and *f.*
prosecute, *v.t.* proseguir, llevar adelante; (*law*, a person) procesar; (*law*, a claim) pedir en juicio
prosecution, *s.* prosecución, *f.*; cumplimiento, *m.*; (*law*) acusación, *f.*; (*law*, party) parte actora, *f.* **in the p. of his duty,** en el cumplimiento de su deber
prosecutor, *s.* demandante, actor, *m.* **Public P.,** fiscal, *m.*
proselyte, *s.* prosélito, *m.*
proselytism, *s.* proselitismo, *m.*
prosody, *s.* prosodia, *f.*
prospect, *s.* perspectiva, *f.*; esperanza, *f.*; probabilidad, *f.*; (in mining) indicio de filón, *m.*; criadero (de oro, etc.), *m. v.i.* explorar; (of a mine) prometer (bien), dar buenas esperanzas. *v.t.* explorar, inspeccionar; examinar. **He is a man with good prospects,** Es un hombre de porvenir
prospective, *a.* en expectativa, futuro; previsor
prospector, *s.* explorador, operador, *m.*
prospectus, *s.* prospecto, programa, *m.*
prosper, *v.i.* prosperar. *v.t.* favorecer, prosperar
prosperity, *s.* prosperidad, *f.*

prosperous, *a.* próspero; favorable

prosperously, *adv.* prósperamente

prostate, *s.* próstata, *f.*

prostitute, *s.* prostituta, *f.* *v.t.* (also *fig.*) prostituir

prostitution, *s.* (also *fig.*) prostitución, *f.*

prostrate, *a.* tendido; postrado; abatido. *v.t.* derribar; arruinar; (by grief, etc.) postrar; (oneself) postrarse

prostration, *s.* postración, *f.*; abatimiento, *m.* **nervous p.,** neurastenia, *f.*

prosy, *a.* aburrido, árido; pedestre, prosaico; verboso, prolijo

protagonist, *s.* protagonista, *m.* and *f.*

protasis, *s.* prótasis, *f.*

protean, *a.* proteico

protect, *v.t.* proteger

protection, *s.* protección, *f.*; defensa, *f.*; garantía, *f.*; abrigo, *m.*; refugio, *m.*; (passport) salvoconducto, *m.*; (*pol.*) proteccionismo, *m.*

protectionism, *s.* proteccionismo, *m.*

protectionist, *s.* proteccionista, *m.* and *f.*

protective, *a.* protector; (*pol.*) proteccionista

protector, *s.* protector, *m.*

protectorate, *s.* protectorado, *m.*

protectress, *s.* protectriz, *f.*

protein, *s.* proteína, *f.*

protest, *v.t.* protestar; (*law*) hacer el protesto de una letra de cambio. *v.i.* declarar; insistir (en); hacer una protesta. *s.* protesta, *f.*; (*law*) protesto, *m.* **under p.,** bajo protesta. **to p. against,** protestar contra

Protestant, *a.* and *s.* protestante (*m.* and *f.*)

Protestantism, *s.* protestantismo, *m.*

protestation, *s.* protestación, *f.*

protester, *s.* el, *m.* (*f.* la) que protesta

protocol, *s.* protocolo, *m.* *v.t.* protocolizar

protoplasm, *s.* protoplasma, *m.*

prototype, *s.* prototipo, *m.*

protract, *v.t.* prolongar; dilatar

protracted, *a.* prolongado; largo

protraction, *s.* prolongación, *f.*

protractor, *s.* (*geom.* and *surv.*) transportador, *m.* **p. muscle,** músculo extensor, *m.*

protrude, *v.t.* sacar fuera. *v.i.* salir fuera; sobresalir

protuberance, *s.* protuberancia, *f.*

protuberant, *a.* protuberante, prominente

proud, *a.* orgulloso; arrogante; noble; glorioso; magnífico; soberbio. **to be p.,** enorgullecerse. **to make p.,** enorgullecer; hacer orgulloso. **to be p. of,** ser orgulloso de, pagarse de, gloriarse en. **p. flesh,** carnosidad, *f.*, bezo, *m.*

proudly, *adv.* con orgullo, orgullosamente

provable, *a.* demostrable

prove, *v.t.* probar; demostrar; (experience) experimentar, sufrir; poner a prueba; (a will) verificar; (show) mostrar; confirmar. *v.i.* resultar, salir (bien or mal)

provenance, *s.* origen, *m.*

Provençal, *a.* provenzal. *s.* provenzal, *m.* and *f.*; (language) provenzal, *m.*

provender, *s.* forraje, *m.*; (*fam.*) provisiones, *f. pl.*

proverb, *s.* refrán, *m.*; proverbio, *m.* **collection of proverbs,** refranero, *m.* **Book of Proverbs,** Proverbios, *m. pl.*

proverbial, *a.* proverbial

proverbially, *adv.* proverbialmente

provide, *v.t.* proporcionar, dar; proveer, surtir, suplir; (stipulate) estipular; preparar (por); tomar precauciones (contra); sufragar los gastos (de); proporcionar medios de vida (a); señalar una pensión (a). **to p. oneself with,** proveerse de

provided (that), *conjunc.* si; a condición de que, siempre que, con tal que

providence, *s.* providencia, *f.*

provident, *a.* próvido, previsor, prudente; económico

providential, *a.* providencial

providentially, *adv.* providencialmente

providently, *adv.* próvidamente, prudentemente

provider, *s.* proveedor (-ra)

province, *s.* provincia, *f.*; esfera, *f.*; función, incumbencia, *f.*

provincial, *a.* provincial, de provincia; provinciano. *s.* provinciano (-na); (*ecc.*) provincial, *m.*

provincialism, *s.* provincialismo, *m.*

provision, *s.* provisión, *f.*; (stipulation) estipulación, *f.*; *pl.* provisions, provisiones, *f. pl.*; víveres, comestibles, *m. pl. v.t.* abastecer, aprovisionar. to make p. for, hacer provisión para, proveer de. to make p. for one's family, asegurar el porvenir de su familia. p. merchant, vendedor (-ra) de comestibles

provisional, *a.* provisional, interino

provisionally, *adv.* provisionalmente

provisioning, *s.* aprovisionamiento, abastecimiento, *m.*

proviso, *s.* condición, estipulación, disposición, *f.*

provisory, *a.* provisional; condicional

provocation, *s.* provocación, *f.*

provocative, *a.* provocativo, provocador

provocatively, *adv.* de un modo provocativo

provoke, *v.t.* provocar; suscitar; incitar, excitar; (irritate) sacar de madre (a), indignar

provoker, *s.* provocador (-ra); instigador (-ra)

provoking, *a.* provocativo; (irritating) enojoso, irritante

provost, *s.* preboste, *m.*; (of a college) director, *m.*; (in Scotland) alcalde, *m.* p.-marshal, capitán preboste, *m.*

prow, *s.* proa, *f.*

prowess, *s.* valor, *m.*, destreza, *f.*; proeza, *f.*

prowl, *v.i.* and *v.t.* rondar; cazar al acecho

prowler, *s.* rondador (-ra); ladrón (-ona)

proximity, *s.* proximidad, *f.*

proximo, *adv.* en (or del) mes próximo

proxy, *s.* poder, *m.*; delegación, *f.*; apoderado, *m.*; delegado (-da); substituto (-ta). to be married by p., casarse por poderes

prude, *s.* mojigata, beata, *f.*

prudence, *s.* prudencia, *f.*

prudent, *a.* prudente

prudently, *adv.* con prudencia

prudery, *s.* mojigatería, beatería, damería, gazmoñería, *f.*

prudish, *a.* mojigato, gazmoño, remilgado

prune, *s.* ciruela pasa, *f.*; color de ciruela, *m. v.t.* podar; (cut) cortar; reducir

pruning, *s.* poda, *f.*; reducción, *f.* p. knife, podadera, *f.*

prurient, *a.* lascivo, lujurioso, salaz

Prussian, *a.* and *s.* prusiano (-na). P. blue, azul de Prusia, *m.*

prussic acid, *s.* acido prúsico, *m.*

pry, *v.i.* escudriñar; acechar, espiar, fisgonear; (meddle) entremeterse, meterse donde no le llaman. *v.t.* See prize

prying, *s.* fisgoneo, *m.*; curiosidad, *f. a.* fisgón, curioso

psalm, *s.* salmo, *m.* to sing psalms, salmodiar

psalmist, *s.* salmista, *m.*

psalmody, *s.* salmodia, *f.*

psaltery, *s.* salterio, *m.*

pseudo-, *a.* seudo. p.-learned, erudito a la violeta

pseudonym, *s.* pseudónimo, *m.*

psittacosis, *s.* psitacosis, *f.*

psychiatrist, *s.* psiquiatro, *m.*

psychiatry, *s.* psiquiatría, *f.*

psychic, *a.* psíquico

psycho-analysis, *s.* psicoanálisis, *m.* or *f.*

psycho-analyst, *s.* psicoanalista, *m.* and *f.*

psycho-analyse, *v.t.* psicoanalizar

psychological, *a.* psicológico

psychologically, *adv.* psicológicamente

psychologist, *s.* psicólogo (-ga)

psychology, *s.* psicología, *f.*

psychopathic, *a.* psicopático

psychosis, *s.* psicosis, *f.*

psychotherapy, *s.* psicoterapia, *f.*

ptomaine poisoning, *s.* intoxicación por ptomaínas, *f.*

puberty, *s.* pubertad, *f.*

pubescent, *a.* púber

pubic, *a.* púbico

pubis, *s.* pubis, *m.*

public, *a.* and *s.* público (*m.*). in p., en público. P. Assistance, asistencia pública, *f.* p. funds, hacienda pública, *f.* p.

health, higiene pública, *f.* **p.-
house,** taberna, *f.* **p. opinión,**
opinión pública, *f.*, (*fam.*) el qué
dirán. **p.-spirited,** patriótico.
p. thoroughfare, vía pública, *f.*
p. works, obras públicas, *f.
pl.*

publican, *s.* tabernero, *m.*

publication, *s.* publicación, *f.*

publicist, *s.* publicista, *m.* and
f.

publicity, *s.* publicidad, *f.*

publicly, *adv.* públicamente

publish, *v.t.* publicar, divulgar,
difundir; (a book, etc.) dar a luz,
dar a la prensa, publicar; (of a
publisher) editar. **to p. abroad,**
pregonar a los cuatro vientos.
to p. banns of marriage,
correr las amonestaciones

publisher, *s.* publicador (-ra); (of
books) editor (-ra)

publishing, *s.* publicación, *f.* **p.
house,** casa editorial, *f.*

puck, *s.* trasgo, *m.*; diablillo,
picaruelo, *m.*

pucker, *v.t.* (one's brow, etc.)
fruncir; (crease) arrugar. *v.i.*
arrugarse. *s.* frunce, *m.*; arruga,
f.; (fold) bolsa, *f.*

puckering, *s.* fruncido, *m.*; arrugas, *f. pl.*

puckish, *a.* travieso

pudding, *s.* pudín, budín, *m.*
black p., morcilla, *f.*

puddle, *s.* charco, *m.*

puerile, *a.* pueril

puerility, *s.* puerilidad, *f.*

puerperal, *a.* puerperal. **p.
fever,** fiebre puerperal, *f.*

puff, *v.t.* and *v.i.* (blow) soplar;
(at a pipe, etc.) chupar; (smoke)
lanzar bocanadas de humo;
(make pant) hacer jadear; (advertise) dar bombo (a); (distend)
hinchar; (make conceited) en-
vanecerse; (of a train, etc.) bufar; resoplar. *s.* soplo, *m.*; (of
smoke, etc.) bocanada, *f.*; (of an
engine, etc.) resoplido, bufido,
m.; (for powder) borla (para
polvos), *f.*; (pastry) bollo, *m.*;
(advertisement) bombo, *m.* **to
be puffed up,** (*fig.*) hincharse,
inflarse. **p. of wind,** ráfaga de
aire, *f.* **p.-ball,** bejín, *m.* **p.-
pastry,** hojaldre, *m.* or *f.* **p.-
sleeve,** manga de bullón, *f.*

puffiness, *s.* hinchazón, *f.*

puffy, *a.* (of the wind) a ráfagas;
(panting) jadeante; (swollen)
hinchado

pug, *s.* (dog) doguino, *m.* **p.-
nosed,** de nariz respingona

pugilism, *s.* boxeo, pugilato, *m.*

pugilist, *s.* pugilista, boxeador,
m.

pugnacious, *a.* pugnaz, belicoso

pugnacity, *s.* pugnacidad, belicosidad, *f.*

pull, *s.* tirón, *m.*; sacudida, *f.*;
golpe, *m.*; (row) paseo en barco,
m.; (with the oars) golpe (de
remos), *m.*; (at a bell) tirón, *m.*;
(bell-rope) tirador, *m.*; (at a
bottle) trago, *m.*; (strain) fuerza,
f.; atracción, *f.*; (struggle) lucha,
f.; (advantage) ventaja, *f.*; (influence) influencia, *f.* **to give a
p.,** tirar (de), dar un tirón (a).
to have plenty of p., (*fam.*)
tener buenas aldabas

pull, *v.t.* tirar (de); (drag) arrastrar; (extract) sacar; (a boat)
remar; (gather) coger; (*print.*)
imprimir. He pulled the trigger
(of his gun), Apretó el gatillo.
He was sitting by the fire
pulling at his pipe, Estaba
sentado cerca del fuego fumando
su pipa. **to p. a hat well down
on the head,** calarse el sombrero.
to p. a person's leg, tomar el
pelo (a). **to p. oneself together,**
componer el semblante, serenarse;
recobrar el aplomo; (tidy oneself)
arreglarse. **to p. apart,** *v.t.* separar; romper en dos. *v.i.* separarse;
romperse en dos. **to p. away,**
v.t. arrancar; quitar. *v.i.* tirar
con esfuerzo. **to p. back,**
tirar hacia atrás; hacer retroceder (a); retener. **to p. down,**
hacer bajar, obligar a bajar;
(objects) bajar; (buildings) derribar, demoler; (humble) humillar; degradar; (weaken) debilitar. **to p. in,** tirar hacia
dentro; hacer entrar; (a horse)
enfrenar; (expenditure) reducir.
to p. off, arrancar; (clothes)
quitarse; (a deal) cerrar (un
trato), concluir con éxito; (win)
ganar. **to p. on,** *v.t.* (gloves,
etc.) meterse, ponerse. *v.i.*
seguir remando. **to p. open,**
abrir; abrir rápidamente. **to p.
out,** hacer salir; obligar a salir;

(teeth, daggers, etc.) sacar; (hair)
arrancar. **to p. round,
through,** *v.t.* ayudar a reponerse (a); sacar de un aprieto.
v.i. restablecerse; reponerse,
cobrar la salud, sanar. **to p.
together,** obrar de acuerdo;
(get on) llevarse (bien or mal).
**He pulled himself together
very quickly,** Se repuso muy
pronto. **to p. up,** *v.t.* montar,
subir; (a horse) sofrenar; (stop)
parar; (by the root) desarraigar,
extirpar; (interrupt) interrumpir; (scold) reñir. *v.i.* parar(se);
(restrain oneself) reprimirse, contenerse

pullet, *s.* polla, *f.*

pulley, *s.* polea, *f.;* (*naut.*) garrucha, *f.* **p. wheel,** roldana, *f.*

pulling, *s.* tracción, *f.;* tirada, *f.;*
arranque, *m.*

pullover, *s.* jersey, *m.*

pullulate, *v.i.* pulular

pulmonary, *a.* pulmonar

pulp, *s.* pulpa, *f.;* (of fruit) carne,
f.; (paper) pasta, *f.;* (of teeth)
bulbo dentario, *m.* *v.t.* reducir a
pulpa; deshacer (el papel). **to
beat to a p.,** (*fam.*) poner como
un pulpo

pulpit, *s.* púlpito, *m.*

pulpy, *a.* pulposo; (*bot.*) carnoso

pulsate, *v.i.* pulsar, latir

pulsation, *s.* pulsación, *f.,* latido,
m.

pulsatory, *a.* pulsante, pulsativo,
latiente

pulse, *s.* pulso, *m.;* pulsación, *f.,*
latido, *m.;* vibración, *f.;* (vegetable) legumbre, *f.* *v.i.* pulsar,
latir; vibrar. **to take a person's p.,** tomar el pulso (a)

pulverization, *s.* pulverización, *f.*

pulverize, *v.t.* pulverizar

puma, *s.* puma, *f.*

pumice, *s.* piedra pómez, *f.*

pummel, *v.t.* aporrear

pump, *s.* (*mech.*) bomba, *f.;* (for
water, etc.) aguatocha, *f.;* (*naut.*)
pompa, *f.;* (slipper) escarpín, *m.*
v.t. bombear, extraer por medio
de una bomba; (inflate) inflar;
(for information) sondear, sonsacar. **hand-p.,** bomba de mano,
f. **to work a p.,** darle a la
bomba

pumpkin, *s.* calabaza, *f.;* (plant)
calabacera, *f.*

pun, *s.* retruécano, *m.*

punch, *s.* (drink) ponche, *m.;*
(blow) puñetazo, golpe, *m.;*
(*mech.*) punzón, *m.;* (for tickets,
etc.) taladro, *m.;* (*fam.*) fuerza, *f.*
v.t. (perforate) taladrar, punzar;
estampar; (hit) dar un puñetazo
(a). **p.-ball,** pelota de boxeo, *f.*
p.-bowl, ponchera, *f.*

Punchinello, *s.* Polichinela, *m.*
Punch and Judy Show, títeres,
m. pl.

punctilious, *a.* formal, puntual,
puntilloso

punctiliousness, *s.* formalidad,
puntualidad, *f.*

punctual, *a.* puntual

punctuality, *s.* puntualidad, *f.*

punctually, *adv.* puntualmente

punctuate, *v.t.* puntuar

punctuation, *s.* puntuación,
f.

puncture, *s.* pinchazo, *m.;* perforación, *f.;* (*surg.*) punción, *f.*
v.t. pinchar; perforar; punzar.
We have a p. in the right tyre,
Tenemos un pinchazo en el
neumático derecho

pungency, *s.* picante, *m.;* acerbidad, mordacidad, *f.*

pungent, *a.* picante; acerbo,
mordaz

Punic, *a.* púnico, cartaginés

punish, *v.t.* castigar; maltratar

punishable, *a.* punible

punishment, *s.* castigo, *m.;* pena,
f.; maltrato, *m.*

punitive, *a.* punitivo

punt, *s.* batea, *f.* *v.t.* impeler una
batea con una pértiga; ir en
batea; (a ball) golpear, dar un
puntapié (a)

puny, *a.* débil, encanijado; insignificante; pequeño

pup, *s.* cachorro (-rra). *v.i.* parir
la perra

pupa, *s.* crisálida, *f.*

pupil, *s.* alumno (-na), discípulo
(-la); (of the eye) pupila, niña del
ojo, *f.;* (law) pupilo (-la). *a.*
escolar. **day p.,** alumno (-na)
externo (-na). **p. teacher,**
maestro (-tra) alumno (-na)

pupilage, *s.* pupilaje, *m.*

puppet, *s.* títere, *m.,* marioneta,
f.; muñeca, *f.;* (person) maniquí,
m. **p. show,** función de títeres, *f.*
p. showman, titiritero, titerero,
m.

puppy, s. perrito (-ta), cachorro (-rra)

purblind, a. ciego; (short-sighted and fig.) miope

purchasable, a. comprable, que puede comprarse; (fig.) sobornable

purchase, v.t. comprar; adquirir; (fig.) lograr, conseguir. s. compra, f.; adquisición, f.; (mech.) apalancamiento, m.; fuerza, f.; (lever) palanca, f., aparejo, m.; (fig.) influencia, f. **p. tax,** impuesto de lujo, m.

purchaser, s. comprador (-ra)

purchasing, s. See **purchase.** **p. power,** poder de adquisición, m.

pure, a. puro. **p.-bred,** de raza

purely, adv. puramente

pureness, s. pureza, f.

purgation, s. purgación, f.

purgative, a. purgativo. s. purga, f.

purgatorial, a. del purgatorio; (expiatory) purgatorio

purgatory, s. purgatorio, m.

purge, s. purgación, f.; (laxative) purga, f.; (pol.) depuración, f.; purificación, f. v.t. purgar; (pol.) depurar; purificar; expurgar

purging, s. purgación, f.; (pol.) depuración, f.; (fig.) purificación, f.

purification, s. purificación, f.

purificatory, a. purificador, purificatorio, que purifica

purifier, s. purificador (-ra)

purify, v.t. purificar; (metals) acrisolar; refinar; depurar; (purge) purgar

purine, s. (chem.) purina, f.

purist, s. purista, m. and f.

puritan, a. and s. puritano (-na)

Puritanism, s. puritanismo, m.

purity, s. pureza, f.

purl, v.i. (of a stream, etc.) murmurar, susurrar. s. (of a stream, etc.) susurro, murmullo, m.

purlieu, s. límite, m.; pl. **purlieus,** alrededores, m. pl., inmediaciones, f. pl.; (slums) barrios bajos, m. pl.

purling, a. murmurante, que susurra, parlero. s. murmullo, susurro, m.

purloin, v.t. hurtar, robar

purple, s. púrpura, f. a. purpúreo. v.t. purpurar, teñir de púrpura. v.i. purpurear

purplish, a. purpurino, algo purpúreo

purport, v.t. dar a entender, querer decir; significar; indicar; parecer; tener el objeto de; pretender. s. importe, m.; sentido, significado, m.; objeto, m.

purpose, s. objeto, m.; propósito, fin, m.; intención, f.; proyecto, m.; designio, m.; determinación, voluntad, f.; efecto, m.; ventaja, utilidad, f. v.i. and v.t. proponerse; pensar, tener el propósito (de), intentar. **It will serve my p.,** Servirá para lo que yo quiero. **for the p. of...,** con el propósito de..., con el fin de... **on p.,** de propósito, expresamente. **to no p.,** inútilmente; en vano

purposeful, a. resuelto; de substancia

purposeless, a. irresoluto, vacilante, vago; sin objeto; inútil

purposely, adv. expresamente, de intento

purr, v.i. ronronear. s. ronroneo, m.

purse, s. bolsa, f.; monedero, portamonedas, m. **to p. one's lips,** apretar los labios

purser, s. (naut.) contador, sobrecargo, m. **purser's office,** contaduría, f.

pursuance, s. cumplimiento, desempeño, m., prosecución, f. **in p. of,** en cumplimiento de; en consecuencia de

pursuant, a. and adv. según; conforme (a), de acuerdo (con); en consecuencia (de)

pursue, v.t. perseguir; seguir; (search) buscar; (hunt) cazar; (a submarine, etc.) dar caza (a); (continue) proseguir, continuar; (an occupation) dedicarse (a), ejercer

pursuer, s. perseguidor (-ra)

pursuit, s. perseguimiento, m.; (search) busca, f.; (hunt) caza, f.; (performance) prosecución, f., desempeño, m.; (employment) ocupación, f. **in p. of,** en busca de. **p. 'plane,** avión de caza, m.

purulence, *s.* purulencia, *f.*
purulent, *a.* purulento
purvey, *v.t.* proveer, surtir, suministrar; abastecer; procurar
purveyance, *s.* suministro, abastecimiento, *m.*; provisión, *f.*
purveyor, *s.* suministrador (-ra),
proveedor (-ra), bastecedor (-ra)
pus, *s.* pus, *m.*
push, *s.* empujón, *m.*; empellón,
m.; impulso, *m.*; (of a person)
empuje, *m.*, energía, *f.*; (attack)
ataque, *m.*; ofensiva, *f.*; (effort)
esfuerzo, *m.*; crisis, *f.*, momento
crítico, *m.* at a push, (*fam.*) en
caso de necesidad; en un aprieto,
si llegara el caso. to give the p.
to, (*fam.*) despedir (a). p.-
bicycle, bicicleta, *f.* p.-button,
botón, *m.*; botón de llamada, *m.*
p.-cart, carretilla de mano, *f.*;
(child's) cochecito de niño, *m.*
push, *v.t.* empujar; (jostle) empellar, dar empellones (a); (a
finger in one's eye, etc.) clavar;
(a button) apretar; (*fig.*, a person)
proteger, ayudar; dar publicidad
(a); (a claim, etc.) insistir en;
(compel) obligar. *v.i.* empujar;
dar empujones, empellar. **I am
pushed for time,** Me falta
tiempo. **He is pushed for
money,** Está apurado por dinero.
**I have pushed my finger in
my eye,** Me he clavado el dedo
en el ojo. to p. against, empujar contra; lanzarse contra;
empellar, dar empellones (a).
to p. aside, away, apartar con
la mano; rechazar, alejar. to p.
back, (hair, etc.) echar hacia
atrás; (people) hacer retroceder;
rechazar. to p. by, pasar. to
p. down, hacer bajar; hacer
caer; (demolish) derribar. to p.
forward, *v.t.* empujar hacia
delante, hacer avanzar; (a plan,
etc.) llevar adelante. *v.i.* adelantarse a empujones; avanzar;
seguir el camino. to p. oneself
forward, (*fig.*) abrirse camino;
entremeterse; darse importancia.
to p. in, *v.t.* empujar; hacer
entrar; clavar, hincar. *v.i.* entrar a la fuerza; entremeterse.
to p. off, *v.t.* apartar con la
mano (a); (*fam.*) quitar de
encima (a). *v.i.* (*naut.*) desatracar; (*fam.*) ponerse en camino.

to p. open, empujar, abrir. to
p. out, *v.t.* empujar hacia fuera;
hacer salir; echar. *v.i.* (*naut.*)
zarpar. to p. through, *v.t.*
(business, etc.) despachar rápidamente; (a crowd) abrirse camino
por. *v.i.* aparecer, mostrarse.
to p. to, cerrar. to p. up,
empujar; hacer subir; (windows, etc.) levantar
pushing, *a.* enérgico, emprendedor; ambicioso; agresivo. by
p. and shoving, a empellones, a
empujones
pusillanimity, *s.* pusilanimidad, *f.*
pusillanimous, *a.* pusilánime
puss, *s.* micho (-cha). P.! P.!
¡Miz, Miz!
pustule, *s.* pústula, *f.*
put, *v.t.* poner; colocar; (pour out)
echar; aplicar; emplear; (estimate) calcular; presentar; (ask)
preguntar; (say) decir; (express)
expresar; (a question) hacer; (a
problem) plantear; (the weight)
lanzar; (rank) estimar. **As the
Spanish put it,** Como dicen los
españoles. **If I may put it so,**
Si puedo expresarlo así, Por así
decirlo. **hard put to it,** en
dificultades, apurado. **How will
you put it to her?** ¿Cómo se lo
vas a explicar a ella? . to put
ashore, echar en tierra (a). to
put a child to bed, acostar a
un niño. to put in order,
arreglar; ordenar. to put out
of joint, dislocar. to put out
of order, estropear. to put to
death, matar; (judicially) ajusticiar. to put about, *v.t.* (a
rumour) diseminar, divulgar;
(worry) preocupar. *v.i.* (*naut.*)
virar, cambiar de rumbo. to
put aside, poner a un lado;
descartar; (omit) omitir, pasar
por alto de; (fears, etc.) desechar.
to put away, quitar; guardar;
poner en salvo; arrinconar;
(thoughts) desechar, ahuyentar;
(save) ahorrar; (banish) despedir,
alejar; (a wife) repudiar, divorciar; (food) tragar. to put
back, *v.t.* echar hacia atrás;
hacer retroceder; (replace) devolver, restituir; (the clock)
retrasar; (retard) retardar, atrasar. *v.i.* volver; (*naut.*) volver a

puerto. **to put down**, depositar; poner en el suelo; (the blinds) bajar; (an umbrella) cerrar; (a rebellion) sofocar; (gambling, etc.) suprimir; (humble) abatir, humillar; degradar; (silence) hacer callar; (reduce) reducir, disminuir; (write) apuntar, anotar; (a name) inscribir; (to an account) poner a la cuenta de; (estimate) juzgar, creer; (impute) atribuir. **to put forth**, (leaves, flowers, sun's rays) echar; (a book) publicar, dar a luz; (a hand) alargar; (an arm) extender; (show) manifestar, mostrar; (strength, etc.) desplegar; (use) emplear. **to put forward**, avanzar; (a clock) adelantar; (a suggestion, etc.) hacer; (propose) proponer; (a case) presentar. **to put oneself forward**, ponerse en evidencia. **to put in**, poner dentro; (a hand, etc.) introducir; (liquids) echar en; (a government) poner en el poder; (an employment) nombrar, colocar; (insert) insertar; (a claim) presentar; (say) decir. **I shall put in two hours' work before bedtime,** Trabajaré por dos horas antes de acostarme. **He put in a good word for you,** Habló en tu favor. **to put in writing,** poner por escrito. **to put in for,** (an employment) solicitar (un empleo); (as a candidate) presentarse como candidato para. **to put into,** meter dentro (de); (words) expresar; (port) arribar, hacer escala en (un puerto). **to put off,** desechar; (garments) quitarse, despojarse (de); (postpone) diferir, aplazar; (evade) evadir, entretener; quitarse de encima (a), desembarazarse (de); (confuse) desconcertar; (discourage) desanimar; quitar el apetito (a). **to put on,** poner sobre; (clothes) ponerse; (pretend) fingir, afectar; poner; (a play) poner en escena; (the hands of a clock) adelantar; (weight) engordar, poner carnes; (add) añadir; (sport, score) hacer; (bet) apostar; (the light) encender; (assume) tomar; (the brake) frenar; (abuse) abusar (de),

engañar. **He put the kettle on the fire,** Puso la tetera en el fuego. **to put on airs and graces,** darse humos. **to put on more trains,** poner más trenes. **to put out,** v.t. (eject) echar, expulsar; hacer salir; poner en la calle; (a tenant) desahuciar; (one's hand) alargar; (one's arm) extender; (one's tongue) sacar; (eyes) saltar; (fire, light) apagar, extinguir; (leaves, etc.) echar; (horns) sacar; (head) asomar, sacar; (use) emplear; (give) entregar, dar; (at interest) dar a interés; (finish) terminar; (dislocate) dislocar; (worry) desconcertar; turbar; poner los nervios en punta (a); (anger) enojar; (inconvenience) incomodar; (a book) publicar; (a boat) echar al mar. v.i. (of a ship) hacerse a la vela, zarpar. **to put out to grass,** mandar a pacer. **We put out to sea,** Nos hicimos a la mar. **to put through,** (perform) desempeñar; concluir, terminar; (thrust) meter; (subject to) someter a; (exercise) ejercitar; (on the telephone) poner en comunicación (con). **to put together,** juntar; (a machine, etc.) montar, armar. **to put two and two together,** atar cabos. **to put up,** v.t. (sails, a flag) izar; (raise a window) levantar, cerrar; (open a window, or an umbrella) abrir; (one's hands, etc.) poner en alto; (one's fists) alzar; (a prayer) ofrecer, hacer; (as a candidate) nombrar; (for sale) poner (a la venta); (the price) aumentar; (a prescription) preparar; (food) conservar; (pack) empaquetar; (a sword) envainar; (lodge) alojar; (a petition) presentar; (build) construir; (mech.) montar; (fam., plan) arreglar. v.i. alojarse. **to put upon,** abusar (de); oprimir; (accuse) imputar, acusar (de). **to put up to,** incitar (a), instigar (a); dar informaciones sobre; poner al corriente (de). **to put up with,** tolerar, soportar, aguantar; resignarse a; contentarse con, conformarse con

putative, a. supuesto; (of relationship) putativo

puteal, s. (of a well) brocal, m.

putrefaction, s; putrefacción, f.

putrefy, v.t. pudrir. v.t. pudrirse, descomponerse

putrid, a. pútrido; (fam.) apestoso

putt, v.t. and v.i. patear. s. golpe con el " putter," m.

puttee, s. polaina, f.

putter, s. putter, m.

putting, s. acción de poner, f.; colocación, f. **p. forward of the clock,** adelanto de la hora, m. **p. off,** tardanza, dilación, f. **p. the weight,** lanzamiento del peso, m. **p. up,** (for office) candidatura, f. **p. green,** pista de golf en miniatura, f.

putty, s. masilla, f. v.t. enmasillar, rellenar con masilla

puzzle, v.t. dejar perplejo; desconcertar; confundir; embrollar. s. problema, m.; dificultad, f.; enigma, m.; (perplexity) perplejidad, f.; (game) rompecabezas, m. **to p. out,** procurar resolver; encontrar la solución de. **to p. over,** pensar en, meditar sobre. **I am puzzled by . . .,** Me trae (or tiene) perplejo . . .

pygmy, a. and s. pigmeo (-eá)

pyjamas, s. pijama, m.

pylon, s. pilón, m.; poste, m.; (in an aerodrome) poste de señales, m.

pylorus, s. píloro, m.

pyorrhœa, s. piorrea, f.

pyramid, s. pirámide, f.

pyramidal, a. piramidal

pyre, s. pira, f.

Pyrenean, a. pirineo, pirenaico

pyrethrum, s. piretro, m.

pyretic, a. pirético

pyridine, s. piridina, f.

pyrites, s. pirita, f.

pyromancy, s. piromancia, f.

pyrometer, s. pirómetro, m.

pyrotechnic, a. pirotécnico

pyrotechnics, s. pirotecnia, f.

pyrotechnist, s. pirotécnico, m.

Pyrrhic, a. pírrico

Pythagorean, a. and s. pitagórico (-ca)

Pythian, a. pitio

python, s. pitón, m.

pythoness, s. pitonisa, f.

Q

q, s. (letter) cu,

quack, v.i. (of a duck) graznar. s. (of a duck) graznido, m.; (charlatan) charlatán, farsante, m.; curandero, m. **q. doctor,** matasanos, medicastro, curandero, m. **q. medicine,** curanderismo, m.

quackery, s. charlatanería, f., charlatanismo, m.

quadragesima, s. cuadragésima, f.

quadragesimal, a. cuadragesimal

quadrangle, s. cuadrángulo, m.; (courtyard) patio, m.

quadrangular, a. cuadrangular

quadrant, s. (geom., ast., etc.) cuadrante, m.

quadratic, a. cuadrático. **q. equation,** cuadrática, ecuación de segundo grado, f.

quadrature, s. (math., ast.) cuadratura, f.

quadrennial, a. cuadrienal

quadriga, s. cuadriga, f.

quadrilateral, a. and s. cuadrilátero (m.)

quadrille, s. cuadrilla, f.; (card game) cuatrillo, m.

quadrillion, s. cuatrillón, m.

quadrisyllabic, a. cuatrisílabo

quadrivalent, a. tetravalente

quadrivium, s. cuadrivio, m.

quadroon, s. cuarterón (-ona)

quadrumanous, a. cuadrúmano

quadruped, a. and s. cuadrúpedo (m.)

quadruple, a. cuádruple. v.t. cuadruplicar. s. cuádruplo, m.

quadruplet, s. serie de cuatro cosas, f.; bicicleta de cuatro asientos, f.; uno (una) de cuatro niños (-as) gemelos (-as)

quadruplication, s. cuadruplicación, f.

quaff, v.t. beber a grandes tragos, vaciar de un trago

quagmire, s. tremedal, pantano, m.; (fig.) cenagal, m.

quail, s. codorniz, f.; (U.S.A.) parpayuela, f. v.i. cejar, retroceder; temblar, acobardarse

quaint, a. pintoresco; curioso; raro; (eccentric) excéntrico, extravagante

quaintly, *adv.* de un modo pintoresco; curiosamente; con extravagancia

quaintness, *s.* lo pintoresco; rareza, singularidad, *f.*; (eccentricity) extravagancia, *f.*

quake, *v.i.* estremecerse, vibrar; temblar. *s.* estremecimiento, *m.*; (of the earth) terremoto, *m.* **to q. with fear,** temblar de miedo

Quaker, *s.* cuáquero (-ra)

Quakerism, *s.* cuaquerismo, *m.*

quaking, *a.* temblón; tembloroso. *s.* temblor, *m.*; estremecimiento, *m.* **q. ash,** álamo temblón, *m.*

quakingly, *adv.* trémulamente

qualifiable, *a.* calificable

qualification, *s.* calificación, *f.*; requisito, *m.*; capacidad, aptitud, *f.*; (reservation) reservación, salvedad, *f.*

qualified, *a.* apto, competente; (of professions) con título universitario; habilitado; limitado

qualify, *v.t.* habilitar; calificar; modificar; suavizar; *v.i.* habilitarse; prepararse; llenar los requisitos

qualifying, *a.* (*gram.*) calificativo

qualitative, *a.* cualitativo

quality, *s.* cualidad, *f.*; calidad, *f.*; propiedad, *f.* **This cloth is of good q.,** Esta tela es de buena calidad. **the q.,** la alta sociedad, la aristocracia

qualm, *s.* náusea, *f.*; mareo, desmayo, *m.*; (of conscience) escrúpulo, remordimiento, *m.*

quandary, *s.* incertidumbre, perplejidad, *f.*; dilema, apuro, *m.* **to be in a q.,** estar en un aprieto, estar entre la espada y la pared

quantitative, *a.* cuantitativo

quantity, *s.* cantidad, *f.*; gran cantidad, *f.* **unknown q.,** incógnita, *f.*

quantum, *s.* cantidad, *f.*; tanto, *m.* **q. theory,** teoría de la quanta, *f.*

quarantine, *s.* cuarentena, *f.* *v.t.* someter a cuarentena

quarrel, *v.i.* pelear, disputar; (scold) reñir; (find fault) criticar. *s.* pelea, disputa, *f.*; (glazier's) diamante de vidriero, *m.* **to pick a q. with,** armar pleito con, reñir con. **to q. with,** reñir con, romper con; quejarse de

quarreller, *s.* reñidor (-ra)

quarrelling, *s.* disputas, altercaciones, *f. pl.*

quarrelsome, *a.* pendenciero, peleador, belicoso

quarrelsomeness, *s* belicosidad, pugnacidad, *f.*

quarry, *s.* cantera, *f.*; (*fig.*) mina, *f.*; (prey) presa, *f.*; víctima, *f.* *v.t.* explotar una cantera; examinar

quarrying, *s.* explotación de canteras, *f.*; cantería, *f.*

quarryman, *s.* cantero, *m.*

quart, *s.* cuarto de galón, *m.*

quartan, *a.* cuartanal. *s.* (fever) cuartana, *f.*

quarter, *s.* (fourth part) cuarta parte, *f.*, cuarto, *m.*; (of a year) trimestre, *m.*; (of an hour, the moon, a ton, an animal, etc.) cuarto, *m.*; (of the compass) cuarta, *f.*; (*naut.*) cuartelada, *f.*; (of a town) barrio, *m.*; (mercy) cuartel, *m.*; (*her.*) cuartel, *m.*; dirección, *f.*; origen, *m.*, fuente, *f.*; *pl.* quarters, vivienda, *f.*; alojamiento, *m.*; (barracks) cuartel, *m.* *v.t.* cuartear; (a body) descuartizar, hacer cuartos (a); (troops) alojar; (in barracks) acuartelar; (*her.*) cuartelar. **a q. of an hour,** un cuarto de hora. **at close quarters,** de cerca. **hind quarters,** cuartos traseros, *m. pl.* **It is a q. to four,** Son las cuatro menos cuarto. **It is a q. past four,** Son las cuatro y cuarto. **q.-day,** primer día de un trimestre, *m.* **q.-deck,** alcázar, *m.*; cuerpo de oficiales de un buque, *m.* **q.-mile,** cuarto de milla, *m.* **q.-plate,** cuarto de placa, *m.* **q.-sessions,** sesión trimestral de los juzgados municipales, *f.* **q.-staff,** barra, *f.* **q.-tone,** cuarto de tono, *m.*

quartering, *s.* (punishment) descuartizamiento, *m.*; (*her.*) cantón, *m.*

quarterly, *a.* trimestral, trimestre. *s.* publicación trimestral, *f.* *adv.* trimestralmente

quartermaster, *s.* (*mil.*) cabo furriel, *m.*; (*nav.*) maestre de víveres, cabo de mar, *m.* **q.-general,** intendente de ejército, *m.*

quartet, *s.* cuarteto, *m.*

quarto, *s.* papel en cuarto, *m.;* libro en cuarto, *m.* **in q.,** en cuarto

quartz, *s.* cuarzo, *m.*

quash, *v.t.* (*law*) anular, derogar; (*fam.*) sofocar, reprimir

quasi, *a.* and *adv.* cuasi

quasimodo, *s.* cuasimodo, *m.*

quatrain, *s.* cuarteta, *f.*

quaver, *v.i.* vibrar; temblar; (trill) trinar, hacer quiebros. *v.t.* decir con voz temblorosa. *s.* vibración, *f.;* trémolo, *m.;* (trill) trino, *m.;* (musical note) corchea, *f.*

quaveringly, *adv.* con voz temblorosa

quavery, *a.* trémulo, tembloroso

quay, *s.* muelle, *m.*

queasiness, *s.* náusea, *f.;* escrupulosidad, *f.*

queasy, *a.* propenso a la náusea; nauseabundo; delicado, escrupuloso

queen, *s.* reina, *f.;* (in a Spanish pack of cards) caballo, *m.;* (in a French or English pack and in chess) reina, *f.* **to q. it,** conducirse como una reina; mandar. **q. bee,** maestra, abeja reina, *f.* **q. cell,** maestril, *m.* **q. mother,** reina madre, *f.* **q. regent,** reina regente, *f.*

queenliness, *s.* majestad de reina, *f.*

queenly, *a.* de reina; regio

queer, *a.* raro; extraño, singular; ridículo; (shady) sospechoso; (ill) malucho, algo enfermo; (mad) chiflado

queerly, *adv.* extrañamente; ridículamente

queerness, *s.* rareza, extrañeza, singularidad, *f.;* ridiculez, *f.*

quell, *v.t.* subyugar; reprimir; apaciguar, calmar

quench, *v.t.* apagar; calmar; satisfacer. **to q. one's thirst,** apagar la sed

quenching, *s.* apagamiento, *m.;* satisfacción, *f.*

quern, *s.* molino de mano, *m.*

querulous, *a.* quejumbroso

querulously, *adv.* quejumbrosamente

querulousness, *s.* hábito de quejarse, *m.;* quejumbre, *f.*

query, *s.* pregunta, *f.;* duda, *f.;* punto de interrogación, *m.* *v.t.*

preguntar; dudar (de); poner en duda. *v.i.* hacer una pregunta; expresar una duda

quest, *s.* busca, *f.;* (adventure) demanda, *f.* **in q. of,** en busca de

question, *s.* pregunta, *f.;* problema, *m.;* asunto, *m.;* cuestión, *f.;* (discussion) debate, *m.,* discusión, *f.* *v.t.* and *v.i.* interrogar; examinar; poner en duda, dudar de; preguntarse; hacer preguntas. **beyond q.,** fuera de duda. **to ask a q.,** hacer una pregunta. **without q.,** sin duda. **It is out of the q.,** Es completamente imposible. **It is a q. of whether . . .,** Se trata de si . . . **q.-mark,** punto interrogante, *m.*

questionable, *a.* cuestionable, discutible, dudoso; equívoco, sospechoso

questionableness, *s.* lo discutible; carácter dudoso, *m.;* carácter sospechoso, *m.*

questioner, *s.* preguntador (-ra); interrogador (-ra)

questioning, *s.* preguntas, *f. pl.;* interrogatorio, *m.*

questioningly, *adv.* interrogativamente

questionnaire, *s.* cuestionario, *m.*

quetzal, *s.* (money and *orn.*) quetzal, *m.*

queue, *s.* coleta, *f.;* cola, *f.* *v.i.* formar cola; hacer cola

quibble, *s.* equívoco, subterfugio, *m.;* sutileza, *f.;* (pun) retruécano, *m.* *v.i.* hacer uso de subterfugios; sutilizar

quibbler, *s.* sofista, *m.* and *f.*

quibbling, *s.* sofistería, *f.,* sofismas, *m. pl.,* sutilezas, *f. pl.*

quick, *a.* vivo; agudo; penetrante; sagaz; rápido, veloz; (ready) pronto; ágil, activo; (light) ligero. *adv.* rápidamente; (soon) pronto. *s.* carne viva, *f.;* (*fig.*) lo vivo. **Be q.!** ¡Date prisa! **He was very q.,** Lo hizo muy aprisa; Volvió (or Fué, according to sense) rápidamente. **the q. and the dead,** los vivos y los muertos. **to cut to the q.,** herir en lo más vivo. **q. march,** paso doble, *m.* **q.-sighted,** de vista aguda; perspicaz. **q. step,** paso rápido, *m.* **q.-tempered,** de genio vivo, colérico. **q. time,**

compás rápido, *m.*; (*mil.*) paso doble, *m.* **q.-witted,** de ingenio agudo

quicken, *v.t.* vivificar; animar; acelerar; excitar, avivar. *v.i.* vivificarse; despertarse; renovarse; acelerarse; (stir) moverse. **to q. one's step,** acelerar el paso

quicklime, *s.* cal viva, *f.*

quickly, *adv.* rápidamente; (soon) pronto; (immediately) en seguida; (promptly) con presteza; vivamente

quickness, *s.* viveza, *f.*; (of wit, etc.) agudeza, *f.*; rapidez, velocidad, *f.*; (promptness) prontitud, *f.*; agilidad, *f.*; (lightness) ligereza, *f.*; (understanding) penetración, sagacidad, *f.*

quicksand, *s.* arena movediza, *f.*; (*fig.*) cenagal, *m.*

quicksilver, *s.* azogue, mercurio, *m. v.t.* azogar

quiescence, *s.* reposo, *m.*; quietud, tranquilidad, *f.*; inactividad, *f.*; pasividad, *f.*

quiescent, *a.* quieto; inactivo; pasivo

quiet, *a.* tranquilo; quieto; silencioso; quedo; monótono; inactivo; (informal) sin ceremonia; (simple) sencillo; (of the mind) sereno; (of colours, etc.) suave. *s.* tranquilidad, quietud, *f.*; silencio, *m.*; paz, *f.*; (of mind) serenidad, *f. v.t.* tranquilizar, sosegar; calmar. **to be q.,** callarse; no hacer ruido. **Be q.!** ¡Estate quieto! ¡A callar!

quietism, *s.* quietismo, *m.*

quietist, *s.* quietista, *m.* and *f.*

quietistic, *a.* quietista

quietly, *adv.* tranquilamente; en silencio; sin ruido; en calma; (simply) sencillamente; dulcemente

quietness, *s.* tranquilidad, quietud, *f.*; calma, *f.*; paz, *f.*; silencio, *m.*

quietus, *s.* (quittance) quitanza, *f.*, finiquito, *m.*; golpe de gracia, *m.*; muerte, *f.*

quill, *s.* pluma de ave, *f.*; (of a feather) cañón, *m.*; (pen) pluma, *f.*; (of a porcupine) púa, *f.* **q.-driver,** cagatintas, *m.*

quilt, *s.* colcha, *f.*, edredón, *m. v.t.* acolchar. **q. maker,** colchero, *m.*

quilting, *s.* acolchamiento, *m.*; colchadura, *f.*

quince, *s.* (tree and fruit) membrillo, *m.* **q. cheese,** carne de membrillo, *f.* **q. jelly,** jalea de membrillo, *f.*

quincentenary, *s.* quinto centenario, *m.*

quinine, *s.* quinina, *f.*

quinquagesima, *s.* quincuagésima, *f.*

quinquereme, *s.* quinquerreme, *f.*

quinsy, *s.* angina, *f.*

quintessence, *s.* quinta esencia, *f.*

quintessential, *a.* quintaesenciado

quintet, *s.* quinteto, *m.*

quintuple, *a.* quíntuplo

quintuplet, *s.* quintupleto, *m.*; uno (una) de cinco niños (-as) gemelos (-as)

quip, *s.* agudeza, salida, *f.*; (hint) indirecta, *f.*; donaire, *m.*, chanza, burla, *f.*

quire, *s.* (of paper) mano (de papel), *f.*

quirk, *s.* (quip) agudeza, salida, *f.*; (quibble) sutileza, evasiva, *f.* (gesture) gesto, *m.*

Quisling, *s.* "quisling," *m.*

quit, *v.t.* abandonar; dejar; renunciar (a). *v.i.* marcharse, (*fam.*) tomar las de Villadiego, poner pies en polvorosa; (slang) dejar de, cesar de. **notice to q.,** aviso de desahucio, *m.*

quite, *adv.* completamente, enteramente; totalmente; del todo; (very) muy; (fairly) bastante. **It is not q. the thing to do,** Esto es algo que no se hace. **Q. so!** ¡Claro!; ¡Eso es!; Se comprende. **It is not q. so good as we hoped,** No es tan bueno como esperábamos. **Peter is q. grown-up,** Pedro está hecho un hombre (or es todo un hombre)

quits, *adv.* quito, descargado. **To be q.,** estar en paz

quittance, *s.* quitanza, *f.*; recibo, *m.*; recompensa, *f.*

quitter, *s.* desertor (-ra); cobarde, *m.* and *f.*

quiver, *v.i.* temblar; vibrar; estremecerse; palpitar; (of light) titilar. *s.* (for arrows) aljaba, *f.*, carcaj, *m.* See also **quivering**

quivering, *a.* tremulante; vibrante; palpitante. *s.* temblor, *m.*; estremecimiento, *m.*

quixotic, *a.* quijotesco

quixotically, *adv.* quijotescamente

quixotism, *s.* quijotismo, *m.*

quiz, *s.* cuestionario, *m.* *v.t.* tomar el pelo (a); burlarse (de); (stare) mirar de hito en hito (a)

quizzical, *a.* burlón; cómico; estrafalario

quizzically, *adv.* burlonamente; cómicamente

quoin, *s.* piedra angular, *f.*; ángulo, *m.*; (wedge) cuña, *f.* *v.t.* meter cuñas (a)

quoit, *s.* tejo, *m.*; *pl.* **quoits,** juego de tejos, *m.*

quondam, *a.* antiguo

quorum, *s.* quórum, *m.* **to form a q.,** hacer un quórum

quota, *s.* cuota, *f.*

quotable, *a.* citable; (Stock Exchange) cotizable

quotation, *s.* citación, *f.*; cita, *f.*; (*com.*) cotización, *f.* **q. marks,** comillas, *f. pl.*

quote, *v.t.* citar; (*com.*) cotizar. *s.* (*fam.*) comilla, *f.*

quoth, *v.t.* **q. I,** dije yo. **q. he,** dijo él

quotient, *s.* cociente, *m.* **intelligence q.,** cociente intelectual, *m.*

R

r, *s.* (letter) erre, *f.*

rabbet, *s.* ranura, *f.*, rebajo, *m.* *v.t.* ensamblar a rebajo. **r.-joint,** junta a rebajo, *f.*

rabbi, *s.* rabí, rabino, *m.* **Grand r.,** gran rabino, *m.*

rabbinical, *a.* rabínico

rabbinism, *s.* rabinismo, *m.*

rabbit, *s.* conejo (-ja). *a.* conejuno, de conejo. *v.i.* cazar conejos. **young r.,** gazapo, *m.* **r.-hutch,** jaula para conejos, *f.* **r.-warren,** conejera, *f.*

rabble, *s.* populacho, vulgo, *m.*, plebe, *f.*

Rabelaisian, *a.* rabelasiano

rabid, *a.* rabioso; fanático; furioso, violento

rabies, *s.* rabia, hidrofobia, *f.*

raccoon, *s.* mapache, *m.*

race, *s.* carrera, *f.*; (current) corriente, *f.*; (prize) premio, *m.*; (breed) raza, *f.*; casta, estirpe, *f.*; (family) linaje, *m.*, familia, *f.*; (scornful) ralea, *f.*; (struggle) lucha, *f.* *v.i.* tomar parte en una carrera; correr de prisa; asistir a concursos de carreras de caballos; (of a machine) dispararse. *v.t.* (hacer) correr; competir en una carrera (con); desafiar a una carrera. **flat r.,** carrera llana, *f.* **mill-r.,** caz, *m.* **to run a r.,** tomar parte en una carrera; (*fig.*) hacer una carrera. **r.-card,** programa de carreras de caballos, *m.* **r. hatred,** odio de razas, *m.* **r.-meeting,** concurso de carreras de caballos, *m.* **r. suicide,** suicidio de la raza, *m.* **r.-track,** pista, *f.*

racecourse, hipódromo, *m.*; estadio, *m.*

racehorse, *s.* caballo de carrera, *m.*

raceme, *s.* racimo, *m.*

racemose, *a.* racimoso

racer, *s.* (horse) caballo de carreras, *m.*; (person) carrerista, *m. and f.*; (car) coche de carreras, *m.*; (boat) yate de carreras, *m.*; (bicycle) bicicleta de carreras, *f.*

rachitic, *a.* raquítico

racial, *a.* racial, de raza

racialism, *s.* rivalidad de razas, *f.*

raciness, *s.* sabor, *m.*; savia, *f.*, picante, *m.*

racing, *s.* carreras, *f. pl.*; (*mech.*) disparo, *m.* *a.* de carreras; hípico. **r. calendar,** calendario de concursos de carreras de caballos, *m.* **r. car,** coche de carreras, *m.* **r. cycle,** bicicleta de carreras, *f.*

rack, *s.* (for hay) percha (del pesebre), *f.*; (in a railway compartment) rejilla, *f.*; (for billiard cues) taquera, *f.*; (for clothes) percha, *f.*; (for torture) potro, *m.*; (*mech.*) cremallera, *f.* *v.t.* poner en el potro, torturar; atormentar. **to be on the r.,** estar en el potro (also *fig.*). **to r. one's brains,** devanarse los sesos, quebrarse la cabeza. **r. and ruin,** ruina total, *f.* **r. railway,** ferrocarril de cremallera, *m.*

racket, s. (*sport*) raqueta, *f.*; (din) barahunda, *f.*; ruido, estrépito, *m.*; confusión, *f.*; (bustle) bullicio, *m.*, agitación, *f.*; (swindle) estafa, *f.*; (binge) parranda, *f.* **to play rackets**, jugar a la raqueta

racking, s. tortura, *f.*; (of wine) trasiego, *m.* *a.* torturante; (of a pain or cough) persistente

racoon, s. mapache, *m.*

racquet, s. See **racket**

racy, *a.* picante; sabroso

radar, s. radar, *m.*

raddled, *a.* pintado de almagre; mal pintado

radial, *a.* radial

radiance, s. resplandor, brillo, *m.*, luminosidad, *f.*

radiant, *a.* radiante; brillante, luminoso. s. (*geom.*) línea radial, *f.* **r. heat**, calor radiante, *m.*

radiantly, *adv.* con resplandor; brillantemente; con alegría

radiate, *v.i.* radiar. *v.t.* irradiar

radiation, s. irradiación, *f.*; (*geom.*) radiación, *f.*

radiator, s. (for central heating and of a car) radiador, *m.*; (stove) calorífero, *m.*

radical, *a.* radical. s. (*math.*, *chem.*) radical, *m.*; (*pol.*) radical, *m.* and *f.*

Radicalism, s. radicalismo, *m.*

radically, *adv.* radicalmente

radio, s. radio, *f.*; radiocomunicación, *f.* **r. amateur**, **r. enthusiast**, radioaficionado (-da). **r. announcer**, locutor (-ra). **r. broadcast**, radioemisión, radiodifusión, *f.* **r. listener**, radioyente, *m.* and *f.* **r. receiver**, (technical) radiorreceptor, *m.*; (usual word) aparato de radio, *m.* **r. transmitter**, radiotransmisor, *m.*

radioactive, *a.* radiactivo

radioactivity, s. radiactividad, *f.*

radiofrequency, s. radiofrecuencia, *f.*

radiogoniometer, s. radiogoniómetro, *m.*

radiogram, s. radiotelegrama, *m.*; radiograma, *m.*; (gramophone) radiogramola, *f.*

radiograph, s. radiografía, *f.* *v.t.* radiografiar

radiographer, s. radiografista, *m.* and *f.*

radiography, s. radiografía, *f.*

radiolocation, s. radiolocación, *f.*

radiologist, s. radiólogo, *m.*

radiology, s. radiología, *f.*

radiometer, s. radiómetro, *m.*

radiometry, s. radiometría, *f.*

radioscopy, s. radioscopia, *f.*

radiotelegram, s. radiotelegrama, *m.*

radiotelegraphic, *a.* radiotelegráfico

radiotelegraphy, s. radiotelegrafía, *f.*

radiotelephony, s. radiotelefonía, *f.*

radiotherapeutics, **radiotherapy**, s. raditerapia, *f.*

radish, s. rábano, *m.* **horse-r.**, rábano picante, *m.*

radium, s. radio, *m.*

radius, s. (*geom.*, *anat.*) radio, *m.*; (of a wheel) rayo, *m.*; (scope) alcance, *m.*

raffia, s. rafia, *f.*

raffish, *a.* disoluto, libertino

raffle, s. rifa, *f.*, sorteo, *m.*; lotería, *f.* *v.t.* rifar, sortear

raffling, s. sorteo, *m.*, rifa, *f.*

raft, s. balsa, *f.*; (timber) armadía, *f.* *v.t.* transportar en balsa; cruzar en balsa

rafter, s. (of a roof) viga, traviesa, *f.*; (raftsman) balsero, *m.*

raftered, *a.* con vigas

rag, s. jirón, guiñapo, *m.*; (for cleaning) paño, trapo, *m.*; (for papermaking) estraza, *f.*; (of smoke, etc.) penacho, *m.*; (newspaper) papelucho, *m.*; *pl.* **rags**, harapos, *m. pl.*; (*fam.*) viejos hábitos, *m. pl.* *v.t.* (tease) tomar el pelo (a); burlarse de; hacer una broma pesada (a). **r.-and-bone-man**, trapero, *m.* **r. doll**, muñeca de trapo, *f.*

ragamuffin, s. galopín, *m.*

rage, s. (anger) cólera, rabia, ira, *f.*; (of the elements) furia, violencia, *f.*; (ardour) entusiasmo, ardor, *m.*; (fashion) boga, moda, *f.*; (craze) manía, *f.*; (of the poet) furor, *m.* *v.i.* (be angry) rabiar, estar furioso; (of the sea) encresparse, alborotarse, enfurecerse; (of wind, fire, animals) bramar, rugir; (of pain) rabiar; (be prevalent) prevalecer, desencadenarse. **to r. against**, protestar furiosamente contra; culpar amarga-

mente (de). **to be all the r.,**
(*fam.*), ser la ultima moda. **to
fly into a r.,** montar en cólera.
to put into a r., hacer rabiar

ragged, *a.* harapiento, andrajoso;
roto; (uneven) desigual; (rugged)
peñascoso, áspero, escabroso;
(serrated) serrado; dentellado;
(of a coastline) accidentado;
(unfinished) inacabado, sin terminar; (of style) descuidado, sin
pulir

raggedness, *s.* harapos, *m. pl.*;
estado andrajoso, *m.*; aspereza,
escabrosidad, *f.*; lo serrado; lo
accidentado; (of style) falta de
elegancia, tosquedad, *f.*

raging, *a.* furioso, rabioso; violento; (roaring) bramante; (of the
sea) bravío; intenso. *s.* furia, *f.*;
violencia, *f.*; intensidad, *f.*

raglan, *s.* raglán, *m.* **r. sleeve,**
manga raglán, *f.*

ragoût, *s.* estofado, *m.*

ragpicker, *s.* trapero (-ra)

ragtime, *s.* música sincopada, *f.*

raid, *s.* incursión, correría, *f.*;
asalto, ataque, *m.*; (by the police)
razzia, *f.*; (by aircraft) bombardeo, *m. v.t.* invadir; atacar,
asaltar; apoderarse de; hacer
una razzia en; (by aircraft)
bombear, bombardear; (pillage)
pillar, saquear. **obliteration r.,**
bombardeo de saturación, *m.*

raider, *s.* corsario, *m.*; atacador,
asaltador, *m.*; (aircraft) avión
enemigo, *m.*

rail, *s.* barra, *f.*; antepecho, *m.*;
(of a staircase) barandilla, *f.*,
pasamano, *m.*; (track) riel, *m.*;
(railway) ferrocarril, *m.*; (of a
ship) barandilla, *f.*; (of a chair)
travesaño, *m. pl.* **rails,** (fence)
cerca, barrera, palizada, *f. v.t.*
cercar con una palizada, poner
cerca a; mandar por ferrocarril.
by r., por ferrocarril. **to run off
the rails,** descarrilar. **to r. at,**
protestar contra; prorrumpir en
invectivas contra, injuriar de
palabra (a)

railing, *s.* barandilla, *f.*; antepecho, *m.*, enrejado, *m.*; (grille)
reja, *f.*; (jeers) burlas, *f. pl.*;
insultos, *m. pl.*, injurias, *f. pl.*;
quejas, *f. pl.*

raillery, *s.* jocosidad, tomadura
de pelo, *f.*; sátiras, *f. pl.*

railway, *s.* ferrocarril, *m.*; vía
férrea, *f.*, camino de hierro, *m.*
a. de ferrocarril, ferroviario.
elevated r., ferrocarril aéreo, *m.*
narrow gauge r., ferrocarril de
vía estrecha, *m.* **r. buffet,**
fonda, *f.* (or restaurante, *m.*) de
estación. **r. carriage,** departamento de tren, *m.* **r. company,**
compañía de ferrocarriles, *f.*
r. crossing, paso a nivel, *m.* **r.
engine,** locomotora, *f.* **r. guard,**
jefe del tren, *m.* **r. guide,** guía
de ferrocarriles, *f.* **r. line,** vía
férrea, *f.* **r. marshalling yard,**
apartadero ferroviario, *m.* **r.
passenger,** viajero (-ra) en un
tren. **r. platform,** andén, *m.*
r. porter, mozo de estación, *m.*
r. siding, vía muerta, *f.* **r.
signal,** disco de señales, *m.* **r.
station,** estación (de ferrocarril),
f. **r. system,** sistema ferroviario, *m.* **r. ticket,** billete de
tren, *m.*

railwayman, *s.* ferroviario, empleado de los ferrocarriles, *m.*

raiment, *s.* ropa, *f.*; (*poet.*)
hábitos, *m. pl.*

rain, *s.* lluvia, *f.* *v.i.* and *v.t.*
llover. **a r. of arrows,** una
lluvia de flechas. **fine r.,** llovizna, *f.* **to r. cats and dogs,**
llover a cántaros. **to r. hard,**
diluviar. **r. cloud,** nubarrón, *m.*
r.-gauge, pluviómetro, *m.*

rainbow, *s.* arco iris, arco de San
Martín, *m.*

raincoat, *s.* abrigo impermeable,
m.

raindrop, *s.* gota de lluvia, *f.*

rainfall, *s.* cantidad llovida, *f.*;
(shower) aguacero, *m.*

rainless, *a.* sin lluvia, seco

rainstorm, *s.* chaparrón, *m.*,
tempestad de lluvia, *f.*

rainwater, *s.* lluvia, *f.*; agua
lluvia, *f.*

rainy, *a.* lluvioso. **r. day,** día de
lluvia, *m.*; (*fig.*) tiempo de
escasez, *m.*

raise, *v.t.* levantar; alzar; (the
hat) quitar; solevantar; (dough)
fermentar; (erect) erigir, edificar;
(dust) levantar; elevar; (promote) ascender; (increase) aumentar; hacer subir; (spirits,
memories) evocar; (the dead)
resucitar; (cause) causar; dar

lugar (a).; hacer concebir; (a question, a point) hacer; plantear; (breed or educate) criar; (a crop) cultivar; (an army) alistar; (gather together) juntar; (a subscription) hacer; (money, etc.) obtener, hallar; (a siege, etc.) levantar, alzar; (a laugh, a protest, etc.) suscitar, provocar; (utter) poner, dar; (a fund) abrir. **to r. oneself**, incorporarse. **He succeeded in raising himself**, Logró alzarse; Logró mejorar su posición. **He raised their hopes unduly**, Les hizo concebir esperanzas desmesuradas. **to r. an objection** (to), poner objeción (a). **to r. an outcry**, armar un alboroto. **to r. a point**, hacer una observación; plantear una cuestión. **to r. a siege**, levantar un sitio. **to r. Cain**, armar lo de Dios es Cristo. **to r. one's voice**, alzar la voz

raised, a. (in relief) en relieve; (embossed) de realce

raiser, s. (breeder) criador (-ra); (cultivator) cultivador (-ra); (educator) educador (-ra); autor (-ra); fundador (-ra); (of objections, etc.) suscitador (-ra)

raisin, s. pasa, f.

raising, s. levantamiento, m.; alzamiento, m.; (of a building, monument) erección, f.; elevación, f.; (increase) aumento, m.; provocación, f.; fundación, f.; (breeding or education) crianza, f.; (of spirits) evocación, f.; (of the dead) resucitación, f.; producción, f.; (of crops) cultivo, m.

rajah, s. rajá, m.

rake, s. (agr.) rastrillo, m., rastra, f.; (for the fire) hurgón, m.; (croupier's) raqueta, f.; (of a mast, funnel) inclinación, f.; (person) tenorio, calavera, m. v.t. (agr.) rastrillar; (a fire, etc.) hurgar; (sweep) barrer; recoger; (ransack) buscar (en); (with fire) enfilar, tirar a lo largo de; (scan) escudriñar. v.i. trabajar con el rastrillo; (slope) inclinarse. **r. off**, tajada, f. **to r. together**, juntar con el rastrillo; amontonar; ahorrar. **to r. up**, (revive) resucitar, desenterrar

raking, s. rastrillaje, m.; (the fire, etc.) hurgonada, f.

rakish, a. (of a ship) de palos muy inclinados, (dissolute) disoluto, libertino; (dashing) elegante

rakishly, adv. disolutamente; elegantemente

rakishness, s. (licentiousness) libertinaje, m., disipación, disolución, f.; (elegance) elegancia, f.

râle, s. estertor, m.

rally, v.t. reunir; (mil.) rehacer; (faculties) concentrar; (tease) tomar el pelo (a). v.i. reunirse; (mil.) rehacerse; (revive) mejorar, recobrar las fuerzas; (of markets, etc.) mejorar. s. reunión, f.

rallying, s. reunión, f.; (of faculties, etc.) concentración, f.; (recovery) mejora, f. **r. point**, punto de reunión, m.

ram, s. (zool.) carnero, morueco, m.; (ast.) Aries, Carnero, m.; (mil., etc.) ariete, m.; (tool) pisón, m.; (nav.) espolón, m. v.t. golpear con ariete o espolón; (of a gun) atacar; apisonar; meter a la fuerza; hacer tragar a la fuerza; (squeeze) apretar; (crowd) atestar

Ramadan, s. ramadán, m.

ramble, v.i. vagar, vagabundear; hacer una excursión. v.t. errar por

rambler, s. excursionista, m. and f.; paseante, m. and f.; (bot.) rosa trepante, f.

rambling, a. (of houses) encantado; laberíntico; (straggly) disperso; (of thought, etc.) incoherente, inconexo. s. vagabundeo, m.; excursiones, f. pl.; paseo, m.; (digression) digresiones, f. pl.; (delirium) desvaríos, m. pl.

ramification, s. ramificación, f.

ramify, v.i. ramificarse, tener ramificaciones. v.t. ramificar; dividir en ramales

rammer, s. pisón de empedrador, m.; baqueta (de fusil), f.; (of a ship) espolón, m.

ramp, s. rampa, f.; (swindle) estafa, f.; (storm, commotion) tormenta, f.

rampage, v.i. alborotarse; bramar

rampant, a. salvaje; (her.) rampante; (of persons) impaciente, furioso; (of plants, growth) lozano, exuberante; desenfrenado; (rife) prevaleciente, predominante

rampart, *s.* muralla, *f.*; terraplén, *m.*; (*fig.*) baluarte, *m.* *v.t.* abaluartar, abastionar

ramrod, *s.* baqueta, *f.*

ramshackle, *a.* destartalado, ruinoso; desvencijado; (badly made) mal hecho

ranch, *s.* rancho, *m.*, hacienda (de ganado), *f.*

rancher, *s.* ranchero, *m.*

rancid, *a.* rancio

rancidness, *s.* rancidez, *f.*

rancorous, *a.* rencoroso

rancour, *s.* rencor, encono, *m.*

random, *s.* azar, *m.* *a.* fortuito, al azar; sin orden ni concierto. **at r.,** a la ventura, al azar; sin pensar; (of shooting) sin apuntar. **to talk at r.,** hablar a trochemoche

range, *s.* línea, hilera, *f.*; (of mountains) cadena, *f.*; serie, *f.*; clase, *f.*; variedad, *f.*; (c. goods) surtido, *m.*; (of a gun, voice, vision, etc.) alcance, *m.*; (area) extensión, área, *f.*; esfera de actividad, *f.*; (scope) alcance, *m.*; (of voice, musical instrument) compás, *m.*; (of colours) gama, *f.*; (for shooting) campo de tiro, *m.*; (for cooking) cocina económica, *f.* **at close r.,** de cerca. **out of r.,** fuera de alcance. **within r.,** al alcance. **r.-finder,** (of guns, cameras) telémetro, *m.* **r. of mountains,** cadena de montañas, *f.*; sierra, *f.*

range, *v.t.* (*poet.*) arreglar; alinear; ordenar; clasificar; (a gun, etc.) apuntar; (place oneself) ponerse; sumarse (a); (roam) recorrer; (scan) escudriñar. *v.i.* extenderse; (roam) vagar; (of plants) crecer (en); variar, fluctuar; oscilar, vacilar; (of guns, etc.) alcanzar; (of the mind) pasar (por); (include) incluir

ranger, *s.* (wanderer) vagabundo, *m.*; (keeper) guardabosque, *m.*; (*mil.*) batidor, *m.*

ranging, *s.* arreglo, *m.*; alineación, *f.*; ordenación, *f.*; clasificación, *f.*; (roving) vida errante, *f.*

rank, *s.* línea, *f.*; fila, *f.*; grado, *m.*; clase, *f.*; rango, *m.*; categoría, *f.*; posición, *f.*; calidad, *f.*; distinción, *f.* *v.t.* ordenar; clasificar; (estimate) estimar; poner (entre). *v.i.* ocupar un

puesto; tener un grado, rango, etc.; estar al nivel (de); ser igual (a); contarse (entre). *a.* (luxuriant) lozano, exuberante; fértil; (thick) espeso; (rancid) rancio; (complete) consumado; completo; (foul-smelling) fétido; (*fig.*) repugnante, aborrecible; (very) muy. **of the first r.,** de primera calidad; de primera clase; de distinción. **the r. and file,** los soldados, la tropa; las masas, la mayoría; los socios ordinarios (de un club, etc.). **to break ranks,** (*mil.*) romper filas. **to rise from the ranks,** ascender de las filas. **to r. high,** ocupar alta posición; ser de los mejores (de). **to r. with,** estar al nivel de; (be numbered among) contarse entre, figurar entre

rankle, *v.i.* (*fig.*) irritar, molestar; envenenarse la vida, hacerse odioso

rankly, *adv.* ranciamente; lozanamente; con exuberancia; abundantemente; groseramente

rankness, *s.* rancidez, *f.*; olor rancio, *m.*; fertilidad, lozanía, *f.*; exuberancia, *f.*, vigor, *m.*; enormidad, *f.*

ransack, *v.t.* (search) registrar; (pillage) saquear; (*fig.*) buscar en

ransacking, *s.* (searching) registro, *m.*; (sacking) saqueo, *m.*

ransom, *s.* rescate, *m.*, redención, *f.*; liberación, *f.* *v.t.* rescatar, redimir

ransomer, *s.* rescatador (-ra)

ransoming, *s.* redención, *f.*; liberación, *f.*

rant, *v.i.* declamar a gritos, vociferar; despotricar (contra); desvariar; hablar por hablar, hablar sin ton ni son. *s.* declamación, vociferación, *f.*; desvarío, *m.*

ranter, *s.* declamador (-ra); agitador populachero, *m.*; predicador chillón, *m.*

ranunculus, *s.* (*bot.*) ranúnculo, *m.*

rap, *s.* golpecito, *m.*; toque, *m.*; (with the knocker) aldabada, *f.*; (worthless trifle) ardite, maravedí, *m.* *v.t. and v.i.* golpear; tocar. **He doesn't care a rap,** No le importa un ardite. **to rap at the door,** tocar a la puerta. **to rap with the**

knuckles, golpear con los nu-
dillos. **to rap out an oath,**
proferir una blasfemia

rapacious, *a.* rapaz

rapaciously, *adv.* con rapacidad

rapacity, *s.* rapacidad, *f.*

rape, *s.* (carrying off) rapto, *m.*;
(*law*) estupro, *m.*; violación, *f.*;
(*bot.*) nabo silvestre, *m.* *v.t.*
(carry off) raptar, robar; violar,
forzar

rapid, *a.* rápido. *s.* rápido, *m.*
r. combustion, combustión
activa, *f.*

rapidity, *s.* rapidez, *f.*

rapidly, *adv.* rápidamente, con
rapidez

rapier, *s.* estoque, *m.*; espadín,
m.

rapine, *s.* rapiña, *f.*

rappee, *s.* rapé, *m.*

rapping, *s.* golpecitos, *m. pl.*;
golpeo, *m.*; toques, *m. pl.*; (of the
knocker) aldabeo, *m.*

rapscallion, *s.* bribón, *m.*

rapt, *past-part.* and *a.* arrebatado;
absorto; extático, extasiado

rapture, *s.* arrebato, *m.*; éxtasis,
m.; transporte, *m.*; embriaguez,
f.; entusiasmo, *m.*

rapturous, *a.* embelesado; extático; entusiasta

rapturously, *adv.* extáticamente;
con entusiasmo

rare, *a.* raro; extraordinario;
exótico; infrecuente

raree-show, *s.* barracón de los
fenómenos, barracón de las atracciones, *m.*

rarefaction, *s.* rarefacción, *f.*

rarefy, *v.t.* rarefacer. *v.i.* rare-
facerse

rarely, *adv.* raramente

rareness, *s.* rareza, *f.*; singularidad, *f.*; infrecuencia, *f.*

rarity, *s.* raridad, *f.*; (uncommonness and rare object) rareza, *f.*

rascal, *s.* sinvergüenza, *m.*; truhán, bribón, pícaro, *m.*; (affectionately) picaruelo, *m.*

rascality, *s.* bellaquería, truhanería, *f.*

rascally, *a.* redomado; vil, ruin,
canallesco

rash, *a.* temerario, precipitado;
imprudente. *s.* erupción, *f.*, salpullido, *m.*

rasher, *s.* magra, *f.*; (of bacon)
torrezno, *m.*

rashly, *adv.* temerariamente,
precipitadamente; imprudentemente, con imprudencia

rashness, *s.* temeridad, precipitación, *f.*; imprudencia, *f.*

rasp, *s.* escofina, *f.*, rallo, *m.*;
sonido áspero, *m.* *v.t.* raspar,
escofinar; (get on one's nerves)
poner los nervios en punta (a)

raspberry, *s.* frambuesa, *f.* **r.-
cane,** frambueso, *m.* **r. jam,**
mermelada de frambuesa, *f.*

rasping, *a.* (of the voice) áspero,
estridente

rat, *s.* rata, *f.*; desertor, *m.*;
(black leg) esquirol, *m.* *v.i.*
cazar ratas; ser desertor; ser
esquirol. **rat-catcher,** cazador
de ratas, *m.* **rat poison,** veneno
para matar ratas, arsénico, *m.*
rat-trap, ratonera, *f.*

ratable, *a.* sujeto a contribución;
imponible; valuable

ratafia, *s.* ratafía, *f.*

rataplan, *s.* rataplán, *m.*

ratchet, *s.* (*mech.*) trinquete, *m.*;
(of a watch) disparador, *m.* **r.-
drill,** carraca, *f.* **r.-wheel,** rueda
dentada con trinquete, *f.*

rate, *s.* velocidad, *f.*; razón, proporción, *f.*; (of exchange) tipo,
m.; tanto, *m.*; precio, *m.*, clase,
f.; modo, *m.*, manera, *f.*; (*naut.*)
clasificación, *f.*; (tax) contribución, *f.*, impuesto, *m.*; *pl.* **rates,**
(of a house) inquilinato, *m.* *v.t.*
tasar; estimar; fijar el precio (a);
(*naut.*) clasificar; imponer una
contribución (de); (scold) reñir.
at a great r., rápidamente,
velozmente. **at a r. of,** a razón
de; a una velocidad de. **at any
r.,** de todos modos; por lo
menos; **sea como fuere. at
this r.,** de este modo; a este paso;
a esa cuenta; en esta proporción;
(with seguir) así. **first-r.,** de
primera clase. **rates and taxes,**
contribuciones e impuestos, *f. pl.*
r. of climb, (*aer.*) velocidad
ascensional, *f.* **r. of exchange,**
tipo de cambio, *m.* **r.-payer,**
contribuyente, *m.* and *f.*

rather, *adv.* más bien; antes;
(more willingly) de mejor gana;
(somewhat) algo, un poco; (perhaps) quizás; mejor dicho; (fairly)
bastante; (very) muy; mucho;
al contrario. **R.!** ¡Ya lo creo!

or r., o más bien. **anything r. than** ..., todo menos ... **He had r.**, Preferiría. **r. than,** antes que, en vez de

ratification, s. ratificación, f.; (of a bill) aprobación, f.

ratifier, s. ratificador (-ra)

ratify, v.t. ratificar

ratifying, s. ratificación, f. a. ratificatorio

rating, s. tasación, f.; valuación, f.; clasificación, f.; impuesto, m., contribución, f.; repartición de impuestos, f.; (of a ship's company) graduación, f.; (scolding) represión, f.

ratio, s. razón, f.; proporción, f. **in direct r.,** en razón directa

ratiocinate, v.i. raciocinar

ratiocination, s. raciocinación, f.

ration, s. ración, f. v.t. racionar. **r.-book,** cartilla de racionamiento, f.

rational, a. racional; razonable, juicioso. s. ser racional, m.

rationalism, s. racionalismo, m.

rationalist, s. racionalista, m. and f.

rationalistic, a. racionalista

rationality, s. racionalidad, f.; justicia, f.

rationalization, s. racionalización, f.; justificación, f.

rationalize, v.t. hacer racional; concebir racionalmente; (math.) quitar los radicales (a); justificar

rationally, adv. racionalmente

rationing, s. racionamiento, m.

ratlin, s. (naut.) rebenque, m.

rattan, s. rota, f., bejuco, m.; junquillo, m.

ratteen, s. ratina, f.

ratter, s. perro ratonero, m.; gato que caza ratas, m.

ratting, s. caza de ratas, f.; deserción, f.

rattle, v.i. hacer ruido; rechinar, crujir; (of loose windows, etc.) zangolotearse; (knock) golpear; tocar; (patter) bailar; sonar; (of the dying) dar un estertor. v.t. (shake) sacudir; hacer vibrar; (jolt) traquetear; (do rapidly) acabar rápidamente; (confuse) aturdir, hacer perder la cabeza (a); desconcertar. **to r. along,** deslizarse (o correr) rápidamente. **to r. off,** (repeat) decir rápidamente; terminar apresura-

damente. **to r. on about,** charlar mucho de, hablar sin cesar sobre

rattle, s. rechinamiento, crujido, m.; zangoloteo, m.; ruido, m.; son (de la lluvia, etc.), m.; (in the throat) estertor, m.; (of a rattlesnake) cascabel, m.; (child's) sonajero, m.; matraca, f.; carraca, f.; (chatter) charla, f. **r.-headed,** de cabeza de chorlito, casquivano

rattlesnake, s. serpiente de cascabel, f., crótalo, m.

rattling, s. See **rattle**

raucous, a. ronco, estridente

raucousness, s. ronquedad, f., estridor, m.

ravage, v.t. devastar; (pillage) saquear; destruir; (spoil) estropear. s. devastación, f.; destrucción, f.; estrago, m.

ravager, s. devastador (-ra); saqueador (-ra)

rave, v.i. desvariar, delirar; (of the elements) bramar, rugir. **to r. about,** hablar con entusiasmo de; delirar por. **to r. against,** vociferar contra, despotricarse contra

ravel, v.t. deshilar, destejer; (fig.) enredar. **to r. out,** deshilarse; (fig.) desenredarse, desenmarañarse

raven, s. cuervo, m. a. negro como el azabache

ravening, a. rapaz, salvaje

ravenous, a. voraz

ravenously, adv. vorazmente

ravenousness, s. voracidad, f.

ravine, s. cañada, f., barranco, cañón, m.

raving, s. delirio, m., desvaríos, m. pl. a. delirante; violento; bravío

ravioli, s. pl. ravioles, m. pl.

ravish, v.t. (carry off) arrebatar, raptar; extasiar, encantar; (rape) violar, forzar

ravisher, s. raptador, m.; violador, m.

ravishing, s. violación, f. a. encantador

ravishment, s. violación, f.; arrobamiento, m.; transporte, éxtasis, m.

raw, a. (of meat, etc., silk, leather, weather) crudo; bruto; (inexpert) bisoño; (of flesh) vivo; (com.) en bruto. **raw-boned,**

huesudo. **raw hand,** novato (-ta). **raw material,** primera materia, f. **raw materials,** materias primas, f. pl. **raw silk,** seda cruda, seda en rama, f. **raw sugar,** azúcar bruto, m.

rawhide, a. de cuero crudo

rawness, s. crudeza, f.; inexperiencia, f.; (of weather) humedad, f.

ray, s. rayo, m.; (line) raya, f.; (radius) radio, m.; (fish) raya, f. **cathode rays,** rayos catódicos, m. pl.

rayon, s. rayón, m.

raze, v.t. arrasar, asolar; demoler; (erase) borrar, tachar

razor, s. navaja, f. **electric r.,** máquina de afeitar eléctrica, f. **safety r.,** máquina de afeitar, f. **slash with a r.,** navajada, f. **r. blade,** hoja de afeitar, f. **r. case,** navajero, m. **r. strop,** suavizador, m.

re, s. (mus.) re, m.; prep. (law) causa, f.; (com.) concerniente a

re, prefix (attached to verb) re-; (after the verb) de nuevo; (followed by infin.) volver a . . . **to re-count,** volver a contar, contar de nuevo, recontar

reabsorb, v.t. resorber

reabsorption, s. reabsorción, resorción, f.

reach, v.t. (stretch out) alargar; extender; alcanzar; llegar hasta; (arrive at) llegar a; (achieve) lograr, obtener. v.i. extenderse; alcanzar; penetrar. s. alcance, m.; extensión, f.; poder, m.; capacidad, f.; (of a river) tabla, f. **as far as the eye could r.,** hasta donde alcanzaba la vista. **He reached home very soon,** Llegó muy pronto a casa. **out of r.,** fuera de alcance. **to r. a deadlock,** llegar a un punto muerto. **within r.,** al alcance. **within easy r.,** de fácil acceso; a corta distancia. **to r. after,** procurar alcanzar; hacer esfuerzos para obtener. **to r. back,** (of time) remontarse. **to r. down,** bajar. **r.-me-downs,** ropa hecha, f.

react, v.i. reaccionar. v.t. hacer de nuevo; (theat.) volver a representar

reaction, s. reacción, f.

reactionary, a. and s. reaccionario (-ia)

reactive, a. reactivo

read, v.t. leer; (a riddle, etc.) adivinar; descifrar; interpretar; (study) estudiar; (the Burial Service, etc.) decir; (correct) corregir; (of thermometers, etc.) marcar. v.i. leer; estudiar; (be written) estar escrito, decir. **The play acts better than it reads,** La comedia es mejor representada que leída. **to r. aloud,** leer en alta voz. **to r. between the lines,** leer entre líneas. **to r. proofs,** corregir pruebas. **to r. to oneself,** leer para sí. **to r. about,** leer; (learn) enterarse de. **to r. again,** volver a leer, leer otra vez. **to r. on,** continuar leyendo. **to r. out,** leer en alta voz. **to r. over,** leer; leerlo todo. **to r. over and over again,** leer muchas veces, leer y releer.

read, past part. leído, etc. **well-r.,** releído; instruido, culto

readability, s. legibilidad, f.; interés, m., amenidad, f.

readable, a. legible; interesante

readdress, v.t. dirigir de nuevo (una carta, etc.); poner la nueva dirección en (una carta, etc.)

reader, s. lector (-ra); (ecc.) lector, m.; (proof) corrector de pruebas, m.; (university) profesor (-ra) auxiliar a cátedra; (book) libro de lectura, m. **to be a great r.,** leer mucho

readily, adv. fácilmente; en seguida, inmediatamente; de buena gana, con placer

readiness, s. prontitud, expedición, f.; buena voluntad, f.; (of speech, etc.) facilidad, f. **in r.,** preparado. **r. of wit,** viveza de ingenio, f.

reading, s. lectura, f.; (erudition) conocimientos, m. pl.; (recital) declamación, f.; (lecture) conferencia, f.; (study) estudio, m.; interpretación, f.; (of a thermometer, etc.) registro, m.; (of a will) apertura, f. **r.-book,** libro de lectura, m. **r.-desk,** atril, m. **r.-glass,** lente para leer, m., carlita, f. **r.-lamp,** lámpara de sobremesa, f. **r.-matter,** material de lectura, m. **r.-room,**

gabinete de lectura, *m.*, sala de lectura, *f.*

readjourn, *v.t.* (a meeting) suspender (la sésión) de nuevo

readjust, *v.t.* reajustar

readjustment, *s.* reajuste, *m.*

readmission, *s.* readmisión, *f.*

readmit, *v.t.* readmitir

ready, *a.* listo, preparado; dispuesto; pronto; (on the point of) a punto de; (easy) fácil; (near at hand) a la mano; (with money) contante; (with wit, etc.) vivo; (available) disponible; (nimble) ágil, ligero. **I am r. to do it,** Estoy dispuesto a hacerlo. **in r. cash,** en dinero contante. **to get r.,** prepararse; (dress) vestirse. **to make r.,** *v.t.* preparar; aprestar; (*print.*) imponer. *v.i.* prepararse, disponerse. **r.-made,** hecho; confeccionado. **r.-made clothing,** ropa hecha, *f.* **r. money,** dinero contante, *m.* **r.-witted,** de ingenio vivo

reaffirm, *v.t.* afirmar de nuevo; reiterar, volver a repetir

reaffirmation, *s.* reiteración, *f.*

reafforestation, *s.* nuevas plantaciones, *f. pl.*

reagent, *s.* reactivo, *m.*

real, *a.* real; verdadero; efectivo; (with silk, etc.) puro; sincero. **r. estate, r. property,** bienes raíces, *m. pl.*

realism, *s.* realismo, *m.*

realist, *s.* realista, *m.* and *f.*

realistic, *a.* realista

reality, *s.* realidad, *f.*; verdad, *f.*

realizable, *a.* realizable; factible

realization, *s.* realización, *f.*; comprensión, *f.*

realize, *v.t.* (understand) darse cuenta de, hacerse cargo de; realizar; (make real) dar vida (a); (accomplish) llevar a cabo; (com.) realizar; (gain) adquirir

really, *adv.* realmente; en verdad; en realidad; en efecto; (frankly) francamente. **R.?** ¿De veras?

realm, *s.* reino, *m.*, dominios, *m. pl.*; (*fig.*) esfera, *f.*

realty, *s.* bienes raíces, *m. pl.*

ream, *s.* resma, *f.*

reanimate, *v.t.* reanimar

reap, *v.t.* segar; (*fig.*) cosechar, recoger

reaper, *s.* segador (-ra); (machine) segadora mecánica, *f.*

reaping, *s.* siega, *f.*; (*fig.*) cosecha, *f.* **r.-machine,** segadora mecánica, *f.*

reappear, *v.i.* reaparecer

reappearance, *s.* reaparición, *f.*

reapplication, *s.* nueva aplicación, *f.*; (of paint, etc.) otra capa, *f.*; (for a post, etc.) nueva solicitud, *f.*

reapply, *v.t.* aplicar de nuevo; (paint, etc.) dar otra capa (de); (for a post, etc.) mandar una nueva solicitud

reappoint, *v.t.* designar de nuevo

rear, *v.t.* (lift) alzar, levantar; (breed, educate) criar; (build) erigir, construir. *v.i.* (of horses) encabritarse, corcovear

rear, *s.* cola, *f.*; parte de atrás, *f.*; parte posterior, *f.*; última fila, *f.*; (background) fondo, *m.*; (*fam.*) trasera, *f.*; (*mil.*) retaguardia, *f.* *a.* de atrás; trasero; último; posterior; de última fila; (*mil.*) de retaguardia. **in the r.,** por detrás; a la cola; a retaguardia. **to bring up the r.,** cerrar la marcha. **r.-admiral,** contraalmirante, *m.* **r.-axle,** eje trasero, *m.* **r.-guard,** retaguardia, *f.* **r. lamp,** faro trasero, *m.* **r. rank,** última fila, *f.* **r. view,** vista por detrás, *f.*; vista posterior, *f.*

rearing, *s.* (breeding) cría, *f.*; (education) crianza, *f.*

rearm, *v.t.* rearmar. *v.i.* rearmarse

rearmament, *s.* rearmamento, *m.*

rearrange, *v.t.* volver a arreglar; arreglar de otra manera; (a literary work) refundir, adaptar

rearrangement, *s.* nuevo arreglo, *m.*; (of a literary work) refundición, adaptación, *f.*

reascend, *v.i.* and *v.t.* subir de nuevo, subir otra vez; montar de nuevo (sobre)

reascent, *s.* nueva ascensión, *f.*

reason, *s.* razón, *f.* *v.i.* and *v.t.* razonar. **to r. out of,** disuadir de. **by r. of,** a causa de, con motivo de; en virtud de. **for this r.,** por esto, por esta razón. **out of all r.,** fuera de razón. **to stand to r.,** ser lógico, estar puesto en razón. **with r.,** con razón. **reasons of state,** razón de estado, *f.*

reasonable, *a.* razonable; racional

reasonableness, *s.* lo razonable; moderación, *f.*; justicia, *f.*; racionalidad, *f.*

reasonably, *adv.* razonablemente; con razón; bastante

reasoner, *s.* razonador (-ra); dialéctico, *m.*

reasoning, *s.* razonamiento, *m.*

reassemble, *v.t.* reunir otra vez. *v.i.* juntarse de nuevo

reassert, *v.t.* afirmar de nuevo, reiterar

reassertion, *s.* reiteración, *f.*

reassess, *v.t.* tasar de nuevo; repartir de nuevo; (a work of art) hacer una nueva apreciación (de)

reassessment, *s.* nueva tasación, *f.*; nuevo repartimiento, *m.*; (of a work of art) nueva estimación, *f.*

reassume, *v.t.* reasumir

reassumption, *s.* reasunción, *f.*

reassurance, *s.* afirmación repetida, *f.*; confianza restablecida, *f.*

reassure, *v.t.* asegurar de nuevo; tranquilizar, confortar

reassuring, *a.* tranquilizador, consolador

rebaptize, *v.t.* rebautizar

rebate, *s.* rebaja, *f.*, descuento, *m.*; reducción, *f.* *v.t.* rebajar, descontar; reducir. **to r. pro rata,** ratear

rebec, *s.* (*mus.*) rabel, *m.*

rebel, *s.* rebelde, *m.* and *f.*, insurrecto (-ta). *v.i.* rebelarse, sublevarse. **r. leader,** cabecilla, *m.*

rebellion, *s.* rebelión, *f.*

rebellious, *a.* rebelde; revoltoso; refractario

rebelliousness, *s.* rebeldía, *f.*

rebind, *v.t.* atar de nuevo; (a book) reencuadernar

rebirth, *s.* renacimiento, *m.*

rebore, *v.t.* (an engine) descarbonizar

reboring, *s.* (of an engine) descarburación, *f.*

reborn, to be, *v.i.* renacer; ser reincarnado

rebound, *a.* (of books) reencuadernado. *v.i.* rebotar; repercutir; (revive) reavivarse. *s.* rebote, resalto, *m.*; reacción, *f.*, rechazo, *m.*

rebuff, *s.* repulsa, *f.*, desaire, *m.*; contrariedad, *f.* *v.t.* rechazar; contrariar

rebuild, *v.t.* reedificar

rebuilding, *s.* reedificación, *f.*

rebuke, *s.* reconvención, reprensión, censura, *f.*, reproche, *m.* *v.t.* reprender, censurar, reprochar

rebukingly, *adv.* en tono de censura; con reprensión, con reprobación

rebut, *v.t.* refutar

rebuttal, *s.* refutación, *f.*

recalcitrance, *s.* terquedad, obstinacia, *f.*; rebeldía, *f.*

recalcitrant, *a.* reacio, recalcitrante

recall, *v.t.* llamar; hacer volver; (dismiss) destituir; (ambassador, etc.) retirar; (remind or remember) recordar; (revoke) revocar. *s.* llamada, *f.*; (*mil.*) toque de llamada, *m.*; (of ambassadors, etc.) retirada, *f.*; (dismissal) destitución, *f.* **beyond r.,** irrevocable; (forgotten) olvidado

recant, *v.t.* retractar, retirar. *v.i.* desdecirse (de), retractarse

recantation, *s.* recantación, *f.*

recapitulate, *v.t.* recapitular, resumir

recapitulation, *s.* recapitulación, *f.*

recapture, *v.t.* volver a prender, hacer prisionero nuevamente; (a place) volver a tomar; (a ship) represar

recast, *v.t.* (metals, a literary work) refundir; (alter) cambiar; (reckon) volver a calcular

recasting, *s.* (metals, a literary work) refundición, *f.*

recede, *v.i.* retroceder; alejarse (de), separarse (de); desviarse (de); retirarse; desaparecer; (diminish) disminuir; (of prices) bajar

receding, *a.* que retrocede, etc.

receipt, *s.* recibo, *m.*; (for money) recibí, *m.*; (recipe) receta, *f.*; *pl.* **receipts,** ingresos, *m. pl.* *v.t.* firmar (or extender) recibo. **on r. of,** al recibir. **to acknowledge the r. of,** acusar recibo de. **r. book,** libro talonario, *m.*

receive, *v.t.* and *v.i.* recibir; admitir, aceptar; acoger; (money) percibir, cobrar; (lodge) hospe-

dar, alojar; (contain) contener.
to be well received, tener
buena acogida

receiver, s. recibidor (-ra); (of
stolen goods) receptador (-ra);
(in bankruptcies) síndico, *m.*;
(for other legal business) receptor, *m.*; (of a telephone) auricular,
m.; (elec.) receptor, *m.*; (rad.)
radiorreceptor, *m.* **to hang up
the r.**, colgar (el auricular)

receivership, s. sindicatura, *f.*;
receptoría, *f.*

receiving, s. recibimiento, *m.*; (of
money, etc.) cobranza, *f.*, percibo, *m.*; (of stolen goods) encubrimiento, *m.* *a.* que recibe;
recipiente; de recepción. **r. set**,
aparato de radio, *m.*

recency, s. lo reciente; novedad,
f.

recent, *a.* reciente; nuevo. **in
r. years**, en estos últimos años

recently, *adv.* recientemente; (before past participles) recién.
until r., hasta hace poco. **r.
painted**, recién pintado

receptacle, s. receptáculo, recipiente, *m.*; (bot.) receptáculo, *m.*

reception, s. recepción, *f.*; recibo,
m.; (welcome) acogida, *f.*; (of
evidence) recepción, *f.* **r. room**,
pieza de recibo, *f.*, gabinete, *m.*

receptive, *a.* receptivo; susceptible

receptiveness, s. sensibilidad,
susceptibilidad, *f.*

recess, s. (holiday) vacaciones, *f.*
pl.; (during school hours) hora de
recreo, *f.*; (fig., heart) seno, *m.*,
entrañas, *f. pl.*; (of the soul,
heart) hondón, *m.*; (in a coastline, etc.) depresión, *f.*; (in a
wall) nicho, *m.*; (alcove) alcoba,
f. **parliamentary r.**, interregno parlamentario, *m.*

recessional, s. himno que se
canta mientras se retiran los
eclesiásticos y el coro, *m.*

Rechabite, s. recabita, *m.* and
f.

recharge, *v.t.* (a gun, etc.) recargar; acusar de nuevo

rechristen, *v.t.* rebautizar

recipe, s. receta, *f.*

recipient, s. recibidor (-ra); el,
m. (*f.* la) que recibe. *a.* recipiente; receptivo

reciprocal, *a.* recíproco

reciprocally, *adv.* recíprocamente

reciprocate, *v.t.* reciprocar;
(mech.) producir movimiento de
vaivén. *v.i.* (mech.) oscilar, tener
movimiento alternativo; corresponder; ser recíproco

reciprocation, s. reciprocación,
f.; reciprocidad, correspondencia,
f.

reciprocity, s. reciprocidad, *f.*

recital, s. narración, relación, *f.*;
enumeración, *f.*; recitación, *f.*;
(mus.) recital, *m.*

recitation, s. recitación, *f.*

recitative, s. recitado, *m.*

recite, *v.t.* recitar, repetir; narrar; declamar. *v.i.* decir una
recitación

reciter, s. recitador (-ra); declamador (-ra)

reckless, *a.* temerario, audaz;
precipitado; descuidado (de);
indiferente (a); excesivo; imprudente

recklessly, *adv.* temerariamente;
descuidadamente; imprudentemente

recklessness, s. temeridad, audacia, *f.*; descuido, *m.*; imprudencia, *f.*; indiferencia, *f.*

reckon, *v.t.* calcular, computar;
contar; enumerar; (believe) considerar, juzgar; (attribute) atribuir; (think) creer (que). **to r.
up**, echar cuentas, calcular. **to
r. with**, contar con; tomar en
serio

reckoner, s. calculador (-ra).
ready r., tablas matemáticas,
f. pl.

reckoning, s. cálculo, *m.*, calculación, *f.*; cuenta, *f.*; (fig.) retribución, *f.*, castigo, *m.*; (naut.)
estima, *f.* **the day of r.**, el día
de ajuste de cuentas; el día del
juicio final. **to be out in one's
r.**, equivocarse en el cálculo;
engañarse en el juicio

reclaim, *v.t.* (land) entarquinar;
(reform) reformar; (tame) domesticar; (claim) reclamar; (restore) restaurar

reclamation, s. (of land) en-
tarquinamiento, *m.*; cultivo, *m.*;
(reform) reformación, *f.*; (restoration) restauración, *f.*; (claim-
ing) reclamación, *f.*

recline, *v.t.* apoyar; recostar;
reclinar; descansar, reposar. *v.i.*

recostarse, reclinarse; estar tumbado; apoyarse; descansar

reclining, *s.* reclinación, *f.* *a.* inclinado; acostado; (of statues) yacente

recluse, *a.* solitario. *s.* recluso (-sa); solitario (-ia); ermitaño, *m.*, anacoreta, *m.* and *f.*

recognition, *s.* reconocimiento, *m.*

recognizable, *a.* que puede reconocerse; identificable

recognizance, *s.* reconocimiento, *m.*; (*law*) obligación, *f.*

recognize, *v.t.* reconocer; confesar

recoil, *s.* reculada, *f.*; (of a gun) culatazo, *m.*; (refusal) rechazo, *m.*; (result) repercusión, *f.*; (repugnance) aversión, repugnancia, *f.* *v.i.* recular; retroceder; repercutir; sentir repugnancia

recoin, *v.t.* acuñar de nuevo

recollect, *v.t.* acordarse de, recordar **to r. oneself,** reponerse, recobrarse

recollection, *s.* recuerdo, *m.*, memoria, *f.*

recommence, *v.t.* and *v.i.* empezar de nuevo

recommend, *v.t.* recomendar; aconsejar; encargar

recommendable, *a.* recomendable

recommendation, *s.* recomendación, *f.*

recommendatory, *a.* recomendatorio

recommender, *s.* el, *m.* (*f.* la) que recomienda

recompense, *s.* recompensa, *f.* *v.t.* recompensar

recomposition, *s.* recomposición, *f.*

reconcilability, *s.* posibilidad de reconciliación, *f.*; compatibilidad, *f.*

reconcilable, *a.* reconciliable; compatible; conciliable

reconcile, *v.t.* reconciliar; (quarrels) componer, ajustar; (opposing theories, etc.) conciliar. **to r. oneself (to),** aceptar; acostumbrarse (a); resignarse (a)

reconciler, *s.* reconciliador (-ra)

reconciliation, *s.* reconciliación, *f.*; (of theories, etc.) conciliación, *f.*

reconciliatory, *a.* reconciliador

recondite, *a.* recóndito

recondition, *v.t.* reacondicionar

reconnaissance, *s.* reconocimiento, *m.*; exploración, *f.* **r. flight,** vuelo de reconocimiento, *m.* **r. 'plane,** aeroplano de reconocimiento, *m.*

reconnoitre, *v.t.* (*mil.*) reconocer; explorar. *v.i.* (*mil.*) practicar un reconocimiento; correr la campaña

reconnoitring, *s.* reconocimiento, *m.* *a.* de reconocimiento

reconquer, *v.t.* reconquistar

reconquest, *s.* reconquista, *f.*

reconsecrate, *v.t.* consagrar de nuevo

reconsider, *v.t.* considerar de nuevo, volver a considerar; volver a discutir

reconsideration, *s.* nueva consideración, *f.*; nueva discusión, *f.*

reconstitute, *v.t.* reconstituir

reconstitution, *s.* reconstitución, *f.*

reconstruct, *v.t.* reconstruir

reconstruction, *s.* reconstrucción, *f.*

reconversion, *s.* reconversión, *f.*

recopy, *v.t.* copiar de nuevo

record, *v.t.* apuntar; inscribir; (recount) contar, escribir; recordar; registrar; (of thermometers, etc.) marcar, registrar; hacer un disco de gramófono de; (radio, cinema) impresionar. *s.* relación, *f.*; crónica, *f.*; historia, *f.*; (soldier's) hoja de servicios, *f.*; (past) antecedentes, *m. pl.*; documento, *m.*; inscripción, *f.*; (entry) partida, *f.*; testimonio, *m.*; (memory) recuerdo, *m.*; registro, *m.*; (gramophone) disco de gramófono, *m.*; (*sport*) "record," *m.*, marca, *f.*; *pl.* **records,** archivos, *m. pl.*; (notes) notas, *f. pl.*; (facts) datos, *m. pl.*; anales, *m. pl.* **Keeper of the Records,** archivero, *m.* **off the r.,** confidencialmente. **on r.,** escrito; registrado; inscrito en los anales de la historia. **to break a r.,** batir el "record." **r.-holder,** plusmarquista, *m.* and *f.*

recorder, *s.* registrador, *m.*; archivero, *m.*; (*law*) juez, *m.*; (historian) historiador, *m.*; (*mus.*) caramillo,. *m.*; (*mech.*) contador, indicador, *m.*; (scientific) aparato registrador, *m.*

recording, *a.* registrador. **r. apparatus,** (cinema, radio, gramophone) máquina de impresionar, *f.*; (scientific) aparato registrador, *m*' **r. van,** carro de sonido, *m.*

recount, *v.t.* contar de nuevo; (tell) referir, narrar, contar

recoup, *v.t.* compensar, indemnizar; recobrar, desquitarse de

recourse, *s.* recurso, *m.* **to have r. to,** recurrir, *a.*

recover, *v.t.* (regain) recobrar; (*fig.*) reconquistar; (retrieve) rescatar; (*law*) reivindicar. *v.i.* reponerse; (in health) recobrar la salud, sanar, curarse; (*law*) ganar un pleito. **to r. consciousness,** volver en sí

recoverable, *a.* recuperable

recovery, *s.* (regaining) recobro, *m.*, recuperación, *f.*; (of money) cobranza, *f.*; (retrieval) rescate, *m.*; (*fig.*) reconquista, *f.*; (from illness) mejoría, convalecencia, *f.*; restablecimiento, *m.*; (*law*) reivindicación, *f.*

recreant, *a.* traidor, falso, desleal. *s.* apóstata, *m.* and *f.*, traidor (-ra)

recreate, *v.t.* recrear

recreation, *s.* recreación, *f.*; (break in schools) recreo, *m.* **r. hall,** sala de recreo, *f.*

recreative, *a.* recreativo

recriminate, *v.i.* recriminar

recrimination, *s.* recriminación, reconvención, *f.*

recriminator, *s.* recriminador (-ra)

recriminatory, *a.* recriminador

recross, *v.t.* volver a cruzar, cruzar de nuevo

recrudesce, *v.i.* recrudecer

recrudescence, *s.* recrudescencia, *f.*

recrudescent, *a.* recrudescente

recruit, *s.* recluta, *m.* *v.t.* reclutar; (restore) reponer

recruiting, *s.* reclutamiento, *m.* **r. office,** caja de reclutamiento, *f.*

rectal, *a.* rectal

rectangle, *s.* rectángulo, *m.*

rectangular, *a.* rectangular

rectifiable, *a.* rectificable

rectification, *s.* rectificación, *f.*

rectifier, *s.* rectificador, *m.*

rectify, *v.t.* rectificar

rectilinear, *a.* rectilíneo

rectitude, *s.* rectitud, *f.*

rector, *s.* (of a university or school) rector, *m.*; (priest) párroco, *m.*

rectorial, *a.* rectoral

rectorship, *s.* rectorado, *m.*

rectory, *s.* rectoría, *f.*

rectum, *s.* recto, *m.*

recumbent, *a.* recostado, reclinado; (of a statue) yacente

recuperable, *a.* recuperable

recuperate, *v.t.* recuperar, recobrar. [*v.i.* restablecerse, reponerse; recuperarse

recuperation, *s.* recuperación, *f.*

recuperative, *a.* recuperativo

recur, *v.i.* presentarse a la imaginación; volver (sobre); presentarse de nuevo, aparecer otra vez; repetirse; reproducirse

recurrence, *s.* reaparición, *f.*; repetición, *f.*

recurrent, *a.* periódico; (*med.*) recurrente

red, *a.* rojo; (of wine) tinto. *s.* color rojo, *m.*; (in billiards) mingo, *m.*, bola roja, *f.*; (*pol.*) rojo, *m.* **to catch red-handed,** coger con el hurto en las manos; coger con las manos en la masa, coger en el acto. **to grow red,** enrojecerse, ponerse rojo; volverse rojo. **red-berried,** con bayas rojas. **red cabbage,** lombarda, *f.* **red cedar,** cedro dulce, *m.* **red corpuscle,** glóbulo rojo, *m.* **Red Cross,** Cruz Roja, *f.* **red currant,** grosella, *f.* **red currant bush,** grossellero, *m.* **red-eyed,** con los ojos inyectados. **red fir,** pino silvestre, *m.* **red flush,** (in the sky) arrebol, *m.* **red-gold,** bermejo; (of hair, etc.) rojo. **red-haired,** pelirrojo, de pelo rojo. **red-handed,** con las manos ensangrentadas; (*fig.*) en el acto. **red-head** (person) pelirrojo (-ja). **red-heat,** incandescencia, *f.* **red-hot,** candente. **Red Indian,** piel roja, *m.* **red-lead,** minio, *m.* **red-letter,** de fiesta; extraordinario. **red-letter day,** día de fiesta, *m.*; día extraordinario, *m.* **red mullet,** salmonete, *m.*, trilla, *f.* **red ochre,** almagre, *m.* **red**

pepper, pimiento, *m.*; (cayenne) pimentón, *m.* **red tape,** balduque, *m.*; formulismo, *m.*; burocracia, *f.* **red wine,** vino tinto, *m.*

redact, *v.t.* redactar

redaction, *s.* redacción, *f.*

redbreast, *s.* petirrojo, *m.*

redden, *v.t.* rojear, enrojecer; pintar de rojo. *v.i.* enrojecerse, ponerse rojo; volverse rojo

reddish, *a.* rojizo

redeem, *v.t.* (a mortgage, bonds, etc.) amortizar; (from pawn) desempeñar; (a promise, etc.) cumplir; libertar; redimir; compensar; (a fault) expiar; (reform) reformar; (rescue) rescatar

redeemable, *a.* redimible; amortizable

redeemer, *s.* rescatador (-ra); salvador (-ra); (*theol.*) Redentor, *m.*

redeeming, *a.* redentor; compensatorio. **r. feature,** compensación, *f.*; rasgo bueno, *m.* **There is no r. feature in his work,** No hay nada bueno en su obra

redemption, *s.* (of a mortgage, etc.) amortización, *f.*; (from pawn) desempeño, *m.*; (of a promise, etc.) cumplimiento, *m.*; (ransom, etc.) rescate, *m.*; (*theol.*) redención, *f.*; compensación, *f.*; (of a fault) expiación, *f.*; reformación, *f.*

redemptive, *a.* redentor

redescend, *v.i.* bajar de nuevo

rediscovery, *s.* nuevo descubrimiento, *m.*

redistribute, *v.t.* distribuir de nuevo, volver a distribuir

redistribution, *s.* nueva distribución, *f.*

redness, *s.* rojez, *f.*, color rojo, *m.*

redolent, *a.* fragante, oloroso; (*fig.*) evocador (de)

redouble, *v.t.* redoblar. *v.i.* redoblarse

redoubling, *s.* redoblamiento, *m.*

redoubt, *s.* reducto, *m.*

redoubtable, *a.* formidable, terrible; valiente

redound, *v.i.* redundar (en)

redress, *v.t.* rectificar; reparar; remediar; hacer justicia (a); corregir

redresser, *s.* remediador (-ra)

redskin, *s.* piel roja, *m.*

reduce, *v.t.* reducir (also *chem., math., med.*); disminuir; (in price) rebajar; abreviar; (exhaust, weaken) agotar; (impoverish) empobrecer; (degrade) degradar. **to r. to the ranks,** (*mil.*) volver a las filas; degradar. **to be in reduced circumstances,** estar en la indigencia

reducible, *a.* reducible

reduction, *s.* reducción (also *math., chem.*), *f.*; (in price) rebaja, *f.*

redundance, *s.* redundancia, *f.*

redundant, *a.* redundante; superfluo, excesivo

reduplicate, *v.t.* reduplicar

reduplication, *s.* reduplicación, *f.*

re-echo, *v.t.* repetir; devolver el son de, hacer reverberar. *v.i.* repercutirse, reverberar

reed, *s.* (*bot.*) caña, *f.*; (arrow) saeta, *f.*; (pipe) caramillo, *m.*; (in wind-instruments) lengüeta, *f.*; (*arch.*) junquillo, *m.*; (in a loom) peine, *m.*; (pastoral poetry) poesía bucólica, *f.* *v.t.* (thatch) bardar con cañas

re-edit, *v.t.* reeditar, volver a editar

reedy, *a.* juncoso, lleno de cañas; (of the voice) silbante

reef, *s.* arrecife, escollo, encalladero, *m.*; (*min.*) filón, *m.*; (*naut.*) rizo, *m.* *v.t.* (*naut.*) arrizar. **to take in reefs,** (*naut.*) hacer el rizo. **r.-knot,** nudo de marino, *m.*

reek, *s.* humo, *m.*; olor, *m.* *v.i.* humear; oler (de); (*fig.*) recordar, hacer pensar (en)

reeky, *a.* humoso

reel, *s.* carrete, *m.*; devanadera, *f.*; (of a fishing rod) carrete, carretel, *m.*; (cinema) cinta, *f.*; (dance) baile escocés, *m.* *v.t.* devanar. *v.i.* tambalear, titubear; (of ships, etc.) cabecear; temblar; oscilar. **to r. about drunkenly,** (of persons) andar haciendo eses, arrimarse a las paredes. **to r. off,** recitar; enumerar; decir rápidamente

re-elect, *v.t.* reelegir

re-election, *s.* reelección, *f.*

re-eligible, *a.* reelegible

reeling, *s.* tambaleo, *m.*; andar vacilante, *m.*; (of a ship, etc.) cabeceo, *m.*; oscilación, *f.*

re-embarcation, *s.* reembarque, *m.*

re-embark, *v.t.* reembarcar. *v.i.* reembarcarse

re-emerge, *v.i.* reaparecer

re-emergence, *s.* reaparición, *f.*

re-enact, *v.t.* revalidar (una ley); decretar de nuevo

re-enactment, *s.* revalidación (de una ley), *f.*; nuevo decreto, *m.*

re-engage, *v.t.* contratar de nuevo

re-engagement, *s.* nuevo contrato, *m.*

re-enlist, *v.t.* and *v.i.* alistar(se) de nuevo

re-enlistment, *s.* reenganche, *m.*

re-enter, *v.t.* volver a entrar (en); reingresar (en)

re-entry, *s.* segunda entrada, *f.*; reingreso, *m.*

re-equip, *v.t.* equipar de nuevo

re-establish, *v.t.* restablecer; restaurar

re-establishment, *s.* restablecimiento, *m.*; restauración, *f.*

reeve, *v.t.* (*naut.*) laborear, guarnir

re-examination, *s.* reexaminación, *f.*; nuevo examen, *m.*; (*law*) nuevo interrogatorio, *m.*

re-examine, *v.t.* reexaminar; (*law*) interrogar de nuevo

re-export, *v.t.* reexportar

re-exportation, *s.* reexportación, *f.*

refashion, *v.t.* volver a hacer; formar de nuevo

refection, *s.* refección, *f.*

refectory, *s.* refectorio, *m.*

refer, *v.t.* atribuir (a); (send) enviar, remitir; (assign) referir (a), relacionar (con). *v.i.* referirse (a); aludir (a); hablar (de)

referee, *s.* árbitro, *m.*; (*law*) juez arbitrador, *m.*; (reference) garante, *m.* and *f.*, fiador (-ra). *v.i.* servir de árbitro

reference, *s.* referencia, *f.*; consulta, *f.*; mención, *f.*; alusión, *f.*; (relation) relación, *f.*; *pl.* references, (*com.*) referencias, *f. pl.* for r., para consulta. in r. to, con referencia a, respecto a, en cuanto a. terms of r., puntos de consulta, *m. pl.* work of r., libro de consulta, *m.*

referendum, *s.* referéndum, *m.*; plebiscito, *m.*

refill, *v.t.* rellenar; rehenchir; (pen) llenar de nuevo con tinta. *s.* (for a pencil) mina de recambio, *f.*

refine, *v.t.* refinar; (metals) acrisolar; (fats) clarificar; (*fig.*) perfeccionar, pulir, refinar

refined, *a.* refinado; fino; culto; cortés; elegante; delicado; (subtle) sutil; (affected) afectado

refinement, *s.* refinamiento, *m.*; finura, *f.*; cultura, *f.*; cortesía, *f.*; elegancia, *f.*; delicadeza, *f.*; (subtlety) sutileza, *f.*; (affectation) afectación, *f.*

refiner, *s.* refinador, *m.*

refinery, *s.* refinería, *f.*

refining, *s.* refinación, *f.*; (*fig.*) refinamiento, *m.*

refit, *v.t.* reparar; (*naut.*) embonar

refitting, *s.* reparación, *f.*; (*naut.*) embonada, *f.*

reflect, *v.t.* reflejar; reflexionar. *v.i.* reflejar; reflexionar (sobre), pensar (en), meditar (sobre). This offer reflects credit on him, Esta oferta le hace honor. to r. on, upon, reflexionar sobre; (disparage) desacreditar; (affect unfavourably) perjudicar

reflecting, *a.* reflector

reflection, *s.* (*phys.*) reflexión, *f.*; reflejo, *m.*; consideración, *f.*, pensamiento, *m.*; (aspersion) censura, *f.*, reproche, *m.* upon mature r., después de pensarlo bien

reflective, *a.* (*phys.*) reflector; reflexivo, pensativo, meditabundo

reflectively, *adv.* reflexivamente

reflector, *s.* reflector, *m.*; (shade) pantalla, *f.*

reflex, *a.* reflejo. *s.* reflejo, *m.*; acción refleja, *f.* r. action, acción refleja, *f.*

refloat, *v.t.* (a ship) poner otra vez a flote, desvarar

reflux, *s.* reflujo, *m.*

refoot, *v.t.* (socks) cabecear

reform, *s.* reforma, *f. a.* de reforma; reformista. *v.t.* reformar; formar de nuevo. *v.i.* reformarse

reformation, *s.* reformación, *f.*; Reformation, Reforma, *f.*

reformatory, *a.* reformatorio, reformador. *s.* reformatorio, *m.*, casa de corrección, *f.*

reformer, *s.* reformador (-ra), reformista, *m.* and *f.*

refract, *v.t.* refractar

refraction, *s.* refracción, *f.*

refractive, *a.* refringente

refractoriness *s.* terquedad, obstinacia, *f.*; rebeldía, indocilidad, *f.*

refractory, *a.* (of substances) refractario; recalcitrante, intratable, rebelde

refrain, *s.* estribillo, estrambote, *m.*

refrain, *v.i.* abstenerse (de), evitar

refresh, *v.t.* refrescar

refreshing, *a.* refrescante; atractivo; estimulante; interesante

refreshment, *s.* (solace) solaz, reposo, *m.*; recreación, *f.*, deleite, *m.*; (food and (or) drink) refresco, *m.* **r.-room,** (on a station) fonda, *f.*

refrigerate, *v.t.* refrigerar; enfriar; refrescar

refrigeration, *s.* refrigeración, *f.*; enfriamiento, *m.* **r. chamber,** cámara frigorífica, *f.*

refrigerative, *a.* refrigerante, frigorífico

refrigerator, *s.* refrigerador, *m.*, nevera, *f.*

refringent, *a.* refringente

refuel, *v.t.* (a furnace) cargar con carbón, etc.; (of a ship) tomar carbón; (of a 'plane, motor vehicle) tomar bencina

refuge, *s.* refugio, *m.*; asilo, *m.*; (resort) recurso, *m.*; subterfugio, *m.*; (traffic island) refugio para peatones, *m.* **to take r.,** refugiarse; resguardarse (de)

refugee, *a.* refugiado. *s.* refugiado (-da)

refulgence, *s.* refulgencia, *f.*

refulgent, *a.* refulgente

refund, *v.t.* reembolsar; devolver

refunding, *s.* reembolso, *m.*; devolución, *f.*

refurbish, *v.t.* restaurar; renovar; (a literary work) refundir

refurnish, *v.t.* amueblar de nuevo

refusal, *s.* negativa, *f.*; (rejection) rechazo, *m.*; (option) opción, *f.*; preferencia, *f.*

refuse, *v.t.* negar; (reject) rechazar. *v.i.* negarse (a), rehusar; (of a horse) resistirse a saltar

refuse, *s.* desecho, *m.*; desperdicios, *m. pl.*; residuo, *m.*; basura, *f. a.* de desecho. **r. dump,** muladar, *m.*

refutable, *a.* refutable

refutation, *s.* refutación, *f.*

refute, *v.t.* refutar

regain, *v.t.* recobrar, recuperar; cobrar; ganar de nuevo; (*fig.*) reconquistar. **to r. one's breath,** cobrar aliento. **to r. consciousness,** volver en sí

regal, *a.* regio, real

regale, *v.t.* regalar, agasajar; recrear, deleitar

regalia, *s.* regalía, *f.*; insignias reales, *f. pl.*; distintivos, *m. pl.*, insignias, *f. pl.*

regalism, *s.* realismo, *m.*

regalist, *s.* realista, *m.* and *f.*

regally, *adv.* regiamente

regard, *v.t.* mirar; observar; considerar; (respect) respetar; (concern) importar, concernir; relacionarse con. *s.* mirada, *f.*; atención, *f.*; (esteem) aprecio, *m.*, estimación, *f.*; respeto, *m.*; veneración, *f.*; (relation) referencia, *f.*; *pl.* regards, recuerdos, saludos, *m. pl.* **He has little r. for their feelings,** Le importan poco sus susceptibilidades. **With kindest regards,** Con mis saludos más afectuosos. **as regards, with r. to,** con referencia a, respecto a, en cuanto a

regardful, *a.* atento (a), cuidadoso (de); que se preocupa (de)

regarding, *prep.* tocante a, en cuanto a, respecto de

regardless, *a.* negligente (de); indiferente (a), insensible (a); que no se interesa (en); que no se inqueta (por); sin preocuparse (de)

regatta, *s.* regata, *f.*

regency, *s.* regencia, *f.*

regeneracy, *s.* regeneración, *f.*

regenerate, *v.t.* regenerar. *a.* regenerado

regeneration, *s.* regeneración, *f.*

regenerative, *a.* regenerador

regenerator, *s.* regenerador (-ra)

regent, *s.* regente, *m.* and *f.*

regicidal, *a.* regicida

regicide, *s.* (act) regicidio, *m.*; (person) regicida, *m.* and *f.*

régime, *s.* régimen, *m.*

regimen, *s.* (*gram., med.*) régimen, *m.*

regiment, s. regimiento, m. v.t. regimentar. **r. of the line,** tropa de línea, f.

regimental, a. de (un) regimiento, perteneciente a un regimiento

regimentals, s. pl. uniforme (militar), m.

regimentation, s. regimentación, f.

region, s. región, f.

regional, a. regional

regionalism, s. regionalismo, m.

regionalist, s. regionalista, m. and f.

regionalistic, a. regionalista

register, s. (record and mech., mus., print.) registro, m.; (of ships, etc.) matrícula, f.; lista, f. v.t. registrar; matricular; (a ship) abanderar; inscribir; (of thermometers, etc.) marcar; (letters) certificar; (luggage) facturar; (in one's mind) grabar; (emotion) mostrar, manifestar. v.i. (at a hotel, etc.) registrarse; (print.) estar en registro. **cash r.,** caja registradora, f. **r. of births, marriages and deaths,** registro civil, m.

registrar, s. registrador, m.; archivero, m.; secretario, m. **r. of births, marriages and deaths,** secretario del registro civil, m. **registrar's office,** oficina del registro civil, f.

registration, s. registro, m.; inscripción, f.; (of a vehicle, etc.) matrícula, f.; (naut.) abanderamiento, m.; (of a letter, etc.) certificación, f. **r. number,** número de matrícula, m.

registry, s. registro, m.; inscripción, f.; matrícula, f. **r. office,** oficina del registro civil, f.; (for servants) agencia doméstica, f.

reglet, s. (arch.) filete, m.; (print.) regleta, f.

regression, s. regresión, f., retroceso, m.

regret, v.t. sentir; lamentar, pesar; arrepentirse (de); (miss) echar de menos (a). s. sentimiento, pesar, m.; (remorse) remordimiento, m. **I r. very much that . . .,** Me pesa mucho que . . ., Siento mucho que . . . **to send one's regrets,** mandar sus excusas

regretful, a. lleno de pesar; arrepentido; lamentable, deplorable. **He was most r. that . . .,** Lamentaba mucho que . . .

regretfully, adv. con pesar

regrettable, a. lamentable, deplorable; doloroso; (with loss, etc.) sensible

regrettably, adv. lamentablemente; sensiblemente

regroup, v.t. arreglar de nuevo; formar de nuevo; reorganizar

regular, a. regular; normal; (ordinary) corriente, común; (in order) en regla; (gram., bot., ecc., mil., geom.) regular. s. (ecc.) regular, m.; (soldier) soldado de línea, m.; (officer) militar de carrera, m.; (client) parroquiano habitual, m.

regularity, s. regularidad, f.

regularization, s. regularización, f.

regularize, v.t. regularizar

regularly, adv. regularmente

regulate, v.t. regular; ajustar, arreglar; (direct) dirigir; reglamentar

regulation, s. regulación, f.; arreglo, m.; (rule) reglamento, m. a. de reglamento; normal

regulative, a. regulador

regulator, s. (mech.) regulador, m.

regurgitate, v.t. and v.i. regurgitar

regurgitation, s. regurgitación, f.

rehabilitate, v.t. rehabilitar

rehabilitation, s. rehabilitación, f.

rehash, v.t. (a literary work, etc.) refundir

rehearing, s. nueva audición, f.; (of a case) revisión, f.

rehearsal, s. (theat.) ensayo, m.; recitación, f.; relación, narración, f. **dress r.,** ensayo general, m.

rehearse, v.t. (theat.) ensayar; recitar; (narrate) narrar; enumerar

reheat, v.t. recalentar

reign, s. reinado, m. v.i. reinar; predominar

reigning, a. reinante; predominante

reimburse, v.t. reembolsar

reimbursement, s. reembolso, m.

reimport, v.t. importar de nuevo, reimportar. s. reimporte, m.

reimportation, *s.* reimportación, *f.*

reimpose, *v.t.* reimponer

reimposition, *s.* reimposición, *f.*

reimprison, *v.t.* encarcelar de nuevo, reencarcelar

reimprisonment, *s.* reencarcelamiento, *m.*

rein, *s.* rienda, *f. v.t.* llevar las riendas (de); (hold back) refrenar. **to give r. to,** (*fig.*) dar rienda suelta (a)

reincarnation, *s.* reencarnación, *f.*

reincorporate, *v.t.* reincorporar

reincorporation, *s.* reincorporación, *f.*

reindeer, *s.* reno, *m.*

reinforce, *v.t.* reforzar; (concrete) armar; fortalecer. **reinforced concrete,** *s.* hormigón armado, *m.*

reinforcement, *s.* reforzamiento, *m.*; (*mil., nav., fig.*) refuerzo, *m.*

reins. See **rein**

reinsert, *v.t.* volver a insertar

reinstall, *v.t.* reinstalar; rehabilitar

reinstalment, *s.* reinstalación, *f.*; rehabilitación, *f.*; restablecimiento, *m.*

reinstate, *v.t.* reponer, restablecer; reinstalar; rehabilitar

reinstatement, *s.* restablecimiento, *m.*; rehabilitación, *f.*

reinsurance, *s.* reaseguro, *m.*

reinsure, *v.t.* reasegurar

reintegrate, *v.t.* reintegrar

reintegration, *s.* reintegración, *f.*

reinter, *v.t.* enterrar de nuevo

reinvest, *v.t.* reinvertir

reinvestment, *s.* reinversión, *f.*

reinvigorate, *v.t.* reanimar, dar nuevo vigor (a)

reinvite, *v.t.* invitar de nuevo (a)

reissue, *s.* nueva emisión, *f.*; (of a book, etc.) nueva edición, reimpresión, *f. v.t.* hacer una nueva emisión (de); reeditar, publicar de nuevo

reiterate, *v.t.* reiterar, repetir

reiteration, *s.* reiteración, *f.*

reiterative, *a.* reiterativo

reject, *v.t.* rechazar, rehusar; repudiar; repulsar; desechar

rejection, *s.* rechazamiento, *m.*; repudiación, refutación, *f.*; repulsa, *f.*

rejoice, *v.t.* alegrar, regocijar. *v.i.* alegrarse (de), regocijarse (de), gloriarse (en)

rejoicing, *s.* regocijo, júbilo, *m.*, alegría, *f.*; algazara, *f.*, fiestas, *f. pl.*

rejoin, *v.t.* and *v.i.* juntar de nuevo; volver a; reunirse con; (reply) contestar, replicar

rejoinder, *s.* contestación, respuesta, *f.*

rejuvenate, *v.t.* rejuvenecer

rejuvenation, *s.* rejuvenecimiento, *m.*

rekindle, *v.t.* encender de nuevo; despertar, reavivar. *v.i.* encenderse de nuevo; reavivarse

relapse, *s.* reincidencia, recaída, *f.*; (*med.*) recidiva, *f. v.i.* reincidir (en); (*med.*) recaer

relapsed, *a.* relapso

relate, *v.t.* (recount) relatar, narrar; relacionar; unir; (of kinship) emparentar. *v.i.* ajustarse (a); referirse (a). **The first fact is not related to the second,** El primer hecho no tiene nada que ver con el segundo

related, *a.* relacionado; (by kinship) emparentado. **John is well-r.,** Juan es de buena familia; Juan es de familia influyente; Juan tiene buenas relaciones

relater, *s.* narrador (-ra)

relation, *s.* (narrative) relación, narración, *f.*; conexión, *f.*; relación, *f.*; (kinship) parentesco, *m.*; (person) pariente (-ta). **in r. to,** con relación a, en cuanto a

relationship, *s.* parentesco, *m.*; conexión, relación, *f.*

relative, *a.* relativo (also *gram.*). *s.* pariente (-ta); *pl.* **relatives,** parientes, *m. pl.*, parentela, *f.*

relatively, *adv.* relativamente

relativism, *s.* relativismo, *m.*

relativity, *s.* relatividad, *f.*

relator, *s.* (*law*) relator, *m.*

relax, *v.t.* relajar; aflojar; soltar; (make less severe) ablandar; (decrease) mitigar. *v.i.* relajarse; aflojar; (rest) descansar

relaxation, *s.* relajación, *f.*; aflojamiento, *m.*; ablandamiento, *m.*; mitigación, *f.*; (rest) descanso, reposo, *m.*; (pastime) pasatiempo, *m.*; (amusement) diversión, *f.*

relaxing, *a.* relajante; (of climate) enervante

relay, *s.* (of horses) parada, *f.*; (shift) tanda, *f.*; relevo, *m.*; (*elec.*) relais, *m.*; (*rad.*) redifusión, *f.* *v.t.* enviar por posta; (*elec.*) reemitir; (*rad.*) retransmitir; (lay again) colocar de nuevo. **r. race,** carrera de equipo, carrera de relevos, *f.*

release, *v.t.* soltar; (hurl) lanzar; (set free) poner en libertad (a); librar (de); absolver; (surrender) renunciar (a); dar al público, poner en circulación; (lease again) realquilar. *s.* soltura, *f.*; lanzamiento, *m.*; liberación, *f.*; (from pain) alivio, *m.*; remisión, *f.*; exoneración, *f.*; publicación, *f.*; (of films) representación, *f.*; (*law*) soltura, *f.*

relegate, *v.t.* relegar

relegation, *s.* relegación, *f.*

relent, *v.i.* ablandarse, enternecerse; ceder

relenting, *s.* enternecimiento, desenojo, *m.*

relentless, *a.* implacable, inexorable; despiadado

relentlessly, *adv.* inexorablemente; sin piedad

relentlessness, *s.* inexorabilidad, *f.*; falta de piedad, *f.*

relet, *v.t.* realquilar

relevance, *s.* conexión, *f.*; pertinencia, *f.*; aplicabilidad, *f.*

relevant, *a.* relativo; pertinente, a propósito, oportuno; aplicable

reliability, *s.* seguridad, *f.*; formalidad, *f.*; confianza, *f.*; exactitud, *f.*; veracidad, *f*

reliable, *a.* seguro; formal; digno de confianza; exacto; veraz

reliably, *adv.* seguramente; de una manera digna de confianza; exactamente

reliance, *s.* confianza, *f.* **to place r. on,** tener confianza en

reliant, *a.* confiado

relic, *s.* vestigio, rastro, *m.*; (*ecc.*) reliquia, *f.*

relict, *s.* viuda, *f.*

relief, *s.* (alleviation) alivio, *m.*; desahogo, *m.*; (help) socorro, *m.*, ayuda, *f.*; beneficencia, *f.*; (*mil.*) relevo, *m.*; (pleasure) placer, *m.*, satisfacción, *f.*; (consolation) consuelo, *m.*; (*law*) remisión, *f.*; (*art*) relieve, *m.* **high r.,** alto relieve,

m. **low r.,** bajo relieve, *m.* **r. map,** mapa en relieve, *m.* **r. train,** tren de socorro, *m.*

relieve, *v.t.* aliviar; aligerar, suavizar; mitigar; (one's feelings, etc.) desahogar; (*mil.* and to take the place of) relevar; (free) librar; (dismiss) destituir; (remove) quitar; (rob) robar; (help) socorrer, remediar; (redeem) redimir; (ornament) adornar; (from a wrong) hacer justicia (a)

relieving, *s.* alivio, *m.*; aligeramiento, *m.*; mitigación, *f.*; (of the feelings) desahogo, *m.*; (*mil.*) relevo, *m.*; (help) socorro, *m.* **r. arch,** sobrearco, *m.*

relight, *v.t.* volver a encender. *v.i.* encenderse de nuevo

religion, *s.* religión, *f.*

religiosity, *s.* religiosidad, *f.*

religious, *a.* religioso; en religión; piadoso; devoto. *s.* religioso (-sa). **r. orders,** órdenes religiosas, *f. pl.* **r. toleration,** libertad de cultos, *f.*

religiously, *adv.* religiosamente

religiousness, *s.* religiosidad, *f.*

relinquish, *v.t.* abandonar; (one's grip) soltar; renunciar; desistir (de), dejar (de); (a post) dimitir (de)

relinquishment, *s.* abandono, *m.*; renuncia, *f.*; dejamiento, *m.*; (of a post) dimisión, *f.*

reliquary, *s.* relicario, *m.*

relish, *s.* gusto, *m.*; sabor, *m.*; (touch, smack) dejo, *m.*; condimento, *m.*; apetito, *m.*, gana, *f.* *v.t.* gustar de; comer con apetito; saborear, paladear; (*fig.*) seducir, atraer, gustar. *v.i.* tener gusto (de). **I do not much r. the idea,** No me seduce la idea

relishing, *s.* saboreo, *m.*; (enjoyment) goce, *m.*, fruición, *f.*; consideración, *f.*

relive, *v.t.* vivir de nuevo, volver a vivir

reload, *v.t.* recargar

reluctance, *s.* repugnancia, desgana, *f.* **with r.,** a regañadientes, de mala gana

reluctant, *a.* poco dispuesto (a), que tiene repugnancia a (hacer algo), sin gana; (forced) forzado artificial; (hesitating) vacilante

reluctantly, *adv.* de mala gana, con repugnancia, a disgusto

rely, *v.i.* contar (con), confiar (en)

remain, *v.i.* quedar; permanecer; (be left over) sobrar; continuar. **I r. yours faithfully . . .,** (in a letter) Queda de Vd. su att. s.s. . . . **It remains to be written,** Queda por escribir

remainder, *s.* resto, *m.*; restos, *m. pl.*, sobras, *f. pl.*; residuo (also *math.*), *m.* **The r.** (persons) **went away,** Los demás se marcharon

remaining, *pres. part.* and *a.* que queda; sobrante

remains, *s. pl.* restos, *m. pl.*; sobras, *f. pl.*, desperdicios, *m. pl.*; ruinas, *f. pl.*

remake, *v.t.* rehacer; reformar

remand, *v.t.* (*law*) reencarcelar. *s.* (*law*) reencarcelamiento, *m.*

remark, *s.* observación, *f.*; nota, *f.*; comentario, *m.* *v.t.* and *v.i.* observar; notar. **to r. on,** comentar, hacer una observación sobre

remarkable, *a.* notable, singular, extraordinario

remarkableness, *s.* singularidad, *f.*, lo extraordinario

remarkably, *adv.* singularmente

remarriage, *s.* segundas nupcias, *f. pl.*, segundo casamiento, *m.*

remarry, *v.t.* volver a casar (a). *v.i.* casarse en segundas nupcias; volver a casarse

remediable, *a.* remediable

remedial, *a.* remediador; curativo, terapéutico

remedy, *s.* remedio, *m.*; recurso, *m.* *v.t.* remediar; curar

remember, *v.t.* recordar; tener presente; acordarse de. *v.i.* acordarse; no olvidarse. **R. me to your mother,** Dale recuerdos míos a tu madre. **If I r. rightly . . .,** Si bien me acuerdo . . . **And r. that I shall do no more! ¡**Y no olvides que no haré más!

remembrance, *s.* recuerdo, *m.*; memoria, *f.*; *pl.* **remembrances,** recuerdos, *m. pl.*

remind, *v.t.* recordar

reminder, *s.* recuerdo, *m.*; (warning) advertencia, *f.* **a gentle r.,** una indirecta, una insinuación

reminisce, *v.i.* (*fam.*) recordar viejas historias

reminiscence, *s.* reminiscencia, *f.*

reminiscent, *a.* evocador, que recuerda; de reminiscencia; que piensa en el pasado. **to be r. of,** recordar; (*fam.*) oler a

reminiscently, *adv.* evocadoramente, como si recordara

remiss, *a.* negligente, descuidado

remission, *s.* remisión, *f.*

remissly, *adv.* negligentemente

remissness, *s.* negligencia, *f.*, descuido, *m.*

remit, *v.t.* remitir; (*com.*) remesar, enviar. *v.i.* (pay) pagar

remittance, *s.* remesa, *f.*, envío, *m.*

remitter, *s.* remitente, *m.* and *f.*

remnant, *s.* resto, *m.*; (of fabric) retal, retazo, *m.*; (relic) vestigio, *m.*, reliquia, *f.* **r. sale,** saldo, *m.*

remodel, *v.t.* rehacer; reformar; modelar de nuevo; (a play, etc.) refundir

remodelling, *s.* reformación, *f.*; (of a play, etc.) refundición, *f.*

remonstrance, *s.* protesta, *f.*; reconvención, *f.*

remonstrate, *v.i.* protestar, objetar. **to r. with,** reprochar, reconvenir

remora, *s.* (*icht.*) rémora, *f.*

remorse, *s.* remordimiento, *m.*

remorseful, *a.* lleno de remordimientos; penitente, arrepentido

remorsefully, *adv.* con remordimiento

remorseless, *a.* sin conciencia, sin remordimientos; despiadado, inflexible

remorselessness, *s.* inexorabilidad, crueldad, dureza, *f.*

remote, *a.* distante, lejano; remoto; aislado; ajeno; (slight) leve, vago. **r. control,** mando a distancia, *m.*

remotely, *adv.* remotamente

remoteness, *s.* distancia, *f.*; aislamiento, *m.*; alejamiento, *m.*; (vagueness) vaguedad, *f.*

remount, *v.t.* subir de nuevo, montar de nuevo; (*mil.*) remontar. *v.i.* (go back to) remontar (a), derivarse (de). *s.* (*mil.*) remonta, *f.*

removable, *a.* que puede quitarse; (of collars, etc.) de quita y pon; transportable; (of officials, etc.) amovible

removal, s. acción de quitar o levantar, f.; sacamiento, m.; separación, f.; eliminación, f.; alejamiento, m.; traslado, m.; (from office, etc.) deposición, f.; supresión, f.; asesinato, m. **r. van**, carro de mudanzas, m.

remove, v.t. quitar; retirar; levantar; sacar; apartar; separar; eliminar; trasladar; (from office) destituir; suprimir; asesinar. v.i. trasladarse. s. grado, m.; distancia, f.; (departure) partida, f. **to r. oneself**, quitarse de en medio. **to r. one's hat**, descubrirse

remunerate, v.t. remunerar

remuneration, s. remuneración, f.

remunerative, a. remunerador

renaissance, s. renacimiento, m. a. renacentista

renal, a. renal

rename, v.t. poner otro nombre (a)

renascent, a. renaciente, que renace

rend, v.t. desgarrar, rasgar; (fig.) lacerar; (split) hender; (fig.) dividir. **to r. from**, arrancar (a). **to r. the air**, (with cries, etc.) llenar el aire

render, v.t. (return) devolver; dar; rendir; (make) hacer; (help, service) prestar; interpretar; (translate) traducir; (fat) derretir y clarificar

rendering, s. versión, f.; interpretación, f.

rendezvous, s. cita, f.; lugar de cita, m.; reunión, f. v.i. reunirse

rending, s. desgarro, m.; hendimiento, m.

renegade, a. renegado. s. renegado (-da)

renew, v.t. renovar; (resume) reanudar; (a lease, etc.) prorrogar

renewable, a. renovable

renewal, s. renovación, f.; (resumption) reanudación, f.; (of a lease, etc.) prorrogación, f.

renewed, a. renovado; nuevo

rennet, s. cuajo, m.

renounce, v.t. renunciar; (a throne) abdicar; renegar (de), repudiar; abandonar. v.i. (law) desistir; (cards) renunciar

renouncement, s. renuncia, f.; (of a throne) abdicación, f.; repudiación, f.

renovate, v.t. renovar; limpiar; restaurar

renovation, s. renovación, f.; limpiadura, f.; restauración, f.

renovator, s. renovador (-ra)

renown, s. renombre, m.; fama, f.

renowned, a. renombrado, famoso

rent, s. (tear) rasgadura, f.; desgarro, m.; abertura, f.; raja, hendedura, f.; (discord) división, f.; (hire) alquiler, m.; arrendamiento, m. v.t. arrendar, alquilar. **r.-free**, sin pagar alquiler

rentable, a. alquilable, arrendable

rental. See rent

renter, s. arrendador (-ra)

rentier, s. rentista, m. and f.

renting, s. alquiler, arrendamiento, m.

renumber, v.t. numerar de nuevo

renunciation, s. renunciación, renuncia, f.

reoccupy, v.t. volver a ocupar, ocupar otra vez

reopen, v.t. abrir de nuevo, volver a abrir. v.i. abrirse nuevamente, abrirse otra vez

reopening, s. reapertura, f.

reorder, v.t. ordenar de nuevo; (com.) volver a pedir. s. (com.) nuevo pedido, m.

reorganization, s. reorganización, f.

reorganize, v.t. reorganizar

reorganizing, a. reorganizador

rep, s. (fabric) reps, m.

repack, v.t. reembalar; reenvasar; volver a hacer (una maleta)

repaint, v.t. pintar de nuevo

repainting, s. nueva pintura, f.

repair, v.t. componer, remendar; reparar; restaurar; rehacer. v.i. (with to) dirigirse a, ir a; acudir a. s. reparación, f.; compostura, f.; restauración, f. **to keep in r.**, conservar en buen estado

repairable, a. que se puede componer

repairer, s. componedor (-ra); restaurador (-ra)

repairing, a. reparador

reparable, a. reparable; remediable

reparation, s. reparación, f.

repartee, s. respuestas, agudezas, f. pl.; (fam.) dimes y diretes, m. pl.

repast, s. comida, f.; (light) colación, f.

repatriate, v.t. repatriar

repatriation, s. repatriación, f.

repay, v.t. reembolsar; recompensar, pagar; pagar en la misma moneda. v.i. pagar. It well repays a visit, Vale la pena de visitarse

repayable, a. reembolsable

repayment, s. reembolso, m.; pago, retorno, m.

repeal, s. abrogación, revocación, f. v.t. abrogar, rescindir, revocar

repeat, v.t. repetir; reiterar; (renew) renovar; duplicar. s. repetición, f.

repeated, a. reiterado; redoblado

repeatedly, adv. reiteradamente, repetidamente

repeater, s. repetidor (-ra); reloj de repetición, m.; arma de repetición, f.

repel, v.t. repeler; ahuyentar; (spurn) rechazar; (phys.) resistir; repugnar

repellent, a. repulsivo

repent, v.t. arrepentirse de. v.i. arrepentirse

repentance, s. arrepentimiento, m., penitencia, f.

repentant, a. arrepentido, penitente, contrito

repentantly, adv. arrepentidamente, con contrición

repeople, v.t. repoblar

repeopling, s. repoblación, f.

repercuss, v.t. repercutir (en)

repercussion, s. repercusión, f.

repercussive, a. repercusivo

repertory, s. repertorio, m.

repetition, s. repetición, f.; recitación, f.

repetitive, a. iterativo

repine, v.i. afligirse (de); quejarse (de); padecer nostalgia

repining, s. pesares, m. pl.; quejas, f. pl., descontento, m.; nostalgia, f.

replace, v.t. (put back) reponer, colocar de nuevo; restituir, devolver; (renew) renovar; (in a post, etc.) reemplazar, substituir

replaceable, a. restituible; renovable; reemplazable

replacement, s. reposición, f.; restitución, devolución, f.; renovación, f.; reemplazo, m.

replant, v.t. replantar

replanting, s. replantación, f.

replenish, v.t. rellenar

replenishment, s. relleno, m.

replete, a. repleto

repletion, s. repleción, f.

replica, s. réplica, f.

reply, s. respuesta, contestación, f. v.i. responder, contestar. Awaiting your r., En espera de sus noticias. in his r., en su respuesta

repolish, v.t. repulir

repopulate, v.t. repoblar

repopulation, s. repoblación, f.

report, s. (rumour) voz, f., rumor, m.; (reputation) fama, f.; (news) noticia, f.; (journalistic) reportaje, m.; (mil., nav. and from school) parte, f.; (weather) boletín, m.; (proceedings) actas, f. pl.; (statement) informe, m.; relación, f.; (of a gun, etc.) detonación, f.; explosión, f. v.t. dar cuenta de, relatar; informar; (measure) registrar; (mil., nav.) dar parte de; comunicar; (journalistic) hacer un reportaje de; (transcribe) transcribir; (accuse) denunciar; quejarse de. v.i. presentar informe; ser reportero; (present oneself) presentarse, comparecer. It is reported that . . ., Se dice que . . .

reporter, s. reportero (-ra); (law) relator, m.

reporting, s. reporterismo, m.

repose, s. reposo, m.; quietud, f.; tranquilidad, serenidad, f. v.t. reposar, descansar; reclinar; (place) poner. v.i. reposar; tener confianza (en); basarse (en)

repository, s. repositorio, depósito, m.; almacén, m.; (furniture) guardamuebles. m.; (person) depositario (-ia)

repoussé (work), s. repujado, m. to work in r., repujar

reprehend, v.t. reprender, reprobar

reprehensible, a. reprensible

reprehension, s. reprensión, f.

represent, v.t. representar; significar

representation, s. representación, f.

representational, *a.* (*art*) realista

representative, *a.* que representa; representativo. *s.* representante, *m.* and *f.*

repress, *v.t.* reprimir

repression, *s.* represión, *f.*

repressive, *a.* represivo

reprieve, *v.t.* (*law*) aplazar la ejecución (de); (*fig.*) dar una tregua (a)

reprimand, *s.* reprimenda, *f.* *v.t.* reprender

reprint, *s.* reimpresión, *f.* *v.t.* reimprimir

reprinting, *s.* reimpresión, *f.*

reprisal, *s.* represalia, *f.* **to take reprisals**, tomar represalias

reproach, *s.* reproche, *m.*; censura, *f.*; (shame) vergüenza, *f.* *v.t.* reprochar; censurar, echar en cara, afear

reproachful, *a.* severo; lleno de reproches; de censura; (shameful) vergonzoso

reproachfully, *adv.* con reprobación, con reprensión, severamente

reproachfulness, *s.* severidad, *f.* **the r. of my gaze**, mi mirada llena de reproches

reprobate, *s.* réprobo (-ba)

reprobation, *s.* reprobación, *f.*

reproduce, *v.t.* reproducir. *v.i.* reproducirse

reproducible, *a.* que puede reproducirse

reproduction, *s.* reproducción, *f.*

reproductive, *a.* reproductor; de reproducción

reproof, *s.* reconvención, *f.*

reprove, *v.t.* censurar, culpar; reprender

reprovingly. See **rebukingly**

reptile, *a.* and *s.* reptil (*m*)

republic, *s.* república, *f.* **the r. of letters**, la república de las letras

republican, *a.* and *s.* republicano (-na)

republicanism, *s.* republicanismo, *m.*

republish, *v.t.* publicar de nuevo; reimprimir

repudiate, *v.t.* repudiar; negar, rechazar

repudiation, *s.* repudiación, *f.*

repugnance, *s.* repugnancia, *f.*

repugnant, *a.* repugnante; contrario; opuesto. **to be r. to**, repugnar (a)

repulse, *v.t.* repulsar, repeler; rebatir, refutar; (refuse) rechazar. *s.* repulsa, *f.*; refutación, *f.*; rechazo, *m.*

repulsion, *s.* (*phys.*) repulsión, *f.*; repugnancia, aversión, *f.*

repulsive, *a.* repulsivo, repugnante, repelente

repulsiveness, *s.* carácter repulsivo, *m.*; aspecto repugnante, *m.*

repurchase, *v.t.* recomprar

reputable, *a.* honrado, respetable, formal

reputation, *s.* reputación, *f.*; fama, *f.*, renombre, *m.* **to have the r. of**, ser reputado como, pasar por

reputed, *a.* supuesto; (with father) putativo

reputedly, *adv.* según la opinión común, según dice la gente

request, *s.* ruego, *m.*, petición, *f.*; instancia, *f.*; solicitud, *f.*; (*com.*) demanda, *f.* *v.t.* pedir, rogar; suplicar; solicitar. **in r.**, en boga; solicitado; en demanda. **on r.**, a solicitud. **r. stop**, (for buses) parada discrecional, *f.*

requiem, *s.* réquiem, *m.* **R. Mass**, misa de difuntos, *f.*

require, *v.t.* exigir, requerir; necesitar; (wish) desear; invitar. *v.i.* ser necesario

required, *a.* necesario; obligatorio

requirement, *s.* deseo, *m.*; requisito, *m.*; formalidad, *f.*; estipulación, *f.*; necesidad, *f.*

requisite, *s.* requisito, *m.* *a.* necesario, requisito, preciso. **to be r.**, ser necesario, ser menester, hacer falta

requisition, *v.t.* (*mil.*) requisar

requisitioning, *s.* requisa, *f.*

requital, *s.* recompensa, *f.*; compensación, satisfacción, *f.*

requite, *v.t.* pagar, recompensar; (affection) corresponder a

reread, *v.t.* releer

reredos, *s.* retablo, *m.*

resale, *s.* reventa, *f.*

rescind, *v.t.* rescindir

rescission, *s.* rescisión, *f.*

rescue, *v.t.* salvar; librar; (*mil.*) rescatar. *s.* socorro, *m.*; salvamento, *m.*; (*mil.*) rescate, *m.* **to go to the r. of**, ir al socorro de.

r. party, expedición de salvamento, *f.*; (*mil.*) expedición de rescate, *f.*

rescuer, *s.* salvador (-ra)

reseal, *v.t.* resellar

research, *s.* investigación, *f. v.t.* investigar

researcher, *s.* investigador (-ra)

reseat, *v.t.* sentar de nuevo

resection, *s.* resección, *f.*

reseda, *s.* (*bot.*) reseda, *f.*

resell, *v.t.* revender

resemblance, *s.* parecido, *m.*, semejanza, *f.* **The two sisters bear a strong r. to each other,** Las dos hermanas se parecen mucho

resemble, *v.t.* parecerse (a). **Mary doesn't r. her mother,** María no se parece a su madre

resent, *v.t.* resentirse de; ofenderse por, indignarse por; tomar a mal

resentful, *a.* resentido; ofendido, indignado, agraviado; vengativo

resentfully, *adv.* con resentimiento; con indignación

resentment, *s.* resentimiento, *m.*

reservation, *s.* reservación, *f.*; reserva, *f.* (also *ecc. law*); territorio reservado, *m.*; santuario, *m.* **mental r.,** reserva mental, *f.*

reserve, *s.* reserva, *f.* (also *mil., nav.*). *v.t.* reservar (also *ecc. law*). *a.* de reserva. **without r.,** sin reserva

reserved, *a.* reservado; callado, taciturno. **r. compartment,** reservado, *m.* **r. list,** (*mil., nav.*) sección de reserva, *f.*

reservedly, *adv.* con reserva

reservist, *s.* reservista, *m.*

reservoir, *s.* depósito, *m.*; cisterna, *f.*, aljibe, tanque, *m.*

reset, *v.t.* montar de nuevo

resettle, *v.t.* repoblar; rehabilitar; (a dispute) llegar a un nuevo acuerdo sobre

resettlement, *s.* repoblación, *f.*; rehabilitación, *f.*; (of a dispute) nuevo acuerdo, *m.*

reshape, *v.t.* reformar

reship, *v.t.* reembarcar

reshipment, *s.* reembarque, *m.*

reshuffle, *v.t.* volver a barajar; (*fig.*) cambiar

reside, *v.i.* residir, habitar; vivir

residence, *s.* residencia, *f.*; permanencia, estada, *f.*; domicilio, *m.*

resident, *a.* residente; (of a servant) que duerme en casa; interno. *s.* residente, *m.* and *f.*; (diplomacy) residente, *m.*

residential, *a.* residencial

residuary, *a.* restante, residual. **r. legatee,** heredero (-ra) universal

residue, *s.* resto, *m.*; (*law, chem.*) residuo, *m.*

residuum, *s.* residuo, *m.*

resign, *v.t.* renunciar (a); ceder; resignar. *v.i.* dimitir. **to r. oneself,** resignarse

resignation, *s.* resignación, *f.*; (from a post) dimisión, *f.* **to send in one's r.,** dimitir

resigned, *a.* resignado

resignedly, *adv.* con resignación

resilience, *s.* elasticidad, *f.*

resilient, *a.* elástico

resin, *s.* resina, *f.*; (solid, for violin bows, etc.) colofonia, *f.*

resinous, *a.* resinoso

resist, *v.t.* and *v.i.* (bear) aguantar; (impede) impedir; (repel, ward off) resistir; rechazar; hacer frente (a); oponerse (a); negarse (a)

resistance, *s.* resistencia, *f.*; aguante, *m.*, tenacidad, *f.*; oposición, *f.*; repugnancia, *f.* **passive r.,** resistencia pasiva, *f.* **r. coil,** (*elec.*) resistencia, *f.* **R. Movement,** movimiento de resistencia, *m.*

resistant, *a.* resistente

resister, *s.* el, *m.* (*f.* la) que resiste

resole, *v.t.* remontar

resoling, *s.* remonta, *f.*

resolute, *a.* resuelto, decidido

resolutely, *adv.* resueltamente

resolution, *s.* resolución, *f.*; (proposal placed before a legislative body, etc.) proposición, *f.*; propósito, *m.*

resolve, *v.t.* resolver. *v.i.* resolverse. *s.* propósito, *m.*; (of character) resolución, firmeza, *f.*

resonance, *s.* resonancia, *f.*; sonoridad, *f.*

resonant, *a.* resonante; reverberante, sonoro

resort, *s.* recurso, *m.*; punto de reunión, *m.*; (frequentation) fre-

cuentación, *f.*; (gathering) concurrencia, *f.*; reunión, *f. v.i.*
acudir (a), acogerse (a); hacer uso
(de); pasar (a); (frequent) frecuentar, concurrir. **health r.**,
balneario, *m.* **holiday r.**, playa
de verano, *f.*; pueblo de veraneo,
m. **in the last r.**, en último
recurso

resound, *v.i.* resonar, retumbar,
retronar; (*fig.*) tener fama, ser
celebrado. *v.t.* hacer reverberar;
(*fig.*) celebrar

resounding, *a.* retumbante, resonante

resource, *s.* recurso, *m.*; (of
character) inventiva, *f.*; *pl.*
resources: recursos, fondos, *m.*
pl.

resourceful, *a.* ingenioso

resourcefully, *adv.* ingeniosamente

resourcefulness, *s.* ingeniosidad,
f.

respect, *s.* respeto, *m.*; consideración, *f.*; (reference, regard) respecto, *m.*; *pl.* **respects,** (greetings) saludos, *m. pl.*; homenaje,
m. v.t. respetar; honrar; (concern, regard) concernir, tocar
(a). **in other respects,** por lo
demás. **in r. of,** tocante a,
respecto a. **in some respects,**
desde algunos puntos de vista.
out of r. for, por consideración a

respectability, *s.* respetabilidad, *f.*

respectable, *a.* respetable; pasable; considerable

respectably, *adv.* respetablemente

respected, *a.* and *part.* respetado;
apreciado, estimado; digno de
respeto, honrado

respecter, *s.* el, *m.* (*f.* la) que
respeta

respectful, *a.* respetuoso

respectfully, *adv.* respetuosamente

respectfulness, *s.* aire respetuoso,
m.; conducta respetuosa, *f.*

respecting, *prep.* con respecto a,
en cuanto a, tocante a; a propósito de

respective, *a.* respectivo; relativo

respectively, *adv.* respectivamente

respirable, *a.* respirable

respiration, *s.* respiración, *f.*

respirator, *s.* respirador, *m.*

respiratory, *a.* respiratorio

respire, *v.t.* and *v.i.* respirar;
exhalar; descansar

respite, *s.* tregua, pausa, *f.*;
respiro, *m.*; (law) espera, *f. v.t.*
dar tregua (a); (postpone) aplazar; (relieve) aliviar

resplendence, *s.* resplandor, *m.*,
refulgencia, *f.*, esplendor, fulgor,
m.

resplendent, *a.* resplandeciente,
refulgente, relumbrante. **He
was r. in a new uniform,** Lucía
(or Ostentaba) un nuevo uniforme. **to be r.,** ser resplandeciente; relumbrar, refulgir

resplendently, *adv.* esplendorosamente

respond, *v.i.* responder (also
ecc.); contestar; (obey) obedecer;
reaccionar

respondent, *s.* (in a suit) demandado (-da)

response, *s.* respuesta, *f.*; (*ecc.*)
responso, *m.*

responsibility, *s.* responsabilidad, *f.*

responsible, *a.* responsable

responsive, *a.* simpático; sensible, sensitivo

responsiveness, *s.* simpatía, *f.*;
sensibilidad, *f.*

rest, *s.* descanso, *m.*; reposo, *m.*;
(the grave) última morada, *f.*;
tranquilidad, paz, *f.*; inacción, *f.*;
(prop) soporte, apoyo, *m.*; base,
f.; (for a lance) ristre, *m.*; (for a
rifle) apoyo, *m.*; (*mus.*) silencio,
m., pausa, *f.*; (in verse) cesura, *f.*
in r., en ristre. **the r.,** el resto;
los demás, los otros. **to set at
r.,** calmar, tranquilizar; (remove) quitar. **r.-cure,** cura de
reposo, *f.* **r.-house,** hospedería,
f.; refugio, *m.* **r.-room,** sala de
descanso, *f.*

rest, *v.i.* reposar, descansar; (lie
down) acostarse, echarse; (stop)
cesar, parar; estar en paz;
apoyarse (en); descansar (sobre);
posar; depender (de); (remain)
quedar. *v.t.* descansar; dar un
descanso (a); (lean) apoyar;
basar (en). **It rests with them,**
Depende de ellos. **May he r. in
peace!** ¡Quien en paz descanse!
to r. assured, estar seguro.
to r. on one's oars, cesar de
remar; descansar

restate, v.t. repetir. afirmar de nuevo

restatement, s. repetición, f.

restaurant, s. restaurante, restorán,·m. **r.-car**, coche comedor, m.

restful, a. descansado; tranquilo, sosegado

resting, s. reposo, m. **last r.-place**, última morada, f. **r.-place**, descansadero, m.; refugio, m.

restitution, s. restitución, f.

restive, a. (of a horse) repropio, ingobernable; inquieto, agitado; impaciente

restiveness, s. inquietud, agitación, f.; impaciencia, f.

restless, a. agitado; inquieto, intranquilo; turbulento; sin reposo; (wakeful) desvelado; (ceaseless) incesante. **r. night**, noche desvelada, noche intranquila, (fam.) noche toledana, f.

restlessly, adv. agitadamente; con inquietud; turbulentamente; incesantemente

restlessness, s. agitación, f.; inquietud, intranquilidad, f.; turbulencia, f.; falta de reposo, f.; (wakefulness) desvelo, m.; movimiento incesante, m.

restock, v.t. (with goods) surtir de nuevo; proveer de nuevo; restablecer; repoblar

restoration, s. restauración, f.; renovación, f.; restablecimiento, m.; (returning) restitución, f.

restorative, a. and s. restaurativo (m.)

restore, v.t. restaurar; restituir; devolver; restablecer; reponer; (repair) reformar, reparar; reconstruir; (to former rank, etc.) rehabilitar. **He restored the book to its place**, Devolvió el libro a su sitio

restorer, s. restaurador (-ra)

restrain, v.t. refrenar; reprimir; (restrict) limitar, restringir; (prevent) impedir; desviar; (detain) recluir. **to r. oneself**, contenerse

restrained, a. moderado, mesurado; sobrio; (of emotion) contenido

restraining, a. restrictivo; moderador, calmante

restraint, s. freno, m.; restricción, f.; limitación, f.; prohibición, f.; compulsión, f.; (reserve) reserva, f.; moderación, f.

restrict, v.t. restringir; limitar

restriction, s. restricción, f.; limitación, f.

restrictive, a. restrictivo

result, s. resultado, m.; consecuencia, resulta, f.; solución, f. v.i. resultar. **as the r. of**, de resultas de

resultant, a. resultante; consecuente. s. resultado, m.; (mech.) resultante, f.

resume, v.t. reasumir; (continue) reanudar, continuar; (summarize) resumir

résumé, s. resumen, m., recapitulación, f.

resummon, v.t. convocar de nuevo (a); citar de nuevo (a)

resumption, s. (renewal) reanudación, f.; reasunción, f.

resurgence, s. resurgimiento, m.

resurrect, v.t. (fam.) desenterrar; resucitar

resurrection, s. resurrección, f.

resuscitate, v.t. and v.i. resucitar

resuscitation,·s. resurrección, f.; renovación, f.; renacimiento, m.

retable, s. retablo, m.

retail, s. venta al por menor, reventa, f. adv. al por menor. v.t. (goods) vender al por menor; revender; (tell) contar; repetir. **r. trade**, comercio al por menor, m.

retailer, s. vendedor (-ra) al por menor; (of a story) narrador (-ra); el, m. (f. la) que cuenta algo

retain, v.t. retener; guardar; conservar; (a barrister) ajustar; (hire) contratar

retainer, s. (dependent) criado, dependiente, m.; partidario, adherente, m.; (fee) honorario, m.; pl. **retainers**, séquito, m., adherentes, m. pl., gente, f.

retake, v.t. volver a tomar; reconquistar

retaking, s. reconquista, f.

retaliate, v.i. vengarse de, desquitarse de. v.t. vengarse, tomar represalias

retaliation, s. represalias, f. pl.; desquite, m., satisfacción, f. **law of r.**, talión, m.

retaliatory, a. de represalias; de desquite

retard, v.t. retardar

retardment, s. retardación, f., retardo, m.

retch, v.i. tener náuseas, procurár vomitar

retching, s. náusea, basca, f.

retell, v.t. repetir, volver a contar

retention, s. retención, f.; conservación, f.

retentive, a. retentivo

retentiveness, s. poder de retención, m.; (memory) retentiva, f.

reticence, s. reticencia, reserva, f.

reticent, a. reservado, inexpresivo, taciturno

reticle, s. (phys.) retículo, m.

reticulate, a. reticular

reticule, s. ridículo, m.

reticulum, s. retículo, m.

retina, s. retina, f.

retinue, s. séquito, acompañamiento, m., comitiva, f.

retire, v.i. retirarse; (to bed) recogerse, acostarse; (from a post) jubilarse. v.t. retirar; jubilar. **to r. from a post,** (mil.) rendir el puesto

retired, a. retirado; (remote) apartado, aislado; (hidden) escondido; (former) antiguo; (from employment, etc.) jubilado; (of an officer) retirado. **to place on the r. list,** jubilar; (mil., nav.) dar el retiro a

retirement, s. retirada, f.; (solitude) apartamiento, aislamiento, m.; retiro, m.; (superannuation) jubilación, f.

retiring, a. que se retira; (from a post) dimitente; (with pension, etc.) de jubilación; (reserved) reservado; modesto

retort, v.i. replicar. v.t. retorcer; devolver (una acusación, etc.). s. réplica, f.; contestación, f.; (chem.) retorta, f.

retouch, v.t. retocar

retrace, v.t. volver a trazar; volver a andar (un camino); (one's steps) volver sobre sus pasos, volver atrás; (in memory) rememorar, recordar; buscar el origen (de); (recount) narrar, contar

retract, v.t. retractar, retirar; (draw back) retraer. v.i. retractarse

retractation, s. retractación, recantación, f.; (drawing back) retracción, f.

retractile, a. retráctil

retraction, s. retracción, f.

retranslate, v.t. hacer una nueva traducción (de)

retransmission, s. retransmisión, f.

retread, v.t. pisar de nuevo; (tyres) recauchetear

retreat, s. retirada, f.; (mil. signal) retreta, f.; (refuge and ecc.) retiro, m. v.i. retirarse; retroceder; refugiarse

retreating, a. que se retira; que retrocede; (mil.) que se bate en retirada

retrench, v.t. reducir; disminuir; v.i. economizar, hacer economías

retrenchment, s. disminución, reducción, f.; economías, f. pl.

retrial, s. (of a person) nuevo proceso, m.; (of a case) revisión, f.

retribution, s. retribución, f.; justo castigo, m., pena merecida, f.

retrievable, a. recuperable, que puede recobrarse; reparable

retrieval, s. recuperación, f.; reparación, f.; (of game) cobra, f.; (of one's character) rehabilitación, f.

retrieve, v.t. (game, of dogs) cobrar; (regain) recobrar, recuperar; restaurar; reparar; restablecer; (one's character) rehabilitar. v.i. cobrar la caza

retriever, s. (dog) perdiguero (-ra)

retroactive, a. retroactivo

retrocede, v.i. retroceder

retrograde, a. retrógrado

retrogression, s. retrogradación, regresión, f.; (med.) retroceso, m.

retrogressive, a. retrógrado

retrospect, s. mirada retrospectiva, f., examen del pasado, m. **in r.,** retrospectivamente

retrospection, s. retrospección, f.

retrospective, a. retrospectivo

retrospectively, adv. retrospectivamente

retroversion, s. retroversión, f.

retry, v.t. (a case) rever; (a person) procesar de nuevo

return, v.i. regresar; volver; reaparecer; presentarse de nuevo; (law) revertir; (answer) contestar, responder. v.t. (give back or put back) devolver; (a ball) restar; (a kindness, visit) pagar; restituir; (reciprocate) corresponder (a); recompensar; contestar (a); dar; rendir; (yield) producir; (a verdict) fallar, pronunciar; (report) dar parte de; anunciar; (exchange) cambiar; (elect) elegir. *s.* regreso, *m.*; vuelta, *f.*; (giving or putting back) devolución, *f.*; pago, *m.*; restitución, *f.*; correspondencia, *f.*; recompensa, *f.*; (reply) respuesta, *f.*; (reappearance) reaparición, *f.*; reinstalación, *f.*; repetición, *f.*; (gain) ganancia, *f.*, provecho, *m.*; rendimiento, *m.*; (exchange) cambio, *m.*; (report) parte oficial, *f.*; informe, *m.*; lista, *f.*; (election) elección, *f.*; *pl.* **returns,** tablas estadísticas, *f. pl.*; (of an election) resultados, *m. pl.* **Many happy returns!** ¡Feliz cumpleaños! **by r. of post,** a vuelta de correo. **on my (his, etc.) r.,** a la vuelta, cuando vuelva. **to r. like for like,** pagar en la misma moneda. **r. journey,** viaje de vuelta, *m.* **r. match,** partido de vuelta, *m.* **r. ticket,** billete de ida y vuelta, *m.*

returnable, *a.* restituible; susceptible a ser devuelto; (on approval) a prueba; (*law*) devolutivo

returning, *a.* que vuelve. *s.* See **return**

reunion, *s.* reunión, *f.*

reunite, *v.t.* reunir. *v.i.* reunirse

revaccinate, *v.t.* revacunar

revaccination, *s.* revacunación, *f.*

reveal, *v.t.* revelar; descubrir

revealer, *s.* revelador (-ra)

revealing, *a.* revelador. *s.* revelación, *f.*; descubrimiento, *m.*

reveille, *s.* (*mil.*) diana, *f.*

revel, *v.i.* divertirse; regocijarse (en), gozarse (en); entregarse (a); (carouse) ir de parranda; emborracharse. *s.* algazara, jarana, *f.*; *pl.* **revels,** fiestas, festividades, *f. pl.*

revelation, *s.* revelación, *f.*; descubrimiento, *m.*; (in the Bible) Apocalipsis, *m.*

reveller, *s.* convidado alegre, *m.*; (at night) trasnochador (-ra); (drunk) borracho (-cha); (masked) máscara, *m.* and *f.*

revelry, *s.* festividades, *f. pl.*, regocijo, *m.*; orgías, *f. pl.*

revenge, *s.* venganza, *f.* *v.t.* vengarse de; desquitarse de

revengeful, *a.* vengativo

revengefully, *adv.* vengativamente

revengefulness, *s.* deseo de venganza, *m.*; carácter vengativo, *m.*

revenger, *s.* vengador (-ra)

revenue, *s.* rentas públicas, *f. pl.*; (treasury) fisco, *m.*; (*com.*) rédito, *m.*, ingresos, *m. pl.*; beneficio, *m.* **Inland R.,** delegación de contribuciones, *f.* **r. officer,** agente fiscal, *m.*

reverberate, *v.t.* and *v.i.* (of sound) retumbar, resonar; (of light, etc.) reverberar

reverberation, *s.* (reflection) reverberación, *f.*; (of sound) retumbo, eco, *m.*

revere, *v.t.* reverenciar, venerar, honrar

reverence, *s.* reverencia, *f.* *v.t.* reverenciar

reverend, *a.* reverendo

reverent, *a.* reverente

reverently, *adv.* reverentemente, con reverencia

reverie, *s.* ensueño, *m.*

revers, *s.* (of a coat, etc.) vueltas, solapas, *f. pl.*

reversal, *s.* inversión, *f.*; (of a verdict) revocación, *f.*

reverse, *v.t.* invertir; (a steam engine) dar contra vapor (a); (a vehicle) poner en marcha atrás; (arms) llevar a la funerala; (a judgment, etc.) revocar. *v.i.* (dancing) dar vueltas al revés. *s.* lo contrario, lo opuesto; (back) dorso, revés, *m.*; (change) cambio, *m.*; (check) revés, *m.*, vicisitud, *f.*; (loss) pérdida, *f.*; (defeat) derrota, *f.*; (*mech.*) marcha atrás, *f.* *a.* inverso; contrario, opuesto. **quite the r.,** todo el contrario. **r. turn,** (of an engine) cambio de dirección, *m.*; (in dancing) vuelta al revés, *f.*

reversible, *a.* reversible

reversion, *s.* reversión, *f.*; (*biol.*) atavismo, *m.*; (of offices) futura, *f.*; (of property) reversión, *f.*

revert, *v.i.* (*law*) revertir; volver (a)

revictual, *v.t.* abastecer de nuevo

review, s. examen, análisis, m.; juicio crítico, m.; (journal and mil.) revista, s.; (criticism) revista, reseña, f.; (law) revisión, f. v.t.. examinar, analizar; (mil., etc.) pasar revista (a); revisar; repasar; (a book, etc.) escribir una revista de; (law) revisar. v.i. escribir revistas

reviewer, s. revistero (-ra), crítico, m.

revile, v.t. injuriar, maldecir, difamar

reviler, s. maldiciente, m., insultador (-ra)

reviling, s. insultos, m. pl., injurias, f. pl.

revisal, s. revisión, f.

revise, v.t. revisar; repasar; corregir; (change) cambiar

reviser, s. revisor, m.; corrector de pruebas, m.

revision, s. revisión, f.; repaso, m.; corrección de pruebas, f.

revisit, v.t. volver a visitar, visitar de nuevo

revival, s. resurgimiento, m.; renovación, f.; (awakening) despertamiento, m.; restablecimiento, m.; resurrección, f.; (of learning) renacimiento, m.; (theat.) reposición, f.; (religious) despertar religioso, m.

revive, v.i. reponerse; restablecerse; resucitar; renovarse; renacer; cobrar fuerzas; (recover consciousness) volver en sí. v.t. hacer revivir; resucitar; restablecer; renovar; restaurar; despertar; (fire, colours) avivar

reviver, s. resucitador (-ra)

revivification, s. revivificación, f.

revivify, v.t. revivificar

revocable, a. revocable

revocation, s. revocación, f.

revoke, v.t. revocar, anular, derogar; (wills) quebrantar. v.i. revocar, anular; (at cards) renunciar. s. (cards) renuncio, m.

revolt, s. rebelión, f. v.i. rebelarse, sublevarse. v.t. repugnar, indignar, dar asco (a)

revolting, a. repugnante, asqueroso; (rebellious) rebelde

revolution, s. revolución, f.; (turn) vuelta, f., giro, m.

revolutionary, a. and s. revolucionario (-ia)

revolutionize, v.t. revolucionar

revolve, v.i. dar vueltas, girar; suceder periódicamente. v.t. hacer girar; (ponder) revolver, discurrir

revolver, s. revólver, m.

revolving, a. giratorio; que vuelve; periódico. r. chair, silla giratoria, f.; r. door, puerta giratoria, f. r. stage, escenario giratorio, m.

revue, s. (theat.) revista, f.

revulsion, s. revulsión, f.

revulsive, a. (med.) revulsivo

rev.-up, v.t. (an engine) calentar

reward, s. recompensa, f.; retribución, f. v.t. recompensar; satisfacer, premiar

rewarding, a. premiador; que recompensa. s. recompensación, f.

rewrite, v.t. escribir de nuevo; volver a escribir; redactar otra vez

rhapsody, s. rapsodia, f.

Rhenish, a. renano

rheometer, s. reómetro, m.

rheostat, s. reóstato, m.

rhetoric, s. retórica, f.

rhetorical, a. retórico; declamatorio

rhetorician, s. retórico (-ca)

rheumatic, a. reumático. r. fever, reumatismo poliarticular agudo, m.

rheumatism, s. reumatismo, reuma, m.

rheumy, a. catarroso; (of the eyes) legañoso

rhinoceros, s. rinoceronte, m.

rhizome, s. rizoma, m.

Rhodian, a. and s. rodio (-ia)

rhododendron, s. rododendro, m.

rhombohedron, s. romboedro, m.

rhomboid, s. romboide, m.

rhombus, s. rombio, m.

rhubarb, s. ruibarbo, m.

rhyme, s. rima, f.; verso, m. v.i. and v.t. rimar. without r. or reason, sin ton ni son; a tontas y a locas

rhymer, s. rimador (-ra)

rhyming, a. rimador

rhythm, s. ritmo, m.

rhythmic, a. rítmico

rhythmically, adv. rítmicamente

rib, s. (anat., bot., aer., naut., arch.) costilla, f.; (of an umbrella or fan) varilla, f.; (in cloth) cordoncillo, m., lista, f.

ribald, *a.* escabroso, ribaldo, indecente

ribaldry, *s.* ribaldería, escabrosidad, indecencia, *f.*

ribbed, *a.* con costillas; (of cloth) listado, con listas

ribbon, *s.* cinta, *f.*; tira, *f.*; (tatter) jirón, *m.* **to tear to ribbons,** hacer jirones

rice, *s.* arroz, *m.* *a.* de arroz; con arroz. **r. field,** arrozal, *m.* **r.-paper,** papel de paja de arroz, *m.* **r.-pudding,** arroz con leche, *m.*

rich, *a.* rico; opulento; (happy) dichoso; (of land, etc.) fértil; abundante; (of objects) magnífico, suntuoso, hermoso; precioso; (of food) exquisito; suculento; (highly seasoned) muy sazonado; (creamy) con mucha nata; (of colours) brillante, vivo. **new r.,** ricacho (-cha). **newly-r.,** advenedizo. **to grow r.,** enriquecerse

riches, *s.* riqueza, *f.*

richly, *adv.* ricamente; abundantemente; magníficamente; bien

richness, *s.* riqueza, *f.*; opulencia, *f.*; (of land, etc.) fertilidad, *f.*; abundancia, *f.*; (of objects) magnificencia, suntuosidad, hermosura, *f.*; preciosidad, *f.*; (of food) gusto exquisito, *m.*; suculencia, *f.*; (piquancy) gusto picante, *m.*; (of colours) viveza, *f.*

rick, *s.* niara, *f.*, almiar, *m.*

rickets, *s.* raquitismo, *m.*

rickety, *a.* (*med.*) raquítico; destartalado, desvencijado; (unsteady) tambaleante; cojo

rickshaw, *s.* riksha, *m.*

ricochet, *s.* rebote, *m.* *v.i.* rebotar

rid, *v.t.* librar (de). **to get rid of,** librarse de; quitarse de encima (a); perder, quitarse; (dismiss) despedir. **to rid oneself of,** librarse de, deshacerse de

riddance, *s.* libramiento, *m.*

riddle, *s.* acertijo, *m.*; enigma, problema, *m.*; misterio, *m.*; (sieve) tamiz de alambre, *m.* *v.t.* (guess) adivinar; (sift) cribar; (with holes) acribillar

ride, *v.i.* (a horse) montar a caballo, cabalgar; pasear a caballo; (a mule, a bicycle) montar en, pasear en; (a vehicle, train) ir en; (a carriage, car) andar en, pasear en; (float) flotar; (on the wind) dejarse llevar por el viento; ser llevado por el viento; (go) ir; (come) venir; (a distance) hacer . . . a caballo, en coche, etc.; (*naut.*) estar al ancla; (*mech.*) tener juego. *v.t.* (a horse, mule, bicycle) montar; ir montado sobre; manejar; (a race) hacer; (float) flotar en; (cleave, the sea, etc.) surcar. *s.* paseo (a caballo, en bicicleta, en coche, etc.), *m.*; viaje (en un autobús, de tren, etc.), *m.*; (bridle path) camino de herradura, *m.*; cabalgata, *f.*, desfile a caballo, *m.* **a r. on horseback,** un paseo a caballo. **They gave me a r. in their car,** Me llevaron a paseo en su auto. **to r. a bicycle,** montar en bicicleta. **to r. rough-shod over,** mandar a la baqueta (a), mandar a puntapiés (a). **to r. side-saddle,** cabalgar a mujeriegas. **to r. at,** embestir con. **to r. away,** marcharse, alejarse; marcharse a caballo, etc. **to r. back,** volver; volver a caballo, en bicicleta, etc. **to r. behind,** seguir a caballo; ir inmediatamente detrás (de); (on the back seat) ocupar el asiento de atrás; (on the same animal) cabalgar en la grupa. **to r. down,** atropellar; (trample) pisotear, pasar por encima de. **to r. on,** seguir su camino. **to r. out,** salir a paseo en caballo, etc.; irse a paseo en coche, etc.; (a storm) hacer frente a, luchar con. **to r. over,** pasar por encima de; recorrer. **to r. up,** *v.i.* llegar, acercarse; (of a tie, etc.) subir. *v.t.* montar

rider, *s.* cabalgador (-ra); jinete, *m.*; persona que va en coche, etc., *f.*; (on a bicycle) ciclista, *m.* and *f.*; (on a motor-cycle) motociclista, *m.* and *f.*; (horse-breaker) domador de caballos, *m.*; (clause) añadidura, *f.*; corolario, *m.*

ridge, *s.* cumbre, cima, *f.*; (of mountains) cordillera, sierra, *f.*; (of a roof, of a nose) caballete, *m.*; (*agr.*) lomo, caballón, *m.*; (wrinkle) arruga, *f.*; (on coins)

cordoncillo, *m.* *v.t.* surcar; formar lomos (en); (wrinkle) arrugar

ridicule, *s.* ridículo, *m.* *v.t.* poner en ridículo, ridiculizar, burlarse (de), mofarse (de)

ridiculous, *a.* ridículo, absurdo

ridiculously, *adv.* absurdamente

ridiculousness, *s.* ridiculez, *f.*

riding, *a.* cabalgante; que va a caballo; montado (a, en, sobre); (*naut.*) al ancla; (in compounds) de equitación; de montar. *s.* equitación, *f.*; paseo a caballo; en bicicleta, etc.; acción de ir a caballo, etc., *f.*; (district) comarca, *f.* **r.-boots**, botas de montar, *f. pl.* **r.-habit**, traje de montar, *m.*; (woman's) amazona, *f.* **r.-master**, profesor de equitación, *m.* **r.-saddle**, silla de montar, *f.* **r.-school**, escuela de equitación, *f.*

rife, *a.* común; corriente; frecuente; prevalente; abundante; general. **r. with**, abundante en; lleno de

Riffian, *a.* and *s.* rifeño (-ña)

riff-raff, *s.* desperdicios, *m. pl.*; (rabble) gentuza, canalla, *f.*

rifle, *s.* rifle, fusil rayado, *m.* *v.t.* robar; (a suitcase, etc.) desvalijar; (a gun) rayar. **r.-range**, campo de tiro, *m.* **r.-sling**, portafusil, *m.* **r.-shot**, fusilazo, *m.*

rifleman, *s.* fusilero, *m.*

rifler, *s.* saqueador (-ra)

rifling, *s.* (robbing) saqueo, robo, *m.*; (of a suitcase, etc.) desvalijamiento, *m.*

rift, *s.* hendedura, abertura, *f.*; grieta, *f.*

rig, *s.* (*naut.*) aparejo, *m.*; (*fam.*) atavío, *m.* *v.t.* (a ship) aparejar; equipar; (elections) falsificar. **to rig out**, proveer de; equipar con; ataviar. **to rig up**, arreglar; armar, construir

rigadoon, *s.* rigadón, *m.*

rigging, *s.* (of a ship) aparejo, *m.*

right, *a.* recto; correcto; conveniente; debido; apropiado; exacto; (opposite of left hand) derecho; (straight) directo; en línea recta; razonable; (true) verdadero, genuino, legítimo; (just) justo; (prudent) prudente; (in health) sano. **All r.!** ¡Está bien! **I feel all r.**, Me siento

perfectamente bien, Estoy bien. **He is the r. man for the job**, Él es el hombre que hace falta para el puesto. **It is the r. word**, Es la palabra apropiada. **on the r.**, a la derecha. **to be r.**, (of persons) tener razón. **to make r.**, poner en orden; arreglar. **r.-angle**, ángulo recto, *m.* **r.-angled**, rectangular. **r.-angled triangle**, triángulo rectángulo, *m.* **r. hand**, *s.* (mano) derecha, diestra, *f.*; derecha, *f.*; (person) brazo derecho, *m.* *a.* de la mano derecha; de la derecha; a la derecha. **r.-handed**, derecho; diestro, hábil. **r. mind**, entero juicio, *m.* **r.-minded**, juicioso, prudente; honrado. **r.-of-way**, derecho a la vía, *m.*

right, *adv.* directamente; inmediatamente; derechamente; correctamente; debidamente; exactamente; bien; (quite, thoroughly) completamente; honradamente; (very) muy. **r. on**, adelante; en frente. **R. about face!** ¡Media vuelta a la derecha! **r. at the bottom**, al fondo; al final; el último (de la clase, etc.). **r. at the end of his speech**, al fin de su discurso. **r. away**, en seguida, inmediatamente

right, *s.* razón, *f.*; verdad, *f.*; justicia, *f.*; (good) bien, *m.*; derecho, *m.*; (not left side) derecha, *f.*; (of political parties) derechas, *f. pl.* **r. and wrong**, el bien y el mal. **All rights reserved**, Derechos reservados. **by rights**, por derecho. **It is on the r.**, Está a la derecha. **to exercise one's r.**, usar de su derecho. **r. of way**, derecho de paso, *m.* **to be in the r.**, tener razón; estar en su derecho

right, *v.t.* enderezar; rectificar; corregir; poner en orden; (*naut.*) enderezar; hacer justicia (a). **to r. wrongs**, deshacer agravios

righteous, *a.* recto, virtuoso, justo; justificado

righteously, *adv.* virtuosamente; justamente

righteousness, *s.* rectitud, integridad, virtud, *f.*; justicia, *f.*

rightful, *a.* justo; legítimo; verdadero

rightfully, *adv.* justamente; legítimamente; verdaderamente

rightfulness, *s.* justicia, *f.*; legitimidad, *f.*; verdad, *f.*

rightly, *adv.* justamente; debidamente; correctamente; bien. **r. or wrongly,** mal que bien

rightness, *s.* rectitud; *f.*; derechura, *f.*; justicia, *f.*; exactitud, *f.*

rigid, *a.* rígido; inflexible; severo, riguroso

rigidity, *s.* rigidez, *f.*; inflexibilidad, *f.*; severidad, *f.*

rigidly, *adv.* rígidamente

rigmarole, *s.* monserga, *f.*, galimatías, *m.*, jerigonza, *f.*

rigor, *s.* rigor, *m.*

rigorous, *a.* riguroso

rigorously, *adv.* rigurosamente

rigour, *s.* rigor, *m.*

rile, *v.t.* (*fam.*) irritar, sacar de tino (a)

rill, *s.* riachuelo, arroyuelo, *m.*

rim, *s.* borde, *m.*; orilla, *f.*; (of a wheel) llanta, *f.*, aro, *m.*

rime, *s.* escarcha, *f.* *v.t.* cubrir con escarcha

rind, *s.* (of fruit) cáscara, corteza, *f.*; (of cheese) costra, *f.*; (of bacon) piel, *f.*

ring, *s.* círculo, *m.*; (round the eyes) ojera, *f.*; (for curtains, etc.) anilla, *f.*; (for the finger) anillo, *m.*, sortija, *f.*; (for children's games, etc.) corro, *m.*; (for the ears) arete, *m.*; (of smoke and for the nose) anillo, *m.*; (for hitching, etc.) argolla, *f.*; (for boxing) cuadrilátero, *m.*; (on a racecourse) picadero, *m.*; (at a circus, bull-fight) ruedo, redondel, *m.*; (*fig.*) arena, *f.*; (group) camarilla, *f.*, grupo, *m.*; (metallic sound) sonido metálico, *m.*; resonancia, *f.*; (tinkle) tintín, *m.*; (of a bell) repique, tañido, son (de la campana), *m.*; (of bells) juego de campanas, *m.*; (of laughter, etc.) ruido, *m.*; (of truth, etc.) apariencia, *f.* **r.-bolt,** (*naut.*) cáncamo, *m.* **r.-finger,** dedo anular, *m.* **r.-master,** director de circo, *m.*

ring, *v.t.* (surround) cercar, rodear; (a bull, etc.) poner un anillo (a); (sound) hacer sonar; sonar; (a door bell, etc.) tocar, apretar; (bells) echar a vuelo; (announce by pealing the bells)

anunciar, proclamar; sonar, tañer. *v.i.* (of bells) sonar; (re-echo) resonar; (of the ears) zumbar; (tinkle) tintinar. **to r. the bell,** tocar la campana; tocar el timbre. **to r. off,** colgar el teléfono. **to r. up,** llamar por teléfono, telefonear

ringing, *s.* acción de tocar las campanas o el timbre, *f.*; toque, *m.*; repique, *m.*; campanilleo, *m.*; (in the ears) zumbido, *m.* *a.* resonante, sonoro. **the r. of the bells,** el son de las campanas

ringleader, *s.* cabecilla, *m.*

ringlet, *s.* rizo, bucle, *m.*

ringworm, *s.* tiña, *f.*

rink, *s.* pista, *f.* **skating-r.,** sala de patinar, *f.*; pista de patinar, *f.*

rinse, *s.* enjuague, *m.*; enjuagadura, *f.*; (of clothes) aclarado, *m.* *v.t.* enjuagar; (clothes) aclarar; lavar

rinsing, *s.* See **rinse**; *pl.* **rinsings,** lavazas, *f. pl. a.* de aclarar

riot, *s.* motín, *m.*; tumulto, *m.*; desorden, *m.*; exceso, *m.*; orgía, *f.*; disipación, *f.* *v.i.* amotinarse; alborotarse; entregarse a la disipación (or al placer); (enjoy) gozar, disfrutar. **to run r.,** hacer excesos; perder el freno; desmandarse; (*fig.*) extenderse por todas partes; crecer en abundancia, cubrir todo

rioter, *s.* amotinador (-ra); alborotador (-ra)

riotous, *a.* sedicioso; bullicioso; disoluto; desordenado; desenfrenado

riotously, *adv.* sediciosamente; bulliciosamente; disolutamente; con exceso

riotousness, *s.* sedición, *f.*; disolución, *f.*; excesos, *m. pl.*, desenfreno, *m.*; desorden, *m.*

rip, *v.t.* rasgar; (unsew) descoser; (wood, etc.) partir; (make) hacer. *v.i.* rasgarse. *s.* rasgón, *m.*; rasgadura, *f.*; desgarro, *m.*; (libertine) calavera, *m.* **to rip off,** arrancar; quitar. **to rip open,** abrir; (an animal) abrir en canal

riparian, *a.* and *s.* ribereño (-ña)

ripe, *a.* maduro; preparado; perfecto, acabado

ripen, *v.t.* and *v.i.* madurar

ripeness, *s.* madurez, *f.*

ripening, *s.* maduración, *f.*

ripping, *s.* rasgadura, *f.*; (unstitching) deshiladura, *f. a.* (*fam.*) estupendo

ripple, *s.* rizo, *m.*; onda, *f.*; (of sound) murmullo, *m. v.t.* rizar. *v.i.* rizarse; murmurar

rippling, *s.* rizado, *m.*; murmullo, *m.*

rip-rap, *s.* (firework) triquitraque, *m.*

rise, *v.i.* ascender; subir; levantarse; ponerse de pie; (of a meeting) suspenderse; (from the dead) resucitar; (grow) crecer; (swell) hincharse; (of sun, moon) salir; (of sound) gradient, price, stock exchange quotations) subir; (of river source) nacer; (in revolt) sublevarse, rebelarse; (to the mind) presentarse, surgir; (appear) aparecer; (of buildings, etc.) elevarse, alzarse; (in the world) mejorar de posición; (originate) originarse (en), proceder (de); (of mercury) alzarse; (of fish) picar. He has risen in my estimation, Ha ganado en mi estimación. She rose early, Ella se levantó temprano. The colour rose in her cheeks, Se le subieron los colores a la cara. to r. to the occasion, estar al nivel de las circunstancias. to r. to one's feet, ponerse de pie. to r. to the bait, morder el anzuelo (also *fig.*). to r. again, levantarse de nuevo; resucitar; renovarse, suscitarse otra vez. to r. above, alzarse por encima de; mostrarse superior a

rise, *s.* ascensión, *f.*; subida, *f.*; levantamiento, *m.*; (in price, temperature) alza, *f.*; (increase) aumento, *m.*; (of the sun, moon) salida, *f.*; (of a river) nacimiento, *m.*; (origin) origen, *m.*; (growth, development) desarrollo, crecimiento, *m.*; (promotion) ascenso, *m.*; (slope) cuesta, *f.*; pendiente, *f.*; (high ground) eminencia, altura, *f.* to give r. to, dar lugar a, causar. r. and fall, subida y baja, *f.*; (of the voice) ritmo, *m.*; (of music) cadencia, *f.*; (of institutions) grandeza y

decadencia, *f.* r. to power, subida al poder, *f.*

riser, *s.* el, *m.* (*f.* la) que se levanta; (of a step) contrahuella, *f.* early r., madrugador (-ra). late r., el, *m.* (*f.* la) que se levanta tarde

risibility, *s.* risibilidad, *f.*

risible, *a.* risible

rising, *s.* subida, *f.*; (of the source of rivers) nacimiento, *m.*; (overflowing of rivers) crecimiento, *m.*; (of sun, moon) salida, *f.*; (from the dead) resurrección, *f.*; (rebellion) sublevación, insurrección, *f.*; (of the tide) crecida, *f.*; (of bread) levadura, *f.*; (of an assembly) suspensión, *f.*; (of a theatre curtain) subida, *f.*; (literary) renacimiento, *m. a.* creciente; naciente; saliente; (promising) de porvenir; (young) joven. the r. generation, los jóvenes, la generación joven. He is r. forty, Raya en los cuarenta. He likes early r., Le gusta madrugar. On the r. of the curtain ..., Al levantarse el telón ... the r. of the moon, la salida de la luna, *f.* the r. tide, la marea creciente

risk, *s.* riesgo, *m.*; peligro, *m. v.t.* arriesgar; atreverse (a), osar. at the r. of, al riesgo de. to take a r., tomar un riesgo; correr peligro. to r. everything on the outcome, jugar el todo por el todo

riskiness, *s.* peligro, *m.*

risky, *a.* arriesgado, peligroso

rissole, *s.* risol, *m.* (*pl.* risoles)

rite, *s.* rito, *m.*

ritual, *a.* ritual. *s.* rito, *m.*, ceremonia, *f.*

ritualism, *s.* ritualismo, *m.*

ritualist, *s.* ritualista, *m.* and *f.*

ritualistic, *a.* ritualista

rival, *s.* rival, *m.* and *f. a.* competidor; rival. *v.t.* rivalizar con, competir con

rivalry, *s.* rivalidad, *f.*

river, *s.* río, *m. a.* del río; fluvial. r.-basin, cuenca de un río, *f.* r.-bed, lecho, cauce (de un río), *m.* r.-god, dios de los ríos, *m.* r.-mouth, ría, *f.* r. port, puerto fluvial, *m.*

riverside, *s.* ribera, orilla de un río, *f. a.* de la(s) orilla(s) de un rio; situado a la orilla de un río; ribereño

rivet, s. remache, roblón, m. v.t. remachar; clavar; (fig.) fijar, concentrar; (fig.) cautivar, absorber

riveter, s. remachador, m.

riveting, s. remachado, remache, m.; (fig.) fijación, concentración, f.; (fig.) absorción, f. **r. machine,** remachadora, f.

rivulet, s. riachuelo, arroyo, m.

road, s. camino, m.; carretera, f.; ruta, f.; pl. **roads,** (naut.) rada, f. **high r.,** camino real, m. **main r.,** carretera, f. **secondary r.,** carretera de segunda clase, f. **on the r. to . . .,** en el camino de . . . **to get out of the r.,** (fam.) quitarse de en medio. **to go by r.,** ir por carretera. **R. up!** Carretera en reparaciones. **r.-book,** guía de carreteras, f. **r. house,** albergue de carretera, m. **r. maker,** constructor de caminos, m.; (navvy) peón caminero, m. **r. making,** construcción de caminos, f. **r. map,** mapa de carreteras, m. **r. sign,** poste indicador del tráfico, m.

roadmender, s. peón caminero, m.

roadside, s. borde del camino, m. a. al lado del camino

roadstead, s. rada, f.

roadster, s. automóvil de turismo, m.; bicicleta de carreras, f.; caballo de aguante, m.; buque fondeado en rada, m.

roadway, s. calzada, carretera, f.

roam, v.i. vagar, vagabundear, andar errante. v.t. errar por

roamer, s. vagabundo (-da), hombre errante, m.

roaming, s. vagabundeo, m.; excursiones, f. pl., paseos, m. pl.; a. errante, vagabundo; nómada

roan, a. roano, sabino. s. caballo roano, m.

roar, v.i. rugir; (of a bull, of the wind, of a person in anger) bramar; dar voces; (of the fire) crepitar; (of cannon) retumbar; (of thunder) estallar. v.t. gritar. s. rugido, bramido, m.; (shout) grito, m.; (of the fire) crepitación, f.; (of cannon, thunder) estallido, m.; (noise) ruido, m.

to r. with laughter, reírse a carcajadas

roaring, s. (of horses) asma de los caballos, f. For other meanings see under **roar.** a. rugiente, bramante; (fam.) magnífico. **to do a r. trade,** hacer un buen negocio

roast, s. asado, m., carne asada, f. a. asado; tostado. v.t. asar; (coffee and to warm one's feet, etc.) tostar; (metals) calcinar; (scold) desollar vivo (a). v.i. asarse; tostarse. **r. beef,** rosbif, m.

roaster, s. asador, m.; (for coffee or peanuts) tostador, m.; (for chestnuts, etc.) tambor, m.

roasting, s. asación, f.; (of coffee) tostado, m.; (of metals) calcinación, f. **r. spit,** asador, m.

rob, v.t. robar; quitar, privar (de). **They have robbed him of his pocket-book,** Le han robado la cartera

robber, s. ladrón (-ona); (footpad) salteador de caminos, m.; (brigand) bandido, m.

robbery, s. robo, m. **It's daylight r.!** ¡Es un desuello! **to commit a r.,** cometer un robo. **r. with violence,** robo armado, m.

robe, s. traje talar, m., toga, f.; (of a monk, nun) hábito, m.; (of a priest, etc.) sotana, f.; (poet.) manto, m.; (infant's) mantillas, f. pl.; pl. **robes,** traje de ceremonia, m. v.t. vestir; cubrir, revestir (de). v.i. vestirse. **bath r.,** albornoz, m.

robin, s. petirrojo, m.

robot, s. hombre mecánico, m.; (aer.) piloto mecánico, m. **traffic r.,** torre del tráfico, f., aparato automático, m. **r. 'plane,** avión sin piloto, m.

robust, a. robusto; fuerte, vigoroso. **to make r.,** robustecer

robustness, s. robustez, f.; vigor, m., fuerza, f.

roc, s. rocho, m.

rochet, s. roquete, m.

rock, s. roca, f.; (in the sea) abrojo, escollo, m.; peña, f., peñasco, m. **as firm as a r.,** como una roca. **to be on the rocks,** (fam.) estar a la cuarta pregunta. **r. bottom,** s. fondo, *m. a.* mínimo, más bajo. **r.-crystal,** cuarzo, *m.* **r.-garden,** jardincito rocoso, jardín alpestre, *m.* **r.-plant,** planta alpestre, *f.* **r.-rose,** heliantemo, *m.* **r.-salt,** sal gema, *f.*

rock, *v.t.* mecer; (shake) hacer temblar, sacudir; (to sleep) arrullar. *v.i.* mecerse, balancearse; tambalearse; agitarse; temblar

rocker, *s.* (of a chair, cradle) balancín, *m.*; (chair) mecedora, *f.*

rockery, *s.* jardincito rocoso, *m.*

rocket, *s.* cohete, volador, *m.* *v.i.* lanzarse. **r.-launching aircraft,** caza lanzacohetes, *f.*

rockiness, *s.* abundancia de rocas, *f.*; fragosidad, escabrosidad, *f.*

rocking, *s.* balanceo, *m.*; (staggering) tambaleo, *m.*; oscilación, *f.*; (of an infant) arrullo, *m.* **r.-chair,** mecedora, *f.* **r.-horse,** caballo balancín, *m.*

rocky, *a.* rocoso; de roca; roqueño; (rough) fragoso, escabroso; (rugged) peñascoso, escarpado. **R. Mountains,** Montañas Rocosas, *f. pl.*

rococo, *s.* rococó, *m.*

rod, *s.* vara, *f.*; bastón de mando, *m.*; (for fishing) caña, *f.*; (measure) pértiga, *f.*; (surveying) jalón, *m.*; palo, *m.*; (for punishment) vergajo, *m.*; (mech.) vástago, *m.* **connecting rod,** biela, *f.* **to fish with rod and line,** pescar con caña

rodent, *a. and s.* roedor, *m.*

roe, *s.* (deer) corzo (-za); (of fish) hueva, *f.* **soft roes,** lechas, *f. pl.*

rogations, *s. pl.* rogativas, rogaciones, *f. pl.*

rogue, *s.* bribón, pícaro, pillo, *m.*; (law) vago, *m.*; (affectionate) picaruelo (-la)

roguery, *s.* truhanería, picardía, *f.*; (knaves) pícaros, *m. pl.*; (mischief) travesuras, *f. pl.* **novel of r.,** novela picaresca, *f.*

roguish, *a.* picaresco, bellaco; (mischievous) travieso, juguetón; malicioso

roguishly, *adv.* como un pícaro; con malicia

roguishness, *s.* picardía, bri-

bonería, bellaquería, *f.*; (mischievousness) travesuras, *f. pl.*; malicia, *f.*

rôle, *s.* papel, *m.*

roll, *s.* rollo, *m.*; (list) rol, *m.*, lista, *f.*; (of bread) panecillo, *m.*; (of a drum) redoble, *m.*; (of thunder) tronido, *m.*; (of cloth) pieza, *f.*; (of tobacco) rollo, *m.*; (of meat, etc.) pastel, *m.*; (of a ship) balanceo, *m.*; *pl.* **rolls,** (records) archivos, *m. pl.* **He has a nautical r.,** Él tiene un andar de marinero. **to call the r.,** pasar lista. **r. film,** película fotográfica, *f.* **r. of honour,** lista de honor, *f.* **r.-on corset,** faja elástica, *f.*, corsé de goma, *m.* **r.-top desk,** buró de cierre enrollable, *m.*

roll, *v.i.* rodar; dar vueltas; (wallow) revolcarse; (of a ship) balancearse, bambolearse; (in money, etc.) nadar; (flow) correr, fluir; (*fig.,* of time) pasar tranquilamente; (of vehicle) rodar; pasar rodando; (of country) ondular; (of the sea) ondear; (of drums) redoblar; (of thunder) retumbar. *v.t.* hacer rodar; arrollar; (a cigarette) liar; (metals) laminar; (move) mover; (the eyes) guiñar (los ojos); (the ground) apisonar; (pastry) aplanar; (of an organ) sonar; (a drum) redoblar. **Mary rolled her eyes heavenwards,** María puso los ojos en blanco. **to r. away,** alejarse; desaparecer; (of time) pasar. **to r. back,** volver; retirarse; desaparecer. **to r. by,** pasar rodando; desaparecer. **to r. down,** bajar rodando, rodar por. **to r. in,** llegar en gran cantidad (or en gran número). **to r. off,** caer de. **to r. on,** seguir su marcha; fluir sin cesar; seguir su curso; (of time) avanzar. **to r. out,** (metal) laminar; (pastry) aplanar; (bring out) sacar; desenrollar. **to r. over,** *v.t.* volcar; tumbar; dar la vuelta (a). *v.i.* dar la vuelta; volverse al otro lado. **to r. up,** arrollar; envolver; (of hedgehogs, etc.) enroscarse, hacerse un ovillo

roller, *s.* rodillo, *m.*; cilindro, *m.*; (wheel, castor) rueda, *f.*; (for flattening the ground) apisonadora, *f.*; (*print.*) rodillo, *m.*; (wave) ola grande, *f.* **r.-bandage**, venda, *f.* **r. canary**, canario de raza flauta, *m.* **r.-skate**, patín de ruedas, *m.* **r.-skating**, patinaje de ruedas, *m.* **r.-towel**, toalla continua, *f.*

rollicking, *a.* alegre, jovial; juguetón

rolling, *a.* rodante; (of landscape) ondulante, quebrado. *s.* rodadura, *f.*; (wallowing) revuelco, *m.*; (of metals) laminación, *f.*; (of a ship) balanceo, *m.*; (rolling up) enrollamiento, *m.* **r.-pin**, rollo, rodillo de pastelero, *m.* **r.-stock**, material móvil ferroviario, *m.*

Romaic, *a.* and *s.* romaico (*m.*)

Roman, *a.* romano, de los romanos; (of noses and *print.*) romano. *s.* romano (-na). **in the R. fashion**, a la romana. **R. Catholic**, *a.* católico; católico apostólico romano. *s.* católico (-ca). **R. Catholicism**, catolicismo, *m.* **R. figures**, números romanos, *m. pl.* **R. nose**, nariz romana, *f.* **R. road**, vía romana, *f.* **R. type**, (*print.*) tipo romano, *m.*

Romance, *a.* (of languages) romance. *s.* (language) romance, *m.*

romance, *s.* novela de caballería, *f.*; romance, *m.*; aventura, *f.*; cuento, *m.*, novela, *f.*; romanticismo, *m.*; (*mus.*) romanza, *f.* *v.i.* inventar ficciones; exagerar

romancer, *s.* romancerista, *m.* and *f.*; mentiroso (-sa), embustero (-ra)

Romanesque, *a.* románico; romanesco

Romanic, *a.* románico; romance

Romanize, *v.t.* romanizar

Romansch, *s.* romanche, *m.*

romantic, *a.* and *s.* romántico (-ca)

romantically, *adv.* románticamente; de un modo romántico

romanticism, *s.* romanticismo, *m.*

romanticist, *s.* romántico (-ca)

Romany, *s.* caló, *m.*

romp, *v.i.* juguetear, brincar, retozar, loquear; correr rápidamente. *s.* locuelo (-la), salta-

paredes, *m.* and *f.*; (game) retozo, *m.* **The horse romped home easily**, El caballo ganó la carrera fácilmente

rompers, *s.* mono, *m.*

romping, *s.* juegos, *m. pl.*, travesuras, *f. pl.*

rondo, *s.* rondó, *m.*

rood, *s.* cruz, *f.*; crucifijo, *m.*; cuarto de acre, *m.* **By the r.!** ¡Por mi santiguada!

roof, *s.* tejado, techado, *m.*; (of a motor-car, bus) tejadillo, *m.*; (of coaches, etc.) imperial, *f.*; cubierta, *f.*; (of the mouth) paladar, *m.*; (bower) enramada, *f.*; (of heaven) bóveda (del cielo), *f.* *v.t.* techar, tejar; (shelter) abrigar. **r.-garden**, azotea, *f.* **r.-gutter**, canalera, *f.*

roofer, *s.* techador, *m.*; constructor de tejados, *m.*

rook, *s.* chova, *f.*, grajo, *m.*; (at chess) torre, *f.* *v.t.* engañar, estafar; (overcharge) desollar vivo (a)

rookery, *s.* manada de grajos, *f.*; colonia de grajos, aves marinas or focas, *f.*

room, *s.* (in a house) habitación, *f.*, cuarto, *m.*; sala, *f.*; cámara, *f.*; (behind a shop) trastienda, *f.*; (space) sitio, espacio, *m.*; lugar, *m.*; (opportunity) oportunidad, *f.*; (cause) motivo, *m.*, causa, *f.* *v.i.* alojarse. **bath-r.**, cuarto de baño, *m.* **dining-r.**, comedor, *m.* **drawing-r.**, salón, *m.* **There is not r. for us in this car**, No cabemos en este coche. **There is still r. for improvement**, Se puede mejorar todavía. **There isn't r. for anything else**, No cabe más. **to be r.**, caber, haber sitio. **to make r.**, hacer sitio

roomed, *a.* (in compounds) de ... habitaciones; de ... salas

roominess, *s.* espaciosidad, amplitud, *f.*; (of garments) holgura, *f.*

roomy, *a.* espacioso, amplio; (of garments) holgado

roost, *s.* percha de gallinero, *f.* *v.i.* dormir en una percha; recogerse. **to rule the r.**, ser el amo del cotarro

rooster, *s.* gallo, *m.*

root, s. raíz, f.; (gram.) radical, m.; (mus.) base, f.; origen, m.; explicación, f. v.t. arraigar; (fig.) fijar, clavar. v.i. echar raíces; (fig.) arraigarse; (of pigs, etc.) hozar, escarbar; revolver. **to r. out,** arrancar de raíz; (fig.) desarraigar; (destroy) extirpar. **cubed r.,** raíz cúbica, f. **from the r.,** (entirely) de raíz. **square r.,** raíz cuadrada, f. **to cut close to the r.,** cortar a raíz

rooted, a. (in compounds) de raíces . . .; arraigado

rooting, s. arraigo, m.; (scratching) hozadura, f.

rootle, v.i. hozar, escarbar

rope, s. soga, cuerda, f.; (hawser) maroma, f.; (naut.) cabo, m.; (tight-rope) cable, m., cuerda de volatinero, f.; (string) ristra, sarta, f.; hilo, m.; pl. ropes, (boxing) cuerdas del cuadrilátero, f. pl. v.t. encordelar, atar con cuerdas. **to r. in,** encerrar; (a person) enganchar, coger. **a r. of pearls,** una sarta de perlas. **to give a person plenty of r.,** dar mucha latitud (a). **to know the ropes,** conocer todos los trucos. **r.-ladder,** escala de cuerda, f. **r.-maker,** cordelero (-ra), soguero, m. **r.-making,** cordelería, soguería, f. **r.-trick,** truco de la cuerda, m. **r.-walk,** cordelería, f. **r.-yarn,** (naut.) filástica, f.

rosaceous, a. rosáceo

rosary, s. rosario, m. **to say the r.,** rezar el rosario

rose, s. rosa, f.; color de rosa, m.; (rosette) roseta, f.; (arch.) rosetón, m.; (of watering-can) pomo, m., roseta, f. a. de rosa, rosado. **to see the world through r.-coloured spectacles,** ver las cosas color de rosa. **to turn to r.,** volverse color de rosa, rosear. **r.-bay,** (bot.) rododafne, adelfa, f. **r.-bush,** rosal, m. **r.-colour,** color de rosa, rosa, m. **r.-coloured,** de color de rosa, rosado. **r.-garden,** rosalera, rosaleda, f. **r. grower,** cultivador (-ra) de rosas. **r. hip,** escaramujo, m. **r. leaf,** hoja de rosa, f.; pétalo de rosa, m. **r.-like,** como una rosa, de rosa. **r.-red,** de color de rosa;

como una rosa, climbing r.-tree, rosal trepador, m. dwarf r.-tree, rosal bajo, m. standard r.-tree, rosal de tallo, m. r.-water, agua de rosas, f. r.-window, rosetón, m., rosa, f. r.-wood, palo de rosa, m.

rosé, a. (of wines) rosado

roseate, a. róseo

rosebud, s. capullo de rosa, m.

rosemary, s. romero, m.

rosette, s. roseta, f.; (arch.) rosetón, m.

rosin, s. (solid, for violin-bows, etc.) colofonia, f.; resina, f. v.t. dar con colofonia; dar con resina

rosiness, s. color de rosa, m.

roster, s. lista, f.; registro, m., matrícula, f.

rostrum, s. tribuna, f.; (zool.) pico, m.; (of a ship) espolón, m.

rosy, a. róseo, rosado; sonrosado; (fig.) de color de rosa, halagüeño; optimista. **r.-cheeked,** con (de) mejillas sonrosadas

rot, s. putrefacción, podredumbre, f.; (in trees) caries, f.; (in sheep) comalía, f.; (slang) patrañas, f. pl., disparates, m. pl. v.i. pudrirse; descomponerse; (fig.) echarse a perder; (slang) decir disparates. v.t. pudrir; (fig.) corromper; (slang) tomar el pelo (a)

rota, s. lista, f.; orden del día, m.

rotary, a. rotativo. **r. printing press,** rotativa, f.

rotate, v.i. girar, dar vueltas; alternarse. v.t. hacer girar

rotating, a. rotativo; giratorio

rotation, s. rotación, f.; turno, m. **in r.,** por turnos. **r. of crops,** rotación de cultivos, f.

rotatory, a. rotatorio

rote, to learn by, v.t. aprender de memoria

rotogravure, s. rotograbado, m.

rotten, a. putrefacto; podrido; (of bones, teeth) cariado; dañado, echado a perder; (fig.) corrompido; (slang) pésimo. **to smell r.,** oler a podredumbre; apestar

rottenness, s. putrefacción, podredumbre, f.; (fig.) corrupción, f.

rotter, s. (slang) perdido, m.

rotting, s. pudrición, f. a. que se pudre

rotund, a. rotundo

rotunda, s. rotonda, f.

rotundity, s. redondez, f.; rotundidad, f.

rouble, s. rublo, m.

roué, s. calavera, libertino, m.

rouge, s. colorete, m. v.t. and v.i. pintar de rojo, poner(se) colorete

rough, a. áspero; duro; (of country) fragoso, escabroso; (uneven) desigual; (stormy) borrascoso, tempestuoso; (of the sea) encrespado, bravo; (of movement) violento; (bristling) erizado; (of the hair) despeinado; (unpolished) tosco; basto; (unskilled, clumsy) torpe; (of sounds, tastes) áspero; (of persons) rudo, inculto; (severe) severo; (of behaviour) brutal; (of manners) brusco; (rude) grosero; (approximate) aproximado. adv. duramente, mal. s. estado tosco, m.; (person) matón, m.; (golf) el "rough." in the r., en bruto; (roughed out) bosquejado. to grow r., (of the sea) encresparse, embravecerse. to take the r. with the smooth, (fig.) aceptar la realidad; tomar lo bueno con lo malo. to r. it, luchar contra las dificultades, pasar apuros; llevar una vida sencilla; vivir mal. to r. out, bosquejar. r. and ready, improvisado; provisional. r. and tumble, s. camorra, pendencia, f. r.-cast, v.t. dar una primera capa de mezcla gruesa (a); bosquejar. r. diamond, diamante bruto (or en bruto) (also fig.), m. r.-draft, borrador, m.; bosquejo, m. r.-haired, (of a dog) de pelo crespo. r.-hewn, modelado toscamente; desbastado; (fig.) cerril, tosco. r.-house, jarana, f. r.-rider, domador (de caballos), m. r.-sketch, bosquejo, esbozo, m. r.-spoken, malhablado

roughen, v.t. poner áspero. v.i. ponerse áspero

roughly, adv. rudamente, toscamente; duramente; brutalmente; bruscamente; (of tastes, sounds) ásperamente; (approximately) aproximadamente, más o menos

roughness, s. aspereza, f.;

dureza, f.; tosquedad, f.; rudeza, f.; (of the sea, wind) braveza, f.; violencia, f.; (of manner) brusquedad, f.; brutalidad, f.; (vulgarity) grosería, f. the r. of the way, la aspereza del camino

roulette, s. ruleta, f.

Roumanian, a. rumano. s. rumano (-na); (language) rumano, m.

round, a. redondo; (plump) rollizo; rotundo, categórico; sonoro a r. sum, una cantidad redonda; un número redondo. to walk at a r. pace, andar a un buen paso. r. dance, baile en ruedo, m. r.-faced, carilleno, de cara redonda. r.-house, cuerpo de guardia, m.; (naut.) tumbadillo, m. r.-shouldered, cargado de espaldas. r. table, mesa redonda, f.; (of King Arthur) Tabla Redonda, f. r. trip, viaje redondo, viaje de ida y vuelta, m. r.-up, rodeo de ganado, m.; arresto, m.

round, s. círculo, m.; esfera, f.; redondez, f.; (slice) rodaja, f.; (of a ladder) peldaño, m.; (patrol and mil.) ronda, f.; circuito, m.; vuelta, f., giro, m.; serie, f.; rutina, f.; (of ammunition) andanada, descarga, f.; (of cartridge) cartucho con bala, m.; (of applause, etc.) salva, f.; (of golf) partido, m.; (in a fight) asalto, m.; (sport) vuelta, f.; (of drinks) ronda, f.; (doctor's) visitas, f. pl.

round, v.t. redondear; (fig., complete) acabar, perfeccionar; (go round) dar vuelta (a); rodear, cercar; (of a ship) doblar. v.i. redondearse. to r. off, redondear; terminar; coronar. to r. up, (cattle) rodear. to r. upon, volverse contra

round, adv. alrededor, en derredor; por todos lados; a la redonda, en torno; en circunferencia; en conjunto (r. is often omitted in Spanish, e.g. I shall come r. to your house, Vendré a tu casa). prep. alrededor de. all the year r., todo el año, el año entero. r. about, a la redonda de, al derredor de; (nearly) cerca de; (of time by the clock) a eso de. **The road is**

closed and we shall have to go r., El camino está cerrado y tendremos que dar una vuelta. **to come r.,** volver; dejarse persuadir; recobrar su buen humor. **to go r.,** (spin) dar vueltas; (of the wind) cambiar. **There is enough to go r.,** Hay bastante para todos

roundabout, a. indirecto; desviado; vago. s. tiovivo, m.; (traffic) redondel, m. **He spoke in a r. way,** Hablaba con circunloquios. **We went there by a r. way,** Fuimos allí dando un rodeo

roundly, adv. en redondo; rotundamente, claramente

roundness, s. redondez, f.; rotundidad, f.

rouse, v.t. despertar; animar; excitar; suscitar, provocar. **to r. oneself,** despertarse; animarse (a hacer algo)

rousing, a. que despierta; (moving) emocionante; (enthusiastic) entusiasta; grande, bueno

rout, s. (rabble) chusma, f.; (party) sarao, m.; (defeat) derrota, f.; (meeting) reunión, f. v.t. derrotar, poner en fuga; vencer

route, s. ruta, f.; camino, m.; itinerario, m. **r. march,** marcha de maniobras, f.

routine, s. rutina, f. a. rutinario, de rutina

rove, v.i. vagar, errar

rover, s. vagabundo (-da); pirata, m.

roving, a. vagabundo, errante; ambulante

row, s. (line) hilera, fila, hila, f.; (in a theatre, etc.) fila, f.; (string) ristra, f.; (in a boat) paseo en bote, m.; (commotion) alboroto, m.; (noise) ruido, m.; (shindy) gresca, camorra, f.; (scolding) regaño, m. v.i. (a boat) remar, bogar. v.t. conducir remando; (scold) regañar. **to be a row,** (shindy) haber la de San Quintín. **to start a row,** (shindy) armar camorra. **row-boat,** bote de remos, m.

rowan, s. fresno alpestre, m.

rowdiness, s. alboroto, m.

rowdy, a. alborotador. s. trafalmejas, m. and f., rufián, m.

rowel, s. estrella de espuela, f.

rower, s. remero (-ra), bogador (-ra)

rowing, a. que rema; de remos. s. deporte del remo, m.; paseo en bote, m. **r.-boat,** bote de remos, m. **r.-club,** club náutico, m. **r.-seat,** bancada, f. **r.-stroke,** bogada, f.

rowlock, s. chumacera, f.

royal, a. real; regio. s. (naut.) sobrejuanete, m. **R. Academy,** Real Academia, f. **r. eagle,** águila real, f. **R. Highness,** Alteza Real, f. **r. letters patent,** cédula real, f. **R. Mail,** mala real, f. **R. Standard,** estandarte real, m.

royalism, s. realismo, m.

royalist, a. and s. realista (m. and f.)

royally, adv. realmente; regiamente

royalty, s. realeza, f.; miembro de la familia real, m.; tanto por ciento de los ingresos, m.; derechos de autor, m. pl.

rub, v.t. frotar, estregar; fregar; rozar; friccionar; (make sore) raspar. **to rub one's hands together,** frotarse las manos. **to rub the wrong way,** frotar a contrapelo. **to rub against,** rozar. **to rub along,** (fam.) ir tirando. **to rub down,** (a horse) bruzar; limpiar; (dry) secar; (wear down) desgastar. **to rub in,** dar fricciones con; frotar con; (an idea, etc.) machacar. **to rub off,** v.t. quitar (frotando); borrar. v.i. borrarse; separarse (de). **to rub out,** v.t. borrar. v.i. borrarse. **to rub up,** (polish) limpiar; (fig.) refrescar

rub, s. frotación, f.; roce, m.; fricción, f.; (fig.) obstáculo, m.; dificultad, f. **to give a rub,** frotar, etc. **rub-a-dub,** rataplán, m.

rubber, a. de caucho, de goma. s. caucho, m., goma, f.; (for erasing) goma de borrar, f.; (masseur) masajista, m. and f.; (at whist, etc.) partida, f.; pl. **rubbers,** zapatos de goma, chanclos, m. pl. **synthetic r.,** caucho artificial, m. **r. band,** goma, banda de goma, f. **r.**

belt, (*mech.*) correa de transmisión de caucho, *f.* **r.-plant, tree,** cauchera, *f.* **r. plantation,** cauchal, *m.* **r. planter,** cauchero, *m.* **r. stamp,** estampilla, *f.*

rubbing, *s.* frotación, *f.*; fricción, *f.*; roce, *m.*; (of floors, dishes, etc.) fregado, *m.*

rubbish, *s.* basura, *f.*; desperdicios, *m. pl.,* desecho, *m.*; (ot goods) pacotilla, *f.*; (nonsense) pamplinas, patrañas, *f. pl.,* disparates, *m. pl.* **r. cart,** carro del basurero, *m.*

rubbishy, *a.* sin valor, malo; (of goods) de pacotilla, de calidad inferior

rubble, *s.* escombros, *m. pl.*; cascote, *m.*; piedra bruta, *f.*

rubefaction, *s.* rubefacción, *f.*

rubicund, *a.* rubicundo

rubicundity, *s.* rubicundez, *f.*

rubidium, *s.* rubidio, *m.*

rubric, *s.* rúbrica, *f.*

ruby, *s.* rubí, *m.* *a.* de rubíes; de rubí. **r. lips,** labios de rubí, *m. pl.*

ruche, *s.* fruncido, *m.* *v.t.* fruncir

ruched, *a.* con fruncidos

rucksack, *s.* mochila, *f.*

rudder, *s.* timón, gobernalle, *m.*

ruddiness, *s.* rubicundez, *f.*; rojez, *f.*; frescura, *f.*

ruddy, *a.* rubicundo; rojo; frescote; (of animals) barcino

rude, *a.* rudo; tosco; vigoroso; grosero, descortés

rudely, *adv.* toscamente; groseramente

rudeness, *s.* rudeza, *f.*; tosquedad, *f.*; grosería, incivilidad, descortesía, *f.*

rudiment, *s.* rudimento, *m.*

rudimentary, *a.* rudimentario

rue, *v.t.* lamentar, llorar. *s.* (*bot.*) ruda, *f.*

rueful, *a.* triste, melancólico; lamentable

ruefully, *adv.* tristemente

ruefulness, *s.* tristeza, *f.*

ruff, *s.* golilla, lechuguilla, *f.*; (of a bird) collarín de plumás, *m.*; (of an animal) collarín de pelo, *m.*

ruffian, *s.* rufián, *m.*

ruffianly, *a.* rufianesco

ruffle, *s.* (*sew.*) volante fruncido, *m.*; (of a bird) collarín de plumas,

m.; (of an animal) collarín de pelo, *m.*; (ripple) rizo, *m.*; (annoyance) irritación, *f.* *v.t.* (ripple) rizar; (pleat) fruncir; (feathers) erizar; (hair) despeinar; agitar; (annoy) irritar, incomodar

ruffling, *s.* (rippling) rizado, *m.*; (pleating) fruncido, *m.*; (of the temper) irritación, *f.*

rug, *s,* (floor) alfombra, *f.*; manta de viaje, *f.* **rug strap,** portamantas, *m.*

Rugby, *s.* fútbol rugby, "rugby," *m.*

rugged, *a.* áspero, escabroso; escarpado, abrupto; (wrinkled) arrugado; tosco; (harsh) duro, severo; inculto; rudo; mal acabado; vigoroso

ruggedness, *s.* aspereza, escabrosidad, *f.*; lo escarpado; dureza, severidad, *f.*; rudeza, *f.*; vigor, *m.*

rugger, *s.* fútbol rugby, *m.*

ruin, *s.* ruina, *f.* *v.t.* arruinar; echar a perder, estropear por completo; (a woman) perder

ruination, *s.* ruina, perdición, *f.*

ruined, *a.* arruinado; en ruinas

ruinous, *a.* ruinoso; en ruinas

ruinously, *adv.* ruinosamente

rule, *s.* regla, *f.*; gobierno, *m.*; autoridad, *f.,* mando, *m.*; administración, *f.*; (reign) reinado, *m.*; (of a court, etc.) orden, *f.*; (for measuring) regla, *f.*; (*print.*) regleta, *f.*; *pl.* **rules,** reglas, *f. pl.*; reglamento, *m.* *v.t.* gobernar; regentar, regir; (control) dominar; (of a chairman, etc.) disponer, decidir; (guide) guiar; (lines) reglar. *v.i.* gobernar; (of a monarch) rcinar; (of prices) mantenerse; estar en boga, prevalecer. **as a r.,** por regla general, en general. **slide-r.,** regla de cálculo, *f.* **to make it a r.,** tener por regla; tener por costumbre; tener por máxima. **to r. out,** excluir; (*law*) no admitir. **to r. over,** (of a king, etc.) reinar sobre. **r. of the road,** reglamento del tráfico, *m.* **r. of thumb,** regla empírica, *f.*; rutina, *f.*

ruler, *s.* gobernador (-ra); soberano (-na); (master) amo (ama); (for ruling lines) regla, *f.*

ruling, *a.* regente; dominante; (current) vigente. *s.* gobierno, *m.*; (law) decisión, *f.*, fallo, *m.*; (with lines) rayado, *m.* **r. pen,** tiralíneas, *m.*

rum, *s.* ron, *m.*

rumba, *s.* rumba, *f.*

rumble, *v.i.* retumbar, tronar; (of vehicles) rugir; crujir. *s.* retumbo, trueno, *m.*; rugido, *m.*; ruido sordo, *m.*; rumor, *m.*; crujido, *m.*

rumbling, *a.* que retumba, etc. *s.* ruido sordo, *m.*; retumbo, *m.*; crujido, *m.*; (in the bowels) rugido, *m.*

ruminant, *a.* and *s.* rumiante (*m.* and *f.*)

ruminate, *v.i.* and *v.t.* rumiar

rumination, *s.* rumia, *f.*; meditación, reflexión, *f.*

rummage, *v.t.* revolver, desordenar, trastornar; explorar. **to r. out,** desenterrar

rumour, *s.* rumor, *m.*, fama, *f.* **It is rumoured that . . .,** Hay rumores de que . . ., La voz corre que . . ., Se dice que . . .

rump, *s.* (of an animal) nalgas, ancas, *f. pl.*; cuarto trasero, *m.*; (of a bird) rabadilla, *f.*; (scornful) culo, *m.*, posaderas, *f. pl.* **r.-steak,** solomillo, *m.*

rumple, *v.t.* arrugar; desordenar

run, *v.i.* correr; acudir; (flee) huir; (rush) precipitarse, lanzarse; (in a race) tomar parte en una carrera; competir; (pass over) deslizarse (por); (of machines) andar, marchar; (of traffic) circular; (leave, of trains, ships, etc.) salir; (ply between) hacer el trayecto entre . . . y . . .; (flow) fluir, correr; (into the sea, of rivers) desembocar (en); (spurt) chorrear, manar; (drip) gotear; (leak) dejar fugar (el agua, etc.); (of colours) correrse; caer; (of tears) correr; derramarse; (of eyes) llorar; (melt) derretirse; (of a sore) supurar; (travel or go) ir; moverse; (work) trabajar; funcionar; (of editions of a book) agotarse; (of a play) representarse; (cross) cruzar; (elapse) correr; transcurrir, pasar; (become) hacerse; (of wording) decir; (be current) correr; (for parliament, etc.)

hacerse candidato; (navigate) navegar; (spread) extenderse; (be) estar; ser; (of thoughts) pasar; (last) durar; (tend) tender (a). *v.t.* (a race, a horse) correr; (drive) conducir; (a business, etc.) administrar; dirigir; (govern) gobernar, regir; (hunt) cazar; perseguir; (water, etc.) hacer correr; (pierce) clavar; introducir; (push) empujar; (one's hand, eye, etc.) pasar; (risks, etc.) correr; (possess) tener; establecer un servicio de (autobuses, etc.); (smuggle) hacer contrabando de. **The ship ran aground,** El barco encalló. **to run dry,** secarse; agotarse. **to run in the family,** estar en la familia. **to run into debt,** endeudarse, contraer deudas. **to run to seed,** granar; agotarse. **Steamers run daily between Barcelona and Mallorca,** Hay servicio diario de vapores entre Barcelona y Mallorca. **A stab of pain ran up his leg,** Sintió un dolor agudo en la pierna. **Feeling was running high,** Los ánimos estaban excitados. **My arrangements ran smoothly,** Mis planes marchaban bien. **Funds are running low,** El dinero escasea. **The tune runs in my head,** Tengo la canción metida en la cabeza. **The message runs like this,** El mensaje reza (dice) así. **He ran his fingers through his hair,** Se mesaba los cabellos. **to run about,** andar de un lado a otro, correr por todas partes; (gad) corretear. **to run across,** cruzar corriendo; (meet) topar con, tropezar con. **to run after,** correr detrás (de); perseguir; buscar. **to run against,** (collide with) dar contra; (meet) tropezar con. **to run at,** abalanzarse hacia, precipitarse sobre; atacar. **to run away,** huir; escaparse; (slip away) escurrirse; (of a horse) dispararse, desbocarse. **to run away with,** huir con, fugarse con; (carry off) arrebatar; (steal) llevarse; (imagine) imaginarse, figurarse; (of temper, etc.) dominar, poseer. **to run back,** volver corriendo;

llegar corriendo; retroceder rápidamente, correr hacia atrás. to run backwards, correr hacia atrás; to run backwards and forwards, ir y venir. to run behind, correr detrás (de); quedarse atrás; (be late) estar atrasado. to run down, v.i. bajar corriendo; descender, bajar; (of a clock) parar; (of a battery) gastarse; (of liquids) correr; fluir; (drop by drop) destilar. v.t. (capture) coger; alcanzar; (a person by a vehicle) atropellar; (a ship) echar a pique; (disparage) hablar mal de. run-down, (in health) agotado; (of a clock) parado. to run for, buscar corriendo; correr para coger (el autobús, etc.); (president, etc.) ser candidato para. to run in, v.i. entrar corriendo. v.t. arrestar; hacer prisionero; (print.) encerrar. to run into, tropezar con; chocar con; (plunge into) meterse de cabeza en; (of sums of money, etc.) ascender a; (of streets, rivers, etc.) desembocar en. to run off, v.i. escaparse corriendo; marcharse corriendo. v.t. deslizarse por; (drain) vaciar; (print.) imprimir; (compose) componer. to run off with, huir con. to run on, correr delante; continuar; (of the mind) pensar en, entregarse a; hablar sin cesar; (print.) recorrer. to run out, v.i. salir corriendo; (of liquids) derramarse; salir; (end) acabarse; agotarse; (project) sobresalir. v.t. (cricket) coger al lanzador fuera de la línea de saque. to run out of, no tener más de, haber terminado. to run over, v.i. rebosar; derramarse. v.t. (of a vehicle) atropellar, pasar por encima de; (peruse) repasar; revisar. to run through, correr por; pasar por; recorrer; (go directly) ir directamente (a); (pierce) traspasar, pasar de parte a parte; (squander) derrochar, malbaratar; (read) hojear, leer por encima. to run up, v.t. (hoist) izar; hacer de prisa; construir rápidamente; (incur) incurrir. v.i. subir corriendo; (of plants) trepar (por); (shrink) encogerse; (of expenses) aumentar. to run up to time, llegar a su hora. to run up against, tropezar con; (opposition, etc.) encontrar.

run, s. carrera, corrida, f.; (excursion) visita, excursión, f.; (cricket) carrera, f.; (walk) paseo, m.; (by train or sea) viaje, m.; (by bus, tram) trayecto, m.; (sea crossing) travesía, f.; (distance run) recorrido, m.; (of events, etc.) curso, m.; marcha, f.; (of markets, etc.) tendencia, f.; (rhythm) ritmo, m.; dirección, f.; distancia, f.; (mus.) serie de notas, f.; serie, f.; duración, f.; (theat.) serie de representaciones, f.; (freedom to use) libre uso, m.; (majority) mayoría, f.; (on a bank) asedio, m.; (on a book, etc.) demanda, f.; (for sheep, etc.) terreno de pasto, m.; (for fowls) gallinero, m. a run of bad luck, una temporada de mala suerte. at a run, corriendo. in the long run, a la larga, al fin y al cabo. on the run, en fuga; ocupado. Prices came down with a run, Los precios bajaron de golpe. take-off run, (aer.) recorrido de despegue, m.

runaway, a. fugitivo; (of a horse) desbocado

rune, s. runa, f.

rung, s. (of a ladder) peldaño, m.; (of a chair) travesaño, m.; (lath) listón, m.

runic, a. rúnico

runner, s. corredor (-ra); (carrier of sedan chair, etc.) silletero, m.; (smuggler) contrabandista, m.; (courier) estafeta, f.; (messenger) mensajero, m.; (ring) anillo movible, pasador corredizo, m.; rueda móvil, f.; (of a sledge) patín, m.; (bot.) tallo rastrero, m. r.-up, el segundo

running, a. corredor; (of water, bank accounts) corriente; (of a knot) corredizo; (of a sore) supurante; (continuous) continuo; (consecutive) consecutivo. s. carrera, f.; marcha, f.; funcionamiento, m.; administración, f.; gobierno, m.; dirección, f.; (flowing) derrame, m.; (of trains, buses, etc.) servicio, m.; (smuggling) contrabando, *m.*; (of a sore) supuración, *f.* **six times r.**, seis veces consecutivas. **The car is in r. order,** El auto está en buen estado. **r. away,** fuga, *f.* **r.-board,** (of a car, etc.) estribo, *m.*; (of a locomotive) plataforma, *f.* **r. costs,** gastos de mantenimiento, *m. pl.*; (railway) gastos de tracción, *m. pl.* **r. fight,** acción de retirada, *f.* **r.-knot,** lazo corredizo, *m.* **r. title,** (*print.*) título de la columna, *m.*

runway, *s.* (for launching a ship) grada, *f.*; (of an airfield) pista de aterrizaje, *f.*

rupee, *s.* rupia, *f.*

rupestrian, *a.* rupestre

rupture, *s.* rompimiento, *m.*, rotura, *f.*; ruptura, *f.*; (*med.*) hernia, *f.*

ruptured, *a.* (*med.*) herniado, quebrado

rupturing, *s.* ruptura, *f.*

rural, *a.* rural, campestre, del campo; agrario

ruse, *s.* artimaña, treta, ardid, *f.*

rush, *s.* (*bot.*) junco, *m.*; acometida, *f.*; ataque *m.*; (of water) torrente, *m.*; (bustle) bullicio, *m.*; (speed) prisa, *f.*; precipitación, *f.*; acceso, *m.*; (crowd) tropel, *m.*, masa, *f.*; (struggle) lucha, *f.*; furia, *f.* *v.i.* precipitarse, lanzarse; agolparse. *v.t.* llevar rápidamente (a); despachar rápidamente; precipitar; (attack) asaltar, atacar; (capture) tomar, capturar; hacer de prisa; (a Bill) hacer aprobar de prisa. **to r. upon,** abalanzarse hacia; embestir. **in a r.,** en tropel, en masa; de prisa. **to r. to a conclusion,** precipitarse a una conclusión. **r.-bottomed,** con asiento de enea. **r. hours,** horas de mayor circulación, *f. pl.* **r. order,** pedido urgente, *m.*

rushy, *a.* juncoso

rusk, *s.* rosquilla, *f.*

russet, *a.* rojizo; rojo. **r. apple,** manzana asperiega, *f.*

Russian, *a.* ruso. *s.* ruso (-sa); (language) ruso, *m.* **R. leather,** piel de Rusia, *f.*

Russianize, *v.t.* rusificar; sovietizar

Russo-, *prefix,* ruso-

rust, *s.* herrumbre. *f.*, orín, *m.*; moho, *m.*; (disease) añublo, tizón, *m.* *v.t.* aherrumbrar; enmohecer. *v.i.* aherrumbrarse; enmohecerse

rustic, *a.* rústico; campesino, aldeano; (scornful) palurdo, grosero. *s.* aldeano, *m.*; (scornful) patán, *m.*

rusticate, *v.i.* rusticar, vivir en el campo. *v.t.* enviar al campo

rustication, *s.* rusticación, *f.*

rusticity, *s.* rusticidad, *f.*

rustiness, *s.* herrumbre, *f.*; enmohecimiento, *m.*; color rojizo, *m.*; falta de práctica, *f.*

rustle, *s.* susurro; *m.*; murmurio, *m.*; (of silk, a dress, etc.) frufrú, *m.*; (of paper, etc.) crujido, *m.* *v.i.* susurrar; murmurar; crujir. *v.t.* (a paper) hacer crujir

rustless, *a.* inoxidable

rustling, *s.* see rustle

rusty, *a.* herrumbroso; enmohecido, mohoso; (red) rojizo; (worn out) usado, viejo; (out of practice) desacostumbrado; (forgotten) olvidado

rut, *s.* rodera, *f.*, bache, surco, *m.*; (*fig.*) sendero trillado, *m.*; (*fig.*) rutina, *f.*; (sexual appetite) celo, *m.* *v.i.* estar en celo

Ruthenian, *a.* ruteno. *s.* ruteno (-na); (language) ruteno, *m.*

ruthless, *a.* inhumano, insensible, despiadado; inexorable, inflexible

ruthlessly, *adv.* inhumanamente; inflexiblemente, inexorablemente

ruthlessness, *s.* inhumanidad, *f.*; inflexibilidad, inexorabilidad, *f.*

rutty, *a.* barrancoso, lleno de roderas

rye, *s.* centeno, *m.* **rye field,** centenar, *m.*

S

s, *s.* (letter) ese, *f.*

sabaean, *a.* and *s.* sabeo (-ea)

sabbatarian, *a.* sabatario

Sabbath, *s.* (Jewish) sábado, *m.*; (Christian) domingo, *m.*

sabbatical, *a.* sabático

Sabine, *a.* and *s.* sabino (-na)

sable, *s.* (animal and fur) marta, *f.*; (*her.*) sable, *m. a.* (*her.*) sable; (*poet.*) negro

SAB 1043 SAF

sabot, s. zueco, zoclo, m.
sabotage, s. sabotaje, m. v.t.
cometer un acto de sabotaje en
saboteur, s. saboteador, m.
sabre, s. sable, m.; (soldier) jinete,
m. v.t. dar sablazos (a), acuchillar.
s. cut, thrust, sablazo, m.
sac, s. (biol.) saco, m.
saccharify, v.t. sacarificar
saccharin, s. sacarina, f.
sachet, s. sachet, m.; bolsa, f.
handkerchief s., bolsa para
pañuelos, f.
sack, s. (bag) saco, m.; (mil.)
saqueo, saco, m. v.t. meter en
sacos; (dismiss) dar pasaporte
(a), despedir; (mil.) saquear. to
get the s., recibir el pasaporte.
to give the s., dar el pasaporte
(a), poner de patitas en la calle
(a). s. coat, saco, m.
sackbut, s. (mus.) sacabuche, m.
sackcloth, s. harpillera, f. to
repent in s. and ashes, ponerse
cenizas en la cabeza
sacking, s. harpillera, f.; (mil.)
saqueo, m.
sacral, a. (anat.) sacro
sacrament, s. sacramento, m.;
Eucaristía, f. the Blessed S.,
el Santísimo Sacramento. to
receive the Holy S., comulgar.
to receive the last sacraments, recibir los sacramentos,
recibir la Extremaunción
sacramental, a. sacramental
sacramentalist, s. sacramentario (-ia)
sacred, a. sagrado; sacro, santo;
consagrado. Nothing is s. to
them, No hay nada sagrado para
ellos, No respetan nada. the S.
Heart, el Sagrado Corazón (de
Jesús). S. to the memory of...
Consagrado a la memoria de ...
s. music, música sagrada, f.
sacredness, s. carácter sagrado,
m.; santidad, f.; inviolabilidad, f.
sacrifice, s. sacrificio, m. v.t. and
v.i. sacrificar. s. of the Mass,
sacrificio del altar, m.
sacrificial, a. sacrificador; del
sacrificio
sacrilege, s. sacrilegio, m.
sacrilegious, a. sacrílego
sacristan, s. sacristán, m.
sacristy, s. sacristía, f.
sacrosanct, a. sacrosanto
sacrum, s. (anat.) sacro, m.

sad, a. triste; melancólico; (of a
mistake) deplorable, funesto;
(fam.) redomado; (pensive) pensativo. How s.! ¡Qué lástima!;
¡Qué triste! It made me s.,
Me entristeció
sadden, v.t. entristecer, acongojar, afligir
saddle, s. (riding) silla de montar,
f.; (of a bicycle, etc.) sillín, m.;
(mech.) silla, f.; (anat.) espalda, f.
v.t. ensillar. to s. with the
responsibility of, echar la
responsabilidad de (a). s. of
mutton, lomo de carnero, m.
s.-bag, alforja, f. s.-cloth,
mantilla de silla, f. s.-tree,
arzón, m.
saddler, s. sillero, guarnicionero,
m.
saddlery, s. guarnicionería, talabartería, f.
Sadducee, s. saduceo (-ea)
sadism, s. sadismo, m.
sadist, s. sadista, m. and f.
sadistic, a. sadístico
sadly, adv. tristemente; (very)
muy
sadness, s. tristeza, melancolía, f.
safe, a. al abrigo (de); seguro;
salvo; (certain) cierto; prudente;
digno de confianza. s. caja de
caudales, f.; (for food) alacena, f.
I stood beneath a tree s. from
the rain, Estaba de pie bajo un
árbol, al abrigo de la lluvia.
to put something in a s. place,
poner algo en salvo; poner algo
en un lugar seguro. s. and
sound, sano y salvo. s.-con-
duct, salvoconducto, m. s.-
keeping, lugar seguro, m.; (of a
person) buenas manos, f. pl.
safeguard, s. protección, garantía, f.; precaución, f. v.t. proteger,
guardar; tomar precauciones
(contra)
safely, adv. seguramente; sin
accidente, sin novedad, sano y
salvo; sin peligro. You may s.
tell him, Puedes decírselo con
toda seguridad. to put (something) away s., poner (algo) en
un lugar seguro
safety, s. seguridad, f. a. de
seguridad; (of locks) de golpe.
a place of s., un lugar seguro.
in s., en salvo, en seguro; con
seguridad. to believe in s.

first, poner la seguridad en primer lugar. **to play for s.**, jugar seguro. **with complete s.**, con toda seguridad. **s.-belt**, (cinto) salvavidas, *m.* **s.-catch**, fiador, *m.* **s.-curtain**, telón de seguridad, telón contra incendios, *m.* **s.-fuse**, espoleta de seguridad, *f.* **s.-glass**, vidrio inastillable, *m.* **s.-island**, refugio para peatones,. *m.* **s.-lamp**, lámpara de seguridad, *f.* **s.-latch**, pestillo de golpe, *m.* **s.-lock**, (of fire-arms) seguro, *m.*; (of doors, etc.) cerradura de seguridad, *f.* **s.-pin**, imperdible, *m.* **s.-razor**, máquina de afeitar, *f.* **s.-valve**, válvula de seguridad, *f.*

saffron, *s.* azafrán, *m.* *a.* azafranado, de color de azafrán.

sag, *v.i.* doblegarse, ceder; inclinarse; (naut.) caer a sotavento; (of prices) bajar; (of spirits, etc.) flaquear

saga, *s.* saga, *f.*; epopeya, *f.*

sagacious, *a.* sagaz, perspicaz; (of animals) sabio

sagacity, *s.* sagacidad, perspicacia, *f.*; (of animals) sagacidad, *f.*

sage, *s.* sabio, *m.*; (bot.) salvia, *f.* *a.* sabio; sagaz; cuerdo

Sagittarius, *s.* Sagitario, *m.*

sago, *s.* sagú, *m.*

said, *a.* antedicho; tal, dicho. No sooner s. than done, Dicho y hecho. **the s. Mr. Martínez**, el tal Sr. Martínez

sail, *s.* (of a ship) vela, *f.*; (sailing-ship) velero, *m.*; (of a windmill) aspa, *f.*; (mech.) ala, *f.*; (trip) paseo en barco. *m. v.i.* navegar; ir en barco; dar un paseo en barco; (leave) salir en barco; zarpar; (of swans, etc.) deslizarse; (of clouds, etc.) flotar. *v.t.* (a ship) gobernar; (the sea) navegar por. **She sailed into the room**, Ella entró majestuosamente en la sala. **The ship sailed at eight knots**, El buque navegaba a ocho nudos. **to go for a s.**, dar un paseo en barco. **to s. round the world**, dar la vuelta al mundo. **to s. the seas**, navegar por los mares. **to set s.**, darse a la vela, zarpar. **to take in the sails**, amainar. **s.-maker**, velero, *m.* **to s. into**,

entrar en. **to s. round**, (the Cape, etc.) doblar. **to s. up**, subir en barco; (of a boat) ir río arriba

sailcloth, *s.* lona, *f.*

sailing, *s.* navegación, *f.*; (departure) salida, *f.* It's all plain s., Todo va viento en popa. **s.-boat**, bote de vela, *m.* **s.-ship**, buque de vela, velero, *m.*

sailor, *s.* marinero, *m.* **John is a bad s.**, Juan se marea fácilmente. **to be a good s.**, no marearse. **s.-blouse**, marinera, *f.* **s.-suit**, traje de marinero, *m.*

saint, *s.* santo (-ta); (before masculine names of Sts., excluding Sts. Dominic and Thomas) San; (fam.) ángel, *m.* **All Saints' Day**, el día de Todos los Santos. **Saint's day**, fiesta de un santo (or de una santa), *f.*; (of a person) santo, *m.* **St. Bernard dog**, perro de San Bernardo, *m.* **St. John the Baptist**, San Juan Bautista. **St. Martin's summer**, el veranillo de San Martín. **St. Vitus's dance**, el baile de San Vito

sainthood, *s.* santidad, *f.*

saintliness, *s.* santidad, *f.*

saintly, *a.* de santo; de santa; santo; (fam.) angelical

sake, *s.* amor, *m.*; causa, *f.* **for God's s.**, por el amor de Dios. **for the s. of**, para; por amor de. **to talk for talking's s.**, hablar por hablar

saker, *s.* (falcon and cannon) sacre, *m.*

salaam, *s.* zalema, *f.* *v.i.* hacer zalemas

salable, *a.* vendible

salaciousness, *s.* salacidad, *f.*

salad, *s.* ensalada, *f.*; (lettuce) lechuga, *f.* **fruit s.**, macedonia de frutas, *f.* **s.-bowl**, ensaladera, *f.* **s.-dressing**, mayonesa, *f.* **s.-oil**, aceite para ensaladas, *m.*

salamander, *s.* salamandra, *f.*

salamé, *s.* (cul.) salchichón, *m.*

salaried, *a.* a sueldo; (of posts) retribuido

salary, *s.* sueldo, salario, *m.*

sale, *s.* venta, *f.*; (auction) almoneda, subasta pública, *f.* **clearance s.**, liquidación, *f.*, saldo, *m.* **to be on s.**, estar de venta. **Piano for s.**, Se vende un piano. **s. price,** precio de venta, *m.*; precio de saldo, *m.*

saleroom, *s.* salón de ventas, *m.*

salesman, *s.* dependiente de tienda, *m.*; (traveller) viajante, *m.*

salesmanship, *s.* arte de vender, *m.* or *f.*

saleswoman, *s.* dependiente de tienda, vendedera, *f.*

Salic, *a.* sálico

salicylate, *s.* salicilato, *m.*

salient, *a.* saliente; (*fig.*) prominente, conspicuo, notable. *s.* saliente, *m.* **s. angle,** ángulo saliente, *m.*

saline, *a.* salino. *s.* (marsh) saladar, *m.*; (*med.*) salino, *m.*

saliva, *s.* saliva, *f.*

salivary, *a.* salival

salivate, *v.i.* salivar

salivation, *s.* salivación, *f.*

sallow, *a.* cetrino, oliváceo, lívido

sallowness, *s.* amarillez, lividez, *f.*; palidez, *f.*

sally, *s.* (*mil.*, etc.) salida, *f.*; (quip) ocurrencia, salida, *f.* *v.i.* hacer una salida, salir. **to s. forth,** ponerse en camino

salmon, *s.* salmón, *m.*; color de salmón, *m.* **s.-net,** salmonera, *f.* **s. trout,** trucha asalmonada, *f.*

salon, *s.* salón, *m.*

saloon, *s.* sala, *f.*; (of a steamer) cámara, *f.*, salón, *m.*; (on train, for sleeping) departamento de coche cama, *m.*; (on train, for dining) coche comedor, *m.*; (*aut.*) coche cerrado, *m.* **billiard s.,** salón de billares, *m.* **dancing s.,** salón de baile, *m.* **hair-dresser's s.,** salón de peluquero, *m.* **s. bar,** bar, *m.*

salsify, *s.* (*bot.*) salsifí, *m.*

salt, *s.* sal, *f.*; (spice) sabor, *m.*; (wit) sal, agudeza, *f.* *a.* salobre, salino; salado; (of land) salitroso. *v.t.* (season) poner sal en; (cure) salar. **kitchen s.,** sal de cocina, *f.* **old s.,** (*fam.*) lobo de mar, *m.* **rock s.,** sal gema, *f.* **sea s.,** sal marina, *f.* **to be not worth one's s.,** no merecer el pan que se come. **to take with a pinch of s.,** creer con cierta reserva. **s.-cellar,** salero, *m.* **s. lagoon,** albufera, *f.* **s. lake,** lago salado, *m.* **s. marsh,** saladar, *m.* **s. meat,** carne salada, cecina, *f.*

s. merchant, salinero, *m.* **s.-mine,** mina de sal, *f.* **s.-spoon,** cucharita de sal, *f.* **s. water,** agua salada, *f.*; agua de mar, *f.* **s.-water fish,** pez de mar, *m.* **s.-works,** salinas, *f. pl.*

saltiness, *s.* sabor de sal, *m.*; salobridad, *f.*

salting, *s.* saladura, *f.*; (salt marsh) saladar, *m.*

saltless, *a.* sin sal, soso, insípido; (*fig.*) soso

saltpetre, *s.* salitre, *m.* **s. bed,** salitral, *m.* **s. works,** salitrería, *f.*

salty, *a.* salado; salobre

salubrious, *a.* salubre, saludable, sano

salubriousness, *s.* salubridad, *f.*

salutary, *a.* saludable, beneficioso

salutation, *s.* salutación, *f.*, saludo, *m.*

salute, *v.t.* and *v.i.* saludar. *s.* saludo, *m.*; (of guns) salva, *f.* **to fire a s.,** hacer salvas, saludar con . . . salvas. **The soldier saluted them,** El soldado les saludó. **to take the s.,** tomar el saludo. **saluting base,** puesto de mando, *m.*

Salvadorean, *a.* and *s.* salvadoreño (-ña)

salvage, *s.* salvamento, *m.* *v.t.* salvar

salvarsan, *s.* (*med.*) salvarsán, *m.*

salvation, *s.* salvación, *f.* **to work out one's own s.,** salvar el alma. **S. Army,** Ejército de la Salvación, *m.*

salve, *s.* pomada, *f.*; (*fig.*) bálsamo, *m.* *v.t.* curar; (overcome) vencer; (soothe) tranquilizar; (*naut.*) salvar. **to s. one's conscience,** tranquilizar la conciencia

salver, *s.* salva, bandeja, *f.*

salvo, *s.* (of guns or applause) salva, *f.*; (reservation) salvedad, reservación, *f.* **s. of applause,** salva de aplausos, *f.*

Samaritan, *a.* and *s.* samaritano (-na)

same, *a.* mismo; igual; parecido; idéntico. *adv.* lo mismo; del mismo modo. **all the s.,** sin embargo; con todo, a pesar de eso. **at the s. time,** al mismo tiempo; a la vez. **just the s.,** igual;

(nevertheless) sin embargo. **He bowed deeply and I did the s.,** Él hizo una profunda reverencia y yo hice lo mismo. **They do not look at things the s. as we do,** No ven las cosas del mismo modo que nosotros. **If it is the s. to her,** Si le es igual a ella. **It's all the s.,** Es igual, Lo mismo da, Es todo uno

sameness, s. identidad, f.; semejanza, f., parecido, m.; monotonía, f.

Samian, a. and s. samio (-ia)

Samothracian, a. and s. samotracio (-ia)

samovar, s samovar, m.

Samoyed, s. samoyedo (-da)

sampan, s. (boat) champán, m.

sample, s. muestra, f.; prueba, f.; ejemplo, m. v.t. sacar una muestra de; (try) probar. **s. book,** muestrario, m.

sampler, s. probador, m.; (of wines) catador, m.; (sew.) dechado, m.

sanatorium, s. sanatorio, m.

sanctification, s. santificación, f.; consagración, f.

sanctify, v.t. santificar; consagrar

sanctimonious, a. santurrón, mojigato, beato

sanctimoniousness, s. beatería, mojigatería, santurronería, f.

sanction, s. sanción, f. v.t. sancionar; autorizar. **to apply sanctions,** (pol.) aplicar sanciones

sanctity, s. santidad, f.; lo sagrado; inviolabilidad, f. **odour of s.,** olor de santidad, f.

sanctuary, s. santuario, m.; (historical) sagrado, m.; refugio, asilo, m. **to take s.,** acogerse a sagrado; refugiarse

sand, s. arena, f.; (for drying writing) arenilla, f.; granos de arena, m. pl.; pl. **sands,** playa, f.; (of life) horas de la vida, f. pl. v.t. arenar. **to plough the s.,** arar en el mar. **s.-bag,** s. saco de arena, m. v.t. (a building) proteger con sacos de arena; (a person) golpear con un saco de arena. **s.-bank,** banco de arena, m., barra, f. **to run on a s.-bank,** encallar. **s.-coloured,** de color de arena. **s.-dune,** médano, m. **s.-paper,** s. papel de lija, m. v.t. pulir con papel de lija, lijar. **s.-pit,** arenal, m. **s. shoes,** alpargatas, f. pl.

sandal, s. sandalia, f.; (ropesoled) alpargata, f. **s.-wood,** sándalo, m.

sandarach gum; s. sandáraca, f.

sandiness, s. naturaleza arenosa, f.; (of hair) color bermejo, m.

sandstone, s. arenisca, f.

sandstorm, s. tempestad de arena, f.; simún, m.

sandwich, s. emparedado, bocadillo, m. v.t. insertar. **I found myself sandwiched between two fat women,** Me encontré aplastado entre dos mujeres gordas. **s.-man,** hombre sándwich, m.

sandy, a. arenoso; sabuloso; (of hair) rojo, rufo, bermejo. **a s. beach,** una playa arenosa

sane, a. de juicio sano; razonable, prudente; sesudo. **He is a very s. person,** Es un hombre con mucho sentido común. **to be s.,** estar en su juicio; (of a policy, etc.) ser prudente, ser razonable

sang-froid, s. sangre fría, f.; aplomo, m.

sanguinary, a. sanguinario

sanguine, a. (of complexion) rubicundo; sanguíneo; optimista, confiado. s. (drawing) sanguina, f. **to be s. about the future,** ser optimista acerca del porvenir, tener confianza en el porvenir

sanhedrim, s. sanedrín, m.

sanitary, a. sanitario; higiénico. **s. inspector,** inspector de sanidad, m. **s. towel,** servilleta higiénica, f., paño higiénico, m.

sanitation, s. higiene, f.; sanidad pública, f.; (apparatus) instalación sanitaria, f.

sanity, s. juicio sano, m.; prudencia, f.; (common sense) sentido común, m., sensatez, f.

sanscrit, a. and s. sánscrito (m.)

Santa Claus, s. (Spanish equivalent) los Reyes Magos

santonine, s. santonina, f.

sap, s. (bot. and fig.) savia, f.; (mil.) zapa, f. v.t. (undermine) debilitar, agotar; (mil.) zapar

sapidity, s. sapidez, f.

sapling, s. arbolillo, m.

saponaceous, a. saponáceo

sapper, s. (mil.) zapador, m.

Sapphic, a. sáfico. S. verse, verso sáfico, m.

sapphire, s. zafiro, m. a. de zafiros; cerúleo, de zafiro

saraband, s. zarabanda, f.

Saracen, a. and s. sarraceno (-na)

sarcasm, s. sarcasmo, m.

sarcastic, a. sarcástico

sarcastically, adv. con sarcasmo, sarcásticamente

sarcophagus, s. sarcófago, m.

sardine, s. sardina, f. packed like sardines, como sardinas en banasta. s.-net, sardinal, m.

Sardinian, a. and s. sardo (-da)

sardonic, a. sardónico

sardonically, adv. sardónica-mente

sardonyx, s. sardónice, f.

sarsaparilla, s. zarzaparrilla, f.

sash, s. (with uniform) faja, f.; (belt) cinto, cinturón, m.; (of a window) cerco, m. s. window, ventana de guillotina, f.

Satan, s. Satanás, m.

satanic, a. satánico

satchel, s. saquito de mano, m., bolsa, f.; (school) vademécum, m.; cartapacio, m., cartera, f.

sate, v.t. saciar, hartar; satisfacer

sateen, s. satén, m.

satellite, s. satélite, m.

satiable, a. saciable

satiate, v.t. saciar, hartar; satis-facer. a. harto; repleto

satiety, s. saciedad, f.

satin, s. raso, m. a. de raso; (glossy) lustroso, terso. v.t. (paper) satinar

satiny, a. arrasado; lustroso, brillante

satire, s. sátira, f.

satiric, a. satírico

satirically, adv. satíricamente

satirist, s. escritor (-ra) satírico (-ca)

satirize, v.t. satirizar

satisfaction, s. satisfacción, f.; (contentment) contento, m., satis-facción, f.; (for sin) expiación, f.; (of a debt) pago, m.; desquite, m.; recompensa, f. to demand s., pedir satisfacción. to give (someone) s., dar contento (a), alegrar

satisfactorily, adv. satisfactoria-mente

satisfactoriness, s. carácter satis-factorio, m., lo satisfactorio

satisfactory, a. satisfactorio; (for sin) expiatorio

satisfy, v.t. satisfacer; (convince) convencer; (allay) tranquilizar, apaciguar. I am satisfied with him, Estoy satisfecho (Estoy contento) con él. The explana-tion did not s. me, La explica-ción no me convenció. to s. oneself that ..., asegurarse de que ... to s. one's thirst, apagar la sed

satisfying, a. que satisface; satis-factorio; (of food) nutritivo

satrap, s. sátrapa, m.

saturate, v.t. saturar (de), em-papar (de); (chem.) saturar; (fig.) imbuir; (fig.) empapar. to s. oneself in, (a subject) empaparse en

saturation, s. saturación, f. s. point, (chem., etc.) punto de saturación, m.

Saturday, s. sábado, m.

Saturn, s. Saturno, m.

saturnalia, s. pl. saturnales, f. pl.

saturnine, a. saturnino, taciturno

satyr, s. sátiro, m.

sauce, s. salsa, f.; (thick fruit) compota, f.; (fam.) insolencia, f. s.-boat, salsera, f.

saucepan, s. cazuela, cacerola, f. double s., baño de María, m.

saucer, s. platillo, m. flying s., platillo volante, m. s.-eyed, con ojos redondos

sauciness, s. impertinencia, in-solencia, f.

saucy, a. respondón, descarado; (cheerful) alegre; (of hats, etc.) coquetón, majo

sauerkraut, s. choucroute, f.

saunter, v.i. pasearse, vagar. s. paseo, m., vuelta, f.

saurian, a. and s. (zool.) saurio (m.)

sausage, s. chorizo, m.; salchicha, f. s.-balloon, globo cautivo, m. s.-curl, bucle, m. s.-machine, choricera, f. s.-maker, choricero (-ra)

savage, a. salvaje; feroz; (cruel) inhumano, cruel; (furious) furio-so. s. salvaje, m. and f.

savagely, adv. bárbaramente; ferozmente; furiosamente

savagery, *s.* salvajismo, *m.*; ferocidad, *f.*; brutalidad, crueldad, *f.*

savannah, *s.* sabana, *f.* **s. dweller**, sabanero (-ra)

save, *v.t.* salvar; (keep) guardar; conservar; reservar; (money, one's clothes, etc.) ahorrar; (time) ganar; (avoid) evitar. *v.i.* salvar; hacer economías; ahorrar. **He saved my life**, Me salvó la vida. **They have saved a room for me**, Me han reservado una habitación. **to s. appearances**, guardar las apariencias. **to s. oneself trouble**, ahorrarse molestias. **to s. the situation**, estar al nivel de las circunstancias

save, *prep.* salvo, excepto, menos. *conjunc.* sino, a menos que; con la excepción de. **all s. one**, todos menos uno. **all the conspirators s. he**, todos los conspiradores con la excepción de él

saving, *a.* frugal, económico; (stingy) tacaño, avaricioso; (clause) condicional. *s.* salvación, *f.*; (of money, time, etc.) ahorro, *m.*, economía, *f.*; *pl.* **savings**, ahorros, *m. pl. prep.* salvo, excepto, fuera de. *conjunc.* con excepción de que, fuera de que. **s. grace**, único mérito, *m.* **savings bank**, caja de ahorros, *f.* **savings fund**, monte pío, *m.*

saviour, *s.* salvador (-ra). **the S.**, el Salvador, el Redentor

savour, *s.* sabor, gusto, *m.*; (aftertaste) dejo, *m.*; (zest) salsa, *f.* *v.i.* saber (a), tener sabor (de); (*fig.*) oler (a). *v.t.* saborear, paladear; (flavour) sazonar

savouriness, *s.* buen sabor, *m.*; (of a district) respetabilidad, *f.*

savoury, *a.* sabroso, apetitoso; (not sweet) no dulce; (of places) respetable; (of reputation, etc.) bueno. *s.* entremés salado, *m.* **s. omelette**, tortilla, *f.*

Savoyard, *a.* saboyano

saw, *s.* (maxim) sentencia, *f.*; (proverb) refrán, decir, *m.*; (tool) sierra, *f.* *v.t.* aserrar; (the air) cortar. *v.i.* usar una sierra. **two-handled saw**, tronzador, *m.* **saw-fish**, pez sierra, *m.* **saw-**

mill, molino de aserrar, *m.* **saw-pit**, aserradero, *m.*

sawdust, *s.* aserrín, *m.*

sawing-horse, *s.* caballete de aserrar, *m.*

sawyer, *s.* aserrador, *m.*

saxifrage, *s.* saxífraga, *f.*

Saxon, *a.* and *s.* sajón (-ona)

saxophone, *s.* saxófono, *m.*

say, *v.t.* decir; recitar. *v.i.* decir. **Let us say that the house is worth £4,000**, Pongamos por ejemplo que la casa vale cuatro mil libras. **He has no say in the matter**, No entra ni sale en el asunto. **I have said my say**, He dicho lo que quería. **They say**, Se dice, Dicen, La gente dice. **You don't say!** ¡Calle!; ¿De veras?; ¡Imposible! **that is to say ...**, es decir ...; esto es ..., a saber ... **to say one's prayers**, rezar, decir sus oraciones. **to say again**, volver a decir; decir otra vez, repetir. **to say over and over again**, repetir muchas veces, decir repetidamente

saying, *s.* decir, *m.*; (proverb) refrán, proverbio, *m.*; (maxim) sentencia, *f.* **As the s. is**, Como suele decirse; Según el refrán. **It goes without s.**, Va sin decir. **It's only a s.**, Es un decir, nada más

scab, *s.* (of a wound) costra, *f.*; (disease) escabro, *m.*; (blackleg) esquirol, *m.*

scabbard, *s.* vaina (de espada), *f.*

scabby, *a.* costroso; (diseased) roñoso, sarnoso

scabies, *s.* sarna, *f.* **s. mite**, arador de la sarna, *m.*

scabious, *s.* (*bot.*) escabiosa, *f.* *a.* (*med.*) escabioso

scaffold, *s.* (in building) andamio, *m.*; (for execution) cadalso, patíbulo, *m.* **to go to the s.**, ir al patíbulo; acabar en el patíbulo

scaffolding, *s.* andamiada, *f.*; (building, scaffold) andamio, *m.*

scald, *v.t.* escaldar; quemar; (instruments) esterilizar. *s.* quemadura, escaldadura, *f.* **to s. oneself**, escaldarse. **scalding hot**, hirviendo

scale, *s.* (of a balance) platillo, *m.*; (*zool.*) escama, *f.*; (*bot.*)

brádtea, *f.*; (*bot.*) hojuela, *f.*; (flake) laminita, *f.*; (*mus.*, *math.*) escala, *f.*; (of charges, etc.) tarifa, *f.*; (of salaries) escalafón, *m.*; (of a thermometer) escala, *f.* *v.t.* escalar; (fish) escamar. **major s.**, escala mayor, *f.* **minor s.**, escala menor, *f.* **on a grand s.**, en gran escala. **on a small s.**, en pequeña escala. **pair of scales**, balanza, *f.*; (for heavy weights) báscula, *f.* **social s.**, escala social, *f.* **The Scales**, (*ast.*) Libra, *f.* **to draw to s.**, dibujar a escala. **to turn the scales**, pesar; (*fig.*) inclinar la balanza. **to s. down**, (*art*, and of charges) reducir

scaling, *s.* (of fish) escamadura, *f.*; (of buildings) desconchadura, *f.*; (ascent) escalamiento, *m.*

scallop, *s.* (*icht.* and badge) venera, *f.*; concha, *f.*; (*sew.*) onda, *f.*, festón, *m.* *v.t.* (*cul.*) guisar en conchas; (*sew.*) ondear, festonear

scalp, *s.* (*anat.*) paricráneo, *m.*; cuero cabelludo, *m.*; (*fig.*) trofeo, *m.* *v.t.* escalpar. **s.-hunter**, cazador de cabelleras, *m.*

scalpel, *s.* escalpelo, *m.*

scaly, *a.* escamoso, conchado; (of boilers) incrustado

scamp, *s.* bribón, granuja, *m.* *v.t.* (work) frangollar

scamper, *v.i.* retozar, brincar; correr. *s.* carrerita, *f.* **to s. off**, salvarse por los pies, huir; marcharse corriendo

scan, *v.t.* (verse) medir, escandir; (examine) escudriñar, examinar; (glance at) dar un vistazo (a)

scandal, *s.* escándalo, *m.*; maledicencia, *f.*; (slander) calumnia, *f.* **to talk s.**, murmurar

scandalize, *v.t.* escandalizar

scandalous, *a.* escandaloso; infame; calumnioso

scandalously, *adv.* escandalosamente

scandalousness, *s.* carácter escandaloso, *m.*

Scandinavian, *a.* escandinavo. *s.* escandinavo (-va); lengua escandinava, *f.*

scansion, *s.* escansión, *f.*

scant, *a.* escaso; insuficiente

scantily, *adv.* insuficientemente

scantiness, *s.* escasez, *f.*; insuficiencia, *f.*

scanty, *a.* insuficiente; escaso; (of hair) ralo; (of crops, etc.) pobre

scapegoat, *s.* víctima propiciatoria, *f.*; **cabeza de turco**, *f.* **to be a s. for**, pagar el pato por

scapegrace, *s.* bribón, *m.*

scapula, *s.* (*anat.*) escápula, *f.*

scapulary, *s.* (*ecc.*) escapulario, *m.*

scar, *s.* cicatriz, *f.*; (*fig.*) señal, *f.* *v.t.* marcar con una cicatriz. **to s. over**, cicatrizarse

scarab, *s.* escarabajo, *m.*; escarabajo sagrado, *m.*

scarce, *a.* escaso; insuficiente; raro. *adv.* (*poet.*) apenas. **to make oneself s.**, largarse, pirarse, escabullirse; ausentarse, esconderse

scarcely, *adv.* apenas; no bien; casi; (with difficulty) a duras penas, con dificultad. **It is s. likely he said that**, No es muy probable que hubiese dicho eso. **There were s. twenty people in the building**, Había apenas veinte personas en el edificio. **S. anyone likes his pictures**, Sus cuadros no gustan a casi nadie

scarcity, *s.* escasez, insuficiencia, *f.*; (famine) carestía, *f.*; (rarity) rareza, *f.*

scare, *v.t.* asustar, espantar, llenar de miedo (a); intimidar. *s.* susto, pánico, *m.*; alarma, *f.* **What a s. I got!** ¡Qué susto me he llevado! **to s. away**, ahuyentar

scarecrow, *s.* espantapájaros, *m.*; (*fam.*) estantigua, *f.*, mamarracho, espantajo, *m.*

scaremonger, *s.* alarmista, *m.* and *f.*

scarf, *s.* bufanda, *f.*; (tie) corbata, *f.*; (*mil.*) faja, *f.*

scarlatina, *s.* (*med.*) escarlatina, *f.*

scarlet, *s.* escarlata, *f.* *a.* de color escarlata. **to turn s.**, (of persons) enrojecerse. **s. fever**, escarlatina, *f.* **s. hat**, (*ecc.*) capelo (cardenalicio), *m.* **s. runner**, (*bot.*) judía verde, *f.*

scatheless, *a.* ileso, sano y salvo

scathing, *a.* mordaz, cáustico

scathingly, *adv.* mordazmente, cáusticamente

scatter, v.t. esparcir, sembrar
con; (benefits, etc.) derramar;
(put to flight) derrotar; dispersar: disipar; (fig.) frustrar;
(squander) derrochar, desparramar. v.i. dispersarse. **The
crowd scattered,** La muchedumbre se dispersó. **s.-brained,**
de cabeza de chorlito, atolondrado

scattered, a. disperso; esparcido

scattering, s. dispersión, f.;
(defeat) derrota, f.; esparcimiento, m.; (small number)
número pequeño, m.

scavenge, v.t. (streets) recoger la
basura, barrer

scavenger, s. (of the streets)
barrendero, m.; (dustman) basurero, m.; (zool.) animal que se
alimenta de carne muerta, m.;
insecto que se alimenta de
estiércol, m. v.t. See **scavenge**

scenario, s. escenario, m.

scene, s. escena, f.; teatro, lugar,
m.; espectáculo, m.; (theat., décor)
decoración, f.; (of a play)
escena, f.; (view) vista, perspectiva, f. **behind the scenes,**
entre bastidores (also fig.). **The
s. is laid . . .,** La acción pasa . . .
to come on the s., entrar en
escena. **to make a s.,** hacer una
escena. **to lose the s.,** perder la
escena. **s.-painter,** s. escenógrafo (-fa). **s.-shifter,** tramoyista, m.

scenery, s. (theat.) decorado, m.;
(landscape) paisaje, m.

scenic, a. dramático; escénico;
pintoresco. **s. railway,** montaña
rusa, f.

scenography, s. escenografía, f.

scent, v.t. perfumar; (smell) oler;
(out) husmear, olfatear; (suspect)
sospechar. s. perfume, m.; fragancia, f., aroma, m.; (smell) olor,
m.; (of hounds) viento, m.; (of
game, etc.) rastro, viento, m.;
(fig., of person) nariz, f.; (trail)
pista, f. **to lose the s.,** perder la
pista. **to s. danger,** oler el
peligro. **to throw off the s.,**
despistar. **s.-bottle,** frasco de
perfume, m. **s.-spray,** pulverizador, m.

scented, a. perfumado; (of roses,
etc.) de olor, oloroso; (in compounds) de . . . olfato. s.
sweet-pea, guisante de olor, m.

scentless, a. sin olor; inodoro

sceptic, s. escéptico (-ca)

sceptical, a. escéptico

scepticism, s. escepticismo, m.

sceptre, s. cetro, m.

schedule, s. lista, f.; programa,
m.; (of taxes) clase, f.; (of trains,
etc.) horario, m. v.t. poner en una
lista; inventariar

scheme, s. plan, m.; proyecto, m.;
diagrama, esquema, m.; (summary) resumen, m.; (of colours,
etc.) combinación, f.; (plot)
intriga, maquinación, f. v.t.
proyectar. v.i. planear, formar
planes; (intrigue) intrigar, conspirar. **colour s.,** combinación
de colores, f.

schemer, s. (plotter) intrigante,
m. and f.

scheming, a. intrigante; astuto.
s. planes, proyectos, m. pl.;
intrigas, maquinaciones, f. pl.

schism, s. cisma, m. or f.

schismatic, a. cismático. s.
cismático (-ca)

scholar, s. (at school) colegial
(-la); (disciple) alumno (-na);
(student) estudiante, m. and f.;
(learned person) erudito (-ta),
hombre de letras, m.; (scholarship holder) becario, m. **to be a
poor s.,** (fig.) ser analfabeto

scholarly, a. de sabio, de hombre
de letras; erudito

scholarship, s. erudición, f.;
saber, m.; (exhibition) beca, f.
s. holder, becario, m.

scholastic, a. escolar, escolástico;
pedante; (medieval) escolástico.
s. escolástico, m. **the s. profession,** el magisterio

school, s. escuela, f.; colegio, m.;
academia, f.; (univ.) departamento, m.; (faculty) facultad, f.;
(of fish) banco, m. v.t. enseñar,
instruir; formar; disciplinar. **in
s.,** en clase. **day s.,** escuela, f.,
colegio, m. **the Florentine s.,**
(of painting) la escuela florentina.
the lower s., los alumnos del
preparatorio. **private s.,** colegio
particular, m. **s.-bag,** vademécum, m. **s.-book,** libro de texto,
m. **s.-days,** los días de escuela;
los años de colegio. **in his s.-
days,** cuando él iba a la escuela.
s.-fees, gastos de la enseñanza,
m. pl., cuota escolar, f.

schoolboy, *s.* muchacho de escuela; colegial, *m.*

schoolfellow, *s.* compañero de colegio, condiscípulo, *m.*

schoolgirl, *s.* colegiala, *f.*

schooling, *s.* educación, enseñanza, *f.*

schoolmaster, *s.* maestro de escuela, profesor, *m.*

schoolmistress, *s.* maestra de escuela, profesora, *f.*

schoolroom, *s.* sala de clase, *f.*

schooner, *s.* (*naut.*) goleta, *f.*

sciatic, *a.* ciático

sciatica, *s.* ciática, *f.*

science, *s.* ciencia, *f.*

scientific, *a.* científico; exacto, sistemático

scientifically, *adv.* científicamente

scientist, *s.* hombre de ciencia, *m.*, científico (-ca)

scimitar, *s.* cimitarra, *f.*

scintilla, *s.* (*fig.*) átomo, vestigio, *m.*

scintillate, *v.i.* centellear, lucir, chispear; (of persons) brillar

scintillation, *s.* destello, centelleo, *m.*; (of wit) relámpago, *m.*

scion, *s.* (sucker) acodo, *m.*; (shoot) vástago, renuevo, *m.*; (human) descendiente, *m.* and *f.* s. of a noble race, vástago de una raza noble, *m.*

scissors, *s. pl.* tijeras, *f. pl.* s.-sharpener, amolador, *m.*

sclerosis, *s.* (*med.*) esclerosis, *f.*

sclerotic, *s.* (*anat.*) esclerótica, *f.*

scoff, *s.* burla, mofa, *f. v.i.* burlarse. to s. at, burlarse de, mofarse de

scoffer, *s.* mofador (-ra); (at religion, etc.) incrédulo (-la)

scoffing, *a.* burlón. *s.* mofas, burlas, *f. pl.*

scold, *s.* virago, *f. v.t.* reñir, reprender

scolding, *s.* reprensión, increpación, *f.*

sconce, *s.* cubo de candelero, *m.*; candelabro de pared, *m.*; cornucopia, *f.*

scone, *s.* bollo, *m.*

scoop, *s.* pala de mano, *f.*; cuchara de draga, *f.*; (boat) achicador, *m.*; (financial) golpe, *m.*; (journalistic) éxito periodístico, *m. v.t.* sacar con pala (de); sacar con cuchara (de); (shares,

etc.) comprar, obtener. to s. out, vaciar; excavar; (bail) achicar

scooter, *s.* (child's) patinete, *m.*; monopatín, *m.*

scope, *s.* alcance, *m.*; esfera de acción, *f.*; lugar, *m.* to give full s. to, dar rienda suelta a. to have full s., tener plena oportunidad; tener todas las facilidades. within the s. of, dentro del alcance de

scorbutic, *a.* (*med.*) escorbútico

scorch, *v.t.* chamuscar; (the skin) tostar; (of the sun) abrasar, quemar; (wither) agostar. to s. along, ir como un relámpago.

scorching, *a.* abrasador, ardiente; (*fig.*) mordaz

score, *s.* (scratch) rasguño, *m.*; señal, *f.*; (crossing out) raya, *f.*; (reckoning) cuenta, *f.*, escote, *m.*; (notch) muesca, *f.*; (*sport*) tanteo, *m.*, puntuación, *f.*; (point) punto, tanto, *m.*; (twenty) veintena, *f.*; (reason) motivo, *m.*, causa, *f.*; respecto, *m.*; (*mus.*) partitura, *f. v.t.* marcar; rayar; (erase) tachar, borrar; (cricket runs, etc.) hacer; (goals) marcar; (points) ganar; (reckon) apuntar; (*mus.*) instrumentar; (for orchestra) orquestar. *v.i.* (be fortunate) llevar la ventaja. to pay off old scores, ajustar cuentas viejas. to s. off someone, ganar un punto (a), triunfar de. upon that s., a ese respecto; por esa causa. Upon what s.? ¿Con qué motivo? s.-board, marcador, *m.*

scorer, *s.* (of a goal, etc.) tanteador, *m.*; (keeper of score) marcador, *m.*

scoria, *s.* escoria, *f.*

scorn, *s.* desprecio, desdén, *m. v.t.* despreciar, desdeñar; reírse de. to s. to do, no dignarse hacer

scornful, *a.* desdeñoso, despreciativo

scornfully, *adv.* desdeñosamente, con desprecio

Scorpio, *s.* Escorpión, *m.*

scorpion, *s.* escorpión, alacrán, *m.*; (*ast.*) Escorpión, *m.*

Scot, *s.* escocés, *m.*

scotch, *v.t.* (kill) matar; (thwart) frustrar; (a wheel) calzar

Scotswoman, *s.* escocesa, *f.*

Scottish, *a.* escocés

scoundrel, *s.* canalla, sinvergüenza, *m.*

scoundrelly, *a.* canallesco, vil

scour, *v.t.* (traverse) recorrer, batir; (pans, etc.) fregar, estregar; (free from) limpiar (de); (of water) arrastrar

scourge, *v.t.* azotar, flagelar; castigar, mortificar. *s.* disciplinas, *f. pl.*; (*fig.*) verdugo, *m.*, plaga, *f.*

scout, *s* (*mil.*) batidor, explorador, *m. v.i.* (*mil.*) explorar, reconocer. *v.t.* (flout) rechazar con desdén. **boy s.,** muchacho explorador, *m.*

scowl, *v.i.* fruncir el ceño. *s.* ceño, *m.* **to s. at,** mirar con ceño

scowling, *a.* amenazador

scragginess, *s.* magrez, flaqueza, *f.*

scraggy, *a.* flaco, magro, descarnado

scramble, *v.i.* trepar. *v.t.* (throw) arrojar; (eggs) revolver. **scrambled eggs,** huevos revueltos, *m. pl.* **to s. for,** andar a la rebatiña por; (for coins, etc.) luchar para. **to s. up,** escalar; subir a gatas

scrap, *s.* pedazo, *m.*; fragmento, *m.*; pizca, brizna, *f.*; (shindy) suiza, camorra, *f.*; (boxing) combate de boxeo, *m.*; *pl.* **scraps,** desperdicios, *m. pl.*; (food) restos de la comida, *m. pl. v.t.* desechar; (expunge) borrar; *v.i.* (fight) armar camorra. **a few scraps of news,** algunas noticias. **Do you mind not coming? Not a s.,** ¿ Te importa el no venir? Ni pizca. **s.-book,** álbum de recortes, *m.*; **s.-heap,** depósito de basura, *m.*; (*fig.*) olvido, *m.* **s. iron,** chatarra, *f.*, hierro viejo, *m.*

scrape, *v.t.* raspar, rascar, raer; (one's shoes) restregar; (a musical instrument) rascar. *s.* rasguño, *m.*; ruido de raspar, *m.*; (predicament) lío, apuro, *m.*; dificultad, *f.* **to s. acquaintance with,** trabar amistad con. **to s. along,** (*fam.*) ir tirando **to s. away,** rascar; quitar. **to s. through,** (an examination) aprobar justo. **to s. together,** amontonar poco a poco

scrappy, *a.* escaso; fragmentario; (incoherent) descosido. **a s. meal,** una comida escasa

scratch, *v.t.* arañar; (the earth) escarbar; (rub) rascar; (a hole) hacer; (sketch) dibujar, trazar; (a horse) retirar de una carrera. *v.i.* arañar; rascar; escarbar; (of a pen) rasguear; (back out) retirarse. *s.* arañazo, *m.*; (of a pen) rasgueo, *m.*; (in a race) línea de salida, *f.*; (in games) cero, *m. a.* improvisado. **The dog scratched at the door,** El perro arañó la puerta. **to come up to s.,** estar al nivel de las circunstancias. **to s. one's head,** rascarse la cabeza. **to s. a person's eyes out,** sacar los ojos con las uñas (a). **to s. the surface of,** (a subject) tratar superficialmente. **to s. out,** tachar

scrawl, *v.i.* hacer garabatos. *v.t.* garabatear, garrapatear. *s.* garabato, *m.*

scream, *v.t.* and *v.i.* chillar. *s.* chillido, *m.* **It was a perfect s.,** Era para morirse de risa. **to s. with laughter,** reírse a carcajadas, morirse de risa

screaming, *s.* chillidos, *m. pl. a.* chillador; (piercing) penetrante, agudo; (funny) divertidísimo

scree, *s.* (*geol.*) deyecciones, *f. pl.*; escombros, *m. pl.*

screech, *v.i.* chillar; (of owls, etc.) ulular; graznar. *s.* chillido, *m.*; ululación, *f.*; graznido, *m.* **s.-owl,** úlula, *f.*

screed, *s.* arenga, *f.*; cita larga, *f.*

screen, *s.* biombo, *m.*; (nonfolding) mampara, *f.*; (*ecc.*) cancel, *m.*; (cinema, television) pantalla, *f.*; (of trees, etc., and *mil.*) cortina, *f.*; (*fig.*, protection) abrigo, *m. v.i.* proteger; (shelter) abrigar; (hide) esconder, ocultar; (a light) proteger con pantalla; (a film) proyectar; (sieve) cribar, cerner; (examine) investigar. **to s. from view,** ocultar a la vista (de), esconder. **s. star,** estrella de la pantalla, *f.*

screw, *s.* tornillo, *m.*; (propeller) hélice, *f.*; vuelta de tornillo, *f.*; presión, *f.*; (miser) tacaño, *m.*; (salary) salario, *m. v.t.* atornillar;

torcer; apretar, oprimir. **He has a s. loose,** Le falta un tornillo. **to s. down,** sujetar con tornillos. **to s. up,** cerrar con tornillos. **to s. up one's courage,** tomar coraje. **to s. up one's eyes,** desojarse, entornar los ojos. **s.-driver,** destornillador, *m.*

scribble, *v.t.* escribir de prisa. *v.i.* garabatear, garrapatear; escribir, ser autor. *s.* garabato, garrapato, *m.*; mala letra, letra ilegible, *f.*; (note) billete, *m.*

scribbler, *s.* el, *m.* (*f.* la) que tiene mala letra; (author) autor (-ra) malo (-la)

scribbling, *s.* garabateo, *m.* **s.-block,** bloque de papel, *m.*

scribe, *s.* escribiente, copista, *m.*; (Jewish history) escriba, *m.*

scrimmage, *s.* reyerta, pelea, camorra, *f.*; (Rugby) mêlée, *f.*

script, *s.* letra cursiva, *f.*; (*print.*) plumilla, *f.*; manuscrito, *m.*; (*law*) escritura, *f.*; examen escrito, *m.*; (film) escenario, *m.*

scriptural, *a.* bíblico

Scripture, *s.* Sagrada Escritura, *f.* **the Scriptures,** la Biblia; (of non-Christian religions) los libros sagrados

scrivener, *s.* chupatintas, *m.*

scrofula, *s.* escrófula, *f.*

scrofulous, *a.* escrofuloso

scroll, *s.* (of paper, etc.) rollo, *m.*; pergamino, *m.*; (flourish) rúbrica, *f.*; (of an Ionic capital) voluta, *f.* **s. of fame,** lista de la fama, *f.*

scrotum, *s.* (*anat.*) escroto, *m.*

scrounge, *v.i.* sablear. *v.t.* dar un sablazo (a); hurtar

scrounger, *s.* sablista, *m.* and *f.*

scrub, *v.t.* fregar; limpiar; restregar. *s.* fregado, *m.*; limpieza, *f.*; fricción, *f.*; (brushwood) matorral, breñal, *m.*, maleza, *f.*

scrubbing, *s.* fregado, *m.* **s.-brush,** cepillo para el suelo, *m.*

scrubby, *a.* (of plants) anémico; (of persons) insignificante, pobre; (of land) cubierto de maleza

scruff, *s.* nuca, *f.*, pescuezo, *m.*

scruple, *s.* escrúpulo, *m.* *v.i.* tener escrúpulos. **to have no scruples,** no tener escrúpulos

scrupulous, *a.* escrupuloso; exacto, meticuloso

scrupulously, *adv.* escrupulosamente; meticulosamente

scrupulousness, *s.* escrupulosidad, *f.*; meticulosidad, *f.*

scrutinize, *v.t.* escudriñar, examinar; (votes) escrutar

scrutinizer, *s.* escudriñador (-ra); (of votes) escrutador (-ra)

scrutinizing, *a.* escrutador

scrutiny, *s.* escrutinio, *m.*

scud, *v.i.* correr; deslizarse; flotar. **to s. before the wind,** ir viento en popa

scuffle, *v.i.* pelear, forcejear, andar a la rebatiña. *s.* refriega, pelea, sarracina, arrebatiña, *f.*

scull, *s.* remo, *m.* *v.i.* remar

scullery, *s.* fregadero, *m.* **s.-maid,** fregona, *f.*

scullion, *s.* pinche, galopillo, *m.*

sculptor, *s.* escultor, *m.* **woman s.,** escultora, *f.*

sculptural, *a.* escultural, escultórico

sculpture, *s.* escultura, *f.* *v.t.* esculpir

scum, *s.* espuma, *f.*; (dregs) heces, *f. pl.* *v.t.* espumar. **s. of the earth,** las heces de la sociedad

scummy, *a.* espumoso

scupper, *s.* (*naut.*) clava, *f.* *v.t.* abrir las clavas (de); (frustrate) frustrar, destruir

scurrility, *s.* grosería, indecencia, *f.*

scurrilous, *a.* grosero, indecente

scurry, *v.i.* echar a correr. *s.* fuga precipitada, *f.*; (of rain) chaparrón, *m.*; (of snow) remolino, *m.* **to s. off,** escabullirse. **to s. through,** hacer de prisa, terminar rápidamente

scurvy, *a.* tiñoso, vil, ruin. *s.* escorbuto, *m.* **a s. trick,** una mala pasada

scut, *s.* (of a rabbit) rabillo, *m.*

scuttle, *s.* (trap-door) escotillón, *m.*; (*naut.*) escotilla, *f.*; (for coal) carbonera, *f.*; (flight) huida precipita, *f.* *v.t.* (a boat) echar a pique. *v.i.* (run away) escabullirse, apretar a correr

scythe, *s.* dalle, *m.*, guadaña, *f.* *v.t.* dallar, segar

sea, *s.* mar, *m.* or *f.*; ola, *f.*; multitud, *f.* **Black, Mediterranean Sea,** Mar Negro, (Mar)

Mediterráneo, m. **at sea**, en el mar; perplejo. **beyond the seas**, allende el mar. **by sea**, por mar. **by the sea**, a la orilla del mar. **high seas**, alta mar, f. **the seven seas**, todos los mares del mundo. **to go to sea**, hacerse marinero. **to put to sea**, hacerse a la mar, hacerse a la vela. **sea-anemone**, anémone de mar, f. **sea-bathing**, baños de mar, m. pl. **sea-breeze**, brisa de mar, f. **sea captain**, capitán de mar, m. **sea chart**, carta de marear, f. **sea-coast**, litoral, m., costa marítima, f. **sea-cow**, manatí, m. **sea dog**, lobo de mar, m. **sea-fight**, combate naval, m. **sea-foam**, espuma de mar, f. **sea-girt**, rodeado por el mar. **sea-going**, de altura; navegante. **sea-going craft**, embarcación de alta mar, f. **sea-green**, verdemar, m. **sea-gull**, gaviota, f. **sea-horse**, caballo marino, m. **sea-legs**, piernas de marino, f. pl. **sea-level**, nivel del mar, m. **sea-lion**, león marino, m. **sea-mist**, bruma, f. **sea-nymph**, nereida, f. **sea-power**, potencia naval, f. **sea-serpent**, serpiente de mar, f. **sea-sick**, mareado. **to be sea-sick**, marearse. **sea-sickness**, mal de mar, m. **sea-trip**, viaje por mar, m. **sea-urchin**, erizo de mar, m. **sea-wall**, dique de mar, m.

seafarer, s. (traveller) viajero (-ra) por mar; (sailor) marinero, m.

seafaring, a. marinero, marino. s. viajes por mar, m. pl.; vida del marinero, f.

seal, s. (zool.) foca, f., lobo marino, m.; piel de foca, f.; sello, m.; (stamp) estampillo, timbre, m.; v.t. sellar; (stamp) estampar; (letters, etc.) cerrar; v.i. cazar focas. **His fate is sealed**, Su suerte está determinada. **His lips were sealed**, Sus labios estaban cerrados. **under my hand and s.**, firmado y sellado por mí. **s.-ring**, sortija de sello, f.

sealing-wax, s. lacre, m.

sealskin, s. piel de foca, f.

seam, s. (sew.) costura, f.; (naut.) costura de los tablones, f.; (anat.) sutura, f.; (surg.) cicatriz, f.; (wrinkle) arruga, f., surco, m.; (geol.) capa, f., yacimiento, m.; (min.) vena, f., filón, m. v.t. coser; juntar; (a face) surcar, arrugar

seaman, s. marinero, m.; hombre de mar, m.; navegante, m. **able-bodied s.**, marinero práctico, m.

seamanlike, a. de marinero, marino; de buen marinero

seamanship, s. marinería, f.; náutica, f.

seamstress, s. costurera, f.

seamy, a. con costuras. **the s. side of life**, el lado peor de la vida

séance, s. sesión, junta, f.; sesión de espiritistas, f.

seaplane, s. hidroavión, hidroplano, m.

seaport, s. puerto de mar, m.

sear, a. marchito. v.t. agostar, secar; (a wound) cauterizar; marchitar, ajar; (a conscience) endurecer

search, v.t. registrar; (a wound) explorar; examinar; escudriñar; investigar. v.i. buscar. s. busca, f.; (of luggage, etc.) reconocimiento, m. **in s. of**, en busca de. **to s. after, for**, buscar; ir al encuentro de. **to s. out**, ir en busca de; preguntar por. **right of s.**, (international law) derecho de visita, m. **s.-party**, pelotón de salvamento, m. **s.-warrant**, auto de reconocimiento, m.

searching, a. escrutador; penetrante; minucioso. **a s. look**, una mirada penetrante. **a s. wind**, un viento penetrante. **a s. question**, una pregunta perspicaz

searchlight, s. reflector, proyector, m.

seashore, s. playa, f.; orilla del mar, f.

seaside, s. orilla del mar, f.; playa, f. **to go to the s.**, ir al mar, ir a la playa

season, s. estación, f.; sazón, f.; temporada, f.; tiempo, m. v.t. (food) sazonar; (wood, wine) madurar; (accustom) acostumbrar, aclimatar; (with wit, etc., salpimentar; (temper) templar, moderar. v.i. madurarse. **at that**

s., a la sazón. **close s.**, veda, *f.*
in s., en sazón; a su tiempo. **out
of s.**, fuera de sazón; fuera de
tiempo, inoportuno. **the dead
s.**, la estación muerta. **the
autumn s.**, el otoño; (for social
functions, etc.) la temporada de
otoño. **s.-ticket**, billete de abono,
m.

seasonable, *a.* de estación; tempestivo, oportuno

seasonably, *adv.* en sazón; oportunamente

seasonal, *a.* estacional; de temporada

seasoned, *a.* (of food) sazonado;
(of wood, etc.) maduro. **highly-
s.**, (of a dish) picante, con
muchas especies

seasoning, *s.* (*cul.*) condimento,
m.; madurez, *f.*; aclimatación.
f.; (*fig.*) salsa, sal, *f.*

seat, *s.* asiento, *m.*; (bench)
banco, *m.*; (chair) silla, *f.*; (in a
cinema, etc.) localidad, *f.*; (*theat.*,
etc., ticket) entrada, *f.*; (of a
person) trasero, *m.*, asentaderas,
f. pl.; (of trousers) fondillos,
m. pl.; (of government, etc.) sede,
capital, *f.*; (of war, etc.) teatro,
m.; (place) sitio, lugar, *m.*;
(house) casa solar, *f.* *v.t.*
sentar; poner en una silla (a);
encontrar sitio; (of buildings)
tener . . . asientos; (a chair)
poner asiento (a). **The hall seats
a thousand**, La sala tiene mil
asientos, Hay mil asientos en la
sala. **Please be seated!** ¡Haga
el favor de sentarse! **to be
seated**, estar sentado; sentarse.
to have a good s., (on a horse)
caer bien a caballo. **to hold a s.
in parliament**, ser diputado a
Cortes. **to keep one's s.**, permanecer sentado. **to take a s.**,
tomar asiento, sentarse. **s.-
back**, respaldo, *m.*

seater, *s.* de . . . asientos. **four-s.**,
automóvil de cuatro asientos,
m.

seawards, *adv.* hacia el mar

seaweed, *s.* alga marina, *f.*

seaworthy, *a.* (of a ship) en
buen estado; marinero

sebaceous, *a.* sebáceo

secede, *v.i.* retirarse (de); separarse (de)

secession, *s.* secesión, *f.*

secessionist, *s.* secesionista, *m.*
and *f.*; (*pol.*) separatista, *m.* and
f. *a.* secesionista; (*pol.*) separatista

secluded, *a.* apartado, retirado;
solitario

seclusion, *s.* reclusión, *f.*; apartamiento, retiro, *m.*; soledad, *f.*

second, *a.* segundo; otro; igual.
adv. en segundo lugar; después.
s. segundo, *m.*; (in a duel)
padrino, *m.*; (helper) ayudante,
m.; (boxing) segundo, *m.*; (railway compartment) departamento de segunda (clase), *m.*;
(*mus.*) segunda, *f.*; (of time)
segundo, *m.*; (moment) instante,
momento, *m.* *v.t.* secundar; (a
motion) apoyar; (*mil.*) ayudar.
the s. of May, el dos de mayo.
James the s., Jaime segundo.
on s. thoughts, después de
pensarlo bien. **every s. day**,
cada dos días. **They live on the
s. floor**, Viven en el segundo piso.
the s. largest, el más grande
menos uno. **to be s. to none**,
no ser inferior a ninguno; (of
persons) no ser inferior a nadie;
no ceder a nadie. **to come off
s.**, llegar el segundo; ser vencido.
seconds hand, (of watch)
segundero, *m.* **s.-in-command**,
segundo, *m.*; subjefe, *m.* **s.-best**,
segundo. **My s.-best hat**, Mi
sombrero número dos. **to come
off s.-best**, salir mal parado,
ser vencido. **s. class**, segunda
clase, *f.* **s.-class**, de segunda
clase; de calidad inferior; mediocre. **s. cousin**, primo (-ma)
segundo (-a). **s. gear**, segunda
velocidad, *f.* **s.-hand**, *a.* usado;
de ocasión; no nuevo. *adv.* de
segunda mano. **s.-hand car**,
un coche de segunda mano.
s.-hand clothing, ropa usada, *f.*
s. lieutenant, (*mil.*) subteniente,
segundo teniente, *m.*; (*nav.*)
alférez de fragata, *m.* **s.-rate**,
a. inferior, mediocre. **s. sight**,
doble vista, *f.*

secondary, *a.* secundario; subordinado; accesorio; poco importante. **s. education**, enseñanza secundaria, *f.*

seconder, *s.* ayudante, *m.*; el, *m.*
(*f.* la) que apoya una proposición

secondly, *adv.* en segundo lugar

secrecy, *s.* secreto, *m.*; reserva, *f.*, silencio, *m.* **in the s. of one's own heart,** en lo más íntimo de su corazón

secret, *a.* secreto; clandestino; (of persons) reservado, taciturno; (secluded) remoto, apartado; oculto; misterioso. *s.* secreto, *m.*; (key) clave, *f.* **a s. code,** un código secreto. **in s.,** en secreto, secretamente. **open s.,** secreto a voces. **to keep a s.,** guardar un secreto. **to keep s.,** tener secreto, ocultar. **s. drawer,** secreto, *m.* **S. Service,** servicio de espionaje, *m.*

secretaire, *s.* secreter, escritorio, *m.*

secretarial, *a.* de secretario. **s. college,** academia comercial, *f.*

secretariat, *s.* secretaría, *f.*

secretary, *s.* secretario (-ia). **private s.,** secretario (-ia) particular. **S. of State,** ministro, *m.*; Ministro de Estado, *m.*

secretaryship, *s.* secretaría, *f.*

secrete, *v.t.* esconder, ocultar; (*med.*) secretar

secretion, *s.* escondimiento, *m.*; (*med.*) secreción, *f.*

secretive, *a.* reservado, callado

secretiveness, *s.* reserva, *f.*

secretly, *adv.* en secreto, secretamente; ocultamente, a escondidas

secretory, *a.* (*med.*) secretorio

sect, *s.* secta, *f.*

sectarian, *a.* and *s.* sectario (-ia)

sectarianism, *s.* sectarismo, *m.*

section, *s.* sección, *f.*; porción, *f.*; subdivisión, *f.*; (of a law) artículo, *m.* *v.t.* seccionar. **conic s.,** sección cónica, *f.*

sectional, *a.* en secciones. **s. bookcase,** biblioteca desmontable, *f.*

sector, *s.* sector, *m.*

secular, *a.* (very old) secular; (lay) seglar; laico; profano. **s. music,** música profana, *f.* **s. school,** escuela laica, *f.*

secularization, *s.* secularización, *f.*

secularize, *v.t.* secularizar

secure, *a.* seguro; (certain) asegurado; (safe) en seguridad; sano y salvo; (firm) firme; fijo;

(confident (in)) confiado (en). *v.t.* asegurar; (insure) garantizar; (lock) cerrar; (confine) prender; (acquire) adquirir, obtener; lograr, conseguir

securely, *adv.* seguramente; en seguridad, sin peligro; con confianza; (firmly) firmemente

security, *s.* seguridad, *f.*; protección, defensa, *f.*; garantía, *f.*; (faith) confianza, *f.*; (com.) fianza, *f.*; (person) fiador, *m.*; *pl.* **securities,** valores, títulos, *m. pl.* **government securities,** papel del Estado, *m.* **to give s.,** (com.) dar fianza. **to stand s. for,** (com.) salir fiador de,

sedan-chair, *s.* silla de manos, *f.*

sedate, *a.* tranquilo, sosegado; formal, serio, grave

sedately, *adv.* sosegadamente; seriamente

sedateness, *s.* sosiego, *m.*, tranquilidad, *f.*; formalidad, compostura, *f.*

sedative, *a.* and *s.* sedativo (*m.*)

sedentary, *a.* sedentario

sedge, *s.* (*bot.*) junco, *m.*

sediment, *s.* sedimento, *m.*

sedimentation, *s.* sedimentación, *f.*

sedition, *s.* sedición, *f.*

seditious, *a.* sedicioso

seduce, *v.t.* seducir

seducer, *s.* seductor, *m.*

seduction, *s.* seducción, *f.*

seductive, *a.* seductivo, atractivo; persuasivo

sedulous, *a.* asiduo, diligente

see, *s.* sede, *f.* **Holy S.,** Santa Sede, *f.*

see, *v.t.* and *v.i.* ver; mirar; (understand) comprender; (visit) visitar; (attend to) atender a; ocuparse de. **He sees the matter quite differently,** Él mira el asunto de un modo completamente distinto, Su punto de vista sobre el asunto es completamente distinto. **You are not fit to be seen,** No eres nada presentable. **See you next Wednesday!** ¡Hasta miércoles próximo! **I see!** ¡Ya! ¡Ahora comprendo! **Let's see!** ¡Vamos a ver! **Shall I see you home?** ¿Quieres que te acompañe a casa? **to go and see,** ir a ver.

to see **red**, echar chispas. **to see the sights**, visitar los monumentos. **to see life**, ver mundo. **to see service**, servir (en el ejército, etc.). **to see about**, atender a; pensar en; ocuparse de. **to see after**, cuidar de; atender (a); ocuparse de. **to see again**, volver a ver. **to see into**, investigar, examinar. **to see off**, (at the station, etc.) ir a despedir; acompañar. **to see out**, (a person) acompañar a la puerta; (a play, etc.) quedarse hasta el fin (de); no dejar el puesto. **to see over**, inspeccionar. **to see through**, (a house, etc.) inspeccionar; (a person) calarle las intenciones; (a mystery) penetrar; (a person through trouble) ayudar. **to see it through**, llevarlo al cabo; quedarse hasta el fin. **to see to**, atender a; ocuparse de; encargarse de. **to see to everything**, encargarse de todo

seed, s. semilla, f.; simiente, f.; (of fruit) pepita, f., grano, m.; (fig.) germen, m.; (offspring) prole, descendencia, f. v.i. granar. v.t. sembrar. **s.-bed**, semillero, m. **s.-pearl**, aljófar, m. **s.-plot**, sementera, f.; (fig.) semillero, m. **s.-time**, tiempo de sembrar, m.

seedling, s. planta de semilla, f.

seedsman, s. tratante en semillas, m.

seedy, a. granado; (of clothes) raído, roto; (of persons) andrajoso, desharrapado; infeliz, desgraciado; (ill) indispuesto, malucho

seeing, s. vista, f.; visión, f. **It is worth s.**, Vale la pena de verse. **s. that . . .**, visto que, dado que, como que. **S. is believing**, Ver es creer

seek, v.t. buscar; solicitar, pretender; (demand) pedir; (investigate) investigar; (to do something) procurar, tratar de. **They are much sought after**, Son muy populares, Están en demanda. **to s. after**, buscar; perseguir. **to s. for**, buscar

seeker, s. el, m. (f. la) que busca; investigador (-ra)

seem, v.i. parecer. **He seemed honest**, Parecía honrado. **It seemed to me**, Me pareció a mí.

It seems that they were both at home last night, Parece ser que ambos de ellos estaban en casa anoche

seeming, a. aparente; supuesto

seemingly, adv. aparentemente; en apariencia

seemliness, s. decoro, m.

seemly, a. decoroso, decente

seep, v.i. filtrar; rezumarse

seer, s. profeta, m.

seesaw, s. columpio, m.; vaivén, m. v.i. columpiarse; balancearse, oscilar. a. de vaivén, oscilante

seethe, v.i. hervir; (fig.) bullir

segment, s. segmento, m.

segregate, v.t. segregar. v.i. segregarse. a. segregado

segregation, s. segregación, f.

seismic, a. sísmico

seismograph, s. sismógrafo, m.

seismological, a. sismológico

seismology, s. sismología, f.

seismometer, s. sismómetro, m.

seize, v.t. (law) embargar; apoderarse de; asir; (a person) prender; coger; (a meaning) comprender; (an occasion, etc.) aprovecharse de; (of emotions) dominar; (of illnesses) atacar. v.i. (mech.) atascarse. **He was seized by fear**, Le dominó el miedo. **to s. the opportunity**, aprovecharse de la oportunidad. **to s. upon a pretext**, valerse de un pretexto

seizure, s. asimiento, m.; (of property) embargo, secuestro, m.; (of a person) captura, f.; arresto, m.; (med.) ataque, m.

seldom, adv. rara vez, raramente; pocas veces

select, a. escogido, selecto; exclusivista. v.t. escoger

selection, s. selección, f. **selections from Cervantes**, trozos escogidos de Cervantes, m. pl. **to make a s. from**, escoger entre. **s. committee**, comité de selección, m.

selective, a. selectivo

selenium, s. (chem.) selenio, m.

selenography, s. selenografía, f.

self, s. mismo (-a), propio (-a); sí mismo (-a), se; personalidad, f.; ser, m. **all by one's s.**, sin ayuda de nadie; solo. **my other s.**, mi otro yo. **my better s.**, mi mejor parte. **the s., el yo. s.-abasement,** humillación de sí mismo, *f.* **s.-acting,** automático. **s.-apparent,** evidente, patente. **s.-appointed,** designado por uno mismo. **s.-assertion,** presunción, *f.* **s.-assertive,** presumido. **s.-assurance,** confianza en sí mismo, *f.;* aplomo, *m.;* (impertinence) cara dura, frescura, *f.* **s.-centred,** egocéntrico. **s.-coloured,** del mismo color; de su color natural. **s.-command,** dominio de sí mismo, *m.;* sangre fría, ecuanimidad, *f.* **s.-complacent,** satisfecho de sí mismo. **s.-conceit,** vanidad, arrogancia, petulancia, *f.* **s.-confidence,** confianza en sí mismo, *f.;* aplomo, *m.* **s.-confident,** seguro de sí mismo, lleno de confianza en sí mismo. **s.-conscious,** turbado, confuso, apocado. **s.-consciousness,** turbación, confusión, *f.,* apocamiento, azoramiento, *m.* **s.-contained,** (of a person) reservado, poco comunicativo; dueño de sí mismo; (of things) completo; (of flats, etc.) independiente; con entrada independiente. **s.-contradictory,** contradictorio. **s.-control,** dominio de sí mismo, *m.;* ecuanimidad, serenidad, sangre fría, *f.* **s.-controlled,** dueño de sí mismo; ecuánime, sereno. **s.-deception,** engaño de sí mismo, *m.;* ilusiones, *f. pl.* **s.-defence,** defensa propia, *f.* **s.-denial,** abnegación, *f.;* renunciación, *f.;* frugalidad, *f.* **s.-destruction,** suicidio, *m.* **s.-determination,** libre albedrío, *m.;* (of peoples) autonomía, *f.;* independencia, *f.* **s.-educating,** autodidacto. **s.-esteem,** respeto para uno mismo, *m.;* amor propio, *m.* **s.-evident,** aparente, que salta a la vista. **s.-explanatory,** que se explica a sí mismo; evidente. **s.-generating,** autógeno. **s.-government,** (of a person) dominio de sí mismo, *m.;* (of a state) autonomía, *f.* **s.-importance,** presunción, petulancia, *f.* **s.-important,** pagado de sí mismo. to be **s.-important,** darse importancia, darse tono. **s.-indul-**

gence, indulgencia con sí mismo, *f.;* (of food, drink, etc.) excesos, *m. pl.,* falta de moderación, *f.* **s.-indulgent,** indulgente con sí mismo; dado a los placeres, sibarita. **s.-interest,** propio interés, *m.* **s.-knowledge,** conocimiento de sí mismo, *m.* **s.-love,** egolatría, *f.* **s.-made man,** hombre que ha llegado a su posición actual por sus propios esfuerzos, *m.* **s.-opinionated,** terco, obstinaz. **s.-portrait,** autorretrato, *m.* **s.-possessed,** dueño de sí mismo; reservado; de sangre fría. **s.-possession,** aplomo, *m.,* sangre fría, serenidad, *f.* **s.-preservation,** protección de sí mismo, *f.* **s.-reliance,** independencia, *f.;* confianza en sí mismo, *f.* **s.-reliant,** independiente; confiado en sí mismo. **s.-reproach,** remordimiento, *m.* **s.-respect,** respeto de sí mismo, *m.;* amor propio, *m.,* dignidad, *f.* **s.-respecting,** que se respeta; que tiene amor propio. **s.-restraint,** dominio de sí mismo, *m.;* moderación, *f.* **s.-righteous,** farisaico. **s.-sacrifice,** abnegación, *f.* **s.-sacrificing,** abnegado. **s.-same,** mismo, idéntico. **s.-satisfaction,** satisfacción de sí mismo, *f.;* vanidad, *f.;* (of desires, etc.) satisfacción, indulgencia, *f.* **s.-satisfied,** satisfecho de sí mismo, pagado de sí mismo. **s.-seeking,** *a.* egoísta, interesado. *s.* egoísmo, *m.* **s.-starter,** (*mech.*) arranque automático, *m.* **s.-styled,** que se llama a sí mismo, supuesto. **s.-sufficiency,** suficiencia, *f.;* presunción, *f.* **s.-sufficient,** que basta a sí mismo; contento de sí mismo. **s.-supporting,** que vive de su propio trabajo; (of an institution, business) independiente. **s.-taught,** autodidacto. **s.-willed,** voluntarioso **selfish,** *a.* egoísta, interesado **selfishly,** *adv.* interesadamente; por egoísmo **selfishness,** *s.* egoísmo, *m.* **sell,** *v.t.* vender; *v.i.* vender; venderse. **They sold him to his enemies,** Le vendieron a sus enemigos. **House to s.,** Se vende una casa. **to s. at a loss,** malvender, vender con pérdida. **to s. for cash,** vender al contado. **to s. retail,** vender al por menor. **to s. wholesale,** vender al por mayor. **to s. one's life dearly,** vender cara la vida. **They sold the chair for £10,** Vendieron la silla por diez libras. **to s. off,** (goods) liquidar, saldar. **to s. out,** vender; agotar. **The best edition is sold out,** La mejor edición está agotada. **All the nylons have been sold out,** Se han vendido todas las medias de nilón (de cristal). **to s. up,** vender

seller, s. vendedor (-ra); comerciante (en), m.

selling, s. venta, f. **s. off,** liquidación, f. **s. price,** precio de venta, m.

selvage, s. (in cloth) orillo, m.

semantics, s. semántica, f.

semaphore, s. semáforo, m. v.t. and v.i. hacer señales semafóricas (a)

semaphoric, a. semafórico

semblance, s. apariencia, f. **to put on a s. of woe,** aparentar ser triste

semen, s. semen, m., esperma, f.

semester, s. semestre, m.

semi, prefix semi; medio. **s.-conscious,** medio consciente. **s.-detached house,** casa doble, f.

semibreve, s. (mus.) semibreve, f.

semicircle, s. semicírculo, m.

semicircular, a. semicircular

semicolon, s. punto y coma, m.

seminarist, s. seminarista, m.

seminary, s. seminario, m.; (for girls) colegio interno, m.

semiquaver, s. semicorchea, f.

Semite, s. semita, m. and f.

Semitic, a. semítico, semita

Semitism, s. semitismo, m.

semitone, s. semitono, m.

semolina, s. sémola, f.

sempiternal, a. sempiterno

senate, s. senado, m.

senator, s. senador, m.

senatorial, a. senatorio

senatorship, s. senaduría, f.

send, v.t. enviar, mandar; (com.) remitir; (a ball) lanzar; (grant) conceder; permitir; (inflict) afligir (con). **I sent Jane for it,** Envié a Juana a buscarlo. **He sent us word that he could not come,** Nos mandó un recado diciéndonos que no podía venir. **to s. mad,** hacer enloquecer. **to s. packing,** mandar a paseo. **to s. again,** volver a mandar. **to s. away,** v.t. enviar; (dismiss) destituir; despedir; (scare off) ahuyentar. v.i. enviar a otra parte. **to s. back,** (goods) devolver; (persons) volver. **to s. down,** hacer bajar; (rain, etc.) mandar, derramar; (a student) suspender, expulsar. **to s. in,** mandar; (persons) hacer entrar, introducir; (food) servir; (a bill) presentar; (one's name) dar. **Please s. him in!** ¡Sírvase de invitarle a entrar! **to s. in one's resignation,** mandar su dimisión. **to s. off,** enviar, mandar; (goods) despachar; (persons) destituir; (scare) ahuyentar. **s.-off,** s. despedida, f. **a good s.-off,** una despedida afectuosa. **to s. on,** (a letter) hacer seguir; (instructions) transmitir. **to s. out,** hacer salir; mandar; (emit) despedir, dar; (new shoots, etc.) echar. **to s. round,** (the hat, etc.) hacer circular. **to s. up,** enviar arriba; mandar subir, hacer subir; mandar, enviar; (a ball) lanzar

sender, s. remitente, m. and f.; (elec.) transmisor, m.

sending, s. envío, m.

Senegalese, a. and s. senegalés (-esa)

seneschal, s. senescal, m.

senile, a. senil

senility, s. senilidad, f.

senior, a. mayor, de mayor edad; más antiguo. **Martínez s.,** Martínez padre. **Charles is Mary's s. by five years,** Carlos es cinco años más viejo que María. **s. member,** decano, m.

seniority, s. ancianidad, f.; antigüedad, f.

senna, s. (bot.) sena, f.

sensation, s. sensación, f.; sentimiento, m.; impresión, f. **to create a s.,** causar una sensación

sensational, a. sensacional

sensationalism, s. (phil.) sensualismo, m.; efectismo, m.

sensationalist, *s.* (*phil.*) sensualista, *m.* and *f.*; efectista, *m.* and *f.*

sense, *s.* sentido, *m.* *v.t.* sentir. **in a s.,** hasta cierto punto; **desde un punto de vista. in the full s. of the word,** en toda la extensión de la palabra. **common s.,** sentido común, *m.* **He has no s. of smell,** No tiene olfato. **the five senses,** los cinco sentidos. **to be out of one's senses,** estar fuera de sí, estar trastornado. **You must be out of your senses!** ¡Debes haber perdido el juicio! ¡Estás loco! **to come to one's senses,** (after unconsciousness) volver en sí; (after folly) recobrar el sentido común. **to talk s.,** hablar con sentido común, hablar razonablemente. **s. organ,** órgano de los sentidos, *m.*

senseless, *a.* (unconscious) sin sentido, insensible; desmayado; (silly) necio, estúpido. **to knock s.,** derribar, tumbar

senselessness, *s.* falta de sentido común, *f.*; locura, absurdidad, *f.*

sensibility, *s.* sensibilidad, *f.*

sensible, *a.* sensible; (conscious) consciente (de); sesudo. **to be s. of,** estar consciente de; estar persuadido de

sensibly, *adv.* sensiblemente; sesudamente, cuerdamente

sensitive, *a.* sensitivo; susceptible (a); impresionable. **s. plant,** sensitiva, *f.*

sensitivity, *s.* sensibilidad, *f.*; susceptibilidad, *f.*; delicadeza, *f.*

sensitize, *v.t.* (*phot.*) sensibilizar

sensory, *a.* sensorio

sensual, *a.* sensual; voluptuoso

sensualism, *s.* sensualismo, *m.*

sensualist, *s.* sensualista, *m.* and *f.*

sensuality, *s.* sensualidad, *f.*

sensually, *adv.* sensualmente

sensuous, *a.* sensorio

sensuousness, *s.* sensualidad, *f.*

sentence, *s.* (*law*) sentencia, *f.*; (penalty) pena, *f.*; (*gram.*) frase, *f.*; (maxim) máxima, sentencia, *f.* *v.t.* sentenciar, condenar. **to pass s.,** pronunciar sentencia, fallar. **under s. of,** bajo pena de

sententious, *a.* sentencioso

sentient, *a.* sensible

sentiment, *s.* sentimiento, *m.*; (sentimentality) sentimentalismo, *m.*; opinión, *f.*

sentimental, *a.* sentimental; (mawkish) sensiblero

sentimentalist, *s.* romántico (-ca), persona sentimental, *f.*

sentimentality, *s.* sentimentalismo, *m.*, sensiblería, *f.*

sentimentalize, *v.t.* idealizar

sentimentally, *adv.* sentimentalmente

sentinel, *s.* centinela, *m.* and *f.*

sentry, *s.* centinela, *m.* **to be on s. duty,** estar de guardia. **s. box,** garita de centinela, *f.*

sepal, *s.* (*bot.*) sépalo, *m.*

separable, *a.* separable

separate, *a.* separado; distinto; independiente. *v.t.* separar; dividir. *v.i.* separarse; (of husband and wife) separarse de bienes y de cuerpos

separately, *adv.* separadamente; aparte

separation, *s.* separación, *f.*; (*law*) separación de bienes y de cuerpos, *f.*

separatism, *s.* separatismo, *m.*

separatist, *a.* and *s.* separatista (*m.* and *f.*)

sepia, *s.* (colour and fish) sepia, *f.*

sepoy, *s.* cipayo, *m.*

sepsis, *s.* sepsia, *f.*

September, *s.* setiembre, septiembre, *m.*

septenary, *a.* septenario

septentrional, *a.* septentrional

septet, *s.* (*mus.*) septeto, *m.*

septic, *a.* séptico

septicæmia, *s.* septicemia, *f.*

septuagenarian, *s.* setentón (-ona); septuagenario (-ia)

septuple, *a.* séptuplo

sepulchral, *a.* sepulcral

sepulchre, *s.* sepulcro, *m.*

sequel, *s.* (of a story, etc.) continuación, *f.*; consecuencia, *f.*; resultado, *m.*

sequence, *s.* sucesión, *f.*; serie, *f.*; orden, *m.* or *f.*; (at cards) serie, *f.*; (*gram.*) correspondencia, *f.*; (*ecc.* and cinema) secuencia, *f.* **s. of tenses,** correspondencia de los tiempos, *f.*

sequestered, *a.* aislado, remoto

sequestrate, *v.t.* secuestrar

sequestration, *s.* secuestro, *m.*

sequin, *s.* lentejuela, *f.*

seraglio, *s.* serrallo, *m.*

seraph, *s.* serafín, *m.*

seraphic, *a.* seráfico

seraphim, *s.* serafín, *m.*

Serbian, *a.* servio. *s.* servio (-ia); (language) servio, *m.*

serenade, *s.* serenata, *f.* *v.t.* dar una serenata (a)

serene, *a.* sereno. His S. Highness, Su Alteza Serenísima

serenely, *adv.* serenamente

serenity, *s.* serenidad, *f.*; tranquilidad, *f.*

serf, *s.* siervo (-va)

serfdom, *s.* servidumbre, *f.*

serge, *s.* estameña, *f.*; (silk) sarga, *f.*

sergeant, *s.* (*mil.*) sargento, *m.*; (police) sargento de policía, *m.* s.-at-arms, macero, *m.* s.-major, sargento instructor, *m.*

sergeantcy, *s.* sargentía, *f.*

serial, *a.* en serie; (of a story) por entregas. *s.* novela por entregas, *f.* s. number, número de serie, *m.*

sericulture, *s.* sericultura, *f.*

series, *s.* serie, *f.*; cadena, *f.*; (*math.*) serie, progresión, *f.* in s., en serie

serious, *a.* serio; sincero; verdadero; (of illness, etc.) grave; importante. He was s. (not laughing) when he said it, Lo dijo en serio. He is very s. about it, Lo toma muy en serio. to grow s., (of persons) ponerse serio; (of events) hacerse grave

seriously, *adv.* seriamente; en serio; gravemente. to take (something) s., tomar (algo) en serio. to take oneself s., tomarse muy en serio

seriousness, *s.* seriedad, *f.*; gravedad, *f.* in all s., en serio, seriamente

sermon, *s* sermón, *m.*

sermonize, *v.t.* and *v.i.* sermonear

serosity, *s.* serosidad, *f.*

serotherapy, *s.* seroterapia, *f.*

serous, *a.* seroso

serpent, *s.* serpiente, *f.*; (*mus.*) serpentón, *m.*

serpentine, *a.* serpentino; (of character) tortuoso. *s.* (*min.*) serpentina, *f.*

serrated, *a.* serrado; dentellado

serried, *a.* apretado, apiñado

serum, *s.* suero, *m.*

servant, *s.* servidor (-ra); (domestic) criado (-da); (employee) empleado (-da); (slave and *fig.*) siervo (-va); *pl* servants, (domestic) servidumbre, *f.*, servicio, *m.* I remain your obedient s., Quedo de Vd. atento y seguro servidor (att. y s.s.). Civil S., empleado del Estado, *m.* general s., criada para todo, *f.* man s., criado, *m.* the s. problem, el problema del servicio. Your s., sir, Servidor de Vd., señor. s.-girl, criada, *f.*

serve, *v.t.* servir (a); ser útil (a); satisfacer; (in a shop) despachar; (an apprenticeship, etc.) hacer; (a prison sentence) cumplir; (treat) tratar; (of stallion) cubrir; (a warrant, etc.) ejecutar; (a notice) entregar; (a ball) servir; (on a jury, etc.) formar parte de; (*naut.*) aforrar. *v.i.* servir; (*mil.*, *nav.*) hacer el servicio. *s.* (*sport*) saque, *m.* It serves you right! ¡Lo tienes merecido! to s. at table, servir a la mesa. to s. as, servir de. to s. out, distribuir; servir

server, *s.* (*ecc.*) acólito, *m.*; (*sport*) saque, *m.*; (tray) bandeja, *f.*; (for fish, etc.) pala, *f.*

service, *s.* servicio, *m.*; (*ecc.*) oficio, *m.*; servicio de mesa, *m.*; (of a writ) entrega, *f.*; (*sport*) saque, *m.* coffee s., juego de café, *m.* diplomatic s., cuerpo diplomático, *m.* At your s., Para servir a Vd., A su disposición. on active s., en acto de servicio; en el campo de batalla. to go into s., (of servants) ir a servir. to render s., prestar servicios. s. tree, serbal, *m.*

serviceable, *a.* (of persons) servicial; (of things) servible, utilizable; útil; práctico; (lasting) duradero

serviette, *s.* servilleta, *f.* s. ring, servilletero, *m.*

servile, *a.* servil

servility, *s.* servilismo, *m.*

serving, *a.* sirviente; al servicio (de). s. maid, criada, *f.* s. table, trinchero, *m.*

servitor, *s.* bedel, *m.*

servitude, *s.* servidumbre, esclavitud, *f.* penal s., cadena perpetua, *f.*

sessile, *a*. (*bot*.) sésil

session, *s*. sesión, *f*.; junta, *f*. **petty sessions**, tribunal de primera instancia, *m*.

set, *v.t.* poner; colocar; fijar; (seeds, etc.) plantar; (bones) reducir, componer; (gems) engastar, montar; (a clock) regular; (sails) desplegar; (the teeth of a saw) trabar, triscar; (congeal) hacer coagular; (a trap) armar; (a snare) tender; (a razor) afilar; (make ready) preparar; (type) componer; (cause) hacer; (*mus*.) poner en música; (*mus*.) adaptar; (order) mandar; (prescribe) dar, asignar; (estimate) estimar, evaluar; (an example, etc.) dar; (establish) establecer, crear. *v.i.* (of the sun, etc.). ponerse; (solidify) coagularse; solidificarse; (of tides) fluir; (of the wind) soplar; (of dogs) hacer punta. **The joke set him laughing**, El chiste le hizo reír. **to set a person's mind at rest**, tranquilizar, sosegar. **to set a trap**, armar lazo. **to set at ease**, poner a sus anchas (a), hacer cómodo (a). **to set at naught**, despreciar. **to set eyes on**, poner los ojos en. **to set fire to**, pegar fuego a, incendiar. **to set free**, poner en libertad, librar (de). **to set in motion**, poner en marcha. **to set one's teeth**, apretar los dientes. **to set people talking**, dar que hablar a la gente. **to set the fashion**, fijar la moda; poner de moda. **to set the alarm at seven o'clock**, poner el despertador a las siete. **to set the table**, poner la mesa. **to set to work**, ponerse a trabajar. **to set about**, *v.i.* (begin) ponerse (a); empezar; (undertake) emprender. *v.t.* (a rumour, etc.) divulgar. **They set about each other**, Empezaron a golpearse, Vinieron a las manos. **to set against**, indisponer (con), enemistar (con); hacer el enemigo (de), ser hostil (a); (balance) oponer, balancear. **to set oneself against**, oponerse a; atacar, luchar contra. **to set aside**, poner a un lado; apartar; (discard) desechar; (omit) omitir, pasar por alto de;

dejar aparte, excluir; (keep) reservar; (money, etc.) ahorrar; (reject) rechazar; (quash) anular. **to set back**, retrasar; hacer retroceder. **set-back**, *s*. revés, *m*.; contrariedad, *f*. **to set before**, poner ante; (facts) exponer; (introduce) presentar. **to set down**, poner en tierra; depositar; (of a 'bus, etc.) dejar; (in writing) poner por escrito; anotar, apuntar; narrar, contar; (attribute) atribuir; (fix) formular; (believe to be) creer. **Passengers are set down at . . .**, Los viajeros pueden apearse en . . . **to set forth**, *v.t.* (one's opinions, etc.) exponer; publicar; (display) exhibir, mostrar; (make) hacer. *v.i.* ponerse en camino. **to set going**, poner en marcha; echar a andar. **to set in**, empezar; (of the tide) fluir. **A reaction has set in**, Se ha hecho sentir una reacción. **to set off**, *v.t.* (explode) hacer estallar; (cause) hacer; (heighten) realzar; hacer resaltar; (counterbalance) contraponer. *v.i.* partir; ponerse en camino. **set-off**, *s*. contraste, *m*., contraposición, *f*. **to set off against**, contraponer. **to set on**, *v.t.* (a dog) azuzar; (incite) instigar, incitar. *v.i.* atacar. **to set out**, *v.t.* (state) exponer, manifestar; (embellish) realzar; (display) arreglar, disponer. *v.i.* ponerse en camino, partir. **to set over**, (rule) tener autoridad sobre, gobernar. **to set to**, (begin to) ponerse a, empezar a; (work) ponerse a trabajar. **set-to**, *s*. lucha, *f*.; (boxing) asalto, *m*.; (quarrel) pelea, riña, *f*. **to set up**, *v.t.* (a monument, etc.) erigir, levantar; (fix) fijar; (apparatus, machinery) montar; (exalt) exaltar; (found) establecer; crear; (propound) exponer; (a howl, etc.) dar; (equip with) proveer de; instalar; (make strong) robustecer; fortificar; (type) componer; (raise) alzar. *v.i.* establecerse; dárselas de. **He sets himself up as a painter**, Se las da de pintor. **to set (a person) up as a model**, poner como modelo (a). **to set up house**, poner casa.

to set up a business, establecer un comercio. **set-up,** s. establecimiento, m.; arreglo, m. **to set upon,** atacar

set, s. (of sun, etc.) puesta, f., ocaso, m.; (of the head, etc.) porte, m.; (of a garment) corte, m.; (of the tide, etc.) dirección, f.; (slant) inclinación, f.; (fig., drift) tendencia, f., movimiento, m.; (of the teeth of a saw) triscamiento, m.; (of men, houses, etc.) grupo, m.; (of tools, golf clubs, china, etc.) juego, m.; (gang) pandilla, camarilla, f.; clase, f.; (dance) tanda, f.; (tennis) partido, f.; (theat.) decoración, f.; (rad.) aparato de radio, m., radio, f. **coffee set,** juego de café, m. **all-mains set,** radio de corriente eléctrica, f. **battery set,** radio de batería, f. **portable set,** radio portátil, f. **the smart set,** el mundo elegante. **to have a shampoo and set,** hacerse lavar y marcar (el pelo). **to make a set,** hacer juego. **to make a dead set at,** hacer un ataque vigoroso (a), atacar resueltamente; procurar insinuarse en el favor de. **set of teeth,** dentadura, f.

set, a. fijo; inmóvil; (of a smile) forzado; (of a task) asignado; (of times) señalado, fijo; (prescribed) prescrito, establecido; (firm) firme; (resolved) resuelto; (well-known) consabido; (obstinate) terco, nada adaptable. **well set-up,** apuesto, bien plantado. **He is very set on doing it,** Se empeña en hacerlo. **to be dead set against,** estar completamente opuesto a. **set phrase,** frase hecha, f. **set-square,** cartabón, m.

settee, s. canapé, m. **s.-bed,** cama turca, f.

setter, s. (perro) sétter, perdiguero, m. **s.-on,** instigador (-ra)

setting, s. (of the sun, etc.) puesta, f.; (of mortar, etc.) fraguado, m.; (of a jelly) solidificación, f.; (of jewels) engaste, m., montadura, f.; (of bones) aliño, m.; (of teeth of saw) traba, f.; (of razor) afiladura, f.; (of a trap) armadura, f.; (of a machine,

etc.) ajuste, m.; (frame) marco, m.; (mus.) arreglo, m.; (theat.) decorado, m.; (emplacement) lecho, m. **the s. sun,** el sol poniente. **s. free,** liberación, f. **s. off,** partida, salida, f. **s. out,** ida, marcha, f.; principio, m. **s.-up,** creación, institución, f.; establecimiento, m.; (of a machine) montaje, m.; (print.) composición, f.

settle, v.t. colocar; asegurar, afirmar; (a country) colonizar; (live in) establecer (en); (populate) poblar; (in a profession, etc.) dar; (install) instalar; (the imagination, etc.) sosegar, calmar; (resolve) resolver; (arrange) disponer, arreglar; (differences) componer, concertar; (an opponent, etc.) confundir; (a bill) saldar, pagar; (a claim) satisfacer; (clarify) depositar, clarificar; (end) poner fin (a). **v.i.** establecerse; (of weather) serenarse; (to work, etc.) empezar a, ponerse a; aplicarse a; (decide) decidirse; (alight) posarse; (of foundations, etc.) asentarse; (of a ship) zozobrar; (of sediment) depositarse; (of liquid) clarificarse. **to s. accounts with,** (fig.) ajustar cuentas con. **to s. down,** establecerse, arraigarse; adaptarse (a); (become calm) sosegarse, calmarse; sentar el juicio; (of foundations) asentarse; (of a ship) zozobrar; (of sediment) depositarse. **to s. in,** v.t. instalar. **v.i.** instalarse. **to s. on,** (choose) escoger; (decide on) decidirse (a). **to s. a pension on,** señalar pensión (a). **to s. up,** v.t. (one's affairs) poner en orden; (bill) pagar, saldar. **v.i.** llegar a un acuerdo; pagar cuentas

settled, a. fijo; permanente; invariable; (of countries) colonizado; (of weather) sereno

settlement, s. (of a country) colonización, f.; (of a dispute) arreglo, ajuste, m.; (of a question) solución, f.; decisión, f.; (of a bill) saldo, pago, m., liquidación, f.; (of an obligation) satisfacción, f.; (colony) colonia, f.; (creation) creación, institución, f.; establecimiento, arraigo, m. **deed of**

s., escritura de donación, *f.*
marriage s., contrato matrimonial, *m.*

settler, *s.* colono, *m.*; colonizador
(-ra)

seven, *a.* and *s.* siete (*m.*). It is
s. o'clock, Son las siete. the
s. deadly sins, los siete pecados
capitales

sevenfold, *a.* séptuplo

seventeen, *a.* diecisiete, diez y
siete. *s.* diecisiete, *m.* She is
just s., Ella acaba de cumplir los
diez y siete

seventeenth, *a.* décimoséptimo;
(of monarchs and of the month)
diez y siete. *s.* décimoséptimo,
m. Louis the S., Luis diez y
siete. the s. of June, el diez y
siete de junio

seventh, *a.* séptimo; (of the
month) siete. *s.* séptimo, *m.*;
séptima parte, *f.*; (*mus.*) séptima,
f. Edward the S., Eduardo
séptimo. the s. of August, el
siete de agosto

seventieth, *a.* septuagésimo,
setentavo. *s.* setentavo, *m.*

seventy, *a.* and *s.* setenta (*m.*)

sever, *v.t.* separar; romper;
dividir

several, *a.* distinto, diferente;
respectivo; varios, *m. pl.* (*f. pl.*
varias); algunos, *m. pl.* (*f. pl.*
algunas)

severally, *adv.* separadamente;
individualmente; independiente-
mente

severance, *s.* separación, *f.*; (of
friendship, etc.) ruptura, *f.*

severe, *a.* severo; riguroso; fuerte;
duro; (of style) austero; (of pain)
agudo; (of illness) grave

severely, *adv.* severamente; intensamente; gravemente

severity, *s.* severidad, *f.*; intensidad, *f.*; (of weather) inclemencia, *f.*; (of illness) gravedad, *f.*

sew, *v.t.* and *v.i.* coser. to sew
on, coser, pegar

sewage, *s.* aguas residuales, *f. pl.*
s. system, alcantarillado, *m.*

sewer, *s.* alcantarilla, cloaca, *f.*,
albañal, *m.*

sewing, *s.* costura, *f.* s. bag,
costurero, *m.* s. cotton, hilo de
coser, *m.* s.-machine, máquina
de coser, *f.* s. silk, torzal, *m.*

sex, *s.* sexo, *m.* the fair sex, el
bello sexo. the weaker sex,
el sexo débil. sex appeal,
atractivo, *m.*

sexagenarian, *s.* sexagenario
(-ia)

sexagesima, *s.* sexagésima, *f.*

sexless, *a.* neutro; frígido

sexologist, *s.* sexólogo (-ga)

sexology, *s.* sexología, *f.*

sextant, *s.* sextante, *m.*

sextet, *s.* sexteto, *m.*

sexton, *s.* sacristán, *m.*; sepulturero, *m.*; (bell-ringer) campanero,
m.

sextuple, *v.t.* sextuplicar

sexual, *a.* sexual

sexuality, *s.* sexualidad, *f.*

sh! *interj.,* ¡Chitón! ¡Chis!

shabbily, *adv.* (of dressing) pobremente; (of treatment) mezquina-
mente

shabbiness, *s.* pobreza, *f.*; estado
andrajoso, *m.*; (of behaviour)
mezquindad, ruindad, *f.*

shabby, *a.* (of persons) desharrapado, andrajoso; (of garments)
raído, roto; (of a neighbourhood,
etc.) pobre; (mean) ruin, mezquino

shack, *s.* choza, *f.*

shackle, *s.* traba, *f.*; *pl.* shackles,
grillos, *m. pl.*, esposas, *f. pl.*;
(*fig.*) cadenas, *f. pl. v.t.* poner
esposas (a), encadenar; (a horse)
apear; (*fig.*) atar; (impede) estorbar

shad, *s.* sábalo, *m.*

shade, *s.* sombra, *f.*; (in a
picture) toque de obscuro, *m.*;
(for the eyes) visera, *f.*; (of a
lamp) pantalla, *f.*; (ghost) espectro, fantasma, *m.*; (of colour)
matiz, *m.*; (tinge) dejo, *m. v.t.*
sombrear, dar sombra (a); (the
face, etc.) proteger, resguardar;
(a drawing) esfumar. in the s.,
a la sombra. 80° in the s.,
ochenta grados a la sombra. to
put (a person) in the s., eclipsar

shadiness, *s.* sombra, *f.*

shading, *s.* sombra, *f.*; (*art*)
degradación, *f.*

shadow, *s.* sombra, *f.*; obscuridad, *f.*; (in a picture) toque
de obscuro, *m. v.t.* sombrear;
obscurecer; (a person) seguir.
to cast a s., proyectar una
sombra. to s. forth, indicar;

símbolizar. **s, show,** sombras chinescas, *f. pl.*

shadowy, *a.* umbroso; vago, indistinto, indefinido

shady, *a.* sombreado, umbrío; sombrío; (of persons, etc.) sospechoso. **It was s. in the wood,** Hacía sombra en el bosque

shaft, *s.* fuste, *m.*; (arrow) flecha, saeta, *f.*, dardo, *m.*; (of a golf club, etc.) mango, *m.*; (of a cart) vara, *f.*; (mech.) árbol, eje, *m.*; (of a column and a feather) cañón, *m.*; (of light) rayo, *m.*; (of a mine) pozo, tiro, *m.*; (air-shaft) conducto de aire, ventilador, *m.* **cam-s.,** árbol de levas, *m.* **driving s.,** árbol motor, *m.*

shaggy, *a.* peludo; lanudo

shagreen, *s.* chagrén, *m.*

shah, *s.* cha, sha, *m.*

shake, *v.t.* sacudir; agitar; hacer temblar; (weaken) debilitar, hacer flaquear. *v.i.* estremecerse; temblar; (trill) trinar. **He managed to s. himself free,** Consiguió librarse por una sacudida. **to s. hands,** darse la mano, estrecharse la mano. **to s. one's finger at,** señalar con el dedo (a). **to s. one's fist at,** amenazar con el puño (a). **to s. one's head,** mover la cabeza; negar con la cabeza. **to s. one's sides, (with laughter)** reírse a carcajadas. **to s. with fear,** temblar de miedo. **to s. down,** sacudir, hacer caer. **s.-down,** *s.* cama improvisada, *f.* **to s. off,** sacudirse; librarse (de), perder; quitar de encima (a). **to s. out, (unfurl)** desplegar; sacudir. **to s. up,** agitar; sacudir; remover

shake, *s.* sacudida, *f.*; (of the head) movimiento (de la cabeza), *m.*; (of the hand) apretón (de manos), *m.*; temblor, *m.*; (mus.) trino, gorjeo, *m.* **in two shakes,** (fam.) en un periquete. **to give a person a good s.,** sacudir violentamente (a)

Shakespearean, *a.* shakespeariano

shakiness, *s.* inestabilidad, *f.*; poca firmeza, *f.*; temblor, *m.*; lo dudoso. **the s. of his voice,** su voz trémula

shaking, *s.* sacudimiento, *m.*; temblor, *m.*; (of windows, etc.) zangoloteo, *m.*

shako, *s.* (mil.) chacó, *m.*

shaky, *a.* inestable; poco firme; (of hands, etc.) tembloroso; (of the voice) trémulo; (of gait) vacilante; dudoso

shale, *s.* esquisto, *m.*

shall, *v. aux.* (expressing simple future) **I s. arrive to-morrow,** Llegaré mañana. **S. we go to the sea next week ?** ¿Iremos al mar la semana próxima ?; (expressing obligation, compulsion) **You s. not go out,** No has de salir, No quiero que salgas. **He s. see her immediately,** Tiene que verla en seguida; (as a polite formula) **S. I go ?** ¿Quiere Vd. que vaya ? **Shall we buy the soap ?** ¿Quiere Vd. que compremos el jabón ?

shallop, *s.* (naut.) chalupa, *f.*

shallot, *s.* (bot.) chalote, *m.*, ascalonia, *f.*

shallow, *a.* poco profundo; (of a receptacle) llano; (of persons) superficial, frívolo; (of knowledge, etc.) superficial, ligero, somero. *s.* bajío, *m.*

shallowness, *s.* poca profundidad, *f.*; superficialidad, *f.*

sham, *v.t.* fingir, simular. *s.* farsa, *f.*; imitación, *f.*; engaño, *m.*; (person) farsante, *m.* *a.* fingido; falso; espurio. **to s. illness,** fingirse enfermo. **to s. dead,** hacer la mortecina. **You're just a s.,** Eres un farsante

shamble, *v.i.* andar arrastrándose. *s.* andar pesado, *m.*; *pl.* **shambles,** matadero, *m.*; (fig.) carnicería, *f.*

shambling, *a.* pesado, lento

shame, *s.* vergüenza, *f.*; ignominia, *f.*; deshonra, *f.* *v.t.* avergonzar; deshonrar. **For s.!** ¡Qué vergüenza! **What a s.!** ¡Qué lástima! **to put to s.,** avergonzar

shamefaced, *a.* (bashful) vergonzoso, tímido; (ashamed) avergonzado

shamefacedly, *adv.* vergonzosamente, tímidamente; con vergüenza

shameful, *a.* vergonzoso, escandaloso; indecente

shamefully, *adv.* escandalosamente

shamefulness, *s.* vergüenza, infamia, *f.*; indecencia, *f.*

shameless, *a.* desvergonzado;
impúdico, indecente

shamelessly, *adv.* desvergon-
zadamente

shamelessness, *s.* desvergüenza,
f.; impudicia, deshonestidad, *f.*

shampoo, *s.* champú, *m.* *v.t.* dar
un champú (a); dar un masaje (a).
dry s., champú seco, *m.*

shamrock, *s.* trébol blanco, *m.*

shank, *s.* zanca, *f.*; (*mech.*)
pierna, *f.*; (handle) mango, *m.*;
(of a button) rabo, *m.*, cola, *f.*

shanty, *s.* choza, *f.*

shape, *s.* forma, *f.*; bulto, *m.*;
fantasma, *m.*; (of a garment)
corte, *m.*; (of a person) talle, *m.*;
(*cul.*) molde, *m.*; (of a hat) forma,
f. *v.t.* formar; (a garment)
cortar; (ideas) dar forma (a);
adaptar; (stone, etc.) labrar;
(one's life) dominar. *v.i.* (of
events) desarrollarse. to go out
of s., perder la forma. to
take s., tomar forma. to s.
one's course, dirigirse (hacia,
a); (*naut.*) dar el rumbo. to s.
well, prometer bien

shaped, *a.* de forma de ..., que
tiene figura de ... pear-s.,
piriforme

shapeless, *a.* informe; disforme

shapelessness, *s.* informidad, *f.*;
deformidad, *f.*

shapeliness, *s.* belleza de forma,
f.; simetría, *f.*

shapely, *a.* bien formado; simétrico

share, *s.* porción, *f.*; parte, *f.*;
cuota, *f.*; contribución, *f.*; (part
ownership) interés, *m.*; (in a
company) acción, *f.* *v.t.* distribuir; compartir; dividir;
tomar parte en. *v.i.* participar
(de); tomar parte (en). to fall
to one's s., tocar, corresponder.
to go shares with, dividir con,
compartir con. to take a s. in
the conversation, tomar parte
en la conversación. paid-up s.,
(*com.*) acción liberada, *f.* to s.
out, repartir, distribuir

shareholder, *s.* accionista, *m.*
and *f.*

sharer, *s.* partícipe, *m.* and *f.*

shark, *s.* (*icht.*) tiburón, *m.*;
(*fam.*) caimán, *m.*

sharp, *a.* (of edges) afilado,
cortante; (of points) punzante,
puntiagudo; (of features, etc.)
anguloso; (of bends, etc.) brusco;
(of outlines, etc.) definido, distinto; (of pain, sound) agudo;
(marked) marcado; (intense) intenso; (of winds, glance, etc.)
penetrante; (of hearing) fino; (of
appetite) bueno; (of showers)
fuerte; (quick) rápido; (clever,
etc.) vivo, listo; perspicaz; (of
children) despierto, precoz; (unscrupulous) astuto, sin escrúpulos; (of criticism, remarks)
mordaz; (of rebukes, sentences,
etc.) severo; (of winters, etc.)
riguroso; (of fighting) encarnizado; (of taste) picante; (sour)
ácido; (*mus.*) sostenido. *adv.*
en punto; puntualmente. *s.*
(*mus.*) sostenido, *m.* at five
o'clock s., a las cinco en punto.
Look s.! ¡Date prisa! s.-edged,
afilado. s.-eyed, con ojos de
lince; de mirada penetrante. s.-
featured, de facciones angu-
losas. s.-nosed, de nariz puntiaguda. s.-pointed, puntiagudo. s. practice, procedi-
mientos poco honrados, *m. pl.*
s.-tongued, de lengua áspera.
s. turn, curva brusca, cuvar
cerrada, *f.* s.-witted, de inteligencia viva, listo

sharpen, *v.t.* (knives) afilar,
amolar; (pencils, etc.) sacar
punta (a); (wits, etc.) despabilar;
(appetite) abrir. This walk has
sharpened my appetite, Este
paseo me ha abierto el apetito.
to s. one's claws, afilarse las
uñas

sharper, *s.* (*fam.*) caballero de
industria, timador, *m.*; (at
cards) fullero, *m.*

sharply, *adv.* claramente; bruscamente; severamente; ásperamente

sharpness, *s.* (of cold, etc.)
intensidad, *f.*; severidad, *f.*;
(cleverness) agudeza, perspicacia,
f.; (of a child) precocidad, *f.*;
(sarcasm, etc.) mordacidad, *f.*;
aspereza; brusquedad, *f.*

sharpshooter, *s.* franco tirador,
m.

shatter, v.t. romper, quebrantar; hacer añicos; (fig.) destrozar. **You have shattered my illusions,** Has destrozado todas mis ilusiones

shave, v.i. afeitar, rasurar; (wood, etc.) acepillar. v.i. afeitarse; (of razors) afeitar. s. afeitada, f. **to have a s.,** hacerse afeitar. **to have a close s.,** (fam.) escapar por un pelo

shaving, s. afeitada, f.; (of wood, etc.) viruta, acepilladura, f. **s.-bowl,** bacía, f. **s.-brush,** brocha de afeitar, f. **s.-glass,** espejo de afeitar, m. **s.-soap,** jabón de afeitar, m. **s.-stick,** barra de jabón de afeitar, f.

shawl, s. chal, m.

she, pers. pron. ella; la; (female) hembra, f.; (translated by fem. ending in the case of animals, etc., e.g. she bear, osa, she cat, gata). **It is she,** Es ella. **she who is dancing,** la que baila

sheaf, s. (of corn, etc.) gavilla, garba, f.; (of arrows) haz, m.; (of papers, etc.) paquete, atado, m. **to bind in sheaves,** agavillar

shear, v.t. (sheep) esquilar, trasquilar; tonsurar; cortar; (cloth) tundir

shearer, s. (of sheep) esquilador, m.

shearing, s. (of sheep) esquileo, m., tonsura, f.; (of cloth) tunda, f. **s. machine,** esquiladora, f. **s. season,** esquileo, m.

shears, s. pl. tijeras grandes, f. pl., cizalla, f.

sheath, s. vaina, f. **s.-knife,** cuchillo de monte, m.

sheathe, v.t. envainar; (naut.) aforrar

shed, v.t. derramar; (skin, etc.) mudar; perder; (remove) quitarse, desprenderse de; (get rid of) deshacerse de. s. cobertizo, sotechado, m.; cabaña, f. **to s. light on,** echar luz sobre, iluminar

sheen, s. lustre, m.; brillo, m.

sheep, s. oveja, f.; carnero, m.; ganado lanar, m. **He is the black s. of the family,** Él es el garbanzo negro de la familia. **to cast sheep's eyes at,** lanzar miradas de carnero degollado.

s. breeder, ganadero, m. **s.-dip,** desinfectante para ganado, m. **s.-dog,** perro de pastor, m. **s.-like,** ovejuno, de oveja. **s.-shearing,** esquileo, m.

sheepfold, s. aprisco, redil, m.

sheepish, a. tímido, vergonzoso; estúpido

sheepishly, adv. tímidamente

sheepishness, s. timidez, cortedad, f.; estupidez, f.

sheepskin, s. piel de carnero, f. **s. jacket,** zamarra, f.

sheer, a. puro; completo, absoluto; (steep) escarpado, acantilado; a pico; (of fabrics) transparente; ligero, fino. adv. completamente; de un golpe; (perpendicularly) a pico. **to s. off,** desviarse; largarse, marcharse

sheet, s. (bed) sábana, f.; (shroud) mortaja, f.; (of paper) hoja, f.; cuartilla, f.; (pamphlet) folleto, m.; (news) periódico, m., hoja, f.; (of metal, etc.) lámina, plancha, f.; (of water, etc.) extensión, f.; (naut.) escota, f. v.t. poner sábanas en; envolver en sábanas; (a corpse) amortajar. **to be as white as a s.,** estar pálido como un muerto. **s. bend,** (knot) nudo de tejedor, m. **s. glass,** vidrio en lámina, m. **s. iron,** hierro en planchas, m.

sheik, s. jeque, m.

shekel, s. (coin) siclo, m.; pl. shekels, dinero, m.

shelf, s. estante, anaquel, m.; (reef) banco de arena, bajío, m.; (of rock) escalón, m. **to be on the s.,** (fam.) quedarse para tía, quedarse para vestir imágenes

shell, s. (of small shellfish) concha, f.; (of tortoise) coraza, f.; (of insects, lobsters, etc.) caparazón, m.; (of a nut) cáscara, f.; (of an egg) cascarón, m.; (of peas, beans) vaina, f.; (com. and mus.) concha, f.; (of a building) casco, m.; (outside) exterior, m.; (empty form) apariencia, f.; (mil.) granada, f. v.t. pelar; (nuts) descascarar; (beans, etc.) desvainar; (mil.) bombardear. **to be under s.-fire,** sufrir un bombardeo. **s. shock,** neurosis de guerra, f.

shellfish, s. crustáceo, m.; (as food) marisco, m.

shelling, s. (mil.) bombardeo, m.

shelter, *s.* abrigo, amparo, *m.*; refugio, *m.*; asilo, *m.* *v.t.* dar asilo (a); abrigar; (defend) amparar, proteger; (hide) esconder. *v.i.* refugiarse; resguardarse; esconderse

sheltered, *a.* abrigado

sheltering, *a.* protector

shelve, *v.t.* (books) poner en un estante; (persons) destituir; (questions, etc.) aplazar, arrinconar; proveer de estantes. *v.i.* (slope) inclinarse, formar declive; (of sea bed) formar escalones

shelving, *a.* inclinado; (of ocean bed) acantilado

shepherd, *s.* pastor, *m.* *v.t.* guardar; guiar, conducir. **s. boy,** zagal, *m.* **shepherd's pouch,** zurrón, *m.*

shepherdess, *s.* pastora, *f.*

sherbet, *s.* sorbete, *m.*

shereef, *s.* jerife, *m.*

sheriff, *s.* (in Gt. Britain) sheriff, *m.*; (U.S.A.) jefe de la policía, *m.*

sherry, *s.* (vino de) jerez, *m.* **dry s.,** jerez seco, *m.*

shield, *s.* escudo, *m.*; (round) rodela, *f.*; (*her.*) escudo de armas, *m.*; (*fig.*) defensa, *f.*, amparo, *m.* *v.t.* proteger, amparar. **to s. a person,** proteger a una persona. **to s. one's eyes from the sun,** proteger los ojos del sol. **s.-bearer,** escudero, *m.*

shift, *v.t.* mover; trasladar; quitar, librarse de; cambiar. *v.i.* moverse; (of the wind) girar; cambiar. *s.* cambio, *m.*; (expedient) recurso, expediente, *m.*; (dodge) artificio, *m.*, trampa, *f.*; (of workmen) tanda, *f.*, turno, *m.* **to make s.,** arreglárselas (para hacer algo); procurar (hacer algo); (manage) ir tirando. **to s. for oneself,** componérselas, arreglárselas. **to s. the scenes,** (*theat.*) cambiar de decoración. **to s. the helm,** (*naut.*) cambiar el timón. **to work in shifts,** trabajar por turnos

shiftiness, *s.* falta de honradez, informalidad, *f.*; astucia, *f.*

shifting, *a.* (of light, etc.) cambiante; (of sand, etc.) movedizo; (of wind) mudable; (of moods) voluble. **s. sand,** arena movediza, *f.*

shiftless, *a.* perezoso; sin energía, ineficaz

shiftlessness, *s.* pereza, *f.*; falta de energía, *f.*

shifty, *a.* (tricky) tramposo, astuto; (dishonest) informal, falso; (of gaze) furtivo. **s.-eyed,** *a.* de mirada furtiva

shilling, *s.* chelín, *m.* **nine shillings in the £,** nueve chelines por libra. **to cut off with a s.,** desheredar

shilly-shally, *s.* irresolución, vacilación, *f.* *v.i.* estar irresoluto, titubear, no saber qué hacer

shimmer, *v.i.* rielar; relucir. *s.* luz trémula, *f.*; resplandor, *m.*; viso, *m.*

shin, *s.* espinilla, *f.*; (of beef) corvejón, *m.* **to s. up,** trepar

shindy, *s.* suiza, reyerta, tasquera, *f.* **to kick up a s.,** armar camorra

shine, *v.i.* brillar; resplandecer, relucir, relumbrar. *v.t.* (shoes) dar lustre (a). *s.* brillo, *m.*; lustre, *m.* **in rain or s.,** en buen o mal tiempo. **to s. with happiness,** radiar felicidad. **to take the s. out of,** eclipsar

shingle, *s.* (pebbles) guijarros, *m. pl.*; cascajo, *m.*; (*carp.*) barda, *f.*; (hair) pelo a la garçonne, *m.*; *pl.* shingles, (*med.*) zona, *f.*, herpe zóster, *m.* *v.t.* (the hair) cortar a la garçonne

shining, *a.* resplandeciente, brillante, reluciente; radiante. **s. with happiness,** radiante de felicidad. **s. example,** ejemplo notable, *m.*

shintoism, *s.* sintoísmo, *m.*

shiny, *a.* brillante; lustroso, terso; (of trousers, etc.) reluciente; (of paper) glaseado

ship, *s.* buque, barco, *m.*; (sailing) velero, *m.* *v.t.* embarcar; (oars) armar. *v.i.* embarcar; (as a member of crew) embarcarse. **on board s.,** a bordo. **to s. a sea,** embarcar agua. **to take s.,** embarcar. **to s. off,** mandar. **ship's boat,** lancha, *f.* **ship's boy,** grumete, *m.* **ship's carpenter,** carpintero de ribera, *m.* **ship's company,** tripulación, *f.* **s.-breaker,** desguazador, *m.* **s.-canal,** canal de navegación, *m.* **s.-load,** cargamento, *m.*

shipbuilder, s. constructor de buques, arquitecto naval, m.

shipbuilding, s. construcción naval, f.

shipment, s. embarque, m.; despacho por mar, m.; (consignment) remesa, f.

shipowner, s. naviero, m.

shipper, s. naviero, m.; importador, m.; exportador, m.

shipping, s. embarque, m.; buques, barcos, m. pl.; (of a country) marina, f. s. agent, consignatario de buques, m. s. company, compañía de navegación, f. s. offices, oficinas de una compañía de navegación, f. pl.

shipshape, a. en buen orden; bien arreglado

shipwreck, s. naufragio, m. v.t. hacer naufragar, echar a pique.

shipwrecked person, s. náufrago (-ga). to be shipwrecked, naufragar

shipyard, s. astillero, varadero, m.

shire, s. condado, m.

shirk, v.t. eludir, esquivar; desentenderse de. v.i. faltar al deber

shirker, s. gandul (-la); persona que no cumple con su deber, f.

shirr, v.t. fruncir

shirt, s. camisa, f. dress s., camisa de pechera dura, f. hair-s., cilicio, m. in one's s.-sleeves, en mangas de camisa. s.-blouse, blusa sencilla, f. s.-collar, cuello de camisa, m. s. factory or shop, camisería, f. shirt-front, pechera, f. s.-maker, camisero (-ra)

shirting, s. tela para camisas, f.

shiver, v.i. temblar, tiritar; dar diente con diente; (of a boat) zozobrar. v.t. (break) hacer añicos, romper; (sails) sacudir. s. temblor, estremecimiento, m.; escalofrío, m.; (of glass, etc.) fragmento, m., astilla, f. You give me the shivers, Me das escalofríos

shivery, a. tembloroso; friolero. I feel s., Tengo escalofríos

shoal, s. (of fish) banco, m.; gran cantidad, f.; (of people) multitud, muchedumbre, f.; (water) bajo fondo, m.; (sand-bank) banco, bajío, m. a. poco profundo.

I know shoals of people in Valencia, Conozco a muchísima gente de Valencia

shock, s. choque, m.; (elec.) conmoción, f.; (med.) shock, m.; (med., stroke) conmoción cerebral, f.; (fright) sobresalto, susto, m. v.t. sacudir, dar una sacudida (a); chocar; escandalizar, horrorizar. v.i. chocar. electric s., conmoción eléctrica, f. She is easily shocked, Ella se escandaliza fácilmente. s. of hair, mata de pelo, f. s. absorber, (mech.) amortiguador, m.; (aut.) amortiguador de los muelles, m. s. troops, tropas de asalto, f. pl., elementos de choque, m. pl.

shocking, a. escandaloso; repugnante, horrible; espantoso. How s.! ¡Qué horror! s. bad, malísimo

shockingly, adv. horriblemente

shod, a. calzado; (of horses) herrado

shoddy, s. pacotilla, f. a. de pacotilla; espurio, falso

shoe, s. zapato, m.; (horse) herradura, f.; (naut., mech.) zapata, f. v.t. (horses) herrar. I should not like to be in his shoes, No me gustaría estar en su pellejo. That is quite another pair of shoes, Eso es harina de otro costal. to cast a s., (of horses) desherrarse, perder una herradura. to put on one's shoes, ponerse los zapatos, calzarse. to remove one's shoes, quitarse los zapatos, descalzarse. wooden shoes, zuecos, m. pl. s.-buckle, hebilla de zapato, f. s.-lace, cordón de zapato, m. s.-leather, cuero para zapatos, m.; calzado, m. s.-scraper, limpiabarros, m., estregadera, f. s.-shop, zapatería, f.

shoeblack, s. betún, m.; (person) limpiabotas, m.

shoehorn, s. calzador, m.

shoemaker, s. zapatero (-ra)

shoemaking, s. fabricación de calzado, zapatería, f.

shoo! interj. ¡fuera! ¡zape! v.t. ahuyentar

shoot, v.t. (throw) lanzar; precipitar; (empty) vaciar; (a rapid) salvar; (rays, etc.) echar; (an arrow, a gun, etc.) disparar; (a person, etc.) pegar un tiro (a); (*sport*) tirar; (*mil.*) fusilar, pasar por las armas; (a film) hacer, impresionar. *v.i.* lanzarse, precipitarse; (of pain) latir; (sprout) brotar; disparar; tirar; (at football). tirar a gol, chutar. **to s. a glance at**, lanzar una mirada (a). **I was shot in the foot,** Una bala me hirió en el pie. **to s. the sun**, (*naut.*) tomar el sol. **to s. ahead**, tomar la delantera. **to s. at**, tirar a. **to s by**, pasar como una bala. **to s. down**, (*aer.*) derribar; matar de un tiro. **to s. up**, (of children) espigarse; (of prices) subir mucho; (of cliffs, etc.) elevarse

shoot, *s.* partida de caza, *f.*; tiro, *m.*; (*bot.*) renuevo, retoño, *m.*

shooting, *s.* tiro, *m.*; caza con escopeta, *f.*; (of guns) tiroteo, *m.*; (of an arrow) disparo, *m.*; (of a film) rodaje, *m.* **to go s.**, ir a cazar con escopeta. **s.-box**, pabellón de caza, *m.* **s. butts**, tiradero, *m.* **s. dog**, perro de caza, *m.* **s.-gallery**, tiro al blanco, *m.* **s. match**, concurso de tiro, *m.* **s. pain**, punzada de dolor, *f.* **s. party**, partida de caza, *f.* **s. practice**, ejercicios de tiro, *m. pl.* **s.-range**, campo de tiro, *m.* **s. star**, estrella fugaz, *f.*

shop, *s.* tienda, *f.*; (workshop) taller, *m. v.i.* ir de compras, ir de tiendas; comprar. **to talk s.**, hablar de negocios. **s.-assistant**, dependiente (-ta). **s.-soiled**, deslucido. **s.-steward**, representante de los obreros de una fábrica o taller, *m.* **s. window**, escaparate, *m.*

shopkeeper, *s.* tendero (-ra)

shoplifter, *s.* ladrón (-ona) de tiendas, ratero (-ra) de las tiendas

shoplifting, *s.* ratería en las tiendas, *f.*

shopper, *s.* comprador (-ra)

shopping, *s.* compra, *f.*; compras, *f. pl.* **to go s.**, ir de compras. **s. basket**, cesta para compras, *f.* **s. centre**, barrio de tiendas, *m.*

shopwalker, *s.* jefe de recepción, *m.*

shore, *s.* orilla, ribera, *f.*; costa, *f.*; (sands) playa, *f.* **off s.**, en alta mar. **on s.**, en tierra. **to come on s.**, desembarcar. **to s. up**, apuntalar, acodalar; (*fig.*) apoyar

short, *a.* corto; (of persons) bajo; breve; (of temper) vivo; insuficiente; distante (de); (brusque) seco; (of money) alcanzado. *adv.* súbitamente; brevemente. *s.* (vowel) vocal breve, *m.*; *pl.* **shorts**, calzones cortos, *m. pl.* **for s.**, para mayor brevedad. **for a s. time**, por poco tiempo. **in a s. time**, dentro de poco. **in s.**, en breve, en resumen, en pocas palabras. **on s. notice**, con poco tiempo de aviso. **s. of**, con la excepción de, menos. **to be s.**, faltar, ser escaso. **to be s. with someone**, tratar con sequedad (a). **to fall s. of expectations**, no cumplir las esperanzas. **to go s. of**, pasarse sin. **to grow s.**, escasear. **s.-circuit**, corto circuito, *m.* **s. cut**, atajo, *m.* **s.-haired**, pelicorto. **s.-handed**, falto de mano de obra. **s.-lived**, de vida corta; efímero, fugaz. **s.-sighted**, corto de vista. **s.-sightedness**, miopía, cortedad de vista, *f.* **s. story**, cuento, *m.* **s.-tempered**, irascible, irritable, de genio vivo. **s.-waisted**, corto de talle. **s.-winded**, corto de resuello; asmático

shortage, *s.* falta, escasez, *f.*; carestía, *f.* **water s.**, carestía de agua, *f.*

shortcoming, *s.* defecto, *m.*; imperfección, *f.*

shorten, *v.t.* acortar; reducir; disminuir; abreviar. *v.i.* acortarse

shorthand, *s.* taquigrafía, estenografía, *f.* *a.* taquigráfico, estenográfico. **to take down in s.**, taquigrafiar. **s. writer**, estenógrafo (-fa); taquígrafo (-fa)

shortly, *adv.* dentro de poco, pronto; brevemente, en resumen, en pocas palabras; (curtly) bruscamente, secamente

shortness, *s.* cortedad, *f.*; brevedad, *f.*; (of a person) pequeñez, *f.*; (lack) falta, *f.*; (of memory, sight) cortedad, *f.*; (brusque-

ness) sequedad, brusquedad, *f.*
s. of breath, falta de aliento,
respiración difícil, *f.*

shot, *s.* perdigón, *m.*; (*fam.*)
perdigones, *m. pl.*; bala, *f.*;
(firing) tiro, *m.*; (person) tirador
(-ra); (stroke, etc.) golpe, *m.*,
tirada, *f.*; (cinema) fotograma,
m. a. (of silk) tornasolado. **at
one s.,** de un tiro. **like a s.,**
(*fig.*) como una bala. **to exchange shots,** tirotearse. **to
fire a s.,** disparar un tiro. **to
have a s. at,** probar suerte.
s.-gun, escopeta, *f.* **s. silk,** seda
tornasolada, *f.*

should, *v. aux.* (expressing
future) **I s. like to go to the
sea,** Me gustaría ir al mar;
(expressing conditional) **I s.
like to see them if I could,** Me
gustaría verlos si pudiera; (expressing obligation) **You s. go
at once,** Debes ir en seguida;
(expressing probability) **They
s. arrive to-morrow,** Seguramente llegarán mañana; (expressing doubt) **If the moment
s. be opportune,** Si el momento fuera oportuno. **I s. just
think so!** ¡Ya lo creo! ¡No lo
dudo!

shoulder, *s.* hombro, *m.*; (of
mutton) espalda, *f.*; (of a hill)
falda, *f.* *v.t.* echar al hombro;
(a responsibility) cargar con,
hacerse responsable para;
(jostle) dar codazos (a). **s. to s.,**
hombro a hombro. **S. arms!**
¡Armas al hombro! **s.-blade,**
omoplato, *m.* **s.-knot,** charretera, *f.* **s.-pad,** hombrera, *f.*
s.-strap, (*mil.*) dragona, *f.*; (of
a dress, etc.) tirante, *m.*; (of a
water carrier, etc.) correón, *m.*

shouldered, *a.* de hombros . . .,
de espaldas . . . **round-s.,**
cargado de espaldas

shout, *v.i.* gritar, hablar a gritos.
v.t. gritar. *s.* grito, *m.* **shouts
of applause,** aclamaciones, *f.pl.*;
aplausos, *m. pl.* **to s. from the
housetops,** pregonar a los cuatro
vientos. **to s. with laughter,**
reírse a carcajadas. **to s. down,**
silbar. **to s. out,** gritar

shouting, *s.* gritos, *m. pl.*, vocerío,
clamor, *m.*; (applause) aclamaciones, *f. pl.*

shove, *v.t.* empujar; poner. *s.*
empujón, *m.* **to s. along,**
empujar. **to s. aside,** empujar a un lado; apartar a
codazos. **to s. away,** rechazar.
to s. back, hacer retroceder.
to s. forward, hacer avanzar,
empujar hacia adelante. **to s.
off,** (a boat) echar afuera. **to s.
out,** empujar hacia fuera

shovel, *s.* pala, *f.* *v.t.* traspalar.
s. hat, sombrero de teja,
m.

shovelful, *s.* palada, *f.*

show, *v.t.* mostrar; hacer ver; (disclose) descubrir; revelar; (exhibit) exhibir; (indicate) indicar; (prove) demostrar, probar;
(conduct) conducir, llevar, guiar;
(explain) explicar; (oneself) presentarse. *v.i.* mostrarse; verse;
parecer. **to s. cause,** mostrar
causa. **to s. fight,** ofrecer
resistencia. **to s. itself,** declararse, asomarse, surgir. **to s.
to the door,** acompañar a la
puerta. **to s. in,** (a person)
hacer entrar, introducir (en). **to
s. off,** *v.t.* exhibir; realzar; (new
clothes, etc.) lucir. *v.i.* darse
importancia; pavonearse. **to
s. out,** (a person) acompañar
a la puerta; (in anger) poner
de patitas en la calle. **to s.
through,** *v.i.* transparentarse.
v.t. conducir por. **to s. up,** *v.t.*
invitar a subir; (a fraud, etc.)
descubrir; (a swindler) desenmascarar; (defects) revelar. *v.i.*
(stand out) destacarse; (be present) asomarse, asistir

show, *s.* (exhibition) exposición,
f.; espectáculo, *m.*; (sign) indicio,
m., señal, *f.*; (ostentation)
pompa, *f.*, aparato, *m.*, ostentación, *f.*; (appearance) apariencia, *f.*; (affair) negocio, *m.*
to give the s. away, echar los
títeres a rodar. **to make a s. of,**
hacer gala de. **s.-case,** escaparate, *m.*, vitrina, *f.* **s. of
hands,** votación por manos
levantadas, *f.* **s.-room,** salón de
muestras, *m.*

shower, *s.* chaparrón, chubasco,
m.; (of spray, etc.) chorro, *m.*;
(of stones, arrows, etc.) lluvia, *f.*;
(of honours) cosecha, *f.* *v.t.* derramar; rociar; mojar; llover.

v.i. chaparrear, llover. **s.-bath,** ducha, *f.*

showery, *a.* lluvioso

showily, *adv.* aparatosamente, con ostentación

showiness, *s.* ostentación, *f.*; esplendor, *m.*, magnificencia, *f.*

showman, *s.* director de un espectáculo de feria, *m.*; titiritero, *m.*; pregonero, *m.*

showy, *a.* vistoso; ostentoso

shrapnel, *s.* shrapnel, *m.*, granada de metralla, *f.*

shred, *s.* fragmento, *m.*; (of cloth) jirón, *m.*; brizna, *f.*; (*fig.*) pizca, *f.* *v.t.* desmenuzar. **to tear in shreds,** hacer pedazos

shrew, *s.* (*zool.*) musaraña, *f.*; (woman) fiera, *f.*

shrewd, *a.* sagaz, perspicaz; prudente; (of the wind) penetrante; (pain) punzante. **to have a s. idea of,** tener una buena idea de

shrewdly, *adv.* sagazmente, con perspicacia; prudentemente

shrewdness, *s.* sagacidad, perspicacia, *f.*; prudencia, *f.*

shrewish, *a.* regañón

shrewishness, *s.* mal genio, *m.*

shriek, *v.i.* chillar, gritar. *v.t.* decir a voces, gritar. *s.* chillido, *m.*; grito agudo, *m.* **shrieks of laughter,** carcajadas, *f. pl.*

shrieking, *s.* gritos, chillidos, *m. pl.*

shrift, to give short, enviar normala (a), enviar a paseo (a)

shrill, *a.* estridente, agudo

shrillness, *s.* estridencia, *f.*

shrimp, *s.* camarón, *m.*, gamba, *f.* *v.i.* pescar camarones

shrine, *s.* relicario, *m.*; sepulcro de santo, *m.*; templete, *m.*, capilla, *f.*; santuario, *m.*

shrink, *v.i.* encogerse; contraerse; disminuir, reducirse. *v.t.* encoger; reducir, disminuir; desaparecer; disiparse. **I shrank from doing it,** Me repugnaba el hacerlo. **to s. away from,** retroceder ante; recular ante; huir de. **to s. back,** recular (ante)

shrinkage, *s.* encogimiento, *m.*; contracción, *f.*; reducción, disminución, *f.*

shrinking, *a.* tímido

shrive, *v.t.* confesar

shrivel, *v.i.* avellanarse; (of persons, through old age) acartonarse, apergaminarse; (wither) marchitarse; arrugarse. *v.t.* arrugar; secar, marchitar

shroud, *s.* sudario, *m.*, mortaja, *f.*; (*naut.*) obenque, *m.* **to wrap in a s.,** amortajar

Shrove Tuesday, *s.* martes de carnaval, *m.*

shrub, *s.* arbusto, *m.*; matajo, *m.*

shrubbery, *s.* arbustos, *m. pl.*, maleza, *f.*; bosquecillo, *m.*

shrug, *v.i.* encogerse de hombros. *s.* encogimiento de hombros, *m.*

shrunken, *a.* contraído; acartonado, apergaminado; seco, marchito

shudder, *v.i.* estremecerse; vibrar. *s.* estremecimiento, *m.*; escalofrío, *m.*; (of an engine, etc.) vibración, *f.*

shuffle, *v.t.* (the feet) arrastrar; (scrape) restregar; (cards) barajar; (papers) mezclar. *v.i.* arrastrar los pies, arrastrarse; (cards) barajar; (*fig.*) tergiversar. *s.* (of the cards) barajadura, *f.*; (*fig.*) evasiva, *f.*; embuste, *m.* **to s. along,** andar arrastrando los pies

shun, *v.t.* evitar, rehuir, esquivar

shunt, *v.t.* (*r.w.*) apartar; (*elec.*) shuntar. *v.i.* (*r.w.*) hacer maniobras

shunting, *s.* (of trains) maniobras, *f. pl.*

shut, *v.t.* and *v.i.* cerrar. **to s. again,** volver a cerrar. **to s. down,** *v.t.* cerrar; (a machine) parar. *v.i.* (of factories, etc.) cerrar. **to s. in,** encerrar; (surround) cercar, rodear. **to s. off,** (water, etc.) cortar; (isolate) aislar (de). **to s. out,** excluir; obstruir, impedir; negar la entrada (a). **to s. up,** *v.t.* cerrar; encerrar; (*fam.*) hacer callar (a). *v.i.* (*fam.*) callarse, cerrar la boca. **to s. oneself up,** encerrarse

shutter, *s.* (window) contraventana, *f.*, postigo, *m.*; (of a camera) obturador, *m.*; (of a fireplace) campana (de hogar), *f.* *v.t.* poner contraventanas (a); cerrar los postigos de

shuttle, *s.* (weaver's, and sewing-machine) lanzadera, *f.* **s.-cock,** volante, *m.*

shy, *a.* (of animals) tímido, salvaje; (of persons) huraño, tímido;

vergonzoso. *v.i.* (of a horse) respingar; (of persons) asustarse (de). *v.t.* (a ball, etc.) lanzar. *s.* (of a horse) respingo, *m.*; (of a ball) lanzamiento, *m.*; (try) prueba, tentativa, *f.* **to fight shy of**, procurar evitar. **to have a shy at**, probar

shyly, *adv.* tímidamente; con vergüenza, vergonzosamente

shyness, *s.* timidez, *f.*; huraña, *f.*; vergüenza, *f.*

Siamese, *a.* siamés. *s.* siamés (-esa); (language) siamés, *m.* **S. cat**, gato siamés, *m.*

Siberian, *a.* and *s.* siberiano (-na)

sibilant, *a.* sibilante

sibyl, *s.* sibila, *f.*

sibylline, *a.* sibilino

Sicilian, *a.* and *s.* siciliano (-na)

sick, *a.* enfermo; mareado. **the s.**, los enfermos. **to be s.**, vomitar; estar enfermo. **to be s. of**, estar harto de. **to feel s.**, sentirse mareado. **to be on the s.-list**, estar enfermo. **s.-bed**, lecho de dolor, *m.* **s.-headache**, migraña, jaqueca, *f.* **s.-leave**, (*mil.*) permiso por enfermedad, *m.* **s.-nurse**, enfermera, *f.*

sicken, *v.i.* caer enfermo, enfermar; (feel sick) marearse; (recoil from) repugnar; (weary of) cansarse (de), aburrirse (de). *v.t.* marear; dar asco (a), repugnar; cansar, aburrir. **It sickens me**, Me da asco. **He is sickening for measles**, Muestra síntomas de sarampión

sickening, *a.* nauseabundo; repugnante; (tedious) fastidioso

sickle, *s.* hoz, segadera, *f.*

sickliness, *s.* falta de salud, *f.*; náusea, *f.*; (paleness) palidez, *f.*

sickly, *a.* enfermizo, achacoso, malucho; (of places, etc.) malsano; (pale) pálido; débil; (of a smell) nauseabundo; (mawkish) empalagoso

sickness, *s.* enfermedad, *f.*; mal, *m.*; náusea, *f.*, mareo, *m.*

side, *s.* lado, *m.*; (hand) mano, *f.*; (of a river, etc.) orilla, *f.*, margen, *m.*; (of a person) costado, *m.*; (of an animal) ijada, *f.*; (of a hill) falda, pendiente, ladera, *f.*; (of a ship) banda, *f.*, costado, *m.*; (aspect) aspecto, *m.*; punto de vista, *m.*; (party) partido, grupo, *m.*; (team) equipo, *m.*; (of descent) lado, *m.* *a.* lateral, de lado; oblicuo. **on all sides**, por todas partes. **on both sides**, por ambos lados. **s. by s.**, lado a lado. **the other s. of the picture**, el revés de la medalla. **to change sides**, cambiar de partido. **to pick sides**, escoger el equipo. **to put on s.**, darse tono, alzar el gallo. **to split one's sides**, desternillarse de risa, reírse a carcajadas. **to s. with someone**, tomar el partido de alguien. **wrong s. out**, al revés. **s.-car**, sidecar, asiento lateral, *m.* **s.-chain**, (*chem.*) cadena lateral, *f.* **s.-dish**, entremés, *m.* **s.-door**, puerta lateral, *f.* **s.-face**, *a.* de perfil. *s.* perfil, *m.* **s.-glance**, mirada de soslayo, *f.* **s.-issue**, cuestión secundaria, *f.* **s.-line**, negocio accesorio, *m.*; ocupación secundaria, *f.*; (*r.w.*) vía secundaria, *f.* **s.-saddle**, silla de señora, silla de montar de lado, *f.* **s.-show**, (at a fair) barraca, *f.*, puesto de feria, *m.*; exhibición secundaria, *f.*; función secundaria, *f.* **s.-table**, trinchero, *m.* **s.-track**, *s.* (*r.w.*) apartadero, *m.* *v.t.* desviar (de), apartar (de). **s.-view**, perfil, *m.* **s.-walk**, acera, *f.* **s.-whiskers**, patillas, *f. pl.*

sidelight, *s.* luz lateral, *f.*; (on a ship) ojo de buey, *m.*; (*fig.*) información incidental, *f.*

sidelong, *adv.* de lado, lateralmente; (of glances) de soslayo. *a.* oblicuo

sidereal, *a.* sidéreo, sideral

siderurgy, *s.* siderurgia, *f.*

sideways, *adv.* oblicuamente, de lado; (edgewise) de soslayo. *a.* de soslayo

siding, *s.* (*r.w.*) apartadero, *m.*

sidle, *v.i.* andar (or ir) de lado. **to s. up to**, acercarse servilmente a; arrimarse (a)

siege, *s.* asedio, sitio, cerco, *m.* **to lay s. to**, poner cerco (a), sitiar, asediar cercar. **to raise a s.**, levantar un sitio

Sienese, *a.* and *s.* sienés (-esa)

sienna, *s.* tierra de siena natural, *f.* **burnt s.,** tierra de siena tostada, *f.*

sieve, *s.* cedazo, tamiz, *m.,* criba, *f.* *v.t.* tamizar, cerner, cribar

sift, *v.t.* (sieve) cerner, cribar; (sugar, etc.) salpicar (con); (a question) escudriñar, examinar minuciosamente

sifting, *s.* cribado, *m.;* (of a question) investigación minuciosa, *f.;* *pl.* **siftings,** cerniduras, *f. pl.*

sigh, *v.i.* suspirar; (of the wind) susurrar. *s.* suspiro, *m.;* (of the wind) susurro, *m.* **to s. for,** suspirar por; lamentar

sighing, *s.* suspiros, *m. pl.;* (of the wind) susurro, *m.*

sight, *s.* vista, *f.;* visión, *f.;* espectáculo, *m.;* (fright) estantigua, *f.* *v.t.* ver, divisar; (aim) apuntar. **front s.,** (of guns) alza, *f.* **short s.,** (of eyes) vista corta, *f.* **at first s.,** a primera vista. **in s.,** a la vista. **in s. of,** a vista de. **out of s.,** que no está a la vista; perdido de vista. **Out of s., out of mind,** Ojos que no ven, corazón que no siente. **to be lost to s.,** perderse de vista. **to lose s. of,** perder de vista (a). **to catch a s. of,** vislumbrar. **to come in s.,** aparecer, asomarse. **to know by s.,** conocer de vista (a). **s.-reading,** lectura a primera vista, *f.*

sightly, *a.* hermoso; deleitable

sightseeing, to go, visitar los monumentos

sightseer, *s.* curioso (-sa); turista, *m.* and *f.*

sign, *s.* señal, *f.;* seña, *f.;* indicio, *m.;* (of the zodiac and *mus.*) signo, *m.;* marca, *f.;* (*ecc.*) símbolo, *m.;* (of a shop, etc.) muestra, *f.,* rótulo, *m.;* (symptom) síntoma, *m.* *v.t.* firmar; indicar; (*ecc.*) persignar. **as a s. of,** en señal de. **to converse by signs,** hablar por señas. **to make the s. of the cross over,** santiguar. **to show signs (of),** dar señas (de); indicar. **s.-painter,** pintor de muestras, *m.*

signal, *s.* señal, *f.* *v.t.* señalar; hacer señas (a). *v.i.* hacer señales. *a.* insigne, notable.

fog-s., señal de niebla, *f.* **landing s.,** (*aer.*) señal de aterrizaje, *f.* **to give the s. for,** dar la señal para. **s.-box,** garita de señales, *f.* **s. code,** (*naut.*) código de señales, *m.*

signalize, *v.t.* señalar, distinguir

signaller, *s.* señalador, *m.*

signally, *adv.* señaladamente, notablemente

signalman, *s.* (*r.w.*) guardavía, *m.*

signatory, *a.* and *s.* signatario (-ia)

signature, *s.* firma, *f.;* (*mus.* and *print.*) signatura, *f.*

signboard, *s.* letrero, *m.,* muestra, *f.*

signet, *s.* sello, *m.* **s.-ring,** anillo de sello, *m.*

significance, *s.* significación, *f.,* significado, *m.;* importancia, *f.*

significant, *a.* significativo, significante; expresivo; importante

significantly, *adv.* significativamente; expresivamente

signify, *v.t.* significar; querer decir; importar. *v.i.* significar, tener importancia; importar

signpost, *s.* indicador de dirección, *m.*

Sikh, *s.* sik, *m.* and *f.* (*pl.* siks)

silage, *s.* forraje conservado en silo, *m.*

silence, *s.* silencio, *m.* *interj.* ¡silencio! *v.t.* hacer callar, imponer silencio (a); silenciar. **to keep s.,** guardar silencio, callarse. **to pass over in s.,** pasar en silencio (por), pasar por alto de. **S. gives consent,** Quien calla otorga

silencer, *s.* (of fire-arms) silencioso, *m.;* (*aut.*) silenciador, silencioso, *m.*

silent, *a.* silencioso. **to become s.,** enmudecer; callar. **to remain s.,** callarse, guardar silencio; permanecer silencioso. **s. partner,** *s.* socio (-ia) comanditario (-ia)

silently, *adv.* silenciosamente, en silencio

Silesian, *a.* and *s.* silesio (-ia)

silhouette, *s.* silueta, *f.* *v.t.* representar en silueta; destacar. **in s.,** en silueta. **to be silhouetted against the sky,** destacarse contra el cielo

silica, s. sílice, f.

silicate, s. silicato, m.

silicum, s. silicio, m.

silk, s. seda, f. a. de seda. **artificial s.,** seda artificial, f. **floss s.,** seda ocal, f. **sewing s.,** seda de coser, f. **twist s.,** seda cordelada, f. **as smooth as s.,** como una seda. **s. growing,** sericultura, f. **s. hat,** sombrero de copa, m. **s. merchandise,** sedería, f. **s. stockings,** medias de seda, f. pl.

silken, a. de seda; sedoso

silkiness, s. carácter sedoso, m.; suavidad, f.

silkworm, s. gusano de seda, m.

silky, a. sedoso; (of wine) suave

sill, s. (of a window) alféizar, antepecho, m.; (of a door) umbral, m.

silliness, s. tontería, estupidez, f.

silly, a. tonto, estúpido; imbécil. s. tonto (-ta). **You are a s. ass,** Eres un imbécil

silo, s. silo, m.

silt, s. aluvión, m., sedimentación, f. **to s. up,** v.t. cegar (or obstruir) con aluvión. v.i. cegarse con aluvión

Silurian, a. silúrico

silver, s. plata, f. a. de plata; argénteo; (of the voice, etc.) argentino. v.t. platear; (mirrors) azogar; (hair) blanquear. **s. birch,** abedul, m. **s. fox,** zorro plateado, m. **s.-grey,** gris perla, m. **s.-haired,** de pelo entrecano. **s.-paper,** papel de estaño, m. **s.-plate,** s. vajilla de plata, f. v.t. platear. **s.-tongued,** de pico de oro; de voz argentina. **s. wedding,** bodas de plata, f. pl.

silversmith, s. platero, m. **silversmith's shop,** platería, f.

silvery, a. plateado, argentado; (of sounds) argentino

simian, a. símico

similar, a. parecido (a), semejante (a); similar; (geom.) semejante. **to be s. to,** asemejarse (a), parecerse (a)

similarity, s. parecido, m., semejanza, similitud, f.

similarly, adv. de un modo parecido, asimismo

simile, s. símil, m.

simmer, v.i. hervir a fuego lento; (fig.) estar a punto de estallar. **to s. down,** (fig.) moderarse poco a poco. **to s. over,** (fig.) estallar

simoniacal, a. simoníaco

simony, s. simonía, f.

simoon, s. simún, m.

simper, v.i. sonreírse bobamente

simpering, s. sonrisilla tonta, f.

simperingly, adv. con sonrisa necia

simple, a. sencillo; simple; ingenuo, inocente; crédulo; (humble) humilde; (mere) mero. **s.-hearted,** inocente, cándido, sin malicia. **s.-minded,** ingenuo; crédulo. **s.-mindedness,** ingenuidad, f.; credulidad, f.

simpleton, s. primo (-ma); papanatas, m., tonto (-ta)

simplicity, s. sencillez, f.; simplicidad, candidez, f.

simplifiable, a. simplificable

simplification, s. simplificación, f.

simplify, v.t. simplificar

simply, adv. sencillamente; simplemente, meramente; absolutamente

simulacrum, s. simulacro, m.

simulate, v.t. fingir, aparentar, simular

simulation, s. simulación, f., fingimiento, m.

simultaneous, a. simultáneo

simultaneously, adv. simultáneamente; al mismo tiempo (que)

simultaneousness, s. simultaneidad, f.

sin, s. pecado, m. v.i. pecar; faltar

since, adv. desde entonces, desde (que). prep. desde. conjunc. desde que, ya que, puesto que. **a long time s.,** hace mucho. **not long s.,** hace poco. **How long is it s. . . . ?** ¿Cuánto tiempo hace que . . . ? **s. then,** desde entonces

sincere, a. sincero

sincerely, adv. sinceramente. **Yours s.,** Su afectísimo . . .

sincerity, s. sinceridad, f.

sine, s. (math.) seno, m.

sinecure, s. sinecura, f.

sinew, s. tendón, m.; pl. sinews, nervio, m., fuerza, f.

sinewy, a. (stringy) fibroso; musculoso, nervudo

sinful, *a.* (of persons) pecador; (of thoughts, acts) pecaminoso

sinfulness, *s.* pecado, *m.*; culpabilidad, perversidad, maldad, *f.*

sing, *v.i.* cantar; (of the ears) zumbar; (of wind, water) murmurar, susurrar; (of a cat) ronronear. *v.t.* cantar. **to s. a child to sleep,** dormir a un niño cantando. **to s. another song,** (*fam.*) bajar el tono. **to s. small,** hacerse el chiquito. **to s. the praises of,** hacer las alabanzas de. **to s. out,** vocear, gritar. **s.-song,** *s.* canturía, *f.*; concierto improvisado, *m. a.* monótono

singe, *v.t.* chamuscar; (a fowl) aperdigar; (hair) quemar las puntas de los cabellos

singer, *s.* cantor (-ra); (professional) cantante, *m.* and *f.*; (bird) ave cantora, *f.*

Singhalese, *a.* and *s.* cingalés (-esa)

singing, *s.* canto, *m.*; (of the ears) zumbido, *m. a.* cantante. **s.-bird,** ave cantora, *f.* **s.-master,** maestro de cantar, *m.*

single, *a.* único; sencillo; solo; simple; (individual) particular; individual; (unmarried) soltero. *s.* (tennis) juego sencillo, individual, *m.* **in s. file,** de reata. **to s. out,** escoger; singularizar. **s. bed,** cama de monja, *f.* **s. bedroom,** habitación individual, habitación con una sola cama, *f.* **s.-breasted,** (of coats) recto. **s. combat,** combate singular, *m.* **s. entry,** (*com.*) partida simple, *f.* **s.-handed,** sin ayuda, solo. **s.-minded,** sin doblez, sincero; de una sola idea. **s. ticket,** billete sencillo, *m.*

singleness, *s.* celibato, *m.*, soltería, *f.* **with s. of purpose,** con un solo objeto

singlet, *s.* camiseta, *f.*

singly, *adv.* separadamente, uno a uno; a solas, solo; sin ayuda

singular, *a.* and *s.* singular (*m.*)

singularity, *s.* singularidad, *f.*

singularly, *adv.* singularmente

sinister, *a.* siniestro

sink, *v.i.* ir al fondo; bajar; hundirse; (of ships) irse a pique, naufragar; sumergirse; disminuir; caer (en); penetrar; (of persons, fires) morir; (of the sun, etc.) ponerse. *v.t.* (a ship) echar a pique; sumergir; hundir; dejar caer; bajar; (wells) cavar; reducir, disminuir; (invest) invertir; (one's identity, etc.) tener secreto; (differences) olvidar; (engrave) grabar. **My heart sank,** Se me cayeron las alas del corazón. **He sank to his knees,** Cayó de rodillas. **He is sinking fast,** Está en las últimas. **Their words began to s. in,** Sus palabras empezaban a tener efecto (or hacer mella). **I found her sunk in thought,** La encontré ensimismada. **to s. one's voice,** bajar la voz. **to s. down on a chair,** dejarse caer en una silla. **to s. into misery,** caer en la miseria. **to s. under,** (a responsibility, etc.) estar agobiado bajo

sink, *s.* (kitchen) fregadero, *m.*; sumidero, *m.*, sentina, *f.* **s. of iniquity,** sentina, *f.*

sinker, *s.* (engraver) grabador (-ra); (of a fishing line) plomada, *f.*

sinking, *s.* hundimiento, *m.*; (of the sun) puesta, *f.*; (of wells) cavadura, *f.*; sumergimiento, *m.* **the s. of a boat,** el hundimiento de un buque. **with s. heart,** con la muerte en el alma. **s. fund,** fondo de amortización, *m.*

sinless, *a.* sin pecado, inocente, puro

sinner, *s.* pecador (-ra)

Sino-Japanese, *a.* chino-japonés

sinologist, *s.* sinólogo, *m.*

sinology, *s.* sinología, *f.*

sinuosity, *s.* sinuosidad, *f.*; flexibilidad, agilidad, *f.*

sinuous, *a.* sinuoso, tortuoso; flexible, ágil

sinus, *s.* (*anat.*, etc.) seno, *m.*

sip, *v.t.* sorber; (wine) saborear, paladear. *s.* sorbo, *m.*

siphon, *s.* sifón, *m. v.t.* sacar con sifón

sir, *s.* señor, *m.*; (British title) sir. **Dear s.,** Muy Señor mío

sire, *s.* (to a monarch) Señor, *m.*; (father) padre, *m.*; (stallion) semental, *m. v.t.* procrear, engendrar

siren, *s.* sirena, *f.* **s. suit,** mono, *m.*

Sirius, *s.* Sirio, *m.*

sirloin, *s.* solomillo, *m.*

sirocco, *s.* siroco, *m.*

sister, *s.* hermana, *f.;* (before nun's christian name) Sor; (hospital) hermana del hospital, *f.;* enfermera, *f.* **s. language,** lengua hermana, *f.* **s. ship,** buque gemelo, *m.* **s.-in-law,** cuñada, hermana política, *f.* **S. of Mercy,** Hermana de la Caridad, *f.*

sisterhood, *s.* hermandad, *f.;* comunidad de monjas, *f.*

sisterly, *a.* de hermana

sit, *v.i.* sentarse; estar sentado; (of birds) posarse; (of hens) empollar; (in Parliament, etc.) ser diputado; (of a committee, etc.) celebrar sesión; (on a committee, etc.) formar parte de; (function funcionar; (of garments, food, and *fig.*) sentar. **to sit a horse,** mantenerse a caballo; montar a caballo. **to sit oneself,** sentarse, tomar asiento. **to sit an examination,** examinarse. **to sit by,** (a person) sentarse (or estar sentado) al lado de. **to sit down under an injustice,** tolerar una injusticia. **to sit for** (a portrait) servir de modelo para; hacerse retratar. **to sit heavy on,** pesar sobre. **to sit tight,** no moverse. **to sit down,** sentarse; (besiege) sitiar. **to sit down to table,** sentarse a la mesa. **to sit on,** sentarse (en or sobre); (eggs) empollar; (a committee, etc.) formar parte de; (investigate) investigar; (snub) dejar aplastado (a). **to sit out,** quedarse hasta el fin (de). **to sit out a dance,** conversar un baile. **to sit up,** incorporarse en la cama; tenerse derecho; (at night) velar; (of dogs, etc.) pedir. **to sit up and take notice,** abrir los ojos. **to sit up in bed,** incorporarse en la cama. **to sit up late,** estar de pie hasta muy tarde

site, *s.* sitio, local, *m.;* (for building) solar, *m.*

sitting, *s.* asentada, *f.;* (of Parliament, etc.) sesión, *f.;* (for a portrait) estadía, *f.;* (of eggs) nidada, *f.* **at a s.,** de una asentada. **s.-room,** sala de estar, *f.*

situated, *a.* situado. How is he s.? ¿Cómo está situado? ¿Cuál es su situación?

situation, *s.* situación, *f.;* (job) empleo, *m.*

six, *a.* and *s.* seis (*m.*). **It is six o'clock,** Son las seis. **Everything is at sixes and sevens,** Todo está en desorden. **six-foot,** de seis pies. **six hundred,** seiscientos (-as)

sixfold, *a.* séxtuplo

sixpence, *s.* seis peniques, *m pl.*

sixpenny, *a.* de seis peniques

sixteen, *a.* and-*s.* diez y seis, dieciséis (*m.*). **John is s.,** Juan tiene dieciséis años

sixteenth, *a.* décimosexto; (of the month) (el) diez y seis; (of monarch) diez y seis. *s.* dieciseisavo, *m.*

sixth, *a.* sexto; (of the month) (el) seis; (of monarchs) sexto. *s.* seisavo, *m.;* sexta parte, *f.;* (*mus.*) sexta, *f.* Henry the S., Enrique sexto. May the s., el seis de mayo

sixtieth, *a.* sexagésimo. *s.* sesentavo, *m.;* sexagésima parte, *f.*

sixty, *a.* and *s.* sesenta (*m.*). **John has turned s.,** Juan ha pasado los sesenta

sizable, *a.* bastante grande

size, *s.* tamaño, *m.;* dimensión, *f.;* (height) altura, *f.;* (measurement) medida, *f.;* talle, *m.;* (in gloves, etc.) número, *m.;* (glue) cola, *f.* *v.t.* clasificar por tamaños; (glaze, etc.) encolar. **to s. up,** tomar las medidas (a).

sizzle, *v.i.* chisporrotear, chirriar. *s.* chisporroteo, chirrido, *m.*

skate, *s.* patín, *m.;* (*icht.*) raya, *f.* *v.i.* patinar

skater, *s.* patinador (-ra)

skating, *s.* patinaje, *m.* **s.-rink,** sala de patinar, *f.;* pista de patinar, *f.*

skein, *s.* madeja, *f.*

skeleton, *s.* esqueleto, *m.;* (of a building) armadura, *f.;* (of a literary work) esquema, *m.* **s. key,** ganzúa, *f.*

sketch, *s.* croquis, apunte, *m.;* (for a literary work) esbozo, esquema, *m.;* (article) cuadro, artículo, *m.;* descripción, *f.;* (*theat.*) entremés, sainete, *m.*

v.t. dibujar; esbozar, bosquejar; trazar; describir. **s.-book,** álbum de croquis, *m.*

sketchily, *adv.* incompletamente

sketching, *s.* arte de dibujar, *m.* or *f.* He likes s., Le gusta dibujar

sketchy, *a.* bosquejado; incompleto; escaso

skewer, *s.* broqueta, *f. v.t.* espetar

ski, *s.* esquí, *m. v.i.* esquiar

skid, *s.* (of a vehicle) patinazo, *m. v.i.* patinar

skidding, *s.* patinaje, *m.*

skier, *s.* esquiador, *m.*

skiff, *s.* esquife, *m.*

ski-ing, *s.* patinaje sobre la nieve, *m.*, el esquiar. to go s., ir a esquiar

skilful, *a.* hábil

skill, *s.* habilidad, *f.*

skilled, *a.* hábil; experto

skim, *v.t.* espumar; (milk) desnatar; (touch lightly) deslizarse sobre, rozar; (a book) hojear

skimp, *v.t.* escatimar; escasear; (work) frangollar. *v.i.* ser parsimonioso

skimpy, *a.* escaso

skin, *s.* tez, *f.*, cutis, *m.*; piel, *f.*; (of fruit) pellejo, *m.*, piel, *f.*; (for wine) odre, pellejo, *m.*; (on milk) espuma, *f. v.t.* despellejar; pelar, mondar; (graze) hacerse daño (a); (*fam.*) desollar. next to one's s., sobre la piel. to s. over, cicatrizarse. to have a thin s., (*fig.*) ser muy susceptible. to save one's s., salvar el pellejo. s.-deep, superficial. s.-tight, escurrido, muy ajustado

skinflint, *s.* avaro (-ra)

skinned, *a.* de ... piel

skinny, *a.* flaco, descarnado, magro

skip, *v.i.* retozar, brincar, saltar; saltar a la comba; (bolt) largarse, escaparse. *v.t.* saltar; (a book) hojear; (omit) omitir; pasar por alto de. *s.* brinco, pequeño salto, *m.*

skipper, *s.* (*naut.*) patrón, *m.*; (*fam.* and *sport*) capitán, *m.*

skipping-rope, *s.* comba, cuerda de saltar, *f.* to play s.-rope, saltar a la comba

skirmish, *v.i.* escaramuzar. *s.* escaramuza, *f.*

skirt, *s.* falda, *f.*; (edge) margen, borde, *m.*, orilla, *f.*; (of a jacket, etc.) faldón, *m. v.t.* ladear; (hug) rodear, ceñir

skirting-board, *s.* zócalo, plinto, *m.*

skit, *s.* sátira, *f.*; parodia, *f.*

skittish, *a.* (of a horse) retozón; (of persons) frívolo; caprichoso

skittle, *s.* bolo, *m.*; *pl.* skittles, juego de bolos, *m.* **s. alley,** pista de bolos, bolera, *f.*

skulk, *v.i.* estar en acecho; esconderse; rondar

skull, *s.* cráneo, *m.*; calavera, *f.* **s.-cap,** gorro, casquete, *m.*; (for ecclesiastics) solideo, *m.*

skunk, *s.* (*zool.*) mofeta, *f.*

sky, *s.* cielo, *m.* to praise to the skies, poner en los cuernos de la luna. **s.-blue,** *s.* azul celeste, *m. a.* de color azul celeste, cerúleo. **s.-high,** hasta las nubes, hasta el cielo. **s.-line,** horizonte, *m.* **s.-scraper,** rascacielos, *m.* **s.-sign,** anuncio luminoso, *m.*

skylark, *s.* alondra, *f.*

skylight, *s.* claraboya, *f.*, tragaluz, *m.*

skywards, *adv.* hacia el cielo

slab, *s.* bloque, *m.*; losa, *f.*; plancha, *f.*

slack, *a.* lento; flojo; (lazy) perezoso; negligente, descuidado; (*com.*) encalmado; débil. *v.i.* ser perezoso. **the s. season,** la estación muerta. to be s. in one's work, ser negligente en el trabajo. to s. off, disminuir sus esfuerzos; dejar de trabajar

slacken, *v.t.* and *v.i.* aflojar; disminuir, reducir. The wind slackened, El viento amainaba (aflojaba). to s. one's efforts, disminuir sus esfuerzos. to s. speed, disminuir la velocidad

slackening, *s.* aflojamiento, *m.*; disminución, *f.*

slacker, *s.* gandul (-la)

slackness, *s.* flojedad, *f.*; pereza, falta de energía, *f.*; negligencia, *f.*; (*com.*) desanimación, *f.*

slacks, *s. pl.* pantalones, *m. pl.*

slag, *s.* escoria, *f.* **s. heap,** escorial, *m.*

slake, *v.t.* (one's thirst and lime) apagar; satisfacer

slam, *v.t.* cerrar de golpe; golpear. *s.* (of a door) portazo, *m.*; golpe, *m.*; (cards) capote, *m.* **He went out and slammed the door,** Salió dando un portazo

slander, *s.* calumnia, *f.* *v.t.* calumniar

slanderer, *s.* calumniador (-ra)

slanderous, *a.* calumnioso

slang, *s.* argot, *m.*, jerga, *f.* *v.t.* poner como un trapo (a), llenar de insultos

slant, *v.i.* estar al sesgo; inclinarse; ser oblicuo. *v.t.* inclinar. *s.* inclinación, *f.*; oblicuidad, *f.* **on the s.,** inclinado; oblicuo

slanting, *a.* al sesgo, inclinado; oblicuo

slap, *v.t.* pegar con la mano. *s.* bofetada, *f.*; palmada, *f.* **to s. on the back,** golpear en la espalda. **s.-dash,** (of persons) irresponsable, descuidado; (of work) chapucero, sin cuidado.

slash, *v.t.* (gash, also sleeves, etc.) acuchillar; cortar; (with a whip) dar latigazos (a). *s.* cuchillada, *f.*; corte, *m.*; latigazo, *m.*

slashing, *a.* mordaz, severo

slat, *s.* tablilla, *f.* *v.i.* (of sails) dar zapatazos, zapatear

slate, *s.* pizarra, *f.*, esquisto, *m.*; (for roofs and for writing) pizarra, *f.* *v.t.* (a roof) empizarrar; (censure) criticar severamente, censurar. **s.-coloured,** apizarrado. **s.** pencil, pizarrín, *m.* **s.** quarry, pizarrería, *f.*, pizarral, *m.*

slater, *s.* pizarrero, *m.*

slating, *s.* empizarrado, *m.*; (criticism) crítica severa, censura, *f.*; (scolding) peluca, *f.*

slattern, *s.* pazpuerca, *f.*

slatternly, *a.* desgarbado, desaliñado

slaughter, *s.* matanza, *f.*; carnicería, *f.* *v.t.* (animals) sacrificar, matar; matar, hacer una carnicería de. **s.-house,** matadero, *m.*

slaughterer, *s.* jifero, carnicero, *m.*

slav, *a.* and *s.* eslavo (-va)

slave, *s.* esclavo (-va). *v.i.* trabajar como un negro. **white s.** traffic, trata de blancas, *f.* **s.-bangle,** esclava, *f.* **s.-driver,** capataz de esclavos, *m.* **s.-trade,** trata de esclavos, *f.*

slaver, *s.* negrero, *m.*

slaver, *v.i.* babear. *s.* baba, *f.*

slavering, *a.* baboso

slavery, *s.* esclavitud, *f.*; trabajo muy arduo, *m.*

slavish, *a.* de esclavo; servil

slavishly, *adv.* como esclava; servilmente

Slavonic, *a.* eslavo. *s.* (language) eslavo, *m.*, lengua eslava, *f.*

slay, *v.t.* matar; asesinar

slayer, *s.* matador (-ra); asesino, *m.* and *f.*

slaying, *s.* matanza, *f.*; asesinato, *m.*

sledge, *s.* trineo, *m.* *v.i.* ir en trineo. *v.t.* transportar por trineo. **s.-hammer,** acotillo, *m.*

sleek, *a.* liso, lustroso; (of general appearance) pulcro, bien aseado, elegante; (of manner) obsequioso

sleekness, *s.* lustre, *m.*, lisura, *f.*; (of an animal) gordura, *f.*; elegancia, *f.*

sleep, *s.* sueño, *m.* *v.i.* dormir; reposar, descansar. *v.t.* dormir. **a deep s.,** un sueño pesado. **He walks in his s.,** Él es un sonámbulo. **to court s.,** conciliar el sueño. **to go to s.,** dormirse; entumecerse. **My foot has gone to s.,** Se me ha dormido (or Se me ha entumecido) el pie. **to send a person to s.,** adormecer. **to s. like a top,** dormir como un lirón. **to s. oneself sober,** dormir la mona. **to s. in,** dormir tarde; dormir en casa. **to s. off,** (a cold, etc.) curarse . . . durmiendo; (drunkenness) dormirla. **to s. on,** *v.t.* (consider) dormir sobre, consultar con la almohada. *v.i.* seguir durmiendo. **to s. out,** dormir fuera de casa; dormir al aire libre

sleeper, *s.* durmiente, *m.* and *f.*; (*r.w.*) traviesa, *f.*; (on a train) coche cama, *m.* **to be a bad s.,** dormir mal. **to be a good s.,** dormir bien.

sleepily, *adv.* soñolientamente

sleepiness, *s.* somnolencia, *f.*; letargo, *m.*

sleeping, *a.* durmiente. *s.* el dormir. **betweens, and waking,** entre duerme y vela. **s.-bag,** saco-cama, *m.* **s.-car,** coche camas, *m.* **s.-draught,** narcótico, *m.* **s.** partner, *s.* socio (-ia) comanditario (-ia). **s.** sickness, enfermedad del sueño, *f.*

sleepless, *a.* (of persons) insomne, desvelado; (unremitting) incansable; (of the sea, etc.) en perpetuo movimiento. **to spend a s. night,** pasar una noche en vela, pasar una noche sin dormir

sleeplessness, *s.* insomnio, *m.*

sleepwalker, *s.* sonámbulo (-la)

sleep-walking, *s.* sonambulismo, *m.*

sleepy, *a.* soñoliento; letárgico. **to be s.,** tener sueño. **s.-head,** lirón, *m.*, marmota, *f.*

sleet, *s.* agua nieve, *f. v.i.* caer agua nieve

sleeve, *s.* manga, *f.*; (of a hose pipe, etc.) manguera, *f.*; (mech.) manguito, *m.* **to have something up one's s.,** traer algo en la manga

sleeved, *a.* con mangas ...; de ... manga(s)

sleeveless, *a.* sin manga

sleigh, *s.* trineo, *m. v.i.* ir en trineo

sleight-of-hand, *s.* prestidigitación, *f.*; juego de manos, *m.*

slender, *a.* delgado; esbelto; tenue; escaso; pequeño; ligero. **Their means are very s.,** Sus recursos son muy escasos. **It is a very s. hope,** Es una esperanza muy remota

slenderness, *s.* delgadez, *f.*; esbeltez, *f.*; tenuidad, *f.*; escasez, *f.*

sleuth, *s.* (dog) sabueso, *m.*; (fam.) detective, *m.*

slice, *s.* lonja, tajada, *f.*; (of fruit) raja, *f.*; (of bread, etc.) rebanada, *f.*; (share) parte, porción, *f.*; (for fish, etc.) pala, *f. v.t.* cortar en tajadas, etc.; rajar; cortar

slick, *a.* hábil, diestro

slide, *v.i.* deslizarse, resbalar; (over a question) pasar por alto de; (into a habit, etc.) caer (en). *s.* resbalón, *m.*; pista de hielo, *f.*; (chute) tobogán, *m.*; (of a microscope) portaobjetos, *m.*; (lantern) diapositiva, *f.*; (for the hair) pasador, *m.*; (of rock, etc.) desprendimiento, *m.*; (mech.) guía, *f.* **to let things s.,** dejar rodar la bola. **s.-rule,** regla de cálculo, *f.*

sliding, *a.* resbaladizo; corredizo; movible. **s.-door,** puerta corrediza, *f.* **s.-roof,** techo corredizo, *m.* **s.-scale,** escala graduada, *f.* **s.-seat,** asiento movible, *m.*; (in a rowing-boat) bancada corrediza, *f.*

slight, *a.* delgado; débil, frágil; ligero; (small) pequeño; escaso; (trivial) insignificante, poco importante. *v.t.* desairar, despreciar. *s.* desaire, desprecio, *m.*; falta de respeto, *f.*

slighting, *a.* despreciativo, de desprecio

slightingly, *adv.* con desprecio

slightly, *adv.* ligeramente; poco. **I only know her s.,** La conozco muy poco. **s. built,** de talle delgado

slightness, *s.* (slimness) delgadez, *f.*; ligereza, *f.*; (triviality) poca importancia, insignificancia, *f.*

slim, *a.* delgado; escaso. *v.i.* adelgazarse. **He has very s. chances of success,** Tiene muy pocas posibilidades de conseguir el éxito

slime, *s.* légamo, limo, lodo, cieno, *m.*; (of a snail) limazo, *m.*; (fig.) cieno, *m.*

sliminess, *s.* limosidad, *f.*; viscosidad, *f.*

slimming, *s.* adelgazamiento, *m.*

slimness, *s.* delgadez, *f.*; escasez, *f.*

slimy, *a.* limoso, legamoso; viscoso; (of persons) rastrero, servil

sling, *v.t.* arrojar, lanzar; tirar con honda; (a sword, etc.) suspender; (lift) embragar; (a limb) poner en cabestrillo. *s.* (for missiles) honda, *f.*; (naut.) balso, *m.*; (for a limb) cabestrillo, *m.*, charpa, *f.*

slink, *v.i.* (away, off) escurrirse, escabullirse

slip, *v.i.* resbalar, deslizar; (stumble) resbalar, tropezar; (fall) caer; (out of place) salirse; (become untied) desatarse; (steal away) escabullirse; (glide) deslizarse; (of years) correr, pasar; (skid) patinar. *v.t.* deslizar; (garments, shoes) ponerse; (dogs, cables) soltar; (an arm round, etc.) pasar; (r.w.) desacoplar; (escape) escaparse de; (free oneself of) librarse de. *s.* resbalón, *m.*; (skid) patinazo, *m.*; (stumble) tropezón, traspié, *m.*; (oversight) inadvertencia, *f.*; (mistake) falta, equivocación, *f.*; (moral lapse) desliz, *m.*; (petticoat) combinación, *f.*; (cover) funda, *f.*; (*bot.*) vástago, *m.*; (*print.*) galerada, *f.*; (of paper) papeleta, *f.*; *pl.* **slips**, (*naut.*) anguilas, *f. pl.* **It slipped my memory,** Se me fué de la memoria. **There's many a s. 'twixt the cup and the lip,** Del dicho al hecho hay muy gran trecho, De la mano a la boca desaparece la sopa. **to give** (someone) **the slip,** escaparse de. **You ought to not let the opportunity s.,** No debes perder la oportunidad. **to let s. a secret,** revelar un secreto. **to let s. an exclamation,** soltar (dar) una exclamación. **to s. into,** colarse en, deslizarse en. **to s. into one's clothes,** vestirse rápidamente. **to s. on,** (a garment) ponerse. **to s. out,** salir a hurtadillas; escaparse; (of information) divulgarse. **s. of a boy,** mozalbete, joven imberbe, *m.* **s. of the tongue,** lapsus linguæ, *m.* **s.-knot,** nudo corredizo, *m.*

slipper, *s.* pantuflo, *m.*; (heelless) chancleta, *f.*; (dancing) zapatilla de baile, *f.* **s.-shaped,** achinelado

slippered, *a.* en zapatillas

slipperiness, *s.* lo resbaladizo; (of persons) informalidad, *f.*

slippery, *a.* resbaladizo; poco firme, inestable; (of persons) informal, sin escrúpulos

slipshod, *a.* descuidado, negligente; poco correcto

slipway, *s.* surtida, *f.*, anguilas, *f. pl.*

slit, *v.t.* cortar; hender, rajar; (the throat) degollar. *s.* cortadura, *f.*; resquicio, *m.* **to s. open,** abrir de un tajo

slither, *v.i.* resbalar; deslizarse

sliver, *s.* raja, *f.*; (of wood) astilla, *f.*; (of cloth) tira, *f.*

slobber, *v.i.* babear; (blubber) gimotear. *s.* baba, *f.*

sloe, *s.* (fruit) endrina, *f.*; (tree) endrino, *m.* **s.-coloured,** endrino. **s.-eyed,** con ojos de mora

slog, *v.t.* golpear duramente. **to s. away,** batirse el cobre, trabajar como un negro

slogan, *s.* grito de batalla, *m.*; reclamo, *m.*; frase hecha, *f.*; mote, *m.*

sloop, *s.* balandra, *f.*

slop, *s.* charco, *m.*; *pl.* **slops,** agua sucia, *f.*; alimentos líquidos, *m. pl.* *v.i.* derramarse, verterse. *v.t.* verter, derramar

slope, *s.* inclinación, *f.*; pendiente, *f.*; (of a mountain, etc.) falda, ladera, cuesta, *f.*; vertiente, *m.* or *f.* *v.i.* inclinarse; estar en declive; bajar (hacia). **to s. down,** declinar

sloping, *a.* inclinado; en declive; (of shoulders) caídos (*m. pl.*)

sloppy, *a.* casi líquido; (muddy) lodoso, lleno de barro; (of work) chapucero; (of persons) baboso, sobón. **s. sentiment,** sensiblería, *f.*

slot, *s.* ranura, muesca, *f.* **s.-machine,** máquina expendedora, *f.*, expendedor, *m.*; (in amusement arcades, etc.) tragaperras, *m.*

sloth, *s.* pereza, indolencia, *f.*; (*zool.*) perezoso, *m.*

slothful, *a.* perezoso, indolente

slouch, *s.* inclinación del cuerpo, *f.* *v.i.* andar cabizbajo, andar arrastrando los pies. **to s. about,** vagar, golfear. **s.-hat,** sombrero gacho, *m.*

slough, *s.* (bog) cenagal, pantano, *m.*, marisma, *f.*; (of a snake) camisa, *f.* *v.t.* (a skin) mudar; (prejudices, etc.) desechar

Slovak, *s.* eslovaco (-ca)

Slovakian, *a.* eslovaco

sloven, *s.* puerco, *m.*; (at work) chapucero, *m.*

Slovene, *a.* and *s.* esloveno (-na)

slovenliness, *s.* desaseo, desaliño, *m.*; (carelessness) descuido, *m.*, negligencia, *f.*; (of work) chapucería, *f.*

slovenly, *a.* desgarbado, desaseado; (careless) descuidado, negligente; (of work) chapucero

slow, *a.* despacio; lento; (stupid) torpe; tardo; (of clocks) atrasado; (boring) aburrido; (inactive) flojo. *adv.* despacio, lentamente. **I was not s. to . . . ,** No tardaba en . . . **The clock**

is ten minutes s., El reloj lleva diez minutos de atraso. **to s. down**, aflojar el paso; ir más despacio. **s.-motion**, velocidad reducida, *f*. **s. train**, tren ómnibus, *m*. **s.-witted**, lerdo tardo

slowcoach, *s*. perezoso (-sa)

slowly, *adv*. despacio, lentamente; poco a poco

slowness, *s*. lentitud, *f*.; (delay) tardanza, *f*.; (stupidity) torpeza, estupidez, *f*.

slug, *s*. babosa, *f*.

sluggard, *s*. gandul (-la), perezoso (-a)

sluggish, *a*. perezoso; (of the market) flojo; (of temperament, etc.) calmoso, flemático; (slow) lento

sluggishness, *s*. pereza, *f*.; (of the market) flojedad, *f*.; (slowness) lentitud, *f*.

sluice, *s*. esclusa, *f*.; canal, *m*., acequia, *f*. **to s. down**, lavar; echar agua sobre; (a person) dar una ducha (a), dar un baño (a). **s.-gate**, compuerta de esclusa, *f*.; tajaderas, *f. pl.*, tablacho, *m*.

slum, *s*. barrio pobre, *m*.; *pl*. **slums**, barrios bajos, *m. pl.*

slumber, *v.i*. dormir; (go to sleep) dormirse, caer dormido; (be latent) estar latente. *s*. sueño, *m*.

slump, *s*. (com.) baja repentina, *f*.; (fig.) baja, *f*. *v.i*. (com.) bajar repentinamente. **the s.**, la crisis económica. **to s. into an arm-chair**, dejarse caer en un sillón

slur, *v.t*. (words) comerse sílabas o letras (de); (in writing) unir (las palabras); (mus., of notes) ligar. **to cast a s. on**, difamar, manchar. **to s. over**, pasar por alto de, omitir, suprimir

slush, *s*. lodo, *m*.; agua nieve, *f*.; (sentimentality) ñoñería, *f*.

slushy, *a*. lodoso, fangoso

slut, *s*. pazpuerca, marrana, *f*.

sly, *a*. astuto, taimado, socarrón; disimulado; (arch) malicioso. **on the sly**, a hurtadillas

slyly, *adv*. astutamente; disimuladamente; (archly) maliciosamente

slyness, *s*. astucia, socarronería, *f*.; disimulo, *m*.; malicia, *f*.

smack, *s*. (taste) sabor, gusto, *m*.; (tinge) dejo, *m*.; (blow) golpe, *m*.; (with the hand) bofetada, palmada, *f*.; (with a whip) latigazo, *m*.; (crack of whip) restallido, chasquido, *m*.; (kiss) beso sonado, *m*.; (boat) lancha de pescar, *f*. *v.i*. (taste of) tener gusto de, saber a; (be tinged with) oler a. *v.t*. (a whip) hacer restallar; (slap) pegar con la mano. **to s. one's lips over**, chuparse los dedos

small, *a*. pequeño; menudo; menor; poco; (petty) mezquino, vulgar. *s*. parte estrecha, *f*. **a s. number**, un pequeño número. **to make a person look s.**, humillar. **to make oneself s.**, hacerse chiquito. **s.-arms**, armas portátiles, *f. pl.* **s. change**, suelto, *m*. **s. craft**, embarcaciones menores, *f. pl.* **s. fry**, pececillos, *m. pl.*; (children) gente menuda, *f*.; gente sin importancia, *f*. **s. hours**, altas horas de la noche, *f. pl.* **s.-minded**, adocenado, de cortos alcances. **s.-talk**, trivialidades, *f. pl.*, charla frívola, *f*.

smallish, *a*. bastante pequeño; más bien pequeño que grande

smallness, *s*. pequeñez, *f*.; escasez, exigüidad, *f*.

smallpox, *s*. viruelas, *f. pl.*

smalt, *s*. esmalte, *m*.

smart, *v.i*. picar; dolerse (de). *s*. escozor, *m*.; dolor, *m*. *a*. severo; vivo; rápido; pronto; (competent) hábil; (clever) listo; (unscrupulous) cuco, astuto; (of personal appearance) majo; elegante, distinguido; (neat) aseado; (fashionable, etc.) de moda: de buen tono. **to s. for**, ser castigado por. **to s. under**, sufrir

smarten, *v.t*. embellecer. *v.i*. (up) ponerse elegante; mejorar. **I must go and s. myself up a little**, Tengo que ir a arreglarme un poco

smartly, *adv*. severamente; vivamente; rápidamente; hábilmente; elegantemente

smartness, *s*. viveza, *f*.; prontitud, rapidez, *f*.; (cleverness) despejo, *m*., habilidad, *f*.; (wittiness) agudeza, *f*.; (astuteness) cuquería, astucia, *f*.; (of dress, etc.) elegancia, *f*.; buen tono, *m*.

smash, *v.t.* romper, quebrar; (a ball, etc.) golpear; (annihilate) destruir; (an opponent) aplastar. *v.i.* romperse, quebrarse; hacerse pedazos; (collide) chocar (con, contra); estallarse (contra); (financially) hacer bancarrota. *s.* rotura, *f.*; quebrantamiento, *m.*; estruendo, *m.*; (financial) quiebra, ruina, *f.*; (car, etc.) accidente, *m.*; desastre, *m.*, catástrofe, *f.* **to s. to atoms,** hacer trizas. **to s. up,** hacer pedazos. **s. and grab raid,** atraco a mano armada, *m.*

smattering, *s.* conocimiento superficial, *m.*, tintura, *f.*, barniz, *m.*

smear, *s.* mancha, *f.*; (biol.) frotis, *m.* *v.t.* embadurnar (de); manchar (con), ensuciar (con); (oneself) untarse; (blur) borrar

smell, *s.* (sense of) olfato, *m.*; (odour) olor, *m.* *v.t.* oler. *v.i.* oler; tener olor; (disagreeably) oler mal, tener mal olor; (stink) apestar. **How good it smells!** ¡Qué bien huele! **to s. of,** oler a. **to s. out,** husmear

smelling, *s.* olfateo, *m.* **s.-bottle,** frasco de sales, *m.* **s.-salts,** sales (inglesas) *f. pl.*

smelt, *v.t.* fundir. *s.* (icht.) eperlano, *m.*

smelter, *s.* fundidor, *m.*

smelting, *s.* fundición, *f.* **s. furnace,** horno de fundición, *m.*

smile, *v.i.* sonreír; reírse. *v.t.* expresar con una sonrisa. *s.* sonrisa, *f.* **Mary smiled her thanks,** María dió las gracias con una sonrisa. **to s. at threats,** reírse de las amenazas

smiling, *a.* sonriente, risueño

smilingly, *adv.* sonriendo, con una sonrisa, con cara risueña

smirch, *v.t.* manchar. *s.* mancha, *f.*

smirk, *v.i.* sonreír con afectación; hacer visajes. *s.* sonrisa afectada, *f.*

smirking, *a.* afectado; sonriente

smite, *v.t.* golpear; (kill) matar; (punish) castigar; (pain) doler; (of bright light, sounds, etc.) herir; (cause remorse) remorder. **My conscience smites me,** Tengo remordimientos de conciencia. **to be smitten by,** (fam.)

estar prendado de. **I was smitten by a desire to smoke,** Me entraron deseos de fumar

smith, *s.* herrero, *m.* **smith's hammer,** destajador, *m.*

smithereens, *s. pl.* añicos, *m. pl.*

smithy, *s.* herrería, *f.*

smock, *s.* blusa, *f.*; (child's) delantal, *m.*

smoke, *s.* humo, *m.* *v.i.* humear; echar humo; (tobacco) fumar. *v.t.* ahumar; ennegrecer; (tobacco) fumar. **smoked glasses,** gafas ahumadas, *f. pl.* **s. helmet,** casco respiratorio, *m.* **s.-screen,** cortina de humo, *f.* **s. signal,** ahumada, *f.* **s.-stack,** chimenea, *f.*

smokeless, *a.* sin humo

smoker, *s.* fumador (-ra)

smoking, *a.* humeante, *s.* el fumar. **S. Prohibited,** Se prohibe fumar. **non-s. compartment,** (r.w.) departamento de no fumadores, *m.* **s.-carriage,** (r.w.) departamento para fumadores, *m.* **s.-room,** fumadero, *m.*

smoky, *a.* humeante; lleno de humo; (black) ahumado

smooth, *a.* liso; igual; (of the skin, etc.) suave; (of water) calmo, tranquilo; (flattering, etc.) lisonjero; obsequioso; afable. *v.t.* allanar; (hair, etc.) alisar; (paths, etc.) igualar. **to s. down,** (a person) tranquilizar, calmar. **to s. over,** (faults) exculpar. **to s. the way for,** allanar el camino para. **s.-faced,** barbilampiño, lampiño, bien afeitado; (fig.) obsequioso, untuoso. **s.-haired,** de pelo liso. **s.-spoken,** de palabras lisonjeras; obsequioso

smoothly, *adv.* lisamente; (of speech) afablemente; con lisonjeras. **Everything was going s.,** Todo iba viento en popa

smoothness, *s.* igualdad, *f.*; lispra, *f.*; (of skin, etc.) suavidad, *f.*; (of water) calma, tranquilidad, *f.*; (of manner, etc.) afabilidad, *f.*

smother, *v.t.* ahogar, sofocar; (a fire) apagar; (cover) envolver, cubrir

smoulder, *v.i.* arder sin llama, arder lentamente; (of passions, etc.) arder; estar latente

smouldering, *a.* que arde lentamente; (*fig.*) latente

smudge, *v.t.* manchar, ensuciar; (blur) borrar. *s.* mancha, *f.*

smug, *a.* satisfecho de sí mismo, pagado de sí mismo; farisaico

smuggle, *v.t.* pasar de contrabando. *v.i.* hacer contrabando

smuggler, *s.* contrabandista, *m.* and *f.*

smuggling, *s.* contrabando, *m.*

smugly, *adv.* con presunción, de un aire satisfecho

smugness, *s.* satisfacción de sí mismo, *f.*; fariseísmo, *m.*

smut, *s.* copo de hollín, *m.*; mancha, *f.*; (disease) tizón, *m.*

smutty, *a.* tiznado; ahumado; (*fam.*) verde

snack, *s.* tentempié, piscolabis, bocado, *m.* **to take a s.,** tomar un piscolabis

snaffle, *s.* filete, *m.* *v.t.* (a horse) refrenar. **s.-bridle,** bridón, *m.*

snag, *s.* (of a tree) tocón, *m.*; (of a tooth) raigón, *m.*; (problem) busilis, *m.*; obstáculo inesperado, *m.*

snail, *s.* caracol, *m.* **at a snail's pace,** a paso de tortuga

snake, *s.* serpiente, *f.* **s.-charmer,** encantador de serpientes, *m.*

snakelike, *a.* de serpiente; serpentino

snap, *v.t.* morder; (break) romper; (one's fingers) castañetear; (a whip) chasquear; (down a lid, etc.) cerrar de golpe; (beaks, etc.) cerrar ruidosamente; (*phot.*) sacar una instantánea de. *v.i.* partirse; quebrarse; hablar bruscamente. *s.* (bite) mordedura, *f.*; golpe seco, *m.*; chasquido, *m.*; rotura, *f.*; (clasp) cierre, *m.*; (of weather) temporada, *f.*; (spirit) vigor, brío, *m.*; (*phot.*) instantánea, *f.* **to s. at,** procurar morder; (an invitation, etc.) aceptar gustoso. **to s. one's fingers at,** (*fig.*) burlarse de. **to s. up,** coger, agarrar; (a person) cortar la palabra (a), interrumpir. **s.-fastener,** botón de presión, *m.*

snapdragon, *s.* dragón, *m.*, becérrima, boca de dragón, *f.*

snappily, *adv.* irritablemente

snappishness, *s.* irritabilidad, *f.*

snappy, *a.* irritable; vigoroso

snapshot, *s.* instantánea, foto, *f.*

snare, *s.* cepo, lazo, *m.*, trampa, *f.*; (*fig.*) red, *f.* *v.t.* coger en el lazo; (*fig.*) enredar

snarl, *v.i.* (of dogs) regañar; (cats, etc.) gruñir. *s.* regañamiento, *m.*; gruñido, *m.*

snarling, *s.* regañamiento, *m.*; gruñidos, *m. pl.* *a.* gruñidor

snatch, *v.t.* asir; agarrar; (enjoy) disfrutar; (an opportunity) tomar, aprovecharse de. *s.* asimiento, agarro, *m.*; (of time) rato, *m.*; instante, *m.*; (of song) fragmento, *m.* **to make a s. at,** procurar agarrar; alargar la mano hacia. **to s. a hurried meal,** comer aprisa. **to s. away,** arrebatar, quitar; (carry off) robar. **to s. up,** coger rápidamente; coger en brazos

sneak, *v.i.* deslizarse (en), colarse (en); (lurk) rondar; (inform) acusar. *s.* mandilón, *m.*; (accuser) acusón (-ona). **to s. off,** escabullirse, irse a hurtadillas. **s.-thief,** *s.* garduño (-ña)

sneaking, *a.* furtivo, ruin, mezquino; secreto

sneer, *v.i.* sonreír irónicamente; burlarse, mofarse. *s.* sonrisa sardónica, sonrisa de desprecio, *f.*; burla, mofa, *f.* **to s. at,** mofarse de, burlarse de; hablar con desprecio de

sneering, *a.* mofador, burlón

sneeringly, *adv.* con una sonrisa sardónica; burlonamente

sneeze, *v.i.* estornudar. *s.* estornudo, *m.* **It's not to be sneezed at,** No es moco de pavo

sniff, *v.i.* respirar fuertemente; resollar. *v.t.* oler, olfatear; aspirar. **to s. at,** oler. **to s. out,** (*fam.*) husmear

snigger, *v.i.* reírse por lo bajo, reírse disimuladamente. *s.* risa disimulada, *f.*

snip, *v.t.* cortar con tijeras; cortar, quitar. *s.* tijeretada, *f.*; (of cloth, etc.) recorte, pedacito, *m.*

snipe, *s.* (*orn.*) agachadiza, *f.* **to s. at,** (*mil.*) pacar

sniper, *s.* (*mil.*) paco, *m.*

snippet, *s.* pedacito, fragmento, *m.*; (of prose, etc.) trocito, *m.*; (of news) noticia, *f.*

snivel, *v.i.* lloriquear, gimotear

snivelling, s. lloriqueo, gimoteo, m. a. llorón; mocoso

snob, s. esnob, m. and f.

snobbery, s. snobismo, m.

snobbish, a. esnob

snood, s. (for the hair) redecilla, f.; (turkey's) moco (de pavo), m.; (fishing) cendal, m.

snoop, v.i. espiar; entremeterse

snooze, v.i. dormitar, echar un sueño. s. sueñecito, m.; (afternoon) siesta, f.

snore, v.i. roncar. s. ronquido, m.

snoring, s. ronquidos, m. pl.

snort, v.i. bufar; resoplar. s. bufido, m.; resoplido, m.

snout, s. hocico, m.; (of a pig) jeta, f.

snow, s. nieve, f. v.i. nevar. v.t. nevar; (fig.) inundar. to s. under (with), inundar con. to be snowed up, estar aprisionado por la nieve. s.-blindness, ceguera causada por la nieve, f. s.-boot, bota para la nieve, f. s.-bound, aprisionado por la nieve; bloqueado por la nieve. s.-capped, coronado de nieve. s.-clad, cubierto de nieve. s.-drift, acumulación de nieve, f. s.-field, ventisquero, m. s.-goggles, gafas ahumadas, f. pl. s.-line, límite de las nieves perpetuas, m. s.-man, figura de nieve, f. s.-plough, quitanieve, m. s.-shoe, raqueta de nieve, f. s.-white, blanco como la nieve

snowball, s. bola de nieves, f.; (bot.) bola de nieve, f.

snowdrop, s. campanilla de invierno, violeta de febrero, f.

snowfall, s. nevada, f.

snowflake, s. copo de nieve, m.

snowstorm, s. ventisca, f.

snowy, a. nevoso; de nieve

snub, v.t. repulsar; desairar, tratar con desdén. s. repulsa, f., desaire, m.; (nose) nariz respingona, f. s.-nosed, de nariz respingona

snuff, v.t. (breathe) oler, olfatear; inhalar; (a candle) atizar, despabilar. s. (of a candle) moco, m., despabiladura, f.; (tobacco) rapé, m. to take s., tomar rapé. to s. out, extinguir. s.-box, tabaquera, f.

snuffers, s. pl. tenacillas, despabiladeras, f. pl.

snuffle, v.i. hacer ruido con la nariz; respirar fuerte; (in speaking) ganguear

snuffling, a. mocoso; (of the voice) gangoso

snug, a. caliente; cómodo; (hidden) escondido. to have a s. income, tener el riñón bien cubierto, ser acomodado

snuggle, v.i. hacerse un ovillo; acomodarse; ponerse cómodo. to s. up to, arrimarse a, apretarse contra

snugly, adv. cómodamente

snugness, s. comodidad, f.

so, adv. así; de este modo, de esta manera; por lo tanto; tanto; (before adjs. and advs. but not before más, mejor, menos, peor, where tanto is used) tan; (in the same way) del mismo modo, de igual modo; (therefore) de modo que, de manera que; (also) también; (approximately) más o menos, aproximadamente. Is that so? ¿De veras? if so..., si así es... He has not yet done so, No lo ha hecho todavía. I told you so! ¡Ya te lo dije yo! So be it! ¡Así sea! so far, hasta aquí; hasta ahora. so forth, etcétera. so much, tanto. So much the worse for them, Tanto peor para ellos. so to speak ..., por decirlo así. so as to, a fin de, para. so long as, con tal que, a condición de que. so on, etcétera. so soon as, tan pronto como. so that, de suerte que, de modo que, para que; con que. so-and-so, s. fulano (-na); mengano (-na). so-called, así llamado, supuesto. so-so, así, regular

soak, v.t. remojar; empapar; (skins) abrevar. v.i. estar en remojo. s. remojo, m.; (rain) diluvio, m.; (booze) borrachera, f. to s. into, filtrar en; penetrar. to s. through, penetrar; filtrar

so-called, así llamado, supuesto.

so-so, así, regular

soaked, a. remojado. He is s. to the skin, Está calado hasta los huesos

soaking, s. remojo, m.; empapamiento, m.

soap, *s.* jabón, *m.* *v.t.* jabonar; (flatter) enjabonar. **a tablet of s.,** una pastilla de jabón. **soft s.,** jabón blando, *m.* **toilet s.,** jabón de tocador, jaboncillo, *m.* **s.-bubble,** burbuja de jabón, *f.* **s. dish,** jabonera, *f.* **s. factory,** jabonería, *f.* **s.-flakes,** copos de jabón, *m. pl.*

soapstone, *s.* esteatita, *f.*

soapsuds, *s. pl.* jabonaduras, *f. pl.*

soapy, *a.* cubierto de jabón; jabonoso

soar, *v.i.* remontarse; (*fig.*) elevarse; (of prices, etc.) subir de golpe

soaring, *s.* remonte, vuelo, *m.*; (*fig.*) aspiración, *f.*; (of prices, etc.) subida repentina, *f.*

sob, *v.i.* sollozar. *s.* sollozo, *m.* **to sob one's heart out,** llorar a lágrima viva. **to sob out,** decir sollozando, decir entre sollozos

sobbing, *s.* sollozos, *m. pl.* *a.* sollozante

sober, *a.* sobrio; moderado; (of colours) obscuro. **s.-minded,** serio; reflexivo

sobriety, *s.* sobriedad, *f.*; moderación, *f.*; seriedad, *f.*; calma, tranquilidad, *f.*

sobriquet, *s.* apodo, *m.*

soccer, *s.* fútbol (Asociación), *m.*

sociability, *s.* sociabilidad, *f.*

sociable, *a.* sociable; amistoso

sociably, *adv.* sociablemente; amistosamente

social, *a.* social; sociable. *s.* reunión, velada, *f.* **s.-democrat,** *a.* and *s.* socialdemócrata (*m.* and *f.*). **s. events,** acontecimientos sociales, *m. pl.* **s. insurance,** previsión social, *f.* **s. services,** servicios sociales, *m. pl.* **s. work,** asistencia social, *f.*

socialism, *s.* socialismo, *m.*

socialist, *a.* socialista, laborista. *s.* socialista, *m.* and *f.*

socialization, *s.* socialización, *f.*

socialize, *v.t.* socializar

socially, *adv.* socialmente

society, *s.* sociedad, *f.*; (fashionable) mundo elegante, *m.*, alta sociedad, *f.*; compañía, *f.* **to go into .s.,** (of girls) ponerse de largo; entrar en el mundo elegante. **s. hostess,** dama de

sociedad, *f.* **s. news,** noticias de sociedad, *f. pl.*

sociological, *a.* sociológico

sociologist, *s.* sociólogo (-ga)

sociology, *s.* sociología; *f.*

sock, *s.* calcetín, *m.*; (for a shoe) plantilla; *f.*

socket, *s.* (*mech.*) encaje, cubo, ojo, *m.*; (of a lamp, and *elec.*) enchufe, *m.*; (of the eye) órbita, cuenca, *f.*; (of a tooth) alvéolo, *m.*; (of a joint) fosa, *f.* **His eyes started out of their sockets,** Sus ojos estaban fuera de su órbita

socle, *s.* (*arch.*) zócalo, *m.*

Socratic, *a.* socrático

sod, *s.* césped, *m.*; (cut) tepe, *m.*

soda, *s.* sosa, *f.* **caustic s.,** sosa cáustica, *f.* **s.-ash,** carbonato sódico, *m.* **s.-fountain,** aparato de aguas gaseosas, *m.* **s.-water,** sifón, *m.*

sodden, *a.* saturado, empapado

sodic, *a.* sódico

sodium, *s.* sodio, *m.*

Sodomite, *s.* sodomita, *m.* and *f.*

sodomy, *s.* sodomía, *f.*

sofa, *s.* sofá, *m.*

soft, *a.* blando; suave; muelle; (flabby) flojo; (of disposition, etc.) dulce; (effeminate) muelle, afeminado; (lenient) indulgente; (easy) fácil; (silly) tonto. **to have a s. spot for,** (a person) tener una debilidad para. **s. coal,** carbón bituminoso, *m.* **s. drink,** bebida no alcohólica, *f.* **s. felt hat,** sombrero flexible, *m.* **s. fruit,** fruta blanda, *f.* **s.-boiled,** (of eggs) pasado por agua; (of persons) inocente, ingenuo. **s.-hearted,** de buen corazón; compasivo, bondadoso. **s.-heartedness,** buen corazón, *m.*, bondad, *f.* **s.-spoken,** de voz suave; que habla con dulzura, meloso. **s. water,** agua blanda, *f.*

soften, *v.t.* ablandar, reblandecer; (weaken) debilitar; (mitigate) mitigar, suavizar; (the heart, etc.) enternecer. *v.i.* reblandecerse; enternecerse

softening, *s.* reblandecimiento, *m.*; (relenting) enternecimiento, *m.*

softly, *adv.* suavemente; dulcemente, tiernamente; sin ruido, silenciosamente

softness, *s.* blandura, *f.*; suavidad, *f.*; (sweetness, etc.) dulzura, *f.*; (of character) debilidad de carácter, *f.*; (silliness) necedad, estupidez, *f.*

soggy, *a.* empapado de agua; saturado

soil, *s.* tierra, *f.*; (country) país, *m.*, tierra, *f.* *v.t.* ensuciar; (*fig.*) manchar. **my native s.**, mi tierra, mi patria

soiled, *a.* sucio. **s. linen**, ropa sucia, *f.*

soirée, *s.* velada, *f.*

sojourn, *v.i.* morar, residir, permanecer. *s.* residencia, permanencia, *f.*

sojourner, *s.* morador (-ra), residente, *m.* and *f.*

sol, *s.* (*mus.*) sol, *m.* **sol-fa**, *s.* solfa, *f.*, solfeo, *m.* *v.t.* solfear

solace, *s.* consuelo, solaz, *m.* *v.t.* consolar; solazar

solar, *a.* solar. **s. plexus**, (*anat.*) plexo solar, *m.* **s. system**, sistema solar, *m.*

solder, *s.* soldadura, *f.* *v.t.* soldar

soldering, *s.* soldadura, *f.*

soldier, *s.* soldado, *m.*; militar, *m.* **He wants to be a s.**, Quiere ser militar

soldierly, *a.* militar; marcial

soldiery, *s.* soldadesca, *f.*

sole, *s.* (of a foot) planta, *f.*; (of a shoe) suela, *f.*; (of a plough) cepa, *f.*; (*icht.*) lenguado, *m.*, suela, *f.* *v.t.* (shoes) solar, poner suela (a). *a.* solo, único; exclusivo. **s. right**, exclusiva, *f.*, derecho exclusivo, *m.*

solecism, *s.* solecismo, *m.*

solely, *adv.* sólo; únicamente, puramente; meramente

solemn, *a.* solemne; grave; serio; (sacred) sagrado. **Why do you look so s.?** ¿Porqué estás tan serio?

solemnity, *s.* solemnidad, *f.*

solemnization, *s.* solemnización, celebración, *f.*

solemnize, *v.t.* solemnizar

solemnly, *adv.* solemnemente; gravemente

solenoid, *s.* (*elec.*) solenoide, *m.*

solicit, *v.t.* solicitar; implorar, rogar encarecidamente

solicitation, *s.* solicitación, *f.*

solicitor, *s.* abogado (-da)

solicitous, *a.* ansioso (de), deseoso (de); solícito, atento; (worried) preocupado

solicitude, *s.* solicitud, *f.*, cuidado, *m.*; (anxiety) preocupación, *f.*

solid, *a.* sólido; macizo; (of persons) serio, formal; (unanimous) unánime. *s.* sólido, *m.* **a s. meal**, una comida fuerte. **He slept for ten s. hours**, Durmió por diez horas seguidas. **s. food**, alimentos sólidos, *m. pl.* **s. geometry**, geometría del espacio, *f.* **s. tyre**, llanta de goma maciza, *f.*

solidarity, *s.* solidaridad, *f.*

solidification, *s.* solidificación, *f.*

solidify, *v.t.* solidificar. *v.i.* solidificarse; congelarse

solidity, *s.* solidez, *f.*; unanimidad, *f.*

solidly, *adv.* sólidamente

soliloquize, *v.i.* soliloquiar, hablar a solas

soliloquy, *s.* soliloquio, *m.*

solitaire, *s.* (diamond and game) solitario, *m.*

solitary, *a.* solitario; solo, aislado, único. **He was in s. confinement for three months**, Estuvo incomunicado durante tres meses. **There is not a s. one**, No hay ni uno

solitude, *s.* soledad, *f.*

solo, *s.* (performance and cards) solo, *m.* **to sing a s.**, cantar un solo. **It was his first s. flight**, Era su primer vuelo a solas

soloist, *s.* solista, *m.* and *f.*

solstice, *s.* solsticio, *m.* **summer s.**, solsticio vernal, *m.*: **winter s.**, solsticio hiemal, *m.*

solubility, *s.* solubilidad, *f.*

soluble, *a.* soluble

solution, *s.* solución, *f.*

solvable, *a.* que se puede resolver, soluble

solve, *v.t.* resolver, hallar la solución de

solvency, *s.* solvencia, *f.*

solvent, *a.* (*com.*) solvente; (*chem.* and *fig.*) disolvente. *s.* disolvente, *m.*

somatic, *a.* somático

somatology, *s.* somatología, *f.*

sombre, *a.* sombrío

sombrely, *adv.* sombríamente

sombreness, *s.* lo sombrío; sobriedad, *f.*; melancolía, *f.*

some, *a.* alguno (-a), algunos (-as); (before a masculine sing. noun) algún; unos (-as); un poco de, algo de; (as a partitive, often omitted, e.g. Give me s. wine, Dame vino); (approximately) aproximadamente, unos (-as). *pron.* algunos (-as), unos (-as); algo, un poco. I should like s. strawberries, Me gustaría comer unas fresas. s. day, algún día. S. say yes, others no, Algunos dicen que sí, otros que no. There are s. sixty people in the garden, Hay unas sesenta personas en el jardín

somebody, someone, *s.* alguien, *m.* and *f.* s. else, otro (-a), otra persona, *f.* S. or other said that the book is worth reading, No sé quién dijo que el libro vale la pena de leerse. to be s., (*fam.*) ser un personaje

somehow, *adv.* de un modo u otro, de alguna manera. S. I don't like them, No sé porqué, pero no me gustan

somersault, *s.* salto mortal, *m.* *v.i.* dar un salto mortal

something, *s.* algo, *m.*, alguna cosa, *f.* *adv.* algún tanto. Would you like s. else? ¿Quiere Vd. otra cosa? He left s. like fifty thousand pounds, Dejó algo así como cincuenta mil libras. He has s. to live for, Tiene para que vivir

sometime, *adv.* algún día, alguna vez; en algún tiempo. *a.* ex-. Come and see me s. soon, Ven a verme algún día de estos. He will have to go abroad s. or another, Tarde o temprano, tiene que ir al extranjero. s. last month, durante el mes pasado

sometimes, *adv.* algunas veces, a veces. s. happy, s. sad, algunas veces feliz y otras triste, ora feliz ora triste

somewhat, *adv.* algo; algún tanto, un tanto; un poco. I am s. busy, Estoy algo ocupado. He is s. of a lady-killer, Él tiene sus puntos de castigador, Él tiene algo de castigador

somewhere, *adv.* en alguna parte. s. about, por ahí. s. else, en otra parte

somnambulism, *s.* somnambulismo, *m.*

somnambulist, *s.* somnámbulo (-la)

somnolence, *s.* somnolencia, *f.*

somnolent, *a.* soñoliento; soporífero

son, *s.* hijo, *m.* **son-in-law,** yerno, hijo político, *m.*

sonata, *s.* sonata, *f.*

song, *s.* canto, *m.*; canción, *f.*; (poem) poema, verso, *m.* It's nothing to make a s. about, No es para tanto. to break into s., ponerse a cantar. to be not worth an old s., no valer un pito. S. of Songs, Cantar de los Cantares, *m.* s.-bird, ave cantora, *f.* s.-book, libro de canciones, *m.* s.-writer, compositor (-ra) de canciones

songster, *s.* ave cantora, *f.*

sonnet, *s.* soneto, *m.*

sonorous, *a.* sonoro

sonorousness, *s.* sonoridad, *f.*

soon, *adv.* pronto; dentro de poco, luego. as s. as, así que, en cuanto, luego que, no bien .. as s. as possible, lo antes posible, cuanto antes. s. after, poco después (de). See you s.! ¡Hasta pronto! sooner or later, tarde o temprano. the sooner the better, cuanto antes mejor. No sooner had he left the house, when ... Apenas había dejado la casa, cuando ... Emily would sooner go to London, Emilia preferiría ir a Londres (A Emilia le gustaría más ir a Londres)

soot, *s.* hollín, *m.* *v.t.* cubrir de hollín

soothe, *v.t.* tranquilizar, calmar; (pain) aliviar, mitigar

soothing, *a.* calmante, tranquilizador, sosegador; (of powders, etc.) calmante

soothingly, *adv.* con dulzura; suavemente; como un consuelo

soothsayer, *s.* adivino (-na), adivinador (-ra)

soothsaying, *s.* adivinanza, *f.*

sooty, *a.* cubierto de hollín; negro como el hollín

sop, s. sopa, f.; (bribe) soborno, m.

sophism, s. sofisma, m.

sophist, s. (hist.) sofista, m.; (quibbler) sofista, m. and f.

sophistic, a. (phil.) sofista; (of persons, arguments) sofístico

sophisticated, a. nada ingenuo; mundano; (cultured) culto

sophistication, s. falta de simplicidad, f.; mundanería, f.; cultura, f.

sophistry, s. sofistería, f.

Sophoclean, a. sofocleo

soporiferous, a. soporífero

soporific, a. soporífico

sopping, a. muy mojado. s. wet, hecho una sopa

soprano, s. (voice and part) soprano, m.; (singer) soprano, tiple, m. and f.

sorcerer, s. encantador, mago, brujo, m.

sorceress, s. hechicera, bruja, f.

sorcery, s. sortilegio, m., hechicería, brujería, f.; encanto, m.

sordid, a. sórdido; (of motives, etc.) ruin, vil

sordidness, s. sordidez, f.; (of motives, etc.) vileza, bajeza, f.

sordine, s. (mus.) sordina, f.

sore, a. doloroso, malo; (sad) triste; (annoyed) enojado; (with need, etc.) extremo. s. llaga, f.; (on horses, etc., caused by girths) matadura, f.; (fig.) herida, f.; recuerdo doloroso, m. to open an old s., (fig.) renovar la herida. running s., úlcera, f. s. throat, dolor de garganta, m.

sorely, adv. grandemente; muy; urgentemente. He was s. tempted, Tuvo grandes tentaciones

soreness, s. dolor, m.; (resentment) amargura, f., resentimiento, m.; (ill-feeling) rencor, m.

sorghum, s. (bot.) zahína, f., sorgo, m.

sorrel, a. alazán. s. (horse) alazán, m.; (bot.) acedera, f.

sorrow, s. pesar, m., aflicción, pesadumbre, f.; tristeza, f. v.i. afligirse; entristecerse. To my great s., Con gran pesar mío. s.-stricken, afligido, agobiado de pena

sorrowful, a. afligido, angustiado; triste

sorrowfully, adv. con pena, tristemente

sorrowing, a. afligido. s. aflicción, f.; lamentación, f.

sort, s. especie, f.; clase, f.; tipo, m. v.t. separar (de); clasificar. a s. of hat, una especie de sombrero. all sorts of, toda clase de. He is a good s., Es un buen chico. He is a queer s., Él es un tipo raro. in some s., hasta cierto punto. I am out of sorts, Estoy destemplado. Nothing of the s.! ¡Nada de eso!

sorter, s. oficial de correos, m.; clasificador (-ra)

sostenuto, a. (mus.) sostenido

sot, s. zaque, pellejo, m.

sotto voce, adv. a sovoz, en voz baja

sough, v.i. gemir, susurrar

soul, s. alma, f.; espíritu, m.; (departed) ánima, f.; (being) ser, m.; (life) vida, f.; (heart) corazón, m. All Souls' Day, Día de los Difuntos, m. He is a good s.! ¡Es un bendito! She is a simple s., Ella es una alma de Dios. Without seeing a living s., Sin ver bicho viviente. Upon my s.! ¡Por mi vida! s. in purgatory, alma en pena, f. s.-stirring, emocionante

soulful, a. sentimental, emocional; espiritual; romántico

soulless, a. sin alma; mecánico

sound, s. sonido, m.; son, m.; ruido, m.; (strait) estrecho, m. v.i. sonar; hacer ruido; resonar; (seem) parecer. v.t. sonar; (the horn, the alarm, musical instrument) tocar; (express) expresar; proclamar; (praise) celebrar; (naut.) hondear; (med.) tentar; (the chest) auscultar; (try to discover) tentar, sondar; (experience) experimentar. to the s. of, al son de. s.-box, (of a gramophone) diafragma, m. s.-detector, fonolocalización de aviones, f. s.-film, película sonora, f. s.-proof, (of radio studios, etc.) aislado de todo sonido. s.-track, (of a film) guía sonora, f. s.-wave, onda sonora, f.

sound, a. sano; (of a person) perspicaz; (reasonable) lógico, razonable; (of a policy, etc.)

prudente; (of an argument, etc.)
válido; (of an investment) seguro;
(solvent) solvente; (good) bueno;
(deep) profundo. *adv.* profundamente, bien

sounding, *s.* (*naut.*) sondeo, *m.*;
pl. **soundings,** sondas, *f. pl.*
a. sonoro. **to take soundings,**
sondar, echar la plomada. **s.-
board,** tabla de armonía, *f.*

soundless, *a.* sin ruido, silencioso

soundly, *adv.* sanamente; juiciosamente, prudentemente; bien;
(deeply) profundamente

soundness, *s.* (of a person) perspicacia, *f.*; (of a policy, etc.)
prudencia, *f.*; (of an argument,
etc.) validez, fuerza, *f.*; (financial) solvencia, *f.*

soup, *s.* sopa, *f.* **clear s.,** con-
sommé, *m.* **thick s.,** puré, *m.*
to be in the s., (*fam.*) estar
aviado. **s.-ladle,** cucharón, *m.*
s.-plate, plato sopero, *m.* **s.-
tureen,** sopera, *f.*

sour, *a.* ácido, agrio; (of milk)
agrio; (of persons, etc.) agrio,
desabrido. *v.t.* agriar. **to go s.,**
volverse agrio. **S. grapes!**
¡Están verdes!

source, *s.* (of a river, etc.)
nacimiento, *m.*; fuente, *f.*; (of
infection) foco, *m.* **to know
from a good s.,** saber de buena
tinta

sourly, *adv.* agriamente

sourness, *s.* acidez, agrura, *f.*;
acrimonia, *f.*

soutane, *s.* sotana, *f.*

south, *s.* sur, *m.*; mediodía, *m.*
a. del sur. *adv.* hacia el sur.
S. African, *a.* and *s.* sudafricano
(-na). **S. American,** *a.* and *s.*
sudamericano (-na). **s.-east,** *s.*
sudeste, *m.* *a.* del sudeste. *adv.*
hacia el sudeste. **s.-easter,**
viento del sudeste, *m.* **s.-
easterly,** *a.* del sudeste; al
sudeste. *adv.* hacia el sudeste.
s.-eastern, del sudeste. **s.-s.-
east,** *s.* sudsudeste, *m.* **s.-s.-
west,** sudsudoeste, *m.* **s.-west,**
s. sudoeste, *m.* *a.* del sudoeste.
adv. hacia el sudoeste. **s.-west
wind,** viento sudoeste, ábrego,
m. **s.-westerly,** *a.* del sudoeste.
adv. hacia el sudoeste. **s.-west-
ern,** *a.* del sudoeste

southerly, *a.* del sur; hacia el sur.
The house has a s. aspect, La
casa está orientada al sur

southern, *a.* del sur; del mediodía;
meridional. **S. Cross,** Cruz, *f.*,
Crucero, *m.* **s. express,** sudexpreso, *m.*

southerner, *s.* habitante del sur,
m.

southward, *a.* del sur; al sur.
adv. hacia el sur

souvenir, *s.* recuerdo, *m.*

sou'wester, *s.* (cap) sueste, *m.*

sovereign, *a.* soberano. *s.* soberano (-na); (coin) soberano, *m.*

sovereignty, *s.* soberanía, *f.*

soviet, *s.* soviet, *m.* *a.* soviético

sovietism, *s.* sovietismo, *m.*

sovietize, *v.t.* sovietizar

sow, *s.* cerda, puerca, marrana, *f.*;
(of a wild boar) jabalina, *f.*; (of
iron) galápago; *m.*

sow, *v.t.* sembrar; esparcir; diseminar

sower, *s.* sembrador (.-ra)

sowing, *s.* sembradura, siembra,
f. **s. machine,** sembradera, *f.*
s. time, tiempo de la siembra, *m.*

soya-bean, *s.* soja, *f.*

spa, *s.* balneario, *m.*; (spring)
manantial mineral, *m.*, caldas,
f. pl.

space, *s.* espacio, *m.*; (of time)
temporada, *f.*; intervalo, *m.*;
(print., mus.) espacio, *m.* *v.t.*
espaciar. **blank s.,** blanco, *m.*
s.-bar, (of a typewriter) tecla de
los espacios, *f.*

spacious, *a.* espacioso; amplio

spaciousness, *s.* espaciosidad, *f.*;
amplitud, *f.*

spade, *s.* pala, azada, *f.*; (cards)
espada, *f.* **to call a s. a s.,**
llamar al pan pan y al vino vino.
s.-work, trabajo preparatorio,
m.

spaghetti, *s.* fideos, macarrones,
m. pl.

spahi, *s.* espahi, *m.*

span, *v.t.* medir a palmos; rodear;
medir; (cross) atravesar, cruzar.
s. palmo, *m.*; espacio, *m.*,
duración, *f.*; (of a bridge) vano,
m.; (of wing, aer., zool.) envergadura, *f.*; (distance) distancia, *f.*
a single s. bridge, un puente de
vano único. **the brief s. of
human life,** la corta duración de
la vida humana

spangle, s. lentejuela, f.; (tinsel) oropel, m. v.t. adornar con lentejuelas; sembrar (de), esparcir (de). **spangled with stars,** sembrado de estrellas

Spaniard, s. español (-la). **a young S.,** un joven español

spaniel, s. perro de aguas, perro sabueso español m.; (cocker) sabueso, m.

Spanish, a. español. s. (language) español, castellano, m. **a S. girl,** una muchacha española. **in the S. fashion,** a la española. **S. American,** a. and s. hispanoamericano (-na). **S. broom,** retama de olor, f. **S. fly,** cantárida, f.

spank, v.t. pegar con la mano, azotar. s. azotazo, m. **to s. along,** correr rápidamente; (of a horse) galopar

spanking, s. azotamiento, vapuleo, m.

spanner, s. llave inglesa, llave de tuercas, f.

spar, s. (naut.) mastel, m.; (min.) espato, m.; (boxing) boxeo, m.; (quarrel) disputa, f. v.i. boxear; (argue) disputar

spare, a. (meagre) frugal, escaso; (of persons) enjuto, flaco; (available) disponible; (extra) de repuesto. s. recambio, m. **s. part,** pieza de recambio, pieza de repuesto, f. **s. room,** cuarto de amigos, m. **s. time,** ratos de ocio, m. pl., tiempo disponible, m. **s. wheel,** rueda de repuesto, f.

spare, v.t. (expense, etc.) escatimar; ahorrar; (do without) pasarse sin; (give) dar; (a life, etc.) perdonar; (avoid) evitar; dispensar de; (grant) hacer gracia de; (time) dedicar. **I cannot s. her,** No puedo estar sin ella. **They have no money to s.,** No tienen dinero de sobra. **to be sparing of,** ser avaro de

sparingly, adv. frugalmente; escasamente. **to eat s.,** comer con frugalidad

spark, s. chispa, f.; (gallant) pisaverde, m. v.i. chispear, echar chispas

sparking, a. chispeante. s. emisión de chispas, f. **s.-plug,** bujía de encendido, f.

sparkle, v.i. centellear, rutilar,

destellar; (fig.) brillar; (of wines) ser espumoso. s. centelleo, destello, m.; (fig.) brillo, m.

sparkling, a. rutilante, centelleante, reluciente; (fig.) brillante, chispeante; (of wines) espumante

sparring-match, s. combate de boxeo amistoso, m.

sparrow, s. gorrión, m. **s.-hawk,** gavilán, esparaván, m.

sparse, a. claro, ralo; esparcido

sparsely, adv. escasamente

Spartan, a. and s. espartano (-na)

spasm, s. espasmo, m.; ataque, m.; acceso, m.

spasmodic, a. espasmódico; intermitente

spasmodically, adv. espasmódicamente

spastic, a. (med.) espasmódico

spat, s. (gaiter) polaina de tela, f.

spate, s. crecida, f.; (fig.) torrente, m. **in s.,** crecido

spatter, v.t. salpicar; (fig., smirch) manchar. v.i. rociar. s. salpicadura, f.; rociada, f.

spatula, s. espátula, f.

spavin, s. esparaván, m.

spawn, v.t. and v.i. desovar; engendrar. s. huevas, f. pl., freza, f.; (offspring) producto, m.

spawning, s. desove, m.

speak, v.i. hablar; pronunciar un discurso; (sound) sonar. v.t. decir; (French, etc.) hablar. **She never spoke to him again,** Ella no volvió a dirigirle la palabra. **roughly speaking,** aproximadamente, más o menos. **Speaking for myself,** En cuanto a mí, Por mi parte. **without speaking,** sin decir nada, sin hablar. **to s. for,** (a person) hablar por. **to s. for itself,** hablar por sí mismo, ser evidente. **to s. one's mind,** decir lo que se piensa. **to s. of,** hablar de. **to s. out,** hablar claro; hablar alto. **to s. up for,** (a person) hablar en favor de (alguien)

speaker, s. el, m. (f. la) que habla; (public) orador (-ra). **The S.,** el Presidente de la Cámara de los Comunes

speaking, a. hablante; para hablar; elocuente, expresivo. s. habla, f.; discurso, m. **They are**

not on s. terms, No se hablan. **within s. distance,** al habla. **s.-trumpet,** portavoz, *m.* **s.-tube,** tubo acústico, *m.*

spear, *s.* lanza, *f.*; (javelin) venablo, *m.*; (harpoon) arpón, *m.* *v.t.* herir con lanza, alancear; (fish) arponear. **s.-head,** punta de la lanza, *f.* **s.-thrust,** lanzada, *f.*

special, *a.* especial; particular; extraordinario. **s.** (train) tren extraordinario, *m.* **s. correspondent,** corresponsal extraordinario, *m.* **s. friend,** amigo (-ga) del alma, amigo íntimo

specialist, *s.* especialista, *m.* and *f.*

speciality, *s.* particularidad, *f.*; especialidad, *f.*

specialization, *s.* especialización, *f.*

specialize, *v.t.* especializar. *v.i.* especializarse

specially, *adv.* especialmente; particularmente; sobre todo

specie, *s.* metálico, *m.*

species, *s.* especie, *f.*; raza, *f.*

specific, *a.* específico; explícito. **s. gravity,** peso específico, *m.*, densidad, *f.*

specifically, *adv.* específicamente; explícitamente

specification, *s.* especificación, *f.*

specify, *v.t.* especificar

specimen, *s.* espécimen, *m.*; ejemplo, *m.*; (fam.) tipo, *m.*

specious, *a.* especioso

speciousness, *s.* plausibilidad, *f.*; apariencia engañosa, *f.*

speck, *s.* pequeña mancha, *f.*; punto, *m.*; átomo, *m.*; (on fruit) maca, *f.*

speckle, *v.t.* motear, manchar

speckled, *a.* abigarrado; con manchas . . .

spectacle, *s.* espectáculo, *m.*; escena, *f.*; *pl.* **spectacles,** gafas, *f. pl.*, anteojos, *m. pl.* **s.-case,** cajita para las gafas, *f.*

spectacled, *a.* con gafas, que lleva gafas

spectacular, *a.* espectacular

spectator, *s.* espectador (-ra)

spectral, *a.* espectral

spectre, *s.* espectro, fantasma, *m.*

spectroscope, *s.* espectroscopio, *m.*

spectrum, *s.* (*phys.*) espectro, *m.*

speculate, *v.i.* especular (sobre, acerca de); (com.) especular (en)

speculation, *s.* especulación, *f.*

speculative, *a.* especulativo

speculator, *s.* especulador (-ra)

speculum, *s.* (surg.) espéculo, *m.*; (mirror) espejo, *m.*

speech, *s.* habla, *f.*; palabra, *f.*; (idiom) lenguaje, *m.*; (language) idioma, *m.*; (gram.) oración, *f.*; (address) discurso, *m.*; disertación, *f.* **part of s.,** parte de la oración, *f.* **to have the gift of s.,** tener el don de la palabra. **to make a s.,** pronunciar un discurso. **s.-day,** distribución de premios, *f.* **s.-maker,** orador (-ra)

speechless, *a.* mudo; sin habla; desconcertado, turbado

speed, *s.* prisa, rapidez, *f.*; velocidad, *f.* *v.t.* dar la bienvenida (a); conceder éxito (a); (accelerate) acelerar. *v.i.* darse prisa; correr a toda prisa; (of arrows) volar. **at full s.,** a toda prisa; a toda velocidad; a todo correr. **maximum s.,** velocidad máxima, *f.* **with all s.,** a toda prisa. **s. of impact,** velocidad del choque, *f.* **s.-boat,** lancha de carrera, *f.* **s.-limit,** velocidad máxima, *f.*, límite de velocidad, *m.*

speedily, *adv.* aprisa, rápidamente; prontamente

speediness, *s.* rapidez, prisa, celeridad, *f.*; prontitud, *f.*

speeding, *s.* exceso de velocidad, *m.* **s. up,** aceleración, *f.*

speedometer, *s.* cuentakilómetros, *m.*

speedway, *s.* pista de ceniza, *f.*

speedwell, *s.* (bot.) verónica, *f.*

speedy, *a.* rápido; pronto

spell, *s.* ensalmo, hechizo, *m.*; encanto, *m.*; (bout) turno, *m.*; (interval) rato, *m.*; temporada, *f.* *v.t.* (a word) deletrear; (a word in writing) escribir; (mean) significar; (be) ser. **a s. of good weather,** una temporada de buen tiempo. **by spells,** a ratos. **to learn to s.,** aprender la ortografía. **s.-bound,** encantado, fascinado; asombrado

spelling, *s.* deletreo, *m.*; ortografía, *f.* **s.-book,** silabario, *m.*; **s. mistake,** falta de ortografía, *f.*

spend, *v.t.* gastar; (time, etc.) pasar; perder; consumir, agotar. *v.i.* gastar, hacer gastos. **to s. oneself**, agotarse

spendthrift, *s.* derrochador (-ra), manirroto (-ta). *a.* despilfarrado, pródigo

spent, *a.* agotado, rendido. **The night is far s.**, La noche está avanzada. **s. bullet**, bala fría, *f.*

sperm, *s.* (*biol.*) esperma, *f.*; (whale) cachalote, *m.*

spermaceti, *s.* esperma de ballena, *f.*

sphere, *s.* esfera, *f.* **s. of influence**, zona de influencia, *f.*

spherical, *a.* esférico

sphinx, *s.* esfinge, *f.* **s.-like**, de esfinge

spice, *s.* especia, *f.*; (*fig.*) sabor, *m.*; (trace) dejo, *m.* *v.t.* especiar. **s. cupboard**, especiero, *m.*

spick and span, *a.* limpio como una patena; (brand-new) flamante; (of persons) muy compuesto

spicy, *a.* especiado; aromático; (*fig.*) picante

spider, *s.* araña, *f.* **spider's web**, telaraña, *f.*

spidery, *a.* de araña; lleno de arañas. **s. writing**, letra de patas de araña, *f.*

spigot, *s.* espiche, *m.*

spike, *s.* punta (de hierro, etc.), *f.*; escarpia, *f.*; (for boots) clavo, *m.*; (*bot.*) espiga, *f.* *v.t.* clavetear; (a cannon) clavar

spikenard, *s.* espicanardo, *m.*

spill, *v.t.* derramar. *s.* (fall) caída, *f.*

spilling, *s.* derramamiento, derrame, *m.*

spin, *v.t.* hilar; (a cocoon) tejer; (a top) bailar; (a ball) tornear; (a coin) lanzar. *v.i.* hilar; girar, bailar. *s.* vuelta, *f.*; paseo, *m.* **to send spinning downstairs**, hacer rodar por la escalera (a). **to s. a yarn**, contar un cuento. **to s. out**, prolongar

spinach, *s.* espinaca, *f.*

spinal, *a.* espinal. **s. anæsthesia**, raquianestesia, *f.* **s. column**, columna vertebral, *f.*

spindle, *s.* huso, *m.*; (*mech.*) eje, *m.* **s.-shaped**, ahusado

spine, *s.* (*anat.*) espinazo, *m.*, columna vertebral, *f.*; (*bot.*)

espina, *f.*; (of a porcupine, etc.) púa, *f.*

spineless, *a.* (*zool.*) invertebrado; (*fig.*) débil

spinet, *s.* espineta, *f.*

spinner, *s.* hilandero (-ra); máquina de hilar, *f.*

spinney, *s.* arboleda, *f.*; bosquecillo, *m.*

spinning, *s.* hilado, *m.*; hilandería, *f.* **s.-machine**, máquina de hilar, *f.* **s.-top**, trompo, *m.*, peonza, *f.* **s.-wheel**, rueca, *f.*

spinster, *s.* soltera, *f.*, **confirmed s.**, solterona, *f.*

spiny, *a.* con púas; espinoso

spiral, *a.* espiral; en espiral. *s.* espiral, *f.*

spirally, *adv.* en espiral

spire, *s.* (of a church) aguja, *f.*; espira, *f.*

spirit, *s.* espíritu, *m.*; alma, *f.*; (ghost) aparecido, fantasma, *m.*; (outstanding person) ingenio, *m.*, inteligencia, *f.*; (disposition) ánimo, *m.*; (courage) valor, espíritu, *m.*; (for a lamp, etc.) alcohol, *m.* **The Holy S.**, El Espíritu Santo. **to be in high spirits**, no caber de contento, saltar de alegría. **to be in low spirits**, estar desalentado, estar deprimido. **to be full of spirits**, ser bullicioso, tener mucha energía. **to keep up one's spirits**, sostener el valor. **to s. away**, quitar secretamente; hacer desaparecer; (kidnap) secuestrar. **s.-level**, nivel de burbuja, *m.* **s.-stove**, cocinilla, *f.*

spirited, *a.* animado, vigoroso, fogoso, animoso, brioso

spiritless, *a.* sin espíritu, apático; flojo, débil; (depressed) abatido, desalentado; (cowardly) sin valor, cobarde

spiritual, *a.* espiritual

spiritualism, *s.* espiritismo, *m.*; (*phil.*) espiritualismo, *m.*

spiritualist, *s.* espiritista, *m.* and *f.*; (*phil.*) espiritualista, *m.* and *f.*

spiritualistic, *a.* espiritista; (*phil.*) espiritualista. **s. séance**, sesión espiritista, *f.*

spirituality, *s.* espiritualidad, *f.*

spiritually, *adv.* espiritualmente

spirituous, *a.* espirituoso

spirt, see **spurt**

spit, *s.* (for roasting) espetón, asador, *m.*; (sand-bank) banco de arena, *m.*; (of land) lengua de tierra, *f.*; (spittle) saliva, *f. v.t.* (skewer) espetar; (saliva, etc.) escupir; (curses, etc.) vomitar. *v.i.* escupir, expectorar; (of a cat) fufear, decir fu; (sputter) chisporrotear; (rain) lloviznar

spite, *s.* malevolencia, mala voluntad, hostilidad, *f.*; rencor, *m.*, ojeriza, *f. v.t.* contrariar, hacer daño (a). **He has a s. against them**, Les tiene rencor. **in s. of**, a pesar de; a despecho de

spiteful, *a.* rencoroso, malévolo

spitefully, *adv.* malévolamente; con rencor; por maldad; por despecho

spitefulness, *s.* malevolencia, *f.*; rencor, *m.*

spitfire, *s.* cascarrabias, *m.* and *f.*, furia, *f.*

spittle, *s.* saliva, *f.*

spittoon, *s.* escupidera, *f.*

spitz, *s.* (dog) perro pomerano, *m.*

splanchnic, *a.* esplácnico

splash, *v.t.* salpicar (de); manchar (con). *v.i.* derramarse, esparcirse; chapotear, chapalear. *s.* chapoteo, *m.*; (of rain, etc.) chapaleteo, *m.*; (stain or patch) mancha, *f.* **John was splashing about in the sea**, Juan chapoteaba en el mar. **to make a s.**, (*fig.*) causar una sensación. **s.-board**, alero, *m.*

splay-footed, *a.* zancajoso

spleen, *s.* (anat.) bazo, *m.*; esplín, *m.*

splendid, *a.* espléndido; magnífico; glorioso; excelente

splendidly, *adv.* espléndidamente; magníficamente; excelentemente

splendour, *s.* resplandor, *m.*; magnificencia, *f.*; (of exploits, etc.) esplendor, brillo, *m.*

splenic, *a.* (anat.) esplénico

splice, *v.t.* (ropes, timbers) empalmar; (marry) unir, casar. *s.* empalme, *m.*

splint, *s.* (surg.) férula, *f.* **to put in a s.**, entablar

splinter, *v.t.* astillar, hacer astillas. *v.i.* hacerse astillas

splintery, *a.* astilloso

split, *v.i.* henderse; resquebrajarse; (of seams) nacerse; abrirse; dividirse. *v.t.* hender; pàrtir; dividir; abrir; (the atom) escindir. *s.* hendedura, *f.*; grieta, *f.*; división, *f.*; (in fabric) rasgón, *m.*; (quarrel) ruptura, *f.* **I have a splitting headache**, Tengo un dolor de cabeza que me trae loco. **to s. one's sides**, reírse a carcajadas, desternillarse de risa. **to s. on a rock**, estrellarse contra una roca. **to s. the difference**, partir la diferencia. **The blow s. his head open**, El golpe le abrió la cabeza. **to s. on**, (*fam.*) delatar, denunciar

splodge, *s.* mancha, *f.*, borrón, *m.*

splutter, *v.i.* chisporrotear; (of a person) balbucir. *s.* chisporroteo, *m.* **to s. out**, decir tartamudeando

spoil, *s.* botín, despojo, *m.*; (of war) trofeo, *m. v.t.* estropear; echar a perder; (diminish) mitigar; (a child) mimar; (injure) dañar; (destroy) arruinar, destruir. *v.i.* estropearse; echarse a perder. **to be spoiling for a fight**, tener ganas de pelearse. **You have spoilt my fun**, Me has aguado la fiesta. **s.-sport**, aguafiestas, *m.* and *f.*

spoilt, *a.* (of a child, etc.) mimado, consentido, malacostumbrado

spoke, *s.* (of a wheel) rayo, *m.*; (of a ladder) travesaño, peldaño, *m.*; (naut.) cabilla (de la rueda del timón), *f.*

spoken, *a.* hablado. **well-s.**, bien hablado; cortés

spokesman, *s.* portavoz, *m.* **to be s.**, llevar la palabra

spoliation, *s.* expoliación, *f.*; despojo, *m.*

spondee, *s.* (metrics) espondeo, *m.*

sponge, *s.* esponja, *f.*; (cadger) gorrón (-ona); (cake) bizcocho, *m. v.t.* limpiar con esponja. **to s.**, (*fam.*) vivir de gorra. **s.-holder**, esponjera, *f.*

sponger, *s.* gorrón (-ona), sablista, *m.* and *f.*

sponginess, *s.* esponjosidad, *f.*

sponging, *s.* esponjadura, *f.*; (*fam.*) sablazo, *m.*

spongy, *a.* esponjoso

sponsor, *s.* garante, *m.* and *f.*; valedor (-ra), patron (-na); (godfather) padrino, *m.*; (godmother) madrina, *f.*

spontaneity, *s.* espontaneidad, *f.*

spontaneous, *a.* espontáneo. **s. combustion,** combustión espontánea, *f.*

spontaneously, *adv.* espontáneamente

spook, *s.* fantasma, espectro, *m.*

spool, *s.* (for thread) bobina, *f.*, carrete, *m.*; (in a sewing machine) canilla, *f.*; (of a fishing rod) carrete, *m.*

spoon, *s.* cuchara, *f. v.t.* sacar con cuchara. *v.i.* (slang) besuquearse. **to s.-feed,** dar de comer con cuchara (a); tratar como un niño (a)

spoonful, *s.* cucharada, *f.*

spoor, *s.* pista, huella de animal, *f.*; rastro, *m.*

sporadic, *a.* esporádico

sporadically, *adv.* esporádicamente

spore, *s.* (*bot.*) espora, *f.*; (*zool.*) germen, *m.*

sporran, *s.* "sporran," *m.*

sport, *s.* deporte, sport, *m.*; deportismo, *m.*; (jest) broma, *f.*; (game) juego, *m.*; (plaything) juguete, *m.*; (pastime) pasatiempo, *m. v.i.* jugar; recrearse, divertirse. *v.t.* llevar; ostentar, lucir. **He is a s.,** Es un buen chico. **to make s. of,** burlarse de. **sports car,** coche de deporte, *m.* **sports ground,** campo de recreo, *m.* **sports jacket,** chaqueta de deporte, americana, *f.* **sports shirt,** camisa corta, *f.*

sporting, *a.* deportista; caballeroso. **I think there is a s. chance,** Me parece que hay una posibilidad de éxito

sportive, *a.* juguetón; bromista

sportsman, *s.* deportista, *m.*; aficionado al sport, *m.*; (*fig.*) caballero, señor, *m.*; buen chico, *m.*

sportsmanlike, *a.* de deportista; caballeroso

spot, *s.* mancha, *f.*; pinta, *f.*; (on the face, etc.) peca, *f.*; grano, *m.*; (place) sitio, *m.*; lugar, *m.*; (of liquor) trago, *m.*; (of food) bocado, *m.*; (of rain) gota, *f. v.t.* manchar; motear; (recognize) reconocer; (understand) darse cuenta de, comprender. **a tender s.,** (*fig.*) debilidad, *f.* **on the s.,** en el acto. **s. ball,** (billiards) pinta, *f.* **s. cash,** dinero contante, *m.*

spotless, *a.* saltando de limpio; sin mancha; inmaculado; puro; virgen

spotlight, *s.* luz del proyector, *f.*; proyector, *m.*

spotted, *a.* (stained) manchado; (of animals, etc.) con manchas; (of garments, etc.) con pintas

spotty, *a.* lleno de manchas; moteado; (pimply) con granos

spouse, *s.* esposo, *m.*; esposa, *f.*

spout, *v.i.* chorrear; (*fam.*) hablar incesantemente. *v.t.* arrojar; vomitar; (*fam.*) declamar, recitar. *s.* (of a jug, etc.) pico, *m.*; (for water, etc.) tubo, *m.*, cañería, *f.*; canalón, *m.*; (gust) ráfaga, nube, *f.* **down s.,** tubo de bajada, *m.*

spouting, *s.* chorreo, *m.*; (*fam.*) declamación, *f.*

sprain, *v.t.* dislocar, torcer. *s.* dislocación, *f.*, esguince, *m.* **Victoria has sprained her foot,** Victoria se ha torcido el pie

sprat, *s.* sardineta, *f.*

sprawl, *v.i.* recostarse (en); extenderse; (of plants) trepar. **He went sprawling,** Cayó cuan largo era

spray, *s.* (branch) ramo, *m.*; (of water, etc.) rocío, *m.*; (of the sea) espuma, *f.*; (mechanical device) pulverizador, *m. v.t.* pulverizar; rociar; regar; (the throat) jeringar

spread, *v.t.* tender; cubrir (de); poner; (stretch out) extender; (open out) desplegar; (of disease, etc.) propagar; diseminar; divulgar, difundir. *v.i.* extenderse; propagarse; difundirse; divulgarse; (become general) generalizarse. *s.* extensión, *f.*; expansión, *f.*; propagación, *f.*; divulgación, *f.*; (*aer.* and of birds) envergadura, *f.* **Carmen s. her hands to the fire,** Carmen extendió las manos al fuego. **The peacock s. its tail,** El pavo real hizo la rueda. **The dove s.**

its **wings**, La paloma desplegó
sus alas. to **s. out**, *v.t.* extender;
desplegar; (scatter) esparcir. *v.i.*
extenderse

spreading, *s.* (of a disease) propagación, *f.*; (of knowledge, etc.)
divulgación, *f.*; expansión, *f.*;
extensión, *f.*

spree, *s.* juerga, parranda, *f.*;
excursión, *f.* to **go on the s.**, ir
de juerga, ir de picos pardos

sprig, *s.* ramita, *f.*; (of heather,
etc.) espiga, *f.*; (scion) vástago, *m.*

sprightliness, *s.* vivacidad, *f.*,
despejo, *m.*; energía, *f.*

sprightly, *a.* vivaracho, despierto; enérgico

spring, *v.i.* saltar, brincar; (become) hacerse; (seek) buscar; (of
plants, water) brotar; (of tears)
arrasar, llenar; (from) originarse
(en), ser causado (por); inspirarse
(en). *v.t.* (a mine) volar; (a trap)
soltar. to **s. a surprise**, dar una
sorpresa. to **s. a surprise on a
person**, coger a la imprevista (a).
to **s. at a person**, precipitarse
sobre. to **s. to one's feet**,
ponerse de pie de un salto.
to **s. back**, saltar hacia atrás;
recular; volver a su sitio. to **s.
open**, abrirse súbitamente. to **s.
up**, (of plants) brotar, crecer; (of
difficulties, etc.) surgir, asomarse

spring, *s.* (jump) salto, brinco,
m.; (of water) fuente, *f.*, manantial, *m.*; (season) primavera,
f.; (of a watch, etc.) resorte, *m.*;
(of a mattress, etc.) muelle, *m.*
a. primaveral. *v.i.* saltar, brincar.
at one s., en un salto. to **give a
s.**, dar un salto. **s.-board**,
trampolín, *m.* **s.-mattress**,
colchón de muelles, *m.* **s.-tide**,
marea viva, *f.*

springiness, *s.* elasticidad, *f.*

springlike, *a.* primaveral

springtime, *s.* primavera, *f.*

sprinkle, *v.t.* esparcir; salpicar;
rociar

sprinkling, *s.* salpicadura, *f.*;
rociadura, *f.*; pequeño número,
m. **a s. of snow**, una nevada
ligera

sprint, *v.i.* sprintar. *s.* sprint, *m.*

sprite, *s.* trasgo, *m.*; hada, *f.*

sprout, *v.i.* brotar, despuntar,
retoñar, tallecer; germinar. *v.t.*
salir. *s.* brote, retoño, pimpollo,

m.; germen, *m.* **Brussels
sprouts**, coles de Bruselas, *f. pl.*

spruce, *a.* peripuesto, muy
aseado, pulido; elegante. *s.* (*bot.*)
pícea, *f.* to **s. oneself up**,
arreglarse, ponerse elegante

spruceness, *s.* aseo, buen parecer,
m., elegancia, *f.*

spry, *a.* activo, ágil

spun glass, *s.* hilacha de vidrio, *f.*

spur, *s.* espuela, *f.*; aguijada, *f.*;
(of a bird) espolón, *m.*; (*bot.*)
espuela, *f.*; (of a mountain range)
espolón, estribo, *m.*; (*fig.*) estímulo, *m.* *v.t.* espolear, picar con
la espuela; calzarse las espuelas;
(*fig.*) estimular, incitar. **on the
s. of the moment**, bajo el
impulso del momento

spurge, *s.* (*bot.*) tártago, *m.*

spurious, *a.* espurio; falso

spurn, *v.t.* rechazar; tratar con
desprecio; menospreciar

spurt, *v.i.* (gush) chorrear, borbotar; brotar, surgir; (in racing,
etc.) hacer un esfuerzo supremo.
v.t. hacer chorrear; lanzar. *s.*
(jet) chorro, *m.*; esfuerzo supremo, *m.*

sputter, *v.i.* chisporrotear; crepitar; (of a pen) escupir; (of a
person) balbucir

sputtering, *s.* chisporroteo, *m.*;
crepitación, *f.*; (of a person)
balbuceo, *m.*

sputum, *s.* esputo, *m.*

spy, *v.t.* observar, discernir. *v.i.*
espiar, ser espía. *s.* espía, *m.* and
f. to **spy out the land**, explorar
el terreno. to **spy upon**, espiar;
seguir los pasos (a). **spy-glass**,
catalejo, *m.*

spying, *s.* espionaje, *m.*

squabble, *s.* disputa, *f.*; riña, *f.*
v.i. pelearse; disputar

squabbling, *s.* riñas, querellas,
f. pl.; disputas, *f. pl.*

squad, *s.* escuadra, *f.*; pelotón, *m.*

squadron, *s.* (*mil.*) escuadrón,
m.; (*nav.*) escuadra, *f.*; (*aer.*)
escuadrilla, *f.*; (of persons) pelotón, *m.* **s.-leader**, comandante, *m.*

squalid, *a.* escuálido; (of quarrels, etc.) sórdido, mezquino

squall, *v.i.* berrear; chillar. *s.*
berrido, *m.*; chillido, *m.*; (storm)
chubasco, turbión, *m.*; (*fig.*)
tormenta, tempestad, *f.*

squalor, *s.* escualidez, *f.*; sordidez, mezquindad, *f.*

squander, *v.t.* derrochar, tirar, desperdiciar; (time, etc.) malgastar

squanderer, *s.* derrochador (-ra)

squandering, *s.* derroche, desperdicio, dispendio, *m.*; (of time, etc.) pérdida, *f.*, desperdicio, *m.*

square, *s.* (*math.*) cuadrado, *m.*; rectángulo, *m.*; (of a chessboard) escaque, *m.*; (of a draughtboard and of graph paper) casilla, *f.*; (in a town) plaza, *f.*; (of troops) cuadro, *m.* *a.* cuadrado; justo; igual; (honest) honrado, formal; (unambiguous) redondo, categórico; (*math.*) cuadrado. **She wore a silk s. on her head,** Ella llevaba un pañuelo de seda en la cabeza. **five s. feet,** cinco pies cuadrados. **nine feet s.,** nueve pies en cuadro. **on the s.,** honradamente. **a s. dance,** contradanza, *f.* **a s. meal,** una buena comida. **s. dealing,** trato limpio, *m.* **The account is s.,** La cuenta está justa. **to get s. with,** desquitarse (de), vengarse de. **s. measure,** medida de superficie, *f.* **s. root,** raíz cuadrada, *f.* **s.-shouldered,** de hombros cuadrados

square, *v.t.* cuadrar; (*carp.*) escuadrar; (arrange) arreglar; (bribe) sobornar; (reconcile) acomodar; (*math.*) cuadrar. *v.i.* conformarse (con), cuadrar (con). **to s. the circle,** cuadrar el círculo. **to s. one's shoulders,** enderezarse. **to s. accounts with,** saldar cuentas con. **to s. up to,** (a person) avanzar belicosamente hacia

squarely, *adv.* en cuadro; directamente; sin ambigüedades, rotundamente; (honestly) de buena fe, honradamente

squareness, *s.* cuadratura, *f.*; (honesty) honradez, buena fe, *f.*

squash, *v.t.* aplastar (also *fig.*, *fam.*). *v.i.* aplastarse; apretarse. *s.* aplastamiento, *m.*; (of fruit, etc.) pulpa, *f.*; (of people) agolpamiento, *m.*; muchedumbre, *f.*; (drink) refresco (de limón, etc.), *m.*

squashy, *a.* blando y húmedo

squat, *v.i.* acuclillarse, agacharse, agazaparse; (on land, etc.) apropiarse sin derecho. *a.* rechoncho

squatter, *s.* intruso (-sa); colono usurpador, *m.*

squaw, *s.* piel roja, *f.*

squawk, *v.i.* graznar; lanzar gritos agudos. *s.* graznido, *m.*; grito agudo, *m.*

squeak, *v.i.* (of carts, etc.) chirriar, rechinar; (of shoes) crujir; (of persons, mice, etc.) chillar; (slang) cantar. *s.* chirrido, crujido, *m.*; chillido, *m.* **to have a narrow s.,** escapar por un pelo

squeaking, *s.* chirrido, rechinamiento, *m.*; crujido, *m.*; (of humans, mice, etc.) chillidos, *m. pl.*

squeal, *v.i.* lanzar gritos agudos, chillar; (complain) quejarse; (slang) cantar. *s.* grito agudo, chillido, *m.*

squealing, *s.* gritos agudos, chillidos, *m. pl.*

squeamish, *a.* que se marea fácilmente; mareado; (nauseated) asqueado; delicado; remilgado

squeamishness, *s.* tendencia a marearse, *f.*; delicadeza, *f.*; remilgos, *m. pl.*

squeeze, *v.t.* apretar; estrujar; (fruit) exprimir; (extort) arrancar; (money from) sangrar. *s.* (of the hand, etc.) apretón, *m.*; estrujón, *m.*; (of fruit juice) algunas gotas (de). **It was a tight s. in the car,** Íbamos muy apretados en el coche. **He was in a tight s.,** Se encontraba en un aprieto. **to s. one's way through the crowd,** abrirse camino a codazos por la muchedumbre. **to s. in,** *v.t.* hacer sitio para. *v.i.* introducirse con dificultad (en)

squelch, *v.i.* gorgotear, chapotear. *v.t.* aplastar

squib, *s.* (firework) rapapiés, buscapiés, *m.*; (lampoon) pasquinada, *f.*

squid, *s.* calamar, *m.*

squint, *s.* estrabismo, *m.*; mirada furtiva, *f.*; (*fam.*) vistazo, *m.*, mirada, *f.* *v.i.* ser bizco; bizcar. **to s. at,** mirar de soslayo. **s.-eyed,** bizco. **to be s.-eyed,** mirar contra el gobierno

squire, s. escudero, m.; hacendado, m. v.t. escoltar, acompañar

squirely, a. escuderil

squirm, v.i. retorcerse; (with embarrassment) no saber dónde meterse. s. retorcimiento, m. **to s. along the ground,** arrastrarse por el suelo

squirrel, s. ardilla, f.

squirt, v.t. (liquids) lanzar. v.i. chorrear, salir a chorros. s. chorro, m.; (syringe) jeringa, f.

stab, v.t. apuñalar, dar de puñaladas (a); herir. s. puñalada, f.; herida, f.; (of pain, and fig.) pinchazo, m. **a s. in the back,** una puñalada por la espalda

stability, s. estabilidad, f.; solidez, firmeza, f.

stabilize, v.t. estabilizar

stable, a. estable; fijo, firme. s. cuadra, caballeriza, f.; (for cows, etc.) establo, m. v.t. poner en la cuadra; alojar. **s.-boy,** mozo de cuadra, m.

stack, s. (of hay) niara, f., almiar, m.; (heap) montón, m.; (of rifles) pabellón, m.; (of a chimney) cañón, m. v.t. (agr.) hacinar; amontonar; (mil.) poner (las armas) en pabellón

stadium, s. estadio, m.

staff, s. vara, f.; (bishop's, and fig.) báculo, m.; (pilgrim's) bordón, m.; (pole) palo, m.; (flagstaff) asta, f.; (of an office, etc.) personal, m.; (editorial) redacción, f.; (corps) cuerpo, m.; (mil.) plana mayor, f., estado mayor, m.; (mus.) pentagrama, m. v.t. proveer de personal. **General S.,** Estado Mayor General, m. **s. officer,** (mil.) oficial de Estado Mayor, m.

stag, s. ciervo, m. **s.-beetle,** ciervo volante, m. **s.-hunting,** caza del ciervo, f.

stage, s. (for workmen) andamio, m.; (of a microscope) porta-objetos, m.; (theat.) escena, f., tablas, f. pl.; teatro, m.; (of development, etc.) etapa, f.; fase, f. v.t. (theat.) poner en escena; (theat.) representar; (a demonstration, etc.) arreglar. **by easy stages,** poco a poco; (of a journey) a pequeñas etapas. **to come on the s.,** salir a la escena. **to go on the s.,** hacerse actor

(actriz), dedicarse al teatro. **s. carpenter,** tramoyista, m. **s.-coach,** diligencia, f. **s.-craft,** arte de escribir para el teatro, f.; arte escénica, f. **s.-direction,** acotación, f. **s.-door,** entrada de los artistas, f. **s.-effect,** efecto escénico, m. **s.-fright,** miedo al público, m. **s.-hand,** tramoyista, sacasillas, metesillas y sacamuertos, m. **s. manager,** director de escena, m. **s.-whisper,** aparte, m.

stager, old, s. veterano, m.

stagger, v.i. tambalear; andar haciendo eses; (hesitate) titubear, vacilar. v.t. desconcertar. s. titubeo, tambaleo, m.; (aer.) decalaje, m. **staggered working hours,** horas de trabajo escalonadas, f. pl.

staggering, a. tambaleante; (surprising) asombroso, sorprendente; (dreadful) espantoso. **a s. blow,** un golpe que derriba

staging, s. (scaffolding) andamio, m.; (theat.) producción, f.; representación, f.; decorado, m.

stagnancy, s. (of water) estancación, f.; (inactivity) estagnación, f.; paralización, f,

stagnant, a. estancado; paralizado. **to be s.,** estar estancado. **s. water,** agua estancada, f.

stagnate, v.i. estancarse; estar estancado; (of persons) vegetar

stagnation, s. (of water) estancación, f.; estagnación, f.; parálisis, f.

staid, a. serio, formal, juicioso

staidness, s. seriedad, formalidad, f.

stain, v.t. manchar; (dye) teñir. s. mancha, f.; colorante, m. **without a s.,** (fig.) sin mancha. **stained glass,** vidrio de color, m. **s.-remover,** quitamanchas, m.

stainless, a. sin mancha; inmaculado, puro

stair, s. escalón, peldaño, m.; escalera, f.; pl. **stairs,** escalera, f. **a flight of stairs,** una escalera; un tramo de escaleras. **below stairs,** escalera abajo. **s.-carpet,** alfombra de escalera, f. **s.-rod,** varilla para alfombra de escalera, f.

staircase, *s.* escalera, *f.* **spiral s.**, escalera de caracol, *f.*

stake, *s.* estaca, *f.*; (for plants) rodrigón, *m.*; (gaming) envite, *m.*, apuesta, *f.*; (in an undertaking) interés, *m.*; *pl.* **stakes**, (prize) premio, *m.*; (race) carrera, *f.* *v.t.* estacar; (plants) rodrigar; (bet) jugar. **at s.**, en juego; en peligro. **to be burnt at the s.**, morir en la hoguera. **to s. one's all**, jugarse el todo por el todo. **to s. a claim**, hacer una reclamación. **to s. out**, jalonar

stalactite, *s.* estalactita, *f.*

stalagmite, *s.* estalagmita, *f.*

stale, *a.* no fresco; (of bread, etc.) duro, seco; (of air) viciado; viejo; pasado de moda; (tired) cansado

stalemate, *s.* (chess, draughts) tablas, *f. pl.*; (fig.) punto muerto, *m.* **to reach a s.**, llegar a un punto muerto

staleness, *s.* rancidez, *f.*; (of bread, etc.) dureza, *f.*; (of news, etc.) falta de novedad, *f.*

stalk, *s.* (bot.) tallo, *m.*; (bot.) pedúnculo, *m.*; (of a glass) pie, *m.* *v.i.* andar majestuosamente; (fig.) rondar. *v.t.* (game) cazar al acecho; (a person) seguir los pasos (a)

stalking-horse, *s.* boezuelo, *m.*; (fig.) pretexto, disfraz, *m.*

stall, *s.* (in a stable) puesto (individual), *m.*; (stable) establo, *m.*; (choir) silla de coro, *f.*; (in a fair, etc.) barraca, *f.*, puesto, *m.*; (theat.) butaca, *f.*; (finger-stall) dedal, *m.* *v.t.* (an engine) cortar accidentalmente. *v.i.* (aut.) pararse de pronto; (aer.) perder velocidad; (of a cart, etc.) atascarse. **pit s.**, (theat.) butaca de platea, *f.*

stalling, *s.* (aut.) parada accidental, *f.*; (aer.) pérdida de velocidad, *f.* **Stop s.!** ¡Déjate de rodeos!

stallion, *s.* semental, *m.*

stalwart, *a.* robusto, fornido; leal; valiente

stalwartness, *s.* robustez, *f.*; lealtad, *f.*; valor, *m.*

stamen, *s.* (bot.) estambre, *m.*

stamina, *s.* resistencia, *f.*

stammer, *v.t.* tartamudear; (hesitate in speaking) titubear, balbucir. *s.* tartamudez, *f.*; titubeo, balbuceo, *m.*

stammerer, *s.* tartamudo (-da)

stammering, *a.* tartamudo; balbuciente. *s.* tartamudeo, *m.*; balbuceo, *m.*

stamp, *v.t.* estampar; imprimir; (documents) timbrar; pegar el sello de correo (a); (characterize) sellar; (fig., engrave) grabar; (coins) acuñar; (press) apisonar; (with the foot) golpear con los pies, patear; (in dancing) zapatear. *s.* (with the foot) patada, *f.*, golpe con los pies, *m.*; (mark, etc.) marca, *f.*; (rubber, etc.) estampilla, *f.*; matasellos, *m.*; cuño, *m.*; (for documents) póliza, *f.*; timbre, *m.*; (for letters) sello, *m.*; (machine) punzón, *m.*; mano de mortero, *f.*; (fig., sign) sello, *m.*; (kind) temple, *m.*, clase, *f.* **The events of that day are stamped on my memory,** Los acontecimientos de aquel día están grabados en mi memoria. **to s. out**, (a fire, etc.) extinguir, apagar; (resistance, etc.) vencer; destruir. **postage-s.**, sello de correos, *m.* **s.-album**, álbum de sellos, *m.* **s.-duty**, impuesto del timbre, *m.* **s.-machine**, expendedor automático de sellos de correo, *m.*

stampede, *s.* fuga precipitada, *f.*; pánico, *m.* *v.i.* huir precipitadamente; (of animals) salir de estampía; huir en desorden. *v.t.* hacer perder la cabeza (a), sembrar el pánico entre

stamping, *s.* selladura, *f.*; (of documents) timbrado, *m.*; (of fabrics, etc.) estampado, *m.*; (with the feet) pataleo, *m.*; (in dancing) zapateo, *m.*

stance, *s.* posición de los pies, *f.*; postura, *f.*

stanch, *v.t.* restañar

stanchion, *s.* puntal, montante, *m.*; (naut.) candelero, *m.*

stand, *v.i.* estar de pie; ponerse de pie, incorporarse; estar; hallarse; sostenerse; ser; ponerse; (halt) parar; (remain) permanecer, quedar. *v.t.* poner; (endure) resistir; tolerar; sufrir; (entertain) convidar. **S.!** ¡Alto! **as things s.**, tal como están las cosas. **I cannot s. any more,** No puedo más. **I cannot s. him,** No le puedo ver. **Nothing stands be-**

tween them and ruin, No hay nada entre ellos y la ruina. I stood him a drink, Le convidé a un trago. How do we s.? ¿Cómo estamos? It stands to reason that..., Es lógico que... Edward stands six feet, Eduardo tiene seis pies de altura. to s. accused of, ser acusado de. to s. godfather (or godmother) to, sacar de pila (a). to s. in need (of), necesitar, tener necesidad (de). to s. on end, (of hair) ponerse de punta, despeluzarse. to s. one in good stead, ser útil, ser ventajoso. to stand one's ground, no ceder, tenerse fuerte. to s. to attention, cuadrarse, permanecer en posición de firmes. to s. well with, tener buenas relaciones con, ser estimado de. to s. aside, tenerse a un lado; apartarse; (in favour of someone) retirarse. to s. back, quedarse atrás; recular, retroceder. to s. by, estar de pie cerca de; estar al lado de; estar presente (sin intervenir); ser espectador; estar preparado; (one's friends) ayudar, proteger; (a promise, etc.) atenerse (a); ser fiel (a); (of a ship) mantenerse listo. s.-by, s. recurso, m. to s. for, representar; simbolizar; (mean) significar; (Parliament, etc.) presentarse como candidato; (put up with) tolerar, sufrir. to s. in, colaborar. to s. in with, estar de acuerdo con, ser partidario de; compartir. to s. off, mantenerse a distancia. to s. out, (in relief, and fig. of persons) destacarse; (be firm) resistir, mantenerse firme; (naut.) gobernar más afuera. S. out of the way! ¡Quítate de en medio! to s. over, (be postponed) quedar aplazado. to s. up, estar de pie; ponerse de pie, incorporarse; tenerse derecho. to s. up against, resistir; oponerse a. to s. up for, defender; volver por. to s. up to, hacer cara a.

stand, s. puesto, m.; posición, actitud, f.; (for taxis, etc.) punto, m.; (in a market, etc.) puesto, m.; (sport) tribuna, f.; (for a band) quiosco, m.; (of a dish, etc.) pie, m.; (mech.) sostén, m.; (opposi-

tion) resistencia, oposición, f. to make a s. against, oponerse resueltamente (a); ofrecer resistencia (a). to take one's s., fundarse (en), apoyarse (en). to take up one's s. by the fire, ponerse cerca del fuego

standard, s. (flag) estandarte, m., bandera, f.; (for gold, weights, etc.) marco, m.; norma, f.; convención, regla, f.; (of a lamp) pie, m.; (pole) poste, m.; columna, f.; (level) nivel, m. a. corriente; normal; típico; clásico. It is a s. type, Es un tipo corriente. gold s., patrón de oro, m. s. author, autor clásico, m. s. formula, fórmula clásica, f. s. of living, nivel de la vida, m. s.-bearer, abanderado, m. s.-lamp, lámpara vertical, f.

standardization, s. (of armaments, etc.) unificación de tipos, f.; (of dyestuffs, medicinals, etc.) control, m., estandardización, f.

standardize, v.t. hacer uniforme controlar

standing, a. de pie, derecho; permanente, fijo; constante. s. posición, f.; reputación, f.; importancia, f.; antigüedad, f. It is a quarrel of long s., Es una riña antigua. s. committee, comisión permanente, f. s. room, sitio para estar de pie, m. s. water, agua estancada, f. standoffish, frío, etiquetero; altanero. stand-offishness, frialdad, f.; altanería, f. standpoint, punto de vista, m.

standstill, s. parada, f.; pausa, f. at a s., parado; (of industry) paralizado

stanza, s. estrofa, estancia, f.

stapes, s. (anat.) estribo, m.

staphylococcus, s. (med.) estafilococo, m.

staple, s. (fastener) grapa, f.; (of wool, etc.) hebra, fibra, f.; producto principal (de un país), m.; (raw material) materia prima, f.; a. principal; más importante; corriente

star, s. (all meanings) estrella, f.; (asterisk) asterisco, m. v.t. estrellar, sembrar de estrellas; marcar con asterisco. v.i. (theat., cinema) presentarse como estrella, ser estrella. stars and

stripes, las barras y las estrellas. **to be born under a lucky s.,** tener estrella. **to see stars,** ver estrellas. **s.-gazing,** observación de las estrellas, *f.*; ensimismamiento, *m.* **s.-spangled,** sembrado de estrellas. **s.-turn,** gran atracción, *f.*

starboard, *s.* (*naut.*) estribor, *m.*

starch, *s.* almidón, *m.* *v.t.* almidonar

starchy, *a.* almidonado; (of food) feculento; (*fig.*) tieso, entonado, etiquetero

stare, *v.i.* mirar fijamente; abrir mucho los ojos. *s.* mirada fija, *f.* **stony s.,** mirada dura, *f.* **to s. at,** (a person) clavar la mirada en; mirar de hito en hito (a). **The explanation stares one in the face,** La explicación salta a la vista (or está evidente). **to s. into space,** mirar las telarañas. **to s. out of countenance,** avergonzar con la mirada

starfish, *s.* estrella de mar, *f.*

staring, *a.* (of colours) chillón, llamativo, encendido. **s. eyes,** ojos saltones, *m. pl.*; ojos espantados, *m. pl.*

stark, *a.* rígido; (*poet.*) poderoso; absoluto. **s. staring mad,** loco de atar. **s.-naked,** en cueros vivos, en pelota

starless, *a.* sin estrellas

starlight, *s.* luz de las estrellas, *f.* *a.* estrellado

starling, *s.* (*orn.*) estornino, tordo de Castilla, *m.*

starry, *a.* estrellado, sembrado de estrellas

start, *v.i.* estremecerse, asustarse; saltar; (set out) salir; ponerse en camino; (of a train, a race) arrancar; ponerse en marcha; (*aer.*) despegar; (begin) empezar; (of timbers) combarse. *v.t.* empezar; (a car, etc.) poner en marcha; (a race) dar la señal de partida; (a hare, etc.) levantar; (cause) provocar, causar; (a discussion, etc.) abrir; iniciar. *s.* (fright) susto, *m.*; (setting out) partida, salida, *f.*; (beginning) principio, comienzo, *m.*; (starting-point of a race) arrancadero, *m.*; (*aer.*) despegue, *m.*; (advantage) ventaja, *f.* **at the s.,** al principio. **for a s.,** para empezar. **from s.**

to finish, desde el principio hasta el fin. **She started to cry,** Ella se puso a llorar. **He has started his journey to Canada,** Ha empezado su viaje al Canadá. **I started up the engine,** Puse el motor en marcha. **to get a s.,** asustarse; tomar la delantera. **to give (a person) a s.,** asustar, dar un susto (a); dar la ventaja (a). **to give (a person) a s. in life,** ayudar a alguien a situarse en la vida. **to make a fresh s. (in life),** hacer vida nueva, empezar la vida de nuevo. **to s. after,** lanzarse en busca de; salir tras. **to s. back,** retroceder; emprender el viaje de regreso; marcharse. **to s. off,** salir, partir; ponerse en camino. **to s. up,** *v.i.* incorporarse bruscamente, ponerse de pie de un salto; (appear) surgir, aparecer. *v.t.* (an engine) poner en marcha

starter, *s.* iniciador (-ra); (for a race) starter, juez de salida, *m.*; (competitor in a race) corredor, *m.*; (of a car, etc.) arranque, *m.*

starting, *s.* (setting out) salida, partida, *f.*; (beginning) principio, *m.*; (fear) estremecimiento, *m.*; susto, *m.* **s.-gear,** palanca de arranque, *f.* **s.-handle,** manivela de arranque, *f.* **s.-point,** punto de partida, *m.*; (*fig.*) arrancadero, *m.* **s.-post,** puesto de salida, *m.*

startle, *v.t.* asustar, sobresaltar, alarmar. **The news startled him out of his indifference,** Las noticias le hicieron salir de su indiferencia

startling, *a.* alarmante; (of dress, etc.) exagerado; (of colours) chillón

starvation, *s.* hambre, *f.*; (*med.*) inanición, *f.* **s. diet,** régimen de hambre, *m.* **s. wage,** ración de hambre, *f.*

starve, *v.i.* morir de hambre; pasar hambre, no tener bastante que comer; no comer. *v.t.* matar de hambre; privar de alimentos (a). **I am simply starving,** Tengo una hambre canina, Muero de hambre. **to s. with cold,** *v.i.* morir de frío. *v.t.* matar de frío

starved, *a.* muerto de hambre, hambriento. **s. of affection,** hambriento de cariño

starving, *a.* que muere de hambre, hambriento

state, *s.* estado, *m.*; condición, *f.*; (anxiety) agitación, ansiedad, *f.*; (social) rango, *m.*; (pomp) magnificencia, pompa, *f.*; (government, etc.) Estado, *m.*; nación, *f. a.* de Estado; de gala, de ceremonia. the married s., el estado matrimonial. a s. of war, un estado de guerra. in s., con gran pompa. to lie in s., (of a body) estar expuesto. s. apartments, habitaciones de gala, *f. pl.* s. banquet, comida de gala, *f.* s. coach, coche de gala, *m.* s. control, control por el Estado, *m.* S. Department, Ministerio de Estado, *m.* s. education, instrucción pública, *f.* s. papers, documentos de Estado, *m. pl.*

state, *v.t.* decir (que), afirmar (que); (one's case, etc.) exponer; explicar; (*math.*) proponer

statecraft, *s.* arte de gobernar, *m.*

stated, *a.* arreglado, indicado; fijo. the s. date, la fecha indicada. at s. intervals, a intervalos fijos

stateliness, *s.* dignidad, *f.*; majestad, *f.*

stately, *a.* majestuoso; imponente; noble; digno

statement, *s.* afirmación, declaración, *f.*; resumen, *m.*; exposición, *f.*; (*law*) deposición, *f.*; (*com.*) estado de cuenta, *m.* to make a s., hacer una declaración

stateroom, *s.* sala de recepción, *f.*; (on a ship) camarote, *m.*

statesman, *s.* hombre de Estado, *m.*

statesmanlike, *a.* de hombre de Estado

statesmanship, *s.* arte de gobernar, *m.*

static, *a.* estático

statics, *s.* estática, *f.*

station, *s.* (place) puesto, sitio, *m.*; (*r.w.* and *ecc.*) estación, *f.*; (social) posición social, *f.*; (*naut.*) apostadero, *m.*; (*surv.*) punto de marca, *m. v.t.* estacionar, colocar, poner. to s. oneself, colocarse. Stations of the Cross, Estaciones, *f. pl.* s.-master, jefe de la estación, *m.*

stationary, *a.* estacionario; inmóvil; (*ast.*) estacional

stationer, *s.* papelero (-ra). stationer's shop, papelería, *f.*

stationery, *s.* papelería, *f.*, efectos de escritorio, *m. pl.*; papel de escribir, *m.*

statistical, *a.* estadístico

statistician, *s.* estadista, *m.*

statistics, *s.* estadística, *f.*

statuary, *a.* estatuario. s. estatuaria, *f.*; estatuas, *f. pl.*; (sculptor) estatuario, *m.*

statue, *s.* estatua, *f.*; imagen, *f.*

statuesque, *a.* escultural

statuette, *s.* figurilla, *f.*

stature, *s.* estatura, *f.*; (moral, etc.) valor, *m.*

status, *s.* (*law*, etc.) estado, *m.*; posición, *f.*; rango, *m.* What is his s. as a physicist? ¿Cómo se le considera entre los físicos? social s., posición social, *f.*; rango social, *m.*

statute, *s.* ley, *f.*; acto legislativo, *m.*; estatuto, *m.*; regla, *f.* s.-book, código legal, *m.*

statutory, *a.* establecido; reglamentario; estatutario

staunch, *a.* leal, fiel; firme, constante. *v.t.* restañar

staunchness, *s.* lealtad, fidelidad, *f.*; firmeza, *f.*

stave, *s.* (of a barrel, etc.) duela, *f.*; (of a ladder) peldaño, *m.*; (stanza) estrofa, *f.*; (*mus.*) pentagrama, *m.* to s. in, abrir boquete en; romper a golpes; quebrar. to s. off, apartar, alejar; (delay) aplazar, diferir; (avoid) evitar; (thirst, etc.) dominar

stay, *v.t.* detener; (a judgment, etc.) suspender. *v.i.* permanecer; quedarse; detenerse; (of weather, etc.) durar; (lodge) hospedarse, vivir. to come to s., venir a ser permanente. to s. a person's hand, parar la mano (a). to s. at home, quedarse en casa. s.-at-home, *a.* casero. s. persona casera, *f.* to s. the course, terminar la carrera. S.! Say no more! ¡Calle! ¡No diga más! to s. away, ausentarse. to s. up, no acostarse; velar. to s. with, quedarse con; alojarse con; quedarse en casa de, vivir con.

stay, s. estancia, permanencia, f.; residencia, f.; (restraint) freno, m.; (law) suspensión, f.; (endurance) aguante, m., resistencia, f.; (naut.) estay, m.; (prop) puntal, m.; (fig.) apoyo, soporte, m.; pl. stays, corsé, m.

stead, s. lugar, m. **in the s. of**, en el lugar de, como substituto de. **It has stood me in good s.**, Me ha sido muy útil

steadfast, a. fijo; constante; firme; tenaz. **s. gaze**, mirada fija, f.

steadfastly, adv. fijamente; con constancia; firmemente; tenazmente

steadfastness, s. fijeza, f.; constancia, f.; firmeza, f.; tenacidad, f.

steadily, adv. firmemente; (without stopping) sin parar; continuamente; (assiduously) diligentemente; (uniformly) uniformemente. **Prices have gone up s.**, Los precios no han dejado de subir. **He looked at it s.**, Lo miraba sin pestañear (or fijamente)

steadiness, s. estabilidad, f.; firmeza, f.; constancia, f.; (of persons) seriedad, formalidad, f.; (of workers) diligencia, asiduidad, f.

steady, a. firme; seguro; fijo; constante; uniforme; continuo; estacionario; (of persons) serio, formal, juicioso; (of workers) diligente, asiduo. v.t. afirmar; (persons) hacer más serio (a); (nerves, etc.) calmar, fortificar a s. job, un empleo seguro. S.! ¡Calma!; (naut.) ¡Seguro! **He steadied himself against the table**, Se apoyó en la mesa

steak, s. tajada, f.; biftec, m.

steal, v.t. robar, hurtar; tomar. v.i. robar, ser ladrón; (glide) deslizarse; (overwhelm) dominar, ganar insensiblemente (a). **to s. a kiss**, robar un beso. **to s. a look at**, mirar de soslayo (or de lado). **to s. away**, escurrirse, escabullirse; marcharse a hurtadillas. **tó s. in**, deslizarse en, colarse en

stealthily, adv. a hurtadillas; a escondidas, furtivamente

stealthiness, s. carácter furtivo, m.

stealthy, a. furtivo; cauteloso

steam, s. vapor, m. a. de vapor. v.i. echar vapor. v.t. (cul.) cocer al vapor; (clothes) mojar; (windows, etc.) empañar. **to have the s. up**, estar bajo presión. **The windows are steamed**, Los cristales están empañados. **s.-boiler**, caldera de vapor, f. **s.-engine**, máquina de vapor, f. **s.-hammer**, maza de fragua, f. **s.-heat**, calefacción por vapor, f. **s.-roller**, apisonadora, f.

steamboat, s. vapor, m.

steamer, s. (cul.) marmita al vacío, f.; (naut.) buque de vapor, m.

steamship, s. buque de vapor, m.

steamy, a. lleno de vapor

steatite, s. esteatita, f.

steed, s. corcel, m.

steel, s. (metal, and poet. sword) acero, m.; (for sharpening) afilón, m. a. de acero; acerado. v.t. acerar; (fig.) endurecer. **to be made of s.**, (fig.) ser de bronce. **He cannot s. himself to do it**, No puede persuadirse a hacerlo. **to s. one's heart**, hacerse duro de corazón. **cold s.**, arma blanca, f. **stainless s.**, acero inoxidable, m. **s.-engraving**, grabado en acero, m.

steelyard, s. romana, f.

steep, a. acantilado, escarpado; precipitoso; (of stairs, etc.) empinado; (of price) exorbitante. v.t. (soak) remojar, empapar; (fig.) absorber; (in a subject) empaparse (en). s. remojo, m. **It's a bit s.!** (fam.) ¡Es un poco demasiado!

steeping, s. remojo, m., maceración, f.

steeple, s. campanario, m., torre, f.; aguja, f.

steeplechase, s. steeplechase, m., carrera de obstáculos, f.

steeplejack, s. reparador de chimeneas, etc., m.

steepness, s. carácter escarpado, m., lo precipitoso

steer, v.t. (naut.) gobernar; (a car, etc.) conducir; (fig.) guiar, conducir. v.i. (naut.) timonear; (naut.) navegar; (aut.) conducir. s. (zool.) novillo, m. **to s. clear of**, evitar. **to s. one's way**

through the crowd, abrirse paso entre la muchedumbre

steerage, s. gobierno, *m.*; (stern) popa, *f.*; (quarters) entrepuente, *m.* **to go s.,** viajar en tercera clase

steering, s. (*naut.*) gobierno, *m.*; (tiller, etc.) gobernalle, timón, *m.*; (of a vehicle) conducción, *f.* **s.-column,** barra de dirección, *f.* **s.-wheel,** (*aut.*) volante de dirección, *m.*; (*naut.*) rueda del timón, *f.*

steersman, s. timonero, *m.*

stellar, *a.* estelar

stem, s. (of a tree) tronco, *m.*; (of a plant) tallo, *m.*; (of a glass, etc.) pie, *m.*; (*mus.*, of a note) rabo, *m.*; (of a pipe) tubo, *m.*; (of a word) radical, *m.* *v.t.* (check) contener; (the tide) ir contra; (the current) vencer; (dam) estancar. **from s. to stern,** de proa a popa

stench, s. tufo, hedor, *m.*, hediondez, *f.*

stencil, s. patrón para estarcir, *m.*; estarcido, *m.* *v.t.* estarcir

stenographer, s. estenógrafo (-fa), taquígrafo (-fa)

stenography, s. estenografía, taquigrafía, *f.*

stentorian, *a.* estentóreo

step, s. paso, *m.*; (footprint) huella, *f.*; (measure) medida, *f.*; (of a stair, etc.) escalón, peldaño, *m.*, grada, *f.*; (of a ladder) peldaño, *m.*; (of vehicles) estribo, *m.*; (grade) escalón, *m.*; (*mus.*) intervalo, *m.* **at every s.,** a cada paso. **flight of steps,** escalera, *f.*; (before a building, etc.) escalinata, *f.* **in steps,** en escalones. **to bend one's steps towards,** dirigirse hacia. **to keep in s.,** llevar el paso. **to take a s.,** dar un paso. **to take steps,** tomar medidas. **s. by s.,** paso a paso; poco a poco. **s.-dance,** baile típico, *m.* **s.-ladder,** escalera de tijera, *f.*

step, *v.i.* dar un paso; pisar; andar. **Please s. in!** Sírvase de entrar. **Will you s. this way, please?** ¡Haga el favor de venir por aquí! **to s. aside,** ponerse a un lado; desviarse; (*fig.*) retirarse (en favor de). **to s. in,** entrar; intervenir (en); (meddle) entrometerse. **He stepped into**

the train, Subió al tren. **to s. on,** pisar. **to s. on board,** (*naut.*) ir a bordo. **to s. out,** salir; (from a vehicle) bajar; (a dance) bailar. **He stepped out a moment ago,** Salió hace un instante

stepbrother, s. hermanastro, medio hermano, *m.*

stepchild, s. hijastro (-ra)

stepdaughter, s. hijastra, *f.*

stepfather, s. padrastro, *m.*

stepmother, s. madrastra, *f.*

steppe, s. estepa, *f.*

stepping-stone, s. pasadera, *f.*; (*fig.*) escabel, escalón, *m.*

stepsister, s. hermanastra, media hermana, *f.*

stepson, s. hijastro, *m.*

stereoscope, s. estereoscopio, *m.*

stereoscopic, *a.* estereoscópico

stereotype, s. estereotipia, *f.*, clisé, *m.* *v.t.* (*print.* and *fig.*) estereotipar

sterile, *a.* estéril; árido

sterility, s. esterilidad, *f.*; aridez, *f.*

sterilization, s. esterilización, *f.*

sterilize, *v.t.* esterilizar

sterilizer, s. esterilizador, *m.*

sterling, *a.* esterlina (*f.*); (*fig.*) genuino. **pound s.,** libra esterlina, *f.*

stern, *a.* severo, austero; duro. s. (*naut.*) popa, *f.*

sternly, *adv.* con severidad, severamente, duramente

sternness, s. severidad, *f.*; dureza, *f.*

sternum, s. (*anat.*) esternón, *m.*

stertorous, *a.* estertoroso

stethoscope, s. estetoscopio, *m.*

stevedore, s. estibador, *m.*

stew, *v.t.* guisar a la cazuela, estofar; (mutton, etc.) hervir; (fruit) cocer. s. estofado, *m.*; (*fam.*) agitación, *f.* **to be in a s.,** (*fam.*) sudar la gota gorda. **stewed fruit,** compota de frutas, *f.* **s.-pot,** cazuela, olla, *f.*, puchero, *m.*

steward, s. administrador, *m.*; mayordomo, *m.*; (provision) despensero, *m.*; (*naut.*) camarero, *m.*

stewardess, s. (*naut.*) camarera, *f*

stick, *v.t.* clavar (en), hundir (en); (put) poner; sacar; (stamps, etc.) pegar; fijar; (endure) resistir; tolerar. *v.i.* clavarse, hundirse; estar clavado; pegarse; (remain) quedar; (in the mud, etc.) atascarse, embarrancarse; (on a reef) encallarse; (in the throat, etc.) atravesarse; (stop) detenerse. It sticks in my throat,(*fam.*) No lo puedo tragar. They cannot s. him, No le pueden ver, No le pueden tragar. Friends always s. together, Los amigos no se abandonan. The nickname stuck to him, El apodo se le quedó. to s. at, persistir en; desistir (ante); pararse (ante); tener escrúpulos sobre. to s. at nothing, no tener escrúpulos. He stuck at his work, Siguió trabajando. to stick down, pegar. to s. out, *v.i.* proyectar; sobresalir. *v.t.* (one's chest) inflar; (one's tongue) sacar. His ears s. out, Tiene las orejas salientes. to s. out for, insistir en su demanda para. to s. to, (one's job) no dejar; (one's plans) adherirse (a); (one's principles) ser fiel (a); (one's friends) no abandonar; (one's word, etc.) cumplir; atenerse a. to s. up, *v.i.* (of hair) erizarse, ponerse de punta; salirse. *v.t.* clavar; (a notice) fijar. to s. up for, (a person) defender

stick, *s.* estaca, *f.*; (for the fire) leña, *f.*; (walking-s.) bastón, *m.*; (of office) vara, *f.*; (of sealing-wax, etc.) barra, *f.*; palo, *m.*; (batón) batuta, *f.*; (of celery) tallo, *m.* in a cleft s., entre la espada y la pared. to give (a person) the s., dar palo (a)

stickiness, *s.* viscosidad, *f.*

sticking-plaster, *s.* esparadrapo, *m.*

stick-in-the-mud, *s.* chapado a la antigua, *m.*

stickler, *s.* rigorista, *m.* and *f.* to be a s. for etiquette, ser etiquetero

sticky, *a.* pegajoso, viscoso; (*fig.*) difícil

stiff, *a.* rígido; inflexible; tieso; (of paste, etc.) espeso; (of manner) distante; (of a bow, etc.) frío; (of a person) almidonado, etiquetero; severo; (of examinations, etc.) difícil; (strong) fuerte; (of price, etc.) alto, exorbitante; (of a shirt front, etc.) duro. s.

with cold, aterido de frío. s. neck, torticolis, *m.* s.-necked, terco, obstinaz

stiffen, *v.t.* reforzar; atiesar; (paste, etc.) hacer más espeso; (*fig.*, strengthen) robustecer; (make more obstinate) hacer más tenaz. *v.i.* atiesarse; endurecerse; (straighten oneself) enderezarse; (of manner) volverse menos cordial; (become firmer) robustecerse; (become more obstinate) hacerse más tenaz. The breeze stiffened, Refrescó el viento

stiffly, *adv.* tiesamente; rígidamente; obstinadamente

stiffness, *s.* rigidez, *f.*; tiesura, *f.*; dureza, *f.*; (of manner) frialdad, *f.*; (obstinacy) terquedad, obstinación, *f.*; (of an examination, etc.) dificultad, *f.*

stifle, *v.t.* ahogar, sofocar; apagar; suprimir

stifling, *a.* sofocante, bochornoso

stigma, *s.* estigma, *m.*

stigmatize, *v.t.* estigmatizar

stile, *s.* (nearest equivalent) portilla con escalones, *f.*

stiletto, *s.* estilete, *m.*

still, *a.* tranquilo; inmóvil; quedo; silencioso; (of wine) no espumoso. *s.* silencio, *m.* in the s. of the night, en el silencio de la noche. Keep s.! ¡Estate quieto! to keep s., quedarse inmóvil, no moverse. s.-birth, nacimiento de un niño muerto, *m.* s.-born, nacido muerto. s. life, (*art*) bodegón, *m.*, naturaleza muerta, *f.*

still, *v.t.* hacer callar, acallar; calmar, tranquilizar; apaciguar; (pain) aliviar

still, *adv.* todavía, aún; (nevertheless) sin embargo, no obstante; (always) siempre. I think she s. visits them every week, Me parece que ella sigue visitándoles cada semana. s. more, aún más

still, *s.* alambique, *m.* salt water s., adrazo, *m.*

stillness, *s.* quietud, tranquilidad, *f.*; silencio, *m.* in the s. of the night, en el silencio de la noche

stilt, *s.* zanco, *m.*

stilted, *a.* ampuloso, campanudo, hinchado

stimulant, *a.* and *s.* estimulante (*m.*)

stimulate, *v.t.* estimular; incitar (a), excitar (a)

stimulating, *a.* estimulante; (encouraging) alentador; (inspiring) sugestivo, inspirador

stimulation, *s.* excitación, *f.*; (stimulus) estímulo, *m.*

stimulus, *s.* estímulo, *m.*; (med.) estimulante, *m.*; (incentive) impulso, incentivo, *m.*; acicate, aguijón, *m.*

sting, *v.t.* picar, pinchar; (of snakes, etc.) morder; (of hot dishes) resquemar; (of hail, etc.) azotar; (pain) atormentar; (provoke) provocar (a), incitar (a). *s.* (zool., organ) aguijón, *m.*; (bot.) púa, *f.*; (of a scorpion) uña, *f.*; (of a serpent) colmillo, *m.*; (pain and wound) pinchazo, *m.*; (serpent's) mordedura, *f.*; (stimulus) acicate, estímulo, *m.*; (torment) tormento, dolor, *m.*

stingily, *adv.* avaramente, tacañamente

stinginess, *s.* tacañería, avaricia, *f.*

stinging, *a.* picante; (fig.) mordaz; (of blows) que duele

stingy, *a.* tacaño, avaro, mezquino

stink, *v.i.* apestar, heder, oler mal. *s.* tufo, *m.*, hediondez, *f.*

stinking, *a.* apestoso, hediondo, fétido, mal oliente

stint, *v.t.* escatimar; limitar. *s.* límite, *m.*, restricción, *f.* **without s.**, sin límite; sin restricción. **He stints himself of bare necessities**, Se niega las meras necesidades de la vida

stipend, *s.* estipendio, salario, *m.*

stipple, *v.t.* (art) puntear. *s.* punteado, *m.*

stipulate, *v.i.* estipular, poner como condición. *v.t.* estipular, especificar. **They stipulated for a five-day week**, Pusieron como condición (or Estipularon) que trabajasen cinco días por semana

stipulation, *s.* estipulación, *f.*; condición, *f.*

stipule, *s.* (bot.) estípula, *f.*

stir, *v.t.* agitar; revolver; (the fire) atizar; (move) mover; (emotionally) conmover, impresionar; (the imagination) estimular. *v.i.* moverse. *s.* movimiento, *m.*;

conmoción, *f.*; (bustle) bullicio, *m.*; sensación, *f.* **Don't s. from your chair**, No te muevas de tu silla. **to make a s.**, causar una sensación. **to s. one's coffee**, revolver el café. **to s. up discontent**, fomentar el descontento

stirring, *a.* conmovedor, emocionante, impresionante; (of times, etc.) turbulento, agitado

stirrup, *s.* estribo, *m.* **s.-cup**, última copa, *f.* **s.-pump**, bomba de mano (para líquidos), *f.*

stitch, *s.* (action) puntada, *f.*; (result) punto, *m.*; (surg.) punto de sutura, *m.*; (pain) punzada, *f.*, pinchazo, *m.* *v.t.* coser; (surg.) suturar

stoat, *s.* armiño, *m.*; (weasel) comadreja, *f.*

stock, *s.* (of a tree) tronco, *m.*; (of a rifle) culata, *f.*; (handle) mango, *m.*; (of a horse's tail) nabo, *m.*; (stem for grafting, etc.) injerto, *m.*; (race) raza, *f.*; (lineage) linaje, *m.*, estirpe, *f.*; (supply) provisión, *f.*; reserva, *f.*; (of merchandise) surtido, *m.*; (cul.) caldo, *m.*; (collar) alzacuello, *m.*; (bot.) alhelí, *m.*; (government) papel del estado, *m.*, valores públicos, *m. pl.*; (financial) valores, *m. pl.*; (of a company) capital, *m.*; *pl.* **stocks**, (hist.) cepo, *m.*; (of goods) existencias, *f. pl.*, stock, *m.* *a.* corriente; del repertorio. **in s.**, en existencia. **live-s.**, ganado, *m.* **rolling-s.**, (r.w.) material móvil ferroviario, *m.* **s. phrase**, frase hecha, *f.* **s. size**, talla corriente, *f.* **to lay in a s. of**, hacer provisión de, almacenar. **to stand s.-still**, quedarse completamente inmóvil. **to take s.**, (com.) hacer inventario. **to take s. of**, inventariar; examinar, considerar. **s.-breeder**, ganadero, *m.* **s.-broker**, corredor de bolsa, bolsista, *m.* **S. Exchange**, Bolsa, *f.* **s.-in-hand**, (com.) existencias, *f. pl.* **s.-in-trade**, (com., etc.) capital, *m.* **s.-raising**, cría de ganados, ganadería, *f.* **s.-taking**, (com.) inventario, *m.*

stock, *v.t.* proveer (de), abastecer (de); (of shops) tener existencia de stockade, s. estacada, empalizada, f. v.t. empalizar

stocking, s. media, f. **nylon stockings**, medias de cristal (or de nilón), f. pl.

stocky, a. rechoncho, doblado, achaparrado

stodgy, a. (of food) indigesto; (of style, etc.) pesado, amazacotado

stoic, a. and s. estoico (-ca).

stoical, a. estoico

stoicism, s. estoicismo, m.

stoke, v.t. (a furnace, etc.) cargar, alimentar; (a fire) echar carbón, etc., en. **s.-hole**, cuarto de fogoneros, m.; (naut.) cámara de calderas, f.

stoker, s. fogonero, m.; (mechanical) cargador, m.

stole, s. (ecc., and of fur, etc.) estola, f.

stolid, a. impasible, imperturbable

stolidity, s. imperturbabilidad, impasibilidad, f.

stolidly, adv. imperturbablemente

stolon, s. (bot.) estolón, m.

stomach, s. estómago, vientre, m.; apetito, estómago, m.; (courage) corazón, valor, m. v.t. digerir; (tolerate) tragar, sufrir. **s.-ache**, dolor de estómago, m. **s.-tube**, sonda gástrica, f.

stomata, s. (bot.) estoma, m.

stomatitis, s. (med.) estomatitis, f.

stone, s. piedra, f.; (gem) piedra preciosa, f.; (of cherries, etc.) hueso, m.; (of grapes, etc.) pepita, f.; (med.) cálculo, m. a. de piedra. v.t. apedrear; (a wall, etc.) revestir de piedra; (fruit) deshuesar. **to pave with stones**, empedrar. **to leave no s. unturned**, no dejar piedra sin remover. **within a stone's throw**, a corta distancia, a un paso. **S. Age**, edad de piedra, f. **s.-breaker**, cantero, picapedrero, m. **s.-cold**, muy frío, completamente frío **s.-deaf**, a. completamente sordo. **s.-fruit**, fruta de hueso, f. **s.-mason**, mazonero, albañil, m.; picapedrero, m. **s.-quarry**, pedrera, cantera, f.

stonecrop, s. (bot.) ombligo de Venus, m.

stonily, adv. fríamente; fijamente, sin pestañear

stoniness, s. lo pedregoso; (of hearts, etc.) dureza, f.; (of stares, etc.) fijeza, inmovilidad, f.

stoning, s. apedreamiento, m., lapidación, f.

stony, a. pedregoso; (of hearts, etc.) duro, insensible, empedernido; (of a stare, etc.) fijo, duro

stook, s. (agr.) tresnal, m.

stool, s. taburete, m.; (fæces) excremento, m.

stoop, v.i. inclinarse, doblarse; encorvarse; ser cargado de espaldas; andar encorvado; (demean oneself) rebajarse (a). v.t. inclinar, doblar. s. inclinación, f.; cargazón de espaldas, f.

stooping, a. inclinado, doblado; (of shoulders) cargado

stop, v.t. (a hole) obstruir, atascar; (a leak) cegar, tapar; (a tooth) empastar; (stanch) restañar; (the traffic, etc.) parar; detener; (prevent) evitar; (discontinue) cesar (de), dejarse de; (cut off) cortar; (end) poner fin (a), acabar con; (payment) suspender. v.i. parar; detenerse; cesar; terminar; (stay) quedarse, permanecer. **I stopped myself from saying what I thought**, Me abstuve de decir lo que pensaba, Me mordí la lengua. **They stopped fifty pesetas out of his wages**, Retuvieron cincuenta pesetas de su sueldo. **They stopped the food-supply**, Cortaron las provisiones. **to s. beating about the bush**, dejarse de historias. **to s. one's ears**, (fig.) taparse los oídos. **to s. payments**, suspender pagos

stop, s. parada, f.; pausa, f.; interrupción, f.; cesación, f.; (of an organ) registro, m. **full s.**, (gram.) punto, m. **tram s.**, parada de tranvía, f. **to come to a full s.**, pararse de golpe; cesar súbitamente. **to put a s. to**, poner fin a, poner coto a, acabar con. **s.-cock**, llave de agua, f., grifo, m. **s.-press news**, noticias de última hora, f. pl. **s.-watch**, cronógrafo, m.

stopgap, s. (person) tapagujeros, m.; substituto, m.

stoppage, *s.* parada, *f.*; cesación, *f.*; suspensión, *f.*; interrupción, *f.*; pausa, *f.*; (obstruction) impedimento, *m.*; obstrucción, *f.* **s. of work,** suspensión de trabajo, *f.*

stopper, *s.* tapón, *m.*; obturador, *m. v.t.* cerrar con tapón, taponar

stopping, *s.* parada, *f.*; cesación, *f.*; suspensión, *f.*; (of a tooth) empaste, *m.* **without s.,** sin parar. **without s. to draw breath,** de un aliento. **s.-place,** paradero, *m.*; (of buses, etc.) parada, *f.* **s. train,** tren ómnibus, *m.* **s. up,** obturación, *f.*

storage, *s.* almacenamiento, *m.*; (charge) almacenaje, *m.*; (place) depósito, *m.* **cold s.,** cámara frigorífica, *f.* **s. battery,** acumulador, *m.*

store, *s.* provisión, *f.*; abundancia, *f.*; reserva, *f.*; (of knowledge, etc.) tesoro, *m.*; (for furniture, etc.) depósito, almacén, *m.*; *pl.* **stores,** (shop) almacenes, *m. pl.*; (food) provisiones, *f. pl.*; (mil., etc.) pertrechos, *m. pl.* *v.t.* proveer; guardar, acumular; tener en reserva; (furniture, etc.) almacenar; (hold) caber en, tomar. **in s.,** en reserva; en depósito, en almacén. **to set s. by,** estimar en mucho; dar importancia a. **to set little s. by,** estimar en poco; conceder poca importancia a. **s.-room,** despensa, *f.*

storehouse, *s.* almacén, *m.*; (fig.) mina; *f.*, tesoro, *m.*

storey, *s.* piso, *m.*

storeyed, *a.* de...pisos. **two-s.,** de dos pisos

stork, *s.* cigüeña, *f.*

storm, *s.* tempestad, tormenta, *f.*, temporal, *m.*; (fig.) tempestad, *f.*; (mil.) asalto, *m. v.t.* (mil.) tomar por asalto, asaltar. *v.i.* (of persons) bramar de cólera. **to take by s.,** tomar por asalto; (fig.) cautivar, conquistar. **s. in a tea-cup,** tempestad en un vaso de agua, *f.* **s.-centre,** centro tempestuoso, *m.* **s.-cloud,** nubarrón, *m.* **s.-cone,** cono, *m.* **s.-signal,** señal de temporal, *f.* **s.-tossed,** *a.* sacudido por la tempestad. **s.-troops,** tropas de asalto, *f. pl.* **s.-window,** contravidriera, *f.*

stormily, *adv.* tempestuosamente; con tormenta

storming, *s.* (mil., etc.) asalto, *m.*; violencia, *f.* **s.-party,** pelotón de asalto, *m.*

stormy, *a.* tempestuoso; de tormenta; (of life, etc.) borrascoso; (of meetings, etc.) tempestuoso

story, *s.* historia, *f.*; cuento, *m.*; anécdota, *f.*; (funny) chiste, *m.*; (plot) argumento, enredo, *m.*; (fib) mentira, *f.* **It's always the same old s.,** Es siempre la misma canción (or historia). **That is quite another s.,** Eso es harina de otro costal. **short s.,** cuento, *m.* **s.-book,** libro de cuentos, *m.* **s.-teller,** cuentista, *m.* and *f.*; (fibber) mentiroso (-sa)

story, *s.* See **storey**

stoup, *s.* copa, *f.*; pila de agua bendita, *f.*

stout, *a.* fuerte; (brave) intrépido, indómito; (fat) gordo, grueso; (firm) sólido, firme; (decided) resuelto; vigoroso. *s.* (drink) cerveza negra, *f.* **s. defence,** defensa resuelta, *f.* **s.-hearted,** valiente, intrépido

stoutly, *adv.* valientemente, vigorosamente; resueltamente

stoutness, *s.* gordura, corpulencia, *f.*; fuerza, *f.*; resolución, *f.*; vigor, *m.*; valor, *m.*

stove, *s.* estufa, *f.*; (open, for cooking) cocina económica, *f.*; (gas, etc., for cooking) cocina, *f.*, fogón, *m.* **s.-pipe,** tubo de la chimenea, *m.*

stow, *v.t.* meter, poner; colocar; (hide) esconder; (cargo) estibar, arrimar

stowaway, *s.* polizón, llovido, *m. v.i.* embarcarse secretamente

strabismus, *s.* (med.) estrabismo, *m.*

straddle, *v.i.* (nav., etc.) graduar el tiro. *v.t.* montar a horcajadas en. **s.-legged,** patiabierto

strafe, *v.t.* bombardear concentradamente; castigar; reñir

straggle, *v.i.* rezagarse; vagar en desorden; dispersarse; estar esparcido; extenderse. **Many cities s. out into the country,** Muchas ciudades se extienden hacia el campo

straggler, *s.* rezagado (-da)

straggling, *a.* disperso; esparcido

straight, *a.* derecho; recto; (of hair) lacio; directo; (tidy) en orden; (frank) franco; (honest) honrado. *adv.* derecho; en línea recta; directamente. **I shall need to put things s.,** Tendré que poner las cosas en orden. **Keep s. on!** ¡Siga Vd. derecho! **out of the s.,** fuera de la plomada. **to go s. to the point,** dejarse de rodeos, ir al grano. **to look s. in the eyes,** mirar derecho en los ojos. **s. away,** inmediatamente, en seguida. **s. out,** sin rodeos

straighten, *v.t.* enderezar; poner derecho; poner en orden; arreglar. *v.i.* ponerse derecho; enderezarse. **to s. one's face,** componer el semblante. **to s. the line,** (*mil.*) rectificar el frente. **to s. out,** poner en orden; (*fig.*) desenredar. **to s. oneself up,** erguirse

straightforward, *a.* honrado, sincero; franco; (simple) sencillo. **s. answer,** respuesta directa, *f.*

straightforwardly, *adv.* honradamente; francamente

straightforwardness, *s.* honradez, integridad, *f.*; franqueza, *f.*; (simplicity) sencillez, *f.*

straightness, *s.* derechura, rectitud, *f.*; (of persons) honradez, probidad, *f.*

straightway, *adv.* al instante, inmediatamente

strain, *v.t.* estirar; forzar; esforzar; (one's eyes) quebrarse; (one's ears) aguzar (el oído); (a muscle, etc.) torcer; (a friendship) pedir demasiado (a), exigir demasiado (de); (a person's patience, etc.) abusar (de); (words) tergiversar; (embrace) abrazar estrechamente (a); (filter) filtrar; (*cul.*) colar. *v.i.* hacer un gran esfuerzo, esforzarse (para). *s.* tirantez, *f.*; tensión, *f.*; (effort) esfuerzo, *m.*; (sprain) torcedura, *f.*; (nervous) tensión nerviosa, *f.*; (*mech.*) esfuerzo, *m.*; (breed) raza, *f.*; (*biol.*) cepa, *f.*; (tendency) tendencia, *f.*; (heredity) herencia, *f.*; rasgo, *m.*, vena, *f.*; (style) estilo, *m.*; (*mus.*) melodía, *f.*; (of mirth, etc.) son, ruido, *m.*; (poetry) poesía, *f.* **to s. a point,** hacer una excepción. **to s. after effect,** buscar demasiado el efecto

strained, *a.* tenso; (of muscles, etc.) torcido; (of smiles, etc.) forzado. **s. relations,** (*pol.*) estado de tirantez, *m.*

strainer, *s.* filtro, *m.*; coladero, *m.*

strait, *s.* (*geog.*) estrecho, *m.* **to be in great straits,** estar en un apuro. **s.-laced,** (*fig.*) de manga estrecha. **s. waistcoat,** camisa de fuerza, *f.*

straiten, *v.t.* estrechar; limitar. **in straitened circumstances,** en la necesidad

strand, *s.* (shore) playa, *f.*; (of a river) ribera, orilla, *f.*; (of rope) cabo, ramal, *m.*; (of thread, etc.) hebra, *f.*; (of hair) trenza, *f.* *v.t.* and *v.i.* (a ship) encallar, varar. **to be stranded,** hallarse abandonado; (by missing a train, etc.) quedarse colgado. **to leave stranded,** abandonar, dejar plantado (a)

strange, *a.* (unknown) desconocido; nuevo; (exotic, etc.) extraño, singular; extraordinario; raro; exótico. **I felt very s. in a s. country,** Me sentía muy solo en un país desconocido. **He is a very s. person,** Él es una persona muy rara

strangely, *adv.* extrañamente, singularmente; de un modo raro

strangeness, *s.* novedad, *f.*; singularidad, *f.*; rareza, *f.*

stranger, *s.* desconocido (-da); (from a foreign country) extranjero (-ra); (from another region, etc.) forastero (-ra). **He is no s. to these problems,** No es ignorante de estos problemas, No desconoce estos problemas

strangle, *v.t.* estrangular; (a sob, etc.) ahogar

stranglehold, to have a (on), tener asido por la garganta; paralizar

strangling, *s.* estrangulación, *f.*

strap, *s.* correa, *f.*; tirante de botas, *m.* *v.t.* atar con correas

strapping, *a.* rozagante, robusto

stratagem, *s.* estratagema, *f.*, ardid, *m.*

strategic, *a.* estratégico

strategically, *adv.* estratégicamente

strategist, *s.* estratego, *m.*

strategy, *s.* estrategia, *f.*

stratification, *s.* estratificación, *f.*

stratosphere, *s.* estratosfera, *f.*

stratum, *s.* (*geol.*) estrato, *m.*, capa, *f.*; (social, etc.) estrato, *m.*

straw, *s.* paja, *f.* **I don't care a s.,** No se me da un bledo. **to be not worth a s.,** no valer un ardite. **to be the last s.,** ser el colmo. **to drink through a s.,** sorber con una paja. **s. hat,** sombrero de paja, *m.* **s.-coloured,** pajizo

strawberry, *s.* (plant and fruit, especially small or wild) fresa, *f.*; (large cultivated) fresón, *m.* **s. bed,** fresal, *m.* **s. ice,** helado de fresa, *m.*

stray, *v.i.* errar, vagar; perderse; (from a path, etc., also *fig.*) descarriarse. *s.* animal perdido, *m.*; niño (-ña) sin hogar. *a.* descarriado, perdido; errante; (sporadic) esporádico

streak, *s.* raya, *f.*; (in wood and stone) vena, *f.*; (of light) rayo, *m.*; (of humour, etc.) rasgo, *m.* *v.t.* rayar. **like a s. of lightning,** como un relámpago

streaky, *a.* rayado; (of bacon) entreverado

stream, *s.* arroyo, riachuelo, *m.*; río, *m.*; (current) corriente, *f.*; (of words, etc.) torrente, *m.* *v.i.* correr, fluir; manar, brotar; (float) flotar, ondear. *v.t.* (blood, etc.) manar, echar. **The tears streamed down Jean's cheeks,** Las lágrimas corrían por las mejillas de Juana. **s.-lined,** fuselado

streamer, *s.* gallardete, *m.*; (on a hat, etc.) cinta colgante, *f.*, siguemepollo, *m.*

streamlet, *s.* arroyuelo, *m.*

street, *s.* calle, *f.* **the man in the s.,** el hombre medio. **s. arab,** golfo, *m.* **s. cries,** gritos de vendedores ambulantes, *m. pl.* **s. entertainer,** saltabanco, *m.* **s. fighting,** luchas en las calles, *f. pl.* **s. musician,** músico ambulante, *m.* **s. sweeper,** barrendero, *m.* **s. walker,** buscona, prostituta, *f.*

strength, *s.* fuerza, *f.*; (of colours, etc.) intensidad, *f.*; (of character) firmeza (de carácter), *f.*; (of will) resolución, decisión, *f.*; (*mil.*) complemento, *m.* **The enemy is in s.,** El enemigo está

presente en gran número. **by sheer s.,** a viva fuerza. **on the s. of,** confiando en, en razón de

strengthen, *v.t.* fortificar; consolidar; reforzar. *v.i.* fortificarse; consolidarse; reforzarse

strengthening, *a.* fortificante; tonificante. *s.* refuerzo, *m.*; fortificación, *f.*; consolidación, *f.*

strenuous, *a.* activo, enérgico; vigoroso; (arduous) arduo

strenuously, *adv.* enérgicamente, vigorosamente

strenuousness, *s.* energía, *f.*, vigor, *m.*; (arduousness) arduidad, *f.*

streptococcus, *s.* (*med.*) estreptococo, *m.*

streptomycine, *s.* (*med.*) estreptomicina, *f.*

stress, *s.* tensión, *f.*; impulso, *m.*; importancia, *f.*, énfasis, *m.*; (*gram.*) acento (tónico), *m.*; acentuación, *f.*; (*mech.*) esfuerzo, *m.* *v.t.* acentuar; poner énfasis en, insistir en. **under s. of circumstance,** impulsado por las circunstancias. **times of s.,** tiempos turbulentos, *m. pl.* **to lay great s. on,** insistir mucho en; dar gran importancia a

stretch, *v.t.* (make bigger) ensanchar; (pull) estirar; (one's hand, etc.) alargar, extender; (knock down) tumbar. *v.i.* ensancharse; dar de sí; ceder; extenderse. **to s. oneself,** estirarse, desperezarse. **to s. as far as,** llegar hasta, extenderse hasta. **to s. a point,** hacer una concesión. **to s. one's legs,** estirar las piernas

stretch, *s.* estirón, *m.*; tensión, *f.*; (of country, etc.) extensión, *f.*; (scope) alcance, *m.* **by a s. of the imagination,** con un esfuerzo de imaginación. **He can sleep for hours at a s.,** Puede dormir durante horas enteras

stretcher, *s.* (for gloves) ensanchador, *m.*; dilatador, *m.*; (for canvas) bastidor, *m.*; (for wounded, etc.) camilla, *f.* **s. bearer,** camillero, *m.*

strew, *v.t.* esparcir; derramar

stricken, *a.* (wounded) herido; (ill) enfermo; (with grief) afligido, agobiado de dolor. **s. in years,** entrado en años

strict, *a.* exacto; estricto; escrupuloso; severo

strictly, *adv.* exactamente; estrictamente; severamente, con severidad. **s. speaking,** en rigor, en realidad

strictness, *s.* exactitud, *f.*; escrupulosidad, *f.*; rigor, *m.*; severidad, *f.*

stricture, *s.* (*fig.*) crítica severa, censura, *f.* **to pass strictures on,** criticar severamente

stride, *v.i.* andar a pasos largos, dar zancadas; cruzar a grandes trancos. *v.t.* cruzar de un tranco; poner una pierna en cada lado de. *s.* zancada, *f.*, paso largo, tranco, *m.* **to s. up and down,** dar zancadas

strident, *a.* estridente; (of colours) chillón

strife, *s.* lucha, *f.*, conflicto, *m.*

strike, *v.t.* golpear; pegar, dar una bofetada (a); (wound) herir; (a coin) acuñar; (a light) encender; (of a snake) morder; (a blow) asestar, dar; (of ships, a rock, etc.) chocar contra; estrellarse contra; (flags) bajar, arriar; (a tent) desmontar; (camp) levantar; (come upon) llegar a; (discover) encontrar por casualidad, tropezar con; hallar, descubrir; (seem) parecer; (impress) impresionar; (of ideas) ocurrirse; (an attitude) tomar, adoptar; (of a clock) dar; (a balance) hacer; (a bargain) cerrar, llegar a; (level) nivelar; (cuttings) enraciar. *v.i.* golpear; (of a clock) dar la hora; (of a ship) encallar; (go) ir; (penetrate) penetrar; (of a cutting) arraigar; (sound) sonar. **He struck the table with his fist,** Golpeó la mesa con el puño. **I was very much struck by the city's beauty,** La belleza de la ciudad me impresionó mucho. **The news struck fear into their hearts,** La noticia les llenó el corazón de miedo. **John struck in with a question about Italy,** Juan interpuso una pregunta sobre Italy. **The clock struck three,** El reloj dió las tres. **The hour has struck,** (*fig.*) Ha llegado la hora. **How did the house s. you?** ¿Qué te pareció la casa? **to s. a bargain,** cerrar un trato. **to s. a blow,** asestar un golpe. **to s. across country,** ir a campo traviesa. **to s. an attitude,** tomar una actitud. **to s. home,** dar en el blanco; herir; herir en lo más vivo; hacerse sentir. **to s. at,** asestar un golpe (a); acometer, embestir; atacar. **to s. down,** derribar; (of illness) acometer. **to s. off,** (a head, etc.) cortar; (a name) borrar, tachar; (print) imprimir. **to s. out,** *v.i.* asestar un golpe (a); (of a swimmer) nadar; echarse, lanzarse. *v.t.* (a word, etc.) borrar, rayar; (begin) iniciar. **to s. through,** (cross out) rayar, tachar; (of the sun's rays, etc.) penetrar. **to s. up,** *v.t.* tocar; empezar a cantar; (a friendship) trabar. *v.i.* empezar a tocar. **to s. up a march,** (*mil.*) batir la marcha

strike, *s.* huelga, *f.* *v.i.* declararse en huelga. **go-slow s.,** trabajo al ralenti, *m.* **lock-out s.,** huelga patronal, *f.* **sit-down s.,** huelga de brazos caídos, *f.* **to go on s.,** declararse en huelga. **s.-breaker,** esquirol, *m.* **s.-pay,** subsidio de huelga, *m.*

striker, *s.* huelguista, *m.* and *f.*

striking, *a.* notable, sorprendente; (impressive) impresionante; que llama la atención; llamativo

string, *s.* bramante, *m.*; cuerda, *f.*; (ribbon) cinta, *f.*; (of beads, etc.) sarta, *f.*; (of onions) ristra, *f.*; (of horses, etc.) reata, *f.*; hilera, *f.*; (of a bridge) cable, *m.*; (of oaths, lies) sarta, serie, *f.*; (of beans) fibra, *f.* *v.t.* encordar; (beads, etc.) ensartar; (beans) quitar las fibras (de). **He is all strung up,** Se le crispan los nervios. **the strings,** los instrumentos de cuerda. **a s. of pearls,** un collar de perlas. **for strings,** (*mus.*) para arco. **to pull strings,** (*fig.*) manejar los hilos. **to s. up,** (an instrument) templar; (a person) pender, ahorcar. **s. beans,** judías verdes, *f. pl.*

stringed, *a.* (of musical instruments) de cuerda. **s. instrument,** instrumento de cuerda, *m.*

stringency, *s.* severidad, *f.*; estrechez, *f.*

stringent, *a.* estricto, severo

stringy, *a.* fibroso; filamentoso; correoso; arrugado

strip, *v.t.* desnudar; despojar (de), quitar; robar; (a cow) ordeñar hasta agotar la leche. *v.i.* desnudarse. *s.* (tatter) jirón, *m.*; tira, lista, *f.*; (of wood) listón, *m.*; (of earth) pedazo, *m.*; (geog., of land) zona, *f.* **to s. off,** *v.t.* quitar; (bark from a tree) descortezar; (one's clothes) despojarse de. *v.i.* desprenderse, separarse

stripe, *s.* raya, lista, *f.*; (mil., etc.) galón, *m.*; (lash) azote, *m.* *v.i.* rayar. **the stripes of the tiger,** las rayas del tigre

striped, *a.* listado, a rayas; con rayas. **s. trousers,** pantalón de corte, *m.*

stripling, *s.* joven imberbe, pollo, mancebo, *m.*

strive, *v.i.* esforzarse (a); pugnar (por, para); trabajar (por); (fight against) luchar contra; pelear con. **He was striving to understand,** Pugnaba por (or Se esforzaba a) comprender

stroke, *s.* (blow) golpe, *m.*; (of the oars) golpe del remo, *m.*, remada, *f.*; (at billiards) tacada, *f.*; (in golf) tirada, *f.*; (in swimming) braza, *f.*; (of a clock) campanada, *f.*; (of a pen) rasgo de la pluma, *m.*; (of a brush) pincelada, *f.*; (mech.) golpe de émbolo, *m.*; (caress) caricia con la mano, *f.* *v.t.* acariciar con la mano. **on the s. of six,** al acabar de dar las seis. **They haven't done a s. of work to-day,** No han hecho absolutamente nada hoy. **to have a s.,** tener un ataque de apoplejía. **s. of genius,** rasgo de ingenio, *m.* **s. of good luck,** racha de buena suerte, *f.*

stroll, *v.i.* pasearse, vagar. *s.* vuelta, *f.*, paseo, *m.* **to go for a s.,** dar una vuelta

stroller, *s.* paseante, *m.* and *f.*

strolling, *a.* errante; ambulante. **s. player,** *s.* comico (-ca) ambulante

strong, *a.* fuerte; vigoroso; robusto; enérgico; firme; poderoso; (of colours) intenso, vivo; (of tea, coffee) cargado; (gram.) fuerte. **The government took s. measures,** El gobierno tomóba medidas enérgicas. **They gave very s. reasons,** Alegaron unas razones muy poderosas. **He is a s. believer in the monarchy,** Cree firmemente en la monarquía. **Grammar is not his s. point,** La gramática no es su fuerte. **The enemy is s. in numbers,** El enemigo es numéricamente fuerte. **The society is four thousand s.,** La sociedad tiene cuatro mil miembros. **s.-box,** caja de caudales, *f.* **s.-man,** hombre fuerte, *m.*; (in a circus) hércules, *m.* **s.-minded,** de espíritu fuerte; independiente. **s.-room,** cámara acorazada, *f.*

stronghold, *s.* fortaleza, *f.*; refugio, *m.*

strongly, *adv.* vigorosamente; fuertemente; firmemente

strop, *s.* (razor) suavizador, *m.* *v.t.* suavizar

strophe, *s.* estrofa, *f.*

structural, *a.* estructural

structurally, *adv.* estructuralmente, desde el punto de vista de la estructura

structure, *s.* estructura, *f.*; edificio, *m.*; construcción, *f.*

struggle, *v.i.* luchar; pelear; disputarse. *s.* lucha, *f.*; combate, *m.*; conflicto, *m.* **to s. to one's feet,** luchar por levantarse. **without a s.,** sin luchar

struggling, *a.* pobre, indigente, que lucha para vivir

strum, *v.t.* (a stringed instrument) rascar; tocar mal

strumpet, *s.* ramera, *f.*

strut, *v.i.* pavonearse. *v.t.* (prop) apuntalar. *s.* pavonada, *f.*; (prop) puntal, *m.* **to s. out,** salir de un paso majestuoso

strychnine, *s.* estricnina, *f.*

stub, *s.* (of a tree) tocón, *m.*; (of a pencil, candle, etc.) cabo, *m.*; pedazo, fragmento, *m.*; (of a cigarette or cigar) colilla, *f.* **s.-book,** talonario, *m.*

stubble, *s.* rastrojo, *m.*; (beard) barba de tres días, *f.*

stubborn, *a.* inquebrantable, tenaz; persistente; (pig-headed) terco, testarudo

stubbornness, *s.* tenacidad, *f.*; terquedad, testarudez, *f.*

stucco, *s.* estuco, *m.* *v.t.* estucar

stud, *s.* (of horses) caballeriza, *f.*; (nail) tachón, *m.*; (for collars) pasador para camisas, *m.* *v.t.* tachonar; sembrar. **dress s.,** botón de la pechera, *m.* **s.-farm,** potrero, *m.*

student, *s.* estudiante, *m.* and *f.* *a.* estudiantil

studied, *a.* estudiado; calculado; (of style) cerebral, reflexivo; (intentional) deliberado

studio, *s.* estudio, *m.* **broadcasting s.,** estudio de emisión, *m.*

studious, *a.* estudioso, aplicado; (deliberate) intencional, deliberate; (eager) solícito, ansioso

studiously, *adv.* estudiosamente; con intención, deliberadamente; solícitamente

study, *s.* estudio, *m.*; solicitud, *f.*, cuidado, *m.*; investigación, *f.*; (room) gabinete, cuarto de trabajo, *m.* *v.t.* ocuparse de, cuidar de, atender a; considerar; estudiar; examinar; (the stars) observar; (try) procurar. *v.i.* estudiar. **in a brown s.,** en Babia. **to make a s. of,** hacer un estudio de, estudiar. **to s. for an examination,** prepararse para un examen

stuff, *s.* substancia, materia, *f.*; (fabric) tela, *f.*, paño, *m.*; (rubbish) cachivaches, *m.* *pl.*, cosas, *f. pl.* *a.* de estofa. *v.t.* henchir; llenar; (cul.) rellenar; (with food) ahitar (de); (cram) atestar, apretar; (furniture) rehenchir; (an animal, bird) disecar; (put) meter, poner. **S. and nonsense!** ¡Patrañas! **to be poor s.,** ser de pacotilla; no valer para nada

stuffiness, *s.* mala ventilación, *f.*; falta de aire, *f.*; calor, *m.*

stuffing, *s.* (of furniture) rehenchimiento, *m.*; (cul.) relleno, *m.*

stuffy, *a.* mal ventilado, poco aireado, ahogado

stultify, *v.t.* hacer inútil; invalidar; hacer ridículo

stumble, *v.i.* tropezar; dar un traspié; (in speaking) tartamudear. *s.* tropezón, *m.*; traspié, *m.* **to s. through a speech,** pronunciar un discurso a tropezones. **to s. against,** tropezar contra. **to s. upon, across,** tropezar con; encontrar por casualidad

stumbling-block, *s.* tropiezo, impedimento, *m.*

stump, *s.* (of a tree) tocón, *m.*; (of an arm, leg) muñón, *m.*; (of a pencil, candle) cabo, *m.*; (of a tooth) raigón, *m.*; (of a cigar) colilla, *f.*; (cricket) poste, montante, *m.*; (art) esfumino, *m.*; (leg) pata, *f.* *v.t.* (disconcert) desconcertar; (art) esfumar; recorrer. **to s. up,** (fam.) pagar

stun, *v.t.* dejar sin sentido (a); aturdir de un golpe (a); (astound) pasmar

stunning, *a.* aturdidor; que pasma; (fam.) estupendo

stunt, *v.t.* impedir el crecimiento de; encanijar. *s.* (advertising) anuncio de. reclamo, *m.*; recurso (para conseguir algo), *m.*; proeza, *f.*

stunted, *a.* (of trees, etc.) enano; (of children) encanijado; (of intelligence) inmaduro

stupefaction, *s.* estupefacción, *f.*; estupor, *m.*

stupefy, *v.t.* atontar, embrutecer; causar estupor (a), asombrar

stupendous, *a.* asombroso; enorme

stupid, *a.* (with sleep, etc.) atontado; (silly) estúpido, tonto. *s.* tonto (-ta)

stupidity, *s.* estupidez, *f.*; tontería, *f.*

stupidly, *adv.* estúpidamente

stupor, *s.* estupor, *m.*

sturdiness, *s.* robustez, *f.*, vigor, *m.*; firmeza, tenacidad, *f.*

sturdy, *a.* robusto, vigoroso, fuerte; firme, tenaz

sturgeon, *s.* (icht.) esturión, *m.*

stutter, *v.i.* tartamudear. *v.t.* balbucir. *s.* tartamudeo, *m.*

stutterer, *s.* tartamudo (-da)

stuttering, *a.* tartamudo; balbuciente. *s.* tartamudeo, *m.*

sty, *s.* (pig) pocilga, *f.*; (med.) orzuelo, *m.*

Stygian, *a.* estigio

style, *s.* (for etching) buril, *m.*;
(*lit., art, arch.,* etc.) estilo, *m.*;
(fashion) moda, *f.*; (model)
modelo, *m.*; (behaviour, etc.)
tono, *m.*; elegancia, *f.*; (kind)
especie, clase, *f.*; (designation)
tratamiento, *m.*; *v.t.* llamar,
nombrar. **the latest styles
from Madrid,** los últimos
modelos de Madrid. **He has a
very individual s.,** Su estilo es
muy personal. **They live in
great s.,** Viven en gran lujo
stylet, *s.* estilete, *m.*
stylish, *a.* elegante
stylishness, *s.* elegancia, *f.*
stylist, *s.* estilista, *m.* and *f.*
stylize, *v.t.* estilizar
suasion, *s.* persuasión, *f.*
suasive, *a.* suasorio, persuasivo
suave, *a.* afable, cortés, urbano;
(of wine) suave
suavity, *s.* afabilidad, urbanidad,
f.
sub-alpine, *a.* subalpino
subaltern, *s.* (*mil.*) subalterno, *m.*
a. subalterno, subordinado
subcommittee, *s.* subcomisión, *f.*
subconscious, *a.* subconsciente.
the s., la subconsciencia
subconsciously, *adv.* subcons-
cientemente
subcutaneous, *a.* subcutáneo
subdivide, *v.t.* subdividir. *v.i.*
subdividirse
subdivision, *s.* subdivisión, *f.*
subdominant, *s.* (*mus.*) subdominante, *f.*
subdue, *v.t.* subyugar, sojuzgar,
vencer; (one's passions) dominar;
(colours, voices) suavizar; (lessen)
mitigar; apagar
subdued, *a.* (of colours) apagado;
(of persons) sumiso; (depressed)
deprimido, melancólico. **in a s.
voice,** en voz baja
sub-editor, *s.* subdirector, *m.*
subheading, *s.* subtítulo, *m*
subhuman, *a.* subhumano
subject, *a.* sujeto; sometido (a);
expuesto (a). *s.* (of a country)
súbdito (-ta); sujeto, *m.*; (of
study) asignatura, materia, *f.*;
(theme) tema, *m.*; (*gram., phil.*)
sujeto, *m. v.t.* subyugar; someter.
**It can only be done s. to his
consent,** Podrá hacerse únicamente si él lo consiente. **He is a
British s.,** Es súbdito británico.

to change the s., cambiar de
conversación. **to s. to criticism,**
criticar (a). **s.-matter,** materia,
f.; (of a letter) contenido, *m.*
subjection, *s.* sujeción, *f.*; sometimiento, *m.* **He was in a state
of complete s.,** Estaba completamente sumiso. **to bring
into s.,** subyugar
subjective, *a.* subjetivo
subjectively, *adv.* subjetiva-
mente
subjectiveness, *s.* subjetividad,
f.
subjectivism, *s.* subjetivismo, *m.*
subjoin, *v.t.* añadir, adjuntar
subjugate, *v.t.* subyugar, someter
subjugation, *s.* subyugación, *f.*
subjunctive, *a.* and *s.* subjuntivo
(*m.*)
sublessee, *s.* subarrendatario
(-ia)
sublet, *v.t.* subarrendar. *s.* subarriendo, *m.*
sublieutenant, *s.* (*nav.*) alférez de
fragata, *m.*
sublimate, *v.t.* sublimar. *s.*
sublimado, *m.*
sublimation, *s.* sublimación, *f.*
sublime, *a.* sublime; absoluto,
completo; extremo. **the s.,** lo
sublime
sublimely, *adv.* sublimemente;
completamente
sublimity, *s.* sublimidad, *f.*
sub-machine gun, *s.* pistola
ametralladora, *f.*
submarine, *a.* submarino. *s.*
submarino, *m.* **midget s.,** submarino enano, submarino de
bolsillo, *m.* **s. chaser,** cazasubmarino, *m.*
submerge, *v.t.* sumergir; inundar.
v.i. sumergirse. **The submarine
submerged,** El submarino se
sumergió
submergence, *s.* sumergimiento,
m., sumersión, *f.*; hundimiento,
m.
submersible, *a.* sumergible
submersion, *s.* sumersión, *f.*;
hundimiento, *m.*
submission, *s.* sometimiento, *m.*;
sumisión, resignación, *f.*; docilidad, *f.*
submissive, *a.* sumiso, dócil,
manso
submissively, *adv.* sumisamente,
con docilidad

submissiveness, s. sumisión, docilidad, f.

submit, v.t. someterse (a); doblarse ante; (a scheme, etc.) someter; presentar; (urge) proponer. v.i. someterse; resignarse; (surrender) rendirse, entregarse. **to s. to arbitration,** someter a arbitraje

subnormal, a. anormal

subordinate, a. subordinado; subalterno, inferior; secundario. s. subordinado (-da). v.t. subordinar.

subordination, s. subordinación, f.

suborn, v.t. sobornar, cohechar

subpœna, s. citación, f. v.t. citar

subscribe, v.t. and v.i. subscribir; (to a periodical, etc.) abonarse (a)

subscriber, s. subscriptor (-ra); abonado (-da)

subscription, s. subscripción, f.; (to a periodical, series of concerts, etc.) abono, m.; (to a club) cuota, f.

subsection, s. subsección, f.

subsequent, a. subsiguiente, subsecuente; posterior. **s. to,** después de, posterior a. **s. upon,** de resultas de

subsequently, adv. más tarde; subsiguientemente; posteriormente

subservience, s. servilidad, f.; utilidad, f.

subservient, a. servil; subordinado; útil

subside, v.i. (of water) bajar; (of ground) hundirse; (of foundations) asentarse; disminuir; calmarse; (be quiet) callarse. **to s. into a chair,** dejarse caer en un sillón

subsidence, s. hundimiento, m.; desplome, derrumbamiento, m.; (of floods) bajada, f.; (of anger, etc.) apaciguamiento, m.

subsidiary, a. subsidiario

subsidize, v.t. subvencionar

subsidy, s. subvención, f., subsidio, m.; prima, f.

subsist, v.i. subsistir

subsistence, s. subsistencia, f.

subsoil, s. subsuelo, m.

substance, s. substancia, f.

substantial, a. substancial; sólido; importante

substantially, adv. substancialmente; sólidamente

substantiate, v.t. establecer, verificar; justificar

substantiation, s. comprobación, verificación, f.; justificación, f.

substantive, a. real, independiente; (gram.) substantivo. s. (gram.) substantivo, m.

substitute, s. substituto (-ta); (material) substituto, m. v.t. substituir, reemplazar. **to be a s. for,** hacer las veces de

substitution, s. substitución, f., reemplazo, m.

substratum, s. substrato, m.

subterfuge, s. subterfugio, m.; evasiva, f.

subterranean, a. subterráneo

subtitle, s. subtítulo, m.; (on films) guión, m.

subtle, a. sutil; delicado; penetrante; (crafty) astuto

subtlety, s. sutileza, f.; delicadeza, f.; (craftiness) astucia, f.

subtly, adv. sutilmente; con delicadeza

subtract, v.t. restar, substraer

subtraction, s. resta, substracción, f.

suburb, s. suburbio, m.; pl. **suburbs,** afueras, f. pl.

suburban, a. suburbano

subvention, s. subvención, f.

subversion, s. subversión, f.

subversive, a. subversivo

subvert, v.t. subvertir

subway, s. pasaje subterráneo, m.

succeed, v.t. seguir (a); suceder (a); heredar. v.i. seguir (a); suceder (a); (be successful) tener éxito. **I did not s. in doing it,** No logré hacerlo. **to s. to the throne,** subir al trono

succeeding, a. subsiguiente; futuro; consecutivo; sucesivo

success, s. éxito, m.; triunfo, m. **to be a s.,** tener éxito

successful, a. que tiene éxito; afortunado, venturoso; próspero. **The film was very s.,** La película tuvo mucho éxito

successfully, adv. con éxito; prósperamente

succession, s. sucesión, f.; (series) serie, f.; (inheritance) herencia, f.; (descendants) descendencia, f. **in s.,** sucesivamente

successive, *a.* sucesivo

successively, *adv.* sucesivamente

successor, *s.* sucesor (-ra)

succinct, *a.* sucinto, conciso

succinctly, *adv.* sucintamente, brevemente, en pocas palabras

succour, *v.t.* socorrer, auxiliar. *s.* socorro, *m.*, ayuda, *f.*

succulence, *s.* suculencia, *f.*

succulent, *a.* suculento

succumb, *v.i.* sucumbir; someterse, ceder

such, *a.* tal; parecido, semejante; así; tanto; (before an adjective, adverb) tan. *s.* el, *m.* (*f.* la) que, los, *m. pl.* (*f. pl.* las) que; tal. **s. men,** tales hombres. **I have never seen s. magnificence,** No he visto nunca tanta magnificencia. **s. an important man,** un hombre tan importante. **s. pictures as these,** cuadros como estos. **S. is life!** ¡ Así es la vida! **science as s.,** la ciencia como tal. **s.-and-s.,** tal y tal

suchlike, *a.* parecido, semejante; de esta clase

suck, *v.t.* chupar; (the breast) mamar; sorber; (of a vacuum cleaner, etc.) aspirar. *s.* chupada, *f.*; succión, *f.* **to s. down,** tragar. **to s. up,** aspirar; absorber

sucker, *s.* (*zool.*) ventosa, *f.*; (*bot.*) acodo, mugrón, *m.*; (greenhorn) primo, *m.*; (pig) lechón, *m.*

sucking-pig, *s.* lechón, cochinillo, *m.*

suckle, *v.t.* amamantar, dar el pecho (a)

suction, *s.* succión, *f.*; aspiración, *f.* **s.-pump,** bomba aspirante, *f.*

Sudanese, *a.* and *s.* sudanés (-esa)

sudden, *a.* súbito; (unexpected) inesperado, impensado; (of bends) brusco. **all of a s.,** de repente; súbitamente

suddenly, *adv.* súbitamente; de pronto, de repente

suddenness, *s.* carácter repentino, *m.*; (of a bend, etc.) brusquedad, *f.*

suds, *s. pl.* jabonaduras, *f. pl.*; espuma, *f.*

sue, *v.t.* (*law*) proceder contra, pedir en juicio; (*law*) demandar; (beg) suplicar. **to sue for peace,** pedir la paz

suède, *s.* ante, *m.* **s. gloves,** guantes de ante, *m. pl.*

suet, *s.* sebo, *m.*

suffer, *v.t.* sufrir, padecer; pasar, experimentar; (tolerate) tolerar, sufrir; (allow) permitir. *v.i.* sufrir. **She suffers from her environment,** Ella es la víctima de su medio ambiente

sufferance, *s.* tolerancia, *f.* **on s.,** por tolerancia

sufferer, *s.* enfermo (-ma); víctima, *f.*

suffering, *s.* sufrimiento, padecimiento, *m.*; dolor, *m.* *a.* sufriente

suffice, *v.i.* ser suficiente, bastar. *v.t.* satisfacer

sufficiency, *s.* suficiencia, *f.*; (of money) subsistencia, *f.*

sufficient, *a.* suficiente, bastante. **to be s.,** bastar, ser suficiente

sufficiently, *adv.* suficientemente, bastante

suffix, *s.* (*gram.*) sufijo, *m.*

suffocate, *v.t.* ahogar, sofocar, asfixiar. *v.i.* sofocarse, asfixiarse

suffocating, *a.* sofocante, asfixiante

suffocation, *s.* sofocación, asfixia, *f.*; ahogo, *m.*

suffrage, *s.* sufragio, *m.*; voto, *m.* **universal s.,** sufragio universal, *m.*

suffragette, *s.* sufragista, *f.*

suffuse, *v.t.* bañar, inundar, cubrir

sufism, *s.* sufismo, *m.*

sugar, *s.* azúcar, *m.* *v.t.* azucarar. **brown s.,** azúcar moreno, *m.* **loaf s.,** azúcar de pilón, *m.* **white s.,** azúcar blanco, *m.* **to s. the pill,** dorar la píldora. **s.-almond,** peladilla, *f.* **s.-basin,** azucarera, *f.* **s.-beet,** remolacha, *f.* **s.-candy,** azúcar candi, *m.* **s.-cane,** caña de azúcar, *f.* **s.-cane syrup,** miel de caña, *f.* **s.-paste,** alfeñique, *m.*, alcorza, *f.* **s.-refinery,** fábrica de azúcar, *f.* **s.-tongs,** tenacillas para azúcar, *f. pl.*

sugary, *a.* azucarado; (*fig.*) meloso, almibarado

suggest, *v.t.* implicar; indicar, dar a entender; sugerir; (advise) aconsejar; (hint) insinuar; (evoke) evocar. **I suggested they should go to London,** Les aconsejé que fueran a Londres.

An idea suggested itself to him, Una idea se le ocurrió

suggestion, *s.* sugestión, *f.*; insinuación, *f.*

suggestive, *a.* sugestivo; estimulante

suicidal, *a.* suicida. s. tendency, tendencia suicida, tendencia al suicidio, *f.*

suicide, *s.* (act) suicidio, *m.*; (person) suicida, *m. and f.* to commit s., suicidarse

suit, *s.* (request) petición, súplica, *f.*; oferta de matrimonio, *f.*; (*law*) pleito, *m.*; (of clothes) traje, *m.*; (cards) palo, *m.*; (of cards held) serie, *f. v.t.* convenir; sentar; ir bien (a); venir bien (a); (adapt) adaptar. S. yourself! ¡Haz lo que quieras! The arrangement suits me very well, El arreglo me viene muy bien. The climate doesn't s. me, El clima no me sienta bien. The colour does not s. you, El color no te va bien. to follow s., seguir el ejemplo (de); (cards) jugar el mismo palo. s.-case, maleta, *f.*

suitability, *s.* conveniencia, *f.*; aptitud, *f.*

suitable, *a.* conveniente; apropiado; apto; a propósito. Not s. for children, No apto para menores. to make s. for, adaptar a las necesidades de

suitably, *adv.* convenientemente; apropiadamente

suite, *s.* (of retainers, etc.) séquito, acompañamiento, *m.*; (of furniture, etc.) juego, *m.*; (*mus.*) suite, *f.* private s., habitaciones particulares, *f. pl.* s. of rooms, apartamento, *m.*

suitor, *s.* (*law*) demandante, *m.*; pretendiente, *m.*

sulk, *v.i.* ponerse malhumorado, ser mohino

sulkiness, *s.* mohina, *f.*, mal humor, *m.*

sulky, *a.* mohino, malhumorado

sullen, *a.* taciturno, hosco; malhumorado, sombrío; (of a landscape, etc.) triste, sombrío

sullenly, *adv.* taciturnamente, hoscamente

sullenness, *s.* taciturnidad, hosquedad, *f.*, mal humor, *m.*

sully, *v.t.* desdorar, empañar; manchar

sulphanilamide, *s.* sulfanilamida, *f.*

sulphate, *s.* sulfato, *m.*

sulphide, *s.* sulfuro, *m.*

sulphite, *s.* sulfito, *m.*

sulphonal, *s.* sulfonal, *m.*

sulphur, *s.* azufre, *m.*

sulphuric, *a.* sulfúrico

sulphurous, *a.* sulfuroso

sultan, *s.* sultán, *m.*

sultana, *s.* sultana, *f.*; pasa de Esmirna, *f.*

sultanate, *s.* sultanía, *f.*

sultriness, *s.* bochorno, calor sofocante, *m.*

sultry, *a.* bochornoso, sofocante

sum, *s.* suma, *f.*; total, *m.*; cantidad, *f.*; (in arithmetic) problema (de aritmética), *m. v.t.* sumar, calcular. in sum, en suma; en resumen. to sum up, recapitular; resumir; (a person) tomar las medidas (a)

summarily, *adv.* someramente; (*law*) sumariamente

summarize, *v.t.* resumir brevemente; compendiar

summary, *a.* somero; (*law*) sumario. *s.* resumen, sumario, compendio, *m.*

summer, *s.* verano, estío, *m.* to spend the s., veranear. s.-house, cenador, *m.* s.-time, verano, *m.*; hora de verano, *f.* s. wheat, trigo tremesino, *m.*

summing-up, *s.* recapitulación, *f.*

summit, *s.* cima, cumbre, *f.*; (*fig.*) apogeo, *m.*

summon, *v.t.* llamar, hacer venir; mandar, requerir; (*law*) citar. to s. up one's courage, cobrar ánimos

summons, *s.* llamamiento, *m.*; (*mil.*) intimación, *f.*; (*law*) citación, *f. v.t.* (*law*) citar

sump, *s.* (of a motor-car) pozo colector, *m.*; (*min.*) sumidero, *m.*

sumptuous, *a.* suntuoso, lujoso, magnífico

sumptuousness, *s.* suntuosidad, magnificencia, *f.*

sun, *s.* sol, *m.* The sun was shining, Hacía sol, El sol brillaba. to bask in the sun, tomar el sol. sun-bathing, baños de sol, *m. pl.* sun-blind, toldo para

el sol, *m.* **sun-bonnet,** capelina,
f. **sun-glasses,** gafas ahumadas,
f. pl. **sun-helmet,** casco colonial,
m. **sun-spot,** *(ast.)* mancha del
sol, *f.;* (freckle) peca, *f.* **sun-
worship,** adoración del sol, *f.*

sunbeam, *s.* rayo de sol, *m.*

sunburn, *s.* quemadura del sol, *f.;*
bronceado, *m.*

sunburnt, *a.* quemado por el sol;
bronceado, tostado por el sol

sundae, *s.* helado de frutas, *m.*

Sunday, *s.* domingo, *m.* **in his S.
best,** en su traje dominguero.
S. school, escuela dominical, *f.*

sunder, *v.t.* dividir en dos, hender; separar

sundew, *s.* *(bot.)* rosolí, *m.*

sundial, *s.* reloj de sol, reloj solar,
m.

sundown, *s.* puesta del sol, *f.*

sundry, *a.* varios (-as). *s. pl.*
sundries, artículos diversos,
m. pl.; *(com.)* varios, *m. pl.* **all
and s.,** todo el mundo, todos y
cada uno

sunflower, *s.* girasol, tornasol, *m.,*
trompeta de amor, *f.*

sunken, *a.* (of eyes, etc.) hundido

sunless, *a.* sin sol

sunlight, *s.* luz del sol, *f.,* rayos
del sol, *m. pl.* **artificial s.,** sol
artificial, *m.* **in the s.,** al sol

sunny, *a.* de sol; bañado de sol;
asoleado; expuesto al sol; (face)
risueño; (of disposition, etc.)
alegre. **to be s.,** hacer sol

sunrise, *s.* salida del sol, *f.* **from
s. to sunset,** de sol a sol

sunset, *s.* puesta del sol, *f.* **at s.,**
a la caída (or puesta) del sol

sunshade, *s.* parasol, quitasol, *m.,*
sombrilla, *f.*

sunshine, *s.* luz del sol, *f.* **in the
s.,** al sol

sunstroke, *s.* insolación, *f.*

sup, *v.t.* sorber. *v.i.* cenar. *s.*
sorbo, *m.*

super, *s.* (actor) comparsa, *m.* and
f.; (film) superproducción, *f.;* (of
a beehive) alza, *f.*

superabundance, *s.* superabundancia, sobreabundancia, *f.*

superabundant, *a.* superabundante, sobreabundante. **to be s.,**
sobreabundar

superannuate, *v.t.* (retire) jubilar

superannuated, *a.* (retired) jubilado; (out-of-date) anticuado

superannuation, *s.* (retirement
and pension) jubilación, *f.*

superb, *a.* magnífico, espléndido

superbly, *adv.* magníficamente

supercargo, *s.* *(naut.)* sobrecargo,
m.

supercharger, *s.* *(aut., aer.)* compresor, *m.*

supercilious, *a.* altanero, altivo,
orgulloso; desdeñoso

superciliousness, *s.* altanería,
altivez, *f.,* orgullo, *m.;* desdén, *m.*

superficial, *a.* superficial

superficiality, *s.* superficialidad,
f.

superficially, *adv.* superficialmente

superfine, *a.* superfino

superfluity, *s.* superfluidad, *f.*

superfluous, *a.* superfluo. **to be
s.,** sobrar

superfortress, *s.* *(aer.)* superfortaleza volante, *f.*

superhuman, *a.* sobrehumano

superimpose, *v.t.* sobreponer

superintend, *v.t.* superentender,
dirigir

superintendent, *s.* superintendente, *m.* and *f.;* director (-ra);
(police) subjefe de la policía, *m.*

superior, *a.* superior; (in number)
mayor; (smug) desdeñoso. *s.*
superior (-ra). **Mother S.,**
(madre) superiora, *f.* **s. to,**
superior a; encima de

superiority, *s.* superioridad, *f.*

superlative, *a.* extremo, supremo; *(gram.)* superlativo. *s.*
(gram.) superlativo, *m.*

superlatively, *adv.* en sumo
grado, superlativamente

superman, *s.* superhombre, *m.*

supernatural, *a.* sobrenatural

supernumerary, *a.* and *s.* supernumerario (-ia)

superposition, *s.* superposición,
f.

superscribe, *v.t.* sobrescribir;
poner el sobrescrito (a)

superscription, *s.* (on letters,
documents) sobrescrito, *m.;*
leyenda, *f.*

supersede, *v.t.* reemplazar; suplantar

supersensible, *a.* suprasensible

superstition, *s.* superstición, *f.*

superstitious, *a.* supersticioso

superstitiously, *adv.* supersti-
ciosamente

supertax, s. impuesto suplementario, m.

supervene, v.i. sobrevenir

supervise, v.t. superentender, vigilar; dirigir

supervision, s. superintendencia, f.; dirección, f.

supervisor, s. superintendente, m. and f.; inspector (-ra); director (-ra)

supine, a. supino; indolente, negligente. s. (gram.) supino, m.

supper, s. cena, f. **The Last S.,** la Última Cena. **to have s.,** cenar. **s.-time,** hora de cenar, f.

supplant, v.t. suplantar; usurpar; reemplazar

supplanter, s. suplantador (-ra)

supple, a. flexible; dócil, manso; (fawning) adulador, servil, lisonjero

supplement, s. suplemento, m.; (of a book) apéndice, m.

supplementary, a. suplementario; adicional

suppleness, s. flexibilidad, f.; docilidad, f.; servilidad, f.

suppliant, a. and s. suplicante (m. and f.)

supplicate, v.t. and v.i. suplicar

supplication, s. suplicación, f.; súplica, f.

supply, v.t. proveer (de); suministrar; proporcionar, dar; (a deficiency) suplir; (a post) llenar; (a post temporarily) reemplazar. s. suministro, surtimiento, m.; provisión, f.; (of electricity, etc.) suministro, m.; (com.) oferta, f.; (person) substituto (-ta); pl. **supplies,** (com.) existencias, f. pl.; (mil.) pertrechos, m. pl.; víveres, m. pl., provisiones, f. pl. **s. and demand,** oferta y demanda, f.

support, v.t. apoyar, sostener; mantener; (endure) soportar; (a cause) apoyar, defender; (corroborate) confirmar, vindicar. s. apoyo, m.; sostén, m.; soporte, m. **to speak in s. of,** defender, abogar por. **to s. oneself,** ganarse la vida, mantenerse

supporter, s. apoyo, m.; defensor (-ra); partidario (-ia)

suppose, v.t. suponer; imaginar(se); creer. **always supposing,** dado que, en el caso de que. **Supposing he had gone out?** ¿Y si hubiera salido? **I don't s. they will go to Spain,** No creo que vayan a España. **He is supposed to be clever,** Él tiene fama de listo

supposed, a. supuesto; que se llama a sí mismo

supposition, s. suposición, hipótesis, f.

suppress, v.t. reprimir; (yawns, etc.) ahogar; contener; (heresies, rebellions, books, etc.) suprimir; (dissemble) disimular, esconder; (a heckler, etc.) hacer callar

suppressed, a. reprimido; contenido; disimulado

suppression, s. represión, f.; supresión, f.; disimulación, f.

suppurate, v.i. supurar

suppuration, s. supuración, f.

supremacy, s. supremacía, f.

supreme, a. supremo; sumo. **with s. indifference,** con suma indiferencia. **S. Court,** tribunal supremo, m.

surcharge, s. sobrecarga, f.

sure, a. seguro; cierto. adv. seguramente. **Be s. to... !** ¡Ten cuidado de... ! ¡No dejes de ... ! **to be s.,** seguramente, sin duda; ¡claro!; (fancy!) ¡no me digas!; ¡qué sorpresa! **I am not so s. of that,** No diría yo tanto. **Come on Thursday for s.,** Venga el jueves sin falta. **It is s. to rain to-morrow,** Seguramente va a llover mañana. **to make s. of,** asegurarse de. **to be (or feel) s.,** estar seguro. **s.-footed,** de pie firme, seguro

surely, adv. seguramente; sin duda, ciertamente; por supuesto

sureness, s. seguridad, f.; certeza, f.

surety, s. garantía, fianza, f.; (person) garante, m. and f. **to go s. for,** ser fiador (de), salir garante (por)

surf, s. resaca, f.; rompiente, m.; oleaje, m. **s.-board,** aquaplano, m. **s.-riding,** patinaje sobre las olas, m.

surface, s. superficie, f.; exterior, m. a. superficial. v.i. (of a submarine) salir a la superficie. **on the s.,** en apariencia

surfeit, s. exceso, m., superabundancia, f.; saciedad, f. v.t. hartar; saciar

surge, *v.i.* (of waves) embravecerse, hincharse; (of crowds)
agitarse, bullir; (of emotions)
despertarse. *s.* (of sea, crowd,
blood) oleada, *f.*; (of anger) ola,
f. **The blood surged into his
face**, La sangre se le subió a las
mejillas

surgeon, *s.* cirujano, *m.*; (*nav.*,
mil.) médico, *m.*

surgery, *s.* cirugía, *f.*; (doctor's)
consultorio, *m.*; (dispensary) dispensario, *m.*

surgical, *a.* quirúrgico

surliness, *s.* mal genio, *m.*,
taciturnidad, *f.*; brusquedad, *f.*

surly, *a.* taciturno, huraño, malhumorado; brusco

surmise, *s.* conjetura, suposición,
f. *v.t.* conjeturar, adivinar;
imaginar, suponer. *v.i.* hacer
conjeturas

surmount, *v.t.* superar, vencer;
coronar

surname, *s.* apellido, *m.* *v.t.*
denominar, nombrar

surpass, *v.t.* superar, exceder;
aventajarse (a); eclipsar

surpassing, *a.* sin par, incomparable

surplice, *s.* sobrepelliz, *f.*

surplus, *s.* exceso, sobrante, *m.*;
(*com.*, of accounts) superávit, *m.*
sale of s. stock, liquidación de
saldos, *f.*

surprise, *s.* sorpresa, *f.*; asombro,
m. *v.t.* sorprender; asombrar.
to s. (someone) **in the act**, coger
en el acto. **to take** (a person) **by
s.**, sorprender (a). **He was
surprised into admitting it**,
Cogido a la imprevista, lo confesó

surprising, *a.* sorprendente

surrealism, *s.* surrealismo, *m.*

surrealist, *a.* and *s.* surrealista
(*m.* and *f.*)

surrender, *v.t.* rendir, entregar;
(goods) ceder, renunciar (a). *v.i.*
rendirse, entregarse; abandonarse. *s.* rendición, capitulación,
f.; entrega, *f.*; (of goods) cesión,
f.; (of an insurance policy) rescate,
m. **to s. oneself to remorse**,
abandonarse (or entregarse) al
remordimiento. **to s. unconditionally**, entregarse a discreción

surreptitious, *a.* subrepticio

surreptitiously, *adv.* subrepti-
ciamente, a hurtadillas

surround, *v.t.* rodear; cercar;
(*mil.*) asediar, sitiar. *s.* borde, *m.*
**Peter was surrounded by his
friends**, Pedro estaba rodeado
por sus amigos

surrounding, *a.* (que está) alrededor de; vecino. **the s.
country**, los alrededores

surroundings, *s. pl.* cercanías,
f. pl., alrededores, *m. pl.*; (environment) medio, *m.*; (medio)
ambiente, *m.*

surtax, *s.* impuesto suplementario, *m.*

surveillance, *s.* vigilancia, *f.*

survey, *v.t.* contemplar, mirar;
(events, etc.) pasar en revista;
estudiar; (land, etc.) apear;
(a house, etc.) inspeccionar. *s.*
vista general, *f.*; inspección, *f.*;
(of facts, etc.) examen, *m.*;
estudio, *m.*; (of land, etc.) apeo, *m.*

surveying, *s.* agrimensura, *f.*

surveyor, *s.* agrimensor, *m.*;
(superintendent) inspector, *m.*;
superintendente, *m.*

survival, *s.* supervivencia, *f.*
s. of the fittest, supervivencia
de los más aptos, *f.*

survive, *v.t.* sobrevivir a. *v.i.*
sobrevivir; (of customs) subsistir,
durar

survivor, *s.* sobreviviente, *m.* and
f.

susceptibility, *s.* susceptibilidad,
f.; tendencia, *f.*; *pl.* **suscepti-
bilities**, sensibilidad, *f.*

susceptible, *a.* susceptible; impresionable; sensible; (to love)
enamoradizo. **He is s. to
bronchitis**, Es susceptible a la
bronquitis

suspect, *a.* and *s.* sospechoso
(-sa). *v.t.* sospechar; dudar;
imaginar, suponer. *v.i.* tener
sospechas

suspend, *v.t.* (all meanings) suspender. **suspended anima-
tion**, muerte aparente, *f.*

suspender, *s.* liga, *f.*; *pl.* **sus-
penders**, (braces) tirantes del
pantalón, *m. pl.* **s.-belt**, faja, *f.*

suspense, *s.* incertidumbre, *f.*
to keep (a person) **in s.**, dejar
en la incertidumbre *f.*

suspension, *s.* suspensión, *f.*
s.-bridge, puente colgante, *m.*
s. of payments, suspensión de
pagos, *f.*

suspicion, s. sospecha, f.; (touch) dejo, m.; cantidad muy pequeña, f. **to be above s.,** estar por encima de toda sospecha. **to be under s.,** estar bajo sospecha. **I had no suspicions . . .,** No sospechaba ...

suspicious, a. (by nature) suspicaz; sospechoso. **to make s.,** hacer sospechar

suspiciously, adv. suspicazmente, desconfiadamente; de un modo sospechoso. **It seems s. like ...,** Tiene toda la apariencia de ...

suspiciousness, s. carácter sospechoso, m., lo sospechoso; suspicacia, f.

sustain, v.t. sostener; mantener; sustentar; apoyar; corroborar, confirmar; (a note) prolongar. **to s. injuries,** recibir heridas

sustenance, s. mantenimiento, m.; sustento, m., alimentos, m. pl.

sutler, s. cantinero, vivandero, m.

suture, s. sutura, f.

suzerain, s. soberano, m.

svelte, a. esbelto, gentil

swab, v.t. (naut.) lampacear; limpiar con lampazo; (surg.) tamponar. s. lampazo, m.; (surg.) torunda, f., tampón, m.

swaddle, v.t. envolver; (infants) fajar

swaddling-clothes, s. pl. pañales, m. pl. **to be still in s.-clothes,** (fig.) estar en mantillas, estar en pañales

swag, s. botín, m.

swagger, v.i. fanfarronear, pavonearse; darse importancia. s. pavoneo, m.; aire importante, m.; (coat) tonto, m. a. majo; de última moda

swaggering, a. fanfarrón, jactancioso; importante

swain, s. zagal, m.; enamorado, m.; pretendiente, amante, m.

swallow, v.t. tragar, engullir. s. trago, m.; sorbo, m.; (orn.) golondrina, f. **to s. an insult** (a story), tragar un insulto (una historia). **to s. one's words,** retractarse. **to s. one's pride,** bajar la cerviz, humillarse. **to s. up,** tragar; absorber. **s.-tailed coat,** frac, m.

swamp, s. pantano, m., marisma,

f. v.t. sumergir; (a boat) echar a pique, hundir; (inundate) inundar

swampy, a. pantanoso

swan, s. cisne, m. **swan's down,** plumón de cisne, m. **s.-song,** canto del cisne, m.

swank, s. pretensiones, f. pl. v.i. darse humos

sward, s. césped, m., hierba, f.

swarm, s. enjambre, m.; (of people) muchedumbre, multitud, f.; tropel, m. v.i. (of bees) enjambrar; (of other insects) pulular; (of people) hormiguear, bullir, pulular. v.t. (climb) trepar. **to s. with,** estar infestado de

swarthiness, s. tez morena, f.; color moreno, m.

swarthy, a. moreno

swashbuckler, s. perdonavidas, matasiete, m.

swashbuckling, a. matamoros, valentón, fanfarrón

swastika, s. svástica, cruz gamada, f.

swathe, v.t. envolver; fajar; (with bandages) vendar

swathing, s. envoltura, f.; (bandages) vendas, f. pl.

sway, v.i. balancearse; oscilar; (stagger, of persons) bambolearse; (totter, of things) tambalearse; (of carriages) cabecear; (gracefully, in walking) cimbrarse. v.t. balancear, mecer; oscilar; hacer tambalear; (influence) influir, inclinar; (govern) regir, gobernar. s. balanceo, m.; oscilación, f.; vaivén, m.; tambaleo, m.; (influence) ascendiente, dominio, m., influencia, f.; (rule) imperio, poder, m. **to hold s. over,** gobernar, regir

swear, v.t. jurar; (law, etc.) declarar bajo juramento. v.i. jurar; (curse) echar pestes, blasfemar. **to s. at,** maldecir. **to s. by,** jurar por; poner fe implícita en. **to be sworn in,** prestar juramento. **to s. in,** tomar juramento (a). **to s. to,** atestiguar

sweat, s. sudor, m.; (fam.) trabajo arduo, m. v.i. sudar. v.t. sudar; hacer sudar; (workers) explotar. **by the s. of one's brow,** con el sudor de la frente. **s.-gland,** glándula sudorípara, *f.*

sweated, *a.* (of persons) explotado; (of labour) mal retribuido

sweater, *s.* sweater, jersey, *m.*

sweating, *s.* transpiración, *f.*; (of workers) explotación, *f.*

sweaty, *a.* sudoroso

Swede, *s.* sueco (-ca); (vegetable) naba, *f.*

Swedish, *a.* sueco. *s.* (language) sueco, *m.*

sweep, *v.i.* extenderse (por); (cleave) surcar; pasar rápidamente (por); invadir; dominar; andar majestuosamente; (with a brush) barrer. *v.t.* barrer; pasar (por); (the strings of a musical instrument) rasguear; (the sea) navegar por; (mines) barrer; (the horizon, etc.) examinar; (a chimney) deshollinar; (with a brush) barrer; (remove) arrebatar; quitar; llevarse; (abolish) suprimir. **to s. along,** *v.t.* (of the current, crowds, etc.) arrastrar. *v.i.* pasar majestuosamente; correr rápidamente (por). **to s. aside,** apartar con la mano; abandonar; (a protest) desoír, no hacer caso de. **to s. away,** barrer; (remove) llevarse; destruir; suprimir. **to s. down,** *v.t.* barrer; (carry) arrastrar. *v.i.* (of cliffs, etc.) bajar; (of an enemy) abalanzarse (sobre); lanzarse (por). **to s. off,** barrer; (a person) llevarse sin perder tiempo; arrebatar con violencia (a). **to be swept off one's feet,** ser arrastrado (por); perder el balance; (of emotion) ser dominado por. **to s. on,** seguir su avance inexorable; seguir su marcha. **to s. up,** recoger, barrer

sweep, *s.* barredura, *f.*; (of a chimney) deshollinador, *m.*; (of the tide) curso, *m.*; (of a scythe, etc.) golpe, *m.*; (range) alcance, *m.*; (fold) pliegue, *m.*; (curve) curva, *f.*; (of water, etc.) extensión, *f.*; (of wings) envergadura, *f.* **with a s. of the arm,** con un gesto del brazo. **to make a clean s. of,** hacer tabla rasa de

sweeping, *a.* completo; comprensivo; demasiado general; radical. **a s. judgment,** un juicio demasiado general. **s. changes,** cambios radicales, *m. pl.* **s. brush,** escoba, *f.*

sweepings, *s. pl.* barreduras, *f. pl.*; residuos, *m. pl.*; (of society) heces, *f. pl.*

sweepstake, *s.* lotería, *f.*

sweet, *a.* dulce; (of scents) oloroso, fragante; (of sounds) melodioso, dulce; (charming) encantador; amable; (pretty) bonito. *s.* bombón, *m.*; golosina, *f.*; (at a meal) (plato) dulce, *m.*; dulzura, *f.*; (beloved) amor, *m.*, querido (-da). **How s. it smells!** ¡Qué buen olor tiene! **the sweets of life,** las dulzuras de la vida. **s.-pea,** guisante de olor, *m.*, haba de las Indias, *f.* **s.-potato,** batata, *f.* **s.-scented,** perfumado, fragante. **s.-tempered,** amable, de carácter dulce. **s.-toothed,** goloso. **s.-william,** (*bot.*) clavel de la China, *m.*

sweetbread, *s.* lechecillas, *f. pl.*

sweeten, *v.t.* azucarar; endulzar. **Cervantes sweetens one's bitter moments,** Cervantes endulza los momentos ásperos

sweetheart, *s.* amante, *m.* and *f.*, amado (-da); (as address) querido (-da)

sweetish, *a.* algo dulce

sweetly, *adv.* dulcemente; (of scents) olorosamente; (of sounds) melodiosamente; (of behaviour, etc.) amablemente

sweetmeat, *s.* bombón, dulce, *m.*

sweetness, *s.* dulzura, *f.*; (of scents) buen olor, *m.*, fragancia, *f.*; (of sounds) melodía, dulzura, *f.*; (of character) bondad, amabilidad, *f.*

swell, *v.i.* hincharse; (of the sea) entumecerse; crecer; aumentarse. *v.t.* hinchar; aumentar. *s.* (of the sea) oleada, *f.*, oleaje, *m.*; (of the ground) ondulación, *f.*; (of sound) crescendo, *m.*; (increase) aumento, *m.*; (dandy) pisaverde, elegante, *m.*; (important person) pájaro gordo, *m.*; (at games, etc.) espada, *m. a.* estupendo; elegantísimo; de primera, excelente. **to suffer from swelled head,** tener humos, darse importancia. **This foot is swollen,** Este pie está hinchado (or tumefacto). **The refugees have swelled the population,** Los refugiados han aumentado la población. **eyes swollen with tears,** ojos arrasados de lágrimas. **to s. with pride,** hincharse de orgullo

swelling, *s.* hinchazón, *f.*; (*med.*) tumefacción, *f.*; (bruise, etc.) chichón, *m.*

swelter, *v.i.* abrasarse; arder. *s.* bochorno, calor sofocante, *m.*

swerve, *v.i.* desviarse; apartarse (de); torcerse. *s.* desvío, *m.*

swift, *a.* rápido, veloz; pronto. *adv.* velozmente, rápidamente. *s.* (*orn.*) vencejo, *m.* **s.-flowing,** (of rivers, etc.) de corriente rápida. **s.-footed,** de pies ligeros

swiftly, *adv.* rápidamente, velozmente

swiftness, *s.* rapidez, velocidad, *f.*; prontitud, *f.*

swim, *v.i.* nadar; flotar; (glide) deslizarse; (fill) inundarse. *v.t.* (a horse) hacer nadar; pasar a nado; nadar. *s.* natación, *f.* **eyes swimming with tears,** ojos inundados de lágrimas. **He enjoys a s.,** Le gusta nadar. **My head swims,** Se me va la cabeza. **Everything swam before my eyes,** Todo parecía bailar ante mis ojos. **to be in the s.,** formar parte (de), ser (de); (be up to date) estar al corriente. **to s. the Channel,** atravesar el canal de la Mancha a nado. **to s. with the tide,** ir con la corriente

swimmer, *s.* nadador (-ra). **He is a bad s.,** Nada mal

swimming, *s.* natación, *f.*; (of the head) vértigo, *m.* **s.-bath,** piscina, *f.* **s.-costume,** traje de baño, *m.* **s.-pool,** piscina al aire libre, *f.*

swindle, *v.t.* engañar, estafar; defraudar (de). *s.* estafa, *f.*, timo, *m.*; engaño, *m.*; impostura, *f.*

swindler, *s.* estafador (-ra), trampeador (-ra); engañador (-ra)

swine, *s.* cerdo, puerco, *m.*; (person) cochino (-na). **a herd of s.,** una manada de cerdos

swineherd, *s.* porquero, *m.*

swing, *v.i.* balancearse; oscilar;

(hang) colgar, pender; columpiarse; girar; dar la vuelta; (of a boat) bornear. *v.t.* balancear; (hang) colgar; (rock) mecer; (in a swing, etc.) columpiar; hacer oscilar; (raise) subir. *s.* oscilación, *f.*; vaivén, *m.*; balanceo, *m.*; (rhythm) ritmo, *m.*; (seat, etc.) columpio, *m.*; (reach) alcance, *m.* **The door swung open,** La puerta se abrió silenciosamente. **He swung the car round,** Dió la vuelta al auto. **He swung himself into the saddle,** Montó de un salto. **to be in full s.,** estar a toda marcha. **to go with a s.,** tener mucho éxito. **s.-boat,** columpio, *m.* **s.-bridge,** puente giratorio, *m.* **s.-door,** puerta giratoria, *f.*

swinging, *a.* oscilante; pendiente; rítmico. *s.* balanceo, *m.*; oscilación, *f.*; vaivén, *m.*; ritmo, *m.* **s. stride,** andar rítmico, *m.*

swinish, *a.* porcuno, de cerdo; cochino, sucio

swipe, *v.t.* golpear duro; aplastar. *s.* golpe fuerte, *m.*

swirl, *v.i.* arremolinarse. *s.* remolino, *m.*

swish, *v.t.* (of an animal's tail) agitar, mover, menear; (of a cane) blandir; (thrash) azotar. *v.i.* silbar; (of water) susurrar; (of a dress, etc.) crujir. *s.* silbo, *m.*; (of water) susurro, murmullo, *m.*; (of a dress, etc.) crujido, *m.*

Swiss, *a.* and *s.* suizo (-za)

switch, *s.* vara, *f.*; (riding) látigo, *m.*; (of hair) trenza, *f.*; (*elec.*) interruptor, *m.*; (*r.w.*) aguja, *f.*; (*r.w.*) siding) desviadero, *m.* *v.t.* azotar; (a train) desviar; (*elec.*) interrumpir; (transfer) trasladar; (of an animal, its tail) remover, mover rápidamente. **to s. off,** (*elec.* and telephone) cortar; (*rad.* and *aut.*) desconectar. **to s. on,** conectar; (a light) poner (la luz); (a radio) encender

switchback, *s.* subida en zigzag, *f.*; (amusement) montañas rusas, *f. pl.*

switchboard, *s.* cuadro de distribución, *m.*

swivel, *s.* torniquete, *m.*; anillo móvil, *m.*; pivote, *m.* *v.i.* girar

sobre un eje; dar una vuelta.
s.-chair, silla giratoria, *f.* **s.-door**, puerta giratoria, *f.*

swoon, *v.i.* desvanecerse, desmayarse. *s.* desmayo, desvanecimiento, *m.*

swoop, *v.i.* calarse, abatirse; (of robbers, etc.) abalanzarse (sobre). *s.* calada, *f.* **at one fell s.**, de un solo golpe

sword, *s.* espada, *f.*; sable, *m.* **to measure swords with**, cruzar espadas con. **to put to the s.**, pasar a cuchillo (a). **s.-arm**, brazo derecho, *m.* **s.-belt**, talabarte, *m.* **s.-cut**, sablazo, *m.* **s.-dance**, danza de espadas, *f.* **s.-fish**, pez espada, *m.*, jifia, *f.* **s.-play**, esgrima, *f.*; manejo de la espada, *m.* **s.-stick**, bastón de estoque, *m.* **s.-thrust**, golpe de espada, *m.*; estocada, *f.*

swordsman, *s.* espadachín, *m.*; esgrimidor, *m.*

swordsmanship, *s.* manejo de la espada, *m.*; esgrima, *f.*

swot, *v.i.* (slang, of students, etc.) empollar. *s.* empollón (-na)

sybarite, *a.* and *s.* sibarita (*m.* and *f.*)

sybaritic, *a.* sibarítico, sibarita

sybaritism, *s.* sibaritismo, *m.*

sycamore, *s.* sicómoro, *m.*; falso plátano, *m.*

sycophancy, *s.* servilismo, *m.*

sycophant, *s.* sicofanta, *m.*

syllabic, *a.* silábico

syllable, *s.* sílaba, *f.*

syllabus, *s.* programa, *m.*; compendio, *m.*

syllepsis, *s.* silepsis, *f.*

syllogism, *s.* silogismo, *m.*

syllogistic, *a.* silogístico

sylph, *s.* sílfide, *f.*, silfo, *m.*; (woman) sílfide, *f.*; (hummingbird) colibrí, *m.* **s.-like**, de sílfide; como una sílfide

sylvan, *a.* selvático, silvestre; rústico

symbiosis, *s.* simbiosis, *f.*

symbol, *s.* símbolo, emblema, *m.*; (*math.*) símbolo, *m.*; (of rank, etc.) insignia, *f.*

symbolical, *a.* simbólico

symbolically, *adv.* simbólicamente

symbolism, *s.* simbolismo, *m.*

symbolist, *s.* simbolista, *m.* and *f.*

symbolize, *v.t.* simbolizar

symmetrical, *a.* simétrico

symmetrically, *adv.* simétricamente

symmetry, *s.* simetría, *f.*

sympathetic, *a.* simpático; compasivo; (of the public, etc.) bien dispuesto. *s.* (*anat.*) gran simpático, *m.* **s. words**, palabras de simpatía, *f. pl.* **s. ink**, tinta simpática, *f.*

sympathetically, *adv.* simpáticamente; con compasión

sympathize, *v.i.* simpatizar (con); (understand) comprender; (condole) compadecerse (de), condolerse (de); dar el pésame

sympathizer, *s.* partidario (-ia)

sympathy, *s.* simpatía, *f.*; compasión, *f.* **Paul is in s. with their aims**, Pablos está de acuerdo con sus objetos. **Please accept my s.**, (on a bereavement) Le acompaña a Vd. en su sentimiento

symphonic, *a.* sinfónico

symphony, *s.* sinfonía, *f.*

symposium, *s.* colección de artículos, *f.*

symptom, *s.* síntoma, *m.*; señal, *f.*, indicio, *m.* **to show symptoms of**, dar indicios de

symptomatic, *a.* sintomático

synæresis, *s.* sinéresis, *f.*

synagogue, *s.* sinagoga, *f.*

synalœpha, *s.* sinalefa, *f.*

synchronism, *s.* sincronismo, *m.*

synchronization, *s.* sincronización, *f.*

synchronize, *v.i.* coincidir, tener lugar simultáneamente; sincronizarse. *v.t.* sincronizar

synchronous, *a.* sincrónico

syncopate, *v.t.* (*gram.*, *mus.*) sincopar

syncopation, *s.* (*mus.*) síncopa, *f.*

syncope, *s.* (*med.*, *gram.*) síncope, *m.*

syndical, *a.* sindical

syndicalism, *s.* sindicalismo, *m.*

syndicalist, *s.* sindicalista, *m.* and *f.*

syndicate, *s.* sindicato, *m.* *v.t.* sindicar

syndication, *s.* sindicación, *f.*

synod, *s.* (*ecc.*) sínodo, *m.*

synonym, *s.* sinónimo, *m.*

synonymous, *a.* sinónimo

synopsis, *s.* sinopsis, *f.*

synoptic, *a.* sinóptico
syntactic, *a.* sintáctico
syntax, *s.* sintaxis, *f.*
synthesis, *s.* síntesis, *f.*
synthetic, *a.* sintético
synthetize, *v.t.* sintetizar
syphilis, *s.* sífilis, *f.*
syphilitic, *a.* and *s.* sifilítico (-ca)
Syracusan, *a.* and *s.* siracusano (-na)
syren. See siren
Syrian, *a.* and *s.* siríaco (-ca), sirio (-ia)
syringa, *s.* (*bot.*) jeringuilla, *f.*
syringe, *s.* jeringa, *f.* *v.t.* jeringar
syrup, *s.* jarabe, *m.*; (for bottling fruit, etc.) almíbar, *m.*
syrupy, *a.* siroposo
system, *s.* sistema, *m.*; régimen *m.*; método, *m.*; (body) organismo, *m.* He has no s. in his work, No tiene método en su trabajo. the nervous s., el sistema nervioso. the feudal s., el feudalismo, el sistema feudal
systematic, *a.* sistemático, metódico
systematically, *adv.* sistemáticamente, metódicamente
systematization, *s.* sistematización, *f.*
systematize, *v.t.* sistematizar
systole, *s.* (*med.*) sístole, *f.*

T

t, *s.* (letter) te, *f.* *a.* en T, en forma de T. T bandage, vendaje en T, *m.* T square, regla T, *f.*
tab, *s.* oreja, *f.*
tabard, *s.* tabardo, *m.*
tabby, *s.* gato romano, *m.*; (female) gata, *f.*; (*fam.*) vieja chismosa, *f.*
tabernacle, *s.* tabernáculo, *m.*; templo, *m.*; (*arch.*) templete, *m.*; (*ecc.*) custodia, *f.*
tabes, *s.* (*med.*) tabes, *f.*
table, *s.* mesa, *f.*; (food) comida, mesa, *f.*; (of the law, weights, measures, contents, etc.) tabla, *f.*; (of land) meseta, *f.*; (of prices) lista, tarifa, *f.* *v.t.* (parliament) poner. sobre la mesa; enumerar, apuntar, hacer

una lista de. to clear the t., alzar (or levantar) la mesa. to lay the t., cubrir (or poner) la mesa. to have a t.-d'hôte meal, tomar el menú. to rise from t., levantarse de la mesa. to sit down to t., ponerse a la mesa. The tables are turned, Se volvió la tortilla. side t., aparador, trinchero, *m.* small t., mesilla, *f.* t. of contents, tabla de materias, *f.*, índice, *m.* t.-centrepiece, centro de mesa, *m.* t.-cloth, mantel, *m.* t.-companion, comensal, *m.* and *f.* t.-knife, cuchillo de mesa, *m.* t.-lamp, quinqué, *m.*; lámpara de mesa, *f.* t.-land, meseta, *f.* t.-leg, pata de una mesa, *f.* t.-linen, mantelería, *f.* t.-napkin, servilleta, *f.* t.-runner, camino de mesa, *m.* t.-spoon, cuchara para los legumbres, *f.* t.-talk, conversación de sobremesa, *f.* t.-turning, mesas que dan vueltas, *f. pl.* t.-ware, artículos para la mesa, *m. pl.*
tableau, *s.* cuadro, *m.* tableaux vivants, cuadros vivos, *m. pl.*
tablespoonful, *s.* cucharada, *f.*
tablet, *s.* tabla, *f.*; (with inscription) tarjeta, losa, lápida, *f.*; (*med.*) comprimido, *m.*, tableta, *f.*; (of soap, chocolate) pastilla, *f.* writing t., taco de papel, *m.*
tabloid, *s.* comprimido, *m.*, pastilla, *f.*
taboo, *s.* tabú, *m.* *a.* prohibido, tabú. *v.t.* declarar tabú, prohibir
tabor, *s.* (*mus.*) tamboril, tamborín, *m.* t. player, tamborilero, *m.*
tabouret, *s.* (stool) taburete, *m.*; (for embroidery) tambor de bordar, *m.*; (*mus.*) tamborilete, *m.*
tabulate, *v.t.* resumir en tablas; hacer una lista de, catalogar
tabulation, *s.* distribución en tablas, *f.*
tachygraphy, *s.* taquigrafía, *f.*
tachymeter, *s.* taquímetro, *m.*
tachymetry, *s.* taquimetría, *f.*
tacit, *a.* tácito
tacitly, *adv.* tácitamente
taciturn, *a.* taciturno, sombrío, reservado, de pocas palabras

taciturnity, s. taciturnidad, *f.*; reserva, *f.*

tack, s. (nail) tachuela, puntilla, *f.*; (sew.) hilván, embaste, *m.*; (naut.) amura, *f.*; (naut.) puño de amura, *m.*; (naut.) bordada, *f.*; (fig.) cambio de política, *m. v.t.* clavar con tachuelas; (sew.) hilvanar, embastar; (fig.) añadir. *v.i.* (naut.) virar; (fig.) cambiar de política, adoptar un nuevo plan de acción. **t. puller,** sacabrocas, *m.*

tackle, s. aparejo, *m.*; maniobra, *f.*; (naut.) cuadernal, *m.*, jarcia, *f.*; (gear) aparejos, avíos, *m. pl.*; (football) carga, *f. v.t.* agarrar, asir; (fig.) atacar, abordar; (football) cargar; (undertake) emprender; (a problem) luchar con. **t.-block,** polea, *f.*

tackling, s. aparejo, *m.*, maniobra, *f.*; (naut.) cordaje, *m.*

tacky, a. pegajoso, viscoso

tact, s. tacto, *m.*, discreción, diplomacia, delicadeza, *f.*

tactful, a. lleno de tacto, diplomático, discreto

tactfully, adv. discretamente, diplomáticamente

tactical, a. táctico

tactically, adv. según la táctica; del punto de vista táctico

tactician, s. táctico, *m.*

tactics, s. pl. táctica, *f.*

tactile, a. táctil; tangible

tactless, a. que no tiene tacto, sin tacto alguno, indiscreto

tactlessly, adv. impolíticamente, indiscretamente

tactlessness, s. falta de tacto, *f.*

tadpole, s. renacuajo, *m.*

taffeta, s. tafetán, *m.*

taffrail, s. (naut.) coronamiento, *m.*

tag, s. herrete, *m.*; (label) marbete, *m.*, etiqueta, *f.*; (of tail) punta del rabo, *f.*; (of boot) tirador de bota, *m.*; (game) marro, *m.*; (rag) arrapiezo, *m.*; (quotation) cita bien conocida, *f.*; (of song, poem) refrán, *m.* **to play t.,** jugar al marro

Tahitian, a. de Taiti

tail, s. cola, *f.*, rabo, *m.*; (plait) trenza, *f.*; (wisp of hair) mechón, *m.*; (of a comet) cola, cabellera, *f.*; (of a note in music) rabito, *m.*; (of a coat) faldon, *m.*; (of a kite)

cola, *f.*; (of the eye), rabo, *m.*; (retinue) séquito, *m.*, banda, *f.*; (of an aeroplane) cola, *f.*; (end) fin, *m.*; (of coin) cruz, *f.*; (line) fila, cola, *f. v.t.* seguir de cerca, pisarle (a uno) los talones. **to t. after,** seguir de cerca. **to t. away,** disminuir; desaparecer, perderse de vista. **to t. on,** unir, juntar. **to turn t.,** volver la espalda, poner los pies en polvorosa. **with the t. between the legs,** con el rabo entre piernas. **t.-board,** (of a cart) escalera, *f.* **t.-coat,** frac, *m.* **t.-end,** extremo, *m.*; fin, *m.*; lo último. **t.-feather,** pena, *f.* **t.-fin,** aleta caudal, *f.*; (aer.) timón de dirección, *m.* **t.-light,** farol trasero, *m.* **t.-piece,** (of a violin, etc.) cola, *f.*; (print.) marmosete, culo de lámpara, *m.* **t. spin** (aer.) barrena de cola, *f.* **t. wind,** viento de cola, *m.*

tailed, a. de rabo. **big-t.,** rabudo, de cola grande. **long-t.,** rabilargo. **short-t.,** rabicorto

tailless, a. rabón, sin rabo

tailor, s. sastre, *m.* **t.-made,** s. traje sastre, *m. a.* de hechura de sastre. **tailor's shop,** sastrería, *f.*

tailoress, s. sastra, *f.*

tailoring, s. sastrería, *f.*; (work) corte, *m.*

taint, s. corrupción, *f.*; infección, *f.*; (blemish) mancha, *f.*; (tinge) dejo, *m. v.t.* corromper, pervertir; inficionar; (meat) corromper. *v.i.* corromperse, inficionarse; (meat) corromperse

take, v.t. tomar; (receive) aceptar; (remove) quitar; (pick up) coger; (grab) asir, agarrar; (math.) restar; (carry) llevar; (a person) traer, llevar; (guide) conducir, guiar; (win) ganar; (earn) cobrar, percibir; obtener; (make prisoner) hacer prisionero, prender; (a town, etc.) tomar, rendir, conquistar; (appropriate) apoderarse de, apropiarse; (steal) robar, hurtar; (ensnare) coger, cazar con trampas; (fish) pescar, coger; (a trick, in cards) hacer (una baza); (an illness) contraer, coger; (by surprise) sorprender, coger desprevenido (a); (attract) atraer; (drink) beber; (a meal) tomar;

(select) escoger; (hire) alquilar; (suppose) suponer; (a journal) estar abonado a; (use) emplear, usar; (impers., require) necesitarse, hacer falta; (purchase) comprar; (assume) adoptar, asumir; (a leap) dar (un salto); (a walk) dar (un paseo); (a look), echar (un vistazo); (measures) tomar (medidas); (the chair) presidir; (understand) comprender; (a photograph) sacar (una fotografía); (believe) creer; (consider) considerar; (a note) apuntar; (jump over) saltar; (time) tomar, emplear. **I t. size three in shoes,** Calzo el número tres. **to t. to be,** (believe) suponer; (mistake) creer equivocadamente. **to t. (a thing) badly,** tomarlo (or llevarlo) a mal. **The book took me two hours to read,** Necesité dos horas para leer el libro, or Leí el libro en dos horas. **And this, I t. it, is Mary?** ¿Y supongo que ésta será María? **to be taken with,** ser entusiasta de; (of persons) estar prendado de. **to t. aback,** desconcertar, coger desprevenido (a). **to t. again,** volver a tomar; llevar otra vez; (a photograph) retratar otra vez. **to t. along,** llevar; traer. **to t. away,** quitar; llevarse. **to t. back,** devolver; (retract) retractar; (receive) recibir (algo) devuelto. **to t. down,** bajar; (a building) derribar; (machinery) desmontar; (hair) deshacerse (el cabello); (swallow) tragar; (in writing) apuntar; (humble) quitar los humos (a), humillar. **to t. for,** creer, imaginar; (a walk, etc.) llevar a; (mistake) creer erróneamente; tomar por. **Whom do you t. me for?** ¿Por quién me tomas? **to t. from,** privar, quitar de; (subtract) restar; substraer de. **to t. in,** (believe) tragar, creer; (sail) acortar las velas; (deceive) engañar; (lead in) hacer entrar; (accept) recibir, aceptar. **to t. off,** quitar; (surgically) amputar; (one's hat, etc.) quitarse (el sombrero); (eyes) sacar; (take away) llevarse; (mimic) imitar; (ridicule) ridiculizar; (unstick) des-

pegar; (discount) descontar. **to t. on,** emprender; aceptar; (at sports) jugar. **to t. on oneself,** encargarse de, tomar por su cuenta, asumir. **to t. out,** sacar; extraer; (remove) quitar; (outside) llevar fuera; (for a walk) llevar a paseo; (obtain) obtener, sacar; (tire) agotar, rendir. **to t. over,** tomar posesión de; asumir; (show) mostrar, conducir por. **to t. up,** subir; (pick up) recoger; tomar; (a challenge, etc.) aceptar; (a dress, etc.) acortar; (absorb) absorber; (of space) ocupar; (of time) ocupar, hacer perder; (buy) comprar; (adopt) dedicarse a; (arrest) arrestar, prender; (criticize) censurar, criticar; (begin) empezar; (resume) continuar

take, v.i. tomar; (be successful) tener éxito; (of vaccination, etc.) prender; (a good (bad) photograph) salir bien (mal). **to t. after,** salir a, parecerse a; (of conduct) seguir el ejemplo de; **to t. off,** salir; (aer.) despegar. **to t. on,** (fam.) lamentarse. **to t. to,** dedicarse a; darse a; (of persons) tomar cariño a; (grow accustomed) acostumbrarse a. **to t. up with,** hacerse amigo de

take, s. toma, f.; cogida, f.; (print.) tomada, f.; (theat.) taquilla, f. **t.-in,** engaño, m. **t.-off,** (aer.) (recorrido de) despegue, m.; caricatura, f.; sátira, f.

taker, s. tomador (-ra)

taking, s. toma, f.; secuestro, m. s. pl. **takings,** ingresos, m. pl.; (theat.) taquilla, entrada, f. a. atractivo, encantador; simpático; (of disease) contagioso

talc, s. (min.) talco, m.

talcum powder, s. talco, polvo de talco, m.

tale, s. (recital) narración, historia, f.; relato, m.; cuento, m.; leyenda, historia, fábula, f.; (number) cuenta, f., número, m.; (gossip) chisme, m. **old wives' t.,** cuento de viejas, m. **to tell a t.,** contar una historia. **to tell tales,** contar cuentos; revelar secretos, chismear

tale-bearer, s. correveidile, m. and f.; chismoso (-sa), soplón (-ona) tale-bearing, s. el chismear, m.

talent, s. (coin) talento, m.; (ability) ingenio, m.; habilidad, f. the best t. in Spain, la flor de la cultura espańñalo

talented, a. talentoso, ingenioso

talisman, s. talismán, m.

talk, v.i. and v.t. hablar, decir. to t. business, hablar de negocios. to t. for talking's sake, hablar por hablar. to t. French, hablar francés. to t. nonsense, decir disparates. to t. too much, hablar demasiado; (fam.) hablar por los codos, irse (a uno) la lengua. to t. about, hablar de; conversar sobre. to t. at, decir algo a alguien para que lo entienda otro. Are you talking at me? ¿Lo dices por mí? to t. away, seguir hablando; disipar. to t. into, persuadir, inducir (a). to t. of, hablar de; charlar sobre. to t. on, hablar acerca de (or sobre); (continue) seguir hablando. to t. out of, disuadir de. to t. out of turn, meterse donde no le llaman, meter la pata. to t. over, hablar de; discutir, considerar. to t. round, persuadir. to t. to, (address) hablar a; (consult) hablar con; (scold) reprender. to t. to each other, hablarse. to t. up, hablar claro

talk, s. conversación, f.; (informal lecture) charla, f.; (empty words) palabras, f. pl.; (notoriety) escándalo, m.; rumor, m. There is t. of..., Se dice que...; Se habla de que. to give a t., dar una charla. to indulge in small t., hablar de cosas sin importancia, hablar de naderías

talkative, a. locuaz, gárrulo, hablador, decidor. to be very t., ser muy locuaz; (fam.) tener mucha lengua

talkativeness, s. locuacidad, garrulidad, f.

talker, s. hablador (-ra), conversador (-ra); (lecturer) orador (-ra); (in a derogatory sense) fanfarrón (-ona), charlatán (-ana). to be a good t., hablar bien, ser buen conversacionista

talking, a. que habla, hablante; (of birds, dolls, etc.) parlero. to

give a good t. to, dar. una peluca (a). t.-film, película sonora, f. t.-machine, fonógrafo, m.

tall, a. alto; (of stories) exagerado. five feet tall, de cinco pies de altura

tallboy, s. cómoda alta, f.

tallith, s. taled, m.

tallness, s. altura, f.; estatura, talla, f.; (of stories) lo exagerado

tallow, s. sebo, m. t. candle, vela de sebo, f. t. chandler, velero (-ra). t.-faced, con cara de color de cera

tallowy, a. seboso

tally, s. tarja, tara, f.; cuenta, f. v.t. llevar la cuenta (de). v.i. estar conforme, cuadrar

talmud, s. talmud, m.

talmudic, a. talmúdico

talon, s. garra, uña, f.; (of a sword) talón, m.

tamable, a. domable, domesticable

tamarind, s. (bot.) tamarindo, m.

tamarisk, s. (bot.) tamarisco, m.

tambour, s. (mus.) tambor, m.; (for embroidery) tambor (or bastidor) para bordar, m.

tambourine, s. pandereta, f.

tame, a. domesticado, manso; (spiritless) sumiso; · (dull) aburrido, soso. v.t. domar, domesticar; (curb) reprimir, gobernar, domar, suavizar. to grow t., domesticarse

tameness, s. mansedumbre, f.; sumisión, timidez, f.

tamer, s. domador (-ra)

taming, s. domadura, f. The T. of the Shrew, La Fierecilla Domada

tam o' shanter cap, s. boina ·escocesa, f.

tamp, v.t. apisonar; (in blasting) atacar (un barreno)

tamper, v.i. (with) descomponer, estropear; (meddle with) meterse con; (witnesses) sobornar; (documents) falsificar

tampon, s. (surg.) tampón, tapón, m. v.t. taponar

tan, v.t. curtir, adobar; (of sun) tostar, quemar; (slang) zurrar. v.i. tostarse por el sol. s. color café claro, m.; bronceado, cutis tostado, m. a. de color café claro

tandem, s. tándem, m.

tang, *s.* (of sword, etc.) espiga, *f.*; (flavour) fuerte sabor, *m.*; (sound) retintín, *m.*

tangent, *a.* and *s.* tangente (*f.*). **to fly off at a t.,** (*fig.*) salir por la tangente

tangerine, *a.* and *s.* tangerino (-na). **t. orange,** naranja mandarina, *f.*

tangible, *a.* tangible; (*fig.*) real

tangle, *s.* embrollo, enredo, nudo, *m.*; (of streets) laberinto, *m.*; (*fig.*) confusión, *f.* *v.t.* embrollar, enmarañar; (entangle) enredar; (*fig.*) poner en confusión, complicar. *v.i.* enmarañarse

tank, *s.* tanque, depósito (de agua, etc.), *m.*; cisterna, *f.*; (as a reservoir) aljibe, estanque, *m.*; (*mil.*) tanque, carro de asalto, *m.*

tankard, *s.* pichel, bock, *m.*

tanker, *s.* petrolero, *m.*

tanned, *a.* bronceado, quemado por el sol, dorado por el sol

tanner, *s.* curtidor, *m.*; (slang) medio chelín, *m.* **tanner's scraper,** descarnador, *m.* **tanner's vat,** noque, *m.*

tannery, *s.* curtiduría; *f.*

tannic, *a.* (*chem.*) tánico. **t. acid,** ácido tánico, *m.*

tannin, *s.* (*chem.*) tanino, *m.*

tanning, *s.* curtido, adobamiento, *m.*

tansy, *s.* (*bot.*) tanaceto, *m.*

tantalize, *v.t.* tentar, atormentar, provocar

tantalizing, *a.* tentador, atormentador; provocativo

tantamount, *a.* equivalente, igual. **to be t. to,** ser equivalente a

tantrum, *s.* pataleta, rabieta, *f.*, berrinche, *m.*

taoism, *s.* taoísmo, *m.*

taoist, *s.* taoísta, *m.* and *f.*

tap, *s.* (blow) pequeño golpe, toque ligero, *m.*; palmadita, *f.*; (for drawing water, etc.) grifo, *m.*, llave, *f.*; (of a barrel) canilla, *f.*; (brew of liquor) clase de vino, *f.*; (tap-room) bar con mostrador, *m.*; (tool) macho de terraja, *m.*; (piece of leather on shoe) tapa, *f.*; *pl.* taps, (*mil.*) toque de apagar las luces, *m.* *v.t.* (strike) golpear ligeramente, dar una palmadita a; (pierce) horadar; (a barrel)

decentar; (*surg.*) hacer una puntura en; (trees) sangrar; (*elec.*) derivar (una corriente); (of water, current) tomar; (information) descubrir; (telephone) escuchar las conversaciones telefónicas. *v.i.* golpear ligeramente. **to tap at the door,** llamar suavemente a la puerta, on tap, en tonel. **screw-tap;** terraja, *f.* **tap-dance,** claqué. *m.* **tap-root,** raíz pivotante, *f.*

tape, *s.* (linen) cinta de hilo, *f.*; (cotton) cinta de algodón, *f.*; (telegraph machine) cinta de papel, *f.*; (surveying) cinta para medir, *f.* **adhesive t.,** cinta adhesiva, *f.* **red t.,** balduque, *m.*; (*fig.*) burocracia, *f.*; formulismo, *m.* **t.-machine,** telégrafo de cotizaciones, bancarias, *m.* **t.-measure,** cinta métrica, *f.*

taper, *s.* bujía, cerilla, *f.*; (*ecc.*) cirio, *m.* *v.i.* ahusarse, rematar en punta. *v.t.* afilar

tapering, *a.* cónico, piramidal; (of fingers) ahusado

tapestried, *a.* cubierto de tapices, tapizado

tapestry, *s.* tapiz, *m.* **t. weaver,** tapicero, *m.*

tapeworm, *s.* tenia, lombriz solitaria, *f.*

tapioca, *s.* tapioca, *f.*

tapir, *s.* (*zool.*) danta, *f.*

tapis, to be on the, estar sobre el tapete

tappet, *s.* (*mech.*) leva, *f.* **t. rod,** varilla percusora, *f.*

tar, *s.* alquitrán, *m.*, brea, *f.* *v.t.* embrear, alquitranar. **to tar and feather,** emplumar. **coal t.,** alquitrán mineral, *m.*

tarantella, *s.* tarantela, *f.*

tarantula, *s.* tarántula, *f.*

tardily, *adv.* tardíamente; lentamente

tardiness, *s.* tardanza, lentitud, *f.*

tardy, *a.* (late) tardío; (slow) lento; (reluctant) desinclinado

tare, *s.* (*bot.*) yero, *m.*; (in the Bible) cizaña, *f.*; (*com.*) tara, *f.*; (of a vehicle) peso en vacío, *m.*

target, *s.* blanco (de tiro), *m.*; (shield) rodela, tarja, *f.* **t. practice,** tiro al blanco, *m.*

tariff, *s.* tarifa, *f.* **to put a t. on,** tarifar

tarlatan, *s.* tarlatana, *f.*

tarmac, *s.* alquitranado, *m.*

tarn, *s.* lago de montaña, *m.*

tarnish, *s.* deslustre, *m.* *v.t.* deslustrar, empañar; (*fig.*) obscurecer, manchar. *v.i.* deslustrarse

tarpaulin, *s.* alquitranado, encerado, *m.*

tarragon, *s.* (*bot.*) estragón, *m.*

tarred, *a.* alquitranado, embreado

tarring, *s.* embreadura, *f.*

tarry, *v.i.* tardar, detenerse

tarsal, *a.* (*anat.*) tarsal

tarsus, *s.* (*anat.*) tarso, *m.*

tart, *a.* ácido, acerbo, agridulce; (*fig.*) áspero. *s.* tarta, *f.*; pastelillo de fruta, *m.*

tartan, *s.* (*naut.*) tartana, *f.*; (plaid) tartán, *m.*

tartar, *s.* (*chem.*) tártaro, *m.*; (in teeth) sarro, tártaro, *m.*; **cream of t.,** (cremor) tártaro, *m.* **t. emetic,** tártaro emético, *m.* **Tartar,** *a.* and *s.* tártaro (-ra)

tartaric, *a.* (*chem.*) tártrico

tartly, *adv.* ásperamente, agriamente

tartness, *s.* acidez, *f.*; (*fig.*) aspereza, *f.*

task, *s.* tarea, labor, *f.*; empresa, *f.*; misión, *f.* **to take to t.,** regañar, censurar. **t.-force,** (naval or military) contingente, *m.*

taskmaster, *s.* el que señala una tarea; amo, *m.*

Tasmanian, *a.* de Tasmania

tassel, *s.* borla, *f.*; (of corn) panoja, espiga, *f.*

taste, *s.* gusto, *m.*; (flavour) sabor, *m.*; (specimen) ejemplo, *m.*, idea, *f.*; (small quantity) un poco, muy poco; (liking) afición, inclinación, *f.*; (of drink) sorbo, trago, *m.*; (tinge) dejo, *m.* *v.t.* (appraise) probar; gustar; (experience) experimentar, conocer. *v.i.* tener gusto, tener sabor. **a matter of t.,** cuestión de gusto. **Each to his own t.,** Entre gustos no hay disputa. **He had not tasted a bite,** No había probado bocado. **in bad (good) t.,** de mal (buen) gusto; de mal (buen) tono. **to have a t. for,** ser aficionado a, gustar de. **to t.,** (*cul.*) a gusto, a sabor. **to t. of,** tener gusto de, saber a

tasted, *a.* (in compounds) de sabor . . .

tasteful, *a.* de buen gusto

tastefully, *adv.* con buen gusto

tastefulness, *s.* buen gusto, *m.*

tasteless, *a.* insípido, soso, insulso; de mal gusto

tastelessness, *s.* insipidez, insulsez, *f.*; mal gusto, *m.*

taster, *s.* catador, *m.*; (vessel) catavino, *m.*

tasting, *s.* saboreo, *m.*, gustación, *f.* *a.* (in compounds) de sabor . . .

tasty, *a.* apetitoso, sabroso

tatter, *s.* andrajo, harapo, *m.*; jirón, *m.* **to tear in tatters,** hacer jirones

tattered, *a.* andrajoso, haraposo

tatting, *s.* frivolité, *m.*

tattoo, *s.* tatuaje, *m.*; (*mil.*) retreta, *f.*; (display) parada militar, *f.* *v.t.* tatuar

tattooing, *s.* tatuaje, *m.*; tamboreo, *m.*

taunt, *s.* mofa, *f.*, insulto, escarnio, *m.* *v.t.* insultar, atormentar. **to t. with,** echar en cara

taunting, *a.* insultante, burlón, insolente

tauntingly, *adv.* burlonamente, insolentemente

taurine, *a.* taurino

tauromachy, *s.* tauromaquia, *f.*

Taurus, *s.* tauro, toro, *m.*

taut, *a.* tieso, tirante, tenso; en regla; (*naut.*) **to make t.,** tesar

tauten, *v.t.* tesar; poner tieso

tautness, *s.* tensión, *f.*

tautological, *a.* tautológico

tautology, *s.* tautología, *f.*

tavern, *s.* taberna, *f.*; (inn) mesón, *m.*, posada, *f.* **t.-keeper,** tabernero, *m.*

tawdrily, *adv.* llamativamente, de un modo cursi

tawdriness, *s.* charrería, *f.*

tawdry, *a.* chillón, charro, cursi

tawny, *a.* leonado

tax, *s.* contribución, gabela, imposición, *f.*; (*fig.*) carga, *f.*; *v.t.* imponer contribuciones (a); (*law*) tasar; (*fig.*) cargar, abrumar. **to tax with,** tachar (de), acusar (de). **direct (indirect) tax,** contribución directa (indirecta), *f.* **tax-collector,** recaudador de contribuciones, *m.* **tax-free,** libre de impuestos. **tax-rate,** tarifa de impuestos, *f.*, cupo, *m.* **tax-register,** lista de contribuyentes, *f.*

taxable, *a.* imponible, sujeto a impuestos

taxation, *s.* imposición de contribuciones (or impuestos), *f.*

taxi, *s.* taxi, *m.* *v.i.* ir en un taxi; (*aer.*) correr por tierra. **t. driver,** chófer de un taxi, *m.* **t. rank,** parada de taxis, *f.*

taxidermist, *s.* taxidermista, *m.* and *f.*

taxidermy, *s.* taxidermia, *f.*

taximeter, *s.* taxímetro, *m.*

taxpayer, *s.* contribuyente, *m.* and *f.*

taxpaying, *a.* tributario, que paga contribuciones

tea, *s.* (liquid) té, *m.*; (meal) merienda, *f.* **to have tea,** tomar el té, merendar. **tea-caddy,** bote para té, *m.* **tea-chest,** caja para té, *f.* **tea-cosy,** cubretetera, *m.* **tea-cup,** taza para té, *f.* **tea-dance,** té baile, *m.* **tea-kettle** or **tea-pot,** tetera, *f.* **tea-leaf,** hoja de té, *f.* **tea-party,** reunión para tomar el té, *f.* **tea-room,** salón de té, *m.* **tea-rose,** rosa de té, *f.* **tea-set,** juego de té, *m.* **tea-strainer,** colador de té, *m.* **tea-time,** hora de té, *f.* **tea-urn,** samowar, *m.*, tetera para hacer té, *f.* **tea-waggon,** carrito para el té, *m.*

teach, *v.t.* (a person) enseñar, instruir; (a subject) enseñar; (to lecture on) ser profesor de; (a lesson) dar una lección (de). **to t. a person Spanish,** enseñar el castellano a alguien. **to t. how to,** enseñar a (followed by infin.)

teachability, *s.* docilidad, *f.*

teachable, *a.* educable; dócil

teacher, *s.* preceptor, *m.*; profesor, maestro, *m.* **woman t.,** profesora, maestra, *f.*

teaching, *s.* enseñanza, *f.*; (belief) doctrina, *f.* *a.* docente. **t. profession,** magisterio, *m.*

teak, *s.* (*bot.*) teca, *f.*; (wood) madera de teca, *f.*

team, *s.* (of horses) tiro, *m.*; (of oxen, mules) par, *m.*, pareja, yunta, *f.*; (*sport*) partido, equipo, *m.*; compañía, *f.*; grupo, *m.* *v.t.* enganchar, uncir. **t.-work,** cooperación, *f.*

teamster, *s.* gañán, *m.*

tear, *v.t.* rasgar; romper; lacerar; (in pieces) hacer pedazos, despedazar; (scratch) arañar; (*fig.*) atormentar. **to t. asunder,** romper; desmembrar. **to t. away,** arrancar, quitar violentamente. **to t. down,** derribar, echar abajo. **to t. off,** arrancar; desgajar. **to t. oneself away,** arrancarse, desgarrarse. **to t. one's hair,** arrancarse los pelos, mesarse. **to t. open,** abrir apresuradamente. **to t. up,** hacer pedazos; (uproot) arrancar, desarraigar.

tear, *v.i.* rasgarse; romper; correr precipitadamente. **to t. along,** correr rápidamente (por). **to t. away,** marcharse corriendo. **to t. down,** bajar corriendo. **to t. into,** entrar corriendo en. **to t. off,** irse precipitadamente, marcharse corriendo. **to t. up,** subir corriendo; llegar corriendo; atravesar rápidamente

tear, *s.* lágrima, *f.*; (drop) gota, *f.* **with tears in one's eyes,** con lágrimas en los ojos. **to shed tears,** llorar, lagrimear. **to wipe away one's tears,** secarse las lágrimas. **t.-drop,** lágrima, *f.* **t.-duct,** conductor lacrimal, *m.* **t.-gas,** gas lacrimante, *m.* **t.-stained,** mojado de lágrimas

tear, *s.* (rent) rasgón, *m.*

tearful, *a.* lloroso, lacrimoso

tearfully, *adv.* con lágrimas en los ojos

tearing, *s.* rasgadura, *f.*, desgarro, *m.*

tease, *v.t.* (card) cardar; (annoy) fastidiar, irritar, molestar; (chaff) tomar el pelo (a), embromar; (pester) importunar. *s.* bromista, *m.* and *f.*

teasel, *s.* (*bot.*) cardencha, *f.* *v.t.* cardar

teaser, *s.* (problem) rompecabezas, *m.*; (person) bromista, *m* and *f.*

teaspoon, *s.* cucharita, *f.*

teaspoonful, *s.* cucharadita, *f.*

teat, *s.* pezón, *m.*; (of animals) teta, *f.*

technical, *a.* técnico. **t. offence,** (*law*) cuasidelito, *m.* **t. school,** escuela industrial, *f.*

technicality, s. carácter técnico, m.; tecnicismo, m.; detalle técnico, m.

technically, adv. técnicamente

technician, s. técnico, m.

technicolour, s. tecnicolor, m.

technique, s. técnica, f.; ejecución, f.; mecanismo, m.

technological, a. tecnológico

technologist, s. tecnólogo, m.

technology, s. tecnología, f.

teddy bear, s. osito de trapo, m.

tedious, a. aburrido, tedioso, pesado

tediously, adv. aburridamente

tediousness, s. aburrimiento, m., pesadez, f.

tedium, s. tedio, m., monotonía, f.

tee, s. (sport) meta, f.; (golf) "tee," m.; (letter) te, f.; cosa en forma de te, f. v.t. (golf) colocar la pelota en el "tee"

teem, v.i. rebosar (de), abundar (en); pulular, hormiguear, estar lleno (de); (with rain) diluviar

teeming, a. prolífico, fecundo. t. with, abundante en, lleno de

teens, s. pl. números y años desde trece hasta veinte; edad de trece a diez y nueve años de edad. to be still in one's t., no haber cumplido aún los veinte

teeter, v.i. balancearse, columpiarse

teethe, v.i. endentecer, echar los dientes

teething, s. dentición, f. t.-ring, chupador, m.

teetotal, a. abstemio

teetotalism, s. abstinencia completa de bebidas alcohólicas, f.

teetotaller, s. abstemio (-ia)

teetotum, s. perinola, f.

tegument, s. tegumento, m.

telecommunication, s. telecomunicación, f.

telegram, s. telegrama, m.

telegraph, s. telégrafo, m. v.i. telegrafiar; (fig.) hacer señas. v.t. telegrafiar, enviar por telégrafo. t. line, línea telegráfica, f. t. office, central de telégrafos, f. t. pole, poste telegráfico, m. t. wire, hilo telegráfico, m.

telegraphic, a. telegráfico

telegraphist, s. telegrafista, m. and f.

telegraphy, s. telegrafía, f. wireless t., telegrafía sin hilos, f.

telemeter, s. telémetro, m.

telemetry, s. telemetría, f.

teleology, s. teleología, f.

telepathic, a. telepático

telepathy, s. telepatía, f.

telephone, s. teléfono, m. v.i. telefonear. v.t. telefonear, llamar por teléfono. to be on the t., (speaking) estar comunicando; (of subscribers) tener teléfono. dial t., teléfono automático, m. t. call, comunicación telefónica, f.; conversación telefónica, f. t. call box, teléfono público, m. t. directory, guía de teléfonos, f. t. exchange, central telefónica, f. t. number, número de teléfono, m. t. operator, telefonista, m. and f. t. receiver, receptor telefónico, m. t. wire, hilo telefónico, m.

telephonic, a. telefónico

telephonist, s. telefonista, m. and f.

telephony, s. telefonía, f. wireless t., telefonía sin hilos, f.

teleprinter, s. teletipo, m.

telescope, s. telescopio, catalejo, m. v.t. enchufar. v.i. enchufarse, meterse una cosa dentro de otra

telescopic, a. telescópico; de enchufe

televise, v.t. transmitir por televisión

television, s. televisión, f.

tell, v.t. contar, narrar; decir; revelar; expresar; (the time, of clocks) marcar; (inform) comunicar, informar; (show) indicar, manifestar; (explain) explicar; distinguir; (order) mandar; (compute) contar. v.i. decir; (have effect) producir efecto. We cannot t., No sabemos. Who can t.? ¿Quién sabe? T. that to the marines!; Cuéntaselo a tu tía! to t. its own tale, hacer ver por sí mismo lo que hay. to t. again, volver a decir; contar otra vez. to t. off, regañar, reñir; (on a mission) despachar, mandar. to t. on, delatar. to t. upon, afectar

teller, s. narrador (-ra); (of votes) escrutador (-ra) de votos; (payer) pagador, m.

telling, a. notable, significante.
s. narración, f.

tell-tale, s. chismoso (-sa), soplón (-ona); (informer) acusón
(-ona); (fig.) indicio, m., señal, f.
a. revelador

tellural, a. telúrico

temerity, s. temeridad, f.

tempᵉr, s. (of metals) temple, m.;
(nature) naturaleza, f., carácter,
m.; espíritu, m.; (mood) humor,
m.; (anger) mal genio, m. v.t.
(of metals) templar; moderar,
mitigar; mezclar. v.i. templarse. bad (good) t., mal (buen)
humor. to keep one's t., no
enojarse, no impacientarse. to
lose one's t., enojarse, perder
la paciencia

tempera, s. (art) templa, f. in
t.; al temple, m.

temperament, s. temperamento,
m.; modo de ser, natural, m.,
naturaleza, índole, f.; (mus.)
temple, m.

temperamental, a. natural, innato; caprichoso

temperamentally, adv. por naturaleza

temperance, s. moderación, templanza, f.; sobriedad, abstinencia, f.

temperate, a. moderado; sobrio;
(of regions) templado. t. zone,
zona templada, f.

temperately, adv. sobriamente

temperateness, s. moderación,
sobriedad, mesura, f.; (of regions)
templanza, f.

temperature, s. temperatura, f.
to have a t., tener fiebre

tempered, a. de humor . . .., de
genio . . . to be good (bad) t.,
ser de buen (mal) humor

tempering, s. temperación, f.

tempest, s. tempestad, borrasca,
f., temporal,m.; (fig.) tormenta,f.

tempestuous, a. tempestuoso,
borrascoso; (fig.) impetuoso,
violento

tempestuousness, s. lo tempestuoso; (fig.) impetuosidad, violencia, f.

Templar, s. templario, m.

temple, s. templo, m.; (anat.)
sien, f.

tempo, s. (mus.) tiempo, m.

temporal, a. temporal; (transient) transitorio, fugaz; (anat.)

temporal. s. (anat.) hueso temporal, m.

temporality, s. temporalidad, f.

temporarily, adv. provisionalmente

temporariness, s. interinidad, f.

temporary, a. provisional, interino

temporize, v.i. ganar tiempo;
contemporizar

temporizing, s. contemporización, f. a. contemporizador

tempt, v.t. tentar; atraer, seducir

temptation, s. tentación, f.;
aliciente, atractivo, m.

tempter, s. tentador (-ra)

tempting, a. tentador, atrayente; seductor

ten, a. diez; (of the clock) las
diez, f. pl.; (of age) diez años,
m. pl. s. diez, m.; (a round
number) decena, f.; ten-
millionth, a. and s. diezmillonésimo (m.). ten months old,
diezmesino. ten syllable, decasílabo. ten thousand, a.
and s. diez mil (m.). There are
ten thousand soldiers, Hay
diez mil soldados. ten-thousandth, a. and s. diezmilésimo
(m.)

tenable, a. sostenible, defendible

tenacious, a. tenaz; (stubborn)
porfiado, obstinaz, terco; (sticky)
adhesivo. to be t. of life, estar
muy apegado a la vida

tenaciously, adv. tenazmente;
porfiadamente

tenacity, s. tenacidad, f.; porfía, f.;
tesón, m.

tenancy, s. inquilinato, m.; tenencia, f.

tenant, s. arrendatario (-ia), inquilino (-na); habitante, m.;
morador (-ra)

tenantry, s. inquilinos, m. pl.

tench, s. (icht.) tenca, f.

tend, v.t. cuidar, atender; guardar; vigilar. v.i. tender; inclinarse (a), propender (a)

tendency, s. tendencia, inclinación, propensión, f.; proclividad, f.

tendentious, a. tendencioso

tender, s. guardián, m.; (com.)
oferta, propuesta, f.; (naut.)
falúa, f.; (of a railway engine)
ténder, m. legal t., moneda
corriente, f.

tender, *a.* tierno; delicado; (of conscience) escrupuloso; (of a subject) espinoso; compasivo, afectuoso, sensible; muelle, blando. **t.-hearted**, compasivo, tierno de corazón

tender, *v.t.* ofrecer; dar; presentar. *v.i.* hacer una oferta. **to t. condolences**, dar el pésame. **to t. one's resignation**, presentar la dimisión. **to t. thanks**, dar las gracias

tenderly, *adv.* tiernamente

tenderness, *s.* ternura, *f.*; sensibilidad, *f.*; delicadeza, *f.*; dulzura, *f.*; indulgencia, *f.*; compasividad, benevolencia, *f.*; escrupulosidad, *f.*; mimo, cariño, *m.*

tendon, *s.* (*anat.*) tendón, *m.* **t. of Achilles**, tendón de Aquiles, *m.*

tendril, *s.* (*bot.*) zarcillo, cirro, *m.*

tenement, *s.* casa de vecindad, *f.*; vivienda, *f.*; (*poet.*) morada, *f.*

tenet, *s.* principio, dogma, *m.*, doctrina, *f.*

tenfold, *a.* décuplo. *adv.* diez veces

tennis, *s.* tenis, *m.* **to play t.**, jugar al tenis. **t. ball**, pelota de tenis, *f.* **t. court**, pista de tenis, *f.* **t. racket**, raqueta de tenis, *f.*

tenon, *s.* (*carp.*) espiga, *f.* *v.t.* espigar

tenor, *s.* curso, *m.*; tenor, contenido, *m.*; (*mus.*) tenor, *m.*; (*mus.*) alto, *m.*; (mus. instrument) viola, *f.* *a.* (*mus.*) de tenor

tense, *s.* (*gram.*) tiempo, *m.* *a.* tirante, estirado, tieso; tenso

tenseness, *s.* tirantez, *f.*; tensión, *f.*

tensile, *a.* tensor; extensible

tension, *s.* tensión, *f.*; (*elec.*) voltaje, *m.*, tensión, *f.*; (of sewing-machine) tensahilo, *m.* **state of t.**, (diplomatic) estado de tirantez, *m.*

tent, *s.* tienda (de campaña), *f.*; (bell) pabellón, *m.*; (*surg.*) tienda, *f.* **oxygen t.**, tienda oxígena, *f.* **to pitch tents**, armar las tiendas de campaña; acamparse. **to strike tents**, plegar tiendas. **t. fly**, toldo de tienda, *m.* **t. maker**, tendero, *m.* **t. peg**, clave que sujeta las cuerdas de una tienda, *f.* **t. pole**, mástil (or montante) de tienda, *m.*

tentacle, *s.* tentáculo, *m.*

tentative, *a.* tentativo. *s.* tentativa, *f.*; ensayo, *m.*

tentatively, *adv.* por vía de ensayo, experimentalmente

tenth, *a.* décimo; (of monarchs) diez; (of the month) (el) diez. *s.* décimo, *m.*; (part) décima parte, *f.*; (*mus.*) decena, *f.*

tenthly, *adv.* en décimo lugar

tenuity, *s.* tenuidad, *f.*; sutilidad, *f.*; delgadez, *f.*

tenuous, *a.* tenue; sutil; delgado; fino

tenure, *s.* tenencia, posesión, *f.*; (duration) duración, *f.*; (of office) administración, *f.*

tepid, *a.* tibio

tepidity, *s.* tibieza, *f.*

teratology, *s.* teratología, *f.*

tercentenary, *s.* tercer centenario, *m.*

tercet, *s.* terceto, *m.*

terentian, *a.* terenciano

term, *s.* (limit) límite, fin, *m.*; (period) plazo, tiempo, período, *m.*; (schools, universities) trimestre, *m.*; (*math.*, *law*, *logic*) término, *m.*; (word) expresión, palabra, *f.* *pl.* **terms**, (conditions) condiciones, *f.* *pl.*; (charges) precios, *m.* *pl.*, tarifa, *f.*; (words) términos, *m.* *pl.*, palabras, *f.* *pl.* *v.t.* llamar, calificar. **for a t. of years**, por un plazo de años. **in plain terms**, en palabras claras. **on equal terms**, en iguales condiciones. **to be on bad (good) terms with**, estar en (or tener) malas (buenas) relaciones con. **to come to terms**, llegar a un acuerdo; hacer las paces. **What are your terms?** ¿Cuáles son sus condiciones?; (price) ¿Cuáles son sus precios? **terms of sale**, condiciones de venta, *f.* *pl.*

termagant, *s.* arpía, fiera, *f.*

terminable, *a.* terminable

terminal, *a.* terminal, final; (of schools, universities) trimestre. *s.* término, *m.*; (*elec.*) borne, *m.*; (schools, universities) examen de fin de trimestre, *m.*; (railway) estación terminal, *f.*; (*arch.* and figure) término, *m.*; (*arch.*) remate, *m.*

terminate, *v.t.* limitar; terminar, concluir, poner fin (a). *v.i.* terminarse, concluirse (por); cesar

termination, *s.* terminación, conclusión, *f.*; fin, *m.*; (*gram.*) terminación, *f.*; cabo, remate, *m.*

terminology, *s.* nomenclatura, terminología, *f.*

terminus, *s.* (railway) estación terminal, *f.*; (*arch.* and figure) término, *m.*; (*arch.*) remate, *m.*; (*myth.*) el dios término

termite, *s.* (*ent.*) termita, *m.*

tern, *s.* terno, *m.*; (*orn.*) golondrina de mar, *f.*

ternary, *a.* ternario, trino. *s.* terno, *m.*

Terpsichorean, *a.* de Terpsícore

terrace, *s.* terraza, *f.* *v.t.* terra- plenar

terraced, *a.* en terrazas; con terrazas

terra-cotta, *s.* terracota, *f.*

terrain, *s.* terreno, campo, *m.*, región, *f.*

terrapin, *s.* tortuga de agua dulce, *f.*

terraqueous, *a.* terráqueo

terreplein, *s.* (*mil.*) terraplén, *m.*

terrestrial, *a.* terrestre, terrenal

terrible, *a.* terrible, pavoroso, espantoso; (*fam.*) tremendo

terribleness, *s.* terribilidad, *f.*, lo horrible

terribly, *adv.* terriblemente

terrier, *s.* terrier, *m.*; (*fam.*) soldado del ejército territorial, *m.*

terrific, *a.* espantoso, terrible; (*fam.*) atroz, tremendo

terrify, *v.t.* aterrorizar, espantar, horrorizar

terrifying, *a.* aterrador, espantoso

territorial, *a.* territorial. *s.* soldado del ejército territorial, *m.*

territoriality, *s.* territorialidad, *f.*

territory, *s.* región, comarca, *f.*; (state) territorio, *m.*; jurisdicción, *f.* **mandated territories,** territorios bajo mandato, *m. pl.*

terror, *s.* terror, pavor, espanto, *m.* **the reign of t.,** el reinado del terror, *m.* **t.-stricken,** espantado, muerto de miedo

terrorism, *s.* terrorismo, *m.*

terrorist, *s.* terrorista, *m.*

terrorization, *s.* aterramiento, *m.*

terrorize, *v.t.* aterrorizar

terse, *a.* conciso, sucinto; seco, brusco

tersely, *adv.* concisamente; secamente

terseness, *s.* concisión, *f.*; brusquedad, *f.*

tertian, *s.* (*med.*) terciana, *f.*

tertiary, *a.* tercero; (*geol.*) terciario. *s.* (*ecc.*) terciario, *m.*

tessellated, *a.* teselado

tessellation, *s.* mosaico, *m.*

tessera, *s.* tesela, *f.*

test, *s.* (proof) prueba, *f.*; examen, *m.*; investigación, *f.*; (standard) criterio, *m.*, piedra de toque, *f.*; (*chem.*) análisis, *m.*; (trial) ensayo, *m.*; (*zool.*) concha, *f.* *v.t.* (*chem.*) ensayar; probar, poner a prueba; examinar; (eyes) graduar (la vista). **to put to the t.,** poner a prueba. **to stand the t.,** soportar la prueba. **t. match,** partido internacional de cricket, *m.* **t. meal,** (*med.*) comida de prueba, *f.* **t. pilot,** (*aer.*) piloto de pruebas, *m.* **t. tube,** tubo de ensayo, *m.*

testament, *s.* testamento, *m.* **New T.,** Nuevo Testamento, *m.* **Old T.,** Antiguo Testamento, *m.*

testamentary, *a.* testamentario

testate, *a.* testado

testator, *s.* testador, *m.* (**testatrix,** testadora, *f.*)

tester, *s.* (canopy) testera, *f.*

testicle, *s.* teste, genital, testículo, *m.*

testification, *s.* testificación, *f.*

testify, *v.t.* and *v.i.* declarar, atestar; (*law*) atestiguar, testificar, dar fe

testily, *adv.* malhumoradamente

testimonial, *s.* recomendación, *f.*; certificado, *m.*; (tribute) homenaje, *m.*

testimony, *s.* testimonio, *m.*, declaración, *f.*; (proof prueba, *f.* **in t. whereof,** en fe de lo cual. **to bear t.,** atestar

testiness, *s.* mal humor, *m.*, irritación, *f.*

testis, *s.* teste, *m.*

testy, *a.* enojadizo, irritable, irascible, quisquilloso

tetanus, *s.* tétano, *m.*

tether, *s.* traba, atadura, maniota, *f.* *v.t.* atar con una correa. **to be at the end of one's t.,**

acabarse la resistencia; acabarse la paciencia

tetrachord, *s.* (*mus.*) tetracordio, *m.*

tetrahedron, *s.* (*geom.*) tetraedro, *m.*

tetrarch, *s.* tetrarca, *m.*

Teuton, *s.* Teutón (-oña)

Teutonic, *a.* teutónico

text, *s.* texto, *m.*; (subject) tema, *m.*; (motto) lema, *m.*; (of a musical composition) letra, *f.* t.-book, libro de texto, *m.*

textile, *a.* textil, de tejer. *s.* textil, *m.*, materia textil, *f.*; tejido, *m.*

textual, *a.* textual

textualist, *s.* textualista, *m.*

textually, *adv.* textualmente

texture, *s.* (material and *biol.*) tejido, *m.*; textura, *f.*

thalamus, *s.* (*anat.*, *bot.*) tálamo, *m.*

thaler, *s.* (old coin) tálero, *m.*

thallium, *s.* (*min.*) talio, *m.*

Thames, *s.* Támesis, *m.* to set the T. on fire, descubrir la pólvora

than, *conjunc.* que; (between "more" or "less" and a number) de; (in comparisons of inequality) que, but que becomes (*a*) del (de la, de los, de las) que if the point of comparison is a noun in the principal clause, which has to be supplied mentally to fill up the ellipsis; (*b*) de lo que if there is no noun to act as a point of comparison, e.g. He was older than I thought, Él era más viejo de·lo que yo pensaba. They have less than they deserve, Tienen menos de lo que merecen.. They lose more money than (the money) they earn, Pierden más dinero del que ganan. He will meet with more opposition than he thought, Va a encontrar más oposición de la que pensaba. I have more books than you, Tengo más libros que tú. She has less than nine and more than five, Ella tiene menos de nueve y más de cinco

thank, *v.t.* agradecer, dar las gracias (a). to t. for, agradecer. I will t. you to be more polite, Le agradecería que fuese más cortés. He has himself to

t. for it, Él mismo tiene la culpa de ello. No, t. you, No, muchas gracias. T. goodness! ¡Gracias a Dios!

thank, *s.* (now in pl. only, thanks) gracias, *f. pl.* a vote of thanks, un voto de gracias. Many thanks! ¡Muchas gracias! to return thanks, dar las gracias. thanks to, merced a, debido a. thanks to you, gracias a ti. t.-offering, ofrecimiento en acción de gracias, *m.*

thankful, *a.* agradecido. I am t. to see, Me alegro de ver, Me es grato ver

thankfully, *adv.* con gratitud, agradecido

thankfulness, *s.* agradecimiento, *m.*; gratitud, *f.*

thankless, *a.* ingrato; desagradecido; desagradable

thanksgiving, *s.* acción de gracias, *f.* t. service, servicio de acción de gracias, *m.*

that, *dem. a.* ese, *m.*; esa, *f.*; aquel, *m.*; aquella, *f.* *dem. pron.* ése, *m.*; ésa, *f.*; eso, *neut.*; aquél, *m.*; aquélla, *f.*; aquello, *neut.*; (standing for a noun) el, *m.*; la, *f.*; lo, *neut.* All t. there is, Todo lo que hay. His temperament is t. of his mother, Su temperamento es el de su madre. We have not.come to t. yet, No hemos llegado a ese punto todavía. T. is what I want to know, Eso es lo que quiero saber. with t., con eso; (thereupon) en eso. Go t. way, Vaya Vd. por allí; Tome Vd. aquel camino. T. is to say . . ., Es decir . . . What do you mean by t.? ¿Qué quieres decir con eso? The novel is not as bad as all t., La novela no es tan mala como todo eso

that, *pron. rel.* que; el cual, *m.*; la cual, *f.*; lo cual, *neut.*; (of persons) a quien, *m.* and *f.*; a quienes, *m.* and *f. pl.*; (with from) de·quien, *m.* and *f.*; de quienes, *m.* and *f. pl.*; (of place) donde. The letter t. I sent you, la carta que te mandé. The box t. John put them in, la caja en la cual los puso Juan. The last time t. I saw her, La última vez que la vi·

that, *conjunc.* que; (of purpose) para que; afin de que; (before infin.) para; (because) porque. **O t.** he would come! ¡Ojalá que viniese! **so t.,** para que; (before infin.) para; (as a result) de manera que; de modo que. **It is better t.** he should not come, Es mejor que no venga. **now t.,** ahora que

thatch, *s.* barda, *f.* *v.t.* bardar

thaumaturgy, *s.* taumaturgia, *f.*

thaw, *s.* deshielo, *m.* *v.t.* deshelar; derretir. *v.i.* deshelarse; derretirse

the, *def. art.* el, *m.*; la, *f.*; lo, *neut.*; los, *m. pl.*; las, *f. pl.*; (before feminine sing. noun beginning with stressed a or ha) el; (untranslated between the name and number of a monarch, pope, ruler, e.g. **Charles the Tenth,** Carlos diez). *adv.* (before a comparative) cuanto, tanto más. **at the or to the,** al, *m.* (also before feminine sing. noun beginning with a or ha); a la, *f.*; a lo, *neut.*; a los, *m. pl.*; a las, *f. pl.* **from the or of the,** del, *m.* (also before feminine sing. noun beginning with stressed a or ha); de la, *f.*; de lo, *neut.*; de los, *m. pl.*; de las, *f. pl.* **the one,** see **one. The sooner the better,** Cuánto antes mejor. **The room will be all the warmer,** El cuarto estará tanto más caliente

theatin, *a.* and *s.(ecc.)* teatino (*m.*)

theatre, *s.* teatro, *m.*; (lecture) anfiteatro, *m.*; (drama) teatro, *m.*, obra dramática, *f.*; (scene) teatro, *m.*, escena, *f.* **t. attendant,** acomodador (-ra)

theatrical, *a.* teatral. *s. pl.* **theatricals,** funciones teatrales, *f. pl.* **amateur theatricals,** función de aficionados, *f.* **t. company,** compañía de teatro, *f.* **t. costumier,** mascarero (-ra), alquilador (-ra) de disfraces. **t. manager,** empresario de teatro, *m.*

theatricality, *s.* teatralidad, *f.*

theatrically, *adv.* teatralmente

theban, *a.* and *s.* tebeo (-ea), tebano (-na)

thee, *pers. pron.* te; (after prep.) ti. **with t.,** contigo

theft, *s.* robo, hurto, *m.*

their, *poss. a.* su, *m.* and *f. sing.*; sus, *pl.*; de ellos, *m. pl.*; de ellas, *f. pl.* **They have t. books,** Ellos tienen sus libros. **I have t. books,** Tengo los libros de ellos.

theirs, *poss. pron.* (el) suyo, *m.*; (la) suya, *f.*; (los) suyos, *m. pl.*; (las) suyas, *f. pl.*; de ellos, *m. pl.*; de ellas, *f. pl.* **These hats are t.,** Estos sombreros son los suyos

theism, *s.* teísmo, *m.*

theist, *s.* teísta, *m.* and *f.*

theistic, *a.* teísta

them, *pers. pron.* ellos, *m. pl.*; ellas, *f. pl.*; (as object of a verb) los, *m. pl.*; las, *f. pl.*; (to them) les

thematic, *a.* temático

theme, *s.* tema, asunto, *m.*; tesis, *f.*; (*mus.*) tema, motivo, *m.*

themselves, *pers. pron. pl.* ellos mismos, *m. pl.*; ellas mismas, *f. pl.* *reflexive pron.* sí; sí mismos; (with a reflexive verb) se. **They have bought t. some sweets,** Se han comprado bombones. **They t. told me about it,** Ellos mismos me lo dijeron. **They left it for t.,** Lo dejaron para sí (mismos)

then, *adv.* (of future time) entonces; (of past time) a la sazón, en aquella época, entonces; (next, afterwards) luego, después, en seguida; (in that case) en este caso, entonces; (therefore) por consiguiente. *a.* de entonces. *s.* entonces, *m.* *conjunc.* (moreover) además; pues. **And what t.?** ¿Y qué pasó después?; ¿Y qué pasará ahora?; ¿Y qué más? **before t.,** antes de entonces. **by t.,** por entonces. **now and t.,** de vez en cuando. **now...t.,** ya...ya, ora...ora. **since t.,** desde aquel tiempo; desde entonces; desde aquella ocasión. **until t.,** hasta entonces; hasta aquella época. **well t.,** bien, pues. **t. and there,** en el acto, en seguida; allí mismo

thence, *adv.* desde allí, de allí; (therefore) por eso, por esa razón, por consiguiente

thenceforth, *adv.* de allí en adelante, desde entonces

theocracy, *s.* teocracia, *f.*

theocratic, *a.* teocrático

theodolite, *s.* teodolito, *m.*

Theodosian, *a.* teodosiano

theologian, s. teólogo, m.
theological, a. teológico, teologal
theologize, v.i. teologizar
theology, s. teología, f.
theorem, s. teorema, m.
theoretical, a. teórico
theoretically, adv. teóricamente, en teoría
theorist, s. teórico, m.
theorize, v.i. teorizar
theory, s. teoría, f.
theosophical, a. teosófico
theosophist, s. teósofo, m.
theosophy, s. teosofía, f.
therapeutic, a. terapéutico. s. **therapeutics,** terapéutica, f.
therapeutist, s. terapeuta, m. and f.
therapy, suffix, terapia, f.
there, adv. allí; ahí, allá; (at that point) en eso; (used pronominally as subject of verb) haber, e.g. T. was once a king, Hubo una vez un rey; What is t. to do here? ¿Qué hay que hacer aquí? interj. ¡vaya!; (I told you so!) ¡ya ves! ¡ya te lo dije yo!; (in surprise) ¡toma!· about t., cerca de allí. down t., allí abajo. in t., allí dentro. on t., allí, encima de . . . (followed by name of object). out t., allí fuera. over t., ahí; allá a lo lejos. to go t. and back, ir y volver. under t., allí abajo; debajo de aquello. up t., allí arriba. T. came a time when . . ., Llegó la hora cuando . . . ¡Allí está! t. is or t. are, hay. t. was or t. were, había, hubo. t. may be, puede haber, quizás habrá. t. must be, tiene que haber. t. will be, habrá. T. will be many people who will buy it, Habrá muchos que lo comprarán. T., t.! (to a child, etc.) ¡Vamos!
thereabouts, adv. (near to a place) cerca de allí, por ahí, allí cerca; (approximately) aproximadamente, cerca de
thereafter, adv. después, después de eso
thereby, adv. (near to that place) por allí cerca; (by that means) con lo cual, de este modo
therefore, adv. por lo tanto, por eso, así, por consiguiente; por esta razón

therein, adv. (inside) allí dentro; (in this, that particular) en esto, en eso, en ese particular
thereinafter, adv. posteriormente, más adelante
thereupon, adv. (in consequence) por consiguiente, por lo tanto; (at that point) luego, en eso; (immediately afterwards) inmediatamente después, en seguida
therm, s. unidad térmica, f.
thermæ, s. pl. termas (de los romanos), f. pl.
thermal, a. termal. t. springs, aguas termales, termas, f. pl.
thermic, a. térmico
thermionic, a. termiónico. (rad.) t. valve, lámpara termiónica, f., tubo termiónico, m.
thermite, s. (ent.) termita, m.
thermodynamics, s. termodinámica, f.
thermoelectric, a. termoeléctrico
thermometer, s. termómetro, m.
thermoscope, s. termoscopio, m.
thermos flask, s. termos, m.
thermostat, s. termostato, m.
thermostatic, a. termostático
thesaurus, s. tesoro, tesauro, m.
these, dem. pron. pl. of this, éstos, m. pl.; éstas, f. pl. dem. a. estos, m. pl.; estas, f. pl. Are not t. your flowers? ¿No son éstas tus flores? T. pictures have been sold, Estos cuadros han sido vendidos
thesis, s. tesis, f.
Thespian, a. dramático
Thessalonian, a. and s. tesalónico (-ca)
theurgy, s. teurgia, f.
thews, s. pl. músculos, m. pl.; (fig.) vigor, m., robustez, f.
they, pers. pron. pl. ellos, m. pl.; ellas, f. pl.; (people) se (followed by sing. verb). T. say, Dicen, Se dice
thick, a. espeso; (big) grueso; (of vapours) denso; (muddy) turbio; (dense, close) tupido apretado; (numerous) numeroso, repetido, continuo; (full of) lleno (de); (of voice) velado, indistinto; (obtuse) estúpido, lerdo; (friendly) íntimo. adv. densamente; continuamente, sin cesar. three feet t., de tres pies de espesor. That's

a bit t.! ¡Eso es un poco demasiado! **to be as t. as thieves,** estar unidos como los dedos de la mano. **t.-lipped,** con labios gruesos, bezudo. **t.-headed,** estúpido, lerdo. **t.-skinned,** de piel gruesa; (zool.) paquidermo; (fig.) sin vergüenza, insensible. **t. stroke,** (of letters) grueso, m.

thick, s. espesor, m.; parte gruesa, f.; lo más denso; (of a fight) lo más reñido; centro, m. **in the t. of,** en el centro (de), en medio de

thicken, v.t. espesar; (increase) aumentar, multiplicar; (cul.) espesar. v.i. espesarse; condensar; aumentar, multiplicarse; (of a mystery, etc.) complicarse; hacerse más denso; (cul.) espesarse

thickening, s. hinchamiento, m.; gordura, f.; (cul. and of paints) espesante, m.

thicket, s. matorral, soto, m., maleza, f.; (grove) boscaje, m.

thickly, adv. densamente; espesamente; continuamente, sin cesar; (of speech) indistintamente

thickness, s. espesor, m.; grueso, m.; densidad, f.; (of liquids) consistencia, f.; (layer) capa, f.; (of speech) dificultad (en el hablar), f.

thickset, a. doblado

thief, s. ladrón (-ona); (in a candle) moco de vela, m. **Stop t.!** ¡Ladrones! **thieves' den,** (fig.) cueva de ladrones, f.

thieve, v.i. hurtar, robar. v.t. robar

thievish, a. ladrón

thigh, s. muslo, m. **t.-bone,** fémur, m.

thimble, s. dedal, m.

thimbleful, s. lo que cabe en un dedal; (fig.) dedada, f.

thin, a. delgado; (lean) flaco; (small) pequeño; delicado; fino; (of air, light) tenue, sutil; (clothes) ligero; (sparse) escaso; transparente; (watery) aguado; (of wine) bautizado; (not close) claro; (of arguments) flojo. v.t. adelgazar; aclarar; (agr.) limpiar; reducir. v.i. adelgazarse; afilarse; reducirse. **somewhat t.,** (of persons) delgaducho, algo flaco.

to grow t., enflaquecer; afilarse. **to make t.,** hacer adelgazar, volver flaco. **t.-clad,** ligero de ropa; mal vestido. **t.-faced,** de cara delgada. **t.-lipped,** de labios apretados. **t.-skinned,** de piel fina; (fig.) sensitivo, sensible

thine. See **theirs.** poss. pron. (el) tuyo, m.; (la) tuya, f.; (los) tuyos, m. pl.; (las) tuyas, f. pl.; tu, m. and f.; tus, m. and f. pl.; de ti. **The fault is t.,** La culpa es tuya or La culpa es de ti

thing, s. cosa, f.; objeto, artículo, m.; (affair) asunto, m.; (contemptuous) sujeto, tipo, m.; (creature) ser, m., criatura, f.; pl. **things,** (belongings) efectos, trastos, m. pl.; (luggage) equipaje, m.; (clothes) trapitos, m. pl.; (circumstances) circunstancias, condiciones, f. pl. **above all things,** ante todo, sobre todo. **a very pretty little t.,** (child) una pequeña muy mona. **As things are,** Tal como están las cosas. **for one t.,** en primer lugar. **Her behaviour is not quite the t.,** La conducta de ella no está bien vista. **It is a bad t. that . . . ,** Lo malo es que . . . **It is a good t. that . . . ,** Menos mal que . . .; Lo bueno es que . . . **No such t.!** ¡No hay tal!; ¡Nada de eso! **Poor t.!** ¡Pobrecito!; (woman) ¡Pobre mujer!; (man) ¡Pobre hombre! **to be just the t.,** venir al pelo. **with one t. and another,** entre unas cosas y otras

think, v.t. and v.i. pensar; (believe) creer; (deem) considerar, juzgar; imaginar; (suspect) sospechar; (opine) ser de opinión (que). **And to t. that . . . !** ¡Y pensar que . . . ! **As you t. fit,** Como usted quiera, Como a usted le parezca bien. **He thought as much,** Él se lo figuraba. **He little thought that . . . !** ¡Cuán lejos estaba de pensar que . . . ! **He thinks nothing of . .,** No le importa . . .; Desprecia, Tiene una opinión bastante mala de. **I don't t. so,** No lo creo. **I should just t. not!** ¡Claro que no! ¡Eso sí que no! **I should just t. so!** ¡Claro! ¡Ya lo creo! **It makes me t. of . . . ,** Me hace pensar en ... **One might t.**, Podría creerse ... **to t. better of something,** cambiar de opinión, considerar mejor. **to t. highly (badly) of,** tener buen (mal) concepto sobre. **to t. over carefully,** pensarlo bien, considerar detenidamente; (*fam.*) consultar con la almohada. **to t. proper,** creer conveniente. **to t. to oneself,** pensar para sí (or entre sí). **to t. too much of oneself,** pensar demasiado en sí; tener demasiada buena opinión de sí mismo; tener humos. **What do you t. about it?** ¿Qué te parece? **to t. about,** (of persons) pensar en; (of things) pensar de (or sobre); meditar, considerar, reflexionar sobre. **to t. for,** pensar por. **to t. of,** pensar en; pensar de (or sobre). **What do you t. of this?** ¿Qué te parece esto? **to t. out,** idear, proyectar, hacer planes para; (a problem) resolver. **to t. over,** pensar; reflexionar sobre, meditar sobre. **I shall t. it over,** Lo pensaré.

thinker, *s.* pensador, *m.*

thinking, *s.* pensamiento, *m.*, reflexión, meditación, *f.*; juicio, *m.*; opinión, *f.*, parecer, *m.* *a.* pensador; inteligente; racional; serio. **To my way of t.,** Según pienso yo, A mi parecer. **way of t.,** modo de pensar, *m.*

thinly, *adv.* delgadamente; esparcidamente; (lightly) ligeramente; poco numeroso

thinness, *s.* delgadez, *f.*; (leanness) flaqueza, *f.*; sutileza, tenuidad, *f.*; (lack) escasez, *f.*; pequeño número, *m.*; poca consistencia, *f.*

third, *a.* tercero (tercer before *m. sing.* noun); (of monarchs) tercero; (of the month) (el) tres. *s.* tercio, *m.*, tercera parte, *f.*; (*mus.*) tercera, *f.* **T. time lucky!** ¡A la tercera va la vencida! **t. class,** *s.* tercera clase, *f.* *a.* de tercera clase. **t. party,** tercera persona, *f.* **t. party insurance,** seguro contra tercera persona, *m.*; **t. person,** tercero (-ra) (*gram.*) tercera persona, *f.* **t.-rate,** de tercera clase

thirdly, *adv.* en tercer lugar

thirst, *s.* sed, *f.*; (*fig.*) deseo, *m.*, ansia, *f.*; entusiasmo, *m.* **to satisfy one's t.,** apagar (or matar) la sed

thirsty, *a.* sediento. **to be t.,** tener sed. **to make t.,** dar sed.

thirteen, *a.* and *s.* trece (*m.*). **t. hundred,** *a.* and *s.* mil trescientos (*m.*)

thirteenth, *a.* décimotercio; (of monarchs) trece; (of month) (el) trece, / *m.* *s.* décimotercio, trezavo, *m.*

thirtieth, *a.* trigésimo; (of month) (el) treinta, *m.* *s.* treintavo, *m.*

thirty, *a.* and *s.* treinta (*m.*). **t.-first,** treinta y uno

this, *dem. a.* este, *m.*; esta, *f.* *dem. pron.* éste, *m.*; ésta, *f.*; esto, *neut.* **by t. time,** a esta hora, ya. **like t.,** de este modo, así. **T. is Wednesday,** Hoy es miércoles. **What is all t.?** ¿Qué es todo esto?

thistle, *s.* cardo, *m.* **t.-down,** papo de cardo, vilano de cardo, *m.*

thistly, *a.* lleno de cardos; espinoso

thither, *adv.* allá, hacia allá; a ese fin. *a.* más remoto

Thomism, *s.* tomismo, *m.*

Thomist, *a.* and *s.* tomista (*m.* and *f.*)

thong, *s.* correa, tira, *f.*

thoracic, *a.* torácico

thorax, *s.* tórax, *m.*

thorium, *s.* (*min.*) torio, *m.*

thorn, *s.* espina, *f.*; (tree) espino, *m.*; (*fig.*) abrojo, *m.*, espina, *f.* **to be a t. in the flesh of,** ser una espina en el costado de. **t. brake,** espinar, *m.*

thornless, *a.* sin espinas

thorny, *a.* espinoso; (*fig.*) difícil, arduo

thorough, *a.* completo; perfecto; (conscientious) concienzudo; (careful) cuidadoso. **t.-bred,** (of animals) de pura raza, de casta; (of persons) bien nacido. **t.-paced,** cabal, consumado

thoroughfare, *s.* vía pública, *f.* **No t.,** Prohibido el paso; Calle cerrada

thoroughly, *adv.* completamente; (of knowing a subject) a fondo; concienzudamente

thoroughness, *s.* perfección, *f.*; minuciosidad, *f.*

those, *dem. a. pl.* of that, esos, *m. pl.*; esas, *f. pl.*; aquellos, *m. pl.*; aquellas, *f. pl. dem. pron.* ésos, *m. pl.*; ésas, *f. pl.*; aquéllos, *m. pl.*; aquéllas, *f. pl.*; (standing for a noun) los, *m. pl.*; las, *f. pl.* t. who, quienes, *m.* and *f. pl.*; los que, *m. pl.*; las que, *f. pl.* t. that or which, los que, *m. pl.*; las que, *f. pl.* Your eyes are t. of your mother, Tus ojos son los de tu madre

thou, *pers. pron.* tú

though, *conjunc.* (followed by subjunc. when doubt is implied or uncertain future time) aunque, bien que; (nevertheless) sin embargo, no obstante; (in spite of) a pesar de que; (but) pero. as t., como si (followed by subjunc.). even t., aunque (followed by subjunc.)

thought, *s.* pensamiento, *m.*; meditación, reflexión, *f.*; opinión, *f.*; consideración, *f.*; idea, *f.*, propósito, *m.*; (care) cuidado, *m.*, solicitud, *f.*; (fam.) pizca, *f.* on second thoughts, después de pensarlo bien. The t. struck him, Se le ocurrió la idea. to collect one's thoughts, orientarse; informarse (de). t.-reading, adivinación del pensamiento, *f.* t.-transference, telepatía, transmisión del pensamiento, *f.*

thoughtful, *a.* pensativo, meditabundo; serio; especulativo; (provident) previsor; (kind) atento, solícito; cuidadoso; (anxious) inquieto, intranquilo

thoughtfully, *adv.* pensativamente; seriamente; (providently) con previsión; (kindly) atentamente, solícitamente

thoughtfulness, *s.* natural reflexivo, *m.*, seriedad, *f.*; (kindness) solicitud, atención, *f.*; (forethought) previsión, *f.*

thoughtless, *a.* irreflexivo; (careless) descuidado, negligente; (unkind) inconsiderado; (silly) necio, estúpido

thoughtlessly, *adv.* sin pensar, irreflexivamente; negligentemente

thoughtlessness, *s.* irreflexión,

f.; descuido, *m.*, negligencia, *f.*; (unkindness) inconsideración, *f.*; (silliness) neciedad, *f.*

thousand, *a.* mil. -s. mil, *m.*; millar, *m.* one t., mil, *m.* one t. three hundred, *a.* mil trescientos, *m. pl.*; mil trescientas, *f. pl. s.* mil trescientos, *m. pl.* two (three) t., dos (tres) mil. by thousands, por millares; por miles. t.-fold, mil veces más

thousandth, *a.* and *s.* milésimo (*m.*)

Thracian, *a.* and *s.* traciano (-na), tracio (-ia)

thrall, *s.* esclavo (-va); esclavitud, *f.*

thrash, *v.t.* azotar, apalear; (agr.) trillar, desgranar; (fam.) triunfar sobre, derrotar. *v.i.* (agr.) trillar el grano; arrojarse, agitarse. (fig.) to t. out, ventilar

thrashing, *s.* apaleamiento, *m.*, paliza, *f.*; (agr.) See threshing

thread, *s.* hilo, *m.*; (fibre) hebra, fibra, *f.*, filamento, *m.*; (of a screw) filete, *m.*; (fig.) hilo, *m. a.* de hilo. *v.t.* (a needle) enhebrar; (beads) ensartar; (make one's way) colarse a través de, atravesar; pasar por. to hang by a t., pender de un hilo. to lose the t. of, (fig.) perder el hilo de

threadbare, *a.* raído; muy usado; (fig.) trivial, viejo

threadlike, *a.* como un hilo, filiforme

threadworm, *s.* oxiurius vermicularis, *m.*, lombriz intestinal, *f.*

threat, *s.* amenaza, *f.*

threaten, *v.t.* and *v.i.* amenazar. to t. with, amenazar con

threatening, *a.* amenazador. *s.* amenazas, *f. pl.*

threateningly, *adv.* con amenazas

three, *a.* and *s.* tres (*m.*); (of the clock) las tres, *f. pl.*; (of one's age) tres años, *m. pl.* t.-colour process, tricromía, *f.* t.-coloured, tricolor. t.-cornered, triangular; (of hats) de tres picos, tricornio. t.-cornered hat, sombrero de tres picos, tricornio, *m.* t. decker, (naut.) navío de tres puentes, *m.*; novela larga, *f.* t. deep, en tres hileras. t. hundred, *a.* and *s.* trescientos (*m.*). t.-hundredth, *a.* and *s.* tricentésimo (*m.*). t.-legged, de

tres patas. **t.-legged stool,**
banqueta, *f.* **t.-per-cents,**
acciones al tres por ciento (3%),
f. pl. **t.-phase,** (*elec.*) trifásico.
t.-ply, (of yarn) triple; (of wood)
de tres capas. **t.-quarter,** de
tres cuartos. **t. quarters of an
hour,** tres cuartos de hora, *m.
pl.* **t.-sided,** trilátero. **t. speed
gear box,** cambio de marcha de
tres velocidades, *m.* **t.-stringed,**
(*mus.*) de tres cuerdos. **t.
thousand,** *a.* tres mil, *m.* or
f. pl.; s. tres mil, *m.*
threefold, *a.* triple
threepence, *s.* tres peniques,
m. pl.
threescore; *a.* and *s.* sesenta
(*m. pl.*)
threesome, *s.* partido de tres, *m.*
threnody, *s.* treno, *m.*
thresh, *v.t.* trillar, desgranar.
v.i. trillar el grano. **to t. out,**
ventilar
threshing, *s.* trilla, *f.* **t. floor,**
era, *f.* **t. machine,** trilladora, *f.*
threshold, *s.* umbral, *m.;* (*psy.*)
limen, *m.;* (*fig.*) comienzo, principio, *m.;* (entrance) entrada, *f.*
to cross the t., atravesar (or
pisar) los umbrales
thrice, *adv.* tres veces
thrift, *s.* frugalidad, parsimonia,
f.
thriftily, *adv.* frugalmente
thriftless, *a.* malgastador, manirroto
thrifty, *a.* frugal, económico
thrill, *s.* estremecimiento, *m.;*
emoción, *f.* *v.t.* conmover, emocionar; penetrar. *v.i.* estremecerse, emocionarse
thriller, *s.* libro, *m.* (or comedia,
f.) sensacional; (detective novel)
novela policíaca, *f.*
thrilling, *a.* sensacional, espeluznante; (moving) emocionante,
conmovedor
thrive, *v.i.* prosperar, medrar;
enriquecerse, tener éxito; (grow)
desarrollarse, robustecerse; florecer; (of plants) acertar
thriving, *a.* próspero; floreciente;
robusto, vigoroso
throat, *s.* garganta, *f.;* orificio,
m.; (narrow entry) paso, *m.*
sore t., dolor de garganta, *m.*
to cut one's t., cortarse la
garganta. **to take by the t.,**

asir (or agarrar) por la garganta
throated, *a.* de garganta..., con
la garganta
throaty, *a.* indistinto, ronco
throb, *s.* latido, *m.;* pulsación, *f.;*
vibración, *f.;* (*fig.*) estremecimiento, *m.* *v.i.* palpitar, latir;
vibrar
throbbing, *s.* pulsación, *f.;*
vibración, *f.* *a.* palpitante;
vibrante. **t. pain,** dolor pun-
gente, *m.*
throe, *s.* dolor, *m.,* agonía; angustia, *f.* **in the throes of,** en
medio de; luchando con; en las
garras de. **throes of childbirth,** dolores de parto, *m. pl.*
throes of death, agonía de la
muerte, *f.*
thrombosis, *s.* (*med.*) trombosis, *f.*
throne, *s.* trono, *m.;* (royal power)
corona, *f.,* poder real, *m.* *v.i.*
elevar al trono. **speech from
the t.,** el discurso de la corona,
m.
throneless, *a.* sin corona
throng, *s.* muchedumbre, multitud, *f.* *v.i.* apiñarse, remolinarse
acudir. *v.t.* atestar, llenar d,
bote en bote
throstle, *s.* (*orn.*) tordo, malvis,
m.
throttle, *s.* (*mech.*) regulador, *m.;*
(*aut.*) estrangulador, *m.;* (*fam.*)
garganta, *f.* *v.t.* estrangular;
(*fig.*) ahogar, suprimir. **to open
(close) the t.,** abrir (cerrar) el
estrangulador
throttling, *s.* estrangulación, *f.*
(also *aut.*)
through, *prep.* por; al través de;
de un lado a otro de; por medio
de; (between) entre; por causa
de; gracias a. *adv.* al través de;
de un lado a otro; (whole) entero,
todo; (from beginning to end)
desde el principio hasta el fin;
(to the end) hasta el fin. *a.* (of
passages, etc.) que va desde...
hasta...; (of trains) directo. **to
look t. the window,** mirar por
la ventana, asomarse a la
ventana. **to be wet t.,** estar
calado hasta los huesos; estar
muy mojado. **to carry t.,** llevar
a cabo. **to fall t.,** caer por; (fail)
fracasar. **to sleep the whole
night t.,** dormir durante toda
la noche, dormir la noche entera.

t. and t., completamente. t. **traffic,** tráfico directo, *m.* t. **train,** tren directo, *m.*
throughout, *prep.* por todo; durante todo. *adv.* completamente; (from beginning to end) desde el principio hasta el fin; (everywhere) en todas partes
throw, *v.t.* arrojar, lanzar, echar; (fire) disparar; (pottery) plasmar; (knock down) derribar; (slough) mudar (la piel); (cast off) despojarse de; (a rider) desmontar; (a glance) echar, dirigir (una mirada, etc.); (silk) torcer; (dice) echar; (light) dirigir, enfocar. to t. **overboard,** *(naut.)* echar al mar; desechar; (desert) abandonar. to t. **about,** esparcir, desparramar; derrochar. to t. **aside,** echar a un lado, desechar; abandonar, dejar. to t. **away,** tirar; desechar; (spend) malgastar, derrochar; (waste) sacrificar; (of opportunities) malograr, perder. to t. **back,** devolver; echar hacia atrás. to t. **down,** derribar, dar en el suelo con; echar abajo; (arms) rendir. to t. **down the glove,** arrojar el guante. to t. **oneself down,** tumbarse, echarse; (descend) echarse abajo. to t. **oneself down from,** arrojarse de. to t. **in,** echar dentro; (give extra) añadir; (the clutch) embragar; insertar; (a remark) hacer (una observación). to t. **off,** despojarse de; quitarse; (refuse) rechazar; sacudirse; (get rid of) despedir; (renounce) renunciar; (exhale) emitir, despedir; (verses) improvisar. to t. **on,** echar sobre; (garments) ponerse. to t. **oneself upon,** lanzarse sobre. to t. **out,** expeler; hacer salir; plantar en la calle; (utter) proferir, soltar; (one's chest) inflar. to t. **over,** (desert) abandonar, dejar. to t. **up,** (build) levantar; lanzar en el aire; (a post, etc.) renunciar (a), abandonar; vomitar
throw, *s.* echada, *f.*; tiro, *m.*; (at dice) lance, *m.*; jugada, *f.*; (wrestling) derribo, *m.* **within**

a stone's t., a tiro de piedra, t.-**back,** retroceso, *m.*; *(biol.)* atavismo, *m.*
thrower, *s.* tirador (-ra), lanzador (-ra)
throwing, *s.* lanzamiento, *m.*, lanzada, *f.* t. **the hammer,** lanzamiento del martillo, *m.*
thrum, *v.t.* and *v.i.* tocar mal; (of keyed instruments) teclear; (of stringed instruments) rascar las cuerdas (de)
thrush, *s.* *(orn.)* tordo, *m.*
thrust, *s.* empujón, *m.*; (with a sword) estocada, *f.*; (fencing) golpe, *m.*; (with a lance) bote, *m.*; ataque, *m.*; asalto, *m.* *v.t.* empujar; (put) meter; (insert) introducir; (pierce) atravesar; (out, through, of the head, etc.) asomar. *v.i.* acometer, atacar; embestir; meterse, introducirse; (intrude) entrometerse; (fencing) dar un golpe. to t. **aside,** empujar a un lado; (proposals) rechazar. to t. **back,** hacer retroceder, empujar hacia atrás; (words) tragarse; (thoughts) apartar, rechazar. to t. **down,** empujar hacia abajo; hacer bajar; *(fig.)* reprimir. to t. **forward,** empujar hacia delante; hacer seguir. to t. **oneself forward,** adelantarse; *(fig.)* ponerse delante de los otros, darse importancia. to t. **in,** introducir; (stick) hincar; (insert) intercalar. to t. **on,** hacer seguir; empujar sobre; (garments) ponerse rápidamente. to t. **oneself in,** introducirse; entrometerse. to t. **out,** echar fuera; hacer salir, echar; expulsar; (the tongue) sacar (la lengua); (the head, etc.) asomar. to t. **through,** atravesar; (pierce) traspasar. to t. **one's way through,** abrirse paso por. to t. **upon,** imponer, hacer aceptar
thud, *s.* sonido sordo, *m.*; golpe sordo, *m.*
thug, *s.* asesino, criminal, *m.*
thumb, *s.* pulgar, *m.* *v.t.* hojear; ensuciar con los dedos. **under the t. of,** *(fig.)* en el poder de. t. **index,** índice pulgar, *m.* t.-**mark,** huella del dedo, *f.* t.-**screw,** tornillo de orejas, *m.*

t.-stall, dedil, *m.* **t.-tack,** chinche, *m.*

thump, *s.* golpe, porrazo, *m.* *v.t.* and *v.i.* golpear, aporrear; (the ground, of rabbits) zapatear

thunder, *s.* trueno, *m.;* (of hooves, etc.) estampido, *m.;* estruendo, *m.* *v.i.* tronar; retumbar; (*fig.*) fulminar. *v.t.* gritar en una voz de trueno, rugir. **to t. along,** avanzar como el trueno; galopar ruidosamente. **t.-clap,** trueno, *m.* **t.-cloud,** nube de tormenta, *f.,* nubarrón, *m.* **t.-storm,** tronada, *f.* **t.-struck,** muerto, estupefacto

thunderbolt, *s.* rayo, *m.*

thunderer, *s.* fulminador, *m.*

Thursday, *s.* jueves, *m.* **Holy T.,** Juéves Santo, *m.*

thus, *adv.* así; de este modo; en estos términos; hasta este punto. **t. far,** hasta ahora; hasta este punto; hasta aquí. **Thus it is that . . .,** Así es que . . .

thwack, *s.* golpe, *m.;* *v.t.* golpear

thwart, *v.t.* frustrar, impedir

thy, *poss. a.* tu, *m.* and *f.;* tus, *m. pl.* and *f. pl.*

thyme, *s.* (*bot.*) tomillo, *m.*

thymol, *s.* timol, *m.*

thymus, *s.* (*anat.*) timo, *m.*

thyroid, *a.* tiroideo. **t. gland,** tiroides, *f.*

thyrsus, *s.* tirso, *m.*

thyself, *poss. pron.* tu mismo, *m.;* tu misma, *f.;* (with prep.) ti mismo, *m.;* ti misma, *f.;* (in a reflexive verb) te

tiara, *s.* tiara, *f.*

Tiberine, *a.* tiberino

Tibetan, *a.* and *s.* tibetano (-na); (language) tibetano, *m.*

tibia, *s.* (*anat.*) tibia, *f.*

tic, *s.* (twitch) tic nervioso, *m.*

tick, *s.* (*ent.*) ácaro, *m.;* (sound) tictac, *m.;* (cover) funda de colchón, *f.;* (*fam.*) fiado, crédito, *m.;* (mark) marca, *f.* *v.i.* hacer tictac. *v.t.* poner una marca contra. **on t.,** (*fam.*) al fiado. **to t. off,** poner una marca contra; (*fam.*) reñir. **to t. over,** (*aut.*) andar, marchar

ticket, *s.* billete, *m.;* (for an entertainment) entrada, localidad, *f.;* (label) etiqueta, *f.;* (pawn) pape-

leta de empeño, *f.;* (for luggage) talón, *m.;* (*pol.,* U.S.A.) candidatura, *f.* *v.t.* marcar. **to take one's t.,** sacar el billete (or for entertainment) la entrada, *f.).* **excursion t.,** billete de excursión, *m.* **return t.,** billete de ida y vuelta, *m.* **season t.,** billete de abono, *m.* **single t.,** billete sencillo, *m.* **t. agency,** (for travel) agencia de viajes, *f.;* (for entertainments) agencia de teatros, *f.* **t. collector** or **inspector,** revisor, *m.* **t. holder,** tenedor de billete, *m.;* abonado (-da). **t. office,** (railway) despacho de billetes, *m.;* taquilla, *f,* **t.-of-leave,** libertad condicional. *f.* **t. punch,** sacabocados, *m;.* (on tramcars) clasificador de billetes, *m.*

ticking, *s.* (sound) tictac, *m.;* (cloth) cotí, *m.*

tickle, *v.t.* hacer cosquillas (a), cosquillear; irritar; (gratify) halagar; (amuse) divertir. *v.i.* tener cosquillas; hacer cosquillas; ser irritante

ticklish, *a.* cosquilloso; (of persons) difícil, vidrioso; (of affairs) espinoso, delicado

tidal, *a.* de marea. **t. wave,** marejada, *f.;* (*fig.*) ola popular, *f.*

tiddly-winks, *s.* juego de la pulga, *m.*

tide, *s.* marea, *f.;* (season) tiempo, *m.,* estación, *f.;* (trend) corriente, *f.;* (progress) curso, *m.;* marcha, *f.* *v.i.* (with over) vencer, superar; aguardar la ocasión. **to go against the t.,** ir contra la corriente. **to go with the t.,** seguir la corriente. **high t.,** marea alta, *f.* **low t.,** marea baja, *f.,* bajamar, *m.* **neap t.,** marea muerta, *f.* **t. mark,** lengua del agua, *f.*

tideless, *a.* sin mareas

tidily, *adv.* aseadamente; en orden, metódicamente

tidiness, *s.* aseo, *m.;* buen orden, *m.*

tidings, *s. pl.* noticias, nuevas, *f. pl.*

tidy, *a.* aseado; metódico, en orden; pulcro; (*fam.*) considerable. *v.t.* poner en orden, asear; limpiar; (oneself) arreglarse

tie, s. lazo, m., atadura, f.; (knot)
nudo, m.; (for the neck) corbata,
f.; (sport) empate, m.; (mus.)
ligado, m.; (arch.) tirante, m.;
(spiritual bond) lazo, m.; (burden)
carga, responsabilidad, f.
tie-pin, alfiler de corbata, m.
tie seller, corbatero (-ra)

tie, v.t. atar; (bind) ligar; (lace)
lacear; (a knot) hacer; (with a
knot) anudar; (unite) unir; (fig.,
bind) constreñir, obligar; (limit)
limitar, restringir; (occupy) ocupar,
entretener; (hamper) estorbar,
impedir. v.i. atarse; (sport)
empatar. **to tie one's tie,**
hacer la corbata. **to tie down,**
atar a; limitar; obligar. **They
tied him down to a chair,** Le
ataron a una silla. **to tie together,**
enlazar, ligar; unir. **to
tie up,** liar, atar; (wrap) envolver;
recoger; (naut.) amarrar,
atracar; (restrict) limitar, restringir;
(invest) invertir

tier, s. fila, hilera, f. **in tiers,**
en gradas; (of a dress) en volantes
tiff, s. disgusto, m.
tiger, s. tigre, m. **t.-cat,** gato
(-ta) atigrado (-da). **t.-lily,** tigridia, f.
tigerish, a. atigrado, de tigre;
salvaje, feroz
tight, a. apretado; (not leaky)
hermético; impermeable; (taut)
tieso, tirante; (narrow) estrecho;
(trim) compacto; (of clothes)
muy ajustado; (shut) bien cerrado;
(naut.) estanco; (risky)
peligroso, difícil; (miserly)
tacaño; (of money, goods) escaso;
(tipsy) borracho. **to be t.-
fisted,** ser·como un puño. **to
hold t.,** agarrar fuerte. **t.
corner,** (fig.) aprieto, lance
apretado, m. **t.-rope,** cuerda de
volatinero, f. **t.-rope walker,**
alambrista, equilibrista, m. and
f.; volatinero (-ra). **t.-rope
walker's pole,** balancín, m.
tighten, v.t. estrechar, apretar;
(stretch) estirar; (of saddle girths)
cinchar. v.i. estrecharse; estirarse
tightly, adv. estrechamente
tightness, s. estrechez, f.; tirantez,
tensión, f.; (feeling of
constriction) opresión, f.; (drunkenness)
emborrachamiento, m.

tights, s. pl. mallas, f. pl.
tigress, s. tigresa, f.
tilbury, s. tílburi, m.
tile, s. teja, f.; (for flooring)
baldosa, losa, f.; (ornamental)
azulejo, m.; (hat) chistera, f.
v.t. tejar; embaldosar. **t. floor,**
enlosado, embaldosado, m. **t.
manufacturer,** tejero, m. **t.
works or yard,** tejar, m.
tiler, s. solador, m.; tejero, m.
till, s. (for money) cajón, m.
v.t. (agr.) cultivar, labrar. prep.
hasta. conjunc. hasta que
tillable, a. laborable
tillage, s. labranza, f., cultivo,
m.; tierra de labrantío, f.
tiller, s. (agr.) labrador, m.;
(bot.) mugrón, renuevo, vástago,
m.; (naut.) caña del timón, f.
tilling, s. (agr.) cultivo, laboreo,
m.
tilt, s. inclinación, f.; ladeo, m.;
(fight) torneo, m., justa, f.
v.t. inclinar; ladear; (a drinking
vessel) empinar. v.i. inclinarse;
ladearse; (fight) justar. **to t.
against,** (fig.) arremeter contra,
atacar. **at full t.,** a todo
correr. **t. hammer,** martinete
de báscula, m. **t.-yard,** palestra,
f.
tilting, s. inclinación, f.; (fighting)
justas, f. pl. a. inclinado
timber, s. madera de construcción,
f.; (trees) árboles de
monte, m. pl.; bosque, m.;
(beam) viga, f.; (naut.) cuaderna,
f. v.t. enmaderar. **t. line,**
límite del bosque maderable, m.
t. merchant, maderero, m.
t. wolf, lobo gris, m. **t. work,**
maderaje, m. **t. yard,** maderería,
f., corral de madera, m.
timbered, a. enmaderado; (with
trees) arbolado
timbre, s. (mus.) timbre, m.·
timbrel, s. (mus.) tamborete,
tamboril, m.
time, s. (in general) tiempo, m.;
(epoch) época, edad, f.; tiempos,
m. pl.; (of the year) estación,
f.; (by the clock) hora, f.;
(lifetime) vida, f.; (particular
moment of time) momento, m.;
(occasion) sazón, ocasión, f.;
(day) día, m.; (time allowed)
plazo, m.; (in repetition) vez, f.;
(mus.) compás, m.; (mil.) paso, m.

v.t. ajustar al tiempo; hacer con oportunidad; (regulate) regular; calcular el tiempo que se emplea en hacer una cosa; (a blow) calcular. **all the t.**, todo el tiempo; continuamente, sin cesar. **a long t.**, mucho tiempo. **a long t. ago,** mucho tiempo ha, hace mucho tiempo. **at a t.**, a la vez, al mismo tiempo; (of period) a una época. **at any t.**, a cualquier hora; en cualquier ocasión; (when you like) cuando gustes. **at no t.**, jamás, nunca. **at some t.**, alguna vez; en alguna época. **at some t. or another,** un día u otro; en una u otra ocasión; en alguna época. **at that t.**, en aquella época; a la sazón; en aquel instante. **at the one t.**, de una vez. **at the present t.**, en la actualidad, al presente. **at the proper t.**, a su debido tiempo; a la hora señalada; a la hora conveniente. **at the same t.**, al mismo tiempo. **at the same t. as,** mientras, a medida que; al mismo instante que. **at times,** a veces, en ocasiones. **behind the times,** (*fig.*) atrasado de noticias; pasado de moda. **behind t.**, atrasado. **by that t.**, para entonces. **every t.**, cada vez; siempre. **for some t.**, durante algún tiempo. **for some t. past,** de algún tiempo a esta parte. **for the t. being,** de momento, por ahora. **from this t.**, desde hoy; desde esta fecha. **from this t. forward,** de hoy en adelante. **from t. to t.**, de vez en cuando, de tarde en tarde. **in a month's t.**, en un mes. **in a short t.**, en breve, dentro de poco. **in good t.**, puntualmente; temprano. **in my t.**, en mis días, en mis tiempos. **in olden times,** antiguamente, en otros tiempos. **in the course of t.**, andando el tiempo, en el transcurso de los años. **in the t. of,** a la época de. **in t.**, (promptly) a tiempo; con el tiempo. **in t. to come,** en el porvenir. **It is t. to . . . ,** Es hora de . . . **many times,** frecuentemente, muchas veces. **Once upon a t.**, Érase una vez, Una vez había, Érase

que érase. **Since t. out of mind,** Desde tiempo inmemorial. **the last (next) t.**, la última (próxima) vez. **this t. of year,** esta estación del año. **T. hangs heavy on his hands,** El tiempo se le hace interminable. **T. flies,** El tiempo vuela. **T. will tell!** ¡El tiempo lo dirá! ¡Veremos lo que veremos! **What t. is it?** ¿Qué hora es? **The t. is . . . ,** La hora es . . . **within a given t.**, dentro de un plazo dado. **to be out of t.**, estar fuera de compás. **to gain t.**, ganar tiempo. **to have a good t.**, pasarlo bien, divertirse. **to have a bad t.**, pasarlo mal; (*fam.*) tener un mal cuarto de hora. **to have no t. to,** no tener tiempo para. **to keep t.**, guardar el compás. **to kill t,** engañar (or entretener) el tiempo. **to mark t.**, marcar el paso; (*fig.*) hacer tiempo. **to pass the t.**, pasar el rato; pasar el tiempo. **to pass the t. of day,** saludar. **to serve one's t.**, (to a trade) servir el aprendizaje; (in prison) cumplir su condena; (*mil.*) hacer el servicio militar. **to take t. to,** tomar tiempo para. **to take t. by the forelock,** asir la ocasión por la melena. **to waste t.**, perder el tiempo. **t. exposure,** pose, *f.* **t. fuse,** espoleta de tiempo, espoleta graduada, *f.* **t.-honoured,** tradicional, consagrado por el tiempo. **t.-keeper,** capataz, *m.*; reloj, *m.* **t.-saving,** que ahorra el tiempo. **t.-server,** lameculos, *m. and f.* **t.-signal,** señales horarias, *f. pl.* **t.-table,** horario, *m.*; itinerario, programa, *m.*; (railway) guía de ferrocarriles, *f.* **t. to come,** porvenir, *m.*, lo venidero

timed, *a.* calculado; (ill-) intempestivo; (well-) oportuno
timeless, *a.* eterno
timeliness, *s.* tempestividad, oportunidad, *f.*
timely, *a.* oportuno
timepiece, *s.* reloj, *m.*
timid, *a.* tímido, asustadizo, medroso; (shy) vergonzoso
timidity, *s.* timidez, *f.*; vergüenza, *f*

timidly, *adv.* tímidamente

timing, *s.* medida del tiempo, *f.*; (*mech.*). regulación, *f.*; (timetable) horario, *m.*

timorous, *a.* timorato, apocado, asustadizo

timorousness, *s.* encogimiento, *m.*, timidez, *f.*

tin, *s.* (metal) estaño, *m.*; (container) lata, *f.*; (sheet) hojalata, *f.*; (money) plata, *f.* *v.t.* estañar; (place in tins) envasar en lata; cubrir con hojalata. **tin-foil,** papel de estaño, *m.* **tin hat,** casco de acero, *m.* **tin opener,** abrelatas, abridor de latas, *m.* **tin-plate,** hojalata, *f.* **tin soldier,** soldado de plomo, *m.* **tin ware,** hojalatería, *f.*

tincture, *s.* tintura, *f.*, tinte, *m.*; (*med.*) tintura, *f.*; (trace) dejo, *m.*; (veneer) capa, *f.* *v.t.* teñir, tinturar

tinder, *s.* yesca, *f.* t. box, yescas, lumbres, *f. pl.*

tinge, *s.* tinte, matiz, *m.*; (*fig.*) dejo, toque, *m.* *v.t.* matizar, tinturar; (*fig.*) tocar

tingle, *s.* picazón, comezón, *f.*; (thrill) estremecimiento, *m.* *v.i.* picar; (of ears) zumbar; (thrill) estremecerse (de); vibrar

tingling, *s.* picazón, *f.*; (of the ears) zumbido, *m.*; (thrill) estremecimiento, *m.*

tinker, *s.* calderero remendón, *m.* *v.t.* remendar. *v.i.* chafallar. to t. with, jugar con

tinkle, *s.* tilín, retintín, *m.*; campanilleo, *m.*; cencerreo, *m.* *v.i.* tintinar. *v.t.* hacer tintinar

tinkling, *s.* retintín, tintineo, *m.*; campanilleo, *m.*

tinman, *s.* hojalatero, *m.*

tinned, *a.* (of food) en lata, en conserva

tinsel, *s.* oropel, *m.*; (cloth) lama de oro o plata, *f.*, brocadillo, *m.*; (*fig.*) oropel, *m.* *a.* de oropel; de brocadillo; (*fig.*) charro. *v.t.* adornar con oropel

tinsmith, *s.* hojalatero, estañador, *m.*

tint, *s.* tinta, *f.*, color, *m.*; matiz, *m.*; tinte, *m.* *v.t.* colorar, teñir; matizar

tinting, *s.* tintura, *f.*, teñido, *m.*

tiny, *a.* diminuto, minúsculo, menudo, chiquito

tip, *s.* punta, *f.*; cabo, *m.*, extremidad, *f.*; (of an umbrella, etc.) regatón, *m.*; (of a lance) borne, *m.*; (of a cigarette) boquilla, *f.*; (of a shoe) puntera, *f.*; (of a finger) yema, *f.*; (for rubbish) depósito de basura, *m.*; (gratuity) propina, *f.*; (information) informe oportuno, *m.*; (tap) golpecito, *m.* **to have on the tip of one's tongue,** tener en la punta de la lengua. **tip-cart,** volquete, *m.* **tip-up seat,** asiento plegable, *m.*

tip, *v.t.* inclinar; volcar, voltear; (drinking vessel) empinar; poner regatón, etc. (a); (*poet.*) tocar, golpear ligeramente; (reward) dar propina (a). *v.i.* inclinarse; (topple) tambalearse; (reward) dar propina. **to tip the wink,** guiñar el ojo (a). **to tip off,** (liquids) echar; hacer caer; (inform) decir en secreto; informar oportunamente. **to tip over,** *v.t.* volcar; hacer caer. *v.i.* volcarse; caer; (of a boat) zozobrar. **to tip up,** *v.t.* (a seat) levantar; (money) proporcionar (el dinero); (upset) volcar; hacer perder el equilibrio. *v.i.* volcarse; (of a seat) levantarse; (lose the balance) perder el equilibrio

tipple, *s.* bebida, *f.* *v.t.* beber, sorber. *v.i.* empinar el codo

tippler, *s.* borracho (-cha)

tipsily, *adv.* como borracho

tipsiness, *s.* borrachera, *f.*

tipsy, *a.* achispado, algo borracho. to be t., estar entre dos luces, estar entre dos velas

tiptoe, (on) *adv.* de puntillas; (*fig.*) excitado, ansioso. to stand on t., ponerse de puntillas, empinarse

tirade, *s.* diatriba, *f.*

tire, *s.* See tyre

tire, *v.t.* cansar, fatigar; (bore) aburrir. *v.i.* cansarse, fatigarse; aburrirse. **to be tired of,** estar cansado de. **to grow tired,** empezar a cansarse. to t. out, rendir de cansancio

tired, *a.* cansado, fatigado. **to be sick and t. of,** estar hasta la coronilla (de), (of persons) con. t. of, cansado de; disgustado de

tiredness, *s.* cansancio, *m.*, fatiga, *f.*; aburrimiento, *m.*

tireless, *a.* infatigable, incansable

tirelessly, *adv.* sin tregua, sin cesar

tiresome, *a.* fastidioso, molesto, pesado; (dull) aburrido

tiresomeness, *s.* pesadez, *f.*, ·fastidio, *m.*; tedio, aburrimiento, *m.*

tiring, *a.* fatigoso

tisane, *s.* tisana, *f.*

tissue, *s.* (cloth) tisú, *m.*, lama, *f.*; (*biol.*) tejido, *m.*; (series) serie, sarta, *f.* **t. paper**, papel de seda, *m.*

tit, *s.* (*orn.*) paro, *m.* **tit for tat**, tal para cual

Titan, *s.* titán, *m.*

titanic, *a.* titánico

titbit, *s.* golosina, *f.*

tithe, *s.* décima, *f.*; fracción, pequeña parte, *f.* *v.t.* diezmar. **t. gatherer**, diezmero (-ra)

titillate, *v.t.* titilar, estimular

titivate, *v.i.* arreglarse

title, *s.* título, *m.*; (right) derecho, *m.*; documento, *m.* **to give a t. to**, intitular; ennoblecer. **t. deeds**, títulos de propiedad, *m. pl.* **t. page**, portada, *f.* **t. role**, papel principal, *m.*

titter, · *v.i.* reírse disimuladamente. *s.* risa disimulada, *f.*

tittle, *s.* adarme, tilde, ápice, *m.*

titular, *a.* titular; nominal

to, *prep.* a; (as far as) hasta; (in the direction of) en dirección a, hacia; (with indirect object) a; (until) hasta; (compared with) en comparación con, comparado con; (against) contra; (according to) según; (as) como; (in) en; (so that,· in order to, for the purpose of) para; (indicating possession) a, de; (of time by the clock) menos; (by) por; (before verbs of motion or which imply motion) a (sometimes para); (before some other verbs) de; en; (before verbs of beginning, inviting, exhorting, obliging) a; (indicating indirect object) a; (before a subjunctive or infinitive indicating future action or obligation) que. **To** is often not translated. With most Spanish infinitives no separate translation is necessary, e.g. leer, decir, to read, to speak. Some verbs are always followed by a preposition (e.g. **to begin to speak**, · empezar a hablar,· etc.). *adv.* (shut) cerrado. **to come to**, volver en sí. **to lie to**, (*naut.*) ponerse ·a la capa. **to and fro**, de un lado a otro. **face to face**, cara a cara. **He has been a good friend to them**, Él ha sido un buen amigo para ellos. **That is new to me**, Eso es nuevo para mí. **He went to London**, Se fué a Londres. **to go to France (Canada)**, ir a Francia (al Canadá). **the road to Madrid**, la carretera de Madrid. **She kept the secret to herself**, Ella guardó el secreto para sí. **to go to the dentist**, ir a casa del dentista. **We give it to them**, Se lo damos a ellos. **It belongs to me**,· Pertenece a· mí. **What does it matter to you?** ¿Qué te importa a ti? **I wish to see him**, Quiero verle. **They did it to help us**, Lo hicieron para ayudarnos. **I have to go to see her**, Tengo que ir a verla. **to this day**, hasta hoy, hasta el presente. **It is a quarter to six**, Son las seis menos cuarto. **to the last shilling**, hasta el último chelín. **the next to me**, el que me sigue

toad, *s.* sapo, *m.*

toadstool, *s.* hongo, *m.* **poisonous t.**, seta venenosa, *f.*

toady, *s.* lameculos, *m.* and *f.*, adulador (-ra), *m.* *v.t.* lamer el culo (a), adular

toast, *s.* (*cul.*) tostada, *f.*; (drink) brindis, *m.* *v.t.* tostar; brindar, beber a la salud de. *v.i.* brindar. **buttered t.**, mantecada, *f.* **t.-rack**, portatostadas, *m.*

toaster, *s.* tostador, *m.*

toasting, *s.* tostadura, *f.*, tueste, *m. a.* de tostar. **t.-fork**, tostadera, *f.*

tobacco, *s.* tabaco, *m.* *a.* tabacalero. **black** or **cut t.**, picadura, *f.* **leaf t.**, tabaco de hoja, *m.* **mild t.**, tabaco flojo, *m.* **pipe t.**, tabaco de pipa, *m.* **plug t.**, tabaco para mascar, *m.* **strong t.**, tabaco fuerte, *m.* **Turkish t.**, tabaco turco, *m.* **Virginian t.**, tabaco rubio, *m.* **t.-pipe**,· pipa (de tabaco), *f.* **t.-pipe cleaner**,

escobillón para limpiar pipas, *m.*
t. plantation, tabacal, *m.* **t.
planter,** tabacalero (-ra). **t.
poisoning,** tabaquismo, *m.* **t.-
pouch** or **jar,** tabaquera, *f.*
tobacconist, *s.* tabaquero (-ra).
tobacconist's shop, tabaquería,
f.
toboggan, *s.* tobogán, *m.* *v.i.*
ir en tobogán. **t. run,** pista de
tobogán, *f.*
toccata, *s.* (*mus.*) tocata, *f.*
tocsin, *s.* rebato, *m.*
today, *adv.* hoy; ahora, actualmente, al presente, hoy día.
s. el día de hoy. **from t.,** desde
hoy. **from t. forward,** de hoy
en adelante
toddle, *v.i.* hacer pinos, empezar
a andar; (stroll) dar una vuelta;
(leave) marcharse
toddy, *s.* ponche, *m.*
toe, *s.* dedo del pie, *m.*; (cloven)
pezuña, *f.*; uña, *f.*; (of furniture)
base, *f.*, pie, *m.*; (of stockings,
shoes) punta, *f.* **He stepped on
my toe,** Me pisó el dedo del pie.
big toe, dedo pulgar del pie,
dedo gordo del pie, *m.* **little t.,**
dedo pequeño del pie, *m.* **to toe
the line,** ponerse en la raya;
(*fig.*) cumplir con su deber. **toe-
cap,** puntera, *f.* **t. toe-dancing,**
baile de puntillas, *m.* **toe-nail,**
uña del dedo del pie, *f.*
toffee, *s.* caramelo, *m.*
toga, *s.* toga, *f.*
together, *adv.* junto; (uninter-
ruptedly) sin interrupción; (in
concert)· simultáneamente, a la
vez, al mismo tiempo; (consecutively) seguido. **t. with,**
con; junto con; en compañía de;
(simultaneously) a la vez que
toil, *s.* labor, *f.*, trabajo, *m.* *pl.*
toils, lazos, *m. pl.*; (*fig.*) redes,
f. pl. *v.i.* trabajar, afanarse.
to t. along, caminar penosamente (por); adelantar con dificultad. **to t. up,** subir penosamente
toiler, *s.* trabajador (-ra)
toilet, *s.* tocado, *m.*; atavío, *m.*;
vestido, *m.*; (w.c.) retrete, excusado, *m.*; (for ladies) tocador, *m.*
to make one's t., arreglarse.
t. case, neceser, *m.* **t.-paper,**
papel higiénico, *m.* **t.-powder,**
polvos de arroz, *m. pl.* **t. roll,**

rollo de papel higiénico, *m.*
t.-set, ·juego de tocador, *m.*
t. soap, jabón de olor, jabón de
tocador, *m.*
toiling, *s.* trabajo duro, *m.*
a. laborioso, trabajador
token, *s.* señal, muestra, *f.*;
prueba, *f.*; (presage) síntoma,
indicio, *m.*; (remembrance) recuerdo, *m.* **as a t. of,** en señal
de; como recuerdo de
tokology, *s.* tocología, *f.*
toledan, *a.* toledano
tolerable, *a.* tolerable, soportable, llevadero; (fairly good)
mediano, mediocre, regular
tolerably, *adv.* bastante
tolerance, *s.* tolerancia, *f.*;
paciencia, indulgencia, *f.*
tolerant, *a.* tolerante; indulgente
tolerate, *v.t.* tolerar, sufrir,
soportar; permitir
toleration, *s.* tolerancia, *f.*; indulgencia, paciencia, *f.* **religious
t.,** libertad de cultos, *f.*
toll, *s.* (of a bell) tañido, doble,
m.; (for passage) peaje, portazgo,
m.; (for grinding) derecho de
molienda, *m.* *v.t.* and *v.i.* doblar, tañer. **to t. the hour,** dar
la hora. **t. call,** conferencia
telefónica interurbana, *f.* **t. gate,**
barrera de peaje, *f.* **t. house,**
oficina de portazgos, *f.*
tolling, *s.* tañido, clamor (de las
campanas), *m.*
Tom, *s.* Tomás, *m.*; (cat) gato, *m.*
Tom, Dick and Harry, Fulano,
Zutano y Mengano
tomahawk, *s.* hacha de guerra de
los indios, *f.*
tomato, *s.* tomate, *m.* **t. plant,**
tomatera, *f.* **t. sauce,** salsa de
tomate, *f.*
tomb, *s.* tumba, *f.*, sepulcro, *m.*
tomboy, *s.* muchachote, torbellino, *m.*
tombstone, *s.* piedra mortuoria,
f., monumento funerario, *m.*
tome, *s.* tomo, volumen, *m.*
tomfoolery, *s.* necedad, tontería,
f.; payasada, *f.*
tommy-gun, *s.* ametralladora
pequeña, *f.*
tomorrow, *adv.* and *s.* mañana
(*f.*). **a fortnight t.,** mañana en
quince. **the day after t.,**
pasado mañana. **t. afternoon
(morning),** mañana por la tarde

(mañana). **T. is Friday,** Mañana es viernes

ton, s. tonelada, *f.*

tonality, s. tonalidad, *f.*

tone, s. tono, *m.*; (*mus., med., art*) tono, *m.*; (of the voice) acento, *m.*, entonación, *f.*; (of musical instruments) sonido, *m.*; (shade) matiz, *m.* *v.t.* entonar; (*phot.*) virar. **to t. down.** *v.t.* (*art, mus.*) amortiguar; (*fig.*) suavizar, modificar. *v.i.* (*art, mus.*) amortiguarse; (*fig.*) suavizarse, modificarse. **to t. in with,** (of colours) *v.t.* armonizar con. *v.i.* armonizarse, corresponder en tono o matiz. **to t. up,** *v.t.* subir de color, intensificar el color de; (*med.*) entonar, robustecer. **t. poem,** poema sinfónico, *m.*

toned, *a.* de voz ...; de sonido ...

tonelessly, *adv.* sin tono; apáticamente

tongs, s. *pl.* tenazas, *f.* *pl.*; tenacillas, *f.* *pl.* **curling t.,** tenacillas para el pelo, *f.* *pl.* **sugar t.,** tenacillas para azúcar, *f.* *pl.*

tongue, s. (*anat.*) lengua, *f.*; (language) idioma, *m.*, lengua, *f.*; (speech) modo de hablar, *m.* habla, *f.*; (*mus.*) lengüeta, *f.*; (of buckle) diente, *m.*; (of shoe) oreja, *f.*; (of land) lengua, *f.*; (of a bell) badajo, *m.*; (flame) lengua, *f.* **My t. ran away with me,** (*fam.*) Se me fué la mula. **to give t.,** ladrar. **to hold one's t.,** cerrar el pico, callarse. **t. of fire,** lengua de fuego, *f.* **t. tied,** con impedimento en el habla; turbado, confuso; mudo. **t.-twister,** trabalenguas, *m.*

-tongued, *a.* de voz ...

tonic, *a.* tónico. s. (*med.*) tónico, reconstituyente, *m.*; (*mus.*) tónica, *f.*

tonight, *adv.* and s. esta noche

tonka bean, s. tonca, sarapia, *f.*

tonnage, s. tonelaje, porte, *m.*; (duty) derecho de tonelaje, *m.*

tonner, s. (*naut.*) de ... toneladas

tonsil, s. amígdala, *f.*

tonsillitis, s. amigdalitis, *f.*

tonsure, s. (*ecc.*) tonsura, *f.* *v.t.* tonsurar

tonsured, *a.* tonsurado

tontine, s. (*com.*) tontina, *f.*

too, *adv.* demasiado; (very) muy; también; además. **too hard,** demasiado difícil, demasiado rígido; (of persons) demasiado duro. **too much,** demasiado. **too often,** con demasiada frecuencia

tool, s. herramienta, *f.*; utensilio, *m.*; instrumento, *m.*; (person) criatura, *f.* *v.t.* labrar con herramienta; (a book) estampar en seco. **t.-bag,** capacho, *m.* **t. box,** caja de herramientas, *f.*

tooling, s. (of books) estampación en seco, *f.*

toot, s. sonido de bocina, *m.* *v.i.* sonar una bocina

tooth, s. diente, *m.*; muela, *f.*; (of comb) púa, *f.*; (taste) gusto, paladar, *m.*; (cog) diente de rueda, *m.*; (of saw) diente, *m.* *v.t.* dentar; mellar. *v.i.* (*mech.*) engranar. **armed to the teeth,** armado hasta los dientes. **double t.,** muela, *f.* **false teeth,** dentadura postiza, *f.* **set of teeth,** dentadura, *f.* **to cut one's teeth,** echar los dientes. **to have a sweet t.,** ser muy goloso. **to show one's teeth,** enseñar los dientes. **t.-brush,** cepillo para los dientes, *m.* **t. drawing,** extracción de un diente, *f.* **t.-paste,** pasta dentífrica, *f.*

toothache, s. dolor de muelas, *m.*

toothed, *a.* con dientes; dentado

toothless, *a.* desdentado, sin dientes; (of combs) sin púas

toothpick, s. mondadientes, *m.*

top, s. (summit) cima, cumbre, *f.*; (of a tree) copa, *f.*; (of the head) coronilla, *f.*; (of a page) cabeza, *f.*; (crest) copete, *m.*, cresta, *f.*; (surface) superficie, *f.*; (of a wall) coronamiento, *m.*; (tip) punta, *f.*; (point) ápice, *m.*; (of a tram, bus) imperial, baca, *f.*; (of a wave) cresta, *f.*; (acme) auge, *m.*; (of a class) primero (de la clase), *m.*; (highest rank) último grado, *m.*; (of a plant) hojas, *f.* *pl.*; (of a piano) cima, *f.*; (*naut.*) cofa, *f.*; (head of a bed, etc.) cabeza, *f.*; (lid) tapadera, *f.*; (toy) trompo, peón, *m.*; (humming) trompa, *f.* *a.* más alto; máximo; (chief) principal, primero. *v.t.* (cover)

cubrir de; (cut off) desmochar;
(come level with) llegar a la
cima de; (rise above) elevarse
por encima (de), coronar, dominar; (be superior to) exceder,
aventajar; (golf) topear.   at
the top, a la cabeza; a la
cumbre. **from top to bottom,**
de arriba abajo. **on top of,**
encima de; (besides) en adición
a, además de. **to be top-dog,**
ser un gallito. **to sleep like a
top,** dormir como un lirón. **top
boots,** botas de campaña, *f. pl.*
top-dog, vencedor, *m.;* poderoso,
m. **top-hat,** sombrero de copa,
m. **top-heavy,** más pesado por
arriba que por abajo
topaz, *s.* topacio, jacinto occidental, *m.*
topcoat, *s.* sobretodo, gabán, *m.*
toper, *s.* borrachín (-ina)
topgallant, *s.* (*naut.*) juanete, *m.*
topic, *s.* asunto, tema, *m.*
topical, *a.* tópico; actual
topknot, *s.* cresta, *f.,* penacho,
m.; (of birds) moño, *m.;* copete,
m.
topmast, *s.* mastelero, *m.*
topmost, *a.* más alto; más
importante
topographer, *s.* topógrafo, *m.*
topographical, *a.* topográfico
topography, *s.* topografía, *f.*
topple, *v.i.* tambalearse, estar al
punto de caer.   **to t. down,**
volcarse; derribarse; caer. **to t.
over,** *v.i.* venirse abajo; perder
el equilibrio. *v.t.* derribar, hacer
caer
topsail, *s.* gavia, *f.*
topsyturvy, *a.* desordenado. *adv.*
en desorden, patas arriba
toque, *s.* toca, *f.*
tor, *s.* pico, tolmo, *m.*
torch, *s.* antorcha, hacha, tea, *f.*
electric t., lamparilla eléctrica, *f.*
t.-bearer, hachero, *m.*
torchlight, *s.* luz de antorcha, *f.*
by t., a la luz de las antorchas
torment, *s.* tormento, *m.,* angustia, *f.;* (torture) tortura, *f.;*
suplicio, *m.;* mortificación, *f.;*
disgusto, *m.*   *v.t.* atormentar,
martirizar; (torture) torturar;
molestar
tormentil, *s.* (*bot.*) tormentila, *f.*
tormentor, *s.* atormentador (-ra)
tornado, *s.* tornado, *m.*

torpedo, *s.* torpedo, *m.;* (*icht.*)
pez torpedo, *m.   v.t.* torpedear.
self-propelling t., torpedo automóvil, *m.*   **t.-boat,** torpedero,
m.   **t.-boat destroyer,** cazatorpedero, contratorpedero, *m.*
t. netting, red contra torpedos, *f.*
t. station, base de torpederos, *f.*
t. tube, tubo lanzatorpedos, *m.*
torpedoing, *s.* torpedeamiento,
torpedeo, *m.*
torpid, *a.* aletargado, entorpe-
cido; (of the mind) torpe, tardo,
apático
torpidity, torpor, *s.* letargo, *m.;*
apatía, *f.*
torrent, *s.* torrente, *m.*
torrential, *a.* torrencial
torrid, *a.* tórrido. **t. zone,** zona
tórrida, *f.*
torsion, *s.* torsión, *f.*
torso, *s.* torso, *m.*
tort, *s.* (*law*) tuerto, *m.*
tortoise, *s.* tortuga, *f.* **t.-shell,**
carey, *m. a.* de carey
tortuous, *a.* tortuoso
tortuousness, *s.* tortuosidad, *f.*
torture, *s.* tortura, *f.,* tormento,
m.; angustia, *f.   v.t.* torturar,
dar tormento (a); martirizar
torturer, *s.* atormentador (-ra)
torturing, *a.* torturador, atormentador; angustioso
toss, *s.* sacudimiento, *m.,* sacudida,
f.; (of the head) movimiento (de
cabeza), *m.;* (bull fighting) cogida,
f.; (from a horse) caída de
caballo, *f. v.t.* echar, lanzar; agitar, sacudir; (of bulls) acornear.
v.i. agitarse; (of plumes, etc.)
ondear; (in a boat) balancearse
a la merced de las olas; jugar a
cara o cruz. **to t. in a blanket,**
mantear, dar una manta (a).
to t. aside, echar a un lado;
abandonar. **to t. off,** beber de un
trago. **to t. up,** jugar a cara o
cruz
tot, *s.* (child) nene (-na); crío (-ía);
(of drink) vaso pequeño, *m.* **to
tot up,** sumar
total, *a.* total; absoluto, completo,
entero. *s.* total, *m.,* suma, *f.*
v.t. sumar.   *v.i.* ascender (a).
t. war, guerra total, *f.*
totalitarian, *a.* totalitario
totality, *s.* totalidad, *f.*
totally, *adv.* totalmente, completamente

totem, s. totem, m.

totemism, s. totemismo, m.

totter, v.i. (of persons) bambolearse; tambalear, estar al punto de caer; (fig.) aproximarse a su fin

tottering, a. vacilante; tambaleante. s. bamboleo, m.; tambaleo, m.

toucan, s. (orn.) tucán, m.

touch, v.t. tocar; (brush against) rozar; (reach) alcanzar; (musical instruments) tocar; (move) emocionar, enternecer; (spur on) aguijar; (food) tomar; (affect) influir, afectar; (arouse) despertar, estimular; (equal) compararse con, igualar; (consider) tratar ligeramente (de); (money) dar un sablazo (a). v.i. tocarse; imponer las manos para curar. **I have not touched a bite,** No he probado bocado. **This touches me nearly,** Esto me toca de cerca. to t. at, hacer escala en, tocar en (un puerto). to t. off, descargar. to t. up, retocar; corregir. to t. upon, (a subject) tratar superficialmente de, tratar ligeramente de; hablar de; considerar

touch, s. (sense of) tacto, m.; (contact) toque, contacto, m.; (brushing) roce, m.; (tap) golpe ligero, m.; palmadita, f.; (of an illness) ataque ligero, m.; (mus.) dedeo, m.; (little) dejo, m.; (test) prueba, f., toque, m.; (art) toque, m., pincelada, f. **by the t.,** a tiento. **in t. with,** en relaciones con; en comunicación con; al corriente de. **to give the finishing t.,** dar la última pincelada; dar el último toque. **t.-line,** (football) línea de toque, línea lateral, f. **t.-me-not,** (fam.) erizo, m. **t.-stone,** piedra de toque, f.

touched, a. emocionado, conmovido

touchiness, s. susceptibilidad, f.

touching, a. patético, conmovedor. prep. tocante a, acerca de. s. tocamiento, m.

touchy, a. susceptible, quisquilloso, vidrioso

tough, a. (hard) duro; vigoroso, fuerte, robusto; resistente; (of character) tenaz, firme; (of a

job) difícil; espinoso. s. chulo, m.

toughen, v.t. endurecer.   v.i. endurecerse

toughness, s. dureza, f.; vigor, m., fuerza, f.; resistencia, f.; tenacidad, firmeza, f.; dificultad, f.

toupee, s. tupé, m.

tour, s. viaje, m., excursión, f. v.i. viajar.   v.t. viajar por. **circular t.,** viaje redondo, m. **on t.,** (theat.) en tour, de gira

touring, a. de turismo. s. turismo, m.; viaje, m. **t. car,** coche de turismo, m.

tourist, s. turista, m. and f.; viajero (-ra). **t. agency,** agencia de turismo, f., patronato de turismo, m. **t. ticket,** billete kilométrico, m.

tourmalin, s. (min.) turmalina, f.

tournament, s. torneo, m., justa, f.; (of games) concurso, m.

tourniquet, s. torniquete, m.

tousle, v.t. despeinar; desordenar el pelo

tout, s. buhonero, m. **to t. for,** pescar, solicitar

tow, s. remolque, m.; (rope) estopa, f. v.t. (naut., aut.) remolcar.   **on tow,** a remolque. **tow-path,** camino de sirga, m. **tow rope,** cable de remolque, m.

towage, s. remolque, m.; (fee) derechos de remolque, m. pl.

towards, prep. hacia, en dirección a; (of time) sobre, cerca de; (concerning) tocante a; (with persons) para, con

towel, s. toalla, f. **roller t.,** toalla continua, f. **t. rail,** toallero, m.

towelling, s. tela para toallas, f.

tower, s. torre, f.; (fortress) fortaleza, f.; (belfry) campanario, m.; (large) torreón, m. v.i. elevarse. **to t. above,** destacarse sobre, sobresalir; (fig.) sobrepujar, superar

towered, a. torreado; de las . . . torres. **high t.,** de las altas torres

towering, a. elevado; dominante; orgulloso; (fig.) violento, terrible

town, s. población, f., pueblo, m.; ciudad, f. **t. clerk,** secretario de ayuntamiento, m. **t. council,** concejo municipal, m. **t. coun-**

cillor, concejero municipal, *m.*
t. crier, pregonero, *m.* **t. hall,**
(casa de) ayuntamiento, casa
consistorial, *f.* **t. house,** casa de
ciudad, *f.* **t. planning,** urbanismo, *m.*; reforma urbana, *f.*
t. wall, muralla, *f.*

townsman, *s.* ciudadano, *m.*

toxæmia, *s.* toxemia, *f.*

toxic, *a.* tóxico

toxicological, *a.* toxicológico

toxicologist, *s.* toxicólogo, *m.*

toxicology, *s.* toxicología, *f.*

toxin, *s.* toxina, *f.*

toy, *s.* juguete, *m.* *v.i.* (with)
jugar con; acariciar. **toy maker,**
fabricante de juguetes, *m.*

toyshop, *s.* juguetería, tienda de
juguetes, *f.*

trace, huella, pista, *f.*, rastro, *m.*;
vestigio, *m.*; indicio, *m.*, evidencia,
f.; (of a harness) tirante, *m.*;
(touch) dejo, *m.*; (of fear, etc.)
sombra, *f.* *v.t.* trazar; (through
transparent paper) calcar; seguir
la pista (de); (write) escribir;
(discern) distinguir; investigar;
descubrir; determinar; (walk)
atravesar, recorrer. **to t. back,**
(of ancestry, etc.) hacer remontar (a)

traceable, *a.* que se puede
trazar; atribuible

tracer, *s.* trazador (-ra). **t.
bullet,** bala luminosa, *f.*

tracery, *s.* tracería, *f.*

trachea, *s.* (*anat.*) tráquea, *f.*

tracheal, *a.* traqueal

tracheotomy, *s.* (*surg.*) traqueotomía, *f.*

trachoma, *s.* (*med.*) tracoma, *f.*

tracing, *s.* calco, *m.*; trazo, *m.*;
seguimiento, *m.* **t.-paper,** papel
de calcar, *m.*

track, *s.* huella, *f.*, rastro, *m.*;
(for racing, etc.) pista, *f.*; (of
wheels) rodada, *f.*; (railway)
vía, *f.*; (of a boat) estela, *f.*; (path)
senda, vereda, *f.*; (sign) señal,
evidencia, *f.*; (course) ruta, *f.*
v.t. rastrear, seguir la pista (de);
(*naut.*) sirgar. **to t. down,** seguir
y capturar. **double t.,** vía doble,
f. **off the t.,** extraviado;
(of a train) descarrilado; (*fig.*) por
los cerros de Úbeda. **side t.,**
desviadero, *m.* **.to keep t. of,**
(*fam.*) no perder de vista (a);
seguir las fortunas de

trackless, *a.* sin camino; sin
huella; (of trams, etc.) sin rieles;
(untrodden) no pisado

tract, *s.* tracto, *m.*; región, *f.*;
(*anat.*) vía, *f.*; (written) tratado, *m.*

tractability, *s.* docilidad, *f.*

tractable, *a.* dócil

traction, *s.* tracción, *f.* **t.-engine,**
máquina de arrastre (or de
tracción), *f.*

tractor, *s.* máquina de arrastre,
f.; tractor, *m.*

trade, *s.* comercio, *m.*; tráfico,
m.; negocio, *m.*; (in transit) trans-
(calling) oficio, *m.*, profesión, *f.*;
(dealers) comerciantes, *m.* and *f.
pl.* *v.i.* comerciar, traficar. *v.t.*
cambiar. **to t. on,** explotar,
aprovecharse de. **by t.,** de oficio,
por profesión. **t.-mark,** marca
de fábrica, *f.* **t.-name,** razón-
social, *f.* **t. price,** precio para el
comerciante, *m.* **t. union,** sindicato, *m.* **T. Union Congress,**
Congreso de Sindicatos, *m.*
t. unionism, sistema de sindicatos obreros, *m.* **t.-winds,**
vientos alisios, *m. pl.*

trader, *s.* comerciante, traficante,
m. and *f.*; mercader, *m.*; (boat)
buque mercante, *m.*

tradesman, *s.* tendero, *m.* **tradesmen's entrance,** puerta de servicio, *f.*

trading, *s.* comercio, tráfico, *m.*
a. mercantil, comerciante, mercante. **t. ship,** buque mercante,
m. **t. station,** factoría, *f.*

tradition, *s.* tradición, *f.*

traditional, *a.* tradicional

traditionalism, *s.* tradicionalismo, *m.*

traditionalist, *s.* tradicionalista,
m. and *f.*

traditionally, *adv.* según tradición, tradicionalmente

traduce, *v.t.* calumniar, denigrar,
vituperar

traducer, *s.* calumniador (-ra)

traffic, *s.* comercio, negocio,
tráfico, *m.*; (in transit) transporte, *m.*; (in movement) circulación, *f.* *v.i.* comerciar,
traficar, negociar. **to cause a
block in the t.,** interrumpir la
circulación. **t. block,** obstrucción del tráfico, *f.*, atasco en la
circulación, *m.* **t. indicator,**
(on a car) indicador de direc-

ción, *m.* **t. island,** refugio para peatones, salvávidas, *m.* **t. lights,** señales luminosas de la circulación, luces del tráfico, *f. pl.* **t. roundabout,** redondel, *m.*

trafficker, *s.* traficante, *m.* and *f.*

tragedian, *s.* trágico, *m.*

tragedy, *s.* tragedia, *f.*

tragic, *a.* trágico

tragically, *adv.* trágicamente

tragi-comedy, *s.* tragicomedia, *f.*

tragi-comic, *a.* tragicómico

trail, *s.* rastro, *m.*, pista, huella, *f.*; (path) sendero, *m.*; (of a comet) cola, cabellera, *f. v.t.* rastrear, seguir el rastro de; (drag) arrastrar; (the anchor) garrar. *v.i.* arrastrar; (of plants) trepar. **on the t. of,** en busca de; siguiendo el rastro de

trailer, *s.* cazador (-ra); perseguidor (-ra); *(aut.)* remolque, *m.*; (cinema) anuncio de próximas atracciones, *m.*; *(bot.)* talle rastrero, *m.*

train, *s.* (railway) tren, *m.*; (of a dress) cola, *f.*; (retinue) séquito, *m.*; (procession) desfile, *m.*, comitiva, *f.*; (series) serie, sucesión, *f.*; (of gunpowder) reguero de pólvora, *m.* **down t.,** tren descendente, *m.* **excursion t.,** tren de excursionistas, *m.* **express t.,** exprés, tren expreso, *m.* **fast t.,** rápido, *m.* **goods t.,** tren de mercancías, *m.* **mail t.,** tren correo, *m.* **next t.,** próximo tren, *m.* **passenger t.,** tren de pasajeros, *m.* **stopping t.,** tren ómnibus, *m.* **through t.,** tren directo, *m.* **up t.,** tren ascendente, *m.* **t.-bearer,** paje que lleva la cola, *m.*; dama de honor, *f.*; (of a cardinal, etc.) caudatario, *m.* **t.-ferry,** buque transbordador, *m.* **t.-oil,** aceite de ballena, *m.* **t. service,** servicio de trenes, *m.*

train, *v.t.* educar; adiestrar; enseñar; *(sport)* entrenar; (firearms) apuntar; (plants) guiar; (accustom) habituar, acostumbrar; (a horse for racing) entrenar; (circus) amaestrar. *v.i.* educarse; adiestrarse; *(sport)* entrenarse

trainer, *s.* (of men and racehorses) entrenador, *m.*; (of performing animals) domador, *m.*

training, *s.* educación, *f.*; enseñanza, instrucción, *f.*; *(sport)* entrenamiento, *m.* **t.-college,** escuela normal, *f.* **t.-ship,** buque escuela, *m.*

trait, *s.* rasgo, *m.*, característica, *f.*

traitor, *s.* traidor, *m.*

traitress, *s.* traidora, *f.*

trajectory, *s.* trayectoria, *f.*

tram, *s.* tranvía, *m. a.* tranviario. **t. conductor,** cobrador de tranvía, *m.* **t. depôt,** cochera de tranvías, *f.* **t. stop,** parada de tranvía, *f.*

trammel, *s.* (of a horse) traba, *f.*; *(fig.)* obstáculo, estorbo, *m. v.t.* trabar; *(fig.)* estorbar, impedir

tramp, *s.* (person) vagabundo (-da); vago (-ga); (walk) caminata, *f.*, paseo largo, *m.*; ruido de pasos, *m.*; *(naut.)* vapor volandero, *m. v.i.* ir a pie; patear; vagabundear. *v.t.* vagar por

trample, *s.* pisoteo, *m.*; (of feet) ruido de pasos, *m. v.t.* pisotear, pisar, hollar. *v.i.* pisar fuerte. **to t. on,** *(fig.)* atropellar humillar

trance, *s.* rapto, arrobamiento, *m.*; *(med.)* catalepsia, *f.*

tranquil, *a.* tranquilo, apacible; sereno, sosegado

tranquillity, *s.* tranquilidad, paz, quietud, *f.*; serenidad, *f.*, sosiego, *m.*; calma, *f.*

tranquillize, *v.t* tranquilizar, sosegar, calmar

tranquillizing, *a.* sosegador, tranquilizador

trans, *prefix* trans-. **t.-Pyrenean,** *a.* transpirenaico. **to t.-ship,** transbordar. **t.-shipment,** transbordo, *m.* **t.-Siberian,** transiberiano

transact, *v.t.* despachar, hacer. *v.i.* despachar un negocio

transaction, *s.* desempeño, *m.*; negocio, *m.*; transacción, operación, *f.*; *pl.* **transactions** (of a society) actas, *f. pl.*

transalpine, *a.* transalpino

transandean, *a.* transandino

transatlantic, *a.* transatlántico. **t. liner,** transatlántico, *m.*

transcend, *v.t.* exceder, superar, rebasar. *v.i.* trascender

transcendence, *s.* superioridad, *f.*; trascendencia, *f.*

transcendental, *a.* trascendental

transcontinental, *a.* transcontinental

transcribe, *v.t.* transcribir, copiar; (*mus.*) transcribir, adaptar

transcriber, *s.* copiador (-ra); (*mus.*) adaptador (-ra)

transcription, *s.* transcripción, copia, *f.,* trasunto, *m.;* (*mus.*) transcripción, adaptación, *f.,* arreglo, *m.*

transept, *s.* (*arch.*) transepto, crucero, *m.*

transfer, *s.* traslado, *m.;* transferencia, *f.,* traspaso, *m.;* (*law*) cesión, enajenación, *f.;* (picture) calcomanía, *f. v.t.* trasladar; transferir; pasar; (*law*) enajenar, ceder; estampar; calcografiar. *v.i.* transbordarse. **deed of t.,** escritura de cesión, *f.* **t.-paper,** papel de calcar, *m.*

transferable, *a.* transferible

transferee, *s.* cesionario (-ia)

transference, *s.* traslado, *m.;* transferencia, *f.;* (*law*) cesión, enajenación; *f.*

transferor, *s.* cesionista, *m.* and *f.*

transfiguration, *s.* transfiguración, *f.*

transfigure, *v.t.* transfigurar, transformar

transfix, *v.t.* traspasar; (*fig.*) paralizar

transfixion, *s.* transfixión, *f.*

transform, *v.t.* transformar; convertir, cambiar. **It is completely transformed,** Está completamente transformado

transformation, *s.* transformación, *f.;* conversión, *f.,* cambio, *m.*

transformative, *a.* transformador

transformer, *s.* (*elec.*) transformador, *m.*

transfuse, *v.t.* transfundir

transfusion, *s.* transfusión, *f.* **blood t.,** transfusión de sangre, *f.*

transgress, *v.t.* exceder, sobrepasar; (violate) contravenir, violar, pecar contra. *v.i.* pecar

transgression, *s.* contravención, transgresión, *f.;* pecado, *m.*

transgressor, *s.* transgresor (-ra), pecador (-ra)

transient, *a.* transitorio, fugaz, pasajero; perecedero

transiently, *adv.* pasajeramente

transit, *s.* tránsito, paso; *m.;* transporte, *m.;* (*ast.*) tránsito, *m.* **in t.,** de tránsito

transition, *s.* transición, *f.;* cambio, *m.;* tránsito, paso, *m.*

transitional, *a.* de transición, transitorio

transitive, *a.* (*gram.*) transitivo, activo. **t. verb,** verbo transitivo, verbo activo, *m.*

transitively, *adv.* transitivamente

transitorily, *adv.* transitoriamente; provisionalmente

transitoriness, *s.* brevedad, *f.,* lo fugaz

transitory, *a.* transitorio, fugaz, pasajero, breve

translatable, *a.* traducible

translate, *v.t.* traducir; interpretar; (transfer) trasladar

translation, *s.* traducción, *f.;* versión, *f.;* traslado, *m.*

translator, *s.* traductor (-ra)

translucence, *s.* translucidez, *f.*

translucent, *a.* translúcido, transparente

transmarine, *a.* transmarino

transmigrate, *v.i.* transmigrar

transmigration, *s.* transmigración, *f.*

transmissibility, *s.* transmisibilidad, *f.*

transmissible, *a.* transmisible

transmission, *s.* transmisión, *f.* (also *rad.*)

transmit, *v.t.* transmitir; remitir, dar

transmitter, *s.* transmisor (-ra); (*rad.*) radiotransmisor, *m.;* (*elec.*) transmisor, *m.*

transmutable, *a.* transmutable

transmutation, *s.* transmutación, *f.*

transmute, *v.t.* transmutar

transoceanic, *a.* transoceánico

transom, *s.* (*carp.*) travesaño, *m.;* (*naut.*) yugo de popa, *m.*

transpacific, *a.* transpacífico

transparency, *s.* transparencia (also *fig.*); diafanidad, *f.;* (picture) transparente, *m.*

transparent, *a.* transparente (also *fig.*); diáfano; (of style) claro, limpio

transpiration, *s.* transpiración, *f.*

transpire, *v.i.* transpirar; rezumarse; hacerse público; (*fam.*) acontecer. *v.t.* exhalar

transplant, *v.t.* trasplantar

transplantation, *s.* trasplante, *m.,* trasplantación, *f.*

transport, s. transporte, m.;
(*naut.*) navío de transporte, m.;
(*aer.*) avión de transporte, m.;
(fit) acceso, paroxismo, m. v.t.
transportar; (convicts) deportar;
(*fig.*) (joy) colmar; (rage) llenar

transportable, a. transportable

transportation, s. transporte,
m.; (convicts) deportación, f.

transporter, s. transportador
(-ra)

transpose, v.t. transponer; (*mus.*)
transportar

transposition, s. transposición, f.

transubstantiation, s. transubstanciación, f.

transversal, a. and s. transversal
(m.)

transverse, a. transverso, transversal

transversely, adv. transversalmente

Transylvanian, a. and s. transilvano (-na)

trap, s. trampa, f.; cepo, m.; (net)
lazo, m., red, f.; (for mice, rats)
ratonera, f.; (*mech.*) sifón de
depósito, m.; pequeño carruaje
de dos ruedas, m.; (door) puerta
caediza, f.; (*theat.*) escotillón, m.;
pl. **traps,** trastos, m. pl.; equipaje, m. v.t. coger con trampa;
hacer caer en el lazo; (*fig.*) tender
el lazo., v.i. armar una trampa;
armar lazo. **to fall into a t.,**
(*fig.*) caer en la trampa. **to pack
one's traps,** liar el hato

trapeze, s. trapecio (de gimnasia),
m.

trapezium, s. (*geom.*) trapecio,
trapezoide, m.

trapper, s. cazador de animales
de piel, m.

trappings, s. pl. arneses, jaeces,
m. pl.; arreos, aderezos, m. pl.,
galas, f. pl.

trappist, a. and s. trapense
(m.)

trash, s. paja, hojarasca, f.; (of
sugar, etc.) bagazo, m.; trastos
viejos, m. pl.; cachivaches, m. pl.;
(literary) paja, f.

trashy, a. de ningún valor,
inútil, despreciable

traumatic, a. (*med.*) traumático

traumatism, s. (*med.*) traumatismo, m.

travail, s. dolores de parto, m. pl.
v.i. estar de parto; trabajar

travel, s. el viajar, viajes, m. pl.
v.i. viajar; ver mundo; (of
traffic) circular, pasar, ir. v.t.
viajar por; recorrer; (with number of miles) hacer. **to t. over,**
viajar por; recorrer. **t. worn,**
fatigado por el viaje

travelled, a. que ha viajado

traveller, s. viajero (-ra); pasajero (-ra). **commercial t.,**
viajante, m. and f. **traveller's
cheque,** cheque de viajeros, m.
traveller's joy, (*bot.*) clemátide, f.

travelling, s. viajes, m. pl.
a. viajero; para (or de) viajar;
(itinerant) ambulante. **t. crane,**
grúa móvil, f. **t. expenses,**
gastos de viaje, m. pl. **t.
requisites,** objetos de viaje,
m. pl. **t. rug,** manta, f. **t. show,**
circo ambulante, m.

traversable, a. atravesable, transitable, practicable

traverse, s. (*carp.*) travesaño,
m.; (*law*) negación, f.; (*mil., arch.*)
través, m.; (crossing) travesía, f.
a. transversal. adv. transversalmente. v.t. atravesar, cruzar;
(*law*) negar

travesty, s. parodia, f. v.t.
parodiar

trawl, v.t. rastrear. v.i. pescar
a la rastra. **t.-net,** red de
arrastre, f.

trawler, s. barco barredero, m.;
pescador a la rastra, m.

trawling, s. pesca a la rastra, f.

tray, s. bandeja, f.; (of a balance)
platillo, m.; (in a wardrobe, etc.)
cajón, m.; (trough) artesa, f.

treacherous, a. traidor, falso,
pérfido, fementido; (of memory)
infiel; engañoso; (of ice, etc.)
peligroso

treacherously, adv. traidoramente, a traición

treachery, s. perfidia, traición,
falsedad, f.

treacle, s. melado, m.

tread, s. pisada, f.; paso, m.; (of
a stair) peldaño, m.; (of a tyre)
pastilla, f.; (walk) andar, porte,
m. v.i. pisar; (trample) pisotear;
hollar; (oppress) oprimir. v.t.
hollar; (a path) abrir; recorrer;
caminar por; bailar. **to t. the
grapes,** pisar las uvas. **to t. the
stage,** pisar las tablas. **to t.
under foot,** hollar; pisotear.

to t. on, pisar. **to t. on one's heels,** pisarle los talones a uno; seguir de cerca.; **to t. out,** (a measure) bailar

treading, s. pisoteo, m.

treadle, s. pedal, m.; (of a loom) cárcola, f.

treadmill, s. molino de rueda de escalones, m.; (fig.) rueda, f.

treason, s. traición, f. **high t.,** alta traición, lesa majestad, f.

treasonable, a. desleal, traidor

treasonably, adv. traidoramente.

treasure, s. tesoro, m.; riqueza, f., caudal, m.; (fig.) perla, f. v.t. atesorar; acumular (or guardar) riquezas; (a memory) guardar. **t. trove,** tesoro hallado, m.

treasurer, s. tesorero (-ra)

treasury, s. tesorería, f.; (government department) Ministerio de Hacienda, m.; (anthology) tesoro, m. **t. bench,** banco del Gobierno, m.

treat, s. (pleasure) gusto, placer, m.; (present) obsequio, m.; (entertainment) fiesta, f. v.t. tratar; (med.) tratar, curar; (regale) obsequiar. v.i. (stand host) convidar; (of) tratar de, versar sobre; (with) negociar con

treatise, s. tesis, monografía, disertación, f., tratado, m.

treatment, s. tratamiento, m.; (of persons) conducta hacia, f., modo de obrar con, m.; (med.) tratamiento, m.; (lit., art.) procedimiento, m., técnica, f.

treaty, s. tratado, pacto, m.; (bargain) contrato, m.

treble, s. (mus.) tiple, m.; voz de tiple, f. a. triple; (mus.) sobreagudo. v.t. triplicar; v.i. triplicarse. **t. clef,** clave de sol, f.

trebling, s. triplicación, f.

tree, s. árbol, m.; (for shoes) horma, f.; (of a saddle) arzón, m. **breadfruit t.,** árbol del pan, m. **Judas t.,** árbol de amor, m. **t. of knowledge,** árbol de la ciencia, m. **t.-covered,** arbolado. **t.-frog,** rana de San Antonio, f.

treeless, a. sin árboles

trefoil, s. trébol, trifolio, m.

trek, v.i. caminar, andar

trellis, s. enrejado, m.; (for plants) espaldera, f. v.t. cercar con un enrejado; construir espalderas

tremble, v.i. temblar; estremecerse; trepidar; vibrar; (sway) oscilar; (of flags) ondear; agitarse; ser tembloroso. **His fate trembled in the balance,** Su suerte estaba en la balanza. **to t. all over,** temblar de pies a cabeza

trembling, s. temblor, m.; estremecimiento, m.; trepidación, f.; vibración, f.; (fear) agitación, ansiedad, f.; temor, m. a. tembloroso; trémulo

tremendous, a. terrible, espantoso; formidable; grande; importante; (fam.) tremendo; enorme

tremendously, adv. terriblemente; (fam.) enormemente

tremor, s. temblor, m.; (thrill) estremecimiento, m.; vibración, f.

tremulous, a. trémulo, tembloroso; vacilante; tímido

tremulously, adv. trémulamente; tímidamente

tremulousness, s. lo tembloroso; vacilación, f.; timidez, f.

trench, s. zanja, f., foso, m.; (for irrigation) acequia, f.; (mil.) trinchera, f. v.t. hacer zanjas (en); acequiar; (mil.) atrincherar. **t.-fever,** tifus exantemático, m. **t.-foot,** pie de trinchera, m. **t.-mortar,** mortero de trinchera, m.

trenchant, a. mordaz

trencher, s. trinchero, m.

trend, s. curso, rumbo, m.; (fig.) tendencia, f.; dirección, f. v.i. (fig.) tender

trepan, v.t. (surg.) trepanar

trepanning, s. (surg.) trepanación, f.

trepidation, s. trepidación, f.

trespass, s. violación de propiedad, f.; ofensa, f.; pecado, m.; (in the Lord's Prayer) deuda, f. v.i. (on land) entrar sin derecho, violar la propiedad; (upon) entrar sin permiso en; (with patience, etc.) abusar de; (against) pecar contra, infringir

trespasser, s. violador (-ra) de la ley de propiedad. **Trespassers will be prosecuted,** Entrada prohibida, Prohibido el paso

tress, s. (plait) trenza, f.; rizo, bucle, m.; pl. **tresses,** cabellera, f.

trestle, *s.* caballete, *m.*; armazón, *m.* **trestle-table,** mesa de caballete, *f.*

triad, *s.* terna, *f.*; (*mus.*) acorde, *m.*

trial, *s.* prueba, *f.*, ensayo, *m.*; examen, *m.*; (experiment) tentativa; *f.*, experimento, *m.*; (misfortune) desgracia, pena, *f.*; (nuisance) molestia, *f.*; (*law*) vista de una causa, *f.* **on t.,** a prueba; (*law*) en proceso. **to bring to t.,** procesar. **to stand one's t.,** ser procesado. **t. run,** marcha de ensayo, *f.* **t. trip,** (*naut.*) viaje de ensayo, *m.*

triangle, *s.* triángulo, *m.* **acute-angled t.,** triángulo acutángulo, *m.* **obtuse-angled t.,** triángulo obtusángulo, *m.* **right-angled t.,** triángulo rectángulo, *m.* **the eternal t.,** el eterno triángulo

triangular, *a.* triangular, triángulo

triangulation, *s.* (in surveying) triangulación, *f.*

tribal, *a.* perteneciente al tribu, de tribu

tribasic, *a.* (*chem.*) tribásico

tribe, *s.* tribu, *f.*

tribesman, *s.* miembro de una tribu, *m.*

tribulation, *s.* tribulación, *f.*; pena, aflicción, desgracia, *f.*

tribunal, *s.* (seat) tribunal, *m.*; (court) juzgado, *m.*; (confessional) confesionario, *m.*

tribunary, *a.* tribúnico

tribunate, *s.* tribunado, *m.*

tribune, *s.* (person) tribuno, *m.*; tribuna, *f.*

tributary, *a.* and *s.* tributario (*m.*)

tribute, *s.* tributo, *m.*; contribución, imposición, *f.*

trice, *s.* tris, soplo, *m.* **in a t.,** en un periquete, en un avemaría, en dos trancos

trichotomy, *s.* tricotomía, *f.*

trick, *s.* (swindle) estafa, *f.*, engaño, *m.*; (ruse) truco, *m.*, estratagema, ardid, *f.*; (mischief) travesura, *f.*; burla, *f.*; (illusion) ilusión, *f.*; (habit) costumbre, *f.*; (affectation) afectación, *f.*; (jugglery) juego de manos, *m.*; (knack) talento, *m.*; (at cards) baza, *f.* *v.t.* engañar, estafar; (with out) adornar, ataviar; (with into) inducir fraudulentamente. *v.i.* trampear. **dirty t.,**

(*fam.*) mala pasada, perrada, *f.* **His memory plays him tricks,** Su memoria le engaña. **to play a t. on,** gastar una broma (a). **to play tricks,** hacer travesuras. **t. riding,** acrobacia ecuestre, *f.*

trickery, *s.* maullería, superchería, *f.*; fraude, engaño, *m.*

trickle, *s.* chorrito, hilo (de agua, etc.) *m.* *v.i.* gotear. **to t. down,** deslizar por, correr por, escurrir por

trickling, *s.* goteo, *m.*; (sound) murmullo, *m.*

trickster, *s.* embustero (-ra), trampeador (-ra). **to be a t.,** ser buena maula

tricky, *a.* informal, maullero; (of things) difícil; complicado; (clever) ingenioso

triclinium, *s.* triclinio, *m.*

tricolour, *a.* tricolor

tricycle, *s.* triciclo, *m.*

trident, *s.* tridente, *m.*

tridentine, *a.* tredentino

tried, *a.* probado

triennial, *a.* trienal

trifle, *s.* (object) baratija, fruslería, *f.*; pequeñez, tontería, bagatela, *f.*; (*cul.*) crema, *f.*; (small amount) pequeña cantidad, *f.*, muy poco (de); (adverbially) algo. *v.i.* entretenerse, jugar. *v.t.* (away) malgastar. **to t. with,** jugar con

trifler, *s.* persona frívola, *f.*; (with affections) seductor (-ra)

trifling, *a.* insignificante, sin importancia, trivial

trigger, *s.* (of a fire-arm) gatillo, *m.*; (*mech.*) tirador, *m.*

triglyph, *s.* (*arch.*) triglifo, *m.*

trigonometric, *a.* trigonométrico

trigonometry, *s.* trigonometría, *f.*

trilby, *s.* sombrero flexible, *m.*

trilingual, *a.* trilingüe

trill, *s.* trino, *m.* *v.i.* trinar

trillion, *s.* trillón, *m.*

trilogy, *s.* trilogía, *f.*

trim, *a.* aseado; bien arreglado; bien ajustado; elegante; bonito; (of sail) orientado. **She has a t. waist,** (*fam.*) Ella tiene un talle juncal. *s.* orden, *m.*; buen estado, *m.*; buena condición, *f.*; (toilet) atavío, *m.* *v.t.* arreglar;

(tidy) asear; pulir; (ornament) ornar, adornar; (adapt) ajustar, adaptar; (sew.) guarnecer; (lamps) despabilar; (a fire) atizar; (hair, moustache) atusar, recortar; (trees) mondar, atusar; (carp.) alisar; (sails) templar, orientar; (distribute weight in a boat) equilibrar; (of quill pens) tajar. v.i. (waver) nadar entre dos aguas. **to t. oneself up,** arreglarse

trimly, adv. aseadamente; lindamente

trimmer, s. guarnecedor (-ra); contemporizador (-ra)

trimming, s. arreglo, m.; guarnición, f.; (on a dress) pasamanería, f.; adorno, m.; (agr.) poda, f.; adaptación, f., ajuste, m.; pl. **trimmings,** accesorios, m. pl.

trimness, s. aseo, buen orden, m.; buen estado, m.; elegancia, lindeza, f.; (slimness) esbeltez, f.

Trinitarian, a. and s. trinitario (-ia)

Trinity, s. Trinidad, f.

trinket, s. joya, alhaja, f.; dije, m., chuchería, baratija, f.

trinomial, a. (math.) de tres términos. s. (math.) trinomio, m.

trio, s. trío, m.

trip, s. excursión, f.; viaje, m.; (slip) traspié, tropiezo, m.; (in wrestling) zancadilla, f.; (mistake) desliz, m. v.i. (stumble) tropezar, caer; (move nimbly) andar airosamente, ir (or correr) ligeramente; (frolic) bailar, saltar; (wrestling, games) echar la zancadilla; (err) equivocarse; cometer un desliz. v.t. (up) hacer caer; echar la zancadilla (a); coger en una falta; hacer desdecirse; coger en un desliz; (naut.) levantar (el ancla)

tripartite, a. tripartito

tripartition, s. tripartición, f.

tripe, s. callos, m. pl.

triphthong, s. triptongo, m.

triplane, s. (aer.) triplano, m.

triple, a. triple. v.t. triplicar. v.i. triplicarse

triplet, s. (poet.) terceto, m.; (mus.) tresillo, m.; cada uno (una) de tres hermanos (hermanas) gemelos (-as)

triplicate, a. triplicado. v.t. triplicar

triplication, s. triplicación, f.

tripod, s. trípode, m.

tripper, s. turista, excursionista, m. and f.

tripping, a. ligero, ágil

trippingly, adv. ligeramente

triptych, s. tríptico, m.

trireme, s. trirreme, m.

trisect, v.t. trisecar

trisection, s. trisección, f.

trismus, s. (med.) trismo, m.

trisyllabic, a. trisílabo

trite, a. vulgar, trivial

triteness, s. trivialidad, vulgaridad, f.

Triton, s. tritón, m.

triumph, s. triunfo, m. v.i. triunfar; (over) triunfar de, vencer

triumphal, a. triunfal. **t. arch,** arco de triunfo, m.

triumphant, a. triunfante, victorioso

triumvir, s. triunviro, m.

triumvirate, s. triunvirato, m.

trivet, s. trébedes, f. pl., trípode, m.

trivial, a. trivial, frívolo; insignificante, sin importancia

triviality, s. trivialidad, frivolidad, f.; insignificancia, f.

trivium, s. trivio, m.

trochaic, a. and s. trocaico (m.)

trochee, s. troqueo, m.

trochlea, s. (anat.) tróclea, f.

trodden, a. trillado, batido

troglodyte, s. and s. troglodita (m. and f.)

troglodytic, a. troglodítico

Trojan, a. and s. troyano (-na). **T. War,** guerra de Troya, f.

trolley, s. (elec.) trole, m.; (for children) carretón, m. **t.-bus,** trolebús, m. **t.-pole,** trole, m.

trollop, s. tarasca, ramera, f.

trombone, s. trombón, m. **t. player,** trombón, m.

troop, s. banda, muchedumbre, f.; (theat.) compañía, f.; (of cavalry) escuadrón, m.; pl. **troops,** (mil.) tropas, f. pl.; ejército, m. v.i. ir en tropel, congregarse; (with away) marcharse en tropel, retirarse; (with out) salir en masa. **fresh troops,** tropas frescas, f. pl. **storm troops,** tropas de asalto, f. pl. **t.-ship,** transporte de guerra, m.

trooper, s. soldado de caballería, m.

trope, s. tropa, m.

trophy, s. trofeo, m.

tropic, a. and s. trópico (m.)

tropical, a. tropical; (figurative) figurativo

tropism, s. tropismo, m.

trot, s. trote, m. v.i. trotar. v.t. hacer trotar. to t. out, (fam.) sacar a relucir

troth, s. fe, f.; palabra, f. to plight one's t., dar palabra de matrimonio, desposarse

trotting, a. trotón. s. trote, m.

troubadour, s. trovador, m. a. trovadoresco

trouble, s. (grief) aflicción, angustia, f.; (difficulty) dificultad, f.; (effort) esfuerzo, m.; pena, desgracia, f.; (annoyance) disgusto, sinsabor, m.; (unrest) confusión, f., disturbio, m.; (illness) enfermedad, f.; mal, m.; (disagreement) desavenencia, f. The t. is . . ., Lo malo es; La dificultad está en que . . . to be in t., estar afligido; estar en un apuro, estar entre la espada y la pared. to be not worth the t., no valer la pena. to stir up t., revolver el ajo; armar un lío. to take the t. to, tomarse la molestia de.

trouble, v.t. turbar; agitar; afligir; inquietar; (badger) importunar; (annoy) molestar; (cost an effort) costar trabajo (e.g. Learning Spanish did not t. him much, No le costó mucho trabajo aprender el castellano). v.i. preocuparse; darse la molestia; inquietarse

troubled, a. agitado; inquieto; preocupado; (of life) accidentado, borrascoso. to fish in t. waters, pescar a río revuelto

troublesome, a. dificultoso; molesto; inconveniente; importuno; fastidioso

trough, s. gamella, f.; (for kneading bread) artesa, f.; (of the waves) seno, m.; (meteorological) mínimo, m. drinking t., abrevadero, m. stone t., pila, f.

trounce, v.t. zurrar, apalear; (fig.) fustigar

troupe, s. compañía, f.

trousers, s. pl. pantalones, m. pl. plus four t., pantalones de golf,

m. pl. striped t., pantalón de corte, m. t. pocket, bolsillo del pantalón, m. t. press, prensa para pantalones, f.

trousseau, s. ajuar de novia, m.

trout, s. trucha, f.

trowel, s. (agr.) almocafre, m.; (mason's) paleta, f., palustre, m.

troy weight, s. peso de joyería, m.

truant, s. novillero, m.; haragán (-ana). a. haragán, perezoso. to play t., (from school) hacer novillos; ausentarse

truce, s. tregua, f.; suspensión, cesación, f.

truck, s. (lorry) camión, m.; carretilla de mano, f.; (railway) vagón de carga, m.; (intercourse) relaciones, f. pl.; (trash) cachivaches, m. pl., cosas sin valor, f. pl.

truckage, s. camionaje, m.; acarreo, m.

truckle, v.i. humillarse, no levantar los ojos. t. bed, carriola, f.

truculence, s. truculencia, agresividad, f.

truculent, a. truculento, agresivo

trudge, v.i. caminar a pie; andar con dificultad, caminar lentamente, andar trabajosamente. s. caminata, f.

trudgeon stroke, s. (swimming) natación a la marinera, f.

true, a. verdadero; real; leal, sincero; fiel; exacto; honesto; genuino; auténtico; alineado, a plomo. adv. realmente; exactamente. t.-bred, de casta legitima. t.-hearted, leal, fiel, sincero

truffle, s. trufa, f. to stuff with truffles, trufar

truism, s. perogrullada, f.

truly, adv. lealmente; realmente, verdaderamente; en efecto, por cierto; sinceramente, de buena fe. Yours t., su seguro servidor (su s.s.)

trump, s. (cards) triunfo, m.; son de la trompeta, m.; (fam.) gran persona, joya, f. v.t. ganar con el triunfo. to t. up, inventar. t.-card, naipe de triunfo, m.

trumpery, a. de pacotilla; ineficaz. s. oropel, m.

trumpet, s. trompeta, f. v.t. trompetear; (fig.) pregonar. v.i.

(of elephant) barritar. **ear.-t.**, trompetilla (acústica), *f.* **speaking t.**, portavoz, *m.* **t. blast**, trompetazo, *m.* **t. shaped**, en trompeta

trumpeter, *s.* trompetero, trompeta, *m.*

trumpeting, *s.* trompeteo, *m.*; (of elephant) barrito, *m.*

truncate, *a.* truncado. *v.t.* truncar

truncheon, *s.* porra (de goma), *f.*; bastón de mando, *m.* **blow with a t.**, porrazo, *m.*

trundle, *v.t.* and *v.i.* rodar

trunk, *s.* (*anat., bot.*) tronco, *m.*; (elephant's) trompa, *f.*; (railway) línea principal, *f.*; baúl, *m.*; cofre, *m.*; *pl.* **trunks**, (Elizabethan, etc.) trusas, *f. pl.*; calzoncillos cortos, *m. pl.* **wardrobe t.**, baúl mundo, *m.* **t.-call**, conferencia telefónica, *f.* **t.-line**, tronco, *m.* **t.-road**, carretera de primera clase, carretera mayor, *f.*

truss, *s.* (*med.*) braguero, *m.*; (of straw, etc.) haz, *m.*; (of blossom) racimo, *m.*; (framework) armazón, *f. v.t.* atar; (*cul.*) espetar; (a building) apuntalar

trust, *s.* fe, confianza, *f.*; deber, *m.*; (*law*) fideicomiso, *m.*; (credit) crédito, *m.*; esperanza, expectación, *f.*; (*com.*) trust, *m. v.t.* tener confianza en; confiar en; esperar; creer; (*com.*) dar crédito (a). *v.i.* confiar; (*com.*) dar crédito. **in t.**, en confianza; en administración, en depósito. **on t.**, al fiado

trustee, *s.* guardián, *m.*; (*law*) fideicomisario, depositario, consignatario, *m.*

trustful, *a.* confiado

trustingly, *adv.* confiadamente

trustworthiness, *s.* honradez, probidad, integridad, *f.*; (of statements) exactitud, *f.*

trustworthy, *a.* digno de confianza, honrado; fidedigno, seguro; exacto

trusty, *a.* leal, fiel; firme, seguro

truth, *s.* verdad, *f.*; realidad, *f.*; exactitud, *f.* **the plain t.**, la pura verdad. **to tell the t.**, decir la verdad

truthful, *a.* veraz; exacto, verdadero

truthfulness, *s.* veracidad, *f.*; exactitud, *f.*

try, *v.t.* and *v.i.* procurar, tratar de; (test) probar, ensayar; (a case, *law*) ver (el pleito); (strain) poner a prueba; (tire) cansar, fatigar; (annoy) molestar, exasperar; (afflict) hacer sufrir, afligir; (attempt) intentar; (judge) juzgar; (the weight of) tomar a pulso; (assay) refinar. *s.* tentativa, *f.*; (football) tiro, *m.* **Try as he would . . .,** Por más que hizo . . . **to try hard to,** hacer un gran esfuerzo para. **to try one's luck,** probar fortuna. **to try on,** (clothes) probarse (un vestido, etc.). **to try out,** poner a prueba, probar. **to try to,** tratar de, procurar

trying, *a.* molesto; fatigoso; irritante; (painful) angustioso, penoso

trypanosome, *s.* (*med.*) tripanosoma, *m.*

trypsin, *s.* (*med.*) tripsina, *f.*

tryst, *s.* cita, *f.*; lugar de cita, *m. v.t.* citar. *v.i.* citarse

tsar, *s.* zar, *m.*

tsetse-fly, *s.* mosca tsetse, *f.*

tub, *s.* cuba, *f.*, artesón, *m.*; cubeta, *f. v.i.* bañarse. **tub thumper,** (*fam.*) gerundio, *m.*

tuba, *s.* (*mus.*) tuba, *f.*

tube, *s.* tubo, *m.*; (railway) metro, ferrocarril subterráneo, *m.*; tubo, *m.*; (*anat.*) trompa, *f.* **Eustachian t.**, (*anat.*) trompa de Eustaquio, *f.* **Fallopian t.**, (*anat.*) trompa de Falopio, *f.* **inner t.**, (*aut.*) cámara de aire, *f.* **speaking t.**, tubo acústico, *m.* **test t.**, tubo de ensayo, *m.*

tuber, *s.* tubérculo, *m.*

tubercle, *s.* (*zool., bot., med.*) tubérculo, *m.*

tubercular, *a.* tuberculoso

tuberculin, *s.* tuberculina, *f.*

tuberculosis, *s.* tuberculosis, *f.*

tuberculous, *a.* tuberculoso

tuberose, *s.* (*bot.*) nardo, *m.*, tuberosa, *f.*

tuberosity, *s.* tuberosidad, *f.*

tuberous, *a.* tuberoso

tubing, *s.* tubería, *f.*

tubular, *a.* tubular

tuck, *s.* (*sew.*) alforza, *f.*; pliegue, *m. v.t.* recoger; (*sew.*) alforzar. *v.i.* hacer alforzas. **to t. in,** (in

bed) arropar; (*fam.*) tragar. **to
t. under,** poner debajo; doblar.
to t. up, (in bed) arropar; (skirt)
sofaldar; (sleeves) arremangar
tucker, *s.* camisolín, *m.*
Tuesday, *s.* martes, *m.* **Shrove
T.,** Martes de Carnaval, *m.*
tuft, *s.* (bunch) manojo, *m.*; (on
the head) copete, moño, *m.*,
cresta, *f.*; (tassel) borla, *f.*;
mechón, *m.*
tug, *s.* tirón, *m.*; sacudida, *f.*;
(boat) remolcador, *m.* *v.t.* tirar
de; halar; sacudir. *v.i.* tirar
con fuerza. **to give a tug,** dar
una sacudida. **tug of war,**
lucha a la cuerda, *f.*
tuition, *s.* instrucción, enseñanza,
f.; lecciones, *f. pl.*
tulip, *s.* tulipán, *m.* **t. wood,**
palo de rosa, *m.*
tulle, *s.* tul, *m.*
tumble, *s.* caída, *f.*; (somersault)
tumbo, *m.*; voltereta, *f.* *v.i.* caer;
(acrobats) voltear, dar saltos.
v.t. hacer caer; desarreglar.
to t. down, venirse abajo; caer
por. **t. down,** ruinoso, destartalado. **to t. off,** caer de. **to t.
out,** *v.t.* hacer salir; arrojar.
v.i. salir apresuradamente. **to t.
over,** *v.t.* tropezar con. *v.i.*
volcarse. **to t. to,** (*fam.*) caer en
la cuenta
tumbler, *s.* (acrobat) volteador
(-ra); vaso para beber, *m.*
tumbrel, *s.* carreta, *f.*
tumefaction, *s.* tumefacción, *f.*
tumid, *a.* túmido, hinchado
tumour, *s.* tumor, *m.*
tumult, *s.* alboroto, tumulto, *m.*;
conmoción, agitación, *f.*; confusión, *f.*
tumultuous, *a.* tumultuoso, alborotado; ruidoso; confuso;
turbulento, violento
tumulus, *s.* túmulo, *m.*
tun, *s.* tonel, *m.*, cuba, *f.* *v.t.*
entonelar, embarrilar
tune, *s.* melodía, *f.*; son, *m.*;
armonía, *f.*; (*fig.*) tono, *m.*; (*fam.*)
suma, *f.* *v.t.* (*mus.*) afinar,
templar; (*rad.*) sintonizar; (up,
an engine) ajustar (un motor).
v.i. (in) sintonizar el receptor;
(up, *mus.*) templar (afinar) los
instrumentos. **in t.,** (*mus.*)
afinado, templado; (*fig.*) armonioso; (agreement) de acuerdo, con-

forme. **out of t.,** (*mus.*) desafinado, destemplado. **to be out
of t.,** desentonar, discordar;
(*fig.*) no armonizar, no estar
en armonía. **to go out of t.,**
desafinar. **to put out of t.,**
destemplar. **to change one's
t.,** (*fam.*) bajar el tono
tuneful, *a.* melodioso
tunefully, *adv.* melodiosamente,
armoniosamente
tunefulness, *s.* melodía, *f.*
tuneless, *a.* disonante, discordante
tuner, *s.* afinador, templador,
m.; (*rad.*) sintonizador, *m.*
tungsten, *s.* tungsteno, *m.*
tunic, *s.* túnica, *f.*
tuning, *s.* afinación, *f.*; (*rad.*)
sintonización, *f.* **t. fork,** diapasón normal, *m.* **t. key,** templador, *m.*
Tunisian, *a.* and *s.* tunecino (-na)
tunnel, *s.* túnel, *m.* *v.t.* hacer (or
construir) un túnel por. *v.i.* hacer
un túnel
tunnelling, *s.* construcción de
túneles, *f.*; horadación, *f.*
tunny, *s.* atún, *m.* **striped t.,**
bonito, *m.* **t. fishery,** almadraba, *f.*
turban, *s.* turbante, *m.*
turbid, *a.* turbio; (*fig.*) confuso,
to make t., enturbiar
turbidity, *s.* turbiedad, *f.*
turbine, *s.* turbina, *f.*
turbot, *s.* rodaballo, *m.*
turbulence, *s.* turbulencia, *f.*;
desorden, *m.*; agitación, *f.*
turbulent, *a.* turbulento; alborotado; (stormy) borrascoso; agitado
turco, *a.* (in compounds) turco
tureen, *s.* sopera, *f.*
turf, *s.* césped, *m.*; (fuel) turba, *f.*;
(racing) carreras de caballos, *f. pl.*
turgid, *a.* turgente, hinchado;
(of style) pomposo
turgidity, *s.* turgencia, *f.*; pomposidad, *f.*
Turk, *s.* turco (-ca). **Turk's
head,** (duster) deshollinador, *m.*;
(*naut.*) cabeza de turco, *f.*
turkey, *s.* (cock) pavo, *m.*; (hen)
pava, *f.* **t. red,** rojo turco, *m.*
Turkish, *a.* turco. *s.* (language)
turco, idioma turco, *m.* **T. bath,**
baño turco, *m.* **T. slipper,**
babucha, *f.* **T. towel,** toalla
rusa, *f.*

turmeric, s. cúrcuma, f. **t. paper,** papel de cúrcuma, m.

turmoil, s. alboroto, tumulto, desorden, m.

turn, s. turno, m.; (twist) torcimiento, m.; (bend) recodo, m., vuelta, f.; (in a river) meandro, .m.; (in a road) viraje, m.; (revolution) vuelta, revolución, f.; (direction) dirección, f.; (in spiral stair) espira, f.; (theat.) número, m.; (change) cambio, m.; vicisitud, f.; (appearance) aspecto, m.; (service) servicio, m.; (nature) índole, naturaleza, f.; (of phrase) giro, m., expresión, f.; (walk) vuelta, f., paseo, m.; (talent) talento, m. **a sharp t.,** (in a road) un viraje rápido. **at every t.,** a cada instante; en todas partes. **bad t.,** flaco servicio, m. **by turns,** por turnos. **good t.,** servicio, favor, m. **in its t.,** a su vez. **in t.,** sucesivamente. **Now it's my t.,** Ahora me toca a mí. **The affair has taken a new t.,** El asunto ha cambiado de aspecto. **to a t.,** (cul.) a la perfección. **to have a t. for,** tener talento para. **to take turns at,** alternar en. **t.-table,** (railway) plataforma, f.; (of a gramophone) disco giratorio, m. **t. up,** barahunda, conmoción, f.; (of trousers) dobladillo (del pantalón), m.

turn, v.t. (on a lathe) tornear; (revolve) dar vueltas a, girar; (a key, door handle, etc.) torcer; (the leaves of a book) hojear; (the brain) trastornar; (a screw) enroscar; (the stomach) revolver (el estómago), marear; (go round) doblar, dar la vuelta a; (change) cambiar, mudar; (translate) traducir, verter; (dissuade) disuadir; (deflect) desviar; (apply) adaptar; (direct, move) volver; (concentrate) dirigir; concentrar; (turn over) volver del revés al derecho; (upside-down) volver lo de arriba abajo; (make) hacer, volver; (make sour) volver agrio; (transform) transformar, convertir; (mil.) envolver. **He has turned thirty,** Ha cumplido los treinta. **He said it without turning a hair,** Lo dijo sin pestañear. **He turned his head,**

Volvió la cabeza. **They have turned the corner,** Han doblado la esquina; (fig.) Han pasado la crisis. **Please t. over,** A la vuelta (de la página). **to t. a deaf ear to,** no dar oídos a, no hacer caso de. **to t. to account,** sacar ventaja (de). **to t. adrift,** dejar a la merced de las olas; echar de casa, poner en la calle; abandonar. **to t. against,** causar aversión, hacer hostil. **to t. aside,** desviar. **to t. away,** despedir; rechazar; (the head, etc.) volver; desviar. **to t. back,** hacer volver; enviar de nuevo; (raise) alzar; (fold) doblar; (the clock) retrasar. **to t. down,** doblar; (gas) bajar; (a glass, etc.) poner boca abajo; (reject) rechazar; (a suitor) dar calabazas (a). **to t. from,** alejar de, desviar de. **to t. in,** doblar hacia dentro; entregar. **to t. in one's toes,** ser patizambo. **to t. inside out,** volver al revés. **to t. into,** (enter) entrar en; (change) cambiar en, transformar en; convertir en; (translate) traducir a. **to t. off,** (dismiss) despedir; (from) desviarse de, dejar; (light) apagar; (water) cortar; (mech.) cerrar; (disconnect) desconectar; (avoid) evitar; (refuse) rechazar. **to t. off the tap,** (water, gas) cerrar la llave (del agua, del gas). **to t. on,** (light) encender; (water, gas, etc.) abrir la llave (del agua, del gas); (steam) dar (vapor); (electric current) establecer (la corriente eléctrica); (eyes) fijar. **to t. out,** (expel) expeler, echar; (dismiss) despedir; (animals) echar al campo; (produce) producir; (dress) vestir; (equip) equipar, guarnecer; (a light) apagar. **to t. over,** (the page) volver (la hoja); (transfer) ceder, traspasar; revolver; (upset) volcar; considerar, pensar. **to t. round,** dar vuelta (a); girar; (empty) descargar. **to t. up,** levantar; apuntar; hacia arriba; (the earth) labrar, cavar; (a glass) poner boca arriba; (one's sleeves, skirt) arremangar; (fold) doblar. **to t. up one's nose at,** mirar con desprecio. **to t. upon,** atacar, volverse contra, acometer; depender de, estribar en. **to t. upside down,** volver lo de arriba abajo; revolver; revolcar **turn,** *v.i.* (in a lathe) tornear; (revolve) girar, dar vueltas; (depend) depender de (de); torcer; volverse; dar la vuelta; girar sobre los talones; dirigirse (a, hacia); (move) mudar de posición; (deviate) desviarse (de); (be changed) convertirse (en); (become) hacerse, venir a ser; (begin) meterse (a); (take to) dedicarse a; (seek help) acudir; (change behaviour) enmendarse, corregirse; (the stomach) revolver (el estómago); (go sour) agriarse, avinagrarse; (rebel) sublevarse. **He turned to the left,** Dió la vuelta a la izquierda; Torció hacia la izquierda. **My head turns,** (with giddiness) Se me va la cabeza. **to t. about,** voltearse, dar la vuelta. **to t. against,** coger aversión (a), disgustarse con; volverse hostil (a). **to t. aside,** desviarse; dejar el camino. **to t. away,** volver la cabeza; apartarse; alejarse. **to t. back,** volver atrás; volver de nuevo; retroceder; volver sobre sus pasos. **to t. down,** doblarse; reducirse. **to t. from,** alejarse de; apartarse de, huir de. **to t. in,** doblarse hacia dentro; (retire) acostarse. **to t. into,** transformarse en; convertirse en. **to t. off,** (depart from) desviarse (de); (fork) torcer, bifurcarse. **to t. out,** estar vuelto hacia fuera; (leave home) salir de casa; (rise) levantarse (de la cama); (arrive) llegar, presentarse; (attend) asistir, acudir; (result) resultar. **to t. over,** mudar (or cambiar) de posición, revolverse; (upset) voltearse, volcarse. **to t. round,** girar; volverse; cambiar de frente; cambiar de dirección, dar la vuelta; (*aut., aer.*) virar; (change views) cambiar de opinión; (change sides) cambiar de partido. **to t. round and round,** dar vueltas, girar. **to t. to,** (apply to) acudir a; (begin) ponerse a; (become) convertirse en; (face)

dirigirse hacia; (address) dirigirse a. **to t. up,** (crop up), surgir, aparecer; (arrive) llegar; (happen) acontecer; (be found again) volver a hallarse, reaparecer; (cards) venir; (of hats) levantar el ala; (of hair, etc.) doblarse. **His nose turns up,** Tiene la nariz respingona
turncoat, *s.* desertor (-ra), renegado (-da). **to become a t.,** volver la casaca
turncock, *s.* pocero, *m.*
turned-up, *a.* (of hats) con el ala levantada; (of noses) respingona
turner, *s.* (craftsman) tornero, torneador, *m.*
turnery, *s.* tornería, *f.*
turning, *s.* (bend) vuelta, *f.*; (turnery) tornería, *f.*; (of milk, etc.) agrura, *f.*; *pl.* **turnings,** (*sew.*) ensanche, *m.* **t.-point,** punto decisivo, *m.*, crisis, *f.*
turnip, *s.* nabo, *m.* **t. field,** nabar, *m.*
turnkey, *s.* llavero de cárcel, *m.*
turnover, *s.* (com.) ventas, *f. pl.*; (*cul.*) pastelillo, *m.*
turnpike, *s.* barrera de portazgo, *f.*
turnstile, *s.* torniquete, *m.*
turpentine, *s.* aguarrás, *m.*, trementina, *f.*
turpitude, *s.* infamia, maldad, *f.*
turquoise, *s.* turquesa, *f.*
turret, *s.* torrecilla, almenilla, *f.*; (*naut.*) torre blindada, *f.*
turreted, *a.* con torres, guarnecido de torres; en forma de torre
turtle, *s.* (dove) tórtolo (-la); (sea) tortuga de mar, *f.* **to turn t.,** voltearse patas arriba; (*naut.*) zozobrar. **t. soup,** sopa de tortuga, *f.*
Tuscan, *a. and s.* toscano (-na)
tusk, *s.* colmillo, *m.*
tusked, *a.* colmilludo
tussle, *s.* lucha, *f.*; agarrada, *f.* *v.i.* luchar, pelear; tener una agarrada
tussock, *s.* copete, manojo, *m.*
tutelage, *s.* tutela, *f.*
tutelar, *a.* tutelar
tutor, *s.* (private) ayo, *m.*; profesor (-ra); (Roman law) tutor, *m.*; (supervisor of studies) preceptor. *v.t.* enseñar, instruir. *v.i.* ser profesor, dar clases

tutorial, *s.* (university) semi-nario, *m.*; (private) clase parti-cular, *f.*

tutoring, *s.* enseñanza, instruc-ción, *f.*

tu-whitt, tu-whoo, *s.* grito del buho, *m.*

twaddle, *s.* disparates, *m. pl.*, tonterías, patrañas, *f. pl.*

twain, *a.* and *s.* dos (*m.*)

twang, *s.* punteado de una cuerda, *m.*; (of a guitar) zumbido, *m.*; (in speech) gangueo, *m.* *v.t.* puntear; (las cuerdas de un instrumento) rasguear. *v.i.* zum-bar. to speak with a t., hablar con una voz gangosa

tweak, *s.* pellizco, *m.*; sacudida, *f.*, tirón, *m.* *v.t.* pellizcar; sacudir, tirar

tweed, *s.* mezcla, *f.*, cheviot, *m.*

tweezers, *s. pl.* pinzas, tenacillas, *f. pl.*

twelfth, *a.* duodécimo; (of the month) (el) doce; (of monarchs) doce. *s.* duodécimo, *m.*; (part) dozavo, *m.*, duodécima parte, *f.* T.-night, Día de Reyes, *m.*, Epifanía, *f.*

twelve, *a.* and *s.* doce (*m.*); (of age) doce años, *m. pl.* t. o'clock, las doce; (mid-day) mediodía, *m.*; (midnight) media noche, *f.*, las doce de la noche. t.-syllabled, dodecasílabo

twentieth, *a.* vigésimo; (of the month) (el) veinte; (of monarchs) veinte, *s.* vigésimo, *m.*; (part) veintavo, *m.*, vigésima parte, *f.*

twenty, *a.* veinte; (of age) veinte años, *m. pl.* *s.* veinte, *m.*; (score) veintena, *f.* t.-first, vigésimo primero; (of date) (el) veintiuno, *m.* (In modern Spanish the ordinals above vigésimo (twentieth) are gener-ally replaced by the cardinals, and even below vigésimo the cardinals are often used, e.g. The twenty-ninth chapter, El capítulo veintinueve.)

twice, *adv.* dos veces. t. as many or as much, el doble

twiddle, *v.t.* jugar con; hacer girar. *v.i.* girar; vibrar. *s.* vuelta, *f.* to t. one's thumbs, dar vuelta a los pulgares, estar mano sobre mano

twig, *s.* ramita, pequeña rama, *f.*

twilight, *s.* crepúsculo, *m.*; media luz, *f.* *a.* crepuscular. in the t., en el crepúsculo; en la media luz. t. sleep, parto sin dolor, *m.*

twill, *s.* sarga, *f.*

twin, *a.* gemelo, mellizo; doble. *s.* gemelo (-la), mellizo (-za); (of objects) pareja, *f.*, par, *m.* t.-engined, bimotor. t. screw, (*naut.*, *aer.*) de dos hélices

twine, *s.* bramante, cordel, *m.*; guita, *f.* *v.t.* enroscar; (weave) tejer; (encircle) ceñir; (round, about) abrazar. *v.i.* (of plants) trepar; entrelazarse; (wind) ser-pentear

twinge, *s.* punzada, *f.*, dolor agudo, *m.*; (*fig.*) remordimiento, tormento, *m.* *v.i.* causar un dolor agudo

twining, *a.* (*bot.*) trepante, voluble. t. plant, planta en-redadera (or trepante), *f.*

twinkle, *v.i.* centellear, chispear, titilar; (of eyes) brillar; (of feet) moverse rápidamente, bailar. *s.* (in the eye) chispa, *f.*

twinkling, *s.* centelleo, *m.*; titila-ción, *f.*; (of the eye) brillo, *m.*; (glimpse) vislumbre, *m.*; (*fig.*) instante, momento, *m.* *a.* titi-lante, centelleador. in a t., en un dos por tres. in the t. of an eye, en un abrir y cerrar de ojos

twirl, *s.* rotación, vuelta, *f.*; pirueta, *f.* *v.t.* hacer girar; voltear; torcer; (a stick, etc.) dar vueltas (a). *v.i.* girar, dar vueltas; dar piruetas

twirp, *s.* (*fam.*) renacuajo, *m.*

twist, *s.* (skein) mecha, *f.*; trenza, *f.*; (yarn) torzal, *m.*; (of tobacco) rollo, *m.*; (of bread) rosca de pan, *f.*; (act of twisting) torcimiento, *m.*, torsión, *f.*; (in a road, etc.) recodo, *m.*, curva, vuelta, *f.*; (pull) sacudida, *f.*; (contortion) regate, esguince, *m.*; (in a wind-ing stair) espira, *f.*; (in ball games) efecto, *m.*; (in a person's nature) peculiaridad, *f.*; falta de franqueza, *f.*; (to words) inter-pretación, *f.* *v.t.* torcer; enros-car; (plait) trenzar; (wring) estrujar; (weave) tejer; (encircle) ceñir; (a stick, etc.) dar vueltas a; (of hands) crispar; (distort) interpretar mal, torcer. *v.i.*

torcerse; enroscarse; (wind) serpentear; dar vueltas; (coil) ensortijarse; (writhe) undular, retorcerse; (of a stair) dar vueltas
twisted, *a.* torcido; (of persons) contrahecho
twisting, *s.* torcimiento, *m.*; torcedura, *f.*; serpenteo, *m.*; (interlacing) entrelazamiento, *m. a.* sinuoso, serpenteado
twit (with), *v.t.* echar en cara
twitch, *s.* sacudida, *f.*, tirón; *m.*; (nervous) contracción nerviosa, *f.* *v.t.* tirar bruscamente, quitar rápidamente; agarrar; (ears, etc.) mover; (hands) crispar, retorcer. *v.i.* crisparse; (of ears, nose) moverse
twitching, *s.* sacudida, *f.*; (contraction) crispamiento, *m.*, contracción nerviosa, *f.*; (pain) punzada, *f.*; (of conscience) remordimiento, *m*
twitter, *s.* piada, *f.*, gorjeo, *m.* *v.i.* piar, gorjear
two, *a.* and *s.* dos (*m.*); (of the clock) (las) dos, *f. pl.*; (of age) dos años, *m. pl. a.* de dos. **in two,** en dos partes. **in two's,** de dos en dos. **one or two,** uno o dos; algunos, *m. pl.*; algunas, *f. pl.* **two against two,** dos a dos: **two by two,** de dos en dos, a pares. **to put two and two together,** atar cabos. **twoedged,** de dos filos. **two-faced,** de dos caras; (*fig.*) de dos haces. **to be two-faced,** hacer a dos caras. **two-headed,** de dos cabezas; bicéfalo. **two hundred,** *a.* and *s.* doscientos (*m.*). **two hundredth,** *a.* ducentésimo. *s.* ducentésima parte, *f.*; doscientos, *m.* **two-legged,** bípedo. **two-ply,** de dos hilos. **two-seater,** *a.* de dos asientos. **two-speed gear box,** cambio de marcha de dos velocidades, *m.* **two-step,** paso doble, *m.* **two of a kind,** (well-matched) tal para cual. **two-way switch,** (*elec.*) interruptor de dos direcciones, *m.*
twofold, *a.* doble. *adv.* doblemente, dos veces
twopence, *s.* dos peniques, *m. pl.*
twopenny, *a.* de dos peniques; (*fig.*) de tres al cuarto
twosome, *s.* partido de dos, *m.*

tying, *s.* ligadura, *f.*; atadura, *f.*
tympanum, *s.* (*anat.*, *arch.*) tímpano, *m.*
type, *s.* tipo, *m.*; (*print.*) carácter, *m.*, letra de imprenta, *f.*, tipo, *m.* *v.t.* and *v.i.* escribir a máquina. **t. case,** caja de imprenta, *f.* **t. founder,** fundidor de letras de imprenta, *m.* **t. foundry,** fundición de tipos, *f.* **t.-setter,** cajista, *m.* and *f.* **t.-setting,** composición tipográfica, *f.*
typewrite, *v.t.* and *v.i.* escribir a máquina
typewriter, *s.* máquina de escribir, *f.*
typewriting, *s.* mecanografía, *f.* *a.* mecanográfico
typewritten, *a.* escrito a máquina
typhoid, *s* tifoidea, fiebre tifoidea, *f.*
typhoon, *s.* tifón, *m.*
typhus, *s.* tifus, tabardillo pintado, *m.*
typical, *a.* típico, característico; simbólico
typify, *v.t.* simbolizar, representar; ser ejemplo de
typist, *s.* mecanografista, *m.* and *f.*; mecanógrafo (*f.*)
typographic, *a.* tipográfico
typography, *s.* tipografía, *f.*
typographer, *s.* tipógrafo, *m.*
tyrannical, *a.* tiránico, despótico
tyrannicide, *s.* (person) tiranicida, *m.* and *f.*; (act) tiranicidio, *m.*
tyrannization, *s.* tiranización, *f.*
tyrannize, *v.i.* tiranizar
tyranny, *s.* tiranía, *f.*, despotismo, *m.*
tyrant, *s.* déspota, *m.* tirano (-na)
tyre, *s.* (of a cart, etc.) llanta, *f.*; (*aut.*) neumático, *m.*; (of a perambulator, etc.) rueda de goma, *f.* **balloon t.,** neumático balón, *m.* **pneumatic t.,** neumático, *m.* **slack t.,** neumático desinflado, *m.* **solid t.,** neumático macizo, *m.* **spare t.,** neumático de recambio (or de repuesto), *m.* **t. burst,** estallido de un neumático, *m.* **t. valve,** válvula de cámara (del neumático), *f.*
Tyrian, *a.* and *s.* tirio (-ia)
Tyrolese, *a.* and *s.* tirolés (-esa)
Tyrrhenian, *a.* tirreno
Tzigany, *a.* and *s.* zíngaro (-ra)

U

u, *s.* (letter) u, *f.* **U-boat,** submarino, *m.* **u-shaped,** en forma de U

ubiquitous, *a.* ubicuo, omnipresente

ubiquity, *s.* ubicuidad, omnipresencia, *f.*

udder, *s.* ubre, teta, mama, *f.*

ugh, *interj.* ¡uf!

ugliness, *s.* fealdad, *f.*; (moral) perversidad, *f.*; (of a situation) peligro, *m.*, lo difícil

ugly, *a.* feo; (morally) repugnante, asqueroso, perverso; (of a situation) peligroso, difícil; (of a wound) grave, profundo; (of a look) amenazador; (*fam.*) desagradable; (of weather) borrascoso. **to make u.,** afear, hacer feo

uhlan, *s.* ulano, *m.*

Ukrainian, *a.* and *s.* ucranio (-ia)

ukulele, *s.* (*mus.*) ukelele, *m.*

ulcer, *s.* úlcera, *f.*

ulcerate, *v.t.* ulcerar. *v.i.* ulcerarse

ulceration, *s.* ulceración, *f.*

ulcerous, *a.* ulceroso

ulna, *s.* (*anat.*) cúbito, *m.*

ulster, *s.* gabán ruso, *m.*

ulterior, *a.* (of place) ulterior; (of time) posterior, ulterior; (of motives) interesado, oculto

ultimate, *a.* último; fundamental, esencial

ultimately, *adv.* por fin, al final; esencialmente

ultimatum, *s.* ultimátum, *m.*

ultimo, *adv.* del mes anterior

ultra, *a.* exagerado, extremo. *prefix* ultra-. **u-red,** ultrarrojo. **u-violet,** ultravioleta

ultramarine, *a.* ultramarino. *s.* azul de ultramar, *m.*

ultramontane, *a.* ultramontano

ululation, *s.* ululación, *f.*, ululato, *m.*

umbel, *s.* (*bot.*) umbela, *f.*

umbelliferous, *a.* (*bot.*) umbelífero

umber, *s.* (pigment) tierra de sombra, *f. a.* pardo oscuro

umbilical, *a.* umbilical

umbilicus, *s.* ombligo, *m.*

umbra, *s.* (*ast.*) cono de sombra, *m.*

umbrage, *s.* (*poet.*) sombra, *f.*; resentimiento, enfado, *m.* **to take u.,** ofenderse, resentirse

umbrella, *s.* paraguas, *m.* **u. maker,** paragüero (-ra). **u. shop,** paragüería, *f.* **u. stand,** paragüero, *m.*

Umbrian, *a.* de Umbría

umpire, *s.* (*sport*) árbitro, *m.*; (*law*) juez arbitrador, tercero en discordia, *m. v.t.* arbitrar

un-, *prefix.* Used before adjectives, adverbs, abstract nouns, verbs and translated in Spanish by in-, des-, no, sin

unabashed, *a.* desvergonzado, descarado, insolente; (calm) sereno, sosegado

unabated, *a.* no disminuido; cabal, entero

unabbreviated, *a.* íntegro, sin abreviar

unable, *a.* incapaz, impotente; (physical defect) imposibilitado. **to be u. to,** no poder, serle a uno imposible. **to be u. to control,** no poder controlar

unabridged, *a.* See **unabbreviated**

unaccented, *a.* sin acento

unacceptability, *s.* lo inaceptable

unacceptable, *a.* inaceptable

unaccepted, *a.* rechazado, no aceptado

unaccommodating, *a.* poco complaciente, nada servicial

unaccompanied, *a.* solo, sin compañía; (*mus.*) sin acompañamiento

unaccomplished, *a.* incompleto, sin terminar, inacabado; (not clever) sin talento

unaccountability, *s.* lo inexplicable; falta de responsabilidad, irresponsabilidad, *f.*

unaccountable, *a.* inexplicable; irresponsable

unaccountably, *adv.* inexplicablemente, extrañamente

unaccredited, *a.* no acreditado, extraoficial

unaccustomed, *a.* no habituado; (unusual) desacostumbrado, insólito, inusitado

unacknowledged, *a.* no reconocido; (of letter) sin contestación, por contestar; no correspondido, sin devolver; (of crimes, etc.) inconfeso, no declarado

unacquainted, *a.* que no conoce; que desconoce, que ignora; no habituado. **to be u. with,** no conocer; ignorar; no estar acostumbrado a

unadaptable, *a.* inadaptable (also of persons)

unadorned, *a.* sin adorno, sencillo

unadulterated, *a.* sin mezcla, no adulterado, natural; genuino, verdadero; puro

unadventurous, *a.* nada aventurero, que no busca aventuras, tímido; tranquilo, sin incidente

unadvisability, *s.* imprudencia, *f.*; inoportunidad, *f.*

unadvisable, *a.* imprudente; inoportuno, no conveniente

unadvisedly, *adv.* imprudentemente

unæsthetic, *a.* antiestético

unaffected, *a.* natural, llano, sin melindres; impasible; genuino, sincero. **u. by,** no afectado por

unaffectedly, *adv.* sin afectación

unaffectedness, *s.* naturalidad, sencillez, *f.*; sinceridad, franqueza, *f.*

unaffiliated, *a.* no afiliado

unafraid, *a.* sin temor

unaided, *a.* sin ayuda, solo, a solas

unaired, *a.* sin ventilar, no ventilado; húmedo, sin airear

unalloyed, *a.* sin mezcla, puro

unalterability, *s.* lo inalterable; constancia, *f.*

unalterable, *a.* inalterable; invariable, constante

unambiguous, *a.* no ambiguo, nada dudoso, claro

unambitious, *a.* sin ambición; modesto

unamusing, *a.* nada divertido

unanimity, *s.* unanimidad, *f.*

unanimous, *a.* unánime

unanimously, *adv.* unánimemente, por unanimidad. **carried u.,** adoptado por unanimidad

unanswerability, *s.* imposibilidad de negar, *f.*; lo irrefutable

unanswerable, *a.* incontestable, incontrovertible, incontrastable, irrefutable

unanswered, *a.* no contestado, sin contestar; (unrequited) no correspondido

unapparent, *a.* no aparente

unappealable, *a.* inapelable

unappeasable, *a.* implacable

unappeased, *a.* no satisfecho; implacable

unappetizing, *a.* no apetitoso; (unattractive) repugnante, feo

unappreciated, *a.* desestimado, no apreciado, tenido en poco; (misunderstood) mal comprendido

unapproachable, *a.* inaccesible

unapproachableness, *s.* inaccesibilidad, *f.*

unappropriated, *a.* no concedido; libre

unapproved, *a.* sin aprobar, no aprobado

unarm, *v.t.* desarmar. *v.i.* desarmarse, quitarse las armas

unarmed, *a.* desarmado; indefenso; (*zool., bot.*) inerme

unarranged, *a.* no arreglado, sin clasificar; (accidental) fortuito, casual

unartistic, *a.* no artístico

unascertainable, *a.* no verificable

unashamed, *a.* sin vergüenza; tranquilo, sereno; insolente, descarado

unasked, *a.* sin pedir; no solicitado; espontáneo; (uninvited) no convidado

unaspirated, *a.* no aspirado

unassailable, *a.* inexpugnable; irrefutable; incontestable

unassisted, *a.* See **unaided**

unassuming, *a.* modesto, sin pretensiones

unattached, *a.* suelto; (*law*) no embargado; (*mil.*) de reemplazo; independiente

unattainable, *a.* inasequible, irrealizable

unattainableness, *s.* imposibilidad de alcanzar (or realizar), *f.*; inaccesibilidad, *f.*

unattended, *a.* solo, sin acompañamiento; (of ill person) sin tratamiento; (of entertainment, etc.) no concurrido

unattested, *a.* sin atestación

unattractive, *a.* poco atrayente, desagradable, antipático, feo

unattractiveness, *s.* fealdad, falta de hermosura, *f.*; lo desagradable

unauthentic, *a.* no auténtico, sin autenticidad; apócrifo

unauthorized, *a.* no autorizado

unavailable, *a.* inaprovechable

unavailing, *a.* inútil, vano

unavenged, *a.* no vengado, sin castigo

unavoidable, *a.* inevitable, preciso, necesario. **to be u.,** no poder evitarse, no tener remedio

unavoidableness, *s.* inevitabilidad, necesidad, *f.*

unavoidably, *adv.* irremediablemente

unaware, *a.* ignorante; inconsciente. **to be u. of,** ignorar, desconocer; no darse cuenta de

unawareness, *s.* ignorancia, *f.*, desconocimiento, *m.*; inconsciencia, *f.*

unawares, *adv.* (by mistake) sin querer, inadvertidamente; (unprepared) de sobresalto, de improviso, inopinadamente. **He caught me u.,** Me cogió desprevenido

unbalance, *v.t.* desequilibrar, hacer perder el equilibrio; (*fig.*) trastornar

unbalanced, *a.* desequilibrado; (*fig.*) trastornado; (*com.*) no balanceado

unballast, *v.t.* deslastrar

unbaptized, *a.* no bautizado, sin bautizar

unbar, *v.t.* desafrancar; (*fig.*) abrir

unbearable, *a.* intolerable, insufrible, inaguantable, inllevable, insoportable

unbearably, *adv.* insoportablemente

unbeatable, *a.* inmejorable

unbeaten, *a.* (of paths) no frecuentado, no pisado; (of armies) no derrotado, no batido; invicto

unbecoming, *a.* impropio, inapropiado, inconveniente; indecoroso, indigno; indecente; (of clothes) que no va bien, que sienta mal

unbelief, *s.* incredulidad, *f.*

unbelievable, *a.* increíble

unbelievably, *adv.* increíblemente

unbeliever, *s.* incrédulo (-la), descreído (-da)

unbeloved, *a.* no amado

unbend, *v.t.* desencorvar, enderezar; entretenerse, descansar; (*naut.,* of sails) desenvergar; (*naut.,* of cables) desamarrar. *v.i.* enderezarse; mostrarse afable

unbending, *a.* inflexible, rígido, tieso; (*fig.*) inexorable, inflexible, duro, terco; (amiable) afable, jovial

unbiassed, *a.* imparcial, ecuánime

unbidden, *a.* espontáneo; (uninvited) no convidado, no invitado

unbind, *v.t.* desligar, desatar; (bandages) desvendar; (books) desencuadernar

unbleached, *a.* crudo, sin blanquear

unblemished, *a.* no manchado; (pure) sin mancha, inmaculado, puro

unblessed, *a.* no bendecido, no consagrado; (accursed) maldito; (unhappy) desdichado

unblushing, *a.* desvergonzado, insolente

unbolt, *v.t.* descerrojar, desempernar

unborn, *a.* sin nacer, no nacido todavía; venidero

unbosom, *v.t.* confesar, declarar. **to u. oneself,** abrir su pecho (a) or (con)

unbought, *a.* no comprado; gratuito, libre; (not bribed) no sobornado

unbound, *a.* suelto, libre; (of books) en rama, no encuadernado

unbounded, *a.* ilimitado, infinito; inmenso

unbowed, *a.* erguido; no encorvado; (undefeated) invicto

unbreakable, *a.* irrompible, inquebrantable

unbridled, *a.* desenfrenado, violento; licencioso

unbroken, *a.* no quebrantado, intacto, entero; continuo, incesante; no interrumpido; (of soil) virgen; (of a horse) indomado; inviolado; (of the spirit) indómito; (of a record) no batido

unbrotherly, *a.* poco fraternal, indigno de hermanos

unbuckle, *v.t.* deshebillar

unburden, *v.t.* descargar; aliviar. **to u. oneself,** (express one's feelings) desahogarse

unburied, *a.* insepulto

unburnt, *a.* no quemado; incombusto

unbusinesslike, *a.* informal; poco comercial, descuidado

unbutton, *v.t.* desabrochar, desabotonar

uncage, *v.t.* desenjaular

uncalled, *a.* no llamado, no invitado. **u.-for,** impertinente; innecesario

uncannily, *adv.* misteriosamente

uncanniness, *s.* lo misterioso

uncanny, *a.* misterioso, horroroso, pavoroso

uncared-for, *a.* abandonado, desatendido, desamparado

uncarpeted, *a.* sin alfombra

uncaught, *a.* no prendido, libre

unceasing, *a.* continuo, incesante, sin cesar, constante

unceasingly, *adv.* incesantemente, sin cesar

uncensored, *a.* no censurado

unceremonious, *a.* sin ceremonia, familiar; descortés, brusco

unceremoniousness, *s.* falta de ceremonia, familiaridad, *f.*; incivilidad, descortesía, *f.*

uncertain, *a.* incierto, dudoso; inseguro; precario; (hesitant) indeciso, vacilante, irresoluto

uncertainly, *adv.* inciertamente

uncertainty, *s.* incertidumbre, duda, *f.*; inseguridad, *f.*; irresolución, *f.*

uncertificated, *a.* sin certificado; (of teachers, etc.) sin título

uncertified, *a.* sin garantía; no garantizado; (of lunatics) sin certificar

unchain, *v.t.* desencadenar

unchallenged, *a.* incontestable

unchangeable, *a.* invariable, inalterable, inmutable

unchangeableness, *s.* invariabilidad, inalterabilidad, *f.*

unchanging, *a.* inmutable, invariable

uncharitable, *a.* nada caritativo, duro; intolerante, intransigente

uncharitableness, *s.* falta de caridad, *f.*; intolerancia, intransigencia

uncharitably, *adv.* sin caridad; con intolerancia

unchaste, *a.* incasto, incontinente; deshonesto, impuro, lascivo

unchecked, *a.* desenfrenado; (unproved) no comprobado; (*com.*) no confrontado

unchivalrous, *a.* nada galante, nada caballeroso

unchristened, *a.* no bautizado, sin bautizar

unchristian, *a.* (heathen) pagano; poco cristiano, indigno de un cristiano, nada caritativo

uncircumcised, *a.* incircunciso

uncircumscribed, *a.* incircunscripto

uncivil, *a.* descortés, incivil

uncivilizable, *a.* reacio a la civilización

uncivilized, *a.* no civilizado, bárbaro, salvaje, inculto

uncivilly, *adv.* descortésmente

unclad, *a.* sin vestir; desnudo

unclasp, *v.t.* (jewellery) desengarzar; desabrochar; (of hands) soltar, separar

unclassifiable, *a.* inclasificable

unclassified, *a.* sin clasificar

uncle, *s.* tío, *m.*; (pawnbroker) prestamista, *m.*

unclean, *a.* sucio, puerco, inmundo; desaseado; impuro, obsceno; (ritually) poluto

uncleanliness, *s.* suciedad, porquería, *f.*; desaseo, *m.*; falta de limpieza, *f.*

uncleanly, *a.* sucio, puerco; desaseado.

uncleanness, *s.* suciedad, *f.*; impureza, obscenidad, inmoralidad, *f.*

unclench, *v.t.* (of hands) abrir

unclouded, *a.* sin nubes, despejado, claro

uncoil, *v.t.* desarrollar. *v.i.* desovillarse; (of snakes) desanillarse

uncollected, *a.* disperso; no cobrado; (in confusion) confuso, desordenado

uncoloured, *a.* incoloro; (*fig.*) imparcial, objetivo, sencillo

uncombed, *a.* despeinado, sin peinar

uncomfortable, *a.* incómodo; (anxious) intranquilo, inquieto, desasosegado, preocupado; (awkward) molesto, difícil, desagradable. **to be u.,** (people) estar incómodo; (anxious) estar preocupado; (of things) ser incómodo

uncomfortableness, *s.* incomodidad, *f.*; malestar, *m.*; intranquilidad, preocupación, *f.*; dificultad, *f.*; lo desagradable

uncomfortably, *adv.* incómodamente; intranquilamente; desagradablemente

uncomforted, *a.* desconsolado; sin consuelo

uncommercial, *a.* no comercial

uncommon, *a.* poco común, extraordinario, singular, raro, extraño; infrecuente; insólito

uncommonly, *adv.* extraordinariamente, muy; infrecuentemente, raramente

uncommonness, *s.* infrecuencia, rareza, *f.*; singularidad, *f.*

uncommunicative, *a.* reservado, poco expresivo

uncommunicativeness, *s.* reserva, *f.*

uncomplaining, *a.* resignado, que no se queja

uncomplainingly, *adv.* con resignación

uncompliant, *a.* sordo, inflexible

uncomplicated, *a.* sencillo, sin complicaciones

uncomplimentary, *a.* descortés, poco halagüeño, ofensivo

uncompromising, *a.* inflexible, estricto, intolerante; irreconciliable

unconcealed, *a.* no oculto; abierto

unconcern, *s.* indiferencia, frialdad, *f.*, desapego, *m.*; (lack of interest) apatía, despreocupación, *f.*; (nonchalance) desenfado, *m.*, frescura, *f.*

unconcerned, *a.* indiferente, frío, despegado; apático, despreocupado; desenfadado, fresco

unconcernedly, *adv.* con indiferencia; sin preocuparse; con desenfado

unconditional, *a.* incondicional, absoluto. **u. surrender,** rendición incondicional, *f.*

unconditionally, *adv.* incondicionalmente; (*mil.*) a discreción

unconfessed, *a.* inconfeso

unconfined, *a.* suelto, libre; ilimitado; sin estorbo

unconfirmed, *a.* no confirmado; (report) sin confirmar

uncongenial, *a.* incompatible, antipático; desagradable, repugnante

uncongeniality, *s.* incompatibilidad, antipatía, *f.*; repugnancia, *f.*; lo desagradable

unconnected, *a.* inconexo; (*mech.*) desconectado; (relationship) sin parentesco; (confused) incoherente

unconquerable, *a.* invencible, indomable, inconquistable

unconquered, *a.* no vencido

unconscientious, *a.* poco concienzudo

unconscionable, *a.* excesivo, desmedido; sin conciencia

unconscious, *a.* inconsciente; (senseless) insensible, sin sentido; espontáneo; (unaware) ignorante. **to be u. of,** ignorar; perder la consciencia de. **to become u.,** perder el sentido

unconsciously, *adv.* inconscientemente, involuntariamente

unconsciousness, *s.* inconsciencia, *f.*; (hypnosis, swoon) insensibilidad, *f.*; (unawareness) ignorancia, falta de conocimiento, *f.*

unconsecrated, *a.* no consagrado

unconsidered, *a.* indeliberado; sin importancia, trivial

unconstitutional, *a.* anticonstitucional, inconstitucional

unconstitutionally, *adv.* inconstitucionalmente

unconstrained, *a.* libre; voluntario; sin freno

uncontaminated, *a.* incontaminado; puro, sin mancha, impoluto

uncontested, *a.* sin oposición

uncontradicted, *a.* sin contradicción; incontestable

uncontrollable, *a.* irrefrenable, incontrolable, inmanejable; (temper) ingobernable; indomable

uncontrolled, *a.* libre, no controlado; desenfrenado, desgobernado

unconventional, *s.* poco convencional; bohemio, excéntrico, extravagante; original

unconventionality, *a.* excentricidad, extravagancia, independencia de ideas, *f.*; (of a design) originalidad, *f.*

unconversant, *a.* poco familiar, poco versado (en)

unconverted, *a.* no convertido; sin transformar ·

unconvinced,· *a.* no convencido

unconvincing, *a.* no convincente; frívolo

uncooked, *a.* crudo, no cocido, sin cocer

uncork, *v.t.* destapar, descorchar, quitar el corcho

uncorrected, *a.* sin corregir, no corregido

uncorroborated, *a.* no confirmado, sin confirmar

uncorrupted, *a.* incorrupto; puro, no · pervertido; (unbribed) no sobornado, honrado

uncorruptible, *a.* incorruptible

uncountable, *a.* innumerable

uncounted, *a.* no contado, sin cuenta

uncouple, *v.t.* soltar; desenganchar, desconectar

uncouth, *a.* grosero, chabacano, tosco, patán

uncouthness, *s.* grosería, tosquedad, patanería, *f.*

uncover, *v.t.* descubrir; (remove lid of) destapar; (remove coverings of) desabrigar, desarropar; (leave unprotected) desamparar; (disclose) revelar, dejar al descubierto. *v.i.* descubrirse, quitar el sombrero

uncovered, *a.* descubierto; desnudo; sin cubierta

uncreated, *a.* increado

uncritical, *a.* sin sentido crítico, poco juicioso

uncross, *v.t.* (of legs) descruzar

uncrossed, *a.* (of cheques) sin cruzar

uncrowned, *a.* antes de ser coronado; sin corona

unction, *s.* unción, *f.*; untadura, *f.*, untamiento, *m.*; (unguent) ·ungüento, *m.*; (zeal) fervor, *m.*; (flattery) insinceridad, hipocresía, *f.*; (relish) gusto, entusiasmo, *m.* Extreme U., Extremaunción, *f.*

unctuous, *a.* untuoso, craso; insincero, zalamero

uncultivable, *a.* incultivable

uncultivated, *a.* inculto, yermo; (barbarous) salvaje, bárbaro; (uncultured) inculto, tosco; no cultivado

uncultured, *a.* inculto, iletrado

uncurbed, *a.* sin freno; (*fig.*) desenfrenado

uncurl, *v.t.* desrizar *v.i.* desrizárse; ·desovillarse

uncurtained, *a.* sin cortinas; con las cortinas recogidas

uncut, *a.* sin cortar, no cortado; (of gems) sin labrar

undamaged, *a.* indemne, sin daño

undated, *a.* sin fecha

undaunted, *a.* intrépido, atrevido

undeceive, *v.t.* desengañar, desilusionar

undecided, *a.* (of question) pendiente, indeciso; dudoso; vacilante, irresoluto

undecipherable, *a.* indescifrable; ilegible

undeclared, *a.* no declarado

undeclinable, *a.* indeclinable

undefended, *a.* indefenso

undeferable, *a.* inaplazable

undefiled, *a.* impoluto, incontaminado; puro

undefinable, *a.* indefinible; inefable, vago

undefined, *a.* indefinido; indeterminado

undelivered, *a.* no recibido; (speech) no pronunciado; (not sent) no enviado

undemonstrative, *a.* poco expresivo, reservado

undeniable, *a.* incontestable, innegable, indudable; excelente; inequívoco, evidente

undeniably, *adv.* indudablemente

undenominational, *a.* sin denominación

undependable, *a.* indigno de confianza

under, *prep.* debajo de; bajo; (in) en; (less than) menos de, menos que; (at the orders of) a las órdenes de, al mando de; (in less time than) en menos de; (under the weight of) bajo el peso de; (at the foot of) al abrigo de; (for less than) por menos de; (at the time of) a la época de, en tiempos de; (according to) según, conforme a; (of monarchs) bajo (or durante) el ·reinado de; (of rank)·inferior a; (in virtue of) en virtud de; (of age) menor de; (with penalty, pretext, etc.) so; en; a (see below for examples); (*agr.*, of fields) plantado de, sembrado de. **u. arms,** bajo las armas. **u.**

contract, bajo contrato. u.
cover, al abrigo, bajo cubierto.
u. cover of, bajo pretexto de, so
color de. u. fire, bajo fuego. u.
oath, bajo juramento. u. pain
of, so pena de. u. sail, a la vela.
u. steam, al vapor. u. way, en
camino; en marcha; en preparación. to be u. an obligation,
deber favores; (to) tener obli-
gacion de; estar obligado a

under, a. inferior; (of rank)
subalterno, subordinado; bajo,
bajero. adv. debajo; abajo; más
abajo; menos; (for less) para
menos; (ill) mal; (insufficient)
insuficiente. to bring u., someter. to keep u., dominar,
subyugar

underact, v.t. hacer un papel sin
fogosidad

underarm, s. sobaco, m. a.
sobacal; (of bowling) de debajo
del brazo. to serve u., sacar
por debajo

underbid, v.t. ofrecer menos
que

underbred, a. mal criado, mal
educado

under-carriage, s. (mech.) bastidor, chasis, m.; (aer.) tren de
aterrizaje, m.

undercharge, v.t. cobrar menos
de lo debido

under-clerk, s. escribiente, m.

underclothes, s. ropa interior, f.,
paños menores, m. pl.

undercurrent, s. corriente
submarina, f.; (fig.) tendencia
oculta, f.

undercut, s. (of meat) filete, m.

under-developed, a. de desarrollo atrasado; (phot.) no revelado lo suficiente

under-dog, s. víctima, f.; débil,
paciente, m.

underdone, a. (of meat) crudo,
medio asado

underdress, v.t. and v.i. vestir(se)
sin bastante elegancia

underestimate, v.t. tasar en
menos; desestimar, menospreciar

underfeed, v.t. alimentar insuficientemente

underfoot, adv. debajo de los pies,
en el suelo

under-gardener, s. mozo jardinero, m.

undergo, v.t. sufrir, padecer,
pasar por

undergraduate, s. estudiante no
graduado, m.

underground, a. subterráneo;
(fig.) oculto, secreto. adv. bajo
tierra, debajo de la tierra; (fig.)
en secreto, ocultamente. s.
sótano, m.; metro, ferrocarril
subterráneo, m.

undergrown, a. enclenque

undergrowth, s. maleza, f.

underhand, adv. (fig.) bajo mano,
ocultamente, a escondidas. a.
(fig.) secreto, oculto

under-housemaid, s. segunda
camarera, f.

under-keeper, s. ayudante de
guardabosques, m.; subdirector
(-ra) (de museo)

underlie, v.t. estar debajo de;
servir de base a, caracterizar

underline, v.t. subrayar

underling, s. subordinado (-da)

underlying, a. fundamental,
básico, esencial

under-master, s. maestro
ayudante, m.

under-mattress, s. colchoneta, f.

undermentioned, a. abajo citado

undermine, v.t. socavar, excavar; minar, destruir poco a
poco

undermining, s. socava, excavación, f.; destrucción, f. a.
minador

underneath, adv. debajo. prep.
bajo, debajo de

undernourished, a. mal alimentado

undernourishment, s. desnutrición, f.

under-officer, s. suboficial, m.

underpaid, a. insuficientemente
retribuido, mal pagado

underpay, v.t. pagar mal, remunerar (or retribuir) deficiente-
mente

underpayment, s. retribución
mezquina, f., pago insuficiente,
m.

underpin, v.t. apuntalar, socalzar

underpopulated, a. con baja
densidad de población

underprivileged, a. menesteroso, pobre, necesitado

underrate, v.t. tasar en menos;
tener en poco, desestimar, menospreciar

underripe, *a.* verde

under-secretary, *s.* subsecretario (-ia)

under-secretaryship, *s.* subsecretaría, *f.*

undersell, *v.t.* vender a un precio más bajo que

underside, *s.* revés, envés, *m.*

undersigned, *a.* infrascrito, suscrito. **the u.,** el abajo firmado, el infrascrito

undersized, *a.* muy pequeño, enclenque, enano

underskirt, *s.* enagua, *f.*; refajo, *m.*

underslung, *a.* (*aut.*) con bajo centro de gravedad

understand, *v.t.* comprender, entender; (know) saber; (be acquainted with) conocer; (hear) oír, tener entendido; (mean) sobrentender. *v.i.* comprender, entender; oír, tener entendido. **to u. each other,** comprenderse. **It being understood that . . .,** Bien entendido que . . .

understandable, *a.* comprensible; inteligible. **It is very u. why he does not wish to come,** Se comprende muy bien porqué no quiere venir

understanding, *s.* (intelligence) entendimiento, *m.*, inteligencia, *f.*; (agreement) acuerdo, *m.*; (knowledge) conocimiento, *m.*; (wisdom) comprensión, sabiduría, *f.* *a.* inteligente; sabio; (sympathetic) comprensivo, simpático. **to come to an u.,** ponerse de acuerdo

understandingly, *adv.* con inteligencia; con conocimiento (de); con simpatía

understate, *v.t.* decir menos que, rebajar, describir sin énfasis

understatement, *s.* moderación, *f.*

understudy, *s.* sobresaliente, *m.* and *f.* *v.t.* sustituir

undertake, *v.t.* comprometerse a, encargarse de; emprender, abarcar, acometer

undertaker, *s.* dueño de funeraria, director de pompas fúnebres, *m.*

undertaking, *s.* empresa, tarea, *f.*; garantía, promesa, *f.*; (funerals) funeraria, *f.*

undertone, *s.* voz baja, *f.*; (art) color tenue (or apagado), *m.* **in an u.,** en voz baja

undervalue, *v.t.* tasar en menos; tener en poco, despreciar

underweight, *a.* de bajo peso, que pesa menos de lo debido, flaco

underworld, *s.* (hell) infierno, averno, *m.*; (slums) hampa, *f.*, fondos bajos de la sociedad, *m. pl.*; heces de la sociedad, *f. pl.*

underwrite, *v.t.* (*com.*) asegurar contra riesgos; reasegurar; obligarse a comprar todas las acciones de una compañía no subscritas por el público, mediante un pago convenido

underwriter, *s.* asegurador, *m.*; reasegurador, *m.*

underwriting, *s.* aseguro, *m.*; reaseguro, *m.*

undeserved, *a.* inmerecido, no merecido

undeserving, *a.* indigno, desmerecedor; que no merece

undesirable, *a.* no deseable; nocivo, pernicioso; (unsuitable) inconveniente

undesired, *a.* no deseado; no solicitado, no buscado

undesirous, *a.* no deseoso

undestroyed, *a.* sin destruir, no destruido, intacto

undetected, *a.* no descubierto

undeveloped, *a.* no desarrollado; rudimentario; inmaturo; (of a country) no explotado, virgen; (*phot.*) no revelado; (of land) sin cultivar

undeviating, *a.* directo; constante, persistente

undigested, *a.* no digerido, indigesto

undignified, *a.* sin dignidad; poco serio; indecoroso

undiluted, *a.* sin diluir, puro

undiminished, *a.* no disminuido, sin disminuir, cabal, íntegro

undimmed, *a.* no obscurecido, brillante

undine, *s.* ondina, *f.*

undiplomatic, *a.* impolítico, indiscreto

undirected, *a.* sin dirección; (of letters) sin señas

undiscernible, *a.* imperceptible, invisible

undiscerning, *a.* sin percepción, obtuso, sin discernimiento

undisciplined, *a.* indisciplinado

undisclosed, *a.* no revelado, secreto

undiscouraged, *a.* animoso, sin flaquear, sin desaliento

undiscovered, *a.* no descubierto, ignoto

undiscriminating, *a.* sin distinción; sin sentido crítico

undisguised, *a.* sin disfraz; abierto, claro

undismayed, *a.* intrépido, impávido; sin desaliento

undisposed, *a.* desinclinado; (of property) no enajenado, no invertido

undisputed, *a.* incontestable, indisputable

undistinguishable, *a.* indistinguible

undistinguished, *a.* (of writers) poco conocido; indistinto; sin distinción

undisturbed, *a.* sin tocar; tranquilo, sereno, impasible

undivided, *a.* indiviso, íntegro; junto; completo, entero

undo, *v.t.* anular; reparar; desatar, deshacer; desasir; abrir

undoing, *s.* anulación, *f.*; (reparation) reparación, *f.*; (opening) abrir, *m.*; ruina, *f.*

undomesticated, *a.* salvaje, no domesticado; poco casero

undone, *a.* and *part.* sin hacer; deshecho; arruinado, perdido. **to come u.,** desatarse. **to leave u.,** dejar sin hacer

undoubted, *a.* indudable, evidente, incontestable

undoubtedly, *adv.* sin duda

undrained, *a.* sin drenaje

undramatic, *a.* no dramático

undreamed, *a.* no soñado. **u. of,** inopinado, no imaginado

undress, *v.t.* desnudar, desvestir. *v.i.* desnudarse. *s.* traje de casa, *m.*; paños menores, *m. pl.*; (*mil.*) traje de cuartel, *m.*

undressed, *a.* desnudo; en paños menores; (of wounds) sin curar; (*com.*) en rama, en bruto

undrinkable, *a.* impotable

undue, *a.* excesivo, indebido; injusto; impropio; (of a bill of exchange) por vencer

undulant, *a.* ondulante. **u. fever,** fiebre mediterránea, fiebre de Malta, *f.*

undulate, *v.i.* ondular; ondear

undulating, *a.* ondulante

undulation, *s.* ondulación, undulación, *f.*, ondeo, *m.*; fluctuación, *f.*

undulatory, *a.* ondulatorio, undoso.

unduly, *adv.* excesivamente, demasiado, indebidamente; injustamente.

undutiful, *a.* desobediente, irrespetuoso

undutifulness, *s.* desobediencia, falta de respeto, *f.*

undying, *a.* inmortal, imperecedero; eterno

unearned, *a.* no ganado; inmerecido

unearth, *v.t.* desenterrar; (*fig.*) descubrir, sacar a luz

unearthing, *s.* desenterramiento, *m.*; (*fig.*) descubrimiento, *m.*, revelación, *f.*

unearthly, *a.* sobrenatural; misterioso, aterrador, espantoso

uneasily, *adv.* con dificultad; incómodamente; inquietamente

uneasiness, *s.* malestar, *m.*; (discomfort) incomodidad, *f.*; (anxiety) inquietud, intranquilidad, *f.*, desasosiego, *m.*

uneasy, *a.* incómodo; inseguro; inquieto, intranquilo, desasosegado; aturdido, turbado. **to become u.,** inquietarse

uneatable, *a.* incomible

uneaten, *a.* no comido

uneconomical, *a.* poco económico, costoso, caro

unedifying, *a.* poco edificante

unedited, *a.* inédito

uneducated, *a.* ignorante; ineducado, inculto, indocto

unembarrassed, *a.* sereno, tranquilo, imperturbable; (financially) sin deudas, acomodado

unemotional, *a.* frío, impasible

unemployable, *a.* sin uso, inservible; (of persons) inútil para el trabajo

unemployed, *a.* sin empleo; (out of work) sin trabajo, parado; desocupado, ocioso; inactivo. *s.* paro obrero, *m.* **the u.,** los sin trabajo

unemployment, *s.* paro forzoso, *m.* **u. benefit,** subvención contra el paro obrero, *f.* **u. insurance,** seguro contra el paro obrero, *m.*

unencumbered, *a.* libre, independiente; (of estates) libre de gravamen; (untaxable) saneado

unending, *a.* perpetuo, eterno, sin fin; inacabable, constante, continuo, incesante

unendurable, *a.* insoportable, insufrible, intolerable

unenlightened, *a.* ignorante

unenterprising, *a.* poco emprendedor, tímido

unenthusiastic, *a.* sin entusiasmo, tibio

unenviable, *a.* no envidiable

unequal, *a.* desigual; inferior; (out of proportion) desproporcionado; injusto; insuficiente; incapaz; (of ground) escabroso. **to be u. to the task,** ser incapaz de la tarea; no tener fuerzas para la tarea

unequalled, *a.* sin igual, incomparable, sin par, único

unequally, *adv.* desigualmente

unequivocal, *a.* inequívoco; redondo, claro, franco

unerring, *a.* infalible; seguro

unerringly, *adv.* infaliblemente; sin equivocarse

unessential, *a.* no esencial

uneven, *a.* desigual; (of roads) escabroso, quebrado; (of numbers) impar; irregular

unevenly, *adv.* desigualmente

unevenness, *s.* desigualdad, *f.*; desnivel, *m.*; escabrosidad, *f.*; irregularidad, *f.*

uneventful, *a.* sin incidentes, sin acontecimientos notables; tranquilo

unexaggerated, *a.* nada exagerado

unexamined, *a.* no examinado, sin examinar

unexampled, *a.* sin igual, sin par

unexceptionable, *a.* intachable, irreprensible; correcto; impecable, perfecto

unexhausted, *a.* no agotado; inexhausto

unexpected, *a.* inesperado, imprevisto, inopinado, impensado; repentino, súbito

unexpectedly, *adv.* inesperadamente; de repente

unexpectedness, *s.* lo inesperado

unexpired, *a.* (of bill of exchange) no vencido; (of lease) no caducado

unexplored, *a.* inexplorado

unexpressed, *a.* no expresado; tácito, sobrentendido

unexpurgated, *a.* sin expurgar, completo

unfading, *a.* inmarcesible, inmarchitable; eterno, inmortal

unfailing, *a.* inagotable; inexhausto; seguro; indefectible

unfailingly, *adv.* siempre, constantemente; sin faltar

unfair, *a.* injusto; vil, bajo, soez; de mala fe, engañoso; (of play) sucio

unfairly, *adv.* injustamente; de mala fe

unfairness, *s.* injusticia, *f.*; mala fe, *f.*

unfaithful, *a.* infiel; desleal; inexacto, incorrecto. **to be u. to,** ser infiel a; faltar a

unfaithfulness, *s.* infidelidad, *f.*; deslealtad, *f.*; inexactitud, *f.*

unfaltering, *a.* sin vacilar; resuelto, firme

unfamiliar, *a.* poco familiar; desconocido. **to be u. with,** ser ignorante de

unfashionable, *a.* pasado de moda, fuera de moda; poco elegante

unfashionableness, *s.* falta de elegancia, *f.*

unfashionably, *adv.* contra la tendencia de la moda; sin elegancia

unfasten, *v.t.* desatar; desabrochar, desenganchar; abrir; aflojar; soltar

unfathomable, *a.* insondable; impenetrable, inescrutable

unfavourable, *a.* desfavorable, adverso, contrario

unfavourably, *adv.* desfavorablemente

unfeathered, *a.* implume, sin plumas

unfeeling, *a.* insensible, impasible, frío; duro, cruel

unfeigned, *a.* sincero, natural, verdadero

unfenced, *a.* descercado, sin tapia; abierto

unfermented, *a.* no fermentado; (of bread) ázimo

unfetter, *v.t.* desencadenar, destrabar; poner en libertad, librar

unfilial, *a.* poco filial, desobediente

unfinished, *a.* incompleto, inacabado; sin acabar; imperfecto

unfit, *a.* incapaz; incompetente, inepto; (unsuitable) impropio; (useless) inservible, inadecuado; (unworthy) indigno; (ill) enfermo, malo. *v.t.* inhabilitar, incapacitar. **u. for human consumption,** impropio para el consumo humano

unfitness, *s.* incapacidad, *f.*; incompetencia, ineptitud, *f.*; impropiedad, *f.*; falta de mérito, *f.*; falta de salud, *f.*

unfix, *v.t.* desprender, despegar, descomponer; soltar. **to come unfixed,** desprenderse

unflagging, *a.* incansable, infatigable; persistente, constante

unflattering, *a.* poco halagüeño

unflinching, *a.* inconmovible, resuelto, firme

unfold, *v.t.* desplegar, desdoblar; tender; abrir; (plans) revelar, descubrir; contar, manifestar. *v.i.* abrirse

unfolding, *a.* que se abre, *s.* despliegue, *m.*; revelación, *f.*; narración, *f.*

unforced, *a.* libre; espontáneo; fácil; natural

unforeseen, *a.* imprevisto, inesperado

unforgettable, *a.* involvidable

unforgivable, *a.* inexcusable, imperdonable

unforgiving, *a.* implacable, que no perdona, inexorable

unforgotten, *a.* no olvidado

unformed, *a.* informe; rudimentario; inmaturo; (inexperienced) inexperto, sin experiencia

unfortunate, *a.* desdichado, infortunado, desgraciado, desventurado. *s.* desdichado (-da); pobre, *m.* and *f.*; (prostitute) perdida, *f.*

unfortunately, *adv.* por desdicha, desgraciadamente

unfounded, *a.* infundado, inmotivado, sin fundamento, injustificado

unframed, *a.* sin marco

unfrequented, *a.* poco frecuentado, solitario, retirado, aislado

unfriendliness, *s.* hostilidad, falta de amistad, frialdad, *f.*; huraña, insociabilidad, *f.*

unfriendly, *a.* hostil, enemigo; (of things, events) perjudicial; huraño, insociable

unfrock, *v.t.* degradar, exclaustrar

unfruitful, *a.* estéril, infecundo; infructuoso, improductivo, vano.

unfulfilled, *a.* incumplido, sin cumplir; malogrado

unfurl, *v.t.* desplegar; (naut.) izar (las velas)

unfurnished, *a.* desamueblado, sin muebles; desprovisto (de), sin

ungainliness, *s.* falta de gracia, torpeza, *f.*, desgarbo, *m.*

ungainly, *a.* desgarbado

ungallant, *a.* poco caballeroso, nada galante

ungenerous, *a.* poco generoso; avaro, tacaño, mezquino; injusto

ungentlemanly, *a.* poco caballeroso, indigno de un caballero

unglazed, *a.* sin vidriar; (paper) sin satinar; deslustrado

ungloved, *a.* sin guante(s)

unglue, *v.t.* desencolar, despegar

ungodliness, *s.* impiedad, *f.*

ungodly, *a.* impío, irreligioso

ungovernable, *a.* ingobernable, indomable; irrefrenable

ungraceful, *a.* desagraciado, desgarbado, sin gracia

ungracious, *a.* desagradable, poco cortés, desdeñoso

ungraciousness, *s.* descortesía, aspereza, inurbanidad, *f.*

ungrammatical, *a.* antigramatical, incorrecto

ungrateful, *a.* ingrato, desagradecido; desagradable, odioso

ungratefulness, *s.* ingratitud, *f.*; lo desagradable

ungrounded, *a.* infundado; sin motivo

ungrudging, *a.* no avaro, liberal; generoso, magnánimo

ungrudgingly, *adv.* de buena gana

unguarded, *a.* indefenso, sin protección; descuidado; indiscreto, imprudente; sin reflexión

unguided, *a.* sin guía

unhallowed, *a.* impío, profano

unhampered, *a.* desembarazado, libre

unhappily, *adv.* desafortunadamente, por desgracia

unhappiness, *s.* infelicidad, desgracia, desdicha, tristeza, *f.*

unhappy, *a.* infeliz, desgraciado, desdichado, triste; (ill-fated) aciago, funesto, malhadado; (remark) inoportuno, inapropiado

unharmed, *a.* ileso, sano y salvo; (of things) indemne, sin daño

unharness, *v.t.* desaparejar; desenganchar; desarmar

unhealthiness, *s.* falta de salud, *f.*; (of place) insalubridad, *f.*

unhealthy, *a.* enfermizo; malsano, insalubre

unheard, *a.* no oído; sin ser escuchado; desconocido. **u.-of,** inaudito, no imaginado

unheeding, *a.* distraído; desatento, sin prestar atención (a); descuidado

unhelpful, *a.* poco servicial; inútil

unhesitating, *a.* resuelto, decidido; pronto, inmediato

unhesitatingly, *adv.* sin vacilar

unhinge, *v.t.* desgoznar, desquiciar; (of the mind) trastornar

unhitch, *v.t.* desenganchar; descolgar

unholy, *a.* impío, sacrílego

unhonoured, *a.* sin que se reconociese sus méritos; despreciado; (cheques) protestado

unhook, *v.t.* desenganchar, desabrochar; descolgar

unhoped-for, *a.* inesperado

unhorse, *v.t.* derribar de caballo

unhurt, *a.* ileso, incólume, sano y salvo; (of things) sin daño

unicellular, *a.* unicelular

unicoloured, *a.* unicolor

unicorn, *s.* unicornio, *m.*

unidentified, *a.* no reconocido, no identificado

unification, *s.* unificación, *f.*

uniform, *a.* uniforme; igual, constante, invariable; homogéneo. *s.* uniforme, *m.* **in full u.,** de gran uniforme. **to make u.,** uniformar, igualar, hacer uniforme

uniformity, *s.* uniformidad, igualdad, *f.*

uniformly, *adv.* uniformemente

unify, *v.t.* unificar; unir

unilateral, *a.* unilateral

unimaginable, *a.* inimaginable, no imaginable

unimaginative, *a.* sin imaginación

unimpaired, *a.* no disminuido; sin alteración; intacto, entero; sin menoscabo

unimpeachable, *a.* irreprochable, intachable

unimportance, *s.* no importancia, insignificancia, trivialidad, *f.*

unimportant, *a.* sin importancia, nada importante, insignificante, trivial

unimpressive, *a.* poco impresionante; nada conmovedor; (of persons) insignificante

uninflammable, *a.* no inflamable, incombustible

uninfluenced, *a.* no afectado (por), libre (de)

uninformed, *a.* ignorante

uninhabitable, *a.* inhabitable

uninhabited, *a.* inhabitado, vacío, desierto

uninjured, *a.* ileso; sin daño

uninspired, *a.* sin inspiración; pedestre, mediocre

uninstructive, *a.* nada instructivo

uninsured, *a.* no asegurado

unintelligent, *a.* nada inteligente, corto de alcances, tonto

unintelligibility, *s.* incomprensibilidad, *f.*, lo ininteligible

unintelligible, *a.* ininteligible, incomprensible

unintentional, *a.* involuntario, inadvertido

unintentionally, *adv.* sin querer, involuntariamente

uninterested, *a.* no interesado, despreocupado

uninteresting, *a.* sin interés, poco interesante, soso

uninterrupted, *a.* ininterrumpido, sin interrupción; continuo, incesante

uninvited, *a.* no invitado, no convidado, sin invitación; (unlooked-for) no buscado

uninviting, *a.* poco atrayente; inhospitalario

union, *s.* unión, *f.*; (mech.) manguito de unión, *m.*; conexión, *f.*; (poverty) asociación, *f.*; (of trade) gremio de oficios, *m.*; sindicato obrero, *m.*; (workhouse) asilo, *m.*; (U.S.A.) Estados Unidos de América, *m. pl.*

unionism, s. unionismo, m.

unionist, s. (*pol.*) unionista, m. and f.

unique, a. único, sin igual, sin par

uniqueness, s. unicidad, f.; lo singular

unisexual, a. unisexual

unison, s. unisonancia, f. **in u.,** al unísono

unit, s. unidad, f. (also *math., mil.*). **u. bookcase,** librería en secciones, f.

Unitarian, a. and s. unitario (-ia)

Unitarianism, s. unitarismo, m.

unite, v.t. unir, juntar; combinar, incorporar; (of countries) unificar; (of energies, etc.) reunir. v.i. unirse, juntarse; reunirse, concertarse; convenirse

united, a. unido; junto. U. Nations, Naciones Unidas, f. pl.

unitedly, adv. unidamente; armoniosamente, de acuerdo

unity, s. unidad, f.; (*math.*) la unidad; unión, f.; conformidad, armonía, f. **the three unities,** las tres unidades

universal, a. universal; general; común. **to make u.,** universalizar, generalizar. **u. joint,** junta universal, f.; (*aut.*) cardán, m.

universality, s. universalidad, f.

universalize, v.t. universalizar

universe, s. universo, m.; creación, f., mundo, m.

university, s. universidad, f. a. universitario. **u. degree,** grado universitario, m.

unjust, a. injusto

unjustifiable, a. injustificable, indisculpable, inexcusable

unjustifiably, adv. injustificadamente, inexcusablemente

unjustly, adv. injustamente, sin razón

unkempt, a. despeinado; desaseado, sucio

unkind, a. nada bondadoso, nada amable; poco complaciente; duro, cruel; desfavorable, nada propicio

unkindly, adv. sin bondad; con dureza, cruelmente

unkindness, s. falta de bondad, f.; severidad, crueldad, dureza, f., rigor, m.; acto de crueldad, m.

unknowable, a. impenetrable, incomprehensible, insondable

unknowingly, adv. sin querer, involuntariamente; sin saberlo; insensiblemente

unknown, a. ignoto, desconocido; (*math.*) incógnito. s. lo desconocido, misterio, m.; (*math.*) incógnita, f.; (person) desconocido (-da), forastero (-ra). (*math.*) **u. quantity,** incógnita, f.

unlabelled, a. sin etiqueta

unlace, v.t. desenlazar; desatar

unladylike, a. indigno (or impropio) de una dama; vulgar, ordinario, cursi

unlamented, a. no llorado, no lamentado

unlatch, v.t. alzar el pestillo de, abrir

unlawful, a. ilegal, ilícito

unlawfulness, s. ilegalidad, f.

unlearn, v.t. olvidar, desaprender

unleash, v.t. soltar

unleavened, a. ázimo

unless, conjunc. a no ser que, a menos que; como no, si no (all followed by subjunc.); salvo, excepto, con excepción de

unlicensed, a. no autorizado, sin licencia

unlike, a. disímil, desemejante; distinto, diferente. prep. a distinción de, a diferencia de, al contrario de. **They are quite u.,** No se parecen en nada

unlikeliness, s. improbabilidad, f.

unlikely, a. improbable, inverosímil; arriesgado

unlikeness, s. desemejanza, diferencia, f.

unlimited, a. ilimitado, infinito, inmenso; sin restricción; excesivo, exagerado

unlined, a. no forrado, sin forro; sin rayas; (of face) sin arrugas

unlit, a. no iluminado, oscuro, sin luz

unload, v.t. descargar; aligerar; (*naut.*) hondear; (of shares) deshacerse de. v.i. descargar

unloading, s. descarga, f., descargue, m.

unlock, v.t. desencerrar, abrir; (*fig.*) revelar, descubrir

unlooked-for, a. inopinado, inesperado

unloose, v.t. desatar; soltar; poner en libertad

unlovable, *a.* indigno del querer; antipático, poco amable; repugnante

unloveliness, *s.* falta de hermosura, fealdad, *f.*

unlovely, *a.* nada hermoso, feo; desagradable

unluckily, *adv.* desafortunadamente, por desgracia

unluckiness, *s.* mala suerte, *f.*; (unsuitability) inoportunidad, *f.*; lo nefasto, lo malo

unlucky, *a.* de mala suerte; desdichado, desgraciado, infeliz; (ill-omened) funesto, nefasto, fatal; inoportuno, inconveniente

unmaidenly, *a.* impropio (or indigno) de una doncella

unman, *v.t.* acobardar, desanimar

unmanageable, *a.* indomable, indócil; ingobernable, inmanejable; (unwieldy) difícil de manejar, pesado

unmannerliness, *s.* mala crianza, descortesía, *f.*

unmannerly, *a.* mal educado, descortés

unmarketable, *a.* invendible

unmarriageable, *a.* incasable

unmarried, *a.* soltero, célibe

unmask, *v.t.* desenmascarar; (*fig.*) quitar la careta (a). *v.i.* quitarse la máscara; (*fig.*) quitarse la careta, descubrirse

unmast, *v.t.* (*naut.*) desarbolar

unmeaning, *a.* sin sentido, vacío, sin significación

unmelodious, *a.* sin melodía, discorde

unmendable, *a.* incomponible

unmentionable, *a.* que no se puede mencionar; indigno de mencionarse

unmerciful, *a.* sin piedad, sin compasión; cruel, despiadado, duro

unmerited, *a.* inmerecido, desmerecido

unmethodical, *a.* poco metódico

unmindful, *a.* olvidadizo; desatento; negligente. **u. of,** sin pensar en, olvidando que

unmistakable, *a.* inequívoco; manifiesto, evidente, indudable

unmistakably, *adv.* indudablemente

unmitigated, *a.* no mitigado; completo, absoluto; (of rogue) redomado

unmixed, *a.* sin mezcla; puro, sencillo; (free) limpio

unmoor, *v.t.* desamarrar

unmoral, *a.* amoral, no moral; sin fin didáctico

unmounted, *a.* desmontado

unmoved, *a.* fijo; (unemotional) impasible, frío; (determined) firme, inflexible, inexorable

unmuffle, *v.t.* desembozar, descubrir

unmusical, *a.* sin afición a la música; sin oído (para la música); inarmónico

unnamable, *a.* que no se puede nombrar, innominable

unnatural, *a.* desnaturalizado; (of vices, etc.) contra natural; innatural; (of style) rebuscado; artificial; inhumano, cruel

unnaturalness, *s.* lo monstruoso; lo innatural; artificialidad, *f.*; inhumanidad, *f.*

unnavigable, *a.* innavegable, no navegable

unnecessarily, *adv.* inútilmente, innecesariamente, sin necesidad

unnecessariness, *s.* inutilidad, *f.*; superfluidad, *f.*; lo innecesario

unnecessary, *a.* innecesario, superfluo, inútil

unneighbourly, *a.* de mala vecindad, impropio de vecinos, poco servicial

unnerve, *v.t.* acobardar quitar el valor, desanimar

unnoticed, *a.* inadvertido, no observado

unobliging, *a.* nada servicial

unobservable, *a.* inobservable

unobservant, *a.* inobservante

unobserved, *a.* sin ser notado, desapercibido

unobtainable, *a.* inalcanzable, inasequible

unobstructed, *a.* no obstruido; sin obstáculos; libre

unobtrusive, *a.* discreto, modesto

unobtrusiveness, *s.* discreción, modestia, *f.*

unoccupied, *a.* (at leisure) desocupado, ocioso, sin ocupación; vacío, vacante, libre; (untenanted) deshabitado

unofficial, *a.* no oficial

unopened, *a.* sin abrir, cerrado; (of exhibitions, etc.) no inaugurado

unopposed, *a.* sin oposición

unorganized, *a.* inorganizado; (*biol.*) inorgánico

unoriginal, *a.* poco original

unorthodox, *a.* heterodoxo

unostentatious, *a.* sencillo, modesto, sin ostentación

unostentatiousness, *s.* sencillez, modestia, falta de ostentación, *f.*

unpack, *v.t.* desempaquetar; (trunks) vaciar; (bales) desembalar. *v.i.* desempaquetar; deshacer las maletas

unpacking, *s.* desembalaje, *m.*

unpaid, *a.* sin pagar, no pagado

unpalatable, *a.* de mal sabor; desagradable

unparalleled, *a.* sin paralelo, sin par, sin igual

unpardonable, *a.* imperdonable, inexcusable, irremisible

unparliamentary, *a.* poco parliamentario

unpatriotic, *a.* antipatriótico

unpaved, *a.* sin empedrar

unperceived, *a.* inadvertido, sin ser notado

unperturbed, *a.* impasible, sin alterarse, sereno

unpick, *v.t.* (*sew.*) descoser

unplait, *v.t.* destrenzar

unpleasant, *a.* desagradable, desapacible; ofensivo; (troublesome) enfadoso, molesto

unpleasantly, *adv.* desagradablemente

unpleasantness, *s.* lo desagradable; disgusto, sinsabor, *m.*; (disagreement) disputa, riña, *f.*

unpleasing, *a.* nada placentero; desagradable, sin atractivos

unplug, *v.t.* desenchufar

unpolished, *a.* sin pulir, tosco, mate; (*fig.*) inculto, cerril. **u. diamond,** diamante en bruto, *m.*

unpolluted, *a.* impoluto, incontaminado; puro, sin pervertir

unpopular, *a.* impopular

unpopularity, *s.* impopularidad, *f.*

unpractical, *a.* impracticable, imposible; (of persons) sin sentido práctico

unpractised, *a.* no practicado; inexperto, inhábil

unpraiseworthy, *a.* inmeritorio

unprecedented, *a.* sin precedente, inaudito

unprejudiced, *a.* sin prejuicios, imparcial

unpremeditated, *a.* sin premeditación, indeliberado, impremeditado

unprepared, *a.* sin preparación, no preparado; desprevenido; desapercibido (unready)

unpreparedness, *s.* falta de preparación, imprevisión, *f.*, desapercibimiento, *m.*

unprepossessing, *a.* poco atrayente, antipático

unpresentable, *a.* impresentable

unpretentious, *a.* sin pretensiones, modesto

unpriced, *a.* sin precio

unprincipled, *a.* sin consciencia, sin escrúpulos

unprinted, *a.* sin imprimir, no impreso

unprocurable, *a.* inalcanzable, inasequible

unproductive, *a.* improductivo; infructuoso, estéril

unproductiveness, *s.* infructuosidad, *f.*; esterilidad, *f.*

unprofessional, *a.* sin profesión; contrario a la ética profesional

unprofitable, *a.* improductivo, infructuoso; sin provecho; inútil; nada lucrativo

unprogressive, *a.* reaccionario

unpromising, *a.* poco halagüeño

unpronounceable, *a.* impronunciable

unpropitious, *a.* desfavorable, nada propicio, nada halagüeño

unprosperous, *a.* impróspero

unprotected, *a.* sin protección; (of persons) indefenso, desválido

unproved, *a.* no probado, sin demostrar

unprovided, *a.* desapercibido, desprovisto. **u. for,** sin provisión (para); sin medios de vida, desamparado

unprovoked, *a.* no provocado, sin provocación; sin motivo

unpublished, *a.* inédito, no publicado, sin publicar

unpunctual, *a.* no puntual, retrasado

unpunctuality, *s.* falta de puntualidad, *f.*, retraso, *m.*

unpunctually, *adv.* sin puntualidad, tarde, con retraso

unpunishable, *a.* no punible

unpunished, *a.* impune, sin castigo

unpurchasable, *a.* que no puede comprarse

unqualified, *a.* incapaz, incompetente; (with professions) sin título; (downright) incondicional, absoluto

unquenchable, *a.* inextinguible, inapagable; insaciable

unquestionable, *a.* indiscutible, indudable, indubitable

unquestionably, *adv.* indudablemente ·

unquiet, *a.* inquieto, intranquilo; agitado

unravel, *v.t.* deshilar; destejer; (a mystery, etc.) desentrañar, desembrollar, descifrar

unravelling, *s.* deshiladura, *f.*; aclaración, *f.*

unreadable, *a.* ilegible

unreadiness, *s.* falta de preparación, *f.*, desapercibimiento, *m.*; lentitud, *f.*

unready, *a.* desapercibido, desprevenido; lento

unreal, *a.* irreal; falso, imaginario, ilusorio; ficticio; artificial; insincero, hipócrita; ideal; incorpóreo

unreality, *s.* irrealidad, *f.*; falsedad, *f.*; artificialidad, *f.*; lo quimérico

unreasonable, *a.* irrazonable, irracional; disparatado, extravagante; (with price, etc.) exorbitante, excesivo

unreasonableness, *s.* irracionalidad, *f.*; exorbitancia, *f.*

unreasonably, *adv.* irracionalmente

unreasoning, *a.* irracional; sin motivo, sin causa

unreceipted, *a.* sin recibo

unrecognizable, *a.* que no puede reconocerse; imposible de reconocer

unrecognized, *a.* no reconocido

unreconciled, *a.* no resignado, no reconciliado

unrectified, *a.* no corregido, sin rectificar

unredeemed, *a.* no redimido; no mitigado; (of pledges) sin desempeñar

unrefined, *a.* no refinado, impuro; inculto, grosero

unreformed, *a.* no reformado

unrefuted, *a.* no refutado

unregenerate, *a.* no regenerado

unregretted, *a.* no llorado, sin lamentar

unrehearsed, *a.* sin preparación; (*theat.*) sin ensayar; (extempore) improvisado

unrelated, *a.* inconexo; (of persons) sin parentesco

unrelenting, *a.* implacable, inflexible, inexorable

unreliability, *s.* incertidumbre, *f.*; el no poder confiar en, informalidad, inestabilidad, *f.*

unreliable, *a.* incierto, dudoso, indigno de confianza; (of persons) informal

unrelieved, *a.* no aliviado; absoluto, complete, total

unremitting, *a.* incansable

unremunerative, *a.* sin remuneración, no remunerado

unrepealed, *a.* vigente

unrepentant, *a.* impenitente

unrepresentative, *a.* poco representativo

unrepresented, *a.* sin representación

unrequited, *a.* no correspondido

unreserved, *a.* no reservado; expresivo, comunicativo, expansivo, franco

unreservedly, *adv.* sin reserva; con toda franqueza

unresisting, *a.* sin oponer resistencia

unresolved, *a.* sin resolverse, vacilante; incierto, dudoso, inseguro; sin solución

unresponsive, *a.* flemático; insensible, sordo

unresponsiveness, *s.* flema, *f.*; insensibilidad, *f.*

unrest, *s.* desasosiego, *m.*, agitación, inquietud, *f.*

unrestful, *a.* agitado, inquieto, intranquilo

unrestrained, *a.* desenfrenado; ilimitado, sin límites; sin reserva

unrestricted, *a.* sin restricción; ilimitado

unrevealed, *a.* no revelado, por descubrir, no descubierto

unrewarded, *a.* sin premio, no recompensado

unrighteous, *a.* injusto, malo, perverso

unrighteousness, *s.* injusticia. *f.*; maldad, perversidad, *f.*

unripe, *a.* verde, inmaturo

unripeness, *s.* falta de madurez, *f.*

unrivalled, *a.* sin igual, sin par

unroll, *v.t.* desarrollar. *v.i.* desarrollarse; (unfold) desplegarse (a la vista)

unromantic, *a.* poco (or nada) romántico

unruffled, *a.* sereno, plácido, ecuánime; no arrugado; (of hair) liso

unruliness, *s.* turbulencia, indisciplina, *f.;* insubordinación, rebeldía, *f.*

unruly, *a.* ingobernable, revoltoso; refractario, rebelde; (of hair) indomable

unsaddle, *v.t.* desensillar; derribar (del caballo, etc.)

unsafe, *a.* inseguro; peligroso; arriesgado; (to eat) nocivo

unsafeness, *s.* inseguridad, *f.;* peligro, riesgo, *m.*

unsaid, *a.* sin decir, no dicho

unsalable, *a.* invendible

unsalaried, *a.* no asalariado

unsalted, *a.* soso, sin sal

unsanctioned, *a.* no permitido, sin sancionar

unsanitary, *a.* antihigiénico

unsatisfactoriness, *s.* lo insatisfactorio

unsatisfactory, *a.* poco (or nada) satisfactorio; no aceptable

unsatisfied, *a.* no satisfecho; descontento; no convencido; (hungry) no harto; (com.) no saldado

unsatisfying, *a.* que no satisface

unsavouriness, *s.* insipidez, *f.,* mal sabor, *m.;* lo desagradable; sordidez, suciedad, *f.*

unsavoury, *a.* insípido, de mal sabor; desagradable; sórdido, sucio

unscalable, *a.* inascendible, virgen

unscathed, *a.* sin daño, ileso

unscented, *a.* sin perfume, sin olor, no fragante

unscholarly, *a.* nada erudito; indigno de un erudito

unscientific, *a.* no científico

unscrew, *v.t.* destornillar. *v.i.* destornillarse

unscrewing, *s.* destornillamiento, *m.*

unscrupulous, *a.* sin escrúpulos, poco escrupuloso, desaprensivo

unscrupulousness, *s.* falta de escrúpulos, desaprensión, *f.*

unseal, *v.t.* desellar, romper (or quitar) el sello (de)

unseasonable, *a.* intempestivo, fuera de sazón; inoportuno, inconveniente. at an u. hour, a una hora inconveniente, a deshora

unseasonableness, *s.* lo intempestivo, inoportunidad, *f.*

unseasonably, *adv.* intempestivamente; a deshora; inoportunamente

unseasoned, *a.* (cul.) sin sazonar, soso; (wood) verde; no maduro, sin madurar

unseat, *v.t.* (from horse) tirar, echar al suelo; (pol.) hacer perder las elecciones parlamentarias

unseaworthy, *a.* innavegable

unseemliness, *s.* falta de decoro, *f.;* indecencia, *f.*

unseemly, *a.* indecoroso, indigno; indecente; impropio

unseen, *a.* invisible; inadvertido; secreto, oculto. *s.* versión al libro abierto, *f.* the u., lo invisible

unselfish, *a.* desinteresado, abnegado, nada egoísta; generoso

unselfishness, *s.* abnegación, *f.;* desinterés, *m.;* generosidad, *f.*

unsentimental, *a.* no sentimental

unserviceable, *a.* inservible, inútil, que no sirve para nada, sin utilidad.

unsettle, *v.t.* desarreglar; desorganizar; hacer inseguro; agitar, perturbar

unsettled, *a.* inconstante, variable; (com.) pendiente, sin pagar; incierto; sin resolver; (of estates) sin solucionar

unshackle, *v.t.* desencadenar

unshakable, *a.* inconmovible, firme

unshapely, *a.* desproporcionado

unshaven, *a.* sin afeitar

unsheathe, *v.t.* desenvainar, sacar

unsheltered, *a.* desabrigado, desamparado; no protegido, sin protección; (of places) sin abrigo, expuesto; (from) sin defensa contra

unship, *v.t.* desembarcar; (the oars) desarmar

unshod, *a.* descalzo; (of a horse) sin herraduras

unshorn, *a.* sin esquilar; intonso

unshrinkable, *a.* que no se encoge

unshrinking, *a.* intrépido; resoluto, sin vacilar

unsightly, *a.* feo, horrible, repugnante, antiestético

unsinkable, *a.* insumergible

unskilled, *a.* inexperto, inhábil, imperito, torpe

unsmokable, *a.* (of tobacco) infumable

unsociability, *s.* insociabilidad, huraña, esquivez, *f.*

unsociable, *a.* insociable, huraño, esquivo, arisco

unsocial, *a.* insocial, antisocial

unsold, *a.* no vendido, sin vender

unsolder, *v.t.* desoldar, desestañar

unsoldierly, *a.* indigno de un soldado; poco marcial

unsophisticated, *a.* ingenuo, inocente, cándido

unsought, *a.* no solicitado; no buscado

unsound, *a.* enfermo; defectuoso; (rotten) podrido; (fallacious) erróneo, poco convincente; (of persons) informal, indigno de confianza; (of religious views) heterodoxo. **of u. mind,** insano

unsoundness, *s.* lo defectuoso; mal estado, *m.;* falsedad, *f.;* informalidad, *f.;* heterodoxia, *f.*

unsparing, *a.* severo, implacable; generoso, pródigo

unspeakable, *a.* indecible, inefable; que no puede mencionarse, horrible

unspecified, *a.* no especificado

unspoilt, *a.* intacto; ileso, indemne; no corrompido; no estropeado; (of children) no mimado

unspoken, *a.* no pronunciado

unsportsmanlike, *a.* indigno de un cazador; indigno de un deportista; nada caballeroso. **to play in an u. way,** jugar sucio

unstable, *a.* inestable; variable; inconstante; vacilante, irresoluto

unstained, *a.* no manchado; no teñido; inmaculado, sin mancha

unstamped, *a.* sin sello; no sellado

unstatesmanlike, *a.* impropio (or indigno) de un hombre de Estado

unsteadiness, *s.* inestabilidad, falta de firmeza, *f.;* inconstancia, *f.*

unsteady, *a.* inestable, inseguro; inconstante

unstick, *v.t.* desapegar

unstitch, *v.t.* desapuntar

unstressed, *a.* sin énfasis; (of syllables) sin acento

unstudied, *a.* no estudiado; natural, espontáneo

unsubstantial, *a.* insubstancial; ligero; irreal, imaginario; incorpóreo; aparente

unsuccessful, *a.* sin éxito; infructuoso. **to be u.,** no tener éxito

unsuccessfully, *adv.* en vano, sin éxito

unsuitability, *s.* impropiedad, *f.;* inconveniencia, incongruencia, *f.;* incapacidad, *f.;* inoportunidad, *f.*

unsuitable, *a.* inapropiado; inconveniente; impropio; inservible; incapaz; inoportuno

unsung, *a.* no cantado; no celebrado en verso

unsupported, *a.* sin apoyo; sin defensa; no favorecido

unsurmountable, *a.* insuperable, infranqueable

unsurpassable, *a.* inmejorable, insuperable

unsurpassed, *a.* sin par

unsuspecting, *a.* no suspicaz, confiado, no receloso

unswerving, *a.* directo; sin vacilar, constante

unsymmetrical, *a.* asimétrico

unsympathetic, *a.* indiferente, incompasivo; antipático

unsystematic, *a.* sin sistema, asistemático, no metódico

untalented, *a.* sin talento

untamed, *a.* indomado, cerril, bravío, no domesticado; desenfrenado, violento

unteach, *v.t.* desenseñar

untenable, *a.* insostenible

untenanted, *a.* desalquilado, deshabitado; vacío, desierto

unthankful, *a.* ingrato, desagradecido

unthinkable, *a.* inconcebible; imposible

unthinking, *a.* sin reflexión; desatento; indiscreto

unthinkingly, *adv.* sin pensar

unthread, *v.t.* deshebrar

untidily, *adv.* en desorden, sin aseo

untidiness, *s.* desorden, *m.*; desaseo, desaliño, *m.*; falta de pulcritud, *f.*

untidy, *a.* desarreglado; desaseado; abandonado; en desorden, sin concierto

untie, *v.t.* desatar, desanudar; (knots) deshacer

until, *prep.* hasta. *conjunc.* hasta que. (The subjunc. is required in clauses referring to future time, e.g. No venga usted hasta que le avise yo, Don't come until I tell you. In clauses referring to past or present time the indicative is generally used, e.g. No la reconocí hasta que se volvió, I didn't recognize her until she turned round)

untilled, *a.* sin cultivar

untimeliness, *s.* inoportunidad, *f.*; lo prematuro

untimely, *a.* inoportuno, intempestivo; prematuro

untiring, *a.* incansable, infatigable

unto, *prep.* hacia

untold, *a.* no revelado; no narrado; sin decir, no dicho; incalculable

untouchable, *a.* que no puede tocarse, intangible; (of castes) intocable

untouched, *a.* sin tocar; intacto, incólume

untrained, *a.* indisciplinado; inexperto; no adiestrado

untranslatable, *a.* intraducible

untravelled, *a.* no frecuentado; (of persons) provinciano

untried, *a.* no experimentado. u. knight, caballero novel, *m.*

untrodden, *a.* no hollado, no frecuentado; inexplorado, virgen

untroubled, *a.* tranquilo, sosegado

untrue, *a.* mentiroso, falso, engañoso; ficticio, imaginario; traidor, desleal; infiel

untrustworthiness, *s.* incertidumbre, inseguridad, *f.*; (of persons) informalidad, *f.*

untrustworthy, *a.* indigno de confianza; incierto, dudoso; desleal

untruth, *s.* mentira, falsedad, *f.*; ficción, *f.*

untruthful, *a.* mentiroso; falso

untruthfulness, *s.* falsedad, *f.*

untwist, *v.t.* destorcer

unused, *a.* no empleado; desacostumbrado; inusitado

unusual, *a.* fuera de lo común, desacostumbrado; extraño, raro, peregrino, extraordinario

unusually, *adv.* excepcionalmente; infrecuentemente

unusualness, *s.* lo insólito; rareza, *f.*

unutterable, *a.* indecible, inexpresable

unvarnished, *a.* sin barnizar; (*fig.*) sencillo

unvarying, *a.* invariable, constante, uniforme

unveil, *v.t.* quitar el velo; (memorial) descubrir; (*fig.*) revelar. *v.i.* quitarse el velo; revelarse, quitarse la careta

unventilated, *a.* sin ventilación; sin aire, ahogado; (of topics) no discutido

unverifiable, *a.* que no puede verificarse

unverified, *a.* sin verificar

unvisited, *a.* no visitado; no frecuentado

unvoiced, *a.* no expresado

unwanted, *a.* no deseado; superfluo, de más

unwarlike, *a.* nada marcial, pacífico

unwarranted, *a.* sin garantía; inexcusable; injustificable

unwary, *a.* incauto, imprudente

unwashed, *a.* sin lavar; sucio

unwatched, *a.* no vigilado

unwavering, *a.* resuelto, firme; inexorable; (gaze) fijo

unwaveringly, *adv.* sin vacilar; inexorablemente

unwearied, *a.* incansable; infatigable

unwelcome, *a.* mal acogido; inoportuno; desagradable

unwell, *a.* indispuesto

unwholesome, *a.* malsano, nocivo, insalubre

unwholesomeness, *s.* insalubridad, *f.*

unwieldiness, *s.* pesadez, dificultad de manejarse, *f.*

unwieldy, *a.* pesado, abultado, difícil de manejar

unwilling, *a.* desinclinado, reluctante

unwillingly, *adv.* de mala gana
unwillingness, *s.* falta de inclinación, repugnancia, *f.*
unwind, *v.t.* desenvolver; (thread) desdevanar, desovillar. *v.i.* desarrollarse; desdevanarse
unwise, *a.* imprudente, indiscreto, incauto; (lacking wisdom) tonto
unwisely, *adv.* imprudentemente, indiscretamente
unwitting, *a.* inconsciente
unwittingly, *adv.* sin darse cuenta
unwomanly, *a.* poco femenino
unwonted, *a.* insólito, inusitado
unworkable, *a.* impráctico
unworkmanlike, *a.* chapucero, charanguero
unworldly, *a.* poco mundano, espiritual
unworn, *a.* sin llevar, nuevo
unworthiness, *s.* indignidad, *f.*
unworthy, *a.* indigno
unwounded, *a.* no herido, sin herida, ileso
unwrap, *v.t.* desenvolver, desempapelar
unwritten, *a.* no escrito. u. law, ley natural, ley tradicional, *f.*
unyielding, *a.* duro, firme; (of persons) inflexible, terco, resuelto, obstinado
unyoke, *v.t.* desuncir, quitar el yugo
up, *adv.* (high) arriba, en alto; (higher) hacia arriba; (out of bed) levantado; (standing) de pie; (finished) concluido, terminado; (of time) llegado; (excited) agitado; (rebellious) sublevado; (of sun, etc.) salido; (come or gone up) subido; (of universities) en residencia; (for discussion) bajo consideración; (abreast of) al lado, al nivel; (incapable) incapaz, incompetente; (ill) enfermo, indispuesto. (For various idiomatic uses of "up" after verbs, see verbs themselves.) *a.* (in a few expressions only) ascendente. *prep.* en lo alto de; hacia arriba de; a lo largo de; (with country) en el interior de; (with current) contra. **to be up in arms,** sublevarse, rebelarse. **to be very hard up,** ser muy pobre, estar a la cuarta pregunta.

to drink up, beberlo todo. **to go or come up,** subir. **to lay up,** acumular. **to speak up,** hablar alto. **He has something up his sleeve,** Tiene algo en la manga. **It is all up,** Todo se acabó, Mi gozo en el pozo. **It is not up to much,** Vale muy poco; No es muy fuerte. **It is up to you,** Tu dirás, Tu harás lo que te parezca. **What is he up to?** ¿Qué está tramando? **What's up?** ¿Qué pasa? ¿Qué hay? **up and down,** *adv.* bajando y subiendo, de arriba abajo; de un lado a otro; por todas partes. **up-and-down,** *a.* fluctuante; (of roads) ondulante; (of life) accidentado, borrascoso. **ups and downs,** vicisitudes, *f. pl.*, altibajos, *m. pl.* **up-grade,** subida, *f.* **up in,** versado en, perito en. **well up in,** fuerte en. **up North,** al norte; en el norte; hacia el norte. **up there,** allí arriba, allí en lo alto. **up to,** hasta; (aware) al corriente de, informado de. **up to date,** *adv.* hasta la fecha. **up-to-date,** *a.* de última moda; al día. **up to now,** hasta ahora. **up train,** tren ascendente. **Up with...!** ¡Arriba! **Up you get!** (to children) ¡Upa!
upbraid, *v.t.* reprender, echar en cara
upbringing, *s.* crianza, educación, *f.*
upcountry, *s.* tierra adentro, *f.*; lo interior (de un país). *a.* de tierra adentro, del interior. *adv.* tierra adentro, hacia el interior
upheaval, *s.* solevantamiento, *m.*; trastorno, *m.*
uphill, *a.* ascendente; penoso, fatigoso, difícil. *adv.* cuesta arriba, pecho arriba
uphold, *v.t.* sostener, apoyar; (help) ayudar, consolar; (protect) defender; (countenance) aprobar; (law) confirmar
upholder, *s.* sostenedor (-ra), defensor (-ra)
upholster, *v.t.* entapizar, tapizar
upholsterer, *s.* tapicero, *m.*
upholstery, *s.* tapicería, *f.*; (of car) almohadillado, *m.*
upkeep, *s.* mantenimiento, *m.*, conservación, *f.*

upland, *s.* tierra alta, *f. a.* alto, elevado

uplift, *v.t.* elevar. *s.* elevación, *f.;* (*fam.*) fervor, *m.*

upon, *prep.* See on

upper, *a. comp.* superior; alto; de arriba. *s.* (of shoe) pala, *f.* (*sport*) **u.-cut,** golpe de abajo arriba, upper-cut, *m.* **U. Egypt,** Alto Egipto, *m.* **u. hand,** dominio, *m.;* superioridad, ventaja, *f.* **U. House,** cámara alta, cámara de los lores, *f.;* senado, *m.* **u. ten,** los diez primeros

uppermost, *a.* más alto, más elevado; predominante, principal; más fuerte. *adv.* en primer lugar; en lo más alto. **to be u.,** predominar

upright, *a.* recto, derecho; vertical; (honourable) honrado, digno, recto. *s.* (stanchion) mástil, soporte, palo derecho, montante, *m. adv.* en pie; derecho

uprightly, *adv.* rectamente, honradamente

uprightness, *s.* rectitud, honradez, probidad, *f.*

uprising, *s.* insurrección, sublevación, *f.*

uproar, *s.* alboroto, tumulto, estrépito, *m.*, conmoción, *f.*

uproarious, *a.* tumultuoso, estrepitoso

uproot, *v.t.* desarraigar; (*fig.*) arrancar; (destroy) extirpar

uprooting, *s.* desarraigo, *m.;* arranque, *m.;* extirpación, *f.*

upset, *v.t.* volcar; (overthrow) derribar, echar abajo; (frustrate) contrariar; desarreglar; (distress) trastornar, turbar; (of food) hacer mal. *v.i.* volcarse. *s.* vuelco, *m.;* trastorno, *m.* **u. price,** tipo de subasta, *m.*

upsetting, *a.* turbante, inquietante

upshot, *s.* resultado, *m.;* consecuencia, *f.*

upside, *s.* lado superior, *m.;* parte superior, *f.;* (of trains) andén ascendente, *m.* **u. down,** al revés, de arriba abajo; en desorden

upstairs, *adv.* arriba, en el piso de arriba; (with go or come) al piso de arriba

upstanding, *a.* gallardo, guapo; **an u. young man (woman),** un buen mozo (una buena moza)

upstart, *s.* arrivista, *m.* and *f.;* advenedizo (-za), insolente, *m.* and *f.;* presuntuoso (-sa)

upstream, *a.* and *adv.* contra la corriente, agua arriba, río arriba

upturned, *a.* (of noses) respingada

upward, *a.* ascendente, hacia arriba

upwards, *adv.* hacia arriba; en adelante. **u. of,** más de

uranium, *s.* (*min.*) uranio, *m.*

Uranus, *s.* (*ast.*) Urano, *m.*

urban, *a.* urbano, ciudadano

urbane, *a.* cortés, urbano, fino

urbanity, *s.* urbanidad, cortesía, finura, *f.*

urbanization, *s.* urbanización, *f.*

urbanize, *v.t.* urbanizar

urchin, *s.* galopín, granuja, pilluelo, *m.*

ureter, *s.* (*anat.*) uréter, *m.*

urethra, *s.* (*anat.*) uretra, *f.*

urge, *v.t.* empujar, impeler; incitar, estimular, azuzar, animar; pedir con urgencia, recomendar con ahinco, instar, insistir (en). *s.* instinto, impulso, *m.;* deseo, *m.;* ambición, *f.*

urgency, *s.* urgencia, *f.;* importancia, perentoriedad, *f.*

urgent, *a.* urgente; importante, apremiante, perentorio. **to be u.,** urgir

urgently, *adv.* urgentemente

uric, *a.* úrico

urinal, *s.* orinal, urinario, *m.*

urinary, *a.* urinario

urinate, *v.i.* orinar

urine, *s.* orín, *m.*

urn, *s.* urna, *f.;* (for coffee) cafetera, *f.;* (for tea) tetera, *f.*

Ursa, *s.* (*ast.*) osa, *f.* **U. Major,** osa mayor, *f.* **U. Minor,** osa menor, *f.*

urticaria, *s.* (*med.*) urticaria, *f.*

Uruguayan, *a.* and *s.* uruguayo (-ya)

us, *pron.* nos; (with prep.) nosotros. **He came towards us,** Vino hacia nosotros

usable, *a.* aprovechable, servible

usage, *s.* (handling) tratamiento, *m.;* uso, *m.*, costumbre, *f.*

use, *s.* uso, *m.;* manejo, empleo, *m.;* (custom) costumbre práctica, *f.*; (need) necesidad, *f.*; (usefulness) aprovechamiento, *m.*; (*law*) usufructo, *m.* **directions for use,** direcciones para el uso, *f. pl.* **in use,** en uso. **out of use,** anticuado; fuera de moda. **to be of no use,** no servir; ser inútil. **to have no use for,** no tener necesidad de ; (*fam.*) tener en poco. **to make use of,** servirse de, aprovechar; (*law*) ejercer. **to put to use,** poner en uso, poner en servicio **use,** *v.t* usar; (employ) emplear; (utilize) servirse de, utilizar; (handle) manejar; hacer uso de; (consume) gastar, consumir; (treat) tratar; practicar. **to use up,** agotar, acabar con; consumir. *v.i. impers.* acostumbrar, soler (e.g. **It used to happen that . . .,** Solía ocurrir que . . .). (" Used to " and the verb which follows are often translated simply by the Imperfect Tense of the following verb, e.g. **I used to see her every day,** La veía todos los días. The use of the verbs acostumbrar or soler to translate " used to " adds emphasis to the statement)

used, *a.* and *past part.* acostumbrado, habituado; empleado; (of clothes) usado. **to become u. to,** acostumbrarse a

useful, *a.* útil; provechoso; servicial

usefully, *adv.* útilmente; con provecho

usefulness, *s.* utilidad, *f.*; valor, *m.*

useless, *a.* inútil; vano, infructuoso. **to render u.,** inutilizar

uselessness, *s.* inutilidad, *f.*

user, *s.* el, *m.* (*f.* la) que usa, comprador (-ra)

usher, *s.* ujier, *m.*; (in a theatre) acomodador (-ra). *v.t.* introducir, anunciar; acomodar

usual, *a.* usual, acostumbrado, habitual; normal, común. **as u.,** como siempre. **in the u. form,** (*com.*) al usado; como de costumbre

usually, *adv.* por lo general, ordinariamente. **We u. go out on Sundays,** Acostumbramos salir los domingos

usufruct, *s.* (*law*) usufructo, *m.*

usurer, *s.* usurero (-ra)

usurious, *a.* usurario

usurp, *v.t.* usurpar; asumir, arrogarse

usurpation, *s.* usurpación, *f.*; arrogación, *f.*

usurper, *s.* usurpador (-ra)

usurping, *a.* usurpador

usury, *s.* usura, *f.* **to practise u.,** usurear, dar (or tomar) a usura

utensil, *s.* utensilio, instrumento, *m.*; herramienta, *f.* **kitchen utensils,** batería de cocina, *f.*

uterine, *a.* (*med.*) uterino

uterus, *s.* útero, *m.*

utilitarian, *a.* utilitario

utilitarianism, *s.* utilitarismo, *m.*

utility, *s.* utilidad, *f.*; ventaja, *f.*, beneficio, provecho, *m.* **u. goods,** artículos fabricados bajo la autorizacion del gobierno, *m. pl.*

utilizable, *a.* utilizable, aprovechable

utilization, *s.* empleo, aprovechamiento, *m.*

utilize, *v.t.* utilizar, servirse de; aprovechar

utmost, *a.* (outermost) extremo; (farthest) más remoto, más distante; (greatest) mayor, más grande. *s.* lo más; todo lo posible. **to do one's u.,** hacer todo lo posible, hacer todo lo que uno pueda

Utopian, *a.* utópico

utter, *a.* completo, total; terminante, absoluto; sumo, extremo. **He is an u. fool,** Es un tonto de capirote

utter, *v.t.* pronunciar, proferir, decir, hablar; (a sigh, cry, etc.) dar; (express) manifestar, expresar, explicar; (coin) poner en circulación; (a libel) publicar; (disclose) revelar, descubrir

utterance, *s.* expresión, manifestación, *f.*; pronunciación, *f.*; (style) lenguaje, *m.*

utterly, *adv.* enteramente, completamente

uttermost, *a.* See **utmost**

uvula, *s.* (*anat.*) úvula, *f.*

uxorious, *a.* uxorio

V

v, *s.* (letter) ve, *f.*; pieza en forma de V, *f.*

vacancy, *s.* vacío, *m.;* vacancia, *f.;* (mental) vacuidad, *f.;* (of offices, posts) vacante, *f.;* (leisure) desocupación, ociosidad, *f.;* (gap, blank) vacío, *m.,* laguna, *f.*

vacant, *a.* vacío; despoblado, deshabitado; (free) libre; (of offices, etc.) vacante; (leisured) ocioso; (absent-minded) distraído; (vague) vago; (foolish) estúpido, estólido

vacantly, *adv.* distraídamente; estúpidamente

vacate, *v.t.* dejar vacío; (a post) dejar; (a throne) renunciar a; dejar vacante; (mil.) evacuar; (law) anular, rescindir

vacation, *s.* (of offices) vacante, *f.;* (holiday) vacación, *f.* **the long v.,** las vacaciones de verano. **to be on a v.,** estar de vacación

vaccinate, *v.t.* vacunar

vaccination, *s.* vacunación, *f.*

vaccine, *s.* vacuna, *f.*

vacillate, *v.i.* (sway) oscilar; (hesitate) vacilar, titubear, dudar

vacillating, *a.* vacilante

vacillation, *s.* vacilación, *f.*

vacuity, *s.* vacuidad, *f.*

vacuous, *a.* desocupado, ocioso; estúpido, vacío

vacuum, *s.* vacío, *m.* **v. brake,** freno al vacío, *m.* **v. cleaner,** aspirador de polvo, *m.* **v. flask,** termos, *m.* **v. pump,** bomba neumática, *f.*

vade-mecum, *s.* vademécum, *m.*

vagabond, *s.* vagabundo (-da); vago, *m.;* (beggar) mendigo (-ga). *a.* vagabundo, errante

vagabondage, *s.* vagabundeo, *m.,* vagancia, *f.*

vagary, *s.* (whim) capricho, antojo, *m.,* extravagancia, *f.;* (of the mind) divagación, *f.*

vagina, *s.* vagina, *f.*

vaginal, *a.* vaginal

vagrancy, *s.* vagancia, *f.*

vagrant, *s.* vago, *m.* *a.* vagabundo, errante

vague, *a.* vago; indistinto; equívoco, ambiguo; (uncertain) incierto

vaguely, *adv.* vagamente

vagueness, *s.* vaguedad, *f.*

vain, *a.* vano; (fruitless) infructuoso; (useless) inútil; (unsub-

stantial) fútil, insubstancial; fantástico; (empty) vacío; (worthless) despreciable; (conceited) vanidoso, presumido. **in v.,** en vano, en balde, inútilmente. **v. about,** orgulloso de

vainglorious, *a.* vanaglorioso

vaingloriousness, *s.* vanagloria, *f.*

vainly, *adv.* vanamente; inútilmente; (conceitedly) vanidosamente, con vanidad

valance, *s.* cenefa, *f.*

vale, *s.* (valley) valle, *m.* *interj.* ¡adiós! *s.* (good-bye) vale, *m.*

valediction, *s.* despedida, *f.;* vale, *m.*

valedictory, *a.* de despedida

Valencian, *a.* and *s.* valenciano (-na)

valency, *s.* (chem.) valencia, *f.*

valerian, *s.* valeriana, *f.*

valet, *s.* criado, *m.* **v. de chambre,** ayuda de cámara, *m.*

valetudinarian, *a.* valetudinario

Valhalla, *s.* Valhala, *m.*

valiant, *a.* valiente, esforzado, animoso, bravo

valiantly, *adv.* valientemente

valid, *a.* válido, valedero; (of laws in force) vigente

validate, *v.t.* validar

validation, *s.* validación, *f.*

validity, *s.* validez, *f.*

validly, *adv.* válidamente

valise, *s.* valija, *f.;* saco de viaje, *m.*

Valkyrie, *s.* Valquiria, *f.*

valley, *s.* valle, *m.*

valorous, *a.* valoroso, esforzudo, intrépido

valour, *s.* valor, *m.,* valentía, *f.*

valse, *s.* vals, *m.*

valuable, *a.* valioso; costoso; precioso; estimable; excelente. *s. pl.* **valuables,** objetos de valor, *m. pl.*

valuableness, *s.* valor, *m.*

valuation, *s.* valuación, tasación, *f.;* estimación, *f.*

valuator, *s.* tasador, *m.*

value, *s.* valor, *m.;* precio, *m.;* estimación, *f.;* importancia, *f.;* (gram., mus.) valor, *m.; pl.* **values,** valores morales, principios, *m. pl. v.t.* tasar, valorar; estimar; apreciar; tener en mucho; hacer caso de; considerar. **to be of v.,** ser de valor

valued, *a.* apreciado, estimado; precioso

valueless, *a.* sin valor; insignificante

valuer, *s.* tasador, *m.*

valve, *s.* (*elec., mech., anat.*) válvula, *f.*; (*bot., zool.*) valva, *f.*

valved, *a.* con válvulas; (in compounds) de . . . válvulas

valvular, *a.* valvular

vamp, *s.* (of a shoe) pala (de zapato), *f.*; (patch) remiendo, *m.*; (*mus.*) acompañamiento improvisado, *m.*; (*fam.*) aventurera, *f. v.t.* (of shoes) poner palas (a); (patch) remendar; (*mus.*) improvisar un acompañamiento; (of a woman) fascinar, engatusar

vampire, *s.* vampiro, *m.*

van, *s.* (*mil., nav., fig.*) vanguardia, *f.*; camión, *m.*; (for delivery) camión de reparto, *m.*; (for furniture) conductora de muebles, *f.*; (removal) carro de mudanzas, *m.*; (mail) camión postal, *m.*; (for bathing) caseta de baño, *f.*; (for guard on trains) furgón de equipajes, *m.*; (railway waggon) vagón, *m.*

vanadium, *s.* vanadio, *m.*

vandal, *a.* and *s.* vándalo (-la); bárbaro (-ra)

vandalism, *s.* vandalismo, *m.*

Vandyke, *s.* cuadro de Vandyke, *m.* **V. beard,** perilla, *f.* **V. collar,** cuello de encaje, *m.*

vane, *s.* (weathercock) veleta, *f.*; (of a windmill) aspa, *f.*; (of a propeller) paleta, *f.*; (of a feather) barba, *f.*; (of a surveying instrument) pínula, *f.*

vanguard, *s.* vanguardia, *f.* **in the v.,** a vanguardia; (*fig.*) en la vanguardia

vanilla, *s.* vainilla, *f.*

vanish, *v.i.* desaparecer; desvanecerse; disiparse

vanishing, *s.* desaparición, *f.*; disipación, *f.* **v. cream,** crema para el cutis, *f.* **v. point,** punto de la vista, *m.*

vanity, *s.* vanidad, *f.* **v. case,** polvera de bolsillo, *f.*

vanquish, *v.t.* vencer, derrotar

vanquisher, *s.* vencedor (-ra)

vantage, *s.* ventaja (also in tennis), *f.* **v.-ground,** posición ventajosa, *f.*

vapid, *a.* insípido, insulso; (of speeches, etc.) soso, aburrido, insípido

vapidity, *s.* insipidez, sosería, *f.*

vaporizable, *a.* vaporizable

vaporization, *s.* vaporización, *f.*

vaporize, *v.t.* vaporizar. *v.i.* vaporizarse

vaporizer, *s.* vaporizador, *m.*

vaporous, *a.* vaporoso

vapour, *s.* vapor, *m.*; *pl.* **vapours,** (hysteria) vapores, *m. pl. v.i.* (boast) jactarse, baladronear; decir disparates. **v. bath,** baño de vapor, *m.*

variability, *s.* variabilidad, *f.*

variable, *a.* variable. *s.* (*math.*) variable, *f.*

variably, *adv.* variablemente

variance, *s.* variación, *f.,* cambio, *m.*; desacuerdo, *m.,* disensión, *f.*; diferencia, contradicción, *f.* **at v.,** en desacuerdo, reñidos; hostil (a), opuesto (a); (of things) distinto (de), en contradicción (con)

variant, *s.* variante, *f.*

variation, *s.* variación, *f.*; cambio, *m.*; variedad, *f.*; diferencia, *f.*; (*mus.,* magnetism) variación, *f.*

varicose, *a.* varicoso

variegate, *v.t.* abigarrar, matizar, salpicar

variegated, *a.* abigarrado; variado; mezclado

variegation, *s.* abigarramiento, *m.*; diversidad de colores, *f.*

variety, *s.* variedad, *f.*; diversidad, *f.*; (choice) surtido, *m.* **v. show,** función de variedades, *f.*

variometer, *s.* variómetro, *m.*

various, *a.* vario, diverso; diferente

variously, *adv.* diversamente

varix, *s.* várice, *f.*

varlet, *s.* lacayo, *m.*; (of a knight) mozo de espuelas, *m.*

varnish, *s.* barniz, *m. v.t.* barnizar; (pottery) vidriar; (conceal) disimular. **copal v.,** barniz copal, *m.* **japan v.,** charol japonés, *m.* **lacquer v.,** laca, *f.* **v. remover,** (for nails) quitaesmalte, *m.*

varnishing, *s.* barnizado, *m.*; (of pottery) vidriado, *m.*

vary, *v.t.* variar; cambiar; diversificar; modificar. *v.i.* variar;

cambiar;· (be different) ser distinto (de); (deviate) desviarse
(de); (disagree) estar en desacuerdo, distar, estar en contradicción. **to v. directly (indirectly)** (*math.*) variar en razón
directa (inversa)

varying, *a.* variante, cambiante,
diverso

vascular, *a.* vascular

vase, *s.* vaso, jarrón, *m.*; urna, *f.*

vaseline, *s.* vaselina, *f.*

vasomotor, *a.* vasomotor

vassal, *s.* vasallo (-lla); esclavo
(-va), siervo (-va). *a.* tributario

vassalage, *s.* vasallaje, *m.*; esclavitud, *f.*

vast, *a.* vasto, extenso; enorme;
grande. *s.* vastedad, inmensidad,
f.

vastly, *adv.* enormemente; muy;
con mucho

vastness, *s.* vastedad, extensión,
f.; inmensidad, *f.*; enormidad, *f.*,
gran tamaño, *m.*; grandeza, *f.*

vat, *s.* cuba, tina, *f.*; alberca,
f., estanque, *m.* **dyeing vat**,
cuba de tintorero, *f.* **tanning
vat**, noque, *m.* **wine vat**, lagar,
m.

vatican, *a.* and *s.* vaticano (*m.*)

vaticinate, *v.t.* and *v.i.* vaticinar,
profetizar

vaticination, *s.* vaticinio, *m.*,
predicción, *f.*

vaudeville, *s.* vaudeville, *m.*,
zarzuela cómica, *f.*

vault, *s.* (*arch.*) bóveda, *f.*;
caverna, *f.*; (for wine) bodega,
cueva, *f.*; (in a bank) cámara
acorazada, *f.*; (in a church)
cripta, *f.*; sepultura, *f.*; (of the
sky) bóveda celeste, *f.*; (leap)
salto, *m.*; voltereta, *f.* *v.i.*
(jump) saltar; (with a pole)
saltar con pértiga; saltar por
encima de; voltear. *v.t.* (*arch.*)
abovedar; saltar

vaulted, *a.* abovedado

vaulter, *s.* saltador (-ra)

vaulting, *s.* construcción de
bóvedas; *f.*; bóvedas, *f. pl.*;
edificio abovedado, *m.*; (jumping) salto, *m.* **v.-horse**, potro de
madera, *m.*

vaunt, *v.i.* jactarse (de), hacer
gala (de); triunfar (sobre). *v.t.*
ostentar, sacar a relucir; (praise)
alabar. *s.* jactancia, *f.*

veal, *s.* ternera, *f.* **v.-cutlet**,
chuleta de ternera, *f.*

vector, *s.* vector, *m.*

Veda, *s.* Veda, *m.*

veer, *v.i.* (of the wind) girar;
(of a ship) virar; (*fig.*) cambiar
(de opinión, etc.). *v.t.* virar

vegetable, *s.* vegetal, *m.*; legumbre, *f.*; *pl.* **vegetables**, (green and
generally cooked) verduras, *f. pl.*;
(raw green) hortalizas, *f. pl.*
v. dish, fuente de legumbres, *f.*
v. garden, huerto de legumbres,
m.; **v. ivory**, marfil vegetal, *m.*
v. kingdom, reino vegetal, *m.*
v. soup, sopa de hortelano, *f.*

vegetal, *a.* vegetal

vegetarian, *a.* and *s.* vegetariano
(-na)

vegetarianism, *s.* vegetarianismo, *m.*

vegetate, *v.i.* vegetar

vegetation, *s.* vegetación, *f.*

vegetative, *a.* vegetativo

vehemence, *s.* vehemencia, *f.*;
violencia, *f.*; impetuosidad, *f.*;
pasión, *f.*, ardor, *m.*

vehement, *a.* vehemente; violento; impetuoso; apasionado

vehemently, *adv.* con vehemencia; violentamente; con impetuosidad; apasionadamente

vehicle, *s.* vehículo, *m.*; (means)
medio, *m.*; instrumento, *m.*

vehicular, *a.* de los vehículos; de
los coches. **v. traffic**, circulación
de los coches, *f.*; los vehículos

veil, *s.* velo, *m.*; (curtain) cortina,
f.; (disguise) disfraz, *m.*; (excuse) pretexto, *m.*; (appearance)
apariencia, *f.* *v.t.* velar; cubrir
con un velo; (hide) tapar,
encubrir; (dissemble) disimular;
(disguise) disfrazar. **to take
the v.**, tomar el velo, profesar

vein,· *s.* (*anat.*, *bot.*) vena, *f.*;
(*geol.*, *min.*) veta, *f.*, filón, *m.*; (in
wood) fibra, hebra, *f.*; (*fig.*,
streak) rasgo, *m.*; (inspiration)
vena, *f.*; (mood) humor, *m.*

veined, **veiny**, *a.* venoso; de
venas; veteado

velar, *a.* velar

velleity, *s.* veleidad, *f.*

vellum, *s.* vitela,· *f.*

velocipede, *s.* velocípedo, *m.*.

velocity, *s.* velocidad, *f.*; rapidez,
f.

velodrome, *s.* velódromo, *m.*

velours, *s.* terciopelo, *m.*

velvet, *s.* terciopelo, *m.* *a.* hecho de terciopelo; aterciopelado

velveteen, *s.* pana, *f.,* velludillo, *m.*

velvety, *a.* aterciopelado

venal, *a.* venal

venality, *s.* venalidad, *f.*

vend, *v.t.* vender

vendor, *s.* vendedor (-ra)

veneer, *v.t.* chapear, taracear; (conceal) disimular, disfrazar. *s.* taraceado, chapeado, *m.;* (plate) chapa, hoja para chapear, *f.;* (*fig.,* gloss) barniz, *m.,* apariencia, *f.*

venerability, *s.* venerabilidad, respetabilidad, *f.*

venerable, *a.* venerable

venerate, *v.t.* venerar, reverenciar

veneration, *s.* veneración, *f.*

venerator, *s.* venerador (-ra)

venereal, *a.* venéreo. **v. disease,** enfermedad venérea, *f.*

Venetian, *a.* and *s.* veneciano (-na). **v. blinds,** persianas, celosías, *f. pl.*

Venezuelan, *a.* and *s.* venezolano (-na)

vengeance, *s.* venganza, *f.*

vengeful, *a.* vengativo

venial, *a.* venial

veniality, *s.* venialidad, *f.*

venison, *s.* venado, *m.*

venom, *s.* veneno, *m.*

venomous, *a.* venenoso; maligno, malicioso

venomously, *adv.* con malignidad, maliciosamente

venomousness, *s.* venenosidad, *f.;* malignidad, *f.*

venous, *a.* venoso

vent, *s.* abertura, *f.;* salida, *f.;* (air-hole) respiradero, *m.;* (in pipes) ventosa, *f.;* (in fire-arms) oído, *m.;* (*anat.*) ano, *m.;* (*fig.,* outlet) desahogo, *m.;* expresión, *f.* *v.t.* dejar escapar; (pierce) agujerear; (discharge) emitir, vomitar; (relieve) desahogar; expresar, dar expresión (a), dar rienda suelta (a)

venter, *s.* (*law*) vientre, *m.*

ventilate, *v.t.* ventilar; discutir

ventilation, *s.* ventilación, *f.*

ventilator, *s.* ventilador, *m.*

ventral, *a.* ventral

ventricle, *s.* ventrículo, *m.*

ventriloquial, *a.* ventrílocuo

ventriloquism, *s.* ventriloquia, *f.*

ventriloquist, *s.* ventrílocuo (-ua)

venture, *s.* ventura, *f.;* riesgo, *m.;* aventura, *f.;* especulación, *f.* *v.t.* arriesgar, aventurar; (stake) jugar; (state) expresar. *v.i.* aventurarse; (dare) atreverse, osar; permitirse. **at a v.,** a la ventura. **to v. on,** arriesgarse a; probar ventura con; lanzarse a; (a remark) permitirse. **to v. out,** atreverse a salir

venturesome, *a.* atrevido, audaz; (dangerous) arriesgado, peligroso

venturesomeness, *s.* atrevimiento, *m.,* temeridad, *f.;* (risk) riesgo, peligro, *m.*

Venus, *s.* (planet) Venus, *m.;* (woman) venus, *f.*

veracious, *a.* veraz, verídico; verdadero

veracity, *s.* veracidad, *f.;* verdad, *f.*

verandah, *s.* veranda, *f.*

verb, *s.* verbo, *m.* **auxiliary v.,** verbo auxiliar, *m.* **intransitive v.,** verbo intransitivo (neutro), *m.* **reflexive v.,** verbo reflexivo, *m.* **transitive v.,** verbo transitivo, *m.*

verbal, *a.* verbal

verbally, *adv.* de palabra, verbalmente

verbatim, *a.* and *adv.* palabra por palabra

verbena, *s.* verbena, *f.*

verbiage, *s.* verbosidad, palabrería, *f.*

verbose, *a.* verboso, prolijo

verbosity, *s.* verbosidad, *f.*

verdancy, *s.* verdura, *f.,* verdor, *m.*

verdant, *a.* verde

verdict, *s.* (*law*) veredicto, fallo, *m.,* sentencia, *f.;* opinión, *f.,* juicio, *m.* **to bring in a v.,** fallar sentencia.

verdigris, *s.* cardenillo, verdín, *m.*

verdure, *s.* verdura, *f.,* verdor, *m.;* (*fig.*) lozanía, *f.*

verge, *s.* (wand) vara, *f.;* (edge) margen, borde, *m.;* (of a lake, etc.) orilla, *f.;* (horizon) horizonte, *m.;* (*fig.*) víspera, *f.,* punto, *m.* **on the v. of,** al margen de, a la orilla de. **to be**

on the v. of, (*fig.*) estar a punto
de; estar en vísperas de

verger, *s.* macero, *m.*; (in a
church) pertiguero, *m.*

verifiable, *a.* verificable

verification, *s.* verificación, *f.*

verifier, *s.* verificador (-ra)

verify, *v.t.* verificar, confirmar;
probar

verily, *adv.* de veras, en verdad

verisimilitude, *s.* verosimilitud,
f.

veritable, *a.* verdadero

veritably, *adv.* verdaderamente

verity, *s.* verdad, *f.*

verjuice, *s.* agraz, *m.*

vermicelli, *s.* fideos, *m. pl.*

vermiform, *a.* vermiforme

vermifuge, *a.* and *s.* vermífugo
(*m.*)

vermilion, *s.* bermellón, *m.*

vermin, *s.* bichos dañinos, *m. pl.*;
(insects) parásitos, *m. pl.*

verminous, *a.* verminoso

vermouth, *s.* vermut, *m.*

vernacular, *a.* vernáculo;
nativo; vulgar. *s.* lengua popular, *f.*; lenguaje vulgar, *m.*

vernal, *a.* vernal, primaveral

veronal, *s.* veronal, *m.*

Veronese, *a.* and *s.* veronés (-esa)

veronica, *s.* verónica, *f.*

versatile, *a.* (*zool.*) versátil; inconstante, voluble; (clever) de
muchos talentos; de muchos
intereses; adaptable; completo,
cabal

versatility, *s.* (cleverness) muchos
talentos, *m. pl.*; adaptabilidad, *f.*

verse, *s.* verso, *m.*; (stanza)
estrofa, *f.*; (in the Bible) versículo, *m.*; (poetry) poesía, *f.*,
versos, *m. pl.* **to make verses**,
escribir versos

versed, *a.* versado, experimentado

versicle, *s.* versículo, *m.*

versification, *s.* versificación, *f.*

versifier, *s.* versificador (-ra)

versify, *v.t.* and *v.i.* versificar

version, *s.* versión, *f.*; traducción, *f.*; interpretación, *f.*

versus, *prep.* contra

vertebra, *s.* vértebra, *f.*

vertebral, *a.* vertebral

vertebrate, *s.* vertebrado, *m.*

vertex, *s.* (*geom.*, *anat.*) vértice,
m.; (*ast.*) cenit, *m.*; cumbre, *f.*

vertical, *a.* vertical

verticality, *s.* verticalidad, *f.*

vertically, *adv.* verticalmente

vertiginous, *a.* vertiginoso

vertigo, *s.* vértigo, *m.*

vervain, *s.* verbena, *f.*

verve, *s.* brío, *m.*, fogosidad, *f.*

very, *a.* mismo; (mere) mero; (true)
verdadero; (with adjective and
comparative) más grande; (*fam.*)
mismísimo; (complete) perfecto,
completo. **The v. thought of
it made him laugh**, Sólo con
pensarlo se rió (or La mera idea le
hizo reírse). **this v. minute**,
este mismísimo instante. **the
v. day**, el mismo día

very, *adv.* muy; mucho; demasiado; (exactly) exactamente; completamente; absolutamente. **He
is v. worried**, Está muy preocupado. **He is not v. well**
(i.e. rather ill) No está demasiado
bien. **This cloth is the v.
best**, Esta tela es la mejor de
todas. **I like it v. much**, Me
gusta muchísimo. **He is v.
much pleased**, Está muy contento. **so v. little**, tan poco;
tan pequeño. **v. well**, muy
bien

vesicle, *s.* vesícula, *f.*

vesper, *s.* estrella vespertina, *f.*,
héspero, *m.*; *pl.* vespers, (*ecc.*)
vísperas, *f. pl.*

vespertine, *a.* vespertino

vessel, *s.* vasija, *f.*, recipiente,
m.; (boat) barco, buque, *m.*;
(*anat.*, *bot.*) vaso, *m.*

vest, *s.* camiseta, *f.*; (waistcoat)
chaleco, *m.* *v.t.* vestir; (with
authority, etc.) revestir de;
(property, etc.) hacer entrega de,
ceder. *v.i.* tener validez; (dress)
vestirse. **vested interests**, intereses creados, *m. pl.* **v.-
pocket**, bolsillo del chaleco, *m.*
v.-pocket camera, vest pocket,
m.

vestal, *a.* vestal; virgen, casto.
s. vestal, *f.*; virgen, *f.*

vestibule, *s.* vestíbulo, *m.*; (ante-
room) antecámara, *f.*; (of a
theatre box) antepalco, *m.*;
(*anat.*) vestíbulo, *m.*

vestige, *s.* vestigio, rastro, *m.*;
sombra, *f.*; (*biol.*) rudimento, *m.*

vestment, *s.* hábito, *m.*; (*ecc.*)
vestidura, *f.*

vestry, *s.* vestuario, *m.*, sacristía, *f.*

vesture, *s.* traje, hábito, *m.*, vestidura, *f.*

Vesuvian, *a.* vesuviano

vetch, *s.* arveja, *f.*

veteran, *a.* veterano; de los veteranos; aguerrido; anciano; experimentado. *s.* veterano (-na)

veterinary, *a.* veterinario. **v. science,** veterinaria, *f.* **v. surgeon,** veterinario, *m.*

veto, *s.* veto, *m.*; prohibición, *f.* *v.t.* poner el veto; prohibir

vex, *v.t.* contrariar, irritar; enojar; (make impatient) impacientar; fastidiar; (afflict) afligir, acongojar; (worry) inquietar

vexation, *s.* contrariedad, irritación, *f.*; enojo, enfado, *m.*; (impatience) impaciencia, *f.*; fastidio, *m.*; aflicción, *f.*; inquietud, *f.*; disgusto, *m.*

vexatious, *a.* irritante; enojoso, enfadoso; fastidioso, molesto

vexatiousness, *s.* fastidio, *m.*, molestia, *f.*; incomodidad, *f.*, contrariedad, *f.*

vexed, *a.* discutido; contencioso; (thorny) espinoso, difícil

vexing, *a.* irritante; molesto; enfadoso

via, *s.* vía, *f.* *prep.* por, por la vía de

viability, *s.* viabilidad, *f.*

viable, *a.* viable

viaduct, *s.* viaducto, *m.*

vial, *s.* frasco, *m.*, ampolleta, *f.*

viand, *s.* vianda, *f.*

viaticum, *s.* viático, *m.*

vibrant, *a.* vibrante

vibrate, *v.i.* vibrar; (of machines) trepidar; oscilar. *v.t.* hacer vibrar, vibrar

vibration, *s.* vibración, *f.*; trepidación, *f.*; oscilación, *f.*

vibrative, *a.* vibratorio

vibrator, *s.* (*elec.*) vibrador, *m.*; (*rad.*) oscilador, *m.*

vicar, *s.* vicario, *m.*; (of a parish) cura, *m.* **v. general,** vicario general, *m.*

vicarage, *s.* vicaría, *f.*

vicarial, *a.* vicario

vicariate, *s.* vicariato, *m.*

vicarious, *a.* vicario; sufrido por otro; experimentado por otro

vicariously, *adv.* por delegación; por substitución

vice, *s.* vicio, *m.*; defecto, *m.*; (in a horse) vicio, resabio, *m.*; (tool) tornillo de banco, *m.* *prefix* vice. **v. admiral,** vicealmirante, *m.* **v. chairman,** vicepresidente (-ta). **v. chancellor,** vicecanciller, *m.* **v. consul,** vicecónsul, *m.* **v. consulate,** viceconsulado, *m.* **v. president,** vicepresidente (-ta)

viceregal, *a.* de virrey

vicereine, *s.* virreina, *f.*

viceroy, *s.* virrey, *m.*

viceroyship, *s.* virreinato, *m.*

viceversa, *adv.* viceversa

vicinity, *s.* vecindad, *f.*; (nearness) cercanía, proximidad, *f.* **to be in the v. of,** estar en la vecindad de

vicious, *a.* vicioso. **v. circle,** círculo vicioso, *m.*

viciously, *adv.* viciosamente

viciousness, *s.* viciosidad, *f.*; (in a horse) resabios, *m. pl.*

vicissitude, *s.* vicisitud, *f.*

vicissitudinous, *a.* accidentado, vicisitudinario

victim, *s.* víctima, *f.*

victimization, *s.* sacrificio, *m.*; tormento, *m.*

victimize, *v.t.* hacer víctima (de); sacrificar; ser víctima (de), sufrir; (cheat) estafar, engañar

victor, *s.* víctor, vencedor, *m.*

victoria, *s.* victoria, *f.*

Victorian, *a.* victoriano

victorious, *a.* victorioso, triunfante. **to be v.,** triunfar, salir victorioso

victoriously, *adv.* victoriosamente, triunfalmente

victory, *s.* victoria, *f.*

victress, *s.* vencedora, *f.*

victual, *s.* vitualla, vianda, *f.*; *pl.* victuals, víveres, *m. pl.*, provisiones, *f. pl.* *v.t.* avituallar; abastecer. *v.i.* tomar provisiones

victualler, *s.* abastecedor (-ra), proveedor (-ra)

victualling, *s.* abastecimiento, *m.*

vide, *Latin imperative* véase

videlicet, *adv.* a saber

vie, *v.i.* (with) competir con; rivalizar con; (with a person for) disputar; luchar con

Viennese, *a. and s.* vienés (-esa)

view, *s.* vista, *f.*; perspectiva, *f.*, panorama, *m.*; (landscape) paisaje, *m.*; escena, *f.*; inspección, *f.*; (judgment) opinión, *f.*, parecer, *m.*; consideración, *f.*; (appearance) apariencia, *f.*; aspecto, *m.*; (purpose) propósito, *m.*, intención, *f.*; (sight) alcance de la vista, *m.*; (show) exposición, *f.* *v.t.* examinar; inspeccionar; (look at) mirar; (see) ver, contemplar; considerar. in v. of, en vista de. in my v., en mi opinión, según creo yo. on v., a la vista. to keep in v., no perder de vista; (*fig.*) no olvidar, tener presente. to take a different v., pensar de un modo distinto. to v. a house, inspeccionar una casa. with a v. to, con el propósito de. v.-finder, enfocador, *m.* v.-point, punto de vista, *m.*

viewer, *s.* espectador (-ra); examinador (-ra)

viewing, *s.* inspección, *f.*, examen, *m.*

vigil, *s.* vela, vigilia, *f.*; (*ecc.*) vigilia, *f.*

vigilance, *s.* vigilancia, *f.*, desvelo, *m.*

vigilant, *a.* vigilante, desvelado

vigilantly, *adv.* vigilantemente

vignette, *s.* viñeta, *f.*

vigorous, *a.* vigoroso, enérgico, fuerte

vigorously, *adv.* con vigor

vigour, *s.* vigor, *m.*, fuerza, *f.*

Viking, *s.* vikingo, *m.*

vile, *a.* vil; bajo; despreciable; infame; (*fam.*) horrible

vilely, *adv.* vilmente; (*fam.*) mal, horriblemente

vileness, *s.* vileza, *f.*; bajeza, *f.*; infamia, *f.*

vilification, *s.* vilipendio, *m.*, difamación, *f.*

vilifier, *s.* difamador (-ra)

vilify, *v.t.* vilipendiar, difamar

villa, *s.* villa, torre, casa de campo, *f.*; hotel, *m.*

village, *s.* aldea, *f.*, pueblo, *m.*

villager, *s.* aldeano (-na)

villain, *s.* (*hist.*) villano, *m.*; malvado, *m.*

villainous, *a.* malvado; infame; vil

villainously, *adv.* vilmente

villainy, *s.* vileza, infamia, maldad, *f.*

vindicate, *v.t.* vindicar, justificar; defender

vindication, *s.* vindicación, justificación, *f.*; defensa, *f.*

vindicative, *a.* vindicativo, vindicador, justificativo

vindicator, *s.* vindicador (-ra)

vindictive, *a.* vengativo; rencoroso

vindictively, *adv.* vengativamente; rencorosamente

vindictiveness, *s.* deseo de venganza, *m.*; rencor, *m.*

vine, *s.* vid, parra, *f.*; (twining plant) enredadera, *f.* v.-arbour, emparrado, *m.* v.-branch, sarmiento, *m.* v.-clad, cubierto de parras. v.-grower, vinicultor, *m.* v.-growing, vinicultura, *f.* v.-leaf, hoja de parra, *f.* v.-pest, filoxera, *f.* v.-stock, cepa, *f.*

vinegar, *s.* vinagre, *m.* v.-cruet, vinagrera, *f.* v.-sauce, vinagreta, *f.*

vinegary, *a.* vinagroso

vineyard, *s.* viña, *f.*, viñedo, *m.* v.-keeper, viñador, *m.*

vinification, *s.* vinificación, *f.*

vinosity, *s.* vinosidad, *f.*

vinous, *a.* vinoso

vintage, *s.* vendimia, *f.*; (of wine) cosecha (de vino), *f.*

vintager, *s.* vendimiador (-ra)

vintner, *s.* vinatero, *m.*

viola, *s.* (*mus.*, *bot.*) viola, *f.* v. player, viola, *m.* and *f.*

violate, *v.t.* (desecrate) profanar; (infringe) contravenir, infringir; (break) romper; (ravish) violar

violation, *s.* profanación, *f.*; (infringement) contravención, *f.*; (rape) violación, *f.*

violator, *s.* violador (-ra); (ravisher) violador, *m.*

violence, *s.* violencia, *f.*

violent, *a.* violento

violently, *adv.* con violencia

violet, *s.* violeta, *f.* *a.* violado. v. colour, violeta, color violado, *m.*

violin, *s.* violín, *m.*

violinist, *s.* violinista, *m.* and *f.*

violoncellist, *s.* violoncelista, *m.* and *f.*

violoncello, *s.* violoncelo, *m.*

viper, *s.* víbora, *f.*

viperish, *a.* viperino

virago, *s.* virago, *f.*

Virgilian, *a.* virgiliano
virgin, *s.* virgen, *f.*; (sign of the zodiac) Virgo, *m.* *a.* virginal; (untouched) virgen. **the V.,** la Virgen. **v. soil,** tierra virgen, *f.*
virginal, *a.* virginal
virginals, *s.* espineta, *f.*
virginity, *s.* virginidad, *f.*
Virgo, *s.* Virgo, *m.*
virile, *a.* viril
virility, *s.* virilidad, *f.*
virtual, *a.* virtual
virtually, *adv.* virtualmente
virtue, *s.* virtud, *f.*
virtuosity, *s.* virtuosidad, *f.*
virtuoso, *s.* virtuoso (-sa)
virtuous, *a.* virtuoso
virtuously, *adv.* virtuosamente
virulence, *s.* virulencia, *f.*
virulent, *a.* virulento
virulently, *adv.* con virulencia
virus, *s.* virus, *m.*
visa, *s.* visado, *m.*
visage, *s.* cara, *f.*, rostro, *m.*; semblante, aspecto, *m.*
viscera, *s.* víscera, *f.*
visceral, *a.* visceral
viscid, *a.* viscoso
viscosity, *s.* viscosidad, *f.*
viscount, *s.* vizconde, *m.*
viscountess, *s.* vizcondesa, *f.*
viscounty, *s.* vizcondado, *m.*
viscous, *a.* viscoso
visé, *s.* visado, *m.* *v.t.* visar
visibility, *s.* visibilidad, *f.* **poor v.,** mala visibilidad, *f.*
visible, *a.* visible; aparente, evidente
visibly, *adv.* visiblemente; a ojos vistas
Visigoth, *s.* visigodo (-da)
Visigothic, *a.* visigodo, visigótico
vision, *s.* visión, *f.*; (eyesight) vista, *f.* **field of v.,** campo visual, *m.*
visionary, *a.* and *s.* visionario (-ia)
visit, *s.* visita, *f.*; (inspection) inspección, *f.*; (doctor's) visita de médico, *f.* *v.t.* visitar; hacer una visita (a); ir a ver; 'inspeccionar; (frequent) frecuentar; (Biblical) visitar. **to be visited by an epidemic,** sufrir una epidemia. **to go visiting,** ir de visita. **to pay a v.,** hacer una visita
visitation, *s.* visita, *f.*; (*ecc.*) visitación, *f.*; (inspection) in-

spección, *f.*; (punishment) castigo, *m.*
visiting, *a.* de visita. **v. card,** tarjeta de visita, *f.* **v. card case,** tarjetero, *m.*
visitor, *s.* visita, *f.*; (official) visitador, *m.*
visor, *s.* visera, *f.*
vista, *s.* vista, perspectiva, *f.*
visual, *a.* visual. **the v. arts,** las artes visuales
visualize, *v.t.* and *v.i.* imaginarse, ver mentalmente
Vitaglass, *s.* vidrio actínico, *m.*
vital, *a.* vital; esencial; trascendental
vitalism, *s.* vitalismo, *m.*
vitality, *s.* vitalidad, *f.*
vitalize, *v.t.* vitalizar, vivificar; reanimar
vitally, *adv.* vitalmente
vitals, *s. pl.* partes vitales, *f. pl.*; (*fig.*) entrañas, *f. pl.*
vitamin, *s.* vitamina, *f.*
vitiate, *v.t.* viciar; corromper, contaminar
viticultural, *a.* vitícola
viticulture, *s.* viticultura, *f.*
vitreous, *a.* vítreo, vidrioso
vitrification, *s.* vitrificación, *f.*
vitrify, *v.t.* vitrificar. *v.i.* vitrificarse
vitriol, *s.* vitriolo, ácido sulfúrico, *m.*
vitriolic, *a.* vitriólico
vituperable, *a.* vituperable
vituperate, *v.t.* vituperar
vituperation, *s.* vituperio, *m.*
vituperative, *a.* vituperador
vivacious, *a.* animado, vivaracho
vivaciously, *adv.* animadamente
vivacity, *s.* vivacidad, animación, *f.*
vivandière, *s.* vivandera, cantinera, *f.*
vivarium, *s.* vivero, *m.*
viva voce, *a.* oral. *s.* examen oral, *m.*
vivid, *a.* vivo; brillante; intenso; (of descriptions, etc.) gráfico
vividly, *adv.* vivamente; brillantemente
vividness, *s.* vivacidad, *f.*; intensidad, *f.*; (strength) fuerza, *f.*
vivification, *s.* vivificación, *f.*
vivify, *v.t.* vivificar, avivar
vivifying, *a.* vivificante
vivisection, *s.* vivisección, *f.*

vixen, s. raposa, zorra, f.; (woman) arpía, f.

viz, adv. a saber

vizier, s. visir, m. **Grand V.,** gran visir, m.

vocabulary, s. vocabulario, m.

vocal, a. vocal. **v. cords,** cuerdas vocales, f. pl.

vocalist, s. cantante, m. and f., voz, f.

vocalization, s. vocalización, f.

vocalize, v.t. vocalizar

vocally, adv. vocalmente

vocation, s. vocación, f.; oficio, m.; empleo, m.; profesión, f.

vocational, a. profesional; práctico. **v. training,** instrucción práctica, f.; enseñanza de oficio, f.

vocative, s. vocativo, m. **in the v. case,** en el vocativo

vociferate, v.t. gritar. v.i. vociferar, vocear

vociferation, s. vociferación, f.

vociferous, a. (noisy) ruidoso; vocinglero, clamoroso

vociferously, adv. ruidosamente; a gritos

vodka, s. vodca, m.

vogue, s. moda, f. **in v.,** en boga, de moda

voice, s. voz, f. v.t. expresar, interpretar, hacerse eco de; hablar. **in a loud v.,** en voz alta. **in a low v.,** en voz baja

voiced, a. (in compounds) de voz . . .; hablado

void, a. (empty) vacío; (vacant) vacante; deshabitado; (lacking in) privado (de), desprovisto (de); (without) sin; (law) inválido, nulo; sin valor. s. vacío, m. v.t. evacuar; (law) anular; invalidar

voile, s. espumilla, f.

volatile, a. volátil; (light) ligero; (changeable) voluble, inconstante

volatility, s. volatilidad, f.; ligereza, f.; volubilidad, f.

volatilization, s. volatilización, f.

volatilize, v.t. volatilizar. v.i. volatilizarse

volcanic, a. volcánico

volcano, s. volcán, m. **extinct v.,** volcán extinto, m.

volition, s. volición, f.; voluntad, f.

volley, s. (of stones, etc.) lluvia, f.; (of fire-arms) descarga, f.; (of cannon, naval guns) andanada, f.; (sport) voleo, m.; (of words, etc.) torrente, m.; (of applause and as a salute) salva, f. v.t. (sport) volear; (abuse, etc.) dirigir. v.i. lanzar una descarga, hacer una descarga

volplane, v.i. planear. s. vuelo planeado, m.

volt, s. (elec.) voltio, m.; (of a horse and in fencing) vuelta, f. **v.-ampere,** voltamperio, m.

voltage, s. voltaje, m. **v. control,** mando del voltaje, m.

voltaic, a. voltaico

Voltairian, a. volteriano

voltmeter, s. voltímetro, m.

volubility, s. garrulidad, locuacidad, f.

voluble, a. gárrulo, locuaz

volume, s. (book) tomo, m.; (amount, size, space) volumen, m.; (of water) caudal (de río), m.; (mass) masa, f.; (of smoke) humareda, f., nubes de humo, f. pl.

volumed, a. (in compounds) en . . . volúmenes, de . . . tomos

volumetric, a. volumétrico

voluminous, a. voluminoso

voluminousness, s. lo voluminoso

voluntarily, adv. voluntariamente

voluntariness, s. carácter voluntario, m.

voluntary, a. voluntario; espontáneo; libre; (charitable) benéfico; (intentional) intencional, deliberado. s. solo de órgano, m.

volunteer, s. (mil.) voluntario (-ia). a. de voluntarios. v.t. ofrecer; contribuir; expresar. v.i. ofrecerse para hacer algo; (mil.) alistarse, ofrecerse a servir como voluntario

volunteering, s. voluntariado, m.

voluptuary, s. voluptuoso (-sa); sibarita, m. and f.

voluptuous, a. voluptuoso

voluptuously, adv. voluptuosamente

voluptuousness, s. voluptuosidad, f.; sensualidad, f.

volute, s. (arch.) voluta, f.

vomica, s. vómica, f.

vomit, *v.t.* and *v.i.* vomitar; arrojar. *s.* vómito, *m.*

vomiting, *s.* vómito, *m.*

voodoo, *s.* vudú, *m.*

voracious, *a.* voraz

voraciously, *adv.* vorazmente

voracity, *s.* voracidad, *f.*

vortex, *s.* torbellino, *m.,* vorágine, *f.;* (*fig.*) vórtice, *m.*

vortical, *a.* vortiginoso

votaress, votary, *s.* devoto (-ta), adorante, *m.* and *f.;* partidario (-ia)

vote, *s.* voto, *m.;* (voting) votación, *f.;* (suffrage) sufragio, *m.;* (election) elección, *f. v.t.* votar; asignar; nombrar; elegir; (consider) tener por. *v.i.* votar, dar el voto. **casting v.,** voto de calidad, *m.* **to put to the v.,** poner a votación. **to v. down,** desechar, rechazar. **v. of confidence,** voto de confianza, *m.* **v. of thanks,** voto de gracias, *m.*

voter, *s.* votante, *m.* and *f.,* votador (-ra); elector (-ra)

voting, *s.* votación, *f.;* elección, *f. a.* de votar; electoral. **v. paper,** papeleta de votación, *f.* **v. place,** colegio electoral, *m.*

votive, *a.* votivo. **v. offering,** exvoto, *m.*

youch, *v.i.* atestiguar, afirmar; garantizar; responder (de)

voucher, *s.* (guarantor) fiador (-ra); (guarantee) garantía, *f.;* (receipt) recibo, *m.;* (proof) prueba, *f.;* documento justificativo, *m.;* vale, bono, *m.*

vouchsafe, *v.t.* conceder, otorgar

vouchsafement, *s.* concesión, *f.,* otorgamiento, *m.*

vow, *s.* voto, *m.;* promesa solemne, *f. v.t.* hacer voto (de), hacer promesa solemne (de); jurar. **to take a vow,** hacer un voto

vowel, *s.* vocal, *f.*

voyage, *s.* viaje (por mar), *m.;* travesía, *f. v.i.* viajar por mar. **Good v.!** ¡Buen viaje!

voyager, *s.* viajero (-ra)

vulcanite, *s.* ebonita, *f.*

vulcanization, *s.* vulcanización, *f.*

vulcanize, *v.t.* vulcanizar

vulgar, *a.* vulgar; (ill-bred) ordinario, cursi; (in bad taste) de mal gusto; trivial; adocenado;
(coarse) grosero. *s.* vulgo, populacho, *m.* **v. fraction,** fracción común, *f.*

vulgarism, *s.* vulgarismo, *m.;* vulgaridad, *f.*

vulgarity, *s.* vulgaridad, *f.;* grosería, *f.;* mal tono, *m.,* cursilería, *f.*

vulgarize, *v.t.* vulgarizar; popularizar

vulgarly, *adv.* vulgarmente; comúnmente; groseramente

Vulgate, *s.* Vulgata, *f.*

vulnerability, *s.* vulnerabilidad, *f.*

vulnerable, *a.* vulnerable

vulpine, *a.* vulpino; astuto

vulture, *s.* buitre, *m.*

vulva, *s.* vulva, *f.*

W

w, *s.* ve doble, *f.*

wabble. See **wobble**

wad, *s.* (of straw, etc.) atado, *m.;* (of notes, etc.) rollo, *m.;* (in a gun) taco, *m. v.t.* (*sew.*) acolchar; (furniture) emborrar; (guns) atacar; (stuff) rellenar

wadding, *s.* borra, *f.;* (lining) entretela, *f.;* (for guns) taco, *m.;* (stuffing) relleno, *m.*

waddle, *s.* anadeo, *m. v.i.* anadear

waddling, *a.* patojo, que anadea

wade, *v.i.* and *v.t.* andar (en el agua, etc.); vadear; (paddle) chapotear. **to w. in,** entrar en (el agua, etc.); (*fig.*) meterse en. **to w. through,** (a book) leer con dificultad; estudiar detenidamente; ir por

wader, *s.* el, *m.* (*f.* la) que vadea; (bird) ave zancuda, *f.;* *pl.* **waders,** botas de vadear, *f. pl.*

wafer, *s.* (host) hostia, *f.;* (for sealing) oblea, *f.;* (for ices) barquillo, *m.*

waffle, *s.* (*cul.*) fruta de sartén, *f.*

waft, *v.t.* llevar por el aire o encima del agua; hacer flotar; (stir) mecer; (of the wind) traer. *s.* (fragrance) ráfaga de olor, *f.*

wag, *s.* (of the tail) coleada, *f.;* movimiento, *m.;* meneo, *m.;* (jester) bromista, *m.* and *f. v.i.* mover ligeramente; agitar; (of

the tail) menear (la cola), colear.
v.i. menearse; moverse; oscilar;
(of the world) ir. And thus the
world wags, Y así va el mundo
wage, wages, *s.* salario, *m.*; (*fig.*)
premio, galardón, *m.* **minimum
wage,** salario mínimo, *m.*
wages clerk, pagador (-ra).
wage-earner, asalariado (-da);
(worker) trabajador (-ra)
wage, *v.t.* emprender; sostener;
hacer. **to w. war,** hacer
guerra
wager, *s.* (bet) apuesta, *f.*; (test)
prueba, *f. v.t.* (bet) apostar;
·(pledge) empeñar. **to lay a w.,**
hacer una apuesta
wages, *s. pl.* See wage
waggish, *a.* zumbón, jocoso;
cómico
waggishness, *s.* jocosidad, *f.*
waggle, *v.t.* menear; mover;
agitar; oscilar. *v.i.* menearse;
moverse; agitarse; oscilar. *s.*
meneo, movimiento, *m.*; oscilación, *f.*
wag(g)on, *s.* carro, *m.*; carreta, *f.*;
(railway) vagón, *m.* **w.-lit,** coche
cama, *m.* **w.-load,** carretada, *f.*;
vagón, *m.*
wag(g)oner, *s.* carretero, *m.*
Wagnerian, *a.* wagneriano
wagonette, *s.* carricoche, *m.*
wagtail, *s.* motacila, aguzanieves,
f.
waif, *s.* niño (-ña) sin hogar;
animal perdido o abandonado,
m.; objeto extraviado, *m.*; objeto
sin dueño, *m.* **waifs and strays,**
niños abandonados, *m. pl.*
wail, *s.* lamento, gemido, *m.*;
(complaint) queja, *f. v.i.* lamentarse, gemir; quejarse (de). *v.t.*
lamentar, deplorar
wailer, *s.* lamentador (-ra)
wailing, *s.* lamentaciones, *f. pl.*,
gemidos, *m. pl. a.* lamentador,
gemidor
wainscot, *s.* entablado de madera, *m. v.t.* enmaderar; poner
friso de madera (a)
waist, *s.* cintura, *f.*; (blouse)
blusa, *f.*; (belt) cinturón, *m.*;
(bodice) corpiño, *m.*; (narrowest
portion) cuello, *m.*, garganta, *f.*;
(naut.) combés, *m.* **w.-band,**
pretina, *f.* **w.-deep,** hasta la
cintura. **w.-line,** cintura, *f.* **w.
measurement,** medida de la

cintura, *f.* **w.-coat,** chaleco,
m. **w. strap,** trincha, *f.*
waisted, *a.* de talle . . .
wait, *v.i.* and *v.t.* esperar, aguardar; (serve) servir. **to keep
waiting,** hacer esperar. **to w.
at table,** servir a la mesa. **to
w. on oneself,** servirse a sí
mismo; cuidarse a sí mismo;
hacer las cosas por sí solo. **to
w. one's time,** aguardar . la
ocasión. **to w. for,** (until)
esperar hasta que; (of persons)
esperar (a), aguardar (a); (in
ambush) acechar. **to w. upon,**
(serve) servir (a); (visit) visitar;
presentar sus respetos (a); (*fig.,*
accompany) acompañar; (follow) seguir a
wait, *s.* espera, *f.*; (pause) pausa,
f., intervalo, *m.*; (ambush) asechanza, *f.; pl.* waits, coro de
nochebuena, *m.* **to lie in w.
for,** estar en acecho para
waiter, *s.* camarero, mozo, *m.*;
(tray) bandeja, *f.*
waiting, *s.* espera, *f. a.* que
espera; de espera; de servicio.
lady-in-w., dama de servicio,
f. **w.-maid,** camarera, doncella, *f.* **w.-room,** sala de espera,
f.; antesala, *f.*
waitress, *s.* camarera, *f.*
waive, *v.t.* renunciar (a); desistir
(de)
wake, *v.i.* estar despierto; despertarse; (watch) velar. *v.t.*
despertar; (a corpse) velar (a).
s. vela, *f.*; vigilia, *f.*; (of a corpse)
velatorio, *m.*; (holiday) fiesta, *f.*;
(of a ship) estela, *f.* **in the w. of,**
(naut.) en la estela de; después
de; seguido por
wakeful, *a.* vigilante; (awake)
despierto. **to be w.,** pasar la
noche en vela
wakefulness, *s.* vigilancia, *f.*;
(sleeplessness) insomnia, *f.*
waken, *v.i.* despertarse. *v.t.*
despertar; (call) llamar
waking, *a.* despierto; de vela.
s. despertar, *m.*; (watching) vela,
f.
wale, *s.* (weal) verdugo, *m.,*
huella de azote, *f. v.t.* azotar
walk, *s.* (pace) paso, *m.*; (modo
de) andar, *m.*; (journey on foot)
paseo, *m.,* vuelta, *f.*; (long)
caminata, *f.*; (promenade) paseo,

m., avenida, *f.*; (path) senda, *f.*; (rank) clase social, *f.*; esfera, *f.*; profesión, *f.*; ocupación, *f.* **quick w.**, paseo rápido, *m.*; (pace) andar rápido, *m.* **to go for a w.**, ir de paseo. **to take a w.**, dar un paseo (or una vuelta), pasear. **to take for a w.**, llevar a paseo, sacar a paseo. **w.-out**, (strike) huelga, *f.* **w.-over**, triunfo, *m.* (or victoria, *f.*) fácil. **w. past**, desfile, *m.*

walk, *v.i.* andar; caminar; ir a pie; (take a walk) pasear, dar un paseo; (of ghosts) aparecer; (behave) conducirse. *v.t.* hacer andar; (take for a walk) sacar a paseo; andar de una parte a otra (de), recorrer; (a specified distance) hacer a pie, andar; (a horse) llevar al paso. **to w. abroad**, dar un paseo; salir. **to w. arm in arm**, ir de bracero. **to w. past**, pasar; (in procession) desfilar. **to w. quickly**, andar de prisa. **to w. slowly**, andar despacio, andar lentamente. **to w. the hospitals**, estudiar en los hospitales. **to w. the streets**, recorrer las calles; vagar por las calles. **to w. about**, pasearse; ir y venir. **to w. after**, seguir (a), ir detrás de. **to w. along**, andar por; recorrer. **to w. away**, marcharse, irse. **to w. away with**, (win) ganar, llevarse; (steal) quitar, tomar, alzarse con. **to w. back**, volver atrás; volver a pie, regresar a pie. **to w. down**, bajar; bajar a pie; andar por. **to w. in**, entrar en; entrar a pie en; (walk about) pasearse en. **to w. on**, seguir andando; (step on) pisar. **to w. out**, salir. **to w. over**, andar por; llevar la victoria (a); triunfar fácilmente sobre. **to w. round**, dar la vuelta a. **to w. round and round**, dar vueltas. **to w. up**, subir andando; subir. **to w. up and down**, dar vueltas, ir y venir.

walker, *s.* (pedestrian) peatón, *m.*; andador (-ra); (promenader) paseante, *m.* and *f.*

walking, *s.* el andar; (excursion on foot) paseo, *m.* *a.* andante; de andar; a pie; ambulante. **at a w. pace**, a un paso de anda-

dura. **w. encyclopædia**, enciclopedia ambulante, *f.* **w.-match**, marcha atlética, *f.* **w.-stick**, bastón, *m.* **w. tour**, excursión a pie, *f.*

Walkyrie, *s.* valquiria, *f.*

wall, *s.* muro, *m.*; (rampart) muralla, *f.*; (*fig.*, and of an organ, cavity, etc.) pared, *f.* **partition w.**, tabique, *m.* **Walls have ears**, Las paredes oyen. **w. lizard**, lagartija, *f.* **w. map**, mapa mural, *m.* **w.-painting**, pintura· mural, *f.* **w.-paper**, papel pintado, *m.* **w. socket**, (*elec.*) enchufe, *m.*

wall, *v.t.* cercar con un muro; amurallar. **to w. in**, murar. **to w. up**, tapiar, tabicar

wallet, *s.* cartera, *f.*; bolsa de cuero, *f.*

wallflower, *s.* alhelí, *m.*

Walloon, *a.* and *s.* valón (-ona)

wallop, *s.* golpe, *m.* *v.t.* tundir, zurrar

wallow, *v.i.* revolcarse; encenagarse; (in riches, etc.) nadar (en). *s.* revuelco, *m.*

walnut, *s.* (tree and wood) nogal, *m.*; (nut) nuez de nogal, *f.*

walrus, *s.* morsa, *f.*

waltz, *s.* vals, *m.* *v.i.* valsar

wan, *a.* ojeroso, descolorido; (of the sky, etc.) pálido, sin color

wand, *s.* vara, *f.*; (conductor's) batuta, *f.* **magic w.**, varita mágica, *f.*

wander, *v.i.* errar, vagar; (deviate) extraviarse; (from the subject) desviarse del asunto; divagar; (be delirious) delirar. *v.t.* vagar por, errar por, recorrer

wanderer, *s.* vagabundo (-da); hombre, *m.* (*f.* mujer) errante; (traveller) viajero (-ra)

wandering, *a.* errante; vagabundo; nómada; (travelling) viajero; (delirious) delirante; (of thoughts, the mind) distraído; (of cells, kidneys, etc.) flotante. *s.* vagancia, *f.*; viaje, *m.*; (delirium) delirio, *m.*; (digression) divagación, *f.*; (of a river, etc.) meandro, *m.* **the w. Jew**, el judío errante

wane, *v.i.* (of the moon, etc.) menguar; (decrease) disminuir; (*fig.*, decay) decaer. *s.* (of the moon) menguante de la luna, *f.*; mengua, *f.*; disminución, *f.*; decadencia, *f.*

waning, *a.* menguante

wanly, *adv.* pálidamente; (*fig.*) tristemente

wanness, *s.* palidez, *f.*; (*fig.*) tristeza, *f.*

want, *v.t.* (lack) carecer de, faltar; (need) necesitar, haber menester de; (require or wish) querer, desear; (demand) exigir; (ought) deber; (do without) pasarse sin. *v.i.* hacer falta; carecer (de); (be poor) estar necesitado. **I don't w. to,** No quiero, No me da la gana. **to be wanted,** hacer falta; (called) ser llamado. **You are wanted on the telephone,** Te llaman al teléfono

wanted, se necesita; (advertisement) demanda, *f.* **Estelle wants me to write a letter,** Estrella quiere que escriba una carta. **What do you w. me to do?** ¿Qué quiere Vd. que haga?; ¿En qué puedo servirle? **What does Paul w.?** ¿Qué quiere Pablo?; (require) ¿Qué necesita Pablo? **He wants (needs) a holiday,** Le hacen falta unas vacaciones, Necesita unas vacaciones

want, *s.* (lack) falta, *f.*; escasez, carestía, *f.*; (need) necesidad, *f.*; (poverty) pobreza, indigencia, *f.*; (absence) ausencia, *f.*; (wish) deseo, *m.*; exigencia, *f.* **in w. of,** por falta de; en la ausencia de. **to be in w.,** estar en la necesidad, ser indigente

wanting, *a.* deficiente (en); falto (de); (scarce) escaso; ausente; (in intelligence) menguado. *prep.* (less) menos; (without) sin. **to be w.,** faltar. **to be w. in,** carecer de

wanton, *a.* (playful) juguetón; (wilful) travieso; (loose) suelto, libre; (unrestrained) desenfrenado; extravagante; excesivo; caprichoso; (dishevelled) en desorden; (reckless) indiscreto; (of vegetation) lozano; (purposeless) inútil; imperdonable; frívolo; (unchaste) disoluto; lascivo. *s.* mujer disoluta, *f.*; ramera, *f.*; (child) niño (-ña) juguetón (-ona)

wantonly, *adv.* innecesariamente; sin motivo; excesivamente; lascivamente

war, *s.* guerra, *f.* *a.* de guerra; guerrero. *v.i.* guerrear. **at war with,** en guerra con. **cold war,** guerra tonta, *f.* **on a war footing,** en pie de guerra. **We are at war,** Estamos en guerra. **to be on the war-path,** (*fig.*, *fam.*) buscar pendencia, tratar de armarla. **to declare war on,** declarar la guerra (a). **to make war on,** hacer la guerra (a). **war to the death,** guerra a muerte, *f.* **war correspondent,** corresponsal en el teatro de guerra, *m.* **war-cry,** alarido de guerra, *m.* **war-dance,** danza guerrera, *f.* **war horse,** caballo de batalla, *m.* **war loan,** empréstito de guerra, *m.* **war-lord,** jefe militar, *m.* **war material,** pertrechos de guerra, *m. pl.*; municiones, *f. pl.* **war memorial,** monumento a los caídos, *m.* **war minister,** Ministro de la Guerra, *m.* **war neurosis,** neurosis de guerra, *f.* **War Office,** Ministerio de la Guerra, *m.* **war 'plane,** avión de guerra, *m.* **war-ship,** barco (or buque) de guerra, *m.* **war-wearied,** agotado por la guerra

warble, *v.t.* and *v.i.* trinar; gorjear; murmurar. *s.* trino, *m.*; gorjeo, *m.*; murmurio, *m.*

ward, *s.* protección, *f.*; (of a minor) pupilo (-la); (of locks, keys) guarda, *f.*; (of a city) barrio, distrito, *m.*; (of a hospital, etc.) sala, *f.*; (of a prison) celda, *f.*; (fencing) guardia, *f.* **w.-room,** cuarto de los oficiales, *m.* **w. sister,** hermana de una sala de hospital, *f.*

ward, *v.t.* proteger, defender. **to w. off,** desviar; evitar

warden, *s.* guardián, *m.*; director (-ra); (of a prison) alcaide, *m.*; (of a church) mayordomo de la iglesia, *m.*; (of a port) capitán, *m.*

warder, *s.* (gaoler) guardián, *m.*; alabardero, guardia, *m.*

wardress, *s.* guardiana, *f.*

wardrobe, *s.* guardarropa, ropero, *m.*; (clothes) ropa, *f.*; (*theat.*) vestuario. *m.* **w. trunk,** baúl mundo, *m.*

ware, s. mercadería, f.; (pottery) loza, f.; pl. **wares,** mercancías, f. pl.

warehouse, s. almacén, m. v.t. almacenar

warehouseman, s. almacenero, m.

warfare, s. guerra, f.; lucha, f.; arte militar, m. or f. **chemical w.,** defensa química, f.

warily, adv. con cautela, cautelosamente; prudentemente

wariness, s. cautela, f.; prudencia, f.

warlike, a. belicoso, guerrero; militar, de guerra; marcial. **war-spirit,** espíritu belicoso, m., marcialidad, f.

warm, a. caliente; (lukewarm) tibio; (hot) caluroso; (affectionate) cordial, cariñoso, afectuoso; (angry) acalorado; (enthusiastic) entusiasta, ardiente; (art) cálido; (of coats, etc.) de abrigo; (fresh) fresco, reciente; (fam.) adinerado. v.t. calentar; (fig.) encender; entusiasmar. v.i. calentarse; (fig.) entusiasmarse (con). **to have a w. at the fire,** calentarse al lado del fuego. **to be w.,** (of things) estar caliente; (of coats, etc.) ser de abrigo; (of the weather) hacer calor; (of people) tener calor. **to grow w.,** calentarse; (grow angry) excitarse, agitarse; (of a discussion) hacerse acalorado. **to keep w.,** conservar caliente; calentar. **to keep oneself w.,** estar caliente, no enfriarse. **to w. up,** calentar. **w.-blooded,** de sangre caliente; ardiente. **w.-hearted,** de buen corazón; generoso; afectuoso, cordial. **w.-heartedness,** buen corazón, m.; generosidad, f.; cordialidad, f.

warming, s. calentamiento, m.; calefacción, f. a. calentador; para calentar. **w.-pan,** calentador, m.

warmly, adv. (affectionately) cordialmente, afectuosamente; con entusiasmo; (angrily) acaloradamente. **to be w. wrapped up,** estar bien abrigado

warmonger, s. propagador (-ra) de guerra

warmth, s. calor, m.

warn, v.t. advertir; prevenir; amonestar; (inform) avisar

warning, s. advertencia, f.; aviso, m.; amonestación, f.; (lesson) lección, f., escarmiento, m.; alarma, f. a. amonestador; de alarma. **to give w.,** prevenir, advertir; (dismiss) despedir. **to take w.,** escarmentar

warningly, adv. indicando el peligro; con alarma; con amenaza

warp, v.t. torcer; combar; (naut.) espiar; (the mind) pervertir. v.i. torcerse; combarse, bornearse; (naut.) espiarse. s. (in a fabric) urdimbre, f.; (in wood) comba, f., torcimiento, m.; (naut.) espía, f. **w. and woof,** trama y urdimbre, f.

warping, s. (of wood) combadura, f.; (weaving) urdidura, f.; (naut.) espía, f.; (of the mind) perversión, f. **w. frame,** urdidera, f.

warrant, s. autoridad, f.; justificación, f.; autorización, f.; garantía, f.; decreto de prisión, m.; orden, f.; (com.) orden de pago, f.; (mil.) nombramiento, m.; motivo, m., razón, f. v.t. justificar; autorizar; garantizar, responder por; asegurar. **pay w.,** boletín de pago, m.

warrantable, a. justificable

warrantor, s. garante, m. and f.

warranty, s. autorización, f.; justificación, f.; (law) garantía, f.

warren, s. (for hunting) vedado, m.; (rabbit) conejera, f.; vivar, m., madriguera, f.

warrior, s. guerrero, m.; soldado, m.

wart, s. verruga, f.

wary, a. cauto, cauteloso; prudente

wash, v.t. lavar; (dishes) fregar; (lave) bañar; (clean) limpiar; (furrow) surcar; (wet) regar, humedecer; (with paint) dar una capa de color o de metal. v.i. lavarse; lavar ropa. **Two of the crew were washed overboard,** El mar arrastró a dos de los tripulantes. **Will this material w.?** ¿Se puede lavar esta tela? ¿Es lavable esta tela? **to w. ashore,** echar a la playa. **to w. one's hands,** lavarse las manos. **to look washed out,** estar ojeroso. **to w. down,** lavar; limpiar; (remove) llevarse; (accompany with drink) regar. **to w. off,** v.t. quitar lavando; hacer desaparecer; borrar; (of waves, etc.) llevarse; (of colour) desteñir. *v.i.* borrarse; desteñirse. to w. up, lavar los platos, fregar la vajilla; (cast up) desechar

wash, *s.* lavadura, *f.*, lavado, *m.*; baño, *m.*; (clothes) ropa para lavar, ropa sucia, *f.*; colada, *f.*; (of the wàves) chapoteo, *m.*; (lotion) loción, *f.*; (coating) capa, *f.*; (silt) aluvión, *m.* w.-basin, palangana, *f.*; lavabo, *m.* w.-board, tabla de lavar, *f.* w.-house, lavadero, *m.* w.-leather, gamuza, badana, *f.* w.-out, fracaso, *m.* w.-stand, aguamanil, lavabo, *m.* w.-tub, cuba de lavar, *f.*

washable, *a.* lavable, que puede ser lavado

washer, *s.* lavador (-ra); (washerwoman) lavandera, *f.*; (machine) lavadora, *f.*; (*mech.*) arandela, *f.*

washerwoman, *s.* lavandera, *f.*

washing, *s.* lavamiento, *m.*; ropa sucia, ropa para lavar, *f.*; ropa limpia, *f.*; ropa, *f.*; (bleaching) blanqueadura, *f.*; (toilet) abluciones, *f. pl.*; (*ecc.*) lavatorio, *m.*; *pl.* washings, lavazas, *f. pl.* There is a lot of w. to be done, Hay mucha ropa para lavar. w.-board, tabla de lavar, *f.* w.-day, día de colada, *m.* w.-machine, lavadora, máquina de lavar, *f.* w.-soda, carbonato sódico, *m.* w.-up, lavado de los platos, *m.* w.-up machine, fregador mecánico de platos, *m.*

wasp, *s.* avispa, *f.* wasp's nest, avispero, *m.* w.-waisted, (of clothes) ceñido, muy ajustado

waspish, *a.* enojadizo, irascible; malicioso; mordaz

wastage, *s.* desgaste, desperdicio, *m.*

waste, *v.t.* desperdiciar, derrochar, malgastar; (time) perder; consumir; corroer; (devastate) asolar, devastar; echar a perder; malograr; disipar; agotar. *v.i.* gastarse; consumirse; perderse. to w. time, perder el tiempo. to w. away, (of persons) demacrarse, consumirse

waste, *s.* (wilderness) yermo, desierto, *m.*; (vastness) inmensi-

dad, vastedad, *f.*; (loss) pérdida, *f.*; (squandering) despilfarro, derroche, *m.*; disminución, *f.*; (refuse) desechos, *m. pl.*; (of cotton, etc.) borra, *f.*; disipación, *f. a.* (of land) sin cultivar; yermo; inútil; desechado, de desecho; superfluo. to lay w., devastar. w. land, yermo, *m.*; tierras sin cultivar, *f. pl.* w. paper, papel usado, papel de desecho, *m.* w.-paper basket, cesto para papeles, *m.* w.-pipe, desaguadero, tubo de desagüe, *m.*

wasteful, *a.* pródigo, derrochador, manirroto; antieconómico; ruinoso; inútil

wastefully, *adv.* pródigamente; antieconómicamente; inútilmente

wastefulness, *s.* prodigalidad, *f.*, despilfarro, *m.*; pérdida, *f.*; gasto inútil, *m.*; falta de economía, *f.*

waster, *s.* gastador (-ra); disipador (-ra); (loafer) golfo, *m.*

watch, *v.i.* velar; mirar. *v.t.* mirar; observar; guardar; (await) esperar; (spy upon) espiar, acechar. to w. for, buscar aguardar. to w. over, vigilar, guardar; (care for) cuidar; proteger

watch, *s.* (at night) vela, *f.*; (wakefulness) desvelo, *m.*; observación, vigilancia, *f.*; (*mil.*) (*naut.*) guardia, *f.*; (sentinel) centinela, *m.*; (watchman) sereno, vigilante, *m.*; (guard) ronda, *f.*; (timepiece) reloj de bolsillo, *m.* to be on the w., estar al acecho, estar al alerta, estar a la mira. to keep w., vigilar. dog w., media guardia, *f.* pocket w., reloj de bolsillo, *m.* wrist w., reloj de pulsera, *m.* w.-case, caja de reloj, relojera, *f.* w.-chain, cadena de reloj, *f.* w.-dog, perro guardián, *m.* w.-glass, cristal de reloj, *m.* w.-making, relojería, *f.* w.-night, noche vieja, *f.* w.-spring, muelle de reloj, *m.*, espiral, *f.* w.-tower, vigía, atalaya, *f.*

watcher, *s.* observador (-ra); espectador (-ra); (at a sick bed) el, *m.* (*f.* la) que vela a un enfermo

watchful, *a.* vigilante, alerto; observador; atento, cuidadoso

watchfully, *adv.* vigilantemente; atentamente

watchfulness, *s.* vigilancia, *f.*; cuidado, *m.*; desvelo, *m.*

watching, *s.* observación, *f.*; (vigil) vela, *f.*

watchmaker, *s.* relojero (-ra).

watchmaker's shop, relojería, *f.*

watchman, *s.* vigilante, sereno, *m.*; guardián, *m.*

watchword, *s.* (password) consigna, contraseña, *f.*; (motto) lema, *m.*

water, *s.* agua, *f.*; (tide) marea, *f.*; (of precious stones) aguas, *f. pl.*; (urine) orina, *f.*; (quality) calidad, clase, *f. a.* de agua; por agua; acuático; hidráulico. **fresh w.,** (not salt) agua dulce, *f.*; agua fresca, *f.* **hard w.,** agua cruda, *f.* **high w.,** marea alta, *f.* **low w.,** marea baja, *f.* **of the first w.,** de primera clase. **running w.,** agua corriente, *f.* **soft w.,** agua blanda, *f.* **to make w.,** (*naut.*) hacer agua; orinar. **to take the waters,** tomar las aguas, **under w.,** *adv.* debajo del agua. *a.* acuático. **w.-bird,** ave acuática, *f.* **w. blister,** ampolla, *f.* **w.-boatman,** chinche de agua, *f.* **w.-borne,** flotante. **w.-bottle,** cantimplora, *f.* **w.-brash,** acedía, *f.* **w.-butt,** barril, *m.*, pipa, *f.* **w.-carrier,** aguador (-ra). **w.-cart,** carro de regar, *m.* **w.-closet,** retrete, excusado, *m.* **w.-colour,** acuarela, *f.* **w.-colour painting,** pintura a la acuarela, *f.* **w.-colourist,** acuarelista, *m.* and *f.* **w.-cooled,** enfriado por agua. **w.-cooler,** cantimplora, *f.* **w.-finder,** zahorí, *m.* **w. front,** (wharf) muelle, *m.*; puerto, *m.*; litoral, *m.* **w.-gauge,** indicador de nivel de agua, *m.*, vara de aforar, *f.* **w.-glass,** vidrio soluble, silicato de sosa, *m.* **w. heater,** calentador de agua, *m.* **w.-ice,** helado, *m.* **w.-level,** nivel de las aguas, *m.* **w.-lily,** nenúfar, *m.*, azucena de agua, *f.* **w.-line,** lengua de agua, *f.*; (of a ship) línea de flotación, *f.* **w.-logged,** anegado en agua. **w.-main,** cañería maestra de agua, *f.* **w. man,** barquero, *m.*

w.-melon, sandía, *f.* **w. mill,** aceña, *f.* **w.-nymph,** náyade, *f.* **w.-pipe,** cañería del agua, *f.* **w. pitcher,** jarro, *m.* **w. plant,** planta acuática, *f.* **w.-polo,** polo acuático, *m.* **w.-power,** fuerza hidráulica, *f.* **w.-rate,** cupo del consumo de agua, *m.* **w. snake,** culebra de agua, *f.* **w. softener,** generador de agua dulce, *m.*; purificador de agua, *m.* **w. spaniel,** perro (-rra) de aguas. **w. sprite,** ondina, *f.* **w.-supply,** abastecimiento de agua, *m.*; traída de aguas, *f.* **w. tank,** depósito para agua, *m.* **w. tower,** arca de agua, *f.* **w. wave,** ondulado al agua, *m.* **w.-way,** canal, río (*m.*) o vía (*f.*) navegable. **w.-wheel,** rueda hidráulica, *f.*, azud, *m.*; (for irrigation) aceña, *f.* **w. wings,** nadaderas, *f. pl.*

water, *v.t.* (irrigate, sprinkle) regar; (moisten) mojar; (cattle, etc.) abrevar; (wine, etc.) aguar; diluir con agua; (bathe) bañar. *v.i.* (of animals) beber agua; (of engines, etc.) tomar agua; (of the eyes, mouth) hacerse agua. **My mouth waters,** Se me hace agua la boca

watercourse, *s.* corriente de agua, *f.*; arroyo, *m.*; río, *m.*; cauce, *m.*; lecho de un río, *m.*

watercress, *s.* berro, mastuerzo, *m.*

watered, *a.* regado, abundante en agua; (of silk) tornasolado

waterfall, *s.* salto de agua, *m.*, cascada, catarata, *f.*

wateriness, *s.* humedad, *f.*; acuosidad, *f.*

watering, *s.* riego, *m.*; irrigación, *f.*; (of eyes) lagrimeo, *m.*; (of cattle, etc.) el abrevar (a); (*naut.*) aguada, *f.* **w.-can,** regadera, *f.* **w.-cart,** carro de regar, *m.* **w.-place,** (for animals) aguadero, *m.*; (for cattle) abrevadero, *m.*; (spa) balneario, *m.*; (by the sea) playa de veraneo, *f.*

watermark, *s.* (in paper) filigrana, *f.*; nivel del agua, *m. v.t.* filigranar

waterproof, *a.* impermeable; a prueba de agua. *s.* impermeable, *m. v.t.* hacer impermeable, impermeabilizar

watershed, s. vertiente, f.; línea divisoria de las aguas, f.; (river-basin) cuenca, f.

waterspout, s. bomba marina, manga, trompa, f.

watertight, a. impermeable, estanco; a prueba de agua; (of arguments, etc.) irrefutable

watertightness, s. impermeabilidad, f.

waterworks, s. establecimiento para la distribución de las aguas, m.; obras hidráulicas, f. pl.

watery, a. (wet) húmedo; acuoso; (of the sky) de lluvia; (of eyes) lagrimoso, lloroso; (sodden) mojado; (of soup, etc.) claro; insípido

watt, s. vatio, m. **w. hour,** vatio hora, m.**w.-meter,** vatímetro, m.

wattage, s. vatiaje, m.

wattle, s. zarzo, m.; (of turkey) barba, f.; (of fish) barbilla, f.

wave, v.i. ondear; ondular; flotar; hacer señales. v.t. (brandish) blandir; agitar; (the hair) ondular; ondear; hacer señales (de). **They waved good-bye to him,** Le hicieron adiós con la mano; Se despidieron de él agitando el pañuelo

wave, s. (of the sea) ola, f.; (phys.) onda, f.; (in hair or a surface) ondulación, f.; (movement) movimiento, m.; (of anger, etc.) ráfaga, f. **long w.,** onda larga, f. **medium w.,** onda media, f. **short w.,** onda corta, f. **sound w.,** onda sonora, f. **to have one's hair waved,** hacerse ondular el pelo. **w. band,** franja undosa, escala de longitudes de onda, f. **w. crest,** cresta de la ola, cabrilla, f. **w.-length,** longitud de onda, f.

wavelet, s. pequeña ola, olita, f.; (ripple) rizo (del agua), m.

waver, v.i. ondear; oscilar; (hesitate) vacilar, titubear; (totter) tambalearse; (weaken) flaquear

waverer, s. irresoluto (-ta), vacilante, m.

wavering, s. vacilación, irresolución, f. a. oscilante; vacilante, irresoluto; flotante

waving, s. ondulación, f.; oscilación, f.; agitación, f.; movimiento, m. a. ondulante; oscilante; que se balancea

wavy, a. ondulado; flotante

wax, s. cera, f.; (cobblers') cerote, m.; (in the ear) cerilla, f. a. de cera. v.t. encerar. v.i. crecer; hacerse; ponerse. **to wax enthusiastic,** entusiasmarse. **waxed paper,** papel encerado, m. **wax chandler,** cerero, m. **wax doll,** muñeca de cera, f. **wax modelling,** modelado en cera, m., ceroplástica, f. **wax taper,** blandón, m.

waxen, a. de cera; como la cera; de color de cera

waxing, s. enceramiento, m.; (of the moon) crecimiento, m.; aumento, m.

waxwork, s. figura de cera, f.

waxy, a. See waxen

way, s. camino, m.; senda, f.; paso, m.; ruta, f.; (railway, etc.) vía, f.; dirección, f.; rumbo, m.; distancia, f.; (journey) viaje, m.; (sea crossing) travesía, f.; avance, progreso, m.; (naut., etc.) marcha, f.; método, m.; modo, m.; (means) medio, m.; manera, f.; (habit) costumbre, f.; (behaviour) conducta, f., modo de obrar, m.; (line of business, etc.) ramo, m.; (state) estado, m., condición, f.; (course) curso, m.; (respect) punto de vista, m.; (particular kind) género, m.; (scale) escala, f. **a long way off,** a gran distancia, a lo lejos. **a short way off,** a poca distancia, no muy lejos. **by way of,** pasando por; por vía de; como; por medio de; a modo de. **by the way,** de paso; durante el viaje; durante la travesía; a propósito, entre paréntesis. **in a small way,** en pequeña escala. **in a way,** hasta cierto punto; desde algunos puntos de vista. **in many ways,** de muchos modos; por muchas cosas. **in no way,** de ningún modo; nada. **in the way,** de por medio. **in the way of,** en cuanto a, tocante a; en materia de. **I went out of my way to,** Dejé el camino para; Me dí la molestia de. **Is this the way to ...?** ¿Es este el camino a ...? **Make way!** ¡Calle! **Milky Way,** vía láctea, f. **on the way,** en camino; al paso; durante el viaje. **once in a**

way, de vez en cuando; en ocasiones. **out of the way,** puesto a un lado; arrinconado; apartado, alejado; (imprisoned) en prisión; fuera del camino; remoto; (unusual) original. **over the way,** en frente; al otro lado (de la calle, etc.). **right of w.,** derecho de paso, *m.* **The ship left on its way to . . .,** El barco zarpó con rumbo a . . . **the Way of the Cross,** vía crucis, *f.* **This way!** ¡Por aquí! De este modo, Así. this way and that, en todas direcciones, por todos lados. This way to . . ., Dirección a . . ., A . . . under way, en camino; en preparación; en marcha. **to bar the way,** cerrar el paso. **to be in the way,** estorbar. **to be out of the way of doing,** haber perdido la costumbre de hacer (algo). **to clear the way,** abrir paso, abrir calle; (*fig.*) preparar el terreno. **to force one's way through,** abrirse paso por. **to find a way,** encontrar un camino; (*fig.*) encontrar medios. **to find one's way,** hallar el camino; orientarse. **to get into the way of,** contraer la costumbre de. **to get under way,** (*naut.*) zarpar, hacerse a la vela; ponerse en marcha. **to give way,** ceder; (break) romper. **to go a long way,** ir lejos; contribuir mucho (a). **to have one's own way,** salir con la suya. **to keep out of the way,** *v.t.* and *v.i.* esconder(se); mantener(se) alejado; mantener(se) apartado. **to lose one's way,** perder el camino; desorientarse; (*fig.*) extraviarse. **to make one's way,** abrirse paso. **to make one's way down,** bajar. **to make one's way round,** dar la vuelta a. **to make one's way up,** subir. **to make way,** hacer lugar; hacer sitio; dar paso (a). **to pay one's way,** ganarse la vida; pagar lo que se debe. **to prepare the way for,** preparar el terreno para. **to put out of the way,** poner a un lado; apartar; (kill) matar; (imprison) poner en la cárcel; hacer cautivo (a). **to see one's way,** poder

ver el camino; poder orientarse; ver el modo de hacer algo; ver cómo se puede hacer algo. **ways and means,** medios y arbitrios, *m. pl.* **way back,** camino de regreso, *m.;* vuelta, *f.* **way down,** bajada, *f.* **way in,** entrada, *f.* way out, salida, *f.* **way round,** camino alrededor, *m.;* solución, *f.;* modo de evitar . . ., *m.* **way through,** paso, *m.* **way up,** subida, *f.*

wayfarer, *s.* transeúnte, *m.* and *f.;* viajero (-ra)

wayfaring, *a.* que va de viaje; errante, ambulante

waylay, *v.t.* asechar, salir al paso (de)

wayside, *s.* borde del camino, *m. a.* (of flowers) silvestre; (by the side of the road) en la carretera

wayward, *a.* caprichoso; desobediente; voluntarioso; travieso; rebelde

waywardness, *s.* desobediencia, indocilidad, *f.;* voluntariedad, *f.;* travesura, *f.;* rebeldía, *f.*

we, *pron.* nosotros, *m. pl.;* nosotras, *f. pl.* (Usually not expressed apart from the verb except for emphasis or for clarity.) **We are in the garden,** Estamos en el jardín. **We have come, but they are not here,** Nosotros hemos venido pero ellos no están aquí

weak, *a.* débil; flojo; frágil; delicado; (insecure) inseguro; (of arguments) poco convincente; (of prices, markets, etc.) flojo, en baja. **w.-eyed,** de vista floja. **w.-kneed,** débil de rodillas; (*fig.*) sin voluntad. **w.-minded,** sin carácter; pusilánime; **w. spot,** debilidad, *f.;* flaco, *m.;* lado débil, *m.;* desventaja, *f.*

weaken, *v.t.* debilitar; (diminish) disminuir. *v.i.* debilitarse; flaquear, desfallecer; (give way) ceder

weakening, *s.* debilitación, *f. a.* debilitante; enervante

weaker, *a. comp.* más débil. **the w. sex,** el sexo débil

weakling, *s.* ser delicado, *m.,* persona débil, *f.;* cobarde, *m.;* (*fam.*) alfeñique, *m.*

weakly, *a.* enfermizo, delicado, enclenque. *adv.* débilmente

weakness, s. debilidad, f.; imperfección, f.

weal, s. bienestar, m.; prosperidad, f.; (blow) verdugo, m:

wealth, s. riqueza, f.; abundancia, f.; bienes, m. pl.

wealthy, a. rico, adinerado, acaudalado; abundante (en)

wean, v.t. destetar, ablactar; separar (de); privar (de); enajenar el afecto de; (of ideas) desaferrar (de)

weaning, s. ablactación, f., destete, m.

weapon, s. arma, f.; pl. weapons, (zool., bot.) medios de defensa, m. pl. **steel w.,** arma blanca, f.

wear, s. uso, m.; gasto, m.; deterioro, m.; (fashion) moda, boga, f. **for hard w.,** para todo uso. **for one's own w.,** para su propio uso. **for evening w.,** para llevar de noche. **for summer w.,** para llevar en verano. **w. and tear,** uso, m.; deterioro natural, m.

wear, v.t. llevar; llevar puesto; traer; usar; (have) tener; (exhibit) mostrar; (be clad in) vestir; (waste) gastar; deteriorar; (make) hacer; (exhaust) agotar, cansar, consumir. v.i. (last) durar; (of persons) conservar(se); (of time) correr; avanzar. **She wears well,** Ella está bien conservada. **to w. one's heart on one's sleeve,** tener el corazón en la mano. **to w. the trousers,** (fig., fam.) llevar los pantalones. **to w. well,** durar mucho. **to w. away,** v.t. gastar, roer; (rub out) borrar; consumir. v.i. (of time) pasar lentamente, transcurrir despacio. **to w. down,** gastar; consumir; reducir; agotar las fuerzas de; destruir; (tire) fatigar. **to w. off,** v.t. destruir; borrar. v.i. quitarse; borrarse; (fig.) desaparecer, pasar. **to w. on,** (of time) transcurrir, correr, pasar. **to w. out,** v.t. usar; romper con el uso; consumir, acabar con; (exhaust) agotar; (tire) rendir. v.i. usarse; romperse con el uso; consumirse

wearable, a. que se puede llevar

wearer, s. el, m. (f. la) que lleva alguna cosa

weariness, s. cansancio, m., fatiga, lasitud, f.; aburrimiento, m.; aversión, repugnancia, f.

wearing, s. uso, m.; desgaste, m. a. (tiring) agotador; cansado. **w. apparel,** ropa, f.

wearisome, a. cansado; laborioso; aburrido, tedioso, pesado

wearisomely, adv. tediosamente

wearisomeness, s. cansancio, m.; aburrimiento, tedio, hastío, m.

weary, a. cansado, fatigado; aburrido; hastiado; impaciente; tedioso, enfadoso. v.t. cansar, fatigar; aburrir; hastiar; molestar. v.i. cansarse, fatigarse; aburrirse. **to w. for,** anhelar, suspirar por; (miss) echar de menos (a). **to w. of,** aburrirse de; (things) impacientarse de; (people) impacientarse con

weasel, s. comadreja, f.

weather, s. tiempo, m.; intemperie, f.; (storm) tempestad, f. a. (naut.) del lado del viento; de barlovento. v.t. (of rain, etc.) desgastar; curtir; secar al aire; (naut.) pasar a barlovento; (bear) aguantar; (survive) sobrevivir a; luchar con. v.i. curtirse a la intemperie. **Andrew is a little under the w.,** Andrés está algo destemplado; (with drink) Andrés tiene una—mona; (depressed) Andrés está melancólico. **to be bad (good) w.,** hacer mal (buen) tiempo. **What is the w. like?** ¿Qué tiempo hace? ¿Cómo está el tiempo? **w.-beaten,** curtido por la intemperie. **w. chart,** carta meteorológica, f. **w. conditions,** condiciones meteorológicas, f. pl. **w. forecast,** pronóstico del tiempo, m. **w.-hardened,** endurecido a la intemperie. **w. prophet,** meteorologista, m. and f. **w. report,** boletín meteorológico, m. **w.-worn,** gastado por la intemperie; curtido por la intemperie

weathercock, s. veleta, f.

weathering, s. desintegración por la acción atmosférica, f.

weave, v.t. tejer; trenzar; entrelazar; (fig.) tejer. v.i. tejer. s. tejido, m.; textura, f.

weaver, *s.* tejedor (-ra)

weaving, *s.* tejido, *m.*; tejeduría, *f.* **w. machine,** telar, *m.*

web, *s.* tejido, *m.*; tela, *f.*; (network) red, *f.*; (spider's) telaraña, *f.*; (of a feather) barba, *f.*; (of birds, etc.) membrana interdigital, *f.*; (of intrigue) red, *f.*; (snarl) lazo, *m.*, trampa, *f.* **web-foot,** pie palmado, *m.* **web-footed,** palmípedo.

webbed, *a.* (of feet) unido por una membrana

wed, *v.t.* casarse con; (join in marriage, cause to marry) casar; (*fig.*) unir. *v.i.* estar casado; casarse

wedded, *a.* casado; matrimonial, conyugal; (*fig.*) unido (a); aficionado (a), entusiasta (de), devoto (de); aferrado (a). **to be w. to one's own opinion,** estar aferrado a su propia opinión

wedding, *s.* boda, *f.*, casamiento, *m.*; (with golden, etc.) bodas, *f. pl.*; (union) enlace, *m.* *a.* de boda, nupcial, matrimonial, conyugal; de novios, de la novia. **golden w.,** bodas de oro, *f. pl.* **silver w.,** bodas de plata, *f. pl.* **w. bouquet,** ramo de la novia, *m.* **w.-breakfast,** banquete de bodas, *m.* **w.-cake,** torta de la boda, *f.*, pan de la boda, *m.* **w.-day,** día de la boda, *m.* **w.-march,** marcha nupcial, *f.* **w.-present,** regalo de boda, *m.* **w.-ring,** anillo de la boda, *m.* **w. trip,** viaje de novios, *m.*

wedge, *s.* cuña, *f.*; (under a wheel) calza, alzaprima, *f.*; (mil.) cuña, mella, *f.*; (of cheese) pedazo, *m.* *v.t.* acuñar, meter cuñas; (a wheel) calzar; (fix) sujetar. **to be the thin end of the w.,** ser el principio, ser el primer paso. **to drive a w.,** (mil.) hacer mella, practicar una cuña. **to w. oneself in,** introducirse con dificultad (en). **w.-shaped,** cuneiforme

wedging, *s.* acuñación, *f.*; calzadura, *f.*

wedlock, *s.* matrimonio, *m.*

Wednesday, *s.* miércoles, *m.*

wee, *a.* pequeñito, chiquito. **a wee bit,** un poquito

weed, *s.* mala hierba, *f.*; tabaco, *m.*; (cigar) cigarro, *m.*; (person)

madeja, *f.*; (*fig.*, evil) cizaña, *f.* *v.t.* sachar, sallar, escardar; (*fig.*) extirpar, arrancar. **w.-grown,** cubierto de malas hierbas. **to w. out,** extirpar; quitar

weeder, *s.* escardador (-ra); (implement) sacho, *m.*

weeding, *s.* escarda, *f.* (also *fig.*)

weedy, *a.* lleno de malas hierbas; (*fig.*) raquítico

week, *s.* semana, *f.* **in a w.,** de hoy en ocho (días); en una semana; después de una semana. **once a w.,** una vez por semana. **a w. ago,** hace una semana. **Michael will come a w. to-day,** Miguel llegará hoy en ocho. **w. in, w. out,** semana tras semana. **w.-day,** día de trabajo, *m.* **w.-end,** fin de semana, *m.* **w.-end case,** saco de noche, *m.*

weekly, *a.* semanal, semanario; de cada semana. *adv.* semanalmente, cada semana. *s.* semanario, *m.*; revista semanal, *f.*

weep, *v.t.* and *v.i.* llorar. **to w. for,** (a person) llorar (a); (on account of) llorar por; (with happiness, etc.) llorar de. **They wept for joy,** Lloraron de alegría

weeping, *s.* lloro, llanto, *m.*, lágrimas, *f. pl.* *a.* lloroso, que llora; (of trees) llorón. **w.-willow,** sauce llorón, *m.*

weevil, *s.* gorgojo, *m.*

weft, *s.* trama, *f.*; (web) red, *f.*

weigh, *v.t.* pesar; (consider) considerar, ponderar, tomar en cuenta; comparar; (the anchor) levar. *v.i.* pesar; ser de importancia. **to w. anchor,** zarpar, levar el ancla, hacerse a la vela. **to w. down,** pesar sobre; sobrecargar; hacer inclinarse bajo; (*fig.*) agobiar. **to be weighed down,** hundirse por su propio peso; (*fig.*) estar agobiado. **to w. out,** pesar. **to w. with,** influir (en). **w.-bridge,** báscula, *f.*

weighing, *s.* pesada, *f.*; (weight) peso, *m.*; (of the anchor) leva, *f.*; (consideration) ponderación, consideración, *f.* **w.-machine,** báscula, *f.*

weight, *s.* peso, *m.*; (heaviness) pesantez, *f.*; cargo, *m.*; (of a clock and as part of a system) pesa, *f.*; (*fig.*) peso, *m.*, im-

portancia, *f. v.t.* cargar; (a
stick) emplomar; aumentar el
peso (de); poner un peso (a).
gross w., peso bruto, *m.*
heavy w., peso pesado, *m.*
light w., peso ligero, *m.* **middle w.**, peso medio, *m.* **net
w.**, peso neto, *m.* **to lose w.**,
adelgazar. **loss of w.**, (of a
person) adelgazamiento, *m.* **to
put on w.**, cobrar carnes, hacerse más gordo. · **to put the w.**,
(*sport*) lanzar el peso. **to
throw one's w. about**, (*fam.*)
darse importancia. **to try the w.
of**, sopesar. **weights and measures**, pesas y medidas, *f. pl.*
weighty, *a.* pesado; (influential)
influyente; importante, de peso;
grave
weir, *s.* presa, esclusa, *f.*; (for
fish) cañal, *m.*
weird, *a.* misterioso, sobrenatural; fantástico; mágico; (queer)
raro, extraño. · **the w. sisters**,
las Parcas
weirdly, *adv.* misteriosamente;
fantásticamente; (queerly) de un
modo raro, extrañamente
weirdness, *s.* misterio, *m.*; cualidad fantástica, *f.*; lo sobrenatural; (queerness) rareza, *f.*
welcome, *a.* bienvenido; (pleasant) grato, agradable. *s.* bienvenida, *f.*; buena acogida, *f.*;
(reception) acogida, *f. v.t.* dar
la bienvenida (a); acoger con
alegría o entusiasmo; agasajar,
festejar; (receive) acoger, recibir;
recibir ·con gusto. **W.!** ¡Bien
venido! **to bid w.**, dar la
bienvenida (a). **You are w.**,
Eres la bienvenida. **You are
w. to it**, Está a su disposición.
welcoming, *a.* acogedor, cordial,
amistoso
weld, *v.t.* soldar; combinar;
unificar
welder, *s.* soldador, *m.*
welding, *s.* soldadura, *f.*; unión,
fusión, *f.*
welfare, *s.* bienestar, bien, *m.*;
(health) salud, *f.*; prosperidad,
f.; intereses, *m. pl.* **w. state**,
Estado socialista, *m.* **w. work**,
trabajo social, *m.*
welkin, *s.* firmamento, *m.*,
bóveda celeste, *f.*, cielo, *m.*
well, *a.* bien; bien de salud;

bueno; conveniente; (advantageous) provechoso; favorable;
(happy) feliz; (healed) curado;
(recovered) repuesto. **I am
very w.**, Estoy muy bien. **to get
w.**, ponerse bien. **to make w.**,
curar. **w. enough**, bastante bien
well, *adv.* bien; (very) muy;
favorablemente; convenientemente; (easily) sin dificultad.
as w., también. **as w. as**, tan
bien como; además de. **That is
all very w. but . . .**, Todo eso
está muy bien pero . . . **to be
w. up in**, estar versado en. **to
get on w. with**, llevarse bien
con. **Very w.!** ¡Está bien!; Muy
bien. **w. and good**, bien está.
w. now, ahora bien. **w. then**,
conque; pues bien. **w.-advised**,
bien aconsejado; prudente. **w.-
aimed**, certero. **w.-appointed**,
bien provisto; (furnished) bien
amueblado. **w.-attended**, concurrido. **w.-balanced**, bien
equilibrado. **w.-behaved**, bien
educado; ·(of animals) manso.
w.-being, bienestar, *m.*; felicidad, *f.* **w.-born**, bien nacido, de
buena familia. **w.-bred**, bien
criado, bien educado; (of animals) de pura raza. **w.-chosen**,
bien escogido. **w.-defined**, bien
definido. **w.-deserved**, bien
merecido. **w.-disposed**, bien
dispuesto; favorable; bien intencionado. **w.-doing**, *s.* el obrar
bien; obras de caridad, *f. pl.*
a. bondadoso, caritativo. **w.-
done**, *a.* bien hecho. *interj.*
¡bravo! **w.-educated**, instruido,
culto. **w.-favoured**, guapo, de
buen parecer. **w.-founded**, bien
fundado. **w.-groomed**, elegante. **w.-grounded**, bien
fundado; bien instruido. **w.-
informed**, instruido; culto,
ilustrado. **w.-intentioned**, bien
intencionado. **w.-known**, bien
conocido; notorio. **w.-meaning**,
bien intencionado. **w.-modu-
lated**, armonioso. **w.-off**, acomodado, adinerado; feliz. **w.-
read**, culto, instruido. **w.-
shaped**, bien hecho; bien formado. **w.-shaped nose**, nariz
perfilada, *f.* **w.-spent**, bien
empleado. **w.-spoken**, bien hablado; bien dicho. **w.-stocked**,

bien provisto. **w.-suited**, apropiado. **w.-timed**, oportuno. **w.-to-do**, acomodado, rico. **w.-wisher**, amigo (-ga). **w.-worn**, raído; (of paths) trillado

well, *s.* pozo, *m.*; (of a stair) caja, *f.*; cañón de escalera, *m.*; (fountain) fuente, *f.*, manantial, *m.*; (of a fishing boat) vivar, *m.*; (of a ship) sentina, *f.* **w.-sinker**, pocero, *m.*

well, *v.i.* chorrear, manar, brotar, fluir

Wellingtons, *s. pl.* botas de goma, *f. pl.*

Welsh, *a.* galés, de Gales. *s.* (language) galés, *m.* **the W.**, los galeses

Welshman, *s.* galés, *m.*

Welshwoman, *s.* galesa, *f.*

welt, *s.* (of shoe) vira, *f.*, cerquillo, *m.*; (in knitting) ribete, *m.*; (weal) verdugo, *m.*

welter, *v.i.* revolcarse; bañarse (en), nadar (en). *s.* confusión, *f.*, tumulto, *m.*; mezcla, *f.* **w.-weight**, peso welter, *m.*

wen, *s.* lobanillo, *m.*

wench, *s.* mozuela, muchacha, *f.*

wend, *v.t.* dirigir, encaminar. *v.i.* ir. **to w. one's way**, dirigir sus pasos, seguir su camino

Wesleyan, *a.* wesleyano, metodista. *s.* metodista, *m.* and *f.*

west, *s.* oeste, *m.*; poniente, *m.*; occidente, *m.* *a.* del oeste; occidental. *adv.* hacia el oeste, a poniente; al occidente. **W. Indian**, de las Antillas, de las Indias Occidentales. **w.-north-w.**, oesnoroeste, *m.* **w.-south-w.**, oessudueste, *m.* **w. wind**, viento del oeste, poniente, *m.*

westerly, *a.* del oeste; hacia el oeste; occidental

western, *a.* occidental; del oeste. *s.* (novel) novela caballista, *f.*

westernized, *a.* influido por el occidente

westernmost, *a.* más al oeste

westward, *a.* que está al oeste. *adv.* hacia el oeste; hacia el occidente

wet, *a.* mojado; húmedo; (rainy) lluvioso. *v.t.* mojar; humedecer. *s.* (rain) lluvia, *f.* **Mind the wet paint!** ¡Cuidado, recién pintado! **to be wet**, estar mojado;

(of the weather) llover. **to get wet**, mojarse. **wet blanket**, (*fig.*) aguafiestas, *m.* and *f.* **wet through**, (of persons) calado, hecho una sopa. **wet-nurse**, nodriza, *f.*

wetness, *s.* humedad, *f.*; (rain) lluvia, *f.*

wetting, *s.* mojada, *f.*; humectación, *f.*; (soaking) remojo, *m.*

whack, *s.* golpe, *m.*; (try) tentativa, *f.*; (portion) porción, parte, *f.* *v.t.* golpear, aporrear, pegar

whale, *s.* ballena, *f.*; sperm w., cachalote, *m.* **w.-oil**, aceite de ballena, *m.*

whalebone, *s.* barbas de ballena, *f. pl.*, ballena, *f.*

whaler, *s.* (man) ballenero, pescador de ballenas, *m.*; (boat) buque ballenero, *m.*

whaling, *a.* ballenero. *s.* pesca de ballenas, *f.* **w.-gun**, cañón arponero, *m.*

wharf, *s.* muelle, embarcadero, descargadero, *m.* *v.t.* amarrar al muelle

wharfage, *s.* muellaje, *m.*

what, *a. pron.* (interrogative and exclamatory) qué; cómo; (relative) que; el que, *m.*; la que, *f.*; lo que, *neut.*; los que, *m. pl.*; las que, *f. pl.*; (which, interrogative) cuál, *m.* and *f.*; cuáles, *m.* and *f. pl.*; (how many) cuantos, *m. pl.*; cuantas, *f. pl.*; (interrogative and exclamatory) cuántos, *m. pl.*; cuántas, *f. pl.*; (how much, interrogative and exclamatory) cuánto, *m.*; cuánta, *f.* **And w. not**, Y qué sé yo qué más. **Make w. changes you will**, Haz los cambios que quieras. **W. confidence he had . . .** La confianza que tenía . . . **W. is this called?** ¿Cómo se llama esto? **W. did they go there for?** ¿Porqué fueron allá? **W. do you take me for?** ¿Por quién me tomas? **That was not w. he said**, No fué eso lo que dijo. **to know what's w.**, saber cuántas son cinco. **You have heard the latest news, w.?** ¿Has oído las últimas noticias, verdad? **W. a pity!** ¡Qué lástima! **W., do you really believe it?** ¿Lo crees de veras? **W. else?** ¿Qué más? **W. for?** ¿Para qué?

what's-his-name, fulano (-na) de tal, *m*. **W. ho!** ¡Hola! **W. if . . . ?** ¿Qué será si . . . ? **W. is the matter?** ¿Qué pasa? ¿Qué hay? **W. though . . .,** Aun cuando . . .; ¿Qué importa qué? **W. with one thing, w. with another,** Entre una cosa y otra

whatever, *a. pron.* cuanto; todo lo que; cualquier cosa que; cualquier. **W. sacrifice is necessary,** Cualquier sacrificio que sea necesario. **W. I have is yours,** Todo lo que tenga es vuestro. **W. happens,** Venga lo que venga. **It is of no use w.,** No sirve absolutamente para nada

wheal, *s.* See weal

wheat, *s.* trigo, *m. a.* de trigo. **summer w.,** trigo tremesino, *m.* **whole w.,** *a.* de trigo entero. **w.-ear,** espiga de trigo, *f.* **w.-field,** trigal, *m.* **w.-sheaf,** gavilla de trigo, *f.*

wheaten, *a.* de trigo; del color del trigo

wheedle, *v.t.* lagotear, engatusar; (flatter) halagar; (with out) sacar con mimos

wheedling, *a.* zalamero, mimoso; marrullero. *s.* lagotería, *f.*, mimos, *m. pl.*; (flattery) halagos, *m. pl.*; marrullería, *f.*

wheel, *s.* rueda, *f.*; (bicycle) bicicleta, *f.*; (for steering a ship) timón, *m.*; rueda del timón, *f.*; (for steering a car) volante, *m.*; (for spinning) rueca, *f.*; (potter's) rueda de alfarero, *f.*; (of birds) vuelo, *m.*; (turn) vuelta, *f.*; (mil.) conversión, *f.* **Catherine w.,** (firework) rueda de Santa Catalina, *f.* **back w.,** rueda trasera, *f.* **front w.,** rueda delantera, *f.* **to break on the w.,** enrodar. **to go on wheels,** ir en ruedas; (*fig.*) ir viento en popa. **to take the w.,** (in a ship) tomar el timón; tomar el volante. **w. of fortune,** rueda de la fortuna, *f.* **w.-chair,** silla de ruedas, *f.* **w.-house,** timonera, *f.* **w.-mark,** rodada, *f.*

wheel, *v.t.* hacer rodar; (push) empujar; (drive) conducir; transportar; llevar; pasear; (turn) hacer girar. *v.i.* girar; dar

vueltas; ir en bicicleta. **to w. about,** cambiar de frente; volverse; cambiar de rumbo

wheelband, *s.* llanta de rueda, *f.*

wheelbarrow, *s.* carretilla, *f.*

wheeled, *a.* de . . . ruedas; con ruedas. **w. chair,** silla de ruedas, *f.*

wheeling, *s.* rodaje, *m.*; (*mil.*) conversión, *f.*; (of birds) vuelos, *m. pl.*, vueltas, *f. pl.* **free-w.,** rueda libre, *f.*

wheelwright, *s.* carpintero de carretas, ruedero, *m.*

wheeze, *v.i.* ser asmático, jadear, respirar fatigosamente, resollar

wheezing, *s.* resuello, jadeo, *m.*; respiración fatigada, *f.*

whelk, *s.* (pimple) granito, *m.*; (shellfish) caracol de mar, *m.*

whelp, *s.* cachorro (-rra). *v.i.* and *v.t.* parir

when, *adv.* cuando (interrogative, cuándo); (as soon as) tan pronto como, en cuanto; (meaning "and then") y luego, y entonces; (although) aunque. **I will see you w. I return,** Te veré cuando vuelva. **W. he came to see me he was already ill,** Cuando vino a verme estaba enfermo ya. **We returned a week ago, since w. I have not been out,** Volvimos hace ocho días y desde entonces no he salido. **Since w.?** ¿Desde cuándo?

whence, *adv.* de donde (interrogative, de dónde); a donde; por donde, de que; por lo que. **W. does he come?** ¿De dónde viene? **W. comes it that?** ¿Cómo es que . . . ?

whenever, *adv.* cuando quiera que, siempre que; cada vez que; todas las veces que; cuando

where, *adv. pron.* donde (interrogative, dónde); en donde; en que (interrogative, en qué); (to where with verbs of motion) adonde (interrogative, adónde); (from where with verbs of motion) de donde (interrogative, de dónde). **W. are you going to?** ¿Adónde va Vd.? **This is w. we get out,** (of a bus, etc.) Nos apeamos aquí

whereabouts, *adv.* (interrogative) dónde; (relative) donde. *s.* paradero, *m.*

whereas, *conjunc.* visto que, ya que; mientras (que)

whereat, *adv.* por lo cual; a lo cual

whereby, *adv.* cómo; por qué; por el cual, con el cual

wherefore, *adv.* (why) por qué; por lo cual. *s.* porqué, *m.*

wherein, *adv.* en donde (interrogative, en dónde); en que (interrogative, en qué)

whereinto, *adv.* en donde; dentro del cual; en lo cual

whereof, *adv.* de que; (whose) cuyo

whereon, *adv.* sobre que; en qué

whereto, *adv.* adonde; a lo que

whereupon, *adv.* dónde; sobre lo cual, con lo cual; en consecuencia de lo cual

wherever, *adv.* dondequiera (que), en cualquier sitio; adondequiera (que). **Sit w. you like**, Siéntate donde te parezca bien

wherewith, *adv.* con que (interrogative, con qué)

wherewithal, *s.* lo necesario; dinero necesario, *m.*

wherry, *s.* chalana, *f.*

whet, *v.t.* (knives, etc.) afilar, amolar, aguzar; (curiosity, etc.) excitar, estimular

whether, *conjunc.* si; que; sea que, ya que. **W. he will or no**, Que quiera, que no quiera. **w. or not**, si o no

whetstone, *s.* afiladera, amoladera, piedra de amolar, *f.*

whetting, *s.* aguzadura, amoladura, *f.*; (of curiosity, etc.) estimulación, excitación, *f.*

whey, *s.* suero de la leche, *m.*

which, *a.* and *pron.* cuál, *m.* and *f.*; cuáles, *m.* and *f. pl.*; que (interrogative, qué); el cual, *m.*; la cual, *f.*; lo cual, *neut.*; los cuales, *m. pl.*; las cuales, *f. pl.*; el que, *m.*; la que, *f.*; lo que, *neut.*; los que, *m. pl.*; las que, *f. pl.*; (who) quien. **all of w.**, todo lo cual, etc. **in w.**, en donde, en el que; donde. **the w.**, el cual, la cual, etc. **W. would you like?** ¿Cuál quieres? **The documents w. I have seen**, Los documentos que he visto. **W. way have we to go?** ¿Por dónde hemos de ir?

whichever, *a.* and *pron.* cualquiera (que), *m.* and *f.*; cuales-

quiera, *m.* and *f. pl.*; el que, *m.*; la que, *f.*; (of persons only) quienquiera (que), *m.* and *f.*; quienesquiera (que), *m.* and *f. pl.* **Give me w. you like**, Dame el que quieras. **I shall take w. of you would like to come**, Me llevaré a cualquiera de Vds. que guste de venir

whiff, *s.* (of air) soplo, *m.*; vaho, *m.*; fragancia, *f.*

while, *s.* rato, *m.*; momento, *m.*; tiempo, *m.* **after a w.**, al cabo de algún tiempo, después de algún tiempo. **a little w. ago**, hace poco. **all this w.**, en todo este tiempo. **at whiles**, a ratos, de vez en cuando. **between whiles**, de cuando en cuando; entre tanto. **It is worth your w. to do it**, Vale la pena de hacerse. **Mary smiled the w.**, María mientras tanto se sonreía

while, *conjunc.* mientras (que); al (followed by an infinitive); al mismo tiempo que; a medida que; (although) aunque; si bien. **W. I was walking down the street**, Mientras andaba por la calle, Al andar yo por la calle. **to w.** (away), pasar, entretener. **to w. away the time**, pasar el rato

whim, *s.* capricho, antojo, *m.*; manía, *f.*; extravagancia, *f.*; fantasía, *f.*

whimper, *s.* quejido, sollozo, gemido, *m.* *v.i.* lloriquear, quejarse, sollozar, gemir

whimpering, *s.* lloriqueo, llanto, *m.* *a.* que lloriquea

whimsical, *a.* antojadizo, caprichoso; fantástico

whimsicality, *s.* capricho, *m.*; extravagancia, *f.*; fantasía, *f.*

whimsically, *adv.* caprichosamente; fantásticamente

whin, *s.* aulaga, *f.*

whine, *v.i.* gimotear, lloriquear; quejarse

whining, *s.* gimoteo, lloriqueo, *m.*; quejumbres, *f. pl.* *a.* que lloriquea; quejumbroso

whinny, *s.* relincho, hin, *m.* *v.i.* relinchar

whip, *v.t.* azotar; pegar; (cul.) batir; (sew.) sobrecoser; (ropes, etc.) ligar; (defeat) vencer. *v.i.* moverse rápidamente. **to w.**

down, *v.i.* bajar volando, bajar corriendo. *v.t.* arrebatar (de). **to w. in,** entrar précipitadamente (en), penetrar apresuradamente (en). **to w. off,** cazar a latigazos, despachar a golpes; (remove) quitar rápidamente; (persons) llevar corriendo, llevar aprisa. **to w. open,** abrir rápidamente. **to w. out,** *v.t.* (draw) sacar rápidamente; (utter) saltar diciendo (que); proferir. *v.i.* escabullirse, escaparse, salir apresuradamente. **to w. round,** volverse de repente. **to w. up,** *v.t.* (horses, etc.) avivar con el látigo; (snatch) coger de repente agarrar; (gather) reunir. *v.i.* (mount) subir corriendo

whip, *s.* azote, zurriago, *m.*; (riding) látigo, *m.* **blow with a w.,** latigazo, *m.* **to have the w.-hand,** mandar, tener la sartén por el mango; tener la ventaja. **w.-cord,** tralla del látigo, *f.*

whippet, *s.* especie de perro (-rra) lebrero (-ra)

whipping, *s.* paliza, *f.*, vapuleo, azotamiento, *m.* **w. post,** picota, *f.* **w. top,** trompo, *m.*, peonza, *f.*

whipple-tree, *s.* balancín, *m.*

whirl, *s.* vuelta, *f.*, giro, *m.*; rotación, *f.*; (*fig.*) torbellino, *m.* *v.i.* girar; dar vueltas; (dance) bailar, danzar. *v.t.* hacer girar; dar vueltas (a); (carry) llevar rápidamente. **to w. along,** volar (por), pasar aprisa (por); dejar atrás los vientos, correr velozmente. **to w. past,** pasar volando (por); pasar como una exhalación. **to w. through,** atravesar rápidamente, cruzar volando

whirligig, *s.* perinola, *f.*; (merry-go-round) tiovivo, *m.*

whirlpool, *s.* vórtice, remolino, *m.*; (*fig.*) vorágine, *f.*

whirlwind, *s.* torbellino, *m.*, manga de viento, *f.*

whirr, *s.* zumbido, *m.*; (of wings) ruido (de las alas), *m.* *v.i.* girar; zumbar

whirring, *s.* zumbido, *m.*; ruido, *m.* *a.* que gira; que zumba

whisk, *s.* cepillo, *m.*; (*cul.*) batidor, *m.*; (movement) movimiento rápido, *m.* *v.t.* (*cul.*) batir; (wag)

menear, mover rápidamente; (with off, away) quitar rápidamente; sacudirse; arrebatar; (take away a person) llevarse (a). *v.i.* moverse rápidamente; andar rápidamente

whiskers, *s. pl.* mostacho, *m.*, patillas, barbas, *f. pl.*; (of a feline) bigotes, *m. pl.*

whiskered, *a.* bigotudo

whisky, *s.* "whisky," *m.*

whisper, *s.* cuchicheo, *m.*; (rumour) voz, *f.*; (of leaves, etc.) susurro, murmullo, *m.* *v.i.* and *v.t.* cuchichear, hablar al oído; (of leaves, etc.) susurrar; (of rumours) murmurar. **in a w.,** al oído, en un susurro

whisperer, *s.* cuchicheador (-ra); (gossip) murmurador (-ra)

whispering, *s.* cuchicheo, *m.*; susurro, *m.*; (gossip) murmurio, *m.* **w. gallery,** galería de los murmullos, *f.*, (*fam.*) sala de los secretos, *f.*

whist, *s.* "whist," *m.* *interj.* ¡chitón!

whistle, *s.* (sound) silbido, silbo, *m.*; (instrument) pito, silbato, *m.*; (*fam.*) gaznate, *m.* *v.i.* and *v.t.* silbar. **blast on the w.,** pitido, *m.* **to w. for,** llamar silbando; (*fam.*) esperar sentado, buscar en vano

whistler, *s.* silbador (-ra)

whistling, *s.* silbido, *m.* *a.* silbador

whit, *s.* pizca, *f.*, bledo, *m.* **not a w.,** ni pizca

Whit, Whitsun, *a.* de Pentecostés. **W. Monday,** lunes de Pentecostés, *m.*

white, *a.* blanco; pálido; puro. *s.* color blanco, blanco, *m.*; (pigment) pintura blanca, *f.*; (whiteness) blancura, *f.*; (of egg) clara (del huevo), *f.*; hombre blanco, *m.* **Elizabeth went w.,** Isabel se puso pálida. **the w.,** (billiards) la blanca. **the w. of the eye,** lo blanco del ojo. **w. ant,** hormiga blanca, termita, *f.* **w. cabbage,** repollo, *m.* **w. caps,** (of waves) cabrillas, *f. pl.*; (of mountains) picos blancos, *m. pl.* **w. clover,** trébol blanco, *m.* **w. corpuscle,** glóbulo blanco, *m.* **w. currant,** grosella blanca, *f.* **w. elephant,** elefante (-ta) blanco (-ca). **w. ensign,** pabellón blanco, *m.* **w.-faced,** de cara pálida. **w. fish,** pescado blanco, *m.* **w. flag,** bandera blanca, *f.* **w.-haired,** de pelo blanco. **w. heat,** calor blanco, *m.,* candencia, *f.;* ardor, *m.* **w. horses,** cabrillas, palomas, *f. pl.* **w.-hot,** incandescente. **W. House,** Casa Blanca, *f.* **w. lead,** albayalde, *m.* **w. lie,** mentirilla, *f.* **w. man,** blanco, hombre de raza blanca, *m.* **w. meat,** carne blanca, pechuga, *f.* **W. Paper,** libro blanco, *m.* **w. sauce,** salsa blanca, *f.* **w. slave,** víctima de la trata de blancas, *f.* **w. slavery,** trata de blancas, *f.* **w. sugar,** azúcar blanco, azúcar de flor, *m.* **w. woman,** mujer de raza blanca, *f.*

whitebait, *s.* boquerones pequeños, *m. pl.*

whiten, *v.t.* blanquear. *v.i.* blanquearse

whiteness, *s.* blancura, *f.;* palidez, *f.;* pureza, *f.;* (*poet.*) nieve, *f.*

whitening, *s.* blanqueo, *m.;* blanco de España, *m.;* blanco para los zapatos, *m.*

whitewash, *v.t.* blanquear, jalbegar, encalar; (*fig.,* of faults) disculpar, justificar

whitewashing, *s.* blanqueo, *m.,* encaladura, *f.*

whither, *adv.* (interrogative) adónde; (with a clause) adonde

whithersoever, *adv.* adondequiera

whiting, *s.* blanco de España, *m.;* blanco para los zapatos, *m.;* (fish) pescadilla, *f.,* merlango, *m.*

whitish, *a.* blanquecino

whitlow, *s.* panadizo, *m.*

Whitsunday, *s.* domingo de Pentecostés, *m.*

Whitsuntide, *s.* pascua de Pentecostés, *f.*

whittle, *s.* navaja, *f.* *v.t.* cercenar, cortar; (sharpen) afilar, sacar punta (a); tallar; (*fig.*) reducir. **to w. away, down,** (*fig.*) reducir a nada

whizz, *s.* silbido, zumbido, *m.* *v.i.* silbar, zumbar

whizzing, *s.* silbido, *m.* *a.* que zumba

who, *pron.* (interrogative) quién, *m.* and *f.;* quiénes, *m.* and *f. pl.;*

(relative) quien, *m.* and *f.;* quienes, *m.* and *f. pl.,* que; (in elliptical constructions the person that, etc.) el que, *m.;* la que, *f.;* los que, *m. pl.;* las que, *f. pl.*

whoa, *interj.* ¡so!

whoever, *pron.* quienquiera (que); cualquiera (que); quien. **Give it to w. you like,** Dáselo a quien te parezca bien

whole, *a.* (healthy) sano; (uninjured) ileso, entero; todo. *s.* todo, *m.;* total, *m.;* totalidad, *f.;* conjunto, *m.* **on the w.,** por regla general, en general; en conjunto. **the w. week,** la semana entera, toda la semana. **w.-hearted,** sincero, genuino; entusiasta. **w.-heartedly,** de todo corazón. **w.-heartedness,** sinceridad, *f.;* entusiasmo, *m.* **w. length,** *a.* de cuerpo entero. **w. number,** número entero, *m.*

wholemeal, *s.* harina de trigo entero, *f.* *a.* de trigo entero

wholeness, *s.* totalidad, *f.;* integridad, *f.;* todo, *m.*

wholesale, *a.* (*com.*) al por mayor; en grueso; (*fig.*) general; en masa. *s.* venta al por mayor, *f.* **w. price,** precio al por mayor, *m.* **w. trade,** comercio al por mayor, *m.*

wholesaler, *s.* comerciante al por mayor, *m.* and *f.,* mercader de grueso, *m.*

wholesome, *a.* sano; saludable; (edifying) edificante

wholesomeness, *s.* sanidad, *f.;* lo sano; lo saludable

wholly, *adv.* completamente, enteramente, totalmente; integralmente; del todo

whom, *pron.* quien; a quien, *m.* and *f.;* a quienes, *m.* and *f. pl.;* (interrogative) a quién, *m.* and *f.;* a quiénes, *m.* and *f. pl.;* al que, *m.;* a la que, *f.;* a los que, *m. pl.;* a las que, *f. pl.* **from w.,** de quien; (interrogative) de quién. **The man w. you saw,** El hombre a quier *r*iste

whoop, *s.* alarido, grito, *m.;* estertor de la tos ferina, *m.* *v.i.* dar gritos, chillar; (whooping-cough) toser

whooping-cough, *s.* tos ferina, coqueluche, *f.*

whore, *s.* puta, ramera, *f.*

whorl, s. (of a shell) espira, f.; (bot.) verticilo, m.; (of a spindle) tortera, f.

whorled, a. (bot.) verticilado; (of shells) en espira

whose, pron. cuyo, m.; cuya, f.; cuyos, m. pl.; cuyas, f. pl.; de quien, m. and f.; de quienes, m. and f. pl.; (interrogative) de quién, de quiénes); **W. daughter is she ?** ¿ De quién es ella la hija ? **This is the writer w. name I always forget,** Este es el autor cuyo nombre siempre olvido

whosoever, pron. See **whoever**

why, adv. (interrogative) por qué; (on account of which) por el cual, m.; por la cual, f.; por lo cual, neut.; por los cuales, m. pl.; por las cuales, f. pl.; (how) cómo. s. el porqué, m. interj. ¡qué! ¡cómo! ¡toma!; si. **not to know the why or wherefore,** no saber el porqué ni el cómo. **Why ! I have just come,** ¡Si no hago más de llegar! **Why not ?** ¿ Por qué no ?; ¡Cómo no!

wick, s. mecha, torcida, f.

wicked, a. malo; malvado, perverso; pecaminoso; malicioso; (mischievous) travieso

wickedly, adv. mal; perversamente; maliciosamente

wickedness, s. maldad, f.; perversidad, f.; pecado, m.; (mischievousness) travesura, f.

wicker, s. mimbre, m. a. de mimbre

wicket, s. postigo, portillo, m.; (half-door) media puerta, f.; (at cricket) meta, f. **w.-keeper,** guardameta, m.

wide, a. ancho; (in measurements) de ancho; vasto; extenso; grande; amplio; (loose) holgado; (distant) lejos; liberal; general, comprensivo. adv. lejos; completamente. **far and w.,** por todas partes. **to be too w.,** ser demasiado ancho; estar demasiado ancho; (of garments) venir muy ancho. **two feet w.,** dos pies de ancho. **w.-awake,** muy despierto; despabilado; vigilante. **w.-eyed,** con los ojos muy abiertos; asombrado. **w.-open,** abierto de par en par

widely, adv. extensamente; generalmente; (very) muy

widen, v.t. ensanchar; extender. v.i. ensancharse; extenderse

widening, s. ensanche, m.; extensión, f.

widespread, a. universal; extenso; esparcido. **to become w.,** generalizarse

widow, s. viuda, f. v.t. dejar viuda; dejar viudo; (fig.) privar. **to be a grass w.,** estar viuda. **to become a w.,** enviudar, perder al esposo. **widow's pension,** viudedad, f. **widow's weeds,** luto de una viuda, m.

widowed, a. viudo

widower, s. viudo, m. **to become a w.,** perder a la esposa, enviudar

widowerhood, widowhood, s. viudez, f.

width, s. anchura, f.; (of cloth) ancho, m.; (of mind) liberalismo, m. **double w.,** (cloth) doble ancho, m.

wield, v.t. (a sceptre) empuñar; (power, etc.) ejercer; (a pen, sword) manejar

wife, s. esposa, mujer, f.; mujer, f.; comadre, f. **husband and w.,** los cónyuges, los esposos. **old wives' tale,** cuento de viejas, m. **The Merry Wives of Windsor,** Las alegres comadres de Windsor. **to take to w.,** contraer matrimonio con, tomar como esposa (a)

wifely, a. de esposa, de mujer casada; de mujer de su casa; conyugal

wig, s. peluca, f.; (hair) cabellera, f. **top wig,** peluquín, m. **wigmaker,** peluquero, m.

wigged, a. con peluca, de peluca

wigging, s. (scolding) peluca, f.

wigwam, s. tienda de indios, f.

wild, a. (of animals, men, land) salvaje; (barren) desierto, yermo; (mountainous) riscoso, montañoso; (of plants, birds) silvestre; montés; (disarranged) en desorden, desarreglado; (complete) absoluto, completo; (dissipated) disipado; vicioso; (foolish) alocado; (of the sea) bravío; (of weather, etc.) borrascoso; (mad with delight, etc.) loco; (frantic, mad) frenético, loco; (with "talk," etc.) extravagante; insensato, desatinado;

(shy) arisco; (incoherent) inconexo, incoherente; (frightened) alarmado, espantado; (wilful) travieso, indomable. *s.* tierra virgen, *f.*; desierto, *m.*; soledad, *f.* It made me w., (angry) Me hizo rabiar. to run w., volver al estado silvestre; (of persons) llevar una vida de salvajes; volverse loco. to shoot w., errar el tiro. to spread like w. fire, propagarse como el fuego. w. beast, fiera, *f.* w. boar, jabalí, *m.* w. cat, gato montés, *m.* w. duck, pato silvestre, *m.* w. goat, cabra montesa, *f.* w.-goose chase, caza infructuosa, *f.*; empresa quimérica, *f.* w. oats, avenas locas, *f. pl.*; (fig.) indiscreciones de la juventud, *f. pl.* to sow one's w. oats, andarse a la flor del berro

wilderness, *s.* desierto, *m.*; yermo, páramo, despoblado, *m.*; soledad, *f.*; (jungle) selva, *f.*; (maze) laberinto, *m.*; infinidad, *f.*

wildly, *adv.* en un estado salvaje; sin cultivo; (rashly) desatinadamente; sin reflexión, sin pensar; (incoherently) incoherentemente; (stupidly, of looking, etc.) tontamente; (in panic) con ojos espantados, con terror en los ojos, alarmado

wildness, *s.* salvajez, *f.*; estado silvestre, *m.*; naturaleza silvestre, *f.*; (ferocity) ferocidad, *f.*; (of the wind, sea) braveza, *f.*; (of the wind) violencia, *f.*; (impetuosity) impetuosidad, *f.*; (of statements, etc.) extravagancia, *f.*; (incoherence) incoherencia, *f.*; (disorder) desorden, *m.*; (wilfulness, of children) travesuras, *f. pl.*; (of the expression) gesto espantado, *m.*

wile, *s.* estratagema, *f.*, engaño, *m.*, ardid, *f.*

wilful, *a.* rebelde, voluntarioso; (of children) travieso; (of crimes, etc.) premeditado

wilfully, *adv.* voluntariamente; intencionadamente; (of committing crimes) con premeditación

wilfulness, *s.* rebeldía, *f.*; (obstinacy) terquedad, obstinación, *f.*

wilily, *adv.* astutamente

wiliness, *s.* astucia, *f.*

will, *s.* voluntad, *f.*; albedrío, *m.*; (wish) deseo, *m.*; (pleasure) discreción, *f.*, placer, *m.*; (legal document) testamento, *m.* Against my w., Contra mi voluntad. at w., a voluntad; a gusto; a discreción. free w., libre albedrío, *m.* of one's own free w., por su propia voluntad. iron w., voluntad de hierro, *f.* last w. and testament, última disposición, última voluntad, *f.* to do with a w., hacer con toda el alma, hacer con entusiasmo. to make one's w., otorgar (hacer) su testamento. w.-power, fuerza de voluntad, *f.*

will, *v.t.* querer; disponer, ordenar; (bequeath) legar, dejar en testamento, mandar; (oblige) sugestionar (a una persona) para que haga algo; hipnotizar. *v.i. aux.* querer; (As a sign of the future it is not translated separately in Spanish) I w. come to-morrow, Vendré mañana. John does not approve, but I *will* go, Juan no lo aprueba pero yo quiero ir. Do what you w., Haga lo que a Vd. le parezca bien, Haga lo que Vd. quiera; Haga lo que haga. Boys w. be boys, Los niños son siempre niños. He w. not (won't) do it, No lo hará; No quiere hacerlo

willing, *a.* dispuesto, inclinado; (serviceable) servicial; deseoso; espontáneo; complaciente; gustoso; (willingly) de buena gana. to be w., estar dispuesto (a), querer; consentir (en)

willingly, *adv.* de buena gana, con gusto

willingness, *s.* buena voluntad, *f.*; deseo de servir, *m.*; complacencia, *f.*; (consent) consentimiento, *m.*

will-o'-the-wisp, *s.* fuego fatuo, *m.*

willow, *s.* sauce, *m.* weeping w., sauce llorón, *m.* w.-pattern china, porcelana de estilo chino, *f.* w. tree, sauce, *m.*

willowy, *a.* lleno de sauces; (slim) cimbreño, esbelto, alto y delgado

willy nilly, *adv.* de buen o mal grado, mal que bien

wilt, *v.i.* (of plants) marchitarse, secarse; (*fig.*) languidecer; ajarse. *v.t.* marchitar; (*fig.*) ajar; hacer languidecer

wily, *a.* astuto, chuzón

wimple, *s.* toca, *f.*

win, *v.t.* ganar; (reach) alcanzar, lograr; (a victory, etc.) llevarse; conquistar. *v.i.* ganar; triunfar. *s.* triunfo, *m.* **to win back,** volver a ganar; recobrar

wince, *v.i.* retroceder, recular; (flinch) quejarse; (of a horse) respingar. *s.* respingo, *m.* **without wincing,** sin quejarse; estoicamente

winch, *s.* cabria, *f.*; (handle) manubrio, *m.*

wind, *s.* viento, *m.*; aire, *m.*; (flatulence) flatulencia, *f.*; (breath) respiración, *f.*, aliento, *m.*; (idle talk) paja, *f.* **breath of w.,** soplo de viento, *m.* **following w.,** viento en popa, *m.* **high w.,** viento alto, viento fuerte, *m.* **land w.,** viento terrenal, *m.* **It's an ill w. that blows nobody good,** No hay mal que por bien no venga. **There is something in the w.,** Hay algo en el aire, Se trama algo. **to get w. of,** husmear. **to sail before the w.,** navegar de viento en popa. **The w. stiffened,** Refrescó el viento. **You took the w. out of his sails,** Le deshinchaste las velas. **w.-instrument,** instrumento de viento, *m.* **w.-proof,** a prueba del viento. **w.-swept,** expuesto a todos los vientos. **w. storm,** huracán, *m.*

wind, *v.i.* serpentear; desfilar lentamente; torcerse. *v.t.* (turn) dar vueltas (a); (a handle) manejar, mover; (a watch) dar cuerda (a); (wool, etc.) devanar, ovillar; (wrap) envolver; (of arms, embrace) rodear (con); (a horn) tocar. **to w. off,** devanar; desenrollar. **to w. round,** (wrap) envolver; (skirt) rodear; (embrace) ceñir con (los brazos); (pass by) pasar por; deslizarse por; (of snakes) enroscarse. **to w. up,** (a watch) dar cuerda (a); (thread) devanar; (conclude) concluir; (*com.*) liquidar; (excite) agitar, emocionar

windbag, *s.* pandero, *m.*, sacamuelas, *m.* and *f.*

winder, *s.* (person) devanador (-ra); (machine) devanadera, *f.*; (of a clock) llave, *f.*

windfall, *s.* fruta caída del árbol, *f.*; (good luck) breva, *f.*; ganancia inesperada, lotería, *f.*

windiness, *s.* tiempo ventoso, *m.*; situación expuesta a todos los vientos, *f.*; (of speech) pomposidad, verbosidad, *f.*

winding, *a.* tortuoso; sinuoso; serpentino; en espiral. *s.* tortuosidad, *f.*; meandro, recoveco, *m.*, vuelta, curva, *f.* **w. sheet,** mortaja, *f.*; sudario, *m.* **w. stair,** escalera de caracol, *f.* **w.-up,** conclusión, *f.*; (*com.*) liquidación, *f.*

windlass, *s.* torno, *m.*

windless, *a.* sin viento

windmill, *s.* molino de viento, *m.*

window, *s.* ventana, *f.*; (of a shop) escaparate, *m.*; (in a train, car, bank, etc.) ventanilla, *f.*; (booking office) taquilla, *f.*; (of a church) vidriera, *f.* **casement w.,** ventana, *f.* **sash w.,** ventana de guillotina, *f.* **small w.,** ventanilla, *f.* **stained glass w.,** vidriera, *f.* **to lean out of the w.,** asomarse a la ventana. **to look out of the w.,** mirar por la ventana. **w. blind,** (Venetian) persiana, *f.*; transparente, *m.*; (against the sun) toldo, *m.* **w.-dresser,** decorador (-ra) de escaparates. **w. frame,** marco de ventana, *m.* **w.-pane,** cristal (de ventana), *m.* **w.-shutter,** contraventana, *f.* **w.-sill,** repisa de la ventana, *f.*, alféizar, *m.*

windpipe, *s.* traquea, *f.*

windscreen, *s.* parabrisas, guardabrisa, *m.* **w.-wiper,** limpiaparabrisas, *m.*

windward, *s.* barlovento, *m.* *a.* de barlovento. *adv.* a barlovento

windy, *a.* ventoso; expuesto al viento; (of style) hinchado, pomposo. **It is w.,** Hace viento

wine, *s.* vino, *m.*; zumo fermentado (de algunas frutas), *m.* *a.* de vino; de vinos; para vino. **in w.,** (*cul.*) en vino; (drunk) ebrio, borracho. **heavy w.,** vino fuerte, *m.* **light w.,** vino ligero, *m.* **local w.,** vino del país, *m.*

matured w., vino generoso, m.
red w., vino tinto, m. thin w.,
vinillo, m. white w., vino blanco,
m. w.-cellar, bodega, cueva, f.
w.-coloured, de color de vino.
w.-cooler, cubo para enfriar
vinos, m. w. country, tierra de
vino, f. w. decanter, garrafa
para vino, f. w.-grower, vinicultor (-ra). w.-growing, s.
vinicultura, f. a. vinícola. w.
lees, zupia, f. w. merchant,
comerciante en vinos, m. and f.,
vinatero, m. w.-press, lagar,
m. w.-taster, catavinos, m.
w. waiter, bodeguero, m.
winebibber, s. bebedor (-ra)
winebottle, s. botella de vino, f.;
(skin) bota, f.
wineglass, s. vaso (para vino), m.,
copa (para vino), f.
wineglassful, s. vaso de vino
(de), m.; copa llena hasta los
bordes, f.
wineskin, s. bota, f., odre,
pellejo, m.
wing, s. (of a bird and zool., arch.,
aer., mil., bot.) ala, f.; (flight)
vuelo, m.; (theat.) bastidor, m.;
(fig.) protección, f. v.t. dar alas
(a); llevar sobre las alas;
(wound) herir en el ala; herir en
el brazo; volar por. v.i. volar.
beating of wings, batir de alas,
aleteo, m. in the wings, (theat.)
entre bastidores. on the w., al
vuelo. to clip a person's
wings, cortar (or quebrar) las
alas (a). under his w., bajo su
protección. w.-case, élitro (de
un insecto), m. w. chair, sillón
con orejas, m. w.-commander,
teniente coronel de aviación, m.
w.-span, (zool. and aer.) envergadura, f. w.-spread, extensión
del ala, f. w.-tip, punta del ala,
f.
winged, a. alado, con alas; (in
compounds) de alas . . .; (swift)
alado; (of style) elevado, alado
wink, v.i. (blink) pestañear; (as
a signal, etc.) guiñar; (of stars,
etc.) titilar, parpadear, centellear.
v.t. guiñar (el ojo). s. pestañeo,
m.; guiño, m. not to sleep a w.,
no pegar los ojos. to take
forty winks, echar una siesta.
to w. at, guiñar el ojo (a);
(ignore) hacer la vista gorda

winking, s. (blinking) parpadeo,
m.; (as a signal) guiños, m. pl.;
(of stars, etc.) titilación, f.,
pestañeo, m. a. (of stars, etc.)
titilante. like w., en un abrir y
cerrar de ojos.
winner, s. ganador (-ra); vencedor (-ra)
winning, a. ganador; vencedor;
(attractive) encantador. s. ganancia, f. w. number, número
vencedor, m. w.-post, meta, f.
w. side, (sport) equipo vencedor,
m.; (politics, etc.) partido vencedor, m.
winnings, s. ganancias, f. pl.
winnow, v.t. aventar, abalear;
(fig.) separar
winnower, s. aventador (-ra)
winnowing, s. abaleo, aventamiento, m.; (fig.) separación, f.
w. fork, bieldo, m. w. machine,
aventador mecánico, m.
winsome, a. sandunguero; dulce,
encantador
winsomeness, s. sandunga, f.;
encanto, m., dulzura, f.
winter, s. invierno, m. a. de invierno; hiemal. v.i. pasar el
invierno, invernar. v.t. (of
cattle, etc.) guardar en invierno.
in w., en invierno, durante el
invierno. w. clothes, ropa de
invierno, f. w. palace, palacio
de invierno, m. w. quarters,
invernadero, m. w. season, invierno, m.; temporada de invierno, f. w. sleep, invernada,
f. w. solstice, solsticio hiemal,
m. w. sports, deportes de
nieve, m. pl. w. wheat, trigo de
invierno, m.
wintry, a. de invierno; invernal;
(of a smile, etc.) glacial
wipe, v.t. limpiar; (rub) frotar;
(dry) secar; (remove) quitar. s.
limpión, m.; (blow) golpe de lado,
m. to w. one's eyes, enjugarse
las lágrimas. to w. off, out, limpiar; (remove) quitar; (erase)
borrar; (kill) destruir completamente, exterminar; (a military
force) destrozar; (a debt) cancelar
wire, s. alambre, m.; hilo metálico,
m.; telégrafo (eléctrico), m.; (fam.)
telegrama, m. v.t. atar con
alambre; (fence) alambrar;
(snare) coger con lazo de alambre;

(of electrical equipment, etc.) instalar; (telegraph) telegrafiar. *v.i.* (telegraph) telegrafiar. barbed w., alambre espinoso, *m.* live w., alambre cargado (de electricidad), *m.*; (person) fuerza viva, *f.* w.-cutters, cortaalambres, *m. pl.* w.-entanglement, (*mil.*) alambrada, *f.* w. fence, alambrera, *f.*, cercado de alambre, *m.* w. gauze, tela metálica, *f.* w. nail, punta de París, *f.* w.-netting, malla de alambre, *f.*; alambrado, *m.* w.-pulling, influencias secretas, *f. pl.*; intrigas políticas, *f. pl.*

wiredraw, *v.t.* estirar (alambre), tirar (el hilo de hierro, plata, etc.); (arguments, etc.) sutilizar

wiredrawer, *s.* estirador, *m.*

wiredrawing, *s.* tirado, *m.*; (*fig.*) sutileza, *f.*

wireless, *a.* sin hilos; (of a message) radiotelegráfico; por radio. *s.* telegrafía sin hilos, *f.*; radiotelefonía, *f.*; (telegram) radiocomunicación, *f.*; (broadcasting) radio, *f.* *v.t.* radiotelegrafiar. Let's listen to the w., Vamos a escuchar la radio. portable w., radio portátil, *f.* w. engineer, ingeniero radiotelegrafista, *m.* w. enthusiast, radioaficionado (-da). w. licence, permiso de radiorreceptor, *m.* w. operator, radiotelegrafista, *m.* and *f.* w. room, cuarto de telegrafía sin hilos, *m.* w. set, aparato de radio, *m.* w. station, estación de radiotelegrafía, *f.*; (broadcasting) radioemisora, *f.* w. telegraph, telégrafo sin hilos, *m.* w. telegraphy, telegrafía sin hilos, radiotelegrafía, *f.* w. telephony, telefonía sin hilos, *f.* w. transmission, radioemisión, *f.*

wiring, *s.* instalación de alambres eléctricos, *f.*

wiry, *a.* semejante a un alambre; (of persons) nervudo

wisdom, *s.* sabiduría, *f.*; (learning) saber, *m.*; (judgment) juicio, *m.* Book of W., Libro de la Sabiduría, *m.* w.-tooth, muela del juicio, *f.*

wise, *a.* sabio; (informed) enterado, informado. a w. man, un sabio. in no w., de ningún modo. The W. Men of the East, los magos. w. guy, (*fam.*) toro corrido, *m.*

wisely, *adv.* sabiamente; prudentemente, con prudencia

wish, *s.* deseo, *m.* Best wishes for the New Year, Los mejores deseos para el Año Nuevo. w.-bone, espoleta, *f.*

wish, *v.t.* querer; desear; ansiar; (with "good morning," etc.) dar. I w. he were here! ¡Ojalá que estuviera aquí! Theresa wishes us to go, Teresa quiere que vayamos. I w. it had happened otherwise, Quisiera que las cosas hubiesen pasado de otra manera. I w. you would make less noise, Me gustaría que hicieses menos ruido. I only w. one thing, Solamente deseo una cosa. I w. you good luck, Te deseo mucha suerte. I wished him a happy Christmas, Le deseé unas Pascuas muy felices, Le felicité las Pascuas. to w. a prosperous New Year, desear un próspero Año Nuevo. to w. good-bye, despedirse (de). to w. good day, dar los buenos días. to w. for, desear

wisher, *s.* el que, *m.* (*f.* la que) desea, deseador (-ra)

wishful, *a.* deseoso; ansioso; ávido. w. thinking, ilusiones, *f. pl.*; optimismo injustificado, optimismo exagerado, *m.*

wisp, *s.* mechón, *m.*; jirón, *m.*; trozo, pedazo, *m.*

wistaria, *s.* vistaria, *f.*

wistful, *a.* ansioso; triste; patético; (envious) envidioso; (regretful) de pesar; (remorseful) de remordimiento; (thoughtful) pensativo

wistfully, *adv.* con ansia; tristemente; patéticamente; con envidia; con pesar; con remordimiento; pensativo

wistfulness, *s.* ansia, *f.*; tristeza, *f.*; (envy) envidia, *f.*; (regret) pesar, *m.*; (remorse) remordimiento, *m.*; (thoughtfulness) lo pensativo, lo distraído

wit, to, *adv.* a saber

wit, *s.* (reason) juicio, *m.*; agudeza, gracia, *f.*, rasgo de ingenio, *m.*; ingenio, *m.*; inteligencia, *f.*, talento, *m.*; (person) hombre de

ingenio, *m.*; mujer de ingenio, *f.*
my five wits, mis cinco sentidos.
to be at one's wits' end, no
saber qué hacer. to live by
one's wits, ser caballero de
industria. to lose one's wits,
perder el juicio

witch, *s.* bruja, *f.* Witches'
Sabbath, aquelarre, *m.* w.-
doctor, hechicero, mago, *m.*
witch-hazel, carpe, *m.*; loción
de carpe, *f.*

witchcraft, *s.* brujería, *f.*; sortilegio, encantamiento, *m.*

witchery, *s.* brujería, *f.*; (*fig.*)
encanto, *m.*, magia, *f.*

with, *prep.* con; en compañía de;
en casa de; (against) contra;
(among) entre; en; (by) por;
(towards) hacia; para con; (according to) según; (notwithstanding) a pesar de; a; (concerning) con respecto a; en el
caso de. Rose is w. Antony,
Rosa está con Antonio. He was
w. his dog, Estaba acompañado
por su perro. He pulled at it
w. both hands, Lo tiró con las
dos manos. filled w. fear,
lleno de miedo. to shiver w.
cold, temblarse de frío. the
girl w. golden hair, la muchacha del pelo dorado. They
killed it w. one blow, Lo
mataron de un solo golpe. It
rests w. you to decide, Tú
tienes que decidirlo; Te toca a tí
el decidirlo. to begin w., para
empezar; empezar por. w. all
speed, a toda prisa. to part
w., desprenderse de; (of people)
despedirse de; separarse de. w.
that ..., (at once) en esto ...

withal, *adv.* además; al mismo
tiempo. *prep.* con

withdraw, *v.t.* retirar; (words)
retractar; (remove) quitar, privar
(de); (a legal action) apartar.
v.i. retirarse; retroceder; apartarse; irse

withdrawal, *s.* retirada, *f.*; (retirement) retiro, *m.*; apartamiento, *m.*

withdrawn, *a.* (abstracted) ensimismado, meditabundo

wither, *v.i.* marchitarse, secarse,
ajarse. *v.t.* marchitar, secar,
ajar; (*fig.*) hacer languidecer,
matar; (snub) avergonzar

withered, *a.* marchito, mustio;
muerto; (of persons) acartonado,
seco

witheredness, *s.* marchitez, *f.*;
sequedad, *f.*

withering, *a.* que marchita;
(scorching) abrasador, ardiente;
(scornful) despreciativo, desdeñoso; (biting) mordaz, cáustico

withers, *s.* cruz, *f.*

withhold, *v.t.* retener; detener;
(restrain) refrenar; apartar; (refuse) negar; abstenerse de; (refuse to reveal) ocultar

withholding, *s.* detención, *f.*;
(refusal) negación, *f.*

within, *adv.* dentro, adentro; en
el interior; en casa; (*fig.*) en su
interior. He stayed w., Se
quedó dentro. Is Mrs. González w.? ¿Está en casa la Sra
González?

within, *prep.* dentro de; el interior de; en; entre; (within
range of) al alcance de; a la
distancia de; (near) cerca de; a
poco de; (of time) en el espacio
de, en; dentro de; (almost) por
poco, casi. He was w. an ace
of being killed, Por poco le
mataron. to be w. hearing,
estar al alcance de la voz. seen
from w., visto desde dentro.
twice w. a fortnight, dos veces
en quince días. w. himself, por
sus adentros, entre sí. w. an
inch of, (*fig.*) a dos dedos de.
w. a few miles of Edinburgh,
a unas millas de Edimburgo.
w. a short distance, en una
corta distancia; a poca distancia

without, *prep.* sin; falto de; (outside) fuera de; (beyond) más
allá de. *adv.* exteriormente; por
fuera; hacia afuera; fuera. It
goes w. saying, No hay que
decir. w. more ado, sin más ni
más. W. my knowledge, Sin
que yo lo supiese. w. regard
for, sin pensar en. w. saying
more, sin decir más

withstand, *v.t.* resistir, oponerse
(a); soportar

withstanding, *s.* resistencia,
oposición (a), *f.*

witless, *a.* sin seso, tonto, necio

witness, *s.* (evidence) testimonio,
m.; (person) testigo, *m.* and *f.*;
espectador (-ra). in w. whereof,

en fe de lo cual. **to bear w.,** atestiguar, dar testimonio. **to bring forward witnesses,** hacer testigos. **w. my hand,** en fe de lo cual, firmo. **w.-box,** puesto de los testigos, *m.* **w. for the defence,** testigo de descargo, *m.* and *f.* **w. for the prosecution,** testigo de cargo, *m.* and *f.*

witness, *v.t.* (show) mostrar, señalar; (see) ser testigo de, ver, presenciar; (*law*) atestiguar. *v.i.* dar testimonio; servir de testigo

witticism, *s.* rasgo de ingenio, donaire, *m.*, agudeza, *f.*

wittily, *adv.* ingeniosamente, donairosamente, agudamente

wittiness, *s.* viveza de ingenio, donosura, *f.*

witty, *a.* salado, gracioso. **w. sally,** agudeza, *f.*

wizard, *s.* mago, hechicero, *m.*

wizardry, *s.* magia, *f.*

wizened, *a.* seco, arrugado; (of persons) acartonado

woad, *s.* hierba pastel, gualda, *f.*

wobble, *v.i.* tambalearse, balancearse; (quiver) temblar; oscilar; (*mech.*) galopar; (stagger) titubear; (*fig.*) vacilar

wobbly, *a.* que se bambolea; inestable; (*fig.*) vacilante

woe, *s.* dolor, *m.*; congoja, aflicción, *f.*; mal, desastre, infortunio, *m.* **Woe is me!** ¡Ay de mí! ¡Desdichado de mí!

woebegone, *a.* angustiado

woeful, *a.* triste; doloroso; funesto

woefully, *adv.* tristemente; dolorosamente

wold, *s.* campiña, llanura, *f.*

wolf, *s.* lobo (-ba). **a w. in sheep's clothing,** un lobo en piel de cordero. **to cry "w., w.,"** gritar "al lobo." **to keep the w. from the door,** ponerse a cubierto del hambre. **w.-cub,** lobezno, *m.* **w.-hound,** perro lobo, *m.* **w. pack,** manada de lobos, *f.*

wolfish, *a.* lobuno, de lobo

wolfram, *s.* volframio, *m.*

woman, *s.* mujer, *f.*; hembra, *f.*; (lady-in-waiting) dama de servicio, *f.* **a fine figure of a w.,** una real hembra. **w. doctor,**

médica, *f.* **w.-hater,** misógino, *m.* **w. of the town,** mujer de la vida airada, *f.* **w. of the world,** mujer de mundo, *f.*

womanhood, *s.* feminidad, *f.*; sexo feminino, *m.*

womanish, *a.* afeminado

womankind, *s.* el sexo femenino, las mujeres

womanliness, *s.* feminidad, *f.*; carácter femenino, *m.*

womanly, *a.* femenino, de mujer

womb, *s.* útero, *m.*, matriz, *f.*; (*fig.*) seno, *m.*

wonder, *s.* maravilla, *f.*; prodigio, *m.*; portento, milagro, *m.*; (surprise) sorpresa, *f.*; admiración, *f.*; asombro, *m.*; (problem) enigma, *m.*; misterio, *m.* *v.i.* admirarse, asombrarse, maravillarse; sorprenderse. *v.t.* (ask oneself) preguntarse; desear saber. **I wondered what the answer would be,** Me preguntaba qué sería la respuesta. **It is no w. that . . .,** No es mucho que . . ., No es sorprendente que . . . **It is one of the wonders of the world,** Es una de las maravillas del mundo. **to work wonders,** hacer milagros. **to w. at,** asombrarse de, maravillarse de; sorprenderse de. **w.-working,** milagroso

wonderful, *a.* maravilloso; magnífico; asombroso; (*fam.*) estupendo

wonderfully, *adv.* maravillosamente; admirablemente

wondering, *a.* de asombro, sorprendido; perplejo

wonderingly, *adv.* con asombro

wonderland, *s.* mundo fantástico, *m.*; reino de las hadas, *m.*; país de las maravillas, *m.* **"Alice in W.,"** Alicia en el país de las maravillas

wonderment, *s.* See **wonder**

wondrous, *a.* maravilloso. *adv.* extraordinariamente

wont, *s.* costumbre, *f.* *v.i.* soler. **As he was w.,** Como solía

won't. See **will not**

wonted, *a.* sólito, acostumbrado

woo, *v.t.* galantear; hacer la corte (a); cortejar; (*fig.*) solicitar; perseguir

wood, *s.* bosque, *m.*; madera, *f.*; (for the fire, etc.) leña, *f.*; (cask) barril, *m. a.* de madera; (of the woods) selvático. **dead w.,** ramas muertas, *f. pl.;* (*fig.*) paja, *f.* **w. alcohol,** alcohol metílico, *m.* **w.-anemone,** anémona de los bosques, *f.* **w.-block floor,** entarimado, *m.* **w.-borer,** xilófago, *m.* **w.-carver,** tallista, *m.* and *f.* **w.-carving,** talla en madera, *f.* **w.-craft,** conocimiento del campo, *m.* **w.-cut,** grabado en madera, *m.* **w.-cutter,** leñador, *m.* **w.-engraver,** grabador (-ra) en madera. **w.-engraving,** grabado al boj, *m.* **w.-fibre,** fibra de madera, *f.* **w.-louse,** cochinilla, *f.* **w.-nymph,** ninfa de los bosques, *f.* **w.-pigeon,** paloma torcaz, *f.* **w.-pile,** pila de leña, leñera, *f.* **w.-pulp,** pulpa de madera, *f.* **w.-shaving,** acepilladura, *f.* **w.-splinter,** tasquil, *m.,* astilla, *f.* **w.-wind,** (*mus.*) madera, *f.* **w.-worm,** carcoma, *f.*

woodbine, madreselva, *f.*

woodcock, *s.* chocha, *f.*

wooded, *a.* provisto de árboles, plantado de árboles, arbolado

wooden, *a.* de madera, de palo; (of smiles) mecánico; (stiff) indiferente, sin emoción; (clumsy) torpe; (of character) inflexible. He has a w. leg, Tiene una pata de palo. **w. beam,** madero, *m.;* viga de madera, *f.* **w. bridge,** pontón, *m.* **w. galley,** (*print.*) galerín, *m.*

woodland, *s.* bosques, *m. pl. a.* de bosque; silvestre

woodpecker, *s.* pájaro carpintero, picamaderos, *m.*

woodshed, *s.* leñera, *f.*

woodwork, *s.* maderaje, *m.;* molduras, *f. pl.;* carpintería, *f.*

woody, *a.* leñoso; arbolado, con árboles. **w. tissue,** tejido leñoso, *m.*

wooer, *s.* pretendiente, galanteador, *m.*

woof, *s.* trama, *f.*

wooing, *s.* galanteo, *m.*

wool, *s.* lana, *f. a.* de lana; lanar. to go w.-gathering, estar distraído. to pull the w. over a person's eyes, engañar como a un chino. **w.-bearing,** lánar. **w.-carding,** cardadura de lana, *f.* **w.-growing,** cría de ganado

lanar, *f.* **w. merchant,** comerciante en lanas, *m.* and *f.,* **lanero,** *m.* **w.-pack,** fardo de lana, *m.* **w. trade,** comercio de lana, *m.*

woollen, *a.* de lana; lanar. *s.* paño de lana, *m.;* género de punta de lana, *m.*

woolliness, *s.* lanosidad, *f.*

woolly, *a.* lanudo, lanoso; de lana; (*bot.*) velloso; (of hair) lanoso, crespo. *s.* género de punta de lana, *m.;* (sweater) jersey, *m.*

woolsack, *s.* fardo de lana, *m.;* asiento del Presidente de la Cámara de los Lores, *m.;* (*fig.*) dignidad de gran canciller, *f.*

word, *s.* palabra, *f.;* (*gram.*) vocablo, *m.;* (*theol.*) verbo, *m.;* (maxim) sentencia, *f.,* dicho, *m.;* (message) recado, *m.;* (news) aviso, *m.,* noticias, *f. pl.;* (*mil.*) command) voz de mando, *f.;* (order) orden, *f.;* (password) contraseña, *f.;* (term) término, *m. v.t.* expresar; formular; (draw up) redactar; escribir. He was as good as his w., Fué hombre de palabra. I do not know how to w. this letter, No sé cómo redactar esta carta. in a w., en una palabra; en resumidas cuentas. by w. of mouth, de palabra. I give you my w. for it, Le doy mi palabra de honor. in other words, en otros términos; en efecto. the W. (of God), el Verbo (de Dios). to have a w. with, hablar con; conversar con; entablar conversación con. to leave w., dejar recado. to have words with, tener palabras con. to keep one's w., cumplir su palabra

wordiness, *s.* palabrería, verbosidad, *f.*

wording, *s.* fraseología, *f.;* expresión, *f.;* estilo, *m.;* (terms) términos, *m. pl.;* (drawing up) redacción, *f.*

wordy, *a.* verboso, prolijo

work, *s.* trabajo, *m.;* (sewing) labor, *f.;* (literary, artistic production and theological) obra, *f.;* (behaviour) acción, *f.,* acto, *m.;* (employment) empleo, *m.;* (business affairs) negocios, *m. pl.;* pl. **works,** obras, fortificaciones, *f.*

pl.; obras públicas, *f. pl.*; construcciones, *f. pl.*; (of a machine) mecanismo, *m.*; motor, *m.*; (factory) fábrica, *f.*, taller, *m.* a w. of art, una obra de arte. w. accident, accidente del trabajo, *m.* w.-bag, bolsa de costura, *f.*, saco de labor, *m.* w.-box, (on legs) costurero, *m.*; (small) neceser de costura, *m.* w.-people, obreros (-as). w.-room, taller, *m.*; (study) estudio, *m.*; (for sewing) cuarto de costura, *m.* w.-table, banco de taller, *m.*; (for writing) mesa de escribir, *f.* work, *v.i.* trabajar; (sew.) hacer labor de aguja, coser; (embroider) bordar; (mech.) funcionar, marchar; (succeed) tener éxito; ser eficaz; (be busy) estar ocupado; (be employed) tener empleo; (of the face) demudarse, torcerse; (ferment) fermentar; (operate) obrar. *v.t.* trabajar; operar, hacer funcionar; mover; (control) manejar; (a mine) explotar; (embroider) bordar; (wood) tallar; (a problem) resolver; calcular; (iron, etc.) labrar; (the soil) cultivar; (a ship) maniobrar; (do) hacer; (bring about) efectuar; traer consigo; producir; (agitate oneself) agitarse, emocionarse, excitarse. to w. in repoussé, repujar. to w. loose, desprenderse. to w. one's passage, trabajar por el pasaje. to w. overtime, trabajar horas extraordinarias. to w. two ways, ser una arma de dos filos. to w. at, trabajar en; ocuparse en; dedicarse a; elaborar. to w. in, *v.t.* introducir; insinuar. *v.i.* combinarse. to w. into, penetrar en. to w. off, usar, emplear; (get rid of) deshacerse de, librarse de. to w. on, upon, influir en; obrar sobre; estar ocupado en. to w. out, *v.t.* calcular; resolver; (a mine, topic, etc.) agotar; (develop) elaborar, desarrollar; trazar, planear; (find) encontrar. *v.i.* llegar (a); resultar; venir a ser. to w. up, crear; (promote) fomentar; producir; (excite) agitar, excitar; (fashion) dar forma (a), labrar; (finish) terminar

workable, *a.* laborable; factible, practicable; (of a mine) explotable

workableness, *s.* practicabilidad, *f.*

workaday, *a.* de todos los días; prosaico

workday, *s.* día de trabajo, *m.*

worker, *s.* trabajador (-ra); (manual) obrero (-ra); (of a machine) operario (-ia). w.-ant, hormiga obrera, *f.* w.-bee, abeja obrera, *f.*

workhouse, *s.* asilo, *m.*

working, *a.* de trabajo; (of capital) de explotación; trabajador, que trabaja; obrero. *s.* trabajo, *m.*; (of a machine, organism, institution) funcionamiento, *m.*; explotación, *f.*; (of a mine) laboreo, *m.*; (of a ship) maniobra, *f.*; (of metal, stone, wood) labra, *f.*; operación, *f.*; (result) efecto, resultado, *m.*; (calculation) cálculo, *m.* Not w., No funciona. to be in w. order, funcionar bien. w.-class, clase obrera, *f.*; pueblo, *m.* w.-clothes, ropa de trabajo, *f.* w.-day, día de trabajo, *m.* w.-hours, horas de trabajo, horas hábiles, *f. pl.* w. hypothesis, postulado, *m.* w.-man, obrero, *m.*; trabajador, *m.* w.-out, elaboración, *f.*; ensayo, *m.* w.-plan, plan de trabajo, *m.* w.-woman, obrera, *f.*; trabajadora, *f.*

workless, *a.* sin trabajo

workman, *s.* obrero, *m.*; (agricultural) labrador, *m.*

workmanlike, *a.* bien hecho, bien acabado; (clever) hábil

workmanship, *s.* trabajo, *m.*; manufactura, *f.*; hechura, *f.*; (cleverness) habilidad, *f.*

works, *s.* fábrica, *f.*

workshop, *s.* taller, *m.*

world, *s.* mundo, *m.* For all the w. as if . . . Exactamente como si . . . to see the w., ver mundo. to treat the w. as one's oyster, ponerse el mundo por montera. w. without end, por los siglos de los siglos. w.-power, potencia mundial; gran potencia, *f.* w.-wide, mundial, universal

worldliness, s. mundanería, f., conocimiento del mundo, m.; frivolidad, vanidad mundana, f.; egoísmo, m.; prudencia, f.

worldly, a. de este mundo; mundano; humano; profano; frívolo. **to be w.-wise,** tener mucho mundo

worm, s. gusano, m.; lombriz, f.; (chem.) serpentín, m.; (of a screw) tornillo sin fin, m.; (person) gusano, m.; (fig.) gusano roedor, remordimiento, m. **intestinal w.,** lombriz intestinal, f. **the w. of conscience,** el gusano de la conciencia. **w.-eaten,** carcomido. **w.-hole,** picadura de gusano, lombriguera, f. **w.-powder,** polvos antihelmínticos, m. pl. **w.-shaped,** vermiforme

worm, v.t. (a dog) dar un vermífugo (a). v.i. arrastrarse como un gusano. **to w. one's way into,** deslizarse en; (fig.) insinuarse en, introducirse en. **to w. out,** (secrets, information) sonsacar

wormwood, s. ajenjo, m.

wormy, a. gusanoso, lleno de gusanos

worn, a. (of garments) raído; estropeado; gastado; (of paths) trillado; (of the face) arrugado, cansado. **w. out,** acabado; muy usado; (tired) rendido; (exhausted) agotado

worrier, s. inquietador (-ra); receloso (-sa); aprensivo (-va)

worry, s. preocupación, inquietud, ansiedad, f.; problema, cuidado, m. v.t. (prey) zamarrear; preocupar, inquietar; molestar; importunar. v.i. estar preocupado, estar intranquilo, inquietarse

worrying, a. inquietante, perturbador; molesto

worse, a. comp. peor; inferior. adv. peor; menos. s. lo peor. **so much the w.,** tanto peor. **to be w. off,** estar peor; estar en peores circunstancias; ser menos feliz. **to be the w. for wear,** ser muy usado; estar ajado; ser ya viejo. **to grow w.,** empeorarse; (of an ill person) ponerse peor. **w. and w.,** de mal en peor, peor que peor. **w. than ever,** peor que nunca

worsen, v.t. agravar, hacer peor; exasperar. v.i. agravarse, empeorarse; exasperarse

worsening, s. agravación, f., empeoramiento, m.; exasperación, f.

worship, s. culto, m.; adoración, f.; veneración, f. v.t. adorar; reverenciar. v.i. adorar; rezar; dar culto ·(a). **place of w.,** edificio de culto, m. **Your W.,** vuestra merced

worshipful, a. venerable, respetable

worshipper, s. adorador (-ra); pl. worshippers, (in a church, etc.) fieles, m. pl., congregación, f.

worshipping, s. adoración, f., culto, m.

worst, a. el (la, etc.) peor; más malo. adv. el (la, etc.) peor. s. el (la, etc.) peor; lo peor. v.t. vencer, derrotar; triunfar sobre. **If the w. comes to the w.,** En el peor de los casos. **The w. of it is that . . .,** Lo peor es que . . . **to have the w. of it,** salir perdiendo, llevar la peor parte

worsted, s. estambre, m. a. de estambre

worth, s. valor, m.; precio, m.; mérito, m. a. (que) vale; de precio de; cuyo valor es de; equivalente a; (que) merece; digno de. **He bought ten pesetas' w. of sweets,** Compró diez pesetas de dulces. **He sang for all he was w.,** Cantó con toda su alma. **It is w. seeing,** Es digno de verse, Vale la pena de verse. **to be w.,** valer. **to be w. while,** valer la pena, merecer la pena

worthily, adv. dignamente

worthiness, s. mérito, valor, m.

worthless, a. sin valor; sin mérito; inútil; malo; (of persons) vil, despreciable, indigno

worthlessness, s. falta de valor, f.; falta de mérito, f.; inutilidad, f.; (of persons) bajeza, vileza, f.

worthy, a. digno de respeto, benemérito, respetable; digno, merecedor; meritorio. s. varón ilustre, hombre célebre, m.; héroe, m.; (fam., iron.) 'tio, m. **to be w. of,** ser digno de, merecer

would, *preterite* and *subjunctive* of **will**. (indicating a conditional tense) **They w. come if . . .,** Vendrían si . . .; (indicating an imperfect tense) **Often he w. sing,** Muchas veces cantaba, Muchas veces solía (or acostumbraba) cantar; (indicating a preterite tense) **Now and then a blackbird w. whistle,** De vez en cuando silbó un mirlo; (expressing wish, desire) **What w. they?** ¿Qué quieren? **The place where I w. be,** El lugar donde quisiera estar. **W. I were at home!** ¡Ojalá que estuviese en casa! **I thought that I w. tell you,** Se me ocurrió la idea de decírselo. **It w. seem that . . .,** Parece ser que . . ., Según parece . . .; Se diría que . . . **He said that he w. never have done it,** Dijo que no lo hubiera hecho nunca. **They w. have been killed if he had not rescued them,** Habrían sido matados si él no los hubiese salvado. **He** *would* **go,** Se empeñó en ir. **He w. not do it,** Rehusó hacerlo, Se resistió a hacerlo; No quiso hacerlo. **This w. probably be the house,** Sin duda esta sería la casa. **W. you be good enough to . . .,** Tenga Vd. la bondad de . . ., Haga el favor de . . .

would-be, *a.* supuesto; llamado; aspirante (a); en esperanza de (followed by infin.); (frustrated) frustrado, malogrado

wound, *s.* herida, *f.* *v.t.* herir; (the feelings) lastimar, lacerar. **deep w.,** herida penetrante, *f.* **the wounded,** los heridos.

wounding, *s.* herida, *f.* *a.* (*fig.*) lastimador

wraith, *s.* fantasma, espectro, *m.*, sombra, *f.*

wrangle, *v.i.* discutir; altercar, disputar acaloradamente; reñir; (bargain) regatear. *s.* argumento, *m.*; disputa, *f.*, altercado, *m.*; riña, *f.*

wrangler, *s.* disputador (-ra); (Cambridge University) laureado en matemáticas, *m.*

wrangling, *s.* disputas, *f. pl.*, altercación, *f.*; (bargaining) regateo, *m.*

wrap, *v.t.* envolver; arrollar; cubrir; abrigar; (conceal) ocultar. *s.* envoltorio, *m.*; abrigo, *m.*; *pl.* **wraps,** abrigos y mantas de viaje, *m. pl.* **W. yourself up well!** ¡Abrígate bien! **to be wrapped up in,** estar envuelto en; (*fig.*) estar entregado a, estar absorto en; (a person) estar embelesado con

wrapper, *s.* envoltura, *f.*; embalaje, *m.*; (of a newspaper) faja, *f.*; (of a book) sobrecubierta, *f.*; (dressing-gown) bata, *f.*, salto de cama, *m.*

wrapping, *s.* envoltura, cubierta, *f.* **w.-paper,** papel de envolver, *m.*

wrath, *s.* ira, *f.*

wrathful, *a.* airado

wrathfully, *adv.* airadamente

wreak, *v.t.* ejecutar; (anger, etc.) descargar. **to w. one's vengeance,** vengarse

wreath, *s.* guirnalda, *f.*; corona, *f.*; trenza, *f.* **funeral w.,** corona funeraria, *f.*

wreathe, *v.t.* trenzar; (entwine) entrelazar (de); (garland) coronar (de), enguirnaldar (con); (encircle) ceñir, rodear; (a face in smiles) iluminar

wreck, *s.* naufragio, *m.*; buque naufragado, *m.*; destrucción, *f.*; (*fig.*) ruina, *f.*; (remains) restos, *m. pl.*; (person) sombra, *f.* *v.t.* hacer naufragar; destruir; (*fig.*) arruinar; hacer fracasar. **I am a complete w.,** (*fam.*) Estoy hecho una ruina. **to be wrecked,** irse a pique, naufragar; (*fig.*) arruinarse; frustrarse

wreckage, *s.* naufragio, *m.*; restos de naufragio, *m. pl.*; ruinas, *f. pl.*; (of a car, 'plane, etc.) restos, *m. pl.*; accidente, *m.*

wrecked, *a.* naufragado

wrecker, *s.* destructor (-ra); (of ships) raquero, *m.*

wren, *s.* reyezuelo, *m.*

wrench, *s.* (jerk) arranque, *m.*; (pull) tirón, *m.*; (sprain) torcedura, *f.*; (tool) llave, *f.*; (pain) dolor, *m.* *v.t.* arrancar; forzar; torcer, dislocar. **He has wrenched his arm,** Se ha torcido el brazo

wrest, *v.t.* arrebatar, arrancar

wrestle, *v.i.* luchar. *s.* lucha grecorromana, *f.;* (*fig.*) lucha, *f.* **to w. with,** (*fig.*) luchar con; luchar contra

wrestler, *s.* luchador, *m.*

wrestling, *s.* lucha grecorromana, *f.* **all-in-w.,** lucha libre, *f.* **w.-match,** lucha, *f.*

wretch, *s.* infeliz; *m.* and *f.;* (ruffian) infame, *m.;* (playful) picaruelo (-la). **a poor w.,** un pobre diablo

wretched, *a.* (unhappy) infeliz, desdichado; miserable; pobre; (ill) enfermo; horrible; malo; mezquino; despreciable; lamentable

wretchedly, *adv.* tristemente; pobremente; muy mal; ruinmente

wretchedness, *s.* infelicidad, desdicha, *f.;* miseria, pobreza, *f.;* escualidez, *f.;* ruindad, *f.*

wriggle, *v.i.* agitarse, moverse; menearse; serpear, culebrear; retorcerse. *s.* See under **wriggling. to w. into,** insinuarse en, deslizarse dentro (de). **to w. out,** escaparse. **to w. out of a difficulty,** extricarse de una dificultad

wriggling, *s.* meneo, *m.;* retorcimiento, *m.;* serpenteo, culebreo, *m.*

wring, *v.t.* torcer; estrujar; exprimir; arrancar; (force) forzar. **to w. one's hands,** restregarse las manos. **to w. the neck of,** torcer el pescuezo (a). **to w. out,** exprimir; estrujar

wringer, *s.* torcedor (-ra); (for clothes) exprimidor de la ropa, *m.*

wringing, *s.* torsión, *f.* **w.-machine,** exprimidor de la ropa, *m.*

wrinkle, *s.* arruga, *f.;* pliegue, *m.;* (*fam.*) noción, *f.* *v.t.* arrugar. *v.i.* arrugarse. **to w. one's brow,** (frown) fruncir el ceño; (in perplexity) arrugar la frente

wrinkling, *s.* arrugamiento, *m.*

wrinkly, *a.* arrugado

wrist, *s.* muñeca, *f.* **w.-band,** tira del puño de la camisa, *f.* **w. bandage,** pulsera, *f.*

wristlet, *s.* pulsera, *f.;* manguito elástico, *m.* **w. watch,** reloj de pulsera, *m.*

writ, *s.* escritura, *f.;* (*law*) decreto judicial, mandamiento, *m.;* orden, *f.;* título ejecutorio, *m.;* hábeas corpus, *m.* **Holy W.,** la Sagrada Escritura. **to issue a w.,** dar orden. **to serve a w.,** notificar una orden. **w. of privilege,** auto de excarcelación, *m.*

write, *v.t.* and *v.i.* escribir; (*fig.*) mostrar. **He writes a good hand,** Tiene buena letra. **I shall w. to them for a list,** Les escribiré pidiendo una lista. **to w. back,** contestar por escrito; contestar a una carta. **to w. down,** poner por escrito; anotar, apuntar; describir. **to w. for,** escribir para; escribir para pedir algo; escribir algo en vez de otra persona. **to w. off,** escribir; escribir rápidamente; cancelar. **to w. on,** seguir escribiendo; escribir sobre. **to w. out,** copiar; redactar. **to w. over again,** escribir de nuevo, escribir otra vez, volver a escribir. **to w. up,** redactar; (*com.*) poner al día; (praise) escribir alabando

writer, *s.* escritor (-ra); autor (-ra). **the present w.,** el que, *m.* (*f.* la que) esto escribe. **writer's cramp,** calambre del escribiente, *m.*

writhe, *v.i.* retorcerse

writhing, *s.* retorsión, *f.*

writing, *s.* escritura, *f.;* (work) escrito, *m.;* inscripción, *f.;* documento, *m.;* (style) estilo, *m.;* (hand) letra, *f.;* el arte de escribir; trabajo literario, *m.* **in one's own w.,** de su propia letra. **in w.,** por escrito. **w.-case,** escribanía, *f.* **w.-desk,** escritorio, *m.* **w.-pad,** taco de papel, *m.* **w.-paper,** papel de escribir, *m.* **w.-table,** mesa de escribir, *f.*

written, *a.* escrito

wrong, *a.* injusto; mal; equivocado, erróneo; inexacto; falso; incorrecto; desacertado; inoportuno. **It is the w. one,** No es el que hacía falta; No es el que quería. **to be in the w. place,** estar mal situado; estar mal colocado. **to be w.,** estar mal; no tener razón; (mistaken) estar equivocado; (of deeds or things) estar mal hecho; (be unjust) ser injusto; (of clocks) andar mal. to do w., hacer mal; obrar mal. to get out of bed on the w. side, levantarse del izquierdo. to go w., (of persons) descarriarse; (of affairs) ir mal; salir mal; frustrarse; (of apparatus) estropearse, no funcionar. We have taken the w. road, Nos hemos equivocado de camino. You were very w. to ..., Has hecho muy mal en ... w.-headed, terco, obstinado; disparatado. w.-headedness, terquedad, obstinación, f. w. number, (telephone) número errado, m. w. side, revés, m.; lado malo, m. w. side out, al envés; al revés

wrong, adv. mal; injustamente; sin razón; incorrectamente; equivocadamente; (inside out) al revés. to get it w., (a sum) calcular mal; (misunderstand) comprender mal

wrong, s. mal, m.; injusticia, f.; perjuicio, m.; ofensa, f., agravio, m.; culpa, f.; error, m. to be in the w., no tener razon; haber hecho mal. to put one in the w., echar la culpa (a), hacer responsable (de).

wrong, v.t. hacer mal (a); perjudicar; ser injusto con; ofender

wrongdoer, s. malhechor (-ra); pecador (-ra); perverso (-sa)

wrongdoing, s. maldad, maleficencia, f.; pecado, m.; injusticia, f.

wrongful, a. injusto; perjudicial; falso

wrongfully, adv. injustamente; falsamente

wrongly, adv. injustamente; erróneamente, equivocadamente; perversamente; mal

wrongness, s. mal, m.; injusticia, f.; falsedad, f.; inexactitud, f., error, m.

wrought, a. forjado; labrado; (hammered) batido; trabajado. w. iron, hierro dulce, hierro forjado, m. w. up, muy excitado, muy agitado, muy nervioso

wry, a. torcido; tuerto; triste; pesimista; desilusionado; irónico. wry face, mueca (f.) de desengaño, de ironía, de disgusto, etc. wry neck, (orn.) torcecuello, m.

wryly, adv. tristemente; irónicamente

wye, s. (letter) ye, i griega, f.; horquilla, cosa en forma de Y, f.

X

x, s. equis, f.

xiphoid, a. (anat.) xifoides

x-ray, v.t. tomar una radiografía (de). x-rays, rayos x, m. pl. x-ray examination, examen con rayos x, m. x-ray photograph, radiografía, f.

xylography, s. xilografía, f.

xylophagous, a. xilófago

xylophone, s. xilófono, m.

Y

y, s. (letter) i griega, ye, f.

yacht, s. yate, m. y. club, club marítimo, m. y. race, regata de yates, f.

yachting, s. deporte de vela, "yachting," m.

yachtsman, s. deportista náutico, yachtsman, m.

yak, s. (zool.) yak, m.

yank, s. tirón, m., sacudida, f. v.t. dar un tirón (a); sacar de un tirón

Yankee, a. and s. yanqui (m. and f.)

yap, v.i. ladrar. s. ladrido, m.

yapping, s. ladridos, m. pl. a. que ladra

yard, s. (measure) yarda, f.; (naut.) verga, f.; corral, m.; (courtyard) patio, m. v.t. acorralar. goods y., estación de mercancías, f. y.-arm, penol (de la verga), m. y.-stick, vara de medir de una yarda, f.

yarn, s. hilaza, f.; hilo, m.; (story) historia, f., cuento, m. to spin a y., contar una historia

yarrow, s. milenrama, f.

yashmak, s. velo, m.

yataghan, s. yatagán, m.

yaw, v.i. (naut.) guiñar; (aer.) serpentear. s. (naut.) guiñada, f.; (aer.) serpenteo, m.

yawl, s. yola, f.; bote, m.

yawn, v.i. bostezar; quedarse con la boca abierta; (of chasms, etc.) abrirse. s. bostezo, m. to stifle a y., ahogar un bostezo

yawning, a. abierto. s. bostezos, m. pl.

ye, pers. pron. vos, vosotros

yea, adv. en verdad, ciertamente; y aun . . . no sólo . . . sino. s. sí, m.

year, s. año, m.; pl. years, años, m. pl., edad, f. We are getting on in years, Nos vamos haciendo viejos. He is five years old, Tiene cinco años. all the y. round, todo el año, el año entero. by the y., al año. every other y., cada dos años, un año sí y otro no. in after years, en años posteriores. last y., el año pasado. next y., el año próximo. y. after y., año tras año. New Y., Año Nuevo, m. to see the New Y. in, ver empezar el Año Nuevo. New Year's Day, día de Año Nuevo, m. A Happy New Y.! ¡Feliz Año Nuevo! y.-book, anuario, m.

yearly, a. anual. adv. anualmente, cada año; una vez al año

yearn, v.i. anhelar, suspirar (por); desear vivamente

yearning, s. sed, ansia, f.; anhelo, deseo vehemente, m. a. ansioso; anhelante; (tender) tierno

yeast, s. levadura, f.

yell, v.i. and v.t. chillar; gritar. s. chillido, m.; grito, m.

yelling, s. chillidos, m. pl.; gritos, m. pl., gritería, f.

yellow, a. amarillo; (of hair) rubio; (cowardly) cobarde; (of Press) sensacionalista. to turn y., v.i. ponerse amarillo; amarillear. v.t. volver amarillo. y. fever, fiebre amarilla, f. y.-hammer, (orn.) emberizo, m.

yellowing, s. amarilleo, m.

yellowish, a. amarillento

yellowness, s. amarillez, f.

yelp, v.i. gañir. s. gañido, m.

yelping, s. gañidos, m. pl.

yeoman, s. pequeño propietario rural, m.; soldado de caballería, m. Y. of the Guard, alabardero de la Casa Real, m.

yes, adv. sí. Yes? ¿De verdad? ¿Y qué pasó después? ¿Y entonces? to say yes, decir que sí; dar el sí. yes-man, sacristán de amén, m.

yesterday, adv. ayer. s. ayer, m. the day before y., anteayer

yet, adv. aún, todavía. as yet, hasta ahora; todavía. He has not come yet, No ha venido todavía. yet again, otra vez

yet, conjunc. sin embargo, no obstante, con todo; pero. The book is well-written and yet I do not like it, El libro está bien escrito, y sin embargo no me gusta

yew, s. tejo, m.; madera de tejo, f.

yield, v.t. producir; dar; (grant) otorgar; (afford) ofrecer; (surrender) ceder. v.i. producir; (submit) rendirse, someterse; (of disease) responder; (give way) flaquear, doblegarse; dar de sí; (consent) consentir (en); (to circumstances, etc.) ceder (a), sucumbir (a). s. producción, f., producto, m.; (com.) rédito, m.; (crop) cosecha, f. to y. to temptation, ceder a la tentación. to y. up, entregar; devolver

yielding, a. flexible; (soft) blando; dócil, sumiso; fácil; condescendiente

yoke, s. yugo, m.; (of oxen) yunta, f.; (for pails) balancín, m.; (of a garment) canesú, m.; (fig.) férula, f., yugo, m. v.t. uncir, acoplar. to throw off the y., sacudir el yugo

yokel, s. patán, rústico, m.

yolk, s. (of an egg) yema, f.

yonder, a. aquel, m.; aquella, f.; aquellos, m. pl.; aquellas, f. pl. adv. allí; allá a lo lejos

yore, s. in days of y., antaño; en otro tiempo

you, pers. pron. nominative, (polite form) usted (Vd.), m. and f.; ustedes (Vds.), m. and f. pl.; (familiar form) (sing.) tu, m. and f.; (plural) vosotros, m. pl.; vosotras, f. pl.; (one) uno, m.; una, f.; se (followed by 3rd pers. sing. of verb). pers. pron. accusative, (polite form) le, m.; la, f.; les, m. pl.; las, f. pl.; a usted, a ustedes; (familiar form) te, m. and f., os, m. and f. pl.;

(after most prepositions) tí, *m.* and *f.*; vosotros, *m. pl.*; vosotras, *f. pl.* Are you there? (telephone) ¡Oiga! I gave the parcel to you, Te (os) di el paquete; Di el paquete a usted (a ustedes). I shall wait for you in the garden, Te (os) esperaré en el jardín; Esperaré a Vds. (a Vd.) en el jardín. This present is for you, Este regalo es para tí (para vosotros, para Vd. (Vds.)). Away with you! ¡Vete! ¡Marcháos! Between you and me, Entre tú y yo. You never can tell, No se sabe nunca, Uno no sabe nunca

young, *a.* joven; nuevo, reciente; inexperto; poco avanzado. *s.* cría, *f.*, hijuelos, *m. pl.* y. blood, (*fam.*) pollo pera, *m.* y. girl, jovencita, *f.* y. man joven, *m.* y. people, jóvenes, *m. pl.* in his y. days, en su juventud. The night is y., La noche está poca avanzada. to grow y. again, rejuvenecer. with y., (of animals) preñada (*f.*)

younger, *a.* más joven; menor. Peter is his y. brother, Pedro es su hermano menor. to look y., parecer más joven

youngish, *a.* bastante joven

youngster, *s.* jovencito, chico, muchacho, *m.*; niño, *m.*

your, *a. poss.* (polite form) su (*pl.* sus), de usted (Vd.), (*pl.* de ustedes (Vds.)); (familiar form) tu (*pl.* vuestro). I have y. papers, Tengo tus (vuestros) papeles; Tengo los papeles de Vd. (or de Vds.). How is y. mother? ¿Cómo está su (tu) madre? It is y. turn, Te toca a ti, Le toca a Vd. (or a Vds.)

yours, *pron. poss.* (polite form) (el) suyo, *m.*; (la) suya, *f.*; (los) suyos, *m. pl.*; (las) suyas, *f. pl.*; el, *m.*; la, *f.*; lo, *neut.*; los, *m. pl.*; las, *f. pl.*; de usted (Vd.), *m.* and *f. sing.* or de ustedes (Vds.), *m.* and *f. pl.*; (familiar form) (el) tuyo, *m.*; (la) tuya, *f.*; (los) tuyos, *m. pl.*; (las) tuyas, *f. pl.*; (el) vuestro, *m.*; (la) vuestra, *f.*; (los) vuestros, *m. pl.*; (las) vuestras, *f. pl.* This is a picture of y., (addressing one person), Este es uno de los cuadros de usted (Vd.), Este es

uno de tus cuadros. This hat is mine, it is not y., Este sombrero es el mío, no es el tuyo. The horse is y., El caballo es tuyo (de Vd.). Y. affectionately, Un abrazo de tu amigo . . . Y. faithfully, Queda de Vd. su att..(atentísimo) s.s. (seguro servidor). Y. sincerely, Quedade Vd. su aff. (afectuoso)

yourself, *pron. pers.* (familiar form *sing.*) tú mismo, *m.*; tú misma, *f.*; (after a preposition) tí, *m.* and *f.*; (polite form) usted (Vd.) mismo, *m.*; usetd misma, *f.*; *pl.* yourselves, (familiar form) vosotros mismos, *m. pl.*; vosotras mismas, *f. pl.*; (polite form) ustedes (Vds.) mismos, *m. pl.*; ustedes mismas, *f. pl.* This is for y., Esto es para tí; Esto es para Vd.

youth, *s.* juventud, *f.*; (man) joven, chico, mozalbete, *m.*; (collectively) jóvenes, *m. pl.*, juventud, *f.*

youthful, *a.* joven, juvenil; de la juventud

yowl, *s.* gañido, aullido, *m. v.i.* gañir, aullar

Yucatan, *a.* yucateco

yucca, *s.* (*bot.*) yuca, *f.*

Yugoslav, *a.* and *s.* See under Jugo Slav

Yule, *s.* Navidad, *f.* y.-log, leño de Navidad, *m.* y.-tide, Navidades, *f. pl.*

Z

z, *s.* (letter) zeda, zeta, *f.*

zeal, *s.* celo, entusiasmo, *m.*; ardor, fervor, *m.*

zealot, *s.* fanático (-ca)

zealous, *a.* celoso, entusiasta

zealously, *adv.* con entusiasmo

zebra, *s.* cebra, *f.*

zenana, *s.* harén indio, *m.*

zenith, *s.* cenit, *m.*; (*fig.*) apogeo, punto culminante, *m.*

zephyr, *s.* céfiro, *m.*, brisa, *f.*

Zeppelin, *s.* zepelín, dirigible, *m.*

zero, *s.* cero, *m.* below z., bajo cero. z. hour, hora de ataque, *f.*

zest, *s.* sabor, gusto, *m.*; entusiasmo, *m.* to eat with z., comer con buen apetito. **to enter on with z.**, emprender con entusiasmo

zigzag, s. zigzag, *m*. *a*. and *adv*. en zigzag. *v.i.* zigzaguear, hacer zigzags, serpentear; (of persons) andar haciendo eses

zinc, s. cinc, *m*. **z. oxide**, óxido de cinc, *m*.

Zion, s. Sión, *m*.

Zionism, s. Sionismo, *m*.

zip, s. (of a bullet) silbido, *m*.; (*fam*.) energía, *f*. **zip fastener**, cierre de cremallera, *m*.

zircon, s. circón, *m*.

zither, s. cítara, *f*.

zodiac, s. zodíaco, *m*.

zonal, *a*. zonal

zone, s. zona, *f*.; faja, *f*.

Zoo, s. jardín zoológico, *m*.

zoological, *a*. zoológico. **Z. garden**, jardín zoológico, *m*.

zoologist, s. zoólogo, *m*.

zoology, s. zoología, *f*.

zoom, s. zumbido, *m*. *v.i.* zumbar; (*aer*.) empinarse

zouave, s. zuavo, *m*.

Zulu, *a*. and s. zulú (*m*. and *f*.)

Abyssinia, Etiopía, f.; Abisinia, f.
Adriatic, the, el (Mar) Adriático
Ægean, the, el (Mar) Egeo
Afghanistan, Afganistán, m.
Africa, África, f.
Albania, Albania, f.
Alexandria, Alejandría, f.
Algeria, Argelia, f.
Algiers, Argel, m.
Alps, the, los Alpes
Alsace, Alsacia, f.
Amazon, River, the, el (Río de las) Amazonas
America, América, f.
Andalusia, Andalucía, f.
Andes, the, los Andes
Antilles, the, las Antillas
Antwerp, Amberes, m.
Apennines, the, los Apeninos
Arabia, Arabia, f.
Argentina, Argentina, f.
Armenia, Armenia, f.
Asia, Asia, f.
Asia Minor, Asia Menor, f.
Athens, Atenas, f.
Atlantic, the, el Atlántico
Atlantis, Atlántida, f.
Australia, Australia, f.
Austria, Austria, f.
Babylon, Babilonia, f.
Bahamas, the, las Islas Bahamas, las Islas Lucayas
Balearic Islands, the, las Islas Baleares
Balkans, the, los Balcanes
Baltic, the, el (Mar) Báltico
Barbadoes, Isla de Barbados, f.
Barbary, Berbería, f.
Barcelona, Barcelona, f.
Basle, Basilea, f.
Basque Provinces, the, las Provincias Vascongadas
Bavaria, Baviera, f.
Bayonne, Bayona, f.
Belgian Congo, the, el Congo Belga
Belgium, Bélgica, f.
Belgrade, Belgrado, m.
Bengal, Bengala, f.
Berlin, Berlín, m.
Bermudas, the, las Islas Bermudas
Berne, Berna, f.
Bethlehem, Belén, m.
Biscay, the Bay of, el Golfo de Vizcaya
Black Forest, the, la Selva Negra
Black Sea, the, el Mar Negro
Bohemia, Bohemia, f.
Bolivia, Bolivia, f.
Bonn, Bona, f.
Bordeaux, Burdeos, m.
Bosphorus, the, el Bósforo
Boulogne, Boloña, f.
Brazil, el Brasil
Bremen, Brema, f.
British Commonwealth, the, la Mancomunidad Británica
Brittany, Bretaña, f.
Bruges, Brujas, f.
Brussels, Bruselas, f.

Bucharest, Bucarest, m.
Bulgaria, Bulgaria, f.
Burgundy, Borgoña, f.
Burma, Birmania, f.
Byzantine Empire, the, el Imperio Bizantino
Byzantium, Bizancio, m.
Cadiz, Cádiz, m.
Cairo, el Cairo
Calcutta, Calcuta, f.
California, California, .
Cambridge, Cambrige, m.
Cameroons, the, el Camerún, los Camarones
Canada, el Canadá
Canary Islands, the, las Islas Canarias
Canterbury, Cantorbery, m.
Cape Horn, Cabo de Hornos, m.
Cape of Good Hope, Cabo de Buena Esperanza, m.
Caribbean Sea, the, el Mar Caribe
Carpathian Mountains, the, los Montes Cárpatos
Carthage, Cartago, m.
Cashmere, Cachemira, f.
Caspian Sea, the, el (Mar) Caspio
Castile, Castilla, f.
Catalonia, Cataluña, f.
Caucasus, the, el Cáucaso
Cevennes, the, los Cevenes
Ceylon, Ceilán, m.
Chaldea, Caldea, f.
Chile, Chile, m.
China, (la) China, f.
Cologne, Colonia, f.
Colombia, Colombia, f.
Constantinople, Constantinopla, f.
Copenhagen, Copenhague, f.
Cordova, Córdoba, f.
Corinth, Corinto, m.
Cornwall, Cornualles, m.
Corsica, Córcega, f.
Corunna, La Coruña, f.
Cracow, Cracovia, f.
Crete, Creta, f.
Crimea, the, la Crimea
Croatia, Croacia, f.
Cyprus, Isla de Chipre, f.
Czechoslovakia, Checoslovaquia, f.
Damascus, Damasco, m.
Danube, the, el (Río) Danubio
Dardanelles, the, los Dardanelos
Dauphiné, the, el Delfinado
Dead Sea, the, el Mar Muerto, el Lago Asfaltites
Delphi, Delfos, m.
Denmark, Dinamarca, f.
Dieppe, Diepa, f.
Dodecannese, the, el Dodecaneso
Dominican Republic, the, la República Dominicana
Dominions, the, los Dominios
Douro, the River, el Duero
Dover, Dóver, m.

Downs, the, las Dunas
Dresden, Dresde, m.
Dunkirk, Dunquerque, m.
East Indies, Indias Orientales, f. pl.
Ecuador, el Ecuador
Edinburgh, Edimburgo, m.
Egypt, Egipto, m.
Eire, Estado libre de Irlanda, m.
England, Inglaterra, f.
English Channel, the, el Canal de la Mancha
Ephesus, Éfeso, m.
Ethiopia, Etiopía, f.
Etna, Mount, el Etna
Finland, Finlandia, f.
Flanders, Flandes, m.
Florence, Florencia, f.
France, Francia, f.
Franche-Comté, Franco-Condado, m.
Friesland, Frisia, f.
Galilee, Galilea, f.
Gascony, Gascuña, f.
Gaul, Galia, f.
Geneva, Ginebra, f.
Genoa, Génova, f.
Germany, Alemania, f.
Gethsemane, Getsemaní, m.
Ghent, Gante, f.
Gold Coast, the, la Costa del Oro
Great Britain, Gran Bretaña, f.
Greece, Grecia, f.
Greenland, Groenlandia, f.
Guernsey, Guernesey, m.
Guiana, Guayana, f.
Guinea, Guinea, f.
Gulf Stream, the, la Corriente del Golfo
Hague, The, La Haya
Haiti, Haití, m.
Hamburg, Hamburgo, m.
Havana, la Habana
Hawaii, Hawai, m.
Hebrides, the, las Hébridas
Hendaye, Hendaya, f.
Himalayas, the, los Himalayas
Holland, Holanda, f.
Holy Land, the, la Tierra Santa
Hungary, Hungría, f.
Iberian Peninsula, the, la Península Ibérica
Iceland, Islandia, f.
India, la India
Indian Ocean, the, el Océano índico
Indonesia, Indonesia, f.
Iraq, Irak, m.
Ireland, Irlanda, f.
Irish Free State, Estado libre de Irlanda, m.
Irish Sea, Mar de Irlanda, f.
Israel, Israel, m.
Italy, Italia, f.
Ithaca, Itaca, f.
Jamaica, Jamaica, f.
Japan, el Japón
Java, Java, f.
Jerusalem, Jerusalén, m.
Jugoslavia, Yugoeslavia, f.

1230a

Jutland, Jutlandia, *f.*
Korea, Corea, *f.*
Lapland, Laponia, *f.*
Latvia, Latvia, *f.*
Lausanne, Lausana, *f.*
Lebanon, the, el Líbano
Leningrad, Leningrado, *m.*
Levant, the, el Levante
Libya, Libia, *f.*
Lisbon, Lisboa, *f.*
Lithuania, Letonia, *f.*
Lombardy, Lombardía, *f.*
London, Londres, *f.*
Low Countries, the, los Países Bajos
Lucerne, Lucerna, *f.*
Luxembourg, Luxemburgo, *m.*
Macedonia, Macedonia, *f.*; Macedón, *m.*
Madagascar, Madagascar, *m.*
Madeira, Madera, *f.*
Madrid, Madrid, *m.*
Majorca, Mallorca, *f.*
Malaya, Malasia, *f.*, Archipiélago Malayo, *m.*
Malta, Malta, *f.*
Manchuria, Manchuria, *f.*
Marseilles, Marsella, *f.*
Martinique, Martinica, *f.*
Matterhorn, the, el Matterhorn
Mauritius, Mauricio, *m.*, Isla de Francia, *f.*
Mecca, la Meca
Mediterranean, the, el Mediterráneo
Mexico, Méjico, *m.*
Middle East, the, el Oriente Medio, el Levante
Minorca, Menorca, *f.*
Mississippi, the, el Misisipí
Missouri, the, el Misuri
Moluccas, the, las Malucas
Morocco, Marruecos, *m.*
Moscow, Moscú, *m.*
Naples, Nápoles, *m.*
Navarre, Navarra, *f.*
Nazareth, Nazaret, *m.*
Netherlands, the, los Países Bajos
Newfoundland, Terranova, *f.*
New Guinea, Nueva Guinea, *f.*
New Orleans, Nueva Orleans, *f.*
New South Wales, La Nueva Gales del Sur
New York, Nueva York, *f.*
New Zealand, Nueva Zelandia, *f.*
Nice, Niza, *f.*
Nile, the, el Nilo
Nineveh, Nínive, *m.*
Normandy, Normandía, *f.*
North America, Norteamérica, América del Norte, *f.*
Norway, Noruega, *f.*

Nova Scotia, Nueva Escocia, *f.*
Oceania, Oceanía, *f.*
Odessa, Odesa, *f.*
Oporto, Oporto, Porto, *m.*
Orkneys, the, las Órcades
Ostend, Ostende, *m.*
Pacific, the, el (Océano) Pacífico
Palestine, Palestina, *f.*
Palmyra, Palmira, *f.*
Panama, el Panamá
Paraguay, el Paraguay
Paris, París, *m.*
Persia, (la) Persia, *f.*
Peru, el Perú
Philippines, the, las (Islas) Filipinas
Poland, Polonia, *f.*
Polynesia, Polinesia, *f.*
Pompeii, Pompeya, *f.*
Porto Rico, Puerto Rico, *m.*
Portugal, Portugal, *m.*
Prague, Praga, *f.*
Provence, Provenza, *f.*
Prussia, Prusia, *f.*
Pyrenees, the, los Pirineos
Rhine, the, el Rin
Rhodes, Rodas, *f.*
Rhodesia, Rodesia, Rhodesia, *f.*
Riviera, the, la Riviera
Rome, Roma, *f.*
Roussillon, Rosellón, *m.*
Rumania, Rumania, *f.*
Russia, Rusia, *f.*
Sahara, the, el Sáhara
Saint Gothard, the, el San Gotardo
Salonika, Salónica, *f.*
Salt Lake, the Great, el Gran Lago Salado
Samothrace, Samotracia, *f.*
Saragossa, Zaragoza, *f.*
Sardinia, Cerdeña, *f.*
Savoy, Saboya, *f.*
Saxony, Sajonia, *f.*
Scandinavia, Escandinavia, *f.*
Scilly Isles, Islas Sorlingues, *f. pl.*
Scotland, Escocia, *f.*
Seine, the, el Sena
Senegal, Senegal, *m.*
Serbia, Servia, *f.*
Shetlands, the, las Islas de Shetland
Siam, Siam, *m.*
Siberia, Siberia, *f.*
Sicily, Sicilia, *f.*
Singapore, Singapur, *m.*
Somaliland, Somalia, *f.*, Somaliland, *m.*
South America, América del Sur, *f.*
South Sea, Mar del Sur, Mar Pacífico, *m.*
Soviet Union, the, la Unión Soviética, *f.*

Spain, España, *f.*
Spanish America, América Española, *f.*
Sparta, Esparta, *f.*
Strait of Magellan, Estrecho de Magallanes, *m.*
Straits Settlements, Establecimientos del Estrecho, *m. pl.*
Strasburg, Estrasburgo, *m.*
Sudan, the, el Sudán
Suez Canal, the, el Istmo de Suez
Sweden, Suecia, *f.*
Switzerland, Suiza, *f.*
Syracuse, Siracusa, *f.*
Syria, Siria, *f.*
Tagus, the River, el Tajo
Tahiti, Taiti, Tahiti, *m.*
Tanganyika, Tangañica, *f.*
Tangier, Tánger, *m.*
Tartary, Tartaria, *f.*
Tasmania, Tasmania, *f.*
Teneriffe, Tenerife, *f.*
Thames, the, el Támesis
Thebes, Tebas, *f.*
Thermopylæ, Termópilas, *pl.*
Thessaly, Tesalia, *f.*
Thrace, Tracia, *f.*
Thuringia, Turingia,.
Tokyo, Tokio, *m.*
Toulon, Tolón, *m.*
Toulouse, Tolosa, *f.*
Transjordan, Transjordania, *f.*
Trinidad, Isla de la Trinidad, *f.*
Tripoli, Trípoli, *m.*
Troy, Troya, *f.*
Tunis, Túnez, *m.*
Turkey, Turquía, *f.*
Tuscany, Toscana, *f.*
Tyre, Tiro, *m.*
Tyrol, the, el Tirol
Tyrrhenian Sea, the, el Mar Tirreno
Ukraine, Ucrania, *f.*
Union of South Africa, Unión Sudafricana, *f.*
United States of America, los Estados Unidos
Urals, the, los Urales
Valencia, Valencia, *f.*
Venezuela, Venezuela, *f.*
Venice, Venecia, *f.*
Vesuvius, Vesubio, *m.*
Vienna, Viena, *f.*
Wales, (País de) Gales, *m.*
Warsaw, Varsovia, *f.*
West Indies, Indias Occidentales, *f. pl.*
Yugoslavia, Yugoeslavia, *f.*
Yukon, the, el Yukón
Zanzibar, Zanzíbar, *m.*
Zion, Sión, *m.*
Zululand, Zululandia, *f.*
Zuyder Zee, the, el Zuyderzée

PROPER NAMES OF PERSONS AND ANIMALS, AND MYTHOLOGICAL NAMES

Abelard, Abelardo
Abraham, Abrahán
Absalom, Absalón
Achilles, Aquiles
Adam, Adán
Adolphus, Adolfo
Æschylus, Esquilo
Æsop, Esopo
Agnes, Inés

Ajax, Ayax
Aladdin, Aladino
Albert, Alberto
Alexander, Alejandro
Alfred, Alfredo
Alice, Alicia
Ambrose, Ambrosio
Amelia, Amalia
Andrew, Andrés

Andromache, Andrómaca
Anne, Ana
Anthony, Antony, Antonio
Apollo, Apolo
Apuleius, Apuleyo
Aquinas, St. Thomas, Santo Tomás de Aquino
Arc, Joan of, Juana de Arco
Arcady, Arcadia, *f.*

Archimedes, Arquimedes
Argonauts, the, los Argonautas
Aristophanes, Aristófanes
Aristotle, Aristóteles
Arthur, Arturo
Augustine, Agustín
Augustus, Augusto
Avernus, Averno, *m.*
Bacchus, Baco
Barbara, Bárbara
Bartholomew, Bartolomé
Basil, Basilio
Beatrice, Beatriz
Beelzebub, Belcebú
Belshazzar, Baltasar
Benedict, Benedicto, Benito
Bernard, Bernardo
Bertha, Berta
Bertram, Beltrán
Blanche, Blanca
Blue Beard, Barba azul
Boccaccio, Bocacio
Boetius, Boecio
Boniface, Bonifacio
Bourbon, the House of, la
   Casa de Borbón
Bridget, Brígida
Brutus, Bruto
Bucephalus, Bucéfalo
Buddha, Buda
Cæsar, César
Caiaphas, Caifás
Cain, Caín
Calvin, Calvino
Camilla, Camila
Canute, Canuto
Caroline, Carolina
Cassandra, Casandra
Catherine, Catalina
Catiline, Catilina
Cato, Catón
Cerberus, Cerbero
Charles, Carlos
Charlemagne, Carlomagno
Charlotte, Carlota
Charon, Caronte
Charybdis, Caribdis
Christ, Cristo
Christine, Cristina
Christopher, Cristóbal
Cicely, Cecilia
Cicero, Cicerón
Cinderella, la Cenicienta
Clara, Clara
Claude, Claudius, Claudio
Clement, Clemente
Columbine, Columbina
Columbus, Colón
Constance, Constanza
Constantine, Constantino
Copernicus, Copérnico
Cornelius, Cornelio
Crœsus, Creso
Cupid, Cupido
Cyclops, Cíclope
Cyprian, Cipriano
Cyril, Cirilo
Dædalus, Dédalo
Daphne, Dafnis
Darius, Darío
Deborah, Débora
Delilah, Dálila
Democritus, Demócrito
Demosthenes, Demóstenes
Diana, Diana
Diocletian, Diocleciano
Diogenes, Diógenes
Dionysus, Dionisio

Dominic, Domingo
Dorothy, Dorotea
Edmund, Edmundo
Edward, Eduardo
Eleanor, Leonor
Elijah, Elías
Elisha, Eliseo
Elizabeth, Isabel
Emily, Emilia
Emmanuel, Manuel
Endymion, Endimión
Enoch, Enoc
Epictetus, Epicteto
Epicurus, Epicuro
Erasmus, Erasmo
Ernest, Ernesto
Esau, Esaú
Esther, Ester
Ethelred, Etelredo
Euclid, Euclides
Eugen, Eugenio
Eustace, Eustaquio
Eve, Eva
Ezekiel, Ezequiel
Ezra, Esdras
Faust, Fausto
Ferdinand, Fernando
Florence, Florencia
Frances, Francisca
Francis, Francisco
Frederick, Federico
Galahad, Galaor
Ganymede, Ganimedes
Genghis Khan, Gengis Kan
Geoffrey, Geofredo
George, Jorge
Gertrude, Gertrudis
Gilbert, Gilberto
Giles, Gil
Godfrey, Godofredo
Goldylocks, Trenza de oro
Gorgons, the, las Gorgonas
Gracchi, the, los Gracos
Grace, Engrácia
Gregory, Gregorio
Habakkuk, Habacuc
Hamilcar, Amílcar
Hannah, Ana
Hannibal, Aníbal
Hapsburgs, the, los Habs-
   burgos
Harlequin, Arlequín
Harry, Enrique
Helen, Elena
Henrietta, Enriqueta
Henry, Enrique
Heraclitus, Heráclito
Hercules, Hércules
Herod, Herodes
Herodotus, Heródoto
Hezekiah, Ezequías
Hilary, Hilario
Homer, Homero
Hop-o-my-thumb, Pulgarcito
Horace, Horacio
Hubert, Huberto
Hugh, Hugo
Iago, Yago
Icarus, Ícaro
Ignatius, Ignacio
Inez, Inés
Iphigenia, Ifigenia
Isabel, Isabel
Isaiah, Isaías
Isidore, Isidro, Isidoro
Jacob, Jacob
James, Jaime
Jane, Juana

Japhet, Jafet
Jasper, Gaspar
Jeremiah, Jeremías
Jerome, Jerónimo
Jesus, Jesús, Jesucristo
John, Juan
Jonah, Jonás
Jonathan, Jonatán
Joseph, José
Jove, Júpiter
Judas, Judas
Judith, Judit
Julian, Julián
Juliet, Julieta
Julius, Julio
Jupiter, Júpiter
Kate, Katharine, Catalina
Launcelot, Lanzarote
Lawrence, Lorenzo
Lazarus, Lázaro
Leander, Leandro
Leonard, Leonardo
Leopold, Leopoldo
Lettice, Leticia
Livy, Livio
Louis, Luis
Louise, Luisa
Lucan, Lucano
Lucretia, Lucrecia
Lucretius, Lucrecio
Lucy, Lucía
Luke, Lucas
Luther, Lutero
Lycurgus, Licurgo
Machiavelli, Maquiavelo
Magdalen, Magdalena
Magi, the, los (Reyes) Magos
Mahomet, Mahoma
Marcus Aurelius, Marco Aure-
   lio
Margaret, Margarita
Marion, Mariana
Marius, Mario
Mark, Marcos
Mars, Marte
Martha, Marta
Martial, Marcial
Mary, María
Matilda, Matilde
Matthew, Mateo
Maurice, Mauricio
Maximilian, Maximiliano
Medusa, Medusa
Mephistopheles, Mefistófeles
Mercury, Mercurio
Michael, Miguel
Michelangelo, Miguel Ángel
Morpheus, Morfeo
Moses, Moisés
Napoleon, Napoleón
Nathaniel, Nataniel
Neptune, Neptuno
Nero, Nerón
Nicholas, Nicolás
Nick, Old, Patillas
Noah, Noé
Octavius, Octavio
Odyssey, the, La Odisea
Œdipus, Edipo
Olympus, Olimpo, *m.*
Orpheus, Orfeo
Otto, Otón
Ovid, Ovidio
Pan, Pan
Parnassus, Parnaso, *m.*
Parthenon, the, el Partenón
Patrick, Patricio
Paul, Pablo

Pauline, Paula
Pegasus, Pegaso
Persephone, Perséfone
Perseus, Perseo
Peter, Pedro
Petrarch, Petrarca
Pharaoh, Faraón
Phidias, Fidias
Philip, Felipe
Pindar, Píndaro
Pius, Pío
Plato, Platón
Plautus, Plauto
Pliny, Plinio
Plutarch, Plutarco
Pluto, Plutón
Pompey, Pompeyo
Pontius Pilate, Poncio Pilatos
Prometheus, Prometeo
Proserpine, Proserpina
Psyche, Psique
Ptolemy, Tolomeo, Ptolomeo
Pythagoras, Pitágoras
Quintilian, Quintiliano
Quixote, Don, Don Quijote
Rachel, Raquel
Raphael, Rafael
Raymond, Raimundo
Rebecca, Rebeca
Red Riding Hood, Caperucita Roja
Richard, Ricardo
Robert, Roberto
Roderick, Rodrigo

Roger, Roger
Roland, Rolando, Orlando
Romulus, Rómulo
Rose, Rosa
Rudolph, Rodolfo
Rupert, Ruperto
Saladin, Saladino
Sallustus, Salusto
Samson, Sansón
Sappho, Safo
Satan, Satanás
Saturn, Saturno
Saul, Saúl
Scipio, Escipión
Scylla, Escila
Sebastian, Sebastián
Seneca, Séneca
Socrates, Sócrates
Solomon, Salomón
Sophia, Sofía
Sophocles, Sófocles
Stephen, Esteban
Stuart, Estuardo
Suetonius, Suetonio
Susan, Susana
Sylvia, Silvia
Tacitus, Tácito
Tamerlane, Tamerlán
Terence, Terencio
Tertullian, Tertuliano
Themistocles, Temístocles
Theobald, Teobaldo
Theocritus, Teócrito

Theodore, Teodoro
Theresa, Teresa
Theseus, Teseo
Thomas, Tomás
Thucydides, Tucídides
Tiberius, Tiberio
Timothy, Timoteo
Titian, Ticiano
Titus, Tito
Tobias, Tobías
Tom Thumb, Pulgarcito
Trajan, Trajano
Trent, Council of, Concilio de Trento, *m.*
Tristram, Tristán
Ulysses, Ulises
Urban, Urbano
Uriah, Urías
Utopia, Utopía
Valentine, Valentín
Venus, Venus
Vespasian, Vespasiano
Vespucci, Vespucio
Victoria, Victoria
Vincent, Vicente
Virgil, Virgilio
Virginia, Virginia
Vulcan, Vulcano
Walter, Gualterio
William, Guillermo
Xenophon, Jenofonte
Zeus, Zeus
Zwingli, Zwinglio

ABBREVIATIONS COMMONLY USED IN ENGLISH WHICH DIFFER FROM THOSE FOUND IN SPANISH, WITH THEIR SPANISH EQUIVALENTS

A

A.C.: Air Corps (Fuerza Aérea, F.A.); (*elec.*) alternating current (corriente alterna, c.a.)
a/c: account (cuenta, cta.)
A.D.: Anno Domini (Año de Cristo, A.C.)
Adj.: Adjutant (Ayudante, Ayte.)
Adm.: Admiral (Almirante, Almte.)
A.R.P.: Air Raid Precautions (Precauciones contra ataques aéreos)
A.V.: Authorized Version (Versión Autorizada, V.A.)
av.: average (promedio, prom.)

B

b.: born (nacido, n.); book (libro, l.)
B.A.: Bachelor of Arts (Bachiller en Artes, Br. en A.)
B.C.: Before Christ (antes de Jesucristo, a. de J.C.)
B.L.: Bachelor of Law (Bachiller en Leyes, Br. en L.)
B/L: bill of lading (conocimiento (conto.) de embarque)
bros.: brothers (hermanos, hnos.)
b.s.: bill of sale (cuenta de ventas, c/vta or c/v)

C

Capt.: Captain (capitán, cap.)
chap.: chapter (capítulo, cap., C.); chaplain (capellán, cappª)
c.i.f.: cost, insurance and freight (coste, seguro y flete, c.s.f.)
Co.: Company (Compañía, Cía.)
C.O.: Commanding Officer (Comandante en Jefe)
C.O.D.: cash on delivery (cóbrese al entregar, C.A.E.)
Col.: Colonel (coronel, cnel.)
Corp.: corporal (cabo); (*com.*) corporation (sociedad anónima, S.A.)
cur.: currency (moneda corriente, m/c or m/cte)

D

d.: date (fecha, fha.); daughter (hija); died (murió, m.)
d.c.: (*elec.*) direct current (corriente continua, c.c.)
D.C.L.: Doctor of Civil Law (Doctor en Derecho Civil)
D.D.: Doctor of Divinity (Doctor en Teología)
D.Litt.: Doctor of Literature (Doctor en Letras, D. en L.)
d.s.: (*com.*) days after sight (días vista, d/v)
D.Sc.: Doctor of Science (Doctor en Ciencias)
D.S.C.: Distinguished Service Cross (Cruz de Servicios Distinguidos)

E

ea.: each (cada uno, c/u)
E. and O.E.: errors and omissions excepted (salvo error u omisión, s.e.u.o.)
e.g.: exempli gratia, for example (por ejemplo, p. ej.)
E.M.F.: electromotive force (fuerza electromotriz, F.E.M.)
Eng.: England (Inglaterra, Ingl.)

F

F.B.I.: Federation of British Industries (Federación de Industrias Británicas, F.I.B.)
f.o.b.: free on board (franco a bordo, f.a.b.)
foll.: following (siguiente, sig.)
Fri.: Friday (viernes)
F.R.S.: Fellow of the Royal Society (Miembro de la Real Sociedad)

G

G.H.Q.: General Headquarters, (*mil.*) Cuartel General, (*com.*, etc.) Oficinas Generales
Gov.: Governor (gobernador, gobᵉ)
Govt.: Government (gobierno, gobᵒ)

1230d

H

h.: hour (hora); height (altura, alt.)

h. and c.: hot and cold (water) (agua fría y caliente)

H.C.F.: (*math.*) highest common factor (máximo factor común)

hdqrs.: headquarters, (*mil.*) cuartel general, (*com.*, etc.) oficinas generales

H.E.: His Excellency (Su Excelencia, S.E.); His Eminence (Su Eminencia, S. Ema); high explosive (alto explosivo)

H.F.: high-frequency (alta frecuencia)

H.H.: His (Her) Highness (Su Alteza, S.A.); His Holiness (Su Santidad, S.S.)

H.M.: His (Her) Majesty (Su Majestad, S.M.)

H.M.S.: Her Majesty's Ship (Barco de la Marina Británica); Her Majesty's Service (Servicio de Su Majestad)

H.R.H.: His (Her) Royal Highness (Su Alteza Real, S.H.R.)

I

I.O.U.: I owe you (pagaré)

I.Q.: Intelligence Quotient (cuociente intelectual)

J

Jr. or jun.: Junior (Hijo)

K

K.G.: Knight of the Garter (Caballero de la Orden de la Jarretera)

Kt.: Knight (Caballero)

L

l.: left (izquierda, izqª); litre (litro, l.)

l.c.: (*print.*) lower case (minúsculas, mín.); letter of credit (carta de crédito)

L.C.M.: (*math.*) least common multiple (mínimo común múltiplo, M.C.M.)

L.D.S.: Licentiate in Dental Surgery (cirujano dentista)

l.h.: left hand (izquierda, izqª)

Lieut. or Lt.: Lieutenant (teniente, tente)

LL.D.: Doctor of Laws (Doctor en Derecho)

Ltd.: Limited (Limitada, Ltda, Sociedad en Comandita, S. en C.)

M

m.: married (casado); metre (metro, m.); minute (minuto, m.)

M.A.: Master of Arts (Maestro en Artes, M. en A.)

M.D.: Doctor of Medicine (Doctor en Medicina)

Mon.: Monday (lunes)

N

nat.: national (nacional, nac.)

N.Z.: New Zéaland (Nueva Zelandia)

O

O.K.: All Correct (correcto; Visto Bueno, Vº Bº)

O.T.: Old Testament (Antiguo Testamento)

P

p.: page (página, pág.); population (población, pob.)

p.c.: per centum (por ciento); post card (tarjeta postal)

pd.: paid (pagado, pagdo)

pharm.: pharmacy (farmacia, farm.); pharmacology (farmacología)

Ph.D.: Doctor of Philosophy (Doctor en Filosofía)

phil.: philosophy (filosofía, fil.); philology (filología)

phot.: photography (fotografía, fot.)

P.S.: postscript (posdata, P.D.)

pt.: part (parte, pte.); payment (pago); pint (pinta)

Pte.: (*mil.*) Private (soldado raso)

P.T.O.: please turn over (A la vuelta)

Q

Q.: Queen (Reina); Question (Pregunta, P.)

Q.M.: Quartermaster (comisario)

R

R.: Railway (ferrocarril, F.C.); Republican (Republicano); right (derecha, drcha.); river (río, R.)

R.A.: Royal Academician (Miembro de la Real Academia de Bellas Artes); Rear-Admiral (Contraalmirante); Royal Artillery (Cuerpo de Artillería)

R.A.C.: Royal Automobile Club (Real Automóvil Club (de España))

R.A.F.: Royal Air Force (Fuerza Real Aérea (de Inglaterra, F.R.A.))

R.C.: Red Cross (Cruz Roja, C.R.); Roman Catholic (católico (romano))

Regt.: Regent (Regente); regiment (regimiento)

Rep.: Representative (representante, rpte.); Report (informe, inf.); Reporter (reportero)

r.h.: right hand (derecha, dcha.)

R.N.: Royal Navy (Marina Real (de Inglaterra))

R.S.P.C.A.: Royal Society for the Prevention of Cruelty to Animals (Sociedad Protectora de Animales y Plantas)

R.S.P.C.C.: Royal Society for the Protection of Cruelty to Children (Sociedad Protectora de Niños)

S

s.: second (segundo, s.); shilling (chelín); singular (sing.); son (hijo, h.); substantive (substantivo, s.)

S.A.: Salvation Army (Ejército de Salvación); South Africa (Sud Africa); South America (Sud América, S.A.)

Sat.: Saturday (sábado)

Sp.: Spanish (español, esp.); Spain (España, Esp.)

S.R.N.: State Registered Nurse (enfermera titulada)

s.s.: screw steamer (vapor, v.)

Sun.: Sunday (domingo)

T

T.A.: telegraphic address (dirección telegráfica)

Thur.: Thursday (jueves, juev.)

Tue.: Tuesday (martes)

U

U.K.: United Kingdom (Reino Unido)

U.S.A.: United States of America (Estados Unidos de América, E.U.A.)

U.S.S.R.: Union of Soviet Socialist Republics (Unión de las Repúblicas Soviéticas Socialistas, U.R.S.S.)

V

v.s.: veterinary surgeon (cirujano veterinario)

W

Wed.: Wednesday (miércoles, miérc.)

W/L: wave length (longitud de onda)

X

Xmas: Christmas (Navidad)

Y

Y.W.C.A.: Young Women's Christian Association (Asociación Cristiana de Mujeres, A.C.M.)

WEIGHTS AND MEASURES (Pesos y Medidas)

Linear Measure (Medidas longitudinales)
1 mile = 1·608 kilómetros
1 yard = 3 feet = 0·914 metros
1 foot = 12 inches = 0·304 metros
1 inch = 24·5 milímetros

Square Measure (Medidas de superficie)
1 square mile = 2·687 kilómetros cuadrados
1 square yard = 9 sq. feet = 0·927 metros cuadrados
1 square foot = 0·103 metros cuadrados
1 square inch = 600 milímetros cuadrados

Liquid Measure (Medidas para líquidos)
1 gallon = 8 pints = 4·545 litros
1 pint = 0·568 litros

Avoirdupois Weights (Pesos avoirdupois)
1 ton = 20 cwt. = 1015 Kilogramos
1 hundredweight = 112 lb. = 50·736 Kilogramos
1 pound = 16 ounces = 0·453 Kilogramos
1 ounce = 28·34 gramos

Apothecaries Weights (Pesos de boticario)
1 lb. = 12 ounces = 453 gramos
1 oz. = 8 drachms = 31·103 gramos
1 drachm = 3 scruples = 3·88 gramos
1 scruple = 20 grains = 1·29 gramos
1 grain = 60 miligramos